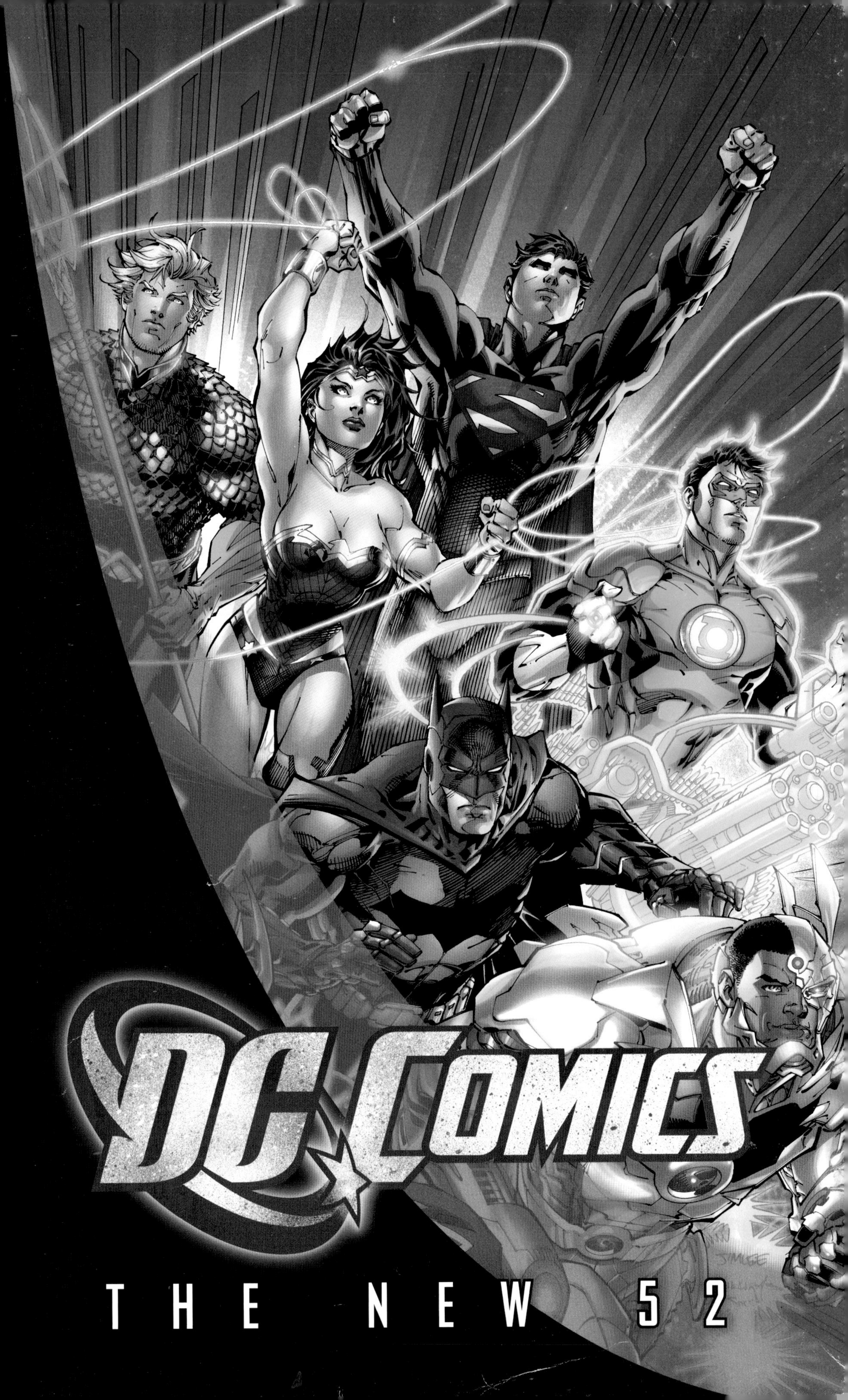
DC COMICS
THE NEW 52

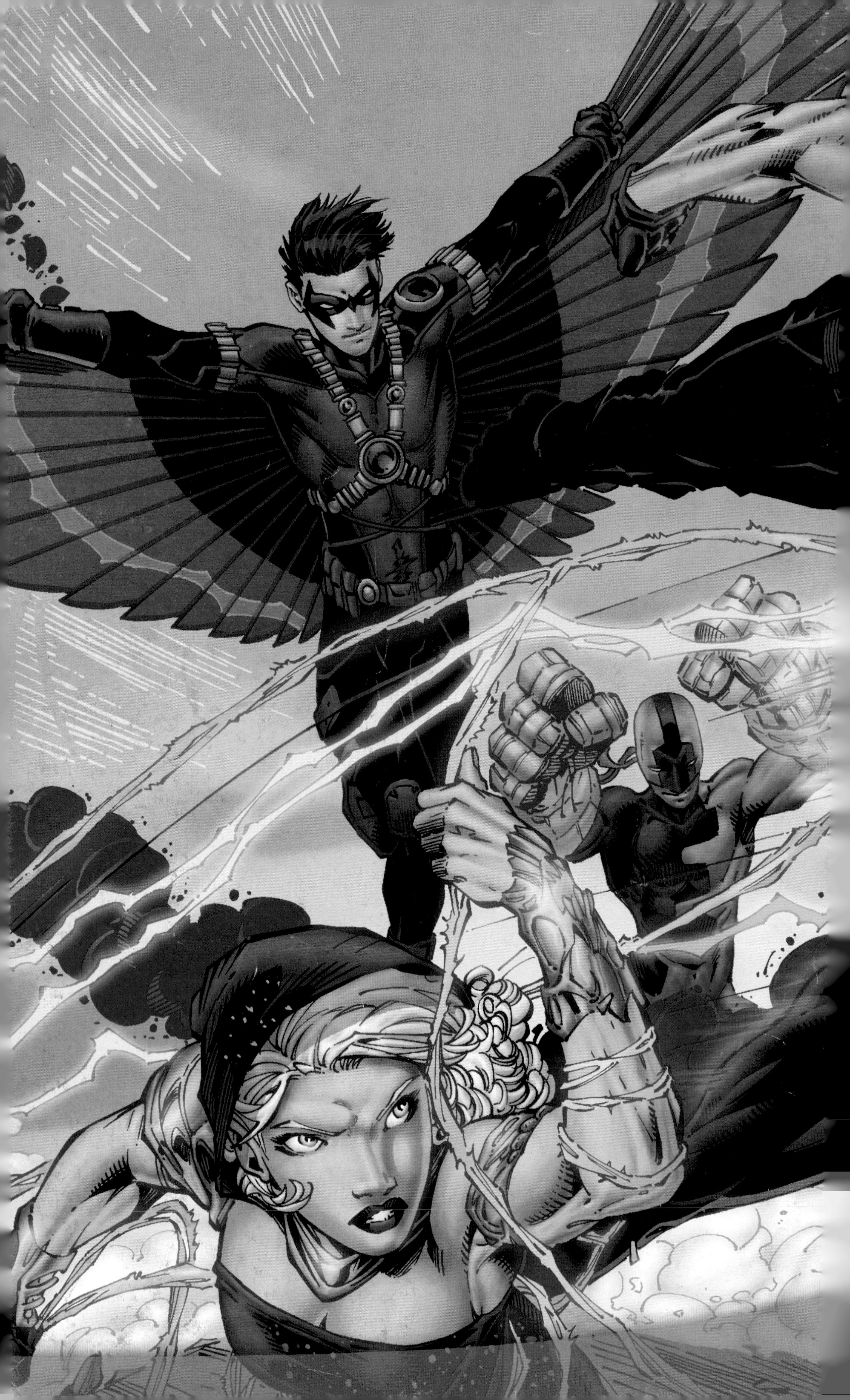

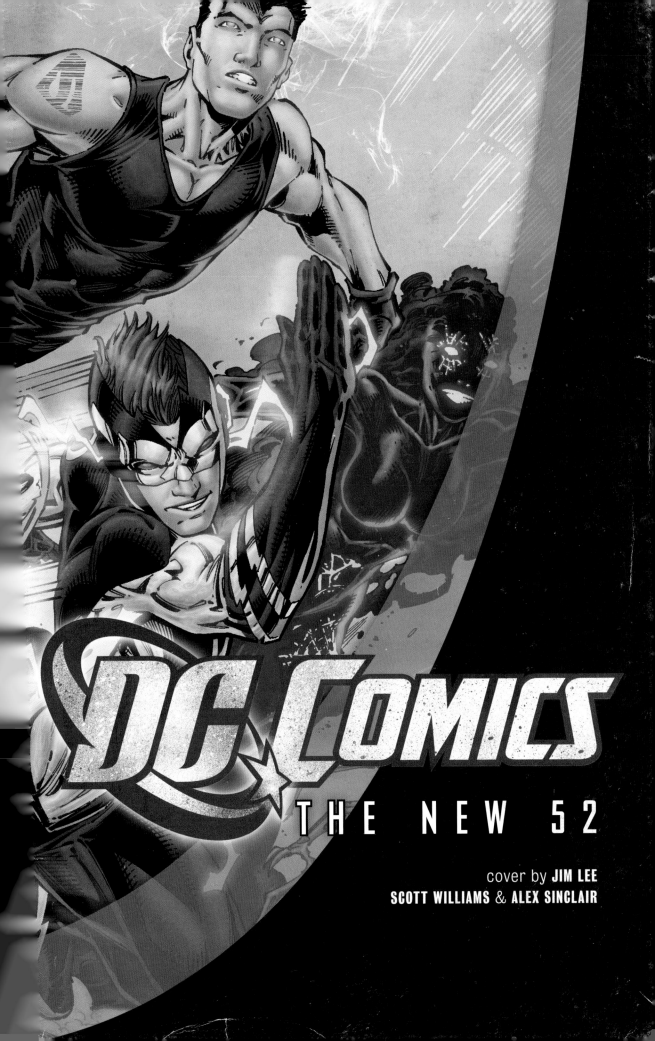

DC COMICS

THE NEW 52

cover by **JIM LEE**

SCOTT WILLIAMS & **ALEX SINCLAIR**

Janelle Asselin, Eddie Berganza, Joey Cavalieri, Bobbie Chase, Chris Conroy, Brian Cunningham, Rachel Gluckstern, Matt Idelson, Mike Marts, Pat McCallum, Wil Moss, Rex Ogle, Harvey Richards Editors – Original Series Katie Kubert, Sean Mackiewicz, Rickey Purdin, Darren Shan, Kate Stewart Assistant Editors – Original Series
Ian Sattler Director – Editorial, Special Projects and Archival Editions Peter Hamboussi Editor Robbin Brosterman Design Director – Books Robbie Biederman Publication Design

Eddie Berganza Executive Editor Bob Harras VP – Editor in Chief

Diane Nelson President Dan DiDio and Jim Lee Co-Publishers Geoff Johns Chief Creative Officer John Rood Executive VP – Sales, Marketing and Business Development
Amy Genkins Senior VP – Business and Legal Affairs Nairi Gardiner Senior VP – Finance Jeff Boison VP – Publishing Operations Mark Chiarello VP – Art Direction and Design
John Cunningham VP – Marketing Terri Cunningham VP – Talent Relations and Services Alison Gill Senior VP – Manufacturing and Operations David Hyde VP – Publicity
Hank Kanalz Senior VP – Digital Jay Kogan VP – Business and Legal Affairs, Publishing Jack Mahan VP – Business Affairs, Talent Nick Napolitano VP – Manufacturing Administration
Sue Pohja VP – Book Sales Courtney Simmons Senior VP – Publicity Bob Wayne Senior VP – Sales

Case art by Jim Lee, Scott Williams, and Alex Sinclair

DC COMICS: THE NEW 52
Published by DC Comics. Cover and compilation Copyright © 2011 DC Comics. All Rights Reserved. Originally published in single magazine form in ACTION COMICS #1, ALL-STAR WESTERN #1, ANIMAL MAN #1, AQUAMAN #1, BATGIRL #1, BATMAN #1, BATMAN AND ROBIN #1, BATMAN: THE DARK KNIGHT #1, BATWING #1, BATWOMAN #1, BIRDS OF PREY #1, BLACKHAWKS #1, BLUE BEETLE #1, CAPTAIN ATOM #1, CATWOMAN #1, DC UNIVERSE PRESENTS #1, DEATHSTROKE #1, DEMON KNIGHTS #1, DETECTIVE COMICS #1, THE FLASH #1, FRANKENSTEIN, AGENT OF S.H.A.D.E. #1, THE FURY OF FIRESTORM #1, GREEN ARROW #1, GREEN LANTERN #1, GREEN LANTERN CORPS #1, GREEN LANTERN: NEW GUARDIANS #1, GRIFTER #1, HAWK AND DOVE #1, I, VAMPIRE #1, JUSTICE LEAGUE #1, JUSTICE LEAGUE DARK #1, JUSTICE LEAGUE INTERNATIONAL #1, LEGION LOST #1, LEGION OF SUPER-HEROES #1, MEN OF WAR #1, MISTER TERRIFIC #1, NIGHTWING #1, O.M.A.C. #1, RED HOOD AND THE OUTLAWS #1, RED LANTERNS #1, RESURRECTION MAN #1, THE SAVAGE HAWKMAN #1, STATIC SHOCK #1, STORMWATCH #1, SUICIDE SQUAD #1, SUPERBOY #1, SUPERGIRL #1, SUPERMAN #1, SWAMP THING #1, TEEN TITANS #1, VOODOO #1, WONDER WOMAN #1 Copyright © 2011 DC Comics. All Rights Reserved.
All characters, their distinctive likenesses and related elements featured in this publication are trademarks of DC Comics. The stories, characters and incidents featured in this publication are entirely fictional. DC Comics does not read or accept unsolicited submissions of ideas, stories or artwork.

DC Comics, 1700 Broadway, New York, NY 10019. A Warner Bros. Entertainment Company
Printed by RR Donnelley, Willard, OH, USA. 11/04/11. First Printing. ISBN: 978-1-4012-3451-5

WELCOME TO THE NEW 52!

In September 2011, DC Comics exploded with 52 new #1 issues! The entire line of comic books was renumbered, with new, innovative storylines featuring our most iconic characters helmed by some of the most creative minds in the industry.

With the NEW 52 there has never been an initiative of this size and purpose before. Not only was this compelling to existing readers, it also gave new readers a precise entry point into the DC Universe.

Enjoy,

Jim Lee, **Dan DiDio** Co-publishers

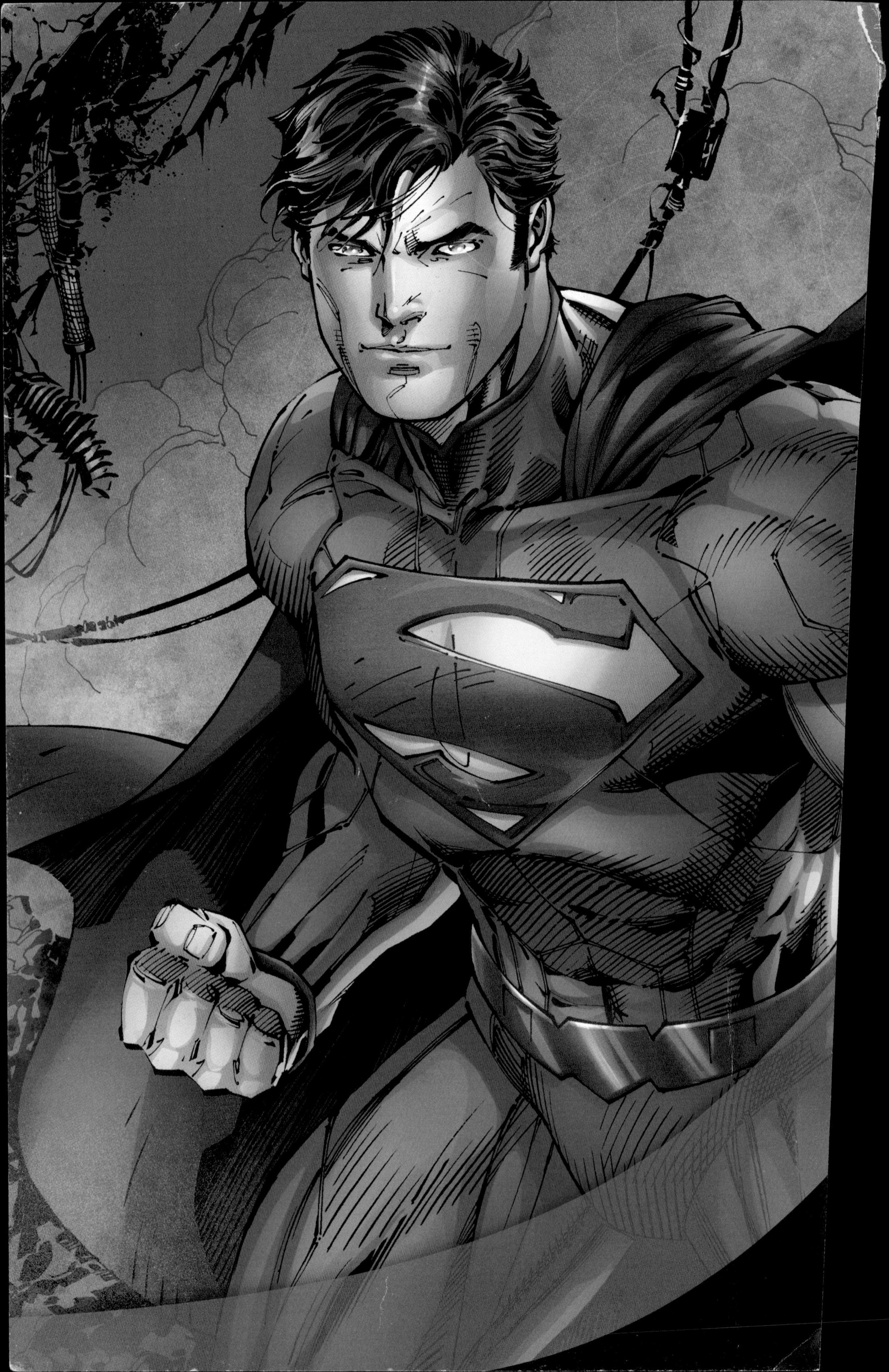

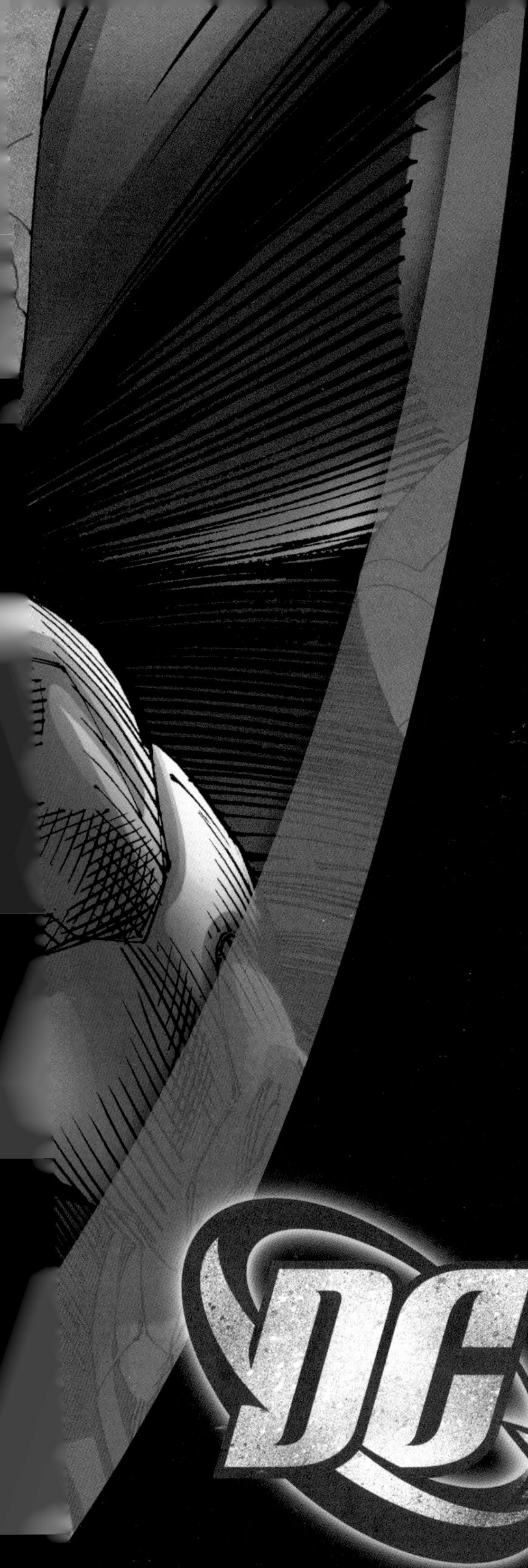

DC COMICS

JUSTICE LEAGUE

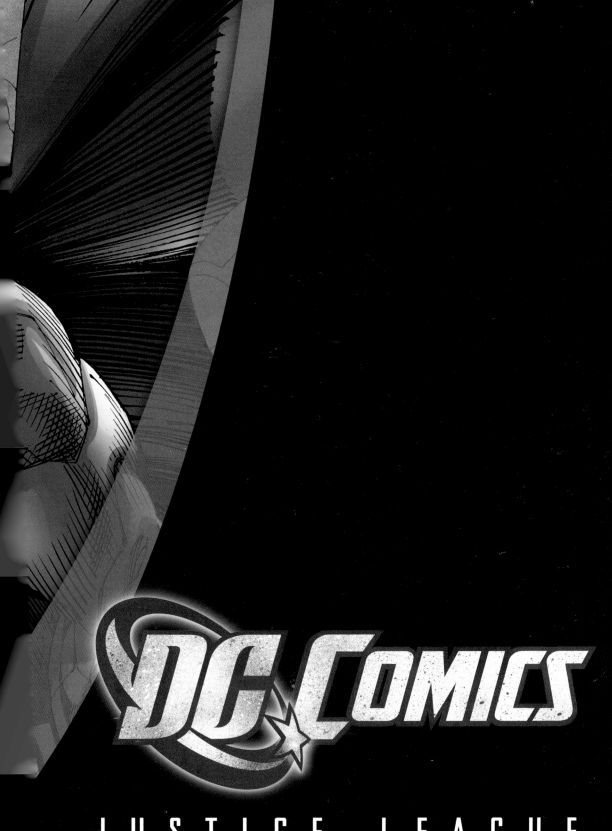

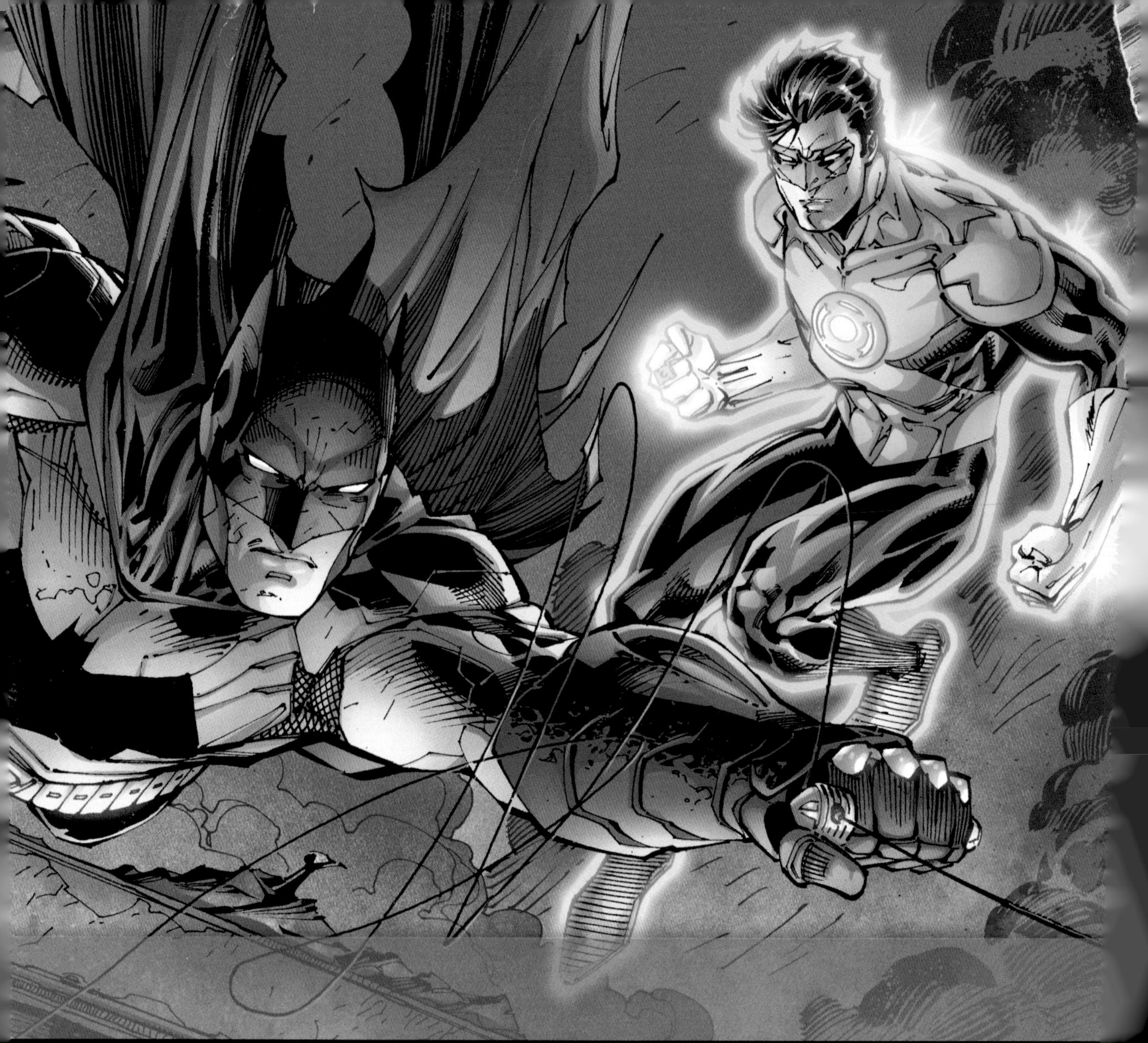

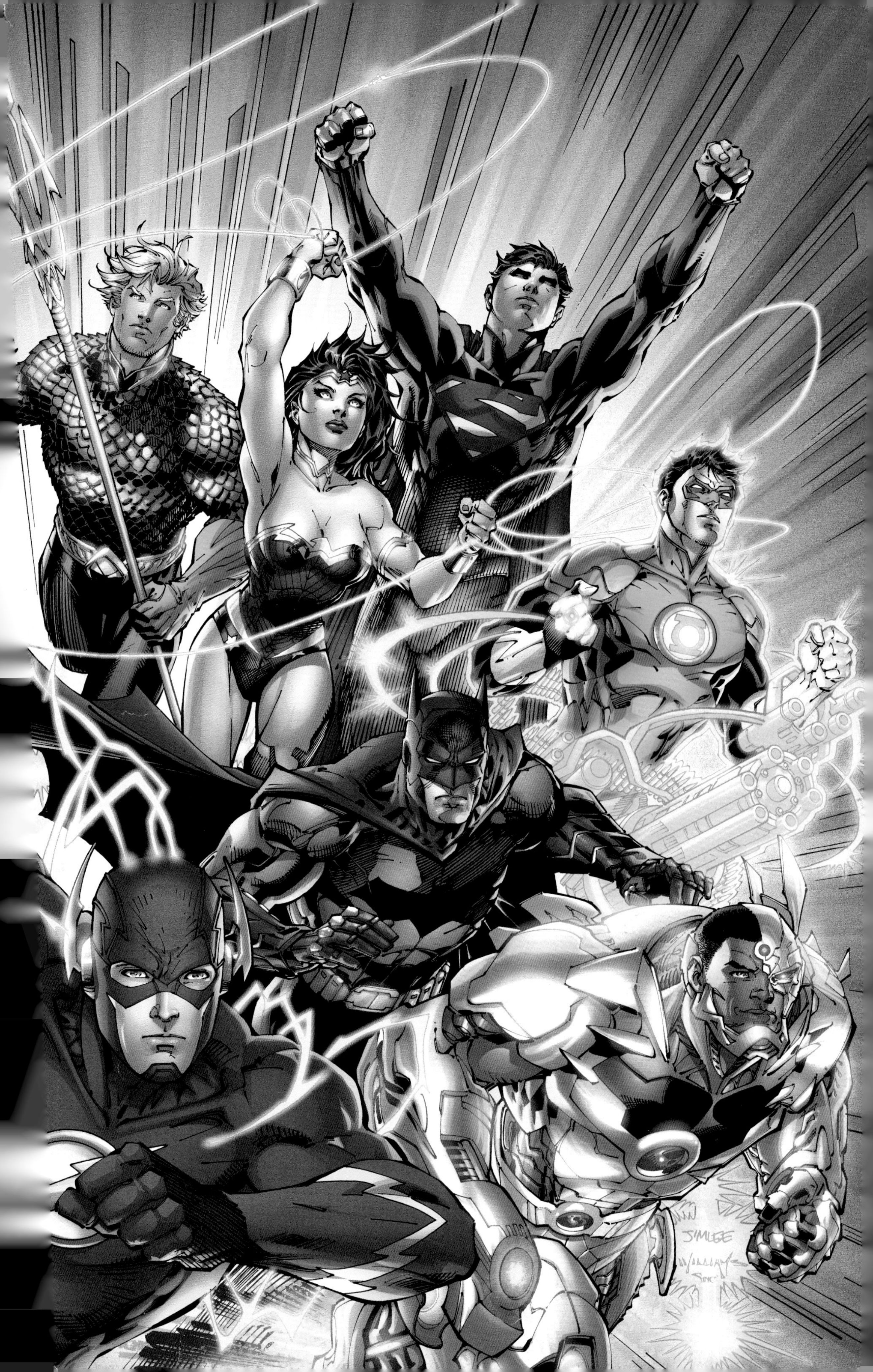

JUSTICE LEAGUE

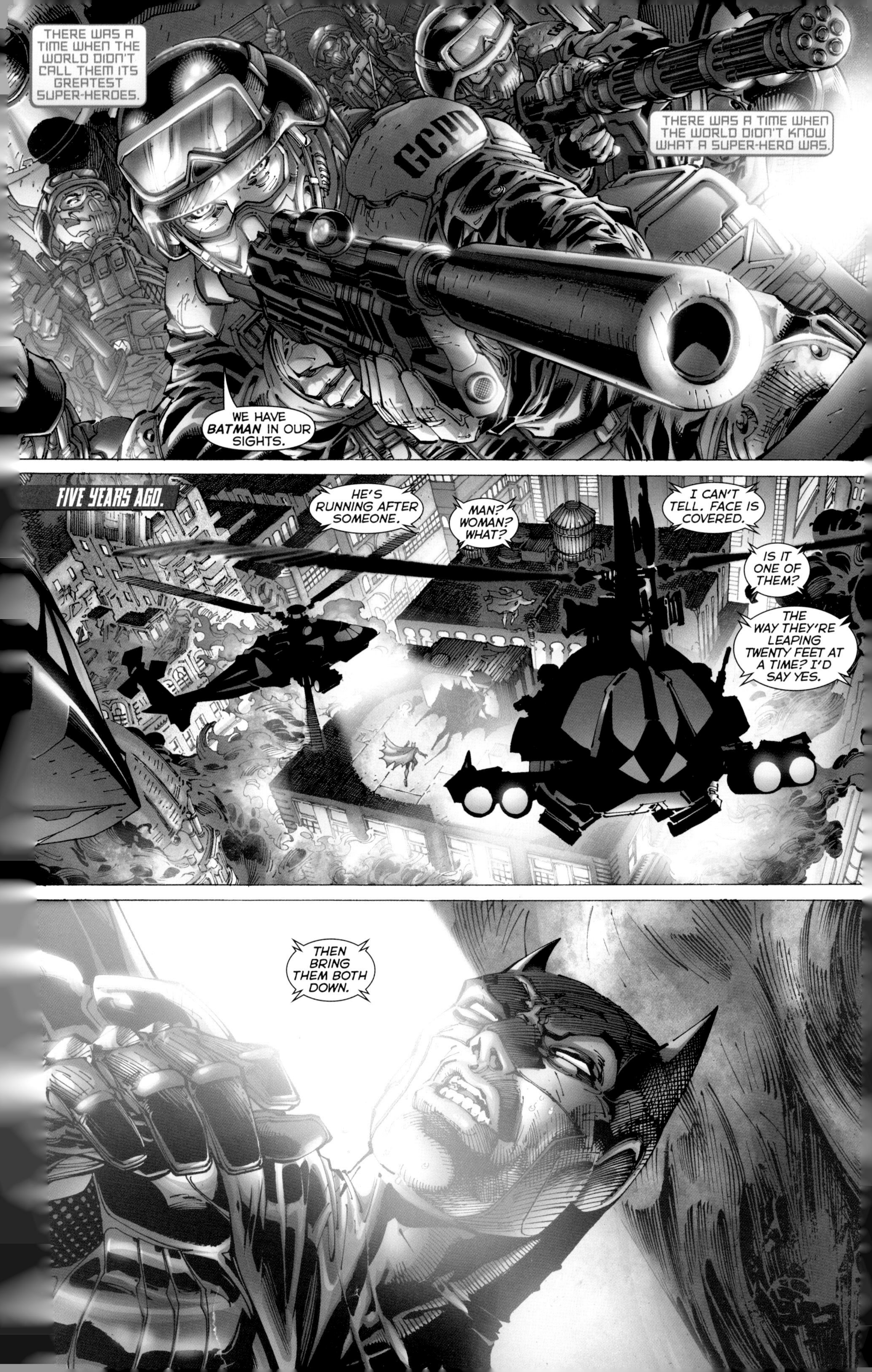

THERE WAS A TIME WHEN THE WORLD DIDN'T CALL THEM ITS GREATEST SUPER-HEROES.
THERE WAS A TIME WHEN THE WORLD DIDN'T KNOW WHAT A SUPER-HERO WAS.
GCPD
WE HAVE BATMAN IN OUR SIGHTS.
FIVE YEARS AGO.
HE'S RUNNING AFTER SOMEONE.
MAN? WOMAN? WHAT?
I CAN'T TELL. FACE IS COVERED.
IS IT ONE OF THEM?
THE WAY THEY'RE LEAPING TWENTY FEET AT A TIME? I'D SAY YES.
THEN BRING THEM BOTH DOWN.

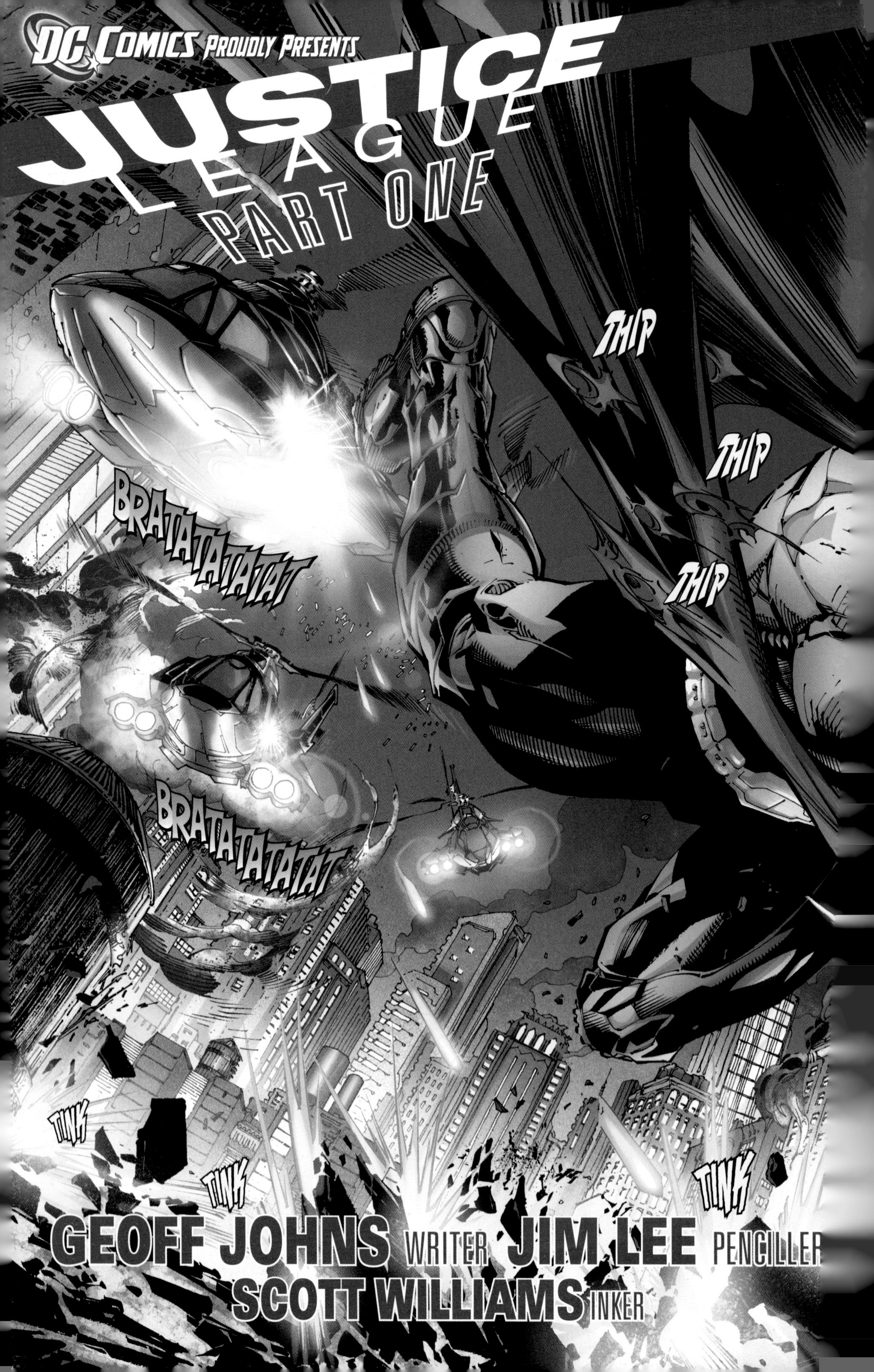
DC COMICS PROUDLY PRESENTS
JUSTICE LEAGUE
PART ONE
THIP
THIP
THIP
BRATATATATATAT
BRATATATATATAT
TINK
TINK
TINK
GEOFF JOHNS WRITER JIM LEE PENCILLER
SCOTT WILLIAMS INKER

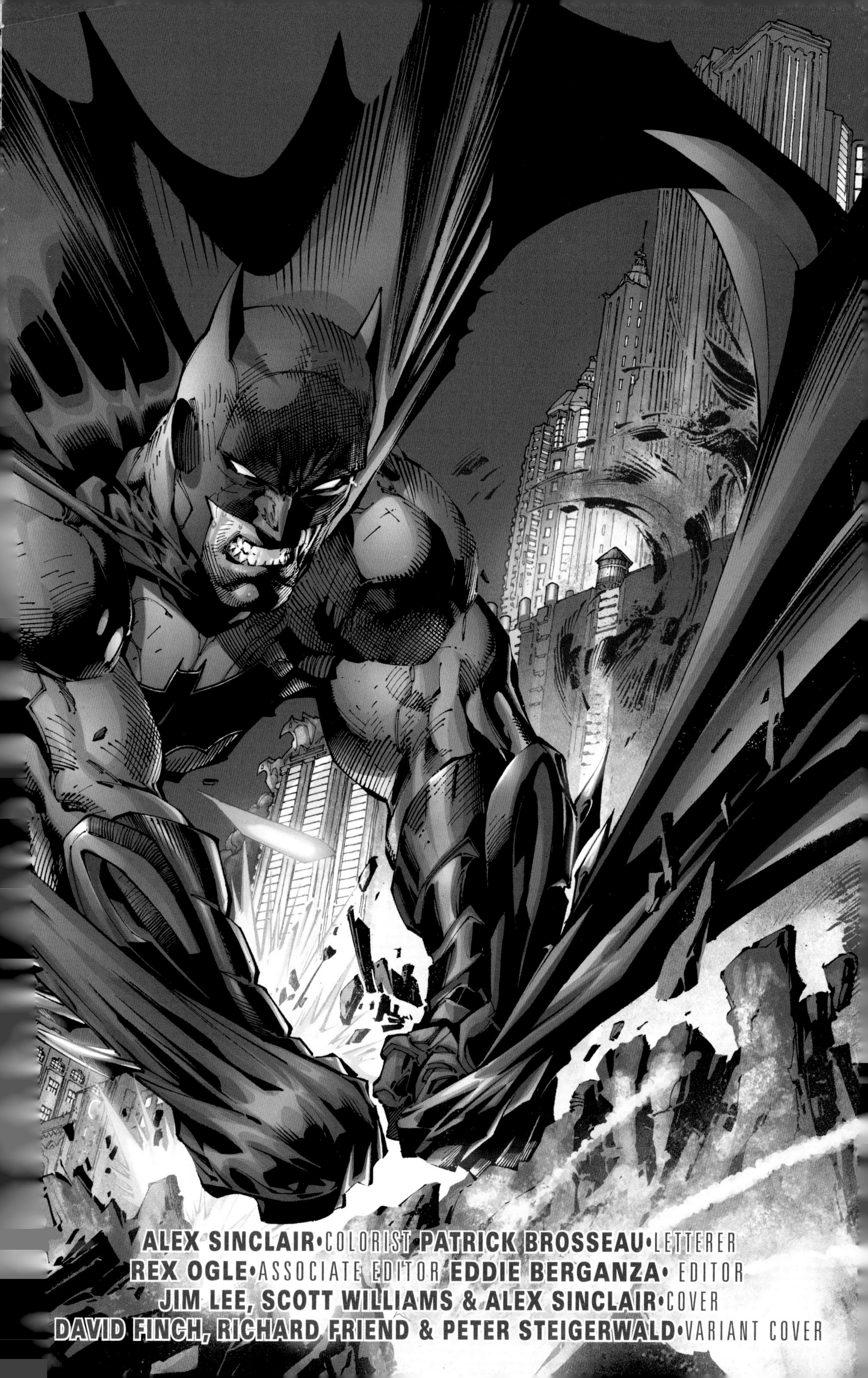
ALEX SINCLAIR•COLORIST PATRICK BROSSEAU•LETTERER
REX OGLE•ASSOCIATE EDITOR EDDIE BERGANZA• EDITOR
JIM LEE, SCOTT WILLIAMS & ALEX SINCLAIR•COVER
DAVID FINCH, RICHARD FRIEND & PETER STEIGERWALD•VARIANT COVER

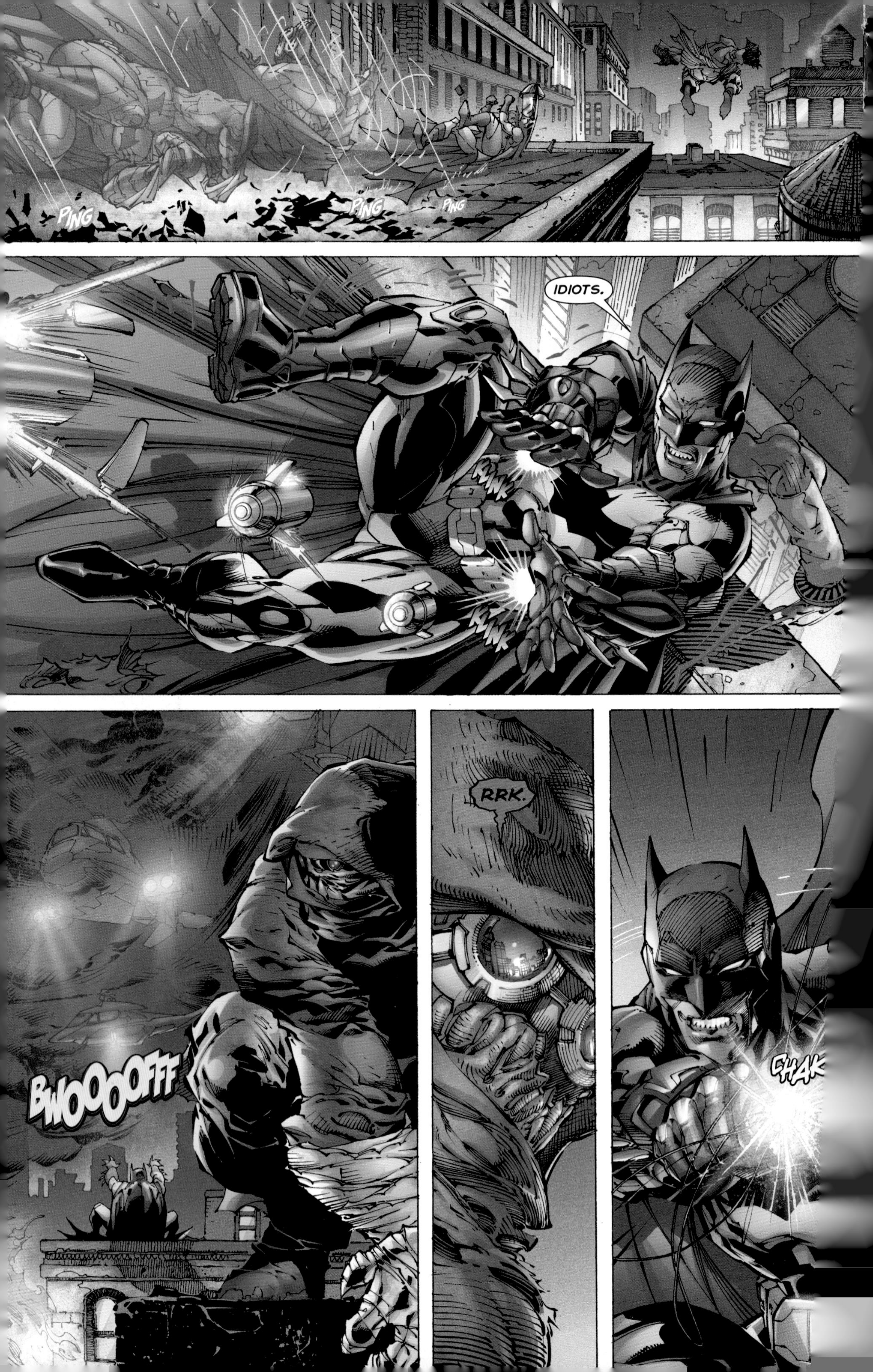
PING
PING
PING
IDIOTS.
KLINK
KLINK
BWOOOOFFF
RRK.
CHAK

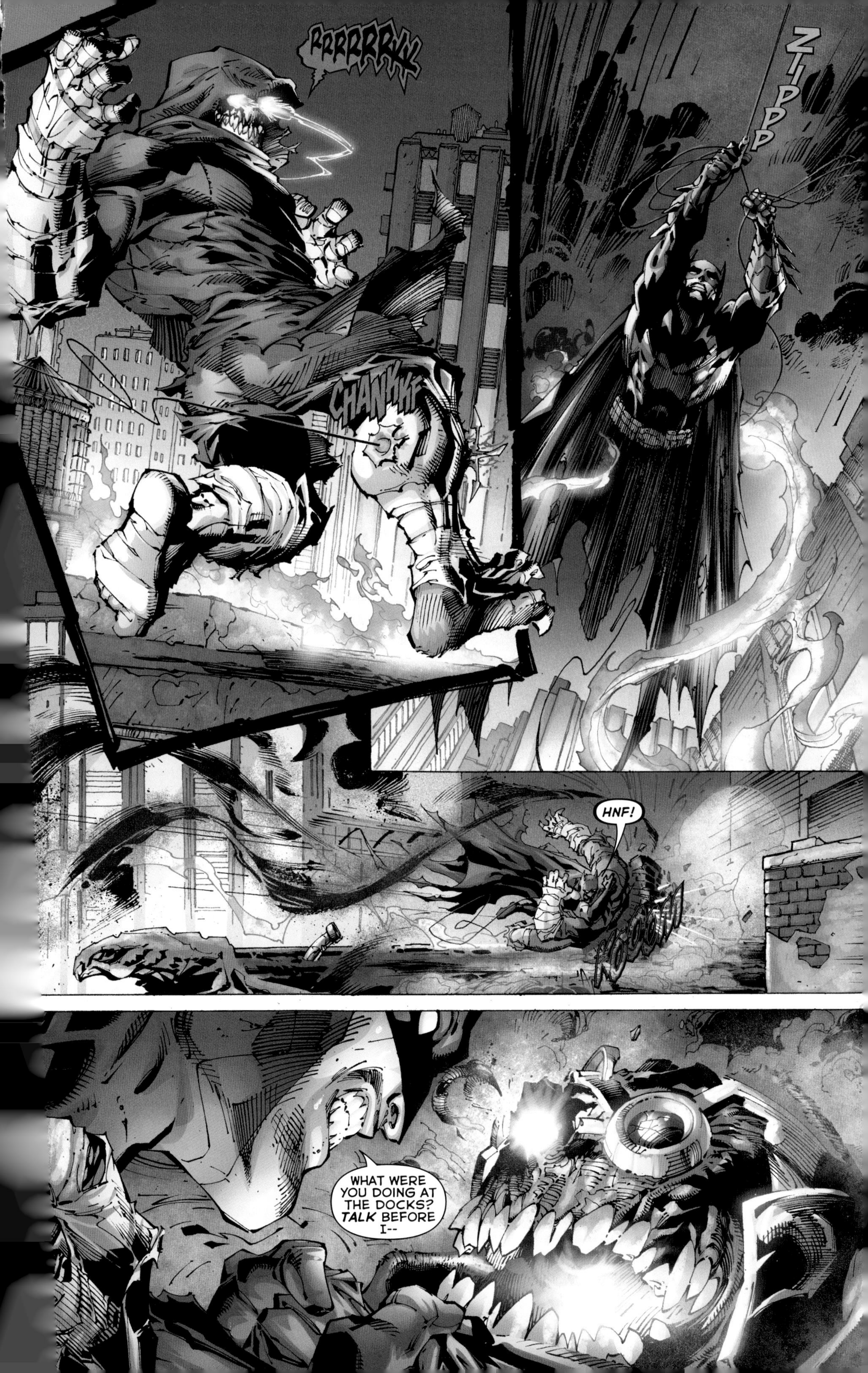
ZIPPPP
HNF!
WHAT WERE YOU DOING AT THE DOCKS? TALK BEFORE I--

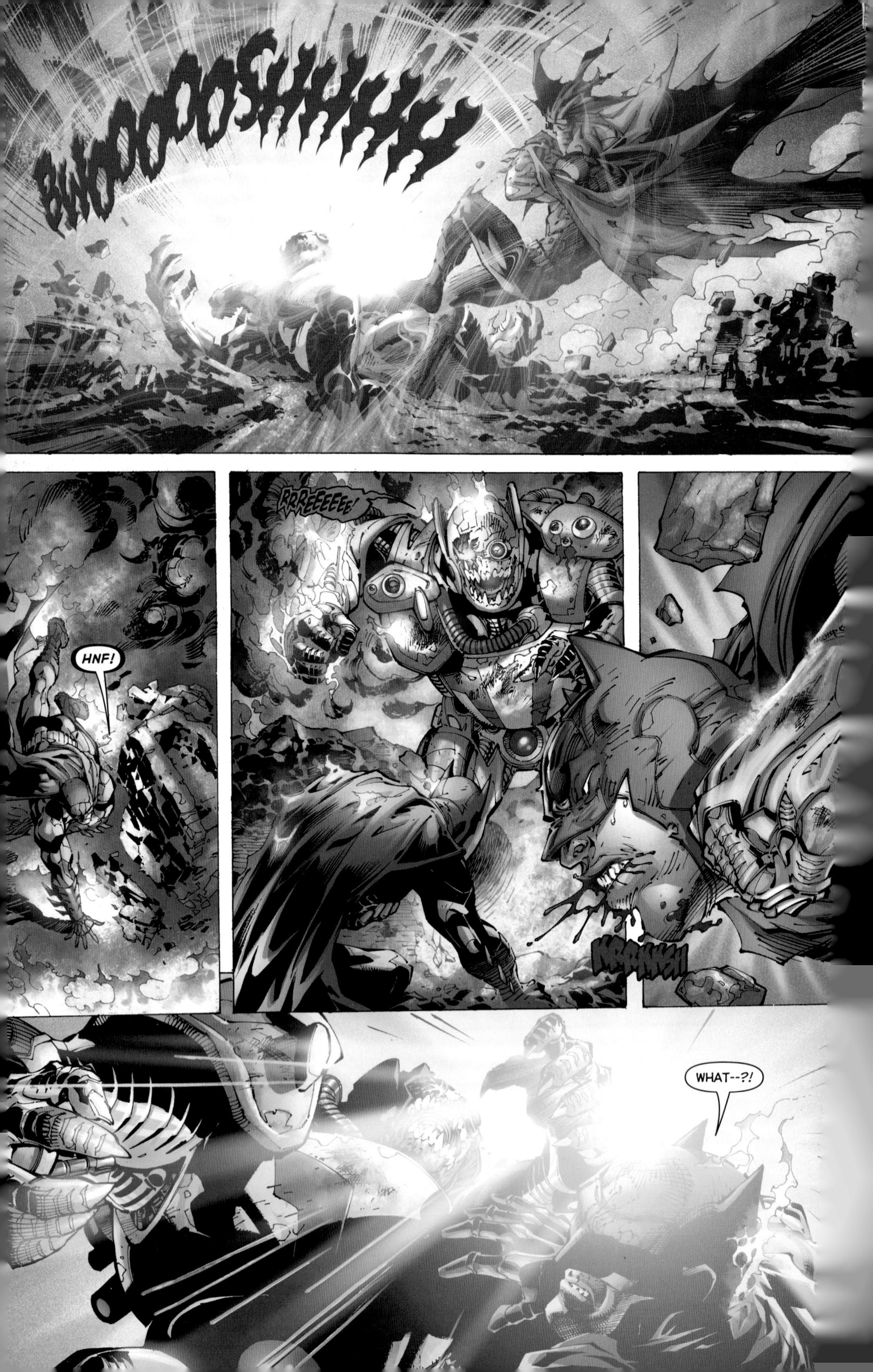
BWOOOOSHHHHH
HNF!
RRREEEEEE!
WHAT--?!

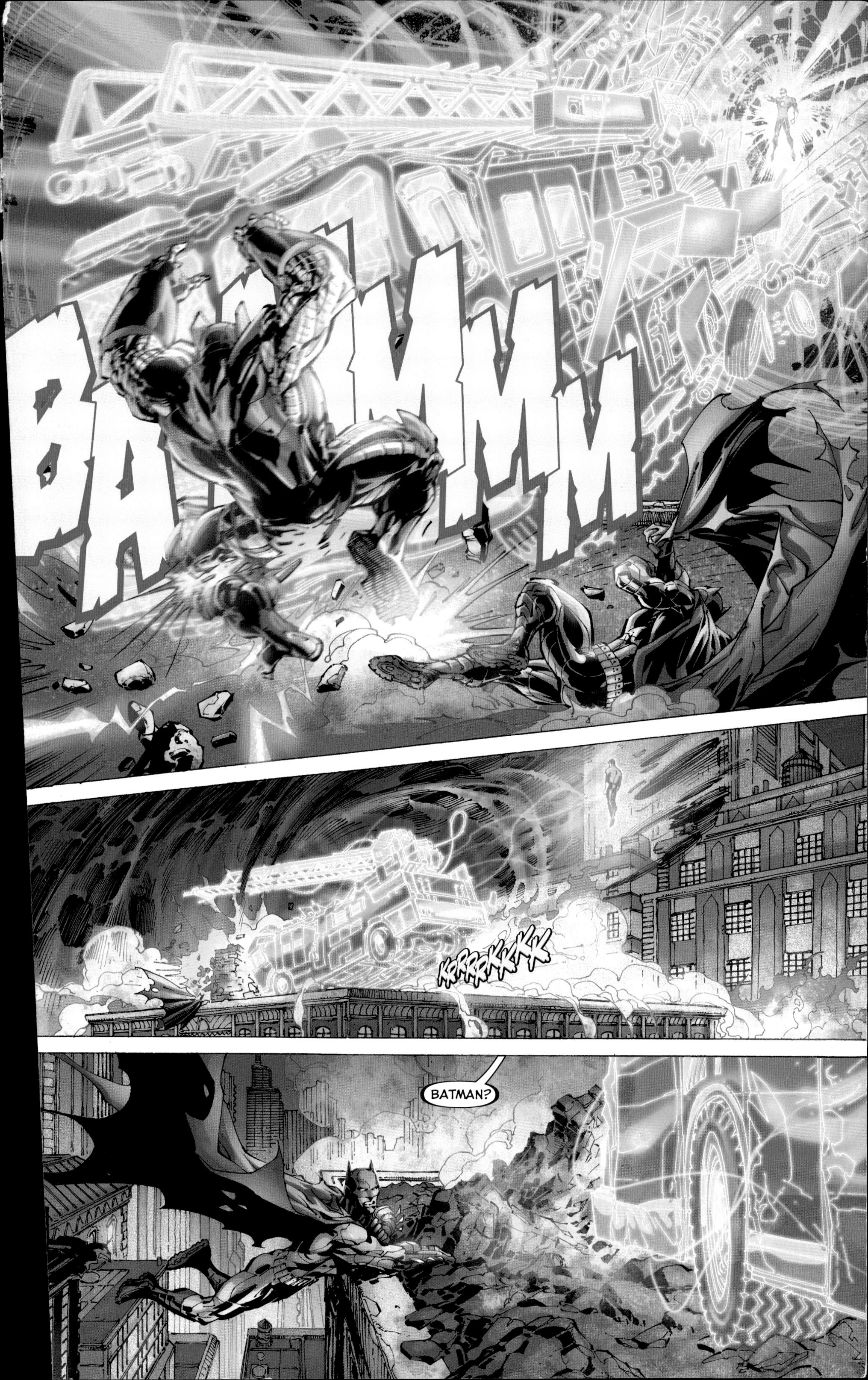
BAMMMM
KRRRRKKKK
BATMAN?

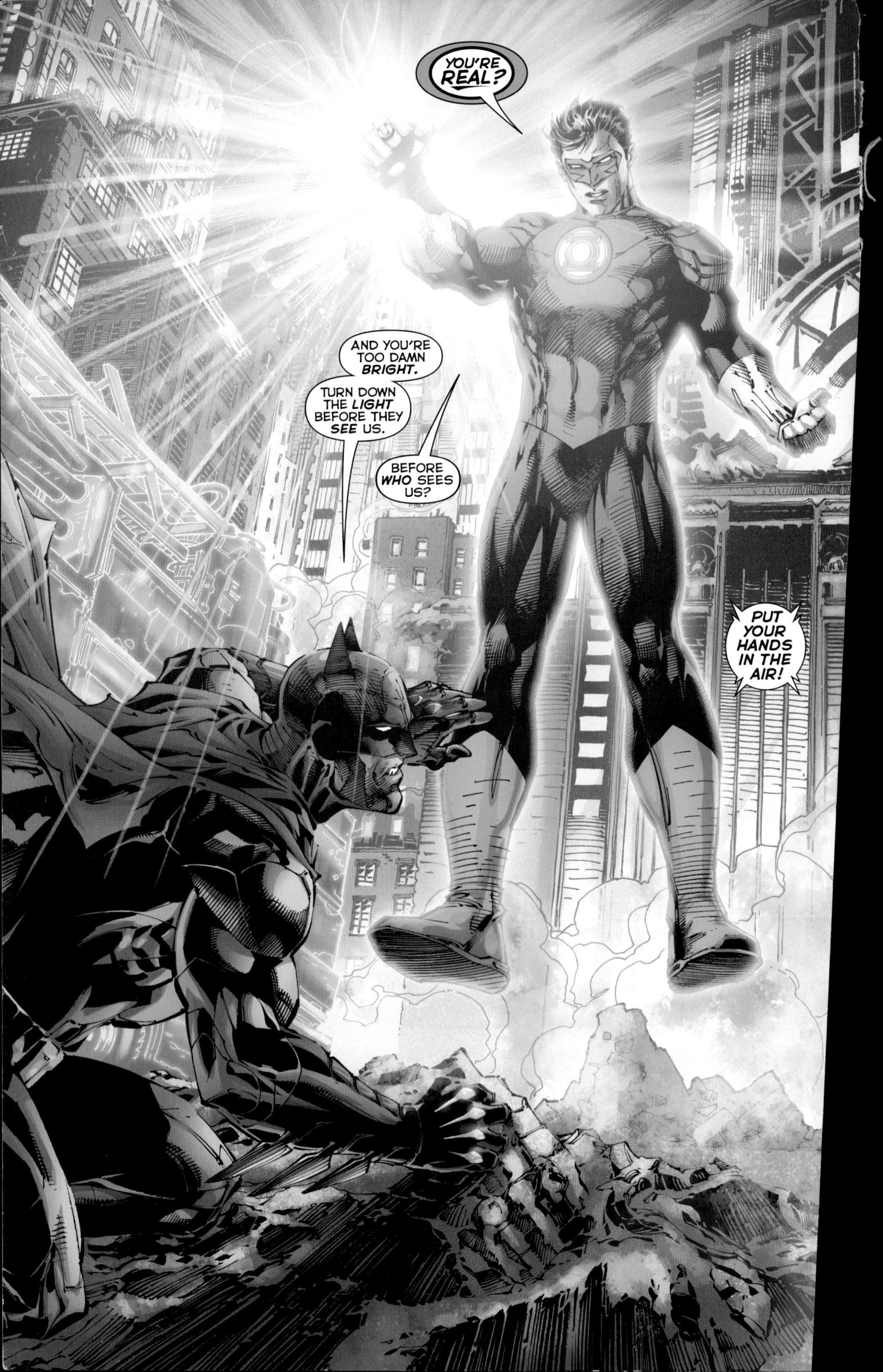
YOU'RE REAL?
AND YOU'RE TOO DAMN BRIGHT.
TURN DOWN THE LIGHT BEFORE THEY SEE US.
BEFORE WHO SEES US?
PUT YOUR HANDS IN THE AIR!

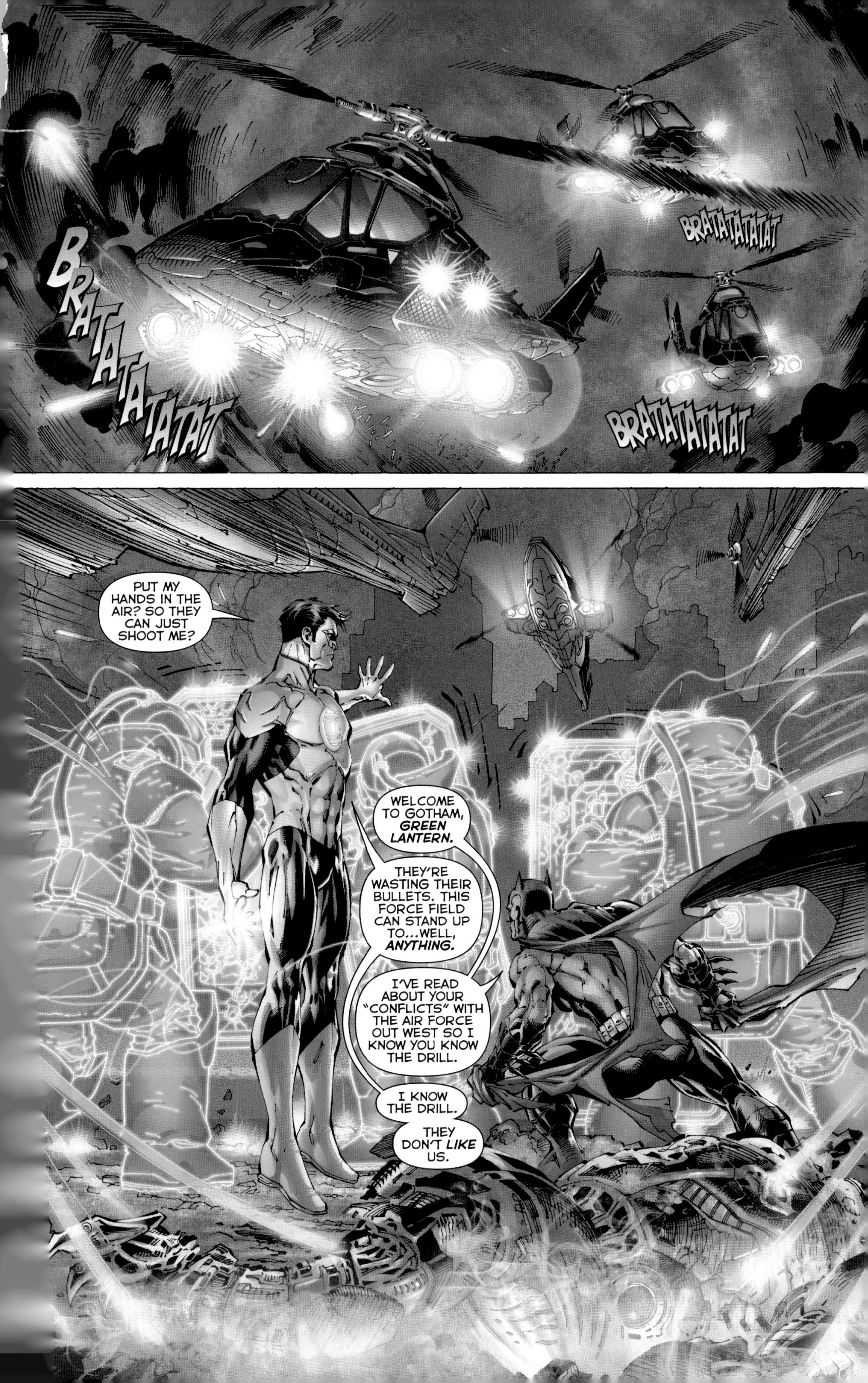
BRATATATATAT
BRATATATATAT
BRATATATATAT
PUT MY HANDS IN THE AIR? SO THEY CAN JUST SHOOT ME?
WELCOME TO GOTHAM, GREEN LANTERN.
THEY'RE WASTING THEIR BULLETS. THIS FORCE FIELD CAN STAND UP TO...WELL, ANYTHING.
I'VE READ ABOUT YOUR "CONFLICTS" WITH THE AIR FORCE OUT WEST SO I KNOW YOU KNOW THE DRILL.
I KNOW THE DRILL.
THEY DON'T LIKE US.

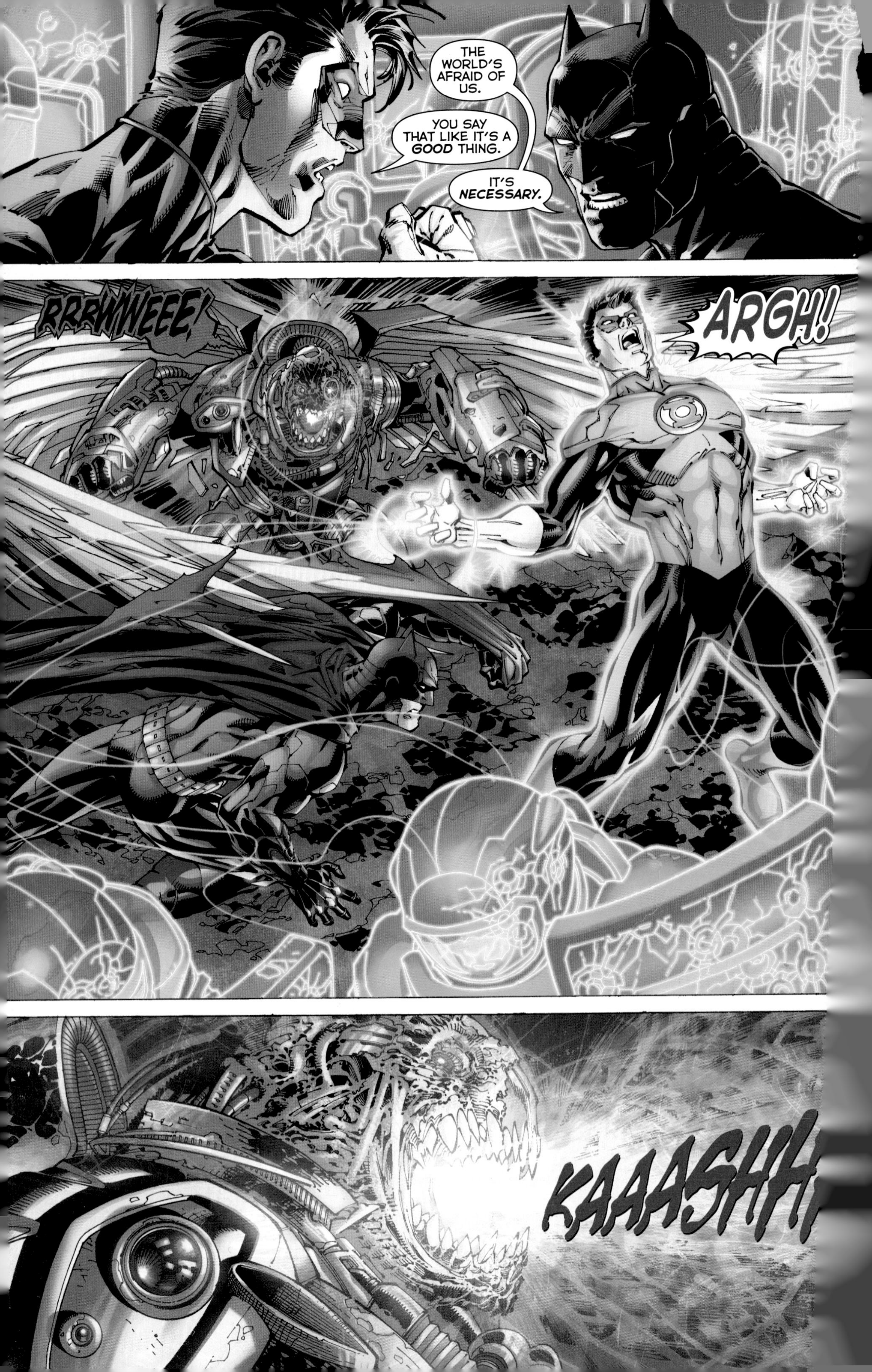
THE WORLD'S AFRAID OF US.
YOU SAY THAT LIKE IT'S A GOOD THING.
IT'S NECESSARY.
RRRWWEEE!
ARGH!
KAAASHH

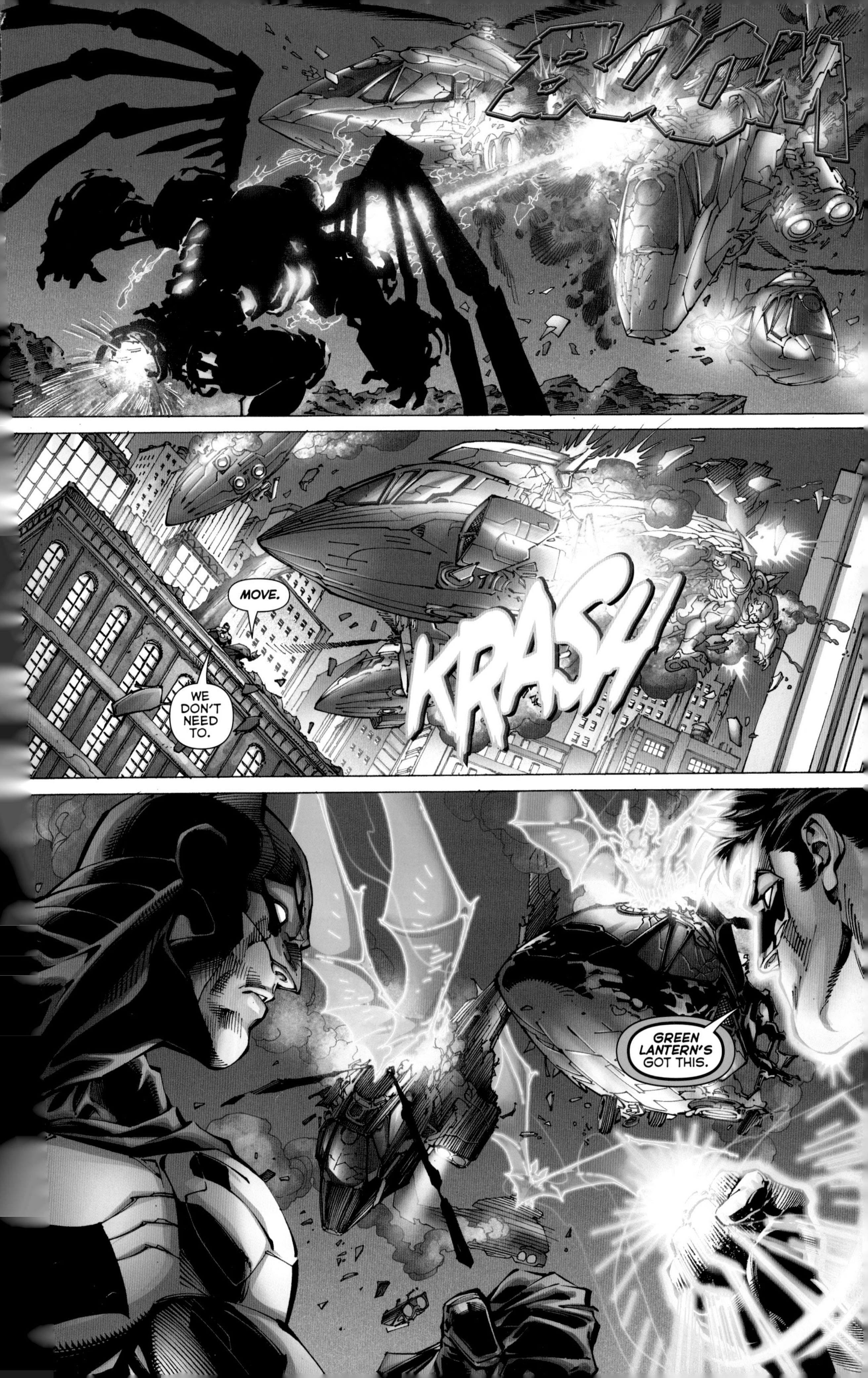

MOVE.
WE DON'T NEED TO.
KRASH
GREEN LANTERN'S GOT THIS.

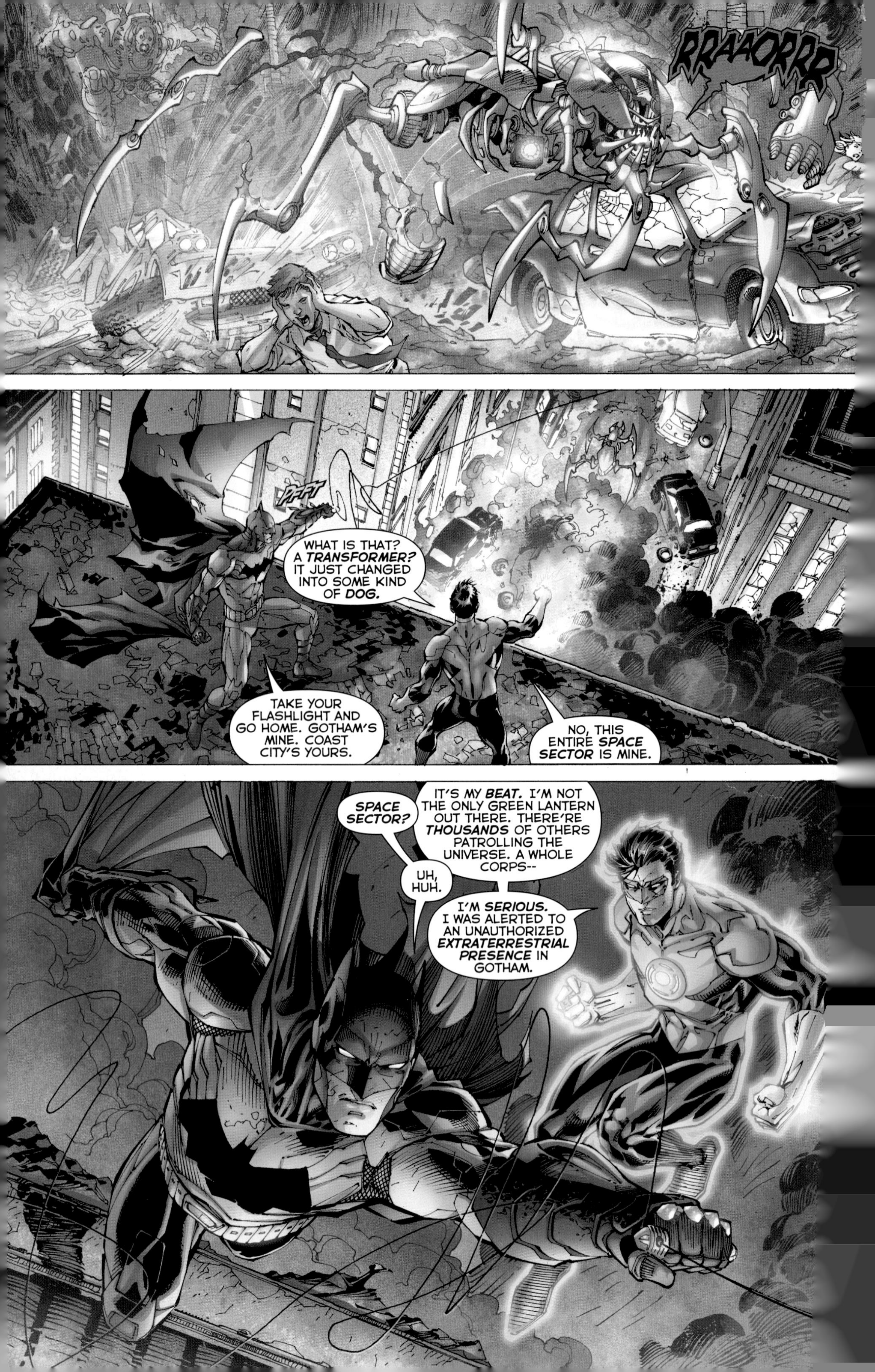
RRAAORRR
PFFT
WHAT IS THAT? A TRANSFORMER? IT JUST CHANGED INTO SOME KIND OF DOG.
TAKE YOUR FLASHLIGHT AND GO HOME. GOTHAM'S MINE. COAST CITY'S YOURS.
NO, THIS ENTIRE SPACE SECTOR IS MINE.
SPACE SECTOR?
IT'S MY BEAT. I'M NOT THE ONLY GREEN LANTERN OUT THERE. THERE'RE THOUSANDS OF OTHERS PATROLLING THE UNIVERSE. A WHOLE CORPS--
UH, HUH.
I'M SERIOUS. I WAS ALERTED TO AN UNAUTHORIZED EXTRATERRESTRIAL PRESENCE IN GOTHAM.

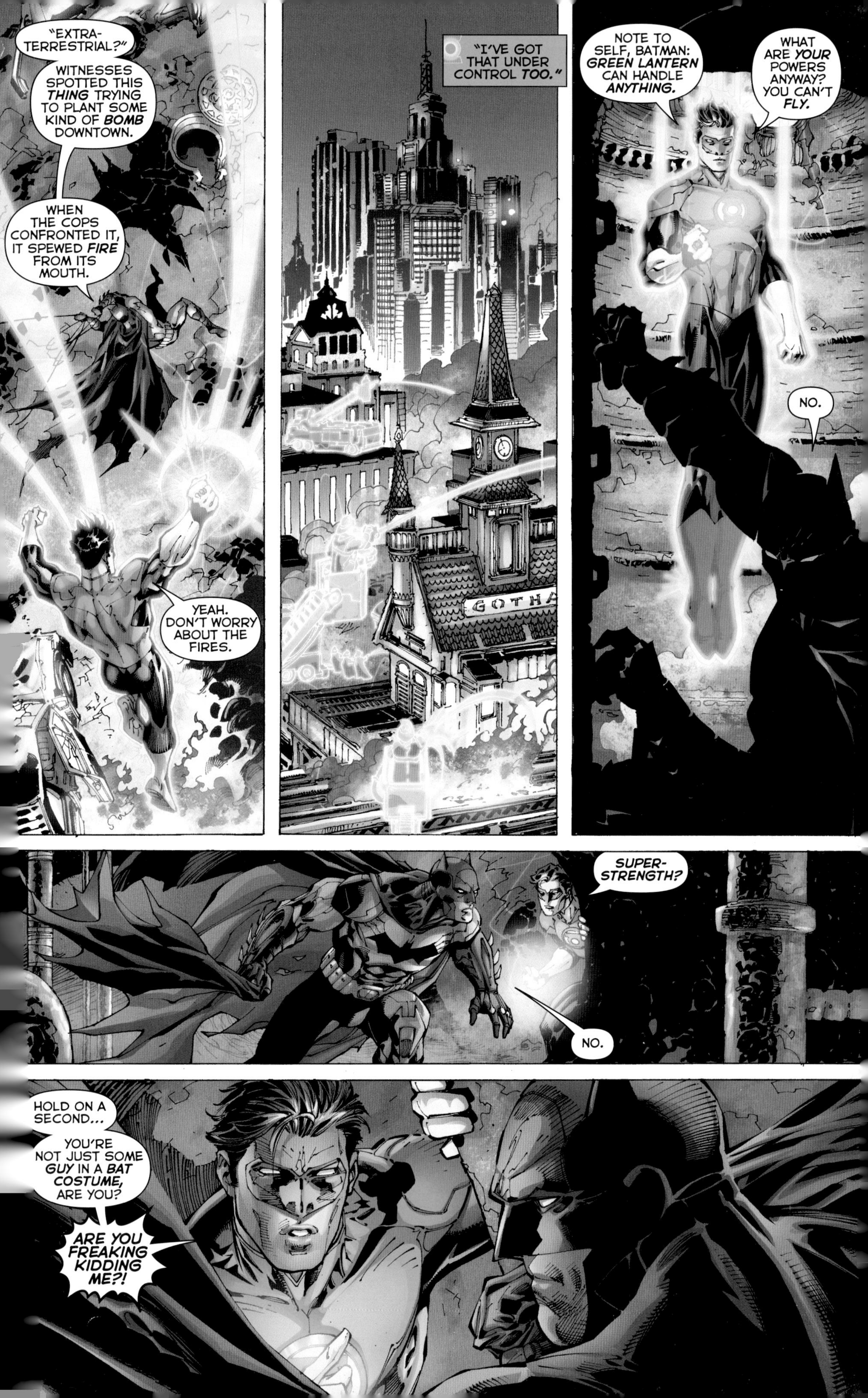
"EXTRA-TERRESTRIAL?"
WITNESSES SPOTTED THIS *THING* TRYING TO PLANT SOME KIND OF *BOMB* DOWNTOWN.
WHEN THE COPS CONFRONTED IT, IT SPEWED *FIRE* FROM ITS MOUTH.
YEAH. DON'T WORRY ABOUT THE FIRES.
"I'VE GOT THAT UNDER CONTROL *TOO.*"
GOTHA
NOTE TO SELF, BATMAN: *GREEN LANTERN* CAN HANDLE *ANYTHING.*
WHAT ARE *YOUR* POWERS ANYWAY? YOU CAN'T *FLY.*
NO.
SUPER-STRENGTH?
NO.
HOLD ON A SECOND...
YOU'RE NOT JUST SOME *GUY* IN A *BAT COSTUME,* ARE YOU?
ARE YOU FREAKING KIDDING ME?!

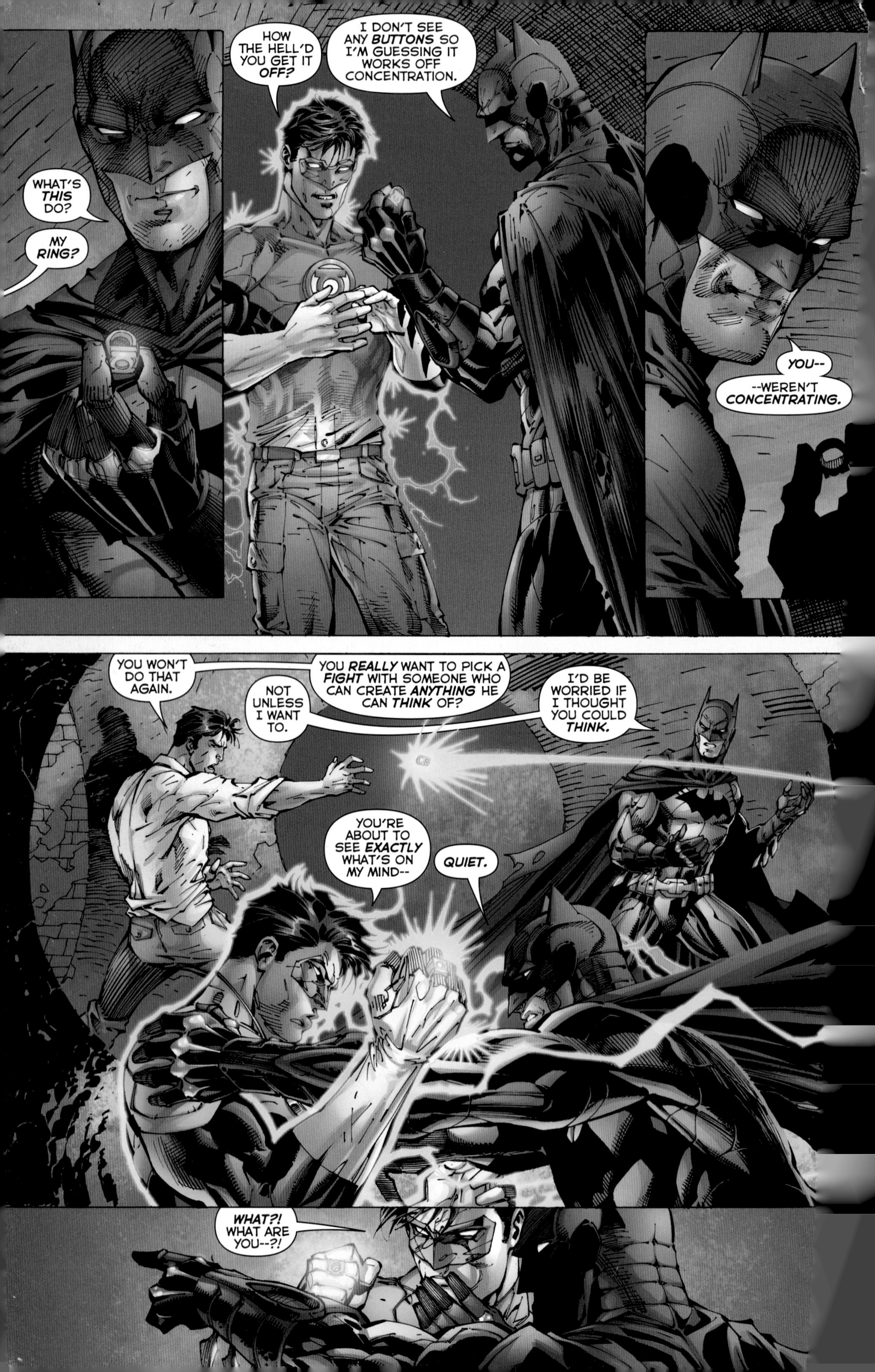
WHAT'S THIS DO?
MY RING?
HOW THE HELL'D YOU GET IT OFF?
I DON'T SEE ANY BUTTONS SO I'M GUESSING IT WORKS OFF CONCENTRATION.
YOU--
--WEREN'T CONCENTRATING.
YOU WON'T DO THAT AGAIN.
YOU REALLY WANT TO PICK A FIGHT WITH SOMEONE WHO CAN CREATE ANYTHING HE CAN THINK OF?
NOT UNLESS I WANT TO.
I'D BE WORRIED IF I THOUGHT YOU COULD THINK.
YOU'RE ABOUT TO SEE EXACTLY WHAT'S ON MY MIND--
QUIET.
WHAT?! WHAT ARE YOU--?!

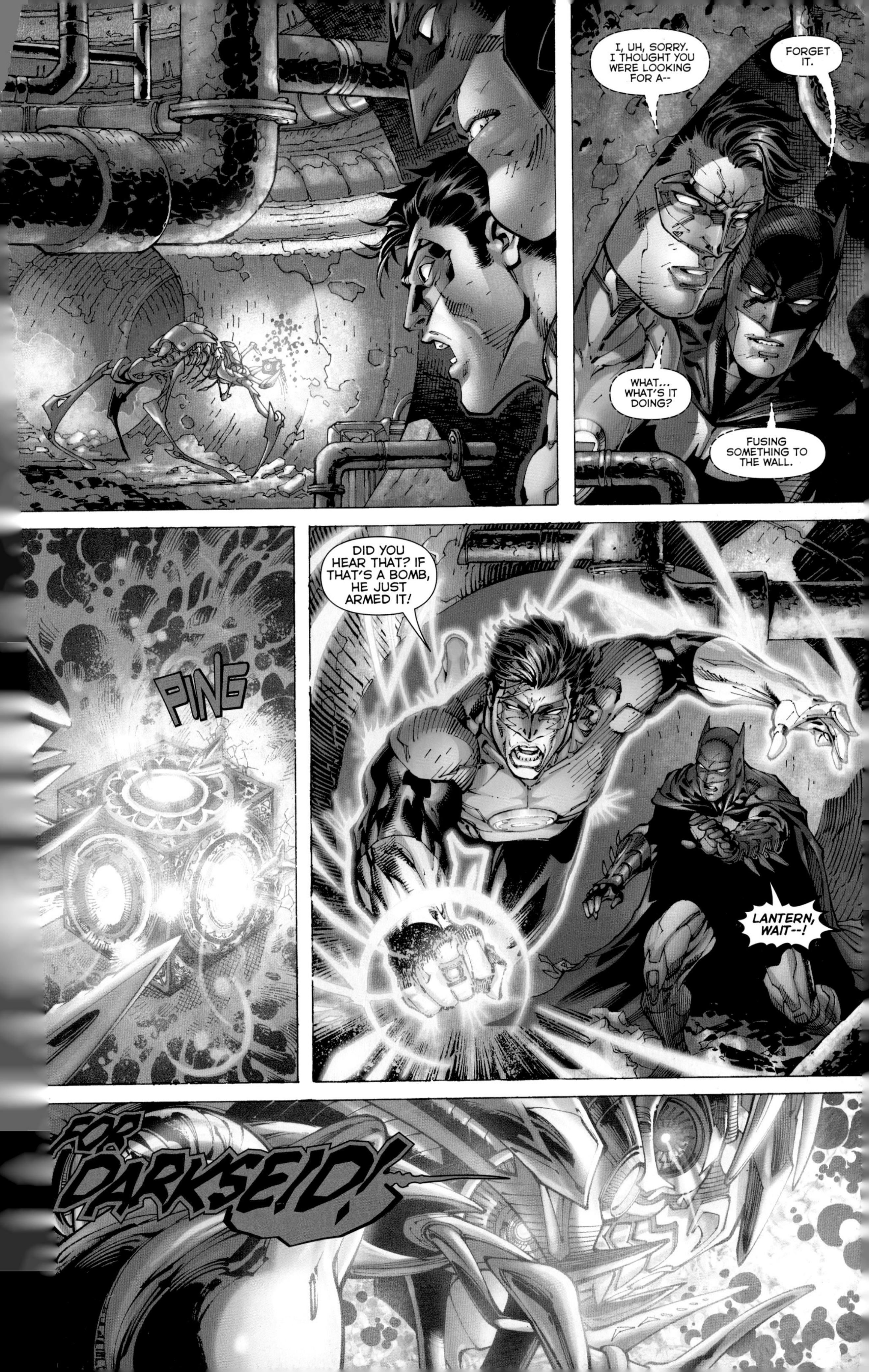
I, UH, SORRY. I THOUGHT YOU WERE LOOKING FOR A--
FORGET IT.
WHAT... WHAT'S IT DOING?
FUSING SOMETHING TO THE WALL.
PING
DID YOU HEAR THAT? IF THAT'S A BOMB, HE JUST ARMED IT!
LANTERN, WAIT--!
FOR DARKSEID!

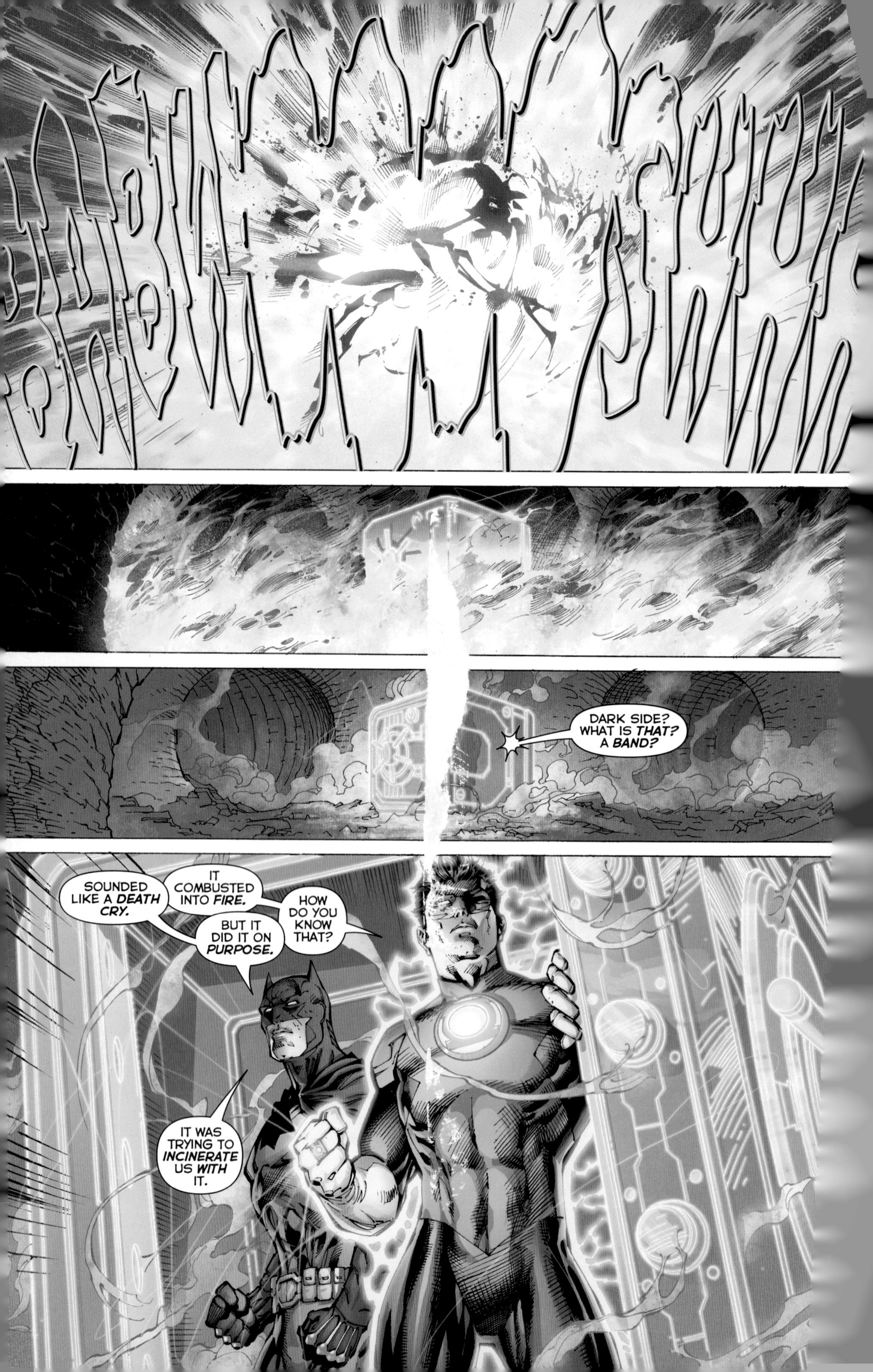
DARK SIDE? WHAT IS THAT? A BAND?
SOUNDED LIKE A DEATH CRY.
IT COMBUSTED INTO FIRE.
BUT IT DID IT ON PURPOSE.
HOW DO YOU KNOW THAT?
IT WAS TRYING TO INCINERATE US WITH IT.

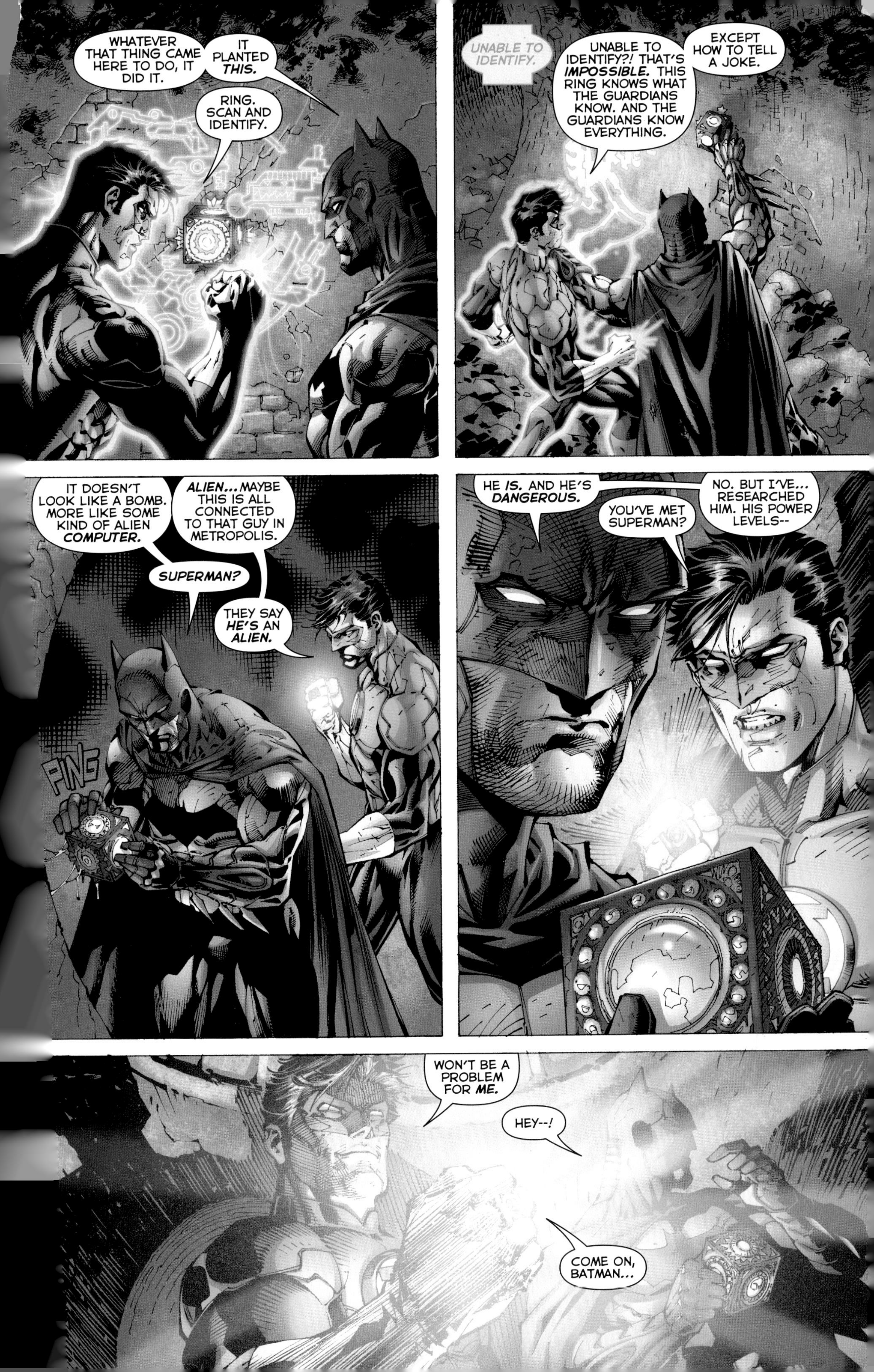
WHATEVER THAT THING CAME HERE TO DO, IT DID IT.
IT PLANTED THIS.
RING. SCAN AND IDENTIFY.
UNABLE TO IDENTIFY.
UNABLE TO IDENTIFY?! THAT'S IMPOSSIBLE. THIS RING KNOWS WHAT THE GUARDIANS KNOW. AND THE GUARDIANS KNOW EVERYTHING.
EXCEPT HOW TO TELL A JOKE.
IT DOESN'T LOOK LIKE A BOMB. MORE LIKE SOME KIND OF ALIEN COMPUTER.
ALIEN... MAYBE THIS IS ALL CONNECTED TO THAT GUY IN METROPOLIS.
SUPERMAN?
THEY SAY HE'S AN ALIEN.
PING
HE IS. AND HE'S DANGEROUS.
YOU'VE MET SUPERMAN?
NO. BUT I'VE... RESEARCHED HIM. HIS POWER LEVELS--
WON'T BE A PROBLEM FOR ME.
HEY--!
COME ON, BATMAN...

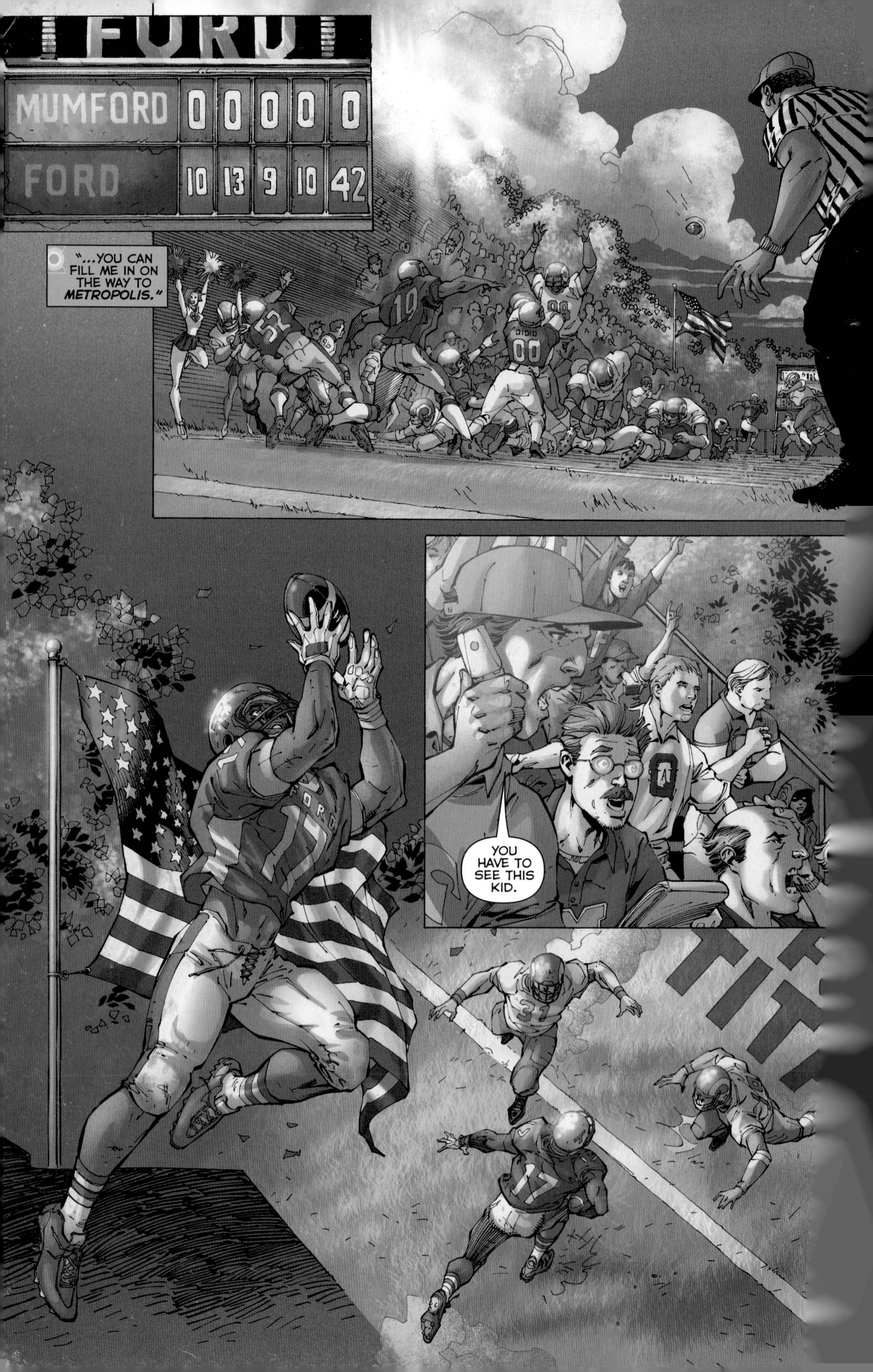
FORD
MUMFORD 0 0 0 0 0
FORD 10 13 9 10 42
"...YOU CAN FILL ME IN ON THE WAY TO METROPOLIS."
YOU HAVE TO SEE THIS KID.

NNFFF!!

TOUCHDOWN!

FORD 10 13 16 48

TIME 00:0

DAMN.

HE'S A TANK.

GET ME COACH CARROLL.

JUST FOUND OUR NEW RECEIVER.

WAY TO GO, VIC!

NEXT STOP: STATE FINALS!

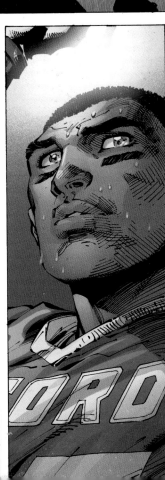

"THERE'S NOTHING VIC STONE LOVES MORE THAN FOOTBALL."

RESERVED

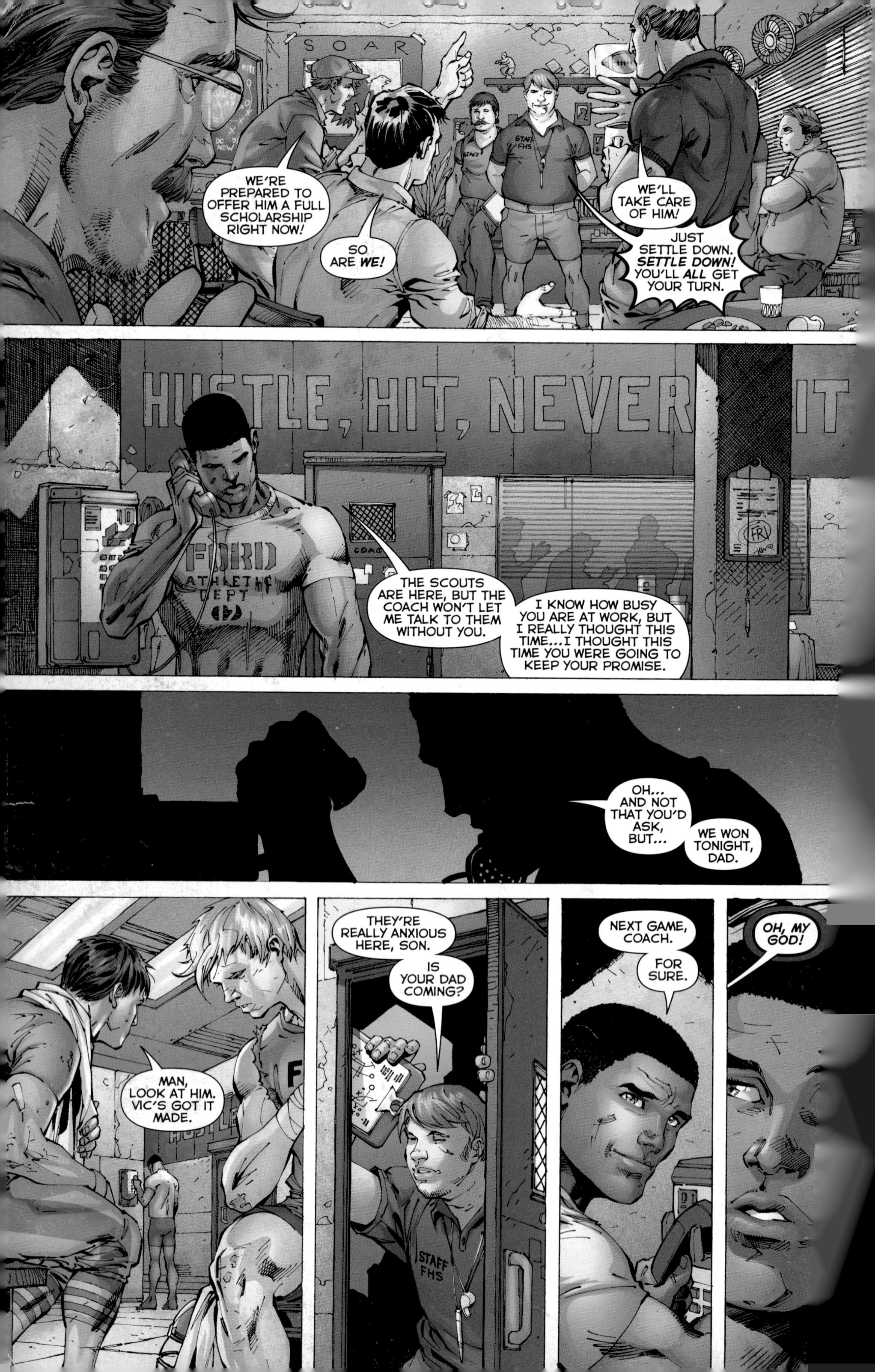

WE'RE PREPARED TO OFFER HIM A FULL SCHOLARSHIP RIGHT NOW!
SO ARE WE!
WE'LL TAKE CARE OF HIM!
JUST SETTLE DOWN. SETTLE DOWN! YOU'LL ALL GET YOUR TURN.
HUSTLE, HIT, NEVER
IT
FORD ATHLETIC DEPT
THE SCOUTS ARE HERE, BUT THE COACH WON'T LET ME TALK TO THEM WITHOUT YOU.
I KNOW HOW BUSY YOU ARE AT WORK, BUT I REALLY THOUGHT THIS TIME...I THOUGHT THIS TIME YOU WERE GOING TO KEEP YOUR PROMISE.
OH... AND NOT THAT YOU'D ASK, BUT...
WE WON TONIGHT, DAD.
MAN, LOOK AT HIM. VIC'S GOT IT MADE.
THEY'RE REALLY ANXIOUS HERE, SON.
IS YOUR DAD COMING?
STAFF FHS
NEXT GAME, COACH.
FOR SURE.
OH, MY GOD!

LOOK!

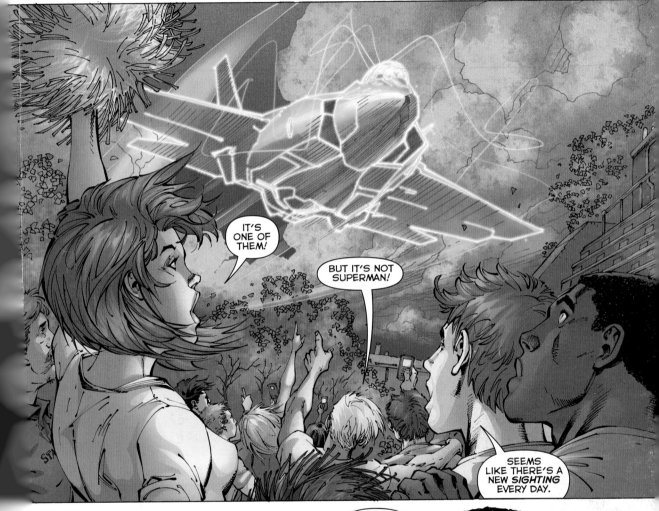

IT'S ONE OF THEM!

BUT IT'S NOT SUPERMAN!

SEEMS LIKE THERE'S A NEW *SIGHTING* EVERY DAY.

OUR DAD *STUDIES* THEM, DOESN'T HE, VIC?

KIND OF.

WHAT'S HE SAY ABOUT THEM? ABOUT *SUPER-HUMANS?*

HE DOESN'T TALK ABOUT THEM.

NOT TO ME.

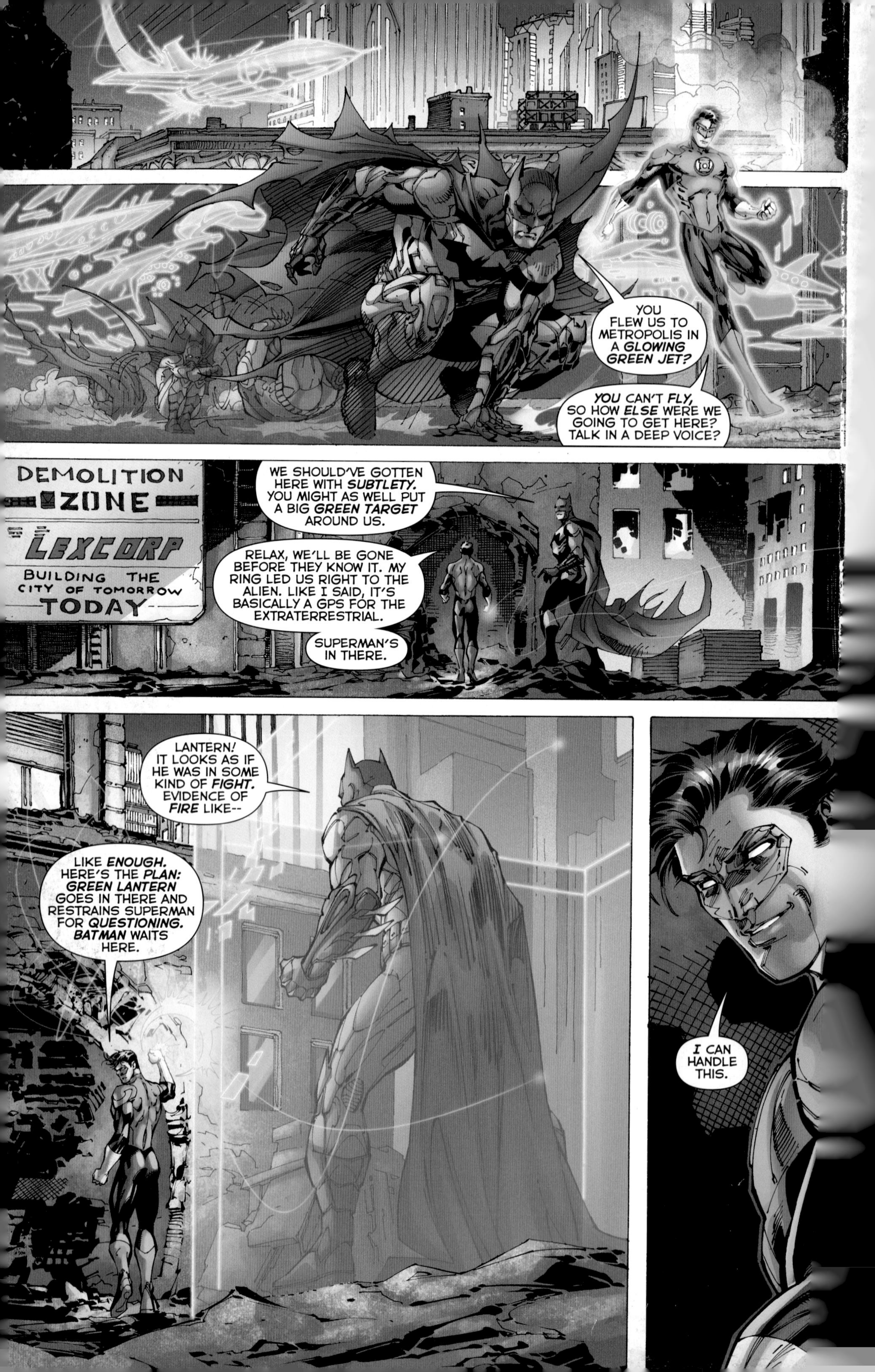
YOU FLEW US TO METROPOLIS IN A GLOWING GREEN JET?
YOU CAN'T FLY, SO HOW ELSE WERE WE GOING TO GET HERE? TALK IN A DEEP VOICE?
DEMOLITION ZONE
LEXCORP
BUILDING THE CITY OF TOMORROW TODAY
WE SHOULD'VE GOTTEN HERE WITH SUBTLETY. YOU MIGHT AS WELL PUT A BIG GREEN TARGET AROUND US.
RELAX, WE'LL BE GONE BEFORE THEY KNOW IT. MY RING LED US RIGHT TO THE ALIEN. LIKE I SAID, IT'S BASICALLY A GPS FOR THE EXTRATERRESTRIAL.
SUPERMAN'S IN THERE.
LANTERN! IT LOOKS AS IF HE WAS IN SOME KIND OF FIGHT. EVIDENCE OF FIRE LIKE--
LIKE ENOUGH. HERE'S THE PLAN: GREEN LANTERN GOES IN THERE AND RESTRAINS SUPERMAN FOR QUESTIONING. BATMAN WAITS HERE.
I CAN HANDLE THIS.

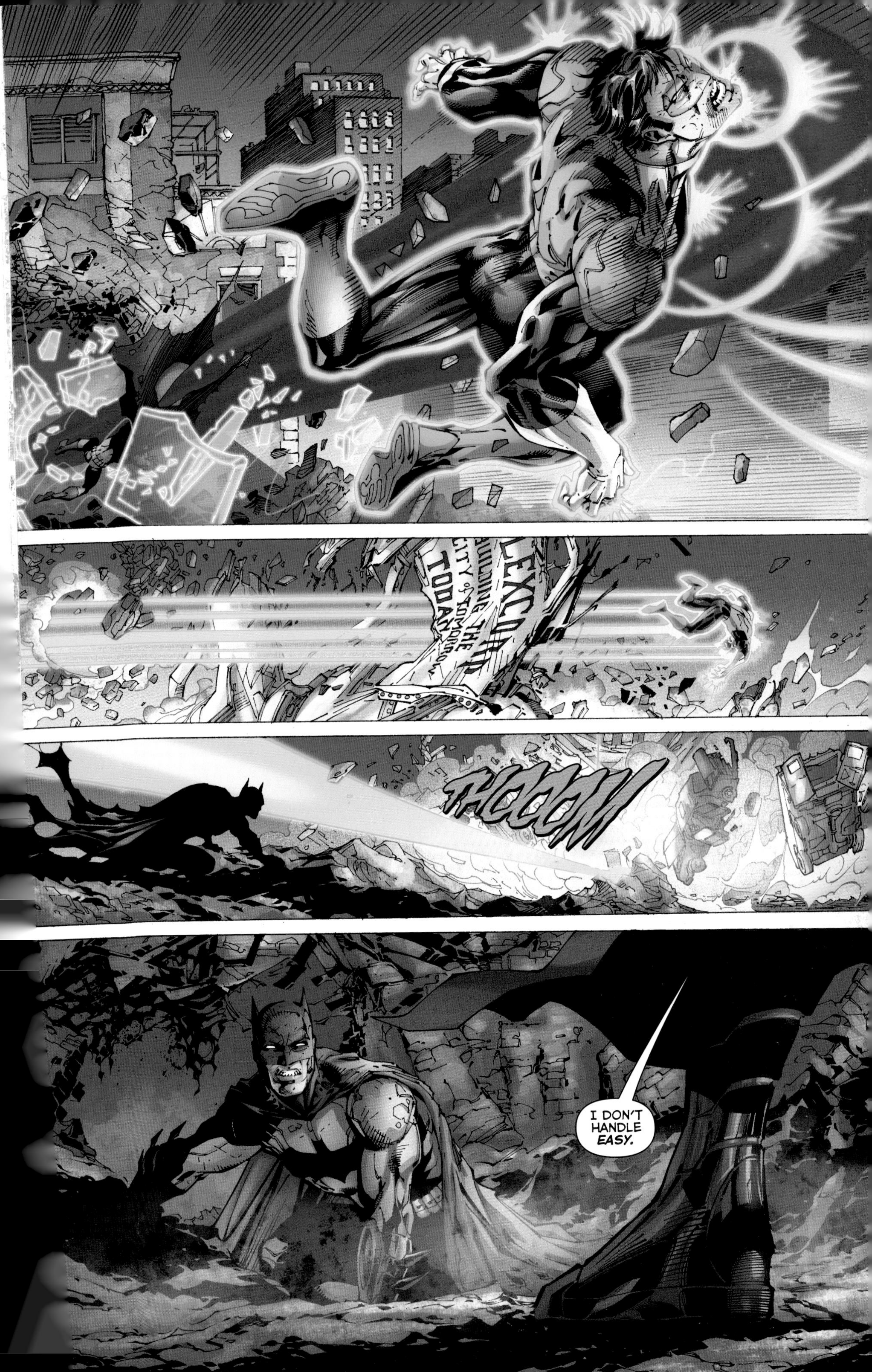
THOOOM
I DON'T HANDLE EASY.

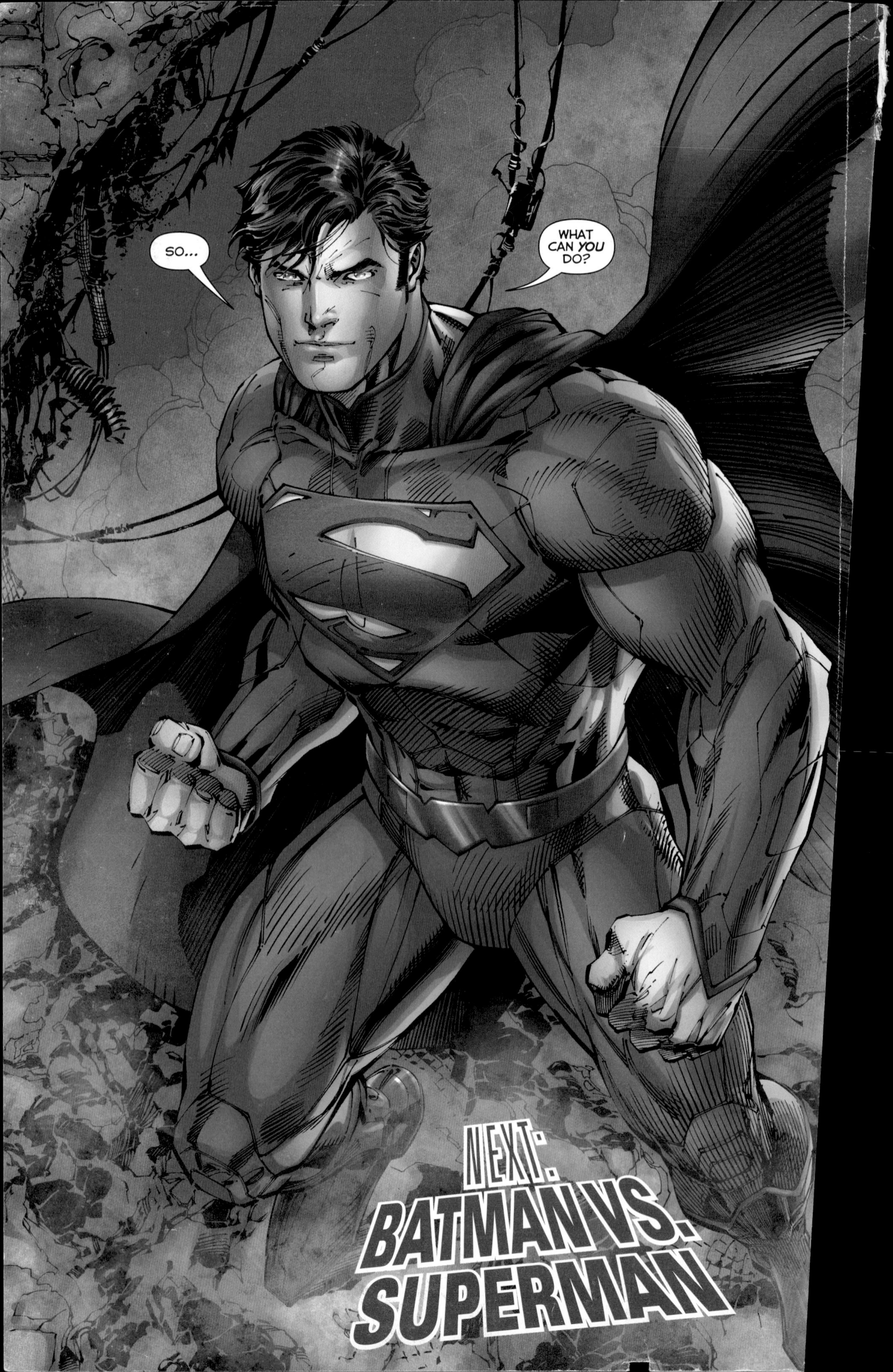
SO...
WHAT CAN YOU DO?
NEXT: BATMAN VS. SUPERMAN

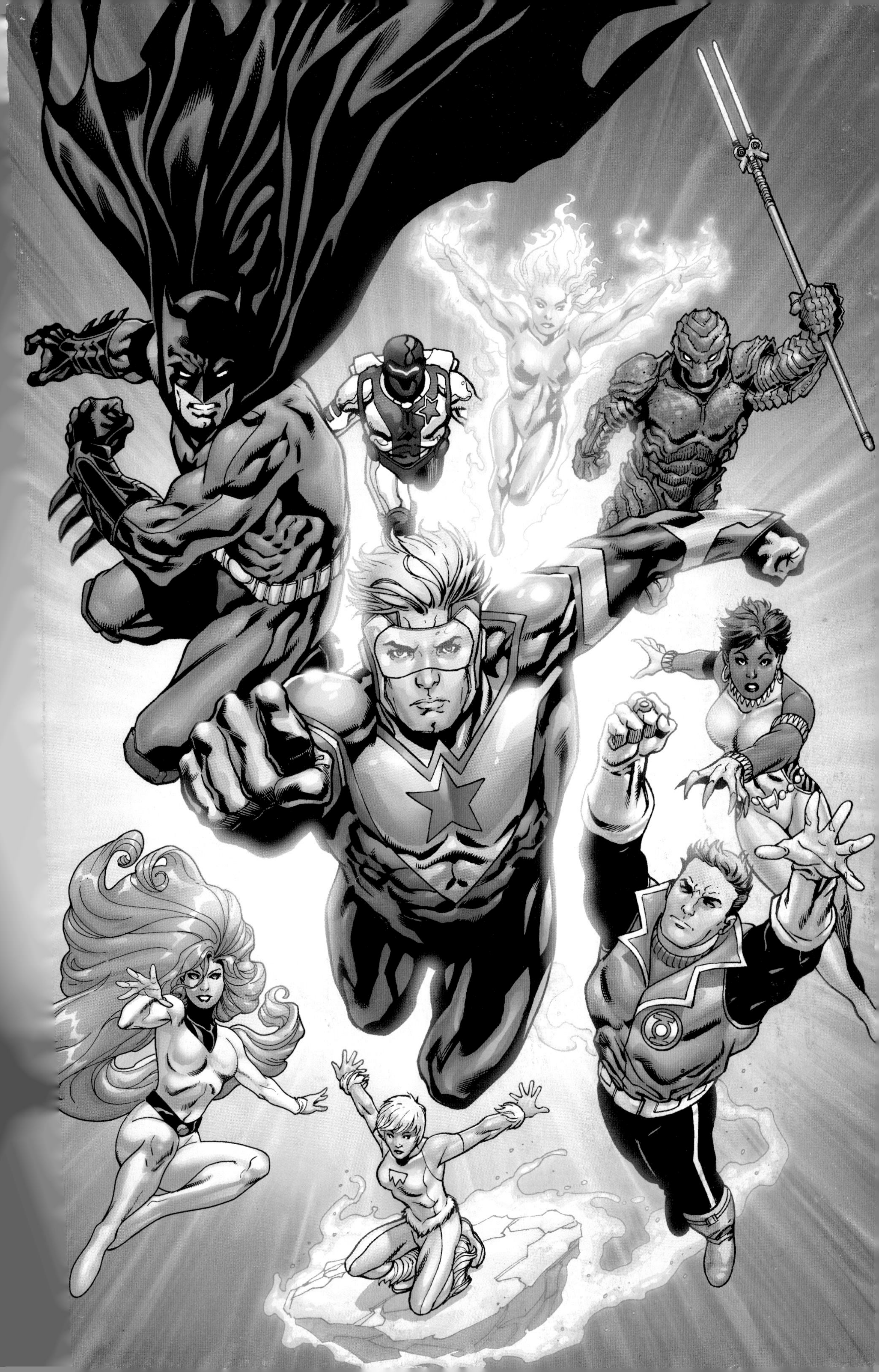

JUSTICE LEAGUE INTERNATIONAL

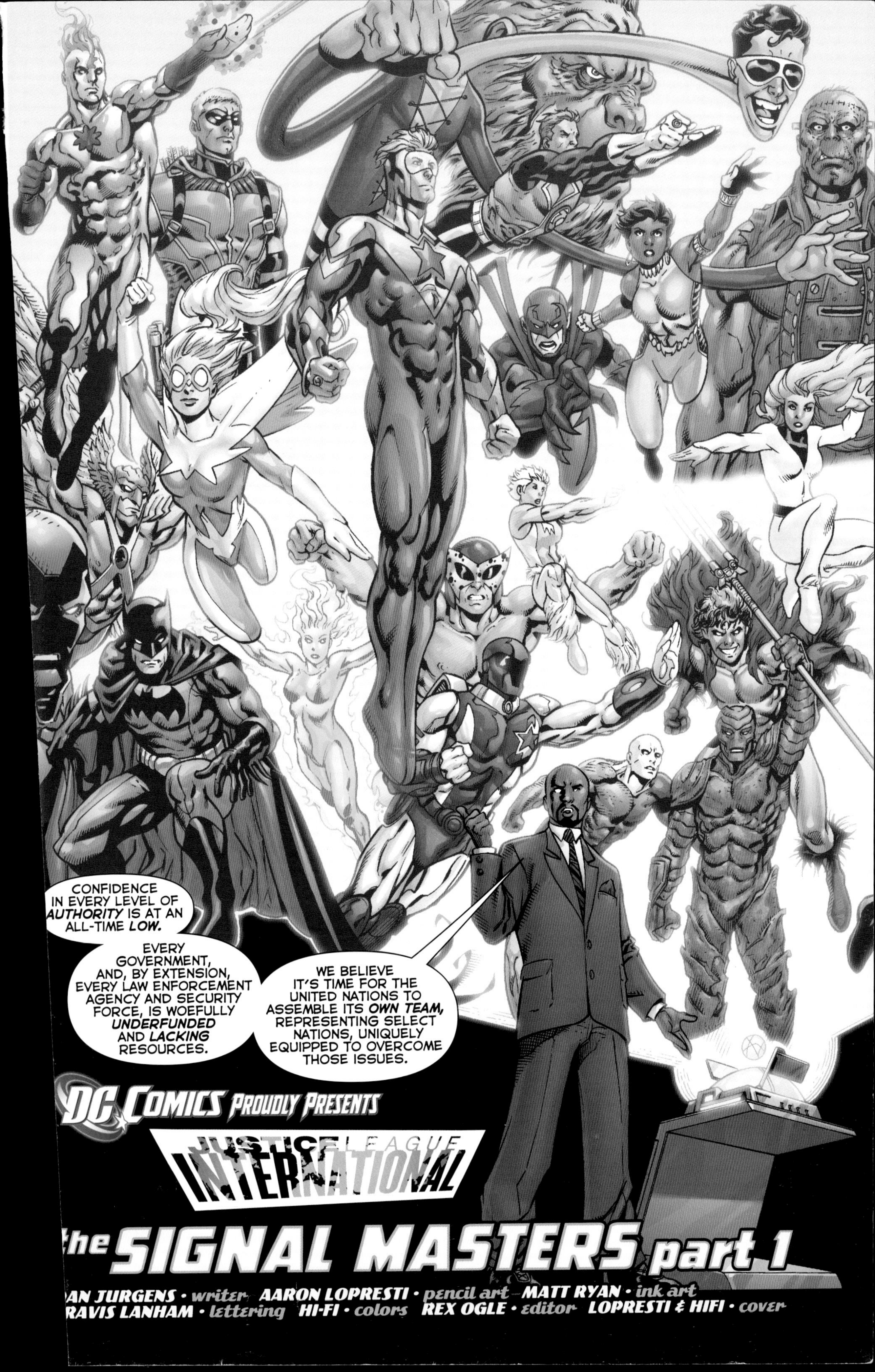

CONFIDENCE IN EVERY LEVEL OF AUTHORITY IS AT AN ALL-TIME LOW.
EVERY GOVERNMENT, AND, BY EXTENSION, EVERY LAW ENFORCEMENT AGENCY AND SECURITY FORCE, IS WOEFULLY UNDERFUNDED AND LACKING RESOURCES.
WE BELIEVE IT'S TIME FOR THE UNITED NATIONS TO ASSEMBLE ITS OWN TEAM, REPRESENTING SELECT NATIONS, UNIQUELY EQUIPPED TO OVERCOME THOSE ISSUES.
DC COMICS PROUDLY PRESENTS
JUSTICE LEAGUE INTERNATIONAL
the SIGNAL MASTERS part 1
AN JURGENS • writer AARON LOPRESTI • pencil art MATT RYAN • ink art
RAVIS LANHAM • lettering HI-FI • colors REX OGLE • editor LOPRESTI & HIFI • cover

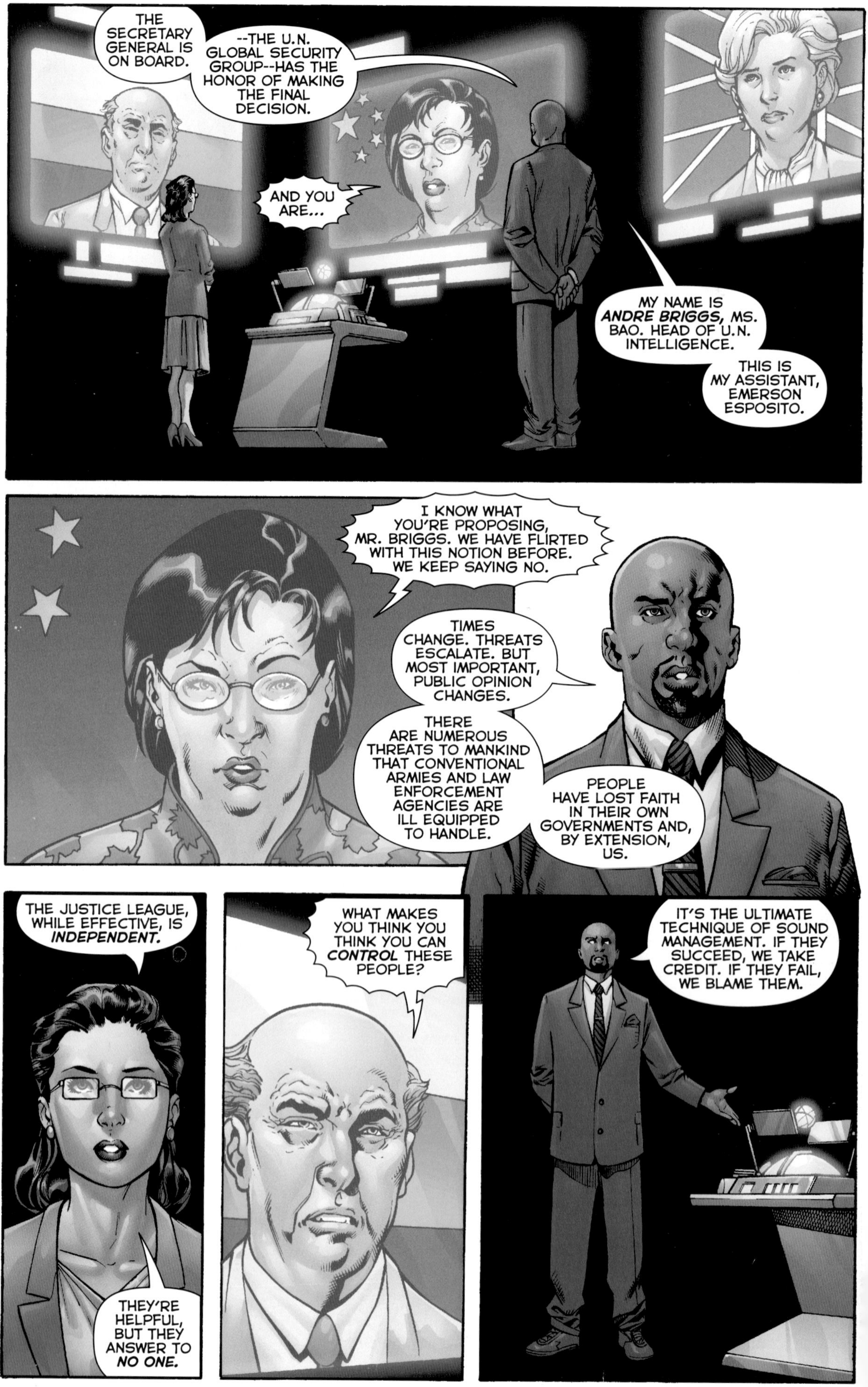
THE SECRETARY GENERAL IS ON BOARD.
--THE U.N. GLOBAL SECURITY GROUP--HAS THE HONOR OF MAKING THE FINAL DECISION.
AND YOU ARE...
MY NAME IS **ANDRE BRIGGS,** MS. BAO. HEAD OF U.N. INTELLIGENCE.
THIS IS MY ASSISTANT, EMERSON ESPOSITO.
I KNOW WHAT YOU'RE PROPOSING, MR. BRIGGS. WE HAVE FLIRTED WITH THIS NOTION BEFORE. WE KEEP SAYING NO.
TIMES CHANGE. THREATS ESCALATE. BUT MOST IMPORTANT, PUBLIC OPINION CHANGES.
THERE ARE NUMEROUS THREATS TO MANKIND THAT CONVENTIONAL ARMIES AND LAW ENFORCEMENT AGENCIES ARE ILL EQUIPPED TO HANDLE.
PEOPLE HAVE LOST FAITH IN THEIR OWN GOVERNMENTS AND, BY EXTENSION, US.
THE JUSTICE LEAGUE, WHILE EFFECTIVE, IS ***INDEPENDENT.***
THEY'RE HELPFUL, BUT THEY ANSWER TO ***NO ONE.***
WHAT MAKES YOU THINK YOU THINK YOU CAN ***CONTROL*** THESE PEOPLE?
IT'S THE ULTIMATE TECHNIQUE OF SOUND MANAGEMENT. IF THEY SUCCEED, WE TAKE CREDIT. IF THEY FAIL, WE BLAME THEM.

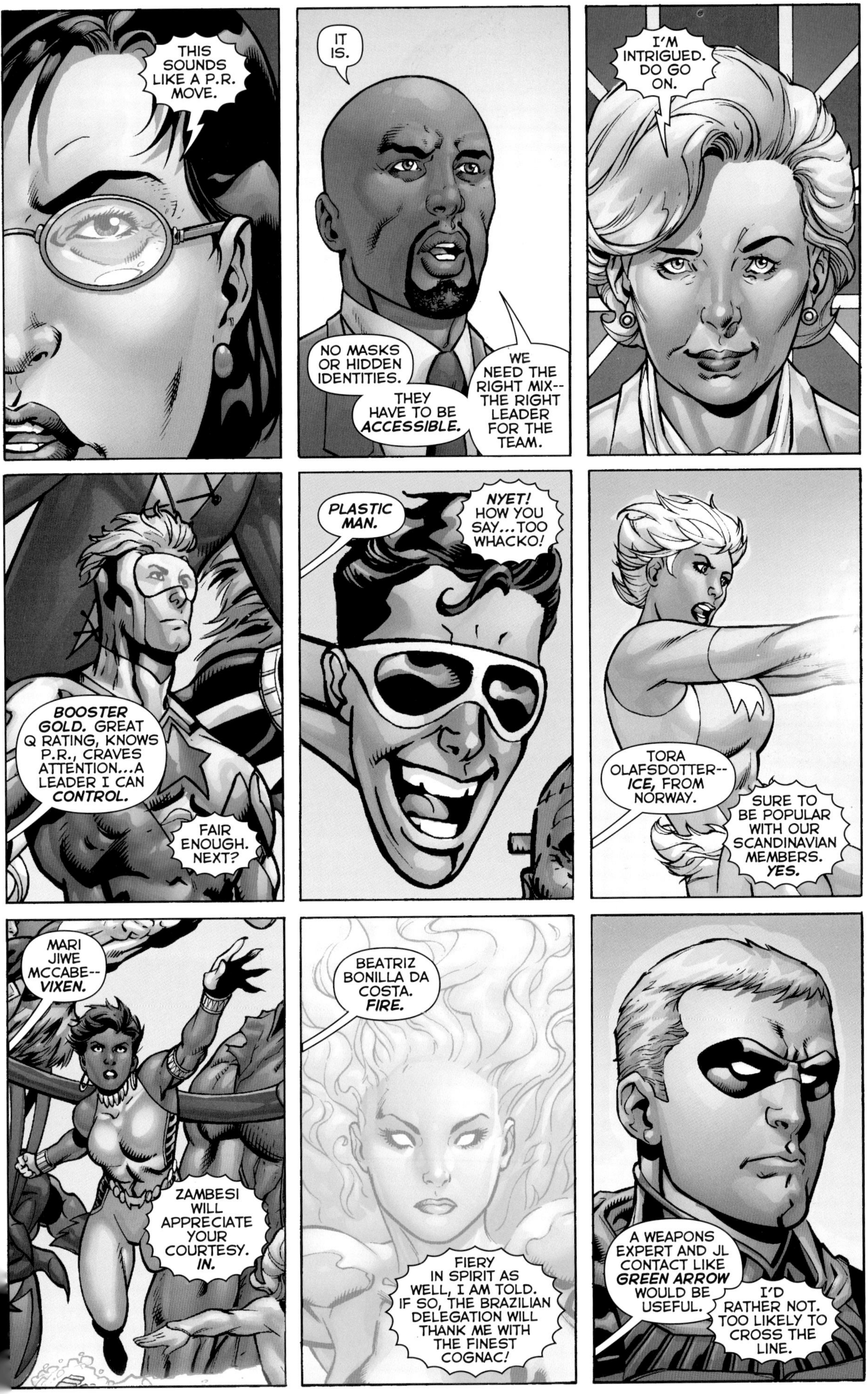
THIS SOUNDS LIKE A P.R. MOVE.
IT IS.
NO MASKS OR HIDDEN IDENTITIES.
THEY HAVE TO BE *ACCESSIBLE.*
WE NEED THE RIGHT MIX-- THE RIGHT LEADER FOR THE TEAM.
I'M INTRIGUED. DO GO ON.
BOOSTER GOLD. GREAT Q RATING, KNOWS P.R., CRAVES ATTENTION...A LEADER I CAN *CONTROL.*
FAIR ENOUGH. NEXT?
PLASTIC MAN.
NYET! HOW YOU SAY...TOO WHACKO!
TORA OLAFSDOTTER-- *ICE,* FROM NORWAY.
SURE TO BE POPULAR WITH OUR SCANDINAVIAN MEMBERS. *YES.*
MARI JIWE MCCABE-- *VIXEN.*
ZAMBESI WILL APPRECIATE YOUR COURTESY. *IN.*
BEATRIZ BONILLA DA COSTA. *FIRE.*
FIERY IN SPIRIT AS WELL, I AM TOLD. IF SO, THE BRAZILIAN DELEGATION WILL THANK ME WITH THE FINEST COGNAC!
A WEAPONS EXPERT AND JL CONTACT LIKE *GREEN ARROW* WOULD BE USEFUL.
I'D RATHER NOT. TOO LIKELY TO CROSS THE LINE.

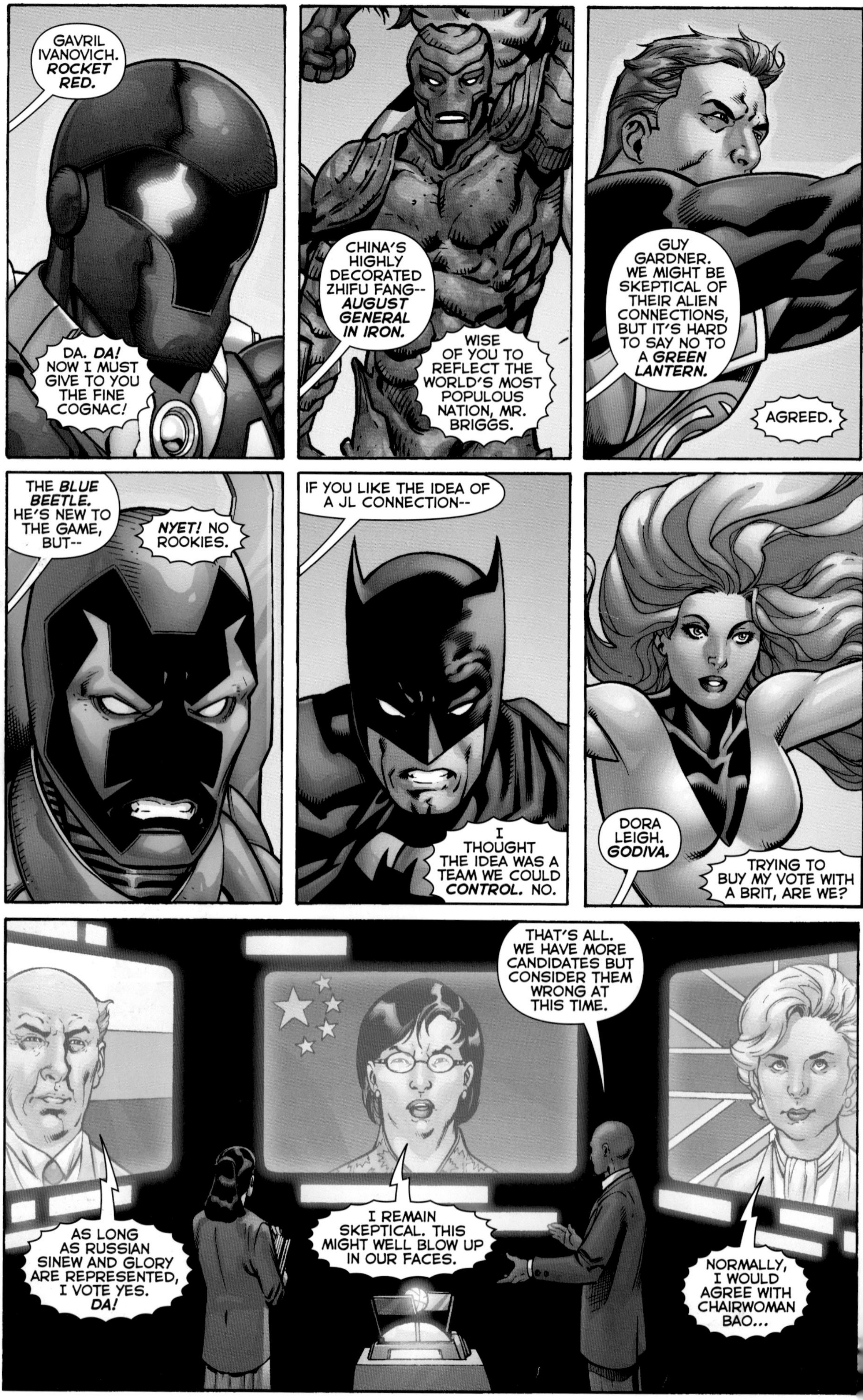
GAVRIL IVANOVICH. ROCKET RED.
DA. DA! NOW I MUST GIVE TO YOU THE FINE COGNAC!
CHINA'S HIGHLY DECORATED ZHIFU FANG-- AUGUST GENERAL IN IRON.
WISE OF YOU TO REFLECT THE WORLD'S MOST POPULOUS NATION, MR. BRIGGS.
GUY GARDNER. WE MIGHT BE SKEPTICAL OF THEIR ALIEN CONNECTIONS, BUT IT'S HARD TO SAY NO TO A GREEN LANTERN.
AGREED.
THE BLUE BEETLE. HE'S NEW TO THE GAME, BUT--
NYET! NO ROOKIES.
IF YOU LIKE THE IDEA OF A JL CONNECTION--
I THOUGHT THE IDEA WAS A TEAM WE COULD CONTROL. NO.
DORA LEIGH. GODIVA.
TRYING TO BUY MY VOTE WITH A BRIT, ARE WE?
THAT'S ALL. WE HAVE MORE CANDIDATES BUT CONSIDER THEM WRONG AT THIS TIME.
AS LONG AS RUSSIAN SINEW AND GLORY ARE REPRESENTED, I VOTE YES. DA!
I REMAIN SKEPTICAL. THIS MIGHT WELL BLOW UP IN OUR FACES.
NORMALLY, I WOULD AGREE WITH CHAIRWOMAN BAO...

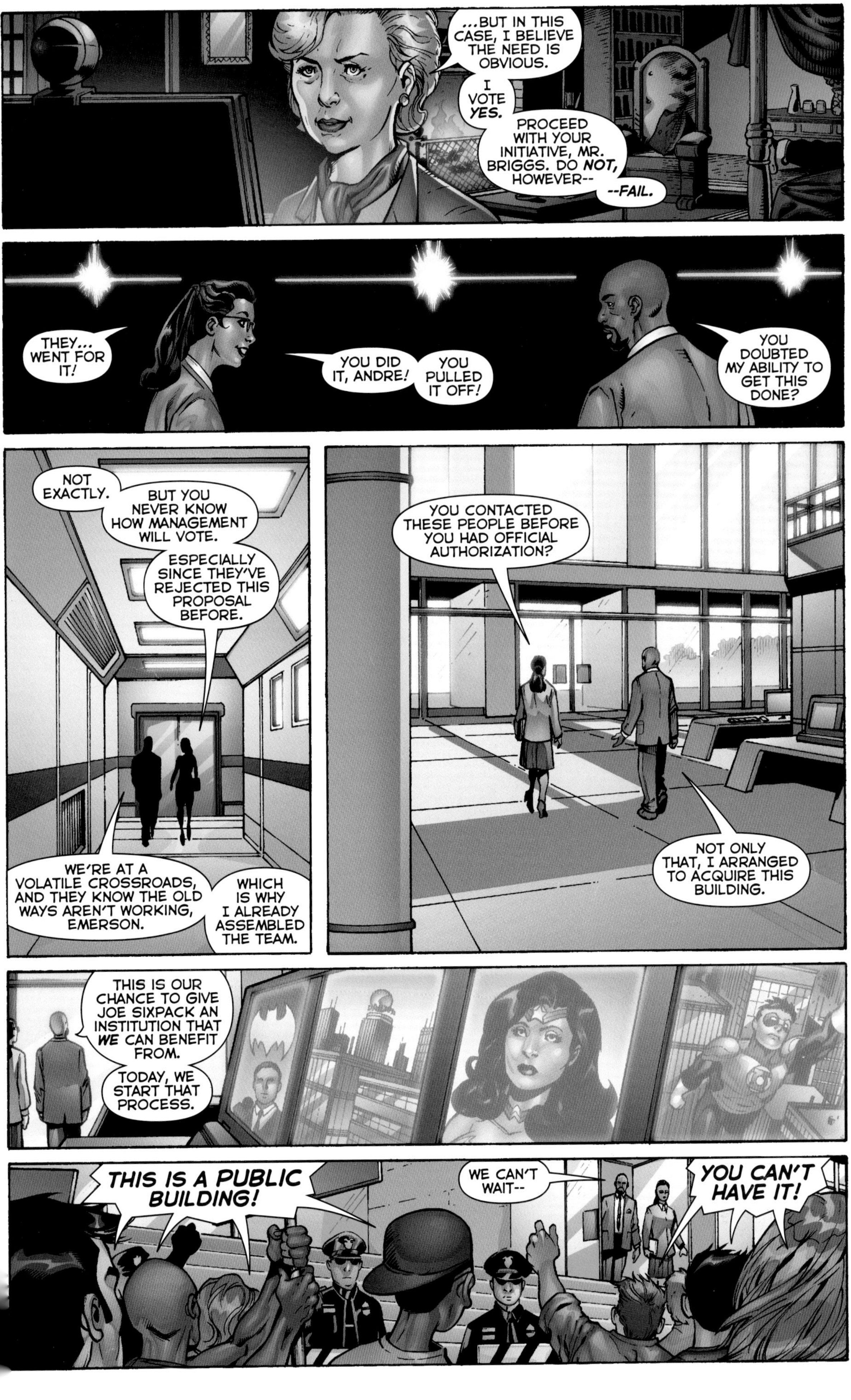
...BUT IN THIS CASE, I BELIEVE THE NEED IS OBVIOUS.
I VOTE *YES.*
PROCEED WITH YOUR INITIATIVE, MR. BRIGGS. DO *NOT,* HOWEVER--
--FAIL.
THEY... WENT FOR IT!
YOU DID IT, ANDRE!
YOU PULLED IT OFF!
YOU DOUBTED MY ABILITY TO GET THIS DONE?
NOT EXACTLY.
BUT YOU NEVER KNOW HOW MANAGEMENT WILL VOTE.
ESPECIALLY SINCE THEY'VE REJECTED THIS PROPOSAL BEFORE.
WE'RE AT A VOLATILE CROSSROADS, AND THEY KNOW THE OLD WAYS AREN'T WORKING, EMERSON.
WHICH IS WHY I ALREADY ASSEMBLED THE TEAM.
YOU CONTACTED THESE PEOPLE BEFORE YOU HAD OFFICIAL AUTHORIZATION?
NOT ONLY THAT, I ARRANGED TO ACQUIRE THIS BUILDING.
THIS IS OUR CHANCE TO GIVE JOE SIXPACK AN INSTITUTION THAT *WE* CAN BENEFIT FROM.
TODAY, WE START THAT PROCESS.
THIS IS A PUBLIC BUILDING!
WE CAN'T WAIT--
YOU CAN'T HAVE IT!

"--FOR SOMETHING REALLY BAD TO HAPPEN."

PERU.

UNITED NATIONS RESEARCH TEAM THREE.

OKAY. EVERYTHING'S SET.

LET'S SEE WHAT WE'RE DEALING WITH.

SEISMIC READINGS HAVE RETURNED TO NORMAL, RACHEL. LIKE NOTHING EVER HAPPENED.

ODD, GIVEN THE HIGH ACTIVITY HERE.

HERE AND THREE OTHER AREAS AROUND THE WORLD--ALL SIMULTANEOUSLY ACTIVE.

NOW THAT OUR TEAMS ARE ON THE GROUND WE SHOULD BE ABLE TO TRACK--

WAIT! I'M GETTING SOMETHING!

ACTIVITY IS BUILDING FAST!

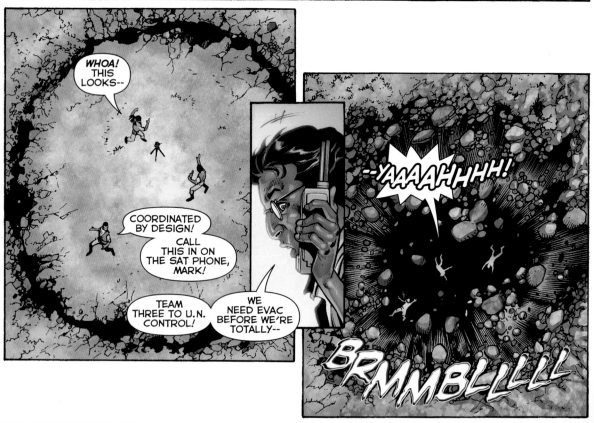

WHOA! THIS LOOKS--

COORDINATED BY DESIGN! CALL THIS IN ON THE SAT PHONE, MARK!

TEAM THREE TO U.N. CONTROL!

WE NEED EVAC BEFORE WE'RE TOTALLY--

--YAAAAHHHH!

BRMMBLLLL

TEAM THREE? ARE YOU THERE?

ARE YOU THERE, TEAM THREE?

HELLO?

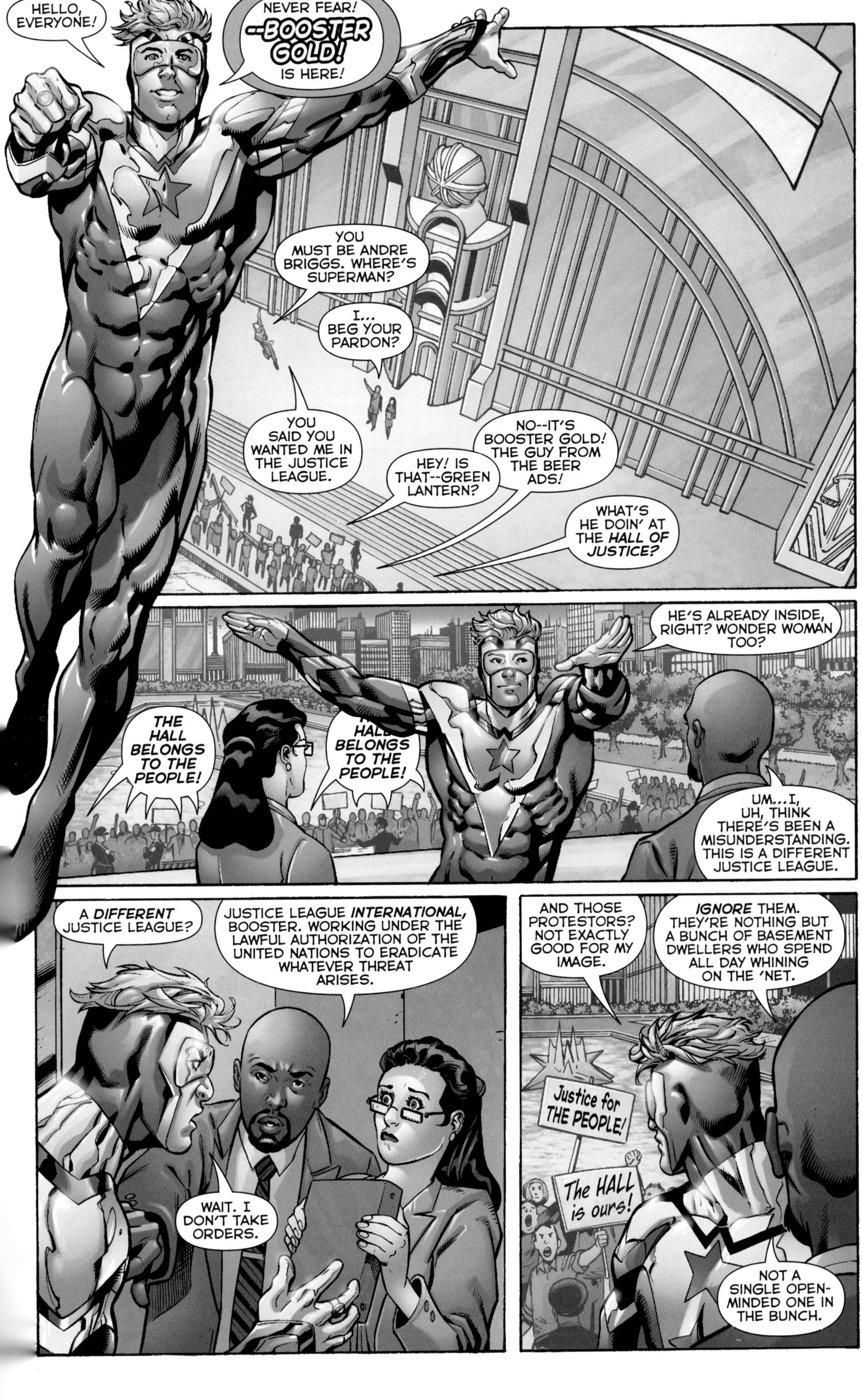

HELLO, EVERYONE!
NEVER FEAR! --BOOSTER GOLD! IS HERE!
YOU MUST BE ANDRE BRIGGS. WHERE'S SUPERMAN?
I... BEG YOUR PARDON?
YOU SAID YOU WANTED ME IN THE JUSTICE LEAGUE.
HEY! IS THAT--GREEN LANTERN?
NO--IT'S BOOSTER GOLD! THE GUY FROM THE BEER ADS!
WHAT'S HE DOIN' AT THE HALL OF JUSTICE?
HE'S ALREADY INSIDE, RIGHT? WONDER WOMAN TOO?
THE HALL BELONGS TO THE PEOPLE!
UM...I, UH, THINK THERE'S BEEN A MISUNDERSTANDING. THIS IS A DIFFERENT JUSTICE LEAGUE.
A DIFFERENT JUSTICE LEAGUE?
JUSTICE LEAGUE INTERNATIONAL, BOOSTER. WORKING UNDER THE LAWFUL AUTHORIZATION OF THE UNITED NATIONS TO ERADICATE WHATEVER THREAT ARISES.
WAIT. I DON'T TAKE ORDERS.
AND THOSE PROTESTORS? NOT EXACTLY GOOD FOR MY IMAGE.
IGNORE THEM. THEY'RE NOTHING BUT A BUNCH OF BASEMENT DWELLERS WHO SPEND ALL DAY WHINING ON THE 'NET.
Justice for THE PEOPLE!
The HALL is ours!
NOT A SINGLE OPEN-MINDED ONE IN THE BUNCH.

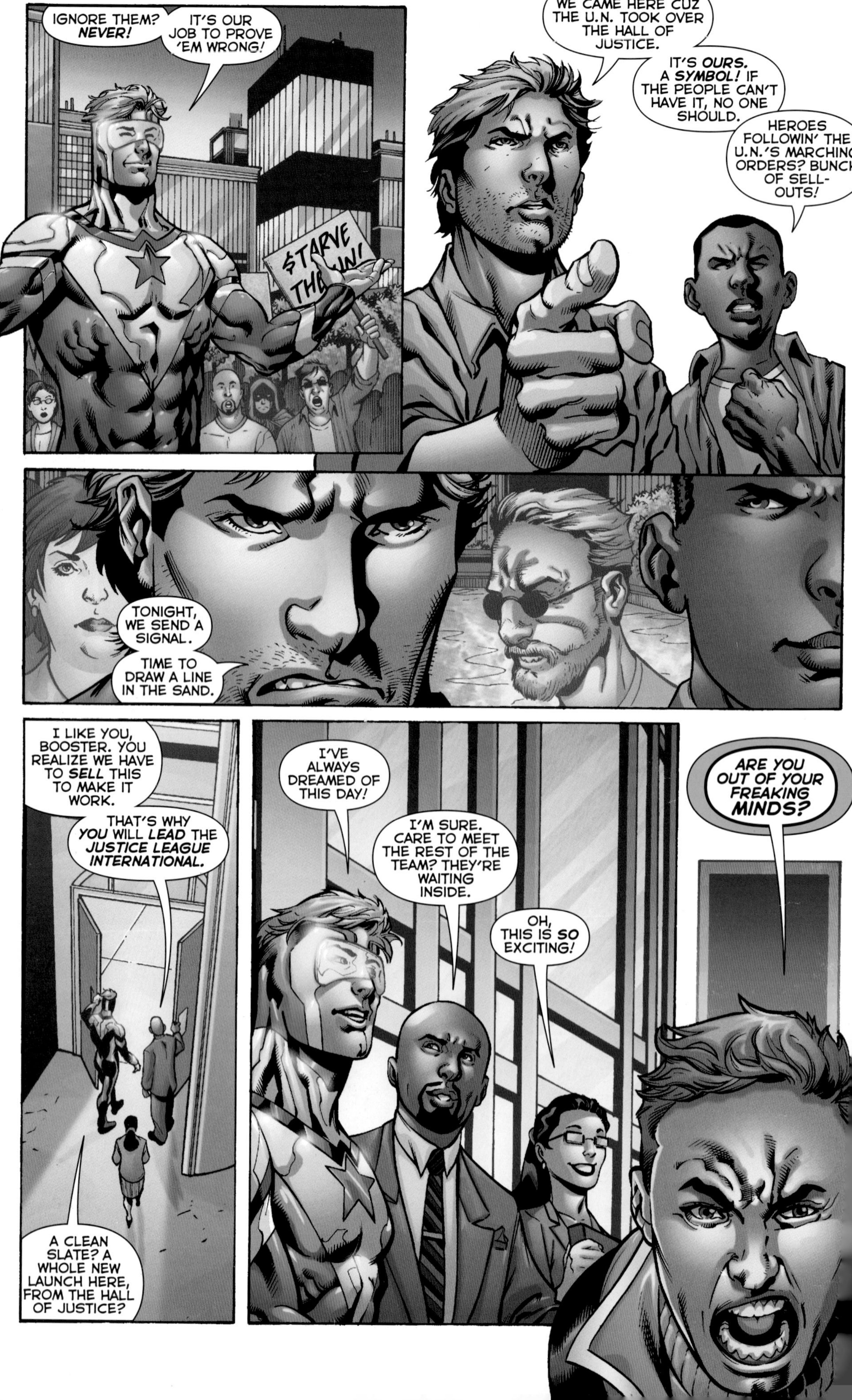
IGNORE THEM? NEVER!
IT'S OUR JOB TO PROVE 'EM WRONG!
$TARVE THE U.N.!
LOOKIT THAT. WE CAME HERE CUZ THE U.N. TOOK OVER THE HALL OF JUSTICE.
IT'S OURS. A SYMBOL! IF THE PEOPLE CAN'T HAVE IT, NO ONE SHOULD.
HEROES FOLLOWIN' THE U.N.'S MARCHING ORDERS? BUNCH OF SELL-OUTS!
TONIGHT, WE SEND A SIGNAL.
TIME TO DRAW A LINE IN THE SAND.
I LIKE YOU, BOOSTER. YOU REALIZE WE HAVE TO SELL THIS TO MAKE IT WORK.
THAT'S WHY YOU WILL LEAD THE JUSTICE LEAGUE INTERNATIONAL.
A CLEAN SLATE? A WHOLE NEW LAUNCH HERE, FROM THE HALL OF JUSTICE?
I'VE ALWAYS DREAMED OF THIS DAY!
I'M SURE. CARE TO MEET THE REST OF THE TEAM? THEY'RE WAITING INSIDE.
OH, THIS IS SO EXCITING!
ARE YOU OUT OF YOUR FREAKING MINDS?

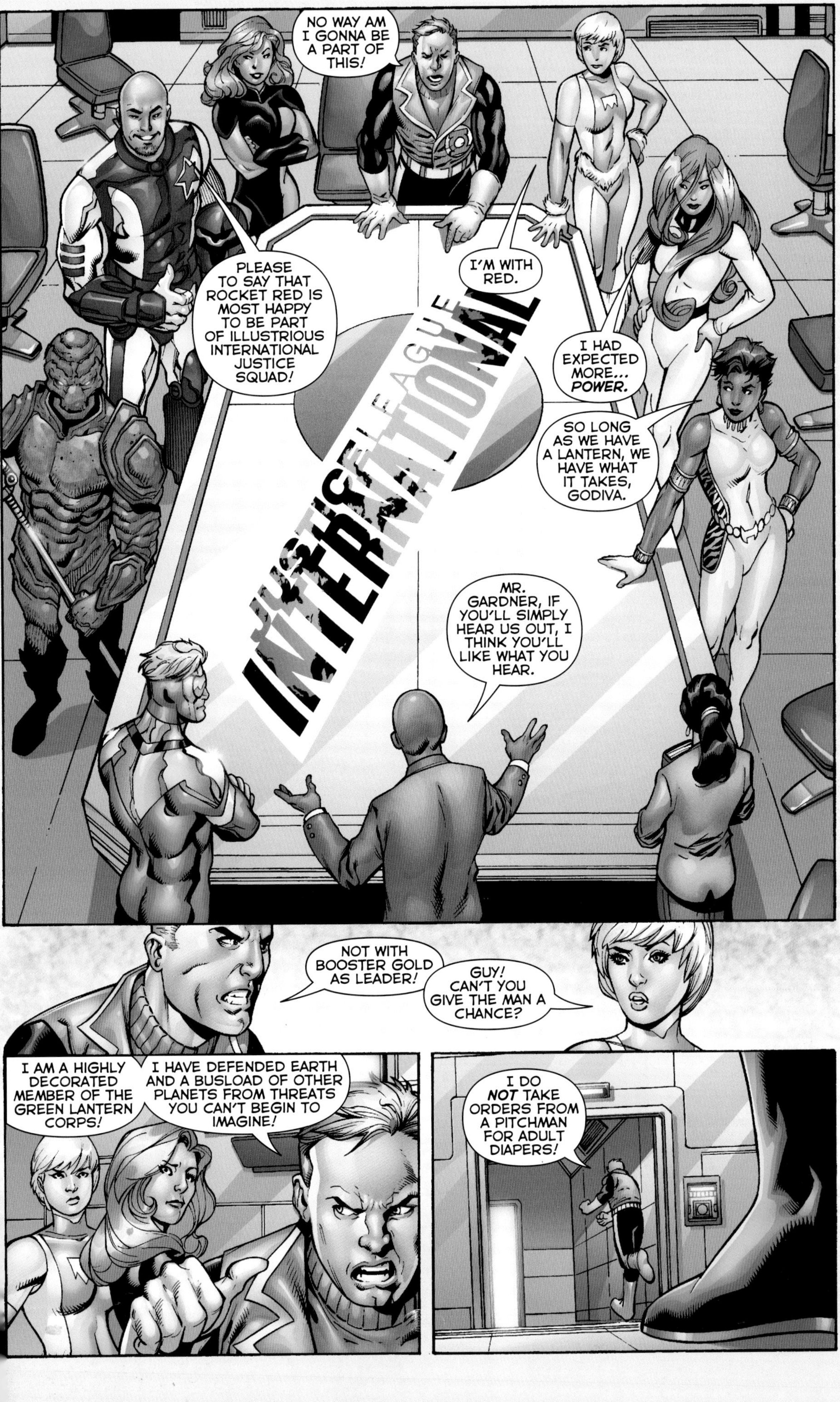
NO WAY AM I GONNA BE A PART OF THIS!
PLEASE TO SAY THAT ROCKET RED IS MOST HAPPY TO BE PART OF ILLUSTRIOUS INTERNATIONAL JUSTICE SQUAD!
I'M WITH RED.
JUSTICE LEAGUE INTERNATIONAL
I HAD EXPECTED MORE... POWER.
SO LONG AS WE HAVE A LANTERN, WE HAVE WHAT IT TAKES, GODIVA.
MR. GARDNER, IF YOU'LL SIMPLY HEAR US OUT, I THINK YOU'LL LIKE WHAT YOU HEAR.
NOT WITH BOOSTER GOLD AS LEADER!
GUY! CAN'T YOU GIVE THE MAN A CHANCE?
I AM A HIGHLY DECORATED MEMBER OF THE GREEN LANTERN CORPS!
I HAVE DEFENDED EARTH AND A BUSLOAD OF OTHER PLANETS FROM THREATS YOU CAN'T BEGIN TO IMAGINE!
I DO NOT TAKE ORDERS FROM A PITCHMAN FOR ADULT DIAPERS!

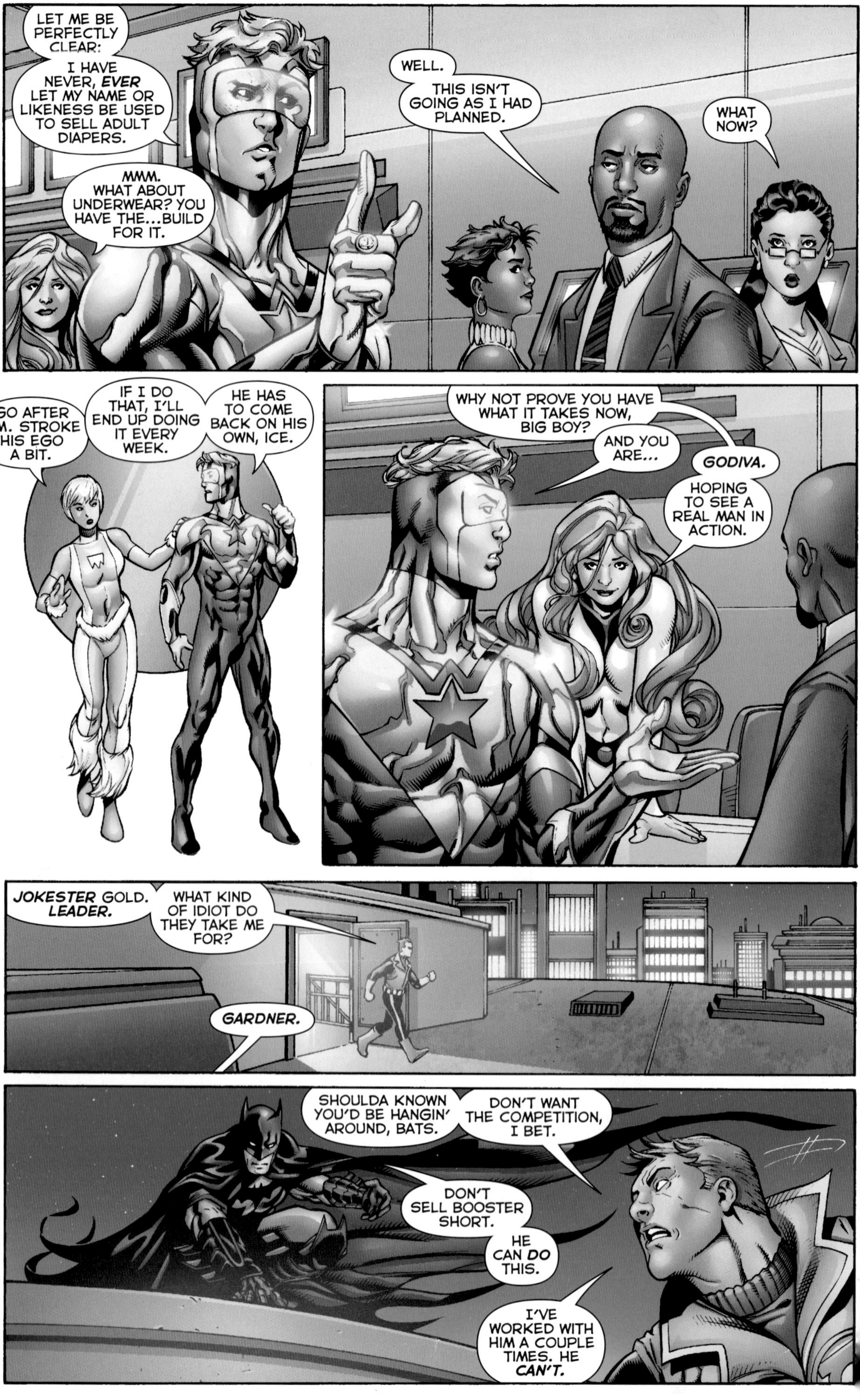
LET ME BE PERFECTLY CLEAR:
I HAVE NEVER, **EVER** LET MY NAME OR LIKENESS BE USED TO SELL ADULT DIAPERS.
MMM. WHAT ABOUT UNDERWEAR? YOU HAVE THE...BUILD FOR IT.
WELL.
THIS ISN'T GOING AS I HAD PLANNED.
WHAT NOW?
GO AFTER HIM. STROKE HIS EGO A BIT.
IF I DO THAT, I'LL END UP DOING IT EVERY WEEK.
HE HAS TO COME BACK ON HIS OWN, ICE.
WHY NOT PROVE YOU HAVE WHAT IT TAKES NOW, BIG BOY?
AND YOU ARE...
GODIVA.
HOPING TO SEE A REAL MAN IN ACTION.
JOKESTER GOLD. **LEADER.**
WHAT KIND OF IDIOT DO THEY TAKE ME FOR?
GARDNER.
SHOULDA KNOWN YOU'D BE HANGIN' AROUND, BATS.
DON'T WANT THE COMPETITION, I BET.
DON'T SELL BOOSTER SHORT.
HE CAN **DO** THIS.
I'VE WORKED WITH HIM A COUPLE TIMES. HE **CAN'T.**

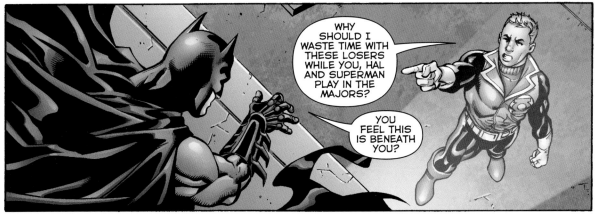

WHY SHOULD I WASTE TIME WITH THESE LOSERS WHILE YOU, HAL AND SUPERMAN PLAY IN THE MAJORS?

YOU FEEL THIS IS BENEATH YOU?

THEY MADE BOOSTER *LEADER.*

NO ONE CAN JUSTIFY THAT.

I KNOW. THE U.N. MUST HAVE SOME *OTHER* MOTIVE. I'M HERE TO FIND OUT WHAT *IT* IS.

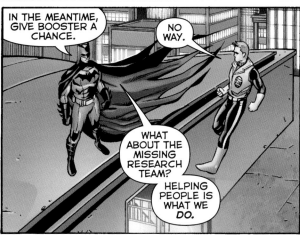

IN THE MEANTIME, GIVE BOOSTER A CHANCE.

NO WAY.

WHAT ABOUT THE MISSING RESEARCH TEAM?

HELPING PEOPLE IS WHAT WE *DO.*

IF BOOSTER GOLD IS AS CAPABLE AS YOU THINK--

--THEY'LL DO JUST FINE WITHOUT ME.

LADIES ND GENTLEMEN, YOUR *RIDE.*

NICE!

AH! IMPRESSIVE RUSSIAN PLANE!

IT'S ACTUALLY AMERICAN MADE, GAVRIL.

CUTTING EDGE ON EVERY LEVEL, COURTESY OF *QUEEN INDUSTRIES.*

UNTIL THEY CRASH. CHINESE AVIATION OFFERS SUPERIOR OPTIONS.

HUMPH. RUSSIAN PLANES *BETTER.*

IRON GENERAL *INSULTS* RUSSIAN ENGINEERING!

I'VE SEEN THEIR FAILURES ON THE BATTLEFIELD, ROCKET RED.

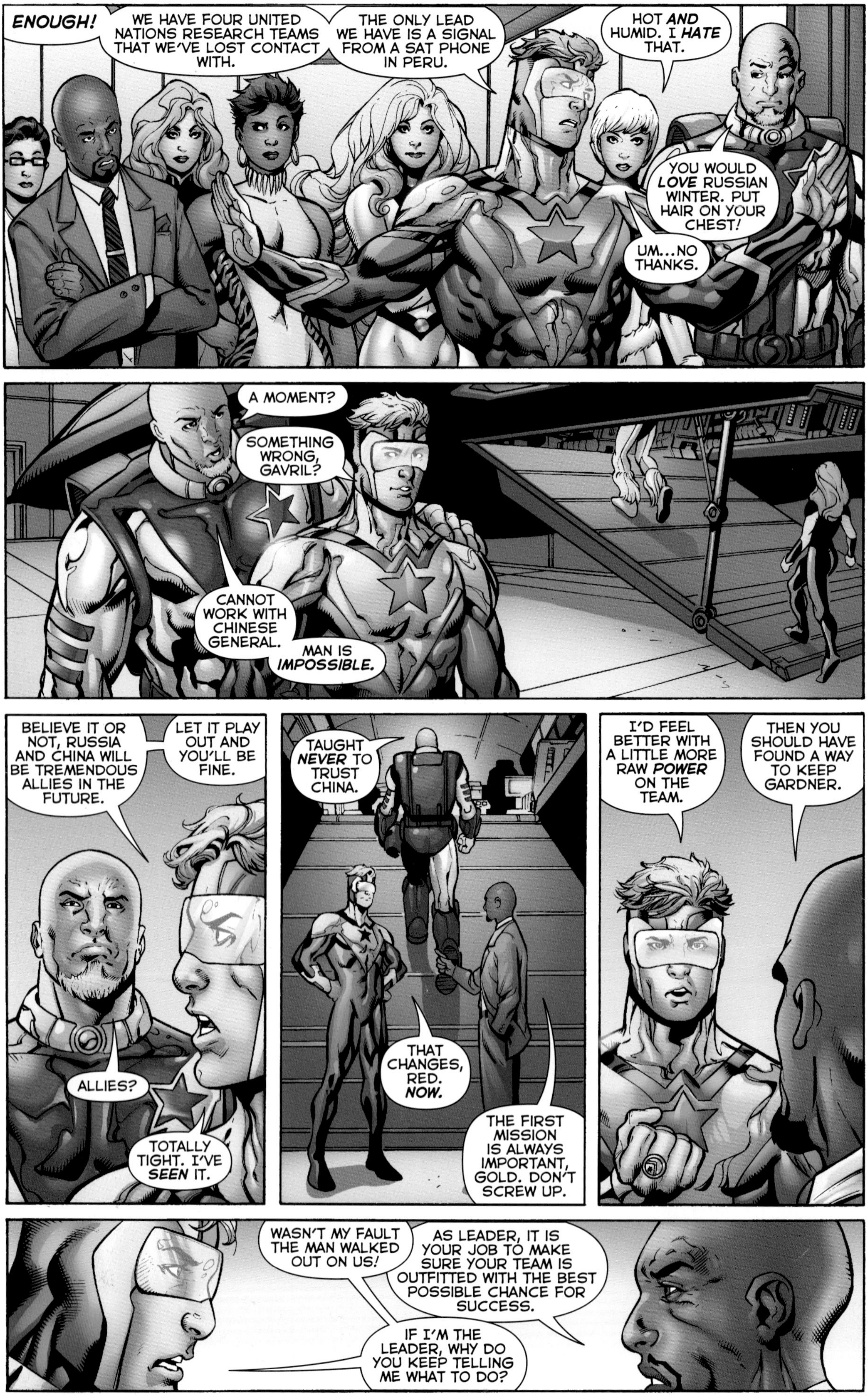
ENOUGH!
WE HAVE FOUR UNITED NATIONS RESEARCH TEAMS THAT WE'VE LOST CONTACT WITH.
THE ONLY LEAD WE HAVE IS A SIGNAL FROM A SAT PHONE IN PERU.
HOT AND HUMID. I HATE THAT.
YOU WOULD LOVE RUSSIAN WINTER. PUT HAIR ON YOUR CHEST!
UM...NO THANKS.
A MOMENT?
SOMETHING WRONG, GAVRIL?
CANNOT WORK WITH CHINESE GENERAL.
MAN IS IMPOSSIBLE.
BELIEVE IT OR NOT, RUSSIA AND CHINA WILL BE TREMENDOUS ALLIES IN THE FUTURE.
LET IT PLAY OUT AND YOU'LL BE FINE.
ALLIES?
TOTALLY TIGHT. I'VE SEEN IT.
TAUGHT NEVER TO TRUST CHINA.
THAT CHANGES, RED. NOW.
THE FIRST MISSION IS ALWAYS IMPORTANT, GOLD. DON'T SCREW UP.
I'D FEEL BETTER WITH A LITTLE MORE RAW POWER ON THE TEAM.
THEN YOU SHOULD HAVE FOUND A WAY TO KEEP GARDNER.
WASN'T MY FAULT THE MAN WALKED OUT ON US!
AS LEADER, IT IS YOUR JOB TO MAKE SURE YOUR TEAM IS OUTFITTED WITH THE BEST POSSIBLE CHANCE FOR SUCCESS.
IF I'M THE LEADER, WHY DO YOU KEEP TELLING ME WHAT TO DO?

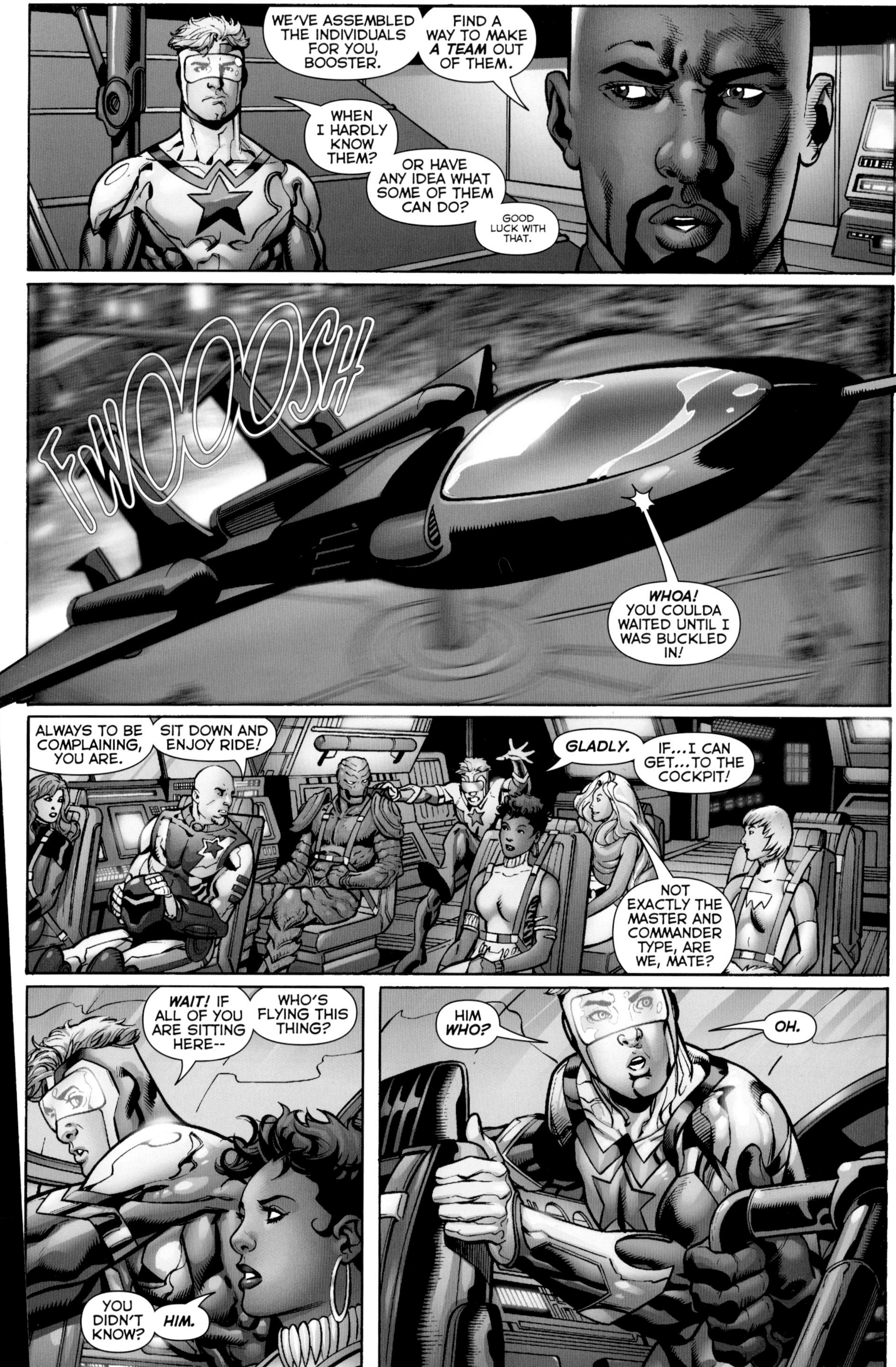
WE'VE ASSEMBLED THE INDIVIDUALS FOR YOU, BOOSTER.
FIND A WAY TO MAKE A TEAM OUT OF THEM.
WHEN I HARDLY KNOW THEM?
OR HAVE ANY IDEA WHAT SOME OF THEM CAN DO?
GOOD LUCK WITH THAT.
FWOOOOSH
WHOA! YOU COULDA WAITED UNTIL I WAS BUCKLED IN!
ALWAYS TO BE COMPLAINING, YOU ARE.
SIT DOWN AND ENJOY RIDE!
GLADLY.
IF...I CAN GET...TO THE COCKPIT!
NOT EXACTLY THE MASTER AND COMMANDER TYPE, ARE WE, MATE?
WAIT! IF ALL OF YOU ARE SITTING HERE--
WHO'S FLYING THIS THING?
YOU DIDN'T KNOW?
HIM.
HIM WHO?
OH.

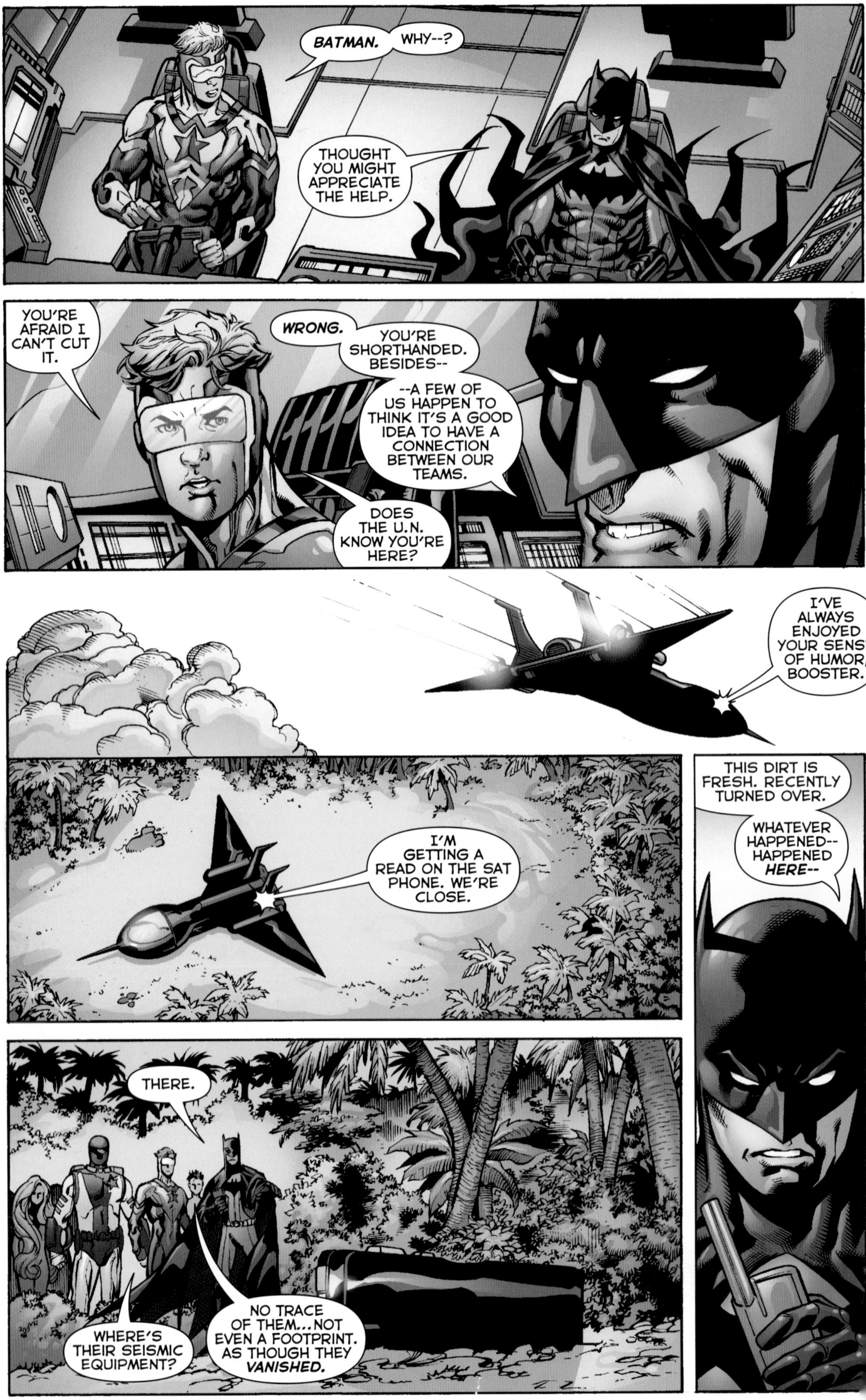
BATMAN.
WHY--?
THOUGHT YOU MIGHT APPRECIATE THE HELP.
YOU'RE AFRAID I CAN'T CUT IT.
WRONG.
YOU'RE SHORTHANDED. BESIDES--
--A FEW OF US HAPPEN TO THINK IT'S A GOOD IDEA TO HAVE A CONNECTION BETWEEN OUR TEAMS.
DOES THE U.N. KNOW YOU'RE HERE?
I'VE ALWAYS ENJOYED YOUR SENSE OF HUMOR, BOOSTER.
I'M GETTING A READ ON THE SAT PHONE. WE'RE CLOSE.
THERE.
WHERE'S THEIR SEISMIC EQUIPMENT?
NO TRACE OF THEM...NOT EVEN A FOOTPRINT. AS THOUGH THEY VANISHED.
THIS DIRT IS FRESH. RECENTLY TURNED OVER.
WHATEVER HAPPENED--HAPPENED HERE--

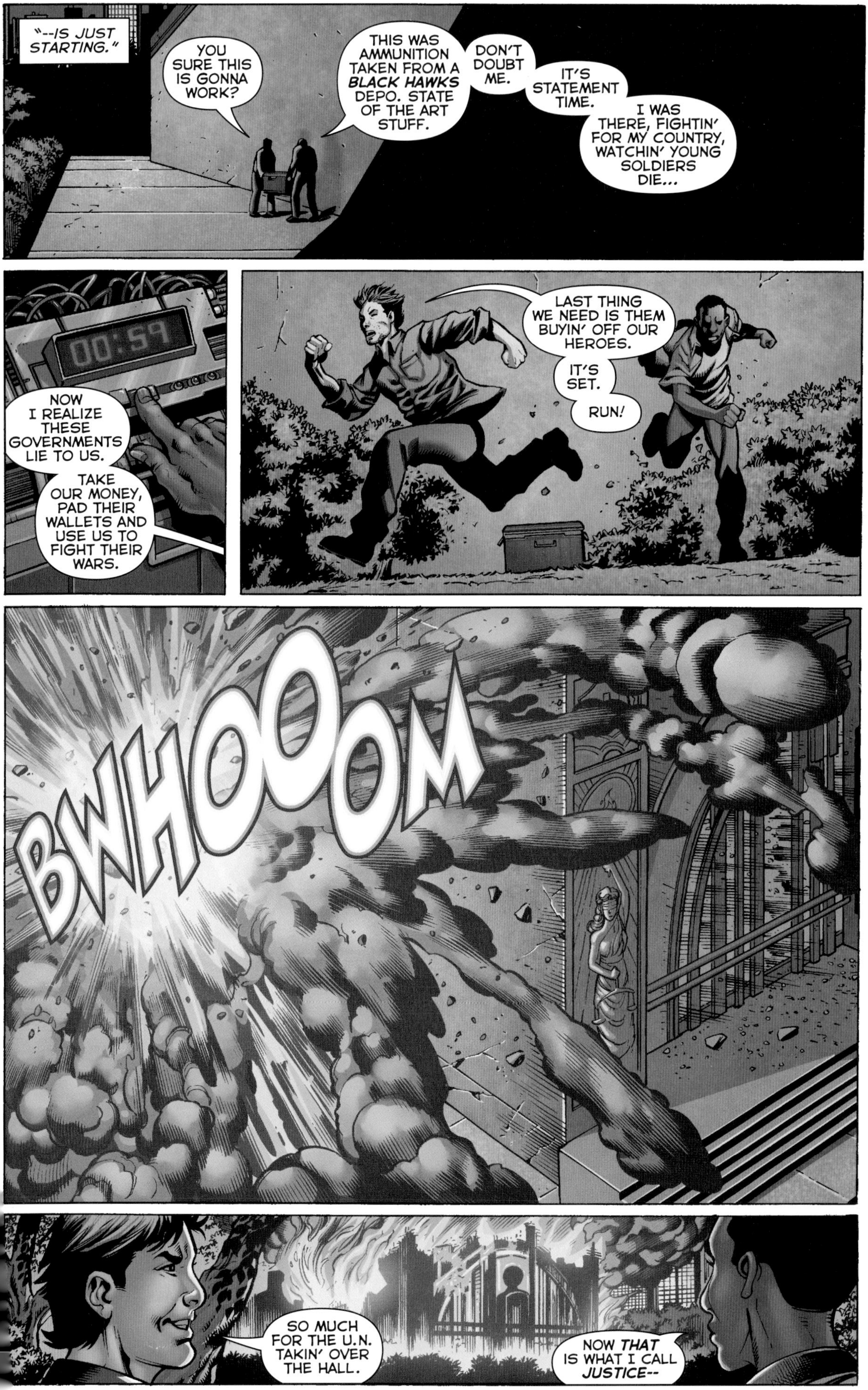
"--IS JUST STARTING."
YOU SURE THIS IS GONNA WORK?
THIS WAS AMMUNITION TAKEN FROM A *BLACK HAWKS* DEPO. STATE OF THE ART STUFF.
DON'T DOUBT ME.
IT'S STATEMENT TIME.
I WAS THERE, FIGHTIN' FOR MY COUNTRY, WATCHIN' YOUNG SOLDIERS DIE...
00:59
NOW I REALIZE THESE GOVERNMENTS LIE TO US.
TAKE OUR MONEY, PAD THEIR WALLETS AND USE US TO FIGHT THEIR WARS.
LAST THING WE NEED IS THEM BUYIN' OFF OUR HEROES.
IT'S SET.
RUN!
BWHOOOOM
SO MUCH FOR THE U.N. TAKIN' OVER THE HALL.
NOW *THAT* IS WHAT I CALL *JUSTICE*--

"--AND SOON THEY WON'T KNOW WHAT HIT THEM."

WILL RUN SCAN. CHECK FOR SIGNS OF TEAM.

HOW? GOING TO OPEN UP A DIALOGUE WITH SOME MONKEYS?

EASY, GODIVA. THE MAN KNOWS HIS JOB.

WHOA. DON'T GET ALL DEFENSIVE, OKAY?

WE SHOULD DISPERSE. IT IS UNWISE TO BE GATHERED IN TIGHT FORMATION.

DETECT NOTHING. RESEARCH TEAM GONE.

SPREAD OUT. TEAMS OF TWO. CIRCULAR SWEEP OF THE AREA, TWO-MILE RADIUS.

SERIOUSLY? YOU BARELY KNOW WHAT SOME OF US--WAIT.

DO YOU HEAR THAT?

EVERYONE BACK!

ASSUME DEFENSE POSTURE!

BROOM

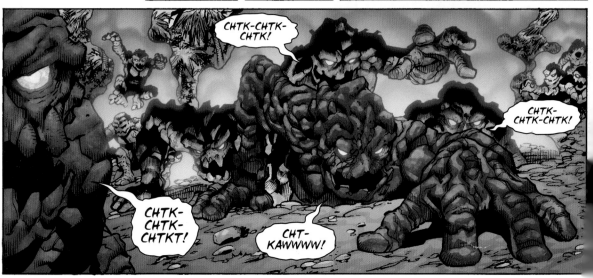

CHTK-CHTK-CHTK!

CHTK-CHTK-CHTK!

CHTK-CHTK-CHTKT!

CHT-KAWWWW!

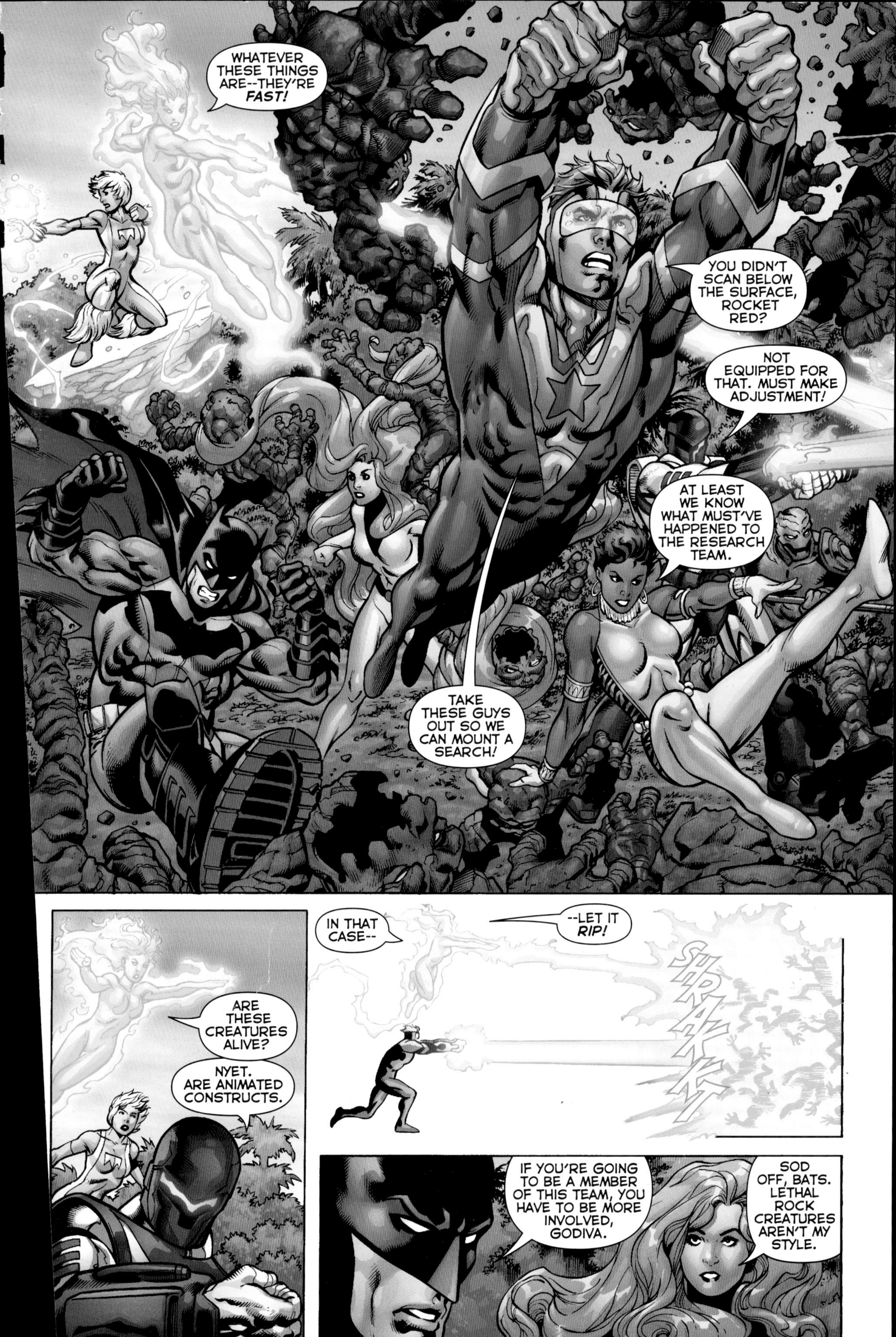
WHATEVER THESE THINGS ARE--THEY'RE *FAST!*
YOU DIDN'T SCAN BELOW THE SURFACE, ROCKET RED?
NOT EQUIPPED FOR THAT. MUST MAKE ADJUSTMENT!
AT LEAST WE KNOW WHAT MUST'VE HAPPENED TO THE RESEARCH TEAM.
TAKE THESE GUYS OUT SO WE CAN MOUNT A SEARCH!
ARE THESE CREATURES ALIVE?
NYET. ARE ANIMATED CONSTRUCTS.
IN THAT CASE--
--LET IT *RIP!*
SHRAKT
IF YOU'RE GOING TO BE A MEMBER OF THIS TEAM, YOU HAVE TO BE MORE INVOLVED, GODIVA.
SOD OFF, BATS. LETHAL ROCK CREATURES AREN'T MY STYLE.

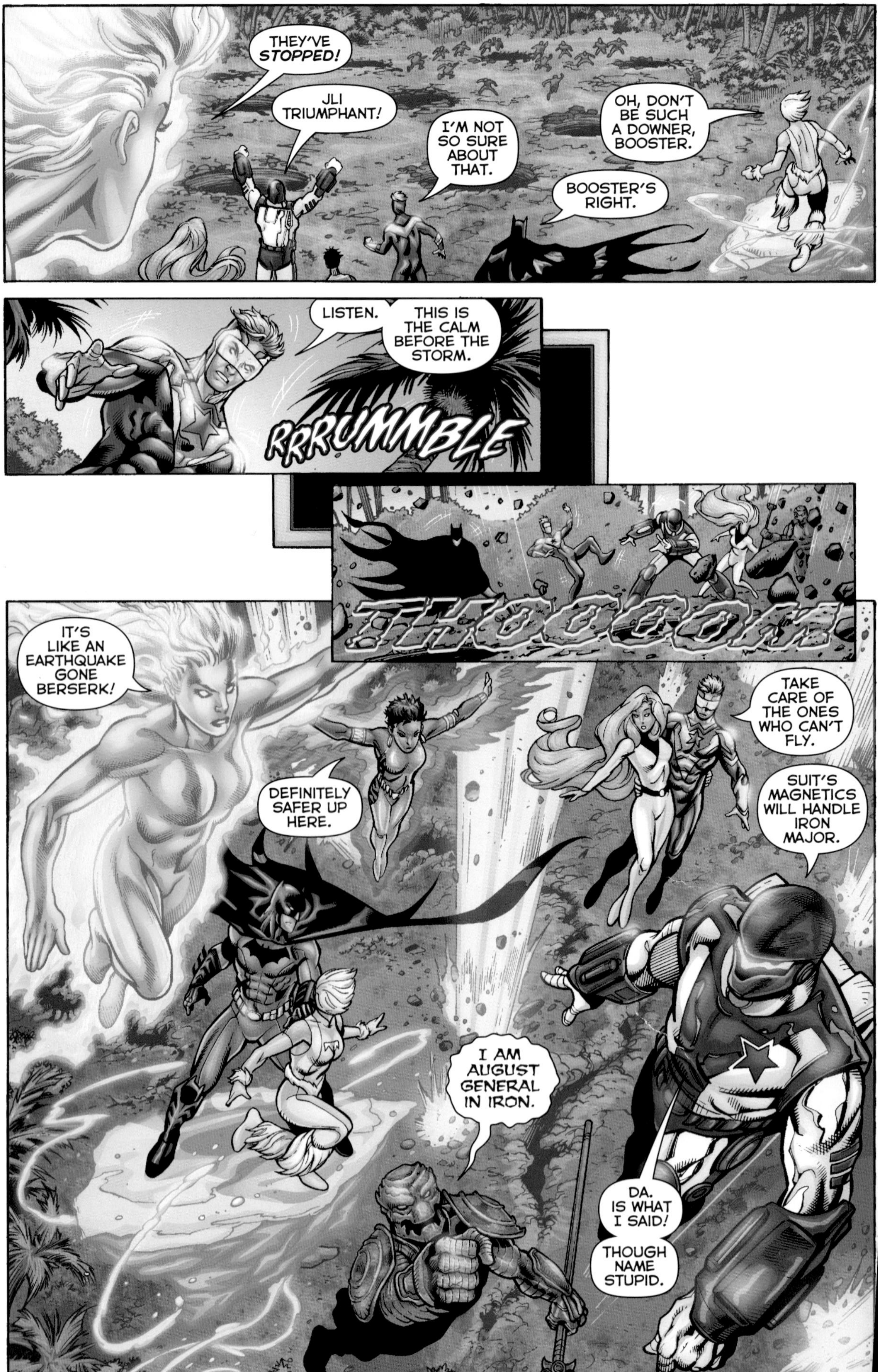
THEY'VE STOPPED!
JLI TRIUMPHANT!
I'M NOT SO SURE ABOUT THAT.
OH, DON'T BE SUCH A DOWNER, BOOSTER.
BOOSTER'S RIGHT.
LISTEN.
THIS IS THE CALM BEFORE THE STORM.
RRRUMMBLE
THOOOOM
IT'S LIKE AN EARTHQUAKE GONE BERSERK!
DEFINITELY SAFER UP HERE.
TAKE CARE OF THE ONES WHO CAN'T FLY.
SUIT'S MAGNETICS WILL HANDLE IRON MAJOR.
I AM AUGUST GENERAL IN IRON.
DA. IS WHAT I SAID!
THOUGH NAME STUPID.

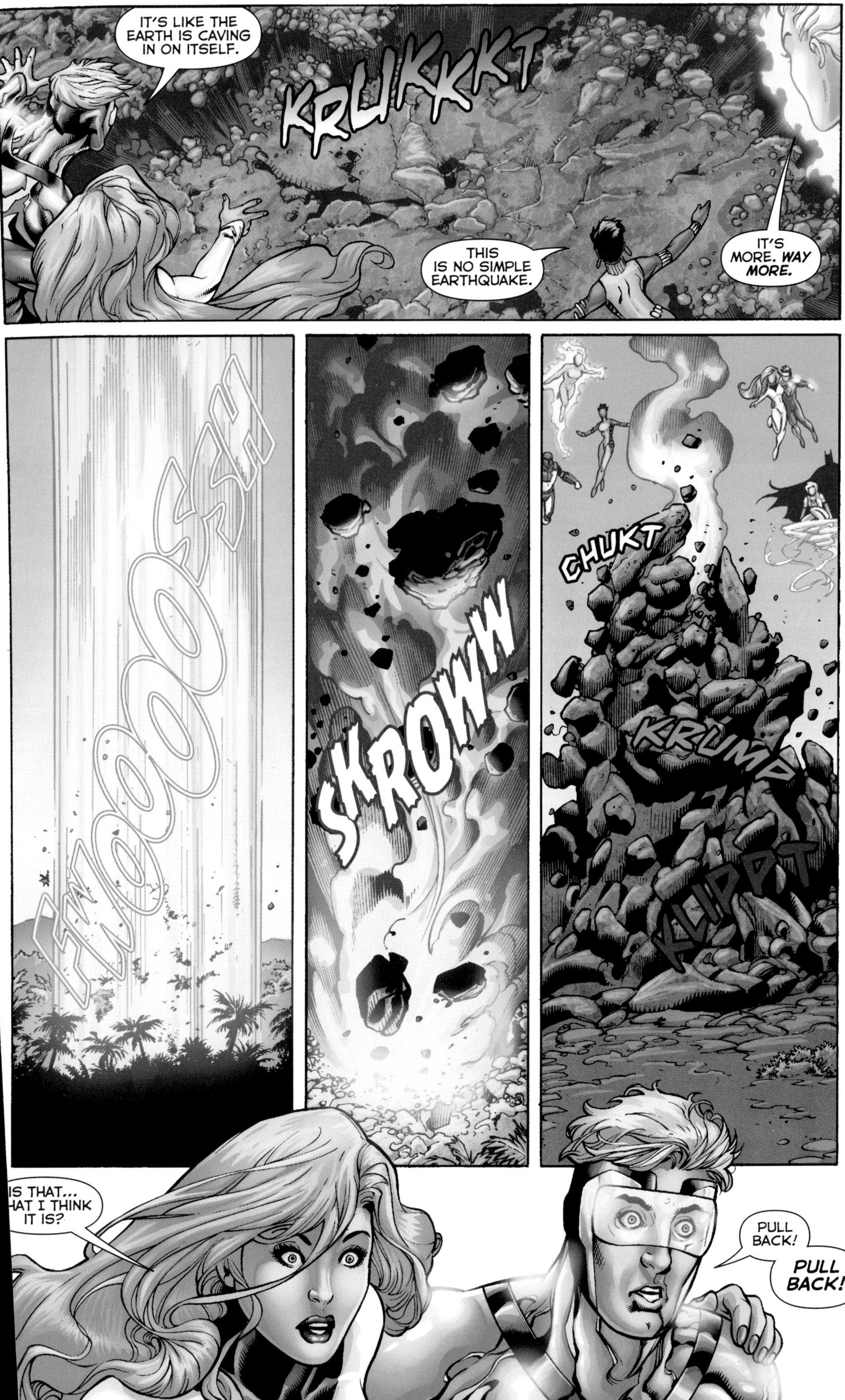
IT'S LIKE THE EARTH IS CAVING IN ON ITSELF.
KRUKKKT
THIS IS NO SIMPLE EARTHQUAKE.
IT'S MORE. WAY MORE.
FWOOOSSH
SKROWW
CHUKT
KRUMP
KLIPPT
IS THAT... WHAT I THINK IT IS?
PULL BACK!
PULL BACK!

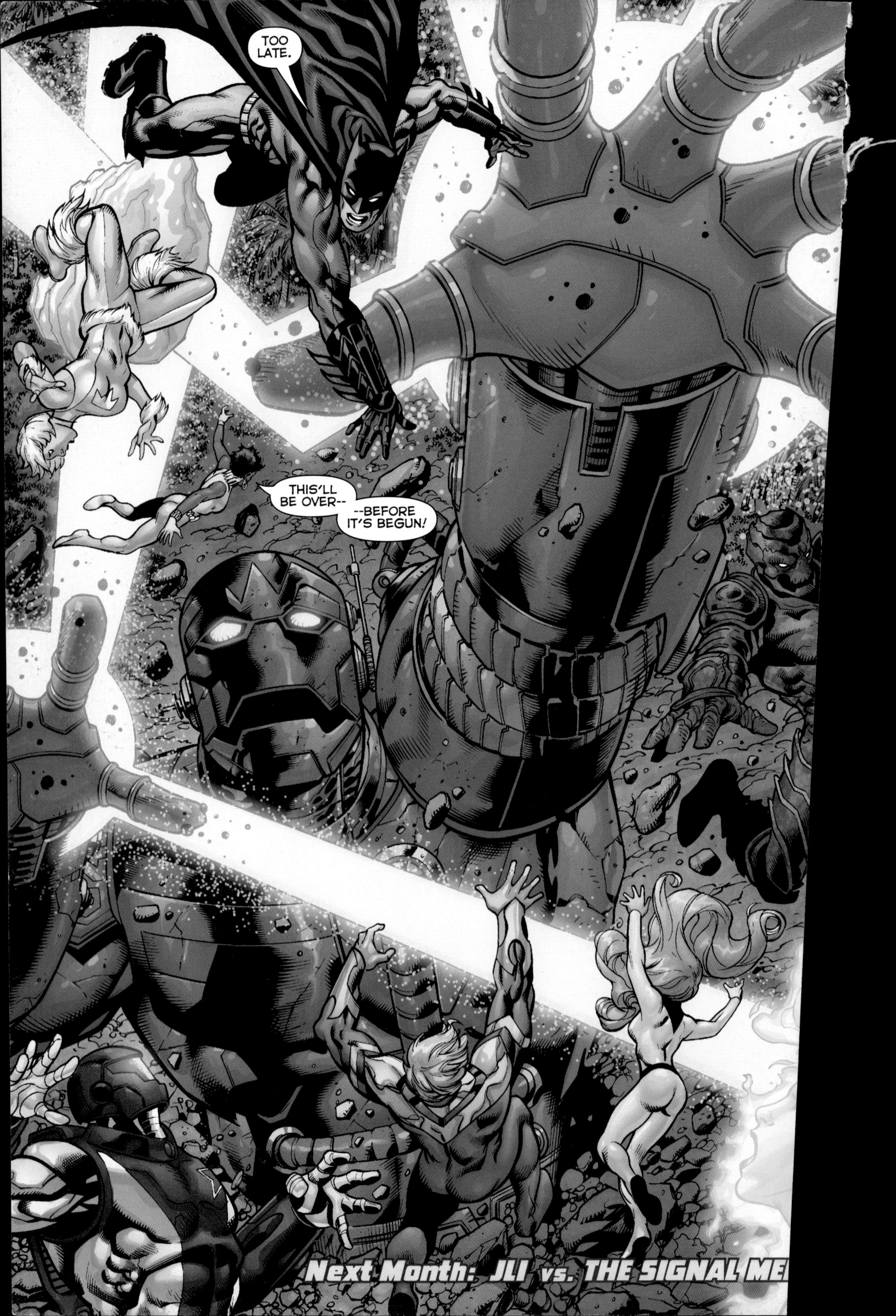
TOO LATE.
THIS'LL BE OVER--
--BEFORE IT'S BEGUN!
Next Month: JLI vs. THE SIGNAL ME

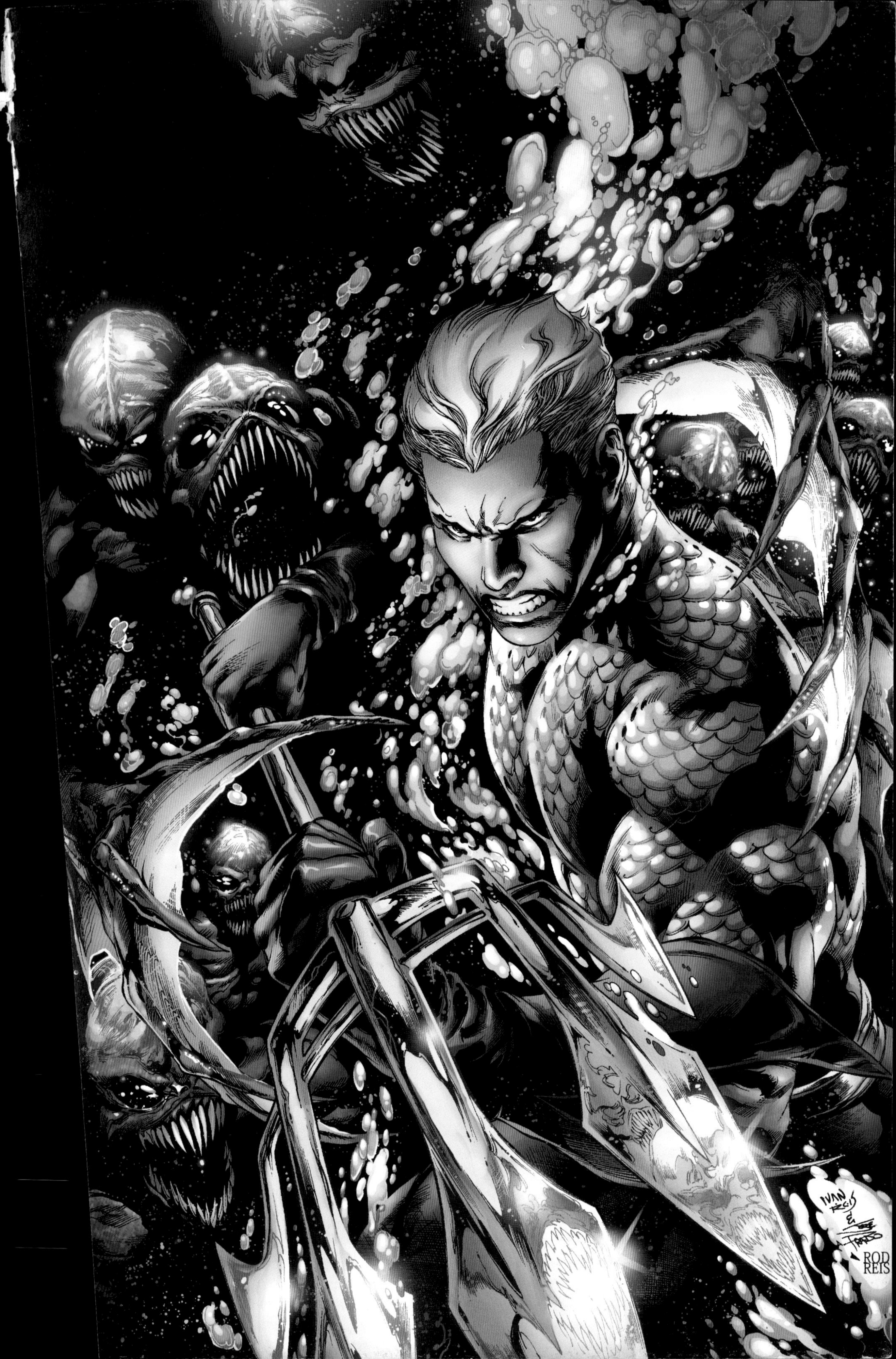
IVAN REIS
ROD REIS

AQUAMAN

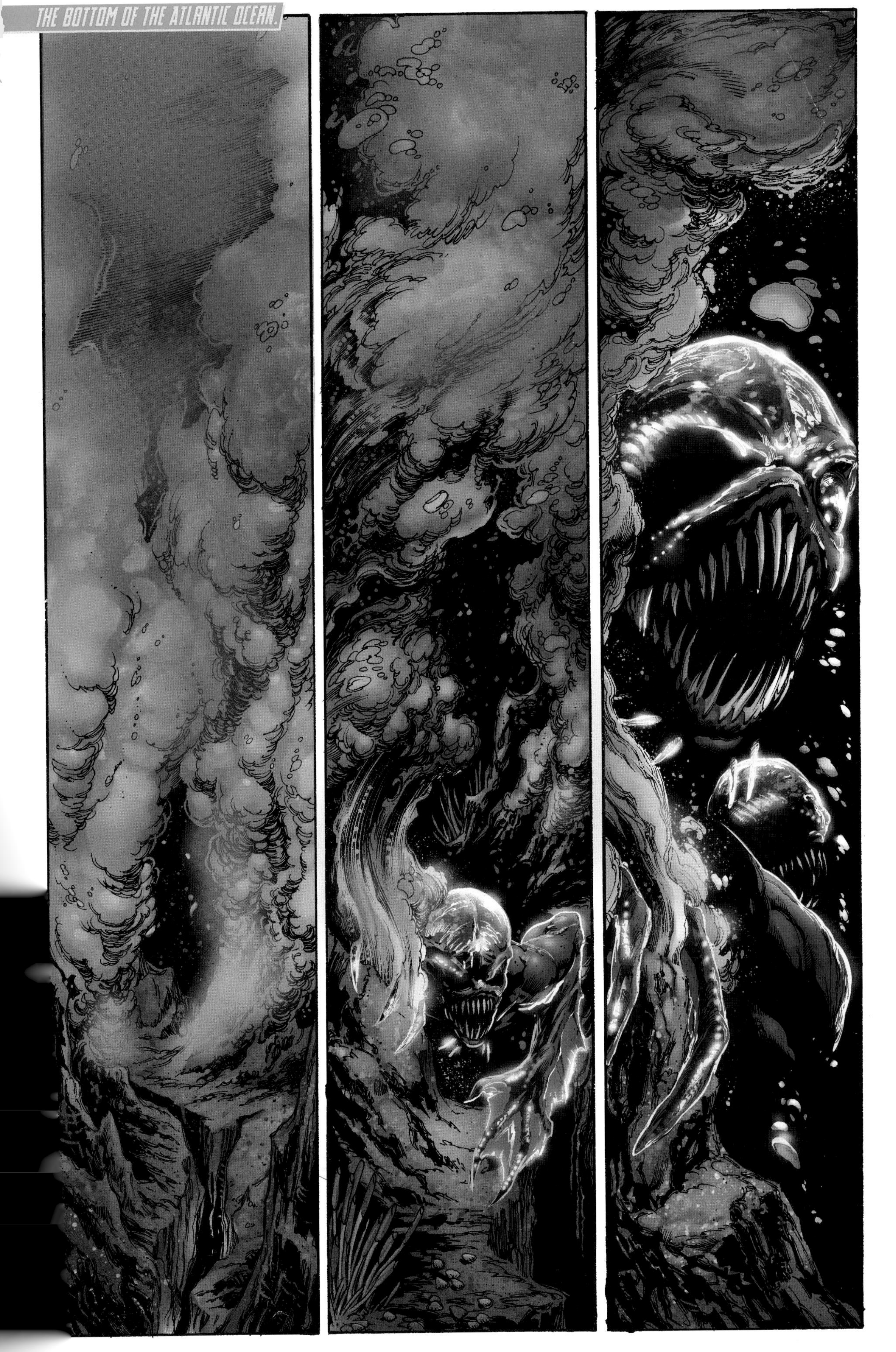
THE BOTTOM OF THE ATLANTIC OCEAN.

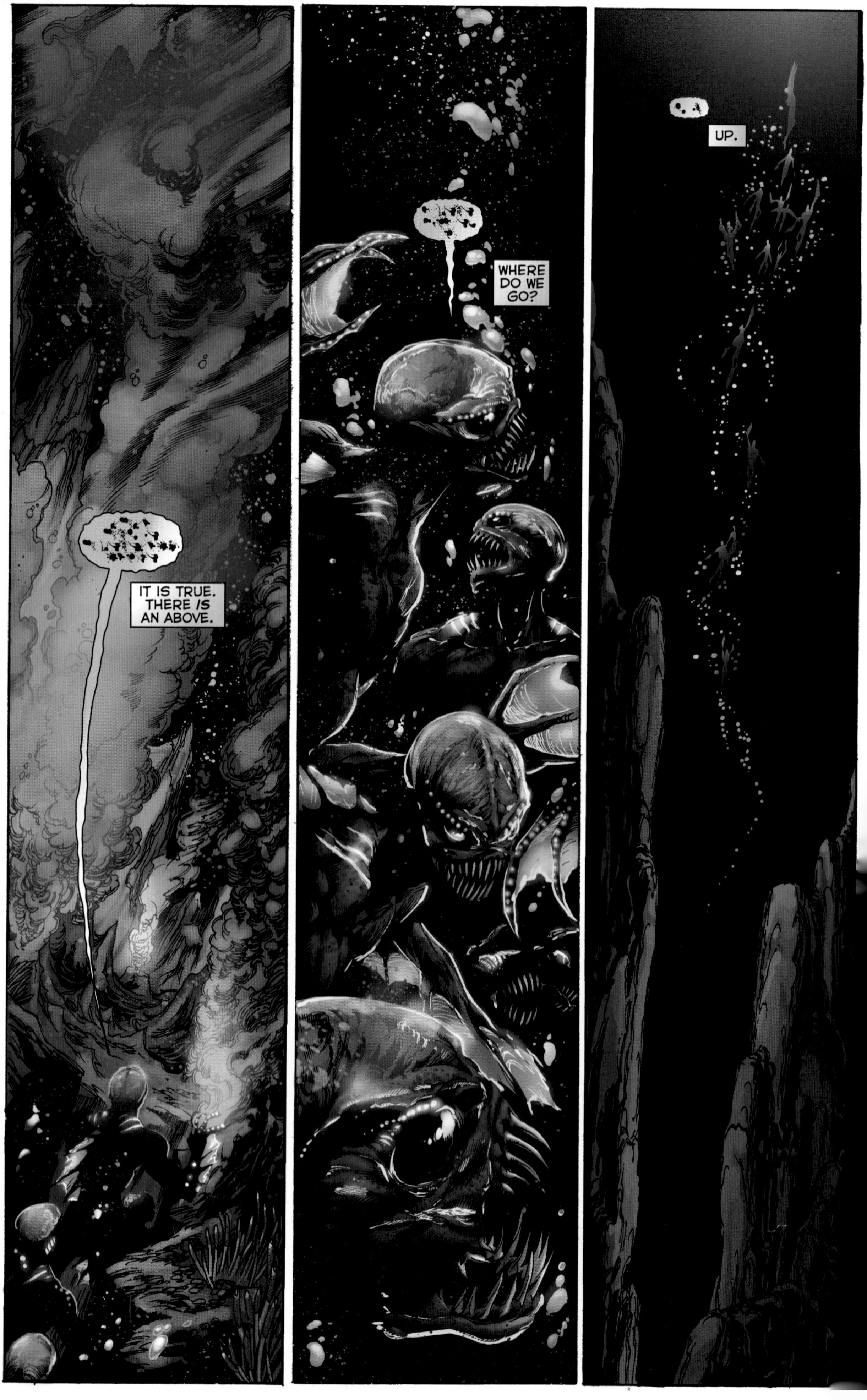
IT IS TRUE. THERE *IS* AN ABOVE.
WHERE DO WE GO?
UP.

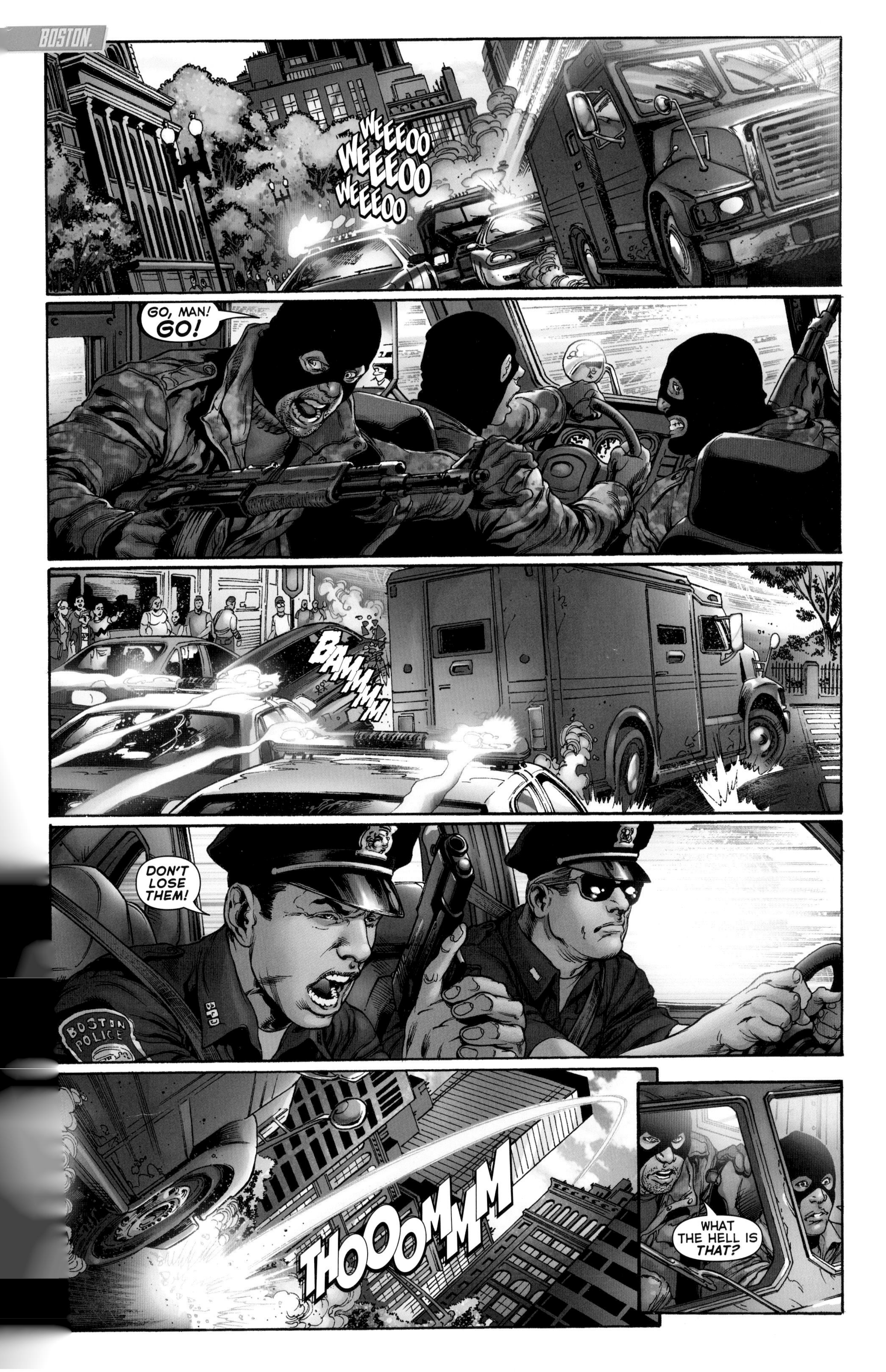
BOSTON.
WEEEOO
WEEEOO
WEEEOO
GO, MAN! GO!
BAMMMM
DON'T LOSE THEM!
THOOOMMM
WHAT THE HELL IS THAT?

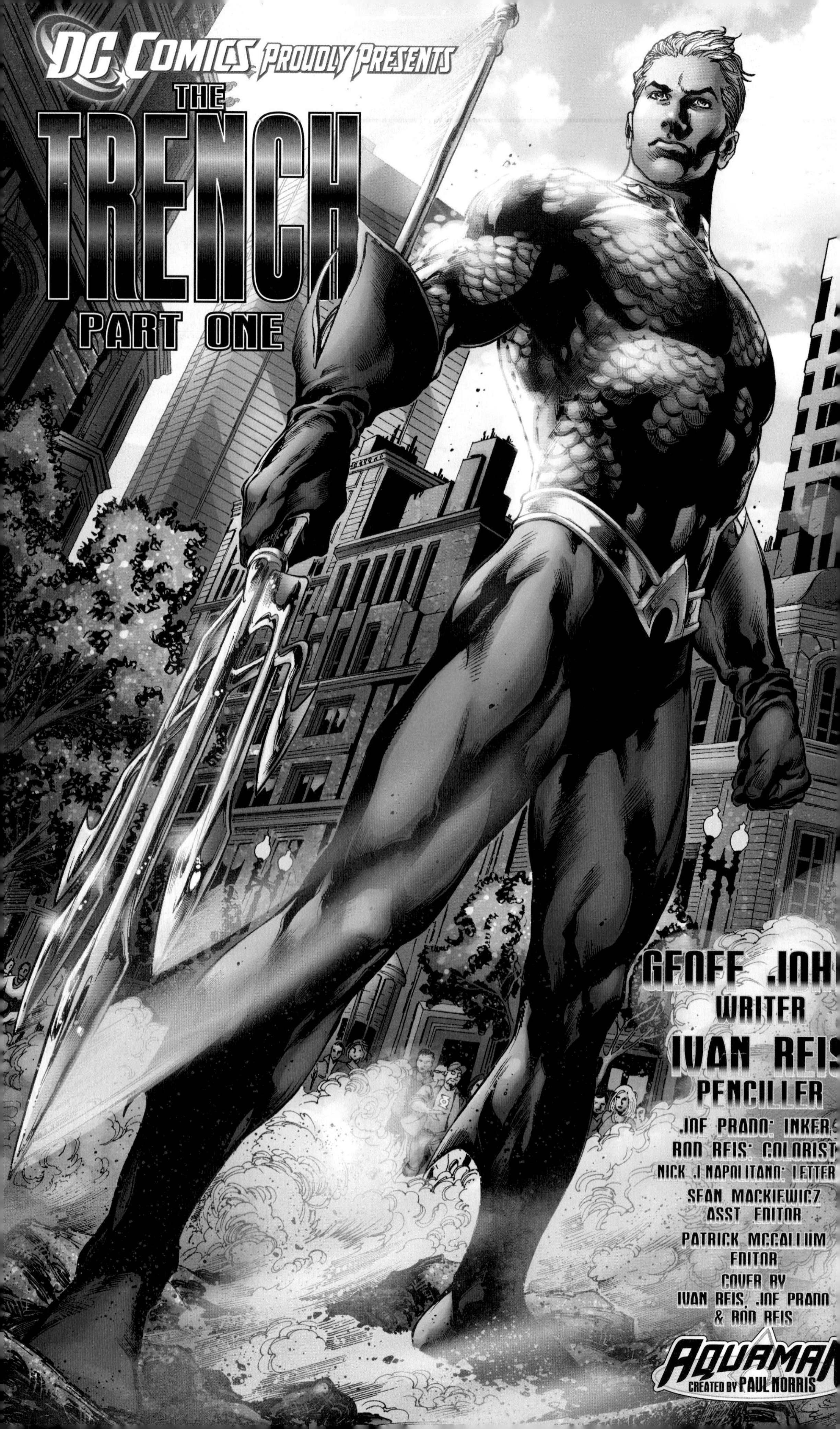
DC COMICS PROUDLY PRESENTS
THE TRENCH
PART ONE
GEOFF JOH
WRITER
IVAN REIS
PENCILLER
JOE PRADO: INKER
ROD REIS: COLORIST
NICK J NAPOLITANO: LETTER
SEAN MACKIEWICZ
ASST EDITOR
PATRICK MCCALLUM
EDITOR
COVER BY
IVAN REIS, JOE PRADO
& ROD REIS
AQUAMAN
CREATED BY PAUL NORRIS

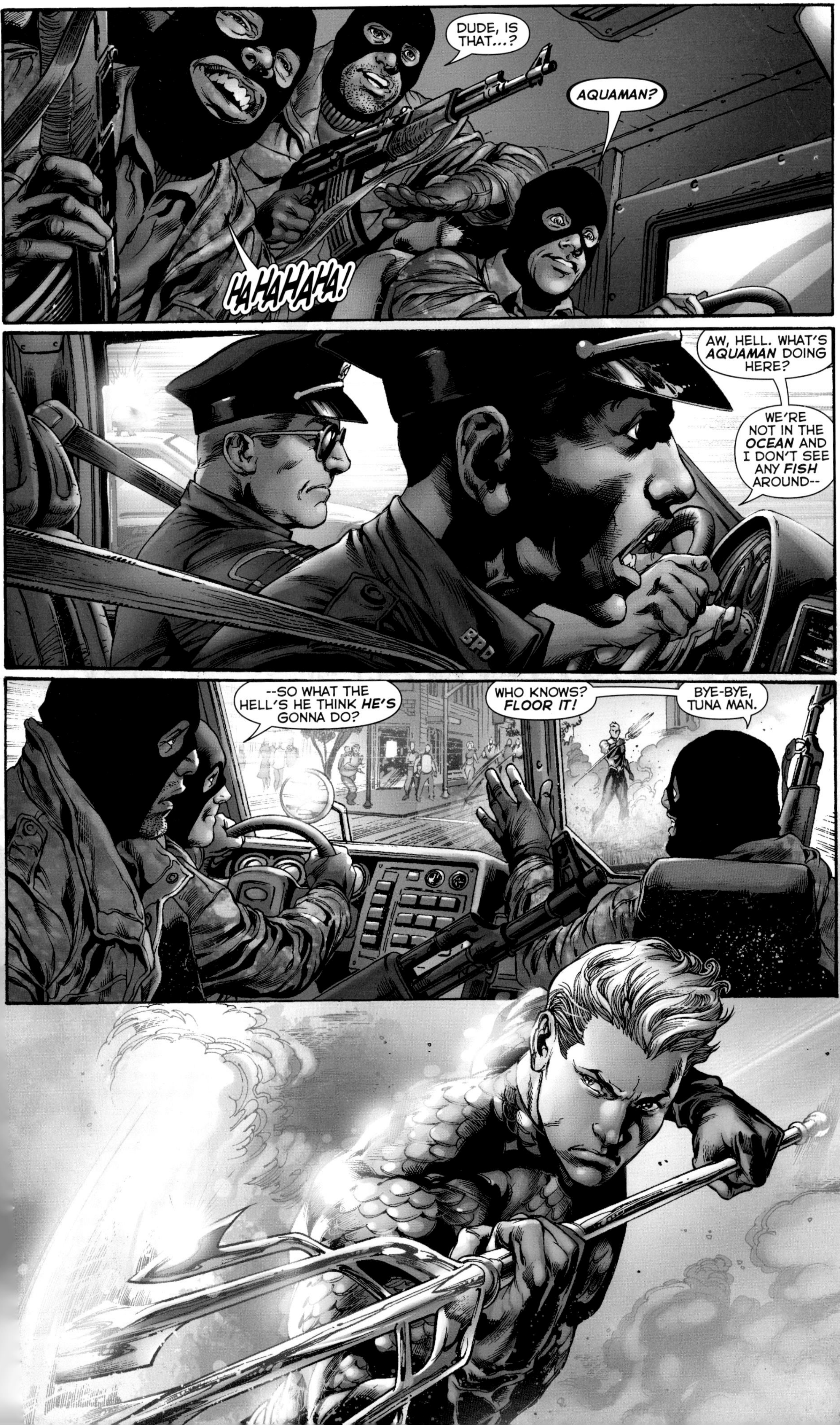
DUDE, IS THAT...?
AQUAMAN?
HAHAHAHA!
AW, HELL. WHAT'S AQUAMAN DOING HERE?
WE'RE NOT IN THE OCEAN AND I DON'T SEE ANY FISH AROUND--
--SO WHAT THE HELL'S HE THINK HE'S GONNA DO?
WHO KNOWS? FLOOR IT!
BYE-BYE, TUNA MAN.

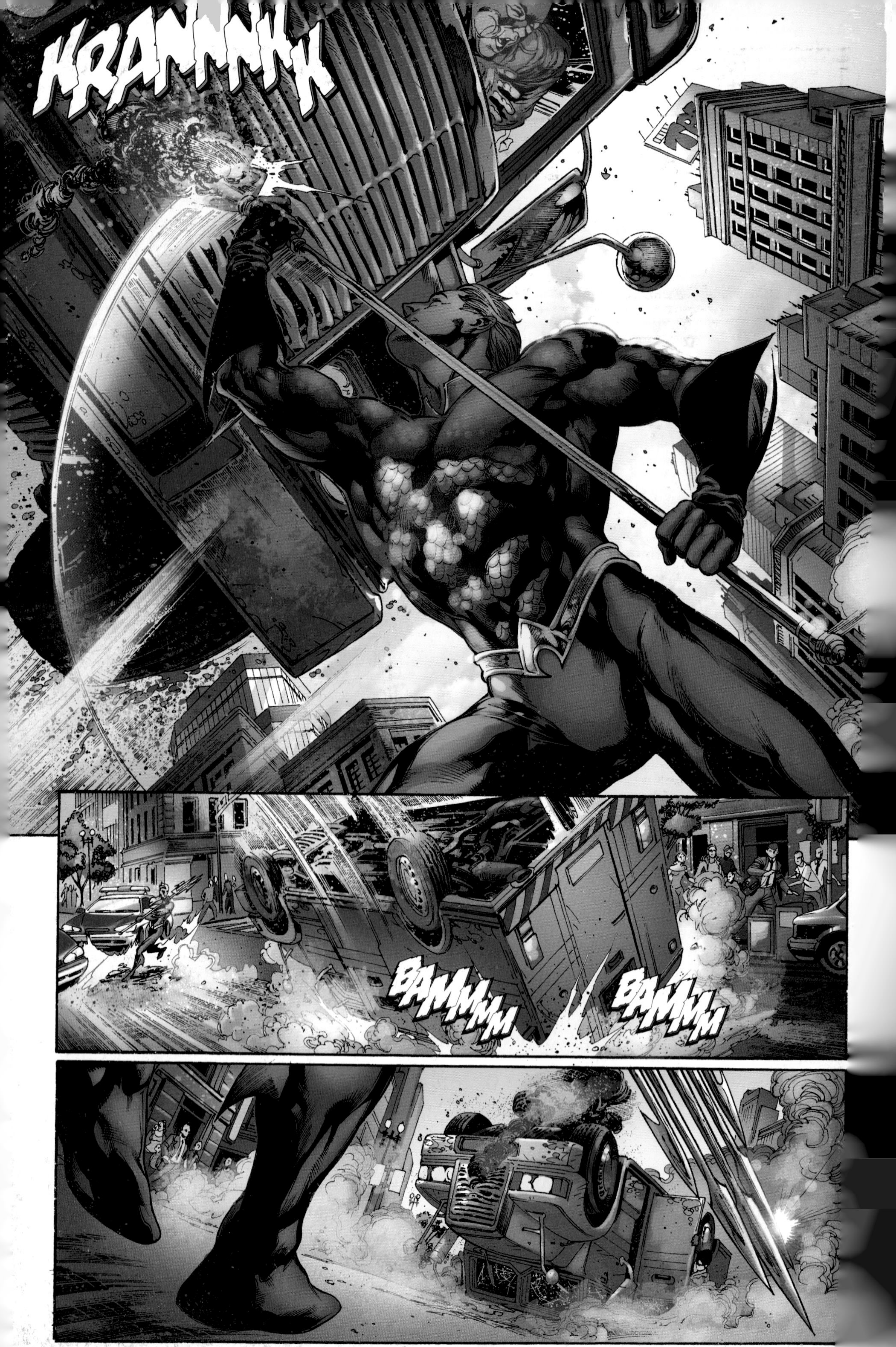
KRANNNKK
BAMMMM
BAMMMM

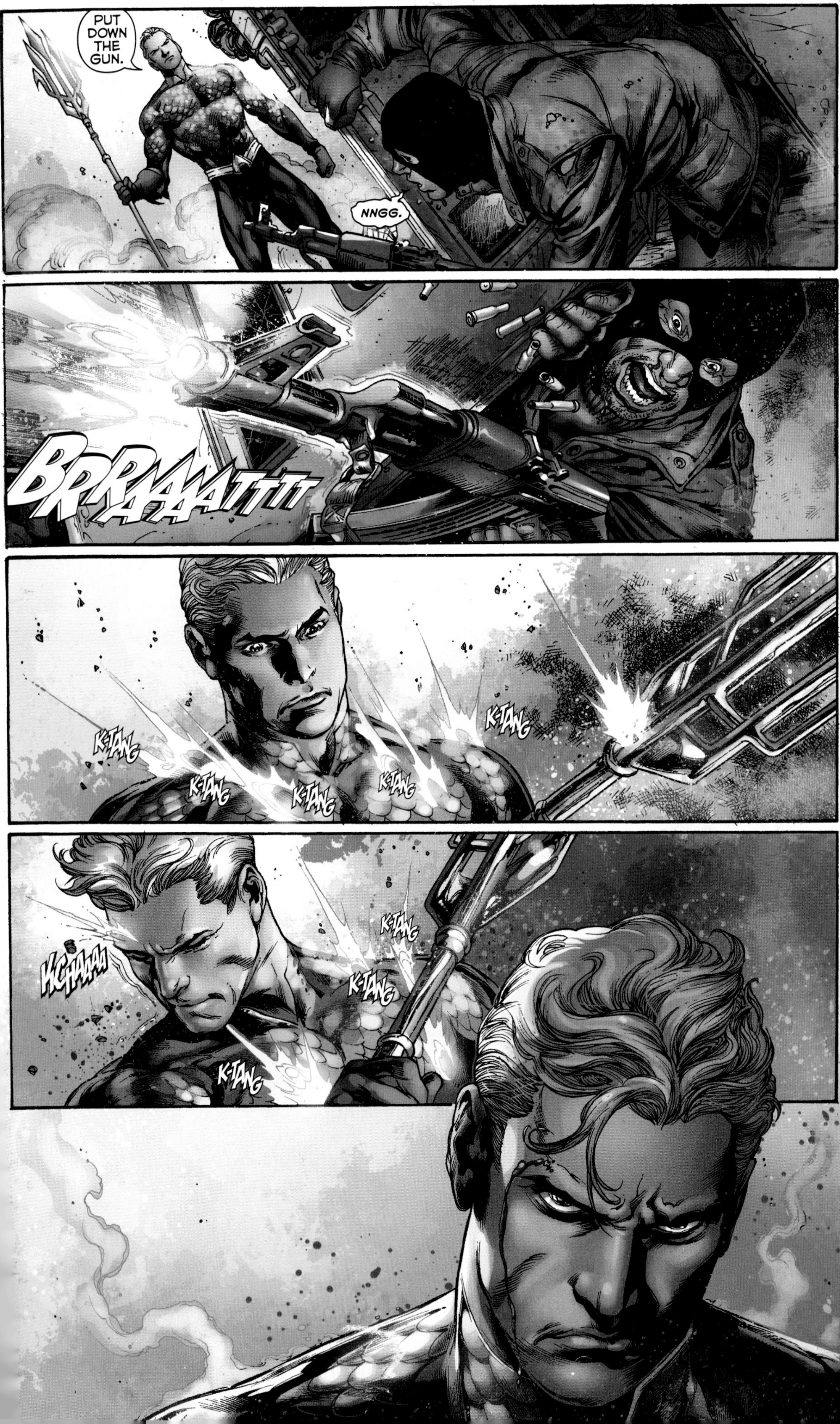
PUT DOWN THE GUN.
NNGG.
BRRAAAATTTT
K-TANG
K-TANG
K-TANG
K-TANG
K-TANG
KCHAAAA
K-TANG
K-TANG
K-TANG

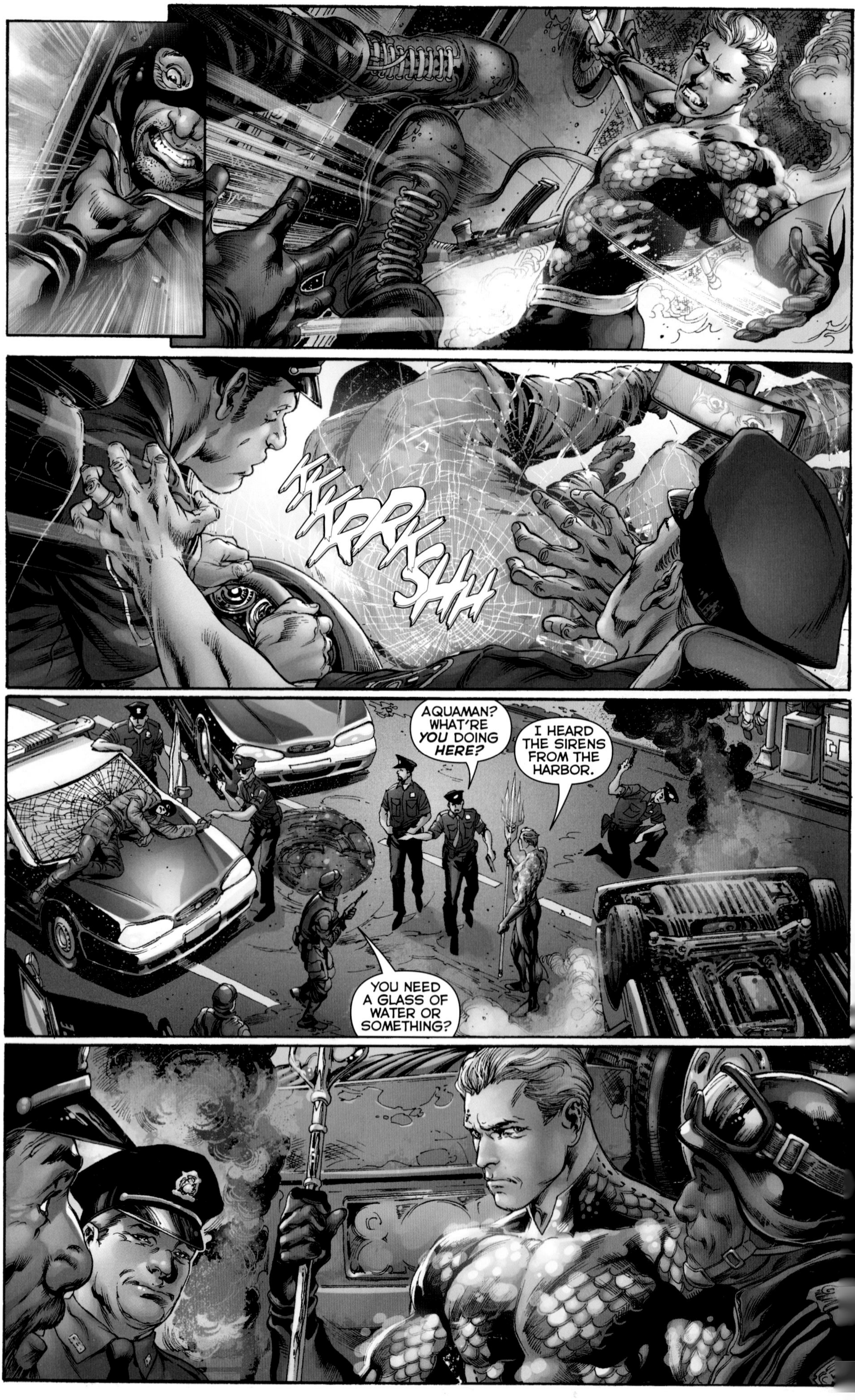
KKKRRKSHH
AQUAMAN? WHAT'RE YOU DOING HERE?
I HEARD THE SIRENS FROM THE HARBOR.
YOU NEED A GLASS OF WATER OR SOMETHING?

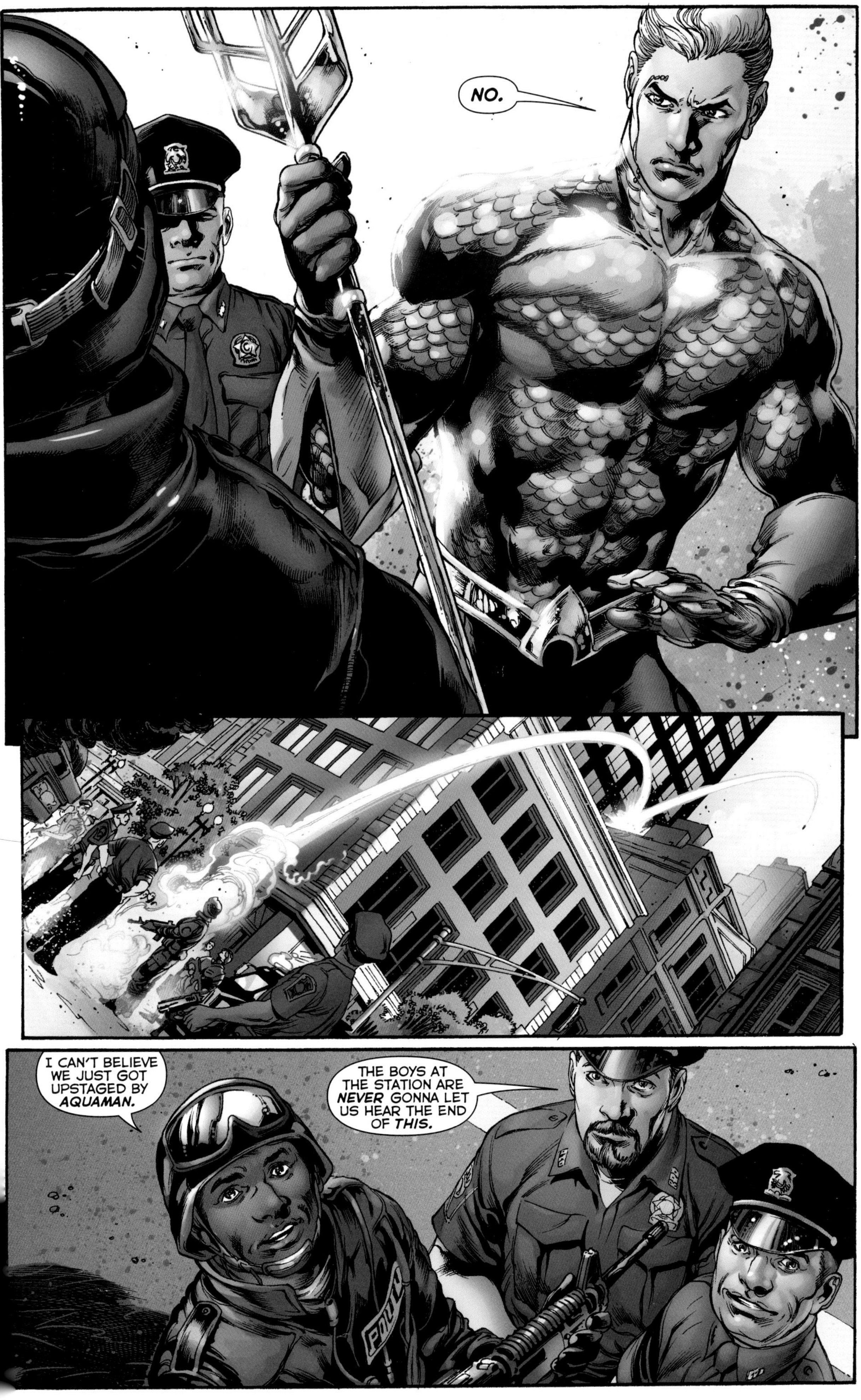
NO.
I CAN'T BELIEVE WE JUST GOT UPSTAGED BY AQUAMAN.
THE BOYS AT THE STATION ARE NEVER GONNA LET US HEAR THE END OF THIS.

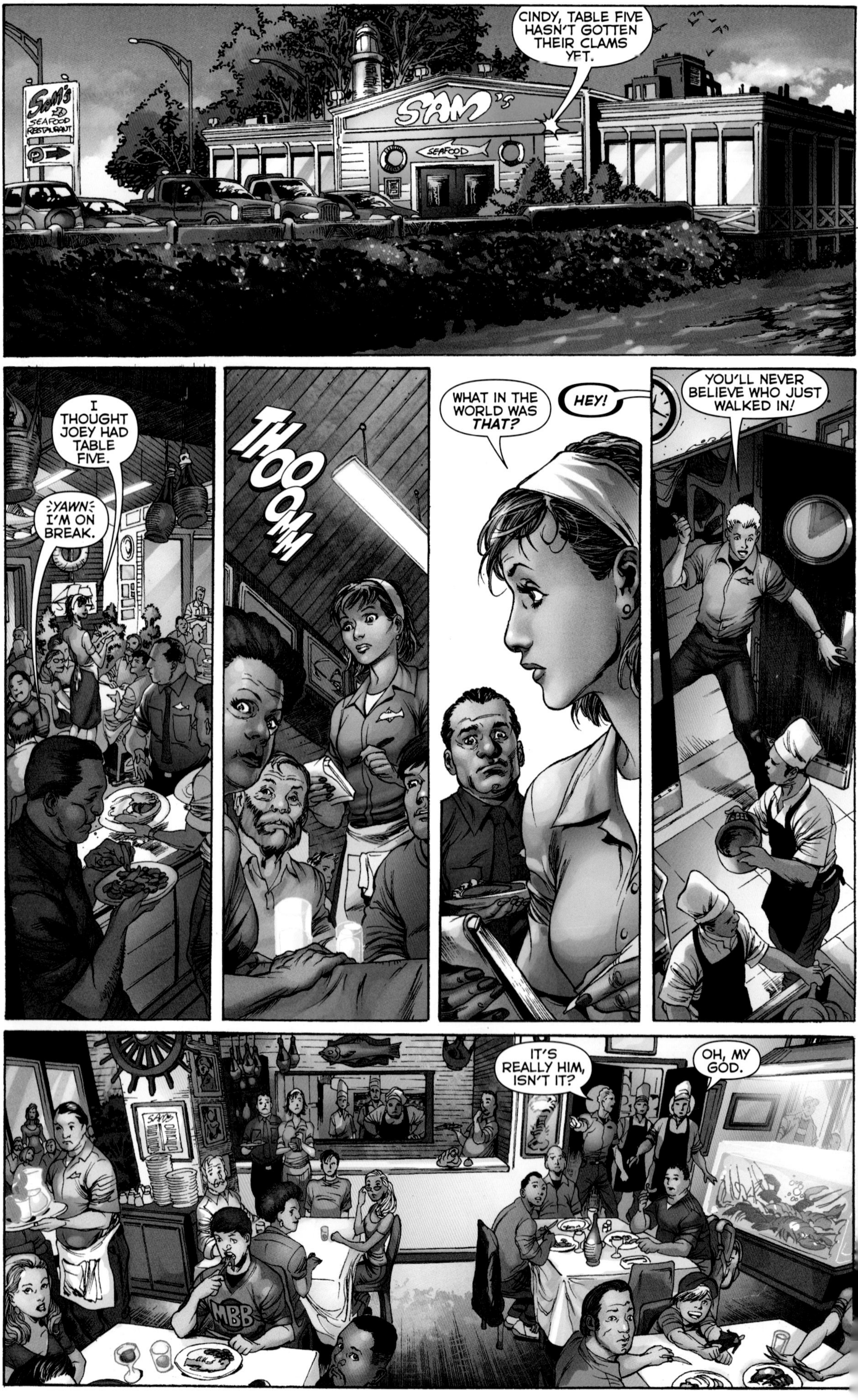
Sam's
SEAFOOD RESTAURANT
P
SAM'S
SEAFOOD
CINDY, TABLE FIVE HASN'T GOTTEN THEIR CLAMS YET.
I THOUGHT JOEY HAD TABLE FIVE.
YAWN I'M ON BREAK.
THOOOMM
WHAT IN THE WORLD WAS THAT?
HEY!
YOU'LL NEVER BELIEVE WHO JUST WALKED IN!
IT'S REALLY HIM, ISN'T IT?
OH, MY GOD.
MBB

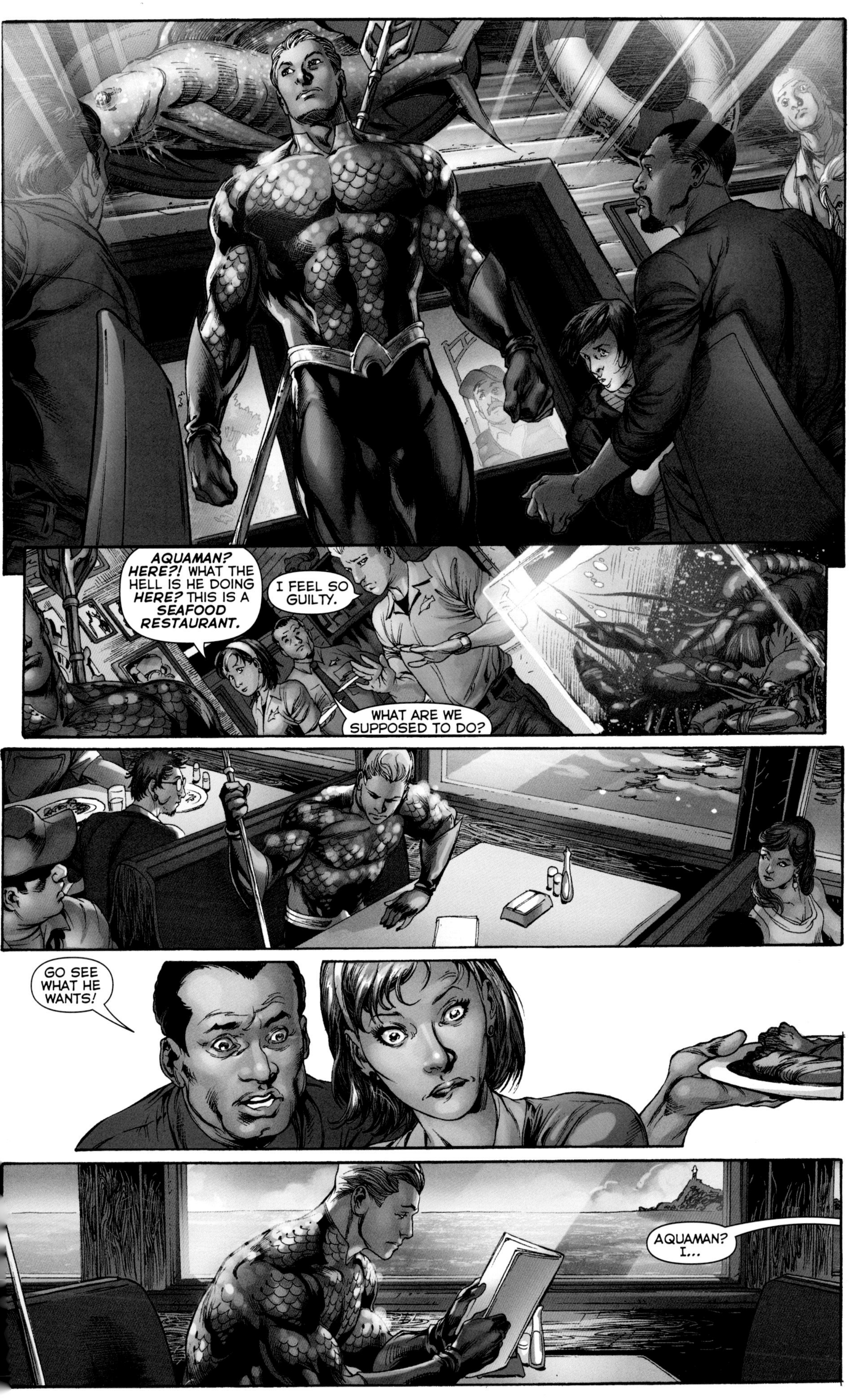
AQUAMAN? HERE?! WHAT THE HELL IS HE DOING HERE? THIS IS A SEAFOOD RESTAURANT.
I FEEL SO GUILTY.
WHAT ARE WE SUPPOSED TO DO?
GO SEE WHAT HE WANTS!
AQUAMAN? I...

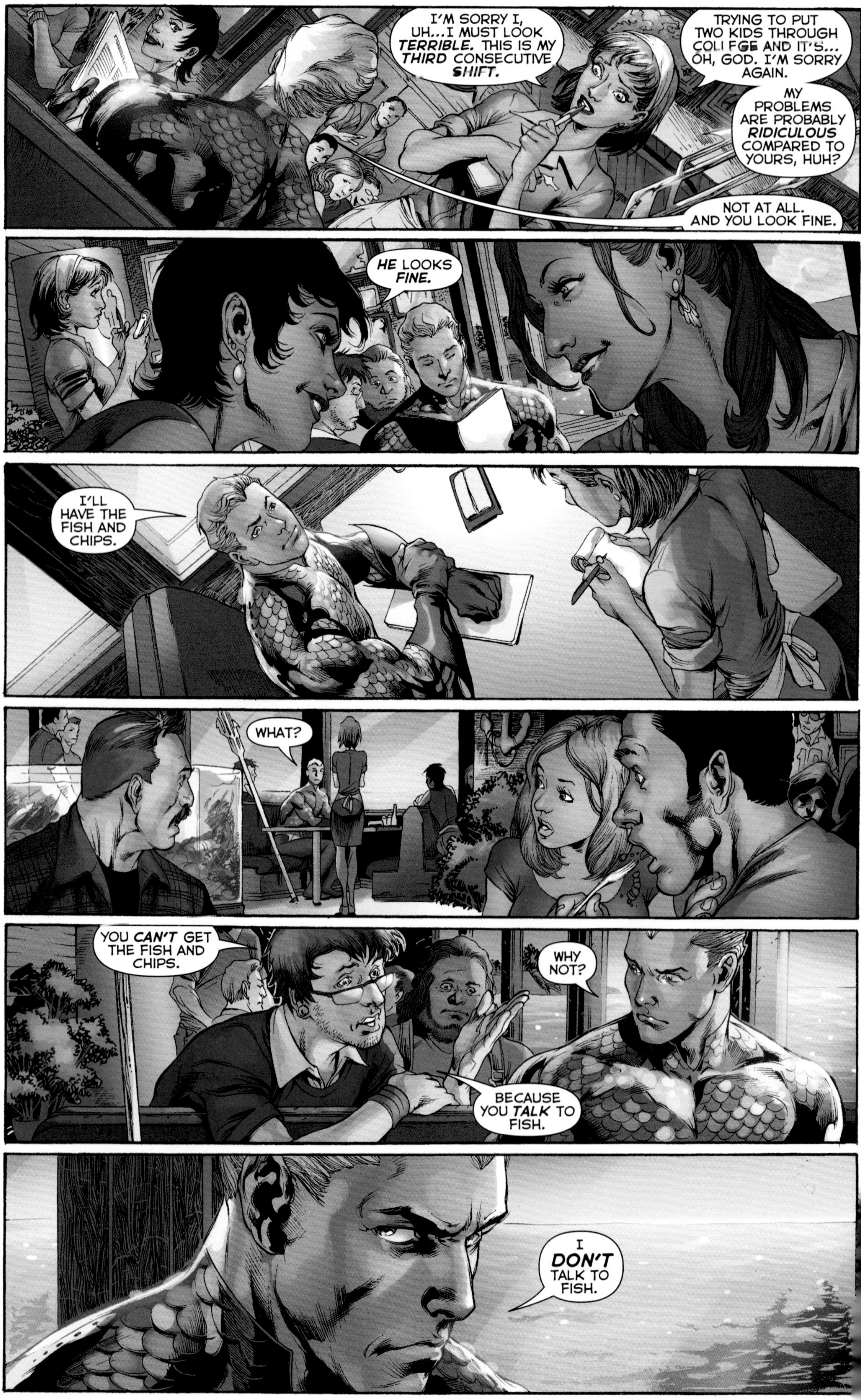
I'M SORRY I, UH...I MUST LOOK TERRIBLE. THIS IS MY THIRD CONSECUTIVE SHIFT.
TRYING TO PUT TWO KIDS THROUGH COLLEGE AND IT'S... OH, GOD. I'M SORRY AGAIN.
MY PROBLEMS ARE PROBABLY RIDICULOUS COMPARED TO YOURS, HUH?
NOT AT ALL. AND YOU LOOK FINE.
HE LOOKS FINE.
I'LL HAVE THE FISH AND CHIPS.
WHAT?
YOU CAN'T GET THE FISH AND CHIPS.
WHY NOT?
BECAUSE YOU TALK TO FISH.
I DON'T TALK TO FISH.

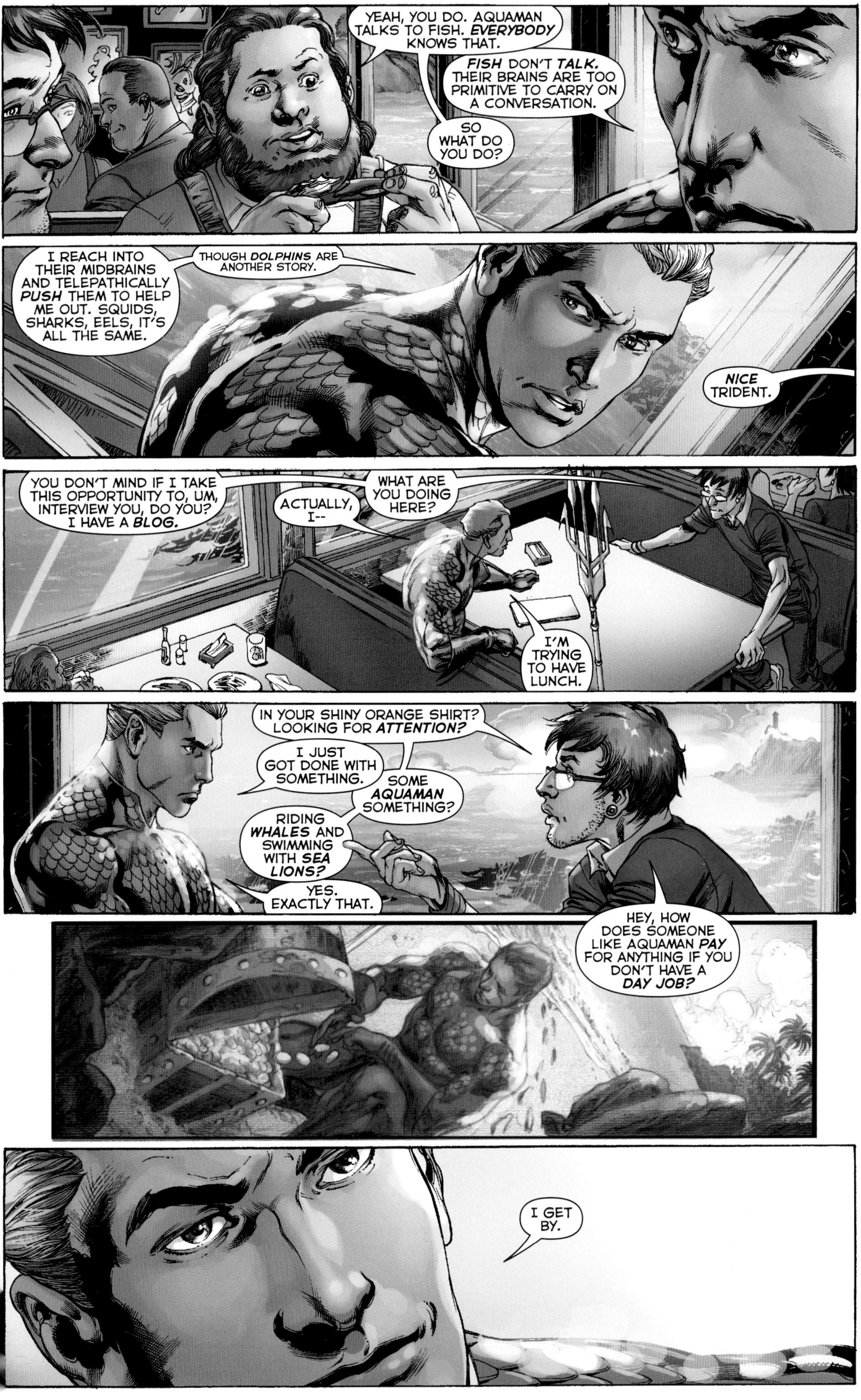

YEAH, YOU DO. AQUAMAN TALKS TO FISH. *EVERYBODY* KNOWS THAT.
FISH DON'T *TALK.* THEIR BRAINS ARE TOO PRIMITIVE TO CARRY ON A CONVERSATION.
SO WHAT DO YOU DO?
I REACH INTO THEIR MIDBRAINS AND TELEPATHICALLY *PUSH* THEM TO HELP ME OUT. SQUIDS, SHARKS, EELS, IT'S ALL THE SAME.
THOUGH *DOLPHINS* ARE ANOTHER STORY.
NICE TRIDENT.
YOU DON'T MIND IF I TAKE THIS OPPORTUNITY TO, UM, INTERVIEW YOU, DO YOU? I HAVE A *BLOG.*
ACTUALLY, I--
WHAT ARE YOU DOING HERE?
I'M TRYING TO HAVE LUNCH.
IN YOUR SHINY ORANGE SHIRT? LOOKING FOR *ATTENTION?*
I JUST GOT DONE WITH SOMETHING.
SOME *AQUAMAN* SOMETHING?
RIDING *WHALES* AND SWIMMING WITH *SEA LIONS?*
YES. EXACTLY THAT.
HEY, HOW DOES SOMEONE LIKE AQUAMAN *PAY* FOR ANYTHING IF YOU DON'T HAVE A *DAY JOB?*
I GET BY.

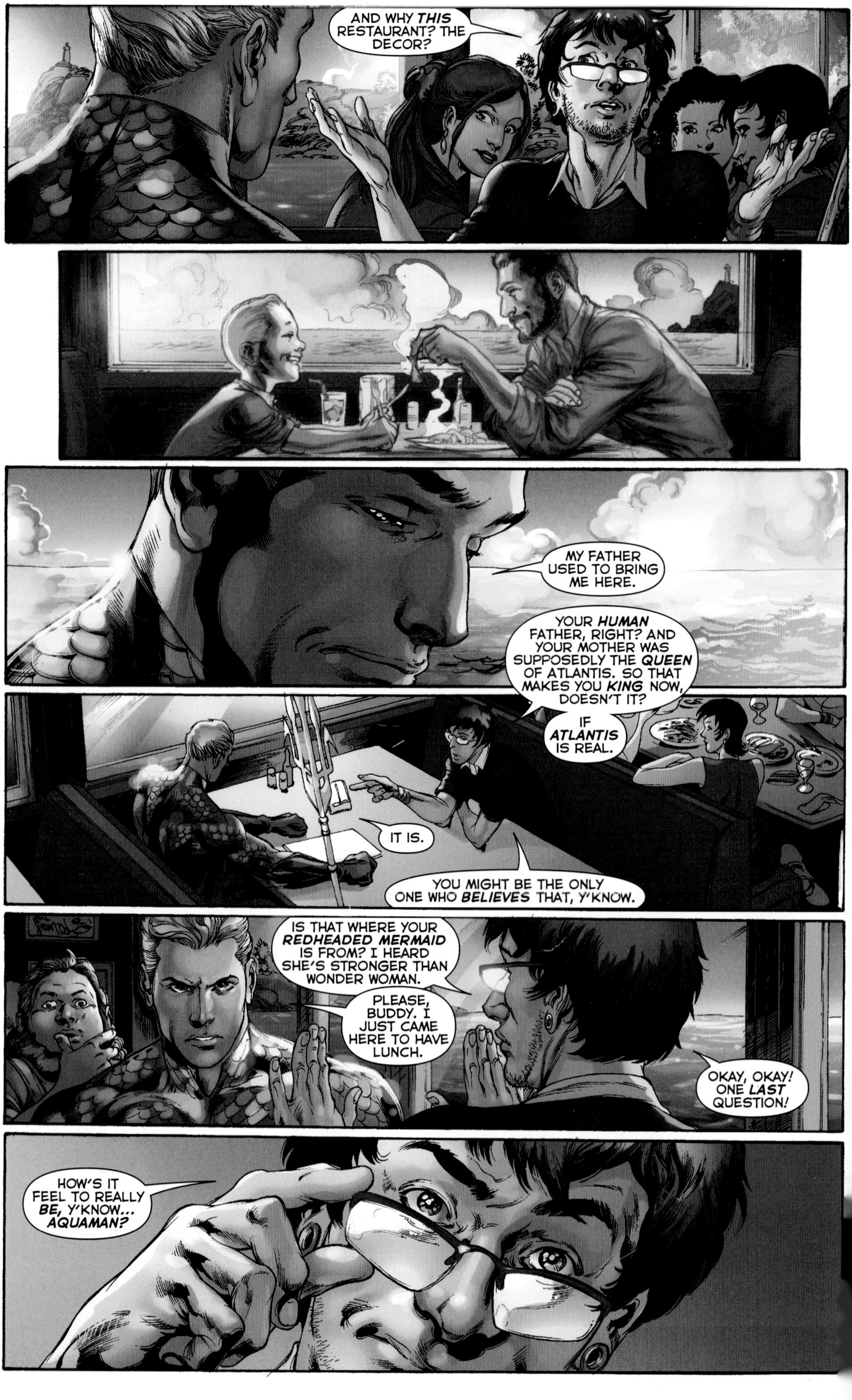

AND WHY *THIS* RESTAURANT? THE DECOR?
MY FATHER USED TO BRING ME HERE.
YOUR *HUMAN* FATHER, RIGHT? AND YOUR MOTHER WAS SUPPOSEDLY THE *QUEEN* OF ATLANTIS. SO THAT MAKES YOU *KING* NOW, DOESN'T IT?
IF *ATLANTIS* IS REAL.
IT IS.
YOU MIGHT BE THE ONLY ONE WHO *BELIEVES* THAT, Y'KNOW.
IS THAT WHERE YOUR *REDHEADED MERMAID* IS FROM? I HEARD SHE'S STRONGER THAN WONDER WOMAN.
PLEASE, BUDDY. I JUST CAME HERE TO HAVE LUNCH.
OKAY, OKAY! ONE *LAST* QUESTION!
HOW'S IT FEEL TO REALLY *BE,* Y'KNOW... *AQUAMAN?*

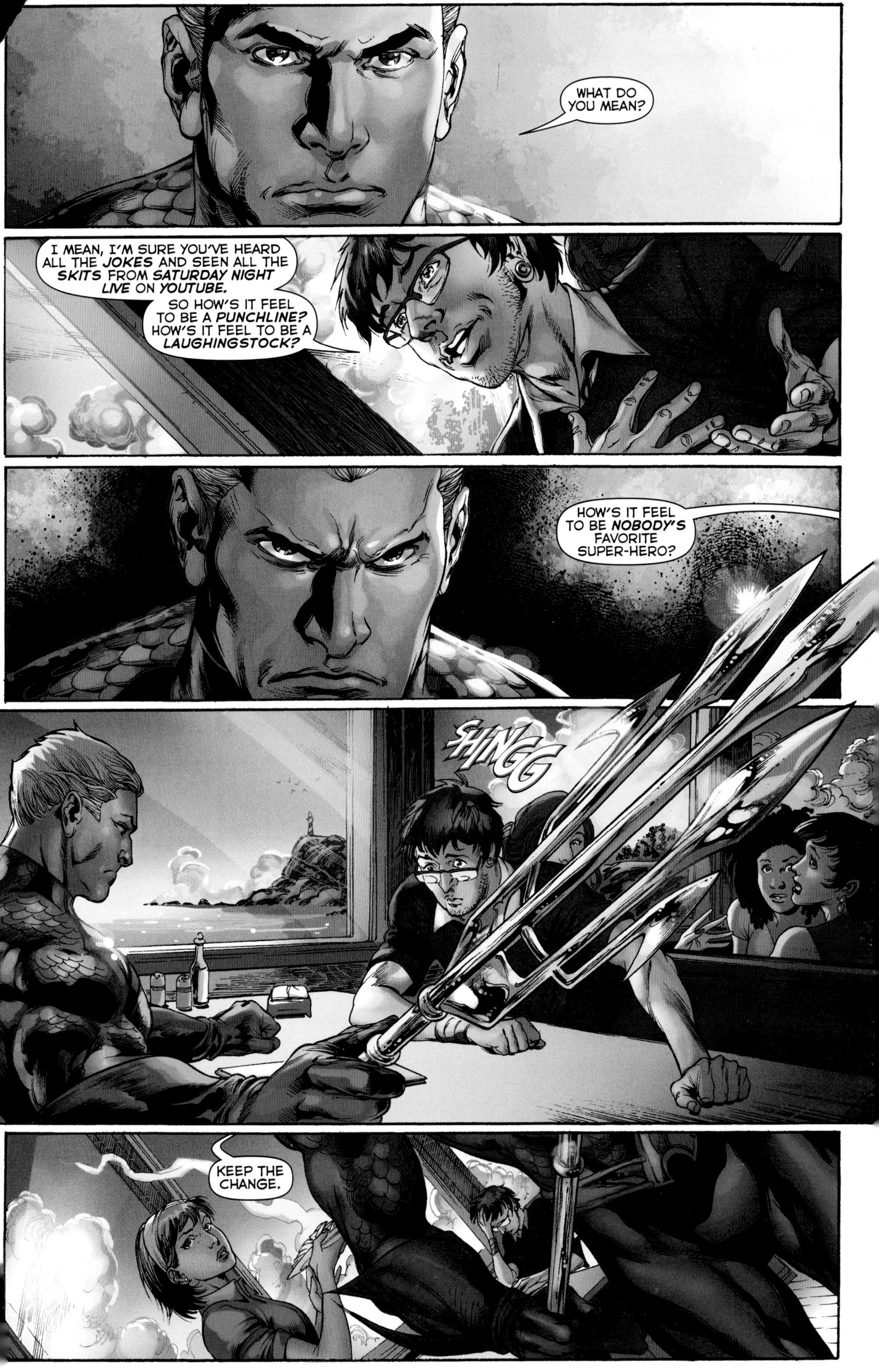

WHAT DO YOU MEAN?
I MEAN, I'M SURE YOU'VE HEARD ALL THE JOKES AND SEEN ALL THE SKITS FROM SATURDAY NIGHT LIVE ON YOUTUBE.
SO HOW'S IT FEEL TO BE A PUNCHLINE? HOW'S IT FEEL TO BE A LAUGHINGSTOCK?
HOW'S IT FEEL TO BE NOBODY'S FAVORITE SUPER-HERO?
SHINGG
KEEP THE CHANGE.

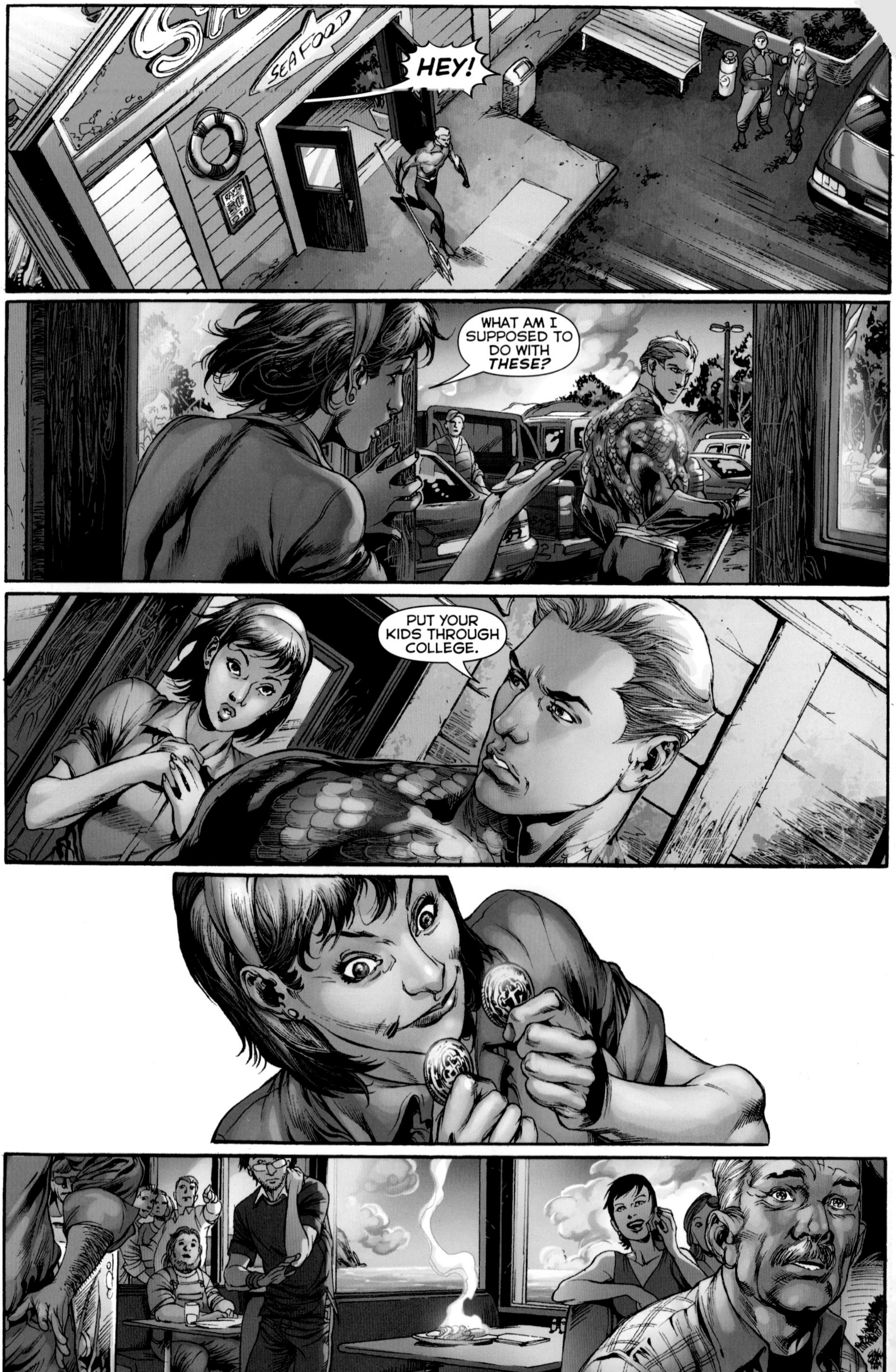
SEAFOOD
HEY!
WHAT AM I SUPPOSED TO DO WITH THESE?
PUT YOUR KIDS THROUGH COLLEGE.

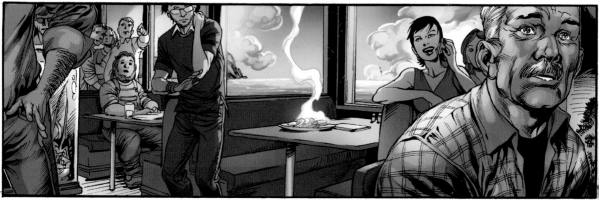

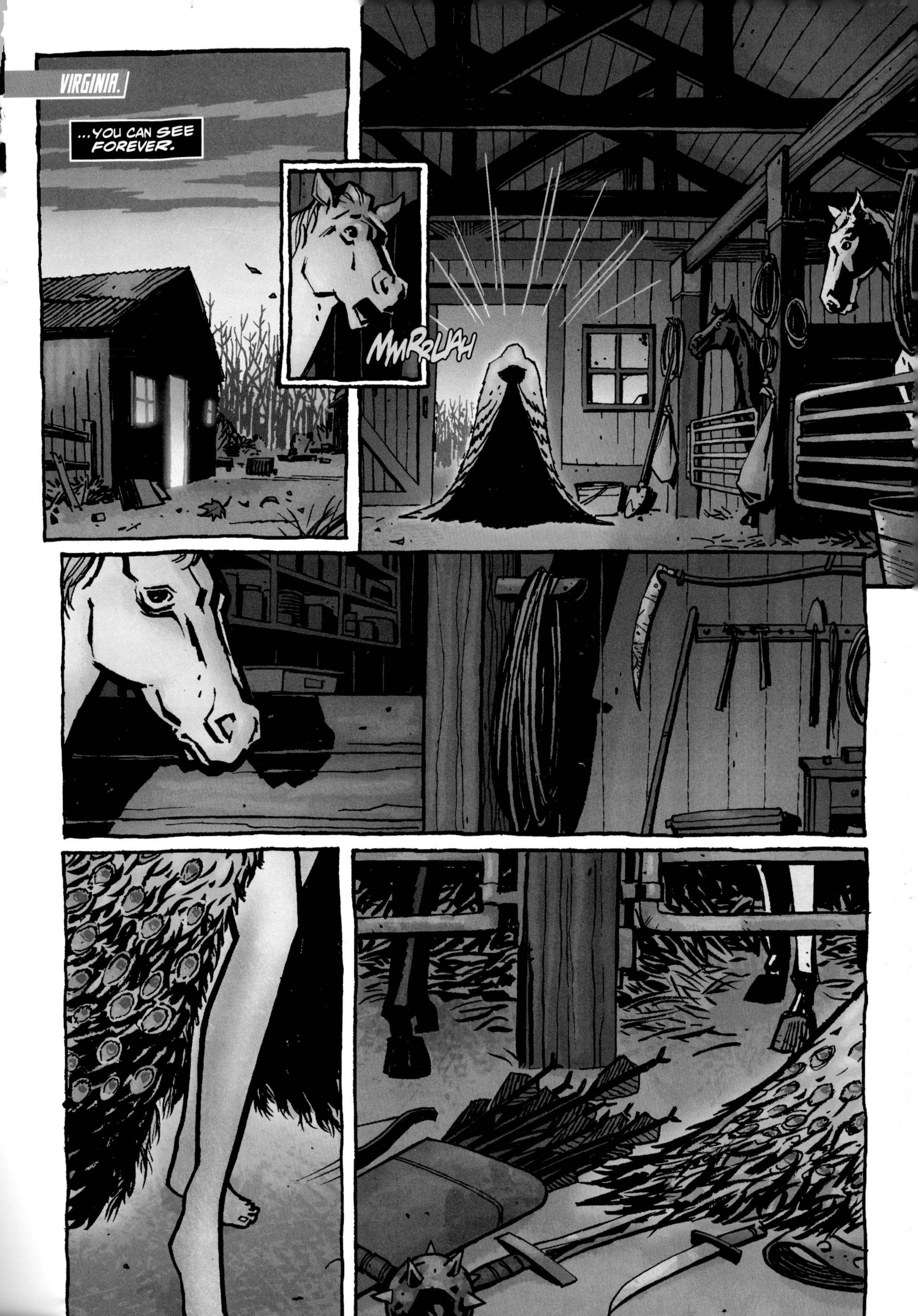

VIRGINIA.
...YOU CAN SEE FOREVER.
MMRRUAH

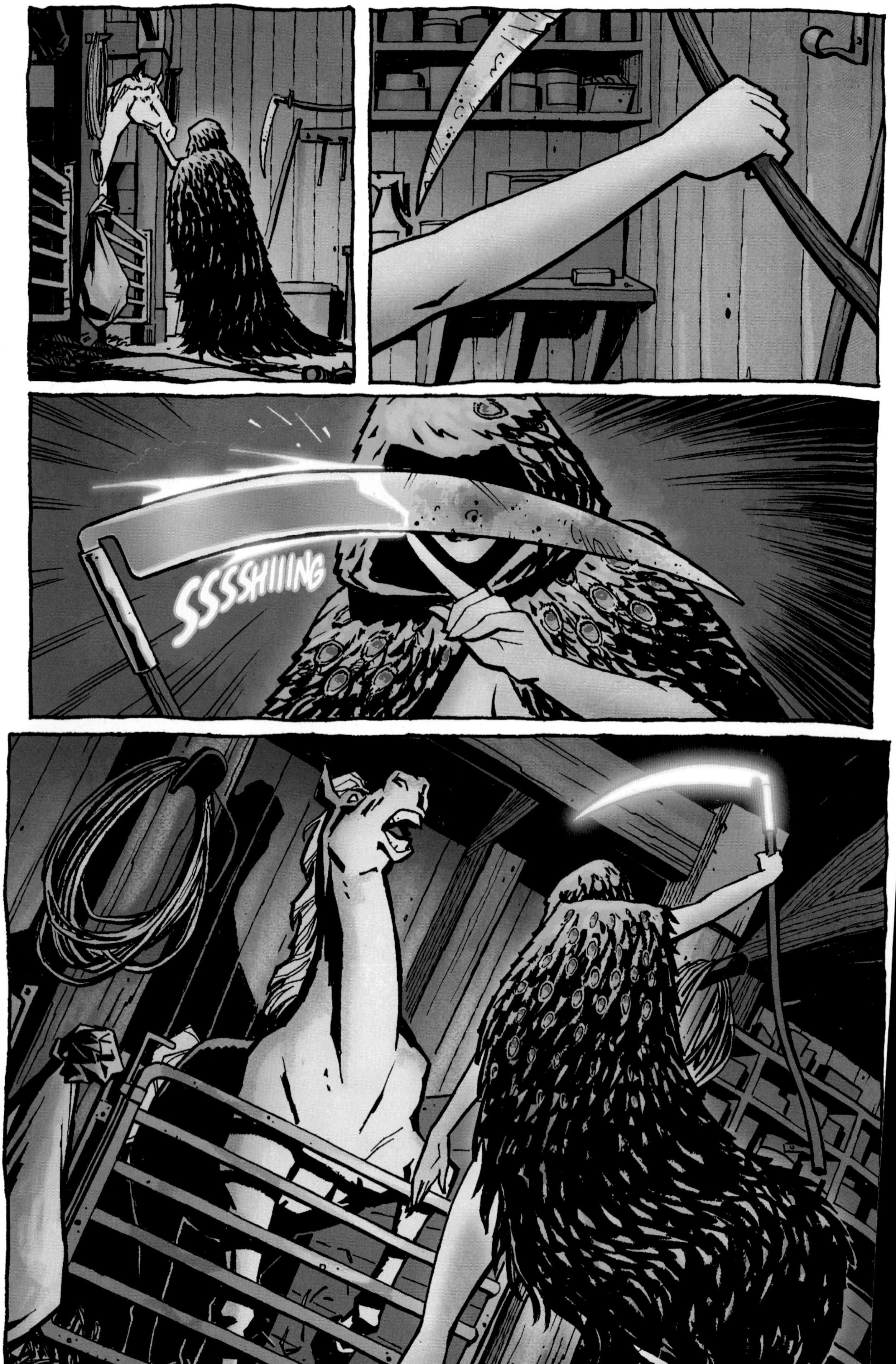
SSSSHIIING

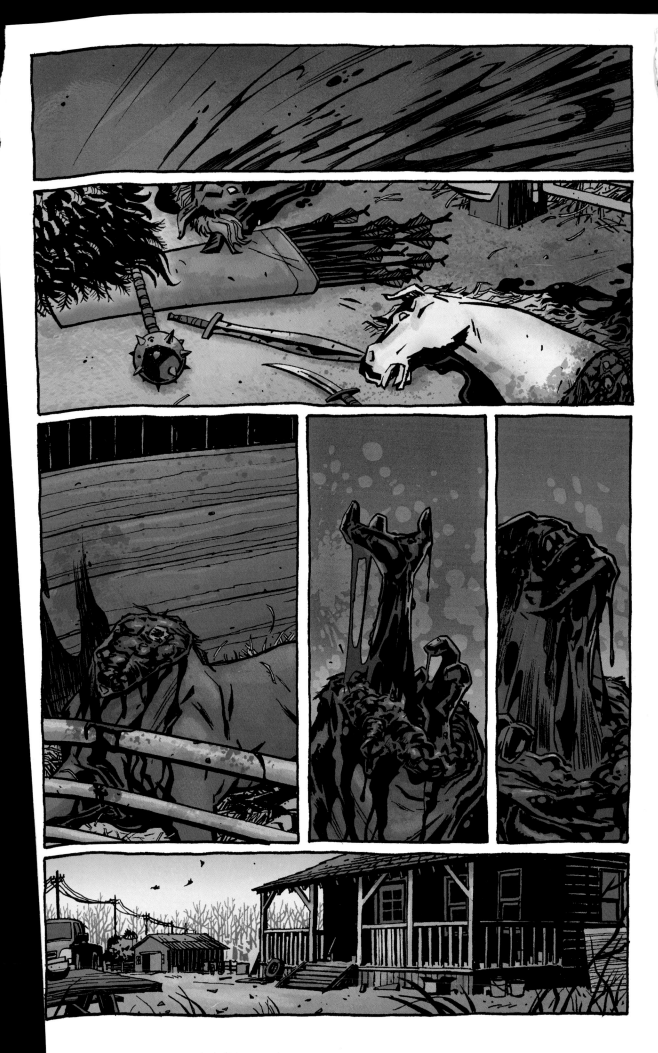

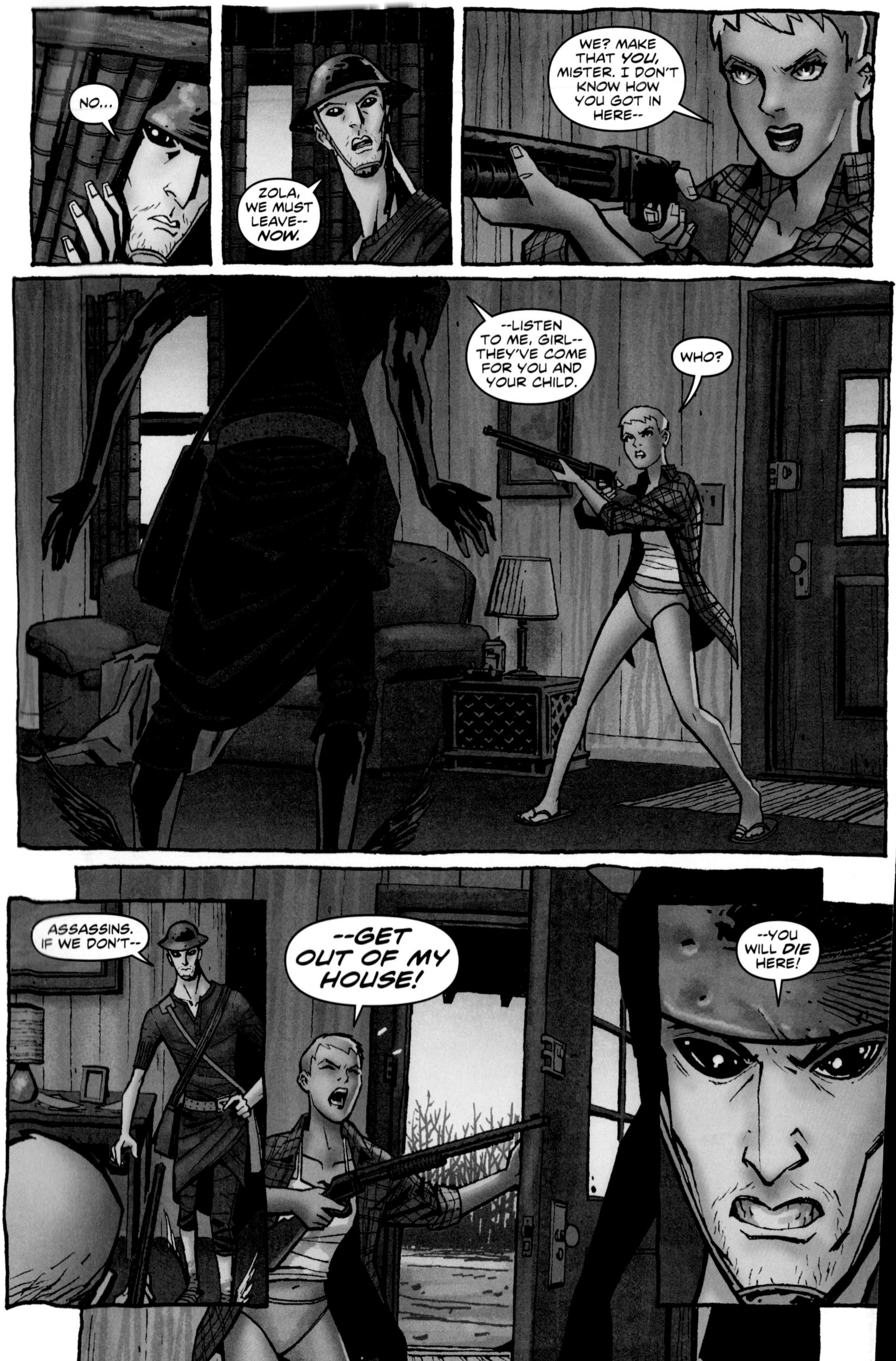
NO...
ZOLA, WE MUST LEAVE-- NOW.
WE? MAKE THAT YOU, MISTER. I DON'T KNOW HOW YOU GOT IN HERE--
--LISTEN TO ME, GIRL-- THEY'VE COME FOR YOU AND YOUR CHILD.
WHO?
ASSASSINS. IF WE DON'T--
--GET OUT OF MY HOUSE!
--YOU WILL DIE HERE!

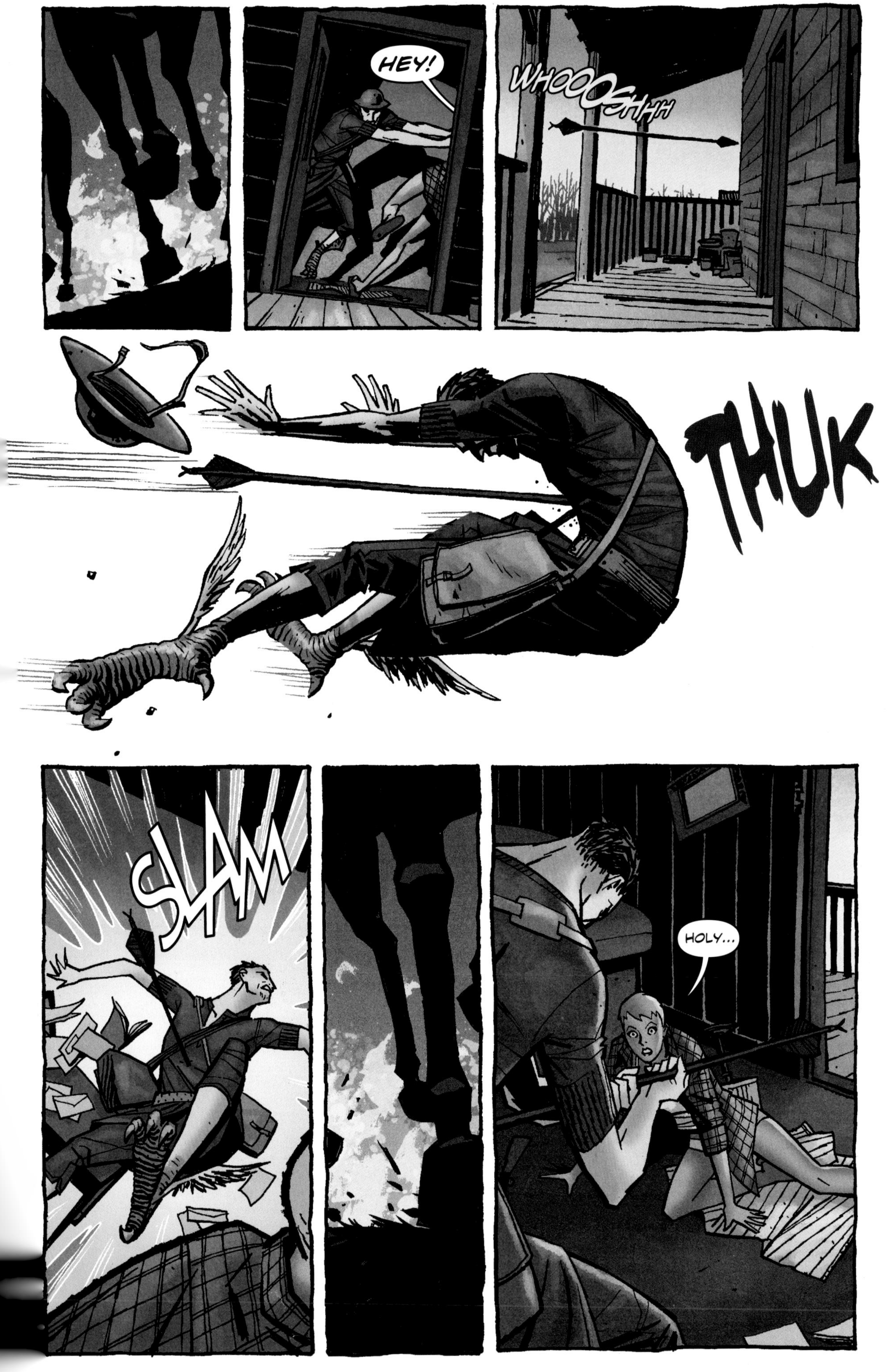
HEY!
WHOOOOSHHH
THUK
SLAM
HOLY...

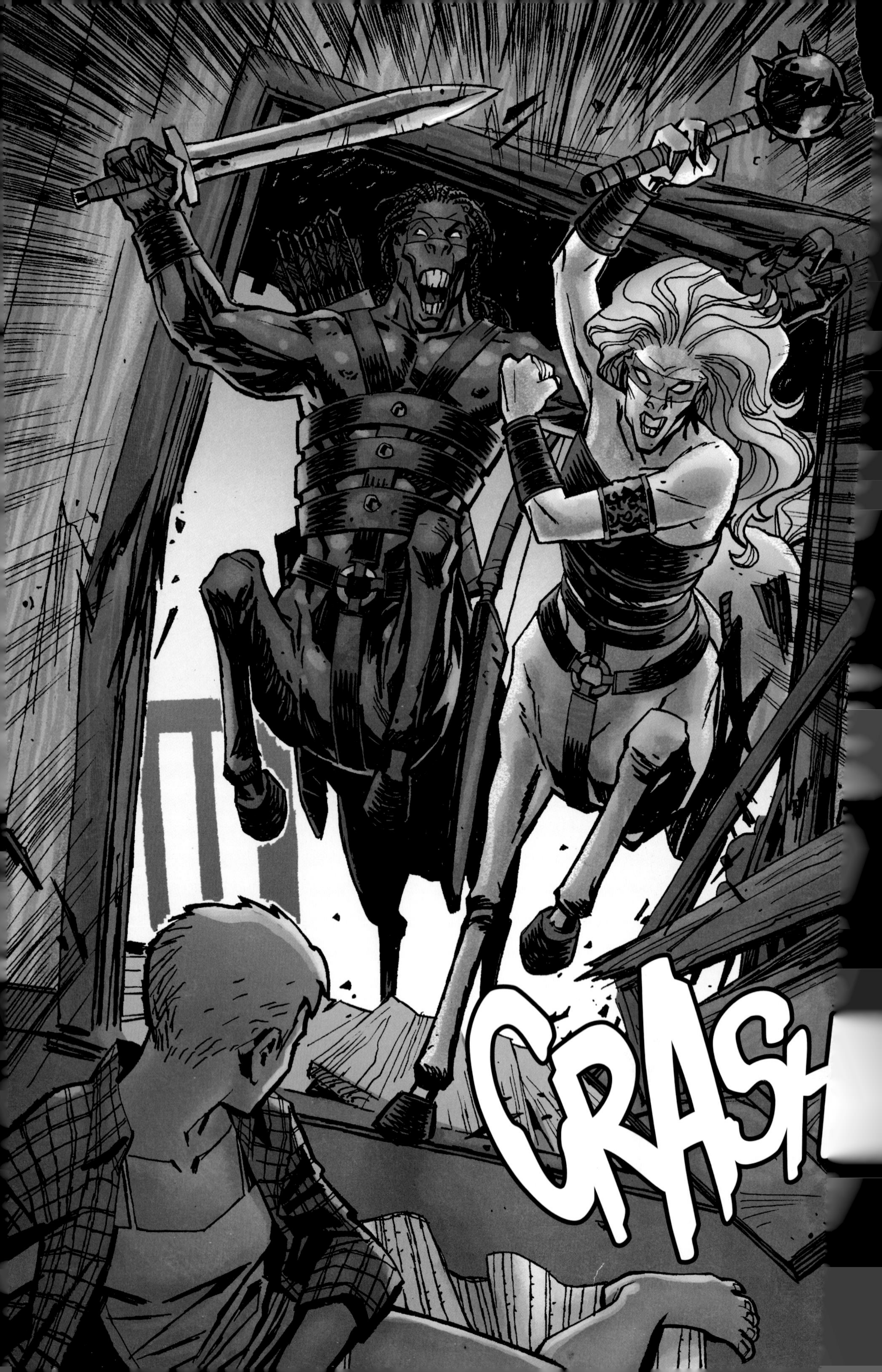
CRASH

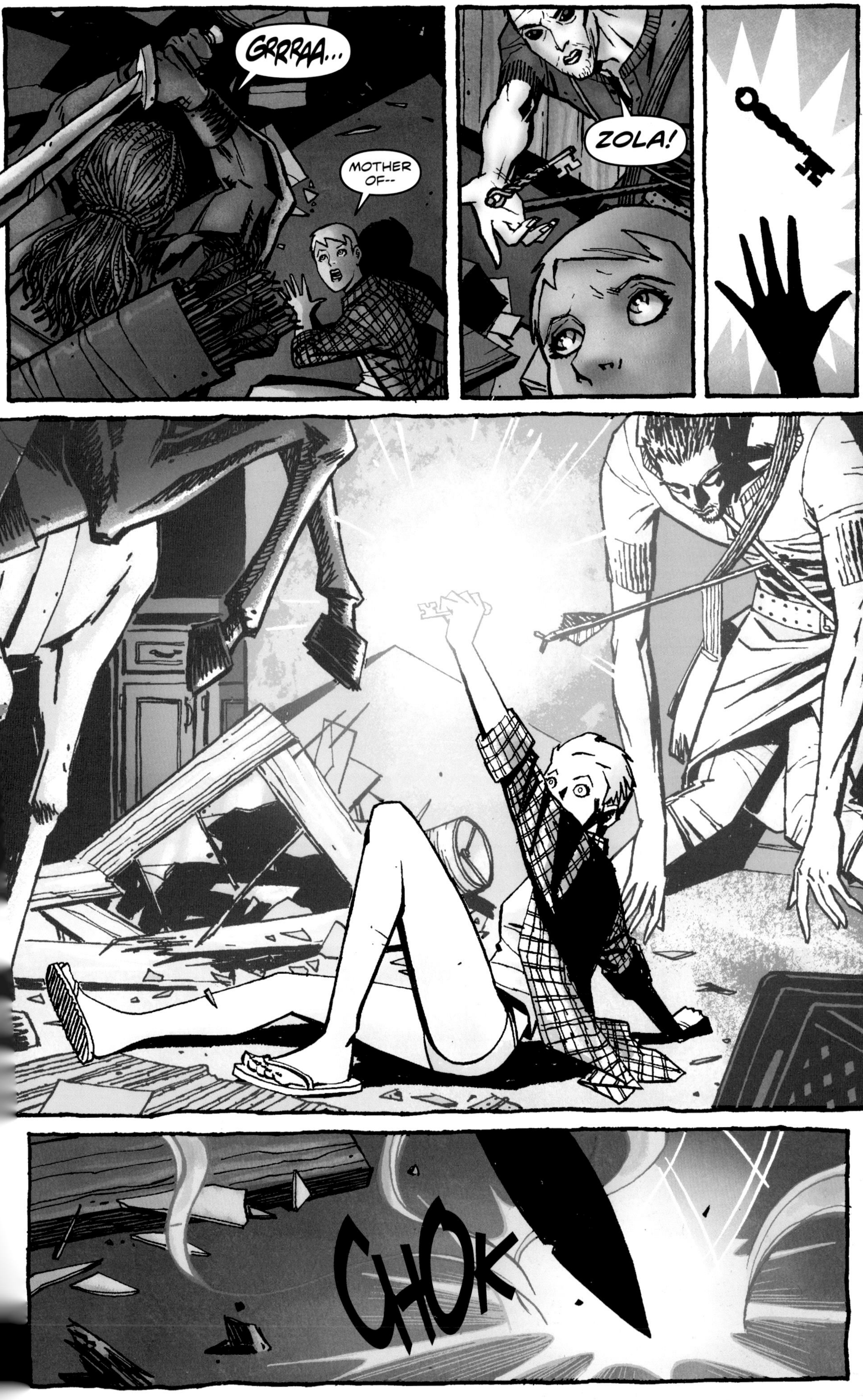
GRRRAA...
MOTHER OF--
ZOLA!
CHOK

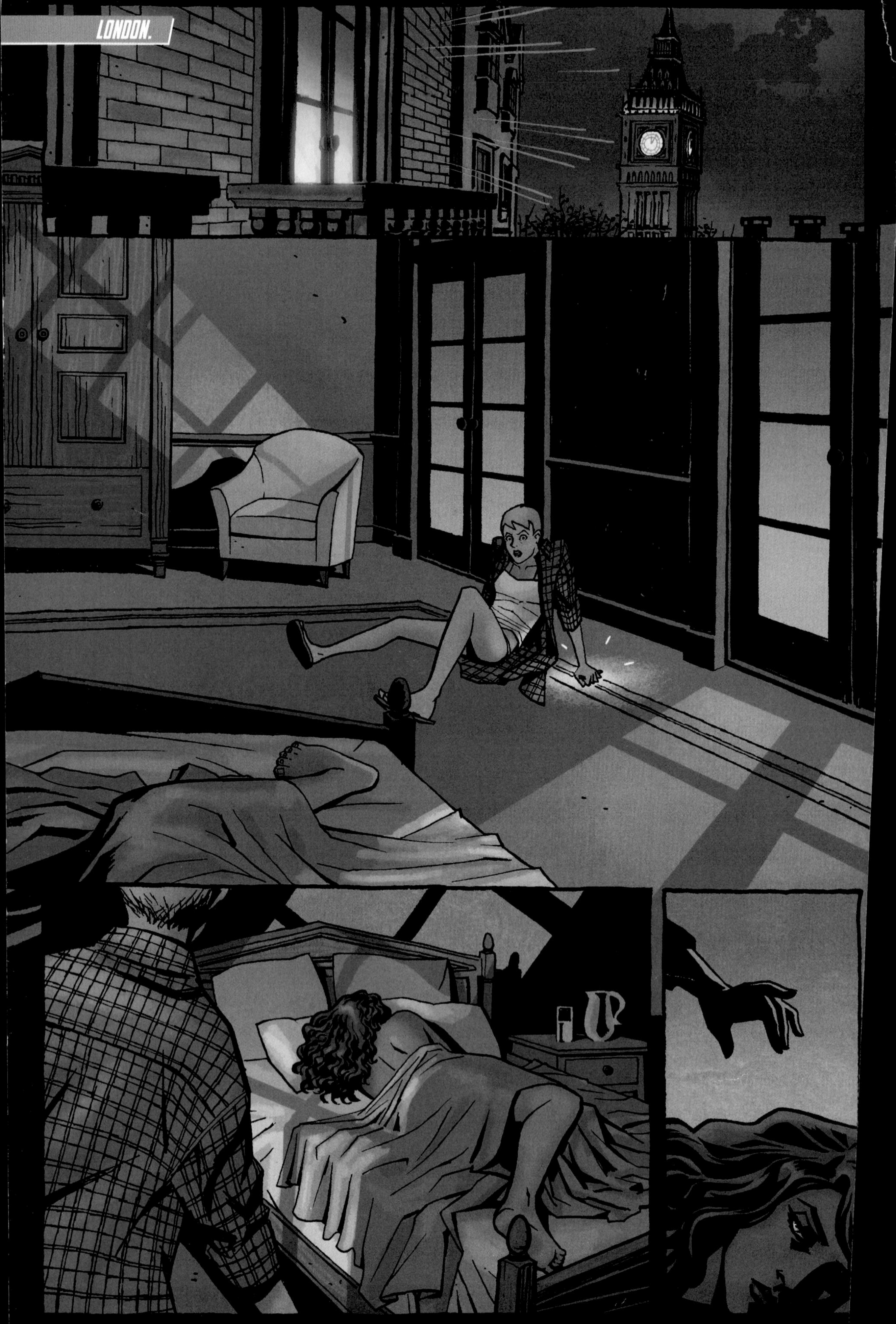
LONDON.

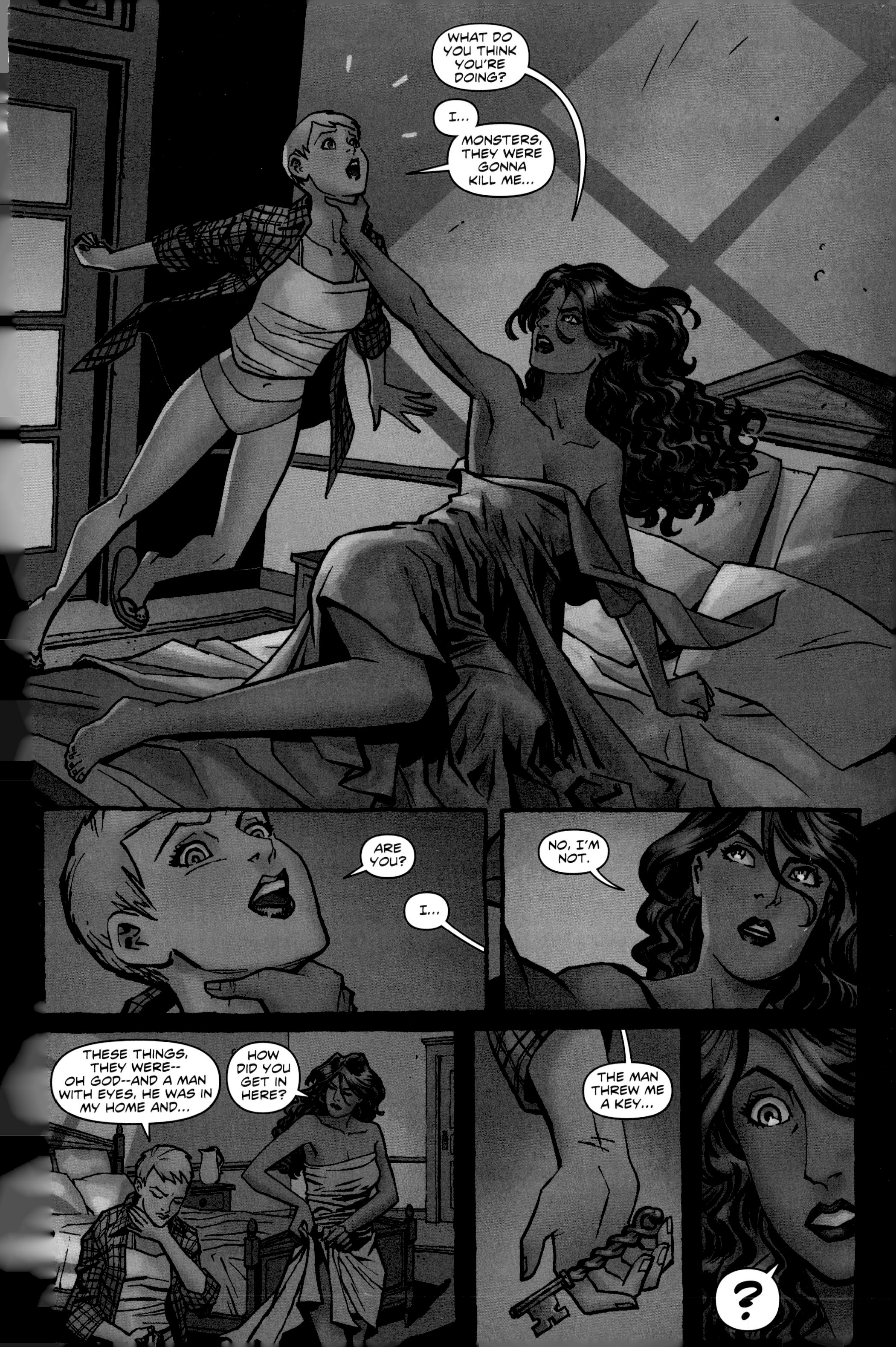
WHAT DO YOU THINK YOU'RE DOING?
I...
MONSTERS, THEY WERE GONNA KILL ME...
ARE YOU?
I...
NO, I'M NOT.
THESE THINGS, THEY WERE-- OH GOD--AND A MAN WITH EYES, HE WAS IN MY HOME AND...
HOW DID YOU GET IN HERE?
THE MAN THREW ME A KEY...
?

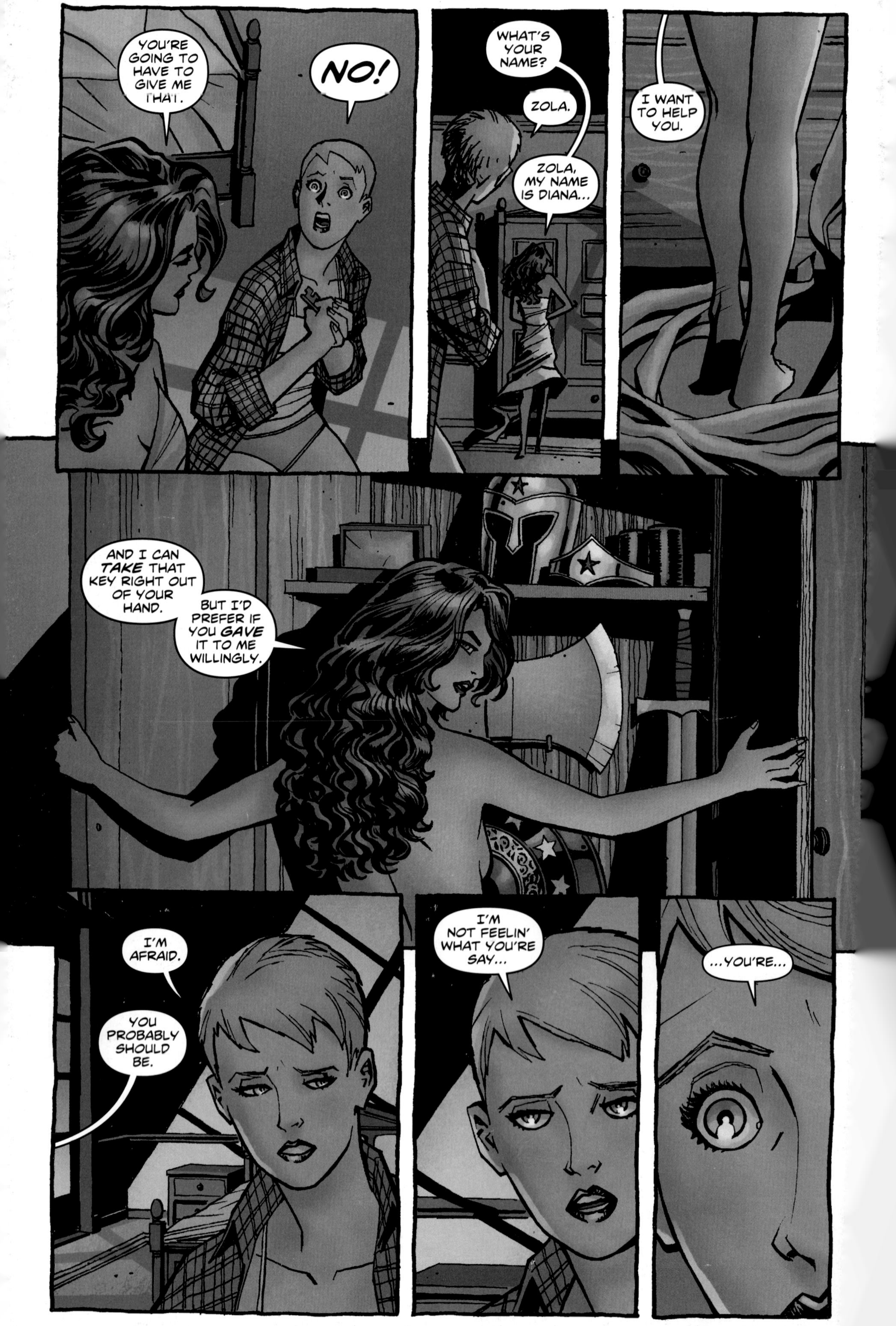

YOU'RE GOING TO HAVE TO GIVE ME THAT.
NO!
WHAT'S YOUR NAME?
ZOLA.
ZOLA, MY NAME IS DIANA...
I WANT TO HELP YOU.
AND I CAN TAKE THAT KEY RIGHT OUT OF YOUR HAND.
BUT I'D PREFER IF YOU GAVE IT TO ME WILLINGLY.
I'M AFRAID.
YOU PROBABLY SHOULD BE.
I'M NOT FEELIN' WHAT YOU'RE SAY...
...YOU'RE...

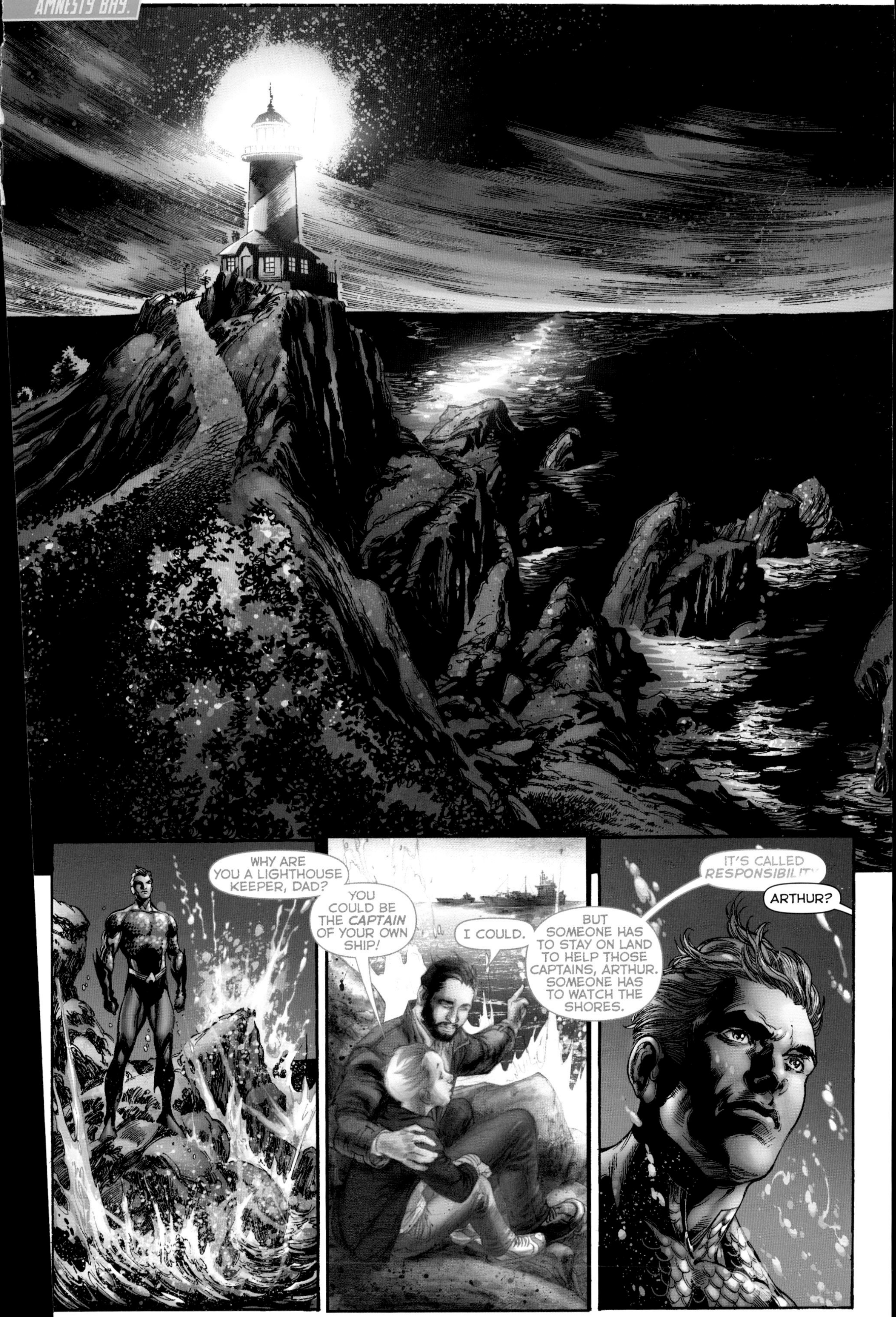
AMNESTY BAY.
WHY ARE YOU A LIGHTHOUSE KEEPER, DAD?
YOU COULD BE THE *CAPTAIN* OF YOUR OWN SHIP!
I COULD.
BUT SOMEONE HAS TO STAY ON LAND TO HELP THOSE CAPTAINS, ARTHUR. SOMEONE HAS TO WATCH THE SHORES.
ARTHUR?

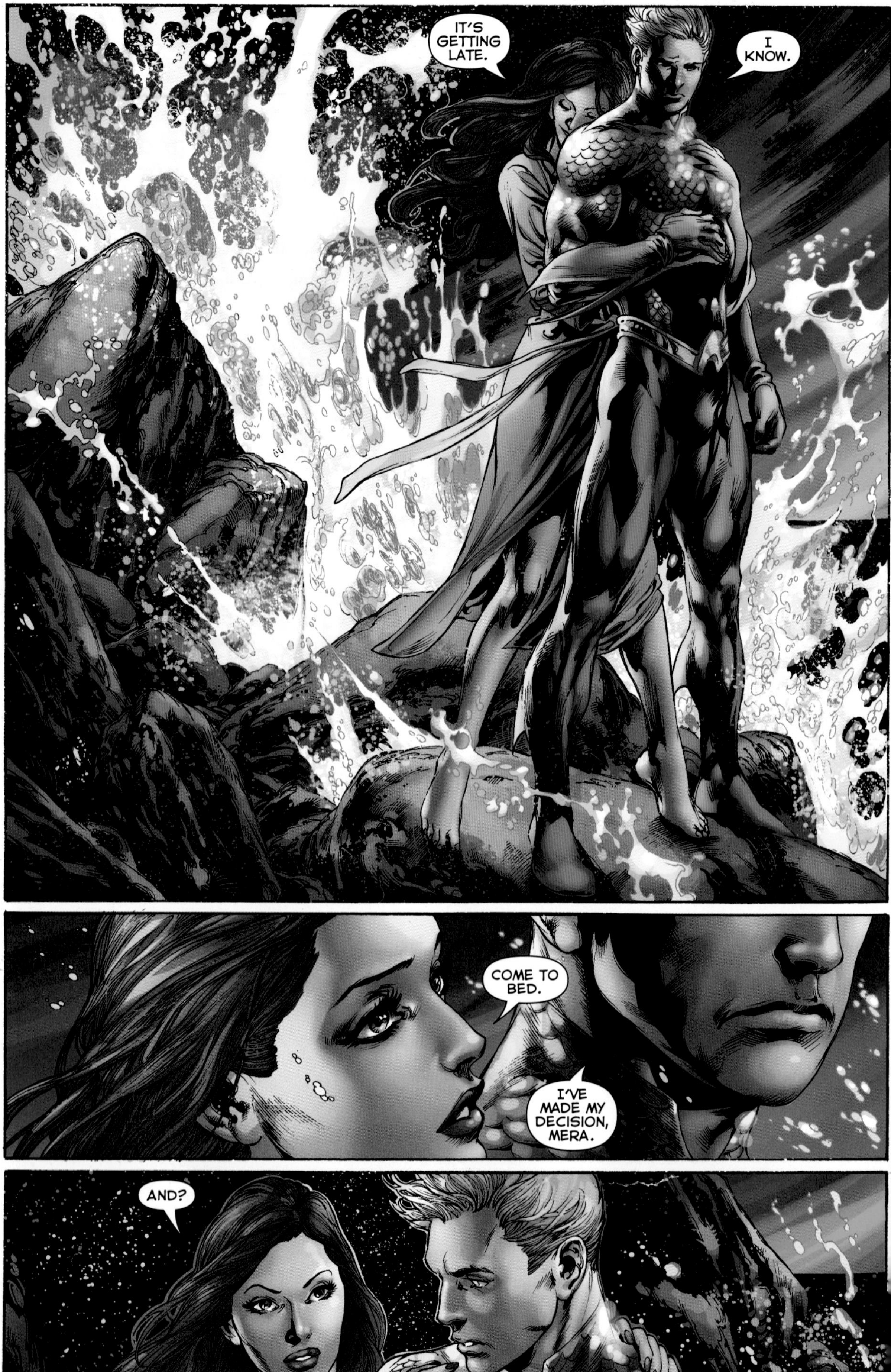
IT'S GETTING LATE.
I KNOW.
COME TO BED.
I'VE MADE MY DECISION, MERA.
AND?

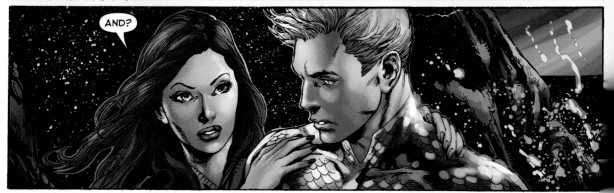

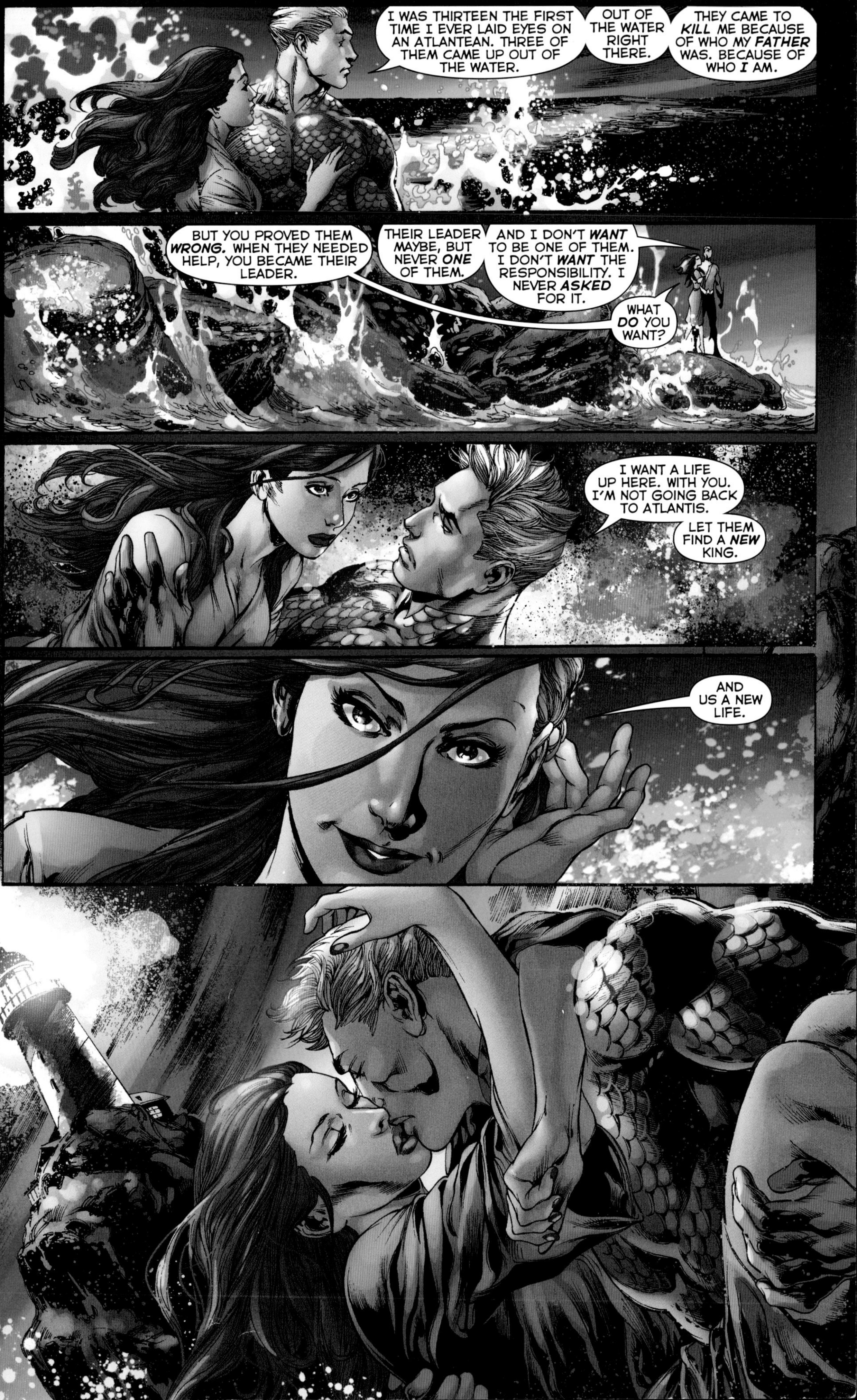
I WAS THIRTEEN THE FIRST TIME I EVER LAID EYES ON AN ATLANTEAN. THREE OF THEM CAME UP OUT OF THE WATER.
OUT OF THE WATER RIGHT THERE.
THEY CAME TO **KILL** ME BECAUSE OF WHO MY **FATHER** WAS. BECAUSE OF WHO **I** AM.
BUT YOU PROVED THEM **WRONG.** WHEN THEY NEEDED HELP, YOU BECAME THEIR LEADER.
THEIR LEADER MAYBE, BUT NEVER **ONE** OF THEM.
AND I DON'T **WANT** TO BE ONE OF THEM. I DON'T **WANT** THE RESPONSIBILITY. I NEVER **ASKED** FOR IT.
WHAT **DO** YOU WANT?
I WANT A LIFE UP HERE. WITH YOU. I'M NOT GOING BACK TO ATLANTIS.
LET THEM FIND A **NEW** KING.
AND US A NEW LIFE.

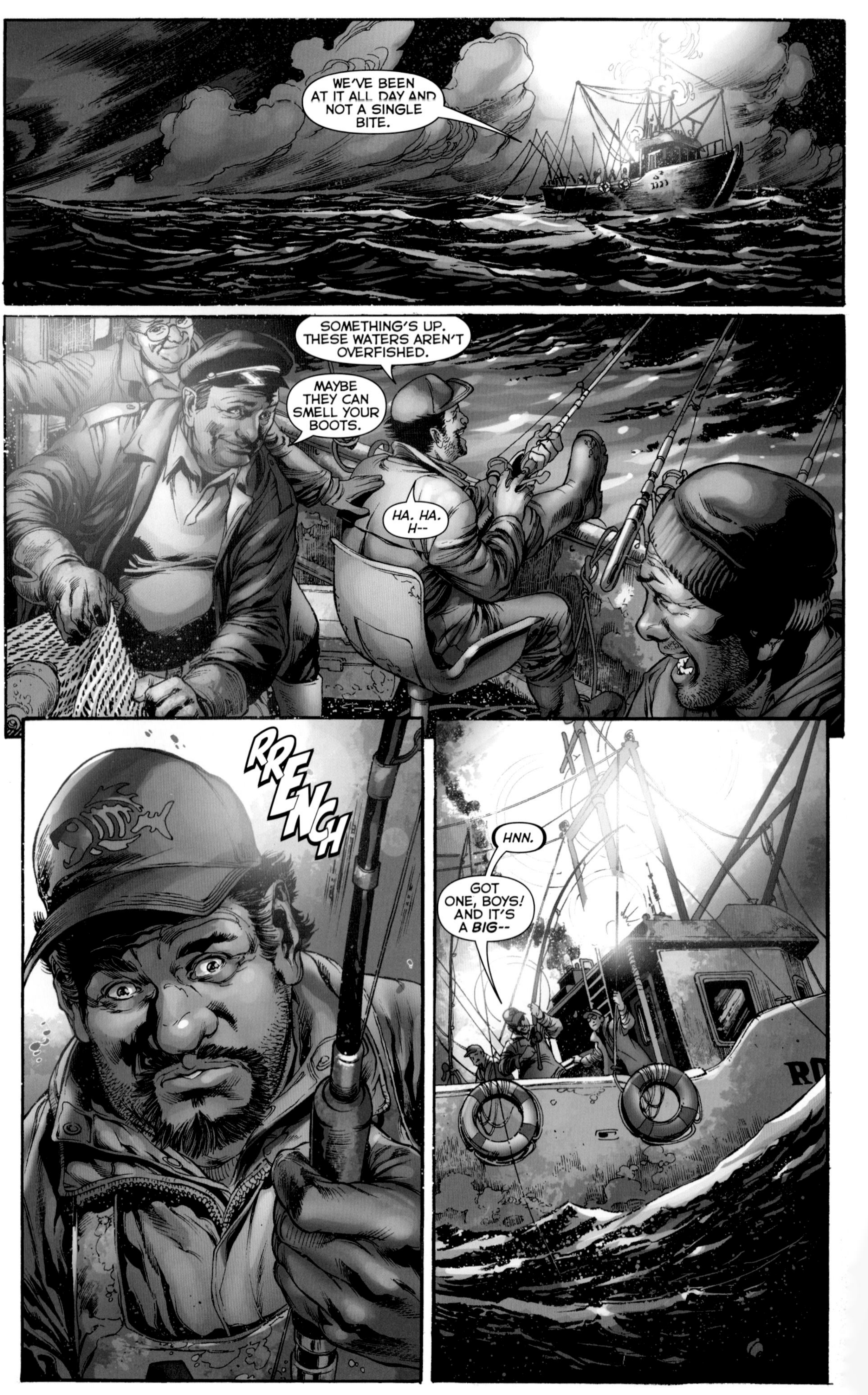
WE'VE BEEN AT IT ALL DAY AND NOT A SINGLE BITE.
SOMETHING'S UP. THESE WATERS AREN'T OVERFISHED.
MAYBE THEY CAN SMELL YOUR BOOTS.
HA. HA. H--
RRENCH
HNN.
GOT ONE, BOYS! AND IT'S A *BIG*--

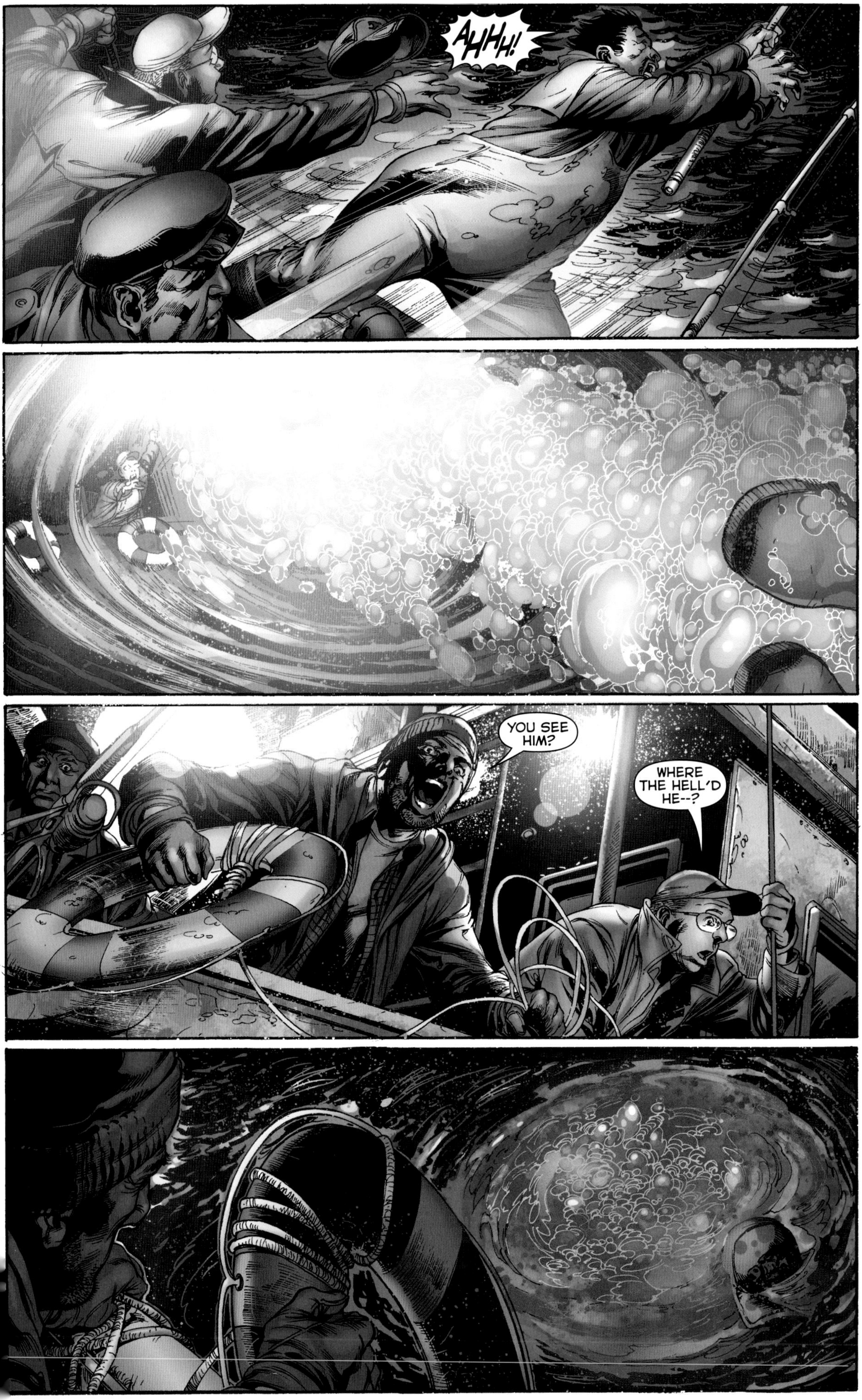
AHHH!
YOU SEE HIM?
WHERE THE HELL'D HE--?

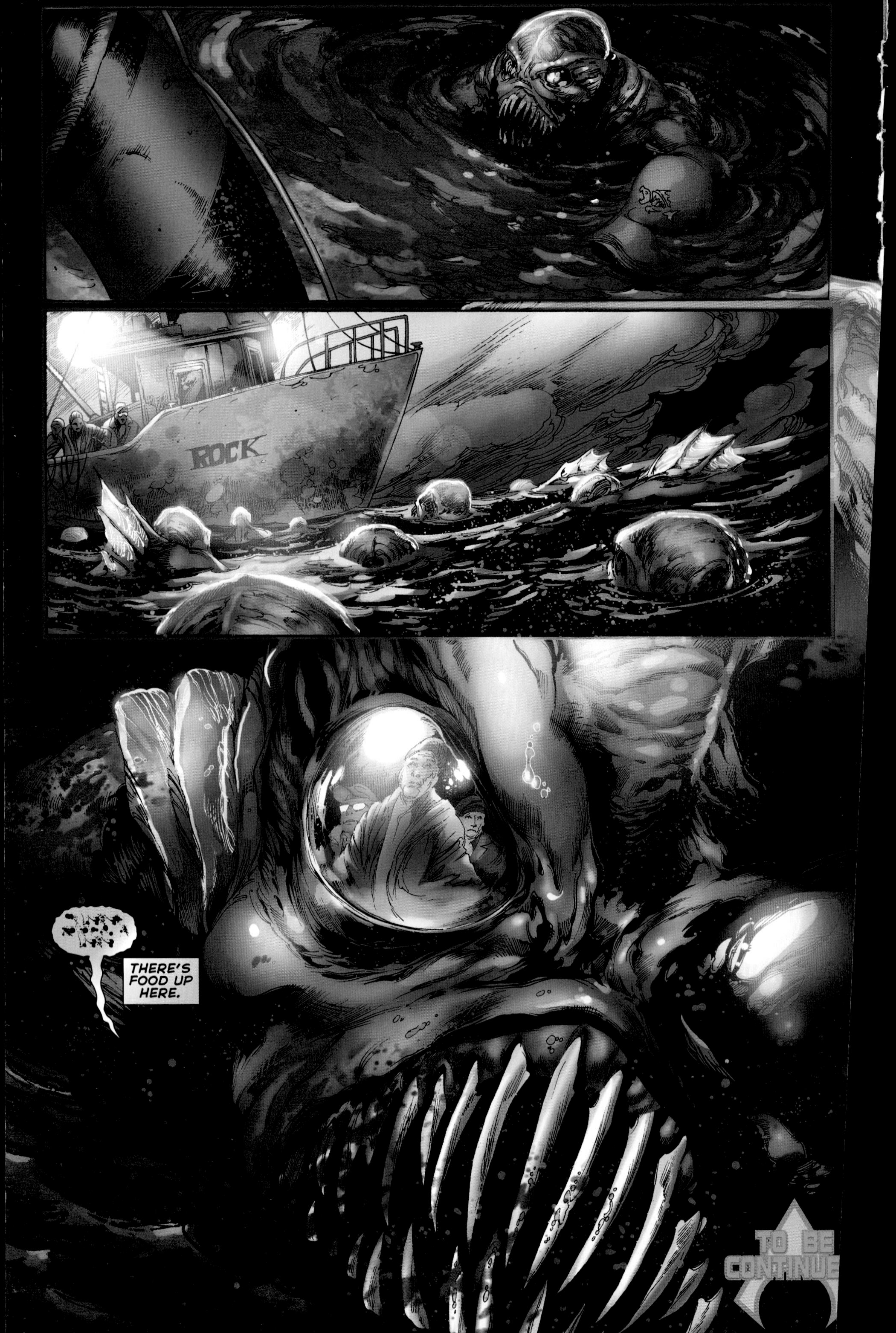
ROCK
THERE'S FOOD UP HERE.
TO BE CONTINUED

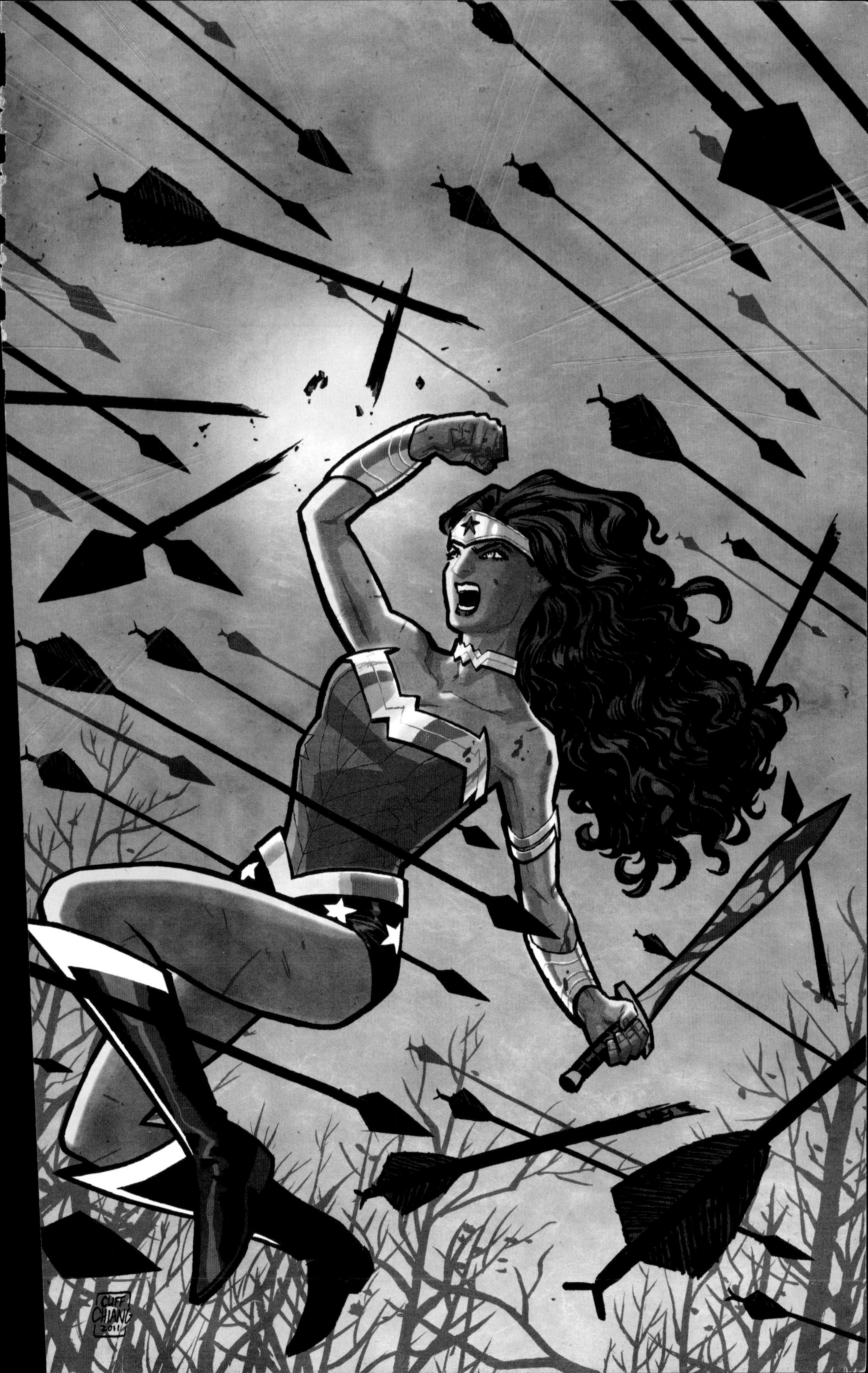
CLIFF
CHIANG
2011

WONDER WOMAN

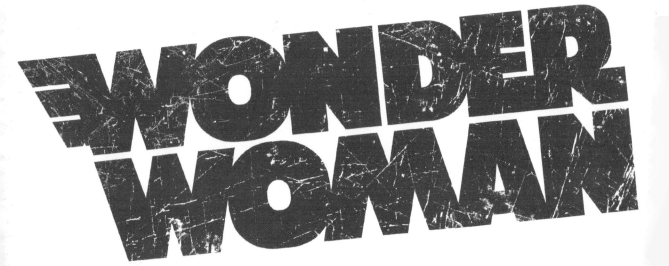

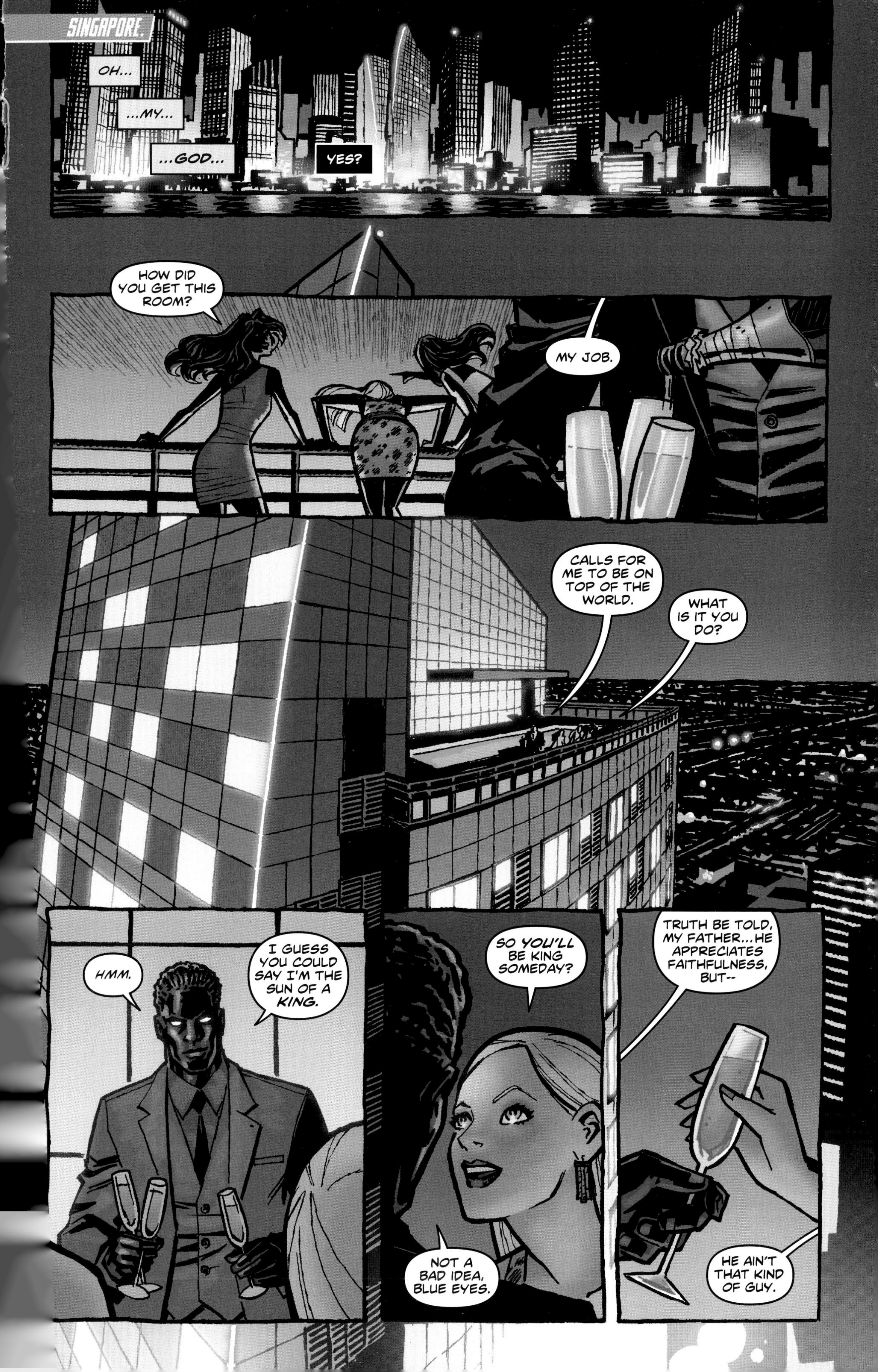
SINGAPORE.
OH...
...MY...
...GOD...
YES?
HOW DID YOU GET THIS ROOM?
MY JOB.
CALLS FOR ME TO BE ON TOP OF THE WORLD.
WHAT IS IT YOU DO?
HMM.
I GUESS YOU COULD SAY I'M THE SUN OF A KING.
SO YOU'LL BE KING SOMEDAY?
NOT A BAD IDEA, BLUE EYES.
TRUTH BE TOLD, MY FATHER...HE APPRECIATES FAITHFULNESS, BUT--
HE AIN'T THAT KIND OF GUY.

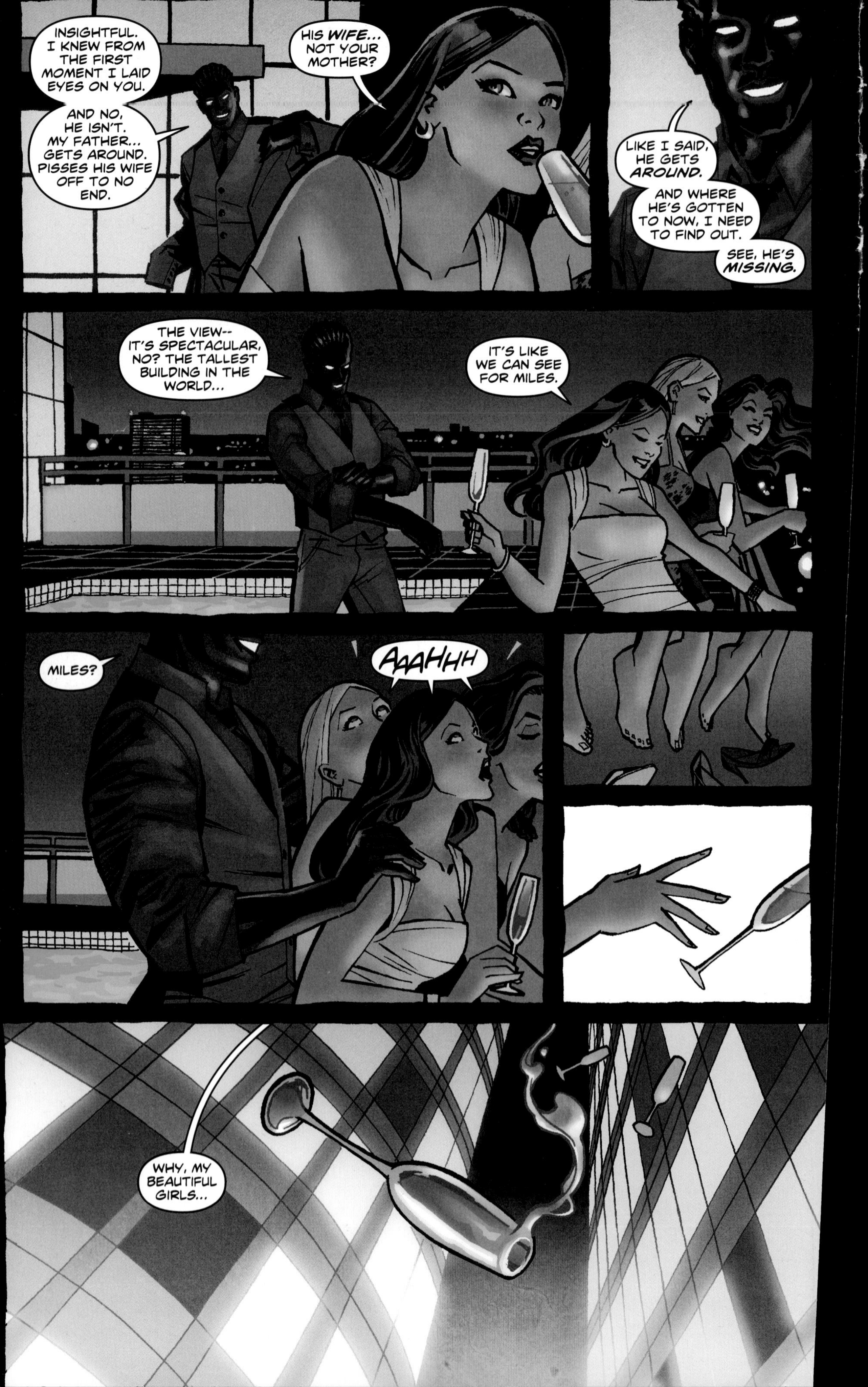
INSIGHTFUL. I KNEW FROM THE FIRST MOMENT I LAID EYES ON YOU.
AND NO, HE ISN'T. MY FATHER... GETS AROUND. PISSES HIS WIFE OFF TO NO END.
HIS WIFE... NOT YOUR MOTHER?
LIKE I SAID, HE GETS AROUND.
AND WHERE HE'S GOTTEN TO NOW, I NEED TO FIND OUT.
SEE, HE'S MISSING.
THE VIEW-- IT'S SPECTACULAR, NO? THE TALLEST BUILDING IN THE WORLD...
IT'S LIKE WE CAN SEE FOR MILES.
MILES?
AAAHHH
WHY, MY BEAUTIFUL GIRLS...

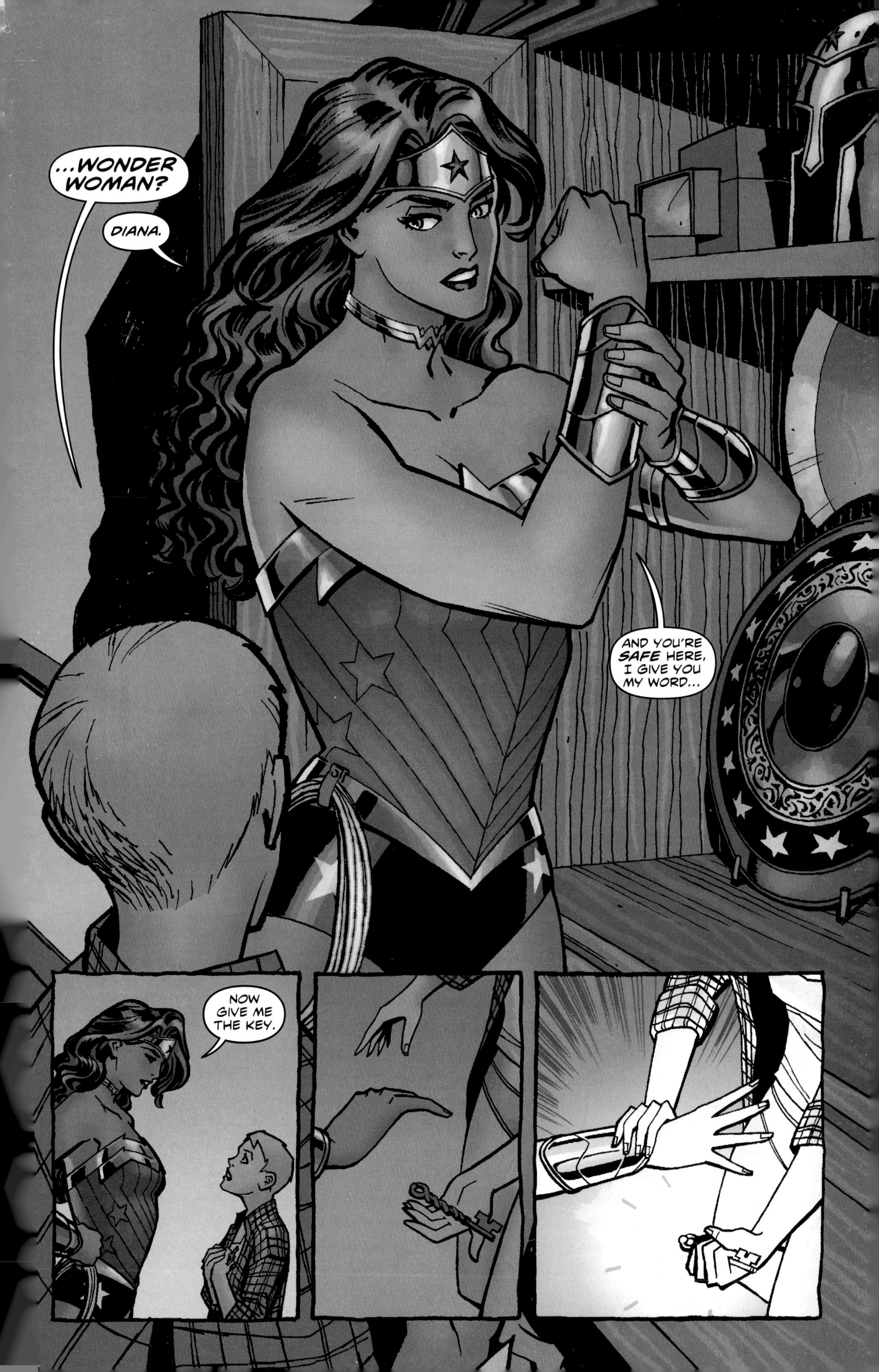

...WONDER WOMAN?
DIANA.
AND YOU'RE SAFE HERE, I GIVE YOU MY WORD...
NOW GIVE ME THE KEY.

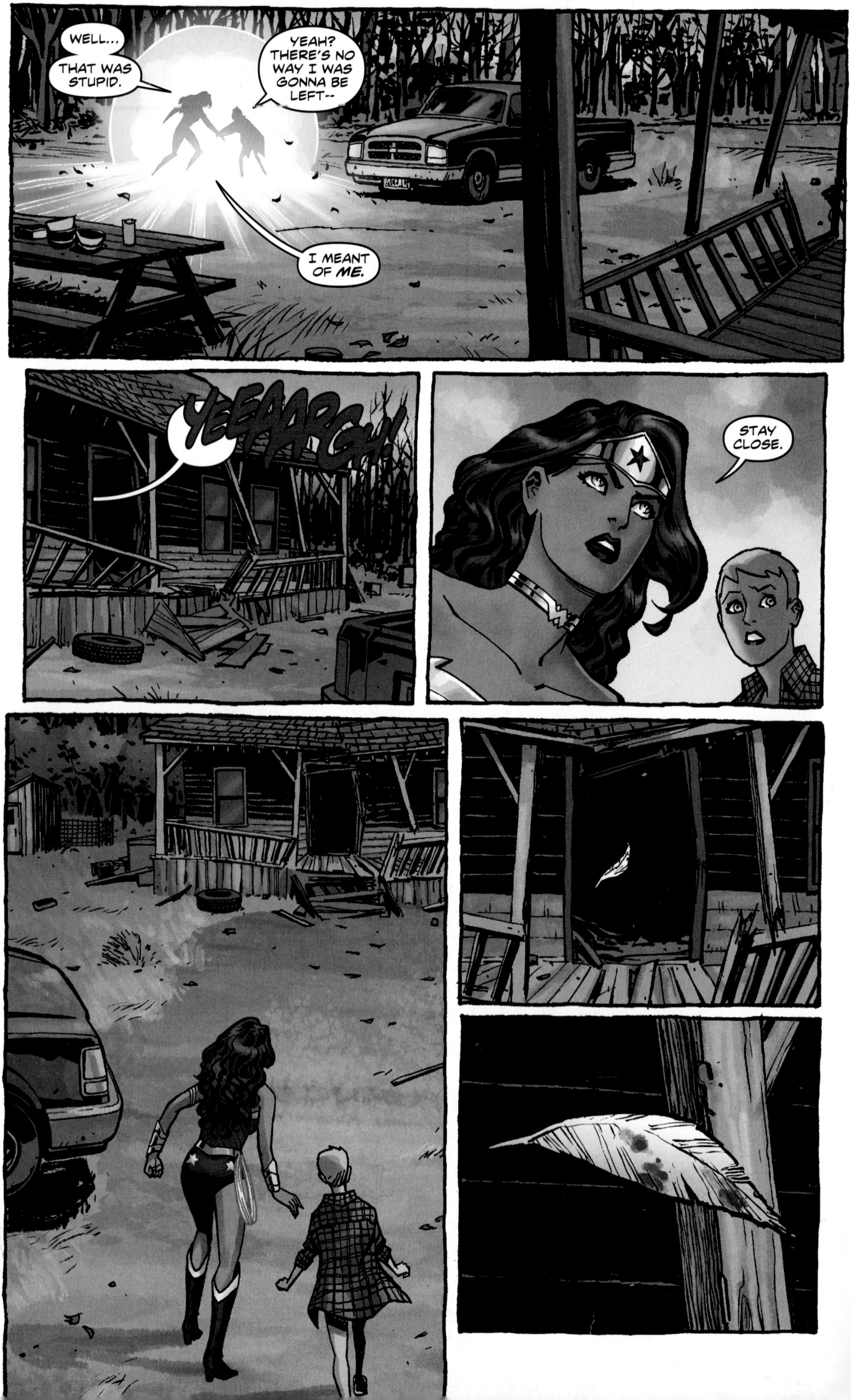
WELL...
THAT WAS STUPID.
YEAH? THERE'S NO WAY I WAS GONNA BE LEFT--
I MEANT OF ME.
YEEAARGH!
STAY CLOSE.

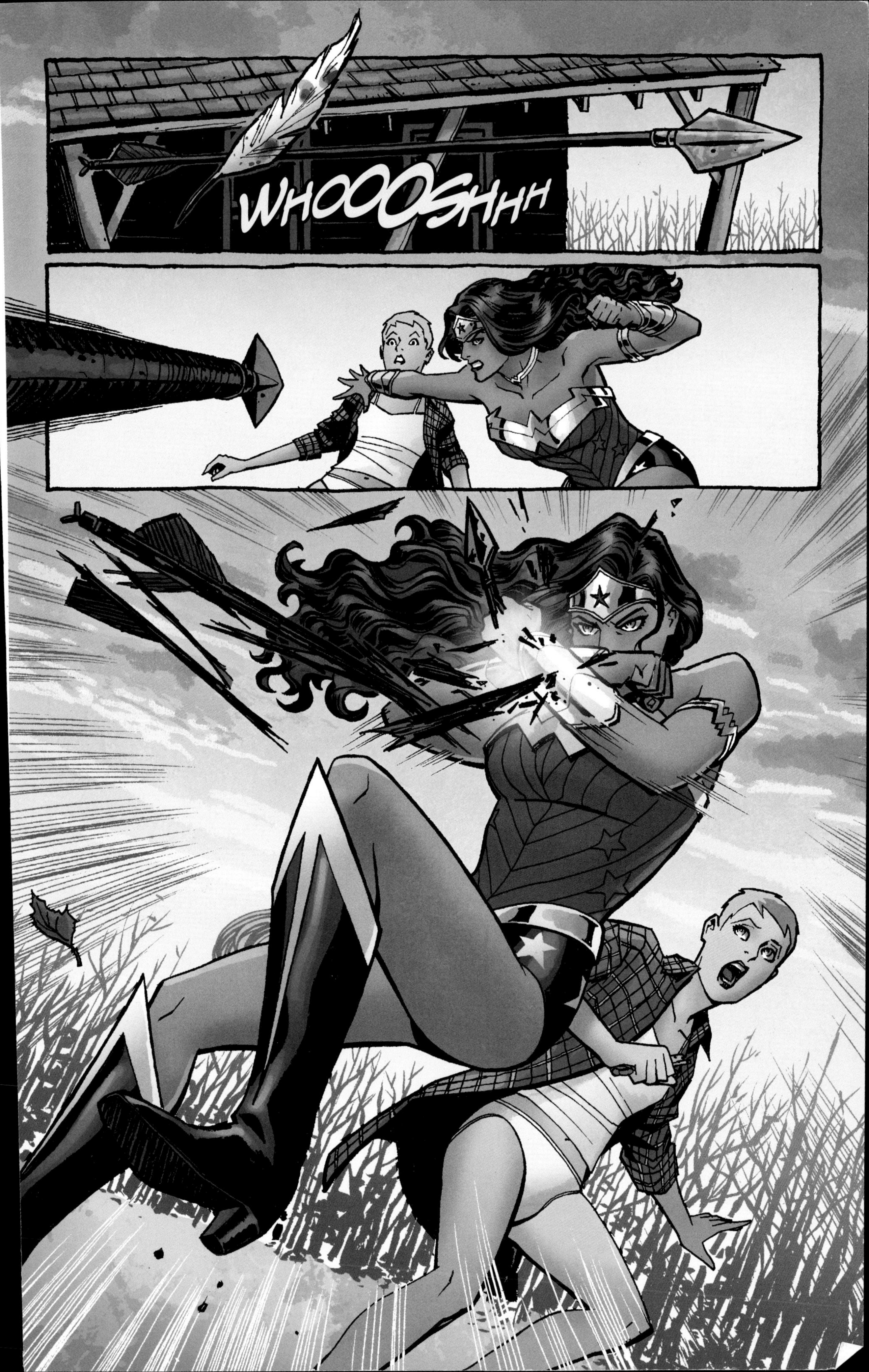
WHOOOSHHH

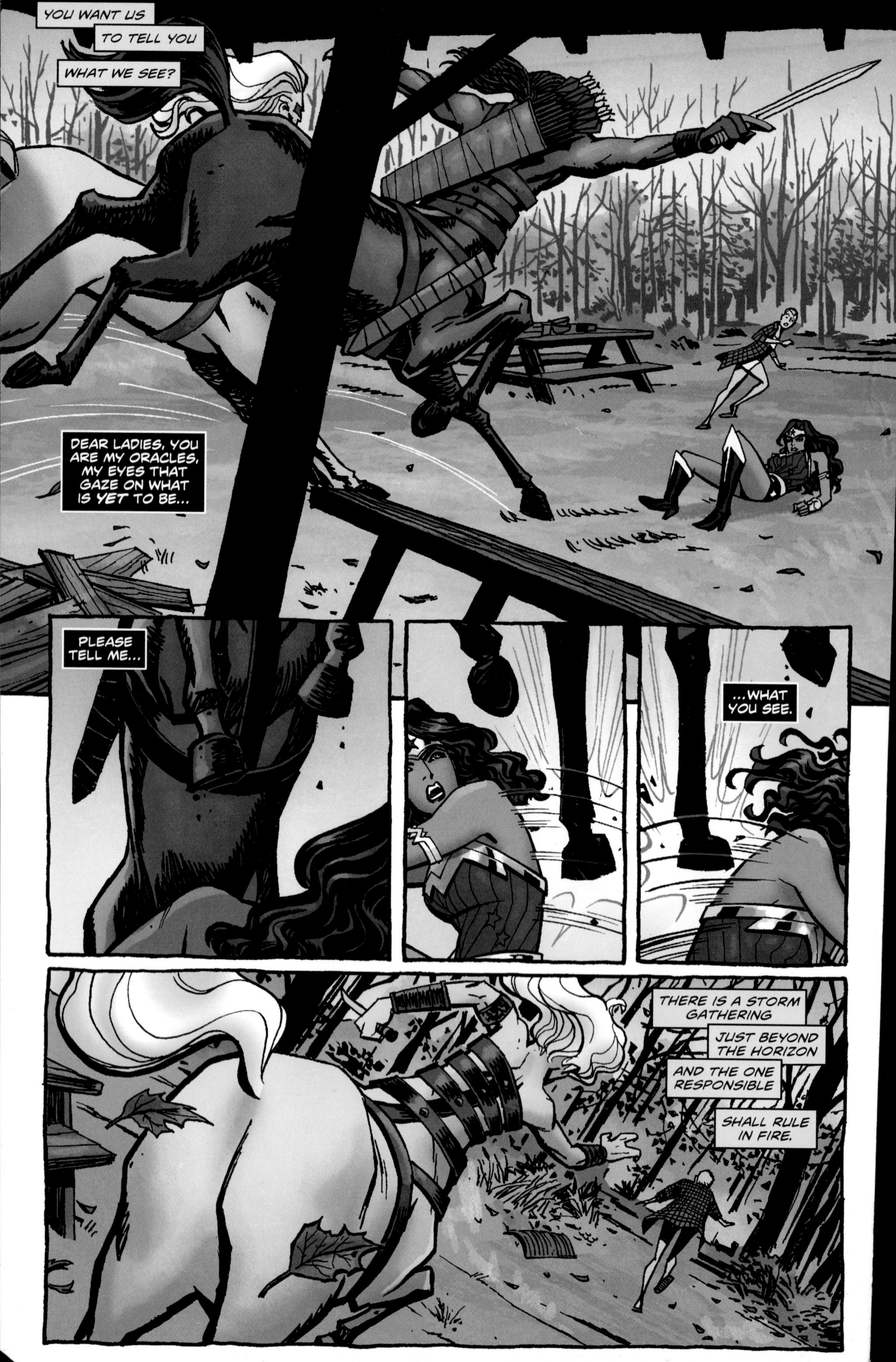
YOU WANT US
TO TELL YOU
WHAT WE SEE?
DEAR LADIES, YOU ARE MY ORACLES, MY EYES THAT GAZE ON WHAT IS YET TO BE...
PLEASE TELL ME...
...WHAT YOU SEE.
THERE IS A STORM GATHERING
JUST BEYOND THE HORIZON
AND THE ONE RESPONSIBLE
SHALL RULE IN FIRE.

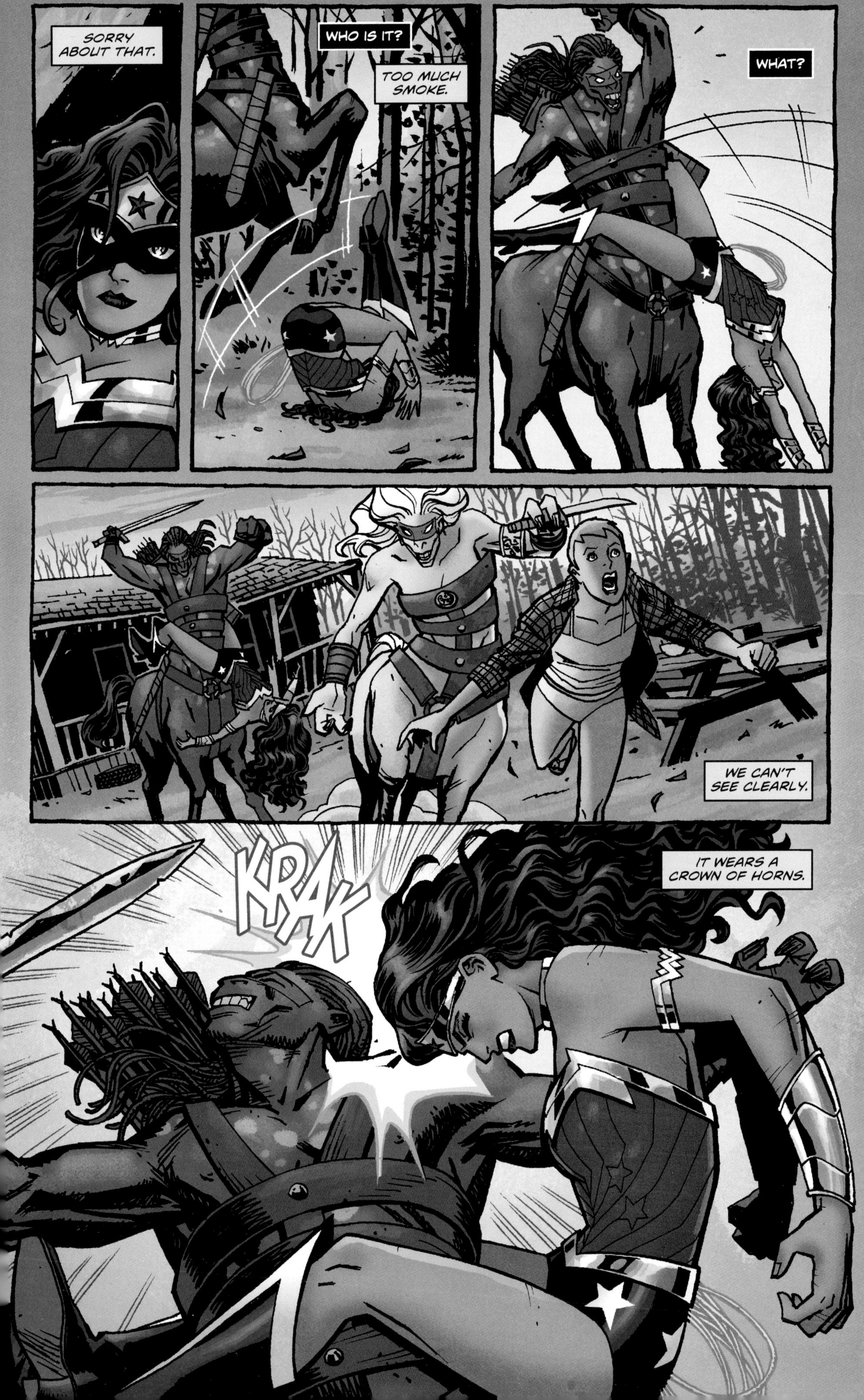
SORRY ABOUT THAT.
WHO IS IT?
TOO MUCH SMOKE.
WHAT?
WE CAN'T SEE CLEARLY.
KRAK
IT WEARS A CROWN OF HORNS.

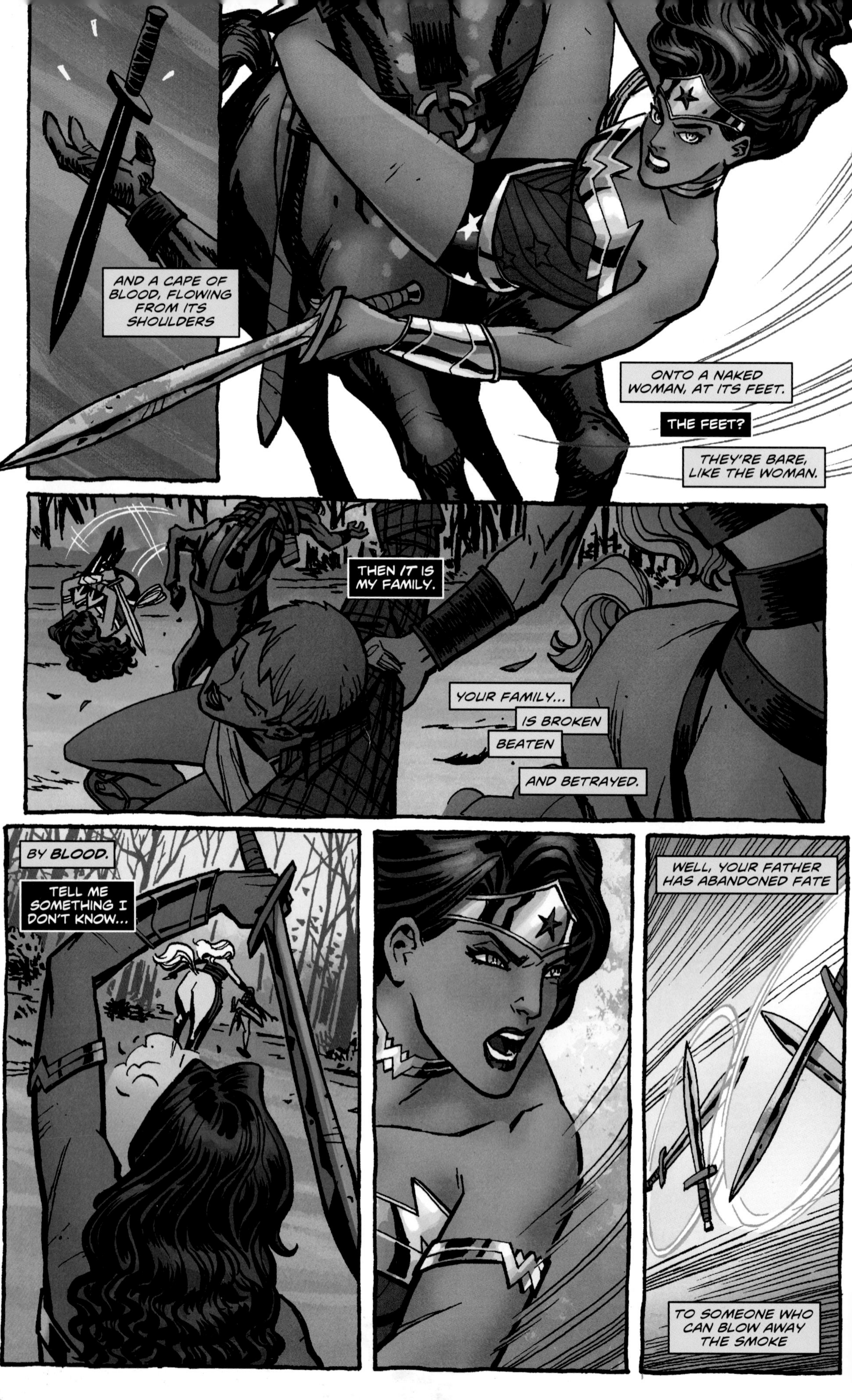
AND A CAPE OF BLOOD, FLOWING FROM ITS SHOULDERS
ONTO A NAKED WOMAN, AT ITS FEET.
THE FEET?
THEY'RE BARE, LIKE THE WOMAN.
THEN *IT* IS MY FAMILY.
YOUR FAMILY...
IS BROKEN
BEATEN
AND BETRAYED.
BY BLOOD.
TELL ME SOMETHING I DON'T KNOW...
WELL, YOUR FATHER HAS ABANDONED FATE
TO SOMEONE WHO CAN BLOW AWAY THE SMOKE

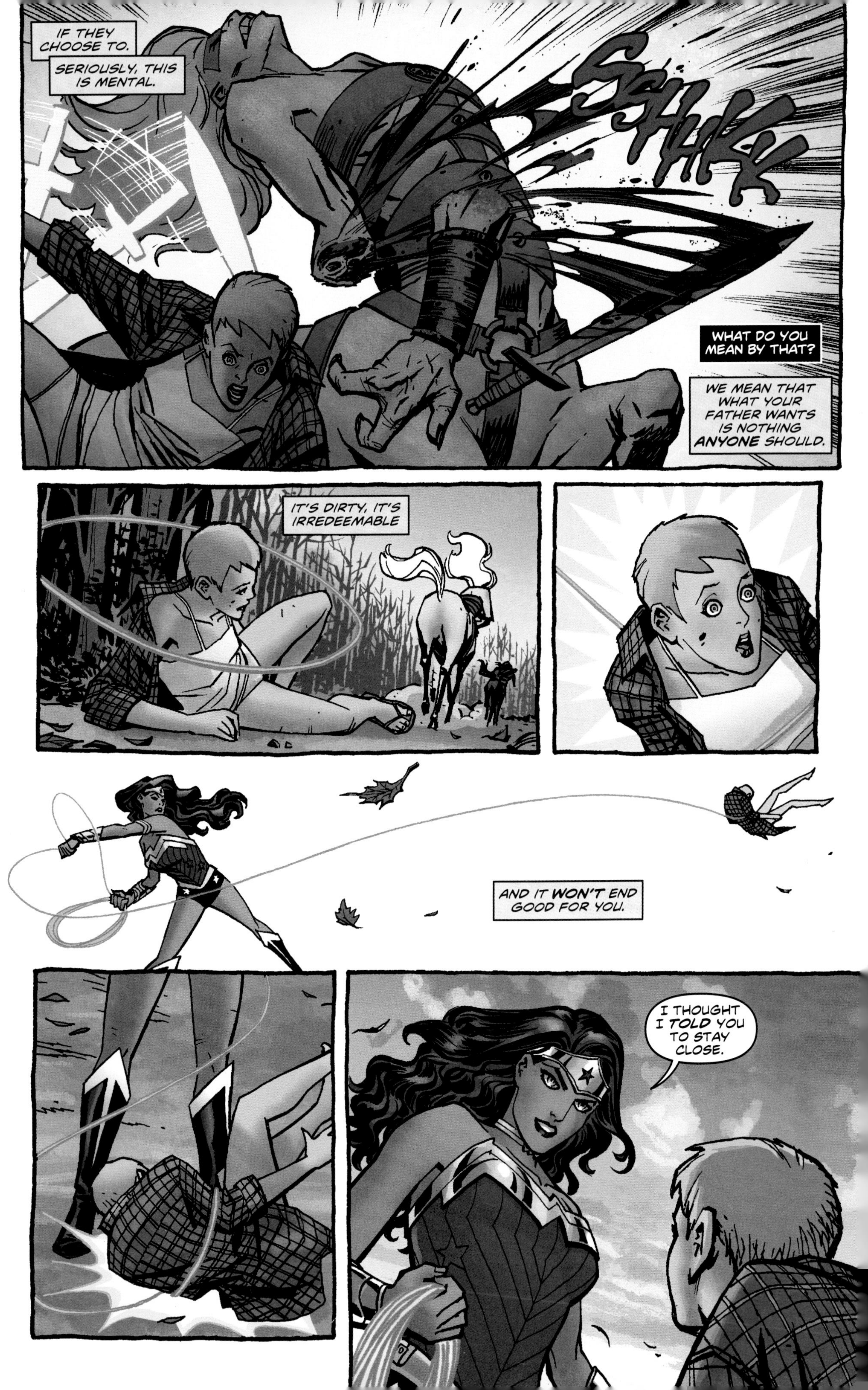
IF THEY CHOOSE TO.
SERIOUSLY, THIS IS MENTAL.
SSHHKK
WHAT DO YOU MEAN BY THAT?
WE MEAN THAT WHAT YOUR FATHER WANTS IS NOTHING ANYONE SHOULD.
IT'S DIRTY, IT'S IRREDEEMABLE
AND IT WON'T END GOOD FOR YOU.
I THOUGHT I TOLD YOU TO STAY CLOSE.

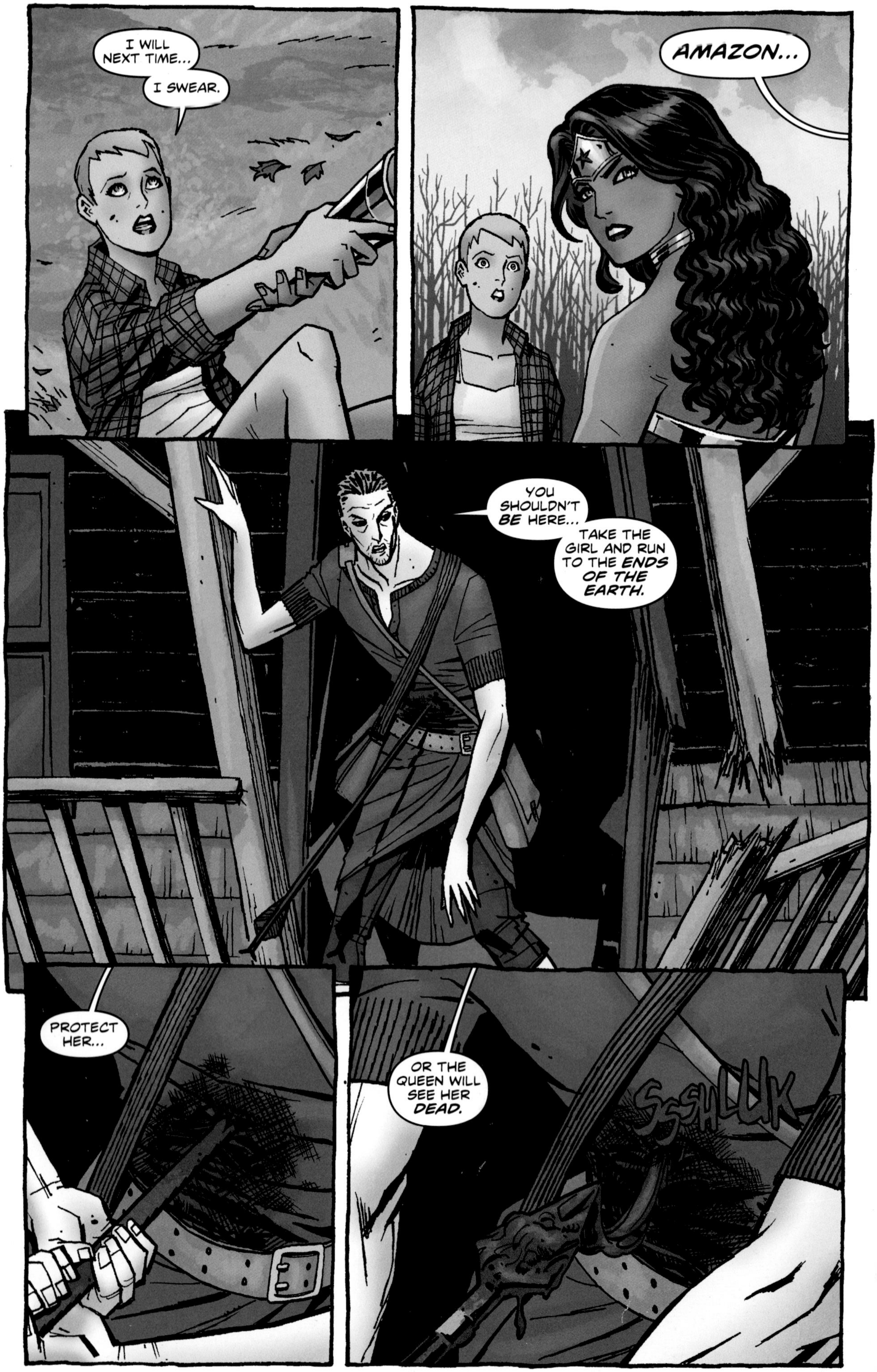
I WILL NEXT TIME...
I SWEAR.
AMAZON...
YOU SHOULDN'T BE HERE...
TAKE THE GIRL AND RUN TO THE ENDS OF THE EARTH.
PROTECT HER...
OR THE QUEEN WILL SEE HER DEAD.
SSSHLUK

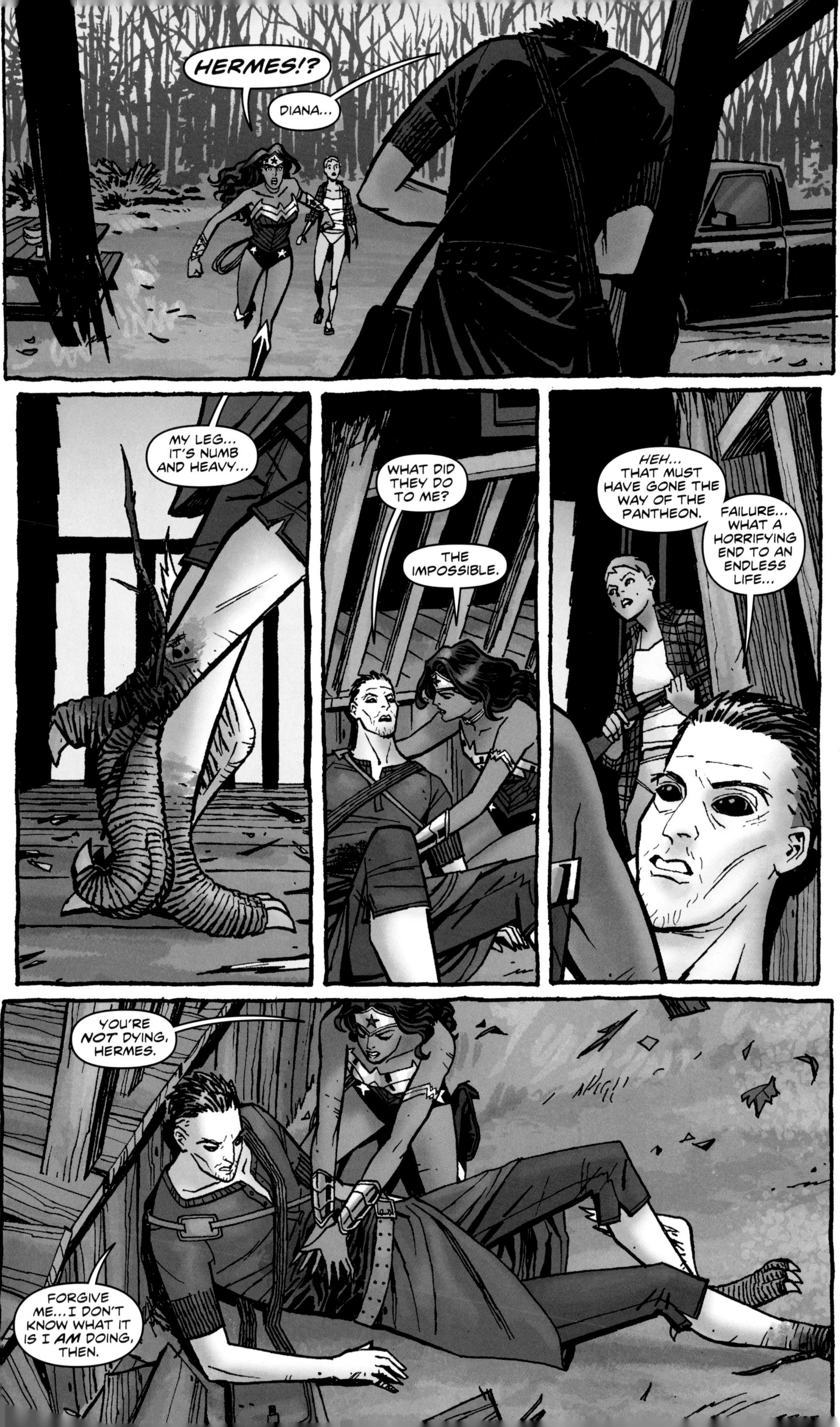

HERMES!?
DIANA...
MY LEG... IT'S NUMB AND HEAVY...
WHAT DID THEY DO TO ME?
THE IMPOSSIBLE.
HEH... THAT MUST HAVE GONE THE WAY OF THE PANTHEON.
FAILURE... WHAT A HORRIFYING END TO AN ENDLESS LIFE...
YOU'RE *NOT* DYING, HERMES.
FORGIVE ME... I DON'T KNOW WHAT IT IS I *AM* DOING, THEN.

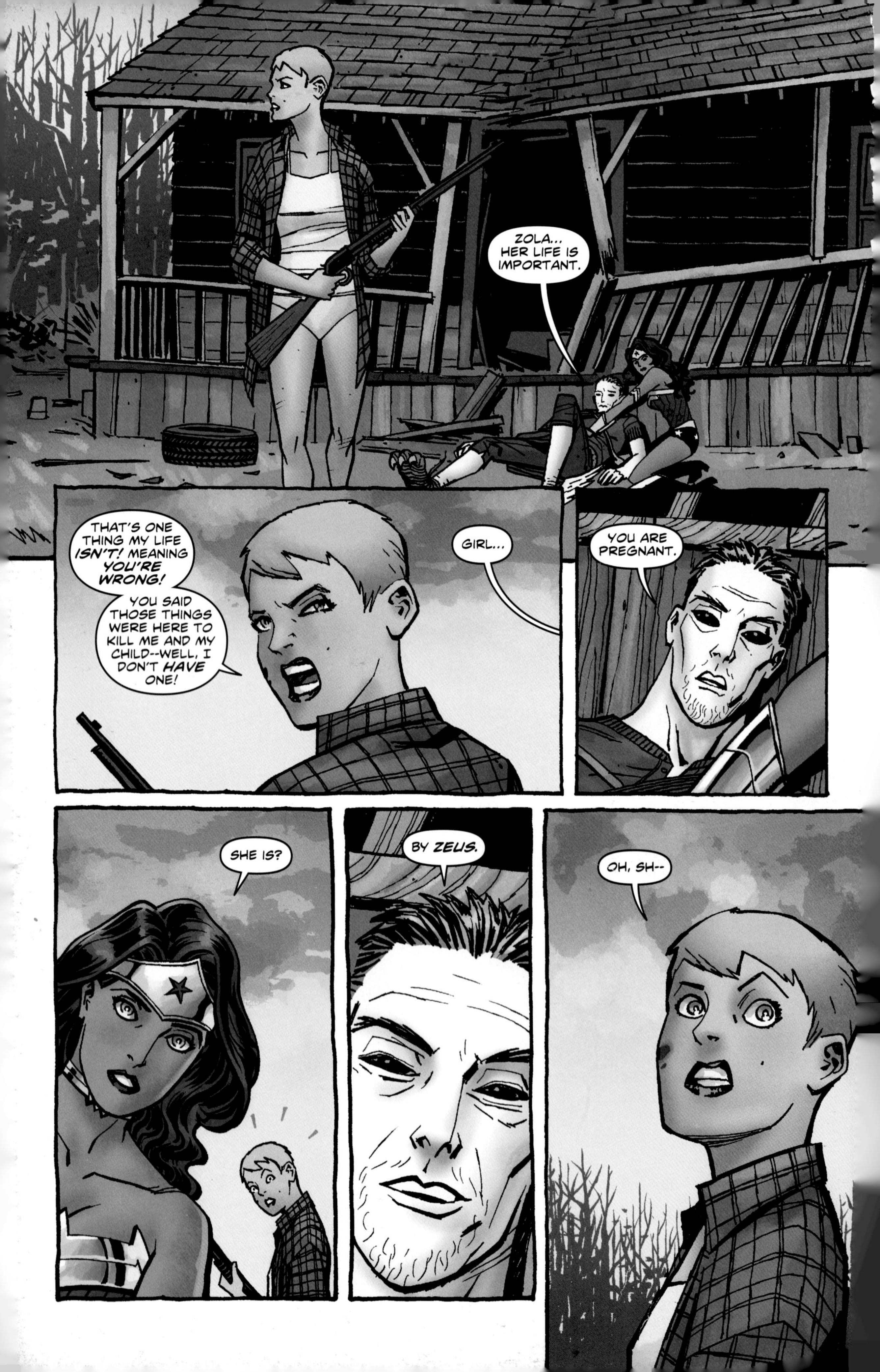
ZOLA... HER LIFE IS IMPORTANT.
THAT'S ONE THING MY LIFE *ISN'T!* MEANING *YOU'RE WRONG!*
YOU SAID THOSE THINGS WERE HERE TO KILL ME AND MY CHILD--WELL, I DON'T *HAVE* ONE!
GIRL...
YOU ARE PREGNANT.
SHE IS?
BY *ZEUS.*
OH, SH--

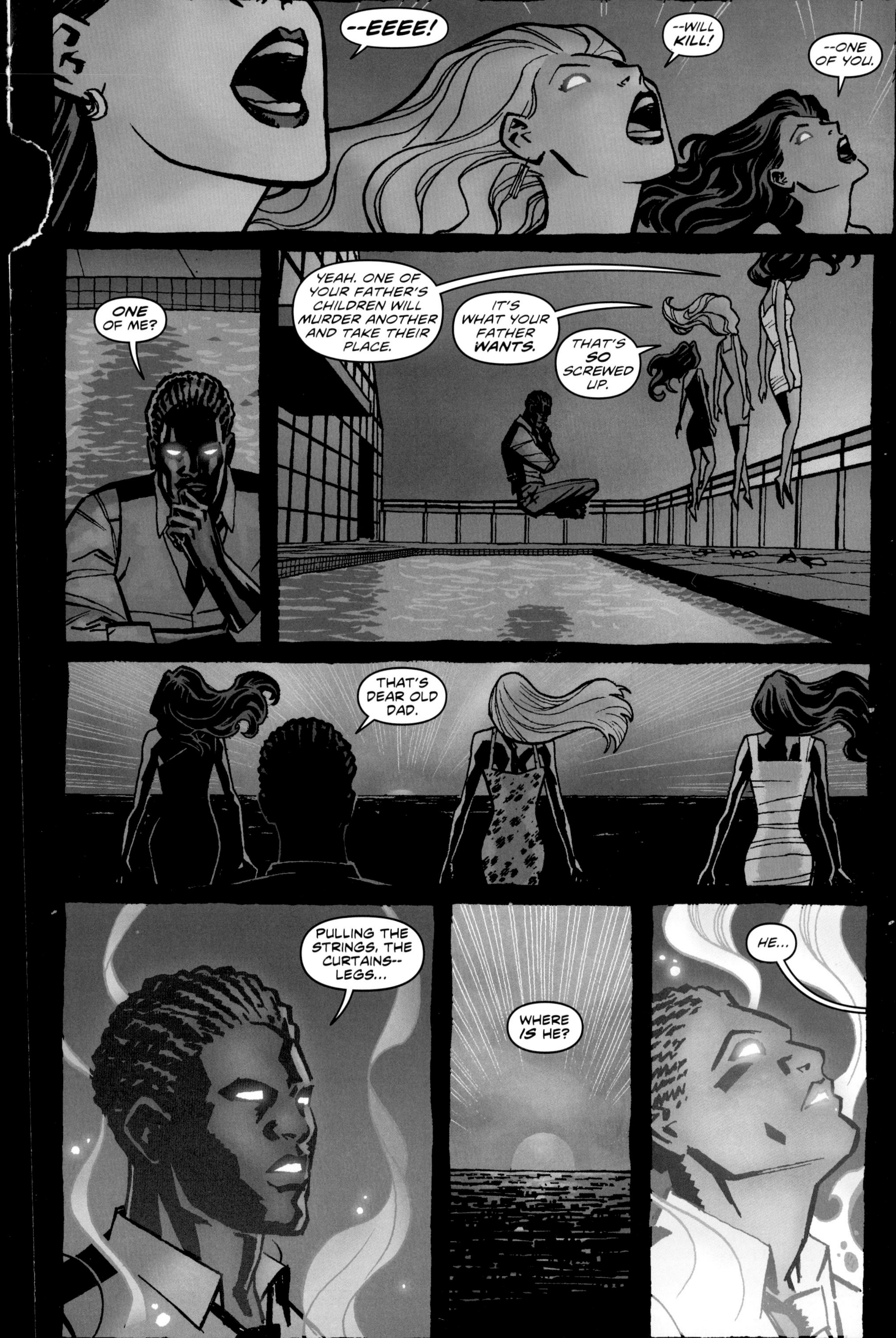
--EEEE!
--WILL KILL!
--ONE OF YOU.
ONE OF ME?
YEAH. ONE OF YOUR FATHER'S CHILDREN WILL MURDER ANOTHER AND TAKE THEIR PLACE.
IT'S WHAT YOUR FATHER WANTS.
THAT'S SO SCREWED UP.
THAT'S DEAR OLD DAD.
PULLING THE STRINGS, THE CURTAINS--LEGS...
WHERE IS HE?
HE...

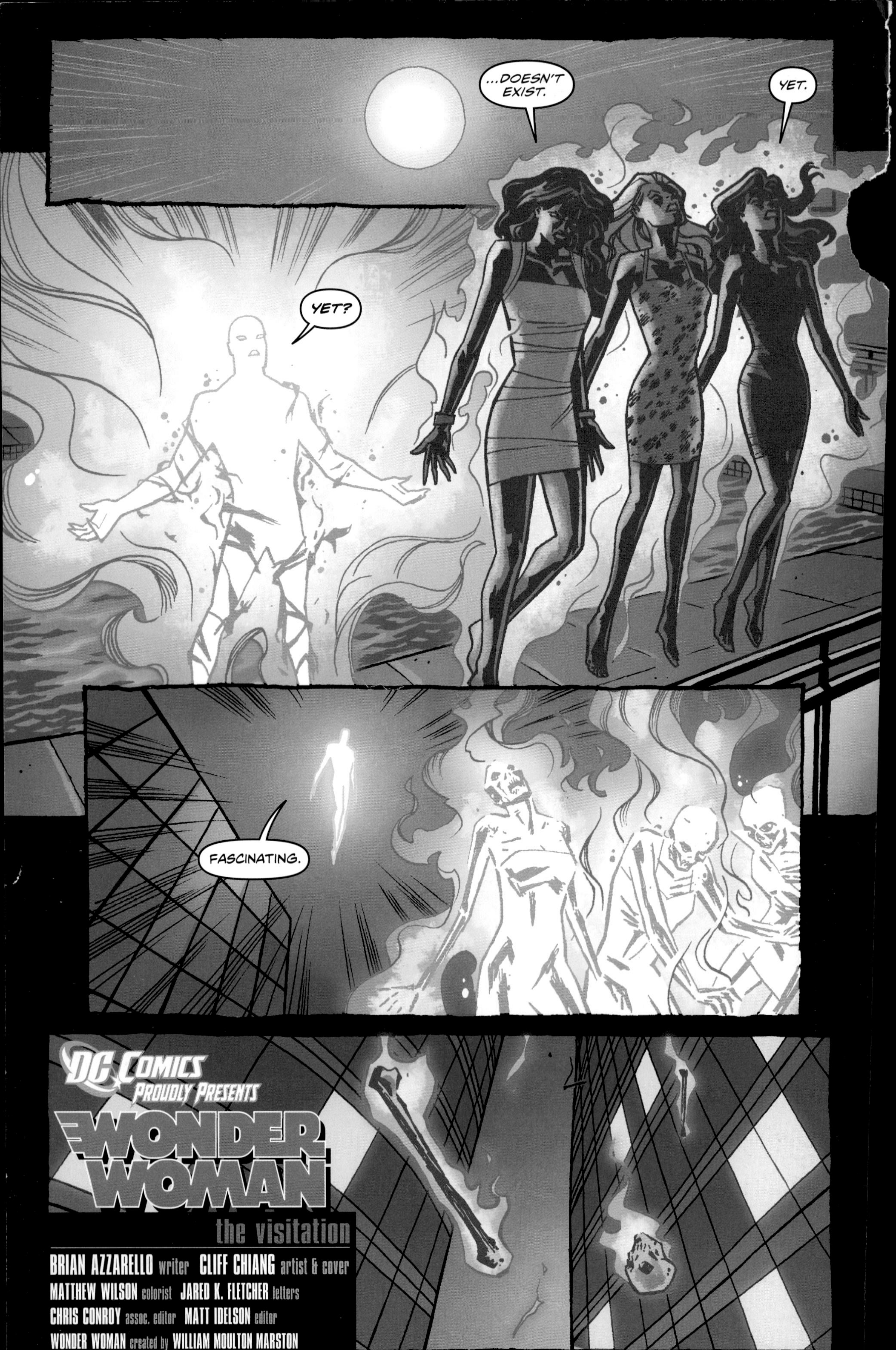
...DOESN'T EXIST.
YET.
YET?
FASCINATING.
DC COMICS
PROUDLY PRESENTS
WONDER WOMAN
the visitation
BRIAN AZZARELLO writer CLIFF CHIANG artist & cover
MATTHEW WILSON colorist JARED K. FLETCHER letters
CHRIS CONROY assoc. editor MATT IDELSON editor
WONDER WOMAN created by WILLIAM MOULTON MARSTON

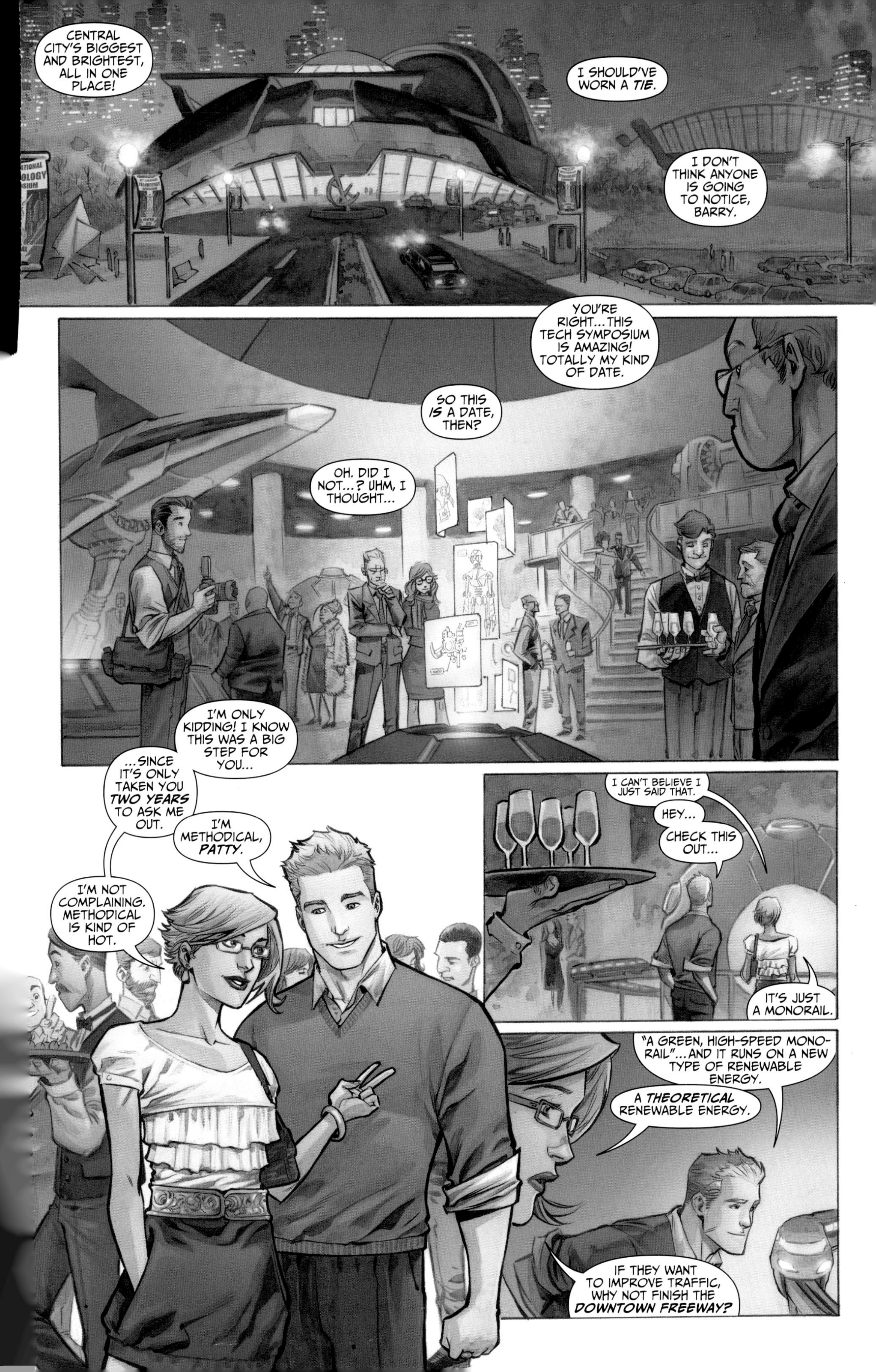
CENTRAL CITY'S BIGGEST AND BRIGHTEST, ALL IN ONE PLACE!
I SHOULD'VE WORN A *TIE*.
I DON'T THINK ANYONE IS GOING TO NOTICE, BARRY.
YOU'RE RIGHT... THIS TECH SYMPOSIUM IS AMAZING! TOTALLY MY KIND OF DATE.
SO THIS *IS* A DATE, THEN?
OH. DID I NOT...? UHM, I THOUGHT...
I'M ONLY KIDDING! I KNOW THIS WAS A BIG STEP FOR YOU...
...SINCE IT'S ONLY TAKEN YOU *TWO YEARS* TO ASK ME OUT.
I'M METHODICAL, *PATTY*.
I'M NOT COMPLAINING. METHODICAL IS KIND OF HOT.
I CAN'T BELIEVE I JUST SAID THAT.
HEY... CHECK THIS OUT...
IT'S JUST A MONORAIL.
"A GREEN, HIGH-SPEED MONO-RAIL"... AND IT RUNS ON A NEW TYPE OF RENEWABLE ENERGY.
A *THEORETICAL* RENEWABLE ENERGY.
IF THEY WANT TO IMPROVE TRAFFIC, WHY NOT FINISH THE *DOWNTOWN FREEWAY?*

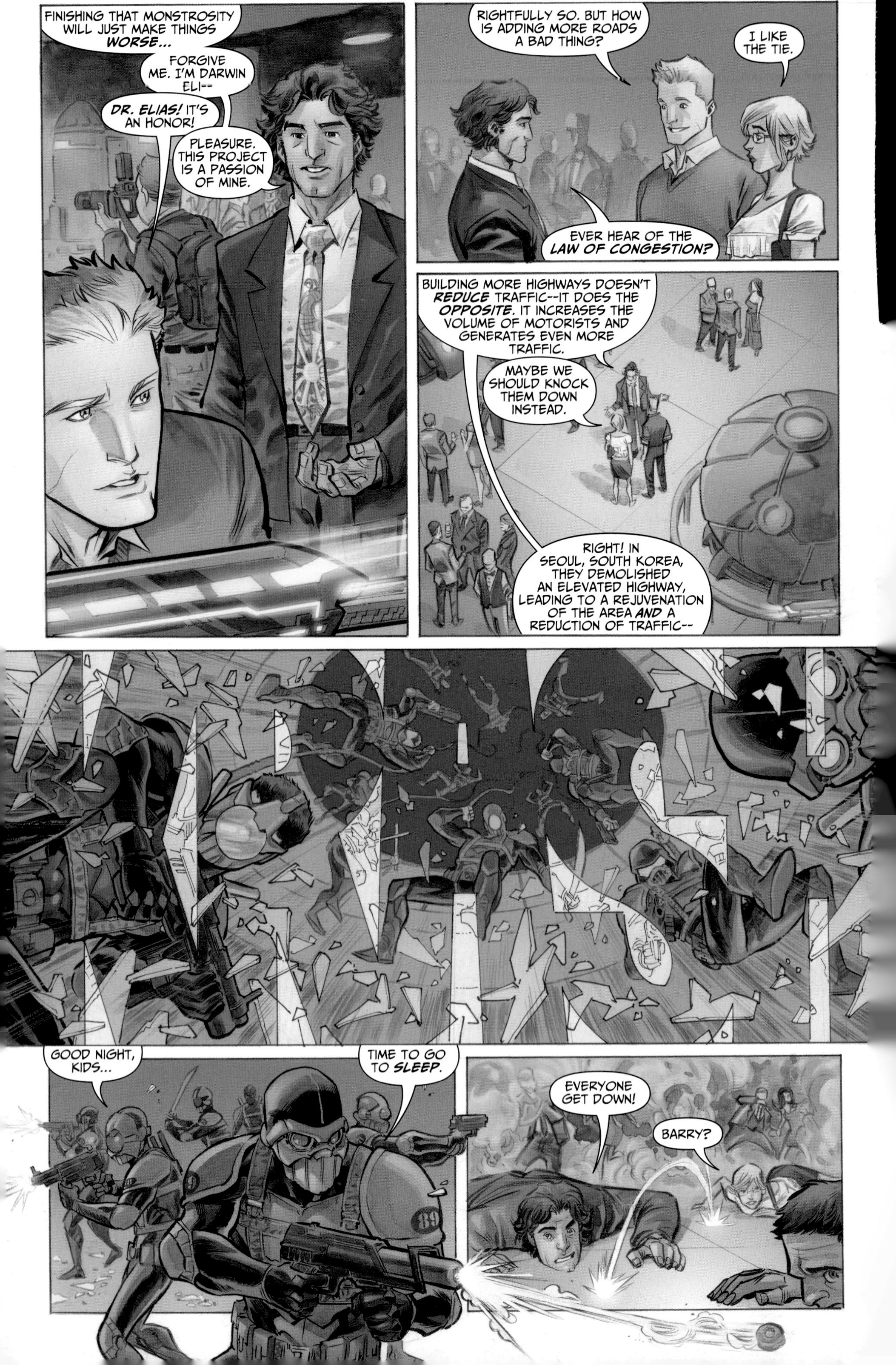
FINISHING THAT MONSTROSITY WILL JUST MAKE THINGS WORSE...
FORGIVE ME. I'M DARWIN ELI--
DR. ELIAS! IT'S AN HONOR!
PLEASURE. THIS PROJECT IS A PASSION OF MINE.
RIGHTFULLY SO. BUT HOW IS ADDING MORE ROADS A BAD THING?
I LIKE THE TIE.
EVER HEAR OF THE LAW OF CONGESTION?
BUILDING MORE HIGHWAYS DOESN'T REDUCE TRAFFIC--IT DOES THE OPPOSITE. IT INCREASES THE VOLUME OF MOTORISTS AND GENERATES EVEN MORE TRAFFIC.
MAYBE WE SHOULD KNOCK THEM DOWN INSTEAD.
RIGHT! IN SEOUL, SOUTH KOREA, THEY DEMOLISHED AN ELEVATED HIGHWAY, LEADING TO A REJUVENATION OF THE AREA AND A REDUCTION OF TRAFFIC--
GOOD NIGHT, KIDS...
TIME TO GO TO SLEEP.
89
EVERYONE GET DOWN!
BARRY?

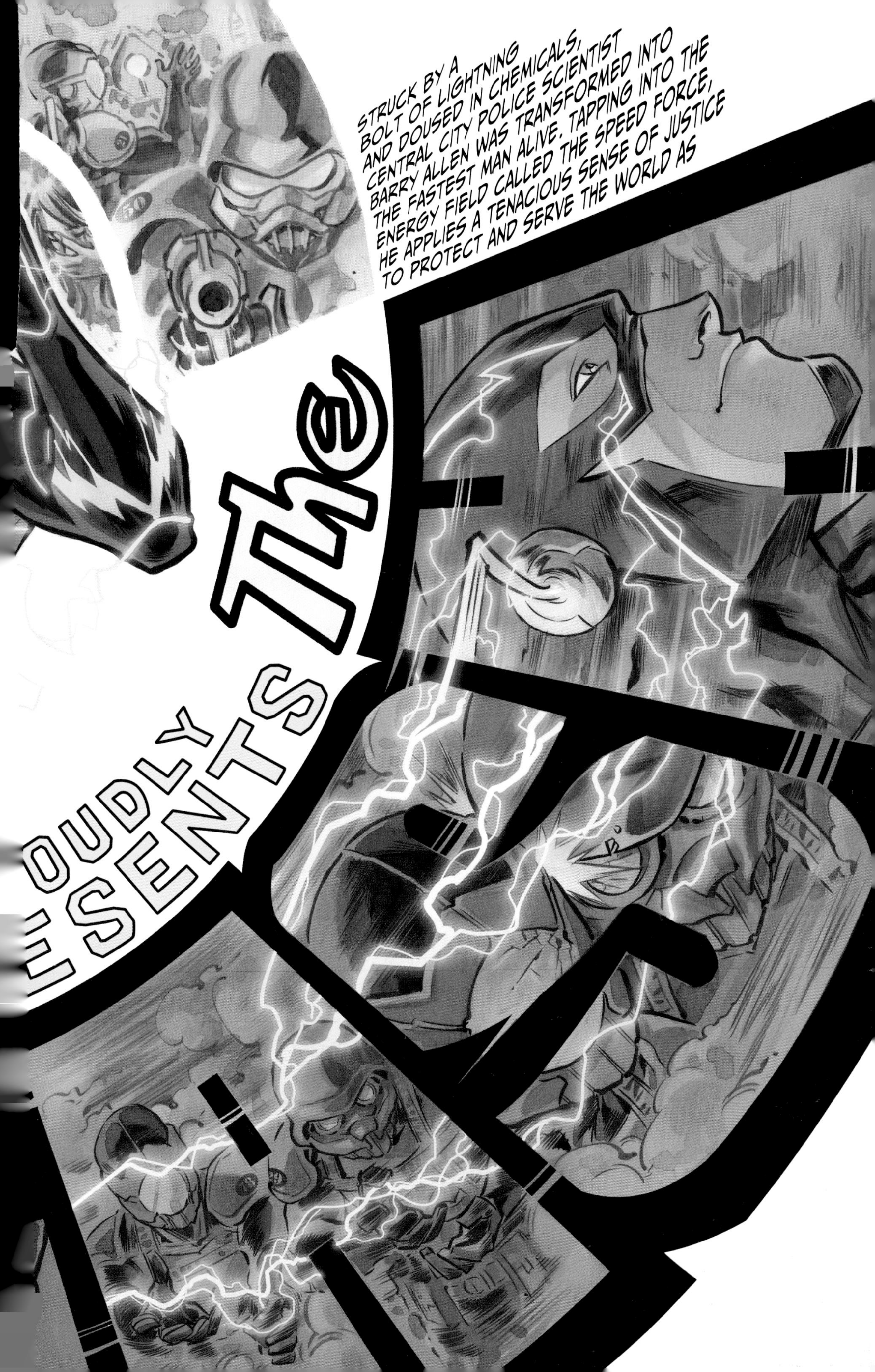
STRUCK BY A BOLT OF LIGHTNING AND DOUSED IN CHEMICALS, CENTRAL CITY POLICE SCIENTIST BARRY ALLEN WAS TRANSFORMED INTO THE FASTEST MAN ALIVE. TAPPING INTO THE ENERGY FIELD CALLED THE SPEED FORCE, HE APPLIES A TENACIOUS SENSE OF JUSTICE TO PROTECT AND SERVE THE WORLD AS
OUDLY
ESENTS
The

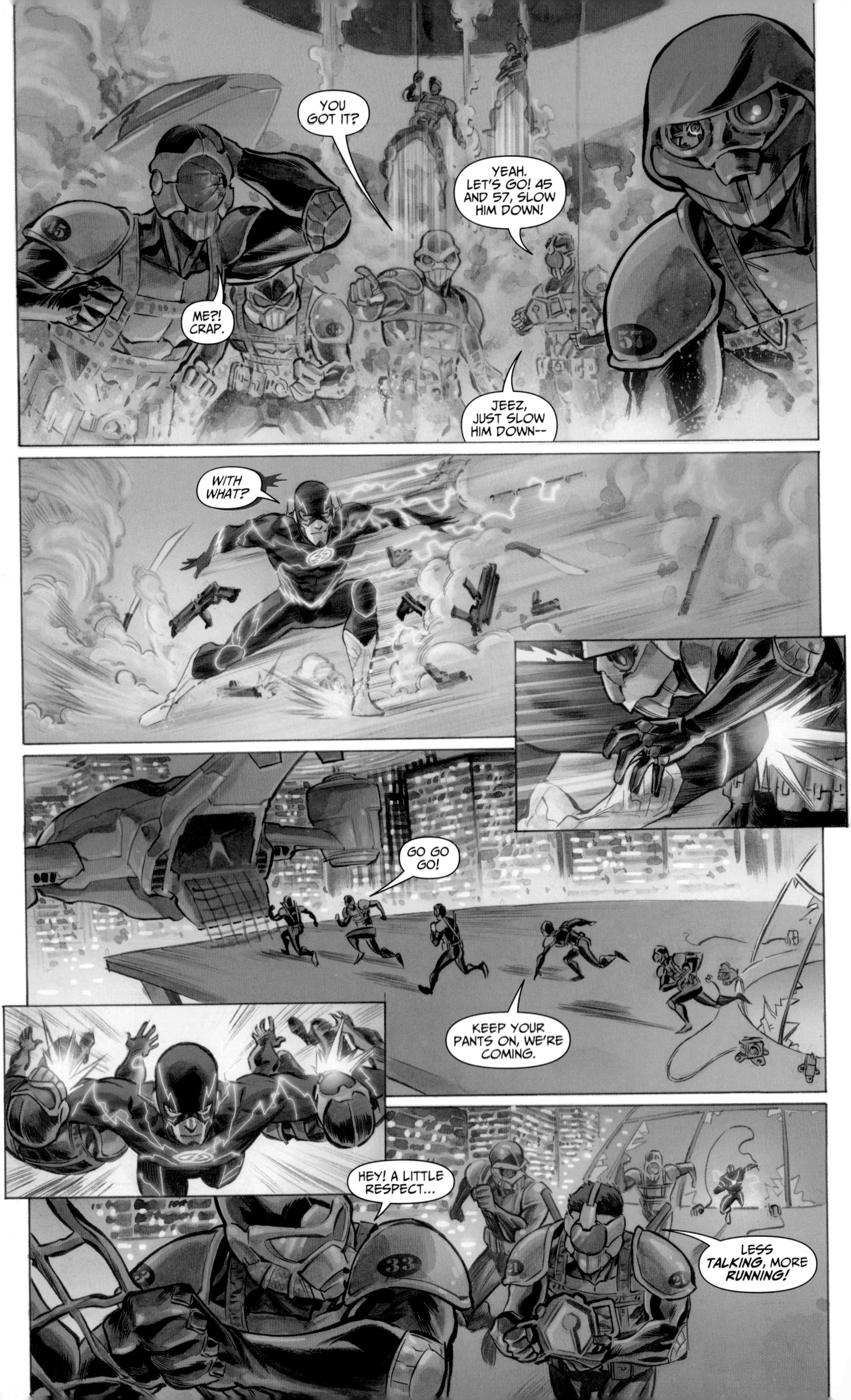
YOU GOT IT?
YEAH. LET'S GO! 45 AND 57, SLOW HIM DOWN!
ME?! CRAP.
JEEZ, JUST SLOW HIM DOWN--
WITH WHAT?
GO GO GO!
KEEP YOUR PANTS ON, WE'RE COMING.
HEY! A LITTLE RESPECT...
LESS TALKING, MORE RUNNING!

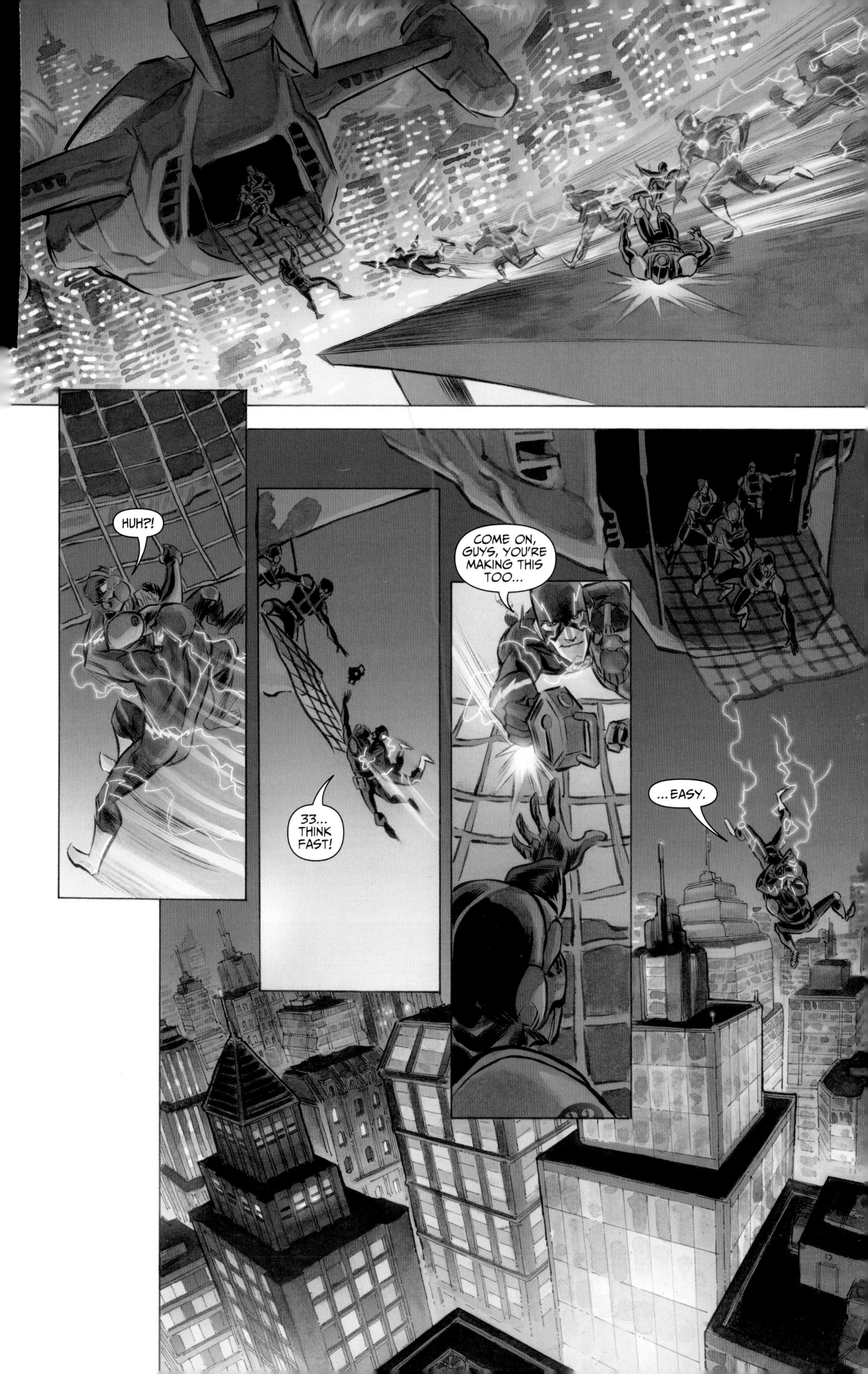
HUH?!
33... THINK FAST!
COME ON, GUYS, YOU'RE MAKING THIS TOO...
...EASY.

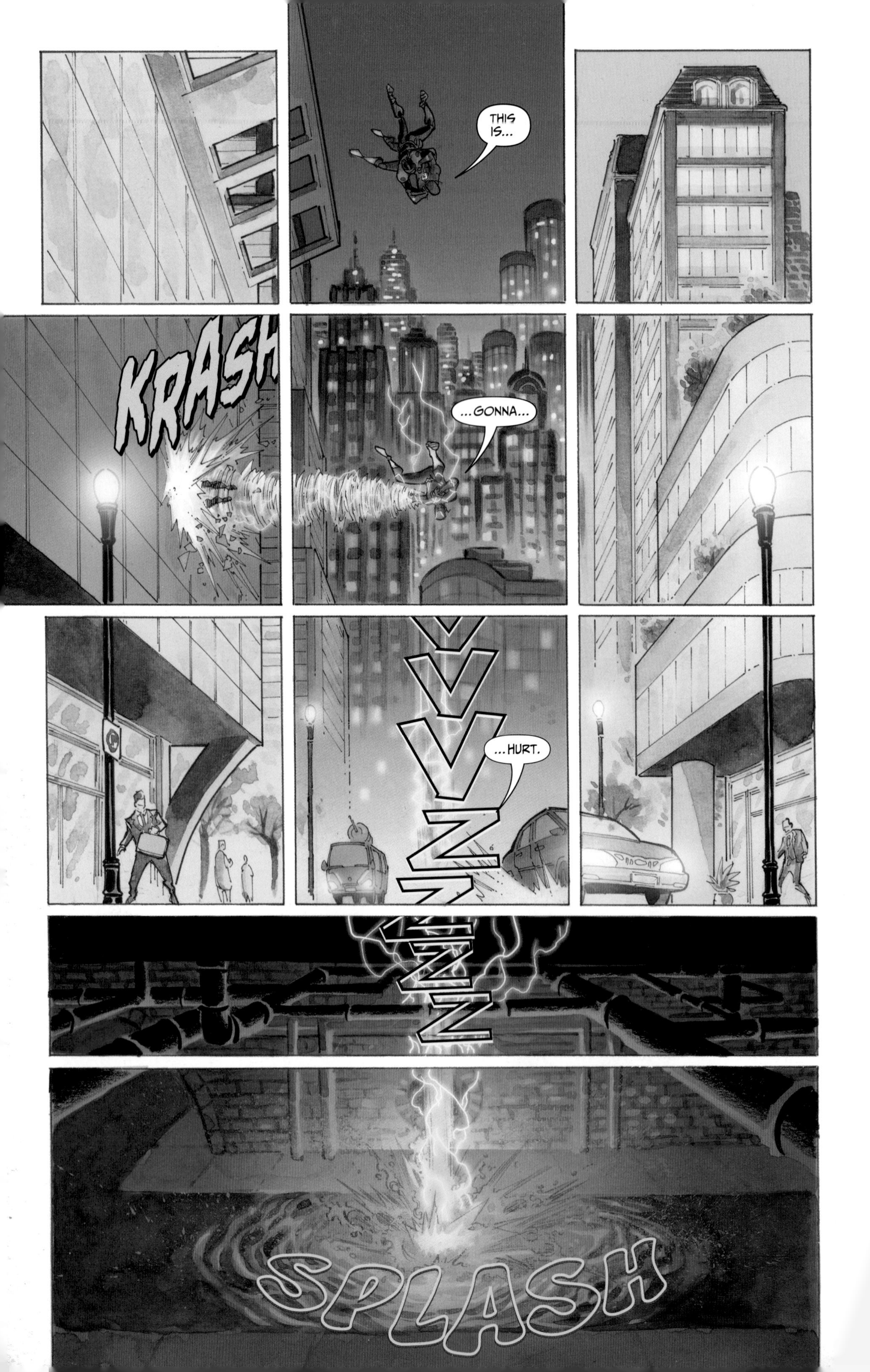
THIS IS...
KRASH
...GONNA...
...HURT.
SPLASH

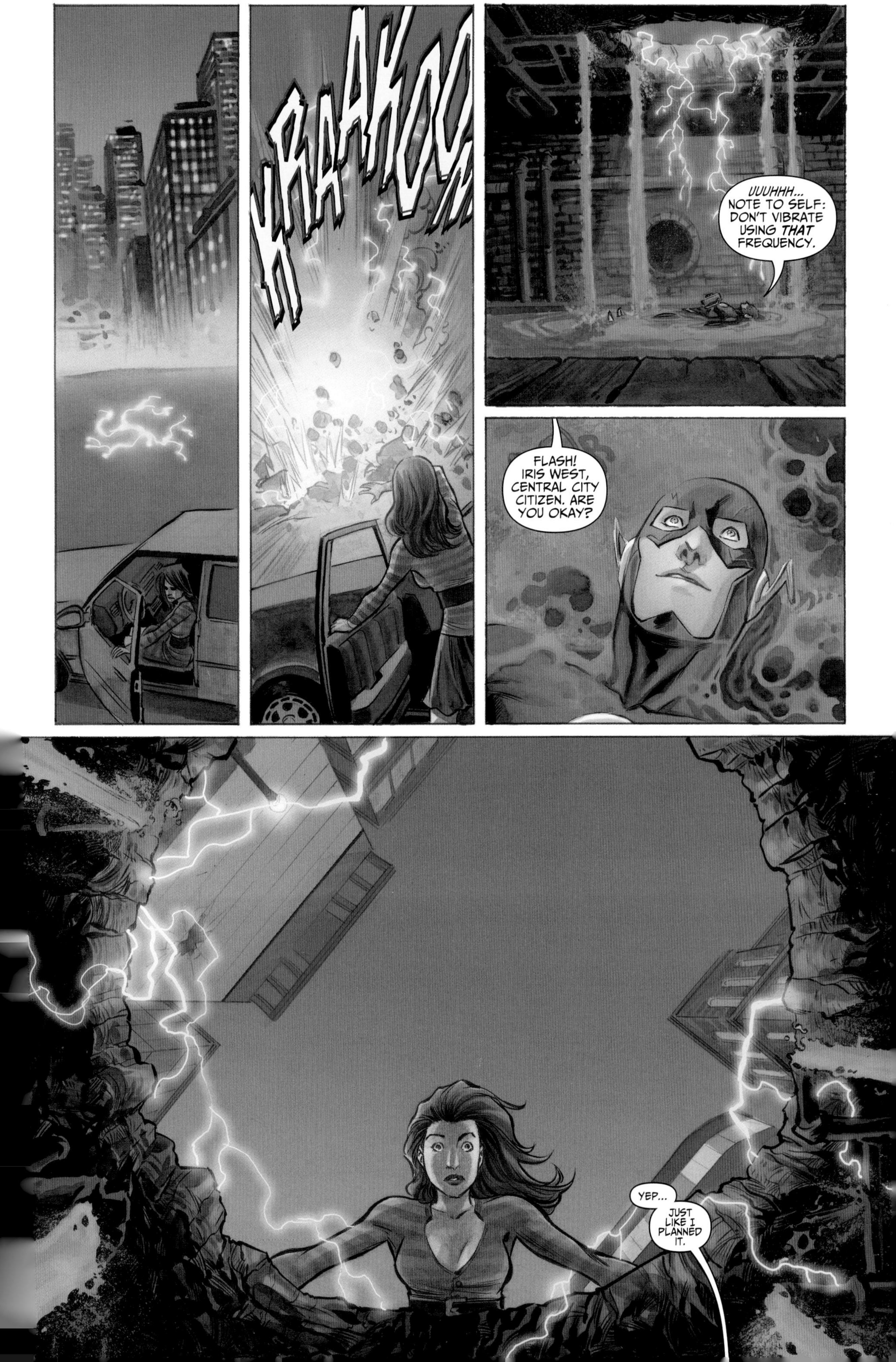

KRAKOOM
UUUHHH... NOTE TO SELF: DON'T VIBRATE USING THAT FREQUENCY.
FLASH! IRIS WEST, CENTRAL CITY CITIZEN. ARE YOU OKAY?
YEP...
JUST LIKE I PLANNED IT.

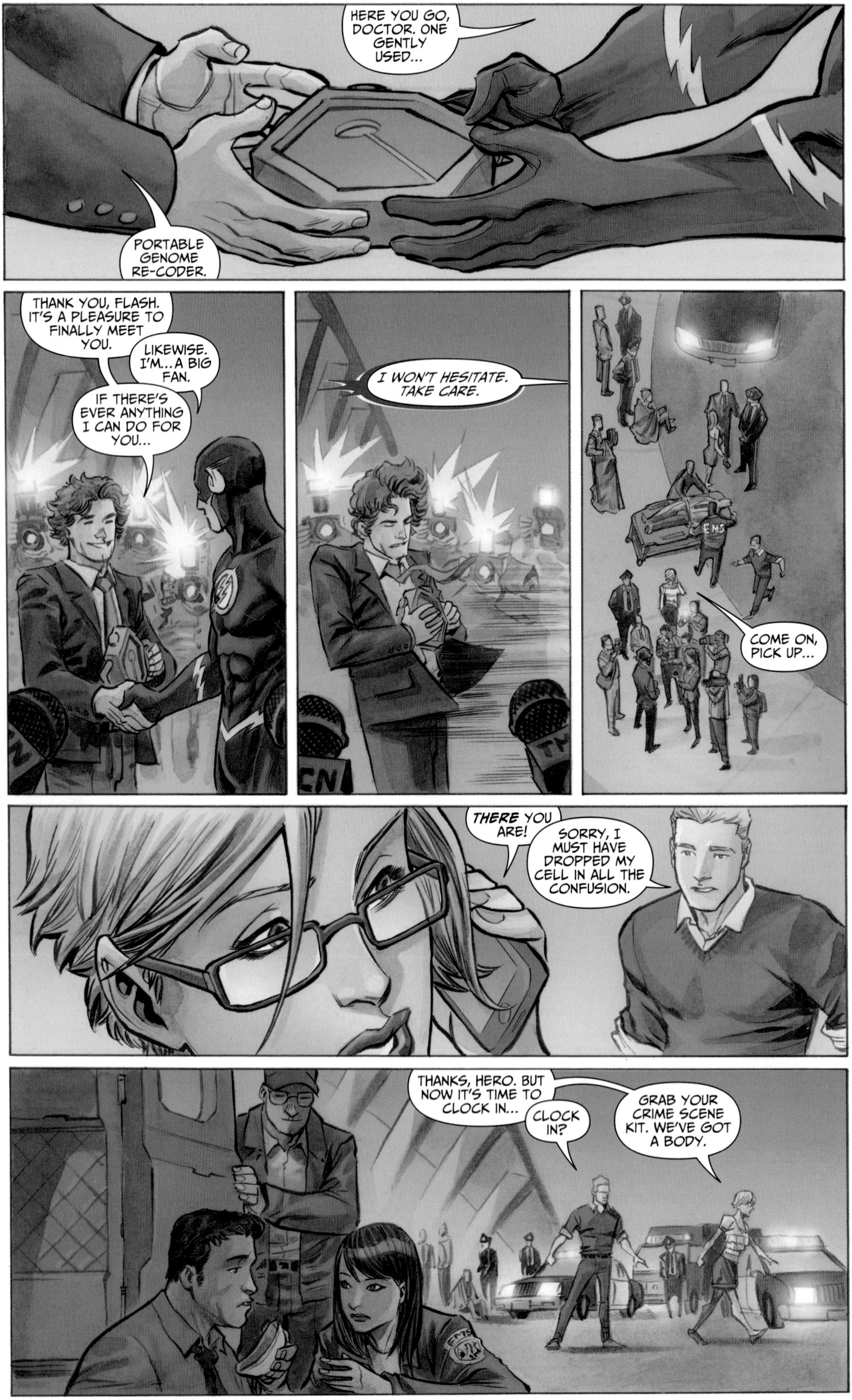
HERE YOU GO, DOCTOR. ONE GENTLY USED...
PORTABLE GENOME RE-CODER.
THANK YOU, FLASH. IT'S A PLEASURE TO FINALLY MEET YOU.
LIKEWISE. I'M...A BIG FAN.
IF THERE'S EVER ANYTHING I CAN DO FOR YOU...
I WON'T HESITATE. TAKE CARE.
COME ON, PICK UP...
EMS
THERE YOU ARE!
SORRY, I MUST HAVE DROPPED MY CELL IN ALL THE CONFUSION.
THANKS, HERO. BUT NOW IT'S TIME TO CLOCK IN...
CLOCK IN?
GRAB YOUR CRIME SCENE KIT. WE'VE GOT A BODY.

LOOK AT THIS... LITTLE PATTY SPIVOT! OUT OF THE LAB COAT AND GETTING HER HANDS DIRTY, FOR A CHANGE.

NICE TO SEE YOU, TOO, TONY. WHAT HAPPENED?

THE FLASH HAPPENED. PUT HIM THROUGH A PLATE GLASS WINDOW.

KILLED ON IMPACT?

WE'LL FIND OUT...

MANUEL?!

HUH? YOU MEAN--

"--YOU KNOW THIS GUY?"

I TOLDJA IT WAS A BAD IDEA.

NO WAY, BARRY. SHE WAS TOTALLY WORTH IT.

WORTH GETTING A BEAT DOWN FROM THE WHOLE RUGBY TEAM, MANUEL?

AT LEAST YOU'RE OUT OF THE DORM FOR ONCE, GETTING FRESH AIR.

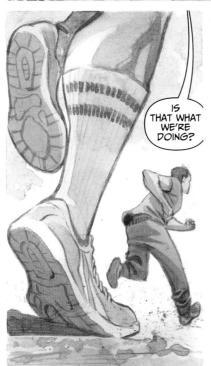

IS THAT WHAT WE'RE DOING?

I THOUGHT WE WERE FLEEING FROM ANOTHER ANGRY MOB...

...INSTEAD OF PREPPING FOR YOUR *HUGE* INTERVIEW TOMORROW.

WHATEVER. YOU KNOW WHAT YOUR PROBLEM IS?

YOU HAVEN'T FOUND SOMEONE WORTH TAKING A BEATING FOR.

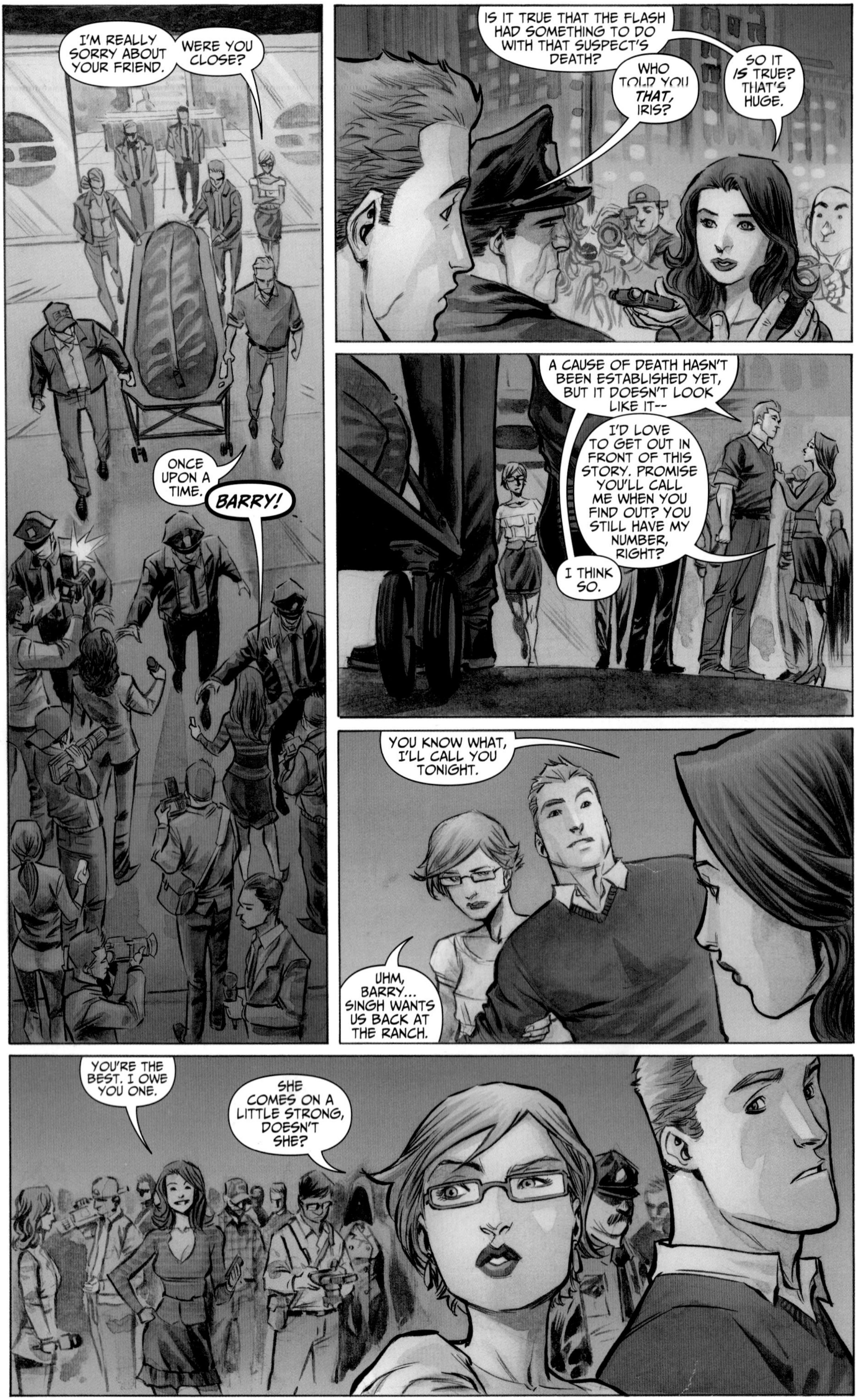
I'M REALLY SORRY ABOUT YOUR FRIEND.
WERE YOU CLOSE?
ONCE UPON A TIME.
BARRY!
IS IT TRUE THAT THE FLASH HAD SOMETHING TO DO WITH THAT SUSPECT'S DEATH?
WHO TOLD YOU THAT, IRIS?
SO IT IS TRUE? THAT'S HUGE.
A CAUSE OF DEATH HASN'T BEEN ESTABLISHED YET, BUT IT DOESN'T LOOK LIKE IT--
I'D LOVE TO GET OUT IN FRONT OF THIS STORY. PROMISE YOU'LL CALL ME WHEN YOU FIND OUT? YOU STILL HAVE MY NUMBER, RIGHT?
I THINK SO.
YOU KNOW WHAT, I'LL CALL YOU TONIGHT.
UHM, BARRY... SINGH WANTS US BACK AT THE RANCH.
YOU'RE THE BEST. I OWE YOU ONE.
SHE COMES ON A LITTLE STRONG, DOESN'T SHE?

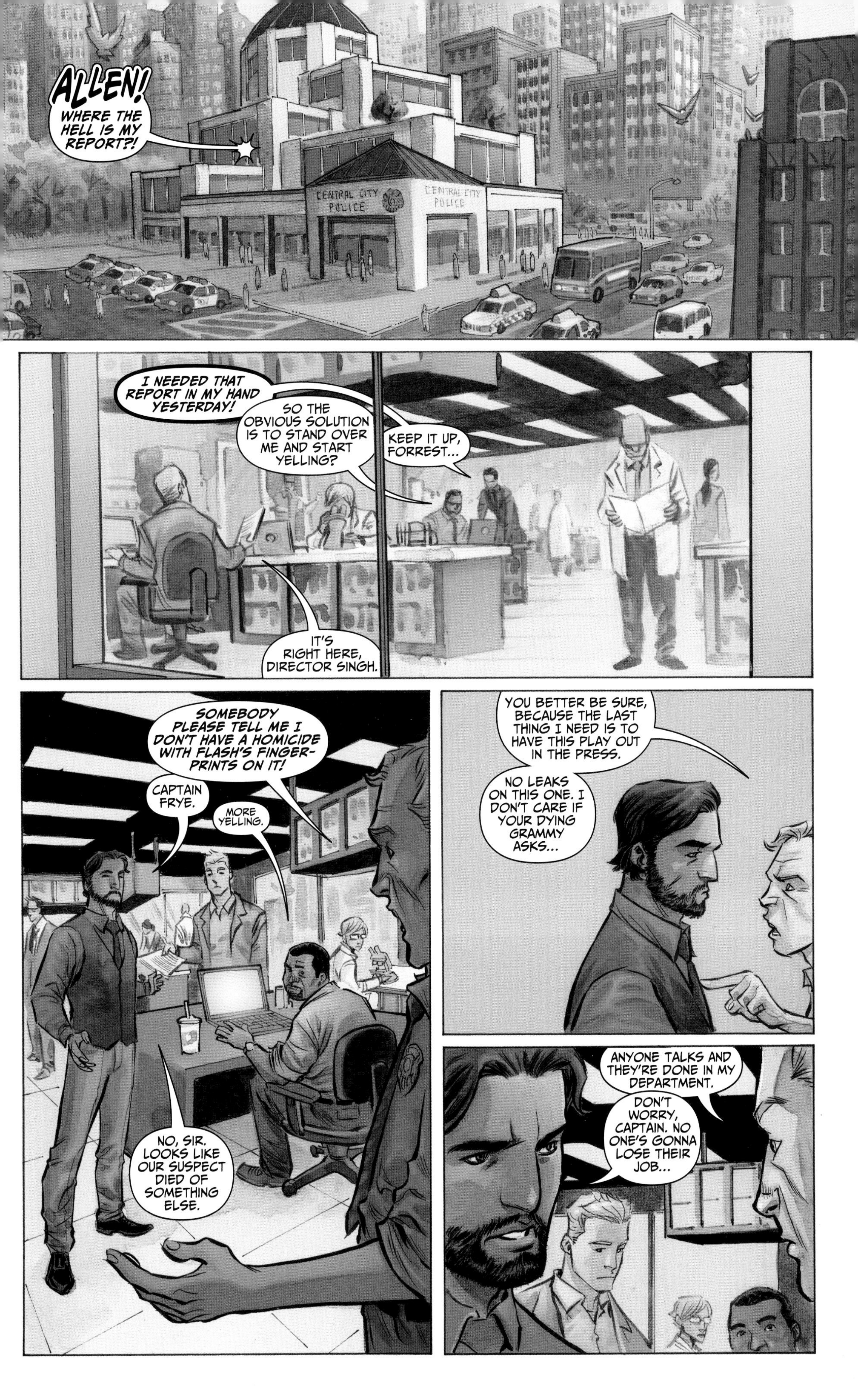

ALLEN! WHERE THE HELL IS MY REPORT?!
CENTRAL CITY POLICE
CENTRAL CITY POLICE
I NEEDED THAT REPORT IN MY HAND YESTERDAY!
SO THE OBVIOUS SOLUTION IS TO STAND OVER ME AND START YELLING?
KEEP IT UP, FORREST...
IT'S RIGHT HERE, DIRECTOR SINGH.
SOMEBODY PLEASE TELL ME I DON'T HAVE A HOMICIDE WITH FLASH'S FINGER-PRINTS ON IT!
CAPTAIN FRYE.
MORE YELLING.
NO, SIR. LOOKS LIKE OUR SUSPECT DIED OF SOMETHING ELSE.
YOU BETTER BE SURE, BECAUSE THE LAST THING I NEED IS TO HAVE THIS PLAY OUT IN THE PRESS.
NO LEAKS ON THIS ONE. I DON'T CARE IF YOUR DYING GRAMMY ASKS...
ANYONE TALKS AND THEY'RE DONE IN MY DEPARTMENT.
DON'T WORRY, CAPTAIN. NO ONE'S GONNA LOSE THEIR JOB...

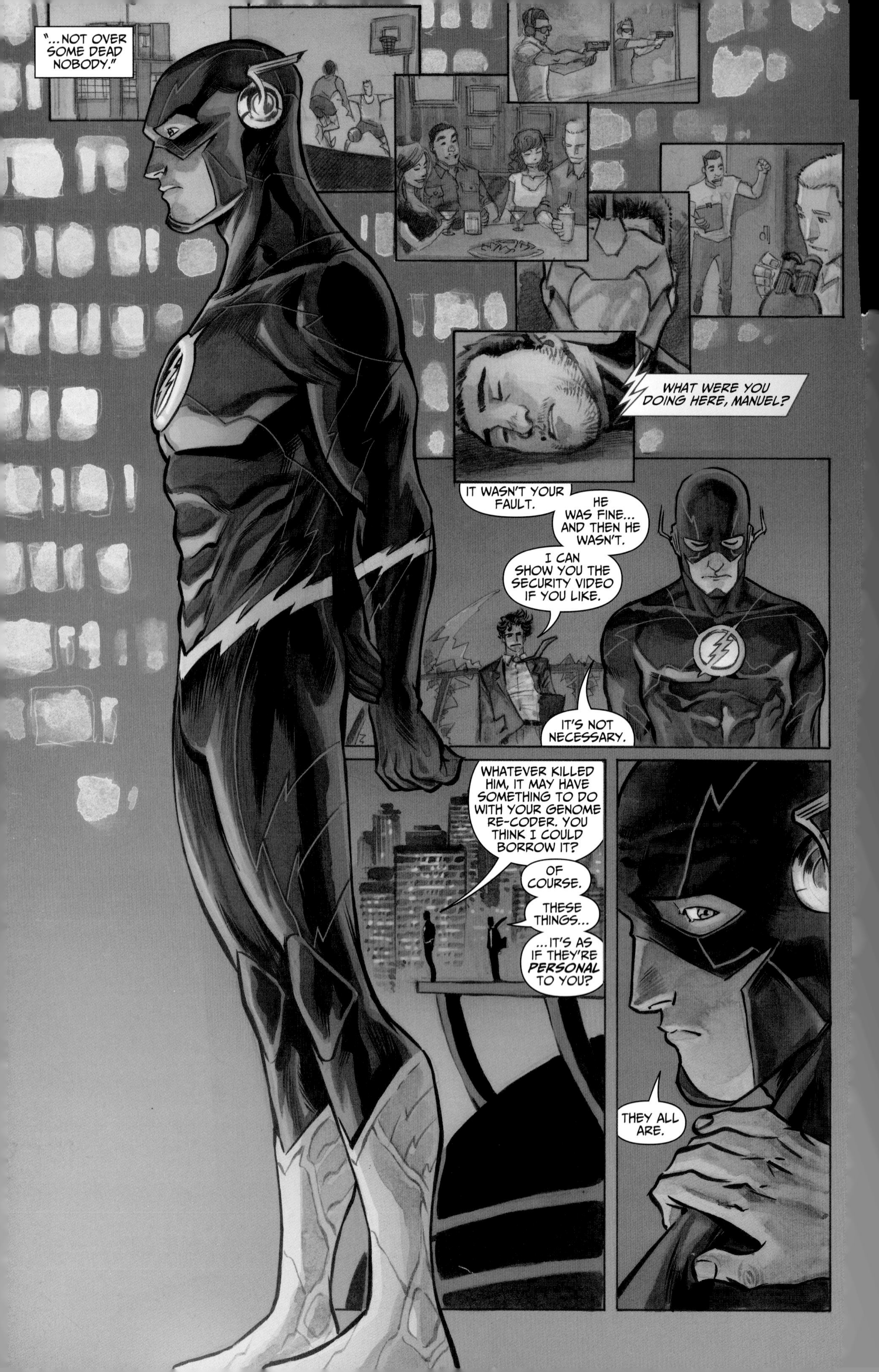
"...NOT OVER SOME DEAD NOBODY."
WHAT WERE YOU DOING HERE, MANUEL?
IT WASN'T YOUR FAULT.
HE WAS FINE... AND THEN HE WASN'T.
I CAN SHOW YOU THE SECURITY VIDEO IF YOU LIKE.
IT'S NOT NECESSARY.
WHATEVER KILLED HIM, IT MAY HAVE SOMETHING TO DO WITH YOUR GENOME RE-CODER. YOU THINK I COULD BORROW IT?
OF COURSE.
THESE THINGS...
...IT'S AS IF THEY'RE PERSONAL TO YOU?
THEY ALL ARE.

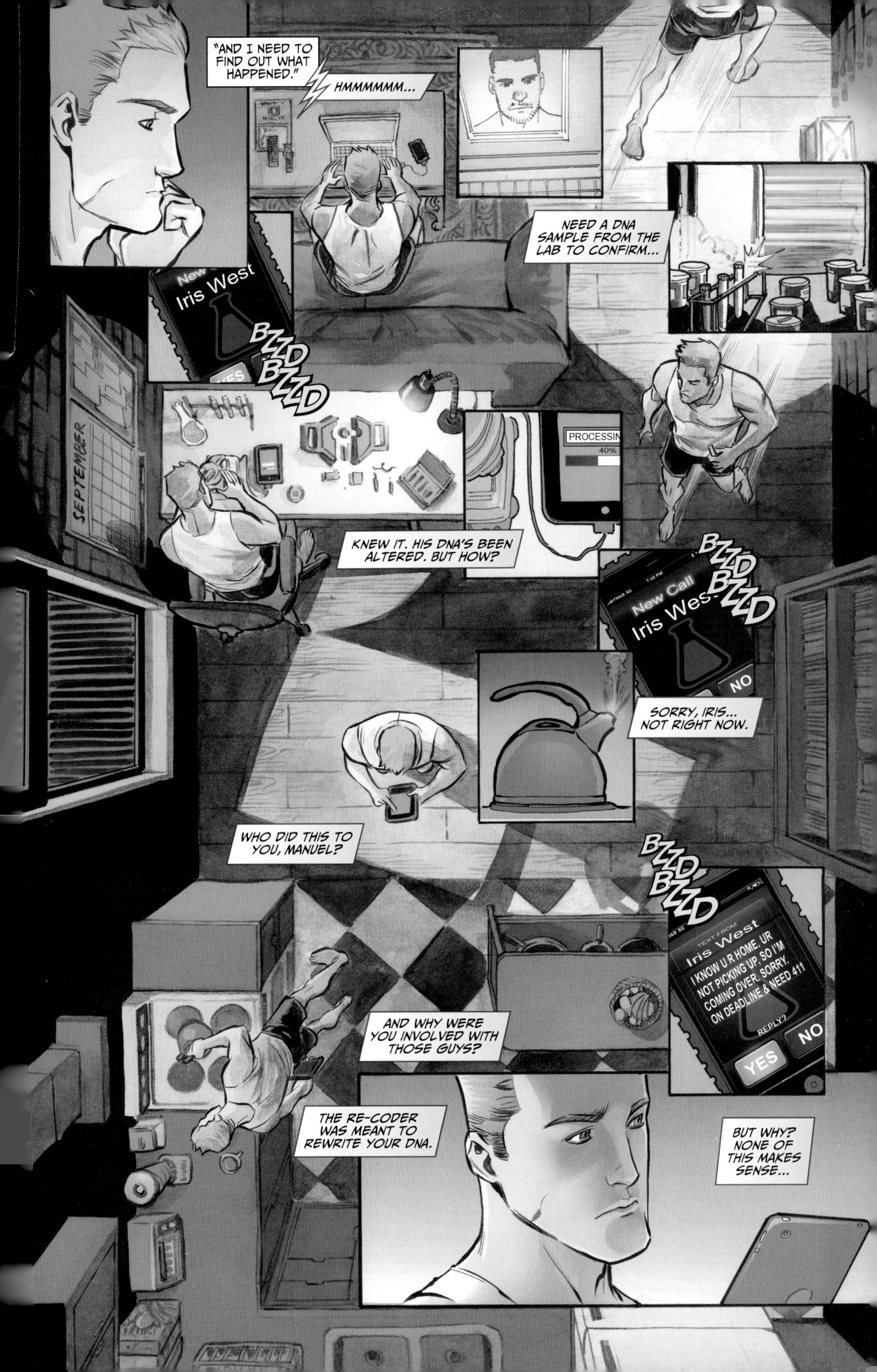
"AND I NEED TO FIND OUT WHAT HAPPENED."
HMMMMMM...
NEED A DNA SAMPLE FROM THE LAB TO CONFIRM...
New
Iris West
BZZZD BZZZD
PROCESSING
40%
KNEW IT. HIS DNA'S BEEN ALTERED. BUT HOW?
New Call
Iris West
BZZZD BZZZD
NO
SORRY, IRIS... NOT RIGHT NOW.
WHO DID THIS TO YOU, MANUEL?
BZZZD BZZZD
TEXT FROM
Iris West
I KNOW U R HOME. UR NOT PICKING UP, SO I'M COMING OVER. SORRY, ON DEADLINE & NEED 411
REPLY?
YES
NO
AND WHY WERE YOU INVOLVED WITH THOSE GUYS?
THE RE-CODER WAS MEANT TO REWRITE YOUR DNA.
BUT WHY? NONE OF THIS MAKES SENSE...

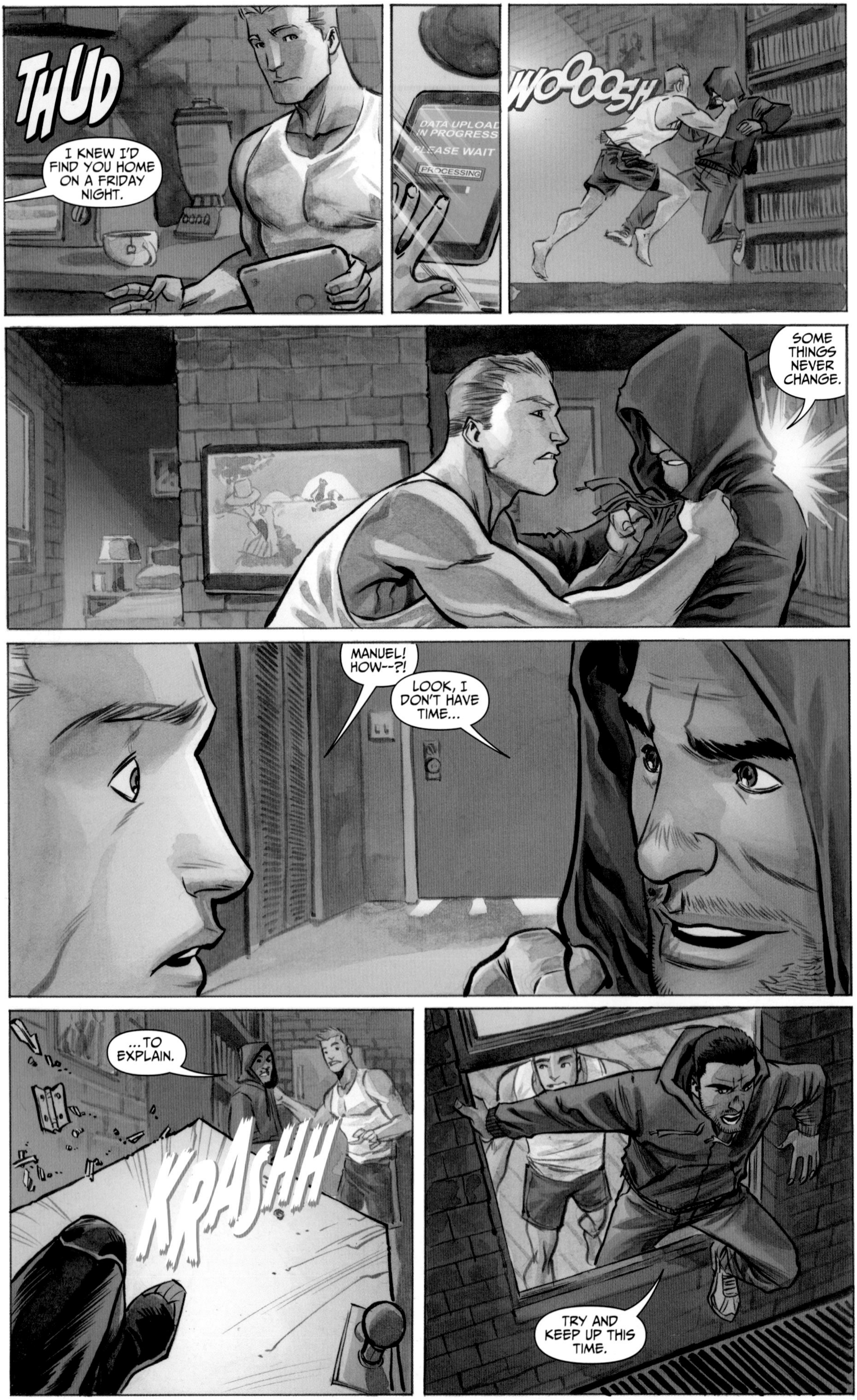
THUD
I KNEW I'D FIND YOU HOME ON A FRIDAY NIGHT.
DATA UPLOAD IN PROGRESS
PLEASE WAIT
PROCESSING
WOOOOSH
SOME THINGS NEVER CHANGE.
MANUEL! HOW--?!
LOOK, I DON'T HAVE TIME...
...TO EXPLAIN.
KRASHH
TRY AND KEEP UP THIS TIME.

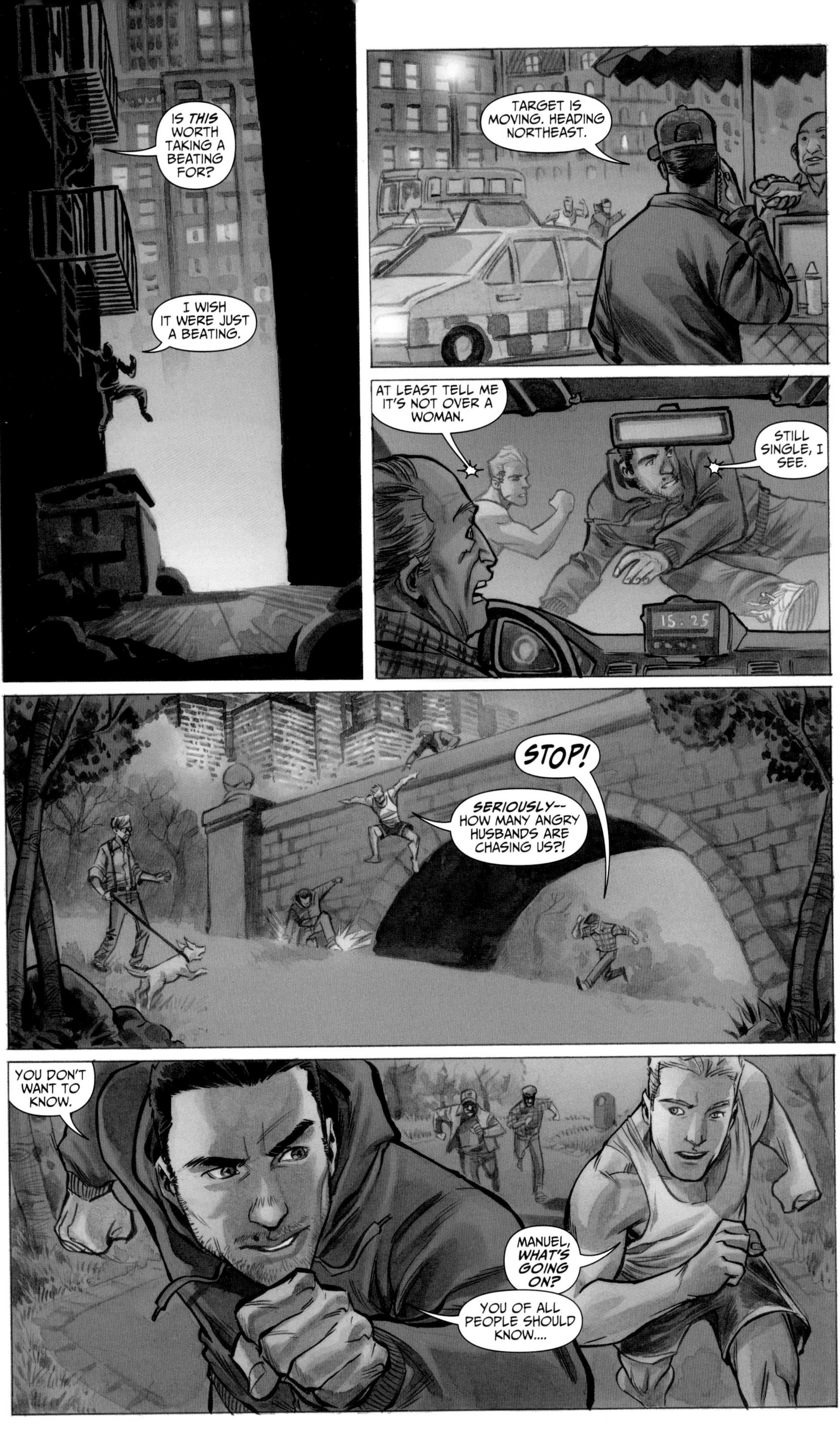
IS *THIS* WORTH TAKING A BEATING FOR?
I WISH IT WERE JUST A BEATING.
TARGET IS MOVING. HEADING NORTHEAST.
AT LEAST TELL ME IT'S NOT OVER A WOMAN.
STILL SINGLE, I SEE.
15.25
STOP!
SERIOUSLY-- HOW MANY ANGRY HUSBANDS ARE CHASING US?!
YOU DON'T WANT TO KNOW.
MANUEL, *WHAT'S GOING ON?*
YOU OF ALL PEOPLE SHOULD KNOW....

...WE'RE ALWAYS RUNNING FROM SOMETHING.

HE'S HALF RIGHT.

MY MOM ONCE TOLD ME THAT "LIFE IS LOCOMOTION..."

"IF YOU'RE NOT MOVING, YOU'RE NOT LIVING."

"BUT THERE COMES A TIME WHEN YOU'VE GOT TO STOP RUNNING *AWAY* FROM THINGS...

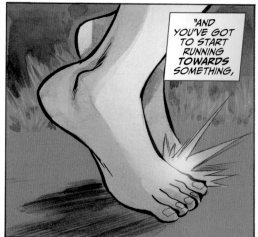

"AND YOU'VE GOT TO START RUNNING *TOWARDS* SOMETHING,

"YOU'VE GOT TO FORGE AHEAD.

BARRY?!

"KEEP MOVING."

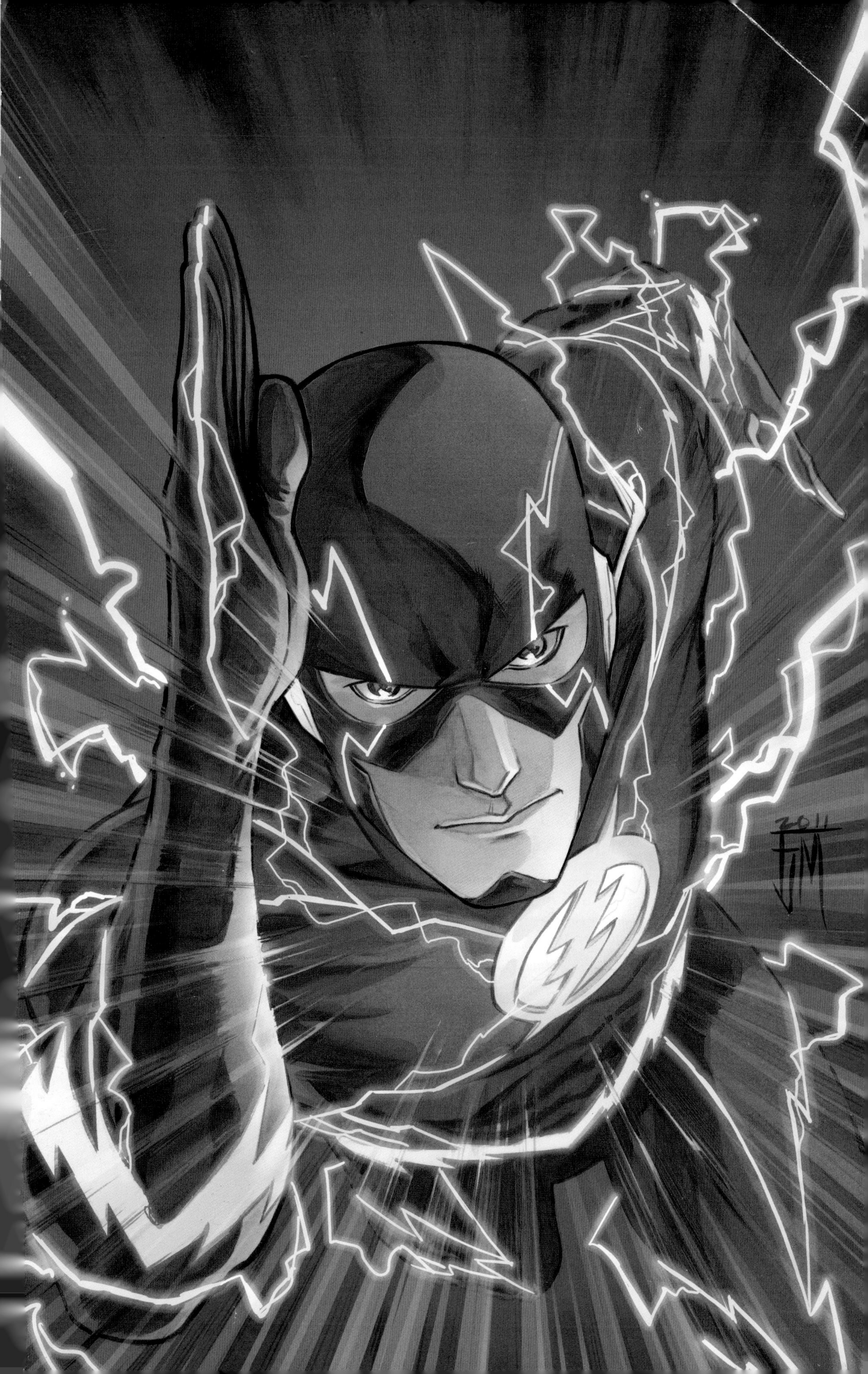

The Flash

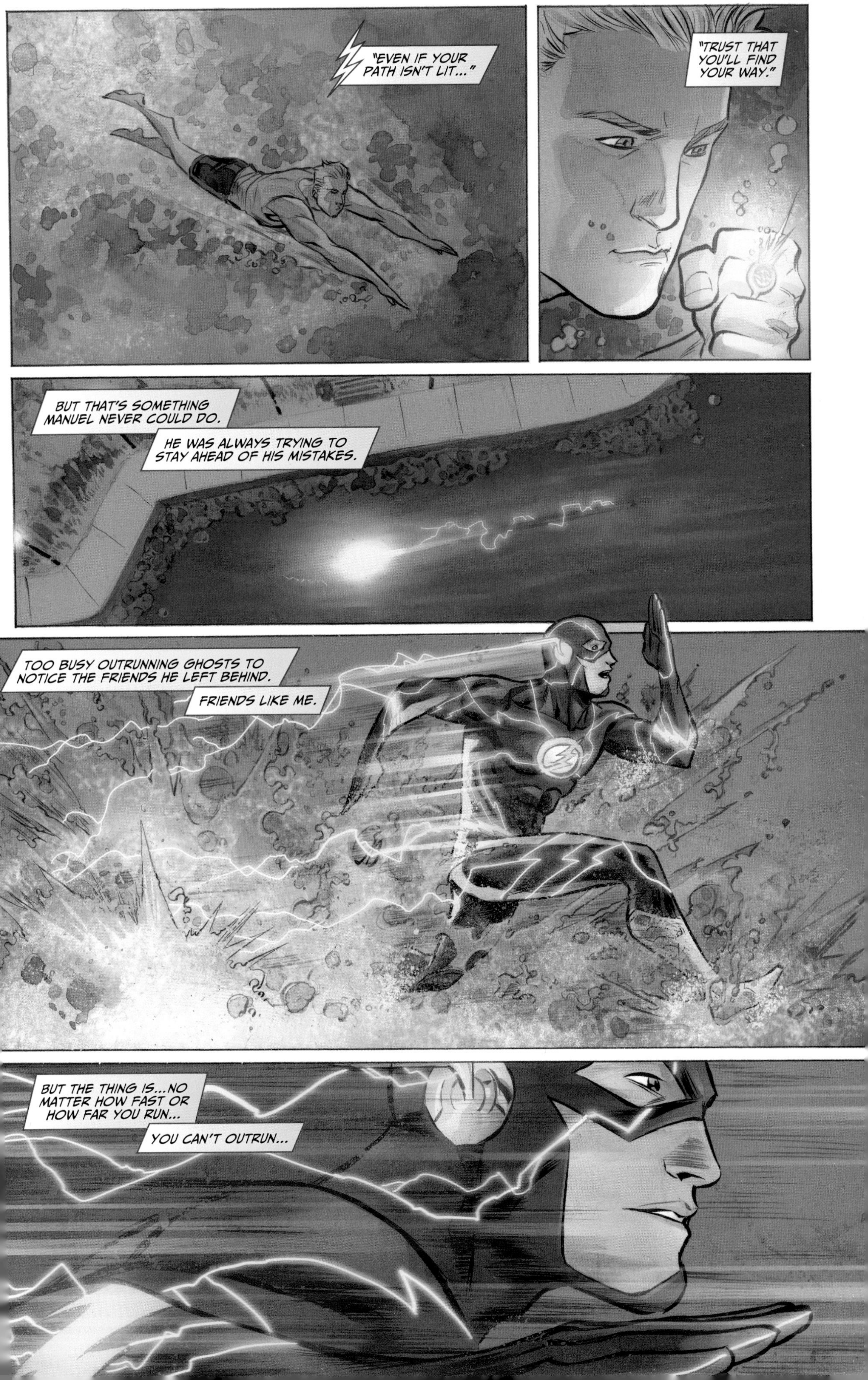
"EVEN IF YOUR PATH ISN'T LIT..."
"TRUST THAT YOU'LL FIND YOUR WAY."
BUT THAT'S SOMETHING MANUEL NEVER COULD DO.
HE WAS ALWAYS TRYING TO STAY AHEAD OF HIS MISTAKES.
TOO BUSY OUTRUNNING GHOSTS TO NOTICE THE FRIENDS HE LEFT BEHIND.
FRIENDS LIKE ME.
BUT THE THING IS...NO MATTER HOW FAST OR HOW FAR YOU RUN...
YOU CAN'T OUTRUN...

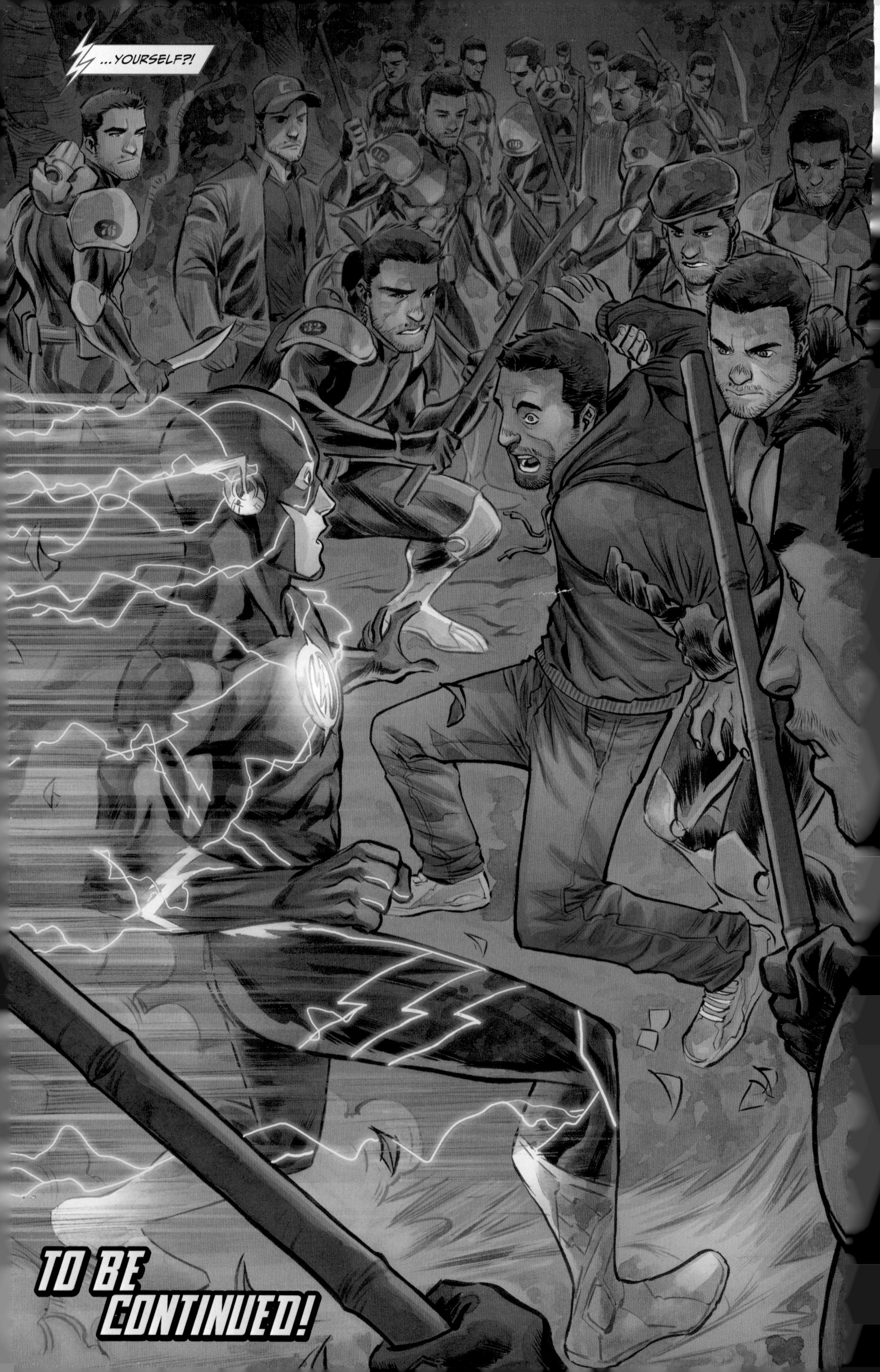
...YOURSELF?!
TO BE CONTINUED!

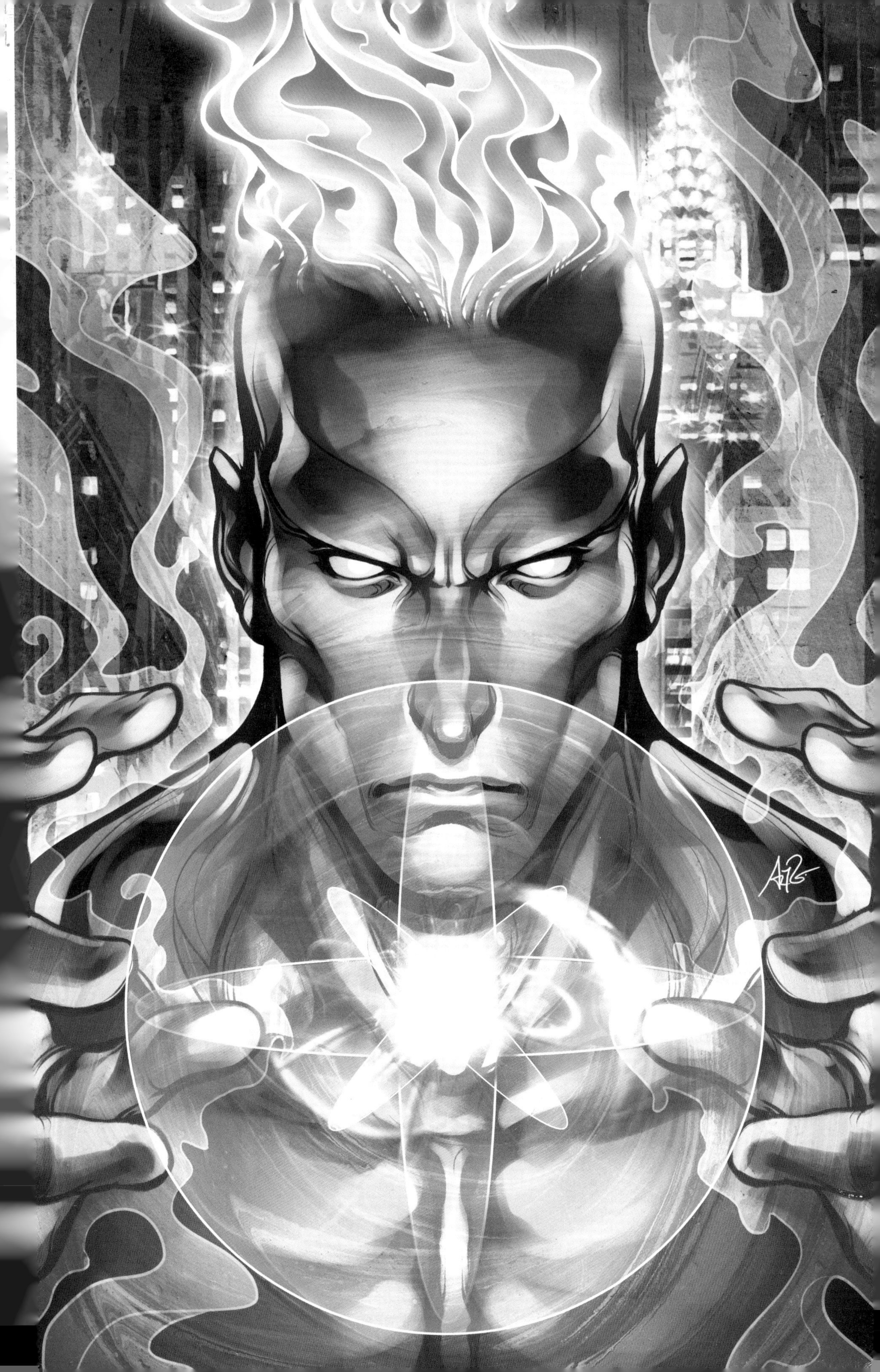

CAPTAIN ATOM

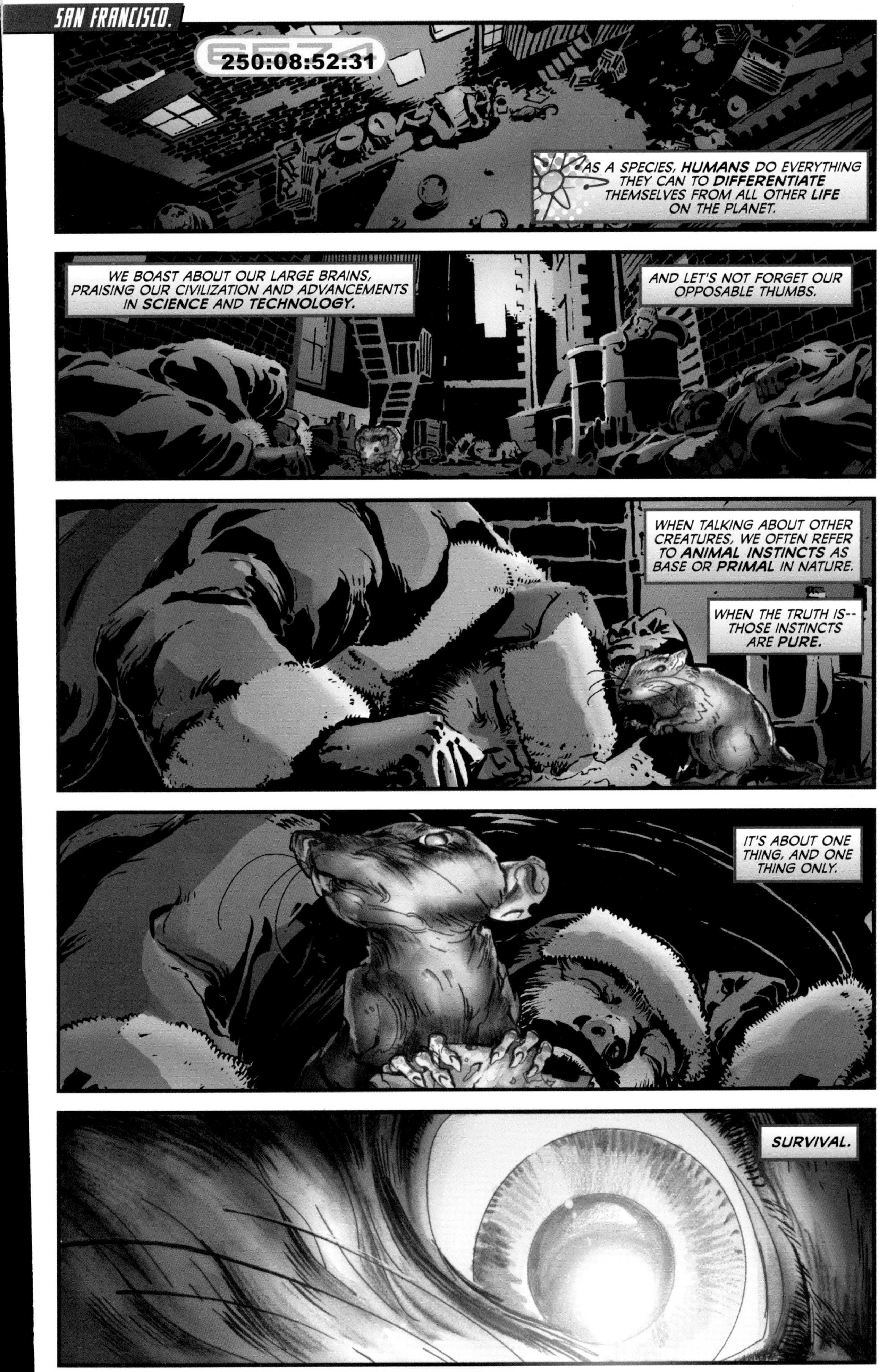
SAN FRANCISCO.
250:08:52:31
AS A SPECIES, HUMANS DO EVERYTHING THEY CAN TO DIFFERENTIATE THEMSELVES FROM ALL OTHER LIFE ON THE PLANET.
WE BOAST ABOUT OUR LARGE BRAINS, PRAISING OUR CIVILIZATION AND ADVANCEMENTS IN SCIENCE AND TECHNOLOGY.
AND LET'S NOT FORGET OUR OPPOSABLE THUMBS.
WHEN TALKING ABOUT OTHER CREATURES, WE OFTEN REFER TO ANIMAL INSTINCTS AS BASE OR PRIMAL IN NATURE.
WHEN THE TRUTH IS-- THOSE INSTINCTS ARE PURE.
IT'S ABOUT ONE THING, AND ONE THING ONLY.
SURVIVAL.

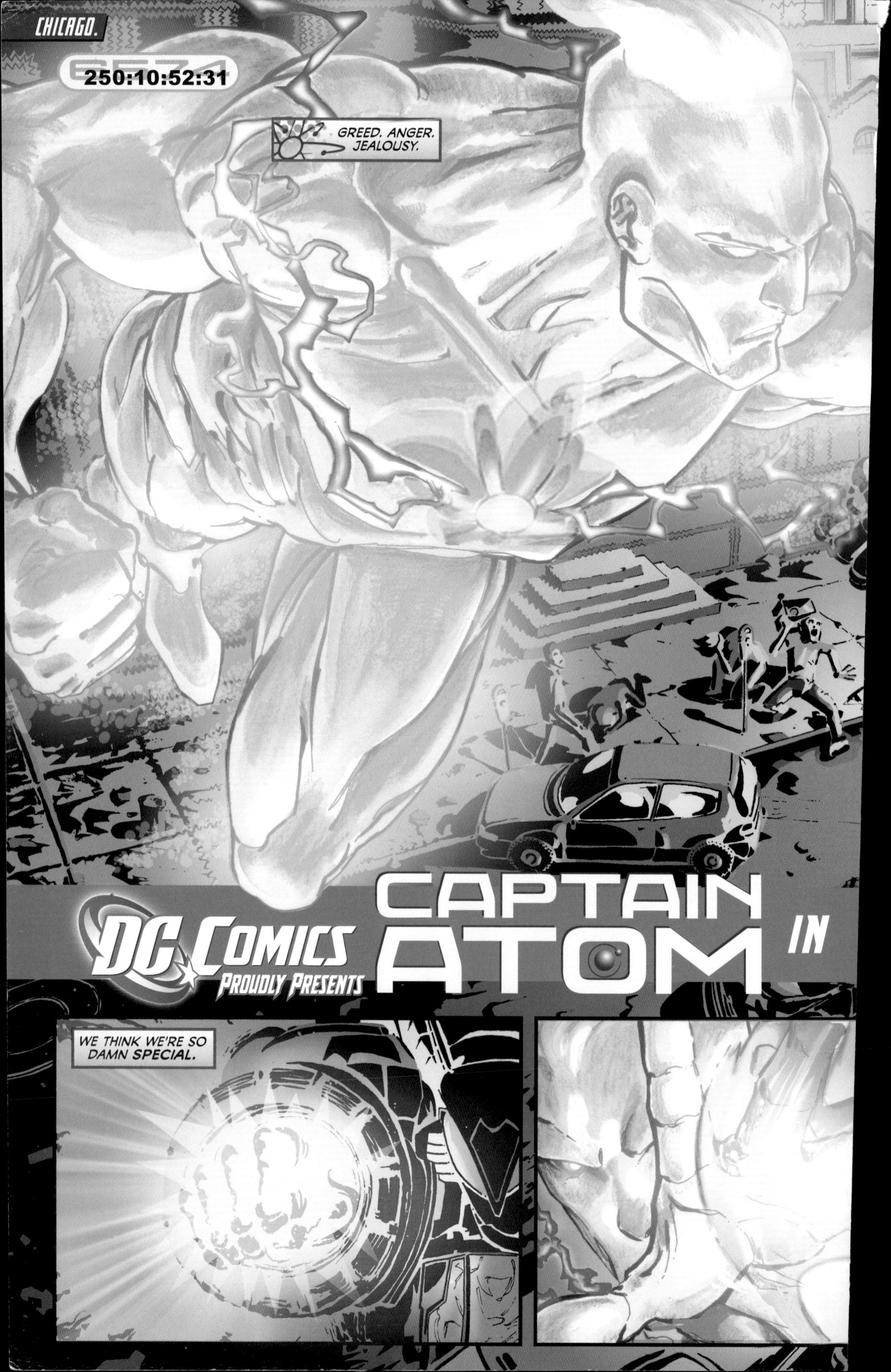
CHICAGO.
250:10:52:31
GREED. ANGER. JEALOUSY.
DC COMICS PROUDLY PRESENTS
CAPTAIN ATOM IN
WE THINK WE'RE SO DAMN SPECIAL.

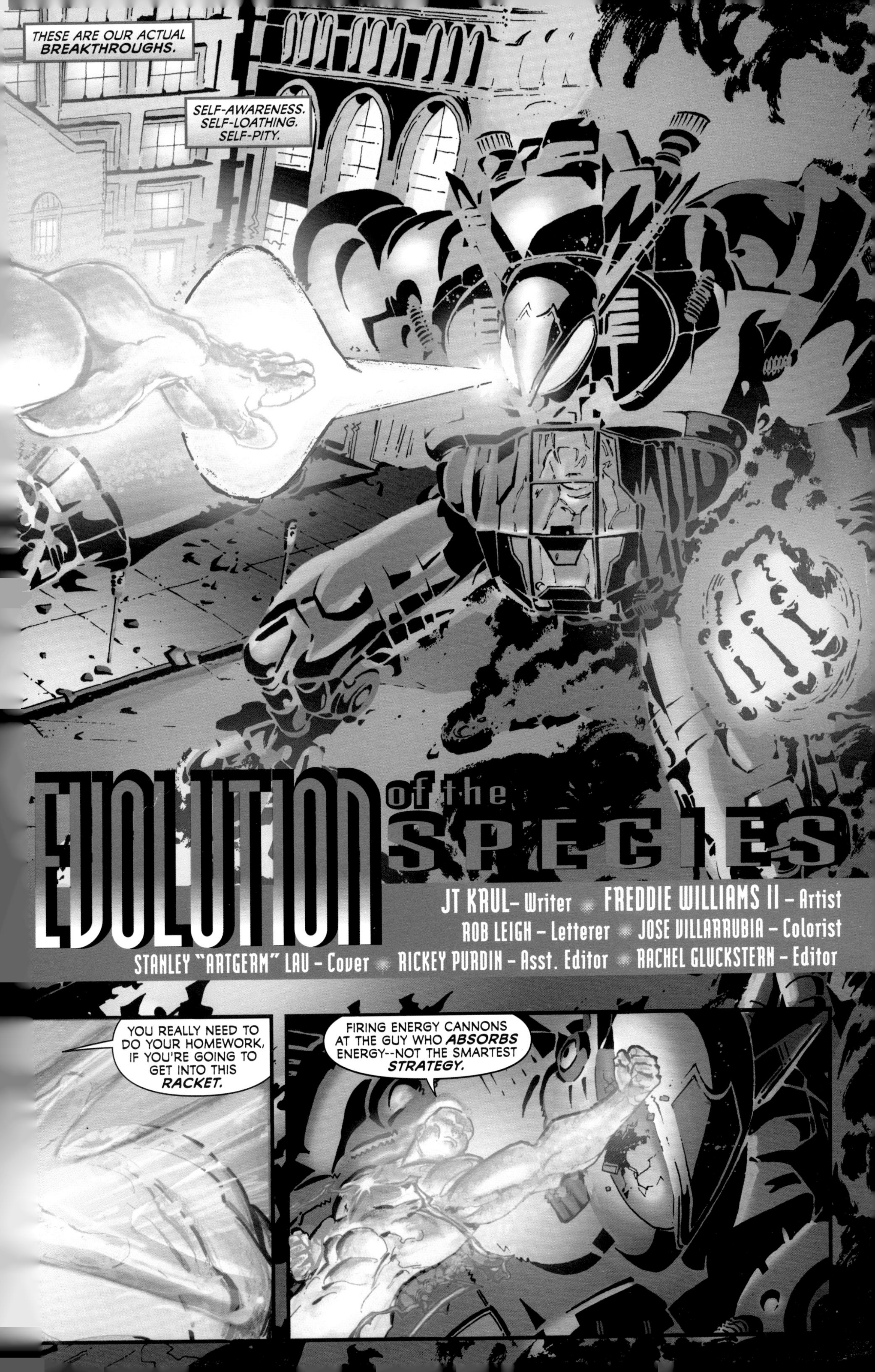

THESE ARE OUR ACTUAL BREAKTHROUGHS.
SELF-AWARENESS. SELF-LOATHING. SELF-PITY.
EVOLUTION of the SPECIES
JT KRUL- Writer FREDDIE WILLIAMS II - Artist
ROB LEIGH - Letterer JOSE VILLARRUBIA - Colorist
STANLEY "ARTGERM" LAU - Cover RICKEY PURDIN - Asst. Editor RACHEL GLUCKSTERN - Editor
YOU REALLY NEED TO DO YOUR HOMEWORK, IF YOU'RE GOING TO GET INTO THIS RACKET.
FIRING ENERGY CANNONS AT THE GUY WHO ABSORBS ENERGY--NOT THE SMARTEST STRATEGY.

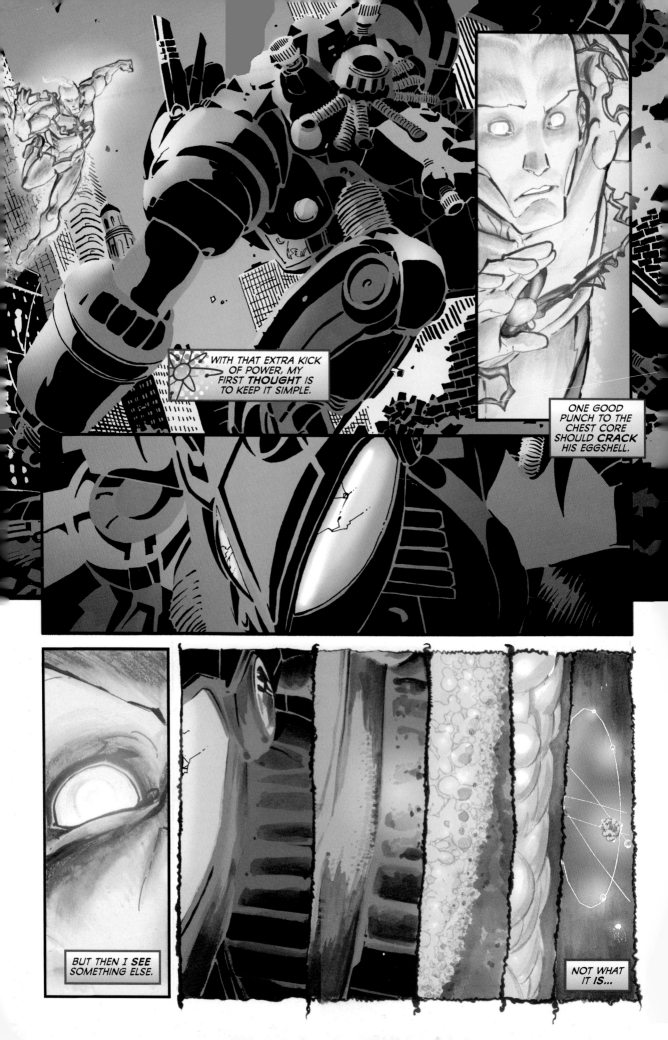

WITH THAT EXTRA KICK OF POWER, MY FIRST **THOUGHT** IS TO KEEP IT SIMPLE.

ONE GOOD PUNCH TO THE CHEST CORE SHOULD **CRACK** HIS EGGSHELL.

BUT THEN I **SEE** SOMETHING ELSE.

NOT WHAT IT **IS**...

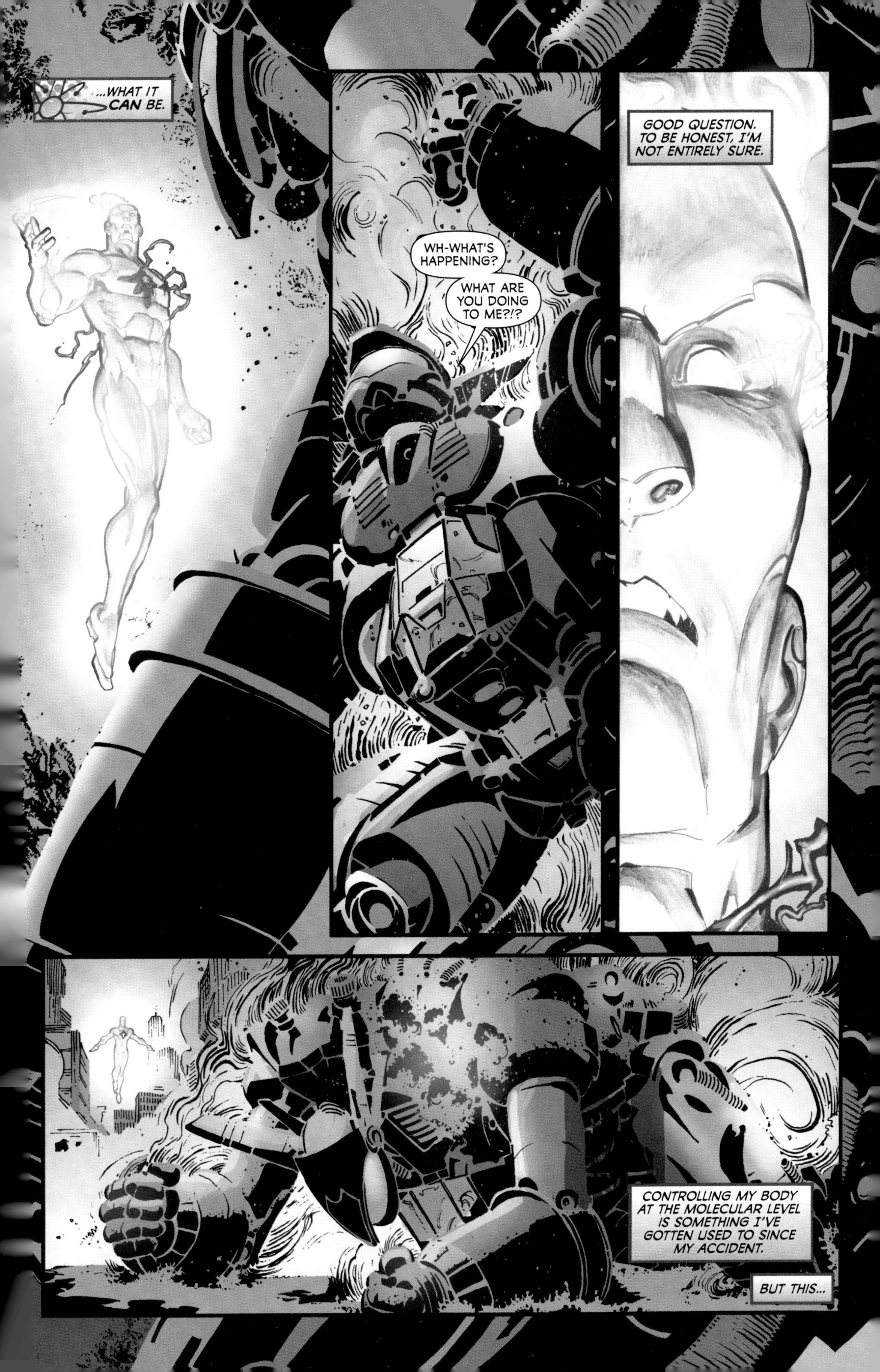
...WHAT IT CAN BE.
WH-WHAT'S HAPPENING?
WHAT ARE YOU DOING TO ME?!?
GOOD QUESTION. TO BE HONEST, I'M NOT ENTIRELY SURE.
CONTROLLING MY BODY AT THE MOLECULAR LEVEL IS SOMETHING I'VE GOTTEN USED TO SINCE MY ACCIDENT.
BUT THIS...

...THIS IS SOMETHING NEW.

THIS IS SCARY.

BECAUSE I THINK I'M LOSING CONTROL.

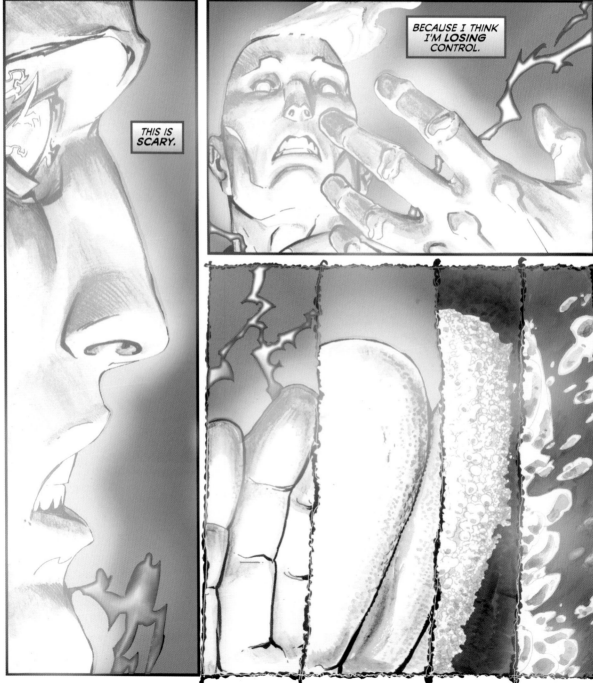

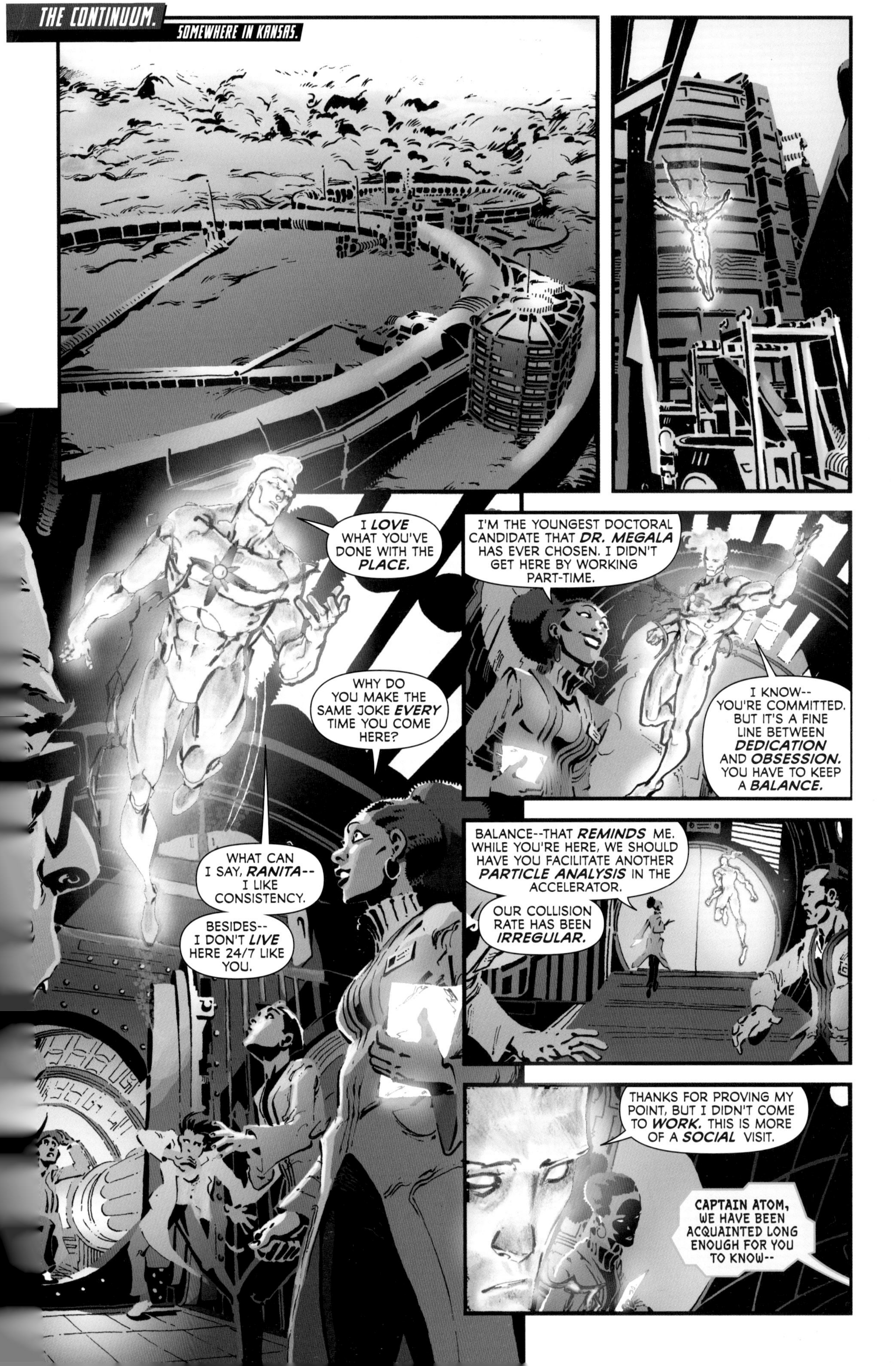
THE CONTINUUM.
SOMEWHERE IN KANSAS.
I LOVE WHAT YOU'VE DONE WITH THE PLACE.
WHY DO YOU MAKE THE SAME JOKE EVERY TIME YOU COME HERE?
WHAT CAN I SAY, RANITA-- I LIKE CONSISTENCY.
BESIDES-- I DON'T LIVE HERE 24/7 LIKE YOU.
I'M THE YOUNGEST DOCTORAL CANDIDATE THAT DR. MEGALA HAS EVER CHOSEN. I DIDN'T GET HERE BY WORKING PART-TIME.
I KNOW-- YOU'RE COMMITTED. BUT IT'S A FINE LINE BETWEEN DEDICATION AND OBSESSION. YOU HAVE TO KEEP A BALANCE.
BALANCE--THAT REMINDS ME. WHILE YOU'RE HERE, WE SHOULD HAVE YOU FACILITATE ANOTHER PARTICLE ANALYSIS IN THE ACCELERATOR.
OUR COLLISION RATE HAS BEEN IRREGULAR.
THANKS FOR PROVING MY POINT, BUT I DIDN'T COME TO WORK. THIS IS MORE OF A SOCIAL VISIT.
CAPTAIN ATOM, WE HAVE BEEN ACQUAINTED LONG ENOUGH FOR YOU TO KNOW--

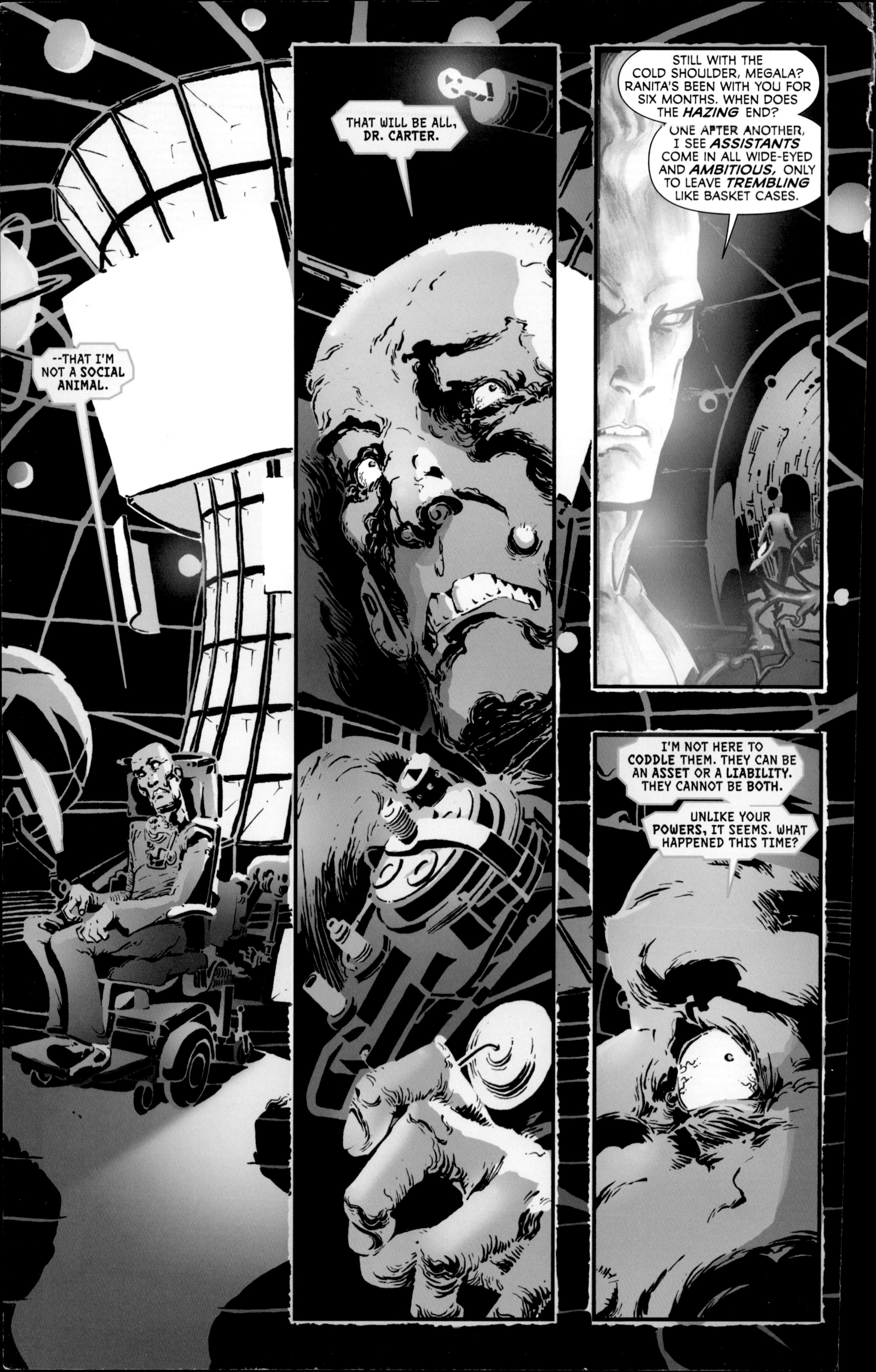
--THAT I'M NOT A SOCIAL ANIMAL.
THAT WILL BE ALL, DR. CARTER.
STILL WITH THE COLD SHOULDER, MEGALA? RANITA'S BEEN WITH YOU FOR SIX MONTHS. WHEN DOES THE HAZING END?
ONE AFTER ANOTHER, I SEE ASSISTANTS COME IN ALL WIDE-EYED AND AMBITIOUS, ONLY TO LEAVE TREMBLING LIKE BASKET CASES.
I'M NOT HERE TO CODDLE THEM. THEY CAN BE AN ASSET OR A LIABILITY. THEY CANNOT BE BOTH.
UNLIKE YOUR POWERS, IT SEEMS. WHAT HAPPENED THIS TIME?

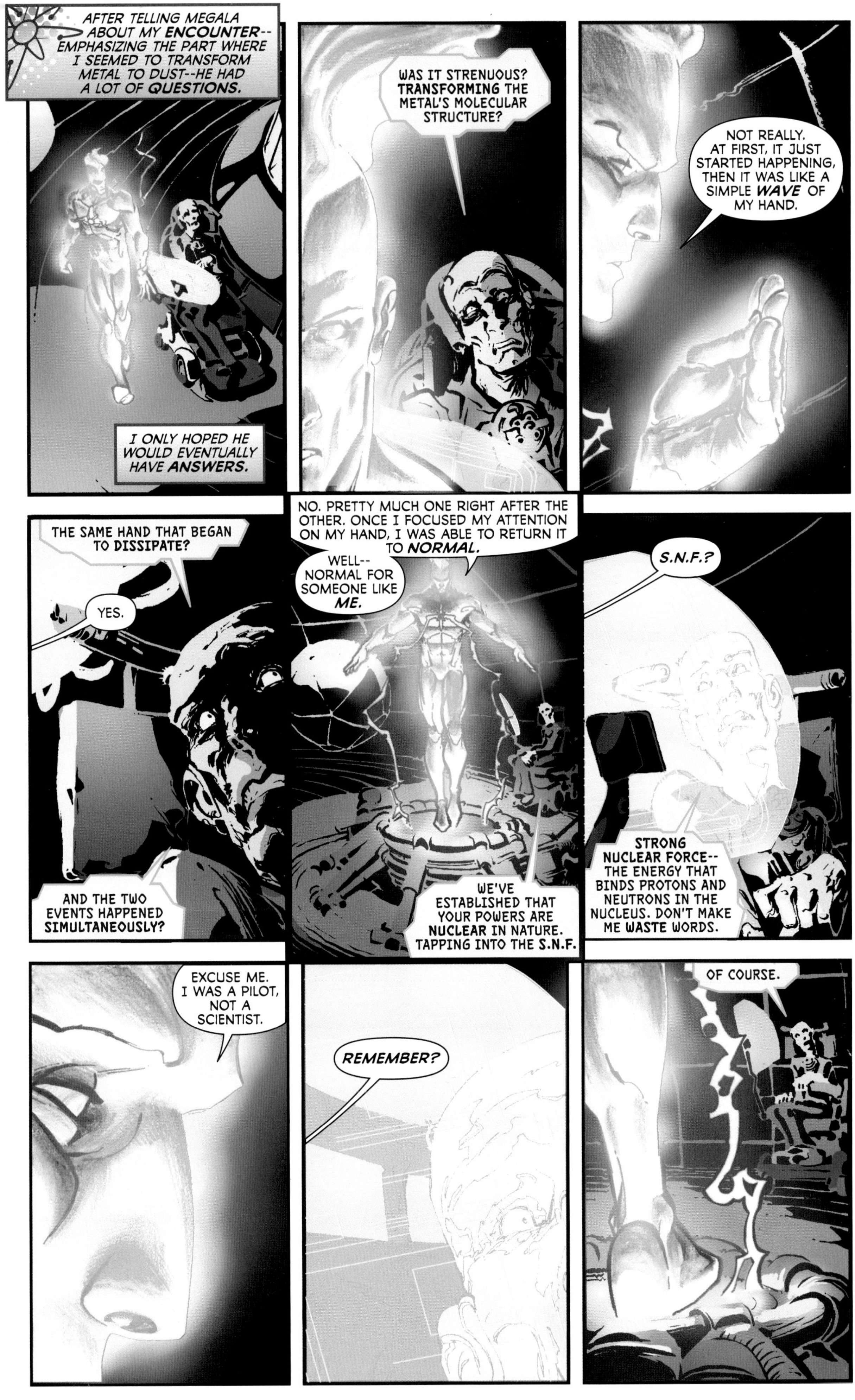
AFTER TELLING MEGALA ABOUT MY ENCOUNTER--EMPHASIZING THE PART WHERE I SEEMED TO TRANSFORM METAL TO DUST--HE HAD A LOT OF QUESTIONS.
I ONLY HOPED HE WOULD EVENTUALLY HAVE ANSWERS.
WAS IT STRENUOUS? TRANSFORMING THE METAL'S MOLECULAR STRUCTURE?
NOT REALLY. AT FIRST, IT JUST STARTED HAPPENING, THEN IT WAS LIKE A SIMPLE WAVE OF MY HAND.
THE SAME HAND THAT BEGAN TO DISSIPATE?
YES.
AND THE TWO EVENTS HAPPENED SIMULTANEOUSLY?
NO. PRETTY MUCH ONE RIGHT AFTER THE OTHER. ONCE I FOCUSED MY ATTENTION ON MY HAND, I WAS ABLE TO RETURN IT TO NORMAL.
WELL--NORMAL FOR SOMEONE LIKE ME.
WE'VE ESTABLISHED THAT YOUR POWERS ARE NUCLEAR IN NATURE. TAPPING INTO THE S.N.F.
S.N.F.?
STRONG NUCLEAR FORCE--THE ENERGY THAT BINDS PROTONS AND NEUTRONS IN THE NUCLEUS. DON'T MAKE ME WASTE WORDS.
EXCUSE ME. I WAS A PILOT, NOT A SCIENTIST.
REMEMBER?
OF COURSE.

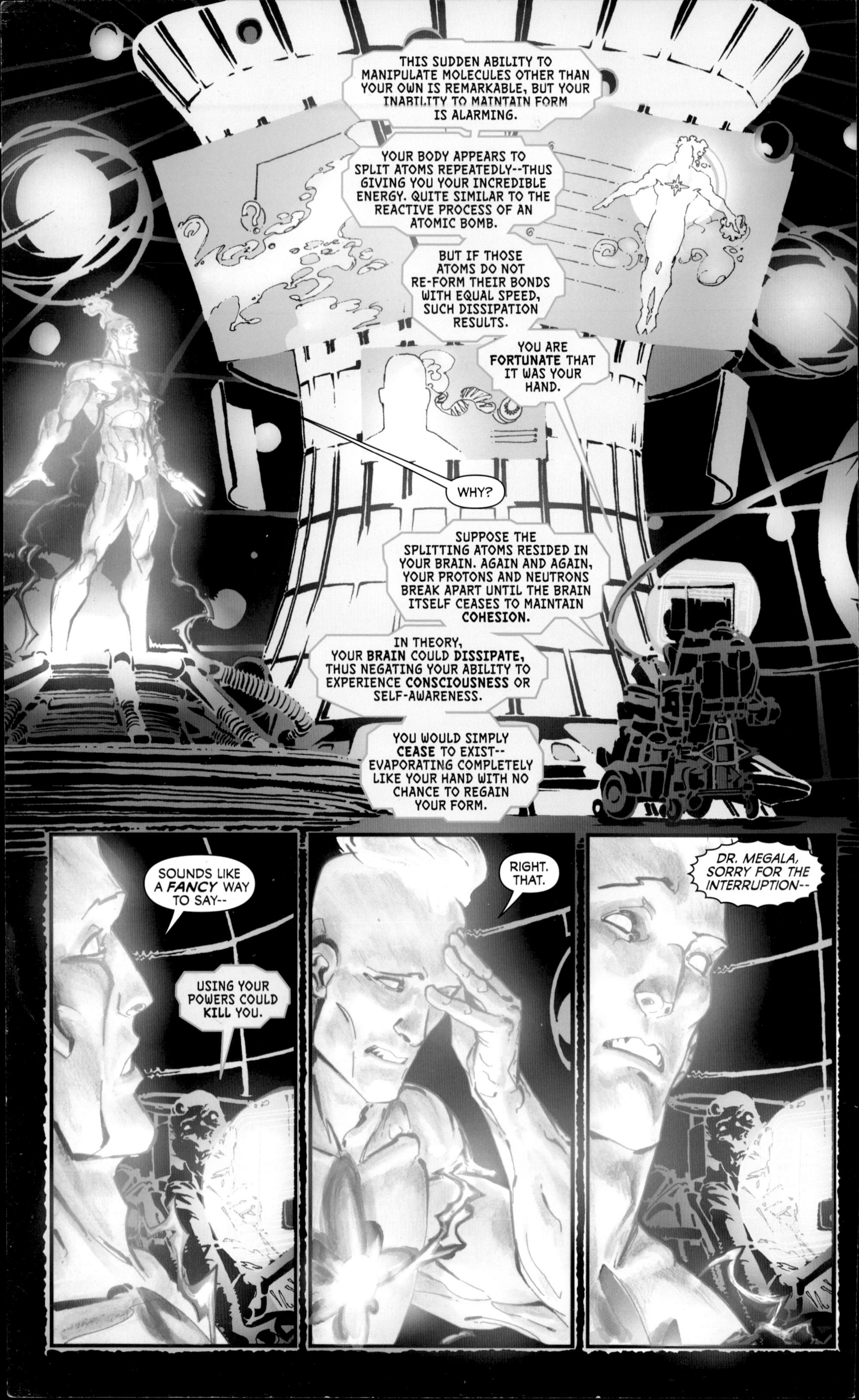
THIS SUDDEN ABILITY TO MANIPULATE MOLECULES OTHER THAN YOUR OWN IS REMARKABLE, BUT YOUR INABILITY TO MAINTAIN FORM IS ALARMING.
YOUR BODY APPEARS TO SPLIT ATOMS REPEATEDLY--THUS GIVING YOU YOUR INCREDIBLE ENERGY. QUITE SIMILAR TO THE REACTIVE PROCESS OF AN ATOMIC BOMB.
BUT IF THOSE ATOMS DO NOT RE-FORM THEIR BONDS WITH EQUAL SPEED, SUCH DISSIPATION RESULTS.
YOU ARE FORTUNATE THAT IT WAS YOUR HAND.
WHY?
SUPPOSE THE SPLITTING ATOMS RESIDED IN YOUR BRAIN. AGAIN AND AGAIN, YOUR PROTONS AND NEUTRONS BREAK APART UNTIL THE BRAIN ITSELF CEASES TO MAINTAIN COHESION.
IN THEORY, YOUR BRAIN COULD DISSIPATE, THUS NEGATING YOUR ABILITY TO EXPERIENCE CONSCIOUSNESS OR SELF-AWARENESS.
YOU WOULD SIMPLY CEASE TO EXIST--EVAPORATING COMPLETELY LIKE YOUR HAND WITH NO CHANCE TO REGAIN YOUR FORM.
SOUNDS LIKE A *FANCY* WAY TO SAY--
USING YOUR POWERS COULD KILL YOU.
RIGHT. THAT.
DR. MEGALA, SORRY FOR THE INTERRUPTION--

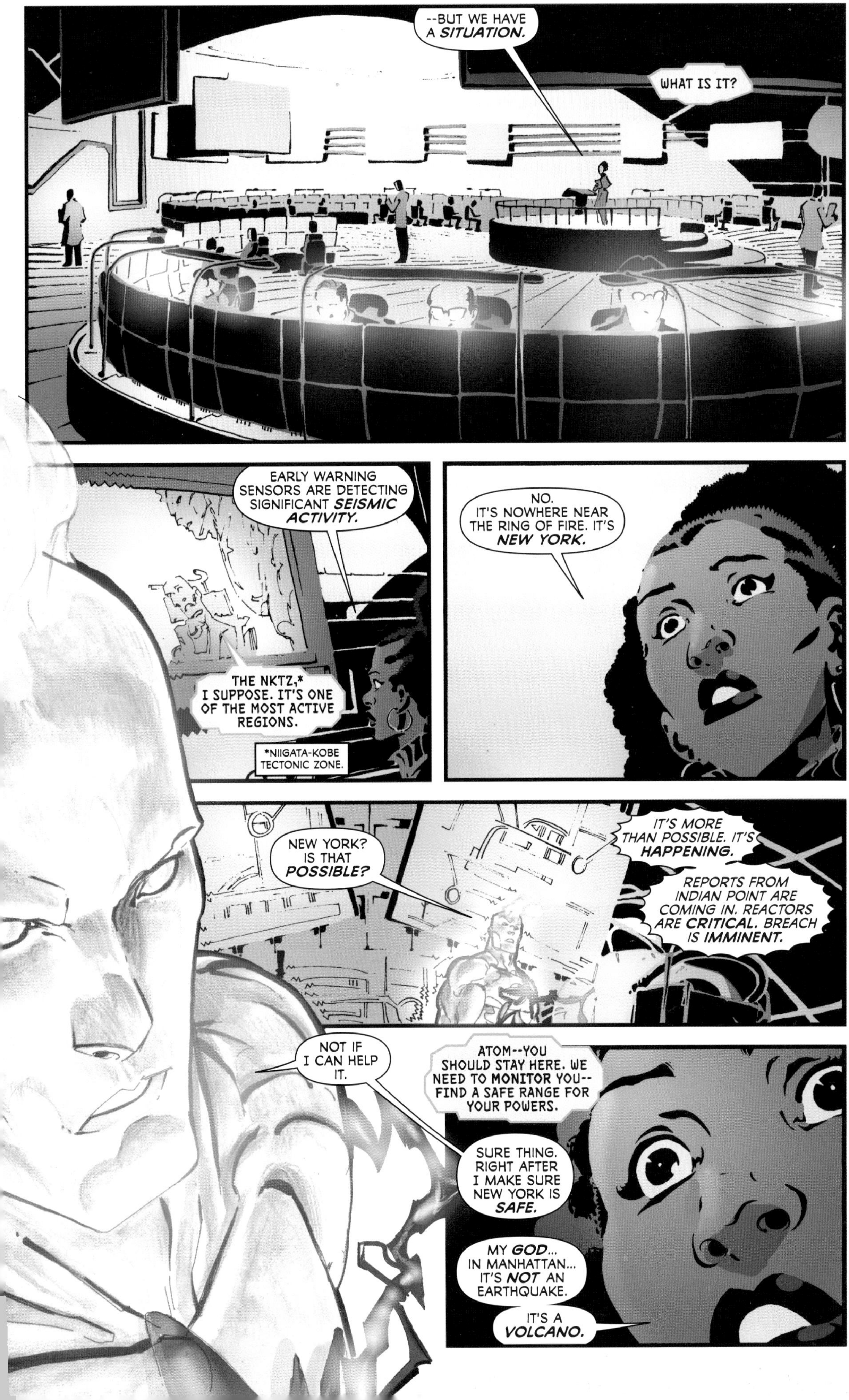
--BUT WE HAVE A SITUATION.
WHAT IS IT?
EARLY WARNING SENSORS ARE DETECTING SIGNIFICANT SEISMIC ACTIVITY.
THE NKTZ,* I SUPPOSE. IT'S ONE OF THE MOST ACTIVE REGIONS.
*NIIGATA-KOBE TECTONIC ZONE.
NO. IT'S NOWHERE NEAR THE RING OF FIRE. IT'S NEW YORK.
NEW YORK? IS THAT POSSIBLE?
IT'S MORE THAN POSSIBLE. IT'S HAPPENING.
REPORTS FROM INDIAN POINT ARE COMING IN. REACTORS ARE CRITICAL. BREACH IS IMMINENT.
NOT IF I CAN HELP IT.
ATOM--YOU SHOULD STAY HERE. WE NEED TO MONITOR YOU--FIND A SAFE RANGE FOR YOUR POWERS.
SURE THING. RIGHT AFTER I MAKE SURE NEW YORK IS SAFE.
MY GOD... IN MANHATTAN... IT'S NOT AN EARTHQUAKE.
IT'S A VOLCANO.

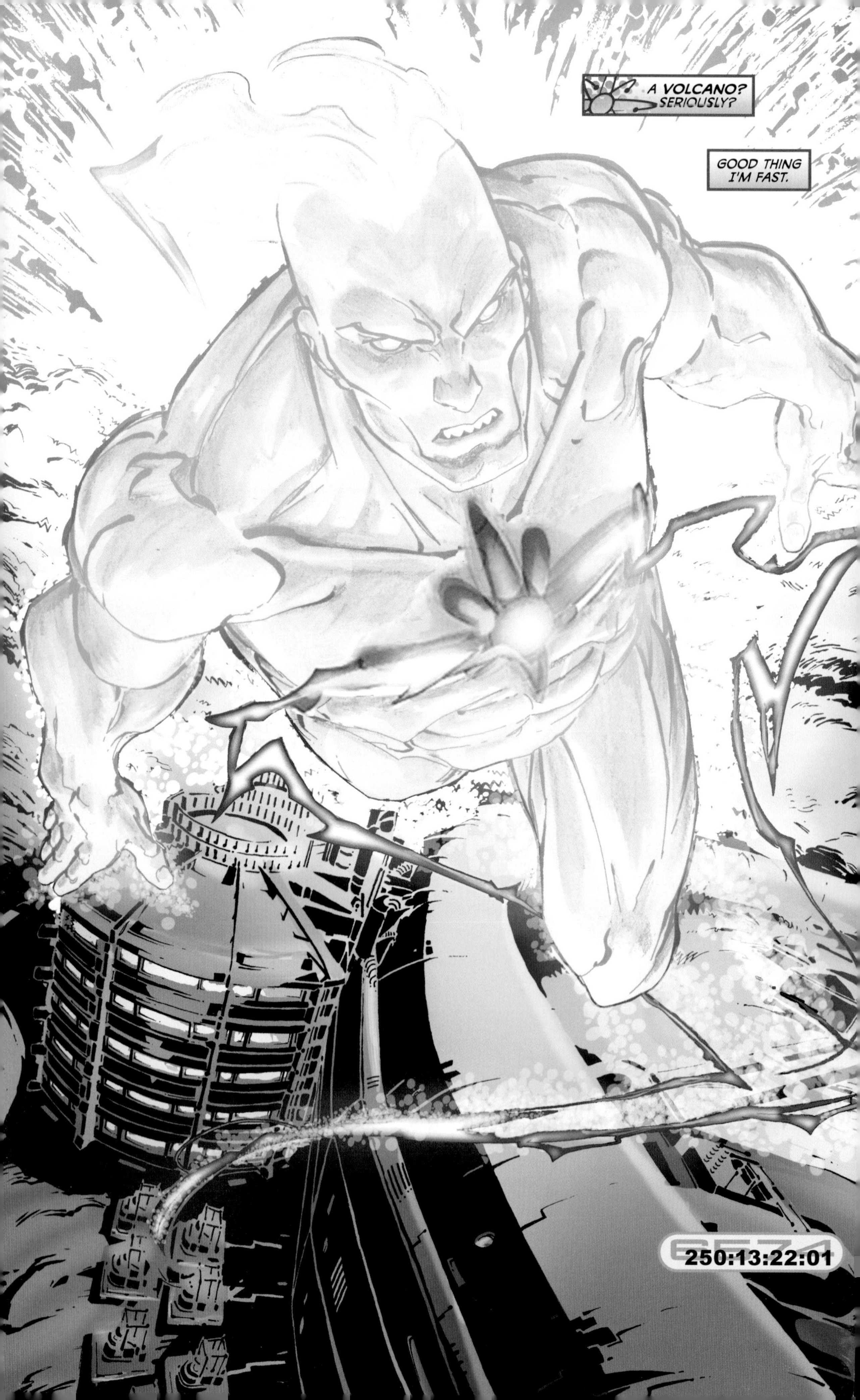
A VOLCANO? SERIOUSLY?
GOOD THING I'M FAST.
250:13:22:01

LOOKS LIKE I'LL HAVE TO STOP THE *MANMADE* DISASTER BEFORE THE *NATURAL* ONE.

A REACTOR *MELTDOWN* AND ENSUING *FALLOUT* COULD JEOPARDIZE MILLIONS OF PEOPLE, MAKING LAVA THE *LEAST* OF THEIR PROBLEMS.

MEGALA'S *WORDS* KEEP FLOATING INSIDE MY *HEAD*--

"USING YOUR POWERS COULD KILL YOU."

GIVEN THE NATURE OF IT, PROBABLY SHOULDN'T USE THE WORDS *FLOATING* AND *HEAD* IN THE SAME SENTENCE.

I'M USED TO *ABSORBING* ENERGY--BUT NOT AT THESE *LEVELS*.

DON'T HAVE A CHOICE.

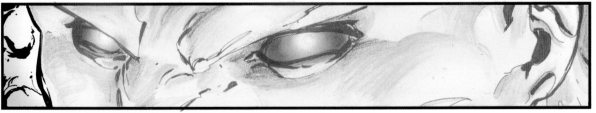

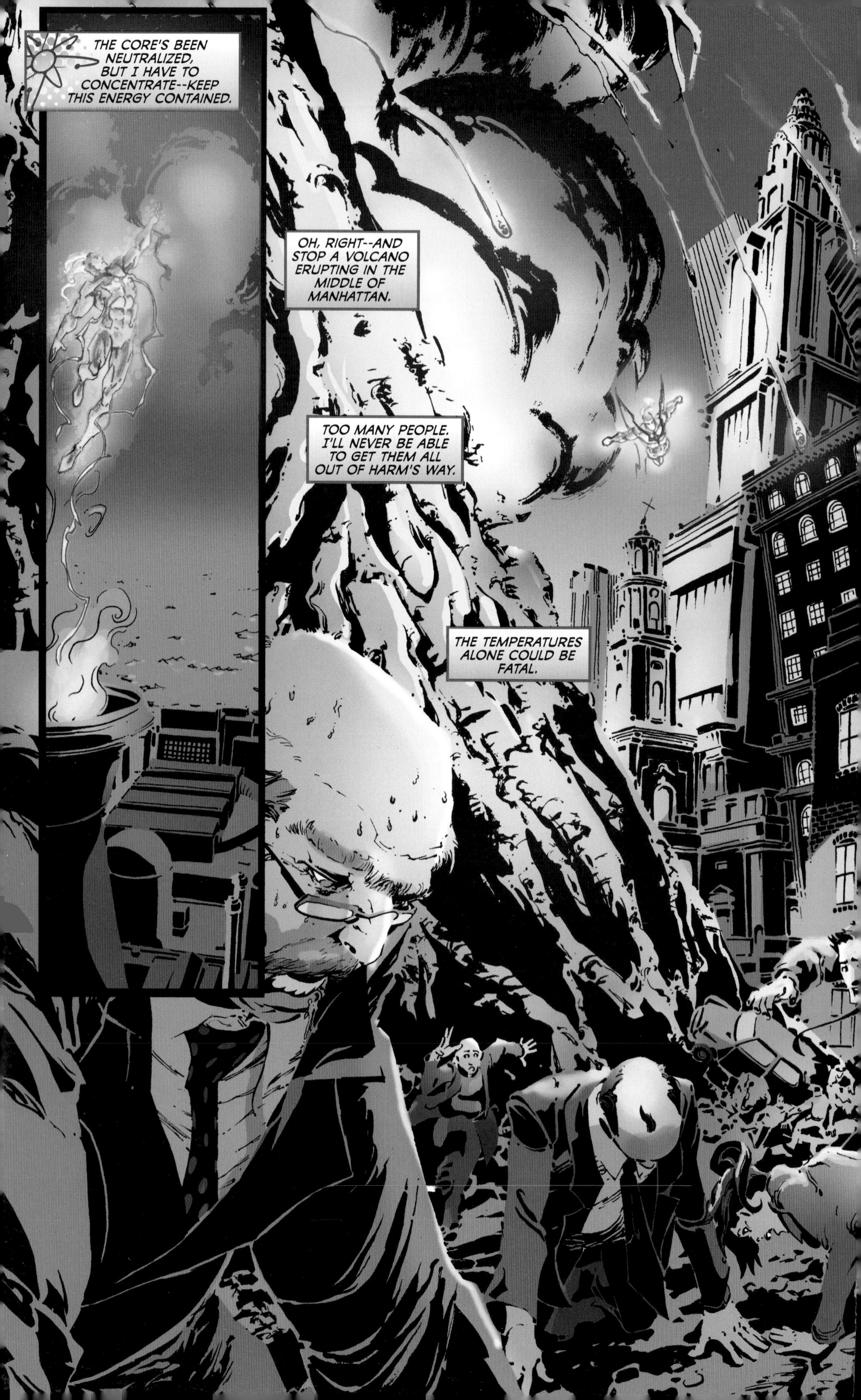
THE CORE'S BEEN NEUTRALIZED, BUT I HAVE TO CONCENTRATE--KEEP THIS ENERGY CONTAINED.
OH, RIGHT--AND STOP A VOLCANO ERUPTING IN THE MIDDLE OF MANHATTAN.
TOO MANY PEOPLE. I'LL NEVER BE ABLE TO GET THEM ALL OUT OF HARM'S WAY.
THE TEMPERATURES ALONE COULD BE FATAL.

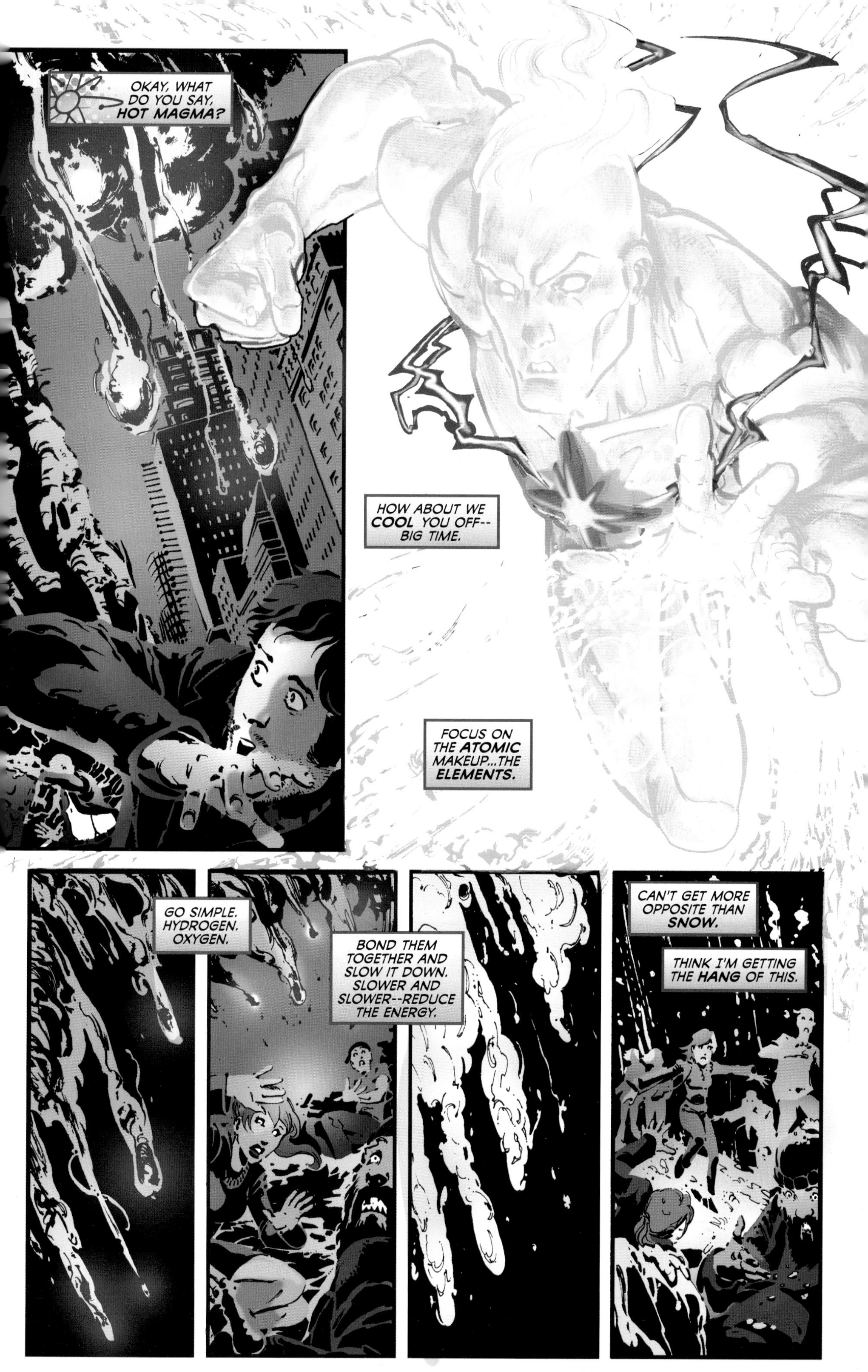
OKAY, WHAT DO YOU SAY, HOT MAGMA?
HOW ABOUT WE COOL YOU OFF-- BIG TIME.
FOCUS ON THE ATOMIC MAKEUP...THE ELEMENTS.
GO SIMPLE. HYDROGEN. OXYGEN.
BOND THEM TOGETHER AND SLOW IT DOWN. SLOWER AND SLOWER--REDUCE THE ENERGY.
CAN'T GET MORE OPPOSITE THAN SNOW.
THINK I'M GETTING THE HANG OF THIS.

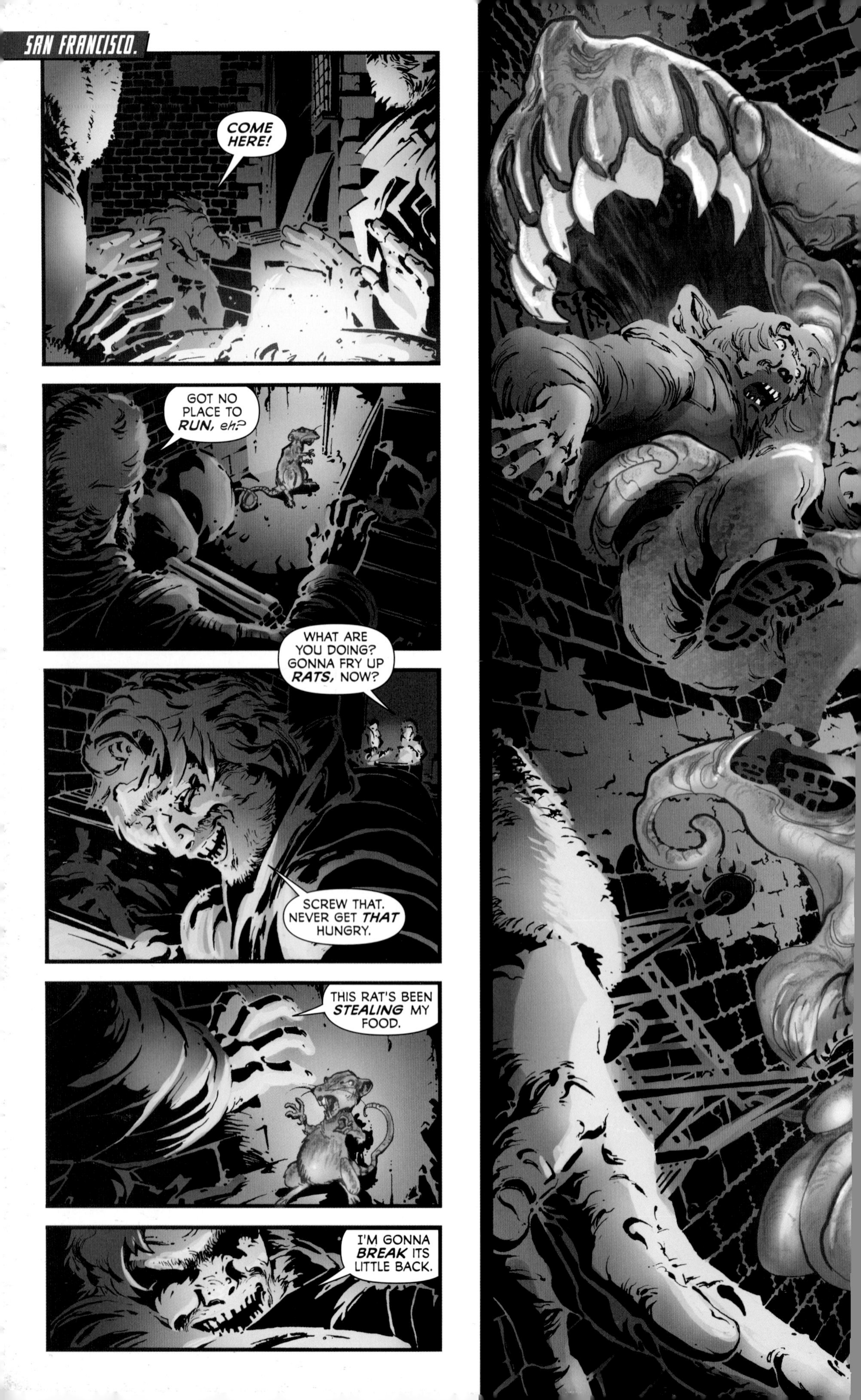
SAN FRANCISCO.
COME HERE!
GOT NO PLACE TO RUN, eh?
WHAT ARE YOU DOING? GONNA FRY UP RATS, NOW?
SCREW THAT. NEVER GET THAT HUNGRY.
THIS RAT'S BEEN STEALING MY FOOD.
I'M GONNA BREAK ITS LITTLE BACK.

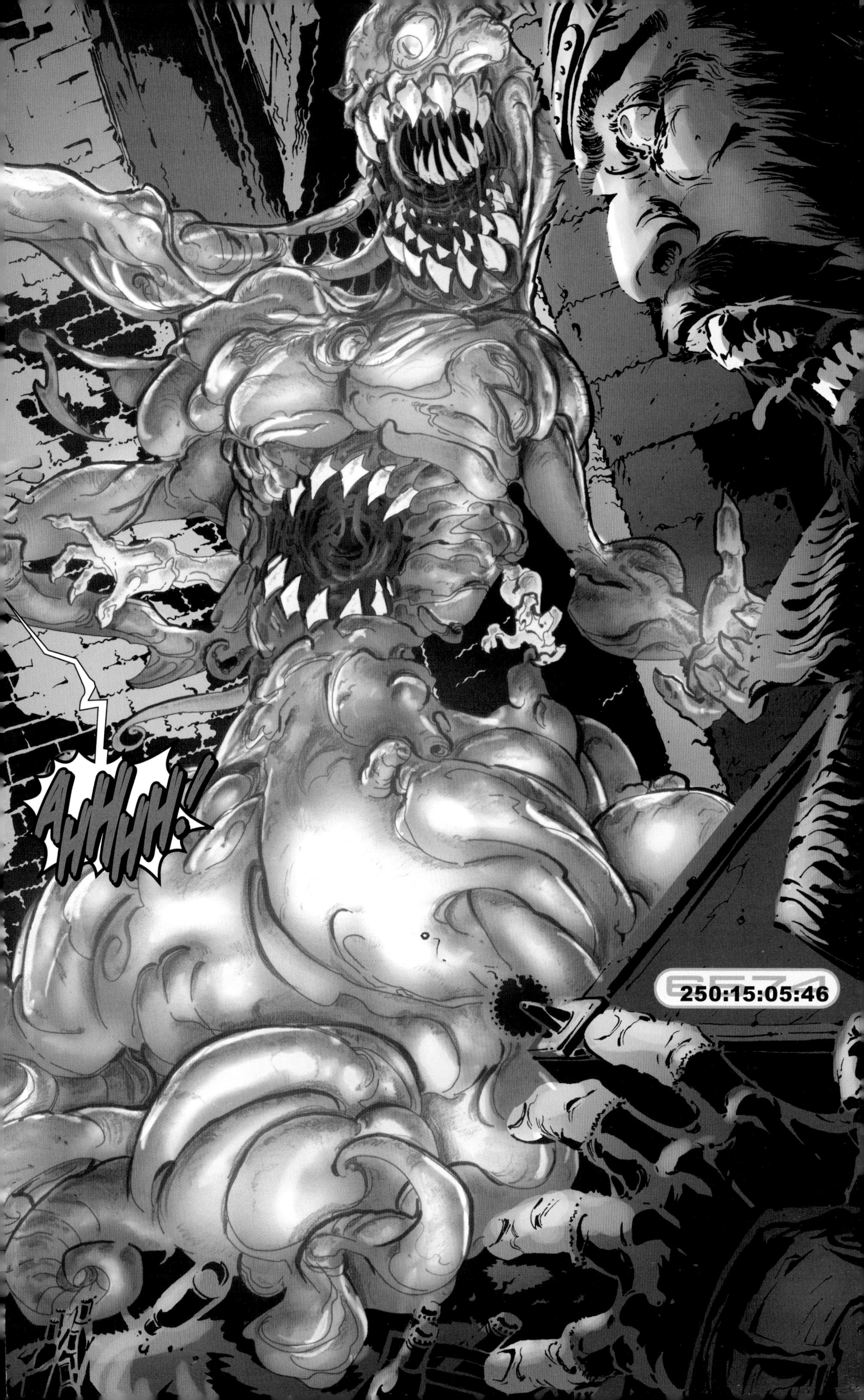
AHHHH!
250:15:05:46

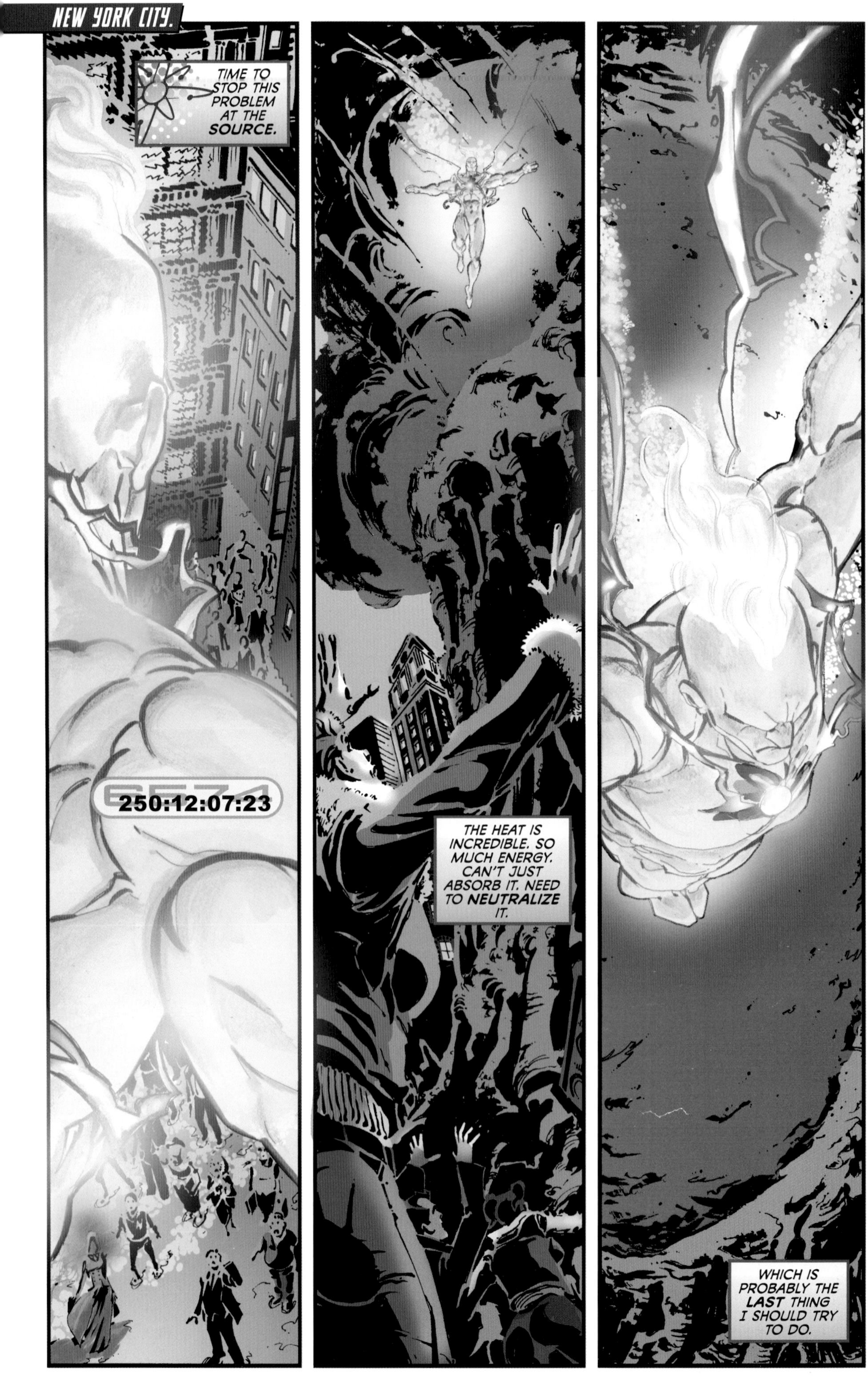
NEW YORK CITY.
TIME TO STOP THIS PROBLEM AT THE SOURCE.
250:12:07:23
THE HEAT IS INCREDIBLE. SO MUCH ENERGY. CAN'T JUST ABSORB IT. NEED TO NEUTRALIZE IT.
WHICH IS PROBABLY THE LAST THING I SHOULD TRY TO DO.

I CAN ALREADY FEEL MY ATOMS *SPLITTING*-- THE ENERGY SPARKING.

AGAIN AND AGAIN, I FEEL LESS AND LESS...*ME*

I'M BURNING FROM THE MAGMA, BUT IT FEELS MORE LIKE A NUMBING COLD.

MY CONNECTION *SLIPS.*

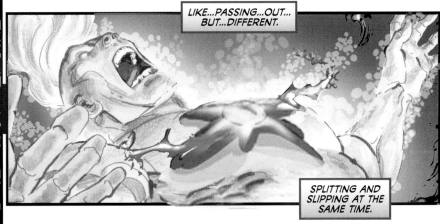

LIKE...PASSING...OUT... BUT...DIFFERENT.

SPLITTING AND SLIPPING AT THE SAME TIME.

MAN, I WISH *MEGALA* WAS WRONG JUST THIS *ONCE.*

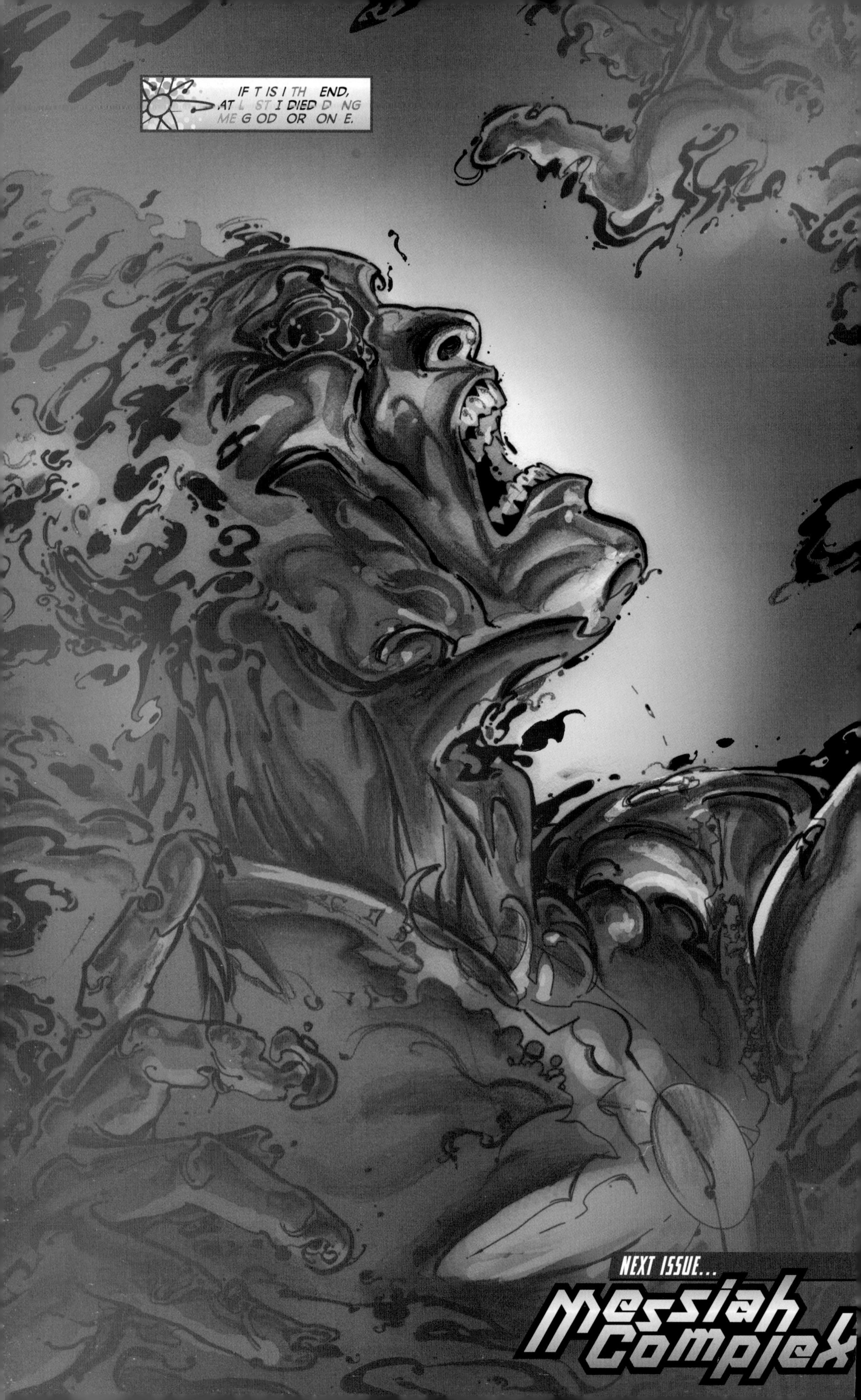
IF T IS I TH END, AT L ST I DIED D NG ME G OD OR ON E.
NEXT ISSUE...
Messiah Complex

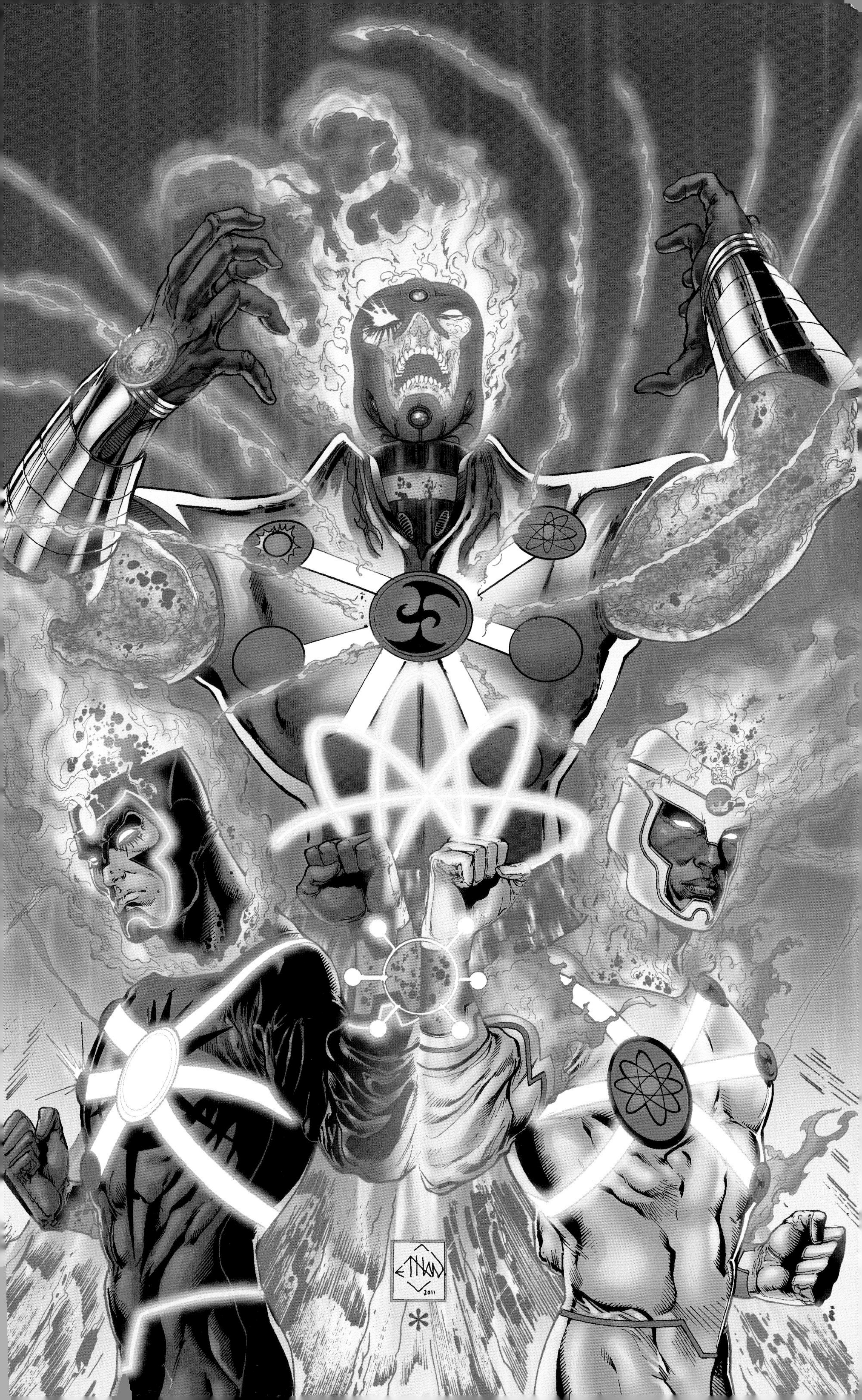

THE FURY OF FIRESTORM
THE NUCLEAR MEN

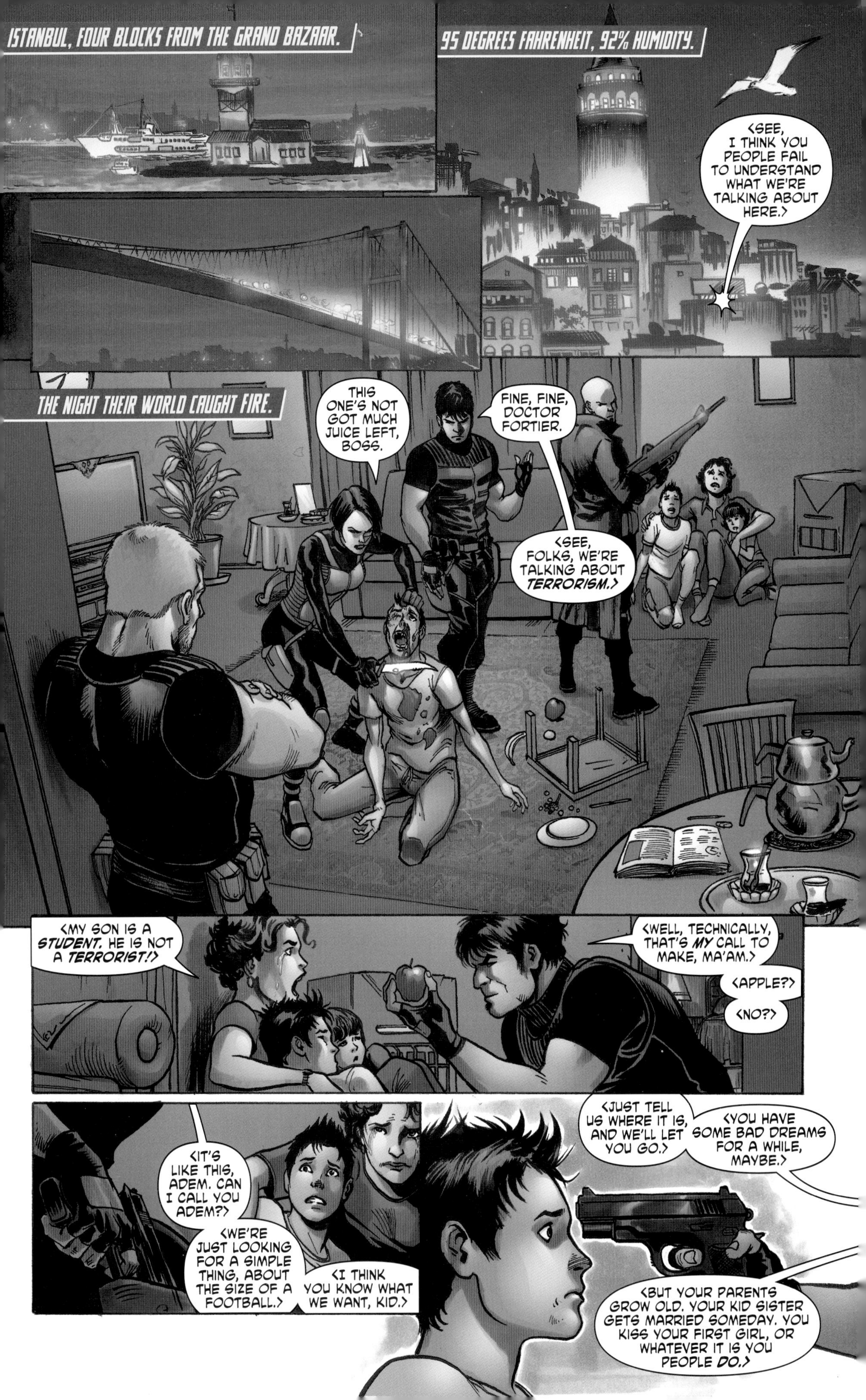
ISTANBUL, FOUR BLOCKS FROM THE GRAND BAZAAR.
95 DEGREES FAHRENHEIT, 92% HUMIDITY.
<SEE, I THINK YOU PEOPLE FAIL TO UNDERSTAND WHAT WE'RE TALKING ABOUT HERE.>
THE NIGHT THEIR WORLD CAUGHT FIRE.
THIS ONE'S NOT GOT MUCH JUICE LEFT, BOSS.
FINE, FINE, DOCTOR FORTIER.
<SEE, FOLKS, WE'RE TALKING ABOUT *TERRORISM*.>
<MY SON IS A *STUDENT*. HE IS NOT A *TERRORIST!*>
<WELL, TECHNICALLY, THAT'S *MY* CALL TO MAKE, MA'AM.>
<APPLE?>
<NO?>
<IT'S LIKE THIS, ADEM. CAN I CALL YOU ADEM?>
<WE'RE JUST LOOKING FOR A SIMPLE THING, ABOUT THE SIZE OF A FOOTBALL.>
<I THINK YOU KNOW WHAT WE WANT, KID.>
<JUST TELL US WHERE IT IS, AND WE'LL LET YOU GO.>
<YOU HAVE SOME BAD DREAMS FOR A WHILE, MAYBE.>
<BUT YOUR PARENTS GROW OLD. YOUR KID SISTER GETS MARRIED SOMEDAY. YOU KISS YOUR FIRST GIRL, OR WHATEVER IT IS YOU PEOPLE *DO*.>

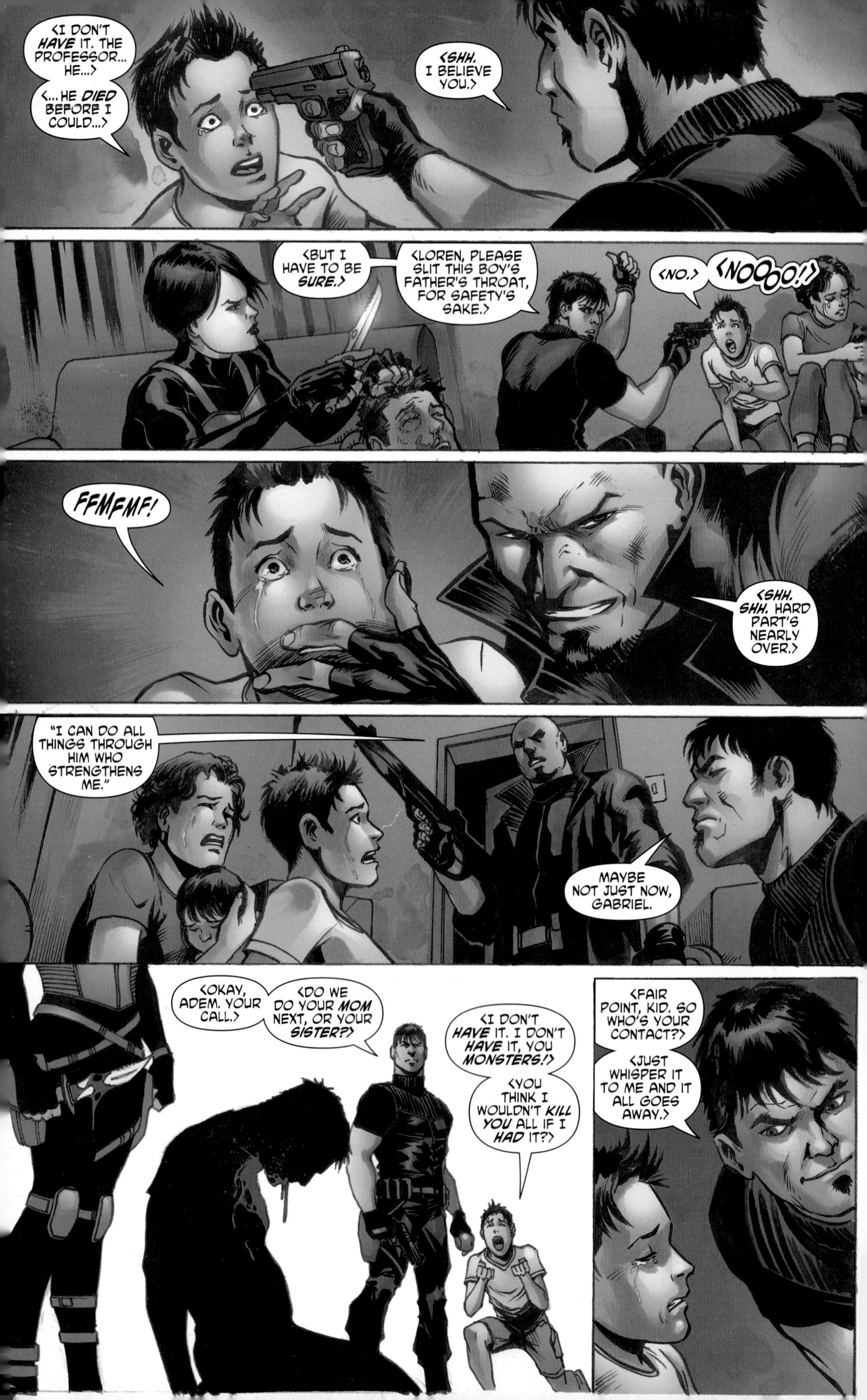

<I DON'T HAVE IT. THE PROFESSOR... HE...>
<...HE DIED BEFORE I COULD...>
<SHH. I BELIEVE YOU.>
<BUT I HAVE TO BE SURE.>
<LOREN, PLEASE SLIT THIS BOY'S FATHER'S THROAT, FOR SAFETY'S SAKE.>
<NO.>
<NOOOO!!>
FFMFMF!
<SHH. SHH. HARD PART'S NEARLY OVER.>
"I CAN DO ALL THINGS THROUGH HIM WHO STRENGTHENS ME."
MAYBE NOT JUST NOW, GABRIEL.
<OKAY, ADEM. YOUR CALL.>
<DO WE DO YOUR MOM NEXT, OR YOUR SISTER?>
<I DON'T HAVE IT. I DON'T HAVE IT, YOU MONSTERS!>
<YOU THINK I WOULDN'T KILL YOU ALL IF I HAD IT?>
<FAIR POINT, KID. SO WHO'S YOUR CONTACT?>
<JUST WHISPER IT TO ME AND IT ALL GOES AWAY.>

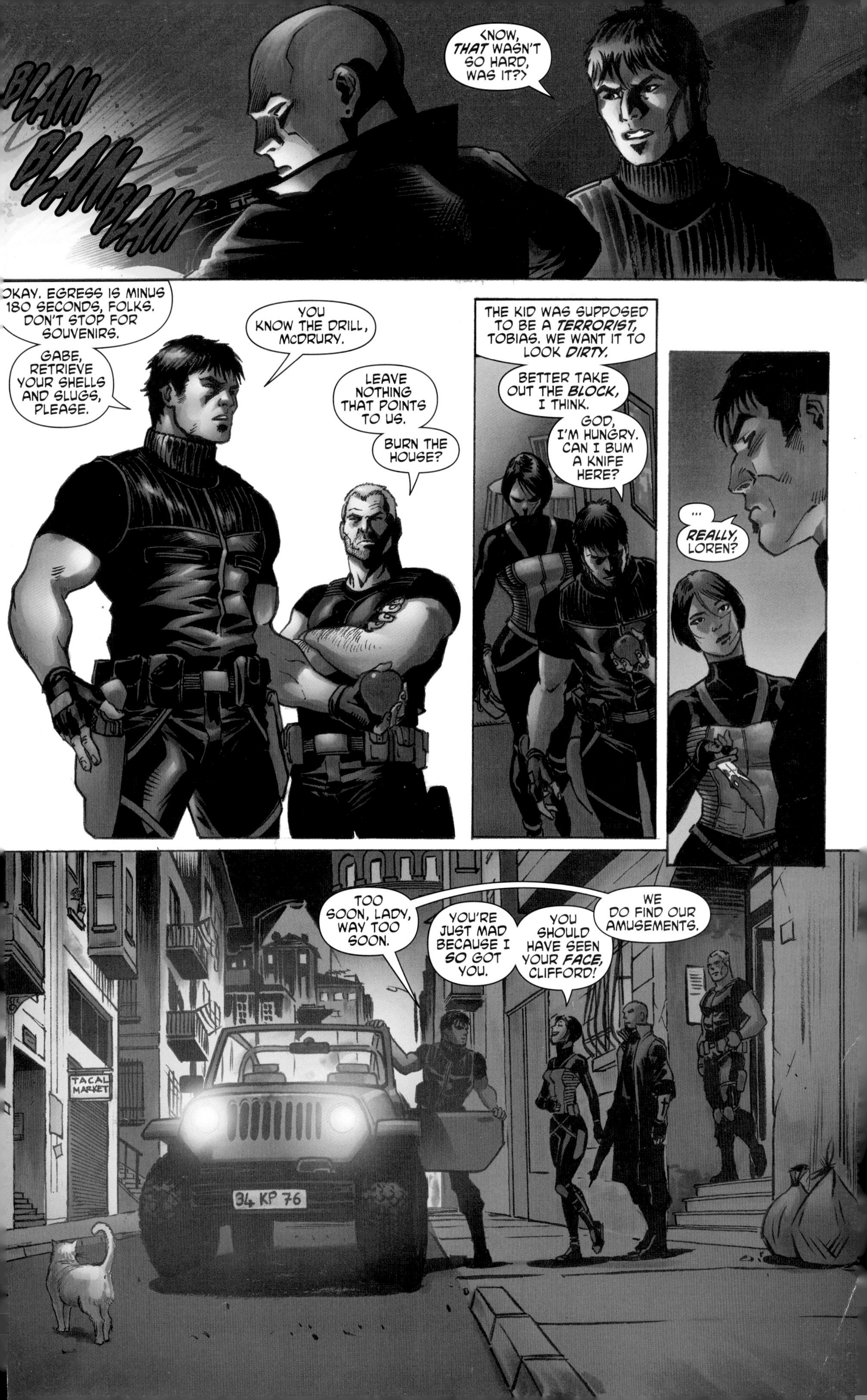

BLAM BLAM BLAM BLAM
<NOW, THAT WASN'T SO HARD, WAS IT?>
OKAY. EGRESS IS MINUS 180 SECONDS, FOLKS. DON'T STOP FOR SOUVENIRS.
GABE, RETRIEVE YOUR SHELLS AND SLUGS, PLEASE.
YOU KNOW THE DRILL, McDRURY.
LEAVE NOTHING THAT POINTS TO US.
BURN THE HOUSE?
THE KID WAS SUPPOSED TO BE A TERRORIST, TOBIAS. WE WANT IT TO LOOK DIRTY.
BETTER TAKE OUT THE BLOCK, I THINK.
GOD, I'M HUNGRY. CAN I BUM A KNIFE HERE?
... REALLY, LOREN?
TOO SOON, LADY, WAY TOO SOON.
YOU'RE JUST MAD BECAUSE I SO GOT YOU.
YOU SHOULD HAVE SEEN YOUR FACE, CLIFFORD!
WE DO FIND OUR AMUSEMENTS.
TACAL MARKET
34 KP 76

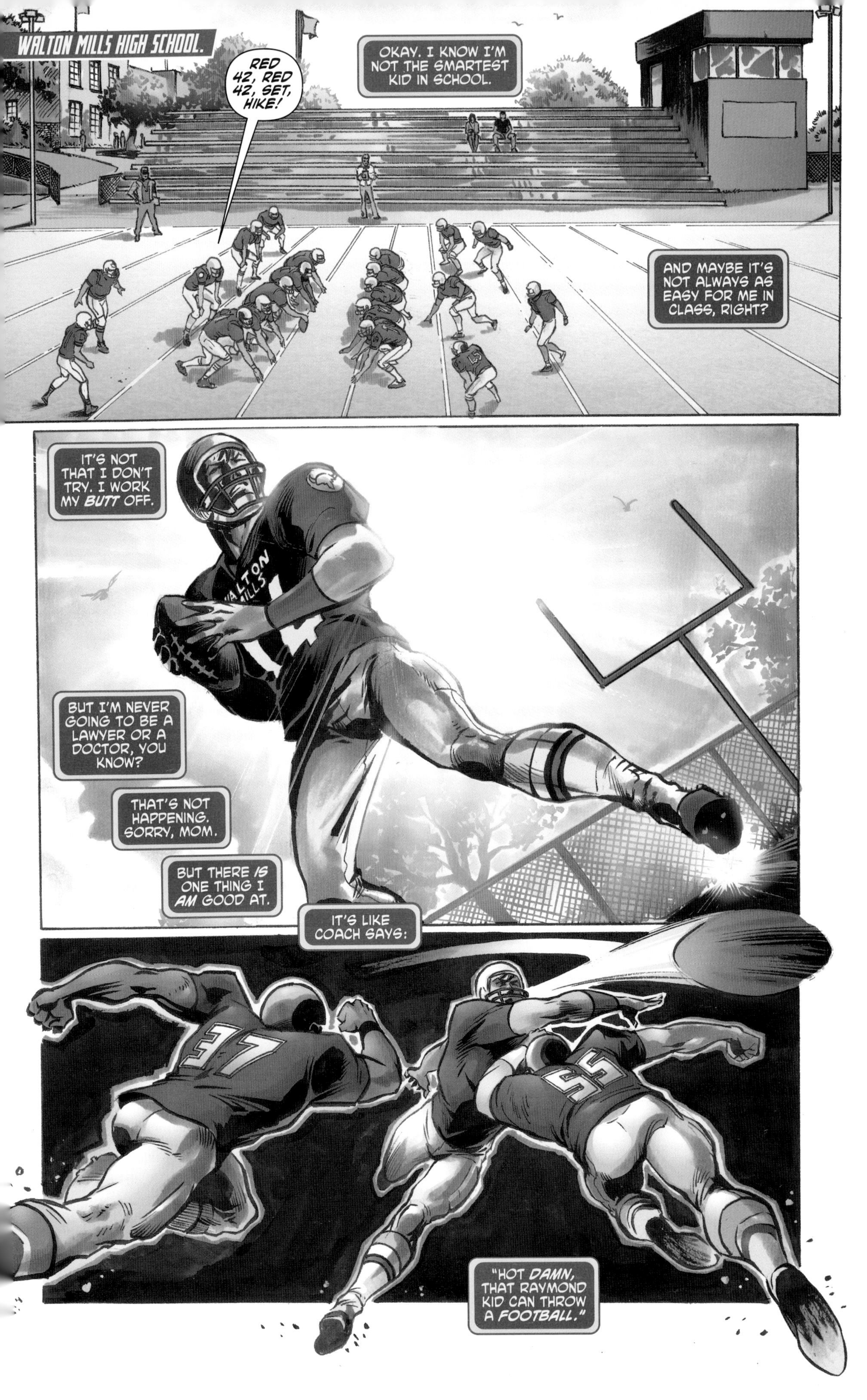
WALTON MILLS HIGH SCHOOL.
RED 42, RED 42, SET, HIKE!
OKAY. I KNOW I'M NOT THE SMARTEST KID IN SCHOOL.
AND MAYBE IT'S NOT ALWAYS AS EASY FOR ME IN CLASS, RIGHT?
IT'S NOT THAT I DON'T TRY. I WORK MY BUTT OFF.
BUT I'M NEVER GOING TO BE A LAWYER OR A DOCTOR, YOU KNOW?
THAT'S NOT HAPPENING. SORRY, MOM.
BUT THERE IS ONE THING I AM GOOD AT.
IT'S LIKE COACH SAYS:
"HOT DAMN, THAT RAYMOND KID CAN THROW A FOOTBALL."

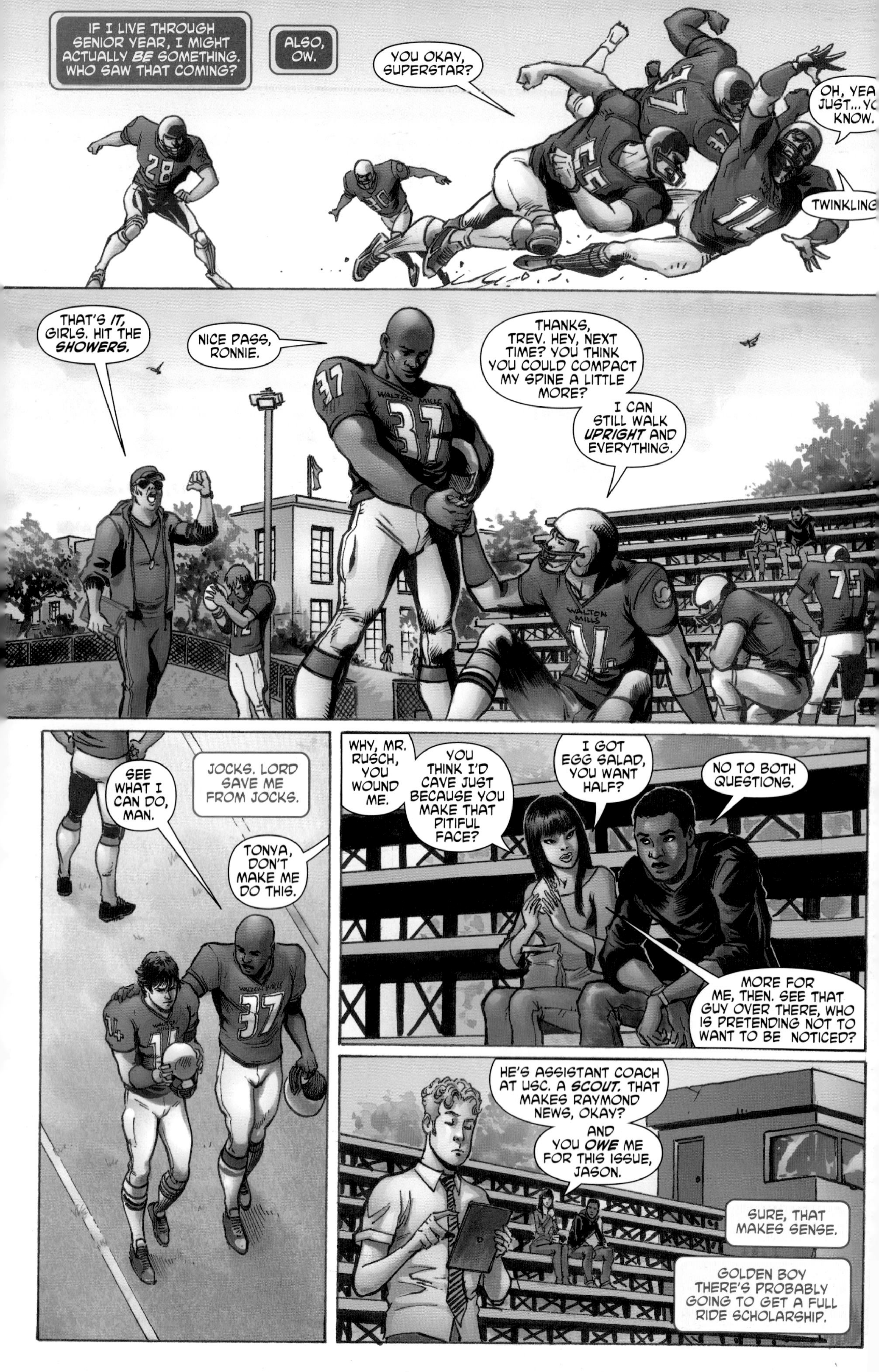
IF I LIVE THROUGH SENIOR YEAR, I MIGHT ACTUALLY *BE* SOMETHING. WHO SAW THAT COMING?
ALSO, OW.
YOU OKAY, SUPERSTAR?
OH, YEA JUST... YO KNOW.
TWINKLING
THAT'S *IT*, GIRLS. HIT THE *SHOWERS.*
NICE PASS, RONNIE.
THANKS, TREV. HEY, NEXT TIME? YOU THINK YOU COULD COMPACT MY SPINE A LITTLE MORE?
I CAN STILL WALK *UPRIGHT* AND EVERYTHING.
SEE WHAT I CAN DO, MAN.
JOCKS. LORD SAVE ME FROM JOCKS.
TONYA, DON'T MAKE ME DO THIS.
WHY, MR. RUSCH, YOU WOUND ME.
YOU THINK I'D CAVE JUST BECAUSE YOU MAKE THAT PITIFUL FACE?
I GOT EGG SALAD, YOU WANT HALF?
NO TO BOTH QUESTIONS.
MORE FOR ME, THEN. SEE THAT GUY OVER THERE, WHO IS PRETENDING NOT TO WANT TO BE NOTICED?
HE'S ASSISTANT COACH AT USC. A *SCOUT.* THAT MAKES RAYMOND NEWS, OKAY?
AND YOU *OWE* ME FOR THIS ISSUE, JASON.
SURE, THAT MAKES SENSE.
GOLDEN BOY THERE'S PROBABLY GOING TO GET A FULL RIDE SCHOLARSHIP.

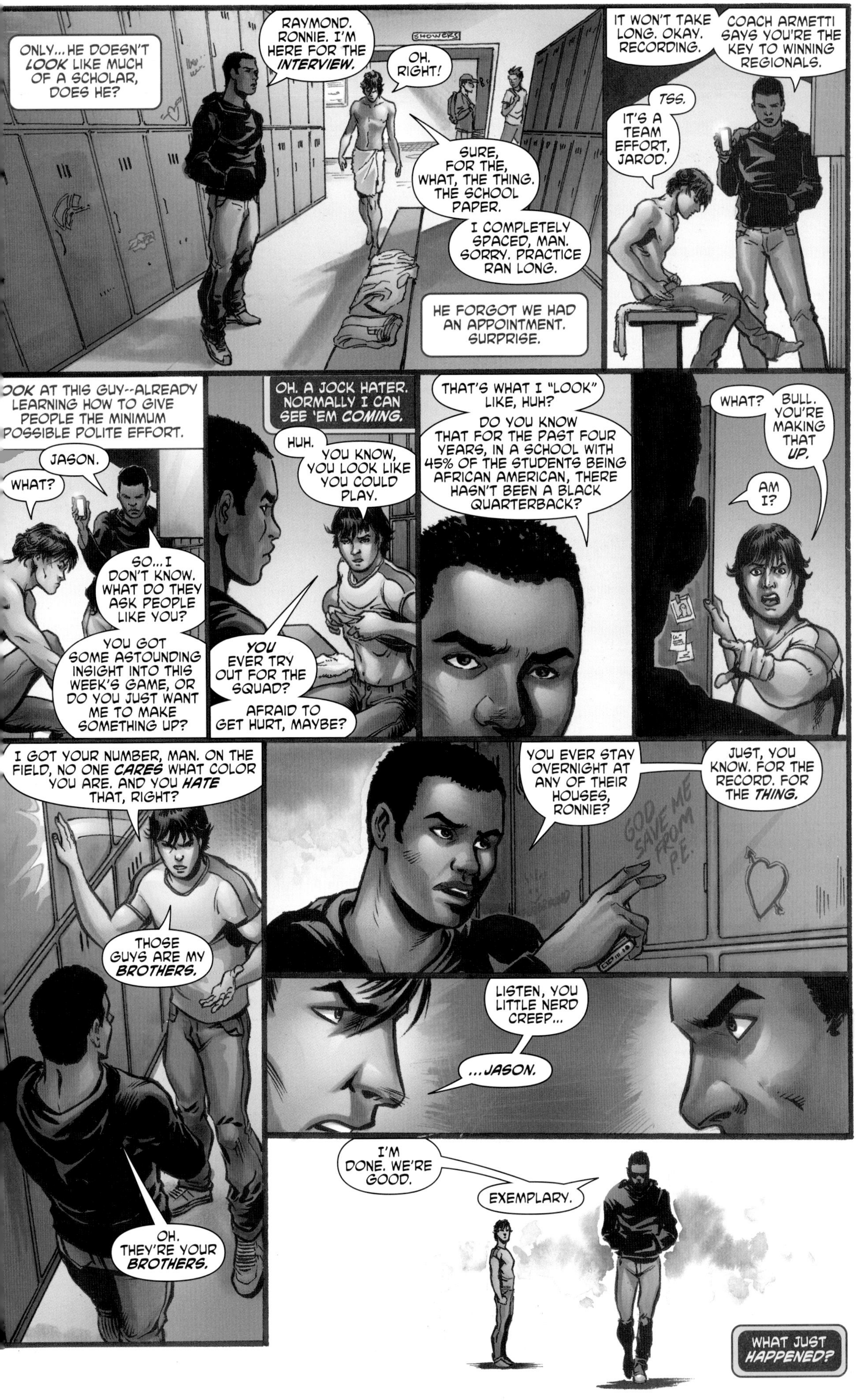
ONLY... HE DOESN'T LOOK LIKE MUCH OF A SCHOLAR, DOES HE?
RAYMOND. RONNIE. I'M HERE FOR THE INTERVIEW.
SHOWERS
OH. RIGHT!
SURE, FOR THE, WHAT, THE THING. THE SCHOOL PAPER.
I COMPLETELY SPACED, MAN. SORRY. PRACTICE RAN LONG.
HE FORGOT WE HAD AN APPOINTMENT. SURPRISE.
IT WON'T TAKE LONG. OKAY. RECORDING.
COACH ARMETTI SAYS YOU'RE THE KEY TO WINNING REGIONALS.
TSS.
IT'S A TEAM EFFORT, JAROD.
OOK AT THIS GUY--ALREADY LEARNING HOW TO GIVE PEOPLE THE MINIMUM POSSIBLE POLITE EFFORT.
JASON.
WHAT?
SO... I DON'T KNOW. WHAT DO THEY ASK PEOPLE LIKE YOU?
YOU GOT SOME ASTOUNDING INSIGHT INTO THIS WEEK'S GAME, OR DO YOU JUST WANT ME TO MAKE SOMETHING UP?
OH. A JOCK HATER. NORMALLY I CAN SEE 'EM COMING.
HUH.
YOU KNOW, YOU LOOK LIKE YOU COULD PLAY.
YOU EVER TRY OUT FOR THE SQUAD?
AFRAID TO GET HURT, MAYBE?
THAT'S WHAT I "LOOK" LIKE, HUH?
DO YOU KNOW THAT FOR THE PAST FOUR YEARS, IN A SCHOOL WITH 45% OF THE STUDENTS BEING AFRICAN AMERICAN, THERE HASN'T BEEN A BLACK QUARTERBACK?
WHAT?
BULL. YOU'RE MAKING THAT UP.
AM I?
I GOT YOUR NUMBER, MAN. ON THE FIELD, NO ONE CARES WHAT COLOR YOU ARE. AND YOU HATE THAT, RIGHT?
THOSE GUYS ARE MY BROTHERS.
OH. THEY'RE YOUR BROTHERS.
YOU EVER STAY OVERNIGHT AT ANY OF THEIR HOUSES, RONNIE?
JUST, YOU KNOW. FOR THE RECORD. FOR THE THING.
GOD SAVE ME FROM P.E.
LISTEN, YOU LITTLE NERD CREEP...
...JASON.
I'M DONE. WE'RE GOOD.
EXEMPLARY.
WHAT JUST HAPPENED?

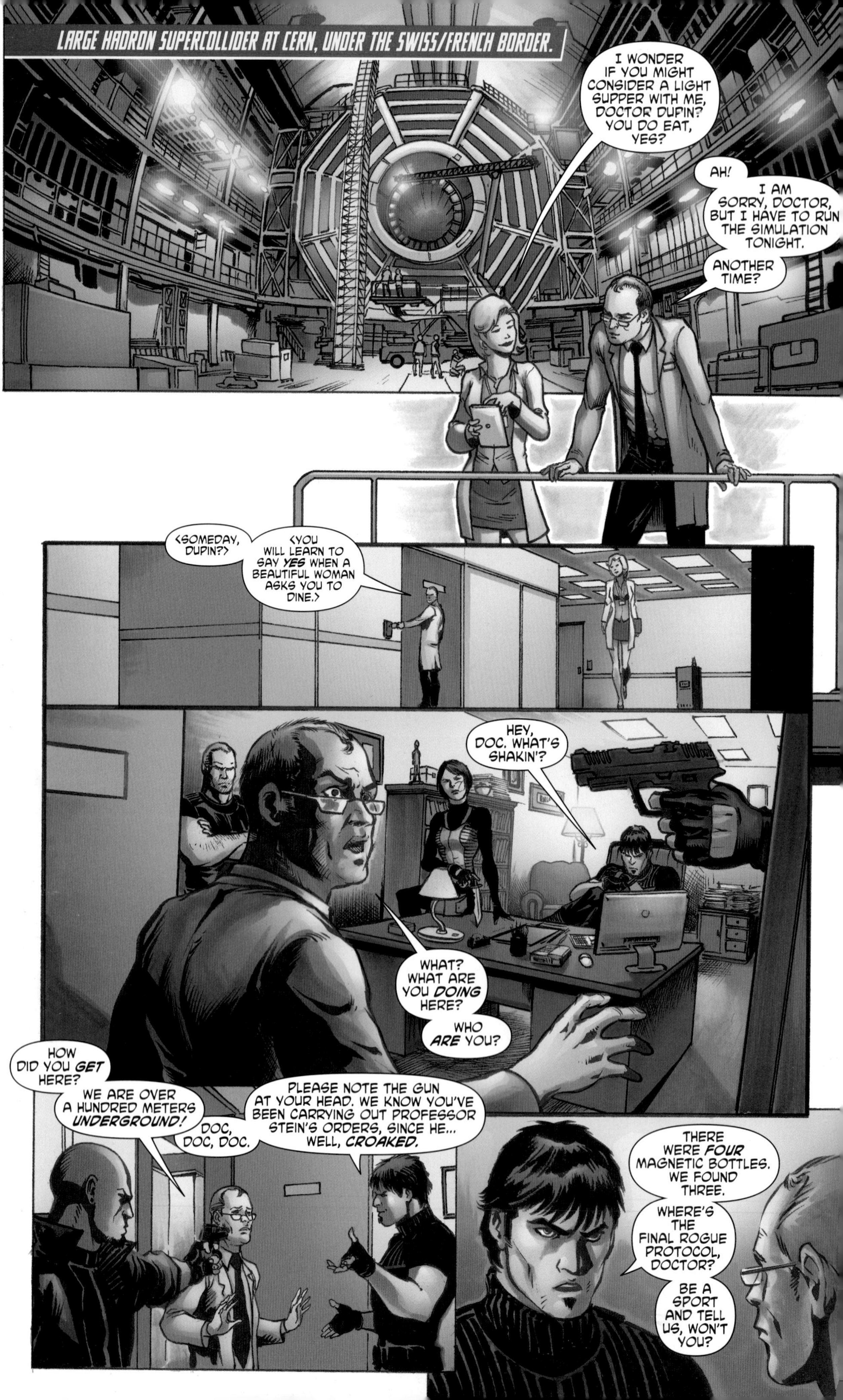
LARGE HADRON SUPERCOLLIDER AT CERN, UNDER THE SWISS/FRENCH BORDER.
I WONDER IF YOU MIGHT CONSIDER A LIGHT SUPPER WITH ME, DOCTOR DUPIN? YOU DO EAT, YES?
AH!
I AM SORRY, DOCTOR, BUT I HAVE TO RUN THE SIMULATION TONIGHT.
ANOTHER TIME?
<SOMEDAY, DUPIN?>
<YOU WILL LEARN TO SAY YES WHEN A BEAUTIFUL WOMAN ASKS YOU TO DINE.>
HEY, DOC. WHAT'S SHAKIN'?
WHAT? WHAT ARE YOU DOING HERE?
WHO ARE YOU?
HOW DID YOU GET HERE?
WE ARE OVER A HUNDRED METERS UNDERGROUND!
DOC, DOC, DOC.
PLEASE NOTE THE GUN AT YOUR HEAD. WE KNOW YOU'VE BEEN CARRYING OUT PROFESSOR STEIN'S ORDERS, SINCE HE... WELL, CROAKED.
THERE WERE FOUR MAGNETIC BOTTLES. WE FOUND THREE.
WHERE'S THE FINAL ROGUE PROTOCOL, DOCTOR?
BE A SPORT AND TELL US, WON'T YOU?

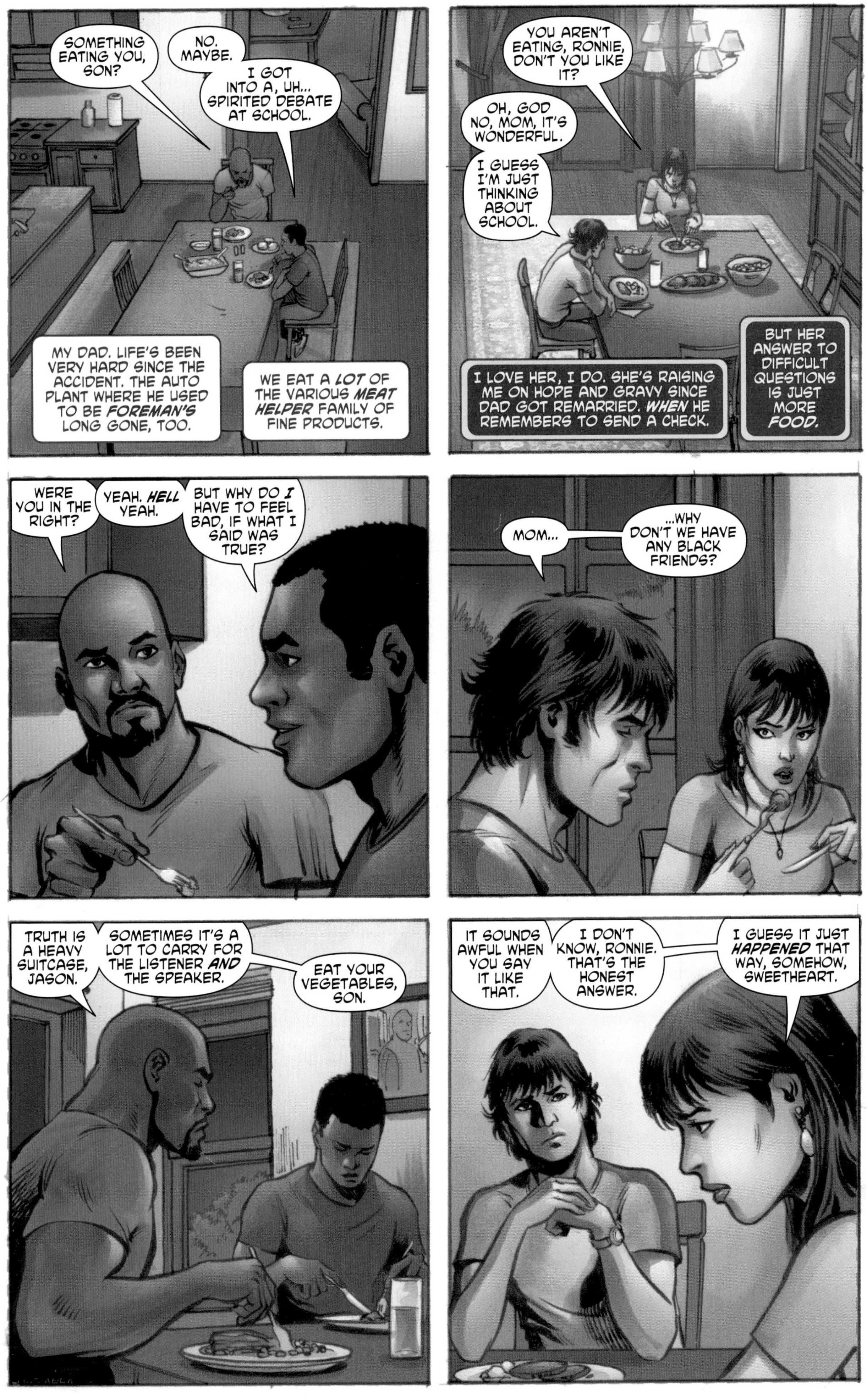
SOMETHING EATING YOU, SON?
NO. MAYBE.
I GOT INTO A, UH... SPIRITED DEBATE AT SCHOOL.
MY DAD. LIFE'S BEEN VERY HARD SINCE THE ACCIDENT. THE AUTO PLANT WHERE HE USED TO BE FOREMAN'S LONG GONE, TOO.
WE EAT A LOT OF THE VARIOUS MEAT HELPER FAMILY OF FINE PRODUCTS.
YOU AREN'T EATING, RONNIE, DON'T YOU LIKE IT?
OH, GOD NO, MOM, IT'S WONDERFUL.
I GUESS I'M JUST THINKING ABOUT SCHOOL.
I LOVE HER, I DO. SHE'S RAISING ME ON HOPE AND GRAVY SINCE DAD GOT REMARRIED. WHEN HE REMEMBERS TO SEND A CHECK.
BUT HER ANSWER TO DIFFICULT QUESTIONS IS JUST MORE FOOD.
WERE YOU IN THE RIGHT?
YEAH. HELL YEAH.
BUT WHY DO I HAVE TO FEEL BAD, IF WHAT I SAID WAS TRUE?
MOM...
...WHY DON'T WE HAVE ANY BLACK FRIENDS?
TRUTH IS A HEAVY SUITCASE, JASON.
SOMETIMES IT'S A LOT TO CARRY FOR THE LISTENER AND THE SPEAKER.
EAT YOUR VEGETABLES, SON.
IT SOUNDS AWFUL WHEN YOU SAY IT LIKE THAT.
I DON'T KNOW, RONNIE. THAT'S THE HONEST ANSWER.
I GUESS IT JUST HAPPENED THAT WAY, SOMEHOW, SWEETHEART.

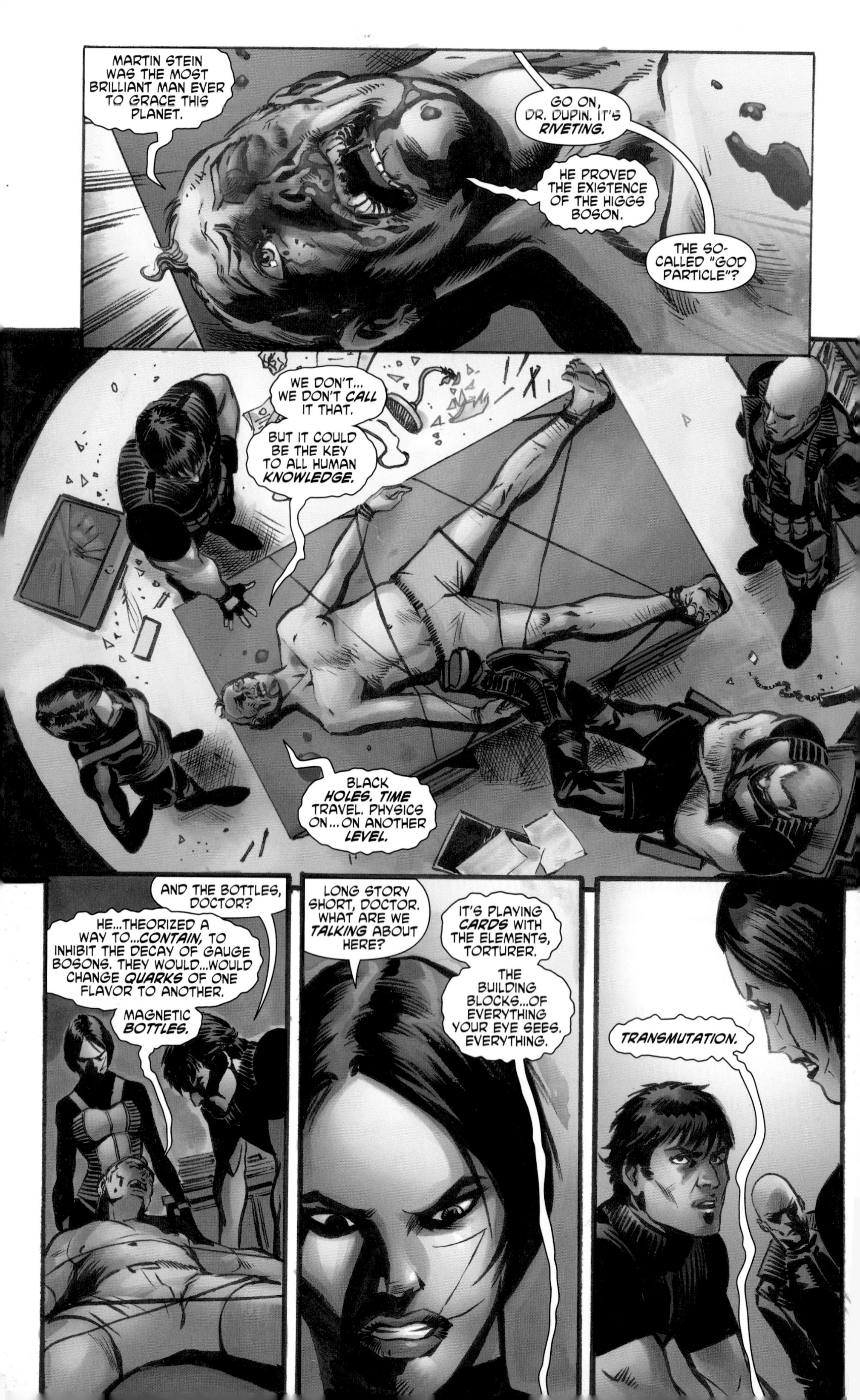
MARTIN STEIN WAS THE MOST BRILLIANT MAN EVER TO GRACE THIS PLANET.
GO ON, DR. DUPIN. IT'S RIVETING.
HE PROVED THE EXISTENCE OF THE HIGGS BOSON.
THE SO-CALLED "GOD PARTICLE"?
WE DON'T... WE DON'T CALL IT THAT.
BUT IT COULD BE THE KEY TO ALL HUMAN KNOWLEDGE.
BLACK HOLES. TIME TRAVEL. PHYSICS ON...ON ANOTHER LEVEL.
AND THE BOTTLES, DOCTOR?
HE...THEORIZED A WAY TO...CONTAIN, TO INHIBIT THE DECAY OF GAUGE BOSONS. THEY WOULD...WOULD CHANGE QUARKS OF ONE FLAVOR TO ANOTHER.
MAGNETIC BOTTLES.
LONG STORY SHORT, DOCTOR. WHAT ARE WE TALKING ABOUT HERE?
IT'S PLAYING CARDS WITH THE ELEMENTS, TORTURER.
THE BUILDING BLOCKS...OF EVERYTHING YOUR EYE SEES. EVERYTHING.
TRANSMUTATION.

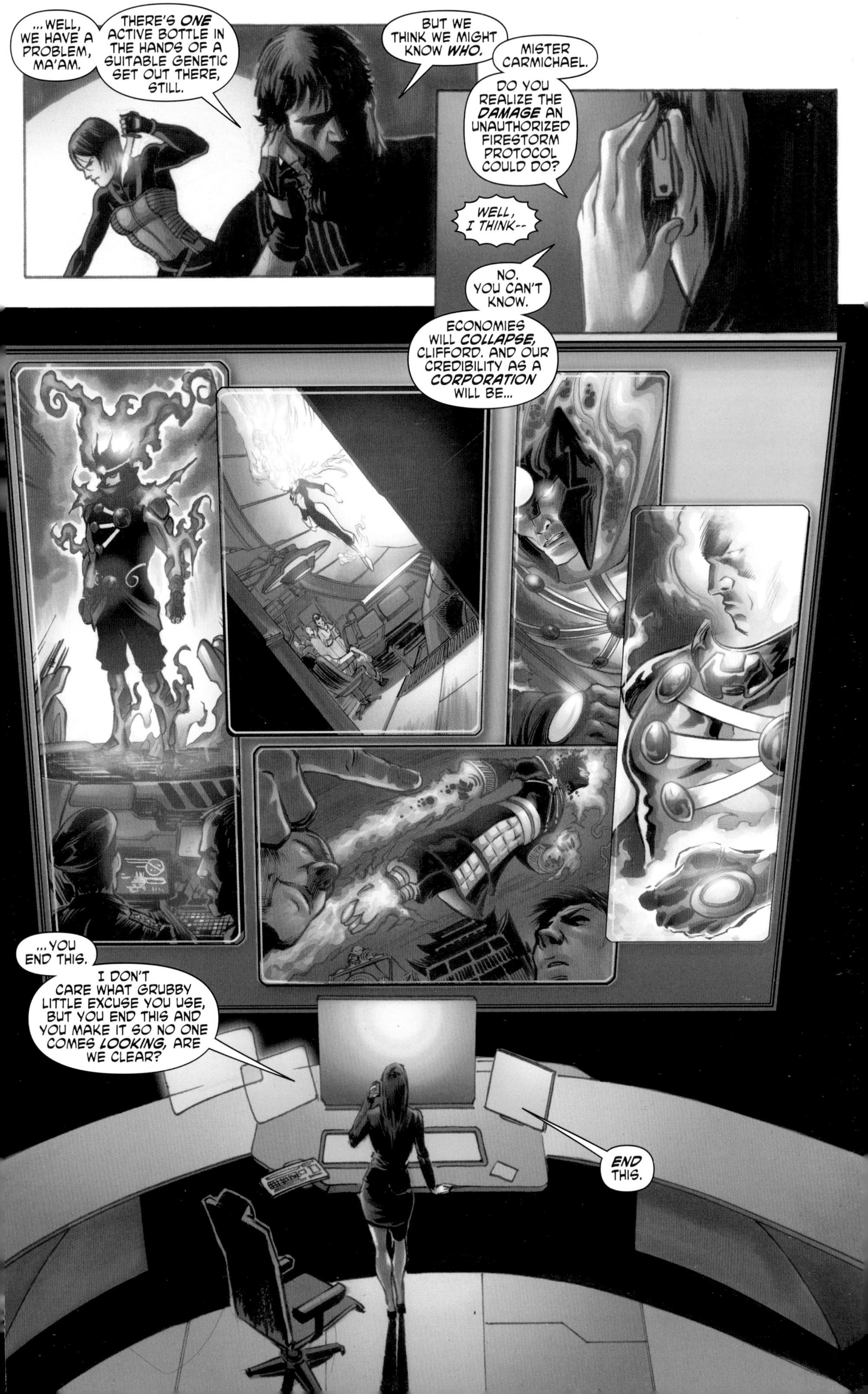
...WELL, WE HAVE A PROBLEM, MA'AM.
THERE'S ONE ACTIVE BOTTLE IN THE HANDS OF A SUITABLE GENETIC SET OUT THERE, STILL.
BUT WE THINK WE MIGHT KNOW WHO.
MISTER CARMICHAEL.
DO YOU REALIZE THE DAMAGE AN UNAUTHORIZED FIRESTORM PROTOCOL COULD DO?
WELL, I THINK--
NO. YOU CAN'T KNOW.
ECONOMIES WILL COLLAPSE, CLIFFORD. AND OUR CREDIBILITY AS A CORPORATION WILL BE...
...YOU END THIS.
I DON'T CARE WHAT GRUBBY LITTLE EXCUSE YOU USE, BUT YOU END THIS AND YOU MAKE IT SO NO ONE COMES LOOKING, ARE WE CLEAR?
END THIS.

THE NEXT EVENING...

GO VIKINGS
WALTON MILLS HIGH

JASON, WHAT IN GOD'S *NAME* WERE YOU THINKING?

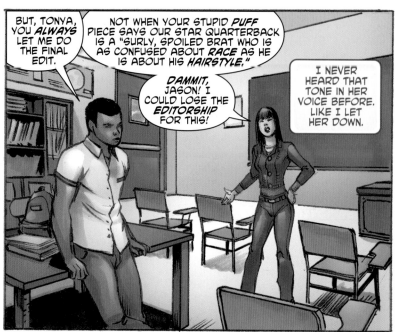

BUT, TONYA, YOU *ALWAYS* LET ME DO THE FINAL EDIT.

NOT WHEN YOUR STUPID *PUFF* PIECE SAYS OUR STAR QUARTERBACK IS A "SURLY, SPOILED BRAT WHO IS AS CONFUSED ABOUT *RACE* AS HE IS ABOUT HIS *HAIRSTYLE*."

DAMMIT, JASON! I COULD LOSE THE *EDITORSHIP* FOR THIS!

I NEVER HEARD THAT TONE IN HER VOICE BEFORE. LIKE I LET HER DOWN.

AND I DON'T HAVE THE GUTS TO TELL HER HOW I *FEEL* ABOUT HER.

AS USUAL.

ALL RIGHT. YOU'RE RIGHT. I MESSED UP.

I'LL...I'LL APOLOGIZE.

WHAT THE HELL, MAYBE I *WAS* TOO ROUGH ON THE GUY.

YOU JERK!

YOU WANT TO SAY THIS CRAP TO ME? SAY IT TO MY *FACE,* YOU GEEK *LOSER!*

COME ON, *RIGHT* NOW!

RONNIE, COME ON, MAN. LET IT *GO.*

I DID *NOTHING* TO YOU. I DIDN'T SAY *ANYTHING* TO DESERVE THIS!

YOU *SURE* ABOUT THAT THERE, BOY BAND?

MAN, WOULD YOU TWO *KNOCK* IT OFF?

THAT'S THE *THING,* TREV--

--I'M NOT SURE WE *CAN.*

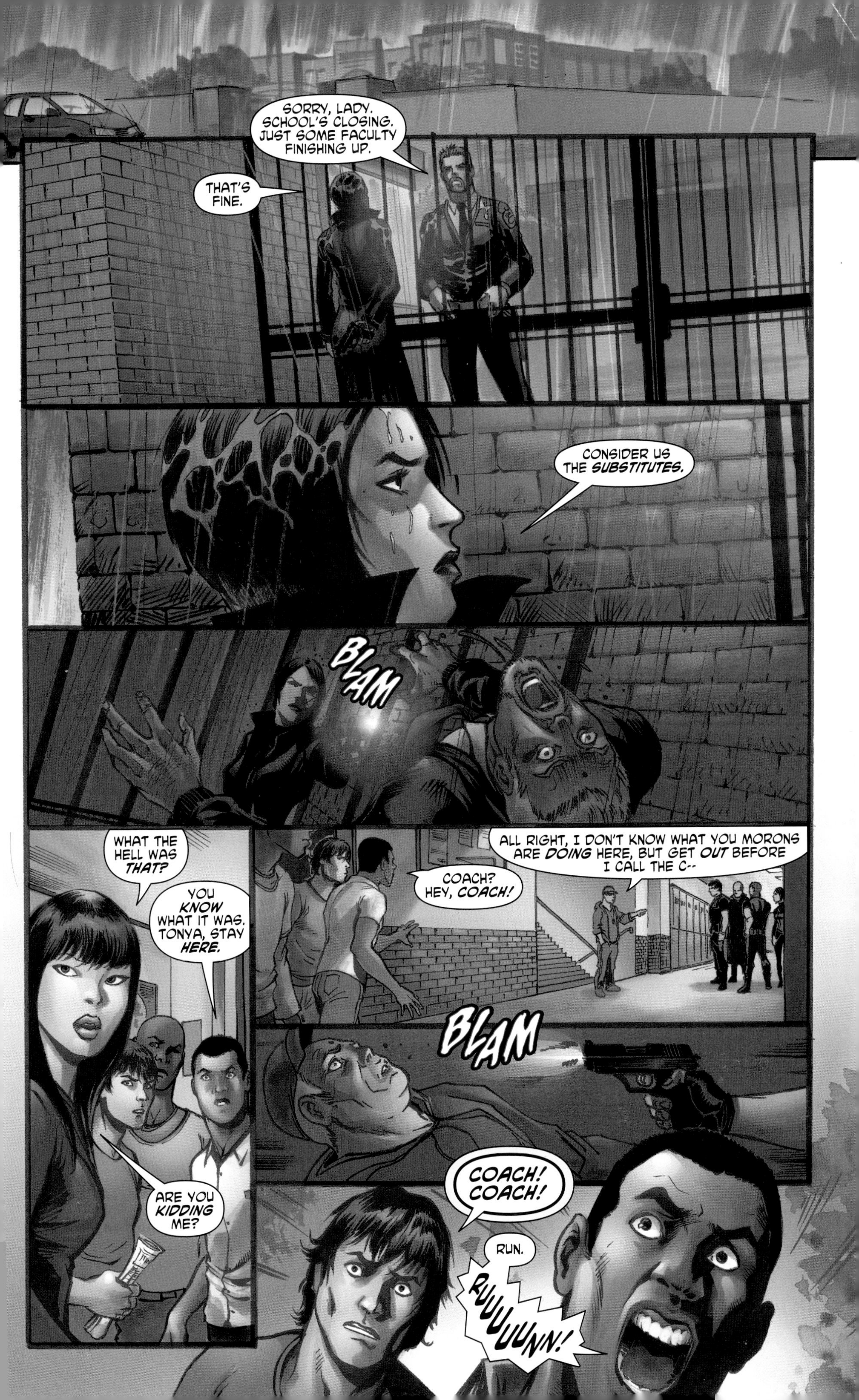
SORRY, LADY. SCHOOL'S CLOSING. JUST SOME FACULTY FINISHING UP.
THAT'S FINE.
CONSIDER US THE *SUBSTITUTES.*
BLAM
WHAT THE HELL WAS *THAT?*
YOU *KNOW* WHAT IT WAS. TONYA, STAY *HERE.*
ARE YOU *KIDDING* ME?
COACH? HEY, *COACH!*
ALL RIGHT, I DON'T KNOW WHAT YOU MORONS ARE *DOING* HERE, BUT GET *OUT* BEFORE I CALL THE C--
BLAM
COACH! COACH!
RUN.
RUUUUUNN!

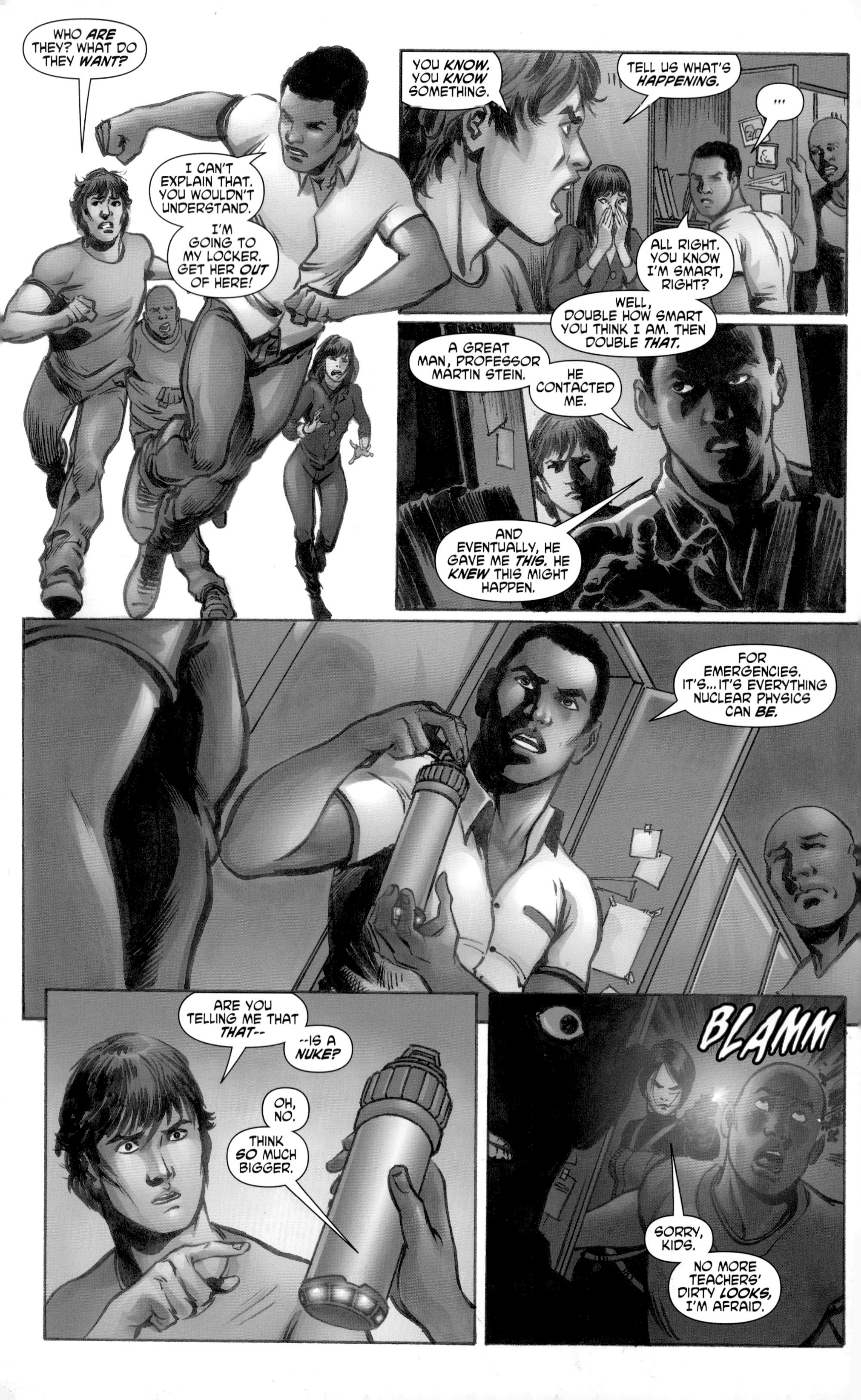
WHO ARE THEY? WHAT DO THEY WANT?
I CAN'T EXPLAIN THAT. YOU WOULDN'T UNDERSTAND.
I'M GOING TO MY LOCKER. GET HER OUT OF HERE!
YOU KNOW. YOU KNOW SOMETHING.
TELL US WHAT'S HAPPENING.
...
ALL RIGHT. YOU KNOW I'M SMART, RIGHT?
WELL, DOUBLE HOW SMART YOU THINK I AM. THEN DOUBLE THAT.
A GREAT MAN, PROFESSOR MARTIN STEIN.
HE CONTACTED ME.
AND EVENTUALLY, HE GAVE ME THIS. HE KNEW THIS MIGHT HAPPEN.
FOR EMERGENCIES. IT'S...IT'S EVERYTHING NUCLEAR PHYSICS CAN BE.
ARE YOU TELLING ME THAT THAT--
--IS A NUKE?
OH, NO.
THINK SO MUCH BIGGER.
BLAMM
SORRY, KIDS.
NO MORE TEACHERS' DIRTY LOOKS, I'M AFRAID.

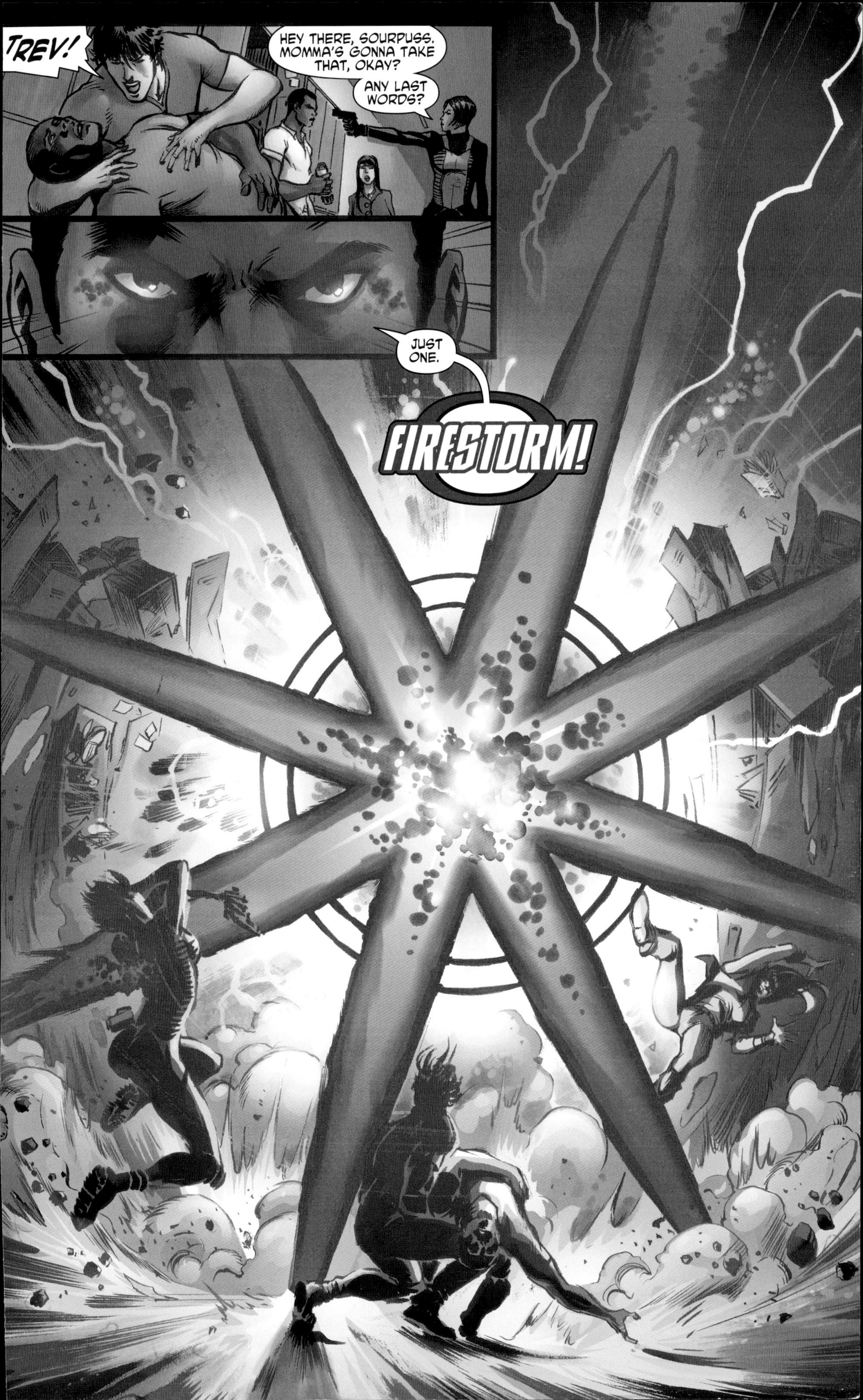
TREV!
HEY THERE, SOURPUSS. MOMMA'S GONNA TAKE THAT, OKAY?
ANY LAST WORDS?
JUST ONE.
FIRESTORM!

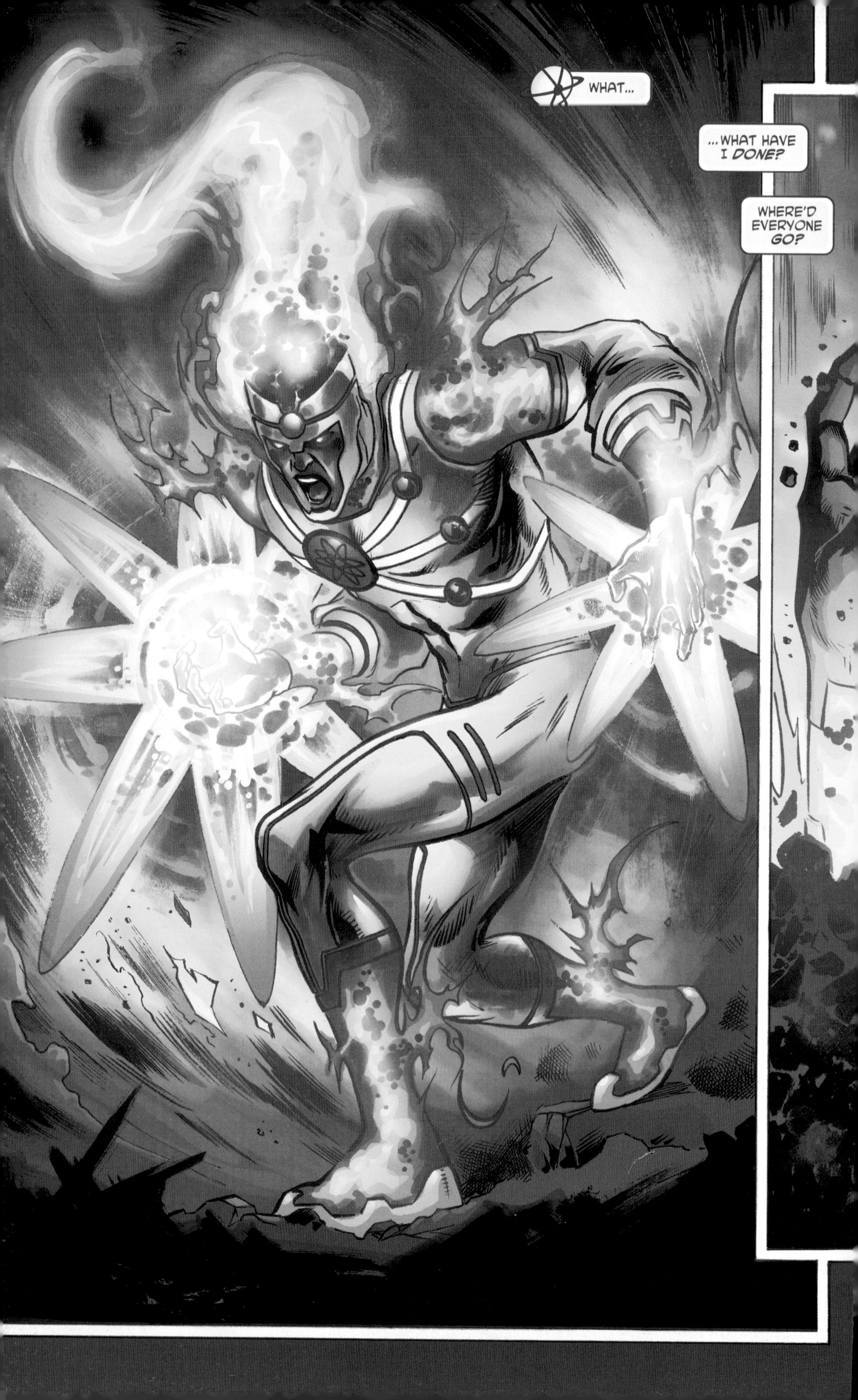
WHAT...
...WHAT HAVE I DONE?
WHERE'D EVERYONE GO?

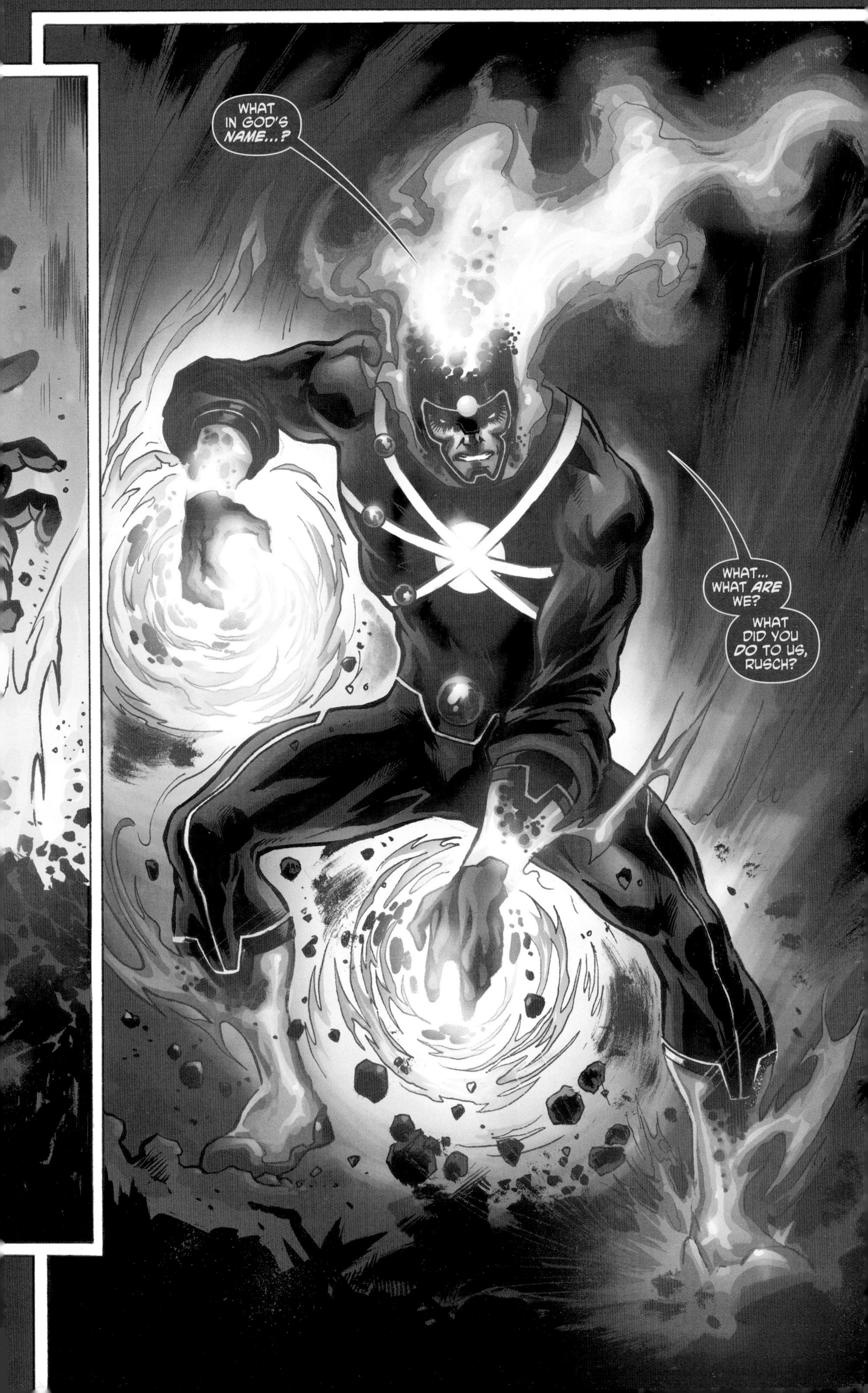
WHAT IN GOD'S *NAME...?*
WHAT... WHAT *ARE* WE?
WHAT DID YOU *DO* TO US, RUSCH?

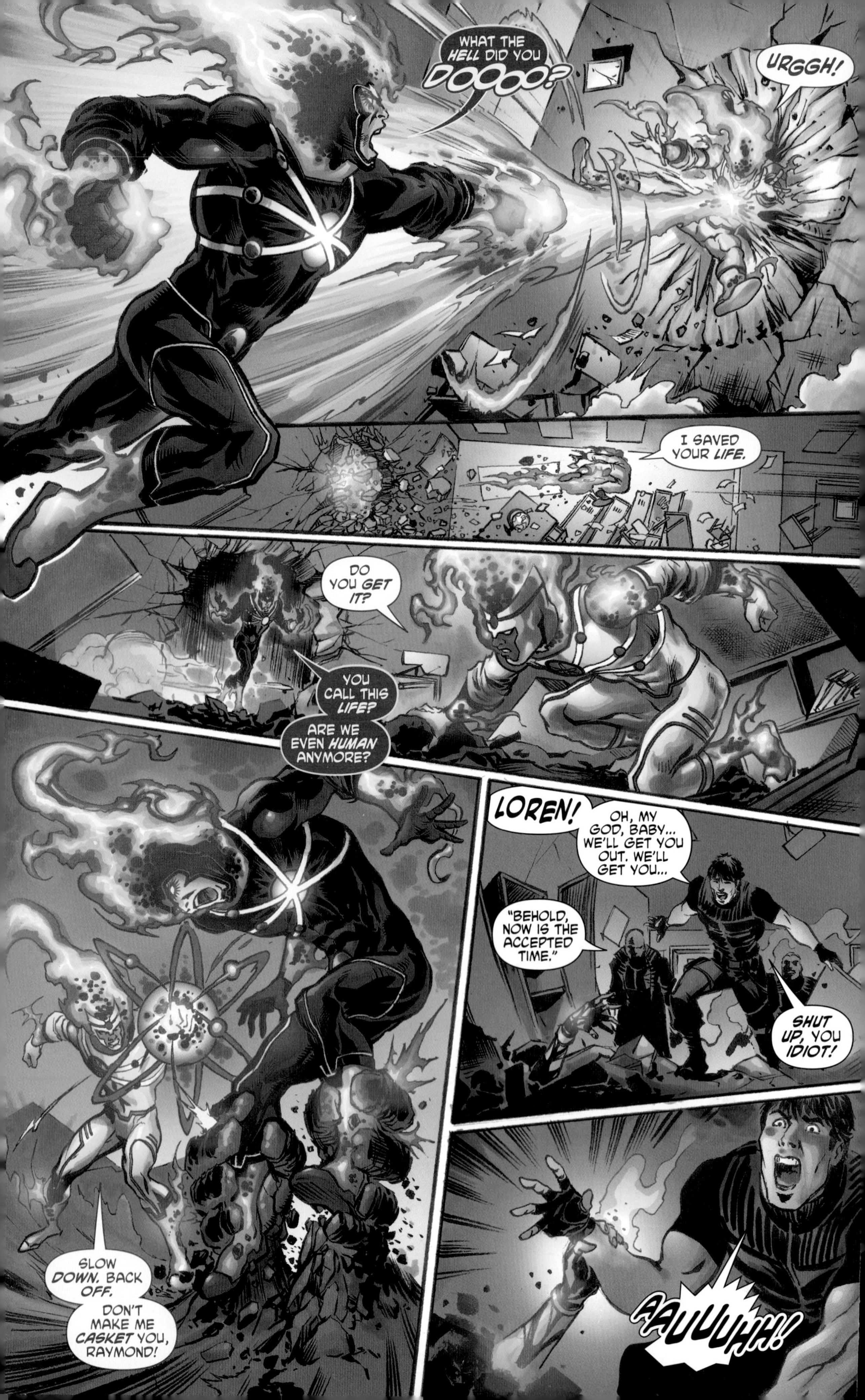
WHAT THE HELL DID YOU DOOOOO?
URGGH!
I SAVED YOUR LIFE.
DO YOU GET IT?
YOU CALL THIS LIFE?
ARE WE EVEN HUMAN ANYMORE?
LOREN!
OH, MY GOD, BABY... WE'LL GET YOU OUT. WE'LL GET YOU...
"BEHOLD, NOW IS THE ACCEPTED TIME."
SHUT UP, YOU IDIOT!
SLOW DOWN. BACK OFF.
DON'T MAKE ME CASKET YOU, RAYMOND!
AAUUUHH!

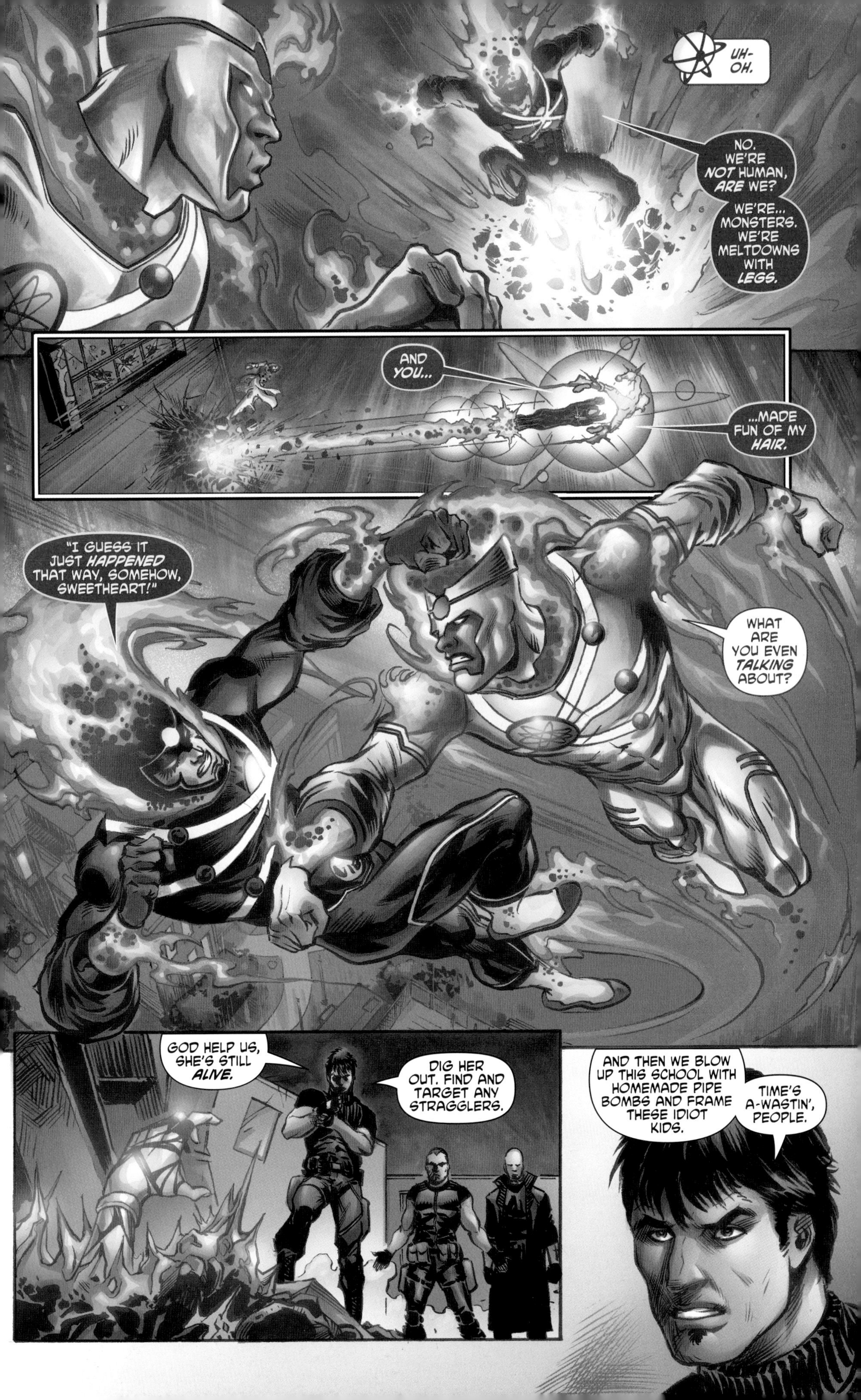

UH-OH.
NO. WE'RE NOT HUMAN, ARE WE?
WE'RE... MONSTERS. WE'RE MELTDOWNS WITH LEGS.
AND YOU...
...MADE FUN OF MY HAIR.
"I GUESS IT JUST HAPPENED THAT WAY, SOMEHOW, SWEETHEART!"
WHAT ARE YOU EVEN TALKING ABOUT?
GOD HELP US, SHE'S STILL ALIVE.
DIG HER OUT. FIND AND TARGET ANY STRAGGLERS.
AND THEN WE BLOW UP THIS SCHOOL WITH HOMEMADE PIPE BOMBS AND FRAME THESE IDIOT KIDS.
TIME'S A-WASTIN', PEOPLE.

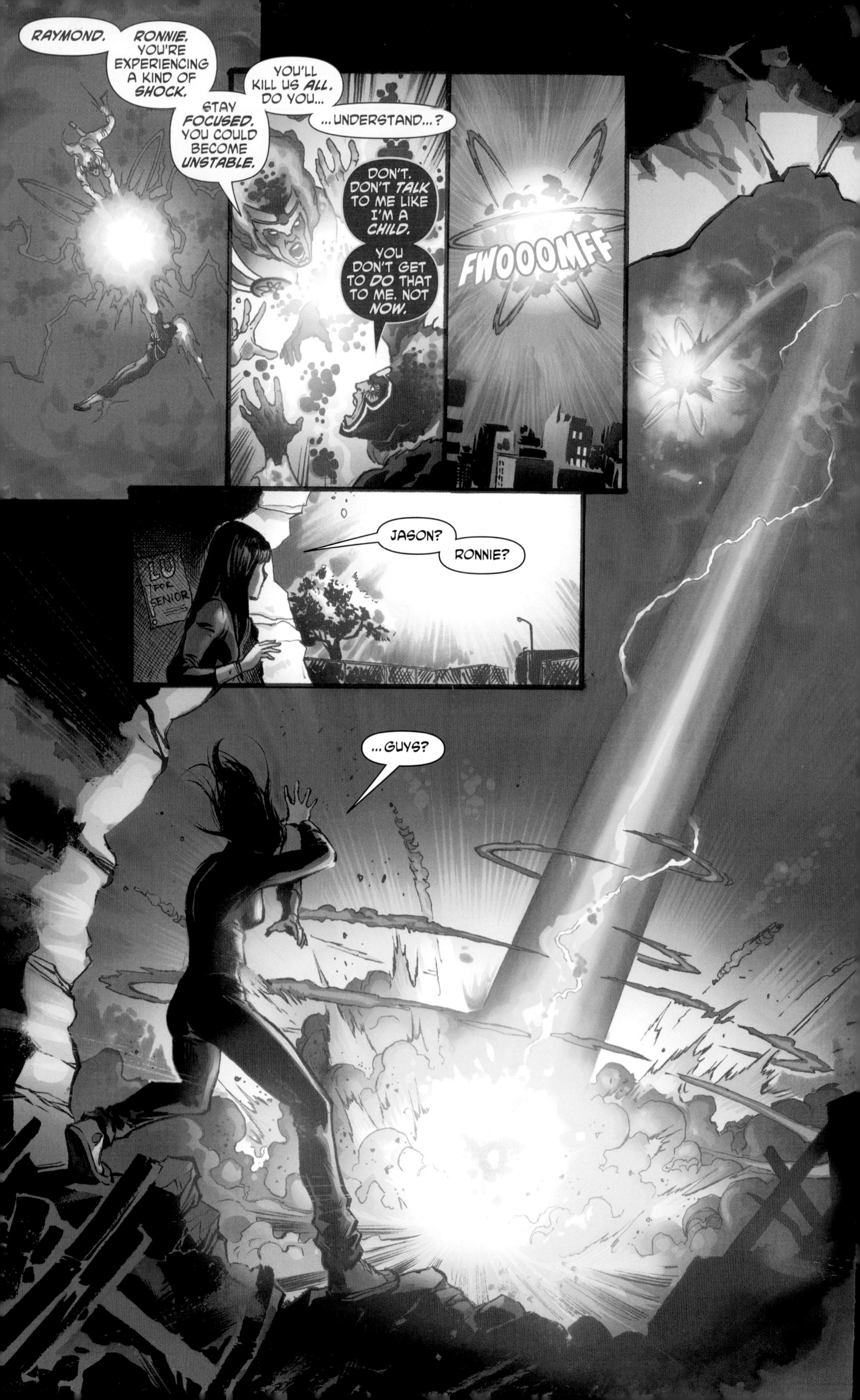
RAYMOND.
RONNIE. YOU'RE EXPERIENCING A KIND OF SHOCK.
STAY FOCUSED. YOU COULD BECOME UNSTABLE.
YOU'LL KILL US ALL. DO YOU...
...UNDERSTAND...?
DON'T. DON'T TALK TO ME LIKE I'M A CHILD.
YOU DON'T GET TO DO THAT TO ME. NOT NOW.
FWOOOMFF
JASON?
RONNIE?
LU FOR SENIOR
...GUYS?

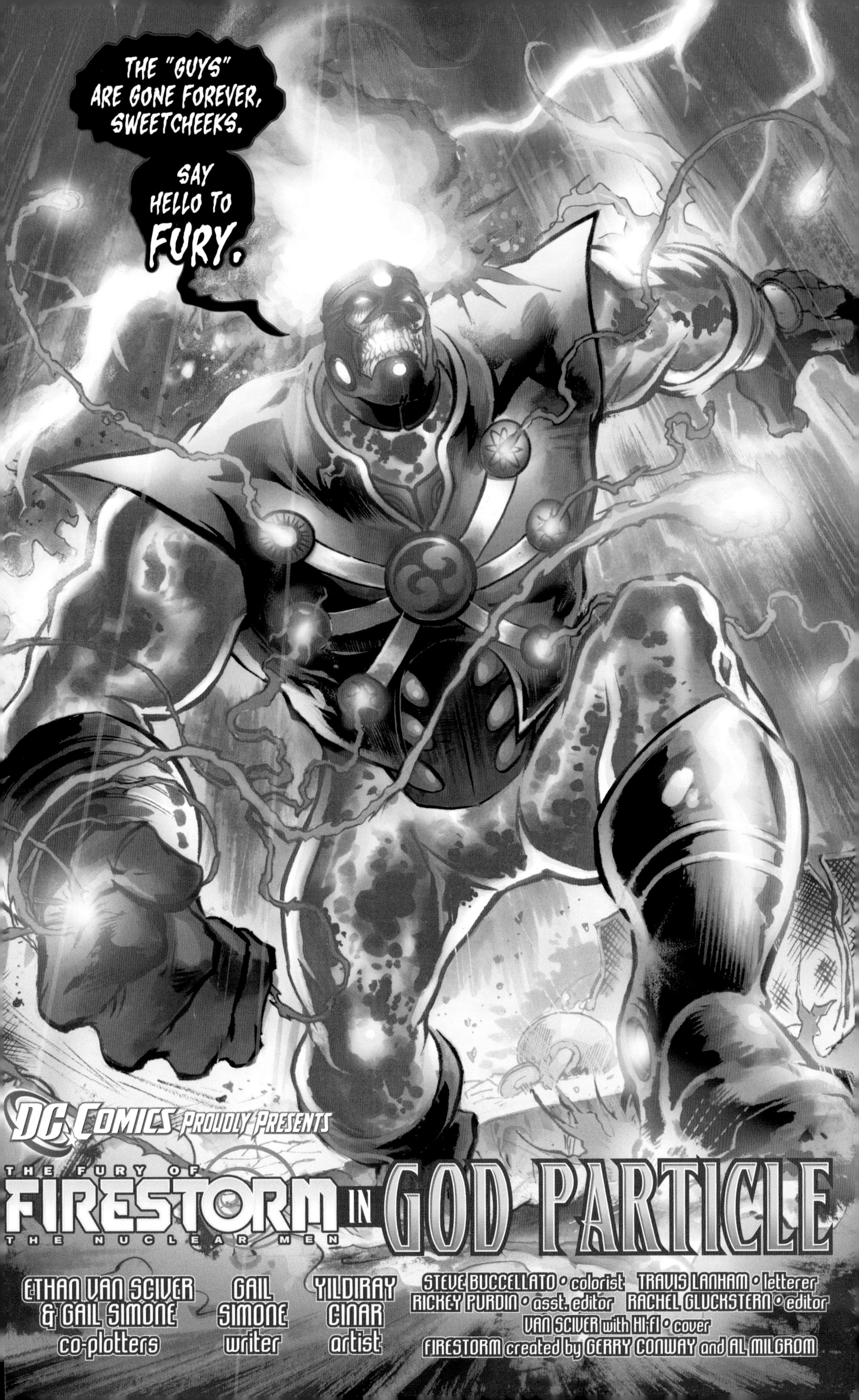

THE "GUYS" ARE GONE FOREVER, SWEETCHEEKS.
SAY HELLO TO FURY.
DC COMICS PROUDLY PRESENTS
THE FURY OF FIRESTORM THE NUCLEAR MEN IN GOD PARTICLE
ETHAN VAN SCIVER & GAIL SIMONE co-plotters
GAIL SIMONE writer
YILDIRAY CINAR artist
STEVE BUCCELLATO • colorist TRAVIS LANHAM • letterer
RICKEY PURDIN • asst. editor RACHEL GLUCKSTERN • editor
VAN SCIVER with HI-FI • cover
FIRESTORM created by GERRY CONWAY and AL MILGROM

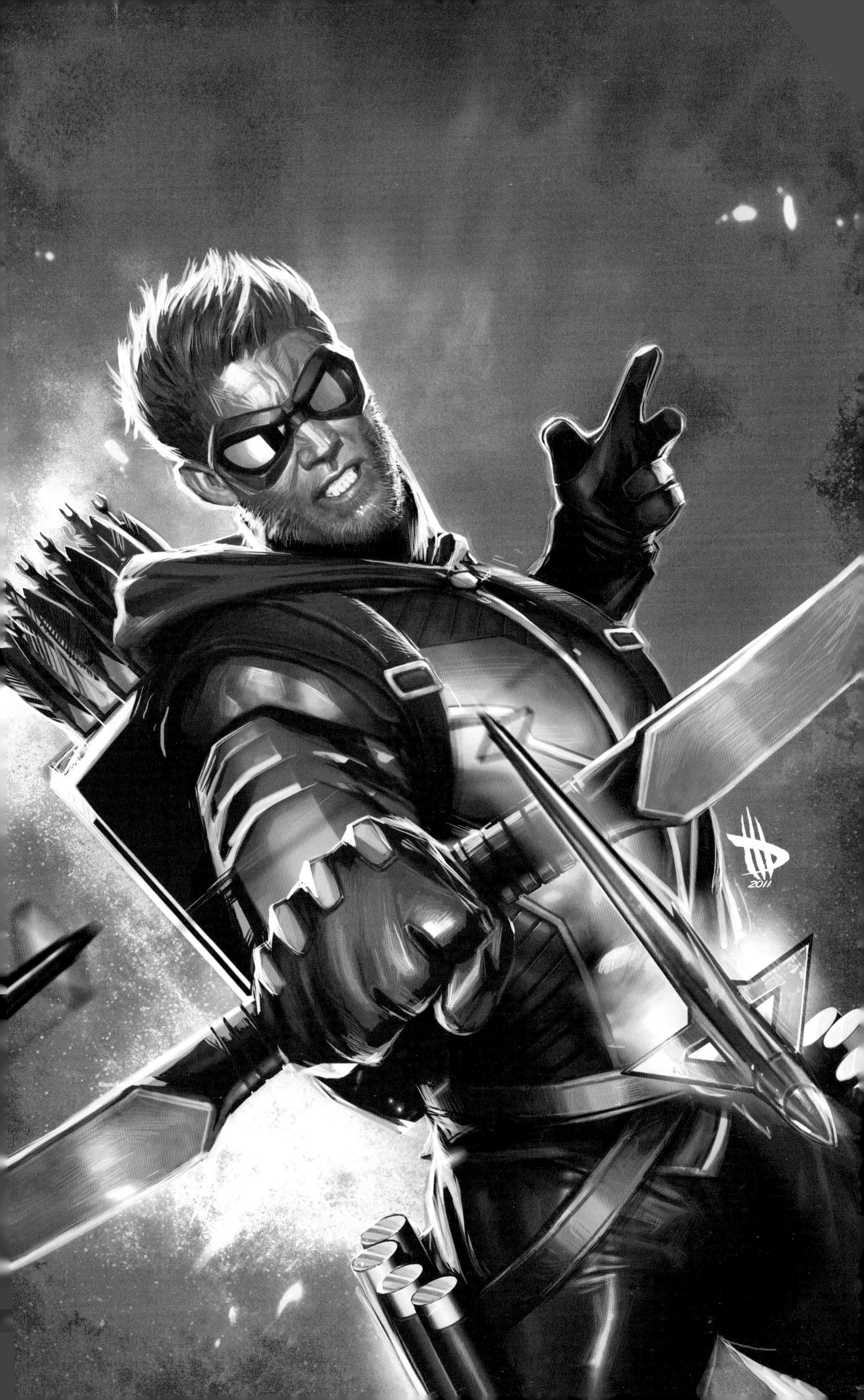

GREEN ARROW

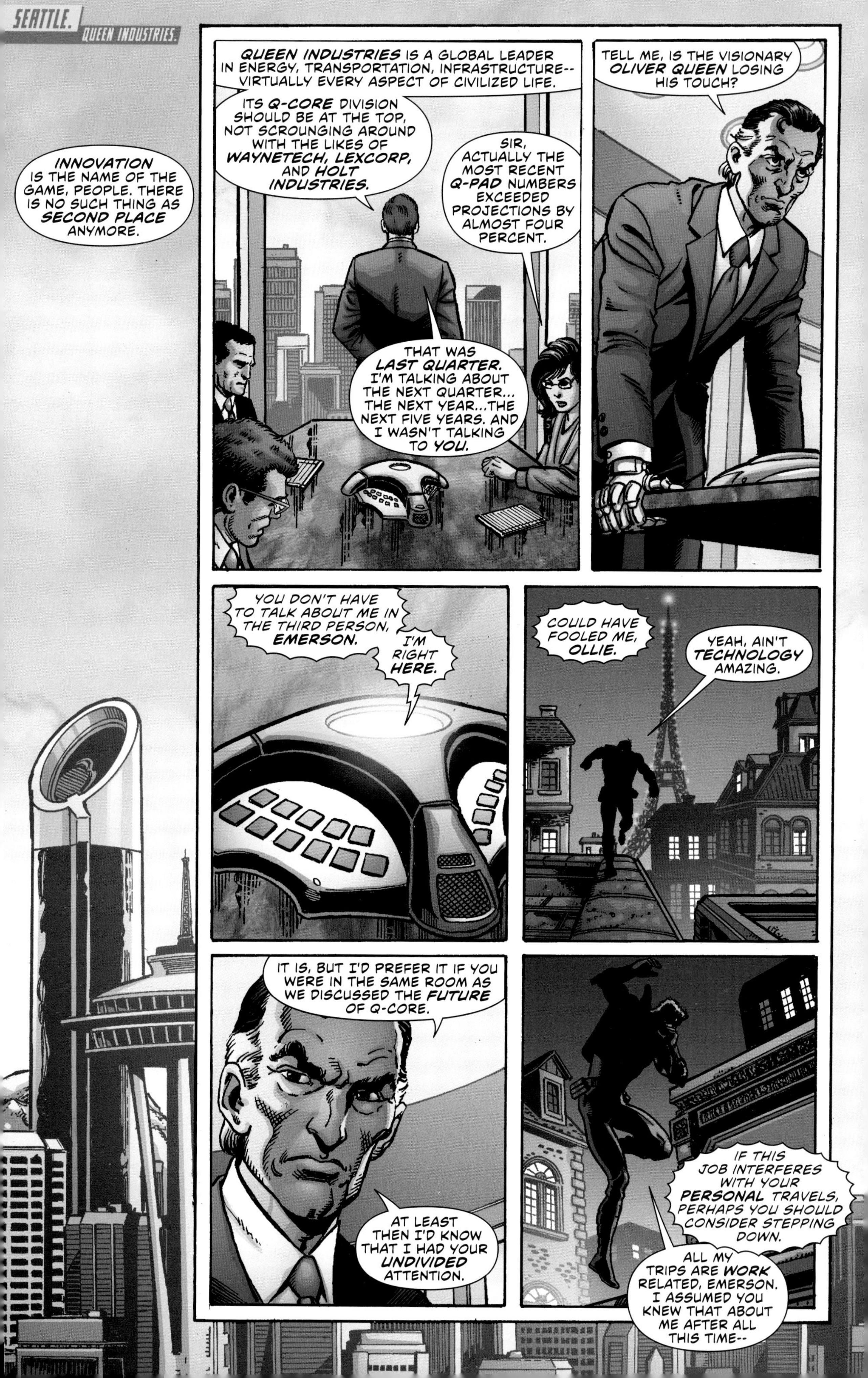
SEATTLE.
QUEEN INDUSTRIES.
INNOVATION IS THE NAME OF THE GAME, PEOPLE. THERE IS NO SUCH THING AS SECOND PLACE ANYMORE.
QUEEN INDUSTRIES IS A GLOBAL LEADER IN ENERGY, TRANSPORTATION, INFRASTRUCTURE-- VIRTUALLY EVERY ASPECT OF CIVILIZED LIFE.
ITS Q-CORE DIVISION SHOULD BE AT THE TOP, NOT SCROUNGING AROUND WITH THE LIKES OF WAYNETECH, LEXCORP, AND HOLT INDUSTRIES.
SIR, ACTUALLY THE MOST RECENT Q-PAD NUMBERS EXCEEDED PROJECTIONS BY ALMOST FOUR PERCENT.
THAT WAS LAST QUARTER. I'M TALKING ABOUT THE NEXT QUARTER... THE NEXT YEAR...THE NEXT FIVE YEARS. AND I WASN'T TALKING TO YOU.
TELL ME, IS THE VISIONARY OLIVER QUEEN LOSING HIS TOUCH?
YOU DON'T HAVE TO TALK ABOUT ME IN THE THIRD PERSON, EMERSON.
I'M RIGHT HERE.
COULD HAVE FOOLED ME, OLLIE.
YEAH, AIN'T TECHNOLOGY AMAZING.
IT IS, BUT I'D PREFER IT IF YOU WERE IN THE SAME ROOM AS WE DISCUSSED THE FUTURE OF Q-CORE.
AT LEAST THEN I'D KNOW THAT I HAD YOUR UNDIVIDED ATTENTION.
IF THIS JOB INTERFERES WITH YOUR PERSONAL TRAVELS, PERHAPS YOU SHOULD CONSIDER STEPPING DOWN.
ALL MY TRIPS ARE WORK RELATED, EMERSON. I ASSUMED YOU KNEW THAT ABOUT ME AFTER ALL THIS TIME--

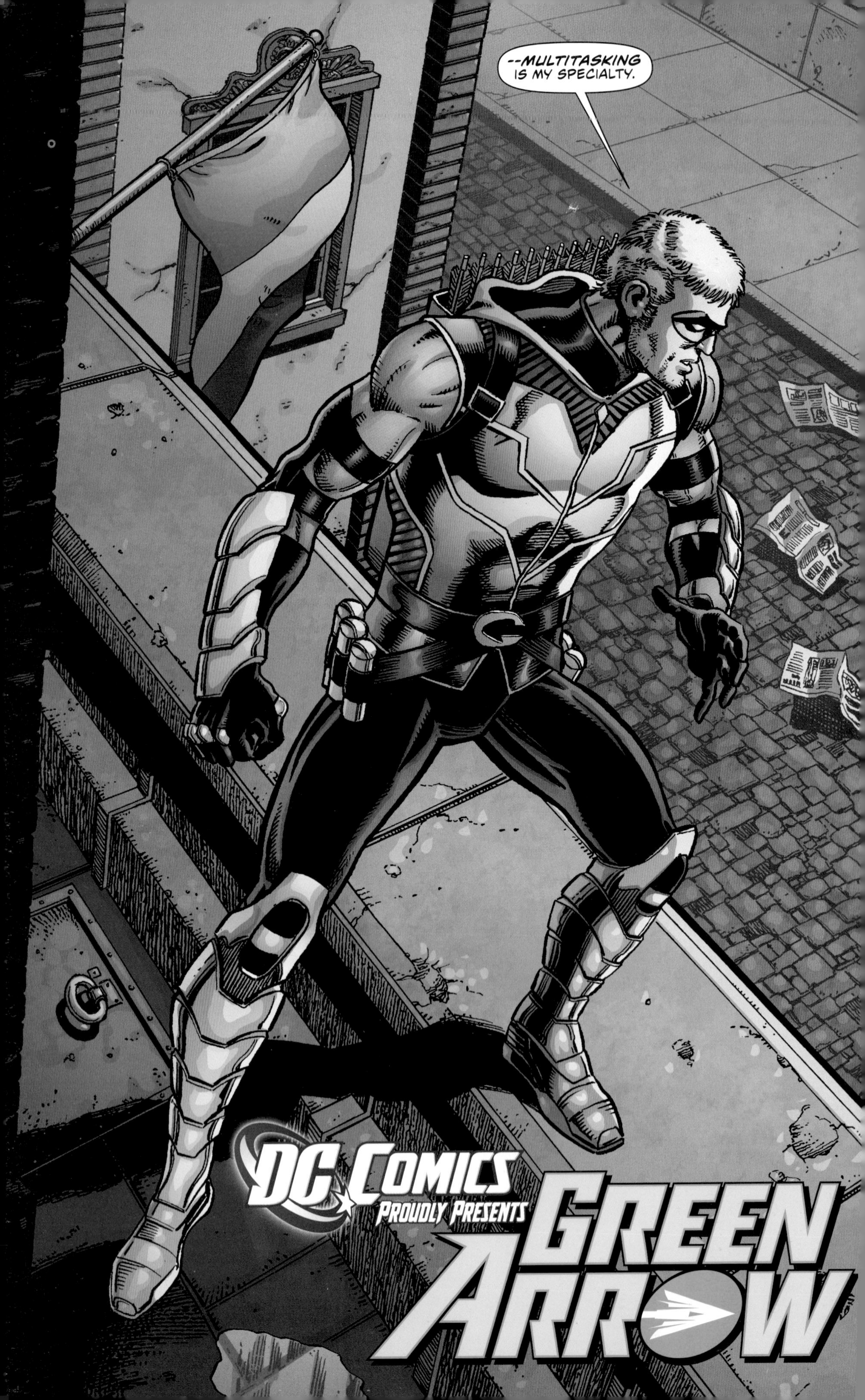
--MULTITASKING IS MY SPECIALTY.
DC COMICS PROUDLY PRESENTS
GREEN ARROW

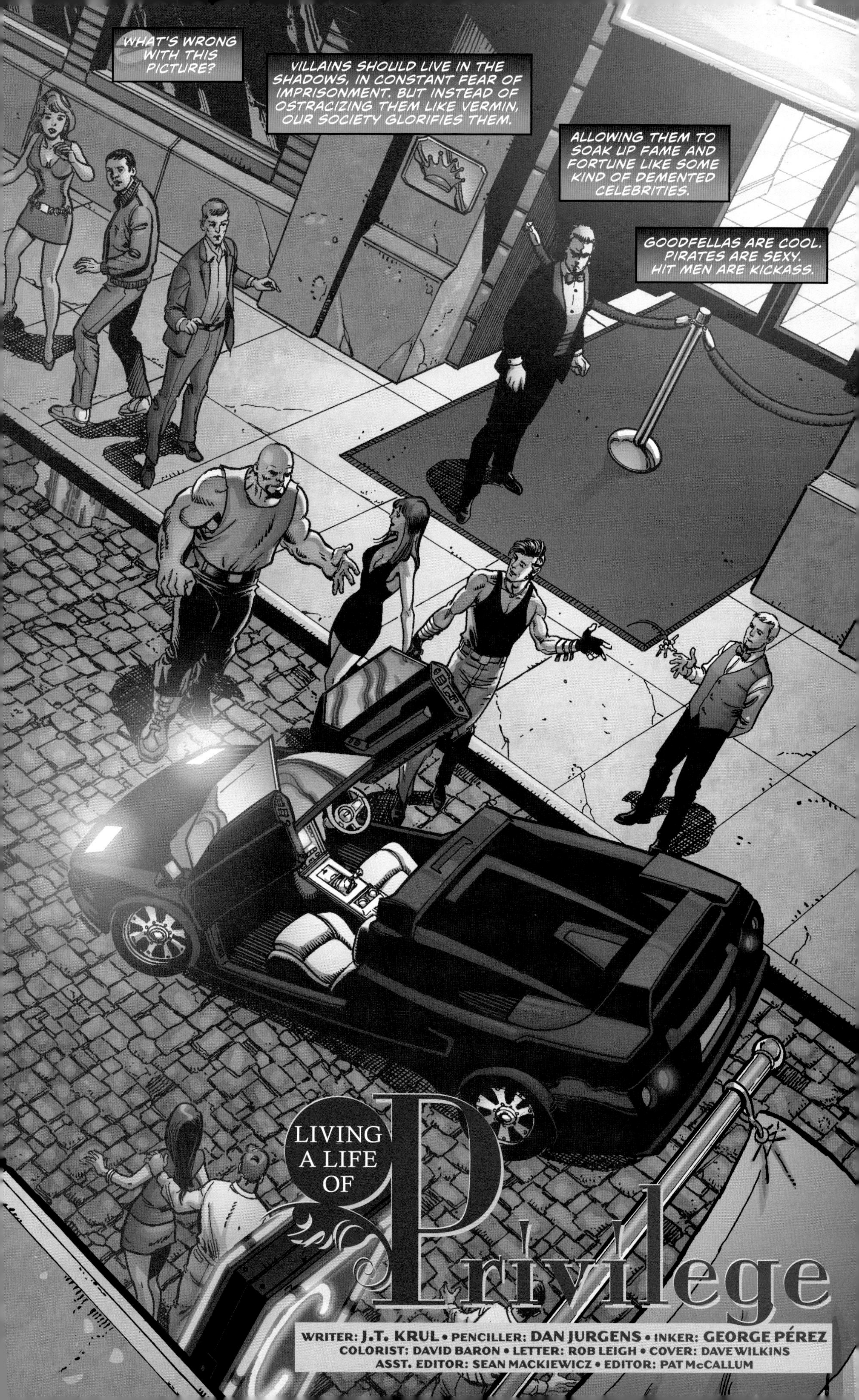
WHAT'S WRONG WITH THIS PICTURE?
VILLAINS SHOULD LIVE IN THE SHADOWS, IN CONSTANT FEAR OF IMPRISONMENT. BUT INSTEAD OF OSTRACIZING THEM LIKE VERMIN, OUR SOCIETY GLORIFIES THEM.
ALLOWING THEM TO SOAK UP FAME AND FORTUNE LIKE SOME KIND OF DEMENTED CELEBRITIES.
GOODFELLAS ARE COOL. PIRATES ARE SEXY. HIT MEN ARE KICKASS.
LIVING A LIFE OF Privilege
WRITER: J.T. KRUL • PENCILLER: DAN JURGENS • INKER: GEORGE PÉREZ
COLORIST: DAVID BARON • LETTER: ROB LEIGH • COVER: DAVE WILKINS
ASST. EDITOR: SEAN MACKIEWICZ • EDITOR: PAT McCALLUM

THAT'S NOT HOW *I* SEE THEM.

NAOMI? YOU THERE?

I'M ALWAYS HERE, OLLIE.

I RECOGNIZE ALL THREE OF THEM FROM THEIR DISTURBING YOUTUBE VIDEOS.

THE BRUTE *DYNAMIX* NEARLY DESTROYED THE LONDON BRIDGE. *DOPPELGANGER* TERRORIZED MILAN DURING FASHION WEEK.

AND *SUPERCHARGE*-- HE BLACKED OUT MONTE CARLO WITH HIS ELECTRICAL POWERS.

LOOKS LIKE YOU GOT BONNIE AND CLYDE AND CLYDE, TONIGHT. A REAL PARTY.

BUT WHAT ARE THEY ALL DOING TOGETHER?

FOR STARTERS, THEY'RE TAKING THE FESTIVITIES TO A BOAT OUT BACK.

I'M ON IT.

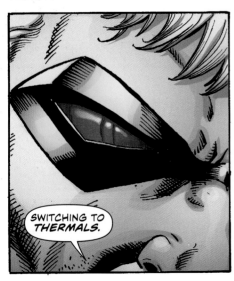

SWITCHING TO THERMALS.

BUT IT'LL BE HARD TO KEEP TRACK OF THEM AMONG THE BUMP AND GRIND ON THE DANCE FLOOR.

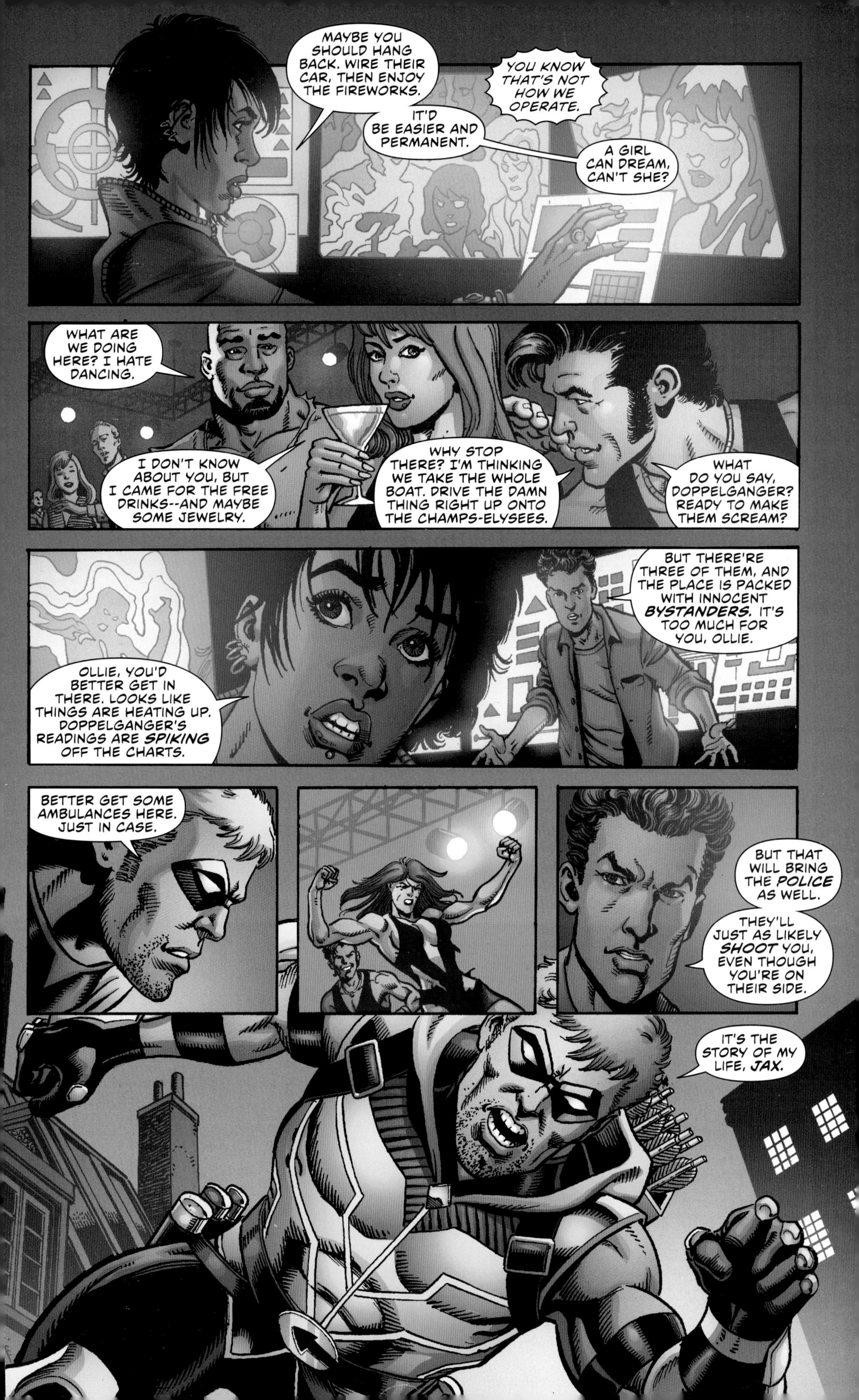
MAYBE YOU SHOULD HANG BACK. WIRE THEIR CAR, THEN ENJOY THE FIREWORKS.
IT'D BE EASIER AND PERMANENT.
YOU KNOW THAT'S NOT HOW WE OPERATE.
A GIRL CAN DREAM, CAN'T SHE?
WHAT ARE WE DOING HERE? I HATE DANCING.
I DON'T KNOW ABOUT YOU, BUT I CAME FOR THE FREE DRINKS--AND MAYBE SOME JEWELRY.
WHY STOP THERE? I'M THINKING WE TAKE THE WHOLE BOAT. DRIVE THE DAMN THING RIGHT UP ONTO THE CHAMPS-ELYSEES.
WHAT DO YOU SAY, DOPPELGANGER? READY TO MAKE THEM SCREAM?
BUT THERE'RE THREE OF THEM, AND THE PLACE IS PACKED WITH INNOCENT BYSTANDERS. IT'S TOO MUCH FOR YOU, OLLIE.
OLLIE, YOU'D BETTER GET IN THERE. LOOKS LIKE THINGS ARE HEATING UP. DOPPELGANGER'S READINGS ARE SPIKING OFF THE CHARTS.
BETTER GET SOME AMBULANCES HERE. JUST IN CASE.
BUT THAT WILL BRING THE POLICE AS WELL.
THEY'LL JUST AS LIKELY SHOOT YOU, EVEN THOUGH YOU'RE ON THEIR SIDE.
IT'S THE STORY OF MY LIFE, JAX.

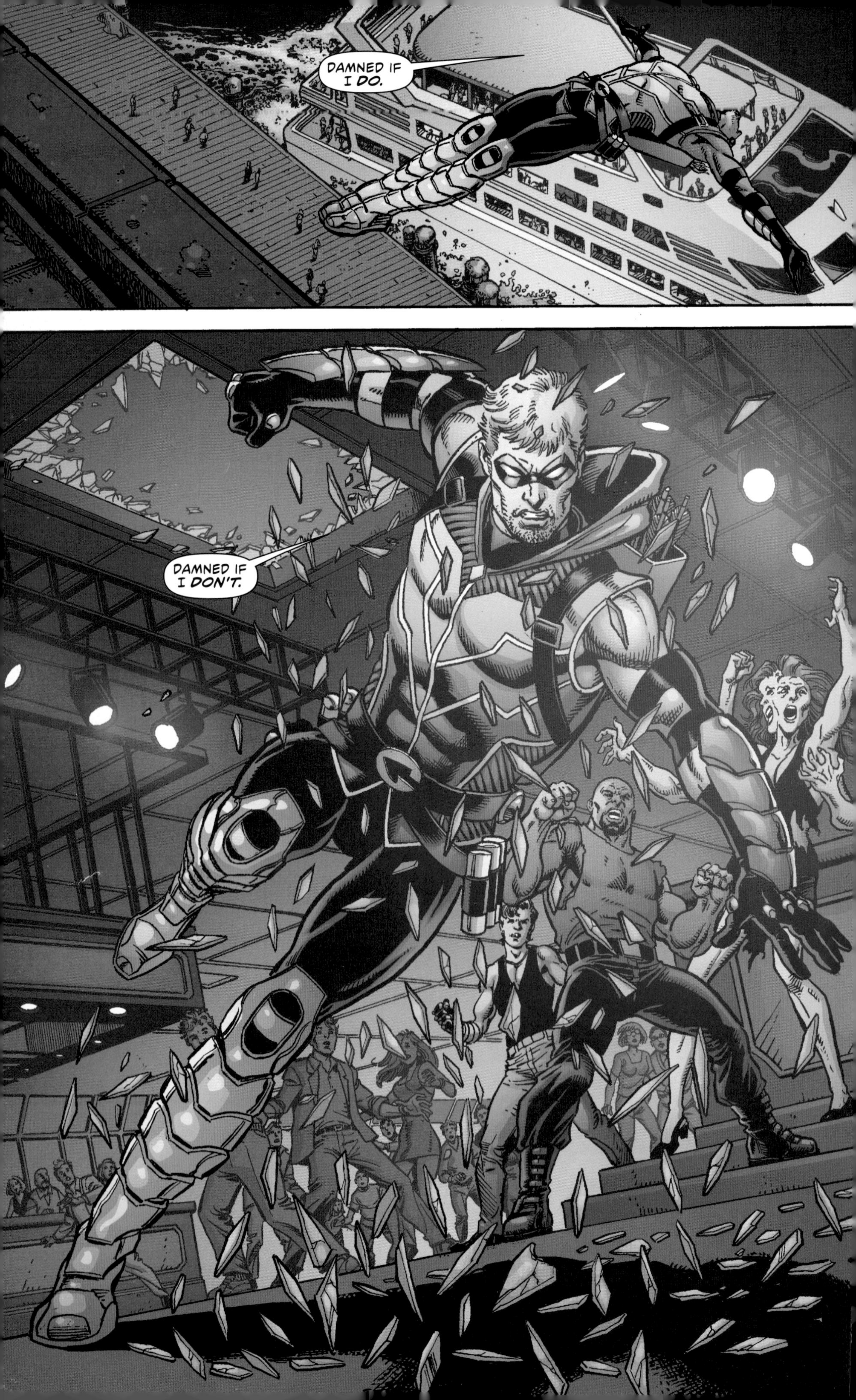

DAMNED IF I DO.
DAMNED IF I DON'T.

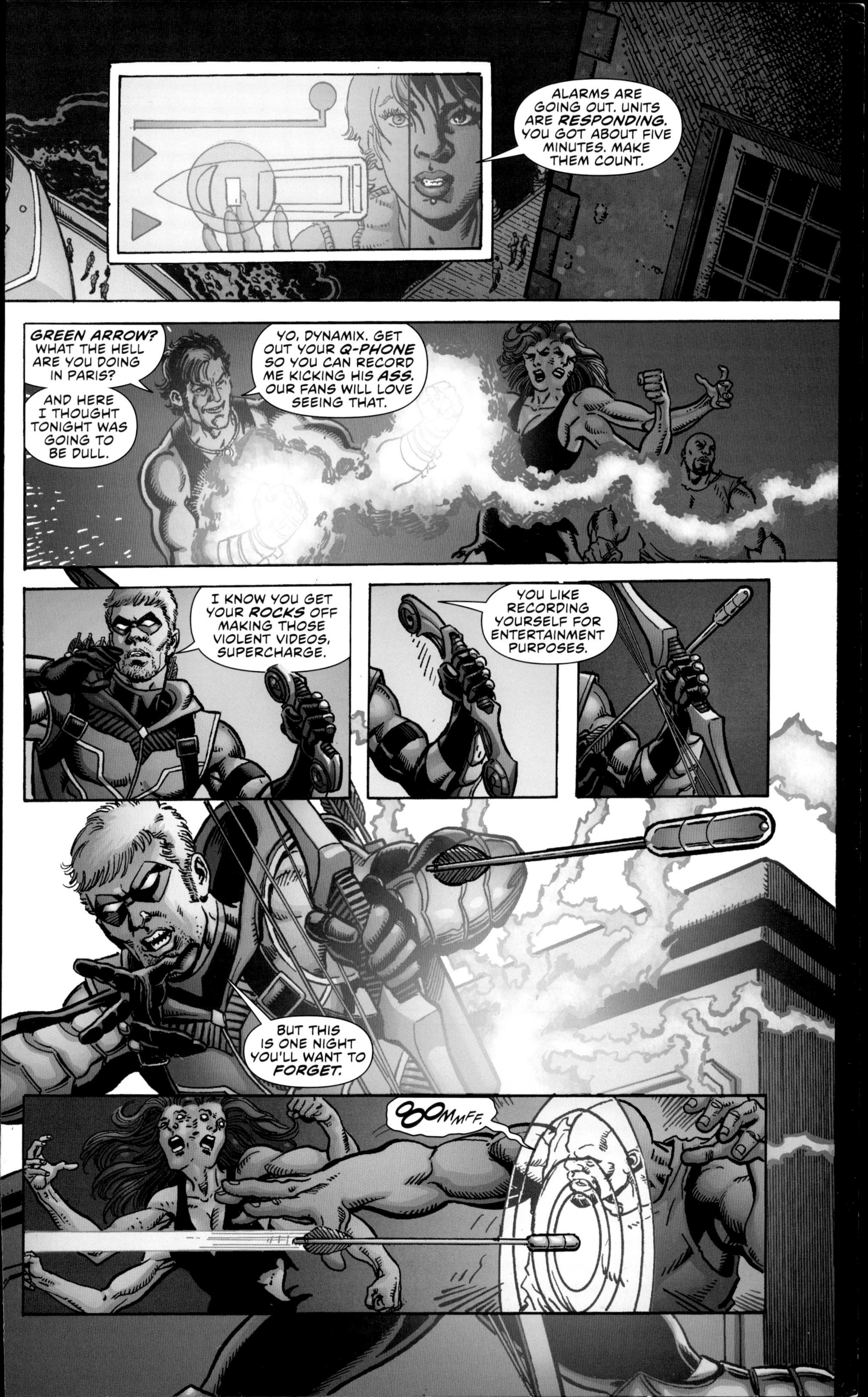
ALARMS ARE GOING OUT. UNITS ARE RESPONDING. YOU GOT ABOUT FIVE MINUTES. MAKE THEM COUNT.
GREEN ARROW? WHAT THE HELL ARE YOU DOING IN PARIS?
AND HERE I THOUGHT TONIGHT WAS GOING TO BE DULL.
YO, DYNAMIX. GET OUT YOUR Q-PHONE SO YOU CAN RECORD ME KICKING HIS ASS. OUR FANS WILL LOVE SEEING THAT.
I KNOW YOU GET YOUR ROCKS OFF MAKING THOSE VIOLENT VIDEOS, SUPERCHARGE.
YOU LIKE RECORDING YOURSELF FOR ENTERTAINMENT PURPOSES.
BUT THIS IS ONE NIGHT YOU'LL WANT TO FORGET.
OOOMMFF.

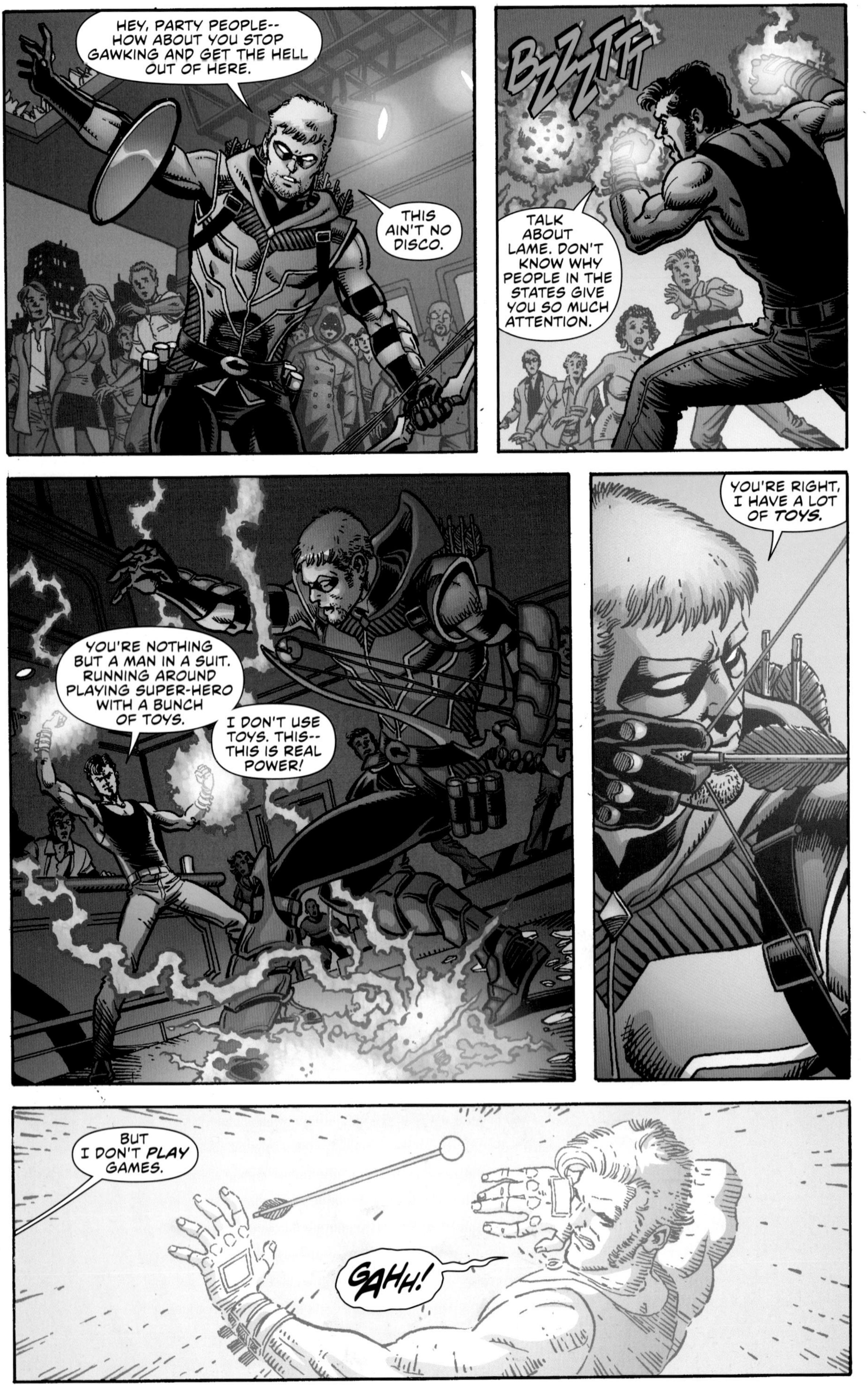
HEY, PARTY PEOPLE-- HOW ABOUT YOU STOP GAWKING AND GET THE HELL OUT OF HERE.
THIS AIN'T NO DISCO.
BZZZTT
TALK ABOUT LAME. DON'T KNOW WHY PEOPLE IN THE STATES GIVE YOU SO MUCH ATTENTION.
YOU'RE NOTHING BUT A MAN IN A SUIT. RUNNING AROUND PLAYING SUPER-HERO WITH A BUNCH OF TOYS.
I DON'T USE TOYS. THIS-- THIS IS REAL POWER!
YOU'RE RIGHT, I HAVE A LOT OF TOYS.
BUT I DON'T PLAY GAMES.
GAHH!

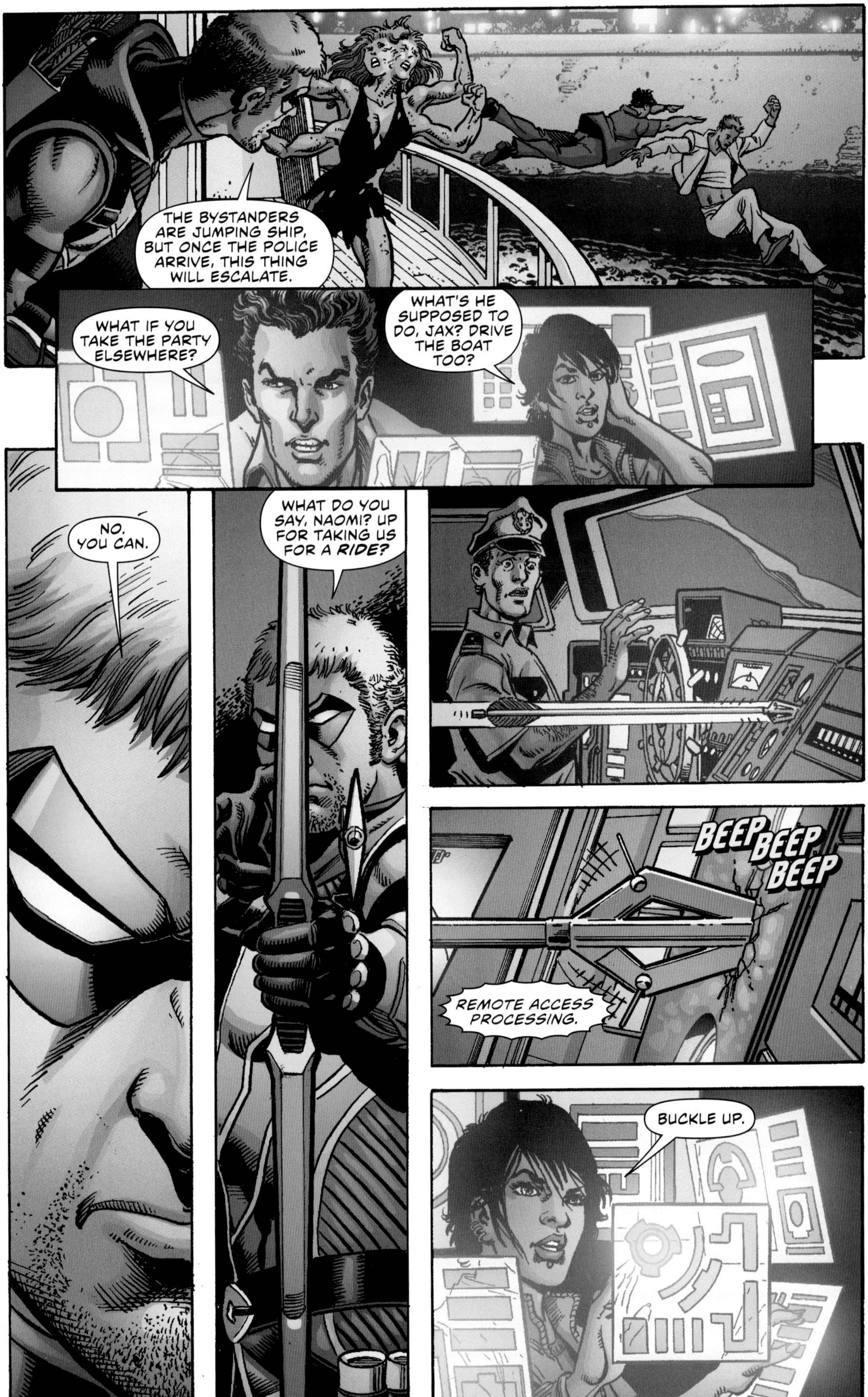
THE BYSTANDERS ARE JUMPING SHIP, BUT ONCE THE POLICE ARRIVE, THIS THING WILL ESCALATE.
WHAT IF YOU TAKE THE PARTY ELSEWHERE?
WHAT'S HE SUPPOSED TO DO, JAX? DRIVE THE BOAT TOO?
NO. YOU CAN.
WHAT DO YOU SAY, NAOMI? UP FOR TAKING US FOR A *RIDE?*
BEEP BEEP BEEP
REMOTE ACCESS PROCESSING.
BUCKLE UP.

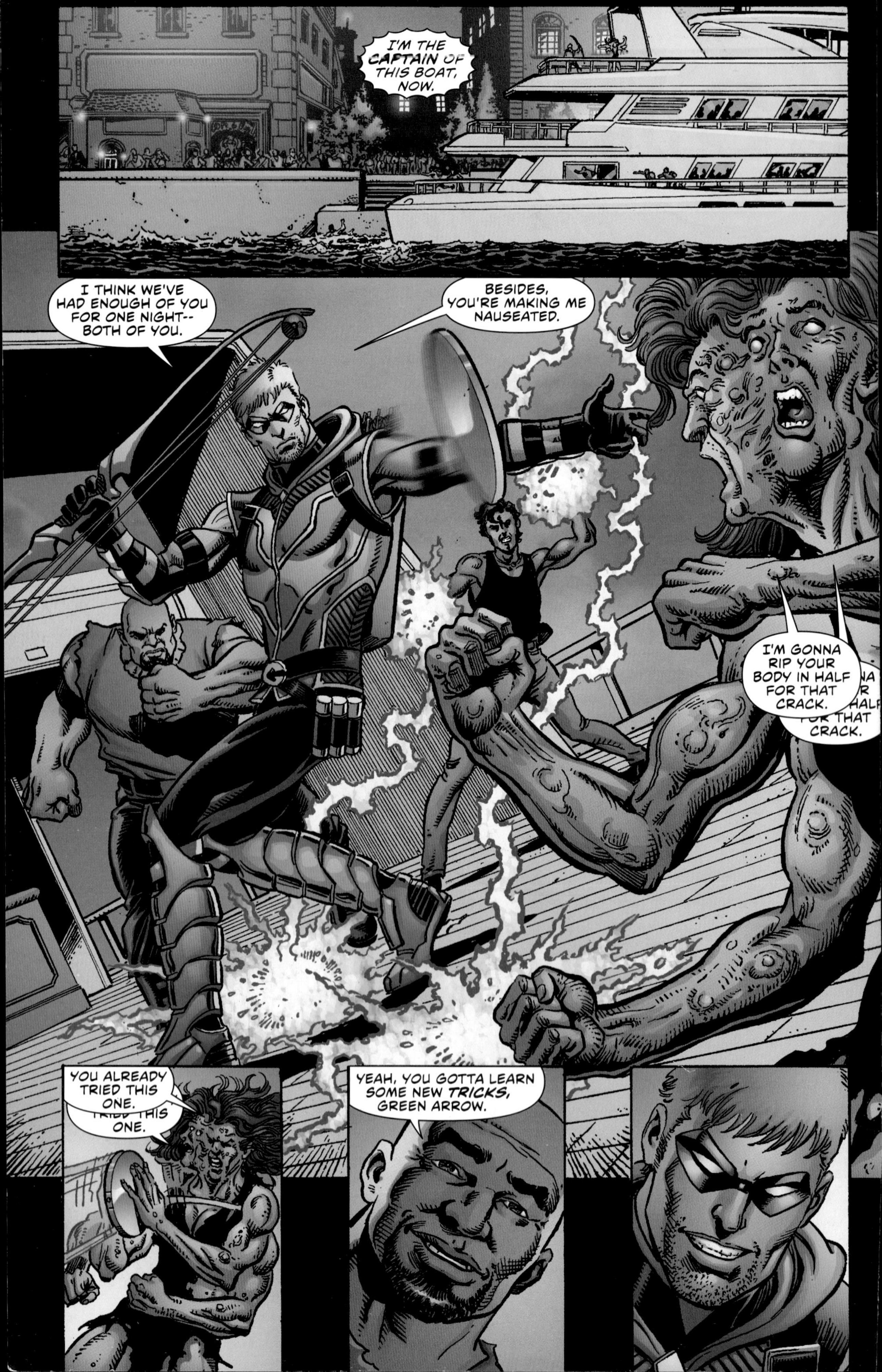
I'M THE CAPTAIN OF THIS BOAT, NOW.
I THINK WE'VE HAD ENOUGH OF YOU FOR ONE NIGHT-- BOTH OF YOU.
BESIDES, YOU'RE MAKING ME NAUSEATED.
I'M GONNA RIP YOUR BODY IN HALF FOR THAT CRACK.
YOU ALREADY TRIED THIS ONE.
YEAH, YOU GOTTA LEARN SOME NEW TRICKS, GREEN ARROW.

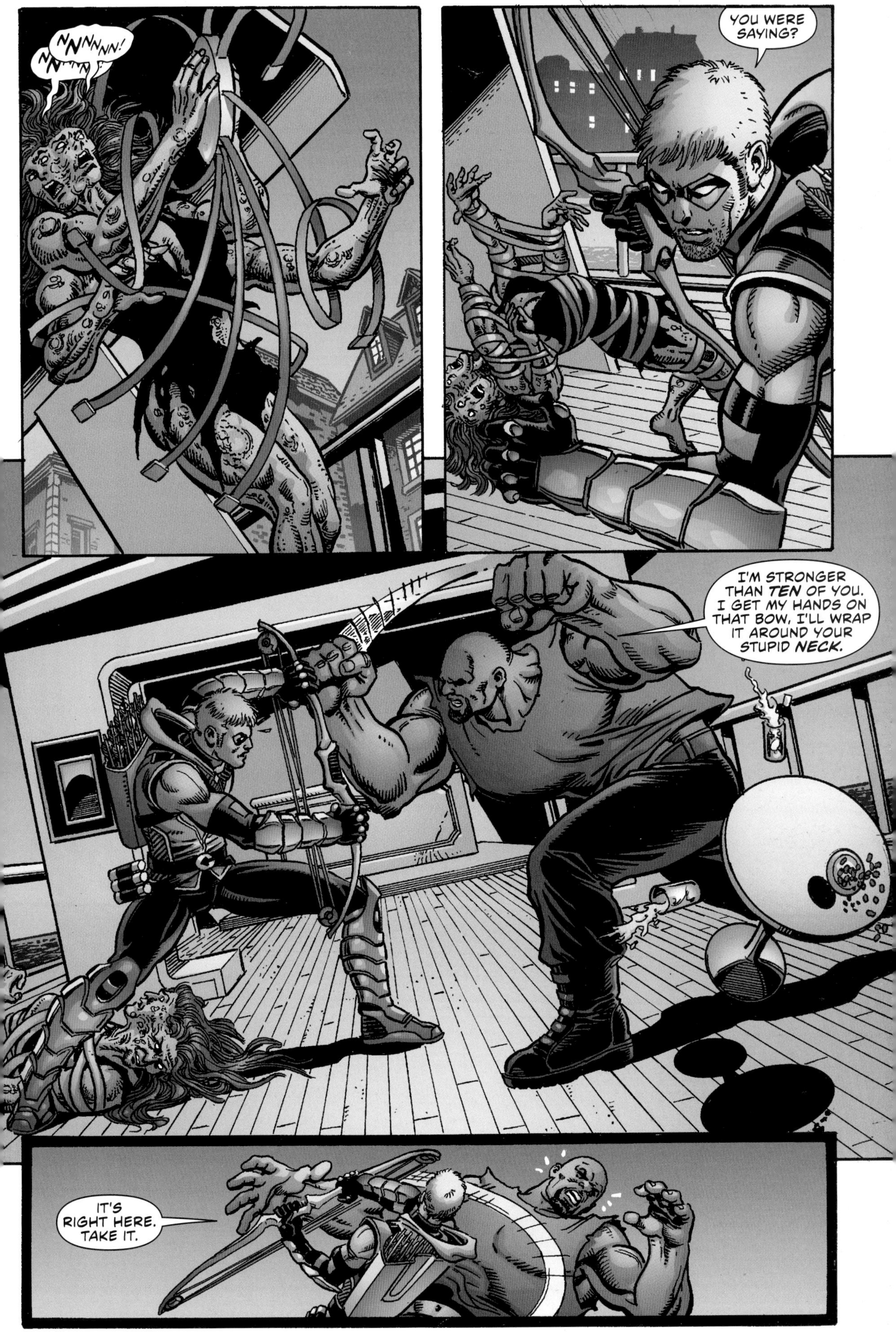
NNNNNN!
NNNNN
YOU WERE SAYING?
I'M STRONGER THAN TEN OF YOU. I GET MY HANDS ON THAT BOW, I'LL WRAP IT AROUND YOUR STUPID NECK.
IT'S RIGHT HERE. TAKE IT.

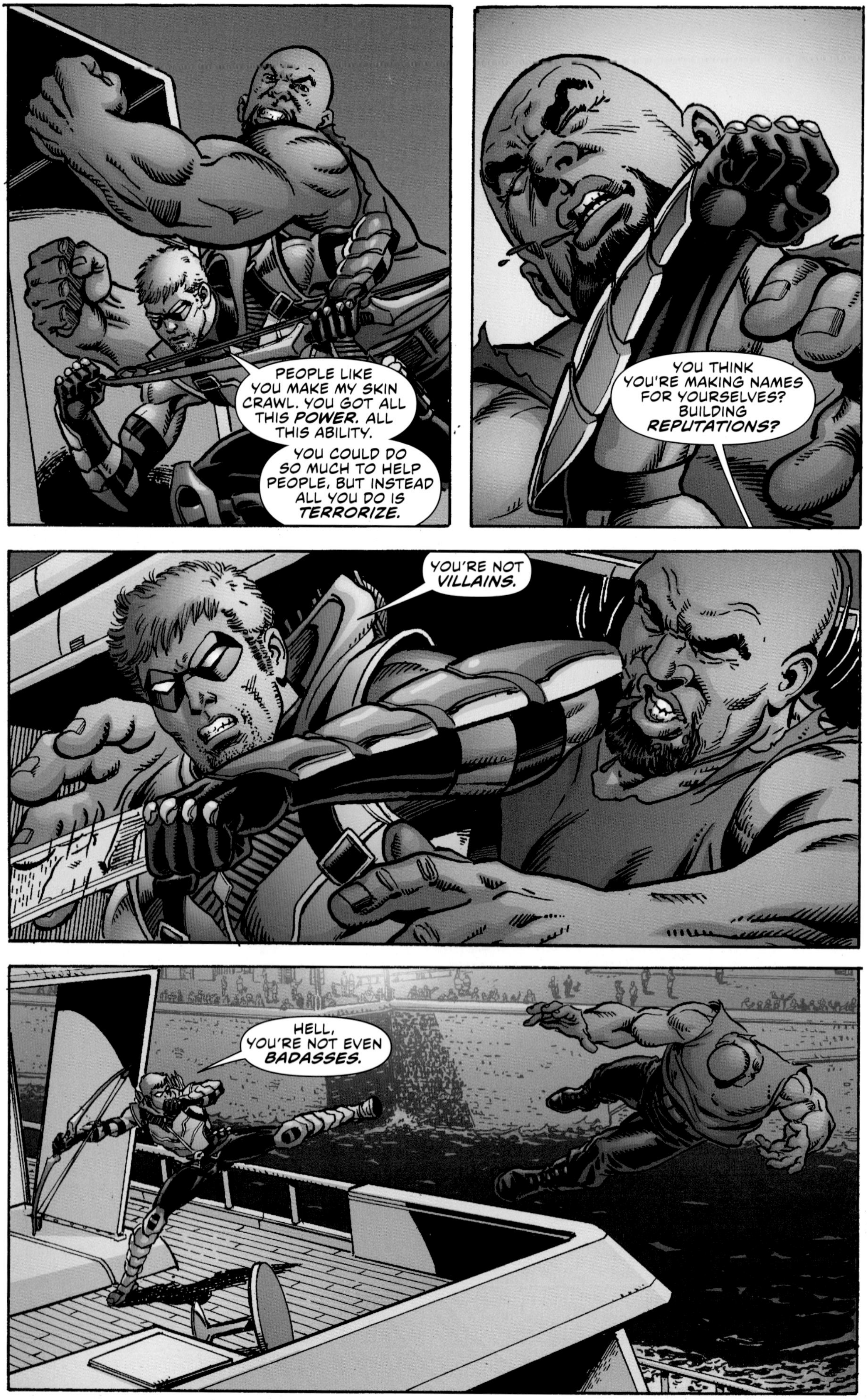
PEOPLE LIKE YOU MAKE MY SKIN CRAWL. YOU GOT ALL THIS POWER. ALL THIS ABILITY.
YOU COULD DO SO MUCH TO HELP PEOPLE, BUT INSTEAD ALL YOU DO IS TERRORIZE.
YOU THINK YOU'RE MAKING NAMES FOR YOURSELVES? BUILDING REPUTATIONS?
YOU'RE NOT VILLAINS.
HELL, YOU'RE NOT EVEN BADASSES.

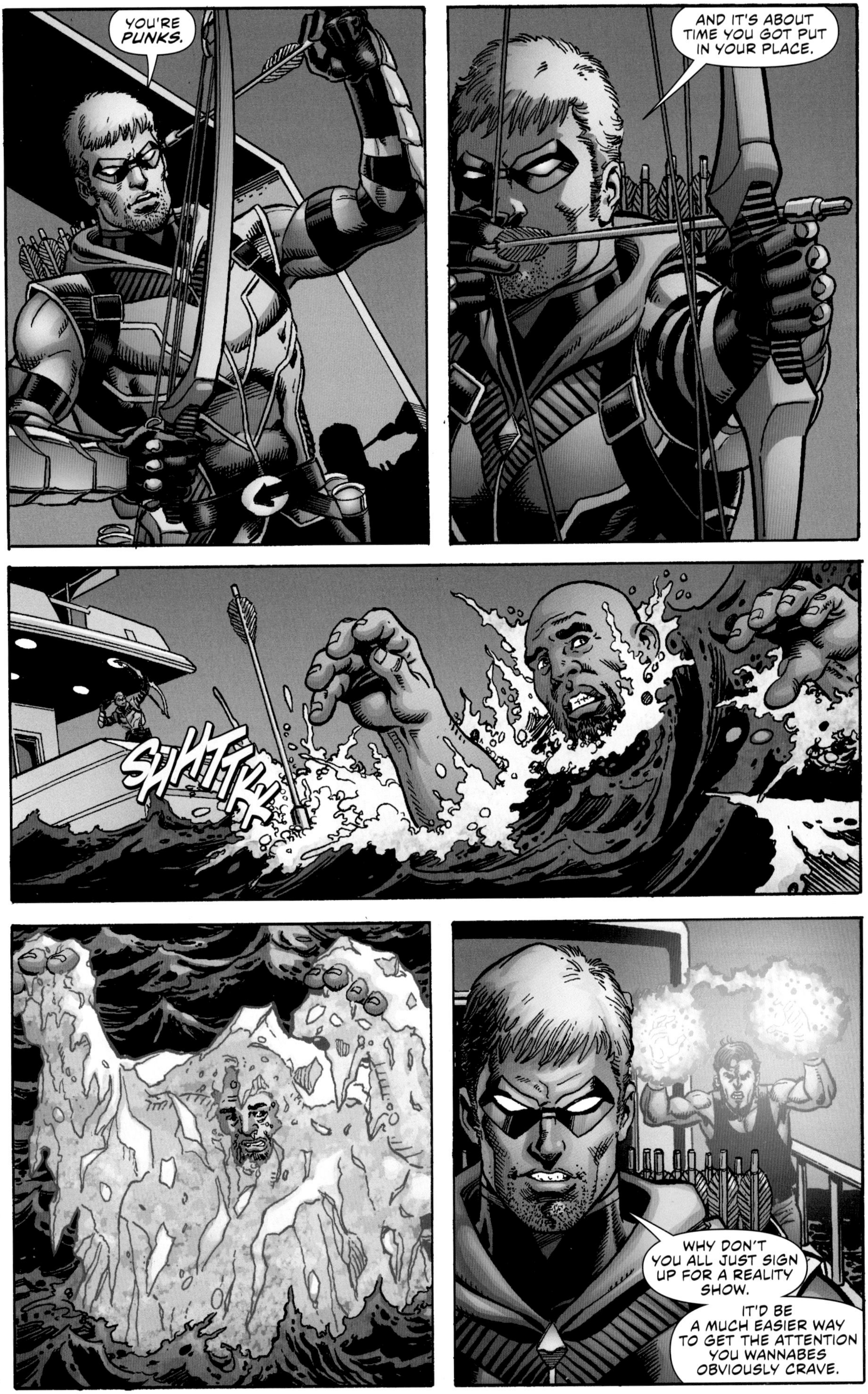

YOU'RE PUNKS.
AND IT'S ABOUT TIME YOU GOT PUT IN YOUR PLACE.
WHY DON'T YOU ALL JUST SIGN UP FOR A REALITY SHOW.
IT'D BE A MUCH EASIER WAY TO GET THE ATTENTION YOU WANNABES OBVIOUSLY CRAVE.

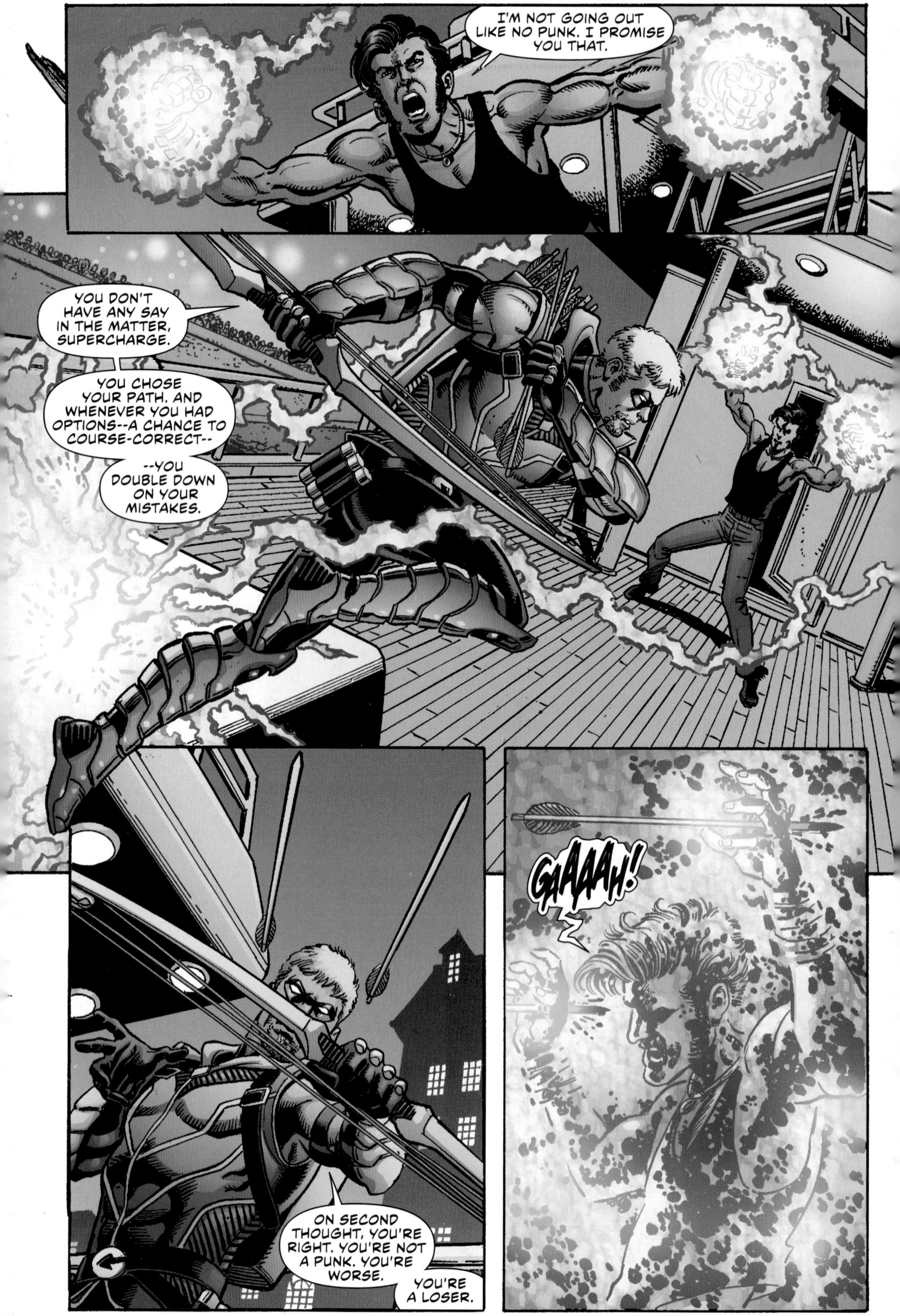

I'M NOT GOING OUT LIKE NO PUNK. I PROMISE YOU THAT.
YOU DON'T HAVE ANY SAY IN THE MATTER, SUPERCHARGE.
YOU CHOSE YOUR PATH. AND WHENEVER YOU HAD OPTIONS--A CHANCE TO COURSE-CORRECT--
--YOU DOUBLE DOWN ON YOUR MISTAKES.
ON SECOND THOUGHT, YOU'RE RIGHT. YOU'RE NOT A PUNK. YOU'RE WORSE.
YOU'RE A LOSER.
GAAAAH!

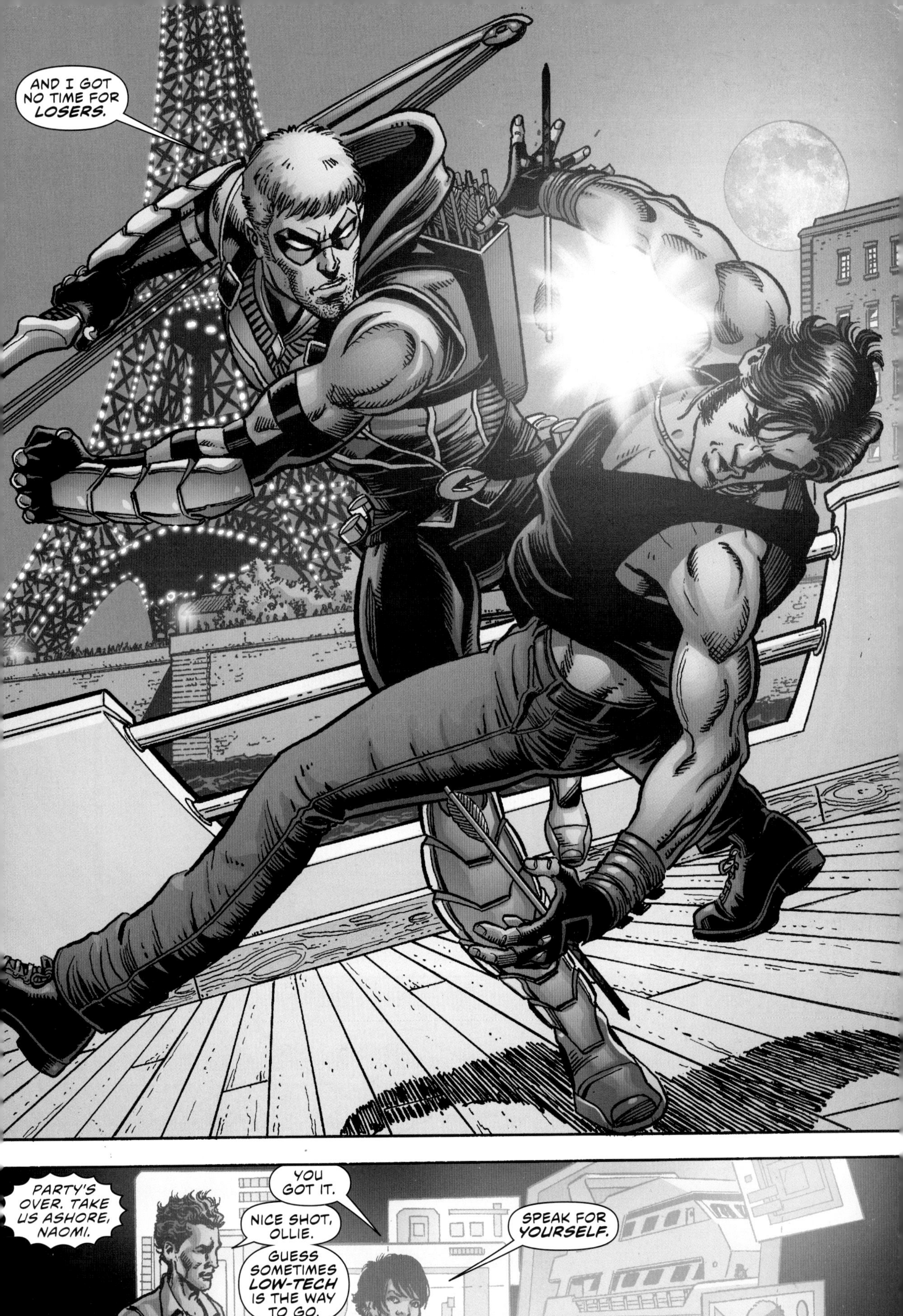
AND I GOT NO TIME FOR LOSERS.

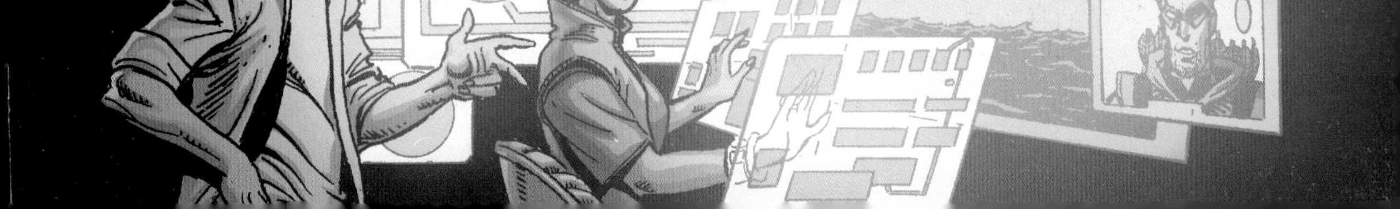
PARTY'S OVER. TAKE US ASHORE, NAOMI.
YOU GOT IT.
NICE SHOT, OLLIE.
GUESS SOMETIMES LOW-TECH IS THE WAY TO GO.
SPEAK FOR YOURSELF.

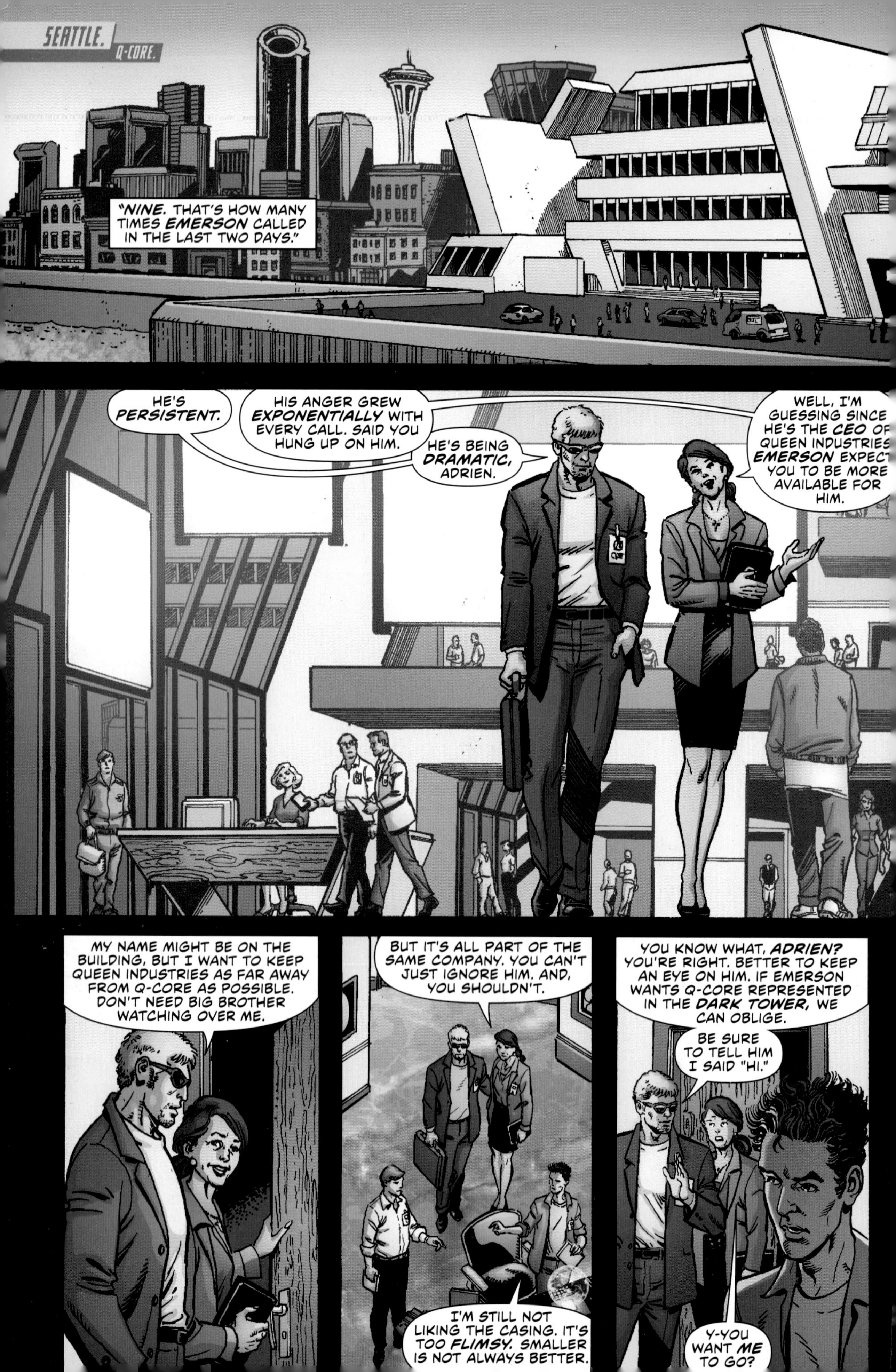

SEATTLE.
Q-CORE.
"NINE. THAT'S HOW MANY TIMES EMERSON CALLED IN THE LAST TWO DAYS."
HE'S PERSISTENT.
HIS ANGER GREW EXPONENTIALLY WITH EVERY CALL. SAID YOU HUNG UP ON HIM.
HE'S BEING DRAMATIC, ADRIEN.
WELL, I'M GUESSING SINCE HE'S THE CEO OF QUEEN INDUSTRIES EMERSON EXPECT YOU TO BE MORE AVAILABLE FOR HIM.
MY NAME MIGHT BE ON THE BUILDING, BUT I WANT TO KEEP QUEEN INDUSTRIES AS FAR AWAY FROM Q-CORE AS POSSIBLE. DON'T NEED BIG BROTHER WATCHING OVER ME.
BUT IT'S ALL PART OF THE SAME COMPANY. YOU CAN'T JUST IGNORE HIM. AND, YOU SHOULDN'T.
I'M STILL NOT LIKING THE CASING. IT'S TOO FLIMSY. SMALLER IS NOT ALWAYS BETTER.
YOU KNOW WHAT, ADRIEN? YOU'RE RIGHT. BETTER TO KEEP AN EYE ON HIM. IF EMERSON WANTS Q-CORE REPRESENTED IN THE DARK TOWER, WE CAN OBLIGE.
BE SURE TO TELL HIM I SAID "HI."
Y-YOU WANT ME TO GO?

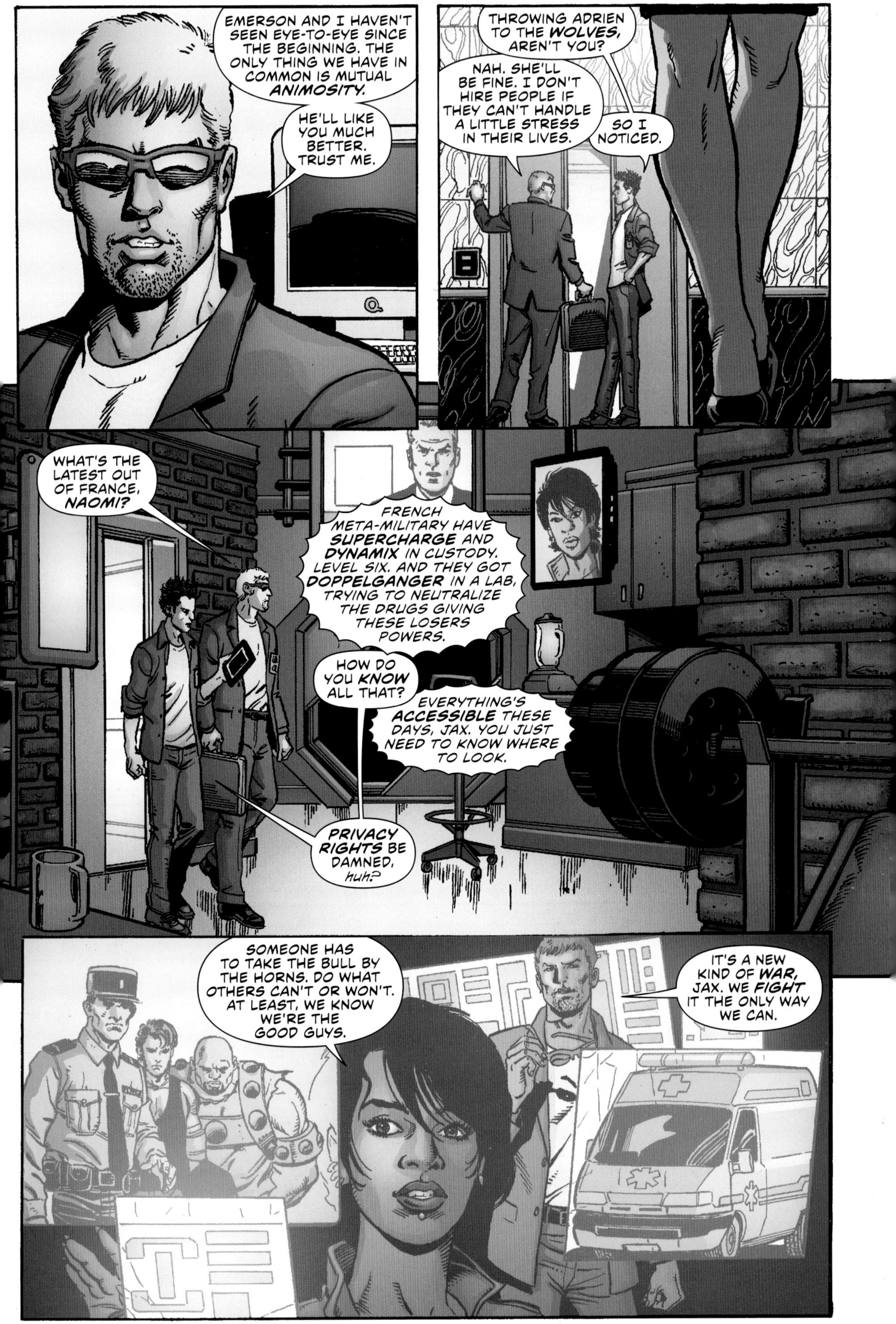
EMERSON AND I HAVEN'T SEEN EYE-TO-EYE SINCE THE BEGINNING. THE ONLY THING WE HAVE IN COMMON IS MUTUAL ANIMOSITY.
HE'LL LIKE YOU MUCH BETTER. TRUST ME.
THROWING ADRIEN TO THE WOLVES, AREN'T YOU?
NAH. SHE'LL BE FINE. I DON'T HIRE PEOPLE IF THEY CAN'T HANDLE A LITTLE STRESS IN THEIR LIVES.
SO I NOTICED.
WHAT'S THE LATEST OUT OF FRANCE, NAOMI?
FRENCH META-MILITARY HAVE SUPERCHARGE AND DYNAMIX IN CUSTODY. LEVEL SIX. AND THEY GOT DOPPELGANGER IN A LAB, TRYING TO NEUTRALIZE THE DRUGS GIVING THESE LOSERS POWERS.
HOW DO YOU KNOW ALL THAT?
EVERYTHING'S ACCESSIBLE THESE DAYS, JAX. YOU JUST NEED TO KNOW WHERE TO LOOK.
PRIVACY RIGHTS BE DAMNED, huh?
SOMEONE HAS TO TAKE THE BULL BY THE HORNS. DO WHAT OTHERS CAN'T OR WON'T. AT LEAST, WE KNOW WE'RE THE GOOD GUYS.
IT'S A NEW KIND OF WAR, JAX. WE FIGHT IT THE ONLY WAY WE CAN.

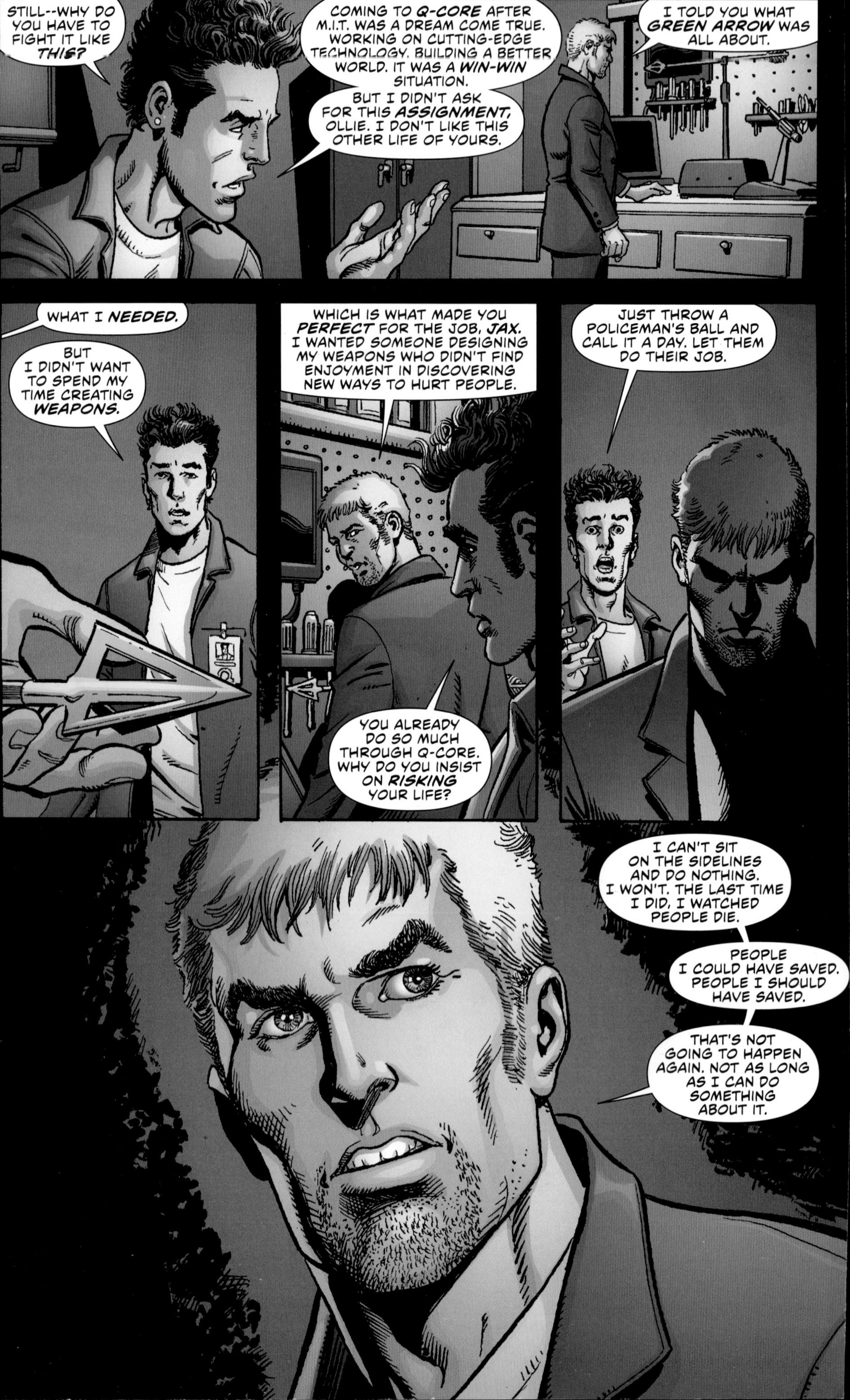

STILL--WHY DO YOU HAVE TO FIGHT IT LIKE THIS?
COMING TO Q-CORE AFTER M.I.T. WAS A DREAM COME TRUE. WORKING ON CUTTING-EDGE TECHNOLOGY. BUILDING A BETTER WORLD. IT WAS A WIN-WIN SITUATION.
BUT I DIDN'T ASK FOR THIS ASSIGNMENT, OLLIE. I DON'T LIKE THIS OTHER LIFE OF YOURS.
I TOLD YOU WHAT GREEN ARROW WAS ALL ABOUT.
WHAT I NEEDED.
BUT I DIDN'T WANT TO SPEND MY TIME CREATING WEAPONS.
WHICH IS WHAT MADE YOU PERFECT FOR THE JOB, JAX. I WANTED SOMEONE DESIGNING MY WEAPONS WHO DIDN'T FIND ENJOYMENT IN DISCOVERING NEW WAYS TO HURT PEOPLE.
YOU ALREADY DO SO MUCH THROUGH Q-CORE. WHY DO YOU INSIST ON RISKING YOUR LIFE?
JUST THROW A POLICEMAN'S BALL AND CALL IT A DAY. LET THEM DO THEIR JOB.
I CAN'T SIT ON THE SIDELINES AND DO NOTHING. I WON'T. THE LAST TIME I DID, I WATCHED PEOPLE DIE.
PEOPLE I COULD HAVE SAVED. PEOPLE I SHOULD HAVE SAVED.
THAT'S NOT GOING TO HAPPEN AGAIN. NOT AS LONG AS I CAN DO SOMETHING ABOUT IT.

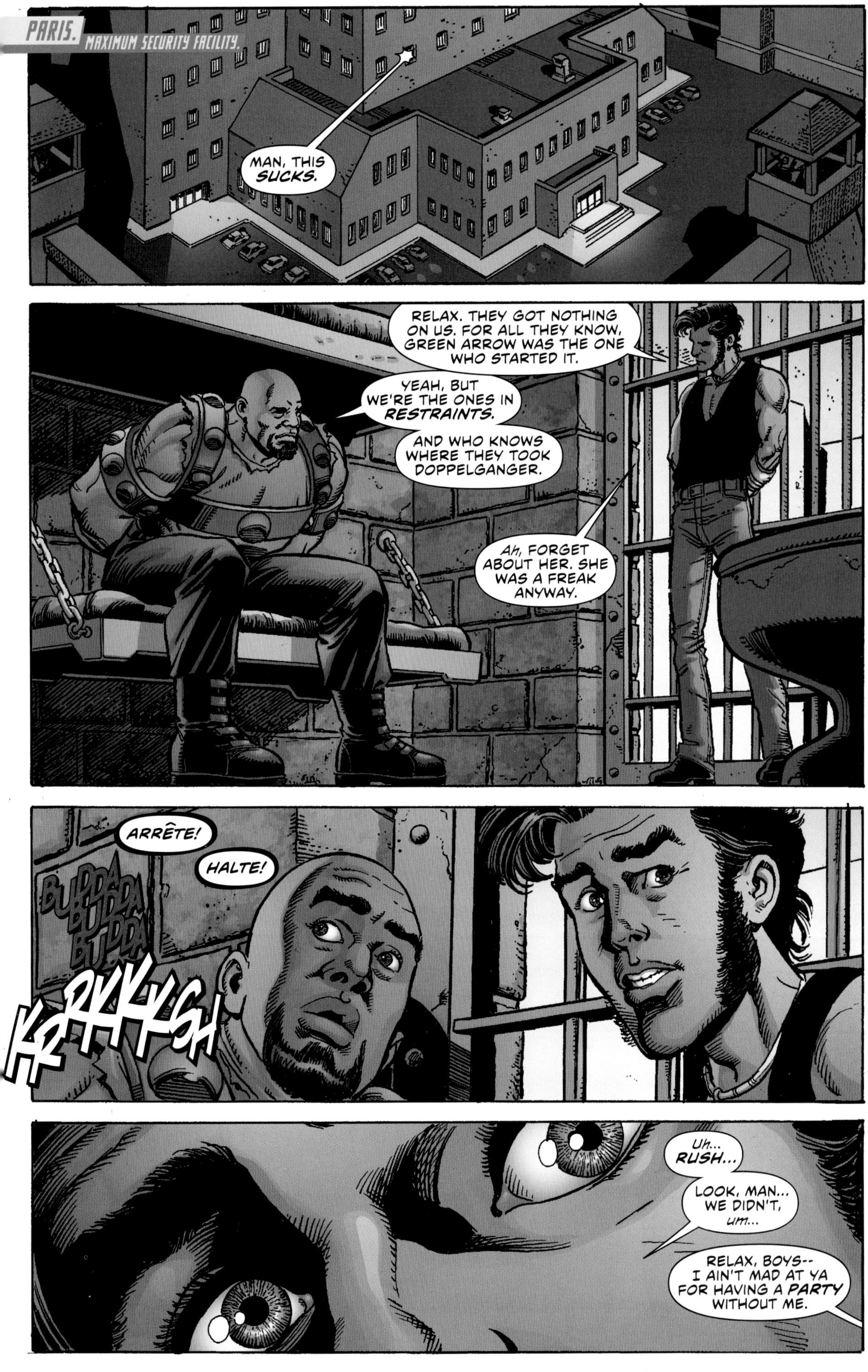
PARIS.
MAXIMUM SECURITY FACILITY.
MAN, THIS SUCKS.
RELAX. THEY GOT NOTHING ON US. FOR ALL THEY KNOW, GREEN ARROW WAS THE ONE WHO STARTED IT.
YEAH, BUT WE'RE THE ONES IN RESTRAINTS.
AND WHO KNOWS WHERE THEY TOOK DOPPELGANGER.
Ah, FORGET ABOUT HER. SHE WAS A FREAK ANYWAY.
ARRÊTE!
HALTE!
BUDDA BUDDA BUDDA
KRRKKKSH
Uh... RUSH...
LOOK, MAN... WE DIDN'T, um...
RELAX, BOYS-- I AIN'T MAD AT YA FOR HAVING A PARTY WITHOUT ME.

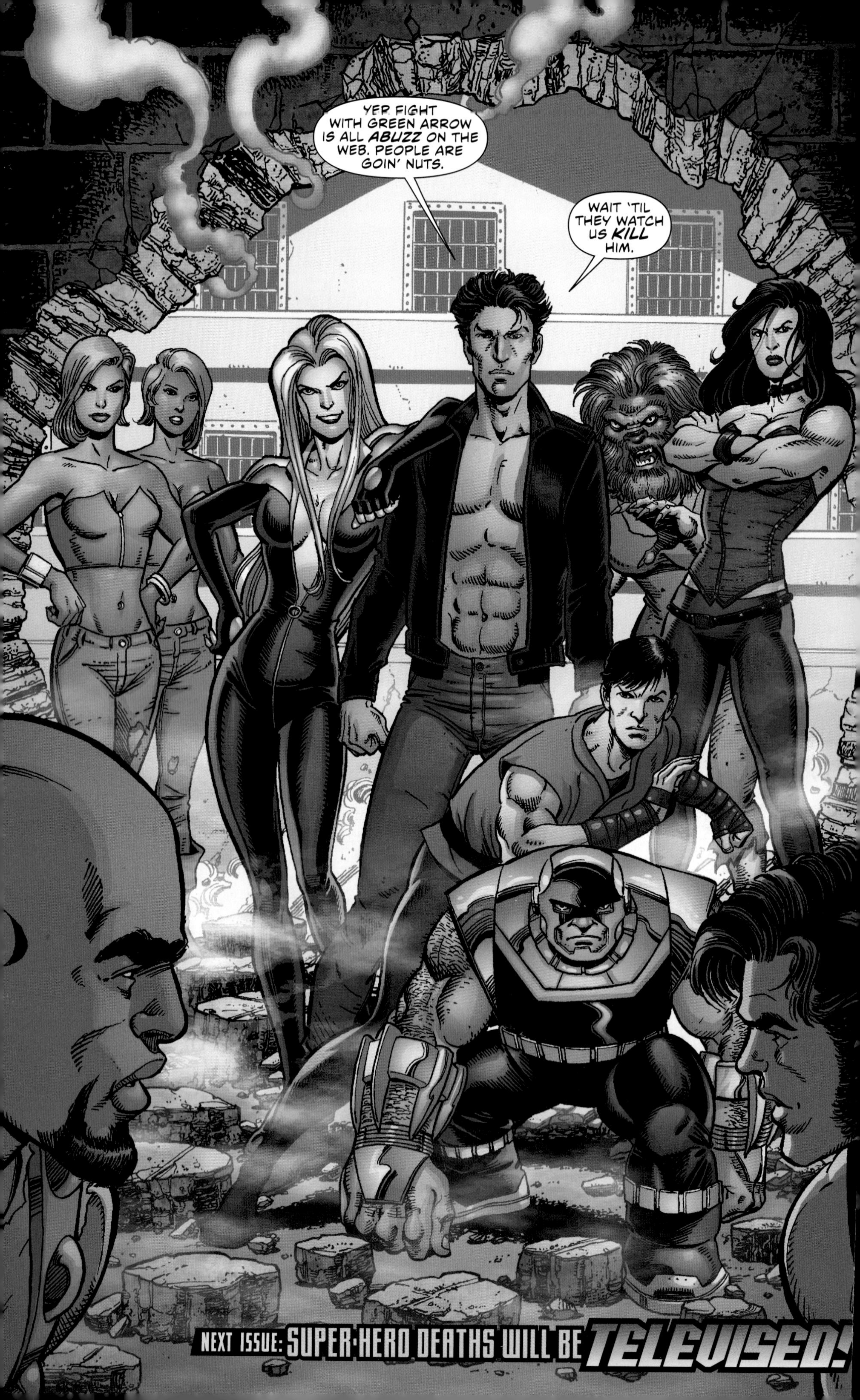
YER FIGHT WITH GREEN ARROW IS ALL ABUZZ ON THE WEB. PEOPLE ARE GOIN' NUTS.
WAIT 'TIL THEY WATCH US KILL HIM.
NEXT ISSUE: SUPER-HERO DEATHS WILL BE TELEVISED!

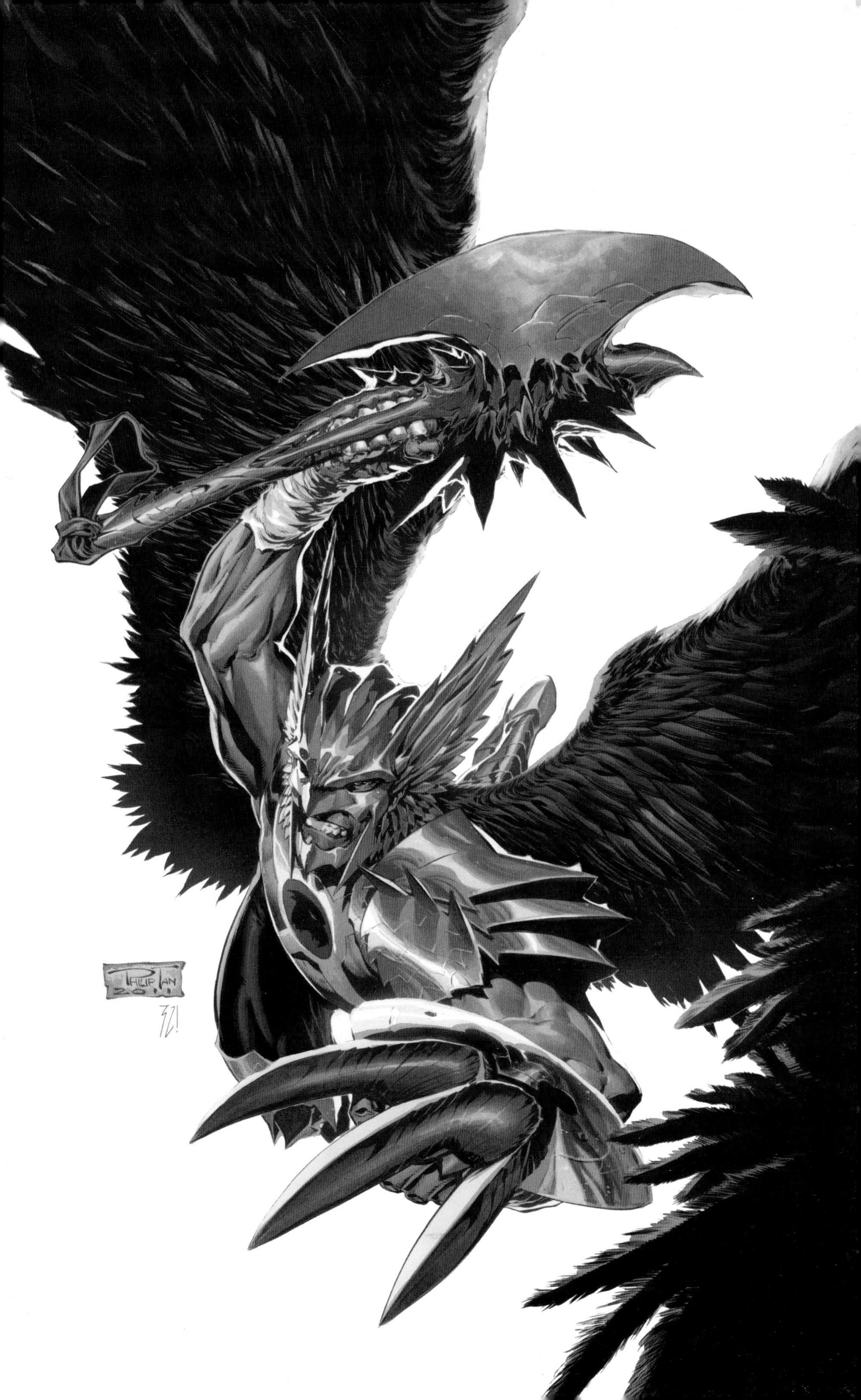
PHILIP TAN 2011

THE SAVAGE HAWKMAN

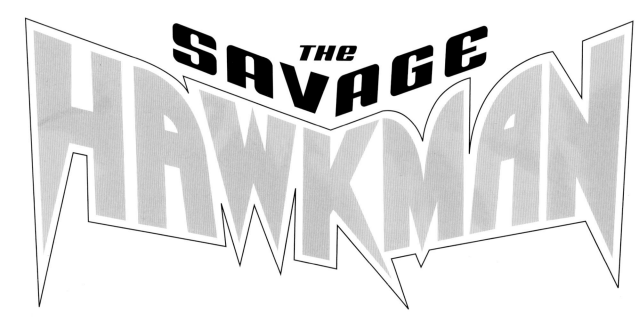

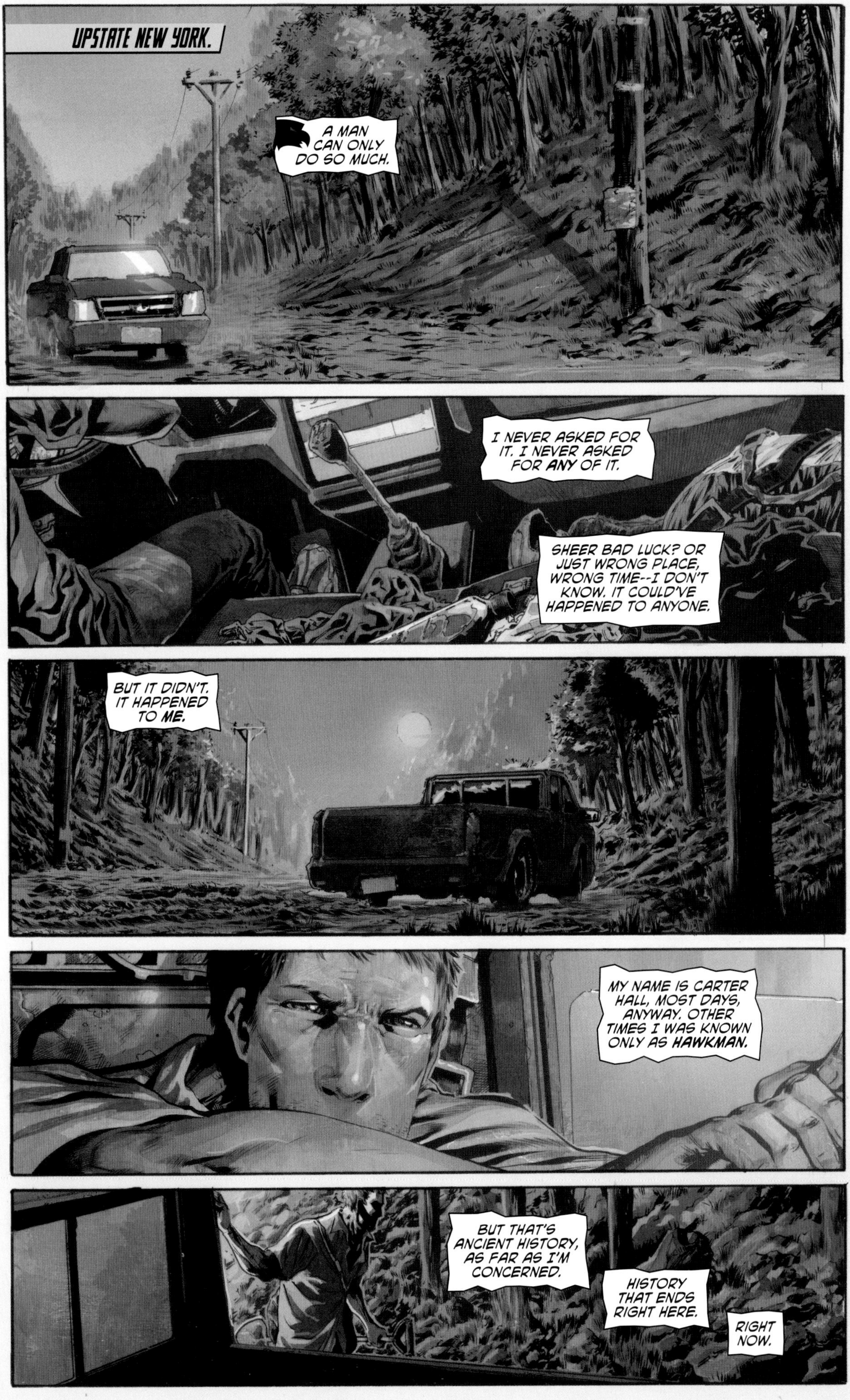
UPSTATE NEW YORK.
A MAN CAN ONLY DO SO MUCH.
I NEVER ASKED FOR IT. I NEVER ASKED FOR ANY OF IT.
SHEER BAD LUCK? OR JUST WRONG PLACE, WRONG TIME--I DON'T KNOW. IT COULD'VE HAPPENED TO ANYONE.
BUT IT DIDN'T. IT HAPPENED TO ME.
MY NAME IS CARTER HALL, MOST DAYS, ANYWAY. OTHER TIMES I WAS KNOWN ONLY AS HAWKMAN.
BUT THAT'S ANCIENT HISTORY, AS FAR AS I'M CONCERNED.
HISTORY THAT ENDS RIGHT HERE.
RIGHT NOW.

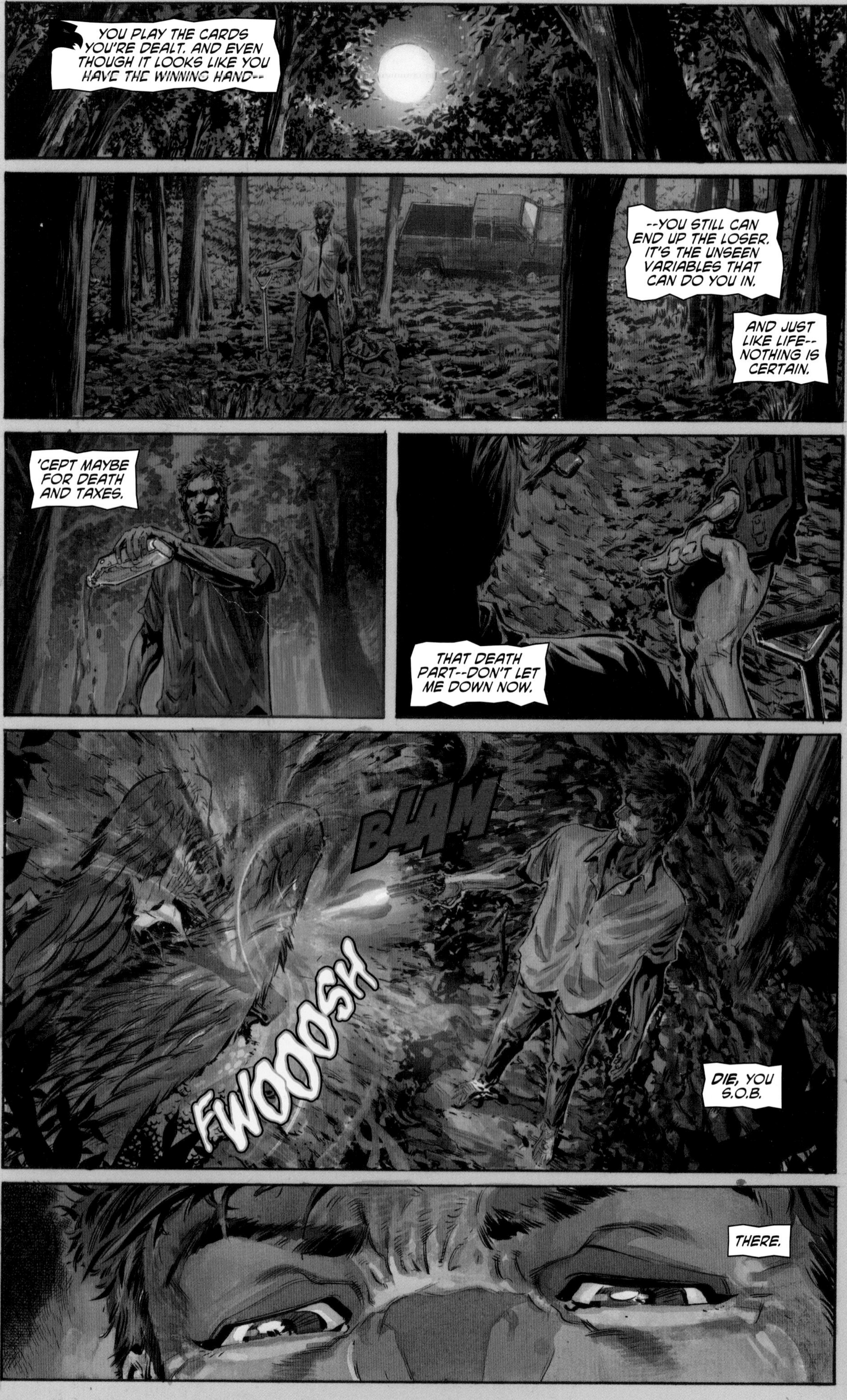
YOU PLAY THE CARDS YOU'RE DEALT. AND EVEN THOUGH IT LOOKS LIKE YOU HAVE THE WINNING HAND--
--YOU STILL CAN END UP THE LOSER. IT'S THE UNSEEN VARIABLES THAT CAN DO YOU IN.
AND JUST LIKE LIFE--NOTHING IS CERTAIN.
'CEPT MAYBE FOR DEATH AND TAXES.
THAT DEATH PART--DON'T LET ME DOWN NOW.
BLAM
FWOOOSH
DIE, YOU S.O.B.
THERE.

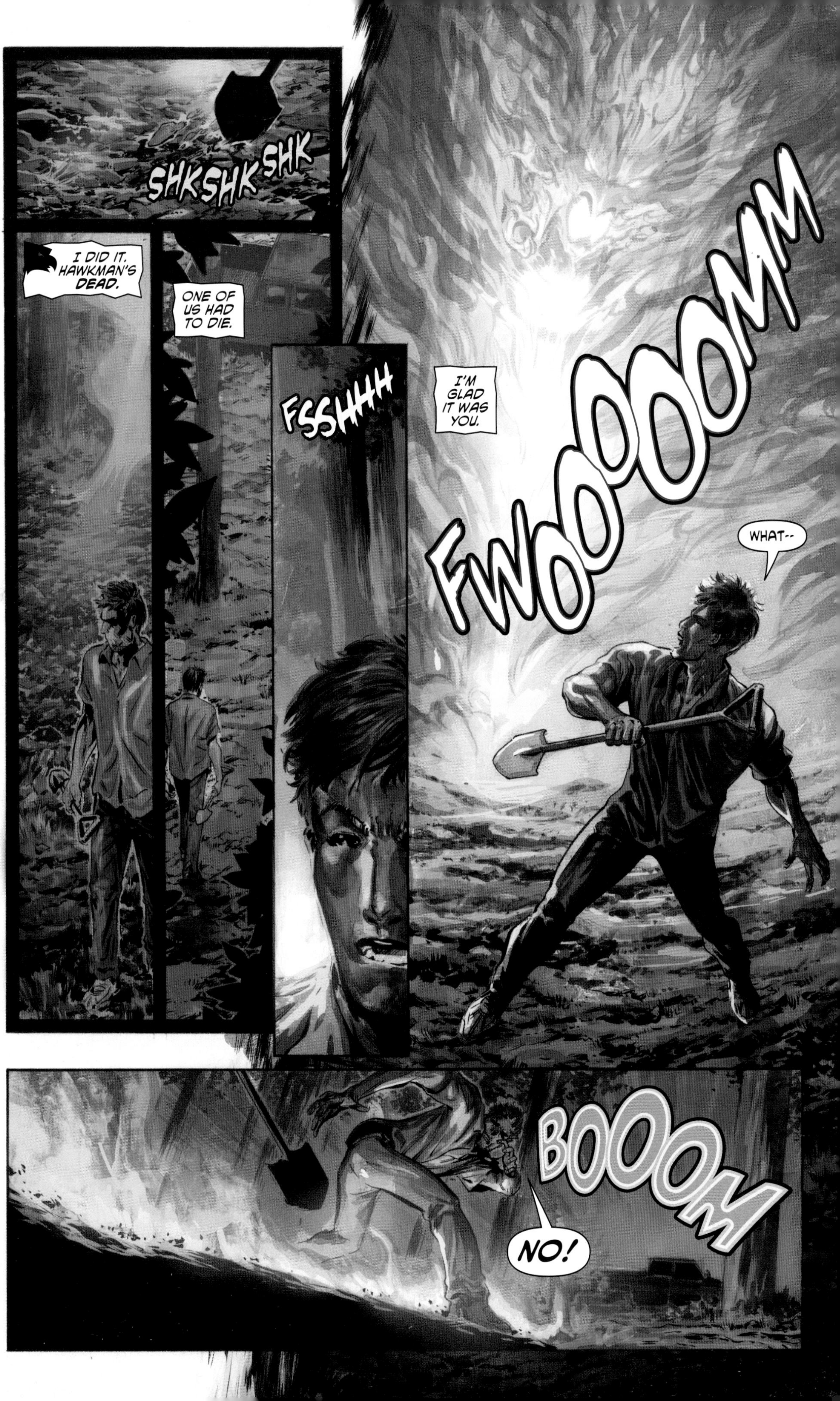
SHKSHK SHK
I DID IT. HAWKMAN'S DEAD.
ONE OF US HAD TO DIE.
FSSHHH
I'M GLAD IT WAS YOU.
FWOOOOOMM
WHAT--
BOOOM
NO!

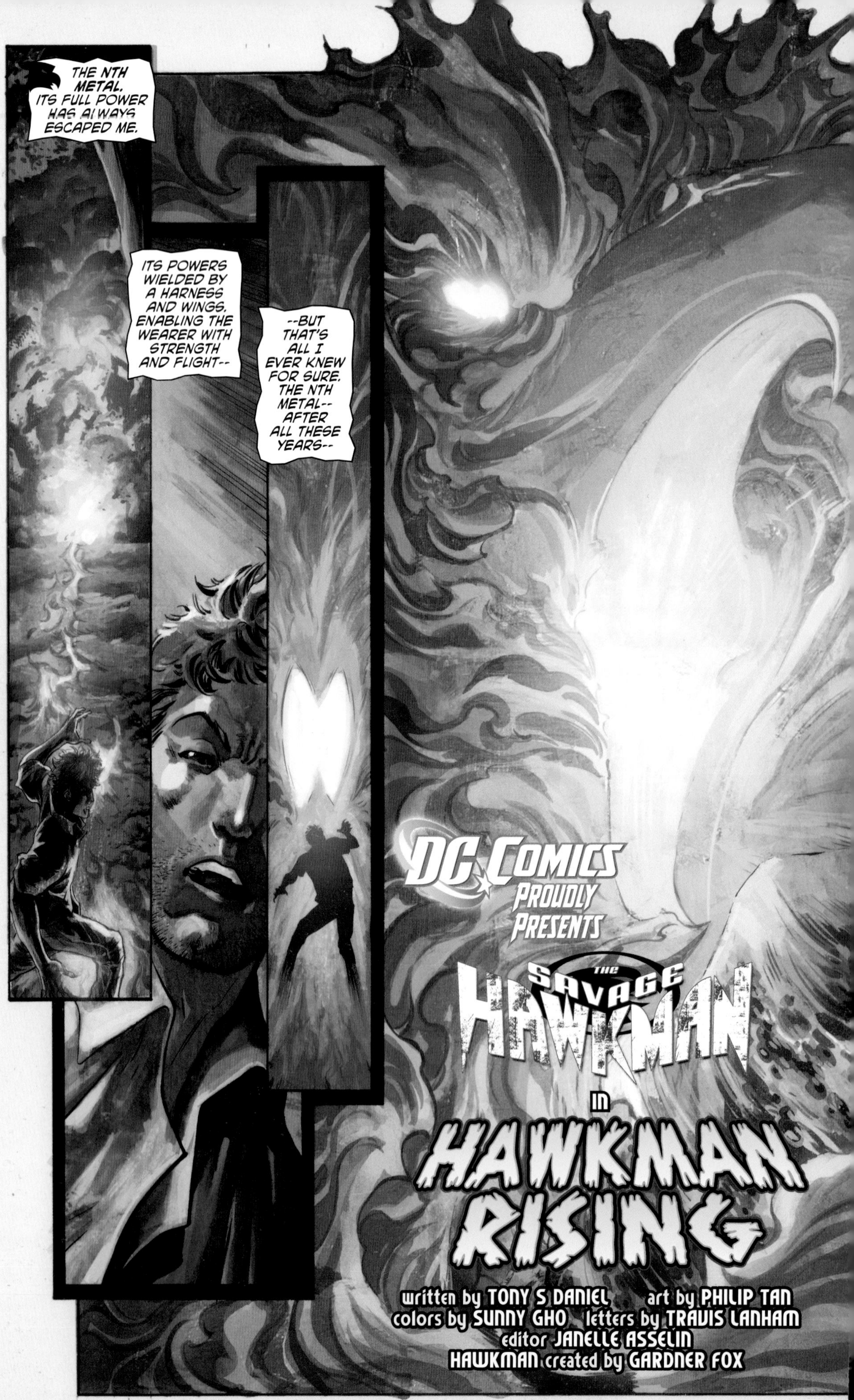
THE NTH METAL. ITS FULL POWER HAS ALWAYS ESCAPED ME.
ITS POWERS WIELDED BY A HARNESS AND WINGS, ENABLING THE WEARER WITH STRENGTH AND FLIGHT--
--BUT THAT'S ALL I EVER KNEW FOR SURE. THE NTH METAL-- AFTER ALL THESE YEARS--
DC COMICS PROUDLY PRESENTS
THE SAVAGE HAWKMAN
IN
HAWKMAN RISING
written by TONY S DANIEL art by PHILIP TAN
colors by SUNNY GHO letters by TRAVIS LANHAM
editor JANELLE ASSELIN
HAWKMAN created by GARDNER FOX

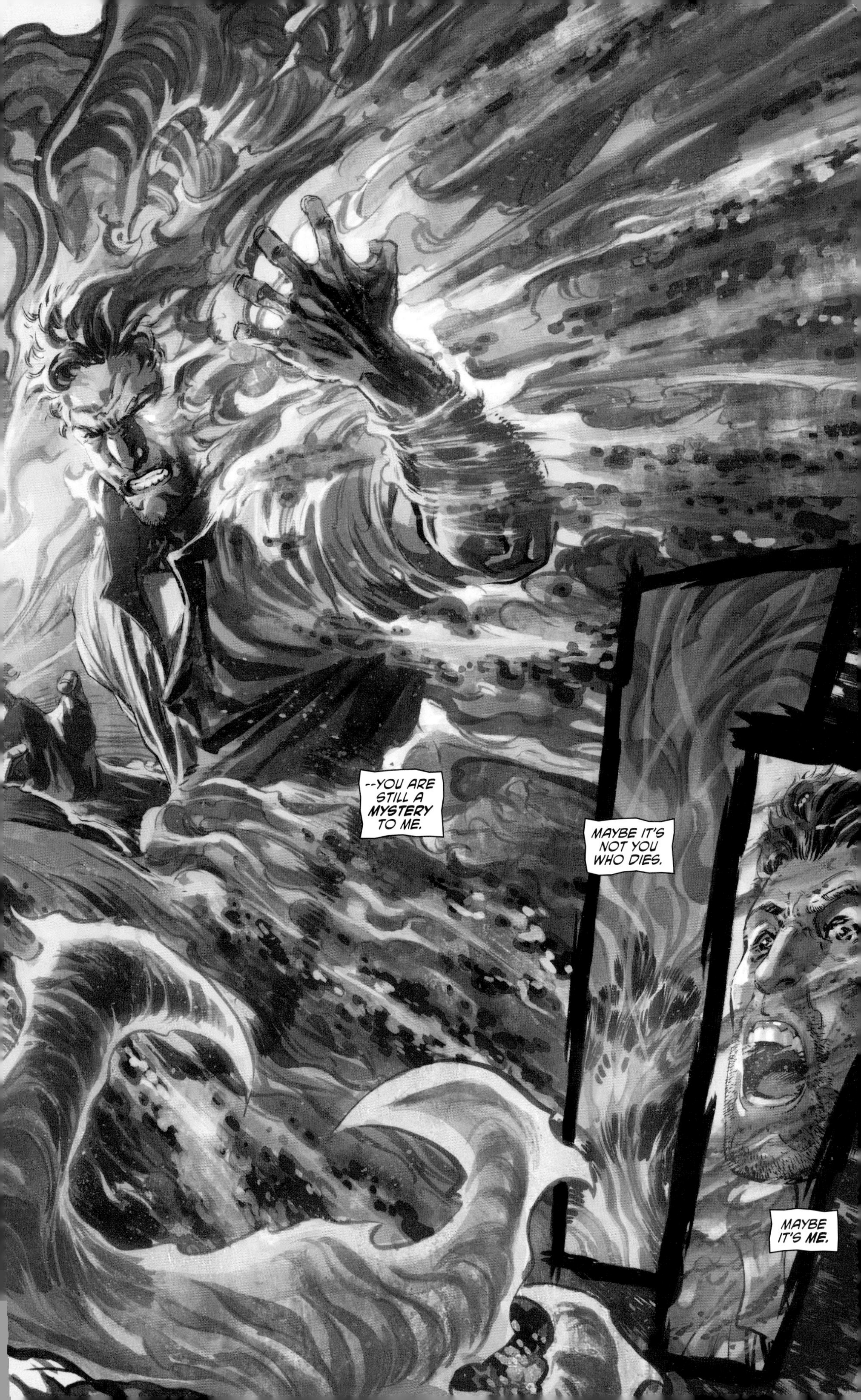
--YOU ARE STILL A MYSTERY TO ME.
MAYBE IT'S NOT YOU WHO DIES.
MAYBE IT'S ME.

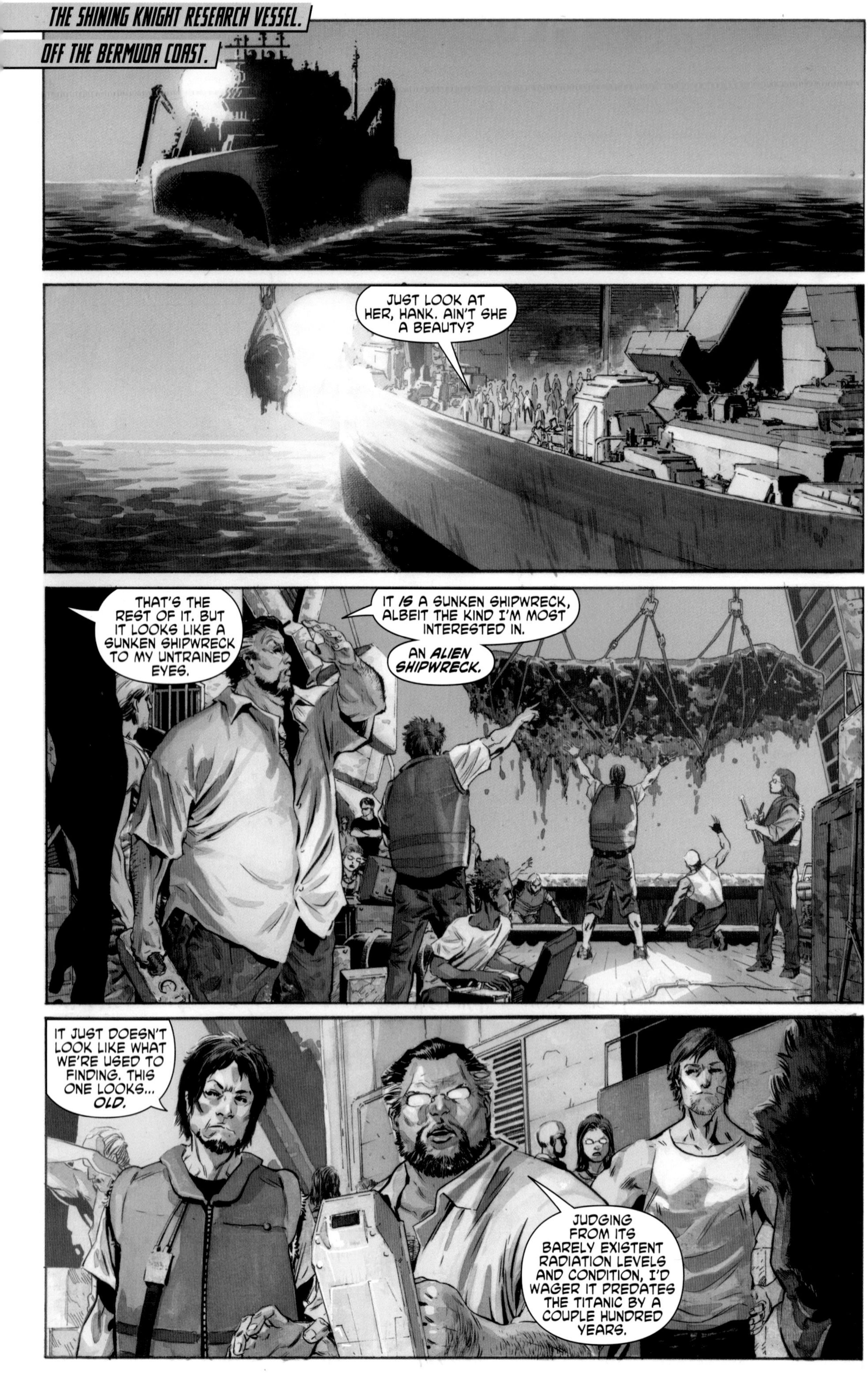
THE SHINING KNIGHT RESEARCH VESSEL.
OFF THE BERMUDA COAST.
JUST LOOK AT HER, HANK. AIN'T SHE A BEAUTY?
THAT'S THE REST OF IT. BUT IT LOOKS LIKE A SUNKEN SHIPWRECK TO MY UNTRAINED EYES.
IT IS A SUNKEN SHIPWRECK, ALBEIT THE KIND I'M MOST INTERESTED IN.
AN ALIEN SHIPWRECK.
IT JUST DOESN'T LOOK LIKE WHAT WE'RE USED TO FINDING. THIS ONE LOOKS... OLD.
JUDGING FROM ITS BARELY EXISTENT RADIATION LEVELS AND CONDITION, I'D WAGER IT PREDATES THE TITANIC BY A COUPLE HUNDRED YEARS.

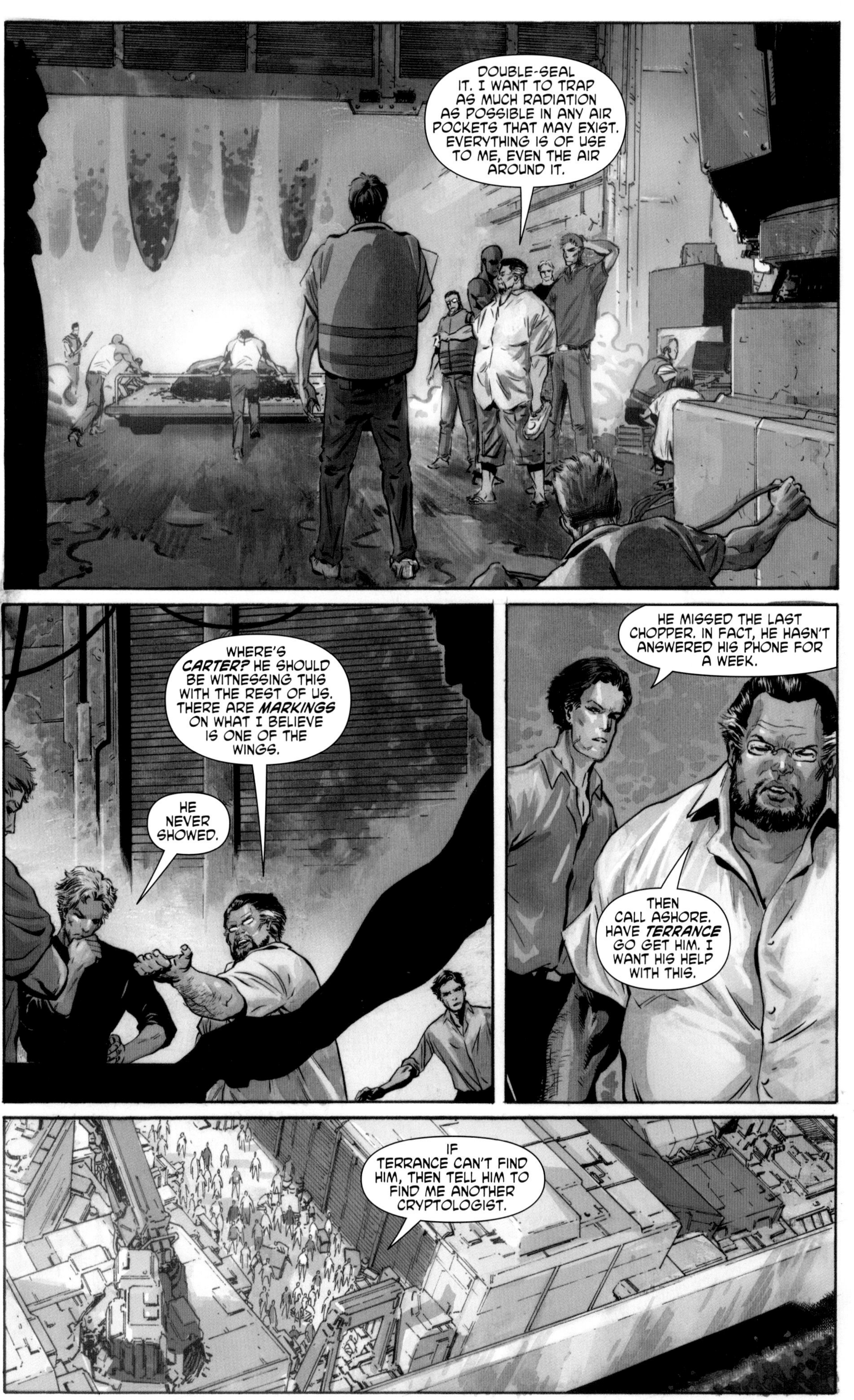

DOUBLE-SEAL IT. I WANT TO TRAP AS MUCH RADIATION AS POSSIBLE IN ANY AIR POCKETS THAT MAY EXIST. EVERYTHING IS OF USE TO ME, EVEN THE AIR AROUND IT.
WHERE'S *CARTER?* HE SHOULD BE WITNESSING THIS WITH THE REST OF US. THERE ARE *MARKINGS* ON WHAT I BELIEVE IS ONE OF THE WINGS.
HE NEVER SHOWED.
HE MISSED THE LAST CHOPPER. IN FACT, HE HASN'T ANSWERED HIS PHONE FOR A WEEK.
THEN CALL ASHORE. HAVE *TERRANCE* GO GET HIM. I WANT HIS HELP WITH THIS.
IF TERRANCE CAN'T FIND HIM, THEN TELL HIM TO FIND ME ANOTHER CRYPTOLOGIST.

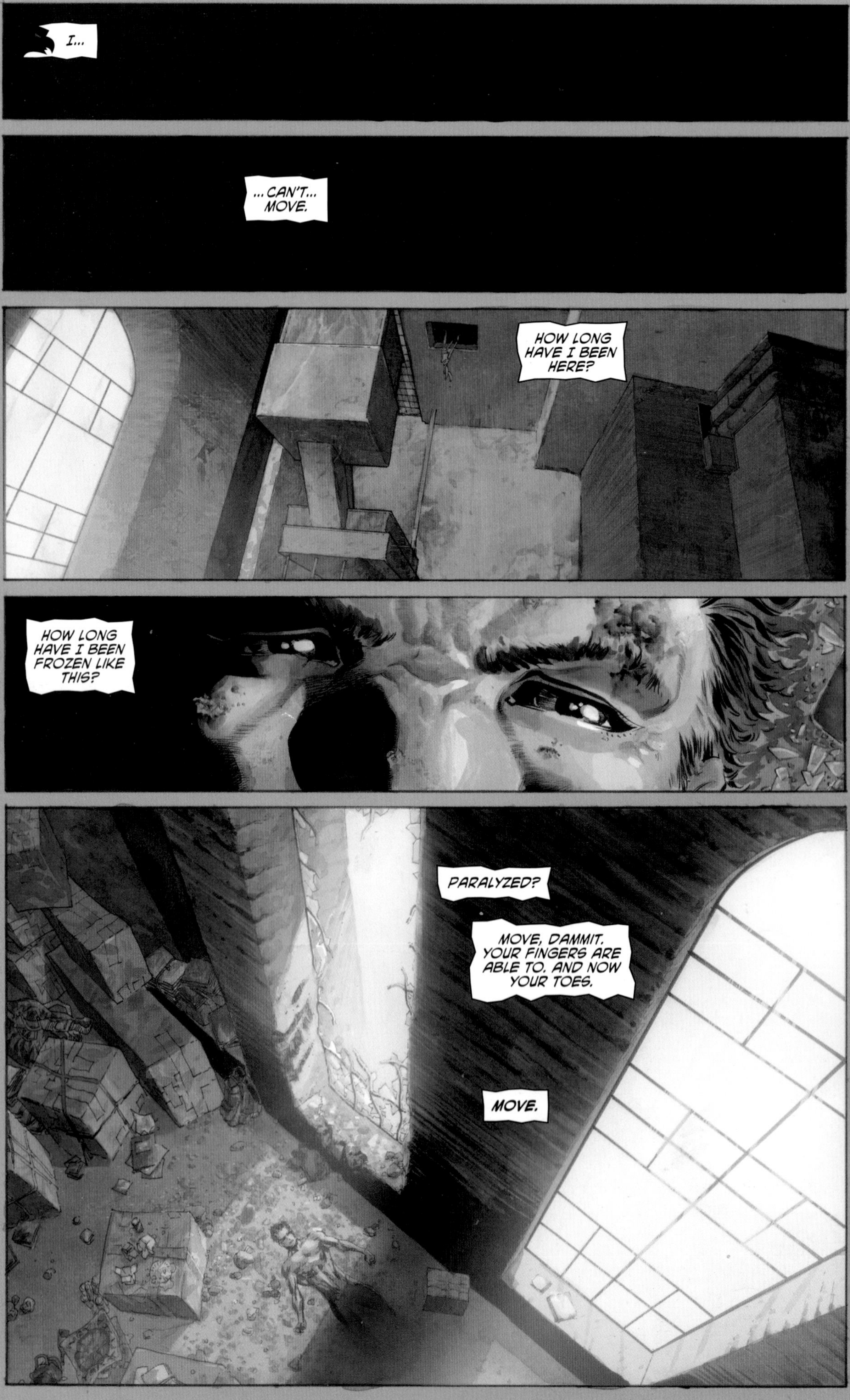
I...
...CAN'T... MOVE.
HOW LONG HAVE I BEEN HERE?
HOW LONG HAVE I BEEN FROZEN LIKE THIS?
PARALYZED?
MOVE, DAMMIT. YOUR FINGERS ARE ABLE TO. AND NOW YOUR TOES.
MOVE.

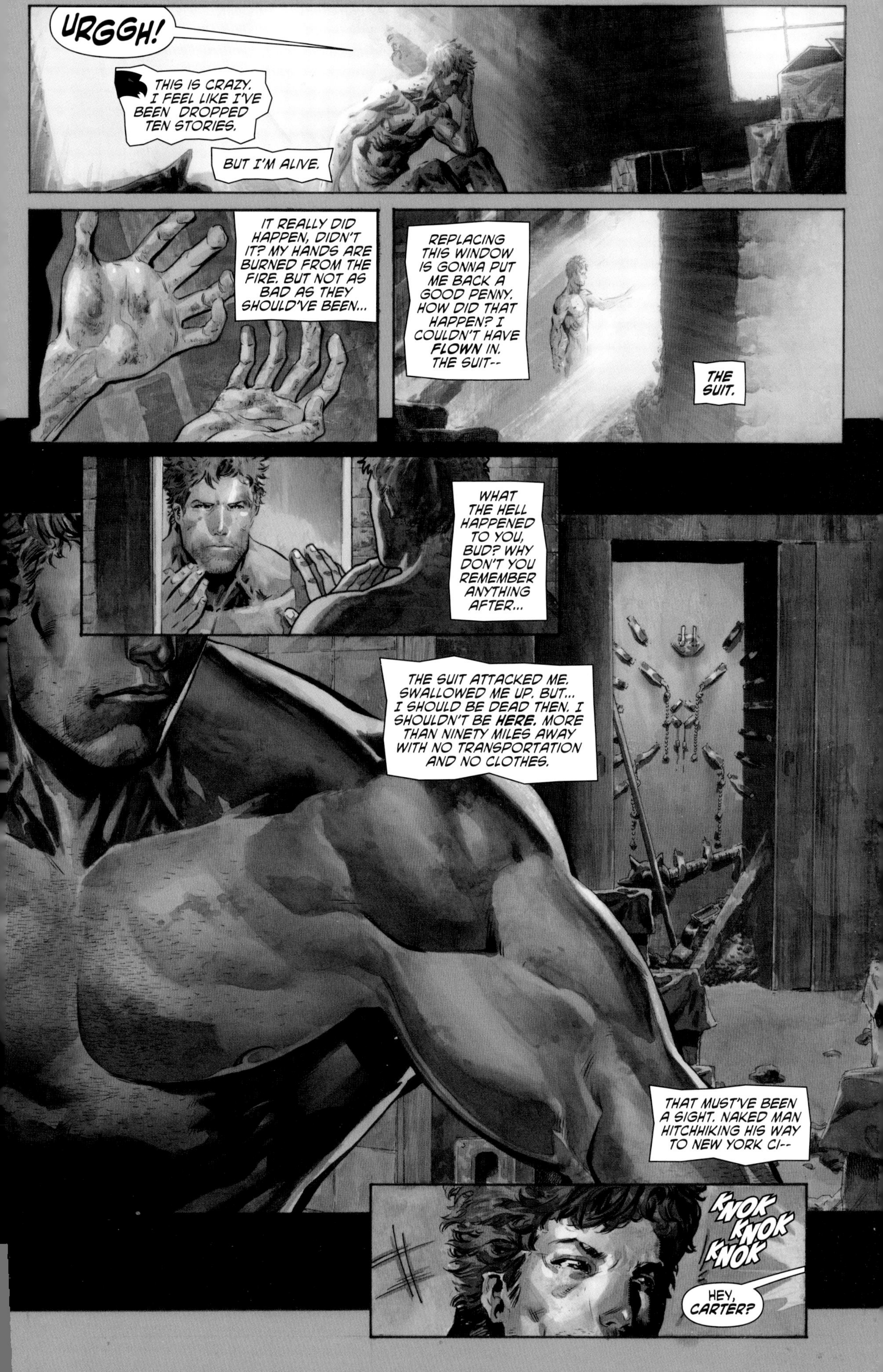
URGGH!
THIS IS CRAZY. I FEEL LIKE I'VE BEEN DROPPED TEN STORIES.
BUT I'M ALIVE.
IT REALLY DID HAPPEN, DIDN'T IT? MY HANDS ARE BURNED FROM THE FIRE. BUT NOT AS BAD AS THEY SHOULD'VE BEEN...
REPLACING THIS WINDOW IS GONNA PUT ME BACK A GOOD PENNY. HOW DID THAT HAPPEN? I COULDN'T HAVE FLOWN IN. THE SUIT--
THE SUIT.
WHAT THE HELL HAPPENED TO YOU, BUD? WHY DON'T YOU REMEMBER ANYTHING AFTER...
THE SUIT ATTACKED ME. SWALLOWED ME UP. BUT... I SHOULD BE DEAD THEN. I SHOULDN'T BE HERE. MORE THAN NINETY MILES AWAY WITH NO TRANSPORTATION AND NO CLOTHES.
THAT MUST'VE BEEN A SIGHT. NAKED MAN HITCHHIKING HIS WAY TO NEW YORK CI--
KNOK KNOK KNOK
HEY, CARTER?

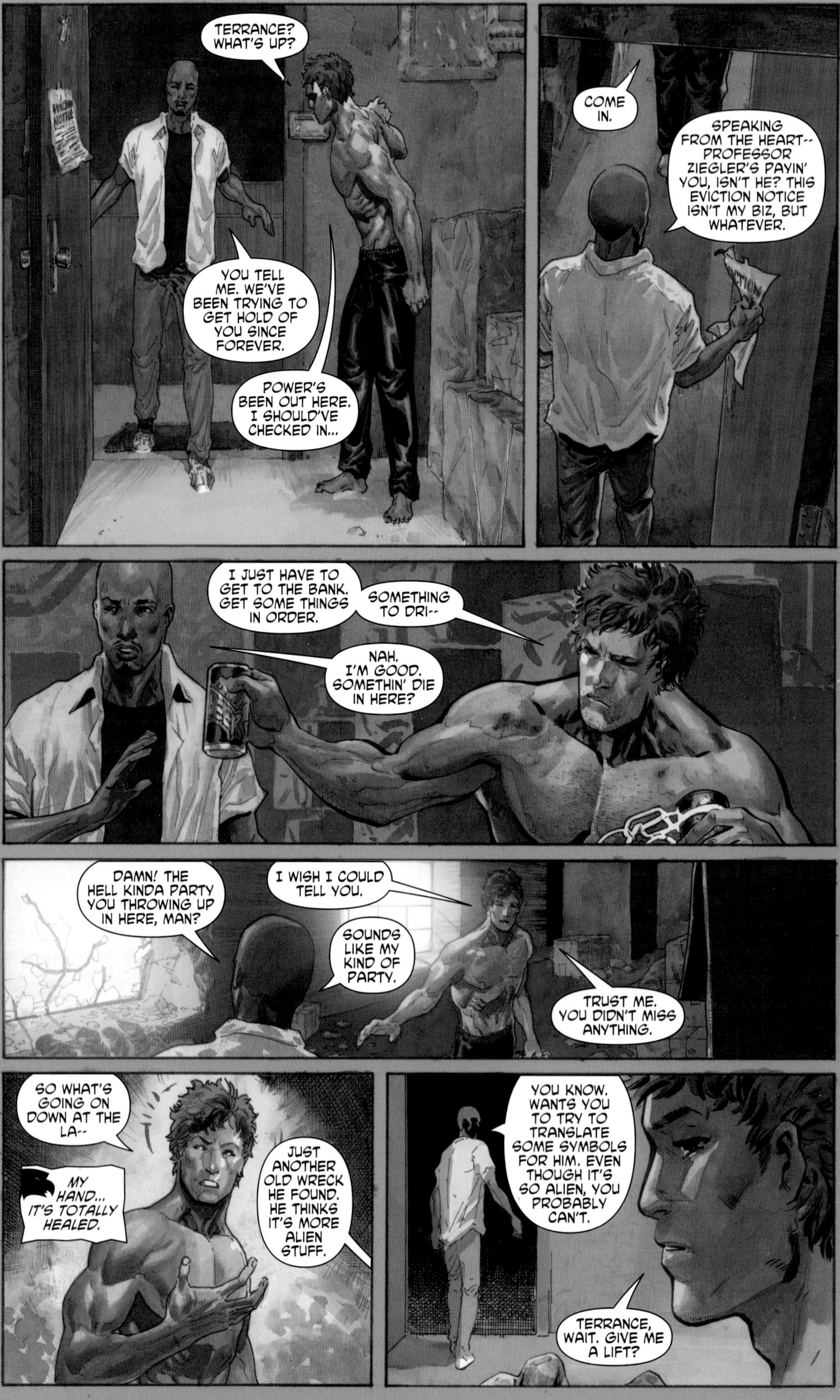
TERRANCE? WHAT'S UP?
YOU TELL ME. WE'VE BEEN TRYING TO GET HOLD OF YOU SINCE FOREVER.
POWER'S BEEN OUT HERE. I SHOULD'VE CHECKED IN...
COME IN.
SPEAKING FROM THE HEART-- PROFESSOR ZIEGLER'S PAYIN' YOU, ISN'T HE? THIS EVICTION NOTICE ISN'T MY BIZ, BUT WHATEVER.
I JUST HAVE TO GET TO THE BANK. GET SOME THINGS IN ORDER.
SOMETHING TO DRI--
NAH. I'M GOOD. SOMETHIN' DIE IN HERE?
DAMN! THE HELL KINDA PARTY YOU THROWING UP IN HERE, MAN?
I WISH I COULD TELL YOU.
SOUNDS LIKE MY KIND OF PARTY.
TRUST ME. YOU DIDN'T MISS ANYTHING.
SO WHAT'S GOING ON DOWN AT THE LA--
MY HAND... IT'S TOTALLY HEALED.
JUST ANOTHER OLD WRECK HE FOUND. HE THINKS IT'S MORE ALIEN STUFF.
YOU KNOW. WANTS YOU TO TRY TO TRANSLATE SOME SYMBOLS FOR HIM. EVEN THOUGH IT'S SO ALIEN, YOU PROBABLY CAN'T.
TERRANCE, WAIT. GIVE ME A LIFT?

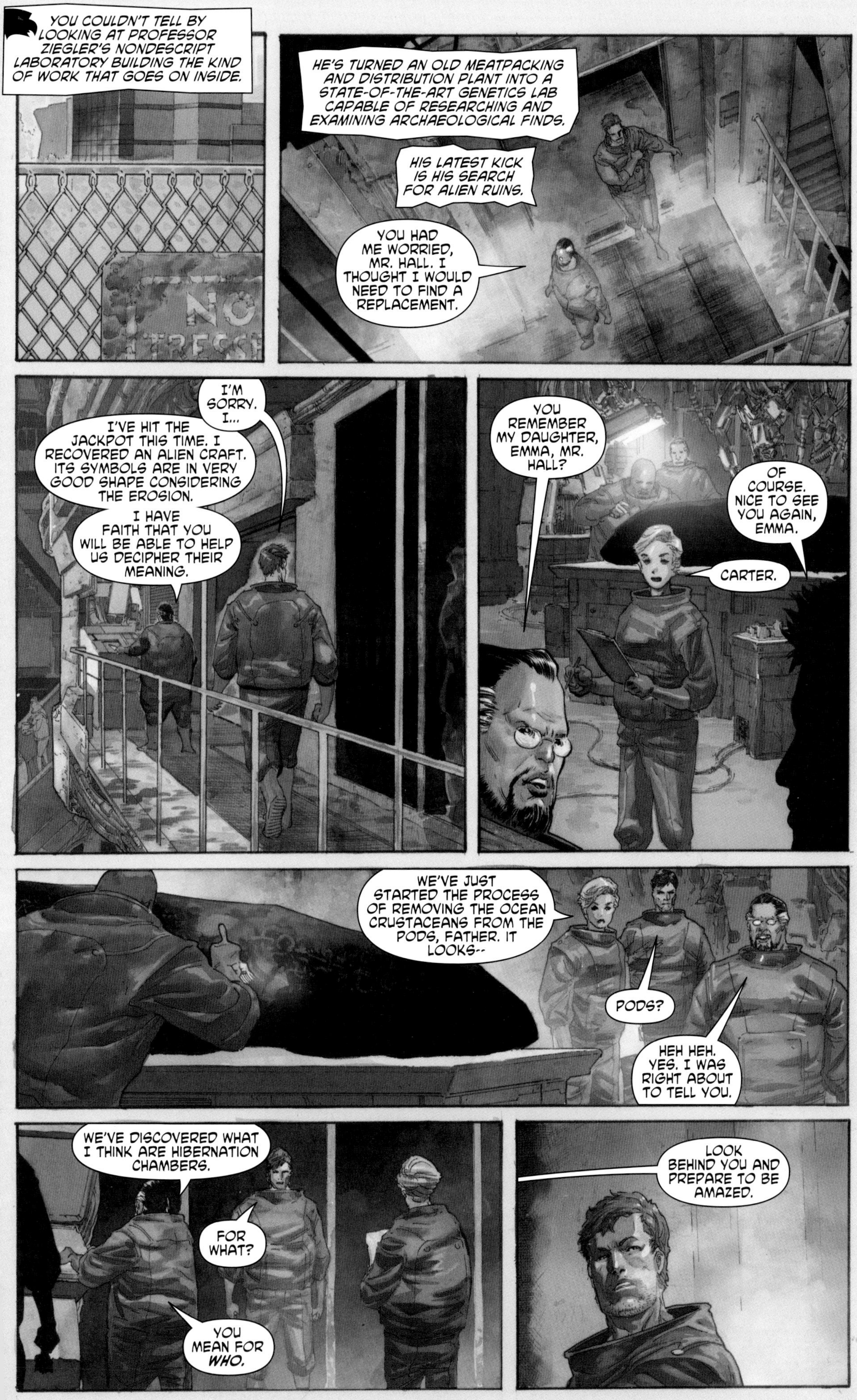

YOU COULDN'T TELL BY LOOKING AT PROFESSOR ZIEGLER'S NONDESCRIPT LABORATORY BUILDING THE KIND OF WORK THAT GOES ON INSIDE.
NO TRESP
HE'S TURNED AN OLD MEATPACKING AND DISTRIBUTION PLANT INTO A STATE-OF-THE-ART GENETICS LAB CAPABLE OF RESEARCHING AND EXAMINING ARCHAEOLOGICAL FINDS.
HIS LATEST KICK IS HIS SEARCH FOR ALIEN RUINS.
YOU HAD ME WORRIED, MR. HALL. I THOUGHT I WOULD NEED TO FIND A REPLACEMENT.
I'M SORRY. I...
I'VE HIT THE JACKPOT THIS TIME. I RECOVERED AN ALIEN CRAFT. ITS SYMBOLS ARE IN VERY GOOD SHAPE CONSIDERING THE EROSION.
I HAVE FAITH THAT YOU WILL BE ABLE TO HELP US DECIPHER THEIR MEANING.
YOU REMEMBER MY DAUGHTER, EMMA, MR. HALL?
OF COURSE. NICE TO SEE YOU AGAIN, EMMA.
CARTER.
WE'VE JUST STARTED THE PROCESS OF REMOVING THE OCEAN CRUSTACEANS FROM THE PODS, FATHER. IT LOOKS--
PODS?
HEH HEH. YES. I WAS RIGHT ABOUT TO TELL YOU.
WE'VE DISCOVERED WHAT I THINK ARE HIBERNATION CHAMBERS.
FOR WHAT?
YOU MEAN FOR *WHO.*
LOOK BEHIND YOU AND PREPARE TO BE AMAZED.

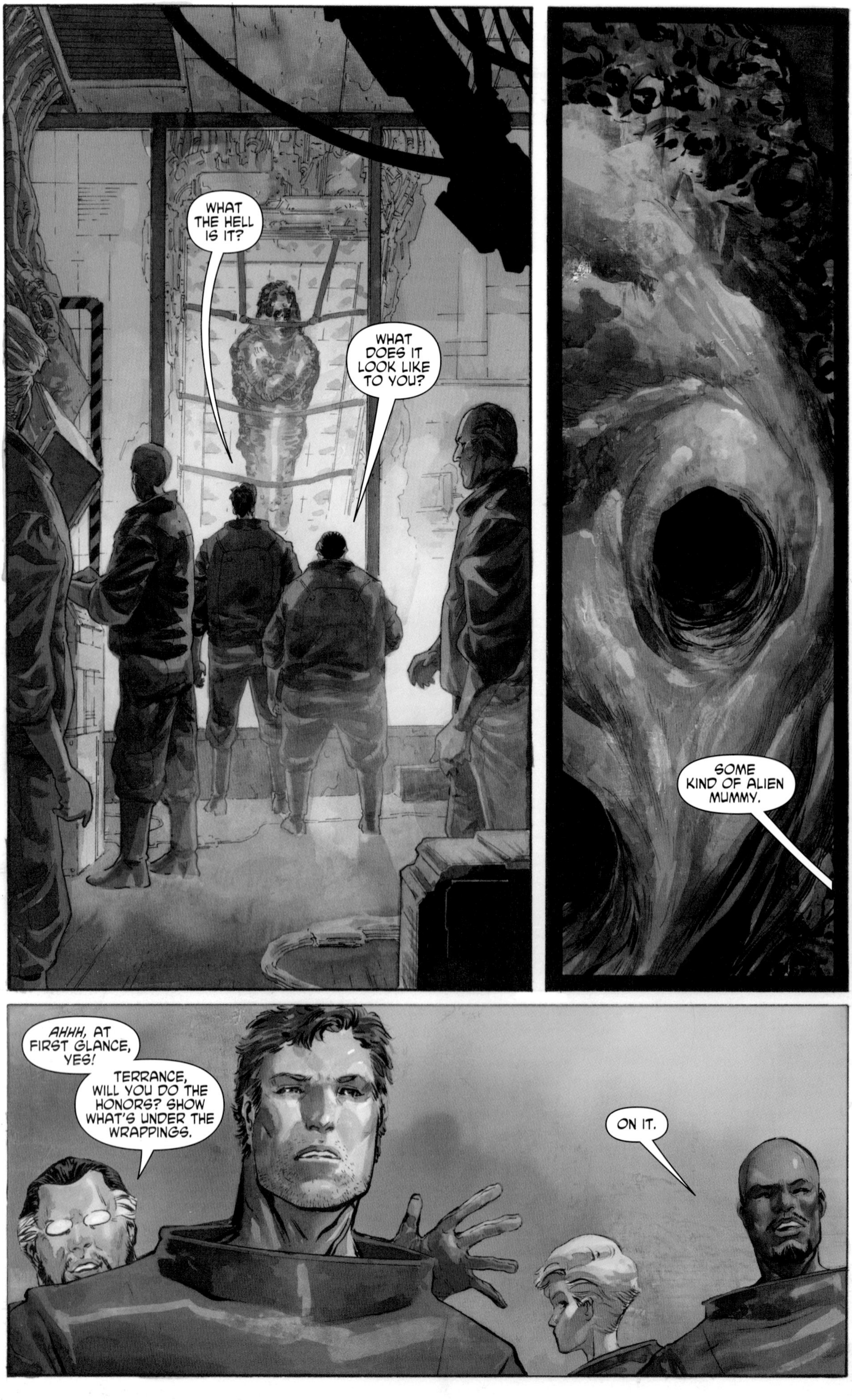
WHAT THE HELL IS IT?
WHAT DOES IT LOOK LIKE TO YOU?
SOME KIND OF ALIEN MUMMY.
AHHH, AT FIRST GLANCE, YES!
TERRANCE, WILL YOU DO THE HONORS? SHOW WHAT'S UNDER THE WRAPPINGS.
ON IT.

IT-- IT LOOKS HUMAN!

WE'RE TAKING A DNA SAMPLE RIGHT NOW. WE'LL KNOW SHORTLY IF INDEED THIS IS A HUMAN BEING.

IT COULD BE AN ALIEN ABDUCTION VICTIM. IF THAT'S THE CASE, YOU MAY HAVE STUMBLED UPON A TREASURE TROVE OF ALIEN/HUMAN CONTACT INFORMATION.

YES, ESPECIALLY IF THEY SUBJECTED THE VICTIM TO ANY SORT OF TESTING. I AM GIDDY WITH--

PROFESSOR ZIEGLER! THE SAMPLE! IT'S DOING SOMETHING!

DAD, LOOK!

DR. BENSON! PUT IT DOWN AND COME OUT!

I--I CAN'T!

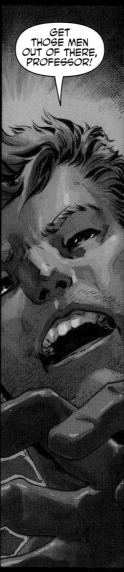
GET THOSE MEN OUT OF THERE, PROFESSOR!

CLSH

GARRRGHH!

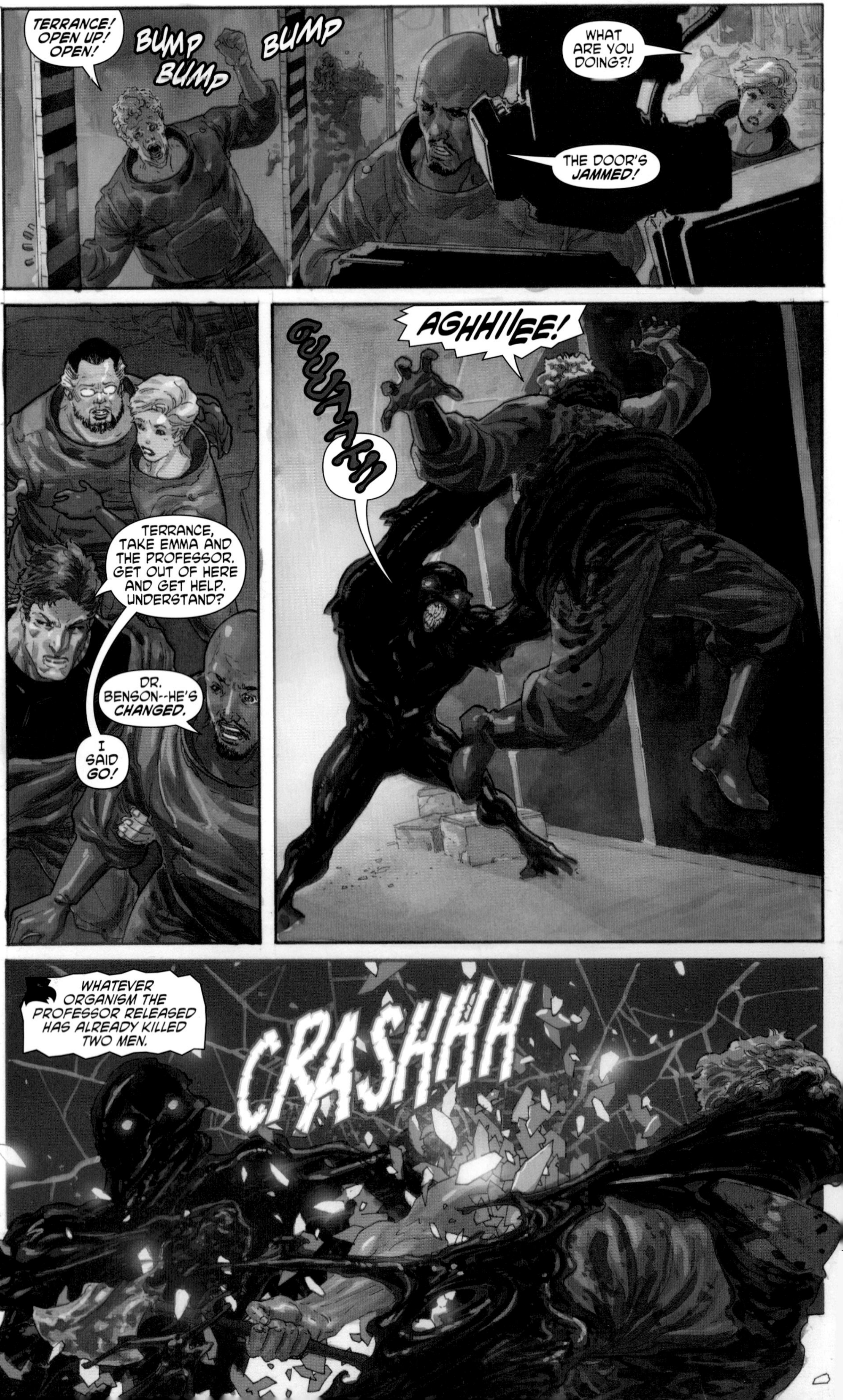
TERRANCE! OPEN UP! OPEN!
BUMP BUMP
BUMP
WHAT ARE YOU DOING?!
THE DOOR'S JAMMED!
TERRANCE, TAKE EMMA AND THE PROFESSOR. GET OUT OF HERE AND GET HELP. UNDERSTAND?
DR. BENSON--HE'S CHANGED.
I SAID GO!
AGHHIIEE!
GUUUNNKH
WHATEVER ORGANISM THE PROFESSOR RELEASED HAS ALREADY KILLED TWO MEN.
CRASHHH

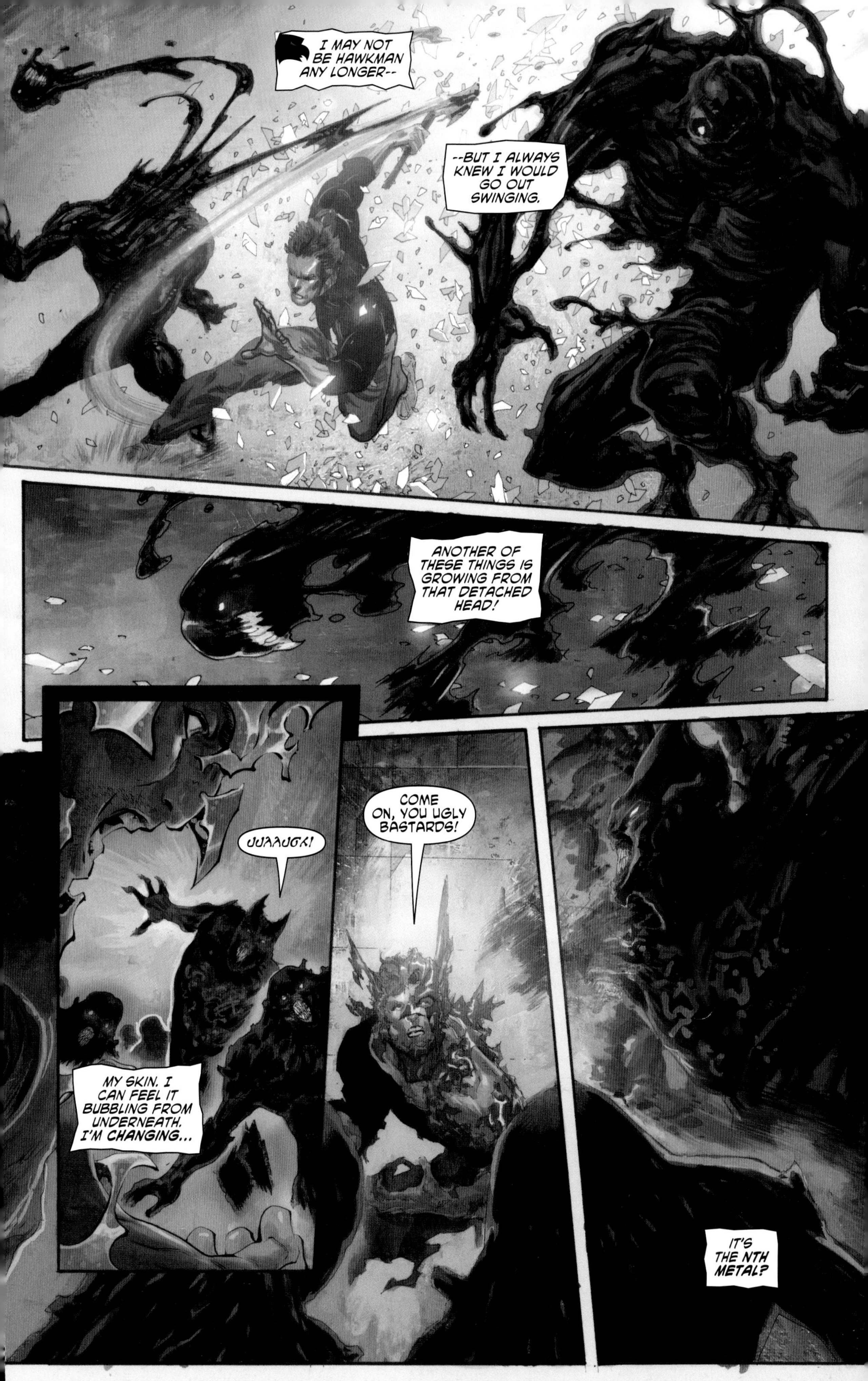
I MAY NOT BE HAWKMAN ANY LONGER--
--BUT I ALWAYS KNEW I WOULD GO OUT SWINGING.
ANOTHER OF THESE THINGS IS GROWING FROM THAT DETACHED HEAD!
UUAAUGK!
MY SKIN. I CAN FEEL IT BUBBLING FROM UNDERNEATH. I'M CHANGING...
COME ON, YOU UGLY BASTARDS!
IT'S THE NTH METAL?

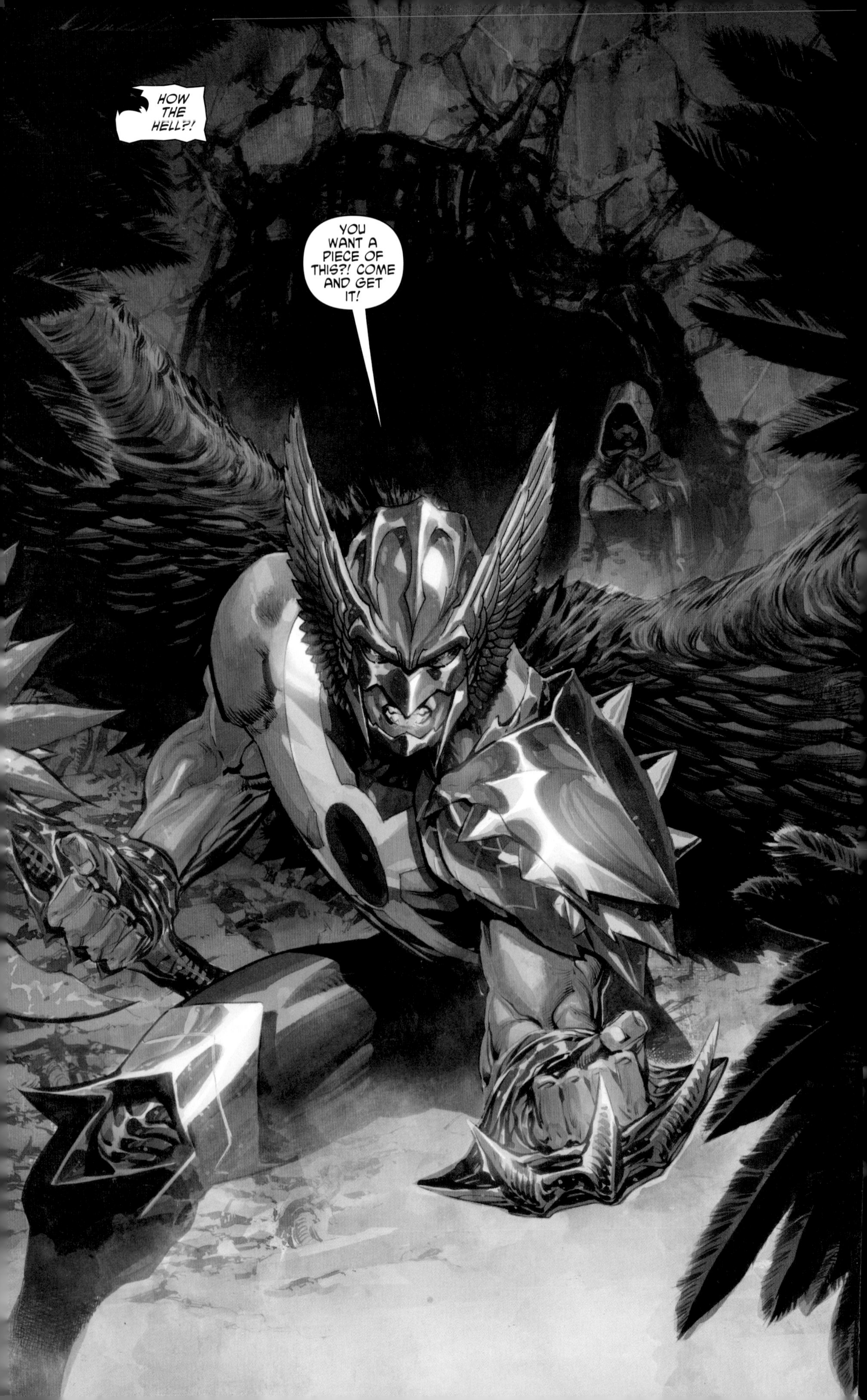
HOW THE HELL?!
YOU WANT A PIECE OF THIS?! COME AND GET IT!

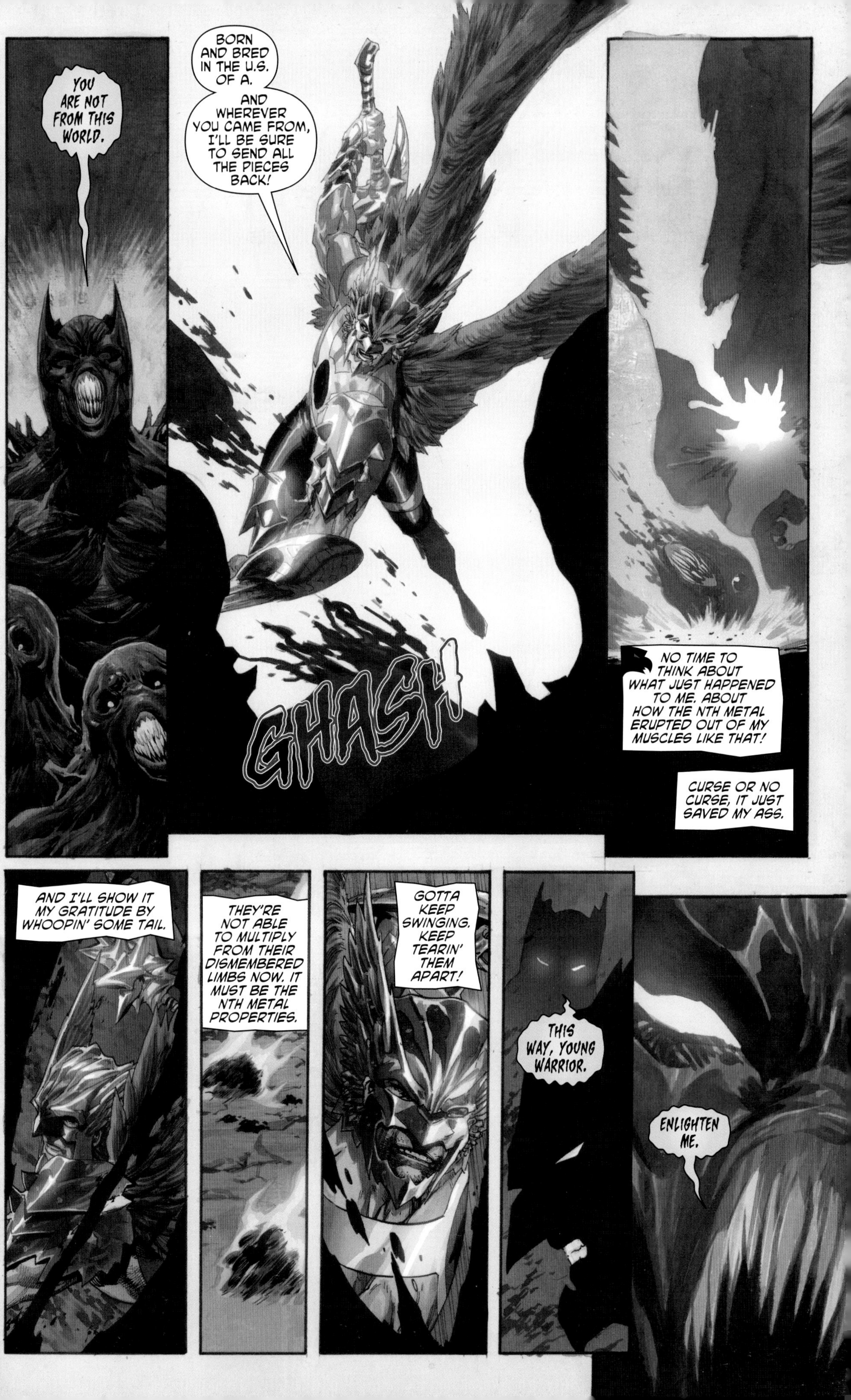
YOU ARE NOT FROM THIS WORLD.
BORN AND BRED IN THE U.S. OF A.
AND WHEREVER YOU CAME FROM, I'LL BE SURE TO SEND ALL THE PIECES BACK!
GHASH
NO TIME TO THINK ABOUT WHAT JUST HAPPENED TO ME. ABOUT HOW THE NTH METAL ERUPTED OUT OF MY MUSCLES LIKE THAT!
CURSE OR NO CURSE, IT JUST SAVED MY ASS.
AND I'LL SHOW IT MY GRATITUDE BY WHOOPIN' SOME TAIL.
THEY'RE NOT ABLE TO MULTIPLY FROM THEIR DISMEMBERED LIMBS NOW. IT MUST BE THE NTH METAL PROPERTIES.
GOTTA KEEP SWINGING. KEEP TEARIN' THEM APART!
THIS WAY, YOUNG WARRIOR.
ENLIGHTEN ME.

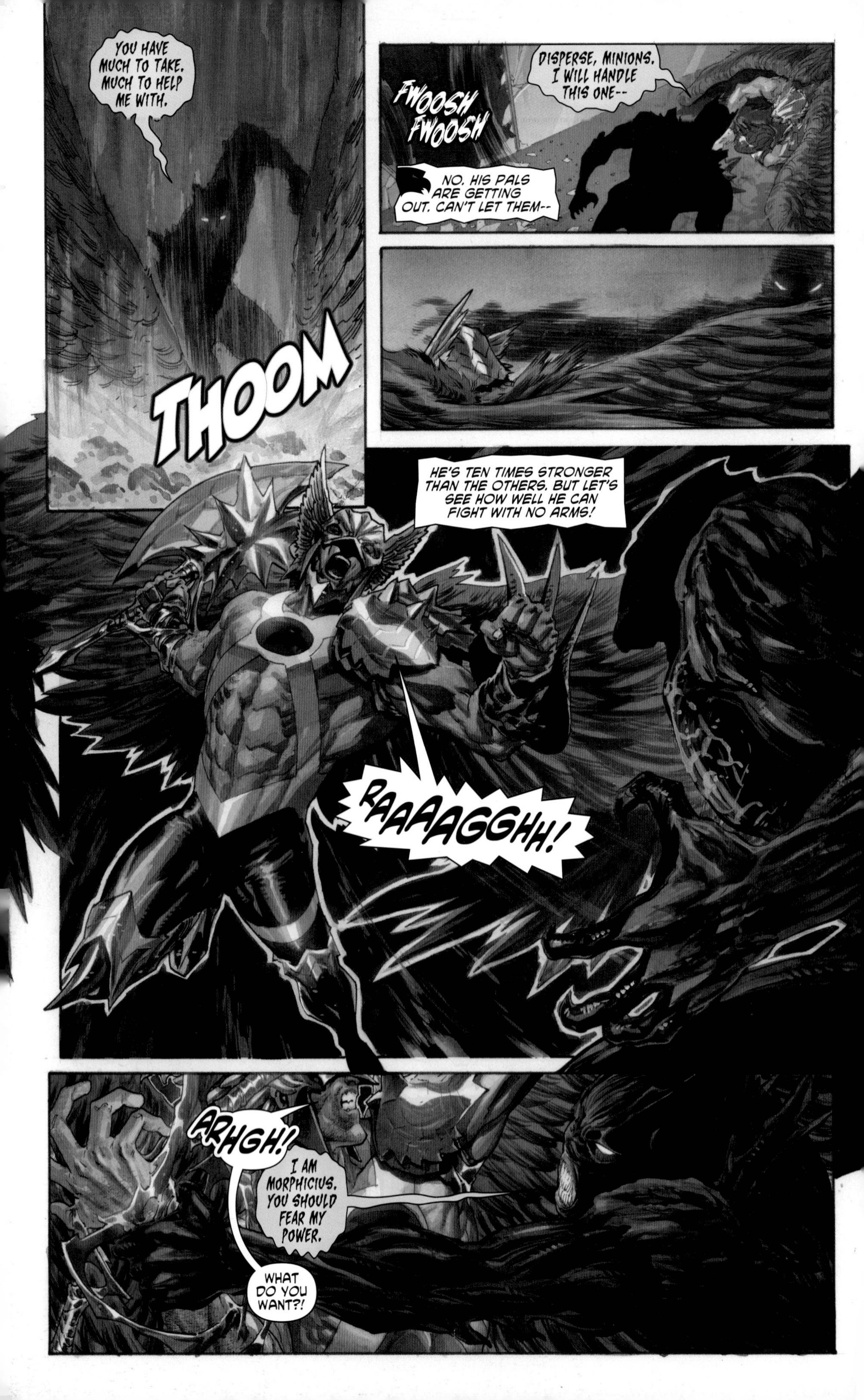
YOU HAVE MUCH TO TAKE. MUCH TO HELP ME WITH.
THOOM
FWOOSH FWOOSH
DISPERSE, MINIONS. I WILL HANDLE THIS ONE--
NO. HIS PALS ARE GETTING OUT. CAN'T LET THEM--
HE'S TEN TIMES STRONGER THAN THE OTHERS. BUT LET'S SEE HOW WELL HE CAN FIGHT WITH NO ARMS!
RAAAAGGHH!
ARHGH!
I AM MORPHICIUS. YOU SHOULD FEAR MY POWER.
WHAT DO YOU WANT?!

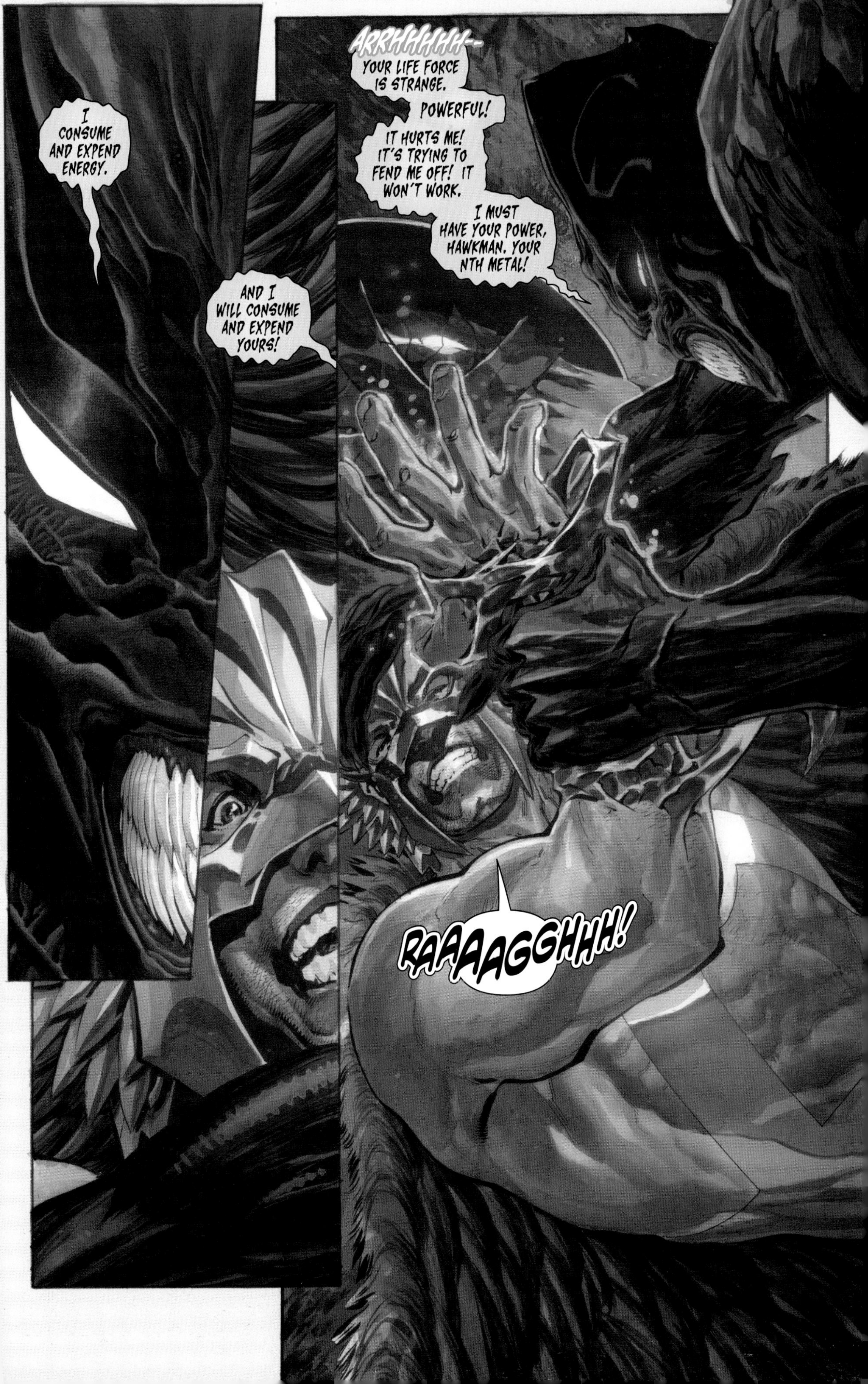
I CONSUME AND EXPEND ENERGY.
AND I WILL CONSUME AND EXPEND YOURS!
ARRHHHHHH--
YOUR LIFE FORCE IS STRANGE.
POWERFUL!
IT HURTS ME! IT'S TRYING TO FEND ME OFF! IT WON'T WORK.
I MUST HAVE YOUR POWER, HAWKMAN. YOUR NTH METAL!
RAAAAGGHHH!

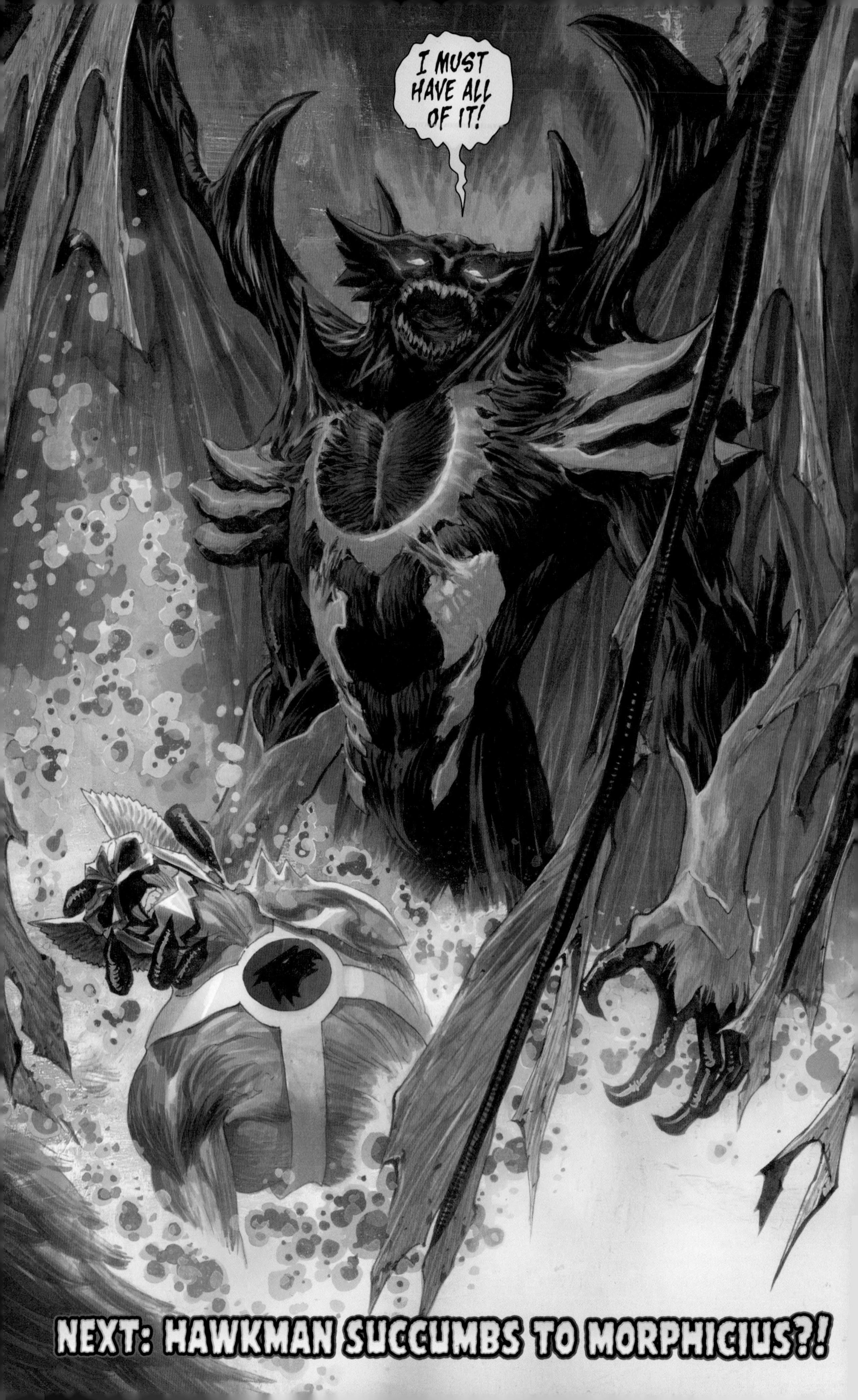
I MUST HAVE ALL OF IT!
NEXT: HAWKMAN SUCCUMBS TO MORPHICIUS?!

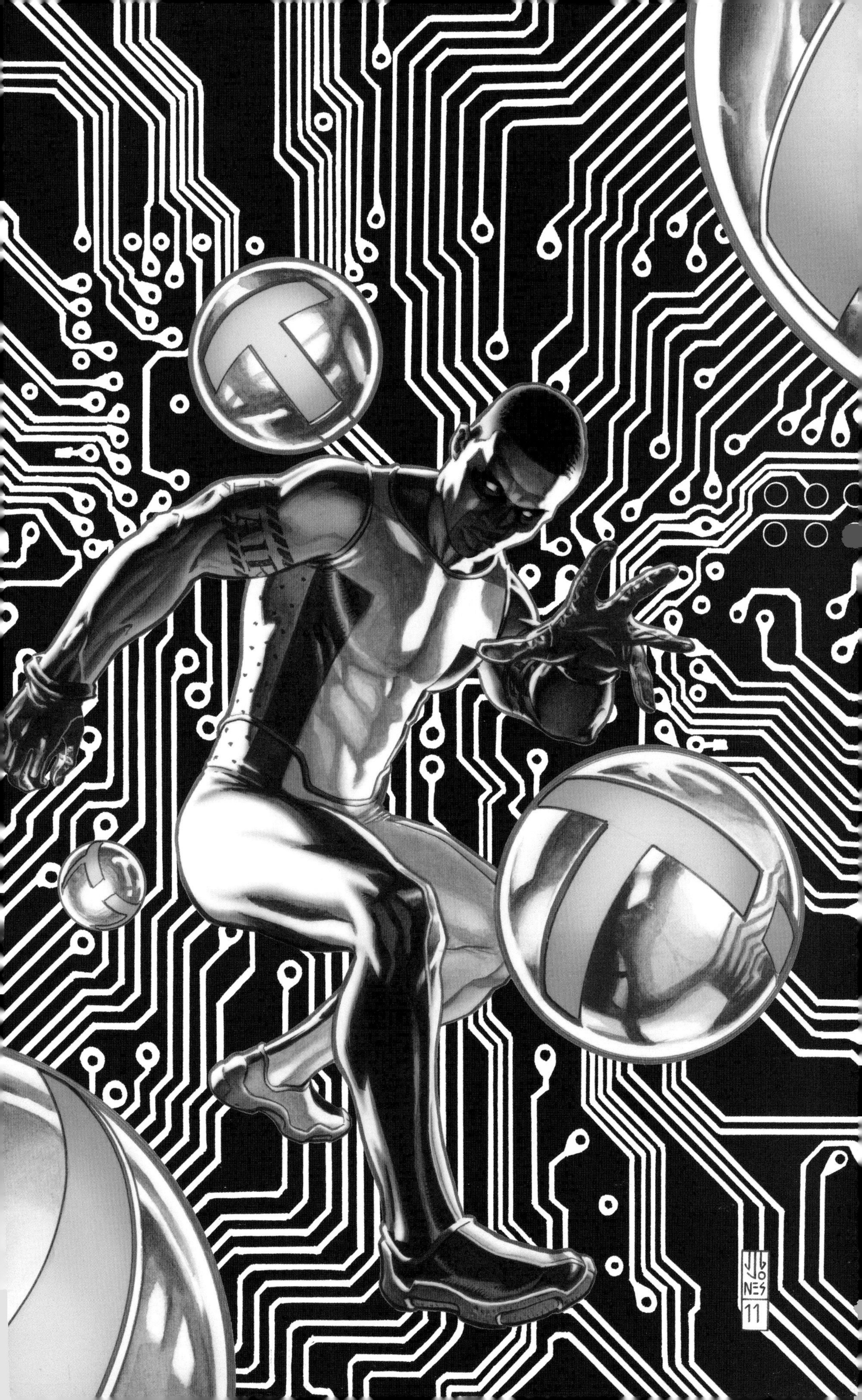
JG JONES 11

MISTER TERRIFIC

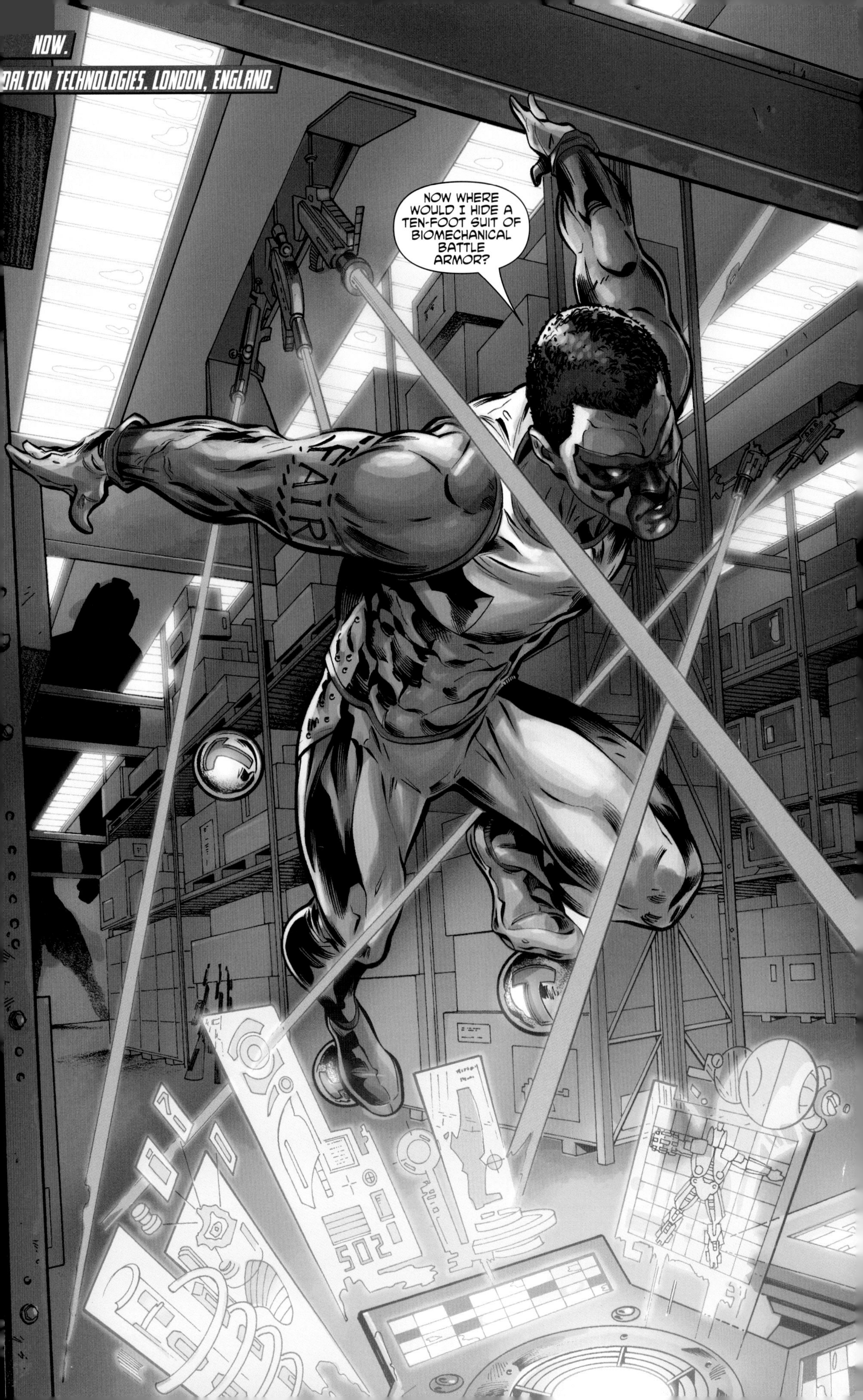
NOW.
DALTON TECHNOLOGIES. LONDON, ENGLAND.
NOW WHERE WOULD I HIDE A TEN-FOOT SUIT OF BIOMECHANICAL BATTLE ARMOR?

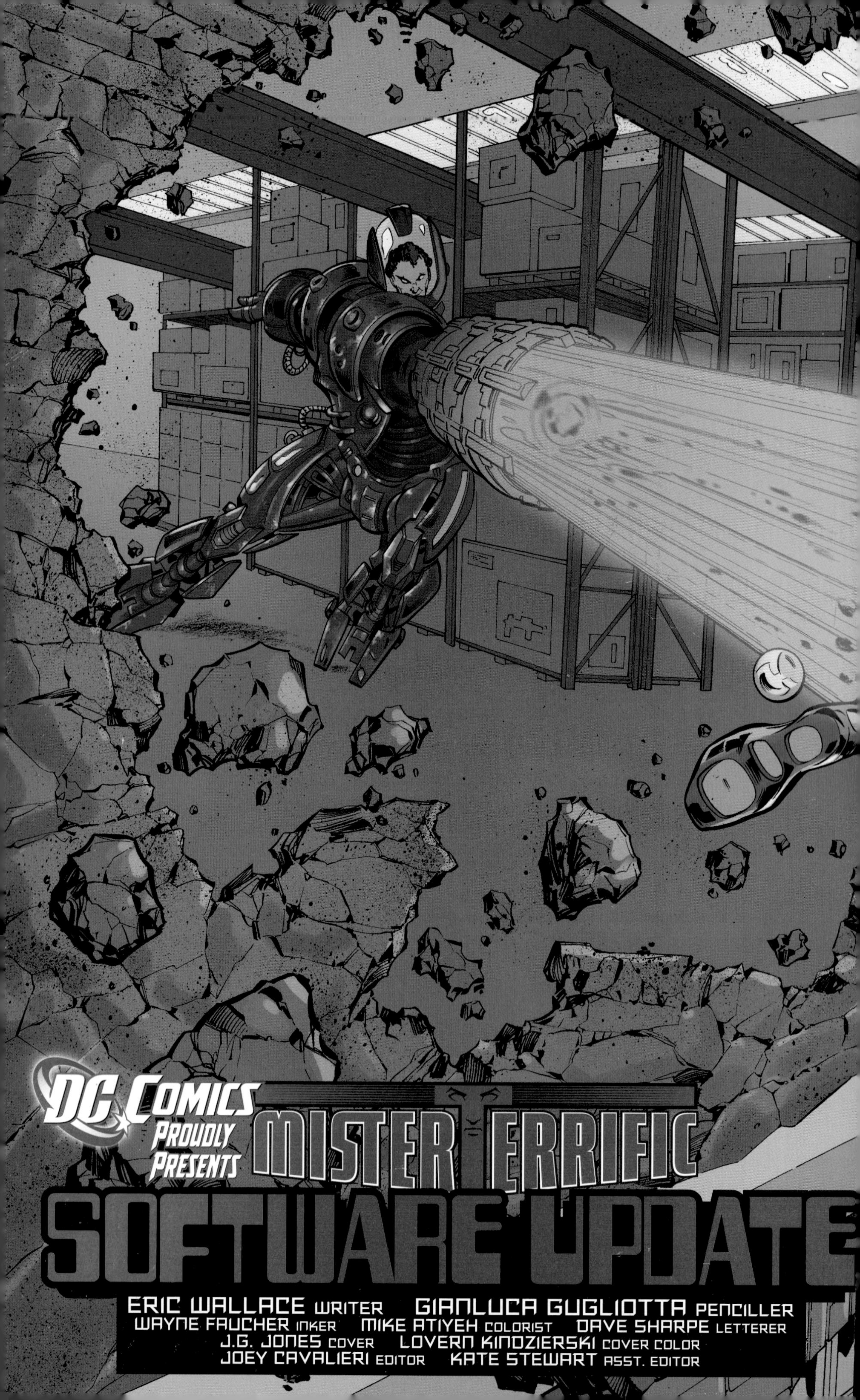
DC COMICS PROUDLY PRESENTS
MISTER TERRIFIC
SOFTWARE UPDATE
ERIC WALLACE WRITER GIANLUCA GUGLIOTTA PENCILLER
WAYNE FAUCHER INKER MIKE ATIYEH COLORIST DAVE SHARPE LETTERER
J.G. JONES COVER LOVERN KINDZIERSKI COVER COLOR
JOEY CAVALIERI EDITOR KATE STEWART ASST. EDITOR

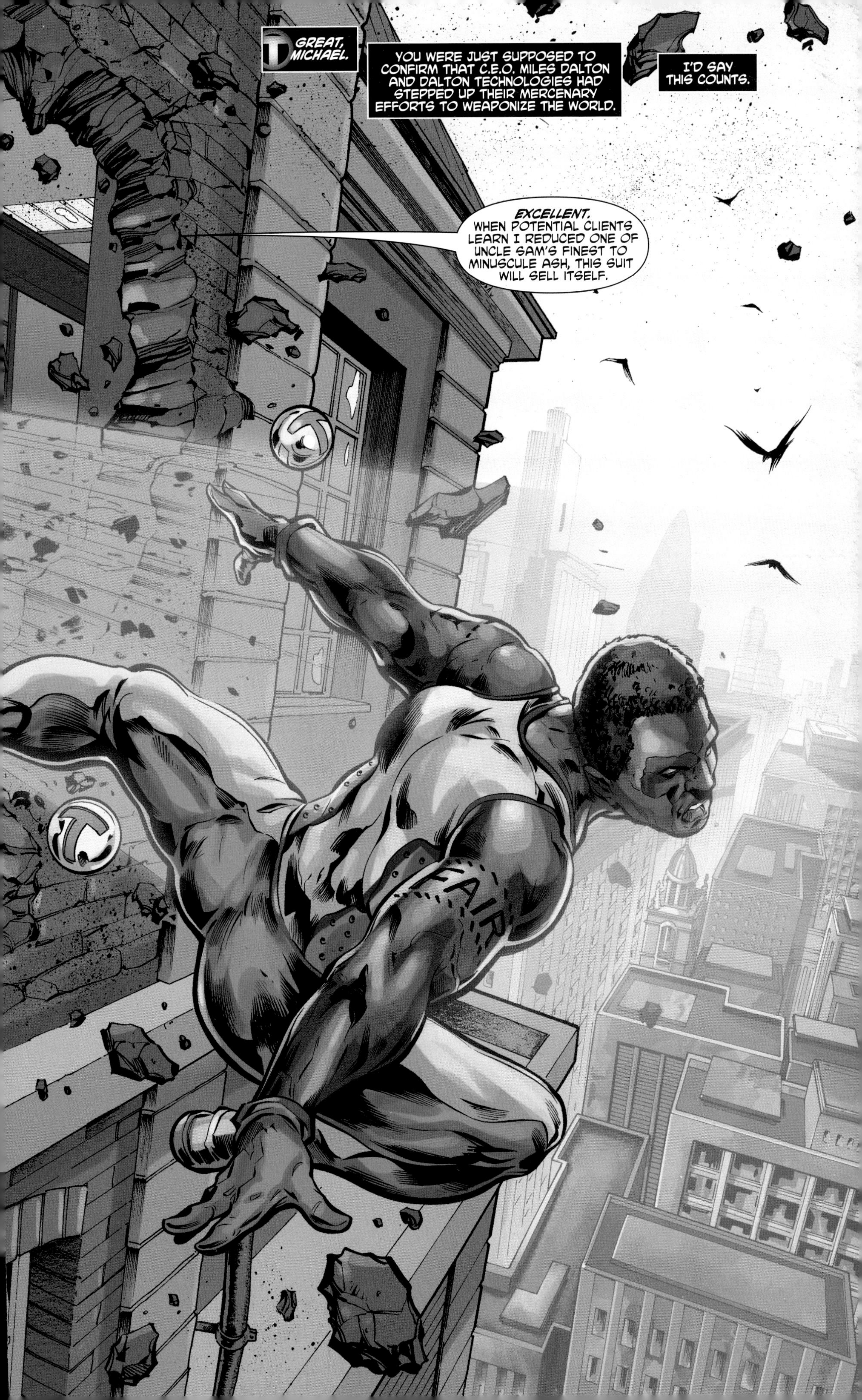
GREAT, MICHAEL.
YOU WERE JUST SUPPOSED TO CONFIRM THAT C.E.O. MILES DALTON AND DALTON TECHNOLOGIES HAD STEPPED UP THEIR MERCENARY EFFORTS TO WEAPONIZE THE WORLD.
I'D SAY THIS COUNTS.
EXCELLENT. WHEN POTENTIAL CLIENTS LEARN I REDUCED ONE OF UNCLE SAM'S FINEST TO MINUSCULE ASH, THIS SUIT WILL SELL ITSELF.
FAIR

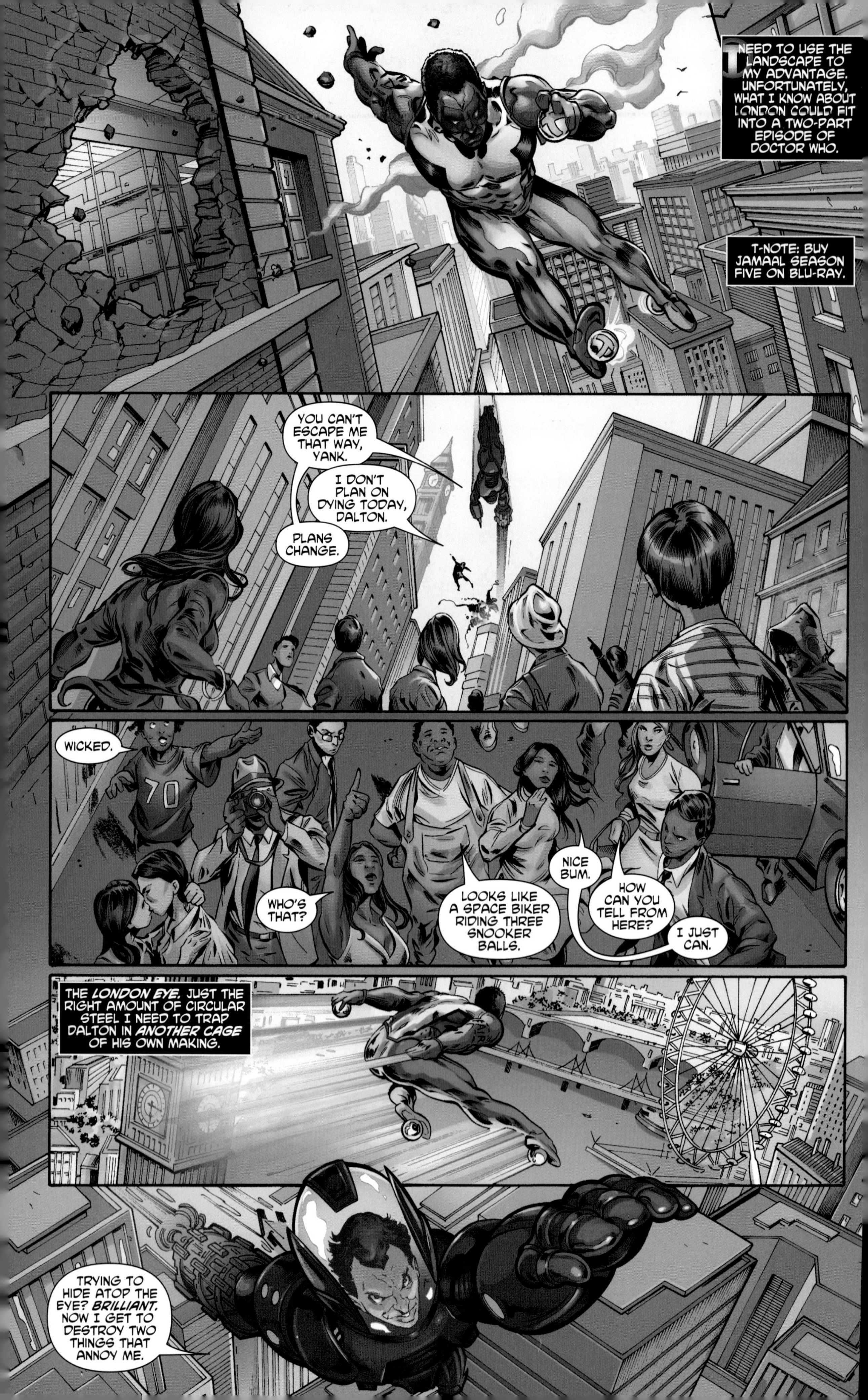
I NEED TO USE THE LANDSCAPE TO MY ADVANTAGE. UNFORTUNATELY, WHAT I KNOW ABOUT LONDON COULD FIT INTO A TWO-PART EPISODE OF DOCTOR WHO.
T-NOTE: BUY JAMAAL SEASON FIVE ON BLU-RAY.
YOU CAN'T ESCAPE ME THAT WAY, YANK.
I DON'T PLAN ON DYING TODAY, DALTON.
PLANS CHANGE.
WICKED.
WHO'S THAT?
LOOKS LIKE A SPACE BIKER RIDING THREE SNOOKER BALLS.
NICE BUM.
HOW CAN YOU TELL FROM HERE?
I JUST CAN.
THE LONDON EYE. JUST THE RIGHT AMOUNT OF CIRCULAR STEEL I NEED TO TRAP DALTON IN ANOTHER CAGE OF HIS OWN MAKING.
TRYING TO HIDE ATOP THE EYE? BRILLIANT. NOW I GET TO DESTROY TWO THINGS THAT ANNOY ME.

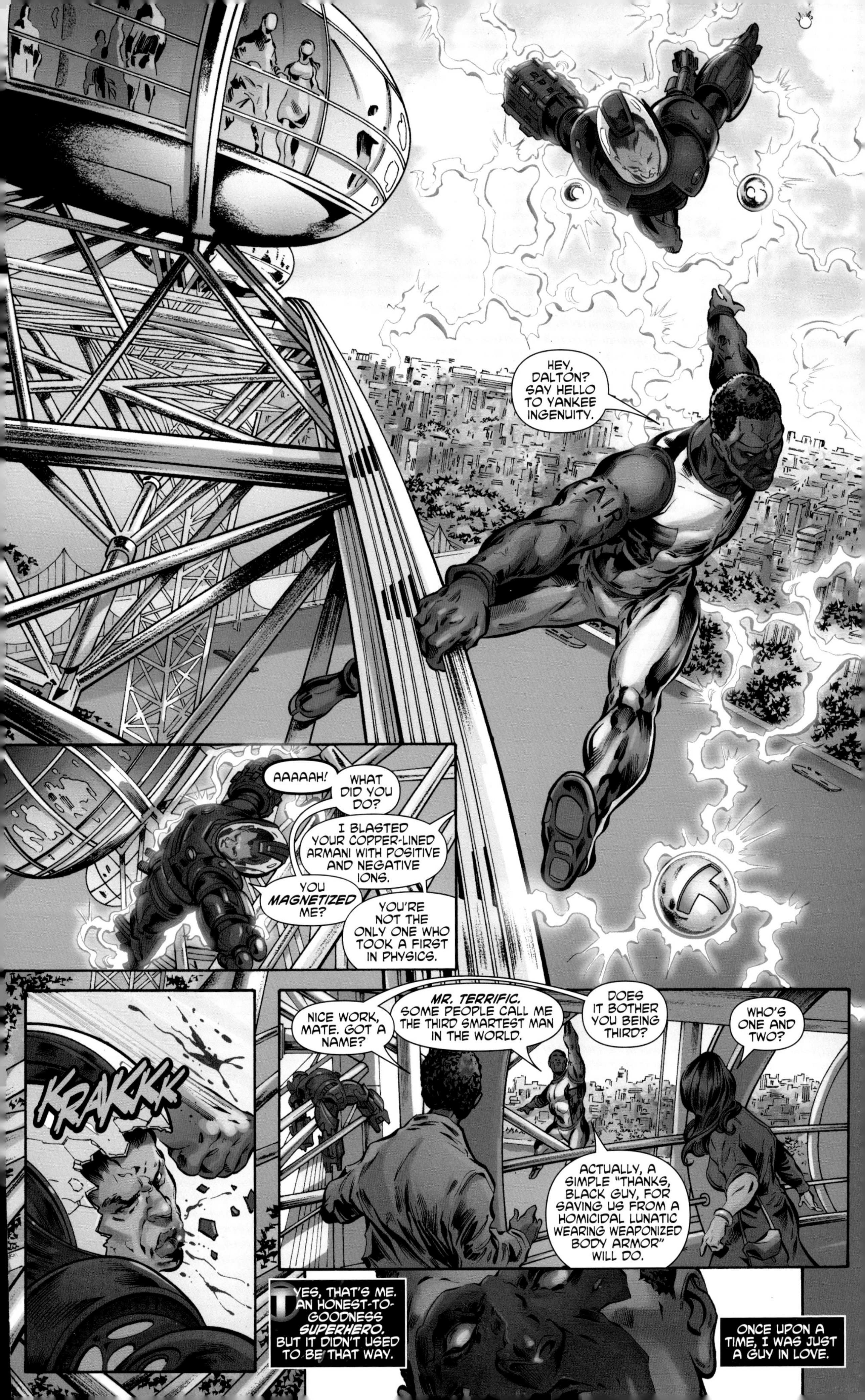
HEY, DALTON? SAY HELLO TO YANKEE INGENUITY.
AAAAAH!
WHAT DID YOU DO?
I BLASTED YOUR COPPER-LINED ARMANI WITH POSITIVE AND NEGATIVE IONS.
YOU *MAGNETIZED* ME?
YOU'RE NOT THE ONLY ONE WHO TOOK A FIRST IN PHYSICS.
KRAKKK
NICE WORK, MATE. GOT A NAME?
MR. TERRIFIC. SOME PEOPLE CALL ME THE THIRD SMARTEST MAN IN THE WORLD.
DOES IT BOTHER YOU BEING THIRD?
WHO'S ONE AND TWO?
ACTUALLY, A SIMPLE "THANKS, BLACK GUY, FOR SAVING US FROM A HOMICIDAL LUNATIC WEARING WEAPONIZED BODY ARMOR" WILL DO.
YES, THAT'S ME. AN HONEST-TO-GOODNESS *SUPERHERO.* BUT IT DIDN'T USED TO BE THAT WAY.
ONCE UPON A TIME, I WAS JUST A GUY IN LOVE.

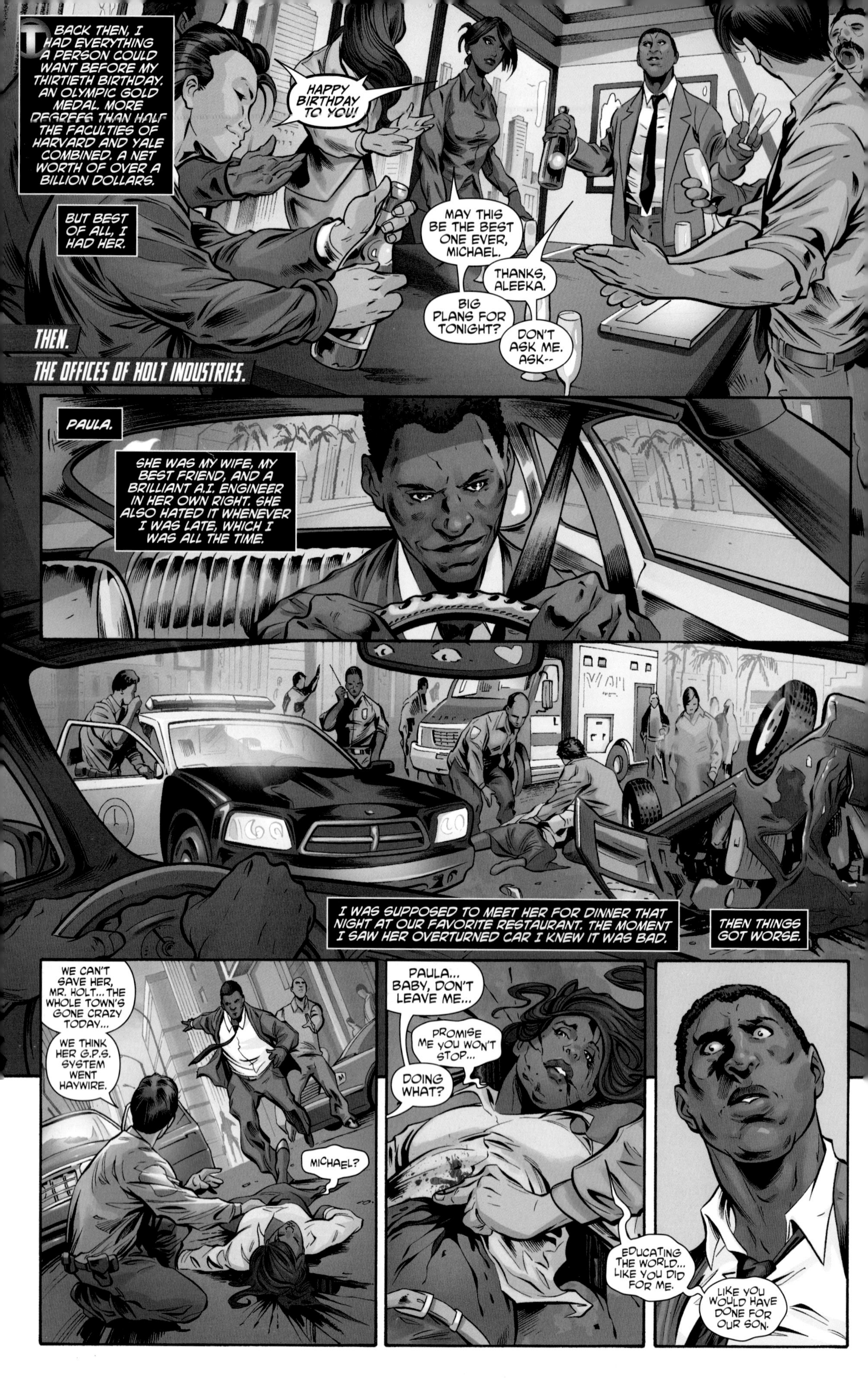
BACK THEN, I HAD EVERYTHING A PERSON COULD WANT BEFORE MY THIRTIETH BIRTHDAY. AN OLYMPIC GOLD MEDAL. MORE DEGREES THAN HALF THE FACULTIES OF HARVARD AND YALE COMBINED. A NET WORTH OF OVER A BILLION DOLLARS.
HAPPY BIRTHDAY TO YOU!
BUT BEST OF ALL, I HAD HER.
MAY THIS BE THE BEST ONE EVER, MICHAEL.
THANKS, ALEEKA.
BIG PLANS FOR TONIGHT?
DON'T ASK ME. ASK--
THEN.
THE OFFICES OF HOLT INDUSTRIES.
PAULA.
SHE WAS MY WIFE, MY BEST FRIEND, AND A BRILLIANT A.I. ENGINEER IN HER OWN RIGHT. SHE ALSO HATED IT WHENEVER I WAS LATE, WHICH I WAS ALL THE TIME.
I WAS SUPPOSED TO MEET HER FOR DINNER THAT NIGHT AT OUR FAVORITE RESTAURANT. THE MOMENT I SAW HER OVERTURNED CAR I KNEW IT WAS BAD.
THEN THINGS GOT WORSE.
WE CAN'T SAVE HER, MR. HOLT... THE WHOLE TOWN'S GONE CRAZY TODAY...
WE THINK HER G.P.S. SYSTEM WENT HAYWIRE.
MICHAEL?
PAULA... BABY, DON'T LEAVE ME...
PROMISE ME YOU WON'T STOP...
DOING WHAT?
EDUCATING THE WORLD... LIKE YOU DID FOR ME.
LIKE YOU WOULD HAVE DONE FOR OUR SON.

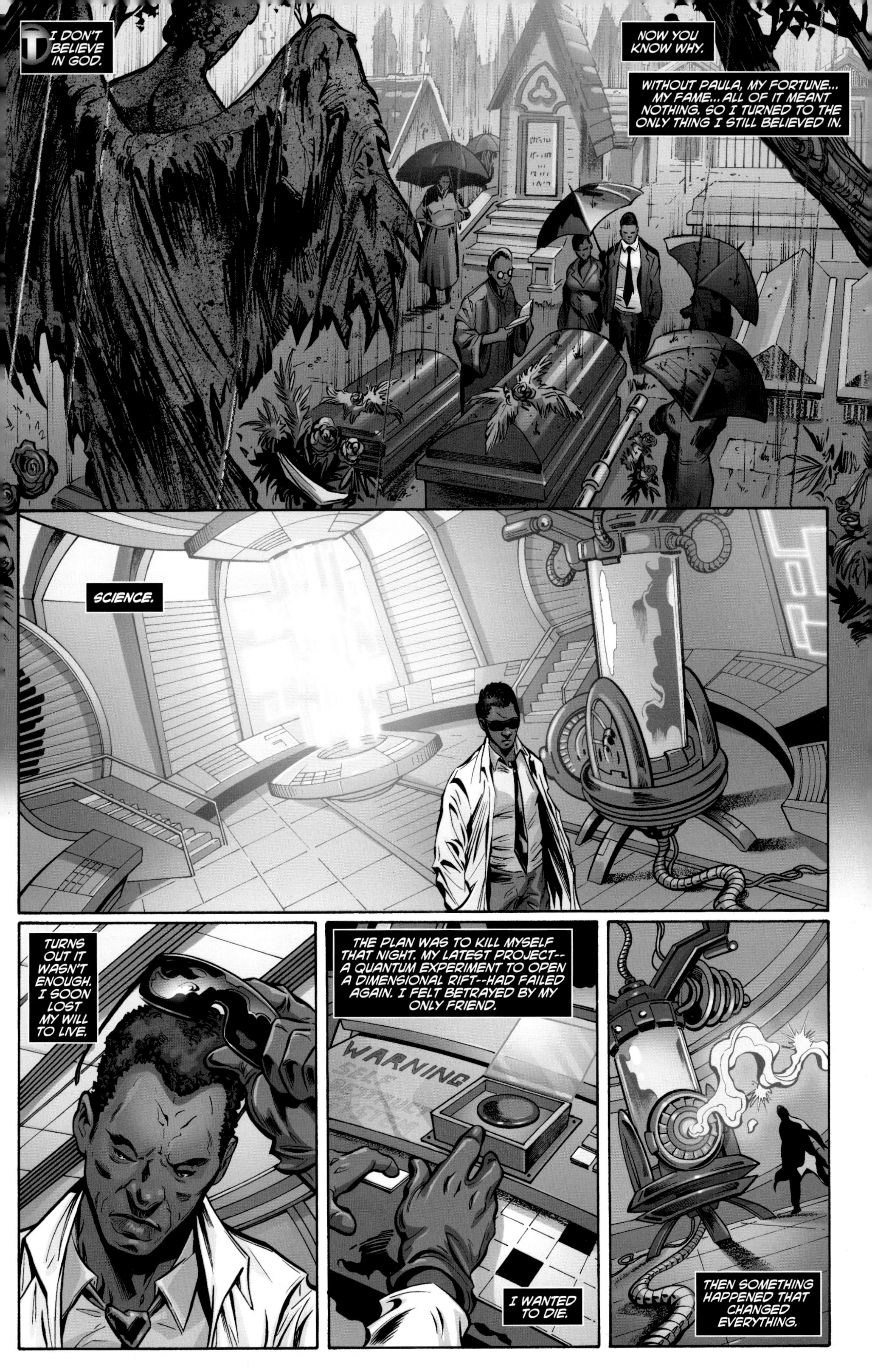
I DON'T BELIEVE IN GOD.
NOW YOU KNOW WHY.
WITHOUT PAULA, MY FORTUNE... MY FAME... ALL OF IT MEANT NOTHING. SO I TURNED TO THE ONLY THING I STILL BELIEVED IN.
SCIENCE.
TURNS OUT IT WASN'T ENOUGH. I SOON LOST MY WILL TO LIVE.
THE PLAN WAS TO KILL MYSELF THAT NIGHT. MY LATEST PROJECT--A QUANTUM EXPERIMENT TO OPEN A DIMENSIONAL RIFT--HAD FAILED AGAIN. I FELT BETRAYED BY MY ONLY FRIEND.
WARNING
SELF DESTRUCT SYSTEM
I WANTED TO DIE.
THEN SOMETHING HAPPENED THAT CHANGED EVERYTHING.

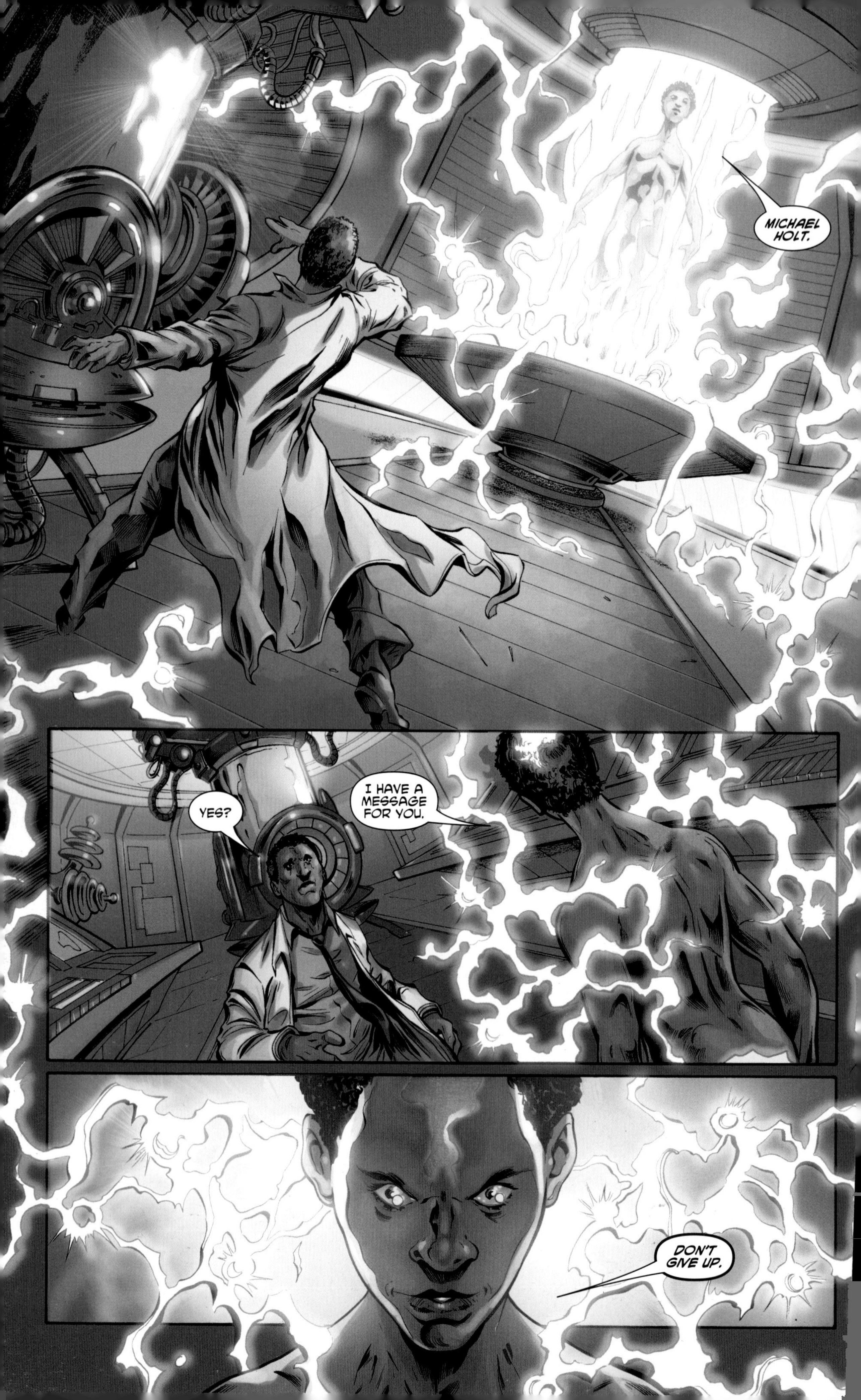
MICHAEL HOLT.
YES?
I HAVE A MESSAGE FOR YOU.
DON'T GIVE UP.

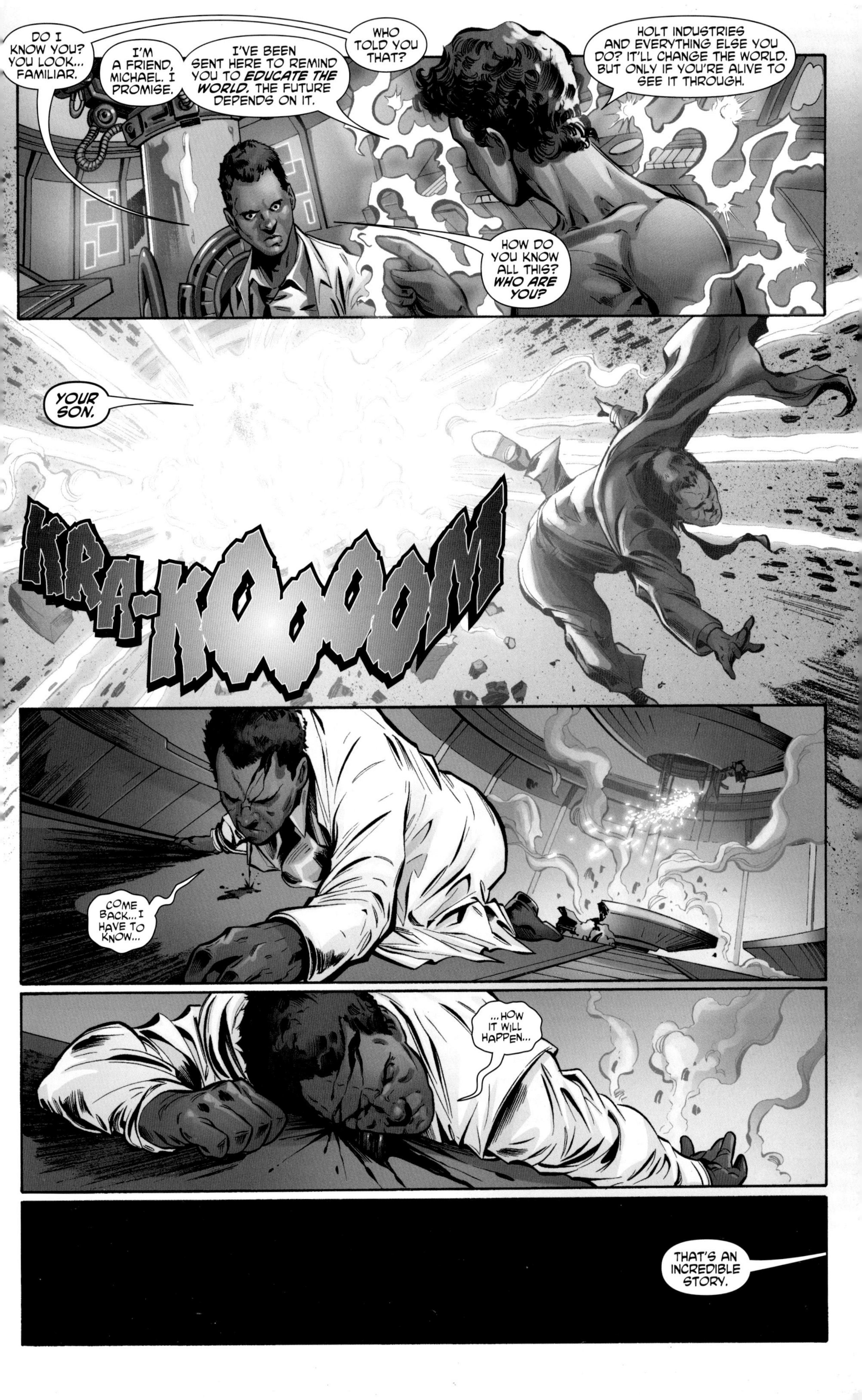
DO I KNOW YOU? YOU LOOK... FAMILIAR.
I'M A FRIEND, MICHAEL. I PROMISE.
I'VE BEEN SENT HERE TO REMIND YOU TO *EDUCATE THE WORLD.* THE FUTURE DEPENDS ON IT.
WHO TOLD YOU THAT?
HOLT INDUSTRIES AND EVERYTHING ELSE YOU DO? IT'LL CHANGE THE WORLD. BUT ONLY IF YOU'RE ALIVE TO SEE IT THROUGH.
HOW DO YOU KNOW ALL THIS? *WHO ARE YOU?*
YOUR SON.
KRA-KOOOOM
COME BACK... I HAVE TO KNOW...
...HOW IT WILL HAPPEN...
THAT'S AN INCREDIBLE STORY.

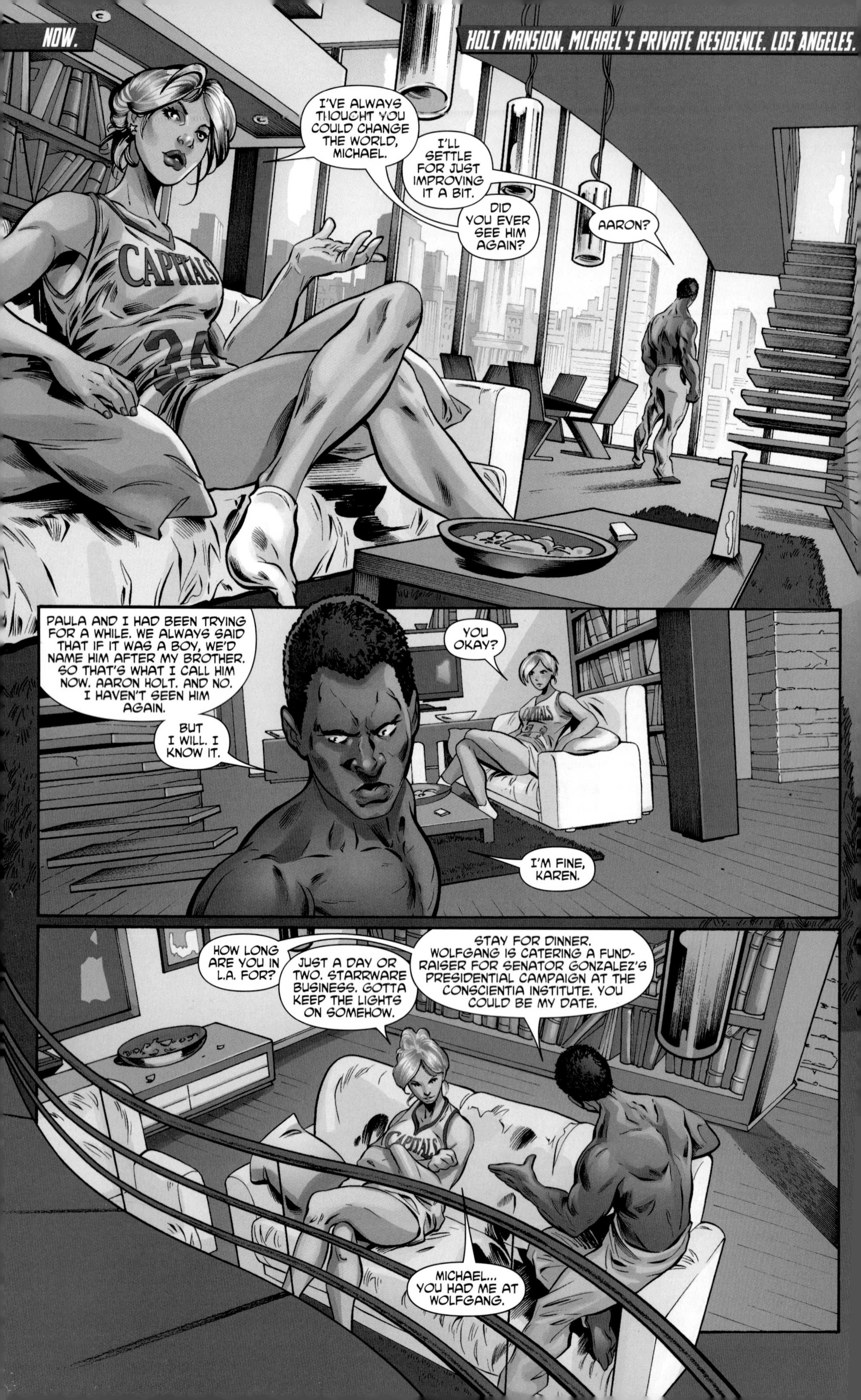
NOW.
HOLT MANSION, MICHAEL'S PRIVATE RESIDENCE. LOS ANGELES.
I'VE ALWAYS THOUGHT YOU COULD CHANGE THE WORLD, MICHAEL.
I'LL SETTLE FOR JUST IMPROVING IT A BIT.
DID YOU EVER SEE HIM AGAIN?
AARON?
CAPITALS
PAULA AND I HAD BEEN TRYING FOR A WHILE. WE ALWAYS SAID THAT IF IT WAS A BOY, WE'D NAME HIM AFTER MY BROTHER. SO THAT'S WHAT I CALL HIM NOW. AARON HOLT. AND NO. I HAVEN'T SEEN HIM AGAIN.
BUT I WILL. I KNOW IT.
YOU OKAY?
I'M FINE, KAREN.
HOW LONG ARE YOU IN L.A. FOR?
JUST A DAY OR TWO. STARRWARE BUSINESS. GOTTA KEEP THE LIGHTS ON SOMEHOW.
STAY FOR DINNER. WOLFGANG IS CATERING A FUND-RAISER FOR SENATOR GONZALEZ'S PRESIDENTIAL CAMPAIGN AT THE CONSCIENTIA INSTITUTE. YOU COULD BE MY DATE.
MICHAEL... YOU HAD ME AT WOLFGANG.

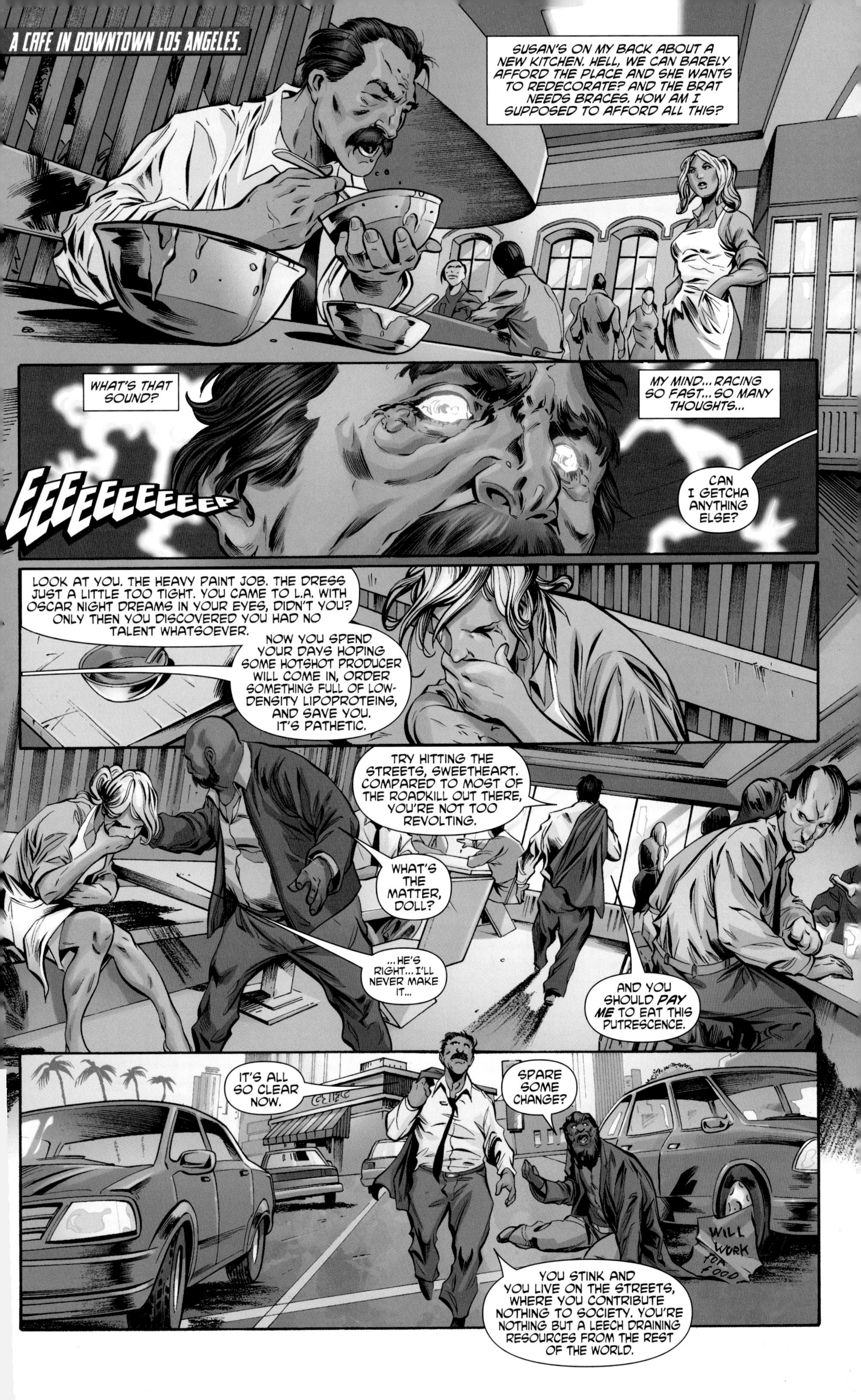
A CAFE IN DOWNTOWN LOS ANGELES.
SUSAN'S ON MY BACK ABOUT A NEW KITCHEN. HELL, WE CAN BARELY AFFORD THE PLACE AND SHE WANTS TO REDECORATE? AND THE BRAT NEEDS BRACES. HOW AM I SUPPOSED TO AFFORD ALL THIS?
WHAT'S THAT SOUND?
EEEEEEEEEEEP
MY MIND... RACING SO FAST... SO MANY THOUGHTS...
CAN I GETCHA ANYTHING ELSE?
LOOK AT YOU. THE HEAVY PAINT JOB. THE DRESS JUST A LITTLE TOO TIGHT. YOU CAME TO L.A. WITH OSCAR NIGHT DREAMS IN YOUR EYES, DIDN'T YOU? ONLY THEN YOU DISCOVERED YOU HAD NO TALENT WHATSOEVER.
NOW YOU SPEND YOUR DAYS HOPING SOME HOTSHOT PRODUCER WILL COME IN, ORDER SOMETHING FULL OF LOW-DENSITY LIPOPROTEINS, AND SAVE YOU. IT'S PATHETIC.
TRY HITTING THE STREETS, SWEETHEART. COMPARED TO MOST OF THE ROADKILL OUT THERE, YOU'RE NOT TOO REVOLTING.
WHAT'S THE MATTER, DOLL?
...HE'S RIGHT... I'LL NEVER MAKE IT...
AND YOU SHOULD PAY ME TO EAT THIS PUTRESCENCE.
IT'S ALL SO CLEAR NOW.
SPARE SOME CHANGE?
WILL WORK FOR FOOD
YOU STINK AND YOU LIVE ON THE STREETS, WHERE YOU CONTRIBUTE NOTHING TO SOCIETY. YOU'RE NOTHING BUT A LEECH DRAINING RESOURCES FROM THE REST OF THE WORLD.

COME BACK HERE, YOU JERK!

OH, MAN.

PROBLEM SOLVED.

"HIS NAME IS EDGAR HOLOWITZ."

LOS ANGELES POLICE DEPARTMENT, HOLLYWOOD DIVISION.

WE CHECKED WITH HIS OFFICE. HE WAS FINE THIS MORNING. THEN THE GUY TAKES A LUNCH BREAK AND SUDDENLY--

--HE GOES NUTS.

HAS HE BEEN WRITING SYMBOLS LIKE THESE ALL DAY?

YUP. LOOKS LIKE SOME KINDA SCIENCE GIBBERISH. FIGURED SINCE THAT'S YOUR BEAT, WE'D BETTER CALL YOU IN.

YOU DID THE RIGHT THING. THIS IS EXACTLY THE KIND OF SITUATION I ENVISIONED WHEN I PROVIDED THE L.A.P.D. WITH A WAY TO CONTACT ME SECURELY. SEE THESE INTEGERS?

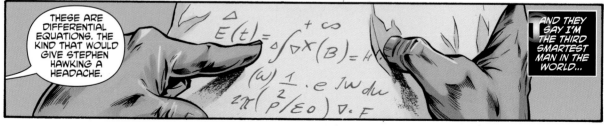

THESE ARE DIFFERENTIAL EQUATIONS. THE KIND THAT WOULD GIVE STEPHEN HAWKING A HEADACHE.

AND THEY SAY I'M THE THIRD SMARTEST MAN IN THE WORLD...

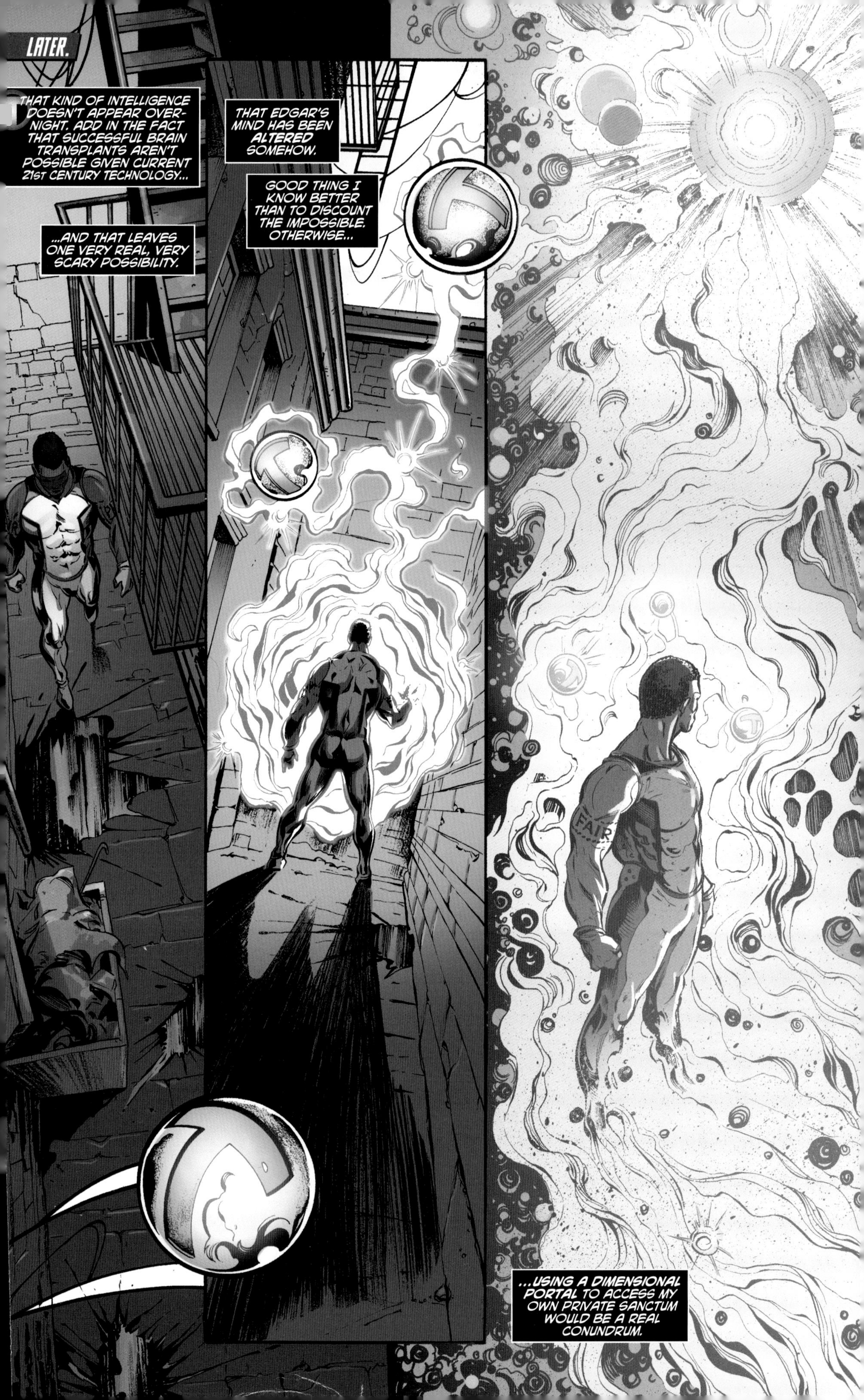
LATER.
THAT KIND OF INTELLIGENCE DOESN'T APPEAR OVER-NIGHT. ADD IN THE FACT THAT SUCCESSFUL BRAIN TRANSPLANTS AREN'T POSSIBLE GIVEN CURRENT 21ST CENTURY TECHNOLOGY...
...AND THAT LEAVES ONE VERY REAL, VERY SCARY POSSIBILITY.
THAT EDGAR'S MIND HAS BEEN ALTERED SOMEHOW.
GOOD THING I KNOW BETTER THAN TO DISCOUNT THE IMPOSSIBLE. OTHERWISE...
...USING A DIMENSIONAL PORTAL TO ACCESS MY OWN PRIVATE SANCTUM WOULD BE A REAL CONUNDRUM.
FAIR

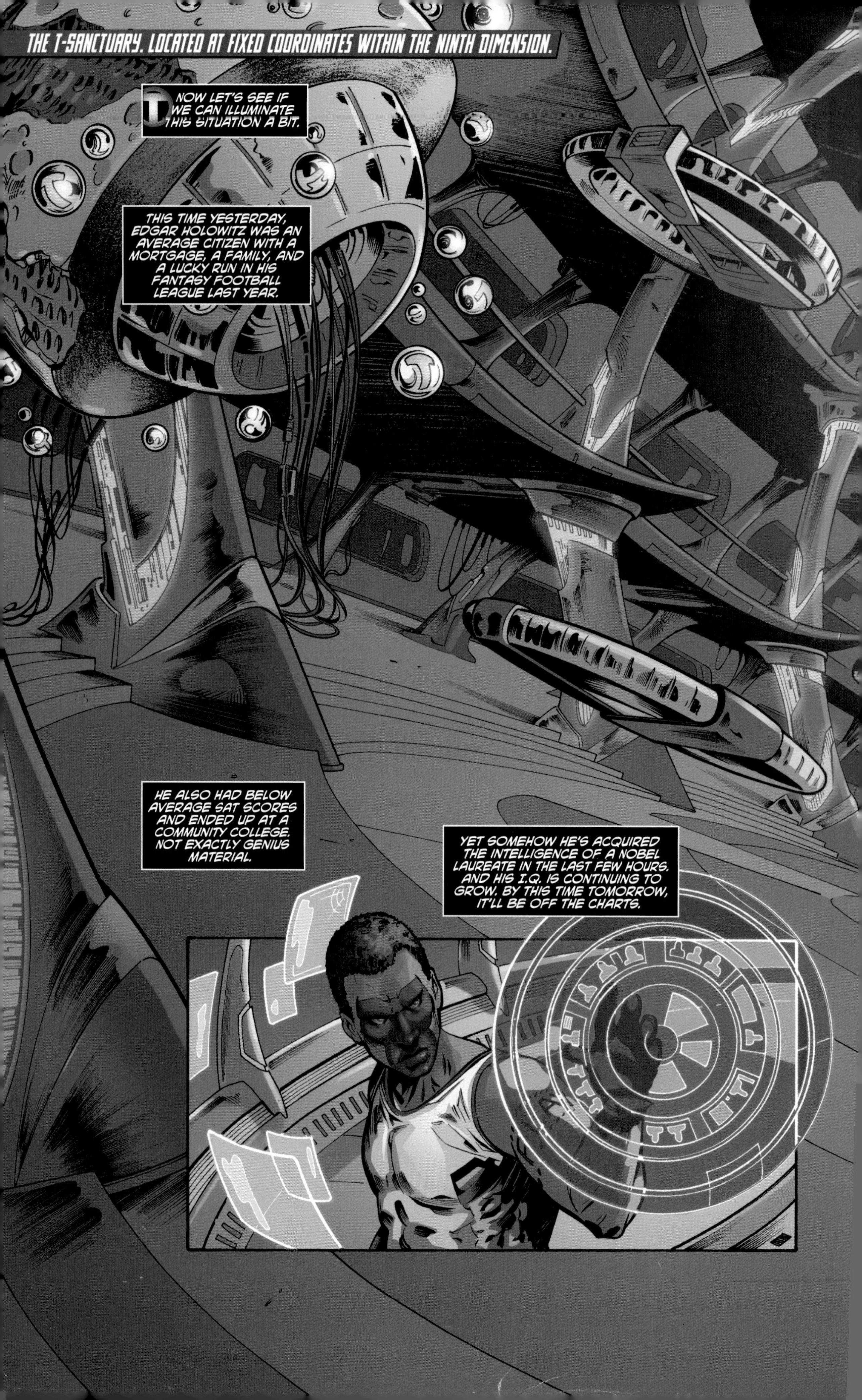
THE T-SANCTUARY. LOCATED AT FIXED COORDINATES WITHIN THE NINTH DIMENSION.
NOW LET'S SEE IF WE CAN ILLUMINATE THIS SITUATION A BIT.
THIS TIME YESTERDAY, EDGAR HOLOWITZ WAS AN AVERAGE CITIZEN WITH A MORTGAGE, A FAMILY, AND A LUCKY RUN IN HIS FANTASY FOOTBALL LEAGUE LAST YEAR.
HE ALSO HAD BELOW AVERAGE SAT SCORES AND ENDED UP AT A COMMUNITY COLLEGE. NOT EXACTLY GENIUS MATERIAL.
YET SOMEHOW HE'S ACQUIRED THE INTELLIGENCE OF A NOBEL LAUREATE IN THE LAST FEW HOURS. AND HIS I.Q. IS CONTINUING TO GROW. BY THIS TIME TOMORROW, IT'LL BE OFF THE CHARTS.

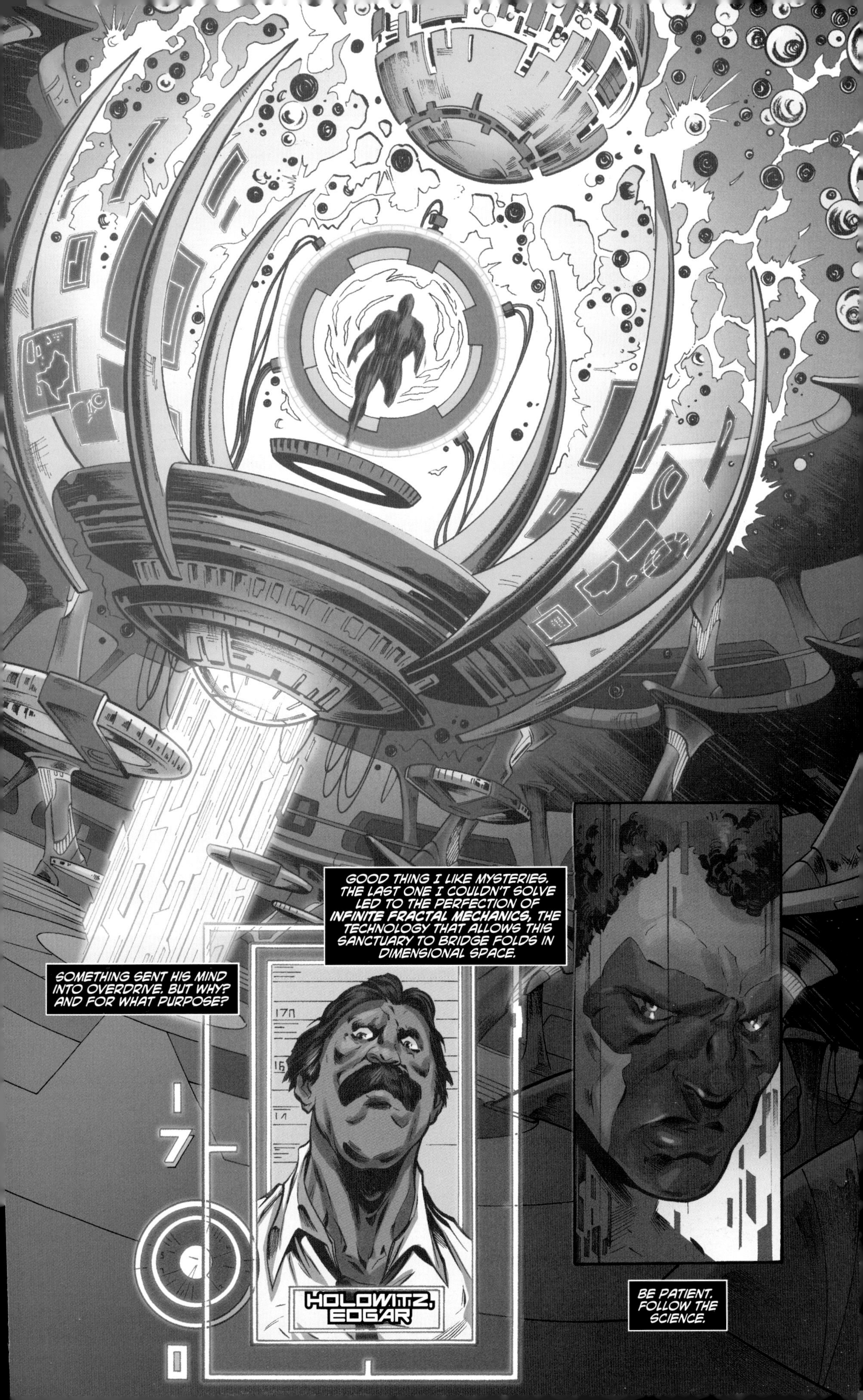
GOOD THING I LIKE MYSTERIES. THE LAST ONE I COULDN'T SOLVE LED TO THE PERFECTION OF INFINITE FRACTAL MECHANICS, THE TECHNOLOGY THAT ALLOWS THIS SANCTUARY TO BRIDGE FOLDS IN DIMENSIONAL SPACE.
SOMETHING SENT HIS MIND INTO OVERDRIVE. BUT WHY? AND FOR WHAT PURPOSE?
HOLOWITZ, EDGAR
BE PATIENT. FOLLOW THE SCIENCE.

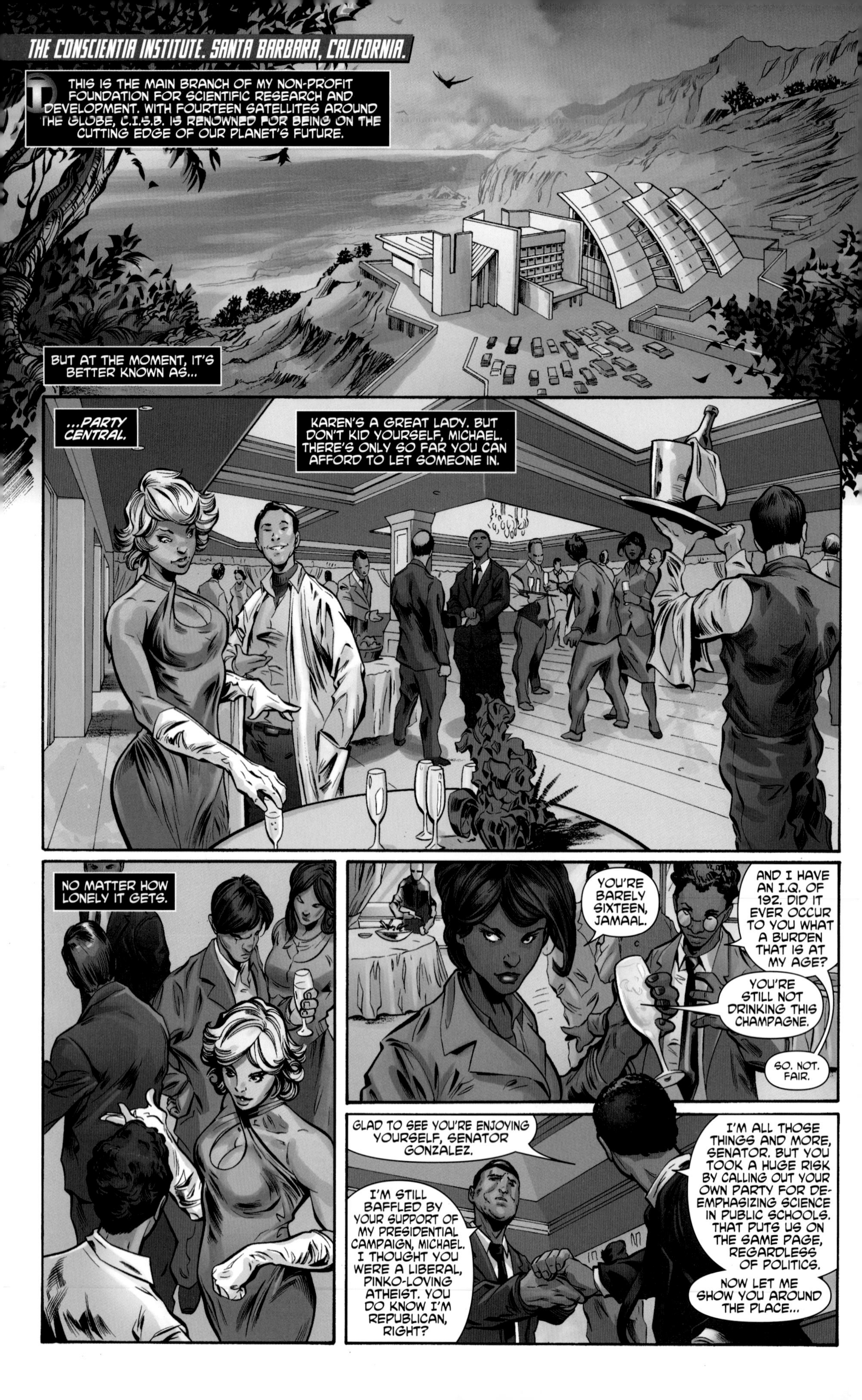
THE CONSCIENTIA INSTITUTE. SANTA BARBARA, CALIFORNIA.
THIS IS THE MAIN BRANCH OF MY NON-PROFIT FOUNDATION FOR SCIENTIFIC RESEARCH AND DEVELOPMENT. WITH FOURTEEN SATELLITES AROUND THE GLOBE, C.I.S.B. IS RENOWNED FOR BEING ON THE CUTTING EDGE OF OUR PLANET'S FUTURE.
BUT AT THE MOMENT, IT'S BETTER KNOWN AS...
...PARTY CENTRAL.
KAREN'S A GREAT LADY. BUT DON'T KID YOURSELF, MICHAEL. THERE'S ONLY SO FAR YOU CAN AFFORD TO LET SOMEONE IN.
NO MATTER HOW LONELY IT GETS.
YOU'RE BARELY SIXTEEN, JAMAAL.
AND I HAVE AN I.Q. OF 192. DID IT EVER OCCUR TO YOU WHAT A BURDEN THAT IS AT MY AGE?
YOU'RE STILL NOT DRINKING THIS CHAMPAGNE.
SO. NOT. FAIR.
GLAD TO SEE YOU'RE ENJOYING YOURSELF, SENATOR GONZALEZ.
I'M STILL BAFFLED BY YOUR SUPPORT OF MY PRESIDENTIAL CAMPAIGN, MICHAEL. I THOUGHT YOU WERE A LIBERAL, PINKO-LOVING ATHEIST. YOU DO KNOW I'M REPUBLICAN, RIGHT?
I'M ALL THOSE THINGS AND MORE, SENATOR. BUT YOU TOOK A HUGE RISK BY CALLING OUT YOUR OWN PARTY FOR DE-EMPHASIZING SCIENCE IN PUBLIC SCHOOLS. THAT PUTS US ON THE SAME PAGE, REGARDLESS OF POLITICS.
NOW LET ME SHOW YOU AROUND THE PLACE...

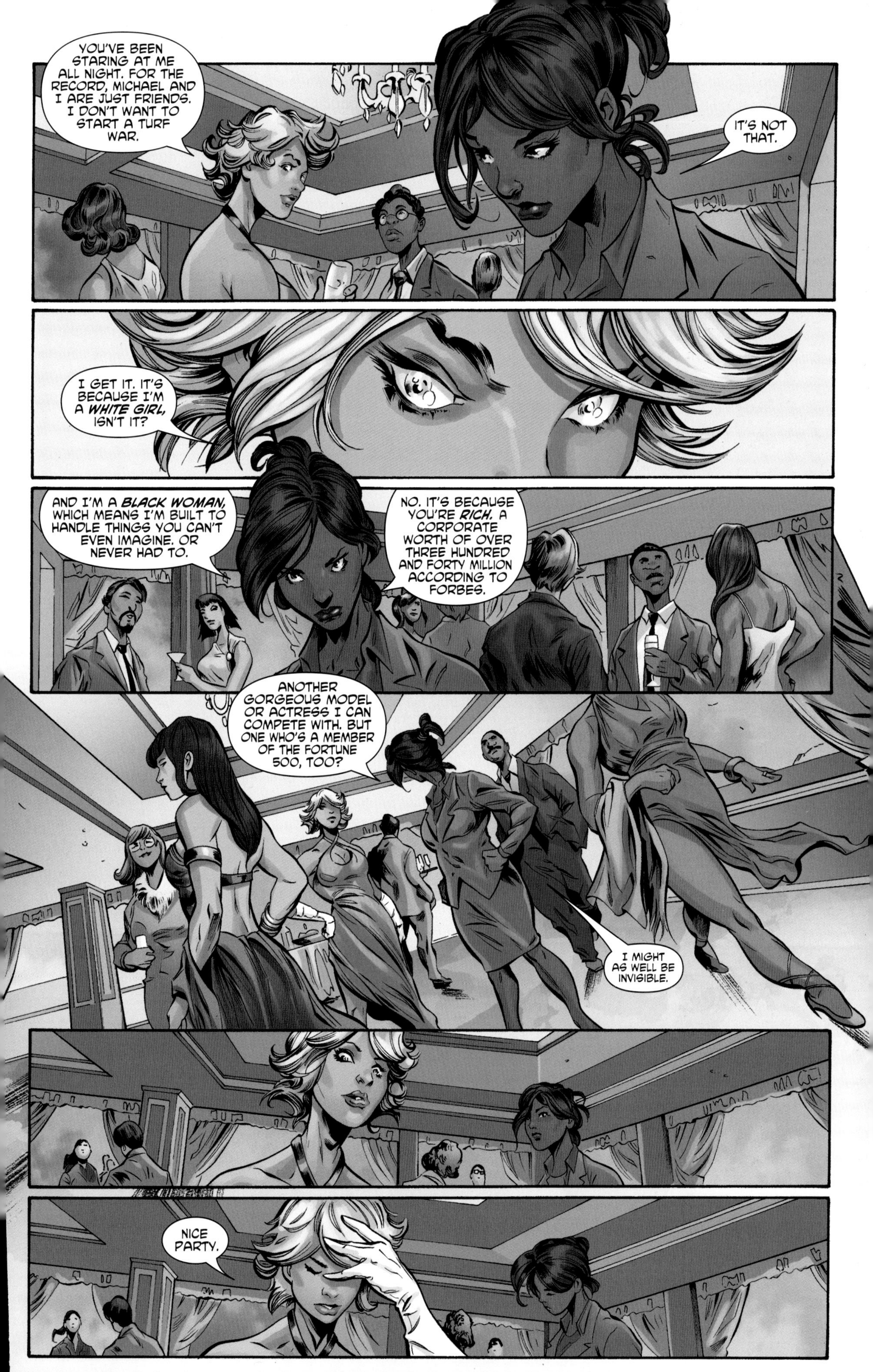
YOU'VE BEEN STARING AT ME ALL NIGHT. FOR THE RECORD, MICHAEL AND I ARE JUST FRIENDS. I DON'T WANT TO START A TURF WAR.
IT'S NOT THAT.
I GET IT. IT'S BECAUSE I'M A WHITE GIRL, ISN'T IT?
AND I'M A BLACK WOMAN, WHICH MEANS I'M BUILT TO HANDLE THINGS YOU CAN'T EVEN IMAGINE. OR NEVER HAD TO.
NO. IT'S BECAUSE YOU'RE RICH. A CORPORATE WORTH OF OVER THREE HUNDRED AND FORTY MILLION ACCORDING TO FORBES.
ANOTHER GORGEOUS MODEL OR ACTRESS I CAN COMPETE WITH. BUT ONE WHO'S A MEMBER OF THE FORTUNE 500, TOO?
I MIGHT AS WELL BE INVISIBLE.
NICE PARTY.

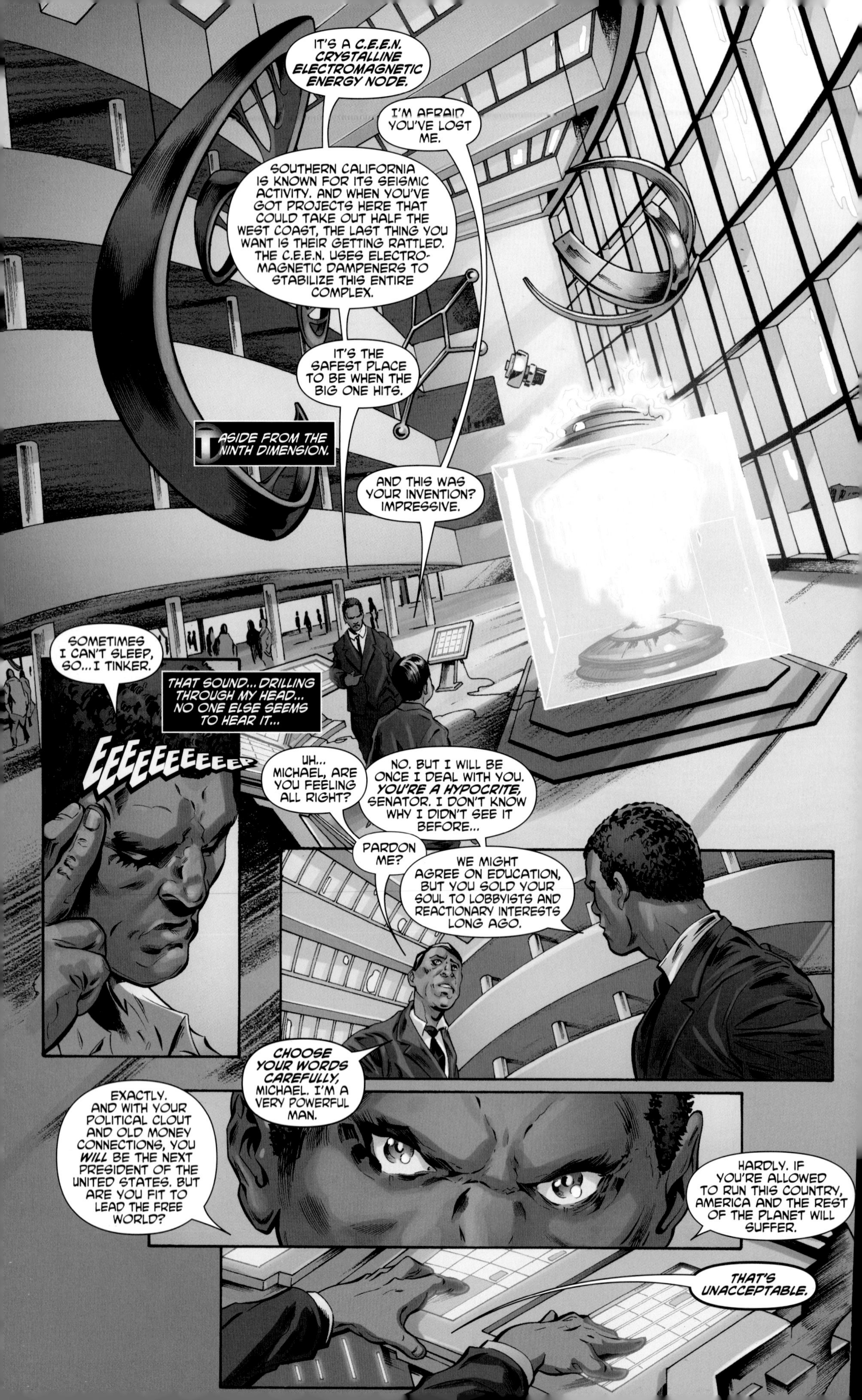
IT'S A C.E.E.N. CRYSTALLINE ELECTROMAGNETIC ENERGY NODE.
I'M AFRAID YOU'VE LOST ME.
SOUTHERN CALIFORNIA IS KNOWN FOR ITS SEISMIC ACTIVITY. AND WHEN YOU'VE GOT PROJECTS HERE THAT COULD TAKE OUT HALF THE WEST COAST, THE LAST THING YOU WANT IS THEIR GETTING RATTLED. THE C.E.E.N. USES ELECTRO-MAGNETIC DAMPENERS TO STABILIZE THIS ENTIRE COMPLEX.
IT'S THE SAFEST PLACE TO BE WHEN THE BIG ONE HITS.
ASIDE FROM THE NINTH DIMENSION.
AND THIS WAS YOUR INVENTION? IMPRESSIVE.
SOMETIMES I CAN'T SLEEP, SO...I TINKER.
THAT SOUND...DRILLING THROUGH MY HEAD... NO ONE ELSE SEEMS TO HEAR IT...
EEEEEEEEEEEP
UH... MICHAEL, ARE YOU FEELING ALL RIGHT?
NO. BUT I WILL BE ONCE I DEAL WITH YOU. YOU'RE A HYPOCRITE, SENATOR. I DON'T KNOW WHY I DIDN'T SEE IT BEFORE...
PARDON ME?
WE MIGHT AGREE ON EDUCATION, BUT YOU SOLD YOUR SOUL TO LOBBYISTS AND REACTIONARY INTERESTS LONG AGO.
CHOOSE YOUR WORDS CAREFULLY, MICHAEL. I'M A VERY POWERFUL MAN.
EXACTLY. AND WITH YOUR POLITICAL CLOUT AND OLD MONEY CONNECTIONS, YOU WILL BE THE NEXT PRESIDENT OF THE UNITED STATES. BUT ARE YOU FIT TO LEAD THE FREE WORLD?
HARDLY. IF YOU'RE ALLOWED TO RUN THIS COUNTRY, AMERICA AND THE REST OF THE PLANET WILL SUFFER.
THAT'S UNACCEPTABLE.

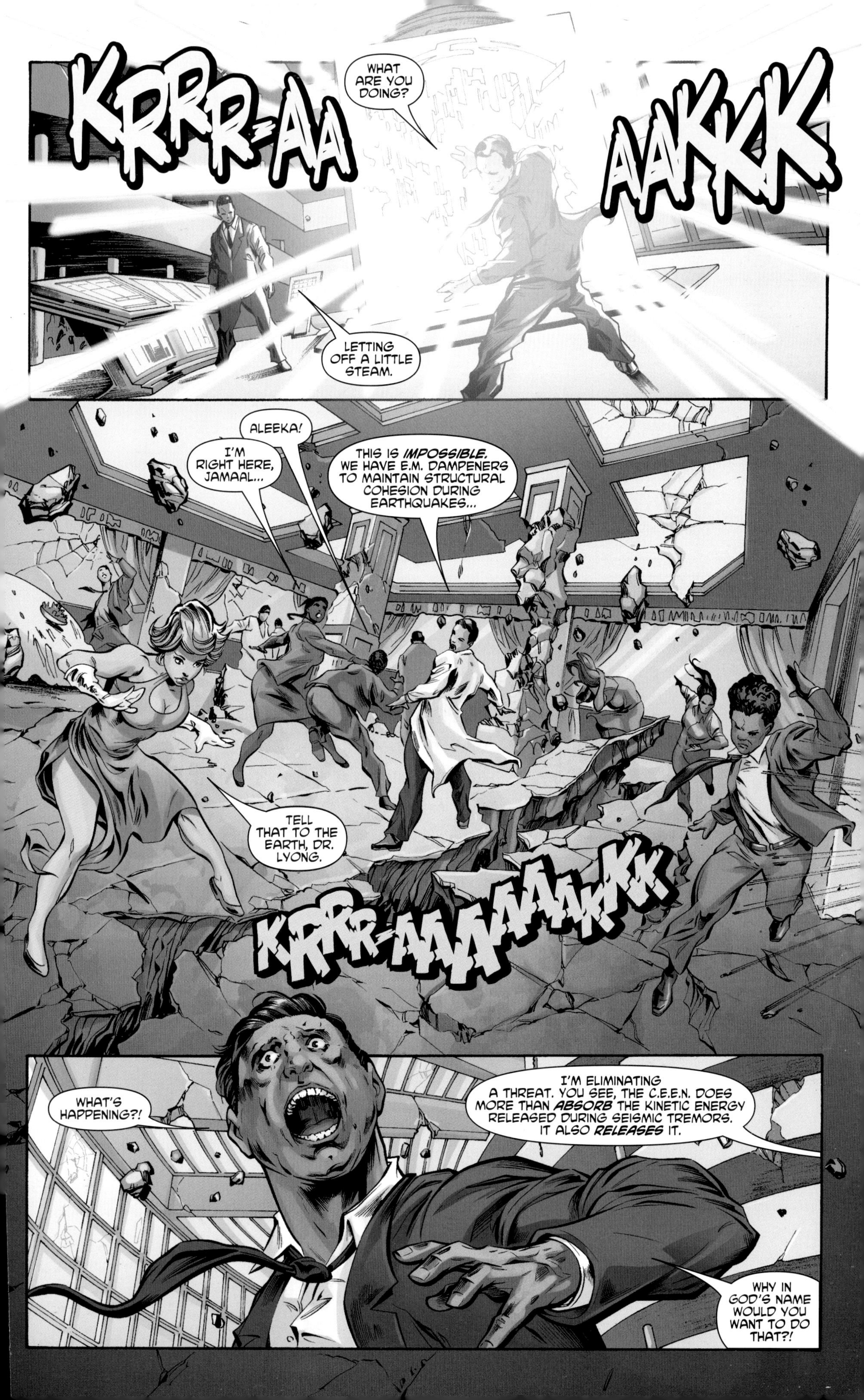
KRRR-AA AAKKK
WHAT ARE YOU DOING?
LETTING OFF A LITTLE STEAM.
ALEEKA!
I'M RIGHT HERE, JAMAAL...
THIS IS *IMPOSSIBLE.* WE HAVE E.M. DAMPENERS TO MAINTAIN STRUCTURAL COHESION DURING EARTHQUAKES...
TELL THAT TO THE EARTH, DR. LYONG.
KRRR-AAAAAAKKK
WHAT'S HAPPENING?!
I'M ELIMINATING A THREAT. YOU SEE, THE C.E.E.N. DOES MORE THAN *ABSORB* THE KINETIC ENERGY RELEASED DURING SEISMIC TREMORS. IT ALSO *RELEASES* IT.
WHY IN GOD'S NAME WOULD YOU WANT TO DO THAT?!

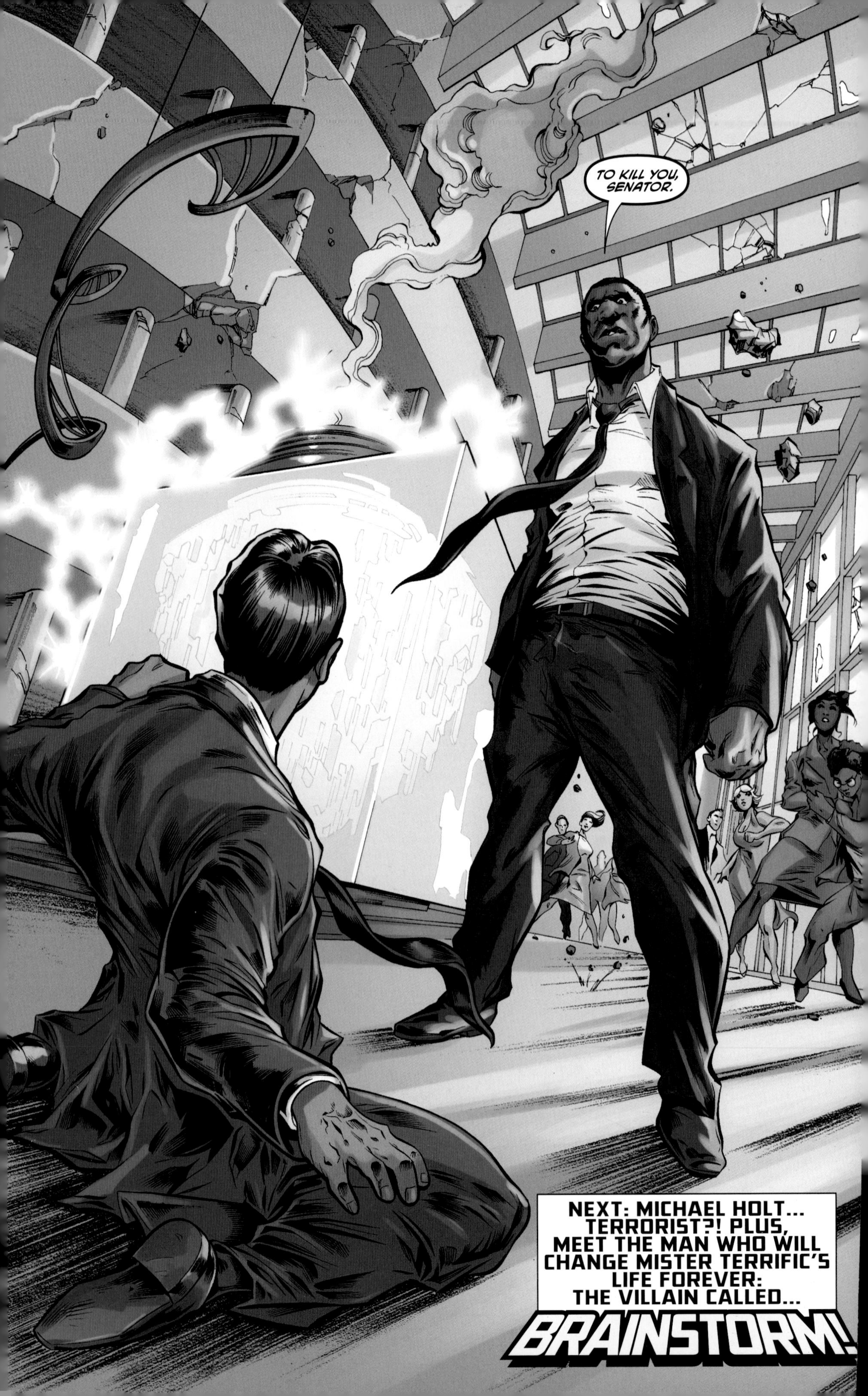
TO KILL YOU, SENATOR.
NEXT: MICHAEL HOLT... TERRORIST?! PLUS, MEET THE MAN WHO WILL CHANGE MISTER TERRIFIC'S LIFE FOREVER: THE VILLAIN CALLED...
BRAINSTORM!

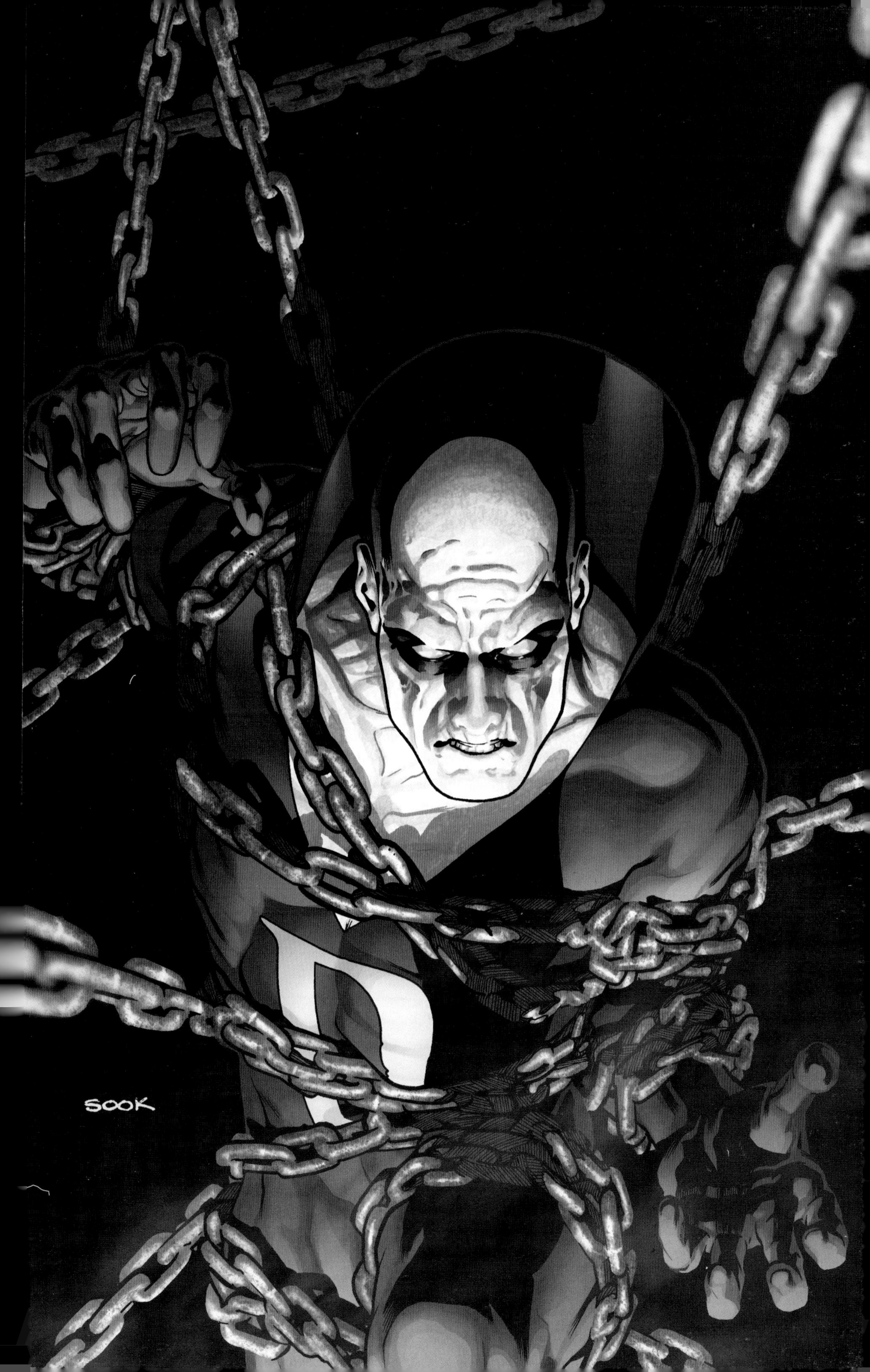
SOOK

DC UNIVERSE PRESENTS:

DEADMAN

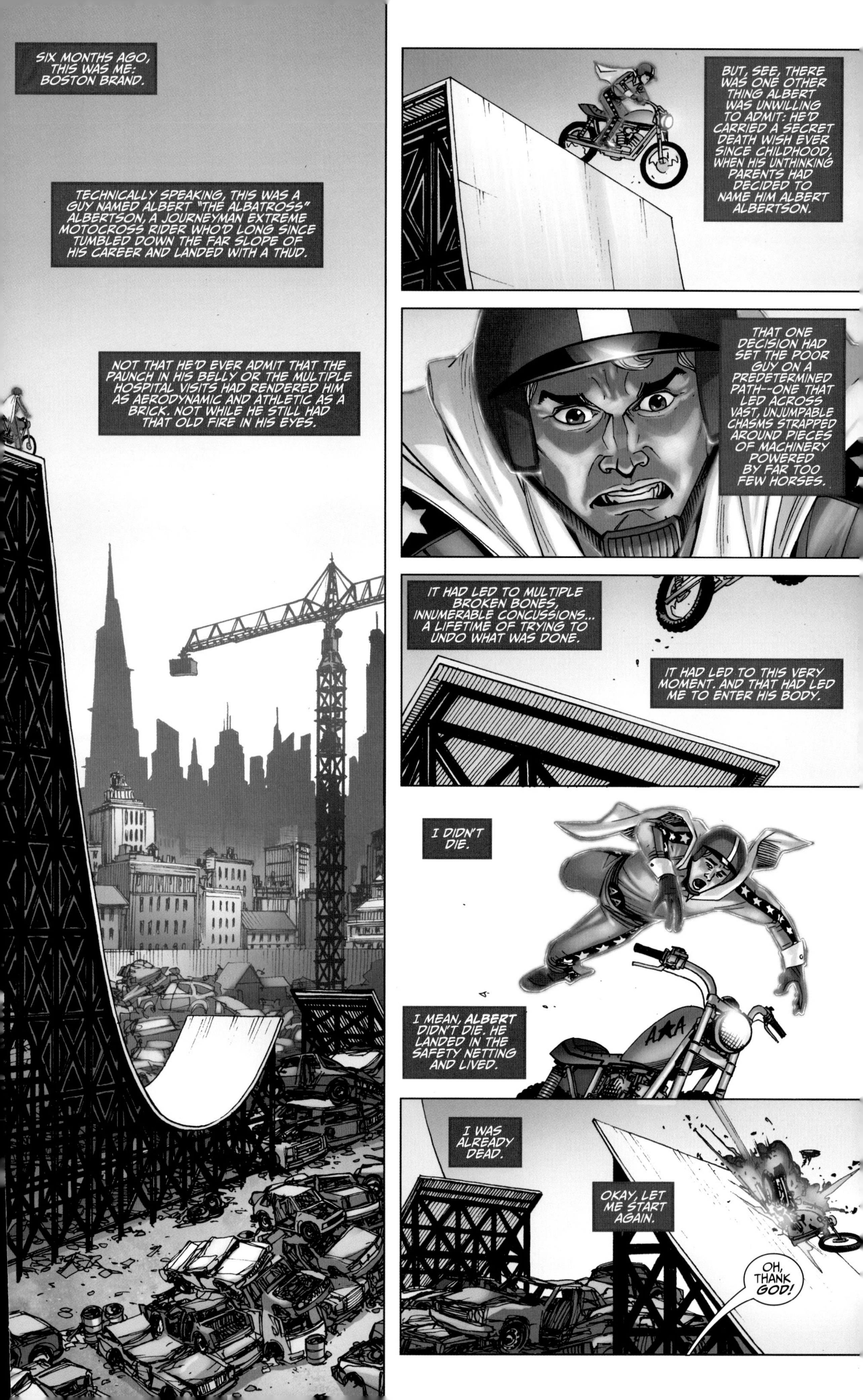
SIX MONTHS AGO, THIS WAS ME: BOSTON BRAND.
TECHNICALLY SPEAKING, THIS WAS A GUY NAMED ALBERT "THE ALBATROSS" ALBERTSON, A JOURNEYMAN EXTREME MOTOCROSS RIDER WHO'D LONG SINCE TUMBLED DOWN THE FAR SLOPE OF HIS CAREER AND LANDED WITH A THUD.
NOT THAT HE'D EVER ADMIT THAT THE PAUNCH IN HIS BELLY OR THE MULTIPLE HOSPITAL VISITS HAD RENDERED HIM AS AERODYNAMIC AND ATHLETIC AS A BRICK. NOT WHILE HE STILL HAD THAT OLD FIRE IN HIS EYES.
BUT, SEE, THERE WAS ONE OTHER THING ALBERT WAS UNWILLING TO ADMIT: HE'D CARRIED A SECRET DEATH WISH EVER SINCE CHILDHOOD, WHEN HIS UNTHINKING PARENTS HAD DECIDED TO NAME HIM ALBERT ALBERTSON.
THAT ONE DECISION HAD SET THE POOR GUY ON A PREDETERMINED PATH--ONE THAT LED ACROSS VAST, UNJUMPABLE CHASMS STRAPPED AROUND PIECES OF MACHINERY POWERED BY FAR TOO FEW HORSES.
IT HAD LED TO MULTIPLE BROKEN BONES, INNUMERABLE CONCUSSIONS... A LIFETIME OF TRYING TO UNDO WHAT WAS DONE.
IT HAD LED TO THIS VERY MOMENT. AND THAT HAD LED ME TO ENTER HIS BODY.
I DIDN'T DIE.
I MEAN, ALBERT DIDN'T DIE. HE LANDED IN THE SAFETY NETTING AND LIVED.
I WAS ALREADY DEAD.
OKAY, LET ME START AGAIN.
OH, THANK GOD!

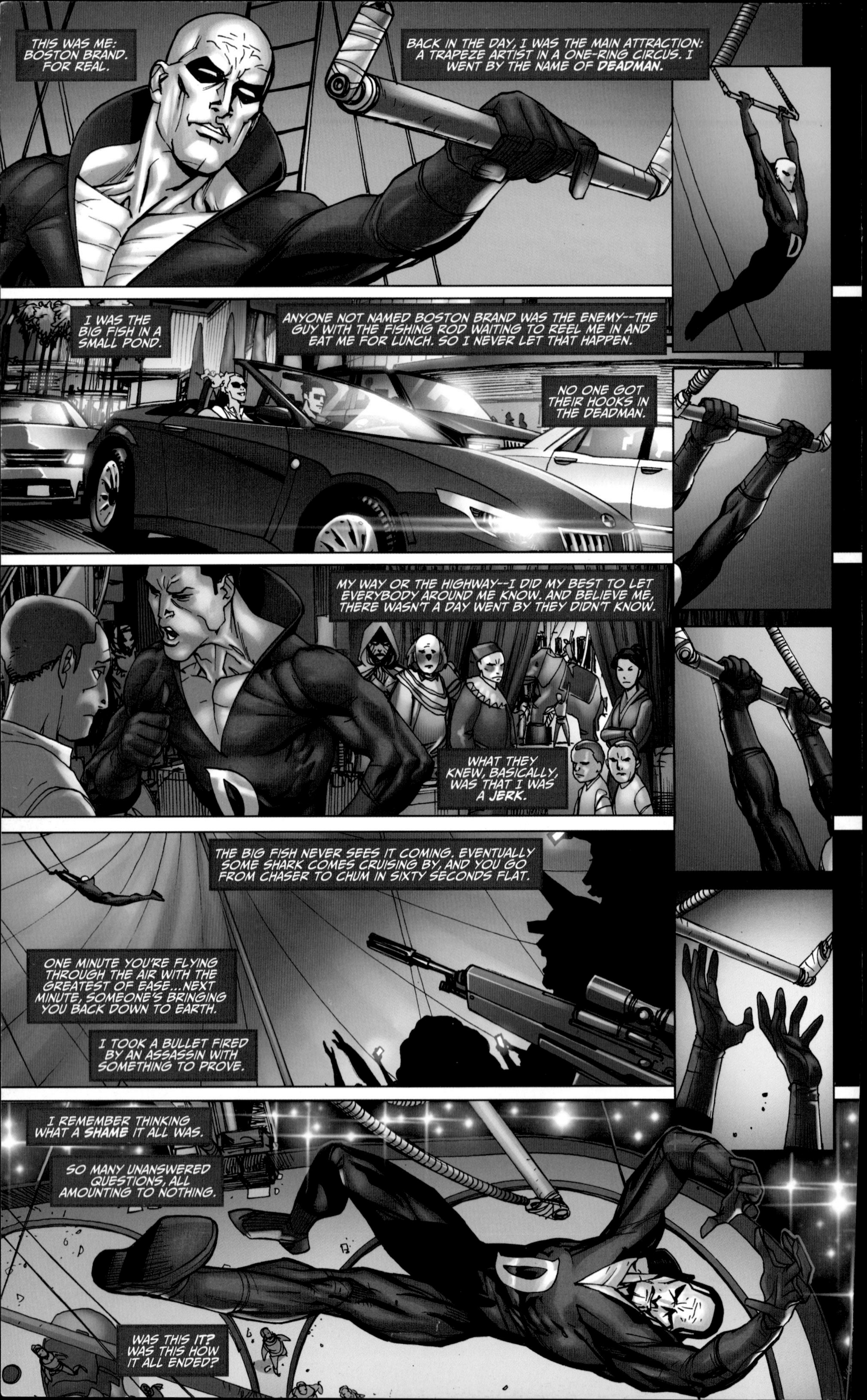
THIS WAS ME: BOSTON BRAND. FOR REAL.
BACK IN THE DAY, I WAS THE MAIN ATTRACTION: A TRAPEZE ARTIST IN A ONE-RING CIRCUS. I WENT BY THE NAME OF DEADMAN.
I WAS THE BIG FISH IN A SMALL POND.
ANYONE NOT NAMED BOSTON BRAND WAS THE ENEMY--THE GUY WITH THE FISHING ROD WAITING TO REEL ME IN AND EAT ME FOR LUNCH. SO I NEVER LET THAT HAPPEN.
NO ONE GOT THEIR HOOKS IN THE DEADMAN.
MY WAY OR THE HIGHWAY--I DID MY BEST TO LET EVERYBODY AROUND ME KNOW. AND BELIEVE ME, THERE WASN'T A DAY WENT BY THEY DIDN'T KNOW.
WHAT THEY KNEW, BASICALLY, WAS THAT I WAS A JERK.
THE BIG FISH NEVER SEES IT COMING. EVENTUALLY SOME SHARK COMES CRUISING BY, AND YOU GO FROM CHASER TO CHUM IN SIXTY SECONDS FLAT.
ONE MINUTE YOU'RE FLYING THROUGH THE AIR WITH THE GREATEST OF EASE...NEXT MINUTE, SOMEONE'S BRINGING YOU BACK DOWN TO EARTH.
I TOOK A BULLET FIRED BY AN ASSASSIN WITH SOMETHING TO PROVE.
I REMEMBER THINKING WHAT A SHAME IT ALL WAS.
SO MANY UNANSWERED QUESTIONS, ALL AMOUNTING TO NOTHING.
WAS THIS IT? WAS THIS HOW IT ALL ENDED?

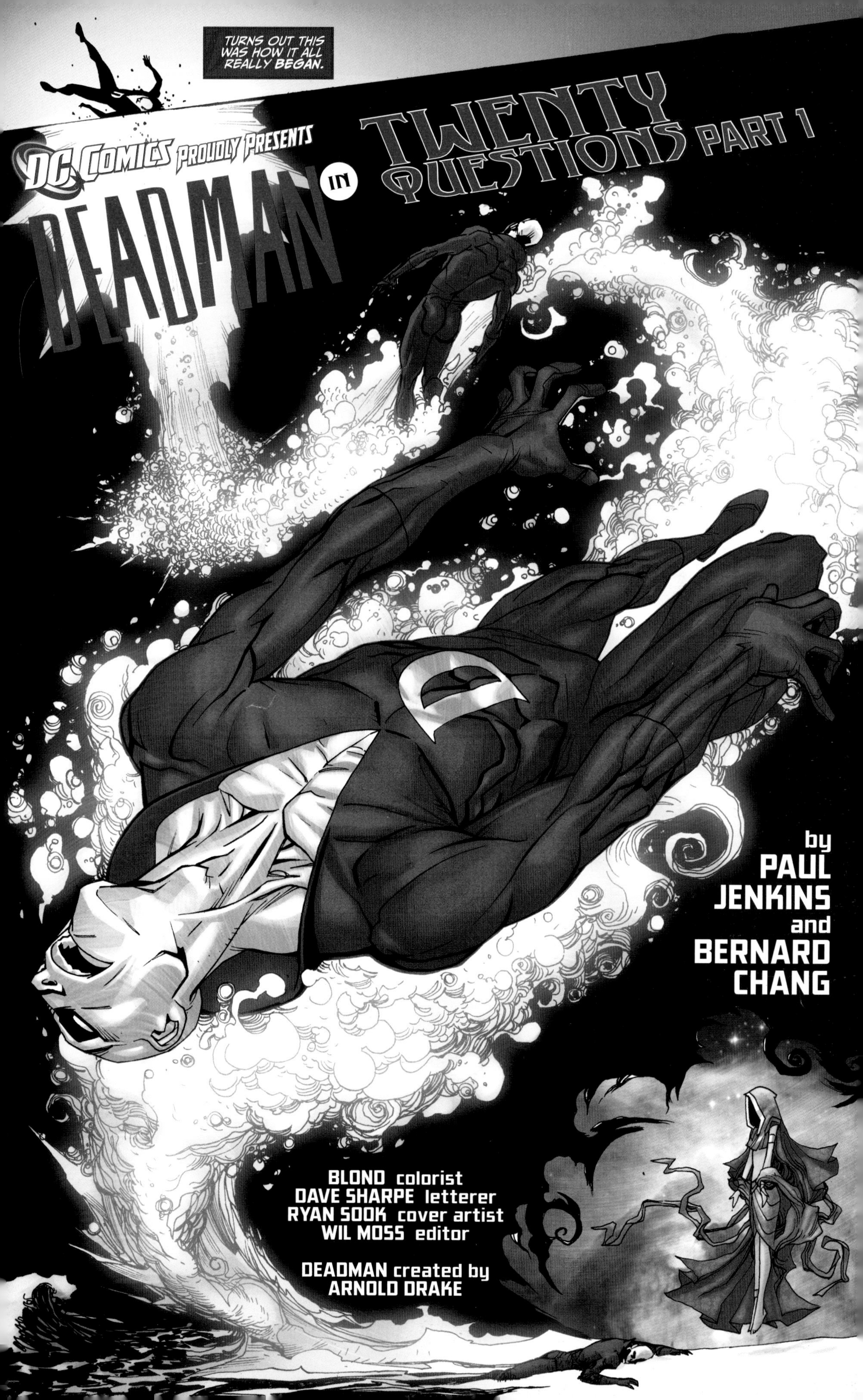

TURNS OUT THIS WAS HOW IT ALL REALLY BEGAN.
DC COMICS PROUDLY PRESENTS
DEADMAN
IN
TWENTY QUESTIONS PART 1
by PAUL JENKINS and BERNARD CHANG
BLOND colorist
DAVE SHARPE letterer
RYAN SOOK cover artist
WIL MOSS editor
DEADMAN created by ARNOLD DRAKE

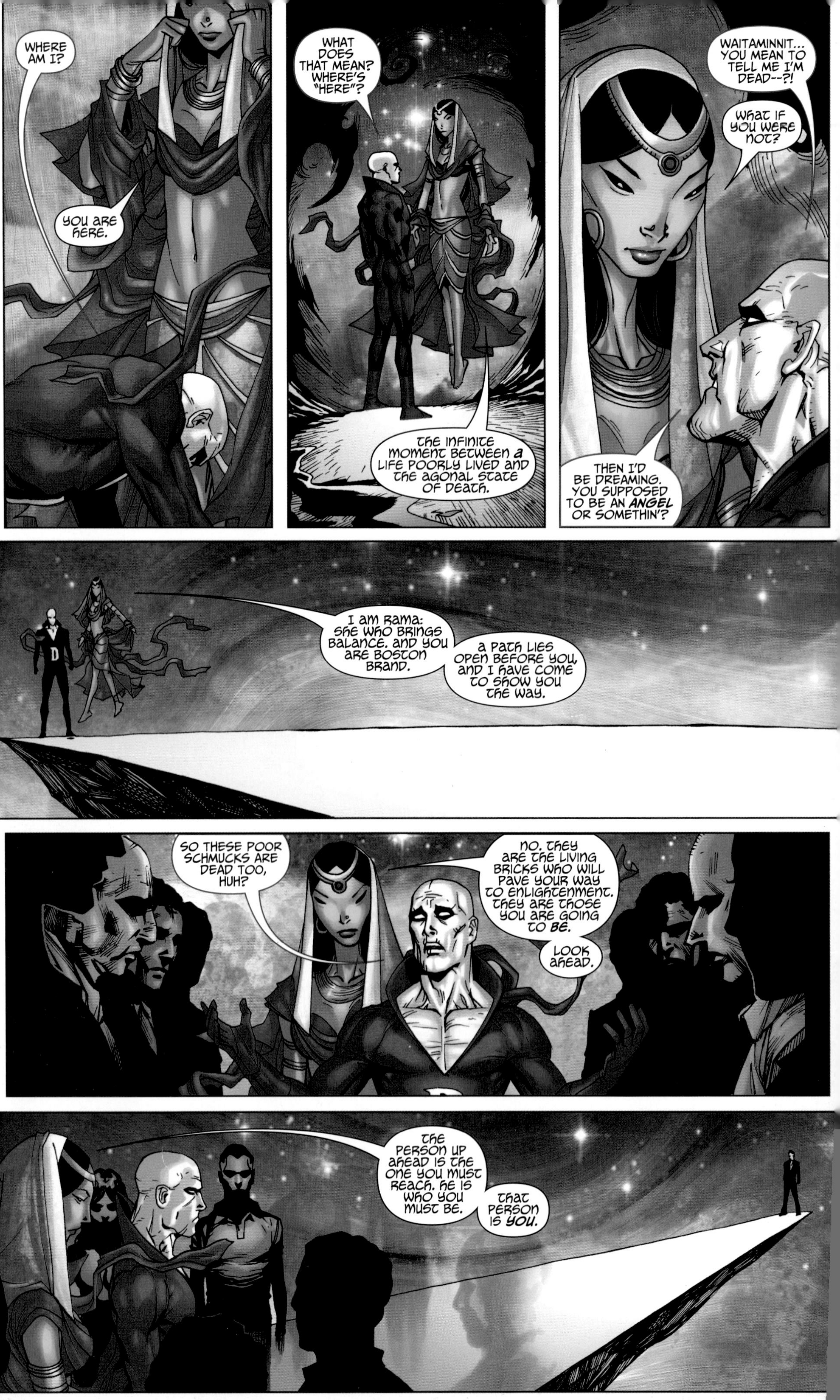
WHERE AM I?
YOU ARE HERE.
WHAT DOES THAT MEAN? WHERE'S "HERE"?
THE INFINITE MOMENT BETWEEN A LIFE POORLY LIVED AND THE AGONAL STATE OF DEATH.
WAITAMINNIT... YOU MEAN TO TELL ME I'M DEAD--?!
WHAT IF YOU WERE NOT?
THEN I'D BE DREAMING. YOU SUPPOSED TO BE AN ANGEL OR SOMETHIN'?
I AM RAMA: SHE WHO BRINGS BALANCE. AND YOU ARE BOSTON BRAND.
A PATH LIES OPEN BEFORE YOU, AND I HAVE COME TO SHOW YOU THE WAY.
SO THESE POOR SCHMUCKS ARE DEAD TOO, HUH?
NO. THEY ARE THE LIVING BRICKS WHO WILL PAVE YOUR WAY TO ENLIGHTENMENT. THEY ARE THOSE YOU ARE GOING TO BE.
LOOK AHEAD.
THE PERSON UP AHEAD IS THE ONE YOU MUST REACH. HE IS WHO YOU MUST BE.
THAT PERSON IS YOU.

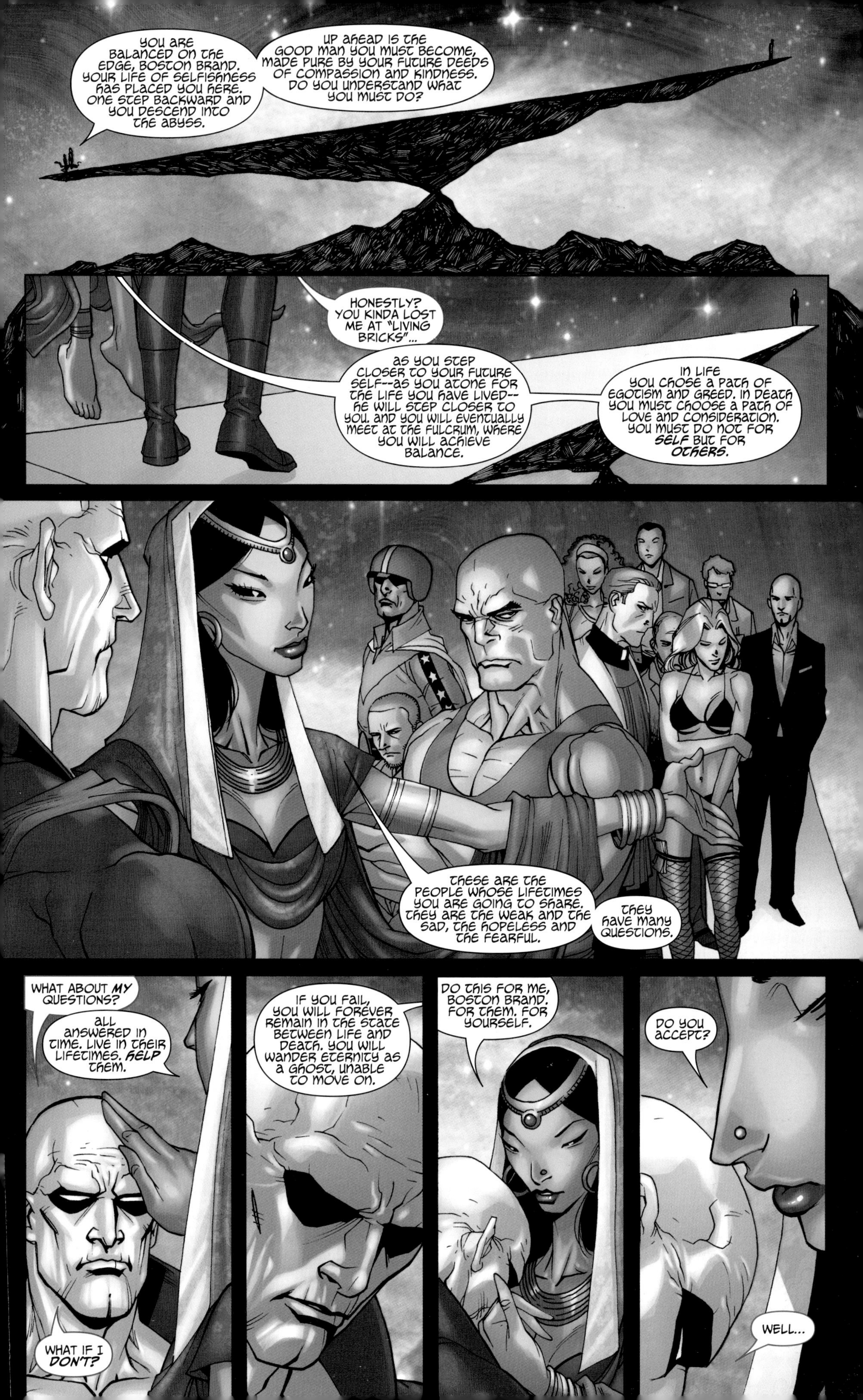
YOU ARE BALANCED ON THE EDGE, BOSTON BRAND. YOUR LIFE OF SELFISHNESS HAS PLACED YOU HERE. ONE STEP BACKWARD AND YOU DESCEND INTO THE ABYSS.
UP AHEAD IS THE GOOD MAN YOU MUST BECOME, MADE PURE BY YOUR FUTURE DEEDS OF COMPASSION AND KINDNESS. DO YOU UNDERSTAND WHAT YOU MUST DO?
HONESTLY? YOU KINDA LOST ME AT "LIVING BRICKS"...
AS YOU STEP CLOSER TO YOUR FUTURE SELF--AS YOU ATONE FOR THE LIFE YOU HAVE LIVED--HE WILL STEP CLOSER TO YOU. AND YOU WILL EVENTUALLY MEET AT THE FULCRUM, WHERE YOU WILL ACHIEVE BALANCE.
IN LIFE YOU CHOSE A PATH OF EGOTISM AND GREED. IN DEATH YOU MUST CHOOSE A PATH OF LOVE AND CONSIDERATION. YOU MUST DO NOT FOR SELF BUT FOR OTHERS.
THESE ARE THE PEOPLE WHOSE LIFETIMES YOU ARE GOING TO SHARE. THEY ARE THE WEAK AND THE SAD, THE HOPELESS AND THE FEARFUL.
THEY HAVE MANY QUESTIONS.
WHAT ABOUT MY QUESTIONS?
ALL ANSWERED IN TIME. LIVE IN THEIR LIFETIMES. HELP THEM.
WHAT IF I DON'T?
IF YOU FAIL, YOU WILL FOREVER REMAIN IN THE STATE BETWEEN LIFE AND DEATH. YOU WILL WANDER ETERNITY AS A GHOST, UNABLE TO MOVE ON.
DO THIS FOR ME, BOSTON BRAND. FOR THEM. FOR YOURSELF.
DO YOU ACCEPT?
WELL...

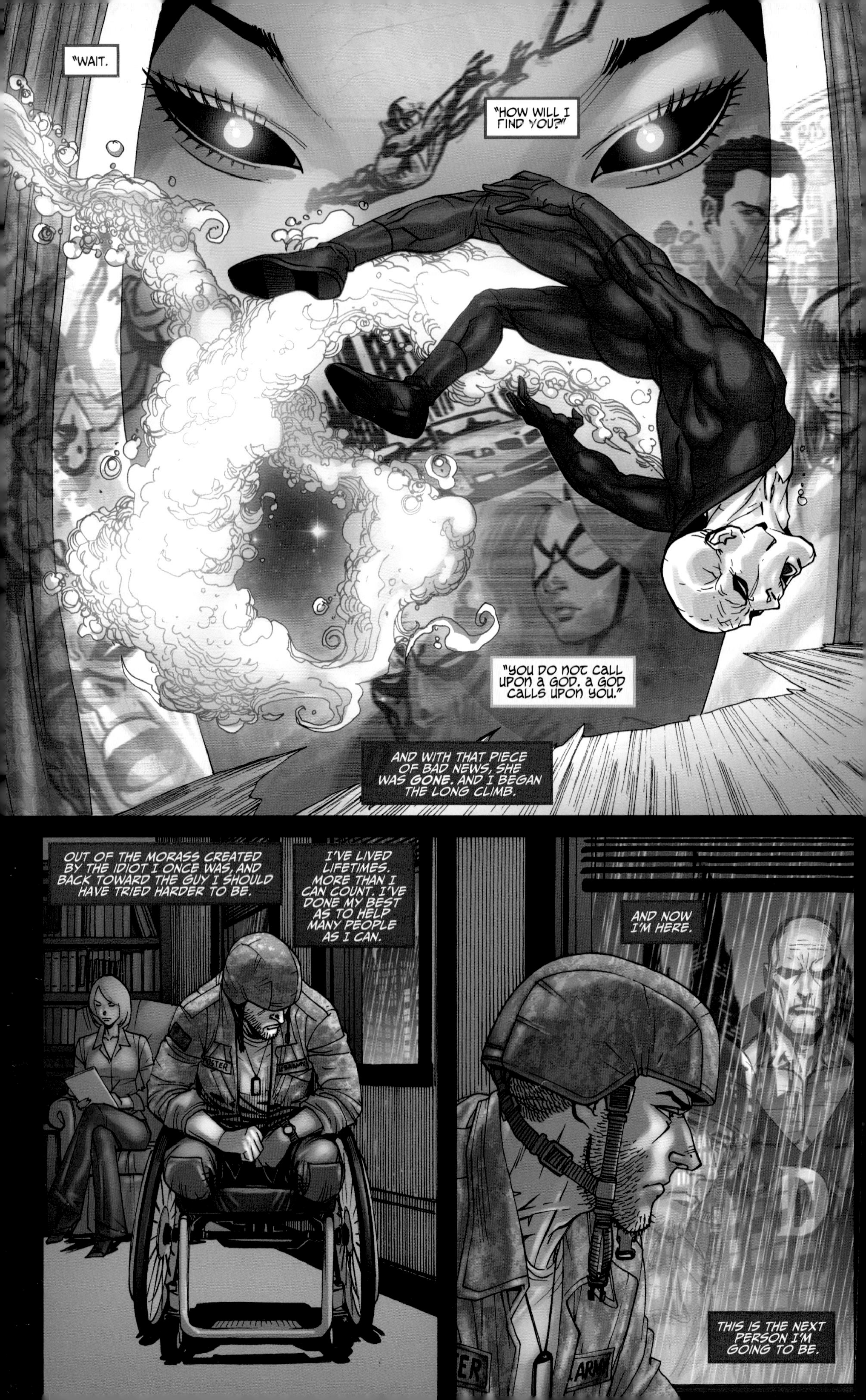
"WAIT.
"HOW WILL I FIND YOU?"
"YOU DO NOT CALL UPON A GOD. A GOD CALLS UPON YOU."
AND WITH THAT PIECE OF BAD NEWS, SHE WAS GONE. AND I BEGAN THE LONG CLIMB.
OUT OF THE MORASS CREATED BY THE IDIOT I ONCE WAS, AND BACK TOWARD THE GUY I SHOULD HAVE TRIED HARDER TO BE.
I'VE LIVED LIFETIMES. MORE THAN I CAN COUNT. I'VE DONE MY BEST AS TO HELP MANY PEOPLE AS I CAN.
AND NOW I'M HERE.
THIS IS THE NEXT PERSON I'M GOING TO BE.

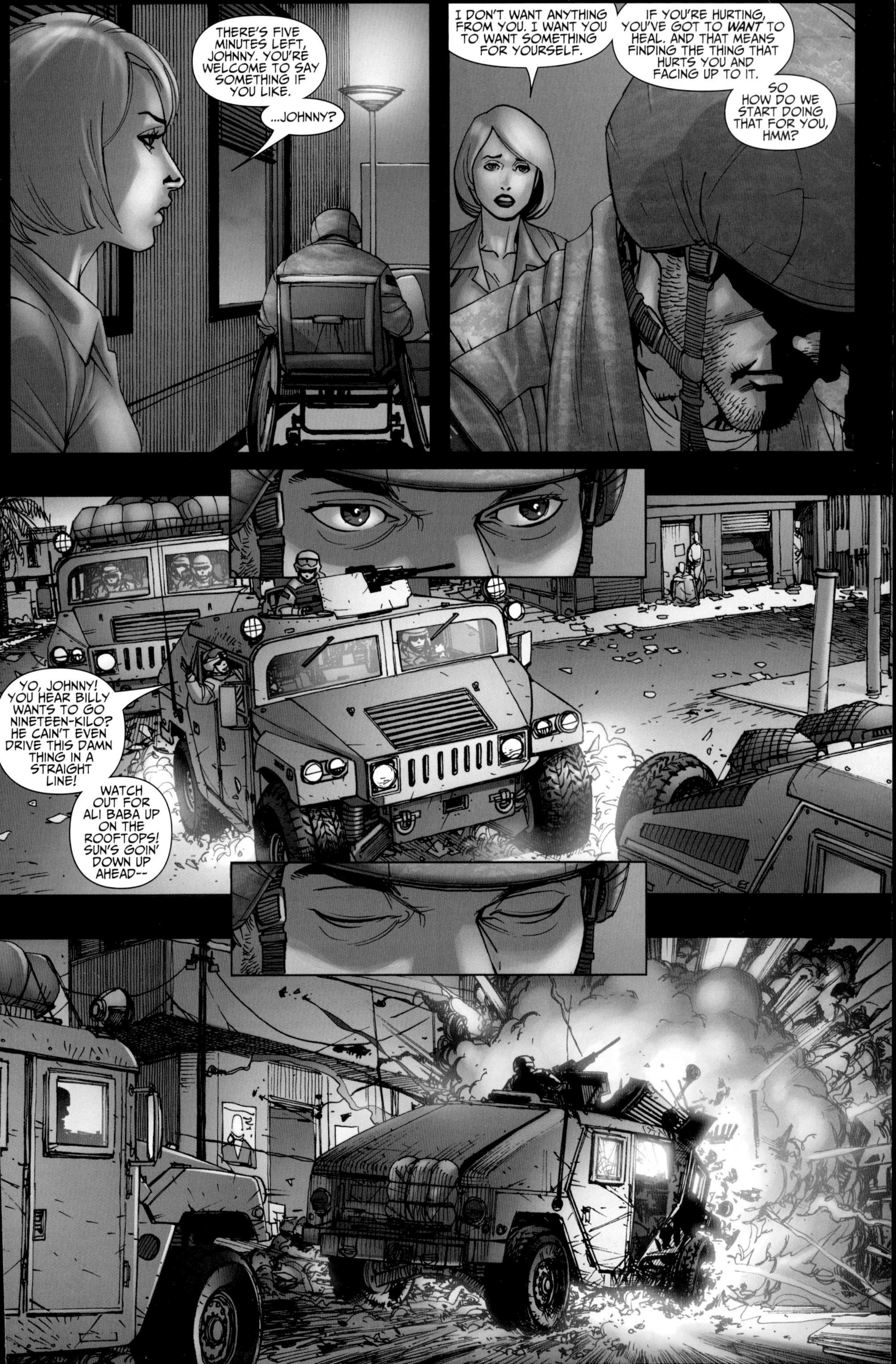

THERE'S FIVE MINUTES LEFT, JOHNNY. YOU'RE WELCOME TO SAY SOMETHING IF YOU LIKE.
...JOHNNY?
I DON'T WANT ANYTHING FROM YOU. I WANT YOU TO WANT SOMETHING FOR YOURSELF.
IF YOU'RE HURTING, YOU'VE GOT TO WANT TO HEAL. AND THAT MEANS FINDING THE THING THAT HURTS YOU AND FACING UP TO IT.
SO HOW DO WE START DOING THAT FOR YOU, HMM?
YO, JOHNNY! YOU HEAR BILLY WANTS TO GO NINETEEN-KILO? HE CAIN'T EVEN DRIVE THIS DAMN THING IN A STRAIGHT LINE!
WATCH OUT FOR ALI BABA UP ON THE ROOFTOPS! SUN'S GOIN' DOWN UP AHEAD--

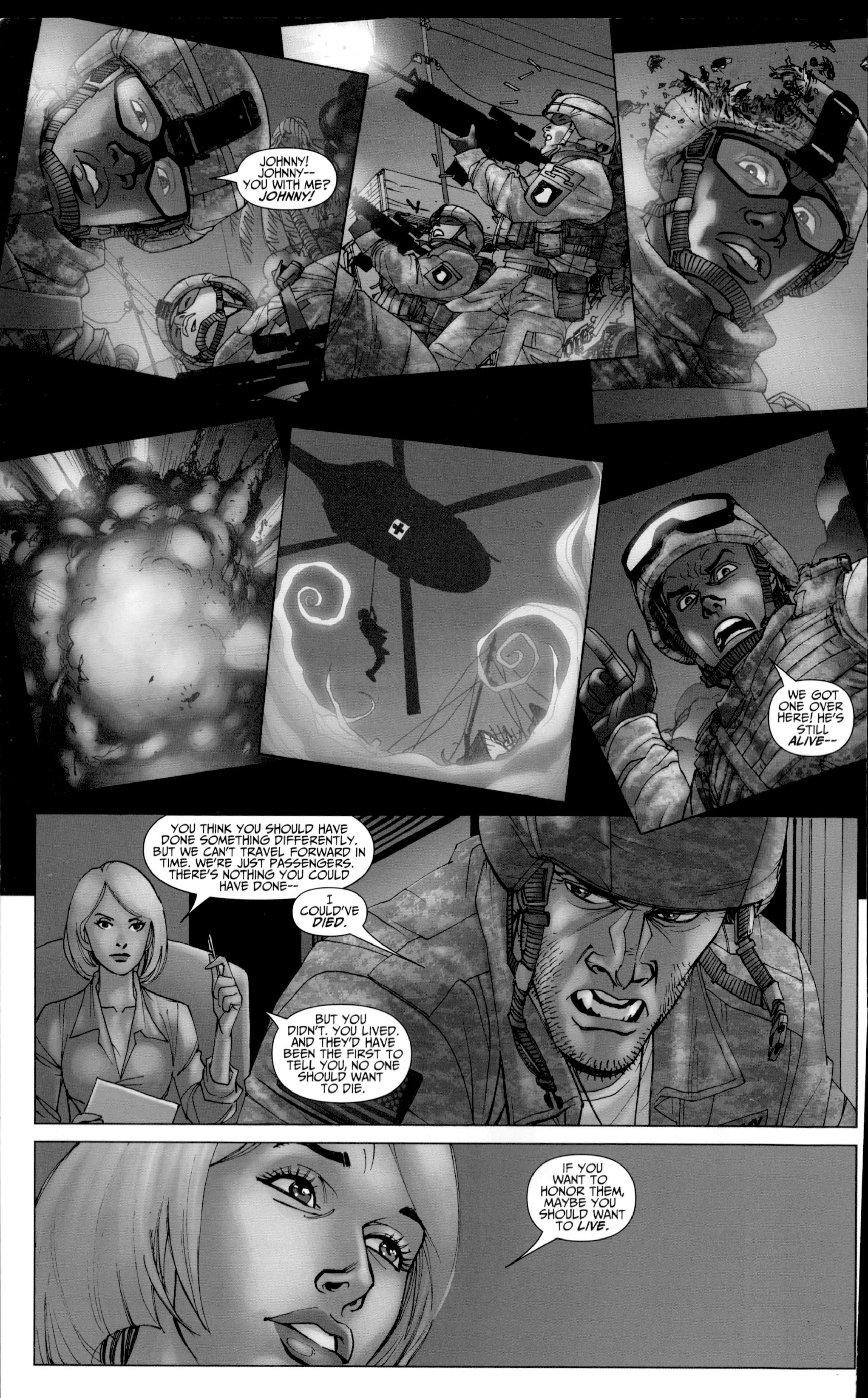
JOHNNY! JOHNNY-- YOU WITH ME? JOHNNY!
WE GOT ONE OVER HERE! HE'S STILL ALIVE--
YOU THINK YOU SHOULD HAVE DONE SOMETHING DIFFERENTLY. BUT WE CAN'T TRAVEL FORWARD IN TIME. WE'RE JUST PASSENGERS. THERE'S NOTHING YOU COULD HAVE DONE--
I COULD'VE DIED.
BUT YOU DIDN'T. YOU LIVED. AND THEY'D HAVE BEEN THE FIRST TO TELL YOU, NO ONE SHOULD WANT TO DIE.
IF YOU WANT TO HONOR THEM, MAYBE YOU SHOULD WANT TO LIVE.

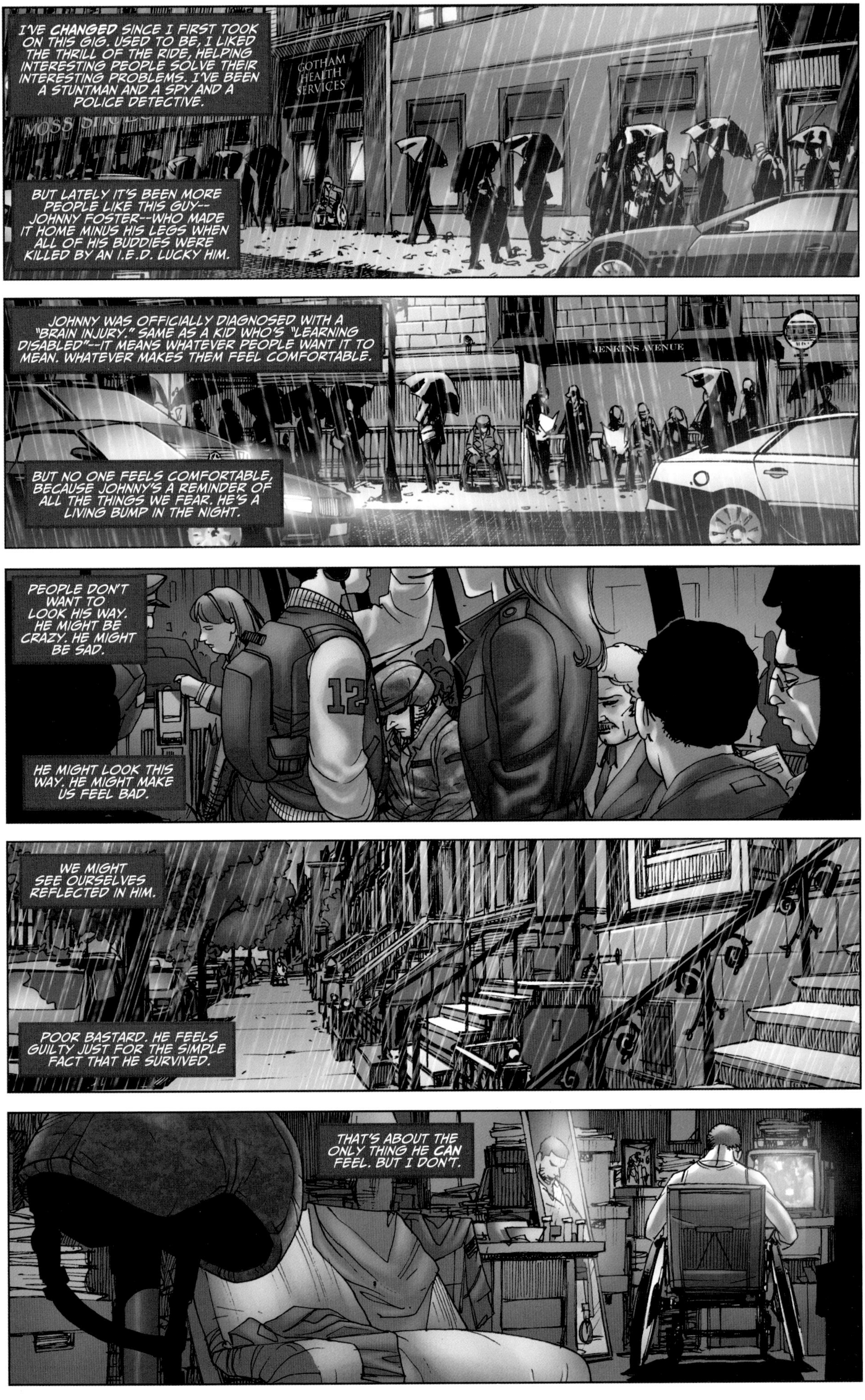
I'VE CHANGED SINCE I FIRST TOOK ON THIS GIG. USED TO BE, I LIKED THE THRILL OF THE RIDE, HELPING INTERESTING PEOPLE SOLVE THEIR INTERESTING PROBLEMS. I'VE BEEN A STUNTMAN AND A SPY AND A POLICE DETECTIVE.
GOTHAM HEALTH SERVICES
BUT LATELY IT'S BEEN MORE PEOPLE LIKE THIS GUY-- JOHNNY FOSTER--WHO MADE IT HOME MINUS HIS LEGS WHEN ALL OF HIS BUDDIES WERE KILLED BY AN I.E.D. LUCKY HIM.
JOHNNY WAS OFFICIALLY DIAGNOSED WITH A "BRAIN INJURY." SAME AS A KID WHO'S "LEARNING DISABLED"--IT MEANS WHATEVER PEOPLE WANT IT TO MEAN. WHATEVER MAKES THEM FEEL COMFORTABLE.
JENKINS AVENUE
BUT NO ONE FEELS COMFORTABLE, BECAUSE JOHNNY'S A REMINDER OF ALL THE THINGS WE FEAR. HE'S A LIVING BUMP IN THE NIGHT.
PEOPLE DON'T WANT TO LOOK HIS WAY. HE MIGHT BE CRAZY. HE MIGHT BE SAD.
12
HE MIGHT LOOK THIS WAY. HE MIGHT MAKE US FEEL BAD.
WE MIGHT SEE OURSELVES REFLECTED IN HIM.
POOR BASTARD. HE FEELS GUILTY JUST FOR THE SIMPLE FACT THAT HE SURVIVED.
THAT'S ABOUT THE ONLY THING HE CAN FEEL. BUT I DON'T.

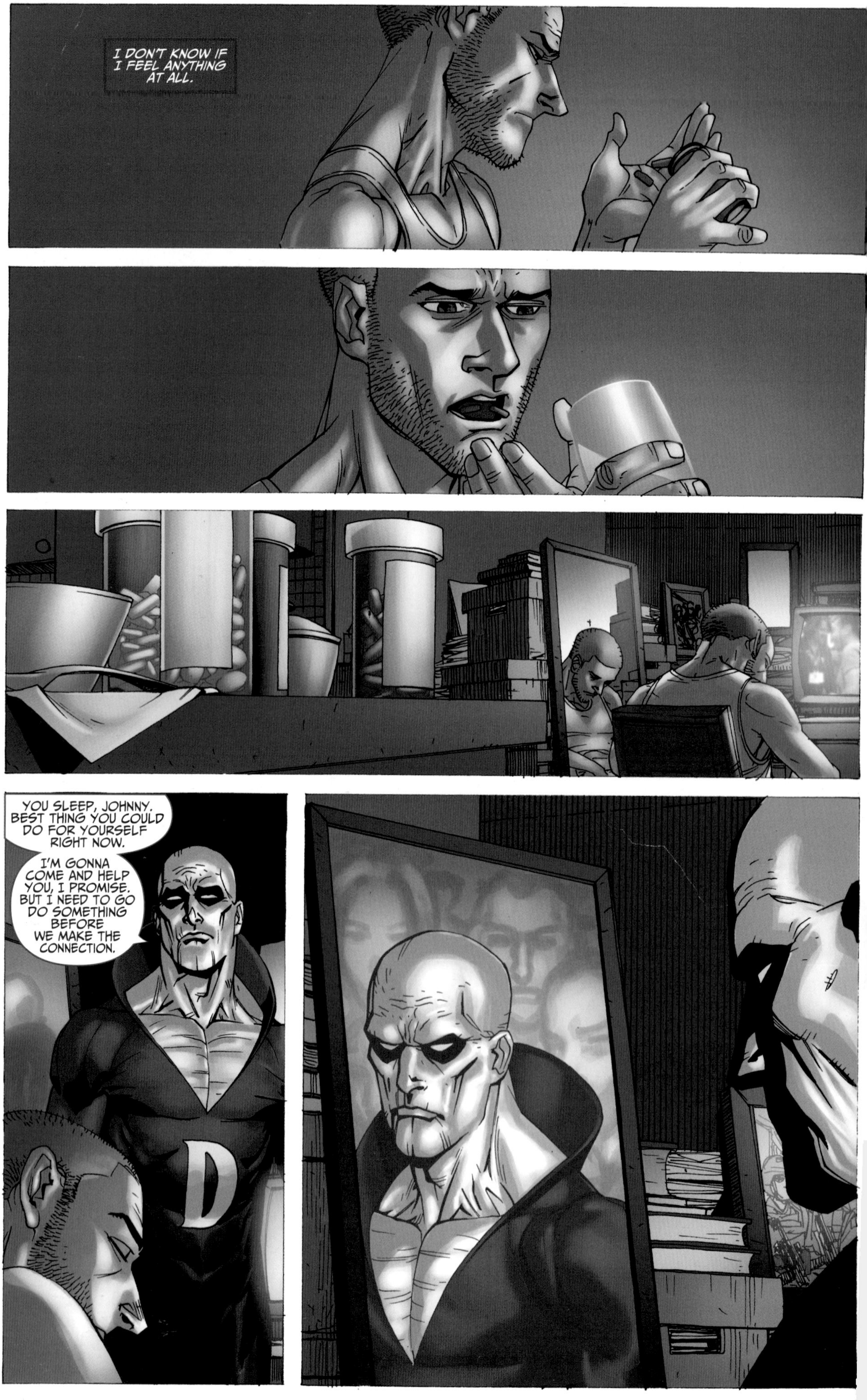
I DON'T KNOW IF I FEEL ANYTHING AT ALL.
YOU SLEEP, JOHNNY. BEST THING YOU COULD DO FOR YOURSELF RIGHT NOW.
I'M GONNA COME AND HELP YOU, I PROMISE. BUT I NEED TO GO DO SOMETHING BEFORE WE MAKE THE CONNECTION.

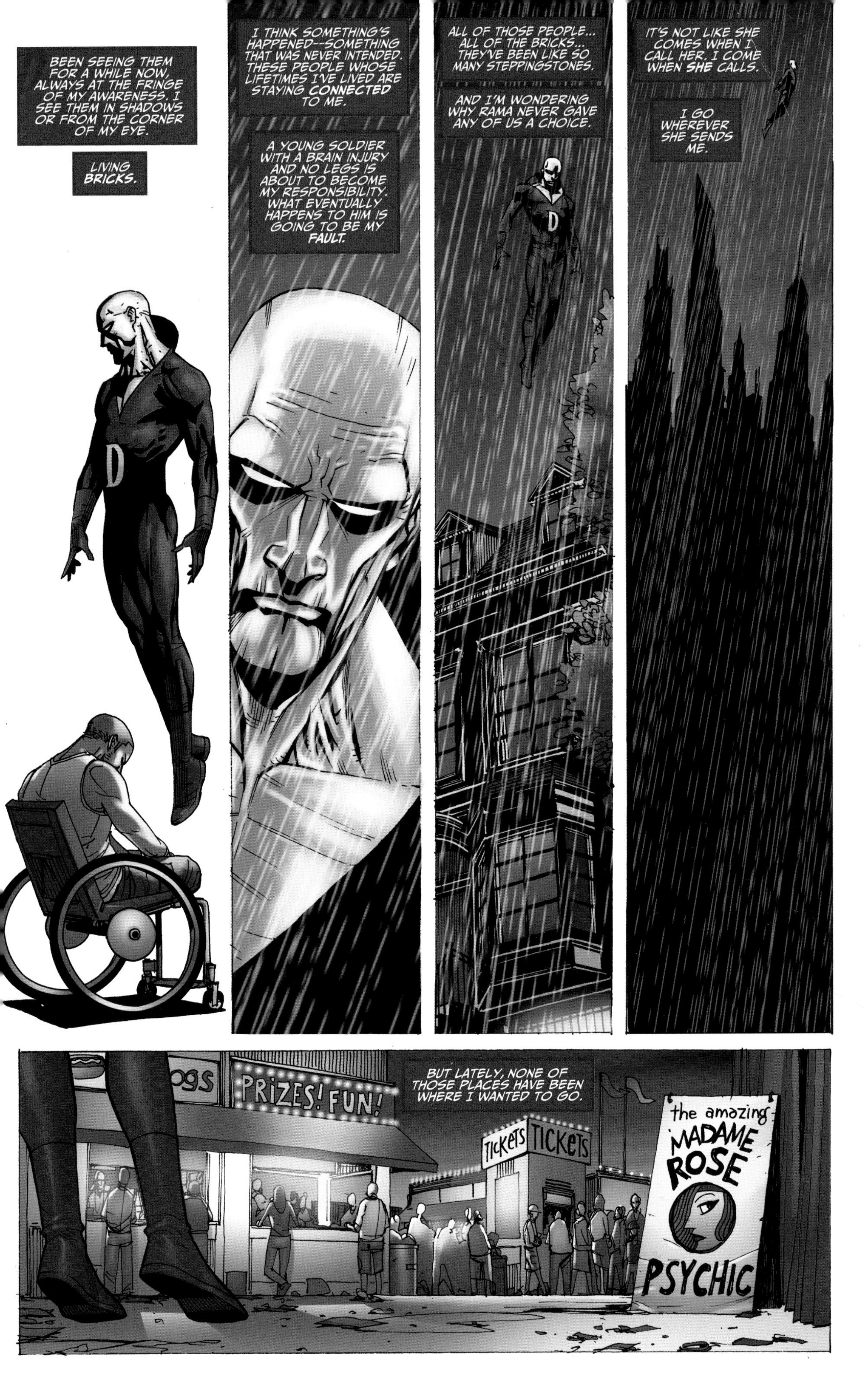
BEEN SEEING THEM FOR A WHILE NOW, ALWAYS AT THE FRINGE OF MY AWARENESS. I SEE THEM IN SHADOWS OR FROM THE CORNER OF MY EYE.
LIVING BRICKS.
I THINK SOMETHING'S HAPPENED--SOMETHING THAT WAS NEVER INTENDED. THESE PEOPLE WHOSE LIFETIMES I'VE LIVED ARE STAYING CONNECTED TO ME.
A YOUNG SOLDIER WITH A BRAIN INJURY AND NO LEGS IS ABOUT TO BECOME MY RESPONSIBILITY. WHAT EVENTUALLY HAPPENS TO HIM IS GOING TO BE MY FAULT.
ALL OF THOSE PEOPLE... ALL OF THE BRICKS... THEY'VE BEEN LIKE SO MANY STEPPINGSTONES.
AND I'M WONDERING WHY RAMA NEVER GAVE ANY OF US A CHOICE.
IT'S NOT LIKE SHE COMES WHEN I CALL HER. I COME WHEN SHE CALLS.
I GO WHEREVER SHE SENDS ME.
OGS
PRIZES! FUN!
BUT LATELY, NONE OF THOSE PLACES HAVE BEEN WHERE I WANTED TO GO.
TICKETS
TICKETS
the amazing MADAME ROSE PSYCHIC

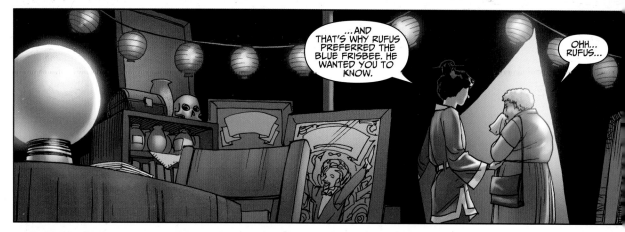

...AND THAT'S WHY RUFUS PREFERRED THE BLUE FRISBEE. HE WANTED YOU TO KNOW.

OHH... RUFUS...

the amazing MADAME

I'M NOT MYSELF LATELY, ROSE. I HAVEN'T ACTUALLY BEEN MYSELF IN A WHILE.

AREN'T YOU A LITTLE YOUNG...?

YOU'D BE SURPRISED.

IT'S ME, ROSE. IT'S BOSTON BRAND. I NEED YOUR HELP.

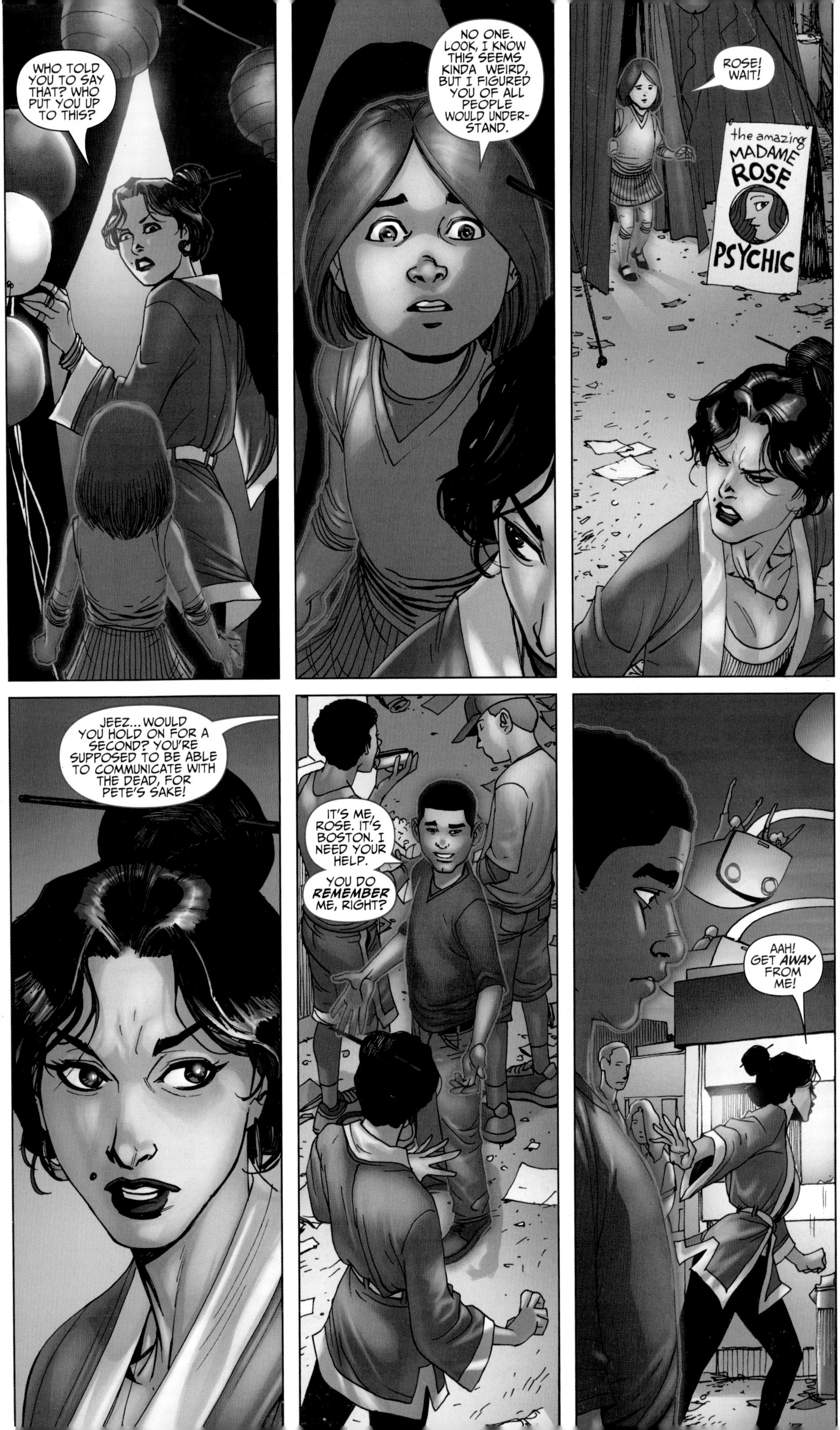
WHO TOLD YOU TO SAY THAT? WHO PUT YOU UP TO THIS?
NO ONE. LOOK, I KNOW THIS SEEMS KINDA WEIRD, BUT I FIGURED YOU OF ALL PEOPLE WOULD UNDER-STAND.
ROSE! WAIT!
the amazing MADAME ROSE PSYCHIC
JEEZ...WOULD YOU HOLD ON FOR A SECOND? YOU'RE SUPPOSED TO BE ABLE TO COMMUNICATE WITH THE DEAD, FOR PETE'S SAKE!
IT'S ME, ROSE. IT'S BOSTON. I NEED YOUR HELP.
YOU DO REMEMBER ME, RIGHT?
AAH! GET AWAY FROM ME!

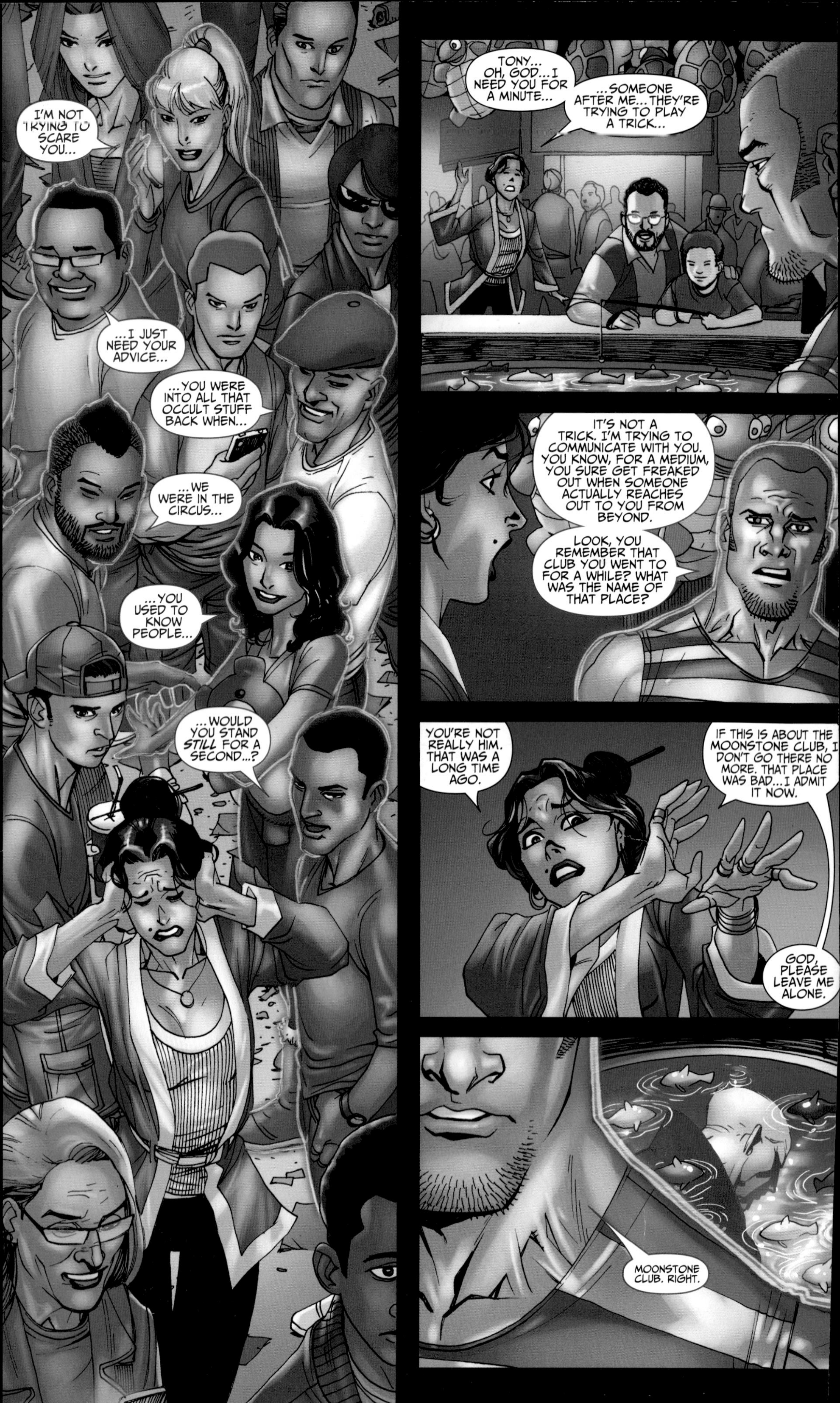
I'M NOT TRYING TO SCARE YOU...
...I JUST NEED YOUR ADVICE...
...YOU WERE INTO ALL THAT OCCULT STUFF BACK WHEN...
...WE WERE IN THE CIRCUS...
...YOU USED TO KNOW PEOPLE...
...WOULD YOU STAND STILL FOR A SECOND...?
TONY... OH, GOD... I NEED YOU FOR A MINUTE...
...SOMEONE AFTER ME... THEY'RE TRYING TO PLAY A TRICK...
IT'S NOT A TRICK. I'M TRYING TO COMMUNICATE WITH YOU. YOU KNOW, FOR A MEDIUM, YOU SURE GET FREAKED OUT WHEN SOMEONE ACTUALLY REACHES OUT TO YOU FROM BEYOND.
LOOK, YOU REMEMBER THAT CLUB YOU WENT TO FOR A WHILE? WHAT WAS THE NAME OF THAT PLACE?
YOU'RE NOT REALLY HIM. THAT WAS A LONG TIME AGO.
IF THIS IS ABOUT THE MOONSTONE CLUB, I DON'T GO THERE NO MORE. THAT PLACE WAS BAD...I ADMIT IT NOW.
GOD, PLEASE LEAVE ME ALONE.
MOONSTONE CLUB. RIGHT.

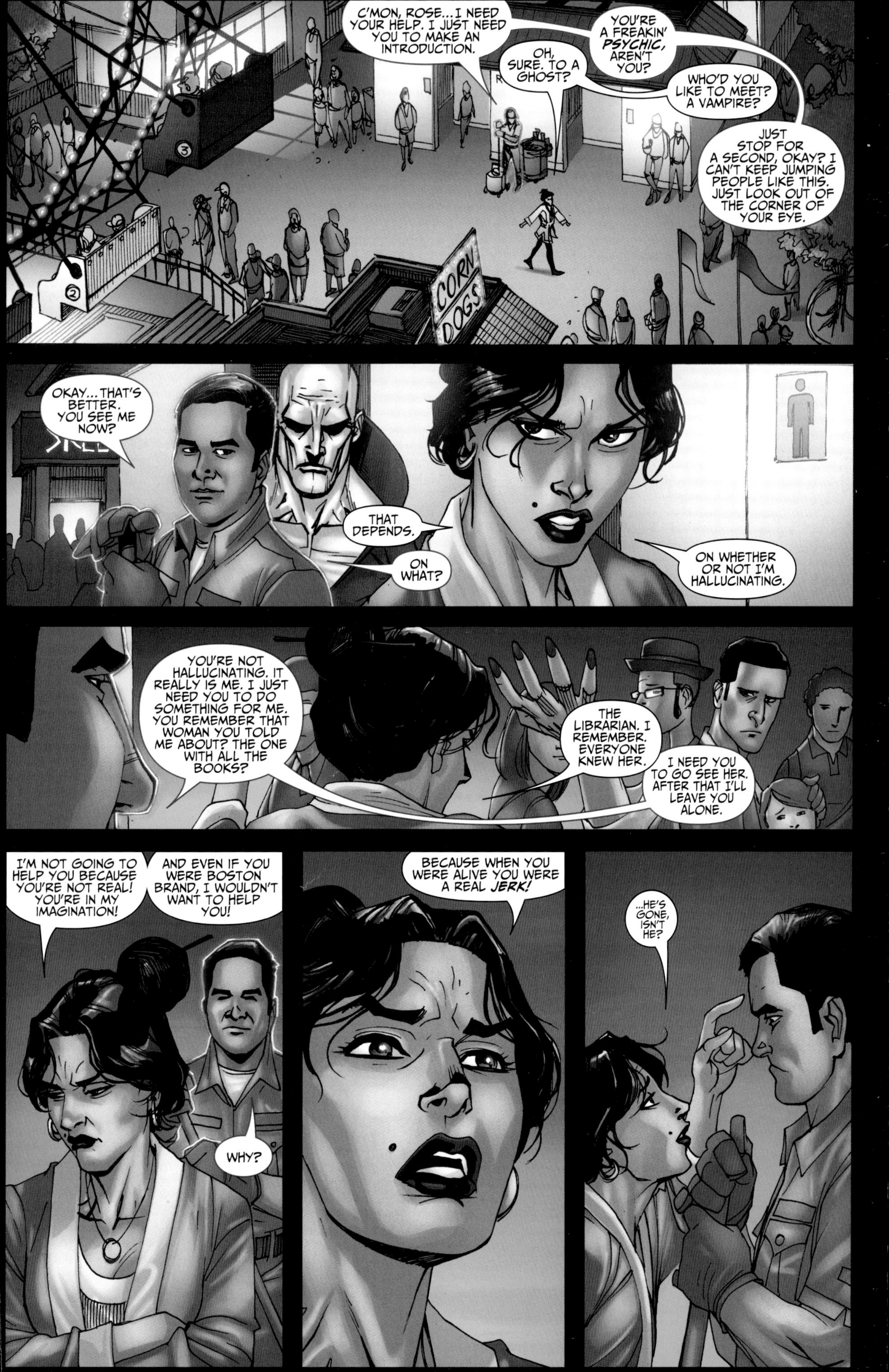
C'MON, ROSE...I NEED YOUR HELP. I JUST NEED YOU TO MAKE AN INTRODUCTION.
OH, SURE. TO A GHOST?
YOU'RE A FREAKIN' PSYCHIC, AREN'T YOU?
WHO'D YOU LIKE TO MEET? A VAMPIRE?
JUST STOP FOR A SECOND, OKAY? I CAN'T KEEP JUMPING PEOPLE LIKE THIS. JUST LOOK OUT OF THE CORNER OF YOUR EYE.
CORN DOGS
OKAY...THAT'S BETTER. YOU SEE ME NOW?
THAT DEPENDS.
ON WHAT?
ON WHETHER OR NOT I'M HALLUCINATING.
YOU'RE NOT HALLUCINATING. IT REALLY IS ME. I JUST NEED YOU TO DO SOMETHING FOR ME. YOU REMEMBER THAT WOMAN YOU TOLD ME ABOUT? THE ONE WITH ALL THE BOOKS?
THE LIBRARIAN. I REMEMBER. EVERYONE KNEW HER.
I NEED YOU TO GO SEE HER. AFTER THAT I'LL LEAVE YOU ALONE.
I'M NOT GOING TO HELP YOU BECAUSE YOU'RE NOT REAL! YOU'RE IN MY IMAGINATION!
AND EVEN IF YOU WERE BOSTON BRAND, I WOULDN'T WANT TO HELP YOU!
WHY?
BECAUSE WHEN YOU WERE ALIVE YOU WERE A REAL JERK!
...HE'S GONE, ISN'T HE?

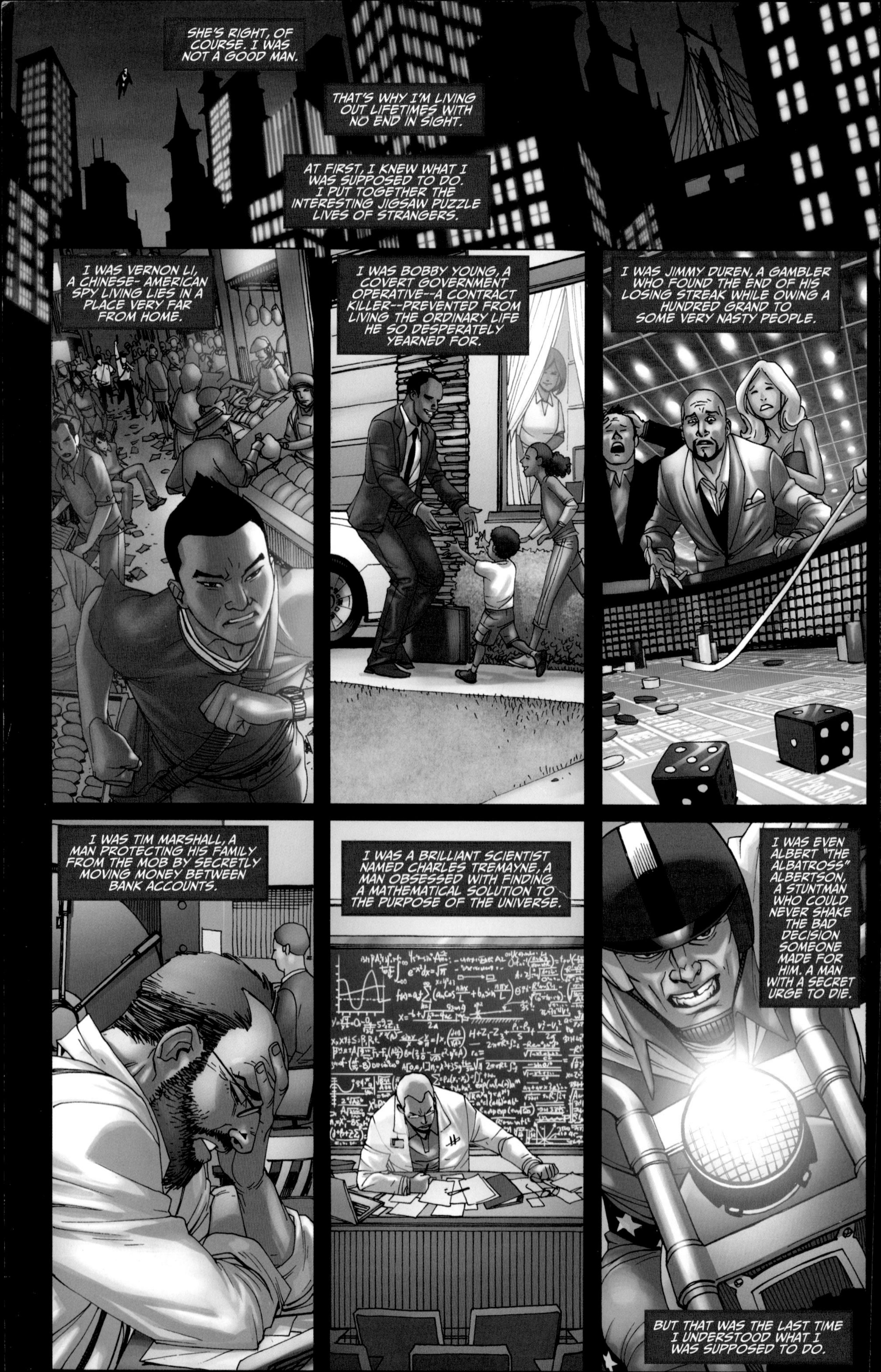

SHE'S RIGHT, OF COURSE. I WAS NOT A GOOD MAN.
THAT'S WHY I'M LIVING OUT LIFETIMES WITH NO END IN SIGHT.
AT FIRST, I KNEW WHAT I WAS SUPPOSED TO DO. I PUT TOGETHER THE INTERESTING JIGSAW PUZZLE LIVES OF STRANGERS.
I WAS VERNON LI, A CHINESE- AMERICAN SPY LIVING LIES IN A PLACE VERY FAR FROM HOME.
I WAS BOBBY YOUNG, A COVERT GOVERNMENT OPERATIVE--A CONTRACT KILLER--PREVENTED FROM LIVING THE ORDINARY LIFE HE SO DESPERATELY YEARNED FOR.
I WAS JIMMY DUREN, A GAMBLER WHO FOUND THE END OF HIS LOSING STREAK WHILE OWING A HUNDRED GRAND TO SOME VERY NASTY PEOPLE.
I WAS TIM MARSHALL, A MAN PROTECTING HIS FAMILY FROM THE MOB BY SECRETLY MOVING MONEY BETWEEN BANK ACCOUNTS.
I WAS A BRILLIANT SCIENTIST NAMED CHARLES TREMAYNE, A MAN OBSESSED WITH FINDING A MATHEMATICAL SOLUTION TO THE PURPOSE OF THE UNIVERSE.
I WAS EVEN ALBERT "THE ALBATROSS" ALBERTSON, A STUNTMAN WHO COULD NEVER SHAKE THE BAD DECISION SOMEONE MADE FOR HIM. A MAN WITH A SECRET URGE TO DIE.
BUT THAT WAS THE LAST TIME I UNDERSTOOD WHAT I WAS SUPPOSED TO DO.

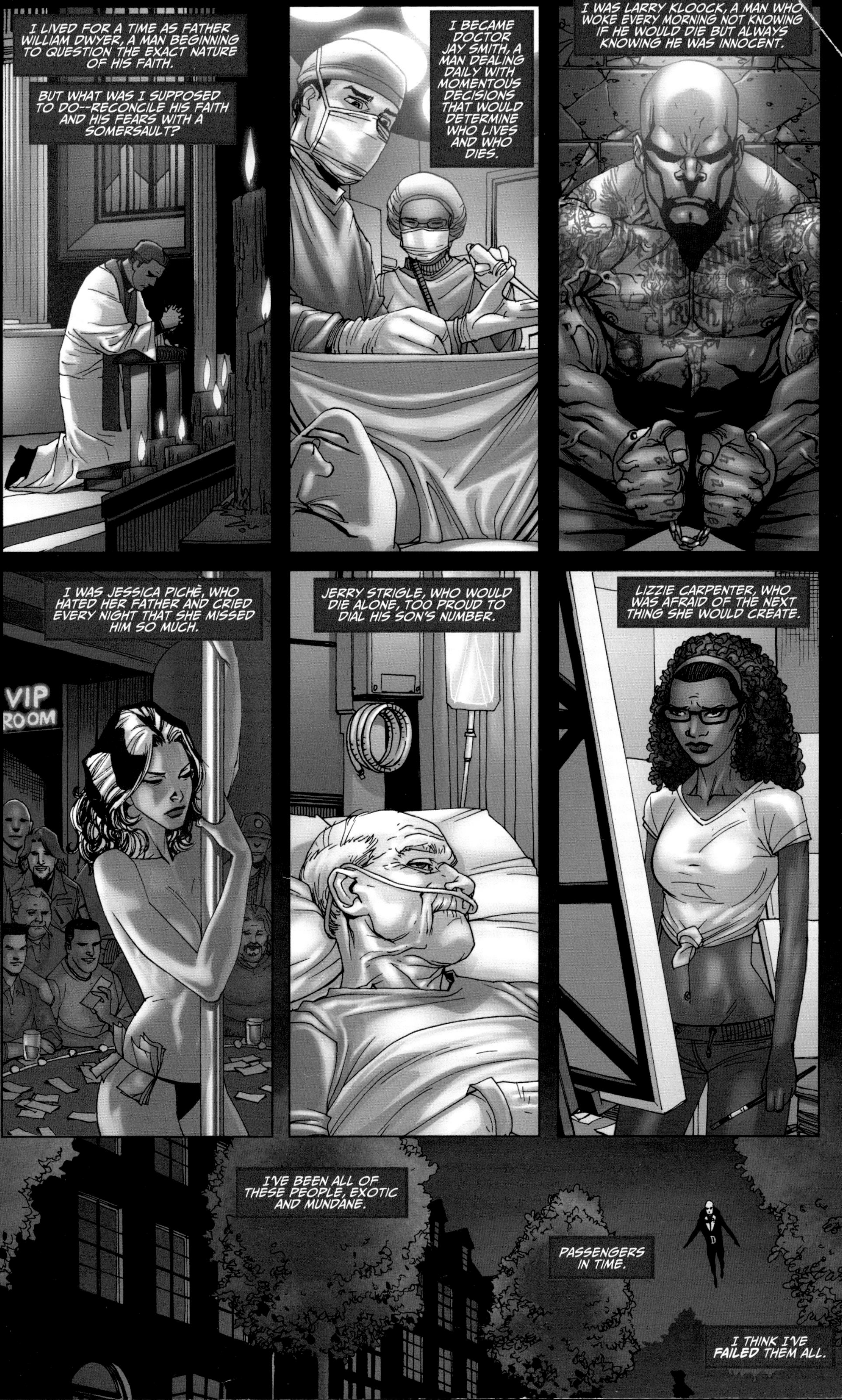
I LIVED FOR A TIME AS FATHER WILLIAM DWYER, A MAN BEGINNING TO QUESTION THE EXACT NATURE OF HIS FAITH.
BUT WHAT WAS I SUPPOSED TO DO--RECONCILE HIS FAITH AND HIS FEARS WITH A SOMERSAULT?
I BECAME DOCTOR JAY SMITH, A MAN DEALING DAILY WITH MOMENTOUS DECISIONS THAT WOULD DETERMINE WHO LIVES AND WHO DIES.
I WAS LARRY KLOOCK, A MAN WHO WOKE EVERY MORNING NOT KNOWING IF HE WOULD DIE BUT ALWAYS KNOWING HE WAS INNOCENT.
I WAS JESSICA PICHÈ, WHO HATED HER FATHER AND CRIED EVERY NIGHT THAT SHE MISSED HIM SO MUCH.
VIP ROOM
JERRY STRIGLE, WHO WOULD DIE ALONE, TOO PROUD TO DIAL HIS SON'S NUMBER.
LIZZIE CARPENTER, WHO WAS AFRAID OF THE NEXT THING SHE WOULD CREATE.
I'VE BEEN ALL OF THESE PEOPLE, EXOTIC AND MUNDANE.
PASSENGERS IN TIME.
I THINK I'VE FAILED THEM ALL.

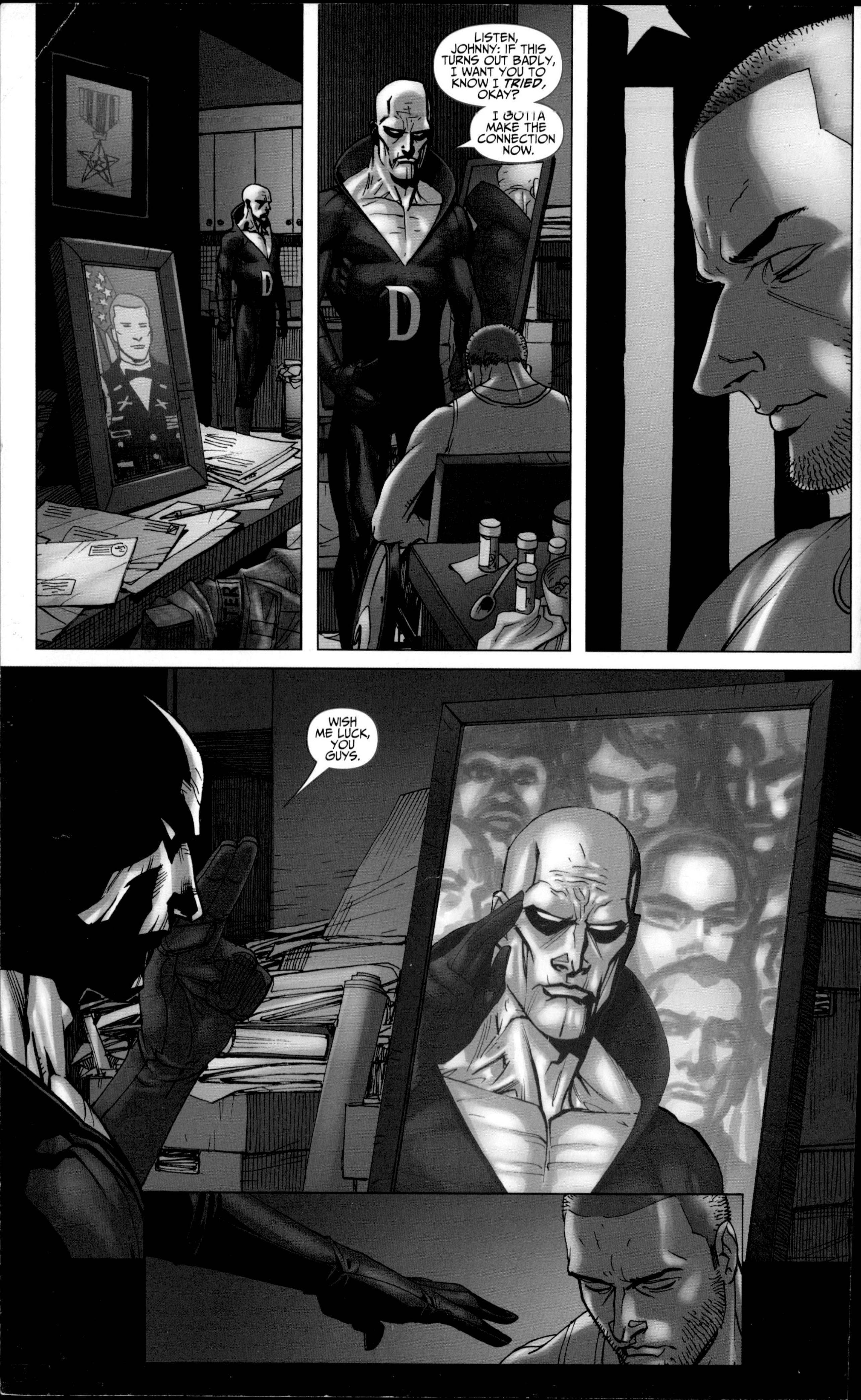
LISTEN, JOHNNY: IF THIS TURNS OUT BADLY, I WANT YOU TO KNOW I *TRIED*, OKAY?
I GOTTA MAKE THE CONNECTION NOW.
WISH ME LUCK, YOU GUYS.

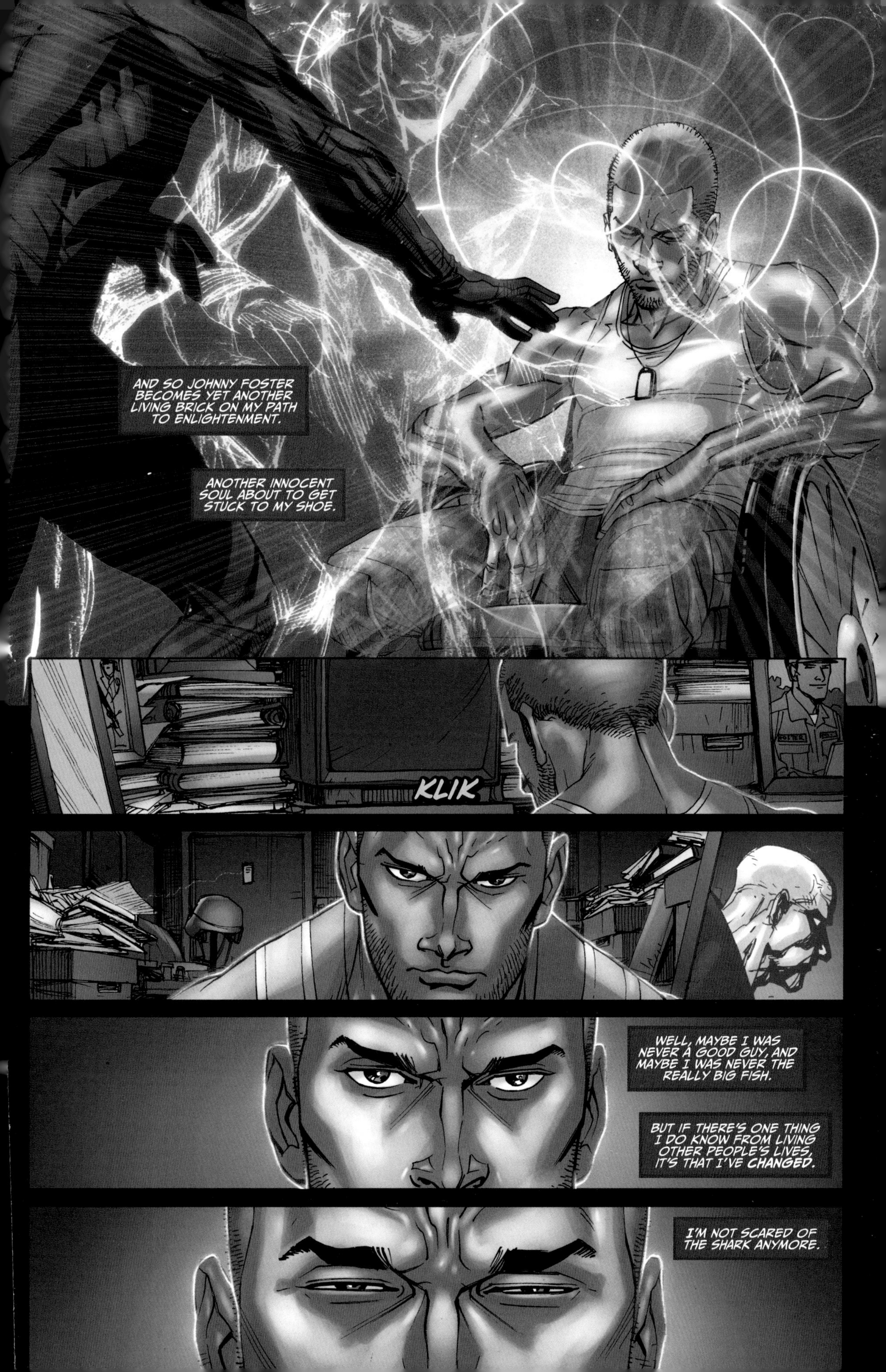
AND SO JOHNNY FOSTER BECOMES YET ANOTHER LIVING BRICK ON MY PATH TO ENLIGHTENMENT.
ANOTHER INNOCENT SOUL ABOUT TO GET STUCK TO MY SHOE.
KLIK
WELL, MAYBE I WAS NEVER A GOOD GUY, AND MAYBE I WAS NEVER THE REALLY BIG FISH.
BUT IF THERE'S ONE THING I DO KNOW FROM LIVING OTHER PEOPLE'S LIVES, IT'S THAT I'VE **CHANGED**.
I'M NOT SCARED OF THE SHARK ANYMORE.

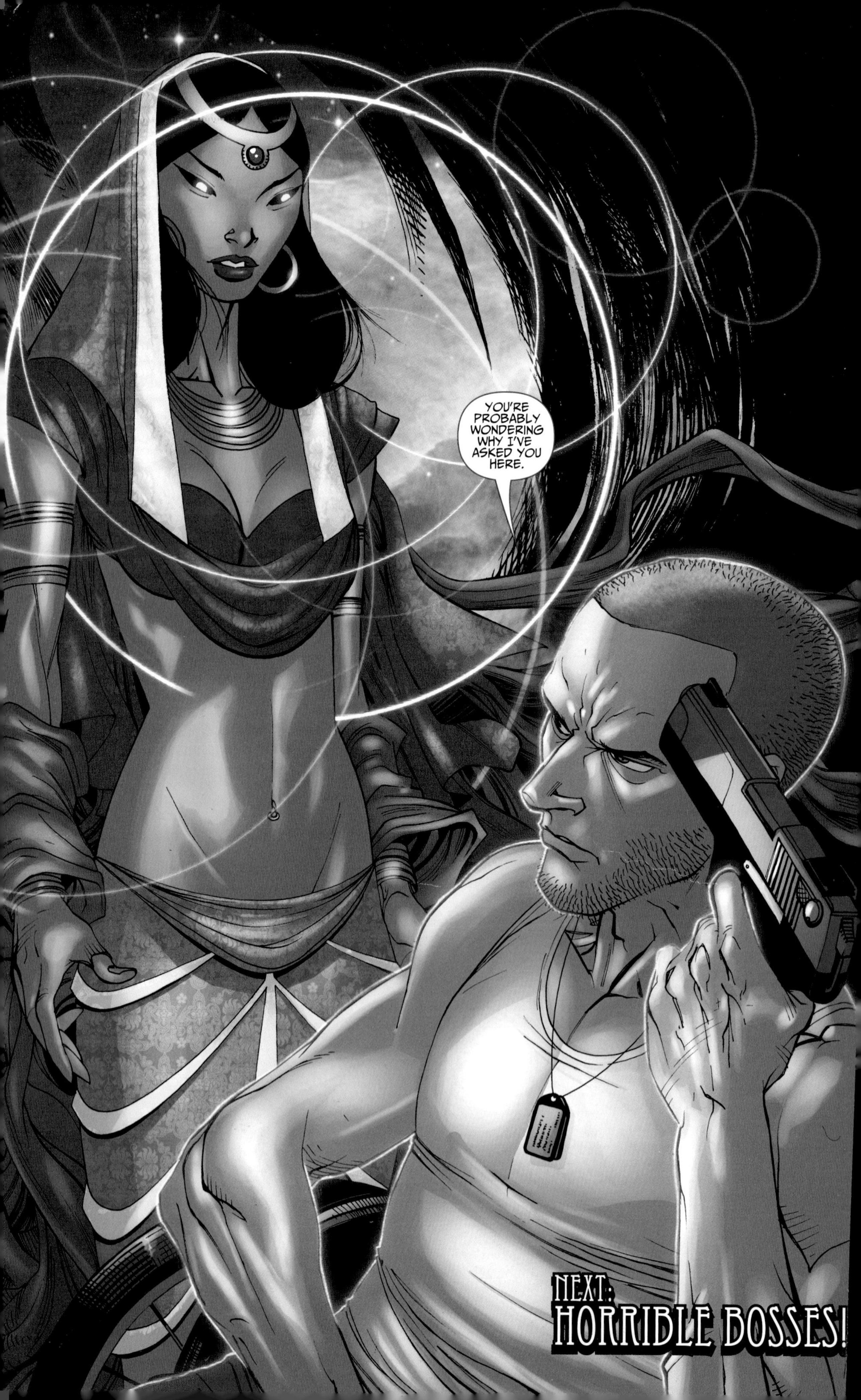
YOU'RE PROBABLY WONDERING WHY I'VE ASKED YOU HERE.
NEXT:
HORRIBLE BOSSES!

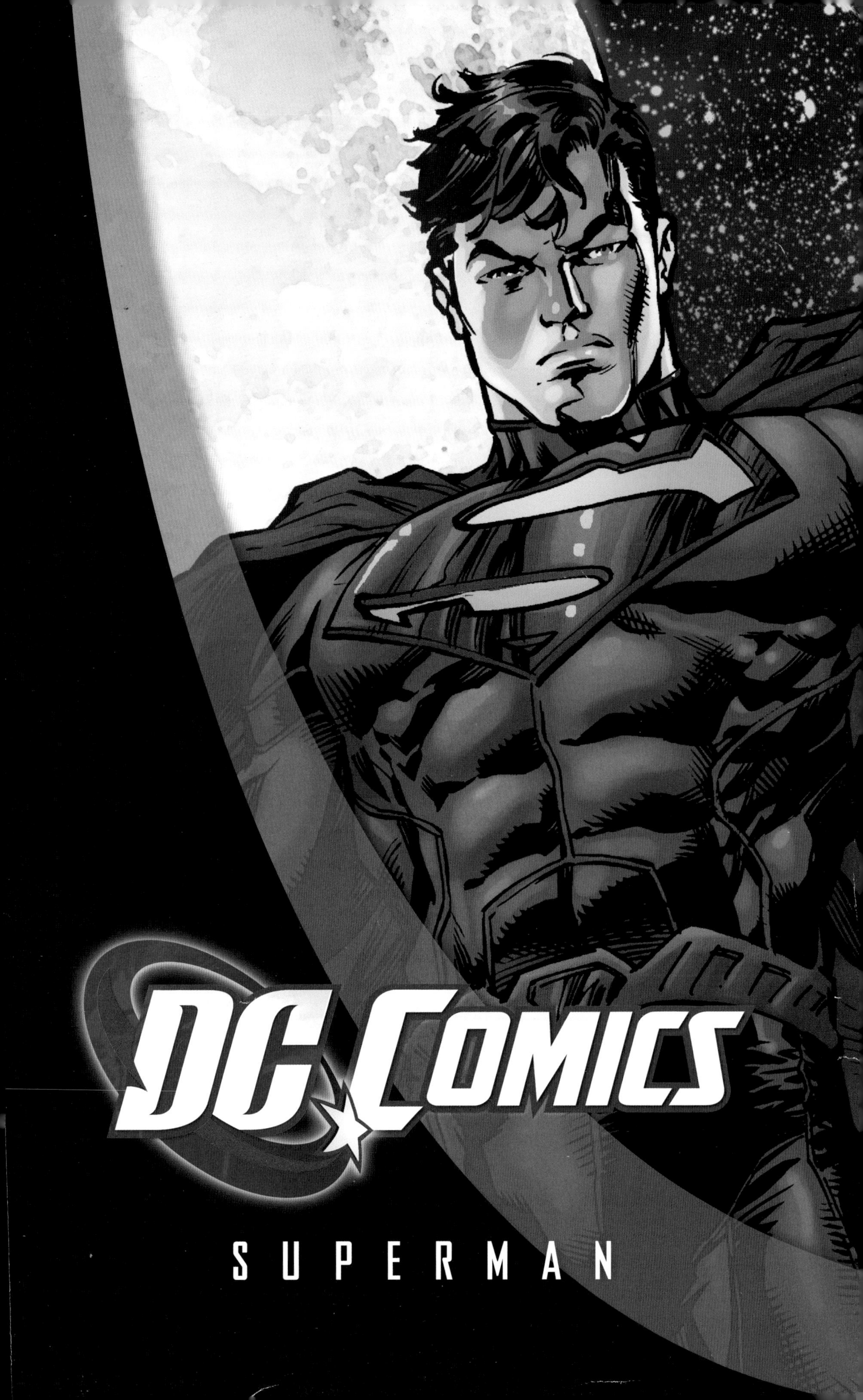
DC COMICS
SUPERMAN

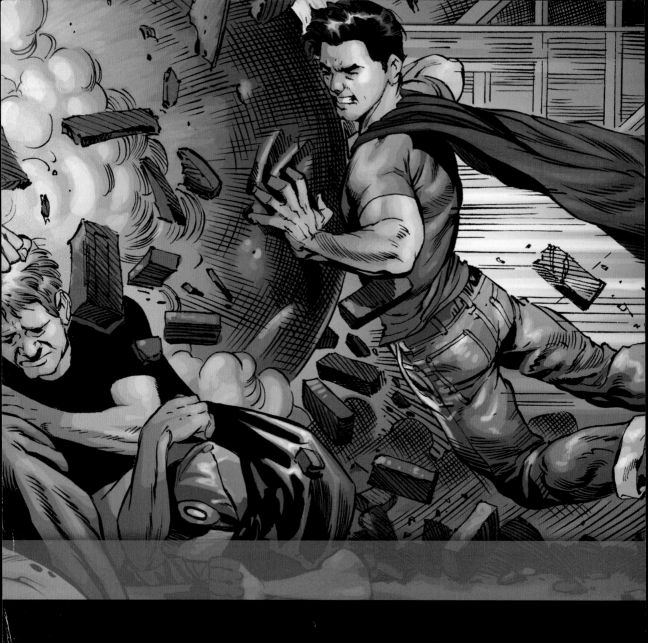

ACTION COMICS #1
Grant Morrison, Rags Morales & Rick Bryant

SUPERMAN #1
George Pérez & Jesús Merino

SUPERBOY #1
Scott Lobdell, R.B. Silva & Rob Lean

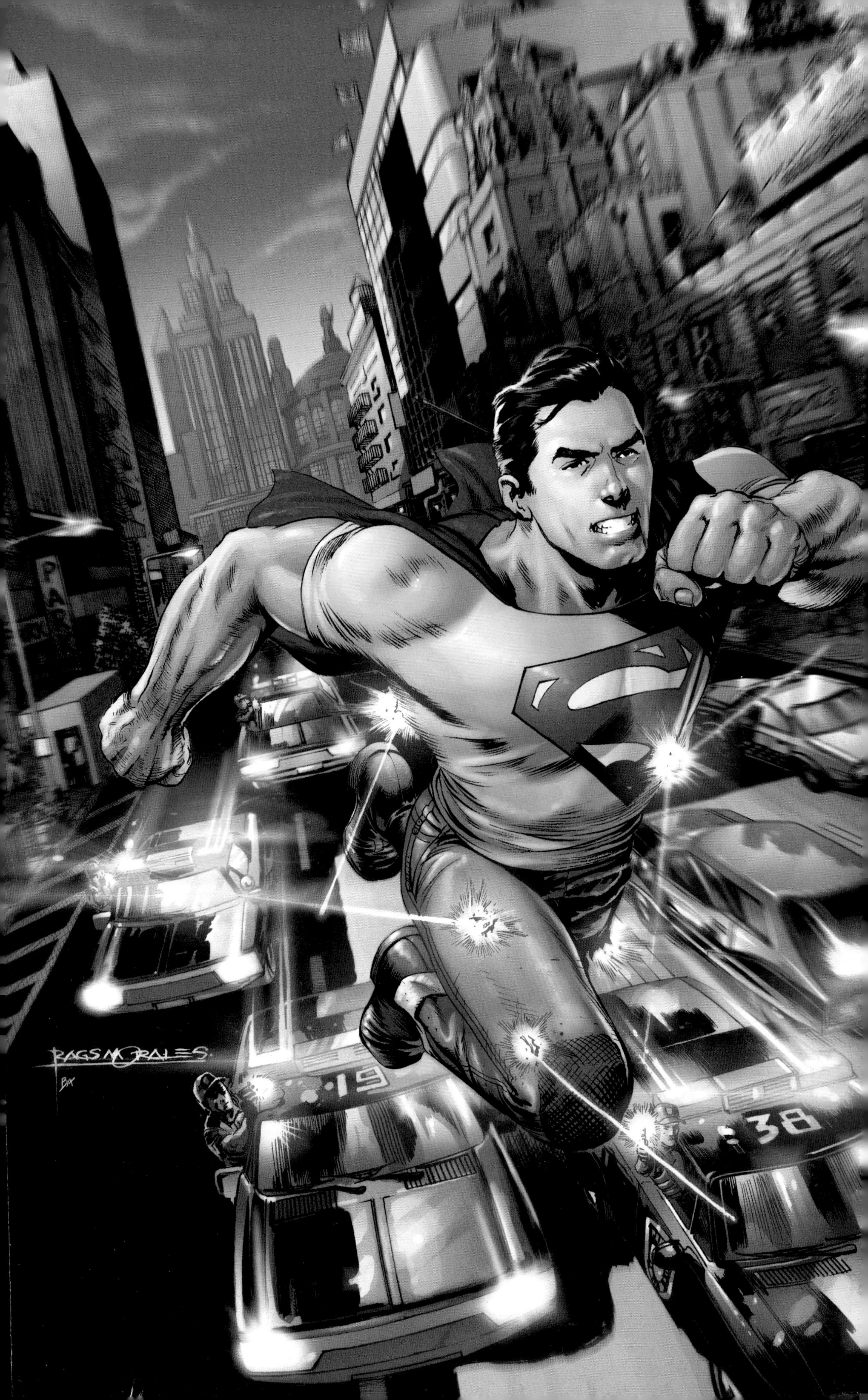
RAGS MORALES
19
38

SUPERMAN

ACTION

COMICS

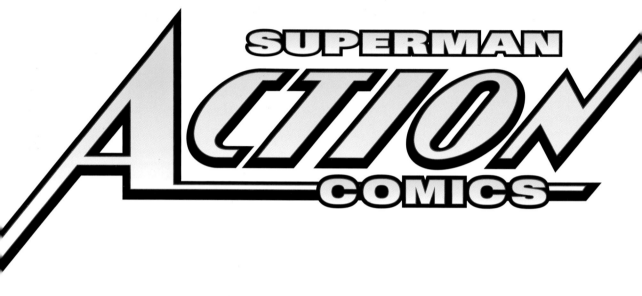

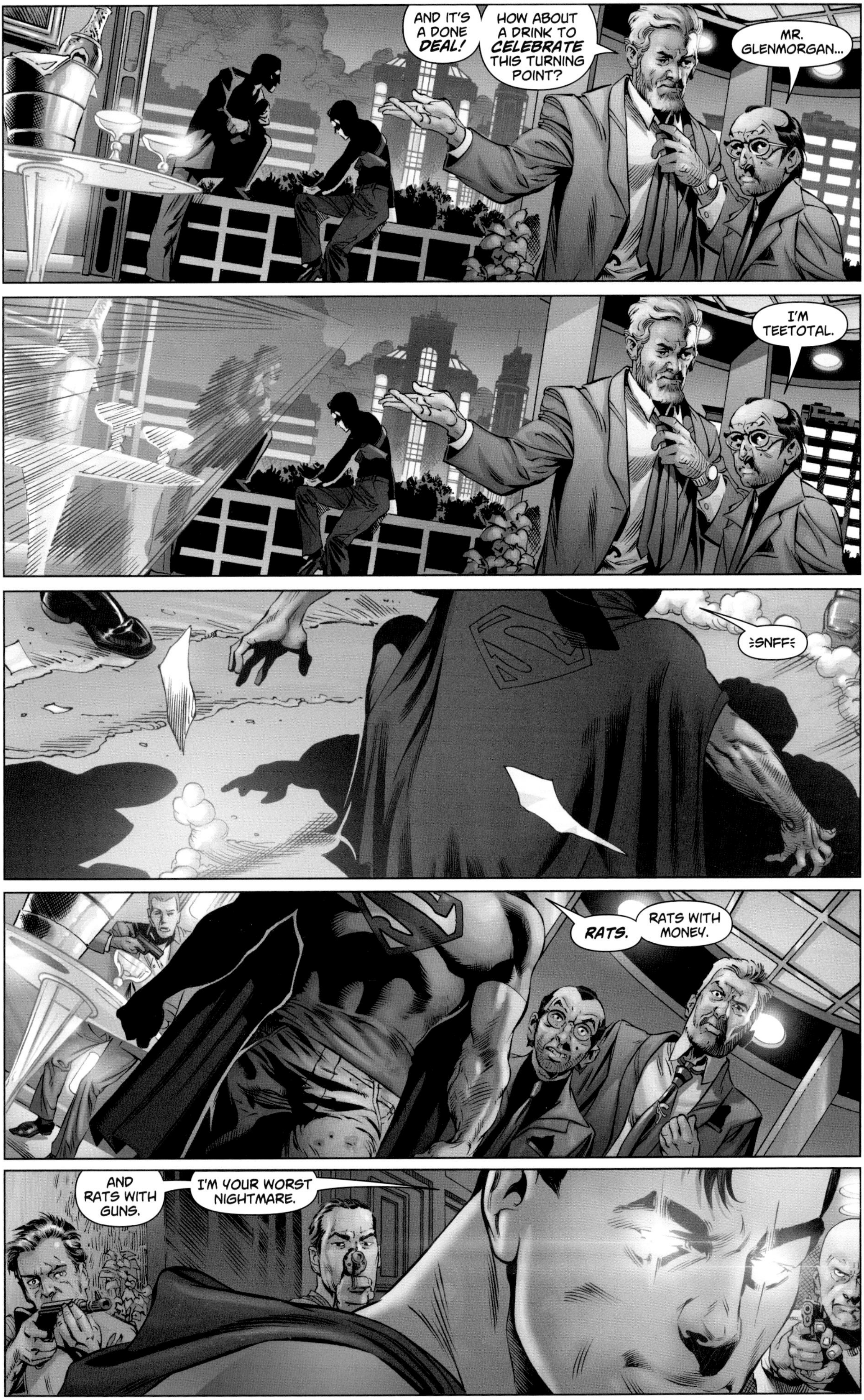
AND IT'S A DONE DEAL!
HOW ABOUT A DRINK TO CELEBRATE THIS TURNING POINT?
MR. GLENMORGAN...
I'M TEETOTAL.
SNFF
RATS.
RATS WITH MONEY.
AND RATS WITH GUNS.
I'M YOUR WORST NIGHTMARE.

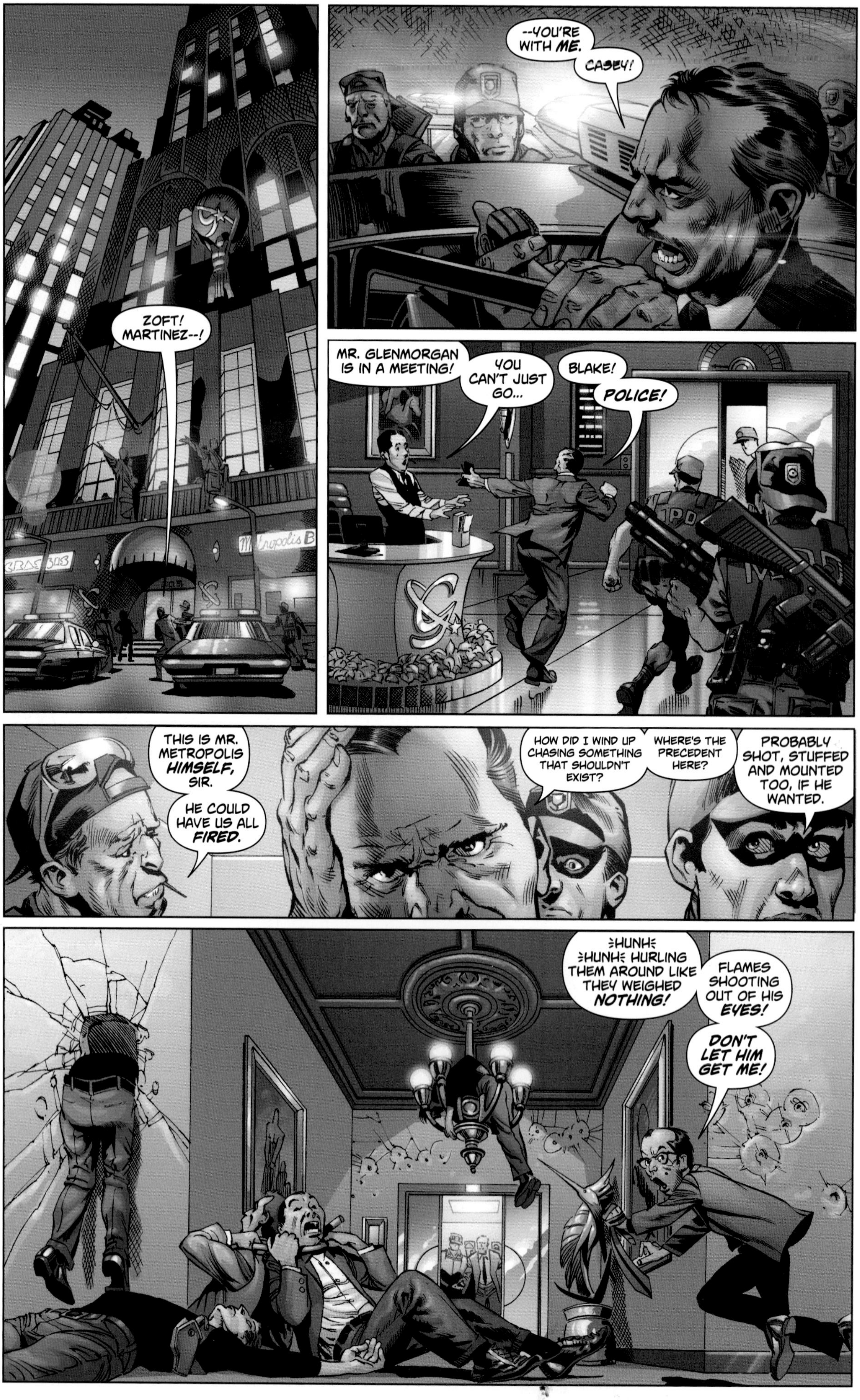
ZOFT! MARTINEZ--!
--YOU'RE WITH ME.
CASEY!
MR. GLENMORGAN IS IN A MEETING!
YOU CAN'T JUST GO...
BLAKE!
POLICE!
THIS IS MR. METROPOLIS HIMSELF, SIR.
HE COULD HAVE US ALL FIRED.
HOW DID I WIND UP CHASING SOMETHING THAT SHOULDN'T EXIST?
WHERE'S THE PRECEDENT HERE?
PROBABLY SHOT, STUFFED AND MOUNTED TOO, IF HE WANTED.
HUNH HUNH HURLING THEM AROUND LIKE THEY WEIGHED NOTHING!
FLAMES SHOOTING OUT OF HIS EYES!
DON'T LET HIM GET ME!

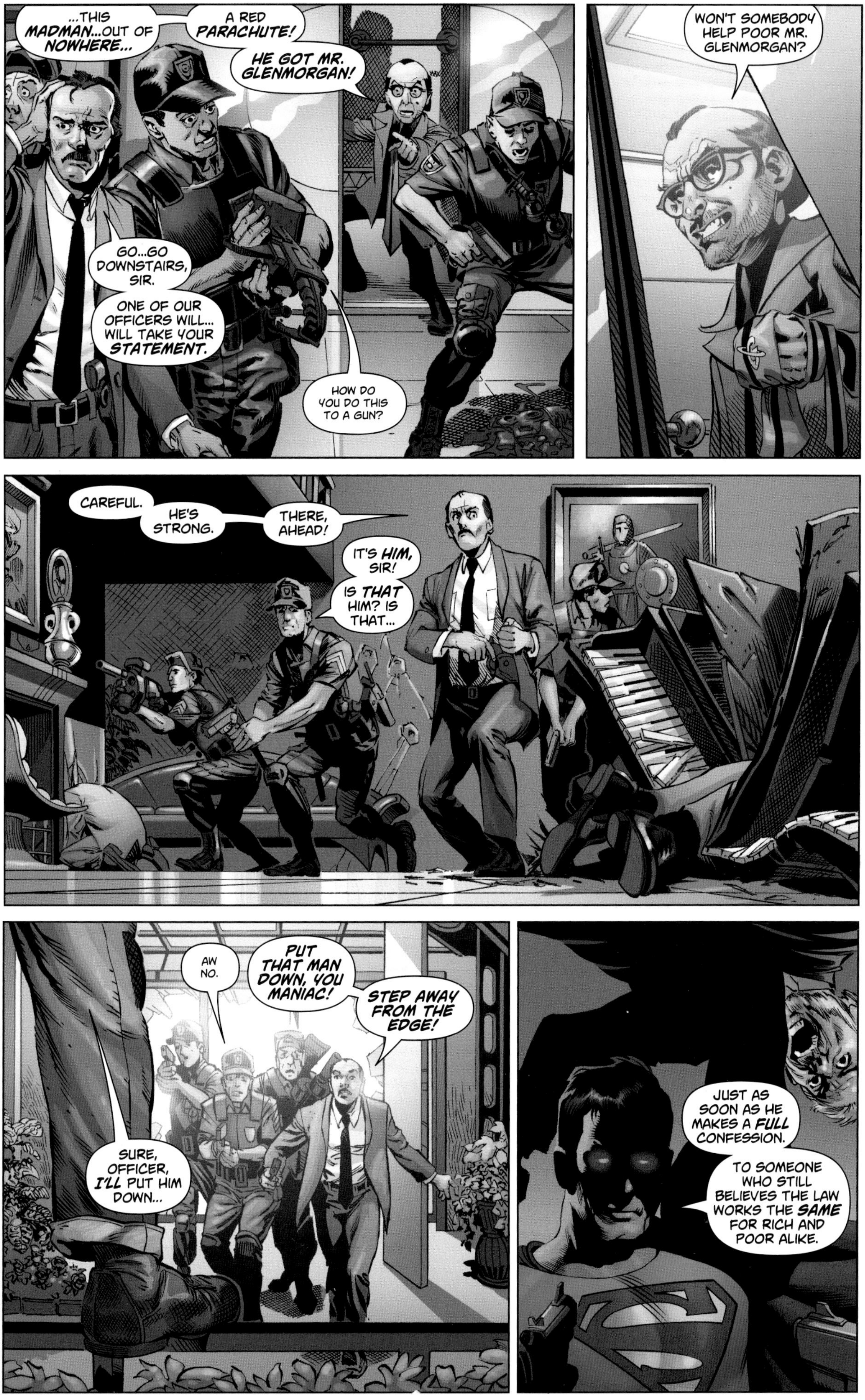

...THIS MADMAN...OUT OF NOWHERE...
A RED PARACHUTE!
HE GOT MR. GLENMORGAN!
GO...GO DOWNSTAIRS, SIR.
ONE OF OUR OFFICERS WILL... WILL TAKE YOUR STATEMENT.
HOW DO YOU DO THIS TO A GUN?
WON'T SOMEBODY HELP POOR MR. GLENMORGAN?
CAREFUL.
HE'S STRONG.
THERE, AHEAD!
IT'S HIM, SIR!
IS THAT HIM? IS THAT...
AW NO.
PUT THAT MAN DOWN, YOU MANIAC!
STEP AWAY FROM THE EDGE!
SURE, OFFICER, I'LL PUT HIM DOWN...
JUST AS SOON AS HE MAKES A FULL CONFESSION.
TO SOMEONE WHO STILL BELIEVES THE LAW WORKS THE SAME FOR RICH AND POOR ALIKE.

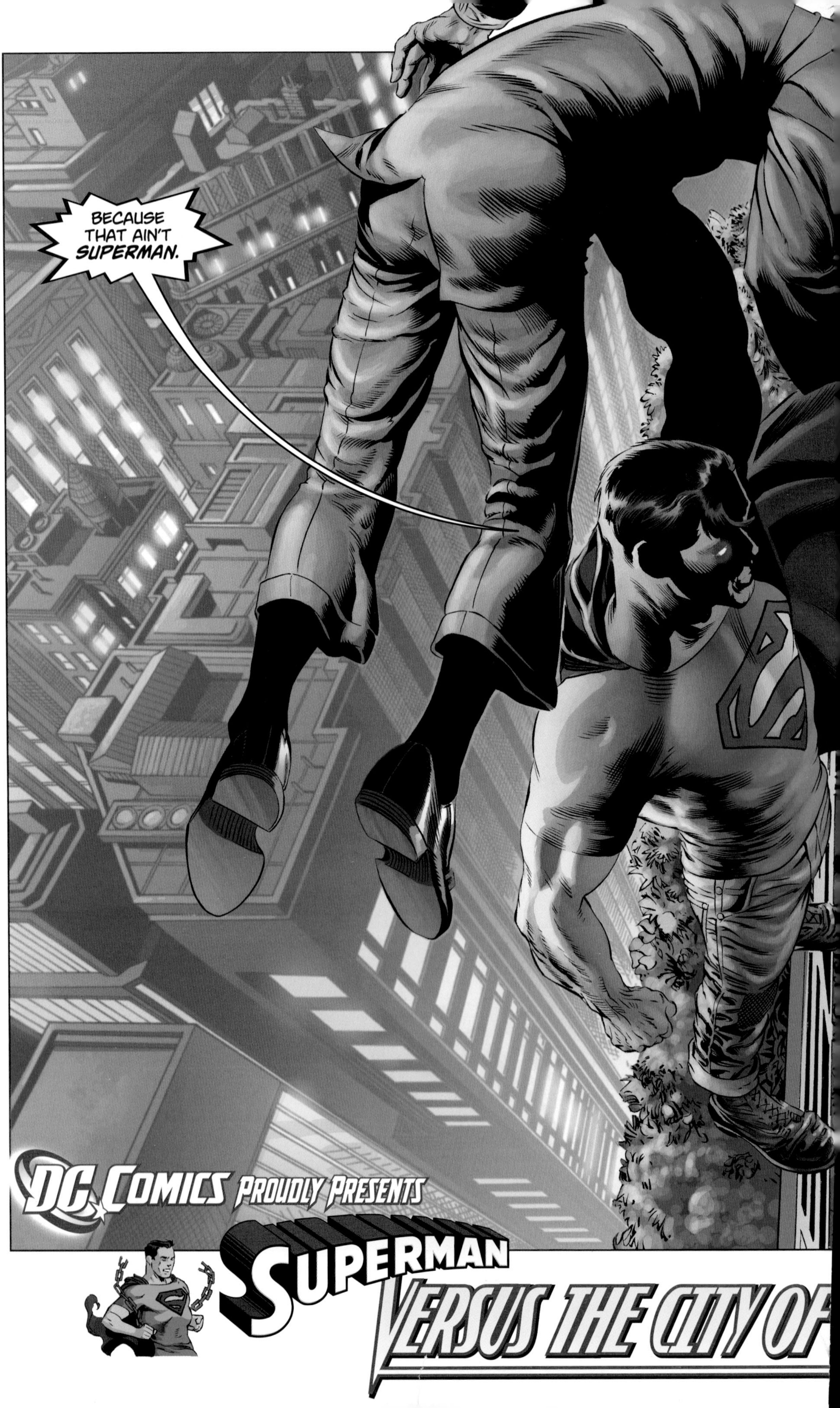
BECAUSE THAT AIN'T SUPERMAN.
DC COMICS PROUDLY PRESENTS
SUPERMAN
VERSUS THE CITY OF

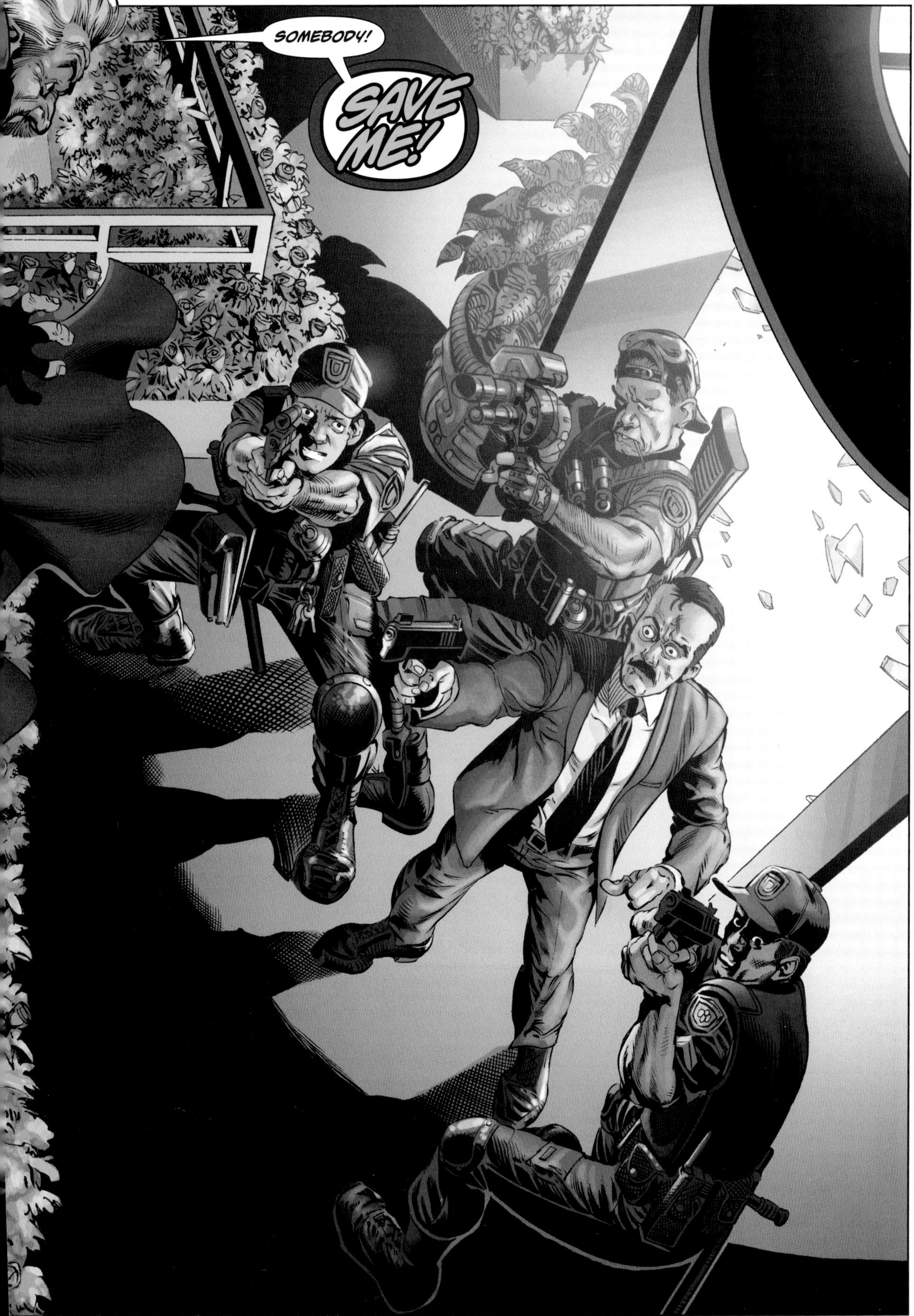

SOMEBODY!
SAVE ME!

TOMORROW

GRANT MORRISON Writer RAGS MORALES Penciller
RICK BRYANT Inker BRAD ANDERSON Colorist PATRICK BROSSEAU Letterer
RAGS MORALES & BRAD ANDERSON Cover JIM LEE, SCOTT WILLIAMS & ALEX SINCLAIR Variant Cover
WIL MOSS Associate Editor MATT IDELSON Editor SUPERMAN Created by JERRY SIEGEL & JOE SHUSTER

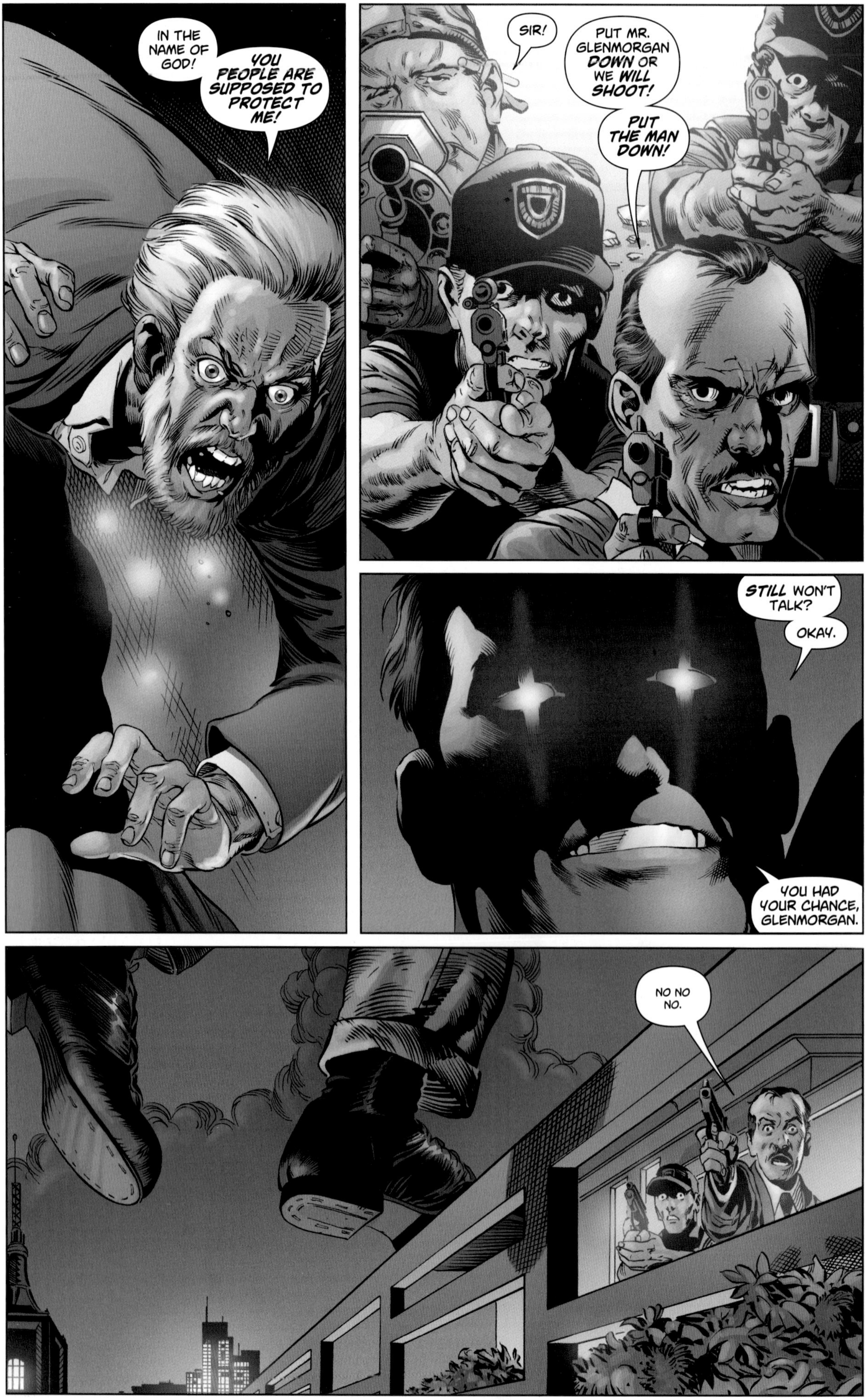
IN THE NAME OF GOD!
YOU PEOPLE ARE SUPPOSED TO PROTECT ME!
SIR!
PUT MR. GLENMORGAN DOWN OR WE WILL SHOOT!
PUT THE MAN DOWN!
STILL WON'T TALK?
OKAY.
YOU HAD YOUR CHANCE, GLENMORGAN.
NO NO NO.

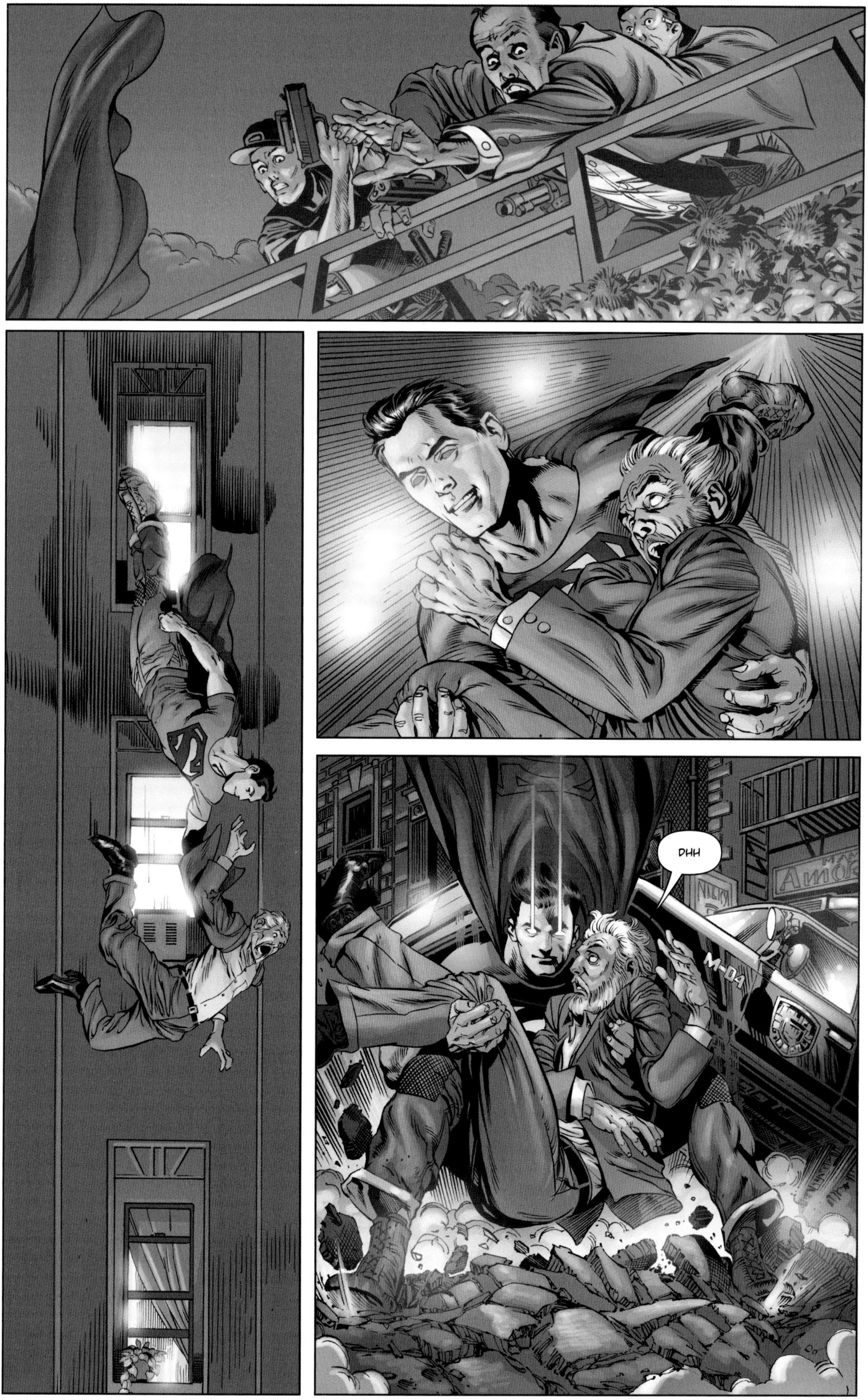
DHH
M-04

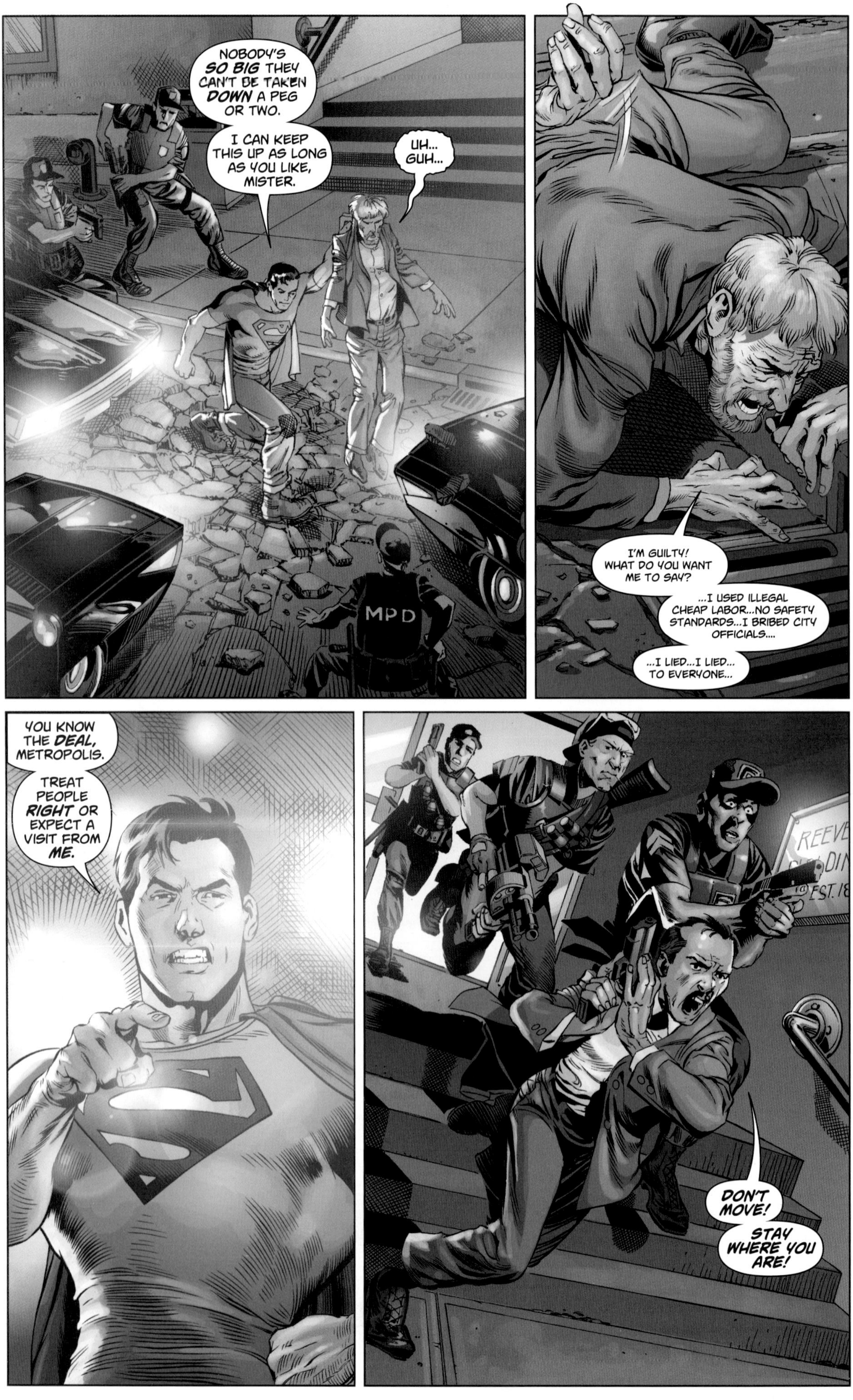
NOBODY'S SO BIG THEY CAN'T BE TAKEN DOWN A PEG OR TWO.
I CAN KEEP THIS UP AS LONG AS YOU LIKE, MISTER.
UH... GUH...
MPD
I'M GUILTY! WHAT DO YOU WANT ME TO SAY?
...I USED ILLEGAL CHEAP LABOR...NO SAFETY STANDARDS...I BRIBED CITY OFFICIALS....
...I LIED...I LIED... TO EVERYONE...
YOU KNOW THE DEAL, METROPOLIS.
TREAT PEOPLE RIGHT OR EXPECT A VISIT FROM ME.
DON'T MOVE!
STAY WHERE YOU ARE!

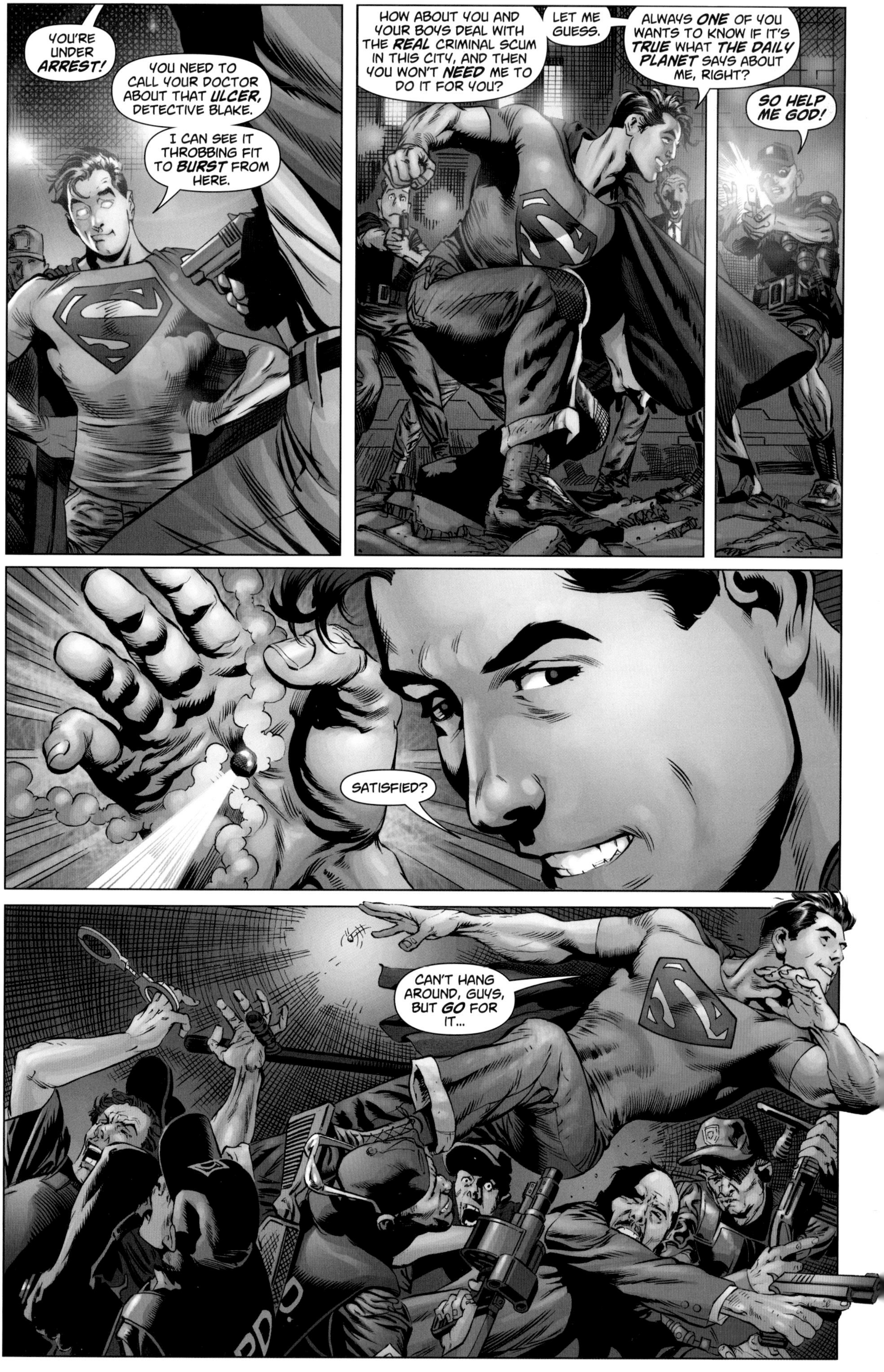
YOU'RE UNDER ARREST!
YOU NEED TO CALL YOUR DOCTOR ABOUT THAT ULCER, DETECTIVE BLAKE.
I CAN SEE IT THROBBING FIT TO BURST FROM HERE.
HOW ABOUT YOU AND YOUR BOYS DEAL WITH THE REAL CRIMINAL SCUM IN THIS CITY, AND THEN YOU WON'T NEED ME TO DO IT FOR YOU?
LET ME GUESS.
ALWAYS ONE OF YOU WANTS TO KNOW IF IT'S TRUE WHAT THE DAILY PLANET SAYS ABOUT ME, RIGHT?
SO HELP ME GOD!
SATISFIED?
CAN'T HANG AROUND, GUYS, BUT GO FOR IT...

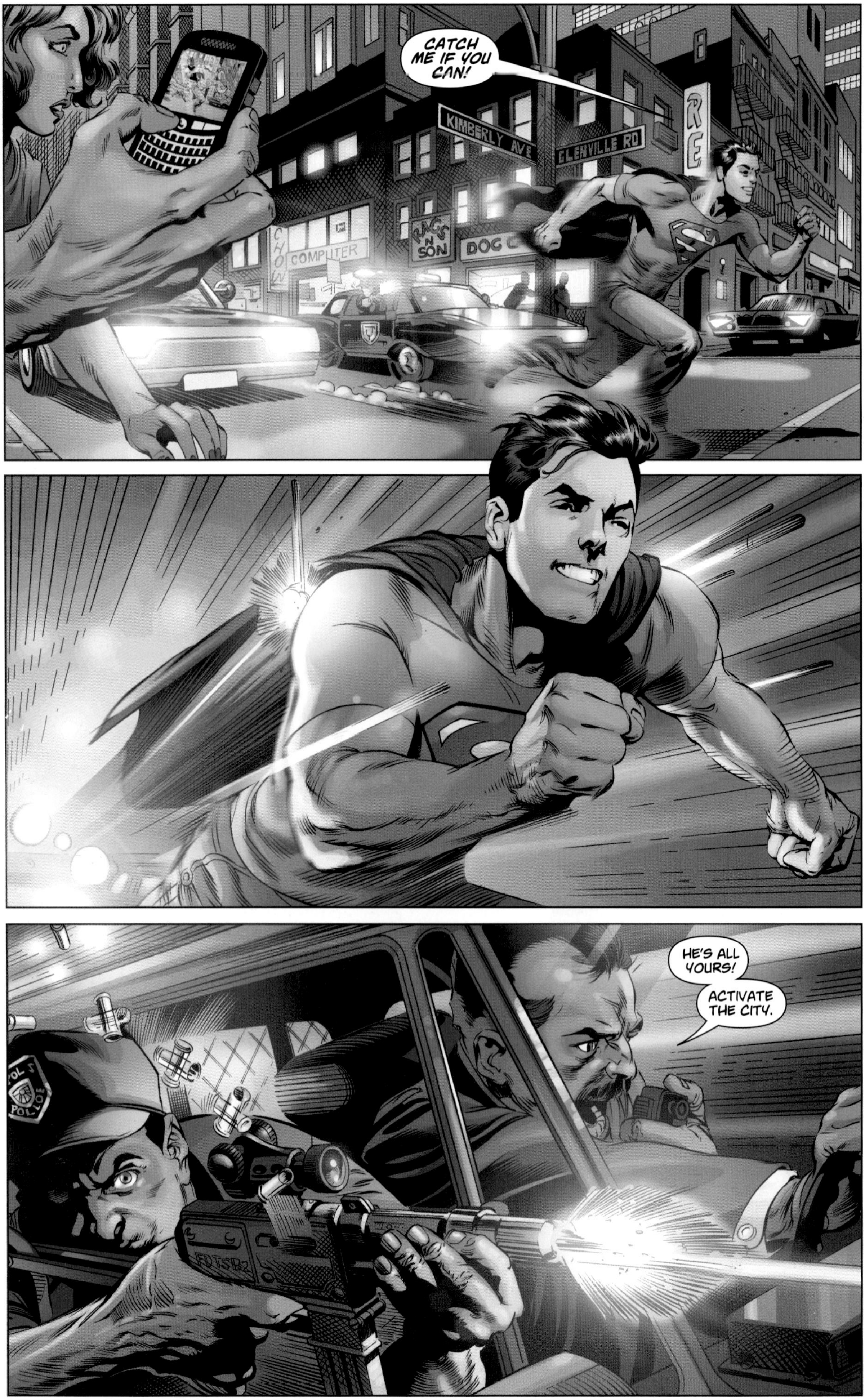
CATCH ME IF YOU CAN!
KIMBERLY AVE
GLENVILLE RD
COMPUTER
RAGS N SON
DOG
HE'S ALL YOURS!
ACTIVATE THE CITY.

THE "SUPERMAN" WHO APPEARED *SIX MONTHS AGO* COULD HURDLE SKYSCRAPERS AND TOSS *TRUCKS* AROUND.

NOW IT'S *FASTER*, NOW IT'S *STRONGER*.

HOW SOON BEFORE IT CAN'T BE *STOPPED*?

19:30

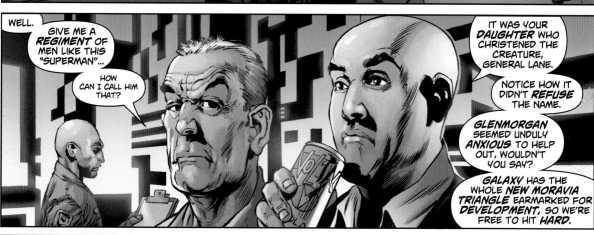

WELL.

GIVE ME A *REGIMENT* OF MEN LIKE THIS "SUPERMAN"...

HOW CAN I CALL HIM THAT?

IT WAS YOUR *DAUGHTER* WHO CHRISTENED THE CREATURE, GENERAL LANE.

NOTICE HOW IT DIDN'T *REFUSE* THE NAME.

GLENMORGAN SEEMED UNDULY *ANXIOUS* TO HELP OUT, WOULDN'T YOU SAY?

GALAXY HAS THE WHOLE *NEW MORAVIA TRIANGLE* EARMARKED FOR *DEVELOPMENT*, SO WE'RE FREE TO HIT *HARD*.

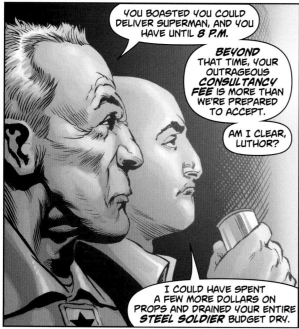

YOU BOASTED YOU COULD DELIVER SUPERMAN, AND YOU HAVE UNTIL *8 P.M.*

BEYOND THAT TIME, YOUR OUTRAGEOUS *CONSULTANCY FEE* IS MORE THAN WE'RE PREPARED TO ACCEPT.

AM I CLEAR, LUTHOR?

I COULD HAVE SPENT A FEW MORE DOLLARS ON *PROPS* AND DRAINED YOUR ENTIRE *STEEL SOLDIER* BUDGET DRY.

BUT I LOVE MY *COUNTRY*, AND IN RETURN ALL I ASK IS *INFORMATION*, SAM.

I CAN *PROVE* TO YOU, ONCE AND FOR ALL, THAT A *MONSTER* WALKS ≶SSPP≷ AMONG US.

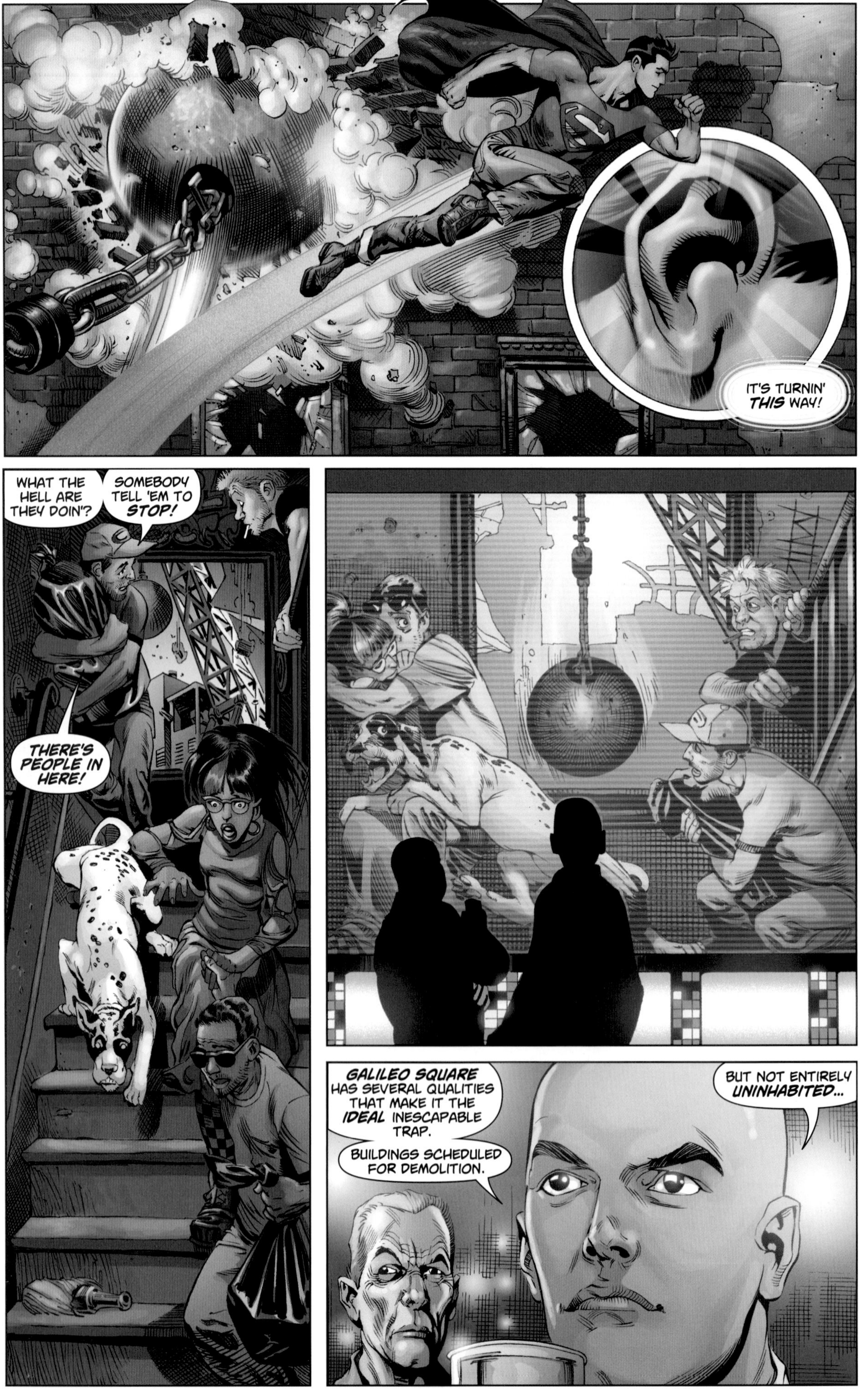
IT'S TURNIN' THIS WAY!
WHAT THE HELL ARE THEY DOIN'?
SOMEBODY TELL 'EM TO STOP!
THERE'S PEOPLE IN HERE!
GALILEO SQUARE HAS SEVERAL QUALITIES THAT MAKE IT THE IDEAL INESCAPABLE TRAP.
BUILDINGS SCHEDULED FOR DEMOLITION.
BUT NOT ENTIRELY UNINHABITED...

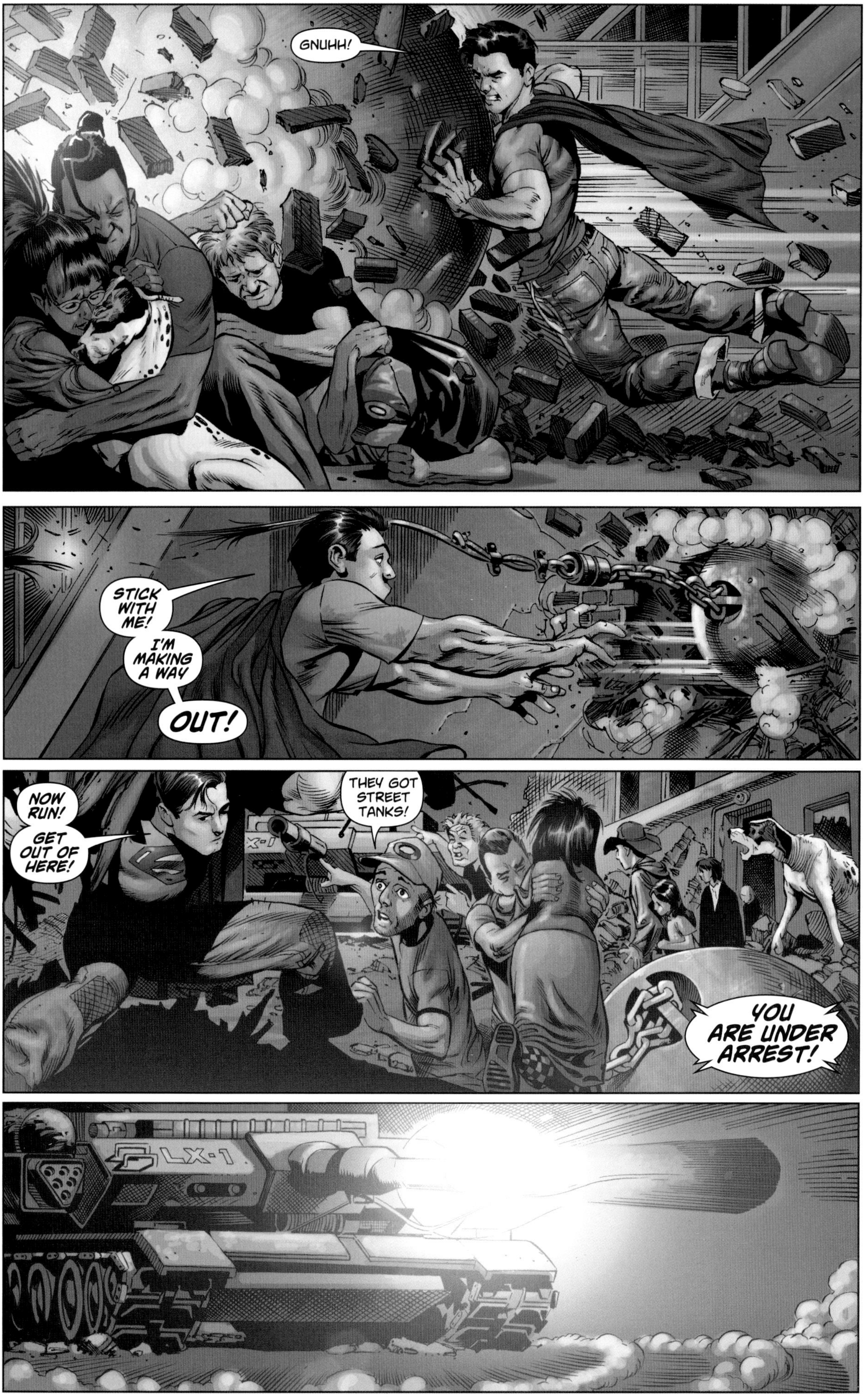
GNUHH!
STICK WITH ME!
I'M MAKING A WAY
OUT!
NOW RUN!
GET OUT OF HERE!
THEY GOT STREET TANKS!
YOU ARE UNDER ARREST!
LX-1

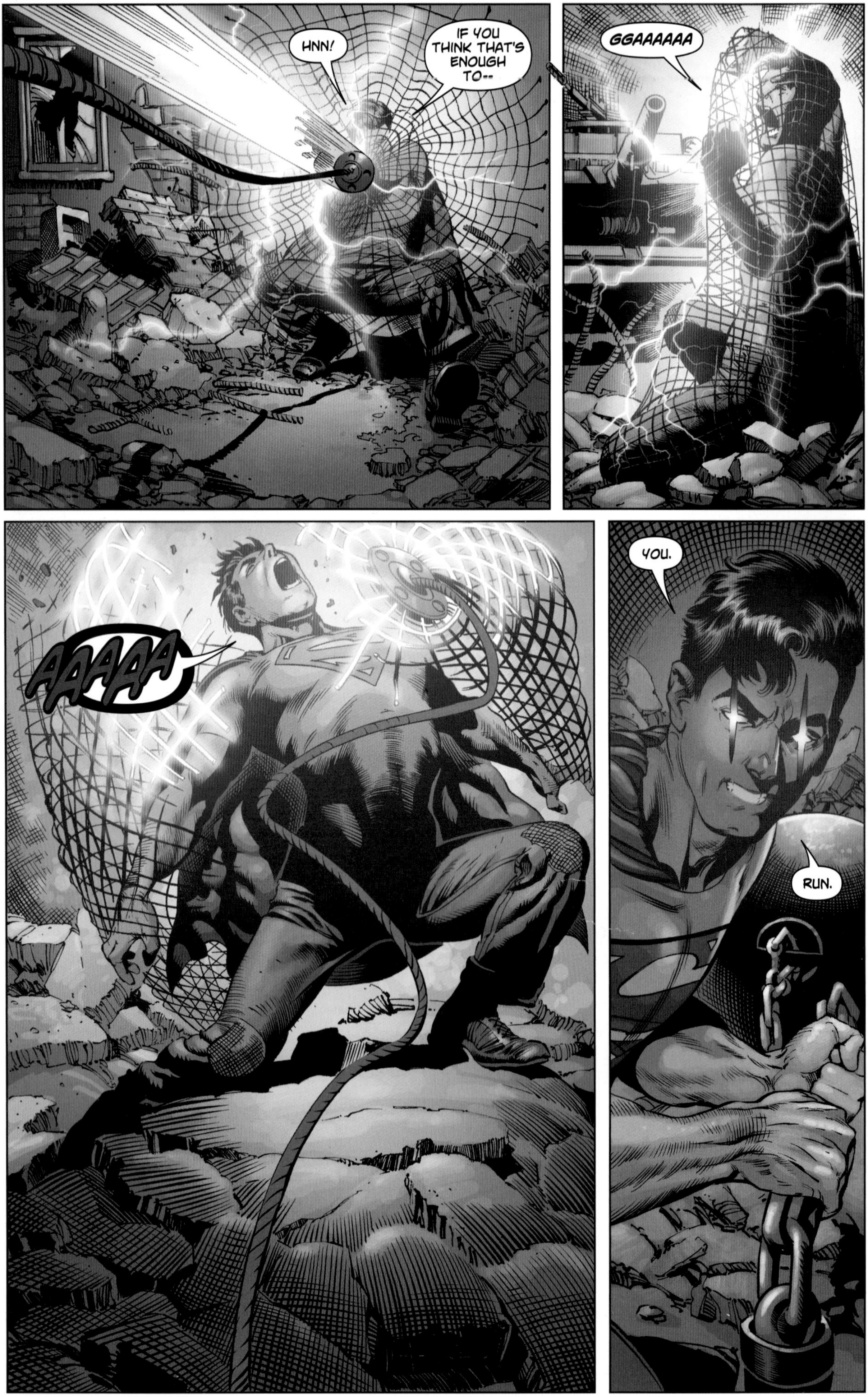
HNN!
IF YOU THINK THAT'S ENOUGH TO--
GGAAAAAA
AAAAA
YOU.
RUN.

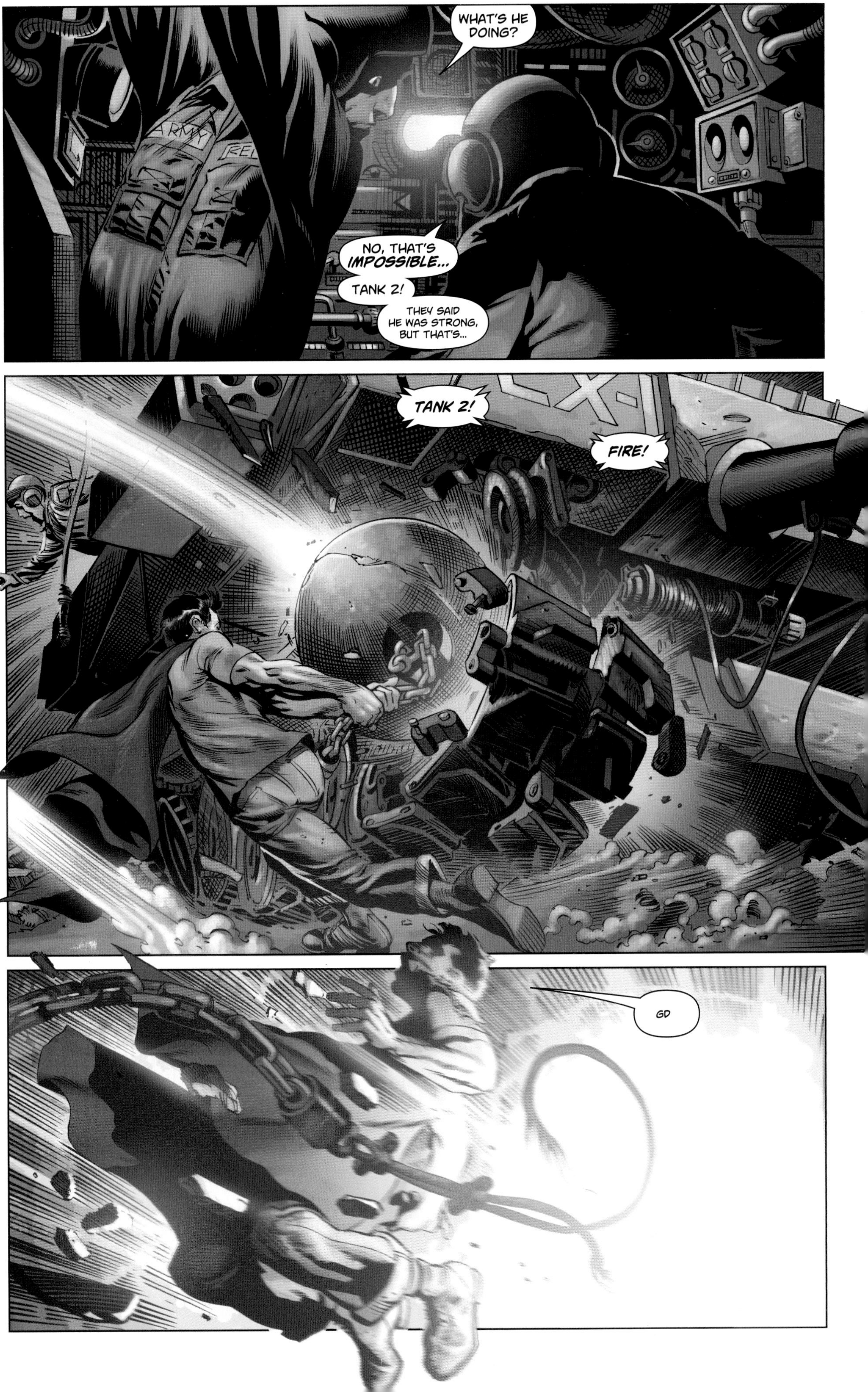
WHAT'S HE DOING?
NO, THAT'S IMPOSSIBLE...
TANK 2!
THEY SAID HE WAS STRONG, BUT THAT'S...
TANK 2!
FIRE!
GD

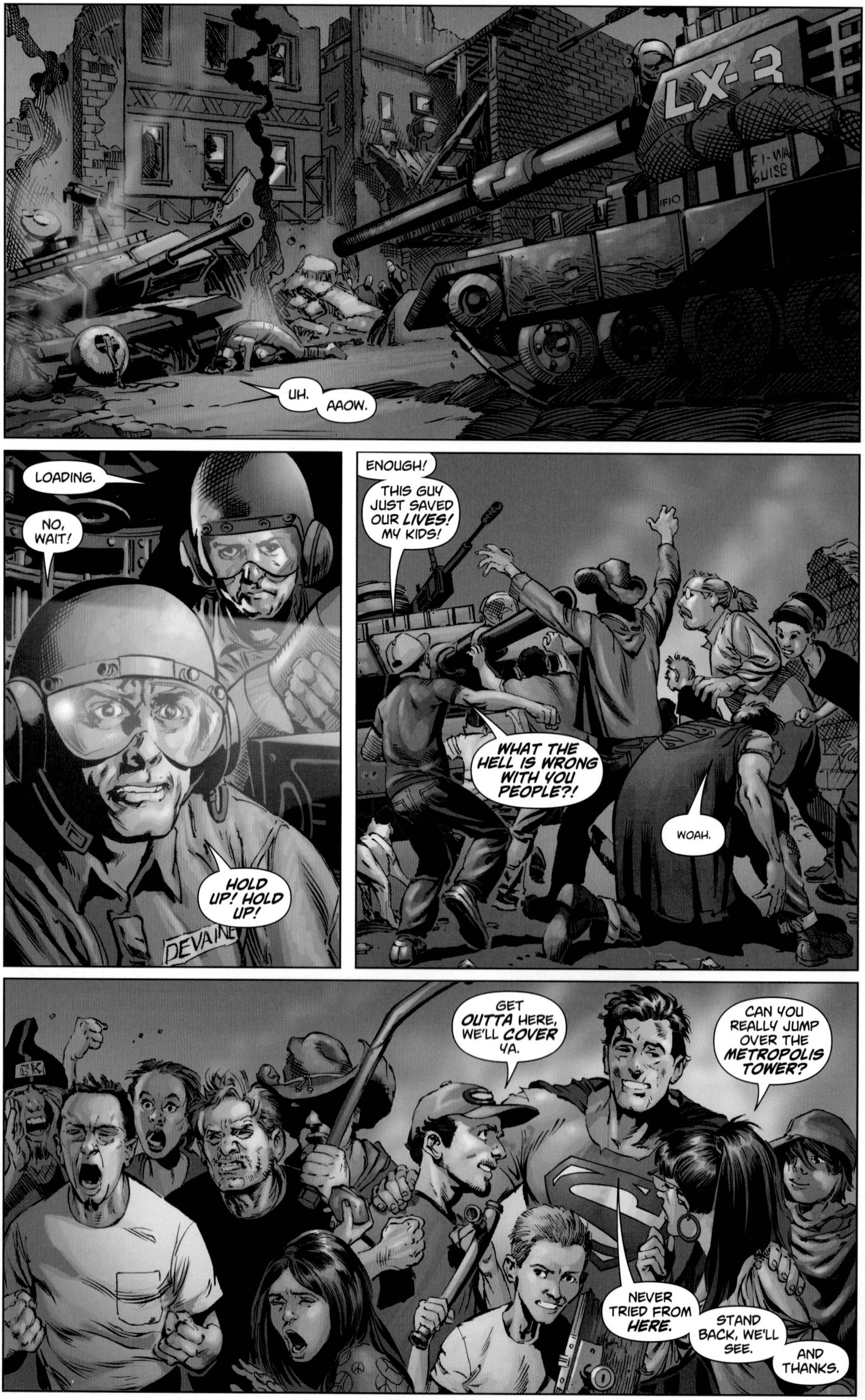
LX-3
UH.
AAOW.
LOADING.
NO, WAIT!
HOLD UP! HOLD UP!
DEVAINE
ENOUGH!
THIS GUY JUST SAVED OUR *LIVES!* MY KIDS!
WHAT THE HELL IS WRONG WITH YOU PEOPLE?!
WOAH.
GET *OUTTA* HERE, WE'LL *COVER* YA.
CAN YOU REALLY JUMP OVER THE *METROPOLIS TOWER?*
NEVER TRIED FROM *HERE.*
STAND BACK, WE'LL SEE.
AND THANKS.

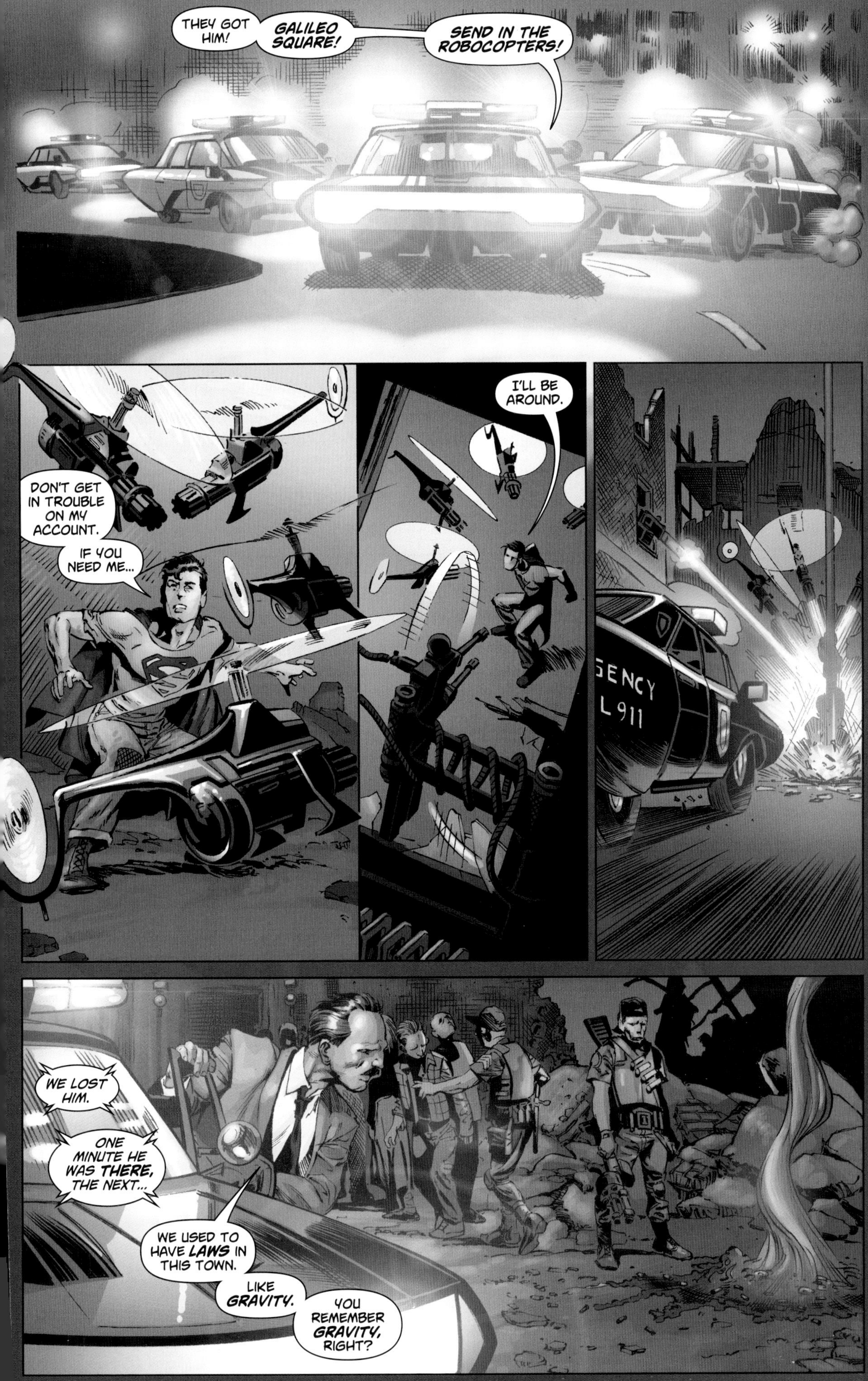
THEY GOT HIM!
GALILEO SQUARE!
SEND IN THE ROBOCOPTERS!
DON'T GET IN TROUBLE ON MY ACCOUNT.
IF YOU NEED ME...
I'LL BE AROUND.
GENCY
L 911
WE LOST HIM.
ONE MINUTE HE WAS THERE, THE NEXT...
WE USED TO HAVE LAWS IN THIS TOWN.
LIKE GRAVITY.
YOU REMEMBER GRAVITY, RIGHT?

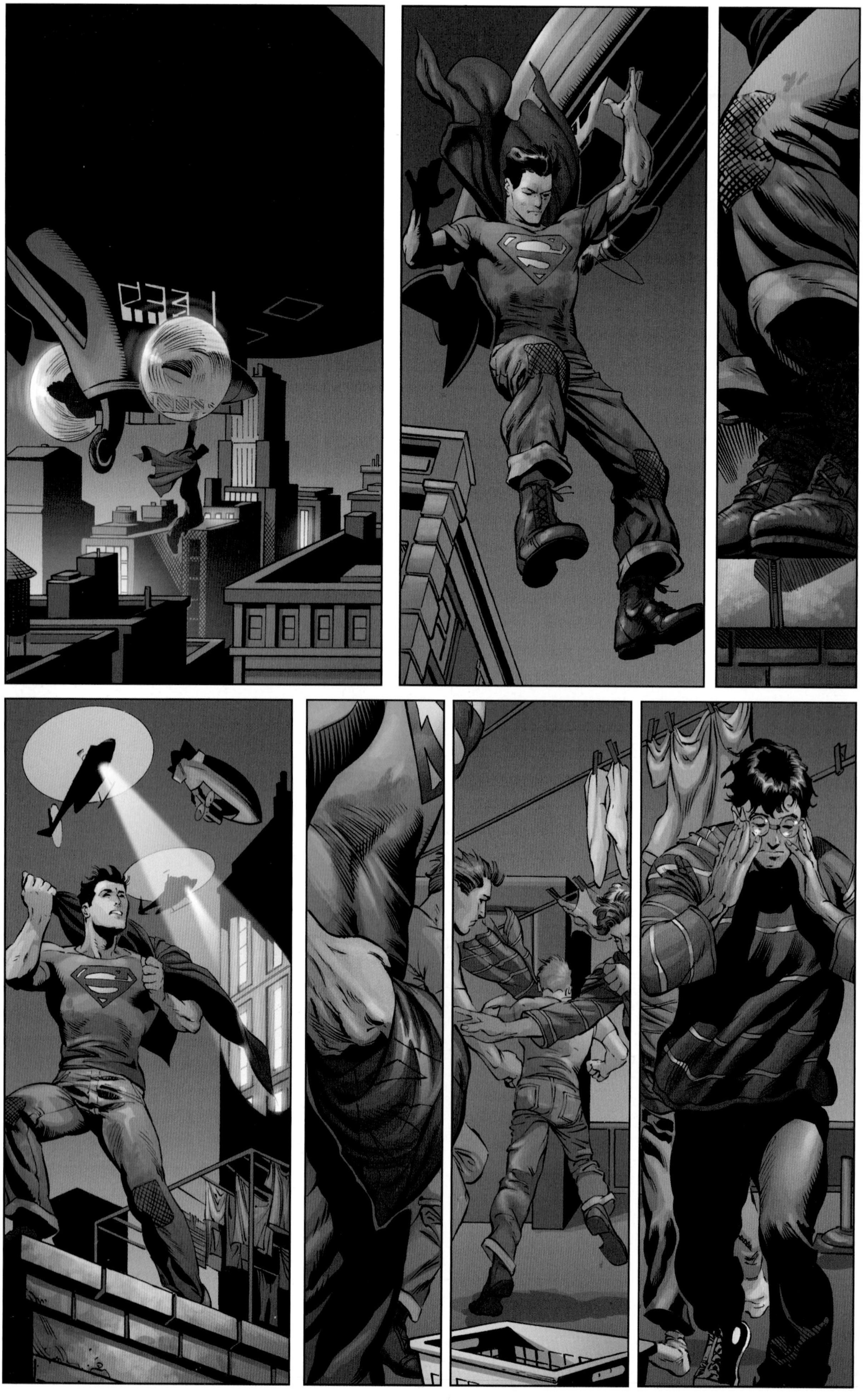

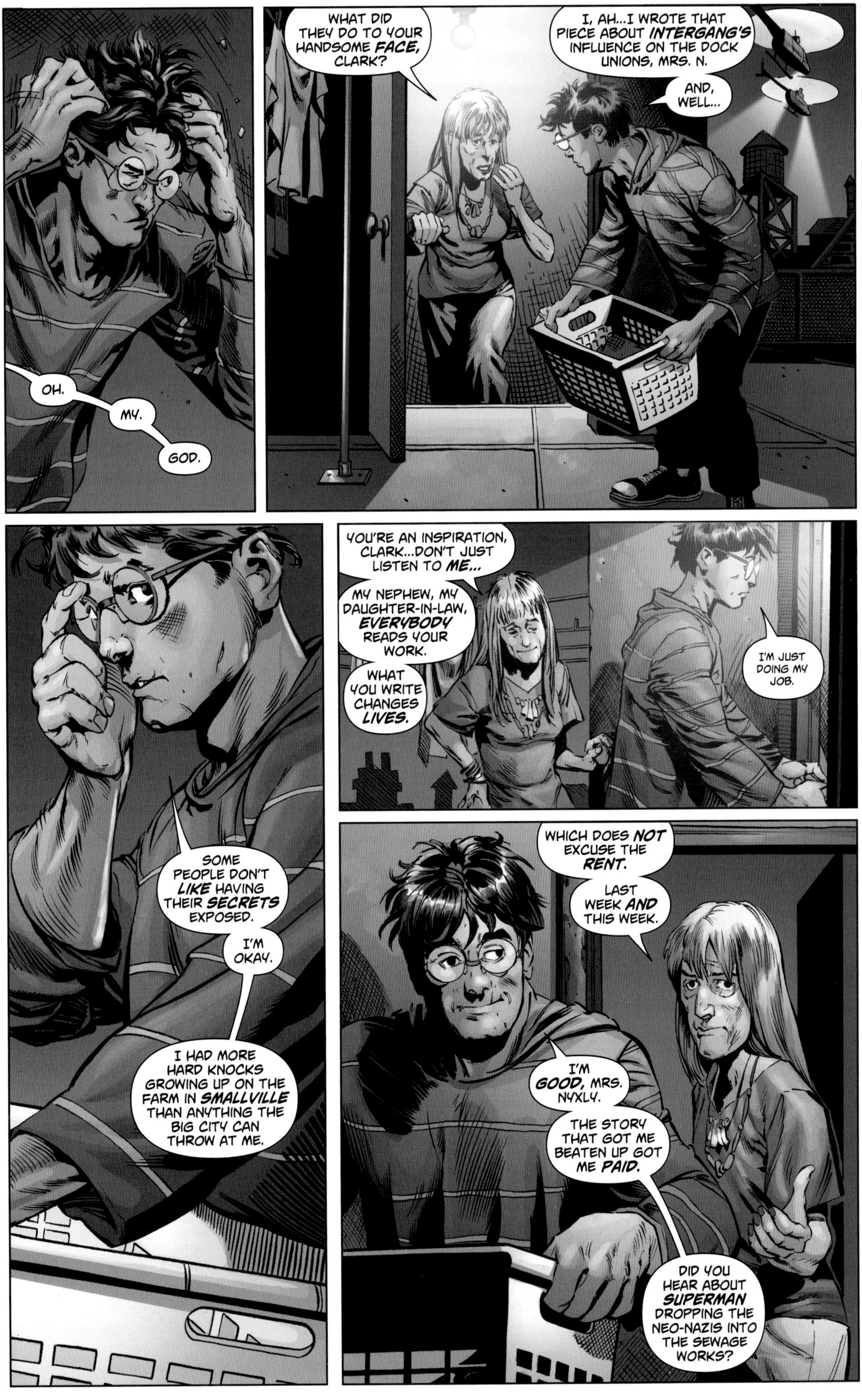
OH.
MY.
GOD.
WHAT DID THEY DO TO YOUR HANDSOME FACE, CLARK?
I, AH...I WROTE THAT PIECE ABOUT INTERGANG'S INFLUENCE ON THE DOCK UNIONS, MRS. N.
AND, WELL...
SOME PEOPLE DON'T LIKE HAVING THEIR SECRETS EXPOSED.
I'M OKAY.
I HAD MORE HARD KNOCKS GROWING UP ON THE FARM IN SMALLVILLE THAN ANYTHING THE BIG CITY CAN THROW AT ME.
YOU'RE AN INSPIRATION, CLARK...DON'T JUST LISTEN TO ME...
MY NEPHEW, MY DAUGHTER-IN-LAW, EVERYBODY READS YOUR WORK.
WHAT YOU WRITE CHANGES LIVES.
I'M JUST DOING MY JOB.
WHICH DOES NOT EXCUSE THE RENT.
LAST WEEK AND THIS WEEK.
I'M GOOD, MRS. NYXLY.
THE STORY THAT GOT ME BEATEN UP GOT ME PAID.
DID YOU HEAR ABOUT SUPERMAN DROPPING THE NEO-NAZIS INTO THE SEWAGE WORKS?

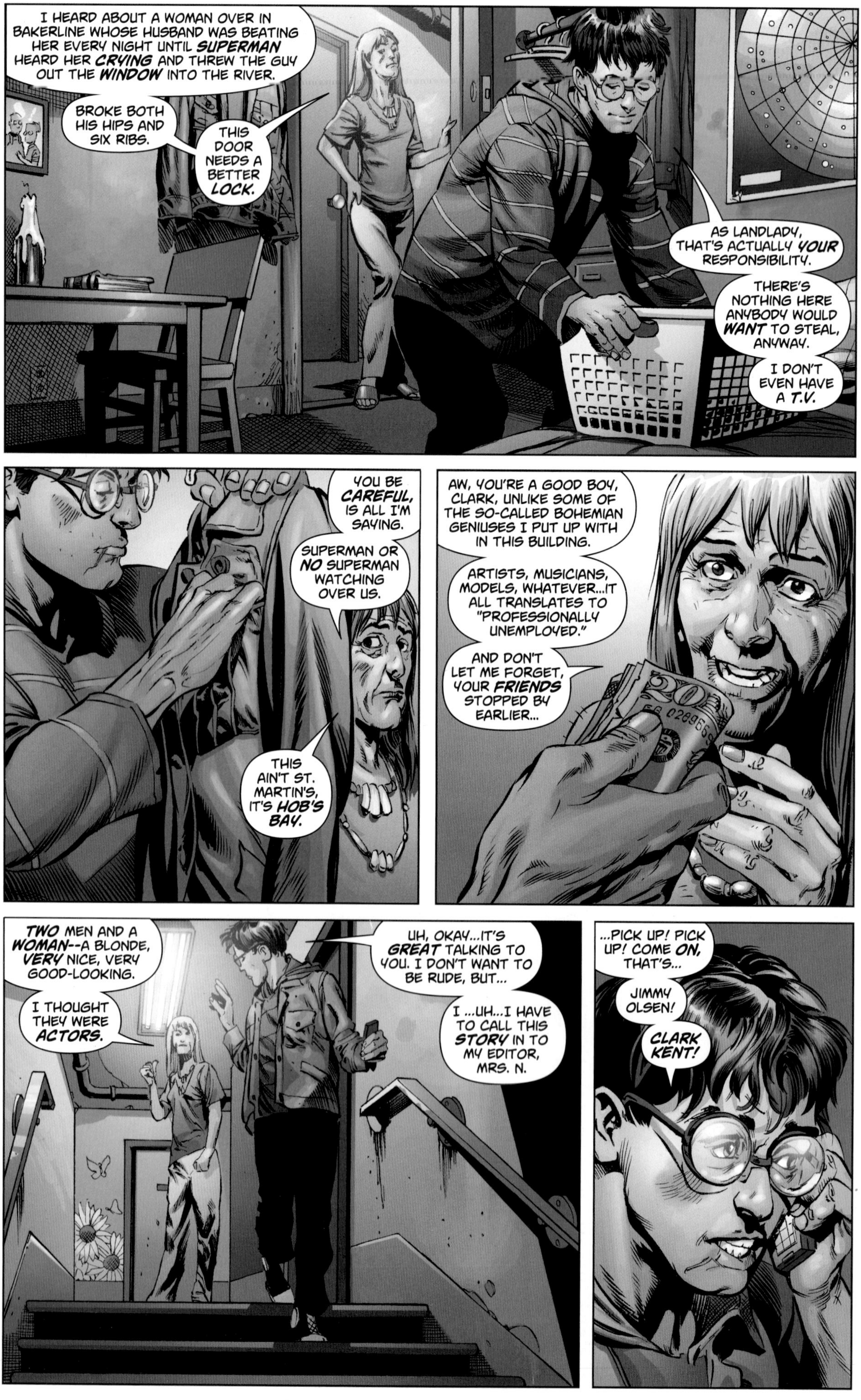
I HEARD ABOUT A WOMAN OVER IN BAKERLINE WHOSE HUSBAND WAS BEATING HER EVERY NIGHT UNTIL SUPERMAN HEARD HER CRYING AND THREW THE GUY OUT THE WINDOW INTO THE RIVER.
BROKE BOTH HIS HIPS AND SIX RIBS.
THIS DOOR NEEDS A BETTER LOCK.
AS LANDLADY, THAT'S ACTUALLY YOUR RESPONSIBILITY.
THERE'S NOTHING HERE ANYBODY WOULD WANT TO STEAL, ANYWAY.
I DON'T EVEN HAVE A T.V.
YOU BE CAREFUL, IS ALL I'M SAYING.
SUPERMAN OR NO SUPERMAN WATCHING OVER US.
THIS AIN'T ST. MARTIN'S, IT'S HOB'S BAY.
AW, YOU'RE A GOOD BOY, CLARK, UNLIKE SOME OF THE SO-CALLED BOHEMIAN GENIUSES I PUT UP WITH IN THIS BUILDING.
ARTISTS, MUSICIANS, MODELS, WHATEVER...IT ALL TRANSLATES TO "PROFESSIONALLY UNEMPLOYED."
AND DON'T LET ME FORGET, YOUR FRIENDS STOPPED BY EARLIER...
TWO MEN AND A WOMAN--A BLONDE, VERY NICE, VERY GOOD-LOOKING.
I THOUGHT THEY WERE ACTORS.
UH, OKAY...IT'S GREAT TALKING TO YOU. I DON'T WANT TO BE RUDE, BUT...
I ...UH...I HAVE TO CALL THIS STORY IN TO MY EDITOR, MRS. N.
...PICK UP! PICK UP! COME ON, THAT'S...
JIMMY OLSEN!
CLARK KENT!

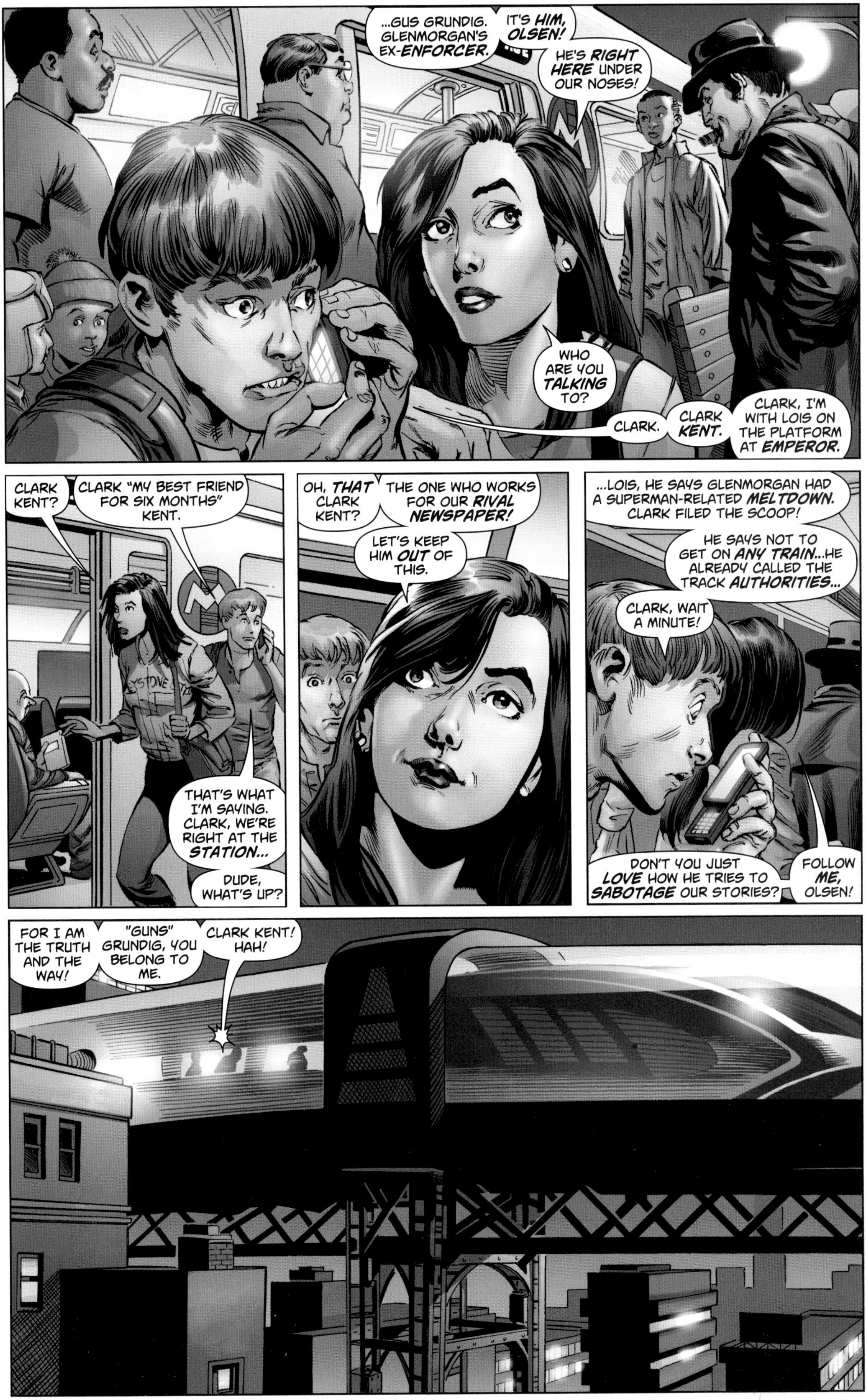
...GUS GRUNDIG. GLENMORGAN'S EX-ENFORCER.
IT'S HIM, OLSEN!
HE'S RIGHT HERE UNDER OUR NOSES!
WHO ARE YOU TALKING TO?
CLARK.
CLARK KENT.
CLARK, I'M WITH LOIS ON THE PLATFORM AT EMPEROR.
CLARK KENT?
CLARK "MY BEST FRIEND FOR SIX MONTHS" KENT.
THAT'S WHAT I'M SAYING. CLARK, WE'RE RIGHT AT THE STATION...
DUDE, WHAT'S UP?
OH, THAT CLARK KENT?
THE ONE WHO WORKS FOR OUR RIVAL NEWSPAPER!
LET'S KEEP HIM OUT OF THIS.
...LOIS, HE SAYS GLENMORGAN HAD A SUPERMAN-RELATED MELTDOWN. CLARK FILED THE SCOOP!
HE SAYS NOT TO GET ON ANY TRAIN...HE ALREADY CALLED THE TRACK AUTHORITIES...
CLARK, WAIT A MINUTE!
DON'T YOU JUST LOVE HOW HE TRIES TO SABOTAGE OUR STORIES?
FOLLOW ME, OLSEN!
FOR I AM THE TRUTH AND THE WAY!
"GUNS" GRUNDIG, YOU BELONG TO ME.
CLARK KENT! HAH!

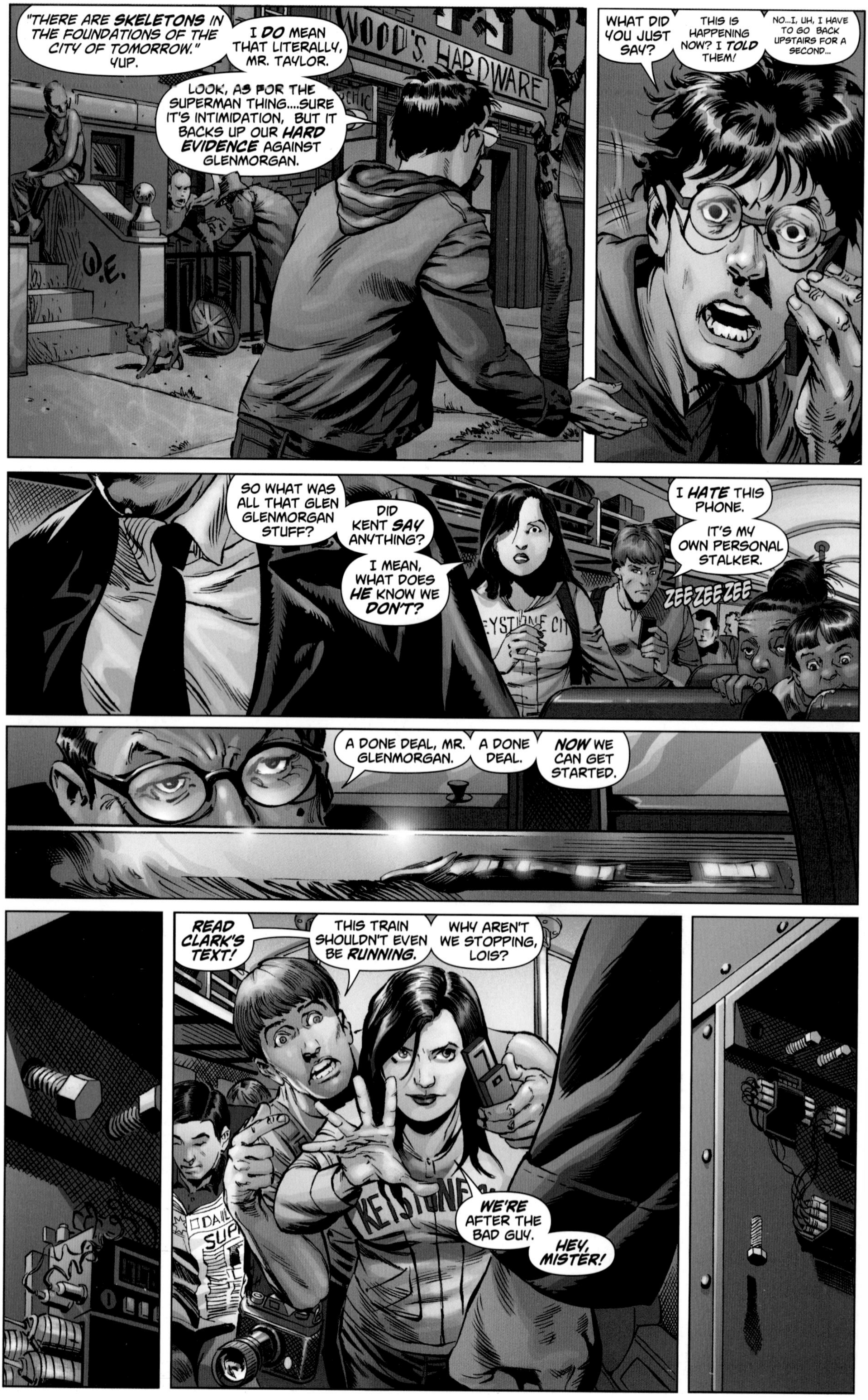

"THERE ARE SKELETONS IN THE FOUNDATIONS OF THE CITY OF TOMORROW." YUP.
I DO MEAN THAT LITERALLY, MR. TAYLOR.
LOOK, AS FOR THE SUPERMAN THING....SURE IT'S INTIMIDATION, BUT IT BACKS UP OUR HARD EVIDENCE AGAINST GLENMORGAN.
WOOD'S HARDWARE
WHAT DID YOU JUST SAY?
THIS IS HAPPENING NOW? I TOLD THEM!
NO...I, UH, I HAVE TO GO BACK UPSTAIRS FOR A SECOND...
SO WHAT WAS ALL THAT GLEN GLENMORGAN STUFF?
DID KENT SAY ANYTHING?
I MEAN, WHAT DOES HE KNOW WE DON'T?
I HATE THIS PHONE.
IT'S MY OWN PERSONAL STALKER.
ZEE ZEE ZEE
A DONE DEAL, MR. GLENMORGAN.
A DONE DEAL.
NOW WE CAN GET STARTED.
READ CLARK'S TEXT!
THIS TRAIN SHOULDN'T EVEN BE RUNNING.
WHY AREN'T WE STOPPING, LOIS?
WE'RE AFTER THE BAD GUY.
HEY, MISTER!

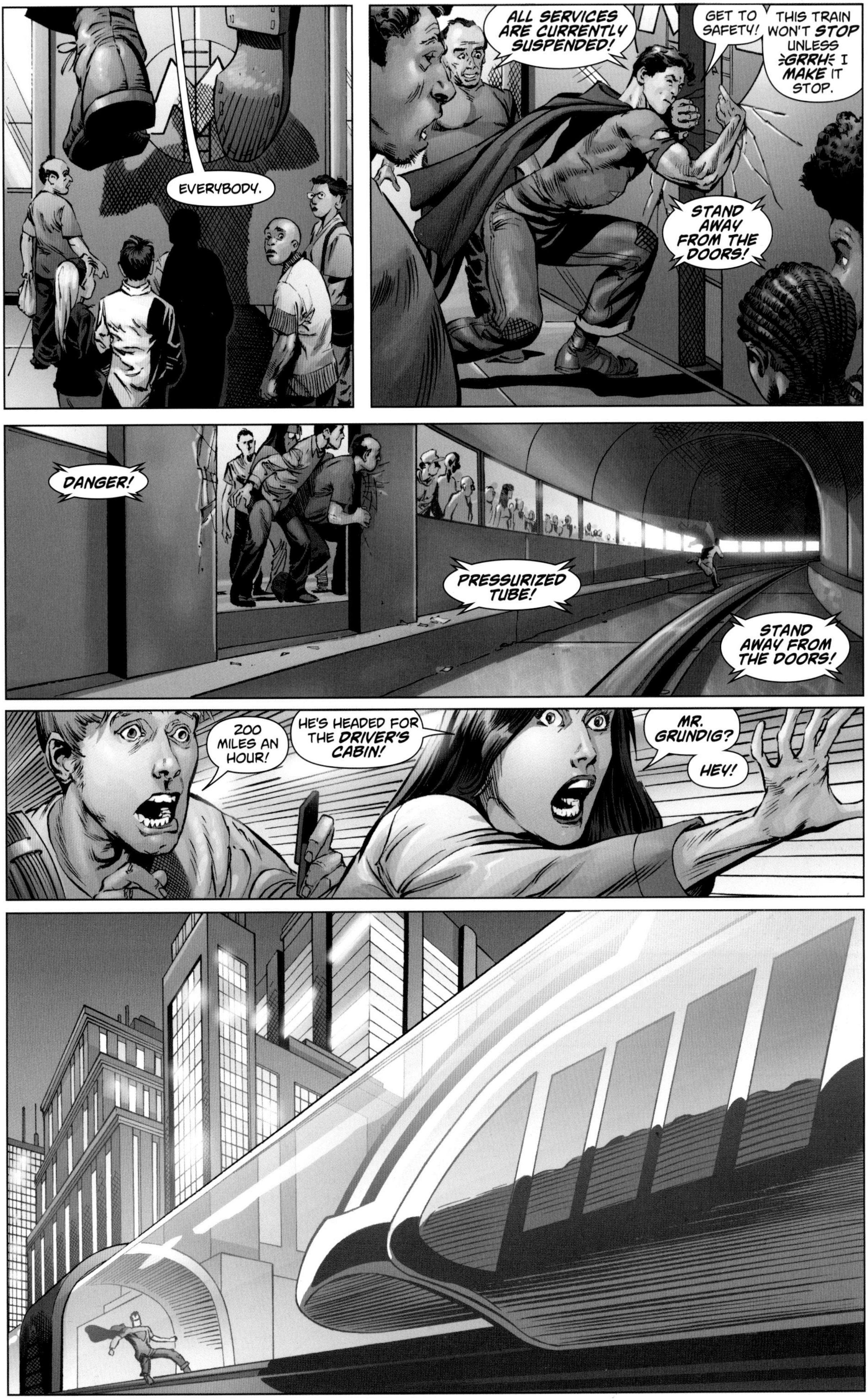
EVERYBODY.
ALL SERVICES ARE CURRENTLY SUSPENDED!
GET TO SAFETY!
THIS TRAIN WON'T STOP UNLESS GRRH I MAKE IT STOP.
STAND AWAY FROM THE DOORS!
DANGER!
PRESSURIZED TUBE!
STAND AWAY FROM THE DOORS!
200 MILES AN HOUR!
HE'S HEADED FOR THE DRIVER'S CABIN!
MR. GRUNDIG?
HEY!

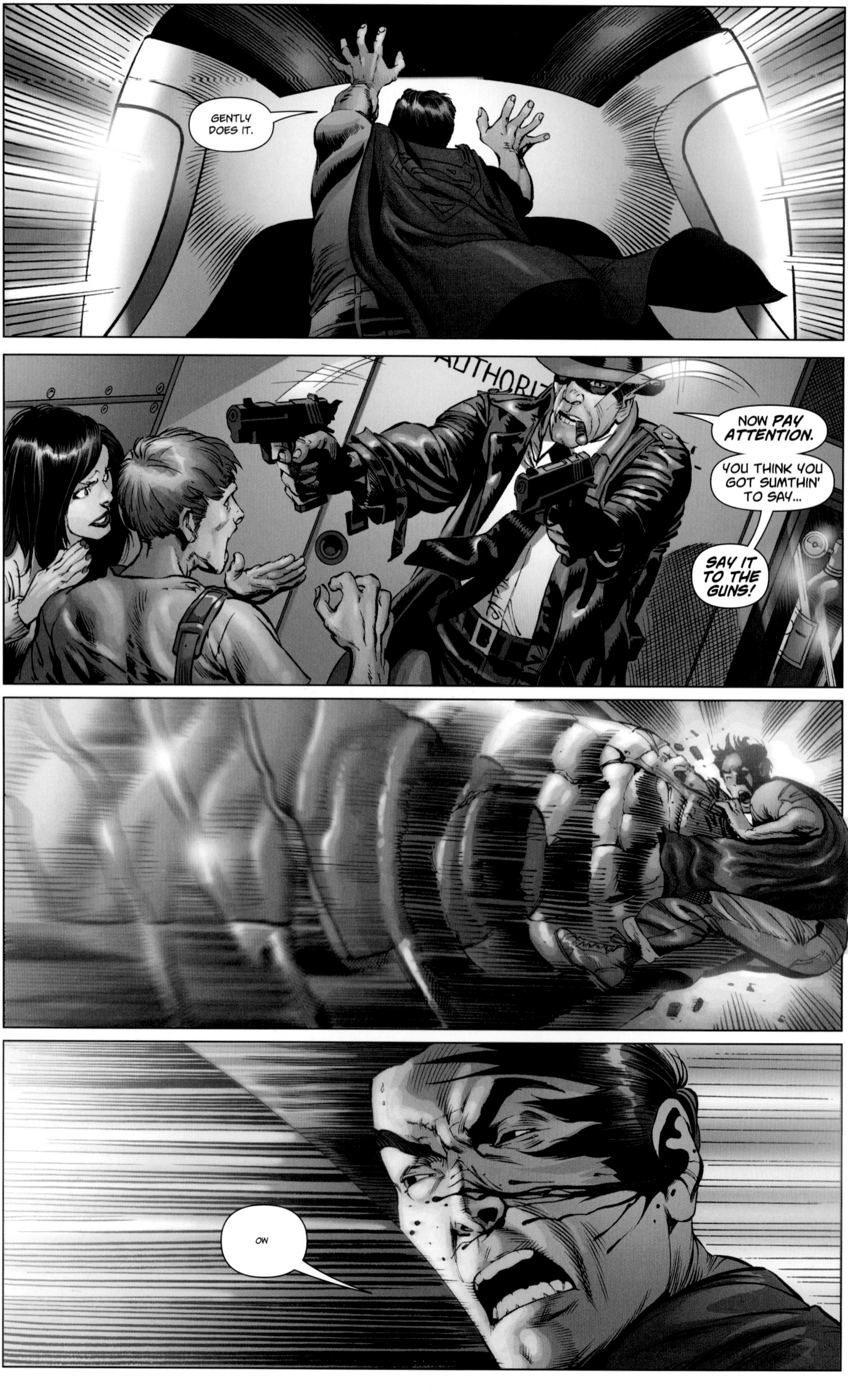
GENTLY DOES IT.
AUTHORIT
NOW PAY ATTENTION.
YOU THINK YOU GOT SUMTHIN' TO SAY...
SAY IT TO THE GUNS!
OW

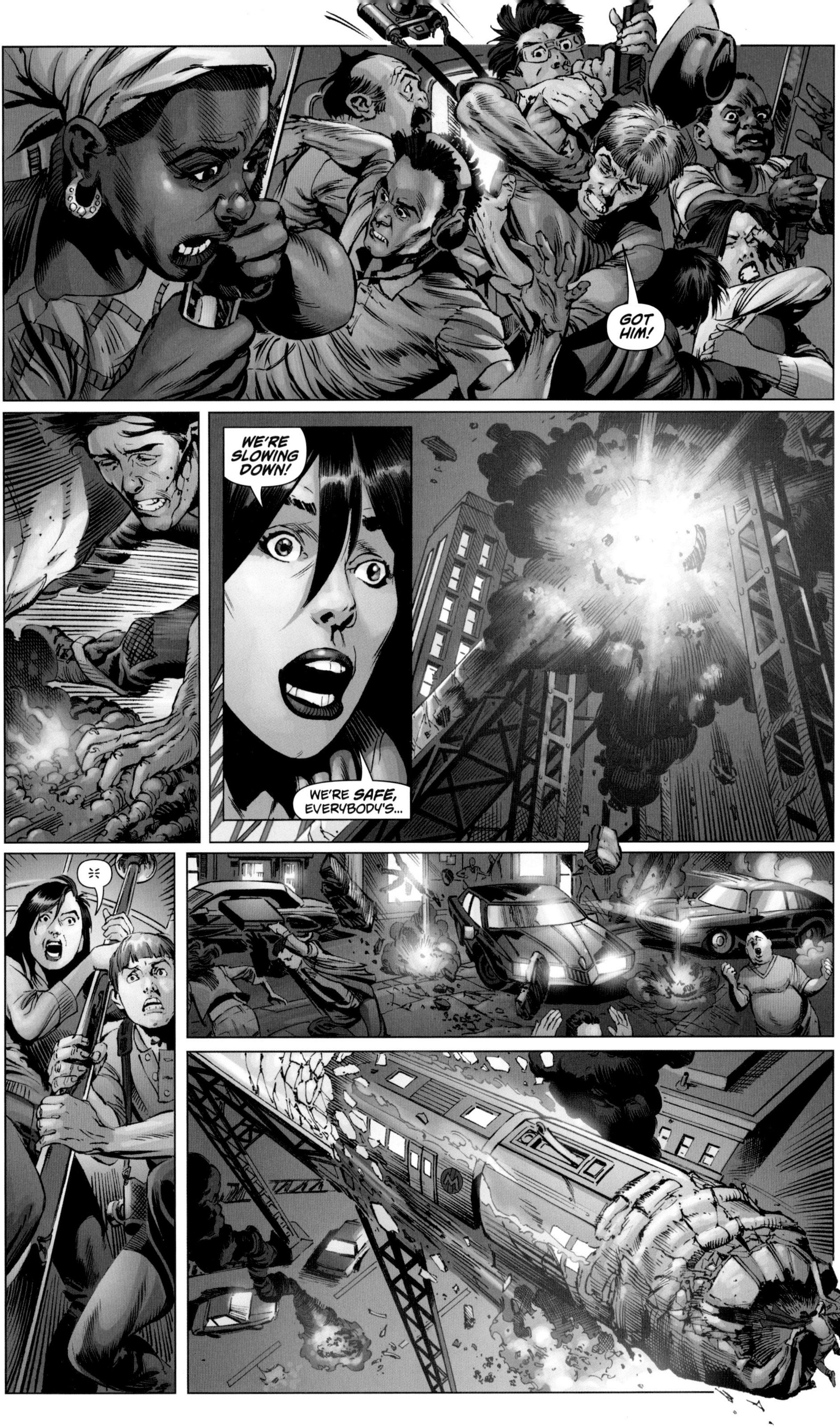

GOT HIM!
WE'RE SLOWING DOWN!
WE'RE SAFE, EVERYBODY'S...

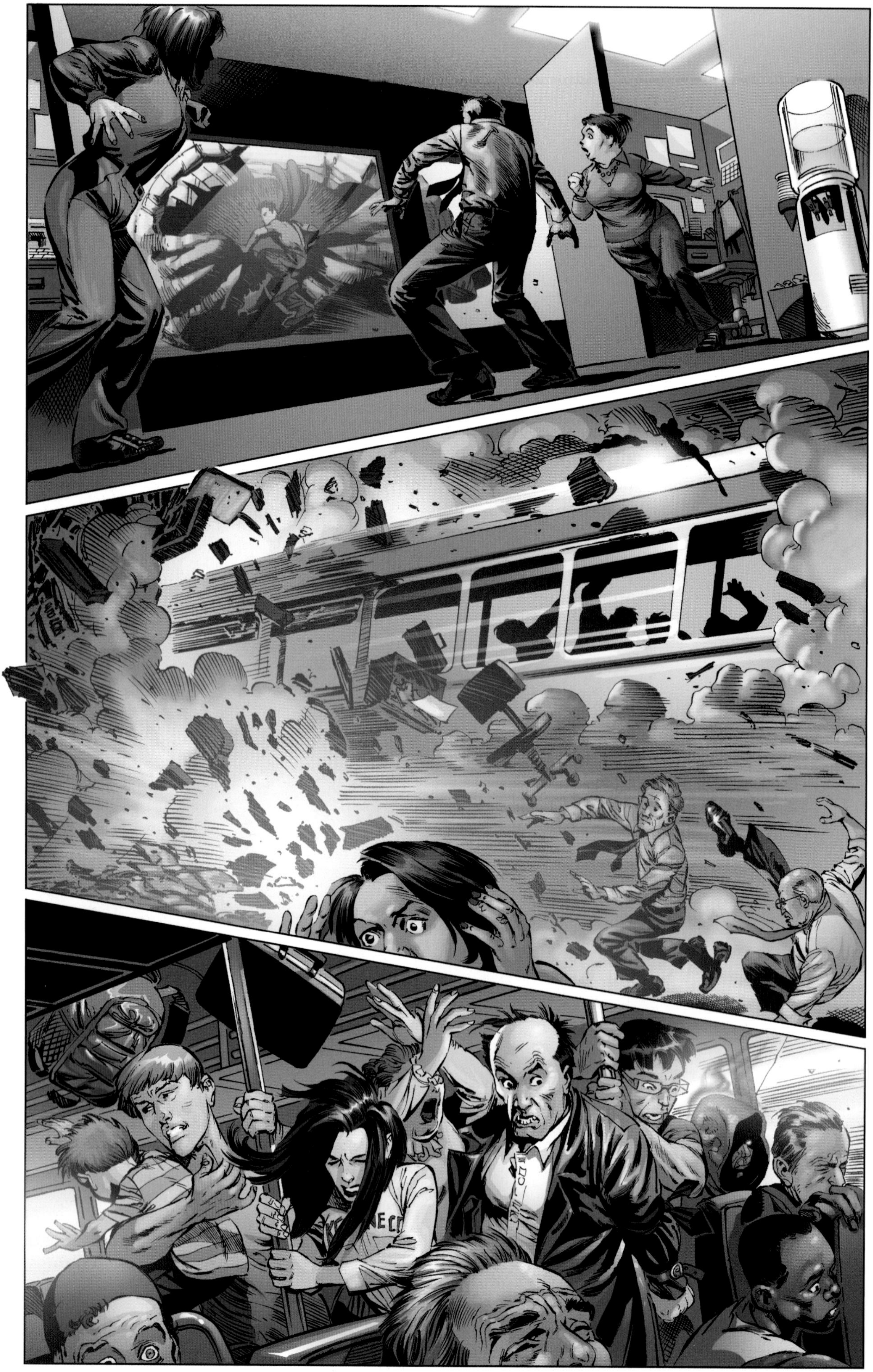

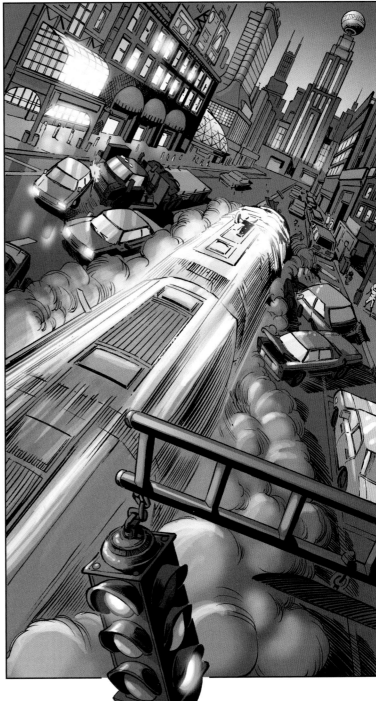

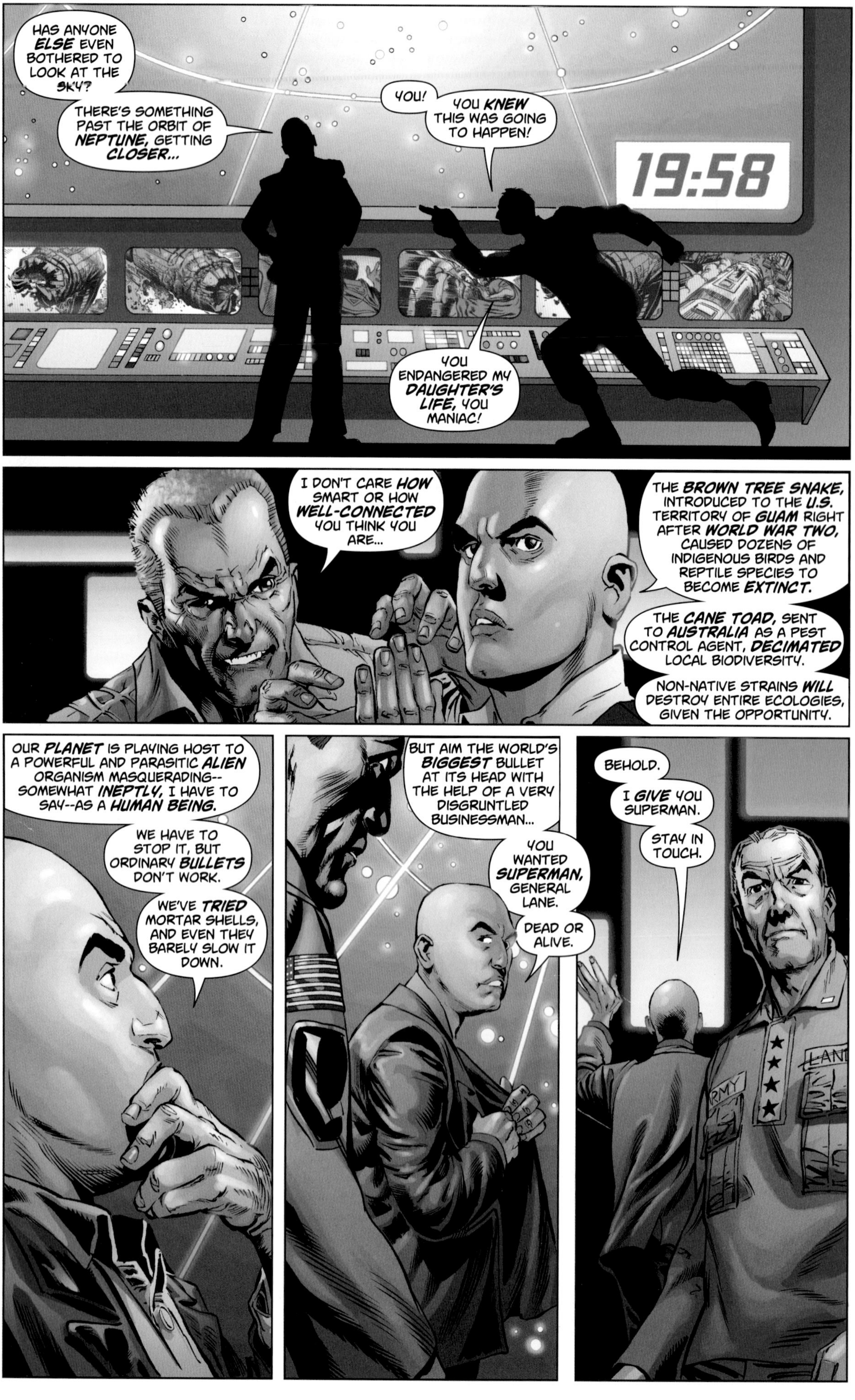

HAS ANYONE ELSE EVEN BOTHERED TO LOOK AT THE SKY?
THERE'S SOMETHING PAST THE ORBIT OF NEPTUNE, GETTING CLOSER...
YOU!
YOU KNEW THIS WAS GOING TO HAPPEN!
19:58
YOU ENDANGERED MY DAUGHTER'S LIFE, YOU MANIAC!
I DON'T CARE HOW SMART OR HOW WELL-CONNECTED YOU THINK YOU ARE...
THE BROWN TREE SNAKE, INTRODUCED TO THE U.S. TERRITORY OF GUAM RIGHT AFTER WORLD WAR TWO, CAUSED DOZENS OF INDIGENOUS BIRDS AND REPTILE SPECIES TO BECOME EXTINCT.
THE CANE TOAD, SENT TO AUSTRALIA AS A PEST CONTROL AGENT, DECIMATED LOCAL BIODIVERSITY.
NON-NATIVE STRAINS WILL DESTROY ENTIRE ECOLOGIES, GIVEN THE OPPORTUNITY.
OUR PLANET IS PLAYING HOST TO A POWERFUL AND PARASITIC ALIEN ORGANISM MASQUERADING--SOMEWHAT INEPTLY, I HAVE TO SAY--AS A HUMAN BEING.
WE HAVE TO STOP IT, BUT ORDINARY BULLETS DON'T WORK.
WE'VE TRIED MORTAR SHELLS, AND EVEN THEY BARELY SLOW IT DOWN.
BUT AIM THE WORLD'S BIGGEST BULLET AT ITS HEAD WITH THE HELP OF A VERY DISGRUNTLED BUSINESSMAN...
YOU WANTED SUPERMAN, GENERAL LANE.
DEAD OR ALIVE.
BEHOLD.
I GIVE YOU SUPERMAN.
STAY IN TOUCH.
ARMY

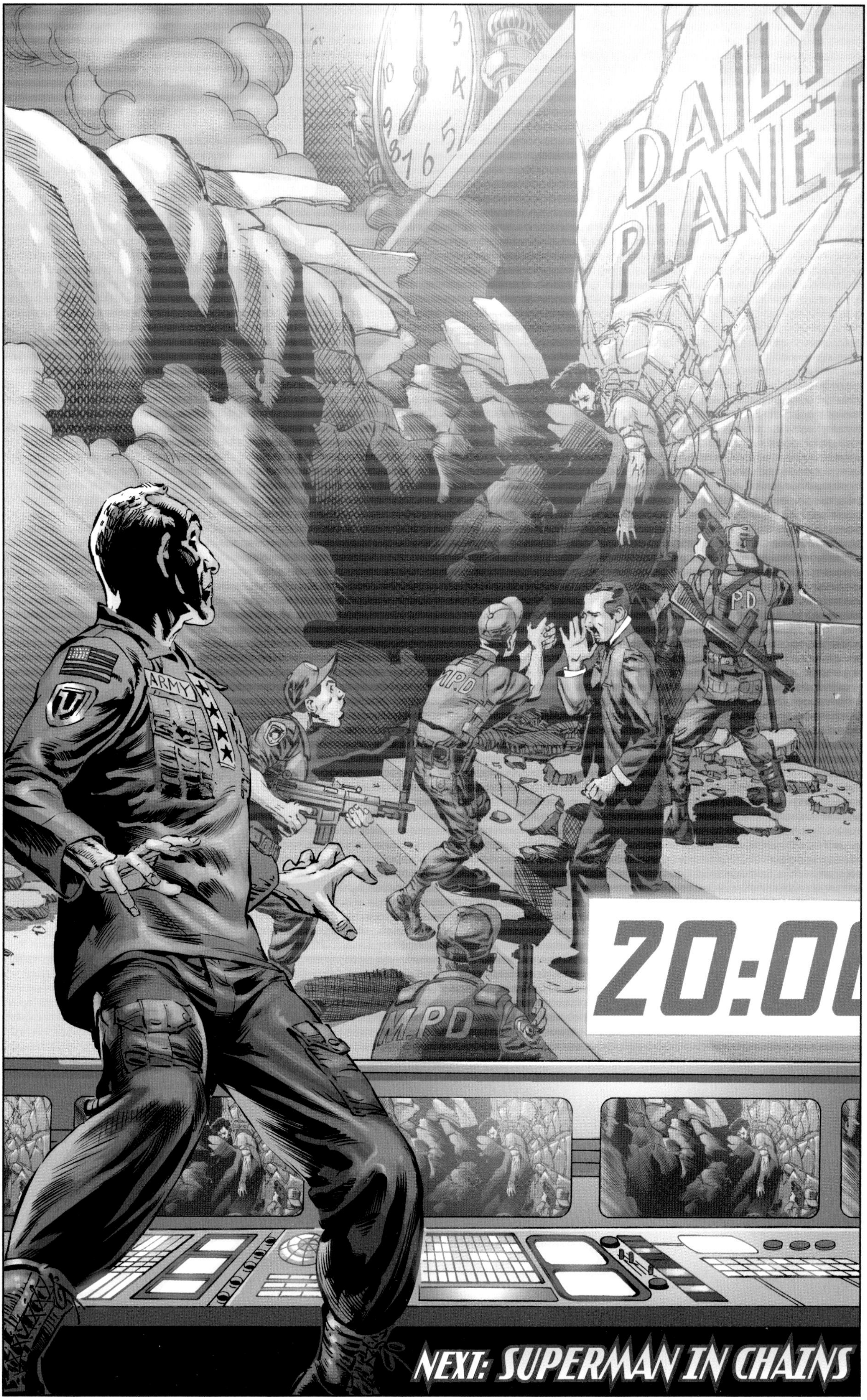
DAILY PLANET
ARMY
M.P.D
P.D.
20:00
NEXT: SUPERMAN IN CHAINS

ACTION COMICS #1
Second printing cover by Rags Morales

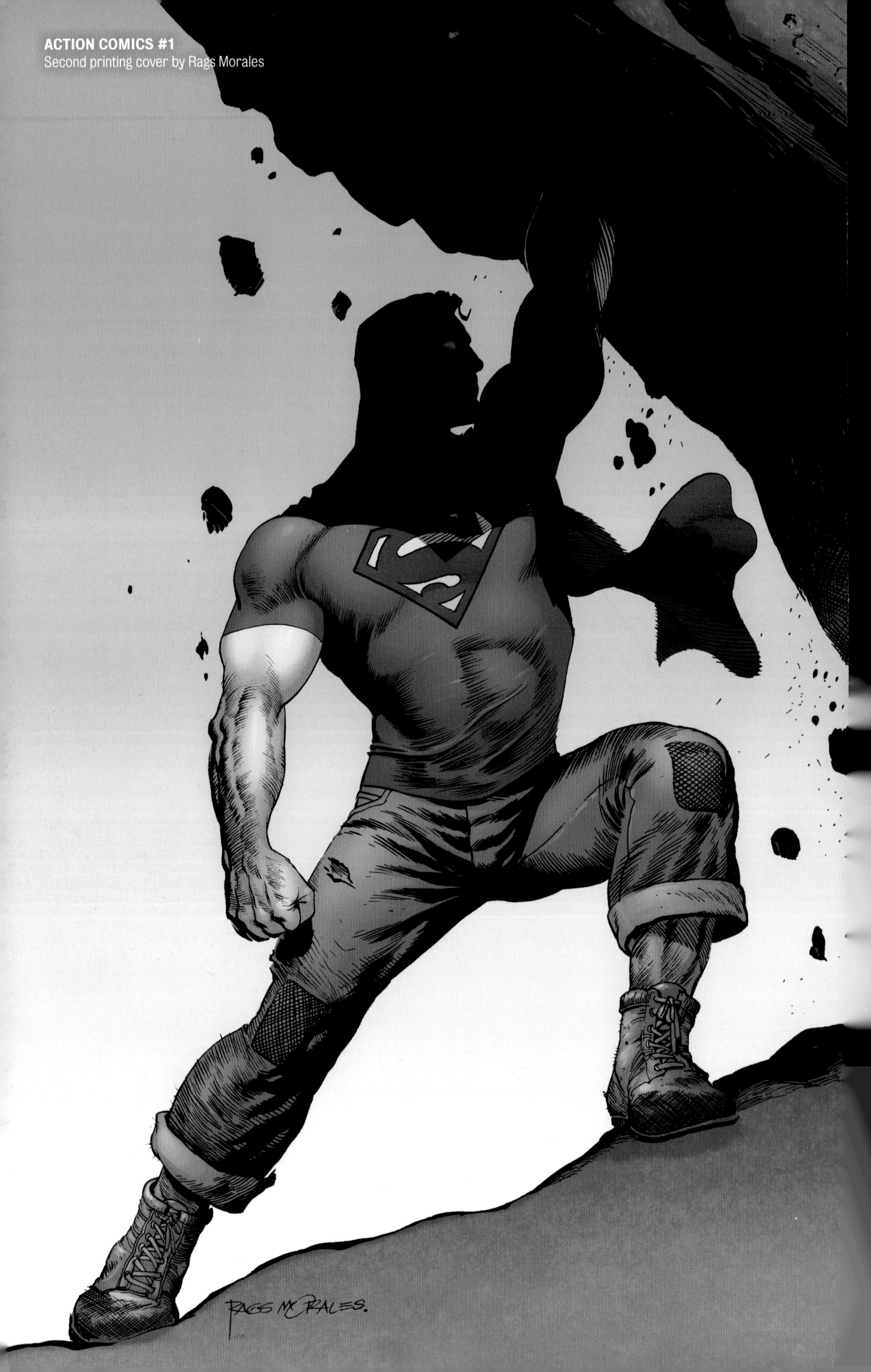
RAGS MORALES.

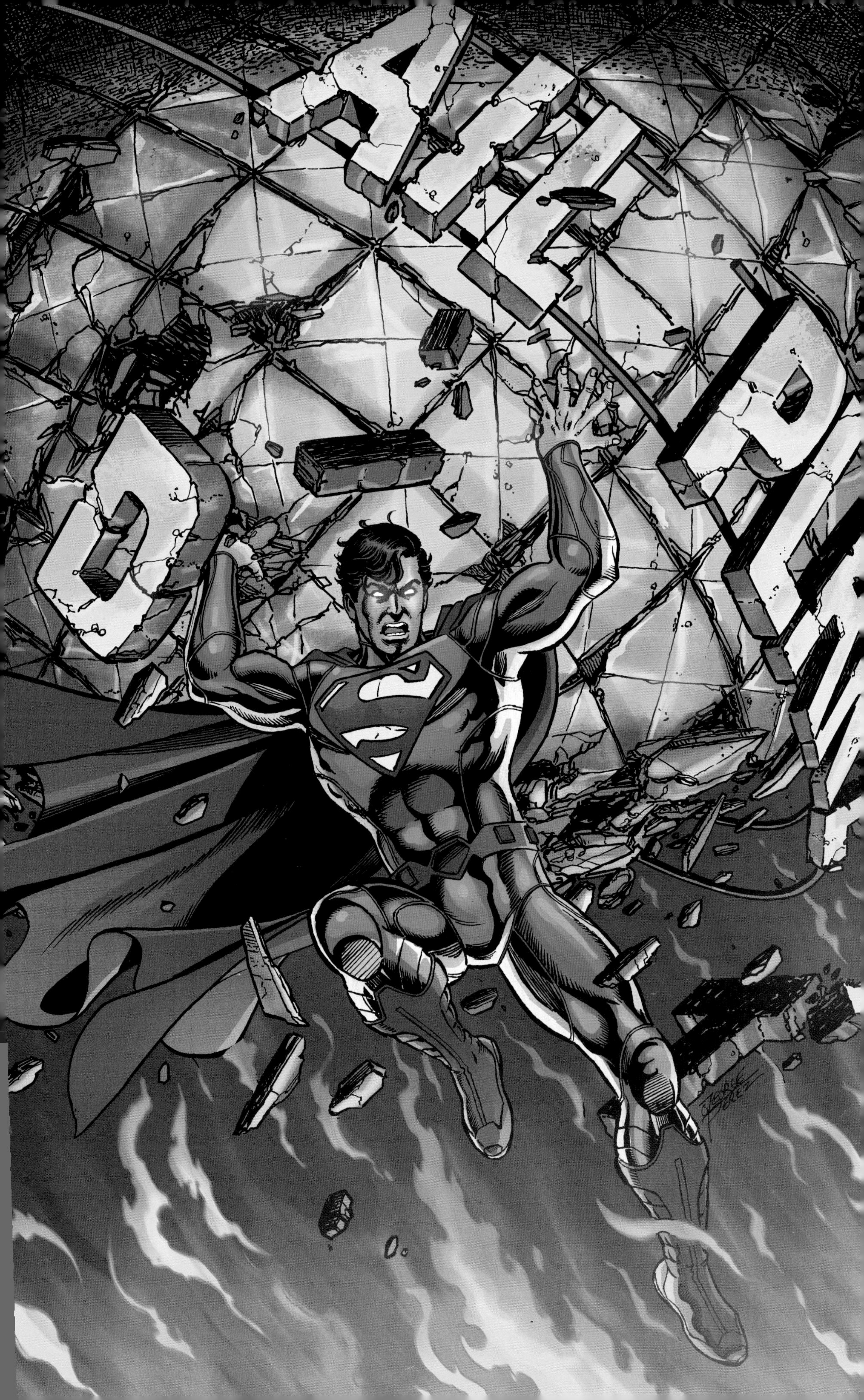

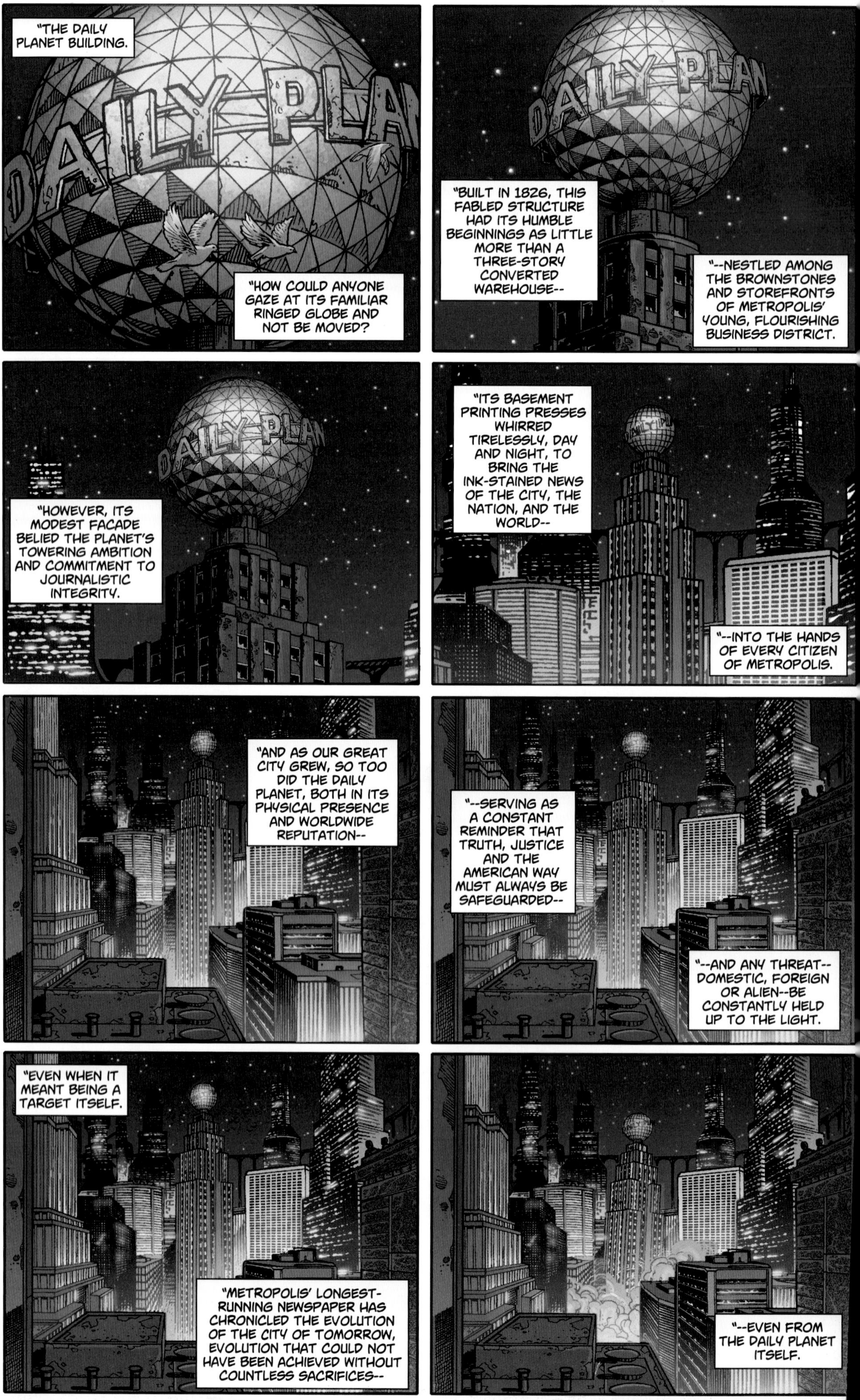
"THE DAILY PLANET BUILDING.
"HOW COULD ANYONE GAZE AT ITS FAMILIAR RINGED GLOBE AND NOT BE MOVED?
"BUILT IN 1826, THIS FABLED STRUCTURE HAD ITS HUMBLE BEGINNINGS AS LITTLE MORE THAN A THREE-STORY CONVERTED WAREHOUSE--
"--NESTLED AMONG THE BROWNSTONES AND STOREFRONTS OF METROPOLIS' YOUNG, FLOURISHING BUSINESS DISTRICT.
"HOWEVER, ITS MODEST FACADE BELIED THE PLANET'S TOWERING AMBITION AND COMMITMENT TO JOURNALISTIC INTEGRITY.
"ITS BASEMENT PRINTING PRESSES WHIRRED TIRELESSLY, DAY AND NIGHT, TO BRING THE INK-STAINED NEWS OF THE CITY, THE NATION, AND THE WORLD--
"--INTO THE HANDS OF EVERY CITIZEN OF METROPOLIS.
"AND AS OUR GREAT CITY GREW, SO TOO DID THE DAILY PLANET, BOTH IN ITS PHYSICAL PRESENCE AND WORLDWIDE REPUTATION--
"--SERVING AS A CONSTANT REMINDER THAT TRUTH, JUSTICE AND THE AMERICAN WAY MUST ALWAYS BE SAFEGUARDED--
"--AND ANY THREAT--DOMESTIC, FOREIGN OR ALIEN--BE CONSTANTLY HELD UP TO THE LIGHT.
"EVEN WHEN IT MEANT BEING A TARGET ITSELF.
"METROPOLIS' LONGEST-RUNNING NEWSPAPER HAS CHRONICLED THE EVOLUTION OF THE CITY OF TOMORROW, EVOLUTION THAT COULD NOT HAVE BEEN ACHIEVED WITHOUT COUNTLESS SACRIFICES--
"--EVEN FROM THE DAILY PLANET ITSELF.

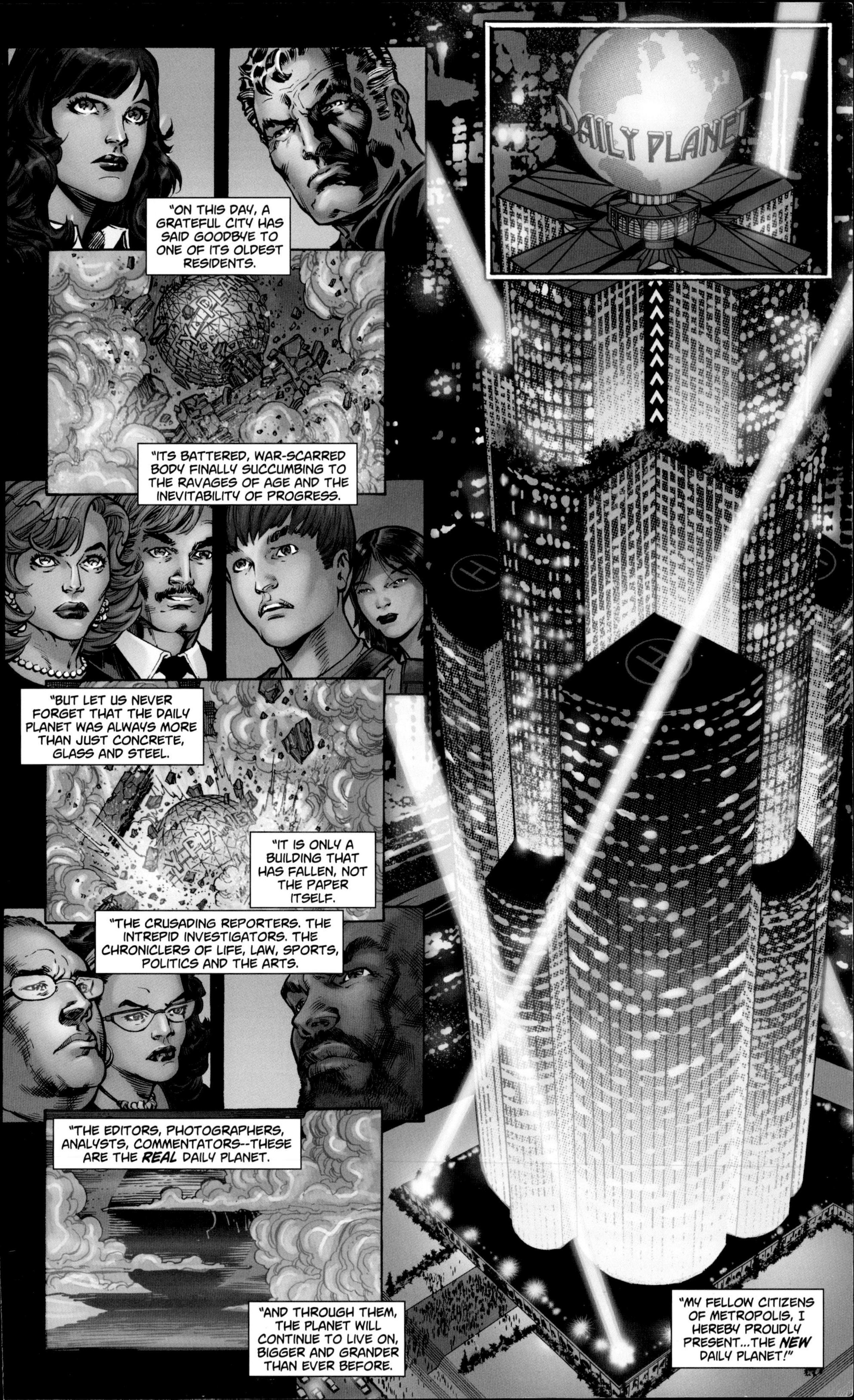
DAILY PLANET
"ON THIS DAY, A GRATEFUL CITY HAS SAID GOODBYE TO ONE OF ITS OLDEST RESIDENTS.
"ITS BATTERED, WAR-SCARRED BODY FINALLY SUCCUMBING TO THE RAVAGES OF AGE AND THE INEVITABILITY OF PROGRESS.
"BUT LET US NEVER FORGET THAT THE DAILY PLANET WAS ALWAYS MORE THAN JUST CONCRETE, GLASS AND STEEL.
"IT IS ONLY A BUILDING THAT HAS FALLEN, NOT THE PAPER ITSELF.
"THE CRUSADING REPORTERS. THE INTREPID INVESTIGATORS. THE CHRONICLERS OF LIFE, LAW, SPORTS, POLITICS AND THE ARTS.
"THE EDITORS, PHOTOGRAPHERS, ANALYSTS, COMMENTATORS--THESE ARE THE *REAL* DAILY PLANET.
"AND THROUGH THEM, THE PLANET WILL CONTINUE TO LIVE ON, BIGGER AND GRANDER THAN EVER BEFORE.
"MY FELLOW CITIZENS OF METROPOLIS, I HEREBY PROUDLY PRESENT...THE *NEW* DAILY PLANET!"

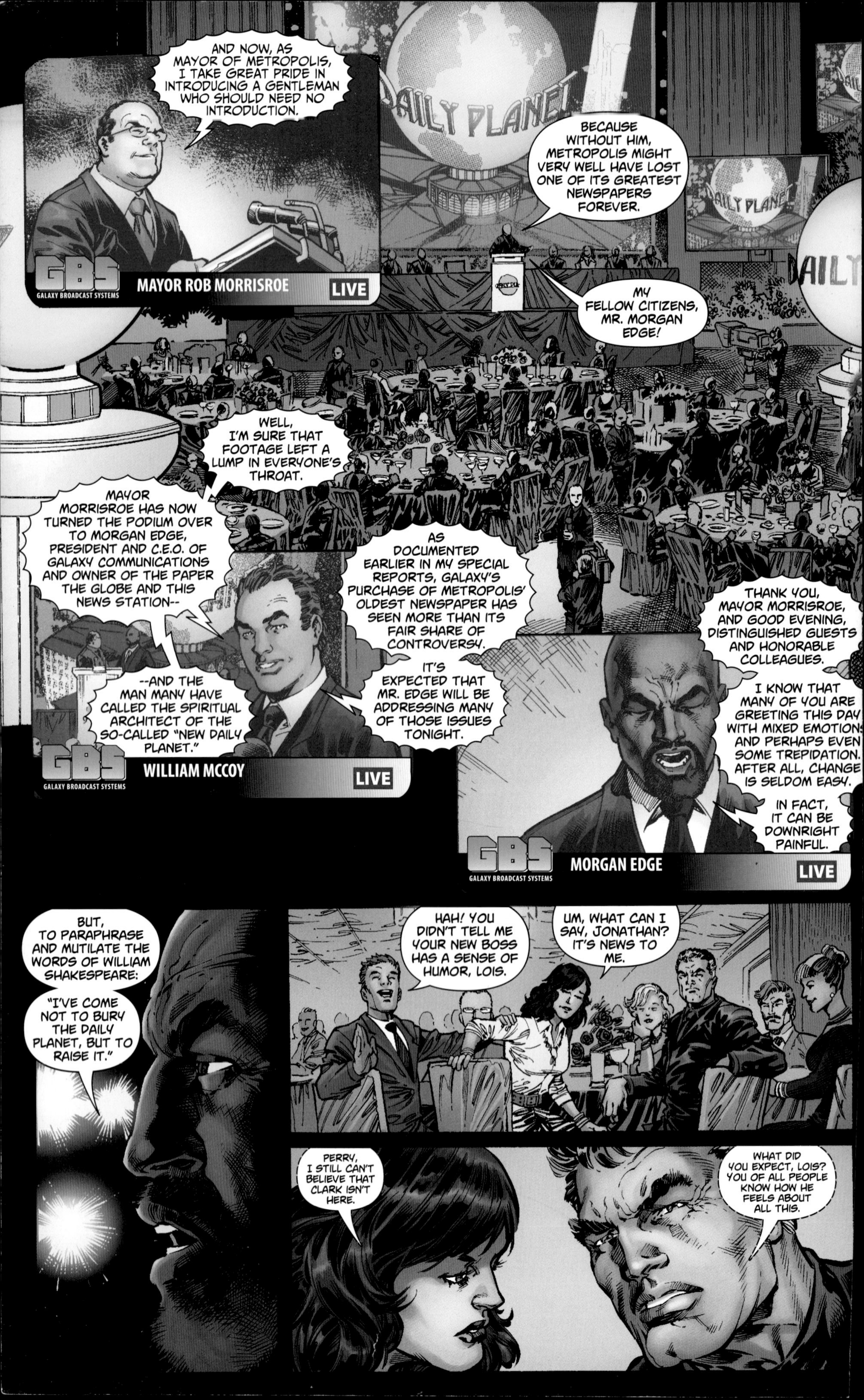
AND NOW, AS MAYOR OF METROPOLIS, I TAKE GREAT PRIDE IN INTRODUCING A GENTLEMAN WHO SHOULD NEED NO INTRODUCTION.
GBS GALAXY BROADCAST SYSTEMS
MAYOR ROB MORRISROE
LIVE
DAILY PLANET
BECAUSE WITHOUT HIM, METROPOLIS MIGHT VERY WELL HAVE LOST ONE OF ITS GREATEST NEWSPAPERS FOREVER.
MY FELLOW CITIZENS, MR. MORGAN EDGE!
WELL, I'M SURE THAT FOOTAGE LEFT A LUMP IN EVERYONE'S THROAT.
MAYOR MORRISROE HAS NOW TURNED THE PODIUM OVER TO MORGAN EDGE, PRESIDENT AND C.E.O. OF GALAXY COMMUNICATIONS AND OWNER OF THE PAPER THE GLOBE AND THIS NEWS STATION--
--AND THE MAN MANY HAVE CALLED THE SPIRITUAL ARCHITECT OF THE SO-CALLED "NEW DAILY PLANET."
AS DOCUMENTED EARLIER IN MY SPECIAL REPORTS, GALAXY'S PURCHASE OF METROPOLIS' OLDEST NEWSPAPER HAS SEEN MORE THAN ITS FAIR SHARE OF CONTROVERSY.
IT'S EXPECTED THAT MR. EDGE WILL BE ADDRESSING MANY OF THOSE ISSUES TONIGHT.
GBS GALAXY BROADCAST SYSTEMS
WILLIAM MCCOY
LIVE
THANK YOU, MAYOR MORRISROE, AND GOOD EVENING, DISTINGUISHED GUESTS AND HONORABLE COLLEAGUES.
I KNOW THAT MANY OF YOU ARE GREETING THIS DAY WITH MIXED EMOTIONS AND PERHAPS EVEN SOME TREPIDATION. AFTER ALL, CHANGE IS SELDOM EASY.
IN FACT, IT CAN BE DOWNRIGHT PAINFUL.
GBS GALAXY BROADCAST SYSTEMS
MORGAN EDGE
LIVE
BUT, TO PARAPHRASE AND MUTILATE THE WORDS OF WILLIAM SHAKESPEARE:
"I'VE COME NOT TO BURY THE DAILY PLANET, BUT TO RAISE IT."
HAH! YOU DIDN'T TELL ME YOUR NEW BOSS HAS A SENSE OF HUMOR, LOIS.
UM, WHAT CAN I SAY, JONATHAN? IT'S NEWS TO ME.
PERRY, I STILL CAN'T BELIEVE THAT CLARK ISN'T HERE.
WHAT DID YOU EXPECT, LOIS? YOU OF ALL PEOPLE KNOW HOW HE FEELS ABOUT ALL THIS.

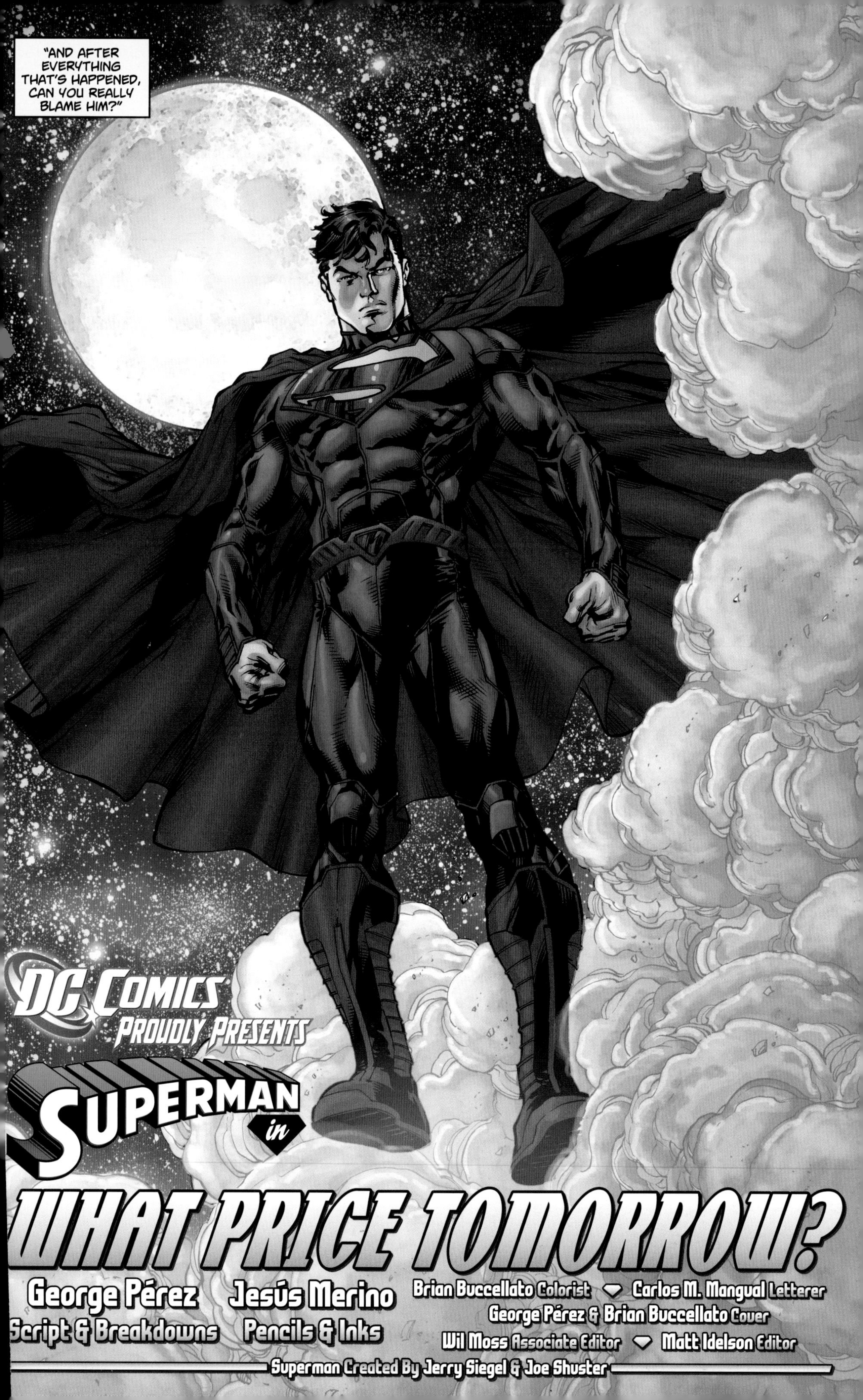
"AND AFTER EVERYTHING THAT'S HAPPENED, CAN YOU REALLY BLAME HIM?"
DC COMICS PROUDLY PRESENTS
SUPERMAN in
WHAT PRICE TOMORROW?
George Pérez Script & Breakdowns
Jesús Merino Pencils & Inks
Brian Buccellato Colorist
Carlos M. Mangual Letterer
George Pérez & Brian Buccellato Cover
Wil Moss Associate Editor
Matt Idelson Editor
Superman Created By Jerry Siegel & Joe Shuster

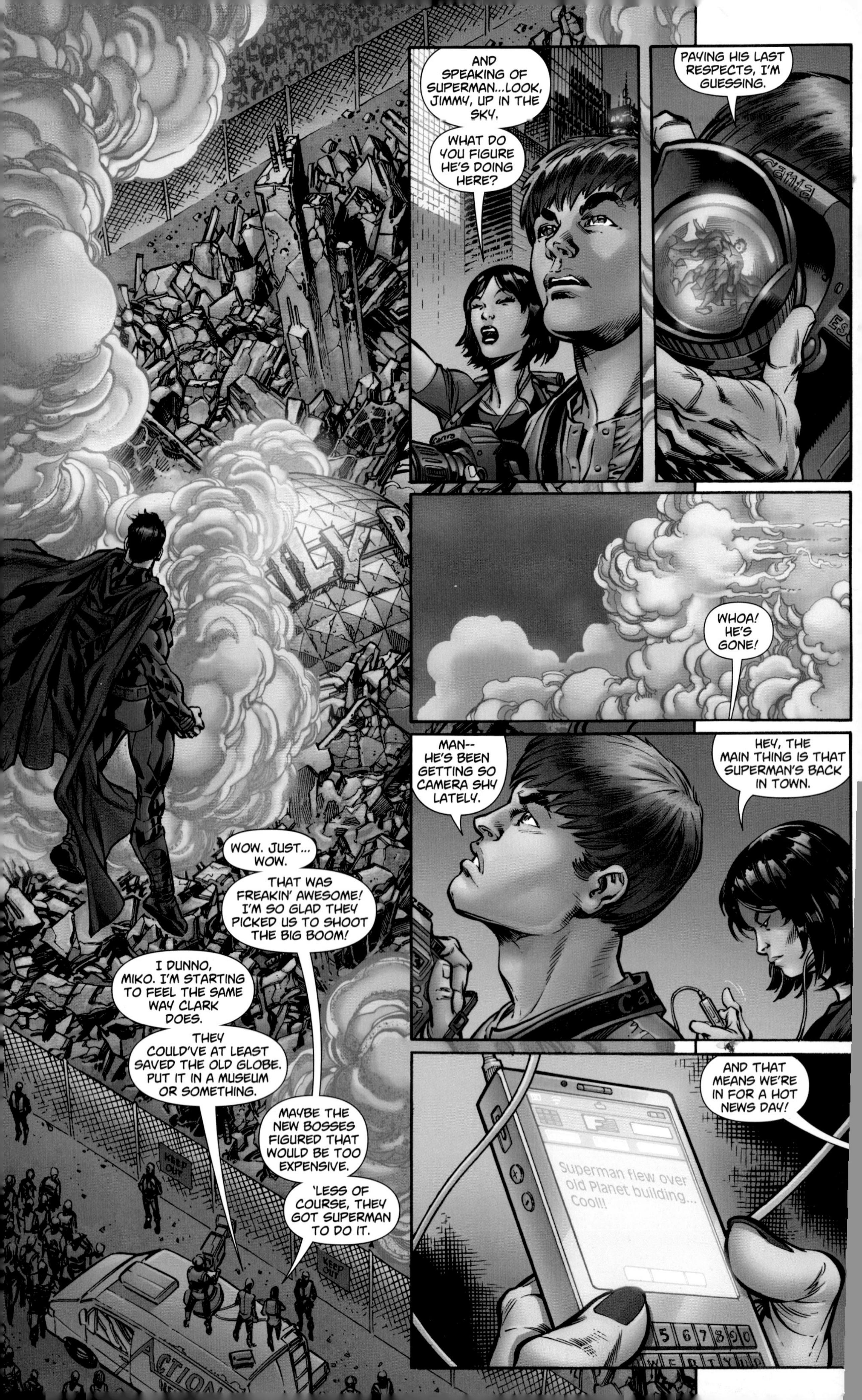

AND SPEAKING OF SUPERMAN...LOOK, JIMMY, UP IN THE SKY.
WHAT DO YOU FIGURE HE'S DOING HERE?
PAYING HIS LAST RESPECTS, I'M GUESSING.
WHOA! HE'S GONE!
MAN-- HE'S BEEN GETTING SO CAMERA SHY LATELY.
HEY, THE MAIN THING IS THAT SUPERMAN'S BACK IN TOWN.
AND THAT MEANS WE'RE IN FOR A HOT NEWS DAY!
Superman flew over old Planet building... Cool!!
WOW. JUST... WOW.
THAT WAS FREAKIN' AWESOME! I'M SO GLAD THEY PICKED US TO SHOOT THE BIG BOOM!
I DUNNO, MIKO. I'M STARTING TO FEEL THE SAME WAY CLARK DOES.
THEY COULD'VE AT LEAST SAVED THE OLD GLOBE. PUT IT IN A MUSEUM OR SOMETHING.
MAYBE THE NEW BOSSES FIGURED THAT WOULD BE TOO EXPENSIVE.
'LESS OF COURSE, THEY GOT SUPERMAN TO DO IT.
KEEP OUT
KEEP OUT

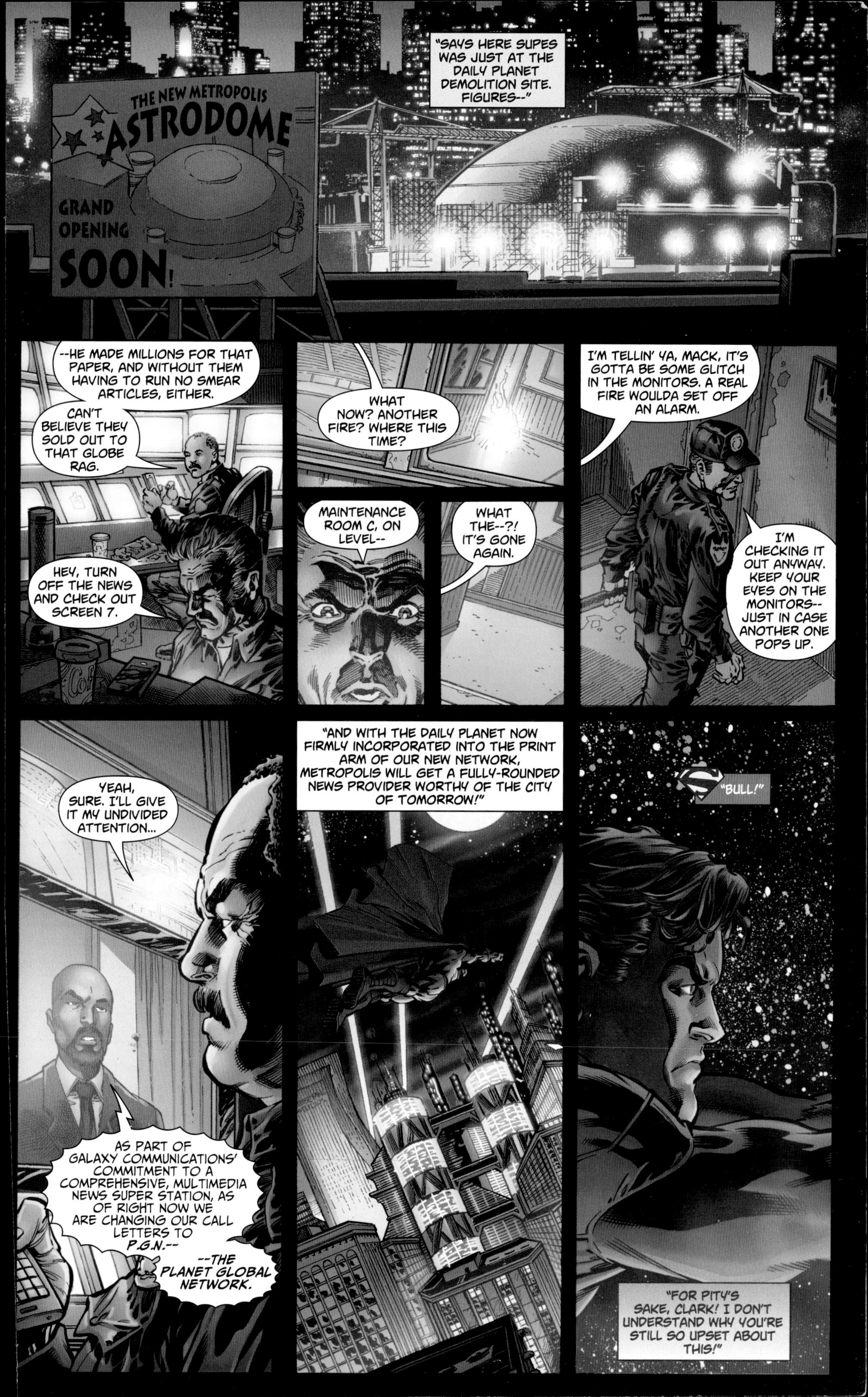
THE NEW METROPOLIS ASTRODOME
GRAND OPENING SOON!
"SAYS HERE SUPES WAS JUST AT THE DAILY PLANET DEMOLITION SITE. FIGURES--"
--HE MADE MILLIONS FOR THAT PAPER, AND WITHOUT THEM HAVING TO RUN NO SMEAR ARTICLES, EITHER.
CAN'T BELIEVE THEY SOLD OUT TO THAT GLOBE RAG.
HEY, TURN OFF THE NEWS AND CHECK OUT SCREEN 7.
WHAT NOW? ANOTHER FIRE? WHERE THIS TIME?
MAINTENANCE ROOM C, ON LEVEL--
WHAT THE--?! IT'S GONE AGAIN.
I'M TELLIN' YA, MACK, IT'S GOTTA BE SOME GLITCH IN THE MONITORS. A REAL FIRE WOULDA SET OFF AN ALARM.
I'M CHECKING IT OUT ANYWAY. KEEP YOUR EYES ON THE MONITORS--JUST IN CASE ANOTHER ONE POPS UP.
YEAH, SURE. I'LL GIVE IT MY UNDIVIDED ATTENTION...
AS PART OF GALAXY COMMUNICATIONS' COMMITMENT TO A COMPREHENSIVE, MULTIMEDIA NEWS SUPER STATION, AS OF RIGHT NOW WE ARE CHANGING OUR CALL LETTERS TO P.G.N.--
--THE PLANET GLOBAL NETWORK.
"AND WITH THE DAILY PLANET NOW FIRMLY INCORPORATED INTO THE PRINT ARM OF OUR NEW NETWORK, METROPOLIS WILL GET A FULLY-ROUNDED NEWS PROVIDER WORTHY OF THE CITY OF TOMORROW!"
"BULL!"
"FOR PITY'S SAKE, CLARK! I DON'T UNDERSTAND WHY YOU'RE STILL SO UPSET ABOUT THIS!"

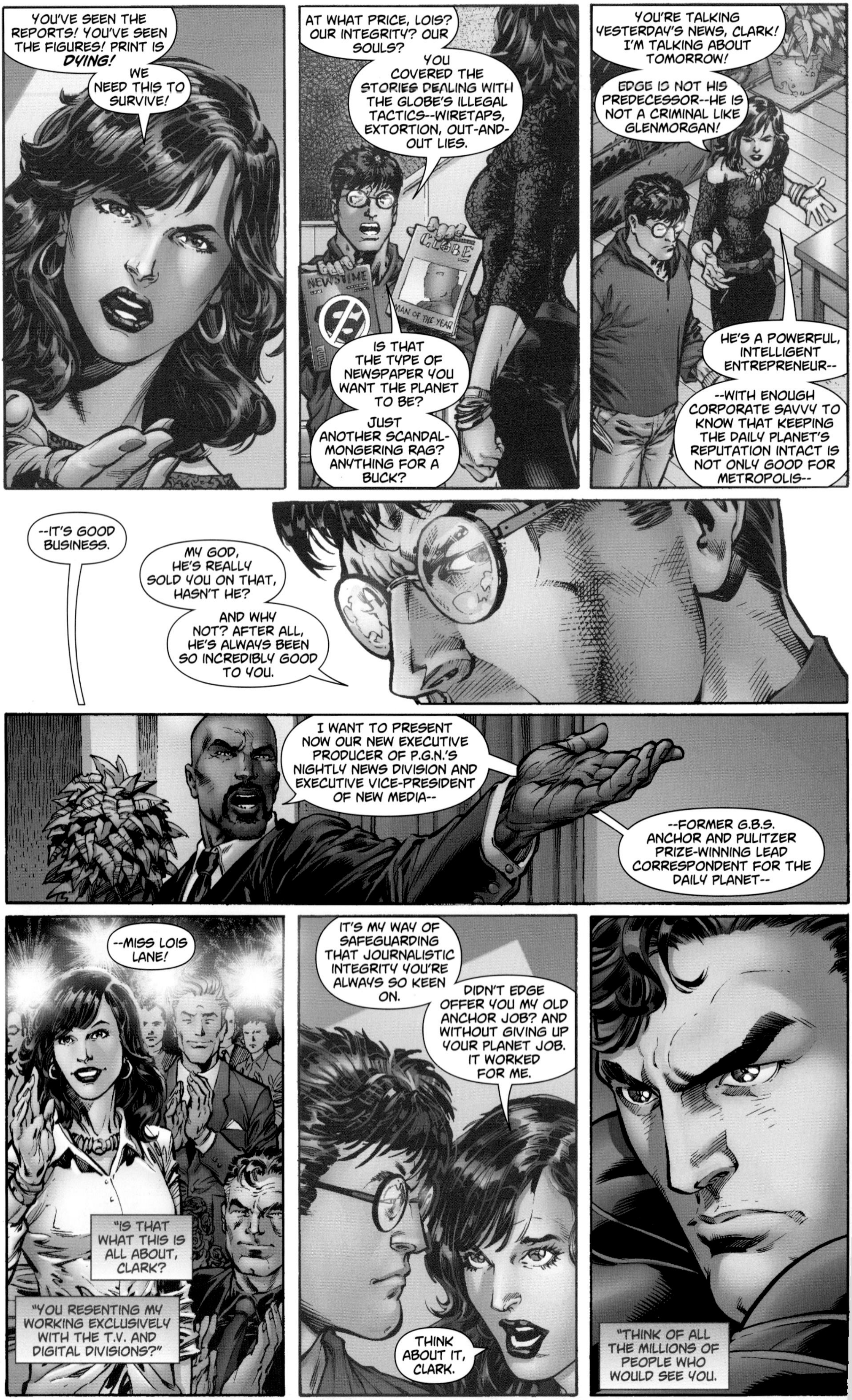
YOU'VE SEEN THE REPORTS! YOU'VE SEEN THE FIGURES! PRINT IS DYING!
WE NEED THIS TO SURVIVE!
AT WHAT PRICE, LOIS? OUR INTEGRITY? OUR SOULS?
YOU COVERED THE STORIES DEALING WITH THE GLOBE'S ILLEGAL TACTICS--WIRETAPS, EXTORTION, OUT-AND-OUT LIES.
GLOBE
NEWSTIME
MAN OF THE YEAR
IS THAT THE TYPE OF NEWSPAPER YOU WANT THE PLANET TO BE?
JUST ANOTHER SCANDAL-MONGERING RAG? ANYTHING FOR A BUCK?
YOU'RE TALKING YESTERDAY'S NEWS, CLARK! I'M TALKING ABOUT TOMORROW!
EDGE IS NOT HIS PREDECESSOR--HE IS NOT A CRIMINAL LIKE GLENMORGAN!
HE'S A POWERFUL, INTELLIGENT ENTREPRENEUR--
--WITH ENOUGH CORPORATE SAVVY TO KNOW THAT KEEPING THE DAILY PLANET'S REPUTATION INTACT IS NOT ONLY GOOD FOR METROPOLIS--
--IT'S GOOD BUSINESS.
MY GOD, HE'S REALLY SOLD YOU ON THAT, HASN'T HE?
AND WHY NOT? AFTER ALL, HE'S ALWAYS BEEN SO INCREDIBLY GOOD TO YOU.
I WANT TO PRESENT NOW OUR NEW EXECUTIVE PRODUCER OF P.G.N.'S NIGHTLY NEWS DIVISION AND EXECUTIVE VICE-PRESIDENT OF NEW MEDIA--
--FORMER G.B.S. ANCHOR AND PULITZER PRIZE-WINNING LEAD CORRESPONDENT FOR THE DAILY PLANET--
--MISS LOIS LANE!
"IS THAT WHAT THIS IS ALL ABOUT, CLARK?
"YOU RESENTING MY WORKING EXCLUSIVELY WITH THE T.V. AND DIGITAL DIVISIONS?"
IT'S MY WAY OF SAFEGUARDING THAT JOURNALISTIC INTEGRITY YOU'RE ALWAYS SO KEEN ON.
DIDN'T EDGE OFFER YOU MY OLD ANCHOR JOB? AND WITHOUT GIVING UP YOUR PLANET JOB. IT WORKED FOR ME.
THINK ABOUT IT, CLARK.
"THINK OF ALL THE MILLIONS OF PEOPLE WHO WOULD SEE YOU.

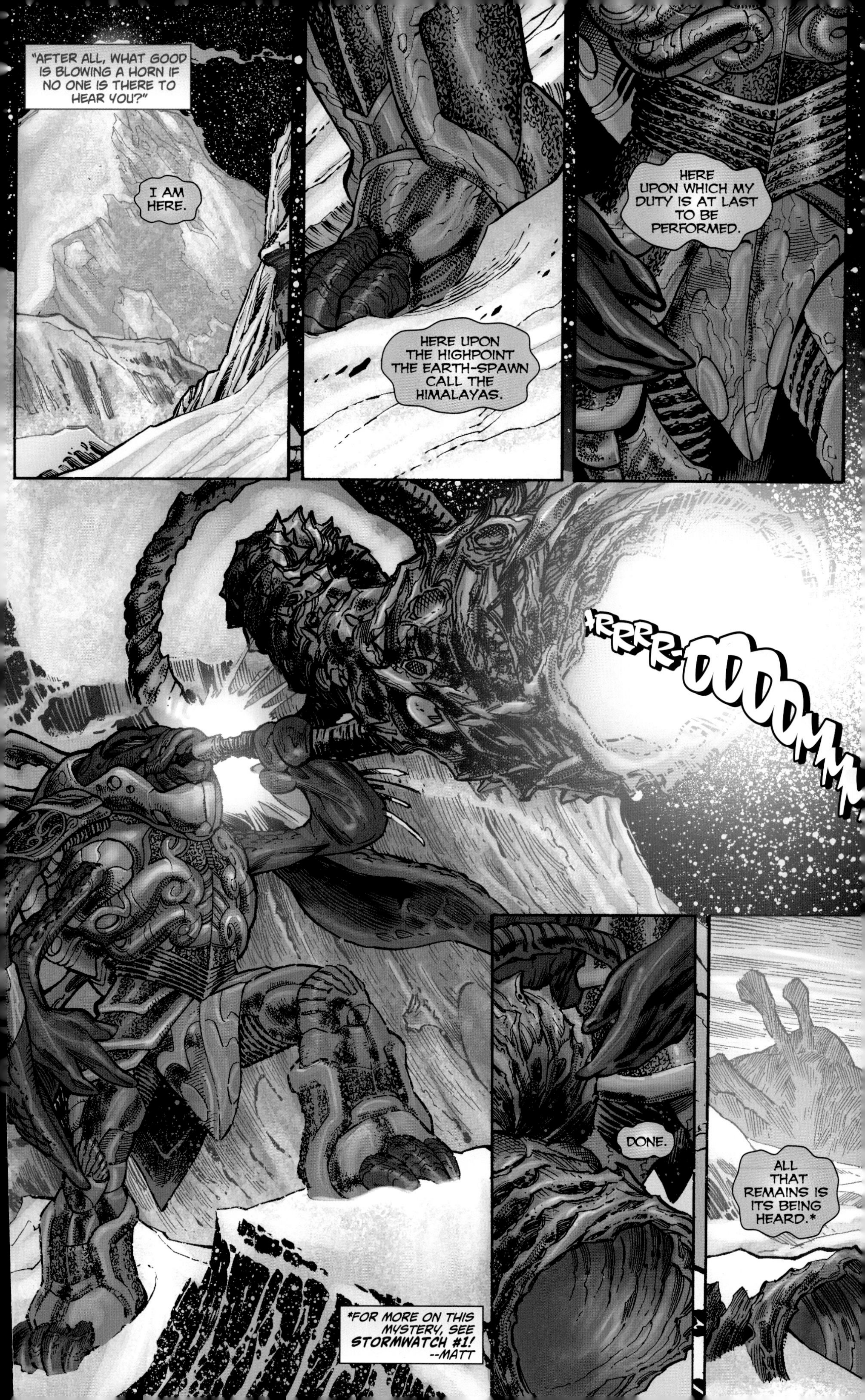
"AFTER ALL, WHAT GOOD IS BLOWING A HORN IF NO ONE IS THERE TO HEAR YOU?"
I AM HERE.
HERE UPON THE HIGHPOINT THE EARTH-SPAWN CALL THE HIMALAYAS.
HERE UPON WHICH MY DUTY IS AT LAST TO BE PERFORMED.
RRRR-OOOOMMM
DONE.
ALL THAT REMAINS IS ITS BEING HEARD.*
*FOR MORE ON THIS MYSTERY, SEE STORMWATCH #1! --MATT

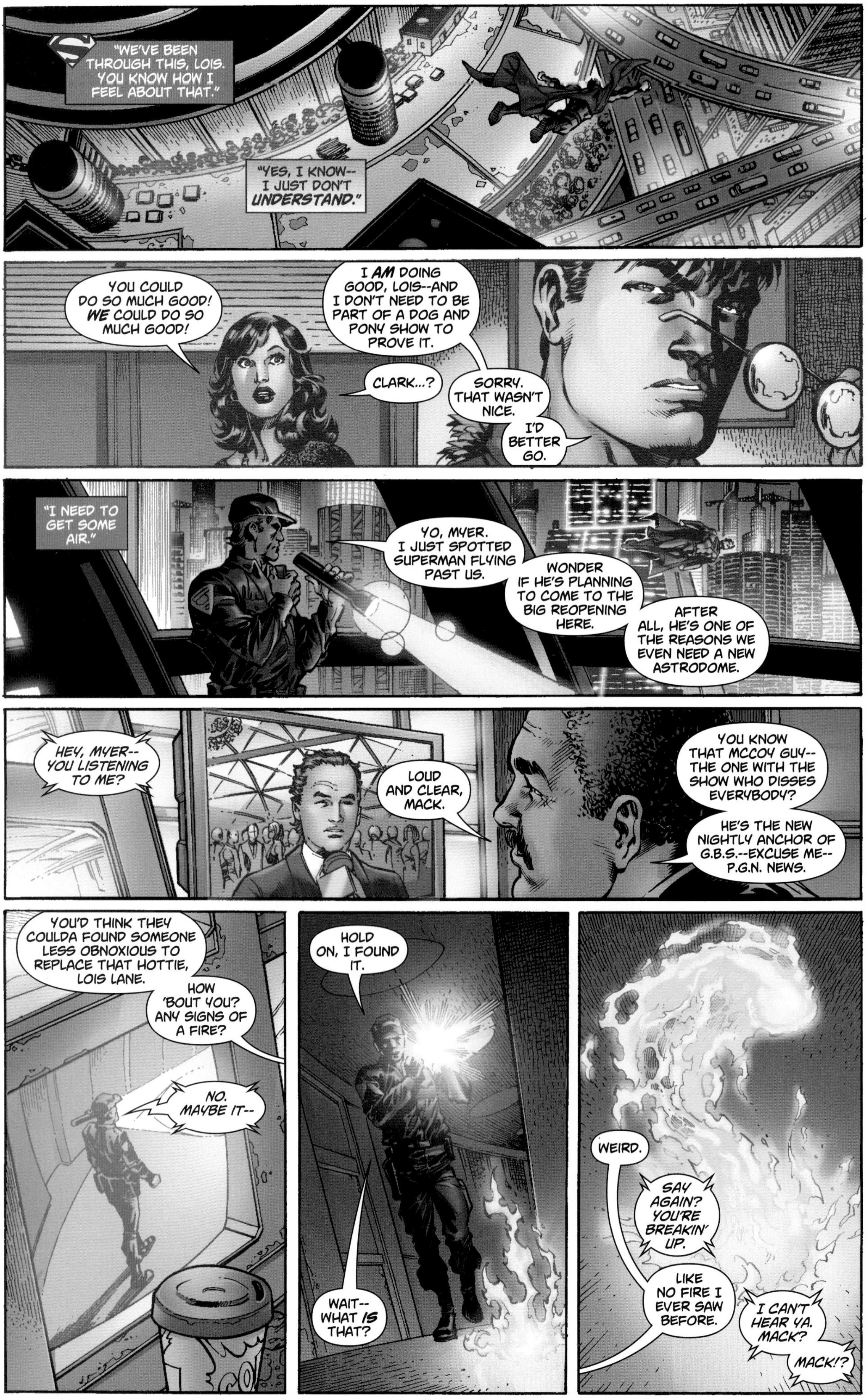
"WE'VE BEEN THROUGH THIS, LOIS. YOU KNOW HOW I FEEL ABOUT THAT."
"YES, I KNOW-- I JUST DON'T UNDERSTAND."
YOU COULD DO SO MUCH GOOD! WE COULD DO SO MUCH GOOD!
I AM DOING GOOD, LOIS--AND I DON'T NEED TO BE PART OF A DOG AND PONY SHOW TO PROVE IT.
CLARK...?
SORRY. THAT WASN'T NICE.
I'D BETTER GO.
"I NEED TO GET SOME AIR."
YO, MYER. I JUST SPOTTED SUPERMAN FLYING PAST US.
WONDER IF HE'S PLANNING TO COME TO THE BIG REOPENING HERE.
AFTER ALL, HE'S ONE OF THE REASONS WE EVEN NEED A NEW ASTRODOME.
HEY, MYER-- YOU LISTENING TO ME?
LOUD AND CLEAR, MACK.
YOU KNOW THAT MCCOY GUY-- THE ONE WITH THE SHOW WHO DISSES EVERYBODY?
HE'S THE NEW NIGHTLY ANCHOR OF G.B.S.--EXCUSE ME-- P.G.N. NEWS.
YOU'D THINK THEY COULDA FOUND SOMEONE LESS OBNOXIOUS TO REPLACE THAT HOTTIE, LOIS LANE.
HOW 'BOUT YOU? ANY SIGNS OF A FIRE?
NO. MAYBE IT--
HOLD ON, I FOUND IT.
WAIT-- WHAT IS THAT?
WEIRD.
SAY AGAIN? YOU'RE BREAKIN' UP.
LIKE NO FIRE I EVER SAW BEFORE.
I CAN'T HEAR YA. MACK?
MACK!?

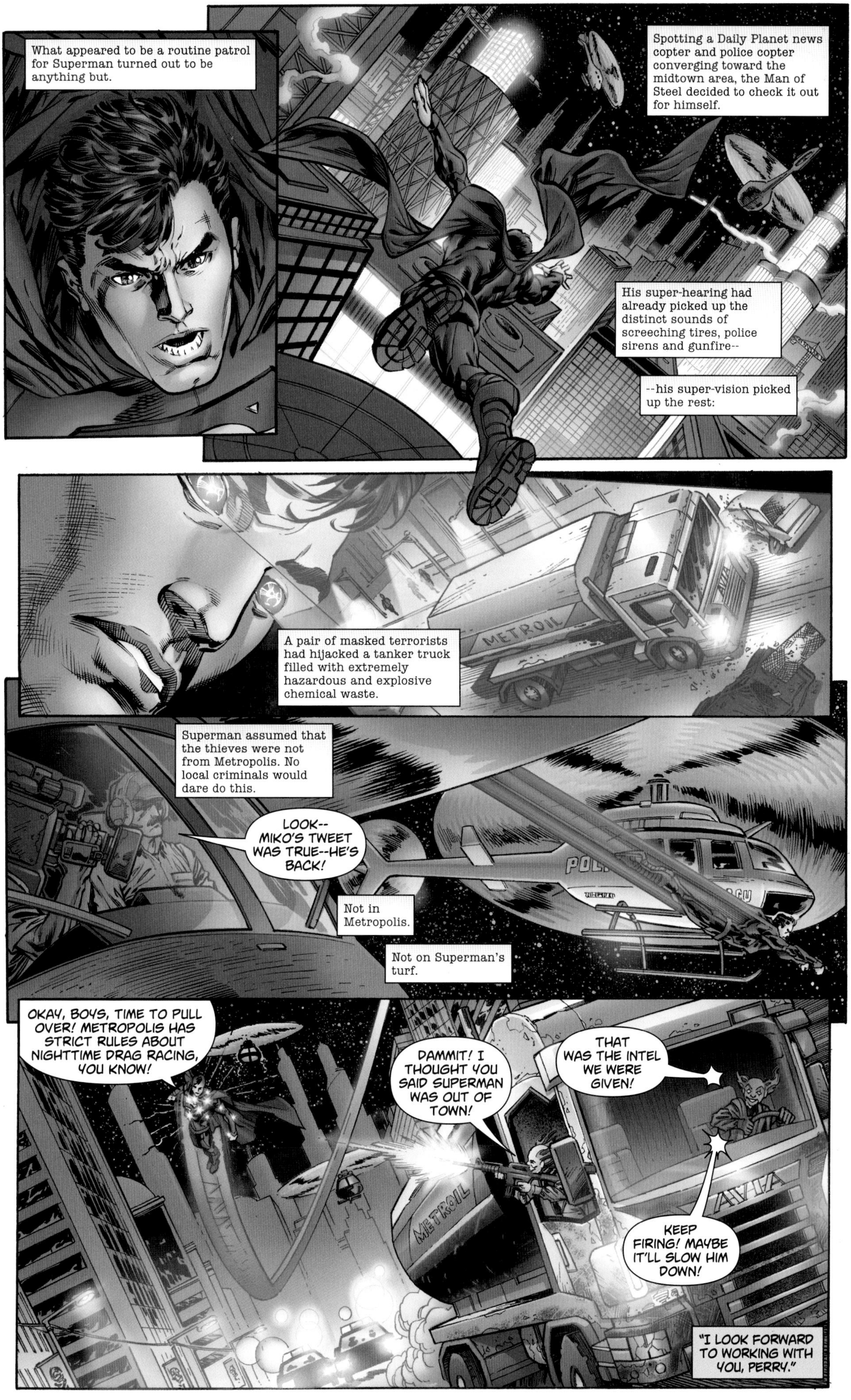

What appeared to be a routine patrol for Superman turned out to be anything but.
Spotting a Daily Planet news copter and police copter converging toward the midtown area, the Man of Steel decided to check it out for himself.
His super-hearing had already picked up the distinct sounds of screeching tires, police sirens and gunfire--
--his super-vision picked up the rest:
METROIL
A pair of masked terrorists had hijacked a tanker truck filled with extremely hazardous and explosive chemical waste.
Superman assumed that the thieves were not from Metropolis. No local criminals would dare do this.
LOOK--MIKO'S TWEET WAS TRUE--HE'S BACK!
Not in Metropolis.
Not on Superman's turf.
OKAY, BOYS, TIME TO PULL OVER! METROPOLIS HAS STRICT RULES ABOUT NIGHTTIME DRAG RACING, YOU KNOW!
DAMMIT! I THOUGHT YOU SAID SUPERMAN WAS OUT OF TOWN!
THAT WAS THE INTEL WE WERE GIVEN!
KEEP FIRING! MAYBE IT'LL SLOW HIM DOWN!
METROIL
"I LOOK FORWARD TO WORKING WITH YOU, PERRY."

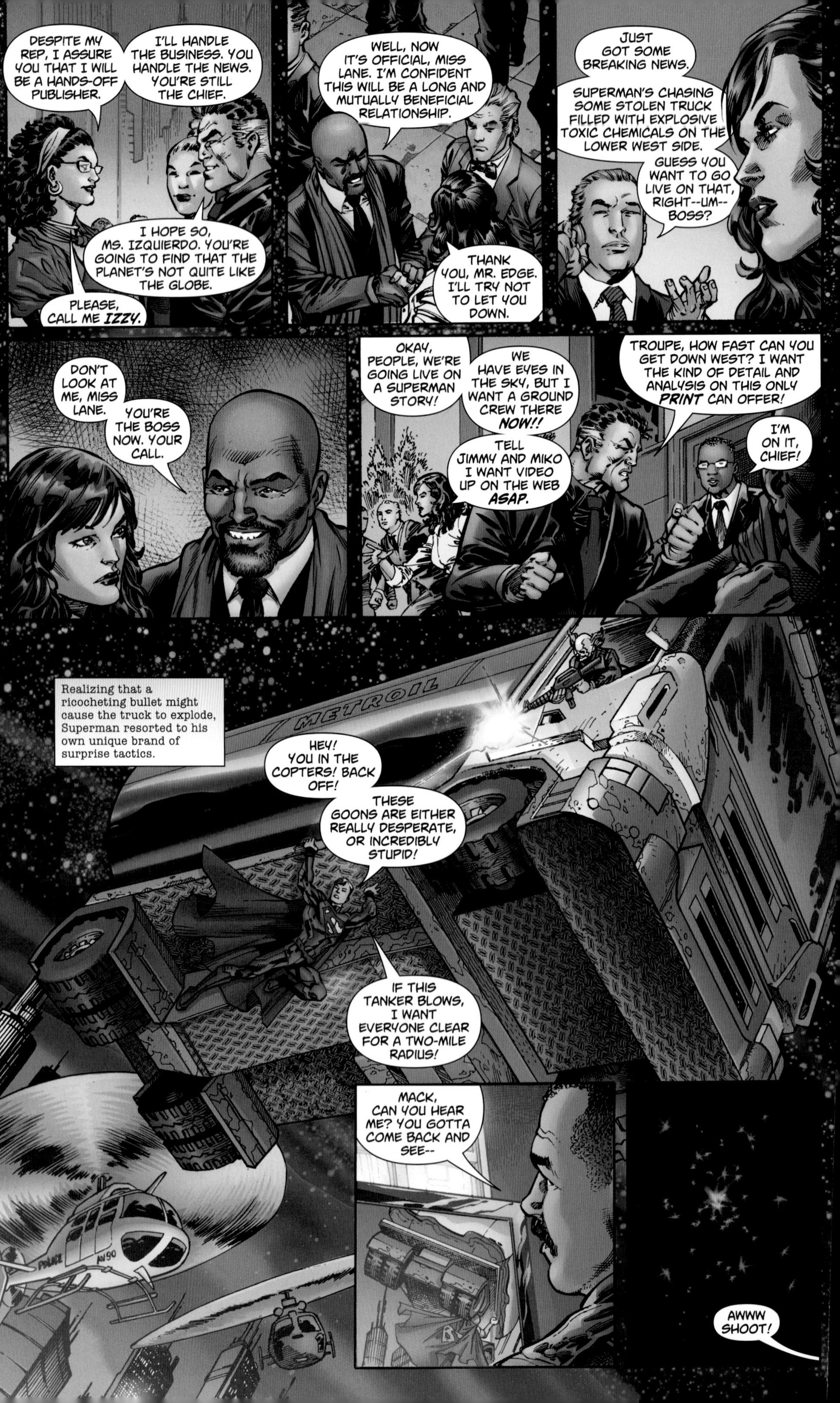

DESPITE MY REP, I ASSURE YOU THAT I WILL BE A HANDS-OFF PUBLISHER.
I'LL HANDLE THE BUSINESS. YOU HANDLE THE NEWS. YOU'RE STILL THE CHIEF.
I HOPE SO, MS. IZQUIERDO. YOU'RE GOING TO FIND THAT THE PLANET'S NOT QUITE LIKE THE GLOBE.
PLEASE, CALL ME IZZY.
WELL, NOW IT'S OFFICIAL, MISS LANE. I'M CONFIDENT THIS WILL BE A LONG AND MUTUALLY BENEFICIAL RELATIONSHIP.
THANK YOU, MR. EDGE. I'LL TRY NOT TO LET YOU DOWN.
JUST GOT SOME BREAKING NEWS.
SUPERMAN'S CHASING SOME STOLEN TRUCK FILLED WITH EXPLOSIVE TOXIC CHEMICALS ON THE LOWER WEST SIDE.
GUESS YOU WANT TO GO LIVE ON THAT, RIGHT--UM--BOSS?
DON'T LOOK AT ME, MISS LANE.
YOU'RE THE BOSS NOW. YOUR CALL.
OKAY, PEOPLE, WE'RE GOING LIVE ON A SUPERMAN STORY!
WE HAVE EYES IN THE SKY, BUT I WANT A GROUND CREW THERE NOW!!
TELL JIMMY AND MIKO I WANT VIDEO UP ON THE WEB ASAP.
TROUPE, HOW FAST CAN YOU GET DOWN WEST? I WANT THE KIND OF DETAIL AND ANALYSIS ON THIS ONLY PRINT CAN OFFER!
I'M ON IT, CHIEF!
Realizing that a ricocheting bullet might cause the truck to explode, Superman resorted to his own unique brand of surprise tactics.
METROIL
HEY! YOU IN THE COPTERS! BACK OFF!
THESE GOONS ARE EITHER REALLY DESPERATE, OR INCREDIBLY STUPID!
IF THIS TANKER BLOWS, I WANT EVERYONE CLEAR FOR A TWO-MILE RADIUS!
MACK, CAN YOU HEAR ME? YOU GOTTA COME BACK AND SEE--
AWWW SHOOT!

MACK, DO YOU READ ME? THE POWER'S GONE OUT OVER HERE. YOU THINK IT COULD HAVE SOMETHING TO DO WITH THAT FIRE?

HELLO? MACK!

DO. YOU. READ. ME?!

MACK? IS THAT YOU? DON'T PLAY WITH ME, MAN.

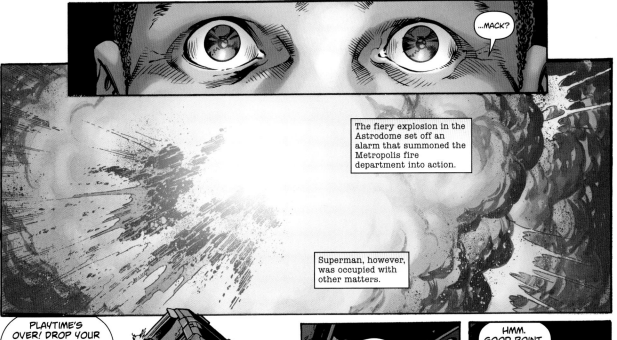

...MACK?

The fiery explosion in the Astrodome set off an alarm that summoned the Metropolis fire department into action.

Superman, however, was occupied with other matters.

PLAYTIME'S OVER! DROP YOUR WEAPONS RIGHT NOW OR I'LL TOSS THIS TIN CAN INTO THE WESTSIDE RIVER!

YOU'RE BLUFFING! YOU DO THAT AND WE'LL BLOW THE TANK!

THE WHOLE METROPOLIS WATER SUPPLY WILL BE CONTAMINATED FOR YEARS!

HMM. GOOD POINT. THANKS.

GUESS I'LL HAVE TO HURL YOU INTO SPACE THEN. JUST AS LONG AS I DON'T HIT A NEWS SATELLITE.

THAT WOULD BE A P.R. NIGHTMARE.

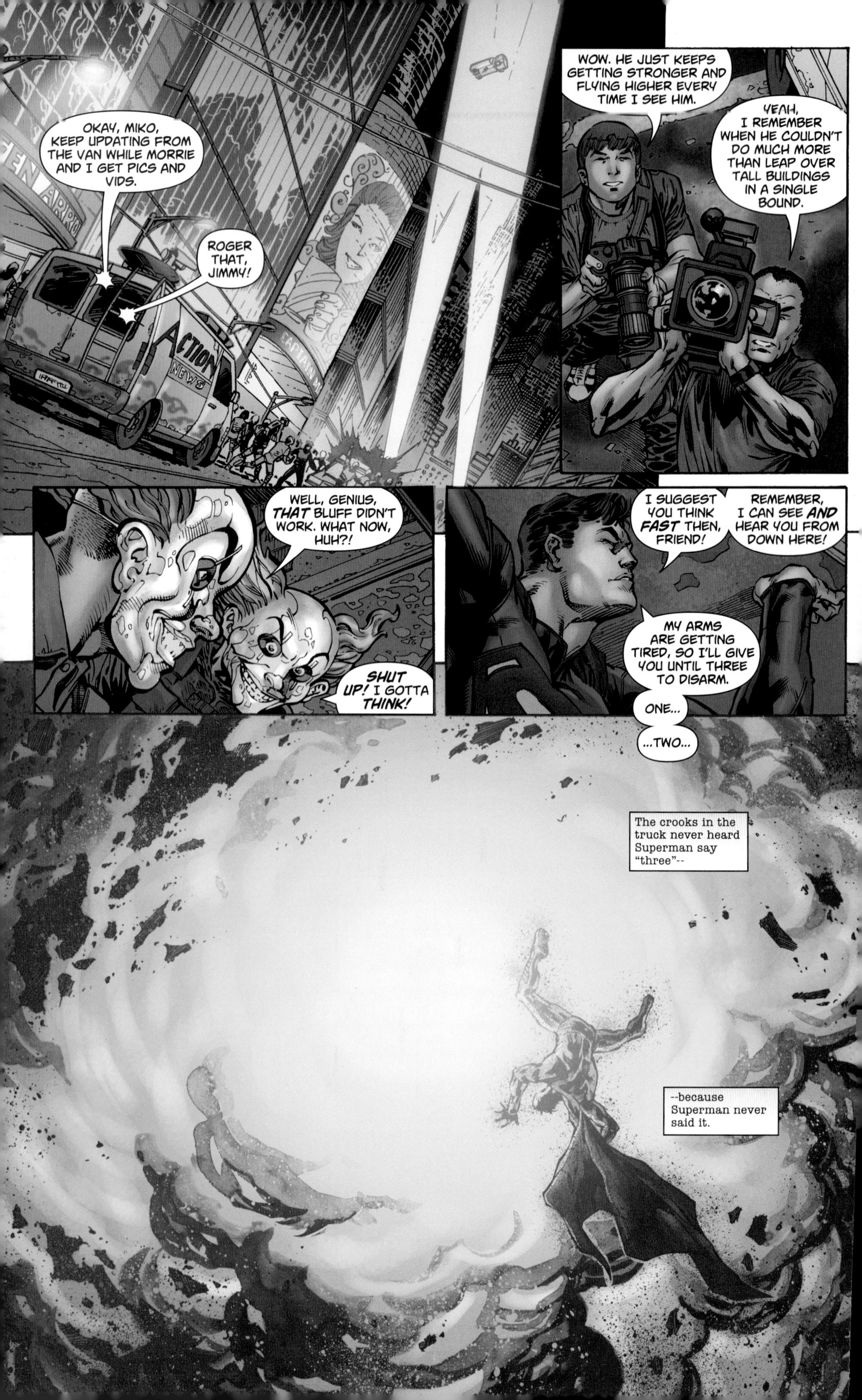
OKAY, MIKO, KEEP UPDATING FROM THE VAN WHILE MORRIE AND I GET PICS AND VIDS.
ROGER THAT, JIMMY!
ACTION NEWS
CAPTAIN M
WOW. HE JUST KEEPS GETTING STRONGER AND FLYING HIGHER EVERY TIME I SEE HIM.
YEAH, I REMEMBER WHEN HE COULDN'T DO MUCH MORE THAN LEAP OVER TALL BUILDINGS IN A SINGLE BOUND.
WELL, GENIUS, *THAT* BLUFF DIDN'T WORK. WHAT NOW, HUH?!
SHUT UP! I GOTTA *THINK!*
I SUGGEST YOU THINK *FAST* THEN, FRIEND!
REMEMBER, I CAN SEE *AND* HEAR YOU FROM DOWN HERE!
MY ARMS ARE GETTING TIRED, SO I'LL GIVE YOU UNTIL THREE TO DISARM.
ONE...
...TWO...
The crooks in the truck never heard Superman say "three"--
--because Superman never said it.

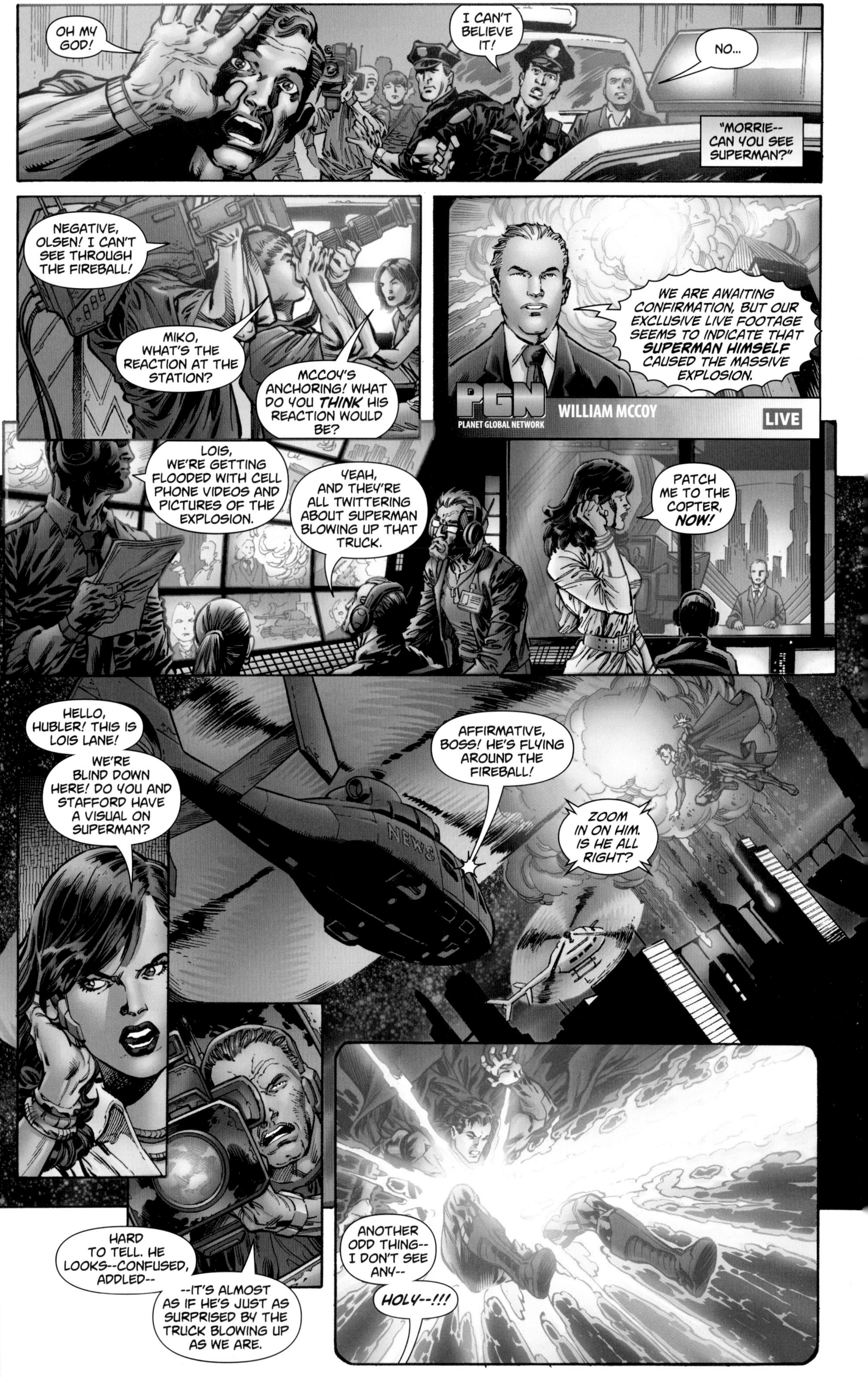

OH MY GOD!
I CAN'T BELIEVE IT!
NO...
"MORRIE-- CAN YOU SEE SUPERMAN?"
NEGATIVE, OLSEN! I CAN'T SEE THROUGH THE FIREBALL!
MIKO, WHAT'S THE REACTION AT THE STATION?
MCCOY'S ANCHORING! WHAT DO YOU THINK HIS REACTION WOULD BE?
WE ARE AWAITING CONFIRMATION, BUT OUR EXCLUSIVE LIVE FOOTAGE SEEMS TO INDICATE THAT SUPERMAN HIMSELF CAUSED THE MASSIVE EXPLOSION.
PGN PLANET GLOBAL NETWORK
WILLIAM MCCOY
LIVE
LOIS, WE'RE GETTING FLOODED WITH CELL PHONE VIDEOS AND PICTURES OF THE EXPLOSION.
YEAH, AND THEY'RE ALL TWITTERING ABOUT SUPERMAN BLOWING UP THAT TRUCK.
PATCH ME TO THE COPTER, NOW!
HELLO, HUBLER! THIS IS LOIS LANE!
WE'RE BLIND DOWN HERE! DO YOU AND STAFFORD HAVE A VISUAL ON SUPERMAN?
AFFIRMATIVE, BOSS! HE'S FLYING AROUND THE FIREBALL!
ZOOM IN ON HIM. IS HE ALL RIGHT?
NEWS
HARD TO TELL. HE LOOKS--CONFUSED, ADDLED--
--IT'S ALMOST AS IF HE'S JUST AS SURPRISED BY THE TRUCK BLOWING UP AS WE ARE.
ANOTHER ODD THING-- I DON'T SEE ANY--
HOLY--!!!

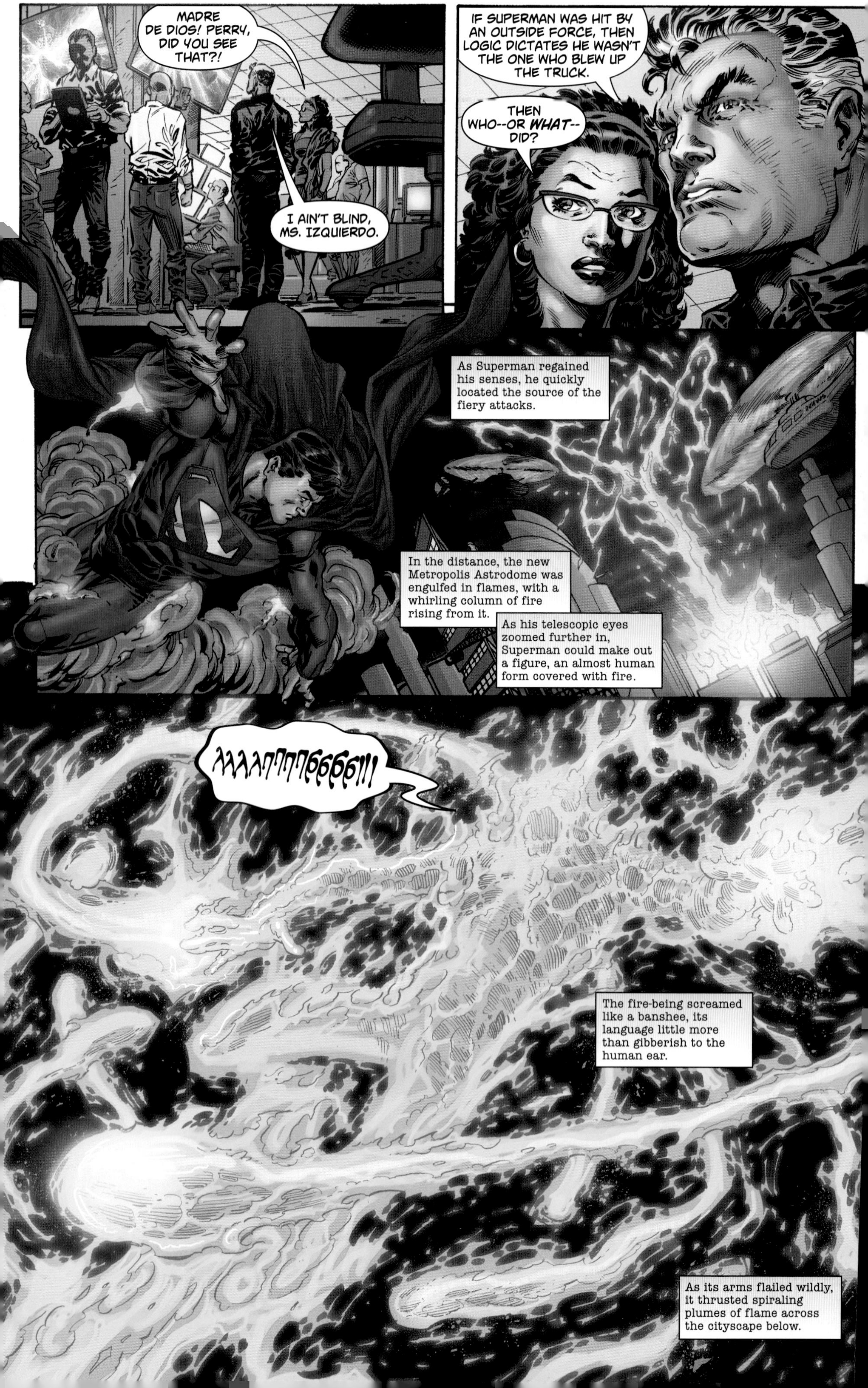
MADRE DE DIOS! PERRY, DID YOU SEE THAT?!
I AIN'T BLIND, MS. IZQUIERDO.
IF SUPERMAN WAS HIT BY AN OUTSIDE FORCE, THEN LOGIC DICTATES HE WASN'T THE ONE WHO BLEW UP THE TRUCK.
THEN WHO--OR WHAT--DID?
As Superman regained his senses, he quickly located the source of the fiery attacks.
In the distance, the new Metropolis Astrodome was engulfed in flames, with a whirling column of fire rising from it.
As his telescopic eyes zoomed further in, Superman could make out a figure, an almost human form covered with fire.
The fire-being screamed like a banshee, its language little more than gibberish to the human ear.
As its arms flailed wildly, it thrusted spiraling plumes of flame across the cityscape below.

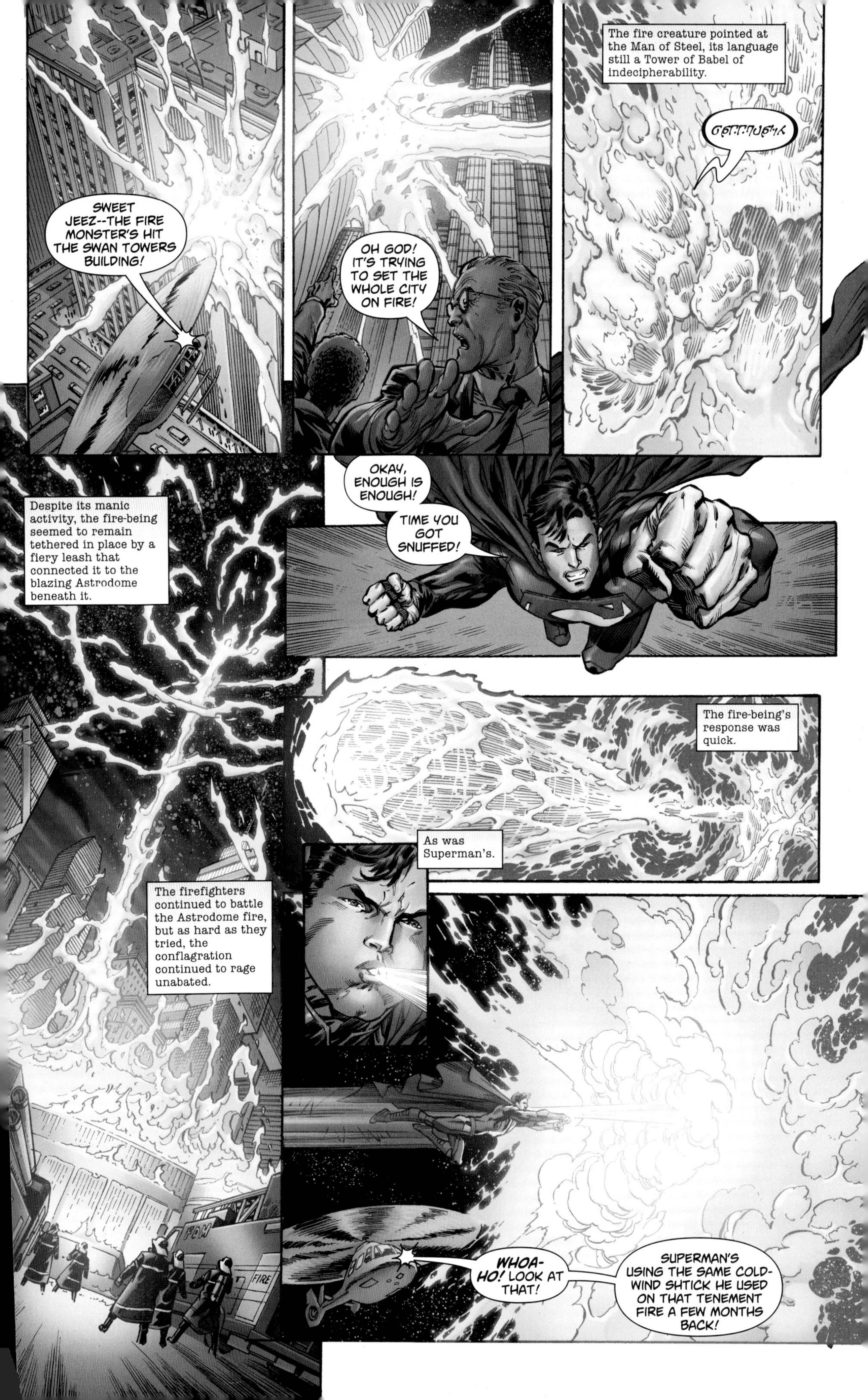
SWEET JEEZ--THE FIRE MONSTER'S HIT THE SWAN TOWERS BUILDING!
OH GOD! IT'S TRYING TO SET THE WHOLE CITY ON FIRE!
The fire creature pointed at the Man of Steel, its language still a Tower of Babel of indecipherability.
Despite its manic activity, the fire-being seemed to remain tethered in place by a fiery leash that connected it to the blazing Astrodome beneath it.
OKAY, ENOUGH IS ENOUGH!
TIME YOU GOT SNUFFED!
The fire-being's response was quick.
As was Superman's.
The firefighters continued to battle the Astrodome fire, but as hard as they tried, the conflagration continued to rage unabated.
WHOA-HO! LOOK AT THAT!
SUPERMAN'S USING THE SAME COLD-WIND SHTICK HE USED ON THAT TENEMENT FIRE A FEW MONTHS BACK!

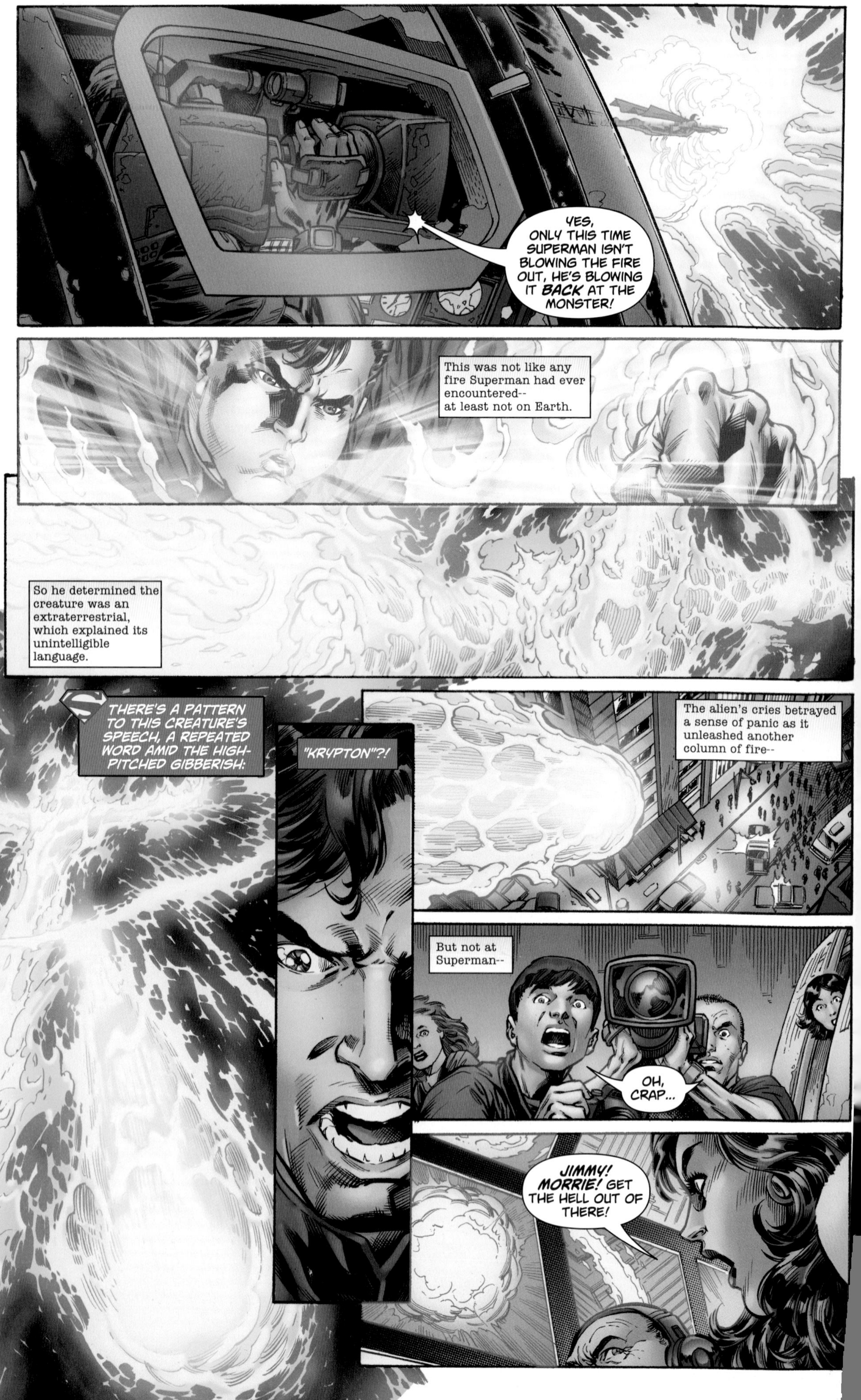
YES, ONLY THIS TIME SUPERMAN ISN'T BLOWING THE FIRE OUT, HE'S BLOWING IT *BACK* AT THE MONSTER!
This was not like any fire Superman had ever encountered-- at least not on Earth.
So he determined the creature was an extraterrestrial, which explained its unintelligible language.
THERE'S A PATTERN TO THIS CREATURE'S SPEECH, A REPEATED WORD AMID THE HIGH-PITCHED GIBBERISH:
"KRYPTON"?!
The alien's cries betrayed a sense of panic as it unleashed another column of fire--
But not at Superman--
OH, CRAP...
JIMMY! MORRIE! GET THE HELL OUT OF THERE!

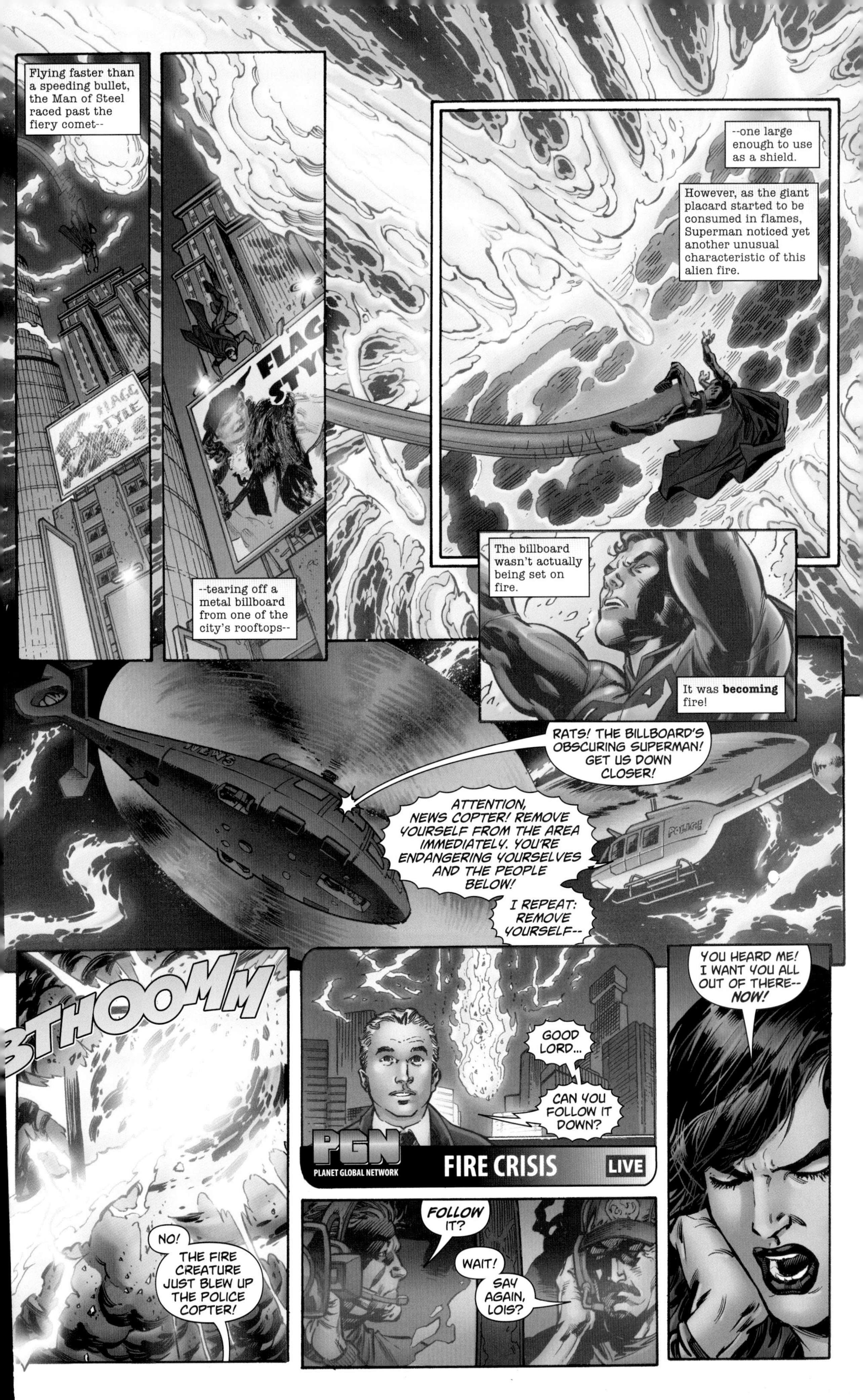
Flying faster than a speeding bullet, the Man of Steel raced past the fiery comet--
--tearing off a metal billboard from one of the city's rooftops--
--one large enough to use as a shield.
However, as the giant placard started to be consumed in flames, Superman noticed yet another unusual characteristic of this alien fire.
The billboard wasn't actually being set on fire.
It was **becoming** fire!
RATS! THE BILLBOARD'S OBSCURING SUPERMAN! GET US DOWN CLOSER!
ATTENTION, NEWS COPTER! REMOVE YOURSELF FROM THE AREA IMMEDIATELY. YOU'RE ENDANGERING YOURSELVES AND THE PEOPLE BELOW!
I REPEAT: REMOVE YOURSELF--
BTHOOMM
NO!
THE FIRE CREATURE JUST BLEW UP THE POLICE COPTER!
GOOD LORD...
CAN YOU FOLLOW IT DOWN?
PGN
PLANET GLOBAL NETWORK
FIRE CRISIS
LIVE
FOLLOW IT?
WAIT!
SAY AGAIN, LOIS?
YOU HEARD ME! I WANT YOU ALL OUT OF THERE-- *NOW!*

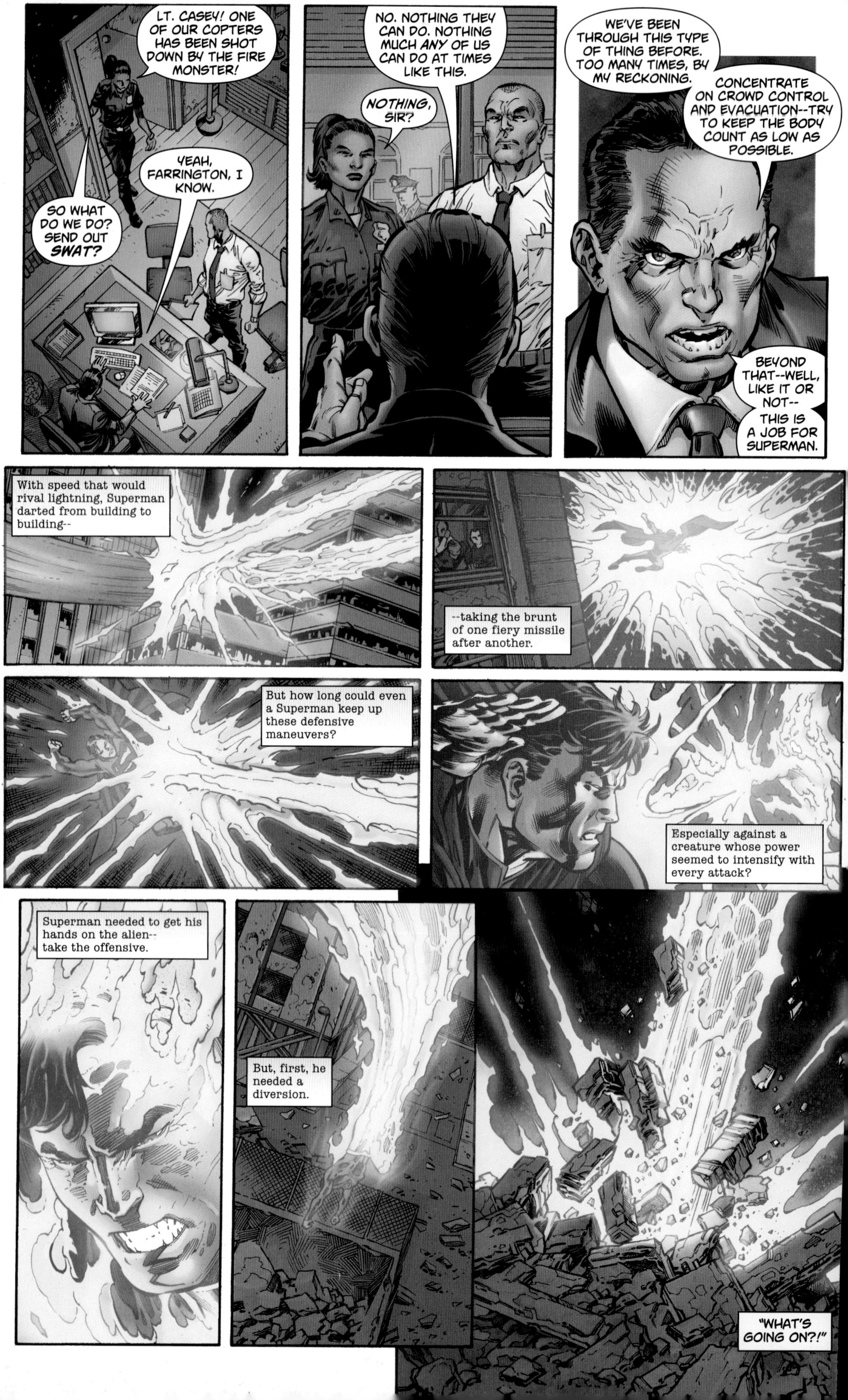
LT. CASEY! ONE OF OUR COPTERS HAS BEEN SHOT DOWN BY THE FIRE MONSTER!
YEAH, FARRINGTON, I KNOW.
SO WHAT DO WE DO? SEND OUT SWAT?
NO. NOTHING THEY CAN DO. NOTHING MUCH ANY OF US CAN DO AT TIMES LIKE THIS.
NOTHING, SIR?
WE'VE BEEN THROUGH THIS TYPE OF THING BEFORE. TOO MANY TIMES, BY MY RECKONING.
CONCENTRATE ON CROWD CONTROL AND EVACUATION--TRY TO KEEP THE BODY COUNT AS LOW AS POSSIBLE.
BEYOND THAT--WELL, LIKE IT OR NOT--
THIS IS A JOB FOR SUPERMAN.
With speed that would rival lightning, Superman darted from building to building--
--taking the brunt of one fiery missile after another.
But how long could even a Superman keep up these defensive maneuvers?
Especially against a creature whose power seemed to intensify with every attack?
Superman needed to get his hands on the alien--take the offensive.
But, first, he needed a diversion.
"WHAT'S GOING ON?!"

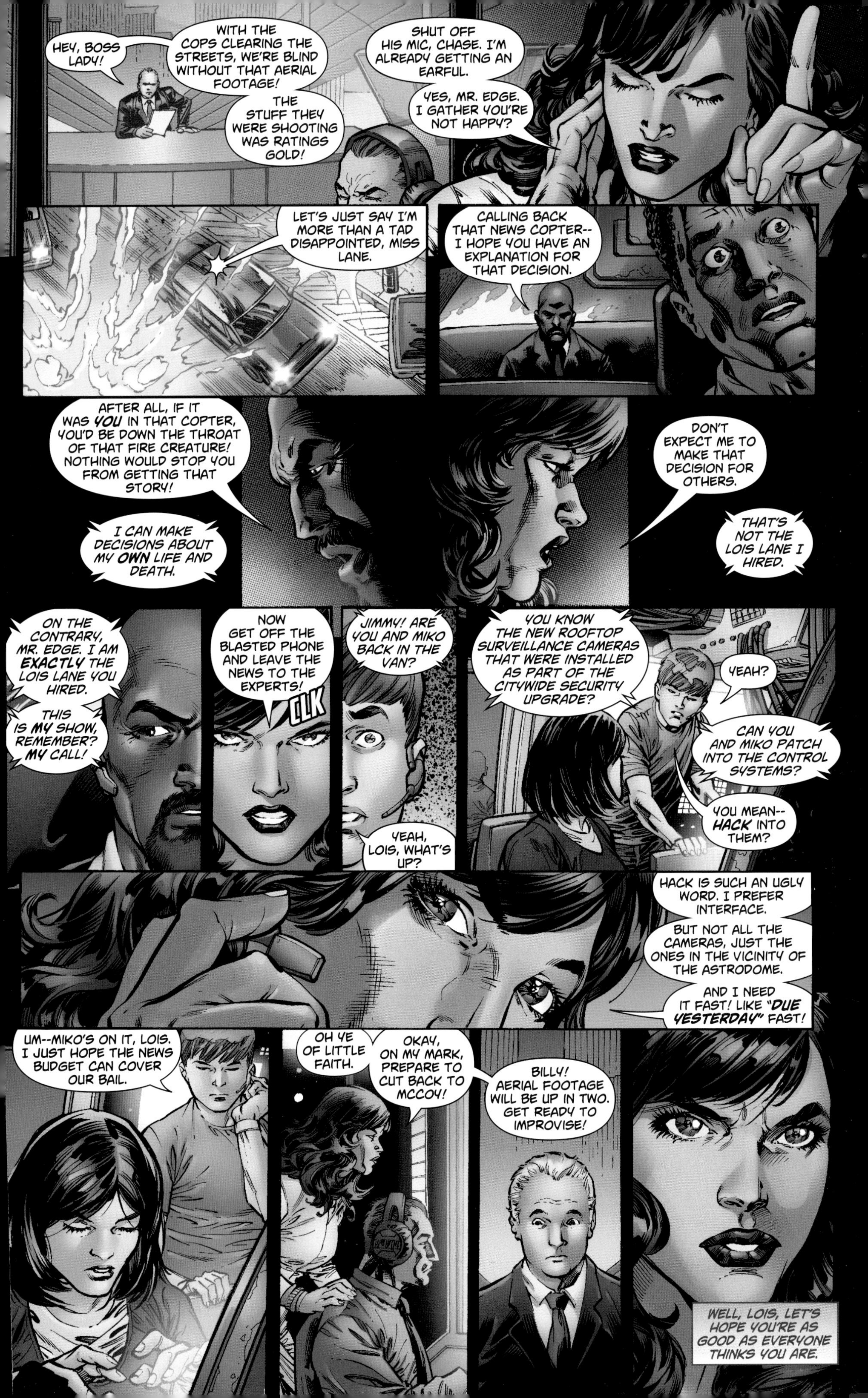

HEY, BOSS LADY!
WITH THE COPS CLEARING THE STREETS, WE'RE BLIND WITHOUT THAT AERIAL FOOTAGE!
THE STUFF THEY WERE SHOOTING WAS RATINGS GOLD!
SHUT OFF HIS MIC, CHASE. I'M ALREADY GETTING AN EARFUL.
YES, MR. EDGE. I GATHER YOU'RE NOT HAPPY?
LET'S JUST SAY I'M MORE THAN A TAD DISAPPOINTED, MISS LANE.
CALLING BACK THAT NEWS COPTER-- I HOPE YOU HAVE AN EXPLANATION FOR THAT DECISION.
AFTER ALL, IF IT WAS YOU IN THAT COPTER, YOU'D BE DOWN THE THROAT OF THAT FIRE CREATURE! NOTHING WOULD STOP YOU FROM GETTING THAT STORY!
I CAN MAKE DECISIONS ABOUT MY OWN LIFE AND DEATH.
DON'T EXPECT ME TO MAKE THAT DECISION FOR OTHERS.
THAT'S NOT THE LOIS LANE I HIRED.
ON THE CONTRARY, MR. EDGE. I AM EXACTLY THE LOIS LANE YOU HIRED.
THIS IS MY SHOW, REMEMBER? MY CALL!
NOW GET OFF THE BLASTED PHONE AND LEAVE THE NEWS TO THE EXPERTS!
CLK
JIMMY! ARE YOU AND MIKO BACK IN THE VAN?
YEAH, LOIS, WHAT'S UP?
YOU KNOW THE NEW ROOFTOP SURVEILLANCE CAMERAS THAT WERE INSTALLED AS PART OF THE CITYWIDE SECURITY UPGRADE?
YEAH?
CAN YOU AND MIKO PATCH INTO THE CONTROL SYSTEMS?
YOU MEAN-- HACK INTO THEM?
HACK IS SUCH AN UGLY WORD. I PREFER INTERFACE.
BUT NOT ALL THE CAMERAS, JUST THE ONES IN THE VICINITY OF THE ASTRODOME.
AND I NEED IT FAST! LIKE "DUE YESTERDAY" FAST!
UM--MIKO'S ON IT, LOIS. I JUST HOPE THE NEWS BUDGET CAN COVER OUR BAIL.
OH YE OF LITTLE FAITH.
OKAY, ON MY MARK, PREPARE TO CUT BACK TO MCCOY!
BILLY! AERIAL FOOTAGE WILL BE UP IN TWO. GET READY TO IMPROVISE!
WELL, LOIS, LET'S HOPE YOU'RE AS GOOD AS EVERYONE THINKS YOU ARE.

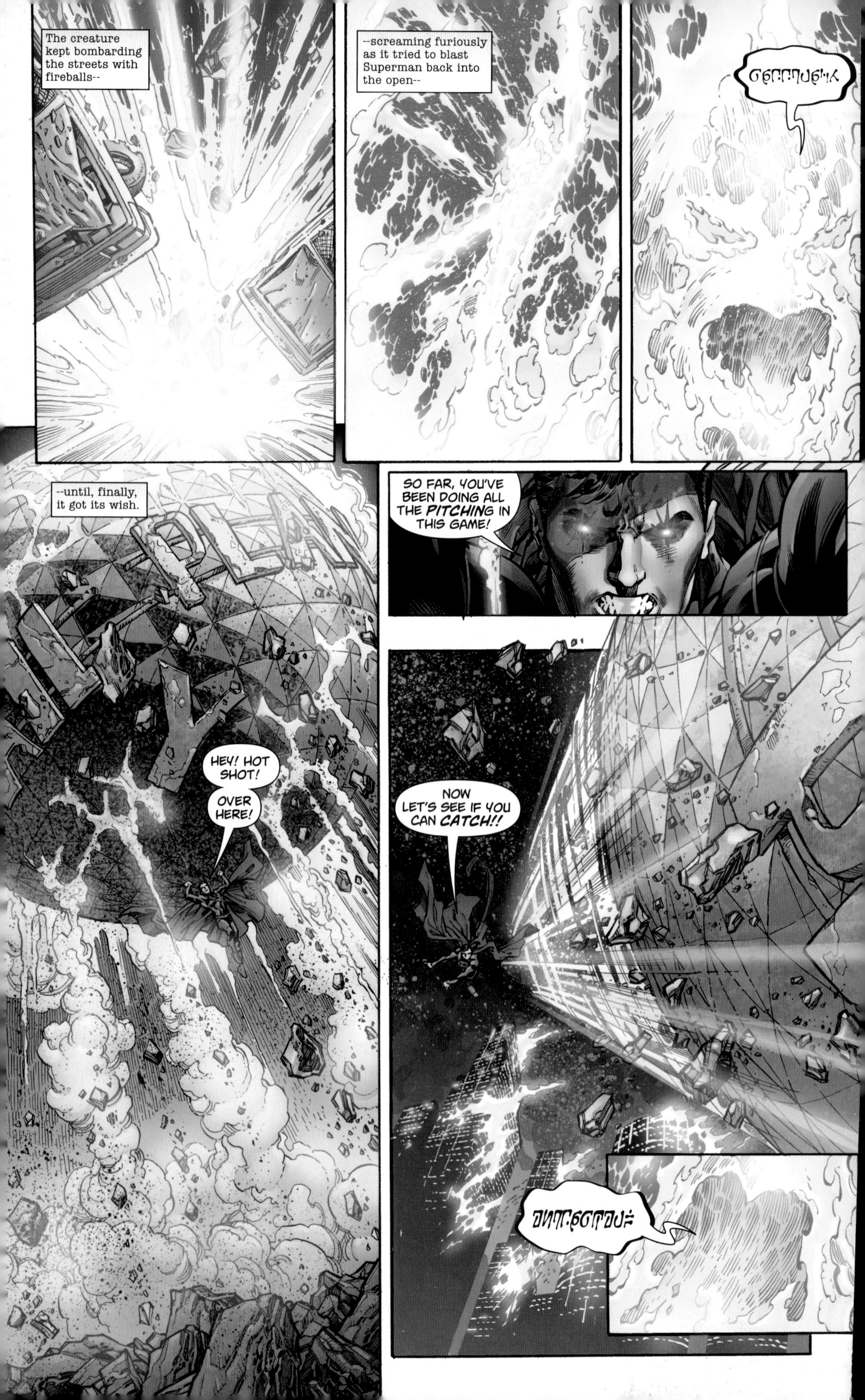
The creature kept bombarding the streets with fireballs--
--screaming furiously as it tried to blast Superman back into the open--
--until, finally, it got its wish.
HEY! HOT SHOT!
OVER HERE!
SO FAR, YOU'VE BEEN DOING ALL THE PITCHING IN THIS GAME!
NOW LET'S SEE IF YOU CAN CATCH!!

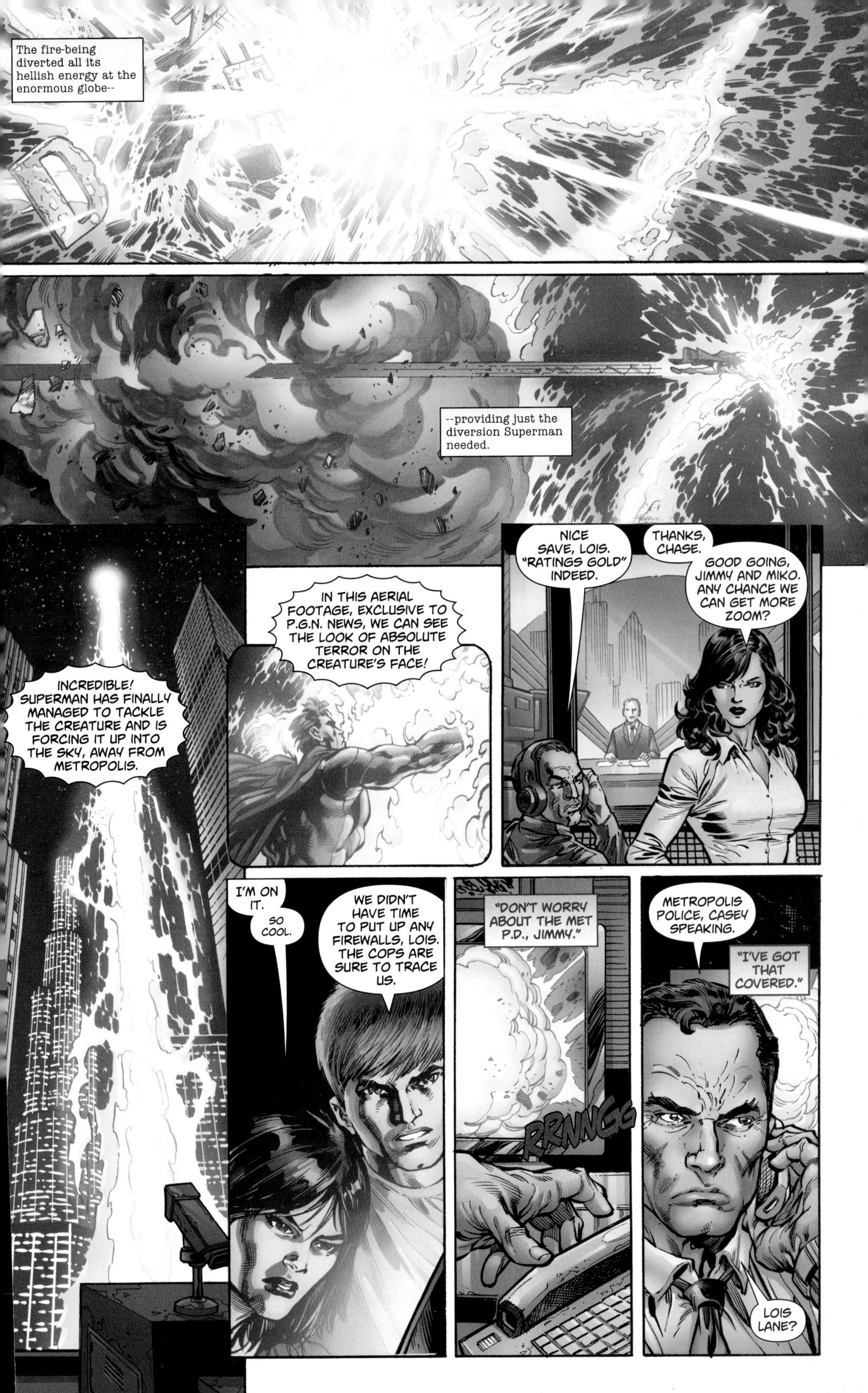

The fire-being diverted all its hellish energy at the enormous globe--
--providing just the diversion Superman needed.
INCREDIBLE! SUPERMAN HAS FINALLY MANAGED TO TACKLE THE CREATURE AND IS FORCING IT UP INTO THE SKY, AWAY FROM METROPOLIS.
IN THIS AERIAL FOOTAGE, EXCLUSIVE TO P.G.N. NEWS, WE CAN SEE THE LOOK OF ABSOLUTE TERROR ON THE CREATURE'S FACE!
NICE SAVE, LOIS. "RATINGS GOLD" INDEED.
THANKS, CHASE.
GOOD GOING, JIMMY AND MIKO. ANY CHANCE WE CAN GET MORE ZOOM?
I'M ON IT.
SO COOL.
WE DIDN'T HAVE TIME TO PUT UP ANY FIREWALLS, LOIS. THE COPS ARE SURE TO TRACE US.
"DON'T WORRY ABOUT THE MET P.D., JIMMY."
RRNNGG
METROPOLIS POLICE, CASEY SPEAKING.
"I'VE GOT THAT COVERED."
LOIS LANE?

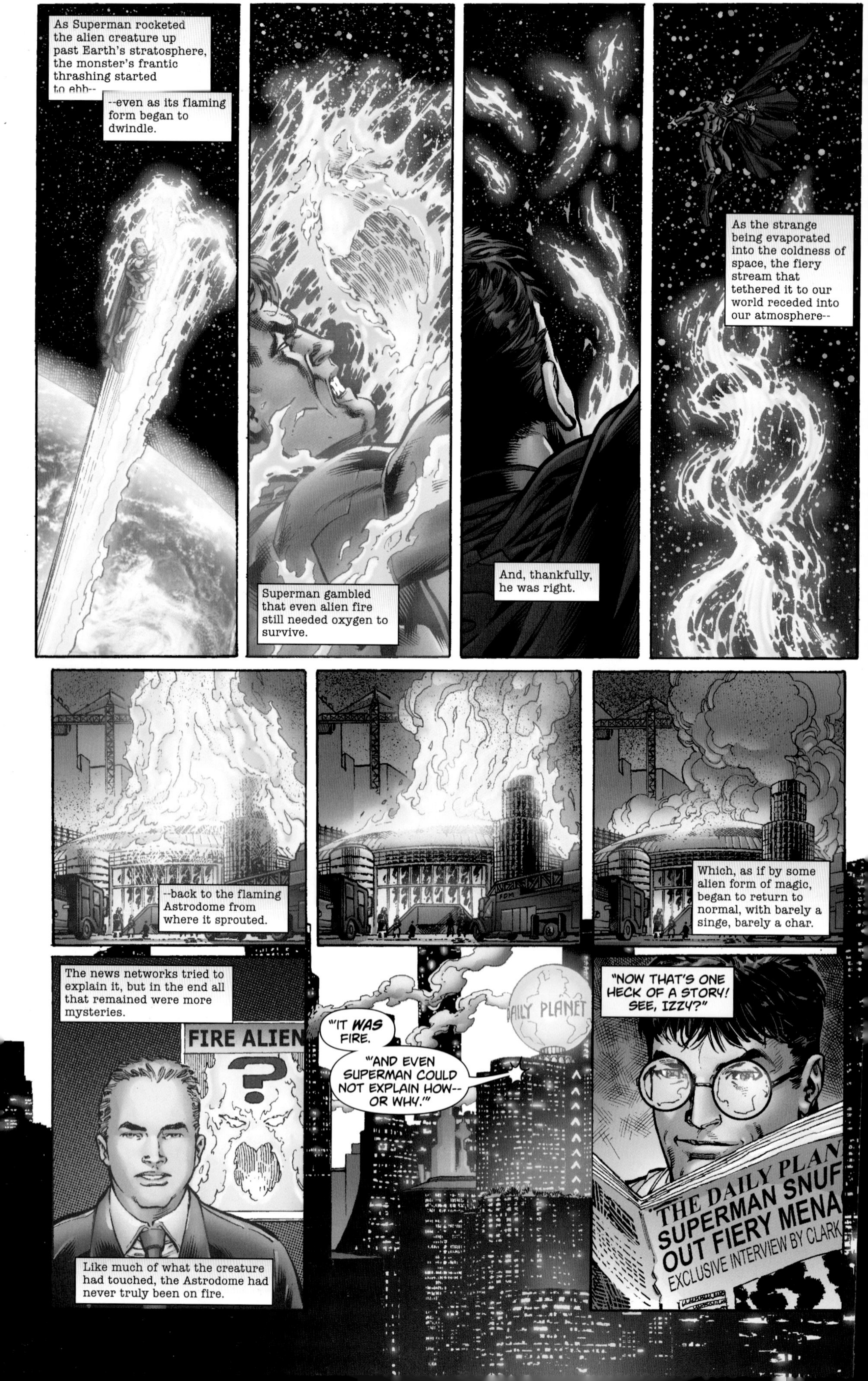

As Superman rocketed the alien creature up past Earth's stratosphere, the monster's frantic thrashing started to ebb--
--even as its flaming form began to dwindle.
Superman gambled that even alien fire still needed oxygen to survive.
And, thankfully, he was right.
As the strange being evaporated into the coldness of space, the fiery stream that tethered it to our world receded into our atmosphere--
--back to the flaming Astrodome from where it sprouted.
Which, as if by some alien form of magic, began to return to normal, with barely a singe, barely a char.
The news networks tried to explain it, but in the end all that remained were more mysteries.
FIRE ALIEN
?
Like much of what the creature had touched, the Astrodome had never truly been on fire.
DAILY PLANET
"IT WAS FIRE.
"AND EVEN SUPERMAN COULD NOT EXPLAIN HOW-- OR WHY."
"NOW THAT'S ONE HECK OF A STORY! SEE, IZZY?"
THE DAILY PLAN
SUPERMAN SNUF OUT FIERY MENA
EXCLUSIVE INTERVIEW BY CLARK

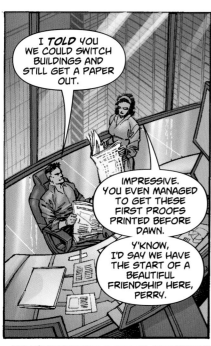

I *TOLD* YOU WE COULD SWITCH BUILDINGS AND STILL GET A PAPER OUT.

IMPRESSIVE. YOU EVEN MANAGED TO GET THESE FIRST PROOFS PRINTED BEFORE DAWN.

Y'KNOW, I'D SAY WE HAVE THE START OF A BEAUTIFUL FRIENDSHIP HERE, PERRY.

I JUST DON'T GET IT, CHIEF. ALL OF US RACED DOWN TO COVER THE ASTRODOME FIRE. HOW DID *KENT* END UP GETTING TOP BILLING ON THIS?!

WE NEVER SAW HIM ANYWHERE NEAR THE AREA.

THE DAILY PLANET
SUPERMAN SNUFFS OUT FIERY MENACE
EXCLUSIVE INTERVIEW BY CLARK KENT

HE SAID HE WAS INVESTIGATING THE LEGALITY OF THE FORCED EVICTIONS AROUND THE ASTRODOME--

--INTERVIEWING PEOPLE IMPACTED BY THAT, WHEN THE FIRE CREATURE ATTACKED.

AS USUAL, IT WAS PURE *LUCK* FOR KENT. HE MAY HAVE A NOSE FOR NEWS, BUT NOT USUALLY THE FRONT PAGE VARIETY.

YEAH, LUCK. CLARK IS SO *FULL* OF IT, ISN'T HE?

WHERE *IS* OUR SMALL-TOWN HERO NOW?

"HE'S GONE TO KISS AND MAKE UP WITH *LOIS.*"

BZZZT

CLARK? WHAT ARE YOU DOING HERE?

OH, I'M SORRY, LOIS. I FIGURED YOU'D STILL BE UP.

IT'S--IT'S OKAY, REALLY. YOU JUST *SURPRISED* ME, THAT'S ALL.

I SAW YOUR STORY ONLINE. CONGRATULATIONS--A FIRST-HAND ACCOUNT FROM SUPERMAN!

IT'S AMAZING HOW METROPOLIS ENDS UP TARGETED BY THREATS OVER AND OVER--

--EVER SINCE HE ARRIVED IN TOWN...

WELL, I CAN'T REALLY SPEAK TO THAT POINT, BUT SPEAKING OF CONGRATULATIONS...

I HEARD ABOUT HOW YOU GOT THE FOOTAGE WITHOUT PUTTING THE COPTER CREW IN HARM'S WAY. MR. EDGE MUST BE THRILLED.

YEAH, WELL, THE LESS SAID ABOUT THAT, THE BETTER.

LOIS, WHAT I REALLY CAME OVER TO SAY IS--

I'M SORRY-- *REALLY* SORRY FOR THE THINGS I SAID.

I GUESS--WELL-- I JUST--

LOIS?

ARE YOU COMING BACK? WHO'S AT THE DOOR?

JUST A FRIEND-- A COLLEAGUE. I TOLD YOU ABOUT HIM. CLARK KENT?

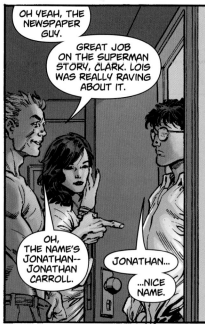

OH YEAH, THE NEWSPAPER GUY.

GREAT JOB ON THE SUPERMAN STORY, CLARK. LOIS WAS REALLY RAVING ABOUT IT.

OH, THE NAME'S JONATHAN-- JONATHAN CARROLL.

JONATHAN...

...NICE NAME.

YOU CATCH LOIS' T.V. COVERAGE?

AND THE RATINGS? THROUGH THE ROOF!

WE WERE JUST... CELEBRATING.

I'M SORRY, LOIS. I DIDN'T KNOW. I SHOULD HAVE CALLED FIRST.

I-I BETTER GO.

SEE YOU TOMORROW, OKAY?

MAYBE YOU SHOULD FIND SOMEONE TO CELEBRATE WITH AS WELL! YOU DESERVE IT!

YEAH. I'LL GO THROUGH MY BLACK BOOK.

G'NIGHT.

GOOD NIGHT, CLARK.

NICE MEETING YOU!

SO, THAT'S CLARK KENT, HUH? HE'S A LOT TALLER THAN I THOUGHT HE'D BE.

YOU AND HE EVER--?

OH NO, NOTHING LIKE THAT.

HE'S SUCH A LONER, NEVER REALLY LETS ANYONE GET CLOSE TO HIM.

I TRIED SETTING HIM UP WITH SOME FRIENDS, BUT--

MAYBE HE'S PINING FOR YOU!

OH, SHUT UP AND GET BACK IN BED!

NEXT: INVISIBLE THREAT!

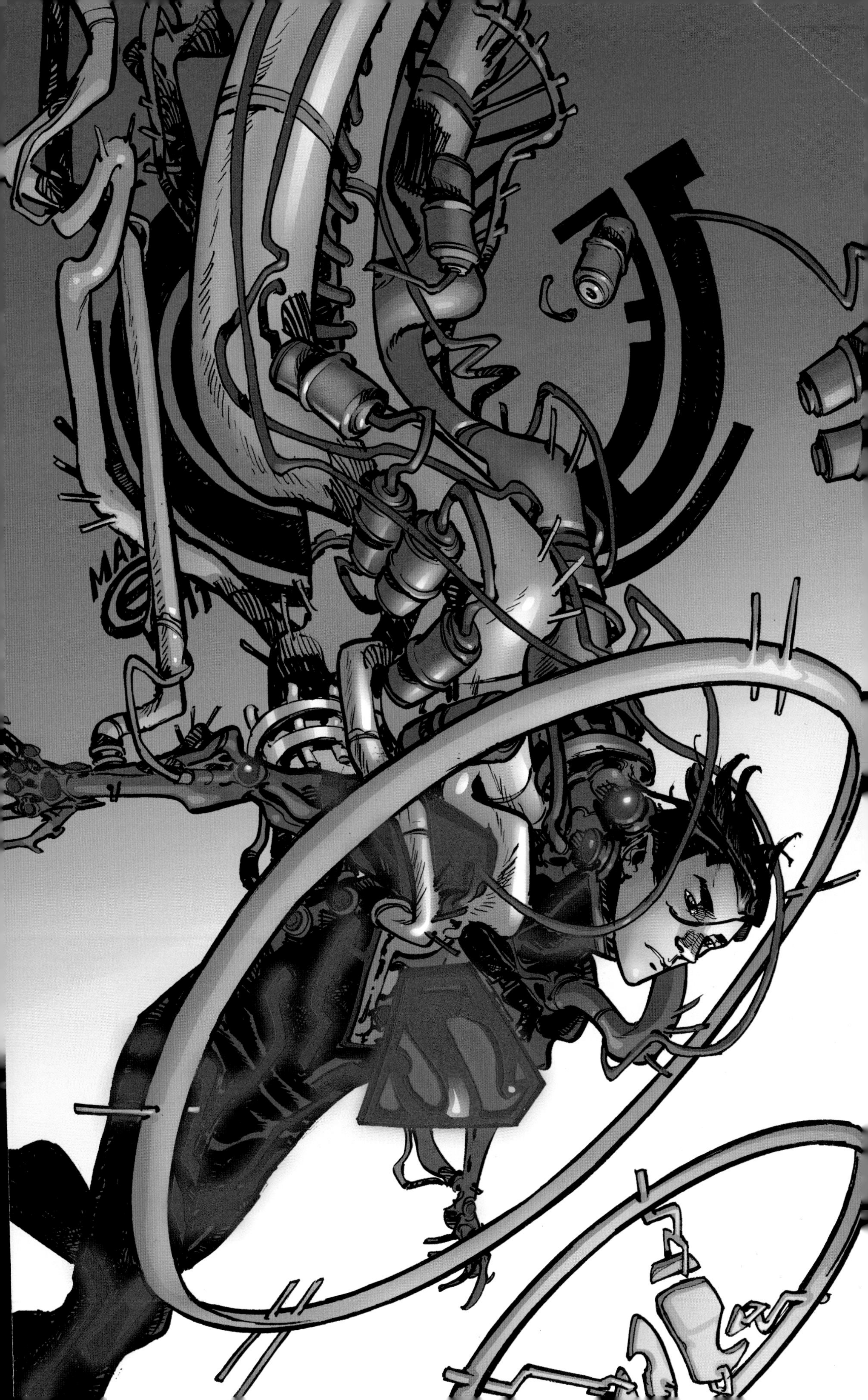

SUPERBOY

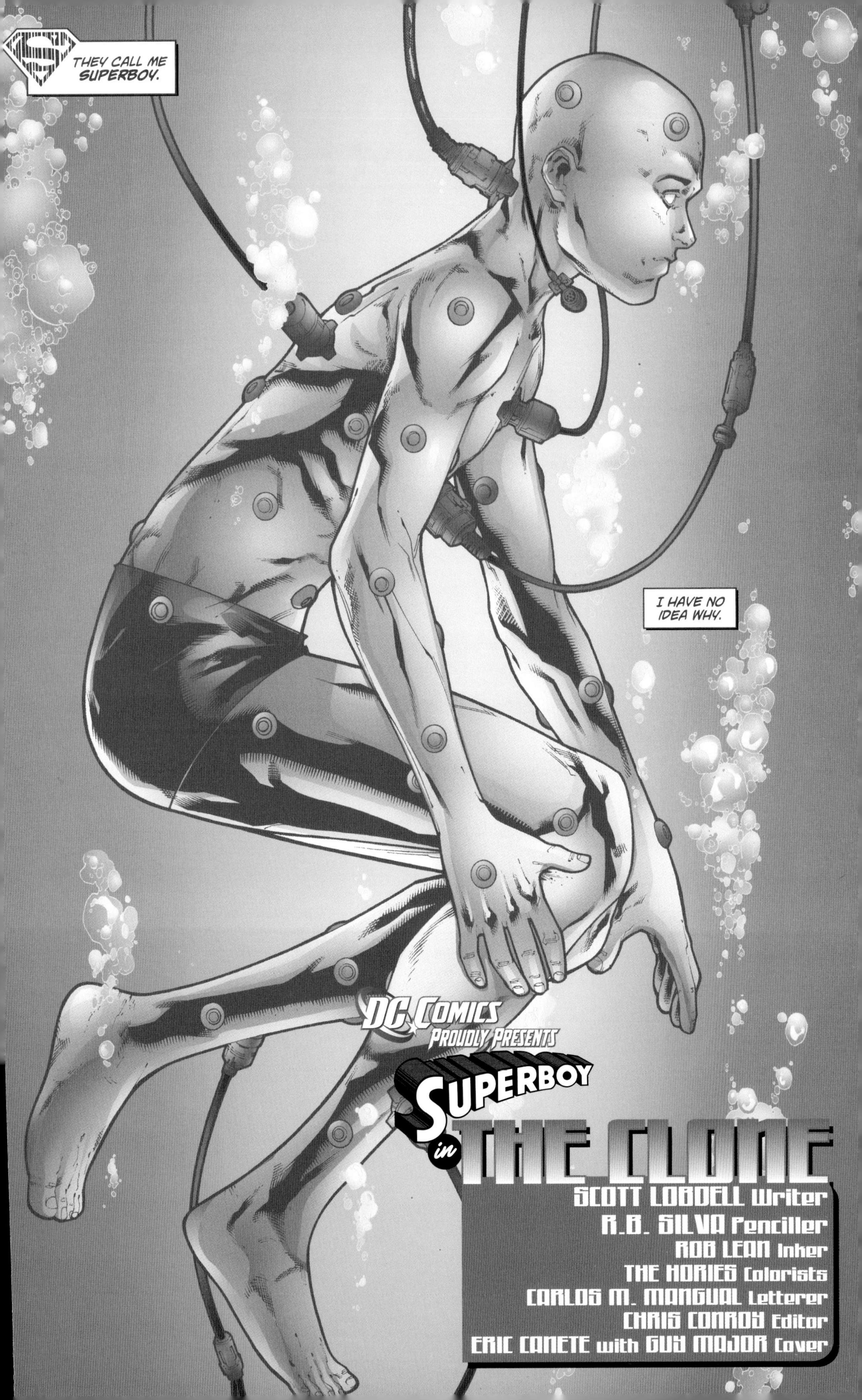

THEY CALL ME SUPERBOY.
I HAVE NO IDEA WHY.
DC COMICS PROUDLY PRESENTS
SUPERBOY in THE CLONE
SCOTT LOBDELL Writer
R.B. SILVA Penciller
ROB LEAN Inker
THE HORIES Colorists
CARLOS M. MANGUAL Letterer
CHRIS CONROY Editor
ERIC CANETE with GUY MAJOR Cover

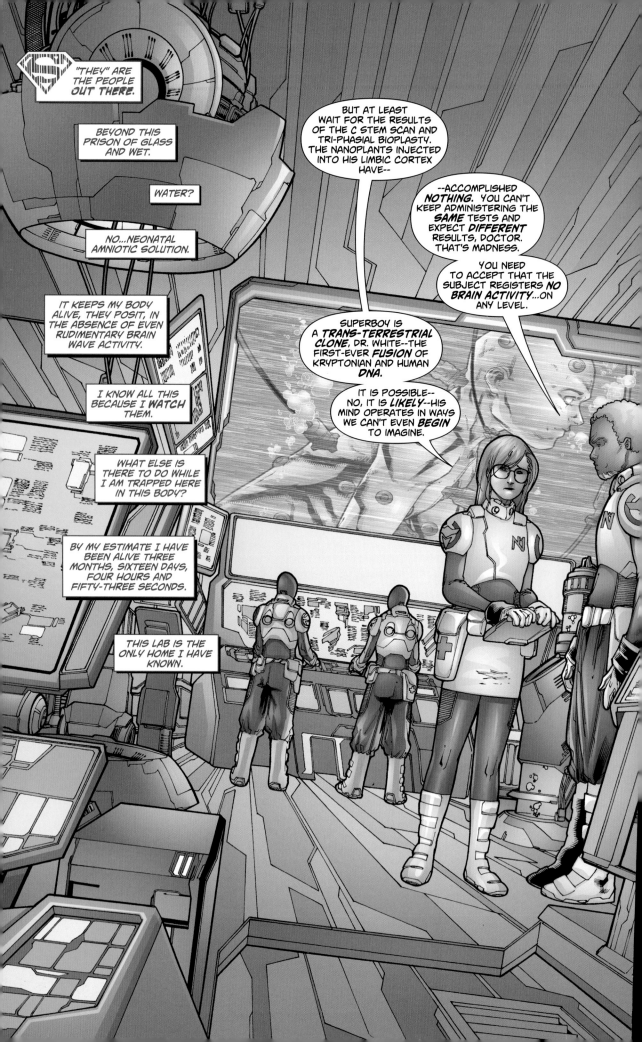

"THEY" ARE THE PEOPLE OUT THERE.

BEYOND THIS PRISON OF GLASS AND WET.

WATER?

NO...NEONATAL AMNIOTIC SOLUTION.

IT KEEPS MY BODY ALIVE, THEY POSIT, IN THE ABSENCE OF EVEN RUDIMENTARY BRAIN WAVE ACTIVITY.

I KNOW ALL THIS BECAUSE I *WATCH* THEM.

WHAT ELSE IS THERE TO DO WHILE I AM TRAPPED HERE IN THIS BODY?

BY MY ESTIMATE I HAVE BEEN ALIVE THREE MONTHS, SIXTEEN DAYS, FOUR HOURS AND FIFTY-THREE SECONDS.

THIS LAB IS THE ONLY HOME I HAVE KNOWN.

BUT AT LEAST WAIT FOR THE RESULTS OF THE C STEM SCAN AND TRI-PHASIAL BIOPLASTY. THE NANOPLANTS INJECTED INTO HIS LIMBIC CORTEX HAVE--

--ACCOMPLISHED *NOTHING.* YOU CAN'T KEEP ADMINISTERING THE *SAME* TESTS AND EXPECT *DIFFERENT* RESULTS, DOCTOR. THAT'S MADNESS.

YOU NEED TO ACCEPT THAT THE SUBJECT REGISTERS *NO BRAIN ACTIVITY*...ON ANY LEVEL.

SUPERBOY IS A *TRANS-TERRESTRIAL CLONE,* DR. WHITE--THE FIRST-EVER *FUSION* OF KRYPTONIAN AND HUMAN *DNA.*

IT IS POSSIBLE-- NO, IT IS *LIKELY*--HIS MIND OPERATES IN WAYS WE CAN'T EVEN *BEGIN* TO IMAGINE.

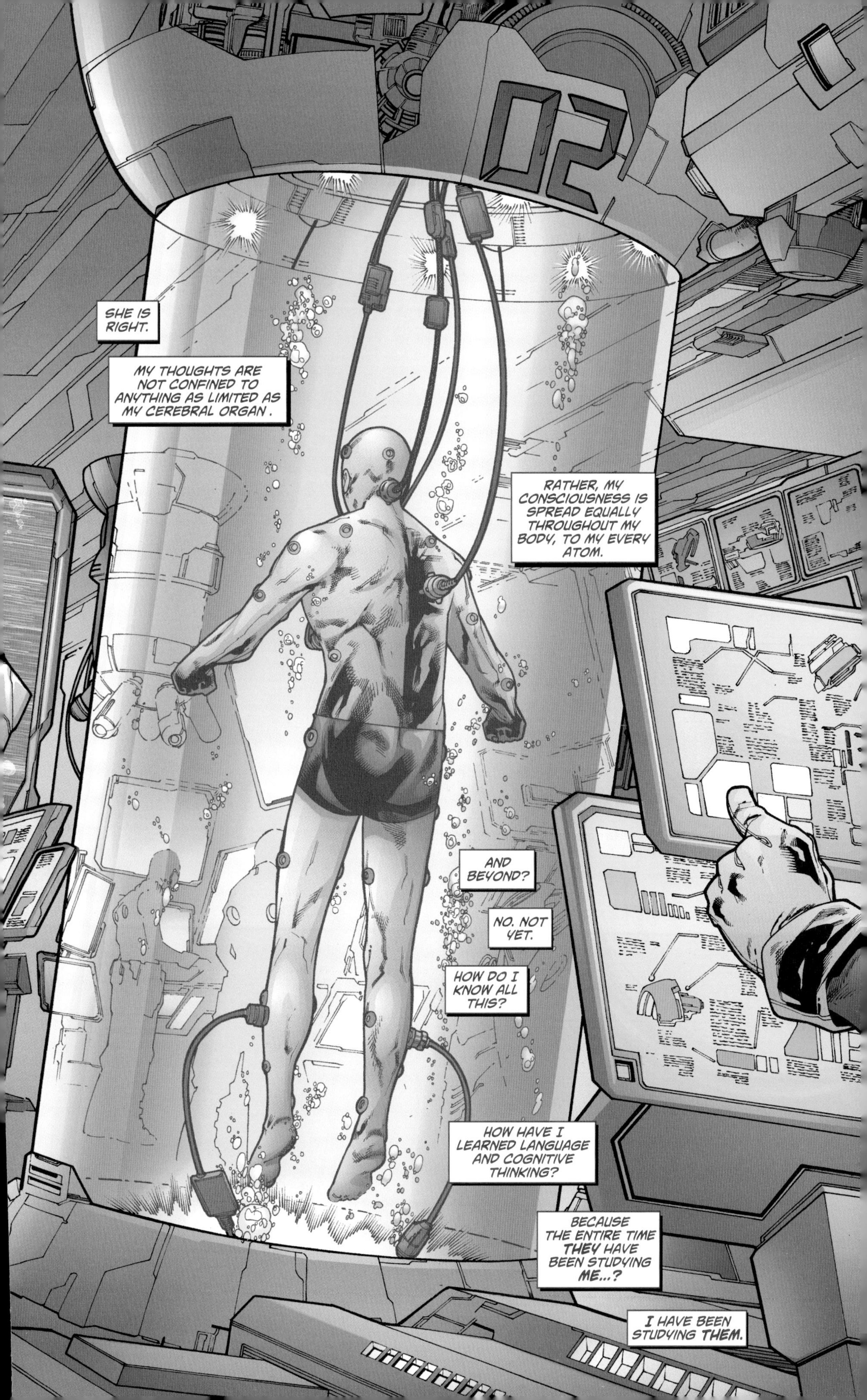
02
SHE IS RIGHT.
MY THOUGHTS ARE NOT CONFINED TO ANYTHING AS LIMITED AS MY CEREBRAL ORGAN.
RATHER, MY CONSCIOUSNESS IS SPREAD EQUALLY THROUGHOUT MY BODY, TO MY EVERY ATOM.
AND BEYOND?
NO. NOT YET.
HOW DO I KNOW ALL THIS?
HOW HAVE I LEARNED LANGUAGE AND COGNITIVE THINKING?
BECAUSE THE ENTIRE TIME THEY HAVE BEEN STUDYING ME...?
I HAVE BEEN STUDYING THEM.

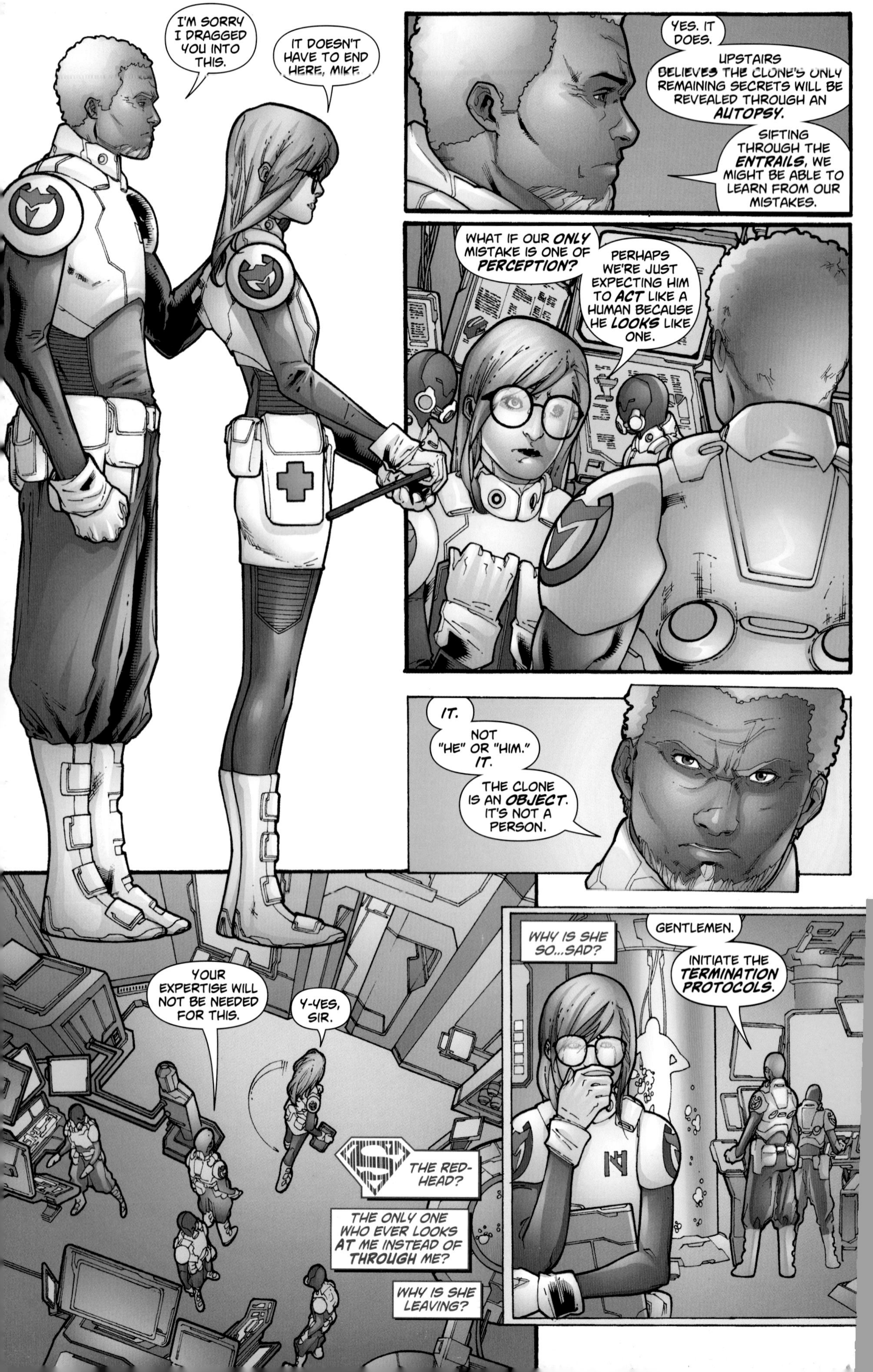
I'M SORRY I DRAGGED YOU INTO THIS.
IT DOESN'T HAVE TO END HERE, MIKE.
YES. IT DOES.
UPSTAIRS BELIEVES THE CLONE'S ONLY REMAINING SECRETS WILL BE REVEALED THROUGH AN AUTOPSY.
SIFTING THROUGH THE ENTRAILS, WE MIGHT BE ABLE TO LEARN FROM OUR MISTAKES.
WHAT IF OUR ONLY MISTAKE IS ONE OF PERCEPTION?
PERHAPS WE'RE JUST EXPECTING HIM TO ACT LIKE A HUMAN BECAUSE HE LOOKS LIKE ONE.
IT.
NOT "HE" OR "HIM." IT.
THE CLONE IS AN OBJECT. IT'S NOT A PERSON.
YOUR EXPERTISE WILL NOT BE NEEDED FOR THIS.
Y-YES, SIR.
THE RED-HEAD?
THE ONLY ONE WHO EVER LOOKS AT ME INSTEAD OF THROUGH ME?
WHY IS SHE LEAVING?
WHY IS SHE SO...SAD?
GENTLEMEN.
INITIATE THE TERMINATION PROTOCOLS.

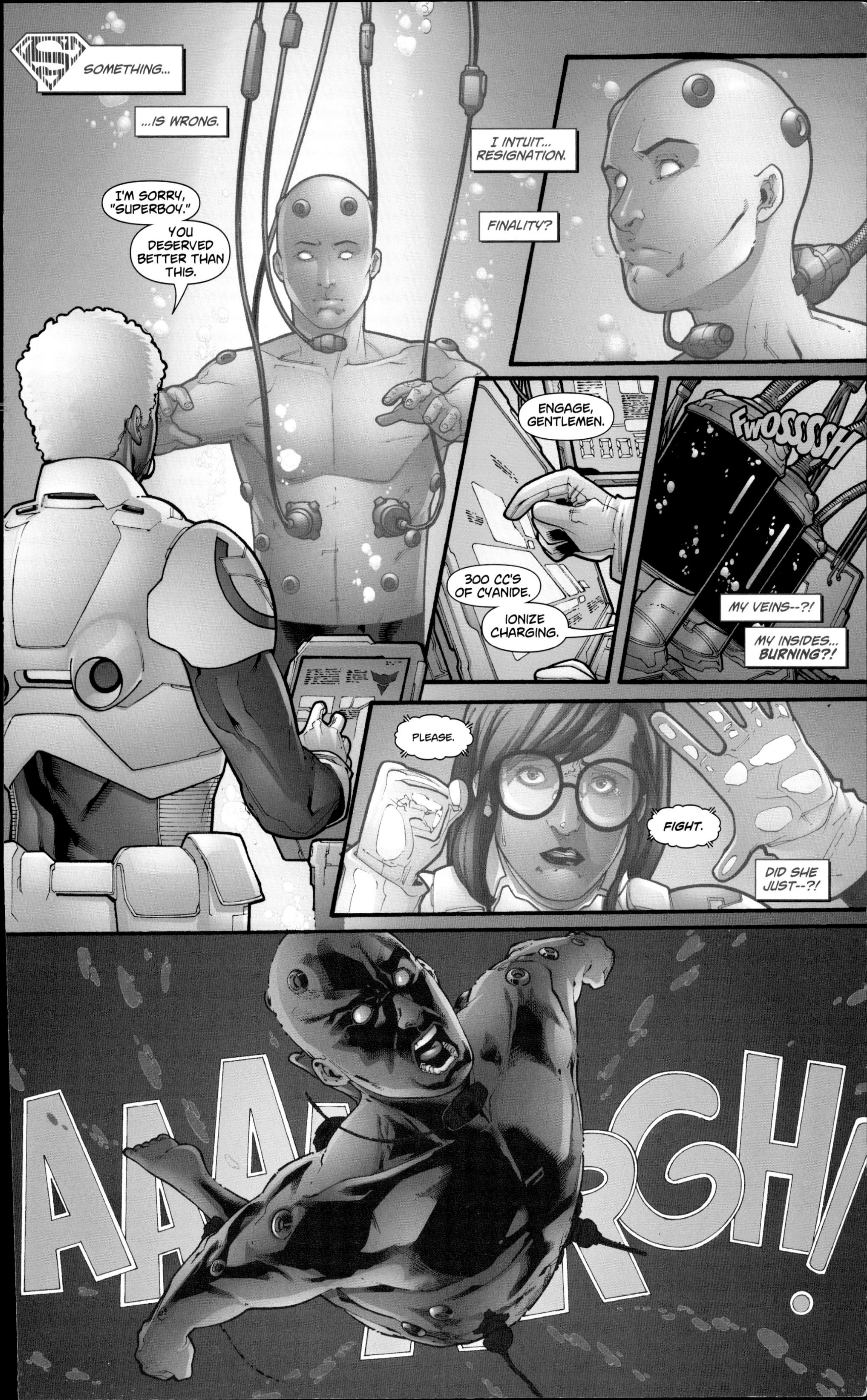
SOMETHING...
...IS WRONG.
I'M SORRY, "SUPERBOY."
YOU DESERVED BETTER THAN THIS.
I INTUIT... RESIGNATION.
FINALITY?
ENGAGE, GENTLEMEN.
300 CC'S OF CYANIDE.
IONIZE CHARGING.
FWOSSSSH
MY VEINS--?!
MY INSIDES... BURNING?!
PLEASE.
FIGHT.
DID SHE JUST--?!
AAARGH!

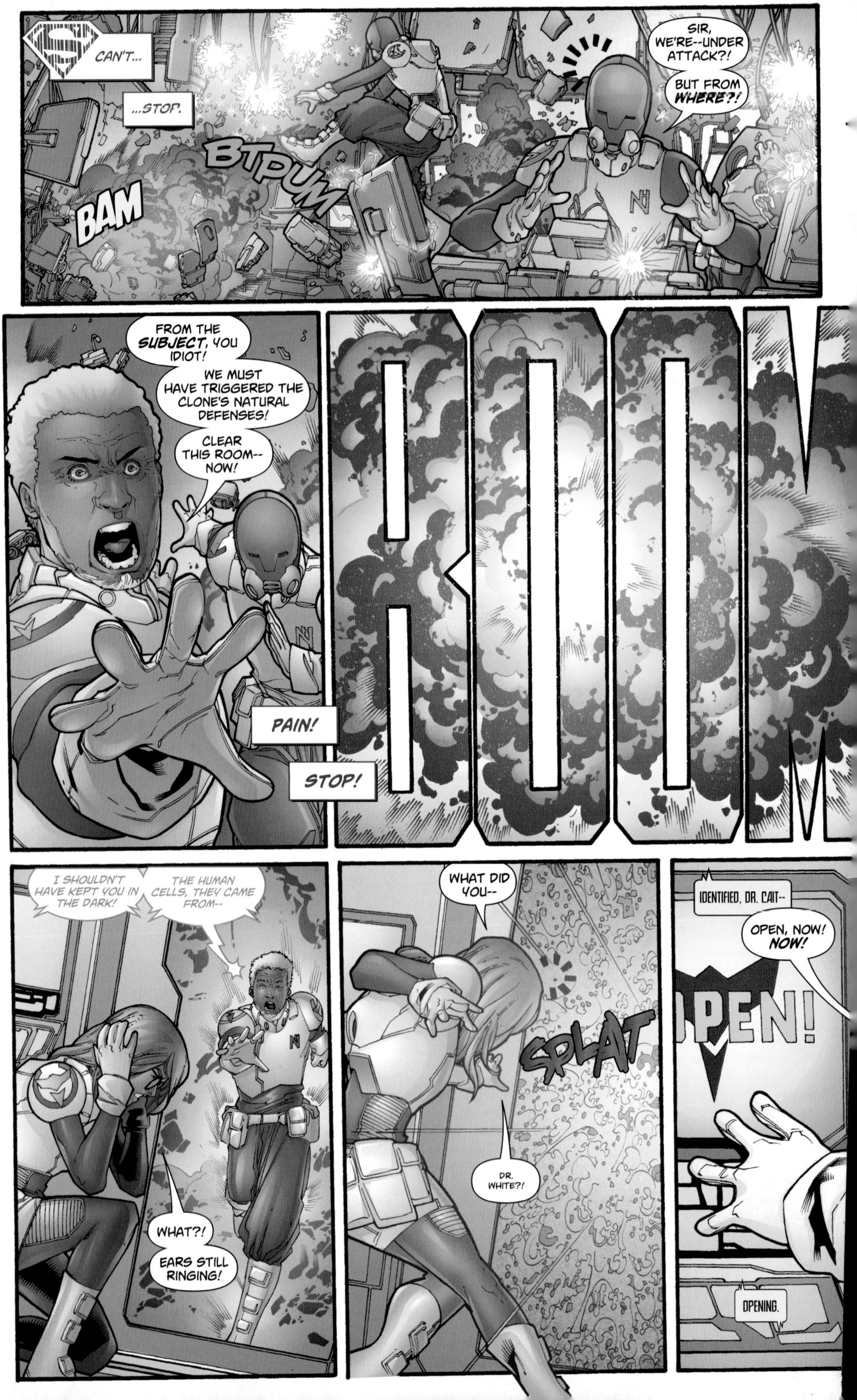
CAN'T...
...STOP.
SIR, WE'RE--UNDER ATTACK?!
BUT FROM WHERE?!
BTPUM
BAM
FROM THE SUBJECT, YOU IDIOT!
WE MUST HAVE TRIGGERED THE CLONE'S NATURAL DEFENSES!
CLEAR THIS ROOM-- NOW!
PAIN!
STOP!
I SHOULDN'T HAVE KEPT YOU IN THE DARK!
THE HUMAN CELLS, THEY CAME FROM--
WHAT?!
EARS STILL RINGING!
WHAT DID YOU--
SPLAT
DR. WHITE?!
IDENTIFIED, DR. CAIT--
OPEN, NOW! NOW!
OPEN!
OPENING.

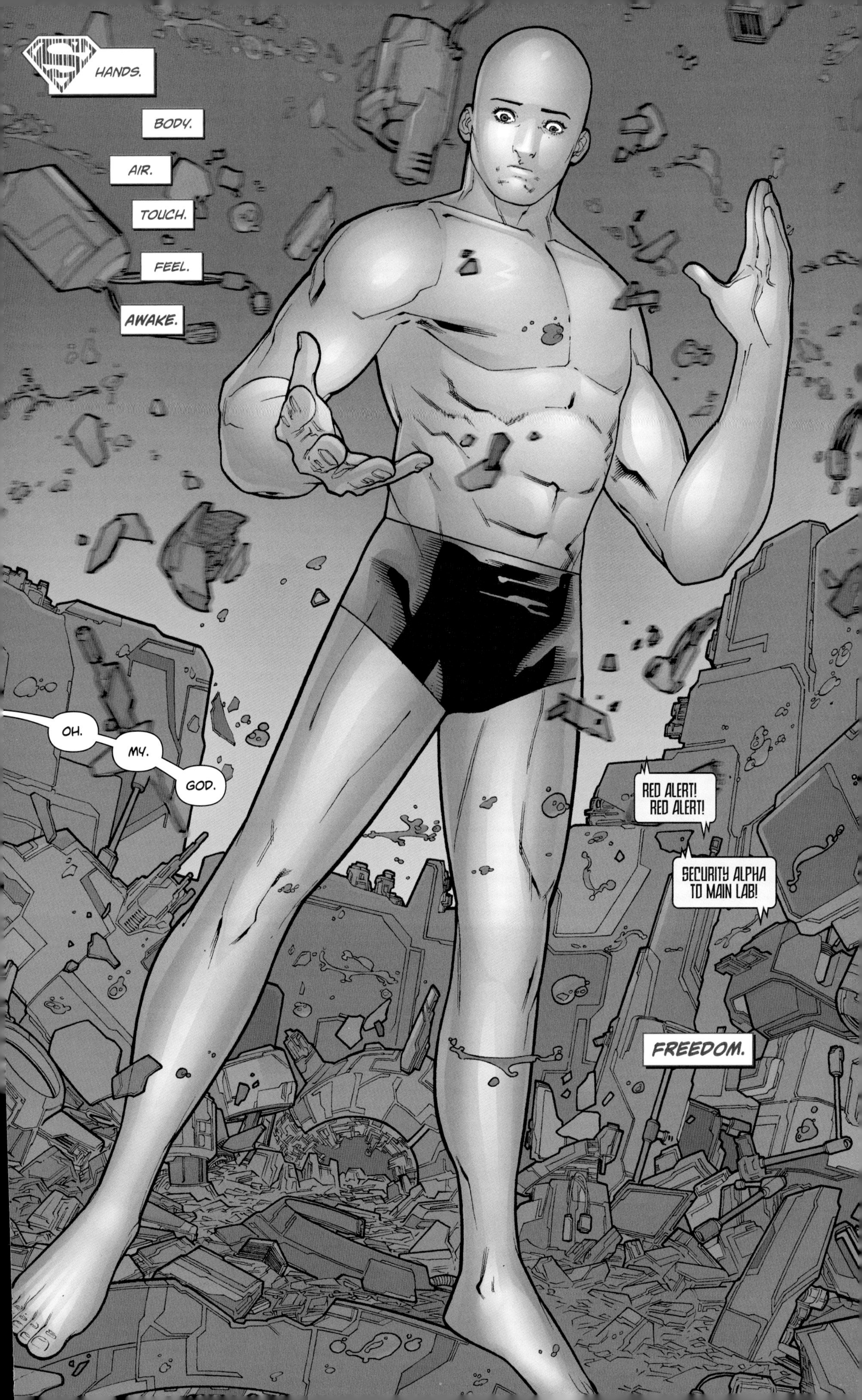
HANDS.
BODY.
AIR.
TOUCH.
FEEL.
AWAKE.
OH.
MY.
GOD.
RED ALERT! RED ALERT!
SECURITY ALPHA TO MAIN LAB!
FREEDOM.

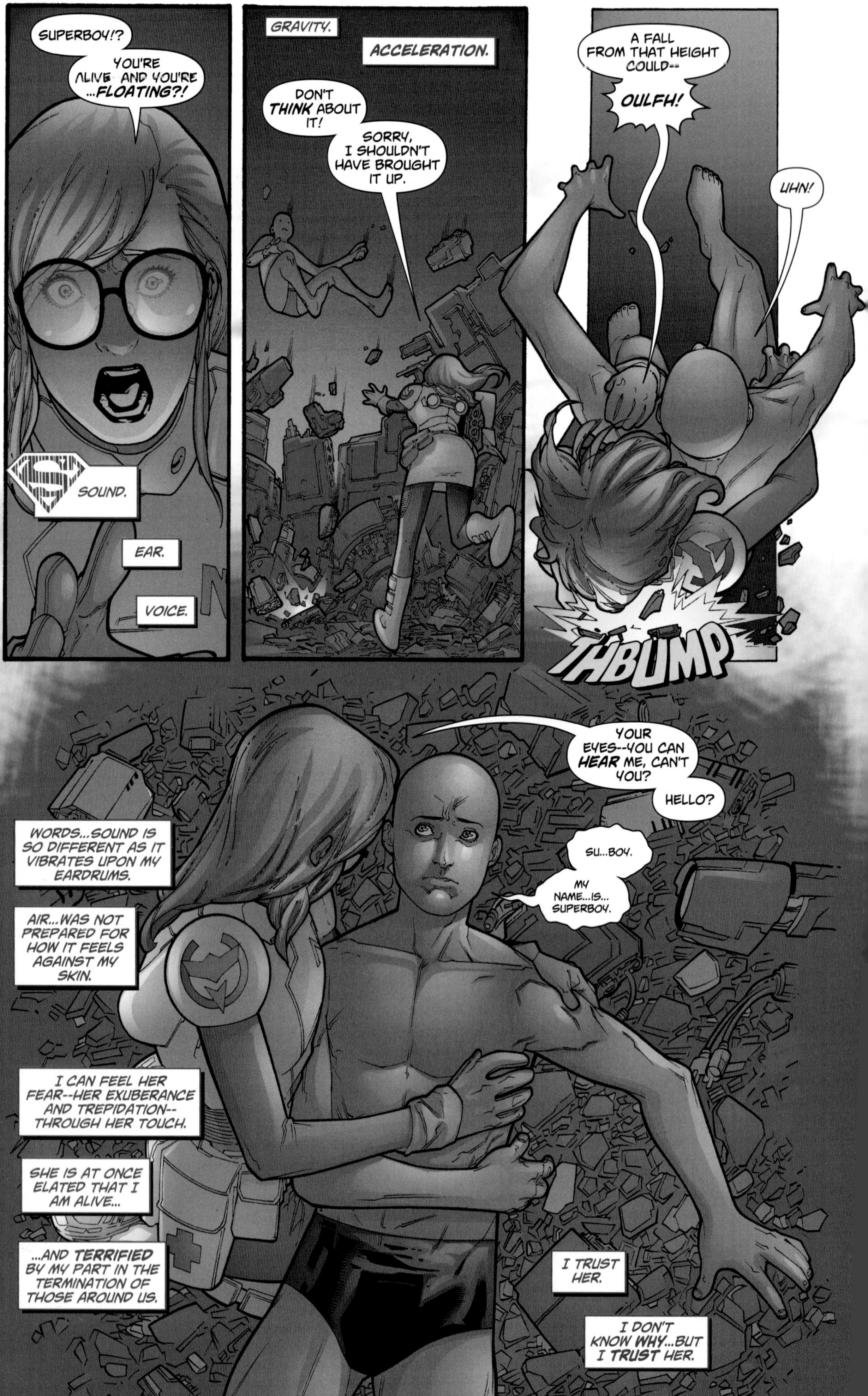

SUPERBOY!?
YOU'RE ALIVE AND YOU'RE ...FLOATING?!
SOUND.
EAR.
VOICE.
GRAVITY.
ACCELERATION.
DON'T THINK ABOUT IT!
SORRY, I SHOULDN'T HAVE BROUGHT IT UP.
A FALL FROM THAT HEIGHT COULD--
OULFH!
UHN!
THBUMP
YOUR EYES--YOU CAN HEAR ME, CAN'T YOU?
HELLO?
WORDS...SOUND IS SO DIFFERENT AS IT VIBRATES UPON MY EARDRUMS.
AIR...WAS NOT PREPARED FOR HOW IT FEELS AGAINST MY SKIN.
SU...BOY.
MY NAME...IS... SUPERBOY.
I CAN FEEL HER FEAR--HER EXUBERANCE AND TREPIDATION--THROUGH HER TOUCH.
SHE IS AT ONCE ELATED THAT I AM ALIVE...
...AND TERRIFIED BY MY PART IN THE TERMINATION OF THOSE AROUND US.
I TRUST HER.
I DON'T KNOW WHY...BUT I TRUST HER.

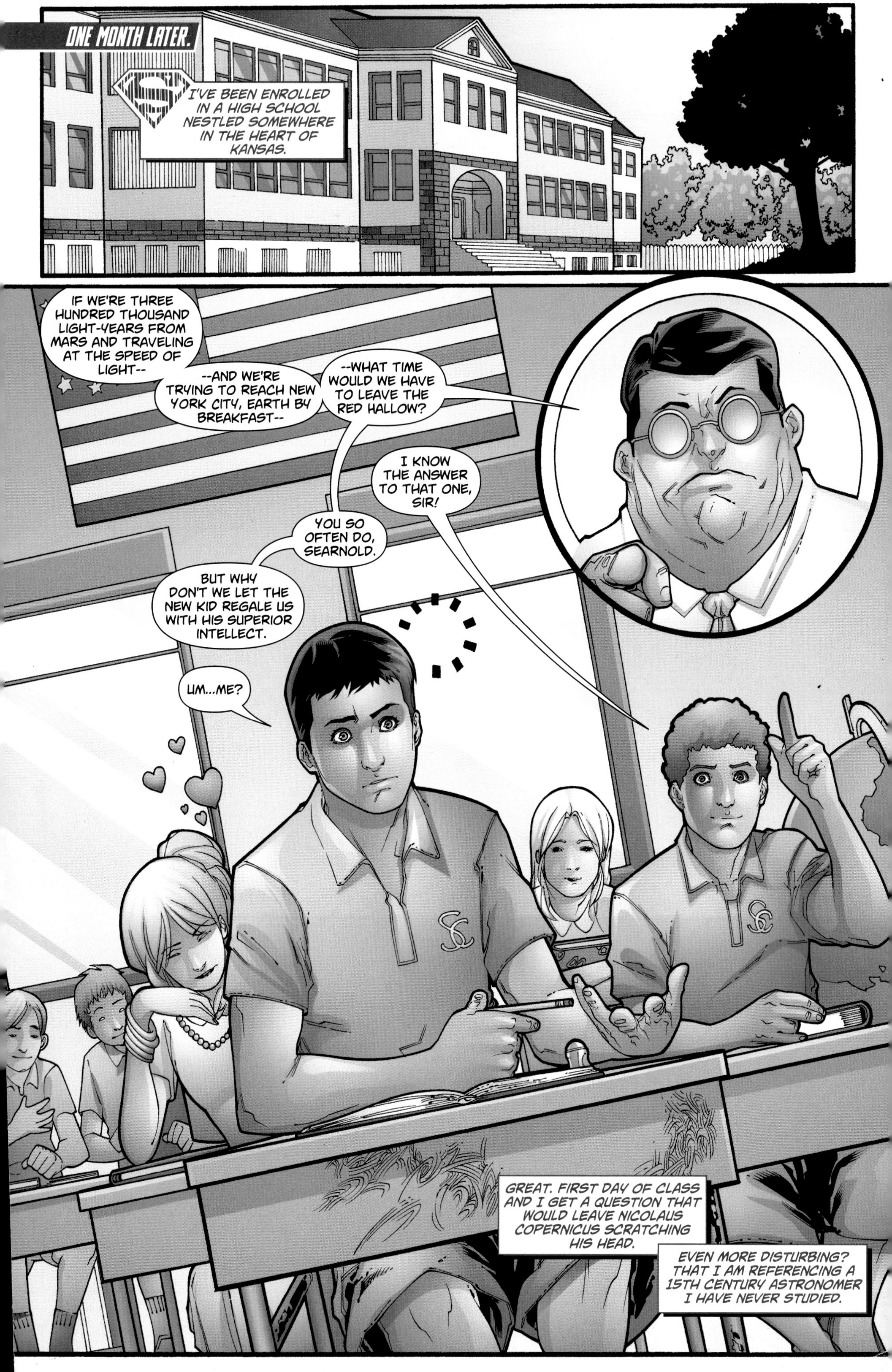
ONE MONTH LATER.
I'VE BEEN ENROLLED IN A HIGH SCHOOL NESTLED SOMEWHERE IN THE HEART OF KANSAS.
IF WE'RE THREE HUNDRED THOUSAND LIGHT-YEARS FROM MARS AND TRAVELING AT THE SPEED OF LIGHT--
--AND WE'RE TRYING TO REACH NEW YORK CITY, EARTH BY BREAKFAST--
--WHAT TIME WOULD WE HAVE TO LEAVE THE RED HALLOW?
I KNOW THE ANSWER TO THAT ONE, SIR!
YOU SO OFTEN DO, SEARNOLD.
BUT WHY DON'T WE LET THE NEW KID REGALE US WITH HIS SUPERIOR INTELLECT.
UM...ME?
GREAT. FIRST DAY OF CLASS AND I GET A QUESTION THAT WOULD LEAVE NICOLAUS COPERNICUS SCRATCHING HIS HEAD.
EVEN MORE DISTURBING? THAT I AM REFERENCING A 15TH CENTURY ASTRONOMER I HAVE NEVER STUDIED.

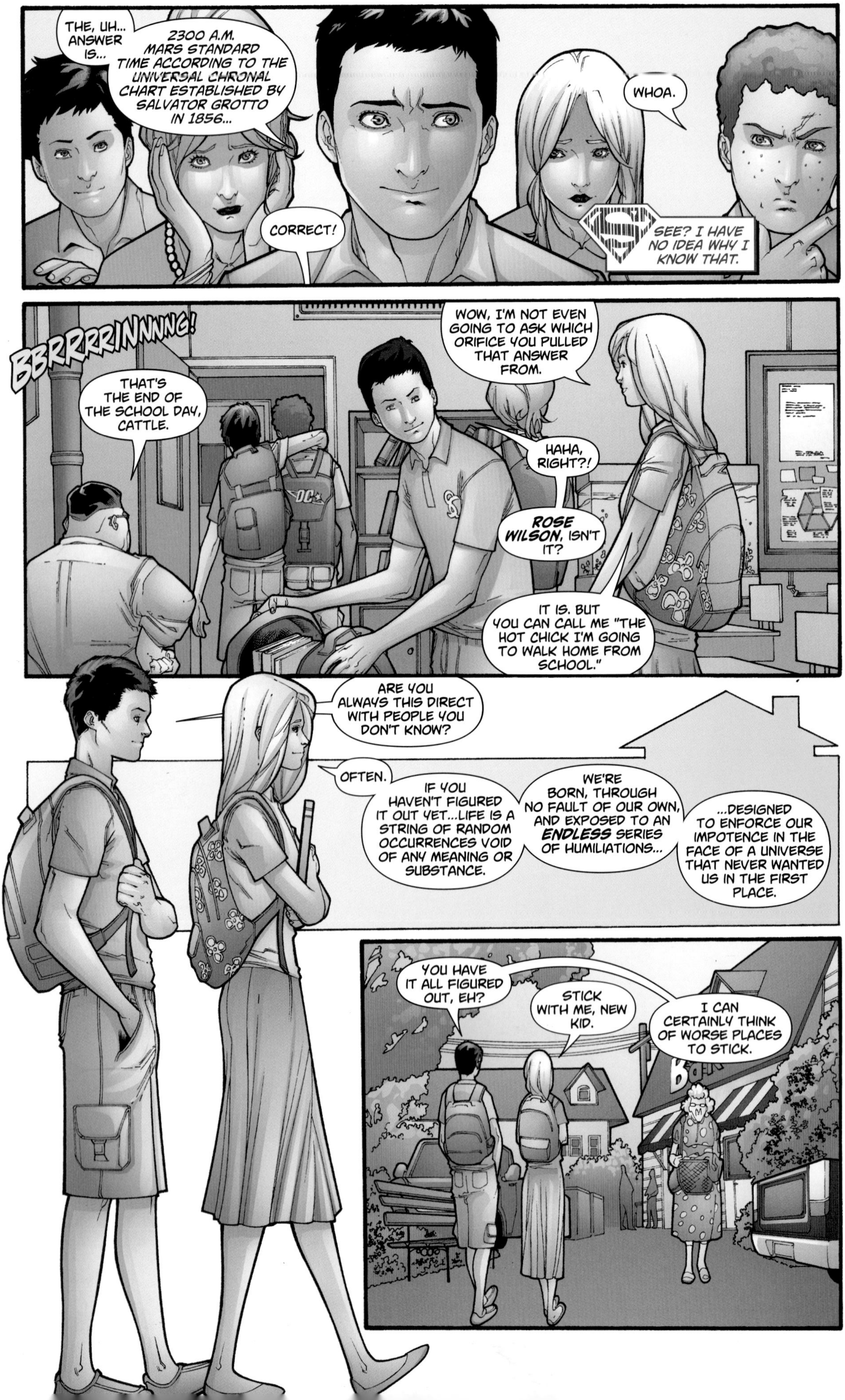
THE, UH... ANSWER IS...
2300 A.M. MARS STANDARD TIME ACCORDING TO THE UNIVERSAL CHRONAL CHART ESTABLISHED BY SALVATOR GROTTO IN 1856...
CORRECT!
WHOA.
SEE? I HAVE NO IDEA WHY I KNOW THAT.
BBRRRRINNNNG!
THAT'S THE END OF THE SCHOOL DAY, CATTLE.
WOW, I'M NOT EVEN GOING TO ASK WHICH ORIFICE YOU PULLED THAT ANSWER FROM.
HAHA, RIGHT?!
ROSE WILSON, ISN'T IT?
IT IS. BUT YOU CAN CALL ME "THE HOT CHICK I'M GOING TO WALK HOME FROM SCHOOL."
ARE YOU ALWAYS THIS DIRECT WITH PEOPLE YOU DON'T KNOW?
OFTEN.
IF YOU HAVEN'T FIGURED IT OUT YET...LIFE IS A STRING OF RANDOM OCCURRENCES VOID OF ANY MEANING OR SUBSTANCE.
WE'RE BORN, THROUGH NO FAULT OF OUR OWN, AND EXPOSED TO AN ENDLESS SERIES OF HUMILIATIONS...
...DESIGNED TO ENFORCE OUR IMPOTENCE IN THE FACE OF A UNIVERSE THAT NEVER WANTED US IN THE FIRST PLACE.
YOU HAVE IT ALL FIGURED OUT, EH?
STICK WITH ME, NEW KID.
I CAN CERTAINLY THINK OF WORSE PLACES TO STICK.

SO WHAT DO YOU THINK OF OUR SLEEPY LITTLE HAMLET?

WORD AROUND SCHOOL IS YOU CAME FROM METROPOLIS--THIS HAS GOT TO BE A LETDOWN.

IT MIGHT BE... BUT I HAVE NO IDEA.

THEY SAY I SUFFERED SOME SORT OF TRAUMATIC BRAIN INJURY. ACCORDING TO THE DOCTORS, I HAVE COGNITIVE AMNESIA.

I REMEMBER HOW TO EAT AND TALK, AND FACTUAL MEMORIES... BUT WHO I AM AND WHERE I LIVED?

NADA.

IT'S EASIER TO EXPLAIN THAN THE *TRUTH*, ANYWAY.

THAT HAS GOT TO SUCK.

IT'S KIND OF LIBERATING, ACTUALLY.

A LOT OF PEOPLE LIVE IN THEIR PAST. I'M FREE TO CONCENTRATE ON ALL THE BEAUTIFUL THINGS RIGHT IN FRONT OF ME.

HELP! PLEASE-- SOMEONE!

HELP!

GOOD TO KNOW.

THIS "CONDITION"... DOES IT AFFECT YOUR PERCEPTIONS OF "RIGHT" AND "WRONG"?

WEIGHTY STUFF LIKE GOOD AND EVIL? EMPATHY AND AMBIVALENCE?

...

I DON'T *THINK* SO.

INTERESTING QUESTION.

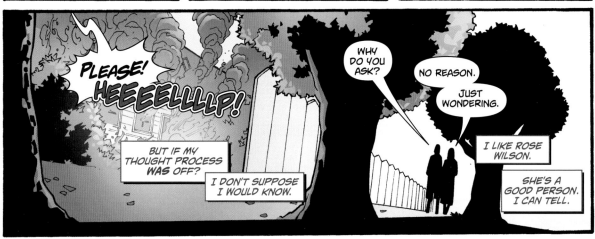

PLEASE! HEEEELLLLP!

BUT IF MY THOUGHT PROCESS *WAS* OFF?

I DON'T SUPPOSE I WOULD KNOW.

WHY DO YOU ASK?

NO REASON. JUST WONDERING.

I LIKE ROSE WILSON.

SHE'S A GOOD PERSON. I CAN TELL.

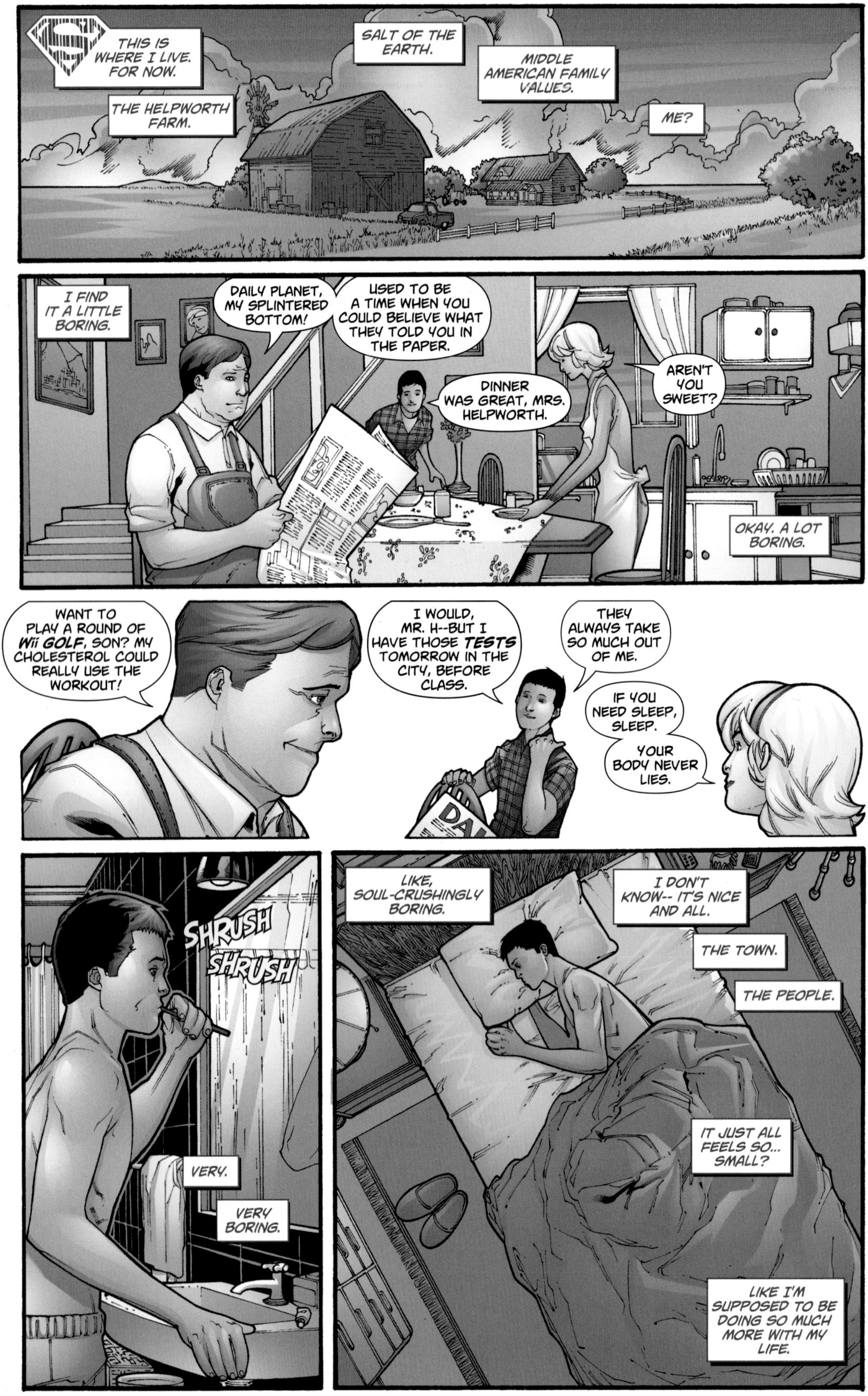
THIS IS WHERE I LIVE. FOR NOW.
THE HELPWORTH FARM.
SALT OF THE EARTH.
MIDDLE AMERICAN FAMILY VALUES.
ME?
I FIND IT A LITTLE BORING.
DAILY PLANET, MY SPLINTERED BOTTOM!
USED TO BE A TIME WHEN YOU COULD BELIEVE WHAT THEY TOLD YOU IN THE PAPER.
DINNER WAS GREAT, MRS. HELPWORTH.
AREN'T YOU SWEET?
OKAY. A LOT BORING.
WANT TO PLAY A ROUND OF Wii GOLF, SON? MY CHOLESTEROL COULD REALLY USE THE WORKOUT!
I WOULD, MR. H--BUT I HAVE THOSE TESTS TOMORROW IN THE CITY, BEFORE CLASS.
THEY ALWAYS TAKE SO MUCH OUT OF ME.
IF YOU NEED SLEEP, SLEEP.
YOUR BODY NEVER LIES.
SHRUSH
SHRUSH
VERY.
VERY BORING.
LIKE, SOUL-CRUSHINGLY BORING.
I DON'T KNOW-- IT'S NICE AND ALL.
THE TOWN.
THE PEOPLE.
IT JUST ALL FEELS SO... SMALL?
LIKE I'M SUPPOSED TO BE DOING SO MUCH MORE WITH MY LIFE.

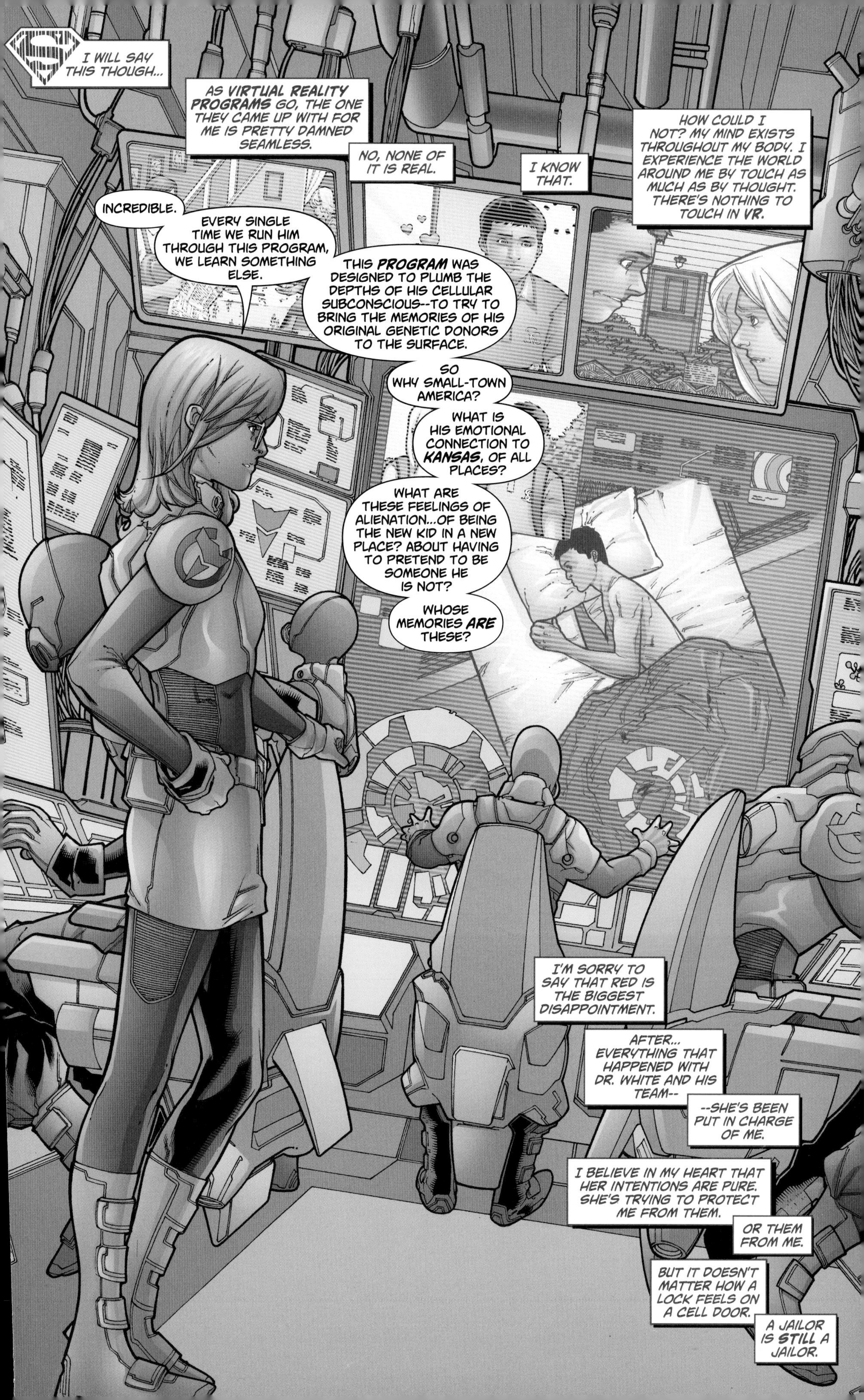

I WILL SAY THIS THOUGH...
AS VIRTUAL REALITY PROGRAMS GO, THE ONE THEY CAME UP WITH FOR ME IS PRETTY DAMNED SEAMLESS.
NO, NONE OF IT IS REAL.
I KNOW THAT.
HOW COULD I NOT? MY MIND EXISTS THROUGHOUT MY BODY. I EXPERIENCE THE WORLD AROUND ME BY TOUCH AS MUCH AS BY THOUGHT. THERE'S NOTHING TO TOUCH IN VR.
INCREDIBLE.
EVERY SINGLE TIME WE RUN HIM THROUGH THIS PROGRAM, WE LEARN SOMETHING ELSE.
THIS PROGRAM WAS DESIGNED TO PLUMB THE DEPTHS OF HIS CELLULAR SUBCONSCIOUS--TO TRY TO BRING THE MEMORIES OF HIS ORIGINAL GENETIC DONORS TO THE SURFACE.
SO WHY SMALL-TOWN AMERICA?
WHAT IS HIS EMOTIONAL CONNECTION TO KANSAS, OF ALL PLACES?
WHAT ARE THESE FEELINGS OF ALIENATION...OF BEING THE NEW KID IN A NEW PLACE? ABOUT HAVING TO PRETEND TO BE SOMEONE HE IS NOT?
WHOSE MEMORIES ARE THESE?
I'M SORRY TO SAY THAT RED IS THE BIGGEST DISAPPOINTMENT.
AFTER... EVERYTHING THAT HAPPENED WITH DR. WHITE AND HIS TEAM--
--SHE'S BEEN PUT IN CHARGE OF ME.
I BELIEVE IN MY HEART THAT HER INTENTIONS ARE PURE. SHE'S TRYING TO PROTECT ME FROM THEM.
OR THEM FROM ME.
BUT IT DOESN'T MATTER HOW A LOCK FEELS ON A CELL DOOR.
A JAILOR IS STILL A JAILOR.

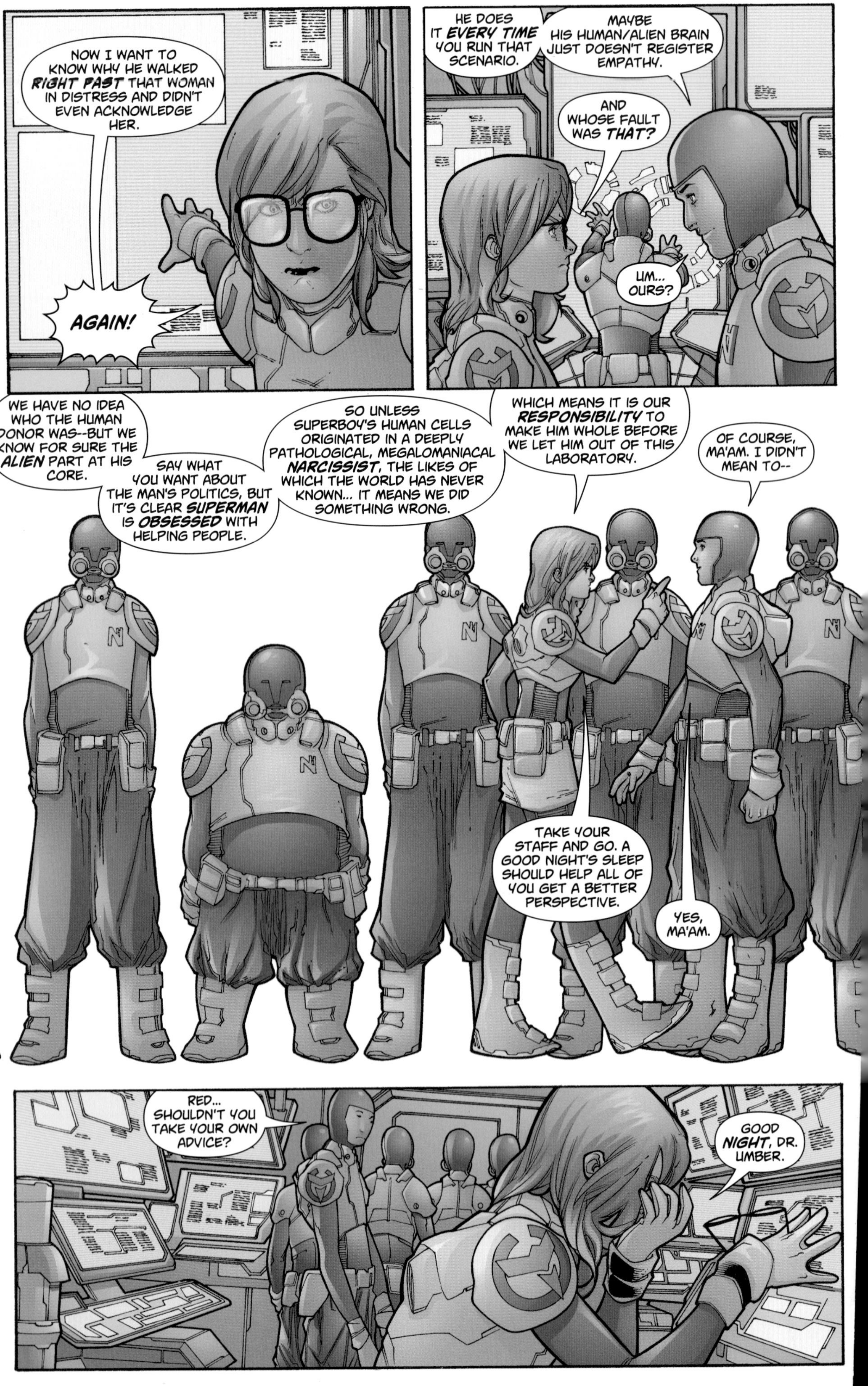
NOW I WANT TO KNOW WHY HE WALKED RIGHT PAST THAT WOMAN IN DISTRESS AND DIDN'T EVEN ACKNOWLEDGE HER.
AGAIN!
HE DOES IT EVERY TIME YOU RUN THAT SCENARIO.
MAYBE HIS HUMAN/ALIEN BRAIN JUST DOESN'T REGISTER EMPATHY.
AND WHOSE FAULT WAS THAT?
UM... OURS?
WE HAVE NO IDEA WHO THE HUMAN DONOR WAS--BUT WE KNOW FOR SURE THE ALIEN PART AT HIS CORE.
SAY WHAT YOU WANT ABOUT THE MAN'S POLITICS, BUT IT'S CLEAR SUPERMAN IS OBSESSED WITH HELPING PEOPLE.
SO UNLESS SUPERBOY'S HUMAN CELLS ORIGINATED IN A DEEPLY PATHOLOGICAL, MEGALOMANIACAL NARCISSIST, THE LIKES OF WHICH THE WORLD HAS NEVER KNOWN... IT MEANS WE DID SOMETHING WRONG.
WHICH MEANS IT IS OUR RESPONSIBILITY TO MAKE HIM WHOLE BEFORE WE LET HIM OUT OF THIS LABORATORY.
OF COURSE, MA'AM. I DIDN'T MEAN TO--
TAKE YOUR STAFF AND GO. A GOOD NIGHT'S SLEEP SHOULD HELP ALL OF YOU GET A BETTER PERSPECTIVE.
YES, MA'AM.
RED... SHOULDN'T YOU TAKE YOUR OWN ADVICE?
GOOD NIGHT, DR. UMBER.

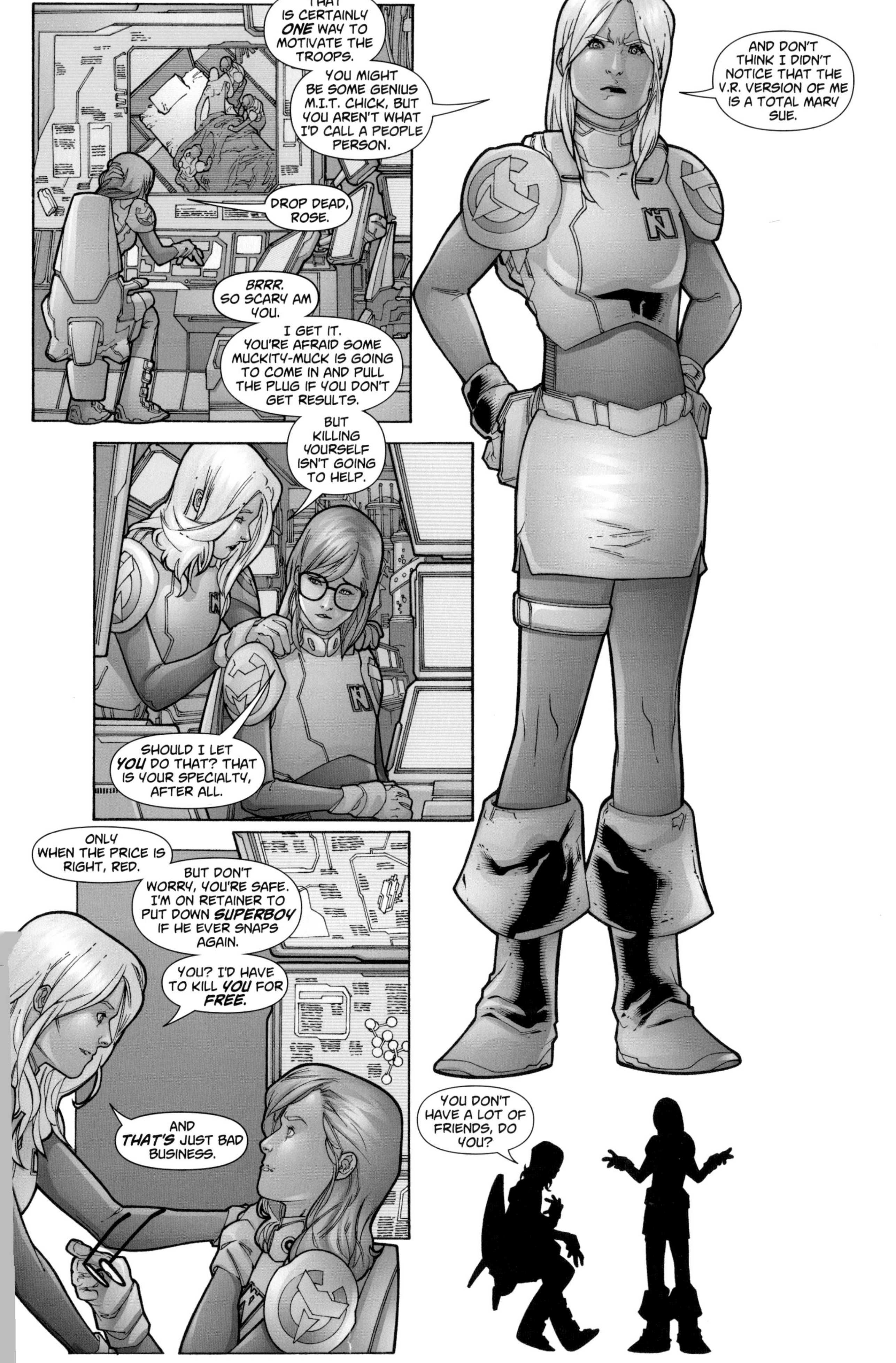

THAT IS CERTAINLY ONE WAY TO MOTIVATE THE TROOPS.
YOU MIGHT BE SOME GENIUS M.I.T. CHICK, BUT YOU AREN'T WHAT I'D CALL A PEOPLE PERSON.
DROP DEAD, ROSE.
BRRR. SO SCARY AM YOU.
I GET IT. YOU'RE AFRAID SOME MUCKITY-MUCK IS GOING TO COME IN AND PULL THE PLUG IF YOU DON'T GET RESULTS.
BUT KILLING YOURSELF ISN'T GOING TO HELP.
SHOULD I LET YOU DO THAT? THAT IS YOUR SPECIALTY, AFTER ALL.
ONLY WHEN THE PRICE IS RIGHT, RED.
BUT DON'T WORRY, YOU'RE SAFE. I'M ON RETAINER TO PUT DOWN SUPERBOY IF HE EVER SNAPS AGAIN.
YOU? I'D HAVE TO KILL YOU FOR FREE.
AND THAT'S JUST BAD BUSINESS.
AND DON'T THINK I DIDN'T NOTICE THAT THE V.R. VERSION OF ME IS A TOTAL MARY SUE.
YOU DON'T HAVE A LOT OF FRIENDS, DO YOU?

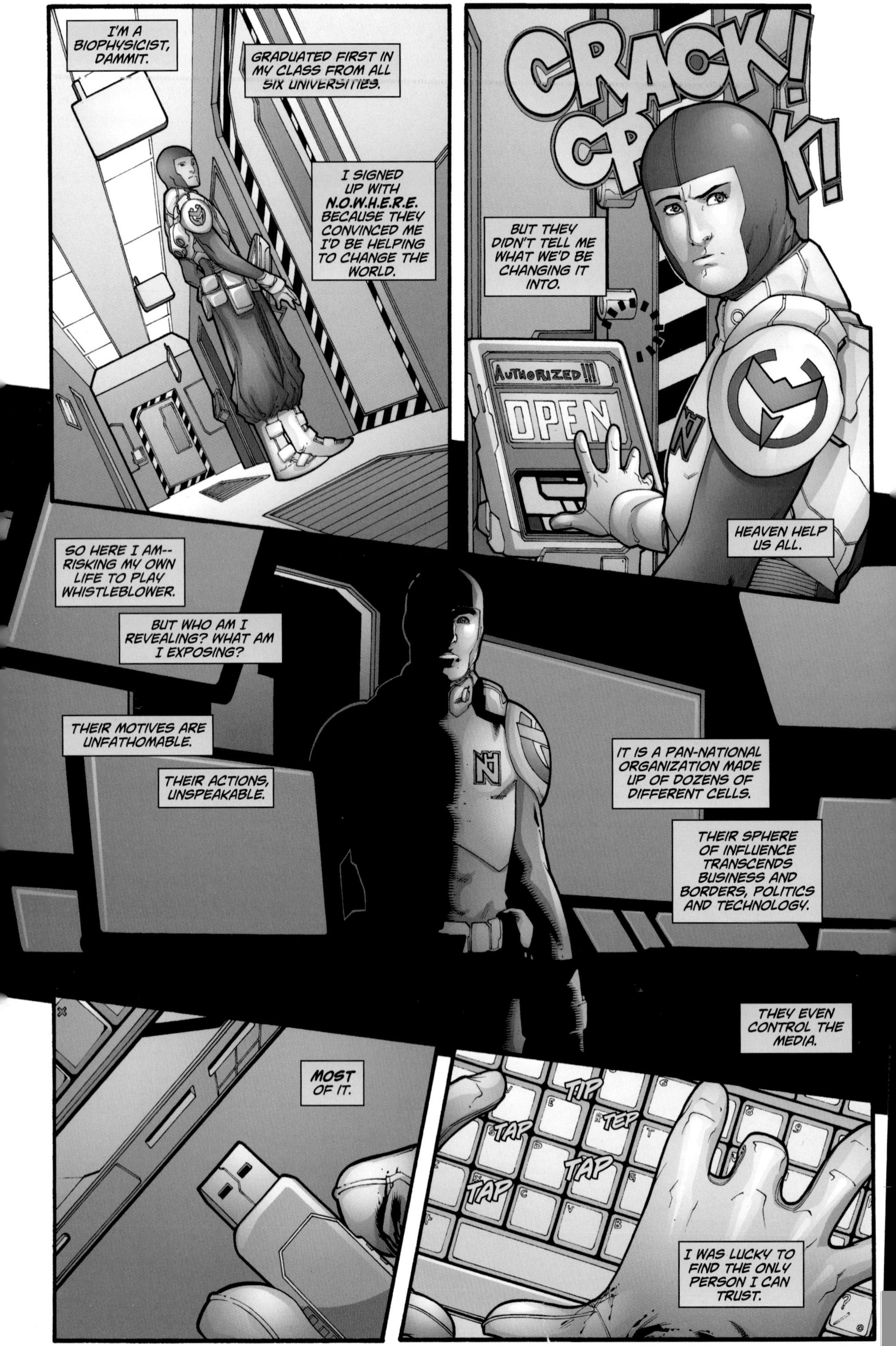
I'M A BIOPHYSICIST, DAMMIT.
GRADUATED FIRST IN MY CLASS FROM ALL SIX UNIVERSITIES.
I SIGNED UP WITH N.O.W.H.E.R.E. BECAUSE THEY CONVINCED ME I'D BE HELPING TO CHANGE THE WORLD.
CRACK! CRACK!
BUT THEY DIDN'T TELL ME WHAT WE'D BE CHANGING IT INTO.
AUTHORIZED!!!
OPEN
HEAVEN HELP US ALL.
SO HERE I AM-- RISKING MY OWN LIFE TO PLAY WHISTLEBLOWER.
BUT WHO AM I REVEALING? WHAT AM I EXPOSING?
THEIR MOTIVES ARE UNFATHOMABLE.
THEIR ACTIONS, UNSPEAKABLE.
IT IS A PAN-NATIONAL ORGANIZATION MADE UP OF DOZENS OF DIFFERENT CELLS.
THEIR SPHERE OF INFLUENCE TRANSCENDS BUSINESS AND BORDERS, POLITICS AND TECHNOLOGY.
THEY EVEN CONTROL THE MEDIA.
MOST OF IT.
TIP
TEP
TAP
TAP
TAP
I WAS LUCKY TO FIND THE ONLY PERSON I CAN TRUST.

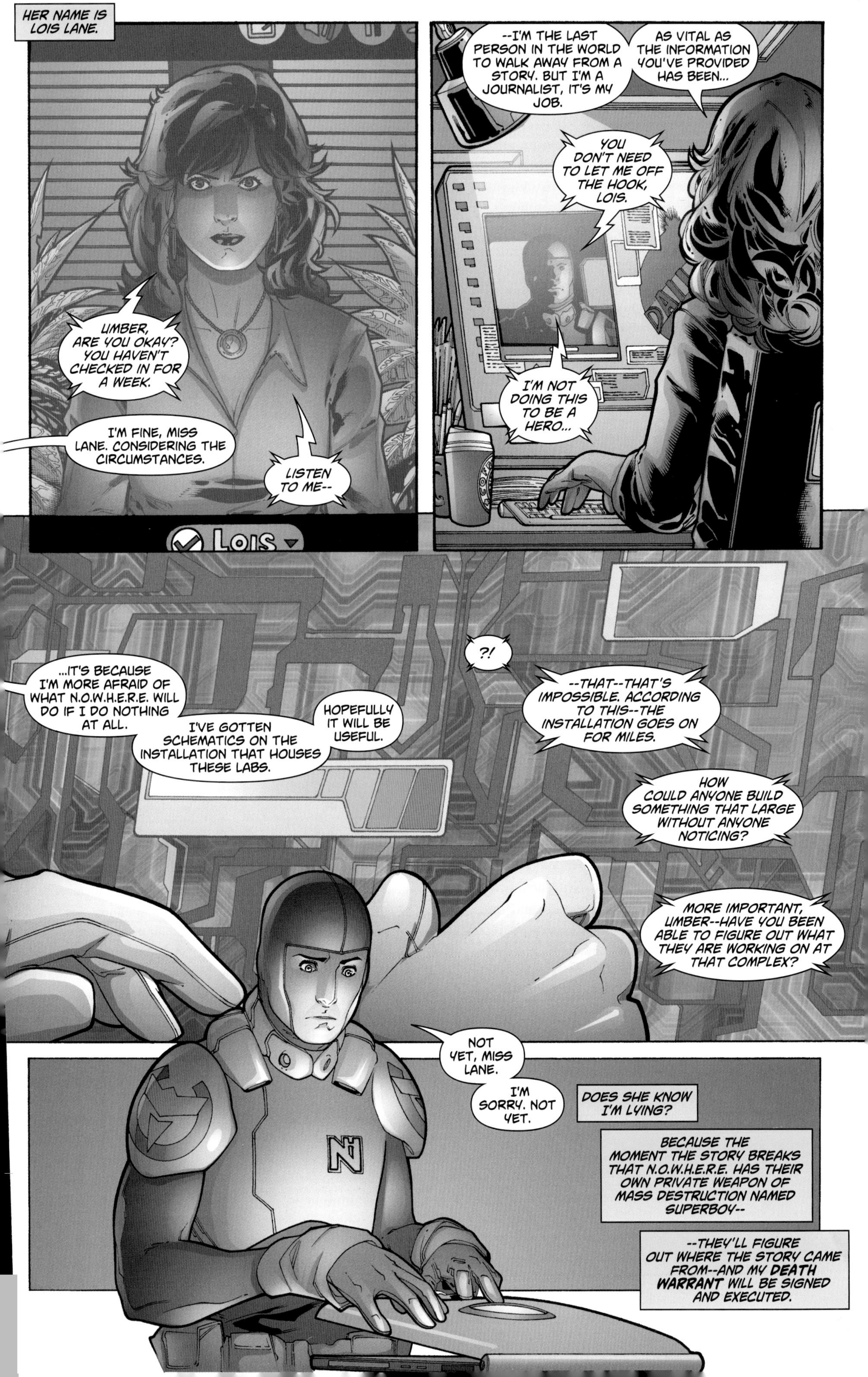

HER NAME IS LOIS LANE.
UMBER, ARE YOU OKAY? YOU HAVEN'T CHECKED IN FOR A WEEK.
I'M FINE, MISS LANE. CONSIDERING THE CIRCUMSTANCES.
LISTEN TO ME--
LOIS
--I'M THE LAST PERSON IN THE WORLD TO WALK AWAY FROM A STORY. BUT I'M A JOURNALIST, IT'S MY JOB.
AS VITAL AS THE INFORMATION YOU'VE PROVIDED HAS BEEN...
YOU DON'T NEED TO LET ME OFF THE HOOK, LOIS.
I'M NOT DOING THIS TO BE A HERO...
...IT'S BECAUSE I'M MORE AFRAID OF WHAT N.O.W.H.E.R.E. WILL DO IF I DO NOTHING AT ALL.
I'VE GOTTEN SCHEMATICS ON THE INSTALLATION THAT HOUSES THESE LABS.
HOPEFULLY IT WILL BE USEFUL.
?!
--THAT--THAT'S IMPOSSIBLE. ACCORDING TO THIS--THE INSTALLATION GOES ON FOR MILES.
HOW COULD ANYONE BUILD SOMETHING THAT LARGE WITHOUT ANYONE NOTICING?
MORE IMPORTANT, UMBER--HAVE YOU BEEN ABLE TO FIGURE OUT WHAT THEY ARE WORKING ON AT THAT COMPLEX?
NOT YET, MISS LANE.
I'M SORRY. NOT YET.
DOES SHE KNOW I'M LYING?
BECAUSE THE MOMENT THE STORY BREAKS THAT N.O.W.H.E.R.E. HAS THEIR OWN PRIVATE WEAPON OF MASS DESTRUCTION NAMED SUPERBOY--
--THEY'LL FIGURE OUT WHERE THE STORY CAME FROM--AND MY DEATH WARRANT WILL BE SIGNED AND EXECUTED.

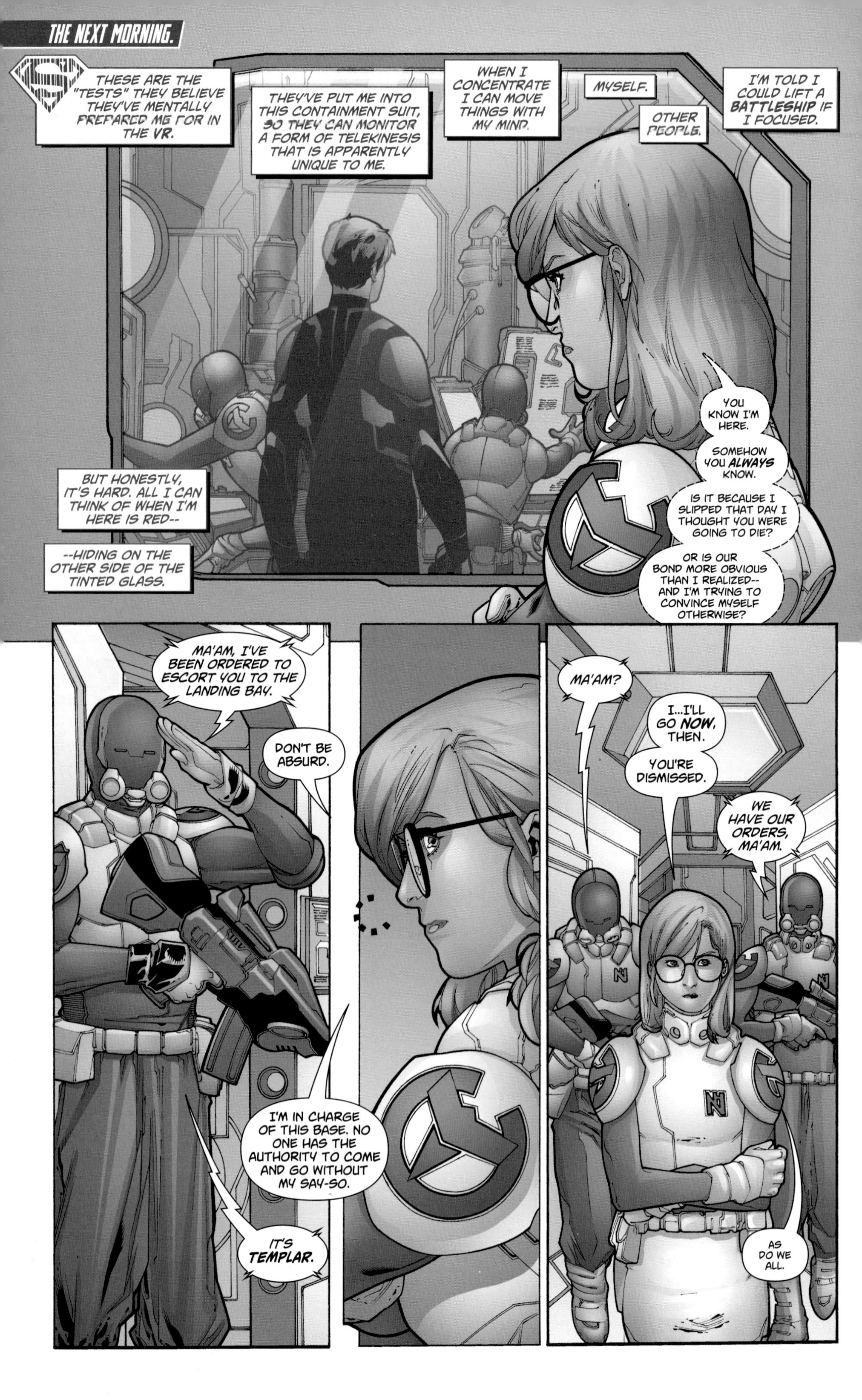
THE NEXT MORNING.
THESE ARE THE "TESTS" THEY BELIEVE THEY'VE MENTALLY PREPARED ME FOR IN THE VR.
THEY'VE PUT ME INTO THIS CONTAINMENT SUIT, SO THEY CAN MONITOR A FORM OF TELEKINESIS THAT IS APPARENTLY UNIQUE TO ME.
WHEN I CONCENTRATE I CAN MOVE THINGS WITH MY MIND.
MYSELF.
OTHER PEOPLE.
I'M TOLD I COULD LIFT A BATTLESHIP IF I FOCUSED.
YOU KNOW I'M HERE.
SOMEHOW YOU ALWAYS KNOW.
IS IT BECAUSE I SLIPPED THAT DAY I THOUGHT YOU WERE GOING TO DIE?
OR IS OUR BOND MORE OBVIOUS THAN I REALIZED-- AND I'M TRYING TO CONVINCE MYSELF OTHERWISE?
BUT HONESTLY, IT'S HARD. ALL I CAN THINK OF WHEN I'M HERE IS RED--
--HIDING ON THE OTHER SIDE OF THE TINTED GLASS.
MA'AM, I'VE BEEN ORDERED TO ESCORT YOU TO THE LANDING BAY.
DON'T BE ABSURD.
I'M IN CHARGE OF THIS BASE. NO ONE HAS THE AUTHORITY TO COME AND GO WITHOUT MY SAY-SO.
IT'S TEMPLAR.
MA'AM?
I...I'LL GO NOW, THEN.
YOU'RE DISMISSED.
WE HAVE OUR ORDERS, MA'AM.
AS DO WE ALL.

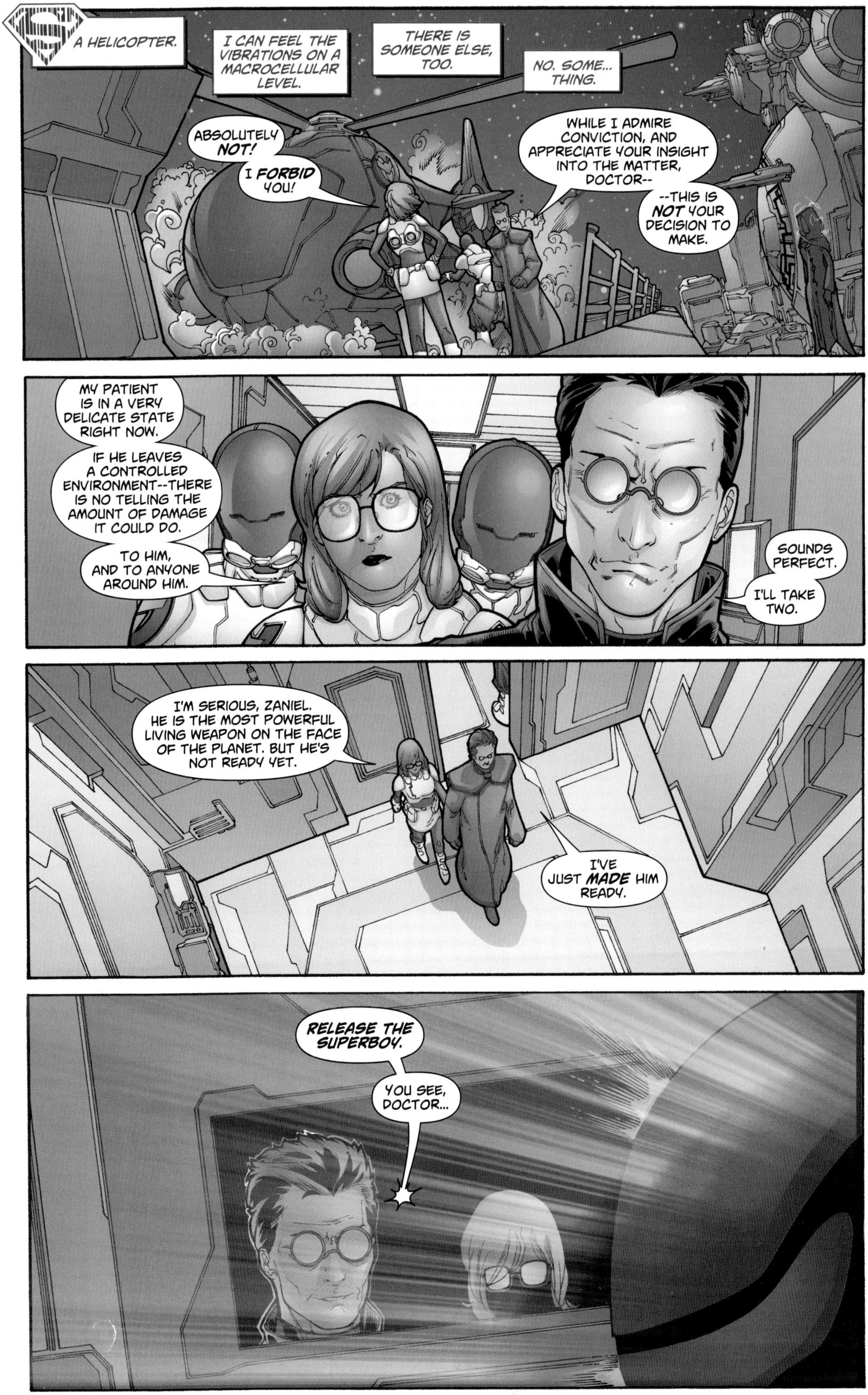
A HELICOPTER.
I CAN FEEL THE VIBRATIONS ON A MACROCELLULAR LEVEL.
THERE IS SOMEONE ELSE, TOO.
NO. SOME... THING.
ABSOLUTELY NOT!
I FORBID YOU!
WHILE I ADMIRE CONVICTION, AND APPRECIATE YOUR INSIGHT INTO THE MATTER, DOCTOR--
--THIS IS NOT YOUR DECISION TO MAKE.
MY PATIENT IS IN A VERY DELICATE STATE RIGHT NOW.
IF HE LEAVES A CONTROLLED ENVIRONMENT--THERE IS NO TELLING THE AMOUNT OF DAMAGE IT COULD DO.
TO HIM, AND TO ANYONE AROUND HIM.
SOUNDS PERFECT.
I'LL TAKE TWO.
I'M SERIOUS, ZANIEL. HE IS THE MOST POWERFUL LIVING WEAPON ON THE FACE OF THE PLANET. BUT HE'S NOT READY YET.
I'VE JUST MADE HIM READY.
RELEASE THE SUPERBOY.
YOU SEE, DOCTOR...

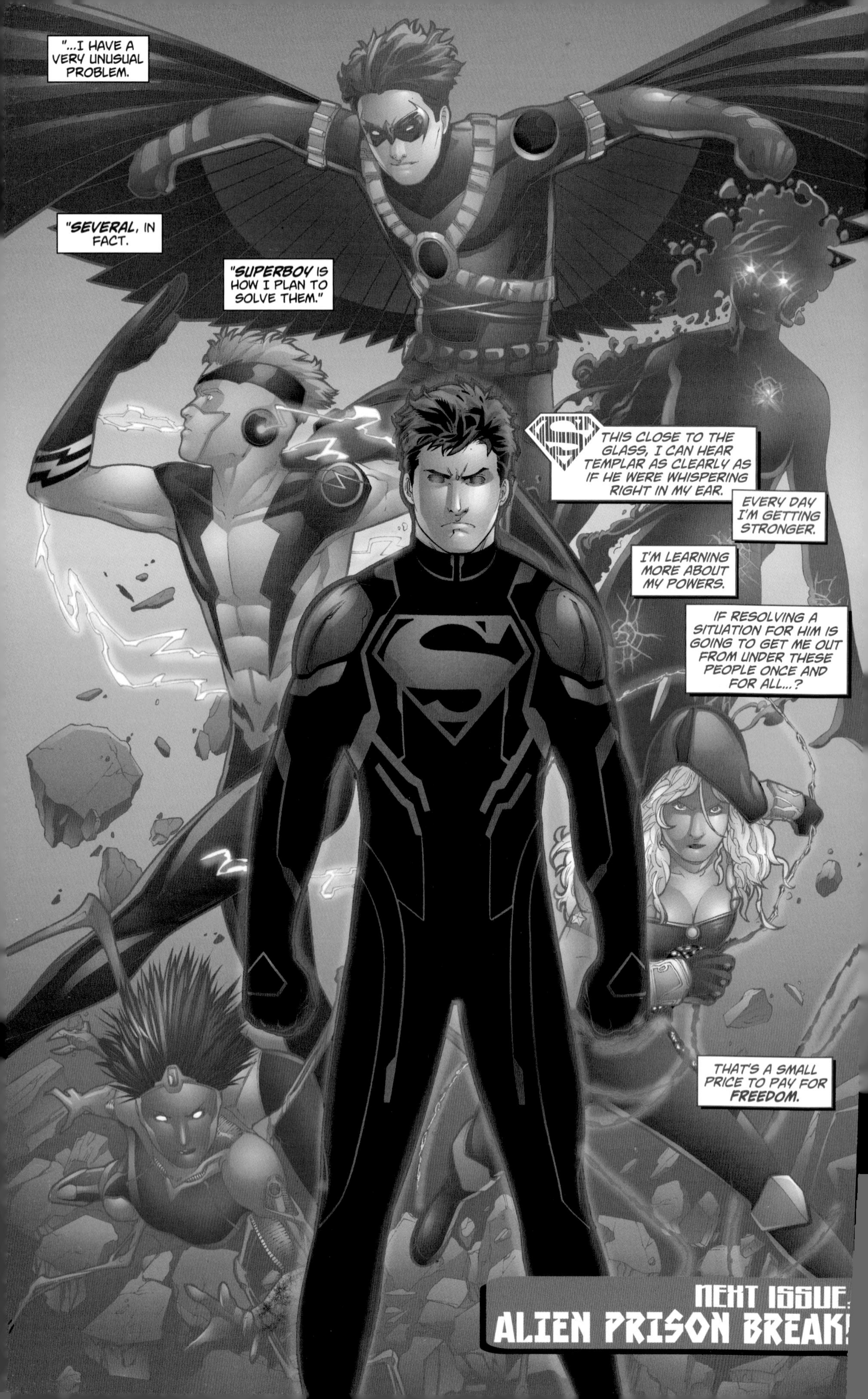
"...I HAVE A VERY UNUSUAL PROBLEM.
"SEVERAL, IN FACT.
"SUPERBOY IS HOW I PLAN TO SOLVE THEM."
THIS CLOSE TO THE GLASS, I CAN HEAR TEMPLAR AS CLEARLY AS IF HE WERE WHISPERING RIGHT IN MY EAR.
EVERY DAY I'M GETTING STRONGER.
I'M LEARNING MORE ABOUT MY POWERS.
IF RESOLVING A SITUATION FOR HIM IS GOING TO GET ME OUT FROM UNDER THESE PEOPLE ONCE AND FOR ALL...?
THAT'S A SMALL PRICE TO PAY FOR FREEDOM.
NEXT ISSUE:
ALIEN PRISON BREAK!

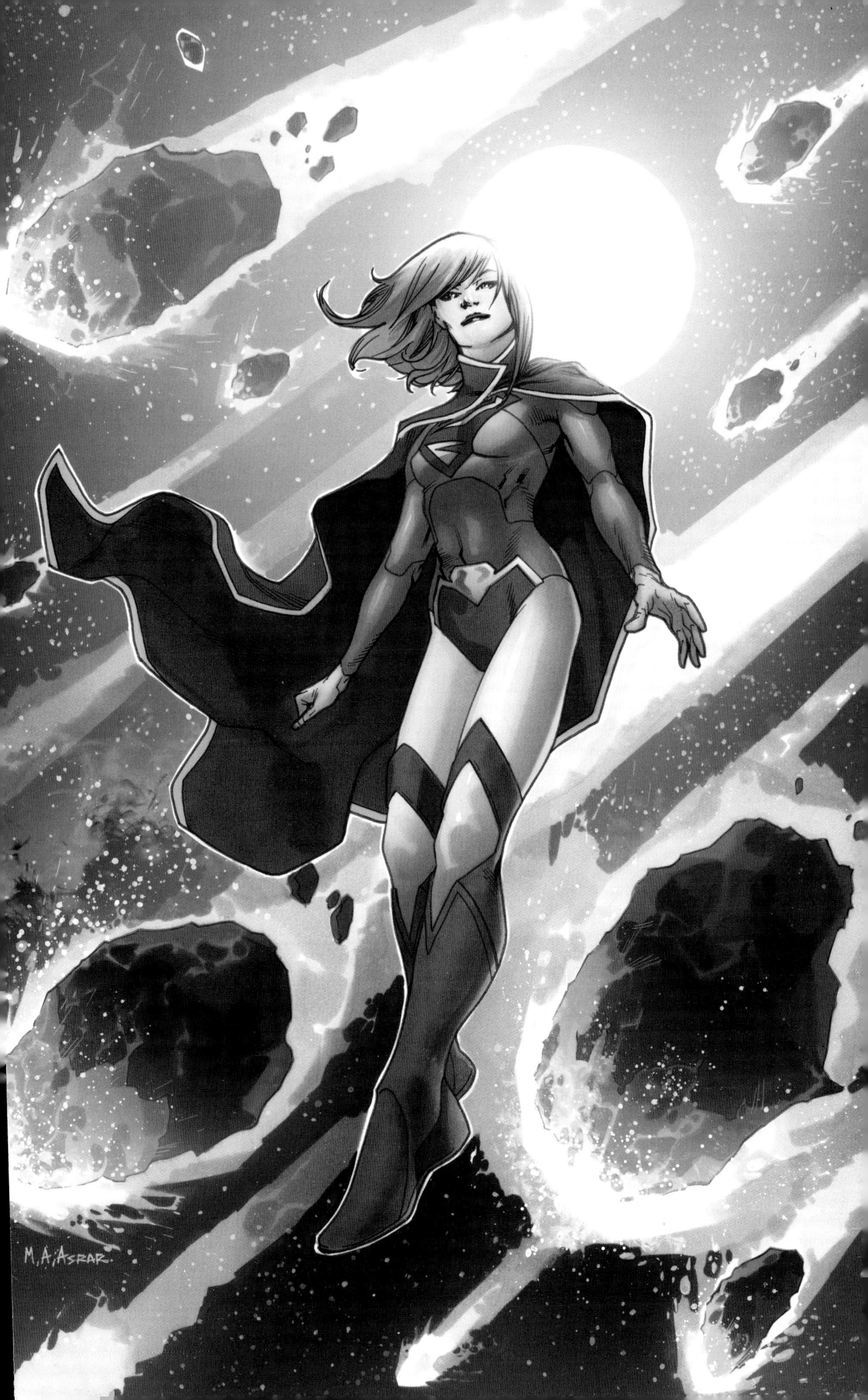
M.A.ASRAR.

SUPERGIRL

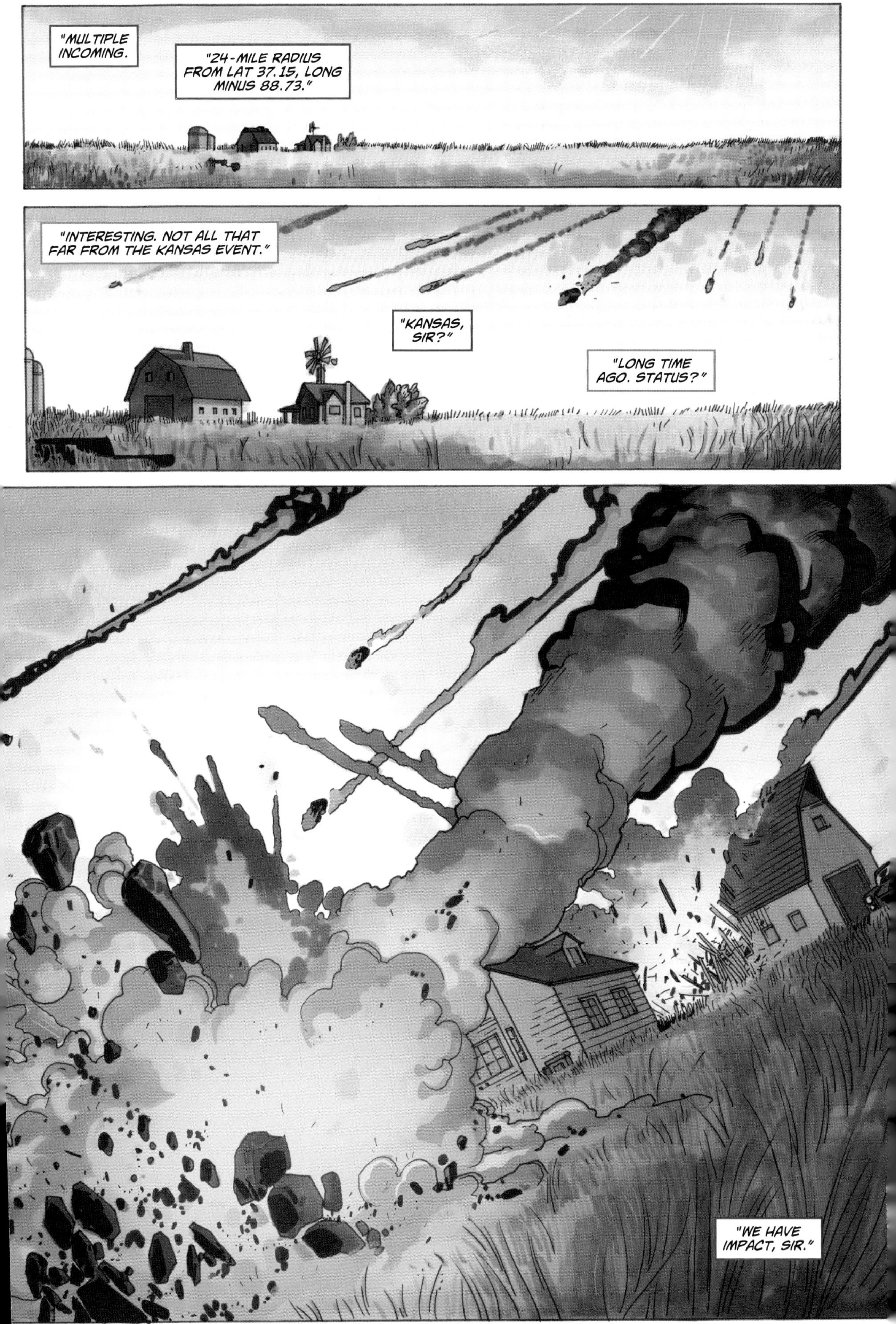
"MULTIPLE INCOMING.
"24-MILE RADIUS FROM LAT 37.15, LONG MINUS 88.73."
"INTERESTING. NOT ALL THAT FAR FROM THE KANSAS EVENT."
"KANSAS, SIR?"
"LONG TIME AGO. STATUS?"
"WE HAVE IMPACT, SIR."

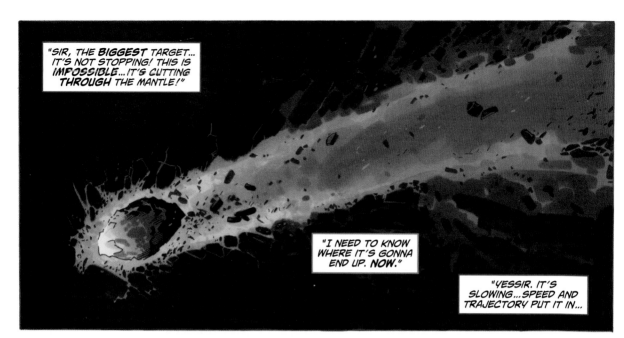

"SIR, THE BIGGEST TARGET... IT'S NOT STOPPING! THIS IS IMPOSSIBLE...IT'S CUTTING THROUGH THE MANTLE!"

"I NEED TO KNOW WHERE IT'S GONNA END UP. NOW."

"YESSIR. IT'S SLOWING...SPEED AND TRAJECTORY PUT IT IN..."

"SIBERIA. ALERT THE RUSSIANS?"

"RUSSIA SIGNED THE VISITOR PROTOCOLS. JUST REMIND THEM TO STAY OUT OF OUR WAY. THEY KNOW WHAT'LL HAPPEN IF THEY DON'T.

"I WANT TWO INTERCEPT TEAMS IN THE AIR BEFORE I FINISH THIS SENTENCE. FULL PACKS, MAX FIRE.

"LET'S GO GET IT."

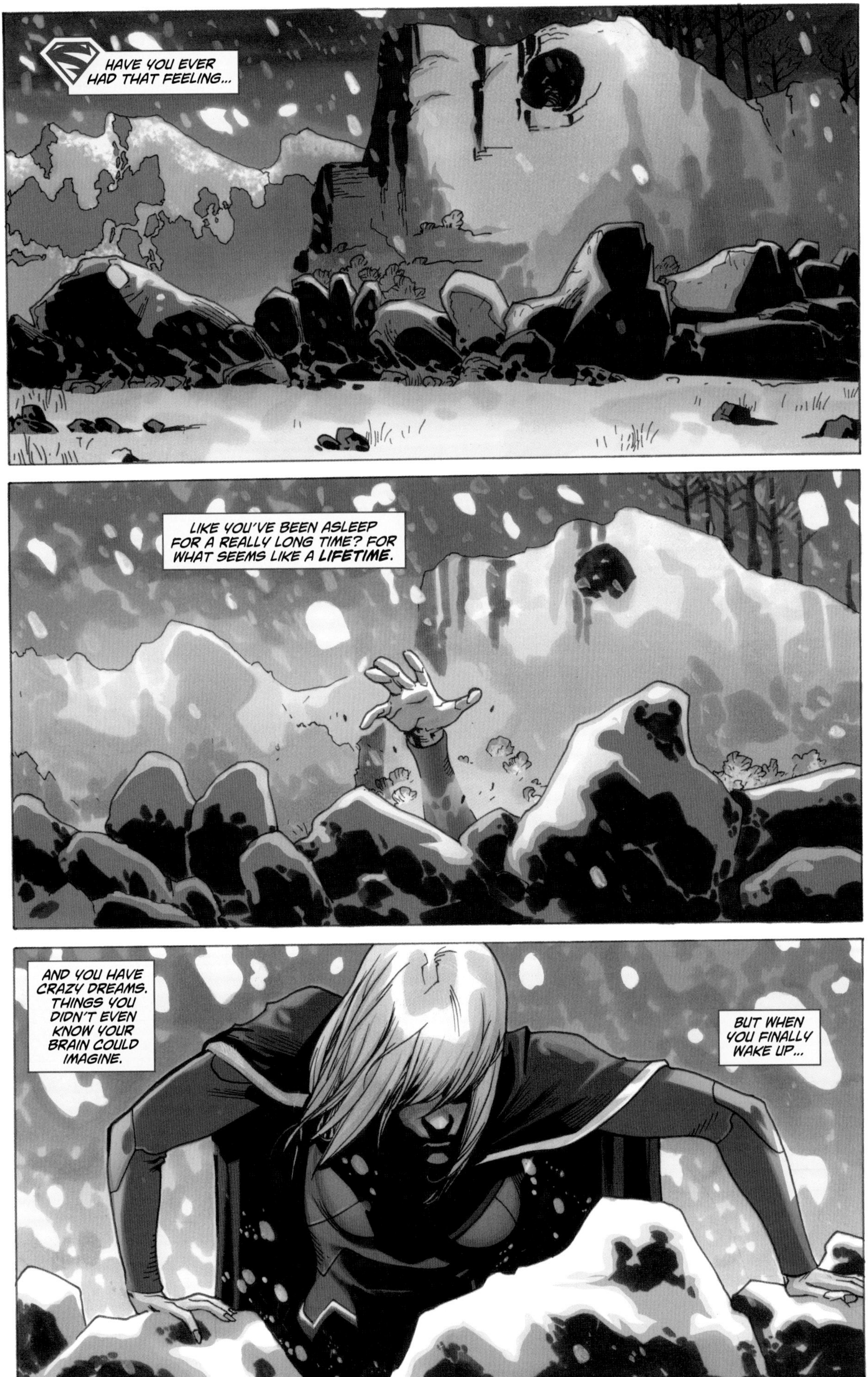
HAVE YOU EVER HAD THAT FEELING...
LIKE YOU'VE BEEN ASLEEP FOR A REALLY LONG TIME? FOR WHAT SEEMS LIKE A **LIFETIME**.
AND YOU HAVE CRAZY DREAMS. THINGS YOU DIDN'T EVEN KNOW YOUR BRAIN COULD IMAGINE.
BUT WHEN YOU FINALLY WAKE UP...

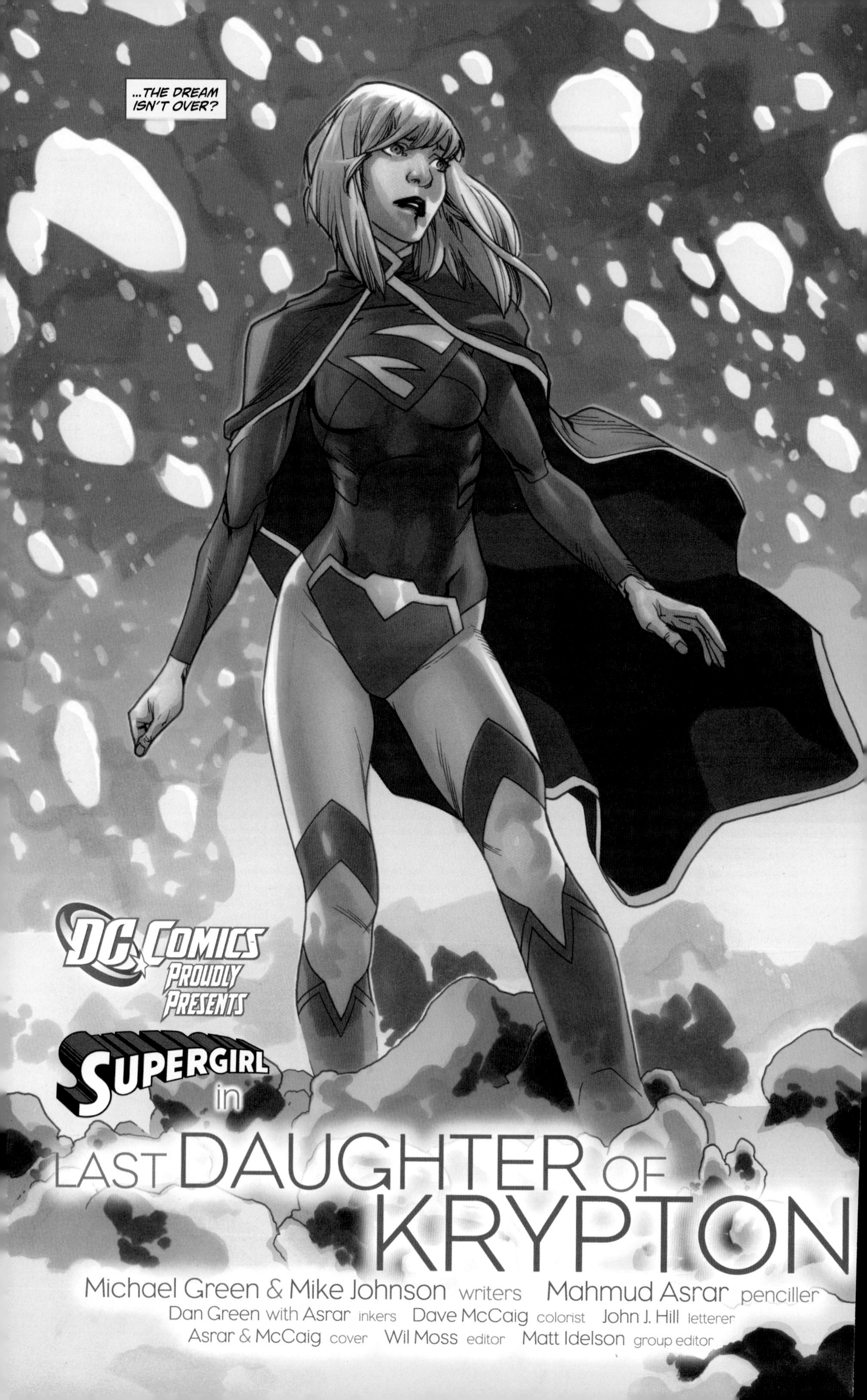
...THE DREAM ISN'T OVER?
DC COMICS PROUDLY PRESENTS
SUPERGIRL in
LAST DAUGHTER OF KRYPTON
Michael Green & Mike Johnson writers Mahmud Asrar penciller
Dan Green with Asrar inkers Dave McCaig colorist John J. Hill letterer
Asrar & McCaig cover Wil Moss editor Matt Idelson group editor

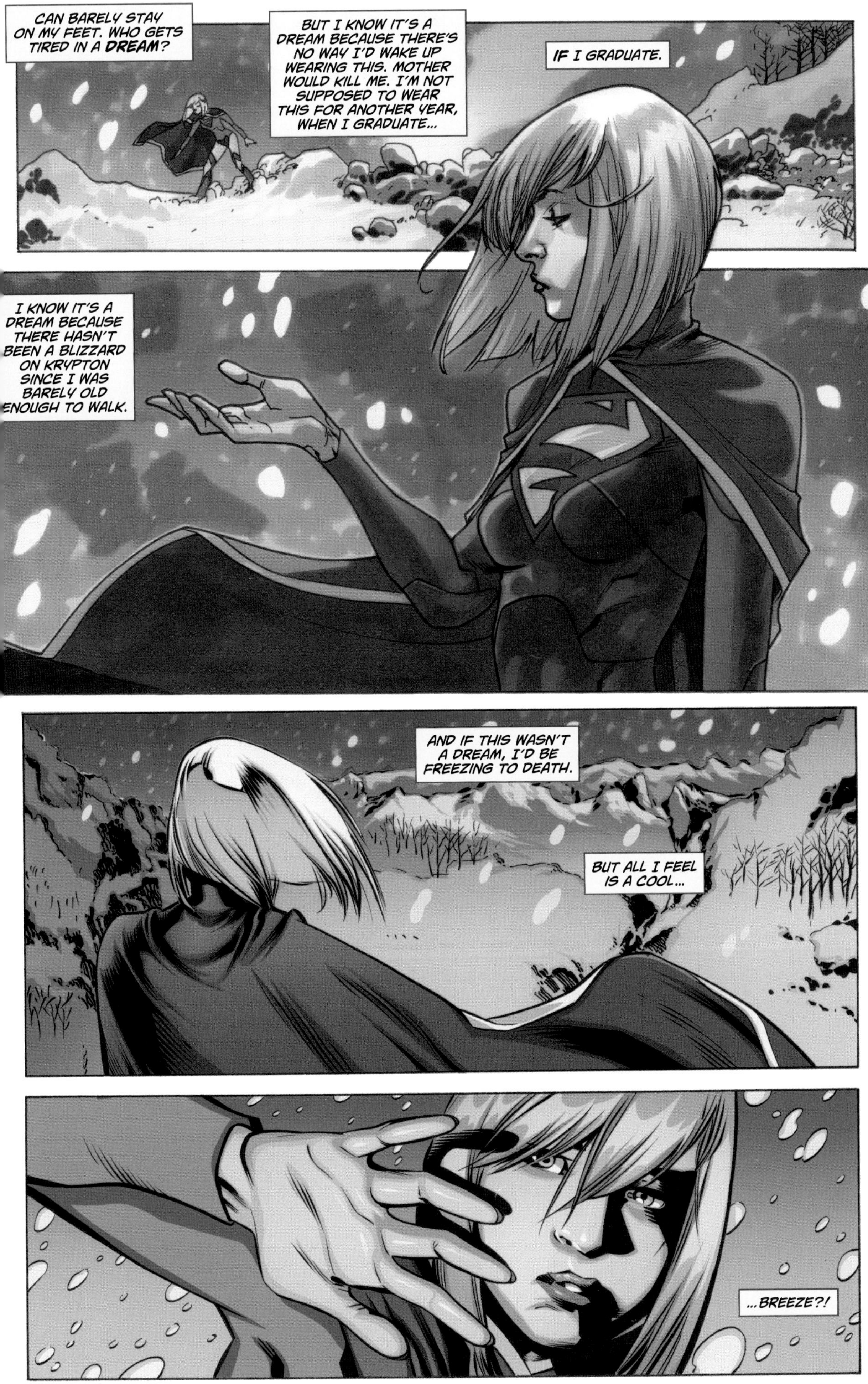

CAN BARELY STAY ON MY FEET. WHO GETS TIRED IN A DREAM?
BUT I KNOW IT'S A DREAM BECAUSE THERE'S NO WAY I'D WAKE UP WEARING THIS. MOTHER WOULD KILL ME. I'M NOT SUPPOSED TO WEAR THIS FOR ANOTHER YEAR, WHEN I GRADUATE...
IF I GRADUATE.
I KNOW IT'S A DREAM BECAUSE THERE HASN'T BEEN A BLIZZARD ON KRYPTON SINCE I WAS BARELY OLD ENOUGH TO WALK.
AND IF THIS WASN'T A DREAM, I'D BE FREEZING TO DEATH.
BUT ALL I FEEL IS A COOL...
...BREEZE?!

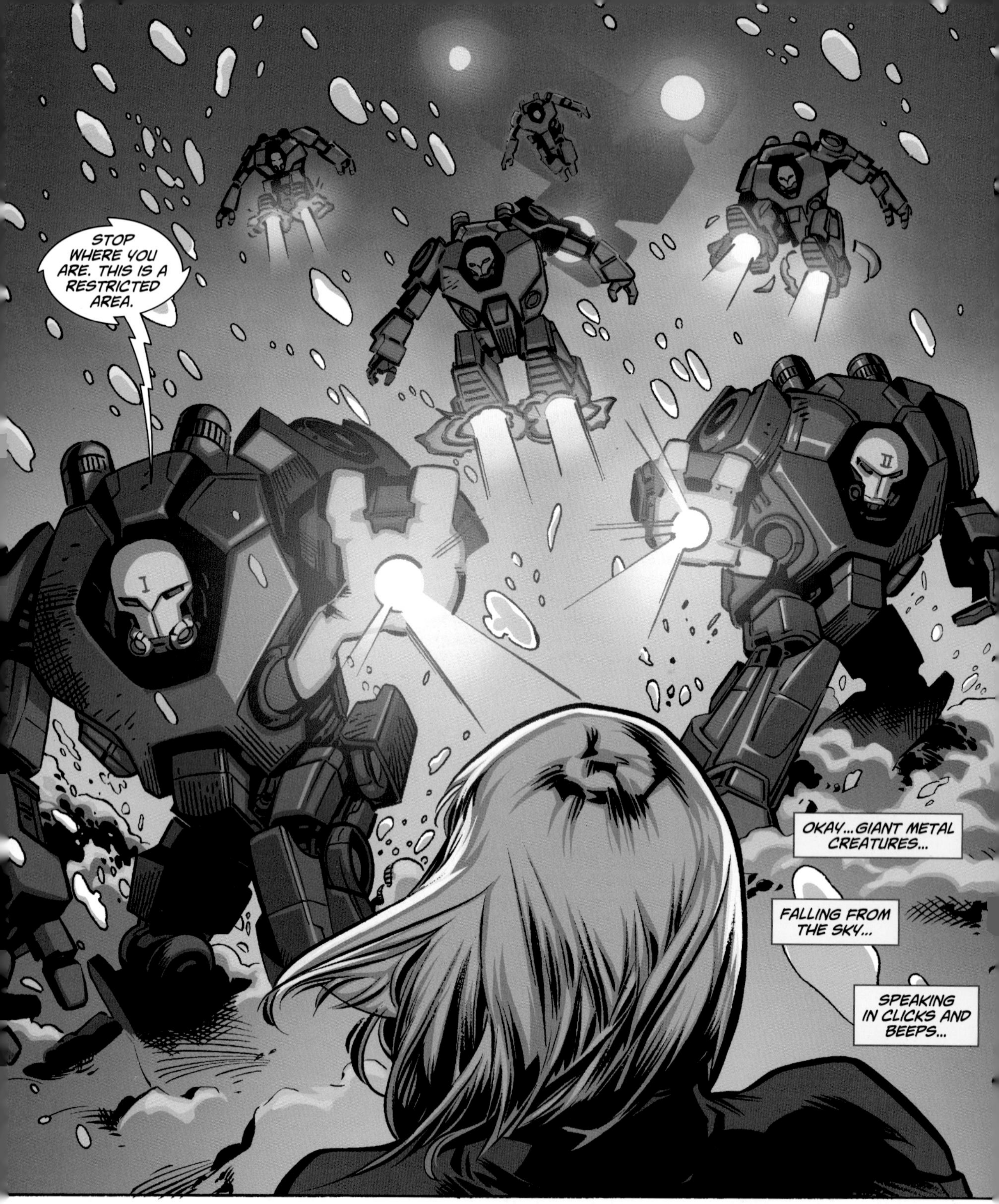
STOP WHERE YOU ARE. THIS IS A RESTRICTED AREA.
OKAY...GIANT METAL CREATURES...
FALLING FROM THE SKY...
SPEAKING IN CLICKS AND BEEPS...

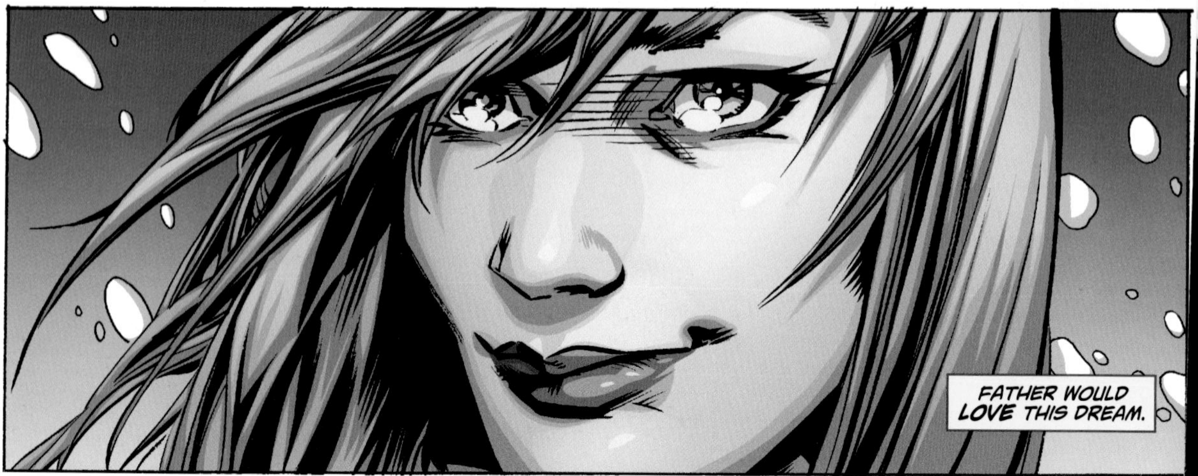
FATHER WOULD LOVE THIS DREAM.

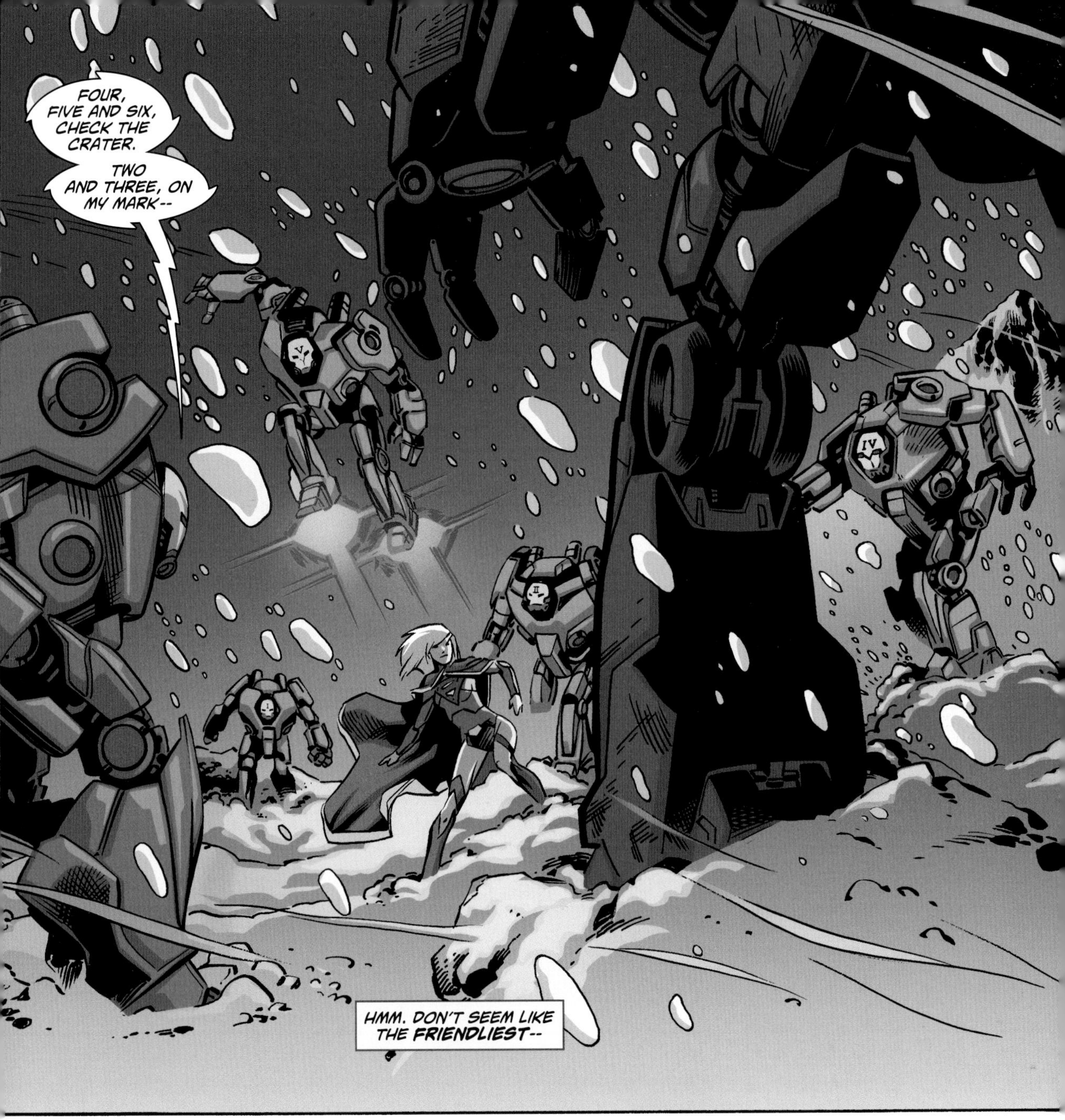
FOUR, FIVE AND SIX, CHECK THE CRATER.
TWO AND THREE, ON MY MARK--
HMM. DON'T SEEM LIKE THE FRIENDLIEST--

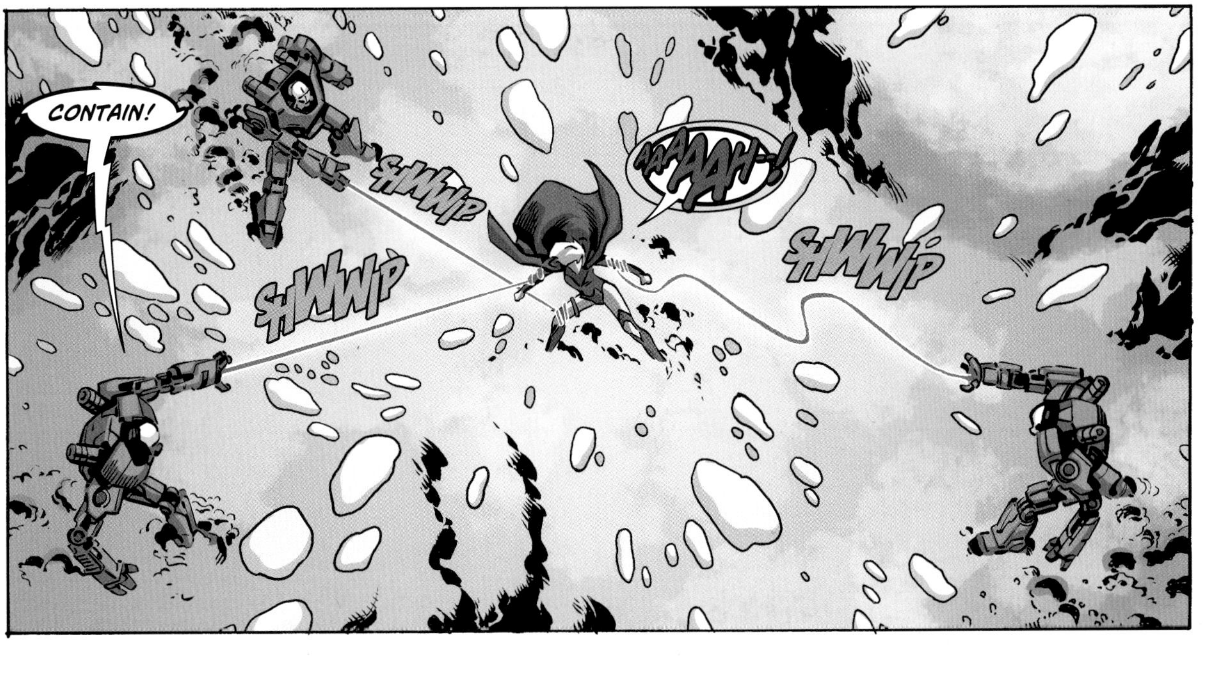
CONTAIN!
SHWWIP
AAAAAH-!
SHWWIP
SHWWIP

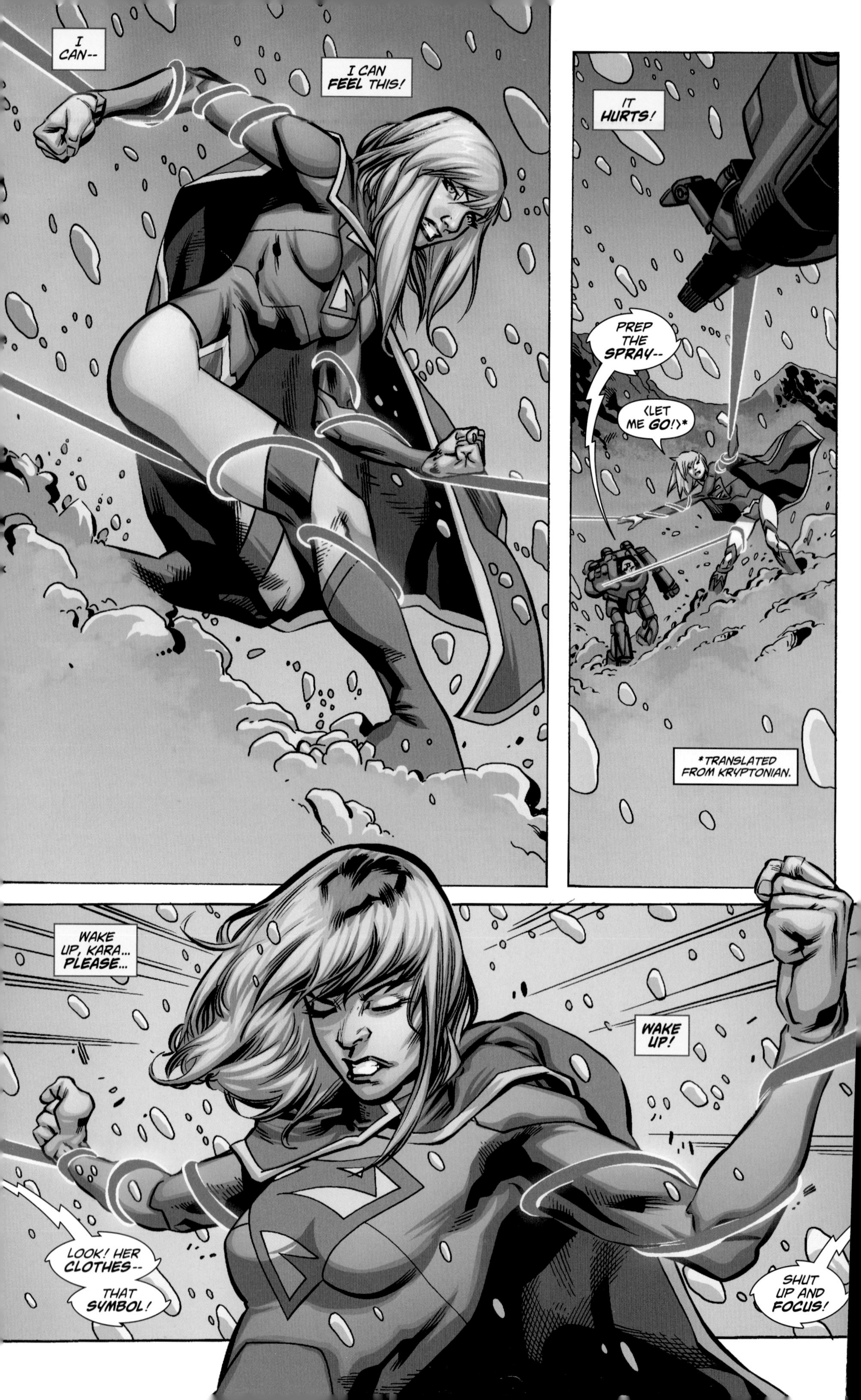
I CAN--
I CAN FEEL THIS!
IT HURTS!
PREP THE SPRAY--
‹LET ME GO!›*
*TRANSLATED FROM KRYPTONIAN.
WAKE UP, KARA... PLEASE...
WAKE UP!
LOOK! HER CLOTHES--
THAT SYMBOL!
SHUT UP AND FOCUS!

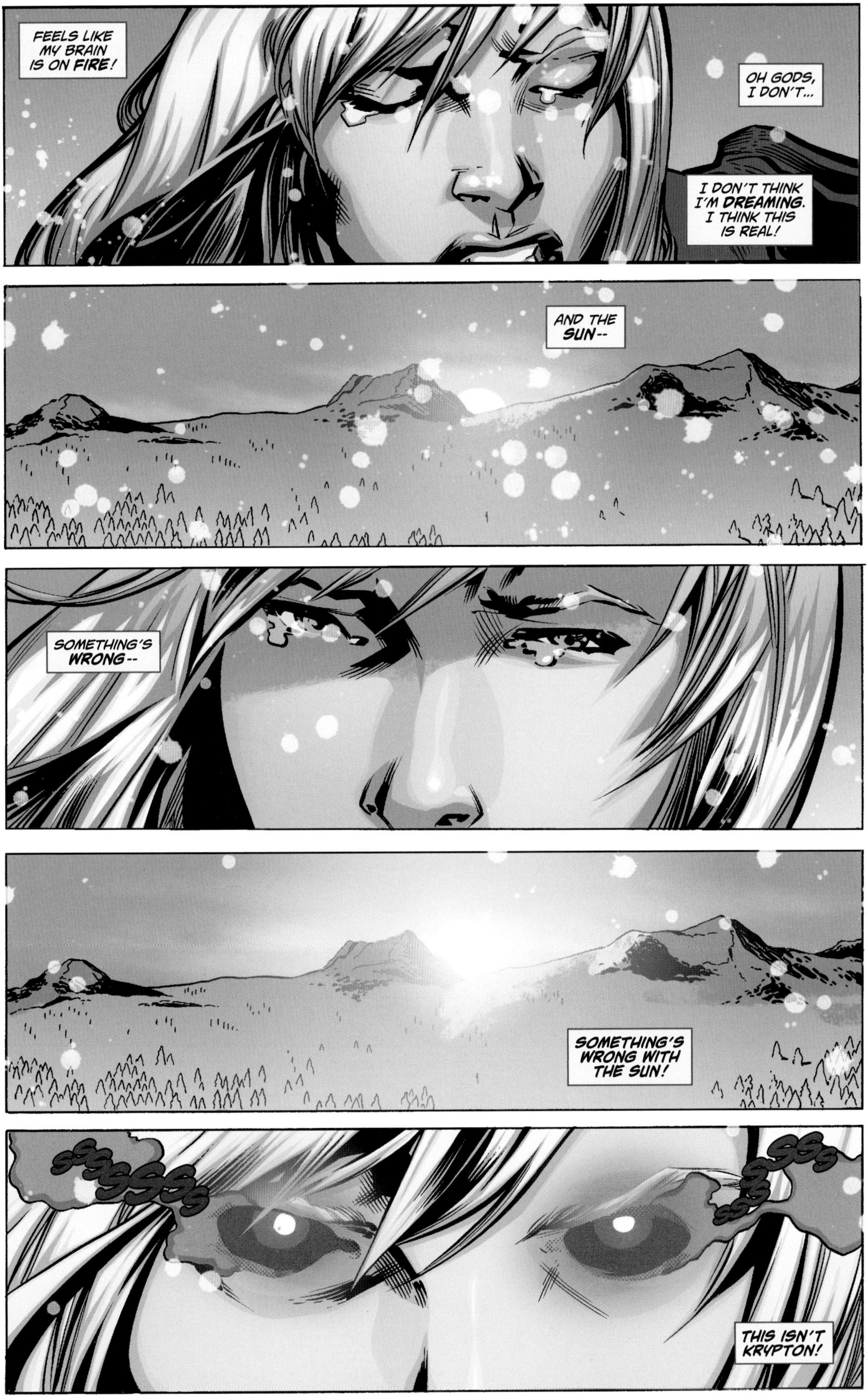
FEELS LIKE MY BRAIN IS ON FIRE!
OH GODS, I DON'T...
I DON'T THINK I'M DREAMING. I THINK THIS IS REAL!
AND THE SUN--
SOMETHING'S WRONG--
SOMETHING'S WRONG WITH THE SUN!
SSSSSSSS
SSSSS
THIS ISN'T KRYPTON!

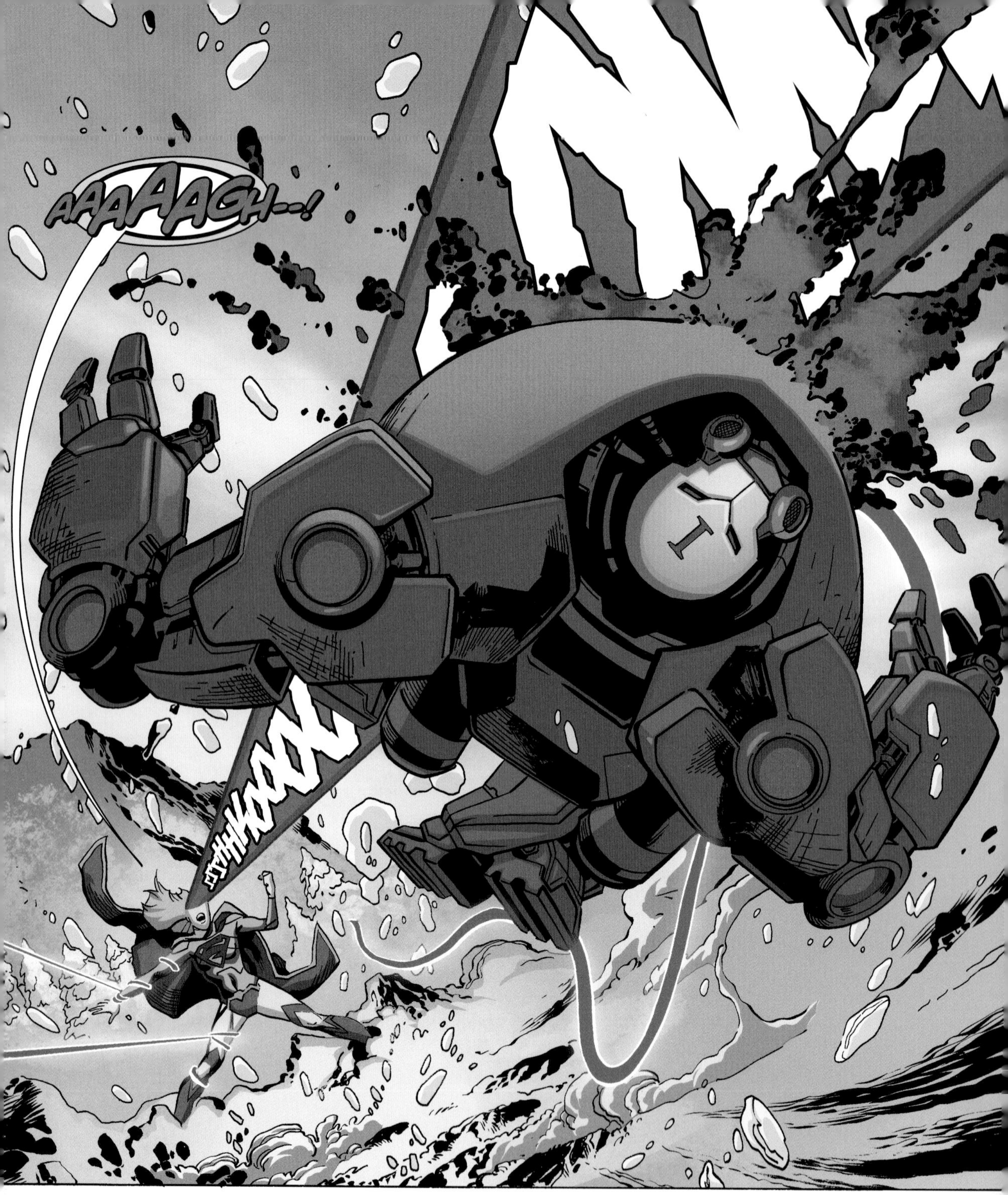
AAAAAAGH--!
THHOOOOOM

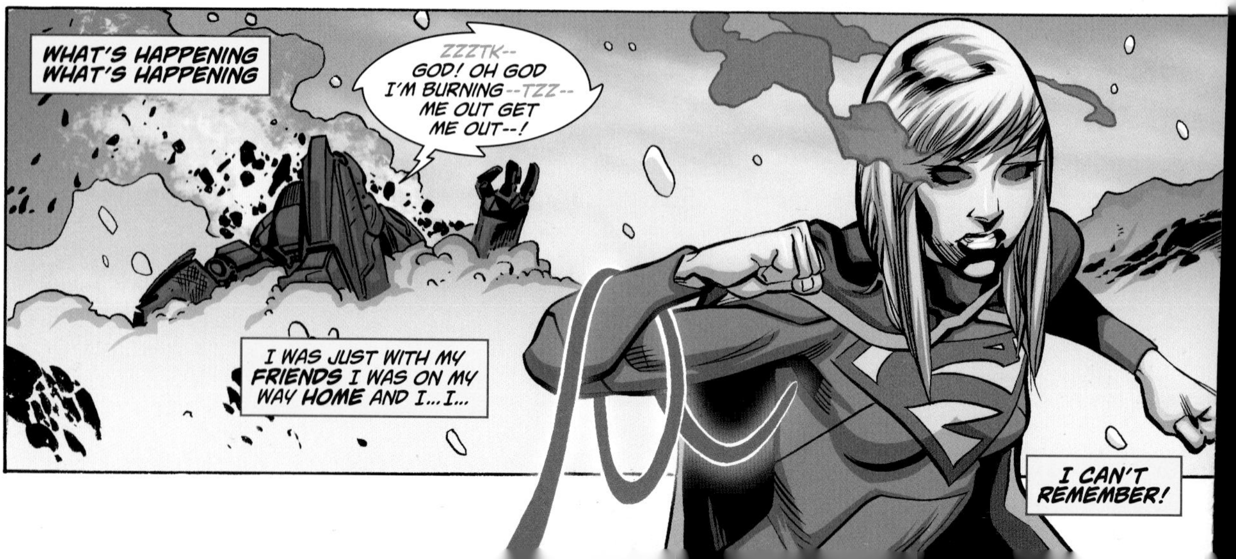
WHAT'S HAPPENING WHAT'S HAPPENING
ZZZTK-- GOD! OH GOD I'M BURNING--TZZ-- ME OUT GET ME OUT--!
I WAS JUST WITH MY FRIENDS I WAS ON MY WAY HOME AND I...I...
I CAN'T REMEMBER!

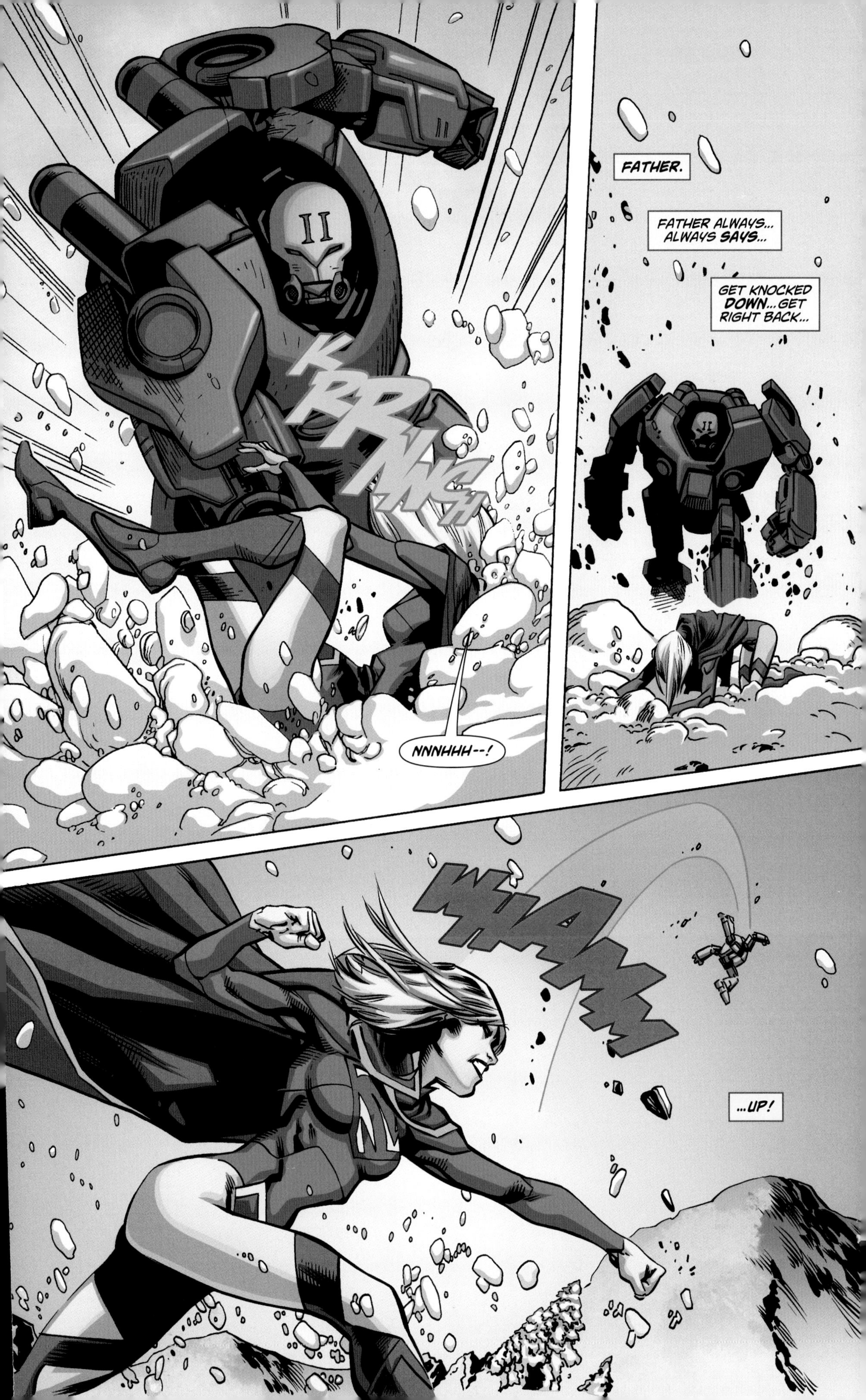
KRRANCH
NNNHHH--!
FATHER.
FATHER ALWAYS... ALWAYS SAYS...
GET KNOCKED DOWN...GET RIGHT BACK...
WHAM
...UP!

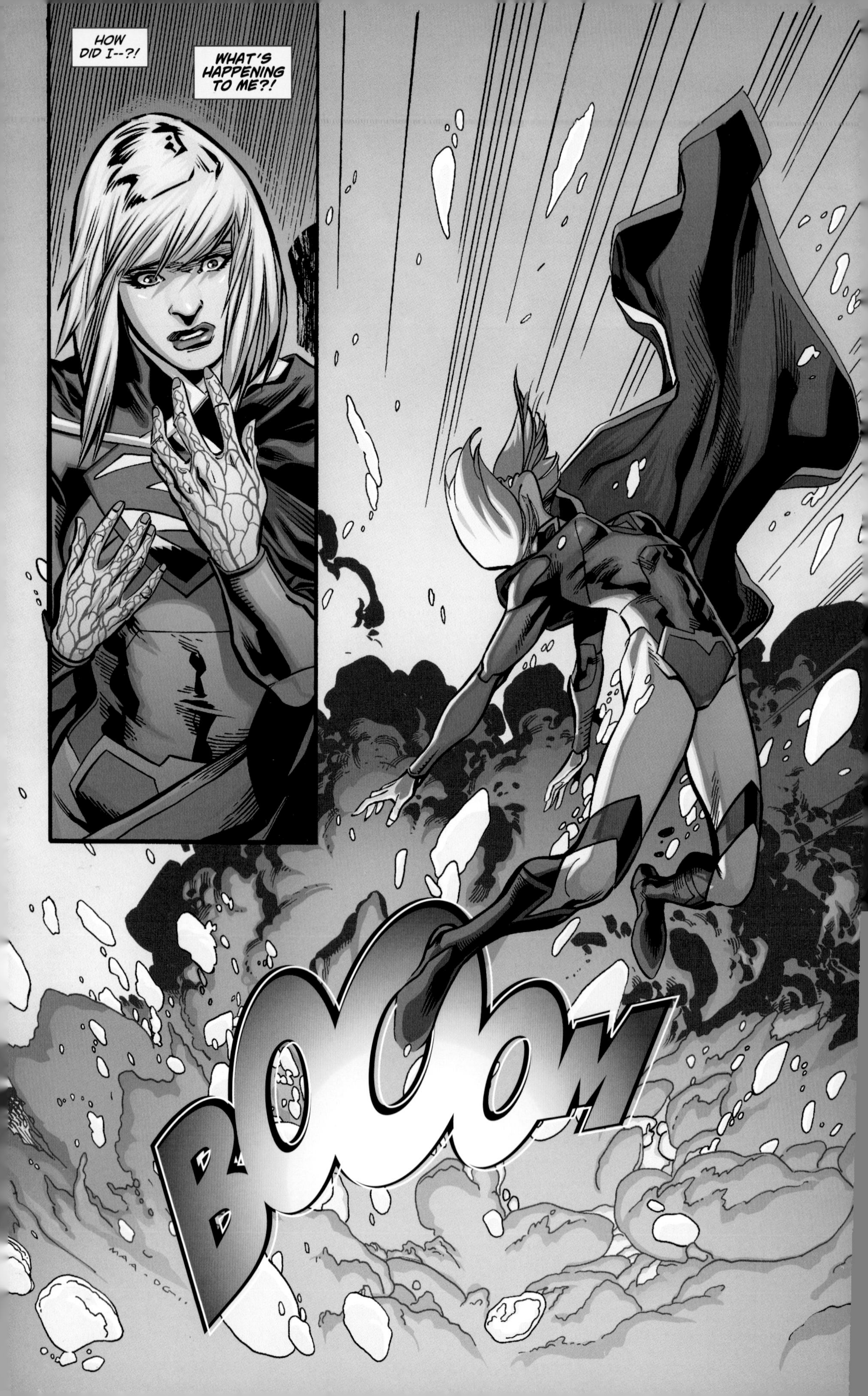
HOW DID I--?!
WHAT'S HAPPENING TO ME?!
BOOOM

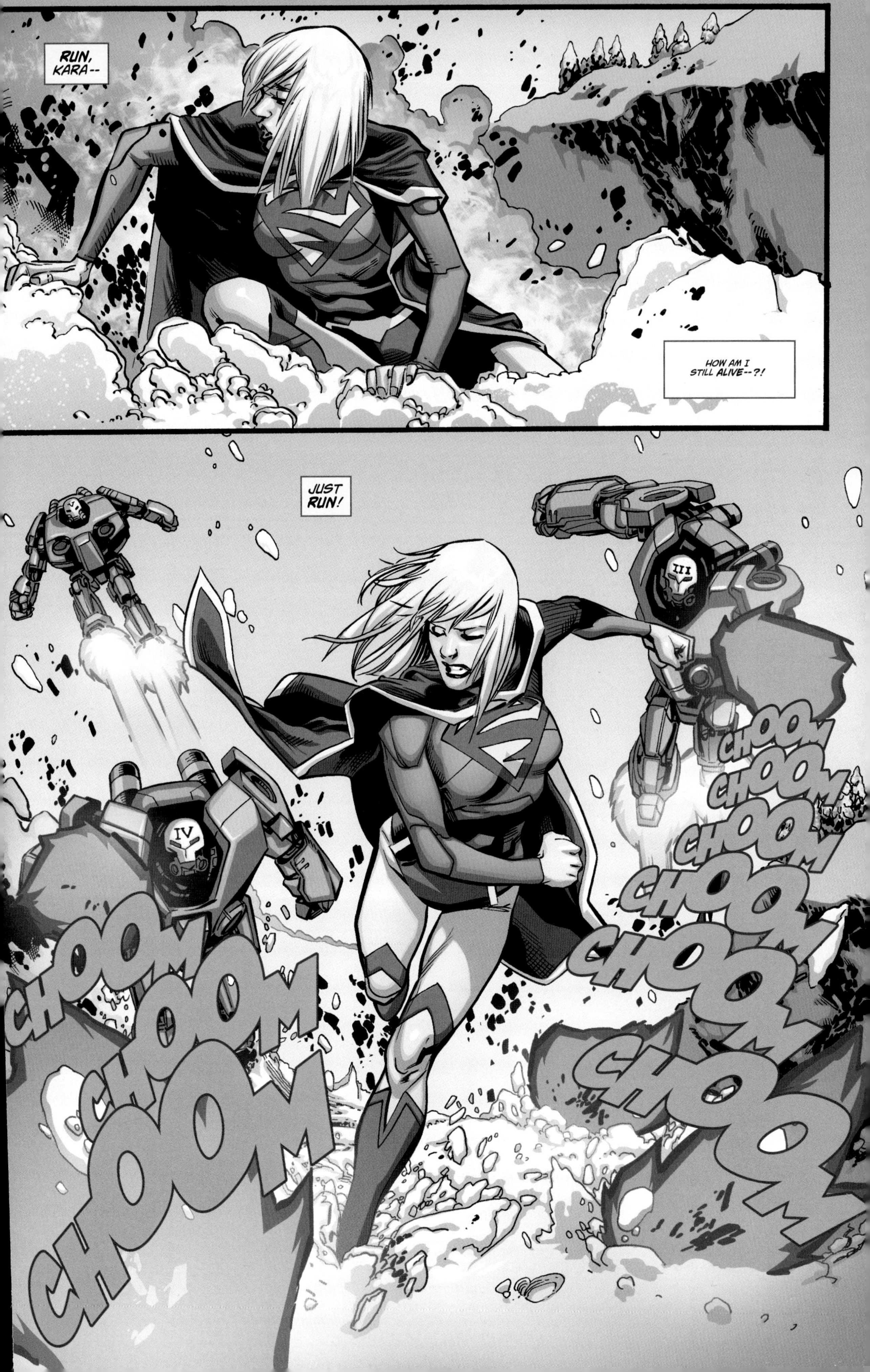
RUN, KARA--
HOW AM I STILL ALIVE--?!
JUST RUN!
CHOOM CHOOM CHOOM
CHOOM CHOOM CHOOM CHOOM CHOOM CHOOM CHOOM

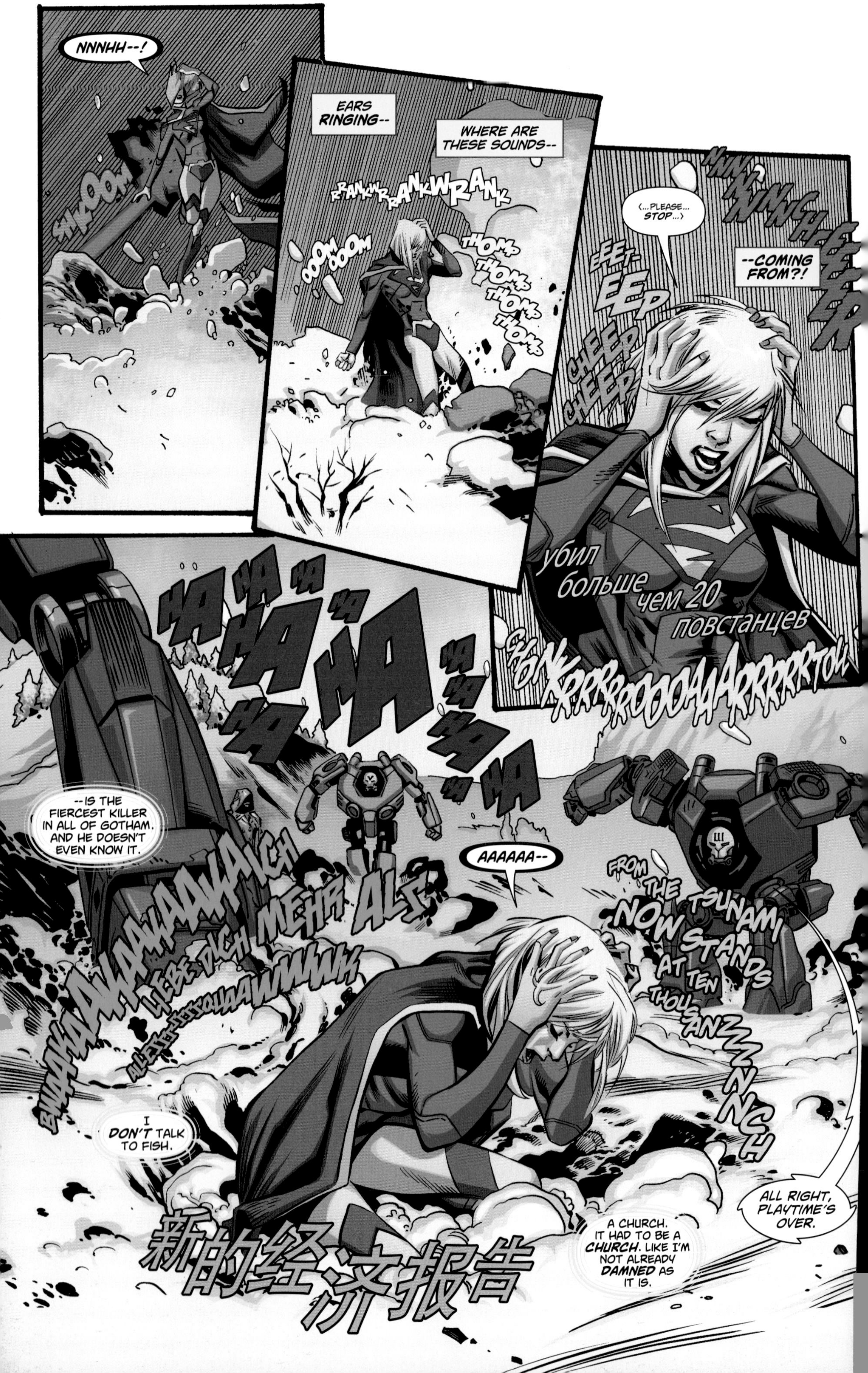
NNNHH--!
SHKOOOM
EARS RINGING--
WHERE ARE THESE SOUNDS--
RRANKWRRANKWRANK
OOOM OOOM
THOMP THOMP THOMP THOMP
‹...PLEASE... STOP...›
--COMING FROM?!
EEEET-EEP
CHEEP CHEEP
убил больше чем 20 повстанцев
HA HA HA HA HA HA HA HA HA HA HA HA HA
--IS THE FIERCEST KILLER IN ALL OF GOTHAM. AND HE DOESN'T EVEN KNOW IT.
AAAAAA--
ICH LIEBE DICH MEHR ALS
FROM THE TSUNAMI NOW STANDS AT TEN THOUSANZZNNCH
I DON'T TALK TO FISH.
新的经济报告
A CHURCH. IT HAD TO BE A CHURCH. LIKE I'M NOT ALREADY DAMNED AS IT IS.
ALL RIGHT, PLAYTIME'S OVER.

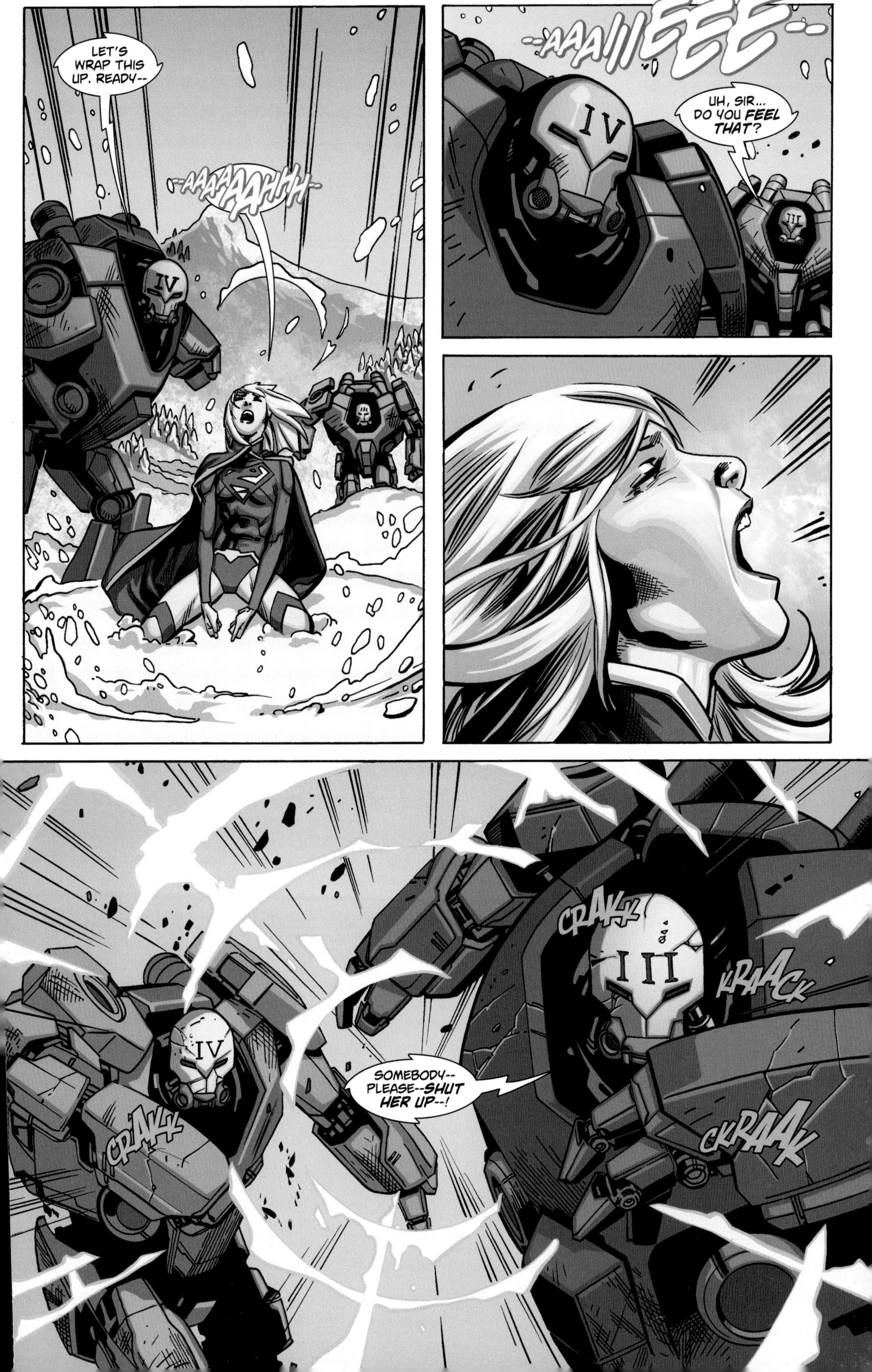
LET'S WRAP THIS UP. READY--
--AAAAAAHHH--
--AAAIIIEEE--
UH, SIR... DO YOU FEEL THAT?
CRAKK
KRAACK
CRAKK
SOMEBODY-- PLEASE--SHUT HER UP--!
CKRAAK

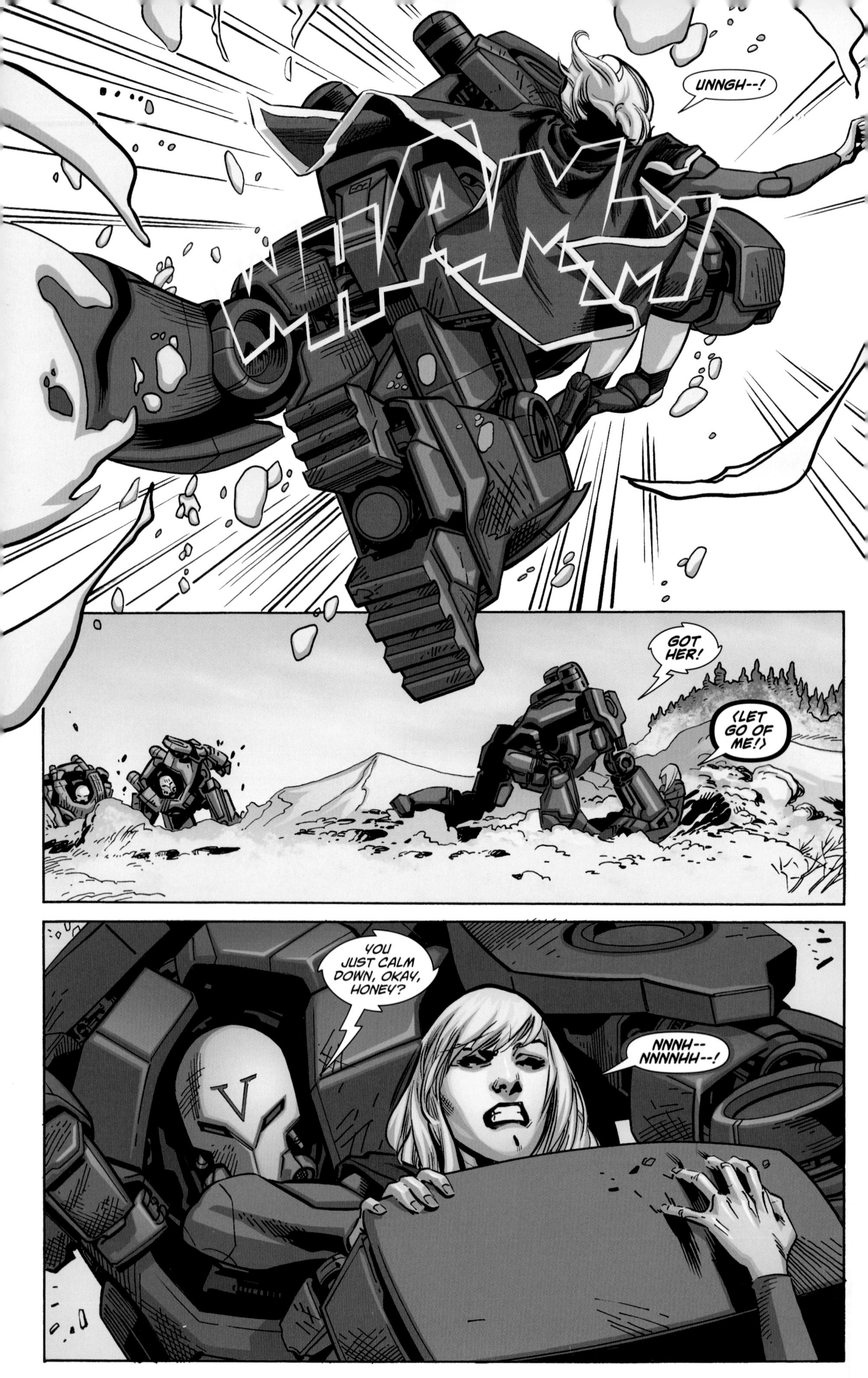
UNNGH--!
WHAM
GOT HER!
‹LET GO OF ME!›
YOU JUST CALM DOWN, OKAY, HONEY?
NNNH-- NNNNHH--!

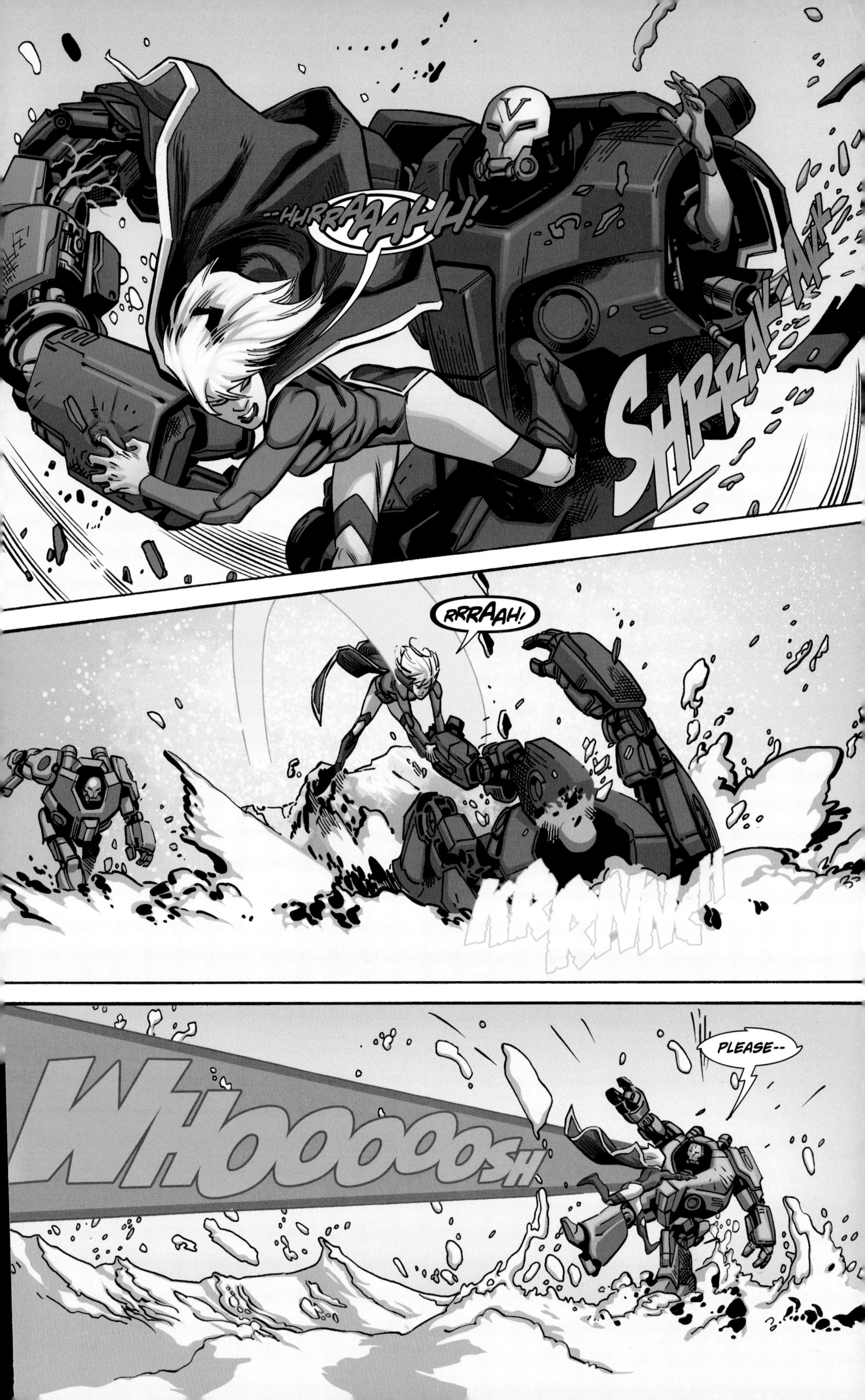
--HHRRAAAHH!
SHRRAK-AKK
RRRAAH!
KRRANNCH
WHOOOOOSH
PLEASE--

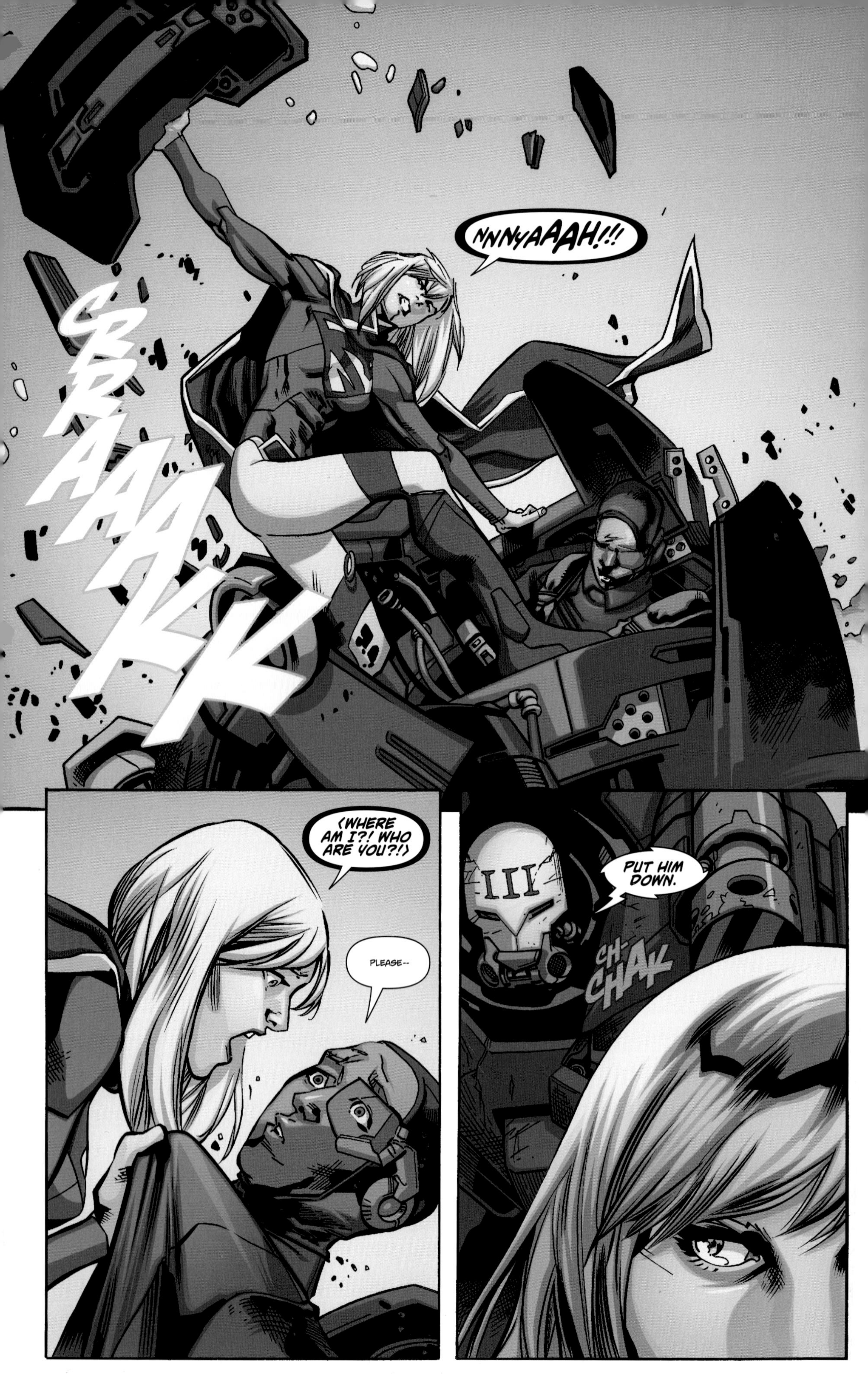
NNNYAAAH!!!
CRRAAAAKK
‹WHERE AM I?! WHO ARE YOU?!›
PLEASE--
PUT HIM DOWN.
CH-CHAK

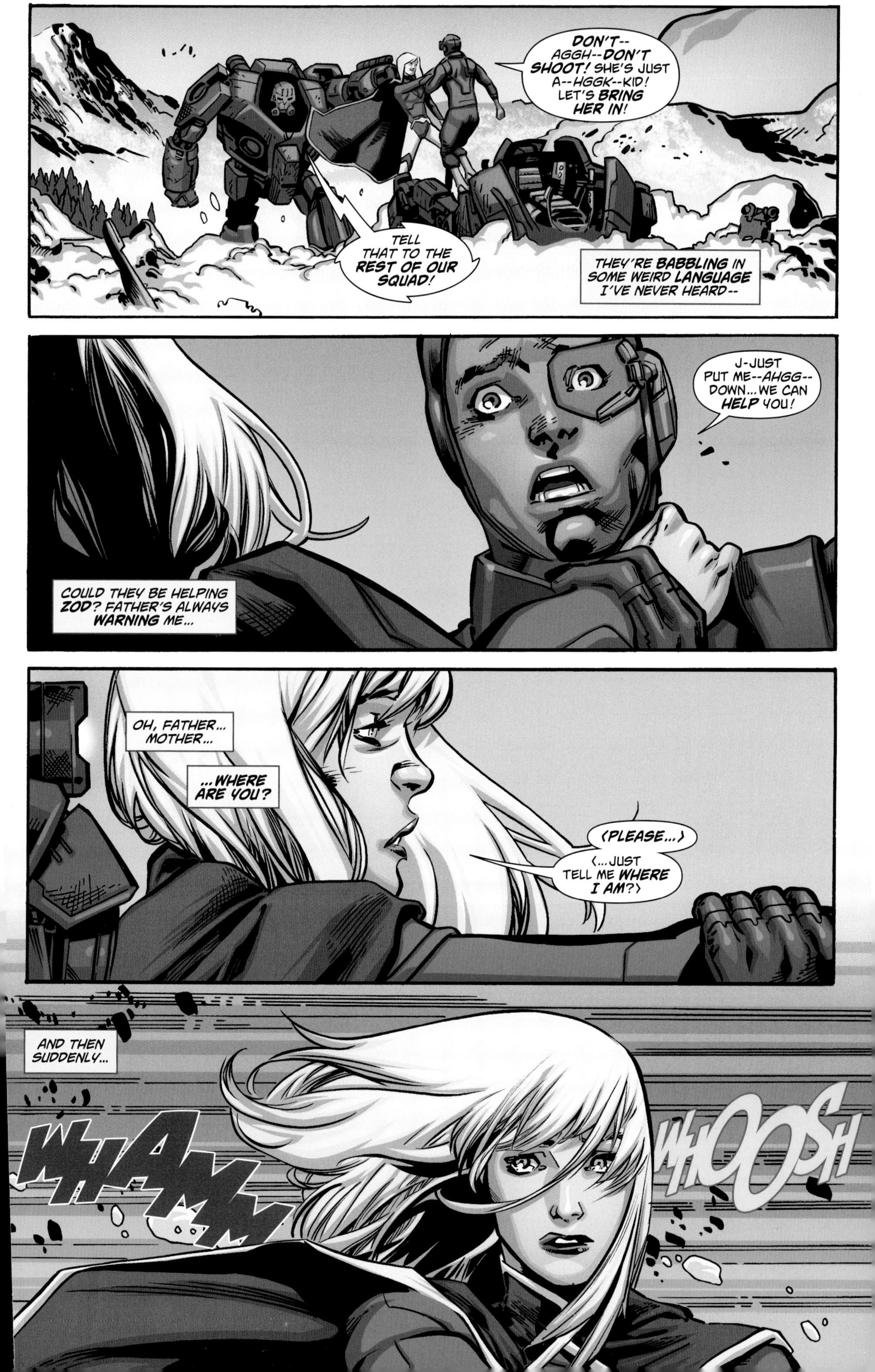
DON'T--AGGH--DON'T SHOOT! SHE'S JUST A--HGGK--KID! LET'S BRING HER IN!
TELL THAT TO THE REST OF OUR SQUAD!
THEY'RE BABBLING IN SOME WEIRD LANGUAGE I'VE NEVER HEARD--
J-JUST PUT ME--AHGG--DOWN...WE CAN HELP YOU!
COULD THEY BE HELPING ZOD? FATHER'S ALWAYS WARNING ME...
OH, FATHER... MOTHER...
...WHERE ARE YOU?
<PLEASE...>
<...JUST TELL ME WHERE I AM?>
AND THEN SUDDENLY...
WHAM
WHOOSH

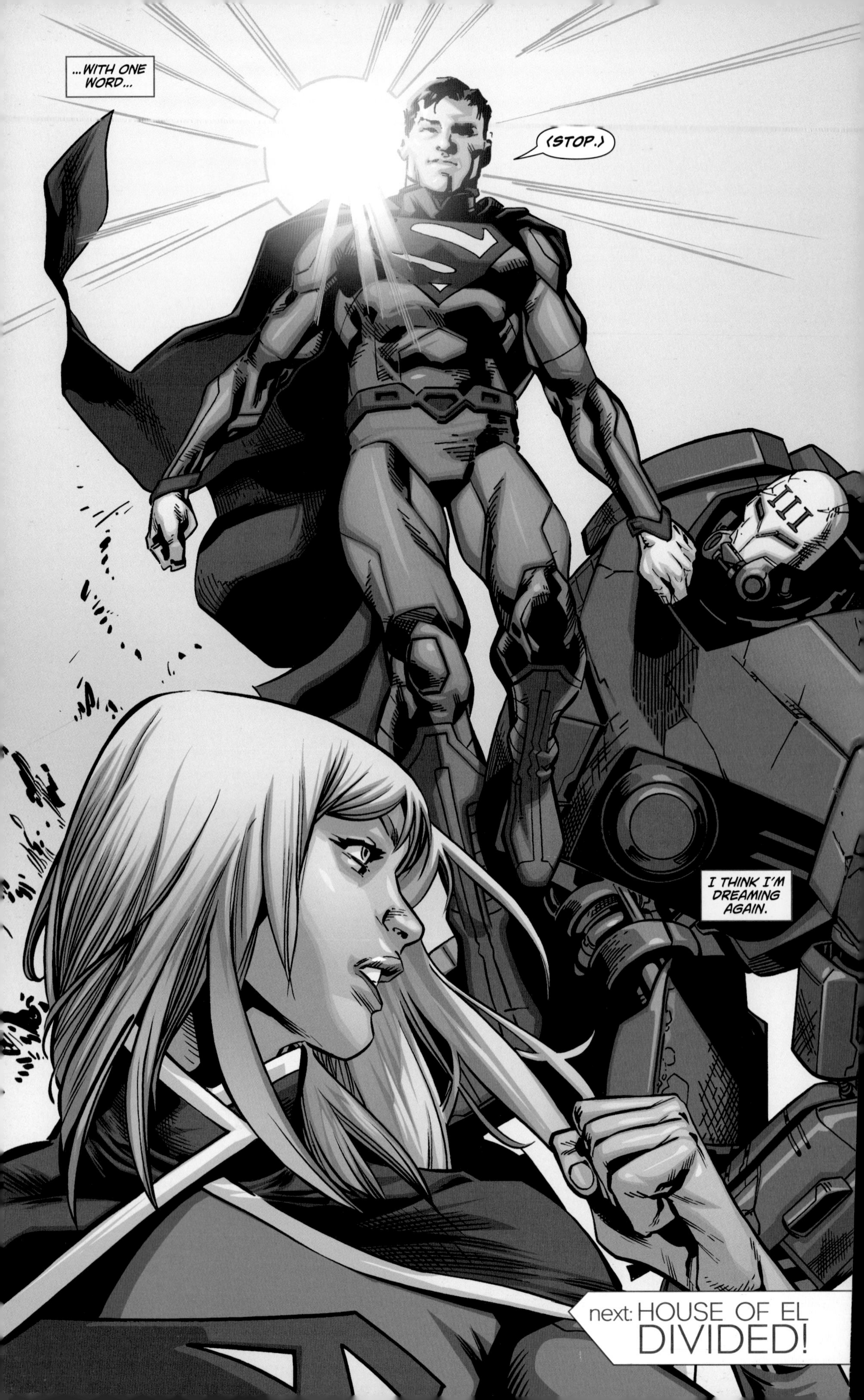
...WITH ONE WORD...
(STOP.)
I THINK I'M DREAMING AGAIN.
next: HOUSE OF EL DIVIDED!

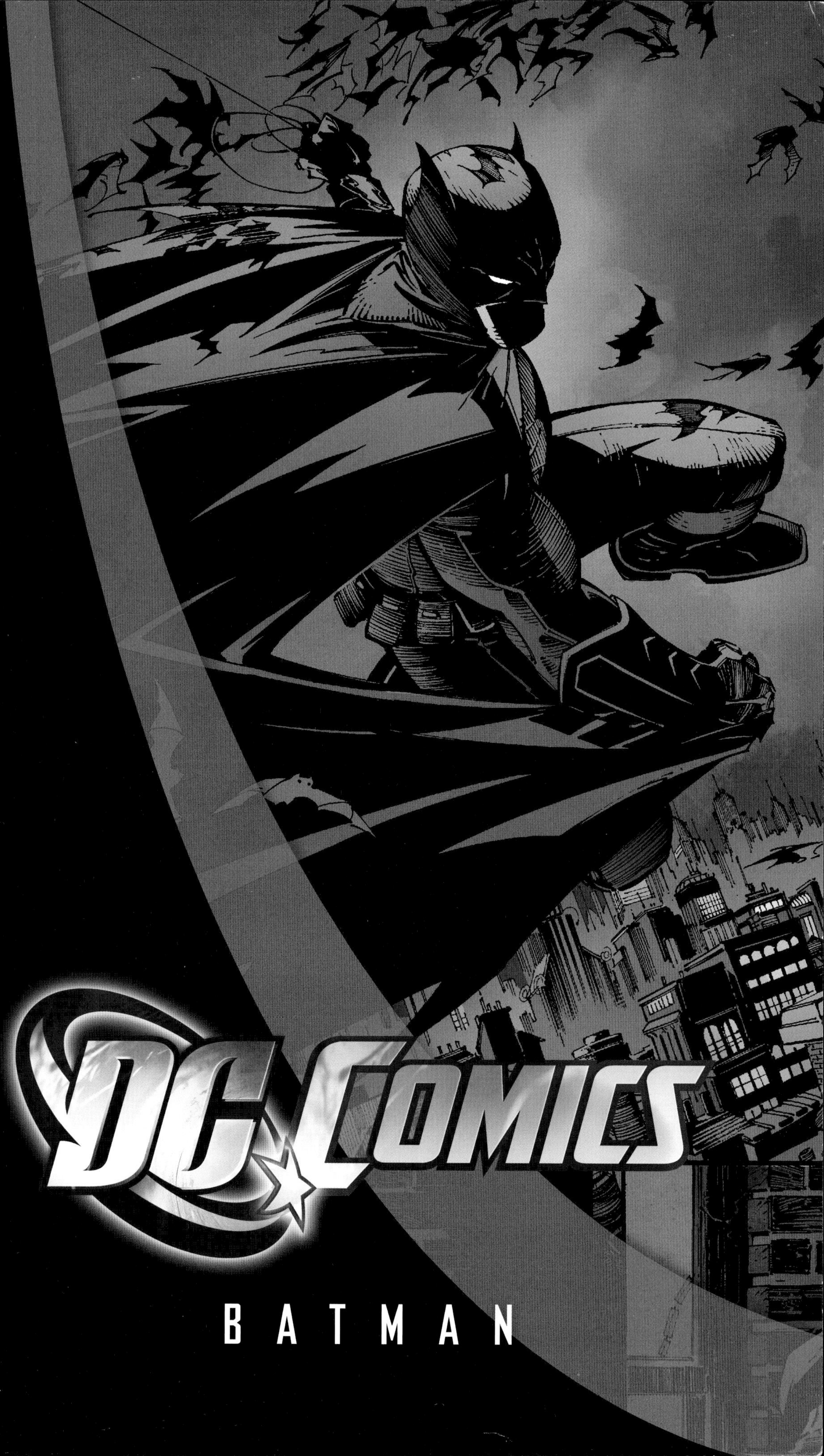

DC COMICS

BATMAN

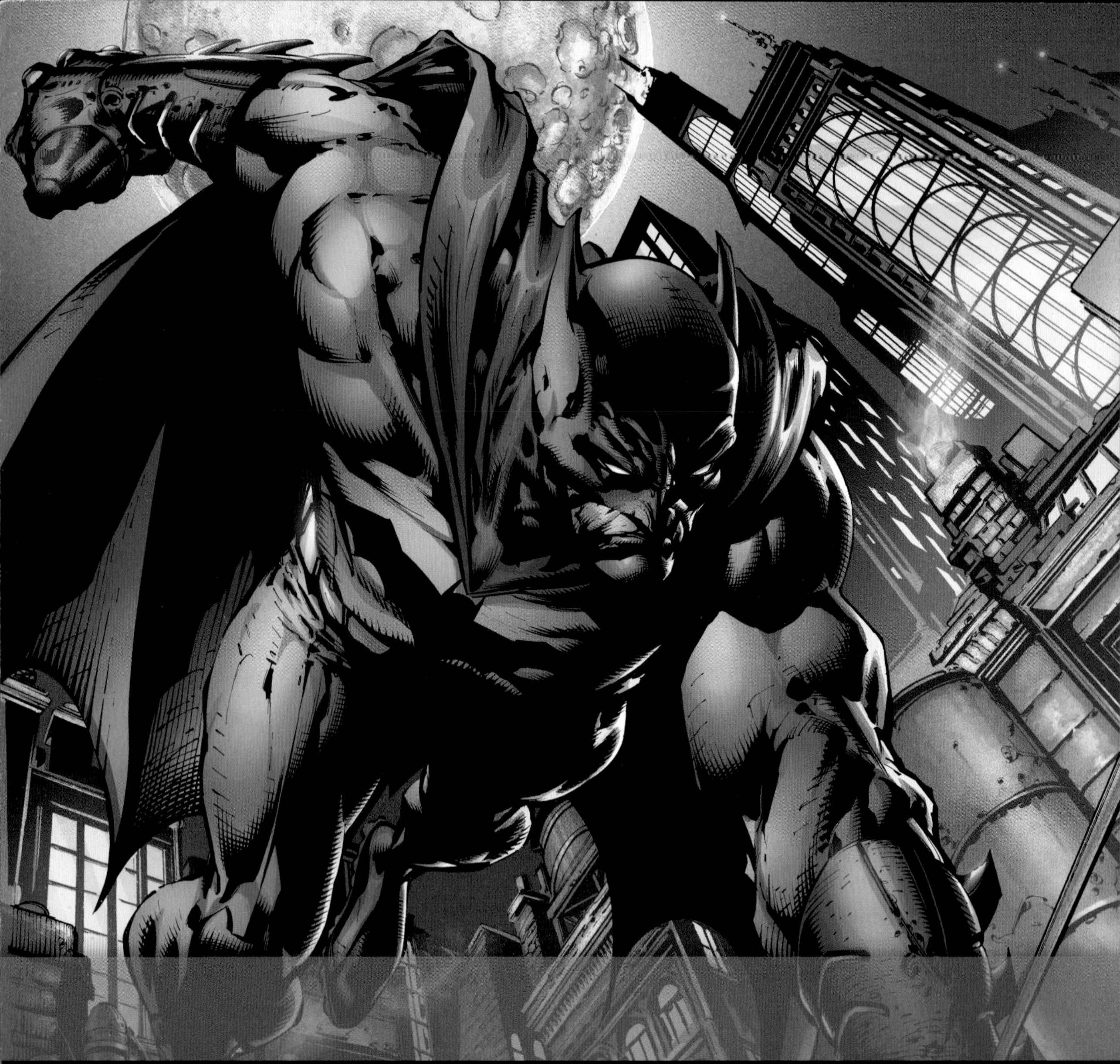

BATMAN #1 Scott Snyder, Greg Capullo & Jonathan Glapion

DETECTIVE COMICS #1 Tony S. Daniel & Ryan Winn

BATWOMAN #1 J.H. Williams III & W. Haden Blackman

BATMAN: THE DARK KNIGHT #1 David Finch, Paul Jenkins & Richard Friend

BATMAN AND ROBIN #1 Peter J. Tomasi, Patrick Gleason & Mick Gray

BATGIRL #1 Gail Simone, Ardian Syaf & Vicente Cifuentes

BATWING #1 Judd Winick & Ben Oliver

CATWOMAN #1 Judd Winick & Guillem March

NIGHTWING #1 Kyle Higgins, Eddy Barrows & J.P. Mayer

BIRDS OF PREY #1 Duane Swierczynski & Jesus Saiz

RED HOOD AND THE OUTLAWS #1 Scott Lobdell & Kenneth Rocafort

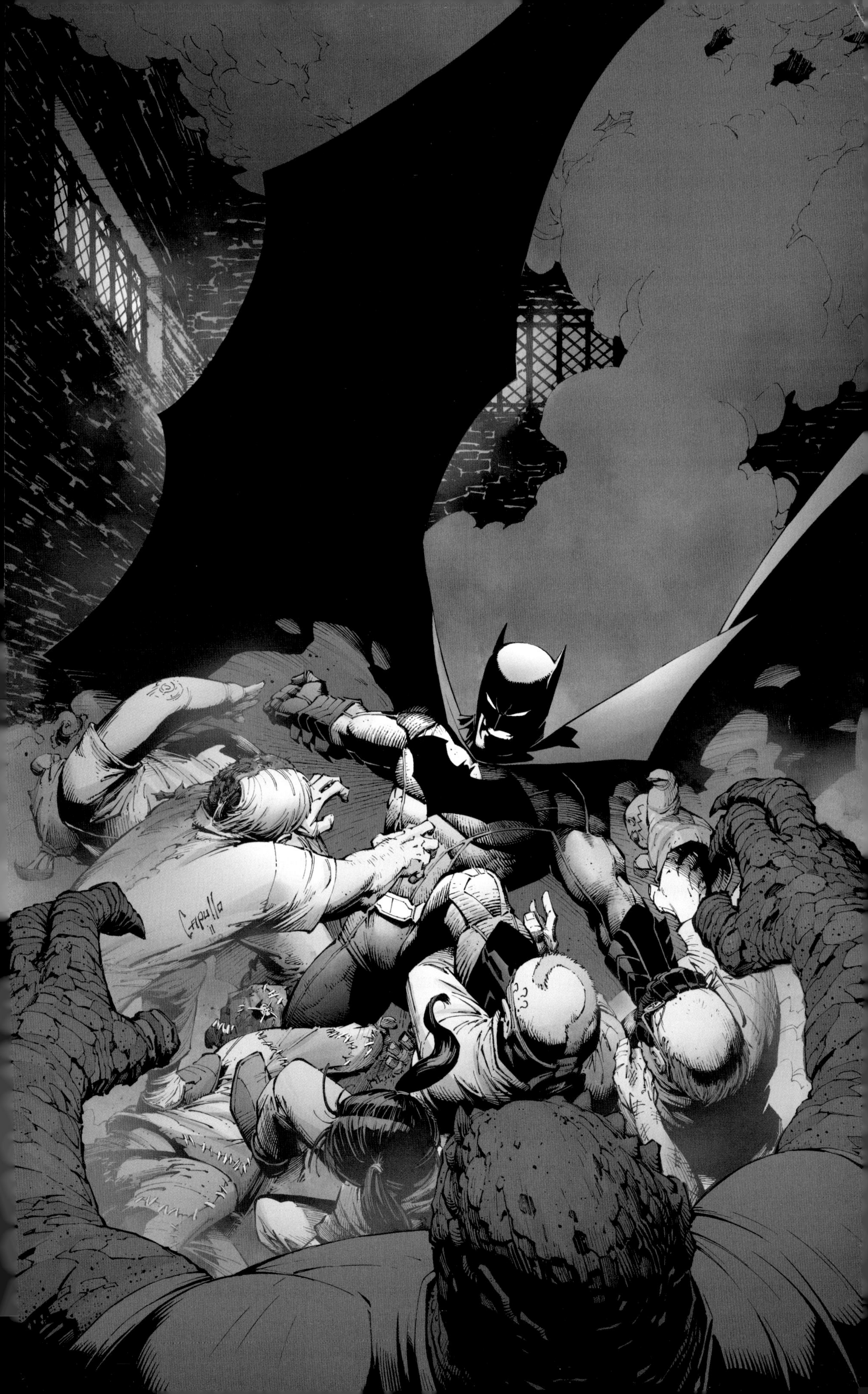
Capullo '11

BATMAN

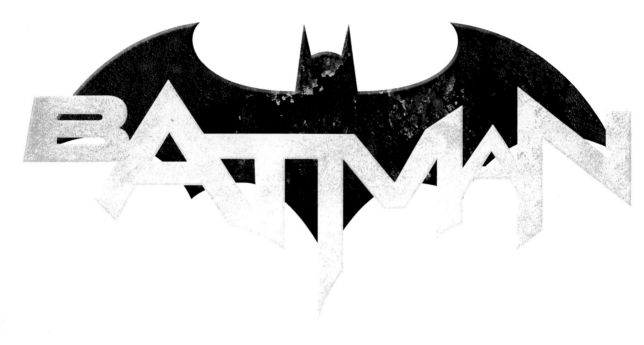

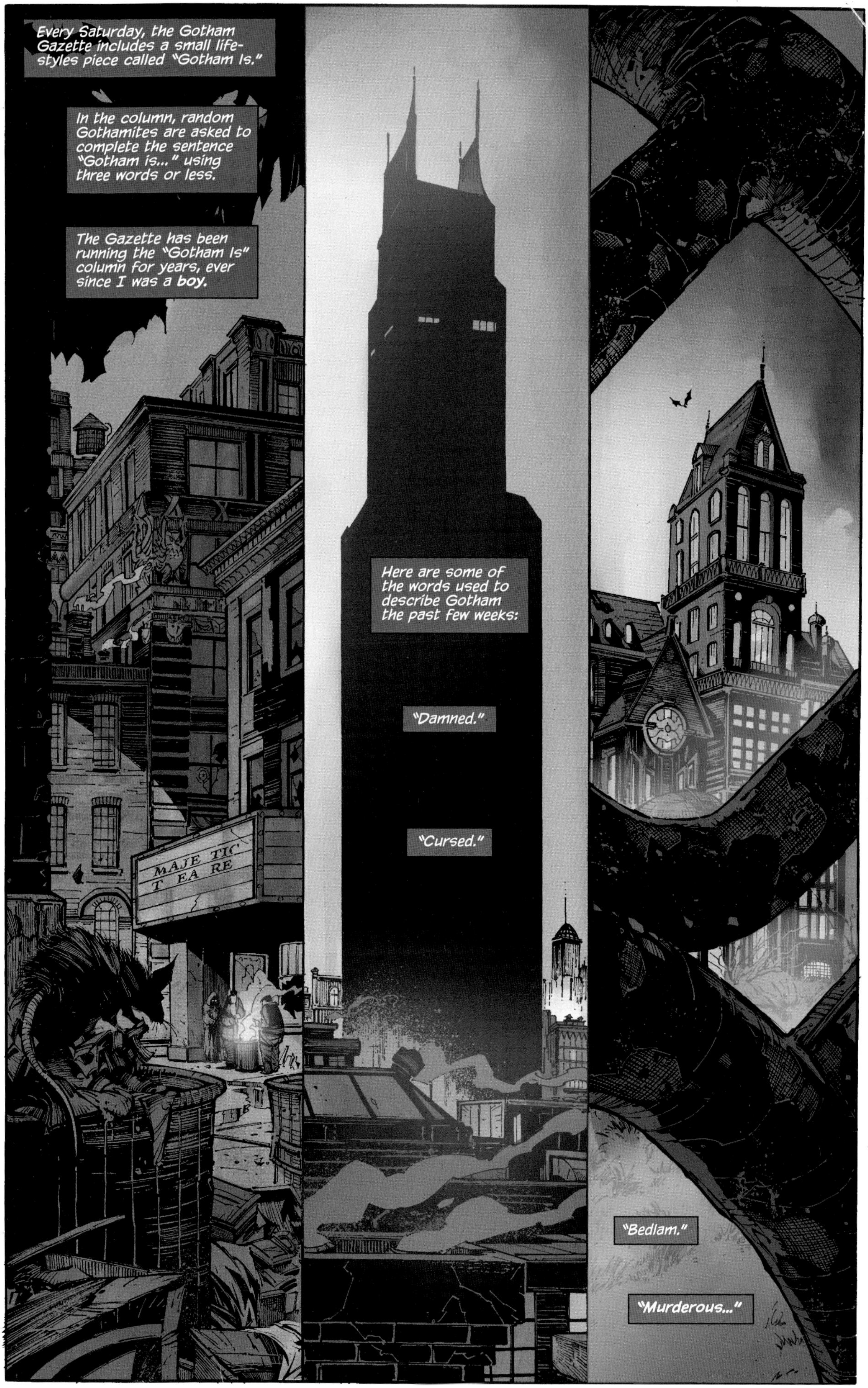
Every Saturday, the Gotham Gazette includes a small life-styles piece called "Gotham Is."
In the column, random Gothamites are asked to complete the sentence "Gotham is..." using three words or less.
The Gazette has been running the "Gotham Is" column for years, ever since I was a **boy.**
MAJE TIC
T EA RE
Here are some of the words used to describe Gotham the past few weeks:
"Damned."
"Cursed."
"Bedlam."
"Murderous..."

DC COMICS PROUDLY PRESENTS

BATMAN

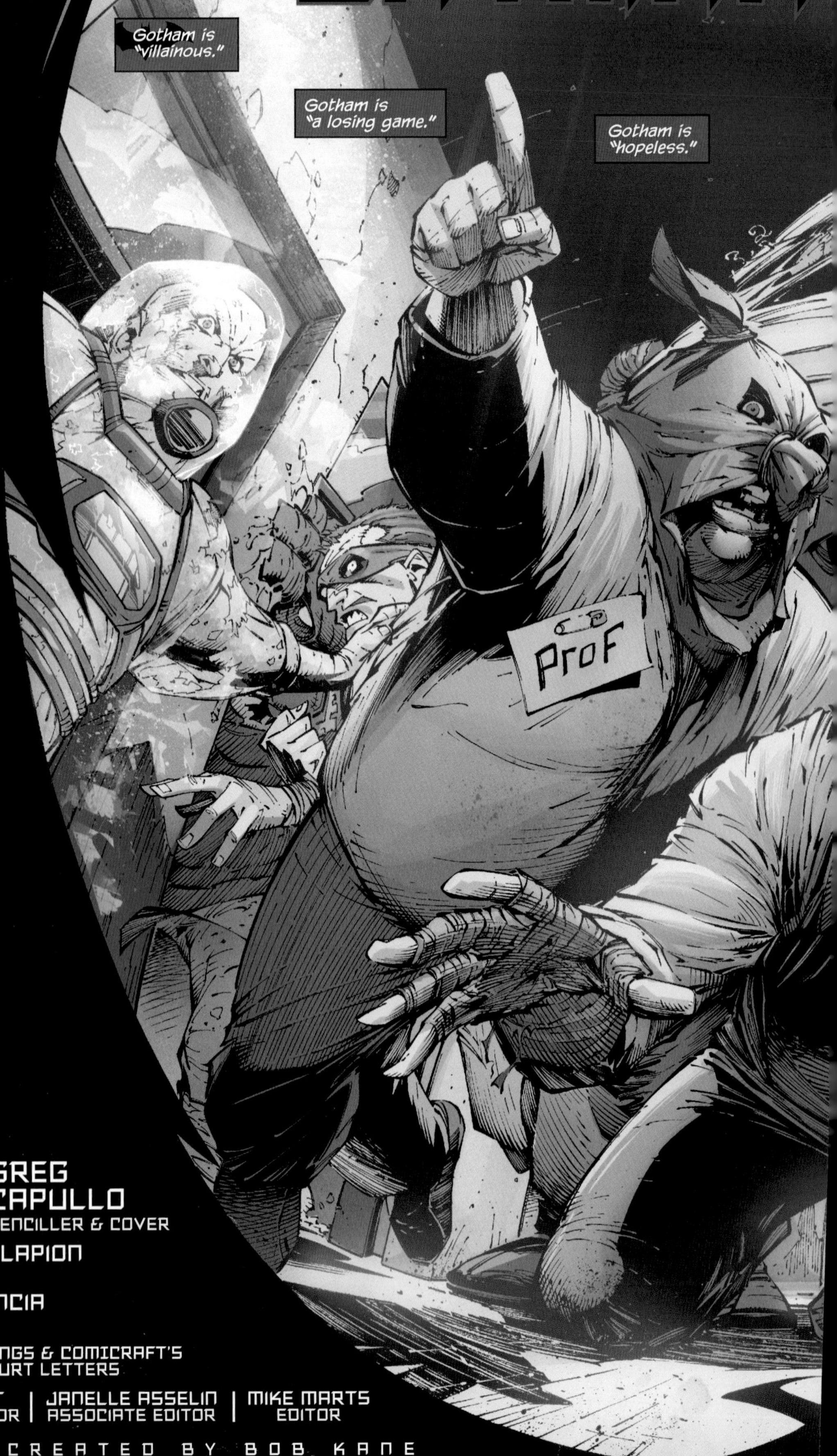

SCOTT SNYDER
WRITER

GREG CAPULLO
PENCILLER & COVER

JONATHAN GLAPION
INKER

FCO PLASCENCIA
COLORS

RICHARD STARKINGS & COMICRAFT'S JIMMY BETANCOURT LETTERS

KATIE KUBERT ASSISTANT EDITOR | JANELLE ASSELIN ASSOCIATE EDITOR | MIKE MARTS EDITOR

BATMAN CREATED BY BOB KANE

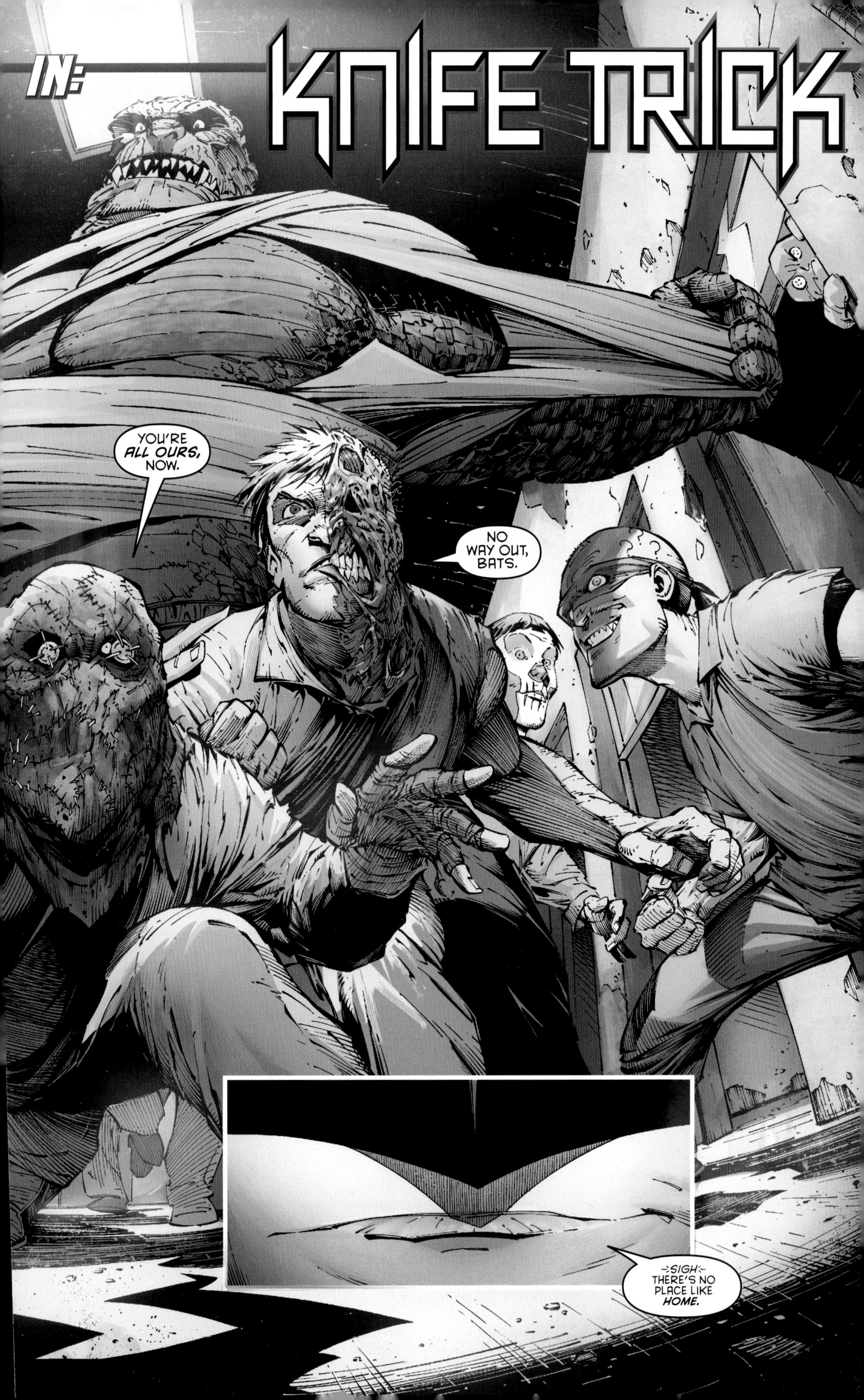
IN:
KNIFE TRICK
YOU'RE ALL OURS, NOW.
NO WAY OUT, BATS.
-SIGH-
THERE'S NO PLACE LIKE HOME.

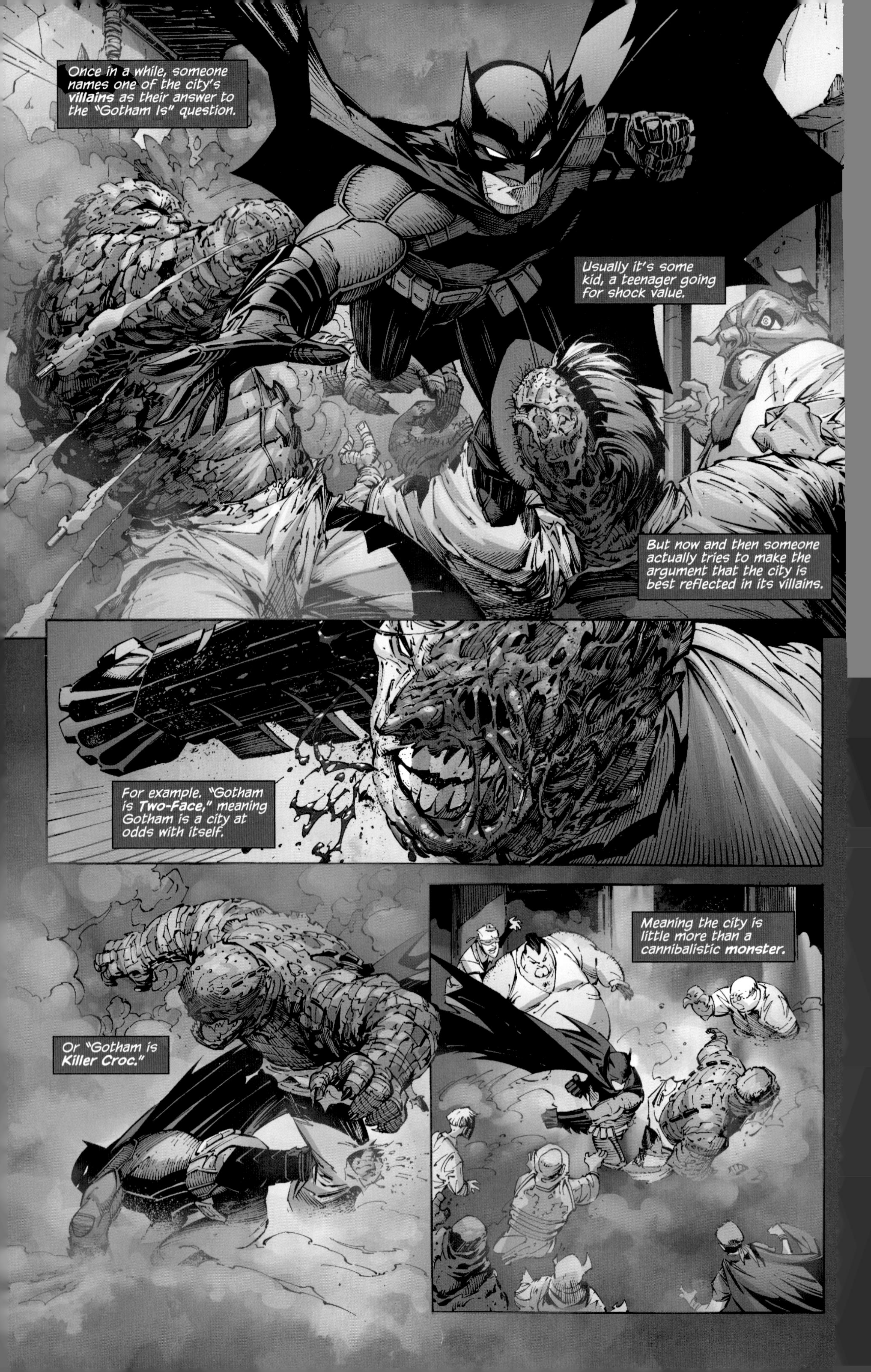

Once in a while, someone names one of the city's **villains** as their answer to the "Gotham Is" question.
Usually it's some kid, a teenager going for shock value.
But now and then someone actually tries to make the argument that the city is best reflected in its villains.
For example, "Gotham is **Two-Face**," meaning Gotham is a city at odds with itself.
Or "Gotham is **Killer Croc.**"
Meaning the city is little more than a cannibalistic **monster.**

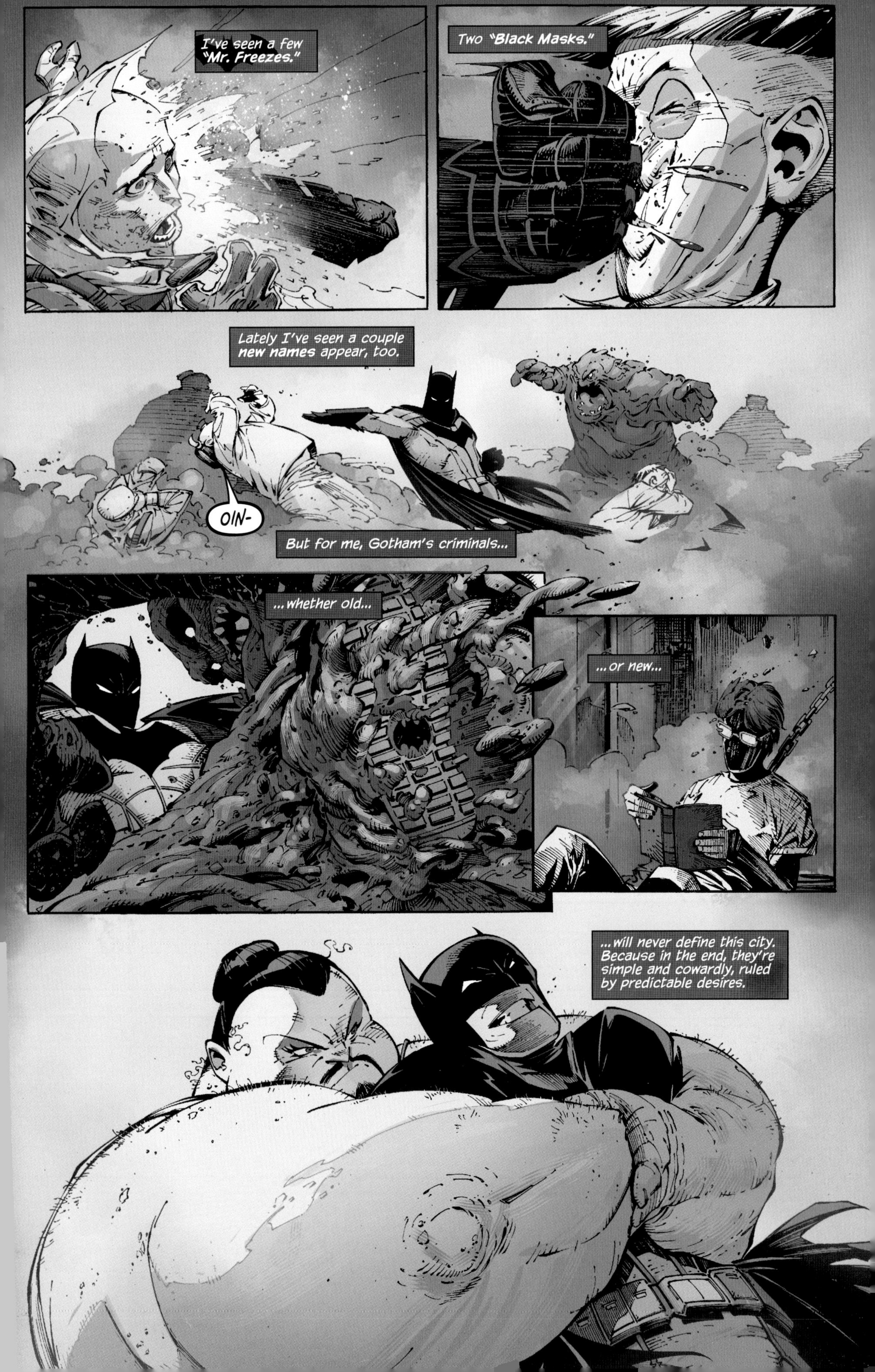
I've seen a few "Mr. Freezes."
Two "Black Masks."
Lately I've seen a couple new names appear, too.
OIN-
But for me, Gotham's criminals...
...whether old...
...or new...
...will never define this city. Because in the end, they're simple and cowardly, ruled by predictable desires.

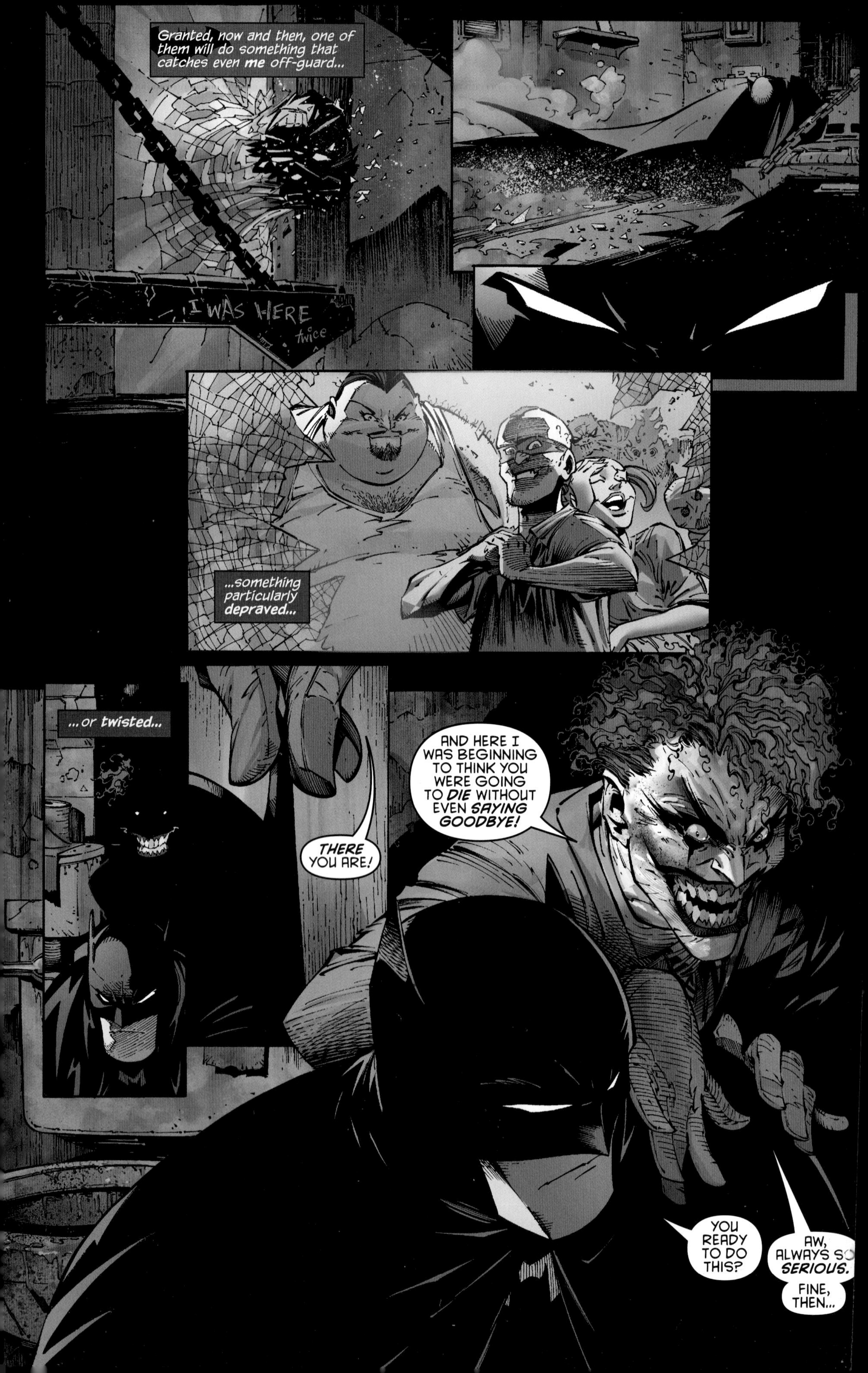
Granted, now and then, one of them will do something that catches even me off-guard...
I WAS HERE twice
...something particularly depraved...
...or twisted...
THERE YOU ARE!
AND HERE I WAS BEGINNING TO THINK YOU WERE GOING TO DIE WITHOUT EVEN SAYING GOODBYE!
YOU READY TO DO THIS?
AW, ALWAYS SO SERIOUS.
FINE, THEN...

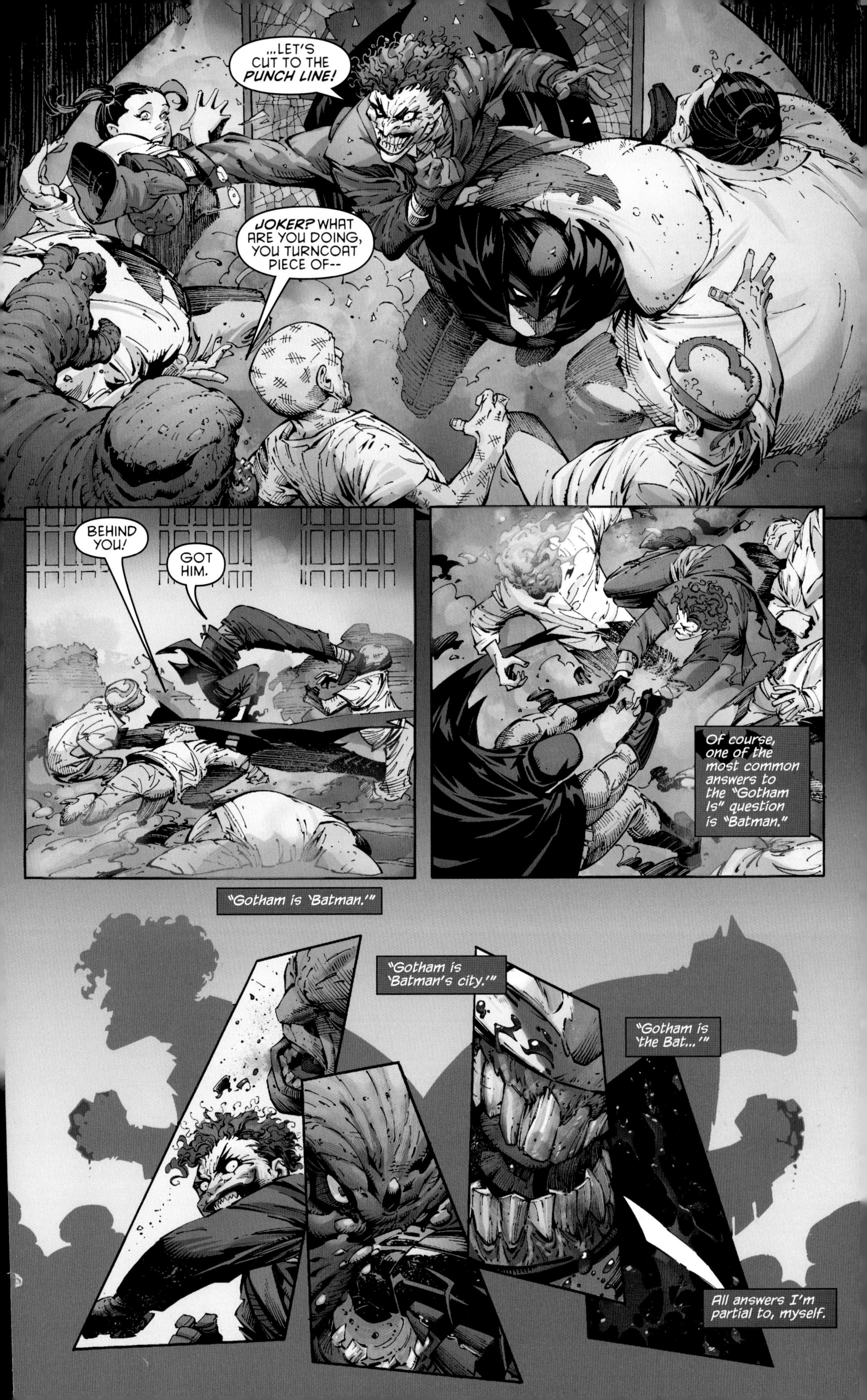
...LET'S CUT TO THE PUNCH LINE!
JOKER? WHAT ARE YOU DOING, YOU TURNCOAT PIECE OF--
BEHIND YOU!
GOT HIM.
Of course, one of the most common answers to the "Gotham Is" question is "Batman."
"Gotham is 'Batman.'"
"Gotham is 'Batman's city.'"
"Gotham is 'the Bat...'"
All answers I'm partial to, myself.

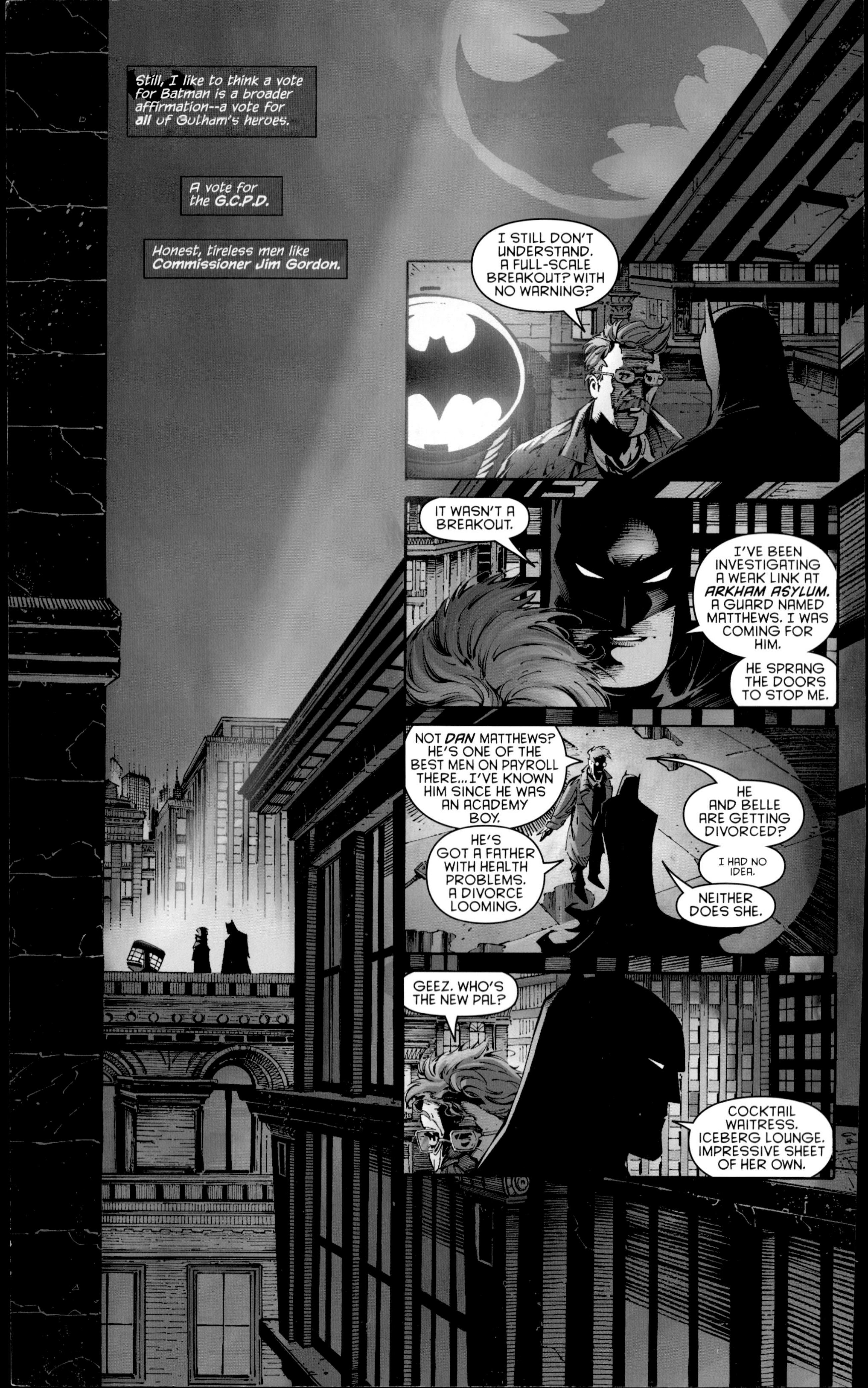
Still, I like to think a vote for Batman is a broader affirmation--a vote for all of Gotham's heroes.
A vote for the G.C.P.D.
Honest, tireless men like Commissioner Jim Gordon.
I STILL DON'T UNDERSTAND. A FULL-SCALE BREAKOUT? WITH NO WARNING?
IT WASN'T A BREAKOUT.
I'VE BEEN INVESTIGATING A WEAK LINK AT ARKHAM ASYLUM. A GUARD NAMED MATTHEWS. I WAS COMING FOR HIM.
HE SPRANG THE DOORS TO STOP ME.
NOT DAN MATTHEWS? HE'S ONE OF THE BEST MEN ON PAYROLL THERE...I'VE KNOWN HIM SINCE HE WAS AN ACADEMY BOY.
HE'S GOT A FATHER WITH HEALTH PROBLEMS. A DIVORCE LOOMING.
HE AND BELLE ARE GETTING DIVORCED?
I HAD NO IDEA.
NEITHER DOES SHE.
GEEZ. WHO'S THE NEW PAL?
COCKTAIL WAITRESS. ICEBERG LOUNGE. IMPRESSIVE SHEET OF HER OWN.

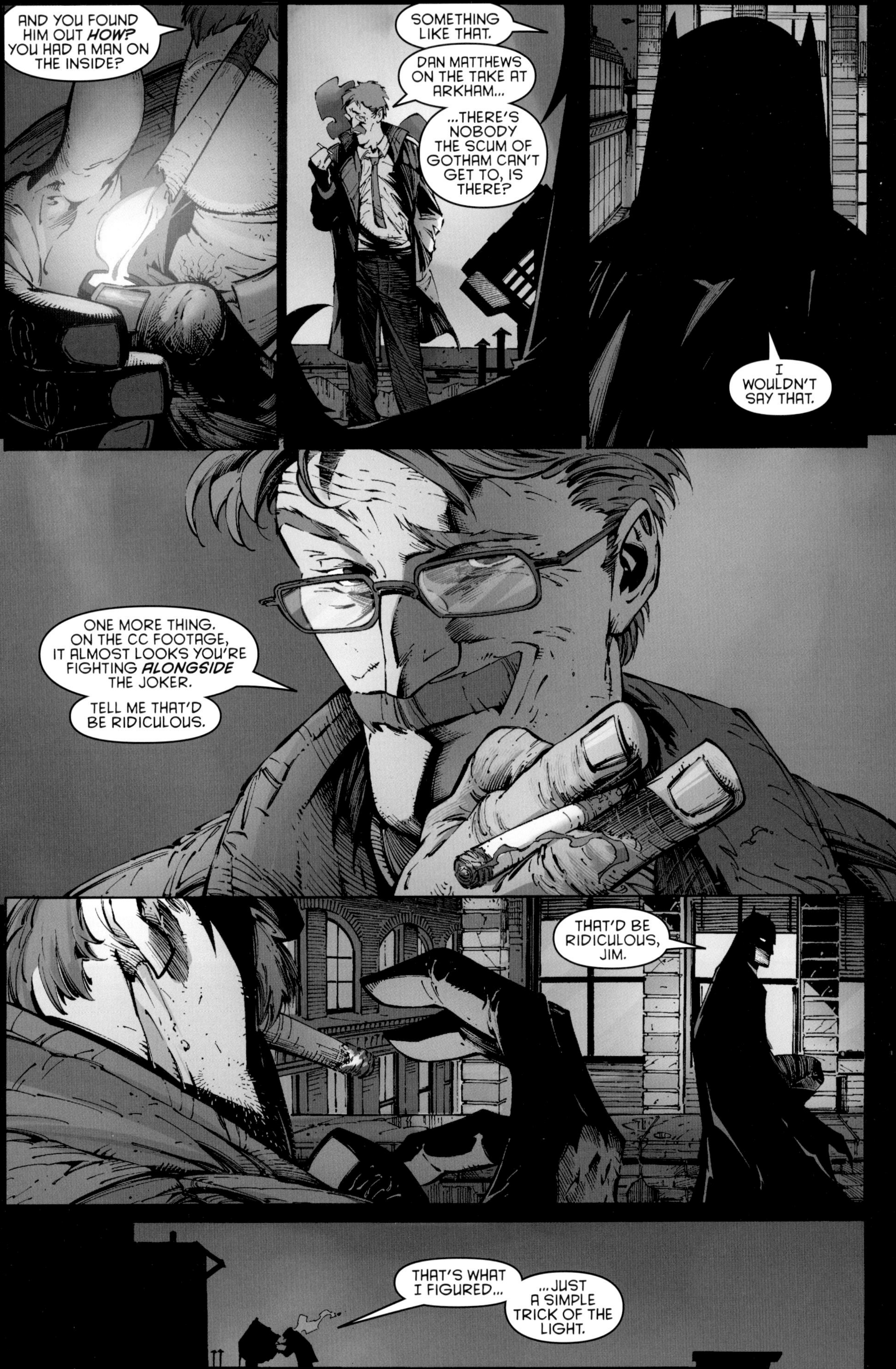
AND YOU FOUND HIM OUT *HOW?* YOU HAD A MAN ON THE INSIDE?
SOMETHING LIKE THAT.
DAN MATTHEWS ON THE TAKE AT ARKHAM...
...THERE'S NOBODY THE SCUM OF GOTHAM CAN'T GET TO, IS THERE?
I WOULDN'T SAY THAT.
ONE MORE THING. ON THE CC FOOTAGE, IT ALMOST LOOKS YOU'RE FIGHTING *ALONGSIDE* THE JOKER.
TELL ME THAT'D BE RIDICULOUS.
THAT'D BE RIDICULOUS, JIM.
THAT'S WHAT I FIGURED...
...JUST A SIMPLE TRICK OF THE LIGHT.

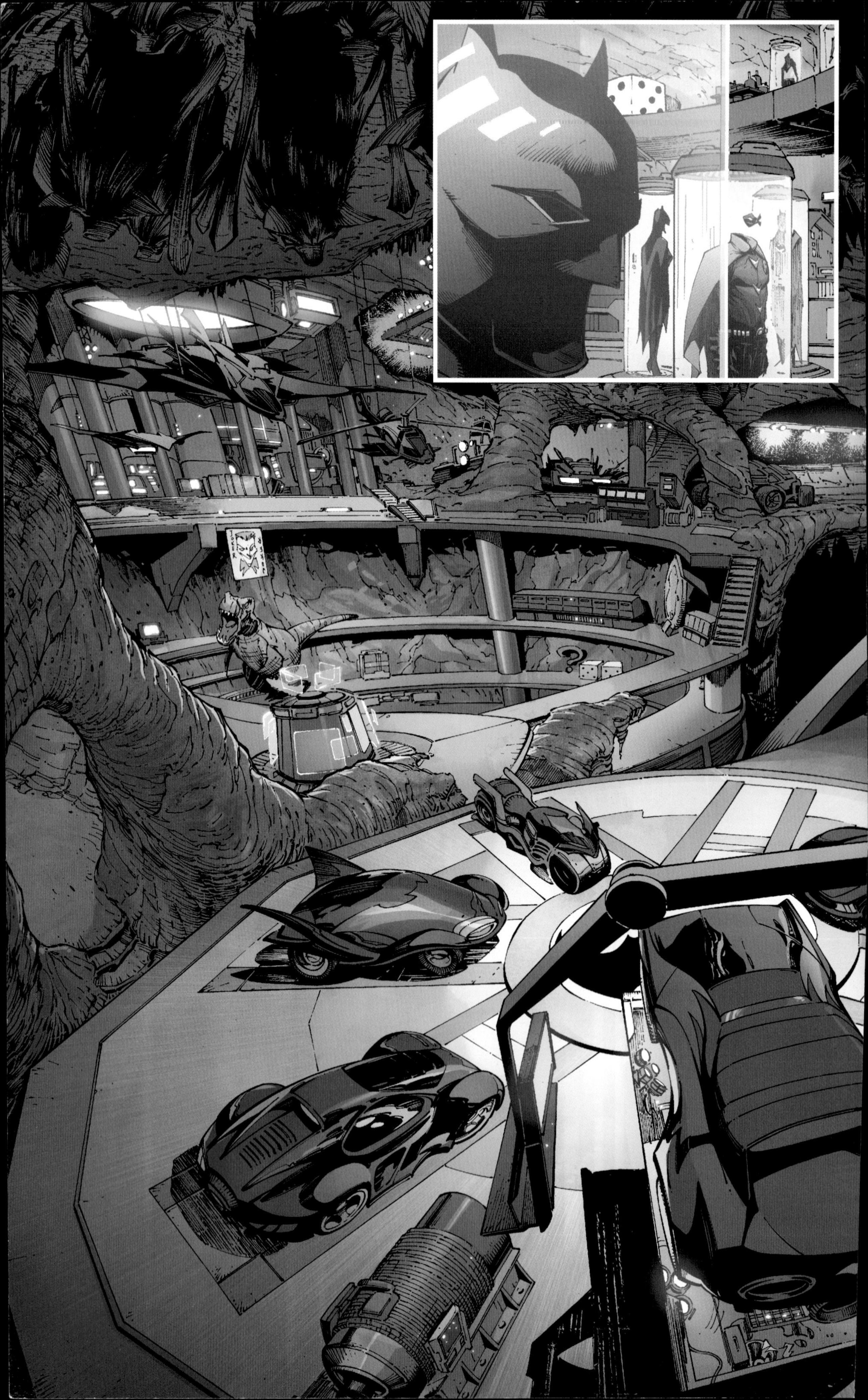

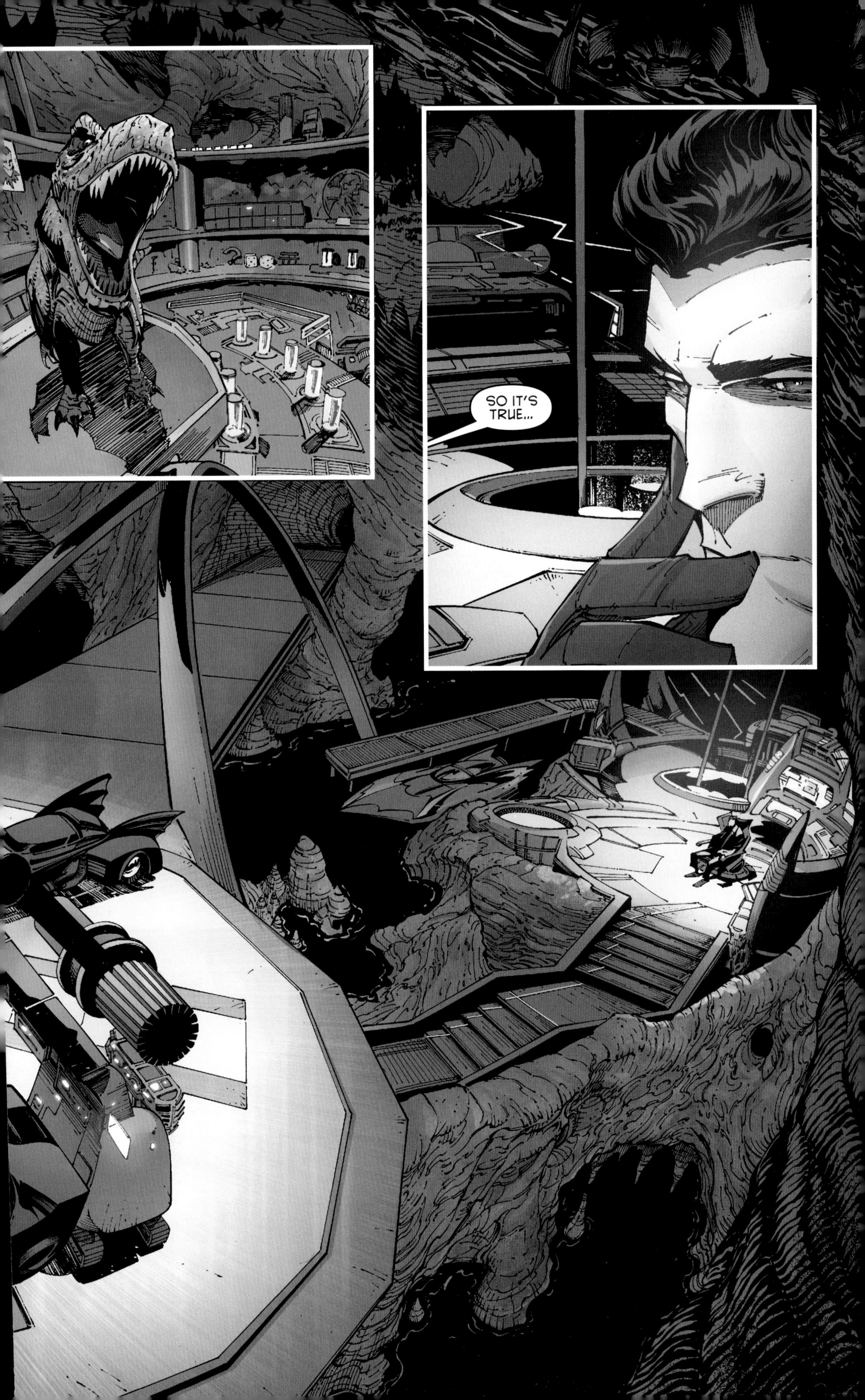
SO IT'S TRUE...

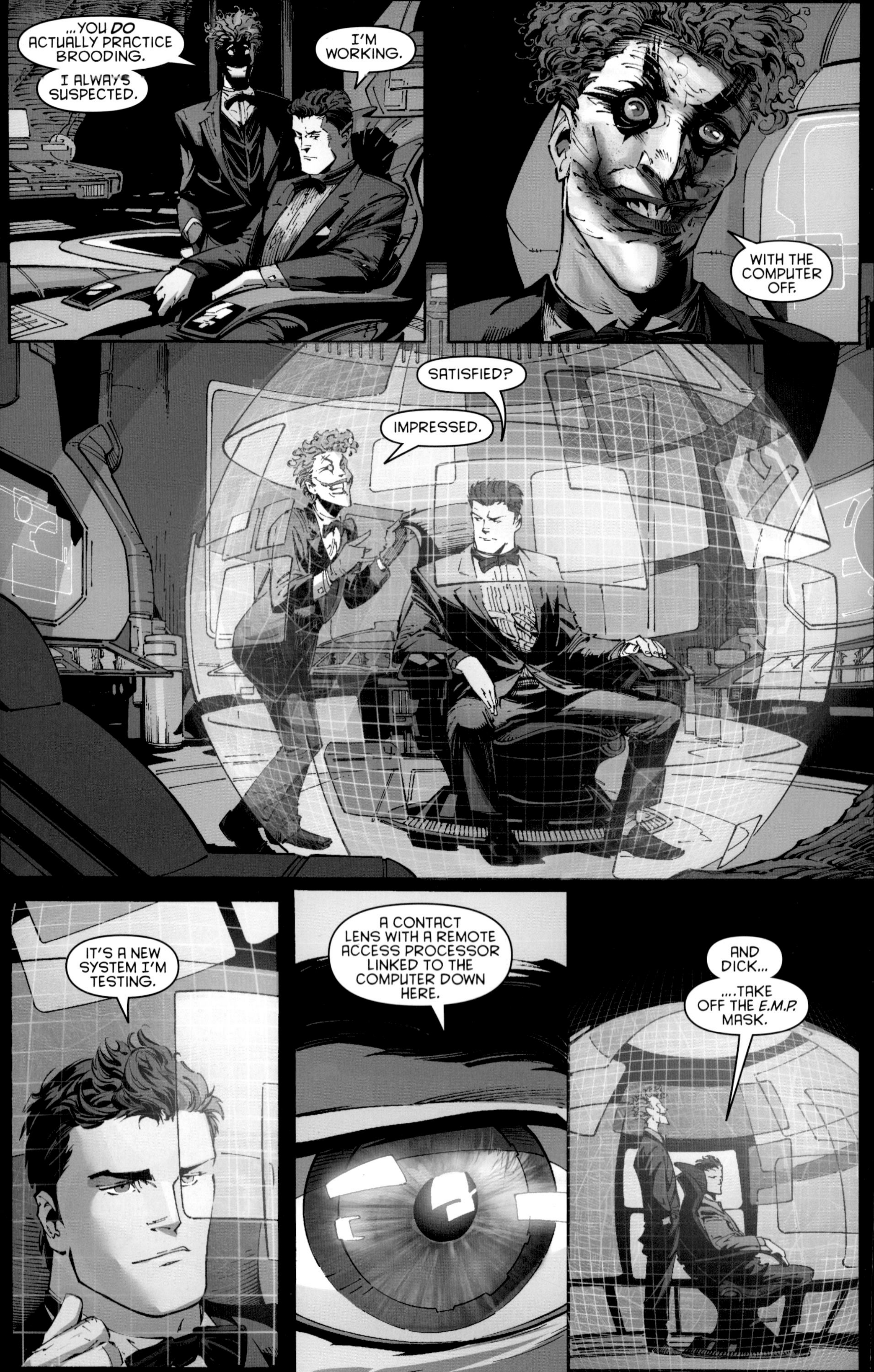
...YOU DO ACTUALLY PRACTICE BROODING.
I ALWAYS SUSPECTED.
I'M WORKING.
WITH THE COMPUTER OFF.
SATISFIED?
IMPRESSED.
IT'S A NEW SYSTEM I'M TESTING.
A CONTACT LENS WITH A REMOTE ACCESS PROCESSOR LINKED TO THE COMPUTER DOWN HERE.
AND DICK...
....TAKE OFF THE E.M.P. MASK.

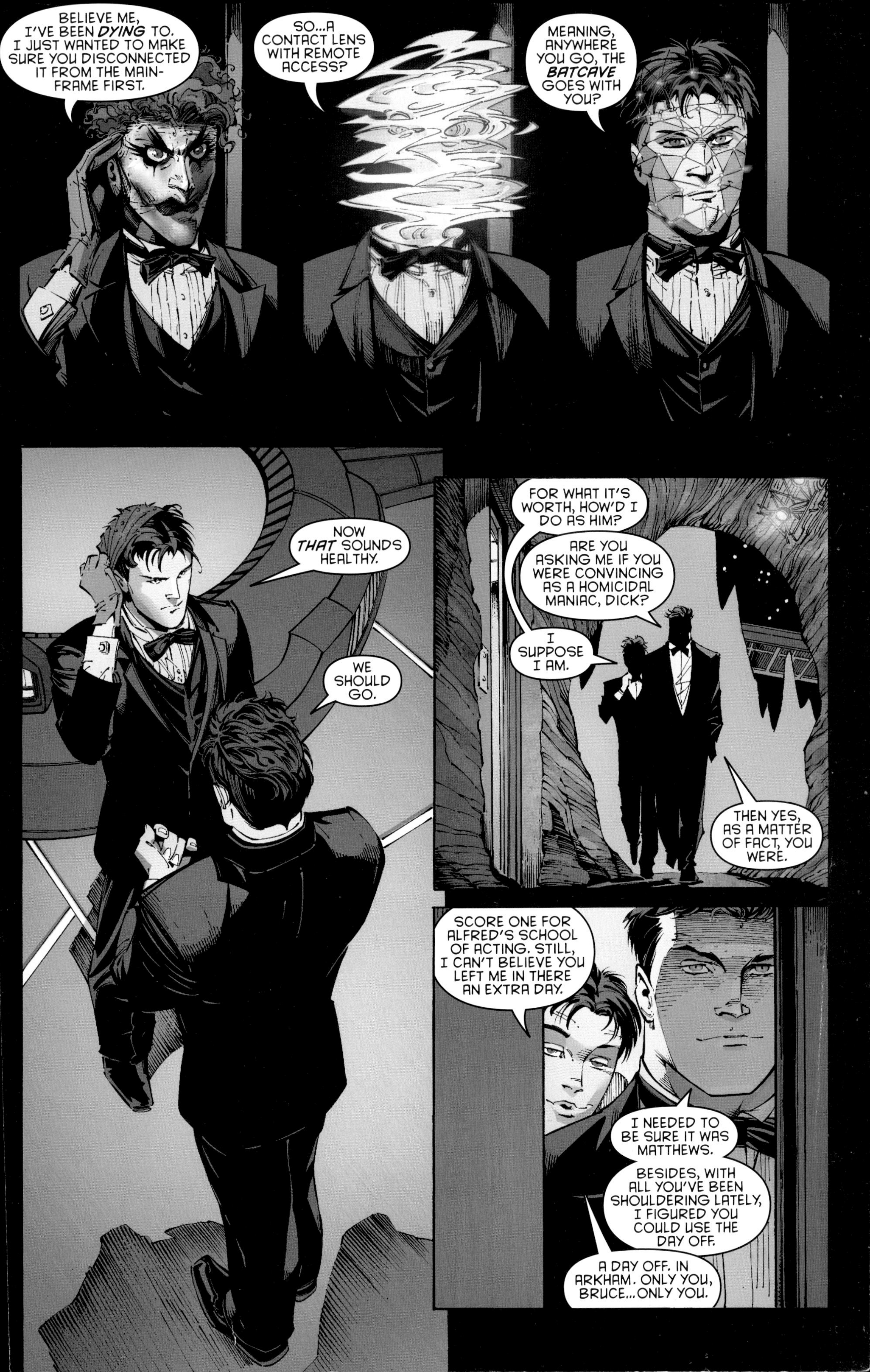
BELIEVE ME, I'VE BEEN DYING TO. I JUST WANTED TO MAKE SURE YOU DISCONNECTED IT FROM THE MAIN-FRAME FIRST.
SO...A CONTACT LENS WITH REMOTE ACCESS?
MEANING, ANYWHERE YOU GO, THE BATCAVE GOES WITH YOU?
NOW THAT SOUNDS HEALTHY.
WE SHOULD GO.
FOR WHAT IT'S WORTH, HOW'D I DO AS HIM?
ARE YOU ASKING ME IF YOU WERE CONVINCING AS A HOMICIDAL MANIAC, DICK?
I SUPPOSE I AM.
THEN YES, AS A MATTER OF FACT, YOU WERE.
SCORE ONE FOR ALFRED'S SCHOOL OF ACTING. STILL, I CAN'T BELIEVE YOU LEFT ME IN THERE AN EXTRA DAY.
I NEEDED TO BE SURE IT WAS MATTHEWS.
BESIDES, WITH ALL YOU'VE BEEN SHOULDERING LATELY, I FIGURED YOU COULD USE THE DAY OFF.
A DAY OFF. IN ARKHAM. ONLY YOU, BRUCE...ONLY YOU.

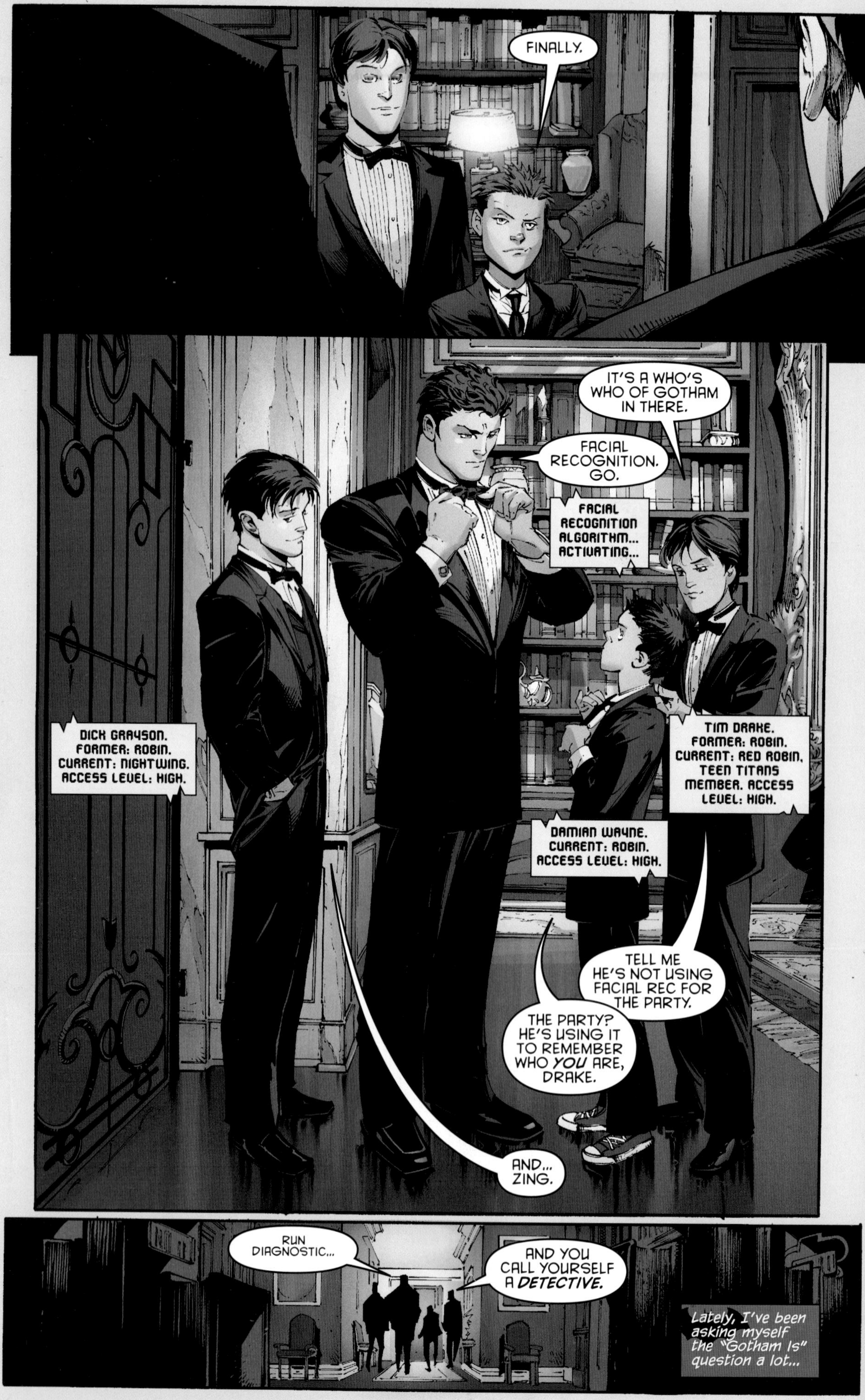
FINALLY.
IT'S A WHO'S WHO OF GOTHAM IN THERE.
FACIAL RECOGNITION. GO.
FACIAL RECOGNITION ALGORITHM... ACTIVATING...
DICK GRAYSON. FORMER: ROBIN. CURRENT: NIGHTWING. ACCESS LEVEL: HIGH.
TIM DRAKE. FORMER: ROBIN. CURRENT: RED ROBIN, TEEN TITANS MEMBER. ACCESS LEVEL: HIGH.
DAMIAN WAYNE. CURRENT: ROBIN. ACCESS LEVEL: HIGH.
TELL ME HE'S NOT USING FACIAL REC FOR THE PARTY.
THE PARTY? HE'S USING IT TO REMEMBER WHO *YOU* ARE, DRAKE.
AND... ZING.
RUN DIAGNOSTIC...
AND YOU CALL YOURSELF A ***DETECTIVE.***
Lately, I've been asking myself the "Gotham Is" question a lot...

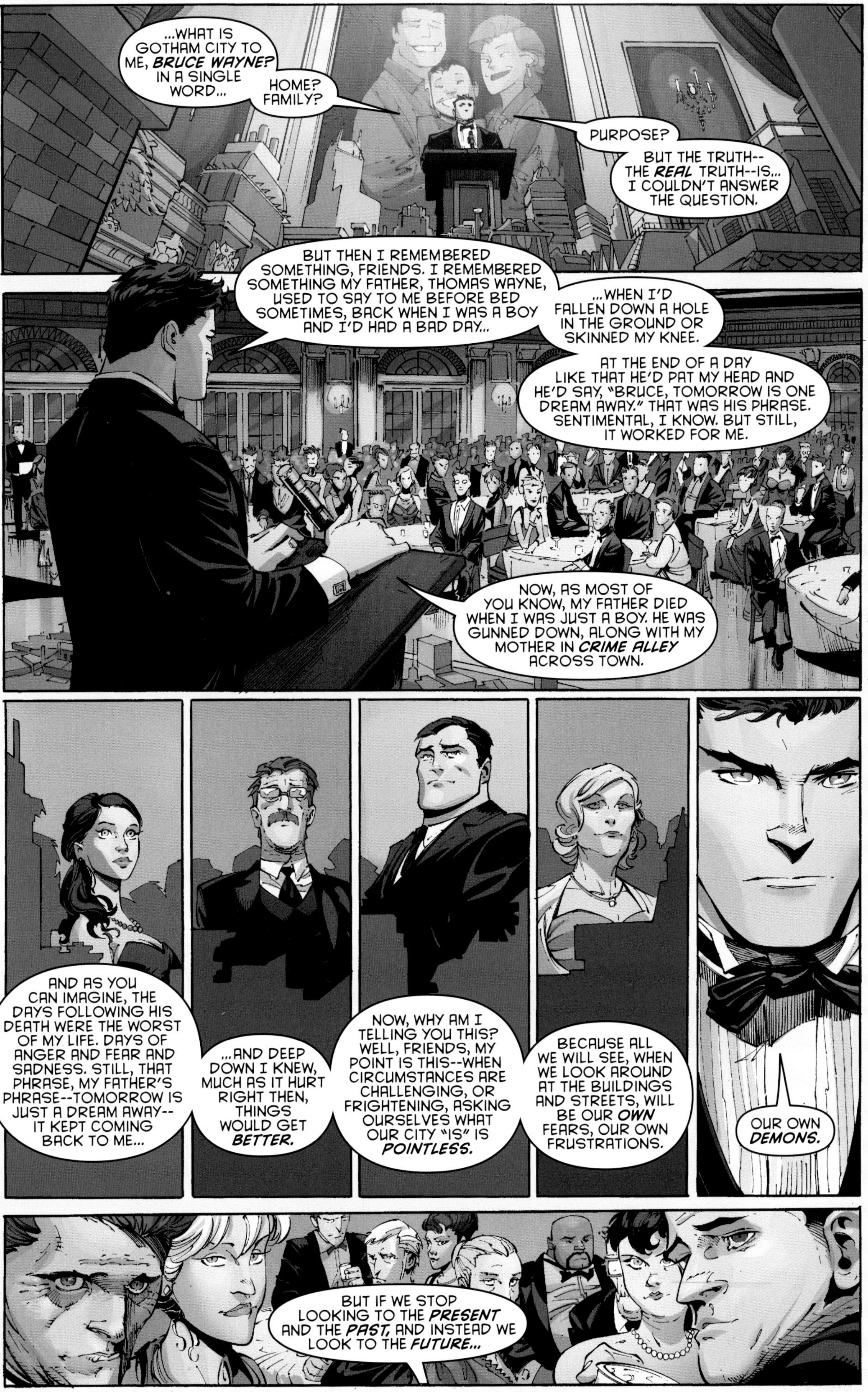
...WHAT IS GOTHAM CITY TO ME, BRUCE WAYNE? IN A SINGLE WORD...
HOME? FAMILY?
PURPOSE?
BUT THE TRUTH--THE REAL TRUTH--IS... I COULDN'T ANSWER THE QUESTION.
BUT THEN I REMEMBERED SOMETHING, FRIENDS. I REMEMBERED SOMETHING MY FATHER, THOMAS WAYNE, USED TO SAY TO ME BEFORE BED SOMETIMES, BACK WHEN I WAS A BOY AND I'D HAD A BAD DAY...
...WHEN I'D FALLEN DOWN A HOLE IN THE GROUND OR SKINNED MY KNEE.
AT THE END OF A DAY LIKE THAT HE'D PAT MY HEAD AND HE'D SAY, "BRUCE, TOMORROW IS ONE DREAM AWAY." THAT WAS HIS PHRASE. SENTIMENTAL, I KNOW. BUT STILL, IT WORKED FOR ME.
NOW, AS MOST OF YOU KNOW, MY FATHER DIED WHEN I WAS JUST A BOY. HE WAS GUNNED DOWN, ALONG WITH MY MOTHER IN CRIME ALLEY ACROSS TOWN.
AND AS YOU CAN IMAGINE, THE DAYS FOLLOWING HIS DEATH WERE THE WORST OF MY LIFE. DAYS OF ANGER AND FEAR AND SADNESS. STILL, THAT PHRASE, MY FATHER'S PHRASE--TOMORROW IS JUST A DREAM AWAY--IT KEPT COMING BACK TO ME...
...AND DEEP DOWN I KNEW, MUCH AS IT HURT RIGHT THEN, THINGS WOULD GET BETTER.
NOW, WHY AM I TELLING YOU THIS? WELL, FRIENDS, MY POINT IS THIS--WHEN CIRCUMSTANCES ARE CHALLENGING, OR FRIGHTENING, ASKING OURSELVES WHAT OUR CITY "IS" IS POINTLESS.
BECAUSE ALL WE WILL SEE, WHEN WE LOOK AROUND AT THE BUILDINGS AND STREETS, WILL BE OUR OWN FEARS, OUR OWN FRUSTRATIONS.
OUR OWN DEMONS.
BUT IF WE STOP LOOKING TO THE PRESENT AND THE PAST, AND INSTEAD WE LOOK TO THE FUTURE...

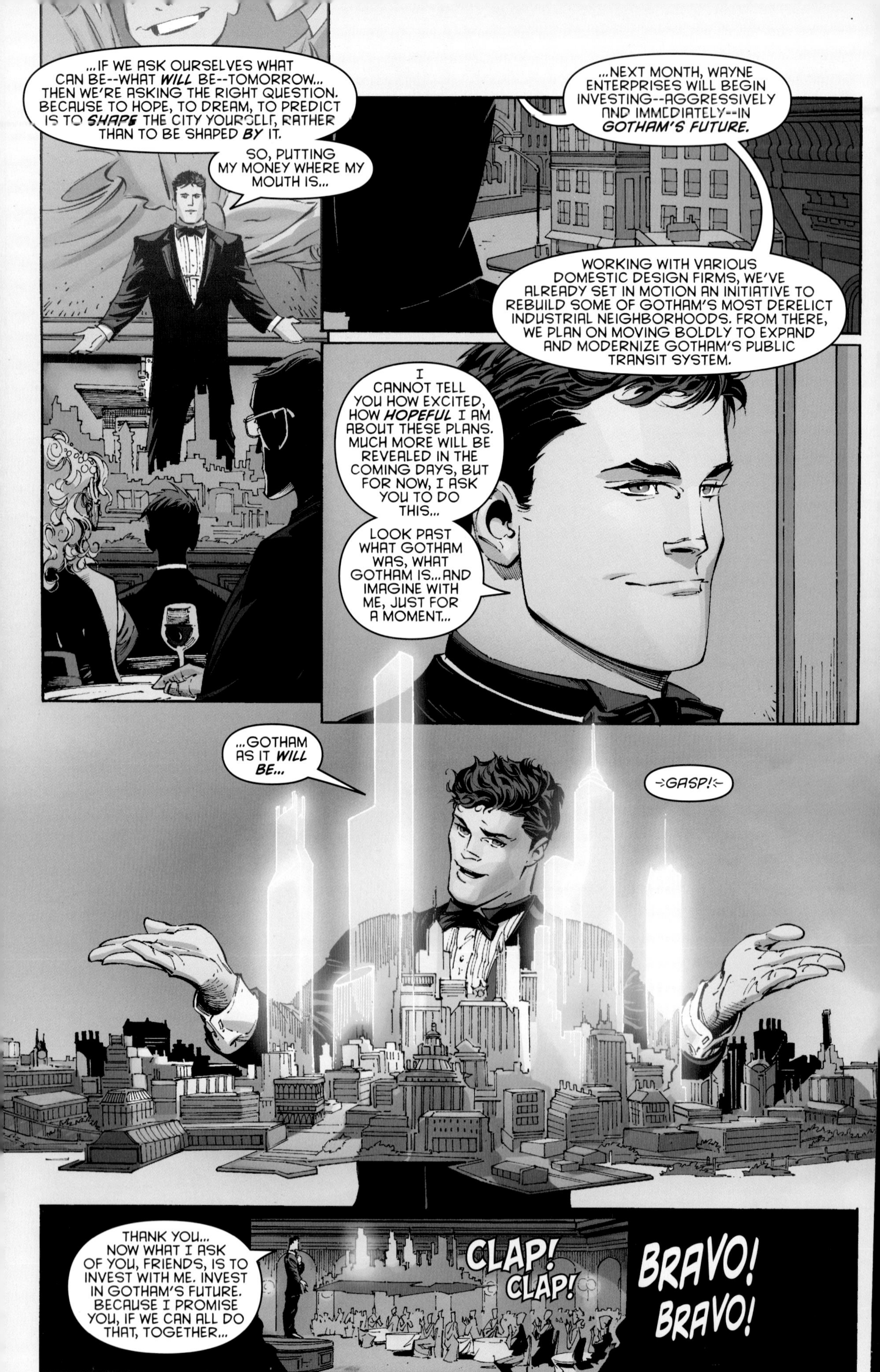
...IF WE ASK OURSELVES WHAT CAN BE--WHAT WILL BE--TOMORROW... THEN WE'RE ASKING THE RIGHT QUESTION. BECAUSE TO HOPE, TO DREAM, TO PREDICT IS TO SHAPE THE CITY YOURSELF, RATHER THAN TO BE SHAPED BY IT.
SO, PUTTING MY MONEY WHERE MY MOUTH IS...
...NEXT MONTH, WAYNE ENTERPRISES WILL BEGIN INVESTING--AGGRESSIVELY AND IMMEDIATELY--IN GOTHAM'S FUTURE.
WORKING WITH VARIOUS DOMESTIC DESIGN FIRMS, WE'VE ALREADY SET IN MOTION AN INITIATIVE TO REBUILD SOME OF GOTHAM'S MOST DERELICT INDUSTRIAL NEIGHBORHOODS. FROM THERE, WE PLAN ON MOVING BOLDLY TO EXPAND AND MODERNIZE GOTHAM'S PUBLIC TRANSIT SYSTEM.
I CANNOT TELL YOU HOW EXCITED, HOW HOPEFUL I AM ABOUT THESE PLANS. MUCH MORE WILL BE REVEALED IN THE COMING DAYS, BUT FOR NOW, I ASK YOU TO DO THIS...
LOOK PAST WHAT GOTHAM WAS, WHAT GOTHAM IS...AND IMAGINE WITH ME, JUST FOR A MOMENT...
...GOTHAM AS IT WILL BE...
GASP!
THANK YOU... NOW WHAT I ASK OF YOU, FRIENDS, IS TO INVEST WITH ME. INVEST IN GOTHAM'S FUTURE. BECAUSE I PROMISE YOU, IF WE CAN ALL DO THAT, TOGETHER...
CLAP! CLAP!
BRAVO! BRAVO!

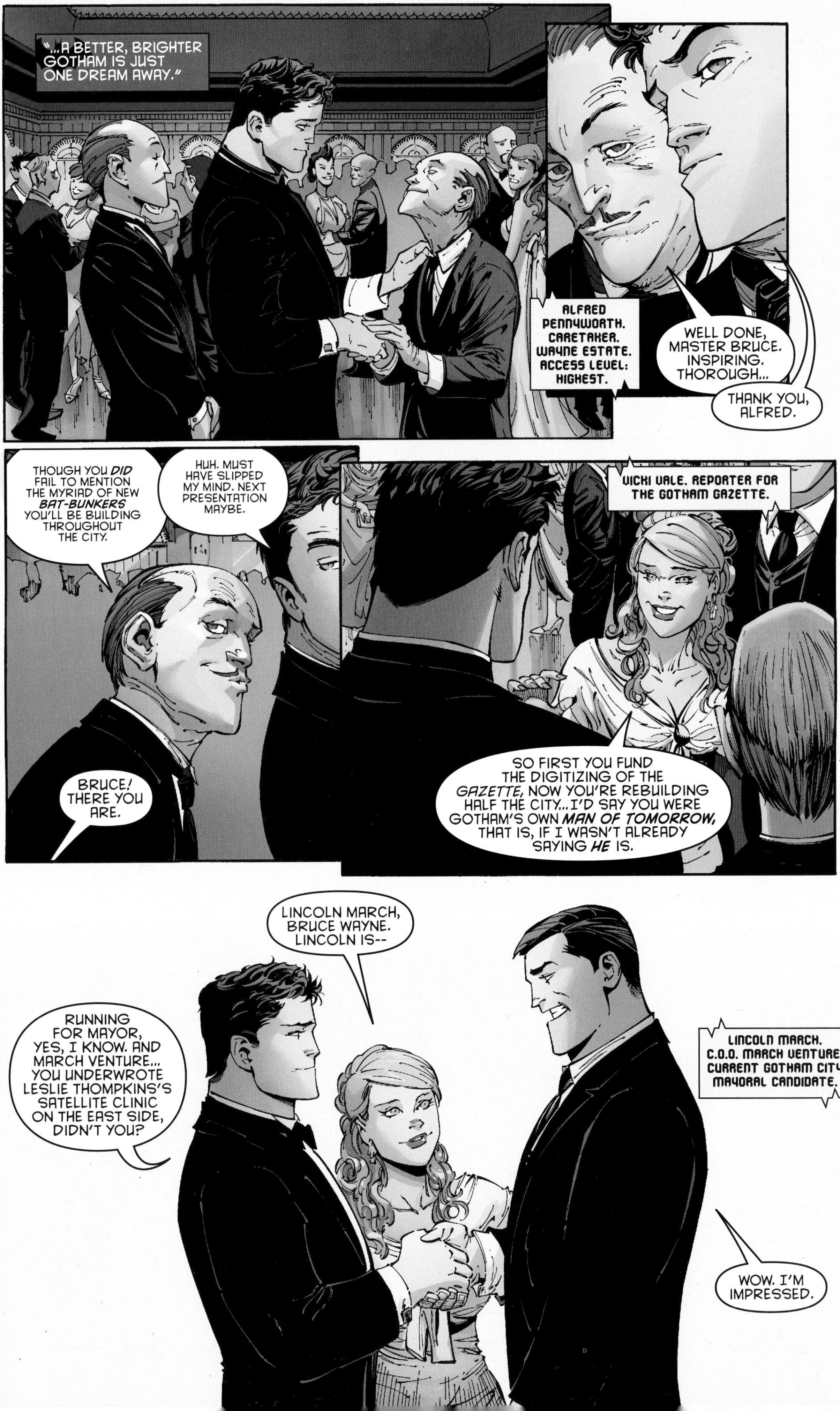
"...A BETTER, BRIGHTER GOTHAM IS JUST ONE DREAM AWAY."
ALFRED PENNYWORTH. CARETAKER. WAYNE ESTATE. ACCESS LEVEL: HIGHEST.
WELL DONE, MASTER BRUCE. INSPIRING. THOROUGH...
THANK YOU, ALFRED.
THOUGH YOU *DID* FAIL TO MENTION THE MYRIAD OF NEW *BAT-BUNKERS* YOU'LL BE BUILDING THROUGHOUT THE CITY.
HUH. MUST HAVE SLIPPED MY MIND. NEXT PRESENTATION MAYBE.
BRUCE! THERE YOU ARE.
VICKI VALE. REPORTER FOR THE GOTHAM GAZETTE.
SO FIRST YOU FUND THE DIGITIZING OF THE *GAZETTE,* NOW YOU'RE REBUILDING HALF THE CITY...I'D SAY YOU WERE GOTHAM'S OWN *MAN OF TOMORROW,* THAT IS, IF I WASN'T ALREADY SAYING *HE* IS.
LINCOLN MARCH, BRUCE WAYNE. LINCOLN IS--
RUNNING FOR MAYOR, YES, I KNOW. AND MARCH VENTURE... YOU UNDERWROTE LESLIE THOMPKINS'S SATELLITE CLINIC ON THE EAST SIDE, DIDN'T YOU?
LINCOLN MARCH. C.O.O. MARCH VENTURE. CURRENT GOTHAM CITY MAYORAL CANDIDATE.
WOW. I'M IMPRESSED.

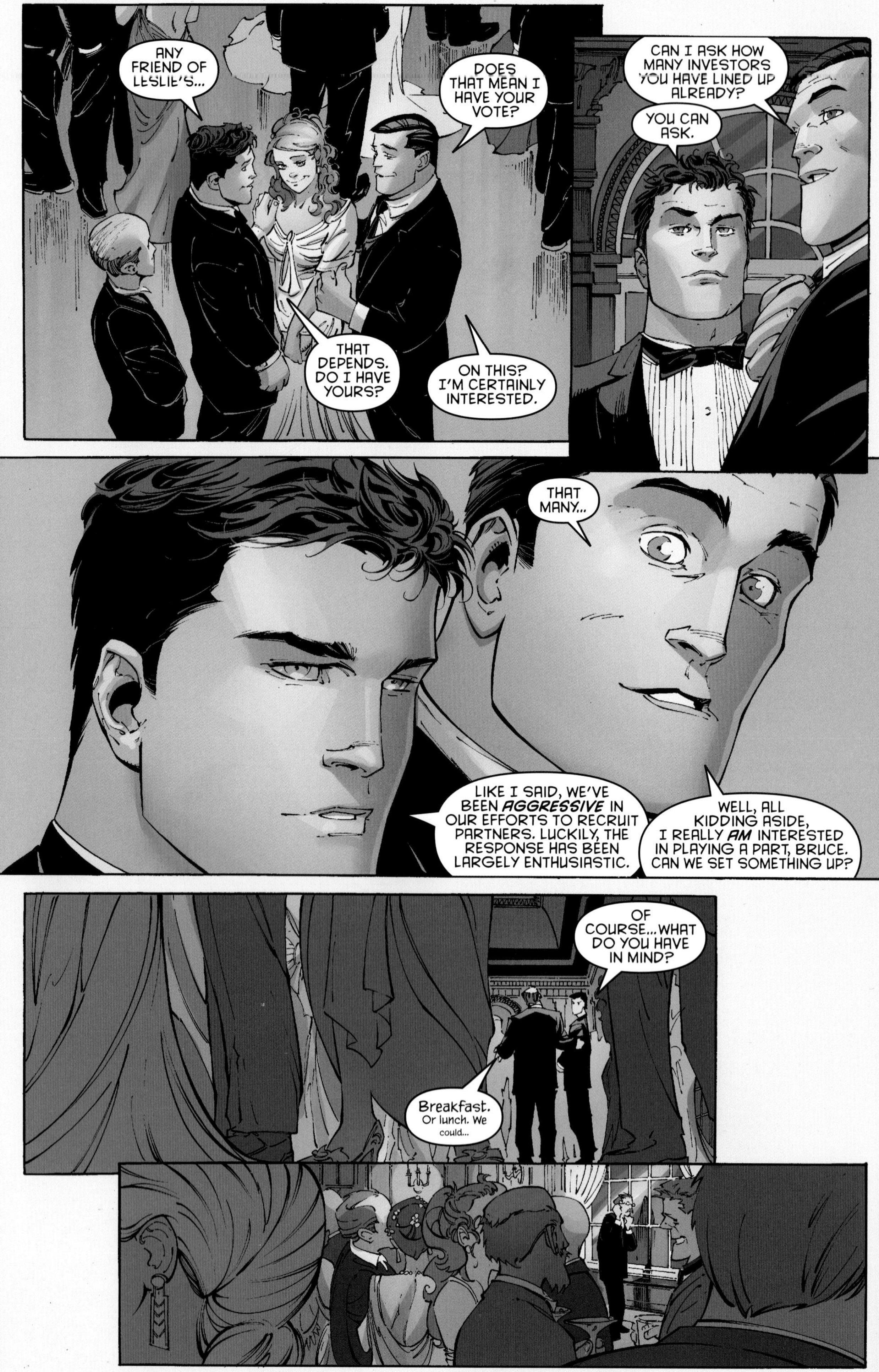
ANY FRIEND OF LESLIE'S...
DOES THAT MEAN I HAVE YOUR VOTE?
THAT DEPENDS. DO I HAVE YOURS?
ON THIS? I'M CERTAINLY INTERESTED.
CAN I ASK HOW MANY INVESTORS YOU HAVE LINED UP ALREADY?
YOU CAN ASK.
THAT MANY...
LIKE I SAID, WE'VE BEEN AGGRESSIVE IN OUR EFFORTS TO RECRUIT PARTNERS. LUCKILY, THE RESPONSE HAS BEEN LARGELY ENTHUSIASTIC.
WELL, ALL KIDDING ASIDE, I REALLY AM INTERESTED IN PLAYING A PART, BRUCE. CAN WE SET SOMETHING UP?
OF COURSE...WHAT DO YOU HAVE IN MIND?
Breakfast. Or lunch. We could...

-:COUGH-COUGH:-
(LIP READ GO).

I'M SORRY. GO ON.

LIP READ ACTIVATING... OCULAR TARGETING TO...

I WAS JUST SAYING I'M ENTHUSIASTIC TO...

HOW MANY STAB WOUNDS? GOD.

ALL RIGHT, I'LL BE RIGHT DOWN. JUST GIVE ME TEN MINUTES TO ESCAPE FROM PLANET OF THE CREPES.

"CREPE." IT'S A PANCAKE. NEVER MIND.

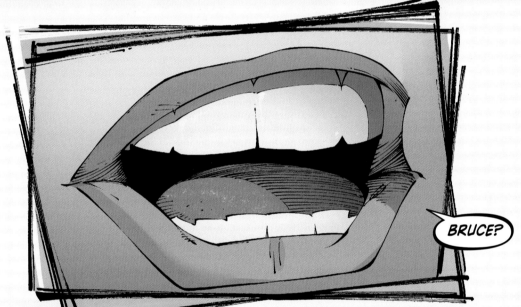

BRUCE?

I'M SORRY, WHAT?

I WAS SAYING I COULD DO AS EARLY AS TOMORROW. LUNCH? TALK ABOUT YOUR PLANS?

OF COURSE. TOMORROW. ALFRED, SET IT UP, WILL YOU? NOW IF YOU'LL EXCUSE ME FOR A MOMENT, LINCOLN...

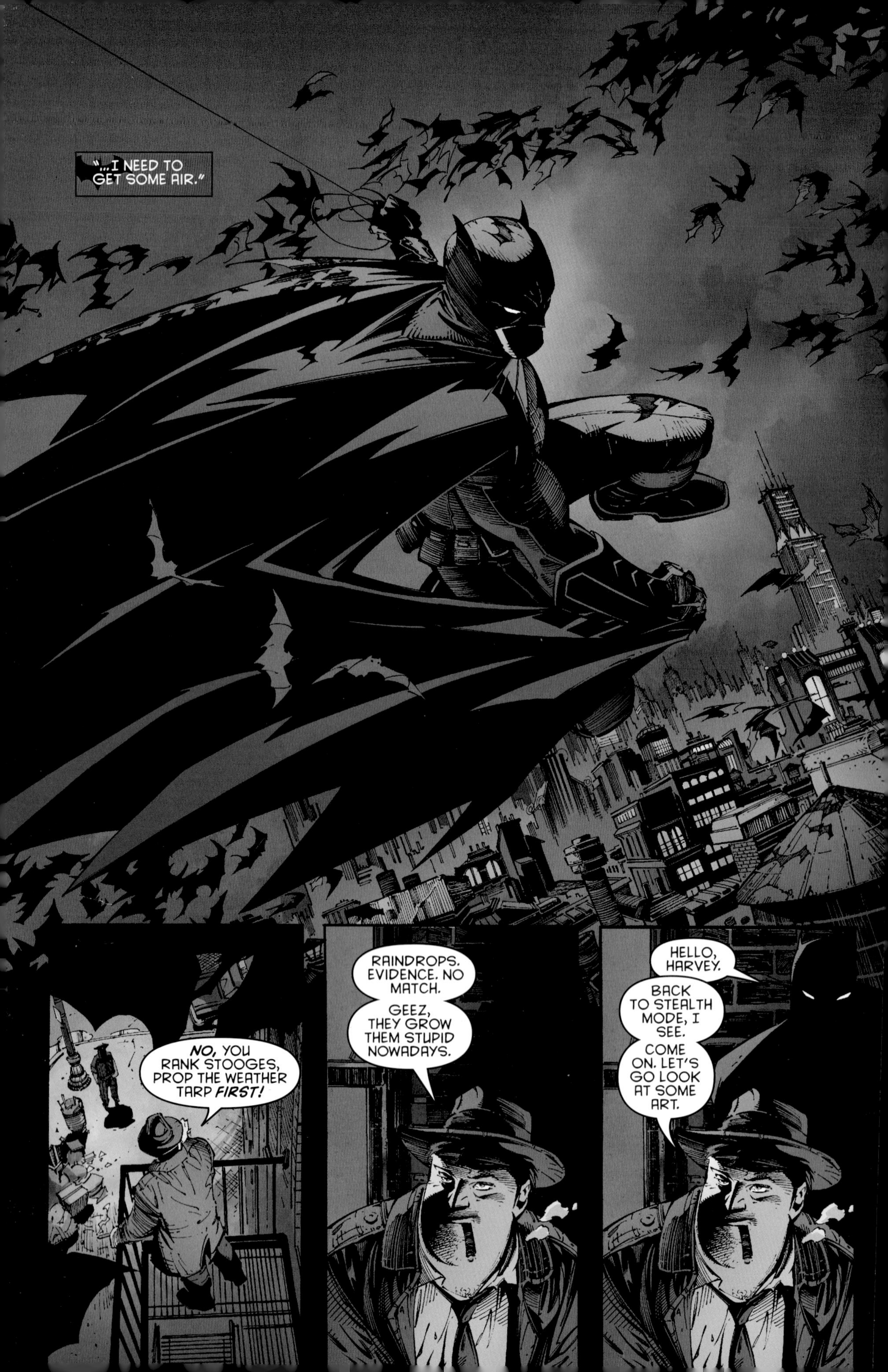
"...I NEED TO GET SOME AIR."
NO, YOU RANK STOOGES, PROP THE WEATHER TARP FIRST!
RAINDROPS. EVIDENCE. NO MATCH.
GEEZ, THEY GROW THEM STUPID NOWADAYS.
HELLO, HARVEY.
BACK TO STEALTH MODE, I SEE.
COME ON. LET'S GO LOOK AT SOME ART.

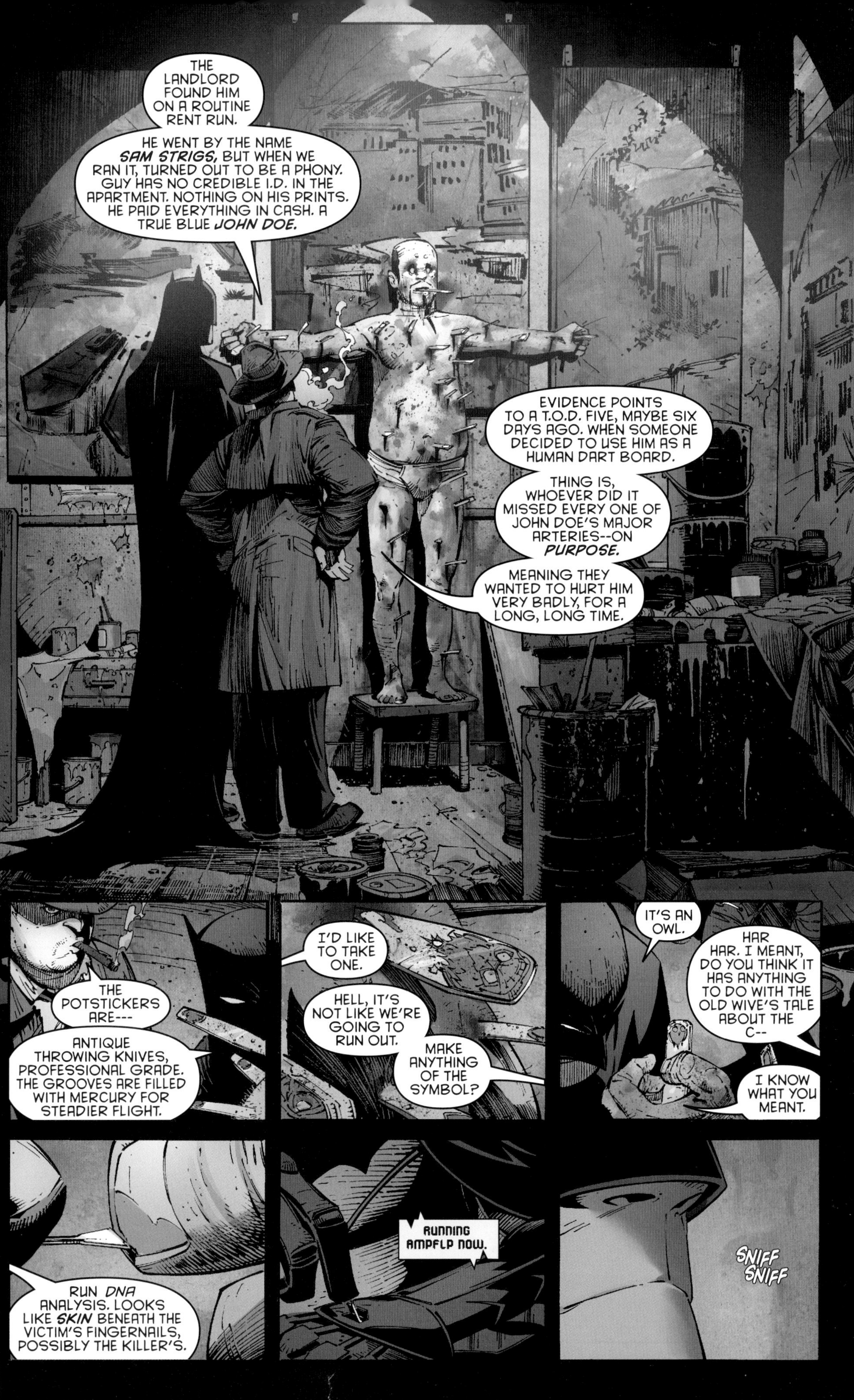
THE LANDLORD FOUND HIM ON A ROUTINE RENT RUN.
HE WENT BY THE NAME SAM STRIGS, BUT WHEN WE RAN IT, TURNED OUT TO BE A PHONY. GUY HAS NO CREDIBLE I.D. IN THE APARTMENT. NOTHING ON HIS PRINTS. HE PAID EVERYTHING IN CASH. A TRUE BLUE JOHN DOE.
EVIDENCE POINTS TO A T.O.D. FIVE, MAYBE SIX DAYS AGO. WHEN SOMEONE DECIDED TO USE HIM AS A HUMAN DART BOARD.
THING IS, WHOEVER DID IT MISSED EVERY ONE OF JOHN DOE'S MAJOR ARTERIES--ON PURPOSE.
MEANING THEY WANTED TO HURT HIM VERY BADLY, FOR A LONG, LONG TIME.
THE POTSTICKERS ARE---
ANTIQUE THROWING KNIVES, PROFESSIONAL GRADE. THE GROOVES ARE FILLED WITH MERCURY FOR STEADIER FLIGHT.
I'D LIKE TO TAKE ONE.
HELL, IT'S NOT LIKE WE'RE GOING TO RUN OUT.
MAKE ANYTHING OF THE SYMBOL?
IT'S AN OWL.
HAR HAR. I MEANT, DO YOU THINK IT HAS ANYTHING TO DO WITH THE OLD WIVE'S TALE ABOUT THE C--
I KNOW WHAT YOU MEANT.
RUN DNA ANALYSIS. LOOKS LIKE SKIN BENEATH THE VICTIM'S FINGERNAILS, POSSIBLY THE KILLER'S.
RUNNING AMPFLP NOW.
SNIFF SNIFF

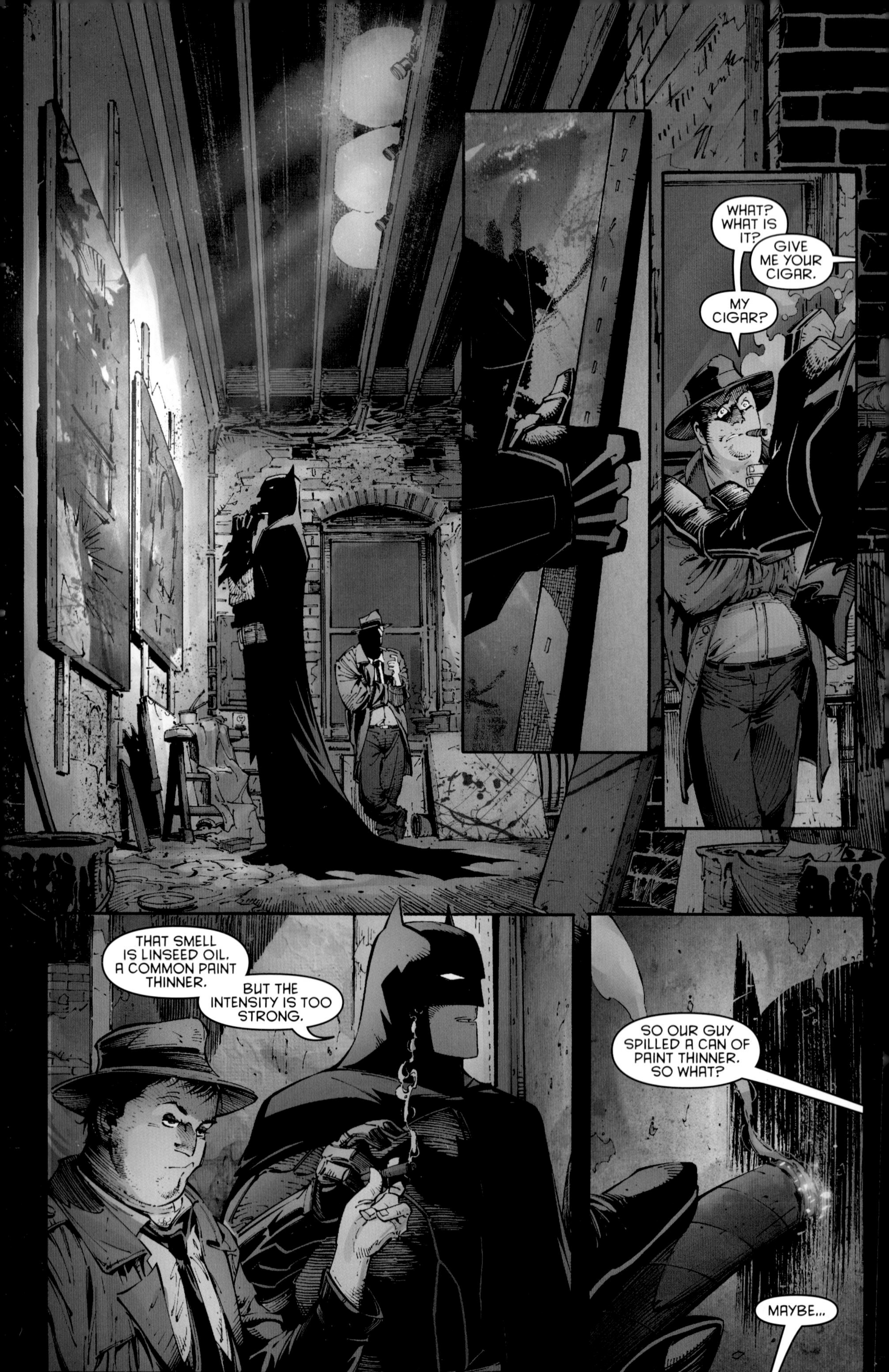
WHAT? WHAT IS IT?
GIVE ME YOUR CIGAR.
MY CIGAR?
THAT SMELL IS LINSEED OIL. A COMMON PAINT THINNER.
BUT THE INTENSITY IS TOO STRONG.
SO OUR GUY SPILLED A CAN OF PAINT THINNER. SO WHAT?
MAYBE...

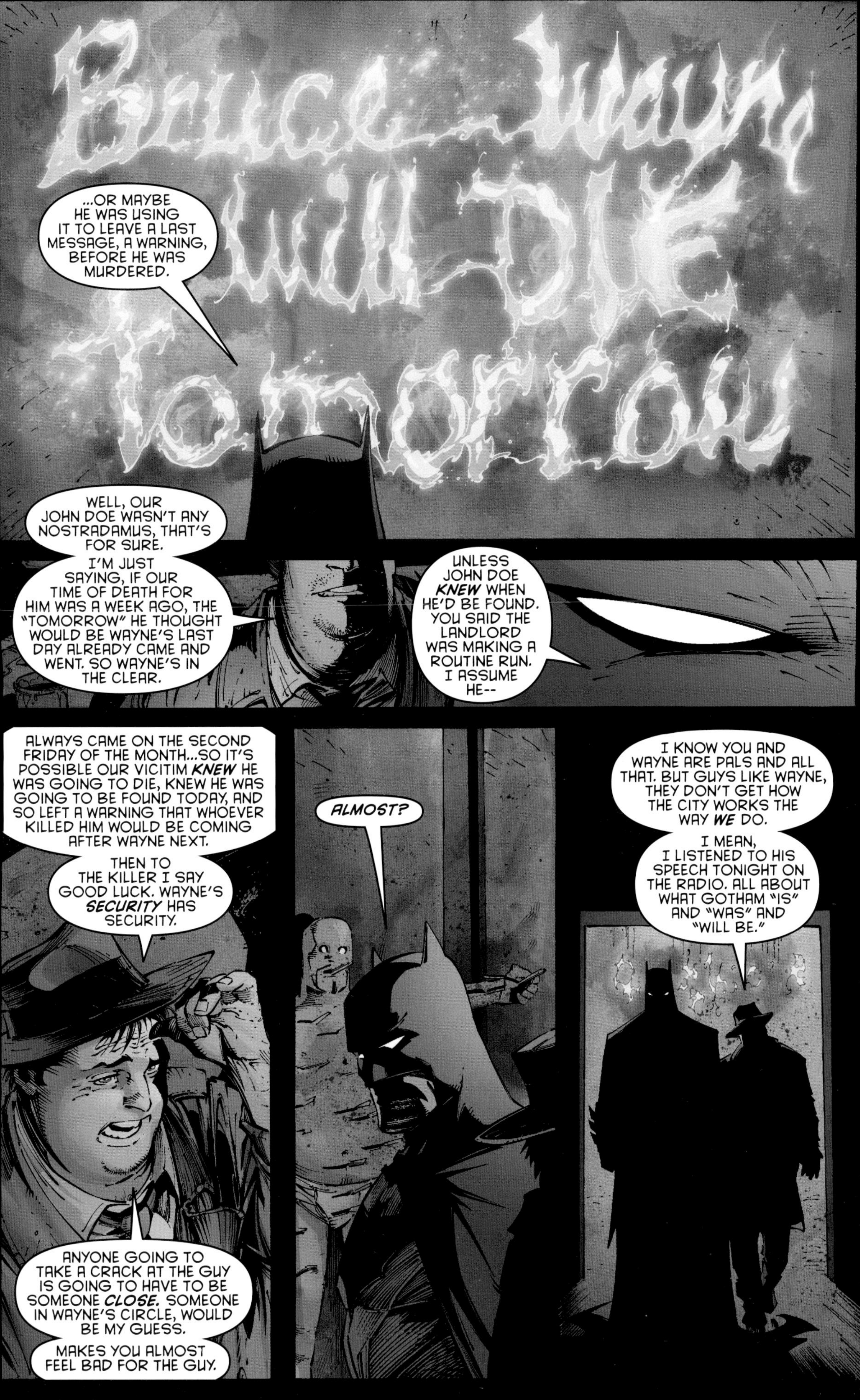
Bruce Wayne will DIE Tomorrow
...OR MAYBE HE WAS USING IT TO LEAVE A LAST MESSAGE, A WARNING, BEFORE HE WAS MURDERED.
WELL, OUR JOHN DOE WASN'T ANY NOSTRADAMUS, THAT'S FOR SURE.
I'M JUST SAYING, IF OUR TIME OF DEATH FOR HIM WAS A WEEK AGO, THE "TOMORROW" HE THOUGHT WOULD BE WAYNE'S LAST DAY ALREADY CAME AND WENT. SO WAYNE'S IN THE CLEAR.
UNLESS JOHN DOE *KNEW* WHEN HE'D BE FOUND. YOU SAID THE LANDLORD WAS MAKING A ROUTINE RUN. I ASSUME HE--
ALWAYS CAME ON THE SECOND FRIDAY OF THE MONTH...SO IT'S POSSIBLE OUR VICITIM *KNEW* HE WAS GOING TO DIE, KNEW HE WAS GOING TO BE FOUND TODAY, AND SO LEFT A WARNING THAT WHOEVER KILLED HIM WOULD BE COMING AFTER WAYNE NEXT.
THEN TO THE KILLER I SAY GOOD LUCK. WAYNE'S *SECURITY* HAS SECURITY.
ANYONE GOING TO TAKE A CRACK AT THE GUY IS GOING TO HAVE TO BE SOMEONE *CLOSE.* SOMEONE IN WAYNE'S CIRCLE, WOULD BE MY GUESS.
MAKES YOU ALMOST FEEL BAD FOR THE GUY.
ALMOST?
I KNOW YOU AND WAYNE ARE PALS AND ALL THAT. BUT GUYS LIKE WAYNE, THEY DON'T GET HOW THE CITY WORKS THE WAY *WE* DO.
I MEAN, I LISTENED TO HIS SPEECH TONIGHT ON THE RADIO. ALL ABOUT WHAT GOTHAM "IS" AND "WAS" AND "WILL BE."

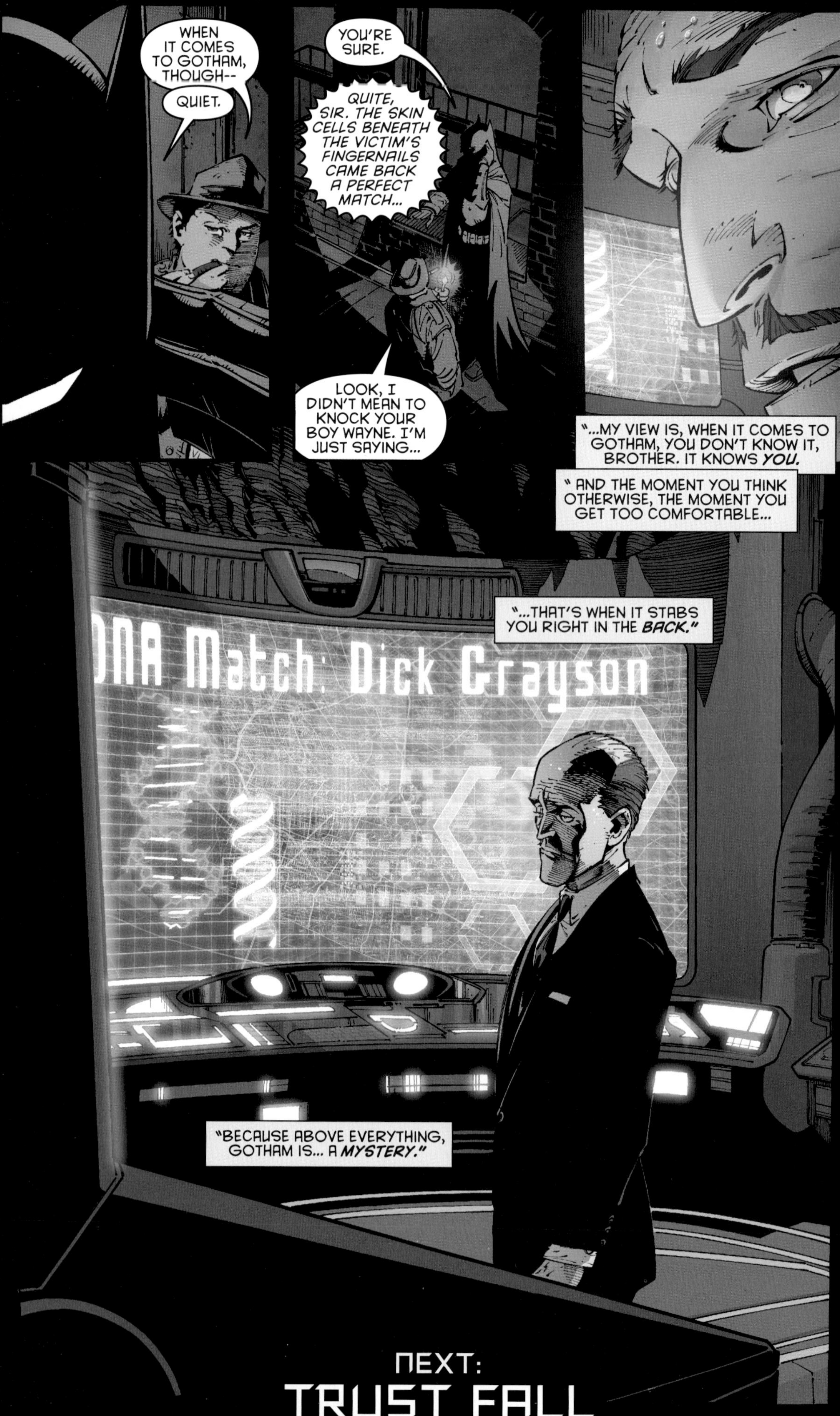
WHEN IT COMES TO GOTHAM, THOUGH--
QUIET.
YOU'RE SURE.
QUITE, SIR. THE SKIN CELLS BENEATH THE VICTIM'S FINGERNAILS CAME BACK A PERFECT MATCH...
LOOK, I DIDN'T MEAN TO KNOCK YOUR BOY WAYNE. I'M JUST SAYING...
"...MY VIEW IS, WHEN IT COMES TO GOTHAM, YOU DON'T KNOW IT, BROTHER. IT KNOWS YOU.
" AND THE MOMENT YOU THINK OTHERWISE, THE MOMENT YOU GET TOO COMFORTABLE...
"...THAT'S WHEN IT STABS YOU RIGHT IN THE BACK."
DNA Match: Dick Grayson
"BECAUSE ABOVE EVERYTHING, GOTHAM IS... A MYSTERY."
NEXT:
TRUST FALL

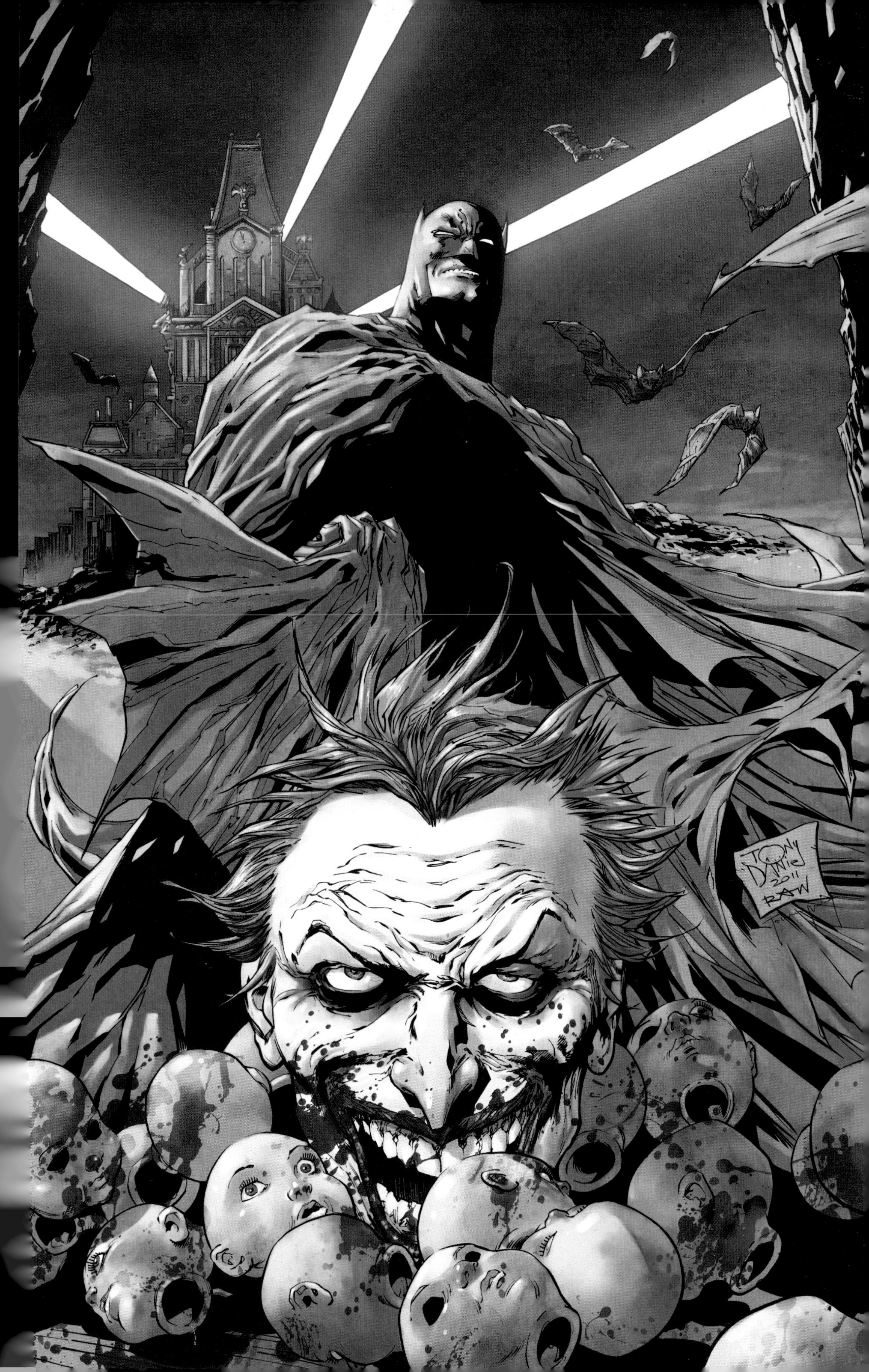
TONY DANIEL 2011 RAW

Batman
DETECTIVE
COMICS

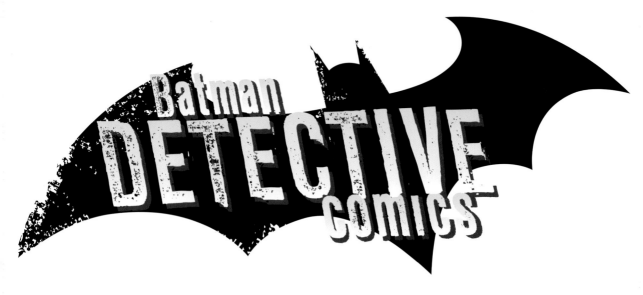

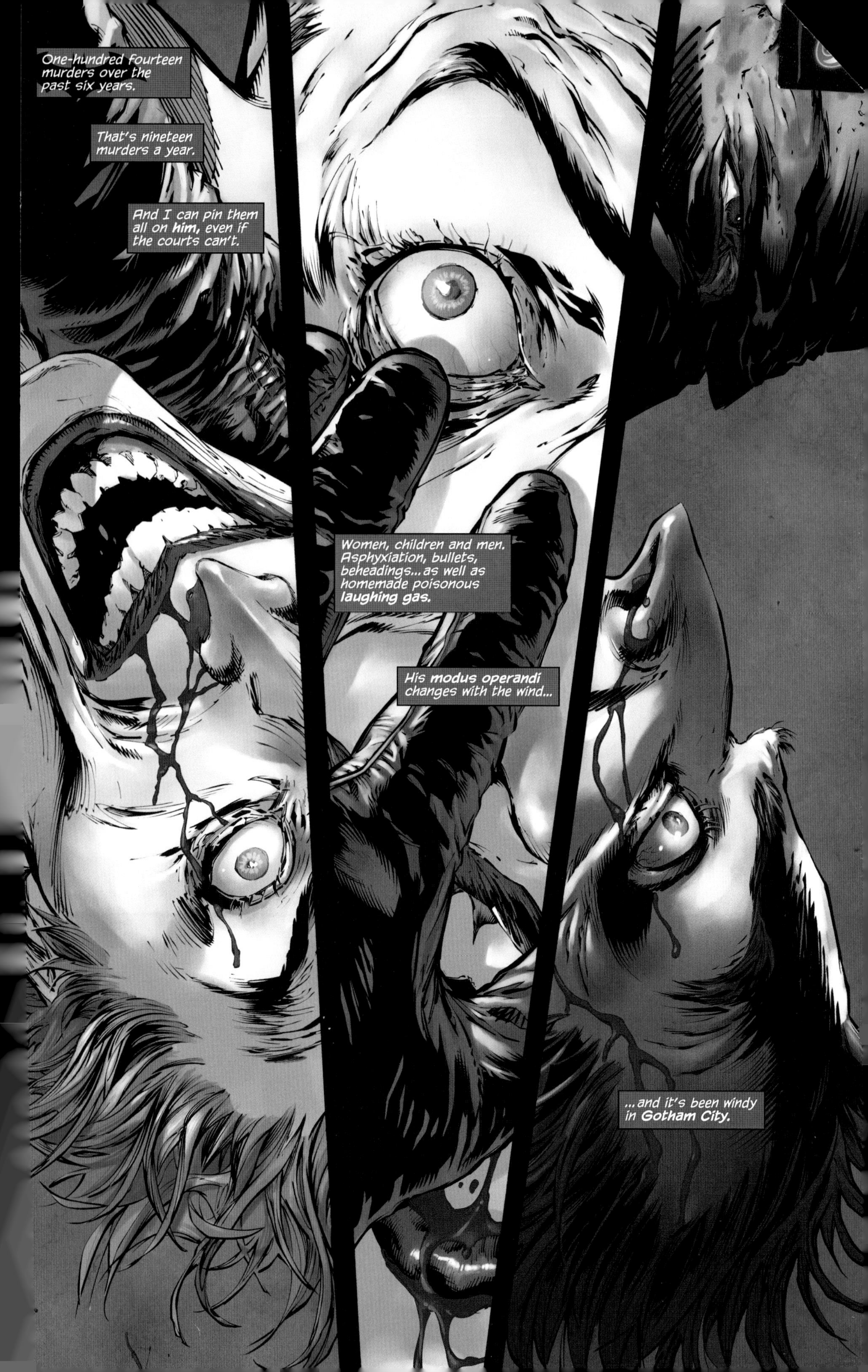
One-hundred fourteen murders over the past six years.
That's nineteen murders a year.
And I can pin them all on **him**, even if the courts can't.
Women, children and men. Asphyxiation, bullets, beheadings...as well as homemade poisonous **laughing gas.**
His **modus operandi** changes with the wind...
...and it's been windy in **Gotham City.**

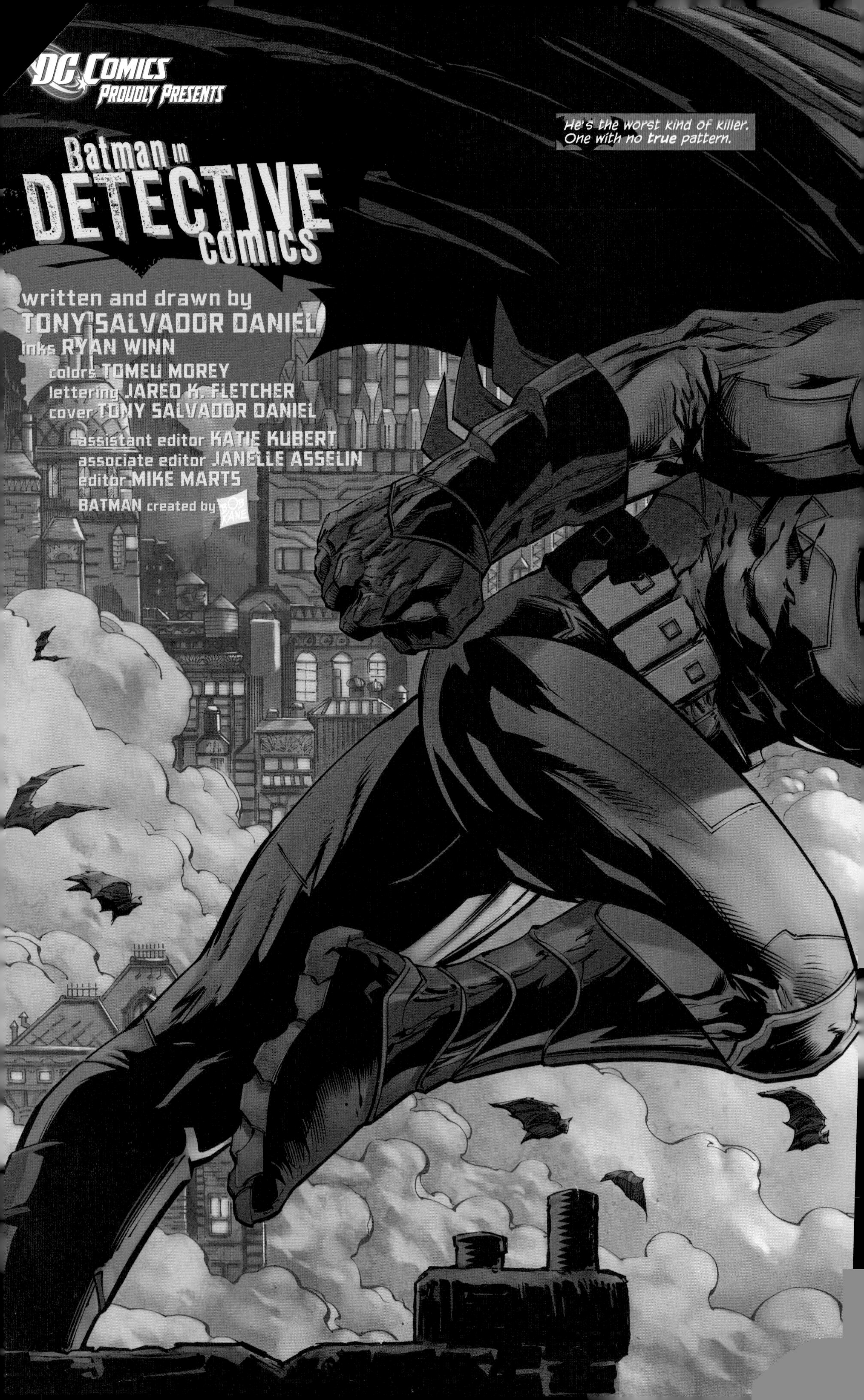
DC COMICS PROUDLY PRESENTS
Batman in DETECTIVE COMICS
written and drawn by TONY SALVADOR DANIEL
inks RYAN WINN
colors TOMEU MOREY
lettering JARED K. FLETCHER
cover TONY SALVADOR DANIEL
assistant editor KATIE KUBERT
associate editor JANELLE ASSELIN
editor MIKE MARTS
BATMAN created by BOB KANE
He's the worst kind of killer. One with no true pattern.

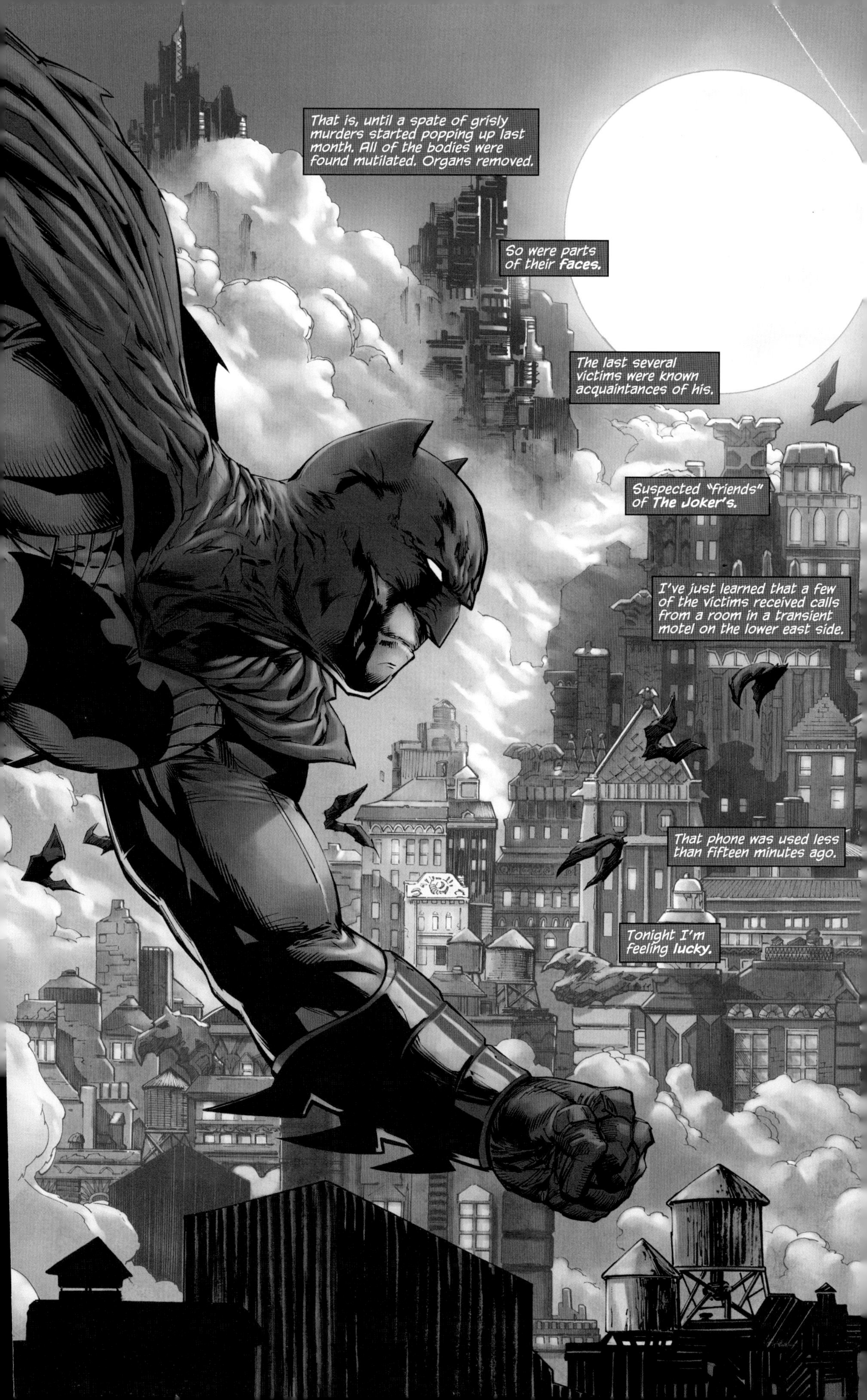
That is, until a spate of grisly murders started popping up last month. All of the bodies were found mutilated. Organs removed.
So were parts of their **faces.**
The last several victims were known acquaintances of his.
Suspected "friends" of **The Joker's.**
I've just learned that a few of the victims received calls from a room in a transient motel on the lower east side.
That phone was used less than fifteen minutes ago.
Tonight I'm feeling **lucky.**

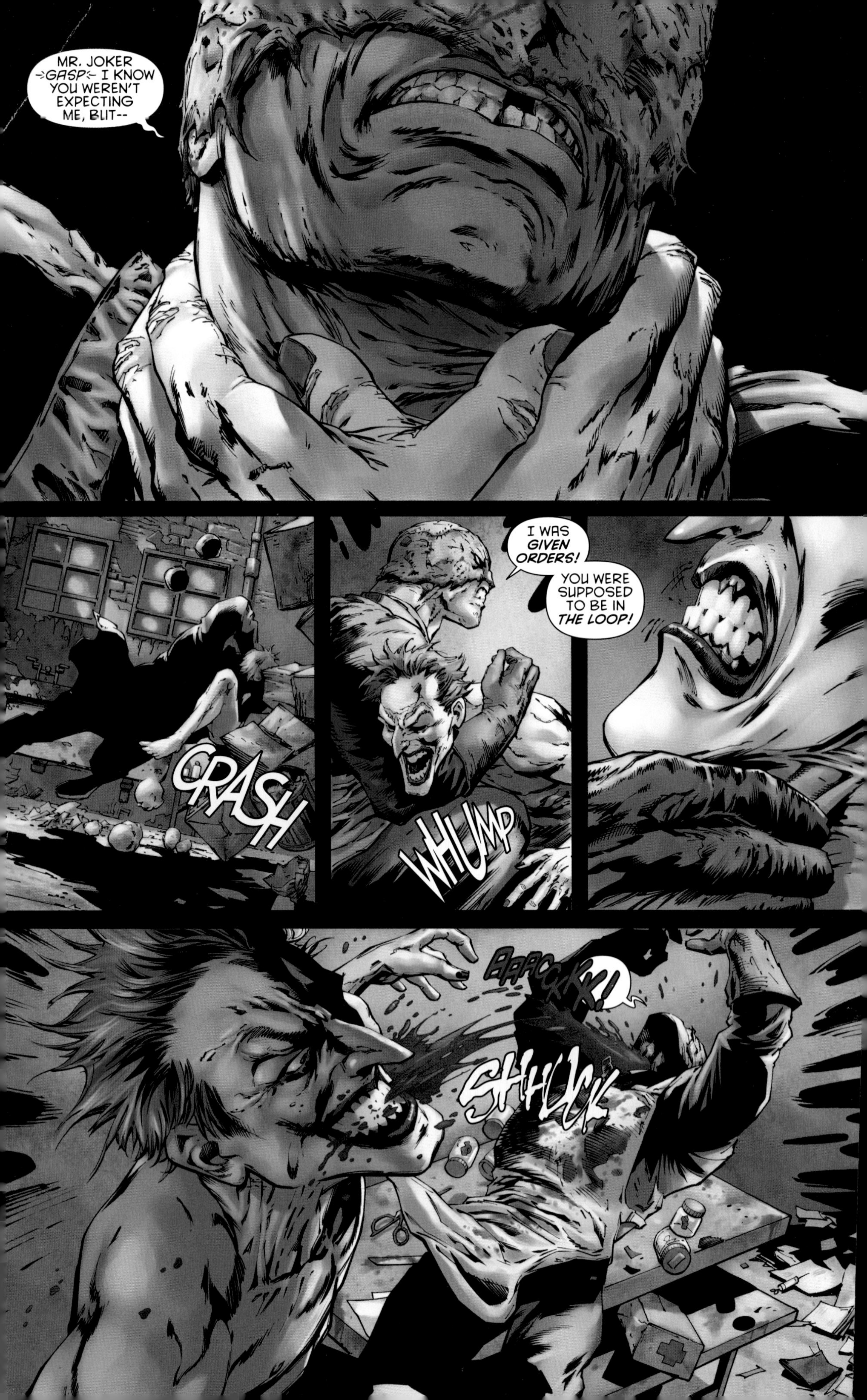
MR. JOKER -GASP- I KNOW YOU WEREN'T EXPECTING ME, BUT--
CRASH
I WAS GIVEN ORDERS!
YOU WERE SUPPOSED TO BE IN THE LOOP!
WHUMP
BAAACKKK!
SHHUCK

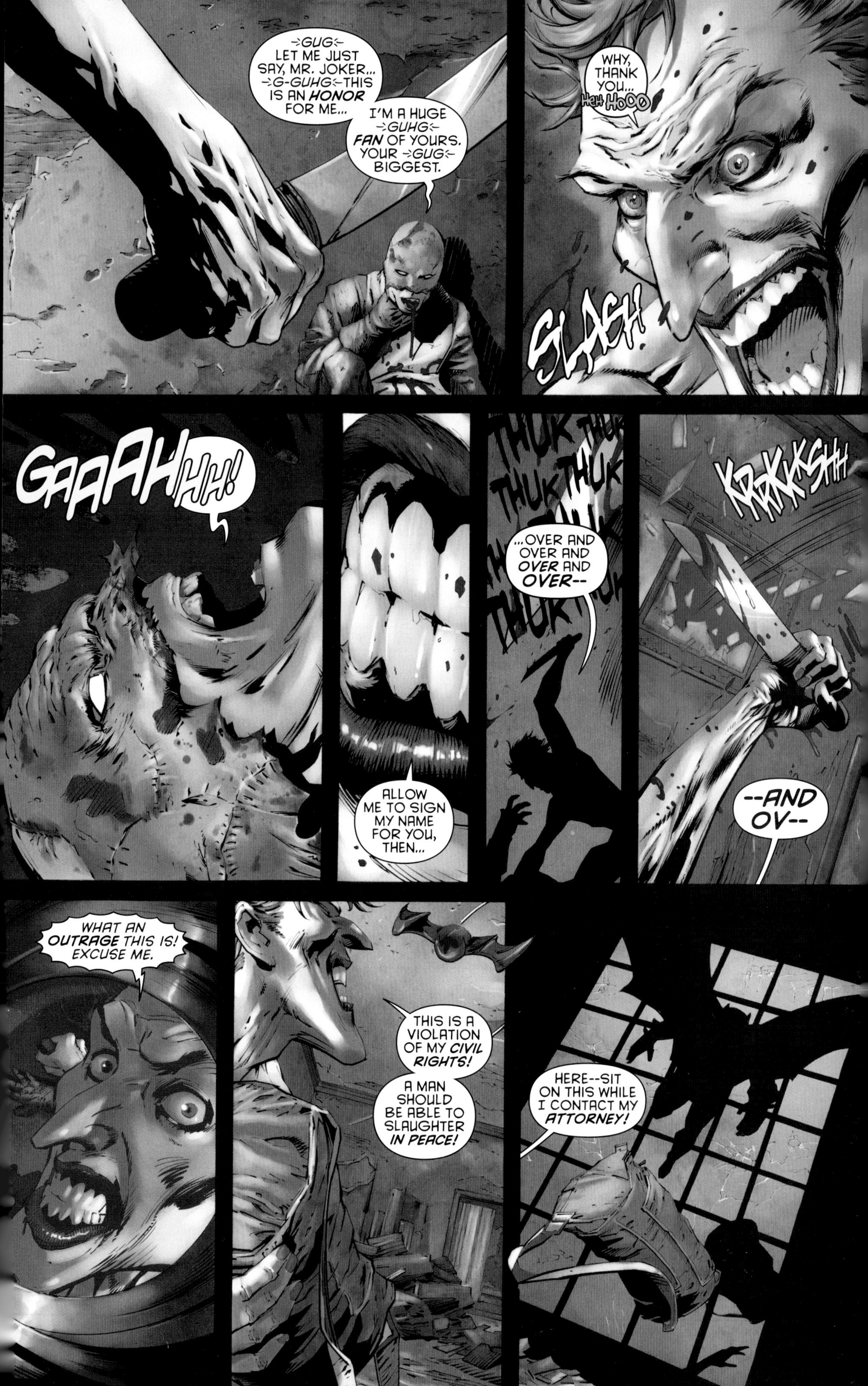

-GUG- LET ME JUST SAY, MR. JOKER... -G-GUHG- THIS IS AN HONOR FOR ME...
I'M A HUGE -GUHG- FAN OF YOURS. YOUR -GUG- BIGGEST.
WHY, THANK YOU... HEH HOOO
SLASH
GAAAHHH!
ALLOW ME TO SIGN MY NAME FOR YOU, THEN...
THUK THUK THUK THUK THUK
...OVER AND OVER AND OVER AND OVER--
KRRKKKSHH
--AND OV--
WHAT AN OUTRAGE THIS IS! EXCUSE ME.
THIS IS A VIOLATION OF MY CIVIL RIGHTS!
A MAN SHOULD BE ABLE TO SLAUGHTER IN PEACE!
HERE--SIT ON THIS WHILE I CONTACT MY ATTORNEY!

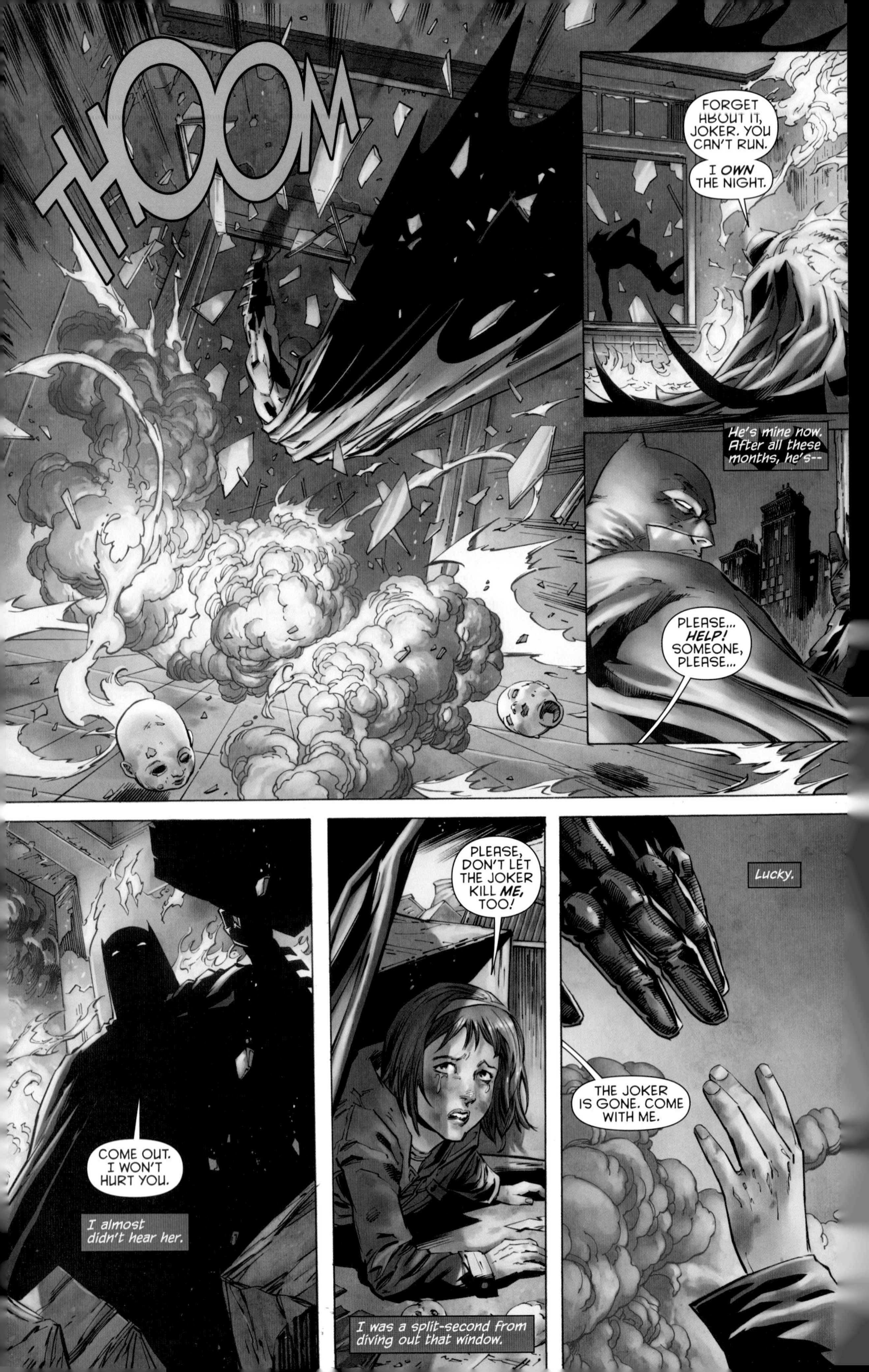
THOOM
FORGET ABOUT IT, JOKER. YOU CAN'T RUN.
I OWN THE NIGHT.
He's mine now. After all these months, he's--
PLEASE... HELP! SOMEONE, PLEASE...
COME OUT. I WON'T HURT YOU.
I almost didn't hear her.
PLEASE, DON'T LET THE JOKER KILL ME, TOO!
I was a split-second from diving out that window.
Lucky.
THE JOKER IS GONE. COME WITH ME.

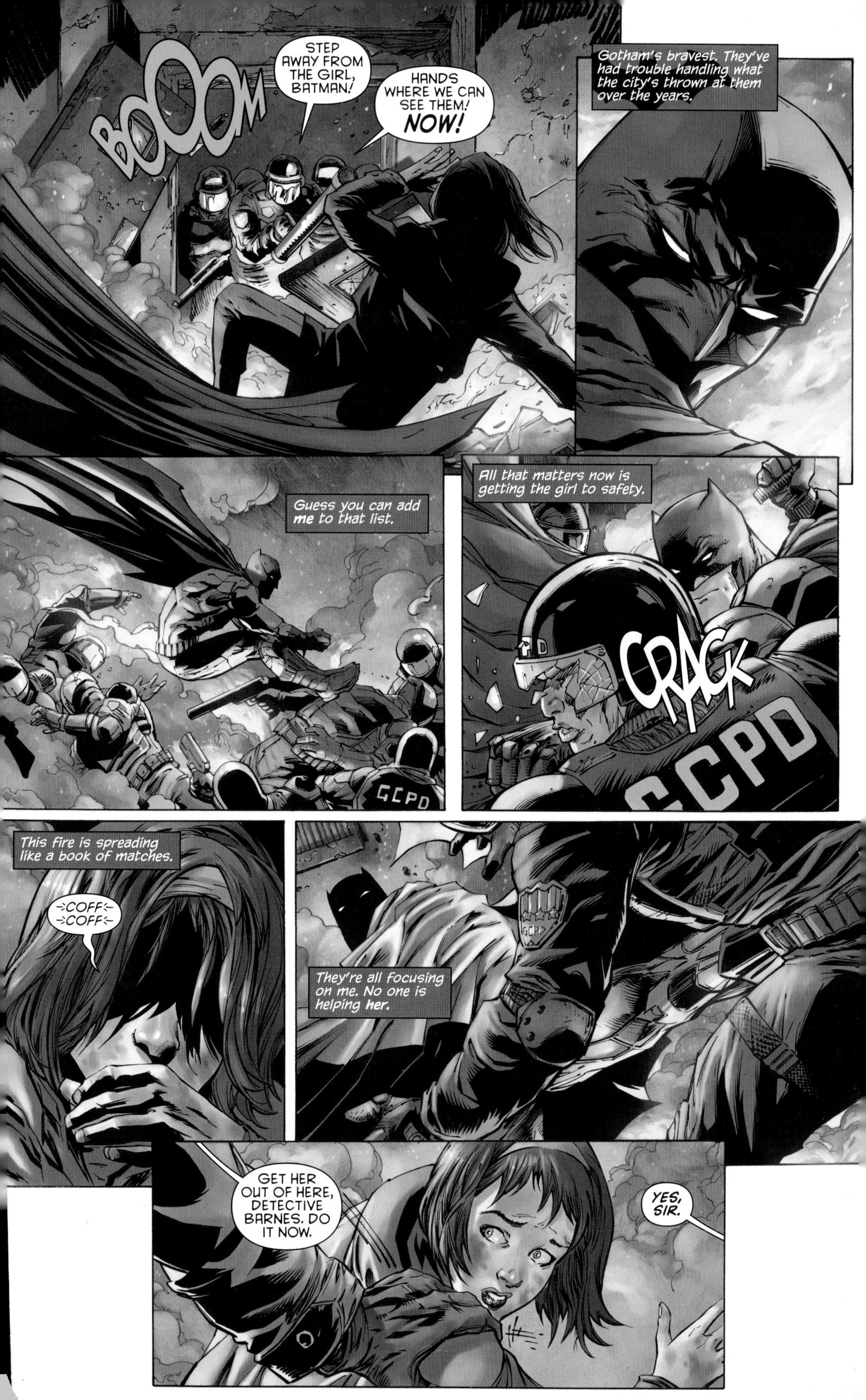
BOOOOM
STEP AWAY FROM THE GIRL, BATMAN!
HANDS WHERE WE CAN SEE THEM! NOW!
Gotham's bravest. They've had trouble handling what the city's thrown at them over the years.
Guess you can add me to that list.
All that matters now is getting the girl to safety.
CRACK
GCPD
This fire is spreading like a book of matches.
COFF COFF
They're all focusing on me. No one is helping her.
GET HER OUT OF HERE, DETECTIVE BARNES. DO IT NOW.
YES, SIR.

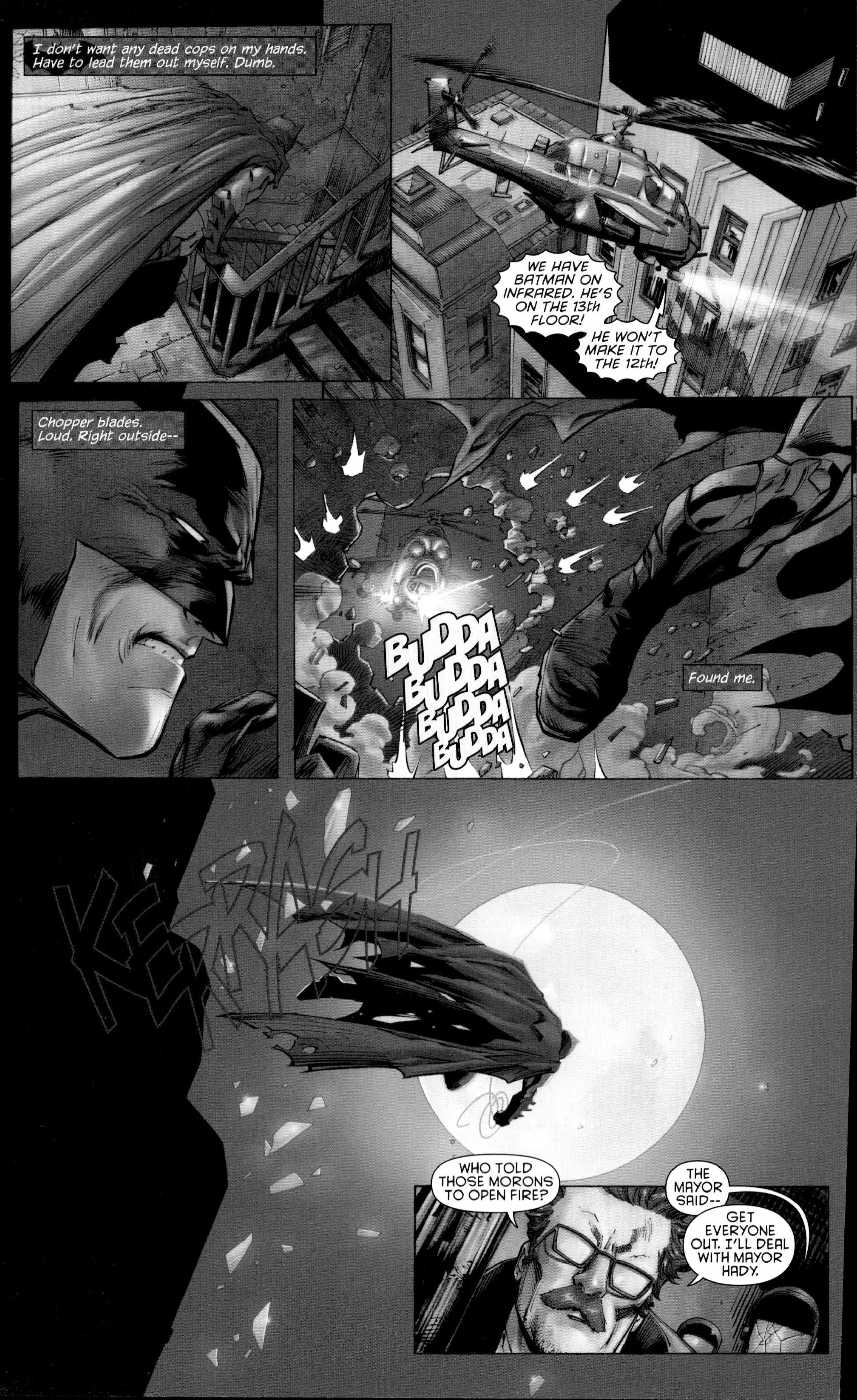
I don't want any dead cops on my hands. Have to lead them out myself. Dumb.
WE HAVE BATMAN ON INFRARED. HE'S ON THE 13th FLOOR!
HE WON'T MAKE IT TO THE 12th!
Chopper blades. Loud. Right outside--
BUDDA BUDDA BUDDA BUDDA
Found me.
KERRASH
WHO TOLD THOSE MORONS TO OPEN FIRE?
THE MAYOR SAID--
GET EVERYONE OUT. I'LL DEAL WITH MAYOR HADY.

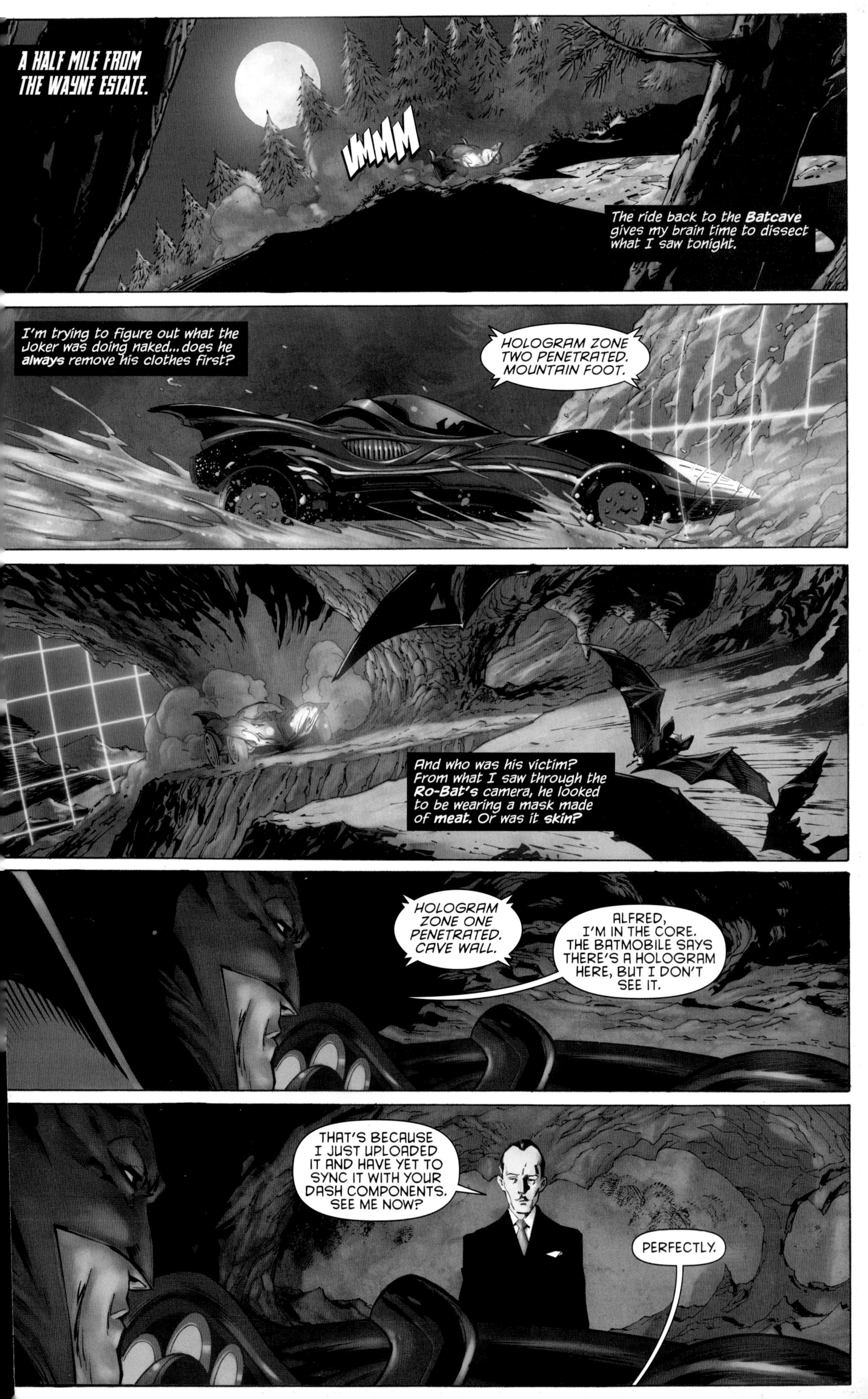
A HALF MILE FROM THE WAYNE ESTATE.
VMMM
The ride back to the Batcave gives my brain time to dissect what I saw tonight.
I'm trying to figure out what the Joker was doing naked... does he always remove his clothes first?
HOLOGRAM ZONE TWO PENETRATED. MOUNTAIN FOOT.
And who was his victim? From what I saw through the Ro-Bat's camera, he looked to be wearing a mask made of meat. Or was it skin?
HOLOGRAM ZONE ONE PENETRATED. CAVE WALL.
ALFRED, I'M IN THE CORE. THE BATMOBILE SAYS THERE'S A HOLOGRAM HERE, BUT I DON'T SEE IT.
THAT'S BECAUSE I JUST UPLOADED IT AND HAVE YET TO SYNC IT WITH YOUR DASH COMPONENTS. SEE ME NOW?
PERFECTLY.

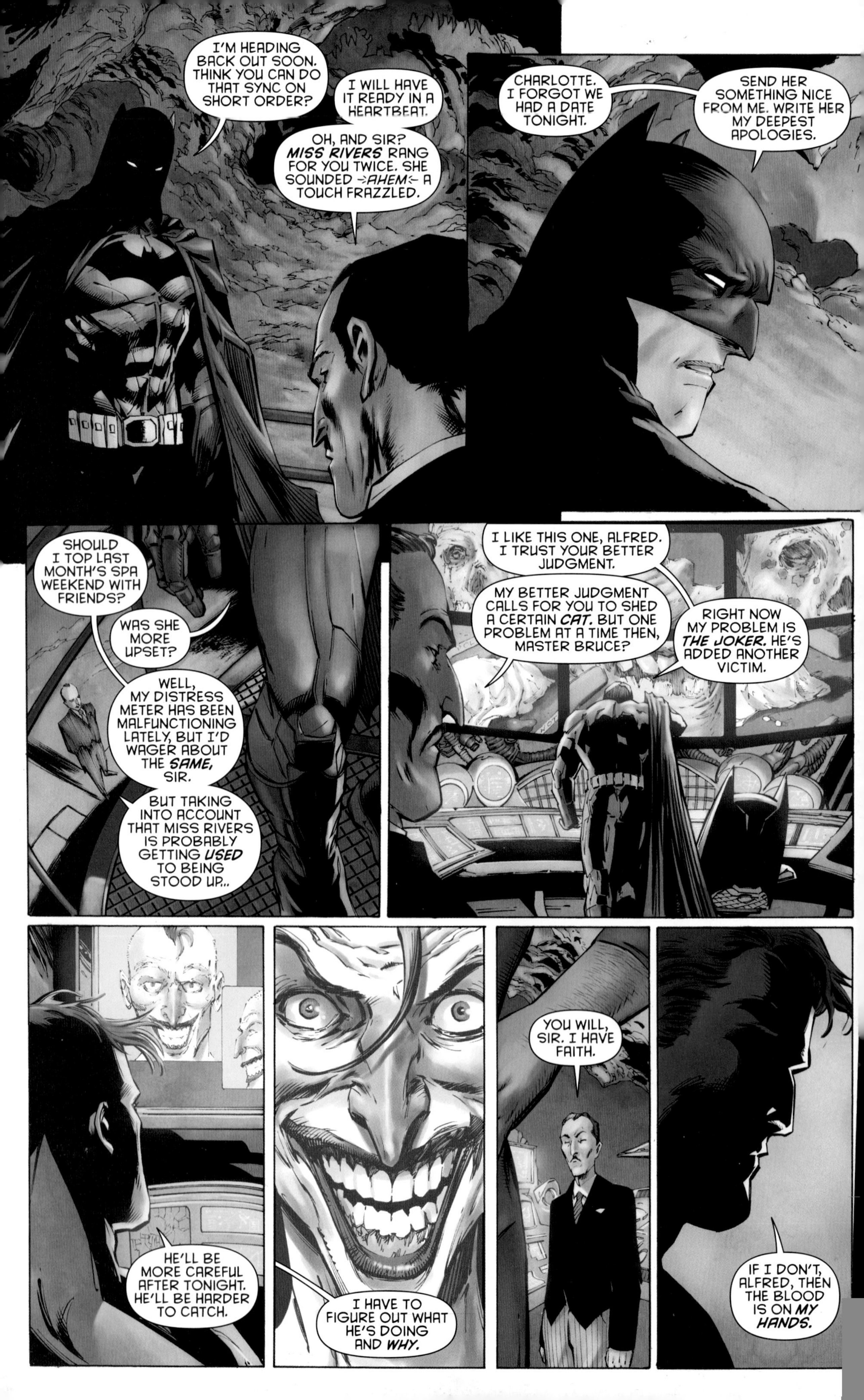
I'M HEADING BACK OUT SOON. THINK YOU CAN DO THAT SYNC ON SHORT ORDER?
I WILL HAVE IT READY IN A HEARTBEAT.
OH, AND SIR? MISS RIVERS RANG FOR YOU TWICE. SHE SOUNDED ⇒AHEM⇐ A TOUCH FRAZZLED.
CHARLOTTE. I FORGOT WE HAD A DATE TONIGHT.
SEND HER SOMETHING NICE FROM ME. WRITE HER MY DEEPEST APOLOGIES.
SHOULD I TOP LAST MONTH'S SPA WEEKEND WITH FRIENDS?
WAS SHE MORE UPSET?
WELL, MY DISTRESS METER HAS BEEN MALFUNCTIONING LATELY, BUT I'D WAGER ABOUT THE SAME, SIR.
BUT TAKING INTO ACCOUNT THAT MISS RIVERS IS PROBABLY GETTING USED TO BEING STOOD UP...
I LIKE THIS ONE, ALFRED. I TRUST YOUR BETTER JUDGMENT.
MY BETTER JUDGMENT CALLS FOR YOU TO SHED A CERTAIN CAT. BUT ONE PROBLEM AT A TIME THEN, MASTER BRUCE?
RIGHT NOW MY PROBLEM IS THE JOKER. HE'S ADDED ANOTHER VICTIM.
HE'LL BE MORE CAREFUL AFTER TONIGHT. HE'LL BE HARDER TO CATCH.
I HAVE TO FIGURE OUT WHAT HE'S DOING AND WHY.
YOU WILL, SIR. I HAVE FAITH.
IF I DON'T, ALFRED, THEN THE BLOOD IS ON MY HANDS.

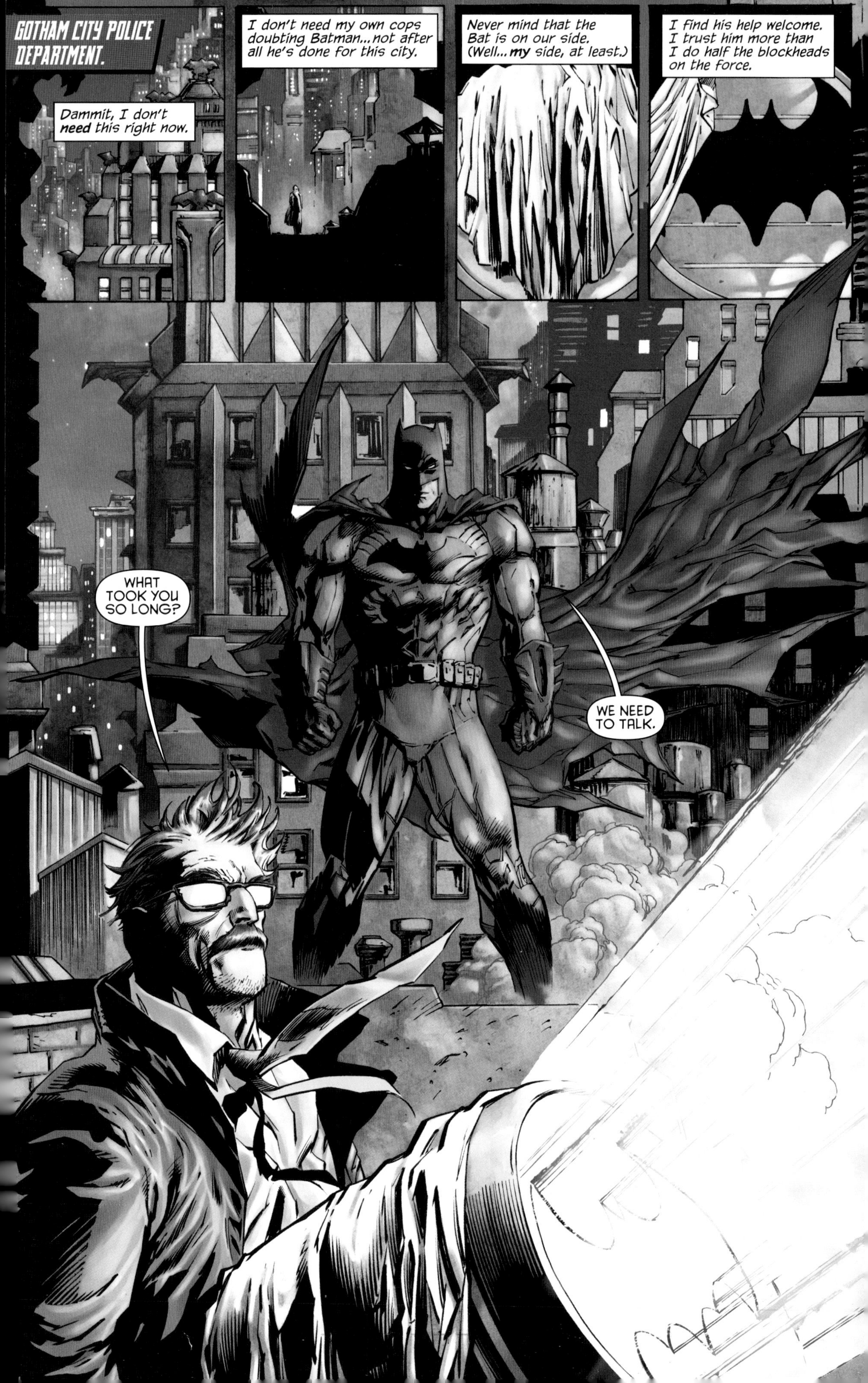
GOTHAM CITY POLICE DEPARTMENT.
Dammit, I don't **need** this right now.
I don't need my own cops doubting Batman...not after all he's done for this city.
Never mind that the Bat is on our side. (Well... **my** side, at least.)
I find his help welcome. I trust him more than I do half the blockheads on the force.
WHAT TOOK YOU SO LONG?
WE NEED TO TALK.

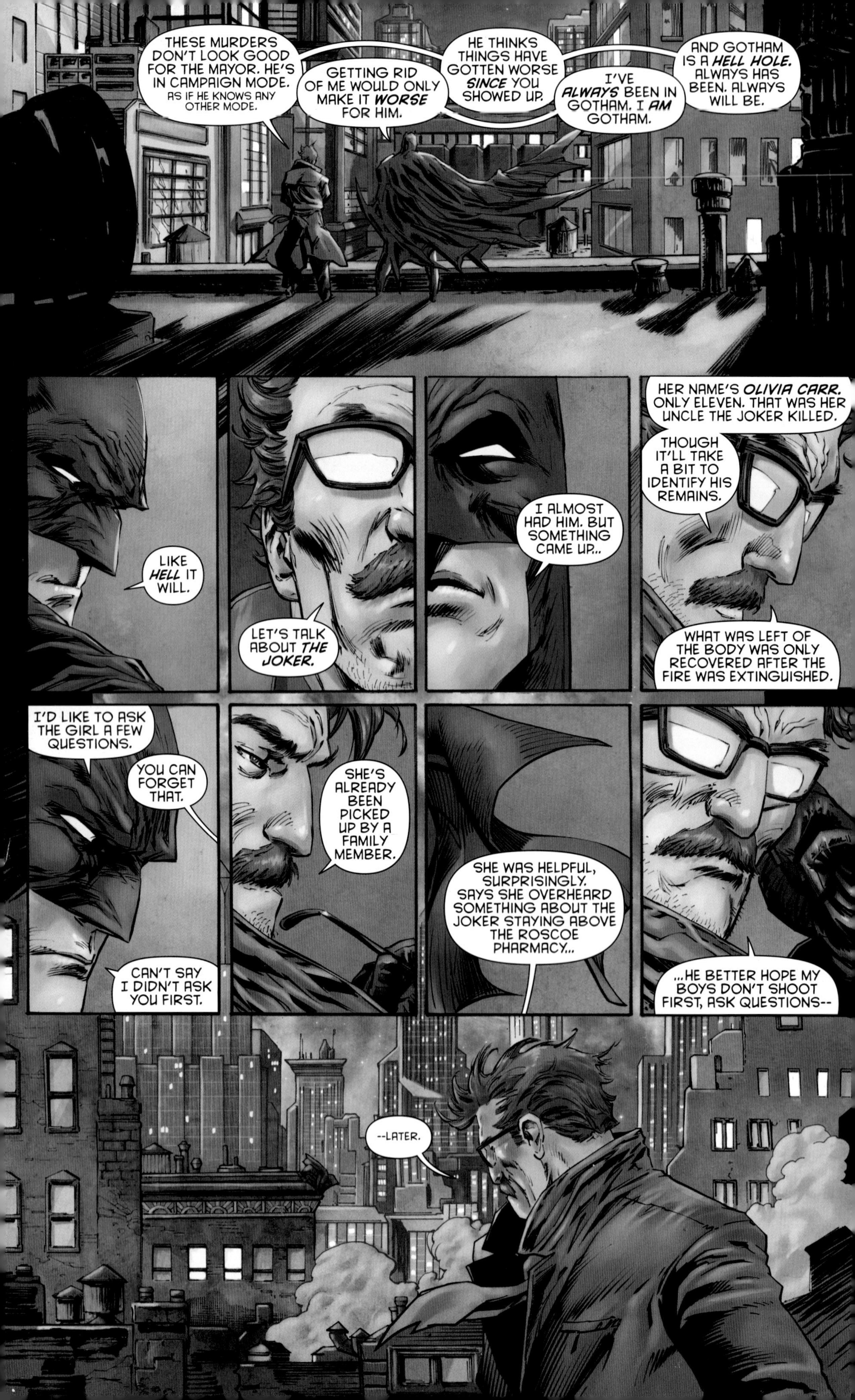

THESE MURDERS DON'T LOOK GOOD FOR THE MAYOR. HE'S IN CAMPAIGN MODE. AS IF HE KNOWS ANY OTHER MODE.
GETTING RID OF ME WOULD ONLY MAKE IT WORSE FOR HIM.
HE THINKS THINGS HAVE GOTTEN WORSE SINCE YOU SHOWED UP.
I'VE ALWAYS BEEN IN GOTHAM. I AM GOTHAM.
AND GOTHAM IS A HELL HOLE. ALWAYS HAS BEEN. ALWAYS WILL BE.
LIKE HELL IT WILL.
LET'S TALK ABOUT THE JOKER.
I ALMOST HAD HIM. BUT SOMETHING CAME UP...
HER NAME'S OLIVIA CARR. ONLY ELEVEN. THAT WAS HER UNCLE THE JOKER KILLED.
THOUGH IT'LL TAKE A BIT TO IDENTIFY HIS REMAINS.
WHAT WAS LEFT OF THE BODY WAS ONLY RECOVERED AFTER THE FIRE WAS EXTINGUISHED.
I'D LIKE TO ASK THE GIRL A FEW QUESTIONS.
YOU CAN FORGET THAT.
CAN'T SAY I DIDN'T ASK YOU FIRST.
SHE'S ALREADY BEEN PICKED UP BY A FAMILY MEMBER.
SHE WAS HELPFUL, SURPRISINGLY. SAYS SHE OVERHEARD SOMETHING ABOUT THE JOKER STAYING ABOVE THE ROSCOE PHARMACY...
...HE BETTER HOPE MY BOYS DON'T SHOOT FIRST, ASK QUESTIONS--
--LATER.

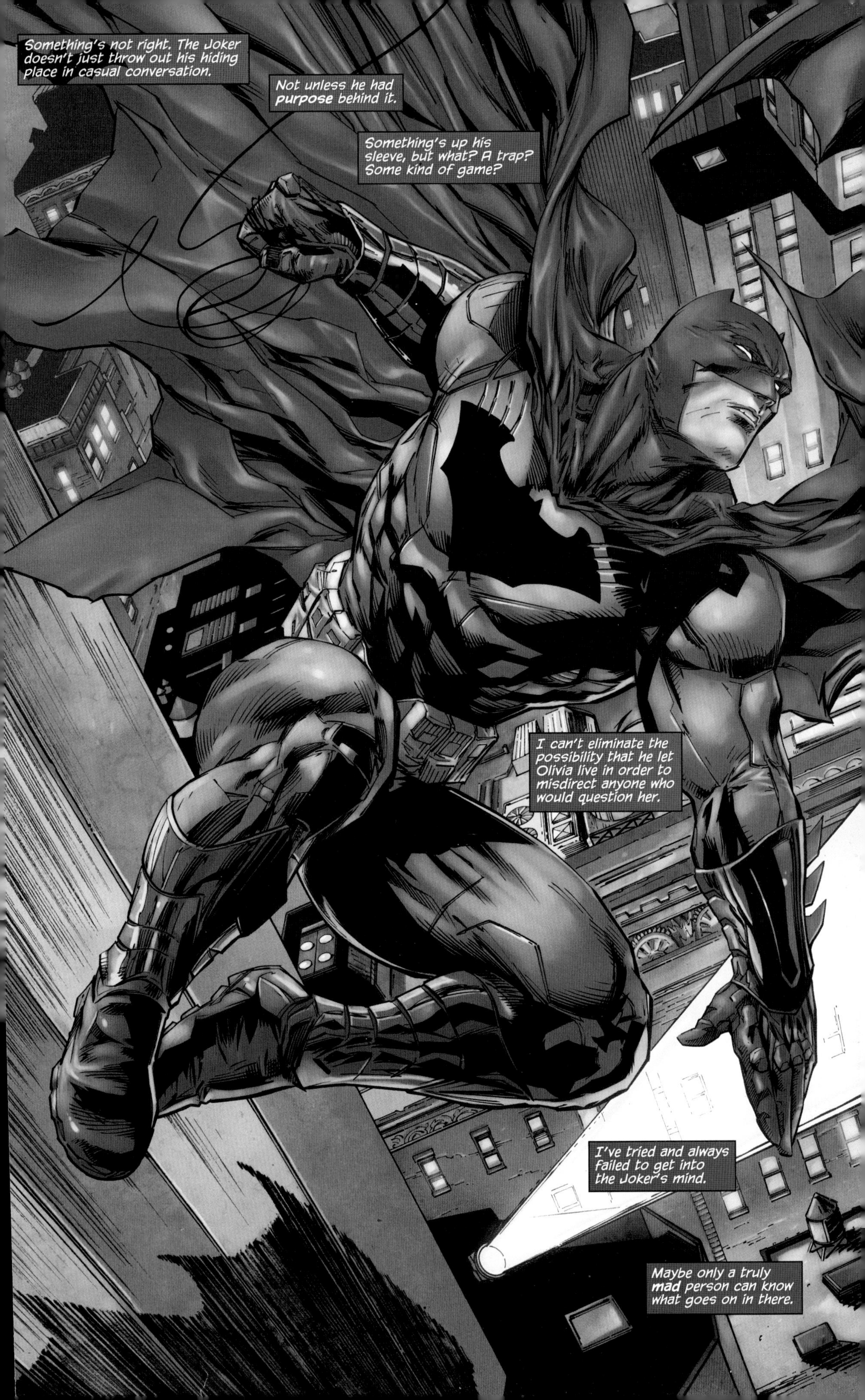
Something's not right. The Joker doesn't just throw out his hiding place in casual conversation.
Not unless he had **purpose** behind it.
Something's up his sleeve, but what? A trap? Some kind of game?
I can't eliminate the possibility that he let Olivia live in order to misdirect anyone who would question her.
I've tried and always failed to get into the Joker's mind.
Maybe only a truly **mad** person can know what goes on in there.

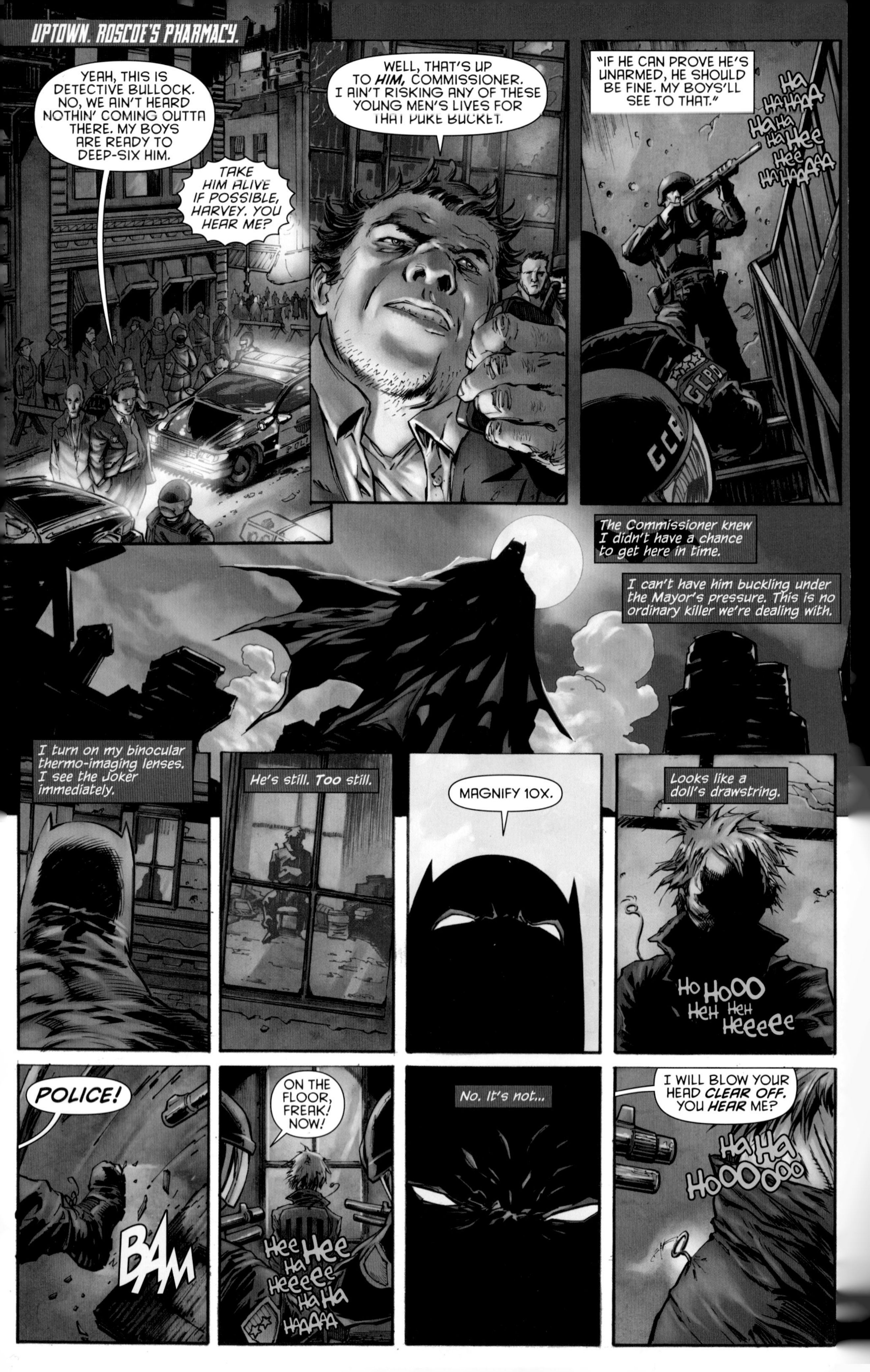
UPTOWN. ROSCOE'S PHARMACY.
YEAH, THIS IS DETECTIVE BULLOCK. NO, WE AIN'T HEARD NOTHIN' COMING OUTTA THERE. MY BOYS ARE READY TO DEEP-SIX HIM.
TAKE HIM ALIVE IF POSSIBLE, HARVEY. YOU HEAR ME?
WELL, THAT'S UP TO *HIM*, COMMISSIONER. I AIN'T RISKING ANY OF THESE YOUNG MEN'S LIVES FOR THAT PUKE BUCKET.
"IF HE CAN PROVE HE'S UNARMED, HE SHOULD BE FINE. MY BOYS'LL SEE TO THAT."
Ha HaHaaa Ha Ha Ha Hee Hee HaHaaaa
GCPD
The Commissioner knew I didn't have a chance to get here in time.
I can't have him buckling under the Mayor's pressure. This is no ordinary killer we're dealing with.
I turn on my binocular thermo-imaging lenses. I see the Joker immediately.
He's still. *Too* still.
MAGNIFY 10X.
Looks like a doll's drawstring.
Ho HoOO Heh Heh Heeeee
POLICE!
BAM
ON THE FLOOR, FREAK! NOW!
Hee Hee Ha Heeeee Ha Ha Haaaaa
No. It's not...
I WILL BLOW YOUR HEAD *CLEAR OFF.* YOU *HEAR* ME?
Ha Ha HoOOOOO

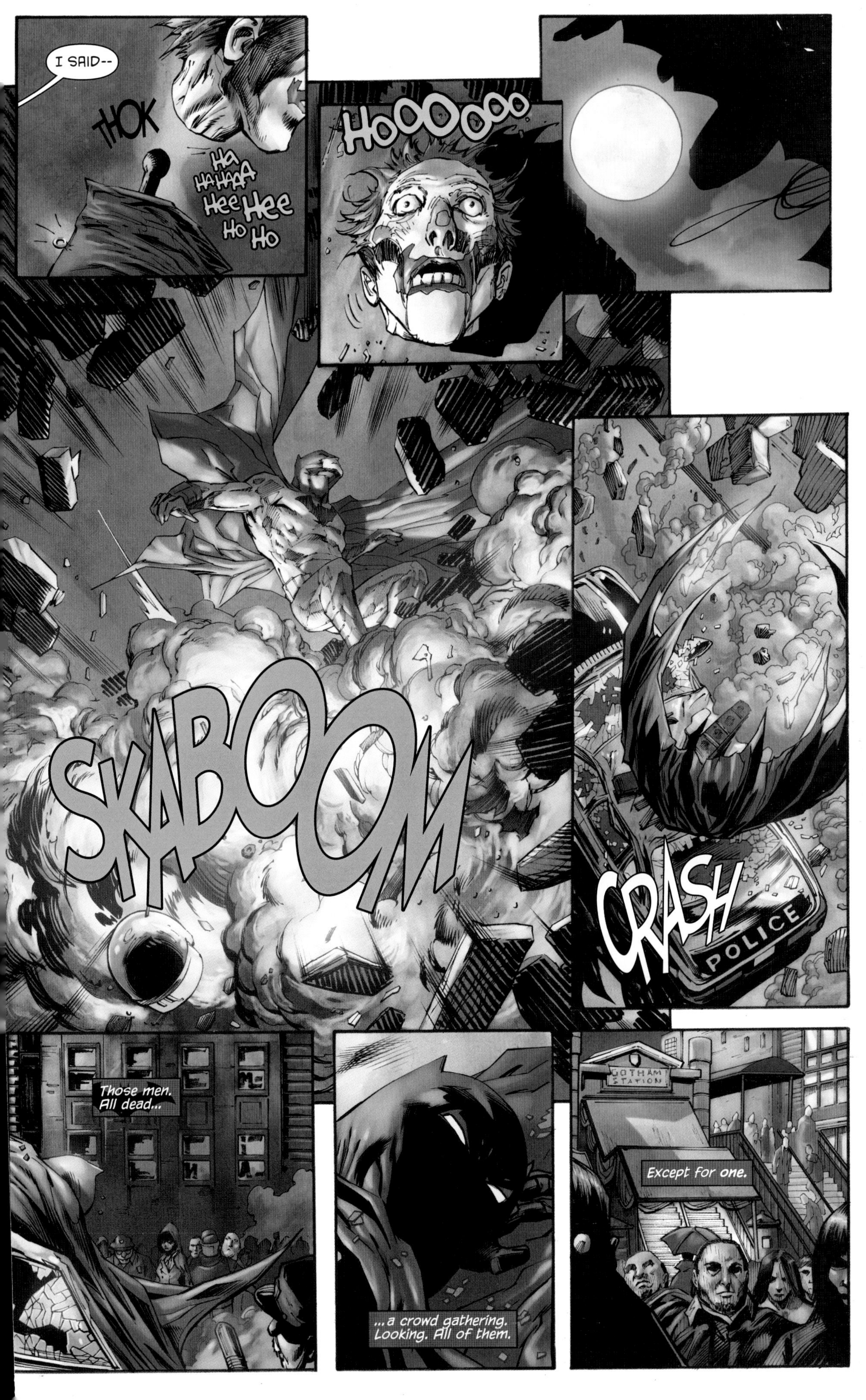
I SAID--
THOK
HA HA HAAA HEE HEE HO HO
HOOOOOO
SKABOOM
CRASH
POLICE
POLICE
Those men. All dead...
...a crowd gathering. Looking. All of them.
GOTHAM STATION
Except for one.

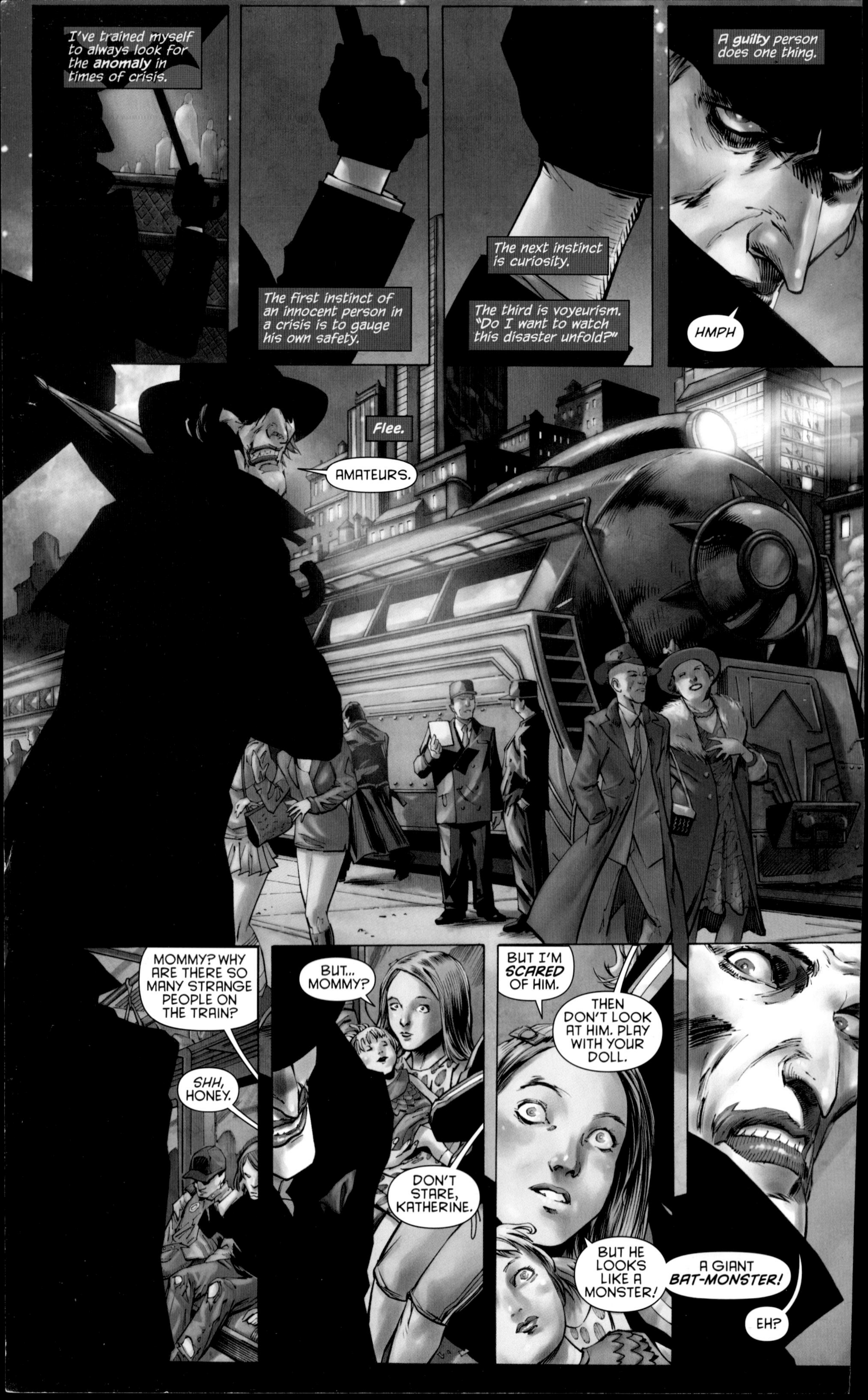
I've trained myself to always look for the **anomaly** in times of crisis.
The first instinct of an innocent person in a crisis is to gauge his own safety.
The next instinct is curiosity.
The third is voyeurism. "Do I want to watch this disaster unfold?"
A **guilty** person does one thing.
HMPH
Flee.
AMATEURS.
MOMMY? WHY ARE THERE SO MANY STRANGE PEOPLE ON THE TRAIN?
SHH, HONEY.
BUT... MOMMY?
DON'T STARE, KATHERINE.
BUT I'M *SCARED* OF HIM.
THEN DON'T LOOK AT HIM. PLAY WITH YOUR DOLL.
BUT HE LOOKS LIKE A MONSTER!
A GIANT *BAT-MONSTER!*
EH?

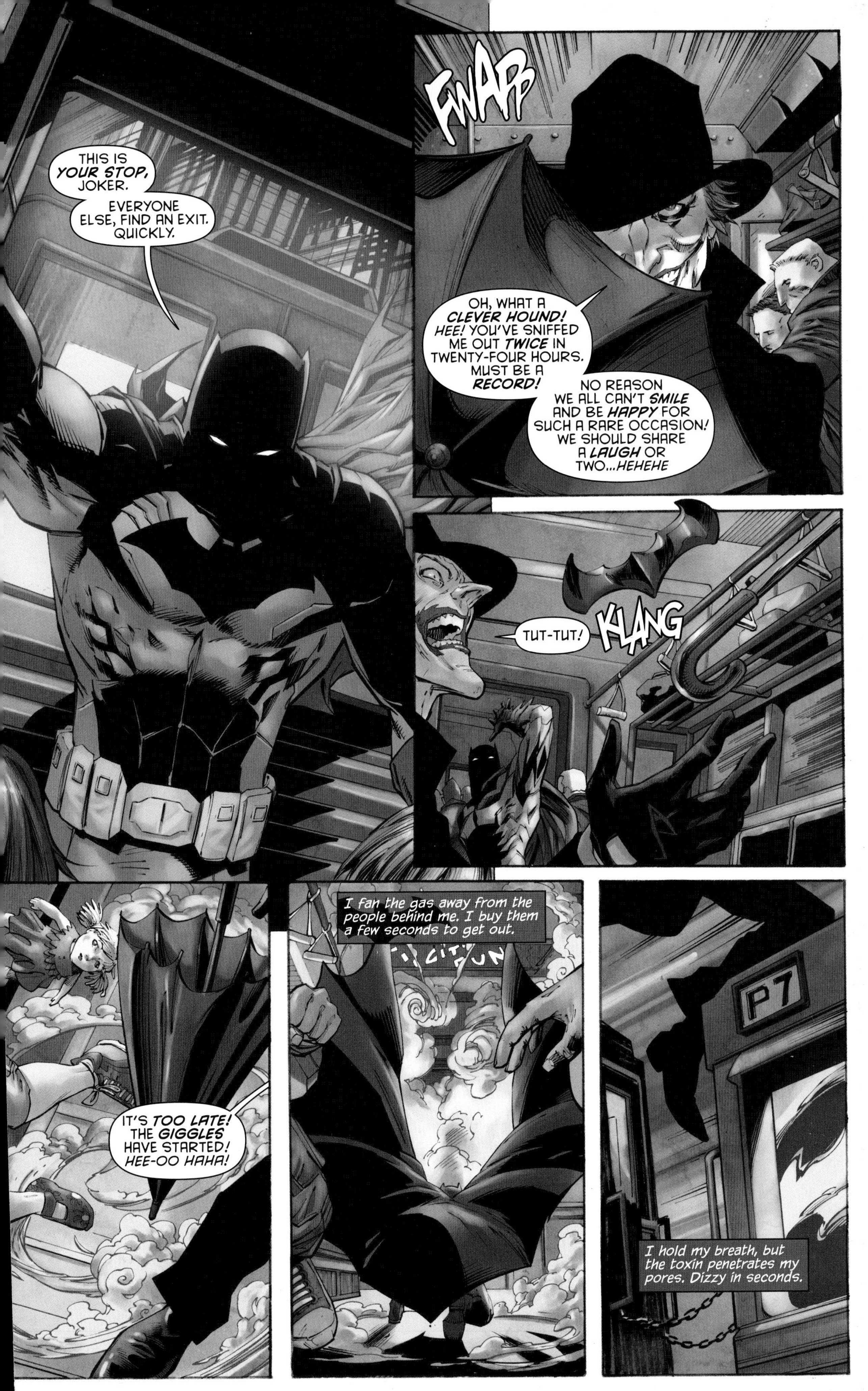
THIS IS YOUR STOP, JOKER.
EVERYONE ELSE, FIND AN EXIT. QUICKLY.
FWAPP
OH, WHAT A CLEVER HOUND! HEE! YOU'VE SNIFFED ME OUT TWICE IN TWENTY-FOUR HOURS. MUST BE A RECORD!
NO REASON WE ALL CAN'T SMILE AND BE HAPPY FOR SUCH A RARE OCCASION! WE SHOULD SHARE A LAUGH OR TWO...HEHEHE
TUT-TUT!
KLANG
IT'S TOO LATE! THE GIGGLES HAVE STARTED! HEE-OO HAHA!
I fan the gas away from the people behind me. I buy them a few seconds to get out.
P7
I hold my breath, but the toxin penetrates my pores. Dizzy in seconds.

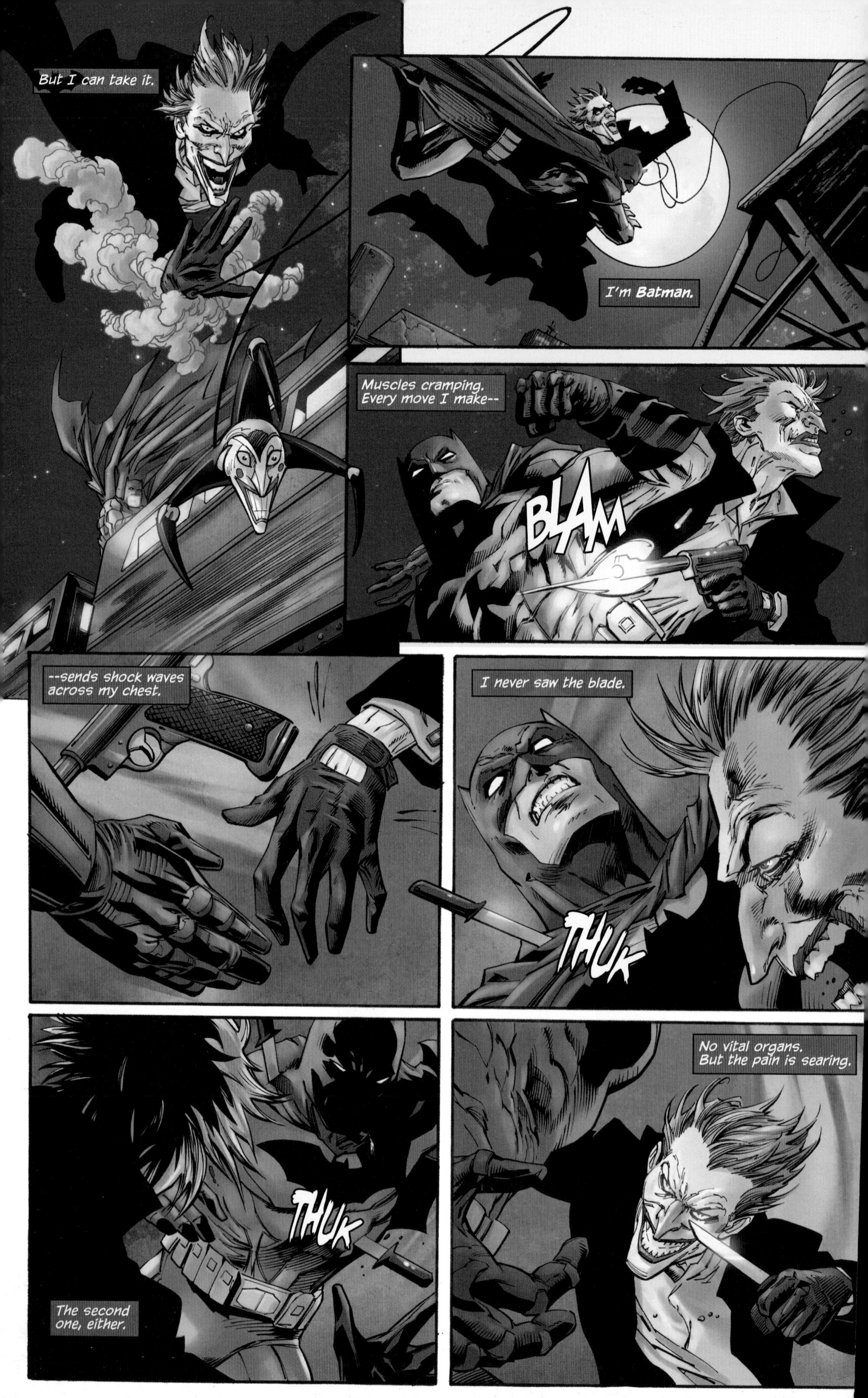
But I can take it.
I'm Batman.
Muscles cramping. Every move I make--
BLAM
--sends shock waves across my chest.
I never saw the blade.
THUK
THUK
The second one, either.
No vital organs. But the pain is searing.

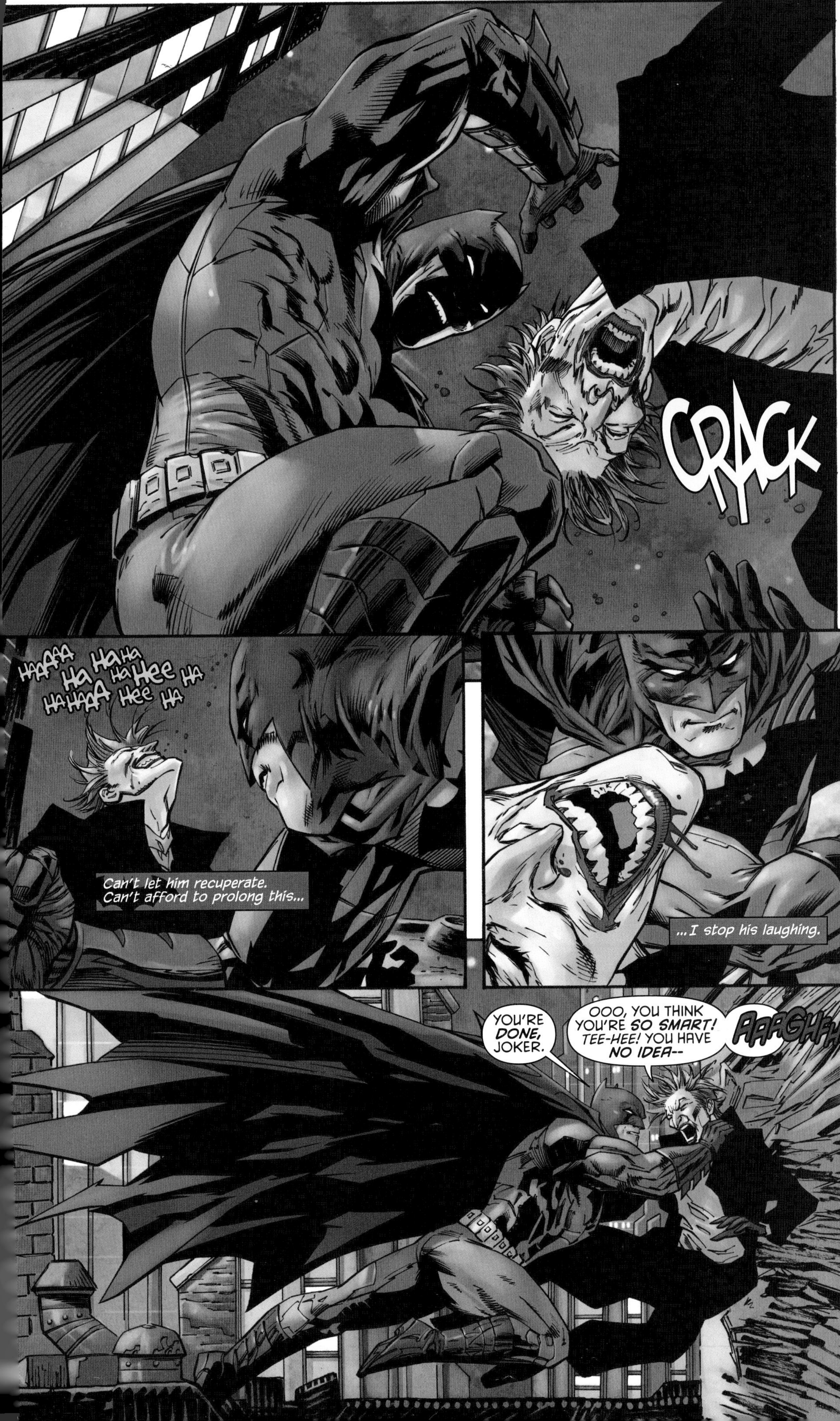
CRACK
HAAAAA HA HAHA HAHA HEE HA HAHAAA HEE HA
Can't let him recuperate. Can't afford to prolong this...
...I stop his laughing.
YOU'RE DONE, JOKER.
OOO, YOU THINK YOU'RE SO SMART! TEE-HEE! YOU HAVE NO IDEA--
AAAGHHH!

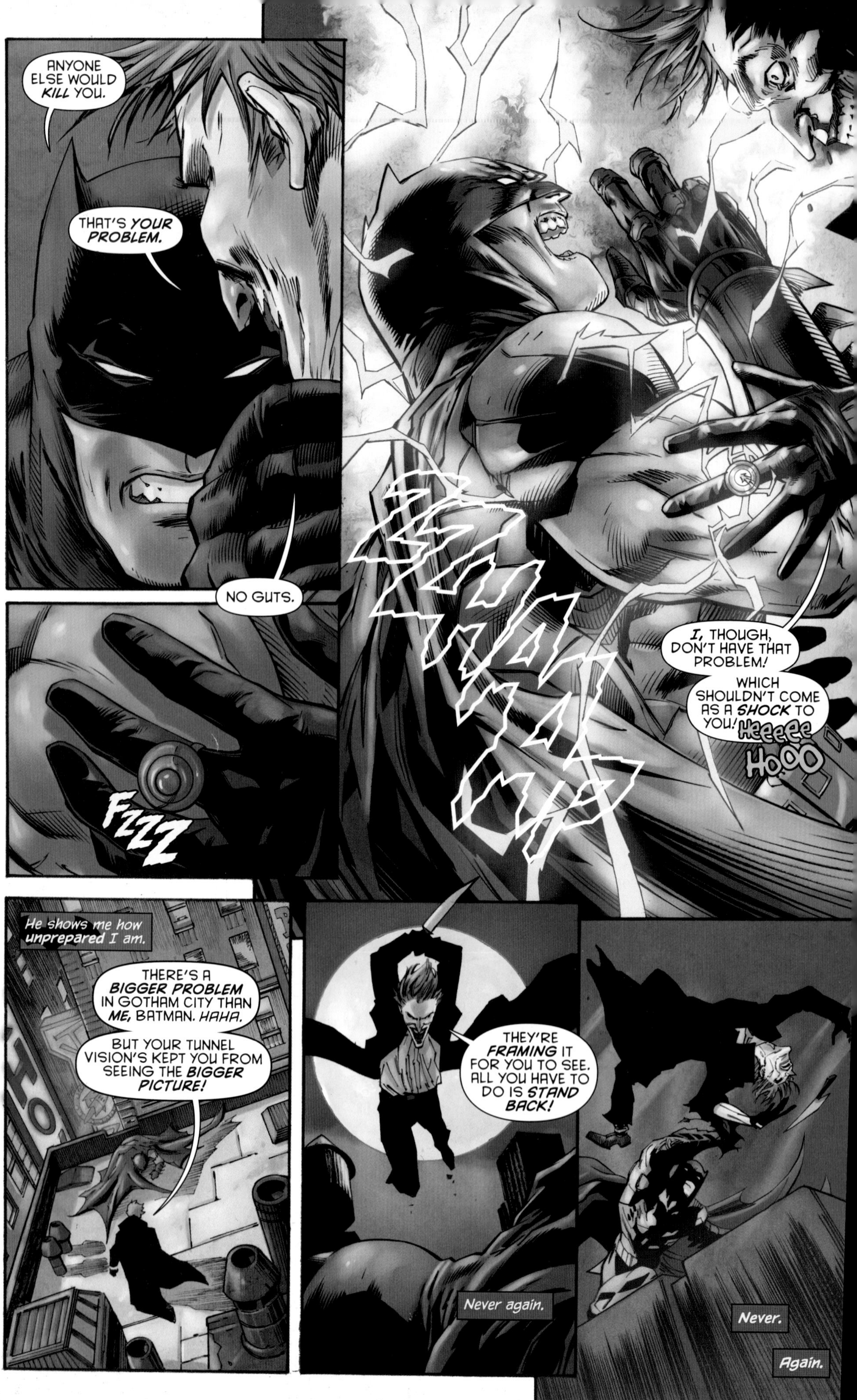

ANYONE ELSE WOULD KILL YOU.
THAT'S YOUR PROBLEM.
NO GUTS.
FZZZ
I, THOUGH, DON'T HAVE THAT PROBLEM!
WHICH SHOULDN'T COME AS A SHOCK TO YOU! HEEEEE HOOO
He shows me how unprepared I am.
THERE'S A BIGGER PROBLEM IN GOTHAM CITY THAN ME, BATMAN. HAHA.
BUT YOUR TUNNEL VISION'S KEPT YOU FROM SEEING THE BIGGER PICTURE!
THEY'RE FRAMING IT FOR YOU TO SEE. ALL YOU HAVE TO DO IS STAND BACK!
Never again.
Never.
Again.

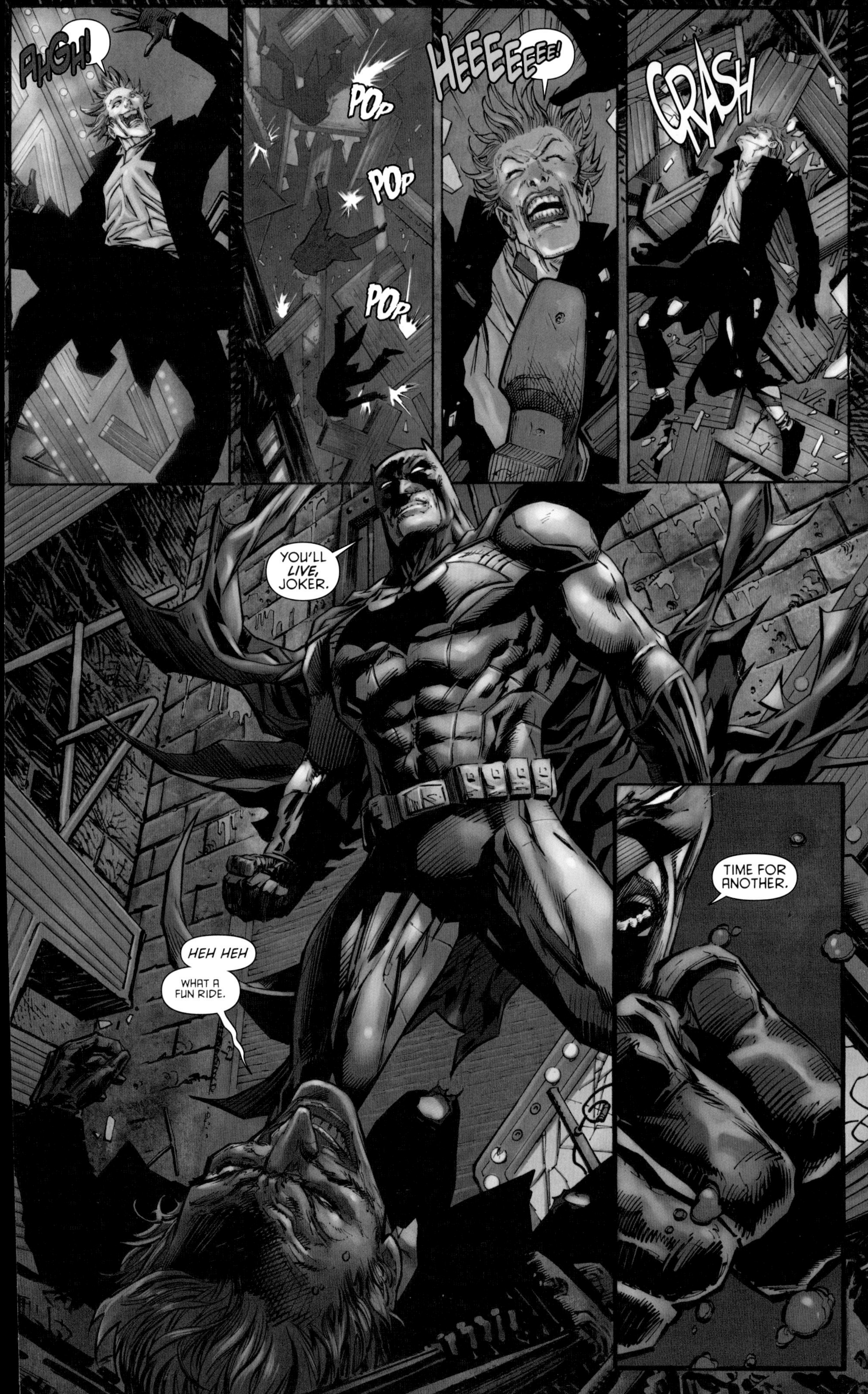
AHGH!
POP
POP
POP
HEEEEEEEE!
CRASH
YOU'LL *LIVE,* JOKER.
HEH HEH
WHAT A FUN RIDE.
TIME FOR ANOTHER.

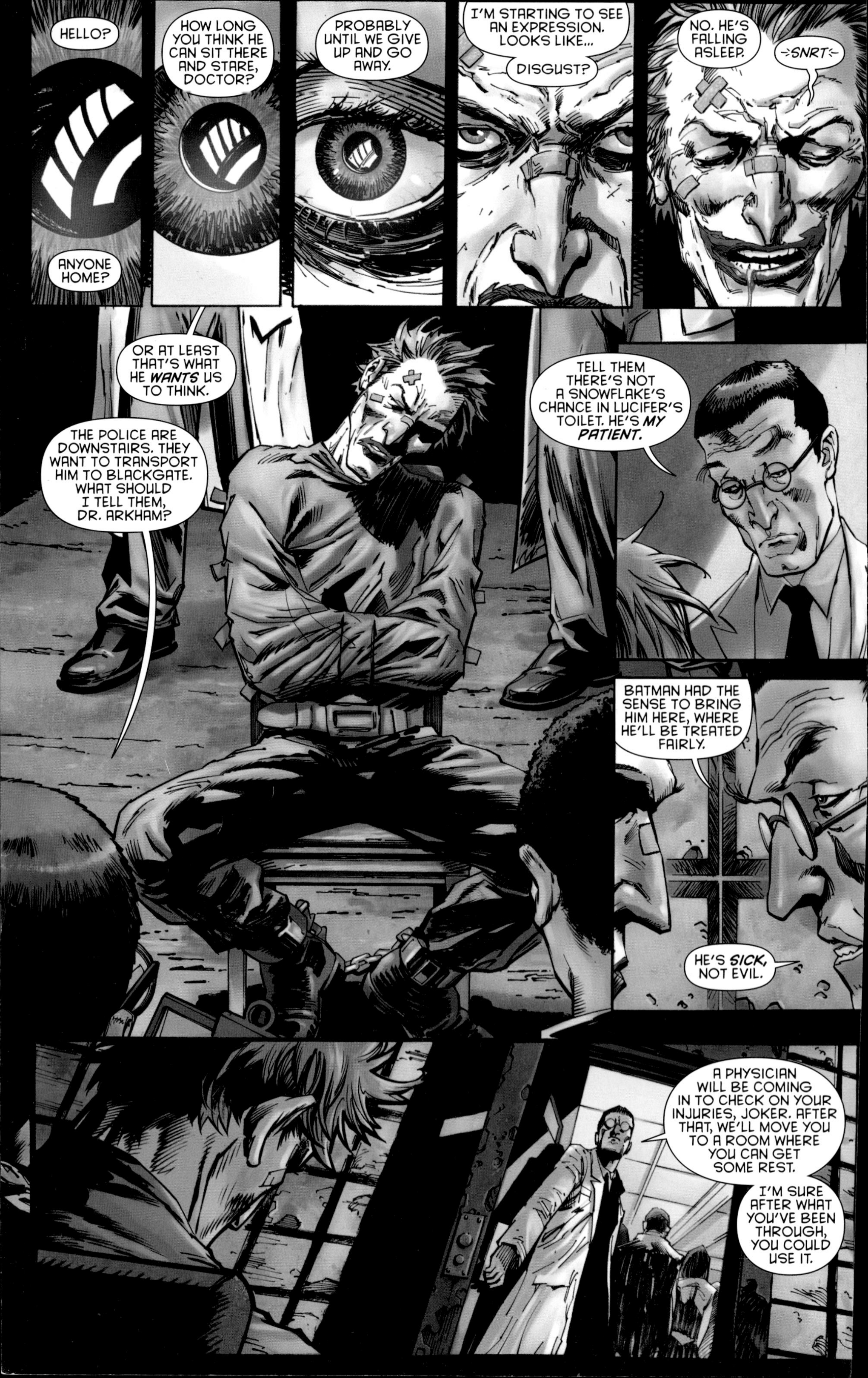
HELLO?
ANYONE HOME?
HOW LONG YOU THINK HE CAN SIT THERE AND STARE, DOCTOR?
PROBABLY UNTIL WE GIVE UP AND GO AWAY.
I'M STARTING TO SEE AN EXPRESSION. LOOKS LIKE...
DISGUST?
NO. HE'S FALLING ASLEEP.
SNRT
OR AT LEAST THAT'S WHAT HE WANTS US TO THINK.
THE POLICE ARE DOWNSTAIRS. THEY WANT TO TRANSPORT HIM TO BLACKGATE. WHAT SHOULD I TELL THEM, DR. ARKHAM?
TELL THEM THERE'S NOT A SNOWFLAKE'S CHANCE IN LUCIFER'S TOILET. HE'S MY PATIENT.
BATMAN HAD THE SENSE TO BRING HIM HERE, WHERE HE'LL BE TREATED FAIRLY.
HE'S SICK, NOT EVIL.
A PHYSICIAN WILL BE COMING IN TO CHECK ON YOUR INJURIES, JOKER. AFTER THAT, WE'LL MOVE YOU TO A ROOM WHERE YOU CAN GET SOME REST.
I'M SURE AFTER WHAT YOU'VE BEEN THROUGH, YOU COULD USE IT.

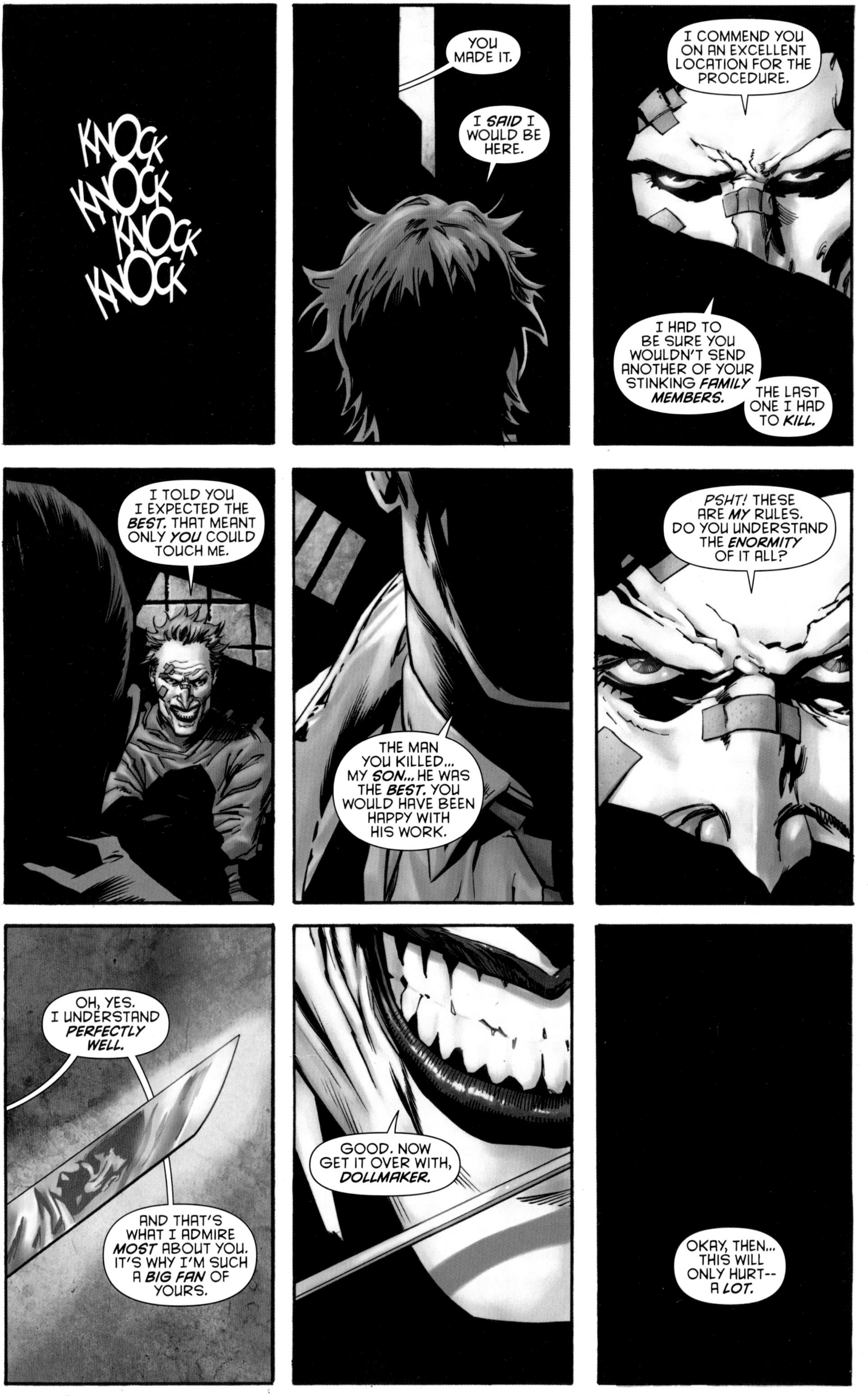
KNOCK KNOCK KNOCK KNOCK
YOU MADE IT.
I *SAID* I WOULD BE HERE.
I COMMEND YOU ON AN EXCELLENT LOCATION FOR THE PROCEDURE.
I HAD TO BE SURE YOU WOULDN'T SEND ANOTHER OF YOUR STINKING *FAMILY MEMBERS.*
THE LAST ONE I HAD TO *KILL.*
I TOLD YOU I EXPECTED THE *BEST.* THAT MEANT ONLY *YOU* COULD TOUCH ME.
THE MAN YOU KILLED... MY *SON...* HE WAS THE *BEST.* YOU WOULD HAVE BEEN HAPPY WITH HIS WORK.
PSHT! THESE ARE *MY* RULES. DO YOU UNDERSTAND THE *ENORMITY* OF IT ALL?
OH, YES. I UNDERSTAND *PERFECTLY WELL.*
AND THAT'S WHAT I ADMIRE *MOST* ABOUT YOU. IT'S WHY I'M SUCH A *BIG FAN* OF YOURS.
GOOD. NOW GET IT OVER WITH, *DOLLMAKER.*
OKAY, THEN... THIS WILL ONLY HURT-- A *LOT.*

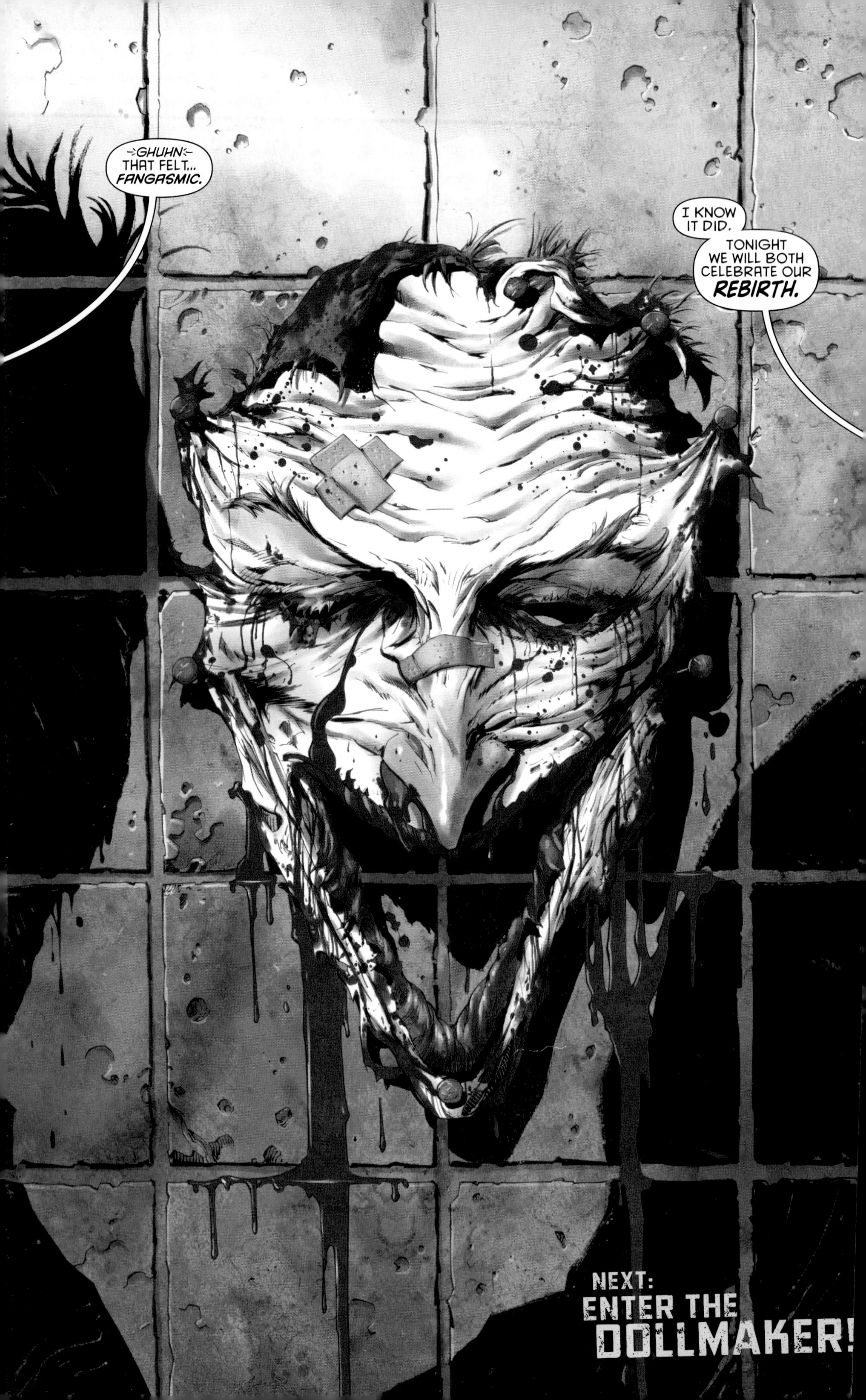

~GHUHN~ THAT FELT... FANGASMIC.
I KNOW IT DID.
TONIGHT WE WILL BOTH CELEBRATE OUR REBIRTH.
NEXT: ENTER THE DOLLMAKER!

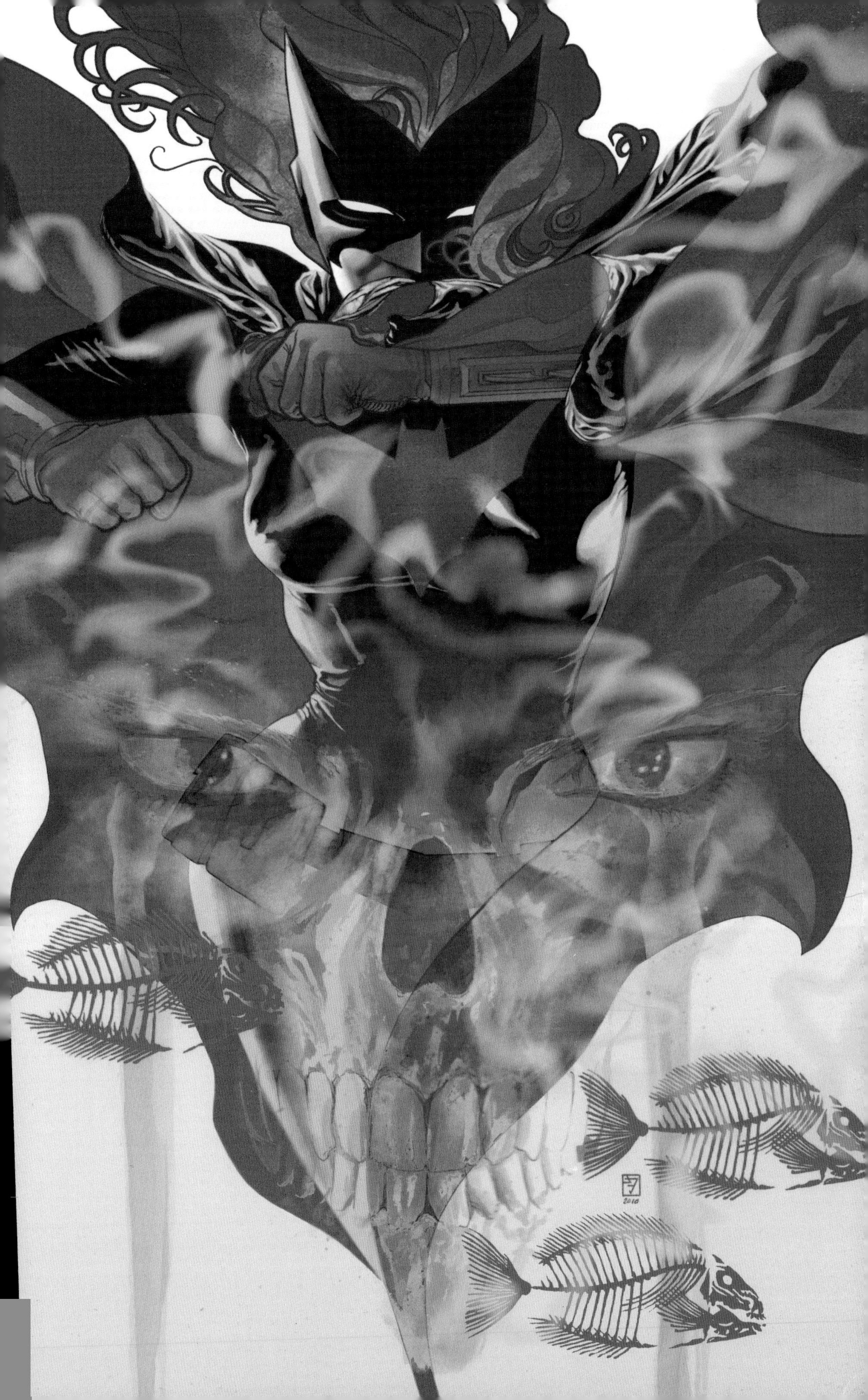

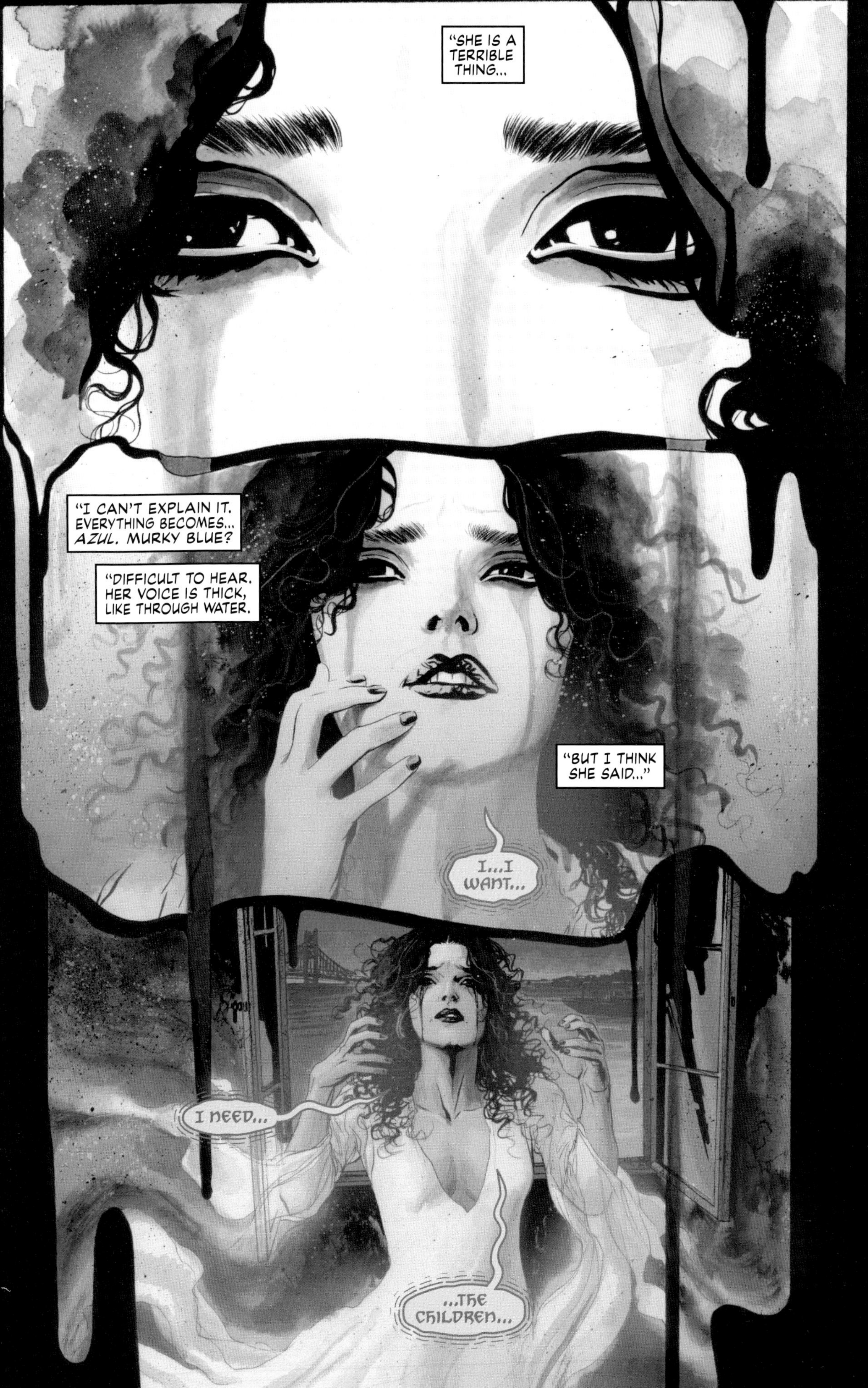
"SHE IS A TERRIBLE THING...
"I CAN'T EXPLAIN IT. EVERYTHING BECOMES... AZUL. MURKY BLUE?
"DIFFICULT TO HEAR. HER VOICE IS THICK, LIKE THROUGH WATER.
"BUT I THINK SHE SAID..."
I...I WANT...
I NEED...
...THE CHILDREN...

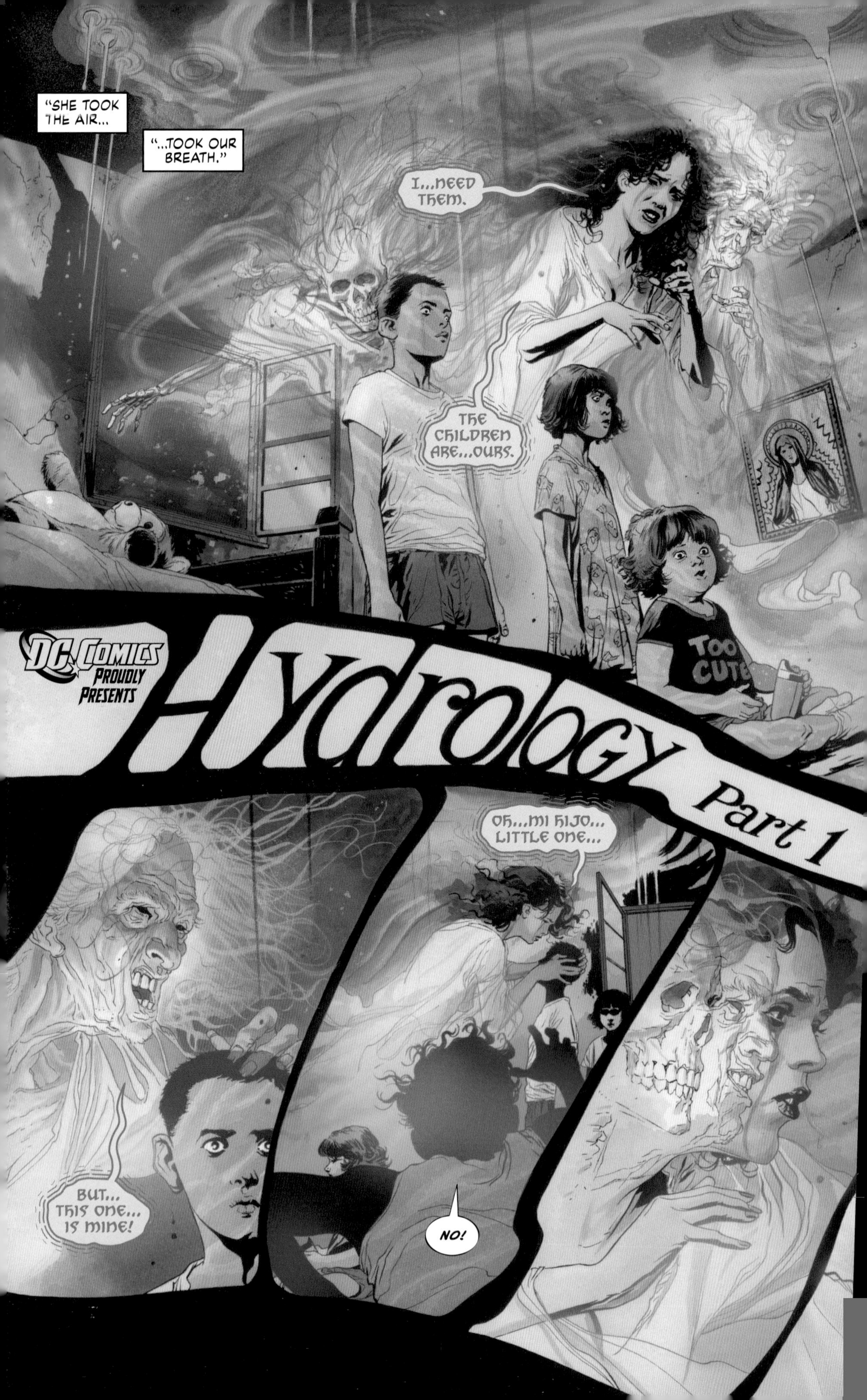
"SHE TOOK THE AIR...
"...TOOK OUR BREATH."
I...NEED THEM.
THE CHILDREN ARE...OURS.
TOO CUTE
DC COMICS PROUDLY PRESENTS
Hydrology Part 1
BUT... THIS ONE... IS MINE!
OH...MI HIJO... LITTLE ONE...
NO!

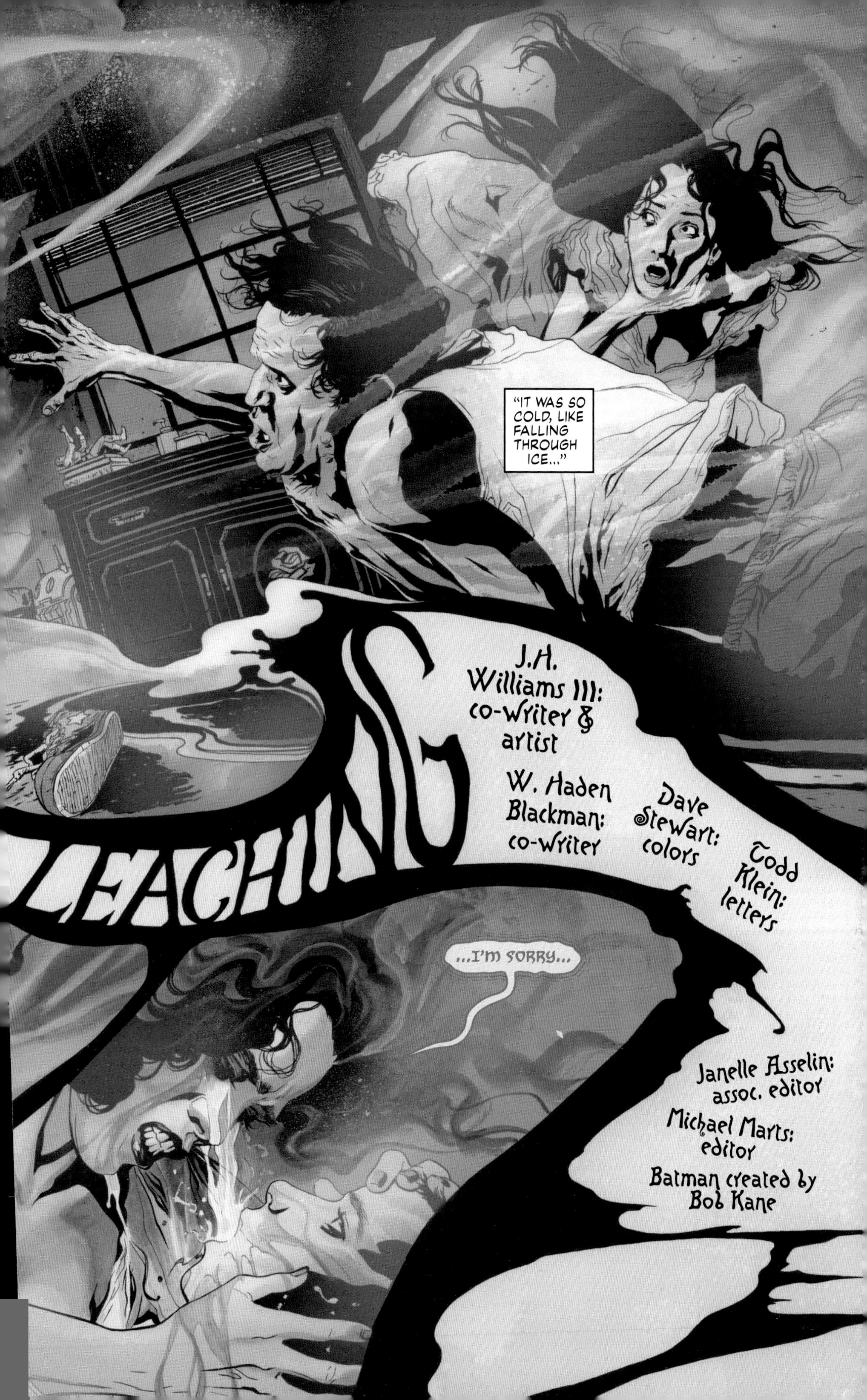
"IT WAS SO COLD, LIKE FALLING THROUGH ICE..."
LEACHING
J.H. Williams III: co-Writer & artist
W. Haden Blackman: co-Writer
Dave Stewart: colors
Todd Klein: letters
...I'M SORRY...
Janelle Asselin: assoc. editor
Michael Marts: editor
Batman created by Bob Kane

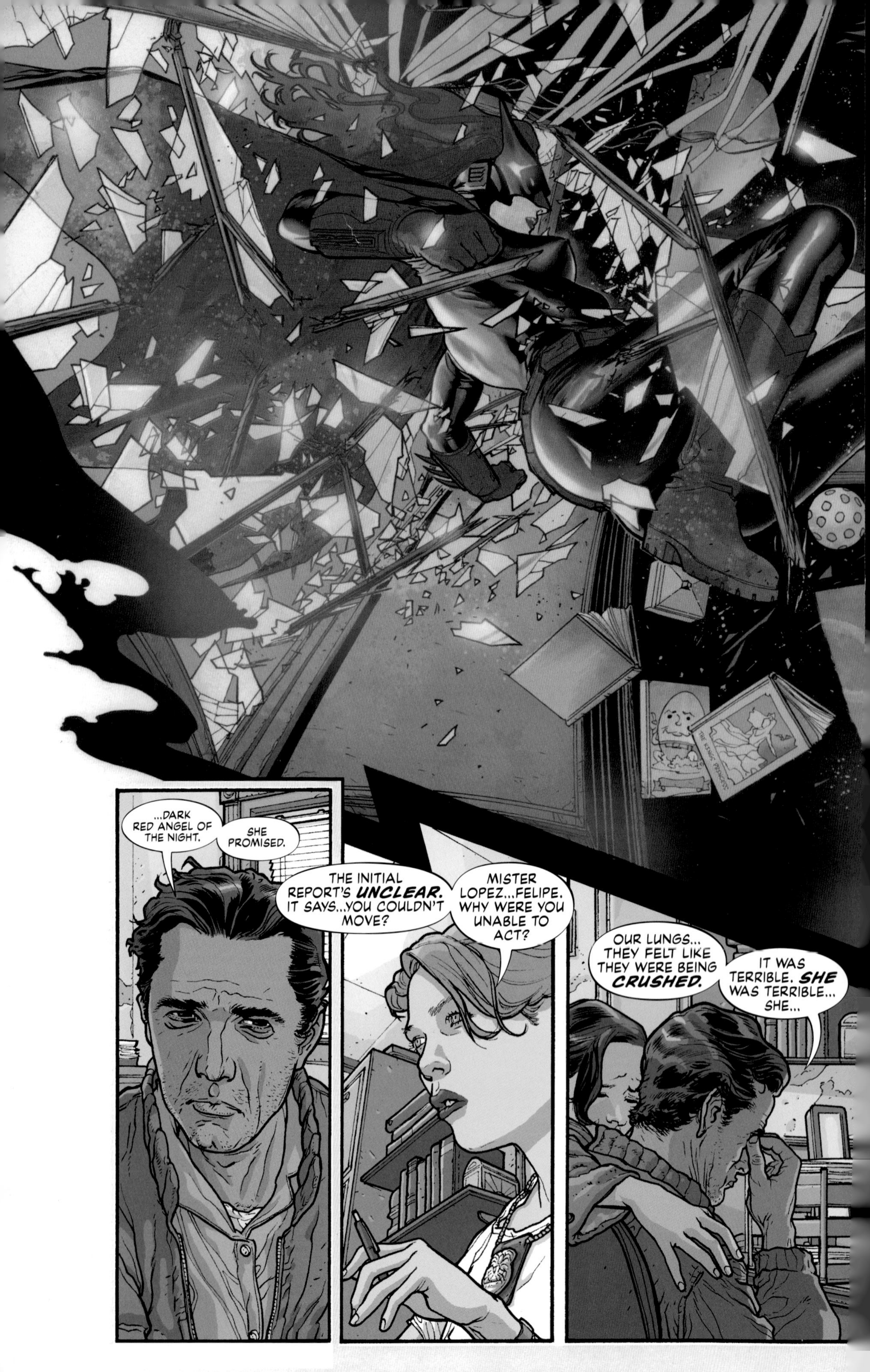
...DARK RED ANGEL OF THE NIGHT.
SHE PROMISED.
THE INITIAL REPORT'S ***UNCLEAR.*** IT SAYS...YOU COULDN'T MOVE?
MISTER LOPEZ...FELIPE. WHY WERE YOU UNABLE TO ACT?
OUR LUNGS... THEY FELT LIKE THEY WERE BEING ***CRUSHED.***
IT WAS TERRIBLE. ***SHE*** WAS TERRIBLE... SHE...

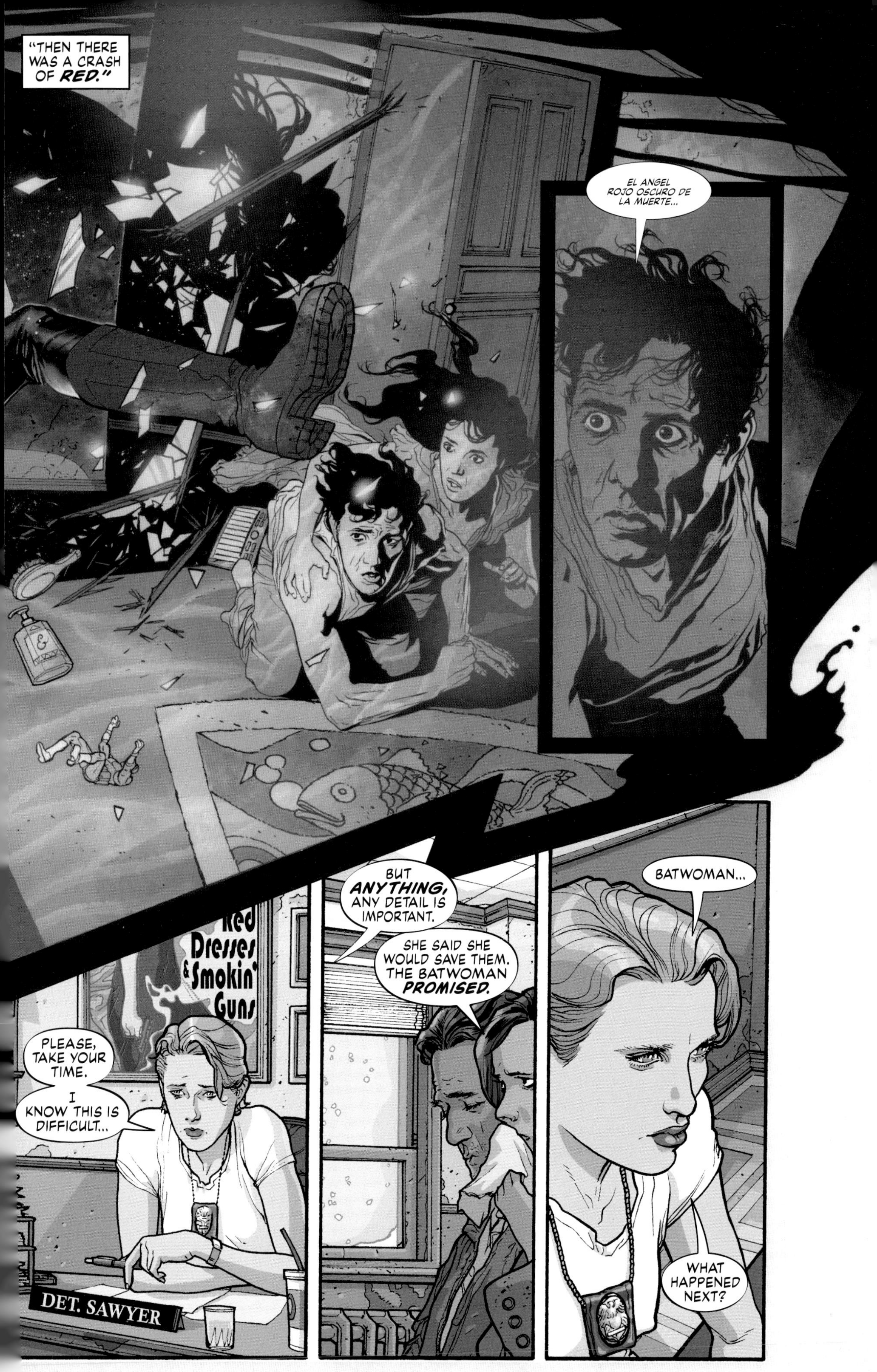
"THEN THERE WAS A CRASH OF **RED.**"
EL ANGEL ROJO OSCURO DE LA MUERTE...
Red Dresses & Smokin' Guns
PLEASE, TAKE YOUR TIME.
I KNOW THIS IS DIFFICULT...
DET. SAWYER
BUT ***ANYTHING,*** ANY DETAIL IS IMPORTANT.
SHE SAID SHE WOULD SAVE THEM. THE BATWOMAN ***PROMISED.***
BATWOMAN...
WHAT HAPPENED NEXT?

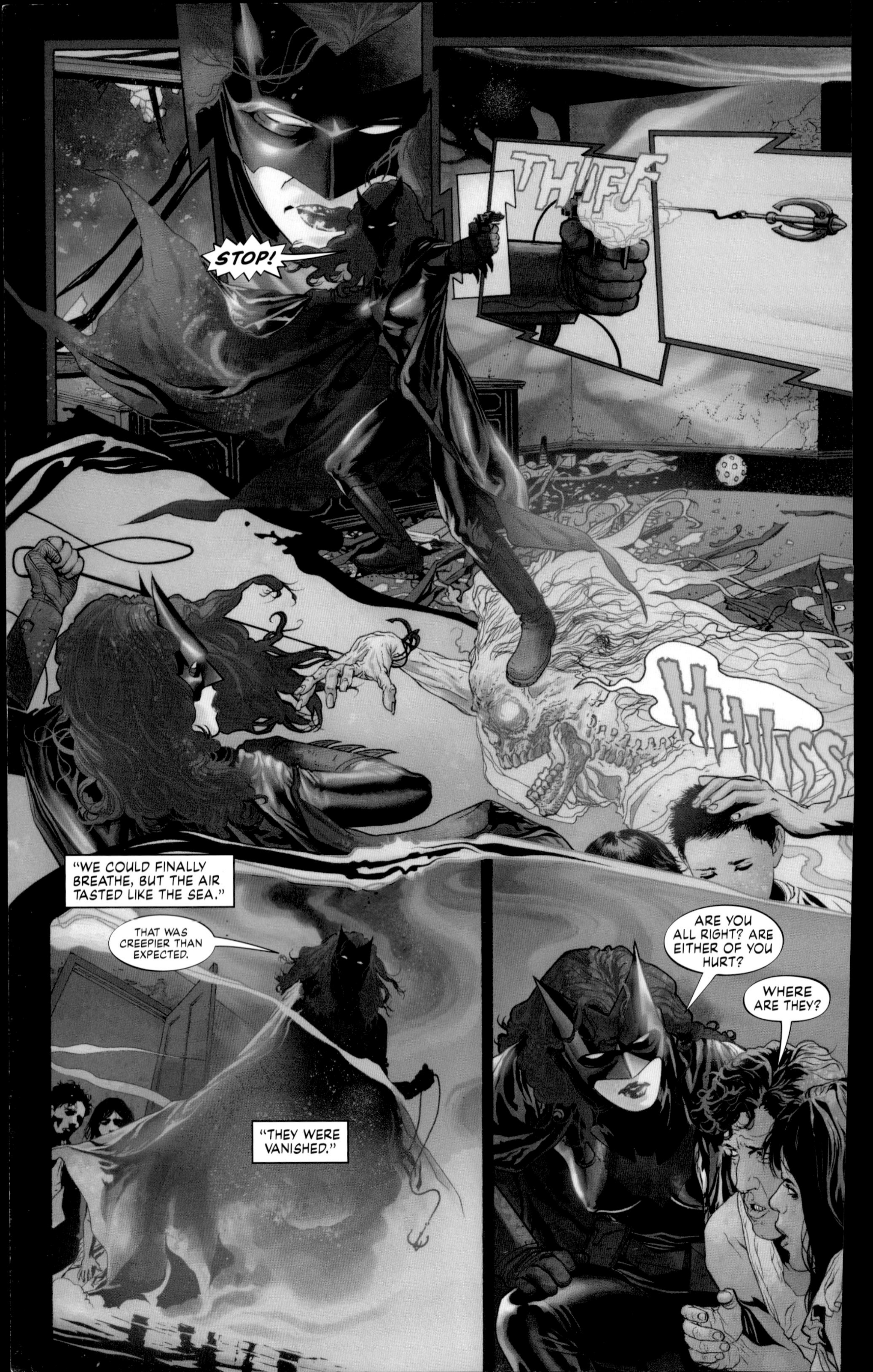
STOP!
THIFF
HHISS
"WE COULD FINALLY BREATHE, BUT THE AIR TASTED LIKE THE SEA."
THAT WAS CREEPIER THAN EXPECTED.
"THEY WERE VANISHED."
ARE YOU ALL RIGHT? ARE EITHER OF YOU HURT?
WHERE ARE THEY?

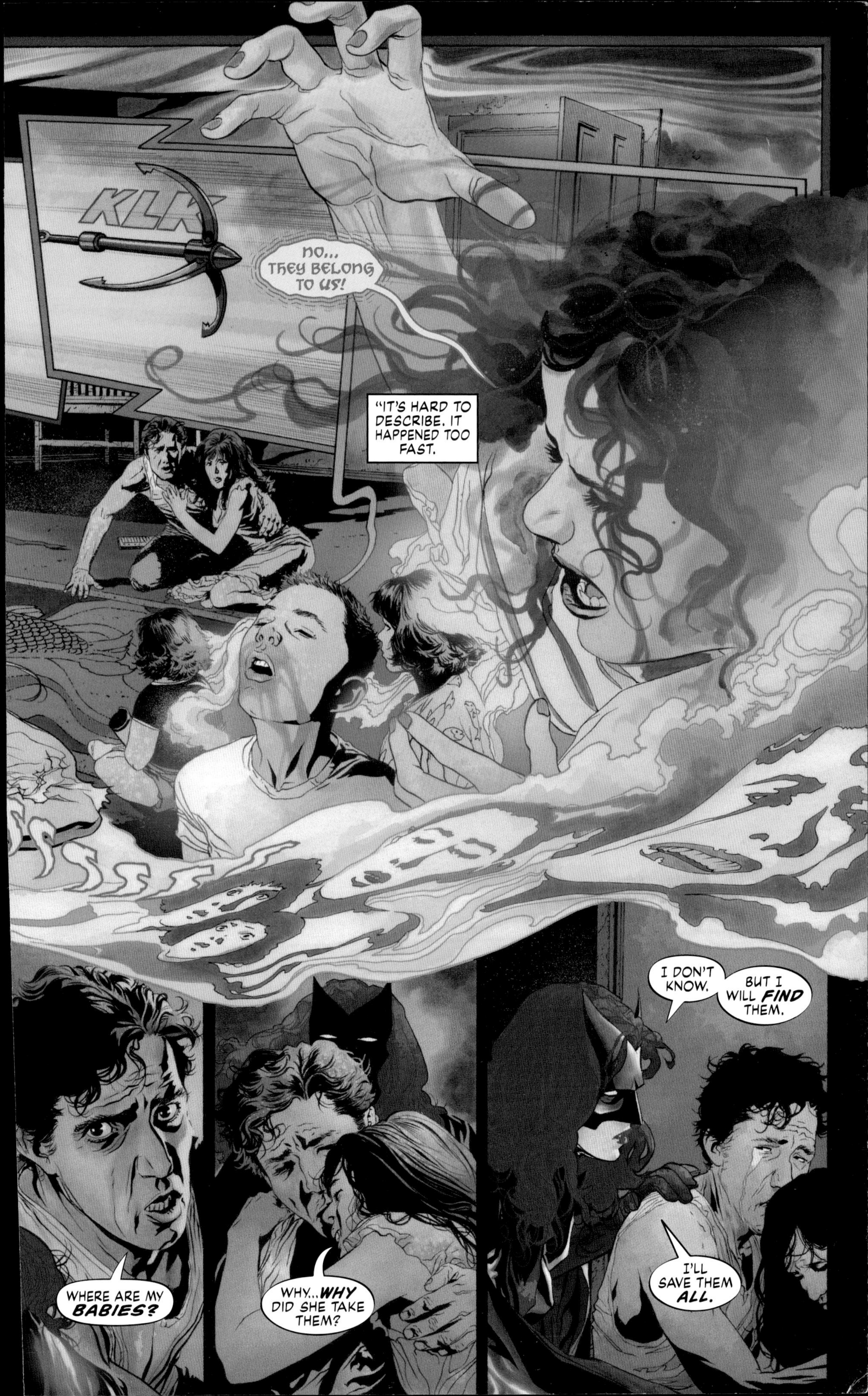
KLK
NO... THEY BELONG TO US!
"IT'S HARD TO DESCRIBE. IT HAPPENED TOO FAST.
WHERE ARE MY BABIES?
WHY...WHY DID SHE TAKE THEM?
I DON'T KNOW.
BUT I WILL FIND THEM.
I'LL SAVE THEM ALL.

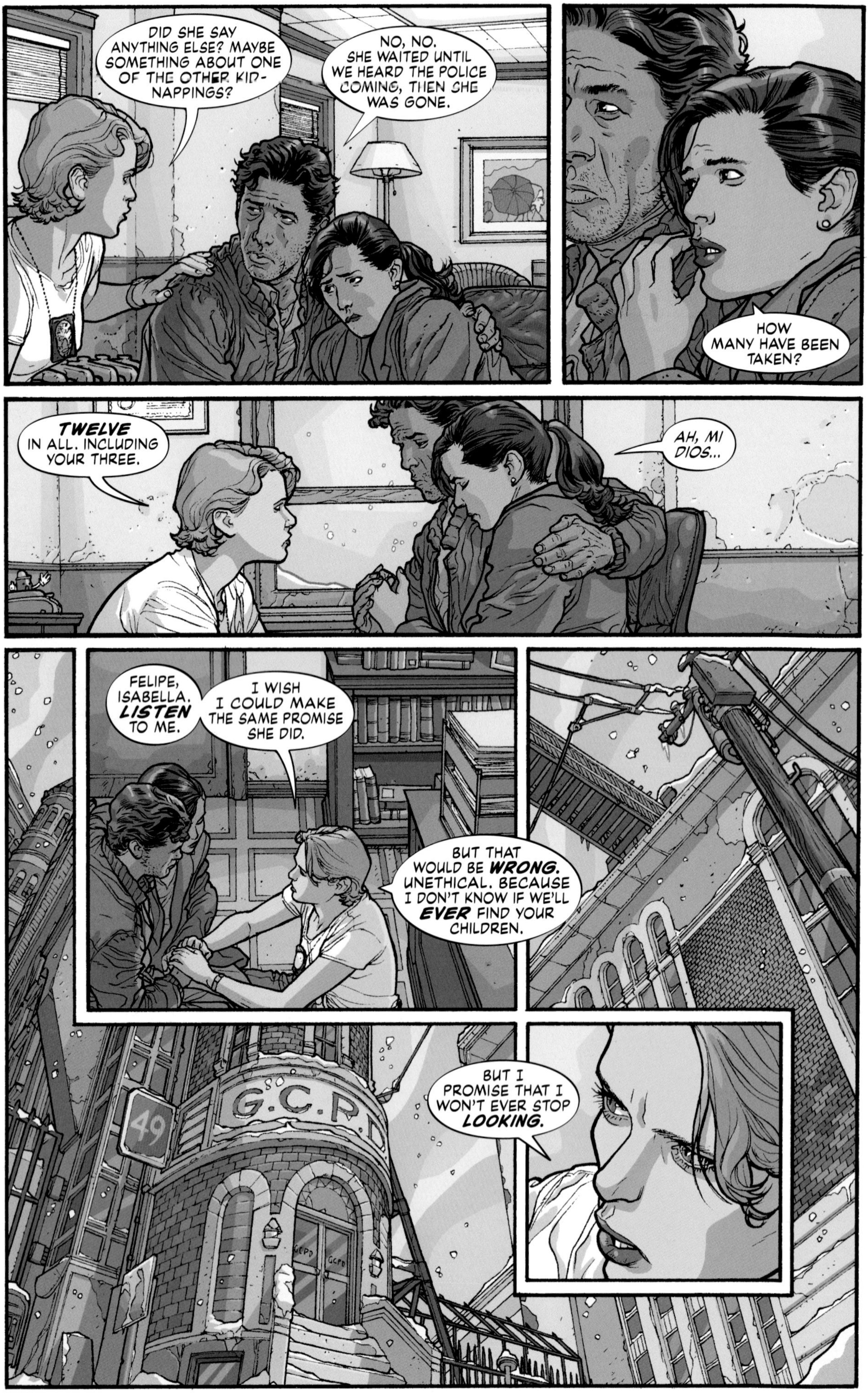
DID SHE SAY ANYTHING ELSE? MAYBE SOMETHING ABOUT ONE OF THE OTHER KID-NAPPINGS?
NO, NO. SHE WAITED UNTIL WE HEARD THE POLICE COMING, THEN SHE WAS GONE.
HOW MANY HAVE BEEN TAKEN?
TWELVE IN ALL. INCLUDING YOUR THREE.
AH, MI DIOS...
FELIPE, ISABELLA. LISTEN TO ME.
I WISH I COULD MAKE THE SAME PROMISE SHE DID.
BUT THAT WOULD BE WRONG. UNETHICAL. BECAUSE I DON'T KNOW IF WE'LL EVER FIND YOUR CHILDREN.
BUT I PROMISE THAT I WON'T EVER STOP LOOKING.
G.C.P.D
49

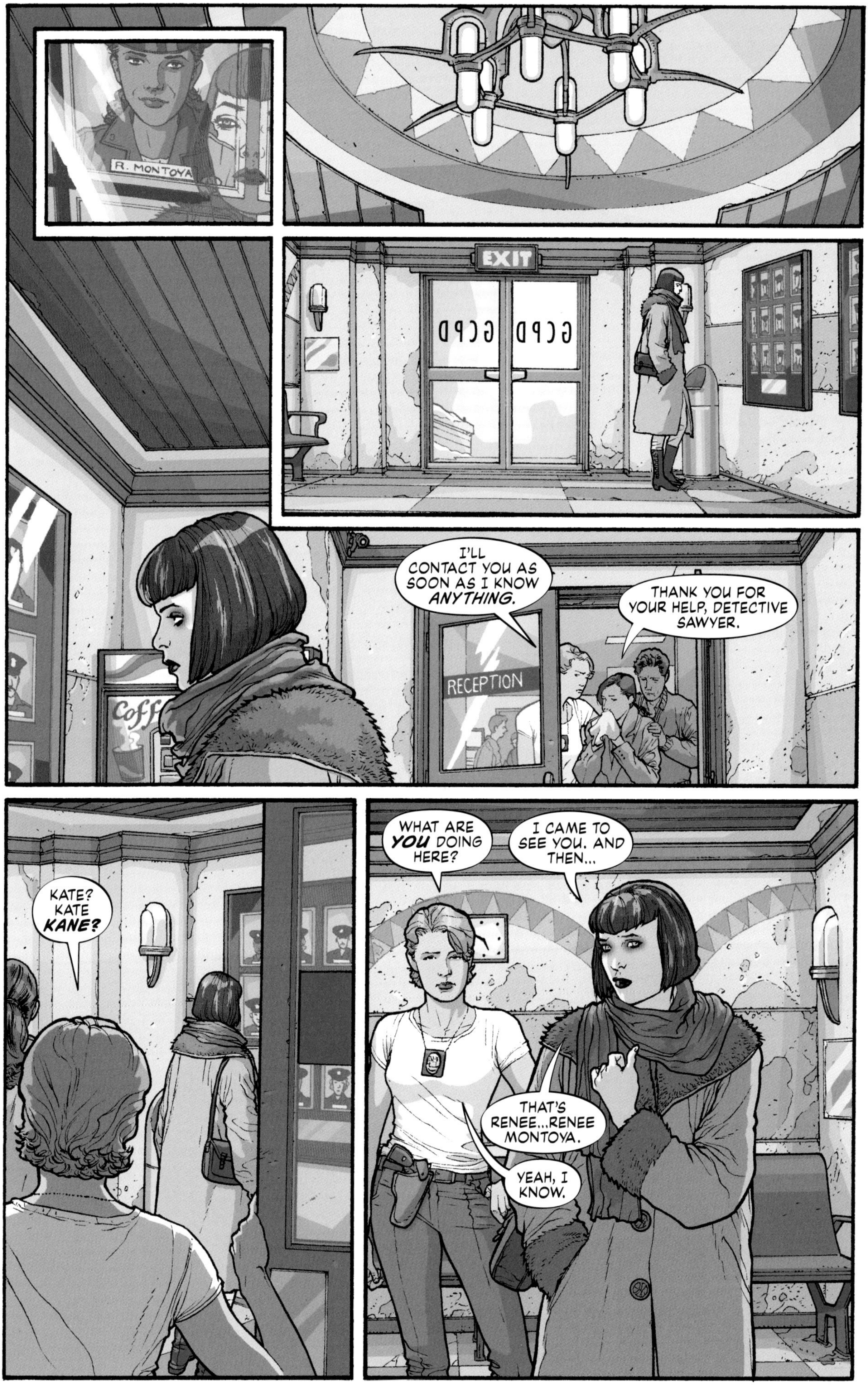
R. MONTOYA
EXIT
GCPD GCPD
I'LL CONTACT YOU AS SOON AS I KNOW *ANYTHING*.
THANK YOU FOR YOUR HELP, DETECTIVE SAWYER.
RECEPTION
KATE? KATE *KANE?*
WHAT ARE *YOU* DOING HERE?
I CAME TO SEE YOU. AND THEN...
THAT'S RENEE...RENEE MONTOYA.
YEAH, I KNOW.

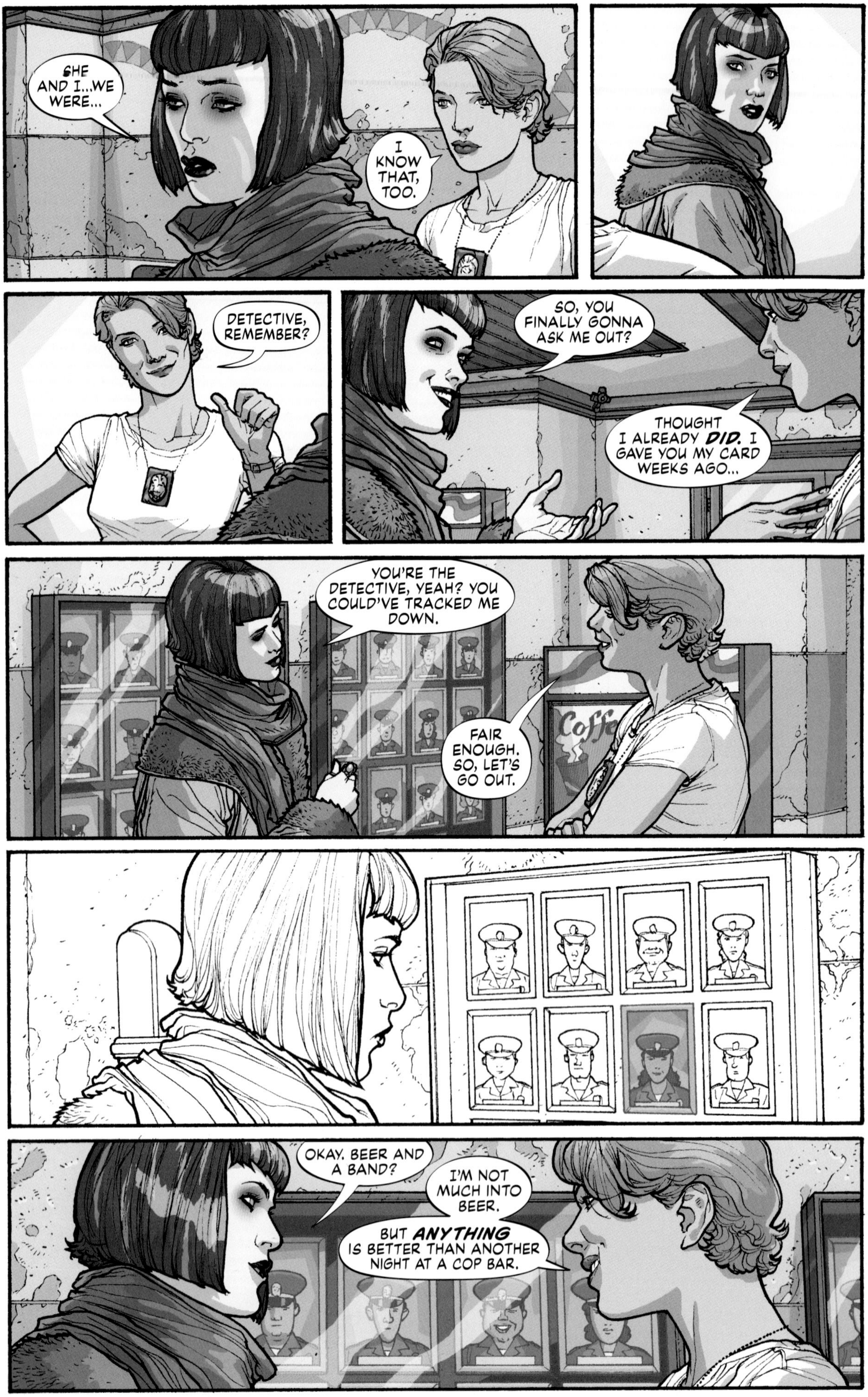
SHE AND I...WE WERE...
I KNOW THAT, TOO.
DETECTIVE, REMEMBER?
SO, YOU FINALLY GONNA ASK ME OUT?
THOUGHT I ALREADY *DID.* I GAVE YOU MY CARD WEEKS AGO...
YOU'RE THE DETECTIVE, YEAH? YOU COULD'VE TRACKED ME DOWN.
FAIR ENOUGH. SO, LET'S GO OUT.
OKAY. BEER AND A BAND?
I'M NOT MUCH INTO BEER.
BUT *ANYTHING* IS BETTER THAN ANOTHER NIGHT AT A COP BAR.

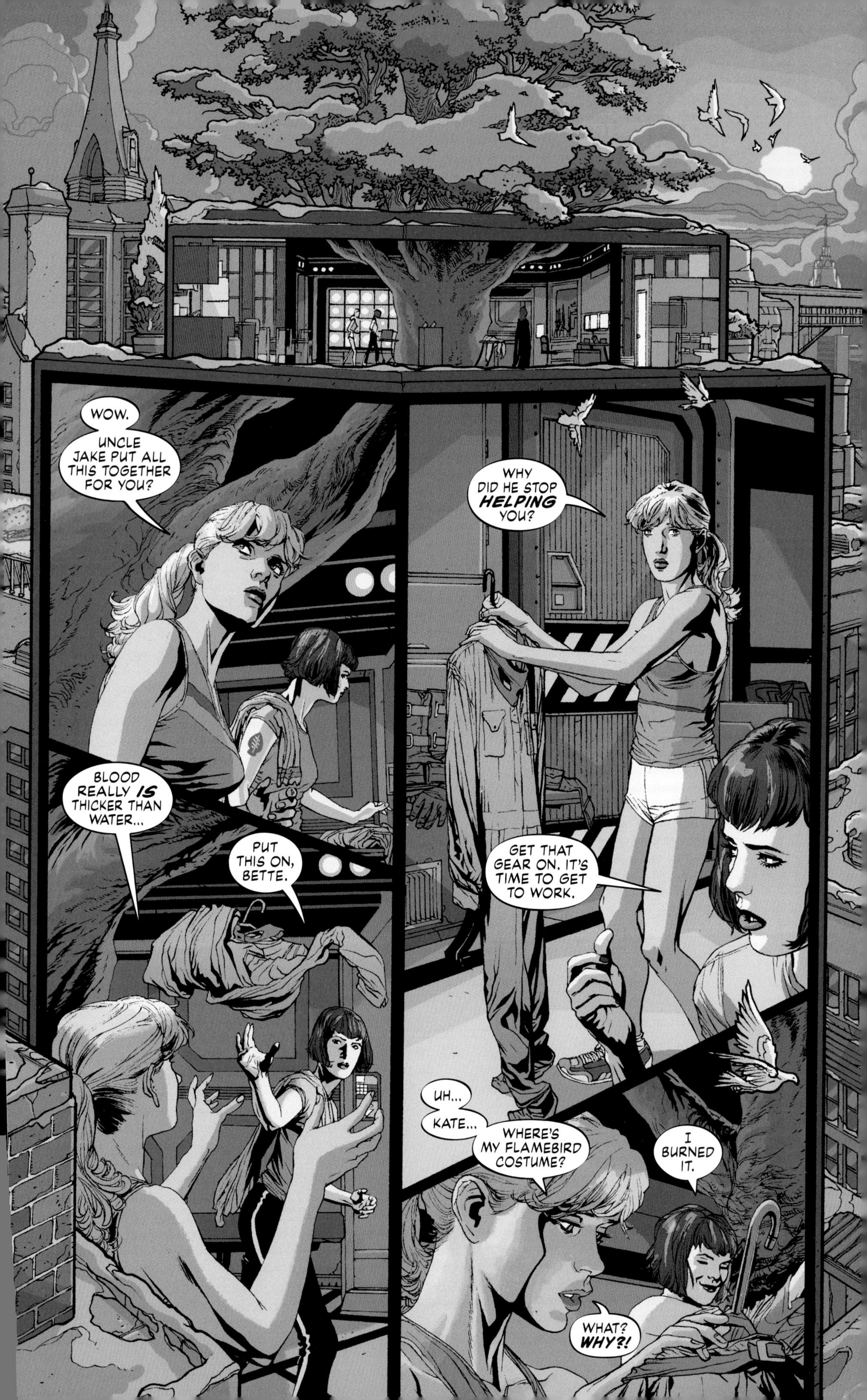
WOW.
UNCLE JAKE PUT ALL THIS TOGETHER FOR YOU?
BLOOD REALLY IS THICKER THAN WATER...
PUT THIS ON, BETTE.
WHY DID HE STOP HELPING YOU?
GET THAT GEAR ON. IT'S TIME TO GET TO WORK.
UH...
KATE...
WHERE'S MY FLAMEBIRD COSTUME?
I BURNED IT.
WHAT? WHY?!

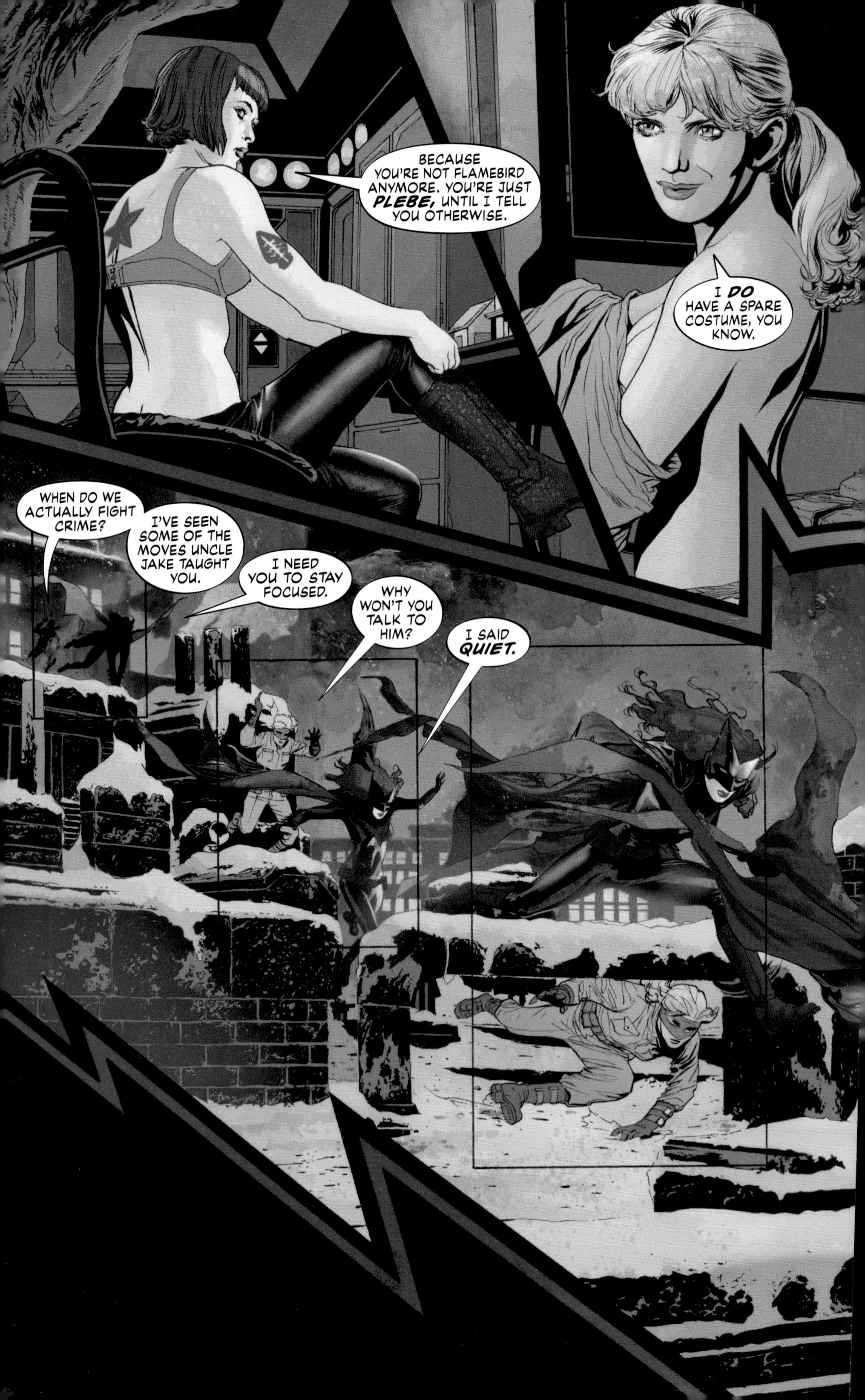
BECAUSE YOU'RE NOT FLAMEBIRD ANYMORE. YOU'RE JUST **PLEBE,** UNTIL I TELL YOU OTHERWISE.
I **DO** HAVE A SPARE COSTUME, YOU KNOW.
WHEN DO WE ACTUALLY FIGHT CRIME?
I'VE SEEN SOME OF THE MOVES UNCLE JAKE TAUGHT YOU.
I NEED YOU TO STAY FOCUSED.
WHY WON'T YOU TALK TO HIM?
I SAID **QUIET.**

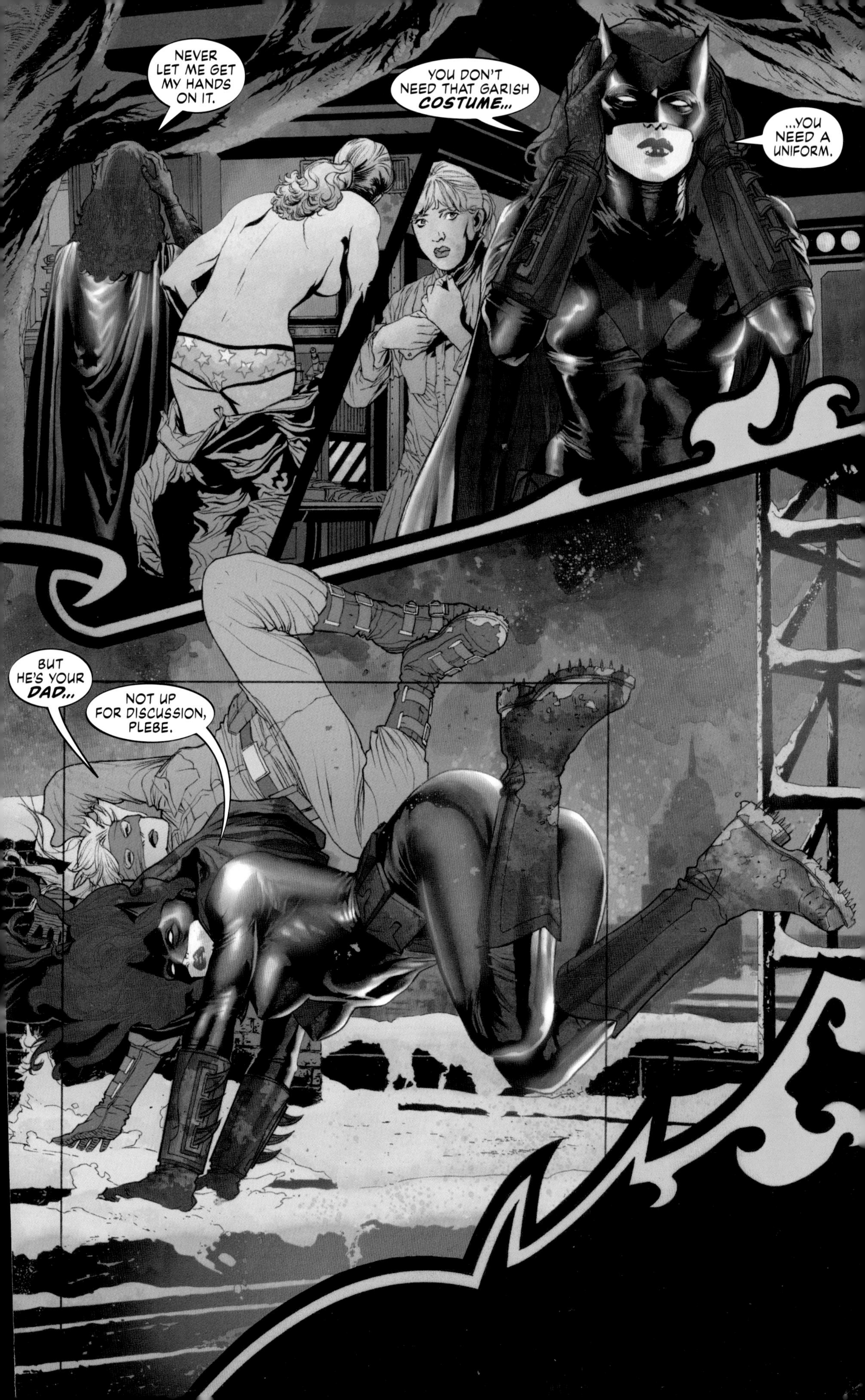
NEVER LET ME GET MY HANDS ON IT.
YOU DON'T NEED THAT GARISH COSTUME...
...YOU NEED A UNIFORM.
BUT HE'S YOUR DAD...
NOT UP FOR DISCUSSION, PLEBE.

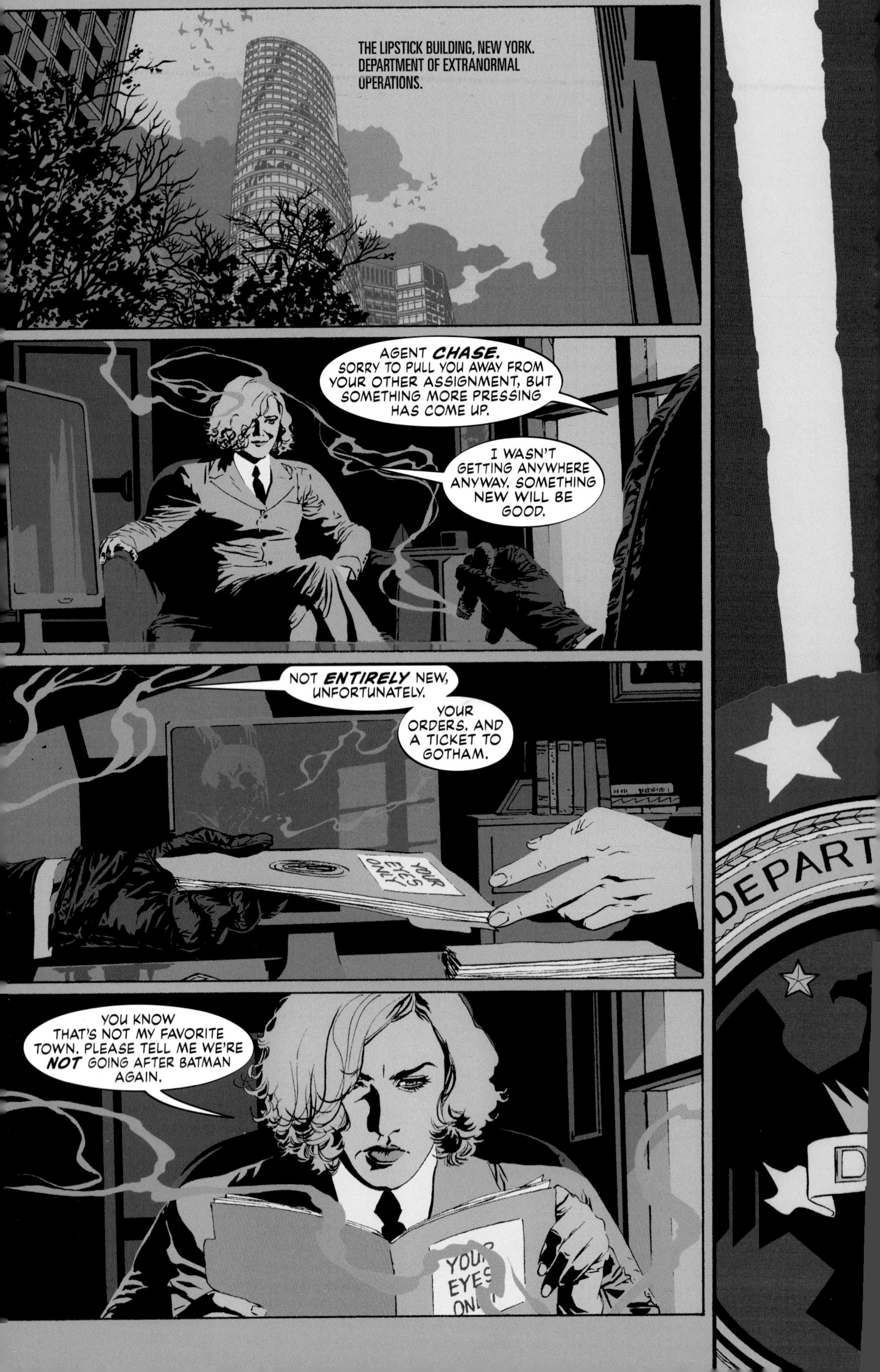
THE LIPSTICK BUILDING, NEW YORK. DEPARTMENT OF EXTRANORMAL OPERATIONS.
AGENT CHASE. SORRY TO PULL YOU AWAY FROM YOUR OTHER ASSIGNMENT, BUT SOMETHING MORE PRESSING HAS COME UP.
I WASN'T GETTING ANYWHERE ANYWAY. SOMETHING NEW WILL BE GOOD.
NOT ENTIRELY NEW, UNFORTUNATELY.
YOUR ORDERS. AND A TICKET TO GOTHAM.
YOUR EYES ONLY
YOU KNOW THAT'S NOT MY FAVORITE TOWN. PLEASE TELL ME WE'RE NOT GOING AFTER BATMAN AGAIN.
DEPART

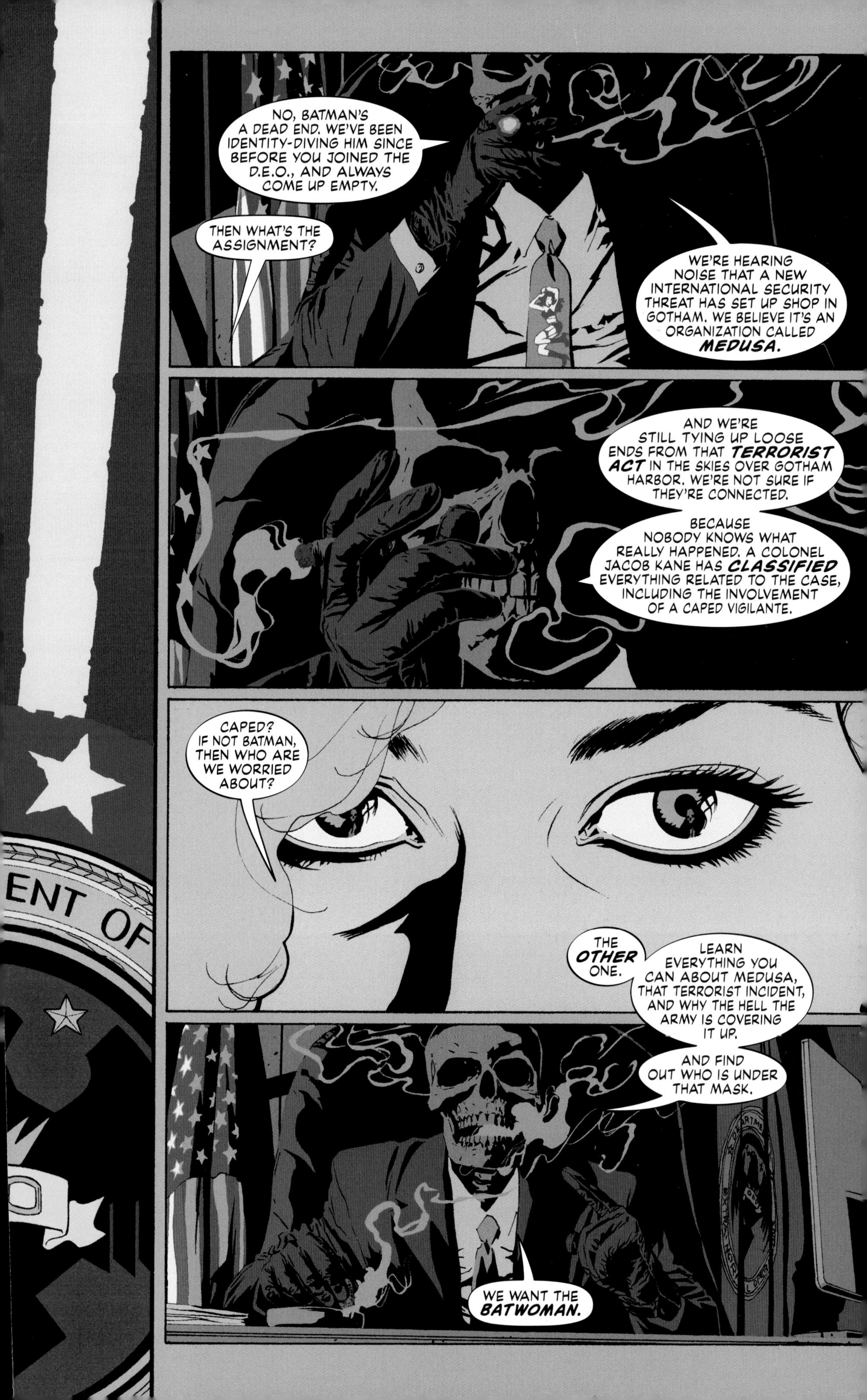

ENT OF
NO, BATMAN'S A DEAD END. WE'VE BEEN IDENTITY-DIVING HIM SINCE BEFORE YOU JOINED THE D.E.O., AND ALWAYS COME UP EMPTY.
THEN WHAT'S THE ASSIGNMENT?
WE'RE HEARING NOISE THAT A NEW INTERNATIONAL SECURITY THREAT HAS SET UP SHOP IN GOTHAM. WE BELIEVE IT'S AN ORGANIZATION CALLED MEDUSA.
AND WE'RE STILL TYING UP LOOSE ENDS FROM THAT TERRORIST ACT IN THE SKIES OVER GOTHAM HARBOR. WE'RE NOT SURE IF THEY'RE CONNECTED.
BECAUSE NOBODY KNOWS WHAT REALLY HAPPENED. A COLONEL JACOB KANE HAS CLASSIFIED EVERYTHING RELATED TO THE CASE, INCLUDING THE INVOLVEMENT OF A CAPED VIGILANTE.
CAPED? IF NOT BATMAN, THEN WHO ARE WE WORRIED ABOUT?
THE OTHER ONE.
LEARN EVERYTHING YOU CAN ABOUT MEDUSA, THAT TERRORIST INCIDENT, AND WHY THE HELL THE ARMY IS COVERING IT UP.
AND FIND OUT WHO IS UNDER THAT MASK.
WE WANT THE BATWOMAN.

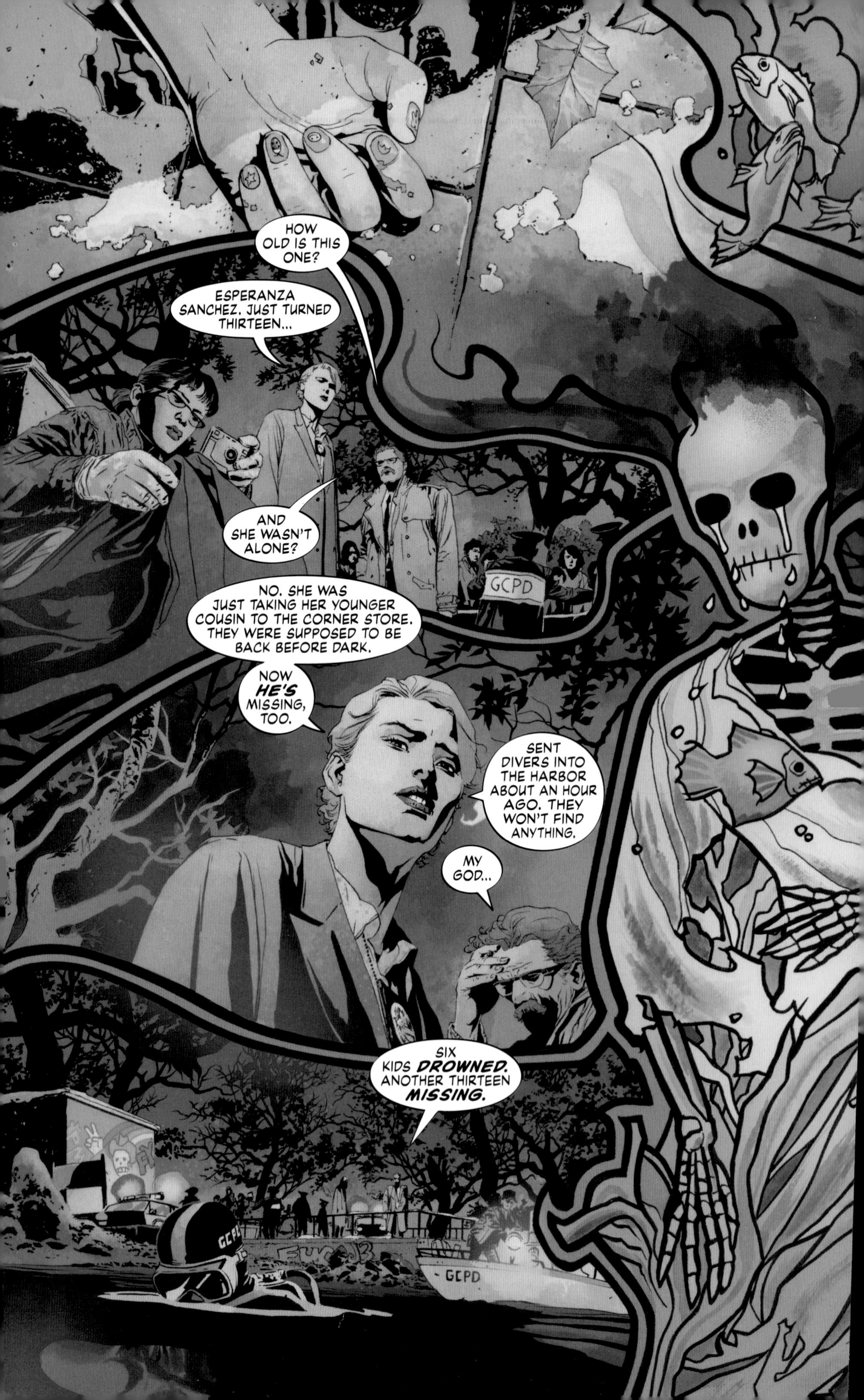
HOW OLD IS THIS ONE?
ESPERANZA SANCHEZ. JUST TURNED THIRTEEN...
AND SHE WASN'T ALONE?
NO. SHE WAS JUST TAKING HER YOUNGER COUSIN TO THE CORNER STORE. THEY WERE SUPPOSED TO BE BACK BEFORE DARK.
NOW HE'S MISSING, TOO.
SENT DIVERS INTO THE HARBOR ABOUT AN HOUR AGO. THEY WON'T FIND ANYTHING.
MY GOD...
SIX KIDS DROWNED. ANOTHER THIRTEEN MISSING.
GCPD
GCPD
GCPD

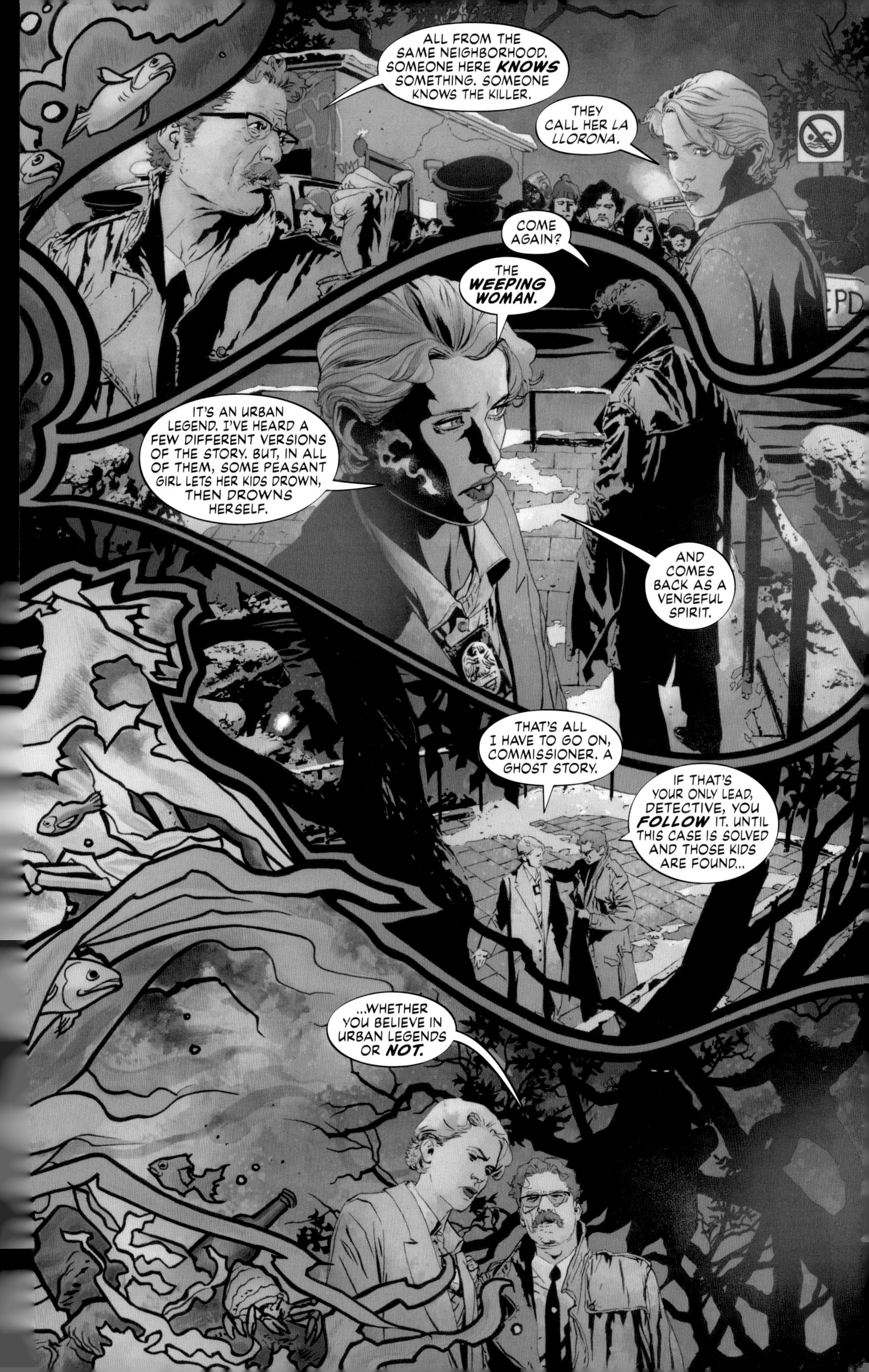
ALL FROM THE SAME NEIGHBORHOOD. SOMEONE HERE KNOWS SOMETHING. SOMEONE KNOWS THE KILLER.
THEY CALL HER LA LLORONA.
COME AGAIN?
THE WEEPING WOMAN.
IT'S AN URBAN LEGEND. I'VE HEARD A FEW DIFFERENT VERSIONS OF THE STORY. BUT, IN ALL OF THEM, SOME PEASANT GIRL LETS HER KIDS DROWN, THEN DROWNS HERSELF.
AND COMES BACK AS A VENGEFUL SPIRIT.
THAT'S ALL I HAVE TO GO ON, COMMISSIONER. A GHOST STORY.
IF THAT'S YOUR ONLY LEAD, DETECTIVE, YOU FOLLOW IT. UNTIL THIS CASE IS SOLVED AND THOSE KIDS ARE FOUND...
...WHETHER YOU BELIEVE IN URBAN LEGENDS OR NOT.

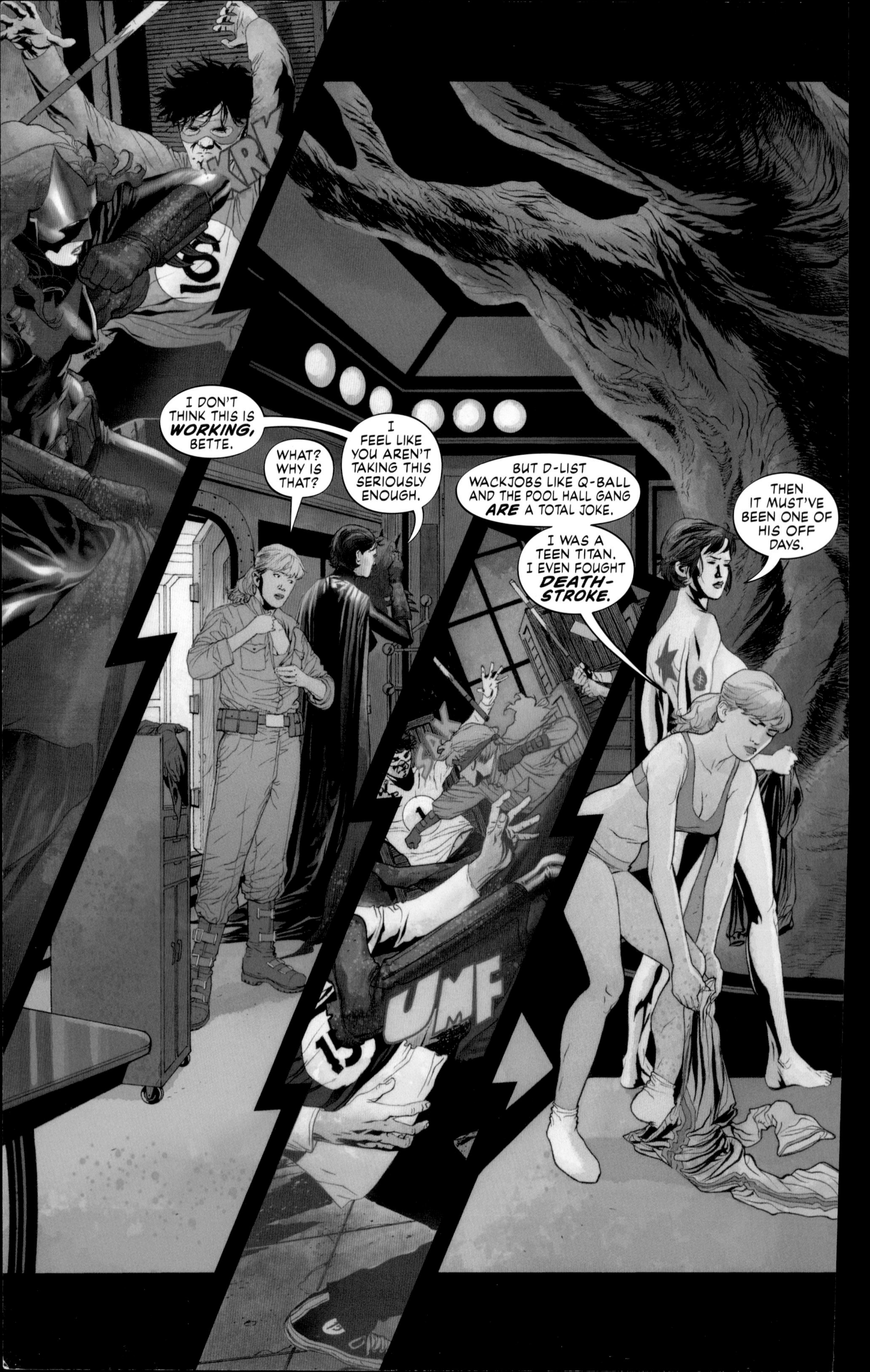
I DON'T THINK THIS IS **WORKING,** BETTE.
WHAT? WHY IS THAT?
I FEEL LIKE YOU AREN'T TAKING THIS SERIOUSLY ENOUGH.
BUT D-LIST WACKJOBS LIKE Q-BALL AND THE POOL HALL GANG **ARE** A TOTAL JOKE.
I WAS A TEEN TITAN. I EVEN FOUGHT **DEATH-STROKE.**
THEN IT MUST'VE BEEN ONE OF HIS OFF DAYS.

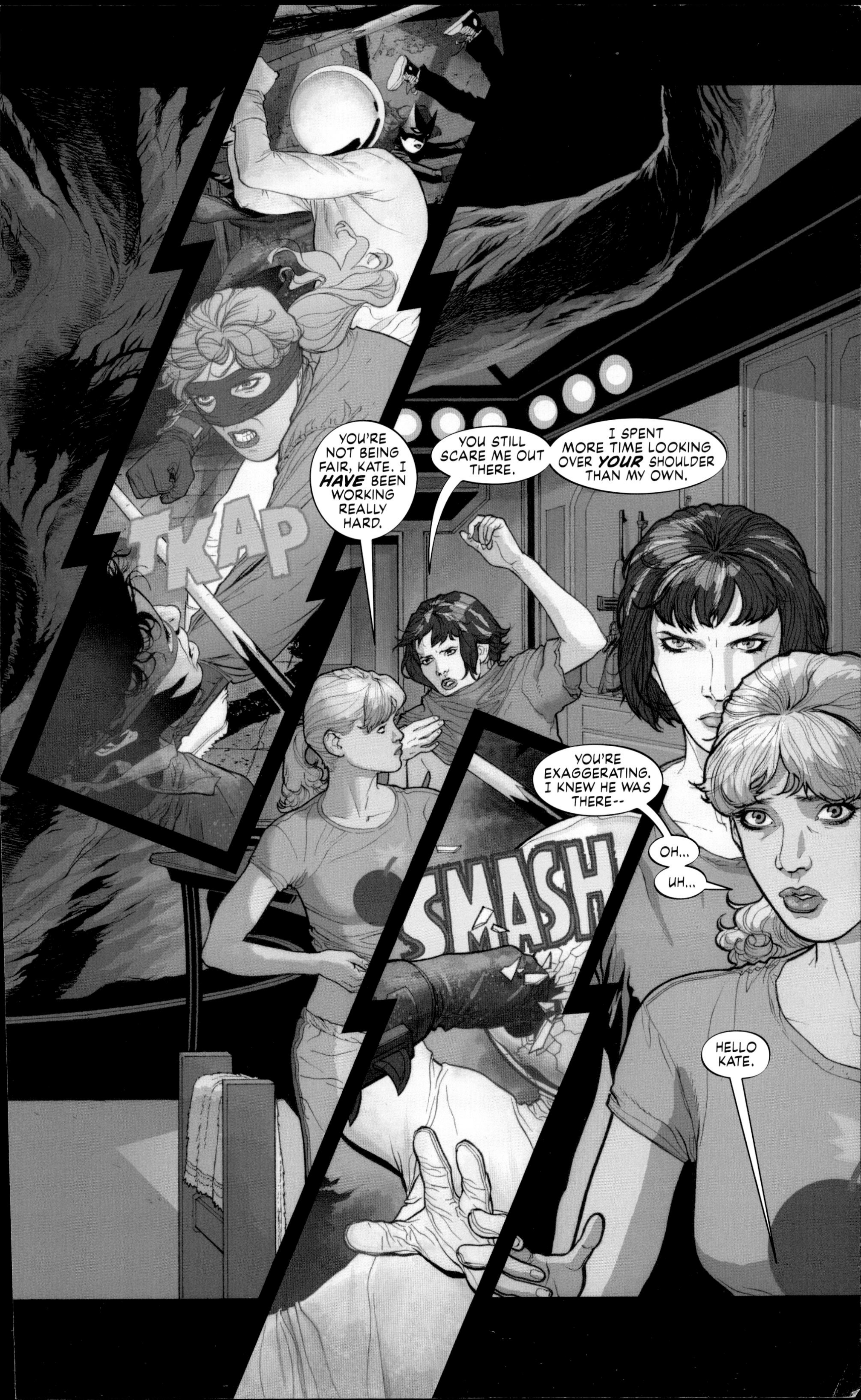
TKAP
YOU'RE NOT BEING FAIR, KATE. I HAVE BEEN WORKING REALLY HARD.
YOU STILL SCARE ME OUT THERE.
I SPENT MORE TIME LOOKING OVER YOUR SHOULDER THAN MY OWN.
SMASH
YOU'RE EXAGGERATING. I KNEW HE WAS THERE--
OH...
UH...
HELLO KATE.

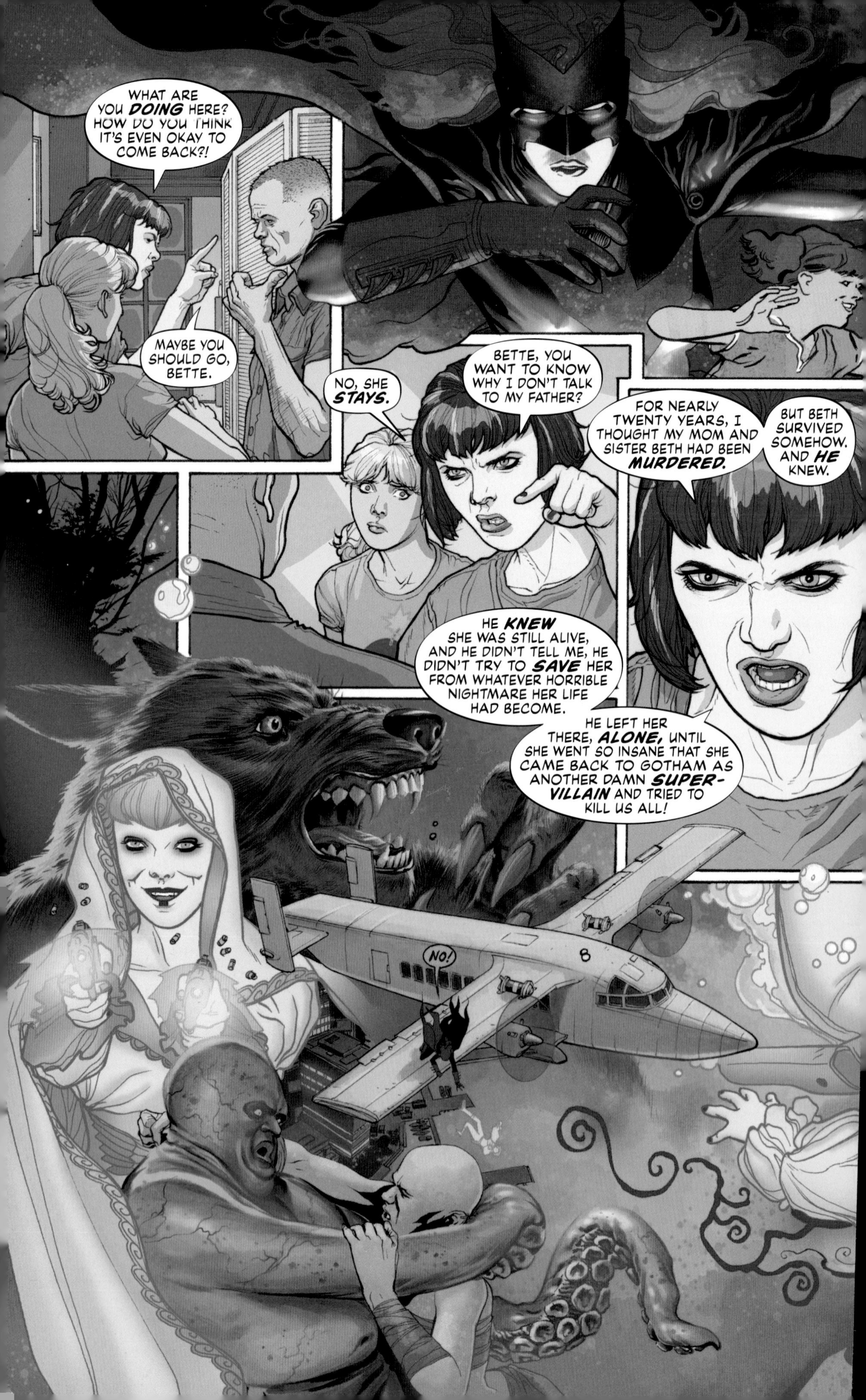
WHAT ARE YOU DOING HERE? HOW DO YOU THINK IT'S EVEN OKAY TO COME BACK?!
MAYBE YOU SHOULD GO, BETTE.
NO, SHE STAYS.
BETTE, YOU WANT TO KNOW WHY I DON'T TALK TO MY FATHER?
FOR NEARLY TWENTY YEARS, I THOUGHT MY MOM AND SISTER BETH HAD BEEN MURDERED.
BUT BETH SURVIVED SOMEHOW. AND HE KNEW.
HE KNEW SHE WAS STILL ALIVE, AND HE DIDN'T TELL ME, HE DIDN'T TRY TO SAVE HER FROM WHATEVER HORRIBLE NIGHTMARE HER LIFE HAD BECOME.
HE LEFT HER THERE, ALONE, UNTIL SHE WENT SO INSANE THAT SHE CAME BACK TO GOTHAM AS ANOTHER DAMN SUPER-VILLAIN AND TRIED TO KILL US ALL!
NO!

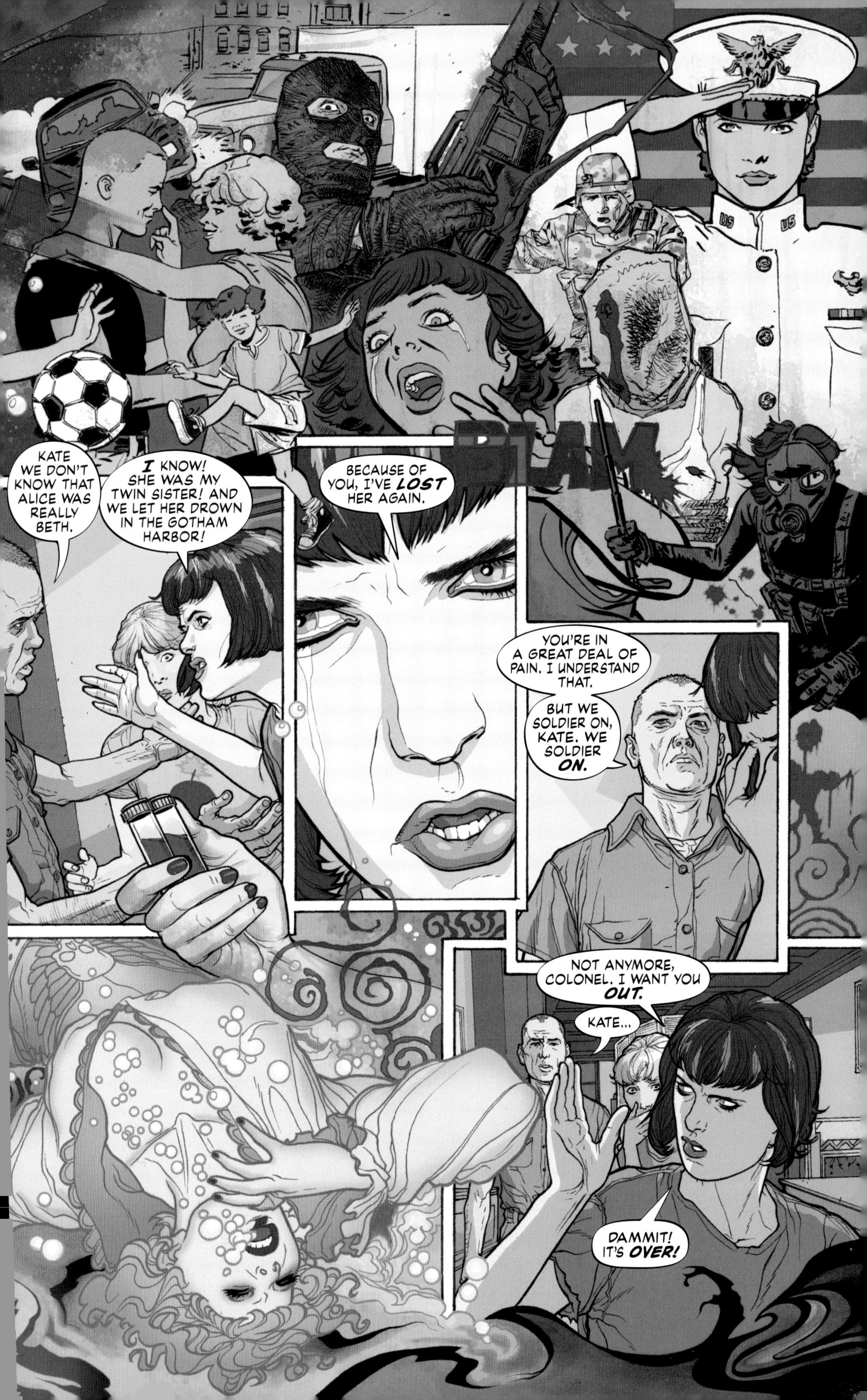
BLAM
KATE WE DON'T KNOW THAT ALICE WAS REALLY BETH.
I KNOW! SHE WAS MY TWIN SISTER! AND WE LET HER DROWN IN THE GOTHAM HARBOR!
BECAUSE OF YOU, I'VE LOST HER AGAIN.
YOU'RE IN A GREAT DEAL OF PAIN. I UNDERSTAND THAT.
BUT WE SOLDIER ON, KATE. WE SOLDIER ON.
NOT ANYMORE, COLONEL. I WANT YOU OUT.
KATE...
DAMMIT! IT'S OVER!

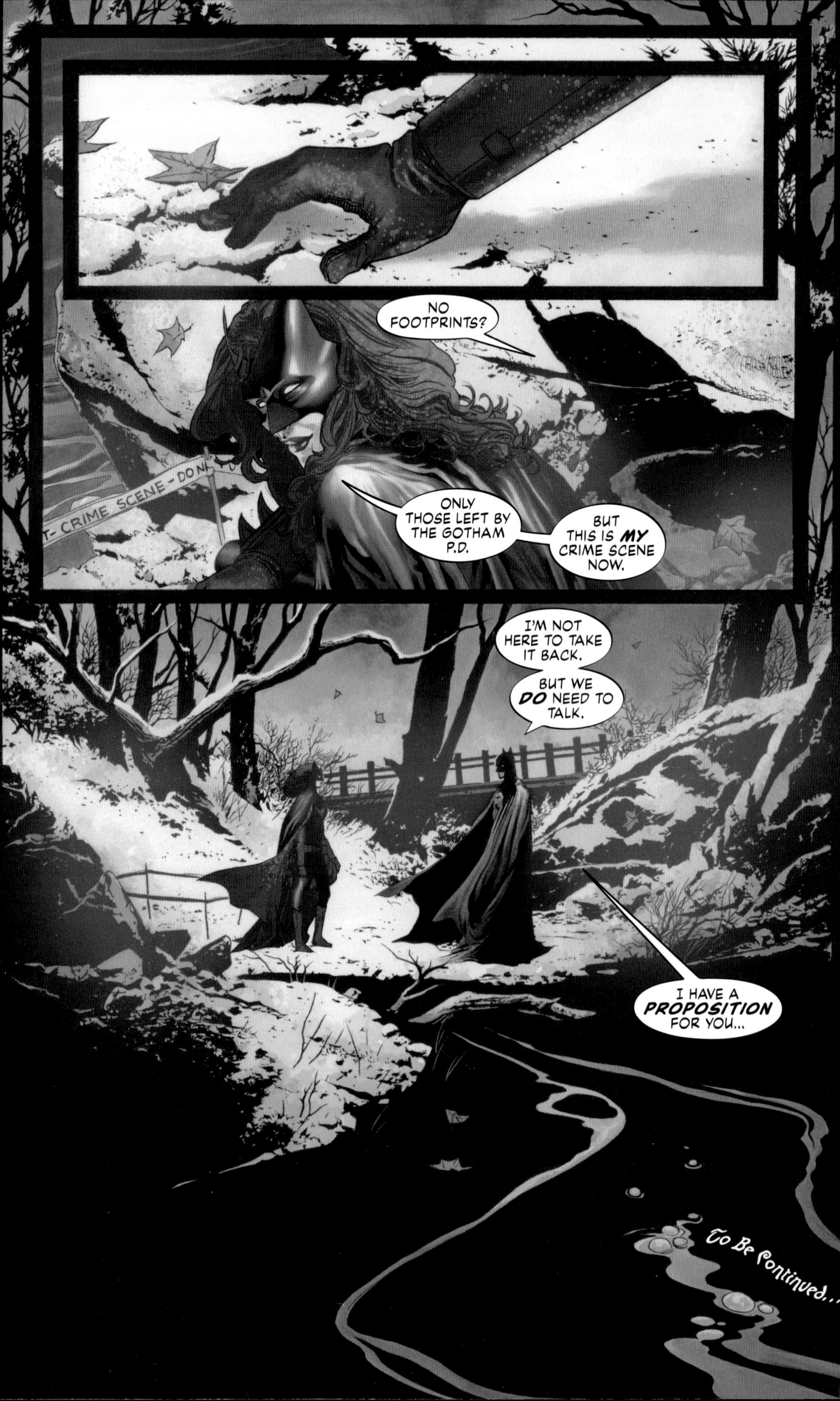

NO FOOTPRINTS?
CRIME SCENE - DO N
ONLY THOSE LEFT BY THE GOTHAM P.D.
BUT THIS IS **MY** CRIME SCENE NOW.
I'M NOT HERE TO TAKE IT BACK.
BUT WE **DO** NEED TO TALK.
I HAVE A **PROPOSITION** FOR YOU...
To Be Continued...

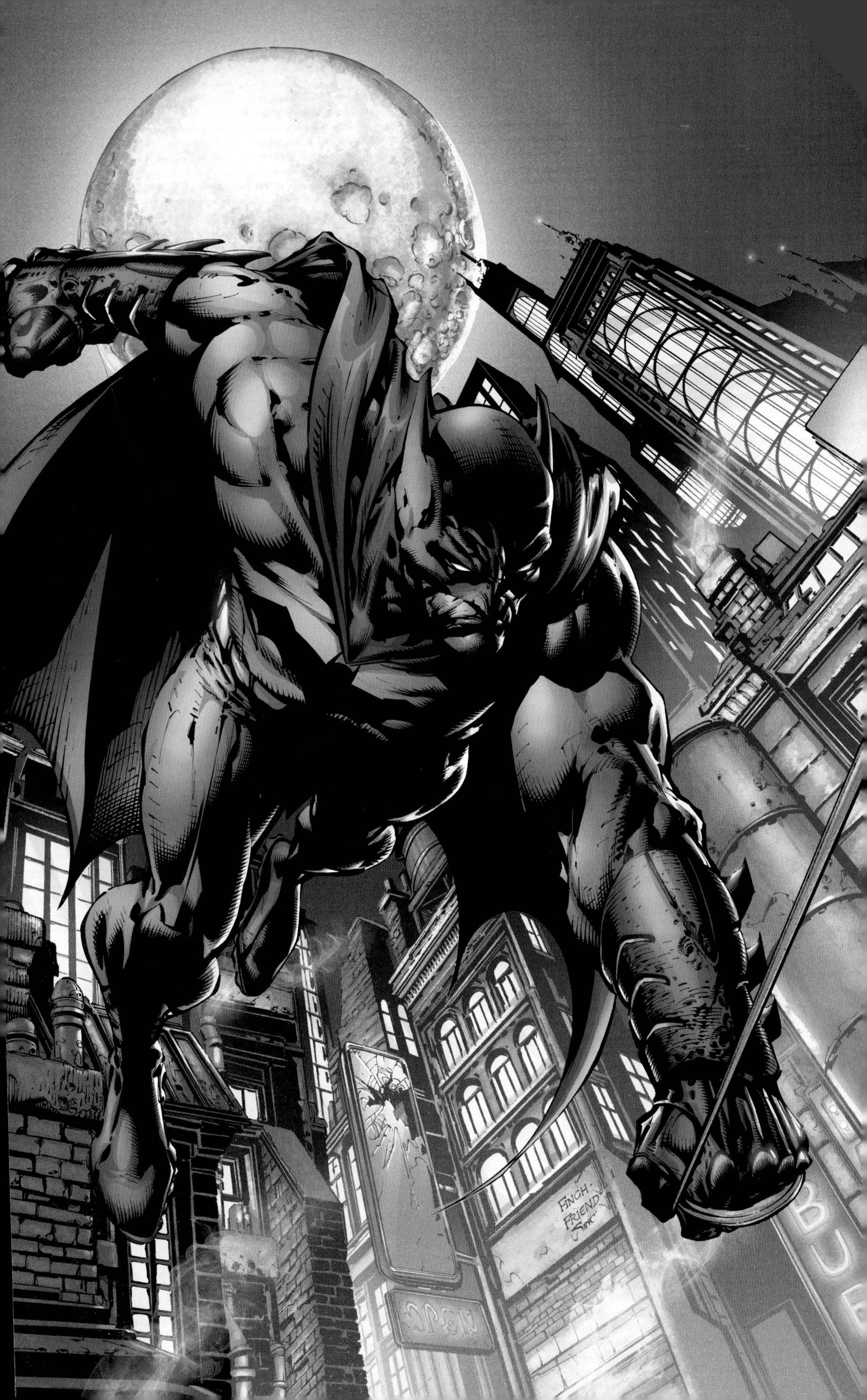
FINCH-
FRIEND
Sinc

BATMAN
THE DARK KNIGHT

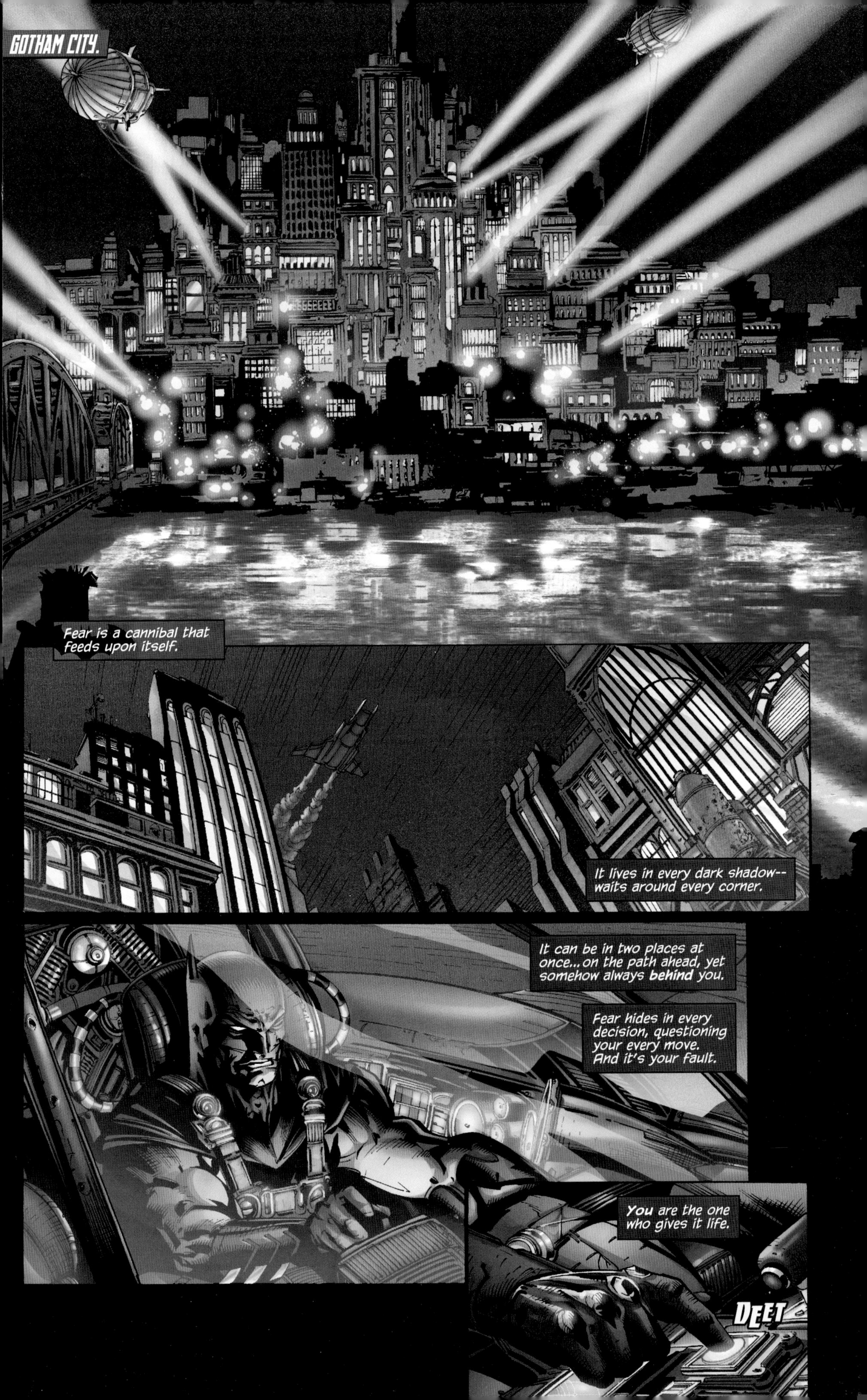

GOTHAM CITY.
Fear is a cannibal that feeds upon itself.
It lives in every dark shadow-- waits around every corner.
It can be in two places at once...on the path ahead, yet somehow always behind you.
Fear hides in every decision, questioning your every move. And it's your fault.
You are the one who gives it life.
DEET

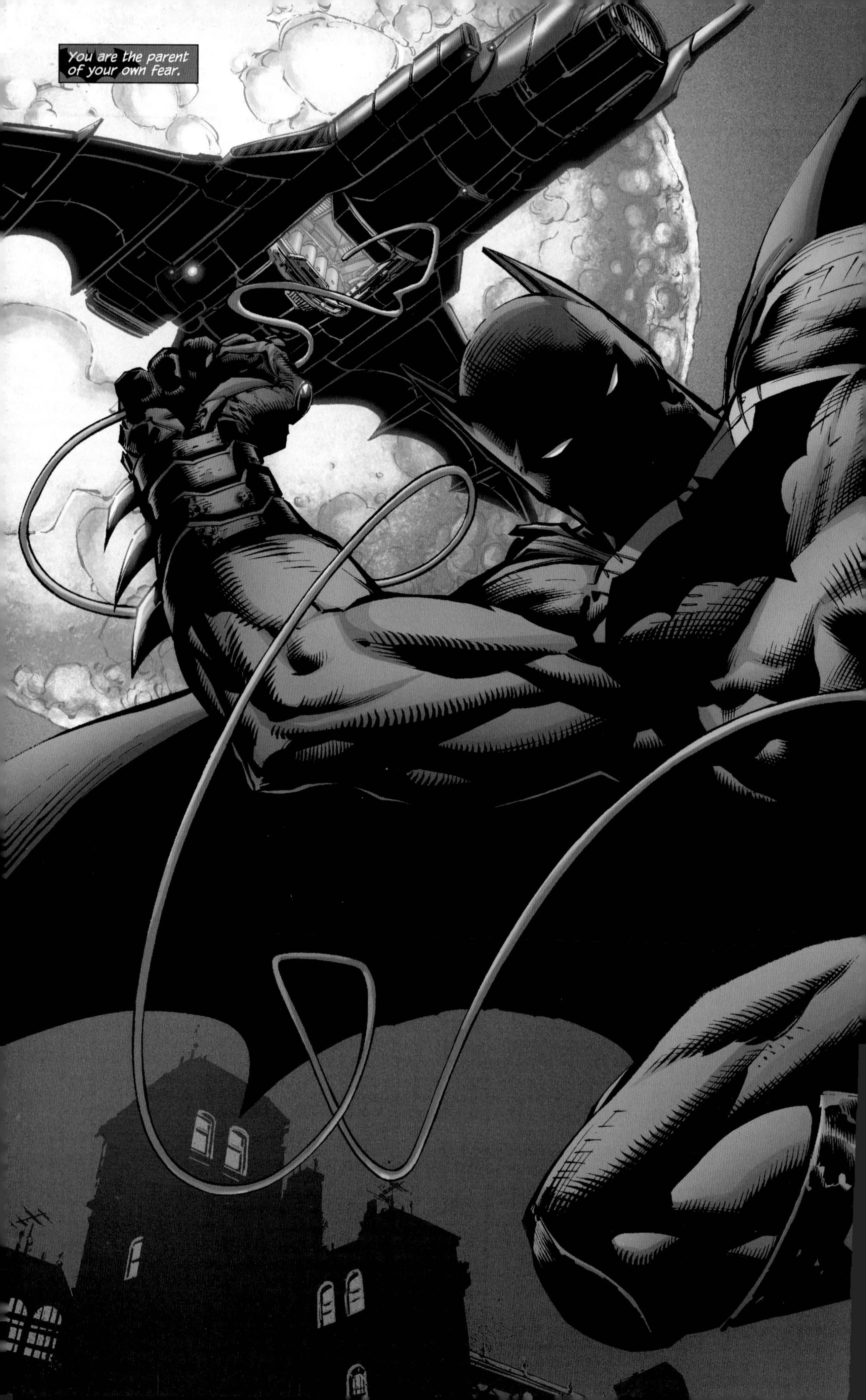
You are the parent of your own fear.

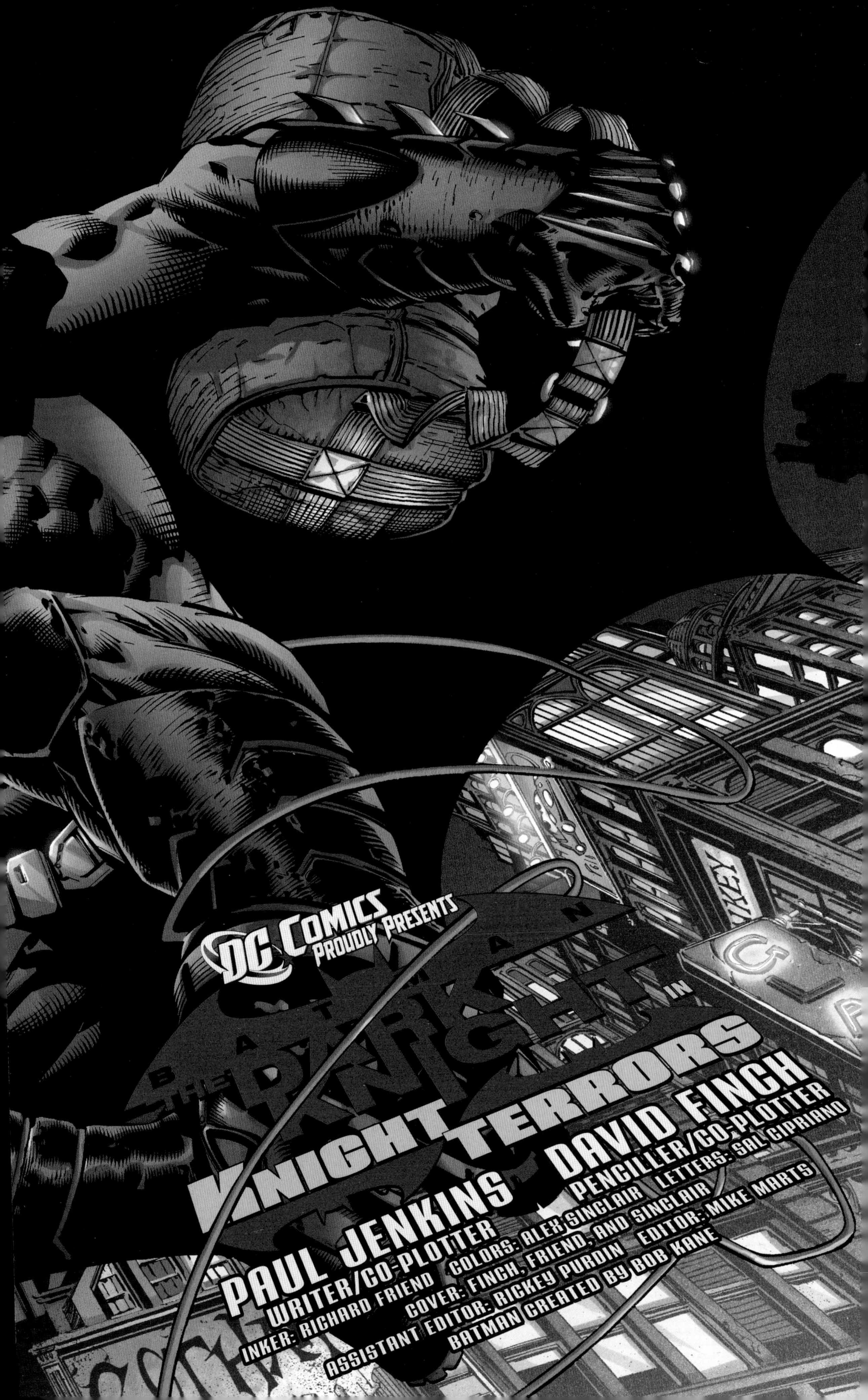
DC COMICS PROUDLY PRESENTS
BATMAN THE DARK KNIGHT IN
KNIGHT TERRORS
PAUL JENKINS WRITER/CO-PLOTTER
DAVID FINCH PENCILLER/CO-PLOTTER
INKER: RICHARD FRIEND COLORS: ALEX SINCLAIR LETTERS: SAL CIPRIANO
COVER: FINCH, FRIEND, AND SINCLAIR
ASSISTANT EDITOR: RICKEY PURDIN EDITOR: MIKE MARTS
BATMAN CREATED BY BOB KANE

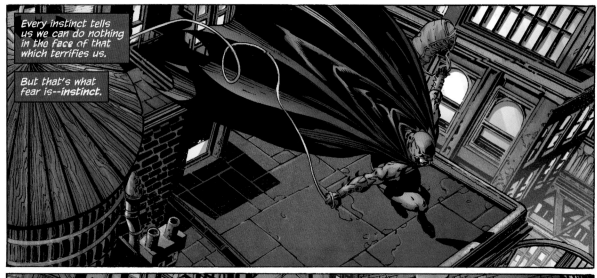

Every instinct tells us we can do nothing in the face of that which terrifies us.

But that's what fear is--*instinct*.

We run because that is our nature. Better to run away and live to fight another day, or so the saying goes.

But if we run, the cannibal feeds and grows stronger.

PAF

Better to run towards your fear. Better still to *face* it.

Stare it in the eye. Make it blink.

Watch it shrink.

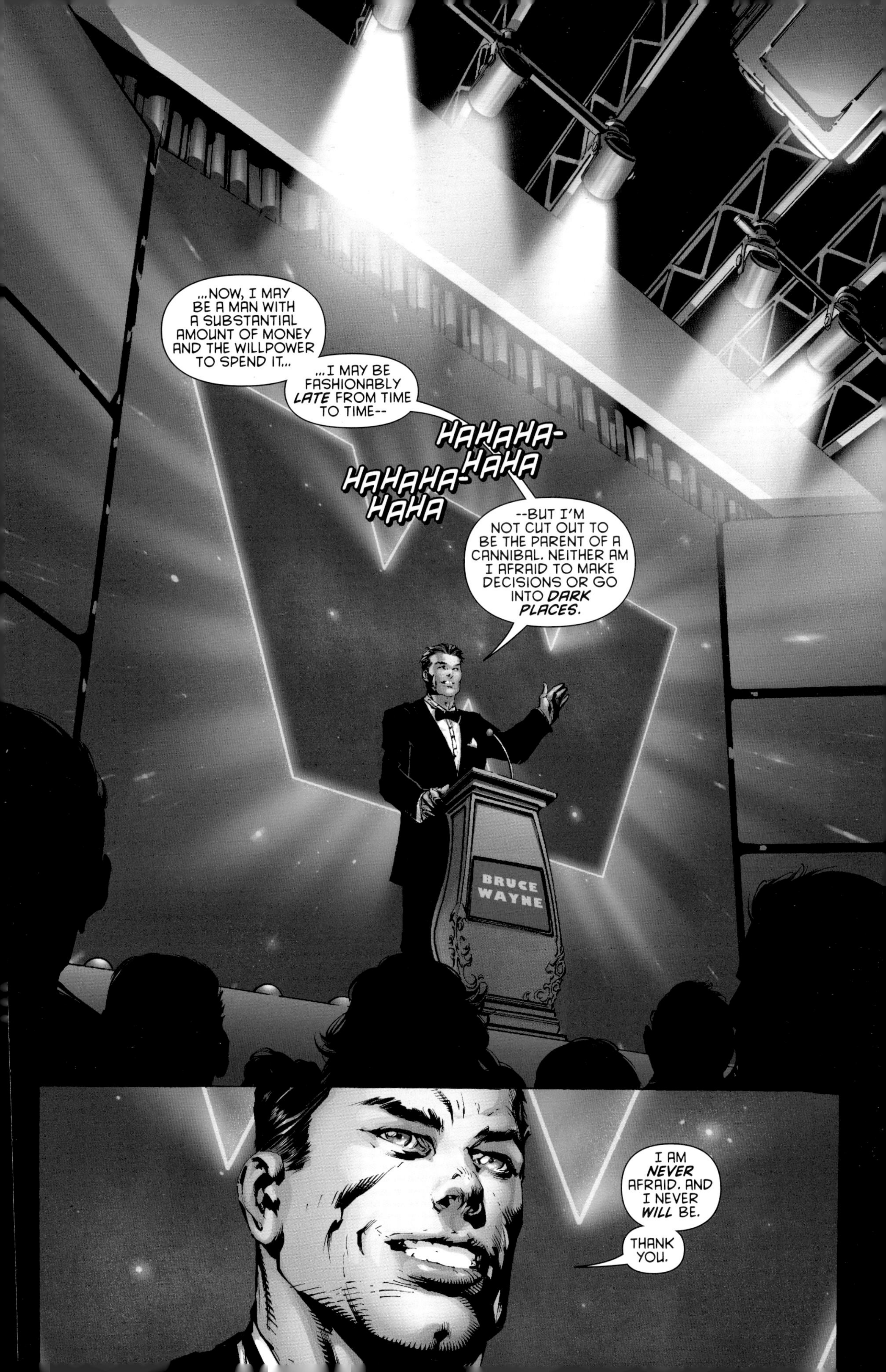
...NOW, I MAY BE A MAN WITH A SUBSTANTIAL AMOUNT OF MONEY AND THE WILLPOWER TO SPEND IT...
...I MAY BE FASHIONABLY *LATE* FROM TIME TO TIME--
HAHAHA-HAHA
HAHAHA-HAHA
--BUT I'M NOT CUT OUT TO BE THE PARENT OF A CANNIBAL. NEITHER AM I AFRAID TO MAKE DECISIONS OR GO INTO *DARK PLACES*.
BRUCE WAYNE
I AM *NEVER* AFRAID. AND I NEVER *WILL* BE.
THANK YOU.

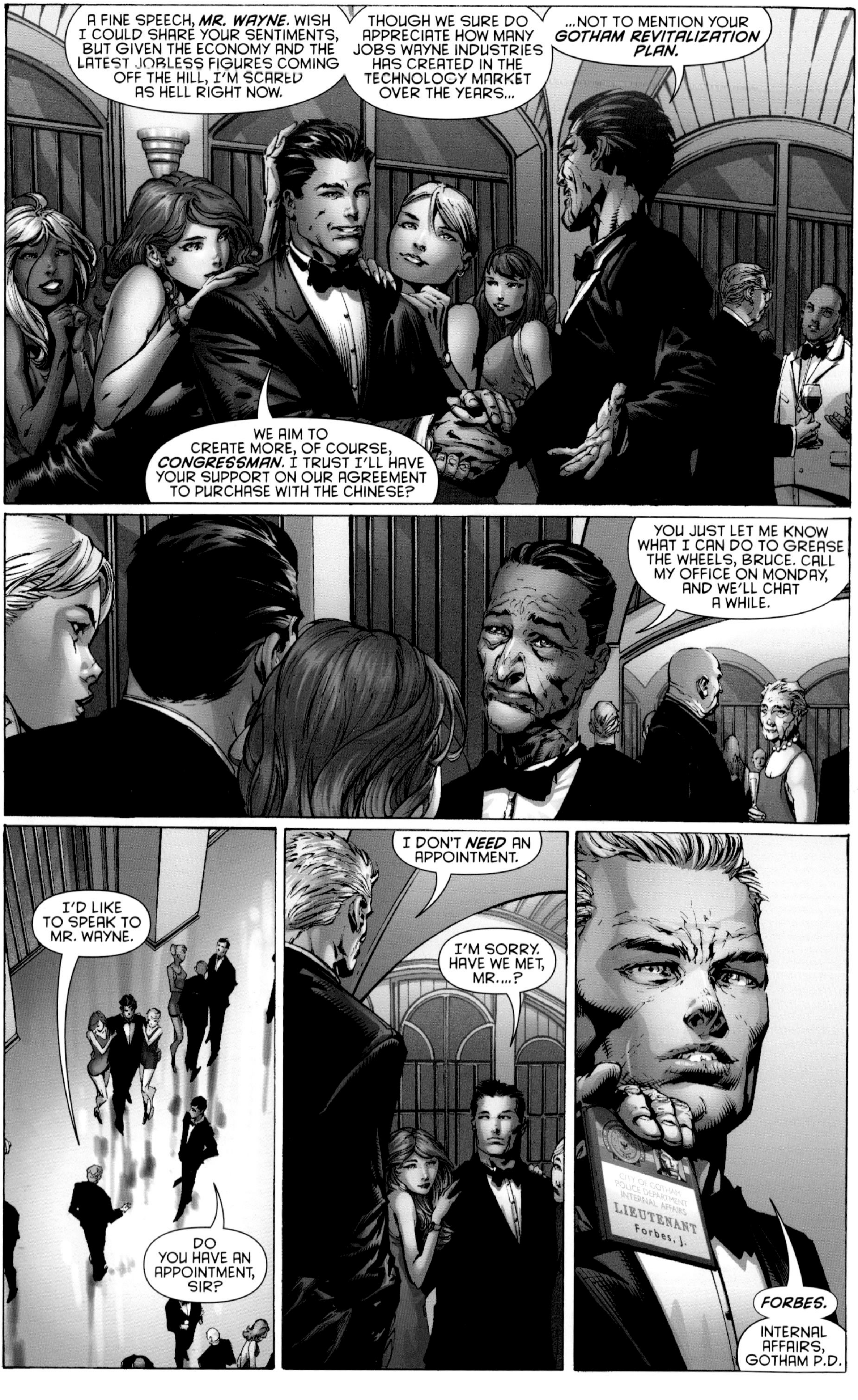
A FINE SPEECH, MR. WAYNE. WISH I COULD SHARE YOUR SENTIMENTS, BUT GIVEN THE ECONOMY AND THE LATEST JOBLESS FIGURES COMING OFF THE HILL, I'M SCARED AS HELL RIGHT NOW.
THOUGH WE SURE DO APPRECIATE HOW MANY JOBS WAYNE INDUSTRIES HAS CREATED IN THE TECHNOLOGY MARKET OVER THE YEARS...
...NOT TO MENTION YOUR GOTHAM REVITALIZATION PLAN.
WE AIM TO CREATE MORE, OF COURSE, CONGRESSMAN. I TRUST I'LL HAVE YOUR SUPPORT ON OUR AGREEMENT TO PURCHASE WITH THE CHINESE?
YOU JUST LET ME KNOW WHAT I CAN DO TO GREASE THE WHEELS, BRUCE. CALL MY OFFICE ON MONDAY, AND WE'LL CHAT A WHILE.
I'D LIKE TO SPEAK TO MR. WAYNE.
DO YOU HAVE AN APPOINTMENT, SIR?
I DON'T NEED AN APPOINTMENT.
I'M SORRY. HAVE WE MET, MR....?
CITY OF GOTHAM POLICE DEPARTMENT INTERNAL AFFAIRS
LIEUTENANT
Forbes, J.
FORBES.
INTERNAL AFFAIRS, GOTHAM P.D.

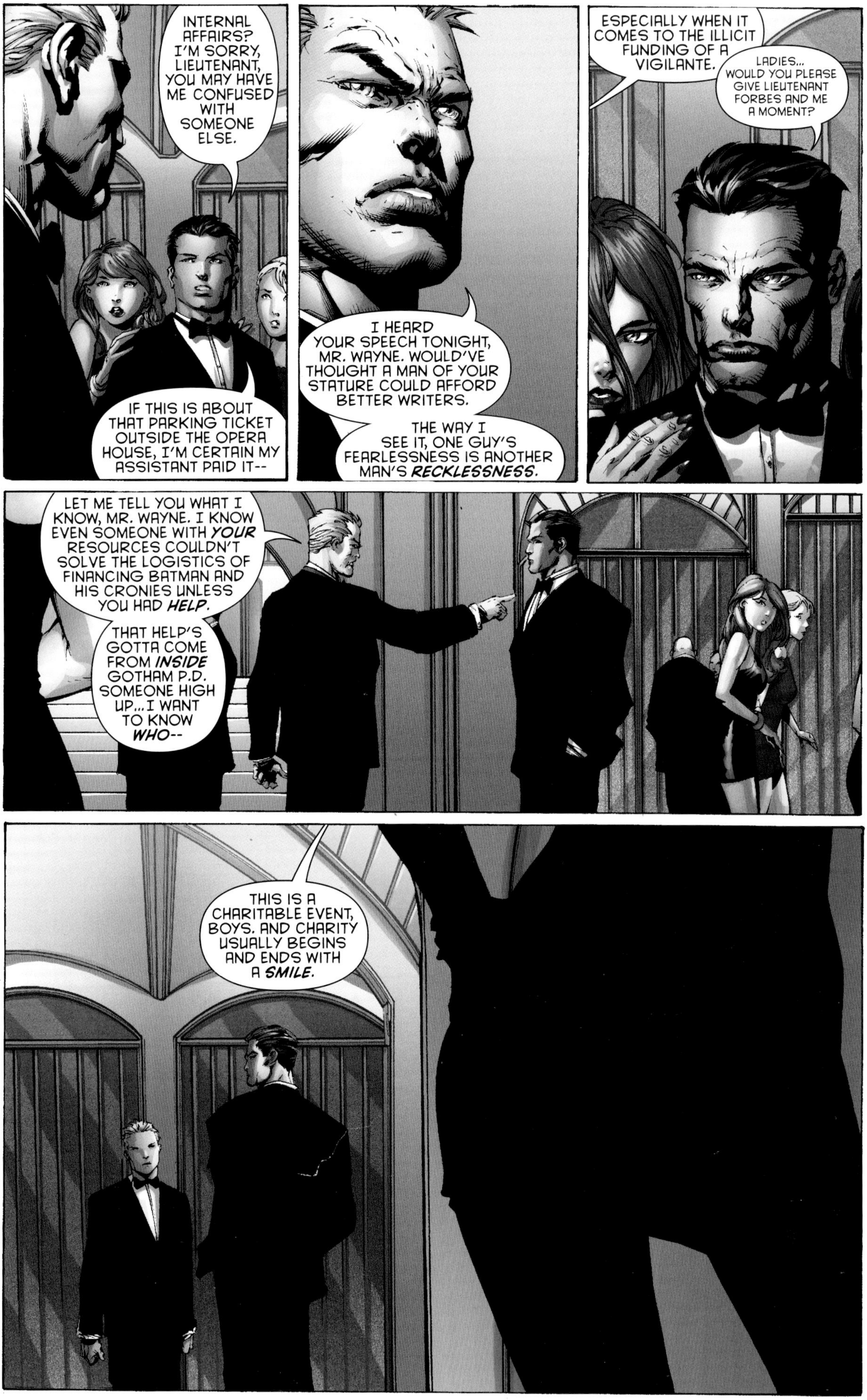
INTERNAL AFFAIRS? I'M SORRY, LIEUTENANT, YOU MAY HAVE ME CONFUSED WITH SOMEONE ELSE.
IF THIS IS ABOUT THAT PARKING TICKET OUTSIDE THE OPERA HOUSE, I'M CERTAIN MY ASSISTANT PAID IT--
I HEARD YOUR SPEECH TONIGHT, MR. WAYNE. WOULD'VE THOUGHT A MAN OF YOUR STATURE COULD AFFORD BETTER WRITERS.
THE WAY I SEE IT, ONE GUY'S FEARLESSNESS IS ANOTHER MAN'S RECKLESSNESS.
ESPECIALLY WHEN IT COMES TO THE ILLICIT FUNDING OF A VIGILANTE.
LADIES... WOULD YOU PLEASE GIVE LIEUTENANT FORBES AND ME A MOMENT?
LET ME TELL YOU WHAT I KNOW, MR. WAYNE. I KNOW EVEN SOMEONE WITH YOUR RESOURCES COULDN'T SOLVE THE LOGISTICS OF FINANCING BATMAN AND HIS CRONIES UNLESS YOU HAD HELP.
THAT HELP'S GOTTA COME FROM INSIDE GOTHAM P.D. SOMEONE HIGH UP...I WANT TO KNOW WHO--
THIS IS A CHARITABLE EVENT, BOYS. AND CHARITY USUALLY BEGINS AND ENDS WITH A SMILE.

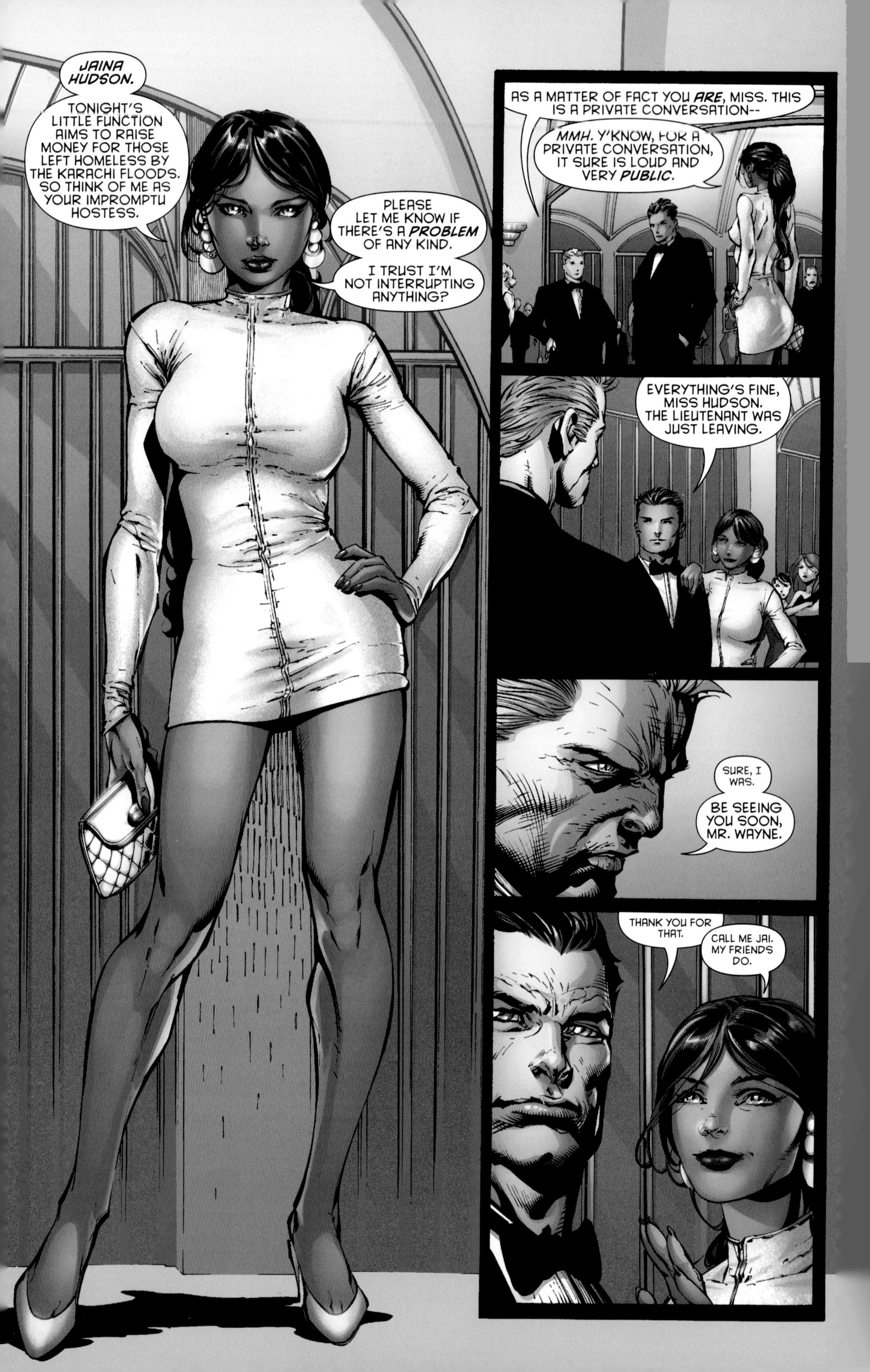
JAINA HUDSON.
TONIGHT'S LITTLE FUNCTION AIMS TO RAISE MONEY FOR THOSE LEFT HOMELESS BY THE KARACHI FLOODS. SO THINK OF ME AS YOUR IMPROMPTU HOSTESS.
PLEASE LET ME KNOW IF THERE'S A *PROBLEM* OF ANY KIND.
I TRUST I'M NOT INTERRUPTING ANYTHING?
AS A MATTER OF FACT YOU *ARE*, MISS. THIS IS A PRIVATE CONVERSATION--
MMH. Y'KNOW, FOR A PRIVATE CONVERSATION, IT SURE IS LOUD AND VERY *PUBLIC.*
EVERYTHING'S FINE, MISS HUDSON. THE LIEUTENANT WAS JUST LEAVING.
SURE, I WAS.
BE SEEING YOU SOON, MR. WAYNE.
THANK YOU FOR THAT.
CALL ME JAI. MY FRIENDS DO.

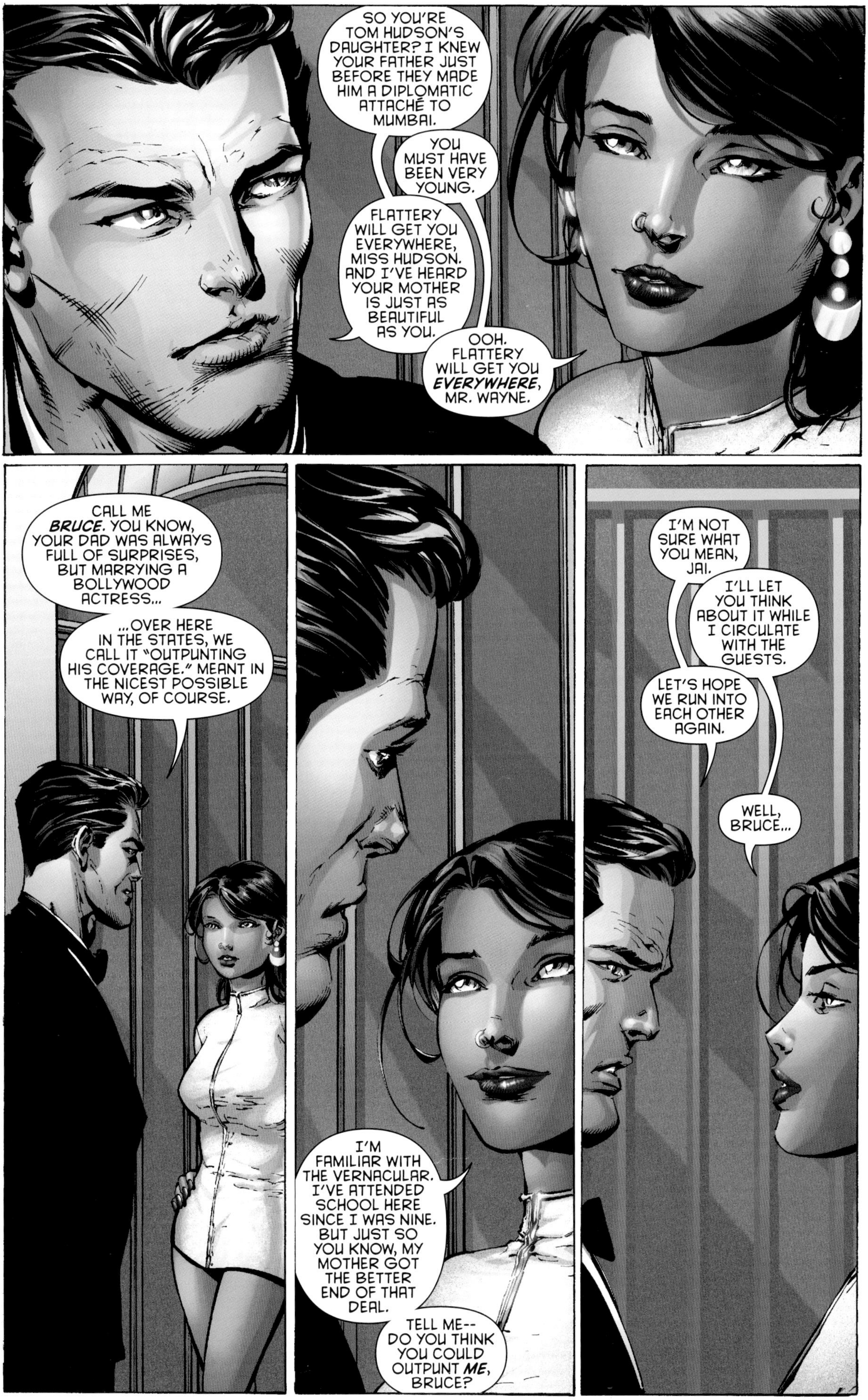
SO YOU'RE TOM HUDSON'S DAUGHTER? I KNEW YOUR FATHER JUST BEFORE THEY MADE HIM A DIPLOMATIC ATTACHÉ TO MUMBAI.
YOU MUST HAVE BEEN VERY YOUNG.
FLATTERY WILL GET YOU EVERYWHERE, MISS HUDSON. AND I'VE HEARD YOUR MOTHER IS JUST AS BEAUTIFUL AS YOU.
OOH. FLATTERY WILL GET YOU *EVERYWHERE*, MR. WAYNE.
CALL ME *BRUCE*. YOU KNOW, YOUR DAD WAS ALWAYS FULL OF SURPRISES, BUT MARRYING A BOLLYWOOD ACTRESS...
...OVER HERE IN THE STATES, WE CALL IT "OUTPUNTING HIS COVERAGE." MEANT IN THE NICEST POSSIBLE WAY, OF COURSE.
I'M FAMILIAR WITH THE VERNACULAR. I'VE ATTENDED SCHOOL HERE SINCE I WAS NINE. BUT JUST SO YOU KNOW, MY MOTHER GOT THE BETTER END OF THAT DEAL.
TELL ME-- DO YOU THINK YOU COULD OUTPUNT *ME*, BRUCE?
I'M NOT SURE WHAT YOU MEAN, JAI.
I'LL LET YOU THINK ABOUT IT WHILE I CIRCULATE WITH THE GUESTS.
LET'S HOPE WE RUN INTO EACH OTHER AGAIN.
WELL, BRUCE...

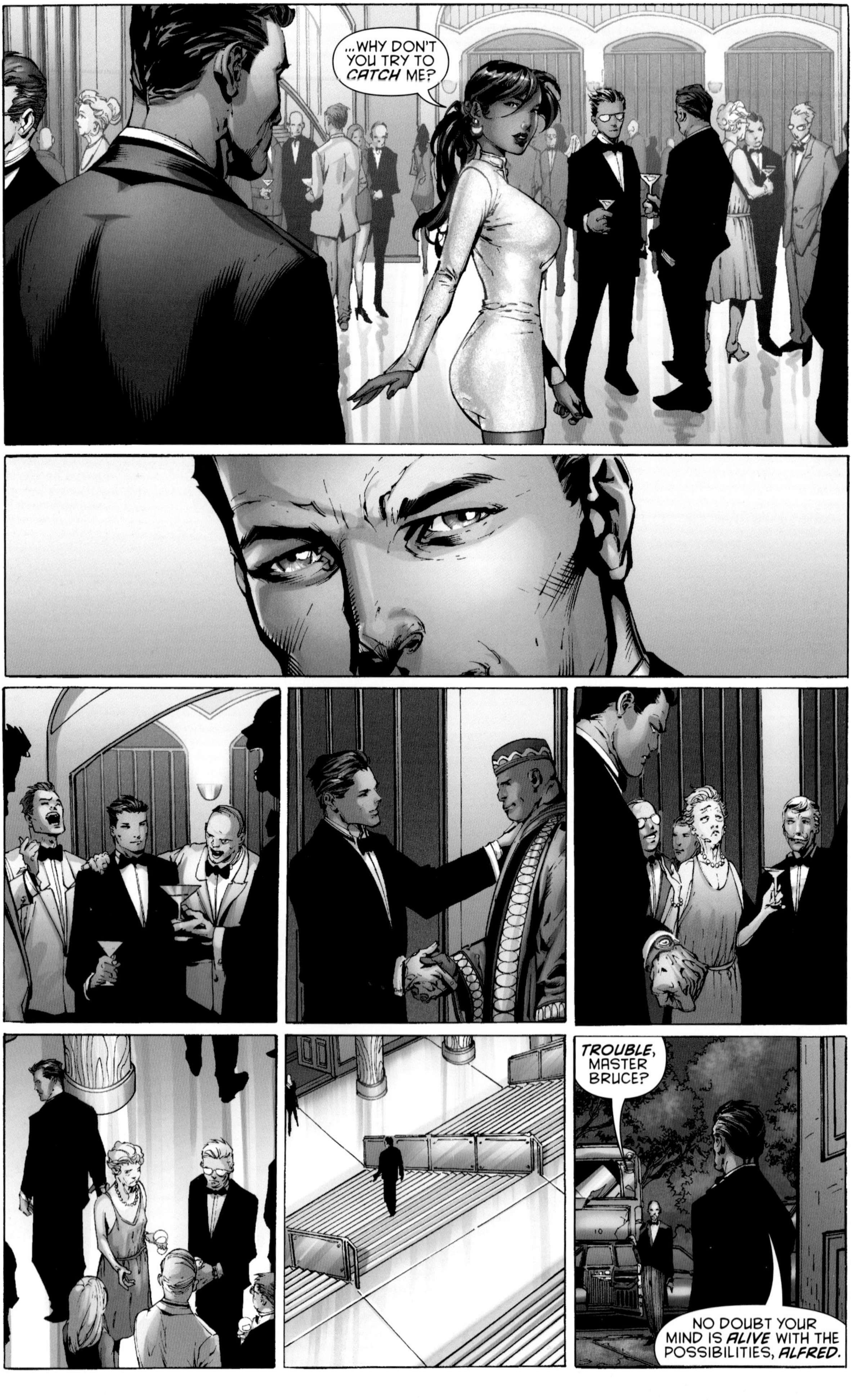
...WHY DON'T YOU TRY TO *CATCH* ME?
TROUBLE, MASTER BRUCE?
NO DOUBT YOUR MIND IS *ALIVE* WITH THE POSSIBILITIES, *ALFRED*.

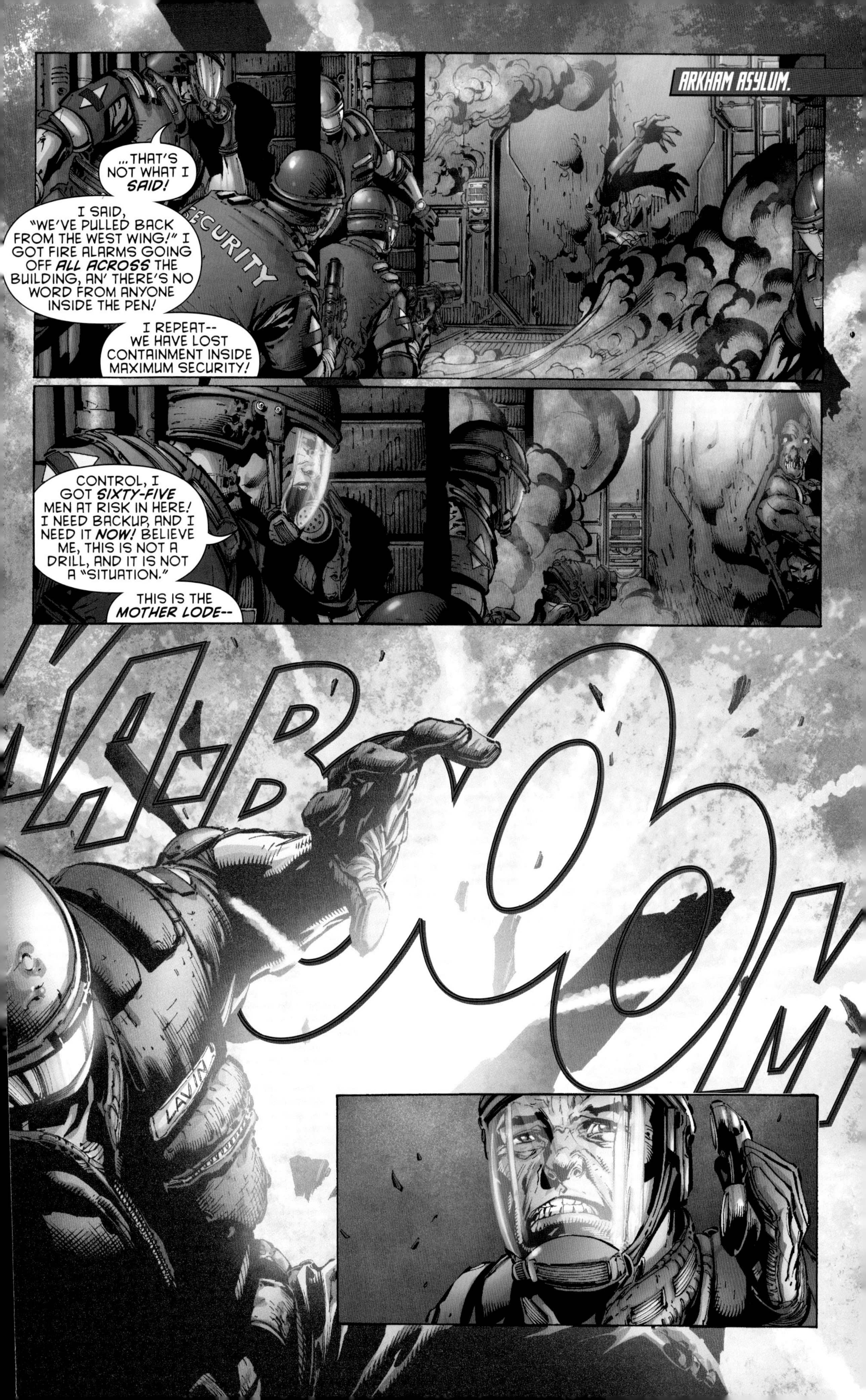

ARKHAM ASYLUM.
...THAT'S NOT WHAT I SAID!
I SAID, "WE'VE PULLED BACK FROM THE WEST WING!" I GOT FIRE ALARMS GOING OFF ALL ACROSS THE BUILDING, AN' THERE'S NO WORD FROM ANYONE INSIDE THE PEN!
I REPEAT-- WE HAVE LOST CONTAINMENT INSIDE MAXIMUM SECURITY!
SECURITY
CONTROL, I GOT SIXTY-FIVE MEN AT RISK IN HERE! I NEED BACKUP, AND I NEED IT NOW! BELIEVE ME, THIS IS NOT A DRILL, AND IT IS NOT A "SITUATION."
THIS IS THE MOTHER LODE--
KABOOOM
LAVIN

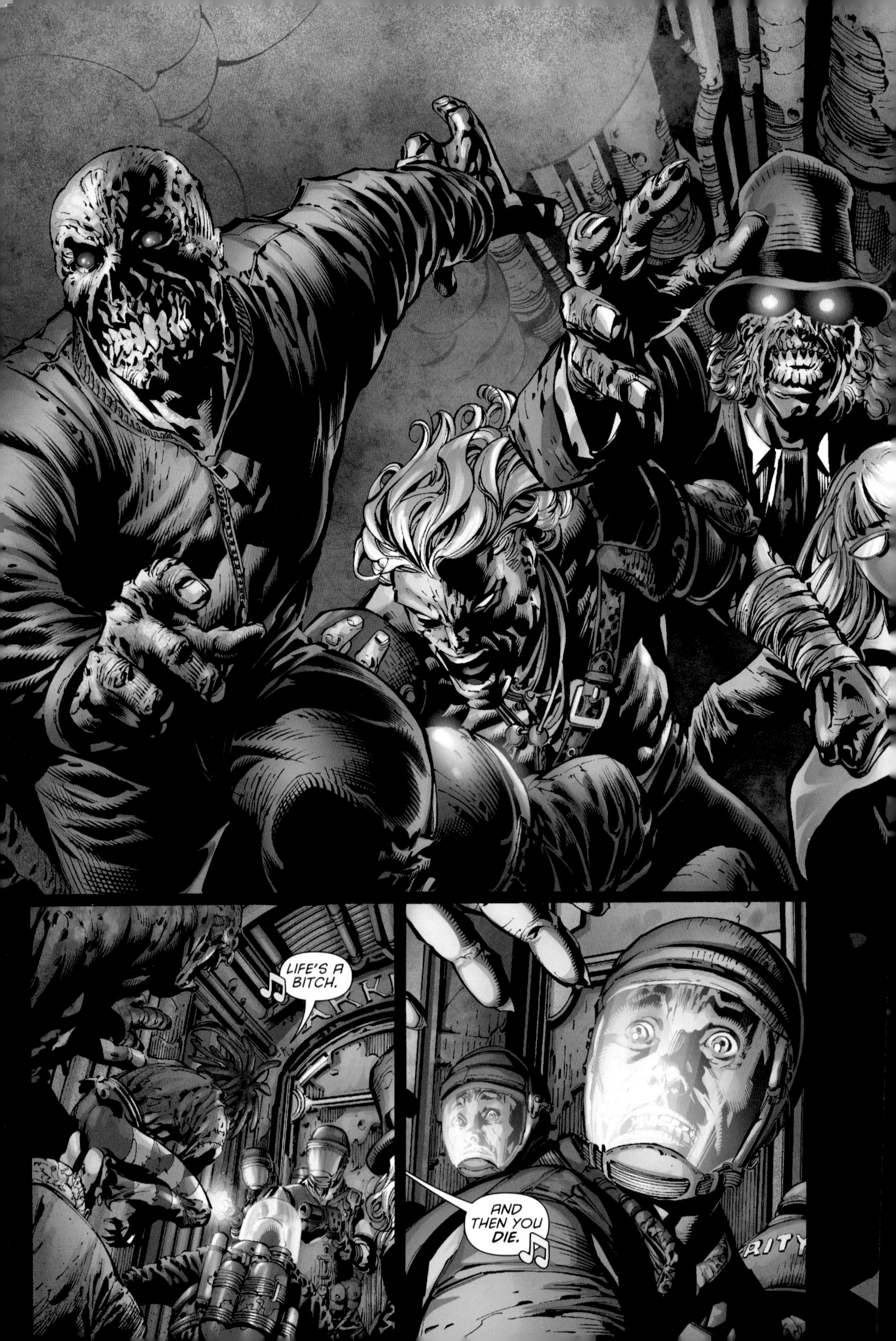
LIFE'S A BITCH.
AND THEN YOU DIE.

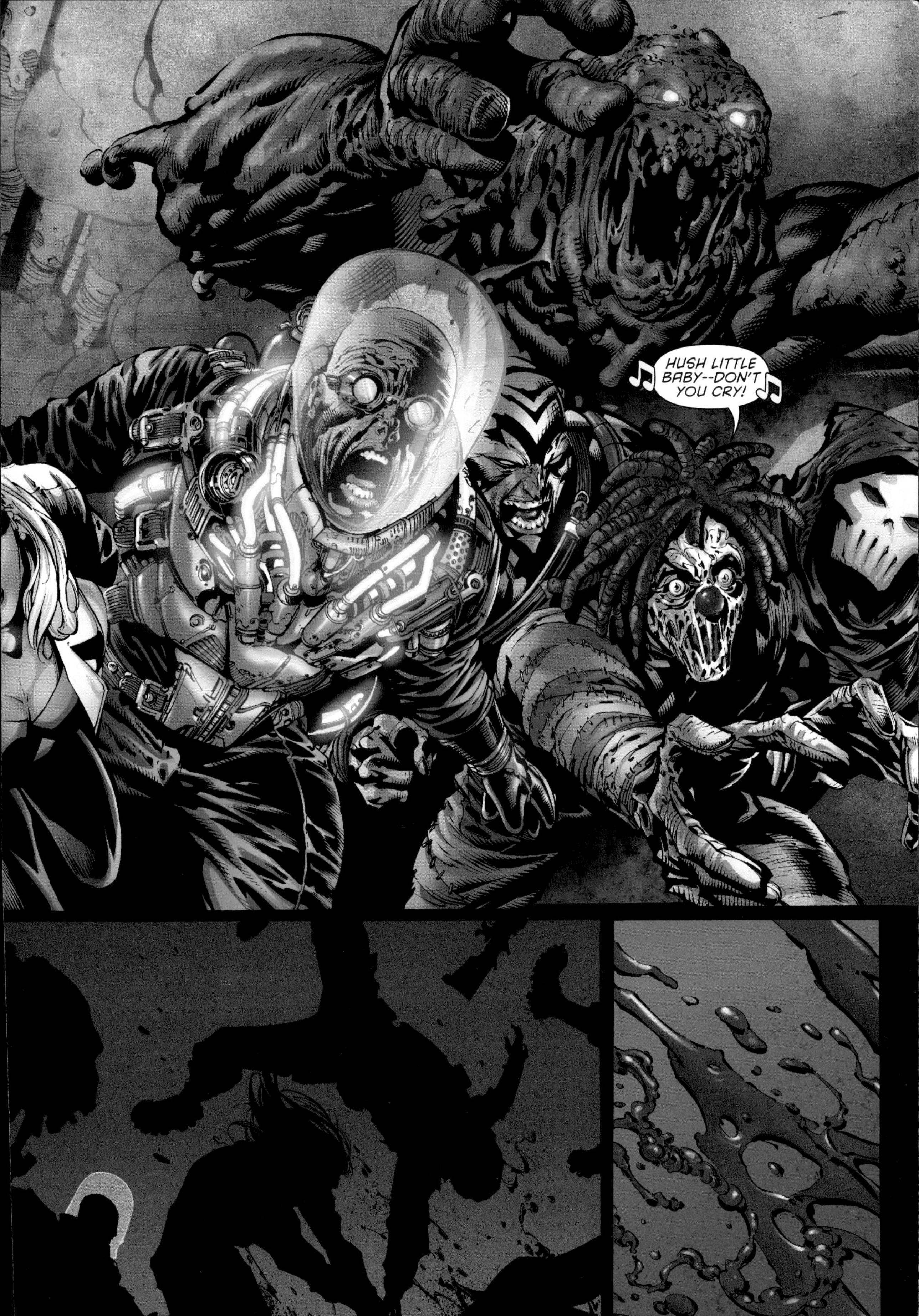
HUSH LITTLE BABY--DON'T YOU CRY!

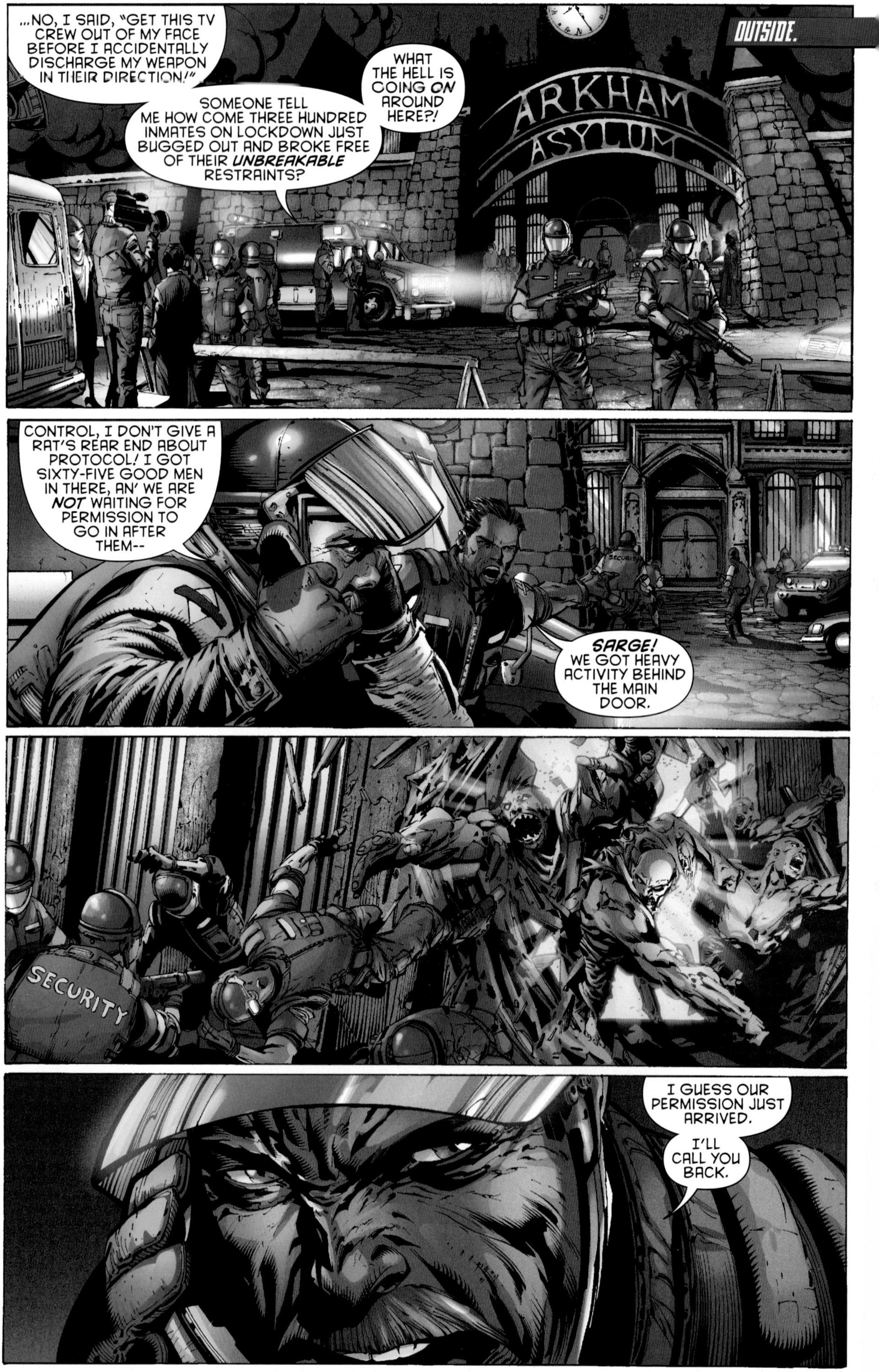
OUTSIDE.
...NO, I SAID, "GET THIS TV CREW OUT OF MY FACE BEFORE I ACCIDENTALLY DISCHARGE MY WEAPON IN THEIR DIRECTION!"
SOMEONE TELL ME HOW COME THREE HUNDRED INMATES ON LOCKDOWN JUST BUGGED OUT AND BROKE FREE OF THEIR *UNBREAKABLE* RESTRAINTS?
WHAT THE HELL IS GOING *ON* AROUND HERE?!
ARKHAM ASYLUM
CONTROL, I DON'T GIVE A RAT'S REAR END ABOUT PROTOCOL! I GOT SIXTY-FIVE GOOD MEN IN THERE, AN' WE ARE *NOT* WAITING FOR PERMISSION TO GO IN AFTER THEM--
SARGE! WE GOT HEAVY ACTIVITY BEHIND THE MAIN DOOR.
SECURITY
I GUESS OUR PERMISSION JUST ARRIVED.
I'LL CALL YOU BACK.

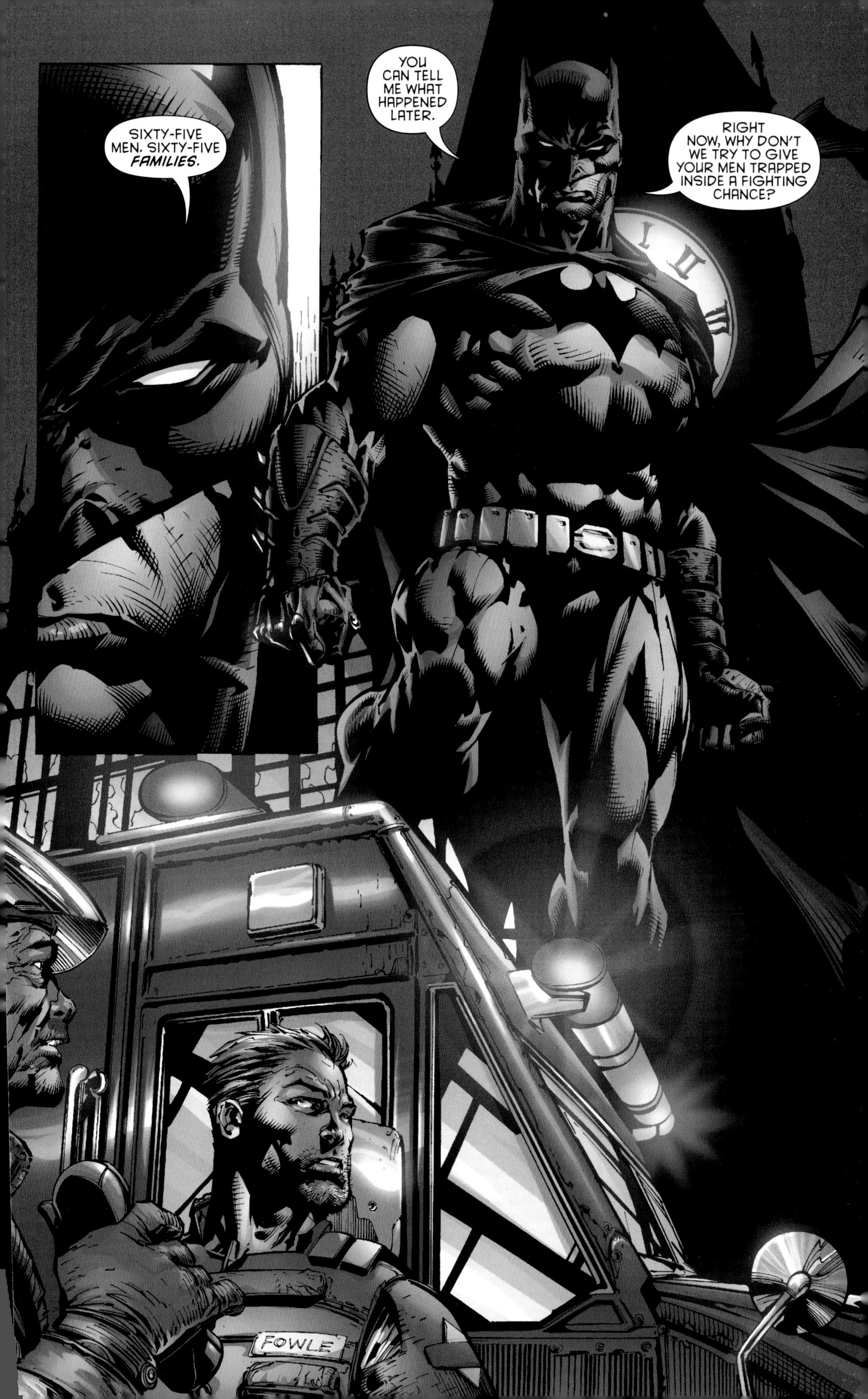
SIXTY-FIVE MEN. SIXTY-FIVE *FAMILIES*.
YOU CAN TELL ME WHAT HAPPENED LATER.
RIGHT NOW, WHY DON'T WE TRY TO GIVE YOUR MEN TRAPPED INSIDE A FIGHTING CHANCE?
FOWLE

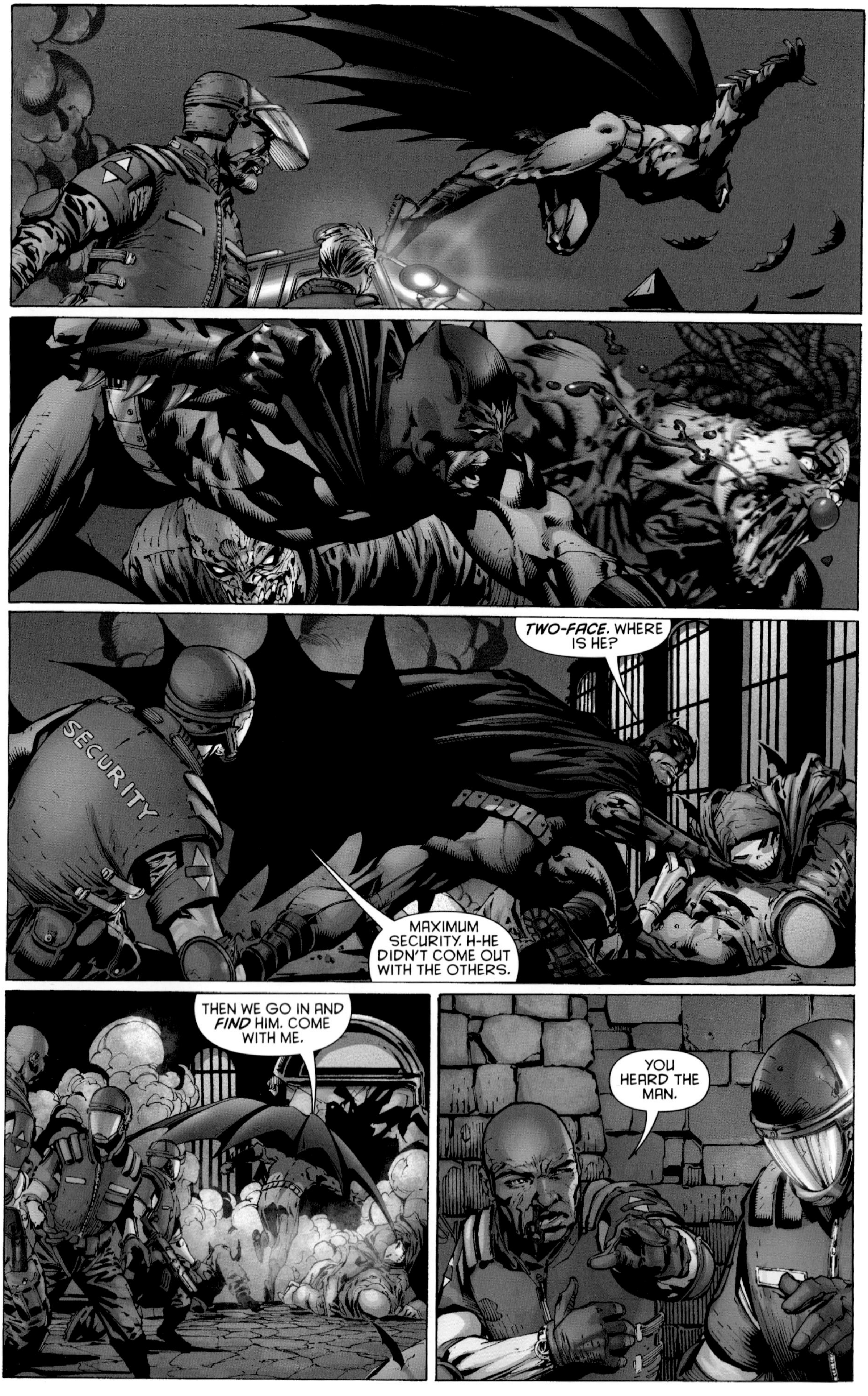
TWO-FACE. WHERE IS HE?
MAXIMUM SECURITY. H-HE DIDN'T COME OUT WITH THE OTHERS.
THEN WE GO IN AND FIND HIM. COME WITH ME.
YOU HEARD THE MAN.

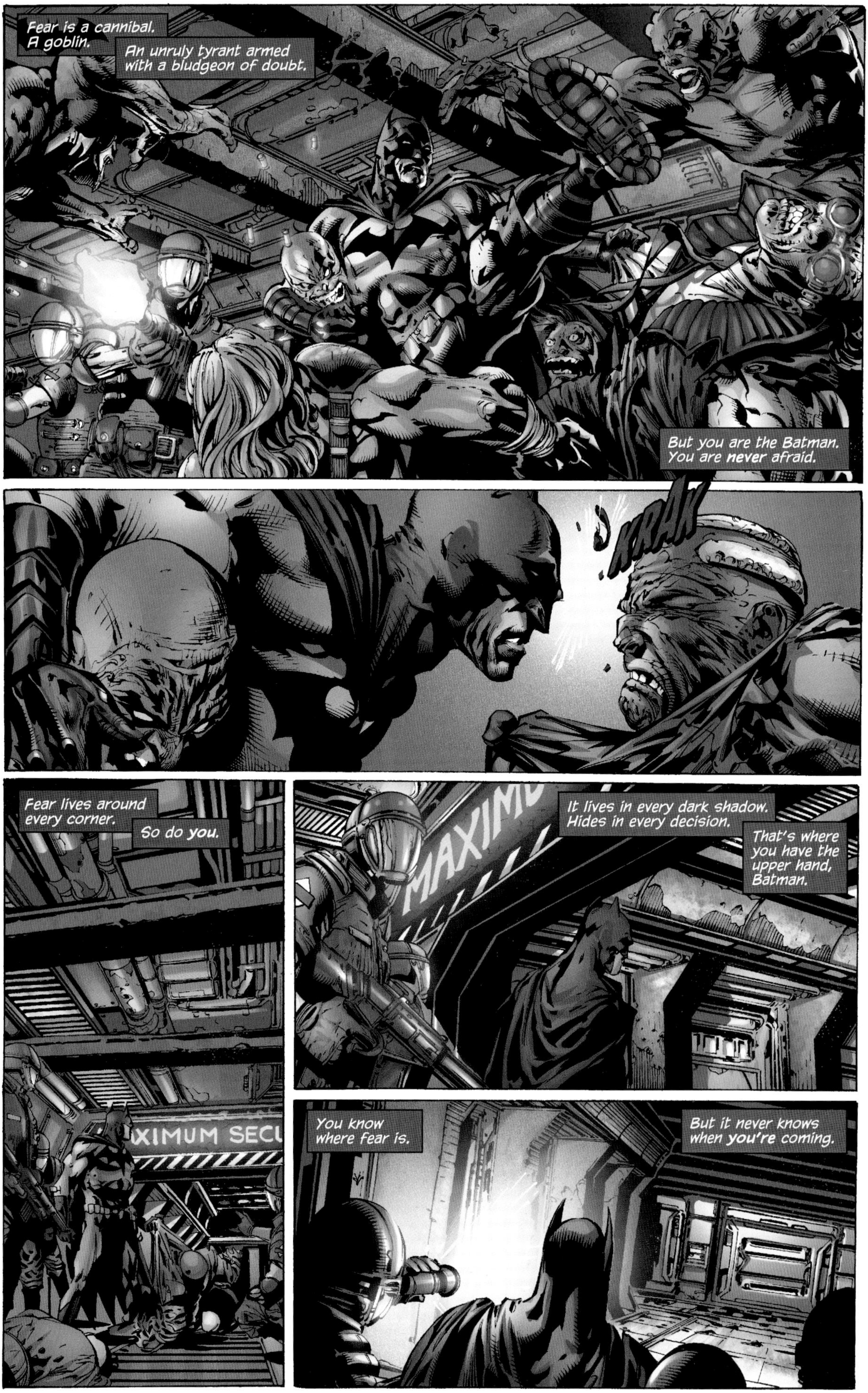
Fear is a cannibal. A goblin.
An unruly tyrant armed with a bludgeon of doubt.
But you are the Batman. You are never afraid.
KRAK
Fear lives around every corner.
So do you.
It lives in every dark shadow. Hides in every decision.
That's where you have the upper hand, Batman.
MAXIMU
XIMUM SECU
You know where fear is.
But it never knows when you're coming.

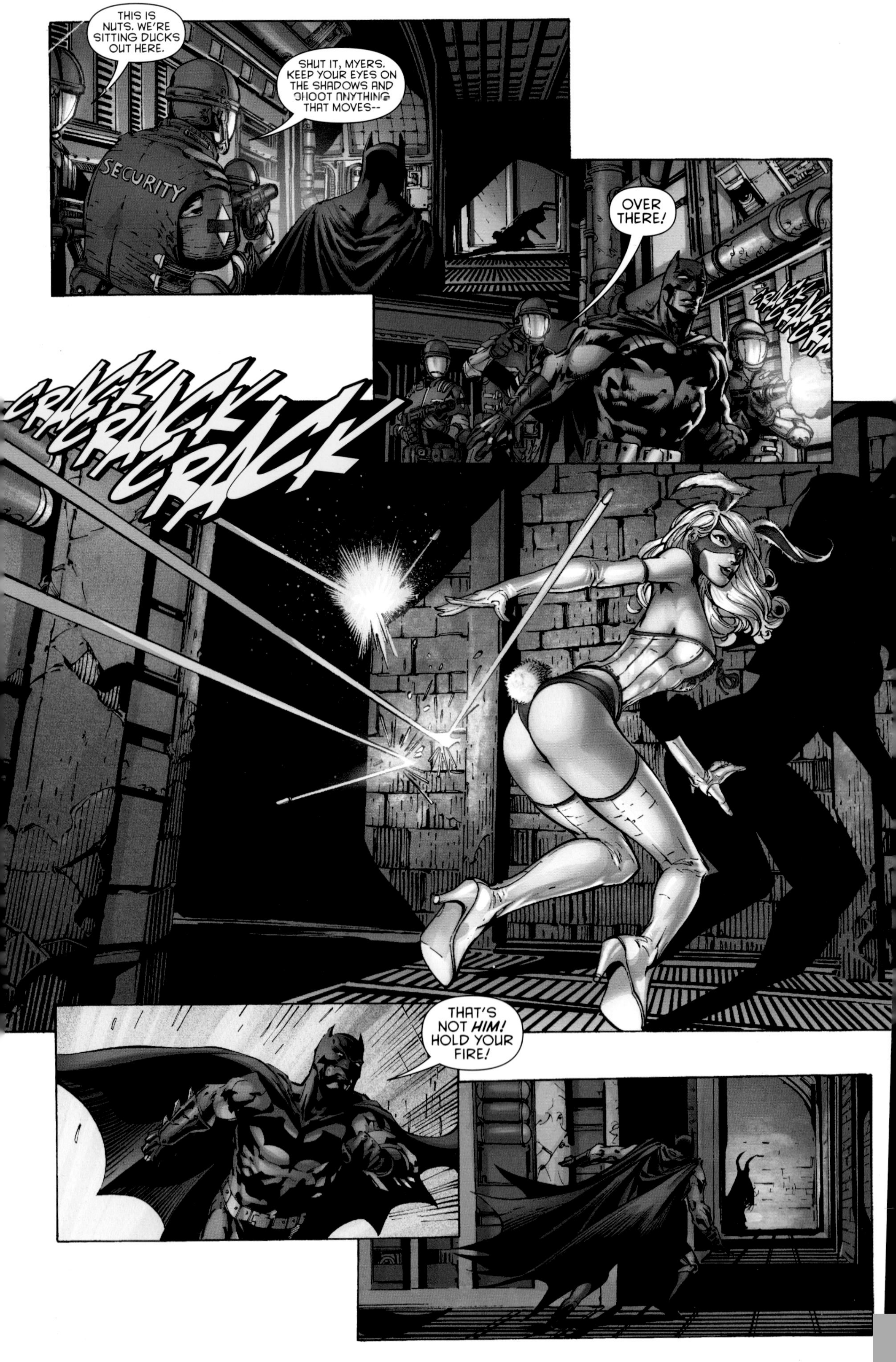

THIS IS NUTS. WE'RE SITTING DUCKS OUT HERE.
SHUT IT, MYERS. KEEP YOUR EYES ON THE SHADOWS AND SHOOT ANYTHING THAT MOVES--
SECURITY
OVER THERE!
CRACKACKACK
CRACKCRACKCRACK
THAT'S NOT *HIM!* HOLD YOUR FIRE!

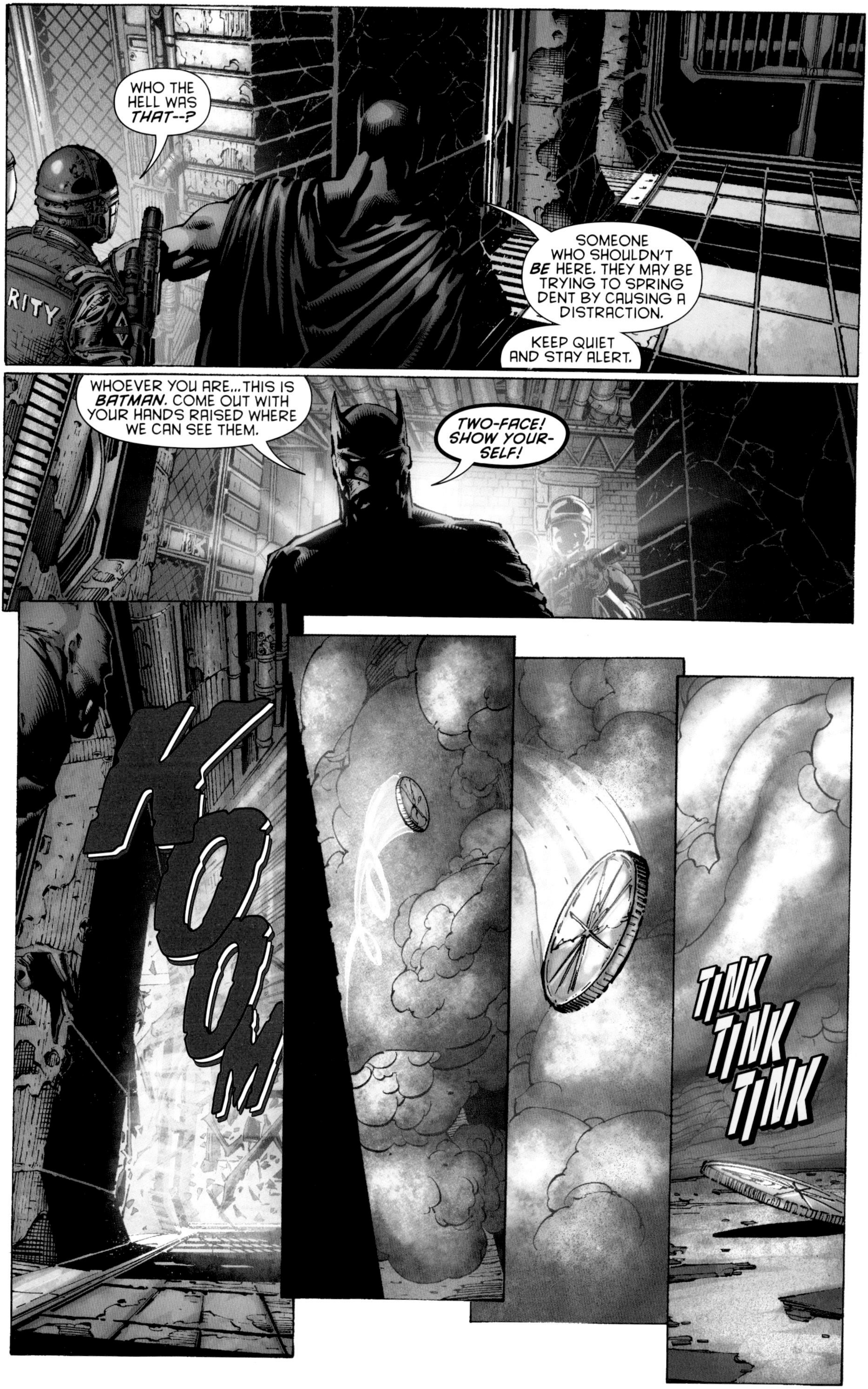

WHO THE HELL WAS *THAT*--?
SOMEONE WHO SHOULDN'T *BE* HERE. THEY MAY BE TRYING TO SPRING DENT BY CAUSING A DISTRACTION.
KEEP QUIET AND STAY ALERT.
RITY
WHOEVER YOU ARE... THIS IS *BATMAN*. COME OUT WITH YOUR HANDS RAISED WHERE WE CAN SEE THEM.
TWO-FACE! SHOW YOUR-SELF!
KOOM
TINK
TINK
TINK

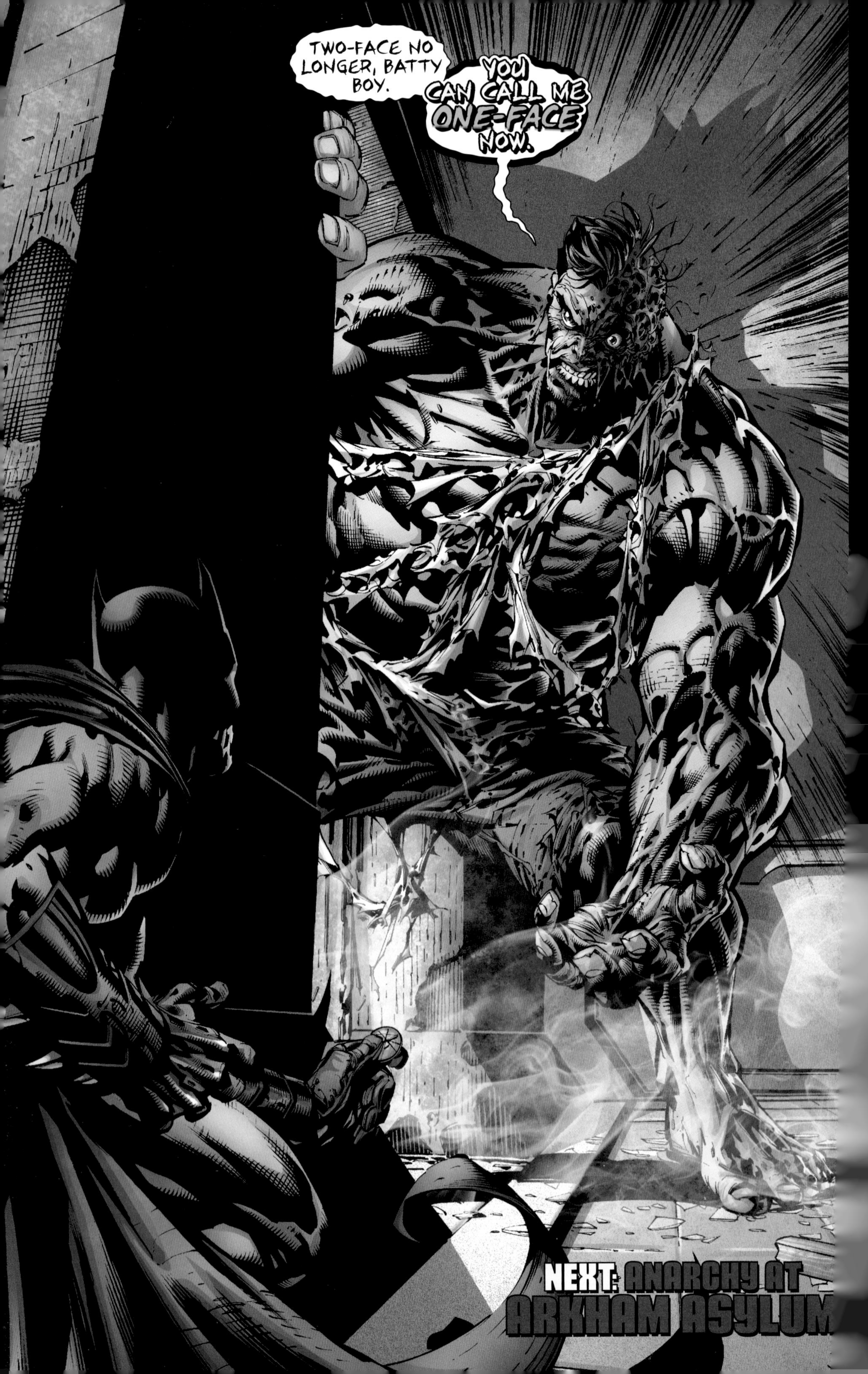
TWO-FACE NO LONGER, BATTY BOY.
YOU CAN CALL ME ONE-FACE NOW.
NEXT: ANARCHY AT ARKHAM ASYLUM

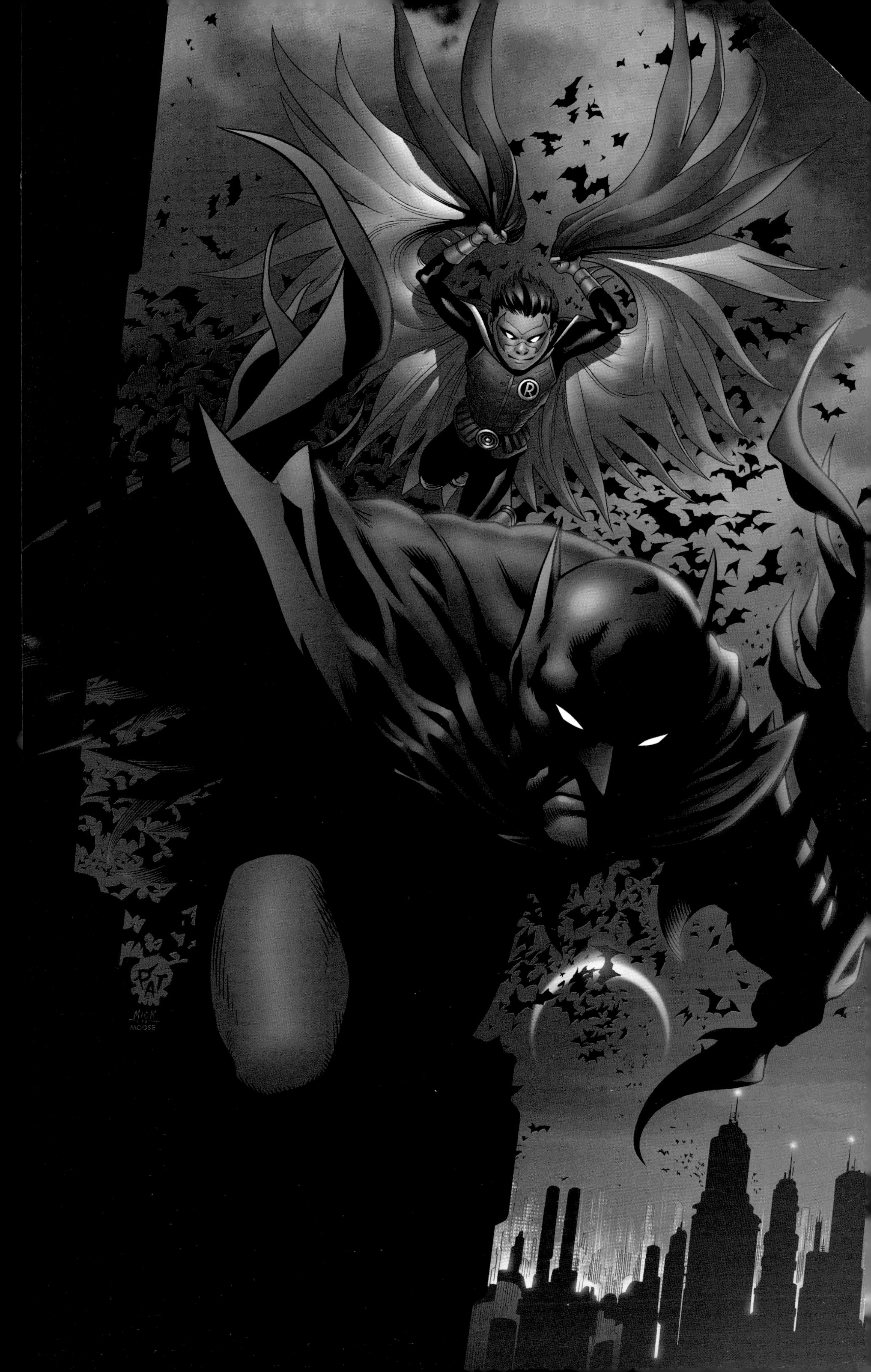

BATMAN AND ROBIN

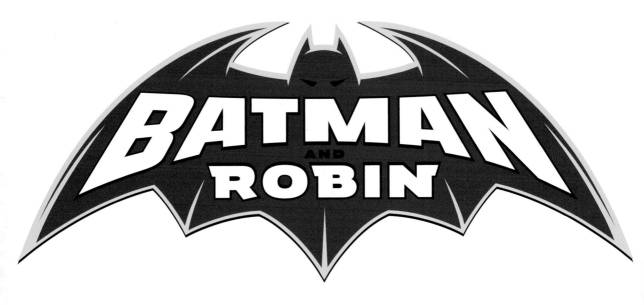

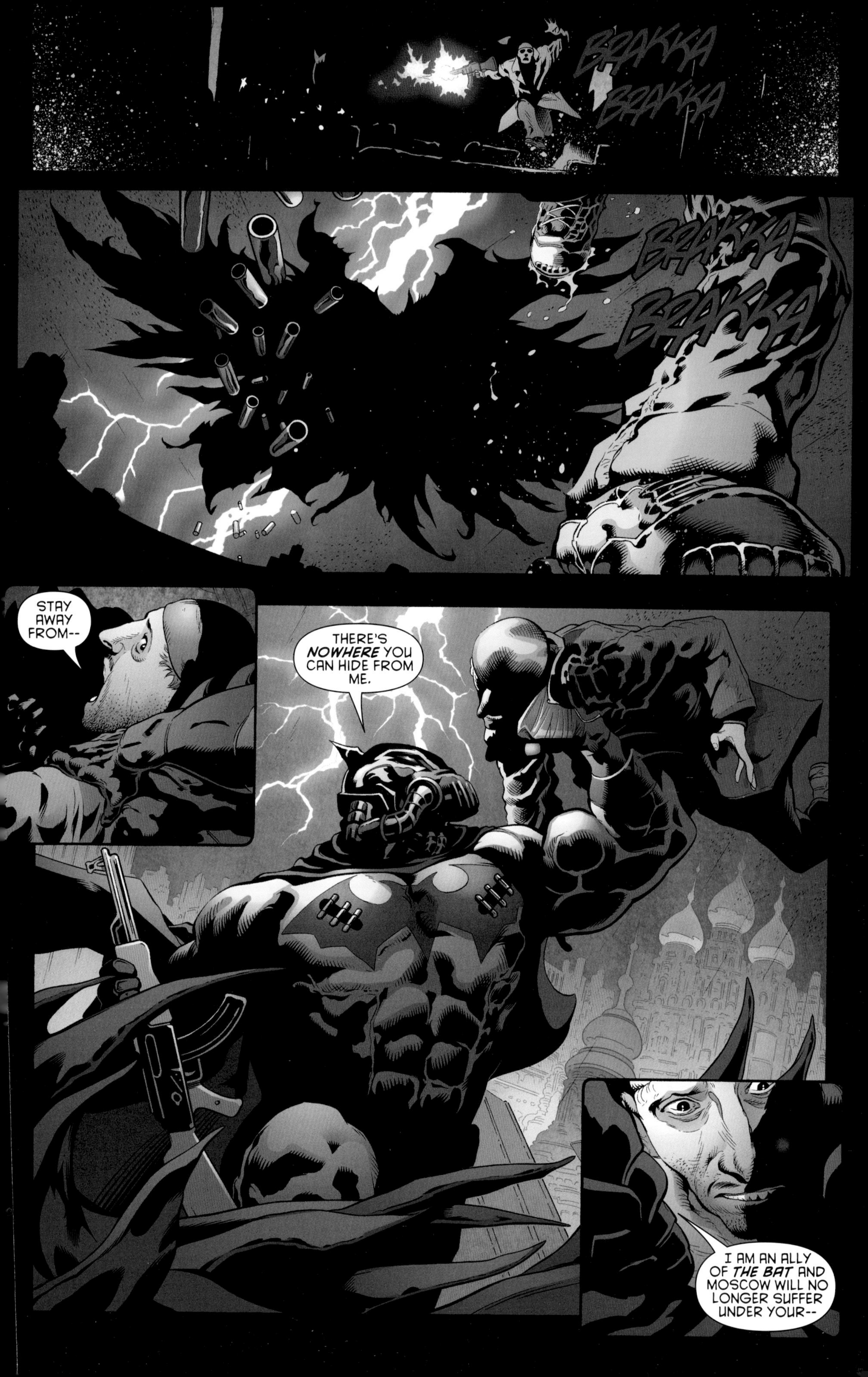
BRAKKA
BRAKKA
BRAKKA
BRAKKA
STAY AWAY FROM--
THERE'S NOWHERE YOU CAN HIDE FROM ME.
I AM AN ALLY OF THE BAT AND MOSCOW WILL NO LONGER SUFFER UNDER YOUR--

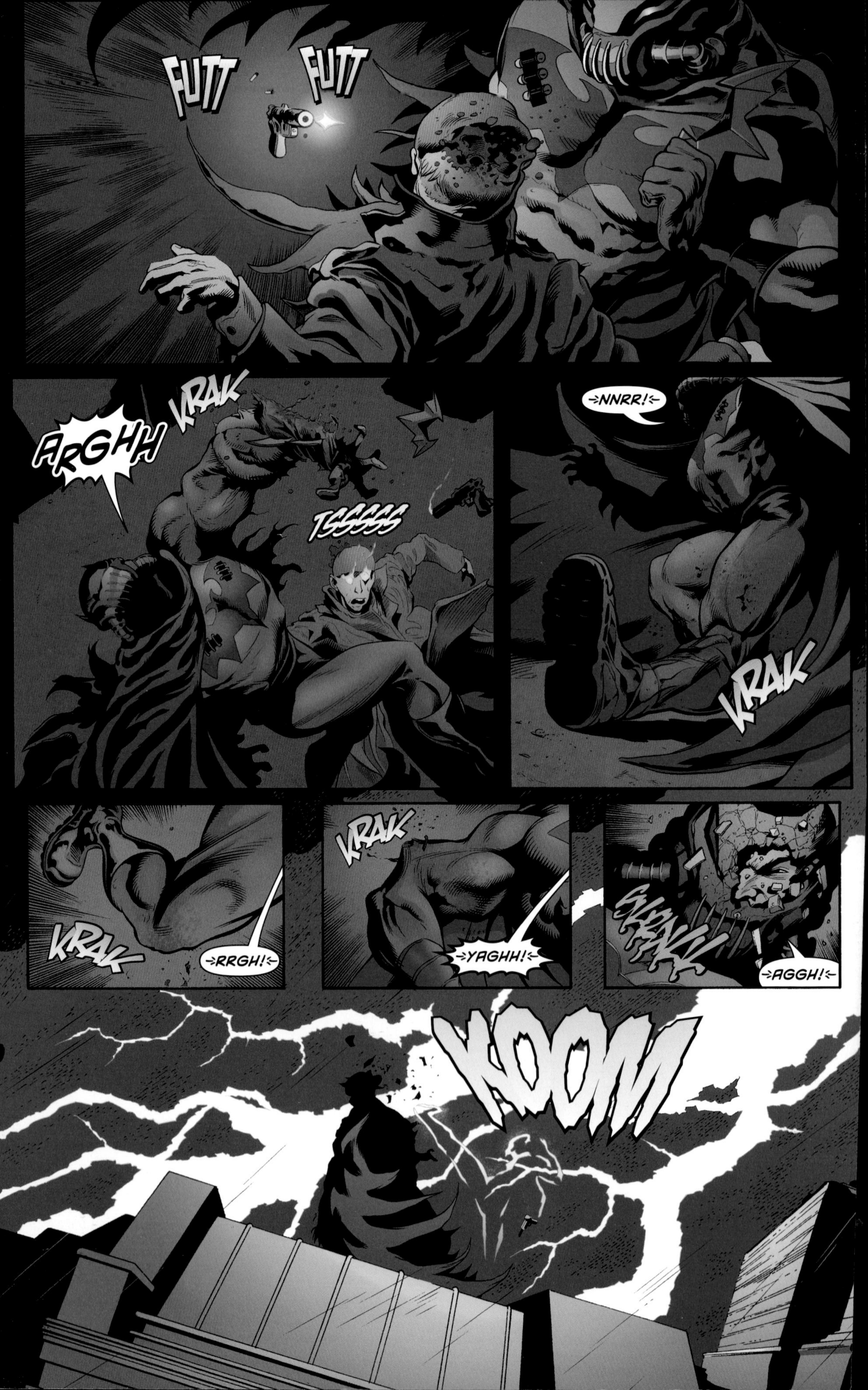
FUTT
FUTT
ARGHH
KRAK
TSSSSS
NNRR!
KRAK
KRAK
RRGH!
KRAK
YAGHH!
AGGH!
KOOM

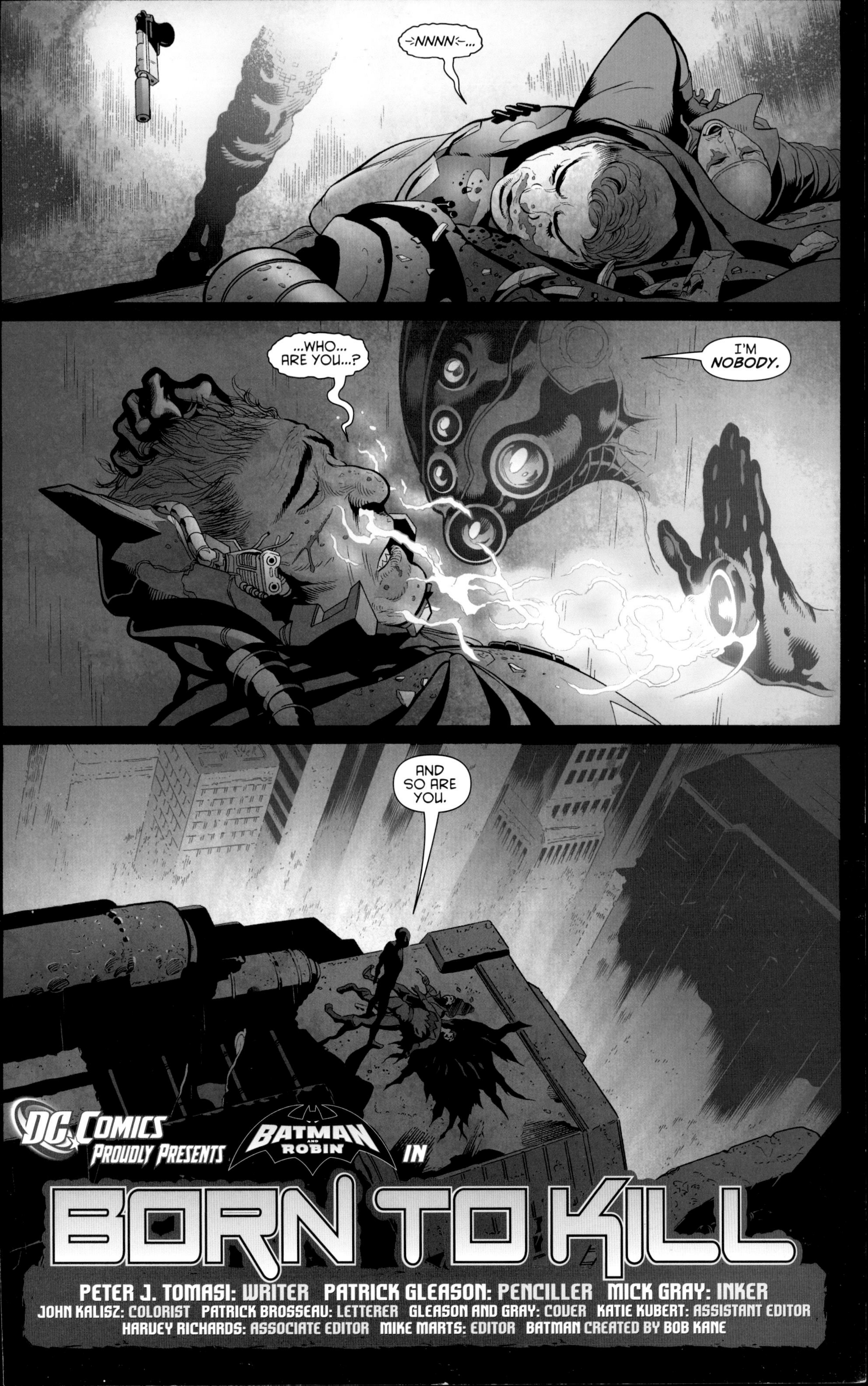
-NNNN-...
...WHO... ARE YOU...?
I'M NOBODY.
AND SO ARE YOU.
DC COMICS PROUDLY PRESENTS
BATMAN AND ROBIN
IN
BORN TO KILL
PETER J. TOMASI: WRITER PATRICK GLEASON: PENCILLER MICK GRAY: INKER
JOHN KALISZ: COLORIST PATRICK BROSSEAU: LETTERER GLEASON AND GRAY: COVER KATIE KUBERT: ASSISTANT EDITOR
HARVEY RICHARDS: ASSOCIATE EDITOR MIKE MARTS: EDITOR BATMAN CREATED BY BOB KANE

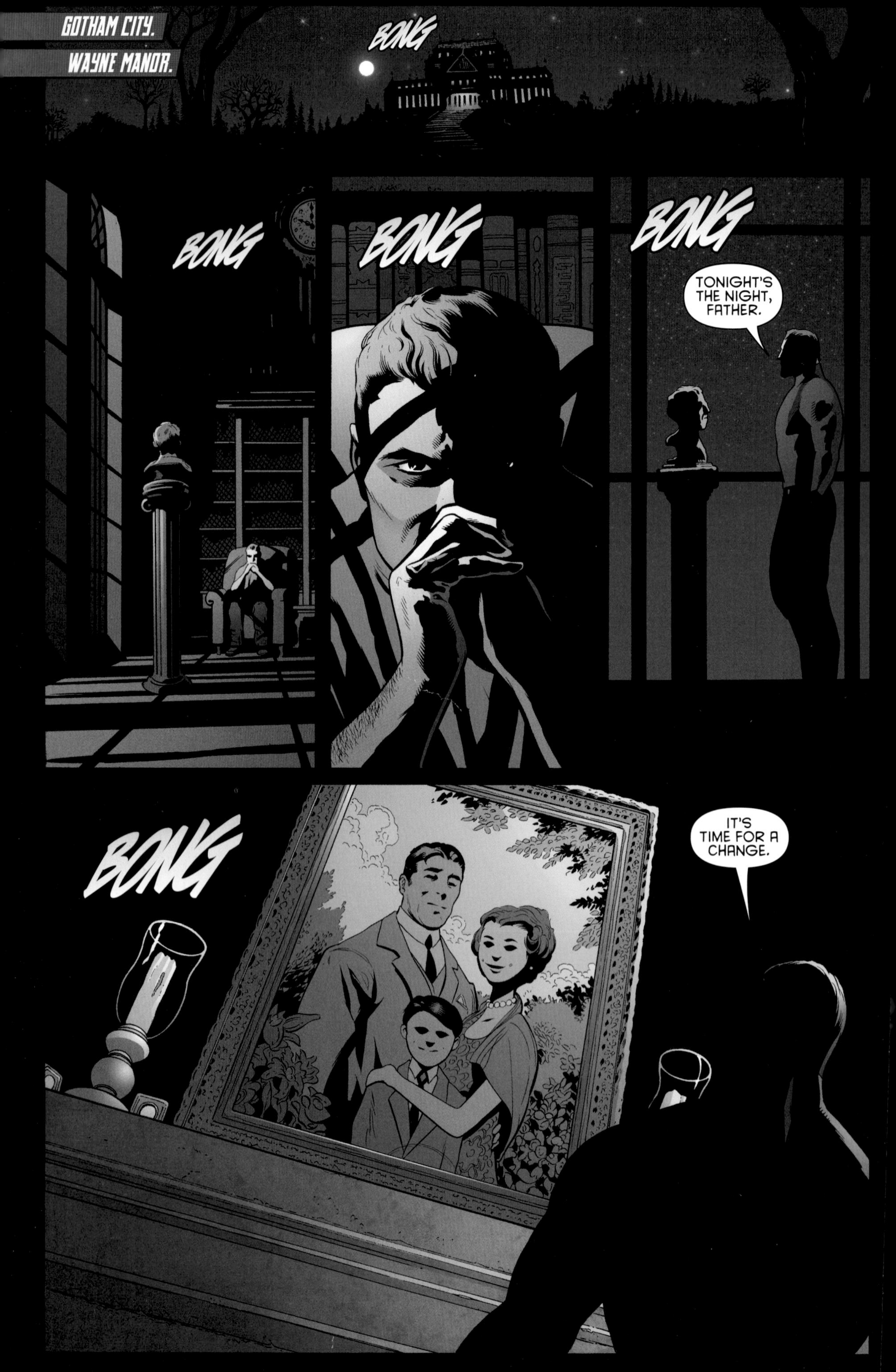
GOTHAM CITY.
WAYNE MANOR.
BONG
BONG
BONG
BONG
TONIGHT'S THE NIGHT, FATHER.
BONG
IT'S TIME FOR A CHANGE.

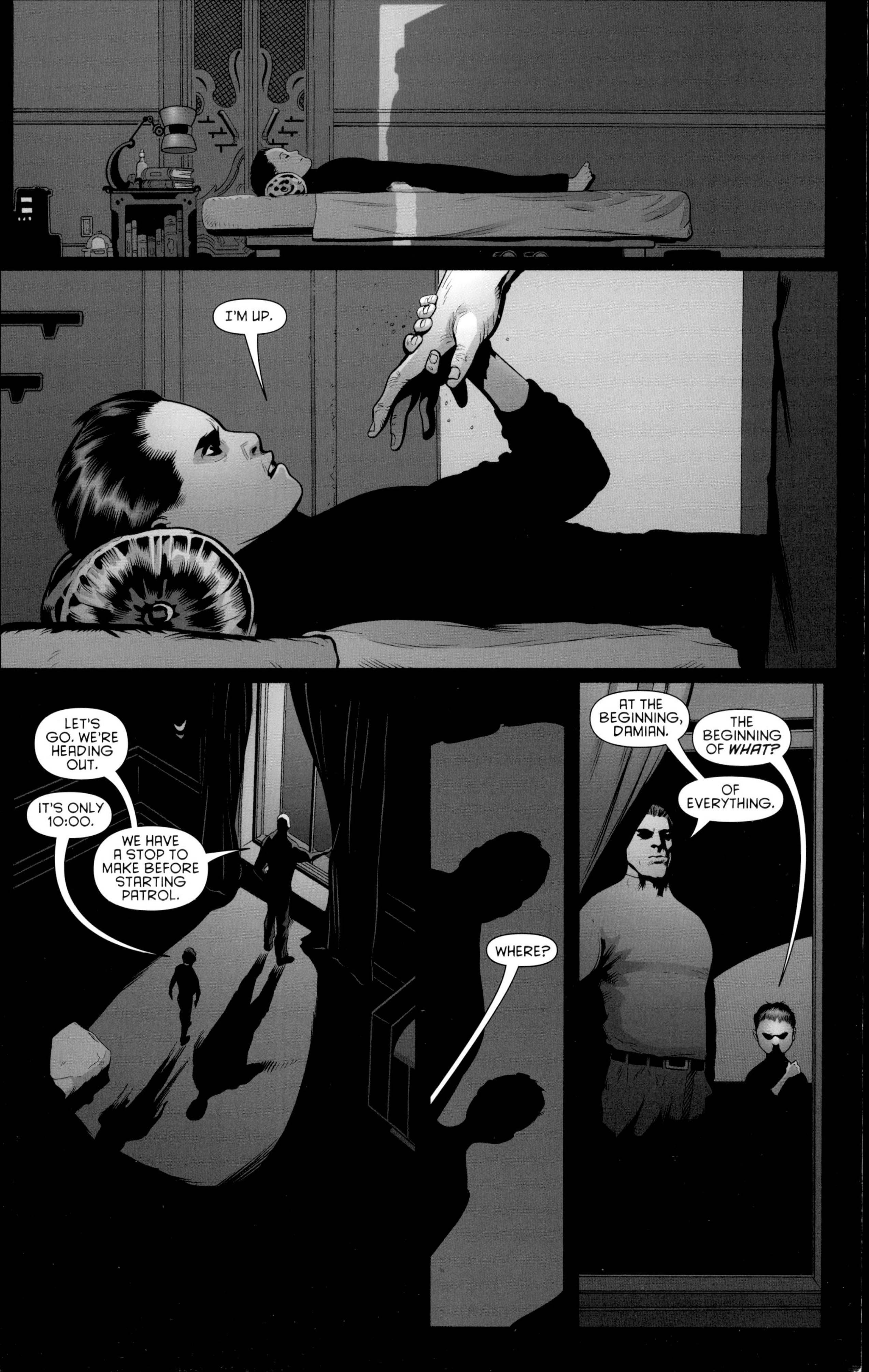
I'M UP.
LET'S GO. WE'RE HEADING OUT.
IT'S ONLY 10:00.
WE HAVE A STOP TO MAKE BEFORE STARTING PATROL.
WHERE?
AT THE BEGINNING, DAMIAN.
THE BEGINNING OF *WHAT?*
OF EVERYTHING.

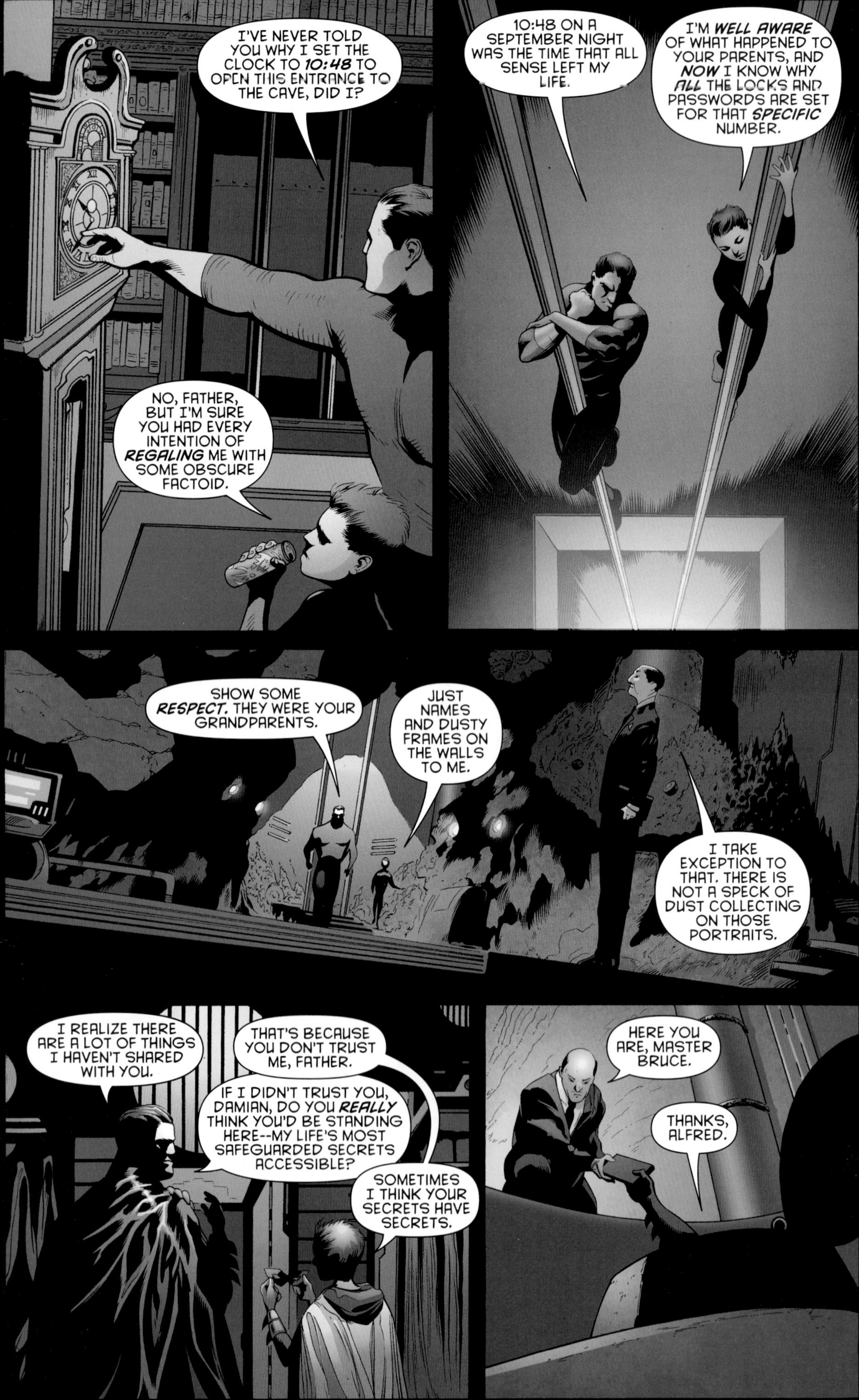

I'VE NEVER TOLD YOU WHY I SET THE CLOCK TO 10:48 TO OPEN THIS ENTRANCE TO THE CAVE, DID I?
NO, FATHER, BUT I'M SURE YOU HAD EVERY INTENTION OF REGALING ME WITH SOME OBSCURE FACTOID.
10:48 ON A SEPTEMBER NIGHT WAS THE TIME THAT ALL SENSE LEFT MY LIFE.
I'M WELL AWARE OF WHAT HAPPENED TO YOUR PARENTS, AND NOW I KNOW WHY ALL THE LOCKS AND PASSWORDS ARE SET FOR THAT SPECIFIC NUMBER.
SHOW SOME RESPECT. THEY WERE YOUR GRANDPARENTS.
JUST NAMES AND DUSTY FRAMES ON THE WALLS TO ME.
I TAKE EXCEPTION TO THAT. THERE IS NOT A SPECK OF DUST COLLECTING ON THOSE PORTRAITS.
I REALIZE THERE ARE A LOT OF THINGS I HAVEN'T SHARED WITH YOU.
THAT'S BECAUSE YOU DON'T TRUST ME, FATHER.
IF I DIDN'T TRUST YOU, DAMIAN, DO YOU REALLY THINK YOU'D BE STANDING HERE--MY LIFE'S MOST SAFEGUARDED SECRETS ACCESSIBLE?
SOMETIMES I THINK YOUR SECRETS HAVE SECRETS.
HERE YOU ARE, MASTER BRUCE.
THANKS, ALFRED.

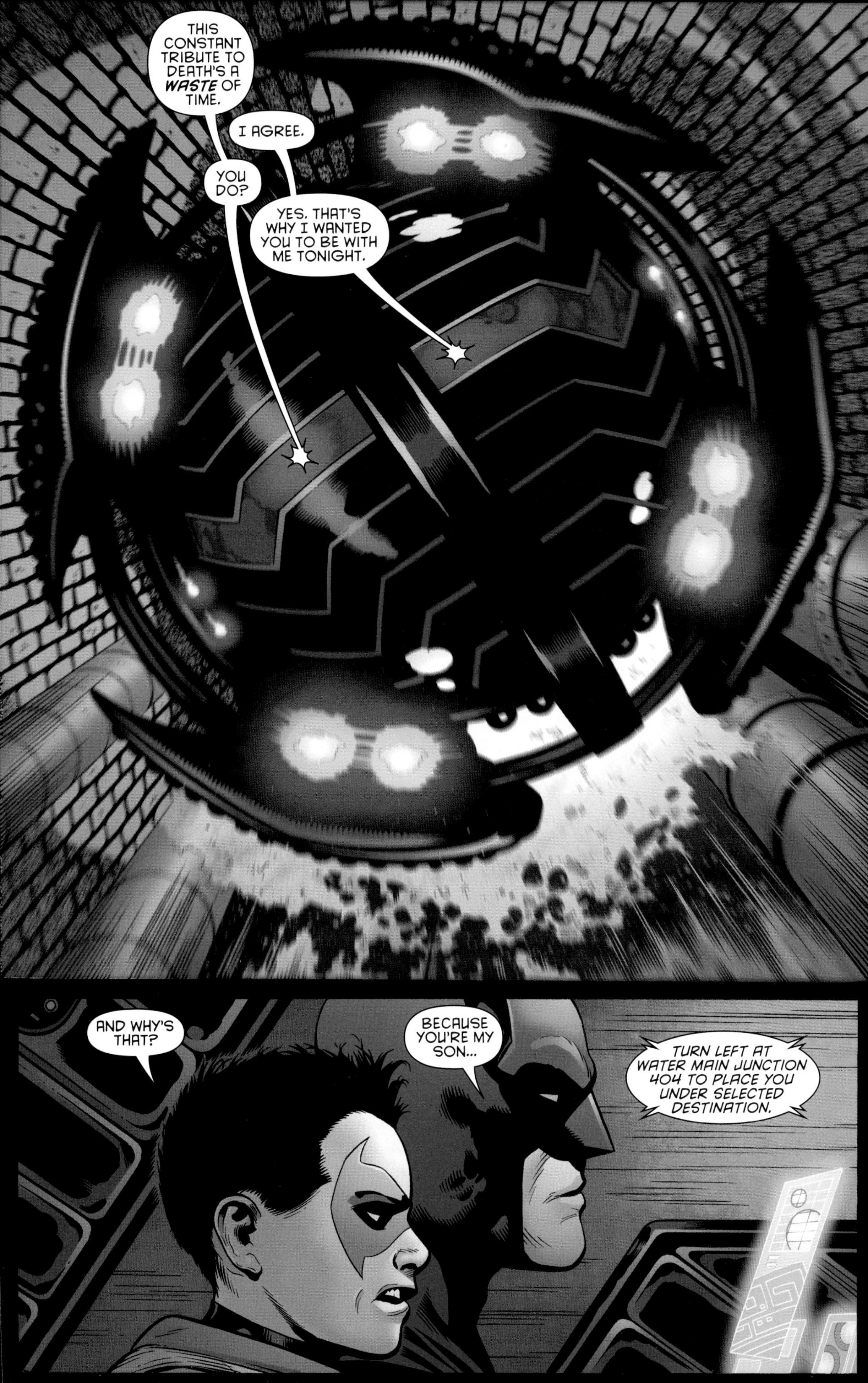
THIS CONSTANT TRIBUTE TO DEATH'S A WASTE OF TIME.
I AGREE.
YOU DO?
YES. THAT'S WHY I WANTED YOU TO BE WITH ME TONIGHT.
AND WHY'S THAT?
BECAUSE YOU'RE MY SON...
TURN LEFT AT WATER MAIN JUNCTION 404 TO PLACE YOU UNDER SELECTED DESTINATION.

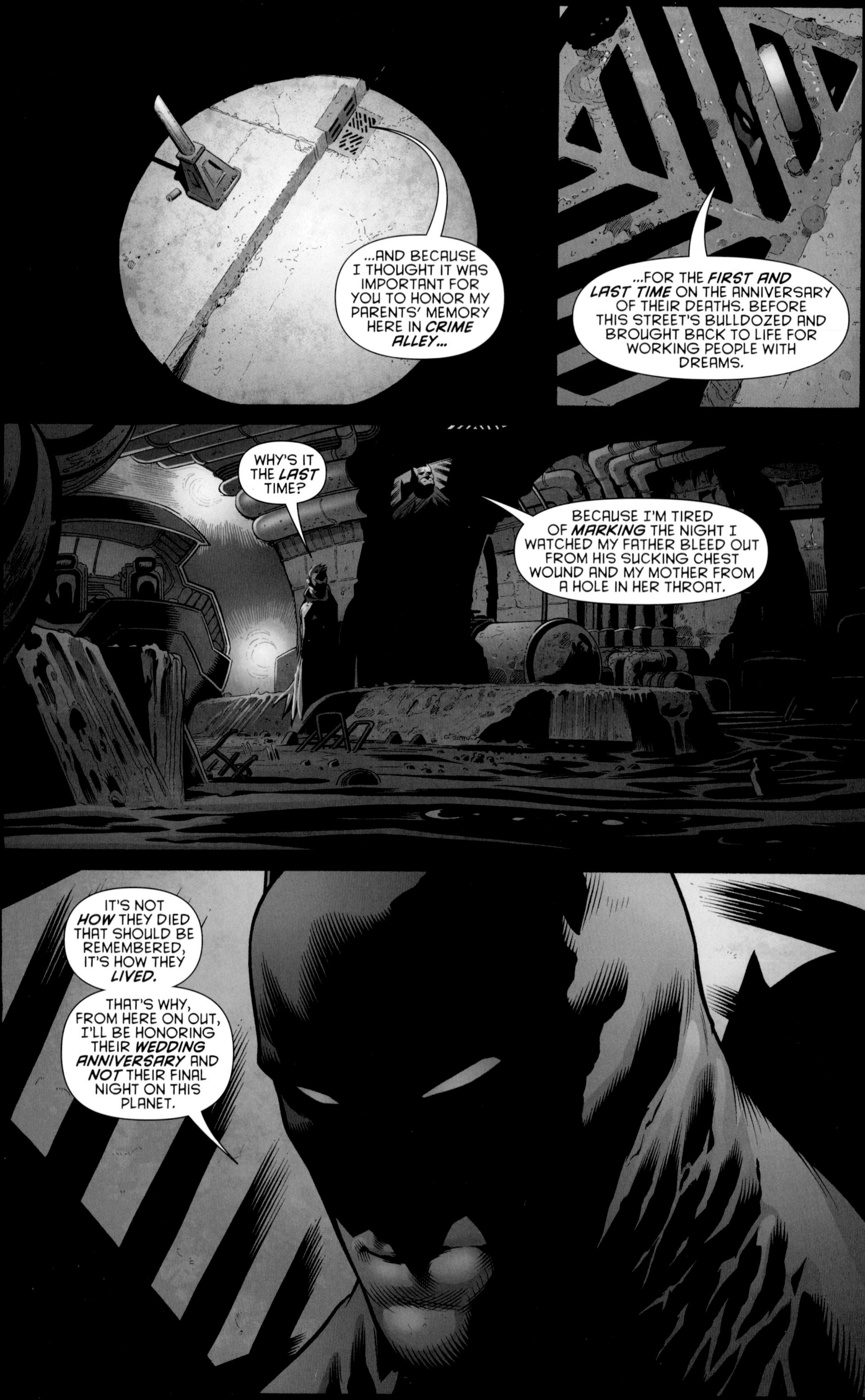
...AND BECAUSE I THOUGHT IT WAS IMPORTANT FOR YOU TO HONOR MY PARENTS' MEMORY HERE IN *CRIME ALLEY...*
...FOR THE *FIRST AND LAST TIME* ON THE ANNIVERSARY OF THEIR DEATHS. BEFORE THIS STREET'S BULLDOZED AND BROUGHT BACK TO LIFE FOR WORKING PEOPLE WITH DREAMS.
WHY'S IT THE *LAST* TIME?
BECAUSE I'M TIRED OF *MARKING* THE NIGHT I WATCHED MY FATHER BLEED OUT FROM HIS SUCKING CHEST WOUND AND MY MOTHER FROM A HOLE IN HER THROAT.
IT'S NOT *HOW* THEY DIED THAT SHOULD BE REMEMBERED, IT'S HOW THEY *LIVED.*
THAT'S WHY, FROM HERE ON OUT, I'LL BE HONORING THEIR *WEDDING ANNIVERSARY* AND *NOT* THEIR FINAL NIGHT ON THIS PLANET.

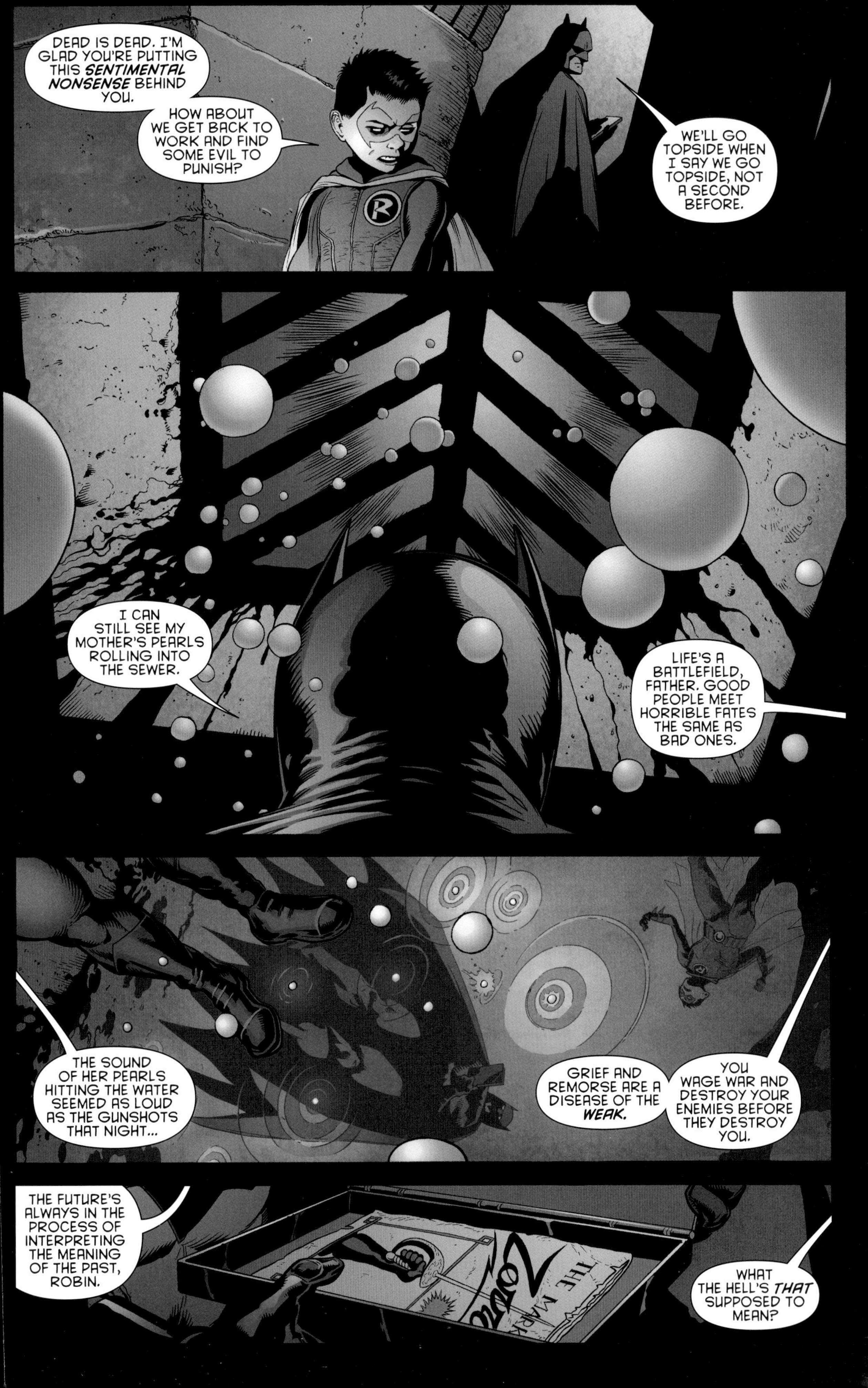
DEAD IS DEAD. I'M GLAD YOU'RE PUTTING THIS **SENTIMENTAL NONSENSE** BEHIND YOU.
HOW ABOUT WE GET BACK TO WORK AND FIND SOME EVIL TO PUNISH?
WE'LL GO TOPSIDE WHEN I SAY WE GO TOPSIDE, NOT A SECOND BEFORE.
I CAN STILL SEE MY MOTHER'S PEARLS ROLLING INTO THE SEWER.
LIFE'S A BATTLEFIELD, FATHER. GOOD PEOPLE MEET HORRIBLE FATES THE SAME AS BAD ONES.
THE SOUND OF HER PEARLS HITTING THE WATER SEEMED AS LOUD AS THE GUNSHOTS THAT NIGHT...
GRIEF AND REMORSE ARE A DISEASE OF THE ***WEAK.***
YOU WAGE WAR AND DESTROY YOUR ENEMIES BEFORE THEY DESTROY YOU.
THE FUTURE'S ALWAYS IN THE PROCESS OF INTERPRETING THE MEANING OF THE PAST, ROBIN.
THE MARK OF ZORRO
WHAT THE HELL'S *THAT* SUPPOSED TO MEAN?

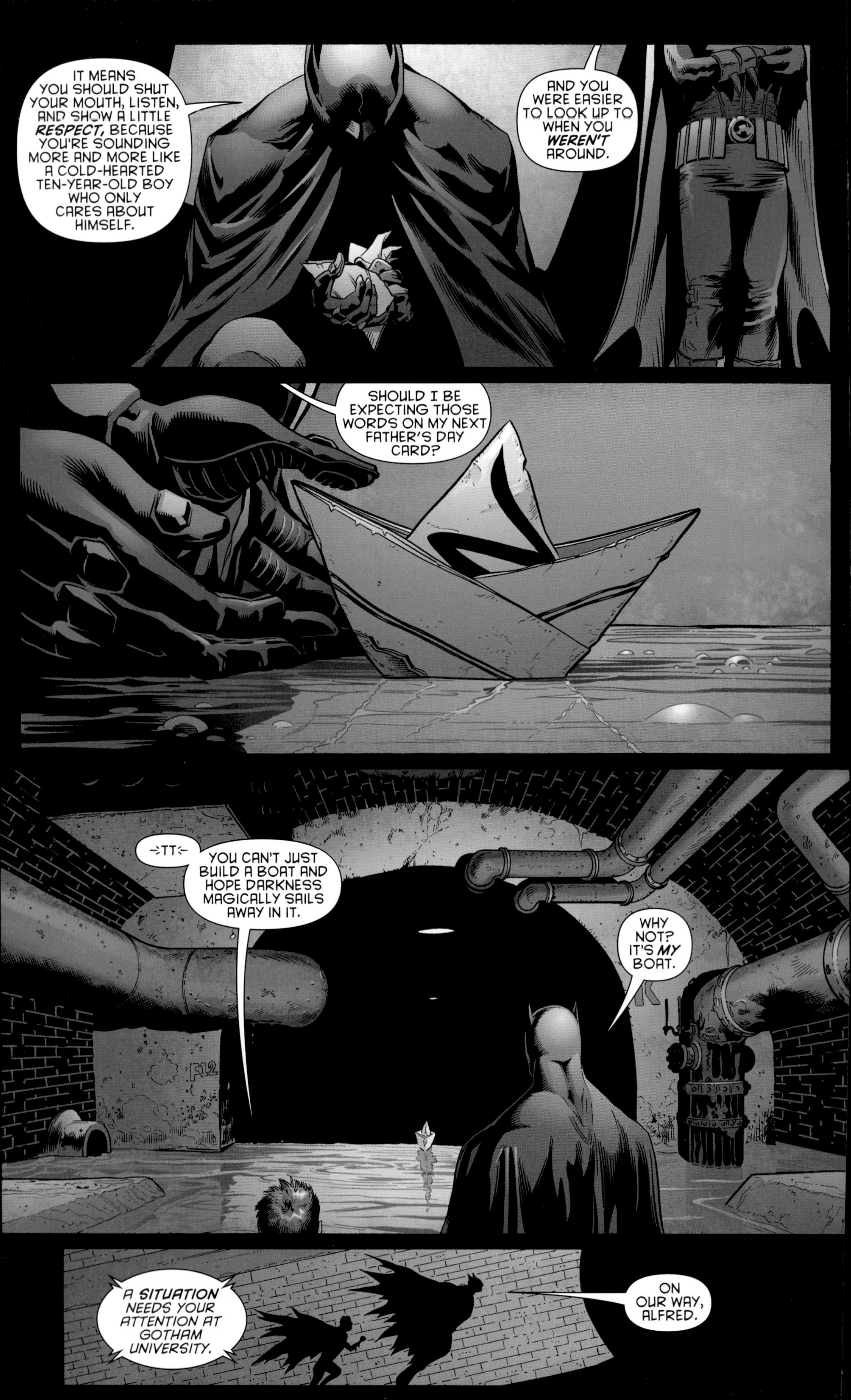
IT MEANS YOU SHOULD SHUT YOUR MOUTH, LISTEN, AND SHOW A LITTLE RESPECT, BECAUSE YOU'RE SOUNDING MORE AND MORE LIKE A COLD-HEARTED TEN-YEAR-OLD BOY WHO ONLY CARES ABOUT HIMSELF.
AND YOU WERE EASIER TO LOOK UP TO WHEN YOU WEREN'T AROUND.
SHOULD I BE EXPECTING THOSE WORDS ON MY NEXT FATHER'S DAY CARD?
-TT-
YOU CAN'T JUST BUILD A BOAT AND HOPE DARKNESS MAGICALLY SAILS AWAY IN IT.
WHY NOT? IT'S MY BOAT.
F12
A SITUATION NEEDS YOUR ATTENTION AT GOTHAM UNIVERSITY.
ON OUR WAY, ALFRED.

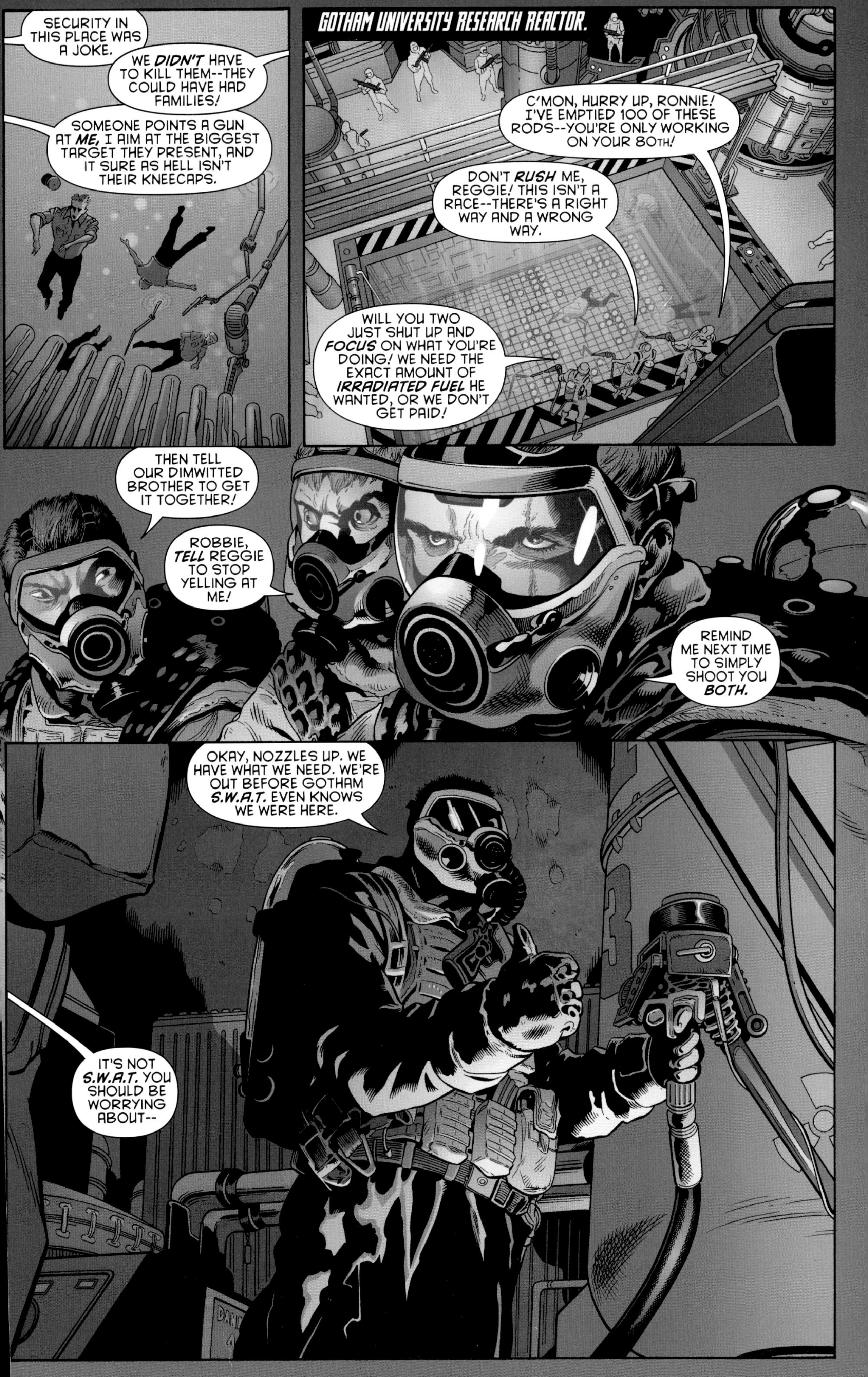
SECURITY IN THIS PLACE WAS A JOKE.
WE DIDN'T HAVE TO KILL THEM--THEY COULD HAVE HAD FAMILIES!
SOMEONE POINTS A GUN AT ME, I AIM AT THE BIGGEST TARGET THEY PRESENT, AND IT SURE AS HELL ISN'T THEIR KNEECAPS.
GOTHAM UNIVERSITY RESEARCH REACTOR.
C'MON, HURRY UP, RONNIE! I'VE EMPTIED 100 OF THESE RODS--YOU'RE ONLY WORKING ON YOUR 80TH!
DON'T RUSH ME, REGGIE! THIS ISN'T A RACE--THERE'S A RIGHT WAY AND A WRONG WAY.
WILL YOU TWO JUST SHUT UP AND FOCUS ON WHAT YOU'RE DOING! WE NEED THE EXACT AMOUNT OF IRRADIATED FUEL HE WANTED, OR WE DON'T GET PAID!
THEN TELL OUR DIMWITTED BROTHER TO GET IT TOGETHER!
ROBBIE, TELL REGGIE TO STOP YELLING AT ME!
REMIND ME NEXT TIME TO SIMPLY SHOOT YOU BOTH.
OKAY, NOZZLES UP. WE HAVE WHAT WE NEED. WE'RE OUT BEFORE GOTHAM S.W.A.T. EVEN KNOWS WE WERE HERE.
IT'S NOT S.W.A.T. YOU SHOULD BE WORRYING ABOUT--

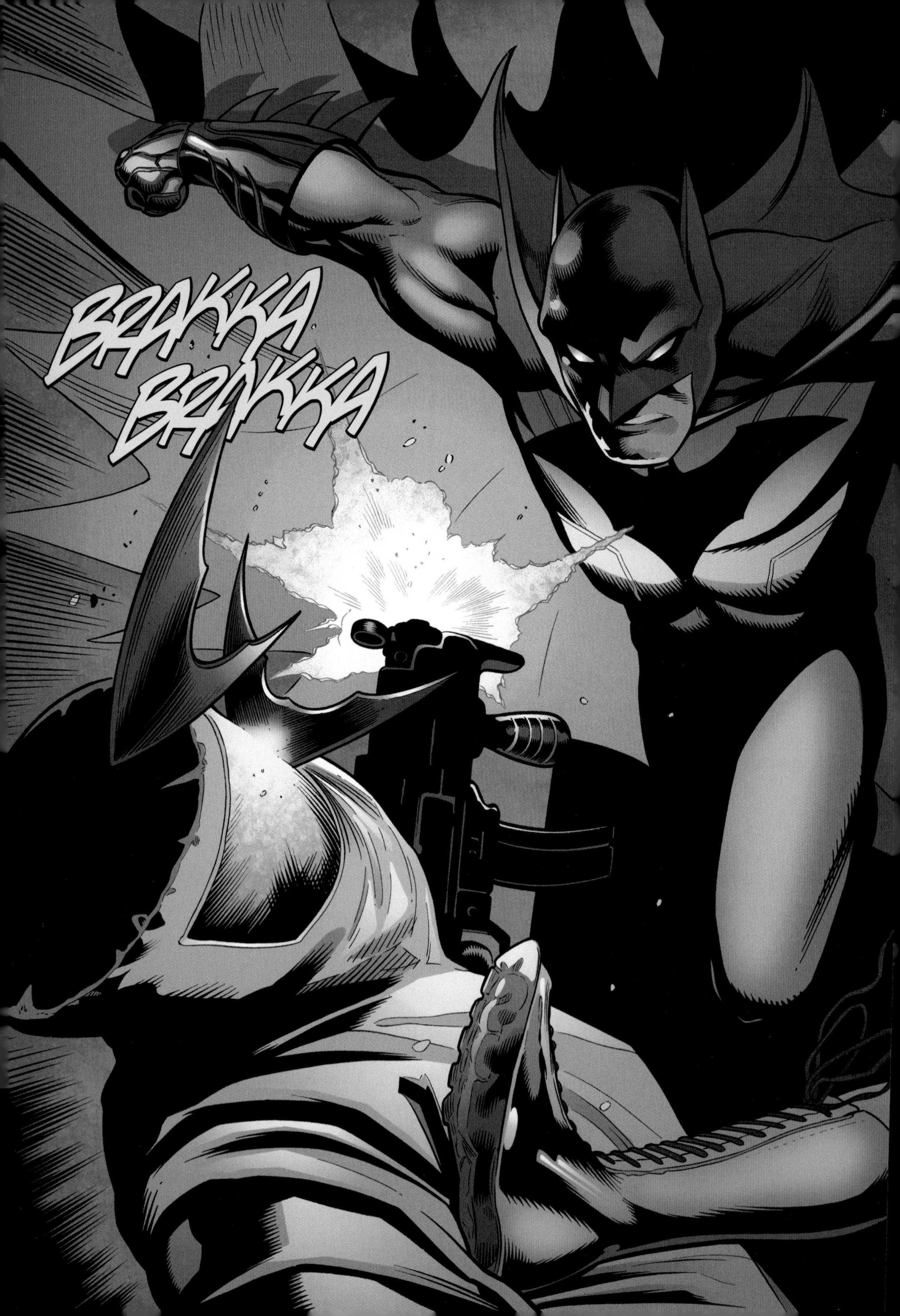
BRAKKA
BRAKKA

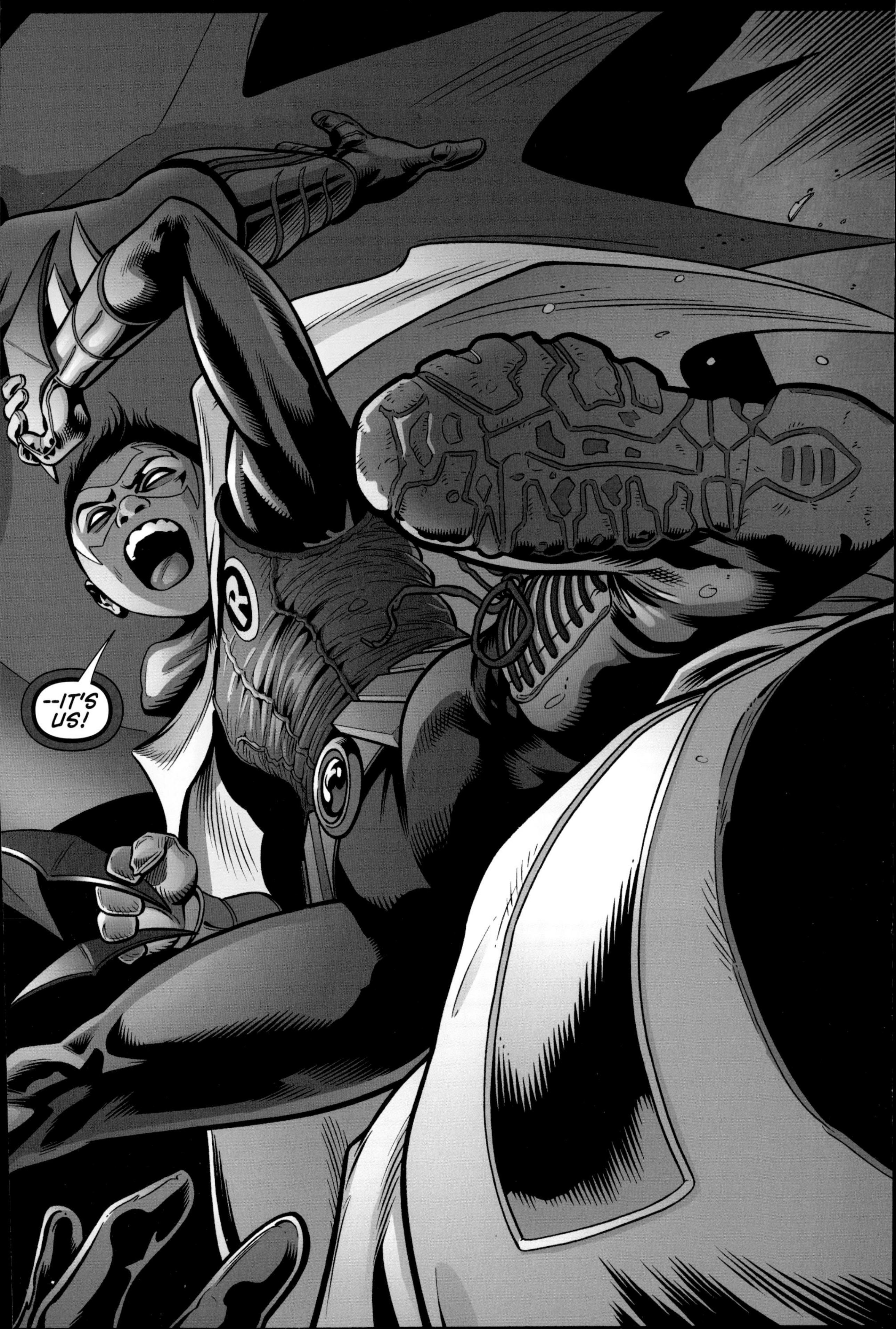
--IT'S US!

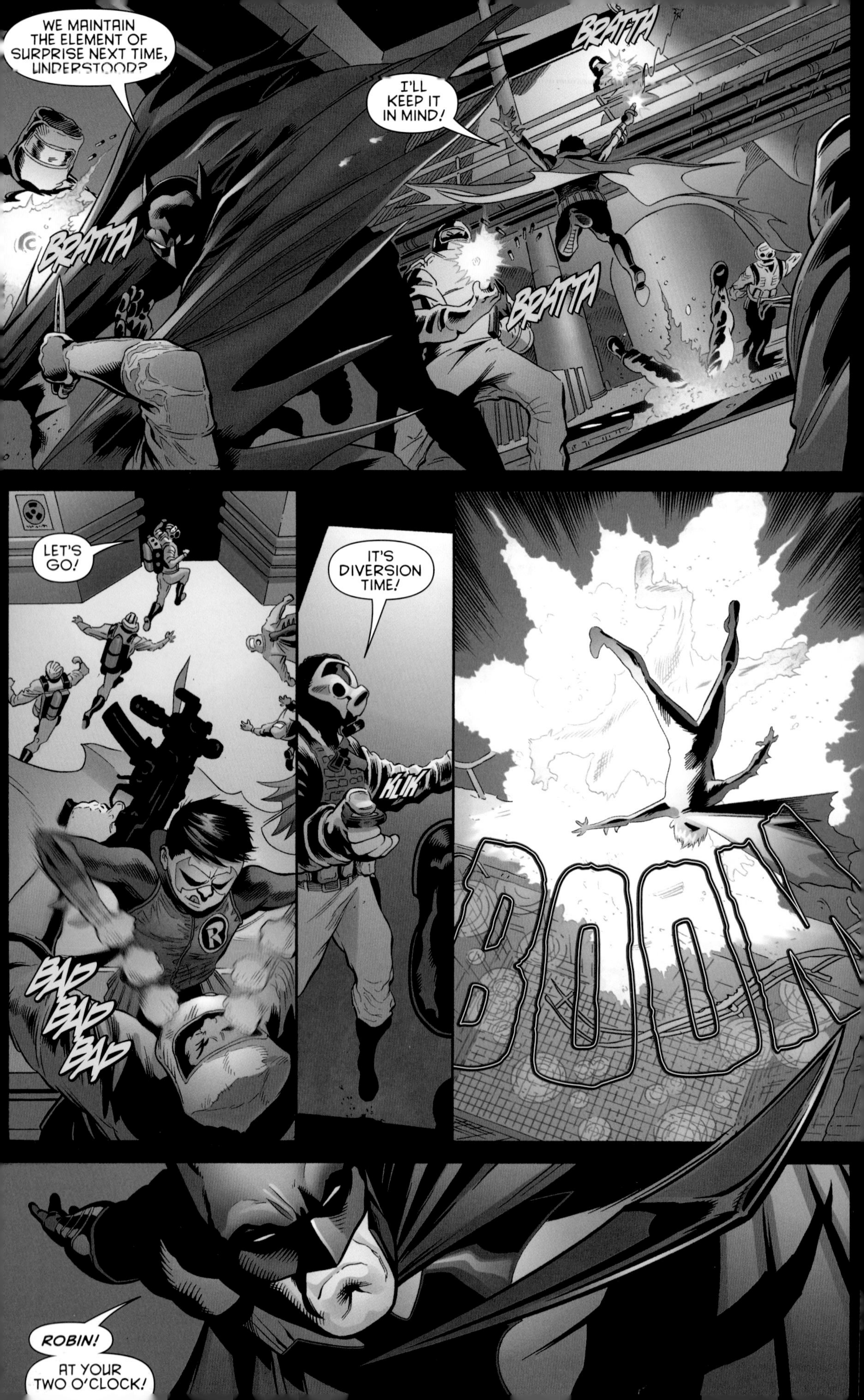

WE MAINTAIN THE ELEMENT OF SURPRISE NEXT TIME, UNDERSTOOD?
BRATTA
I'LL KEEP IT IN MIND!
BRATTA
BRATTA
LET'S GO!
BAP BAP BAP
IT'S DIVERSION TIME!
KLIK
BOOM
ROBIN!
AT YOUR TWO O'CLOCK!

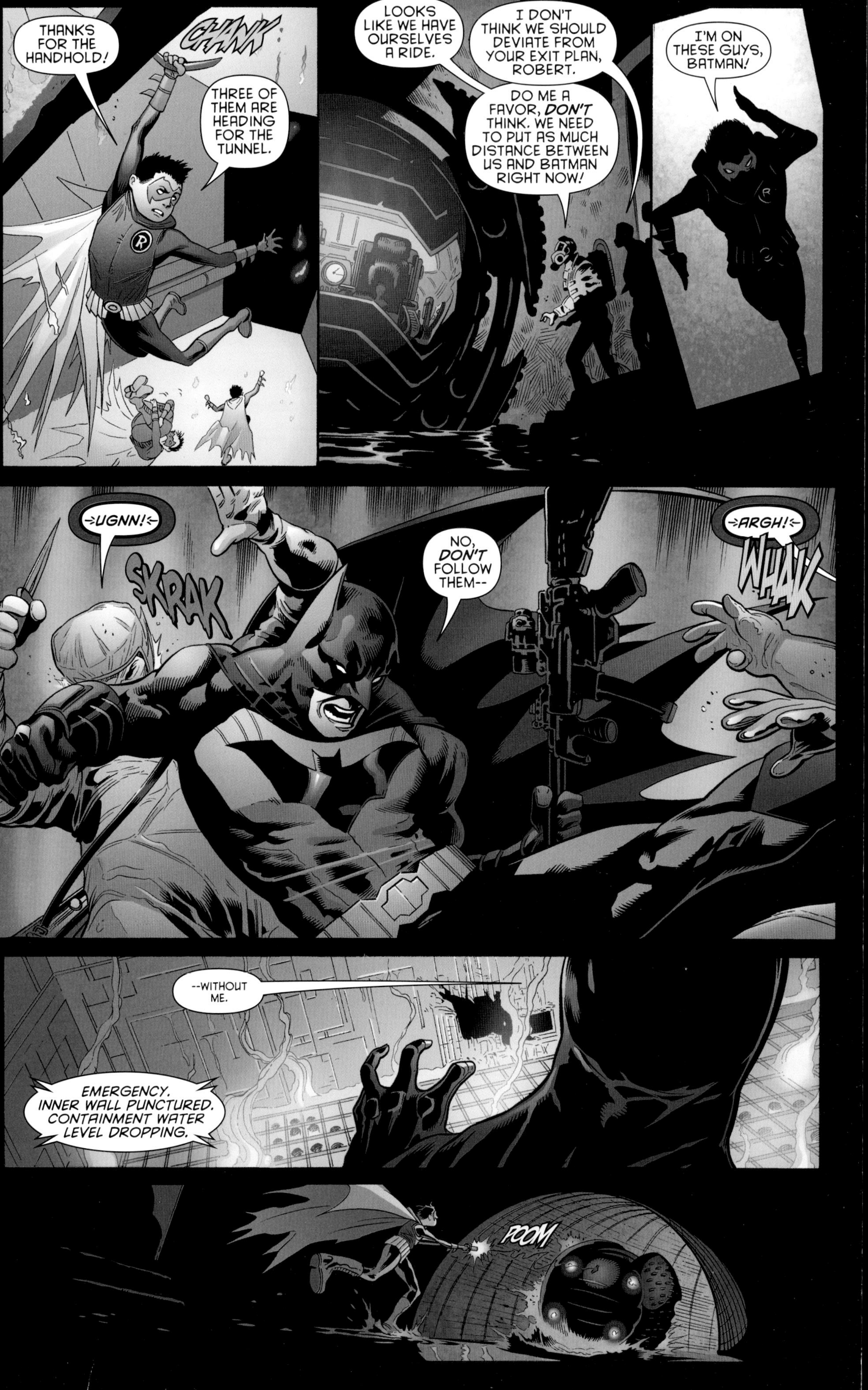
THANKS FOR THE HANDHOLD!
CHANK
THREE OF THEM ARE HEADING FOR THE TUNNEL.
LOOKS LIKE WE HAVE OURSELVES A RIDE.
I DON'T THINK WE SHOULD DEVIATE FROM YOUR EXIT PLAN, ROBERT.
DO ME A FAVOR, DON'T THINK. WE NEED TO PUT AS MUCH DISTANCE BETWEEN US AND BATMAN RIGHT NOW!
I'M ON THESE GUYS, BATMAN!
UGNN!
SKRAK
NO, DON'T FOLLOW THEM--
ARGH!
WHAK
--WITHOUT ME.
EMERGENCY. INNER WALL PUNCTURED. CONTAINMENT WATER LEVEL DROPPING.
POOM

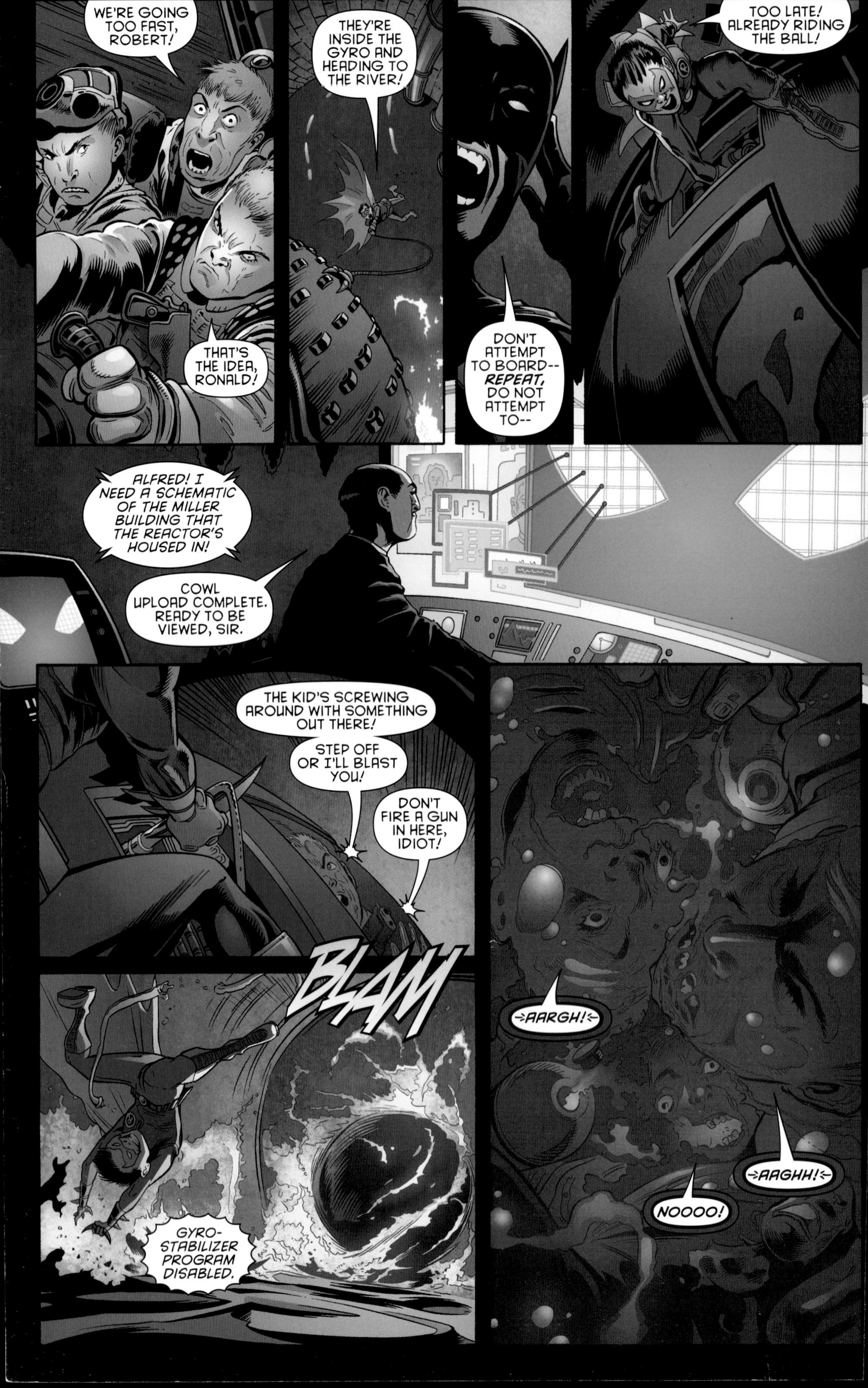
WE'RE GOING TOO FAST, ROBERT!
THAT'S THE IDEA, RONALD!
THEY'RE INSIDE THE GYRO AND HEADING TO THE RIVER!
DON'T ATTEMPT TO BOARD-- REPEAT, DO NOT ATTEMPT TO--
TOO LATE! ALREADY RIDING THE BALL!
ALFRED! I NEED A SCHEMATIC OF THE MILLER BUILDING THAT THE REACTOR'S HOUSED IN!
COWL UPLOAD COMPLETE. READY TO BE VIEWED, SIR.
THE KID'S SCREWING AROUND WITH SOMETHING OUT THERE!
STEP OFF OR I'LL BLAST YOU!
DON'T FIRE A GUN IN HERE, IDIOT!
BLAM
GYRO-STABILIZER PROGRAM DISABLED.
AARGH!
AAGHH!
NOOOO!

POOM

FSSSS

I'M SEALING THE CONTAINMENT RUPTURE, ALFRED.

POOM

CONTACT COMMISSIONER GORDON AND GET A *N.A.I.R.* TEAM HERE NOW--

TWEET

PUSH OFF THAT WALL! FASTER, ADAMS!

BOOM
BOOM
BOOM
BOOM

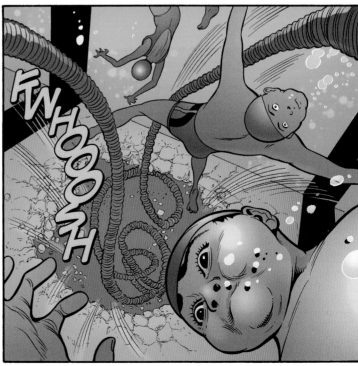

FTWHOOOM

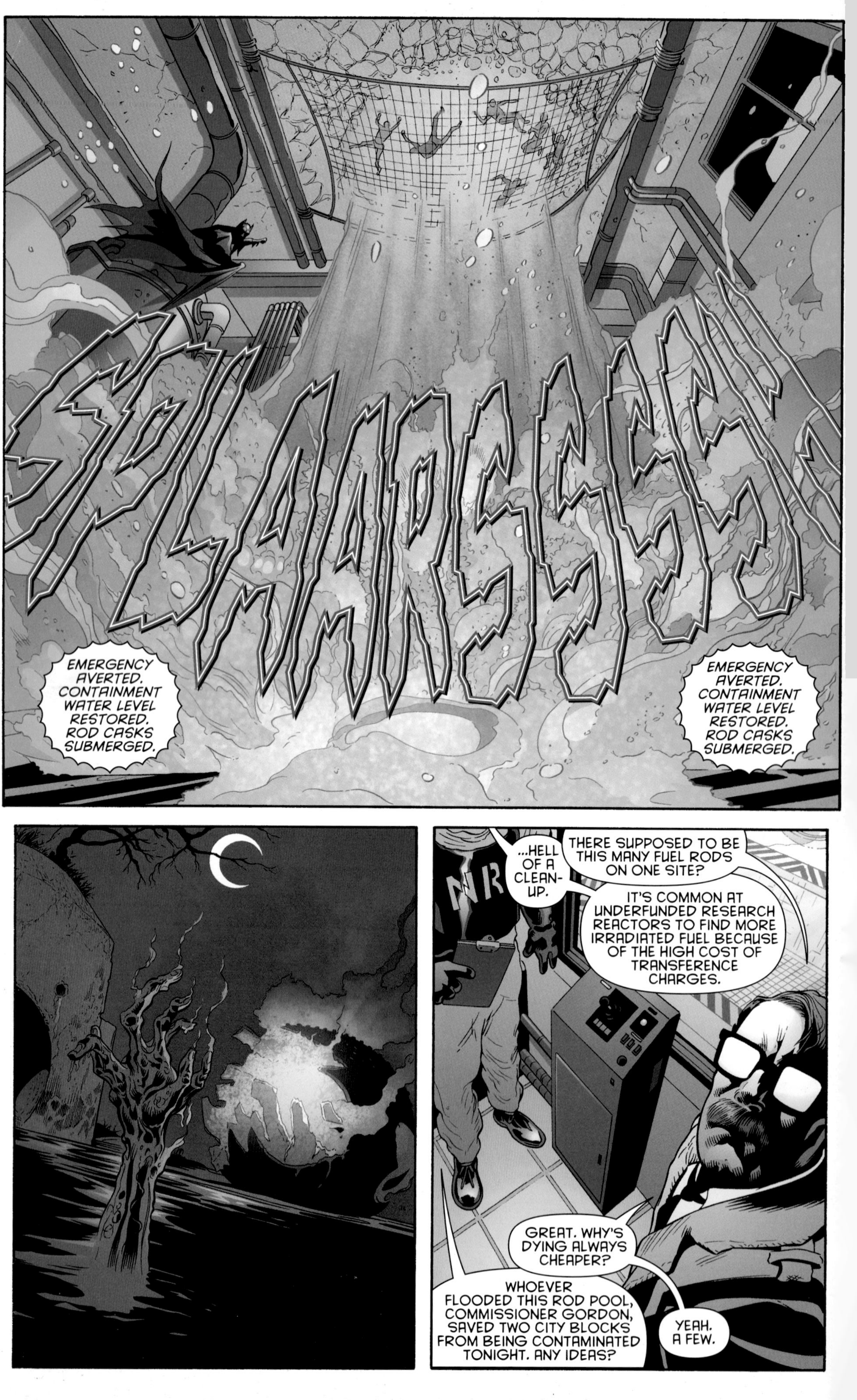
EMERGENCY AVERTED. CONTAINMENT WATER LEVEL RESTORED. ROD CASKS SUBMERGED.
EMERGENCY AVERTED. CONTAINMENT WATER LEVEL RESTORED. ROD CASKS SUBMERGED.
...HELL OF A CLEAN-UP.
THERE SUPPOSED TO BE THIS MANY FUEL RODS ON ONE SITE?
IT'S COMMON AT UNDERFUNDED RESEARCH REACTORS TO FIND MORE IRRADIATED FUEL BECAUSE OF THE HIGH COST OF TRANSFERENCE CHARGES.
GREAT. WHY'S DYING ALWAYS CHEAPER?
WHOEVER FLOODED THIS ROD POOL, COMMISSIONER GORDON, SAVED TWO CITY BLOCKS FROM BEING CONTAMINATED TONIGHT. ANY IDEAS?
YEAH. A FEW.

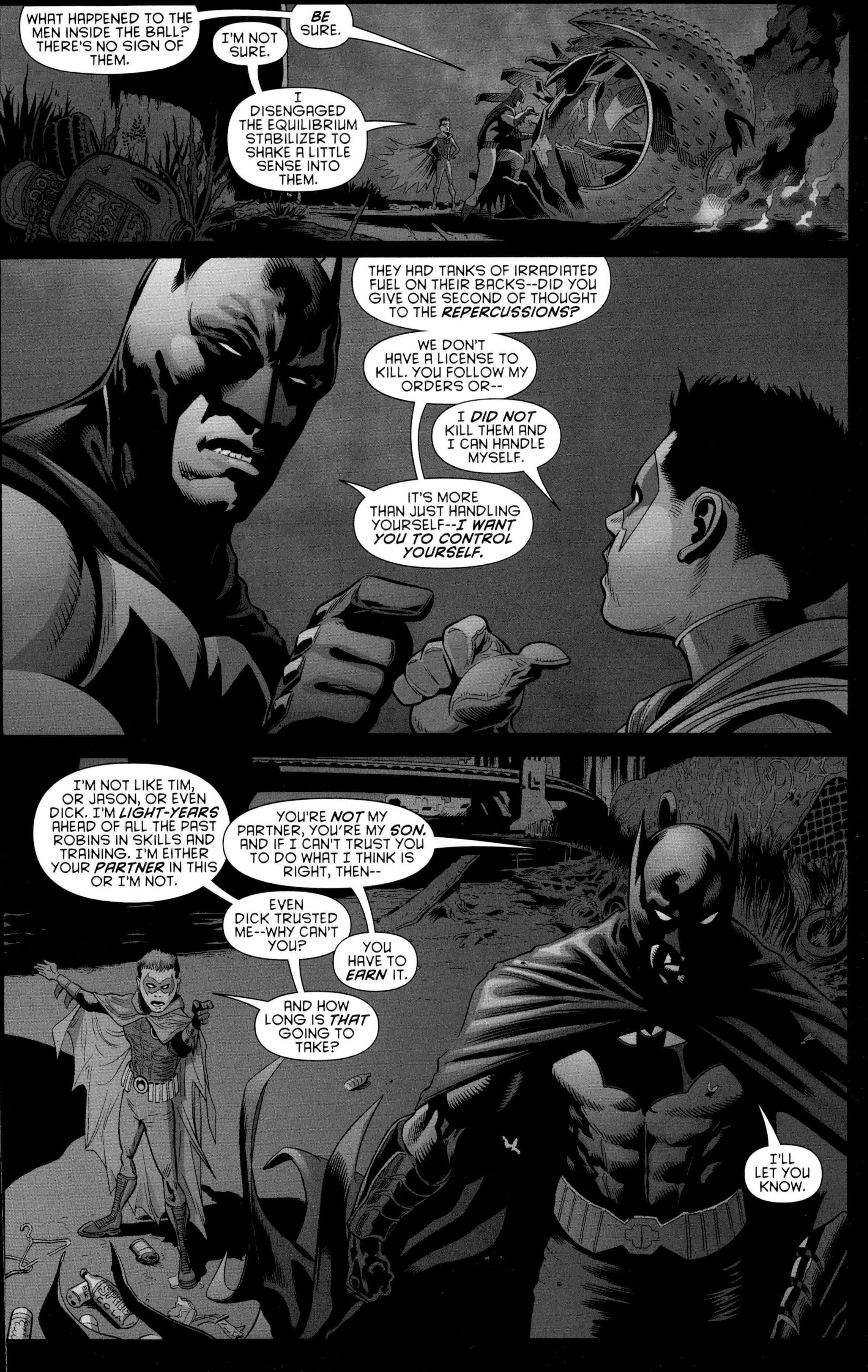
WHAT HAPPENED TO THE MEN INSIDE THE BALL? THERE'S NO SIGN OF THEM.
I'M NOT SURE.
BE SURE.
I DISENGAGED THE EQUILIBRIUM STABILIZER TO SHAKE A LITTLE SENSE INTO THEM.
THEY HAD TANKS OF IRRADIATED FUEL ON THEIR BACKS--DID YOU GIVE ONE SECOND OF THOUGHT TO THE REPERCUSSIONS?
WE DON'T HAVE A LICENSE TO KILL. YOU FOLLOW MY ORDERS OR--
I DID NOT KILL THEM AND I CAN HANDLE MYSELF.
IT'S MORE THAN JUST HANDLING YOURSELF--I WANT YOU TO CONTROL YOURSELF.
I'M NOT LIKE TIM, OR JASON, OR EVEN DICK. I'M LIGHT-YEARS AHEAD OF ALL THE PAST ROBINS IN SKILLS AND TRAINING. I'M EITHER YOUR PARTNER IN THIS OR I'M NOT.
YOU'RE NOT MY PARTNER, YOU'RE MY SON. AND IF I CAN'T TRUST YOU TO DO WHAT I THINK IS RIGHT, THEN--
EVEN DICK TRUSTED ME--WHY CAN'T YOU?
YOU HAVE TO EARN IT.
AND HOW LONG IS THAT GOING TO TAKE?
I'LL LET YOU KNOW.

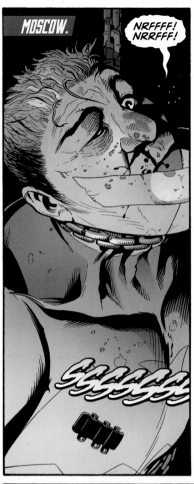

MOSCOW.

NRFFFF! NRRFFF!

RRRGFFF! RRRGFF!

MY APOLOGIES, I EXPECTED YOU TO REMAIN *UNCONSCIOUS* FOR THIS. YOU MUST COME FROM HARDY STOCK.

SSSSSSS

SSSSSSS

NAARR! RRAFFF!

I'M *ERASING* YOU.

NRRRRRRR!

IT'LL BE LIKE YOU *NEVER* EXISTED AT ALL.

SSSSSSS

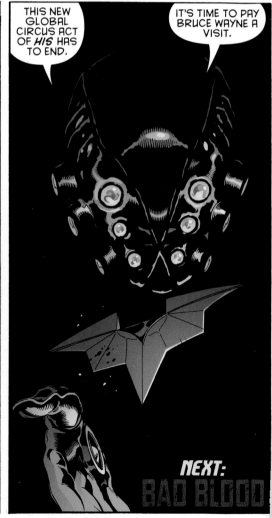

THIS NEW GLOBAL CIRCUS ACT OF *HIS* HAS TO END.

IT'S TIME TO PAY BRUCE WAYNE A VISIT.

NEXT: BAD BLOOD

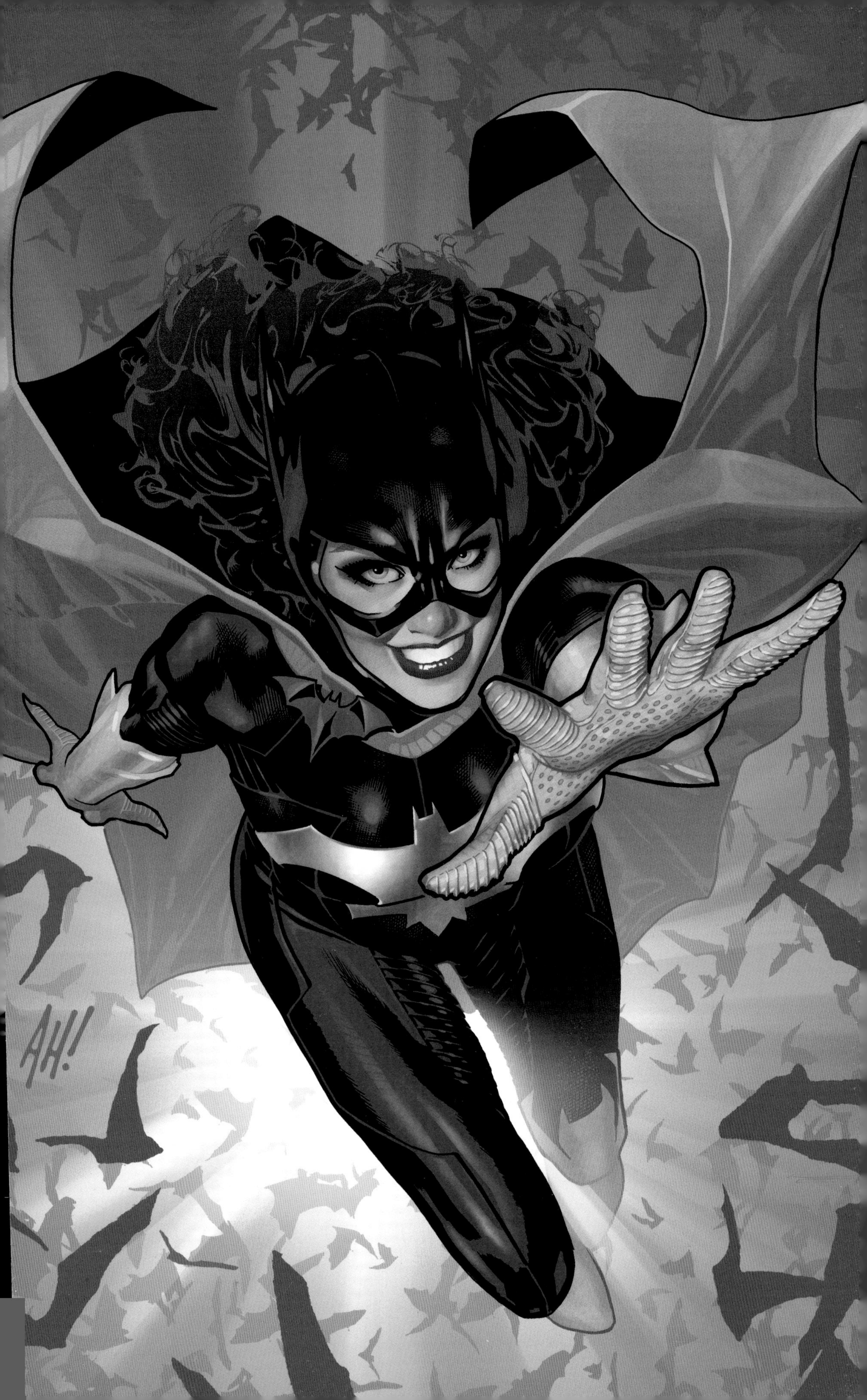
AH!

BATGIRL

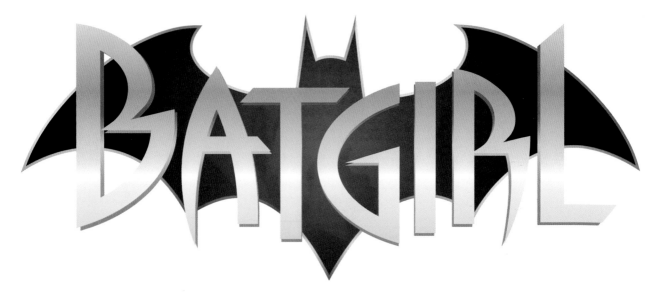

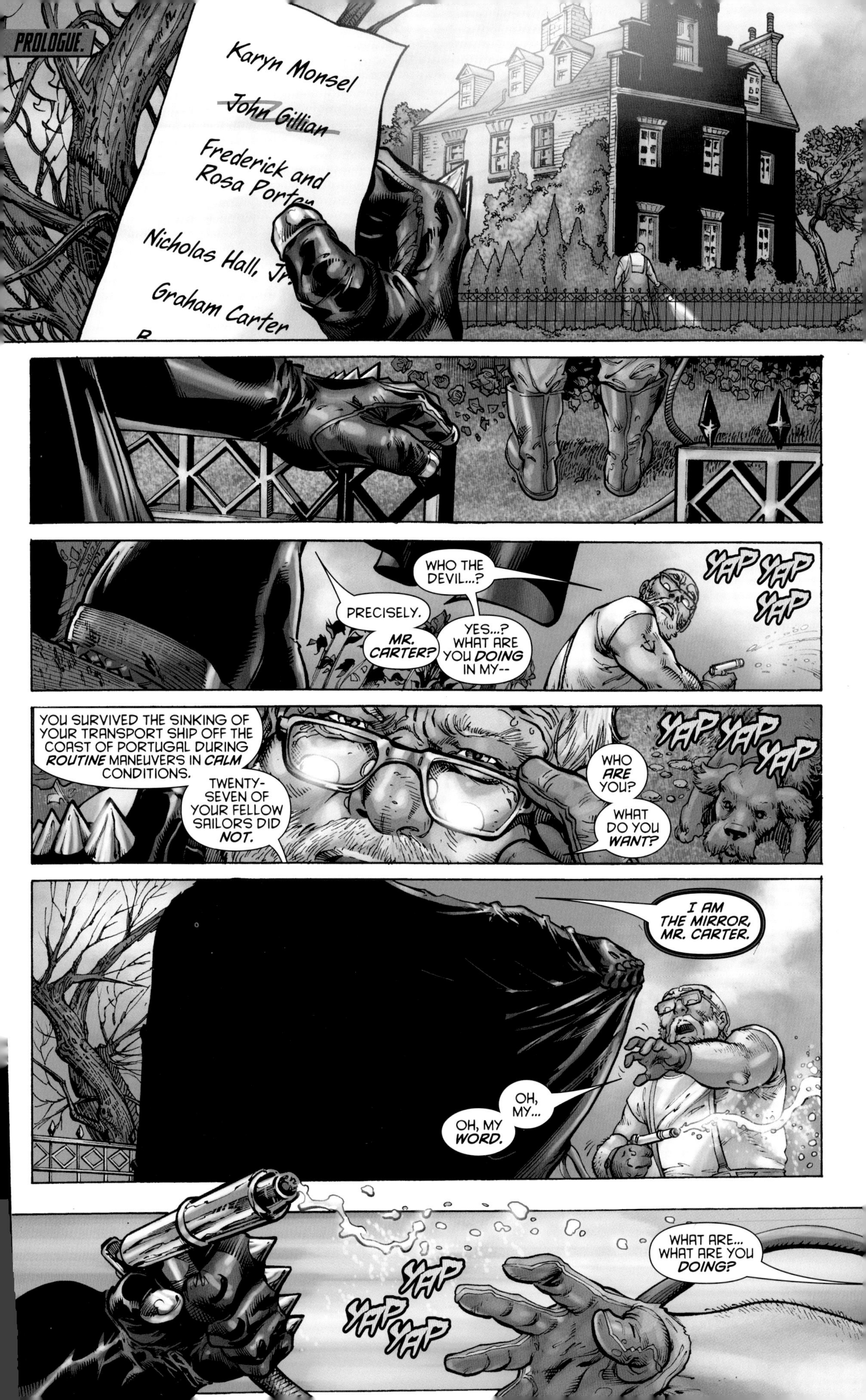
PROLOGUE.
Karyn Monsel
John Gillian
Frederick and Rosa Porter
Nicholas Hall, Jr.
Graham Carter
WHO THE DEVIL...?
PRECISELY.
MR. CARTER?
YES...? WHAT ARE YOU DOING IN MY--
YAP YAP YAP
YOU SURVIVED THE SINKING OF YOUR TRANSPORT SHIP OFF THE COAST OF PORTUGAL DURING ROUTINE MANEUVERS IN CALM CONDITIONS.
TWENTY-SEVEN OF YOUR FELLOW SAILORS DID NOT.
WHO ARE YOU?
WHAT DO YOU WANT?
YAP YAP YAP
I AM THE MIRROR, MR. CARTER.
OH, MY...
OH, MY WORD.
WHAT ARE... WHAT ARE YOU DOING?
YAP YAP YAP

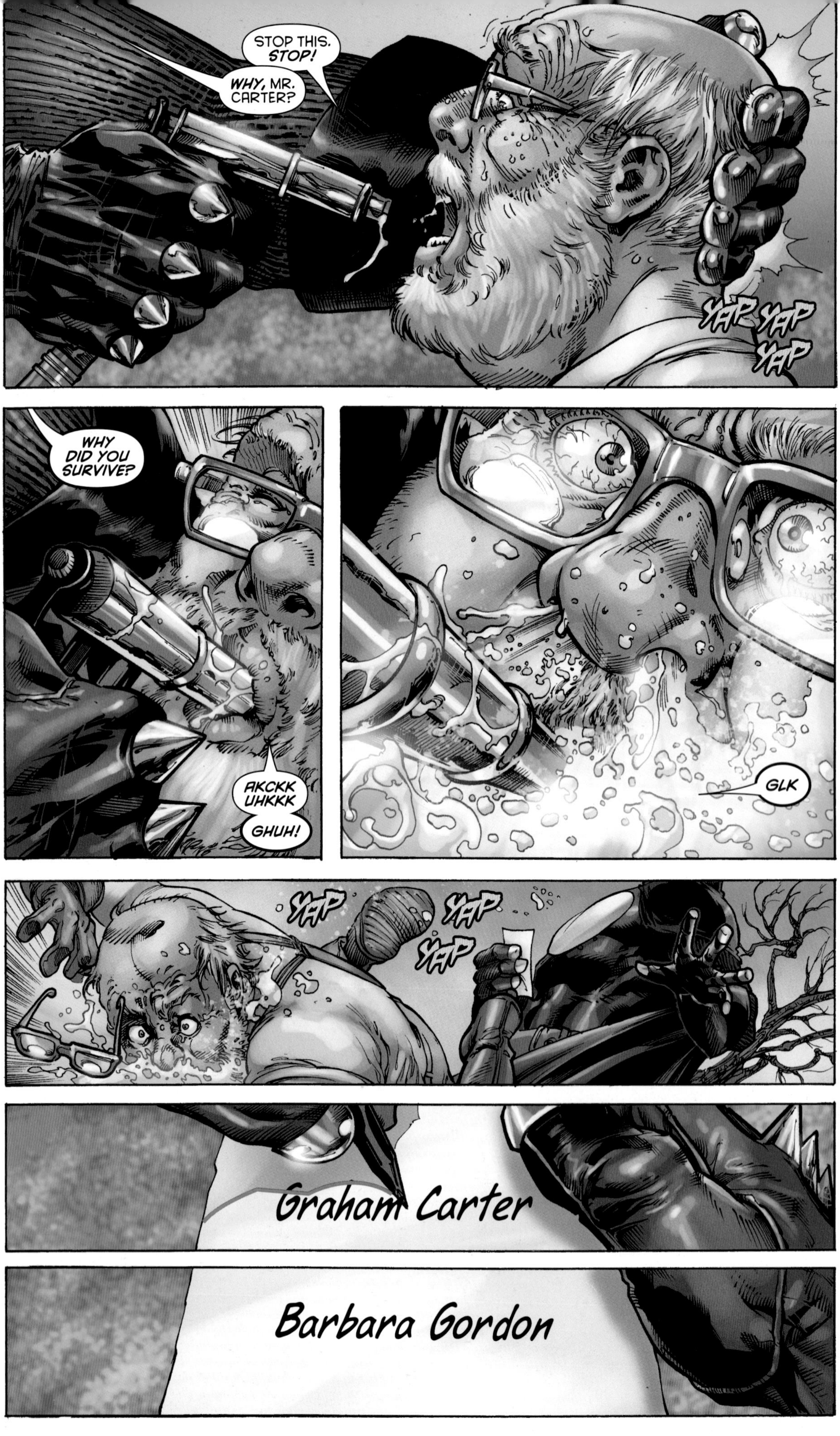

STOP THIS. STOP!
WHY, MR. CARTER?
YAP YAP YAP
WHY DID YOU SURVIVE?
AKCKK UHKKK
GHUH!
GLK
YAP YAP YAP
Graham Carter
Barbara Gordon

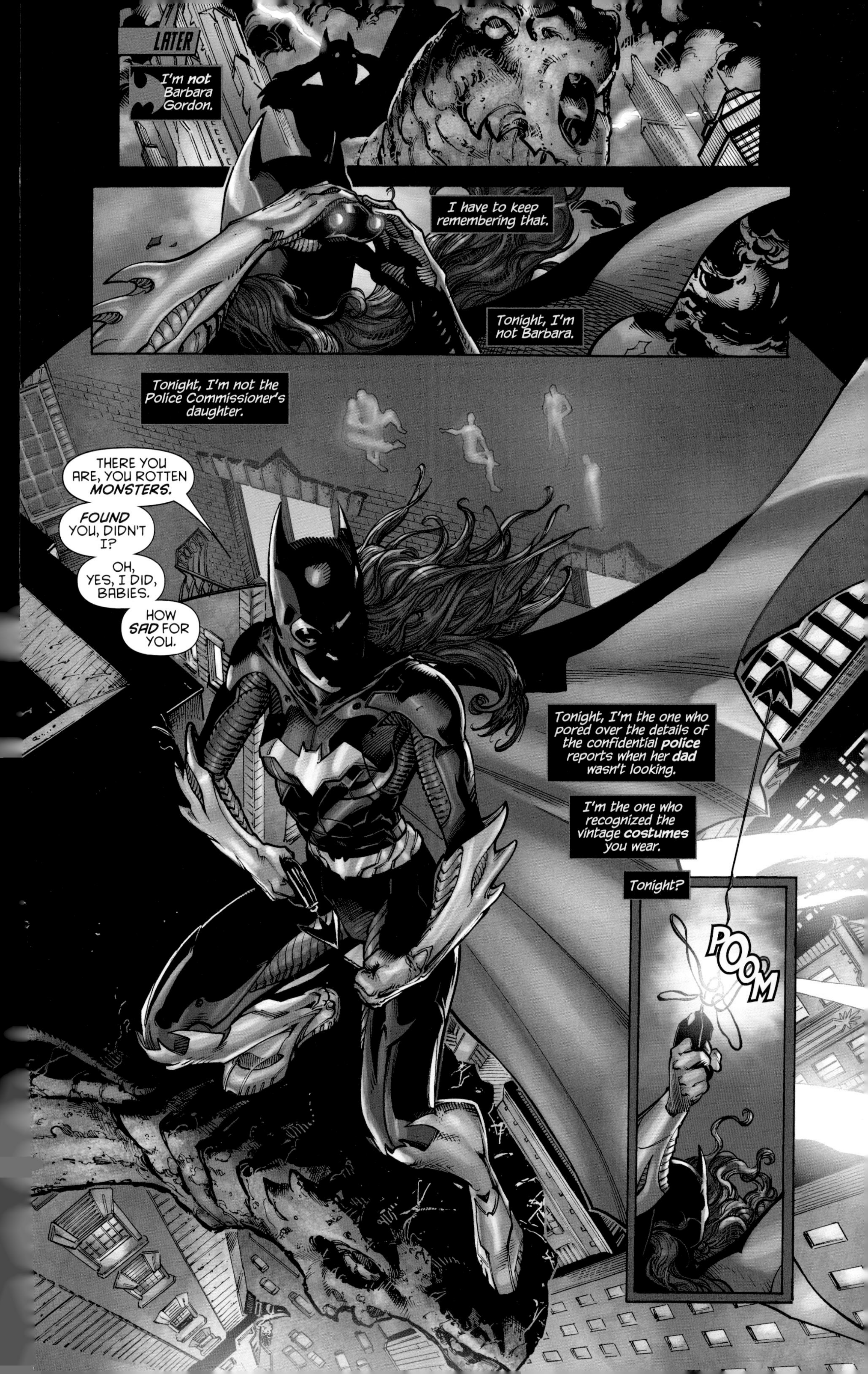
LATER
I'm not Barbara Gordon.
I have to keep remembering that.
Tonight, I'm not Barbara.
Tonight, I'm not the Police Commissioner's daughter.
THERE YOU ARE, YOU ROTTEN MONSTERS.
FOUND YOU, DIDN'T I?
OH, YES, I DID, BABIES.
HOW SAD FOR YOU.
Tonight, I'm the one who pored over the details of the confidential police reports when her dad wasn't looking.
I'm the one who recognized the vintage costumes you wear.
Tonight?
POOM

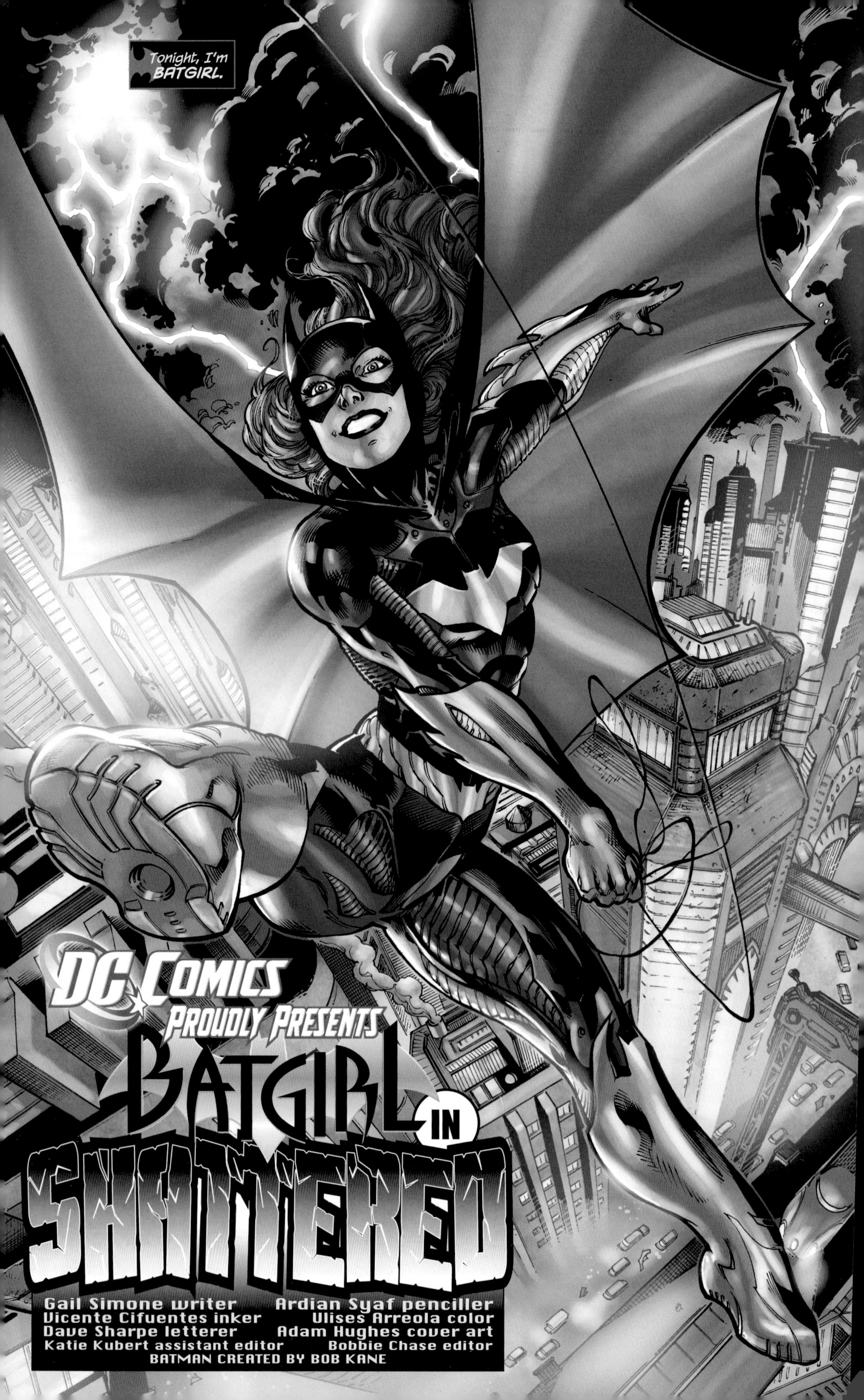
Tonight, I'm BATGIRL.
DC COMICS PROUDLY PRESENTS
BATGIRL IN
SHATTERED
Gail Simone writer Ardian Syaf penciller
Vicente Cifuentes inker Ulises Arreola color
Dave Sharpe letterer Adam Hughes cover art
Katie Kubert assistant editor Bobbie Chase editor
BATMAN CREATED BY BOB KANE

"HAVE YOU EVER WANTED SOMETHING SO BADLY THAT IT WAS ALL YOU THOUGHT ABOUT, DAY AND NIGHT?"

"TO BE FREE, I MEAN. UNFETTERED. WITHOUT THE CHAINS THAT HOLD US DOWN."

YOU CAN'T CALL IT A DREAM, EVEN. IT'S A NEED. A *NECESSITY*.

SO DEEP, IT'S IN THE BLOOD. IT'S IN THE *BONES*.

THAT'S HOW I FEEL ABOUT *HOME INVASION* AND *MURDER*.

PLEASE. PLEASE, JUST *LEAVE*. WE WON'T...WE WON'T...

WHO *ARE* YOU?

OH, WHERE ARE MY MANNERS?

I'M SORRY, I THOUGHT YOU KNEW.

DANNY, GIVE THE ORTEGAS THE SCRAPBOOK, WOULD YOU?

WE'RE THE BRISBY KILLERS.

FAMILY MASSACRE IN GOTHAM SUBURB
Jack Ryder
World Associated Press and Times

Only Surviving Daughter Returns to Gruesome Scene

Tonight, the peaceful Gotham suburb of Brisby is quiet for the most tragic reason possible. Brisby is the retirement community of choice for former members of the Gotham City Police Force, and is known as an area local criminals stay well clear of. However, tragedy managed to find one family even in this quiet, [...] in what witnesses say [...] shocking

"BRISBY KILLERS" LIKELY PERPETRATORS IN SECOND BLOODBATH
Central News Desk

Breaking News, Central News Desk
In a horrifying scene that alarmed even the most hardened of state troopers, a second family was found killed in the Brisby area outside of Gotham City lines early Thursday morning when neighbors were alerted by the terrified barking of the family's beloved pet dog. The bodies were posed in a grotesque mockery of
(CONT. PAGE TWO)

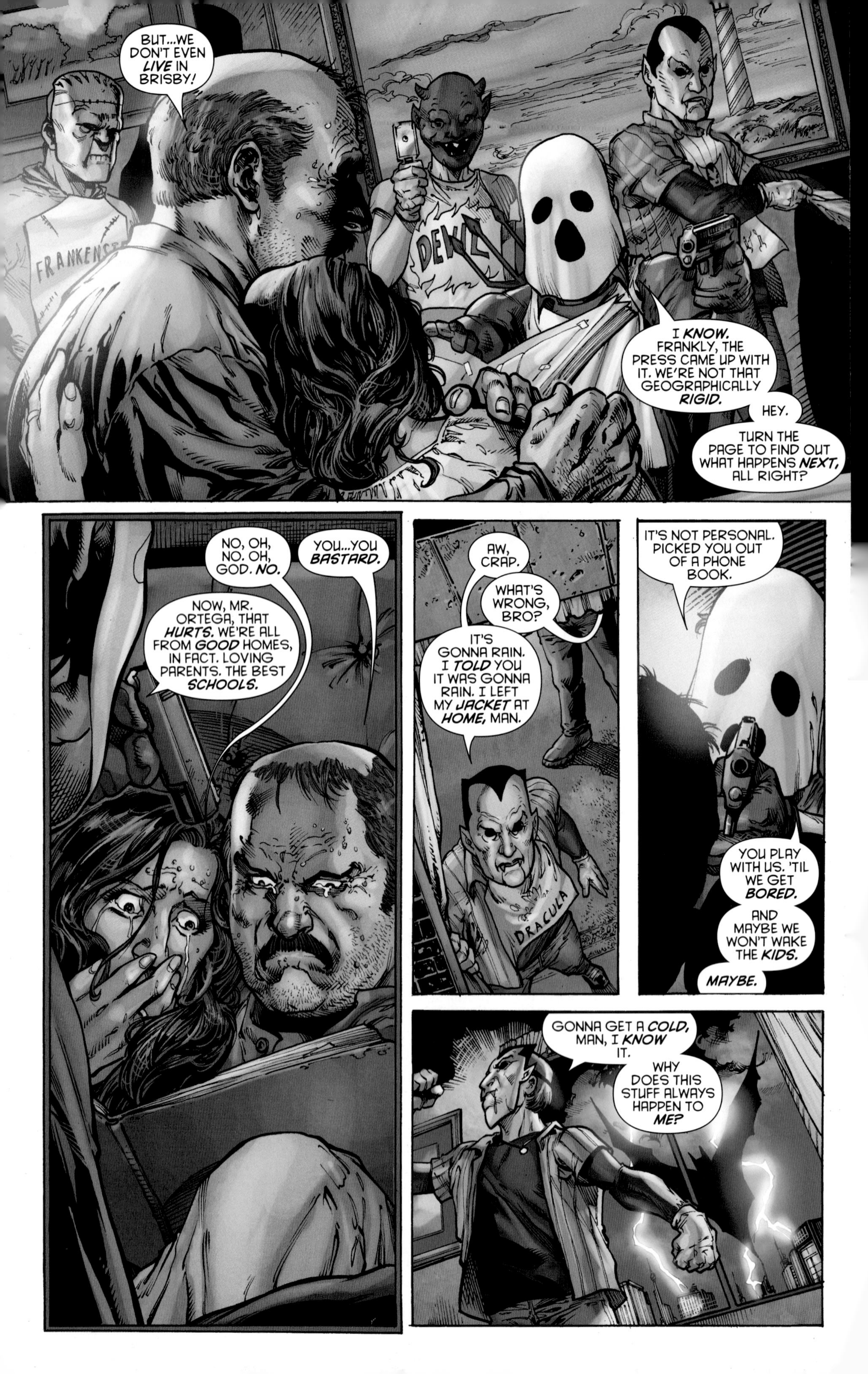

BUT...WE DON'T EVEN LIVE IN BRISBY!
FRANKENST
DEVIL
I KNOW. FRANKLY, THE PRESS CAME UP WITH IT. WE'RE NOT THAT GEOGRAPHICALLY RIGID.
HEY.
TURN THE PAGE TO FIND OUT WHAT HAPPENS NEXT, ALL RIGHT?
NO, OH, NO. OH, GOD. NO.
YOU...YOU BASTARD.
NOW, MR. ORTEGA, THAT HURTS. WE'RE ALL FROM GOOD HOMES, IN FACT. LOVING PARENTS. THE BEST SCHOOLS.
AW, CRAP.
WHAT'S WRONG, BRO?
IT'S GONNA RAIN. I TOLD YOU IT WAS GONNA RAIN. I LEFT MY JACKET AT HOME, MAN.
DRACULA
IT'S NOT PERSONAL. PICKED YOU OUT OF A PHONE BOOK.
YOU PLAY WITH US. 'TIL WE GET BORED.
AND MAYBE WE WON'T WAKE THE KIDS.
MAYBE.
GONNA GET A COLD, MAN, I KNOW IT.
WHY DOES THIS STUFF ALWAYS HAPPEN TO ME?

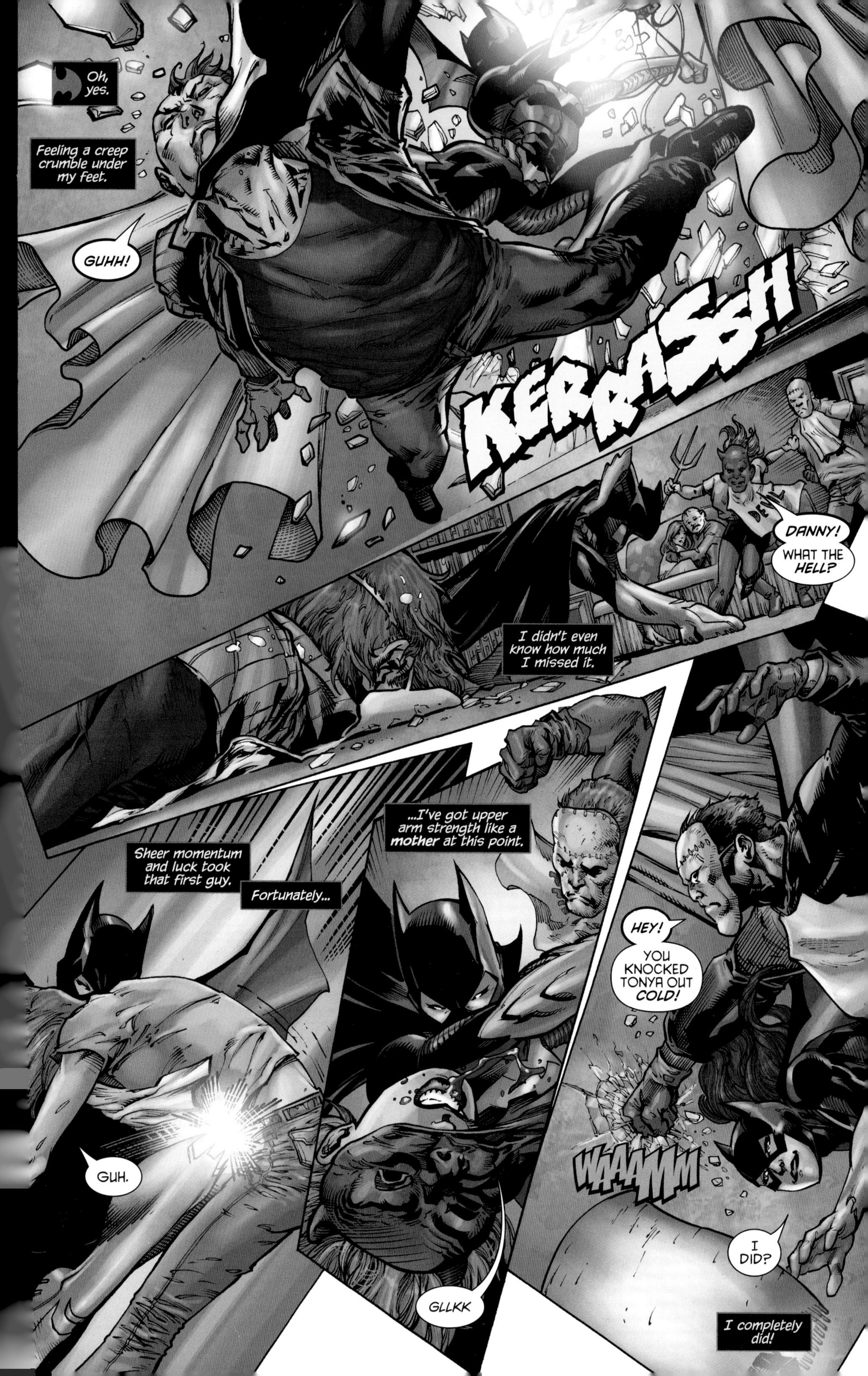

Oh, yes.
Feeling a creep crumble under my feet.
GUHH!
KERRASSH
DANNY! WHAT THE HELL?
I didn't even know how much I missed it.
Sheer momentum and luck took that first guy.
Fortunately...
...I've got upper arm strength like a mother at this point.
GUH.
GLLKK
HEY!
YOU KNOCKED TONYA OUT COLD!
WAAAMM
I DID?
I completely did!

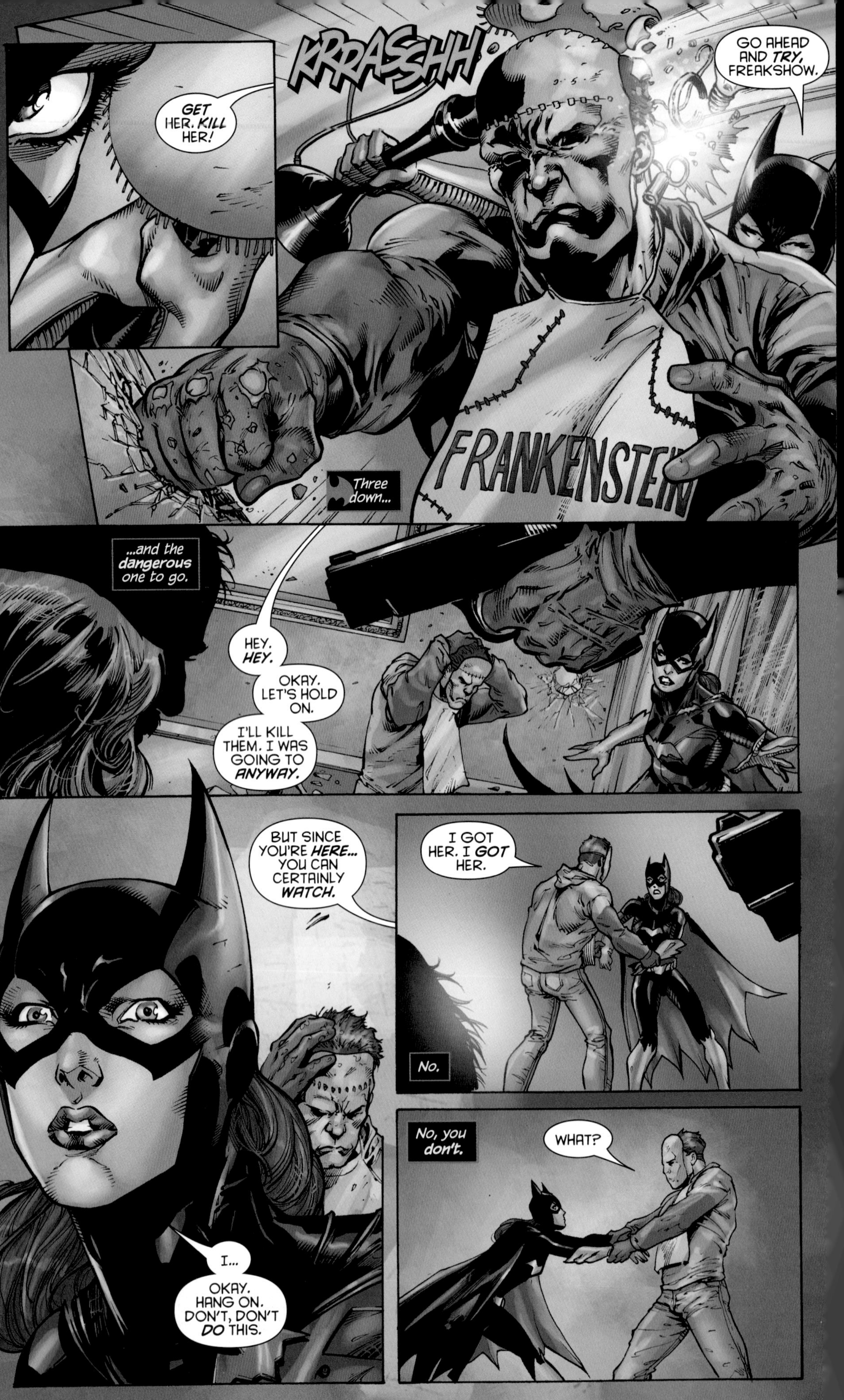
GET HER. KILL HER!
KRRASHH
GO AHEAD AND TRY, FREAKSHOW.
FRANKENSTEIN
Three down...
...and the dangerous one to go.
HEY. HEY.
OKAY. LET'S HOLD ON.
I'LL KILL THEM. I WAS GOING TO ANYWAY.
BUT SINCE YOU'RE HERE... YOU CAN CERTAINLY WATCH.
I...
OKAY. HANG ON. DON'T, DON'T DO THIS.
I GOT HER. I GOT HER.
No.
No, you don't.
WHAT?

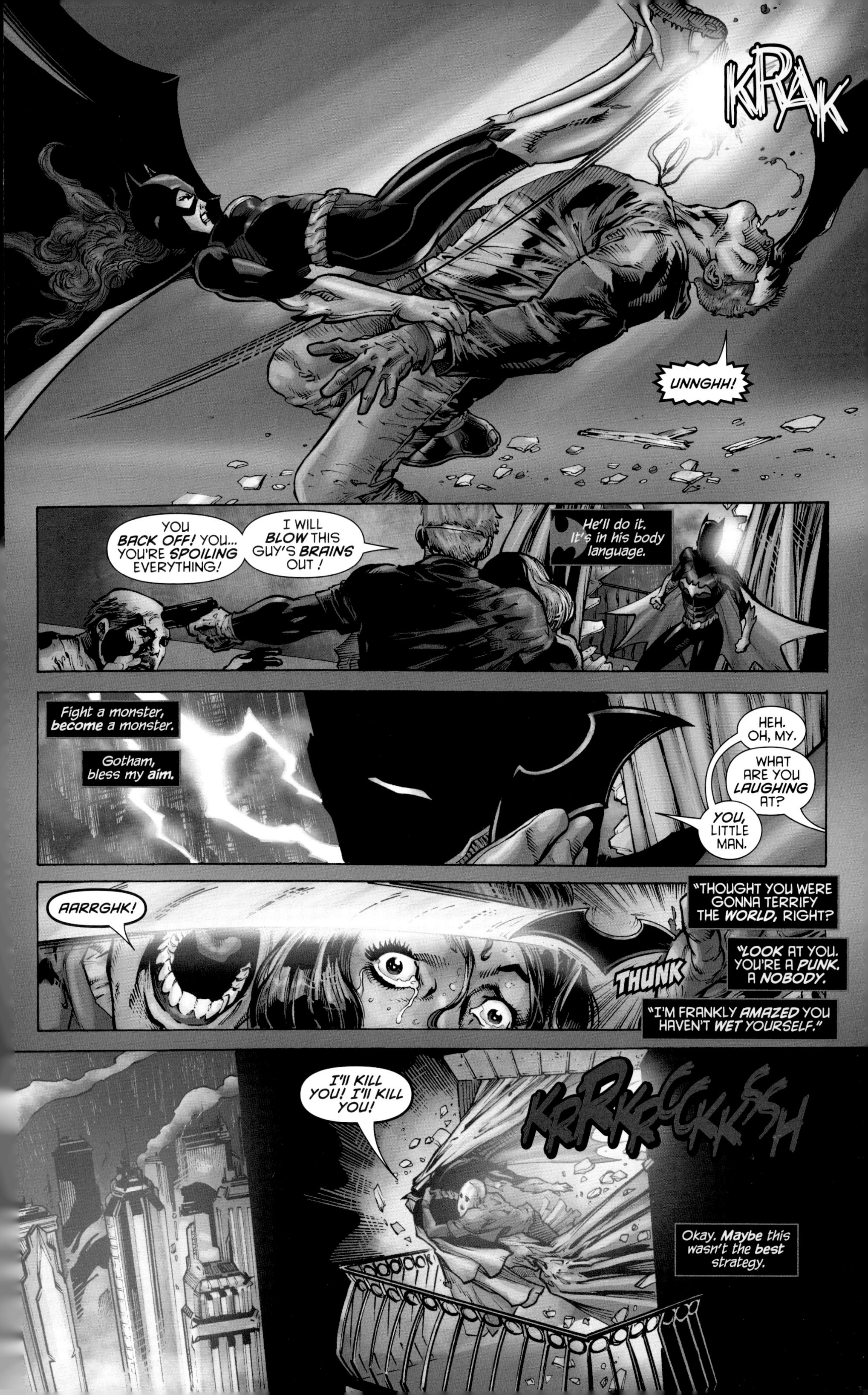
KRAK
UNNGHH!
YOU BACK OFF! YOU... YOU'RE SPOILING EVERYTHING!
I WILL BLOW THIS GUY'S BRAINS OUT!
He'll do it. It's in his body language.
Fight a monster, become a monster.
Gotham, bless my aim.
HEH. OH, MY.
WHAT ARE YOU LAUGHING AT?
YOU, LITTLE MAN.
AARRGHK!
"THOUGHT YOU WERE GONNA TERRIFY THE WORLD, RIGHT?
"LOOK AT YOU. YOU'RE A PUNK. A NOBODY.
THUNK
"I'M FRANKLY AMAZED YOU HAVEN'T WET YOURSELF."
I'LL KILL YOU! I'LL KILL YOU!
KRRKKCCKKSSH
Okay. Maybe this wasn't the best strategy.

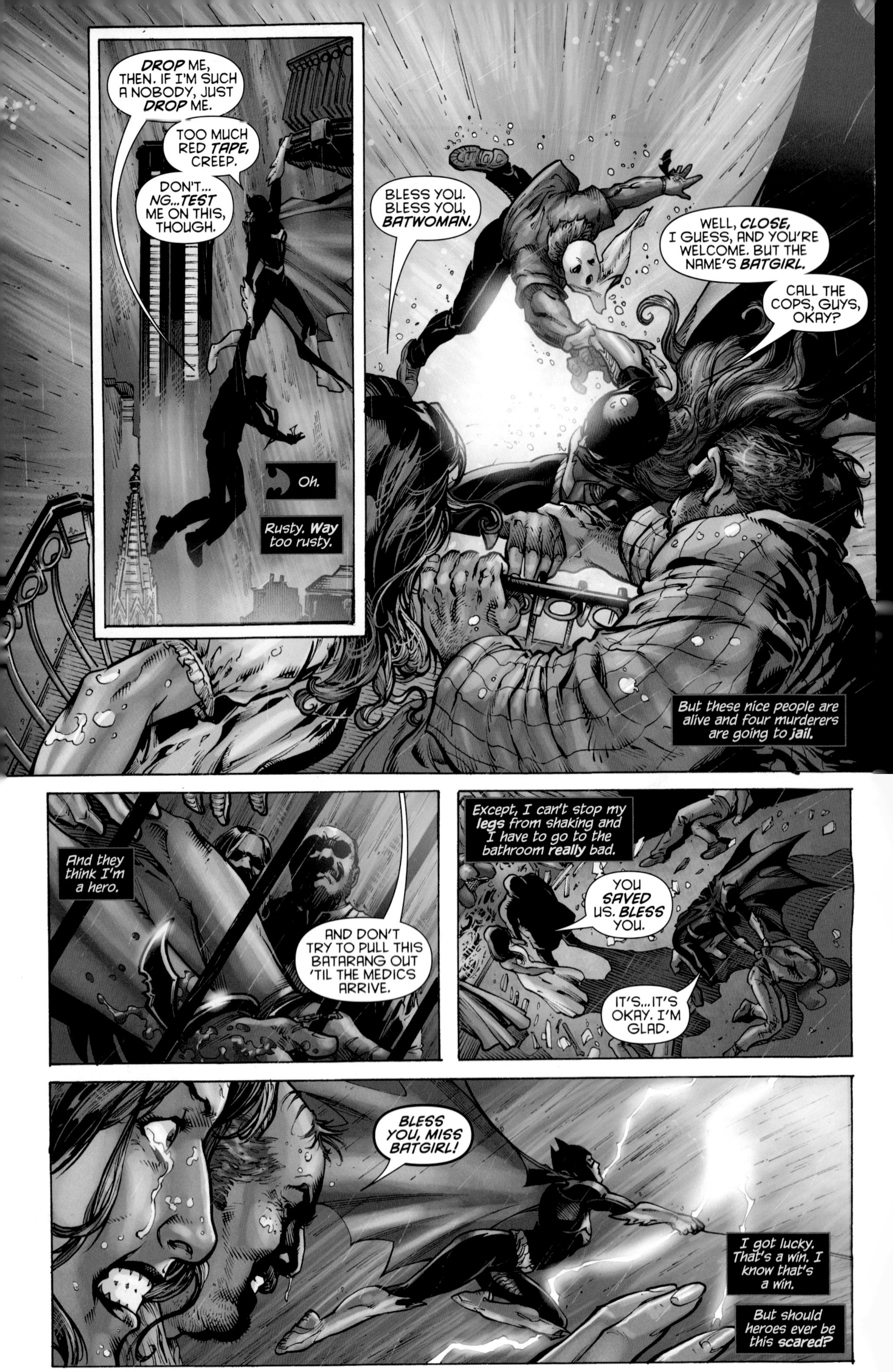
DROP ME, THEN. IF I'M SUCH A NOBODY, JUST DROP ME.
TOO MUCH RED TAPE, CREEP.
DON'T... NG...TEST ME ON THIS, THOUGH.
Oh.
Rusty. Way too rusty.
BLESS YOU. BLESS YOU, BATWOMAN.
WELL, CLOSE, I GUESS, AND YOU'RE WELCOME. BUT THE NAME'S BATGIRL.
CALL THE COPS, GUYS, OKAY?
But these nice people are alive and four murderers are going to jail.
And they think I'm a hero.
AND DON'T TRY TO PULL THIS BATARANG OUT 'TIL THE MEDICS ARRIVE.
Except, I can't stop my legs from shaking and I have to go to the bathroom really bad.
YOU SAVED US. BLESS YOU.
IT'S...IT'S OKAY. I'M GLAD.
BLESS YOU, MISS BATGIRL!
I got lucky. That's a win. I know that's a win.
But should heroes ever be this scared?

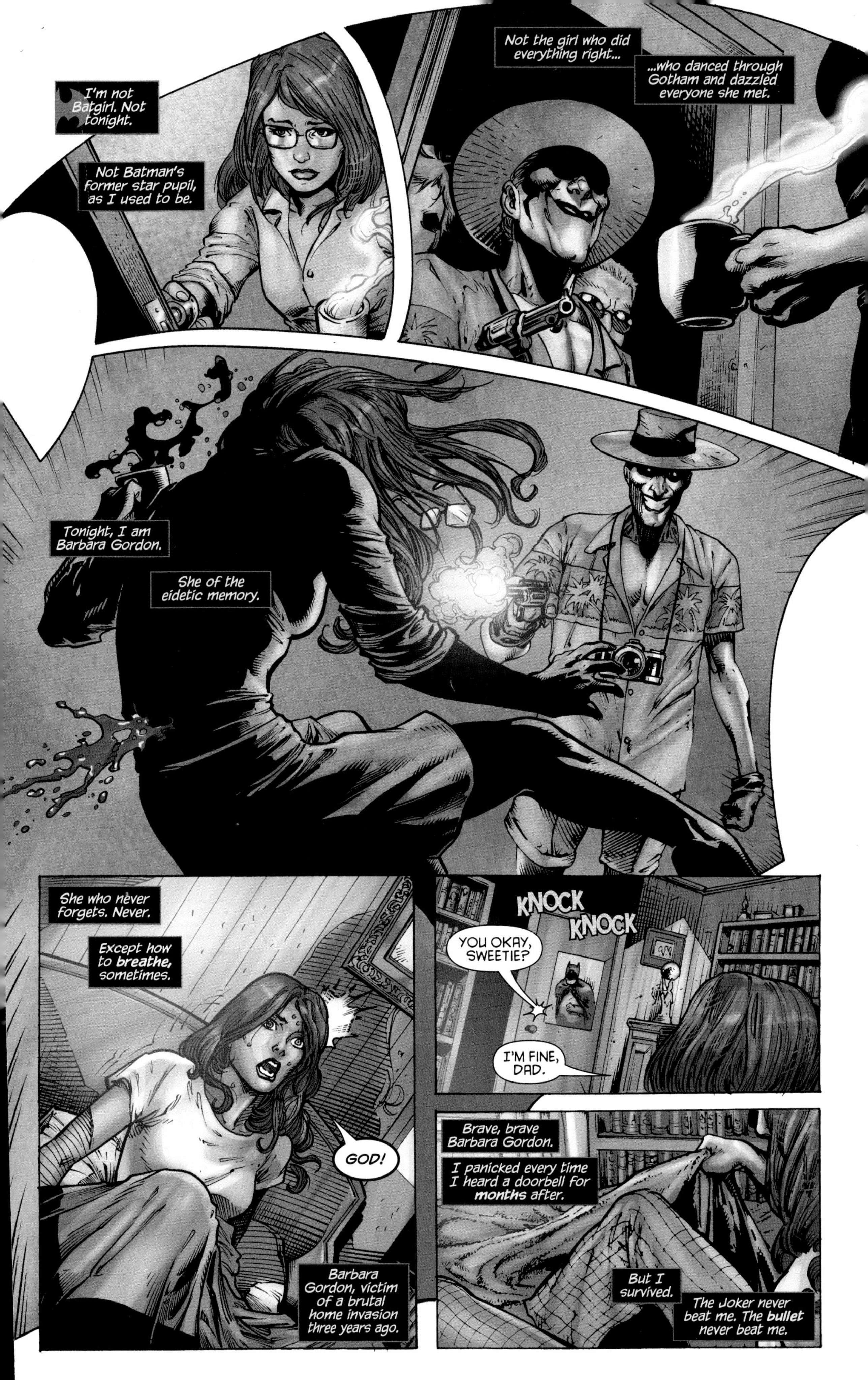

I'm not Batgirl. Not tonight.
Not Batman's former star pupil, as I used to be.
Not the girl who did everything right...
...who danced through Gotham and dazzled everyone she met.
Tonight, I am Barbara Gordon.
She of the eidetic memory.
She who never forgets. Never.
Except how to **breathe,** sometimes.
GOD!
Barbara Gordon, victim of a brutal home invasion three years ago.
KNOCK
KNOCK
YOU OKAY, SWEETIE?
I'M FINE, DAD.
Brave, brave Barbara Gordon.
I panicked every time I heard a doorbell for **months** after.
But I survived.
The Joker never beat me. The **bullet** never beat me.

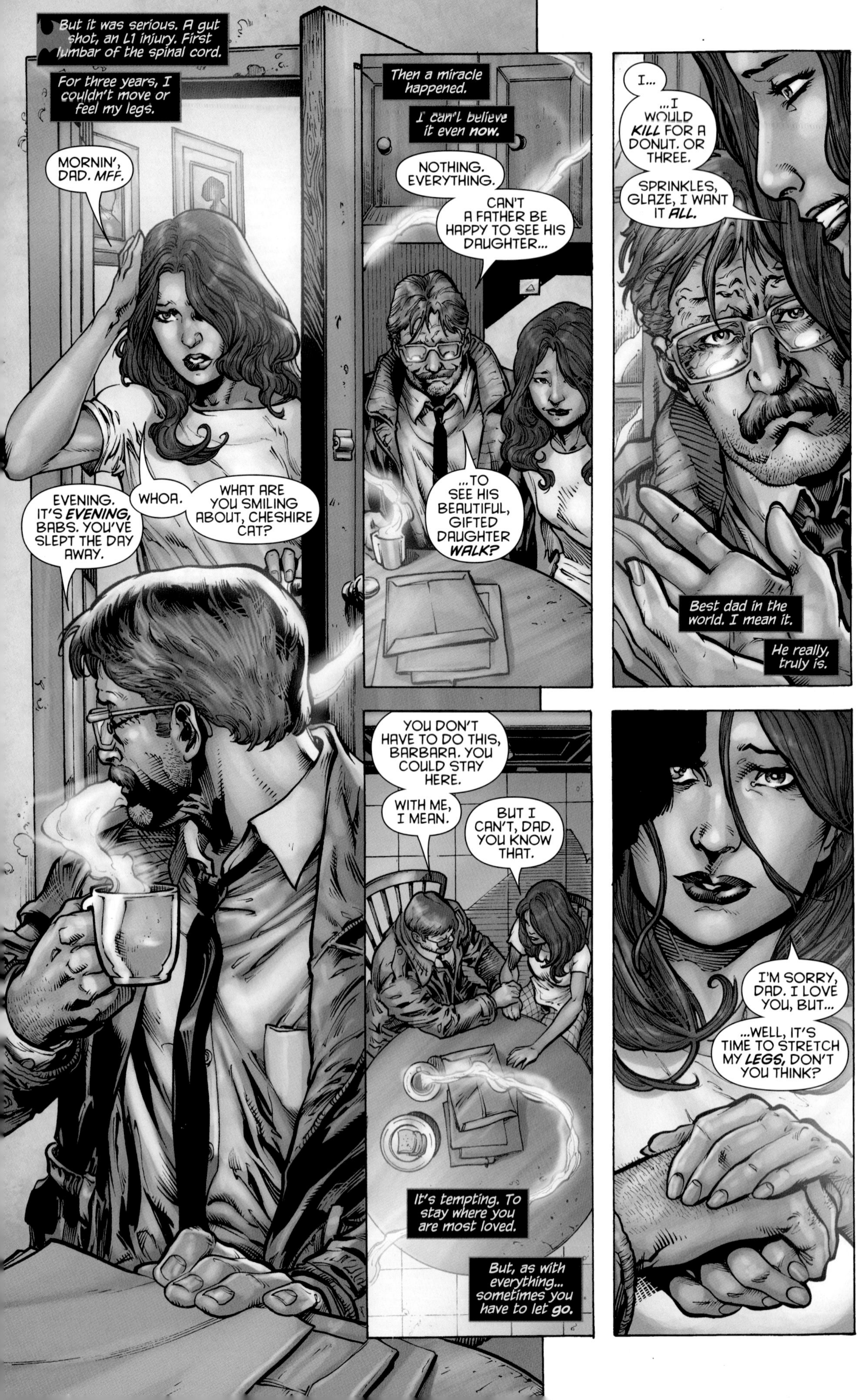
But it was serious. A gut shot, an L1 injury. First lumbar of the spinal cord.
For three years, I couldn't move or feel my legs.
MORNIN', DAD. MFF.
EVENING. IT'S EVENING, BABS. YOU'VE SLEPT THE DAY AWAY.
WHOA.
WHAT ARE YOU SMILING ABOUT, CHESHIRE CAT?
Then a miracle happened.
I can't believe it even now.
NOTHING. EVERYTHING.
CAN'T A FATHER BE HAPPY TO SEE HIS DAUGHTER...
...TO SEE HIS BEAUTIFUL, GIFTED DAUGHTER WALK?
I...
...I WOULD KILL FOR A DONUT. OR THREE.
SPRINKLES, GLAZE, I WANT IT ALL.
Best dad in the world. I mean it.
He really, truly is.
YOU DON'T HAVE TO DO THIS, BARBARA. YOU COULD STAY HERE.
WITH ME, I MEAN.
BUT I CAN'T, DAD. YOU KNOW THAT.
It's tempting. To stay where you are most loved.
But, as with everything... sometimes you have to let go.
I'M SORRY, DAD. I LOVE YOU, BUT...
...WELL, IT'S TIME TO STRETCH MY LEGS, DON'T YOU THINK?

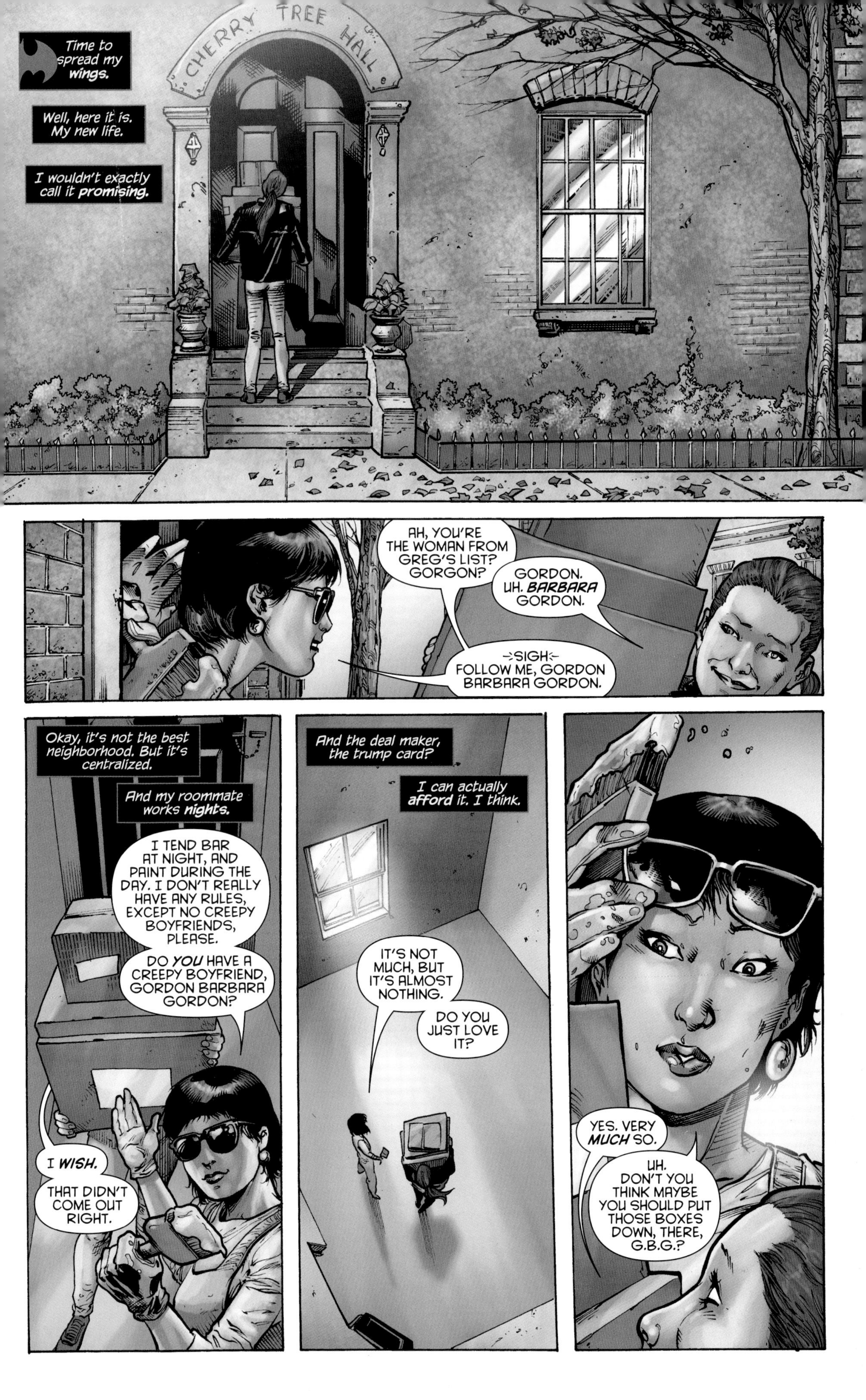

CHERRY TREE HALL
Time to spread my wings.
Well, here it is. My new life.
I wouldn't exactly call it promising.
AH, YOU'RE THE WOMAN FROM GREG'S LIST? GORGON?
GORDON. UH. BARBARA GORDON.
-SIGH- FOLLOW ME, GORDON BARBARA GORDON.
Okay, it's not the best neighborhood. But it's centralized.
And my roommate works nights.
I TEND BAR AT NIGHT, AND PAINT DURING THE DAY. I DON'T REALLY HAVE ANY RULES, EXCEPT NO CREEPY BOYFRIENDS, PLEASE.
DO YOU HAVE A CREEPY BOYFRIEND, GORDON BARBARA GORDON?
I WISH.
THAT DIDN'T COME OUT RIGHT.
And the deal maker, the trump card?
I can actually afford it. I think.
IT'S NOT MUCH, BUT IT'S ALMOST NOTHING.
DO YOU JUST LOVE IT?
YES. VERY MUCH SO.
UH. DON'T YOU THINK MAYBE YOU SHOULD PUT THOSE BOXES DOWN, THERE, G.B.G.?

COME ON, I'LL HELP. THEN I'LL MAKE SOME TEA AND WE CAN DISCOVER WHAT THINGS WE BOTH HATE.

REALLY? THAT'D BE... THAT'D BE NICE.

BUT JUST FAIR WARNING, OKAY?

I'M KINDA AN ACTIVIST.

ALL GOOD?

FIGHT THE POWER!

It took a while, after the shooting, to let strangers back in.

It'd be nice to have someone to have tea with.

WE'RE ALL GOOD.

HECTIC, HECTIC DAY.

BUT ALL, ALL GOOD.

IF I COULD JUST GET FIVE MINUTES ALONE WITH THAT MURDERING SCUZZ...

SACRED HANDS OF GOD HOSPITAL

WELL, FIRST, YOU KNOW HE'S ASLEEP, RIGHT?

SECOND, OUR LITTLE THRILL KILLER GOT HIMSELF A SLASHED HAND AND A SNOOTFUL OF MEDS.

WAIT 'TIL HIS LAWYER SHOWS, MEL.

MY SHIFT STARTS IN TWENTY, BUT I CAN HELP YOU UNPACK. THIS YOUR VAN?

YES. NO. WAIT.

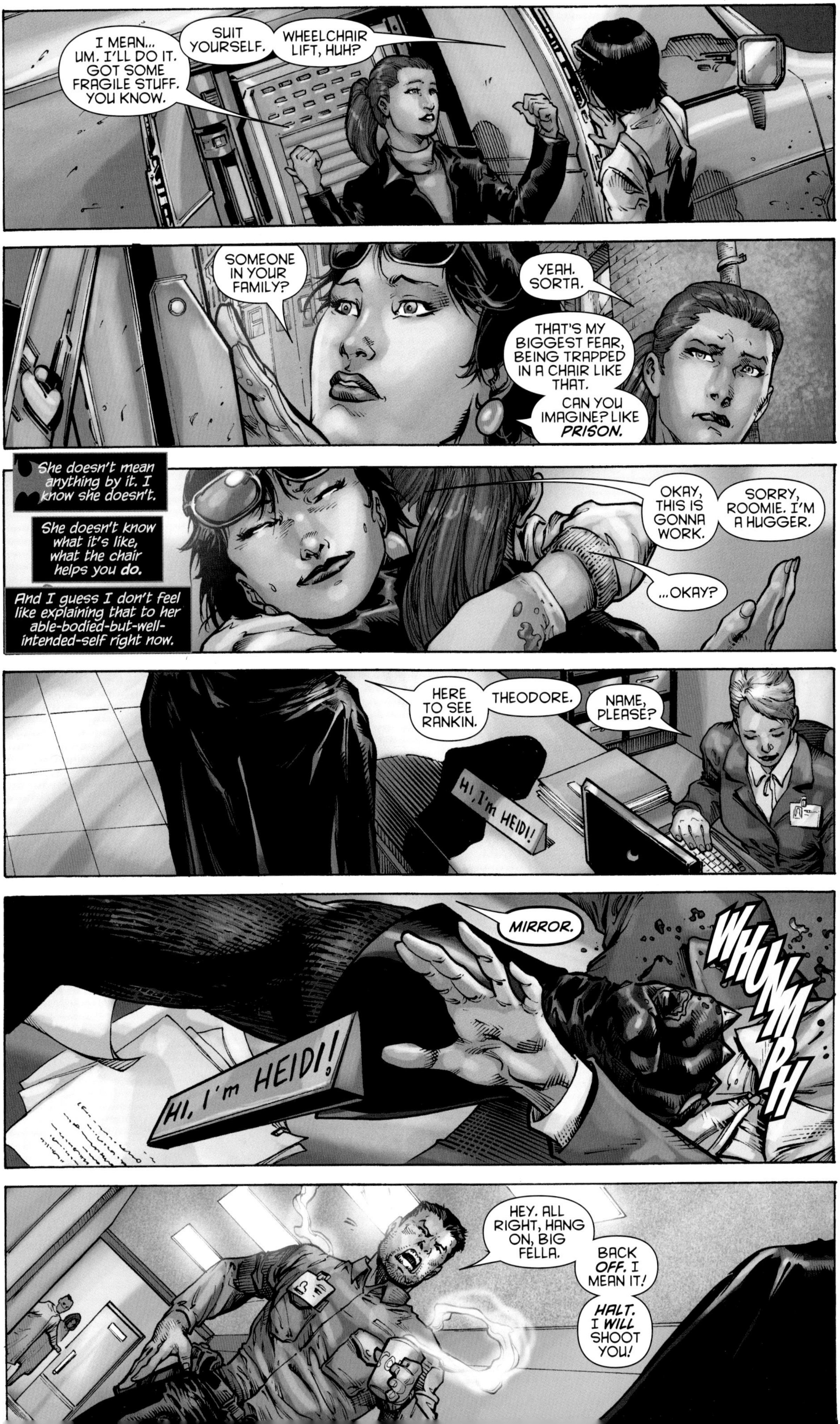

I MEAN... UM. I'LL DO IT. GOT SOME FRAGILE STUFF. YOU KNOW.
SUIT YOURSELF.
WHEELCHAIR LIFT, HUH?
SOMEONE IN YOUR FAMILY?
YEAH. SORTA.
THAT'S MY BIGGEST FEAR, BEING TRAPPED IN A CHAIR LIKE THAT.
CAN YOU IMAGINE? LIKE PRISON.
She doesn't mean anything by it. I know she doesn't.
She doesn't know what it's like, what the chair helps you do.
And I guess I don't feel like explaining that to her able-bodied-but-well-intended-self right now.
OKAY, THIS IS GONNA WORK.
SORRY, ROOMIE. I'M A HUGGER.
...OKAY?
NAME, PLEASE?
THEODORE.
HERE TO SEE RANKIN.
HI, I'm HEIDI!
MIRROR.
WHUMMPH
HI, I'm HEIDI!
HEY. ALL RIGHT, HANG ON, BIG FELLA.
BACK OFF. I MEAN IT!
HALT. I WILL SHOOT YOU!

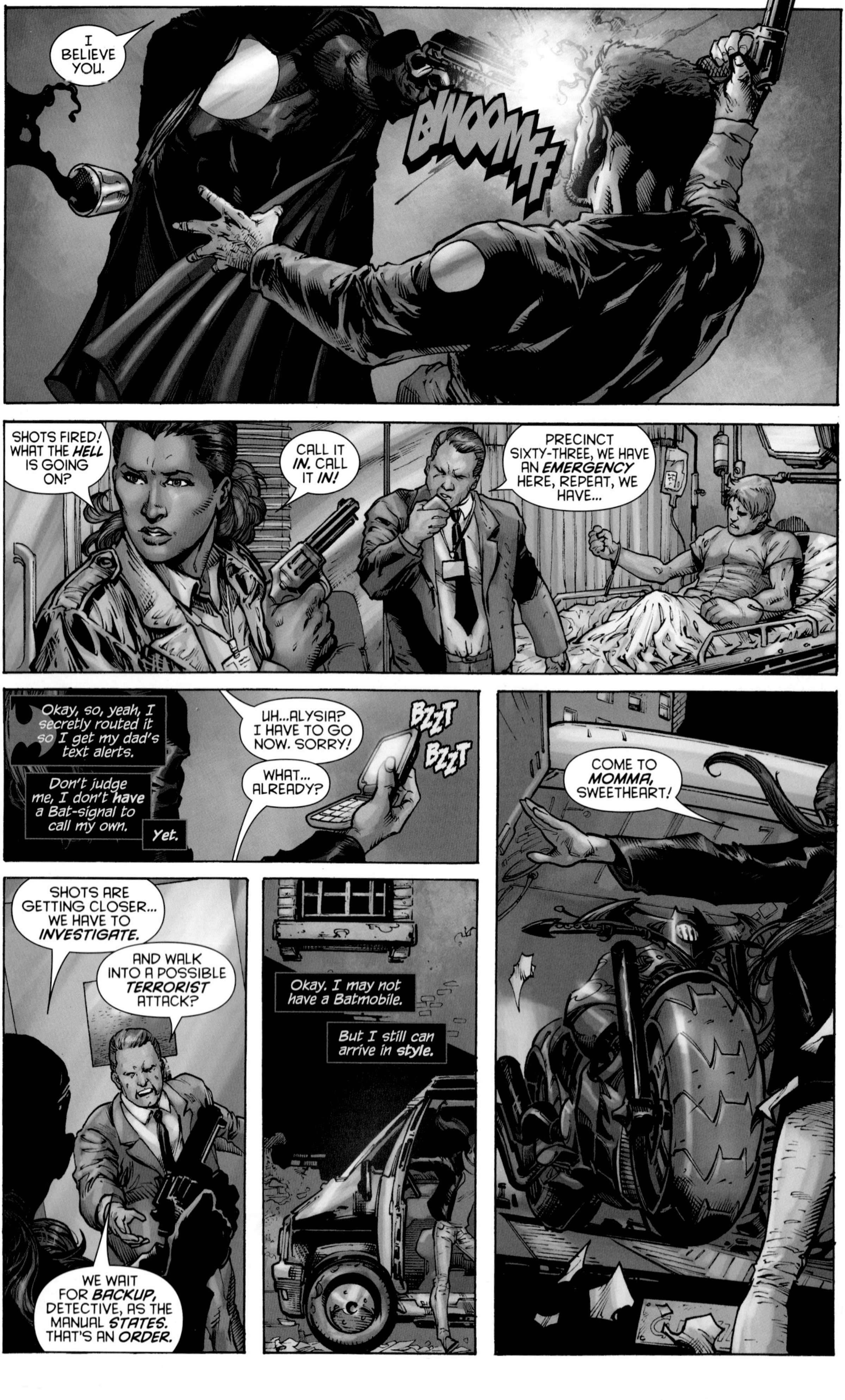

I BELIEVE YOU.
BWOOMFF
SHOTS FIRED! WHAT THE HELL IS GOING ON?
CALL IT IN. CALL IT IN!
PRECINCT SIXTY-THREE, WE HAVE AN EMERGENCY HERE, REPEAT, WE HAVE...
Okay, so, yeah, I secretly routed it so I get my dad's text alerts.
Don't judge me, I don't have a Bat-signal to call my own.
Yet.
UH...ALYSIA? I HAVE TO GO NOW. SORRY!
WHAT... ALREADY?
BZZT
BZZT
COME TO MOMMA, SWEETHEART!
SHOTS ARE GETTING CLOSER... WE HAVE TO INVESTIGATE.
AND WALK INTO A POSSIBLE TERRORIST ATTACK?
WE WAIT FOR BACKUP, DETECTIVE, AS THE MANUAL STATES. THAT'S AN ORDER.
Okay. I may not have a Batmobile.
But I still can arrive in style.

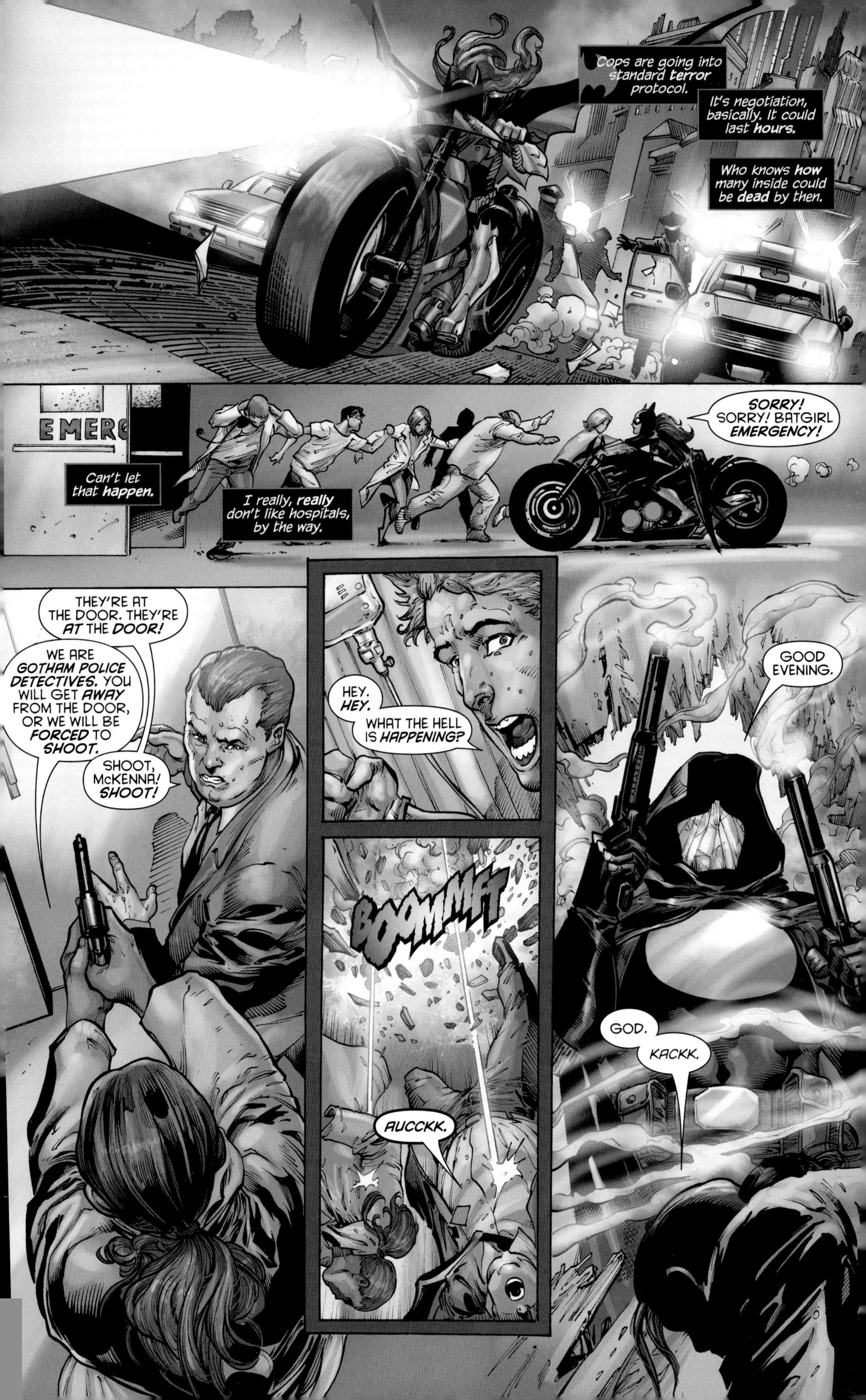
Cops are going into standard terror protocol.
It's negotiation, basically. It could last hours.
Who knows how many inside could be dead by then.
EMERG
Can't let that happen.
I really, really don't like hospitals, by the way.
SORRY! SORRY! BATGIRL EMERGENCY!
THEY'RE AT THE DOOR. THEY'RE AT THE DOOR!
WE ARE GOTHAM POLICE DETECTIVES. YOU WILL GET AWAY FROM THE DOOR, OR WE WILL BE FORCED TO SHOOT.
SHOOT, McKENNA! SHOOT!
HEY. HEY.
WHAT THE HELL IS HAPPENING?
BOOMMFT
AUCCKK.
GOOD EVENING.
GOD.
KACKK.

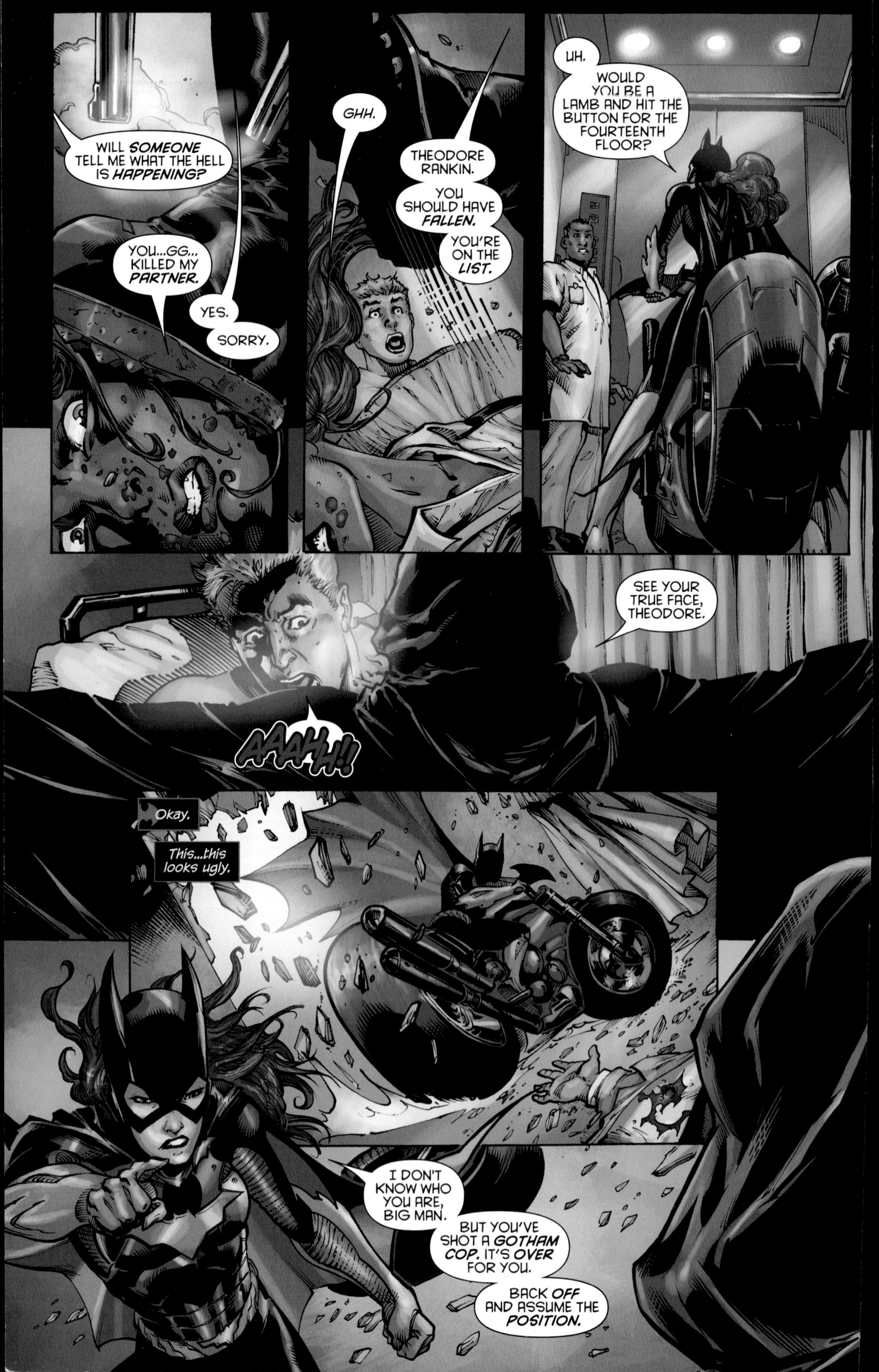

WILL *SOMEONE* TELL ME WHAT THE HELL IS *HAPPENING?*
YOU...GG... KILLED MY *PARTNER.*
YES.
SORRY.
GHH.
THEODORE RANKIN.
YOU SHOULD HAVE *FALLEN.*
YOU'RE ON THE *LIST.*
UH.
WOULD YOU BE A LAMB AND HIT THE BUTTON FOR THE FOURTEENTH FLOOR?
SEE YOUR TRUE FACE, THEODORE.
AAAHH!!
Okay.
This...this looks ugly.
I DON'T KNOW WHO YOU ARE, BIG MAN.
BUT YOU'VE SHOT A *GOTHAM COP.* IT'S *OVER* FOR YOU.
BACK *OFF* AND ASSUME THE *POSITION.*

I DON'T THINK SO.

Oh.

The gun. It's...it's pointed right... right at the same...

HELP! HE'S GOING TO KILL ME!

TAKE HIM DOWN. WHOEVER YOU ARE, TAKE HIM OUT! HE KILLED MY PARTNER!

He's going to shoot me.

I can't... I can't...

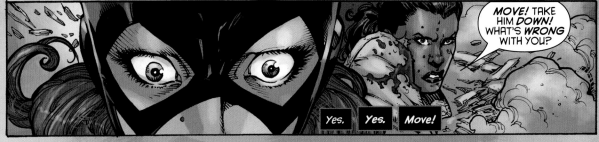

MOVE! TAKE HIM DOWN! WHAT'S WRONG WITH YOU?

Yes. Yes. Move!

I froze. He pointed that gun at my spine, and I froze!

TOO LATE.

LITTLE GIRL.

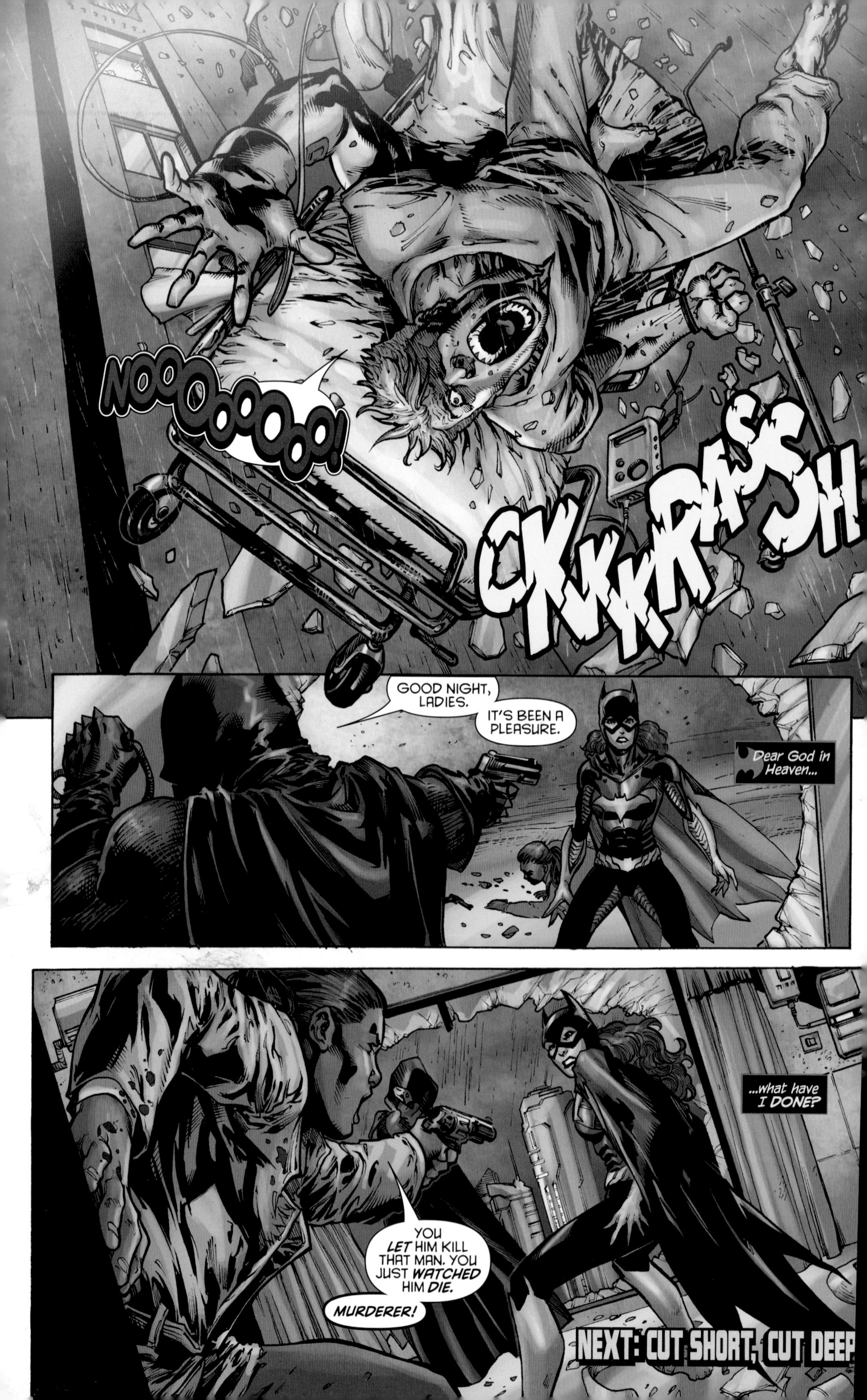

NOOOOOOOOO!
CKKKRASH
GOOD NIGHT, LADIES.
IT'S BEEN A PLEASURE.
Dear God in Heaven...
...what have I DONE?
YOU LET HIM KILL THAT MAN. YOU JUST WATCHED HIM DIE.
MURDERER!
NEXT: CUT SHORT, CUT DEEP

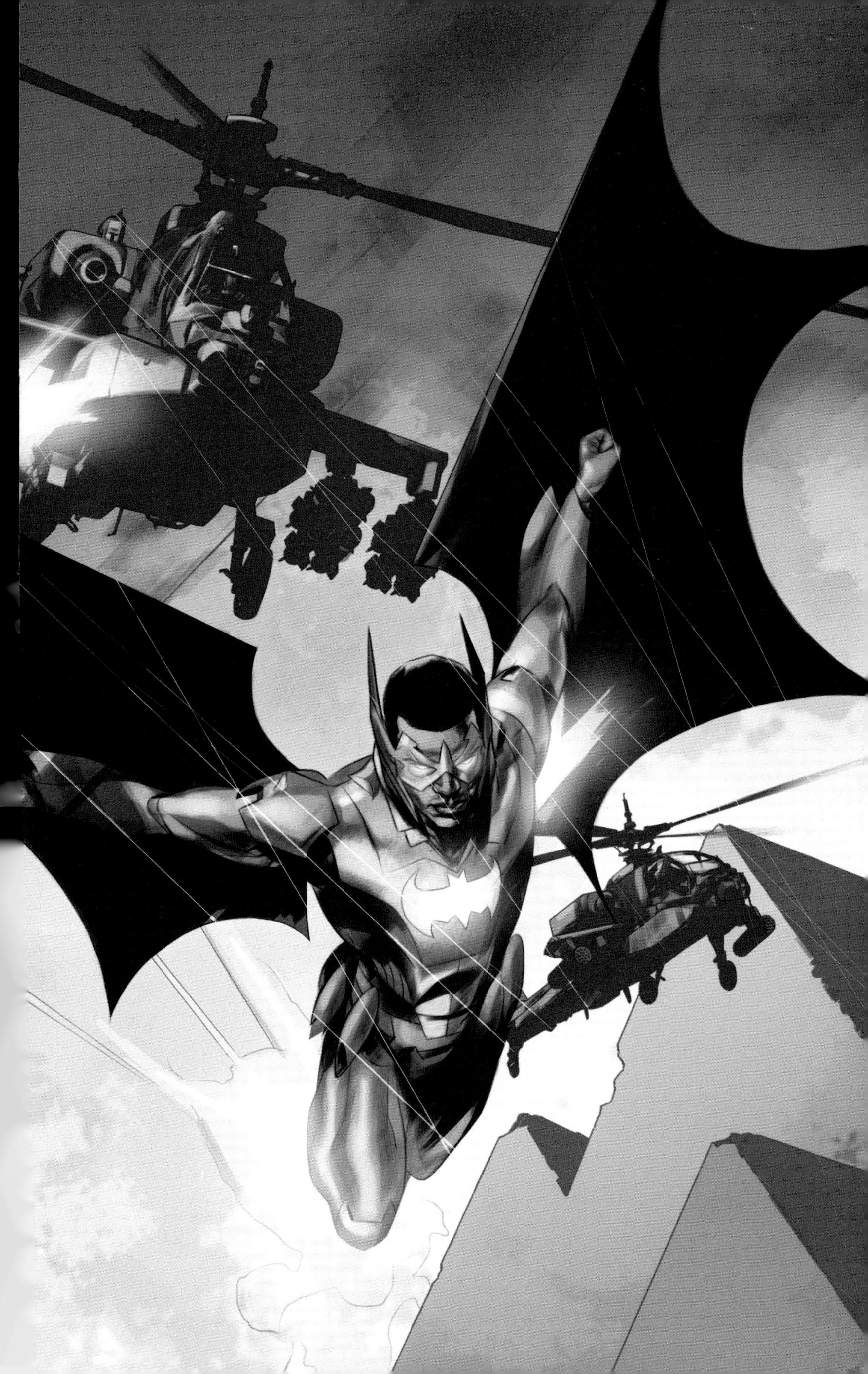

BATWING

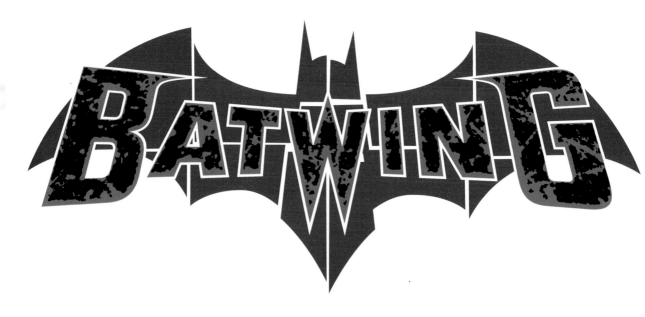

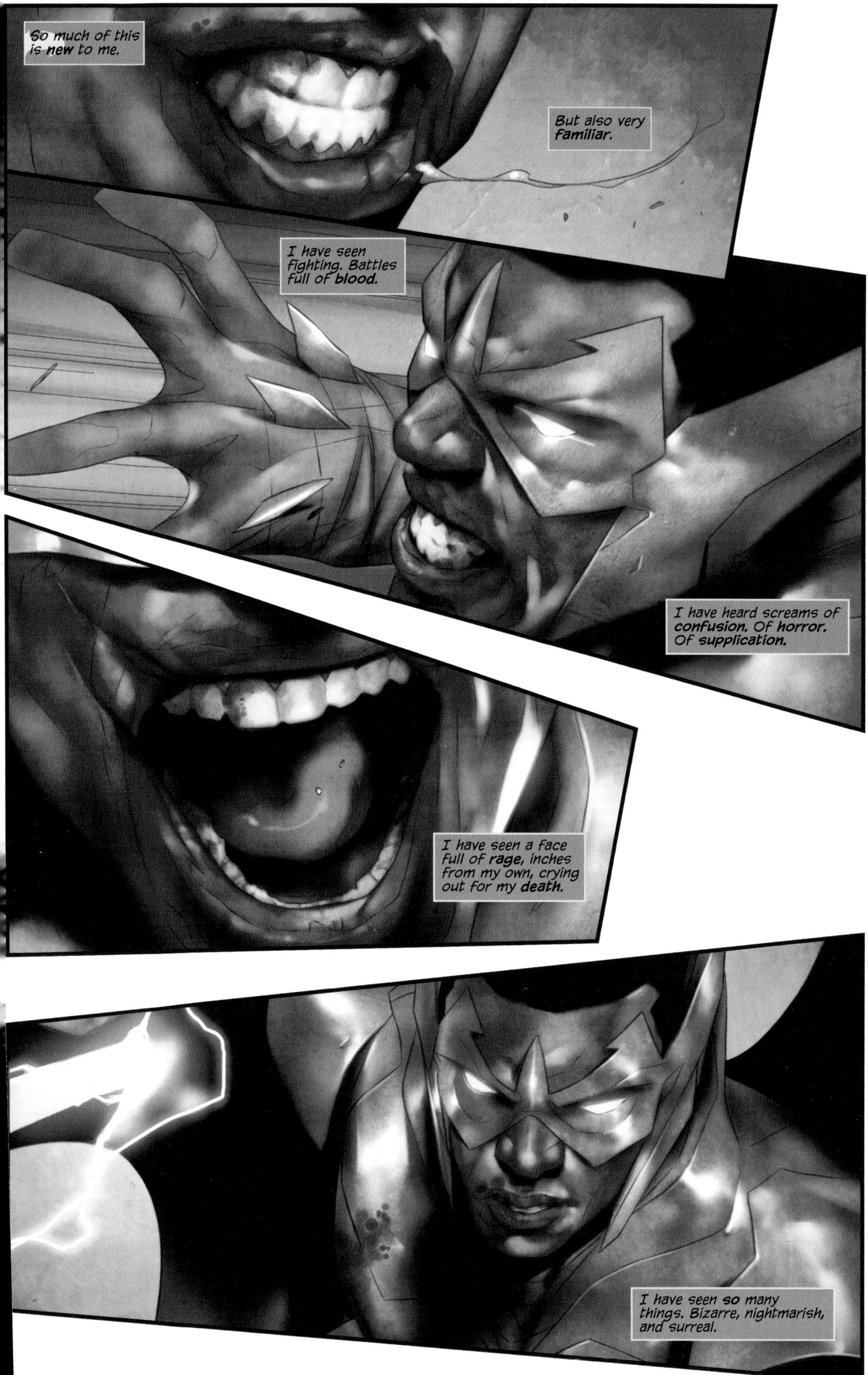
So much of this is **new** to me.
But also very **familiar**.
I have seen fighting. Battles full of **blood**.
I have heard screams of **confusion**. Of **horror**. Of **supplication**.
I have seen a face full of **rage**, inches from my own, crying out for my **death**.
I have seen **so** many things. Bizarre, nightmarish, and surreal.

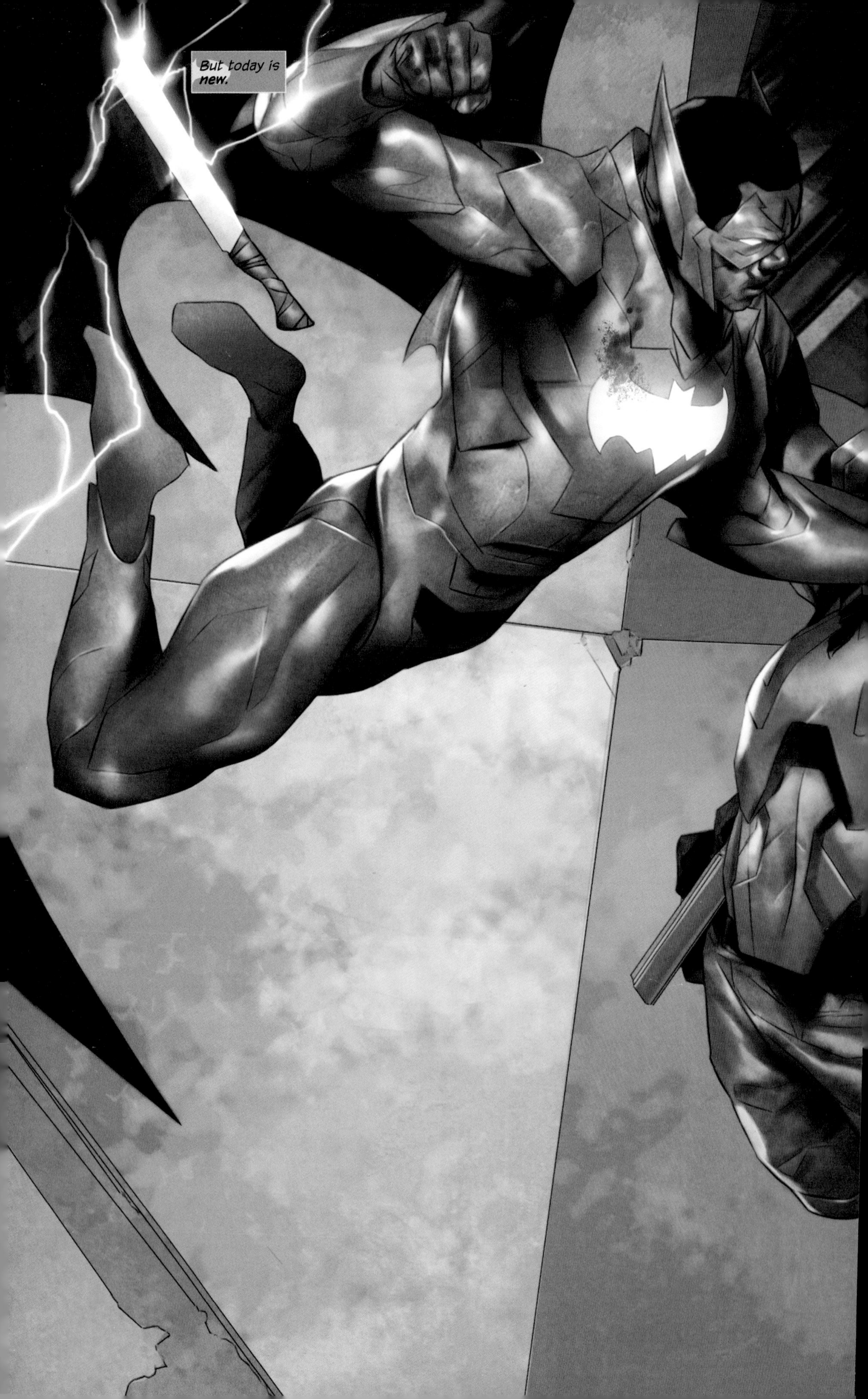
But today is new.

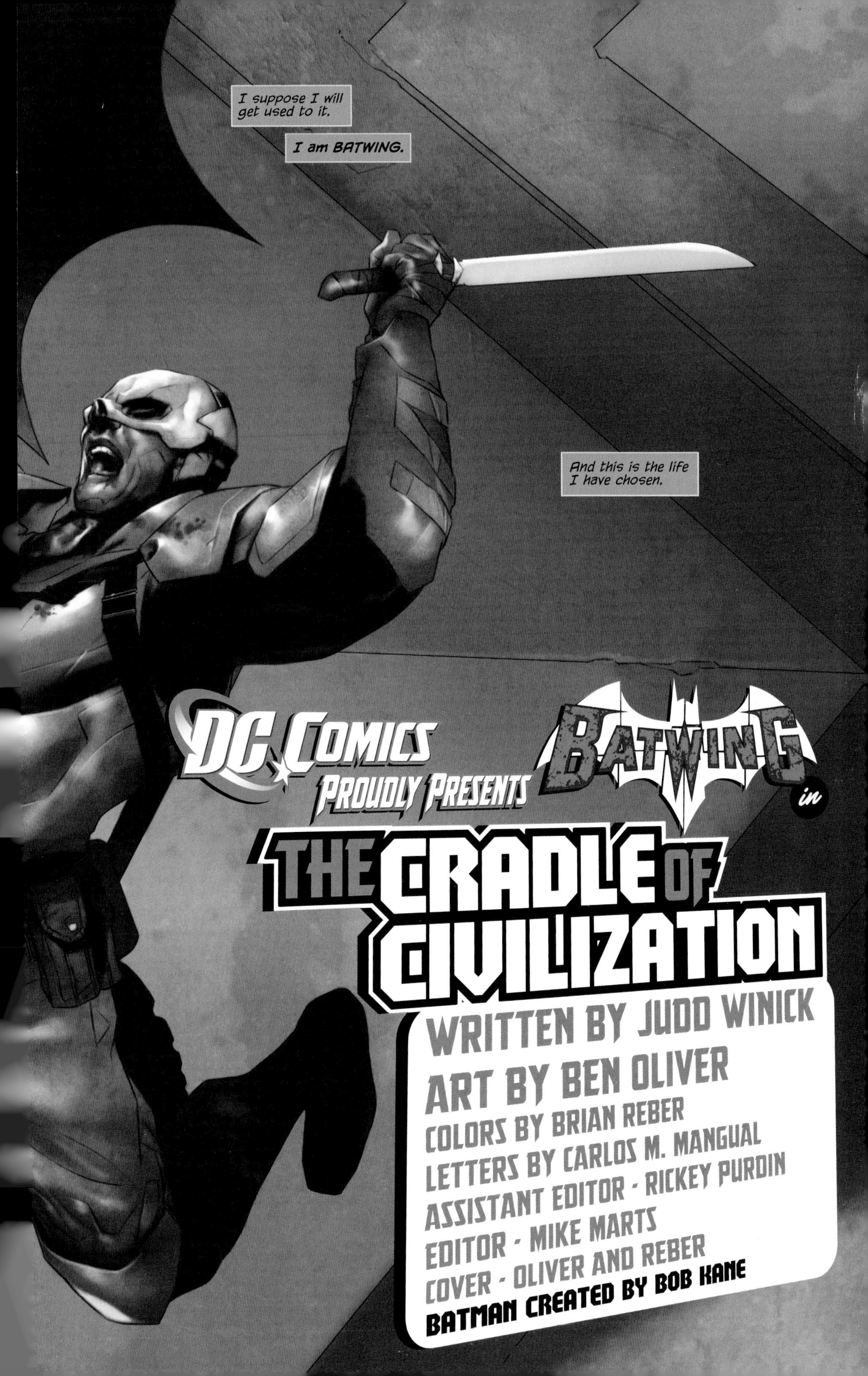

I suppose I will get used to it.
I am BATWING.
And this is the life I have chosen.
DC COMICS PROUDLY PRESENTS
BATWING in
THE CRADLE OF CIVILIZATION
WRITTEN BY JUDD WINICK
ART BY BEN OLIVER
COLORS BY BRIAN REBER
LETTERS BY CARLOS M. MANGUAL
ASSISTANT EDITOR - RICKEY PURDIN
EDITOR - MIKE MARTS
COVER - OLIVER AND REBER
BATMAN CREATED BY BOB KANE

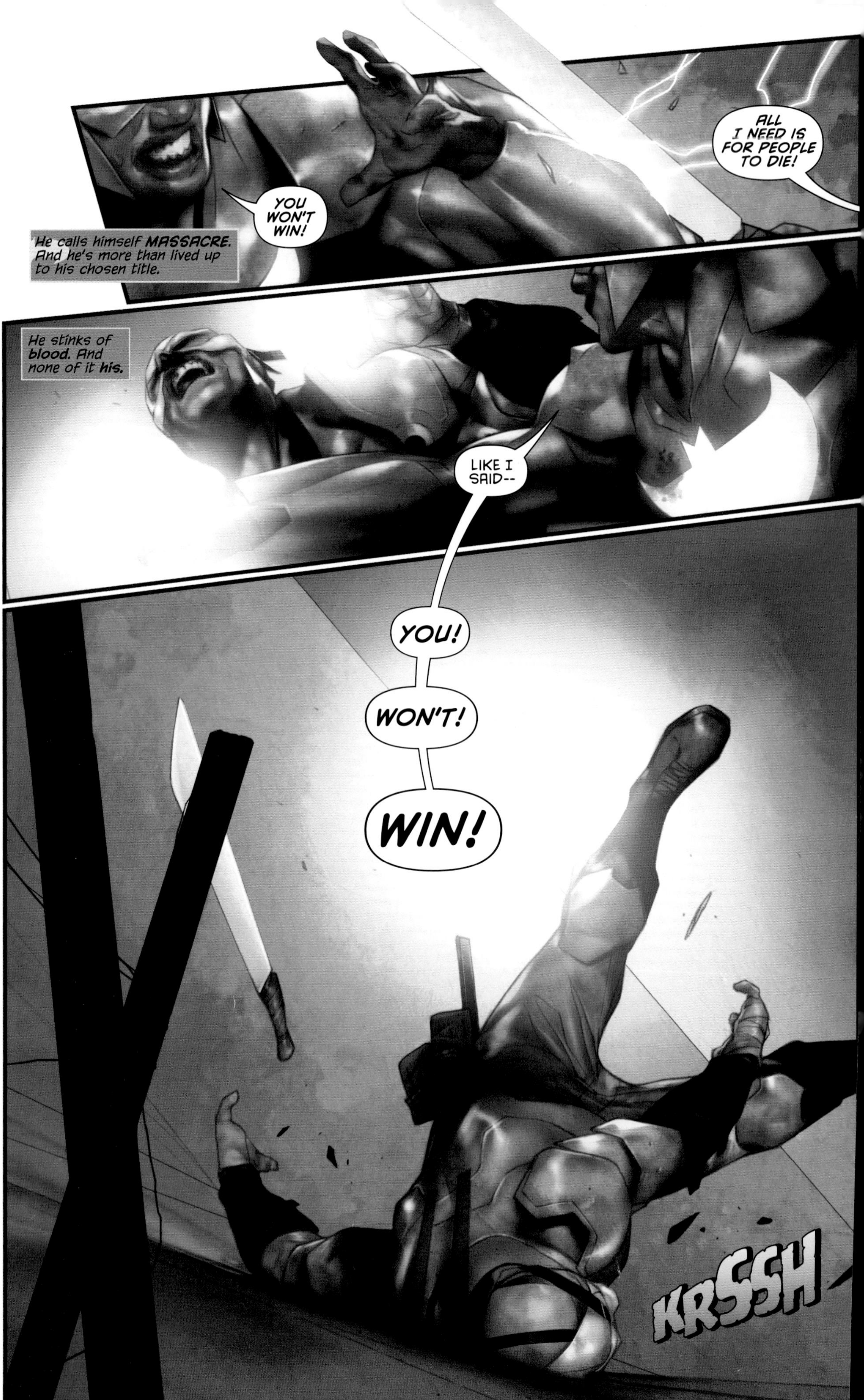

ALL I NEED IS FOR PEOPLE TO DIE!
YOU WON'T WIN!
He calls himself MASSACRE. And he's more than lived up to his chosen title.
He stinks of blood. And none of it his.
LIKE I SAID--
YOU!
WON'T!
WIN!
KRSSH

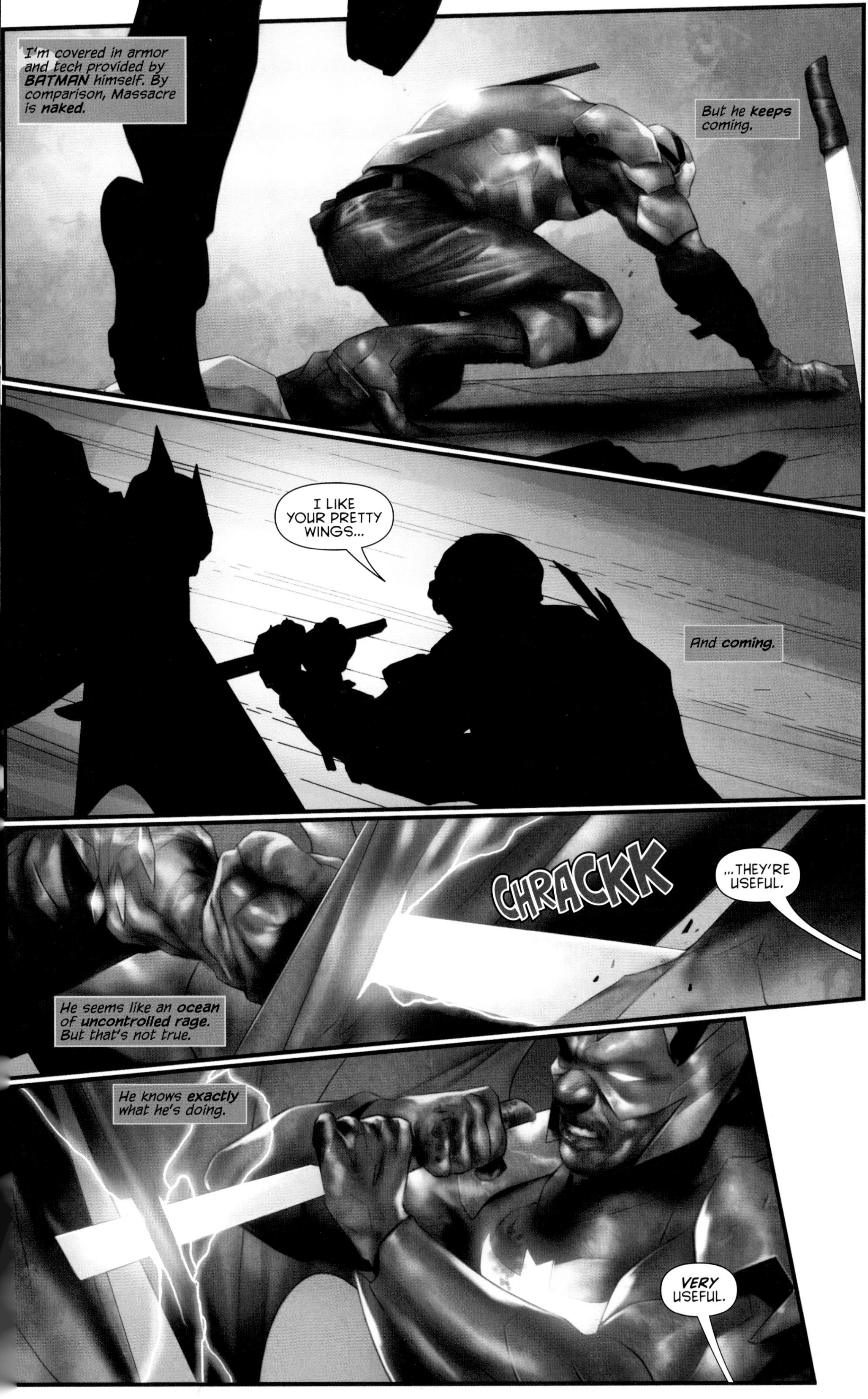
I'm covered in armor and tech provided by BATMAN himself. By comparison, Massacre is naked.
But he keeps coming.
I LIKE YOUR PRETTY WINGS...
And coming.
CHRACKK
...THEY'RE USEFUL.
He seems like an ocean of uncontrolled rage. But that's not true.
He knows exactly what he's doing.
VERY USEFUL.

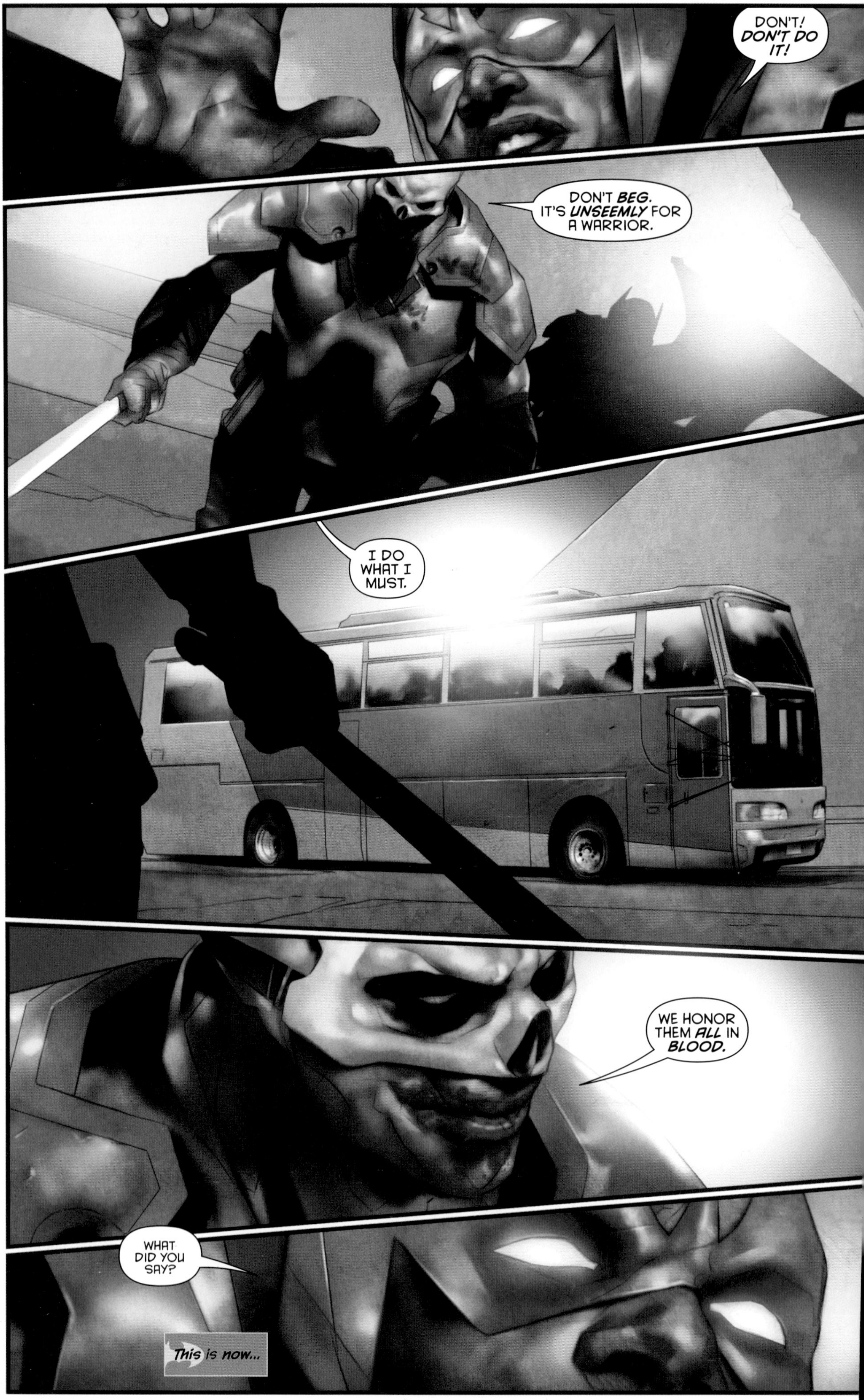
DON'T! DON'T DO IT!
DON'T BEG. IT'S UNSEEMLY FOR A WARRIOR.
I DO WHAT I MUST.
WE HONOR THEM ALL IN BLOOD.
WHAT DID YOU SAY?
This is now...

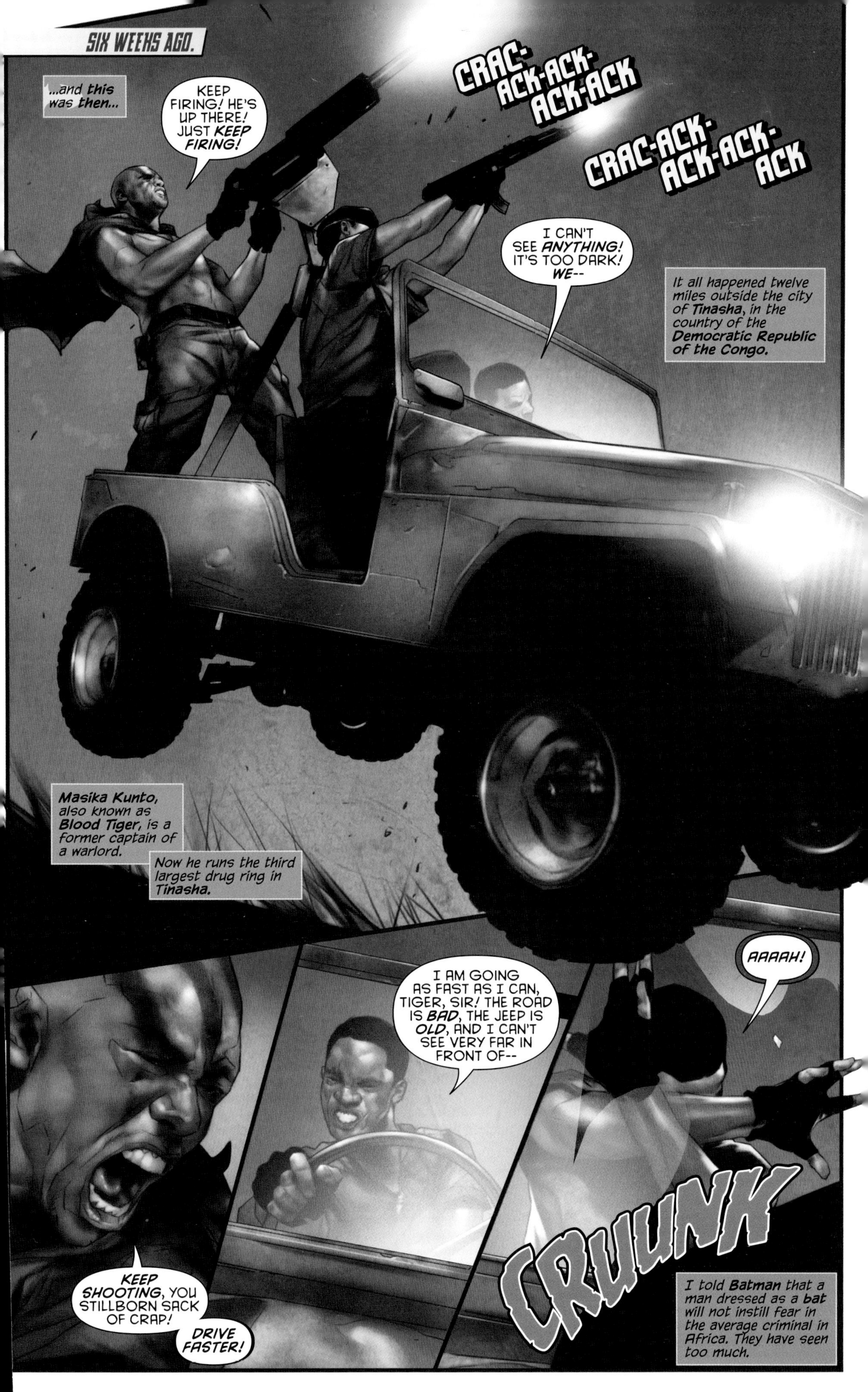
SIX WEEKS AGO.
...and this was then...
KEEP FIRING! HE'S UP THERE! JUST KEEP FIRING!
CRAC-ACK-ACK-ACK-ACK
CRAC-ACK-ACK-ACK-ACK
I CAN'T SEE ANYTHING! IT'S TOO DARK! WE--
It all happened twelve miles outside the city of Tinasha, in the country of the Democratic Republic of the Congo.
Masika Kunto, also known as Blood Tiger, is a former captain of a warlord.
Now he runs the third largest drug ring in Tinasha.
KEEP SHOOTING, YOU STILLBORN SACK OF CRAP!
DRIVE FASTER!
I AM GOING AS FAST AS I CAN, TIGER, SIR! THE ROAD IS BAD, THE JEEP IS OLD, AND I CAN'T SEE VERY FAR IN FRONT OF--
AAAAH!
CRUUNK
I told Batman that a man dressed as a bat will not instill fear in the average criminal in Africa. They have seen too much.

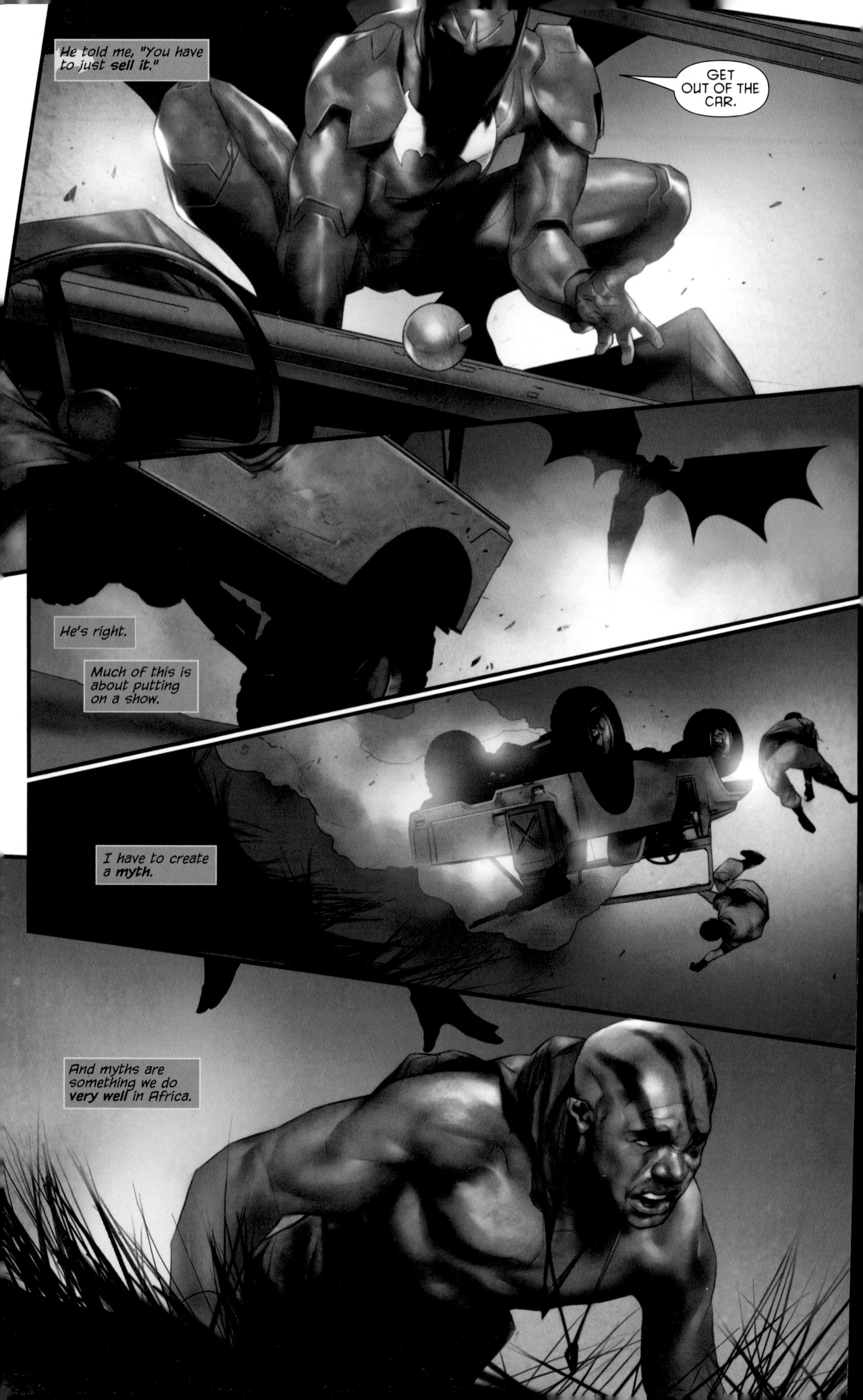
He told me, "You have to just **sell it.**"
GET OUT OF THE CAR.
He's right.
Much of this is about putting on a show.
I have to create a **myth**.
And myths are something we do **very well** in Africa.

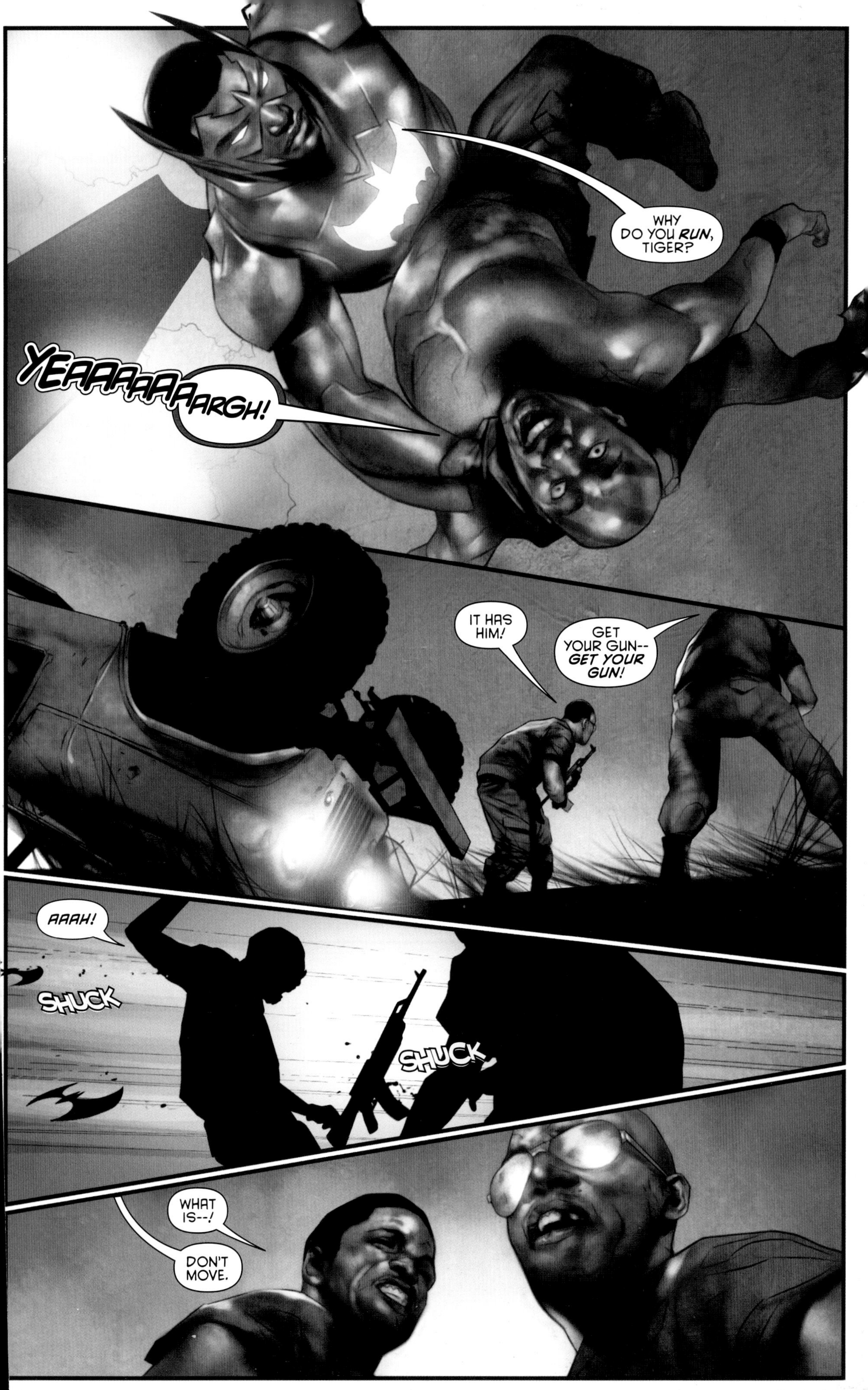
WHY DO YOU RUN, TIGER?
YEAAAAAAAARGH!
IT HAS HIM!
GET YOUR GUN-- GET YOUR GUN!
AAAH!
SHUCK
SHUCK
WHAT IS--!
DON'T MOVE.

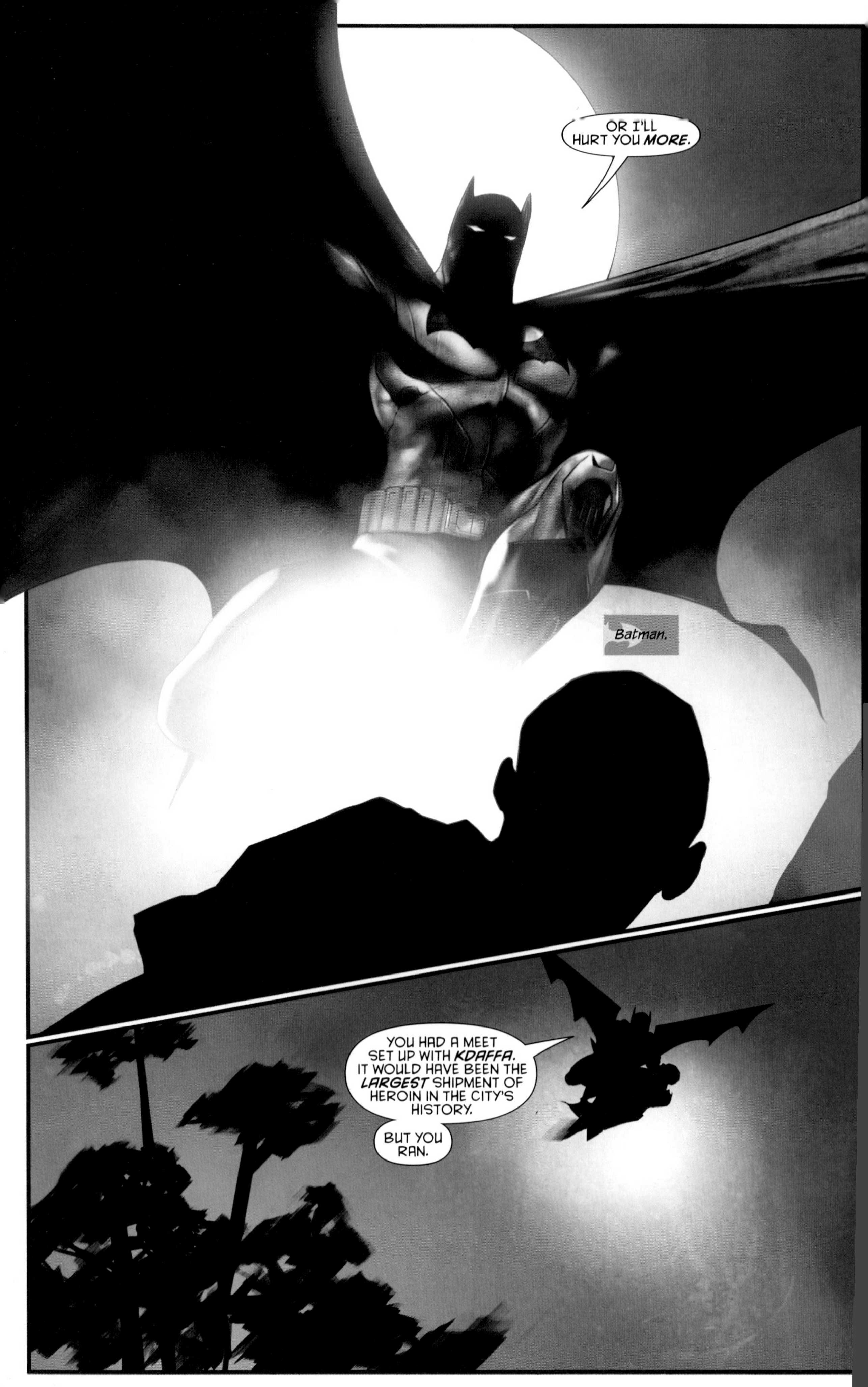
OR I'LL HURT YOU MORE.
Batman.
YOU HAD A MEET SET UP WITH KDAFFA. IT WOULD HAVE BEEN THE LARGEST SHIPMENT OF HEROIN IN THE CITY'S HISTORY.
BUT YOU RAN.

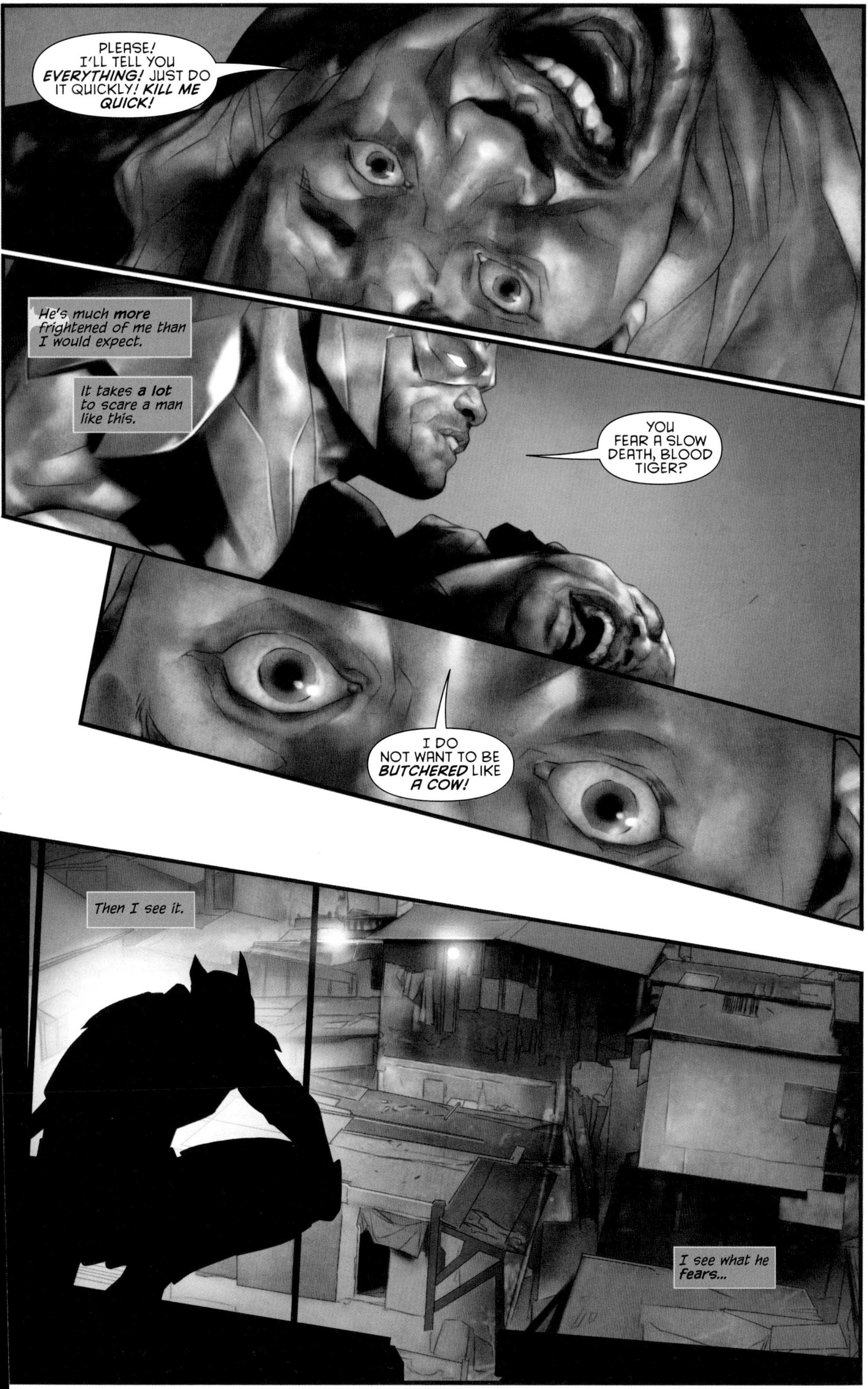
PLEASE! I'LL TELL YOU EVERYTHING! JUST DO IT QUICKLY! KILL ME QUICK!
He's much more frightened of me than I would expect.
It takes a lot to scare a man like this.
YOU FEAR A SLOW DEATH, BLOOD TIGER?
I DO NOT WANT TO BE BUTCHERED LIKE A COW!
Then I see it.
I see what he fears...

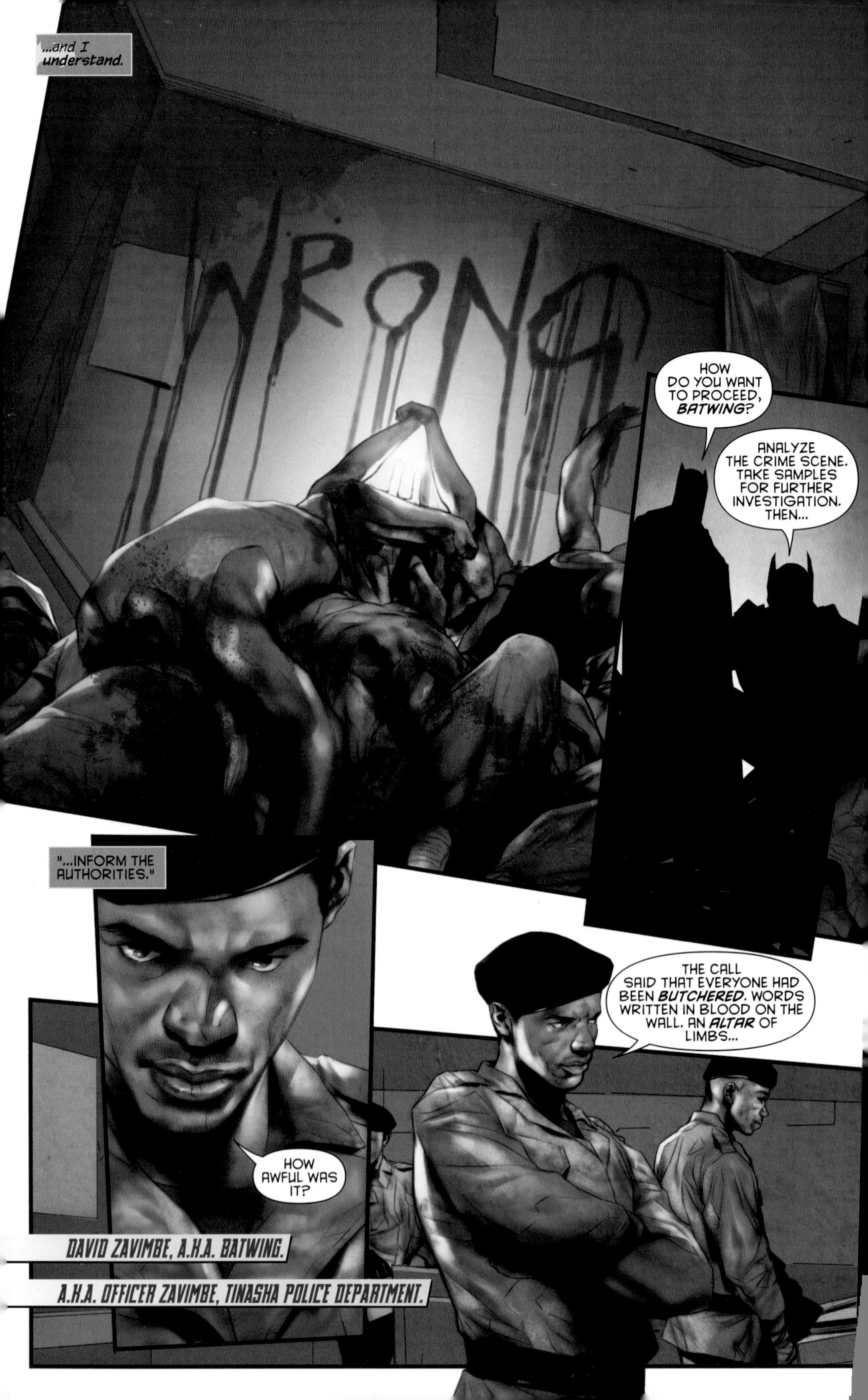
...and I understand.
WRONG
HOW DO YOU WANT TO PROCEED, *BATWING*?
ANALYZE THE CRIME SCENE. TAKE SAMPLES FOR FURTHER INVESTIGATION. THEN...
"...INFORM THE AUTHORITIES."
THE CALL SAID THAT EVERYONE HAD BEEN *BUTCHERED*. WORDS WRITTEN IN BLOOD ON THE WALL. AN *ALTAR* OF LIMBS...
HOW AWFUL WAS IT?
DAVID ZAVIMBE, A.K.A. BATWING.
A.K.A. OFFICER ZAVIMBE, TINASHA POLICE DEPARTMENT.

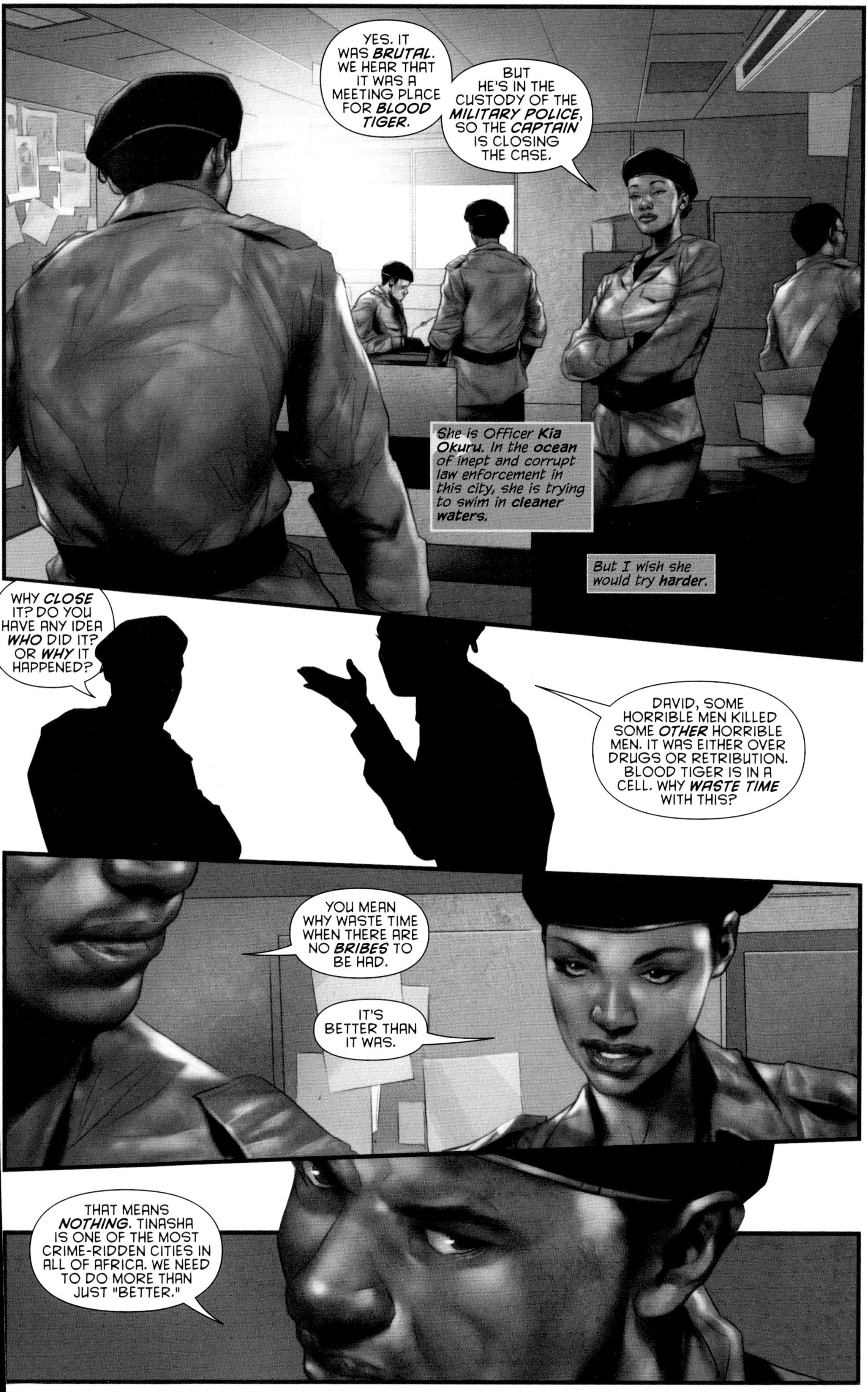
YES. IT WAS BRUTAL. WE HEAR THAT IT WAS A MEETING PLACE FOR BLOOD TIGER.
BUT HE'S IN THE CUSTODY OF THE MILITARY POLICE, SO THE CAPTAIN IS CLOSING THE CASE.
She is Officer Kia Okuru. In the ocean of inept and corrupt law enforcement in this city, she is trying to swim in cleaner waters.
But I wish she would try harder.
WHY CLOSE IT? DO YOU HAVE ANY IDEA WHO DID IT? OR WHY IT HAPPENED?
DAVID, SOME HORRIBLE MEN KILLED SOME OTHER HORRIBLE MEN. IT WAS EITHER OVER DRUGS OR RETRIBUTION. BLOOD TIGER IS IN A CELL. WHY WASTE TIME WITH THIS?
YOU MEAN WHY WASTE TIME WHEN THERE ARE NO BRIBES TO BE HAD.
IT'S BETTER THAN IT WAS.
THAT MEANS NOTHING. TINASHA IS ONE OF THE MOST CRIME-RIDDEN CITIES IN ALL OF AFRICA. WE NEED TO DO MORE THAN JUST "BETTER."

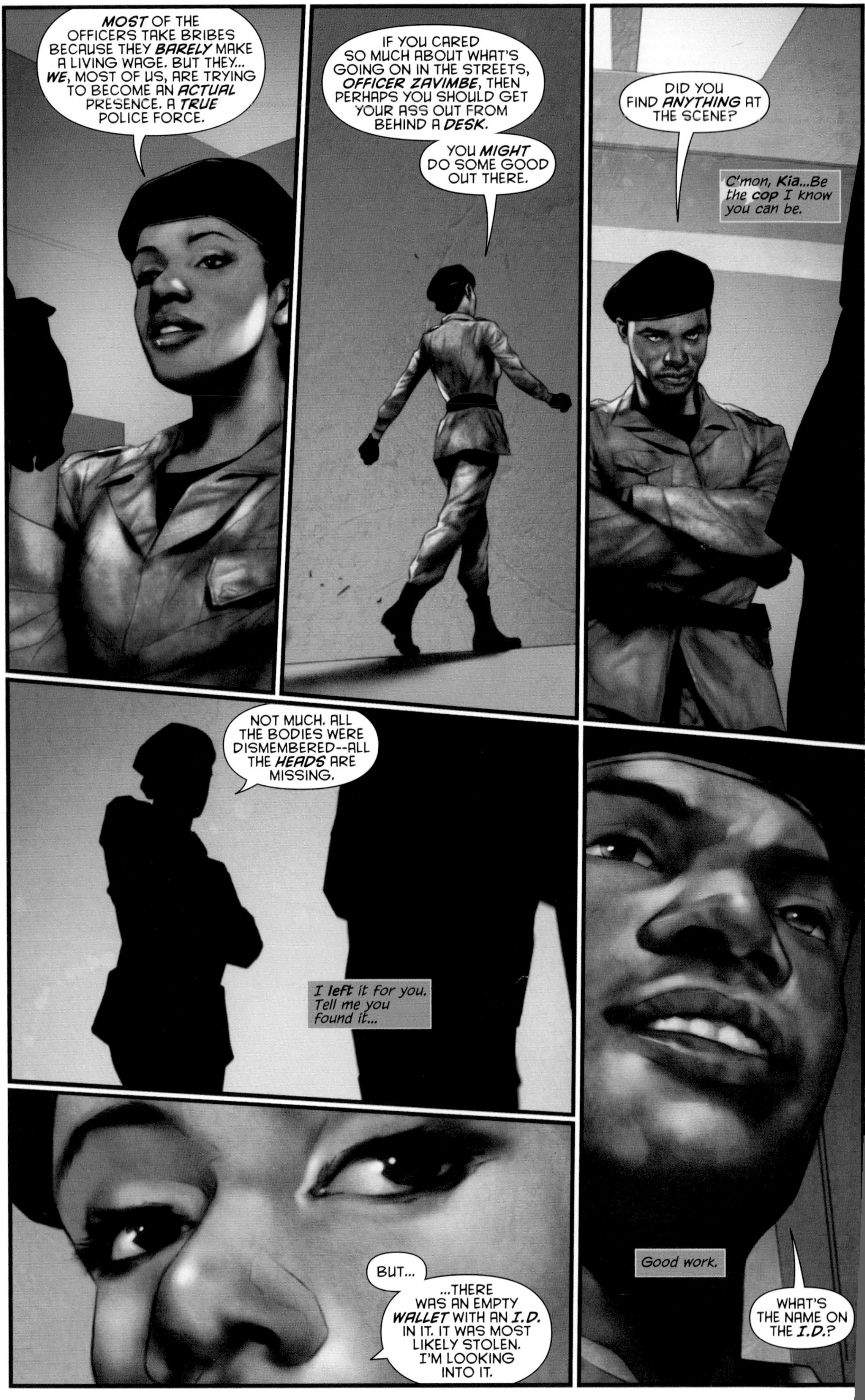
MOST OF THE OFFICERS TAKE BRIBES BECAUSE THEY BARELY MAKE A LIVING WAGE. BUT THEY... WE, MOST OF US, ARE TRYING TO BECOME AN ACTUAL PRESENCE. A TRUE POLICE FORCE.
IF YOU CARED SO MUCH ABOUT WHAT'S GOING ON IN THE STREETS, OFFICER ZAVIMBE, THEN PERHAPS YOU SHOULD GET YOUR ASS OUT FROM BEHIND A DESK.
YOU MIGHT DO SOME GOOD OUT THERE.
DID YOU FIND ANYTHING AT THE SCENE?
C'mon, Kia...Be the cop I know you can be.
NOT MUCH. ALL THE BODIES WERE DISMEMBERED--ALL THE HEADS ARE MISSING.
I left it for you. Tell me you found it...
BUT...
...THERE WAS AN EMPTY WALLET WITH AN I.D. IN IT. IT WAS MOST LIKELY STOLEN. I'M LOOKING INTO IT.
Good work.
WHAT'S THE NAME ON THE I.D.?

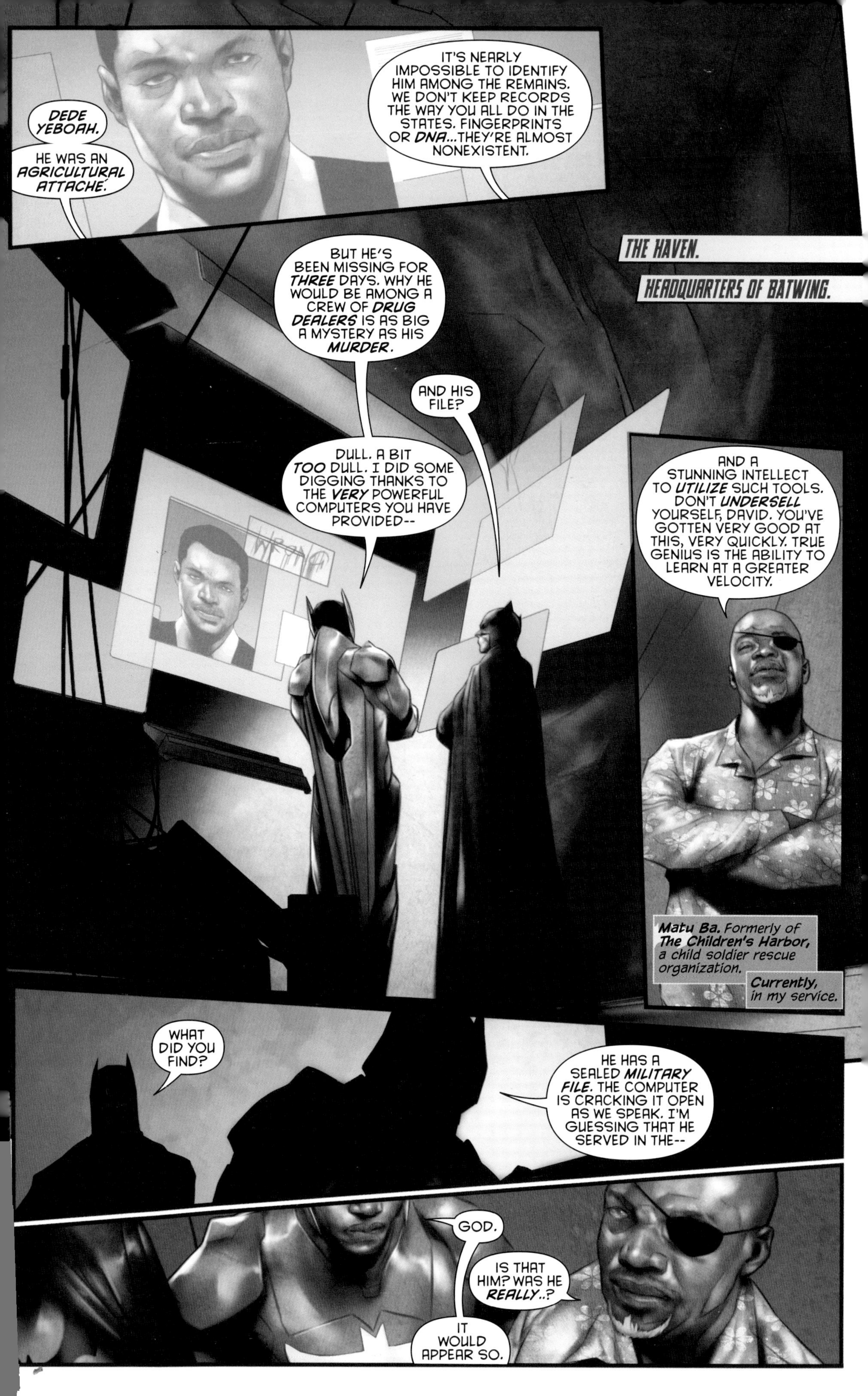
DEDE YEBOAH.
HE WAS AN AGRICULTURAL ATTACHÉ.
IT'S NEARLY IMPOSSIBLE TO IDENTIFY HIM AMONG THE REMAINS. WE DON'T KEEP RECORDS THE WAY YOU ALL DO IN THE STATES. FINGERPRINTS OR DNA...THEY'RE ALMOST NONEXISTENT.
THE HAVEN.
HEADQUARTERS OF BATWING.
BUT HE'S BEEN MISSING FOR THREE DAYS. WHY HE WOULD BE AMONG A CREW OF DRUG DEALERS IS AS BIG A MYSTERY AS HIS MURDER.
AND HIS FILE?
DULL. A BIT TOO DULL. I DID SOME DIGGING THANKS TO THE VERY POWERFUL COMPUTERS YOU HAVE PROVIDED--
AND A STUNNING INTELLECT TO UTILIZE SUCH TOOLS. DON'T UNDERSELL YOURSELF, DAVID. YOU'VE GOTTEN VERY GOOD AT THIS, VERY QUICKLY. TRUE GENIUS IS THE ABILITY TO LEARN AT A GREATER VELOCITY.
Matu Ba. Formerly of The Children's Harbor, a child soldier rescue organization.
Currently, in my service.
WHAT DID YOU FIND?
HE HAS A SEALED MILITARY FILE. THE COMPUTER IS CRACKING IT OPEN AS WE SPEAK. I'M GUESSING THAT HE SERVED IN THE--
GOD.
IS THAT HIM? WAS HE REALLY..?
IT WOULD APPEAR SO.

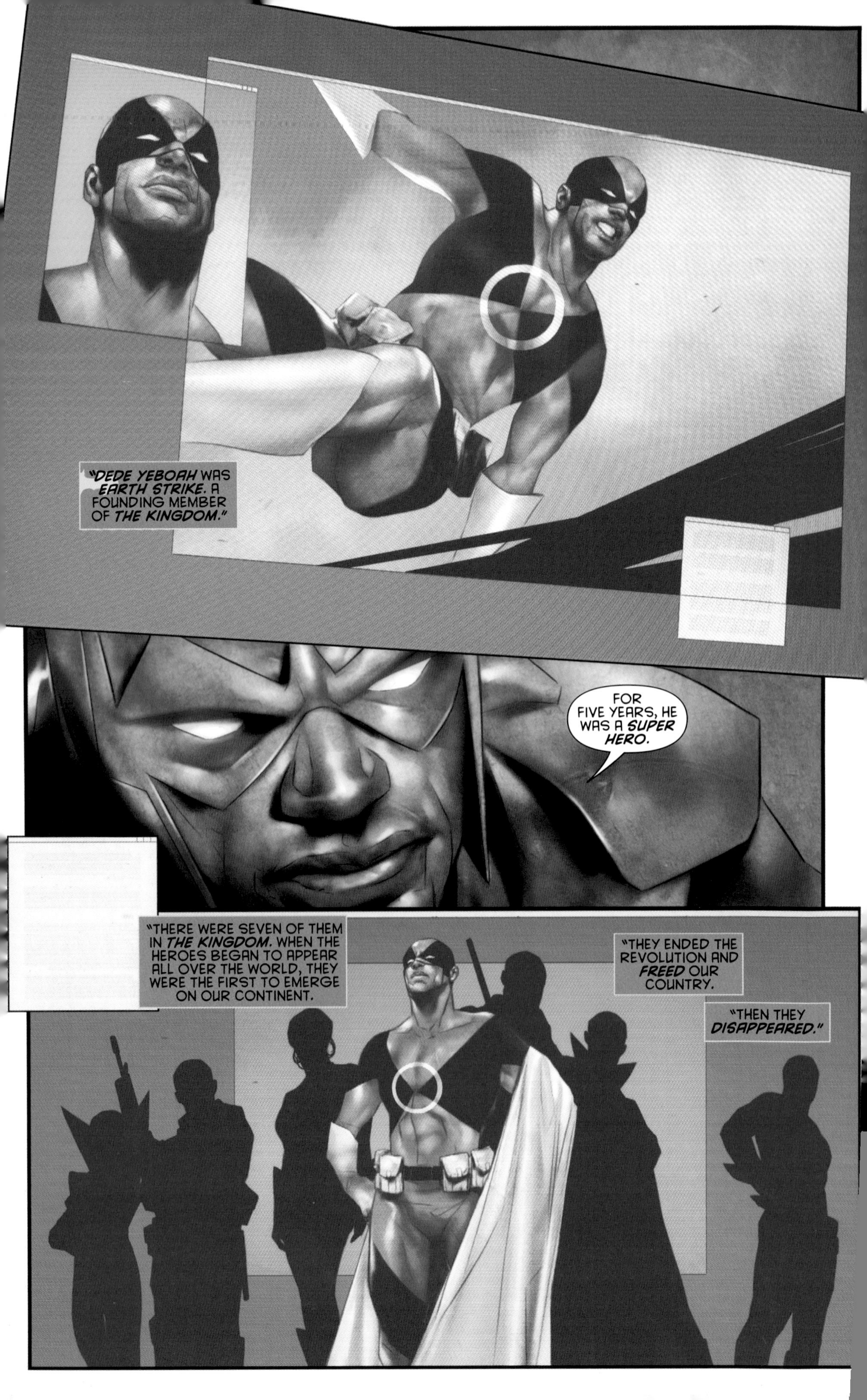

"DEDE YEBOAH WAS EARTH STRIKE. A FOUNDING MEMBER OF THE KINGDOM."
FOR FIVE YEARS, HE WAS A SUPER HERO.
"THERE WERE SEVEN OF THEM IN THE KINGDOM. WHEN THE HEROES BEGAN TO APPEAR ALL OVER THE WORLD, THEY WERE THE FIRST TO EMERGE ON OUR CONTINENT.
"THEY ENDED THE REVOLUTION AND FREED OUR COUNTRY.
"THEN THEY DISAPPEARED."

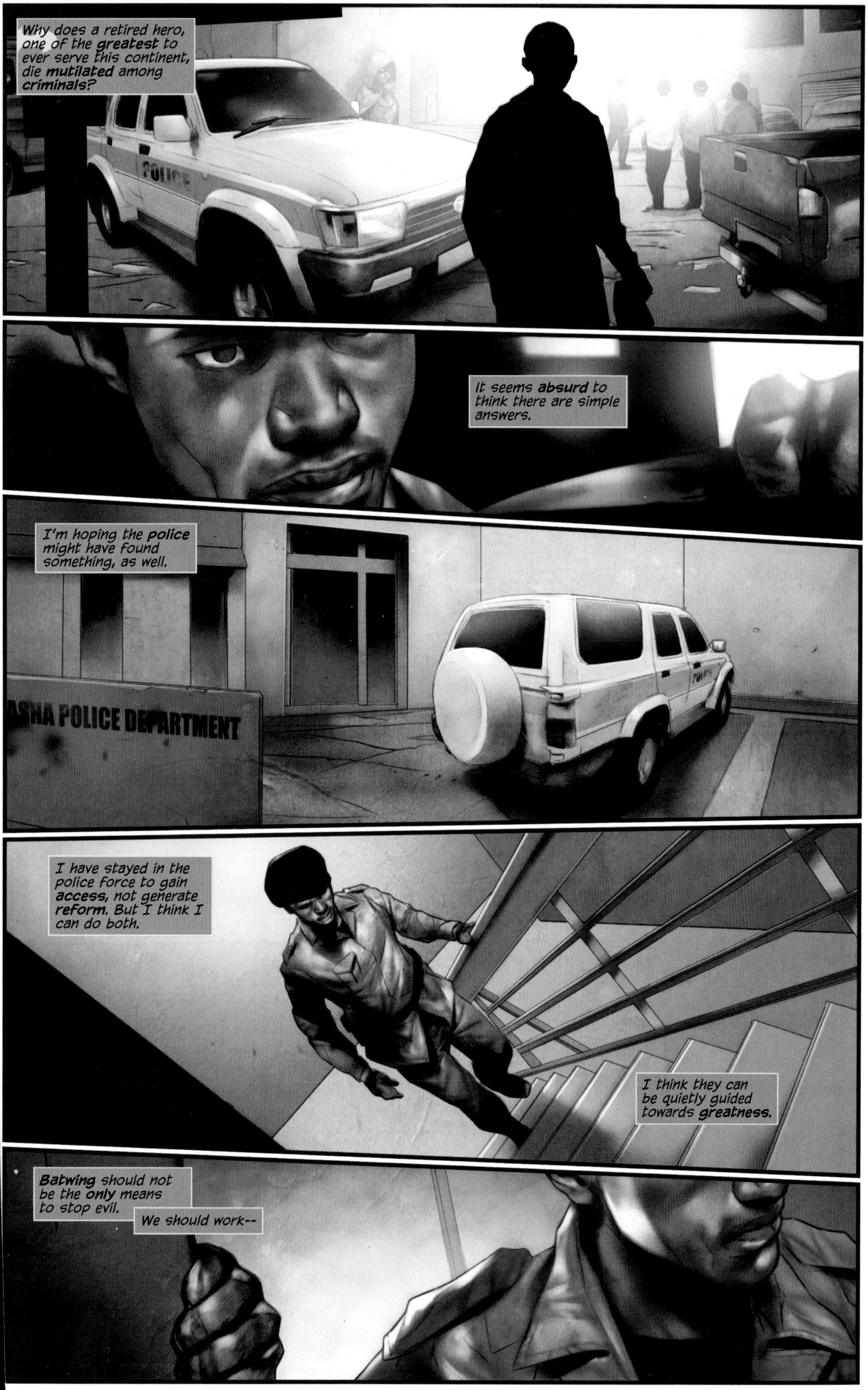
Why does a retired hero, one of the greatest to ever serve this continent, die mutilated among criminals?
POLICE
It seems absurd to think there are simple answers.
I'm hoping the police might have found something, as well.
ASHA POLICE DEPARTMENT
I have stayed in the police force to gain access, not generate reform. But I think I can do both.
I think they can be quietly guided towards greatness.
Batwing should not be the only means to stop evil.
We should work--

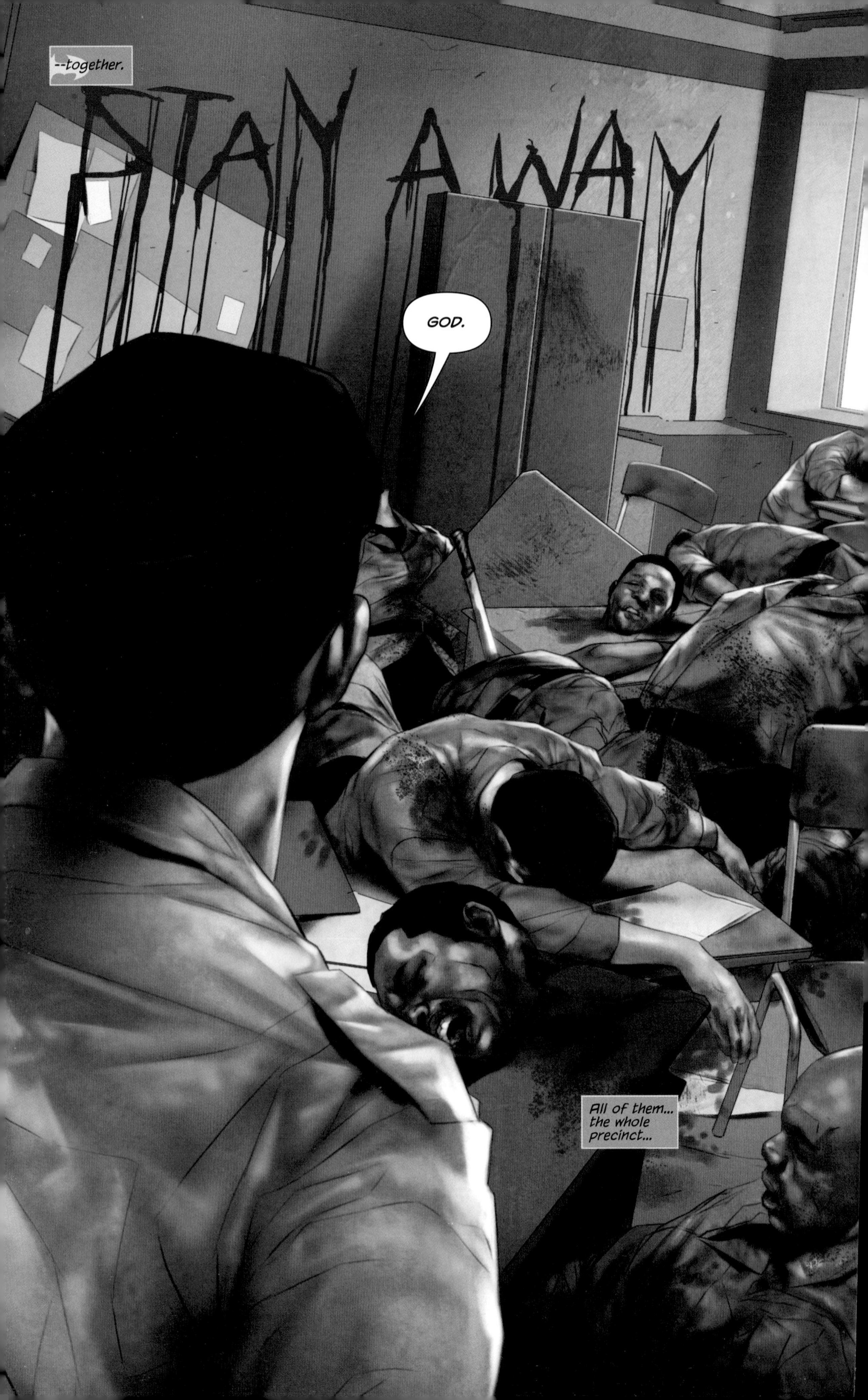
--together.
STAY AWAY
GOD.
All of them... the whole precinct...

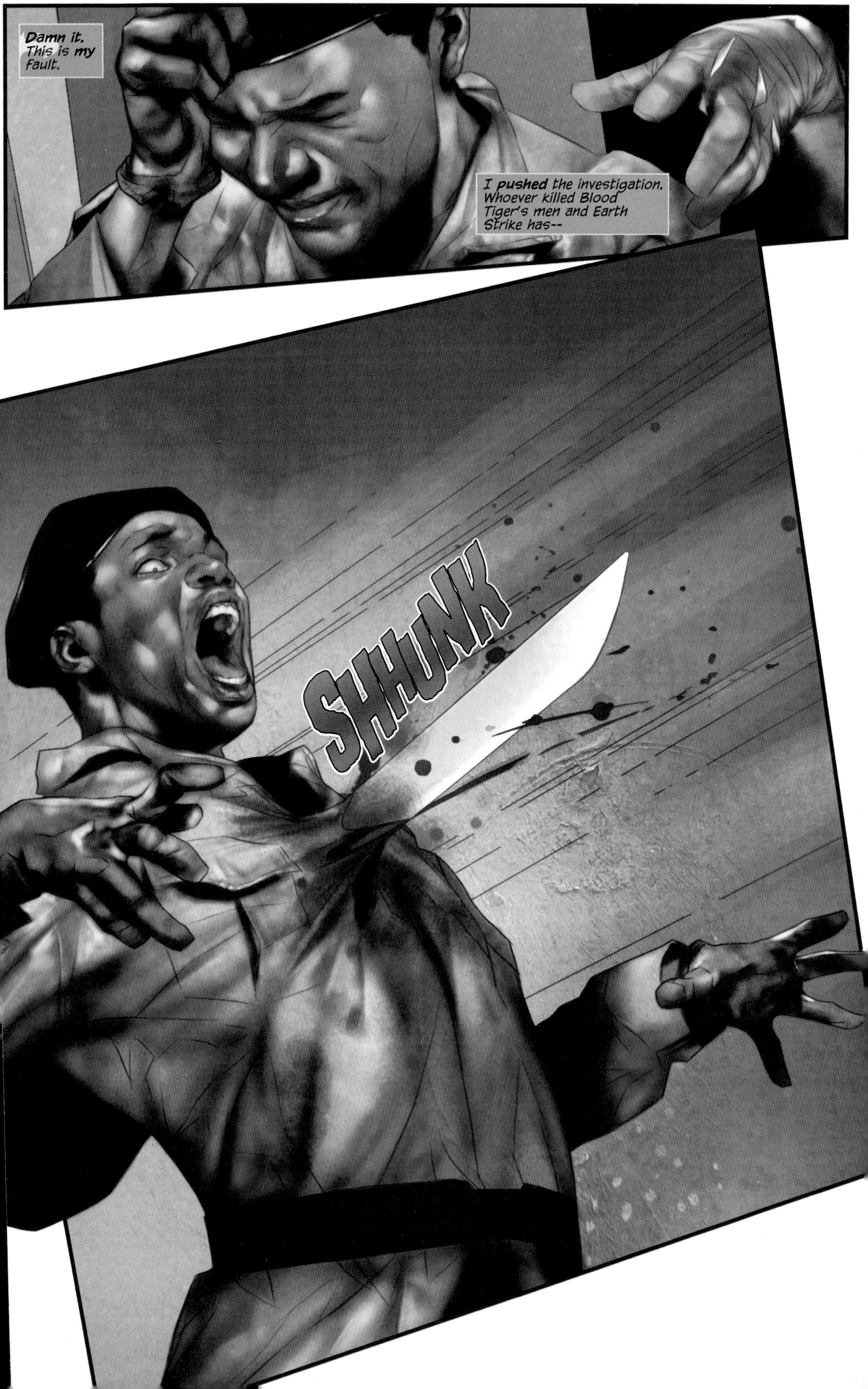
Damn it. This is my fault.
I pushed the investigation. Whoever killed Blood Tiger's men and Earth Strike has--
SHHUNK

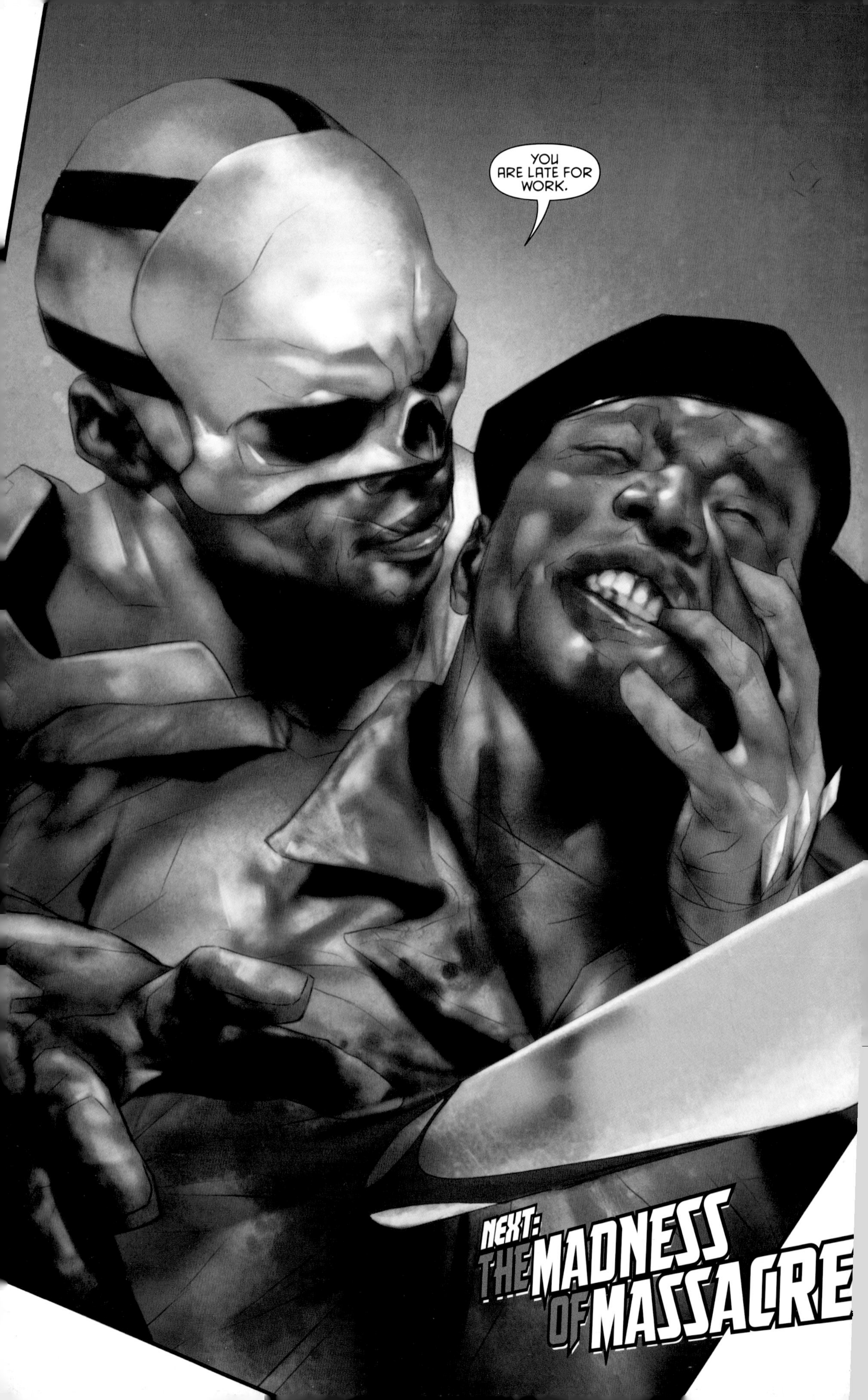
YOU ARE LATE FOR WORK.
NEXT: THE MADNESS OF MASSACRE

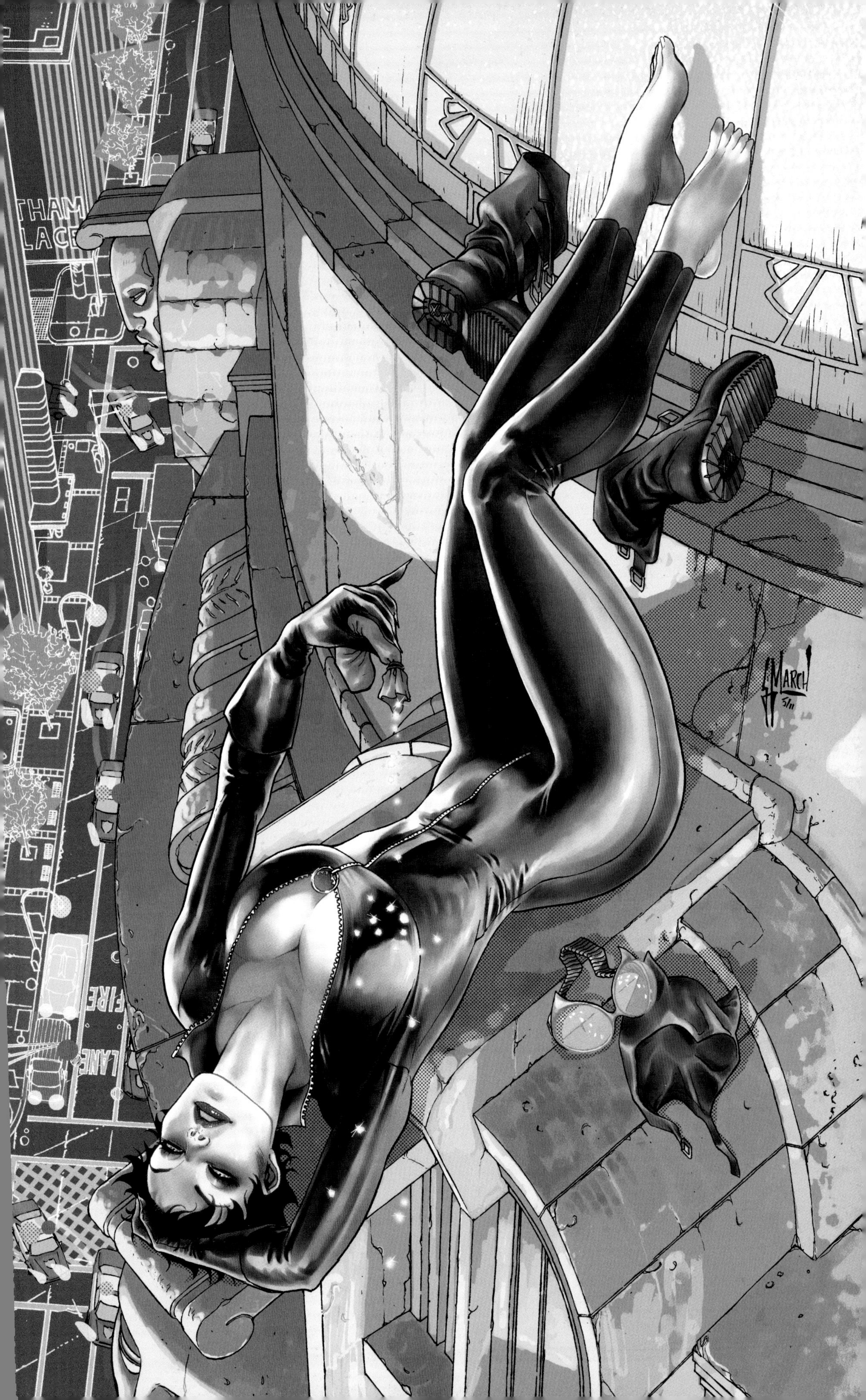

FIRE
LANE

CATWOMAN

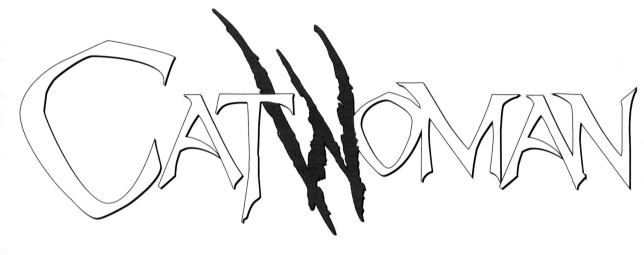

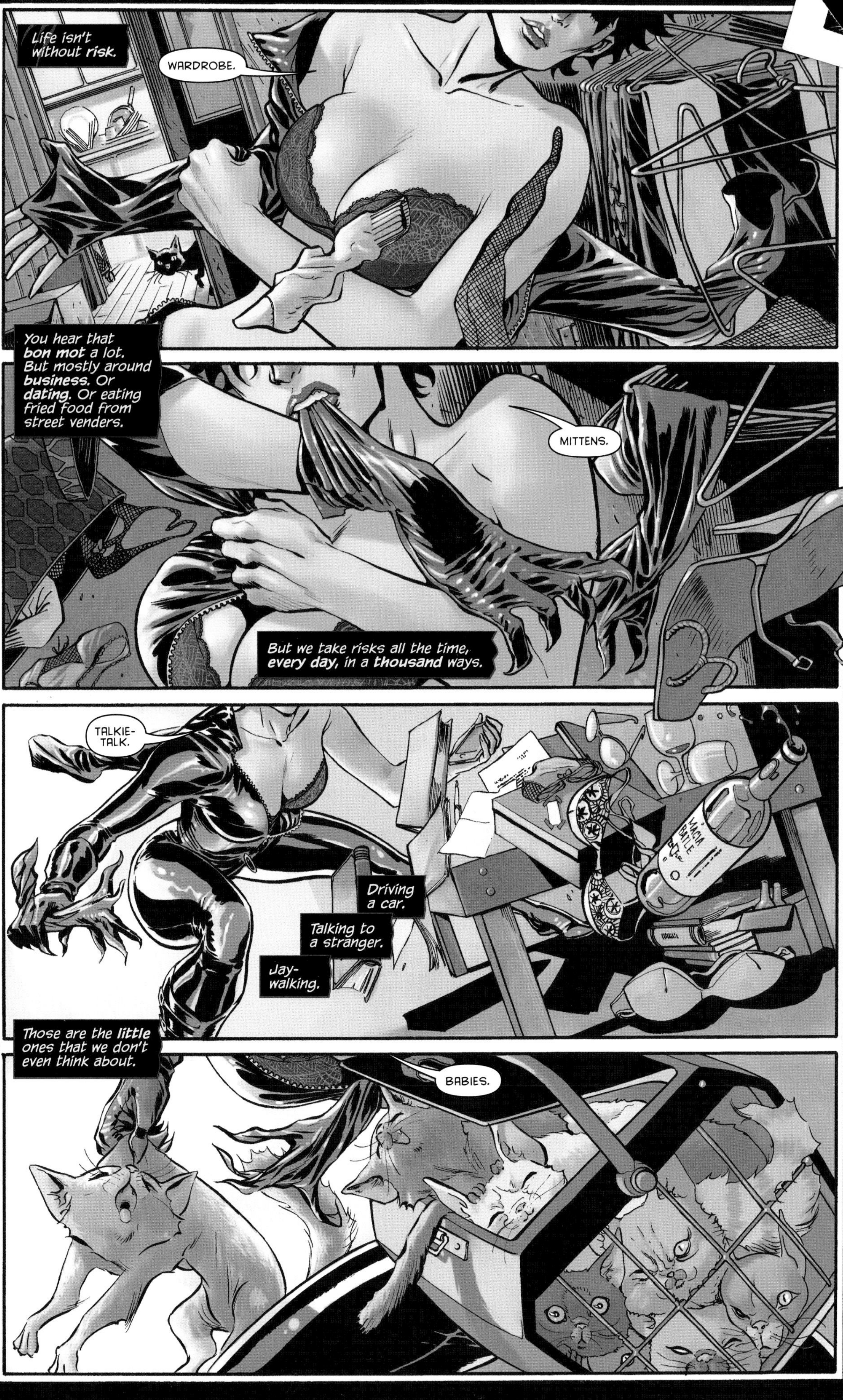

Life isn't without risk.
WARDROBE.
You hear that bon mot a lot. But mostly around business. Or dating. Or eating fried food from street venders.
MITTENS.
But we take risks all the time, every day, in a thousand ways.
TALKIE-TALK.
Driving a car.
Talking to a stranger.
Jay-walking.
Those are the little ones that we don't even think about.
BABIES.

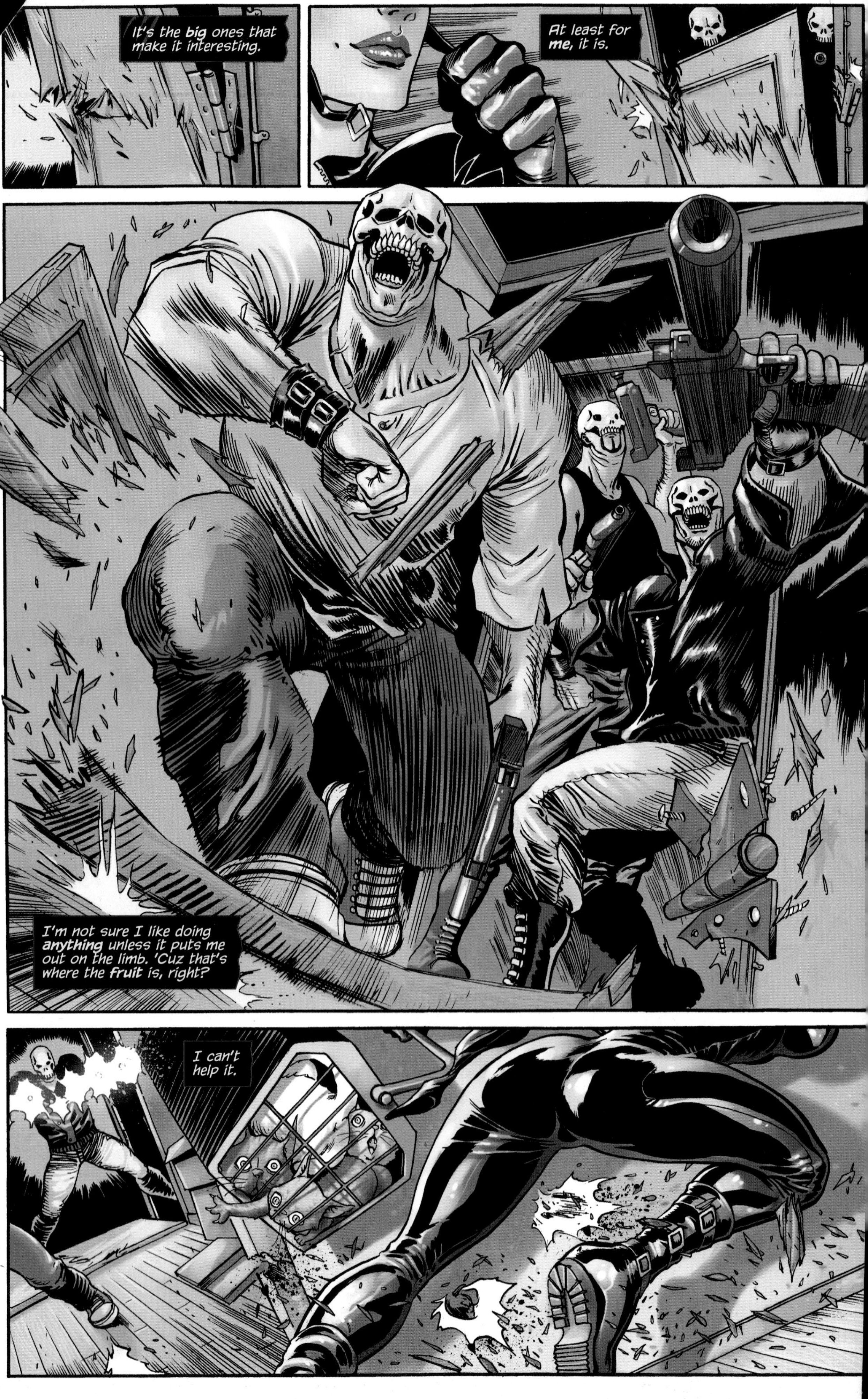

It's the big ones that make it interesting.
At least for me, it is.
I'm not sure I like doing anything unless it puts me out on the limb. 'Cuz that's where the fruit is, right?
I can't help it.

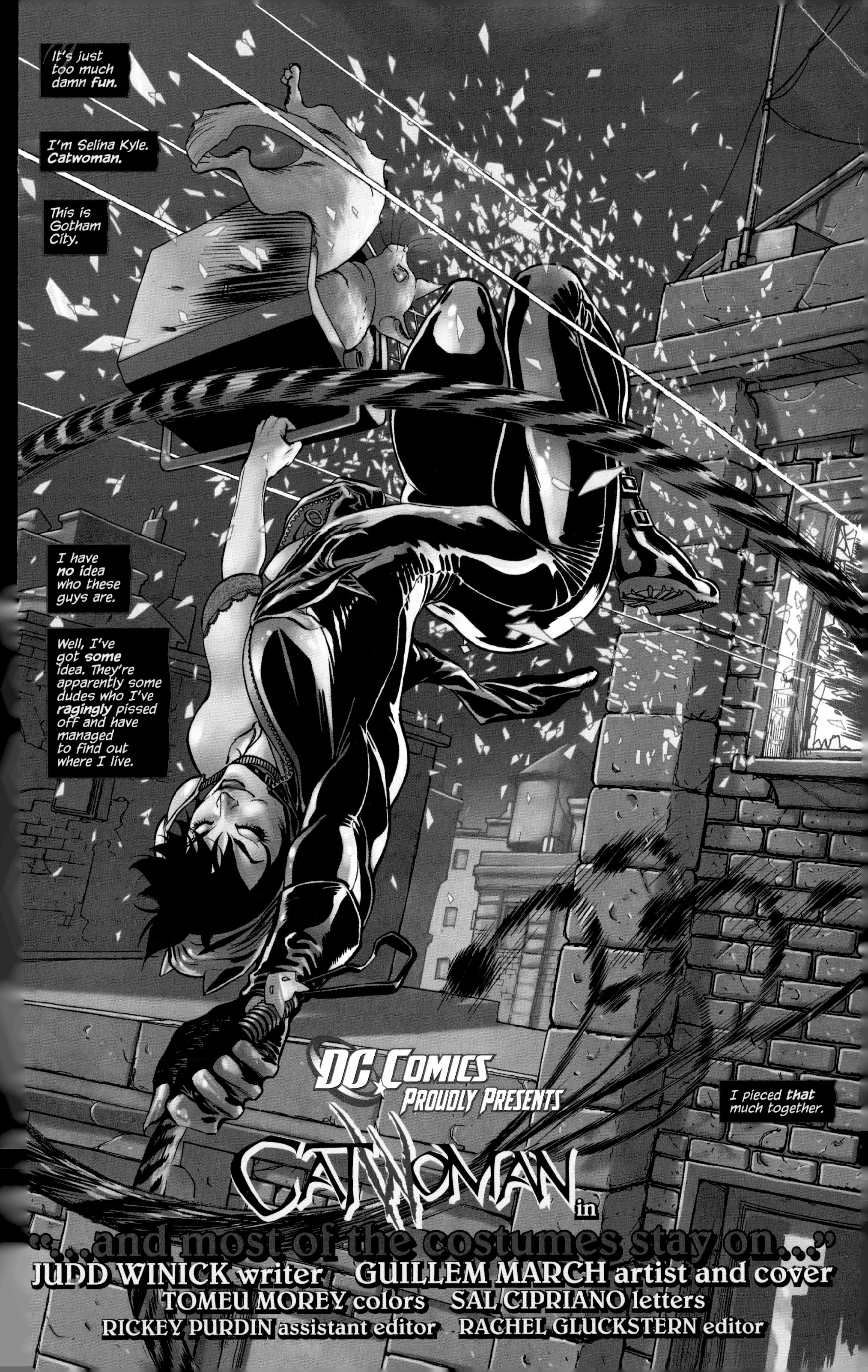

It's just too much damn fun.
I'm Selina Kyle. Catwoman.
This is Gotham City.
I have no idea who these guys are.
Well, I've got some idea. They're apparently some dudes who I've ragingly pissed off and have managed to find out where I live.
I pieced that much together.
DC COMICS PROUDLY PRESENTS
CATWOMAN in
"...and most of the costumes stay on..."
JUDD WINICK writer GUILLEM MARCH artist and cover
TOMEU MOREY colors SAL CIPRIANO letters
RICKEY PURDIN assistant editor RACHEL GLUCKSTERN editor

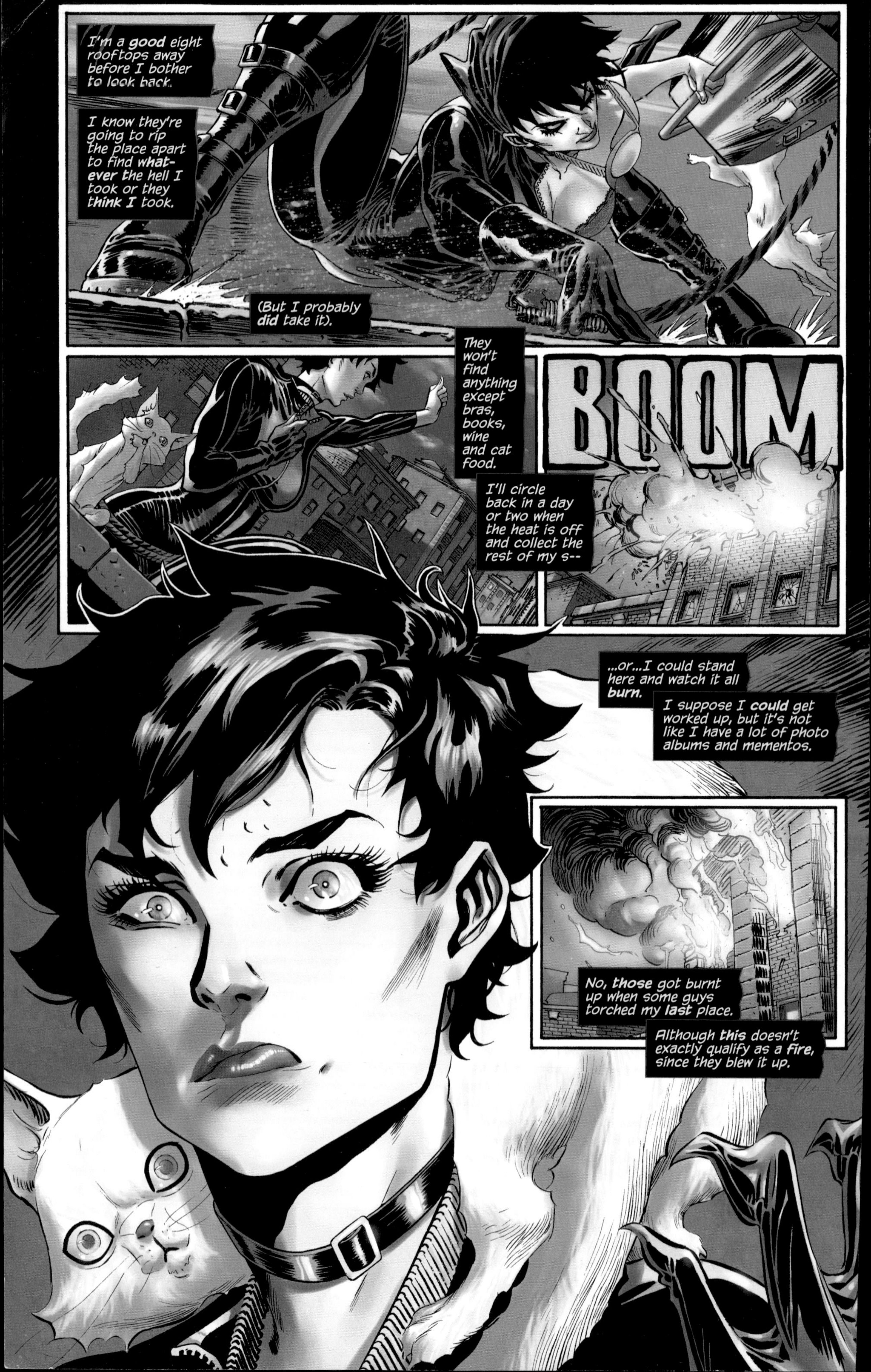

I'm a good eight rooftops away before I bother to look back.
I know they're going to rip the place apart to find whatever the hell I took or they think I took.
(But I probably did take it).
They won't find anything except bras, books, wine and cat food.
BOOM
I'll circle back in a day or two when the heat is off and collect the rest of my s--
...or...I could stand here and watch it all burn.
I suppose I could get worked up, but it's not like I have a lot of photo albums and mementos.
No, those got burnt up when some guys torched my last place.
Although this doesn't exactly qualify as a fire, since they blew it up.

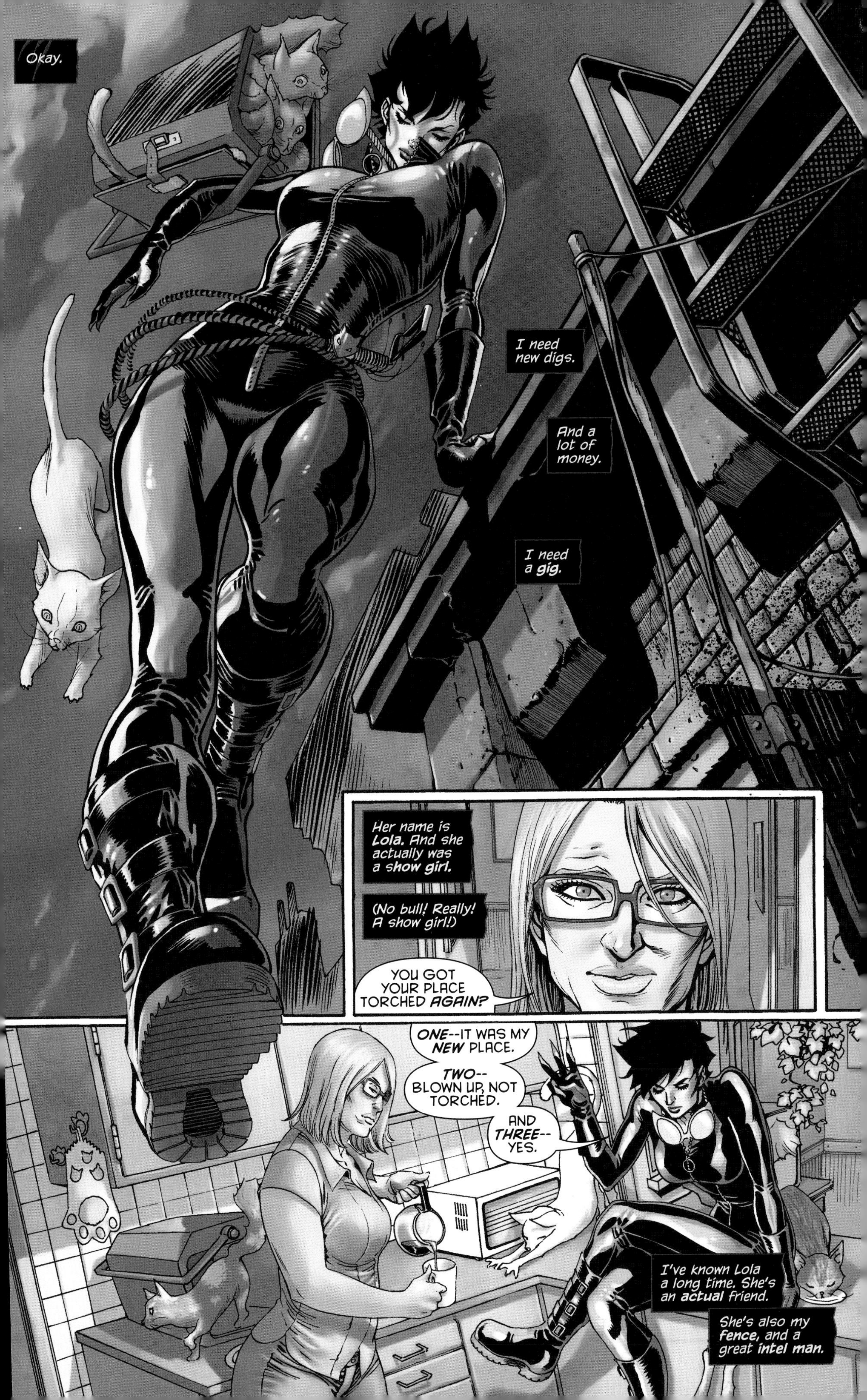

Okay.
I need new digs.
And a lot of money.
I need a gig.
Her name is Lola. And she actually was a show girl.
(No bull! Really! A show girl!)
YOU GOT YOUR PLACE TORCHED AGAIN?
ONE--IT WAS MY NEW PLACE.
TWO--BLOWN UP, NOT TORCHED.
AND THREE--YES.
I've known Lola a long time. She's an actual friend.
She's also my fence, and a great intel man.

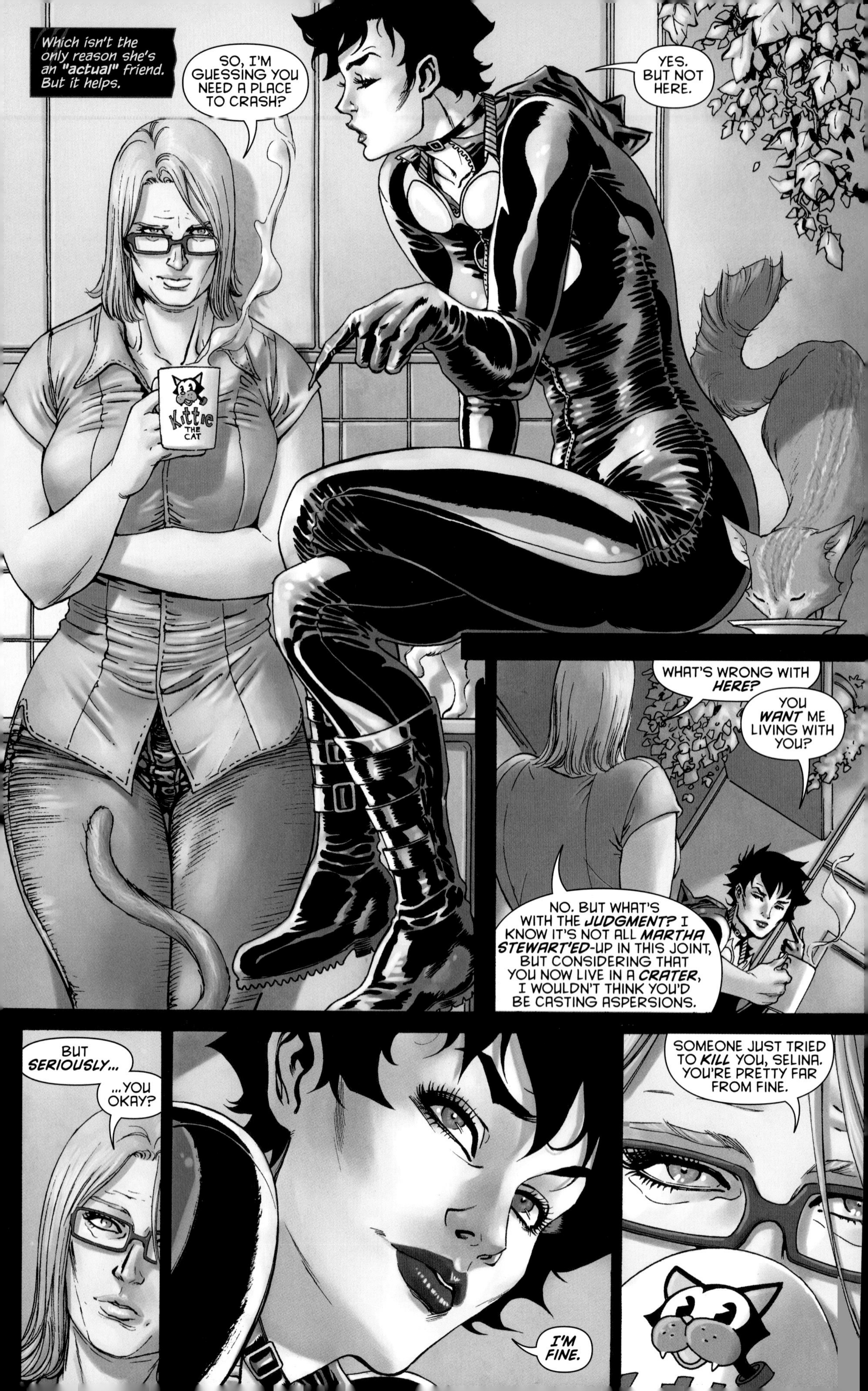

Which isn't the only reason she's an "actual" friend. But it helps.
SO, I'M GUESSING YOU NEED A PLACE TO CRASH?
YES. BUT NOT HERE.
Kittie THE CAT
WHAT'S WRONG WITH HERE?
YOU WANT ME LIVING WITH YOU?
NO. BUT WHAT'S WITH THE JUDGMENT? I KNOW IT'S NOT ALL MARTHA STEWART'ED-UP IN THIS JOINT, BUT CONSIDERING THAT YOU NOW LIVE IN A CRATER, I WOULDN'T THINK YOU'D BE CASTING ASPERSIONS.
BUT SERIOUSLY...
...YOU OKAY?
I'M FINE.
SOMEONE JUST TRIED TO KILL YOU, SELINA. YOU'RE PRETTY FAR FROM FINE.

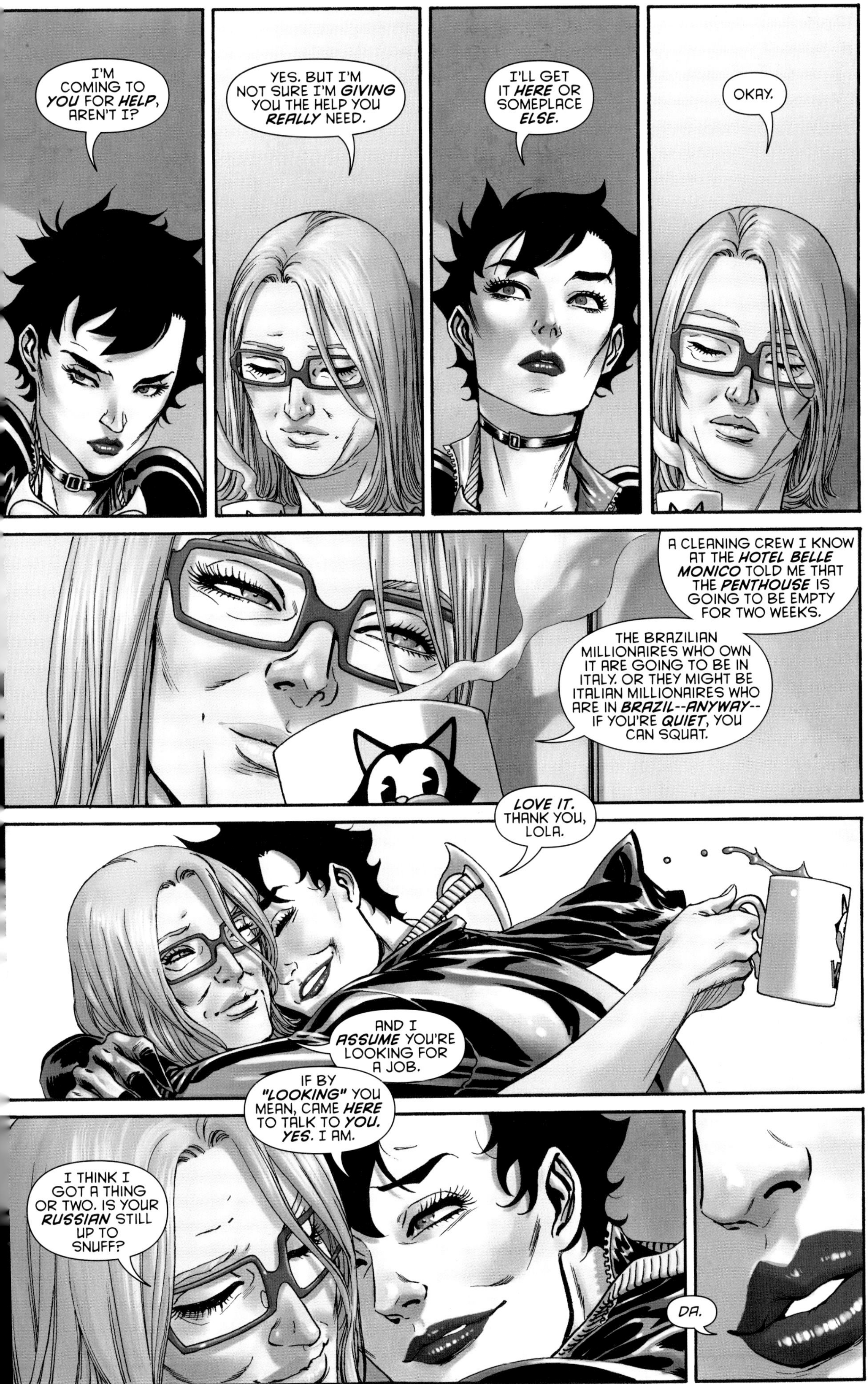
I'M COMING TO YOU FOR HELP, AREN'T I?
YES. BUT I'M NOT SURE I'M GIVING YOU THE HELP YOU REALLY NEED.
I'LL GET IT HERE OR SOMEPLACE ELSE.
OKAY.
A CLEANING CREW I KNOW AT THE HOTEL BELLE MONICO TOLD ME THAT THE PENTHOUSE IS GOING TO BE EMPTY FOR TWO WEEKS.
THE BRAZILIAN MILLIONAIRES WHO OWN IT ARE GOING TO BE IN ITALY. OR THEY MIGHT BE ITALIAN MILLIONAIRES WHO ARE IN BRAZIL--ANYWAY--IF YOU'RE QUIET, YOU CAN SQUAT.
LOVE IT. THANK YOU, LOLA.
AND I ASSUME YOU'RE LOOKING FOR A JOB.
IF BY "LOOKING" YOU MEAN, CAME HERE TO TALK TO YOU. YES. I AM.
I THINK I GOT A THING OR TWO. IS YOUR RUSSIAN STILL UP TO SNUFF?
DA.

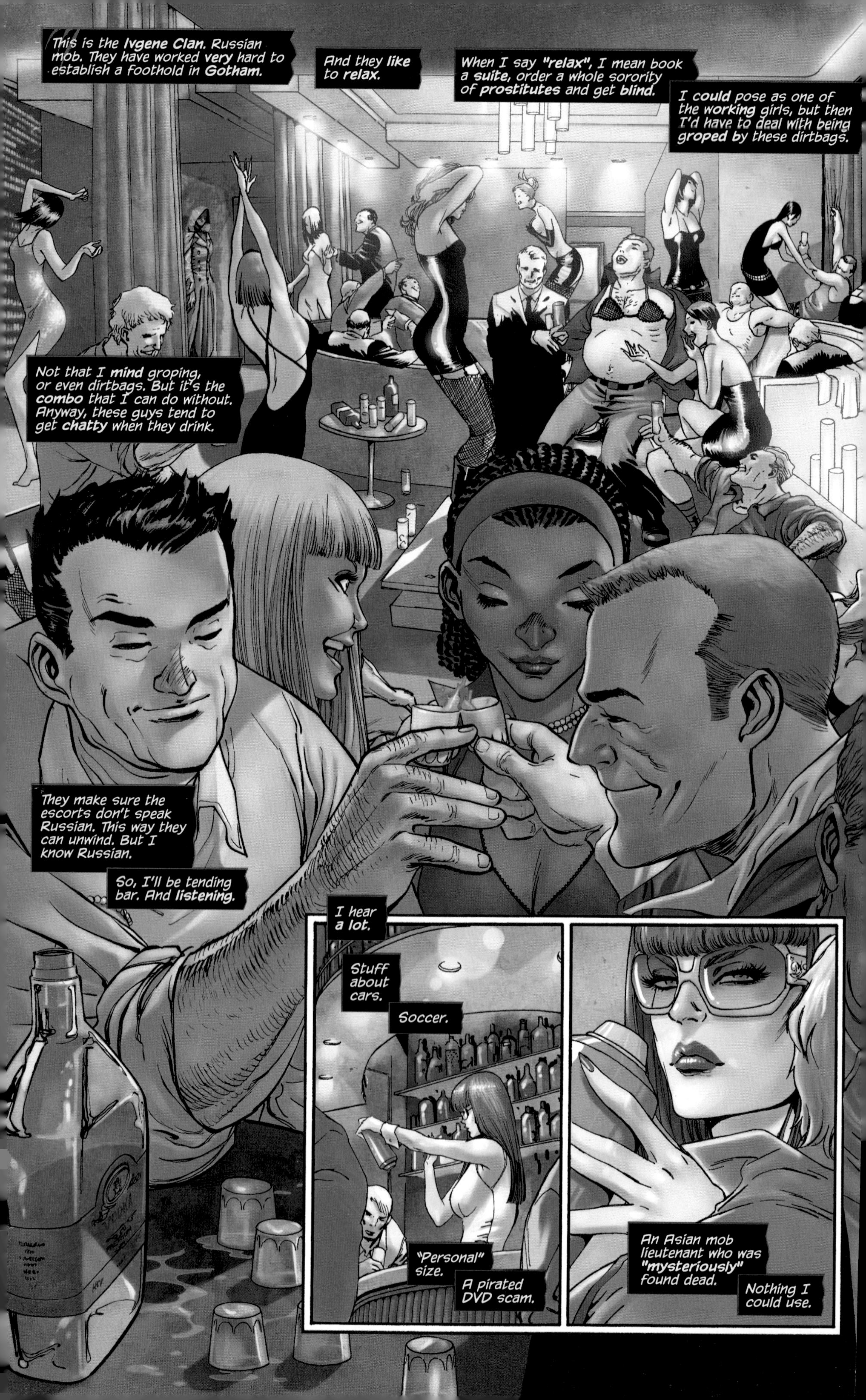
This is the Ivgene Clan. Russian mob. They have worked very hard to establish a foothold in Gotham.
And they like to relax.
When I say "relax", I mean book a suite, order a whole sorority of prostitutes and get blind.
I could pose as one of the working girls, but then I'd have to deal with being groped by these dirtbags.
Not that I mind groping, or even dirtbags. But it's the combo that I can do without. Anyway, these guys tend to get chatty when they drink.
They make sure the escorts don't speak Russian. This way they can unwind. But I know Russian.
So, I'll be tending bar. And listening.
I hear a lot.
Stuff about cars.
Soccer.
"Personal" size.
A pirated DVD scam.
An Asian mob lieutenant who was "mysteriously" found dead.
Nothing I could use.

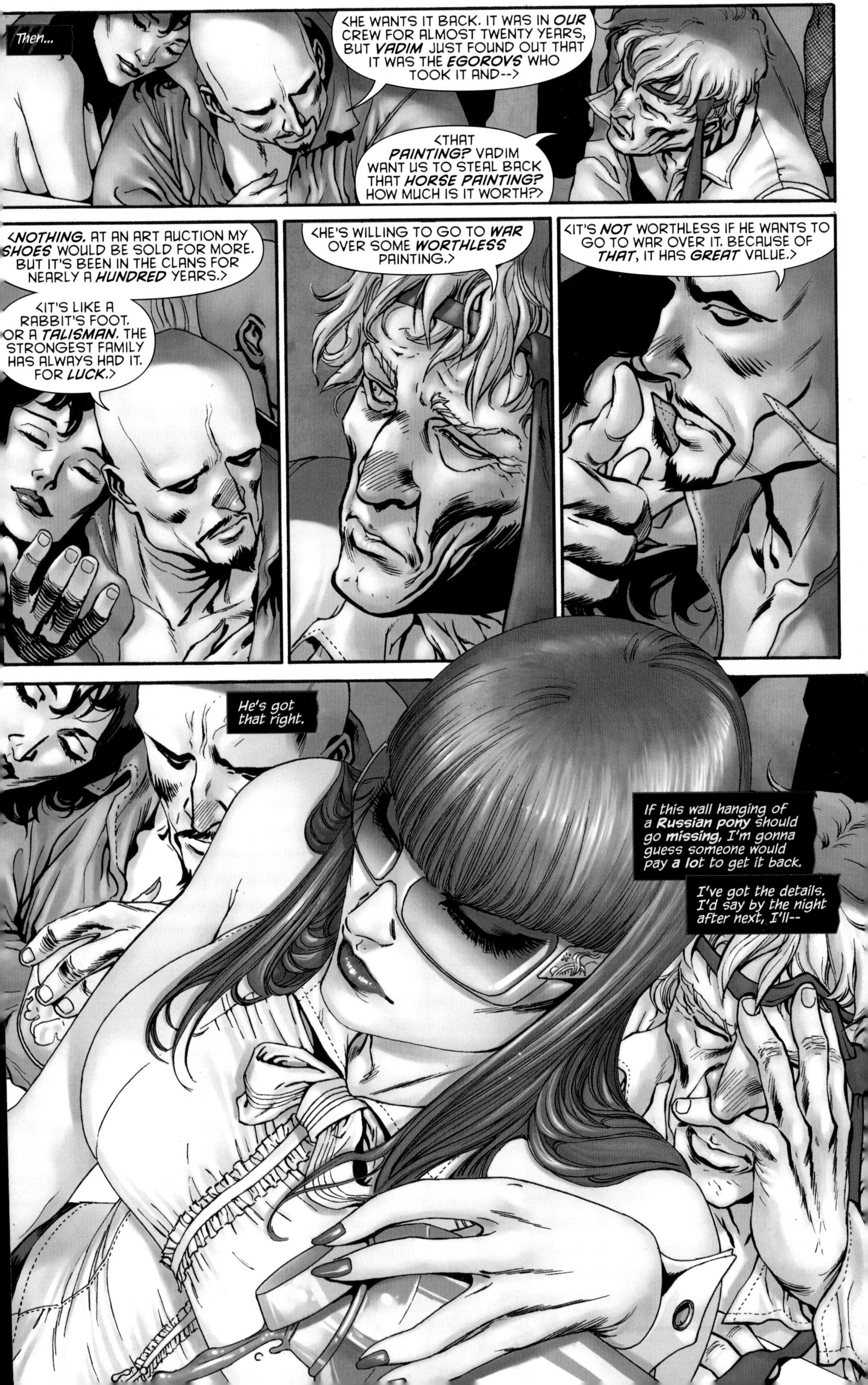
Then...
<HE WANTS IT BACK. IT WAS IN OUR CREW FOR ALMOST TWENTY YEARS, BUT VADIM JUST FOUND OUT THAT IT WAS THE EGOROVS WHO TOOK IT AND-->
<THAT PAINTING? VADIM WANT US TO STEAL BACK THAT HORSE PAINTING? HOW MUCH IS IT WORTH?>
<NOTHING. AT AN ART AUCTION MY SHOES WOULD BE SOLD FOR MORE. BUT IT'S BEEN IN THE CLANS FOR NEARLY A HUNDRED YEARS.>
<IT'S LIKE A RABBIT'S FOOT. OR A TALISMAN. THE STRONGEST FAMILY HAS ALWAYS HAD IT. FOR LUCK.>
<HE'S WILLING TO GO TO WAR OVER SOME WORTHLESS PAINTING.>
<IT'S NOT WORTHLESS IF HE WANTS TO GO TO WAR OVER IT. BECAUSE OF THAT, IT HAS GREAT VALUE.>
He's got that right.
If this wall hanging of a Russian pony should go missing, I'm gonna guess someone would pay a lot to get it back.
I've got the details. I'd say by the night after next, I'll--

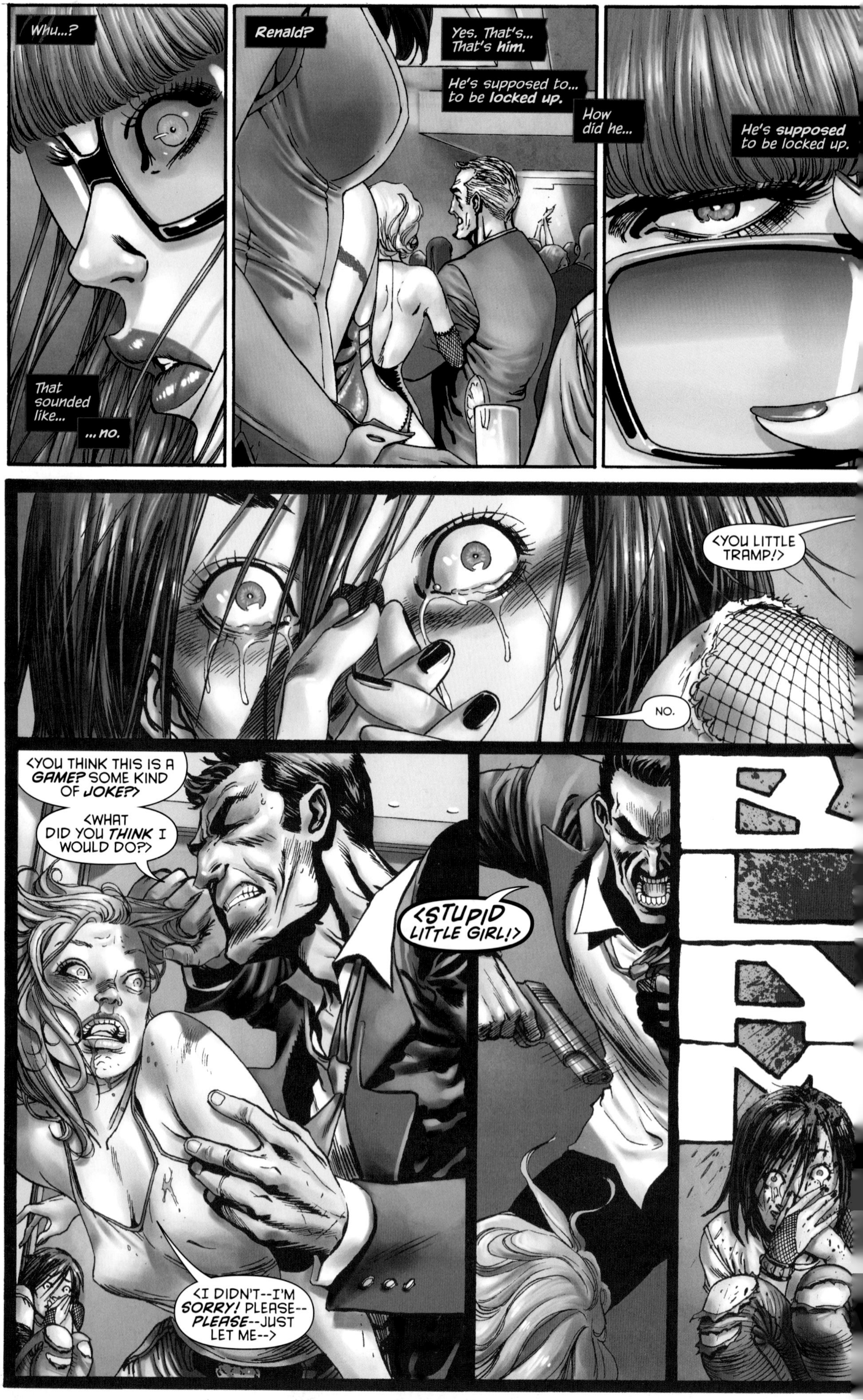

Whu...?
That sounded like...
...no.
Renald?
Yes. That's... That's him.
He's supposed to... to be locked up.
How did he...
He's supposed to be locked up.
<YOU LITTLE TRAMP!>
NO.
<YOU THINK THIS IS A GAME? SOME KIND OF JOKE?>
<WHAT DID YOU THINK I WOULD DO?>
<STUPID LITTLE GIRL!>
<I DIDN'T--I'M SORRY! PLEASE--PLEASE--JUST LET ME-->

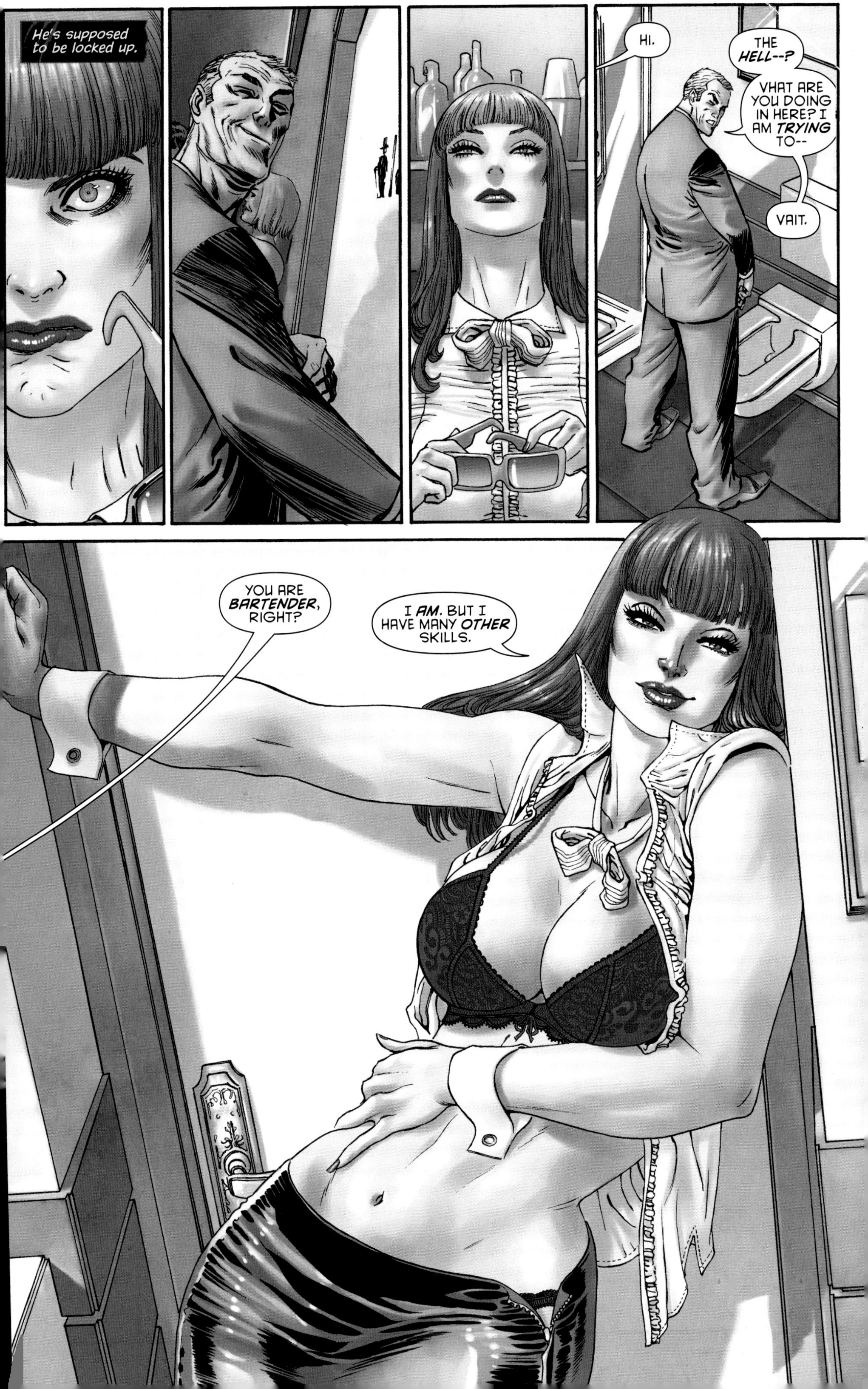

He's supposed to be locked up.
HI.
THE *HELL--?*
VHAT ARE YOU DOING IN HERE? I AM *TRYING* TO--
VAIT.
YOU ARE *BARTENDER*, RIGHT?
I *AM*. BUT I HAVE MANY *OTHER* SKILLS.

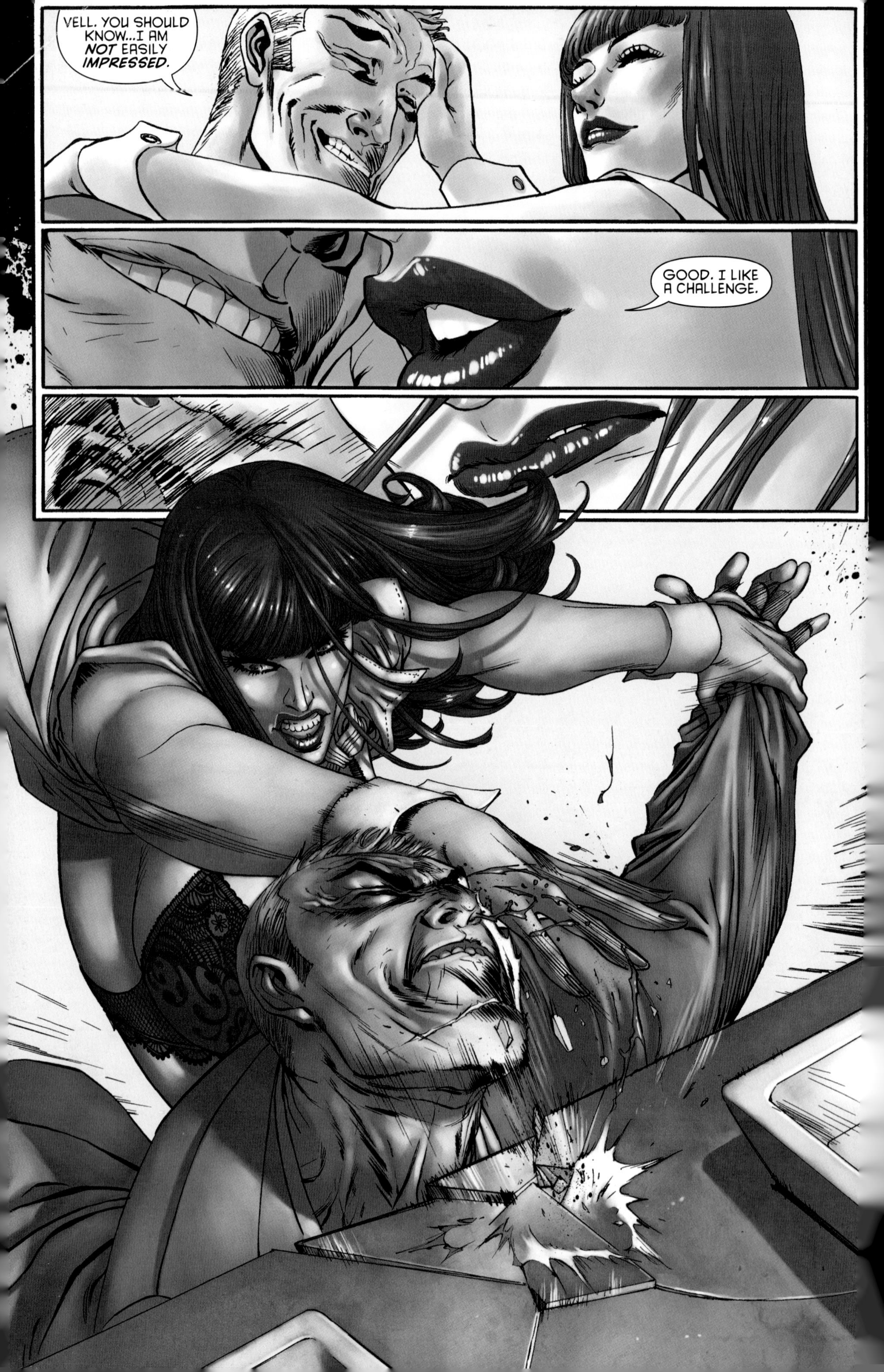
VELL. YOU SHOULD KNOW...I AM *NOT* EASILY *IMPRESSED*.
GOOD. I LIKE A CHALLENGE.

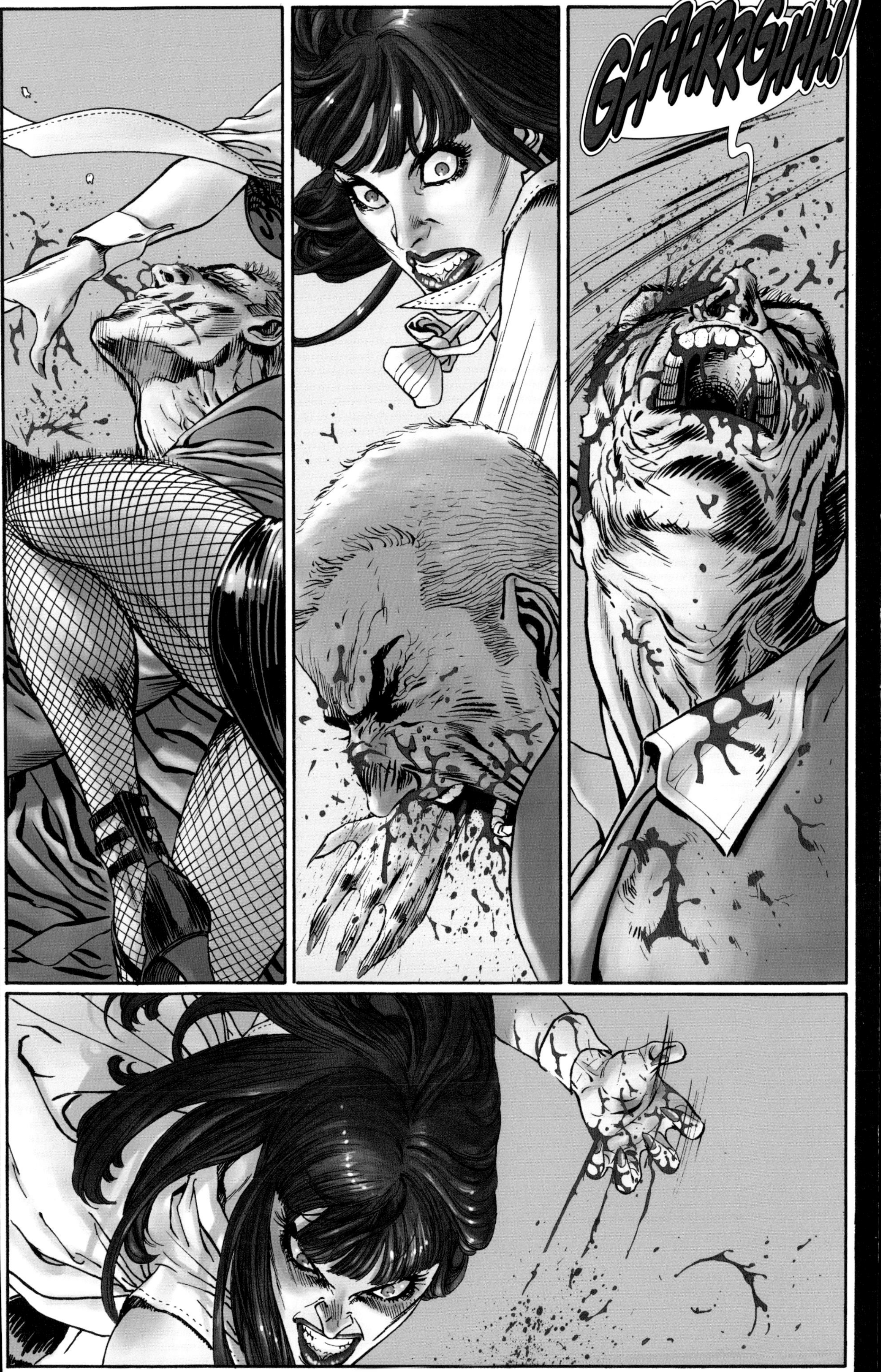
GAAARRGHHH!

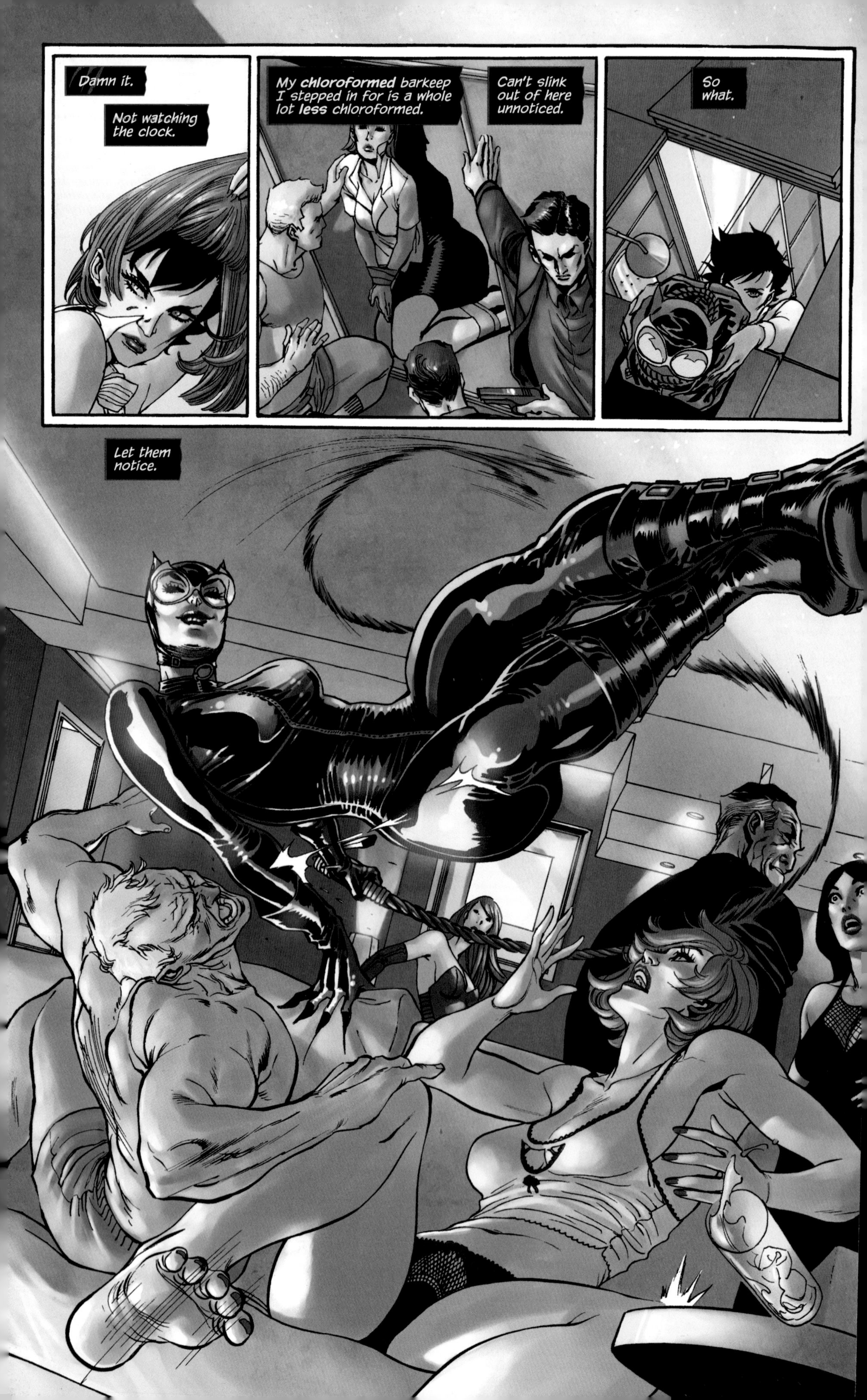

Damn it.
Not watching the clock.
My **chloroformed** barkeep I stepped in for is a whole lot **less** chloroformed.
Can't slink out of here unnoticed.
So what.
Let them notice.

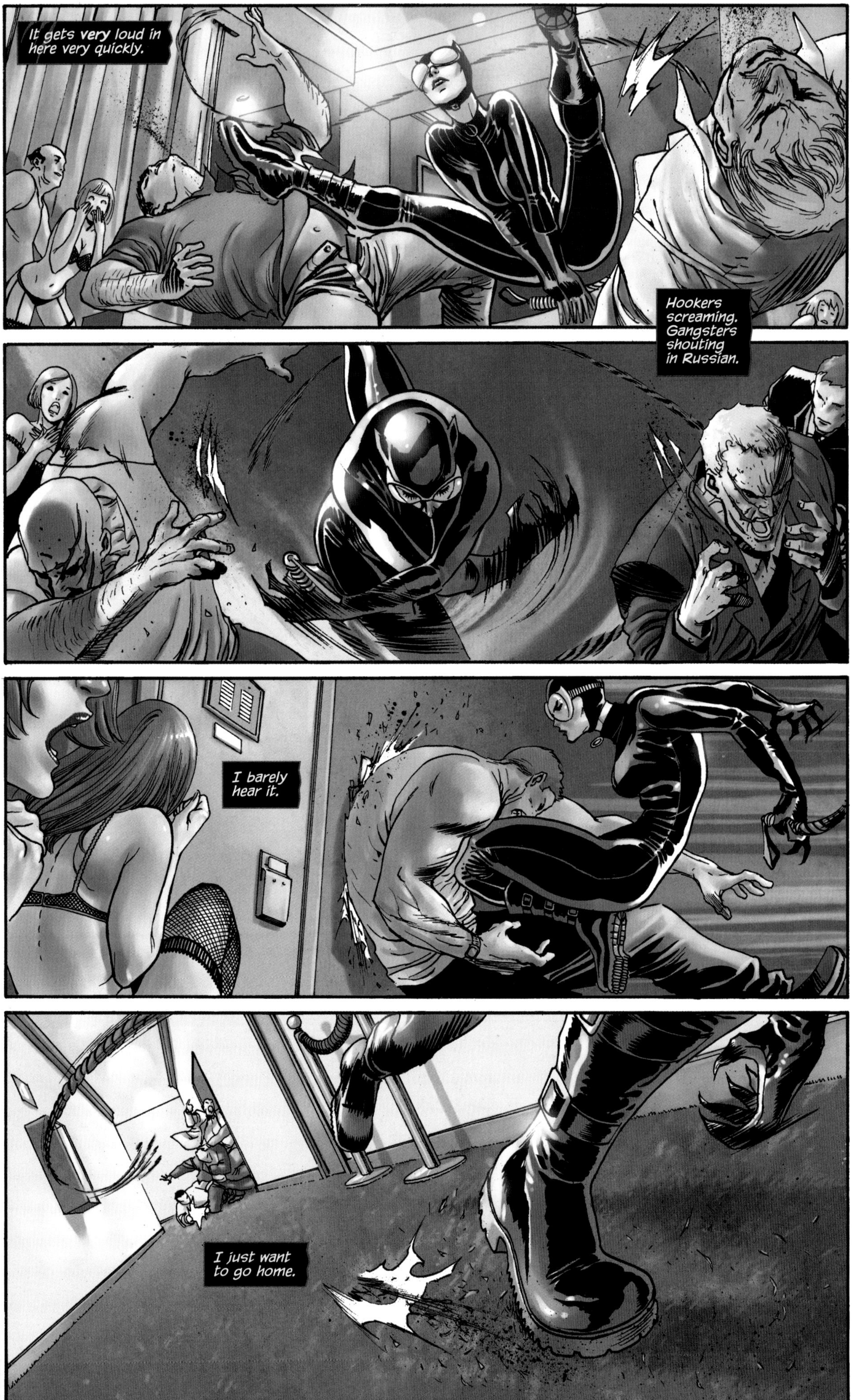
It gets very loud in here very quickly.
Hookers screaming. Gangsters shouting in Russian.
I barely hear it.
I just want to go home.

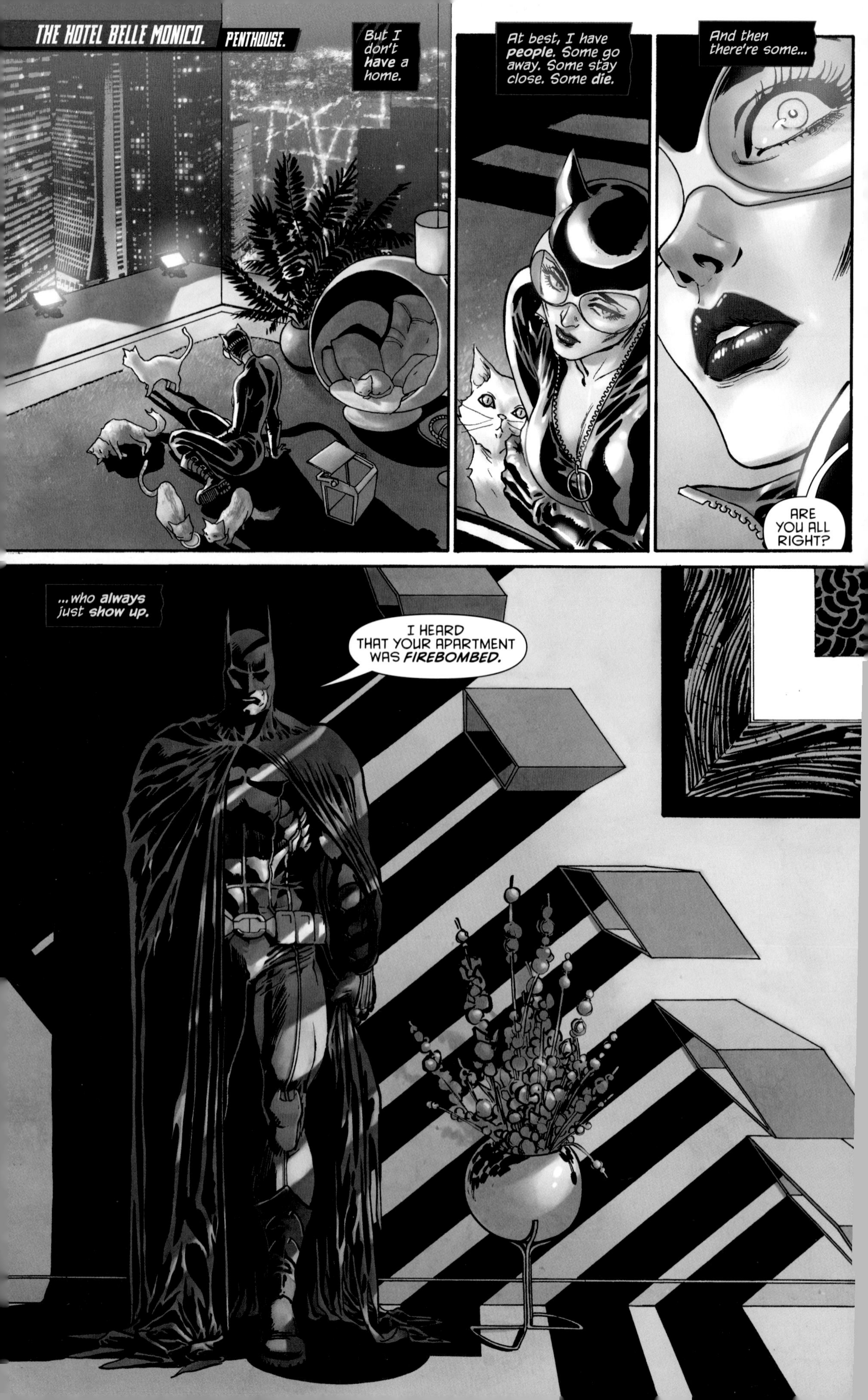

THE HOTEL BELLE MONICO.
PENTHOUSE.
But I don't have a home.
At best, I have people. Some go away. Some stay close. Some die.
And then there're some...
ARE YOU ALL RIGHT?
...who always just show up.
I HEARD THAT YOUR APARTMENT WAS FIREBOMBED.

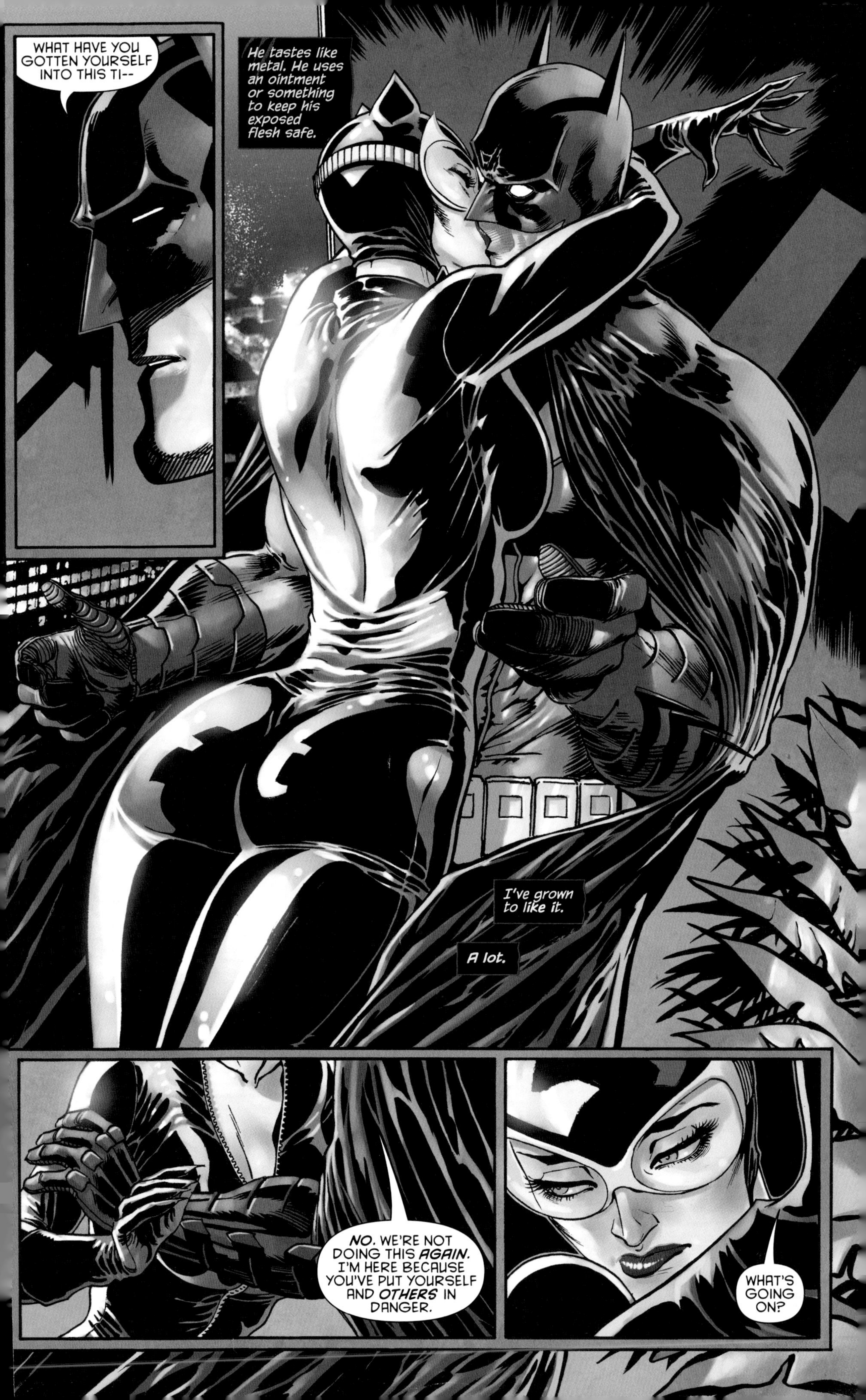
WHAT HAVE YOU GOTTEN YOURSELF INTO THIS TI--
He tastes like metal. He uses an ointment or something to keep his exposed flesh safe.
I've grown to like it.
A lot.
NO. WE'RE NOT DOING THIS AGAIN. I'M HERE BECAUSE YOU'VE PUT YOURSELF AND OTHERS IN DANGER.
WHAT'S GOING ON?

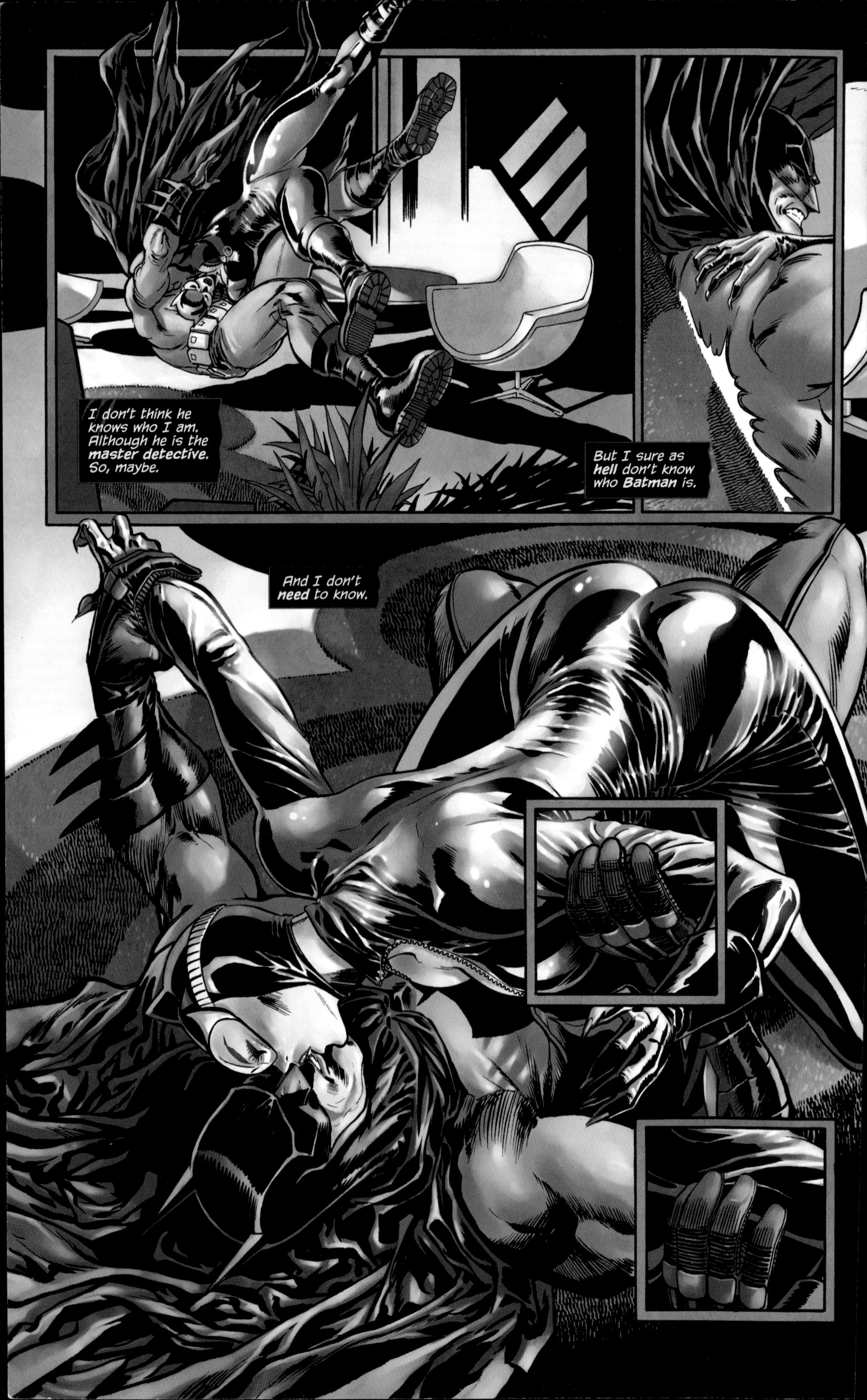

I don't think he knows who I am. Although he is the **master detective.** So, maybe.
But I sure as **hell** don't know who **Batman** is.
And I don't **need** to know.

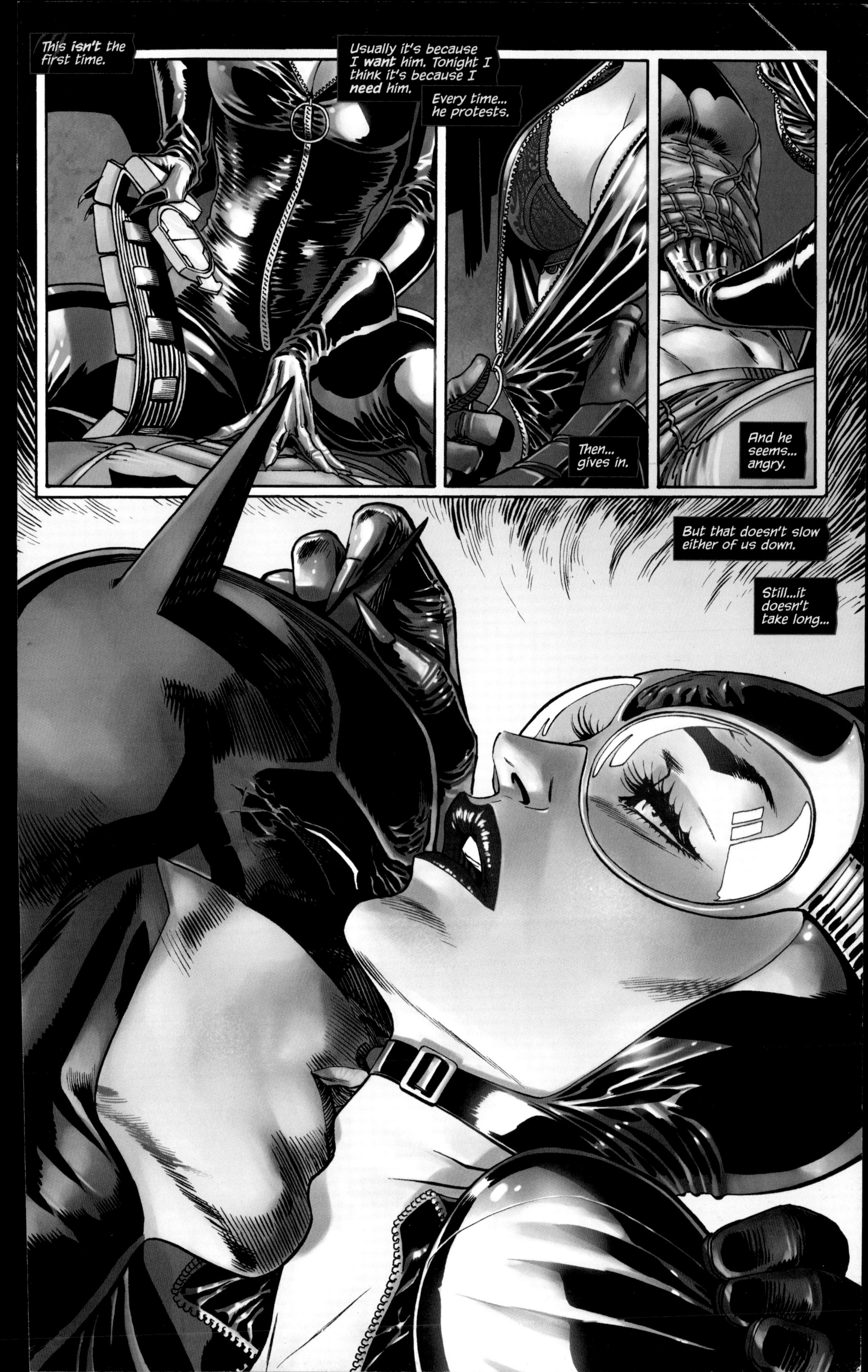

This isn't the first time.
Usually it's because I want him. Tonight I think it's because I need him.
Every time... he protests.
Then... gives in.
And he seems... angry.
But that doesn't slow either of us down.
Still...it doesn't take long...

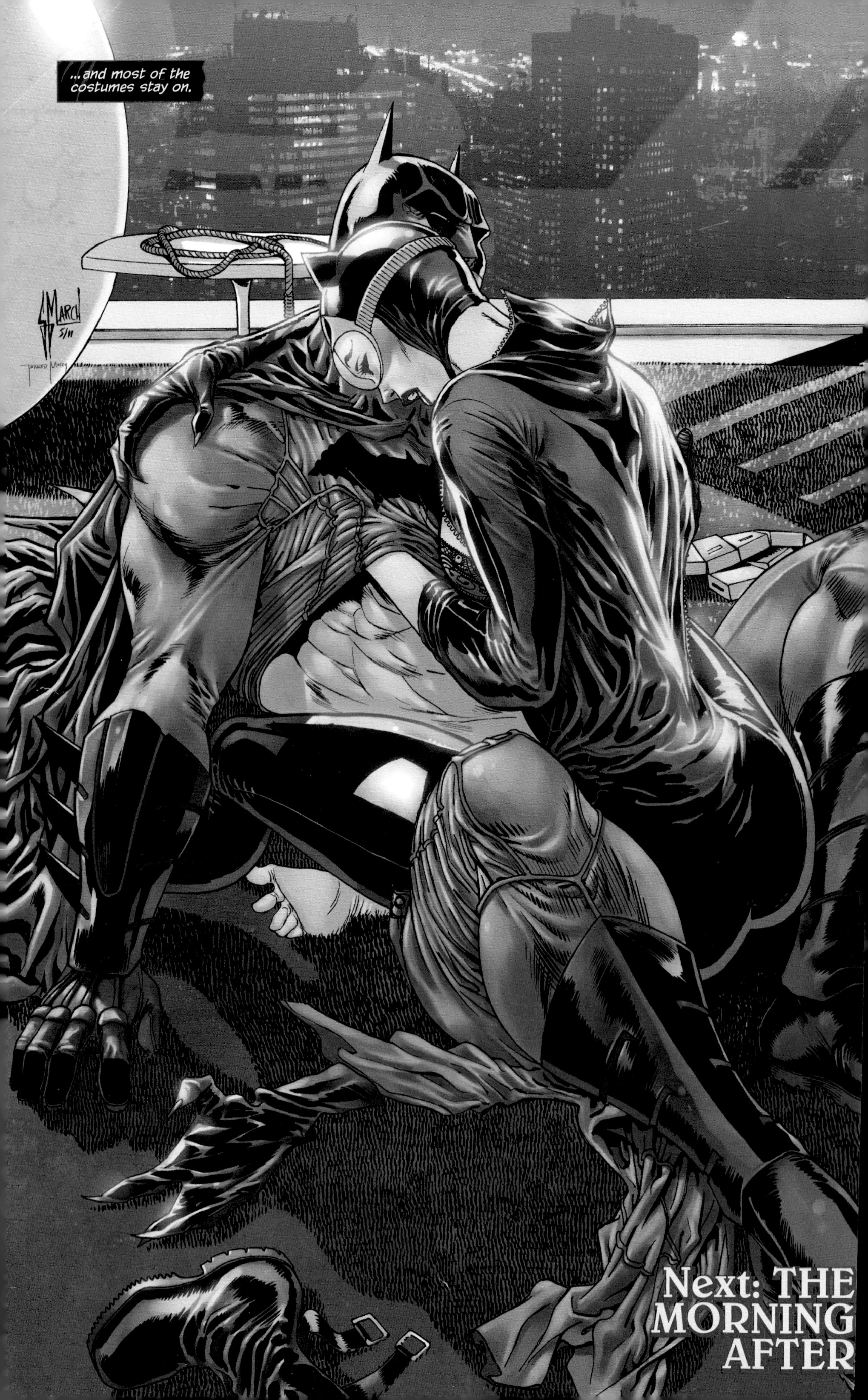
...and most of the costumes stay on.
Next: THE MORNING AFTER

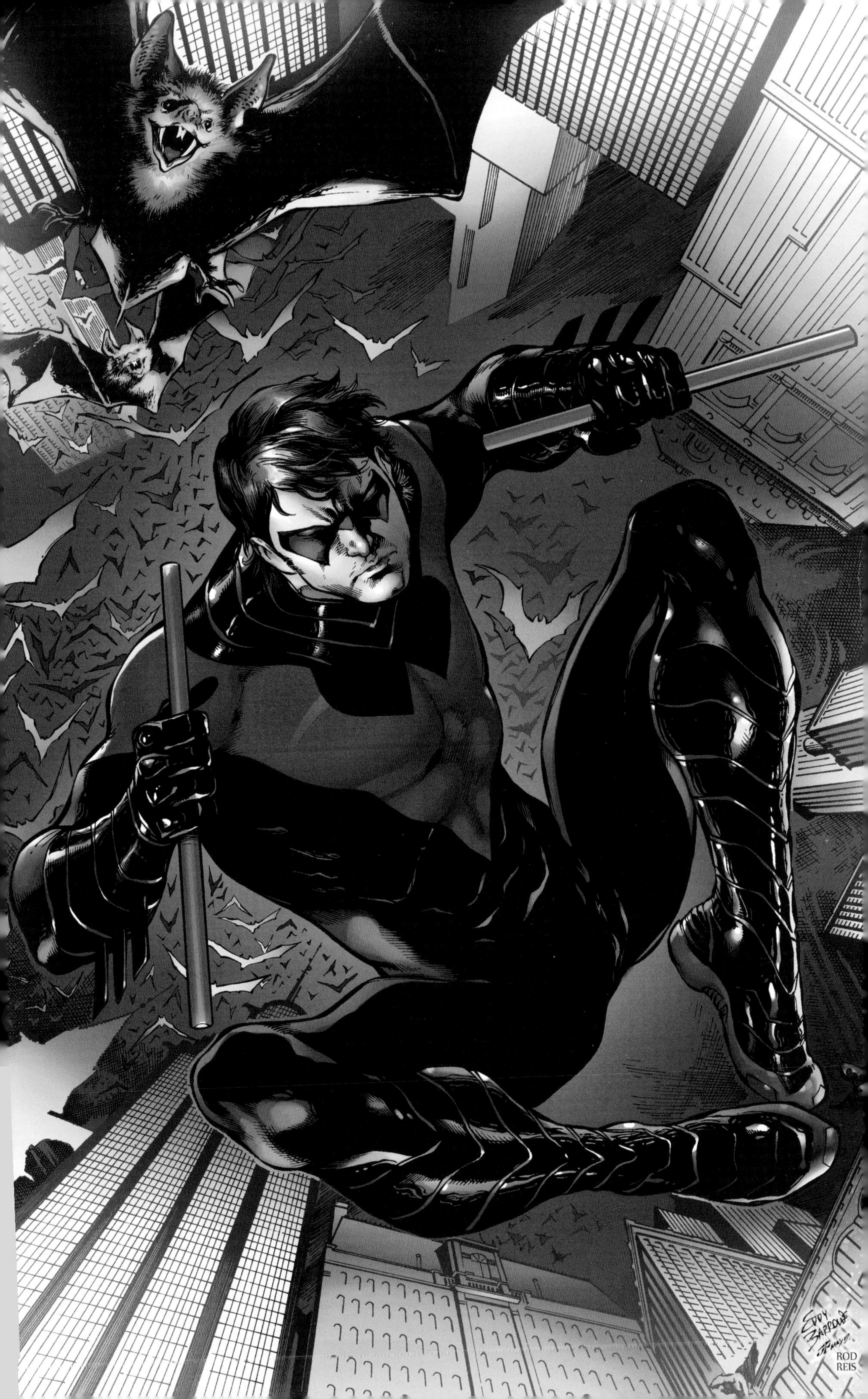
ROD
REIS

NIGHTWING

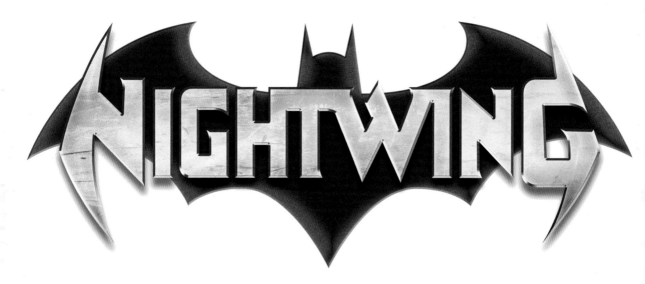

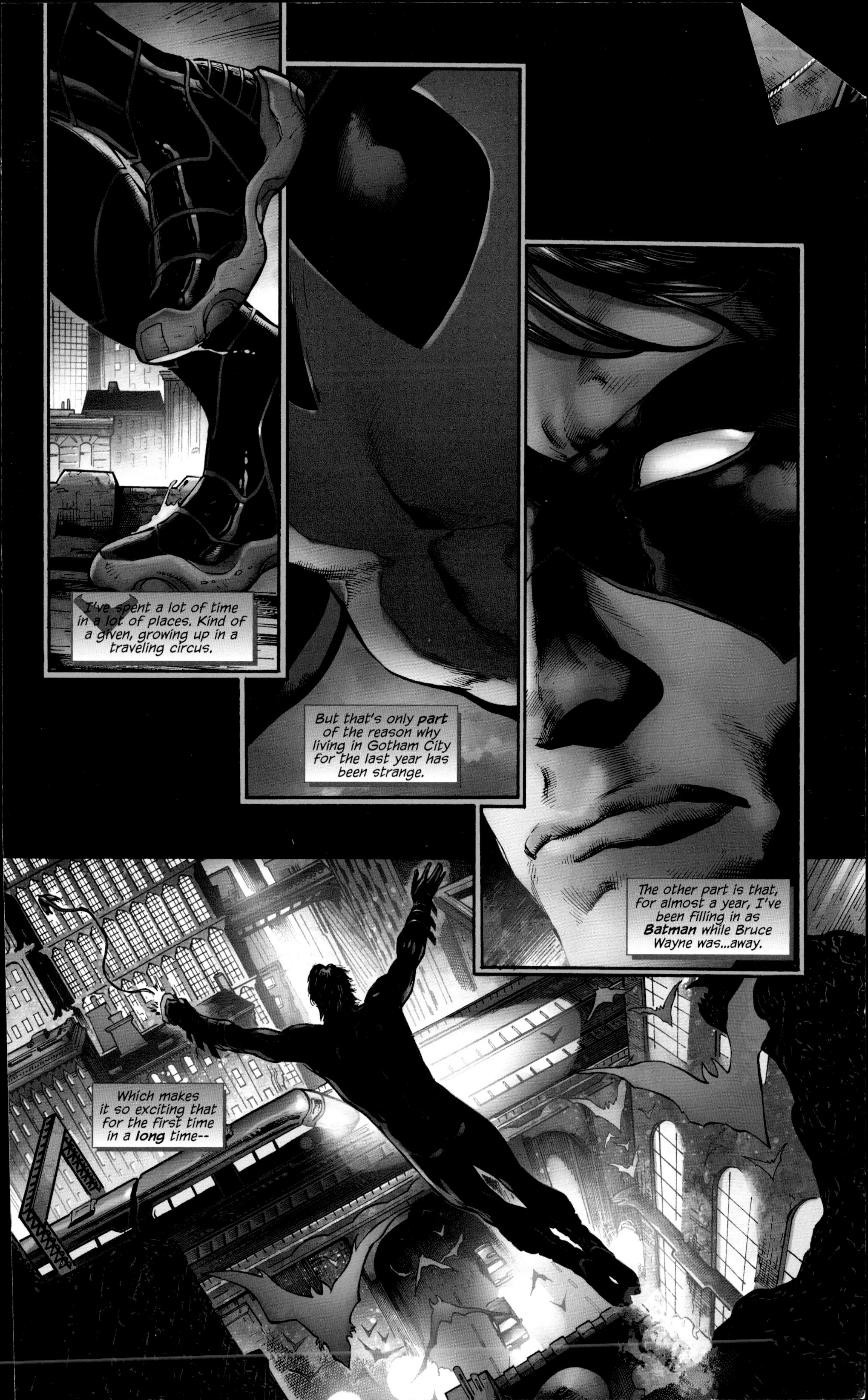
I've spent a lot of time in a lot of places. Kind of a given, growing up in a traveling circus.
But that's only **part** of the reason why living in Gotham City for the last year has been strange.
The other part is that, for almost a year, I've been filling in as **Batman** while Bruce Wayne was...away.
Which makes it so exciting that for the first time in a **long** time--

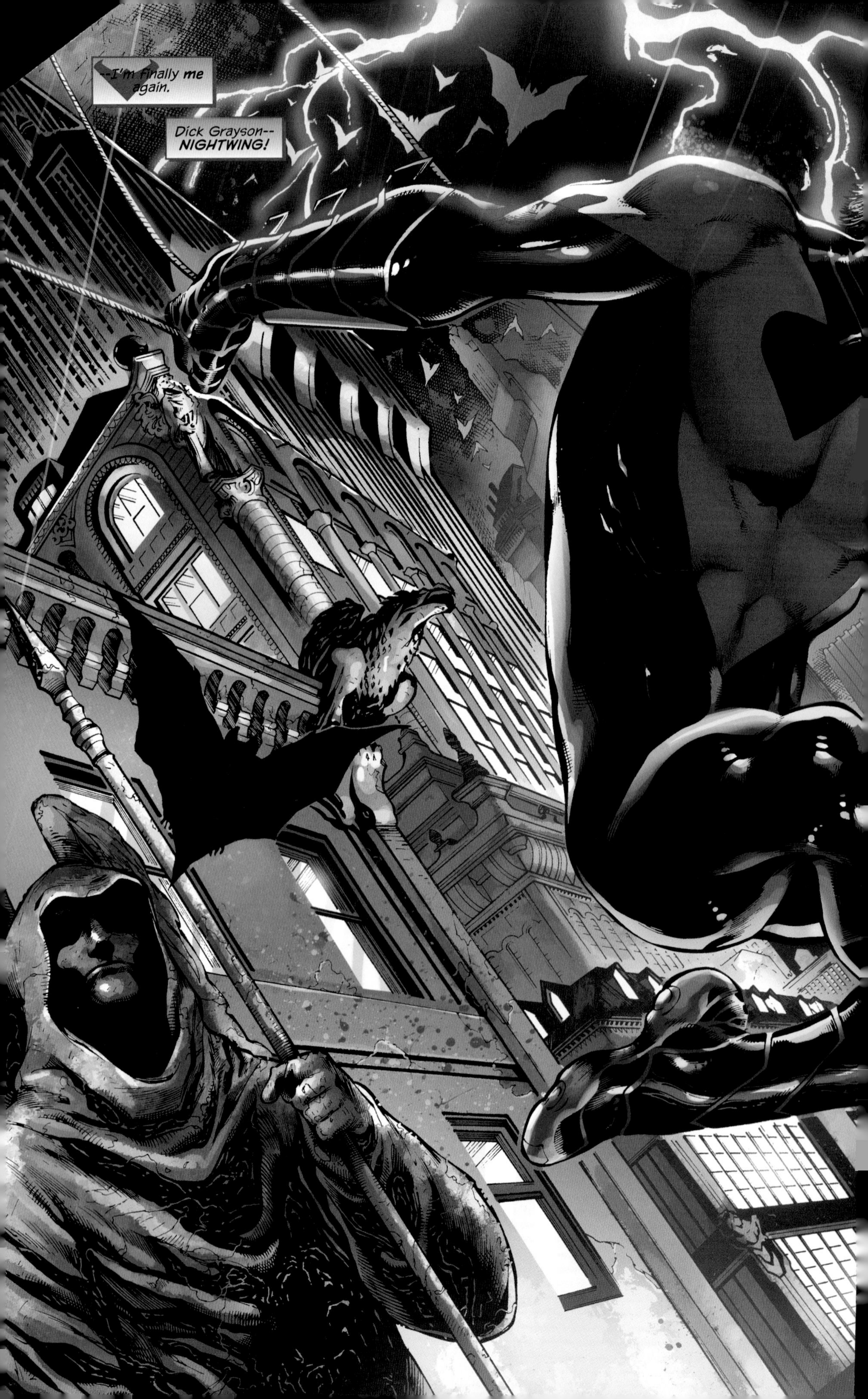
--I'm finally me again.
Dick Grayson-- NIGHTWING!

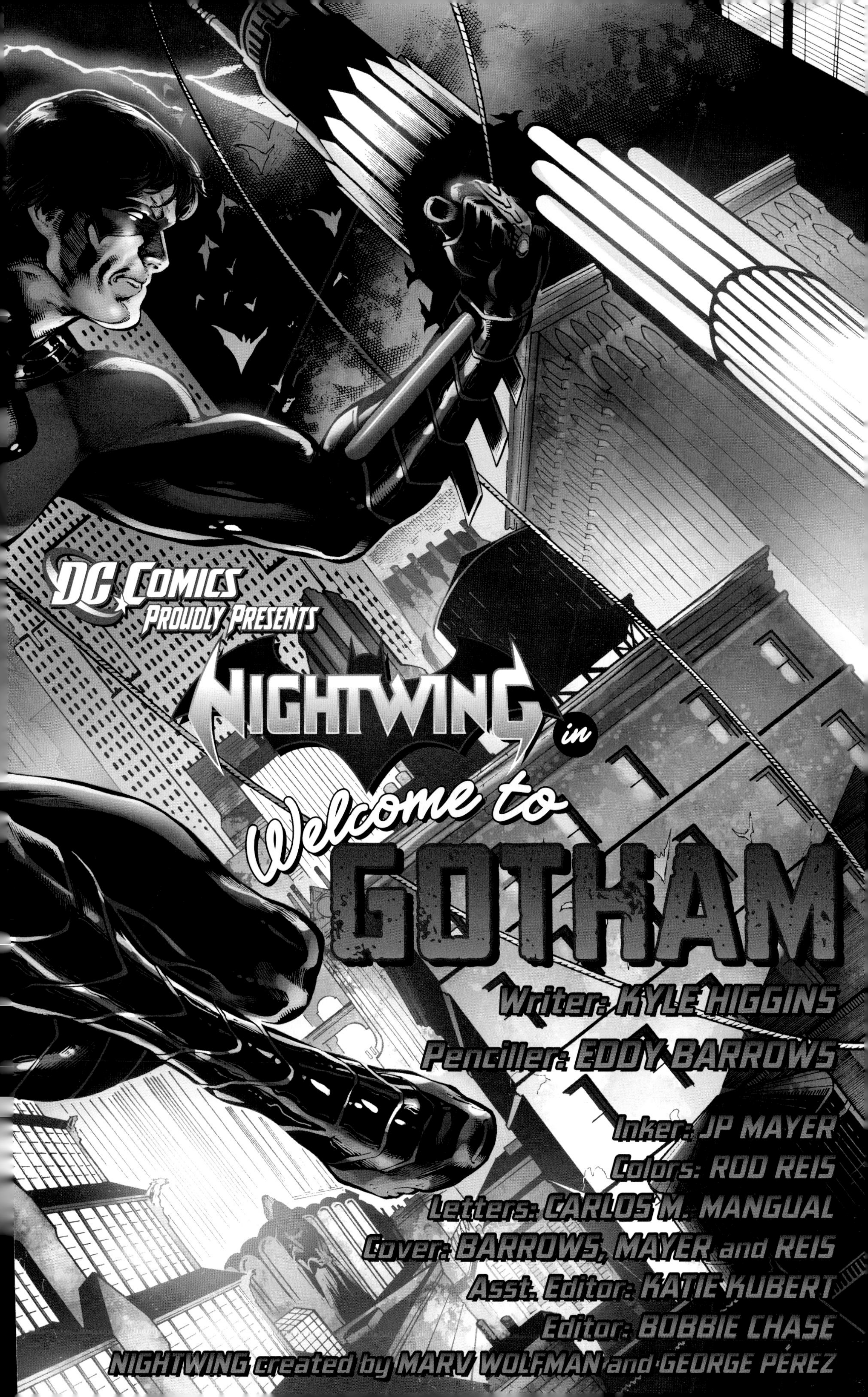
DC COMICS PROUDLY PRESENTS
NIGHTWING in
Welcome to GOTHAM
Writer: KYLE HIGGINS
Penciller: EDDY BARROWS
Inker: JP MAYER
Colors: ROD REIS
Letters: CARLOS M. MANGUAL
Cover: BARROWS, MAYER and REIS
Asst. Editor: KATIE KUBERT
Editor: BOBBIE CHASE
NIGHTWING created by MARV WOLFMAN and GEORGE PÉREZ

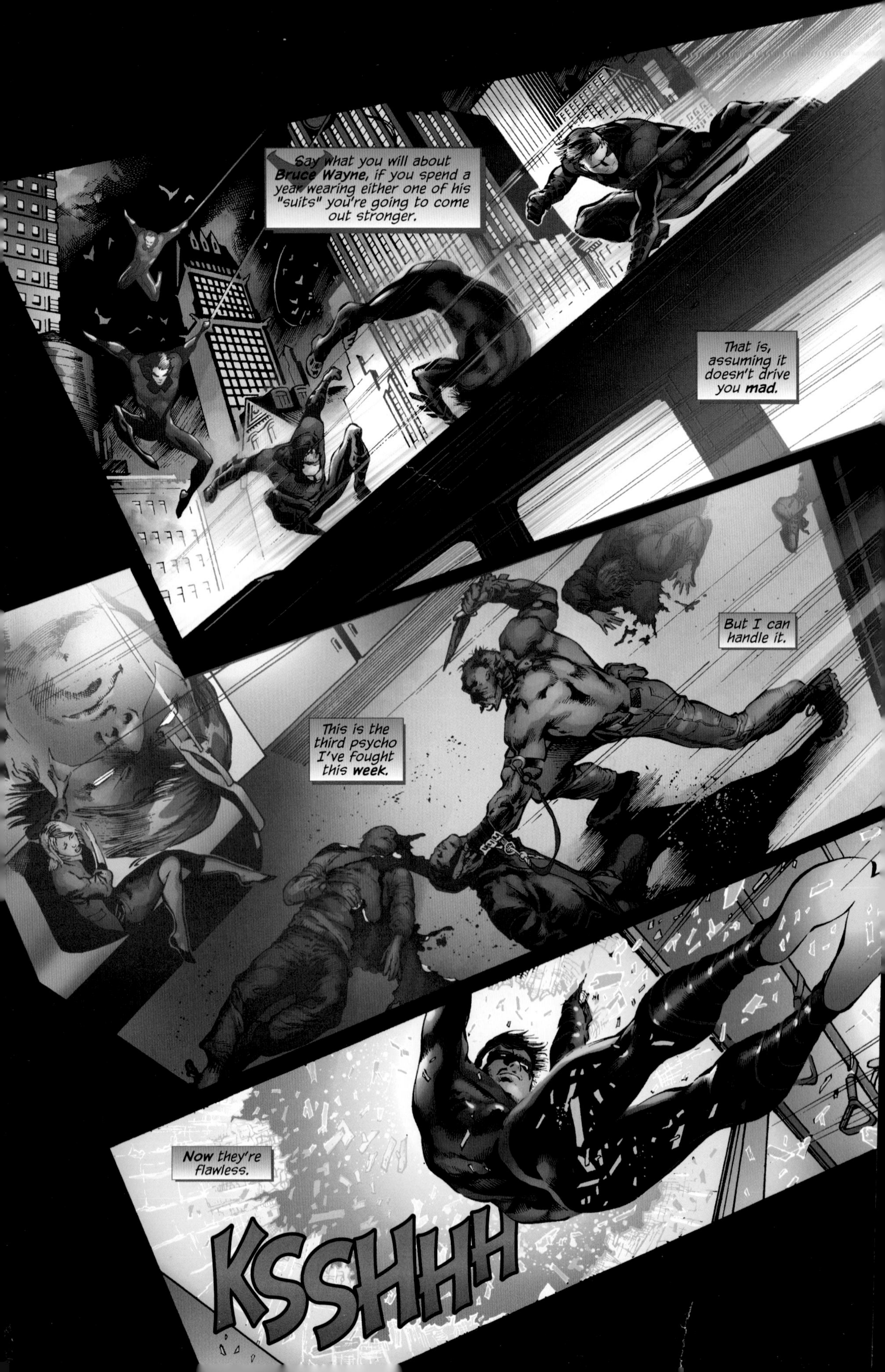

Say what you will about Bruce Wayne, if you spend a year wearing either one of his "suits" you're going to come out stronger.
That is, assuming it doesn't drive you mad.
But I can handle it.
This is the third psycho I've fought this week.
Now they're flawless.
KSSHHH

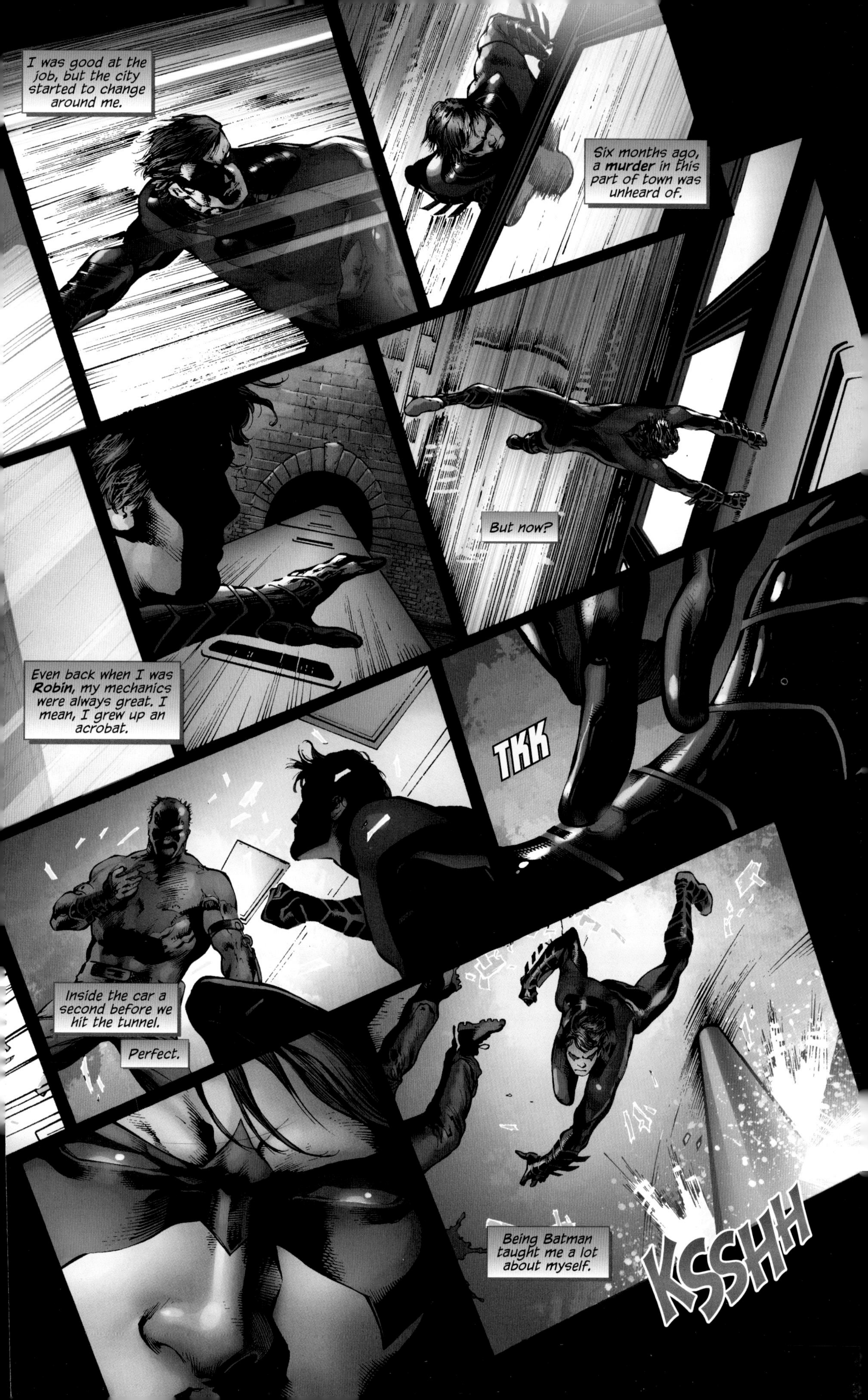
I was good at the job, but the city started to change around me.
Six months ago, a **murder** in this part of town was unheard of.
But now?
Even back when I was **Robin**, my mechanics were always great. I mean, I grew up an acrobat.
TKK
Inside the car a second before we hit the tunnel.
Perfect.
Being Batman taught me a lot about myself.
KSSHH

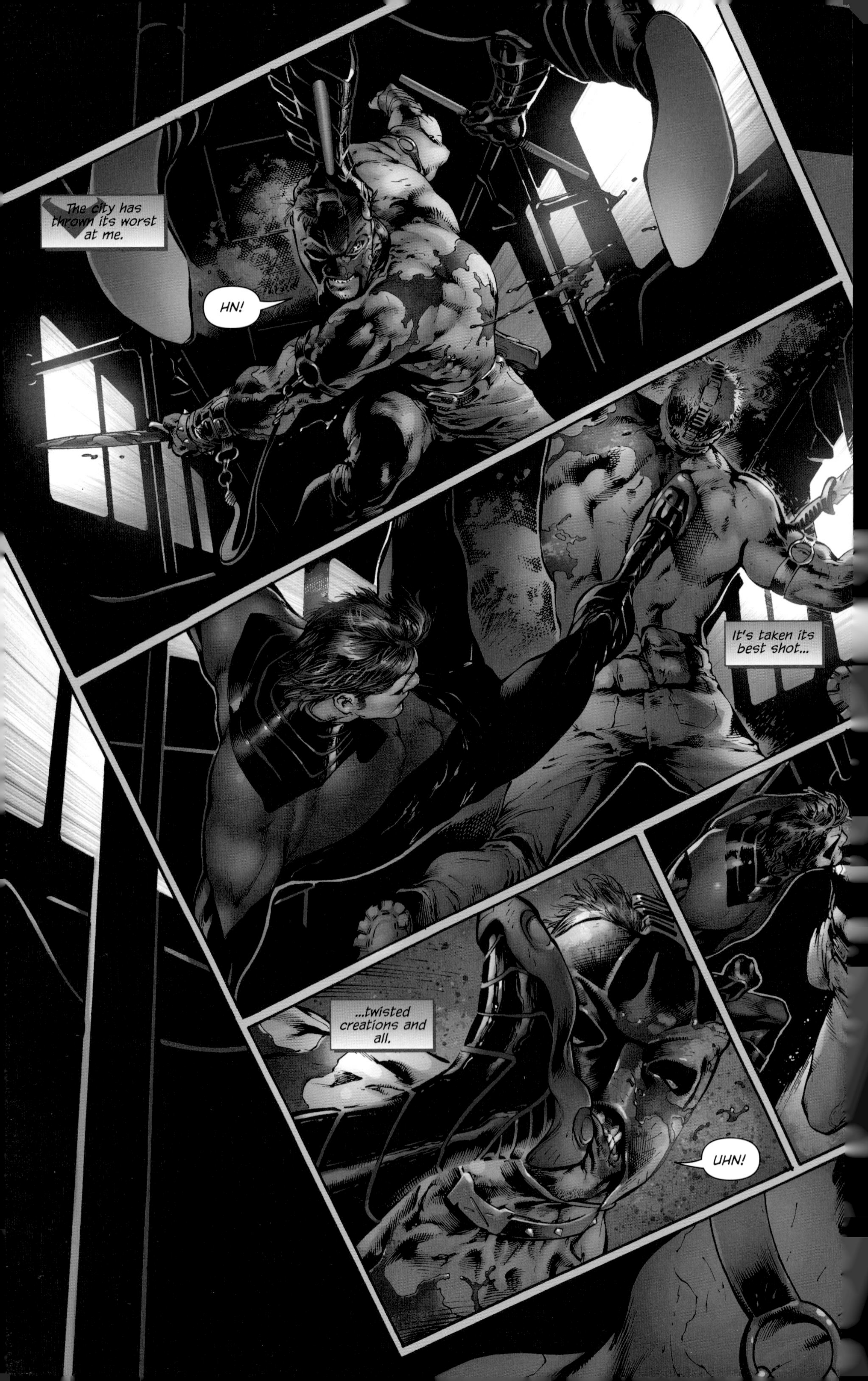
The city has thrown its worst at me.
HN!
It's taken its best shot...
...twisted creations and all.
UHN!

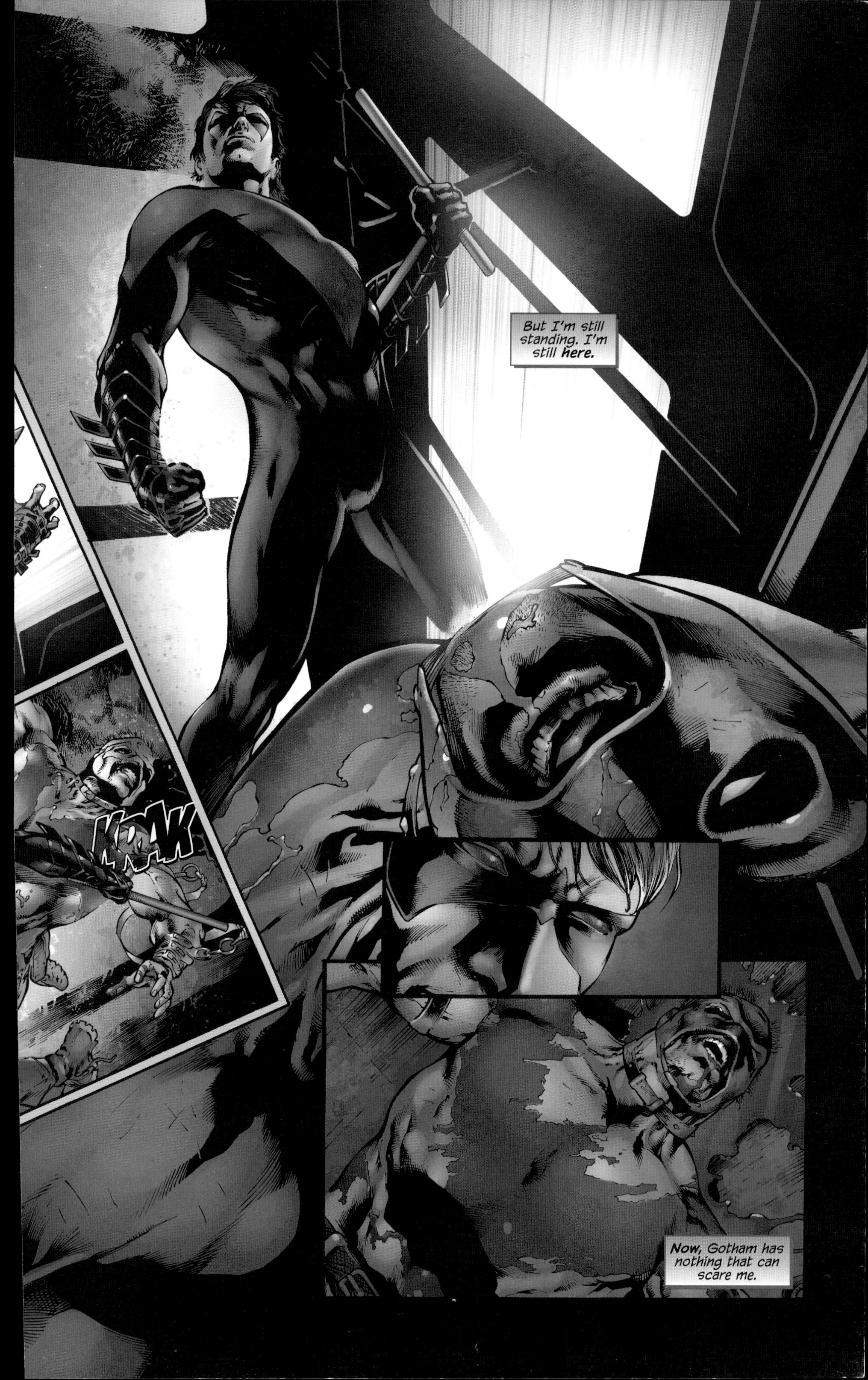
But I'm still standing. I'm still **here.**
KRAK
Now, Gotham has nothing that can scare me.

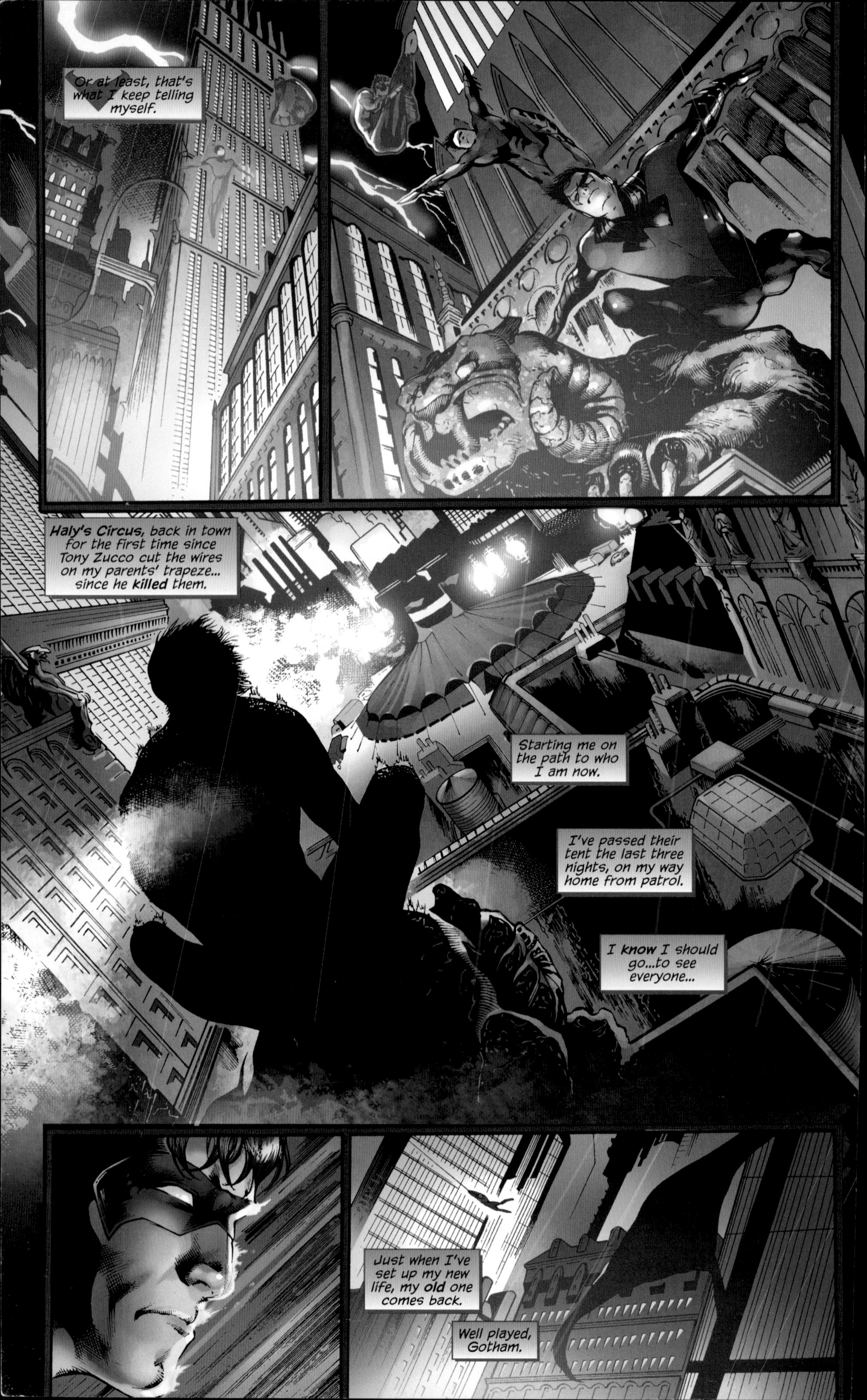
Or at least, that's what I keep telling myself.
Haly's Circus, back in town for the first time since Tony Zucco cut the wires on my parents' trapeze... since he killed them.
Starting me on the path to who I am now.
I've passed their tent the last three nights, on my way home from patrol.
I know I should go...to see everyone...
Just when I've set up my new life, my old one comes back.
Well played, Gotham.

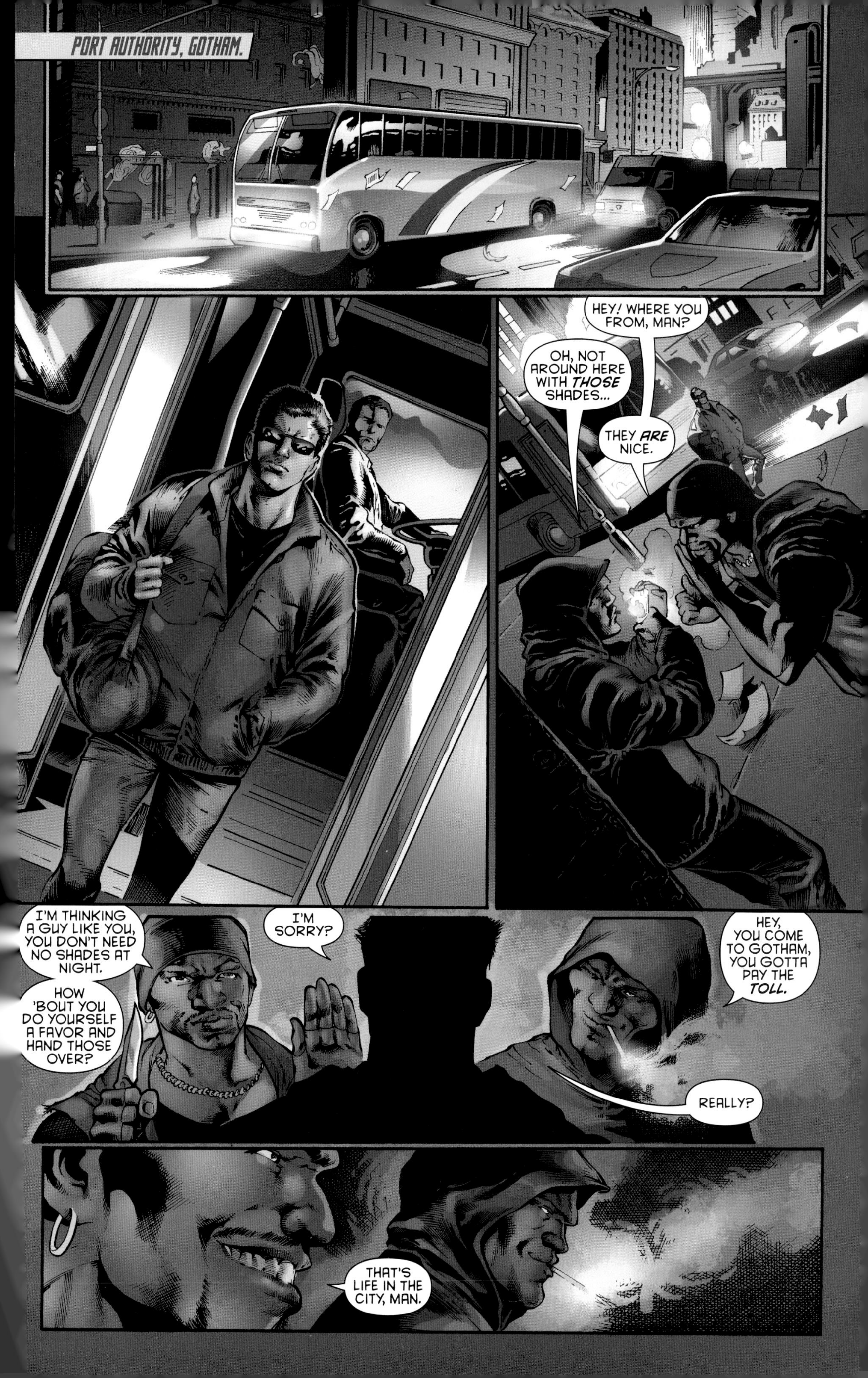
PORT AUTHORITY, GOTHAM.
HEY! WHERE YOU FROM, MAN?
OH, NOT AROUND HERE WITH THOSE SHADES...
THEY ARE NICE.
I'M THINKING A GUY LIKE YOU, YOU DON'T NEED NO SHADES AT NIGHT.
HOW 'BOUT YOU DO YOURSELF A FAVOR AND HAND THOSE OVER?
I'M SORRY?
HEY, YOU COME TO GOTHAM, YOU GOTTA PAY THE TOLL.
REALLY?
THAT'S LIFE IN THE CITY, MAN.

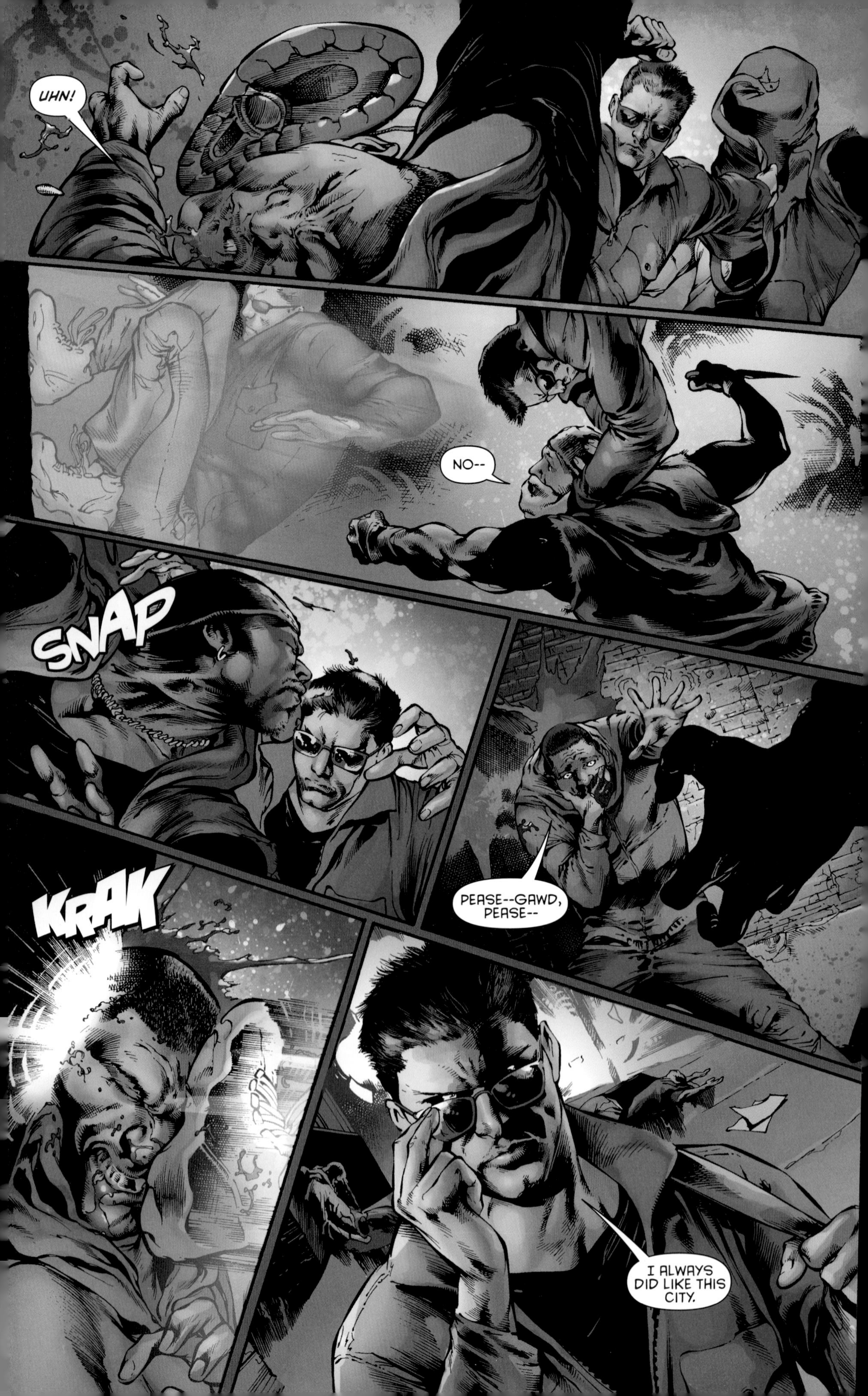
UHN!
NO--
SNAP
PEASE--GAWD, PEASE--
KRAK
I ALWAYS DID LIKE THIS CITY.

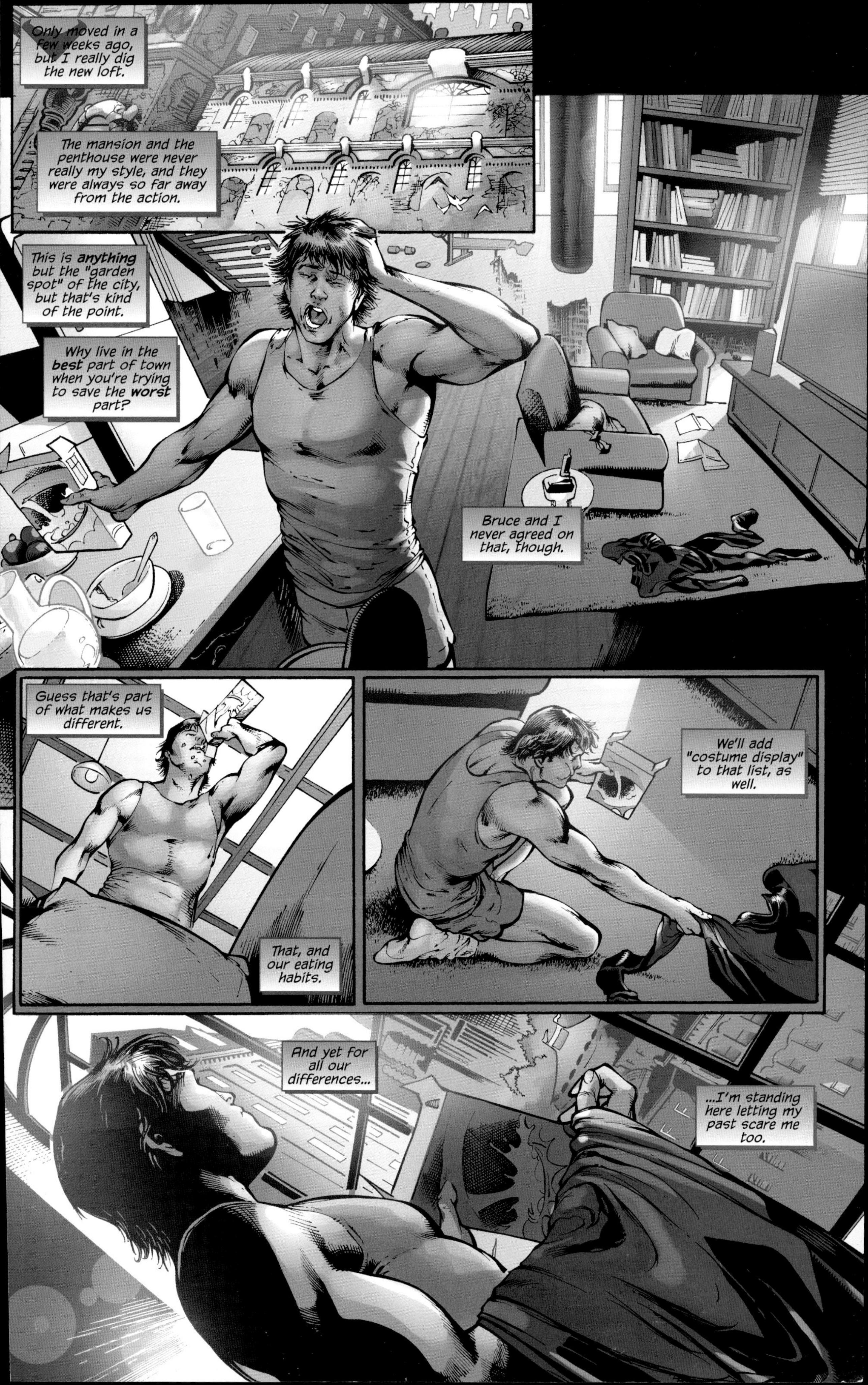

Only moved in a few weeks ago, but I really dig the new loft.
The mansion and the penthouse were never really my style, and they were always so far away from the action.
This is **anything** but the "garden spot" of the city, but that's kind of the point.
Why live in the **best** part of town when you're trying to save the **worst** part?
Bruce and I never agreed on that, though.
Guess that's part of what makes us different.
That, and our eating habits.
We'll add "costume display" to that list, as well.
And yet for all our differences...
...I'm standing here letting my past scare me too.

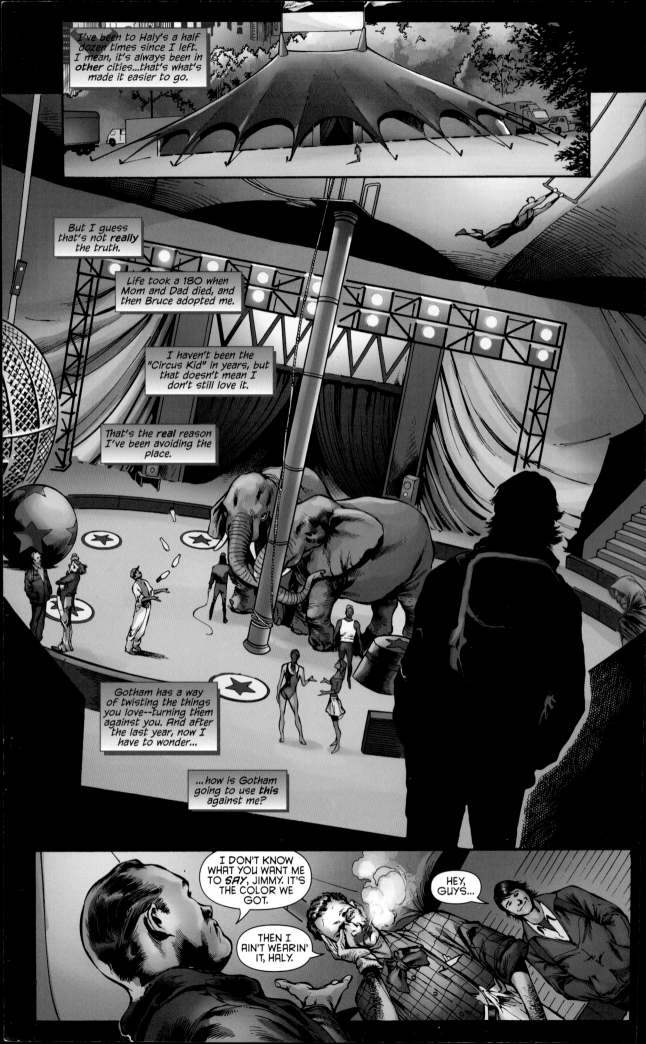

I've been to Haly's a half dozen times since I left. I mean, it's always been in *other* cities...that's what's made it easier to go.

But I guess that's not *really* the truth.

Life took a 180 when Mom and Dad died, and then Bruce adopted me.

I haven't been the "Circus Kid" in years, but that doesn't mean I don't still love it.

That's the *real* reason I've been avoiding the place.

Gotham has a way of twisting the things you love--turning them against you. And after the last year, now I have to wonder...

...how is Gotham going to use *this* against me?

I DON'T KNOW WHAT YOU WANT ME TO *SAY*, JIMMY. IT'S THE COLOR WE GOT.

THEN I AIN'T WEARIN' IT, HALY.

HEY, GUYS...

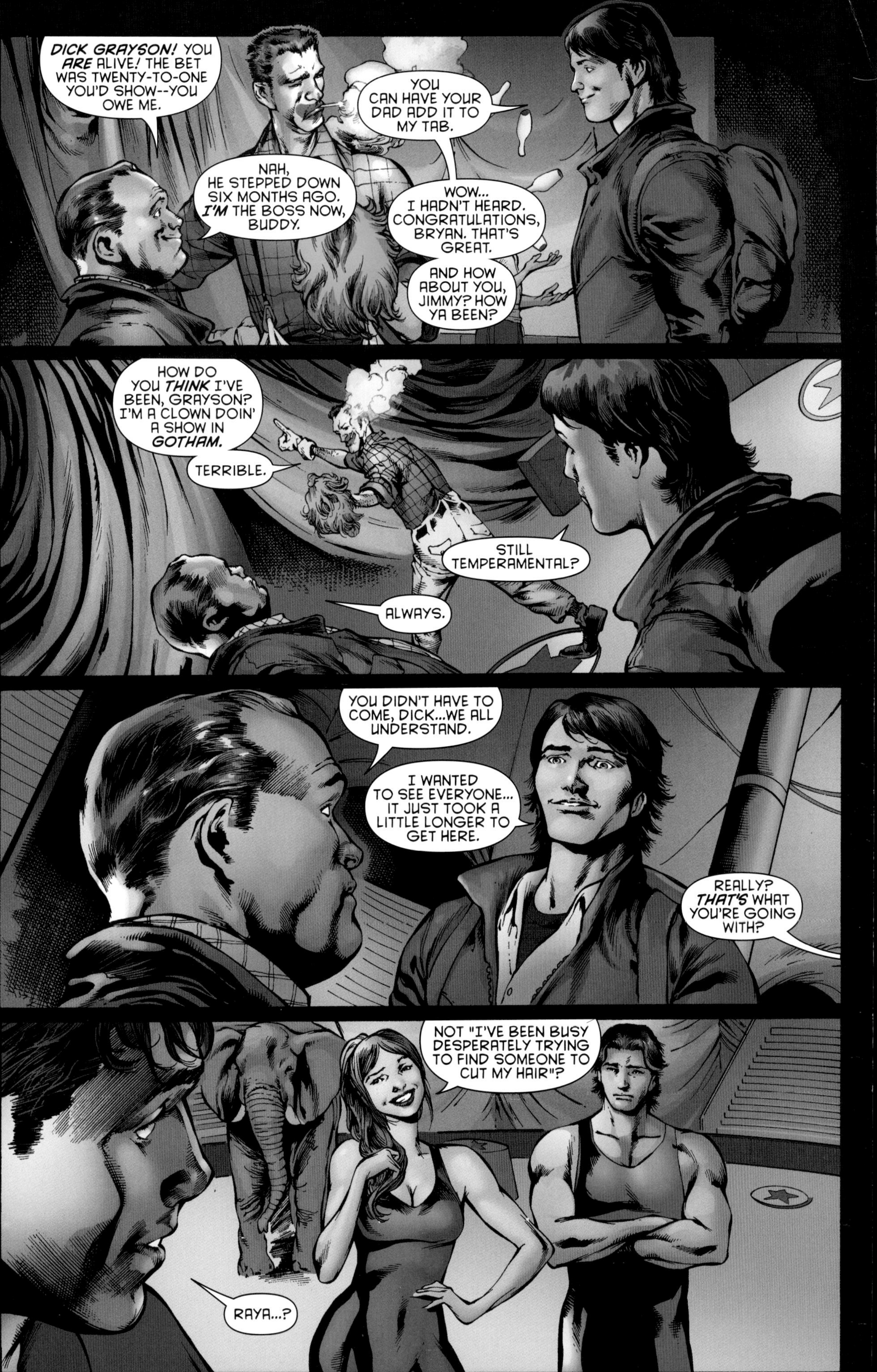
DICK GRAYSON! YOU ARE ALIVE! THE BET WAS TWENTY-TO-ONE YOU'D SHOW--YOU OWE ME.
YOU CAN HAVE YOUR DAD ADD IT TO MY TAB.
NAH, HE STEPPED DOWN SIX MONTHS AGO. I'M THE BOSS NOW, BUDDY.
WOW... I HADN'T HEARD. CONGRATULATIONS, BRYAN. THAT'S GREAT.
AND HOW ABOUT YOU, JIMMY? HOW YA BEEN?
HOW DO YOU THINK I'VE BEEN, GRAYSON? I'M A CLOWN DOIN' A SHOW IN GOTHAM.
TERRIBLE.
STILL TEMPERAMENTAL?
ALWAYS.
YOU DIDN'T HAVE TO COME, DICK...WE ALL UNDERSTAND.
I WANTED TO SEE EVERYONE... IT JUST TOOK A LITTLE LONGER TO GET HERE.
REALLY? THAT'S WHAT YOU'RE GOING WITH?
NOT "I'VE BEEN BUSY DESPERATELY TRYING TO FIND SOMEONE TO CUT MY HAIR"?
RAYA...?

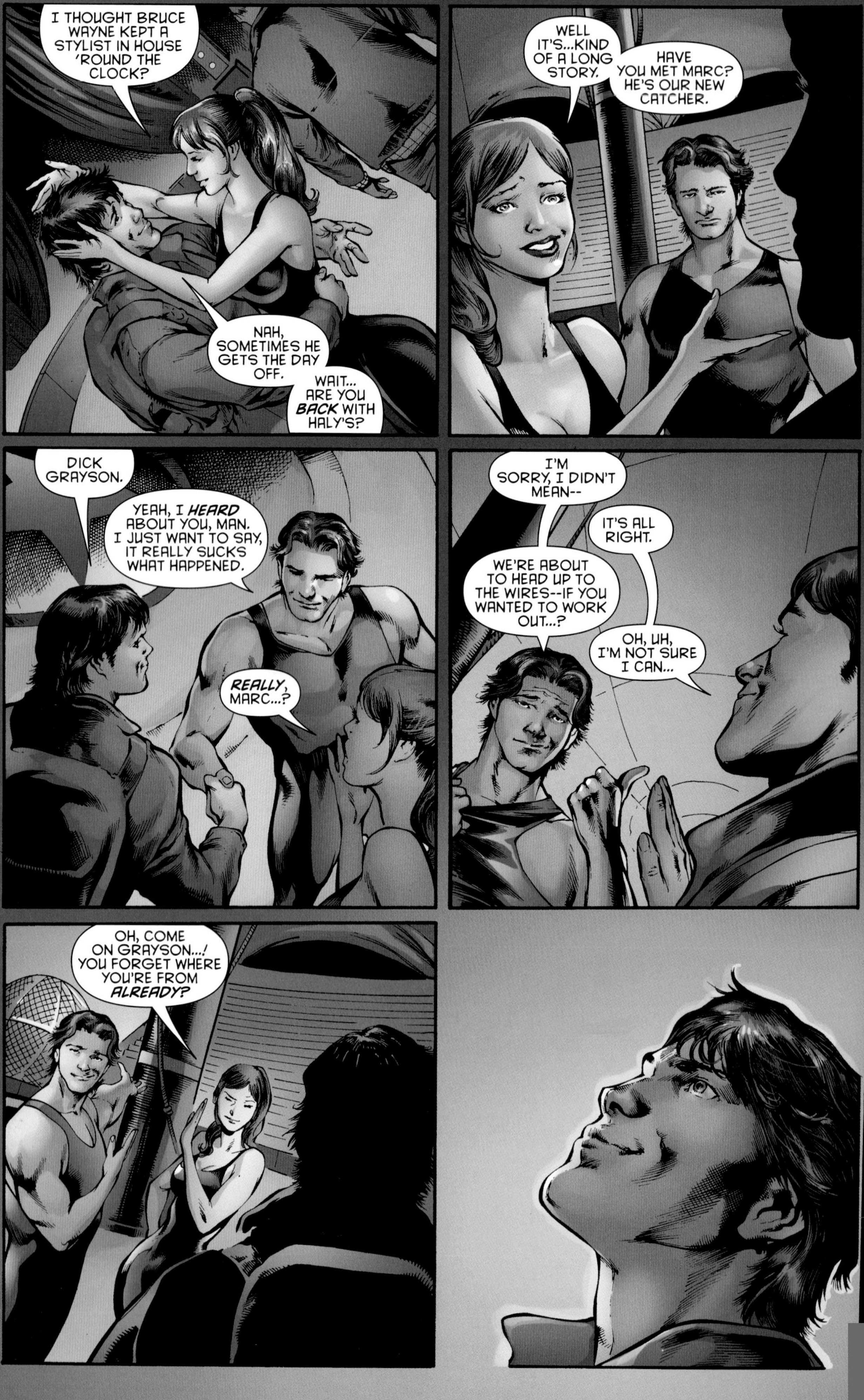
I THOUGHT BRUCE WAYNE KEPT A STYLIST IN HOUSE 'ROUND THE CLOCK?
NAH, SOMETIMES HE GETS THE DAY OFF.
WAIT... ARE YOU *BACK* WITH HALY'S?
WELL IT'S...KIND OF A LONG STORY.
HAVE YOU MET MARC? HE'S OUR NEW CATCHER.
DICK GRAYSON.
YEAH, I *HEARD* ABOUT YOU, MAN. I JUST WANT TO SAY, IT REALLY SUCKS WHAT HAPPENED.
REALLY, MARC...?
I'M SORRY, I DIDN'T MEAN--
IT'S ALL RIGHT.
WE'RE ABOUT TO HEAD UP TO THE WIRES--IF YOU WANTED TO WORK OUT...?
OH, UH, I'M NOT SURE I CAN...
OH, COME ON GRAYSON...! YOU FORGET WHERE YOU'RE FROM *ALREADY*?

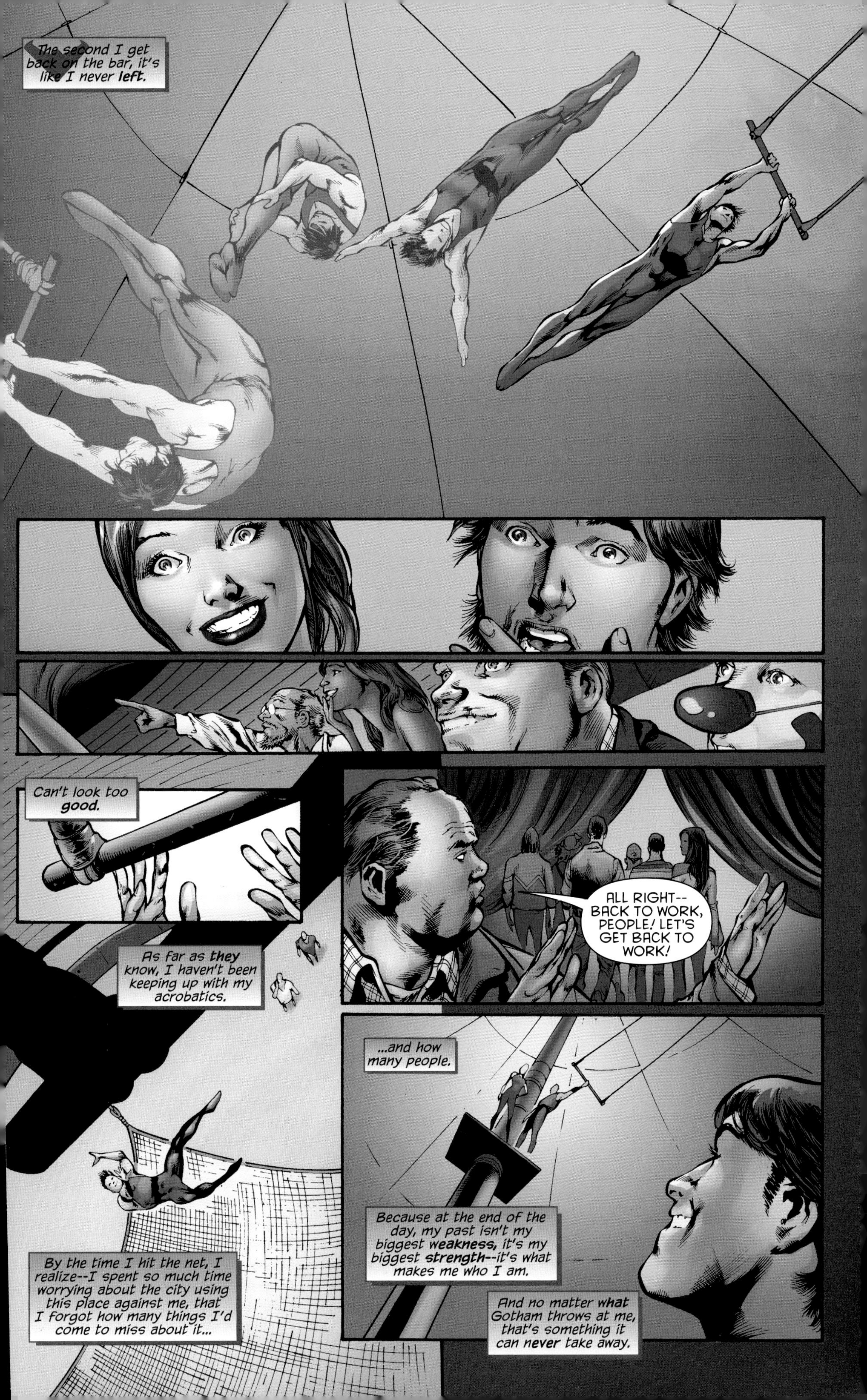

The second I get back on the bar, it's like I never left.
Can't look too good.
ALL RIGHT-- BACK TO WORK, PEOPLE! LET'S GET BACK TO WORK!
As far as they know, I haven't been keeping up with my acrobatics.
By the time I hit the net, I realize--I spent so much time worrying about the city using this place against me, that I forgot how many things I'd come to miss about it...
...and how many people.
Because at the end of the day, my past isn't my biggest weakness, it's my biggest strength--it's what makes me who I am.
And no matter what Gotham throws at me, that's something it can never take away.

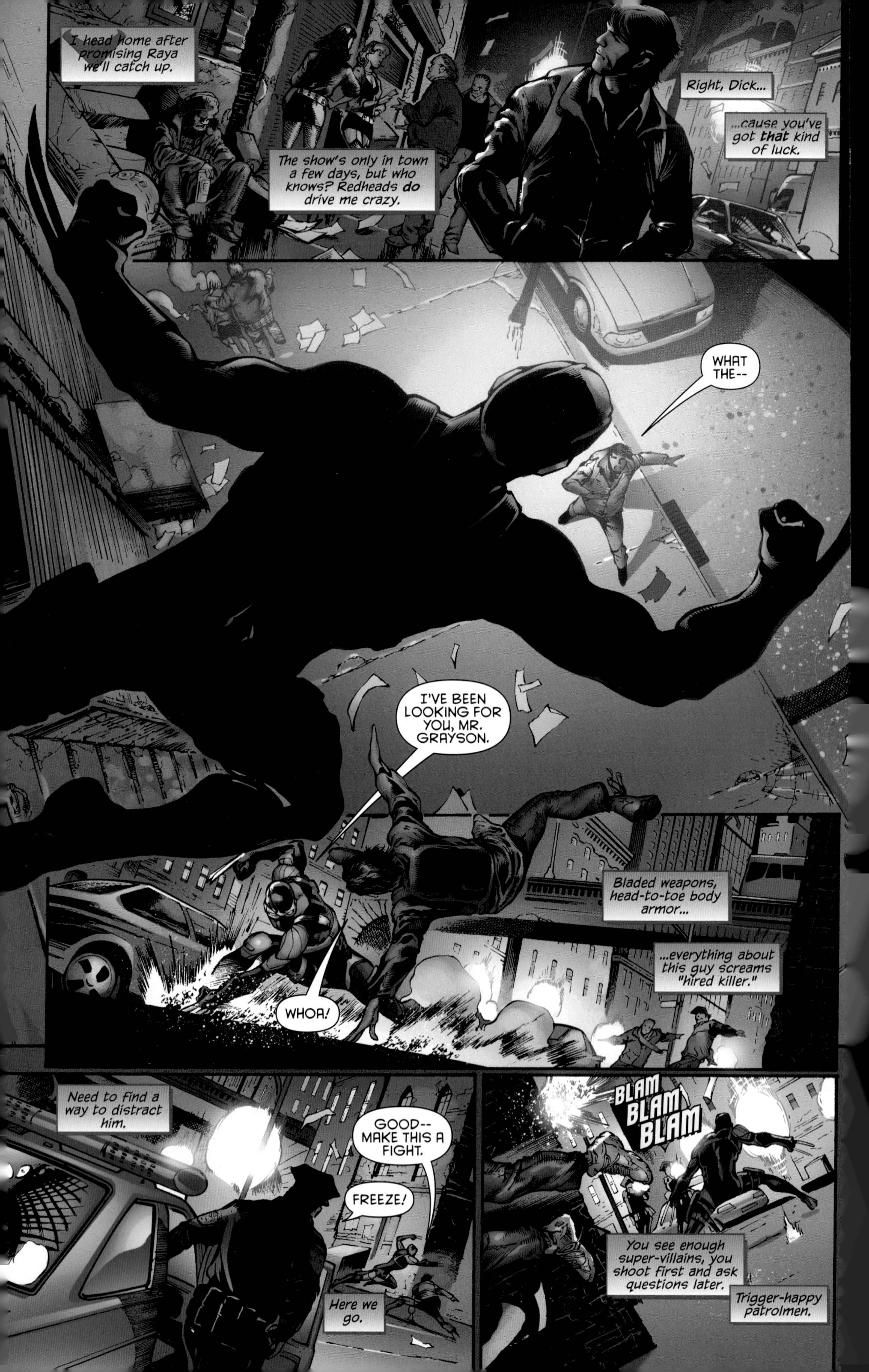
I head home after promising Raya we'll catch up.
The show's only in town a few days, but who knows? Redheads **do** drive me crazy.
Right, Dick...
...cause you've got **that** kind of luck.
WHAT THE--
I'VE BEEN LOOKING FOR YOU, MR. GRAYSON.
WHOA!
Bladed weapons, head-to-toe body armor...
...everything about this guy screams "hired killer."
Need to find a way to distract him.
GOOD-- MAKE THIS A FIGHT.
FREEZE!
Here we go.
BLAM BLAM BLAM
You see enough super-villains, you shoot first and ask questions later.
Trigger-happy patrolmen.

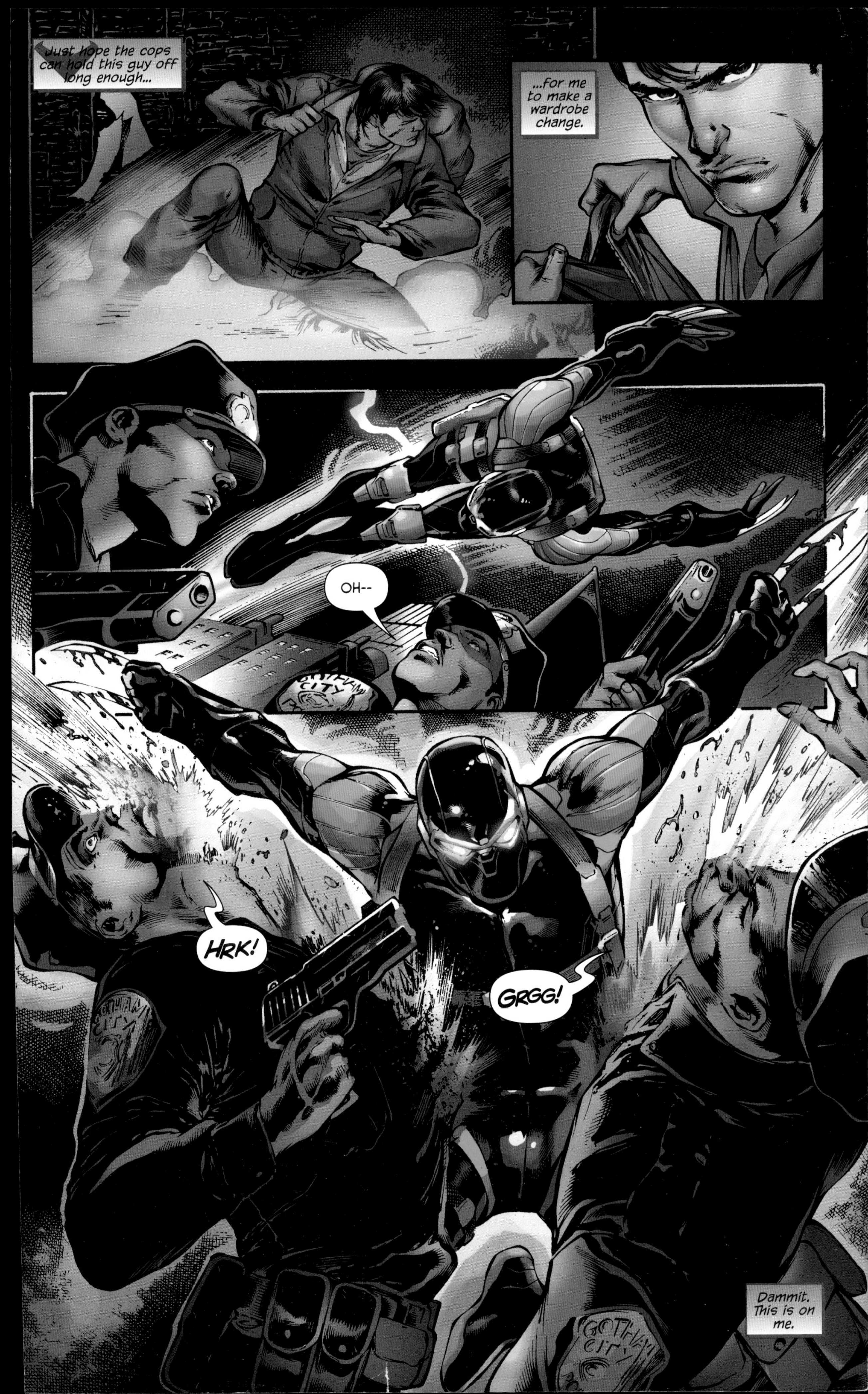
Just hope the cops can hold this guy off long enough...
...for me to make a wardrobe change.
OH--
HRK!
GRGG!
Dammit. This is on me.

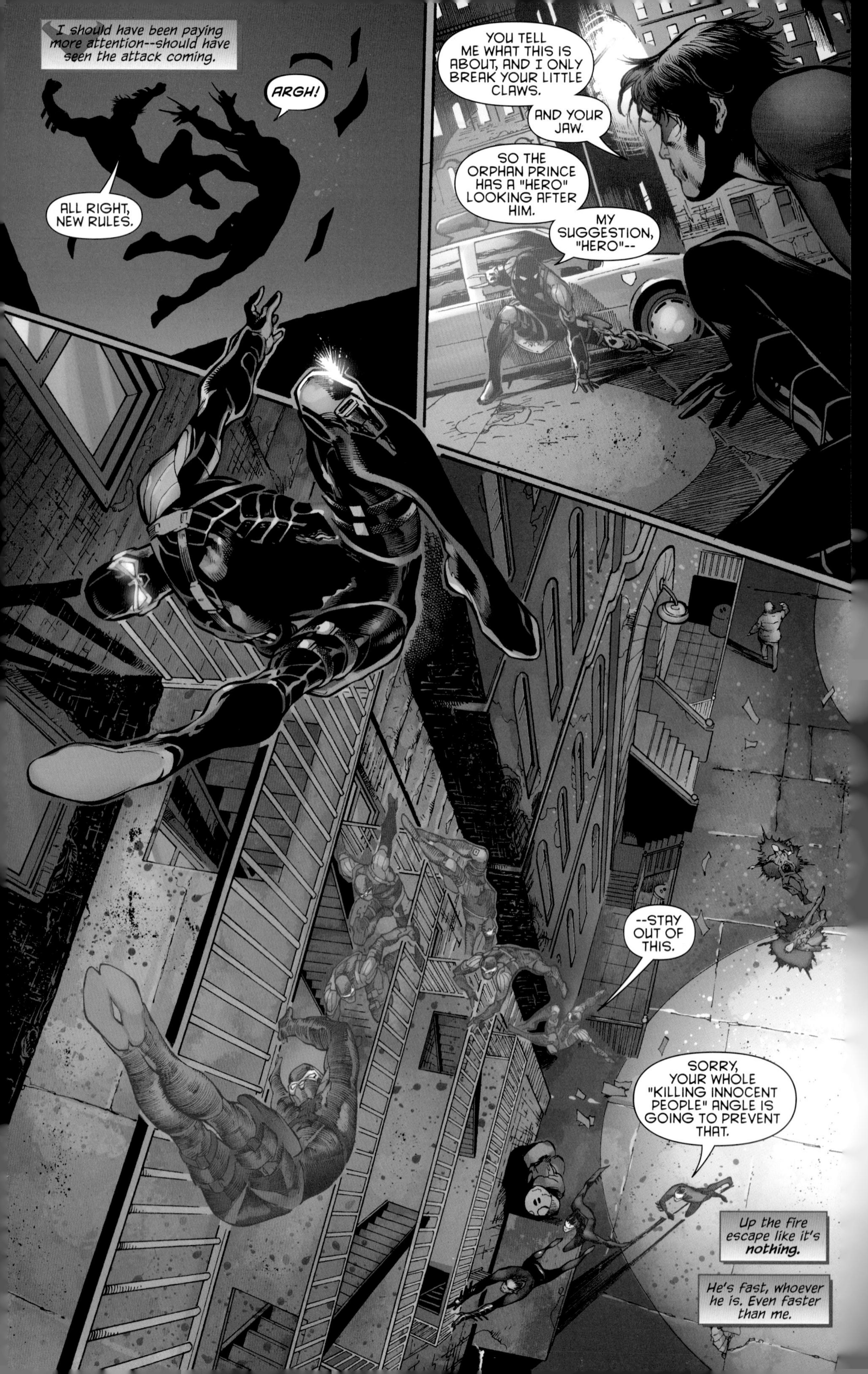

I should have been paying more attention--should have seen the attack coming.
ARGH!
ALL RIGHT, NEW RULES.
YOU TELL ME WHAT THIS IS ABOUT, AND I ONLY BREAK YOUR LITTLE CLAWS.
AND YOUR JAW.
SO THE ORPHAN PRINCE HAS A "HERO" LOOKING AFTER HIM.
MY SUGGESTION, "HERO"--
--STAY OUT OF THIS.
SORRY, YOUR WHOLE "KILLING INNOCENT PEOPLE" ANGLE IS GOING TO PREVENT THAT.
Up the fire escape like it's ***nothing.***
He's fast, whoever he is. Even faster than me.

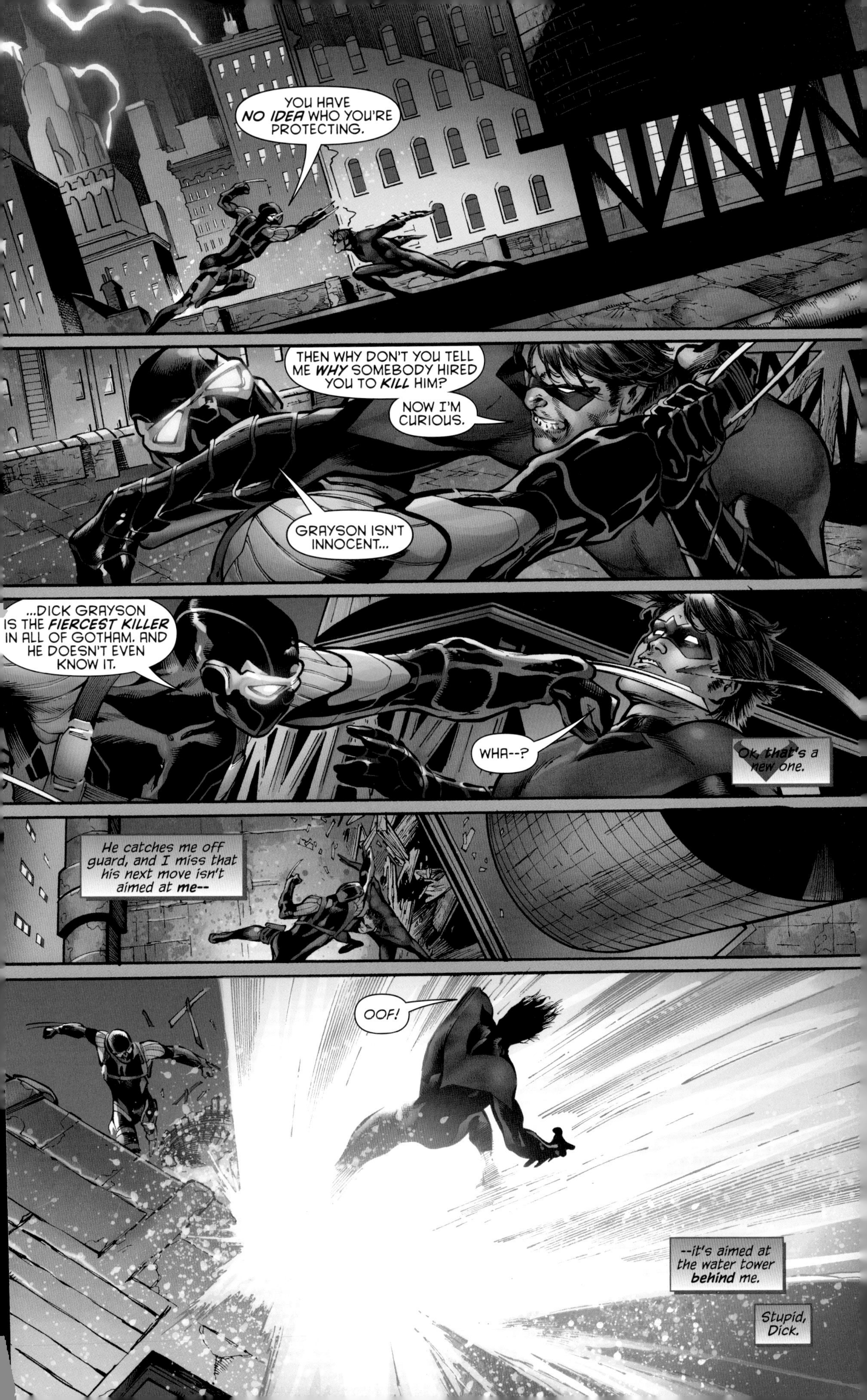
YOU HAVE NO IDEA WHO YOU'RE PROTECTING.
THEN WHY DON'T YOU TELL ME WHY SOMEBODY HIRED YOU TO KILL HIM?
NOW I'M CURIOUS.
GRAYSON ISN'T INNOCENT...
...DICK GRAYSON IS THE FIERCEST KILLER IN ALL OF GOTHAM. AND HE DOESN'T EVEN KNOW IT.
WHA--?
Ok, that's a new one.
He catches me off guard, and I miss that his next move isn't aimed at me--
OOF!
--it's aimed at the water tower behind me.
Stupid, Dick.

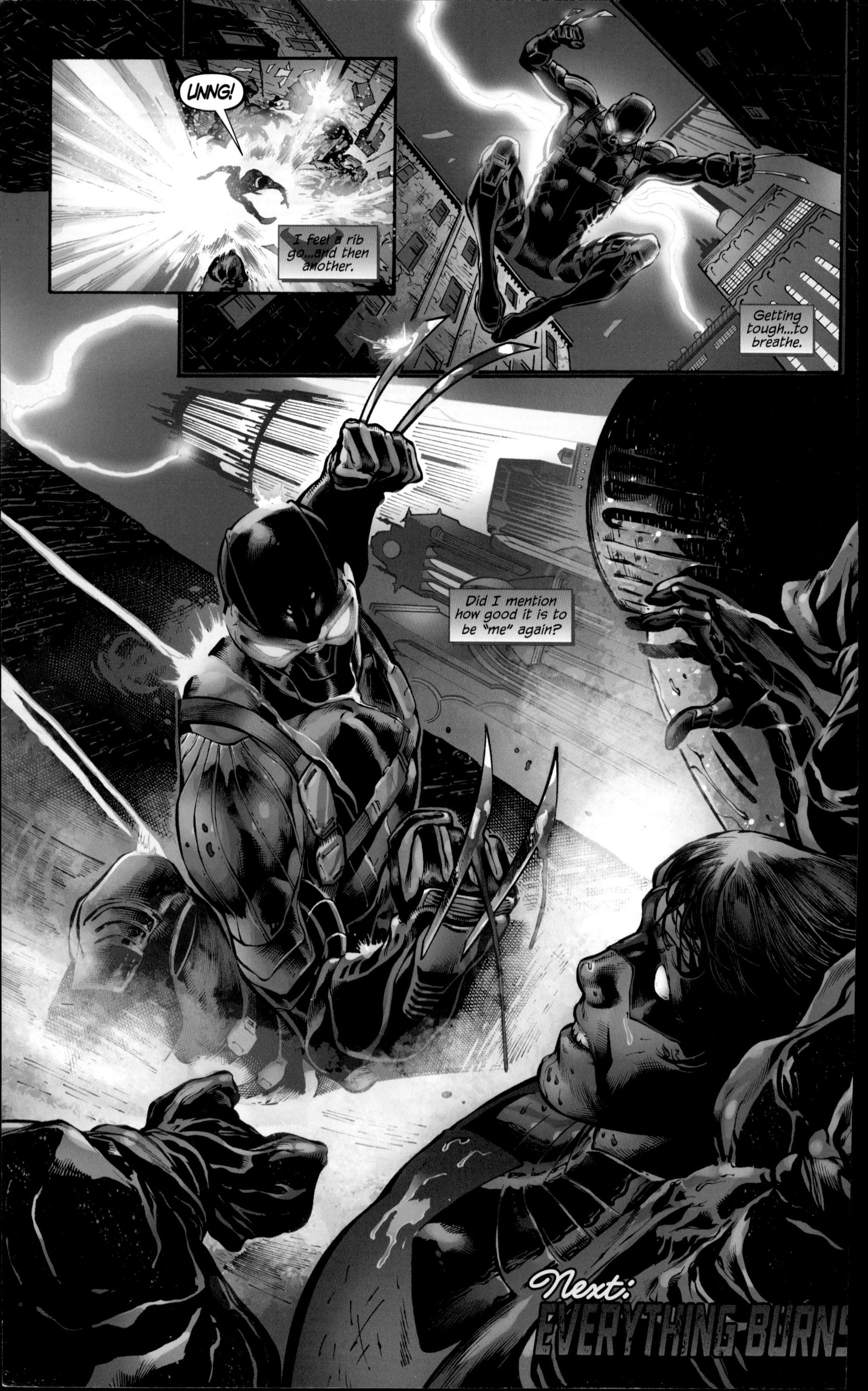
UNNG!
I feel a rib go...and then another.
Getting tough...to breathe.
Did I mention how good it is to be "me" again?
Next:
EVERYTHING BURNS

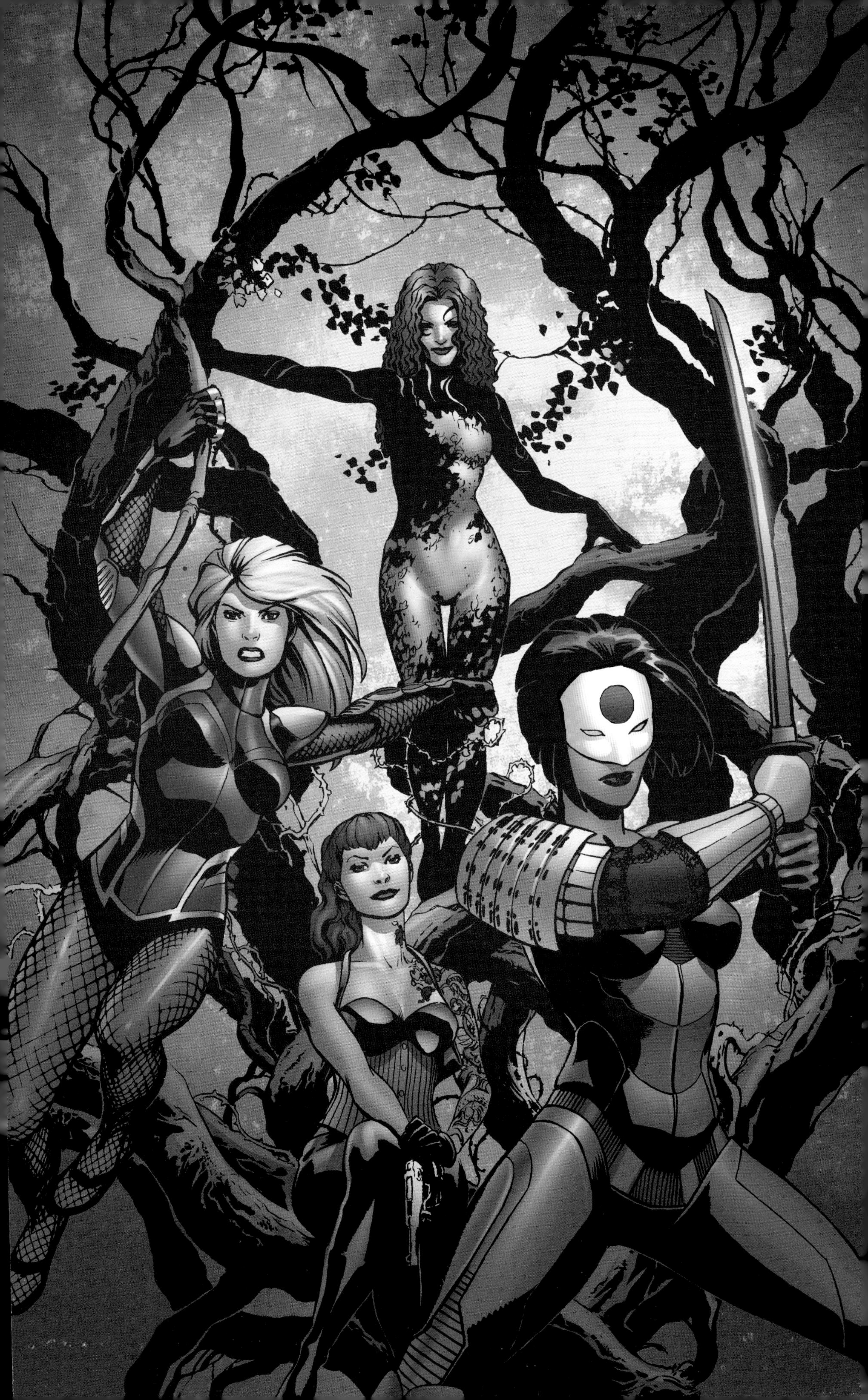

BIRDS OF PREY

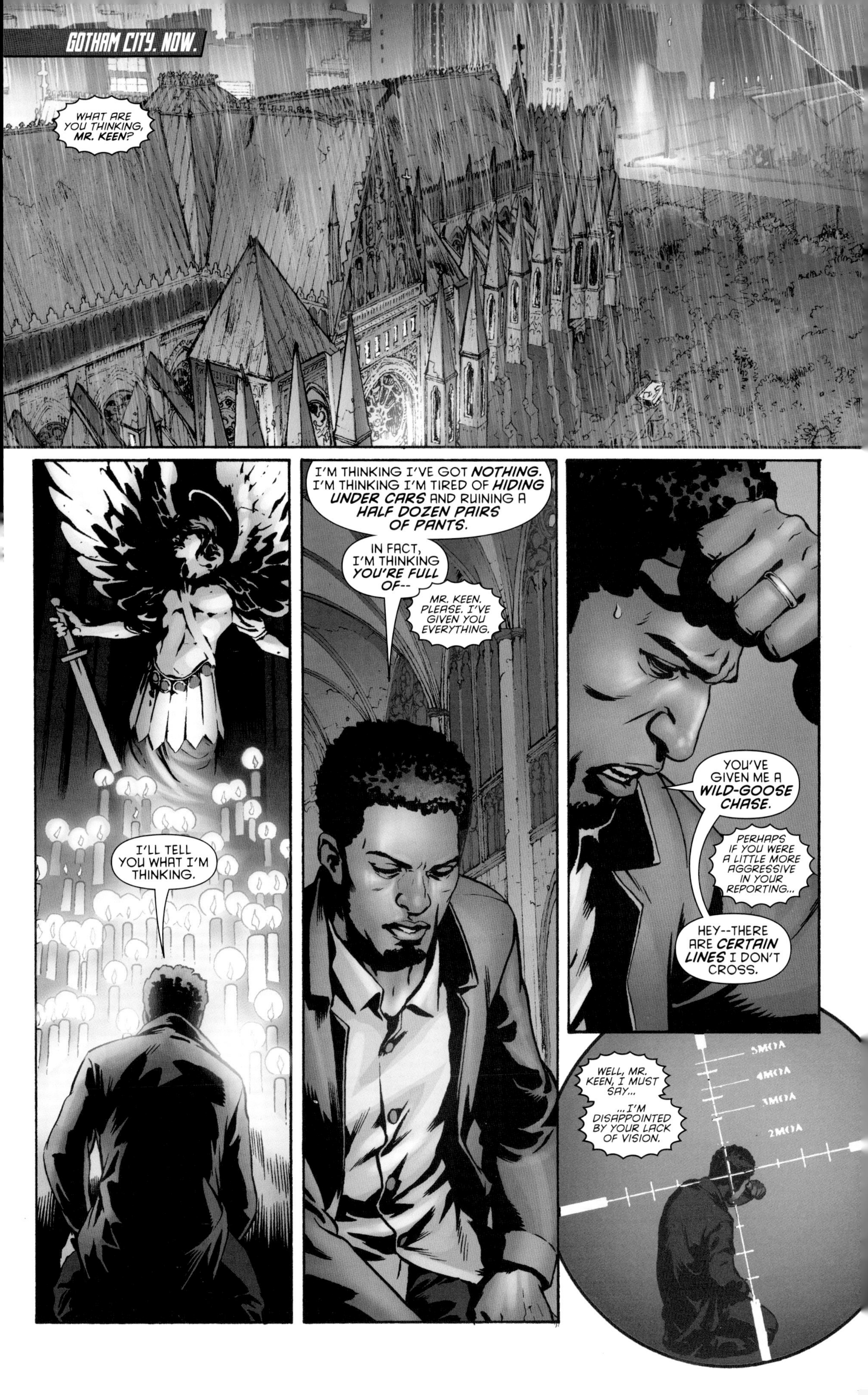
GOTHAM CITY. NOW.
WHAT ARE YOU THINKING, MR. KEEN?
I'LL TELL YOU WHAT I'M THINKING.
I'M THINKING I'VE GOT NOTHING. I'M THINKING I'M TIRED OF HIDING UNDER CARS AND RUINING A HALF DOZEN PAIRS OF PANTS.
IN FACT, I'M THINKING YOU'RE FULL OF--
MR. KEEN. PLEASE. I'VE GIVEN YOU EVERYTHING.
YOU'VE GIVEN ME A WILD-GOOSE CHASE.
PERHAPS IF YOU WERE A LITTLE MORE AGGRESSIVE IN YOUR REPORTING...
HEY--THERE ARE CERTAIN LINES I DON'T CROSS.
5MOA
4MOA
3MOA
2MOA
WELL, MR. KEEN, I MUST SAY...
...I'M DISAPPOINTED BY YOUR LACK OF VISION.

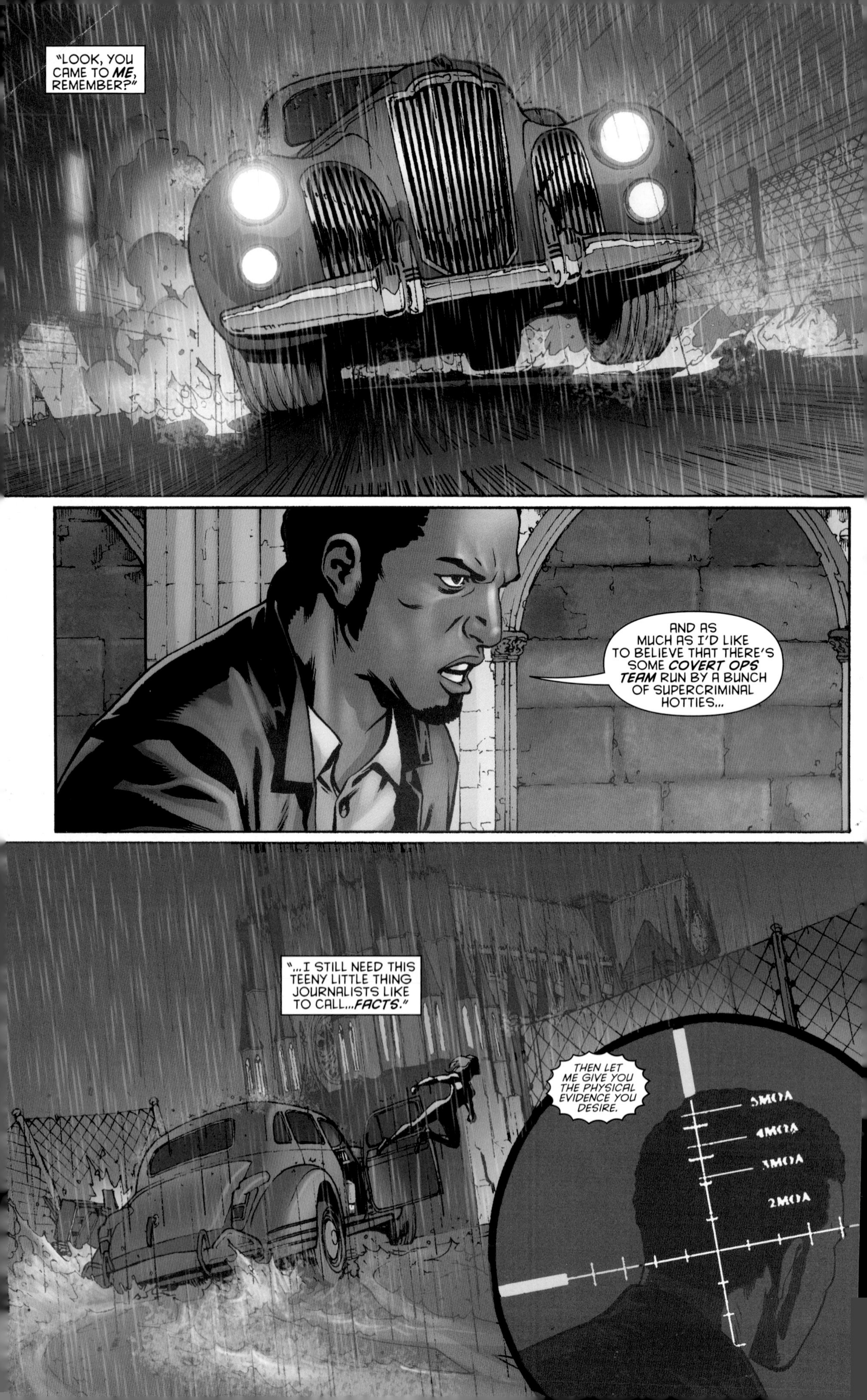
"LOOK, YOU CAME TO *ME*, REMEMBER?"
AND AS MUCH AS I'D LIKE TO BELIEVE THAT THERE'S SOME *COVERT OPS TEAM* RUN BY A BUNCH OF SUPERCRIMINAL HOTTIES...
"...I STILL NEED THIS TEENY LITTLE THING JOURNALISTS LIKE TO CALL...*FACTS*."
THEN LET ME GIVE YOU THE PHYSICAL EVIDENCE YOU DESIRE.
5MOA
4MOA
3MOA
2MOA

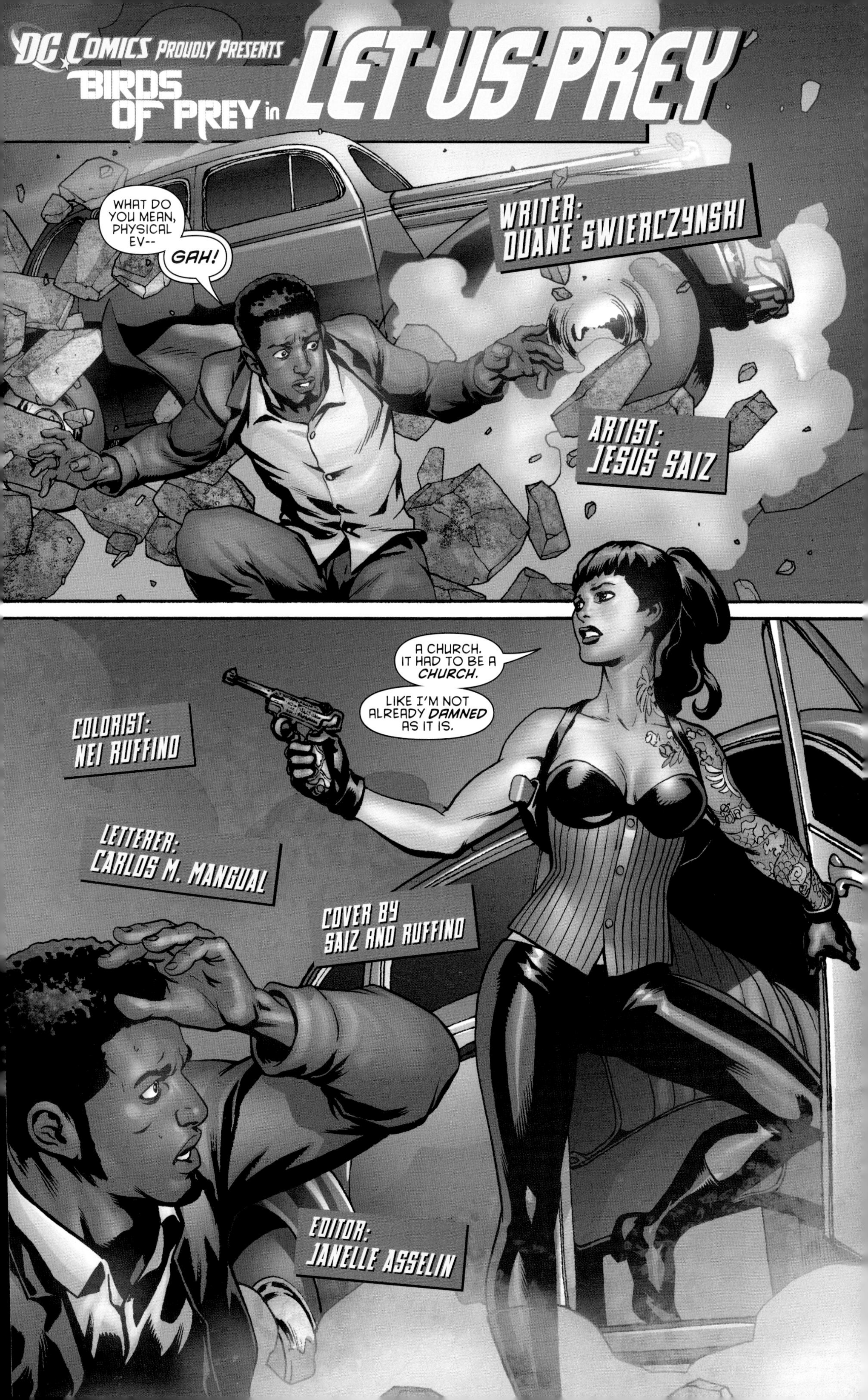
DC COMICS PROUDLY PRESENTS
BIRDS OF PREY in
LET US PREY
WHAT DO YOU MEAN, PHYSICAL EV--
GAH!
WRITER: DUANE SWIERCZYNSKI
ARTIST: JESUS SAIZ
A CHURCH. IT HAD TO BE A CHURCH.
LIKE I'M NOT ALREADY DAMNED AS IT IS.
COLORIST: NEI RUFFINO
LETTERER: CARLOS M. MANGUAL
COVER BY SAIZ AND RUFFINO
EDITOR: JANELLE ASSELIN

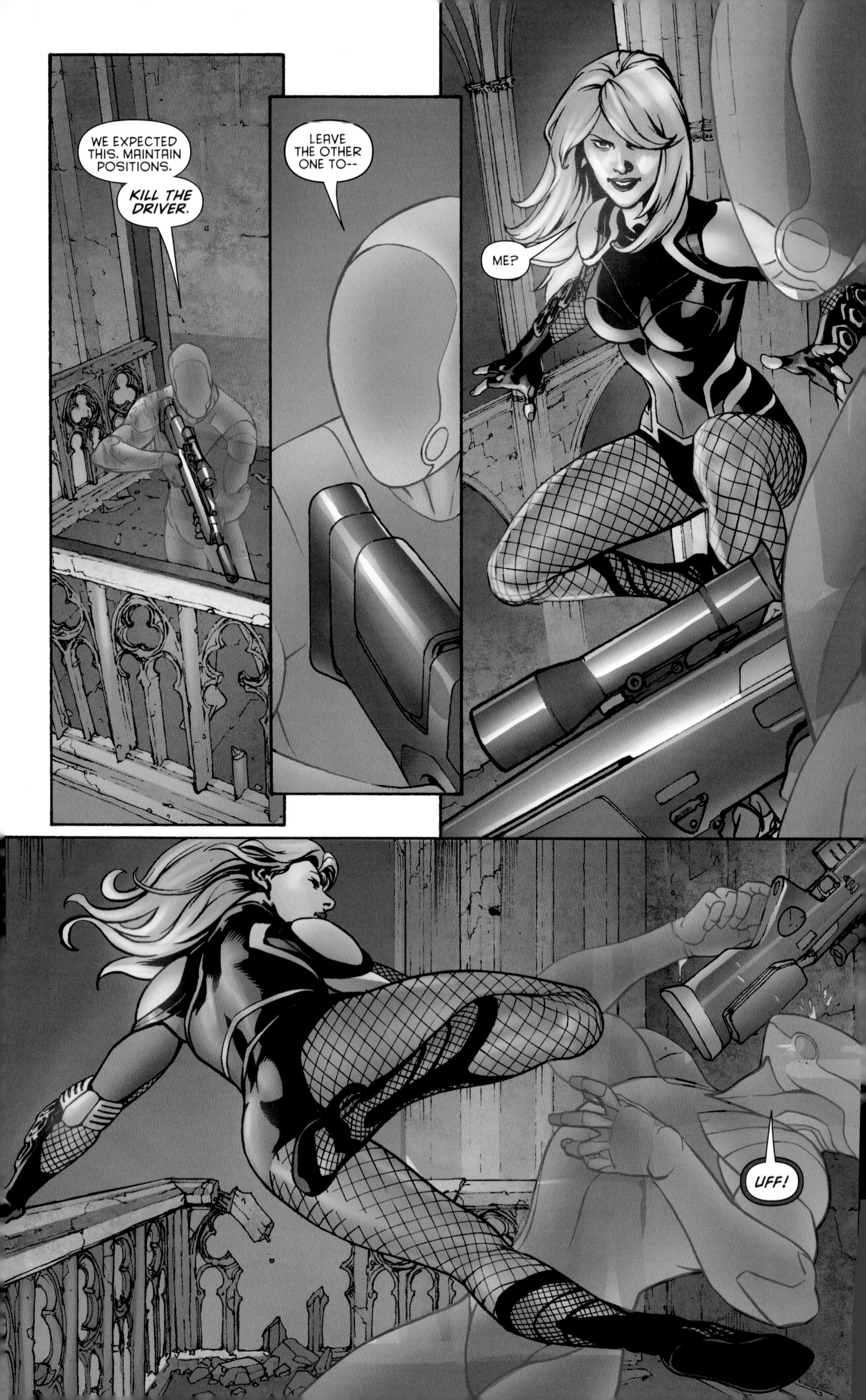
WE EXPECTED THIS. MAINTAIN POSITIONS.
KILL THE DRIVER.
LEAVE THE OTHER ONE TO--
ME?
UFF!

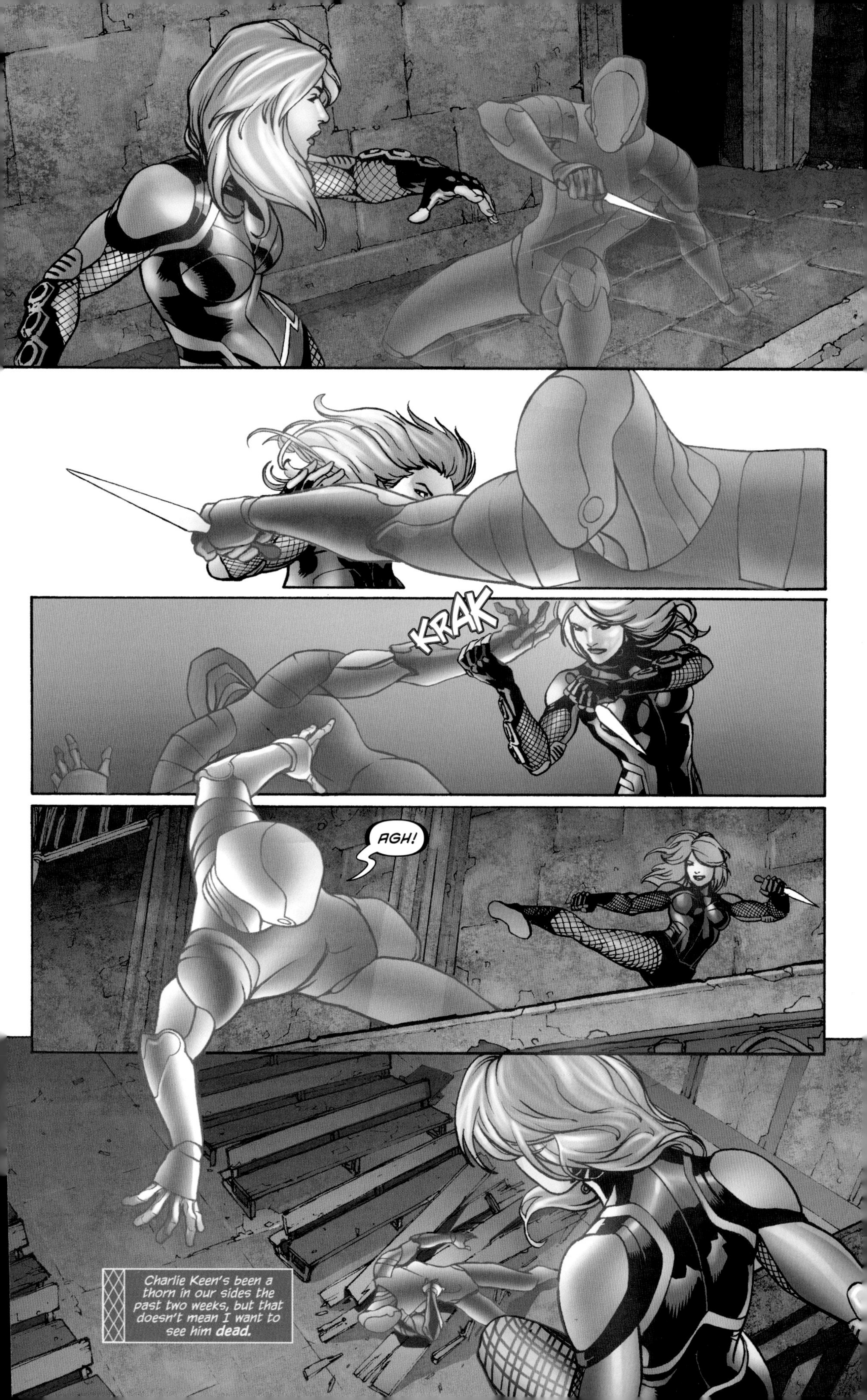
KRAK
AGH!
Charlie Keen's been a thorn in our sides the past two weeks, but that doesn't mean I want to see him dead.

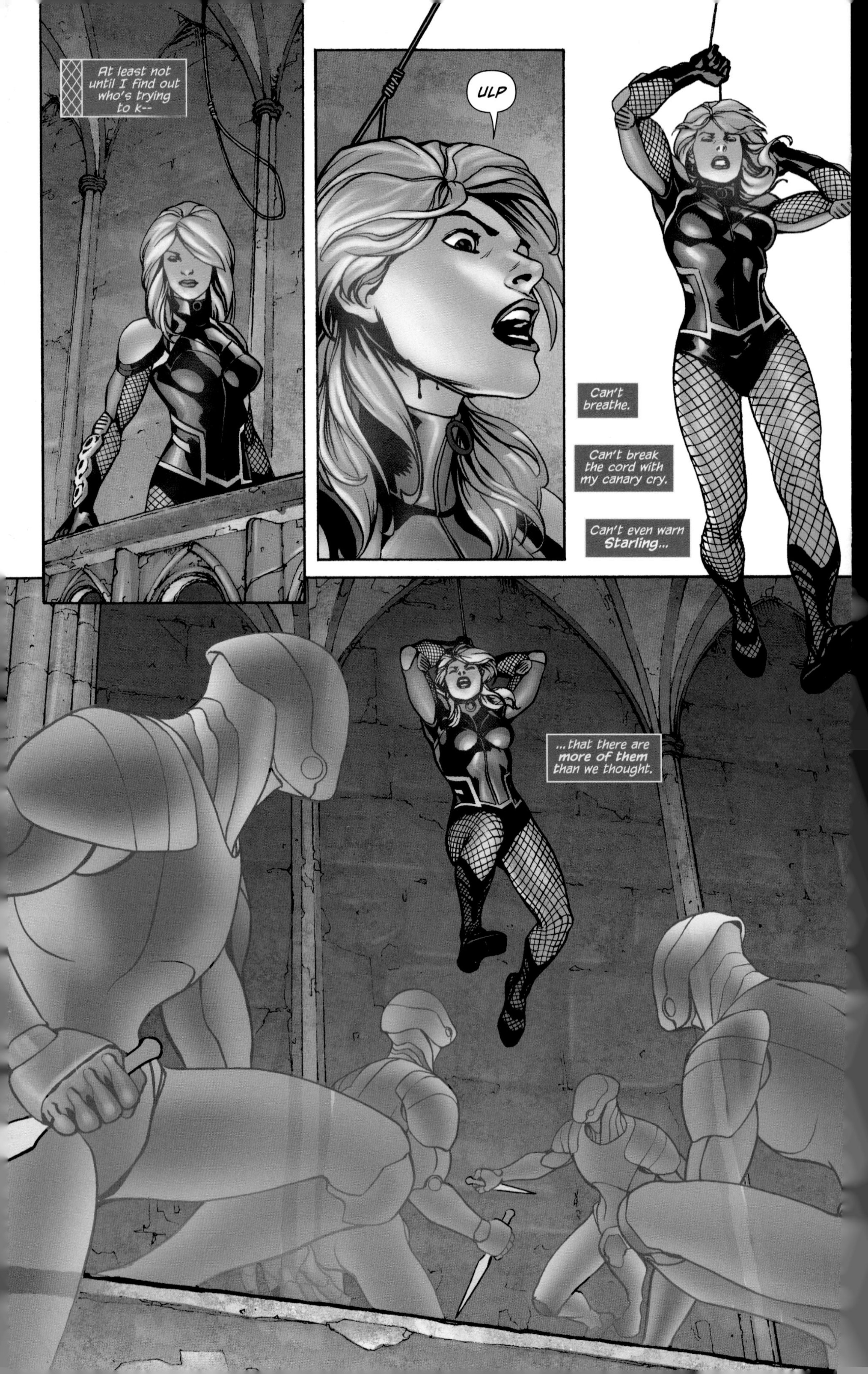

At least not until I find out who's trying to k--
ULP
Can't breathe.
Can't break the cord with my canary cry.
Can't even warn Starling...
...that there are more of them than we thought.

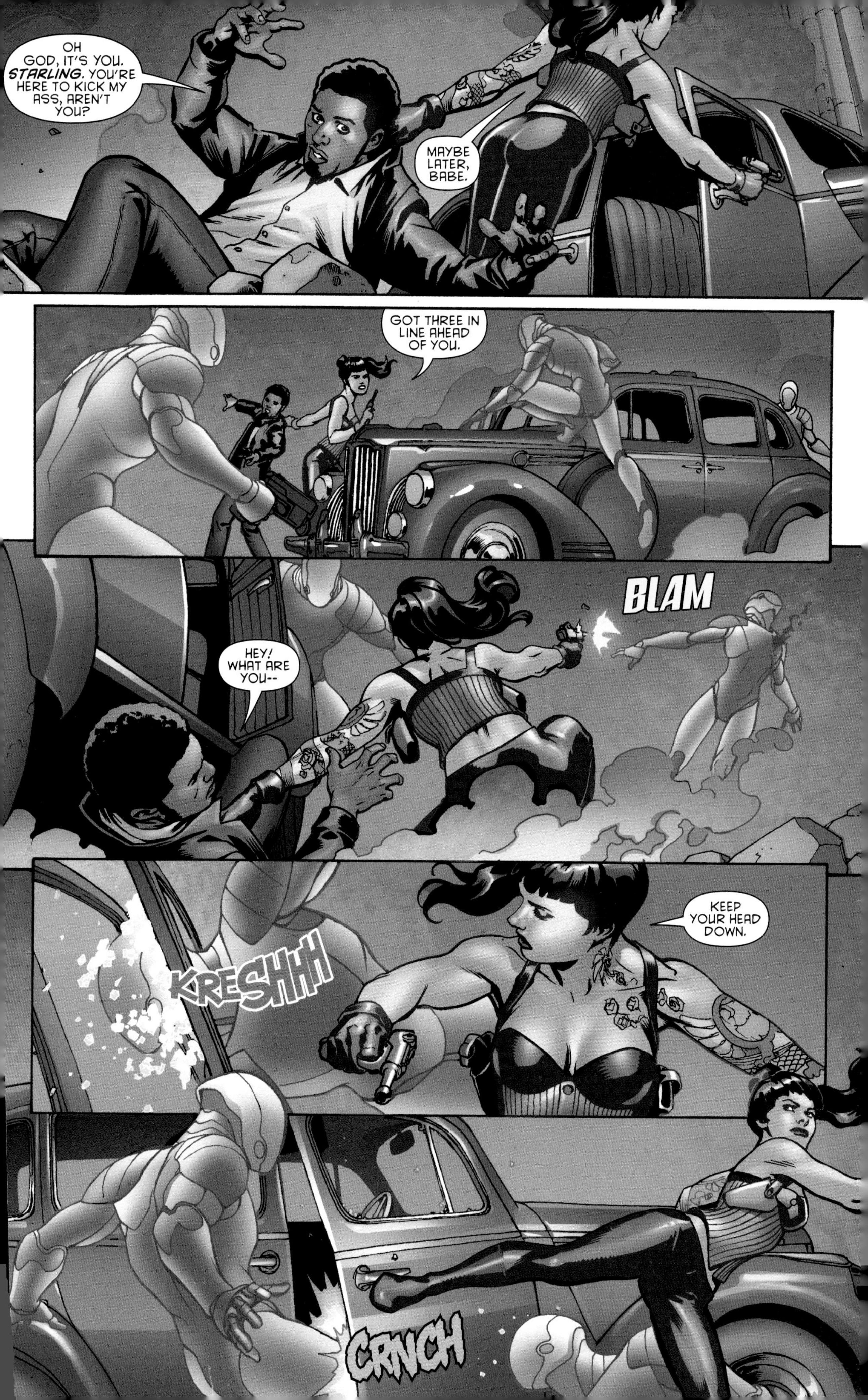

OH GOD, IT'S YOU. STARLING. YOU'RE HERE TO KICK MY ASS, AREN'T YOU?
MAYBE LATER, BABE.
GOT THREE IN LINE AHEAD OF YOU.
BLAM
HEY! WHAT ARE YOU--
KRESHHH
KEEP YOUR HEAD DOWN.
CRNCH

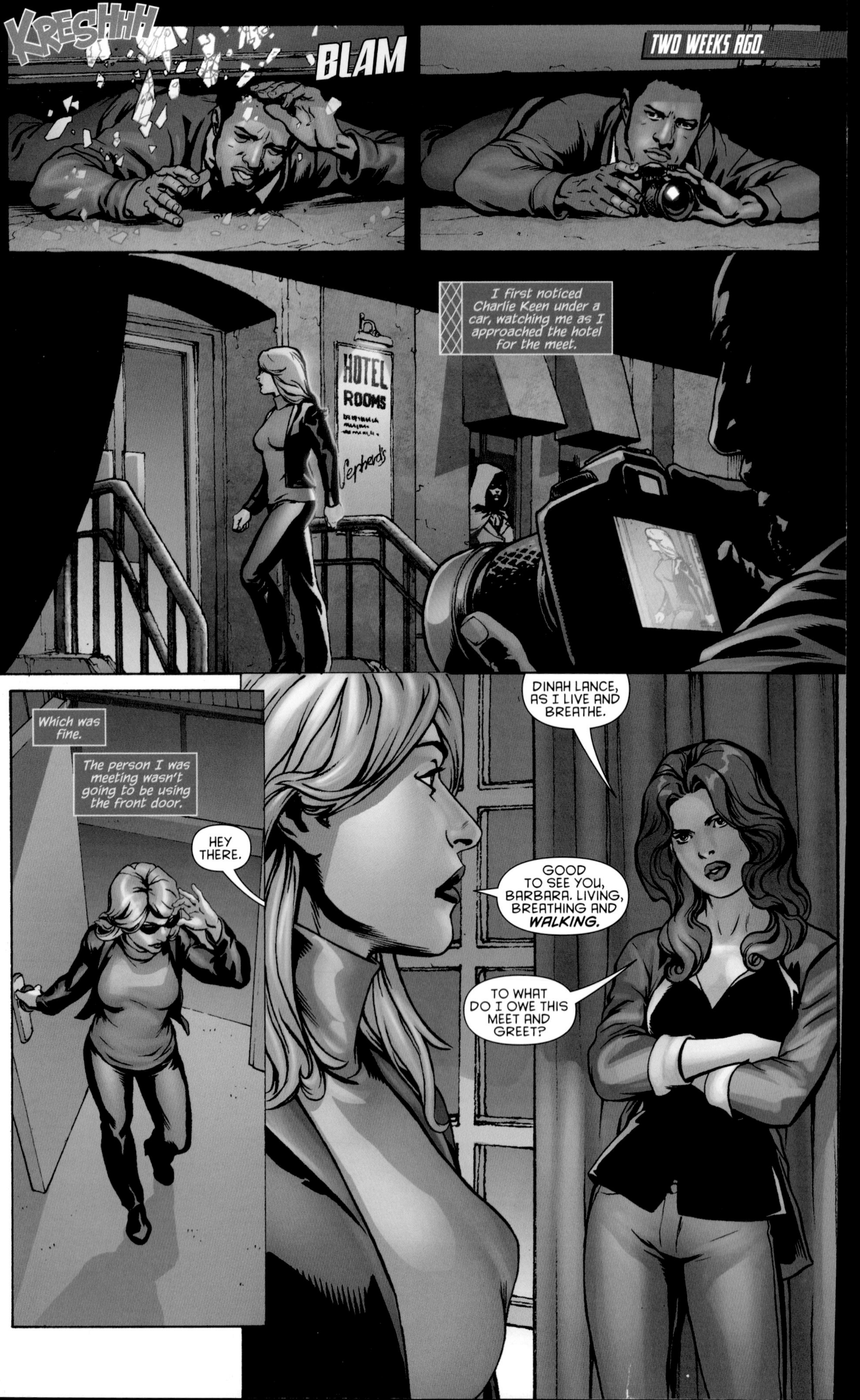
KRESHHH
BLAM
TWO WEEKS AGO.
I first noticed Charlie Keen under a car, watching me as I approached the hotel for the meet.
HOTEL ROOMS
Which was fine.
The person I was meeting wasn't going to be using the front door.
HEY THERE.
DINAH LANCE, AS I LIVE AND BREATHE.
GOOD TO SEE YOU, BARBARA. LIVING, BREATHING AND WALKING.
TO WHAT DO I OWE THIS MEET AND GREET?

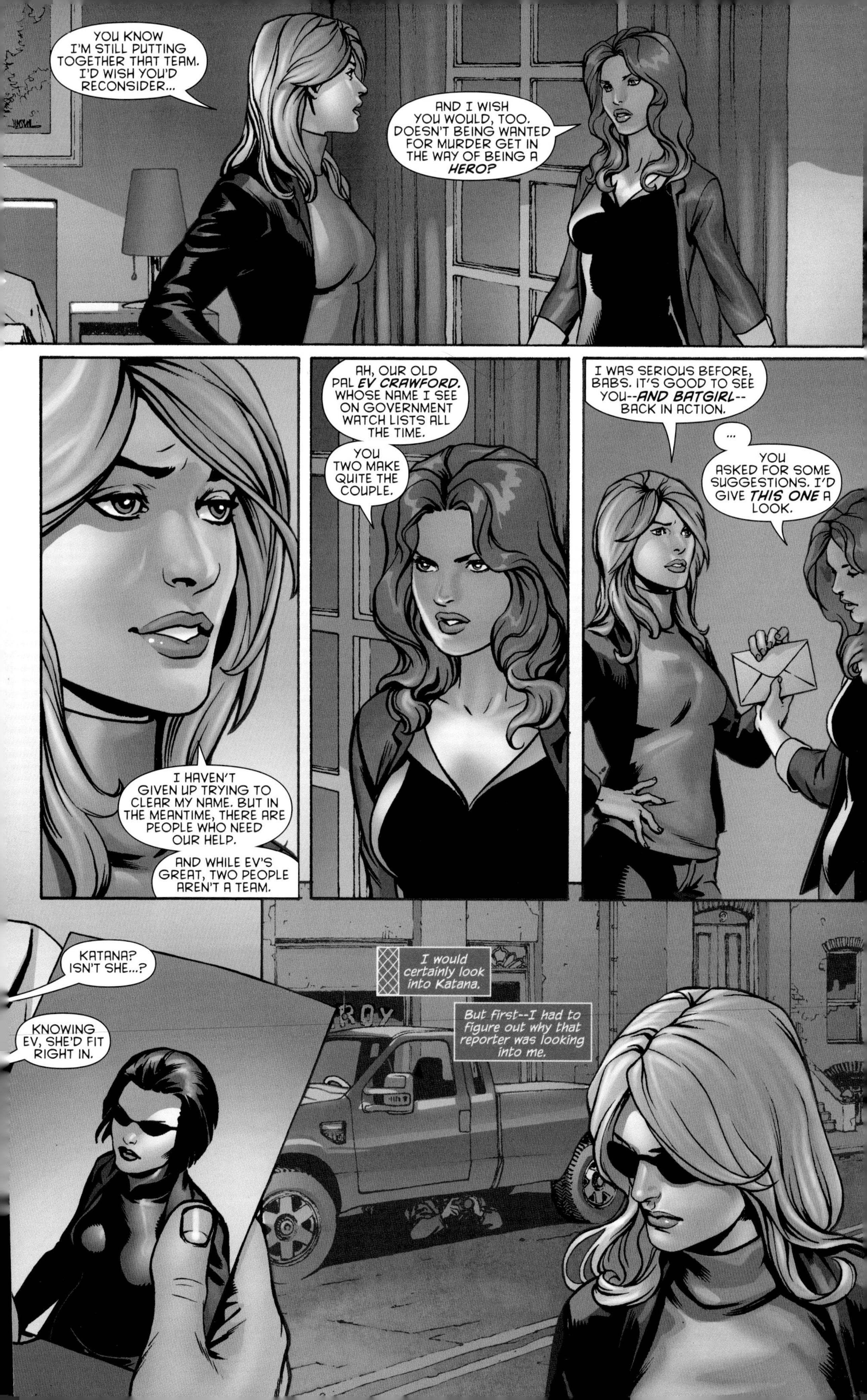

YOU KNOW I'M STILL PUTTING TOGETHER THAT TEAM. I'D WISH YOU'D RECONSIDER...
AND I WISH YOU WOULD, TOO. DOESN'T BEING WANTED FOR MURDER GET IN THE WAY OF BEING A HERO?
I HAVEN'T GIVEN UP TRYING TO CLEAR MY NAME. BUT IN THE MEANTIME, THERE ARE PEOPLE WHO NEED OUR HELP.
AND WHILE EV'S GREAT, TWO PEOPLE AREN'T A TEAM.
AH, OUR OLD PAL EV CRAWFORD. WHOSE NAME I SEE ON GOVERNMENT WATCH LISTS ALL THE TIME.
YOU TWO MAKE QUITE THE COUPLE.
I WAS SERIOUS BEFORE, BABS. IT'S GOOD TO SEE YOU--AND BATGIRL--BACK IN ACTION.
...
YOU ASKED FOR SOME SUGGESTIONS. I'D GIVE THIS ONE A LOOK.
KATANA? ISN'T SHE...?
KNOWING EV, SHE'D FIT RIGHT IN.
I would certainly look into Katana.
But first--I had to figure out why that reporter was looking into me.

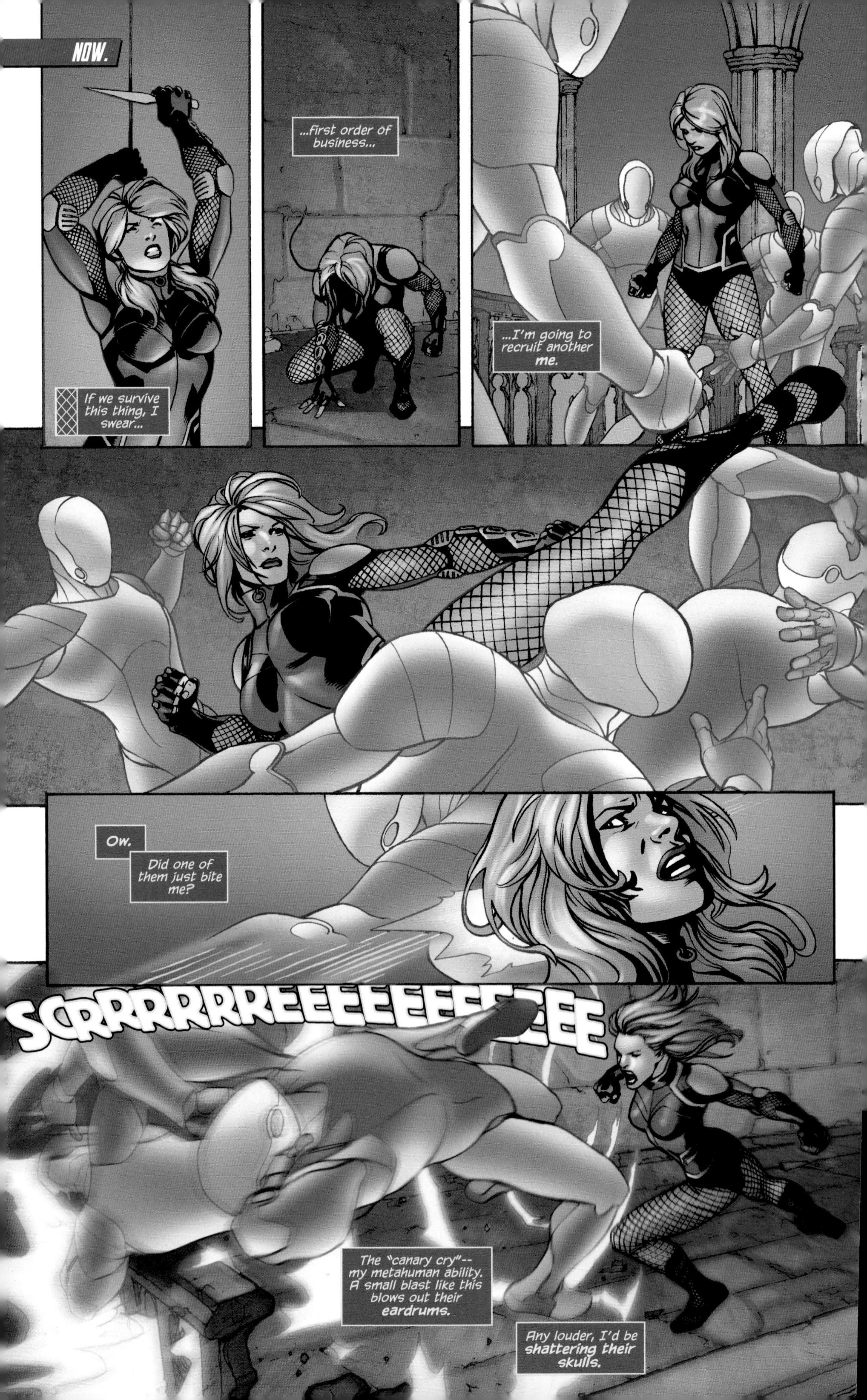
NOW.
If we survive this thing, I swear...
...first order of business...
...I'm going to recruit another me.
Ow.
Did one of them just bite me?
SCRRRRRREEEEEEEEEEEE
The "canary cry"-- my metahuman ability. A small blast like this blows out their eardrums.
Any louder, I'd be shattering their skulls.

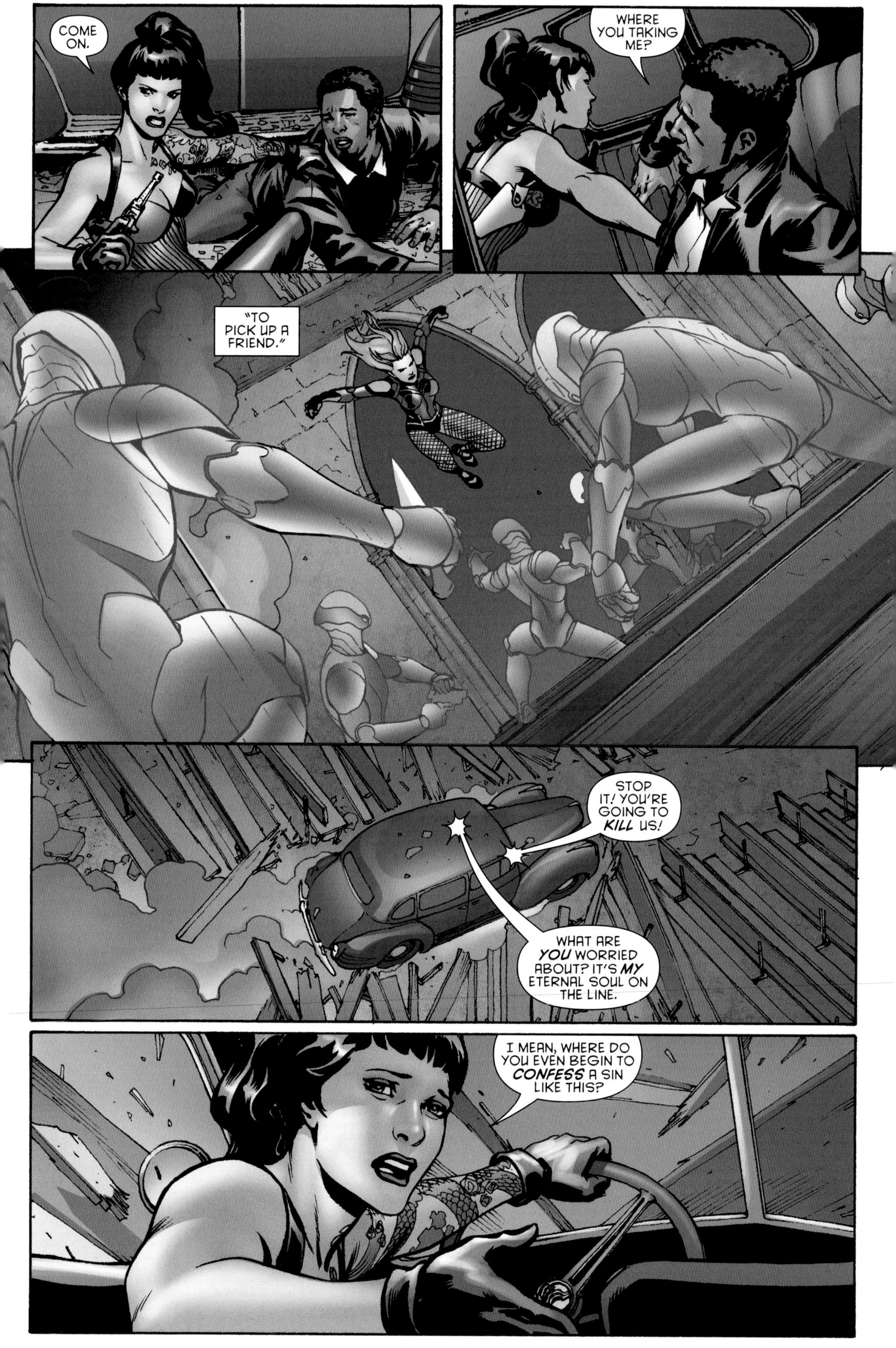
COME ON.
WHERE YOU TAKING ME?
"TO PICK UP A FRIEND."
STOP IT! YOU'RE GOING TO KILL US!
WHAT ARE YOU WORRIED ABOUT? IT'S MY ETERNAL SOUL ON THE LINE.
I MEAN, WHERE DO YOU EVEN BEGIN TO CONFESS A SIN LIKE THIS?

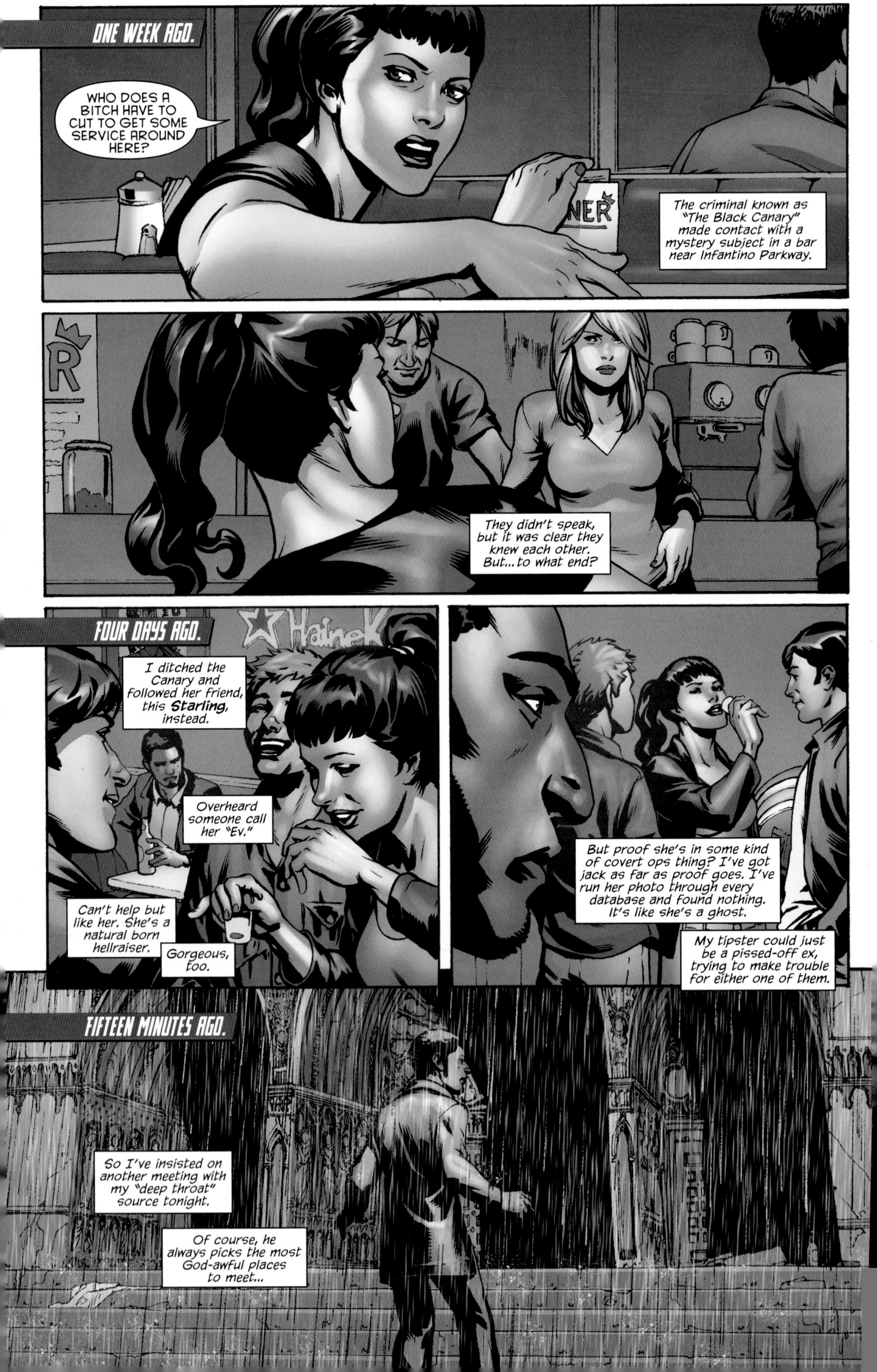
ONE WEEK AGO.
WHO DOES A BITCH HAVE TO CUT TO GET SOME SERVICE AROUND HERE?
The criminal known as "The Black Canary" made contact with a mystery subject in a bar near Infantino Parkway.
They didn't speak, but it was clear they knew each other. But...to what end?
FOUR DAYS AGO.
I ditched the Canary and followed her friend, this Starling, instead.
Overheard someone call her "Ev."
Can't help but like her. She's a natural born hellraiser.
Gorgeous, too.
But proof she's in some kind of covert ops thing? I've got jack as far as proof goes. I've run her photo through every database and found nothing. It's like she's a ghost.
My tipster could just be a pissed-off ex, trying to make trouble for either one of them.
FIFTEEN MINUTES AGO.
So I've insisted on another meeting with my "deep throat" source tonight.
Of course, he always picks the most God-awful places to meet...

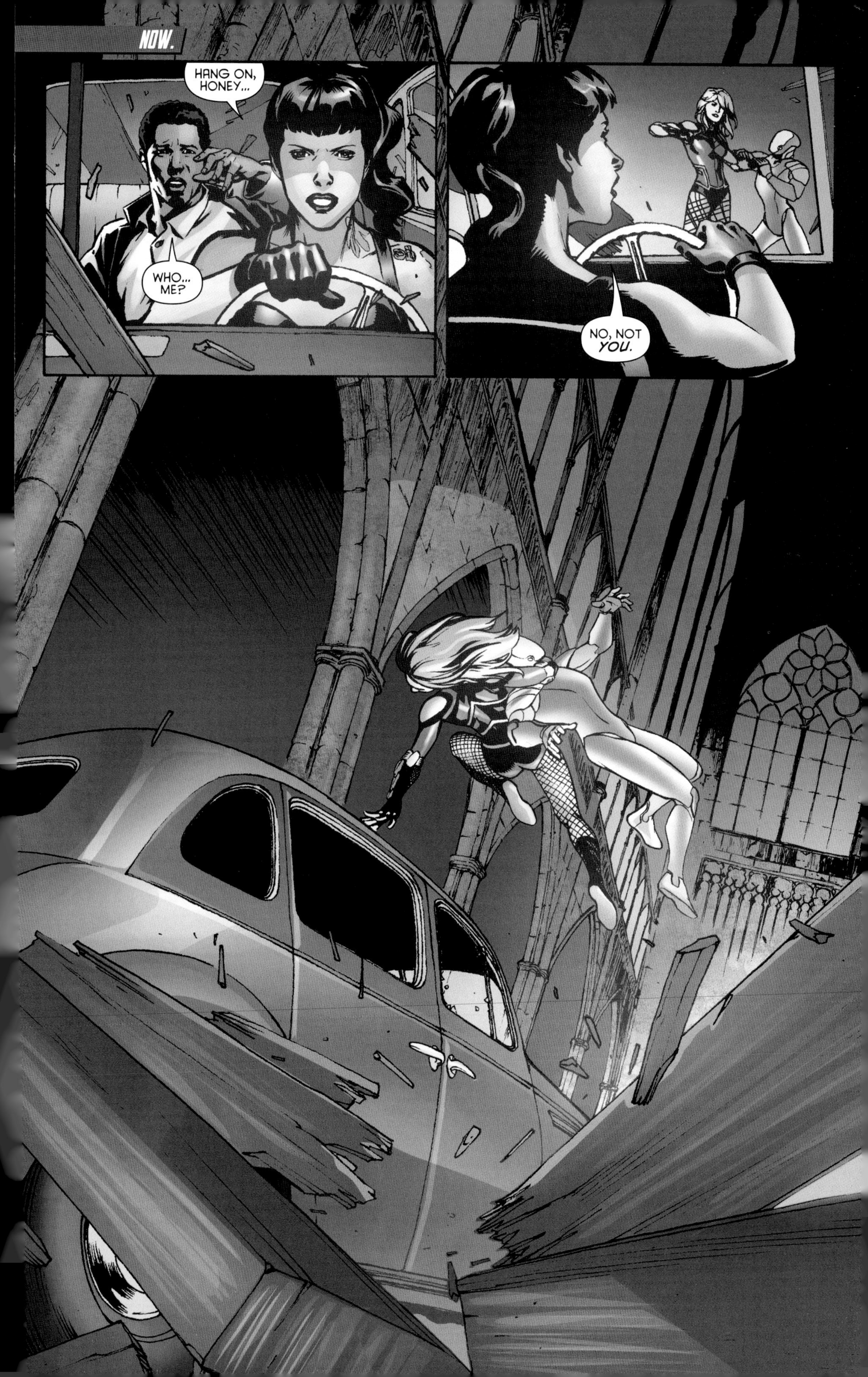
NOW.
HANG ON, HONEY...
WHO... ME?
NO, NOT *YOU*.

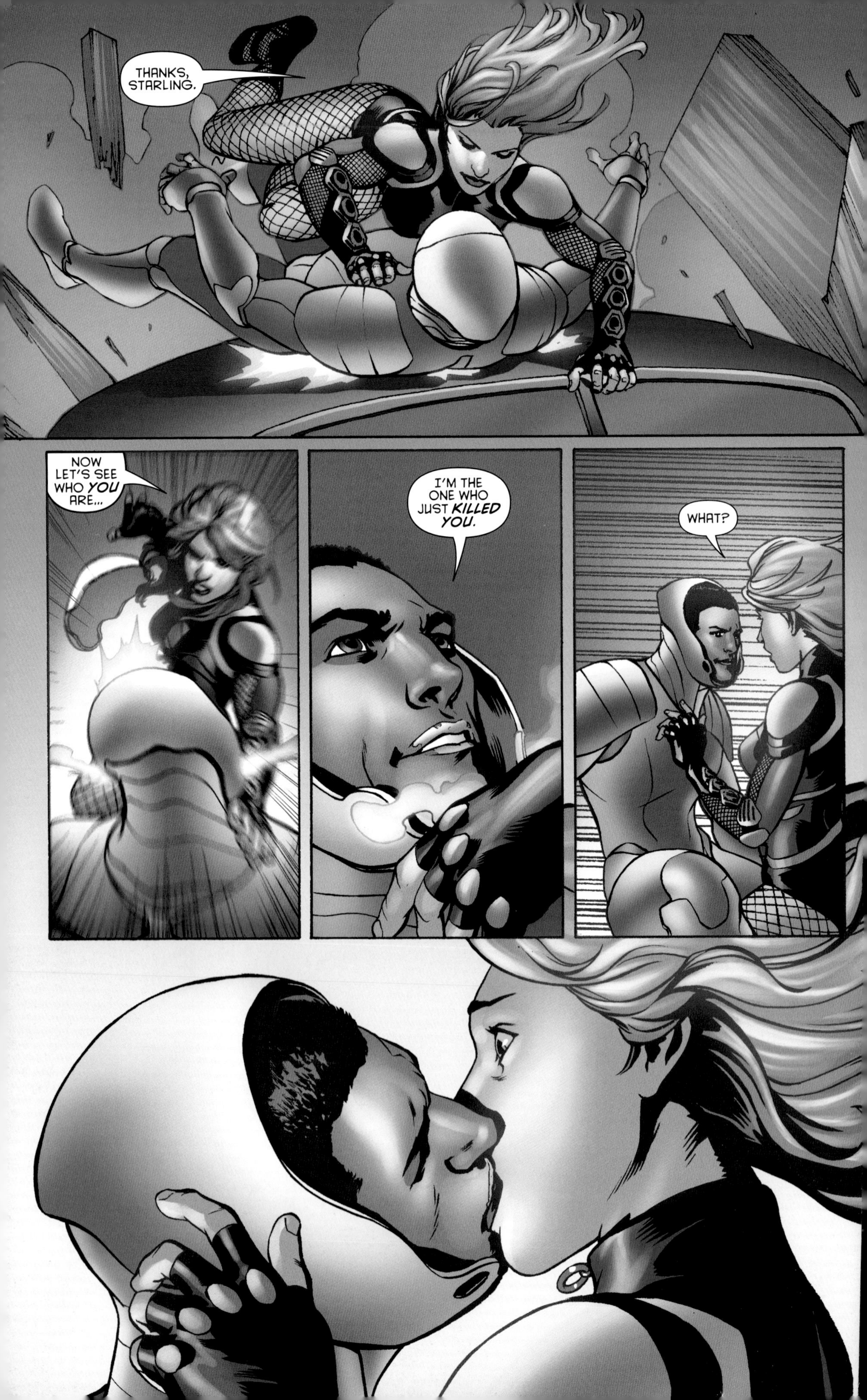
THANKS, STARLING.
NOW LET'S SEE WHO *YOU* ARE...
I'M THE ONE WHO JUST *KILLED YOU*.
WHAT?

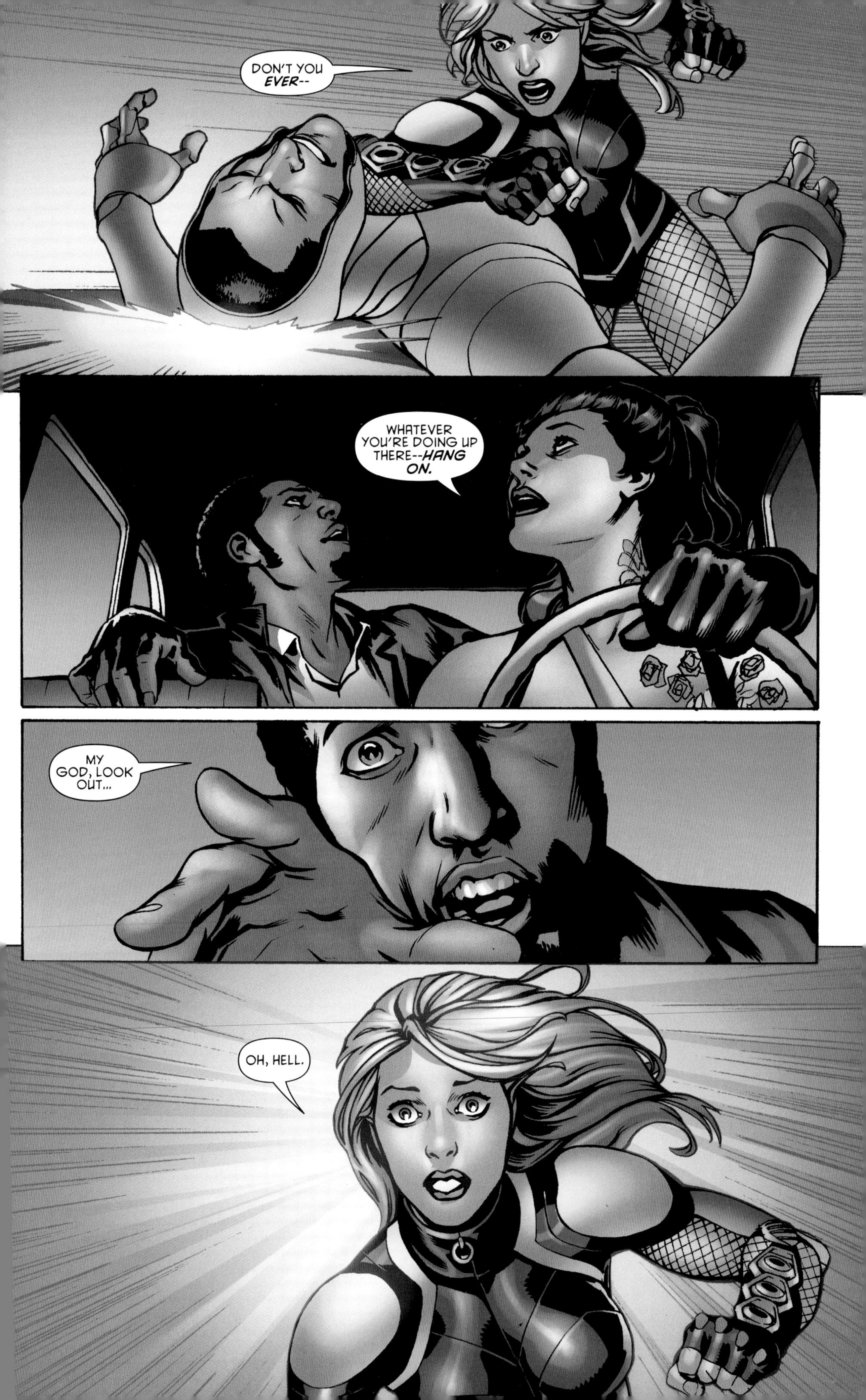
DON'T YOU *EVER*--
WHATEVER YOU'RE DOING UP THERE--*HANG ON.*
MY GOD, LOOK OUT...
OH, HELL.

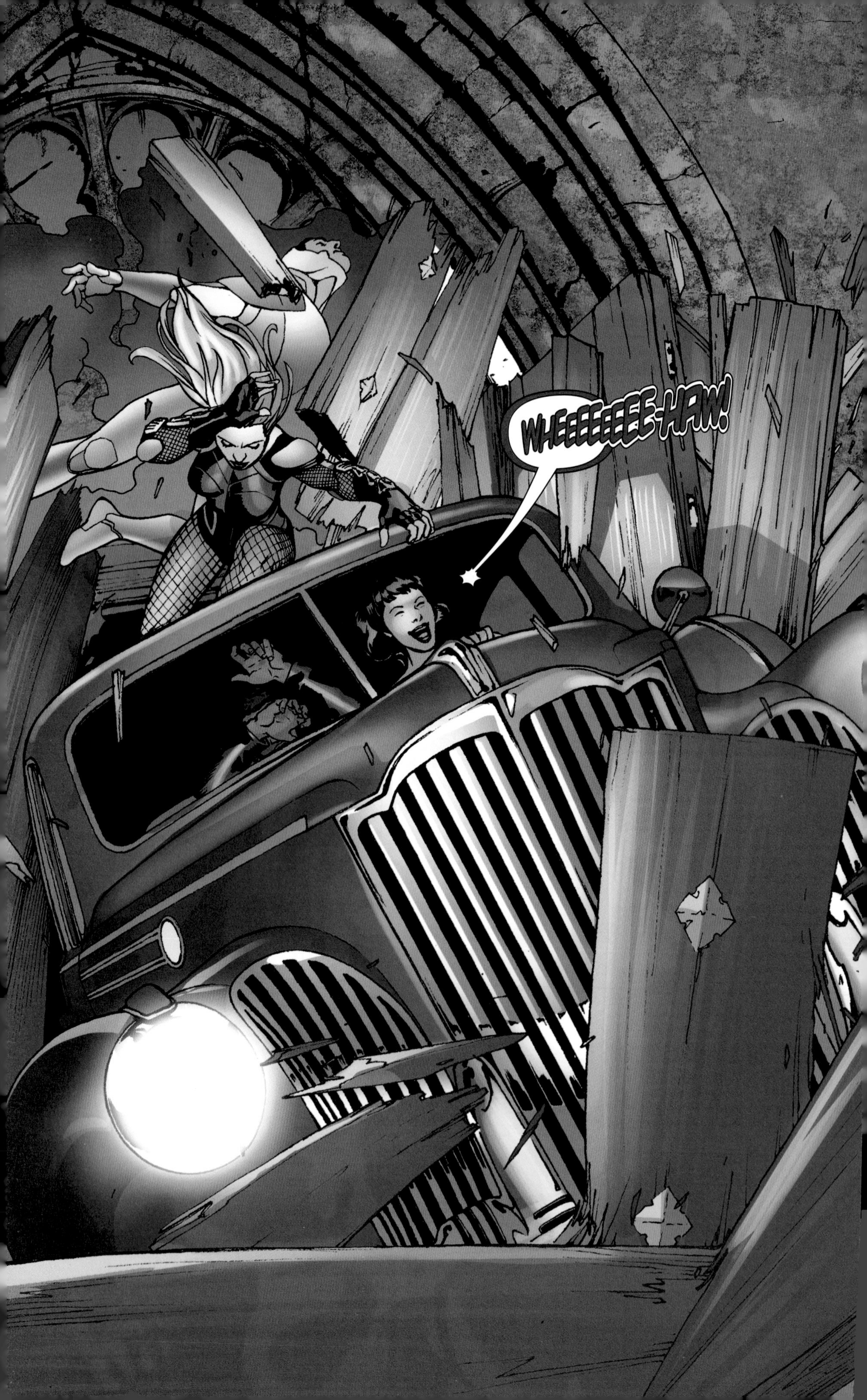
WHEEEEEEEE-HAW!

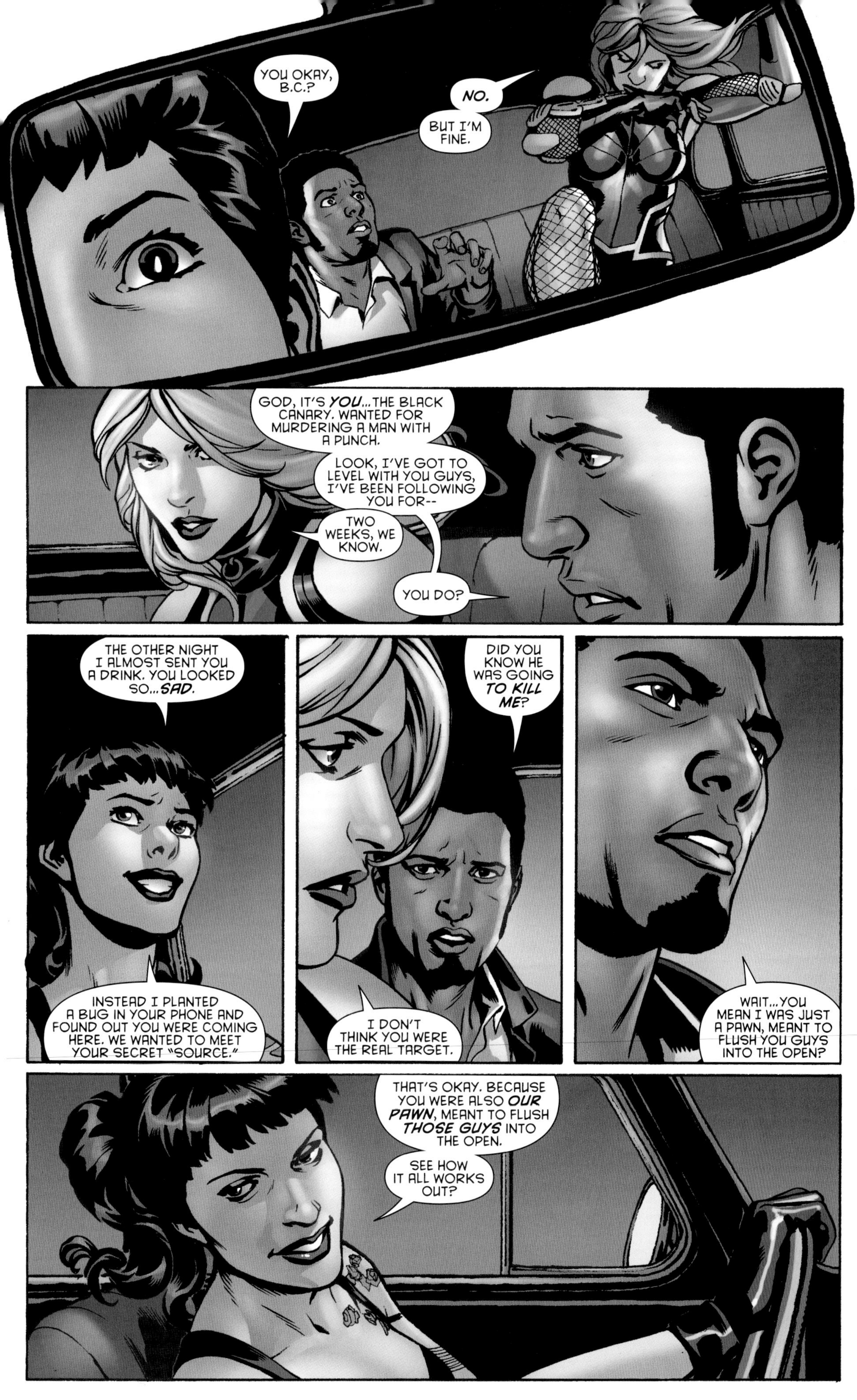

YOU OKAY, B.C.?
NO.
BUT I'M FINE.
GOD, IT'S YOU... THE BLACK CANARY. WANTED FOR MURDERING A MAN WITH A PUNCH.
LOOK, I'VE GOT TO LEVEL WITH YOU GUYS, I'VE BEEN FOLLOWING YOU FOR--
TWO WEEKS, WE KNOW.
YOU DO?
THE OTHER NIGHT I ALMOST SENT YOU A DRINK. YOU LOOKED SO... SAD.
INSTEAD I PLANTED A BUG IN YOUR PHONE AND FOUND OUT YOU WERE COMING HERE. WE WANTED TO MEET YOUR SECRET "SOURCE."
DID YOU KNOW HE WAS GOING TO KILL ME?
I DON'T THINK YOU WERE THE REAL TARGET.
WAIT... YOU MEAN I WAS JUST A PAWN, MEANT TO FLUSH YOU GUYS INTO THE OPEN?
THAT'S OKAY. BECAUSE YOU WERE ALSO OUR PAWN, MEANT TO FLUSH THOSE GUYS INTO THE OPEN.
SEE HOW IT ALL WORKS OUT?

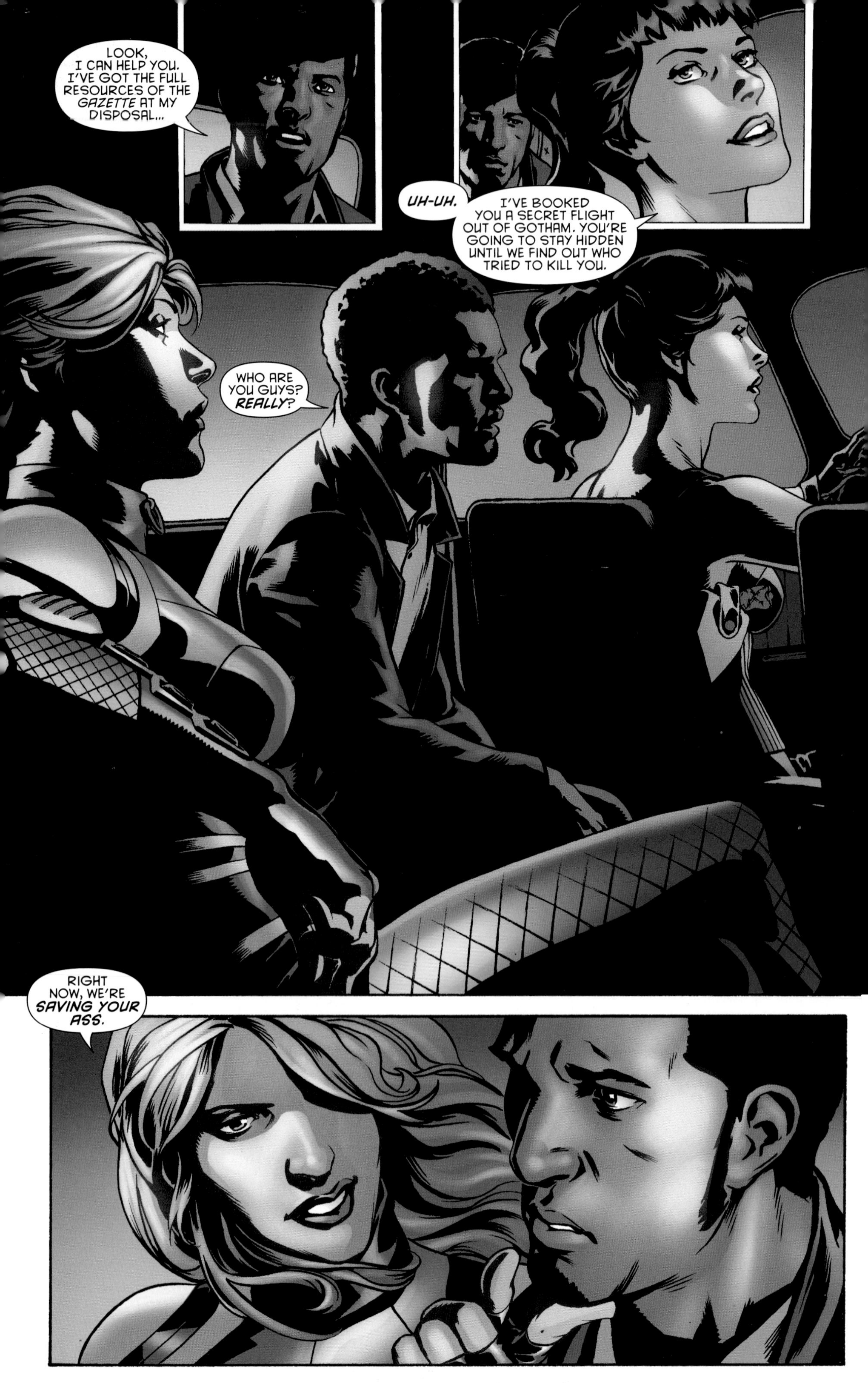
LOOK, I CAN HELP YOU. I'VE GOT THE FULL RESOURCES OF THE *GAZETTE* AT MY DISPOSAL...
UH-UH.
I'VE BOOKED YOU A SECRET FLIGHT OUT OF GOTHAM. YOU'RE GOING TO STAY HIDDEN UNTIL WE FIND OUT WHO TRIED TO KILL YOU.
WHO ARE YOU GUYS? ***REALLY***?
RIGHT NOW, WE'RE ***SAVING YOUR ASS***.

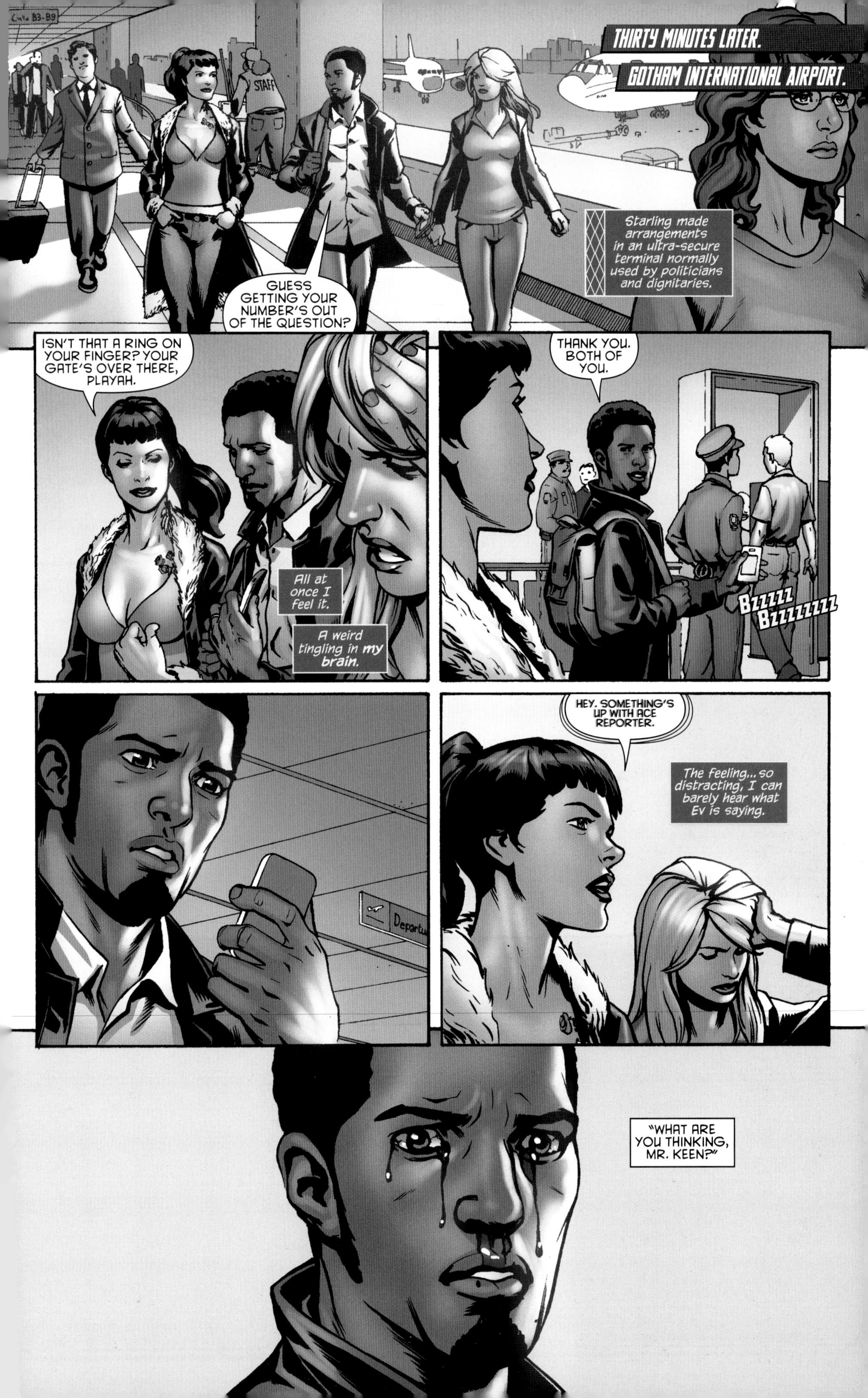
THIRTY MINUTES LATER.
GOTHAM INTERNATIONAL AIRPORT.
Starling made arrangements in an ultra-secure terminal normally used by politicians and dignitaries.
GUESS GETTING YOUR NUMBER'S OUT OF THE QUESTION?
ISN'T THAT A RING ON YOUR FINGER? YOUR GATE'S OVER THERE, PLAYAH.
All at once I feel it.
A weird tingling in my brain.
THANK YOU. BOTH OF YOU.
Bzzzzz Bzzzzzzzz
HEY. SOMETHING'S UP WITH ACE REPORTER.
The feeling... so distracting, I can barely hear what Ev is saying.
"WHAT ARE YOU THINKING, MR. KEEN?"

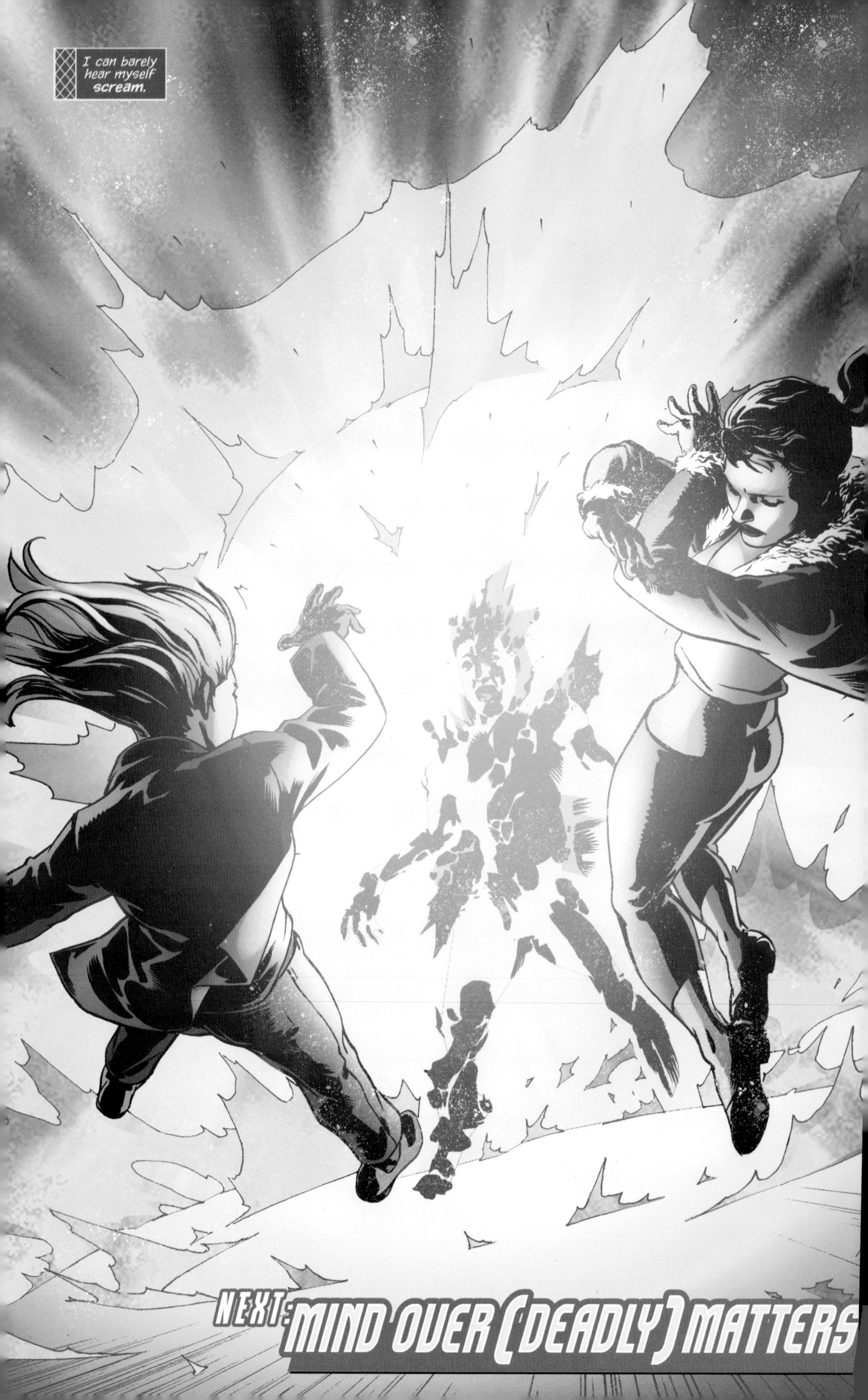
I can barely hear myself scream.
NEXT: MIND OVER (DEADLY) MATTERS

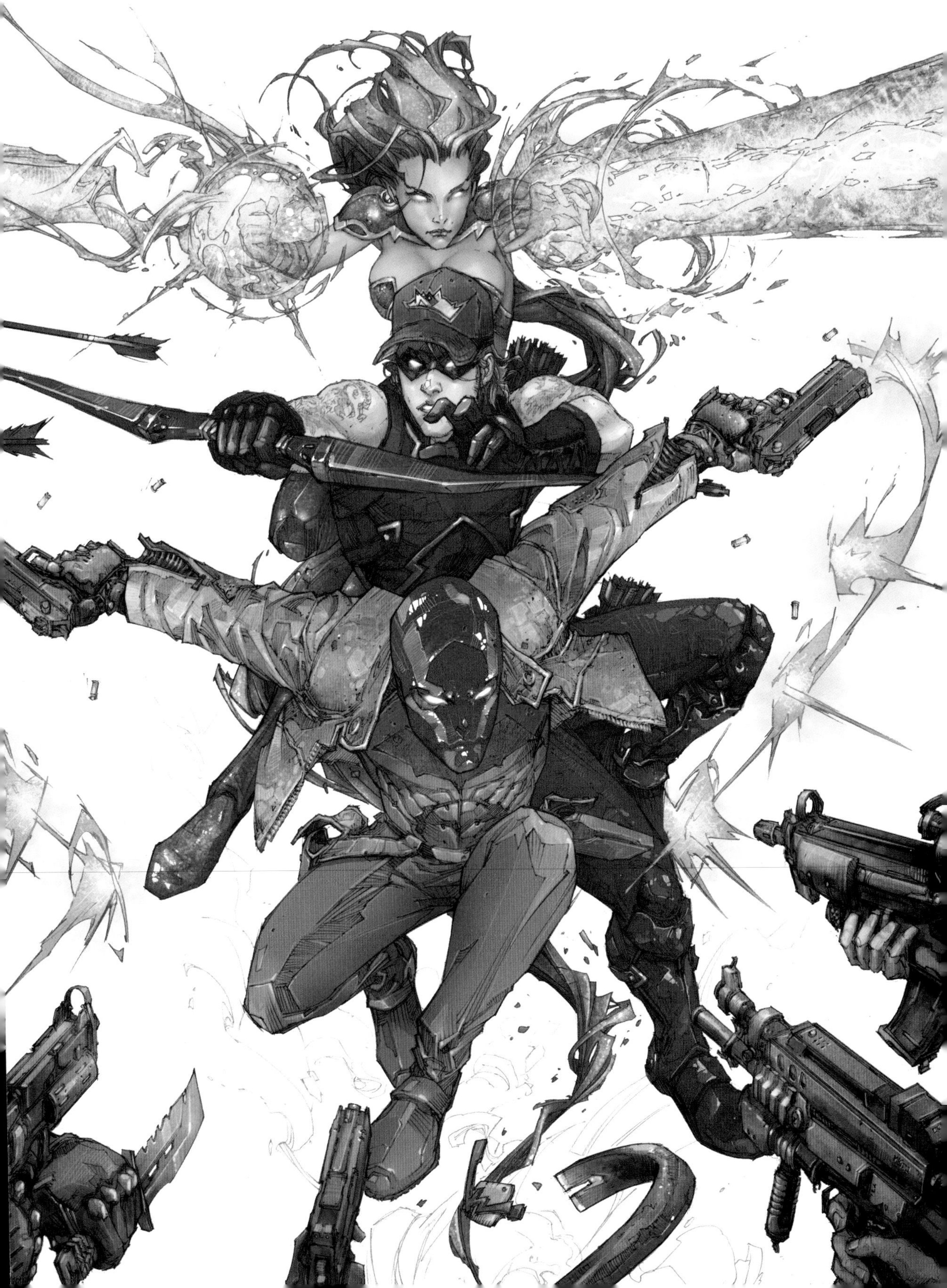

RED HOOD AND THE OUTLAWS

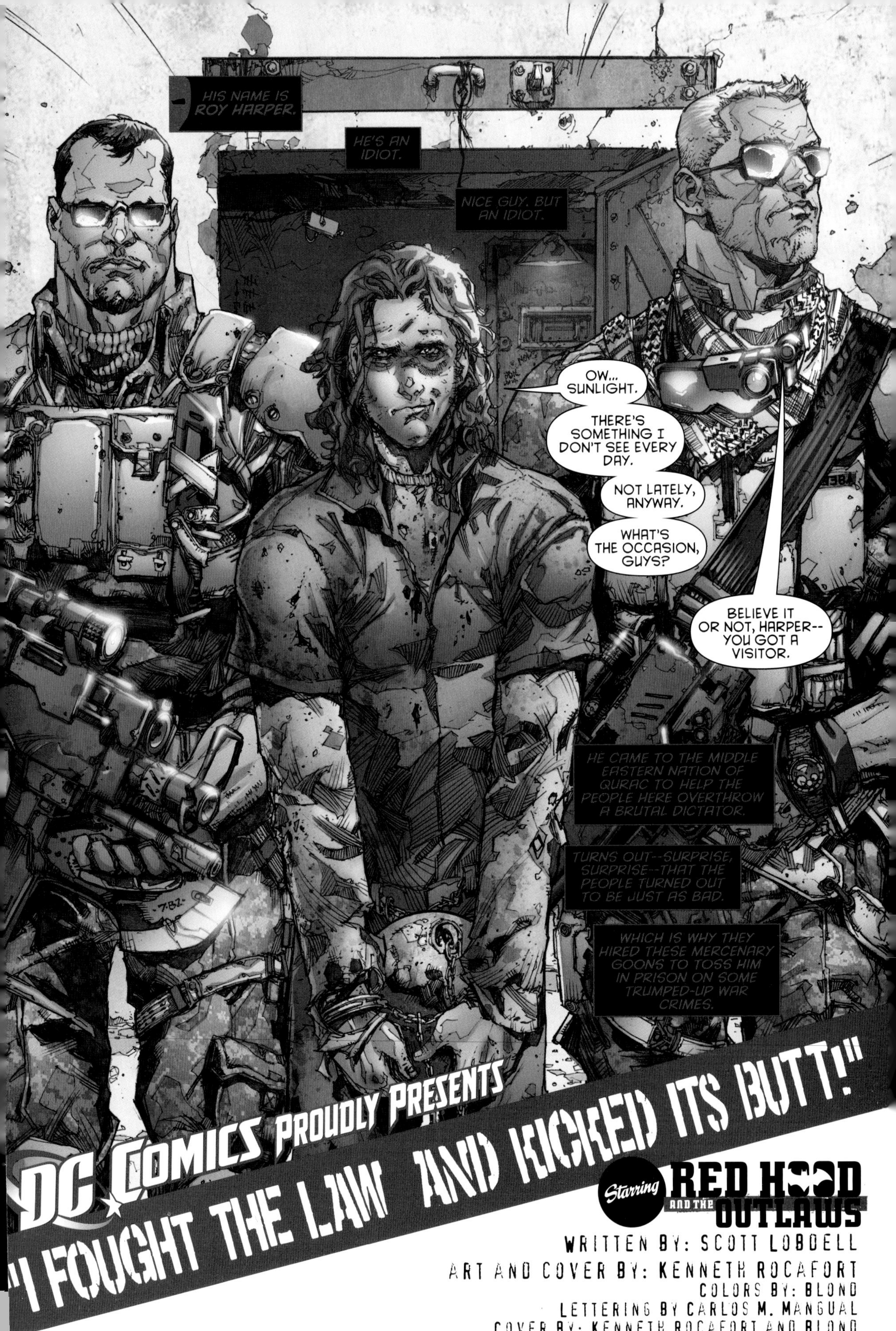
HIS NAME IS ROY HARPER.
HE'S AN IDIOT.
NICE GUY. BUT AN IDIOT.
OW... SUNLIGHT.
THERE'S SOMETHING I DON'T SEE EVERY DAY.
NOT LATELY, ANYWAY.
WHAT'S THE OCCASION, GUYS?
BELIEVE IT OR NOT, HARPER-- YOU GOT A VISITOR.
HE CAME TO THE MIDDLE EASTERN NATION OF QURAC TO HELP THE PEOPLE HERE OVERTHROW A BRUTAL DICTATOR.
TURNS OUT--SURPRISE, SURPRISE--THAT THE PEOPLE TURNED OUT TO BE JUST AS BAD.
WHICH IS WHY THEY HIRED THESE MERCENARY GOONS TO TOSS HIM IN PRISON ON SOME TRUMPED-UP WAR CRIMES.
DC COMICS PROUDLY PRESENTS
"I FOUGHT THE LAW AND KICKED ITS BUTT!"
Starring RED HOOD AND THE OUTLAWS
WRITTEN BY: SCOTT LOBDELL
ART AND COVER BY: KENNETH ROCAFORT
COLORS BY: BLOND
LETTERING BY CARLOS M. MANGUAL
COVER BY: KENNETH ROCAFORT AND BLOND
ASSISTANT EDITOR: KATIE KUBERT
EDITOR: BOBBIE CHASE
*WITH A SPECIAL THANK YOU TO JESSICA ROCAFORT!

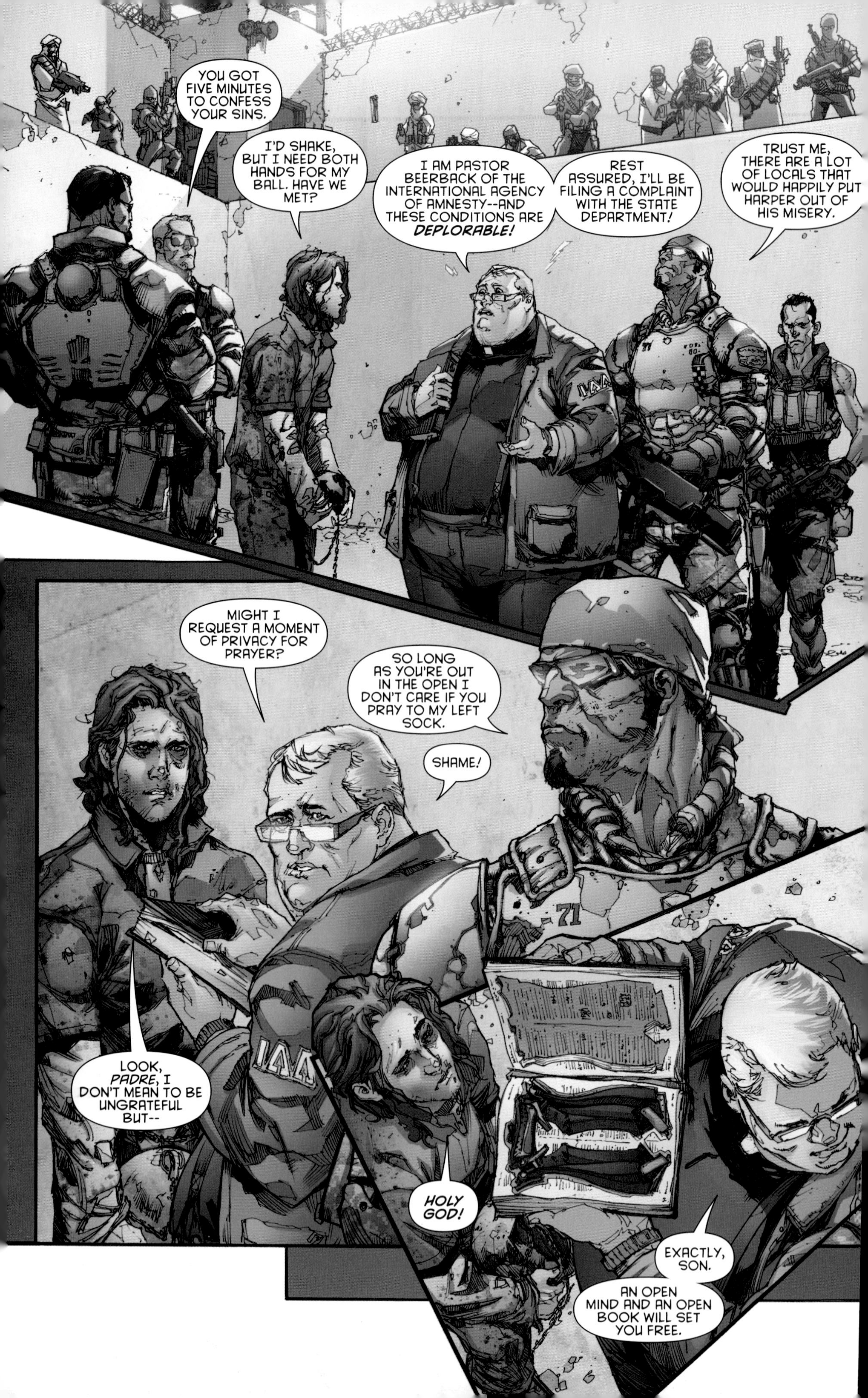
YOU GOT FIVE MINUTES TO CONFESS YOUR SINS.
I'D SHAKE, BUT I NEED BOTH HANDS FOR MY BALL. HAVE WE MET?
I AM PASTOR BEERBACK OF THE INTERNATIONAL AGENCY OF AMNESTY--AND THESE CONDITIONS ARE *DEPLORABLE!*
REST ASSURED, I'LL BE FILING A COMPLAINT WITH THE STATE DEPARTMENT!
TRUST ME, THERE ARE A LOT OF LOCALS THAT WOULD HAPPILY PUT HARPER OUT OF HIS MISERY.
MIGHT I REQUEST A MOMENT OF PRIVACY FOR PRAYER?
SO LONG AS YOU'RE OUT IN THE OPEN I DON'T CARE IF YOU PRAY TO MY LEFT SOCK.
SHAME!
LOOK, *PADRE*, I DON'T MEAN TO BE UNGRATEFUL BUT--
HOLY GOD!
EXACTLY, SON.
AN OPEN MIND AND AN OPEN BOOK WILL SET YOU FREE.

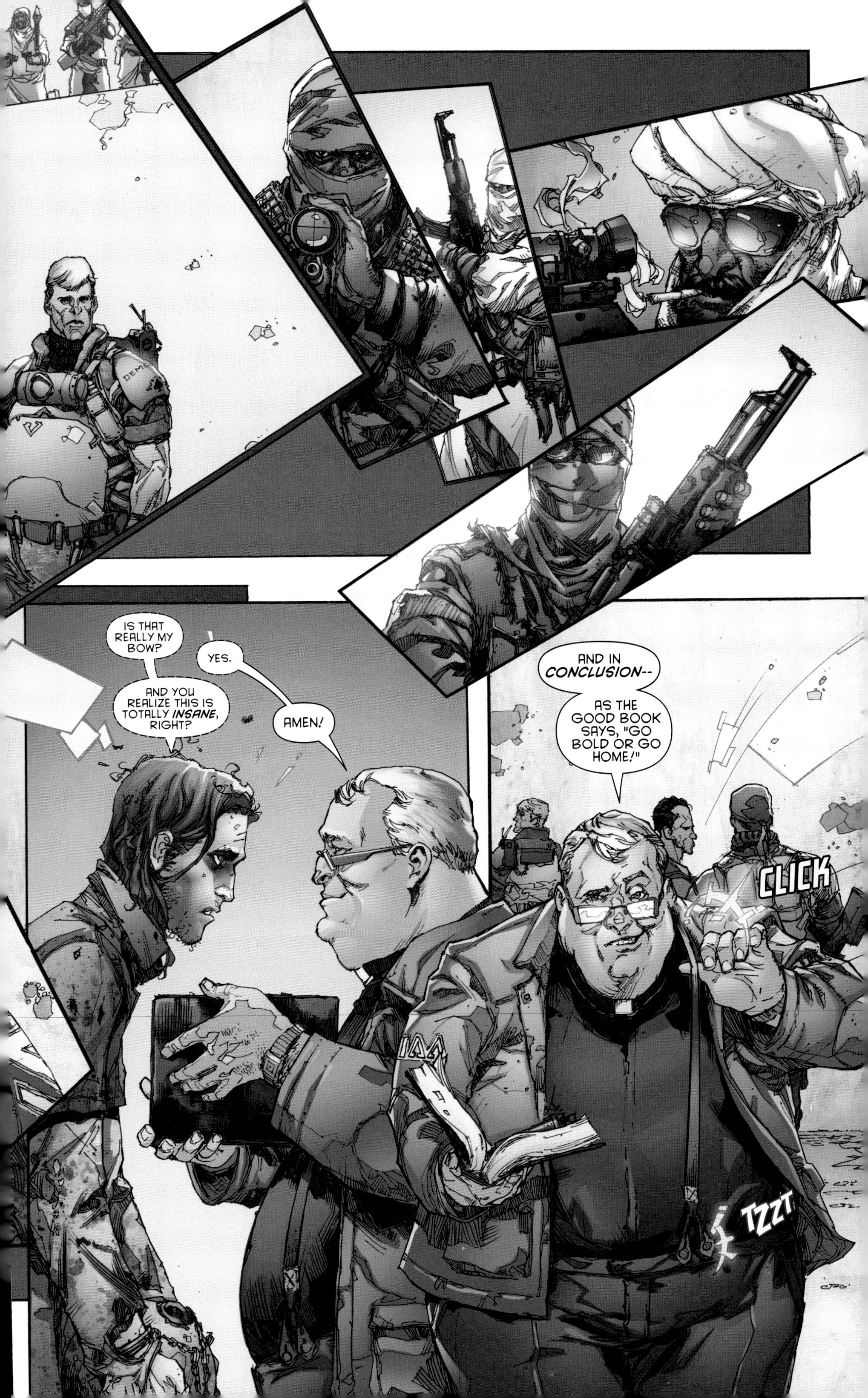
IS THAT REALLY MY BOW?
YES.
AND YOU REALIZE THIS IS TOTALLY *INSANE*, RIGHT?
AMEN!
AND IN *CONCLUSION*--
AS THE GOOD BOOK SAYS, "GO BOLD OR GO HOME!"
CLICK
TZZT

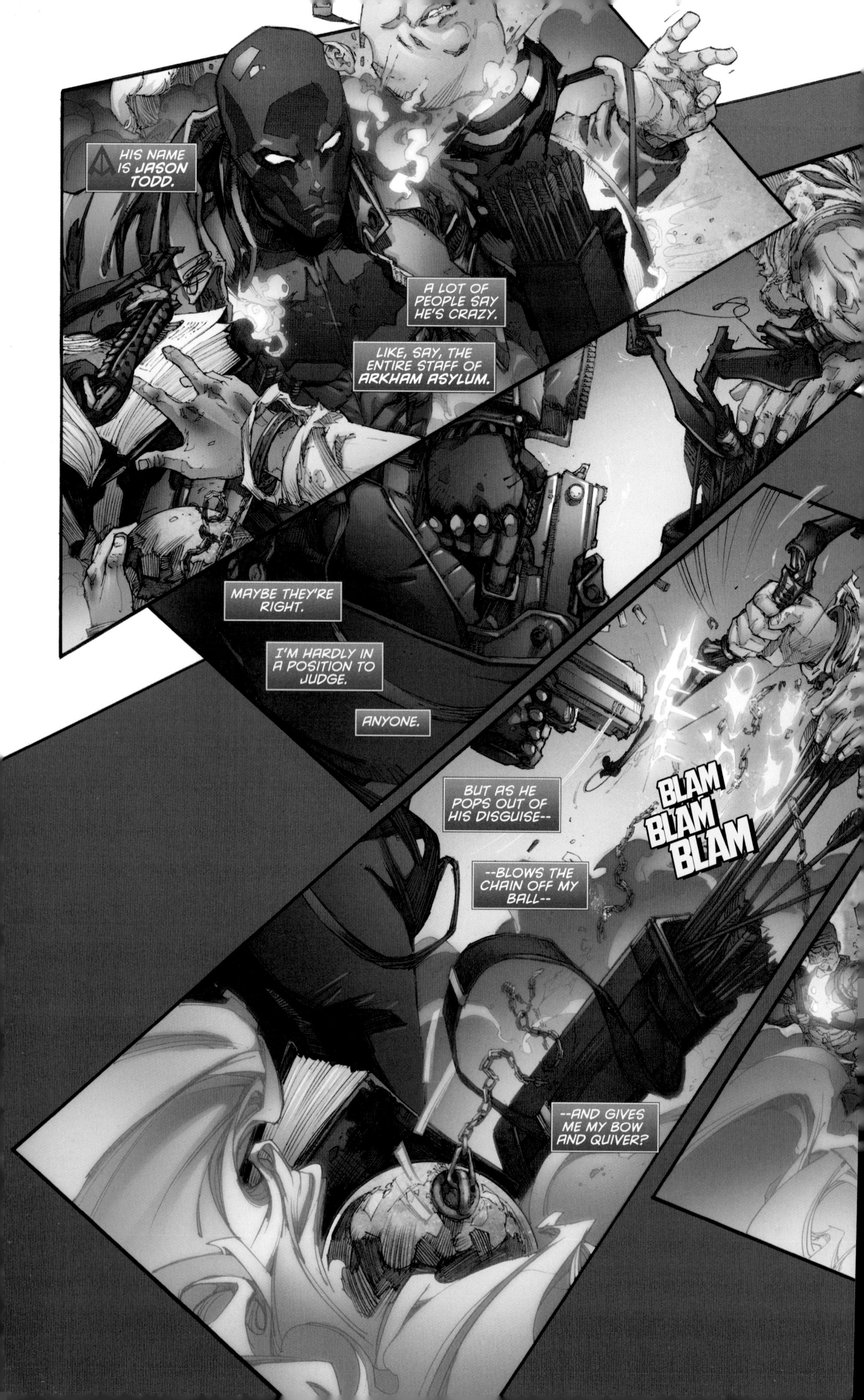
HIS NAME IS JASON TODD.
A LOT OF PEOPLE SAY HE'S CRAZY.
LIKE, SAY, THE ENTIRE STAFF OF ARKHAM ASYLUM.
MAYBE THEY'RE RIGHT.
I'M HARDLY IN A POSITION TO JUDGE.
ANYONE.
BUT AS HE POPS OUT OF HIS DISGUISE--
BLAM BLAM BLAM
--BLOWS THE CHAIN OFF MY BALL--
--AND GIVES ME MY BOW AND QUIVER?

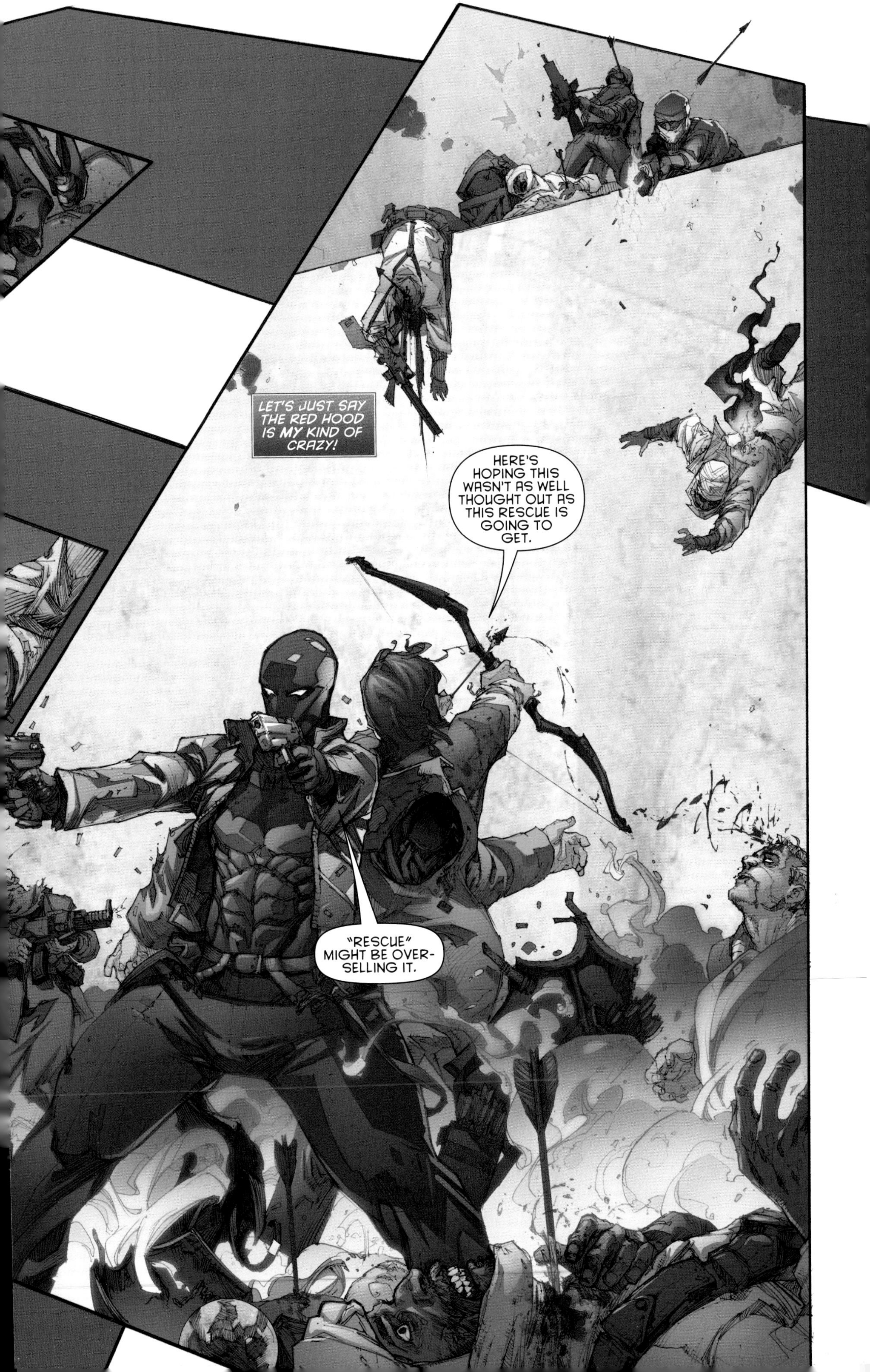
LET'S JUST SAY THE RED HOOD IS MY KIND OF CRAZY!
HERE'S HOPING THIS WASN'T AS WELL THOUGHT OUT AS THIS RESCUE IS GOING TO GET.
"RESCUE" MIGHT BE OVER-SELLING IT.

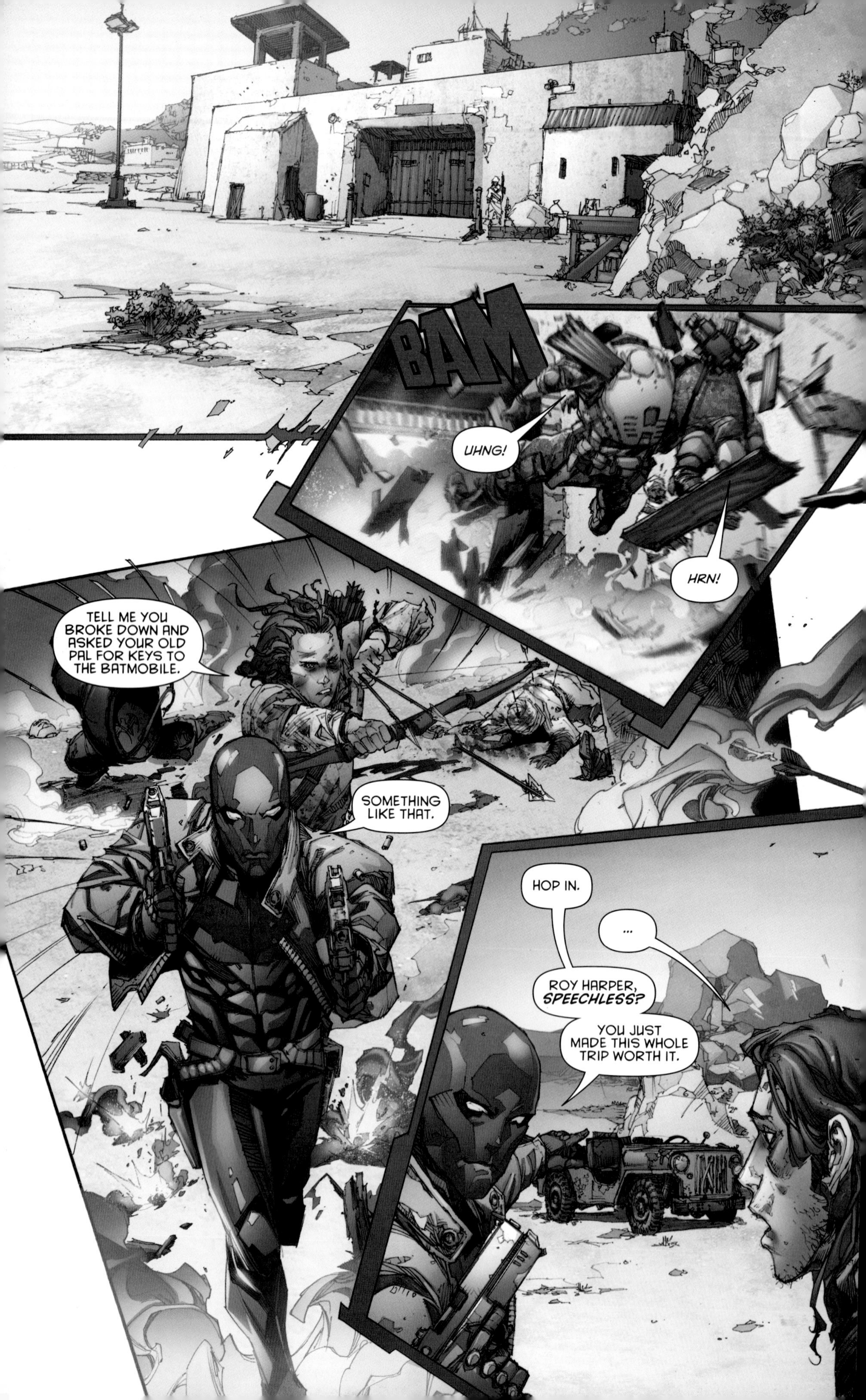
BAM
UHNG!
HRN!
TELL ME YOU BROKE DOWN AND ASKED YOUR OLD PAL FOR KEYS TO THE BATMOBILE.
SOMETHING LIKE THAT.
HOP IN.
...
ROY HARPER, SPEECHLESS?
YOU JUST MADE THIS WHOLE TRIP WORTH IT.

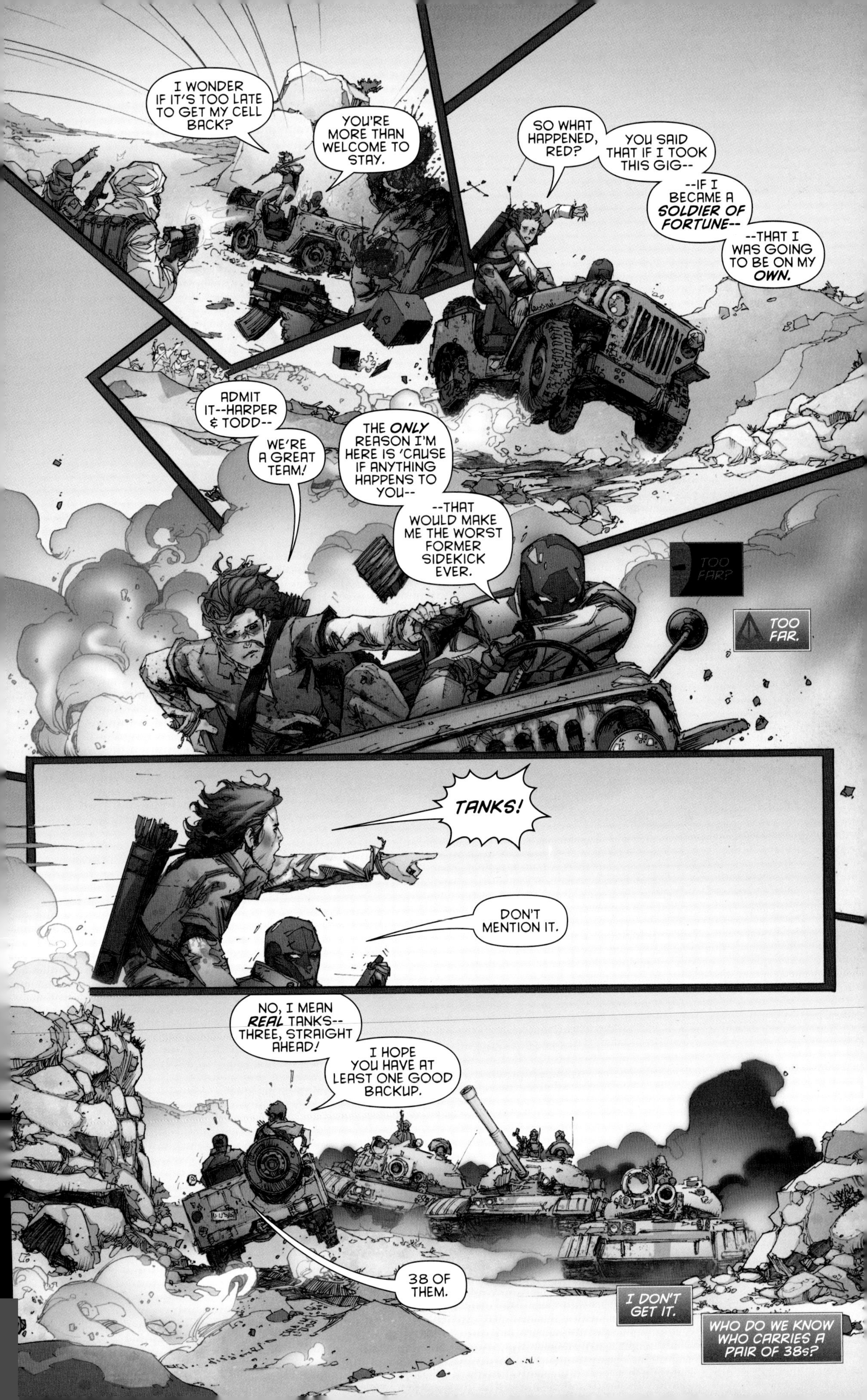
I WONDER IF IT'S TOO LATE TO GET MY CELL BACK?
YOU'RE MORE THAN WELCOME TO STAY.
SO WHAT HAPPENED, RED?
YOU SAID THAT IF I TOOK THIS GIG--
--IF I BECAME A SOLDIER OF FORTUNE--
--THAT I WAS GOING TO BE ON MY OWN.
ADMIT IT--HARPER & TODD--
WE'RE A GREAT TEAM!
THE ONLY REASON I'M HERE IS 'CAUSE IF ANYTHING HAPPENS TO YOU--
--THAT WOULD MAKE ME THE WORST FORMER SIDEKICK EVER.
TOO FAR?
TOO FAR.
TANKS!
DON'T MENTION IT.
NO, I MEAN REAL TANKS--THREE, STRAIGHT AHEAD!
I HOPE YOU HAVE AT LEAST ONE GOOD BACKUP.
38 OF THEM.
I DON'T GET IT.
WHO DO WE KNOW WHO CARRIES A PAIR OF 38s?

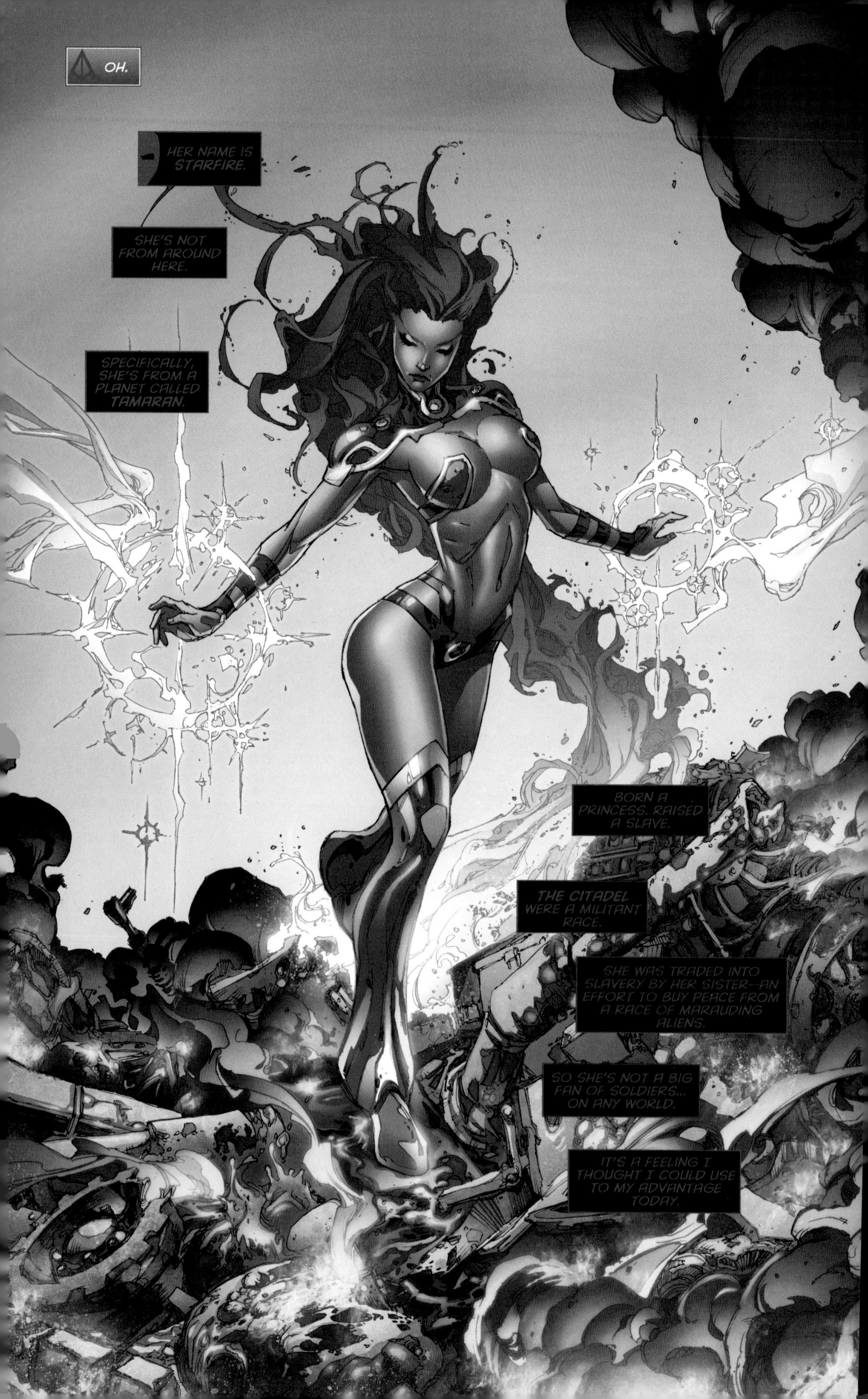
OH.
HER NAME IS STARFIRE.
SHE'S NOT FROM AROUND HERE.
SPECIFICALLY, SHE'S FROM A PLANET CALLED TAMARAN.
BORN A PRINCESS. RAISED A SLAVE.
THE CITADEL WERE A MILITANT RACE.
SHE WAS TRADED INTO SLAVERY BY HER SISTER--AN EFFORT TO BUY PEACE FROM A RACE OF MARAUDING ALIENS.
SO SHE'S NOT A BIG FAN OF SOLDIERS... ON ANY WORLD.
IT'S A FEELING I THOUGHT I COULD USE TO MY ADVANTAGE TODAY.

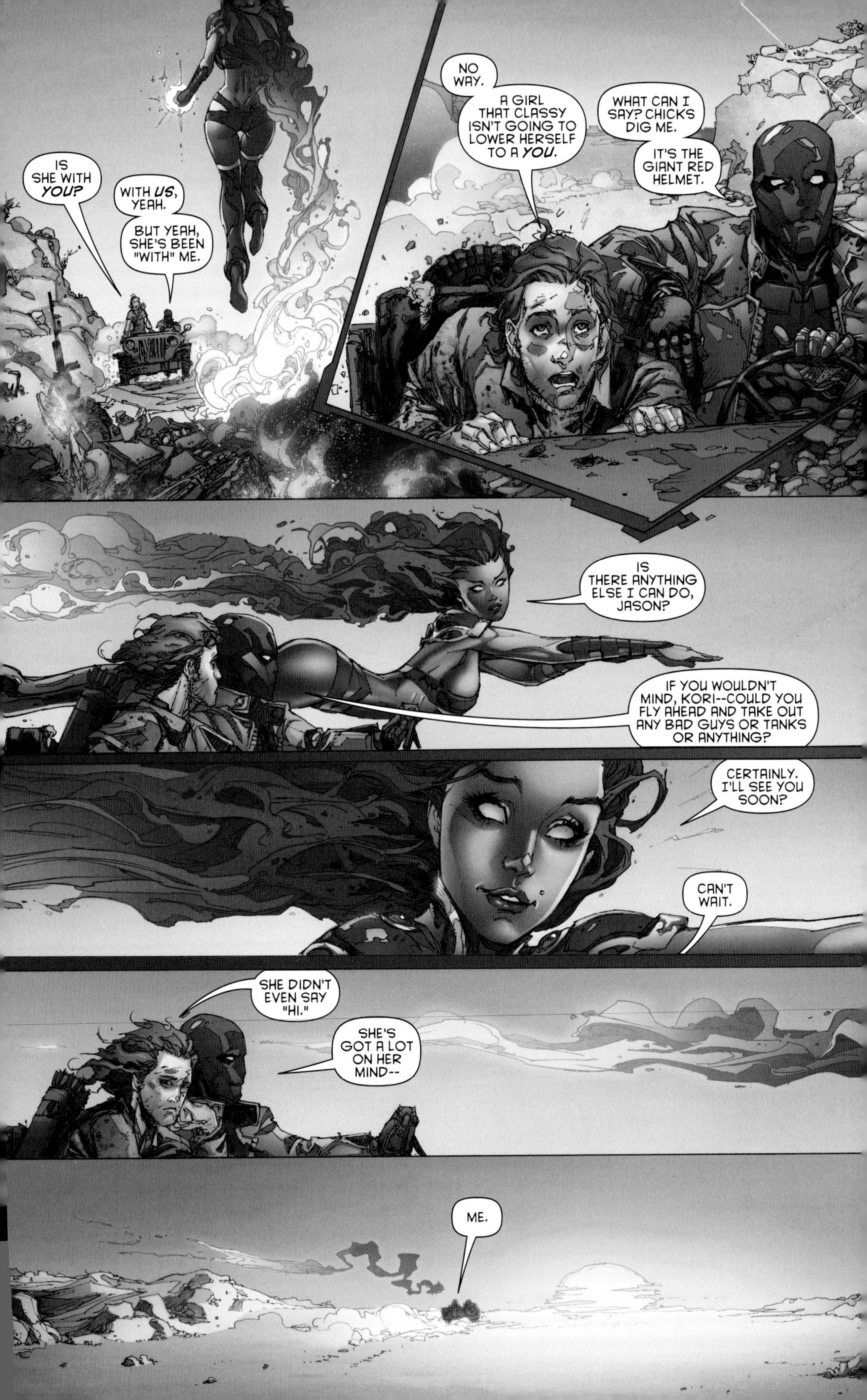
IS SHE WITH *YOU?*
WITH *US*, YEAH.
BUT YEAH, SHE'S BEEN "WITH" ME.
NO WAY.
A GIRL THAT CLASSY ISN'T GOING TO LOWER HERSELF TO A *YOU.*
WHAT CAN I SAY? CHICKS DIG ME.
IT'S THE GIANT RED HELMET.
IS THERE ANYTHING ELSE I CAN DO, JASON?
IF YOU WOULDN'T MIND, KORI--COULD YOU FLY AHEAD AND TAKE OUT ANY BAD GUYS OR TANKS OR ANYTHING?
CERTAINLY. I'LL SEE YOU SOON?
CAN'T WAIT.
SHE DIDN'T EVEN SAY "HI."
SHE'S GOT A LOT ON HER MIND--
ME.

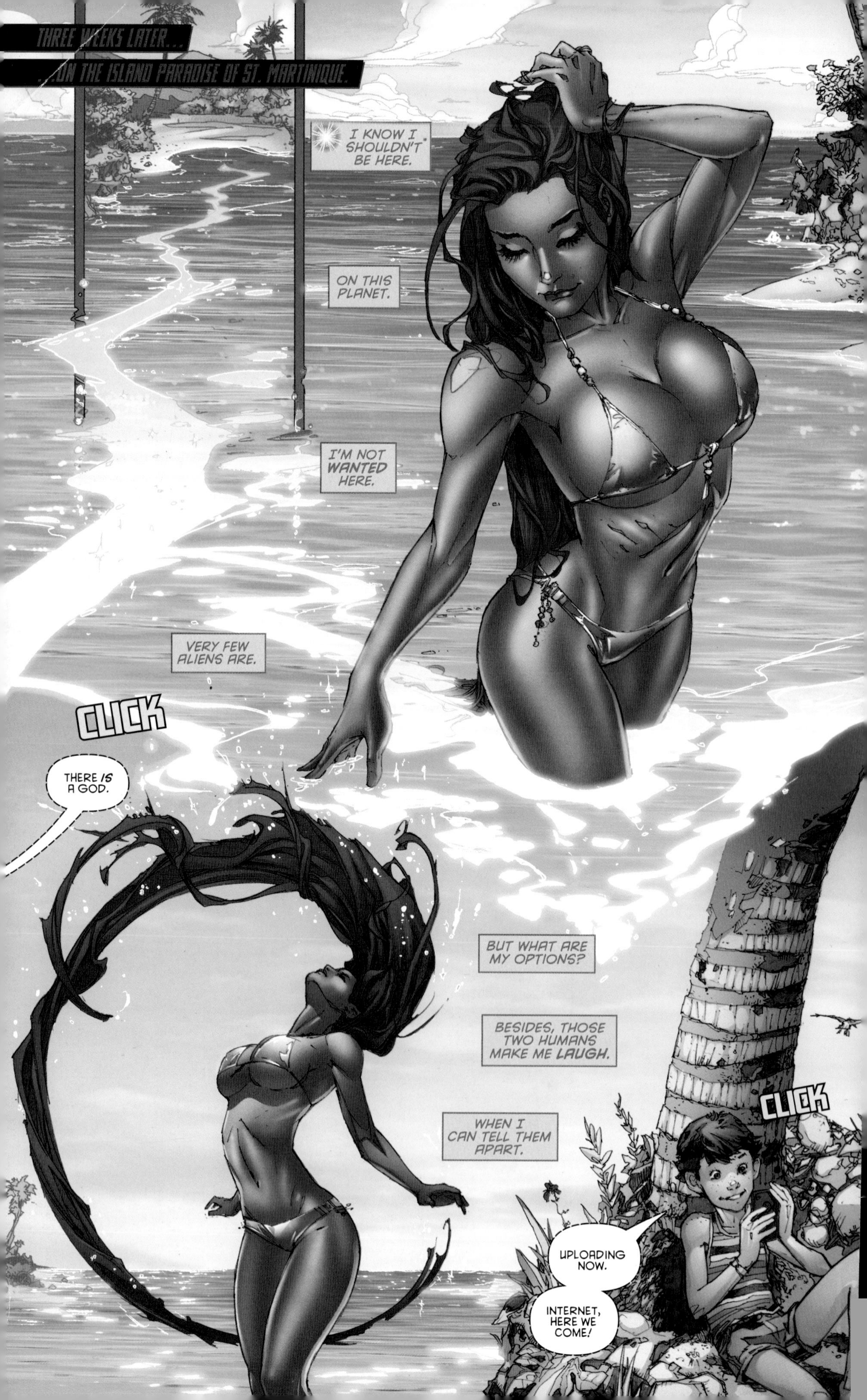
THREE WEEKS LATER...
...ON THE ISLAND PARADISE OF ST. MARTINIQUE.
I KNOW I SHOULDN'T BE HERE.
ON THIS PLANET.
I'M NOT WANTED HERE.
VERY FEW ALIENS ARE.
CLICK
THERE IS A GOD.
BUT WHAT ARE MY OPTIONS?
BESIDES, THOSE TWO HUMANS MAKE ME LAUGH.
WHEN I CAN TELL THEM APART.
CLICK
UPLOADING NOW.
INTERNET, HERE WE COME!

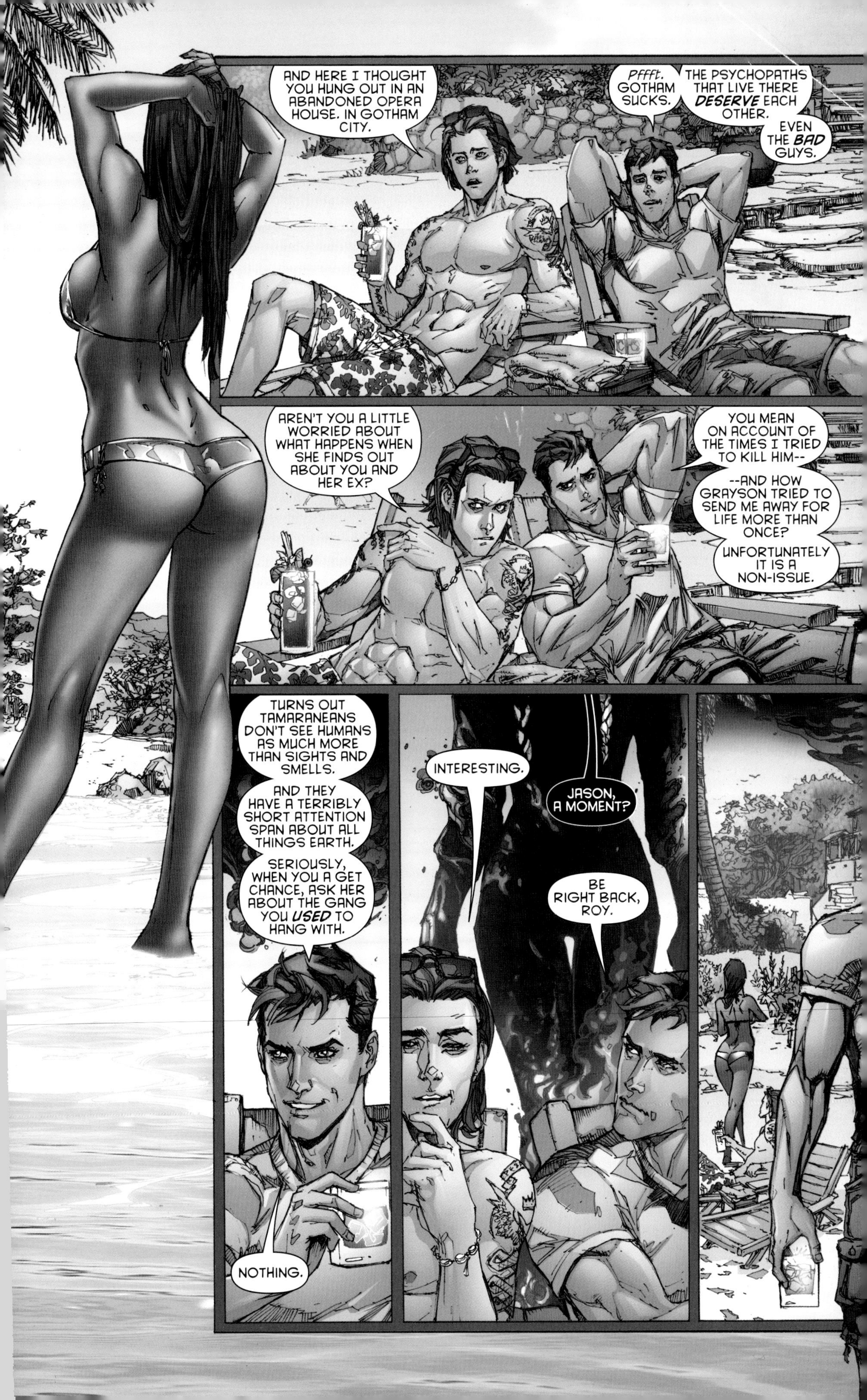
AND HERE I THOUGHT YOU HUNG OUT IN AN ABANDONED OPERA HOUSE. IN GOTHAM CITY.
Pfffft. GOTHAM SUCKS.
THE PSYCHOPATHS THAT LIVE THERE DESERVE EACH OTHER.
EVEN THE BAD GUYS.
AREN'T YOU A LITTLE WORRIED ABOUT WHAT HAPPENS WHEN SHE FINDS OUT ABOUT YOU AND HER EX?
YOU MEAN ON ACCOUNT OF THE TIMES I TRIED TO KILL HIM--
--AND HOW GRAYSON TRIED TO SEND ME AWAY FOR LIFE MORE THAN ONCE?
UNFORTUNATELY IT IS A NON-ISSUE.
TURNS OUT TAMARANEANS DON'T SEE HUMANS AS MUCH MORE THAN SIGHTS AND SMELLS.
AND THEY HAVE A TERRIBLY SHORT ATTENTION SPAN ABOUT ALL THINGS EARTH.
SERIOUSLY, WHEN YOU A GET CHANCE, ASK HER ABOUT THE GANG YOU USED TO HANG WITH.
NOTHING.
INTERESTING.
JASON, A MOMENT?
BE RIGHT BACK, ROY.

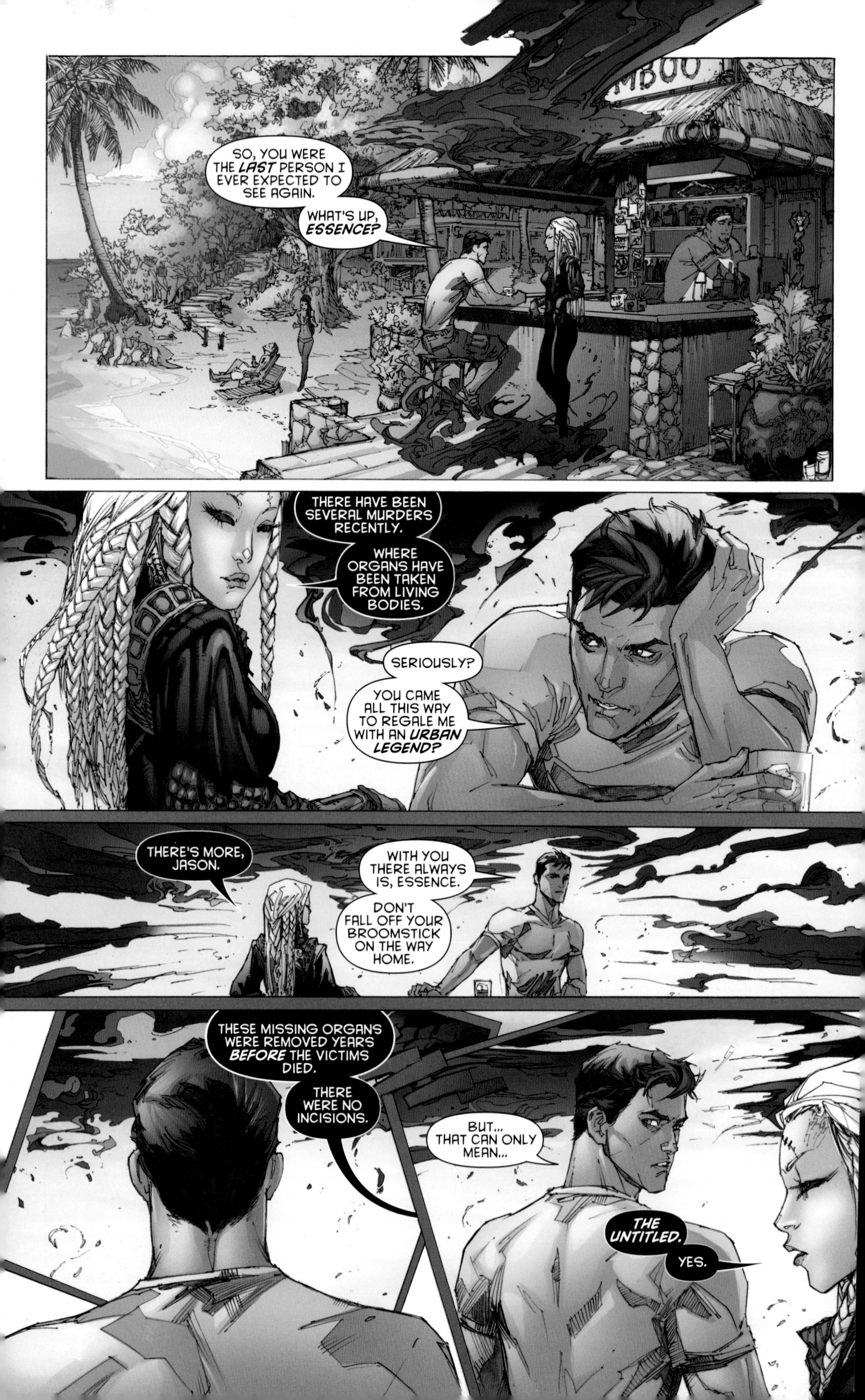

MBOO
SO, YOU WERE THE LAST PERSON I EVER EXPECTED TO SEE AGAIN.
WHAT'S UP, ESSENCE?
THERE HAVE BEEN SEVERAL MURDERS RECENTLY.
WHERE ORGANS HAVE BEEN TAKEN FROM LIVING BODIES.
SERIOUSLY?
YOU CAME ALL THIS WAY TO REGALE ME WITH AN URBAN LEGEND?
THERE'S MORE, JASON.
WITH YOU THERE ALWAYS IS, ESSENCE.
DON'T FALL OFF YOUR BROOMSTICK ON THE WAY HOME.
THESE MISSING ORGANS WERE REMOVED YEARS BEFORE THE VICTIMS DIED.
THERE WERE NO INCISIONS.
BUT... THAT CAN ONLY MEAN...
THE UNTITLED.
YES.

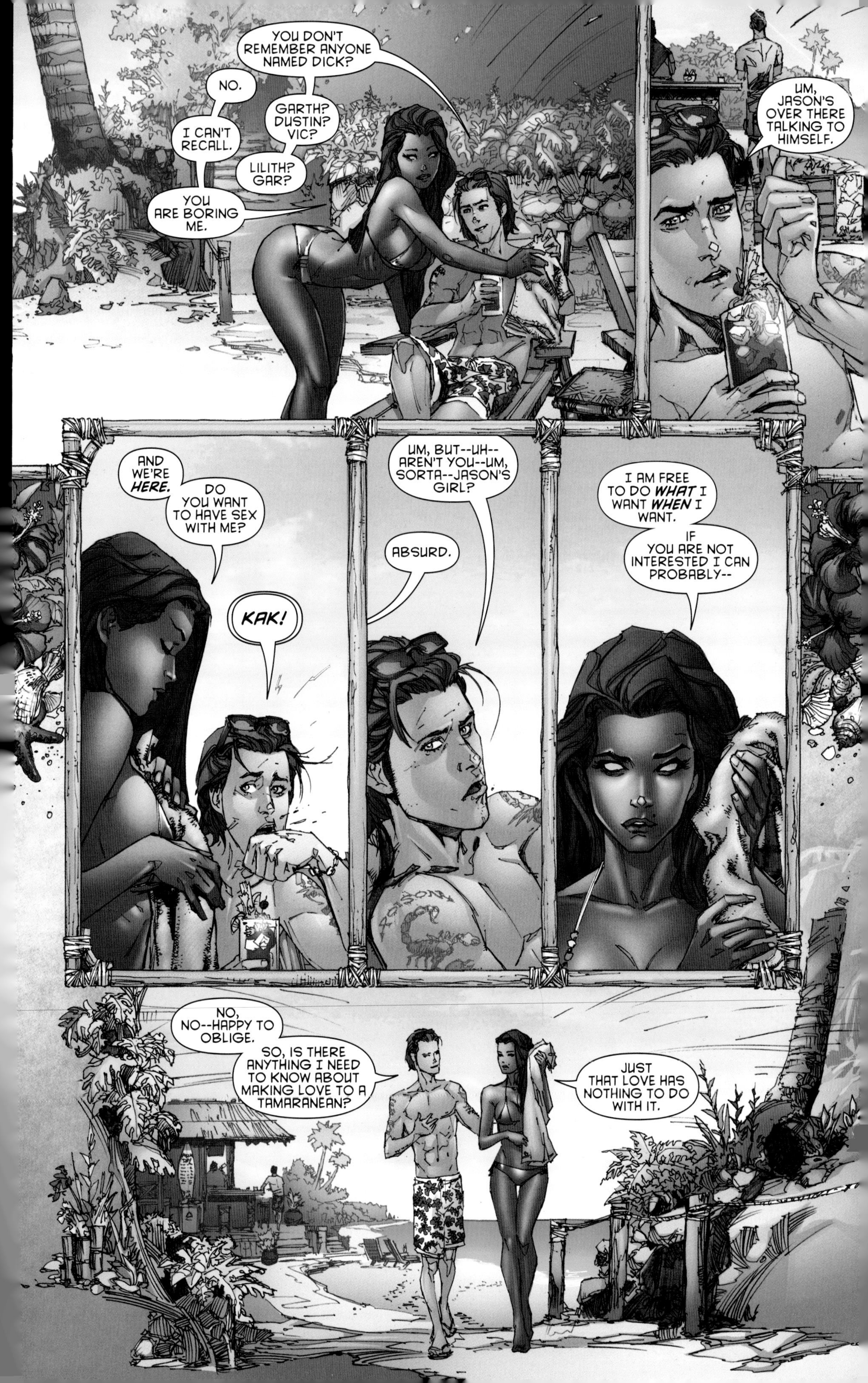
YOU DON'T REMEMBER ANYONE NAMED DICK?
NO.
I CAN'T RECALL.
GARTH? DUSTIN? VIC?
LILITH? GAR?
YOU ARE BORING ME.
UM, JASON'S OVER THERE TALKING TO HIMSELF.
AND WE'RE HERE.
DO YOU WANT TO HAVE SEX WITH ME?
KAK!
UM, BUT--UH--AREN'T YOU--UM, SORTA--JASON'S GIRL?
ABSURD.
I AM FREE TO DO WHAT I WANT WHEN I WANT.
IF YOU ARE NOT INTERESTED I CAN PROBABLY--
NO, NO--HAPPY TO OBLIGE.
SO, IS THERE ANYTHING I NEED TO KNOW ABOUT MAKING LOVE TO A TAMARANEAN?
JUST THAT LOVE HAS NOTHING TO DO WITH IT.

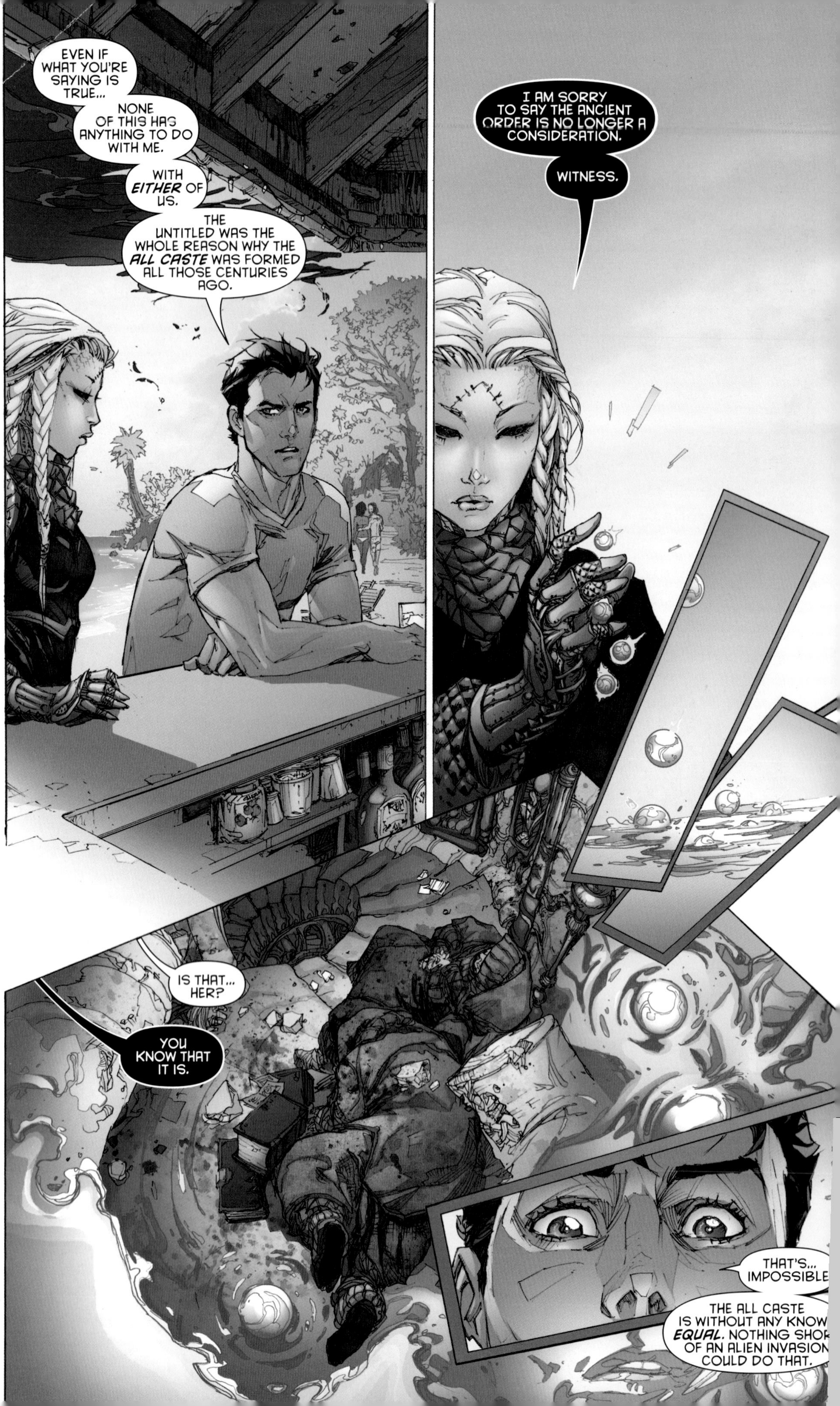
EVEN IF WHAT YOU'RE SAYING IS TRUE...
NONE OF THIS HAS ANYTHING TO DO WITH ME.
WITH EITHER OF US.
THE UNTITLED WAS THE WHOLE REASON WHY THE ALL CASTE WAS FORMED ALL THOSE CENTURIES AGO.
I AM SORRY TO SAY THE ANCIENT ORDER IS NO LONGER A CONSIDERATION.
WITNESS.
IS THAT... HER?
YOU KNOW THAT IT IS.
THAT'S... IMPOSSIBLE
THE ALL CASTE IS WITHOUT ANY KNOW EQUAL. NOTHING SHOR OF AN ALIEN INVASION COULD DO THAT.

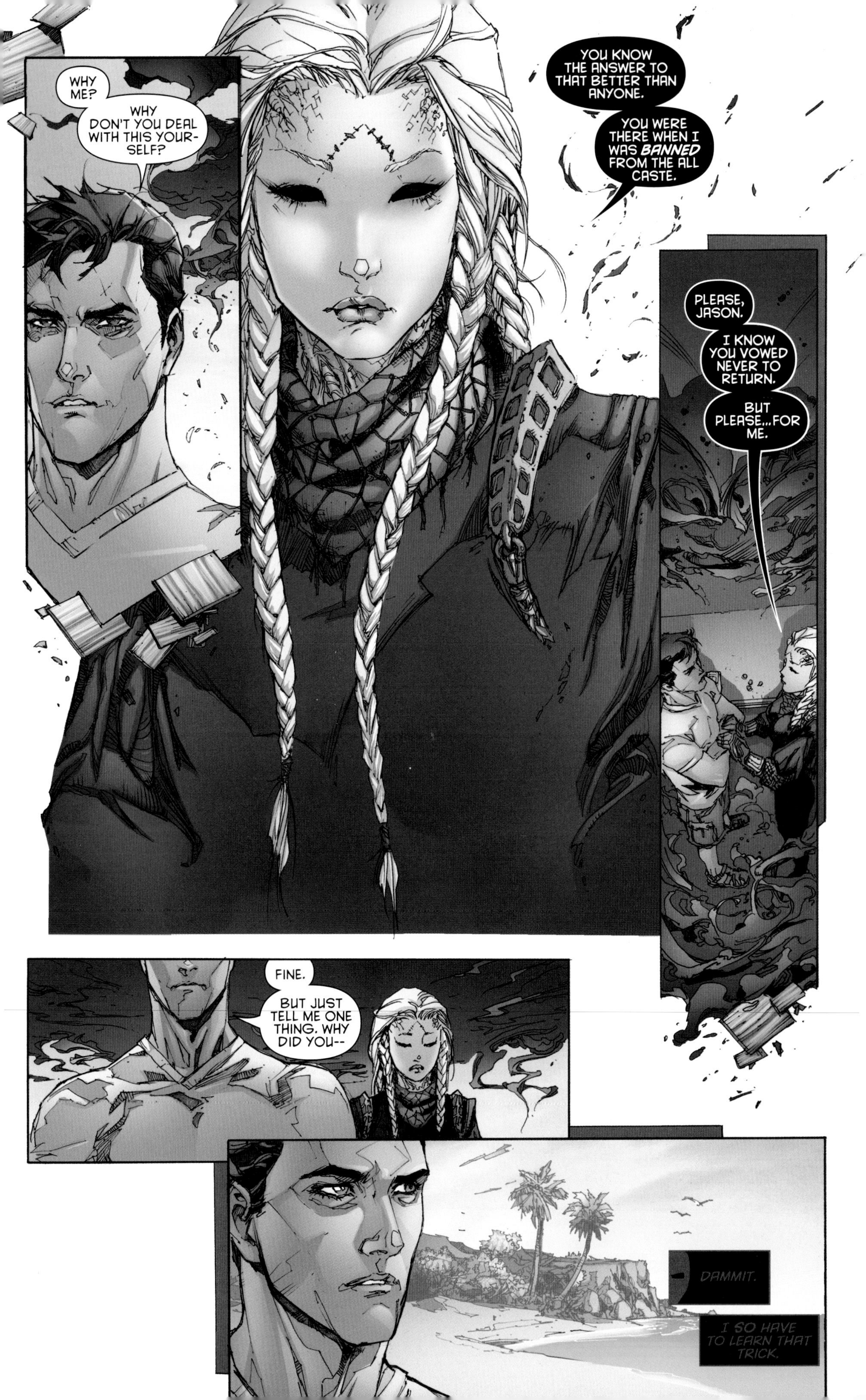
WHY ME?
WHY DON'T YOU DEAL WITH THIS YOUR-SELF?
YOU KNOW THE ANSWER TO THAT BETTER THAN ANYONE.
YOU WERE THERE WHEN I WAS BANNED FROM THE ALL CASTE.
PLEASE, JASON.
I KNOW YOU VOWED NEVER TO RETURN.
BUT PLEASE...FOR ME.
FINE.
BUT JUST TELL ME ONE THING. WHY DID YOU--
DAMMIT.
I SO HAVE TO LEARN THAT TRICK.

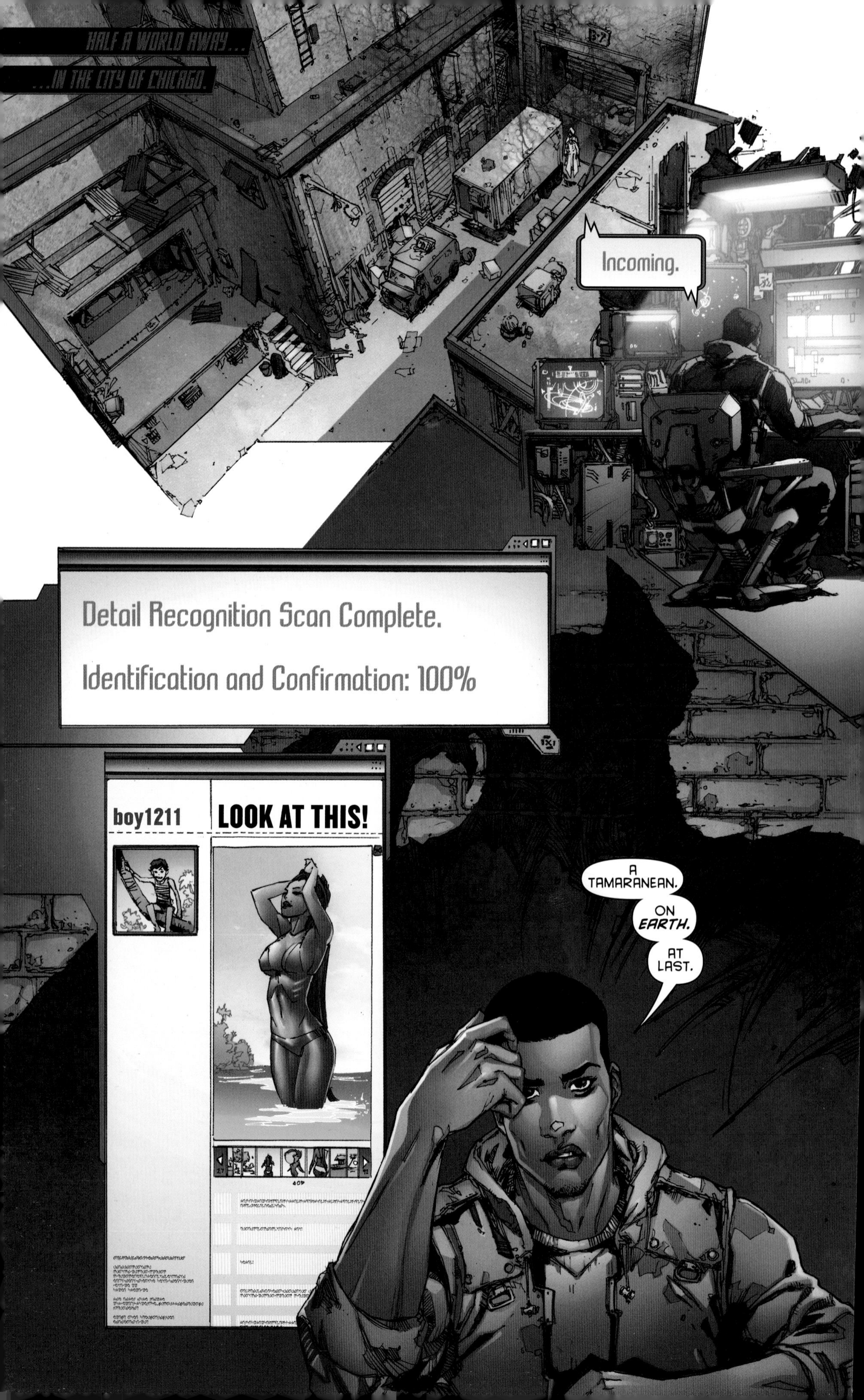

HALF A WORLD AWAY...
...IN THE CITY OF CHICAGO.
Incoming.
Detail Recognition Scan Complete.
Identification and Confirmation: 100%
boy1211
LOOK AT THIS!
A TAMARANEAN.
ON *EARTH.*
AT LAST.

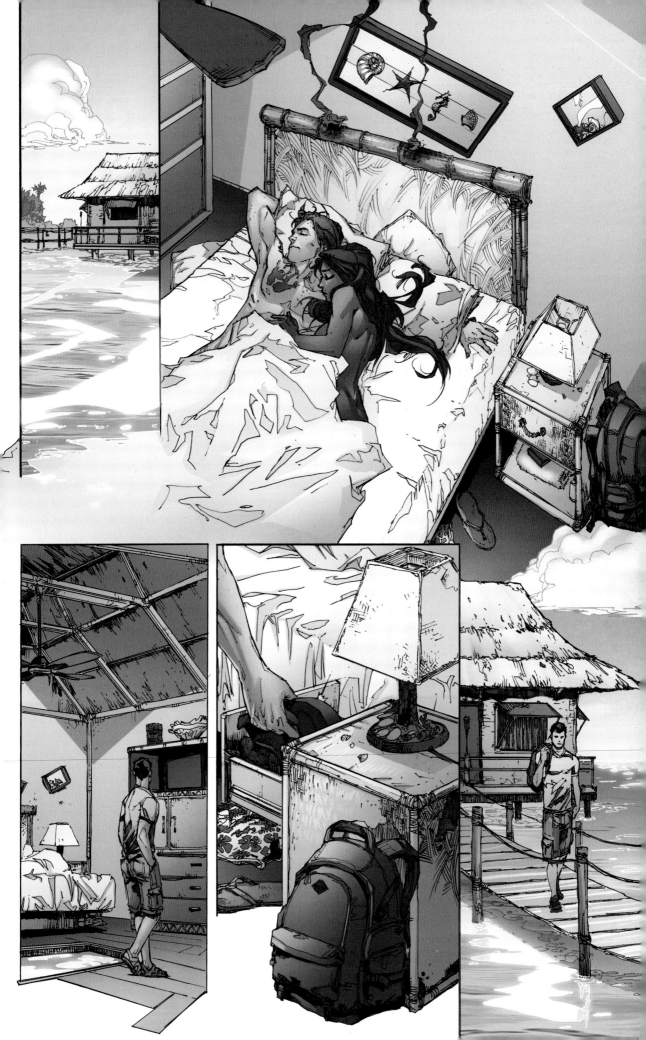

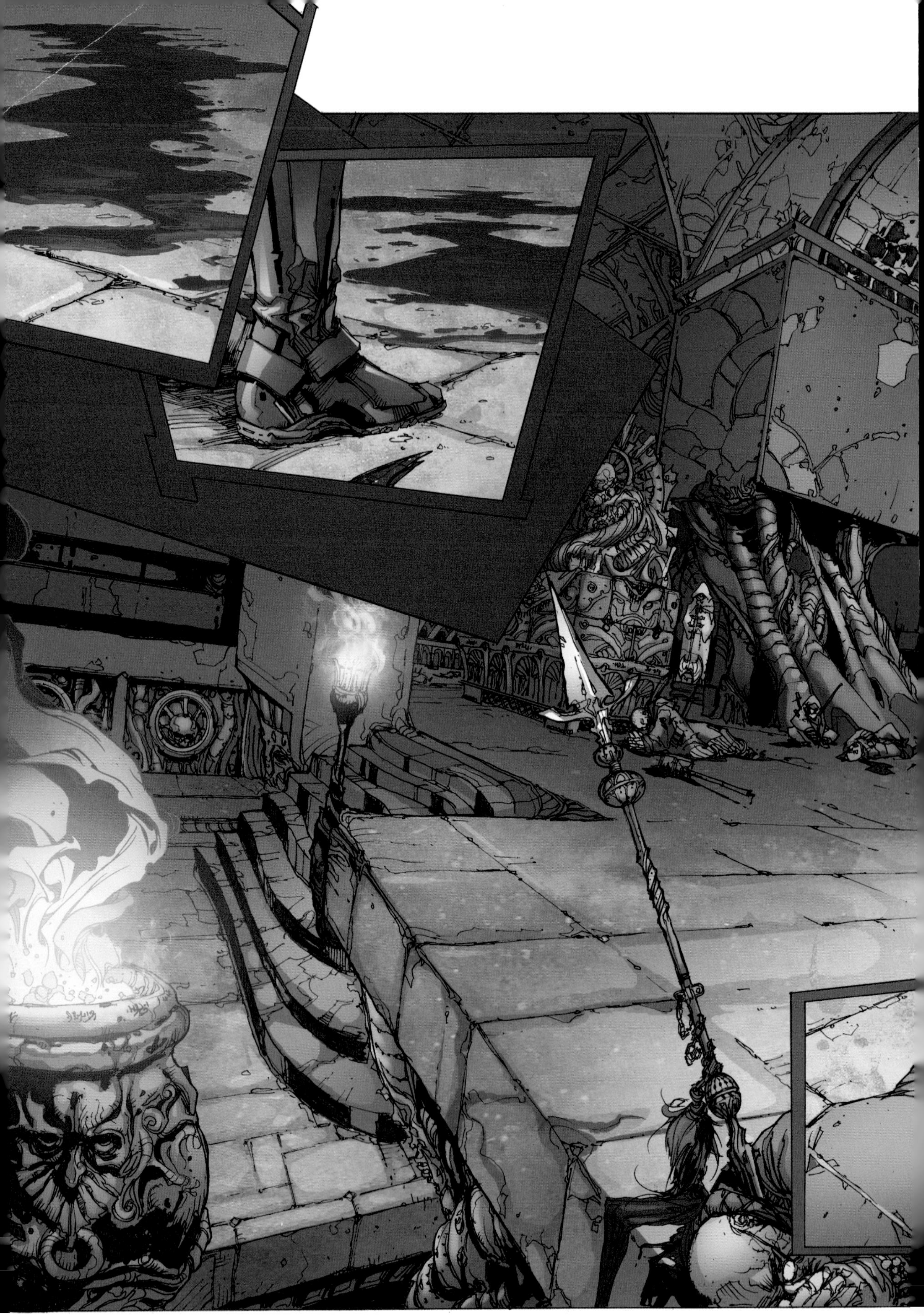

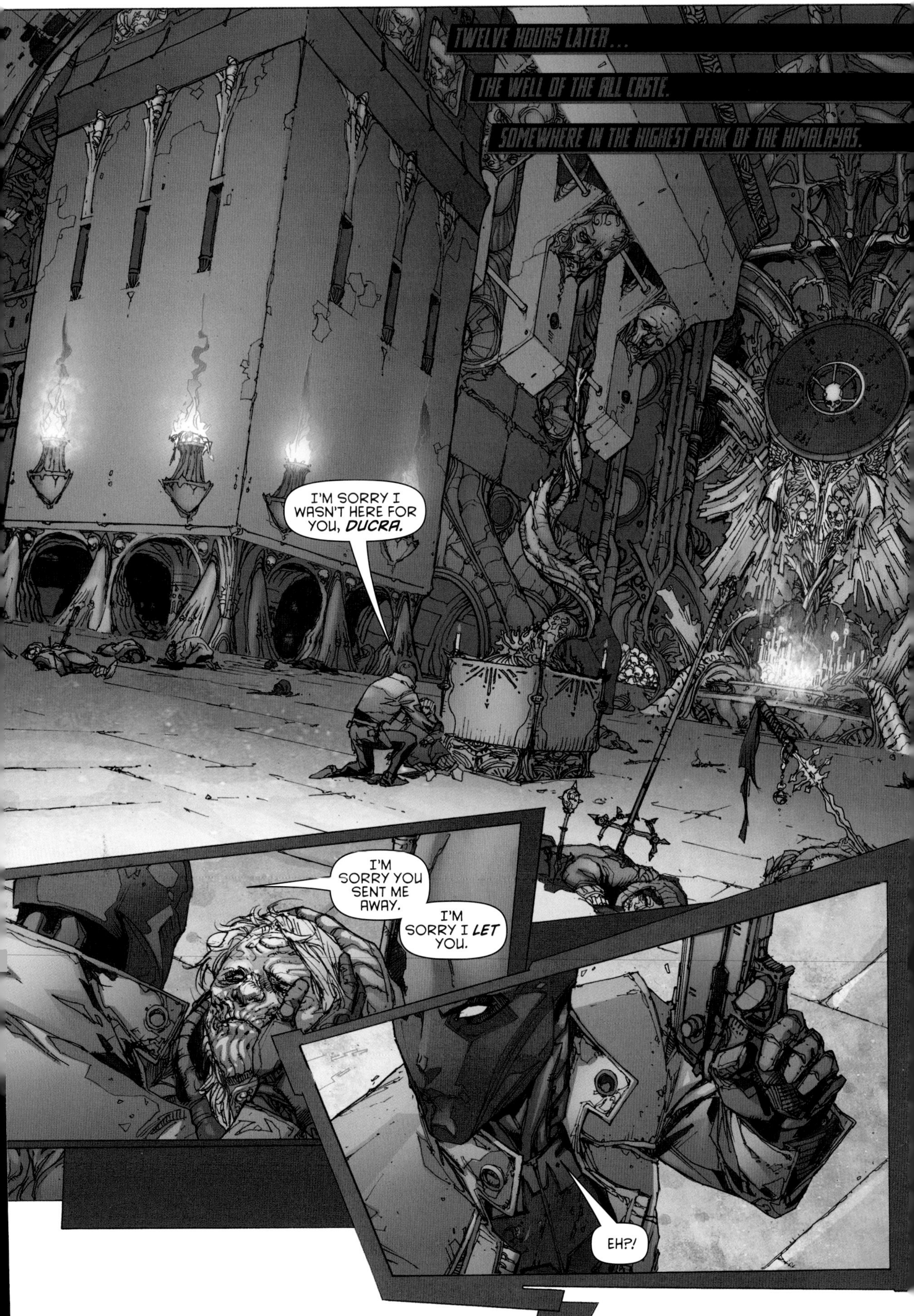
TWELVE HOURS LATER...
THE WELL OF THE ALL CASTE.
SOMEWHERE IN THE HIGHEST PEAK OF THE HIMALAYAS.
I'M SORRY I WASN'T HERE FOR YOU, DUCRA.
I'M SORRY YOU SENT ME AWAY.
I'M SORRY I LET YOU.
EH?!

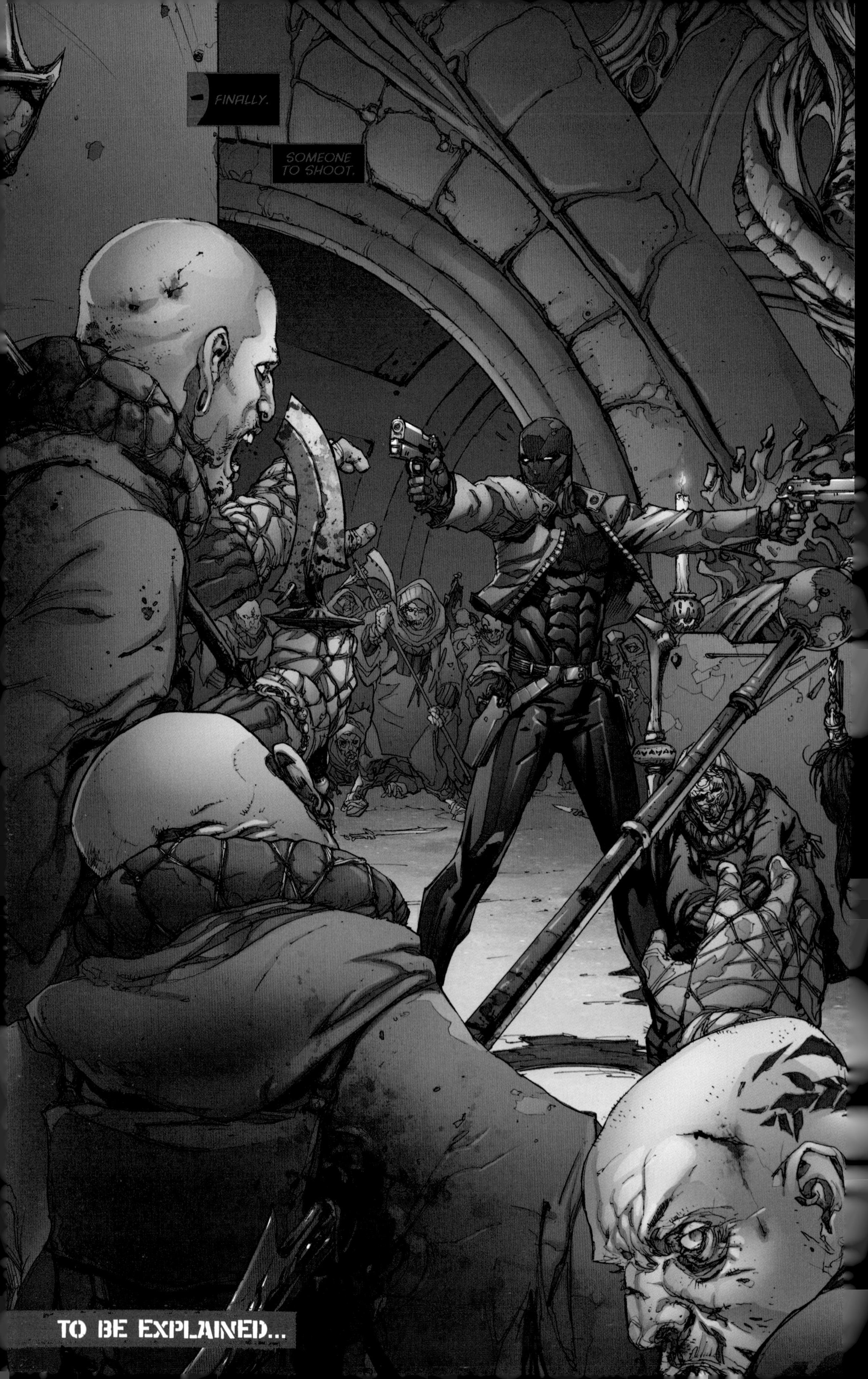
FINALLY.
SOMEONE TO SHOOT.
TO BE EXPLAINED...

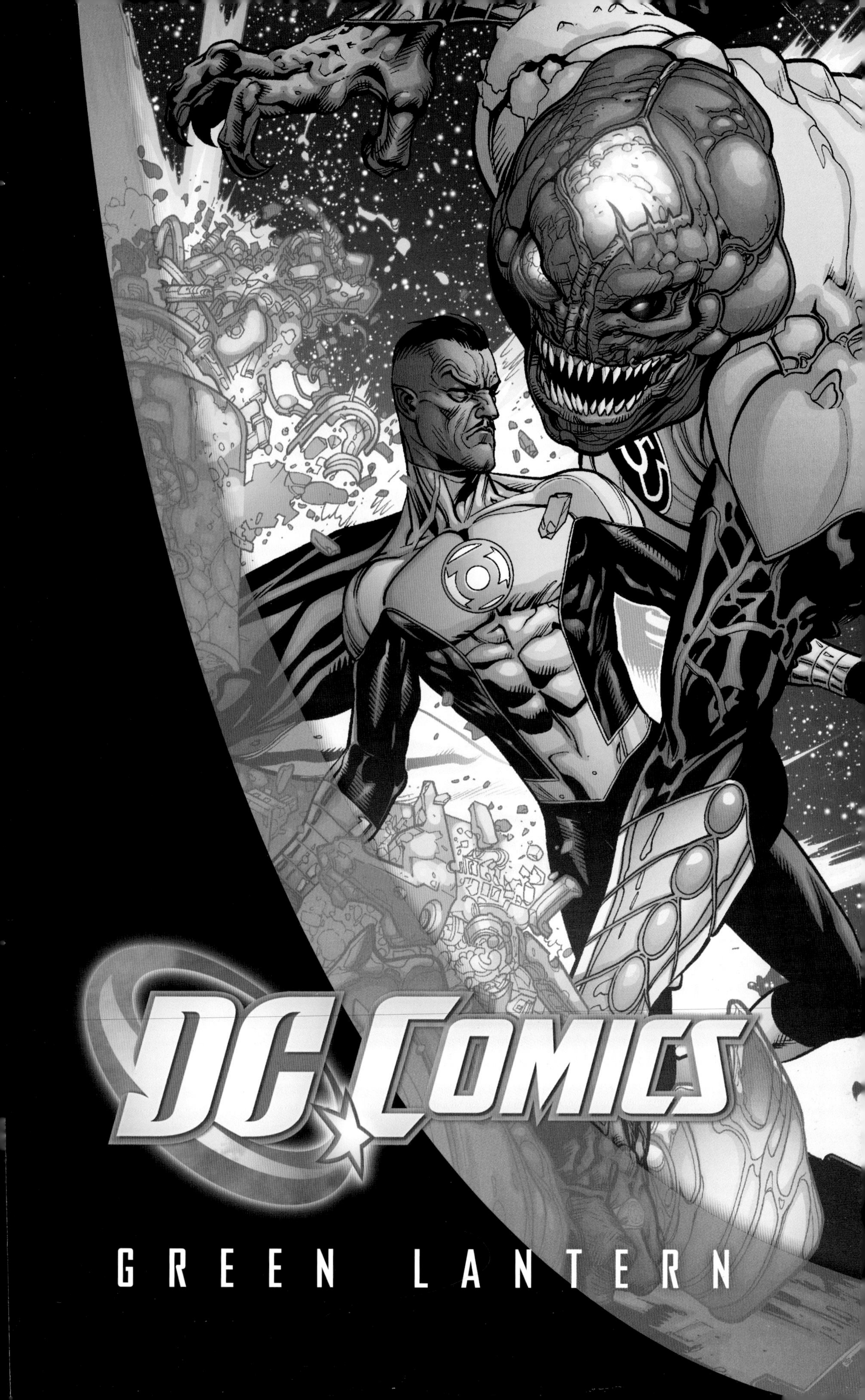
DC COMICS
GREEN LANTERN

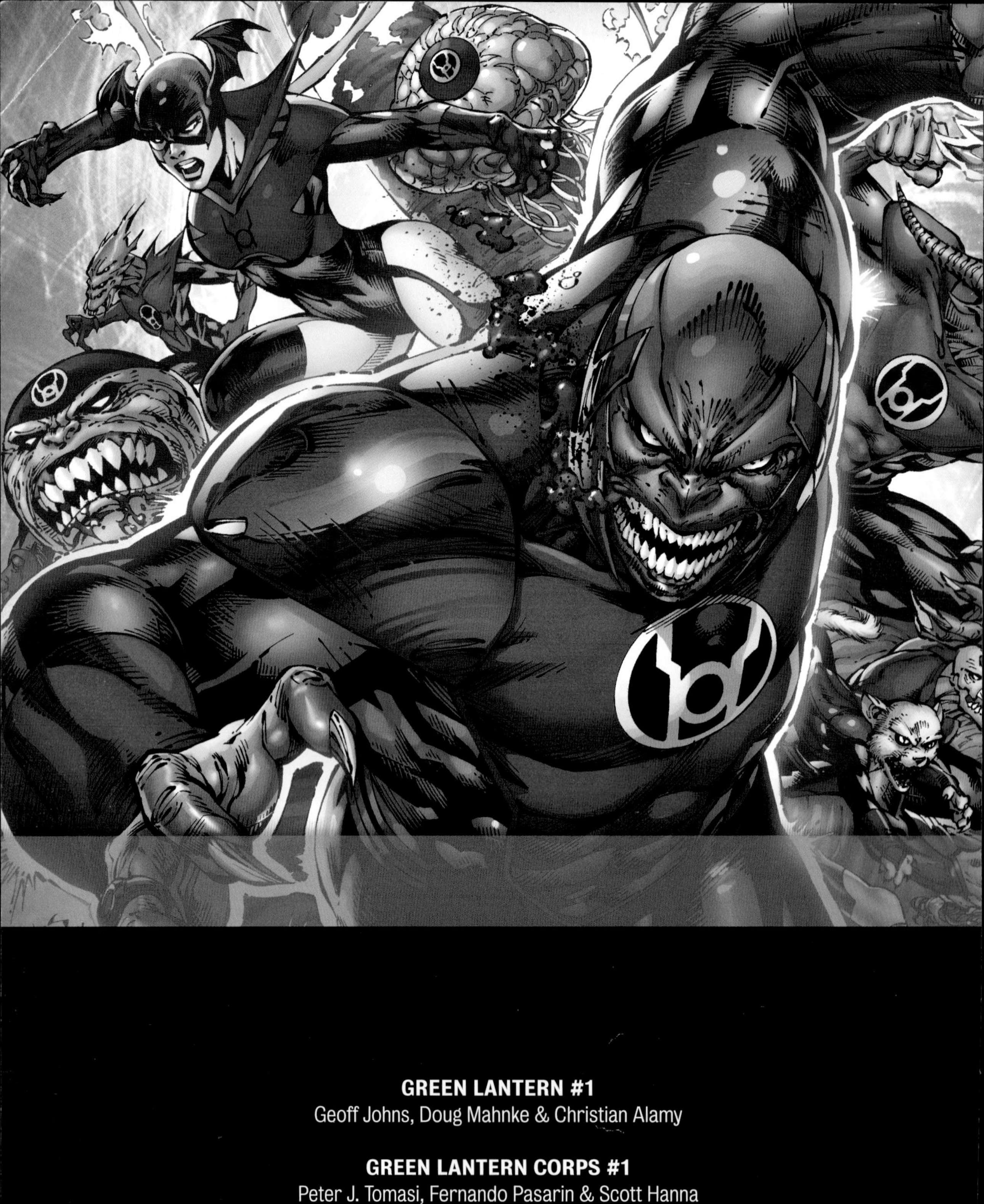

GREEN LANTERN #1
Geoff Johns, Doug Mahnke & Christian Alamy

GREEN LANTERN CORPS #1
Peter J. Tomasi, Fernando Pasarin & Scott Hanna

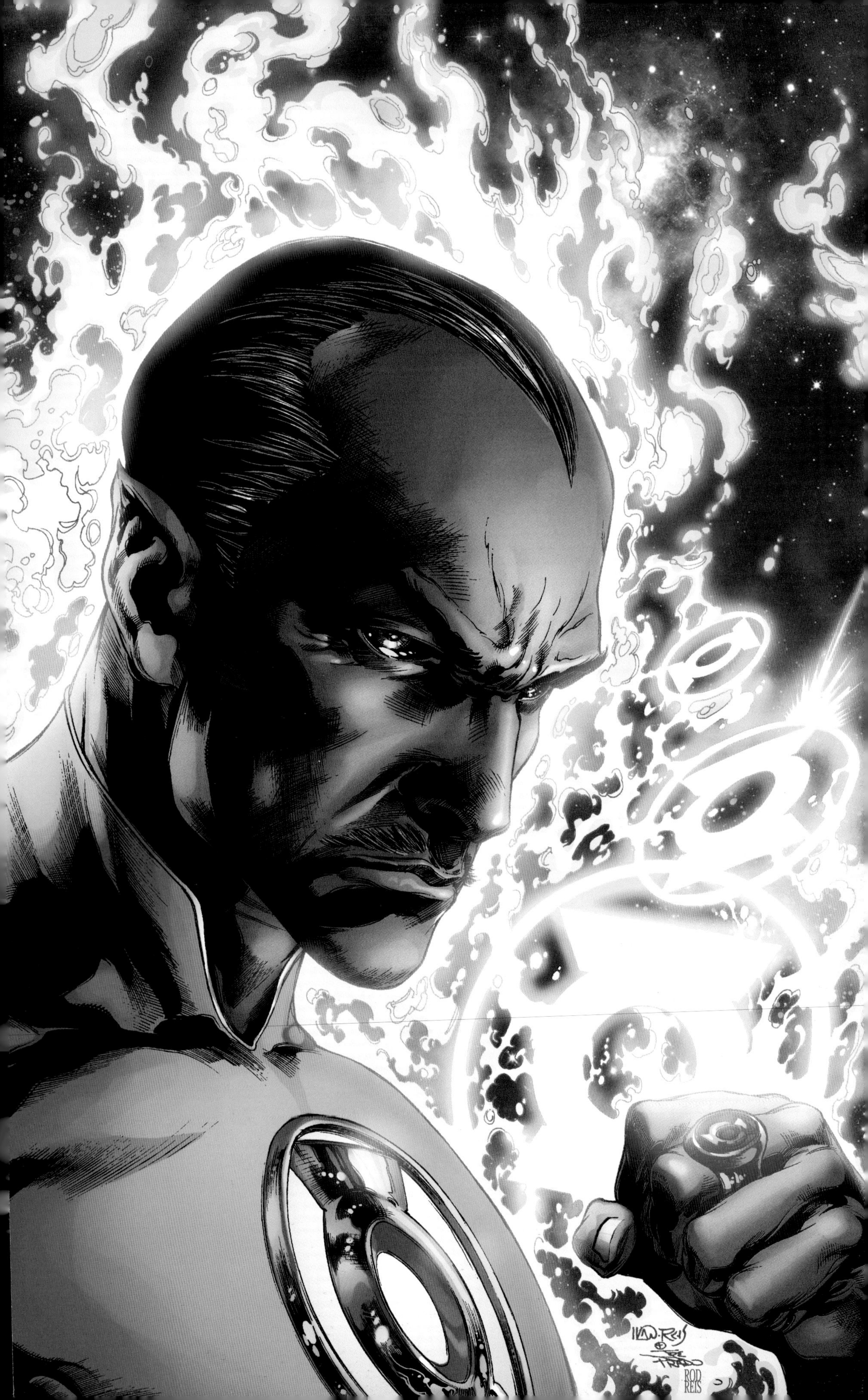
ROD REIS

GREEN LANTERN

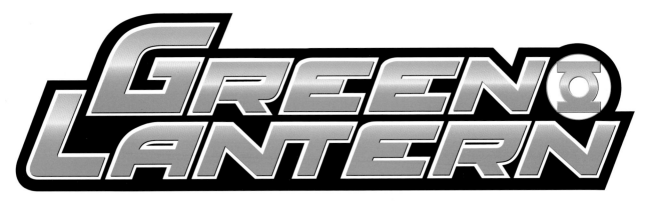

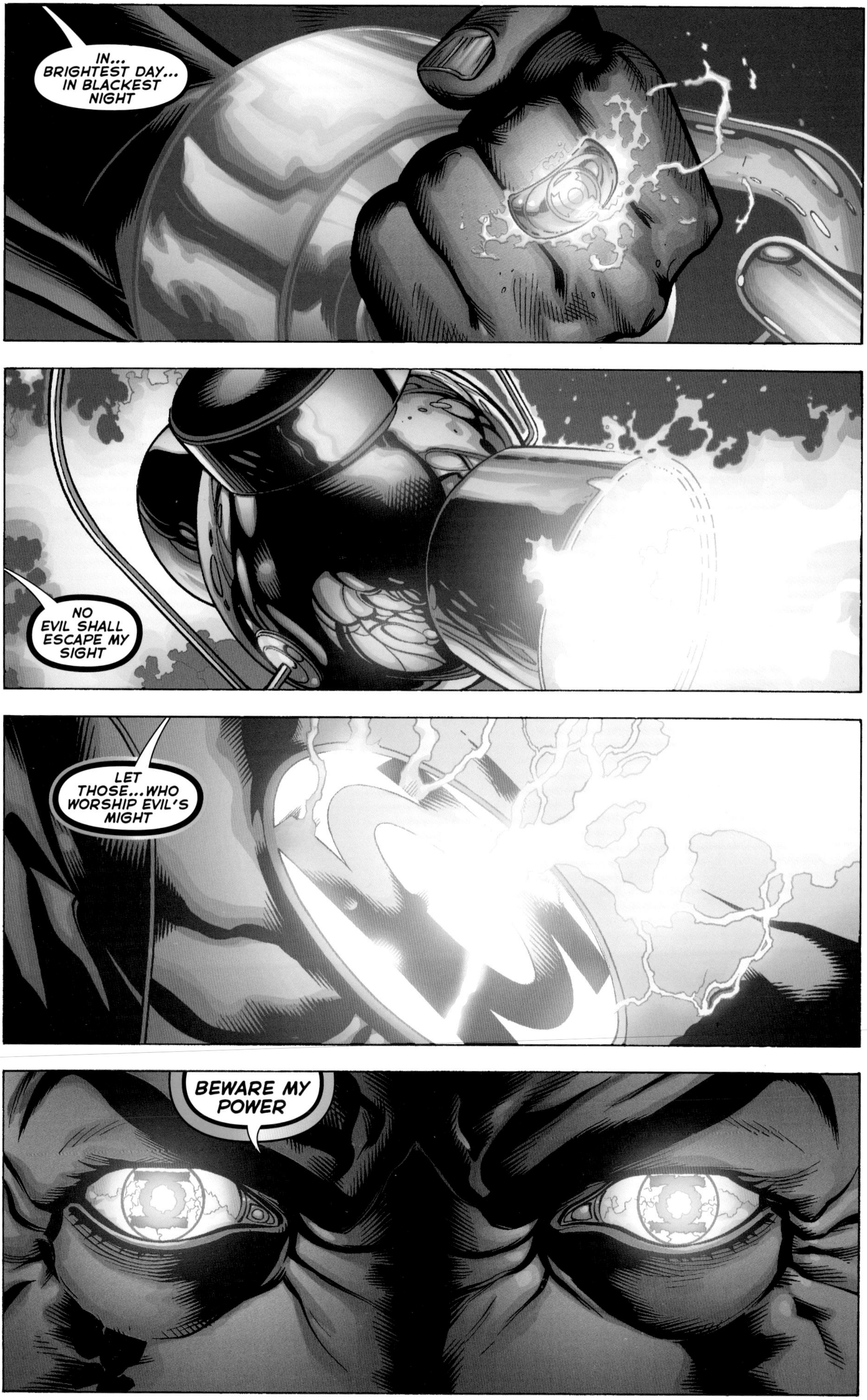
IN... BRIGHTEST DAY... IN BLACKEST NIGHT
NO EVIL SHALL ESCAPE MY SIGHT
LET THOSE...WHO WORSHIP EVIL'S MIGHT
BEWARE MY POWER

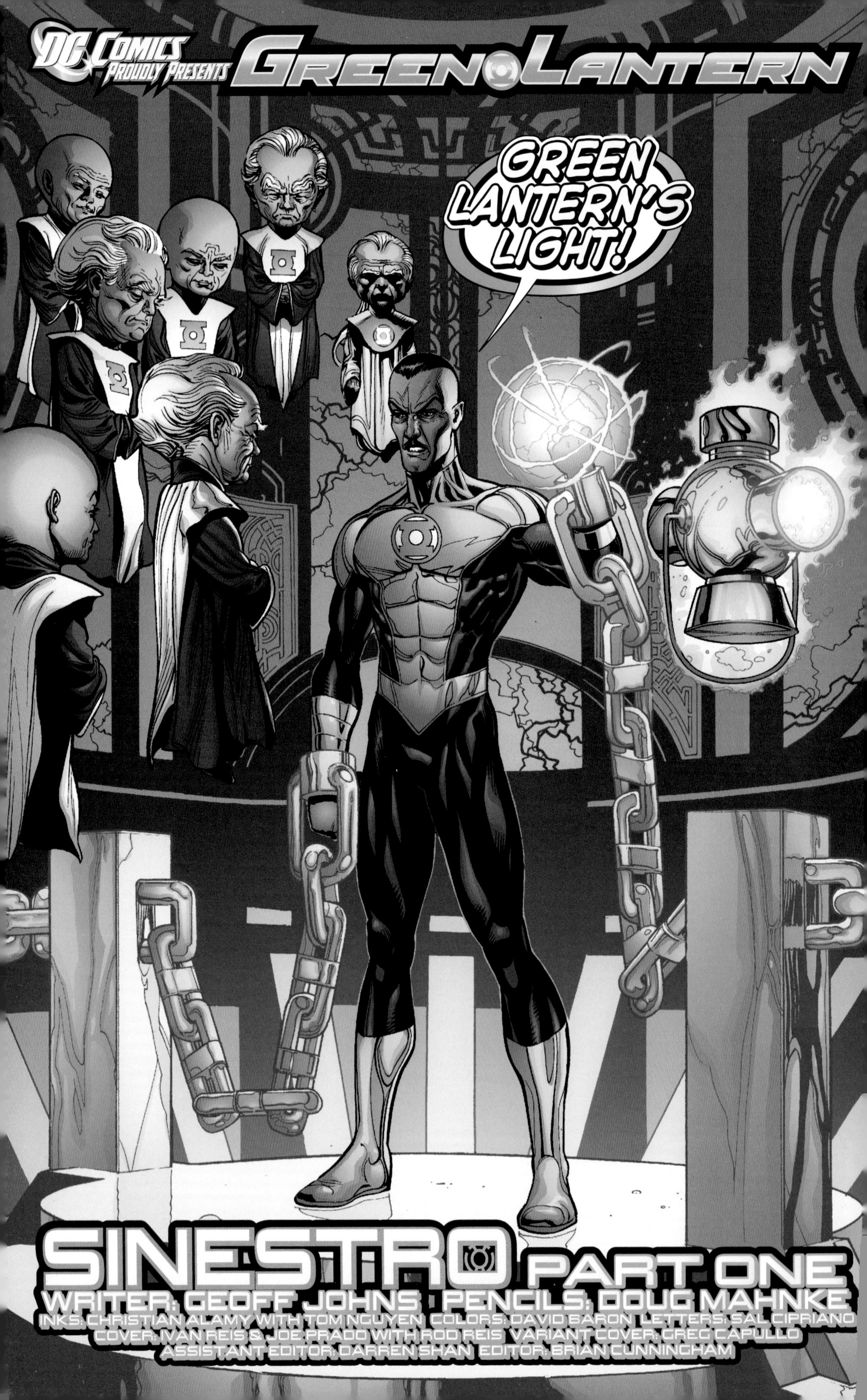
DC COMICS PROUDLY PRESENTS GREEN LANTERN
GREEN LANTERN'S LIGHT!
SINESTRO PART ONE
WRITER: GEOFF JOHNS PENCILS: DOUG MAHNKE
INKS: CHRISTIAN ALAMY WITH TOM NGUYEN COLORS: DAVID BARON LETTERS: SAL CIPRIANO
COVER: IVAN REIS & JOE PRADO WITH ROD REIS VARIANT COVER: GREG CAPULLO
ASSISTANT EDITOR: DARREN SHAN EDITOR: BRIAN CUNNINGHAM

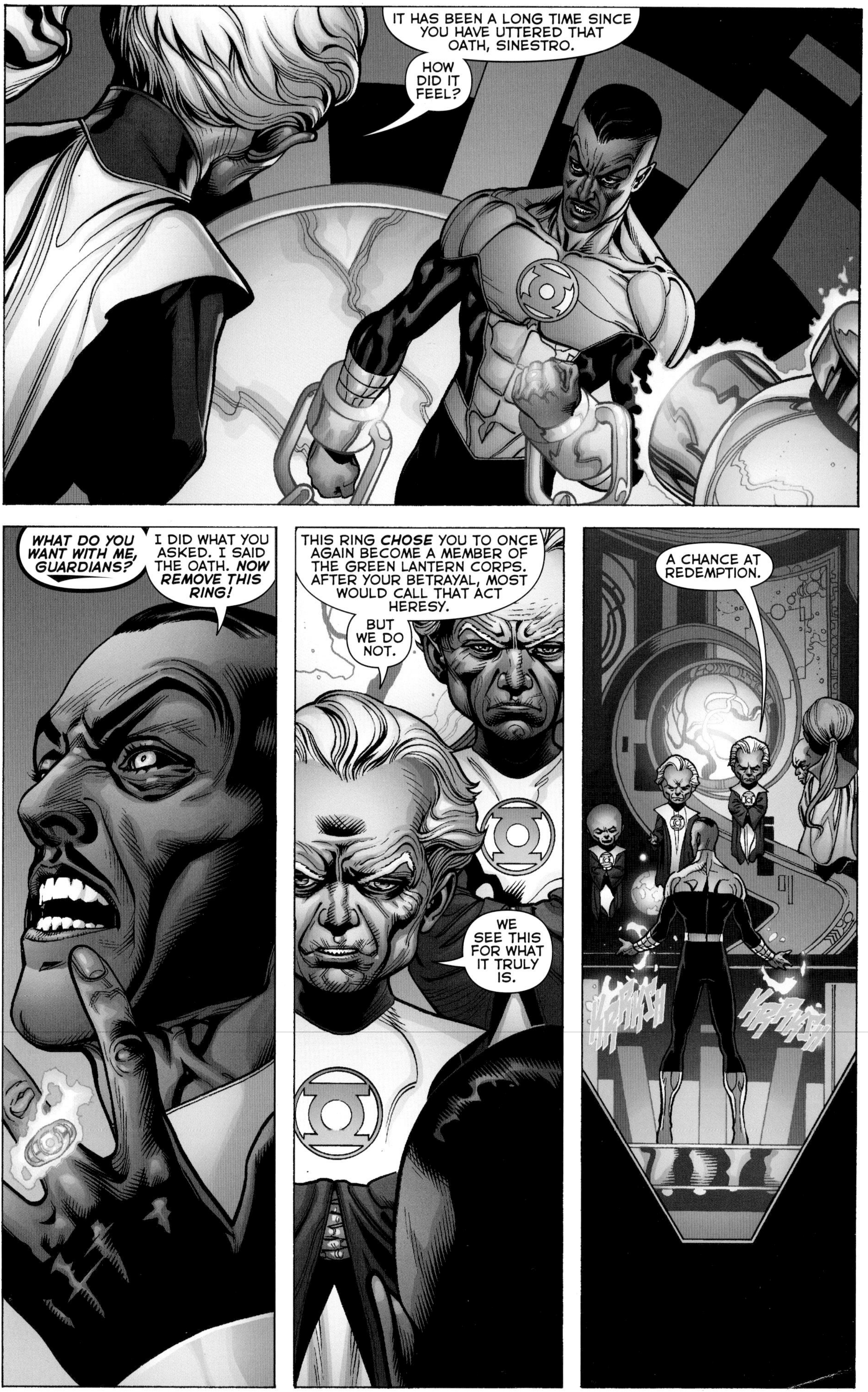
IT HAS BEEN A LONG TIME SINCE YOU HAVE UTTERED THAT OATH, SINESTRO.
HOW DID IT FEEL?
WHAT DO YOU WANT WITH ME, GUARDIANS?
I DID WHAT YOU ASKED. I SAID THE OATH. NOW REMOVE THIS RING!
THIS RING CHOSE YOU TO ONCE AGAIN BECOME A MEMBER OF THE GREEN LANTERN CORPS. AFTER YOUR BETRAYAL, MOST WOULD CALL THAT ACT HERESY.
BUT WE DO NOT.
WE SEE THIS FOR WHAT IT TRULY IS.
A CHANCE AT REDEMPTION.
KRRKSH
KRRKSH

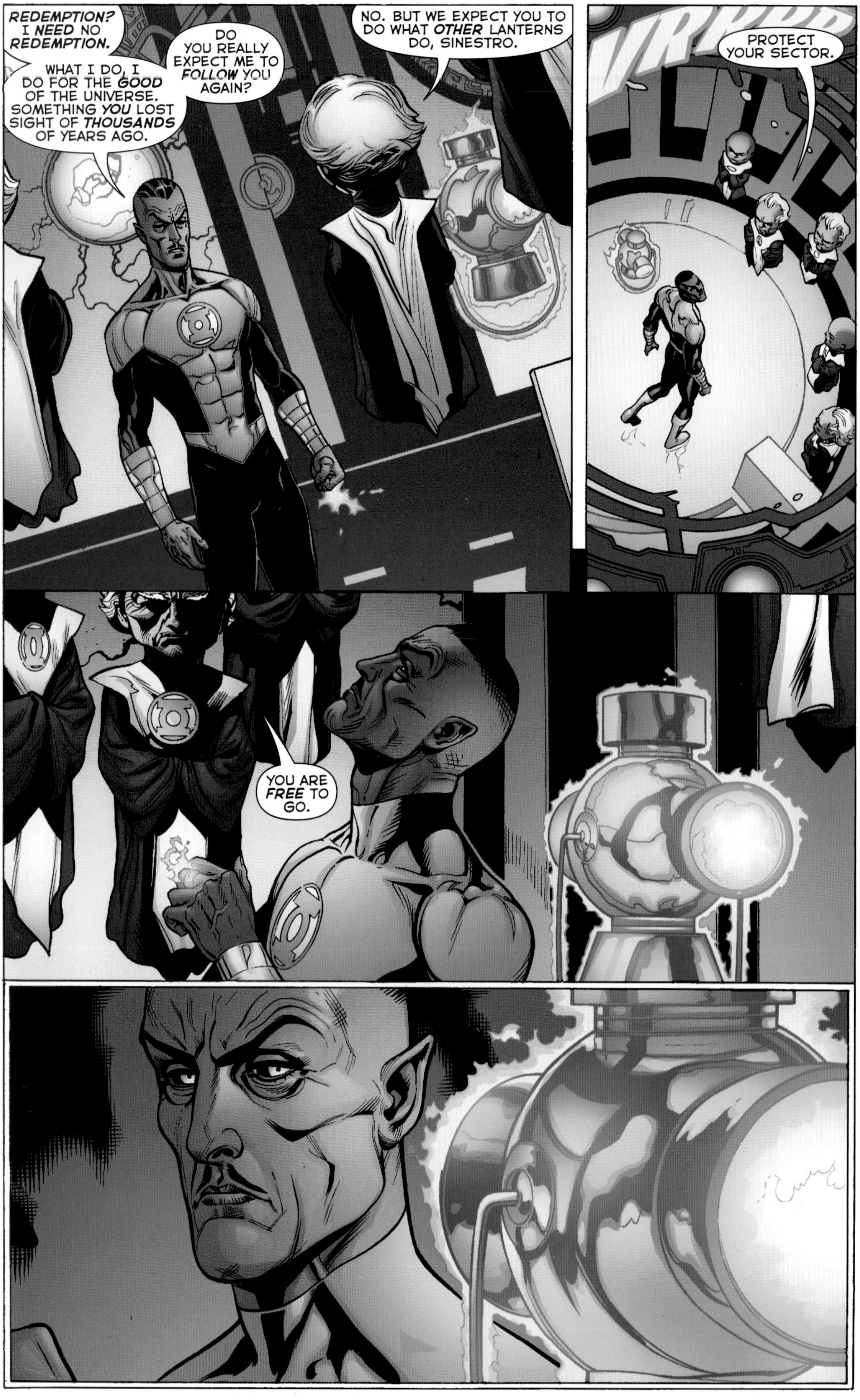
REDEMPTION? I NEED NO REDEMPTION.
WHAT I DO, I DO FOR THE GOOD OF THE UNIVERSE. SOMETHING YOU LOST SIGHT OF THOUSANDS OF YEARS AGO.
DO YOU REALLY EXPECT ME TO FOLLOW YOU AGAIN?
NO. BUT WE EXPECT YOU TO DO WHAT OTHER LANTERNS DO, SINESTRO.
PROTECT YOUR SECTOR.
YOU ARE FREE TO GO.

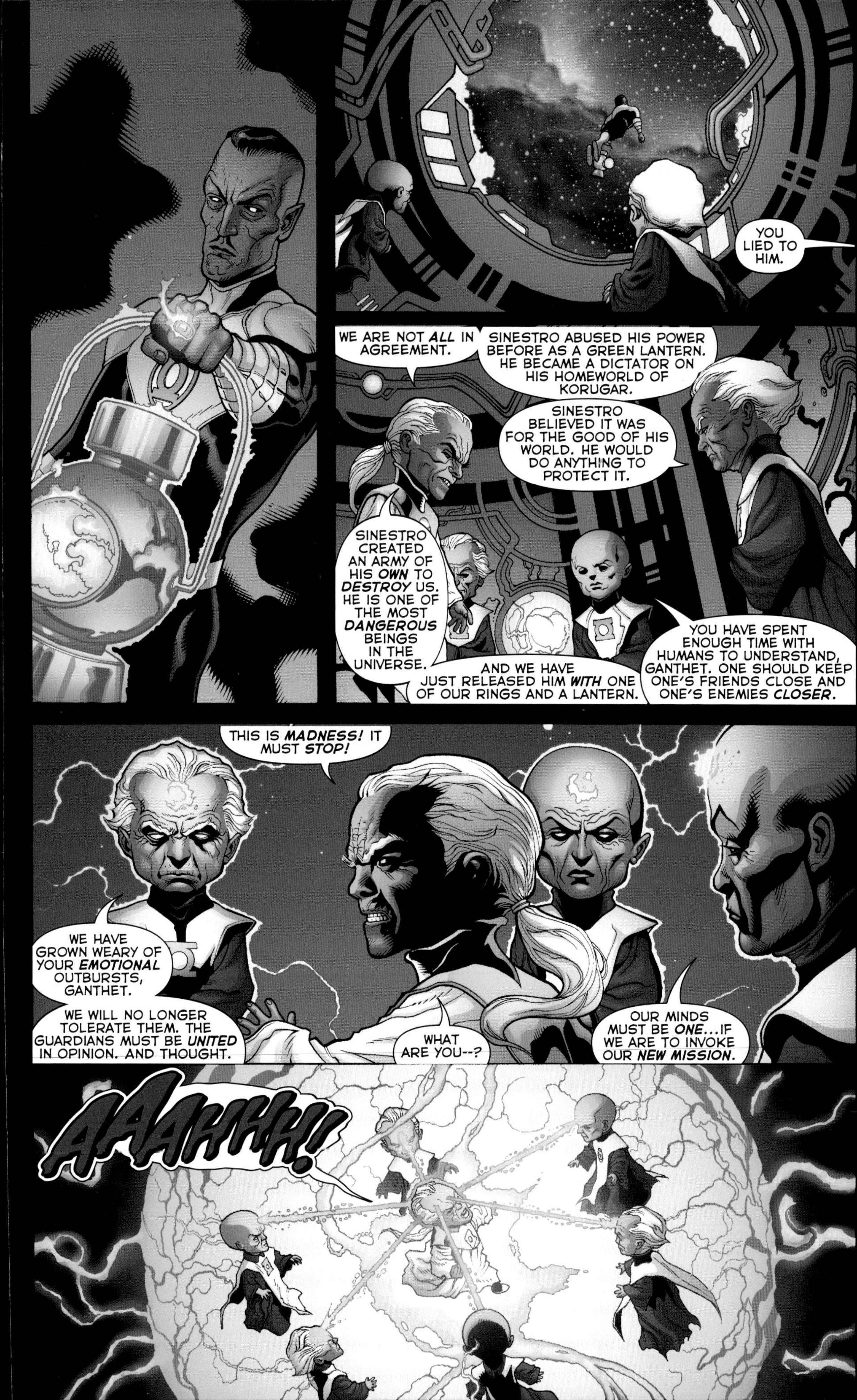
YOU LIED TO HIM.
WE ARE NOT ALL IN AGREEMENT.
SINESTRO ABUSED HIS POWER BEFORE AS A GREEN LANTERN. HE BECAME A DICTATOR ON HIS HOMEWORLD OF KORUGAR.
SINESTRO BELIEVED IT WAS FOR THE GOOD OF HIS WORLD. HE WOULD DO ANYTHING TO PROTECT IT.
SINESTRO CREATED AN ARMY OF HIS OWN TO DESTROY US. HE IS ONE OF THE MOST DANGEROUS BEINGS IN THE UNIVERSE.
AND WE HAVE JUST RELEASED HIM WITH ONE OF OUR RINGS AND A LANTERN.
YOU HAVE SPENT ENOUGH TIME WITH HUMANS TO UNDERSTAND, GANTHET. ONE SHOULD KEEP ONE'S FRIENDS CLOSE AND ONE'S ENEMIES CLOSER.
THIS IS MADNESS! IT MUST STOP!
WE HAVE GROWN WEARY OF YOUR EMOTIONAL OUTBURSTS, GANTHET.
WE WILL NO LONGER TOLERATE THEM. THE GUARDIANS MUST BE UNITED IN OPINION. AND THOUGHT.
WHAT ARE YOU--?
OUR MINDS MUST BE ONE...IF WE ARE TO INVOKE OUR NEW MISSION.
AAAHHH!

HEY!

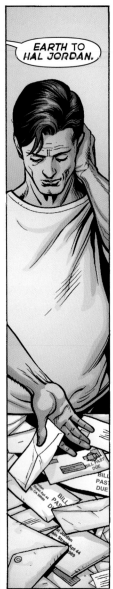

EARTH TO HAL JORDAN.

MR. JORDAN--?

I'M TRYING TO FIND MY CHECKBOOK.

NO. NO MORE CHECKS. THEY NEVER CLEAR.

THIS ONE WILL.

YOU SAID THAT THE LAST TIME. YOU'RE ALREADY TWO MONTHS BEHIND--

I'VE BEEN OUT OF TOWN.

I WANT *THREE MONTHS'* RENT, MR. JORDAN. RIGHT *NOW.* IN *CASH.*

I DON'T HAVE THAT KIND OF CASH ON ME, GARY.

THEN GRAB YOUR A.T.M. CARD AND GET IN YOUR CAR.

I'LL DRIVE.

I DON'T HAVE A CAR.

HELP!

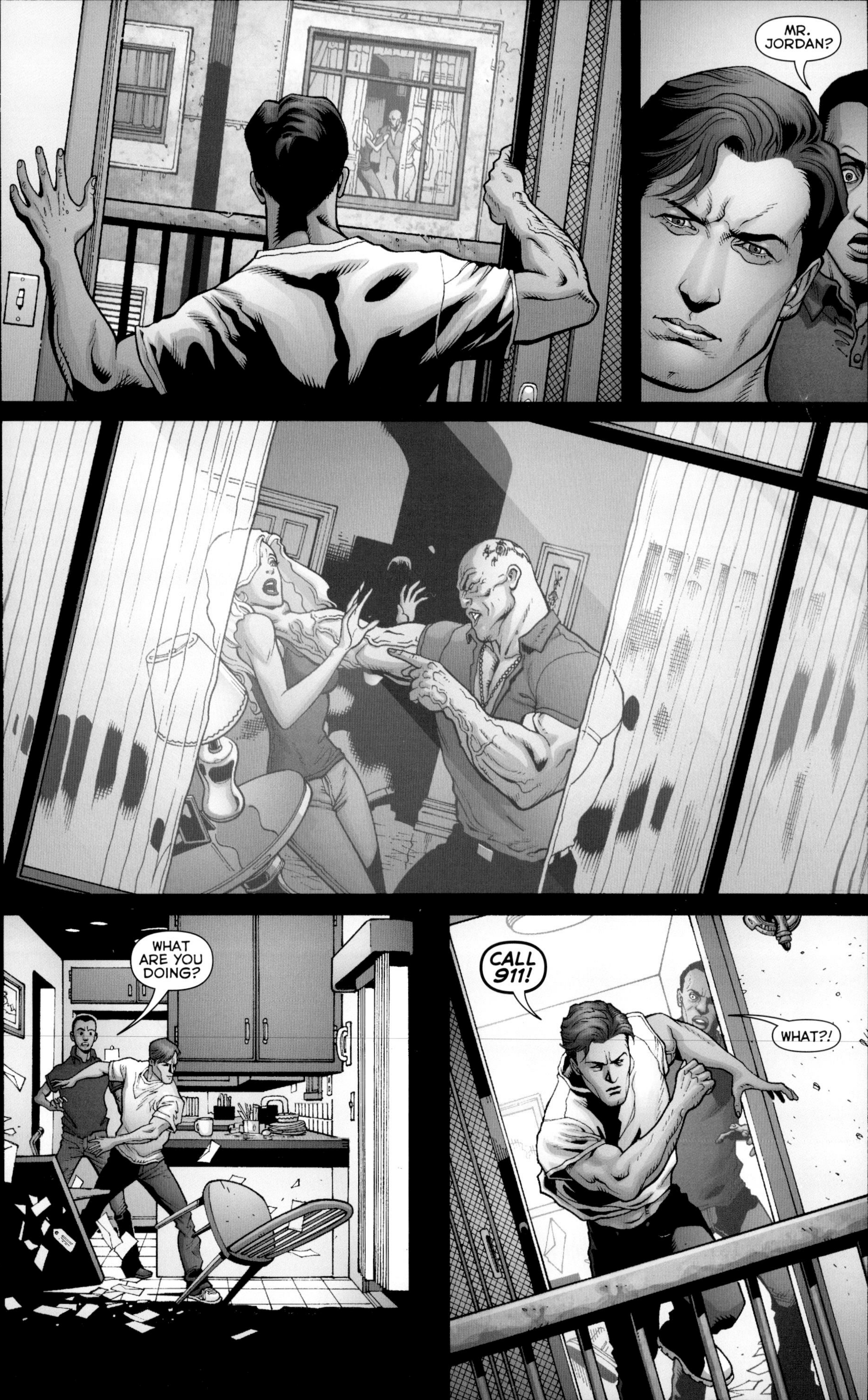
MR. JORDAN?
WHAT ARE YOU DOING?
CALL 911!
WHAT?!

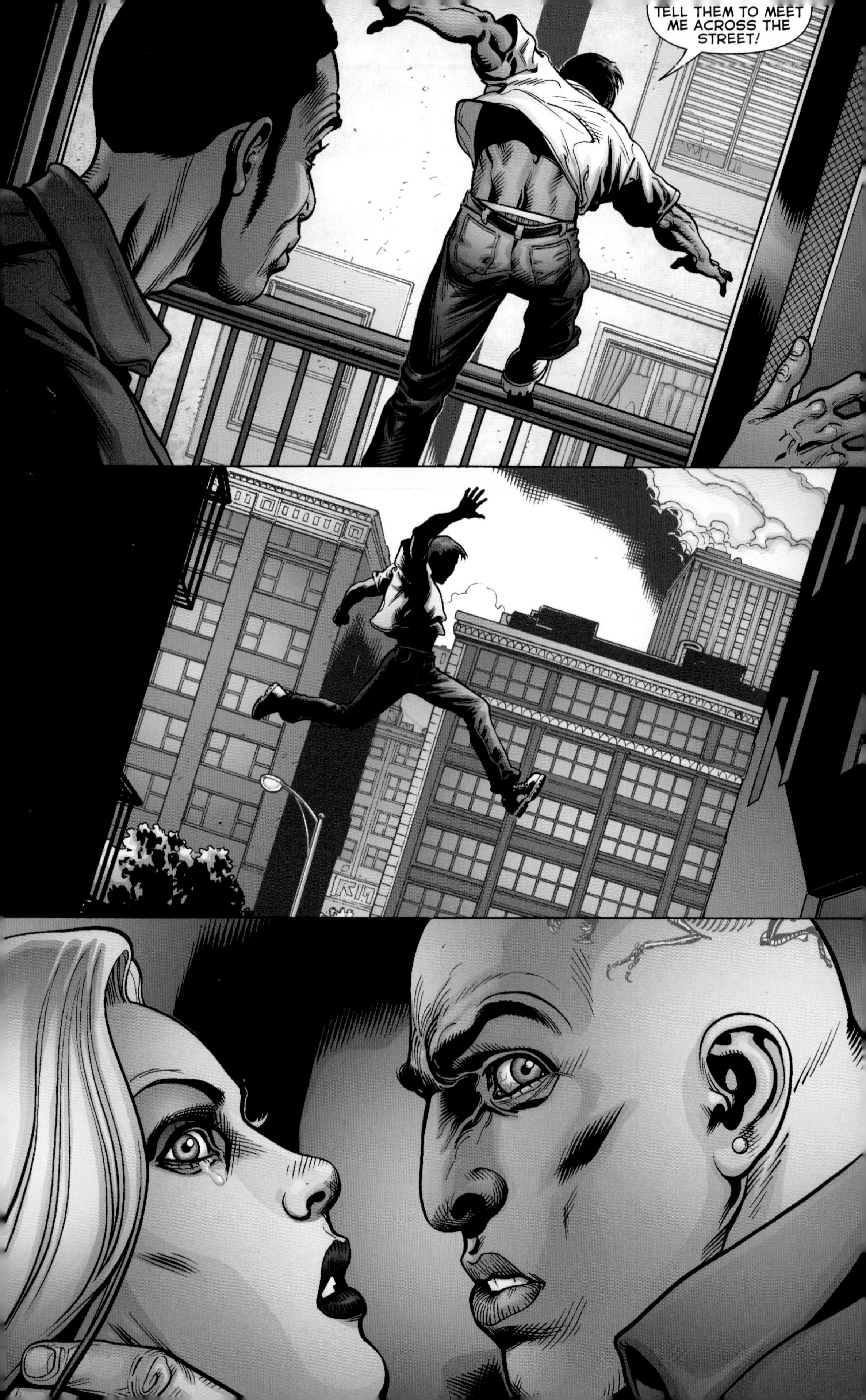
TELL THEM TO MEET ME ACROSS THE STREET!

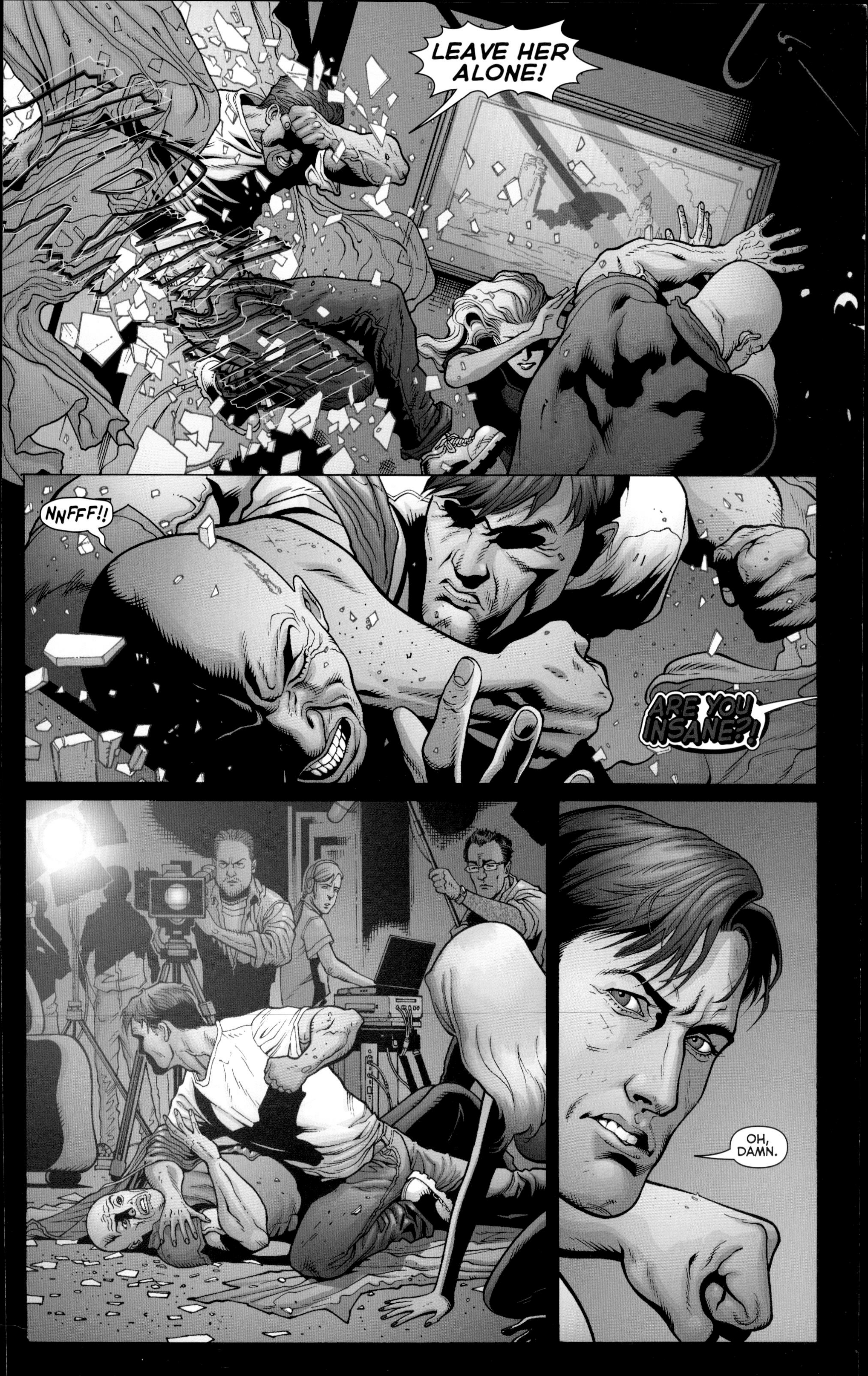
LEAVE HER ALONE!
NNFFF!!
ARE YOU INSANE?!
OH, DAMN.

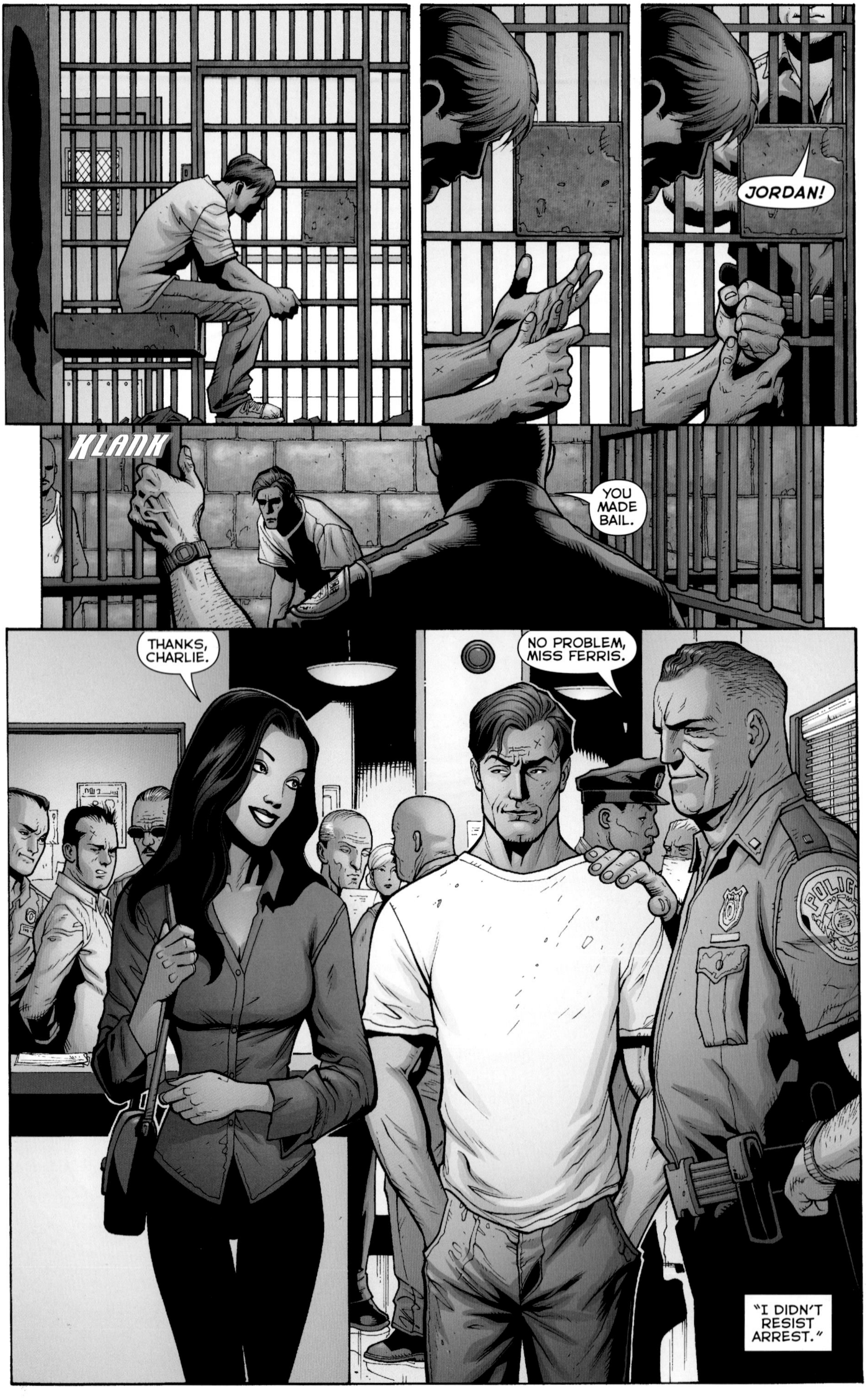
JORDAN!
KLANK
YOU MADE BAIL.
THANKS, CHARLIE.
NO PROBLEM, MISS FERRIS.
"I DIDN'T RESIST ARREST."

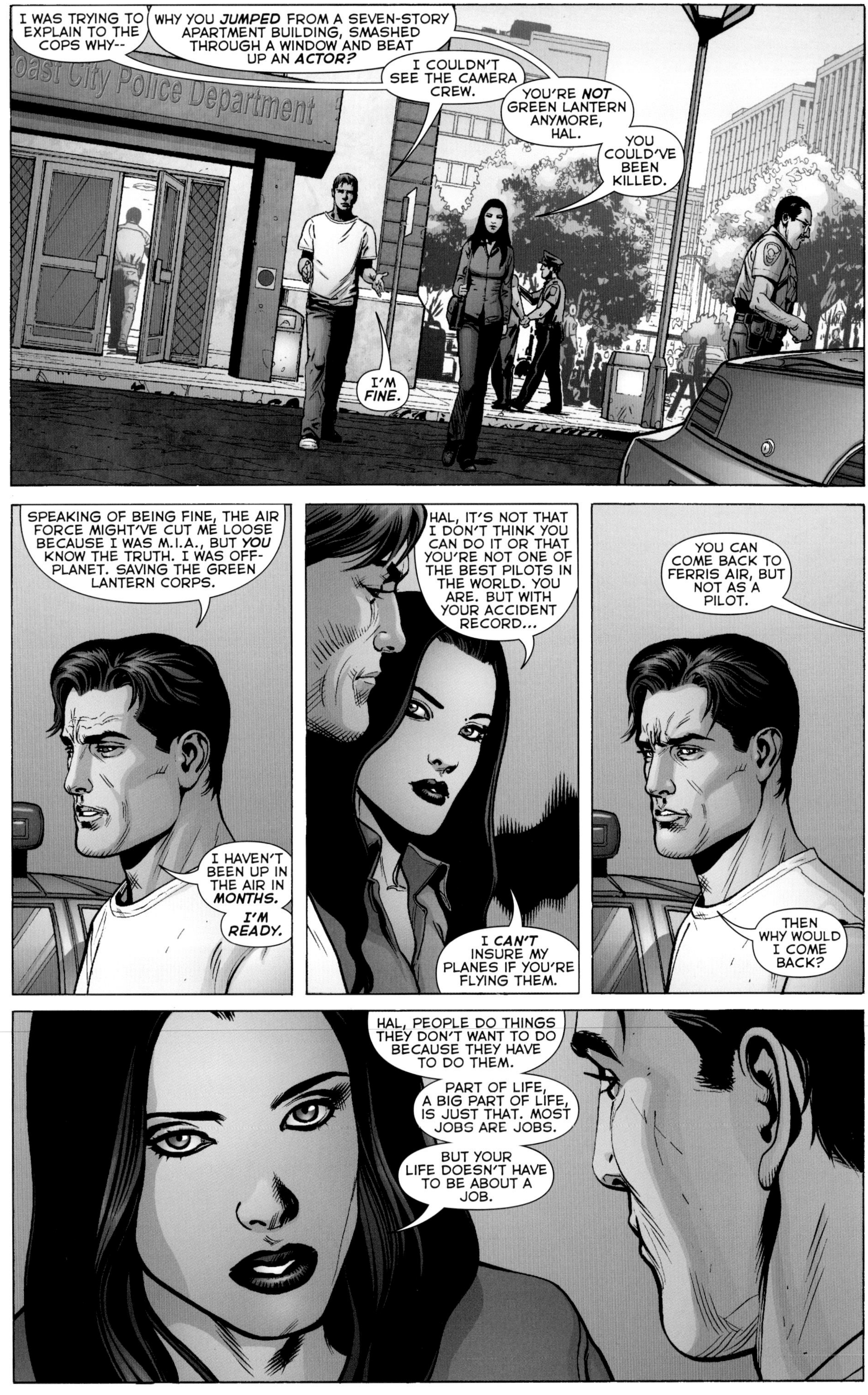

Coast City Police Department
I WAS TRYING TO EXPLAIN TO THE COPS WHY--
WHY YOU JUMPED FROM A SEVEN-STORY APARTMENT BUILDING, SMASHED THROUGH A WINDOW AND BEAT UP AN ACTOR?
I COULDN'T SEE THE CAMERA CREW.
YOU'RE NOT GREEN LANTERN ANYMORE, HAL.
YOU COULD'VE BEEN KILLED.
I'M FINE.
SPEAKING OF BEING FINE, THE AIR FORCE MIGHT'VE CUT ME LOOSE BECAUSE I WAS M.I.A., BUT YOU KNOW THE TRUTH. I WAS OFF-PLANET. SAVING THE GREEN LANTERN CORPS.
I HAVEN'T BEEN UP IN THE AIR IN MONTHS.
I'M READY.
HAL, IT'S NOT THAT I DON'T THINK YOU CAN DO IT OR THAT YOU'RE NOT ONE OF THE BEST PILOTS IN THE WORLD. YOU ARE. BUT WITH YOUR ACCIDENT RECORD...
I CAN'T INSURE MY PLANES IF YOU'RE FLYING THEM.
YOU CAN COME BACK TO FERRIS AIR, BUT NOT AS A PILOT.
THEN WHY WOULD I COME BACK?
HAL, PEOPLE DO THINGS THEY DON'T WANT TO DO BECAUSE THEY HAVE TO DO THEM.
PART OF LIFE, A BIG PART OF LIFE, IS JUST THAT. MOST JOBS ARE JOBS.
BUT YOUR LIFE DOESN'T HAVE TO BE ABOUT A JOB.

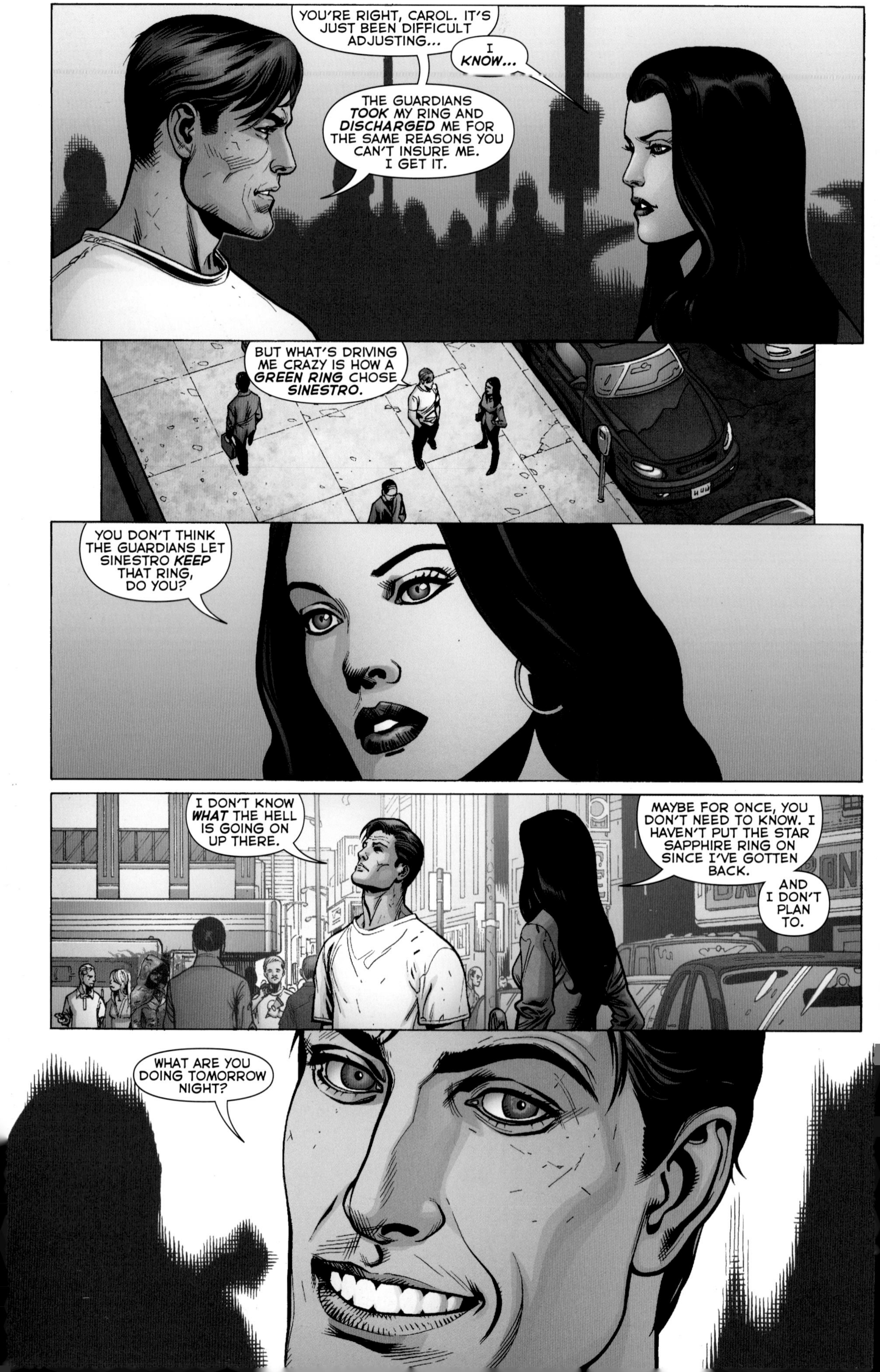
YOU'RE RIGHT, CAROL. IT'S JUST BEEN DIFFICULT ADJUSTING...
I KNOW...
THE GUARDIANS TOOK MY RING AND DISCHARGED ME FOR THE SAME REASONS YOU CAN'T INSURE ME. I GET IT.
BUT WHAT'S DRIVING ME CRAZY IS HOW A GREEN RING CHOSE SINESTRO.
YOU DON'T THINK THE GUARDIANS LET SINESTRO KEEP THAT RING, DO YOU?
I DON'T KNOW WHAT THE HELL IS GOING ON UP THERE.
MAYBE FOR ONCE, YOU DON'T NEED TO KNOW. I HAVEN'T PUT THE STAR SAPPHIRE RING ON SINCE I'VE GOTTEN BACK.
AND I DON'T PLAN TO.
WHAT ARE YOU DOING TOMORROW NIGHT?

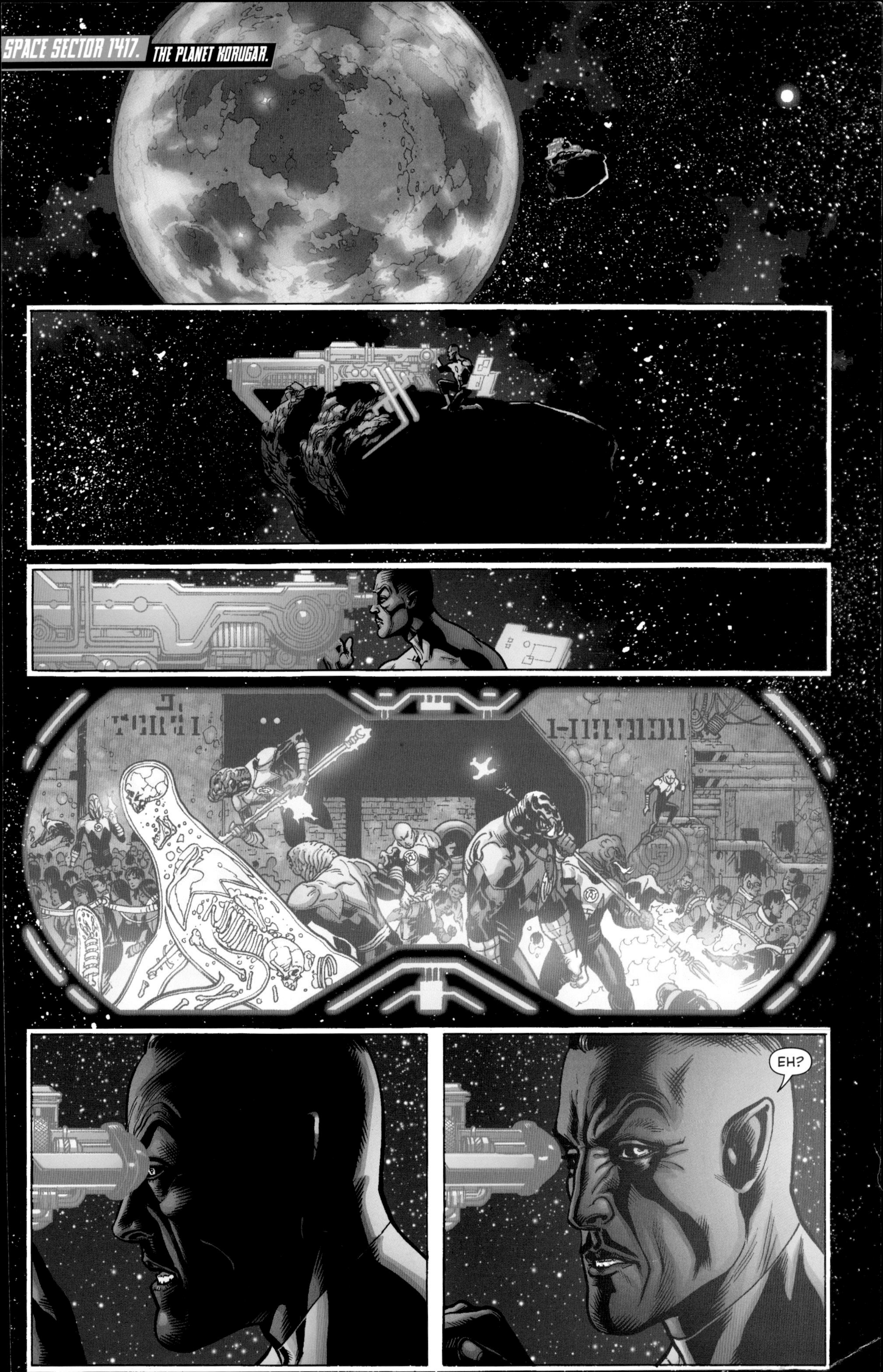
SPACE SECTOR 1417.
THE PLANET KORUGAR.
EH?

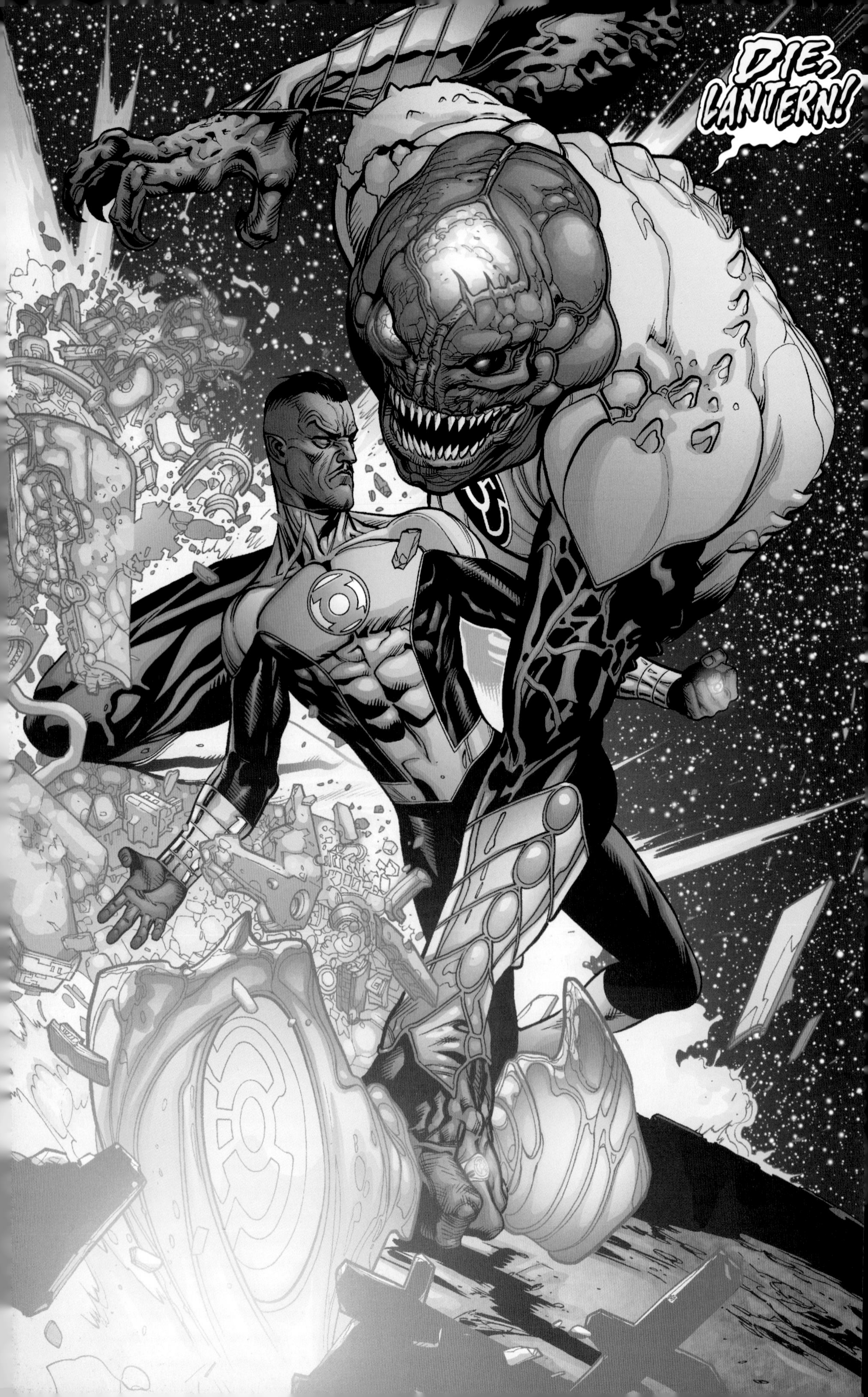
DIE, LANTERN!

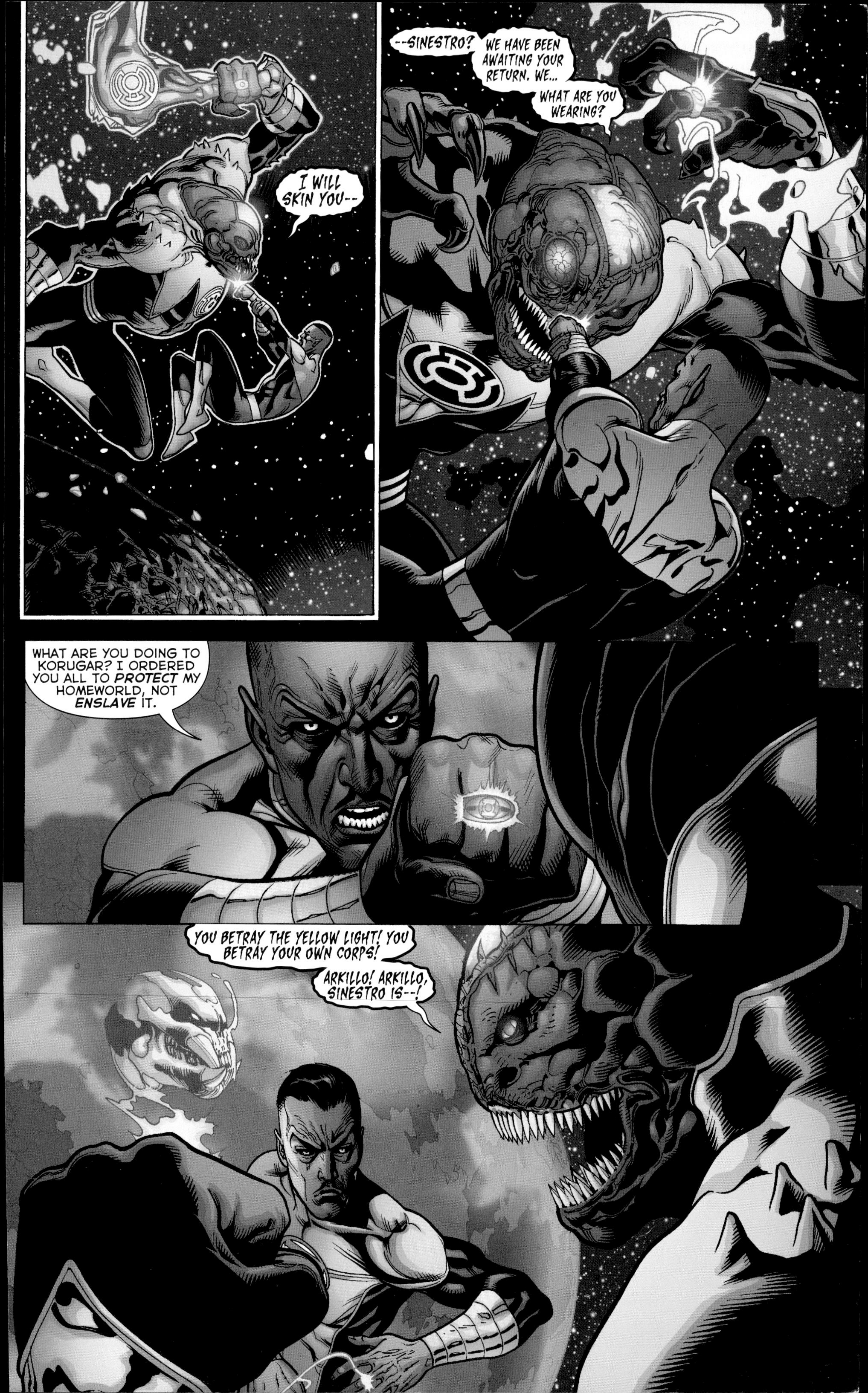
I WILL SKIN YOU--
--SINESTRO?
WE HAVE BEEN AWAITING YOUR RETURN. WE...
WHAT ARE YOU WEARING?
WHAT ARE YOU DOING TO KORUGAR? I ORDERED YOU ALL TO *PROTECT* MY HOMEWORLD, NOT *ENSLAVE* IT.
YOU BETRAY THE YELLOW LIGHT! YOU BETRAY YOUR OWN CORPS!
ARKILLO! ARKILLO, SINESTRO IS--!

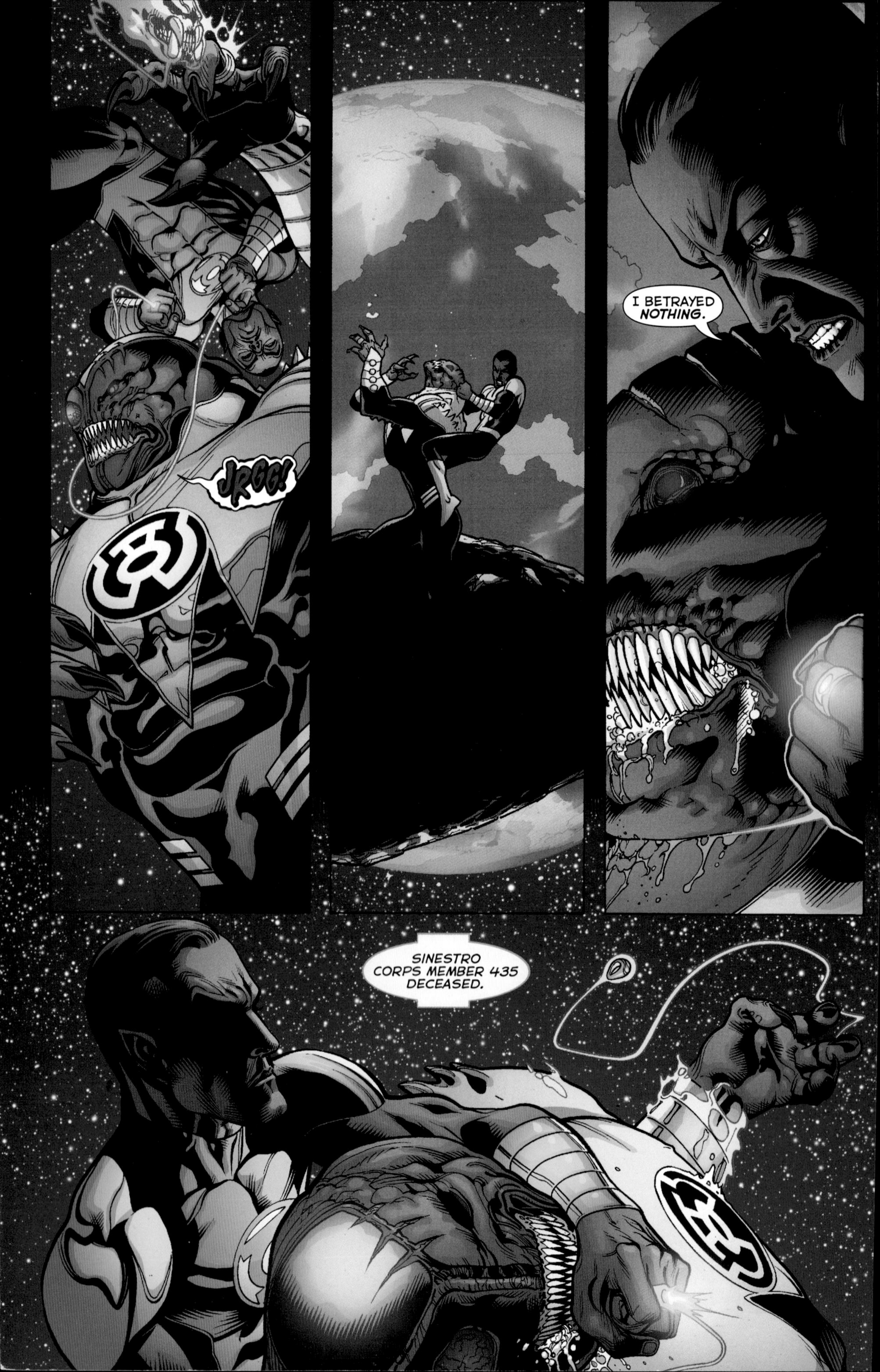
JRGG!
I BETRAYED NOTHING.
SINESTRO CORPS MEMBER 435 DECEASED.

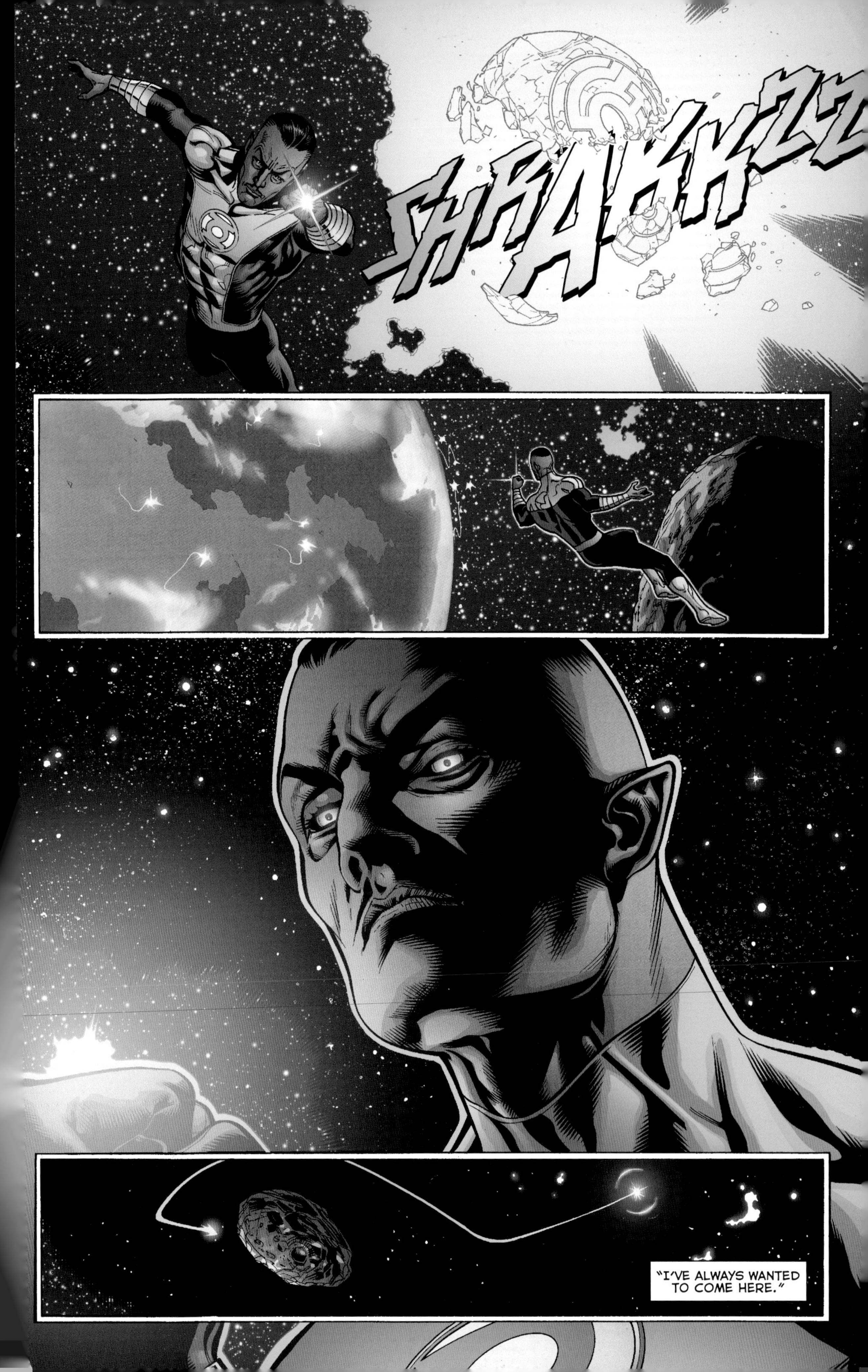
SHRAKKZZ
"I'VE ALWAYS WANTED TO COME HERE."

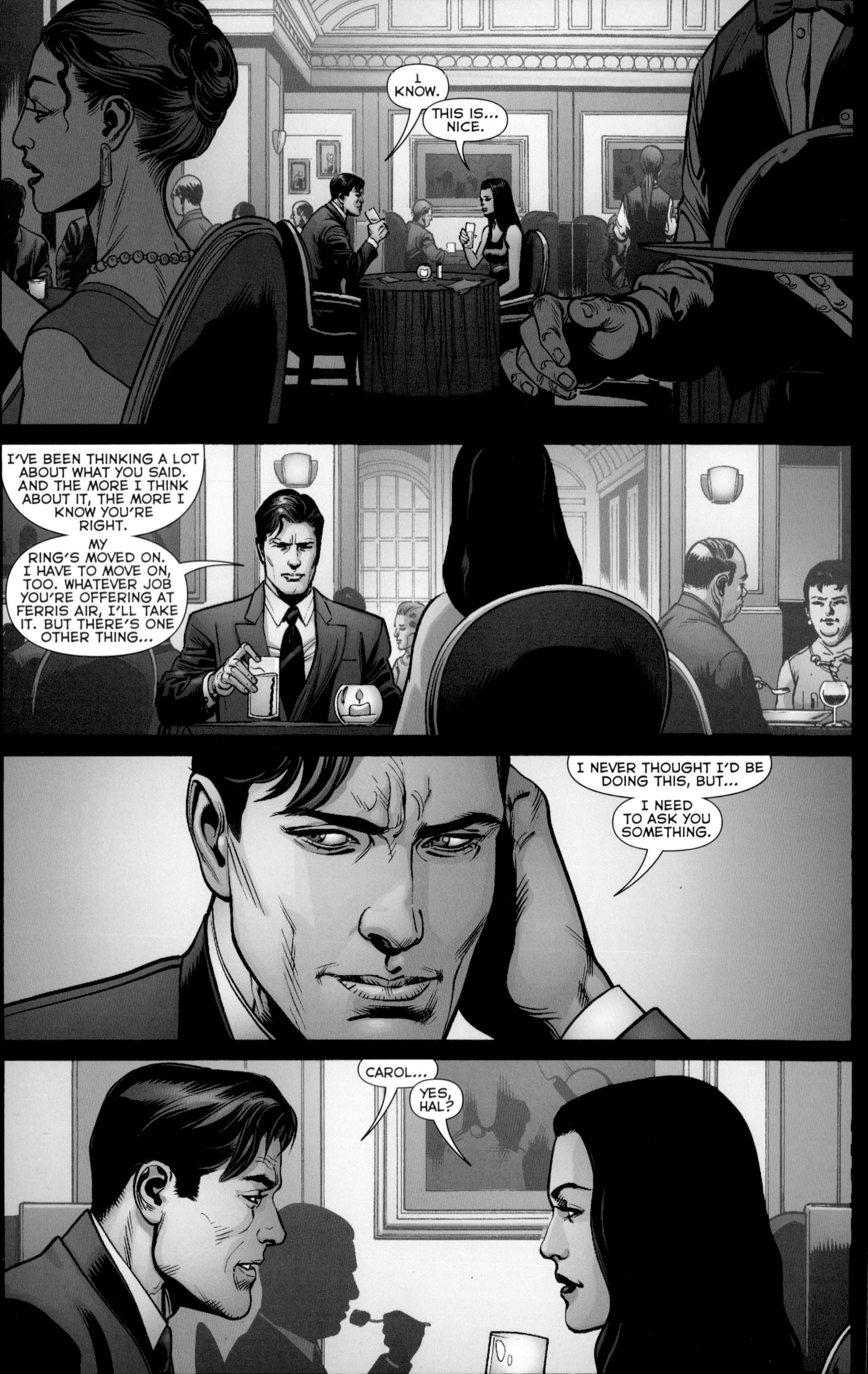
I KNOW.
THIS IS... NICE.
I'VE BEEN THINKING A LOT ABOUT WHAT YOU SAID. AND THE MORE I THINK ABOUT IT, THE MORE I KNOW YOU'RE RIGHT.
MY RING'S MOVED ON. I HAVE TO MOVE ON, TOO. WHATEVER JOB YOU'RE OFFERING AT FERRIS AIR, I'LL TAKE IT. BUT THERE'S ONE OTHER THING...
I NEVER THOUGHT I'D BE DOING THIS, BUT...
I NEED TO ASK YOU SOMETHING.
CAROL...
YES, HAL?

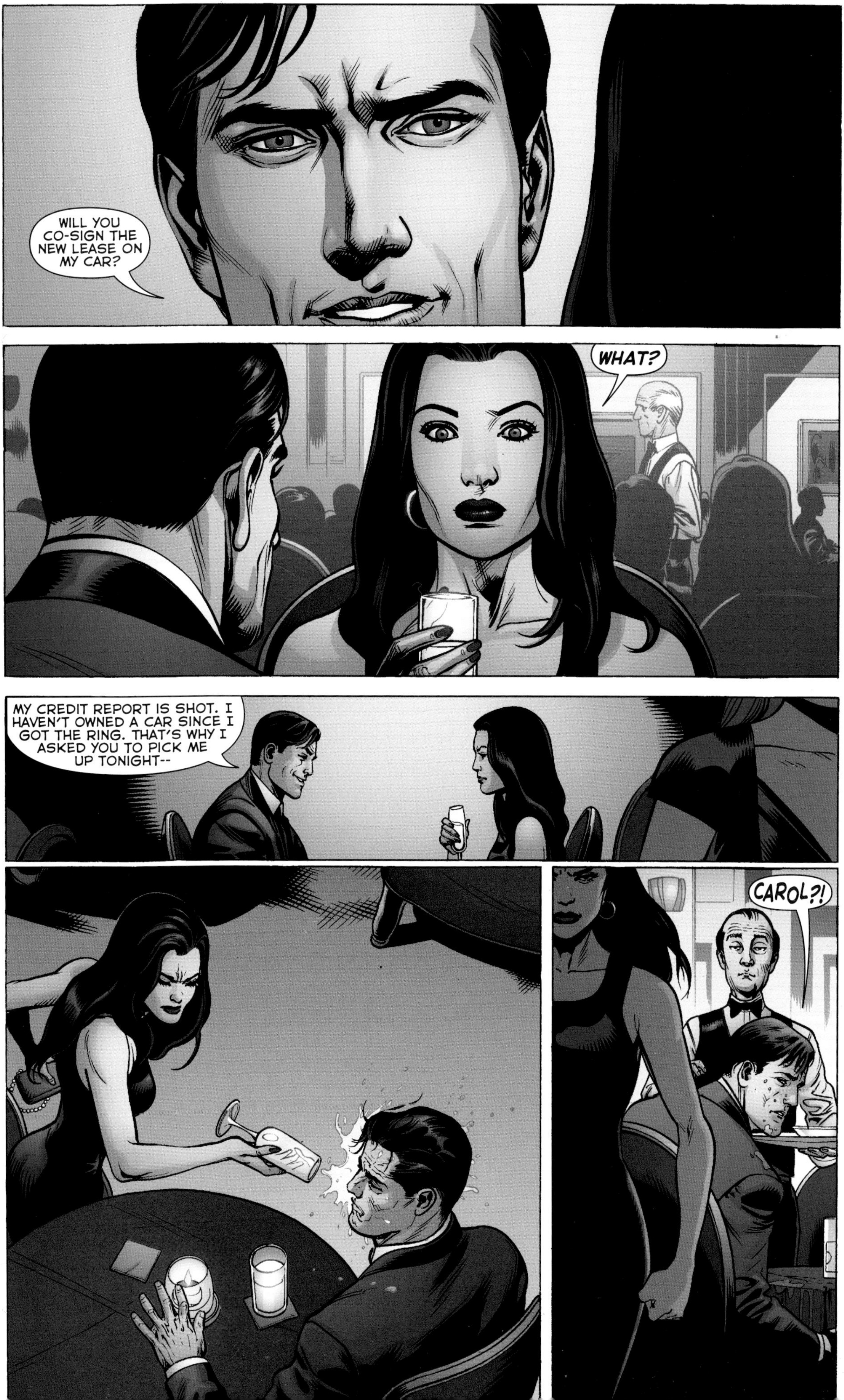
WILL YOU CO-SIGN THE NEW LEASE ON MY CAR?
WHAT?
MY CREDIT REPORT IS SHOT. I HAVEN'T OWNED A CAR SINCE I GOT THE RING. THAT'S WHY I ASKED YOU TO PICK ME UP TONIGHT--
CAROL?!

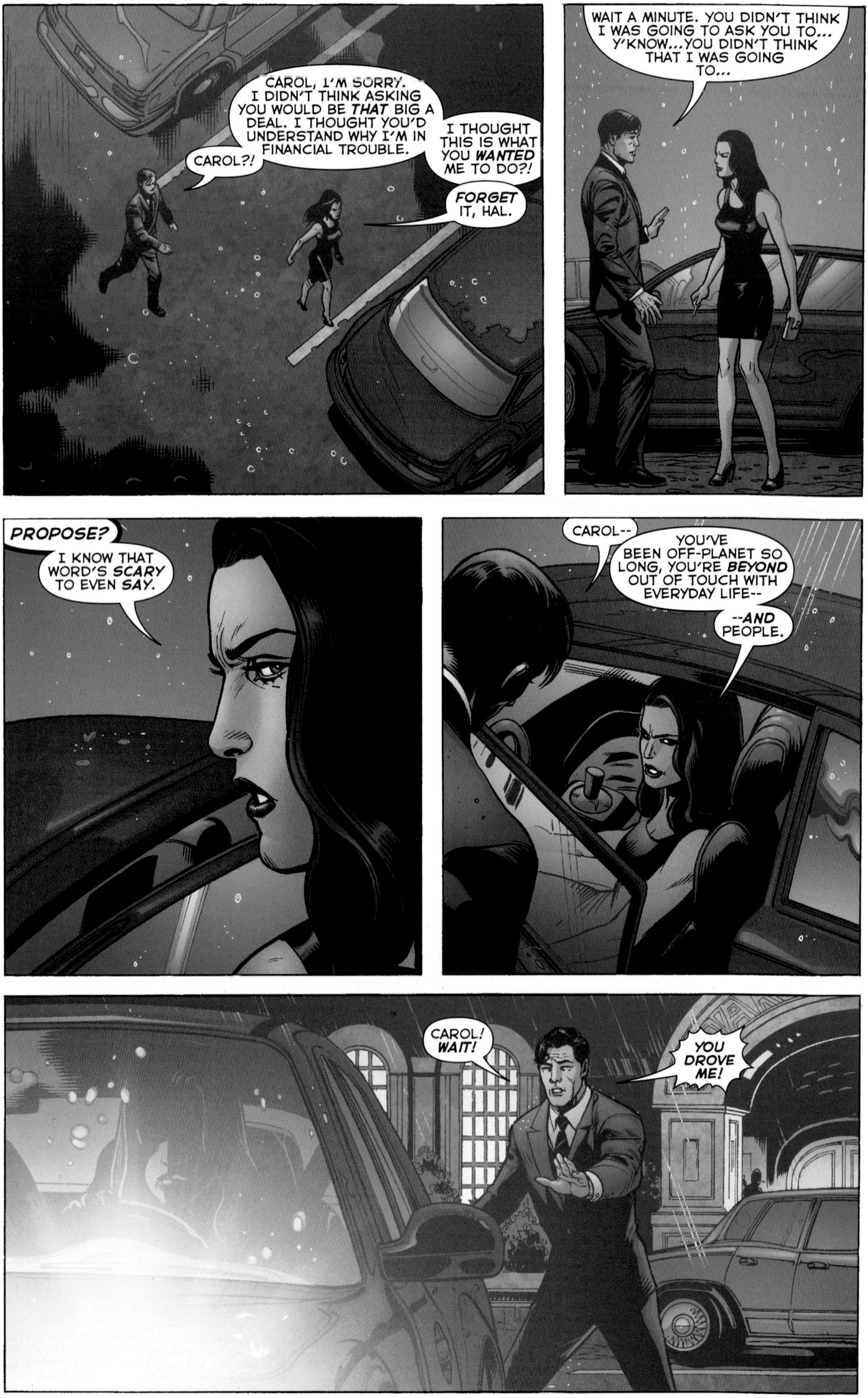
CAROL, I'M SORRY. I DIDN'T THINK ASKING YOU WOULD BE THAT BIG A DEAL. I THOUGHT YOU'D UNDERSTAND WHY I'M IN FINANCIAL TROUBLE.
CAROL?!
I THOUGHT THIS IS WHAT YOU WANTED ME TO DO?!
FORGET IT, HAL.
WAIT A MINUTE. YOU DIDN'T THINK I WAS GOING TO ASK YOU TO... Y'KNOW...YOU DIDN'T THINK THAT I WAS GOING TO...
PROPOSE?
I KNOW THAT WORD'S SCARY TO EVEN SAY.
CAROL--
YOU'VE BEEN OFF-PLANET SO LONG, YOU'RE BEYOND OUT OF TOUCH WITH EVERYDAY LIFE--
--AND PEOPLE.
CAROL! WAIT!
YOU DROVE ME!

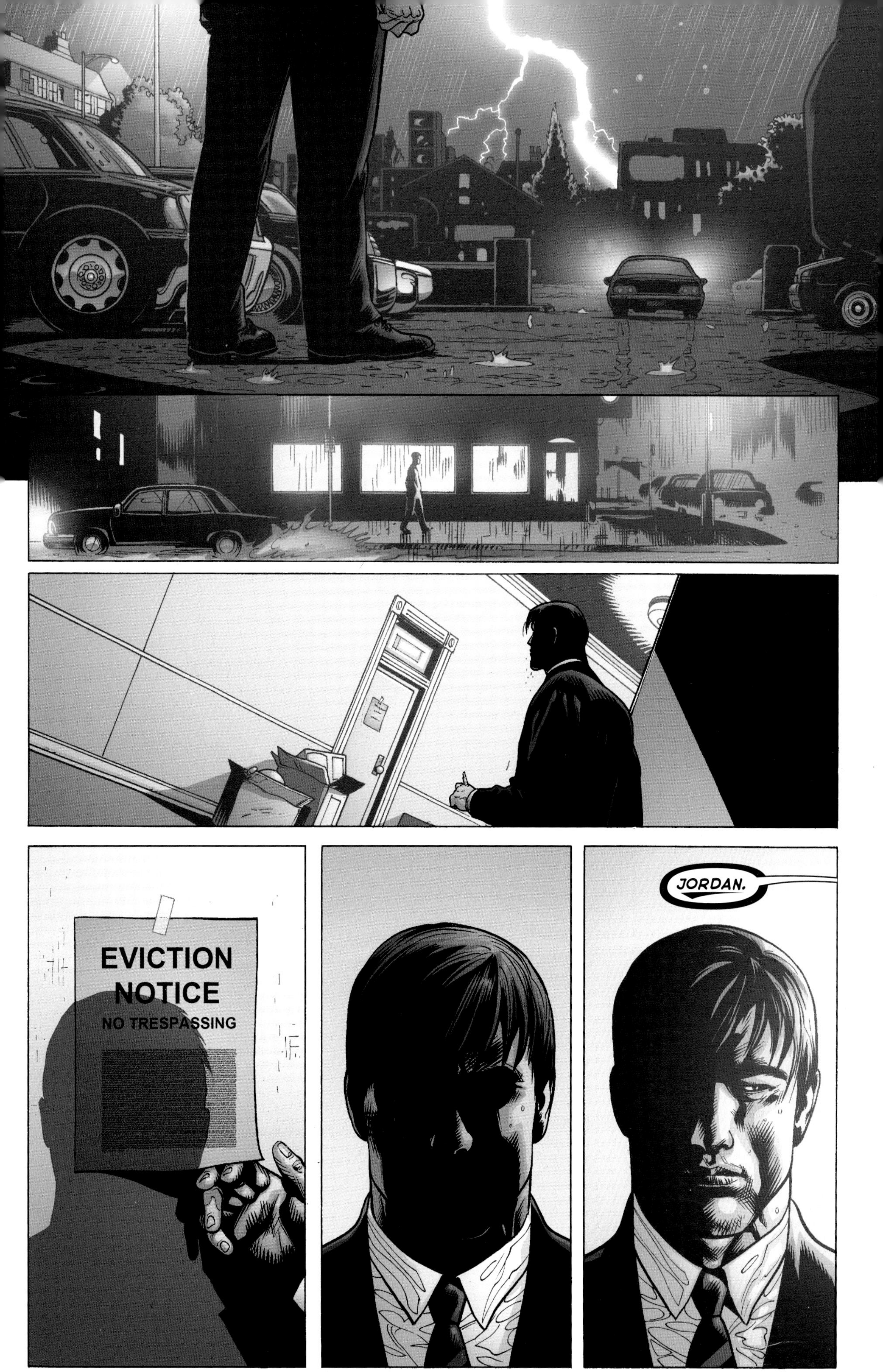
EVICTION NOTICE
NO TRESPASSING
JORDAN.

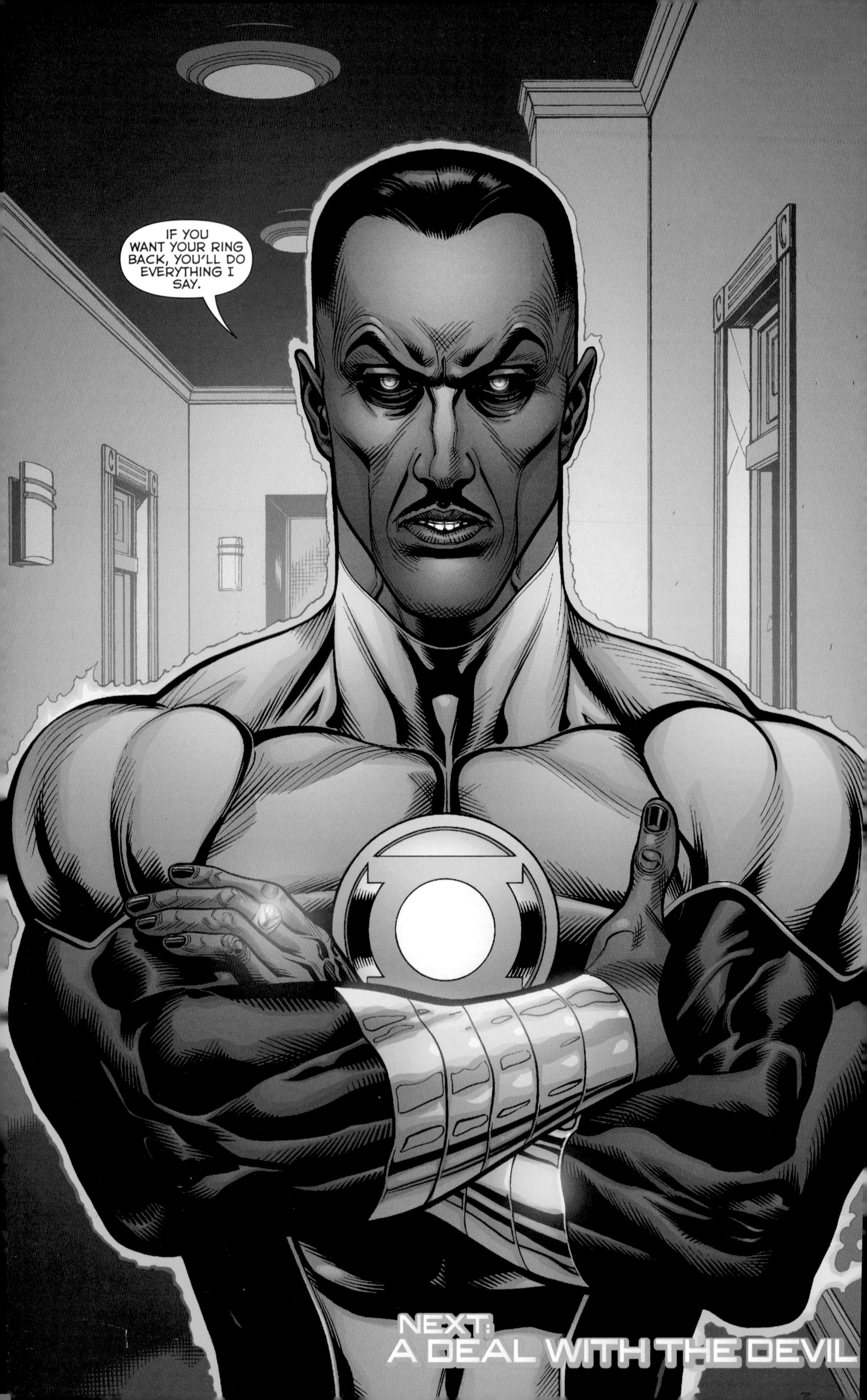
IF YOU WANT YOUR RING BACK, YOU'LL DO EVERYTHING I SAY.
NEXT: A DEAL WITH THE DEVIL

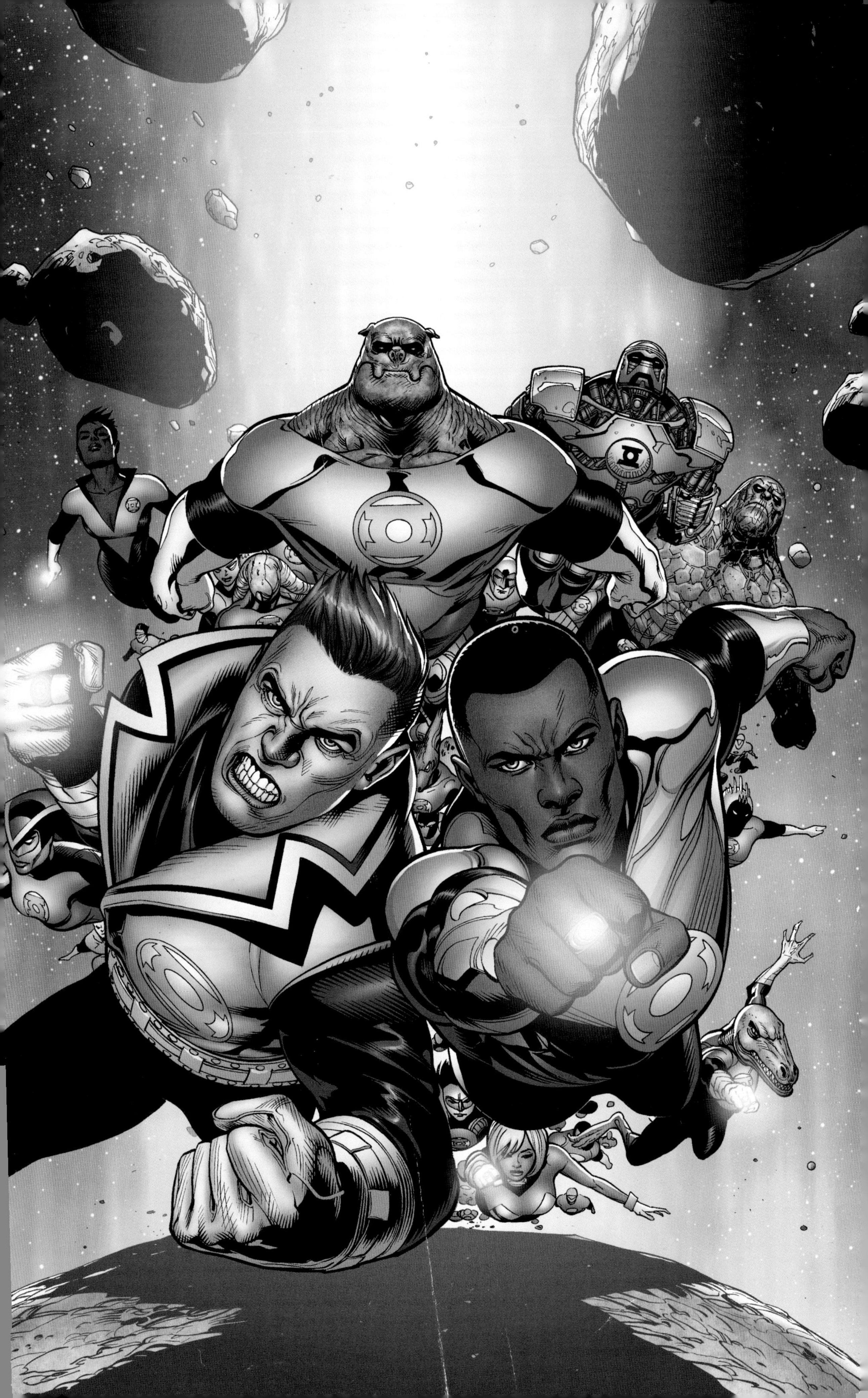

GREEN LANTERN CORPS

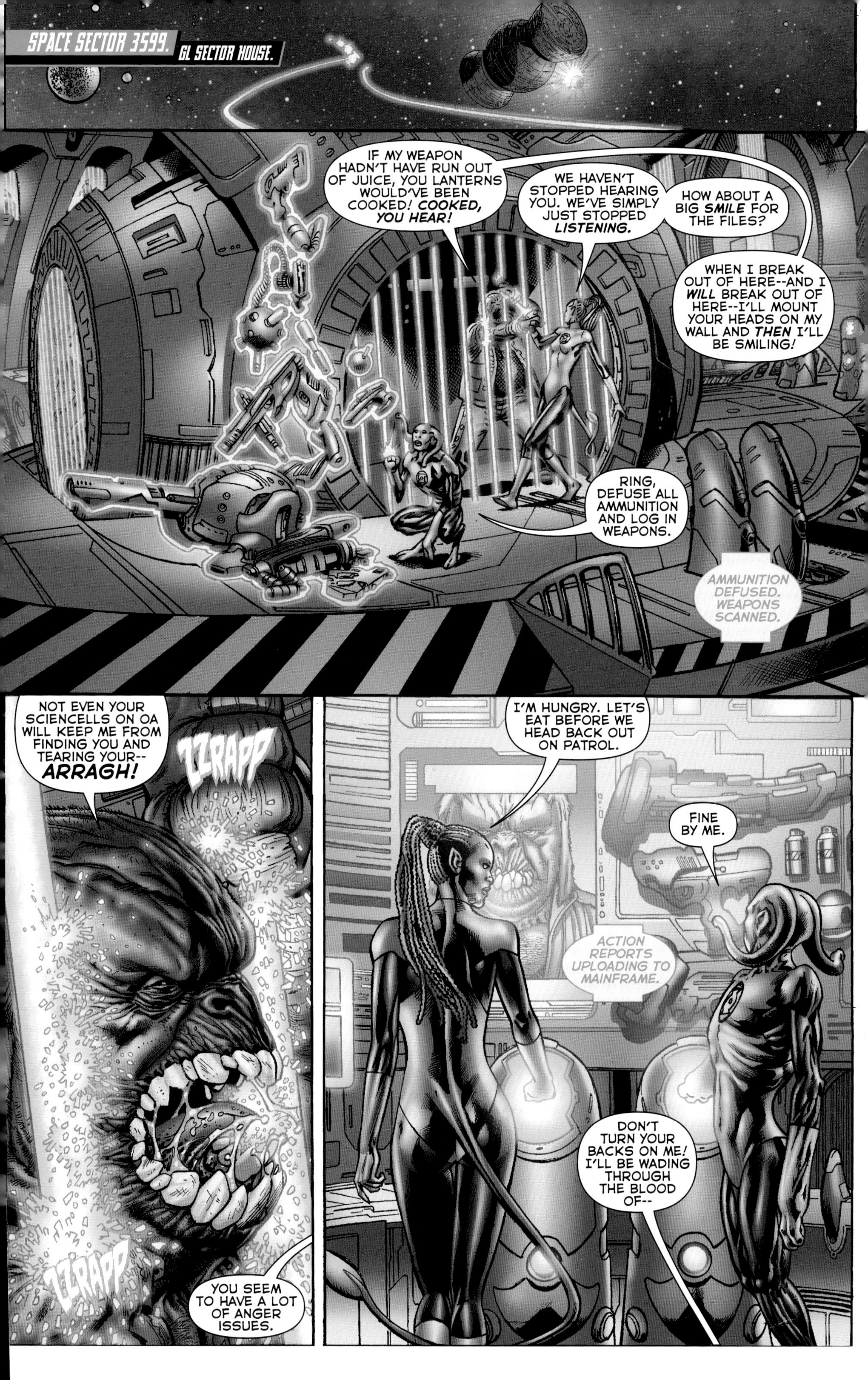
SPACE SECTOR 3599.
GL SECTOR HOUSE.
IF MY WEAPON HADN'T HAVE RUN OUT OF JUICE, YOU LANTERNS WOULD'VE BEEN COOKED! COOKED, YOU HEAR!
WE HAVEN'T STOPPED HEARING YOU. WE'VE SIMPLY JUST STOPPED LISTENING.
HOW ABOUT A BIG SMILE FOR THE FILES?
WHEN I BREAK OUT OF HERE--AND I WILL BREAK OUT OF HERE--I'LL MOUNT YOUR HEADS ON MY WALL AND THEN I'LL BE SMILING!
RING, DEFUSE ALL AMMUNITION AND LOG IN WEAPONS.
AMMUNITION DEFUSED. WEAPONS SCANNED.
NOT EVEN YOUR SCIENCELLS ON OA WILL KEEP ME FROM FINDING YOU AND TEARING YOUR-- ARRAGH!
ZZRAPP
ZZRAPP
YOU SEEM TO HAVE A LOT OF ANGER ISSUES.
I'M HUNGRY. LET'S EAT BEFORE WE HEAD BACK OUT ON PATROL.
FINE BY ME.
ACTION REPORTS UPLOADING TO MAINFRAME.
DON'T TURN YOUR BACKS ON ME! I'LL BE WADING THROUGH THE BLOOD OF--

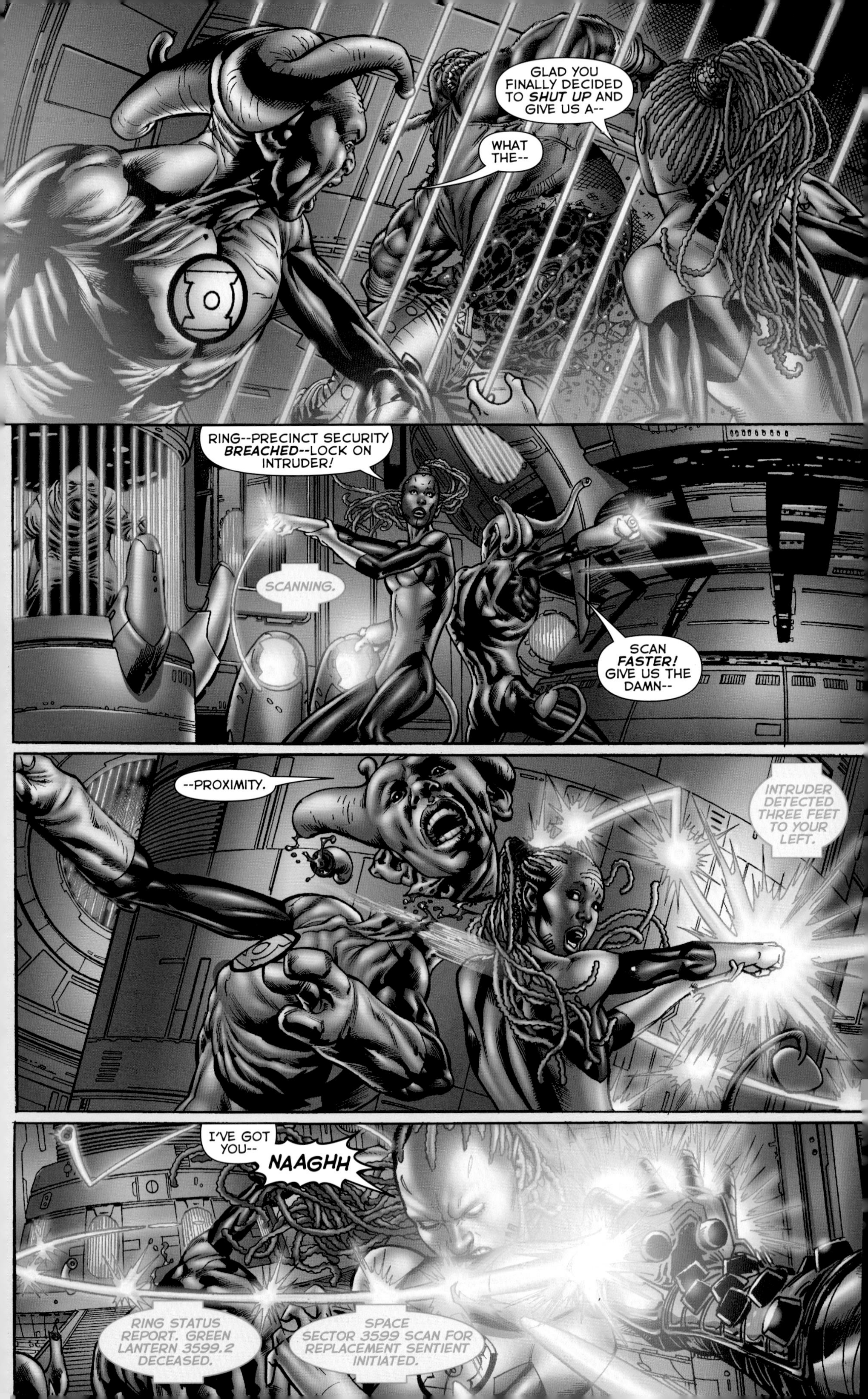
GLAD YOU FINALLY DECIDED TO SHUT UP AND GIVE US A--
WHAT THE--
RING--PRECINCT SECURITY BREACHED--LOCK ON INTRUDER!
SCANNING.
SCAN FASTER! GIVE US THE DAMN--
--PROXIMITY.
INTRUDER DETECTED THREE FEET TO YOUR LEFT.
I'VE GOT YOU--
NAAGHH
RING STATUS REPORT. GREEN LANTERN 3599.2 DECEASED.
SPACE SECTOR 3599 SCAN FOR REPLACEMENT SENTIENT INITIATED.

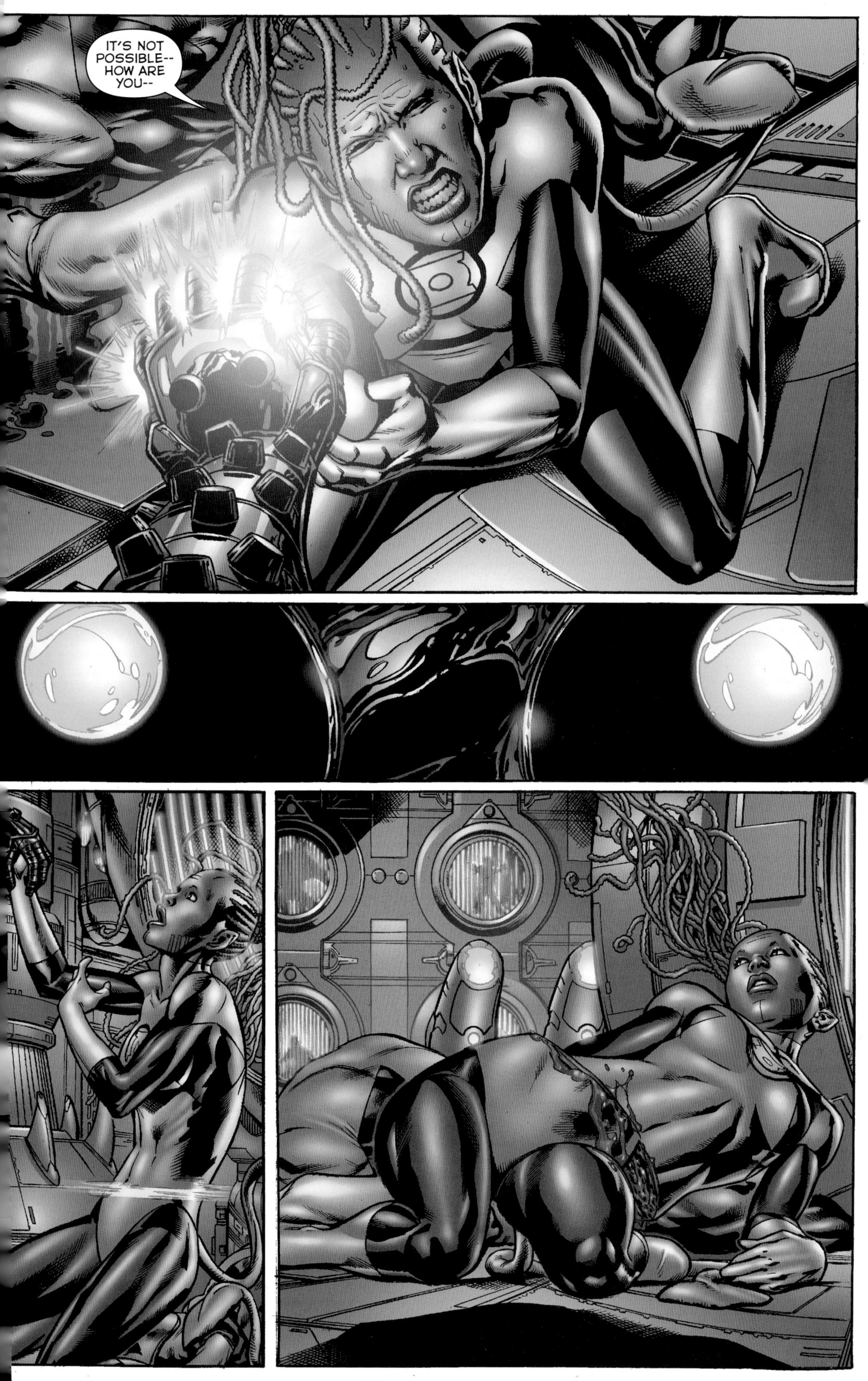
IT'S NOT POSSIBLE-- HOW ARE YOU--

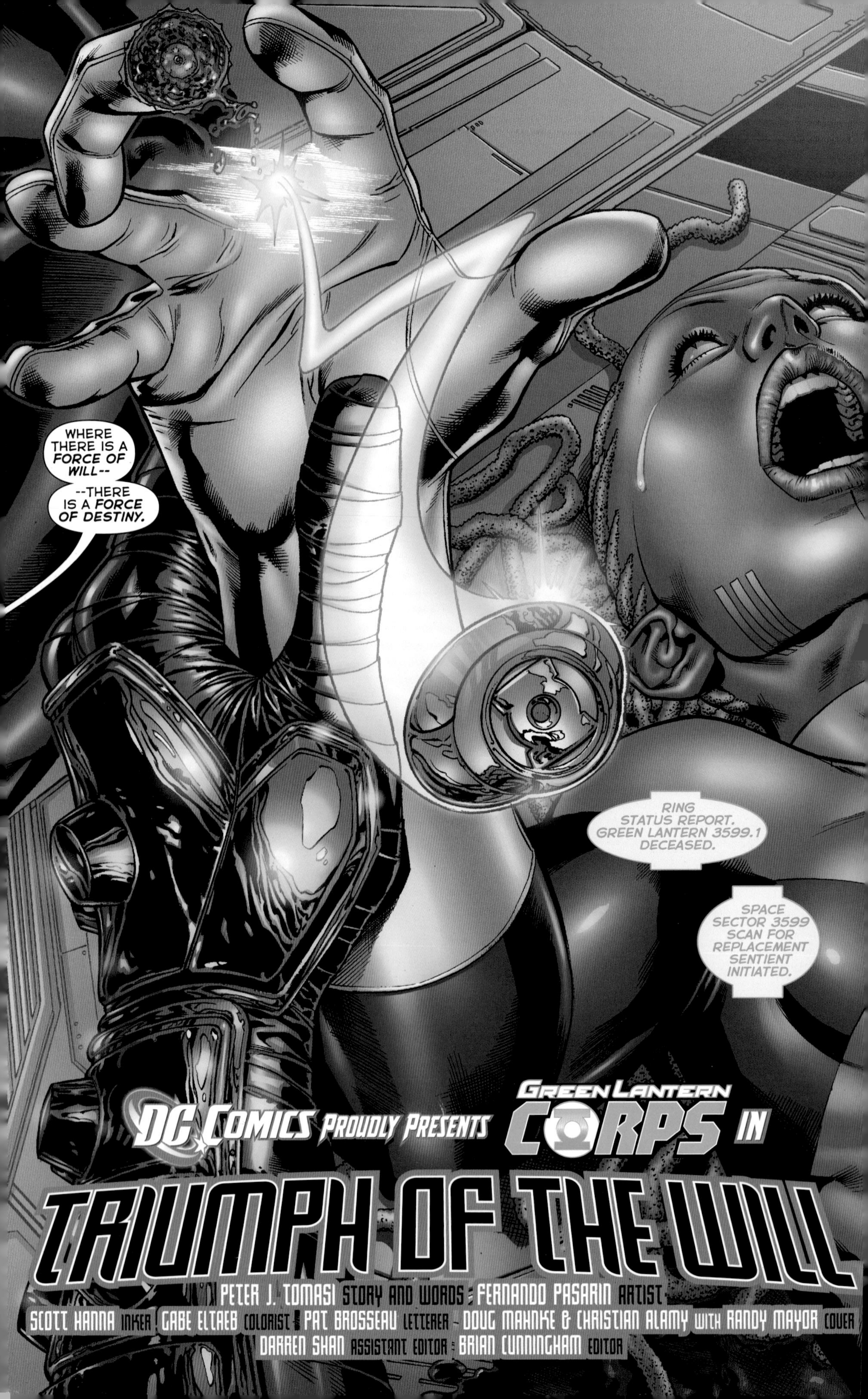
WHERE THERE IS A FORCE OF WILL--
--THERE IS A FORCE OF DESTINY.
RING STATUS REPORT. GREEN LANTERN 3599.1 DECEASED.
SPACE SECTOR 3599 SCAN FOR REPLACEMENT SENTIENT INITIATED.
DC COMICS PROUDLY PRESENTS GREEN LANTERN CORPS IN
TRIUMPH OF THE WILL
PETER J. TOMASI STORY AND WORDS · FERNANDO PASARIN ARTIST
SCOTT HANNA INKER · GABE ELTAEB COLORIST · PAT BROSSEAU LETTERER · DOUG MAHNKE & CHRISTIAN ALAMY WITH RANDY MAYOR COVER
DARREN SHAN ASSISTANT EDITOR · BRIAN CUNNINGHAM EDITOR

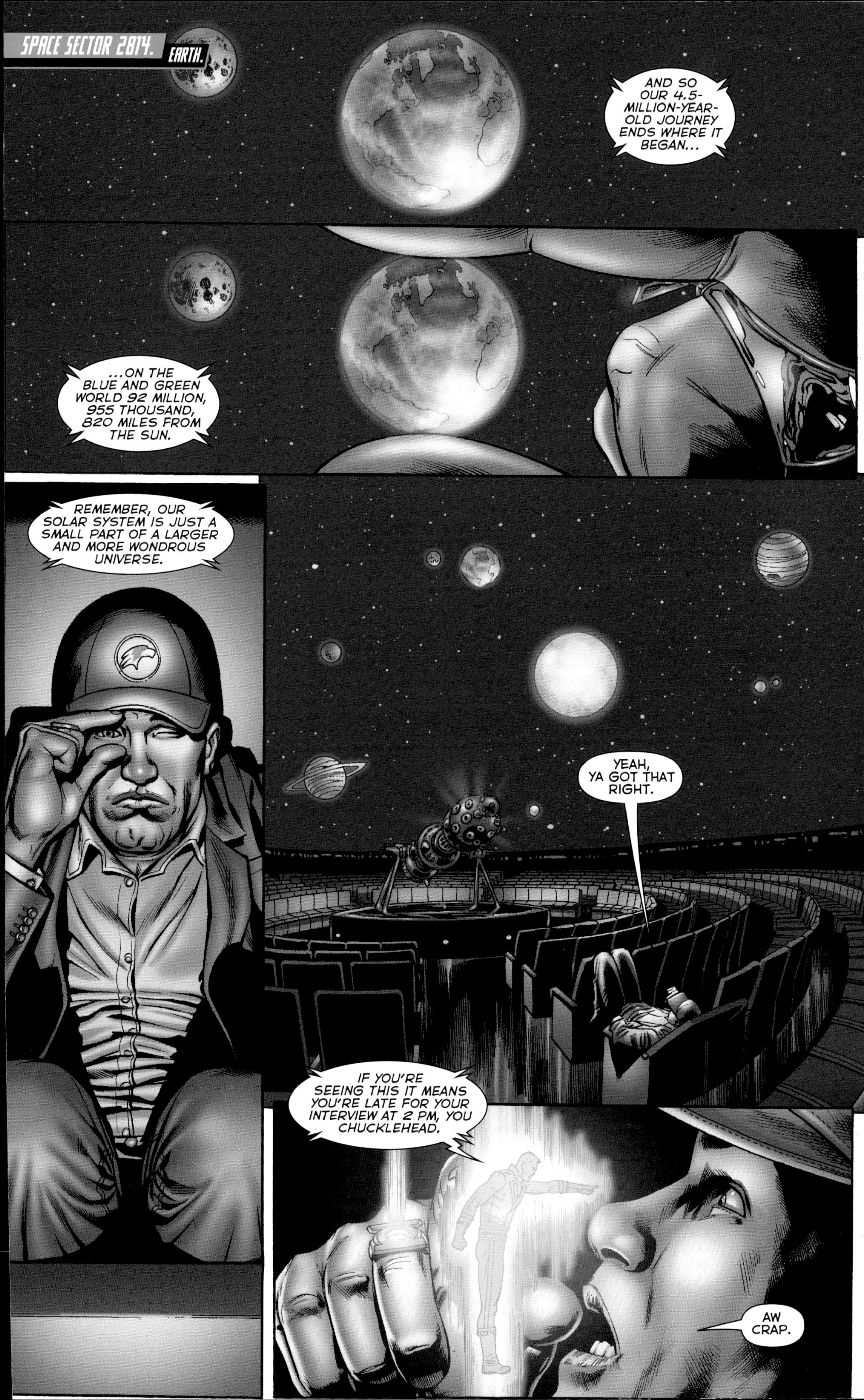
SPACE SECTOR 2814.
EARTH.
AND SO OUR 4.5-MILLION-YEAR-OLD JOURNEY ENDS WHERE IT BEGAN...
...ON THE BLUE AND GREEN WORLD 92 MILLION, 955 THOUSAND, 820 MILES FROM THE SUN.
REMEMBER, OUR SOLAR SYSTEM IS JUST A SMALL PART OF A LARGER AND MORE WONDROUS UNIVERSE.
YEAH, YA GOT THAT RIGHT.
IF YOU'RE SEEING THIS IT MEANS YOU'RE LATE FOR YOUR INTERVIEW AT 2 PM, YOU CHUCKLEHEAD.
AW CRAP.

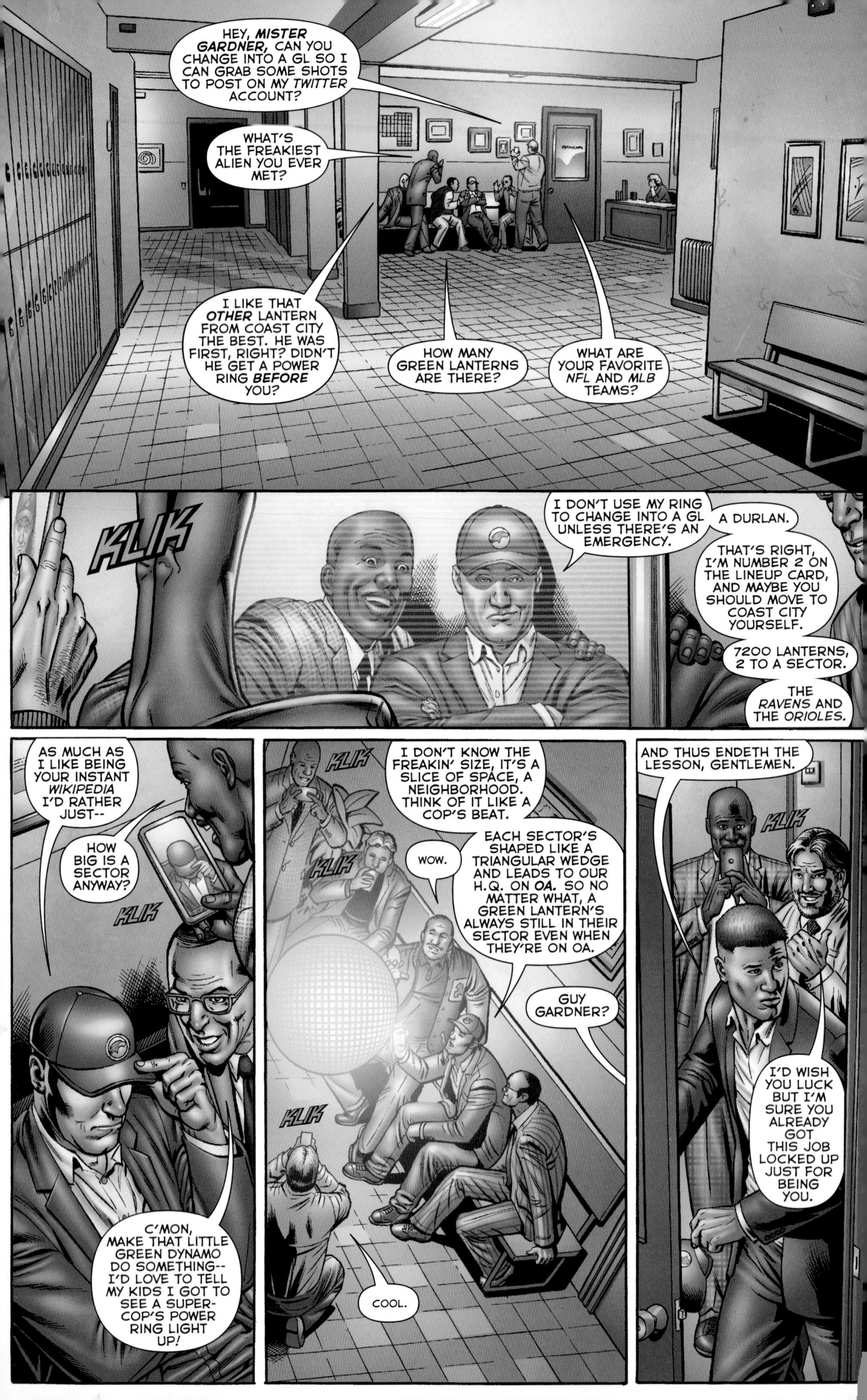
HEY, MISTER GARDNER, CAN YOU CHANGE INTO A GL SO I CAN GRAB SOME SHOTS TO POST ON MY TWITTER ACCOUNT?
WHAT'S THE FREAKIEST ALIEN YOU EVER MET?
I LIKE THAT OTHER LANTERN FROM COAST CITY THE BEST. HE WAS FIRST, RIGHT? DIDN'T HE GET A POWER RING BEFORE YOU?
HOW MANY GREEN LANTERNS ARE THERE?
WHAT ARE YOUR FAVORITE NFL AND MLB TEAMS?
KLIK
I DON'T USE MY RING TO CHANGE INTO A GL UNLESS THERE'S AN EMERGENCY.
A DURLAN.
THAT'S RIGHT, I'M NUMBER 2 ON THE LINEUP CARD, AND MAYBE YOU SHOULD MOVE TO COAST CITY YOURSELF.
7200 LANTERNS, 2 TO A SECTOR.
THE RAVENS AND THE ORIOLES.
AS MUCH AS I LIKE BEING YOUR INSTANT WIKIPEDIA I'D RATHER JUST--
HOW BIG IS A SECTOR ANYWAY?
KLIK
C'MON, MAKE THAT LITTLE GREEN DYNAMO DO SOMETHING-- I'D LOVE TO TELL MY KIDS I GOT TO SEE A SUPER-COP'S POWER RING LIGHT UP!
KLIK
I DON'T KNOW THE FREAKIN' SIZE, IT'S A SLICE OF SPACE, A NEIGHBORHOOD. THINK OF IT LIKE A COP'S BEAT.
KLIK
WOW.
EACH SECTOR'S SHAPED LIKE A TRIANGULAR WEDGE AND LEADS TO OUR H.Q. ON OA. SO NO MATTER WHAT, A GREEN LANTERN'S ALWAYS STILL IN THEIR SECTOR EVEN WHEN THEY'RE ON OA.
GUY GARDNER?
KLIK
COOL.
AND THUS ENDETH THE LESSON, GENTLEMEN.
KLIK
I'D WISH YOU LUCK BUT I'M SURE YOU ALREADY GOT THIS JOB LOCKED UP JUST FOR BEING YOU.

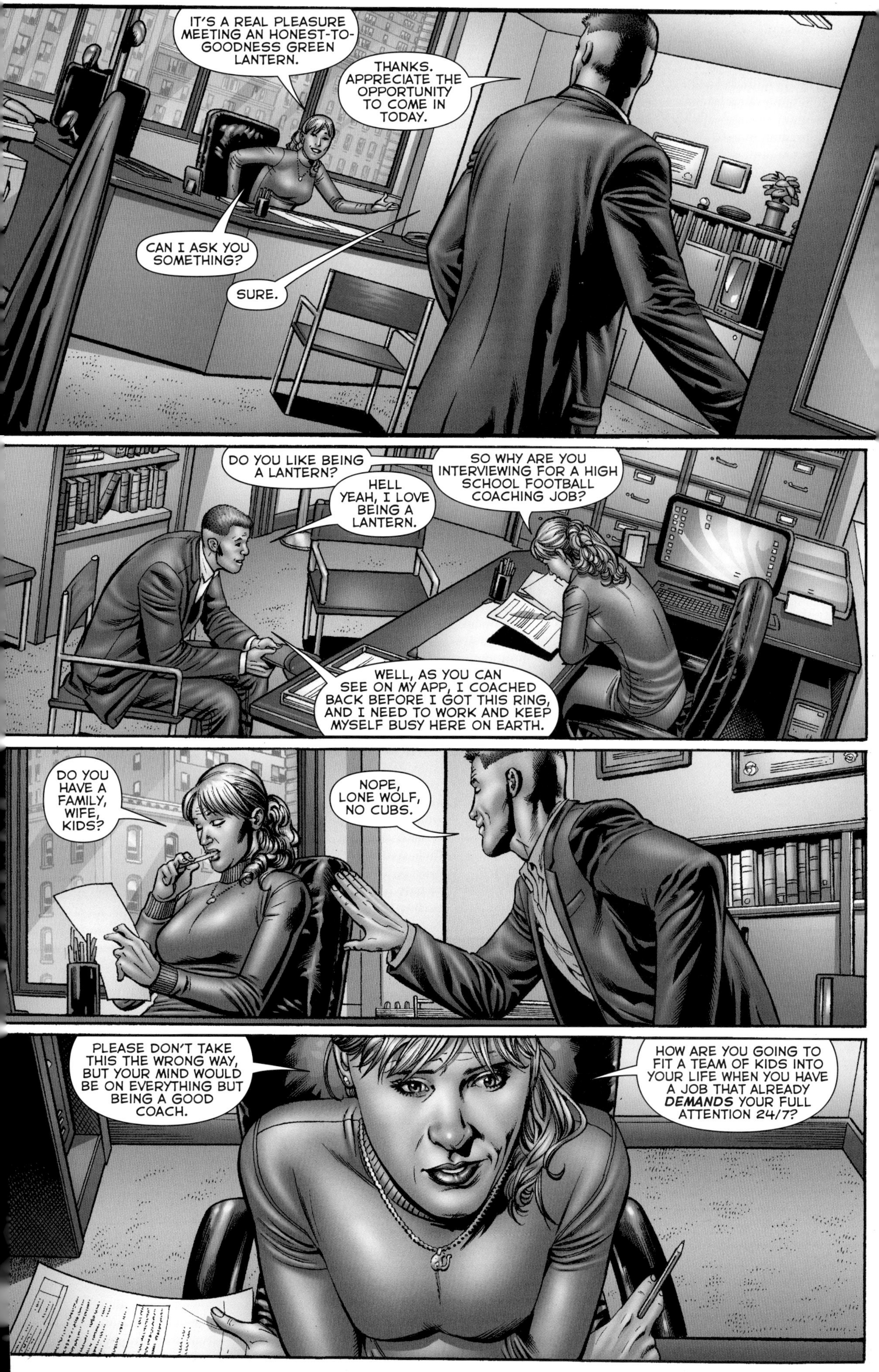
IT'S A REAL PLEASURE MEETING AN HONEST-TO-GOODNESS GREEN LANTERN.
THANKS. APPRECIATE THE OPPORTUNITY TO COME IN TODAY.
CAN I ASK YOU SOMETHING?
SURE.
DO YOU LIKE BEING A LANTERN?
HELL YEAH, I LOVE BEING A LANTERN.
SO WHY ARE YOU INTERVIEWING FOR A HIGH SCHOOL FOOTBALL COACHING JOB?
WELL, AS YOU CAN SEE ON MY APP, I COACHED BACK BEFORE I GOT THIS RING, AND I NEED TO WORK AND KEEP MYSELF BUSY HERE ON EARTH.
DO YOU HAVE A FAMILY, WIFE, KIDS?
NOPE, LONE WOLF, NO CUBS.
PLEASE DON'T TAKE THIS THE WRONG WAY, BUT YOUR MIND WOULD BE ON EVERYTHING BUT BEING A GOOD COACH.
HOW ARE YOU GOING TO FIT A TEAM OF KIDS INTO YOUR LIFE WHEN YOU HAVE A JOB THAT ALREADY *DEMANDS* YOUR FULL ATTENTION 24/7?

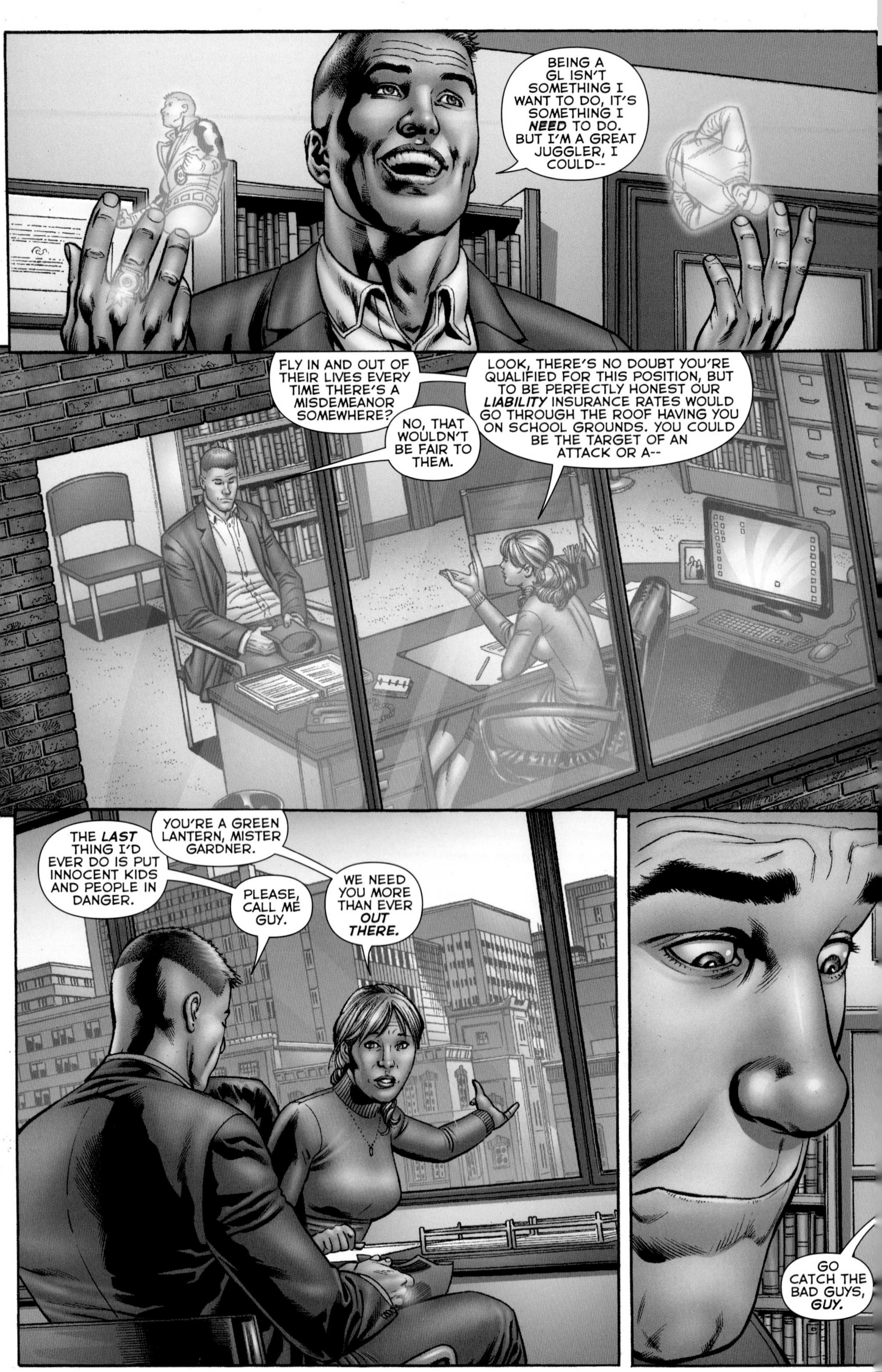
BEING A GL ISN'T SOMETHING I WANT TO DO, IT'S SOMETHING I NEED TO DO. BUT I'M A GREAT JUGGLER, I COULD--
FLY IN AND OUT OF THEIR LIVES EVERY TIME THERE'S A MISDEMEANOR SOMEWHERE?
LOOK, THERE'S NO DOUBT YOU'RE QUALIFIED FOR THIS POSITION, BUT TO BE PERFECTLY HONEST OUR LIABILITY INSURANCE RATES WOULD GO THROUGH THE ROOF HAVING YOU ON SCHOOL GROUNDS. YOU COULD BE THE TARGET OF AN ATTACK OR A--
NO, THAT WOULDN'T BE FAIR TO THEM.
THE LAST THING I'D EVER DO IS PUT INNOCENT KIDS AND PEOPLE IN DANGER.
YOU'RE A GREEN LANTERN, MISTER GARDNER.
PLEASE, CALL ME GUY.
WE NEED YOU MORE THAN EVER OUT THERE.
GO CATCH THE BAD GUYS, GUY.

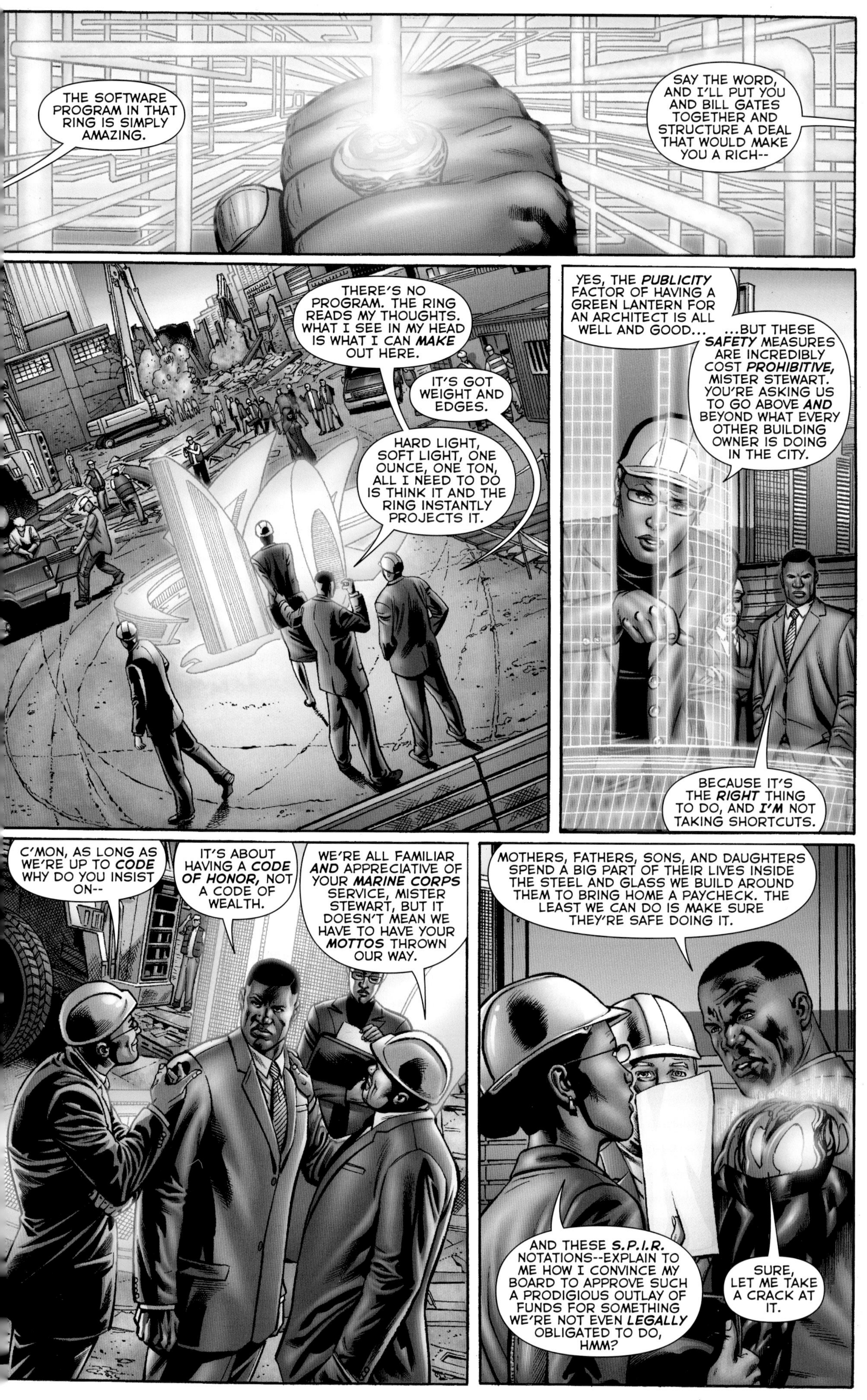
THE SOFTWARE PROGRAM IN THAT RING IS SIMPLY AMAZING.
SAY THE WORD, AND I'LL PUT YOU AND BILL GATES TOGETHER AND STRUCTURE A DEAL THAT WOULD MAKE YOU A RICH--
THERE'S NO PROGRAM. THE RING READS MY THOUGHTS. WHAT I SEE IN MY HEAD IS WHAT I CAN MAKE OUT HERE.
IT'S GOT WEIGHT AND EDGES.
HARD LIGHT, SOFT LIGHT, ONE OUNCE, ONE TON, ALL I NEED TO DO IS THINK IT AND THE RING INSTANTLY PROJECTS IT.
YES, THE PUBLICITY FACTOR OF HAVING A GREEN LANTERN FOR AN ARCHITECT IS ALL WELL AND GOOD...
...BUT THESE SAFETY MEASURES ARE INCREDIBLY COST PROHIBITIVE, MISTER STEWART. YOU'RE ASKING US TO GO ABOVE AND BEYOND WHAT EVERY OTHER BUILDING OWNER IS DOING IN THE CITY.
BECAUSE IT'S THE RIGHT THING TO DO, AND I'M NOT TAKING SHORTCUTS.
C'MON, AS LONG AS WE'RE UP TO CODE WHY DO YOU INSIST ON--
IT'S ABOUT HAVING A CODE OF HONOR, NOT A CODE OF WEALTH.
WE'RE ALL FAMILIAR AND APPRECIATIVE OF YOUR MARINE CORPS SERVICE, MISTER STEWART, BUT IT DOESN'T MEAN WE HAVE TO HAVE YOUR MOTTOS THROWN OUR WAY.
MOTHERS, FATHERS, SONS, AND DAUGHTERS SPEND A BIG PART OF THEIR LIVES INSIDE THE STEEL AND GLASS WE BUILD AROUND THEM TO BRING HOME A PAYCHECK. THE LEAST WE CAN DO IS MAKE SURE THEY'RE SAFE DOING IT.
AND THESE S.P.I.R. NOTATIONS--EXPLAIN TO ME HOW I CONVINCE MY BOARD TO APPROVE SUCH A PRODIGIOUS OUTLAY OF FUNDS FOR SOMETHING WE'RE NOT EVEN LEGALLY OBLIGATED TO DO, HMM?
SURE, LET ME TAKE A CRACK AT IT.

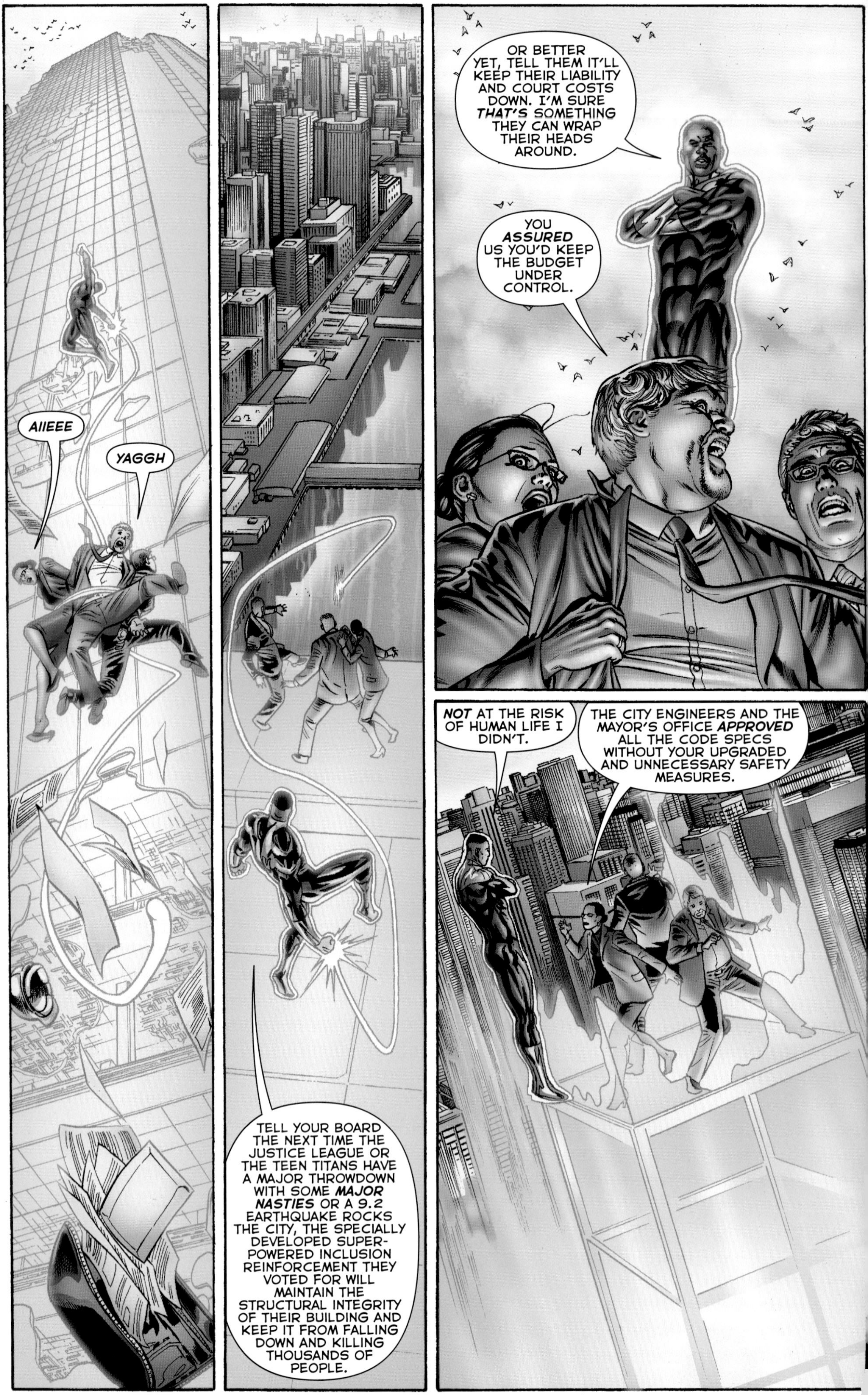

AIIEEE
YAGGH
TELL YOUR BOARD THE NEXT TIME THE JUSTICE LEAGUE OR THE TEEN TITANS HAVE A MAJOR THROWDOWN WITH SOME *MAJOR NASTIES* OR A 9.2 EARTHQUAKE ROCKS THE CITY, THE SPECIALLY DEVELOPED SUPER-POWERED INCLUSION REINFORCEMENT THEY VOTED FOR WILL MAINTAIN THE STRUCTURAL INTEGRITY OF THEIR BUILDING AND KEEP IT FROM FALLING DOWN AND KILLING THOUSANDS OF PEOPLE.
OR BETTER YET, TELL THEM IT'LL KEEP THEIR LIABILITY AND COURT COSTS DOWN. I'M SURE *THAT'S* SOMETHING THEY CAN WRAP THEIR HEADS AROUND.
YOU *ASSURED* US YOU'D KEEP THE BUDGET UNDER CONTROL.
NOT AT THE RISK OF HUMAN LIFE I DIDN'T.
THE CITY ENGINEERS AND THE MAYOR'S OFFICE *APPROVED* ALL THE CODE SPECS WITHOUT YOUR UPGRADED AND UNNECESSARY SAFETY MEASURES.

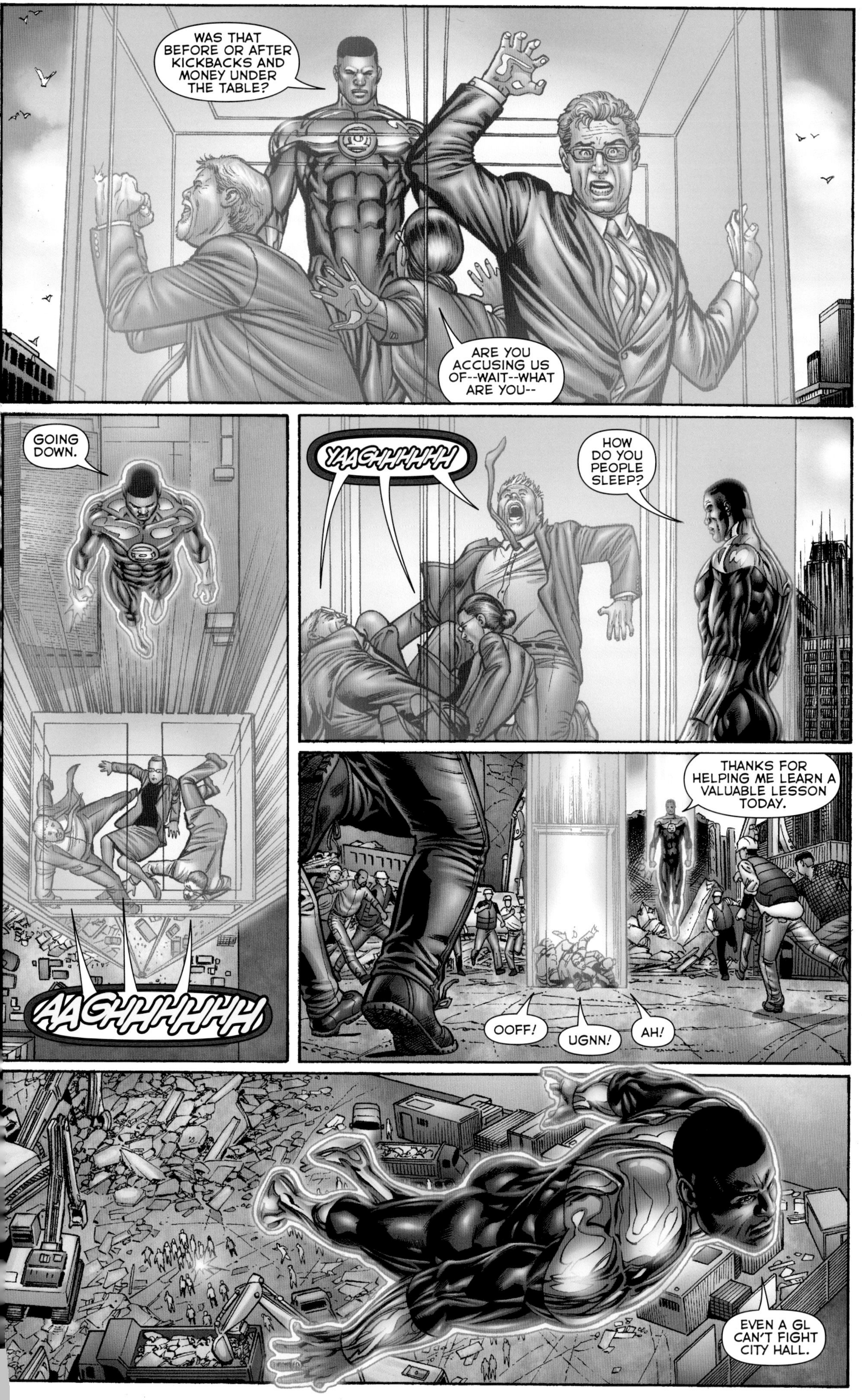
WAS THAT BEFORE OR AFTER KICKBACKS AND MONEY UNDER THE TABLE?
ARE YOU ACCUSING US OF--WAIT--WHAT ARE YOU--
GOING DOWN.
AAGHHHHHH
YAAGHHHHH
HOW DO YOU PEOPLE SLEEP?
THANKS FOR HELPING ME LEARN A VALUABLE LESSON TODAY.
OOFF!
UGNN!
AH!
EVEN A GL CAN'T FIGHT CITY HALL.

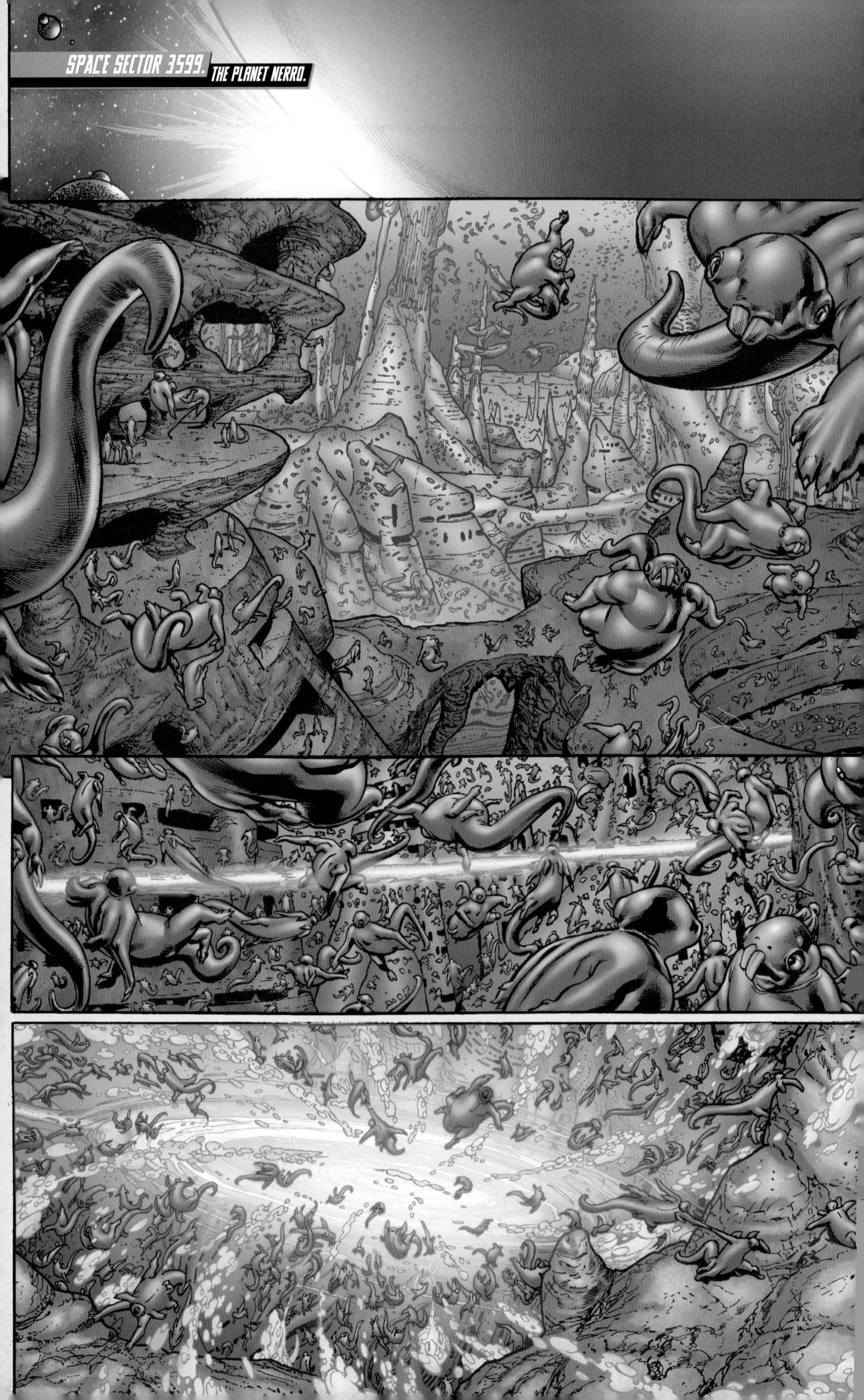
SPACE SECTOR 3599.
THE PLANET NERRO.

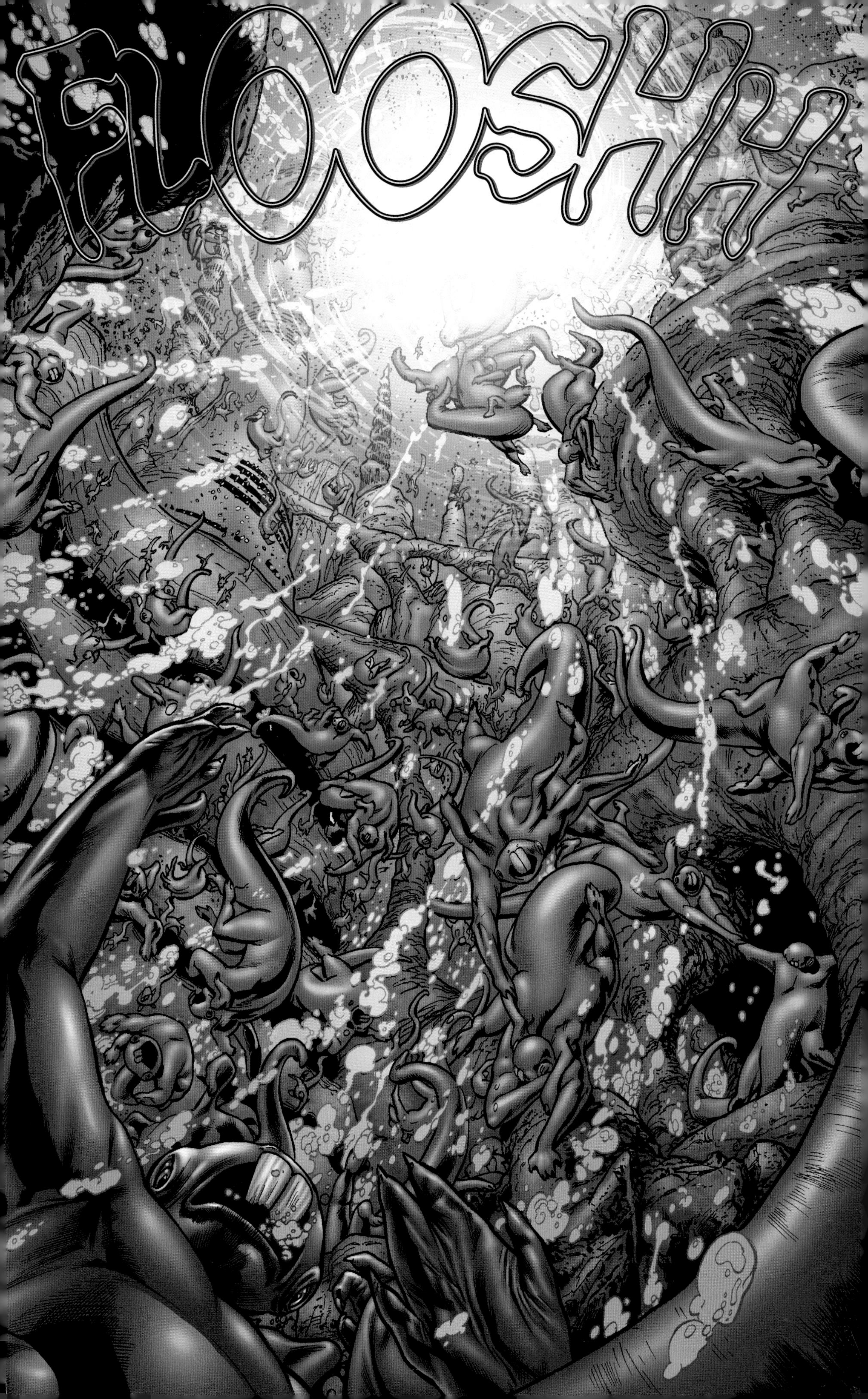
FLOOSHHH

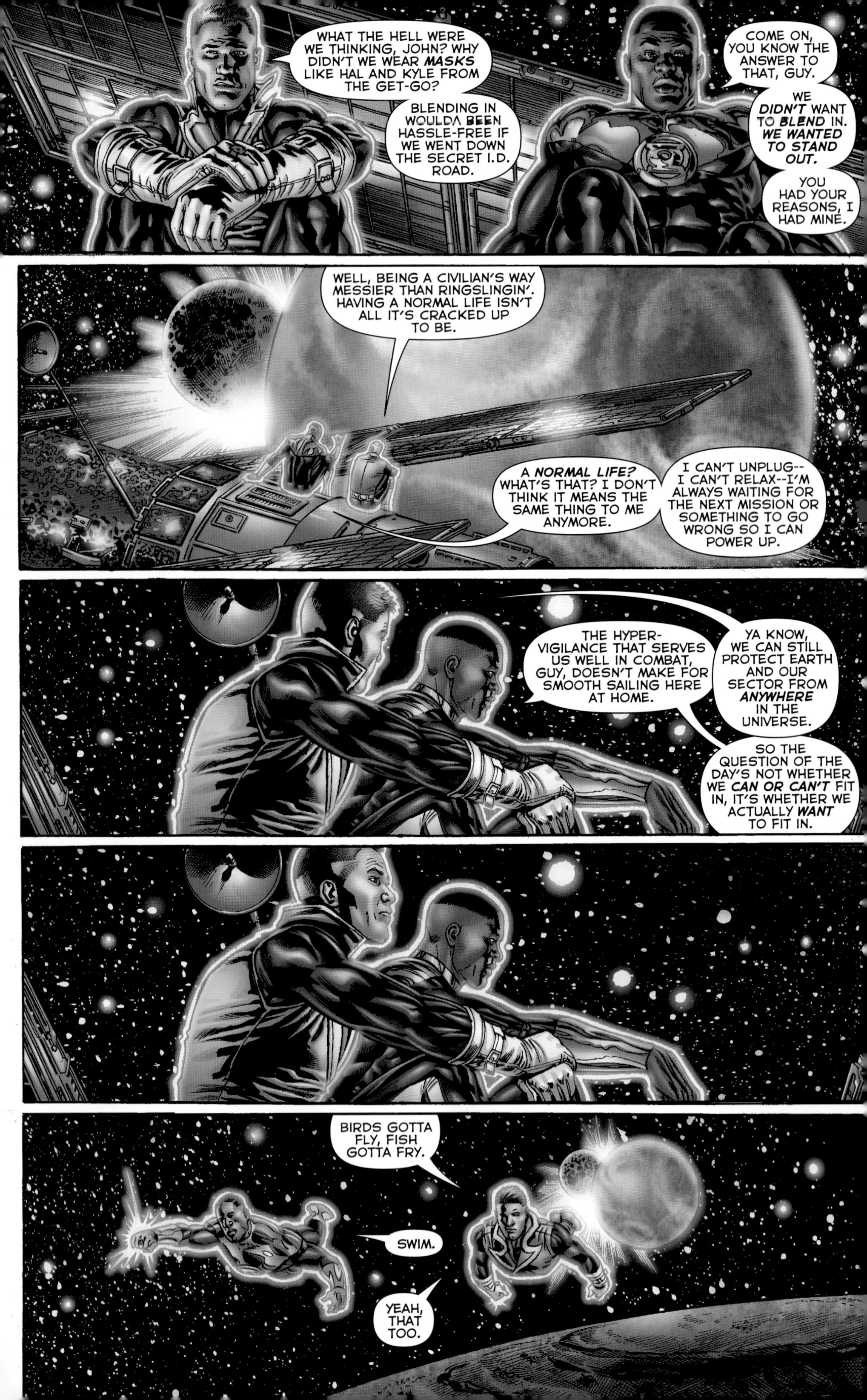
WHAT THE HELL WERE WE THINKING, JOHN? WHY DIDN'T WE WEAR *MASKS* LIKE HAL AND KYLE FROM THE GET-GO?
BLENDING IN WOULDA BEEN HASSLE-FREE IF WE WENT DOWN THE SECRET I.D. ROAD.
COME ON, YOU KNOW THE ANSWER TO THAT, GUY.
WE *DIDN'T* WANT TO *BLEND* IN. *WE WANTED TO STAND OUT.*
YOU HAD YOUR REASONS, I HAD MINE.
WELL, BEING A CIVILIAN'S WAY MESSIER THAN RINGSLINGIN'. HAVING A NORMAL LIFE ISN'T ALL IT'S CRACKED UP TO BE.
A *NORMAL LIFE?* WHAT'S THAT? I DON'T THINK IT MEANS THE SAME THING TO ME ANYMORE.
I CAN'T UNPLUG-- I CAN'T RELAX--I'M ALWAYS WAITING FOR THE NEXT MISSION OR SOMETHING TO GO WRONG SO I CAN POWER UP.
THE HYPER-VIGILANCE THAT SERVES US WELL IN COMBAT, GUY, DOESN'T MAKE FOR SMOOTH SAILING HERE AT HOME.
YA KNOW, WE CAN STILL PROTECT EARTH AND OUR SECTOR FROM *ANYWHERE* IN THE UNIVERSE.
SO THE QUESTION OF THE DAY'S NOT WHETHER WE *CAN OR CAN'T* FIT IN, IT'S WHETHER WE ACTUALLY *WANT* TO FIT IN.
BIRDS GOTTA FLY, FISH GOTTA FRY.
SWIM.
YEAH, THAT TOO.

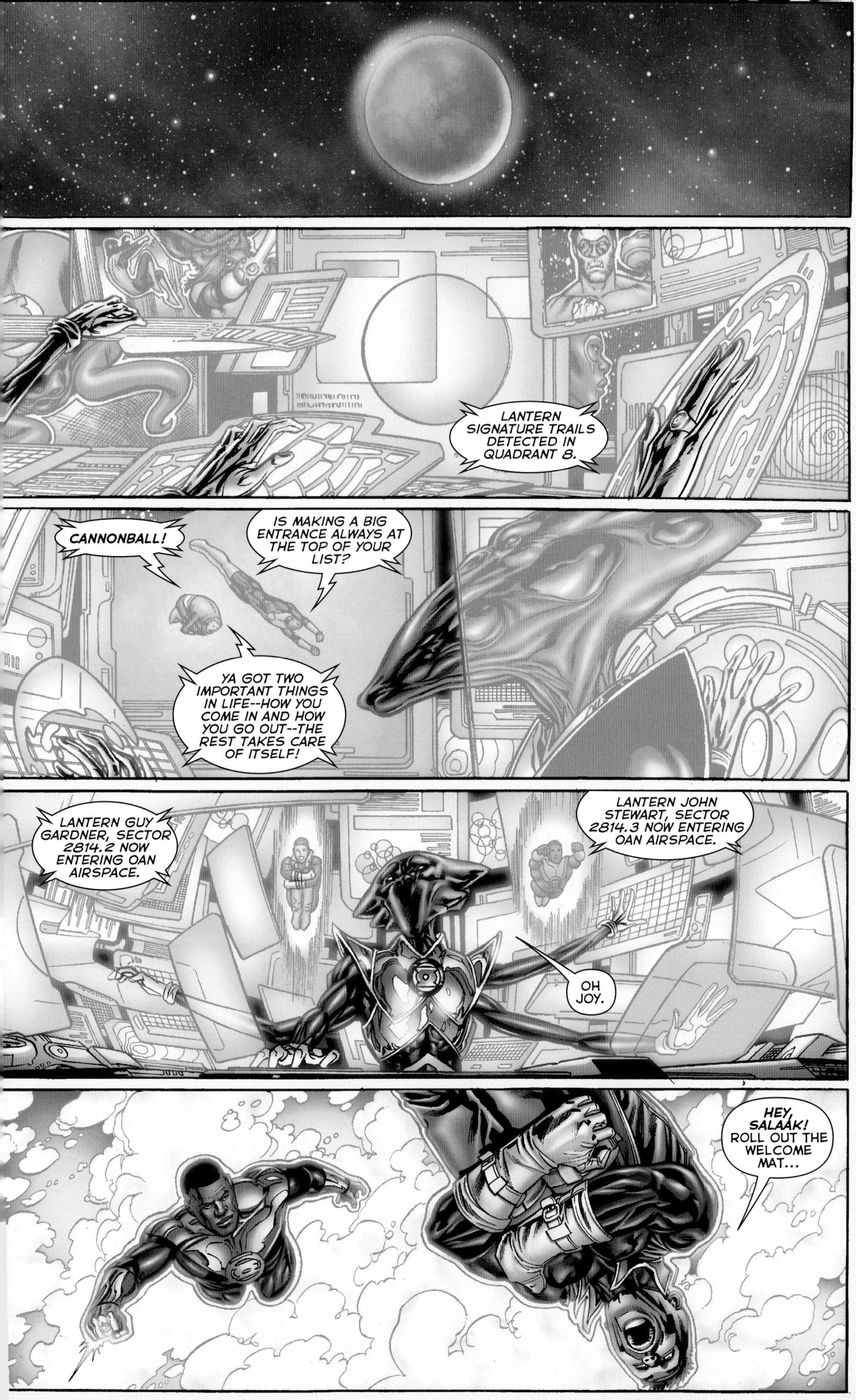
LANTERN SIGNATURE TRAILS DETECTED IN QUADRANT 8.
CANNONBALL!
IS MAKING A BIG ENTRANCE ALWAYS AT THE TOP OF YOUR LIST?
YA GOT TWO IMPORTANT THINGS IN LIFE--HOW YOU COME IN AND HOW YOU GO OUT--THE REST TAKES CARE OF ITSELF!
LANTERN GUY GARDNER, SECTOR 2814.2 NOW ENTERING OAN AIRSPACE.
LANTERN JOHN STEWART, SECTOR 2814.3 NOW ENTERING OAN AIRSPACE.
OH JOY.
HEY, SALAAK! ROLL OUT THE WELCOME MAT...

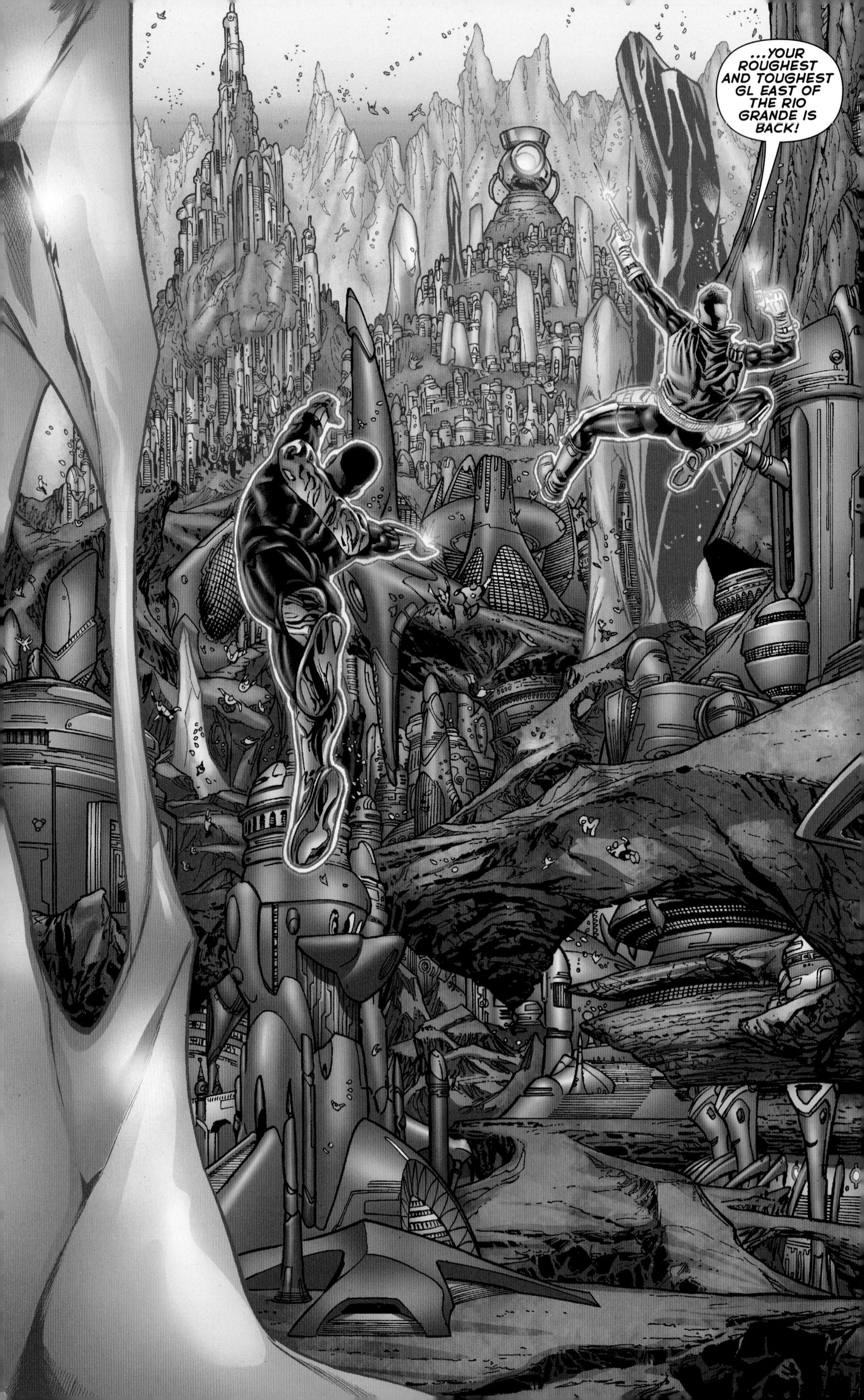
...YOUR ROUGHEST AND TOUGHEST GL EAST OF THE RIO GRANDE IS BACK!

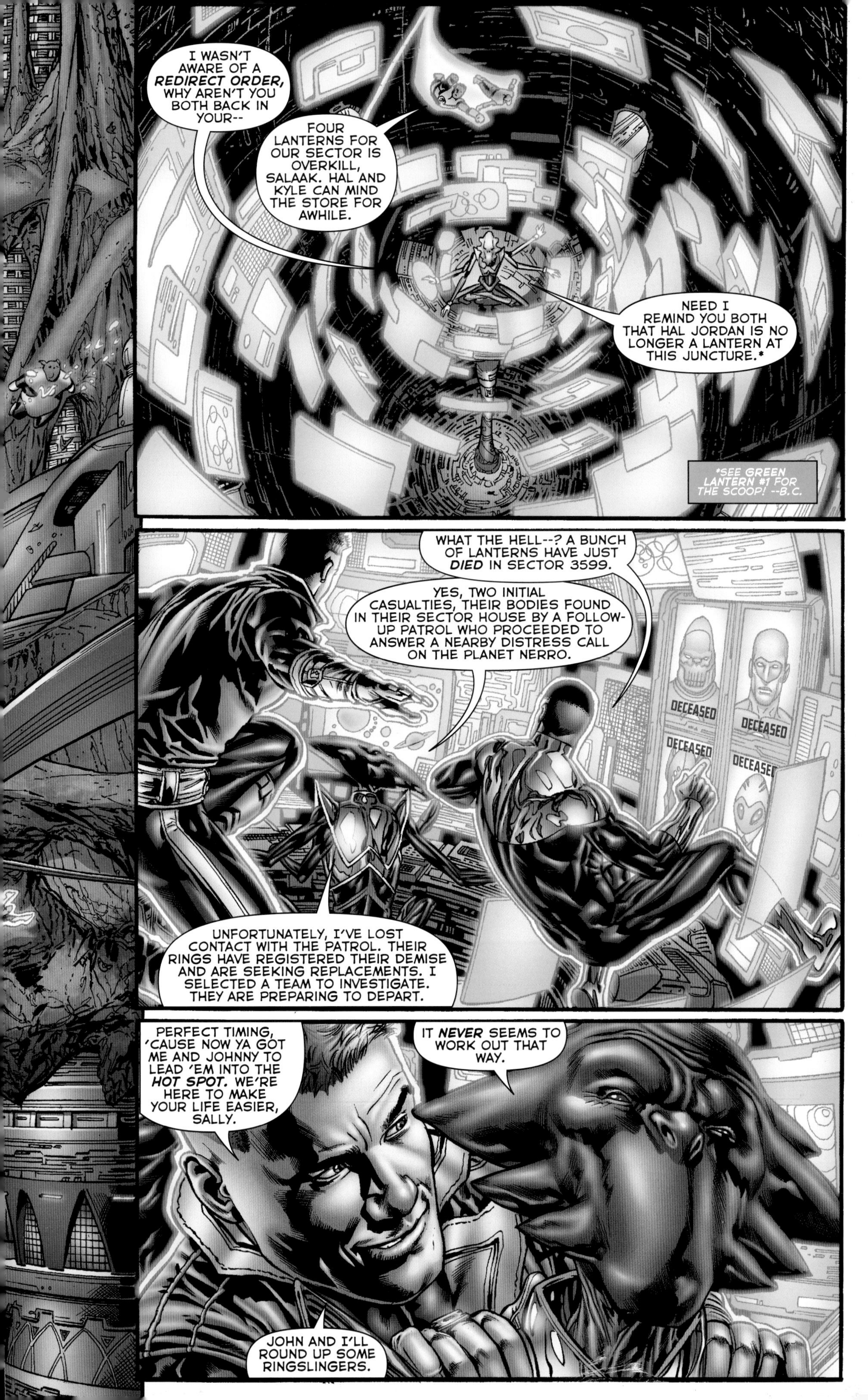
I WASN'T AWARE OF A REDIRECT ORDER, WHY AREN'T YOU BOTH BACK IN YOUR--
FOUR LANTERNS FOR OUR SECTOR IS OVERKILL, SALAAK. HAL AND KYLE CAN MIND THE STORE FOR AWHILE.
NEED I REMIND YOU BOTH THAT HAL JORDAN IS NO LONGER A LANTERN AT THIS JUNCTURE.*
*SEE GREEN LANTERN #1 FOR THE SCOOP! --B.C.
WHAT THE HELL--? A BUNCH OF LANTERNS HAVE JUST DIED IN SECTOR 3599.
YES, TWO INITIAL CASUALTIES, THEIR BODIES FOUND IN THEIR SECTOR HOUSE BY A FOLLOW-UP PATROL WHO PROCEEDED TO ANSWER A NEARBY DISTRESS CALL ON THE PLANET NERRO.
DECEASED
DECEASED
DECEASED
DECEASED
UNFORTUNATELY, I'VE LOST CONTACT WITH THE PATROL. THEIR RINGS HAVE REGISTERED THEIR DEMISE AND ARE SEEKING REPLACEMENTS. I SELECTED A TEAM TO INVESTIGATE. THEY ARE PREPARING TO DEPART.
PERFECT TIMING, 'CAUSE NOW YA GOT ME AND JOHNNY TO LEAD 'EM INTO THE HOT SPOT. WE'RE HERE TO MAKE YOUR LIFE EASIER, SALLY.
IT NEVER SEEMS TO WORK OUT THAT WAY.
JOHN AND I'LL ROUND UP SOME RINGSLINGERS.

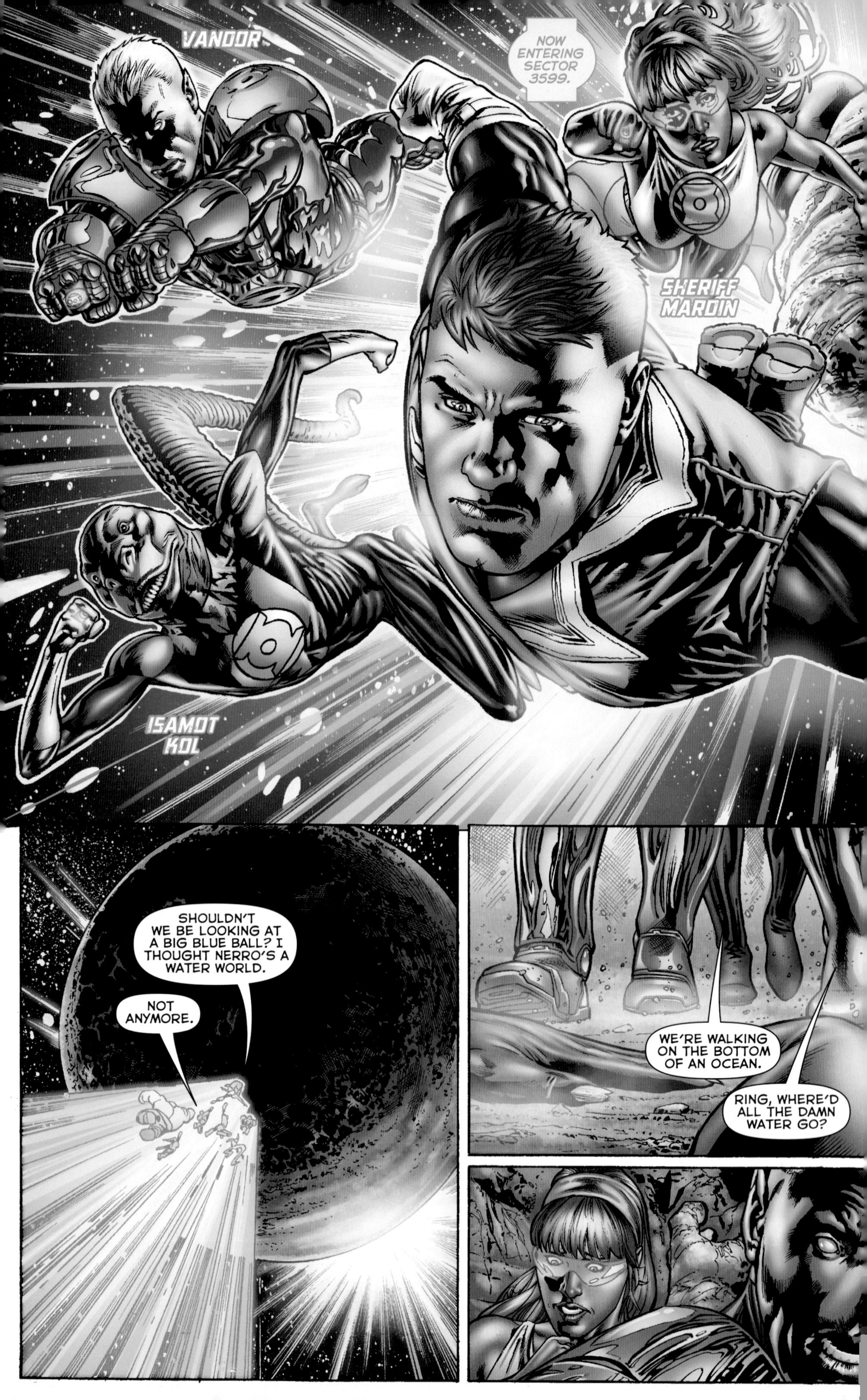
VANDOR
NOW ENTERING SECTOR 3599.
SHERIFF MARDIN
ISAMOT KOL
SHOULDN'T WE BE LOOKING AT A BIG BLUE BALL? I THOUGHT NERRO'S A WATER WORLD.
NOT ANYMORE.
WE'RE WALKING ON THE BOTTOM OF AN OCEAN.
RING, WHERE'D ALL THE DAMN WATER GO?

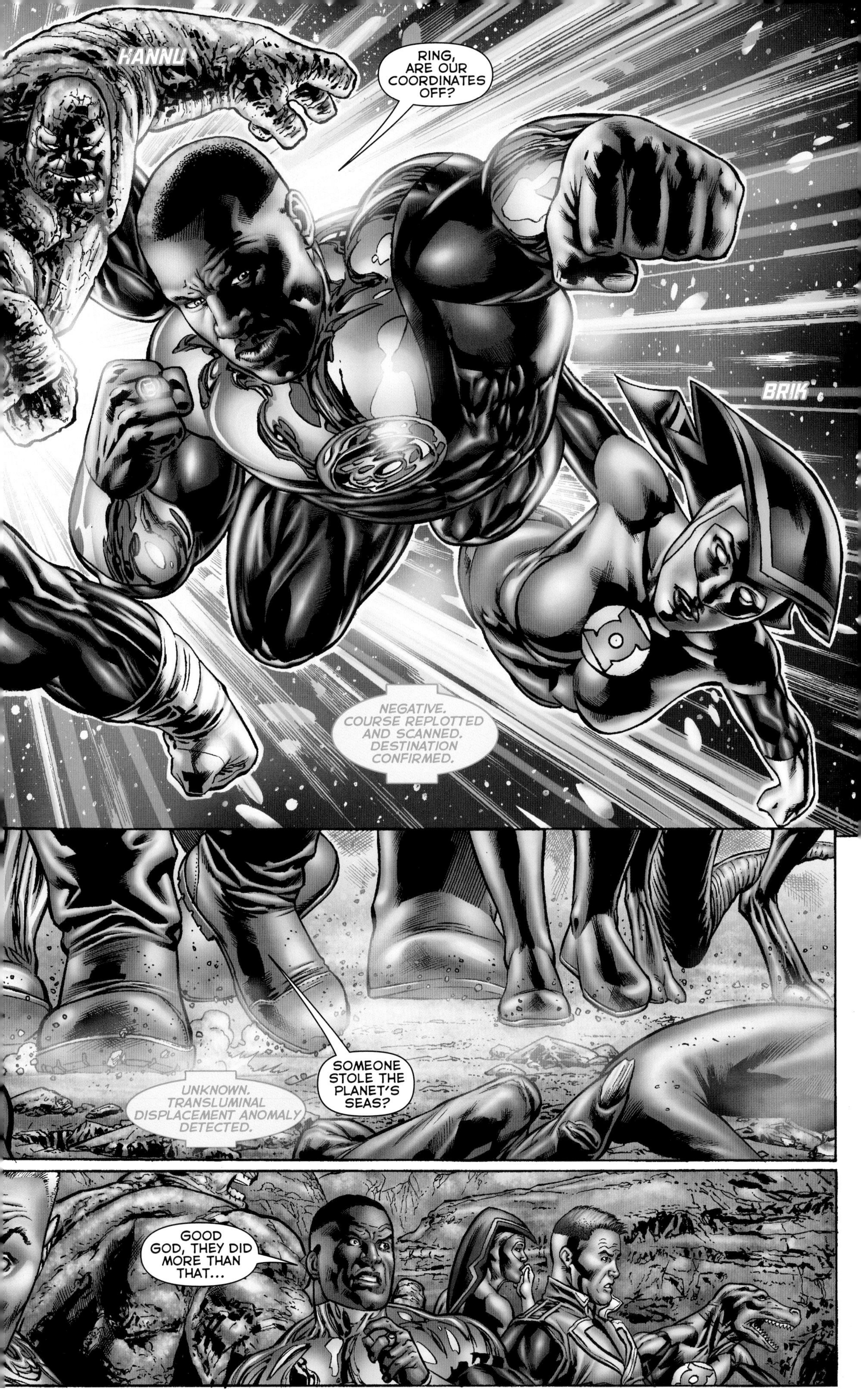
HANNU
RING, ARE OUR COORDINATES OFF?
BRIK
NEGATIVE. COURSE REPLOTTED AND SCANNED. DESTINATION CONFIRMED.
SOMEONE STOLE THE PLANET'S SEAS?
UNKNOWN. TRANSLUMINAL DISPLACEMENT ANOMALY DETECTED.
GOOD GOD, THEY DID MORE THAN THAT...

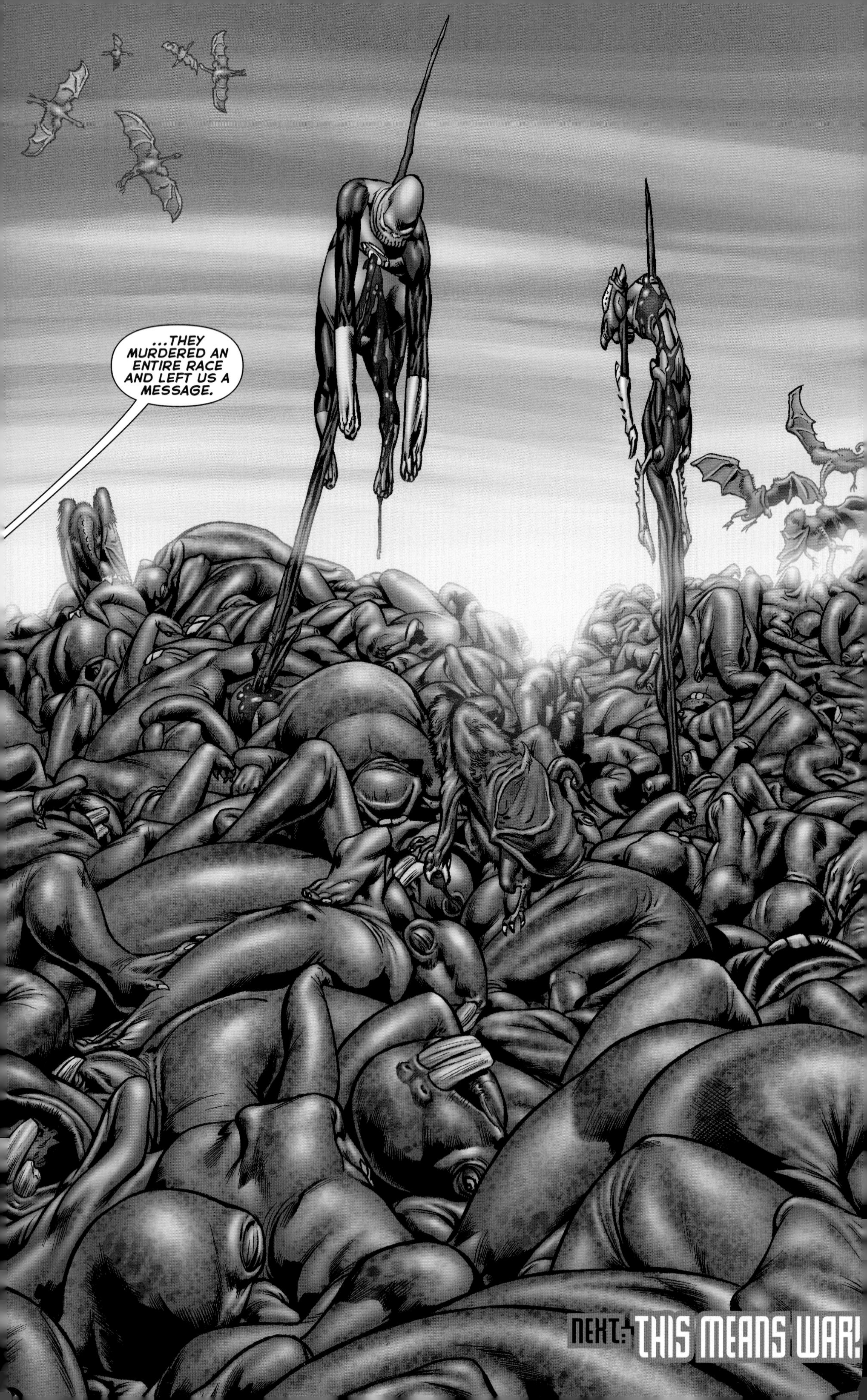
...THEY MURDERED AN ENTIRE RACE AND LEFT US A MESSAGE.
NEXT: THIS MEANS WAR!

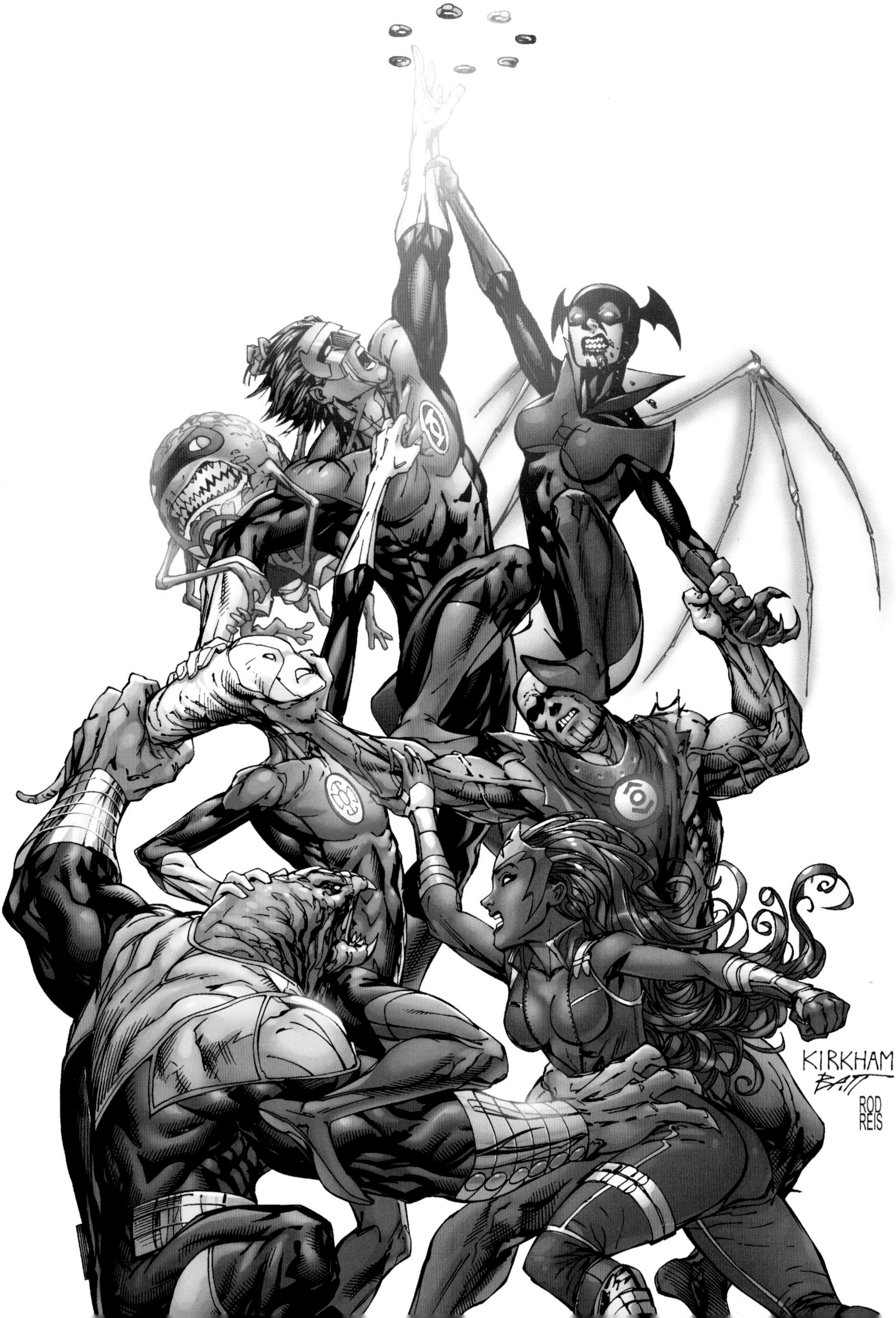
KIRKHAM
BATT
ROD
REIS

GREEN LANTERN NEW GUARDIANS

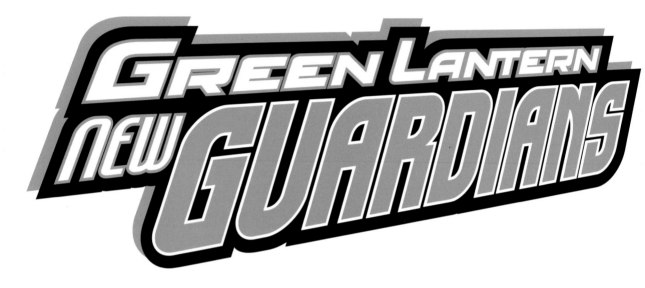

DC COMICS PROUDLY PRESENTS

GREEN LANTERN NEW GUARDIANS PART ONE

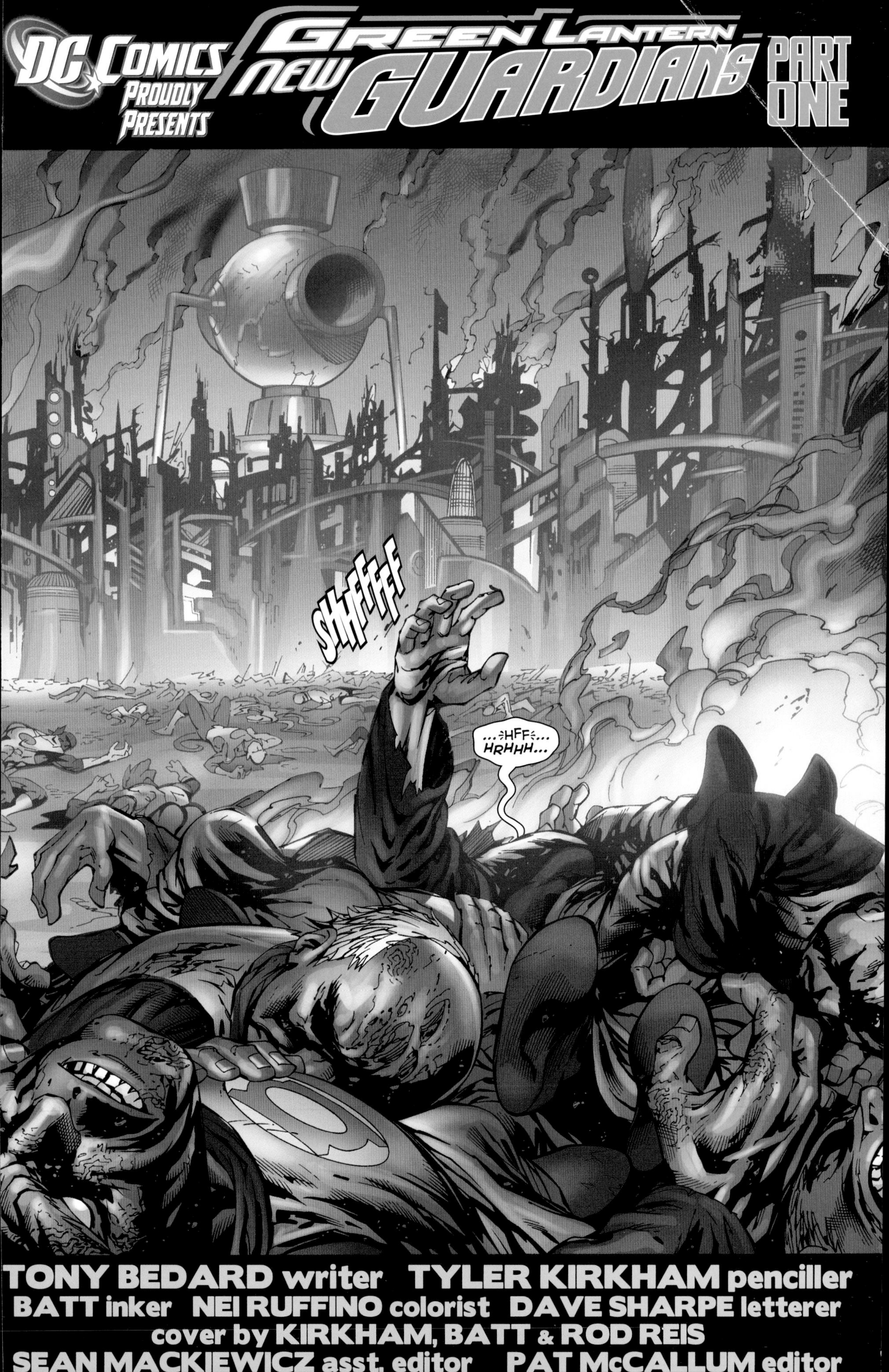
SHFFFFFF
...SHFF...
HRHHH...

TONY BEDARD writer **TYLER KIRKHAM** penciller
BATT inker **NEI RUFFINO** colorist **DAVE SHARPE** letterer
cover by **KIRKHAM, BATT & ROD REIS**
SEAN MACKIEWICZ asst. editor **PAT McCALLUM** editor

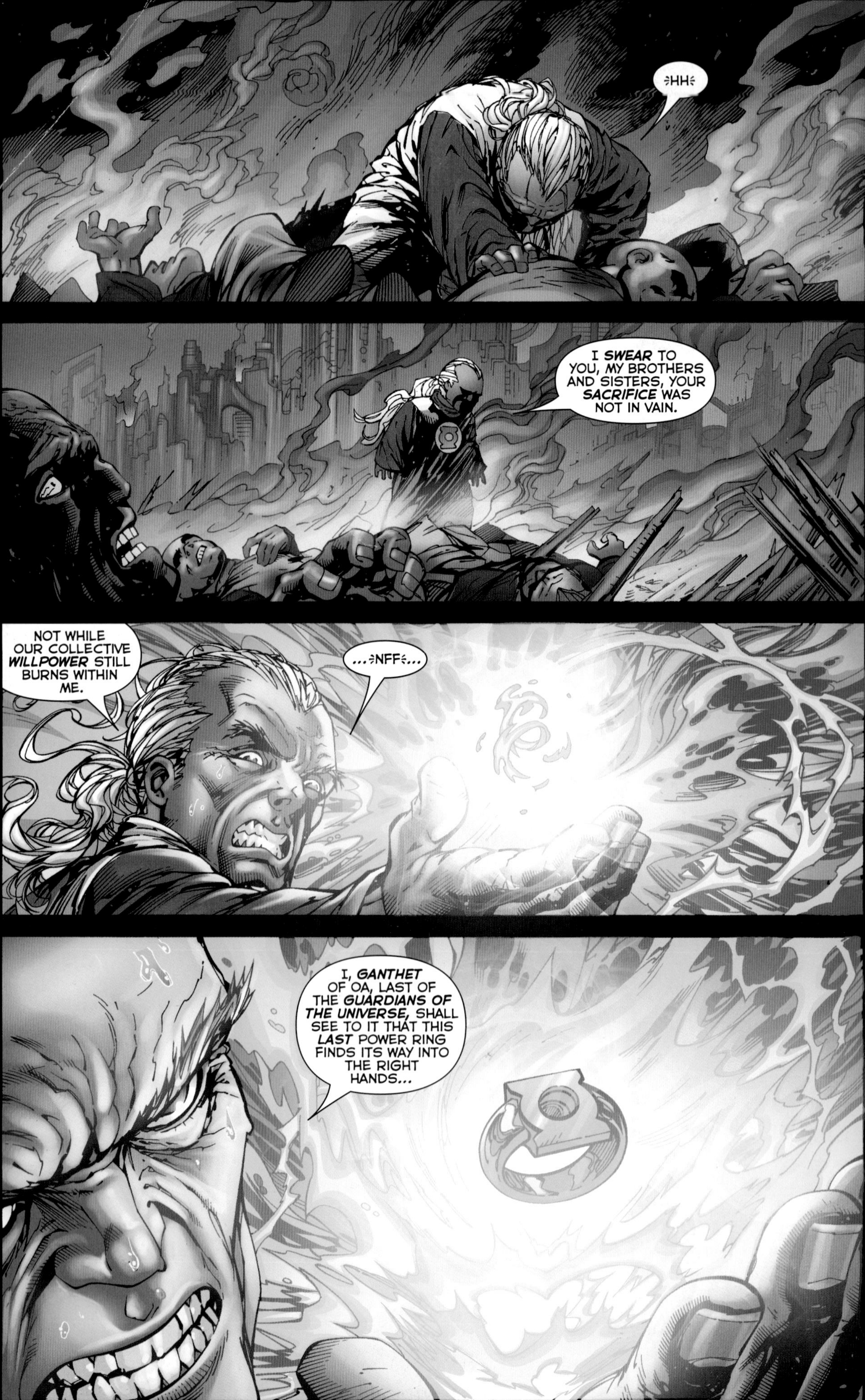
HH
I SWEAR TO YOU, MY BROTHERS AND SISTERS, YOUR SACRIFICE WAS NOT IN VAIN.
NOT WHILE OUR COLLECTIVE WILLPOWER STILL BURNS WITHIN ME.
...NFF...
I, GANTHET OF OA, LAST OF THE GUARDIANS OF THE UNIVERSE, SHALL SEE TO IT THAT THIS LAST POWER RING FINDS ITS WAY INTO THE RIGHT HANDS...

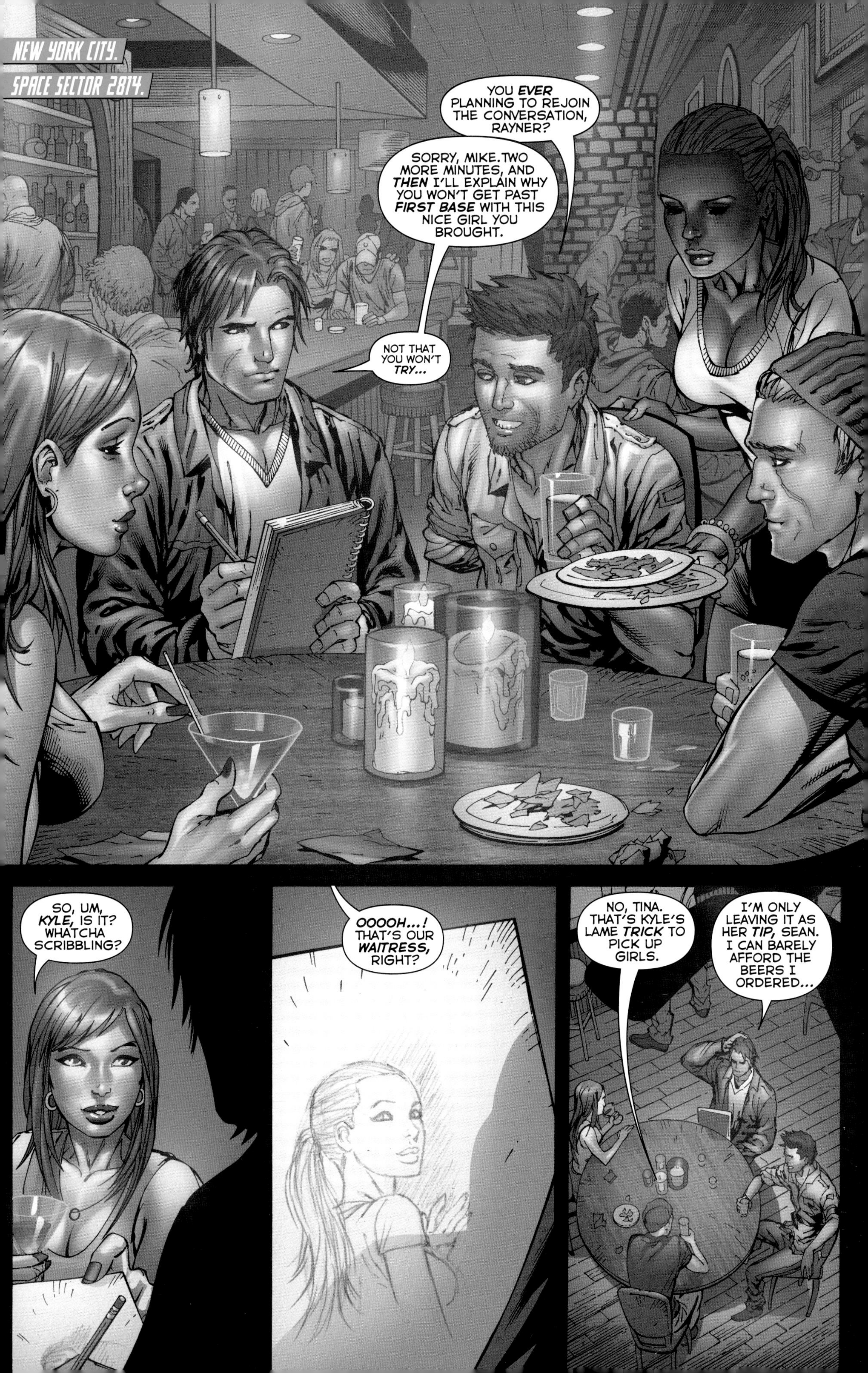
NEW YORK CITY.
SPACE SECTOR 2814.
YOU EVER PLANNING TO REJOIN THE CONVERSATION, RAYNER?
SORRY, MIKE. TWO MORE MINUTES, AND THEN I'LL EXPLAIN WHY YOU WON'T GET PAST FIRST BASE WITH THIS NICE GIRL YOU BROUGHT.
NOT THAT YOU WON'T TRY...
SO, UM, KYLE, IS IT? WHATCHA SCRIBBLING?
OOOOH...! THAT'S OUR WAITRESS, RIGHT?
NO, TINA. THAT'S KYLE'S LAME TRICK TO PICK UP GIRLS.
I'M ONLY LEAVING IT AS HER TIP, SEAN. I CAN BARELY AFFORD THE BEERS I ORDERED...

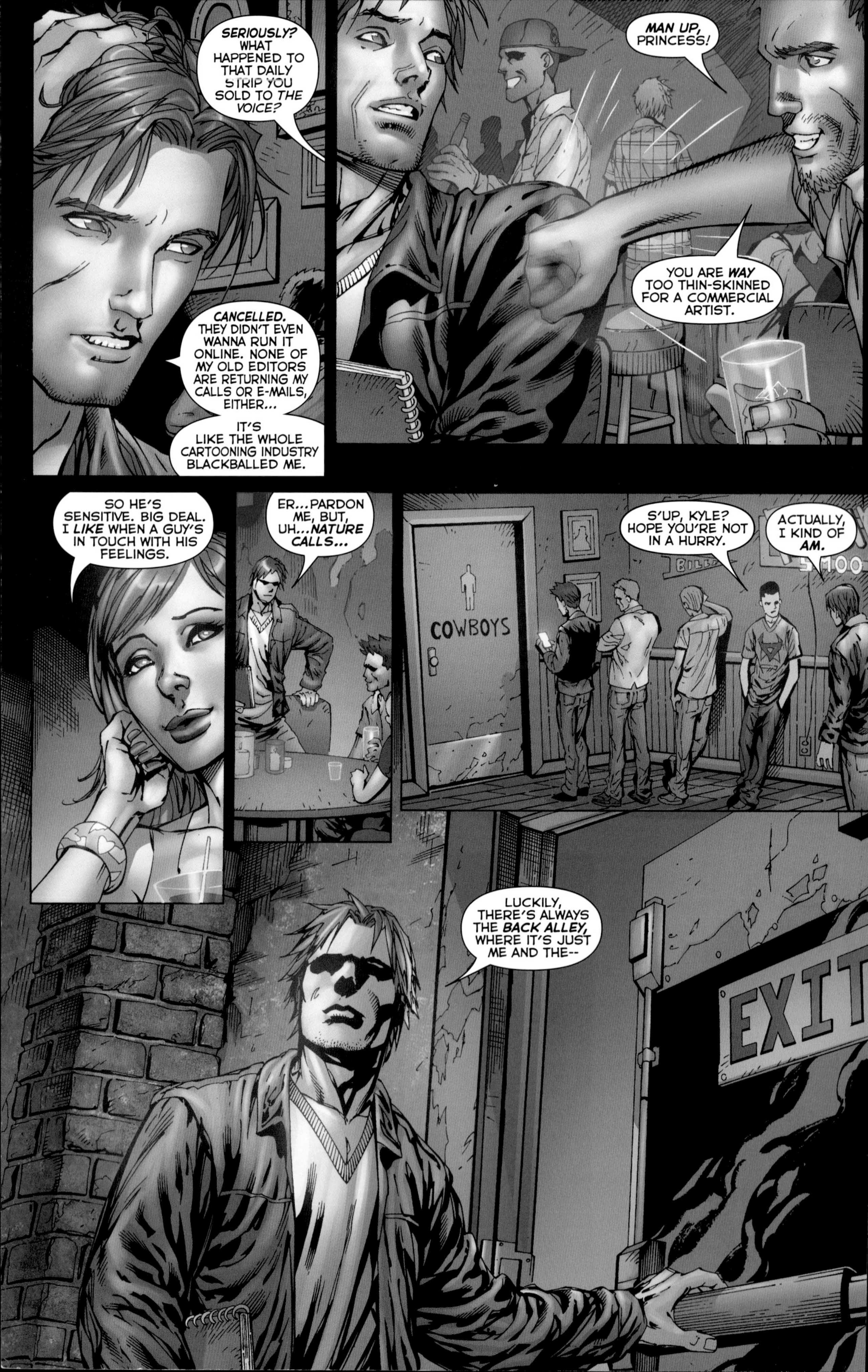
SERIOUSLY? WHAT HAPPENED TO THAT DAILY STRIP YOU SOLD TO THE VOICE?
CANCELLED. THEY DIDN'T EVEN WANNA RUN IT ONLINE. NONE OF MY OLD EDITORS ARE RETURNING MY CALLS OR E-MAILS, EITHER...
IT'S LIKE THE WHOLE CARTOONING INDUSTRY BLACKBALLED ME.
MAN UP, PRINCESS!
YOU ARE WAY TOO THIN-SKINNED FOR A COMMERCIAL ARTIST.
SO HE'S SENSITIVE. BIG DEAL. I LIKE WHEN A GUY'S IN TOUCH WITH HIS FEELINGS.
ER...PARDON ME, BUT, UH...NATURE CALLS...
COWBOYS
S'UP, KYLE? HOPE YOU'RE NOT IN A HURRY.
ACTUALLY, I KIND OF AM.
LUCKILY, THERE'S ALWAYS THE BACK ALLEY, WHERE IT'S JUST ME AND THE--
EXIT

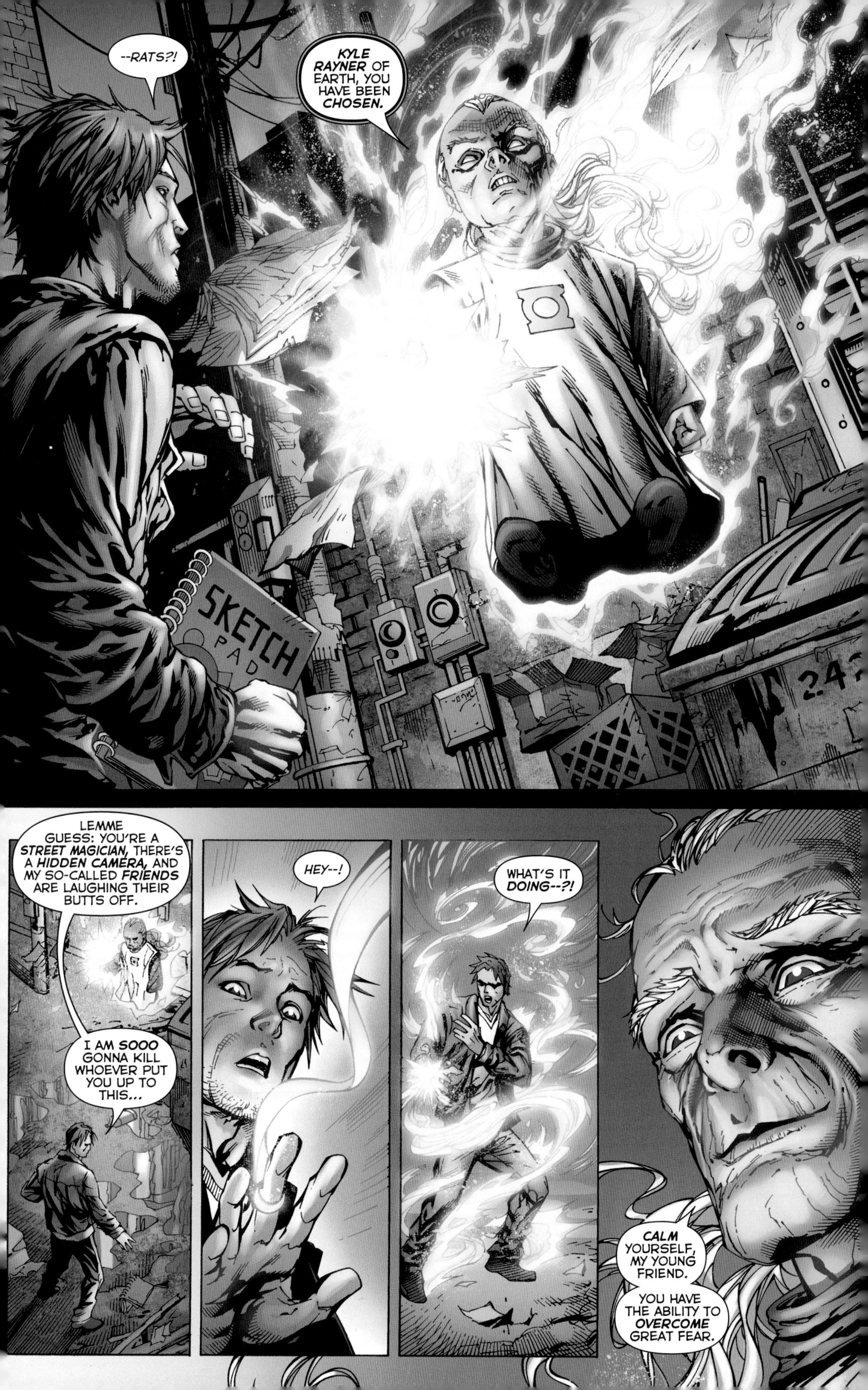
--RATS?!
KYLE RAYNER OF EARTH, YOU HAVE BEEN CHOSEN.
SKETCH PAD
LEMME GUESS: YOU'RE A STREET MAGICIAN, THERE'S A HIDDEN CAMERA, AND MY SO-CALLED FRIENDS ARE LAUGHING THEIR BUTTS OFF.
I AM SOOO GONNA KILL WHOEVER PUT YOU UP TO THIS...
HEY--!
WHAT'S IT DOING--?!
CALM YOURSELF, MY YOUNG FRIEND.
YOU HAVE THE ABILITY TO OVERCOME GREAT FEAR.

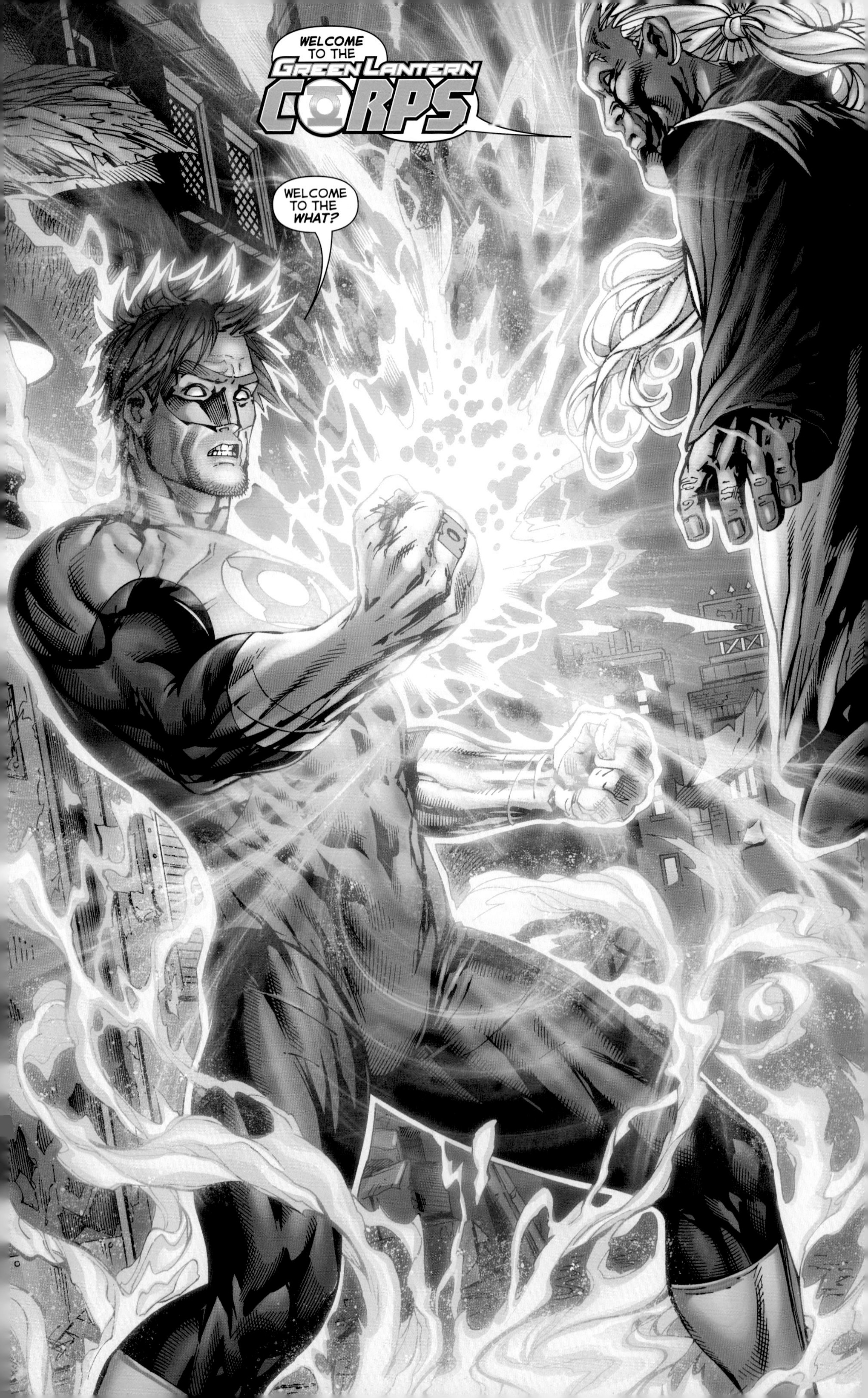
WELCOME TO THE GREEN LANTERN CORPS
WELCOME TO THE WHAT?

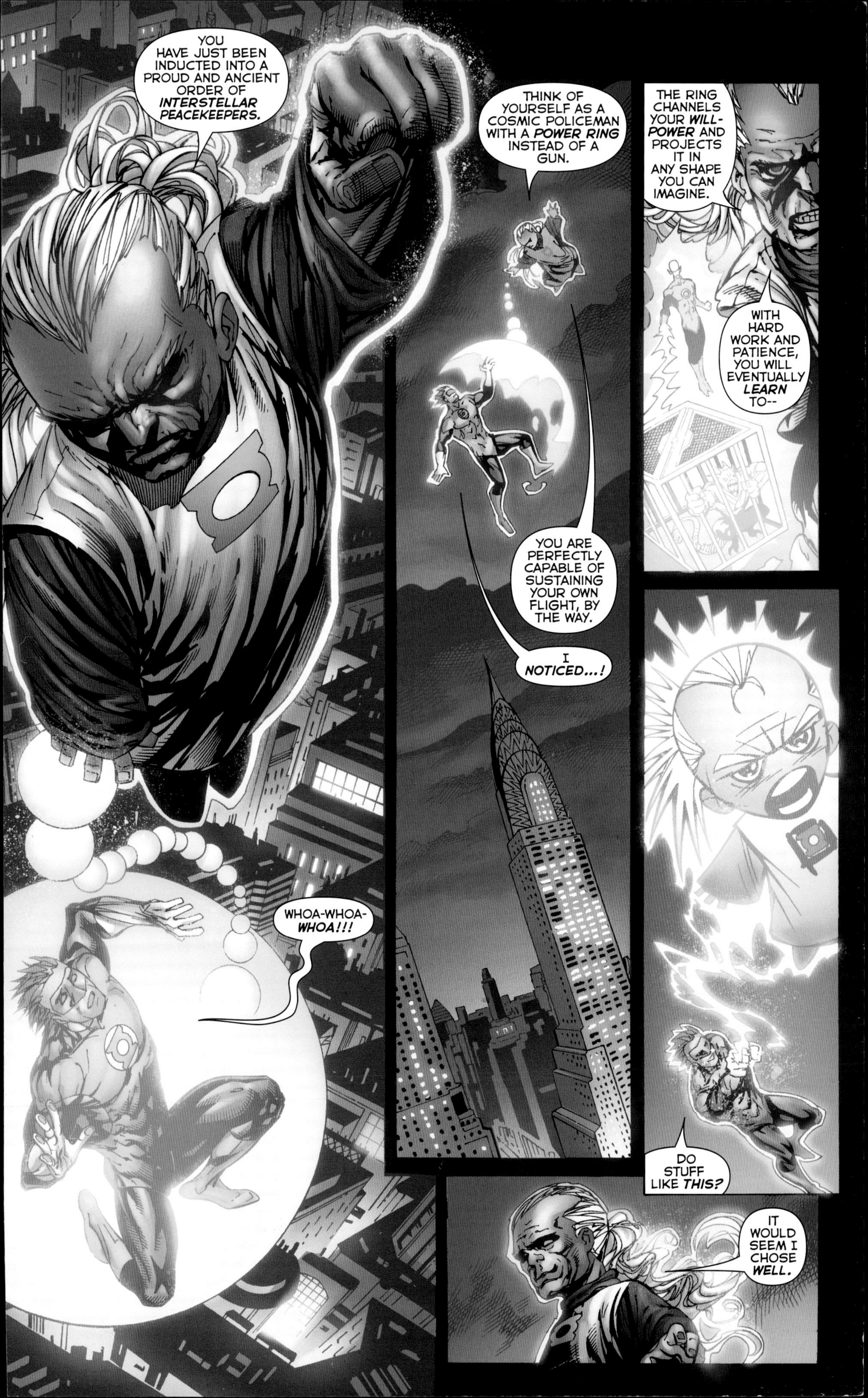
YOU HAVE JUST BEEN INDUCTED INTO A PROUD AND ANCIENT ORDER OF INTERSTELLAR PEACEKEEPERS.
WHOA-WHOA-WHOA!!!
THINK OF YOURSELF AS A COSMIC POLICEMAN WITH A POWER RING INSTEAD OF A GUN.
YOU ARE PERFECTLY CAPABLE OF SUSTAINING YOUR OWN FLIGHT, BY THE WAY.
I NOTICED...!
THE RING CHANNELS YOUR WILL-POWER AND PROJECTS IT IN ANY SHAPE YOU CAN IMAGINE.
WITH HARD WORK AND PATIENCE, YOU WILL EVENTUALLY LEARN TO--
DO STUFF LIKE THIS?
IT WOULD SEEM I CHOSE WELL.

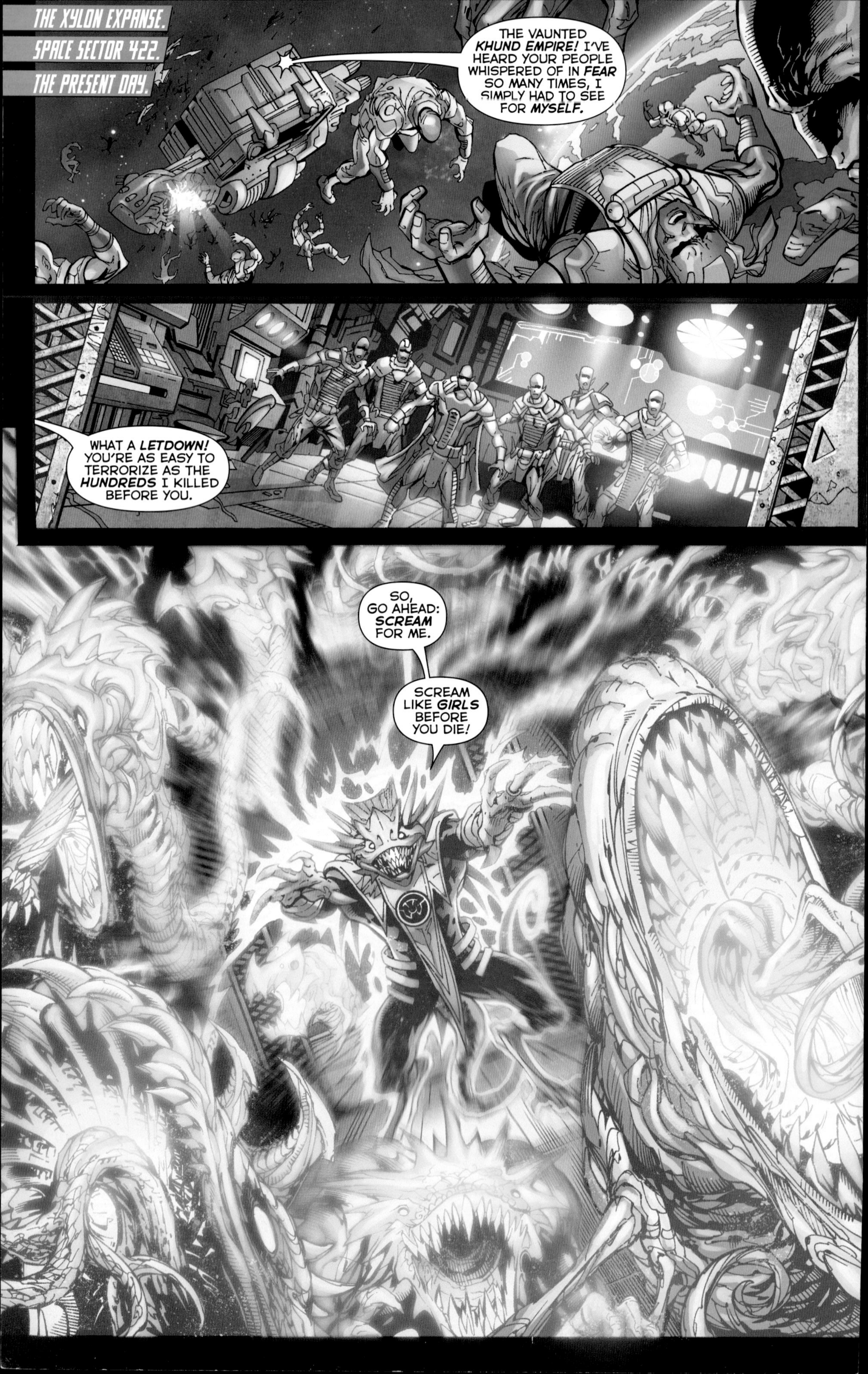
THE XYLON EXPANSE.
SPACE SECTOR 422.
THE PRESENT DAY.
THE VAUNTED KHUND EMPIRE! I'VE HEARD YOUR PEOPLE WHISPERED OF IN FEAR SO MANY TIMES, I SIMPLY HAD TO SEE FOR MYSELF.
WHAT A LETDOWN! YOU'RE AS EASY TO TERRORIZE AS THE HUNDREDS I KILLED BEFORE YOU.
SO, GO AHEAD: SCREAM FOR ME.
SCREAM LIKE GIRLS BEFORE YOU DIE!

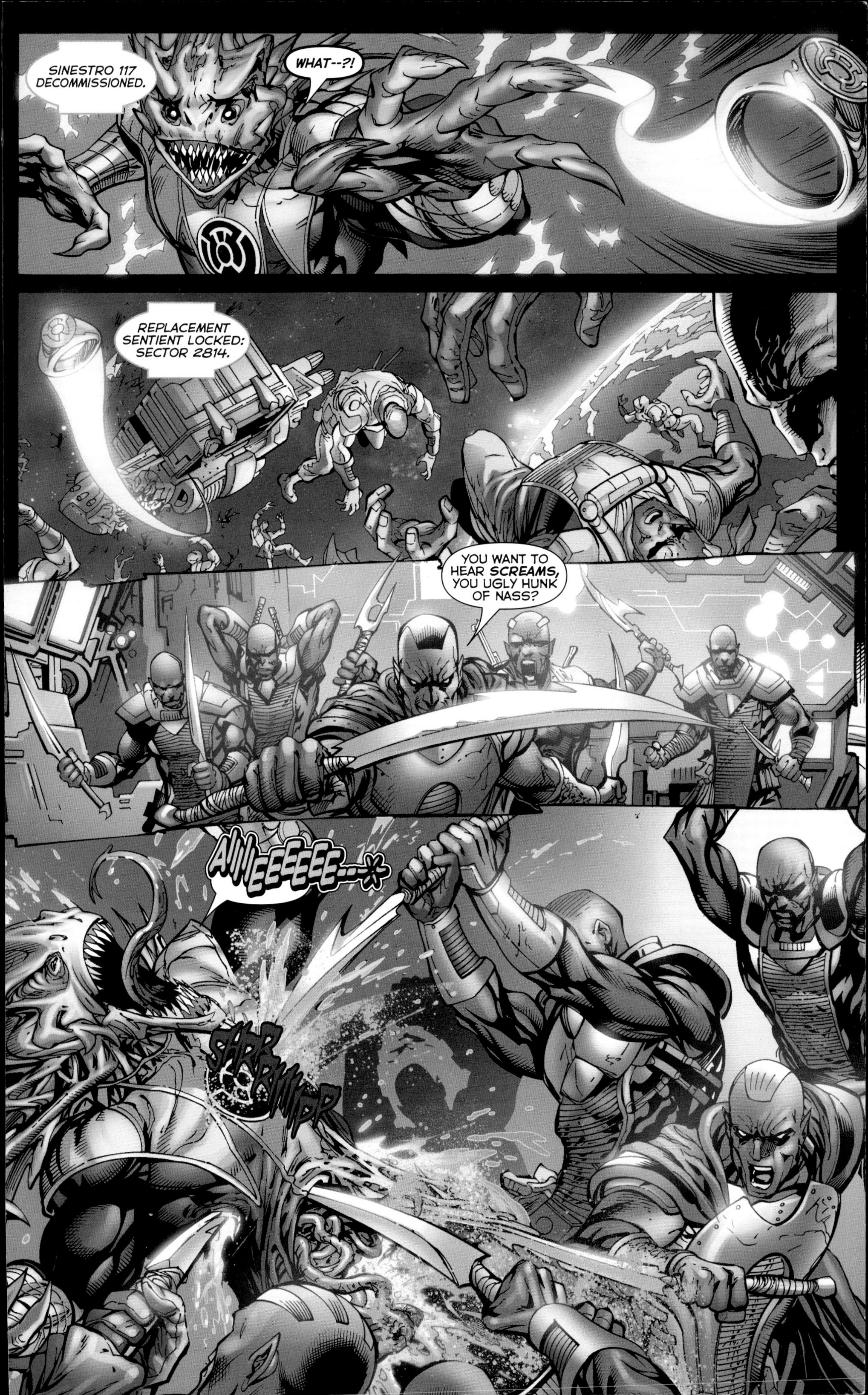
SINESTRO 117 DECOMMISSIONED.
WHAT--?!
REPLACEMENT SENTIENT LOCKED: SECTOR 2814.
YOU WANT TO HEAR SCREAMS, YOU UGLY HUNK OF NASS?
AIIIEEEEEEE--*
SHRRRINNPP

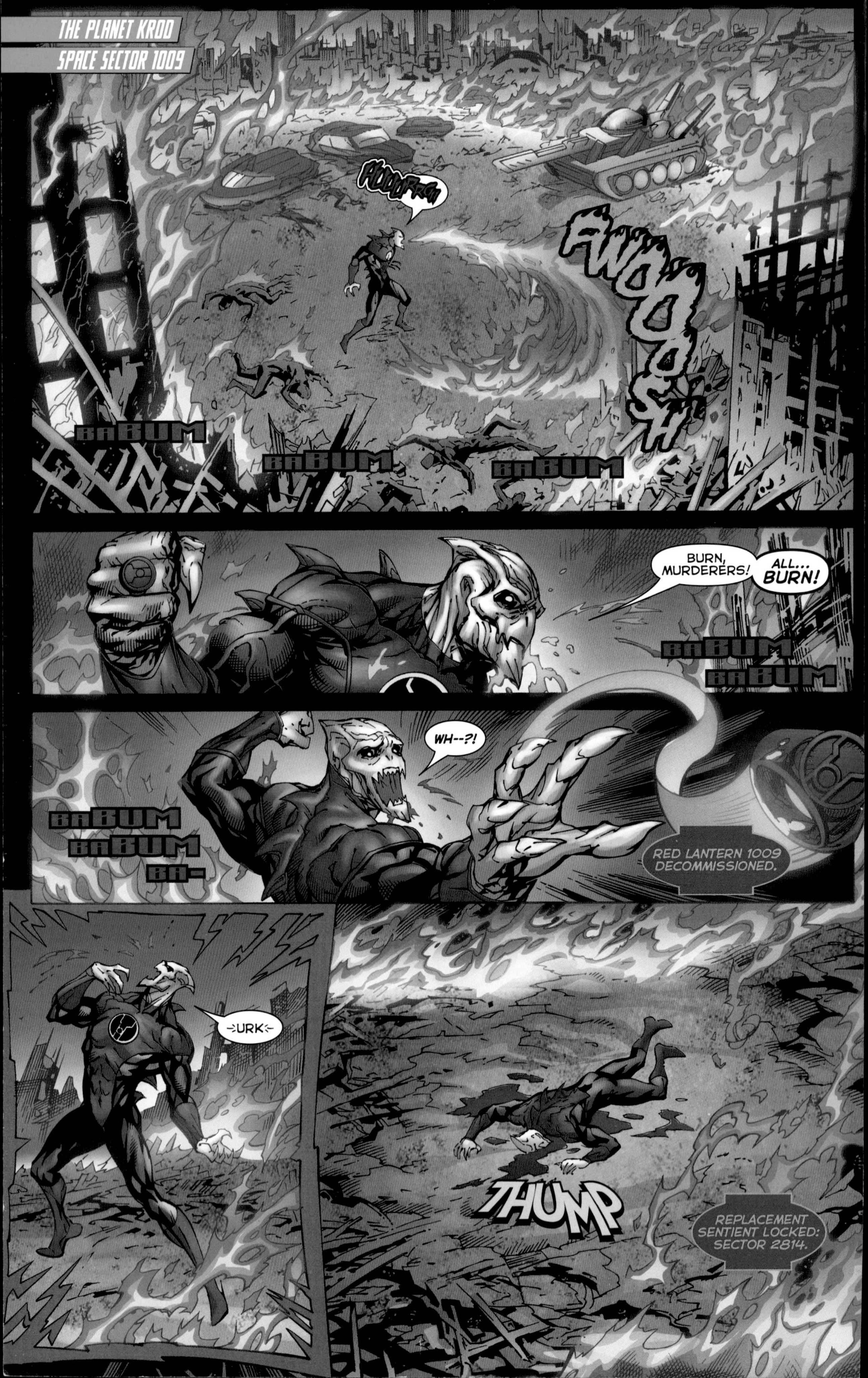
THE PLANET KROD
SPACE SECTOR 1009
FWOOOSH
BABUM
BABUM
BABUM
BURN, MURDERERS!
ALL... BURN!
BABUM
BABUM
WH--?!
BABUM
BABUM
BA-
RED LANTERN 1009 DECOMMISSIONED.
URK
THUMP
REPLACEMENT SENTIENT LOCKED: SECTOR 2814.

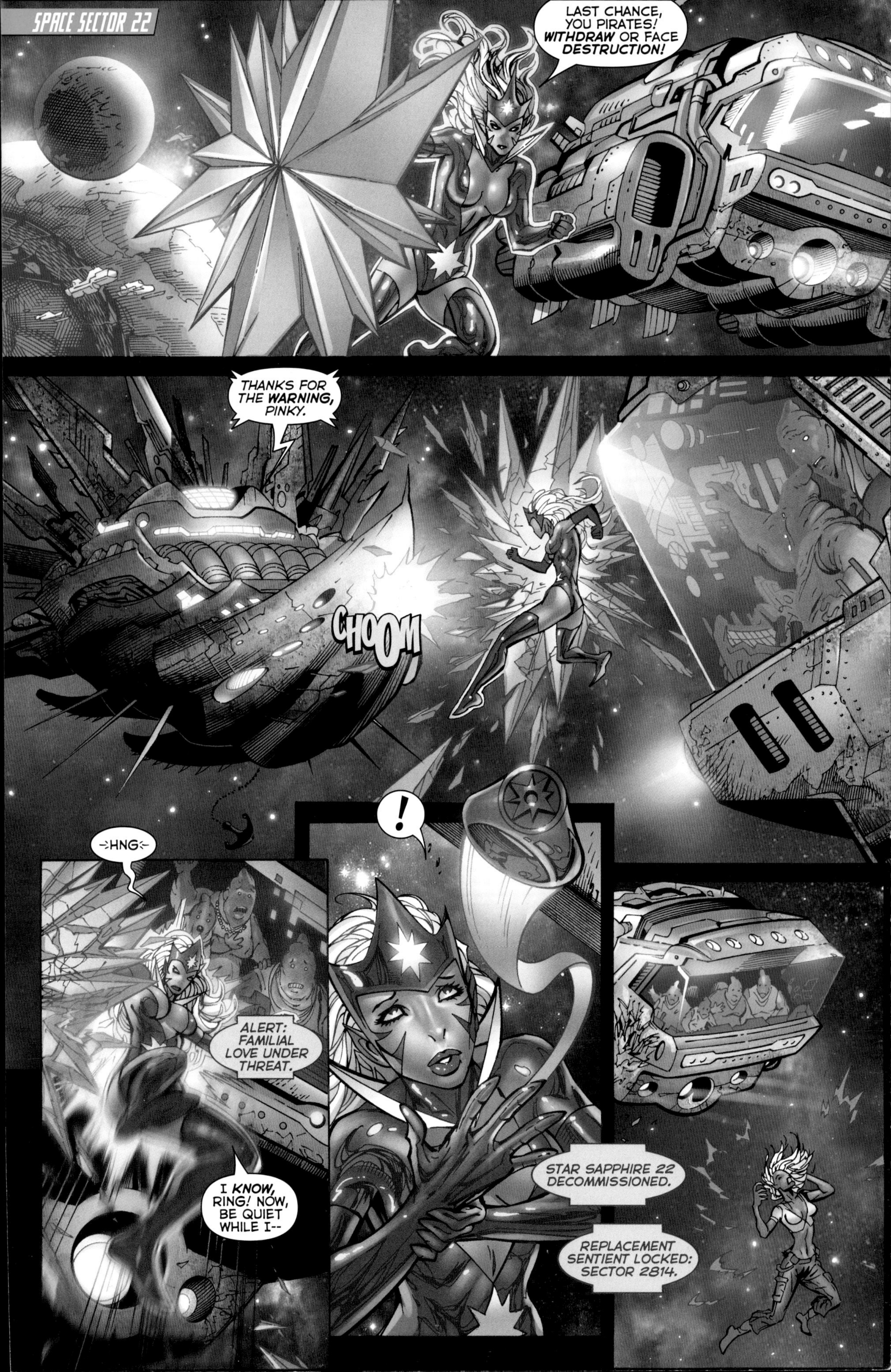
SPACE SECTOR 22
LAST CHANCE, YOU PIRATES! WITHDRAW OR FACE DESTRUCTION!
THANKS FOR THE WARNING, PINKY.
CHOOM
-HNG-
ALERT: FAMILIAL LOVE UNDER THREAT.
I KNOW, RING! NOW, BE QUIET WHILE I--
!
STAR SAPPHIRE 22 DECOMMISSIONED.
REPLACEMENT SENTIENT LOCKED: SECTOR 2814.

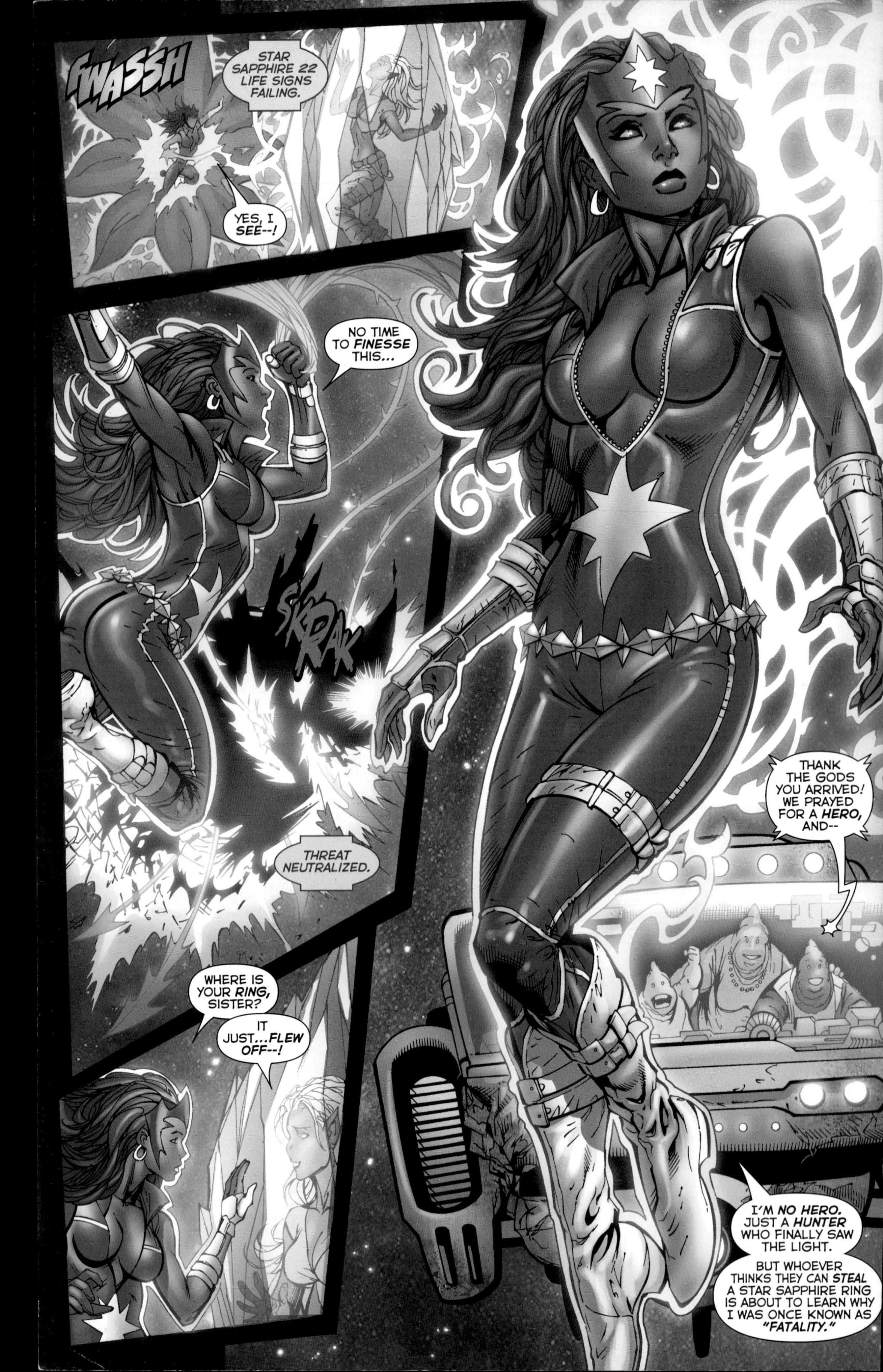
FWASSH
STAR SAPPHIRE 22 LIFE SIGNS FAILING.
YES, I *SEE*--!
NO TIME TO *FINESSE* THIS...
SKRAK
THREAT NEUTRALIZED.
WHERE IS YOUR *RING,* SISTER?
IT JUST...*FLEW OFF*--!
THANK THE GODS YOU ARRIVED! WE PRAYED FOR A *HERO,* AND--
I'M *NO HERO.* JUST A *HUNTER* WHO FINALLY SAW THE LIGHT.
BUT WHOEVER THINKS THEY CAN *STEAL* A STAR SAPPHIRE RING IS ABOUT TO LEARN WHY I WAS ONCE KNOWN AS *"FATALITY."*

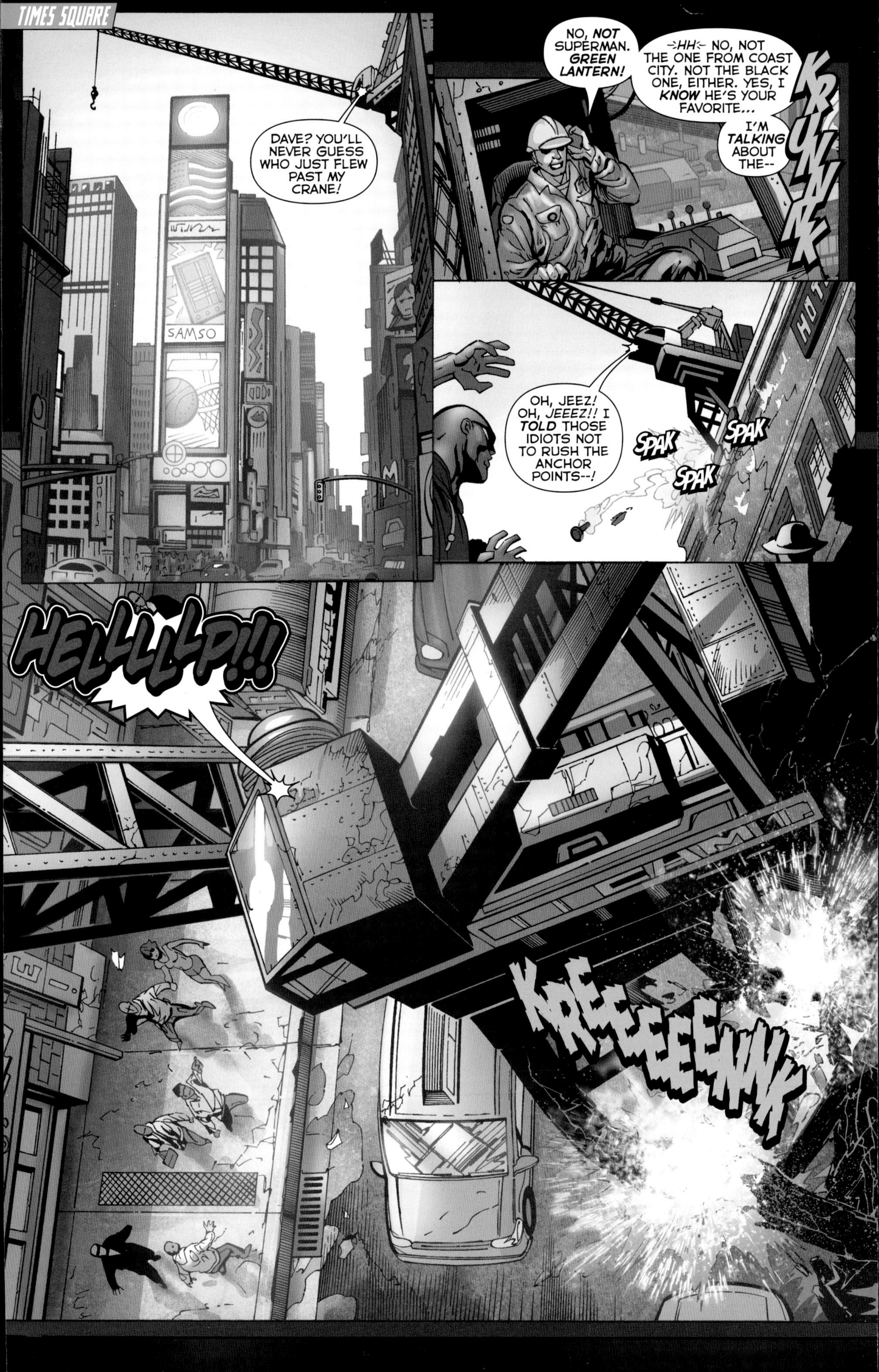

TIMES SQUARE
DAVE? YOU'LL NEVER GUESS WHO JUST FLEW PAST MY CRANE!
NO, NOT SUPERMAN. GREEN LANTERN!
-HH- NO, NOT THE ONE FROM COAST CITY. NOT THE BLACK ONE, EITHER. YES, I KNOW HE'S YOUR FAVORITE...
I'M TALKING ABOUT THE--
KRUNNNK
OH, JEEZ! OH, JEEEZ!! I TOLD THOSE IDIOTS NOT TO RUSH THE ANCHOR POINTS--!
SPAK
SPAK
SPAK
HELLLLLP!!!
KREEEEEENNK

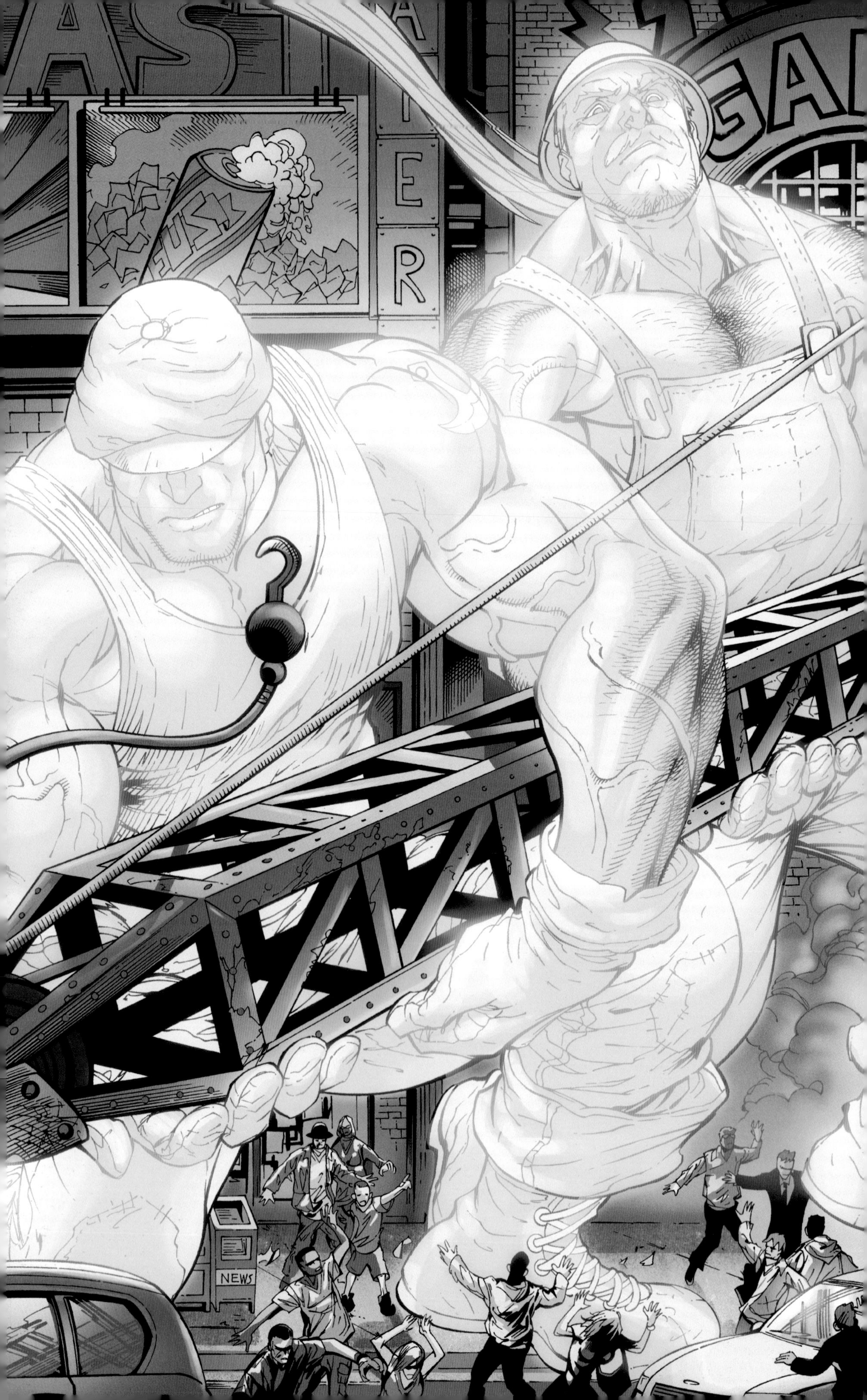
NEWS

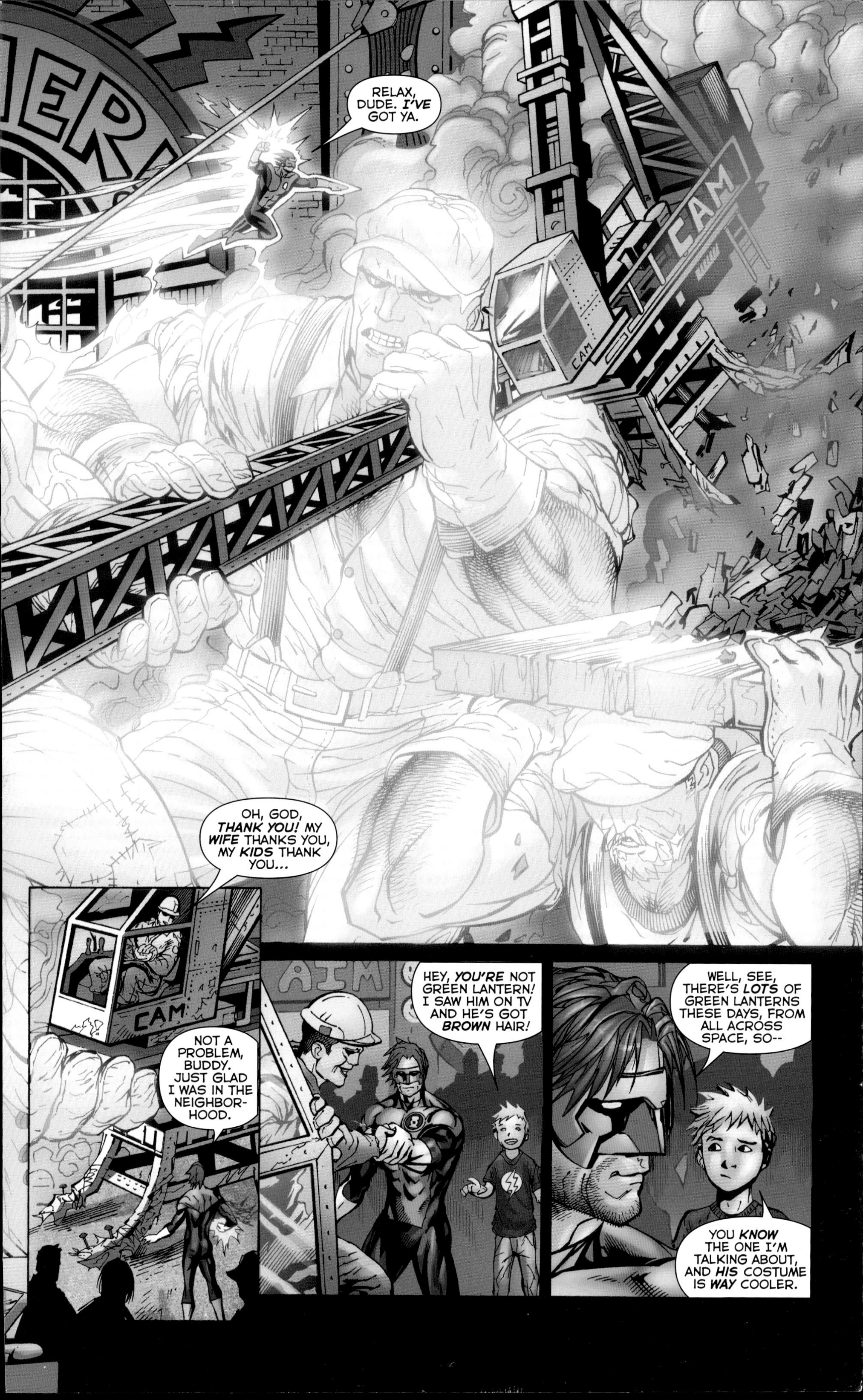

RELAX, DUDE. I'VE GOT YA.
OH, GOD, THANK YOU! MY WIFE THANKS YOU, MY KIDS THANK YOU...
NOT A PROBLEM, BUDDY. JUST GLAD I WAS IN THE NEIGHBOR-HOOD.
HEY, YOU'RE NOT GREEN LANTERN! I SAW HIM ON TV AND HE'S GOT BROWN HAIR!
WELL, SEE, THERE'S LOTS OF GREEN LANTERNS THESE DAYS, FROM ALL ACROSS SPACE, SO--
YOU KNOW THE ONE I'M TALKING ABOUT, AND HIS COSTUME IS WAY COOLER.

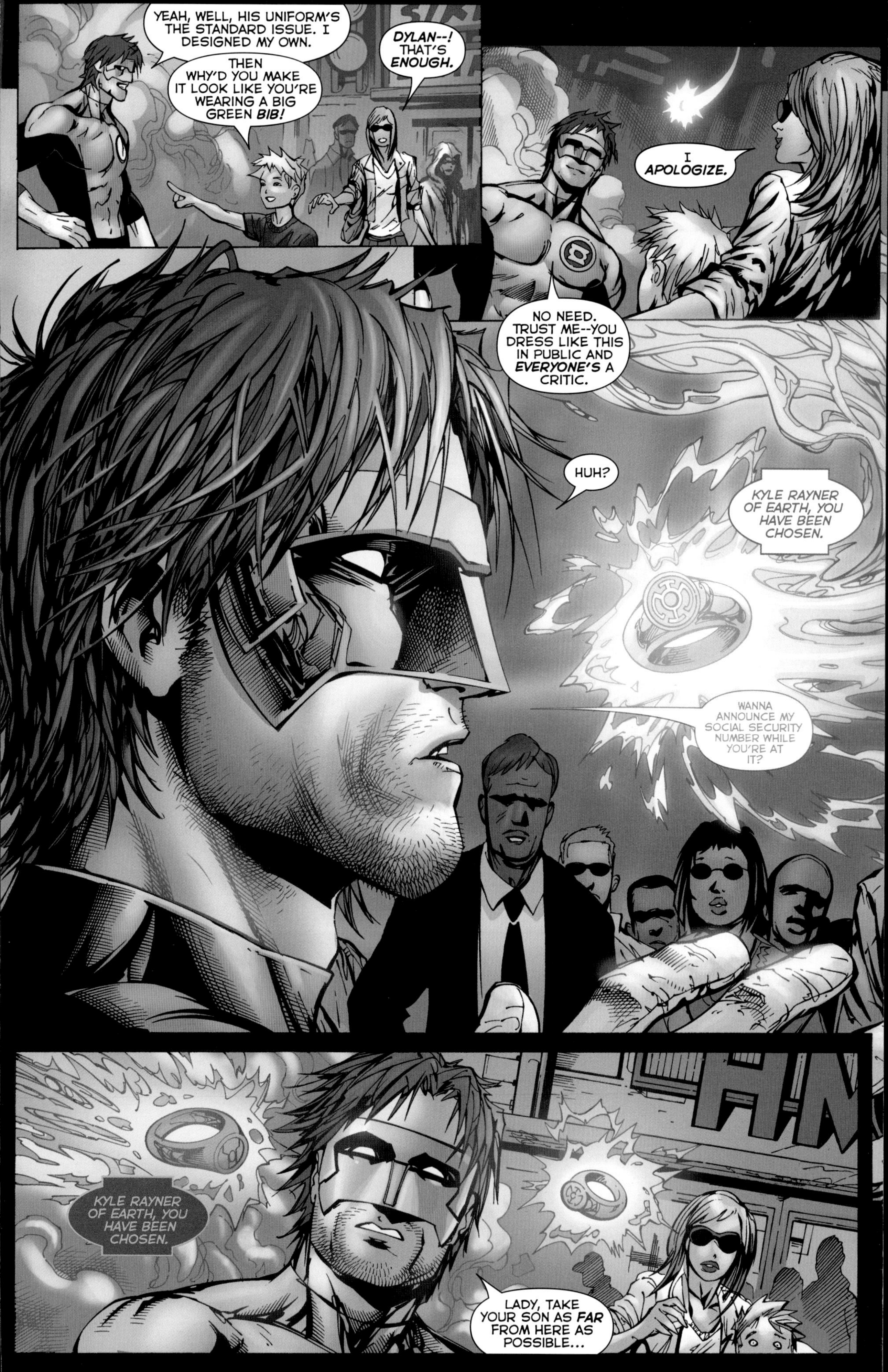
YEAH, WELL, HIS UNIFORM'S THE STANDARD ISSUE. I DESIGNED MY OWN.
THEN WHY'D YOU MAKE IT LOOK LIKE YOU'RE WEARING A BIG GREEN BIB!
DYLAN--! THAT'S ENOUGH.
I APOLOGIZE.
NO NEED. TRUST ME--YOU DRESS LIKE THIS IN PUBLIC AND EVERYONE'S A CRITIC.
HUH?
KYLE RAYNER OF EARTH, YOU HAVE BEEN CHOSEN.
WANNA ANNOUNCE MY SOCIAL SECURITY NUMBER WHILE YOU'RE AT IT?
KYLE RAYNER OF EARTH, YOU HAVE BEEN CHOSEN.
LADY, TAKE YOUR SON AS FAR FROM HERE AS POSSIBLE...

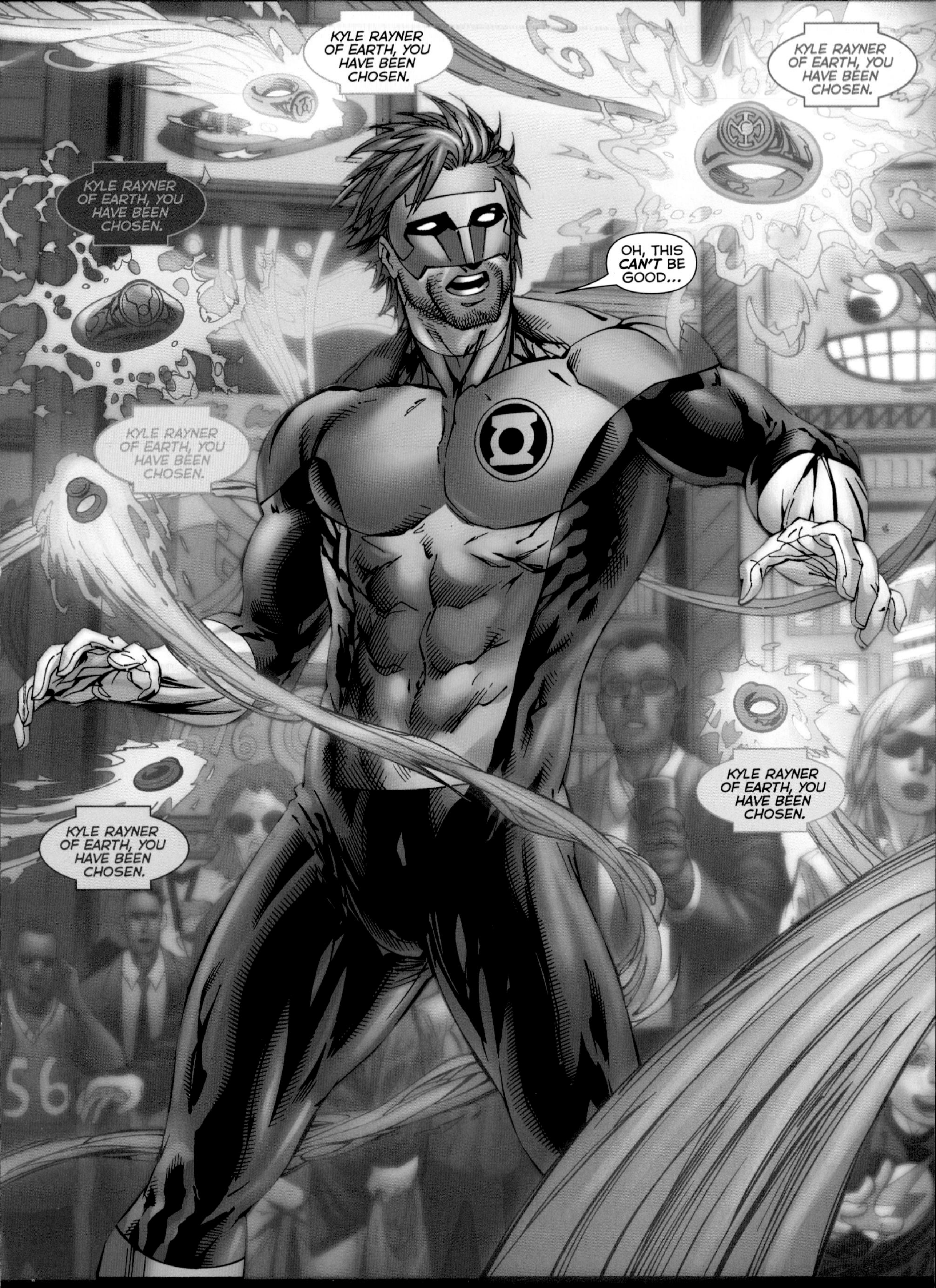
KYLE RAYNER
OF EARTH, YOU
HAVE BEEN
CHOSEN.
KYLE RAYNER
OF EARTH, YOU
HAVE BEEN
CHOSEN.
KYLE RAYNER
OF EARTH, YOU
HAVE BEEN
CHOSEN.
OH, THIS
CAN'T BE
GOOD...
KYLE RAYNER
OF EARTH, YOU
HAVE BEEN
CHOSEN.
KYLE RAYNER
OF EARTH, YOU
HAVE BEEN
CHOSEN.
KYLE RAYNER
OF EARTH, YOU
HAVE BEEN
CHOSEN.

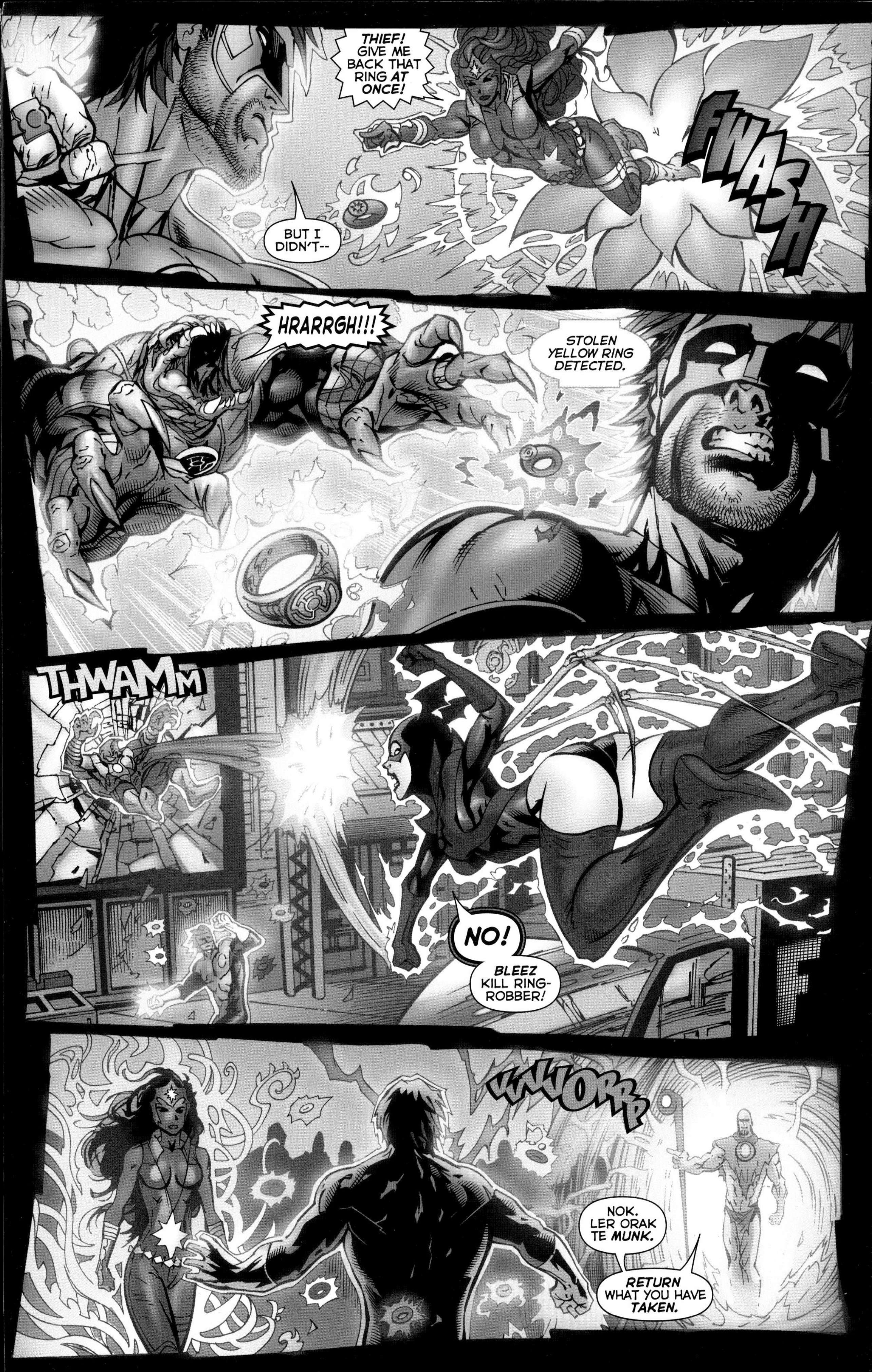
THIEF! GIVE ME BACK THAT RING AT ONCE!
FWASH
BUT I DIDN'T--
HRARRGH!!!
STOLEN YELLOW RING DETECTED.
THWAMM
NO!
BLEEZ KILL RING-ROBBER!
VWORRP
NOK. LER ORAK TE MUNK.
RETURN WHAT YOU HAVE TAKEN.

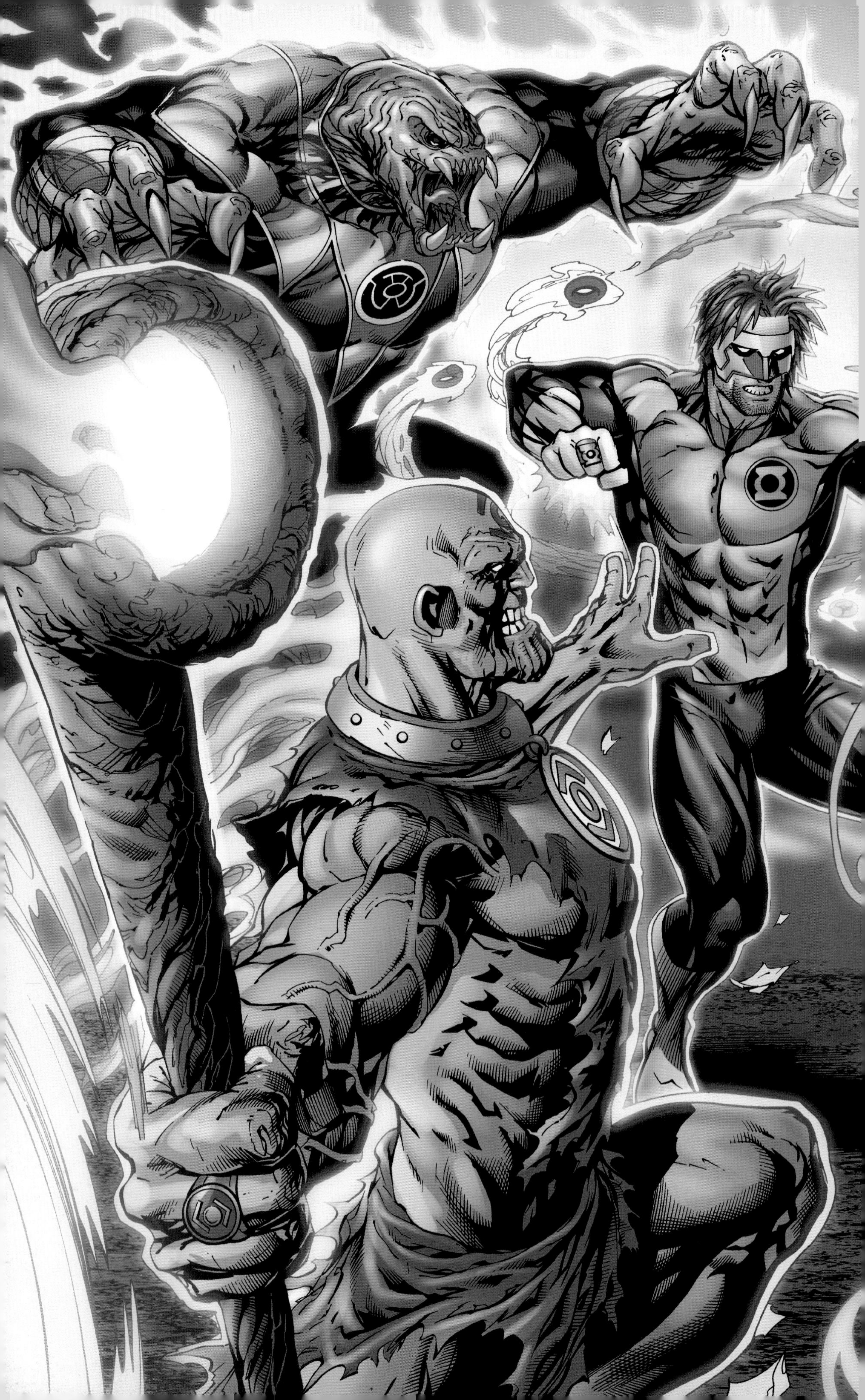

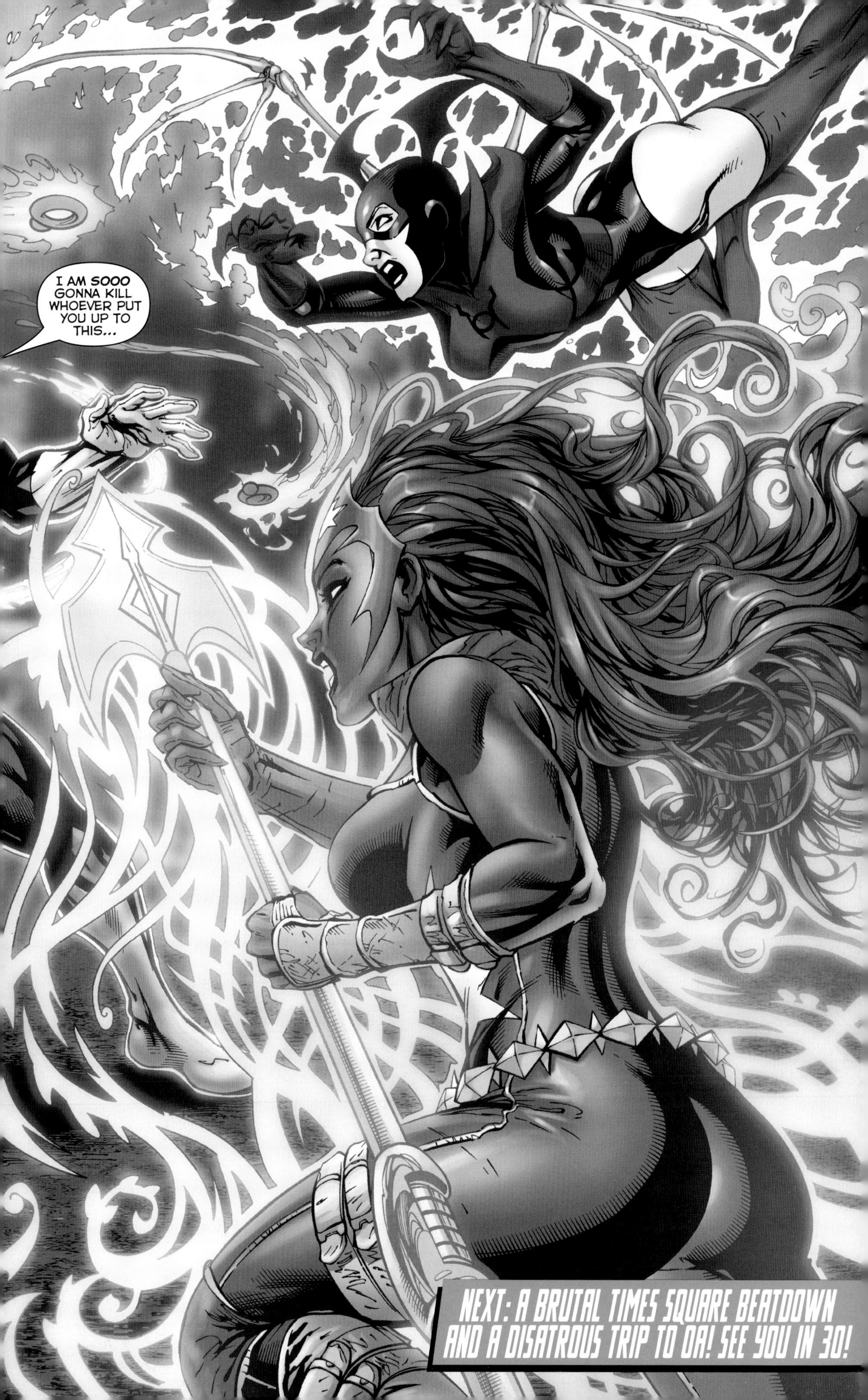
I AM SOOO GONNA KILL WHOEVER PUT YOU UP TO THIS...
NEXT: A BRUTAL TIMES SQUARE BEATDOWN AND A DISATROUS TRIP TO OA! SEE YOU IN 30!

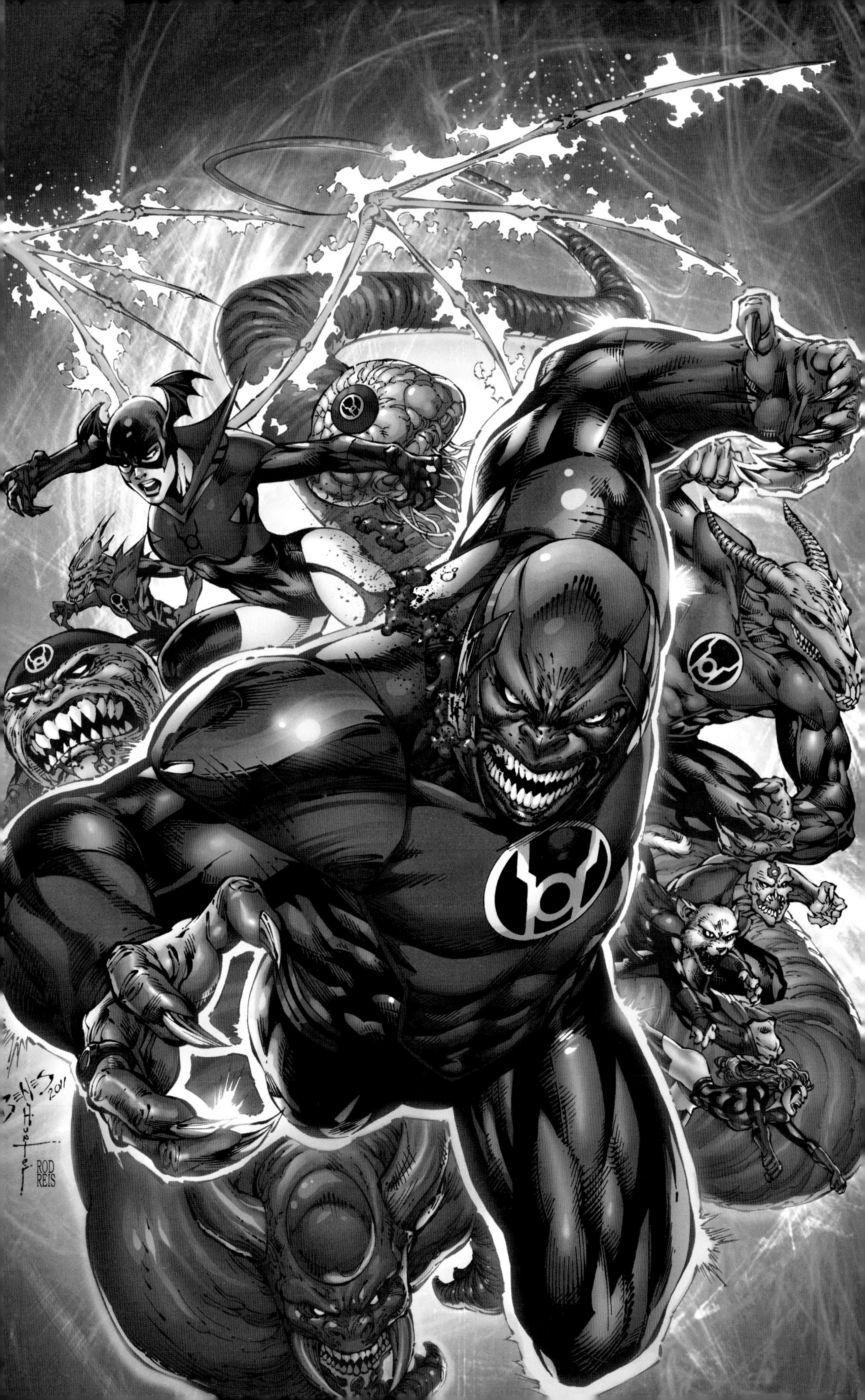
BENES 2011
Hunter!
ROD REIS

RED LANTERNS

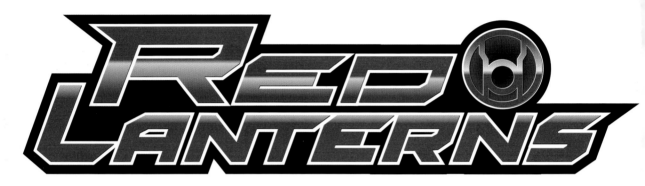

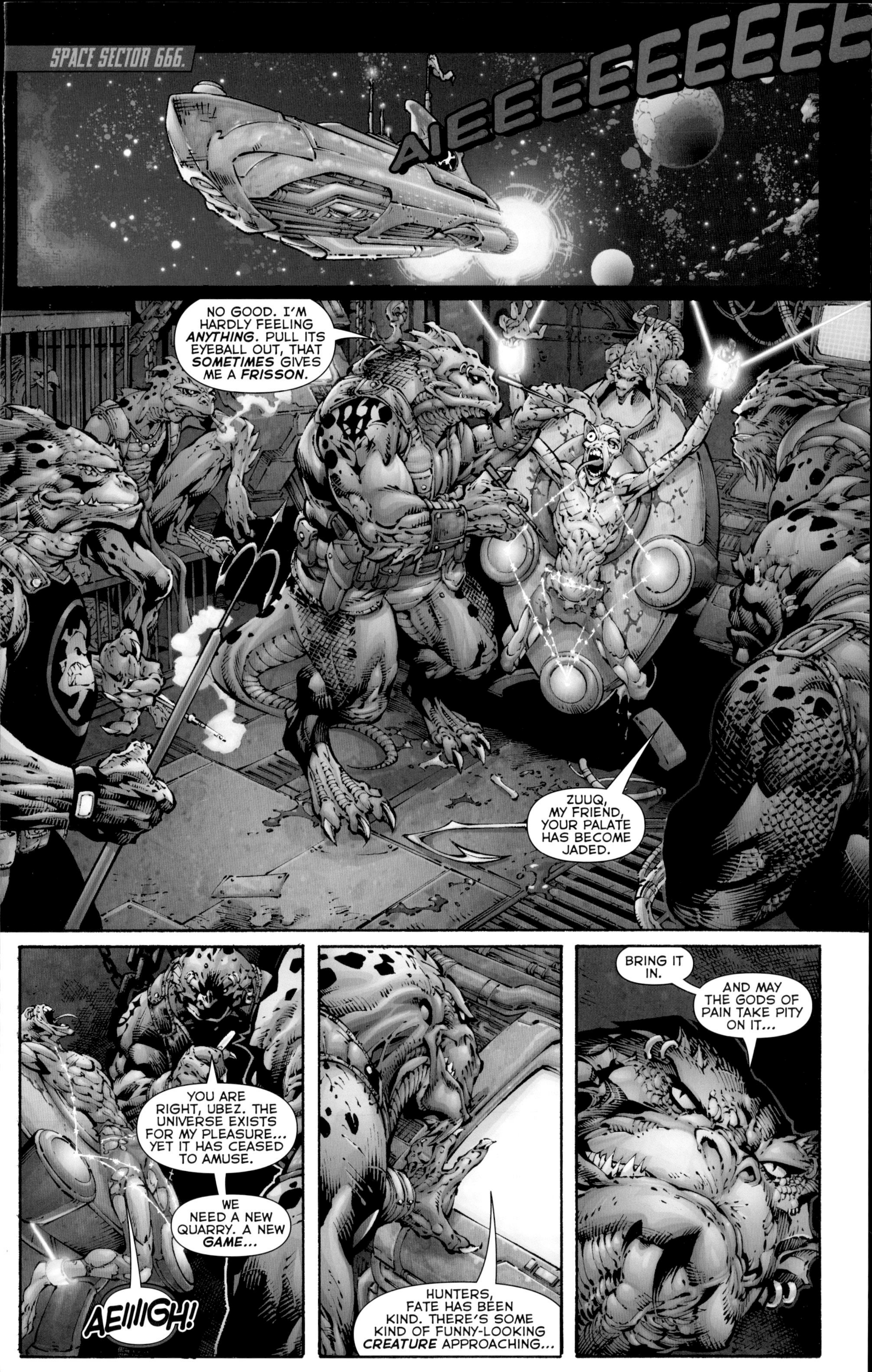

SPACE SECTOR 666.
AIEEEEEEEEEEEE
NO GOOD. I'M HARDLY FEELING ANYTHING. PULL ITS EYEBALL OUT, THAT SOMETIMES GIVES ME A FRISSON.
ZUUQ, MY FRIEND, YOUR PALATE HAS BECOME JADED.
YOU ARE RIGHT, UBEZ. THE UNIVERSE EXISTS FOR MY PLEASURE... YET IT HAS CEASED TO AMUSE.
WE NEED A NEW QUARRY. A NEW GAME...
AEIIIIGH!
HUNTERS, FATE HAS BEEN KIND. THERE'S SOME KIND OF FUNNY-LOOKING CREATURE APPROACHING...
BRING IT IN.
AND MAY THE GODS OF PAIN TAKE PITY ON IT...

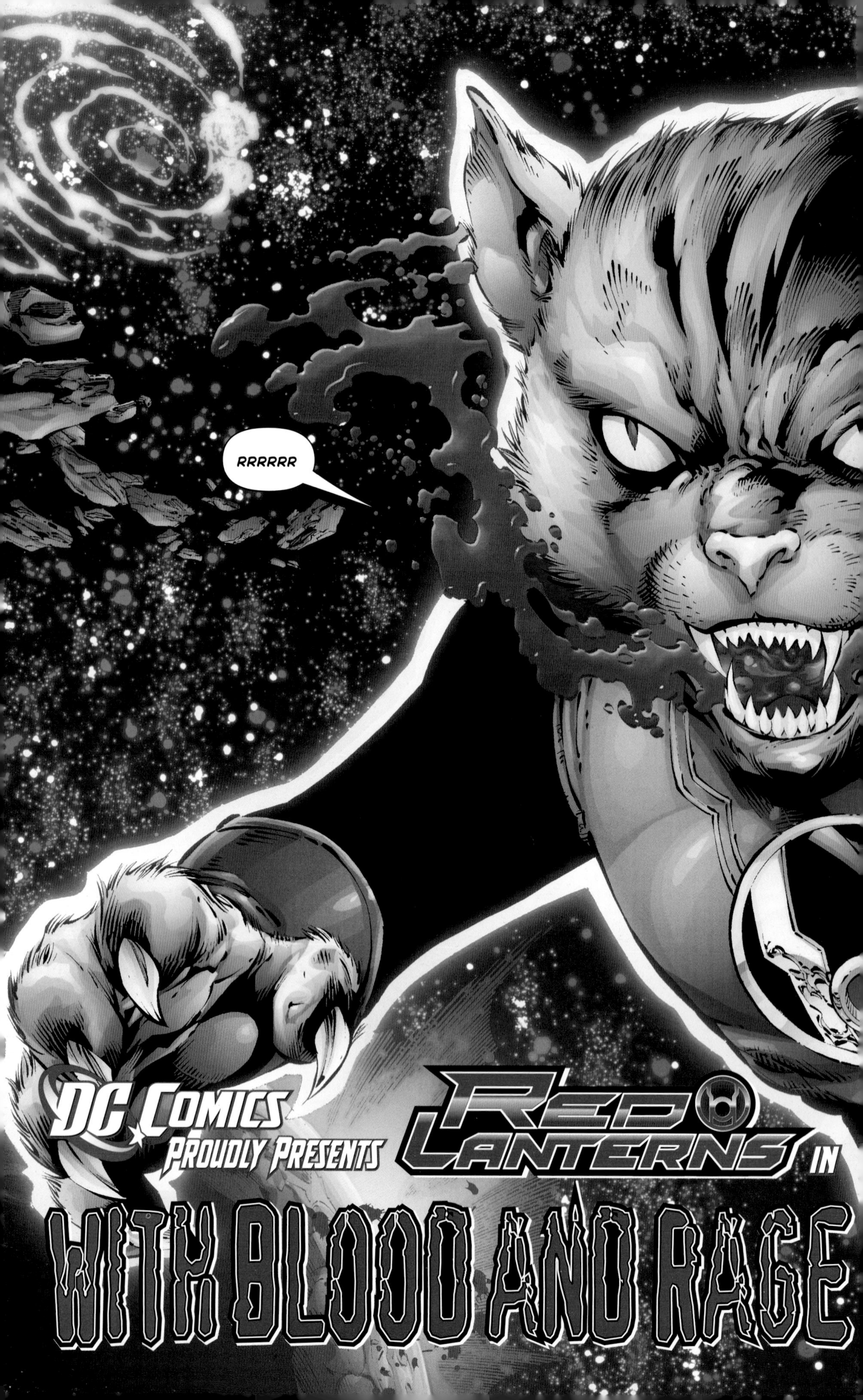
RRRRRR
DC COMICS PROUDLY PRESENTS
RED LANTERNS IN
WITH BLOOD AND RAGE

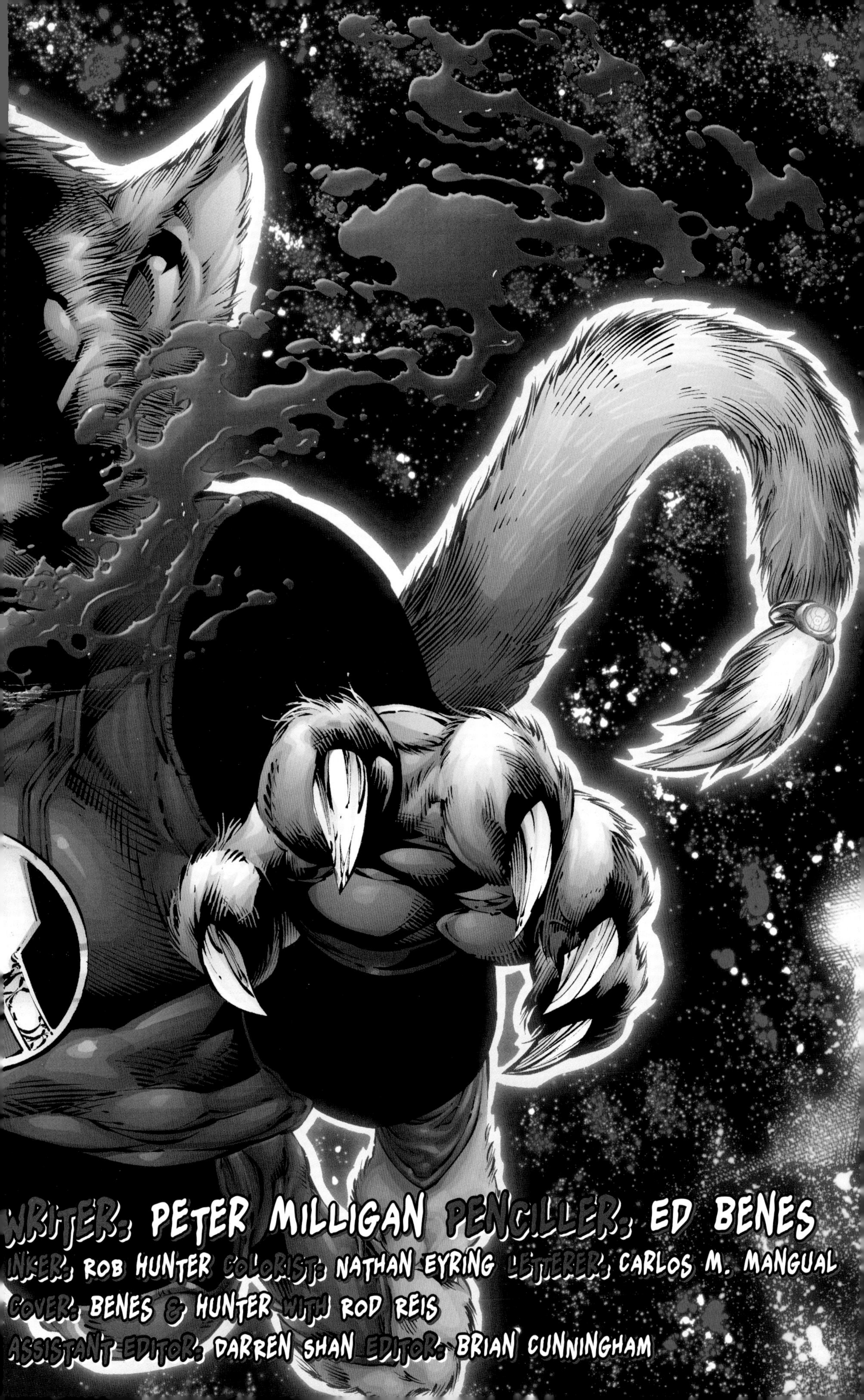

WRITER: PETER MILLIGAN PENCILLER: ED BENES
INKER: ROB HUNTER COLORIST: NATHAN EYRING LETTERER: CARLOS M. MANGUAL
COVER: BENES & HUNTER WITH ROD REIS
ASSISTANT EDITOR: DARREN SHAN EDITOR: BRIAN CUNNINGHAM

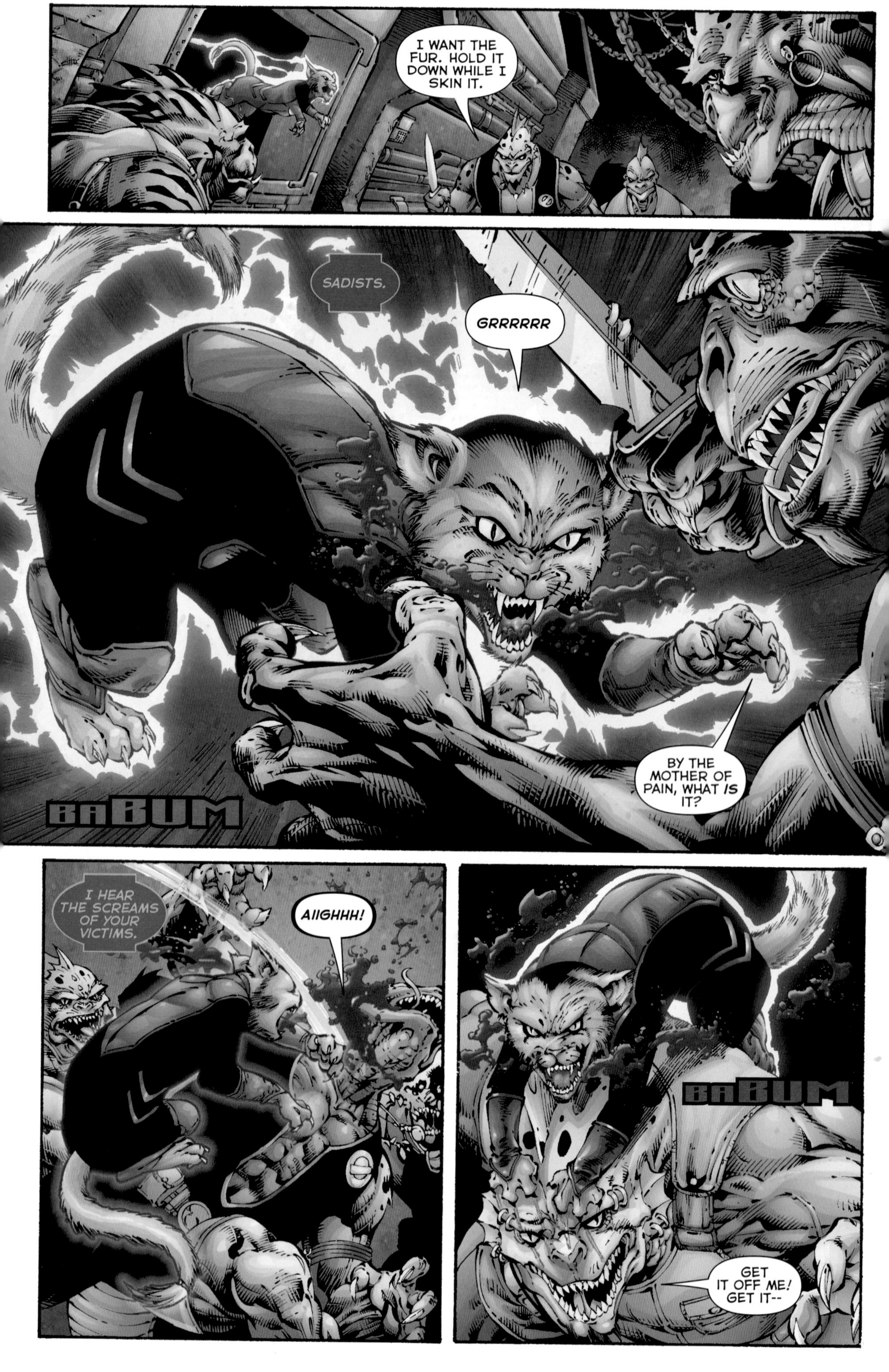
I WANT THE FUR. HOLD IT DOWN WHILE I SKIN IT.
SADISTS.
GRRRRRR
BY THE MOTHER OF PAIN, WHAT IS IT?
BABUM
I HEAR THE SCREAMS OF YOUR VICTIMS.
AIIGHHH!
BABUM
GET IT OFF ME! GET IT--

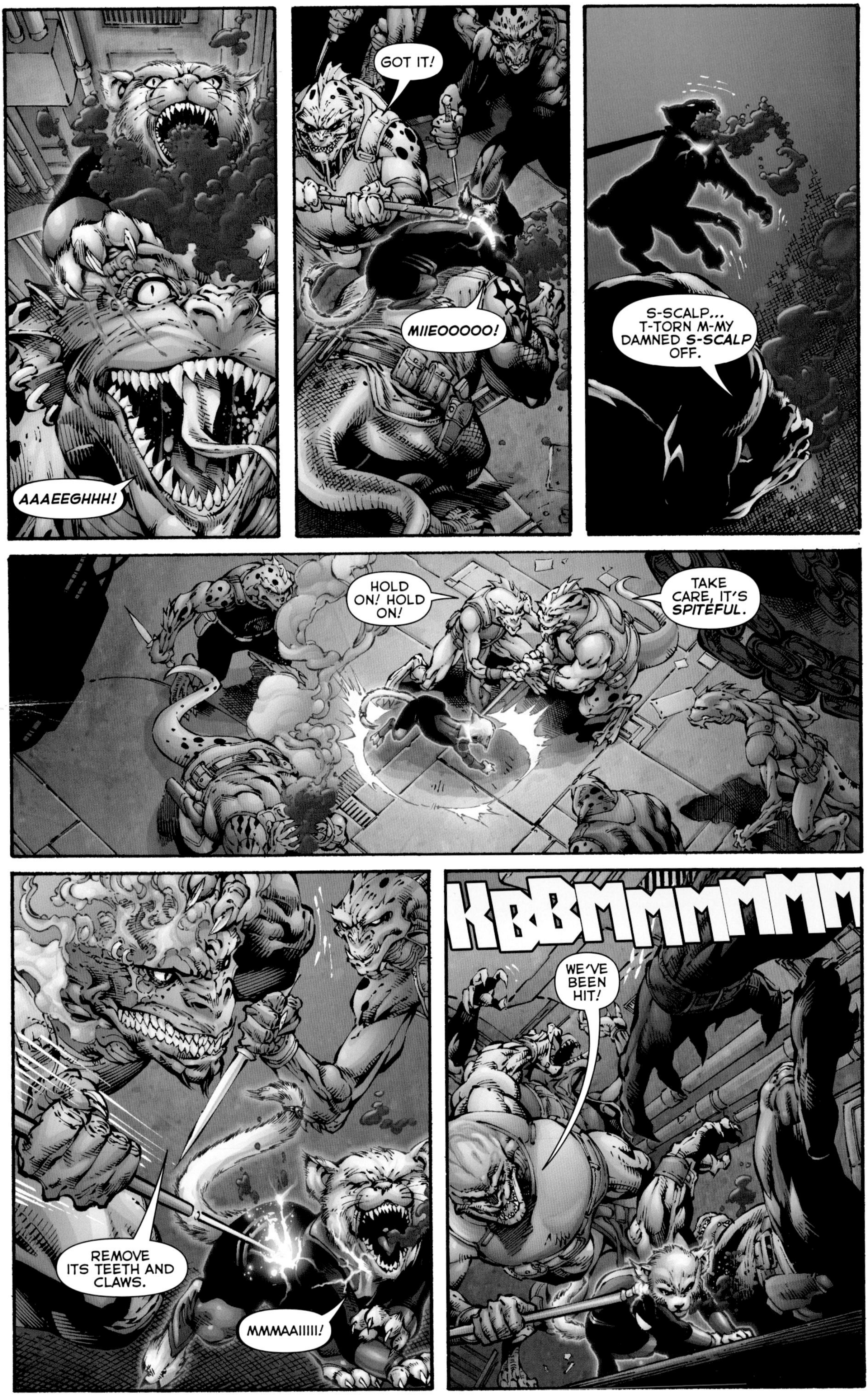
AAAEEGHHH!
GOT IT!
MIIEOOOOO!
S-SCALP... T-TORN M-MY DAMNED S-SCALP OFF.
HOLD ON! HOLD ON!
TAKE CARE, IT'S SPITEFUL.
REMOVE ITS TEETH AND CLAWS.
MMMAAIIIII!
KBBMMMMMMM
WE'VE BEEN HIT!

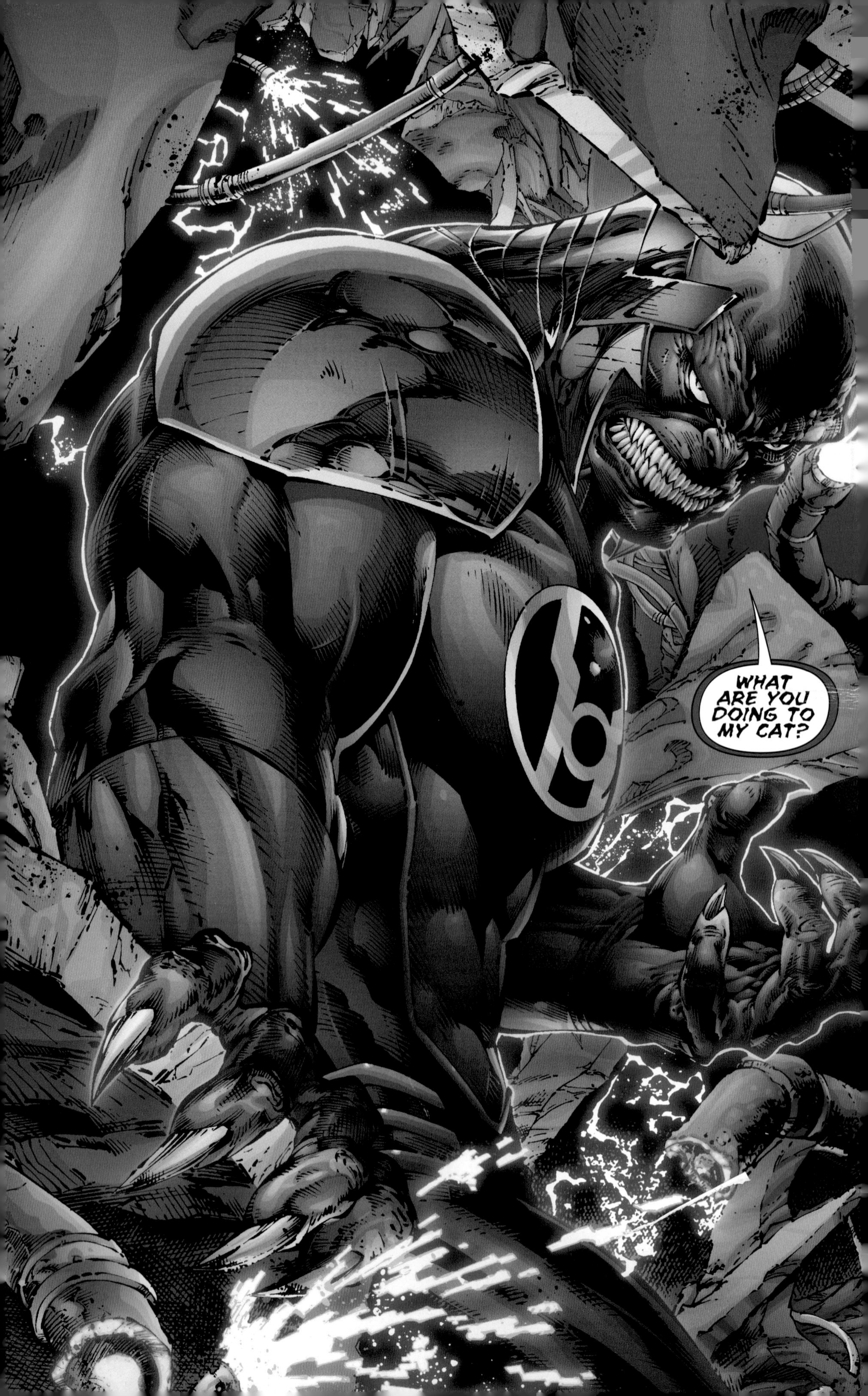
WHAT ARE YOU DOING TO MY CAT?

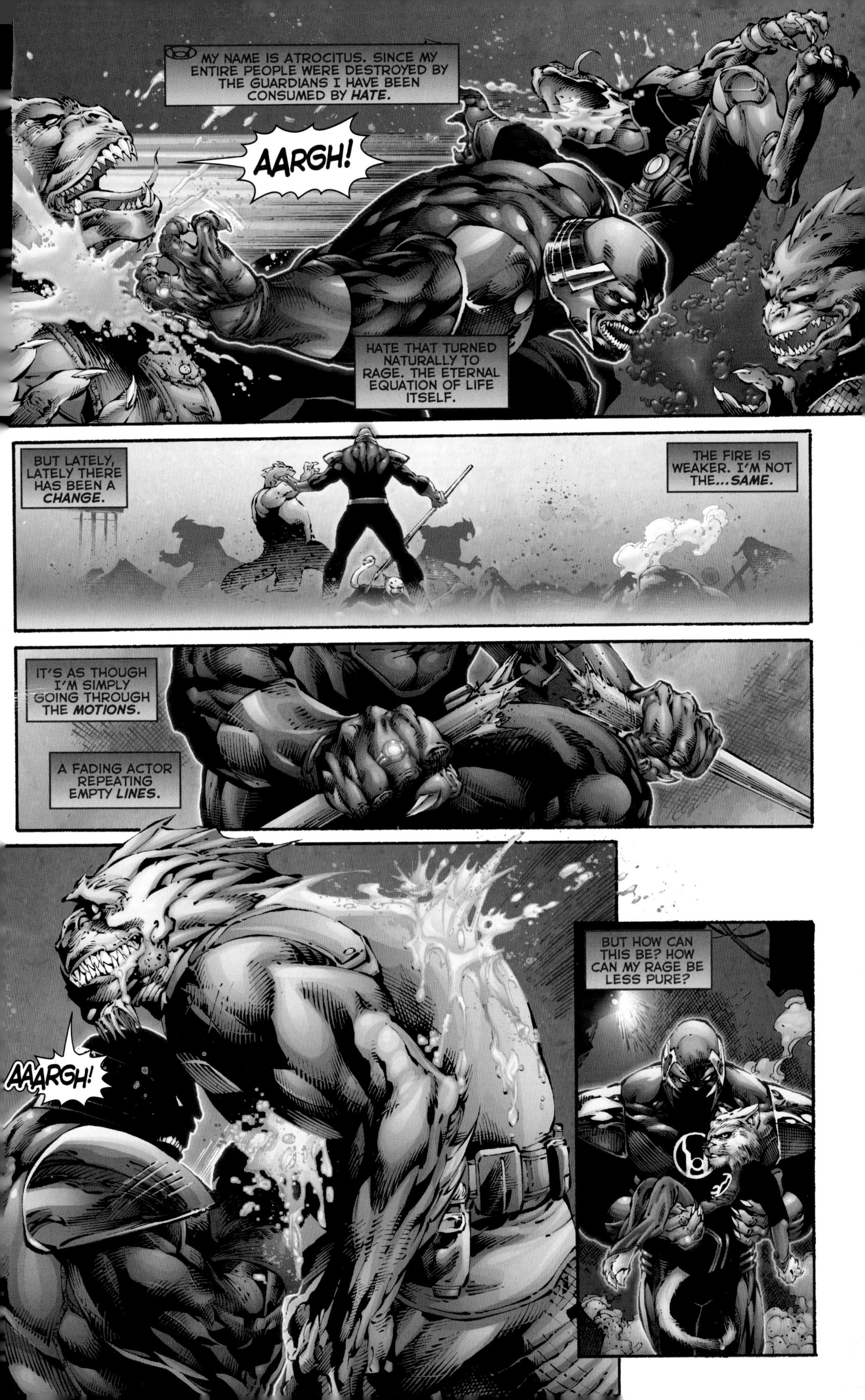
MY NAME IS ATROCITUS. SINCE MY ENTIRE PEOPLE WERE DESTROYED BY THE GUARDIANS I HAVE BEEN CONSUMED BY HATE.
AARGH!
HATE THAT TURNED NATURALLY TO RAGE. THE ETERNAL EQUATION OF LIFE ITSELF.
BUT LATELY, LATELY THERE HAS BEEN A CHANGE.
THE FIRE IS WEAKER. I'M NOT THE...SAME.
IT'S AS THOUGH I'M SIMPLY GOING THROUGH THE MOTIONS.
A FADING ACTOR REPEATING EMPTY LINES.
AAARGH!
BUT HOW CAN THIS BE? HOW CAN MY RAGE BE LESS PURE?

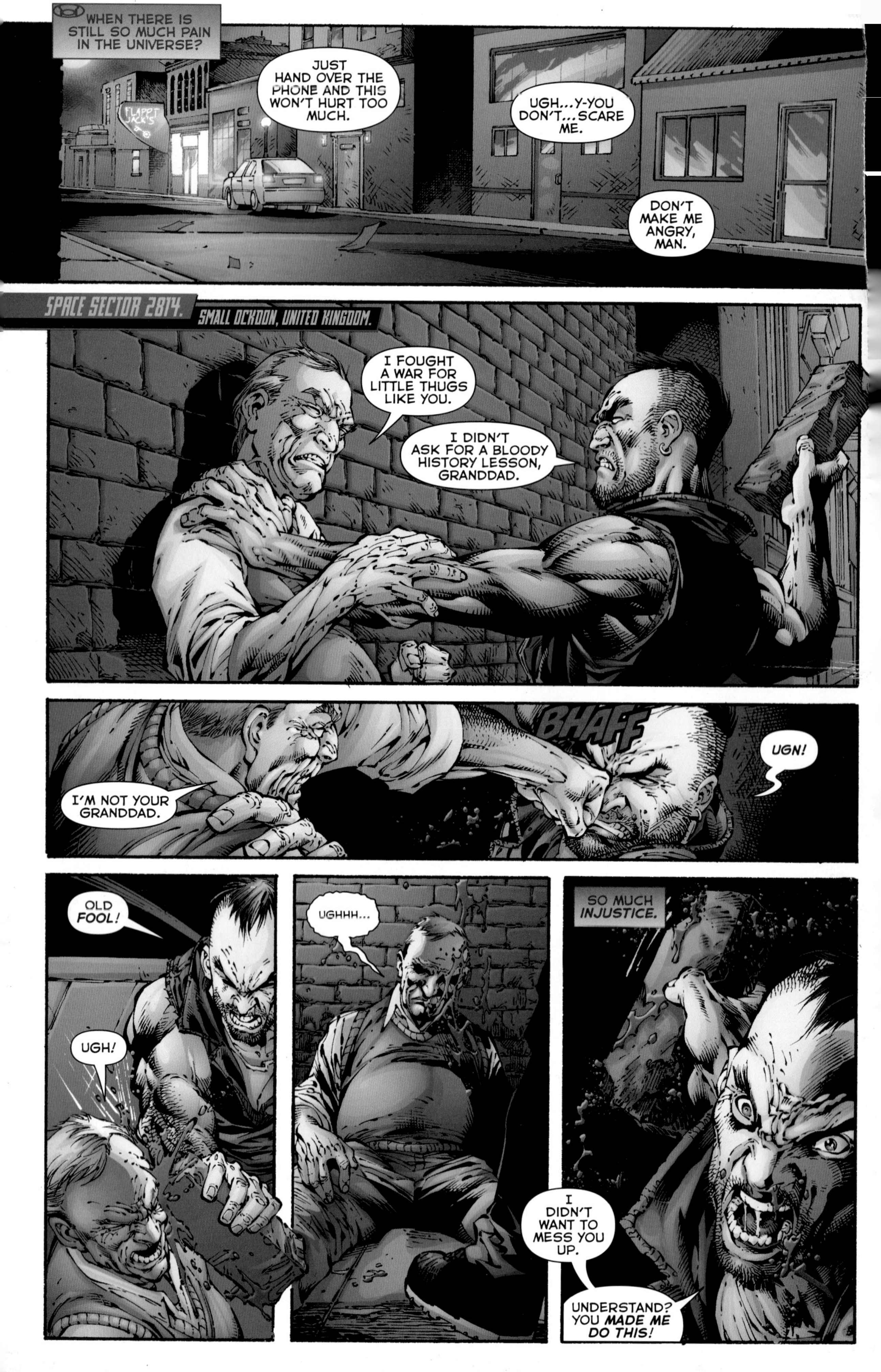
WHEN THERE IS STILL SO MUCH PAIN IN THE UNIVERSE?
FLAPPY JACK'S
JUST HAND OVER THE PHONE AND THIS WON'T HURT TOO MUCH.
UGH...Y-YOU DON'T...SCARE ME.
DON'T MAKE ME ANGRY, MAN.
SPACE SECTOR 2814.
SMALL OCKDON, UNITED KINGDOM.
I FOUGHT A WAR FOR LITTLE THUGS LIKE YOU.
I DIDN'T ASK FOR A BLOODY HISTORY LESSON, GRANDDAD.
BHAFF
UGN!
I'M NOT YOUR GRANDDAD.
OLD FOOL!
UGH!
UGHHH...
SO MUCH INJUSTICE.
I DIDN'T WANT TO MESS YOU UP.
UNDERSTAND? YOU MADE ME DO THIS!

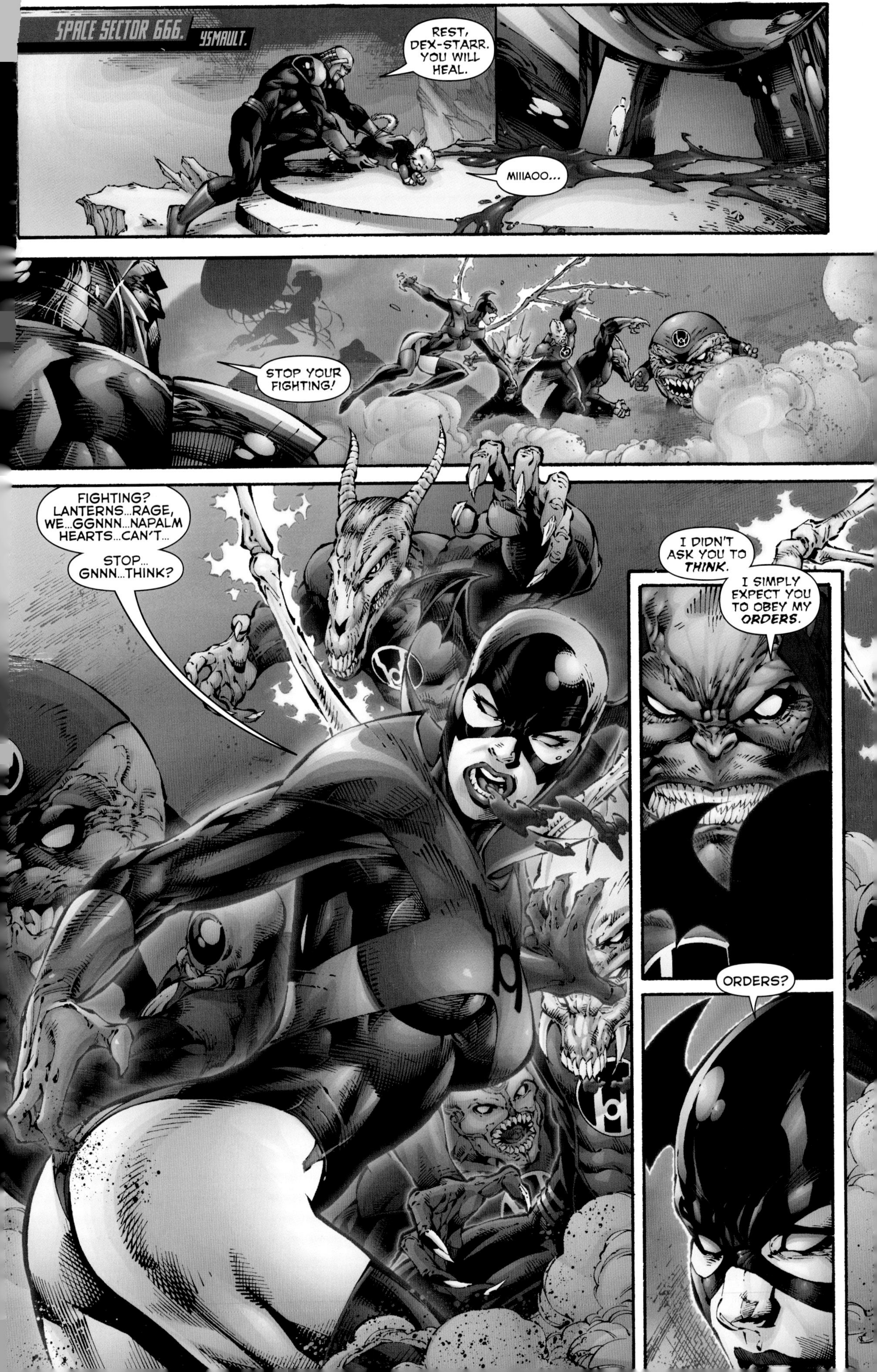
SPACE SECTOR 666. YSMAULT.
REST, DEX-STARR. YOU WILL HEAL.
MIIIAOO...
STOP YOUR FIGHTING!
FIGHTING? LANTERNS...RAGE, WE...GGNNN...NAPALM HEARTS...CAN'T...
STOP... GNNN...THINK?
I DIDN'T ASK YOU TO THINK.
I SIMPLY EXPECT YOU TO OBEY MY ORDERS.
ORDERS?

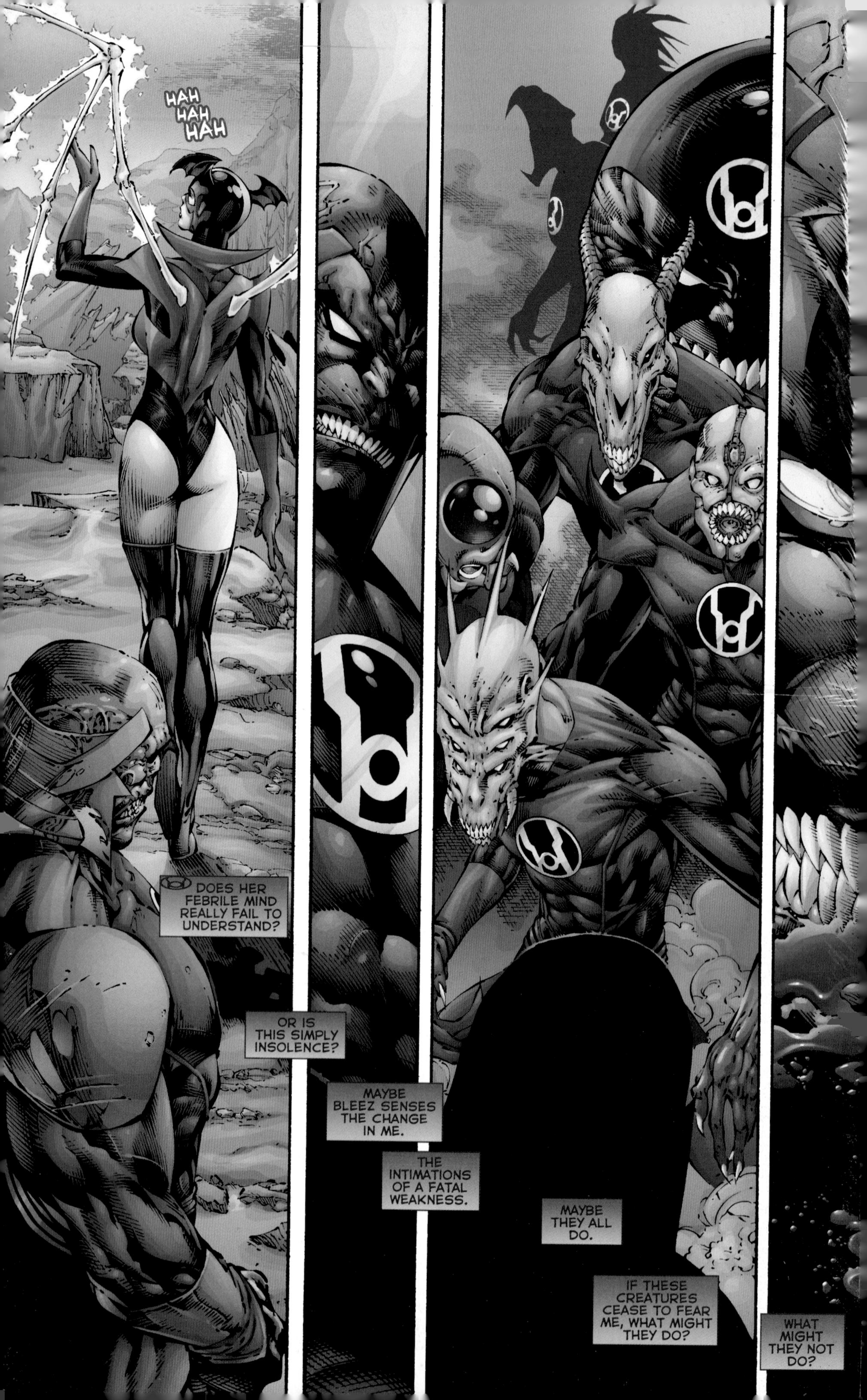

HAH HAH HAH
DOES HER FEBRILE MIND REALLY FAIL TO UNDERSTAND?
OR IS THIS SIMPLY INSOLENCE?
MAYBE BLEEZ SENSES THE CHANGE IN ME.
THE INTIMATIONS OF A FATAL WEAKNESS.
MAYBE THEY ALL DO.
IF THESE CREATURES CEASE TO FEAR ME, WHAT MIGHT THEY DO?
WHAT MIGHT THEY NOT DO?

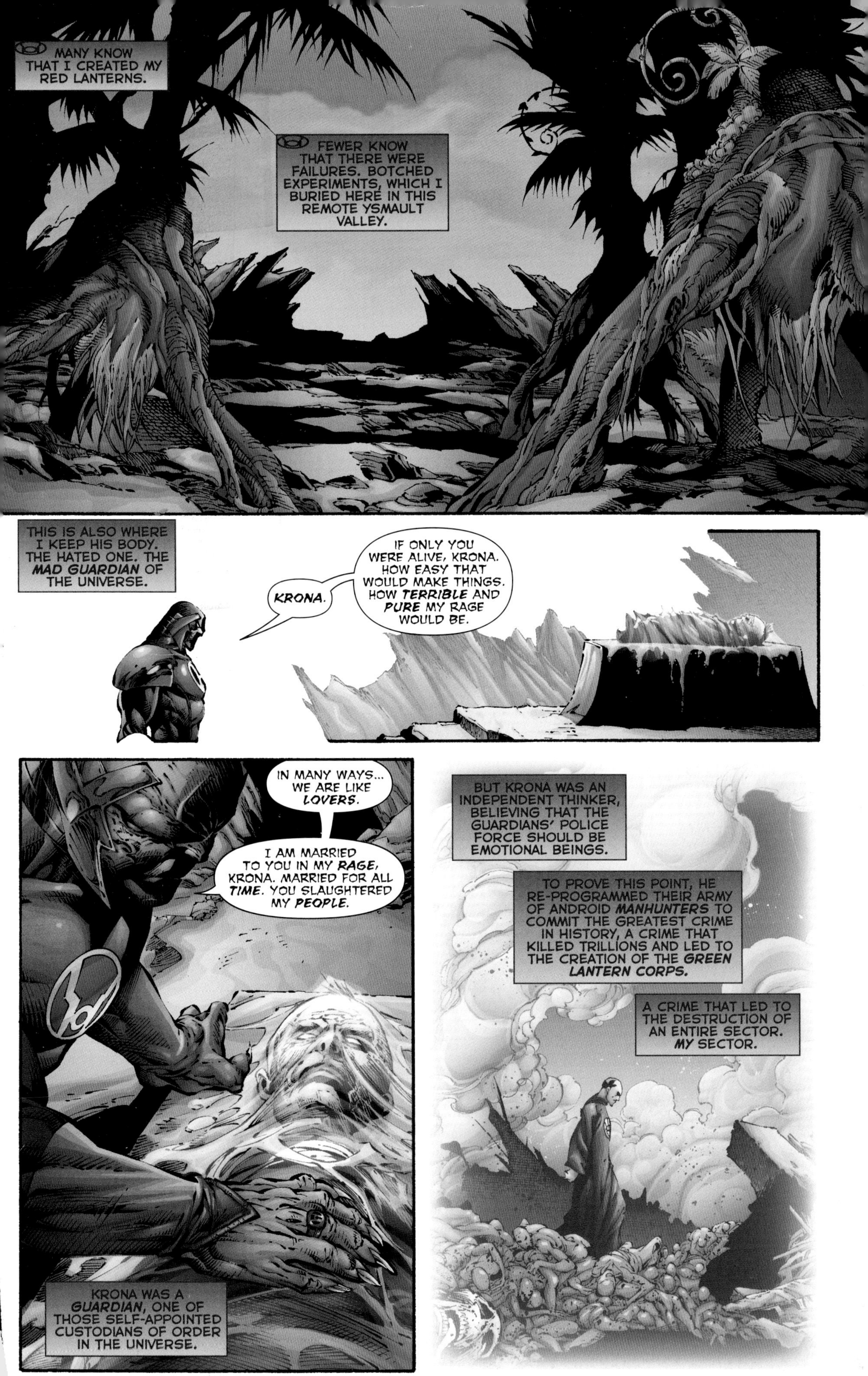
MANY KNOW THAT I CREATED MY RED LANTERNS.
FEWER KNOW THAT THERE WERE FAILURES. BOTCHED EXPERIMENTS, WHICH I BURIED HERE IN THIS REMOTE YSMAULT VALLEY.
THIS IS ALSO WHERE I KEEP HIS BODY. THE HATED ONE. THE MAD GUARDIAN OF THE UNIVERSE.
KRONA.
IF ONLY YOU WERE ALIVE, KRONA. HOW EASY THAT WOULD MAKE THINGS. HOW TERRIBLE AND PURE MY RAGE WOULD BE.
IN MANY WAYS... WE ARE LIKE LOVERS.
I AM MARRIED TO YOU IN MY RAGE, KRONA. MARRIED FOR ALL TIME. YOU SLAUGHTERED MY PEOPLE.
KRONA WAS A GUARDIAN, ONE OF THOSE SELF-APPOINTED CUSTODIANS OF ORDER IN THE UNIVERSE.
BUT KRONA WAS AN INDEPENDENT THINKER, BELIEVING THAT THE GUARDIANS' POLICE FORCE SHOULD BE EMOTIONAL BEINGS.
TO PROVE THIS POINT, HE RE-PROGRAMMED THEIR ARMY OF ANDROID MANHUNTERS TO COMMIT THE GREATEST CRIME IN HISTORY, A CRIME THAT KILLED TRILLIONS AND LED TO THE CREATION OF THE GREEN LANTERN CORPS.
A CRIME THAT LED TO THE DESTRUCTION OF AN ENTIRE SECTOR. MY SECTOR.

AND LIKE A LOVER, I AM JEALOUS. YOU WERE MEANT TO BE MINE. BUT ANOTHER TOOK YOU.

...THE GREEN LANTERN NAMED HAL JORDAN. HE STOLE YOU FROM ME!

MY VENGEANCE FOREVER *DENIED.*

I WOULD MAKE A BLOOD PROPHECY TO UNDERSTAND WHERE ALL THIS MIGHT END.

BUT SINCE MY FEELINGS OF MALAISE I HAVE BEEN UNWILLING. HOW IRONIC, A MAN SCARRED BY THE PAST.

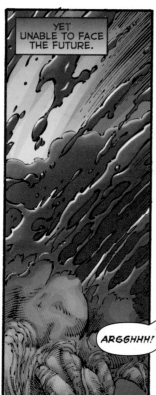

YET UNABLE TO FACE THE FUTURE.

ARGGHHH!

A NEARBY FEVER POD EXPLODES.

THE PAIN. UNBEARABLE. IT'S HAPPENING.

BURNING.

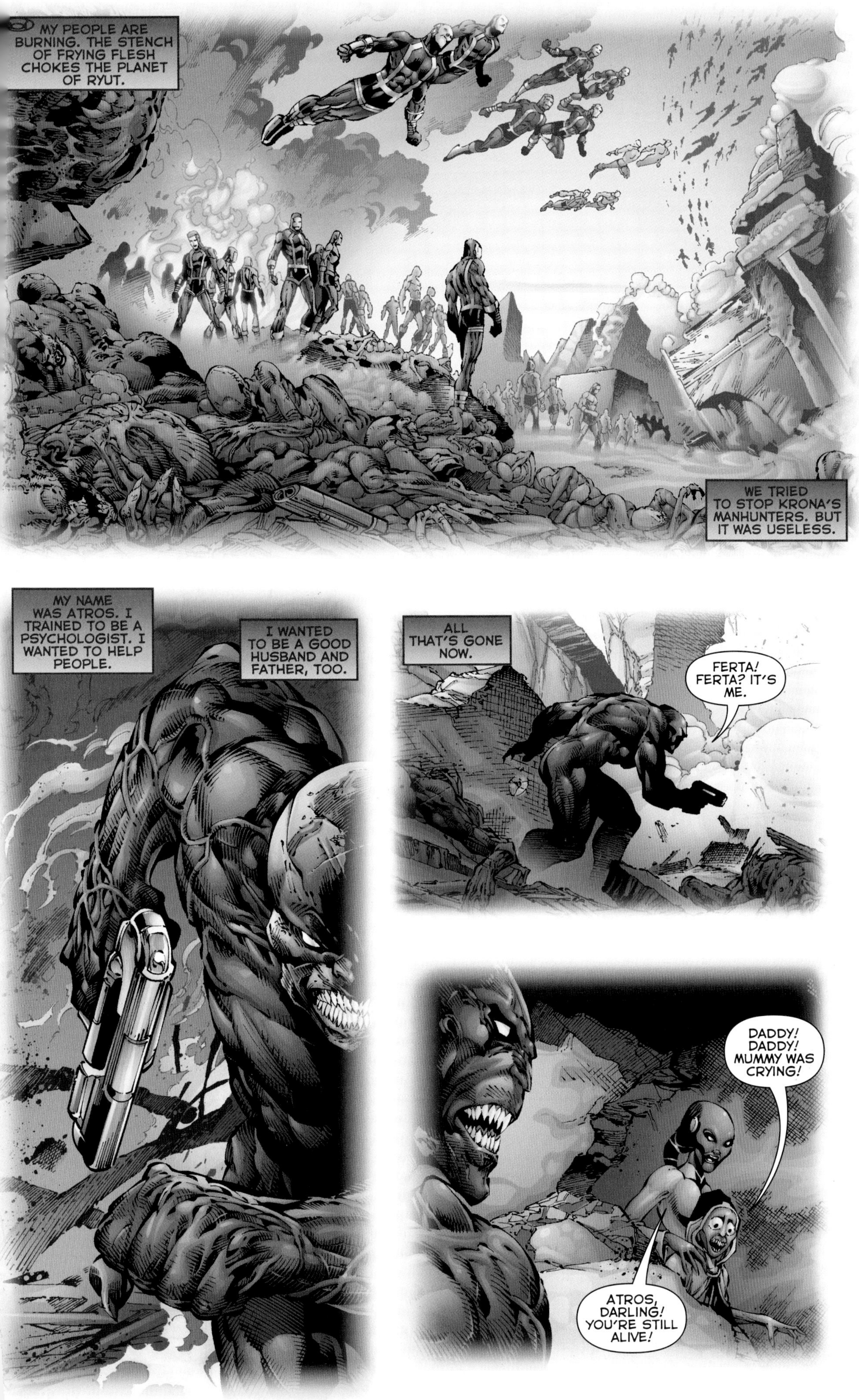
MY PEOPLE ARE BURNING. THE STENCH OF FRYING FLESH CHOKES THE PLANET OF RYUT.
WE TRIED TO STOP KRONA'S MANHUNTERS. BUT IT WAS USELESS.
MY NAME WAS ATROS. I TRAINED TO BE A PSYCHOLOGIST. I WANTED TO HELP PEOPLE.
I WANTED TO BE A GOOD HUSBAND AND FATHER, TOO.
ALL THAT'S GONE NOW.
FERTA! FERTA? IT'S ME.
DADDY! DADDY! MUMMY WAS CRYING!
ATROS, DARLING! YOU'RE STILL ALIVE!

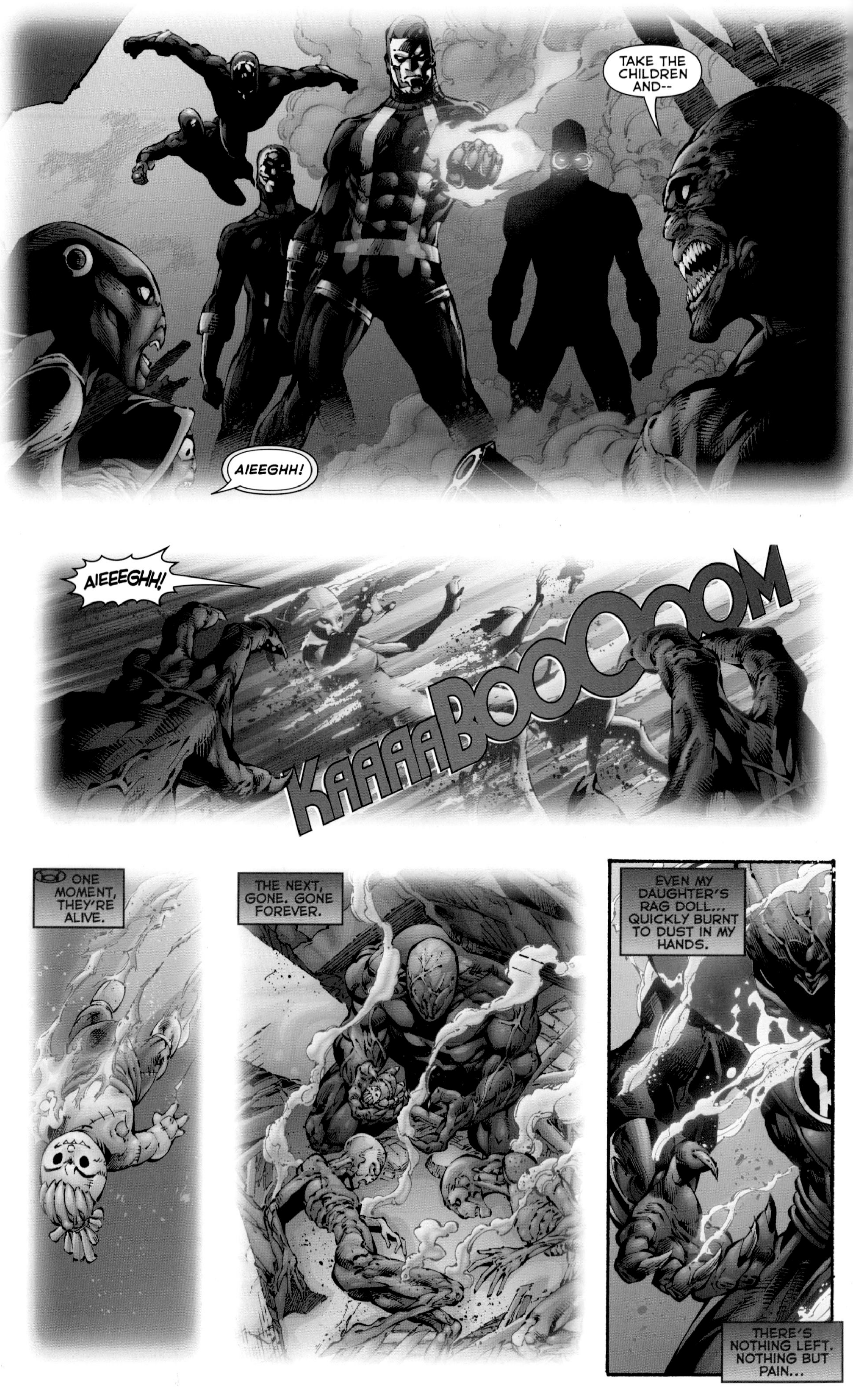

TAKE THE CHILDREN AND--
AIEEGHH!
AIEEEGHH!
KAAAABOOOOOOM
ONE MOMENT, THEY'RE ALIVE.
THE NEXT, GONE. GONE FOREVER.
EVEN MY DAUGHTER'S RAG DOLL... QUICKLY BURNT TO DUST IN MY HANDS.
THERE'S NOTHING LEFT. NOTHING BUT PAIN...

NOTHING BUT ANGER.

GRANDDAD...

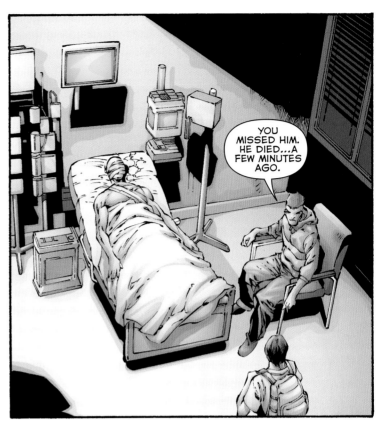

YOU MISSED HIM. HE DIED...A FEW MINUTES AGO.

HE WAS AN OLD MAN. WHO COULD DO SOMETHING LIKE THIS?

THE WORLD'S *FULL* OF PEOPLE WHO COULD DO STUFF LIKE THIS, BRO. MAYBE THAT'S SOMETHING THEY DON'T TEACH YOU AT UNIVERSITY.

RAY, NOW'S NOT THE TIME.

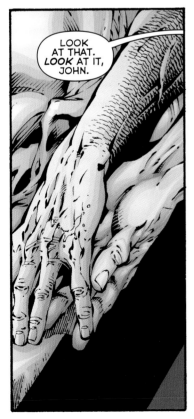

LOOK AT THAT. *LOOK* AT IT, JOHN.

WH-WHAT AM I LOOKING AT?

SCRAPES. ON HIS KNUCKLES. GRANDDAD PUT UP A *FIGHT*.

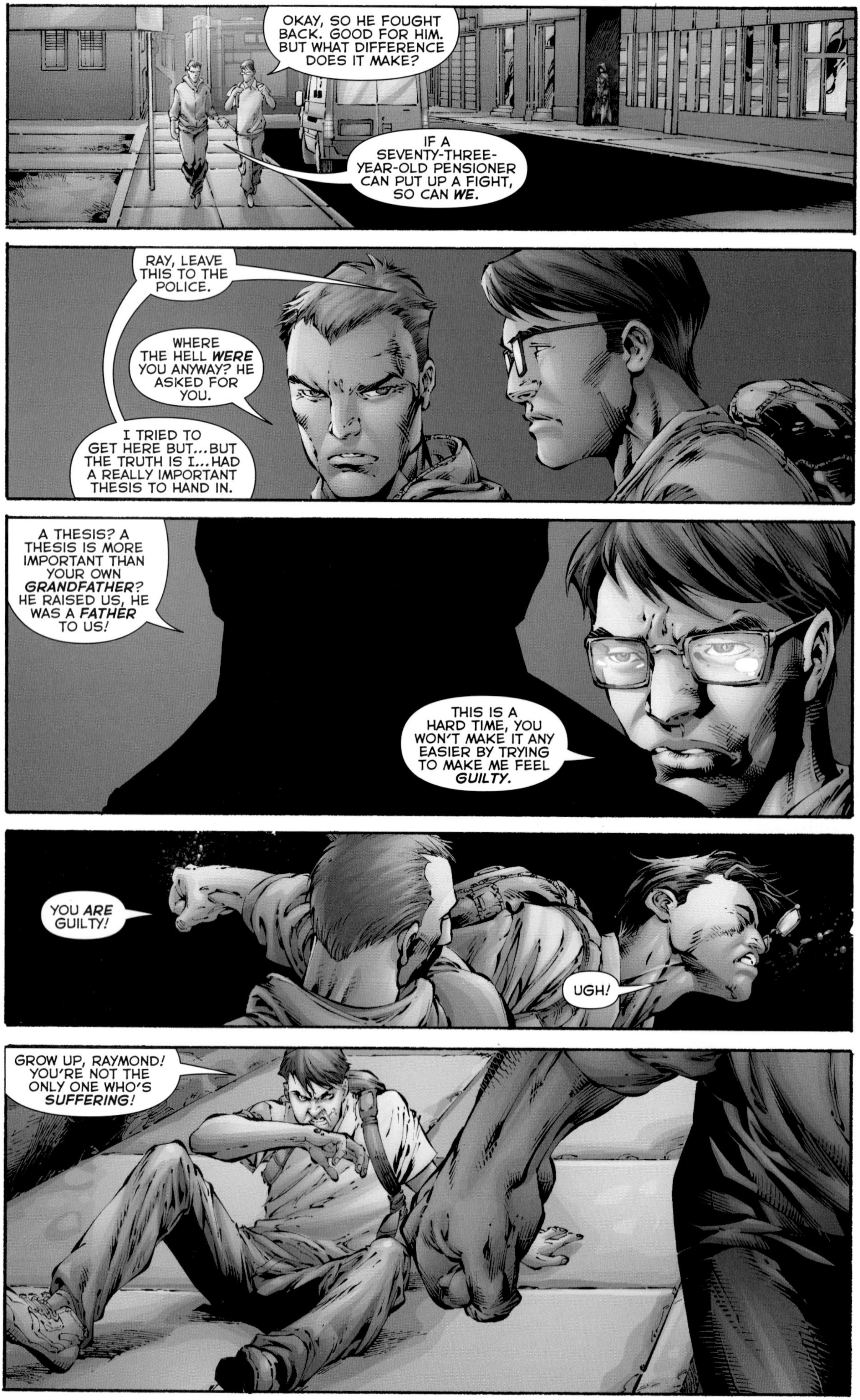

OKAY, SO HE FOUGHT BACK. GOOD FOR HIM. BUT WHAT DIFFERENCE DOES IT MAKE?
IF A SEVENTY-THREE-YEAR-OLD PENSIONER CAN PUT UP A FIGHT, SO CAN WE.
RAY, LEAVE THIS TO THE POLICE.
WHERE THE HELL WERE YOU ANYWAY? HE ASKED FOR YOU.
I TRIED TO GET HERE BUT...BUT THE TRUTH IS I...HAD A REALLY IMPORTANT THESIS TO HAND IN.
A THESIS? A THESIS IS MORE IMPORTANT THAN YOUR OWN GRANDFATHER? HE RAISED US, HE WAS A FATHER TO US!
THIS IS A HARD TIME, YOU WON'T MAKE IT ANY EASIER BY TRYING TO MAKE ME FEEL GUILTY.
YOU ARE GUILTY!
UGH!
GROW UP, RAYMOND! YOU'RE NOT THE ONLY ONE WHO'S SUFFERING!

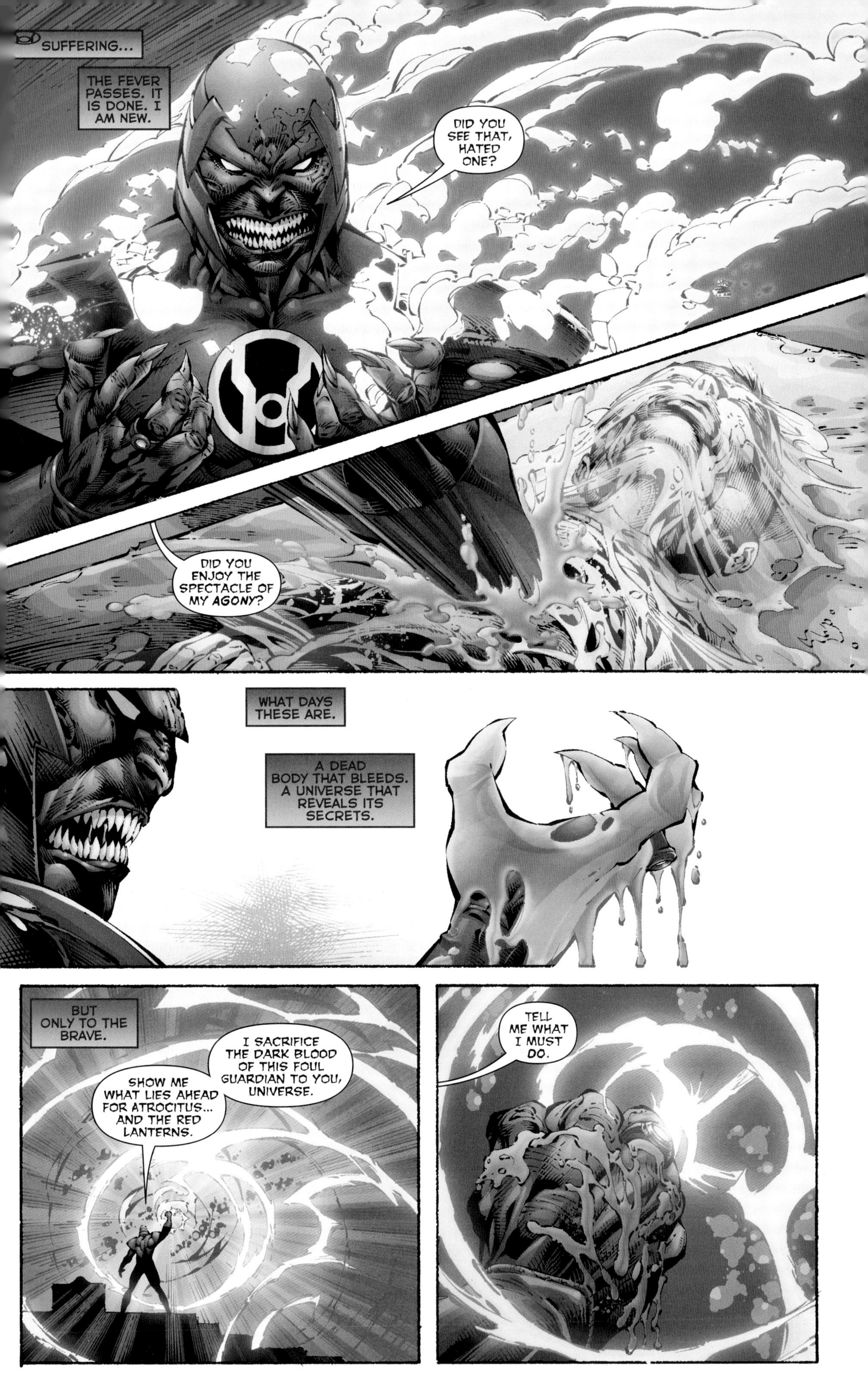
SUFFERING...
THE FEVER PASSES. IT IS DONE. I AM NEW.
DID YOU SEE THAT, HATED ONE?
DID YOU ENJOY THE SPECTACLE OF MY AGONY?
WHAT DAYS THESE ARE.
A DEAD BODY THAT BLEEDS. A UNIVERSE THAT REVEALS ITS SECRETS.
BUT ONLY TO THE BRAVE.
I SACRIFICE THE DARK BLOOD OF THIS FOUL GUARDIAN TO YOU, UNIVERSE.
SHOW ME WHAT LIES AHEAD FOR ATROCITUS... AND THE RED LANTERNS.
TELL ME WHAT I MUST DO.

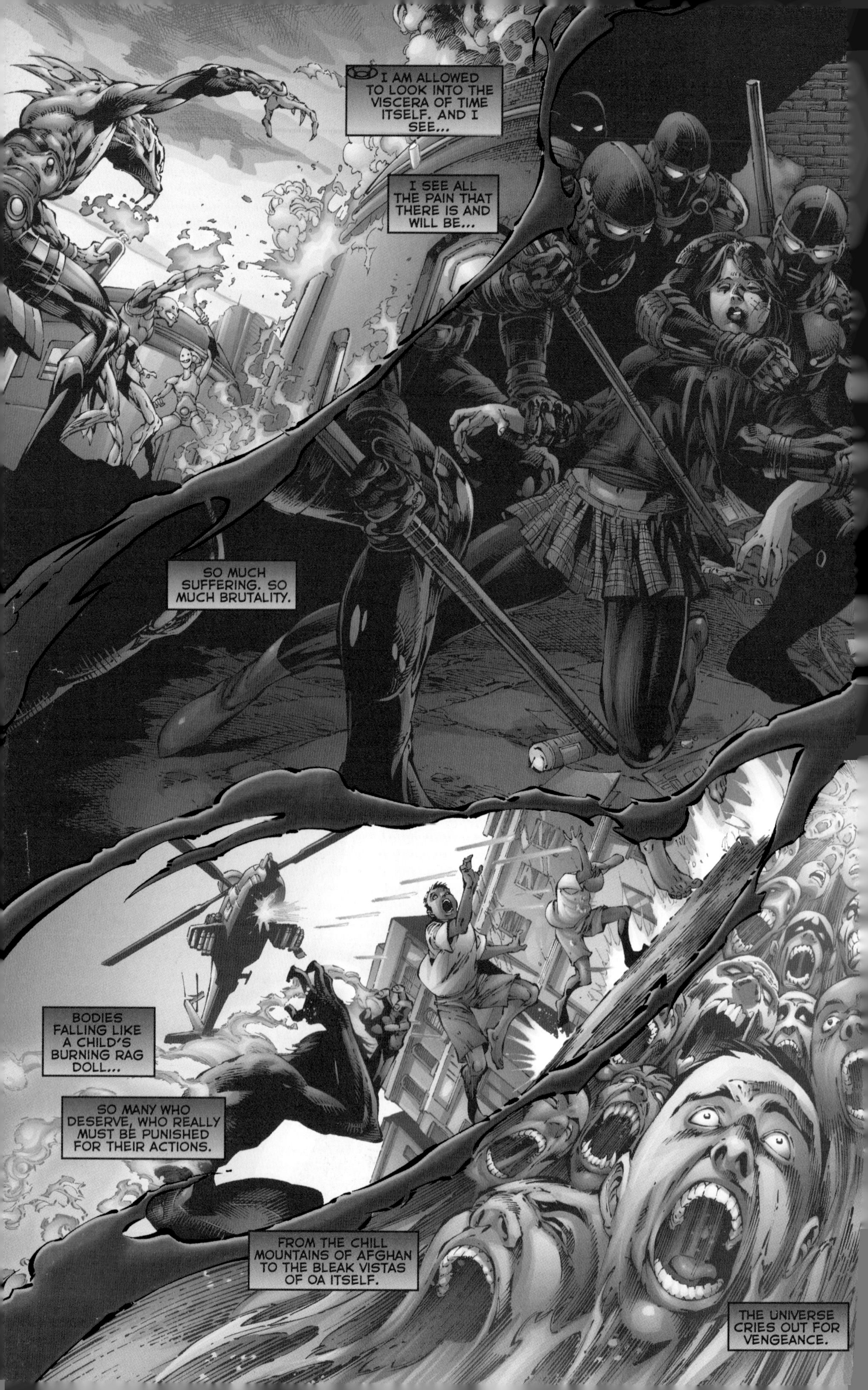
I AM ALLOWED TO LOOK INTO THE VISCERA OF TIME ITSELF. AND I SEE...
I SEE ALL THE PAIN THAT THERE IS AND WILL BE...
SO MUCH SUFFERING. SO MUCH BRUTALITY.
BODIES FALLING LIKE A CHILD'S BURNING RAG DOLL...
SO MANY WHO DESERVE, WHO REALLY MUST BE PUNISHED FOR THEIR ACTIONS.
FROM THE CHILL MOUNTAINS OF AFGHAN TO THE BLEAK VISTAS OF OA ITSELF.
THE UNIVERSE CRIES OUT FOR VENGEANCE.

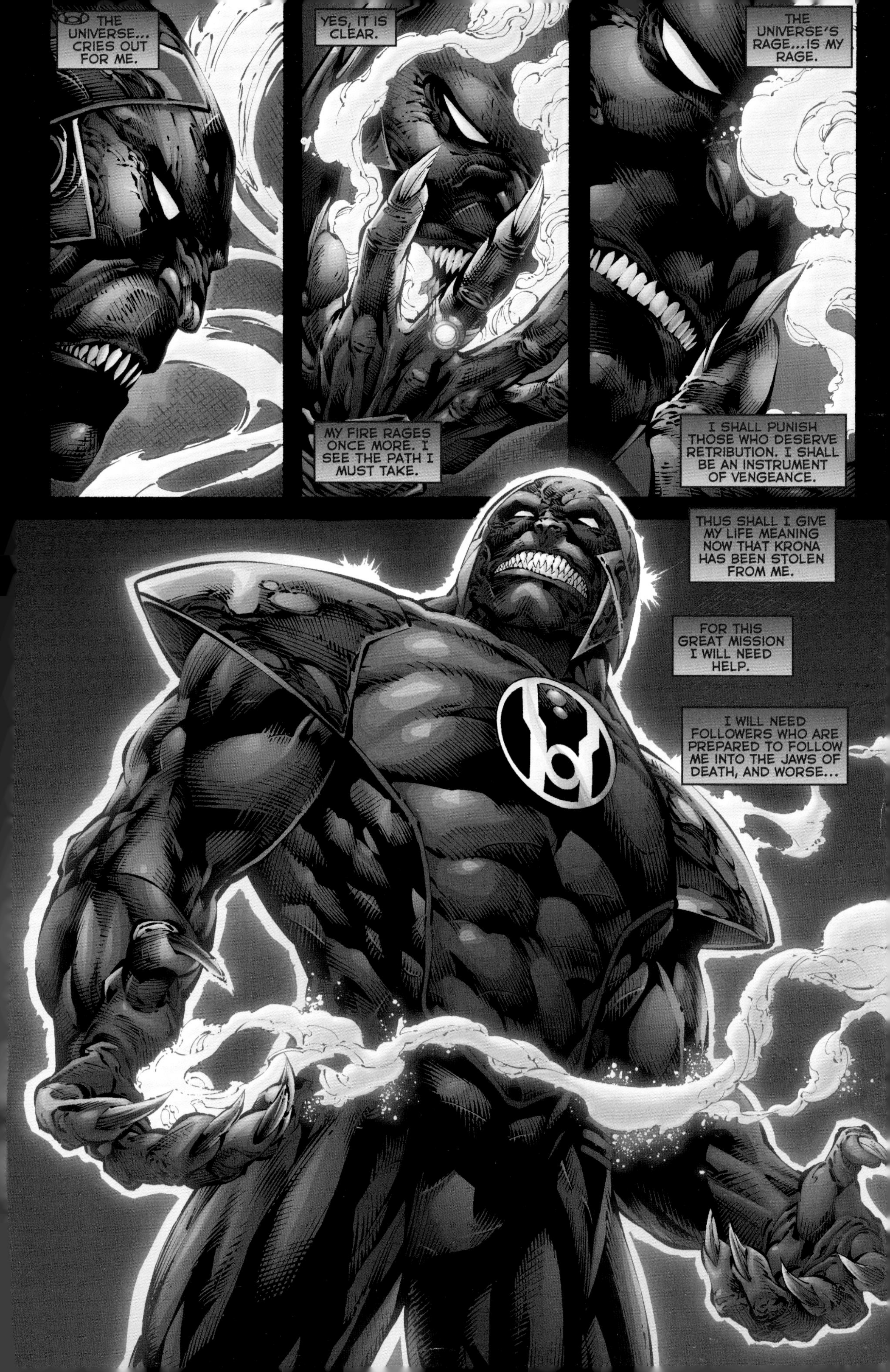
THE UNIVERSE... CRIES OUT FOR ME.
YES, IT IS CLEAR.
MY FIRE RAGES ONCE MORE. I SEE THE PATH I MUST TAKE.
THE UNIVERSE'S RAGE...IS MY RAGE.
I SHALL PUNISH THOSE WHO DESERVE RETRIBUTION. I SHALL BE AN INSTRUMENT OF VENGEANCE.
THUS SHALL I GIVE MY LIFE MEANING NOW THAT KRONA HAS BEEN STOLEN FROM ME.
FOR THIS GREAT MISSION I WILL NEED HELP.
I WILL NEED FOLLOWERS WHO ARE PREPARED TO FOLLOW ME INTO THE JAWS OF DEATH, AND WORSE...

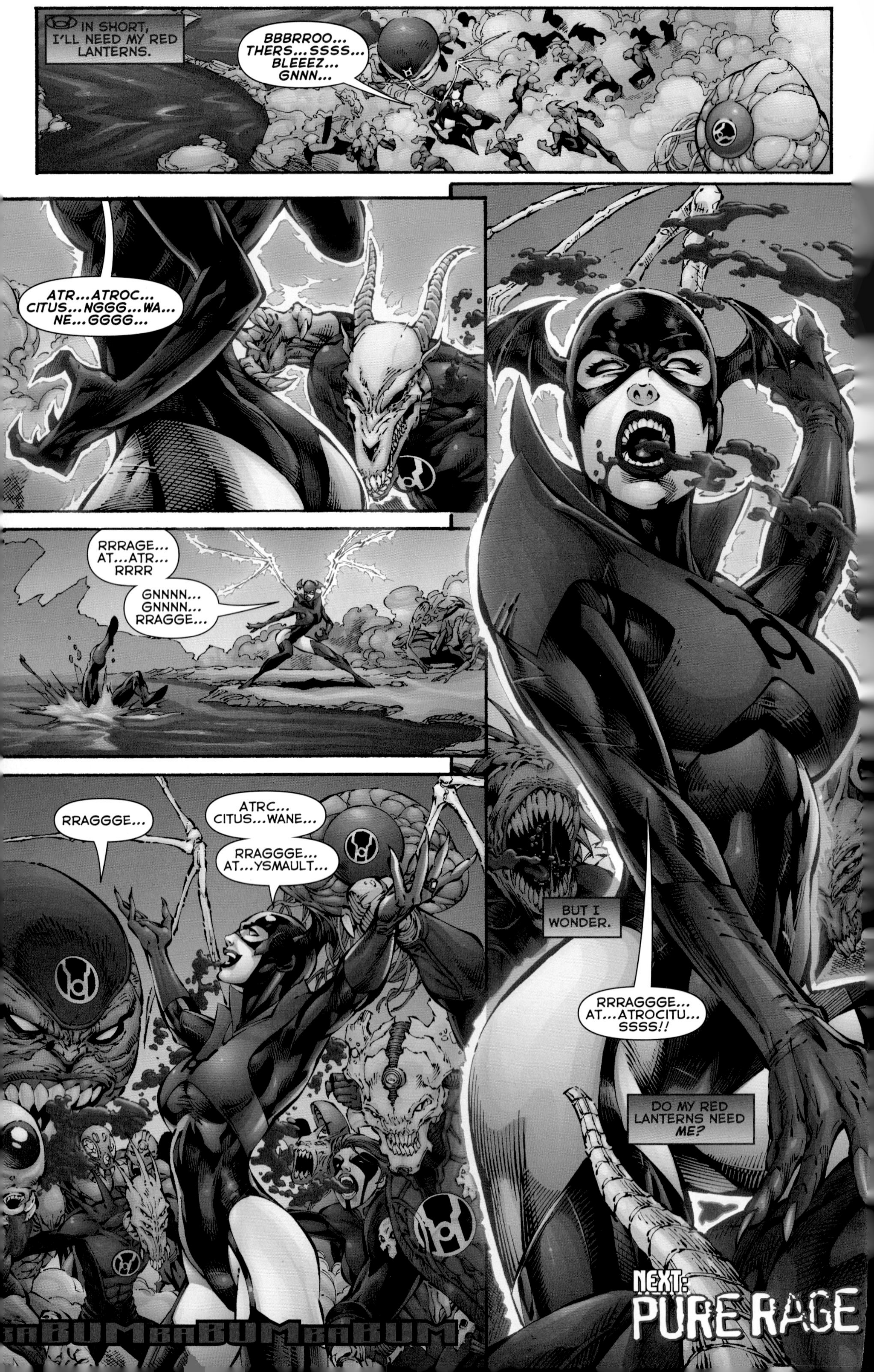
IN SHORT, I'LL NEED MY RED LANTERNS.
BBBRROO... THERS...SSSS... BLEEEZ... GNNN...
ATR...ATROC... CITUS...NGGG...WA... NE...GGGG...
RRRAGE... AT...ATR... RRRR
GNNNN... GNNNN... RRAGGE...
RRAGGGE...
ATRC... CITUS...WANE...
RRAGGGE... AT...YSMAULT...
BUT I WONDER.
RRRAGGGE... AT...ATROCITU... SSSS!!
DO MY RED LANTERNS NEED ME?
NEXT: PURE RAGE

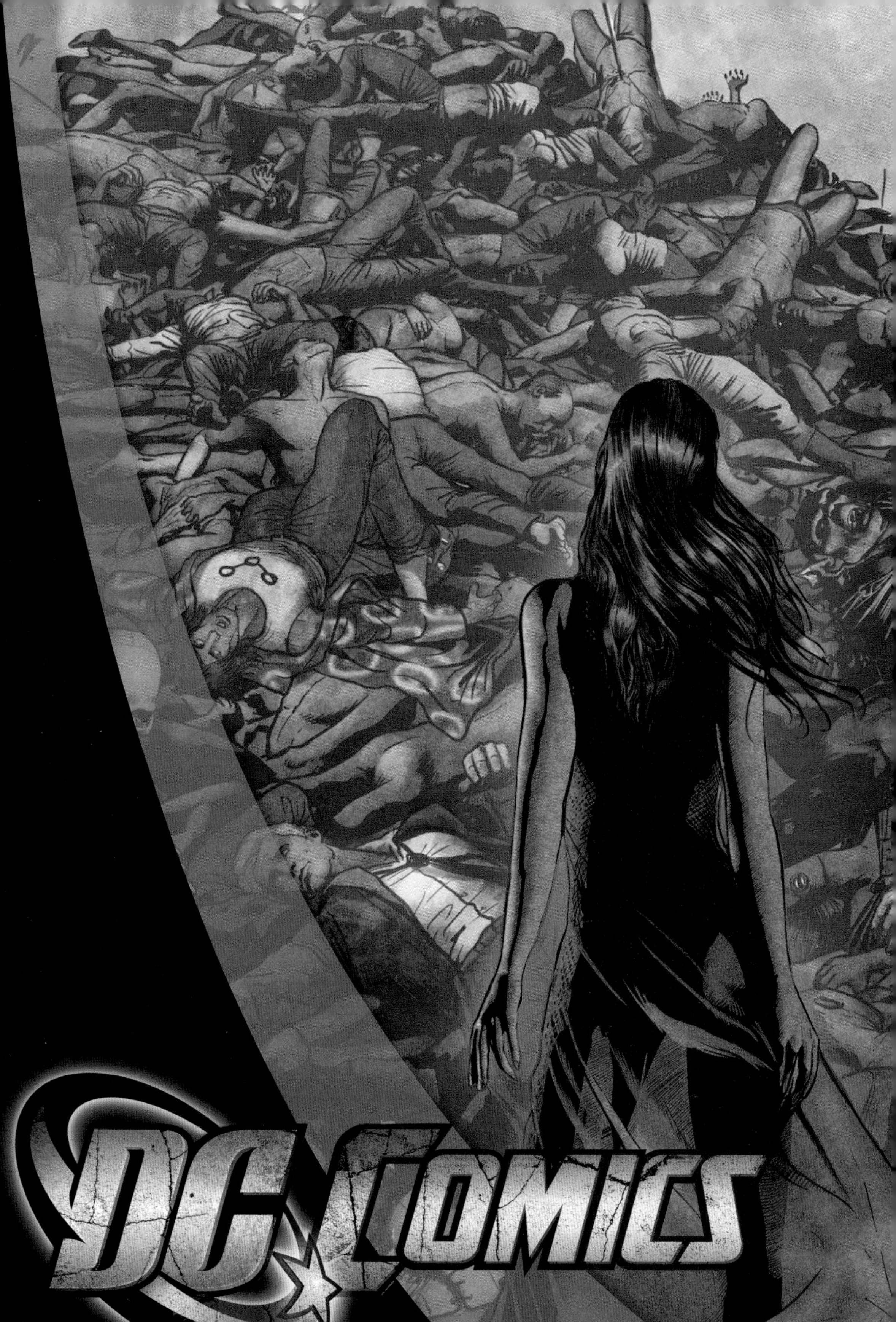

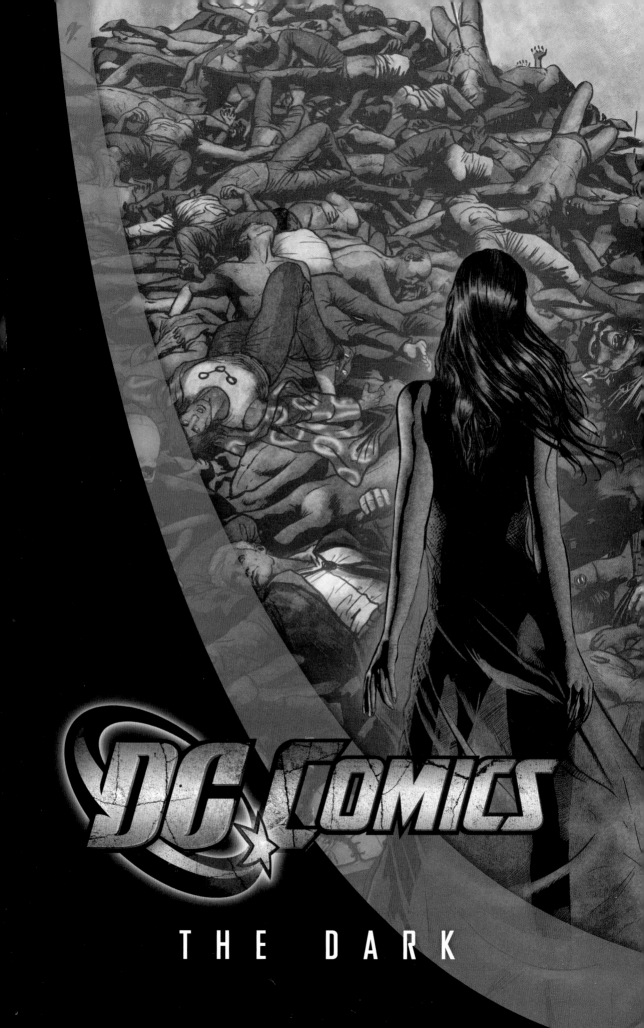

DC COMICS

THE DARK

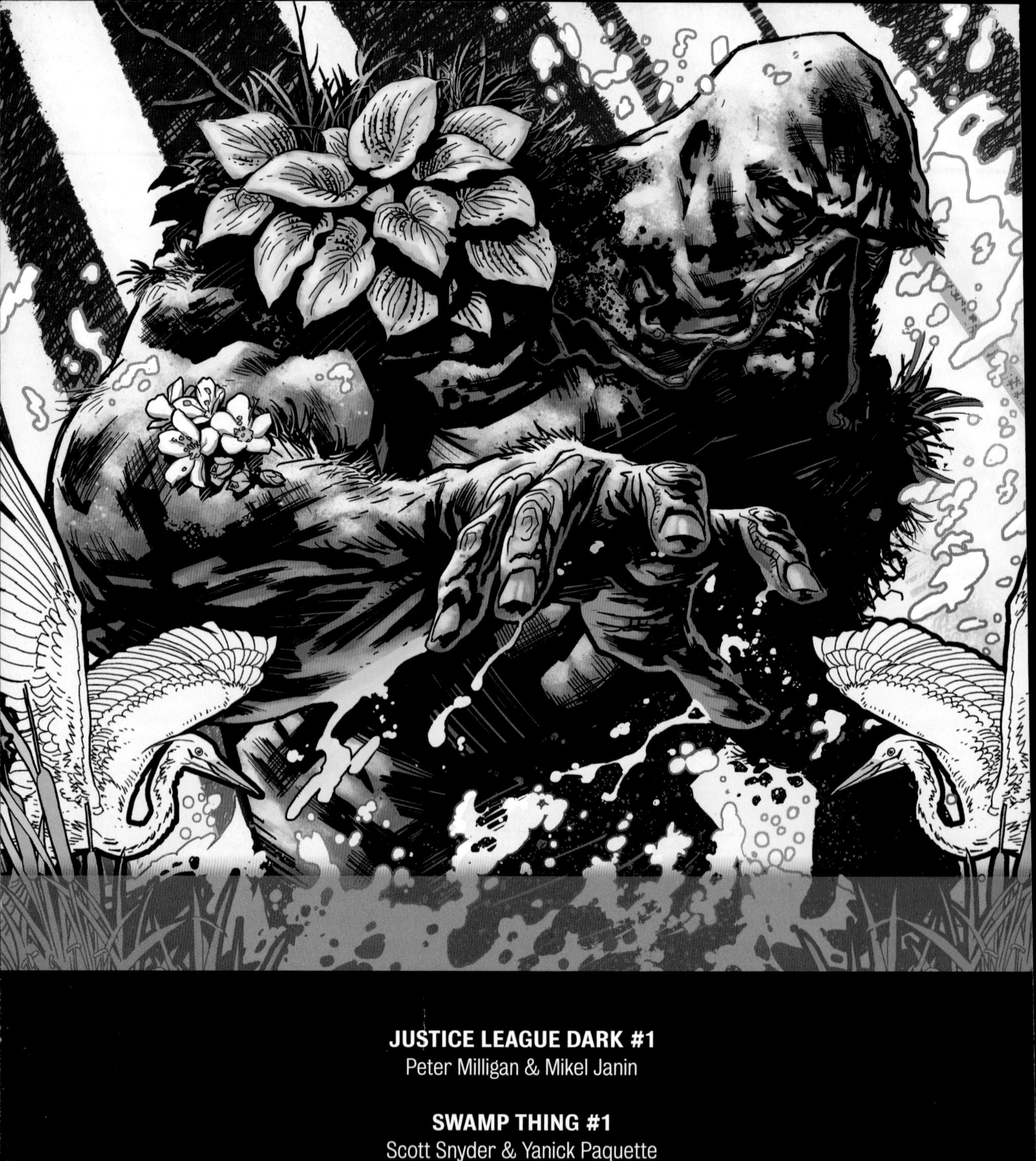

JUSTICE LEAGUE DARK #1
Peter Milligan & Mikel Janin

SWAMP THING #1
Scott Snyder & Yanick Paquette

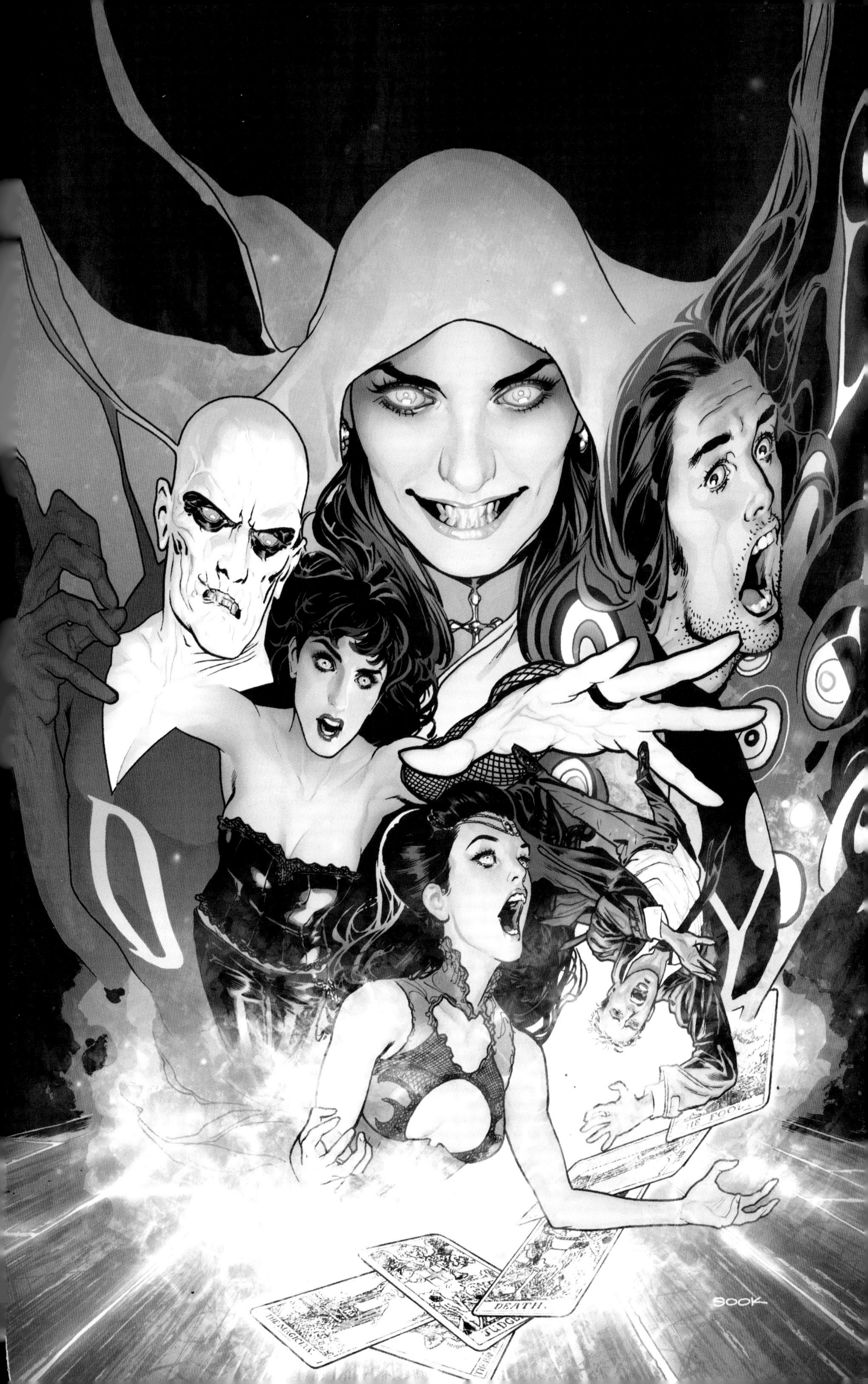
HE FOOL
DEATH.
THE MAGICIAN.
JUDGE
SOOK

JUSTICE LEAGUE DARK

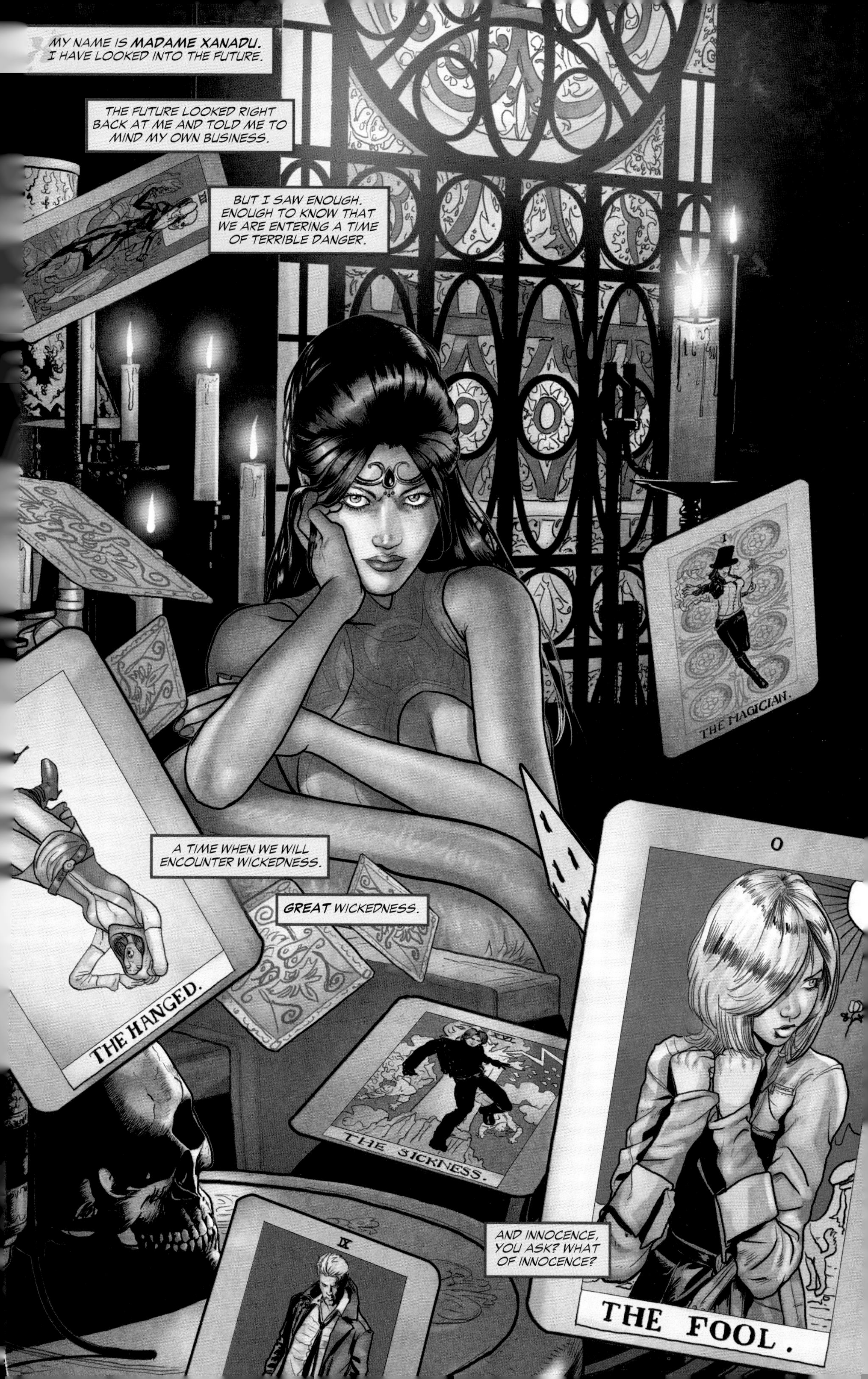

MY NAME IS MADAME XANADU. I HAVE LOOKED INTO THE FUTURE.
THE FUTURE LOOKED RIGHT BACK AT ME AND TOLD ME TO MIND MY OWN BUSINESS.
BUT I SAW ENOUGH. ENOUGH TO KNOW THAT WE ARE ENTERING A TIME OF TERRIBLE DANGER.
THE MAGICIAN.
A TIME WHEN WE WILL ENCOUNTER WICKEDNESS.
GREAT WICKEDNESS.
O
THE HANGED.
THE SICKNESS.
AND INNOCENCE, YOU ASK? WHAT OF INNOCENCE?
THE FOOL.

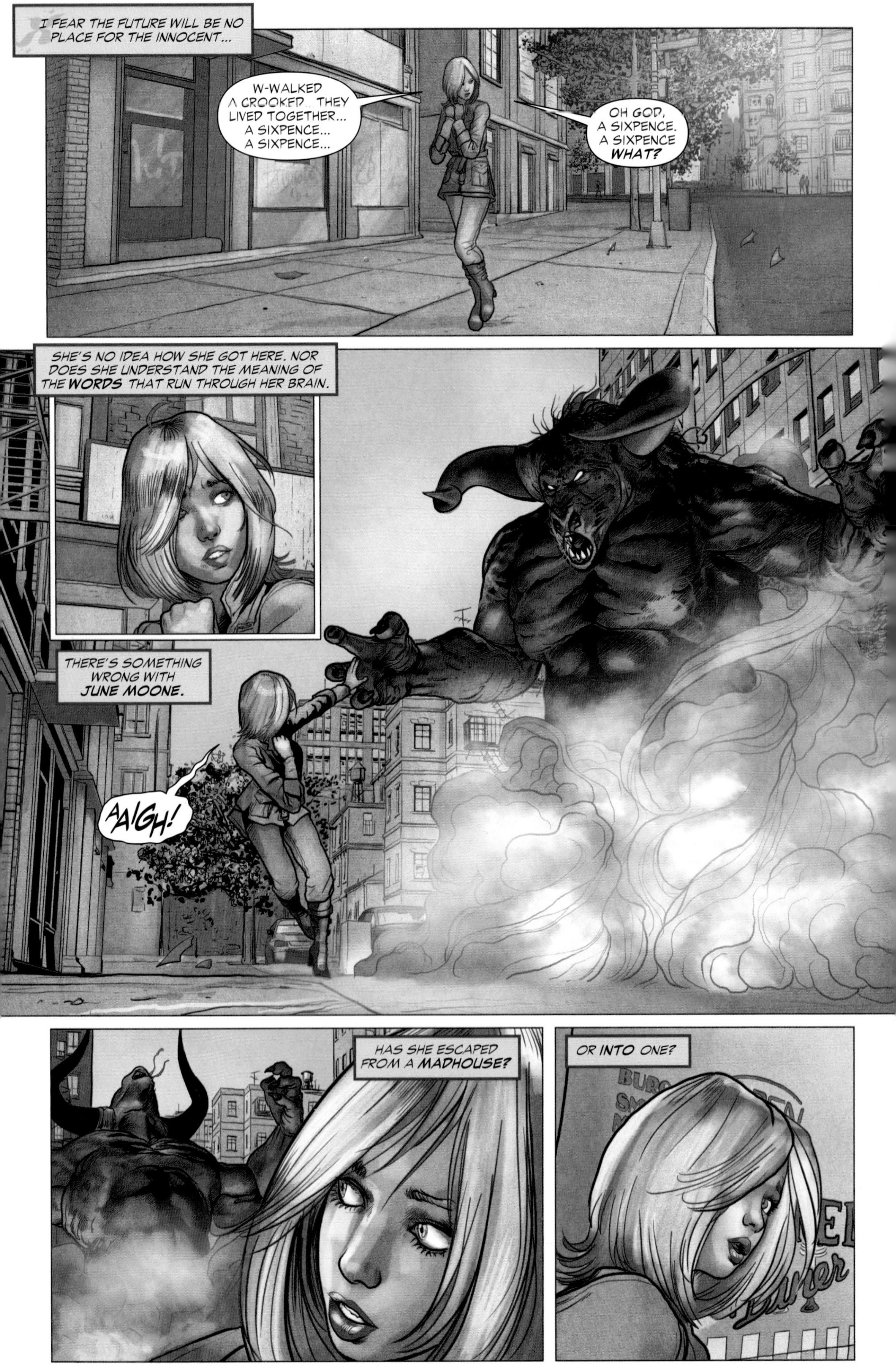
I FEAR THE FUTURE WILL BE NO PLACE FOR THE INNOCENT...
W-WALKED A CROOKED... THEY LIVED TOGETHER... A SIXPENCE... A SIXPENCE...
OH GOD, A SIXPENCE. A SIXPENCE WHAT?
SHE'S NO IDEA HOW SHE GOT HERE. NOR DOES SHE UNDERSTAND THE MEANING OF THE WORDS THAT RUN THROUGH HER BRAIN.
THERE'S SOMETHING WRONG WITH JUNE MOONE.
AAIGH!
HAS SHE ESCAPED FROM A MADHOUSE?
OR INTO ONE?

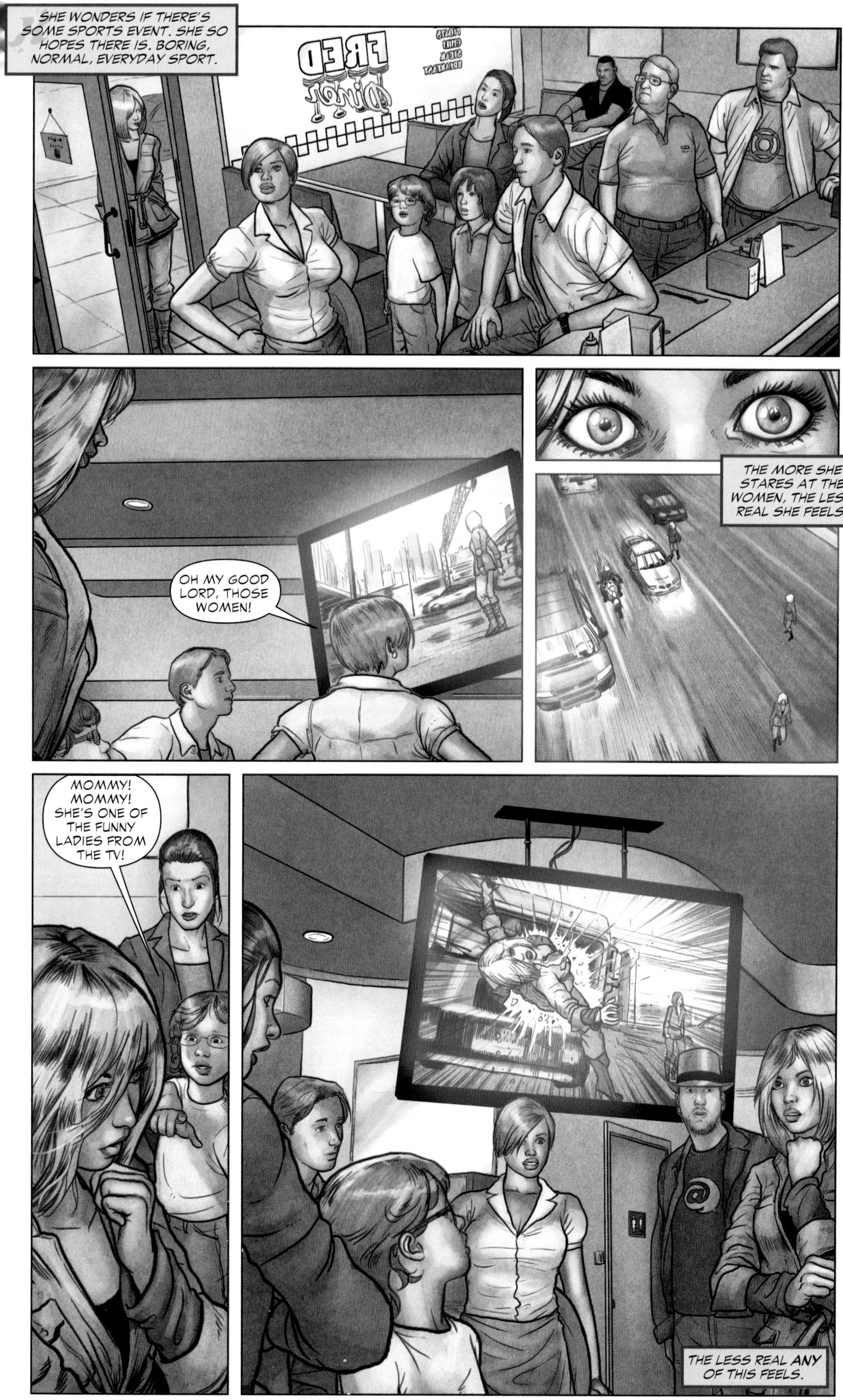
SHE WONDERS IF THERE'S SOME SPORTS EVENT. SHE SO HOPES THERE IS. BORING, NORMAL, EVERYDAY SPORT.
FRED Diner
OH MY GOOD LORD, THOSE WOMEN!
THE MORE SHE STARES AT THE WOMEN, THE LESS REAL SHE FEELS.
MOMMY! MOMMY! SHE'S ONE OF THE FUNNY LADIES FROM THE TV!
THE LESS REAL ANY OF THIS FEELS.

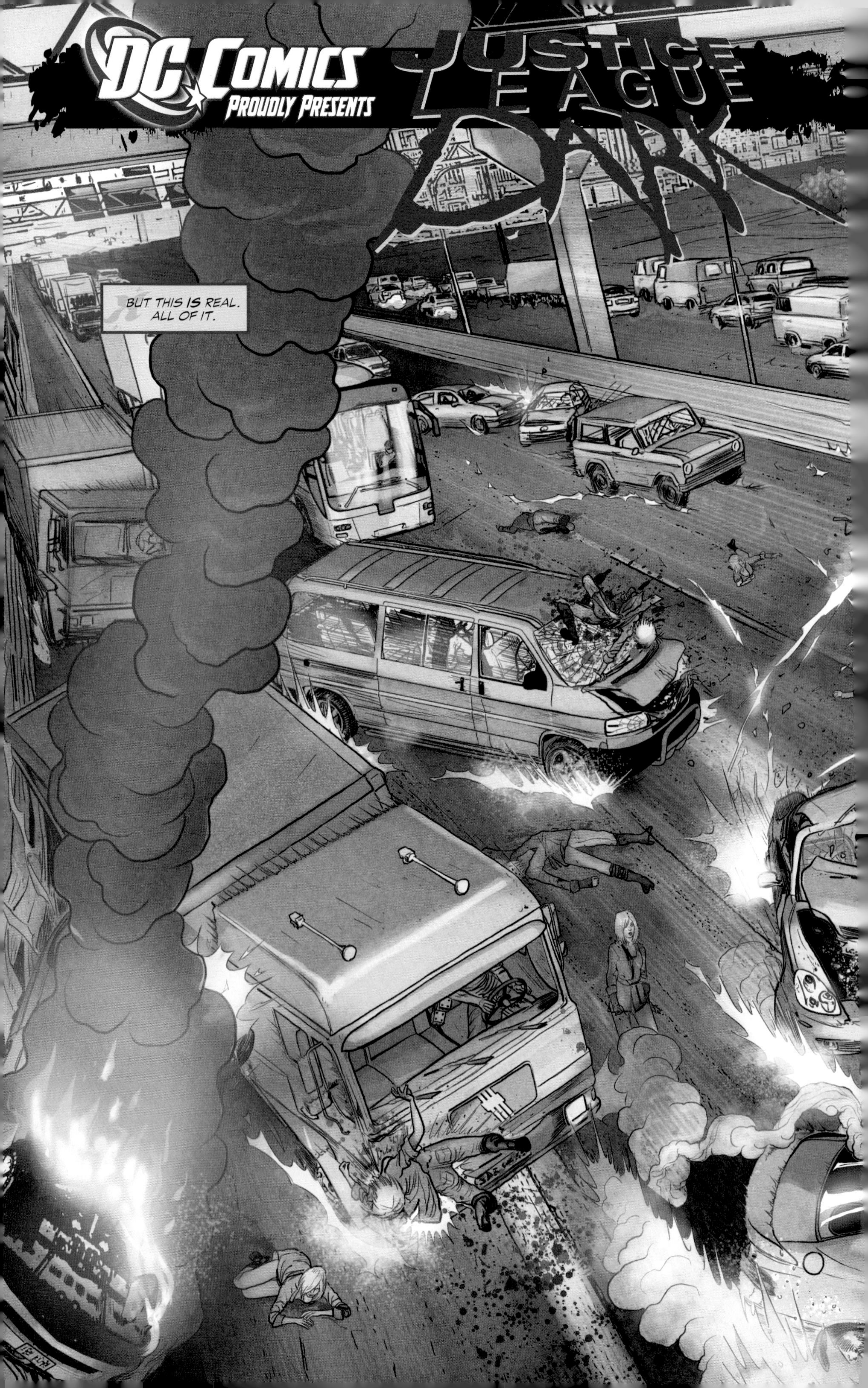
DC COMICS PROUDLY PRESENTS
JUSTICE LEAGUE DARK
BUT THIS IS REAL. ALL OF IT.

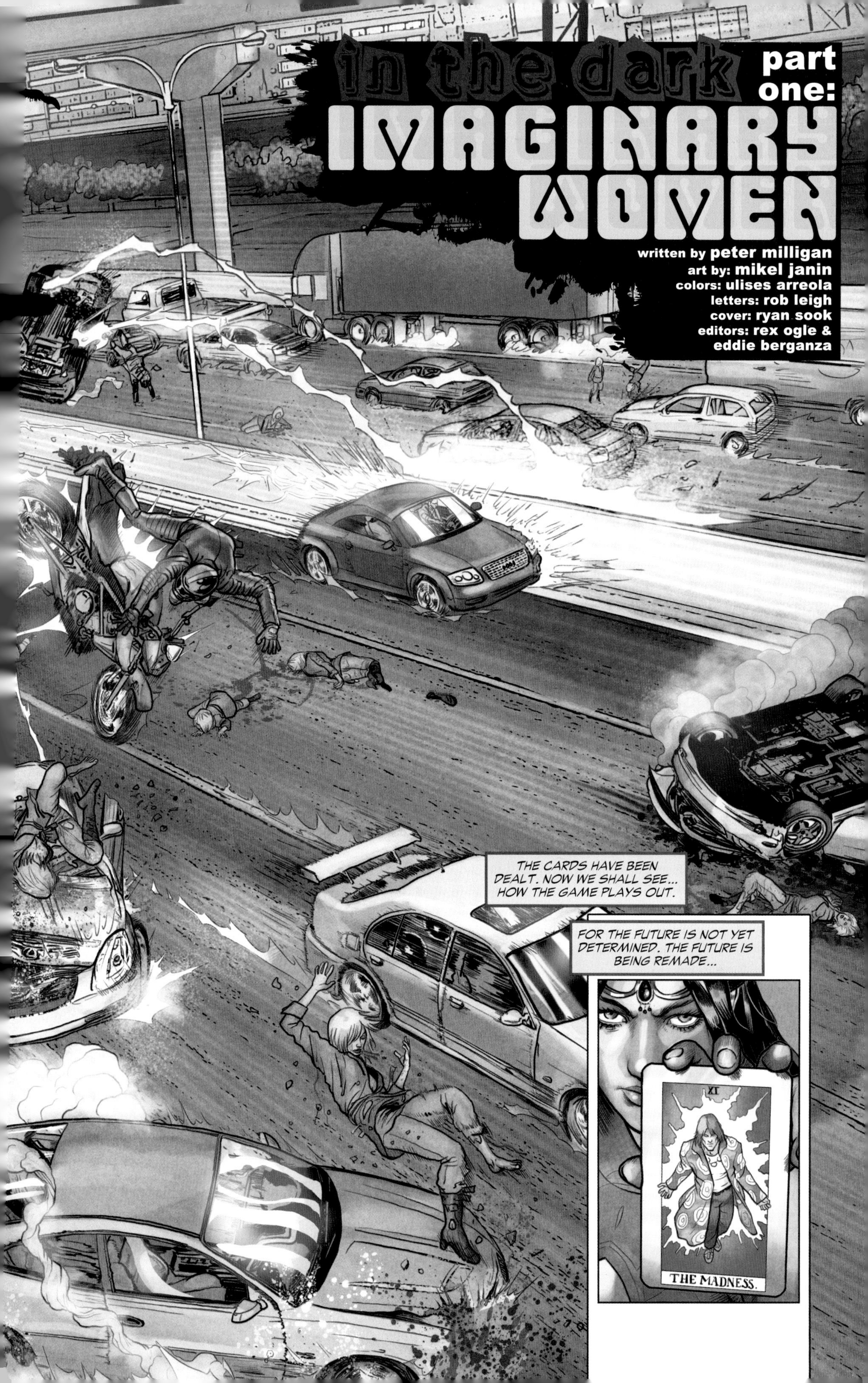
in the dark
part one:
IMAGINARY WOMEN
written by peter milligan
art by: mikel janin
colors: ulises arreola
letters: rob leigh
cover: ryan sook
editors: rex ogle & eddie berganza
THE CARDS HAVE BEEN DEALT. NOW WE SHALL SEE... HOW THE GAME PLAYS OUT.
FOR THE FUTURE IS NOT YET DETERMINED. THE FUTURE IS BEING REMADE...
XI
THE MADNESS.

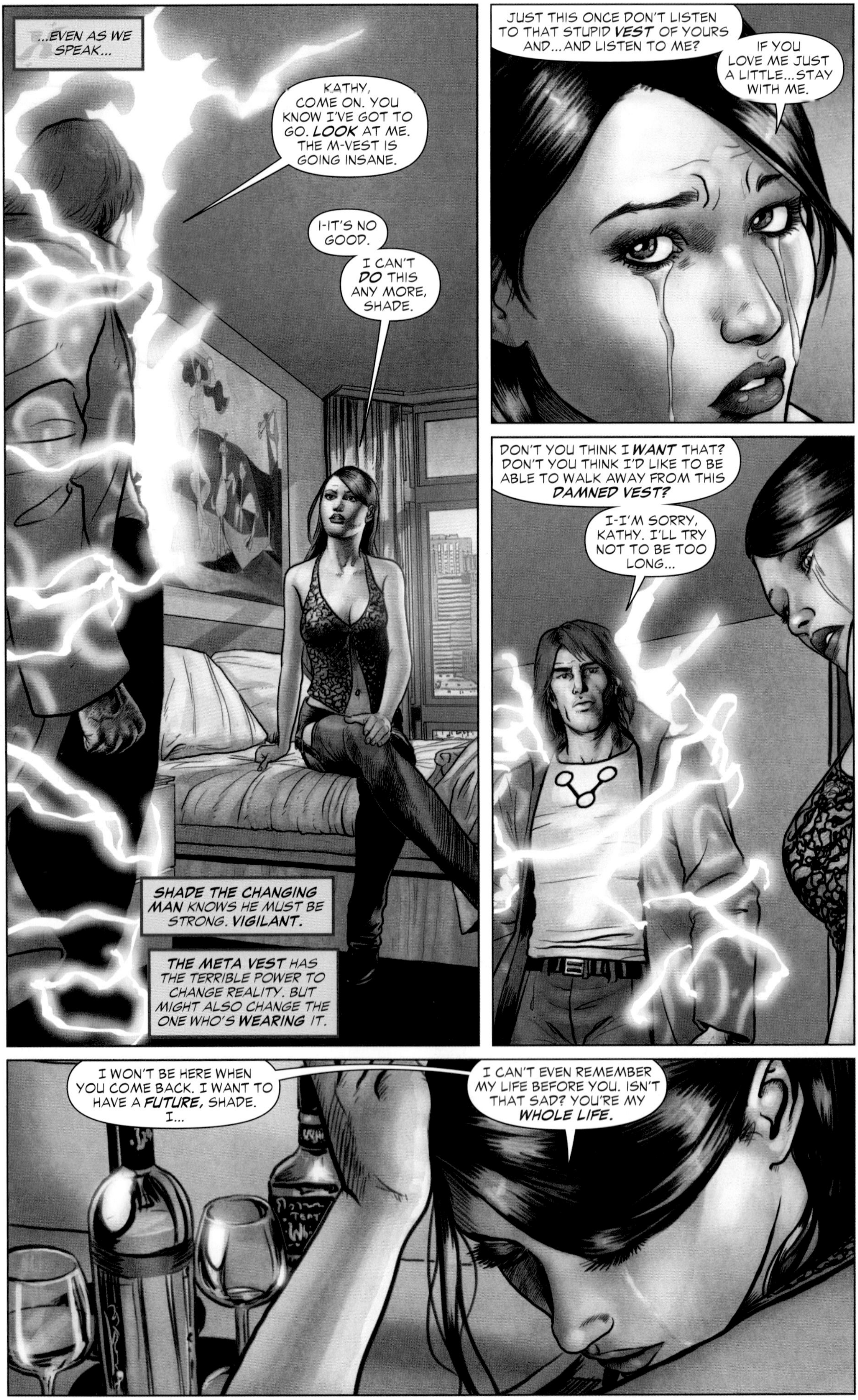
...EVEN AS WE SPEAK...
KATHY, COME ON. YOU KNOW I'VE GOT TO GO. **LOOK** AT ME. THE M-VEST IS GOING INSANE.
I-IT'S NO GOOD.
I CAN'T **DO** THIS ANY MORE, SHADE.
SHADE THE CHANGING MAN KNOWS HE MUST BE STRONG. **VIGILANT.**
THE META VEST HAS THE TERRIBLE POWER TO CHANGE REALITY. BUT MIGHT ALSO CHANGE THE ONE WHO'S **WEARING** IT.
JUST THIS ONCE DON'T LISTEN TO THAT STUPID **VEST** OF YOURS AND...AND LISTEN TO ME?
IF YOU LOVE ME JUST A LITTLE...STAY WITH ME.
DON'T YOU THINK I **WANT** THAT? DON'T YOU THINK I'D LIKE TO BE ABLE TO WALK AWAY FROM THIS **DAMNED VEST?**
I-I'M SORRY, KATHY. I'LL TRY NOT TO BE TOO LONG...
I WON'T BE HERE WHEN YOU COME BACK. I WANT TO HAVE A **FUTURE,** SHADE. I...
I CAN'T EVEN REMEMBER MY LIFE BEFORE YOU. ISN'T THAT SAD? YOU'RE MY **WHOLE LIFE.**

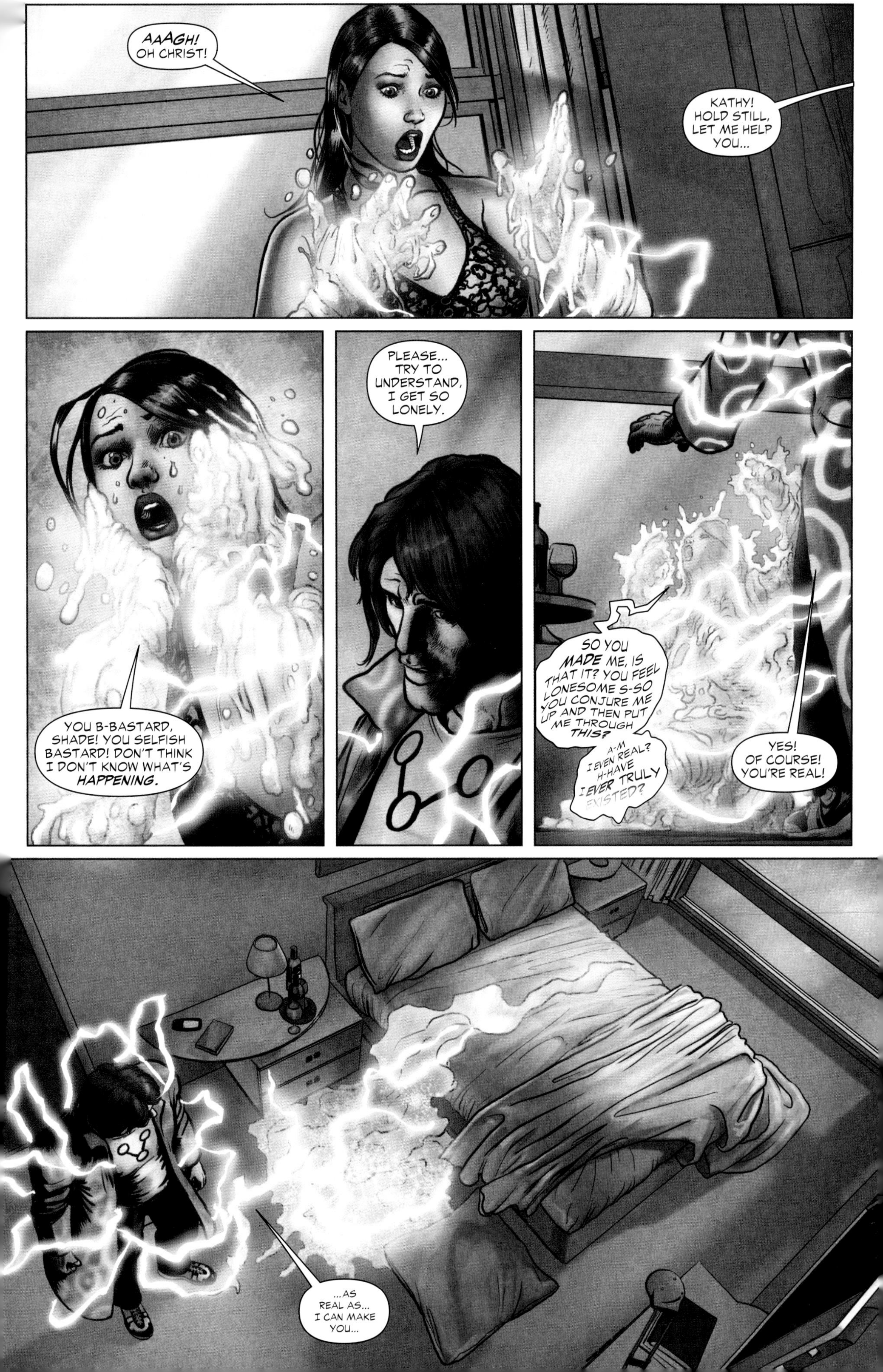
AAAGH! OH CHRIST!
KATHY! HOLD STILL, LET ME HELP YOU...
YOU B-BASTARD, SHADE! YOU SELFISH BASTARD! DON'T THINK I DON'T KNOW WHAT'S HAPPENING.
PLEASE... TRY TO UNDERSTAND, I GET SO LONELY.
SO YOU MADE ME, IS THAT IT? YOU FEEL LONESOME S-SO YOU CONJURE ME UP AND THEN PUT ME THROUGH THIS?
A-M I EVEN REAL? H-HAVE I EVER TRULY EXISTED?
YES! OF COURSE! YOU'RE REAL!
...AS REAL AS... I CAN MAKE YOU...

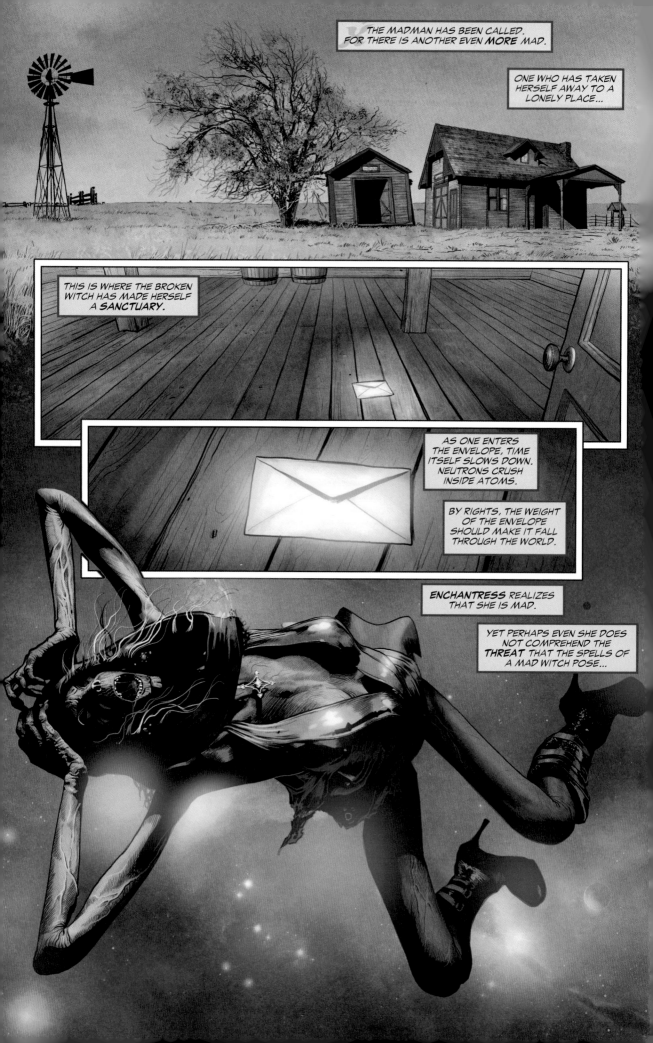

THE MADMAN HAS BEEN CALLED. FOR THERE IS ANOTHER EVEN **MORE** MAD.

ONE WHO HAS TAKEN HERSELF AWAY TO A LONELY PLACE...

THIS IS WHERE THE BROKEN WITCH HAS MADE HERSELF A **SANCTUARY.**

AS ONE ENTERS THE ENVELOPE, TIME ITSELF SLOWS DOWN. NEUTRONS CRUSH INSIDE ATOMS.

BY RIGHTS, THE WEIGHT OF THE ENVELOPE SHOULD MAKE IT FALL THROUGH THE WORLD.

ENCHANTRESS REALIZES THAT SHE IS MAD.

YET PERHAPS EVEN SHE DOES NOT COMPREHEND THE **THREAT** THAT THE SPELLS OF A MAD WITCH POSE...

IN A NEIGHBORING TOWN, A SHOWER OF **BOOKS** IN A DEAD LANGUAGE KILL SIX PEOPLE.

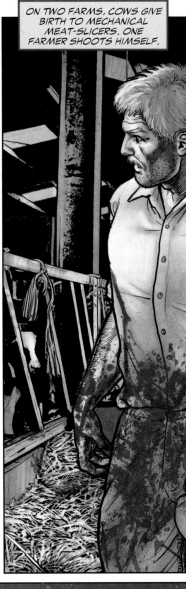

ON TWO FARMS, COWS GIVE BIRTH TO MECHANICAL MEAT-SLICERS. ONE FARMER SHOOTS HIMSELF.

THE LOCAL POWER STATION THREATENS TO EXPLODE WHEN IT IS IMBUED WITH **CONSCIOUSNESS**...

AND GETS **BORED.**

AND THERE ARE STILL THOSE WHO DO NOT KNOW IF IT'S THEY OR THE WORLD THAT'S INSANE...

"JUNE MOONE..."

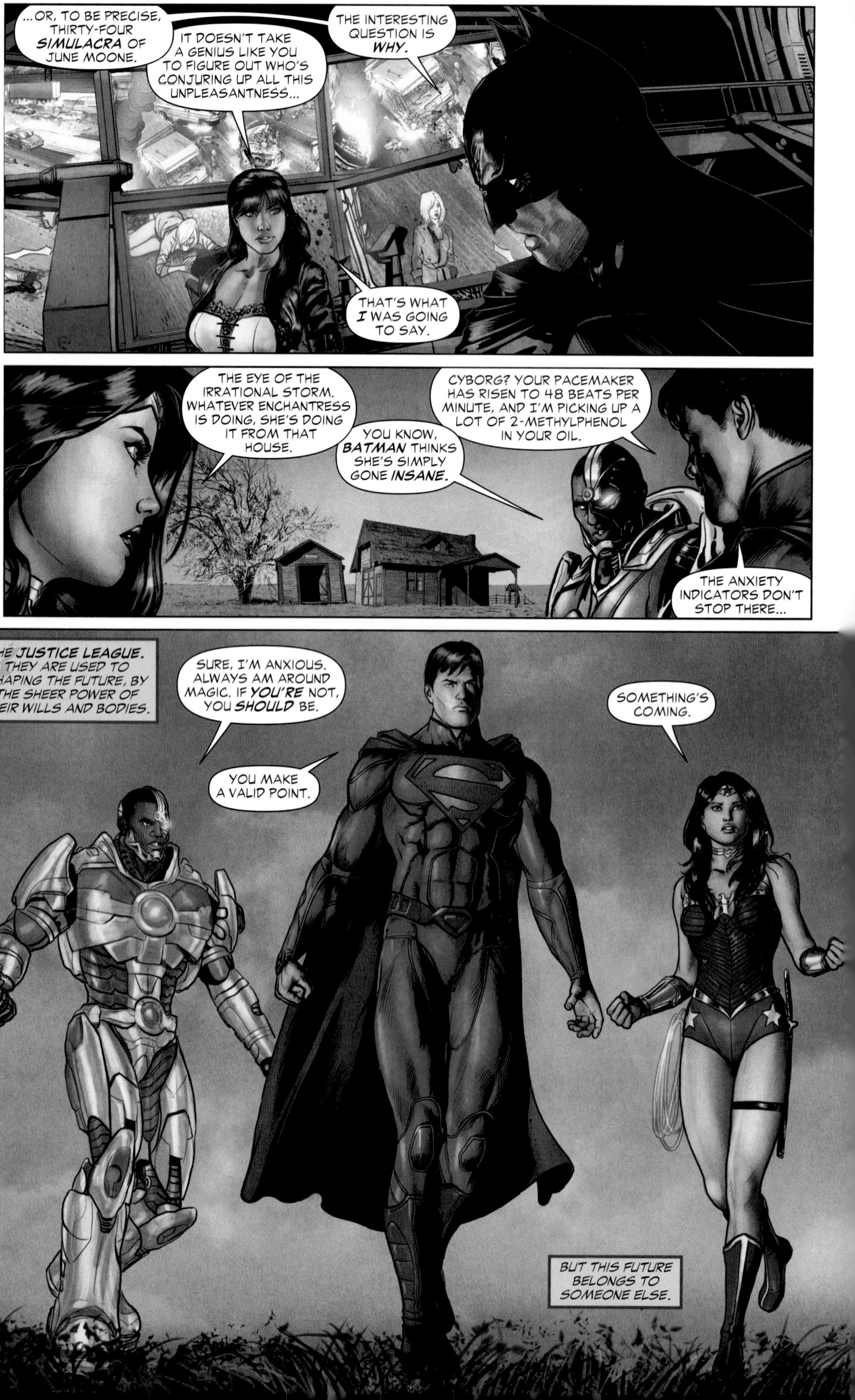
...OR, TO BE PRECISE, THIRTY-FOUR SIMULACRA OF JUNE MOONE.
IT DOESN'T TAKE A GENIUS LIKE YOU TO FIGURE OUT WHO'S CONJURING UP ALL THIS UNPLEASANTNESS...
THE INTERESTING QUESTION IS WHY.
THAT'S WHAT I WAS GOING TO SAY.
THE EYE OF THE IRRATIONAL STORM. WHATEVER ENCHANTRESS IS DOING, SHE'S DOING IT FROM THAT HOUSE.
YOU KNOW, BATMAN THINKS SHE'S SIMPLY GONE INSANE.
CYBORG? YOUR PACEMAKER HAS RISEN TO 48 BEATS PER MINUTE, AND I'M PICKING UP A LOT OF 2-METHYLPHENOL IN YOUR OIL.
THE ANXIETY INDICATORS DON'T STOP THERE...
THE JUSTICE LEAGUE. THEY ARE USED TO SHAPING THE FUTURE, BY THE SHEER POWER OF THEIR WILLS AND BODIES.
SURE, I'M ANXIOUS. ALWAYS AM AROUND MAGIC. IF YOU'RE NOT, YOU SHOULD BE.
YOU MAKE A VALID POINT.
SOMETHING'S COMING.
BUT THIS FUTURE BELONGS TO SOMEONE ELSE.

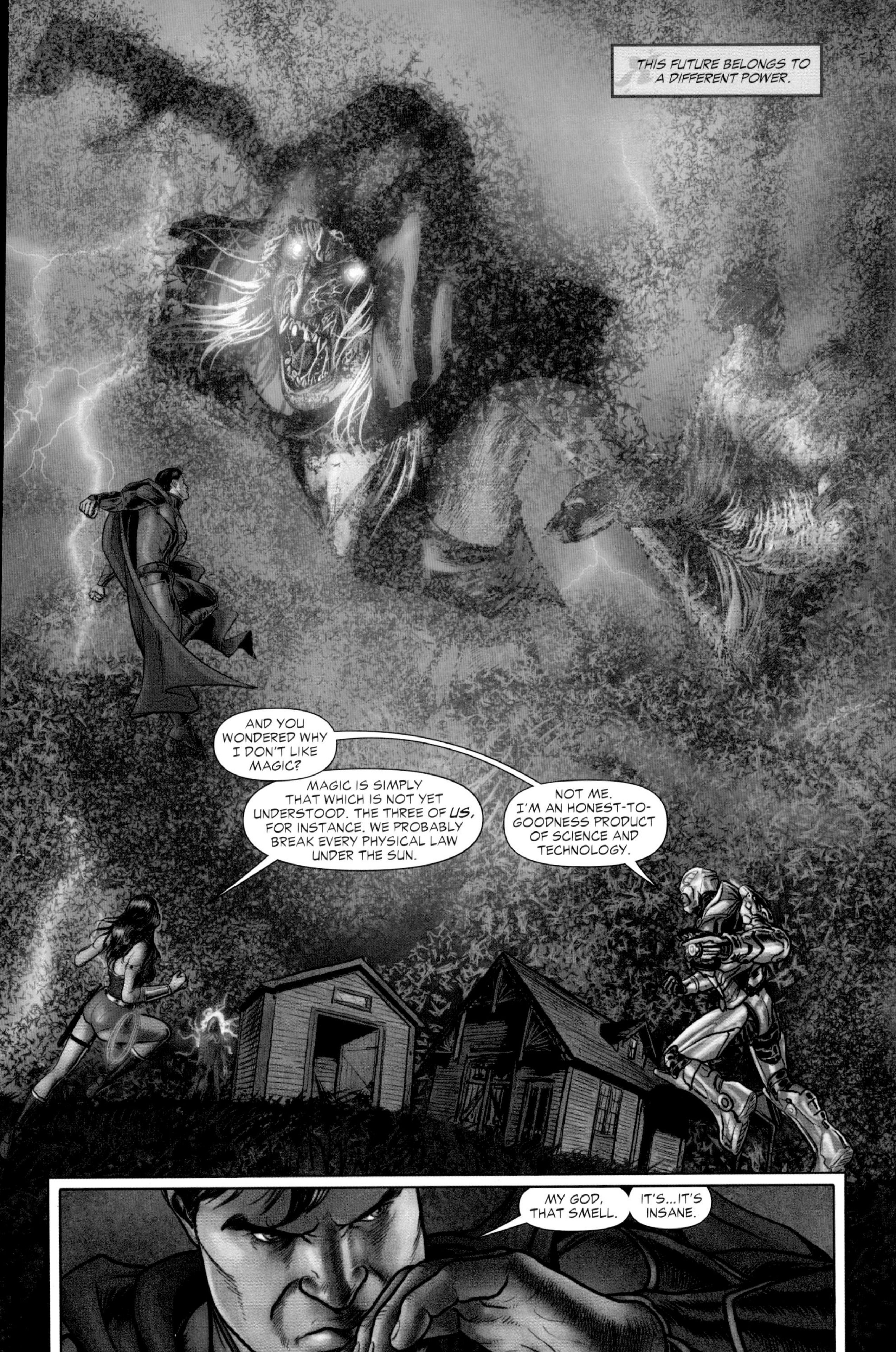
THIS FUTURE BELONGS TO A DIFFERENT POWER.
AND YOU WONDERED WHY I DON'T LIKE MAGIC?
MAGIC IS SIMPLY THAT WHICH IS NOT YET UNDERSTOOD. THE THREE OF US, FOR INSTANCE. WE PROBABLY BREAK EVERY PHYSICAL LAW UNDER THE SUN.
NOT ME. I'M AN HONEST-TO-GOODNESS PRODUCT OF SCIENCE AND TECHNOLOGY.

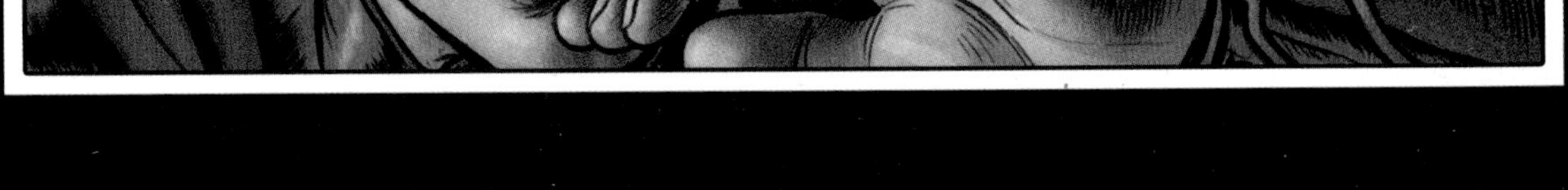
MY GOD, THAT SMELL.
IT'S...IT'S INSANE.

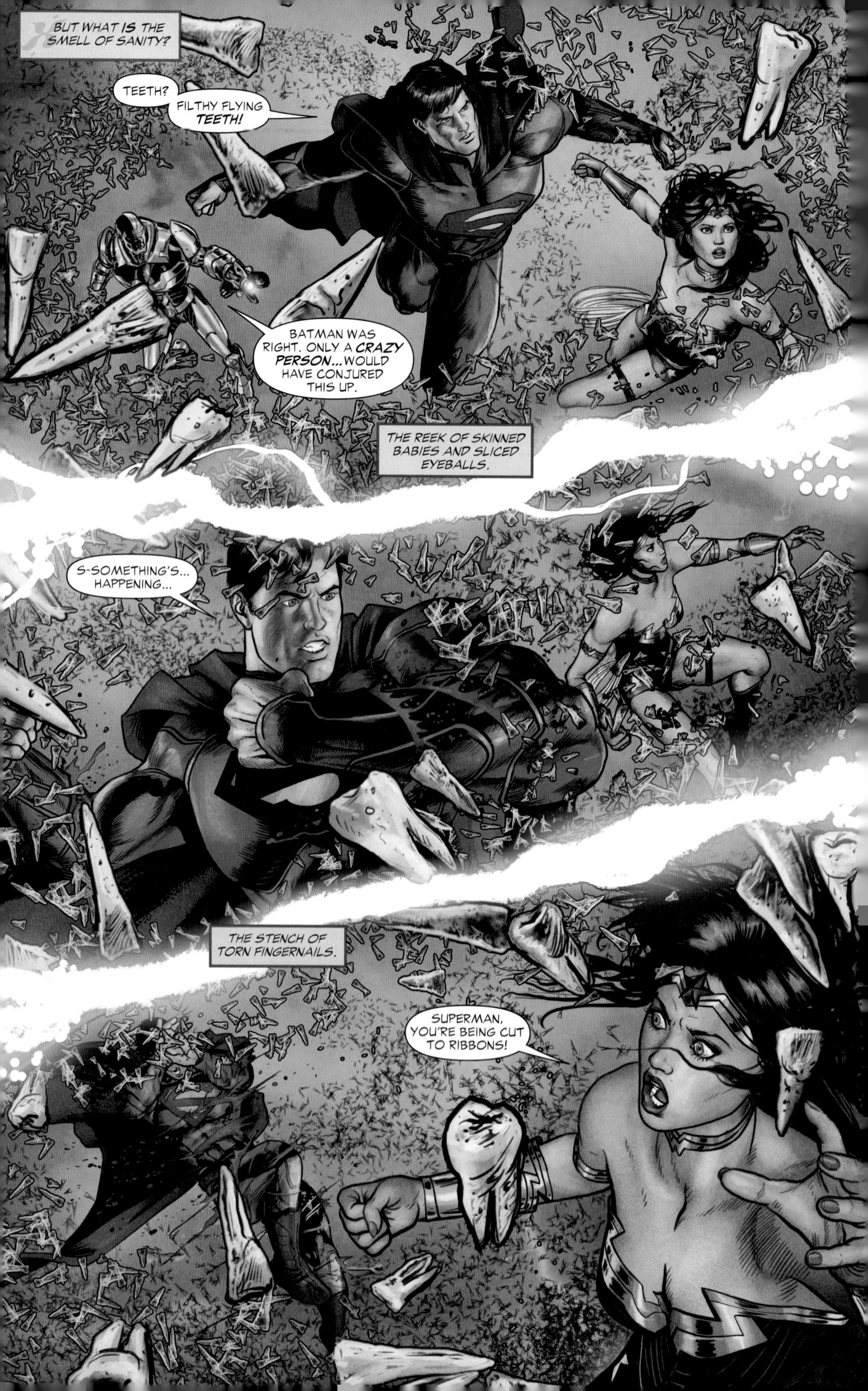
BUT WHAT IS THE SMELL OF SANITY?
TEETH?
FILTHY FLYING TEETH!
BATMAN WAS RIGHT. ONLY A CRAZY PERSON...WOULD HAVE CONJURED THIS UP.
THE REEK OF SKINNED BABIES AND SLICED EYEBALLS.
S-SOMETHING'S... HAPPENING...
THE STENCH OF TORN FINGERNAILS.
SUPERMAN, YOU'RE BEING CUT TO RIBBONS!

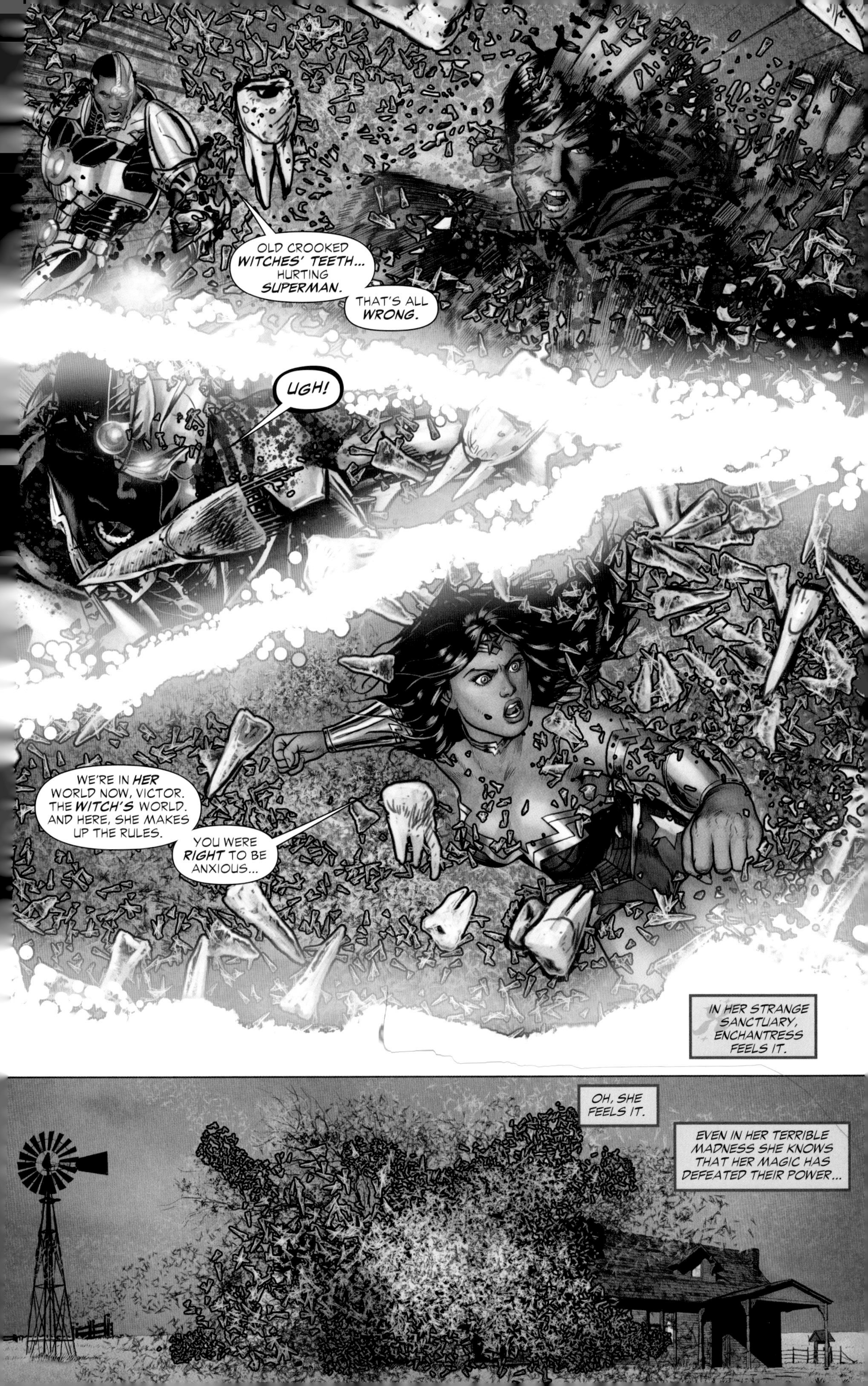
OLD CROOKED WITCHES' TEETH... HURTING SUPERMAN.
THAT'S ALL WRONG.
UGH!
WE'RE IN HER WORLD NOW, VICTOR. THE WITCH'S WORLD. AND HERE, SHE MAKES UP THE RULES.
YOU WERE RIGHT TO BE ANXIOUS...
IN HER STRANGE SANCTUARY, ENCHANTRESS FEELS IT.
OH, SHE FEELS IT.
EVEN IN HER TERRIBLE MADNESS SHE KNOWS THAT HER MAGIC HAS DEFEATED THEIR POWER...

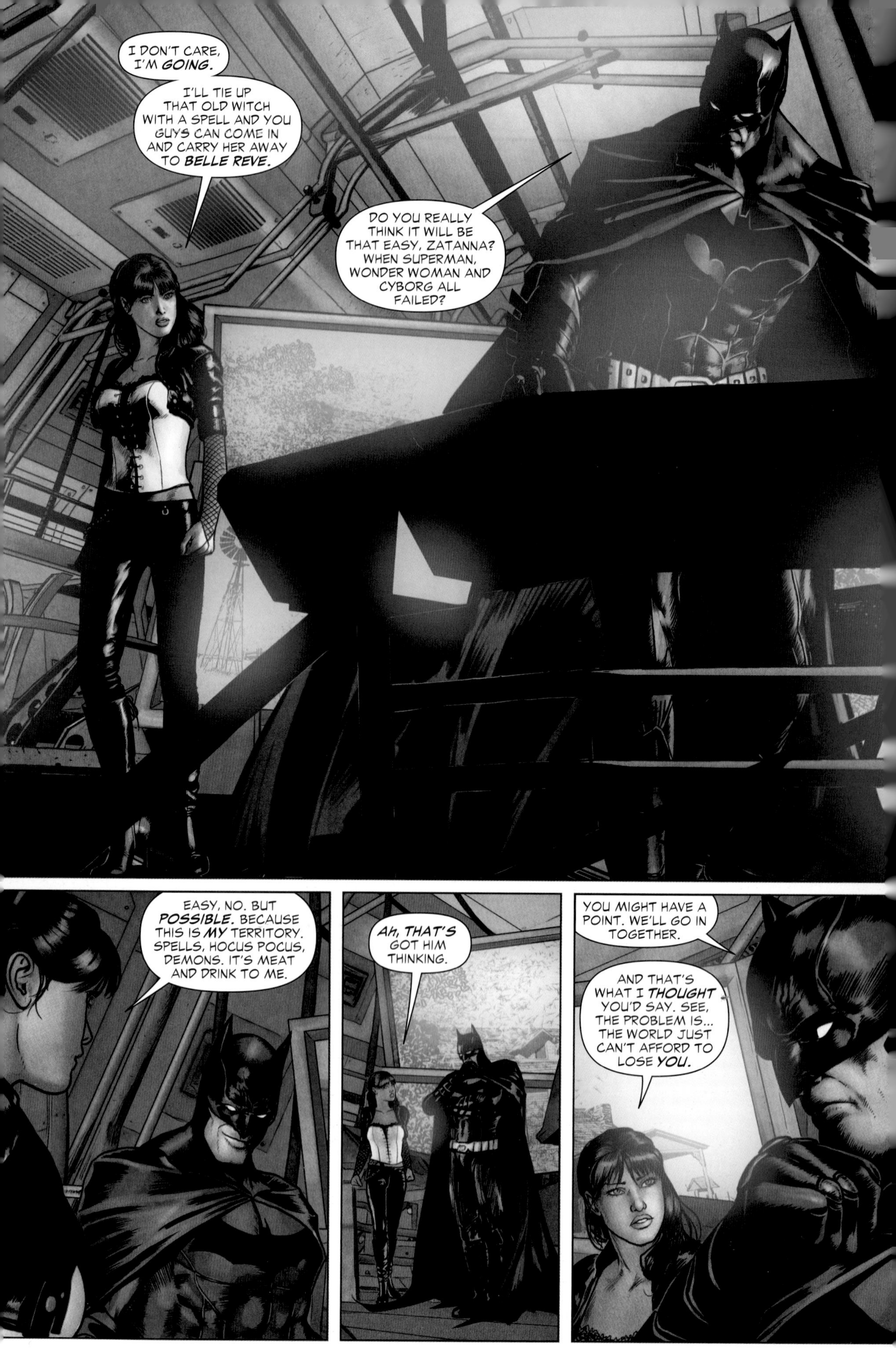

I DON'T CARE, I'M *GOING.*
I'LL TIE UP THAT OLD WITCH WITH A SPELL AND YOU GUYS CAN COME IN AND CARRY HER AWAY TO *BELLE REVE.*
DO YOU REALLY THINK IT WILL BE THAT EASY, ZATANNA? WHEN SUPERMAN, WONDER WOMAN AND CYBORG ALL FAILED?
EASY, NO. BUT *POSSIBLE.* BECAUSE THIS IS *MY* TERRITORY. SPELLS, HOCUS POCUS, DEMONS. IT'S MEAT AND DRINK TO ME.
Ah, THAT'S GOT HIM THINKING.
YOU MIGHT HAVE A POINT. WE'LL GO IN TOGETHER.
AND THAT'S WHAT I *THOUGHT* YOU'D SAY. SEE, THE PROBLEM IS... THE WORLD JUST CAN'T AFFORD TO LOSE *YOU.*

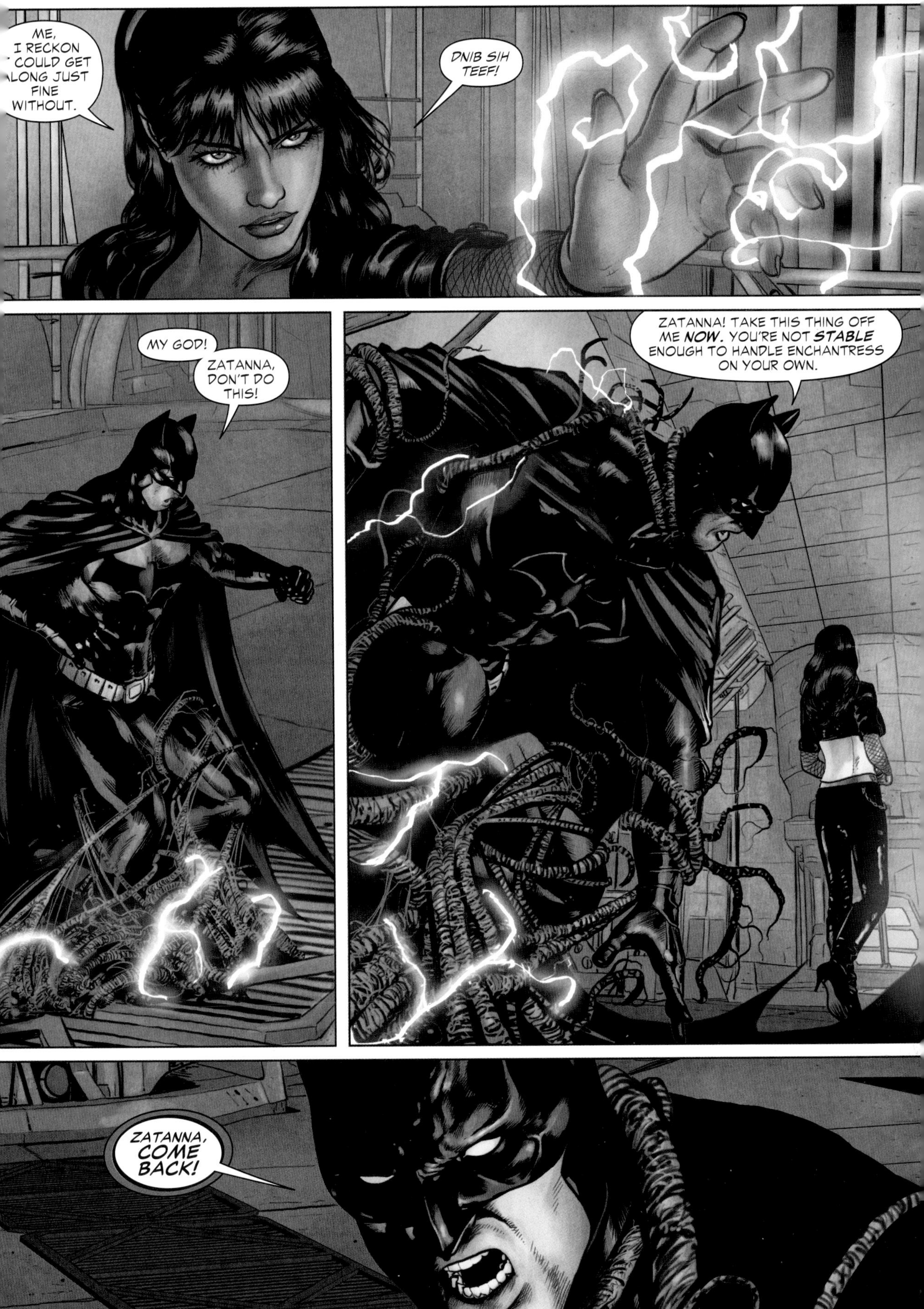
ME, I RECKON I COULD GET ALONG JUST FINE WITHOUT.
DNIB SIH TEEF!
MY GOD!
ZATANNA, DON'T DO THIS!
ZATANNA! TAKE THIS THING OFF ME NOW. YOU'RE NOT STABLE ENOUGH TO HANDLE ENCHANTRESS ON YOUR OWN.
ZATANNA, COME BACK!

MY NAME'S **JOHN CONSTANTINE**, SO YOU'D BETTER HOLD YOUR NOSES NOW.

A FEW MOMENTS AGO I WAS SCAMMING THIS RICH GEEZER IN **BRIGHTON**. HE WANTED TO CONTACT HIS DEAD WIFE. **I** WANTED UP TO PAY MY RENT.

INSTEAD OF THE WIFE, I GOT A SCARY VISION OF A **GIRL** I USED TO KNOW, SHE HAD THIS CUTE WAY OF SAYING THINGS BACKWARDS.

AND THEN I GOT SWEPT AWAY BY THIS...THIS **MAGICAL VORTEX.**

OH CHRIST! OH, NOOOOOAHH!

NAH, NOT MY USUAL BOLLOCKS. THIS WAS THE **REAL BLOODY THING.**

LONDON

I ♥ LONDON

I ♥ LONDON

I ♥ LONDON

I ♥ LONDON

Z-ZATANNA...

WHAT THE HELL HAVE YOU GOT YOURSELF MIXED UP IN, GIRL?

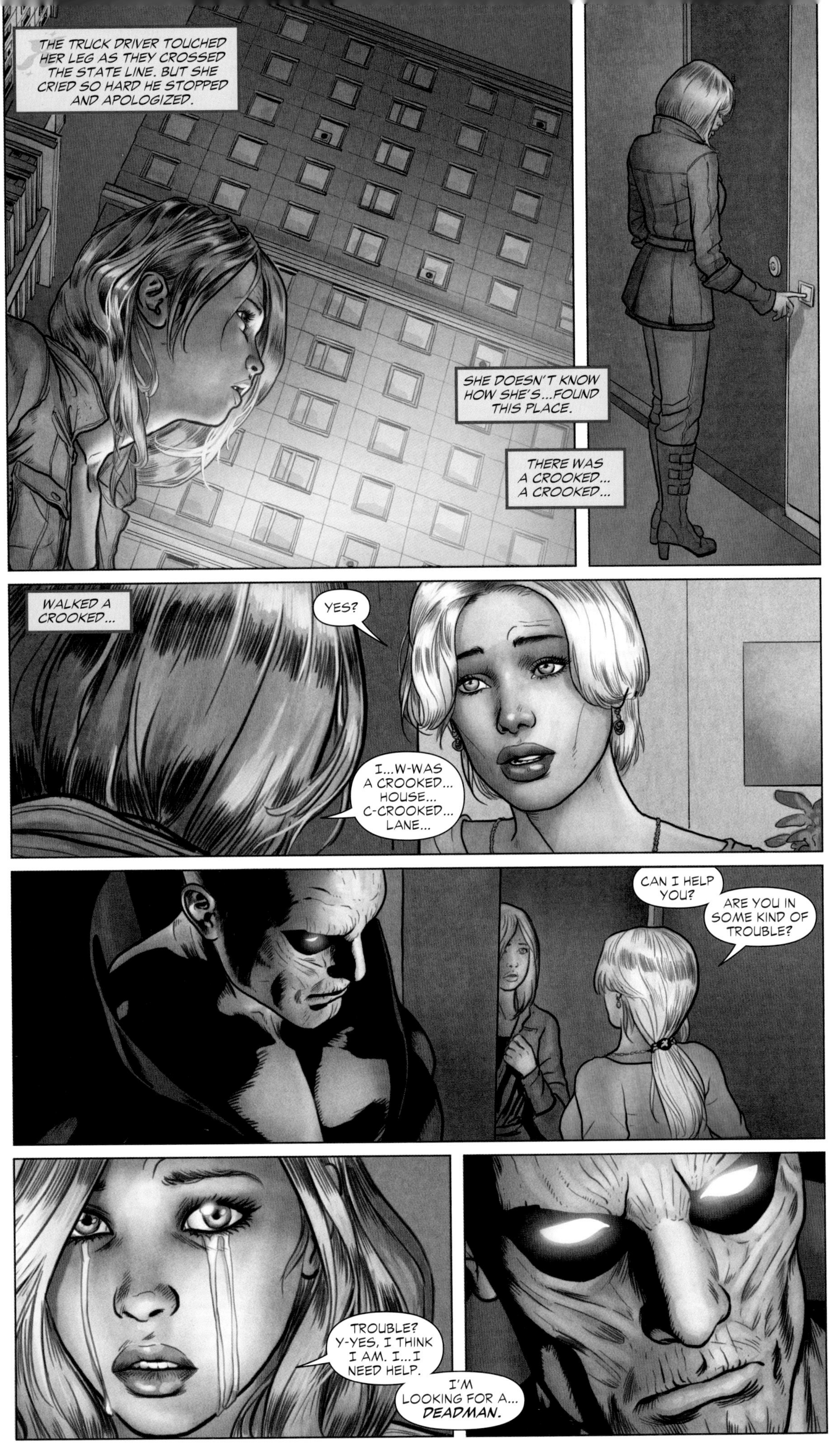
THE TRUCK DRIVER TOUCHED HER LEG AS THEY CROSSED THE STATE LINE. BUT SHE CRIED SO HARD HE STOPPED AND APOLOGIZED.
SHE DOESN'T KNOW HOW SHE'S...FOUND THIS PLACE.
THERE WAS A CROOKED... A CROOKED...
WALKED A CROOKED...
YES?
I...W-WAS A CROOKED... HOUSE... C-CROOKED... LANE...
CAN I HELP YOU?
ARE YOU IN SOME KIND OF TROUBLE?
TROUBLE? Y-YES, I THINK I AM. I...I NEED HELP.
I'M LOOKING FOR A... DEADMAN.

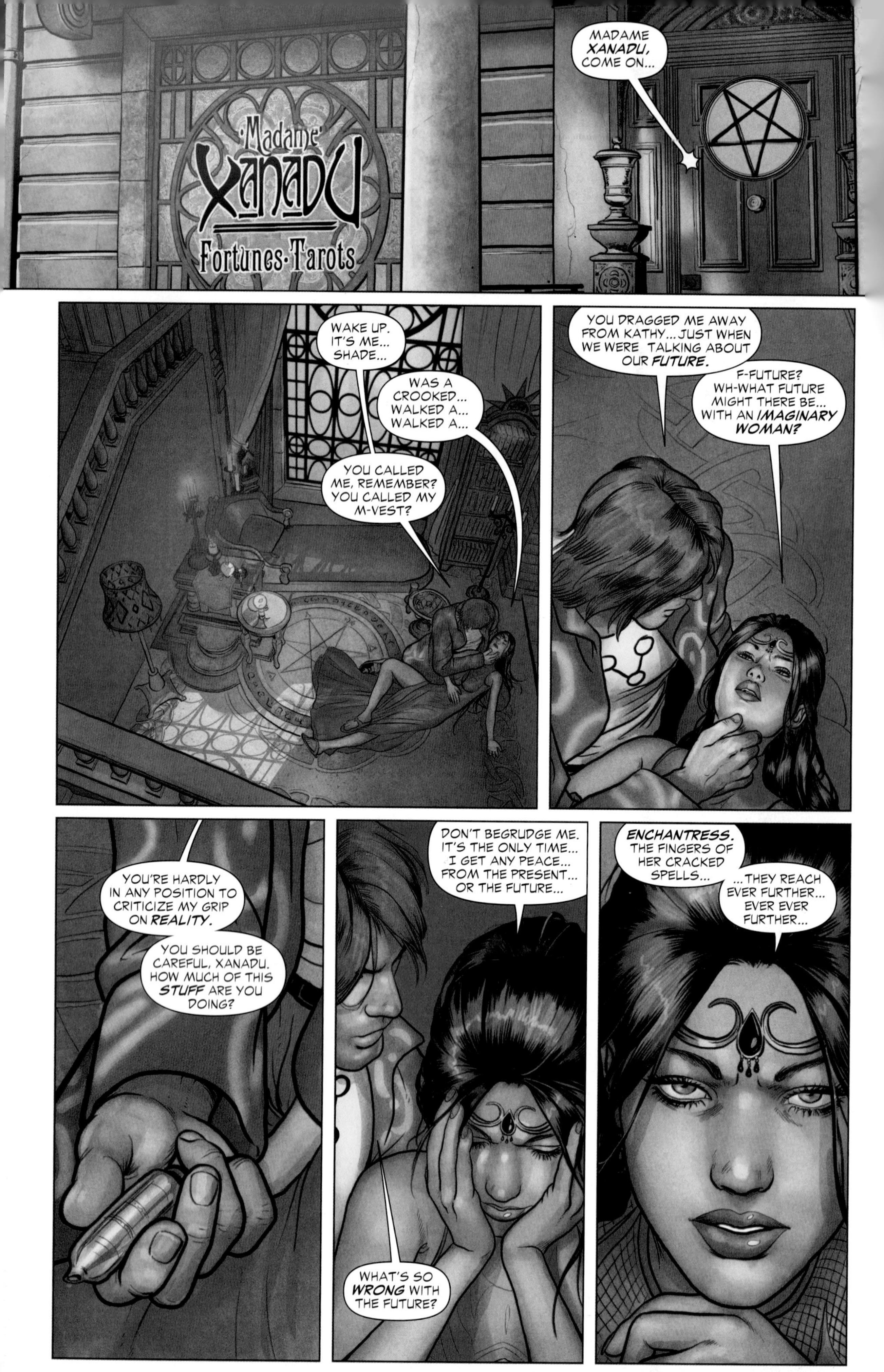
·Madame·
XANADU
Fortunes·Tarots
MADAME XANADU, COME ON...
WAKE UP. IT'S ME... SHADE...
WAS A CROOKED... WALKED A... WALKED A...
YOU CALLED ME, REMEMBER? YOU CALLED MY M-VEST?
YOU DRAGGED ME AWAY FROM KATHY... JUST WHEN WE WERE TALKING ABOUT OUR FUTURE.
F-FUTURE? WH-WHAT FUTURE MIGHT THERE BE... WITH AN IMAGINARY WOMAN?
YOU'RE HARDLY IN ANY POSITION TO CRITICIZE MY GRIP ON REALITY.
YOU SHOULD BE CAREFUL, XANADU. HOW MUCH OF THIS STUFF ARE YOU DOING?
DON'T BEGRUDGE ME. IT'S THE ONLY TIME... I GET ANY PEACE... FROM THE PRESENT... OR THE FUTURE...
WHAT'S SO WRONG WITH THE FUTURE?
ENCHANTRESS. THE FINGERS OF HER CRACKED SPELLS...
...THEY REACH EVER FURTHER... EVER EVER FURTHER...

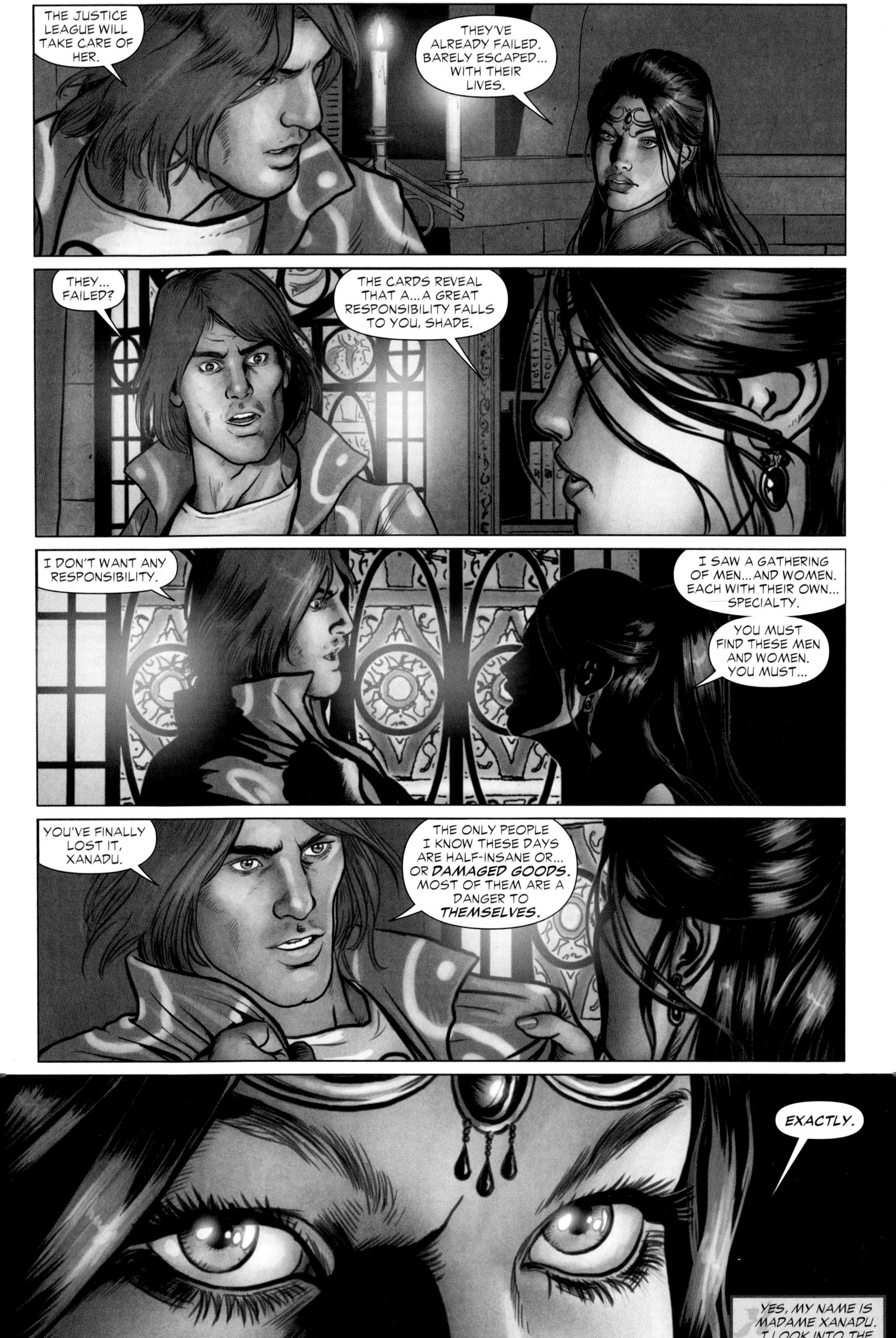
THE JUSTICE LEAGUE WILL TAKE CARE OF HER.
THEY'VE ALREADY FAILED. BARELY ESCAPED... WITH THEIR LIVES.
THEY... FAILED?
THE CARDS REVEAL THAT A... A GREAT RESPONSIBILITY FALLS TO YOU, SHADE.
I DON'T WANT ANY RESPONSIBILITY.
I SAW A GATHERING OF MEN... AND WOMEN. EACH WITH THEIR OWN... SPECIALTY.
YOU MUST FIND THESE MEN AND WOMEN. YOU MUST...
YOU'VE FINALLY LOST IT, XANADU.
THE ONLY PEOPLE I KNOW THESE DAYS ARE HALF-INSANE OR... OR DAMAGED GOODS. MOST OF THEM ARE A DANGER TO THEMSELVES.
EXACTLY.
YES, MY NAME IS MADAME XANADU. I LOOK INTO THE FUTURE...

AND THE FUTURE LOOKS RIGHT BACK AT ME...
XANADU, WHAT IS IT?
WHAT ARE YOU LOOKING AT?
NEXT: THE WAR AGAINST ENCHANTRESS BEGINS.

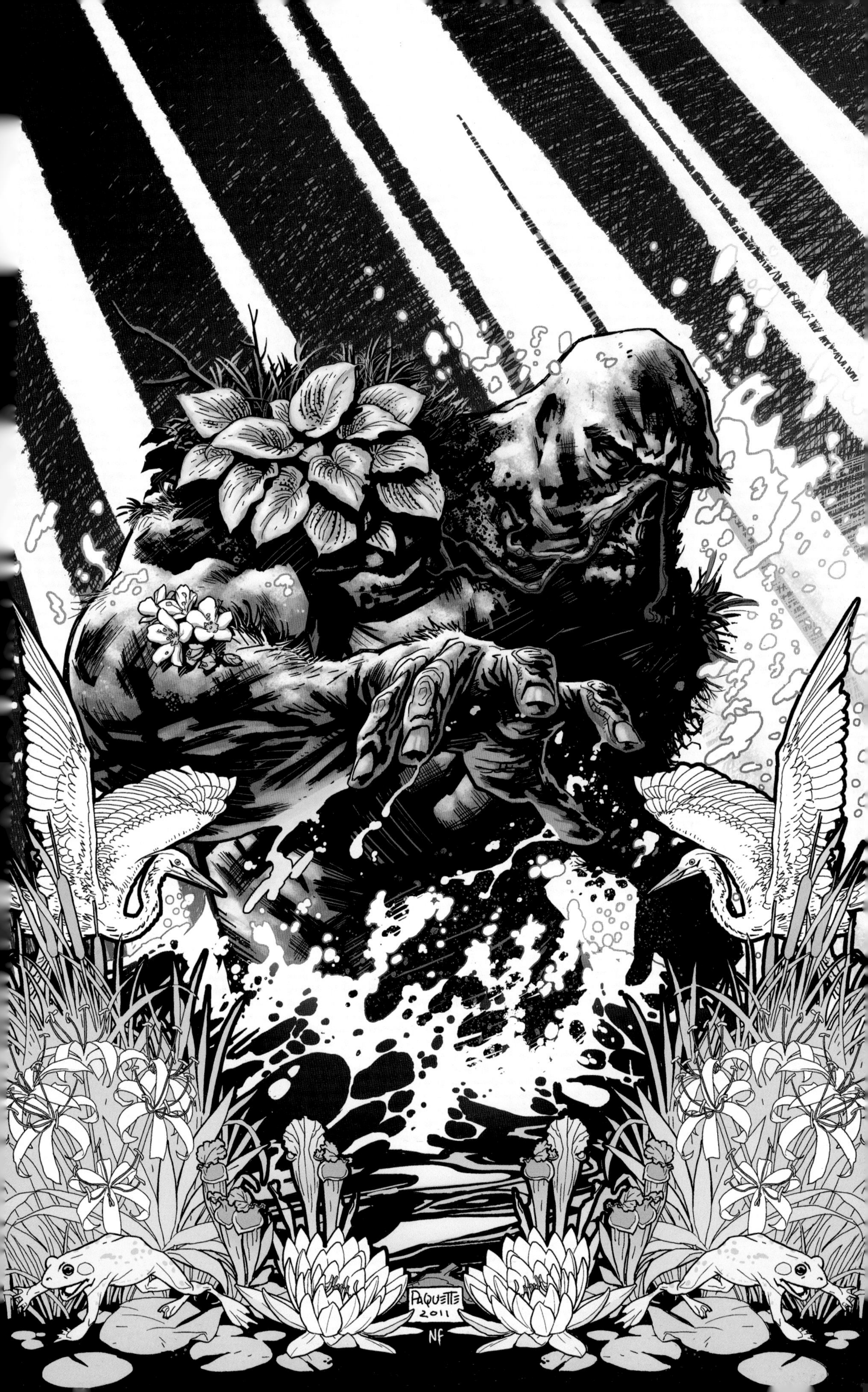
PAQUETTE
2011
NF

SWAMP THING

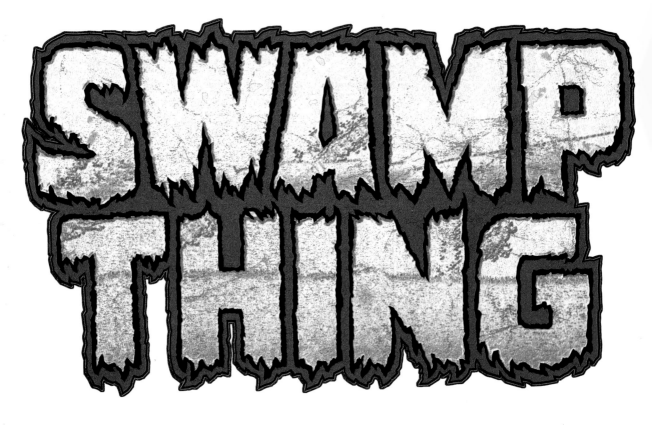

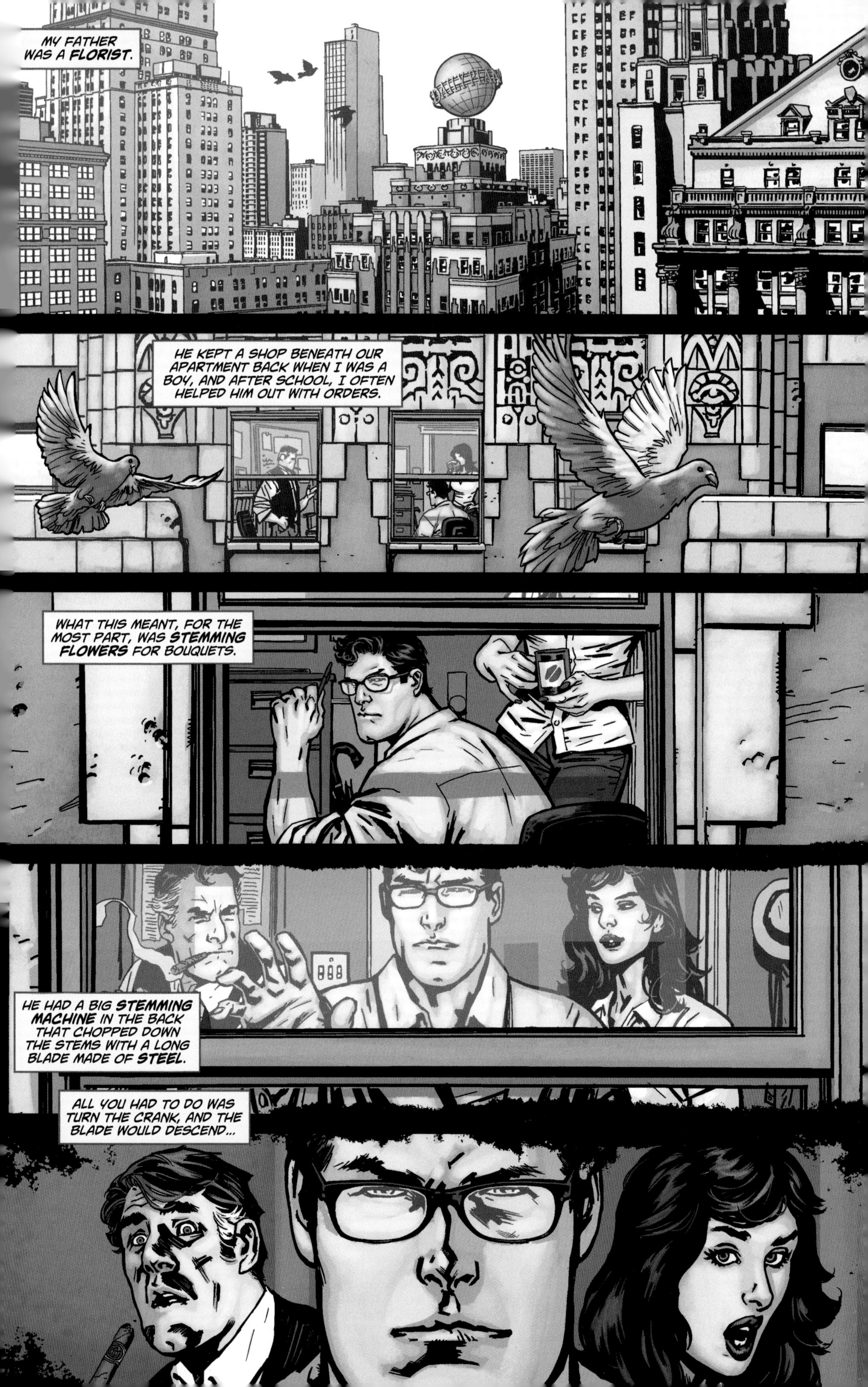
MY FATHER WAS A **FLORIST**.
HE KEPT A SHOP BENEATH OUR APARTMENT BACK WHEN I WAS A BOY, AND AFTER SCHOOL, I OFTEN HELPED HIM OUT WITH ORDERS.
WHAT THIS MEANT, FOR THE MOST PART, WAS **STEMMING FLOWERS** FOR BOUQUETS.
HE HAD A BIG **STEMMING MACHINE** IN THE BACK THAT CHOPPED DOWN THE STEMS WITH A LONG BLADE MADE OF **STEEL**.
ALL YOU HAD TO DO WAS TURN THE CRANK, AND THE BLADE WOULD DESCEND...

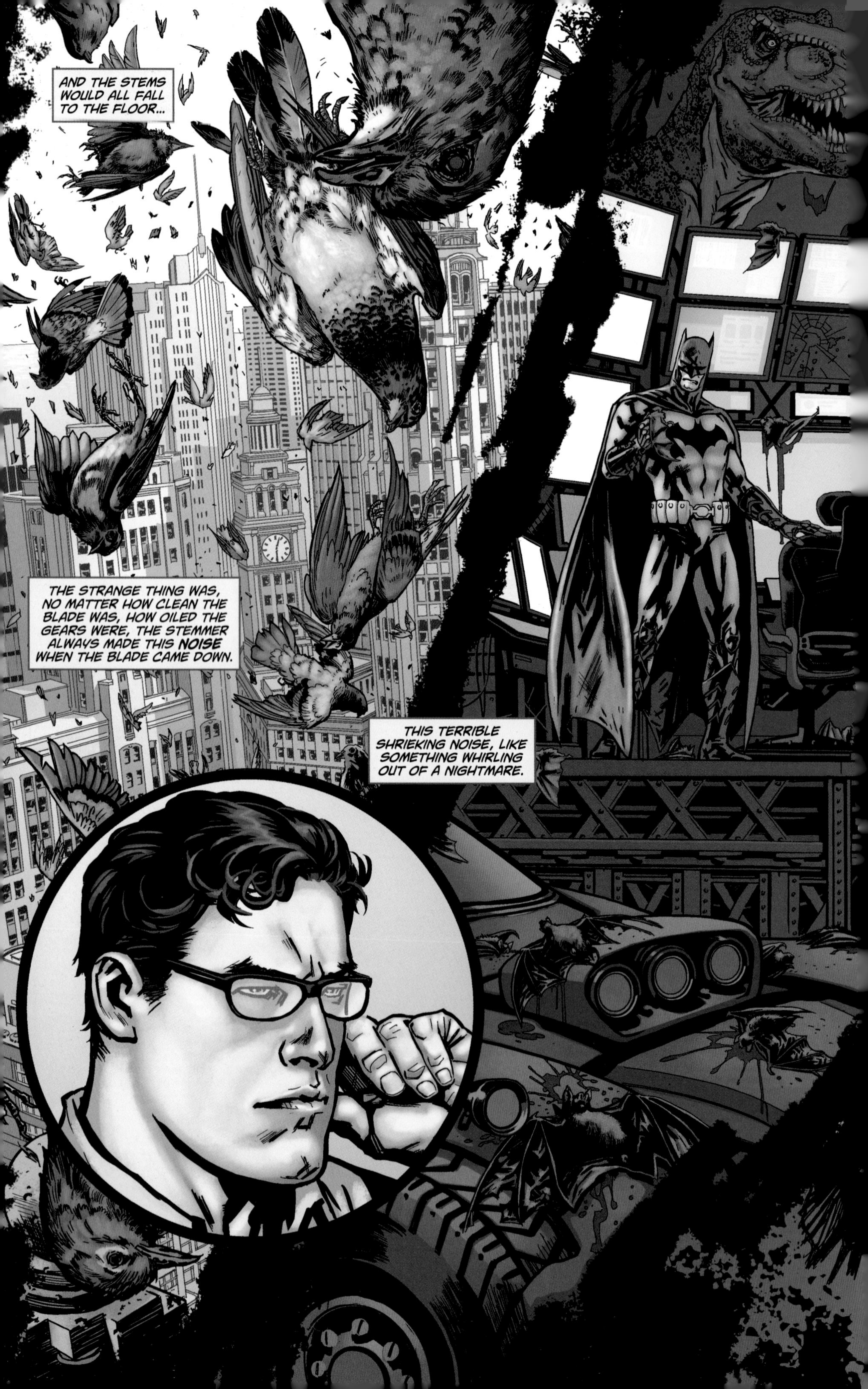
AND THE STEMS WOULD ALL FALL TO THE FLOOR...
THE STRANGE THING WAS, NO MATTER HOW CLEAN THE BLADE WAS, HOW OILED THE GEARS WERE, THE STEMMER ALWAYS MADE THIS NOISE WHEN THE BLADE CAME DOWN.
THIS TERRIBLE SHRIEKING NOISE, LIKE SOMETHING WHIRLING OUT OF A NIGHTMARE.

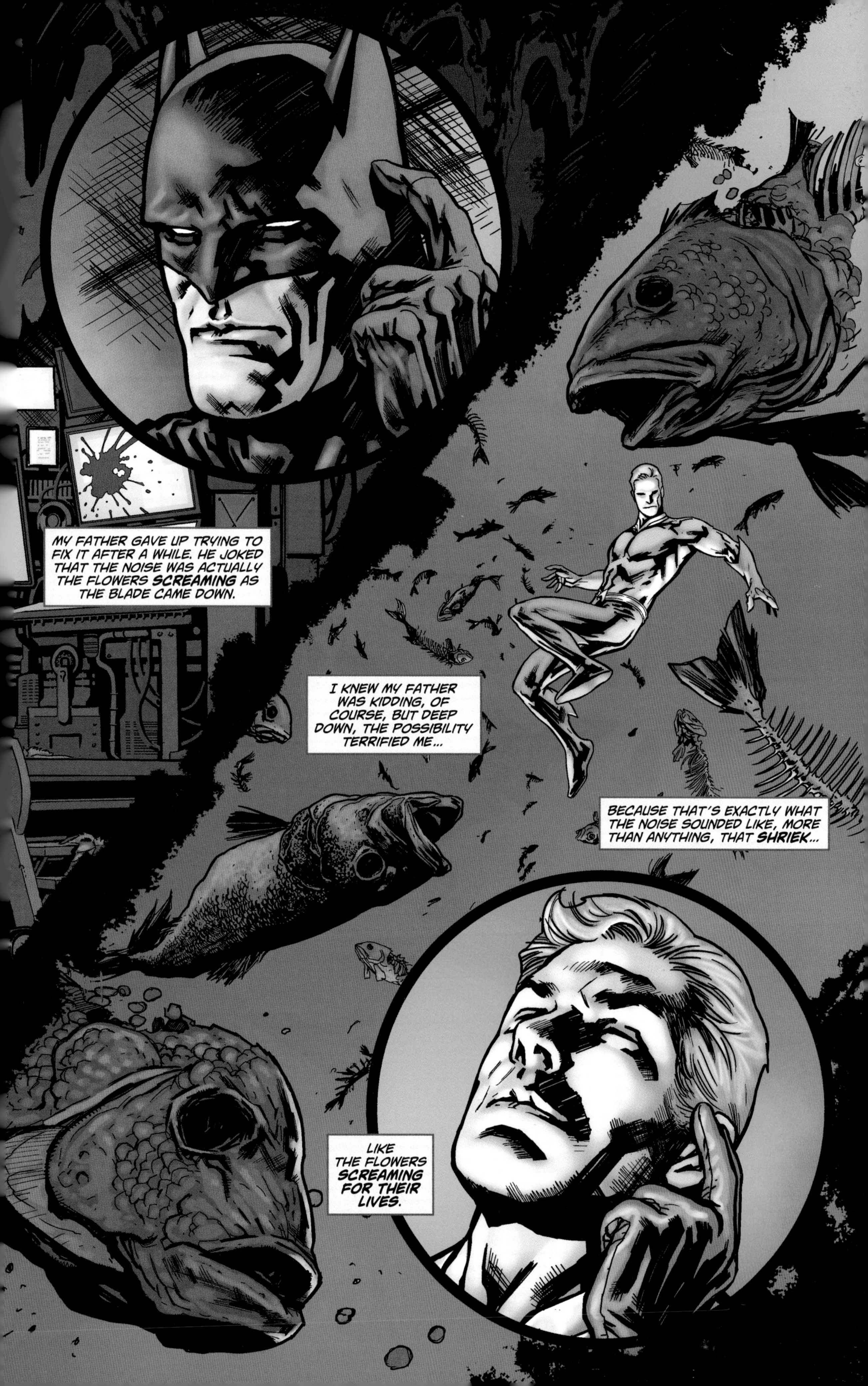
MY FATHER GAVE UP TRYING TO FIX IT AFTER A WHILE. HE JOKED THAT THE NOISE WAS ACTUALLY THE FLOWERS SCREAMING AS THE BLADE CAME DOWN.
I KNEW MY FATHER WAS KIDDING, OF COURSE, BUT DEEP DOWN, THE POSSIBILITY TERRIFIED ME...
BECAUSE THAT'S EXACTLY WHAT THE NOISE SOUNDED LIKE, MORE THAN ANYTHING, THAT SHRIEK...
LIKE THE FLOWERS SCREAMING FOR THEIR LIVES.

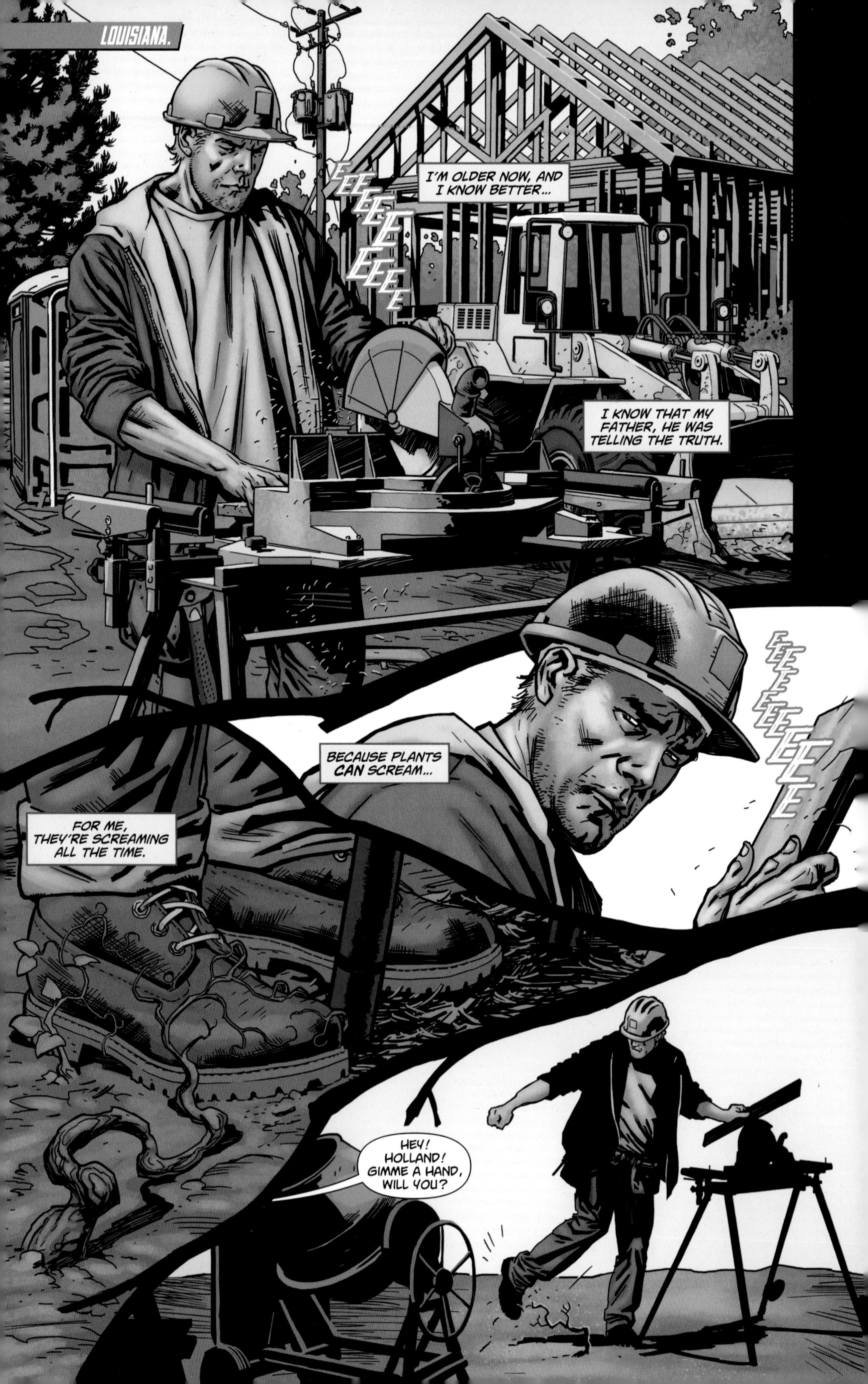
LOUISIANA.
EEEEEEEEEEEE
I'M OLDER NOW, AND I KNOW BETTER...
I KNOW THAT MY FATHER, HE WAS TELLING THE TRUTH.
EEEEEEEEEEE
BECAUSE PLANTS CAN SCREAM...
FOR ME, THEY'RE SCREAMING ALL THE TIME.
HEY! HOLLAND! GIMME A HAND, WILL YOU?

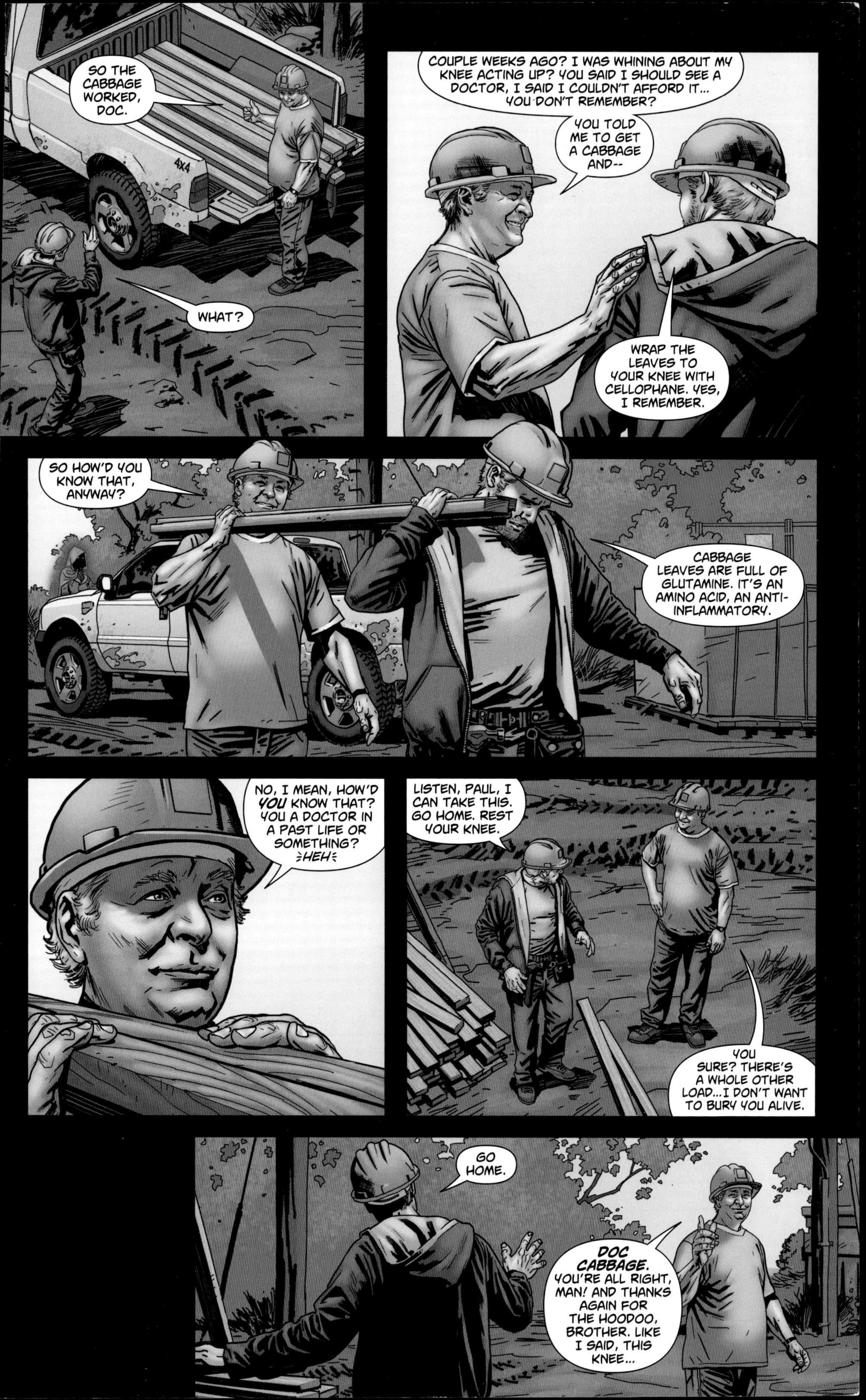
SO THE CABBAGE WORKED, DOC.
WHAT?
COUPLE WEEKS AGO? I WAS WHINING ABOUT MY KNEE ACTING UP? YOU SAID I SHOULD SEE A DOCTOR, I SAID I COULDN'T AFFORD IT... YOU DON'T REMEMBER?
YOU TOLD ME TO GET A CABBAGE AND--
WRAP THE LEAVES TO YOUR KNEE WITH CELLOPHANE. YES, I REMEMBER.
SO HOW'D YOU KNOW THAT, ANYWAY?
CABBAGE LEAVES ARE FULL OF GLUTAMINE. IT'S AN AMINO ACID, AN ANTI-INFLAMMATORY.
NO, I MEAN, HOW'D *YOU* KNOW THAT? YOU A DOCTOR IN A PAST LIFE OR SOMETHING? *HEH*
LISTEN, PAUL, I CAN TAKE THIS. GO HOME. REST YOUR KNEE.
YOU SURE? THERE'S A WHOLE OTHER LOAD...I DON'T WANT TO BURY YOU ALIVE.
GO HOME.
DOC CABBAGE. YOU'RE ALL RIGHT, MAN! AND THANKS AGAIN FOR THE HOODOO, BROTHER. LIKE I SAID, THIS KNEE...

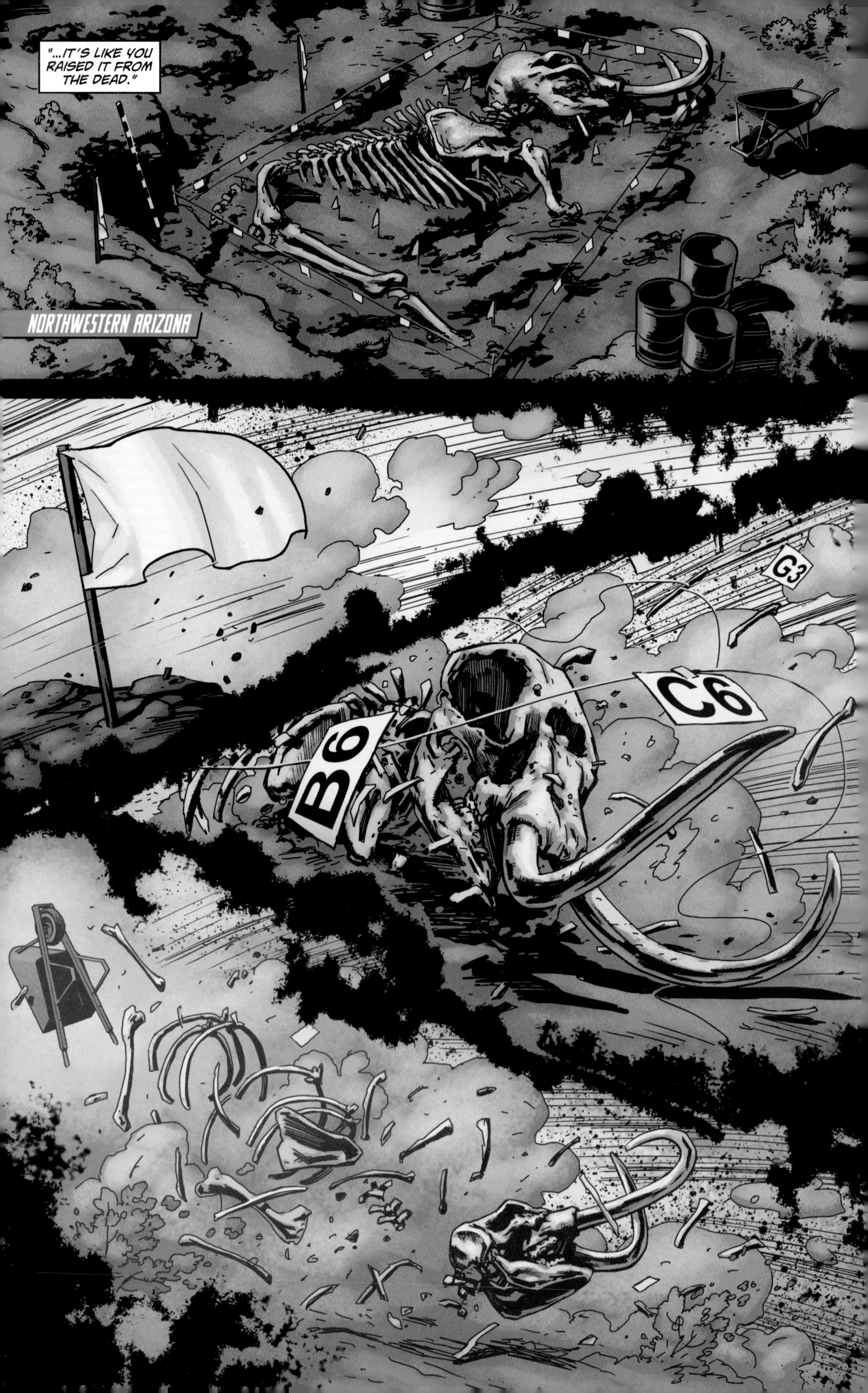
"...IT'S LIKE YOU RAISED IT FROM THE DEAD."
NORTHWESTERN ARIZONA
G3
C6
B6

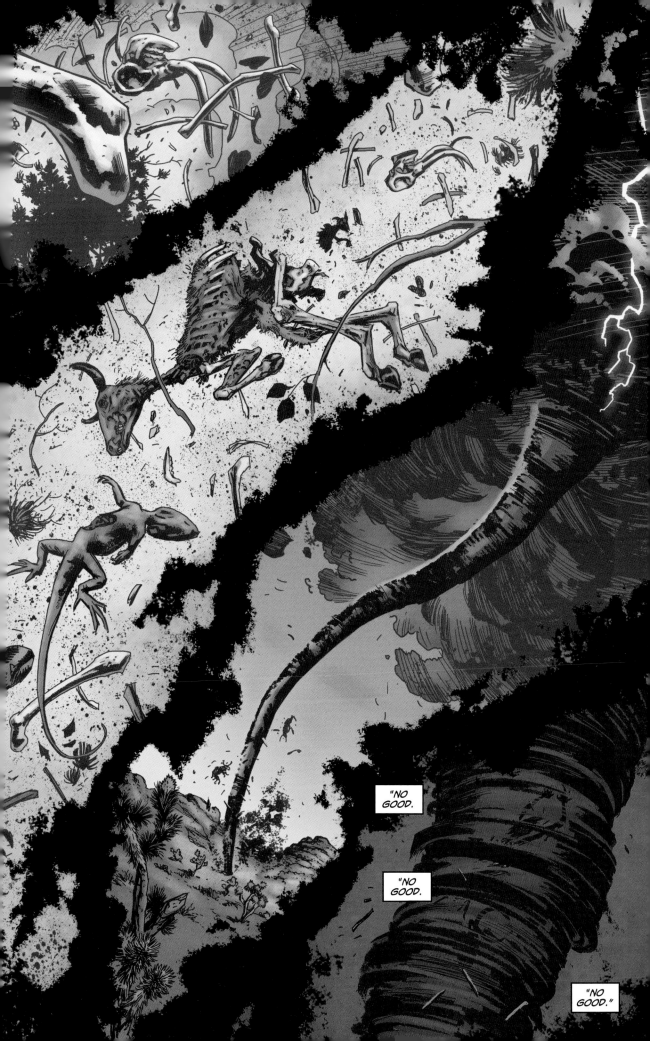

"NO GOOD.

"NO GOOD.

"NO GOOD."

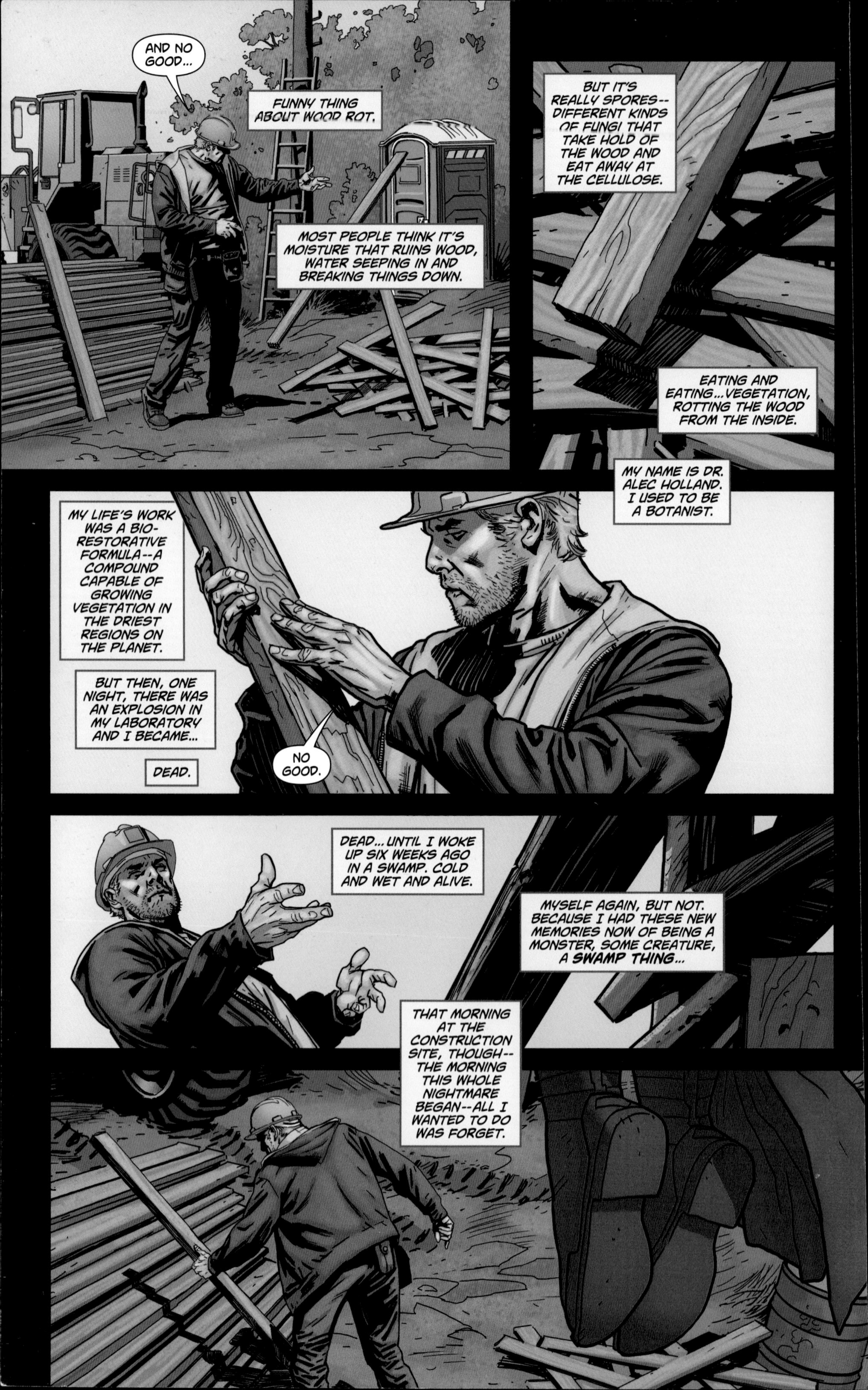
AND NO GOOD...
FUNNY THING ABOUT WOOD ROT.
MOST PEOPLE THINK IT'S MOISTURE THAT RUINS WOOD, WATER SEEPING IN AND BREAKING THINGS DOWN.
BUT IT'S REALLY SPORES-- DIFFERENT KINDS OF FUNGI THAT TAKE HOLD OF THE WOOD AND EAT AWAY AT THE CELLULOSE.
EATING AND EATING...VEGETATION, ROTTING THE WOOD FROM THE INSIDE.
MY NAME IS DR. ALEC HOLLAND. I USED TO BE A BOTANIST.
MY LIFE'S WORK WAS A BIO-RESTORATIVE FORMULA--A COMPOUND CAPABLE OF GROWING VEGETATION IN THE DRIEST REGIONS ON THE PLANET.
BUT THEN, ONE NIGHT, THERE WAS AN EXPLOSION IN MY LABORATORY AND I BECAME...
DEAD.
NO GOOD.
DEAD... UNTIL I WOKE UP SIX WEEKS AGO IN A SWAMP. COLD AND WET AND ALIVE.
MYSELF AGAIN, BUT NOT. BECAUSE I HAD THESE NEW MEMORIES NOW OF BEING A MONSTER, SOME CREATURE, A SWAMP THING...
THAT MORNING AT THE CONSTRUCTION SITE, THOUGH-- THE MORNING THIS WHOLE NIGHTMARE BEGAN--ALL I WANTED TO DO WAS FORGET.

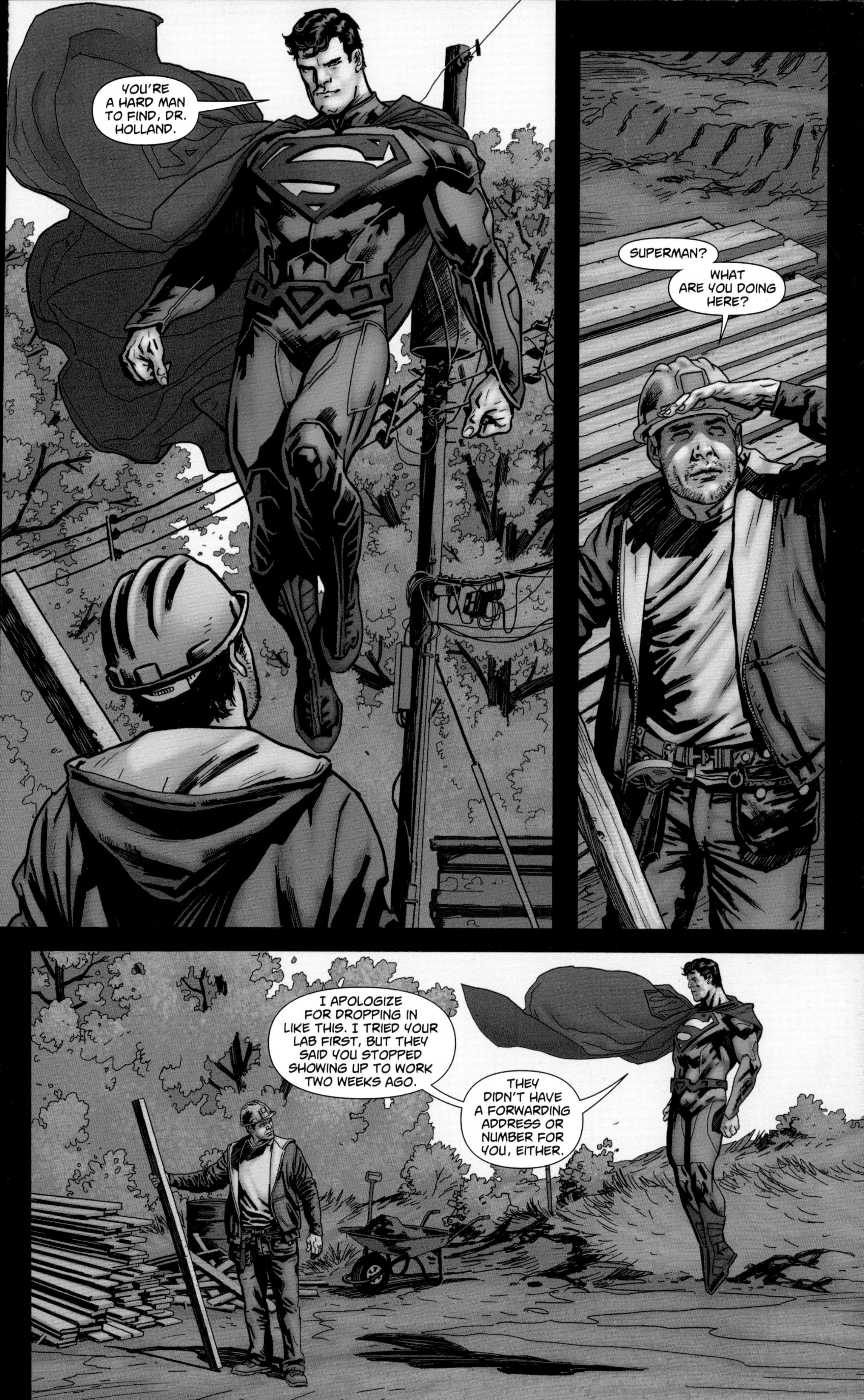
YOU'RE A HARD MAN TO FIND, DR. HOLLAND.
SUPERMAN?
WHAT ARE YOU DOING HERE?
I APOLOGIZE FOR DROPPING IN LIKE THIS. I TRIED YOUR LAB FIRST, BUT THEY SAID YOU STOPPED SHOWING UP TO WORK TWO WEEKS AGO.
THEY DIDN'T HAVE A FORWARDING ADDRESS OR NUMBER FOR YOU, EITHER.

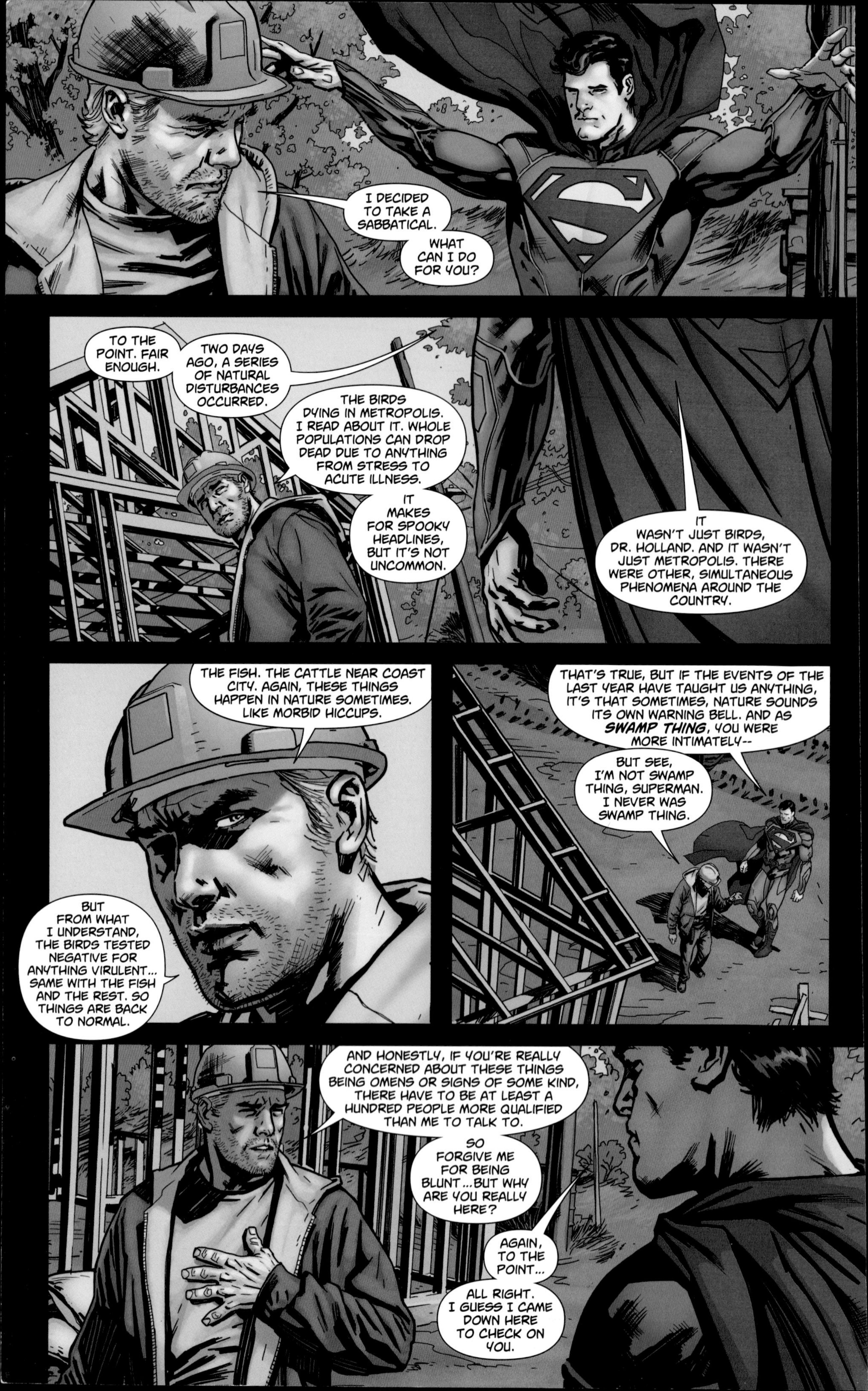
I DECIDED TO TAKE A SABBATICAL.
WHAT CAN I DO FOR YOU?
TO THE POINT. FAIR ENOUGH.
TWO DAYS AGO, A SERIES OF NATURAL DISTURBANCES OCCURRED.
THE BIRDS DYING IN METROPOLIS. I READ ABOUT IT. WHOLE POPULATIONS CAN DROP DEAD DUE TO ANYTHING FROM STRESS TO ACUTE ILLNESS.
IT MAKES FOR SPOOKY HEADLINES, BUT IT'S NOT UNCOMMON.
IT WASN'T JUST BIRDS, DR. HOLLAND. AND IT WASN'T JUST METROPOLIS. THERE WERE OTHER, SIMULTANEOUS PHENOMENA AROUND THE COUNTRY.
THE FISH. THE CATTLE NEAR COAST CITY. AGAIN, THESE THINGS HAPPEN IN NATURE SOMETIMES. LIKE MORBID HICCUPS.
BUT FROM WHAT I UNDERSTAND, THE BIRDS TESTED NEGATIVE FOR ANYTHING VIRULENT... SAME WITH THE FISH AND THE REST. SO THINGS ARE BACK TO NORMAL.
THAT'S TRUE, BUT IF THE EVENTS OF THE LAST YEAR HAVE TAUGHT US ANYTHING, IT'S THAT SOMETIMES, NATURE SOUNDS ITS OWN WARNING BELL. AND AS SWAMP THING, YOU WERE MORE INTIMATELY--
BUT SEE, I'M NOT SWAMP THING, SUPERMAN. I NEVER WAS SWAMP THING.
AND HONESTLY, IF YOU'RE REALLY CONCERNED ABOUT THESE THINGS BEING OMENS OR SIGNS OF SOME KIND, THERE HAVE TO BE AT LEAST A HUNDRED PEOPLE MORE QUALIFIED THAN ME TO TALK TO.
SO FORGIVE ME FOR BEING BLUNT... BUT WHY ARE YOU REALLY HERE?
AGAIN, TO THE POINT...
ALL RIGHT. I GUESS I CAME DOWN HERE TO CHECK ON YOU.

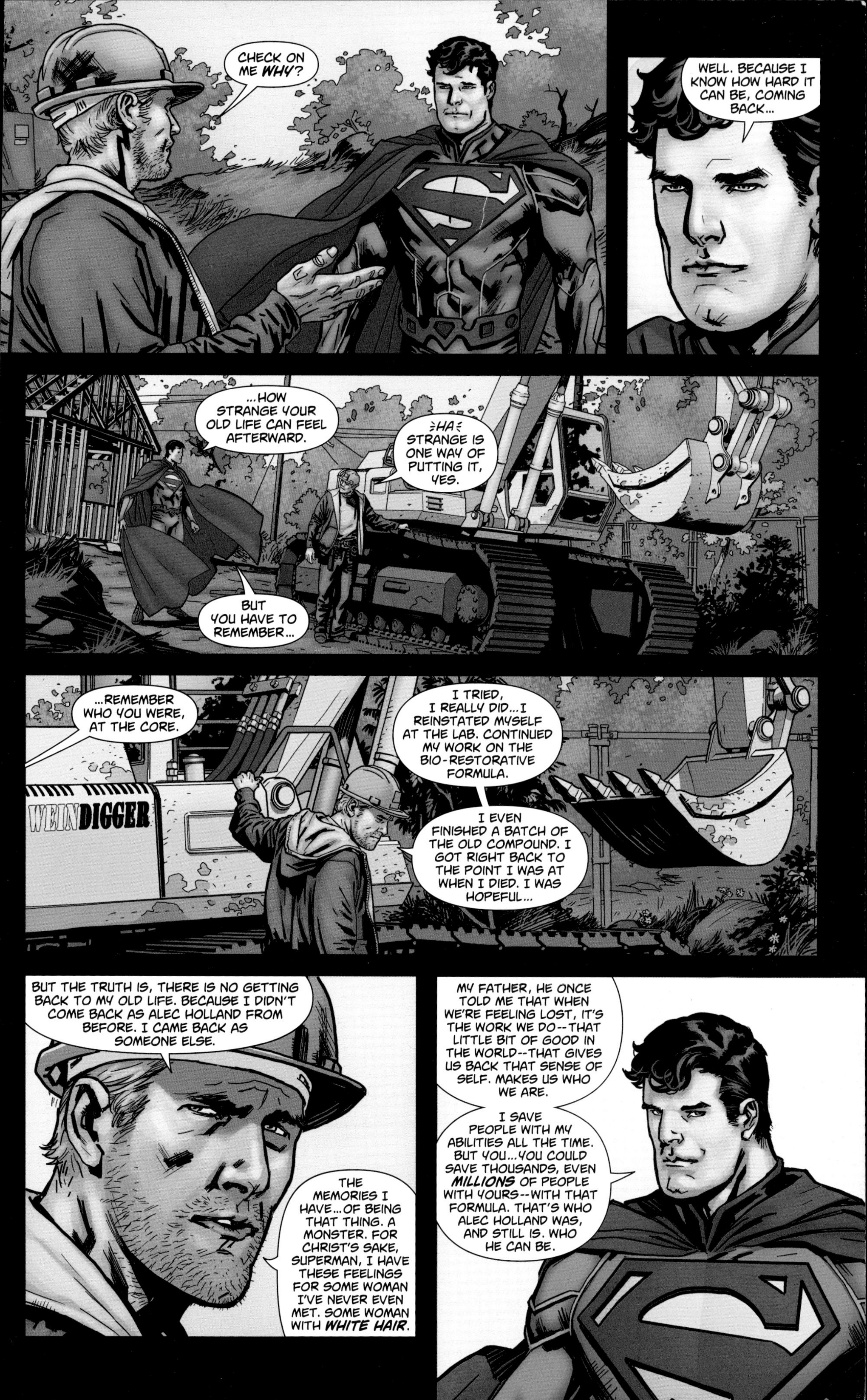
CHECK ON ME WHY?
WELL. BECAUSE I KNOW HOW HARD IT CAN BE, COMING BACK...
...HOW STRANGE YOUR OLD LIFE CAN FEEL AFTERWARD.
HA STRANGE IS ONE WAY OF PUTTING IT, YES.
BUT YOU HAVE TO REMEMBER...
...REMEMBER WHO YOU WERE, AT THE CORE.
WEINDIGGER
I TRIED, I REALLY DID...I REINSTATED MYSELF AT THE LAB. CONTINUED MY WORK ON THE BIO-RESTORATIVE FORMULA.
I EVEN FINISHED A BATCH OF THE OLD COMPOUND. I GOT RIGHT BACK TO THE POINT I WAS AT WHEN I DIED. I WAS HOPEFUL...
BUT THE TRUTH IS, THERE IS NO GETTING BACK TO MY OLD LIFE. BECAUSE I DIDN'T COME BACK AS ALEC HOLLAND FROM BEFORE. I CAME BACK AS SOMEONE ELSE.
THE MEMORIES I HAVE...OF BEING THAT THING. A MONSTER. FOR CHRIST'S SAKE, SUPERMAN, I HAVE THESE FEELINGS FOR SOME WOMAN I'VE NEVER EVEN MET. SOME WOMAN WITH WHITE HAIR.
MY FATHER, HE ONCE TOLD ME THAT WHEN WE'RE FEELING LOST, IT'S THE WORK WE DO--THAT LITTLE BIT OF GOOD IN THE WORLD--THAT GIVES US BACK THAT SENSE OF SELF. MAKES US WHO WE ARE.
I SAVE PEOPLE WITH MY ABILITIES ALL THE TIME. BUT YOU...YOU COULD SAVE THOUSANDS, EVEN MILLIONS OF PEOPLE WITH YOURS--WITH THAT FORMULA. THAT'S WHO ALEC HOLLAND WAS, AND STILL IS. WHO HE CAN BE.

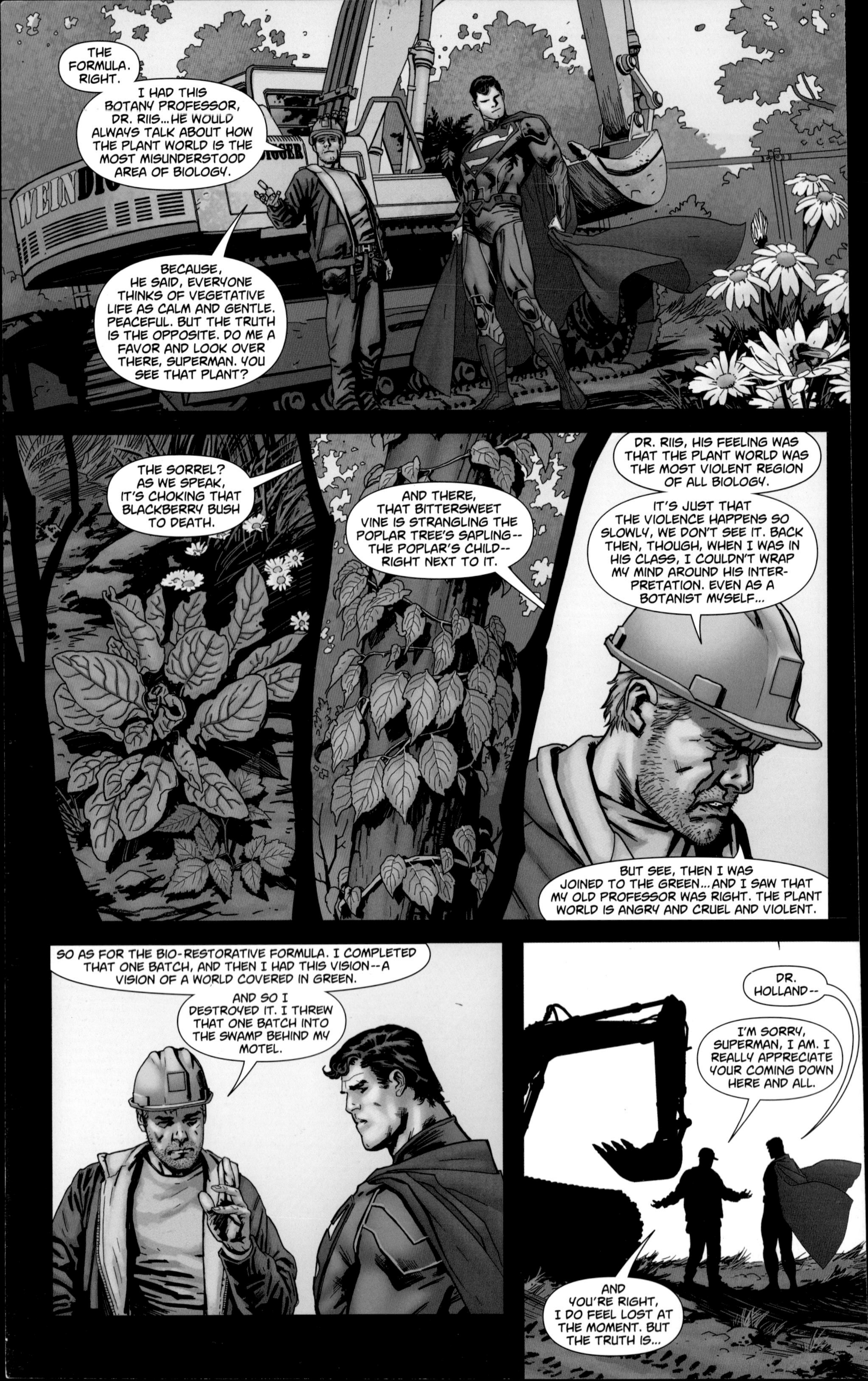
THE FORMULA. RIGHT.
I HAD THIS BOTANY PROFESSOR, DR. RIIS...HE WOULD ALWAYS TALK ABOUT HOW THE PLANT WORLD IS THE MOST MISUNDERSTOOD AREA OF BIOLOGY.
BECAUSE, HE SAID, EVERYONE THINKS OF VEGETATIVE LIFE AS CALM AND GENTLE. PEACEFUL. BUT THE TRUTH IS THE OPPOSITE. DO ME A FAVOR AND LOOK OVER THERE, SUPERMAN. YOU SEE THAT PLANT?
THE SORREL? AS WE SPEAK, IT'S CHOKING THAT BLACKBERRY BUSH TO DEATH.
AND THERE, THAT BITTERSWEET VINE IS STRANGLING THE POPLAR TREE'S SAPLING-- THE POPLAR'S CHILD-- RIGHT NEXT TO IT.
DR. RIIS, HIS FEELING WAS THAT THE PLANT WORLD WAS THE MOST VIOLENT REGION OF ALL BIOLOGY.
IT'S JUST THAT THE VIOLENCE HAPPENS SO SLOWLY, WE DON'T SEE IT. BACK THEN, THOUGH, WHEN I WAS IN HIS CLASS, I COULDN'T WRAP MY MIND AROUND HIS INTER-PRETATION. EVEN AS A BOTANIST MYSELF...
BUT SEE, THEN I WAS JOINED TO THE GREEN... AND I SAW THAT MY OLD PROFESSOR WAS RIGHT. THE PLANT WORLD IS ANGRY AND CRUEL AND VIOLENT.
SO AS FOR THE BIO-RESTORATIVE FORMULA. I COMPLETED THAT ONE BATCH, AND THEN I HAD THIS VISION--A VISION OF A WORLD COVERED IN GREEN.
AND SO I DESTROYED IT. I THREW THAT ONE BATCH INTO THE SWAMP BEHIND MY MOTEL.
DR. HOLLAND--
I'M SORRY, SUPERMAN, I AM. I REALLY APPRECIATE YOUR COMING DOWN HERE AND ALL.
AND YOU'RE RIGHT, I DO FEEL LOST AT THE MOMENT. BUT THE TRUTH IS...

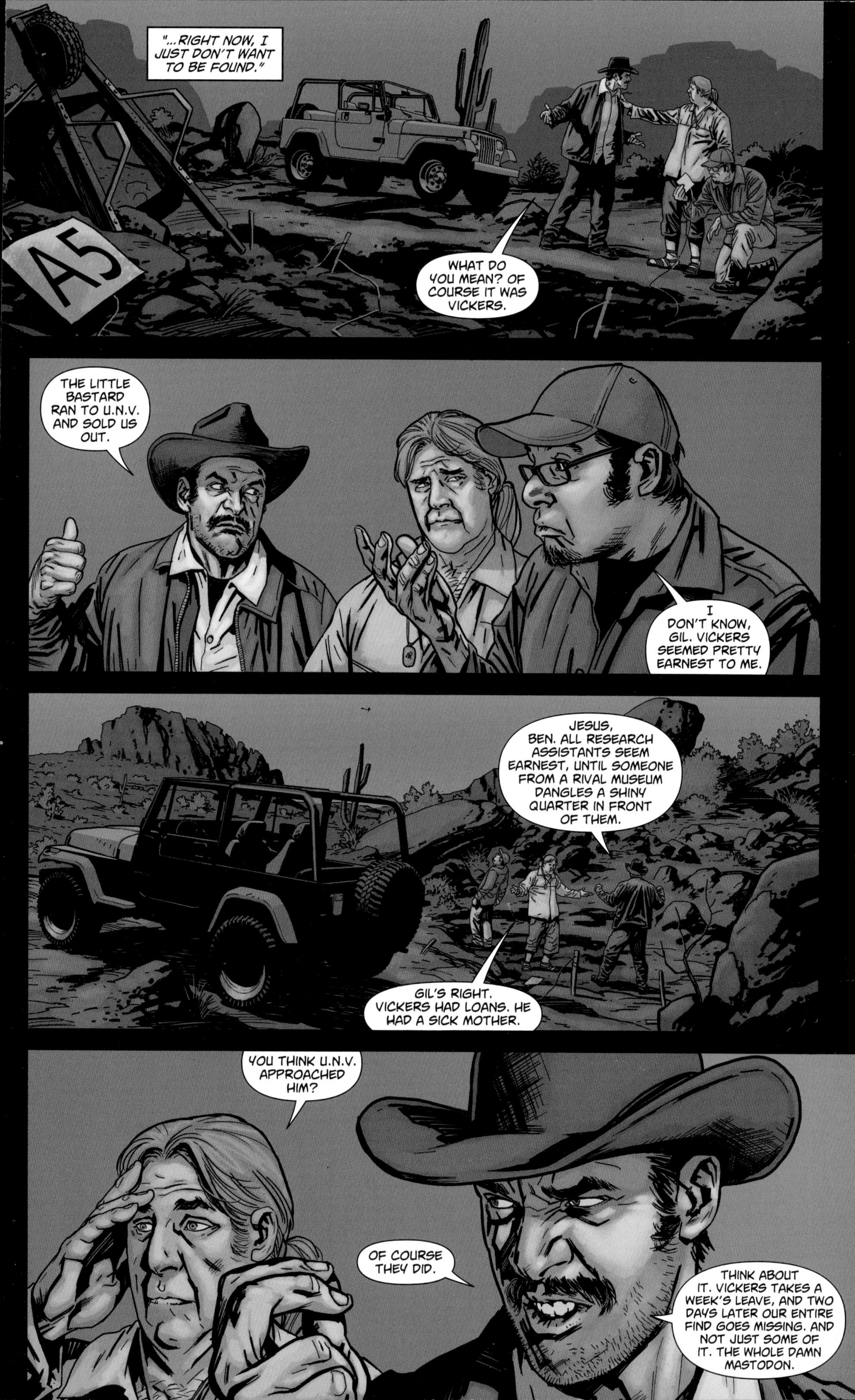
"...RIGHT NOW, I JUST DON'T WANT TO BE FOUND."
A5
WHAT DO YOU MEAN? OF COURSE IT WAS VICKERS.
THE LITTLE BASTARD RAN TO U.N.V. AND SOLD US OUT.
I DON'T KNOW, GIL. VICKERS SEEMED PRETTY EARNEST TO ME.
JESUS, BEN. ALL RESEARCH ASSISTANTS SEEM EARNEST, UNTIL SOMEONE FROM A RIVAL MUSEUM DANGLES A SHINY QUARTER IN FRONT OF THEM.
GIL'S RIGHT. VICKERS HAD LOANS. HE HAD A SICK MOTHER.
YOU THINK U.N.V. APPROACHED HIM?
OF COURSE THEY DID.
THINK ABOUT IT. VICKERS TAKES A WEEK'S LEAVE, AND TWO DAYS LATER OUR ENTIRE FIND GOES MISSING. AND NOT JUST SOME OF IT. THE WHOLE DAMN MASTODON.

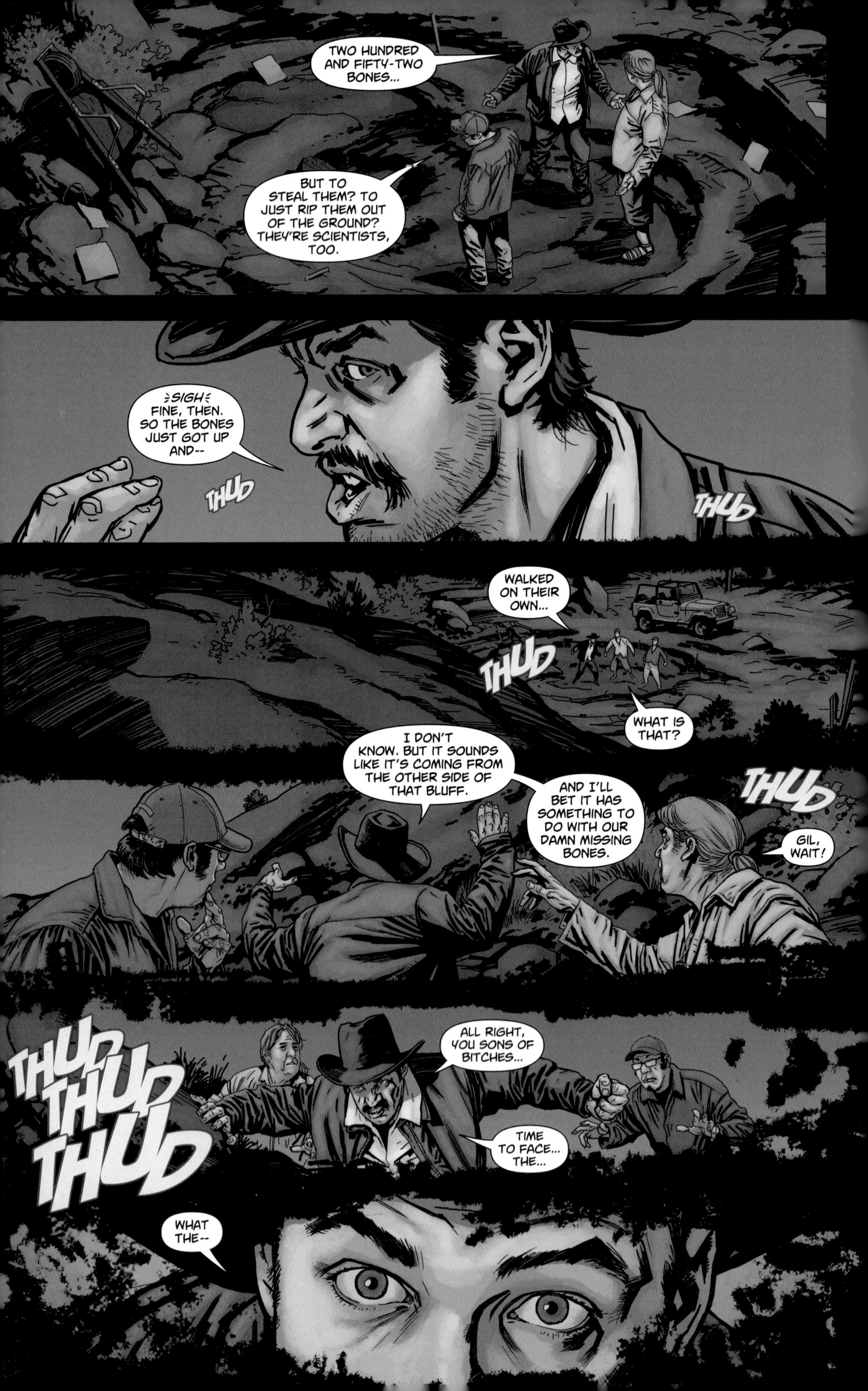
TWO HUNDRED AND FIFTY-TWO BONES...
BUT TO STEAL THEM? TO JUST RIP THEM OUT OF THE GROUND? THEY'RE SCIENTISTS, TOO.
SIGH
FINE, THEN. SO THE BONES JUST GOT UP AND--
THUD
THUD
WALKED ON THEIR OWN...
THUD
WHAT IS THAT?
I DON'T KNOW. BUT IT SOUNDS LIKE IT'S COMING FROM THE OTHER SIDE OF THAT BLUFF.
AND I'LL BET IT HAS SOMETHING TO DO WITH OUR DAMN MISSING BONES.
THUD
GIL, WAIT!
THUD THUD THUD
ALL RIGHT, YOU SONS OF BITCHES...
TIME TO FACE... THE...
WHAT THE--

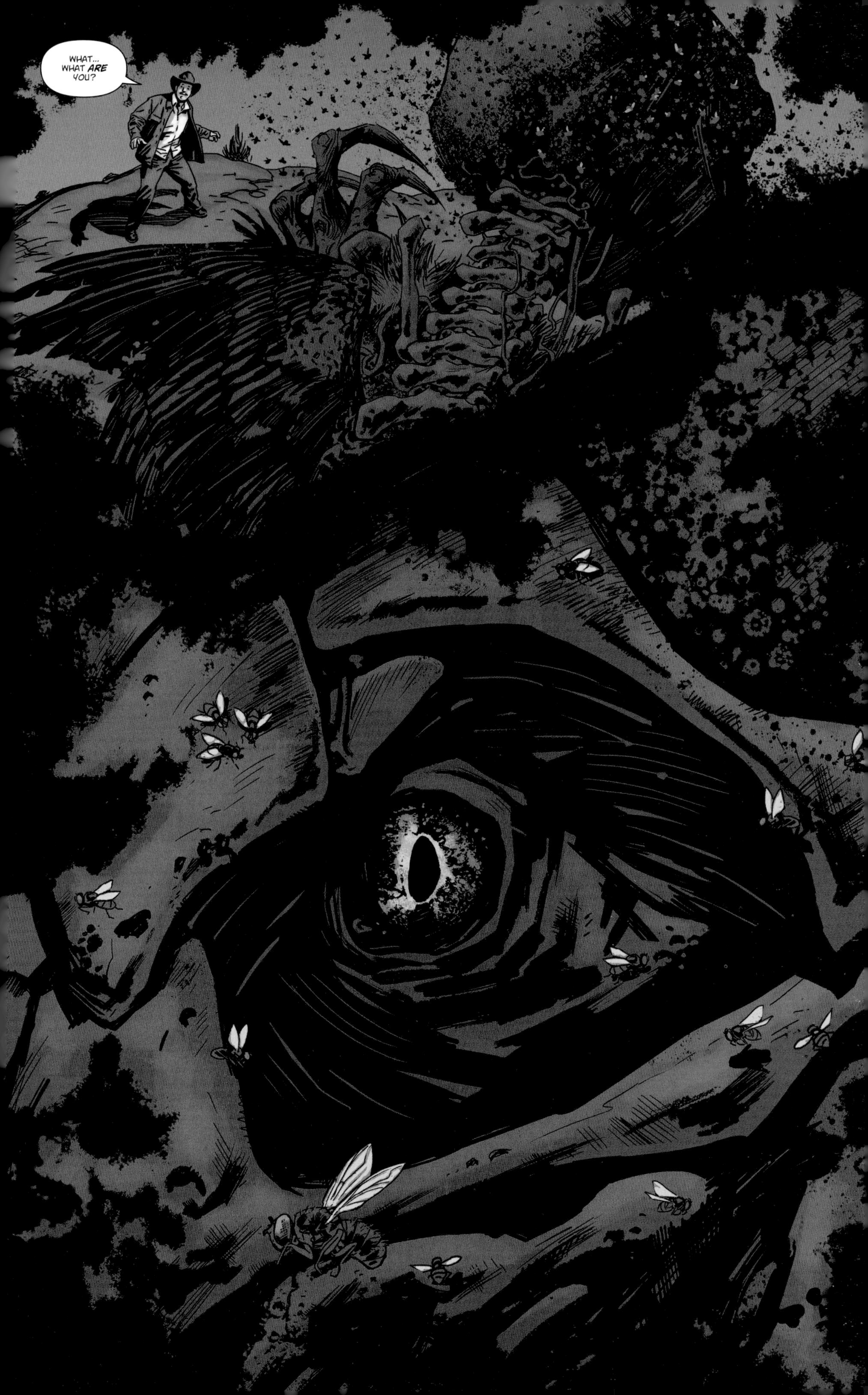
WHAT... WHAT ARE YOU?

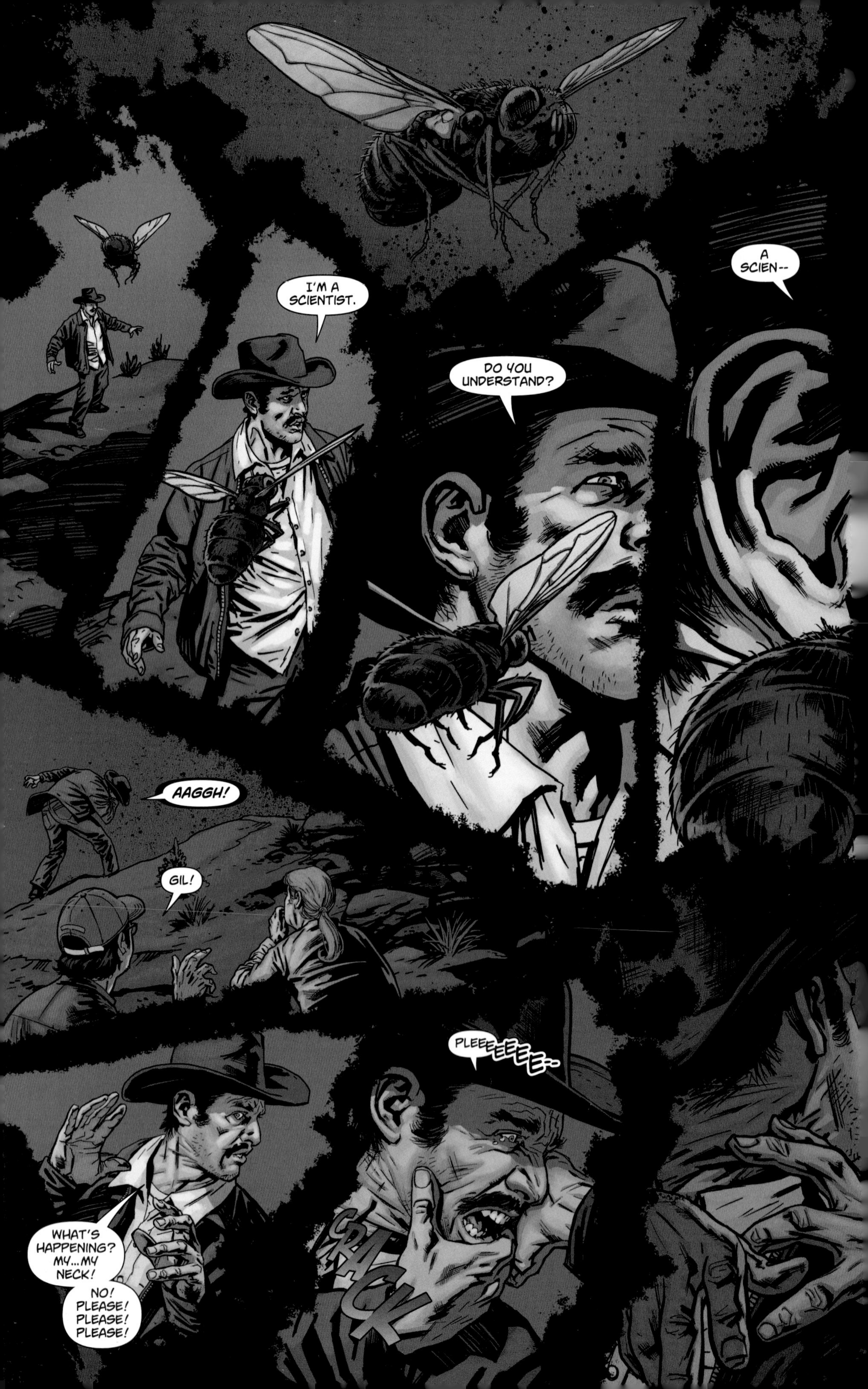
I'M A SCIENTIST.
DO YOU UNDERSTAND?
A SCIEN--
AAGGH!
GIL!
WHAT'S HAPPENING? MY...MY NECK!
NO! PLEASE! PLEASE! PLEASE!
PLEEEEEEE--
CRACK

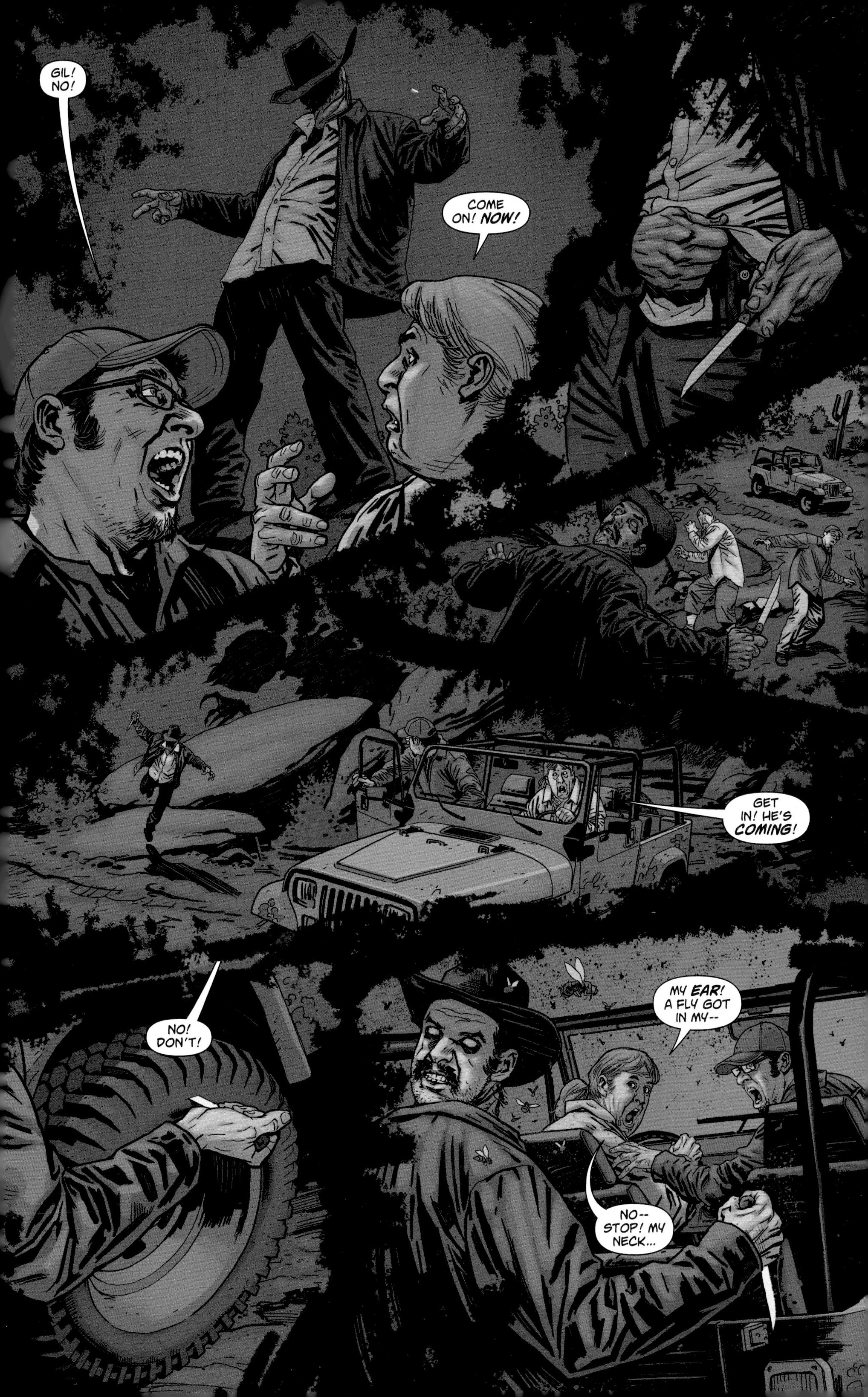
GIL! NO!
COME ON! NOW!
GET IN! HE'S COMING!
NO! DON'T!
MY EAR! A FLY GOT IN MY--
NO-- STOP! MY NECK...

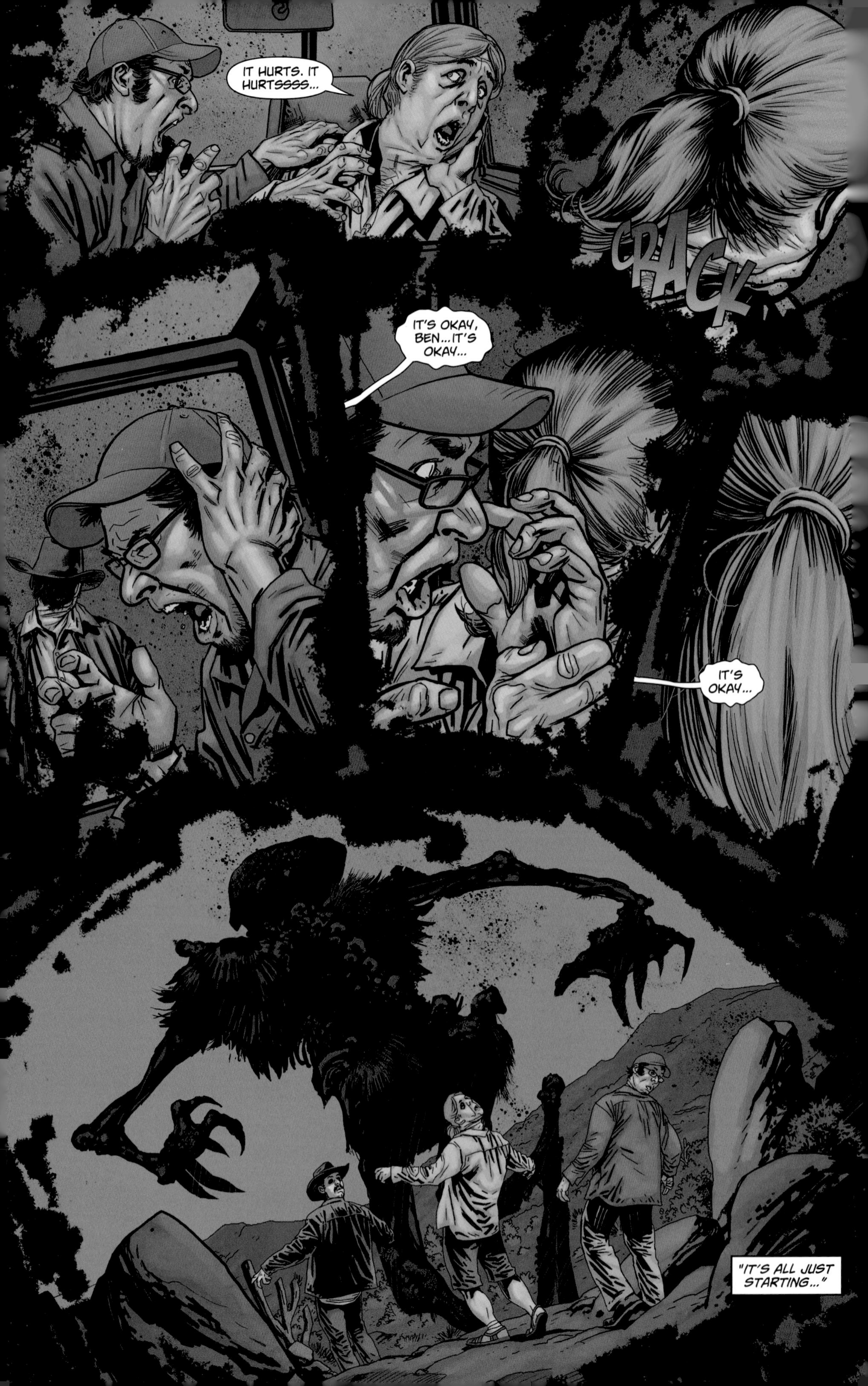
IT HURTS. IT HURTSSSS...
CRACK
IT'S OKAY, BEN...IT'S OKAY...
IT'S OKAY...
"IT'S ALL JUST STARTING..."

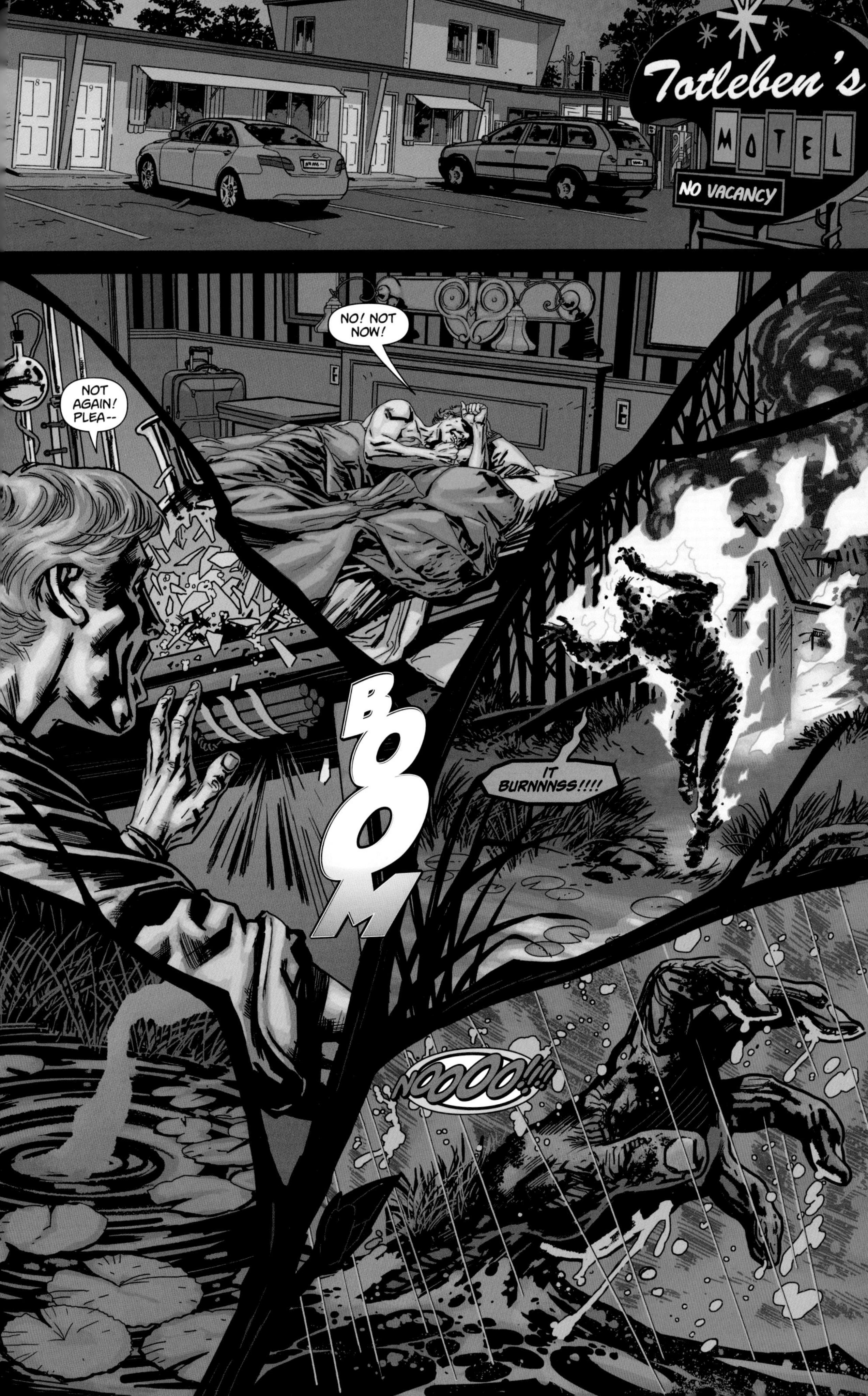
Totleben's
MOTEL
NO VACANCY
NOT AGAIN! PLEA--
NO! NOT NOW!
BOOM
IT BURNNNSS!!!!
NOOOOO!!!

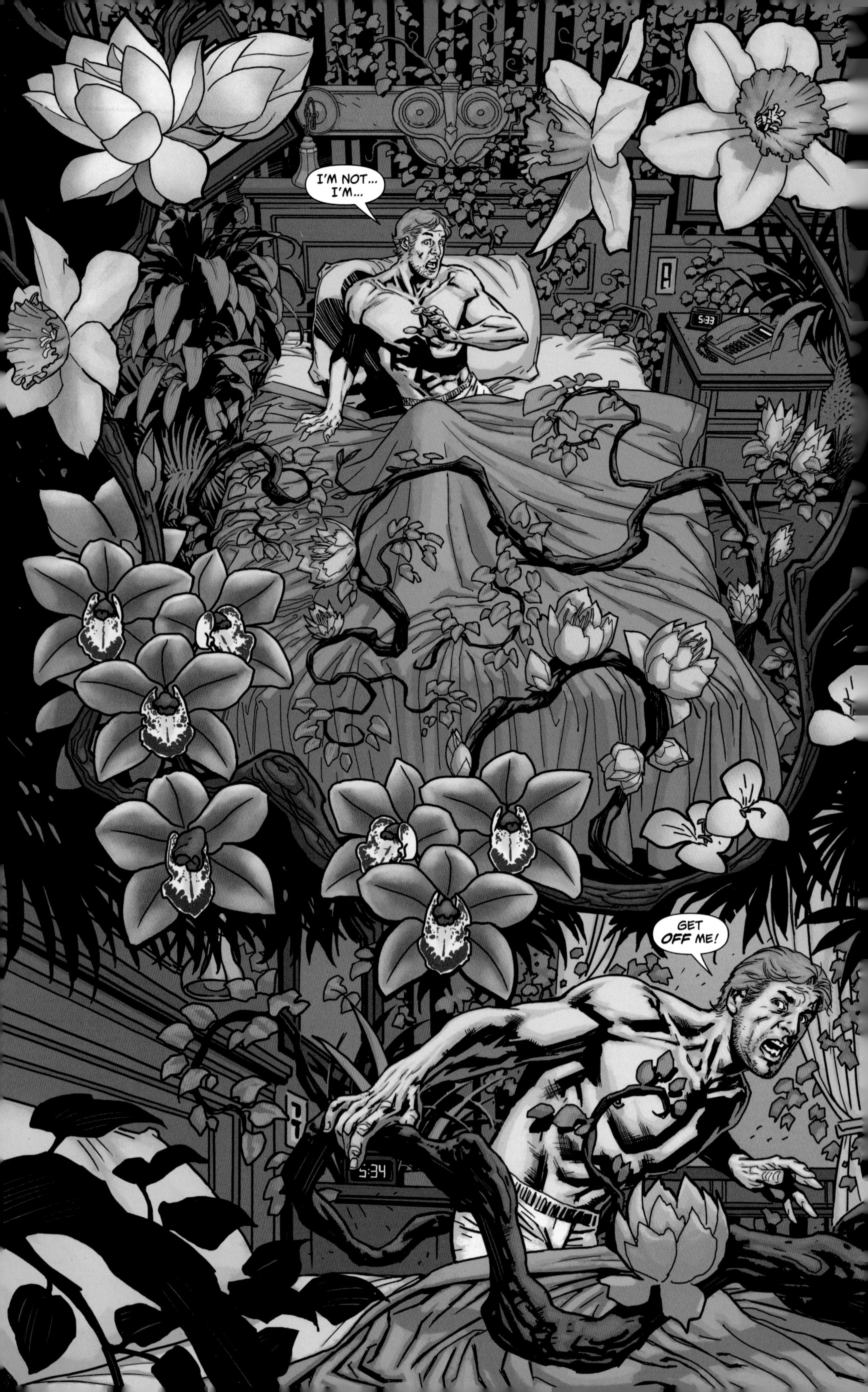
I'M NOT...
I'M...
5:33
GET
OFF ME!
5:34

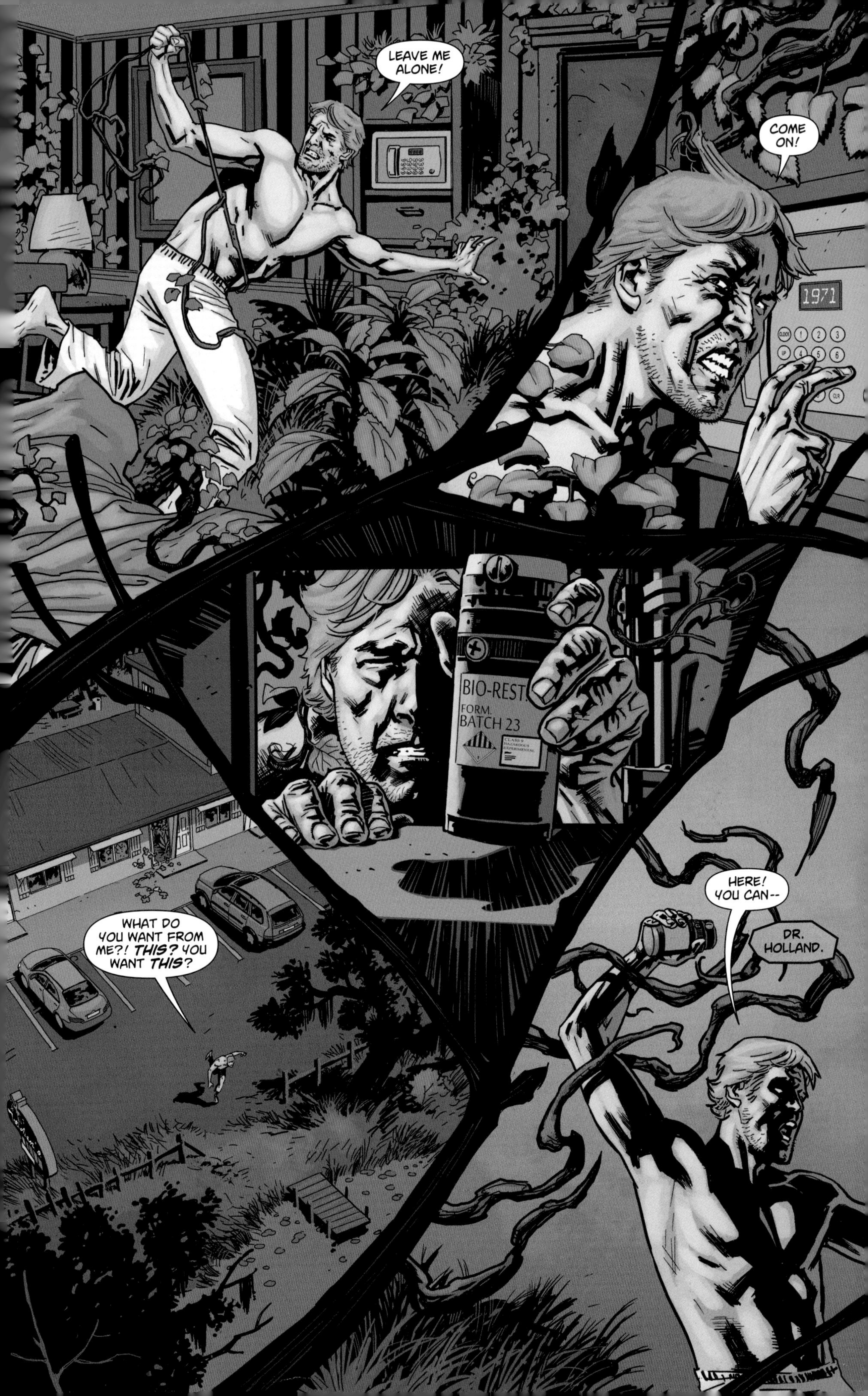
LEAVE ME ALONE!
COME ON!
1971
BIO-REST.
FORM.
BATCH 23
WHAT DO YOU WANT FROM ME?! THIS? YOU WANT THIS?
HERE! YOU CAN--
DR. HOLLAND.

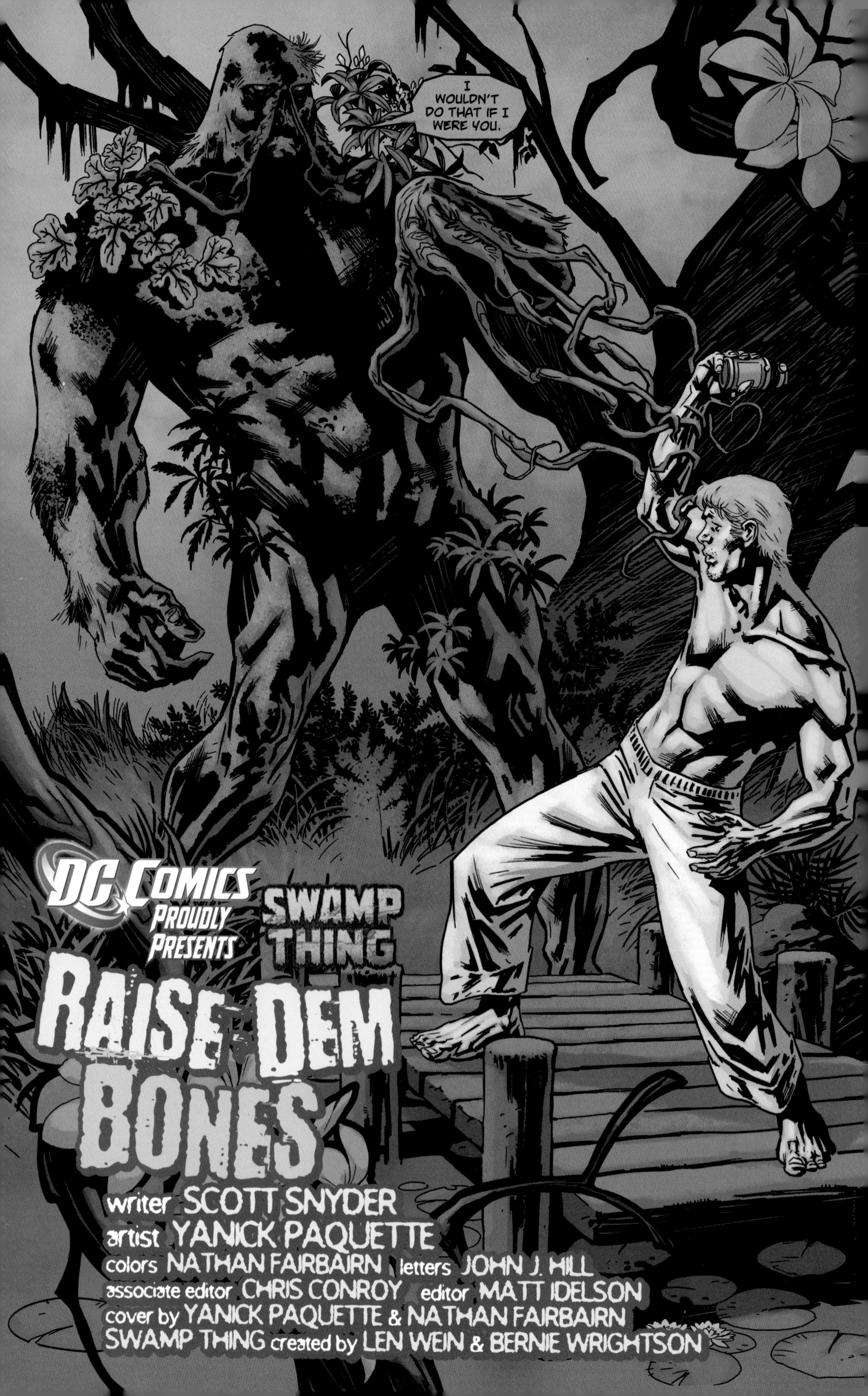
I WOULDN'T DO THAT IF I WERE YOU.
DC COMICS PROUDLY PRESENTS
SWAMP THING
RAISE DEM BONES
writer SCOTT SNYDER
artist YANICK PAQUETTE
colors NATHAN FAIRBAIRN letters JOHN J. HILL
associate editor CHRIS CONROY editor MATT IDELSON
cover by YANICK PAQUETTE & NATHAN FAIRBAIRN
SWAMP THING created by LEN WEIN & BERNIE WRIGHTSON

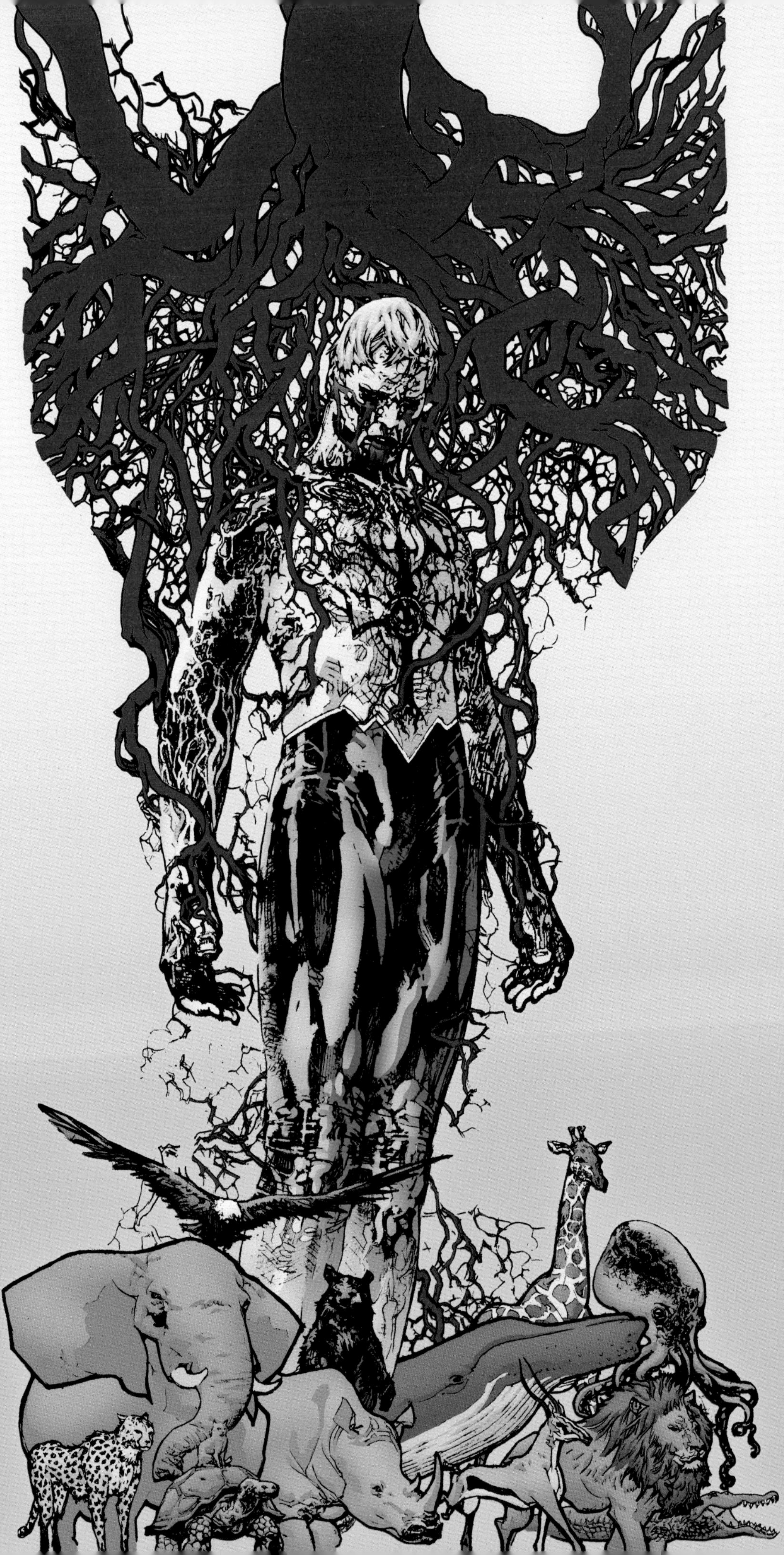

Animal Man

BUDDY BAKER
[SUPERHERO/ACTOR/ACTIVIST]

"I REALIZED I COULD MAKE MORE OF A DIFFERENCE EDUCATING PEOPLE ON ANIMAL RIGHTS THAN I COULD BY PUNCHING OUT A SUPER VILLAIN, YOU KNOW? IT WAS KIND OF A NATURAL PROGRESSION. AN EVOLUTION."

O*ver the last three years, San Diego-based family man Buddy Baker has perhaps been better known as the goggles-wearing superhero "Animal Man." But more recently, Baker's on-again, off-again career as a costumed crimefighter has given way to a new role, that of an animal rights activist and spokesperson. Baker's iconic image has even been adopted by youth culture. His politics and past exploits have made him something of a poster boy for the young left-wing hipster crowd. Perhaps most surprising, though, is Baker's current turn in front of the movie cameras, starring in indie-darling Ryan Daranovsky's edgy drama "Tights," playing, what else, a washed-up superhero determined to go down fighting. The Believer caught up with Buddy in his favorite vegan restaurant in downtown L.A.*
—Jeff Lemire

THE BELIEVER: You seem to be a guy who can't sit still. You started out as a Hollywood stunt man, then you popped up as a superhero, and now you're an actor. Yet you've been happily married for almost a decade. How do you reconcile that inherent restlessness with the stability of your family life?

BUDDY BAKER: Well, I don't know if I'd say I'm restless. I just kind of like to roll with the punches, you know. I take opportunities as they present themselves. When I got my superpowers, becoming a hero just seemed like the thing to do. And that led to all kinds of new experiences, and really opened my eyes to the injustices facing animals in our world. I realized I could make more of a difference educating people on animal rights than I could by punching out a super villain, you know? It was kind of a natural progression. An evolution.

BLVR: Yes, but then, why the decision to return to the film world after so many years away? And why as an actor this time instead of coming back as a stunt man, where you got your start?

BB: Again, the opportunity just sort of presented itself. My superhero "career" hadn't really been going anywhere in the last couple of years. Like I said, I had sort of become more of a spokesman than a superman. Flying around space and catching maniacs in funny costumes was never really my thing, although I did do my fair share of that [laughs]. But

anyway, Ryan [Daranovsky] contacted my agent out of the blue and asked if I'd be interested in reading for the role. Once I heard about the project, and realized how perfect it was for me, I couldn't turn it down. I thought it would be fun.

BLVR: So is this a one-time thing? Or are you going to actively pursue more acting roles? You must be aware that there is already some Oscar buzz surrounding you.

BB: Hell, I really don't know. I've been offered other things, but nothing I really cared for. It was fun, a great experience, but who knows what's next?

BLVR: Let's switch gears for a minute. Your image, specifically your iconic look with the skintight suit with the stylized "A" on the front as Animal Man, has become something of a flag for youth culture of late. How does it feel to have your face plastered on kids' dorm rooms and T-shirts all over the country?

BB: It's weird [laughs]. My wife makes fun of me every time she sees a kid wearing one of those Animal Man "Evolve or Die" T-shirts. But the truth is, I think it's pretty great, you know. If my time as Animal Man has helped open people's eyes to the fact that we share this planet with all other creatures, and that we are all connected…then I'm not complaining.

BLVR: I have to ask, do you get any money for all those T-shirts?

BB: Sigh…no, not a penny [laughs]. I think that's what really ticked Ellen (my wife) off [laughs]. But come on… I was a punk when I was that age. The whole DIY, bootleg thing is a part of who I am. I'm certainly not going to go after anyone to get cash.

BLVR: Finally, you seem to speak about your time as Animal Man as if it were a thing of the past. You've barely been active lately. Is your time as a legitimate superhero over?

BB: No. Not at all. Animal Man will always be a big part of who I am. I may not go out on regular patrols like I used to, but I'll never give it up. As long as the world still needs Animal Man, he'll be around.

Illustration by Travel Foreman

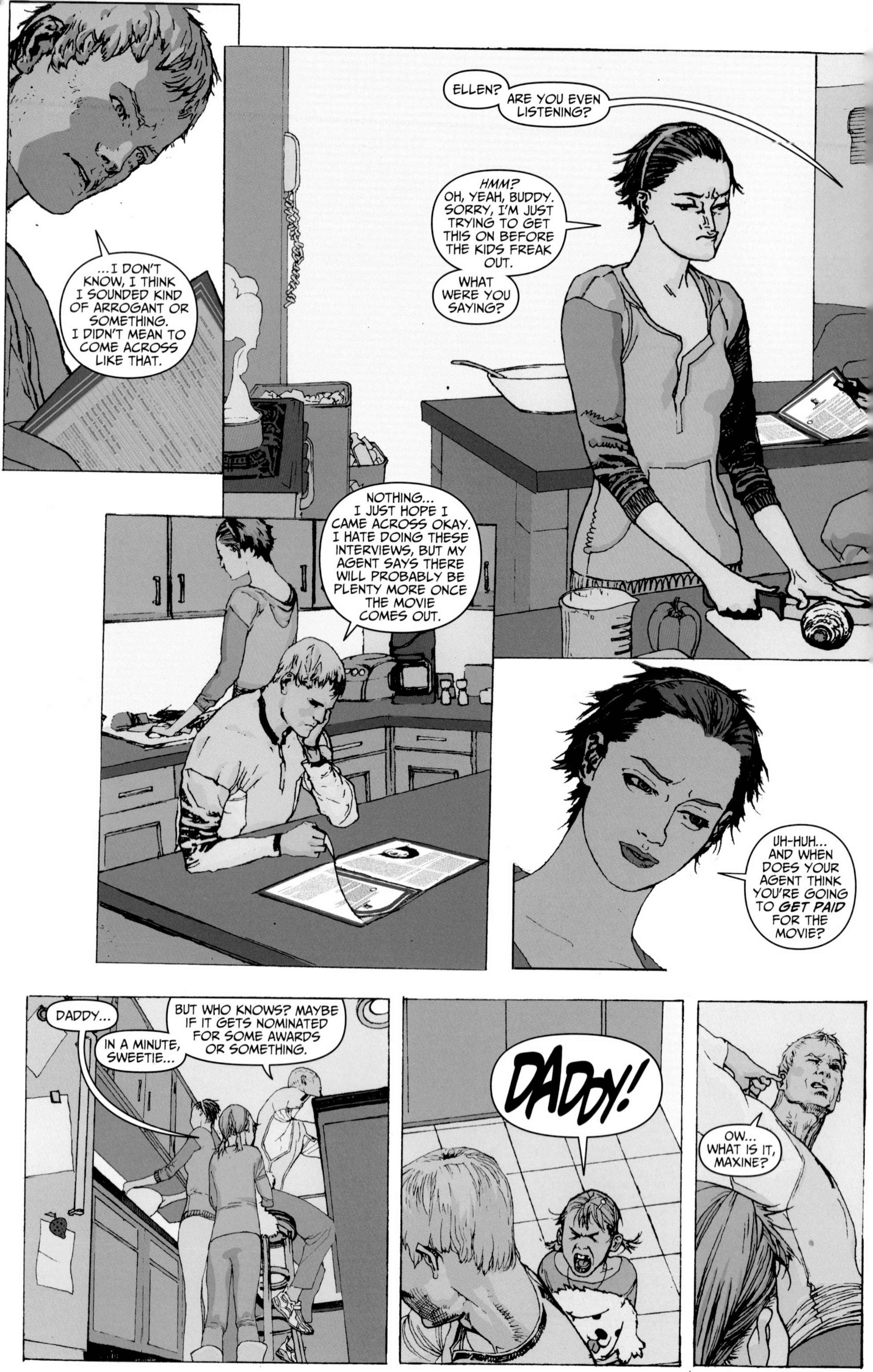
...I DON'T KNOW, I THINK I SOUNDED KIND OF ARROGANT OR SOMETHING. I DIDN'T MEAN TO COME ACROSS LIKE THAT.
ELLEN?
ARE YOU EVEN LISTENING?
HMM? OH, YEAH, BUDDY. SORRY, I'M JUST TRYING TO GET THIS ON BEFORE THE KIDS FREAK OUT.
WHAT WERE YOU SAYING?
NOTHING... I JUST HOPE I CAME ACROSS OKAY. I HATE DOING THESE INTERVIEWS, BUT MY AGENT SAYS THERE WILL PROBABLY BE PLENTY MORE ONCE THE MOVIE COMES OUT.
UH-HUH... AND WHEN DOES YOUR AGENT THINK YOU'RE GOING TO GET PAID FOR THE MOVIE?
DADDY...
IN A MINUTE, SWEETIE...
BUT WHO KNOWS? MAYBE IF IT GETS NOMINATED FOR SOME AWARDS OR SOMETHING.
DADDY!
OW... WHAT IS IT, MAXINE?

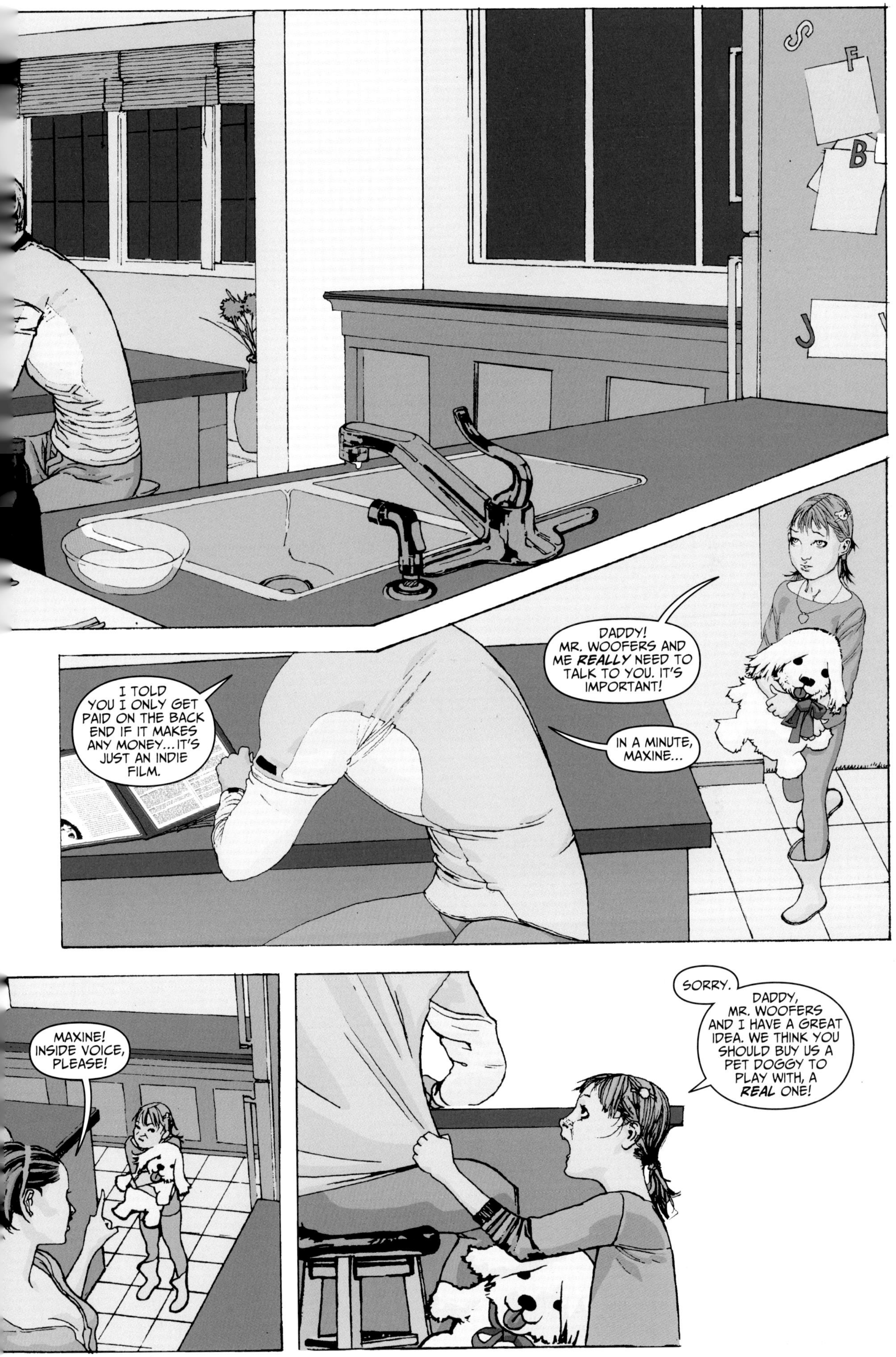
DADDY! MR. WOOFERS AND ME REALLY NEED TO TALK TO YOU. IT'S IMPORTANT!
I TOLD YOU I ONLY GET PAID ON THE BACK END IF IT MAKES ANY MONEY... IT'S JUST AN INDIE FILM.
IN A MINUTE, MAXINE...
MAXINE! INSIDE VOICE, PLEASE!
SORRY.
DADDY, MR. WOOFERS AND I HAVE A GREAT IDEA. WE THINK YOU SHOULD BUY US A PET DOGGY TO PLAY WITH, A REAL ONE!
F
B
J

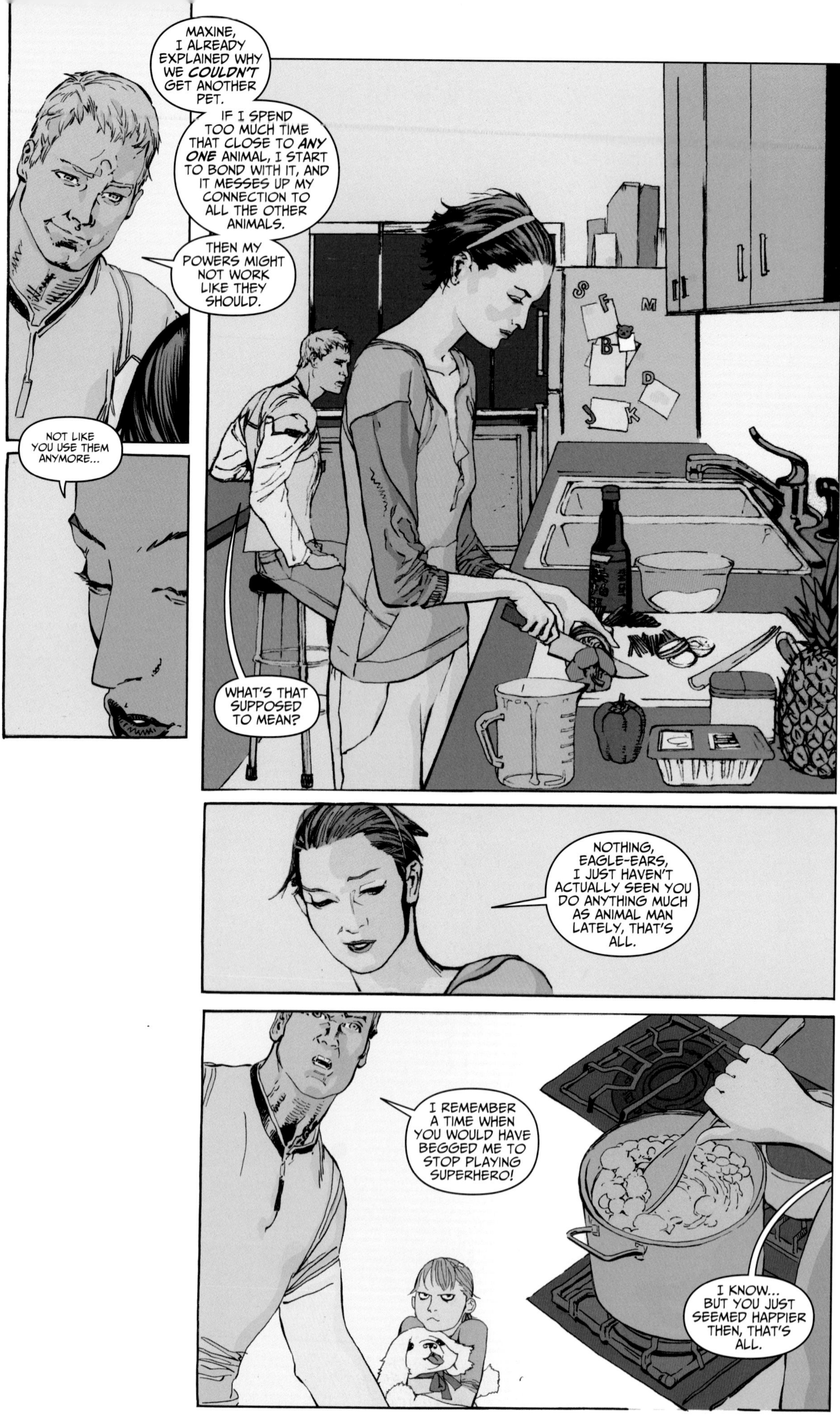
MAXINE, I ALREADY EXPLAINED WHY WE COULDN'T GET ANOTHER PET.
IF I SPEND TOO MUCH TIME THAT CLOSE TO ANY ONE ANIMAL, I START TO BOND WITH IT, AND IT MESSES UP MY CONNECTION TO ALL THE OTHER ANIMALS.
THEN MY POWERS MIGHT NOT WORK LIKE THEY SHOULD.
NOT LIKE YOU USE THEM ANYMORE...
WHAT'S THAT SUPPOSED TO MEAN?
NOTHING, EAGLE-EARS, I JUST HAVEN'T ACTUALLY SEEN YOU DO ANYTHING MUCH AS ANIMAL MAN LATELY, THAT'S ALL.
I REMEMBER A TIME WHEN YOU WOULD HAVE BEGGED ME TO STOP PLAYING SUPERHERO!
I KNOW... BUT YOU JUST SEEMED HAPPIER THEN, THAT'S ALL.

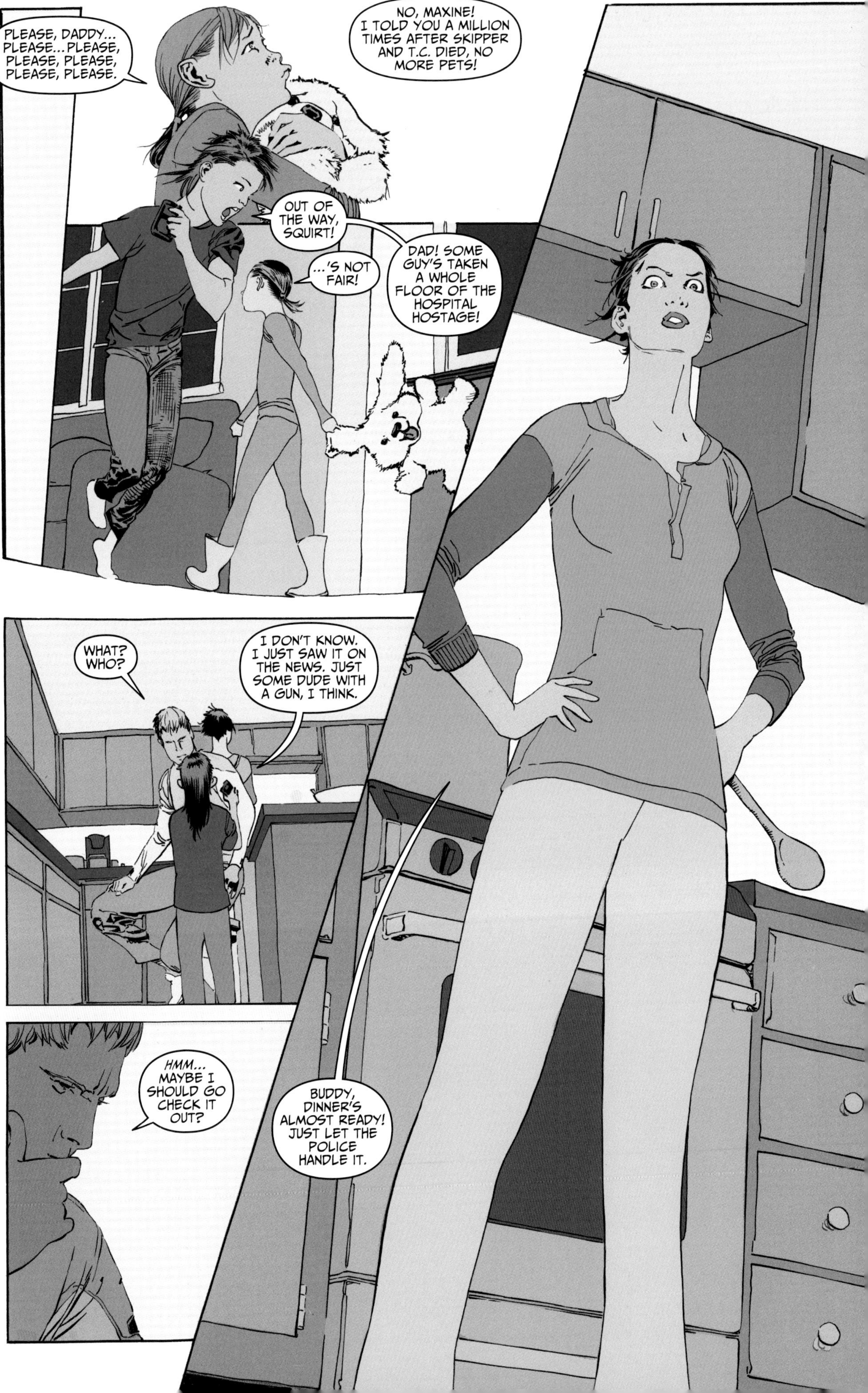
PLEASE, DADDY... PLEASE...PLEASE, PLEASE, PLEASE, PLEASE, PLEASE.
NO, MAXINE! I TOLD YOU A MILLION TIMES AFTER SKIPPER AND T.C. DIED, NO MORE PETS!
OUT OF THE WAY, SQUIRT!
...'S NOT FAIR!
DAD! SOME GUY'S TAKEN A WHOLE FLOOR OF THE HOSPITAL HOSTAGE!
WHAT? WHO?
I DON'T KNOW. I JUST SAW IT ON THE NEWS. JUST SOME DUDE WITH A GUN, I THINK.
HMM... MAYBE I SHOULD GO CHECK IT OUT?
BUDDY, DINNER'S ALMOST READY! JUST LET THE POLICE HANDLE IT.

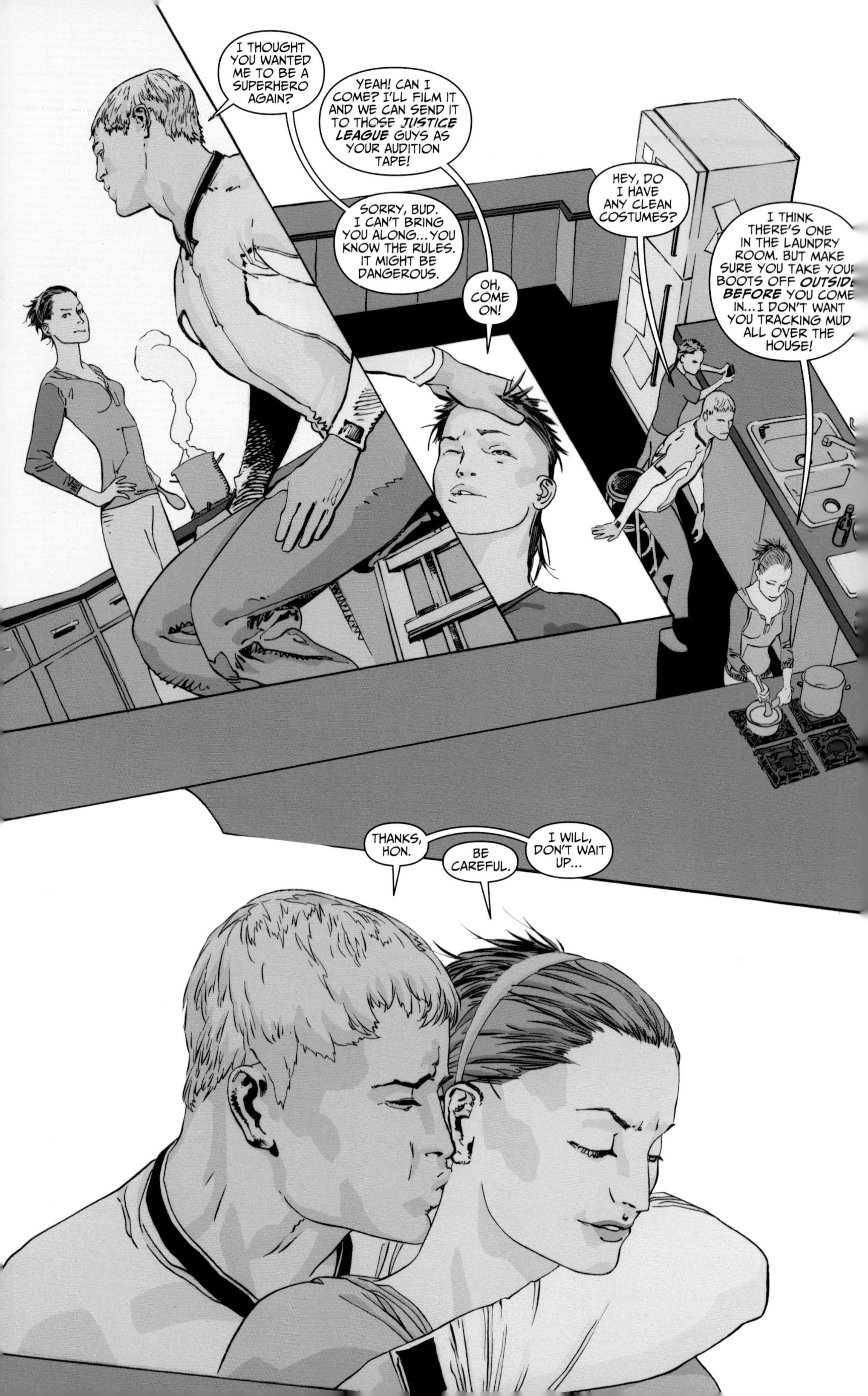
I THOUGHT YOU WANTED ME TO BE A SUPERHERO AGAIN?
YEAH! CAN I COME? I'LL FILM IT AND WE CAN SEND IT TO THOSE JUSTICE LEAGUE GUYS AS YOUR AUDITION TAPE!
SORRY, BUD. I CAN'T BRING YOU ALONG...YOU KNOW THE RULES. IT MIGHT BE DANGEROUS.
OH, COME ON!
HEY, DO I HAVE ANY CLEAN COSTUMES?
I THINK THERE'S ONE IN THE LAUNDRY ROOM. BUT MAKE SURE YOU TAKE YOUR BOOTS OFF OUTSIDE BEFORE YOU COME IN...I DON'T WANT YOU TRACKING MUD ALL OVER THE HOUSE!
THANKS, HON.
BE CAREFUL.
I WILL, DON'T WAIT UP...

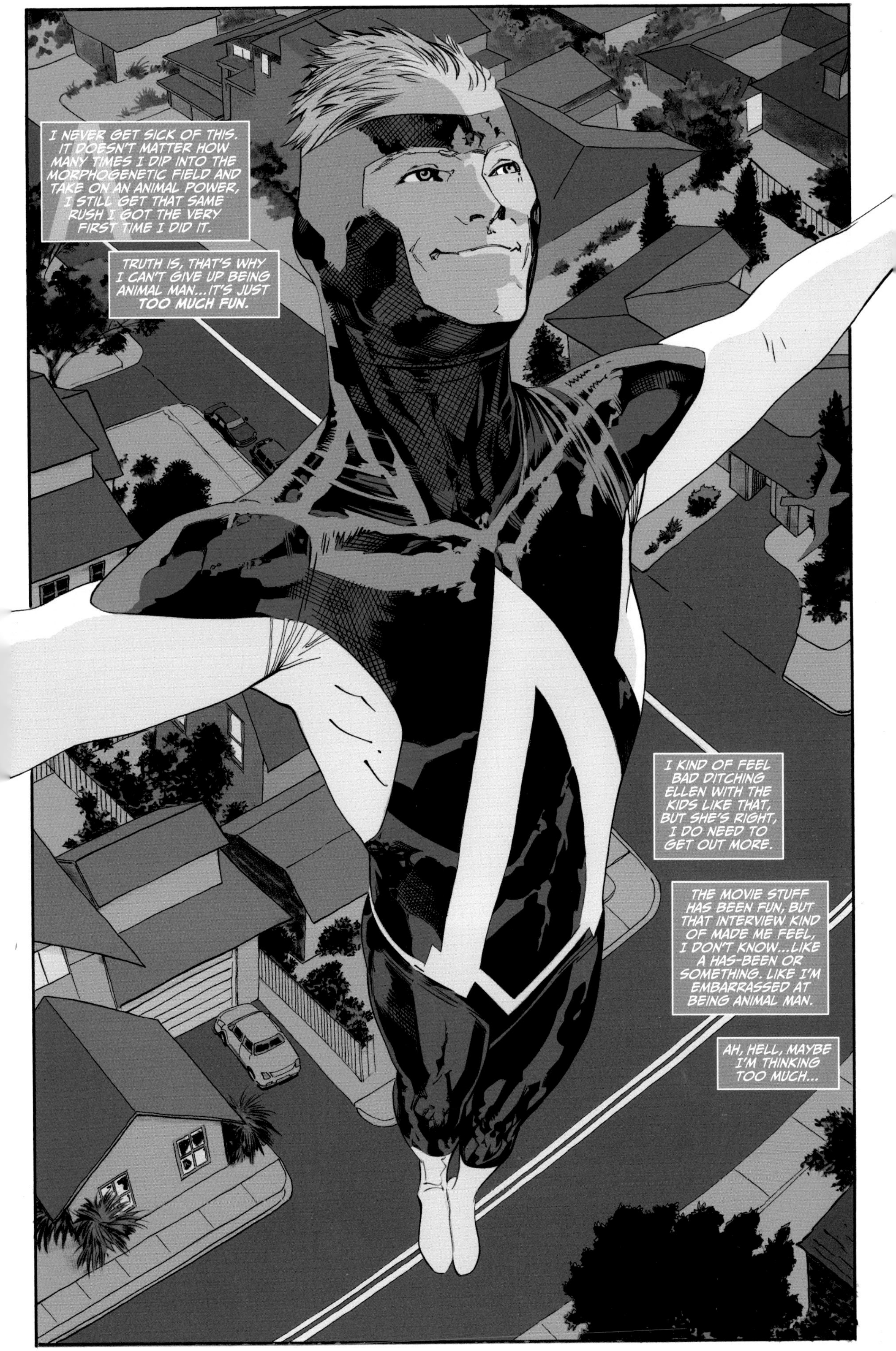
I NEVER GET SICK OF THIS. IT DOESN'T MATTER HOW MANY TIMES I DIP INTO THE MORPHOGENETIC FIELD AND TAKE ON AN ANIMAL POWER, I STILL GET THAT SAME RUSH I GOT THE VERY FIRST TIME I DID IT.
TRUTH IS, THAT'S WHY I CAN'T GIVE UP BEING ANIMAL MAN...IT'S JUST TOO MUCH FUN.
I KIND OF FEEL BAD DITCHING ELLEN WITH THE KIDS LIKE THAT, BUT SHE'S RIGHT, I DO NEED TO GET OUT MORE.
THE MOVIE STUFF HAS BEEN FUN, BUT THAT INTERVIEW KIND OF MADE ME FEEL, I DON'T KNOW...LIKE A HAS-BEEN OR SOMETHING. LIKE I'M EMBARRASSED AT BEING ANIMAL MAN.
AH, HELL, MAYBE I'M THINKING TOO MUCH...

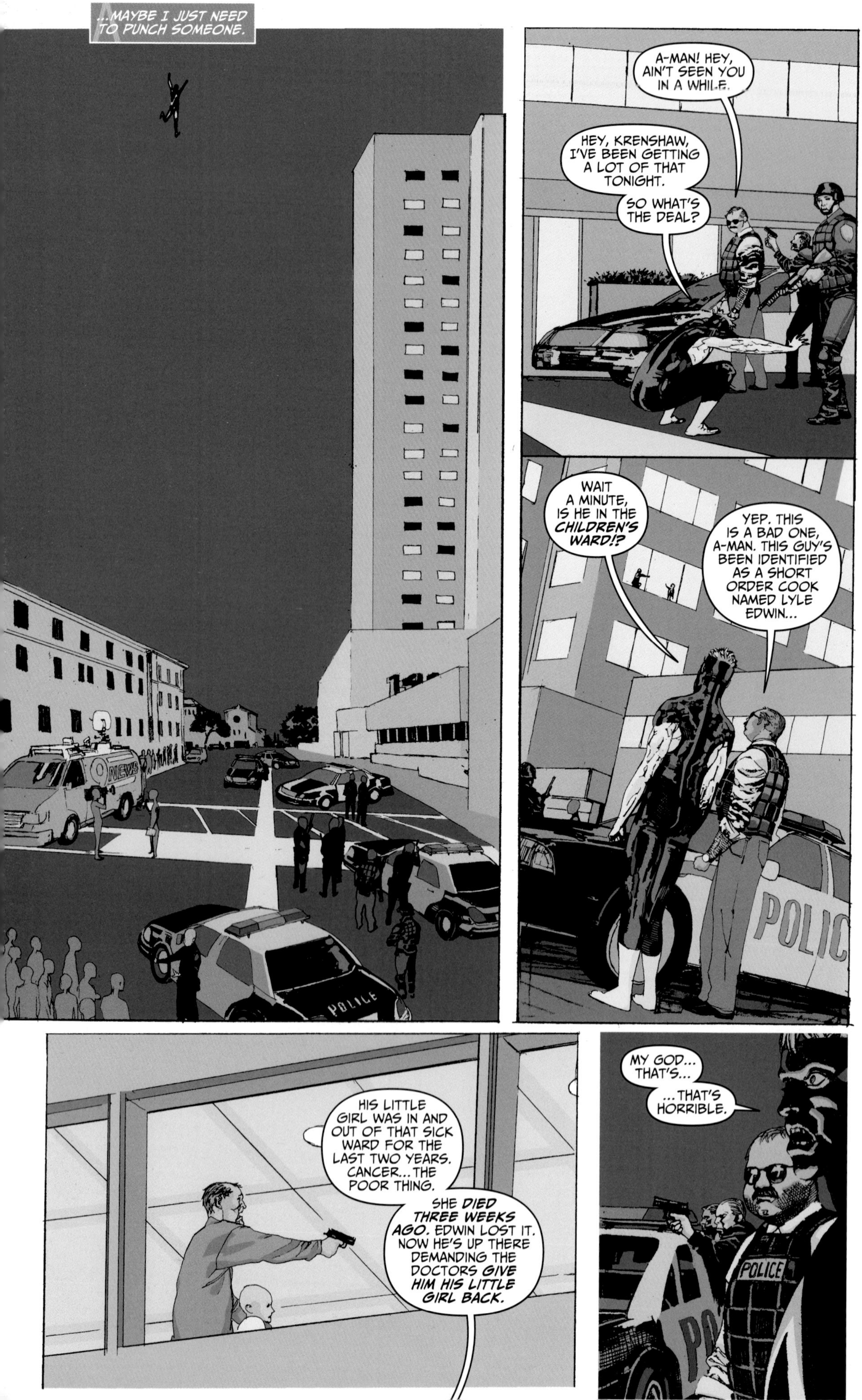
...MAYBE I JUST NEED TO PUNCH SOMEONE.
NEWS
POLICE
A-MAN! HEY, AIN'T SEEN YOU IN A WHILE.
HEY, KRENSHAW, I'VE BEEN GETTING A LOT OF THAT TONIGHT.
SO WHAT'S THE DEAL?
WAIT A MINUTE, IS HE IN THE CHILDREN'S WARD!?
YEP. THIS IS A BAD ONE, A-MAN. THIS GUY'S BEEN IDENTIFIED AS A SHORT ORDER COOK NAMED LYLE EDWIN...
POLIC
HIS LITTLE GIRL WAS IN AND OUT OF THAT SICK WARD FOR THE LAST TWO YEARS. CANCER... THE POOR THING.
SHE DIED THREE WEEKS AGO. EDWIN LOST IT. NOW HE'S UP THERE DEMANDING THE DOCTORS GIVE HIM HIS LITTLE GIRL BACK.
MY GOD... THAT'S...
...THAT'S HORRIBLE.
POLICE
PO

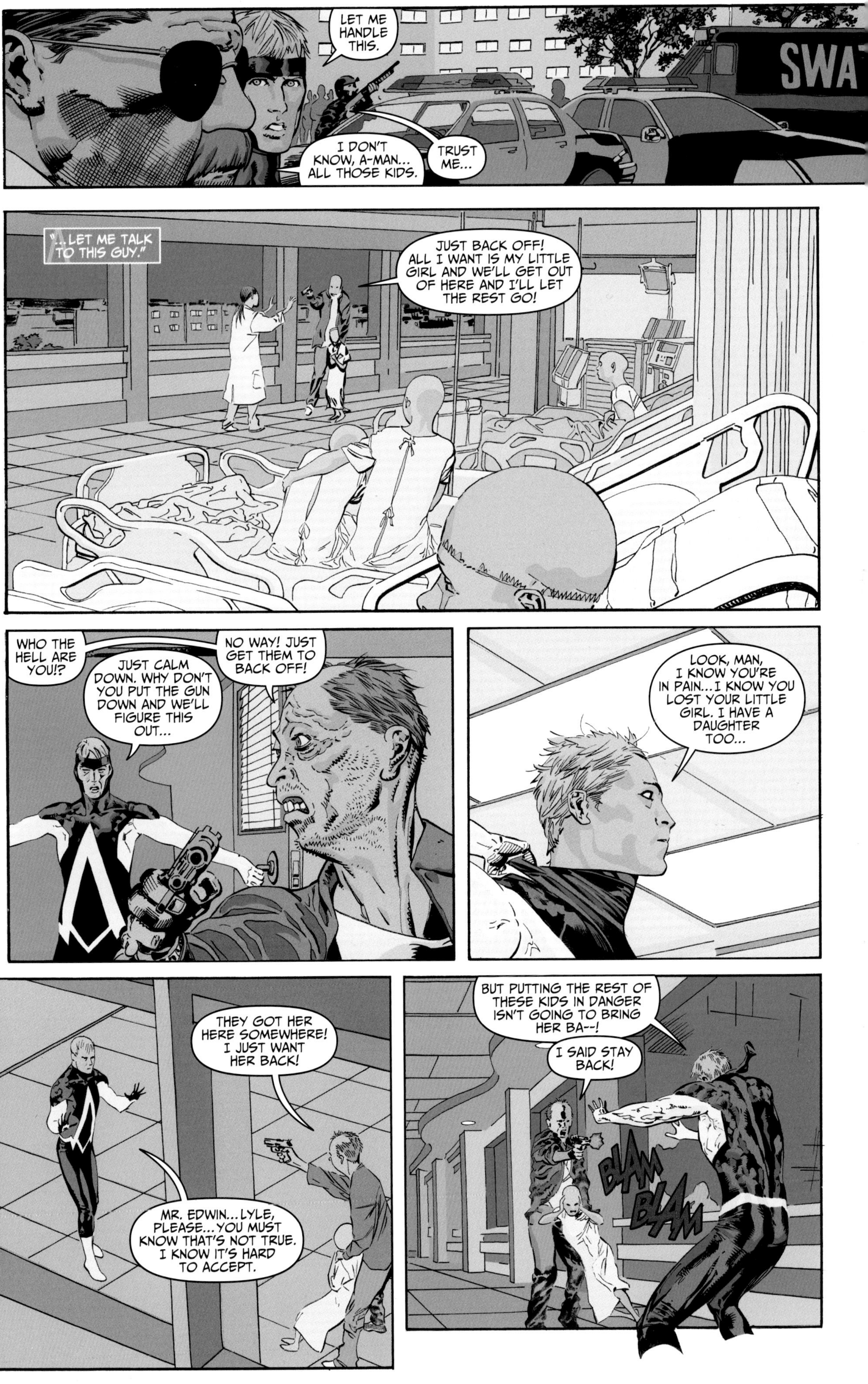
LET ME HANDLE THIS.
SWAT
I DON'T KNOW, A-MAN... ALL THOSE KIDS.
TRUST ME...
"...LET ME TALK TO THIS GUY."
JUST BACK OFF! ALL I WANT IS MY LITTLE GIRL AND WE'LL GET OUT OF HERE AND I'LL LET THE REST GO!
WHO THE HELL ARE YOU!?
JUST CALM DOWN. WHY DON'T YOU PUT THE GUN DOWN AND WE'LL FIGURE THIS OUT...
NO WAY! JUST GET THEM TO BACK OFF!
LOOK, MAN, I KNOW YOU'RE IN PAIN...I KNOW YOU LOST YOUR LITTLE GIRL. I HAVE A DAUGHTER TOO...
THEY GOT HER HERE SOMEWHERE! I JUST WANT HER BACK!
MR. EDWIN...LYLE, PLEASE...YOU MUST KNOW THAT'S NOT TRUE. I KNOW IT'S HARD TO ACCEPT.
BUT PUTTING THE REST OF THESE KIDS IN DANGER ISN'T GOING TO BRING HER BA--!
I SAID STAY BACK!
BLAM
BLAM

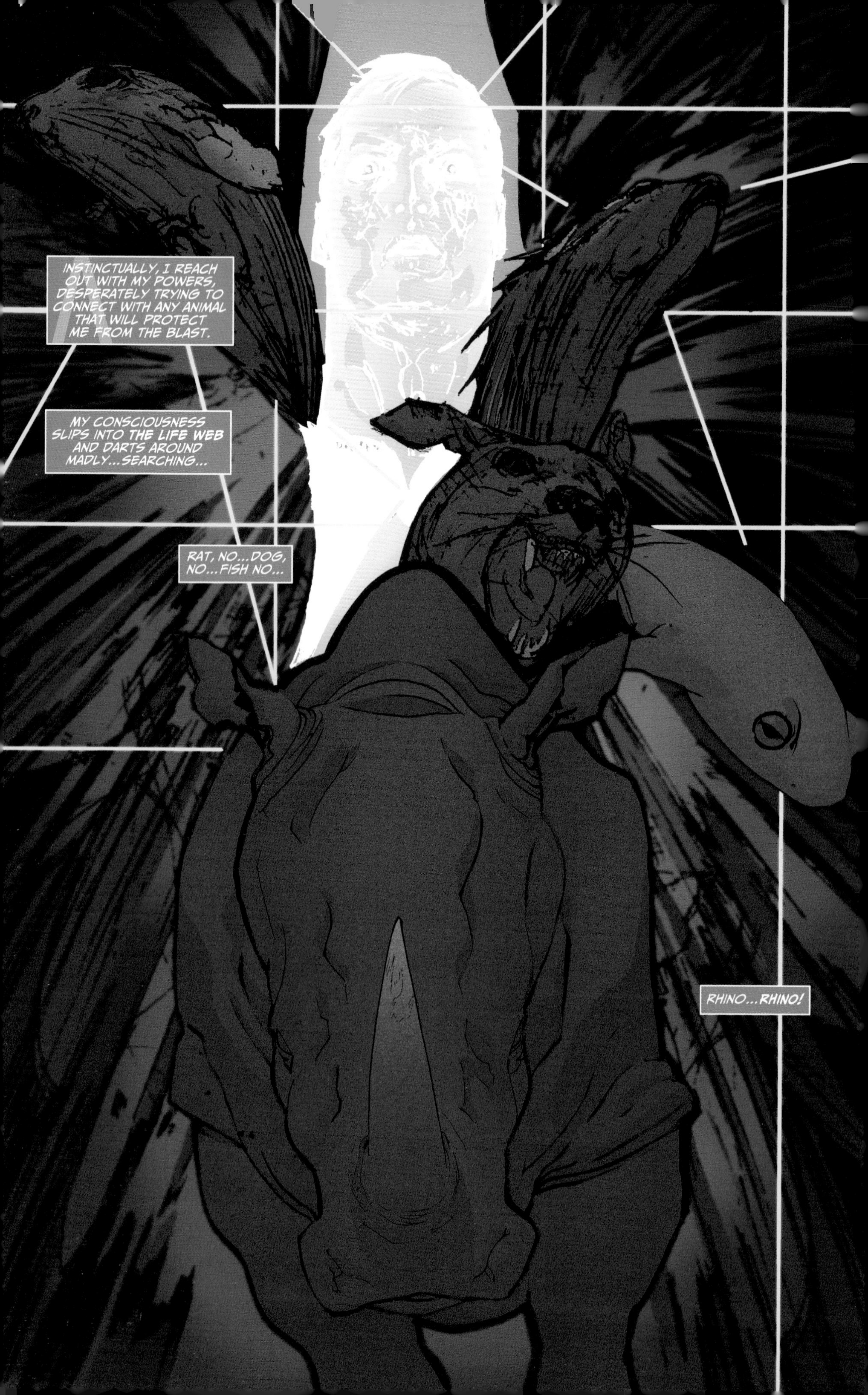
INSTINCTUALLY, I REACH OUT WITH MY POWERS, DESPERATELY TRYING TO CONNECT WITH ANY ANIMAL THAT WILL PROTECT ME FROM THE BLAST.
MY CONSCIOUSNESS SLIPS INTO THE LIFE WEB AND DARTS AROUND MADLY...SEARCHING...
RAT, NO...DOG, NO...FISH NO...
RHINO...RHINO!

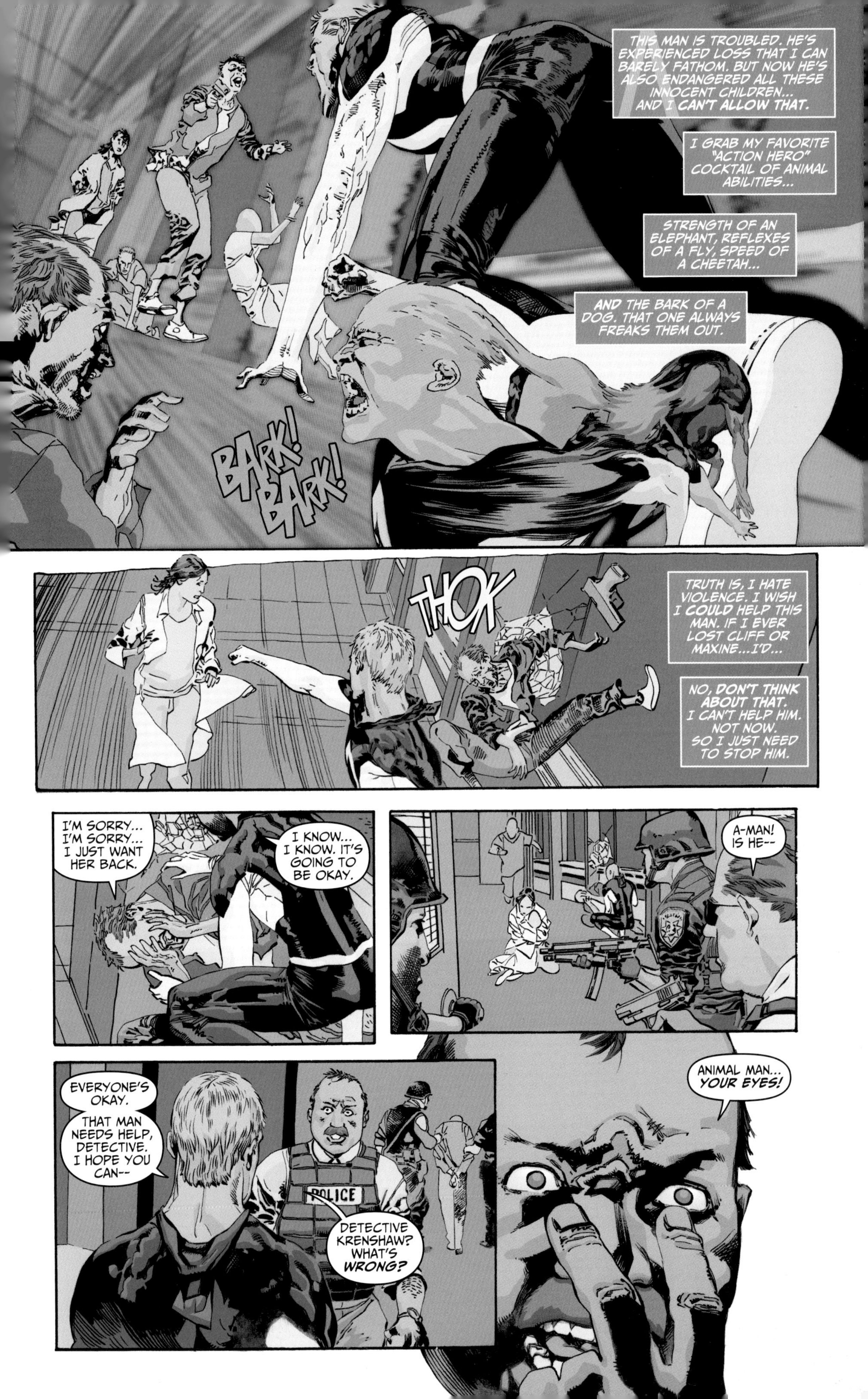
THIS MAN IS TROUBLED. HE'S EXPERIENCED LOSS THAT I CAN BARELY FATHOM. BUT NOW HE'S ALSO ENDANGERED ALL THESE INNOCENT CHILDREN... AND I CAN'T ALLOW THAT.
I GRAB MY FAVORITE "ACTION HERO" COCKTAIL OF ANIMAL ABILITIES...
STRENGTH OF AN ELEPHANT, REFLEXES OF A FLY, SPEED OF A CHEETAH...
AND THE BARK OF A DOG. THAT ONE ALWAYS FREAKS THEM OUT.
BARK! BARK!
THOK
TRUTH IS, I HATE VIOLENCE. I WISH I COULD HELP THIS MAN. IF I EVER LOST CLIFF OR MAXINE...I'D...
NO, DON'T THINK ABOUT THAT. I CAN'T HELP HIM. NOT NOW. SO I JUST NEED TO STOP HIM.
I'M SORRY... I'M SORRY... I JUST WANT HER BACK.
I KNOW... I KNOW. IT'S GOING TO BE OKAY.
A-MAN! IS HE--
EVERYONE'S OKAY.
THAT MAN NEEDS HELP, DETECTIVE. I HOPE YOU CAN--
POLICE
DETECTIVE KRENSHAW? WHAT'S WRONG?
ANIMAL MAN... YOUR EYES!

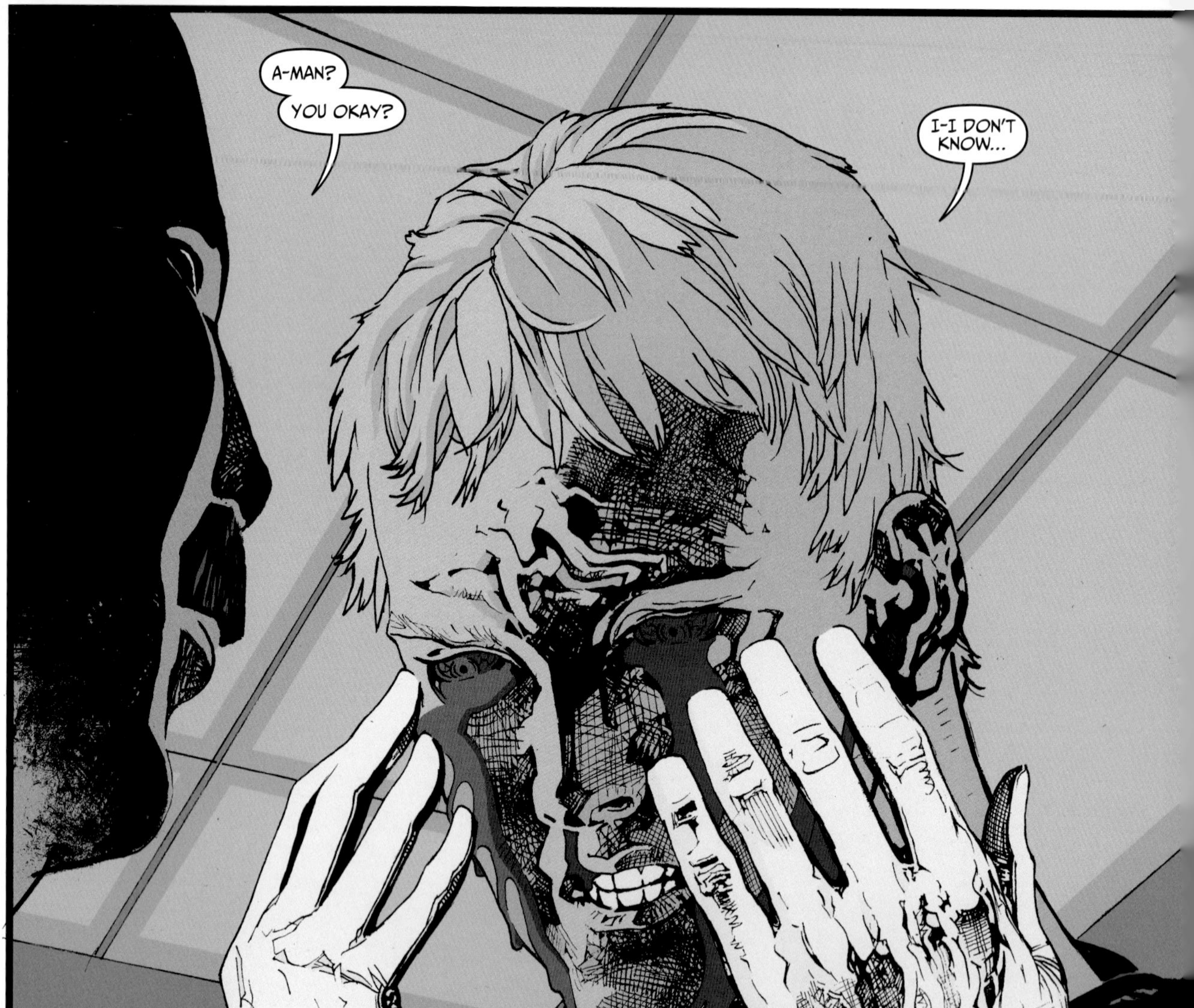
A-MAN?
YOU OKAY?
I-I DON'T KNOW...

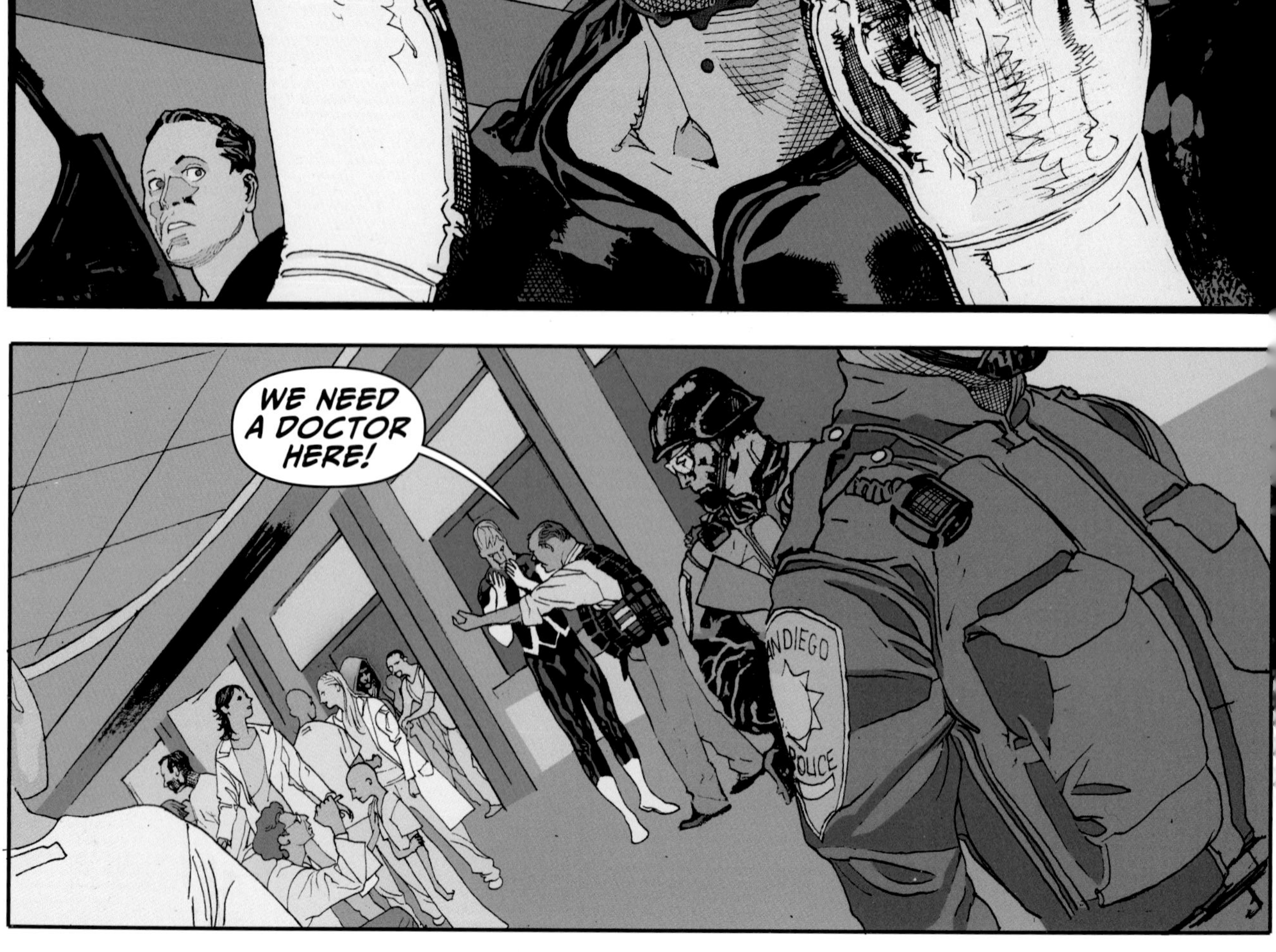
WE NEED A DOCTOR HERE!

THERE DOESN'T SEEM TO BE *ANYTHING* WRONG. I DON'T KNOW WHERE THE BLOOD CAME FROM. THERE ARE NO WOUNDS... NO SORES.

AS FAR AS I CAN TELL, YOU'RE HEALTHY AS A HORSE.

I'M TELLING YOU, DOC, I FEEL FINE. IN FACT I FEEL *BETTER* THAN I HAVE IN A WHILE. STRONG... ALERT.

IF ANYTHING, MY CONNECTION TO THE LIFE WEB HASN'T FELT THAT STRONG IN A WHILE.

I ADMIT, I'M NOT VERY EXPERIENCED IN DEALING WITH SUPERHUMANS, BUT I'D STILL LIKE TO DO SOME MORE TESTS.

IF IT'S ALL THE SAME TO YOU, I'D RATHER COME BACK TOMORROW...

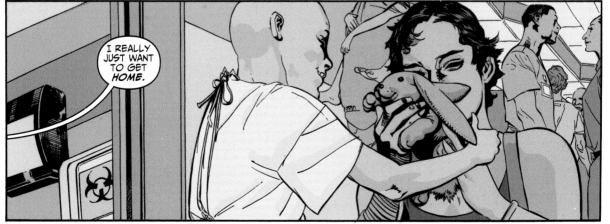

I REALLY JUST WANT TO GET *HOME.*

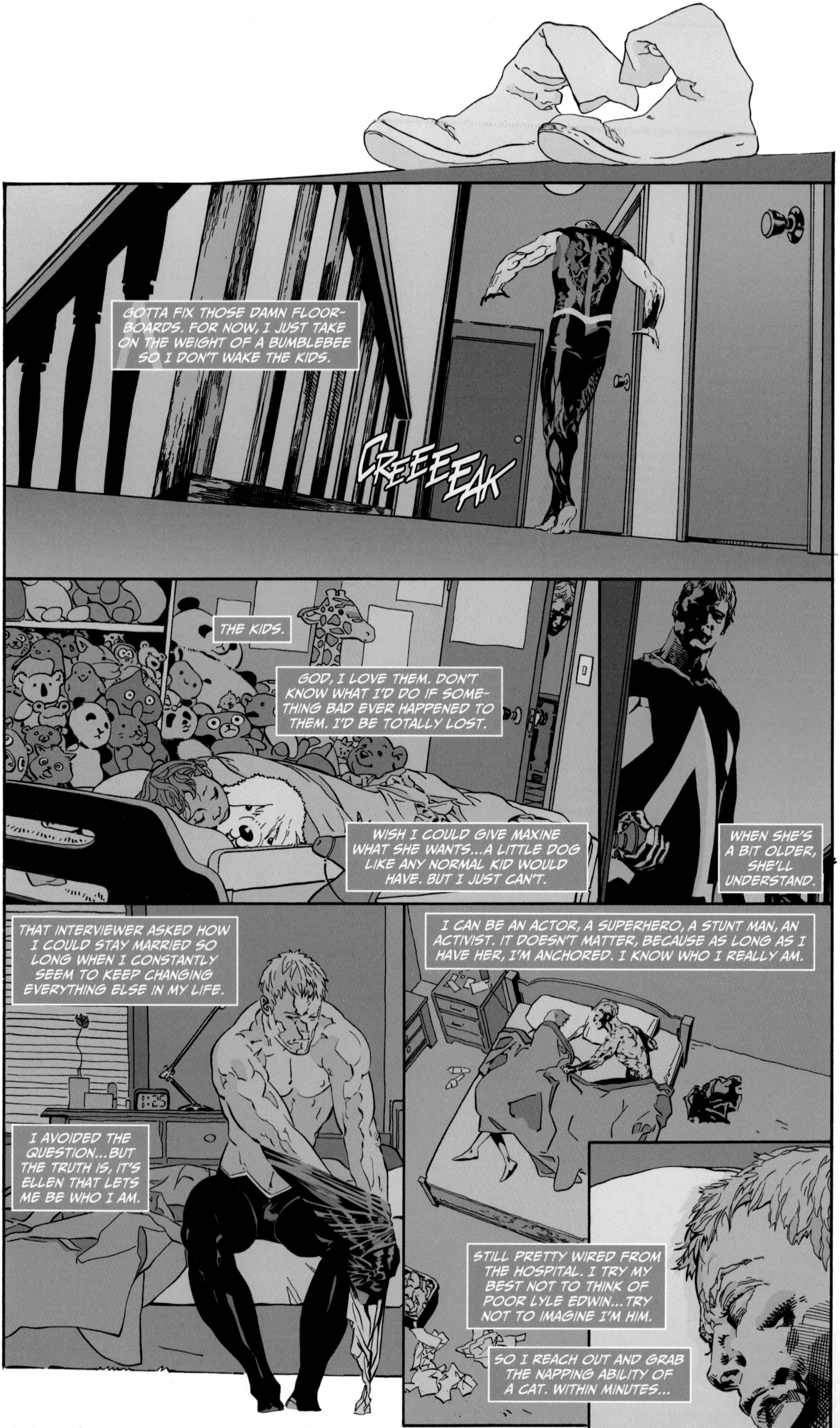
GOTTA FIX THOSE DAMN FLOOR-BOARDS. FOR NOW, I JUST TAKE ON THE WEIGHT OF A BUMBLEBEE SO I DON'T WAKE THE KIDS.
CREEEEAK
THE KIDS.
GOD, I LOVE THEM. DON'T KNOW WHAT I'D DO IF SOME-THING BAD EVER HAPPENED TO THEM. I'D BE TOTALLY LOST.
WISH I COULD GIVE MAXINE WHAT SHE WANTS...A LITTLE DOG LIKE ANY NORMAL KID WOULD HAVE. BUT I JUST CAN'T.
WHEN SHE'S A BIT OLDER, SHE'LL UNDERSTAND.
THAT INTERVIEWER ASKED HOW I COULD STAY MARRIED SO LONG WHEN I CONSTANTLY SEEM TO KEEP CHANGING EVERYTHING ELSE IN MY LIFE.
I AVOIDED THE QUESTION...BUT THE TRUTH IS, IT'S ELLEN THAT LETS ME BE WHO I AM.
I CAN BE AN ACTOR, A SUPERHERO, A STUNT MAN, AN ACTIVIST. IT DOESN'T MATTER, BECAUSE AS LONG AS I HAVE HER, I'M ANCHORED. I KNOW WHO I REALLY AM.
STILL PRETTY WIRED FROM THE HOSPITAL. I TRY MY BEST NOT TO THINK OF POOR LYLE EDWIN...TRY NOT TO IMAGINE I'M HIM.
SO I REACH OUT AND GRAB THE NAPPING ABILITY OF A CAT. WITHIN MINUTES...

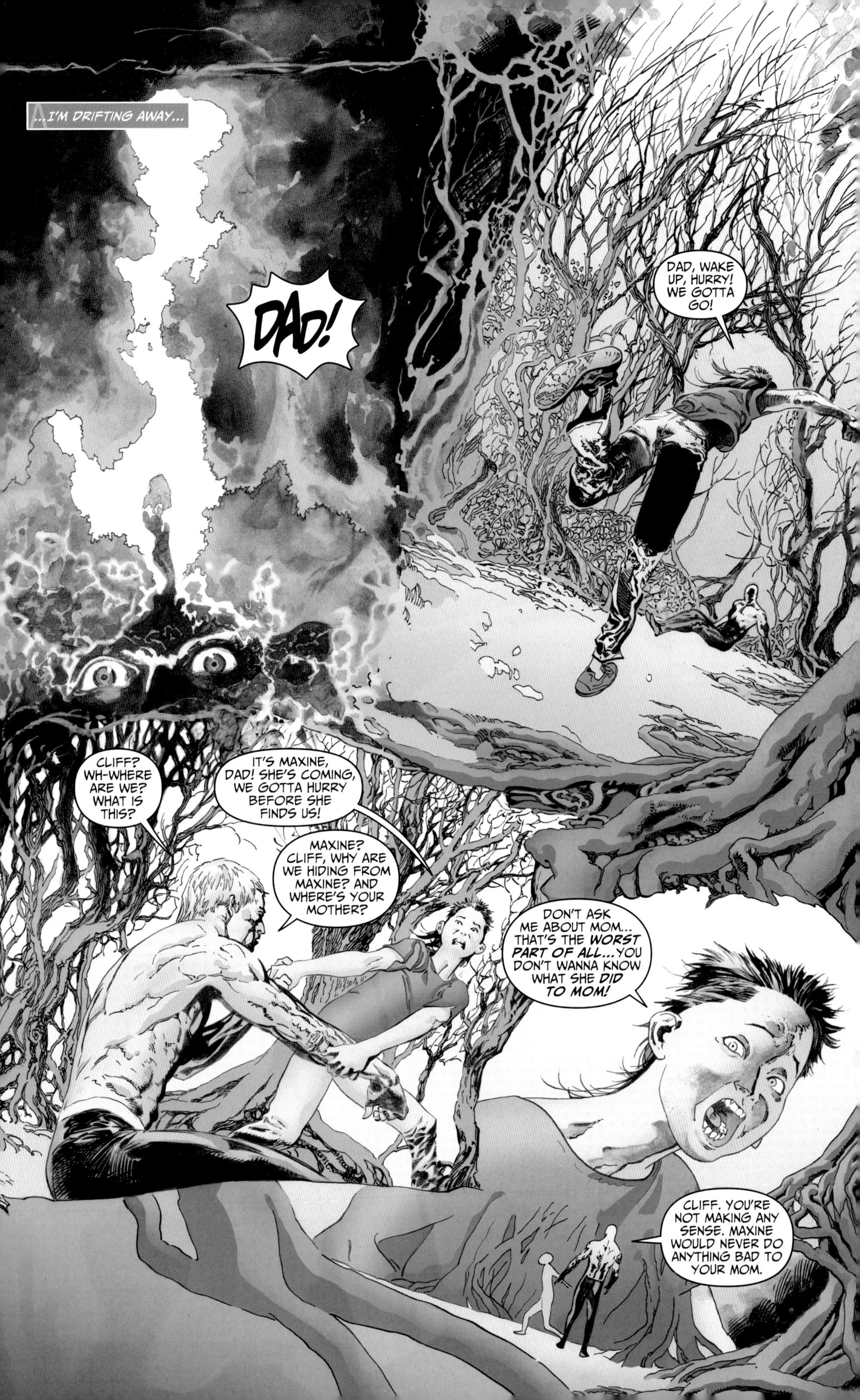
...I'M DRIFTING AWAY...
DAD!
DAD, WAKE UP, HURRY! WE GOTTA GO!
CLIFF? WH-WHERE ARE WE? WHAT IS THIS?
IT'S MAXINE, DAD! SHE'S COMING, WE GOTTA HURRY BEFORE SHE FINDS US!
MAXINE? CLIFF, WHY ARE WE HIDING FROM MAXINE? AND WHERE'S YOUR MOTHER?
DON'T ASK ME ABOUT MOM... THAT'S THE WORST PART OF ALL... YOU DON'T WANNA KNOW WHAT SHE DID TO MOM!
CLIFF. YOU'RE NOT MAKING ANY SENSE. MAXINE WOULD NEVER DO ANYTHING BAD TO YOUR MOM.

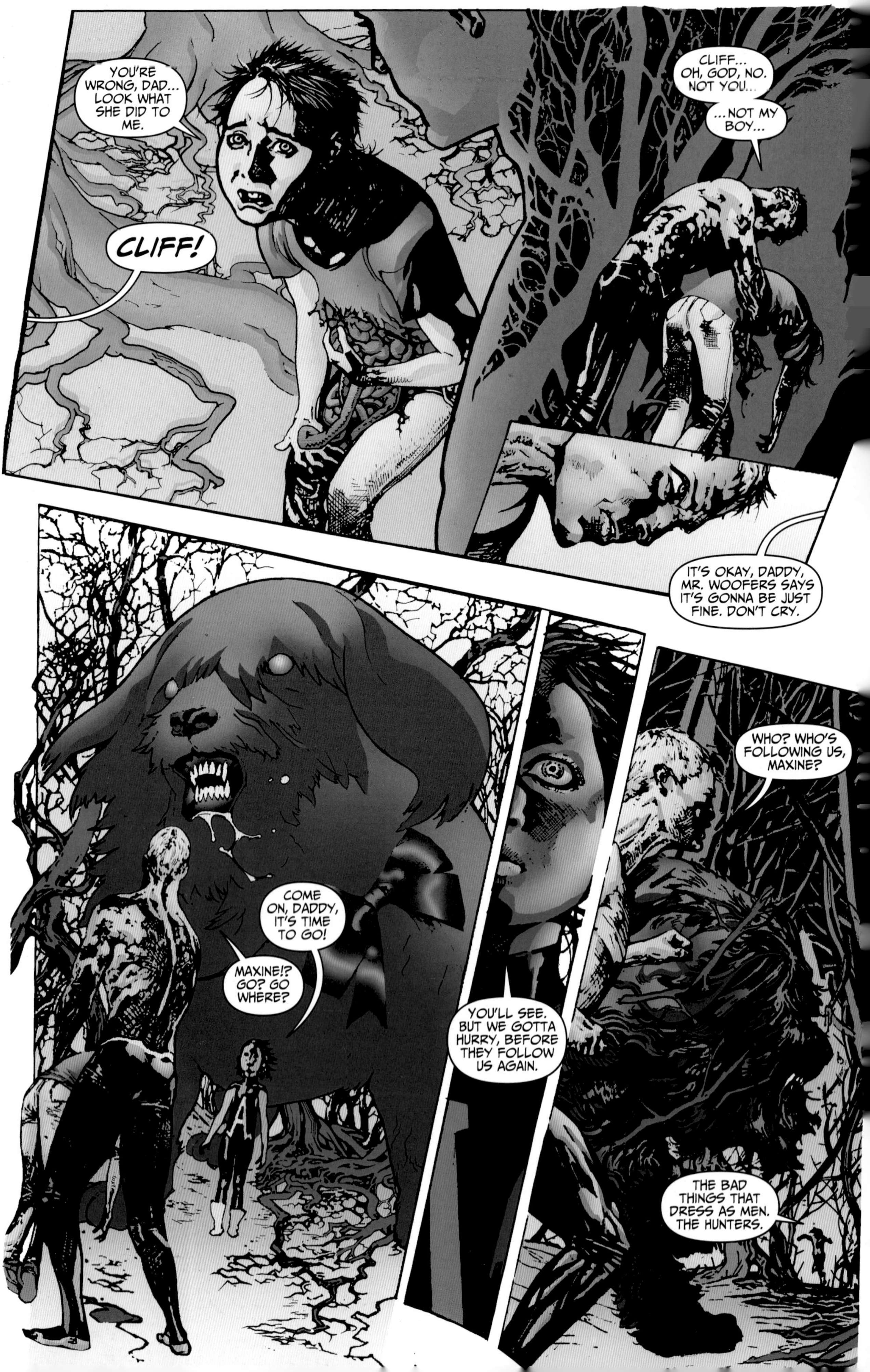
YOU'RE WRONG, DAD... LOOK WHAT SHE DID TO ME.
CLIFF!
CLIFF... OH, GOD, NO. NOT YOU...
...NOT MY BOY...
IT'S OKAY, DADDY, MR. WOOFERS SAYS IT'S GONNA BE JUST FINE. DON'T CRY.
COME ON, DADDY, IT'S TIME TO GO!
MAXINE!? GO? GO WHERE?
YOU'LL SEE. BUT WE GOTTA HURRY, BEFORE THEY FOLLOW US AGAIN.
WHO? WHO'S FOLLOWING US, MAXINE?
THE BAD THINGS THAT DRESS AS MEN. THE HUNTERS.

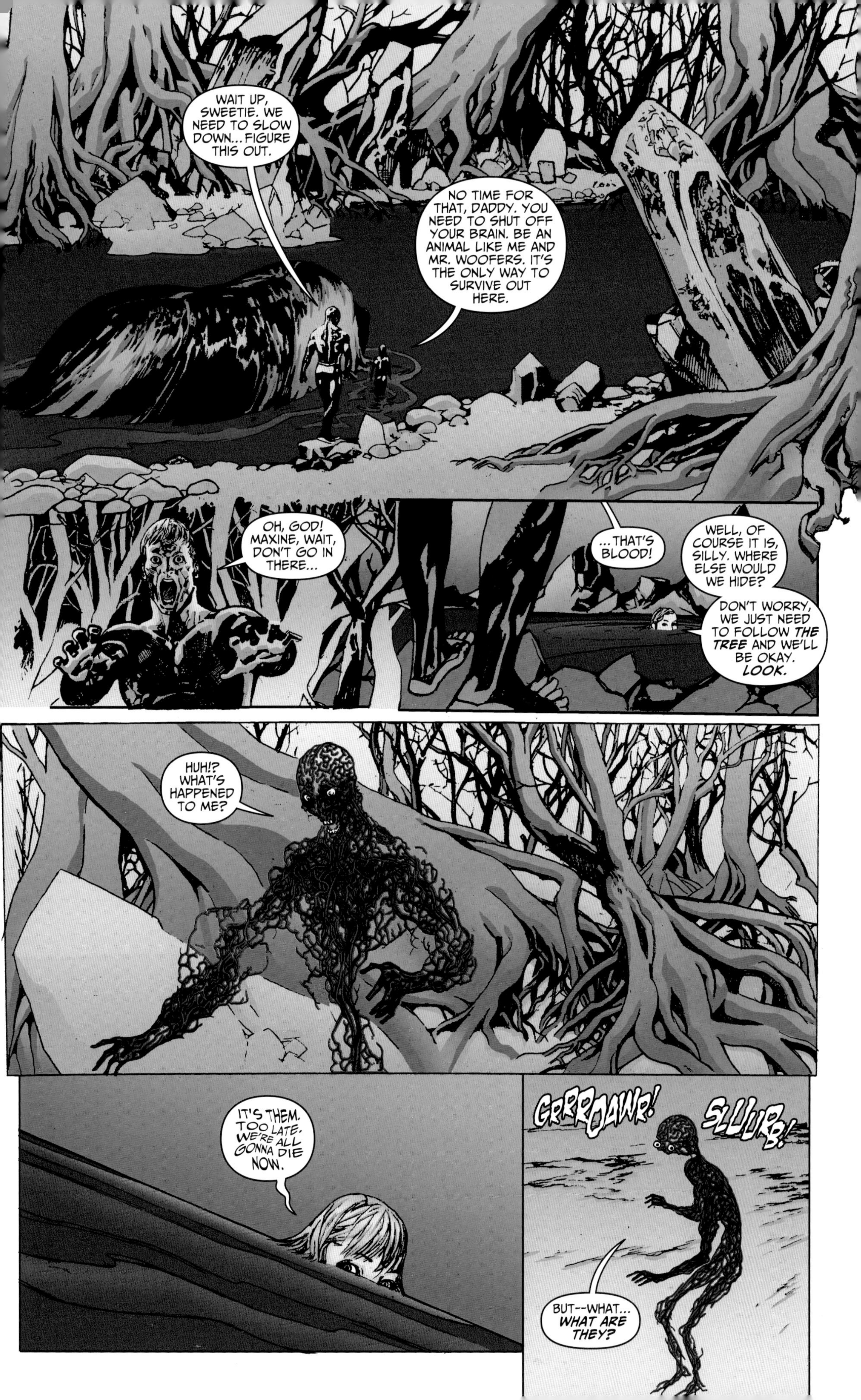
WAIT UP, SWEETIE. WE NEED TO SLOW DOWN... FIGURE THIS OUT.
NO TIME FOR THAT, DADDY. YOU NEED TO SHUT OFF YOUR BRAIN. BE AN ANIMAL LIKE ME AND MR. WOOFERS. IT'S THE ONLY WAY TO SURVIVE OUT HERE.
OH, GOD! MAXINE, WAIT, DON'T GO IN THERE...
...THAT'S BLOOD!
WELL, OF COURSE IT IS, SILLY. WHERE ELSE WOULD WE HIDE?
DON'T WORRY, WE JUST NEED TO FOLLOW THE TREE AND WE'LL BE OKAY. LOOK.
HUH!? WHAT'S HAPPENED TO ME?
IT'S THEM. TOO LATE. WE'RE ALL GONNA DIE NOW.
GRRROAWR!
SLUURB!
BUT--WHAT... WHAT ARE THEY?

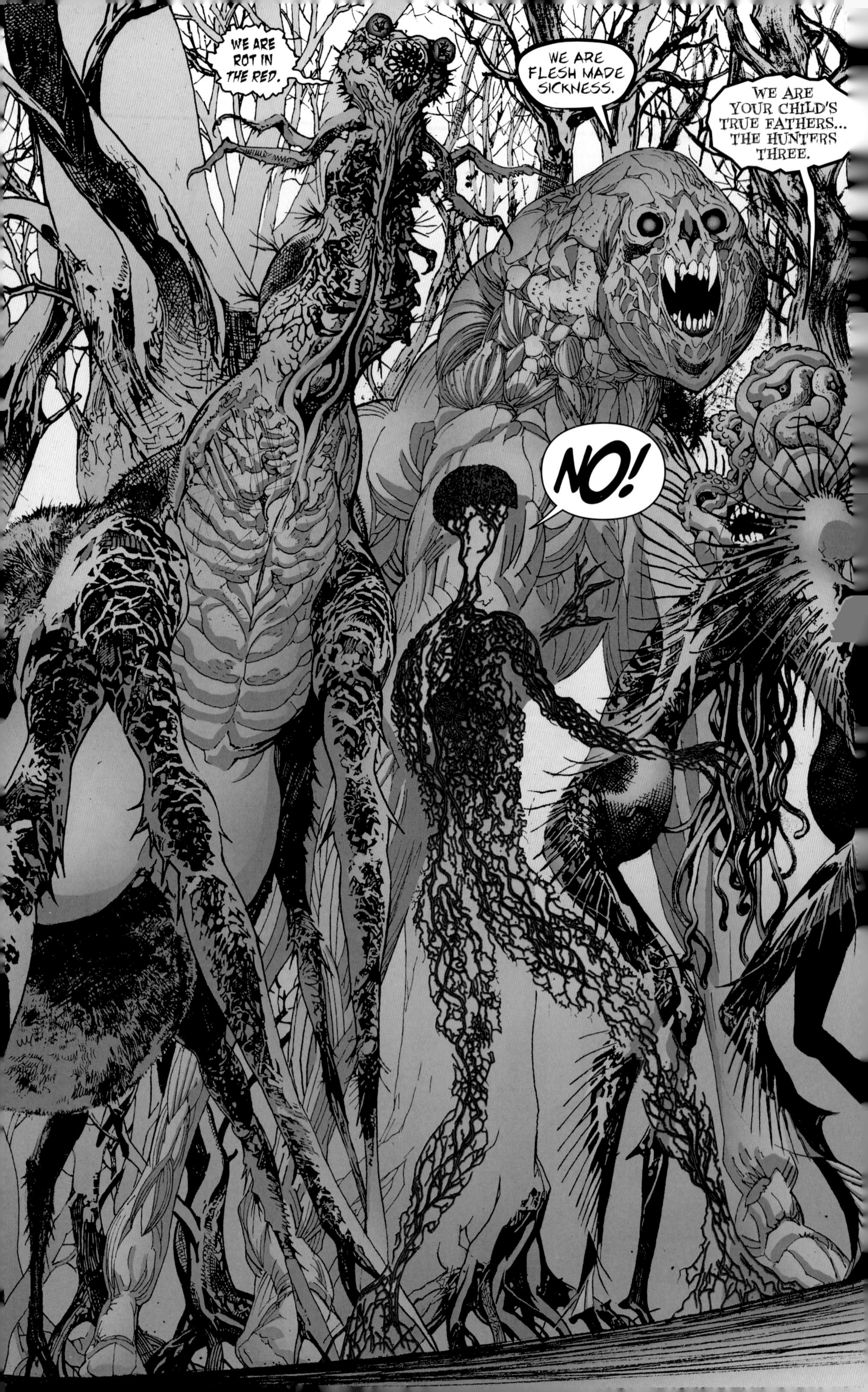
WE ARE ROT IN THE RED.
WE ARE FLESH MADE SICKNESS.
WE ARE YOUR CHILD'S TRUE FATHERS... THE HUNTERS THREE.
NO!

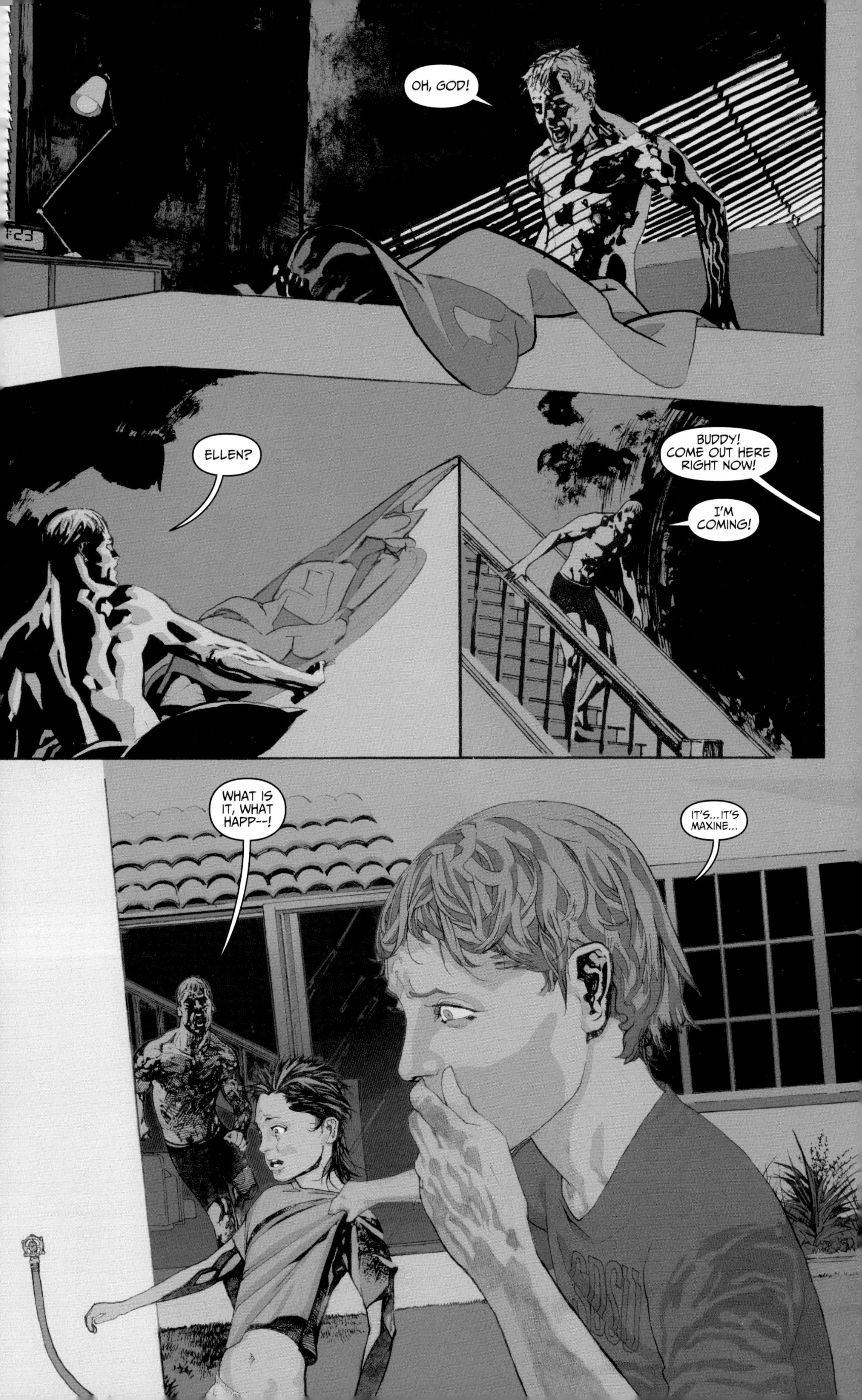
OH, GOD!
ELLEN?
BUDDY! COME OUT HERE RIGHT NOW!
I'M COMING!
WHAT IS IT, WHAT HAPP--!
IT'S...IT'S MAXINE...

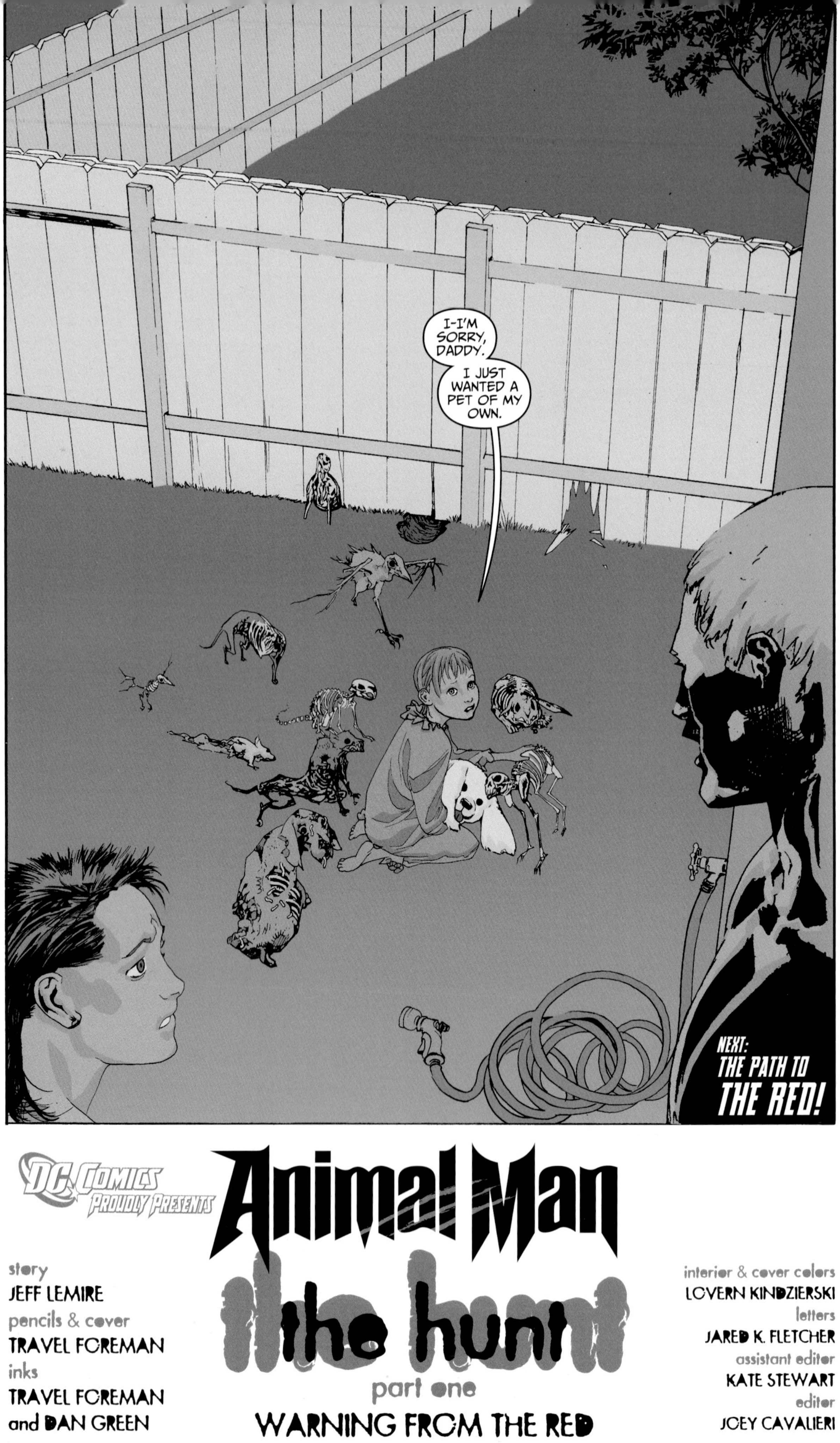
I-I'M SORRY, DADDY.
I JUST WANTED A PET OF MY OWN.
NEXT: THE PATH TO THE RED!

DC COMICS PROUDLY PRESENTS

Animal Man

the hunt

part one
WARNING FROM THE RED

story
JEFF LEMIRE
pencils & cover
TRAVEL FOREMAN
inks
TRAVEL FOREMAN
and DAN GREEN
interior & cover colors
LOVERN KINDZIERSKI
letters
JARED K. FLETCHER
assistant editor
KATE STEWART
editor
JOEY CAVALIERI

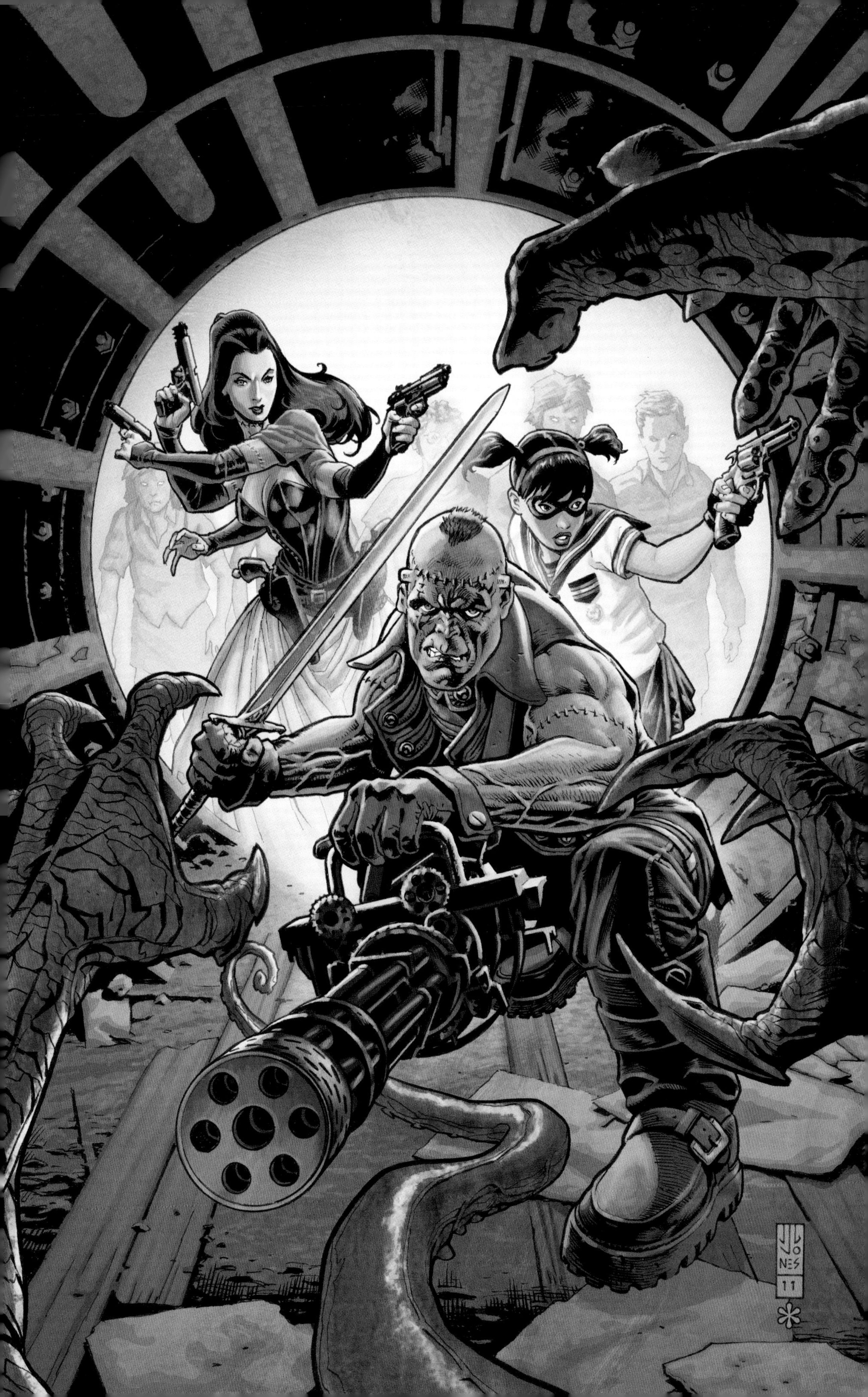

FRANKENSTEIN
AGENT OF S.H.A.D.E.

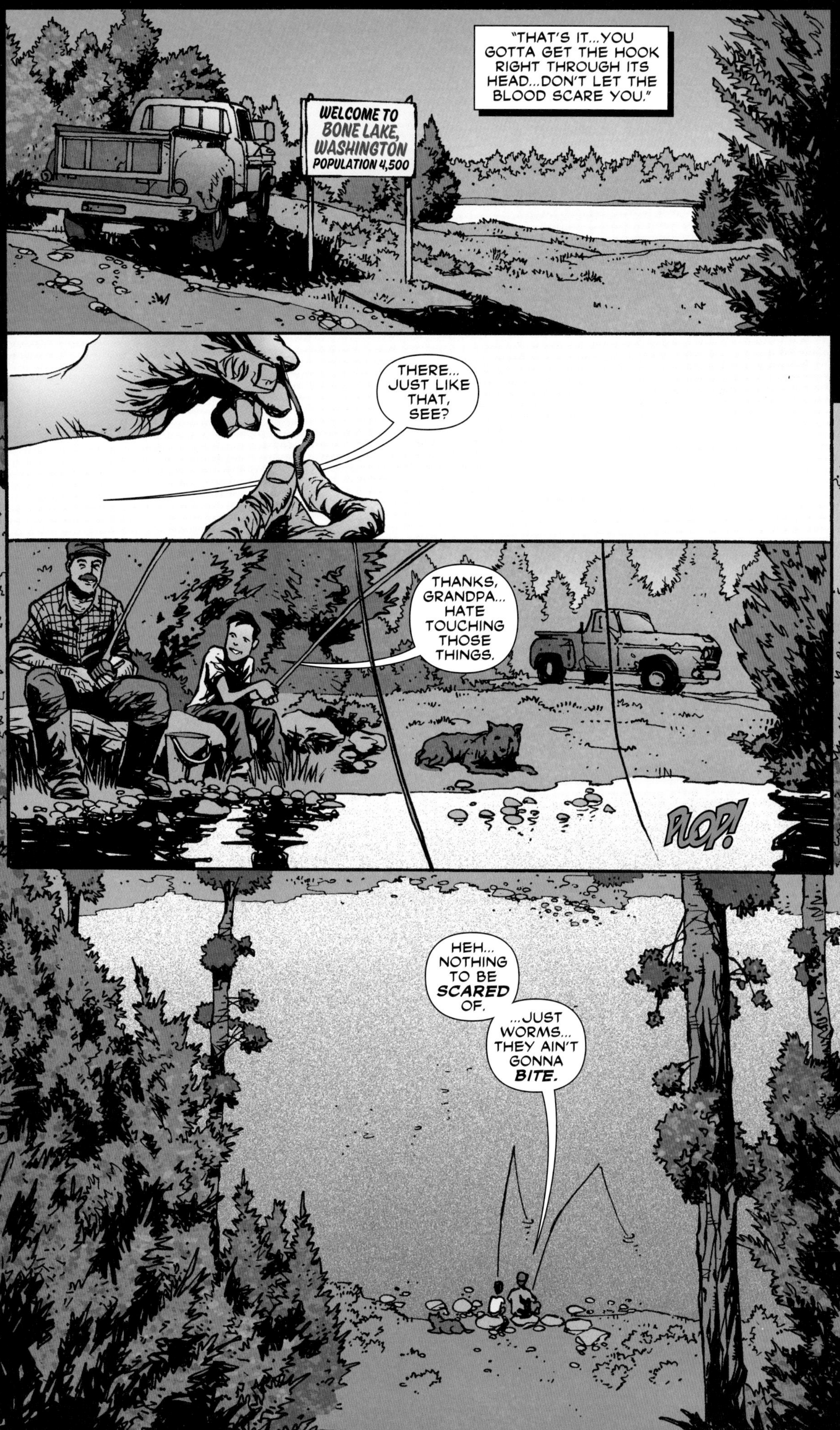

"THAT'S IT...YOU GOTTA GET THE HOOK RIGHT THROUGH ITS HEAD...DON'T LET THE BLOOD SCARE YOU."
WELCOME TO BONE LAKE, WASHINGTON POPULATION 4,500
THERE... JUST LIKE THAT, SEE?
THANKS, GRANDPA... HATE TOUCHING THOSE THINGS.
PLOP!
HEH... NOTHING TO BE SCARED OF.
...JUST WORMS... THEY AIN'T GONNA BITE.

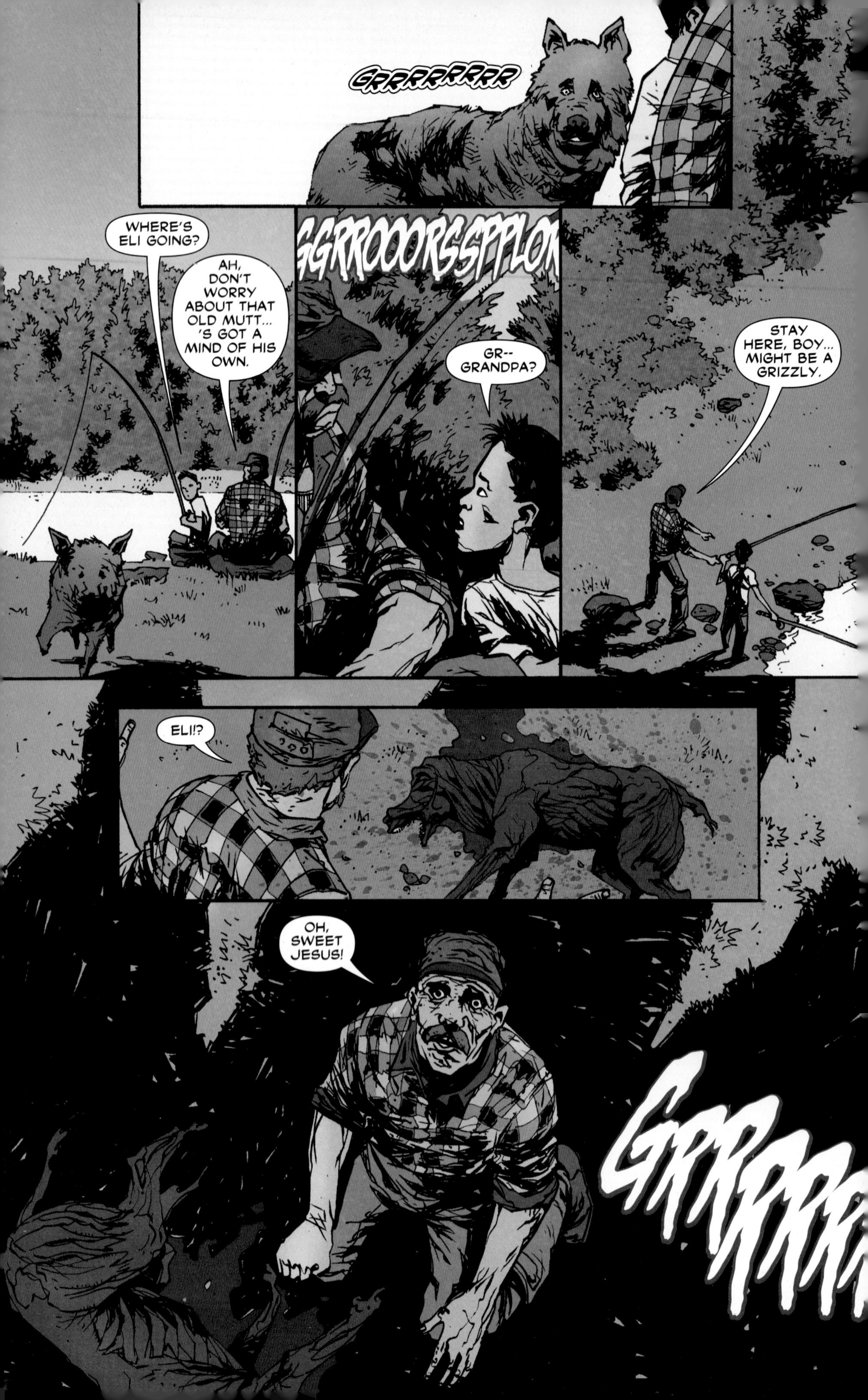
GRRRRRRRR
WHERE'S ELI GOING?
AH, DON'T WORRY ABOUT THAT OLD MUTT... 'S GOT A MIND OF HIS OWN.
GGRROOORSSPPLOK
GR-- GRANDPA?
STAY HERE, BOY... MIGHT BE A GRIZZLY.
ELI!?
OH, SWEET JESUS!
GRRRRR

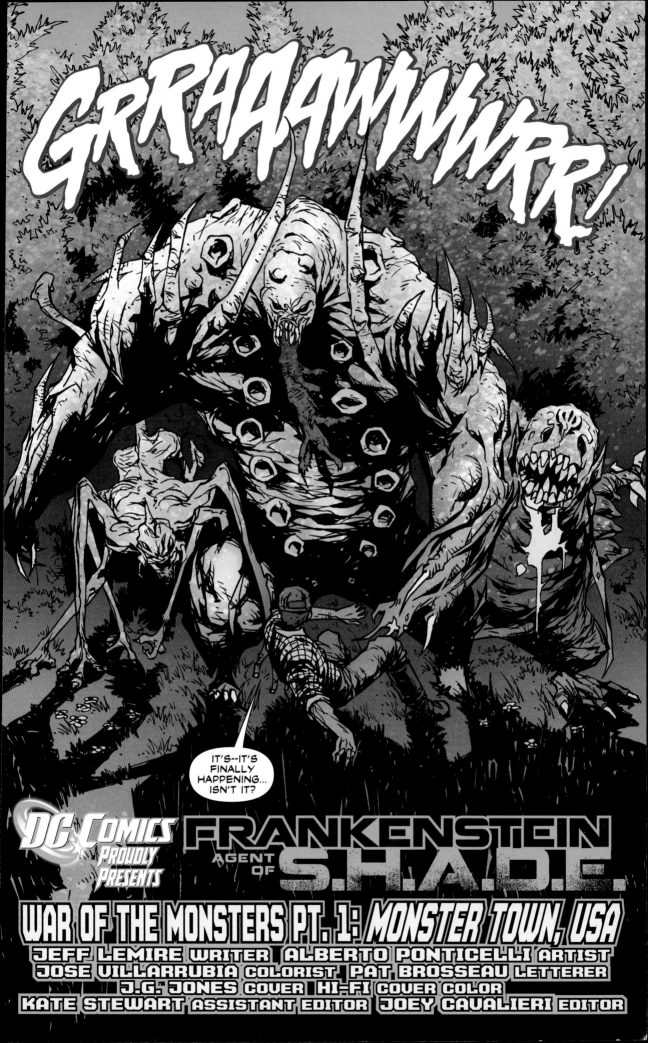

GRRAAAWWWRR!

IT'S--IT'S FINALLY HAPPENING... ISN'T IT?

DC Comics PROUDLY PRESENTS

FRANKENSTEIN AGENT OF **S.H.A.D.E.**

WAR OF THE MONSTERS PT. 1: *MONSTER TOWN, USA*

JEFF LEMIRE WRITER   ALBERTO PONTICELLI ARTIST
JOSE VILLARRUBIA COLORIST   PAT BROSSEAU LETTERER
J.G. JONES COVER   HI-FI COVER COLOR
KATE STEWART ASSISTANT EDITOR   JOEY CAVALIERI EDITOR

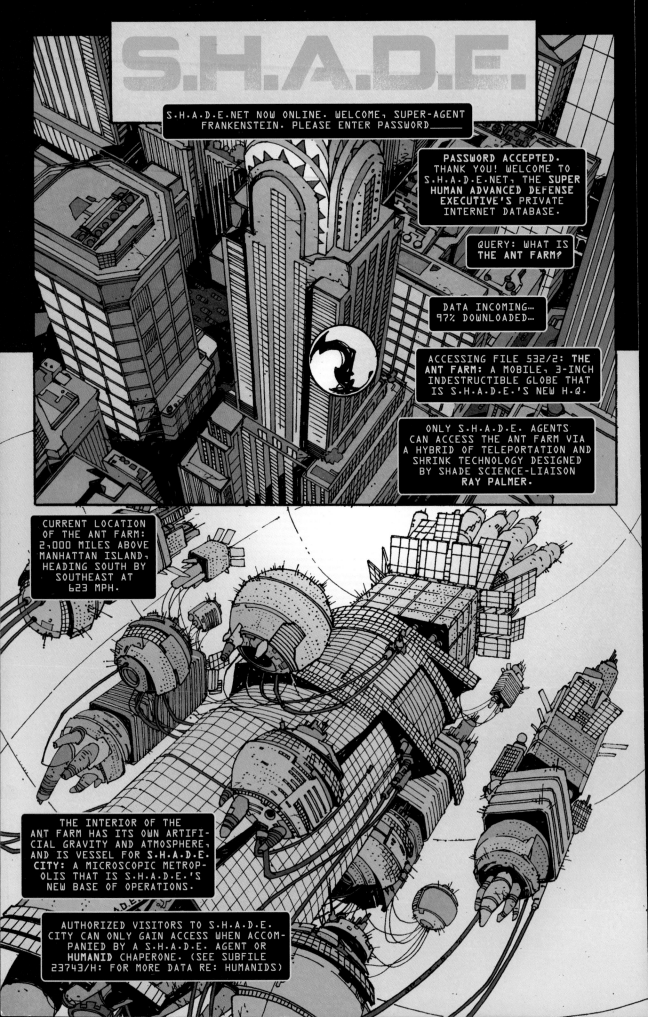

S.H.A.D.E.

S·H·A·D·E·NET NOW ONLINE. WELCOME, SUPER-AGENT FRANKENSTEIN. PLEASE ENTER PASSWORD____

PASSWORD ACCEPTED. THANK YOU! WELCOME TO S·H·A·D·E·NET, THE SUPER HUMAN ADVANCED DEFENSE EXECUTIVE'S PRIVATE INTERNET DATABASE.

QUERY: WHAT IS THE ANT FARM?

DATA INCOMING... 97% DOWNLOADED...

ACCESSING FILE 532/2: THE ANT FARM: A MOBILE, 3-INCH INDESTRUCTIBLE GLOBE THAT IS S·H·A·D·E·'S NEW H.Q.

ONLY S·H·A·D·E· AGENTS CAN ACCESS THE ANT FARM VIA A HYBRID OF TELEPORTATION AND SHRINK TECHNOLOGY DESIGNED BY SHADE SCIENCE-LIAISON RAY PALMER.

CURRENT LOCATION OF THE ANT FARM: 2,000 MILES ABOVE MANHATTAN ISLAND, HEADING SOUTH BY SOUTHEAST AT 623 MPH.

THE INTERIOR OF THE ANT FARM HAS ITS OWN ARTIFICIAL GRAVITY AND ATMOSPHERE, AND IS VESSEL FOR S·H·A·D·E· CITY: A MICROSCOPIC METROPOLIS THAT IS S·H·A·D·E·'S NEW BASE OF OPERATIONS.

AUTHORIZED VISITORS TO S·H·A·D·E· CITY CAN ONLY GAIN ACCESS WHEN ACCOMPANIED BY A S·H·A·D·E· AGENT OR HUMANID CHAPERONE. (SEE SUBFILE 23743/H: FOR MORE DATA RE: HUMANIDS)

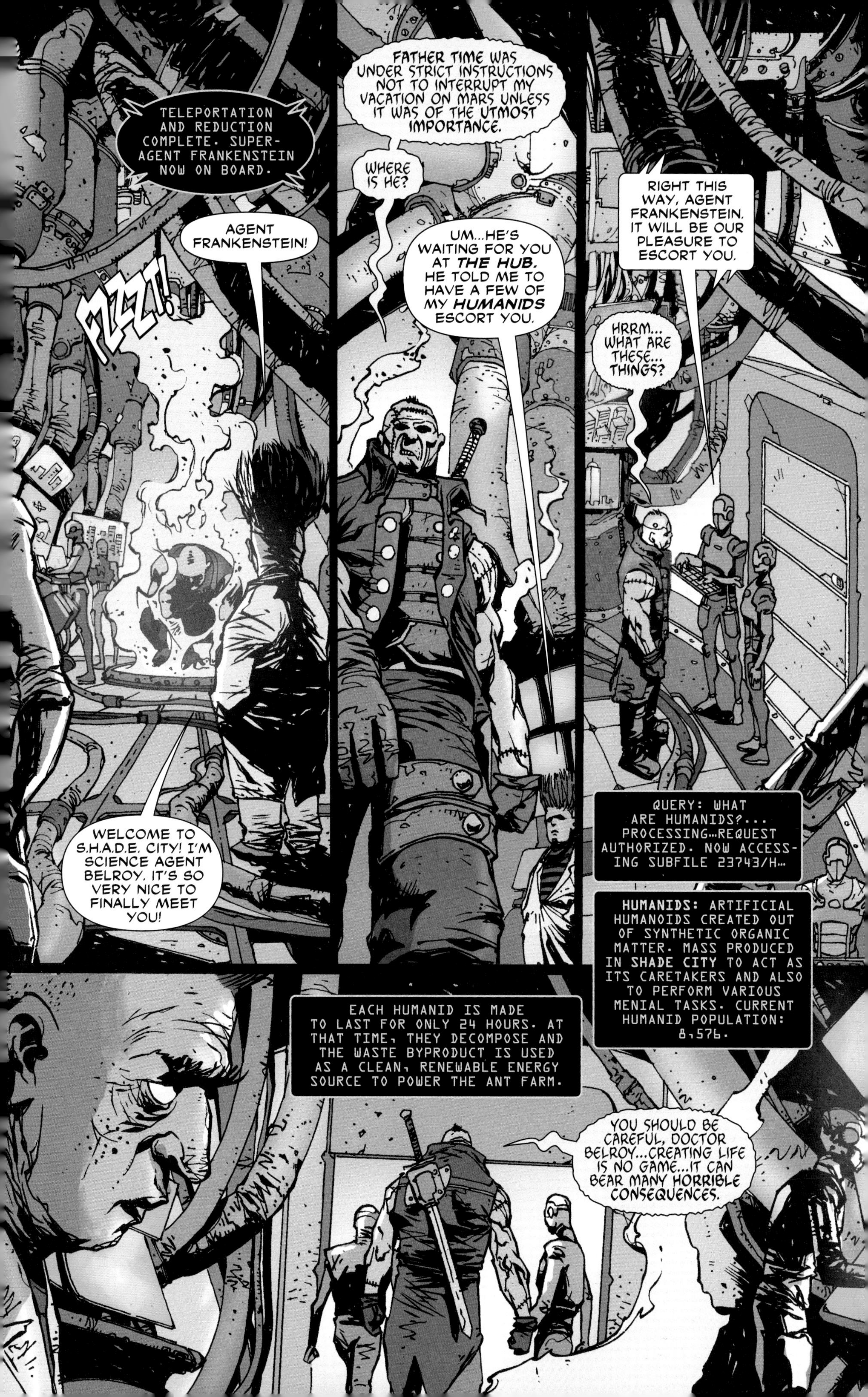

TELEPORTATION AND REDUCTION COMPLETE. SUPER-AGENT FRANKENSTEIN NOW ON BOARD.
AGENT FRANKENSTEIN!
FZZZT!
WELCOME TO S.H.A.D.E. CITY! I'M SCIENCE AGENT BELROY. IT'S SO VERY NICE TO FINALLY MEET YOU!
FATHER TIME WAS UNDER STRICT INSTRUCTIONS NOT TO INTERRUPT MY VACATION ON MARS UNLESS IT WAS OF THE UTMOST IMPORTANCE.
WHERE IS HE?
UM...HE'S WAITING FOR YOU AT THE HUB. HE TOLD ME TO HAVE A FEW OF MY HUMANIDS ESCORT YOU.
RIGHT THIS WAY, AGENT FRANKENSTEIN. IT WILL BE OUR PLEASURE TO ESCORT YOU.
HRRM... WHAT ARE THESE... THINGS?
QUERY: WHAT ARE HUMANIDS?... PROCESSING...REQUEST AUTHORIZED. NOW ACCESSING SUBFILE 23743/H...
HUMANIDS: ARTIFICIAL HUMANOIDS CREATED OUT OF SYNTHETIC ORGANIC MATTER. MASS PRODUCED IN SHADE CITY TO ACT AS ITS CARETAKERS AND ALSO TO PERFORM VARIOUS MENIAL TASKS. CURRENT HUMANID POPULATION: 8,576.
EACH HUMANID IS MADE TO LAST FOR ONLY 24 HOURS. AT THAT TIME, THEY DECOMPOSE AND THE WASTE BYPRODUCT IS USED AS A CLEAN, RENEWABLE ENERGY SOURCE TO POWER THE ANT FARM.
YOU SHOULD BE CAREFUL, DOCTOR BELROY...CREATING LIFE IS NO GAME...IT CAN BEAR MANY HORRIBLE CONSEQUENCES.

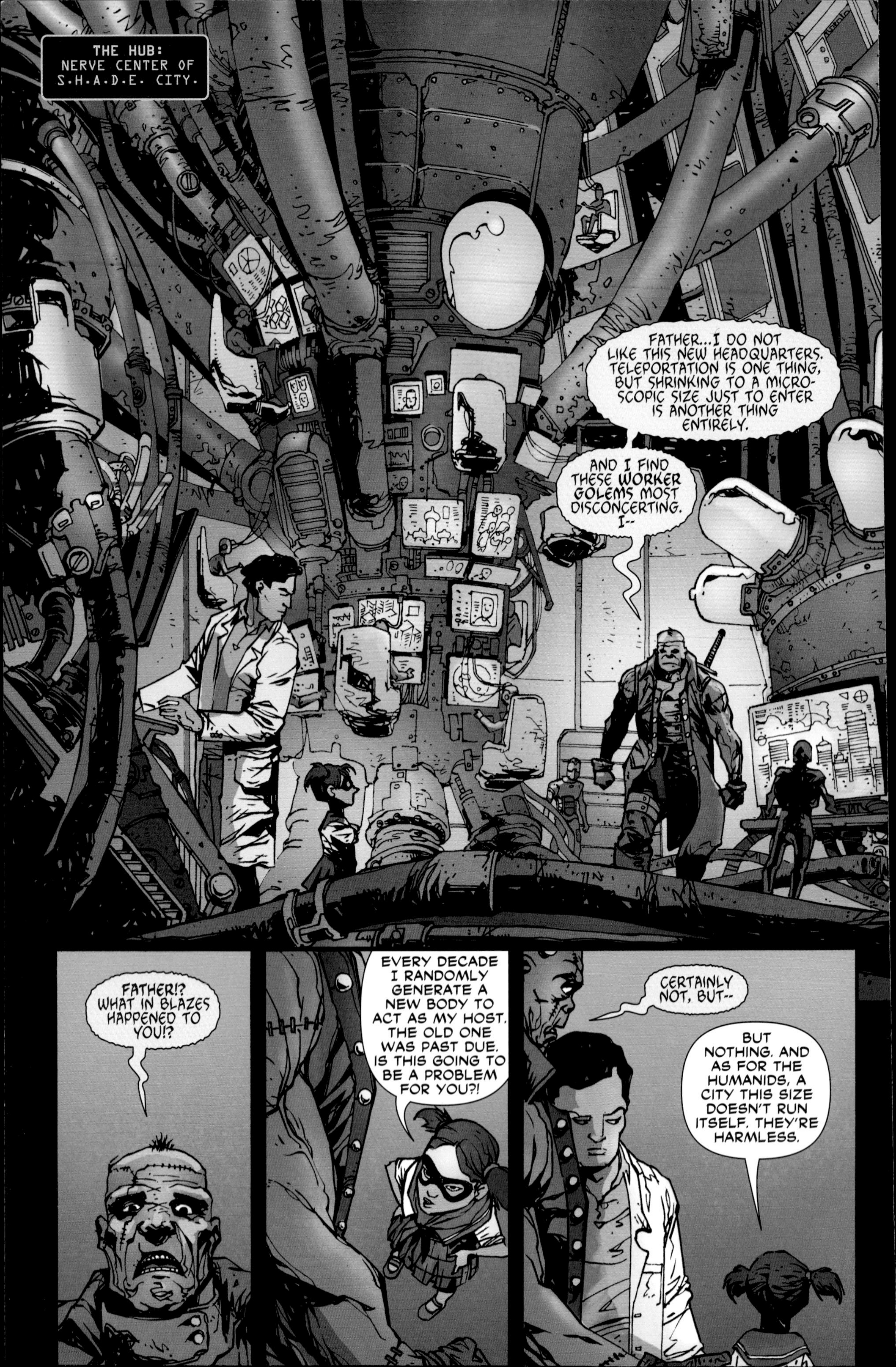
THE HUB: NERVE CENTER OF S.H.A.D.E. CITY.
FATHER...I DO NOT LIKE THIS NEW HEADQUARTERS. TELEPORTATION IS ONE THING, BUT SHRINKING TO A MICRO-SCOPIC SIZE JUST TO ENTER IS ANOTHER THING ENTIRELY.
AND I FIND THESE WORKER GOLEMS MOST DISCONCERTING. I--
FATHER!? WHAT IN BLAZES HAPPENED TO YOU!?
EVERY DECADE I RANDOMLY GENERATE A NEW BODY TO ACT AS MY HOST. THE OLD ONE WAS PAST DUE. IS THIS GOING TO BE A PROBLEM FOR YOU?!
CERTAINLY NOT, BUT--
BUT NOTHING. AND AS FOR THE HUMANIDS, A CITY THIS SIZE DOESN'T RUN ITSELF. THEY'RE HARMLESS.

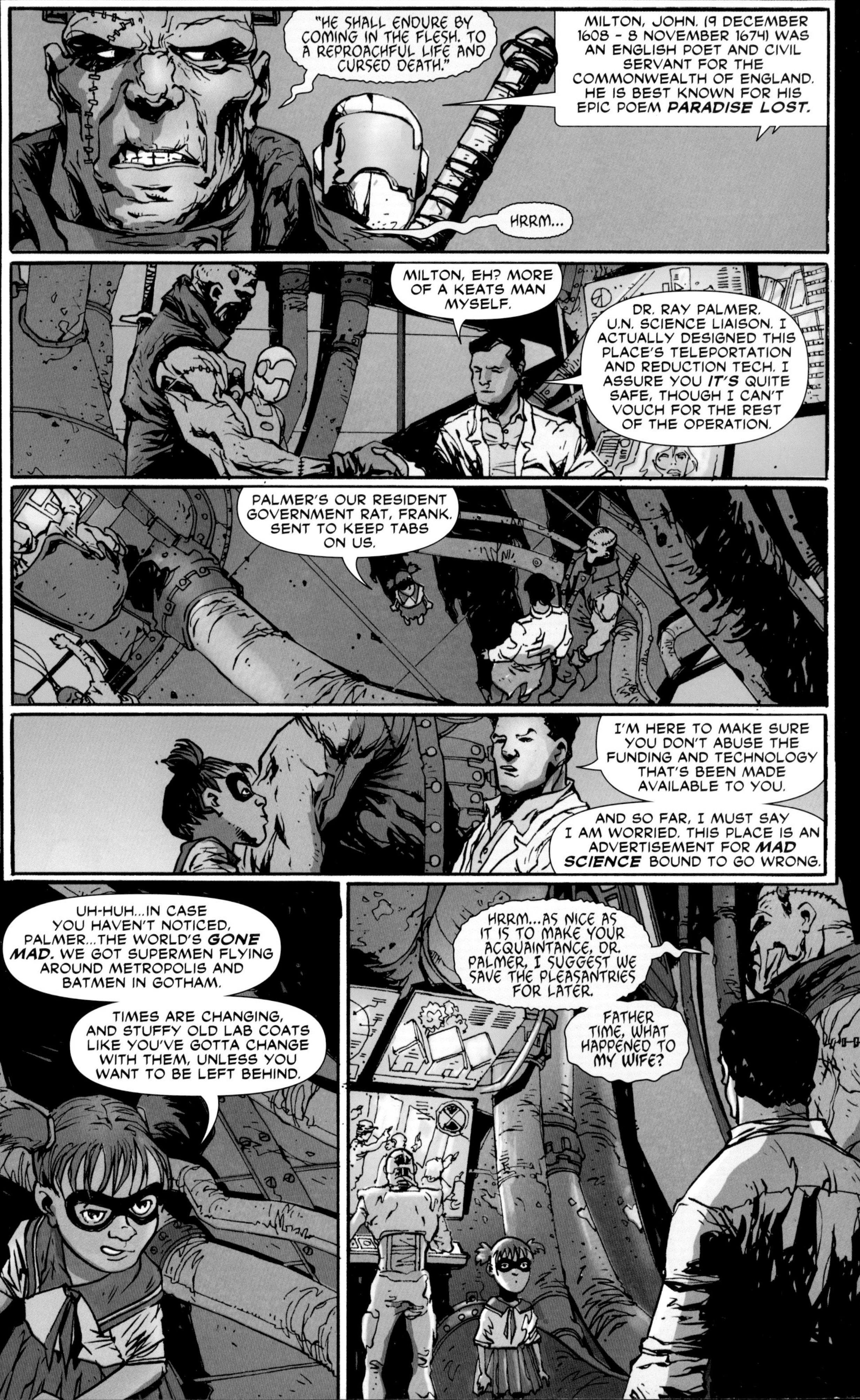
"HE SHALL ENDURE BY COMING IN THE FLESH. TO A REPROACHFUL LIFE AND CURSED DEATH."
MILTON, JOHN. (9 DECEMBER 1608 - 8 NOVEMBER 1674) WAS AN ENGLISH POET AND CIVIL SERVANT FOR THE COMMONWEALTH OF ENGLAND. HE IS BEST KNOWN FOR HIS EPIC POEM *PARADISE LOST.*
HRRM...
MILTON, EH? MORE OF A KEATS MAN MYSELF.
DR. RAY PALMER. U.N. SCIENCE LIAISON. I ACTUALLY DESIGNED THIS PLACE'S TELEPORTATION AND REDUCTION TECH. I ASSURE YOU *IT'S* QUITE SAFE, THOUGH I CAN'T VOUCH FOR THE REST OF THE OPERATION.
PALMER'S OUR RESIDENT GOVERNMENT RAT, FRANK. SENT TO KEEP TABS ON US.
I'M HERE TO MAKE SURE YOU DON'T ABUSE THE FUNDING AND TECHNOLOGY THAT'S BEEN MADE AVAILABLE TO YOU.
AND SO FAR, I MUST SAY I AM WORRIED. THIS PLACE IS AN ADVERTISEMENT FOR *MAD SCIENCE* BOUND TO GO WRONG.
UH-HUH...IN CASE YOU HAVEN'T NOTICED, PALMER...THE WORLD'S *GONE MAD.* WE GOT SUPERMEN FLYING AROUND METROPOLIS AND BATMEN IN GOTHAM.
TIMES ARE CHANGING, AND STUFFY OLD LAB COATS LIKE YOU'VE GOTTA CHANGE WITH THEM, UNLESS YOU WANT TO BE LEFT BEHIND.
HRRM...AS NICE AS IT IS TO MAKE YOUR ACQUAINTANCE, DR. PALMER, I SUGGEST WE SAVE THE PLEASANTRIES FOR LATER.
FATHER TIME, WHAT HAPPENED TO **MY WIFE?**

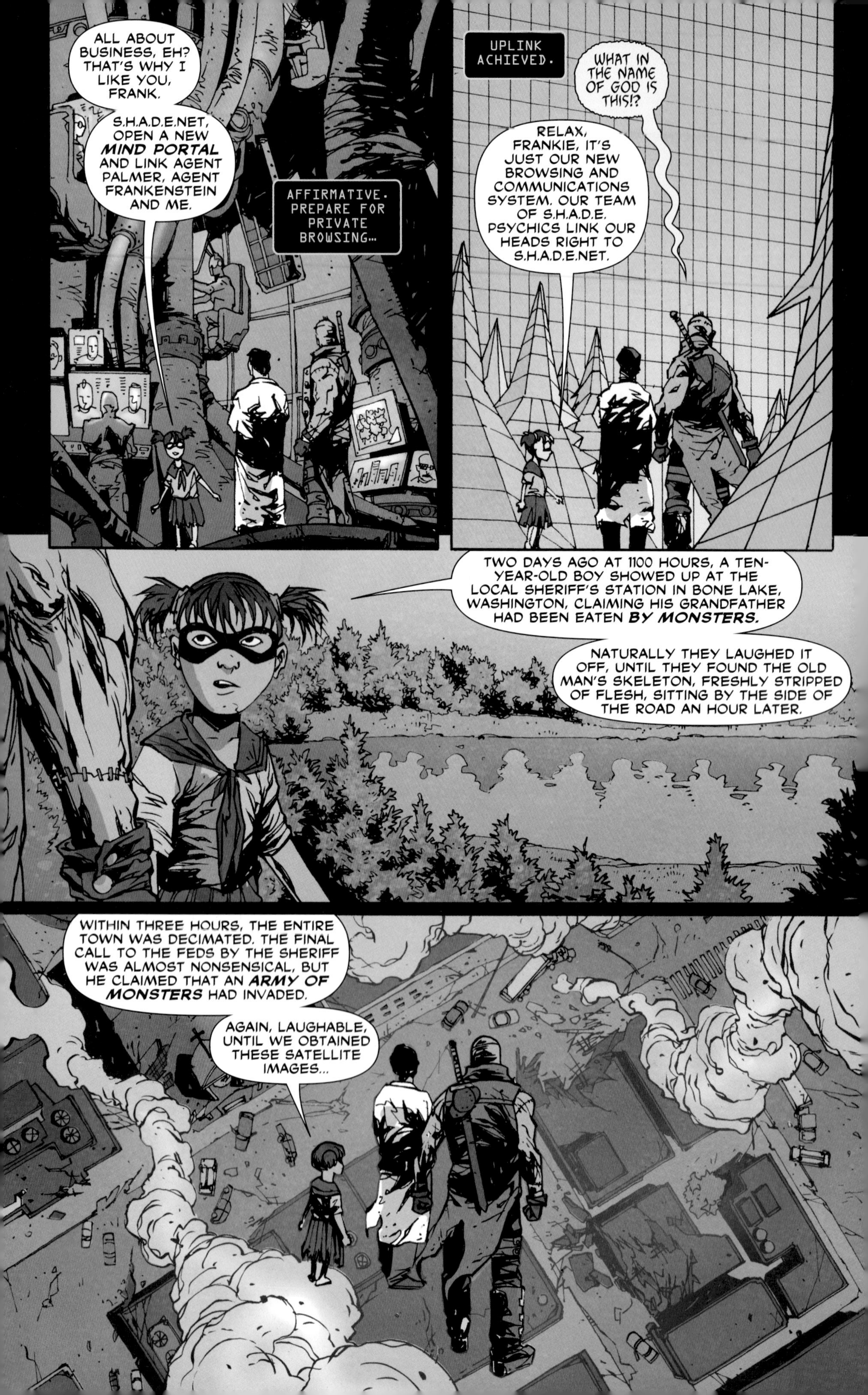
ALL ABOUT BUSINESS, EH? THAT'S WHY I LIKE YOU, FRANK.
S.H.A.D.E.NET, OPEN A NEW *MIND PORTAL* AND LINK AGENT PALMER, AGENT FRANKENSTEIN AND ME.
AFFIRMATIVE. PREPARE FOR PRIVATE BROWSING...
UPLINK ACHIEVED.
WHAT IN THE NAME OF GOD IS THIS!?
RELAX, FRANKIE, IT'S JUST OUR NEW BROWSING AND COMMUNICATIONS SYSTEM. OUR TEAM OF S.H.A.D.E. PSYCHICS LINK OUR HEADS RIGHT TO S.H.A.D.E.NET.
TWO DAYS AGO AT 1100 HOURS, A TEN-YEAR-OLD BOY SHOWED UP AT THE LOCAL SHERIFF'S STATION IN BONE LAKE, WASHINGTON, CLAIMING HIS GRANDFATHER HAD BEEN EATEN *BY MONSTERS.*
NATURALLY THEY LAUGHED IT OFF, UNTIL THEY FOUND THE OLD MAN'S SKELETON, FRESHLY STRIPPED OF FLESH, SITTING BY THE SIDE OF THE ROAD AN HOUR LATER.
WITHIN THREE HOURS, THE ENTIRE TOWN WAS DECIMATED. THE FINAL CALL TO THE FEDS BY THE SHERIFF WAS ALMOST NONSENSICAL, BUT HE CLAIMED THAT AN *ARMY OF MONSTERS* HAD INVADED.
AGAIN, LAUGHABLE, UNTIL WE OBTAINED THESE SATELLITE IMAGES...

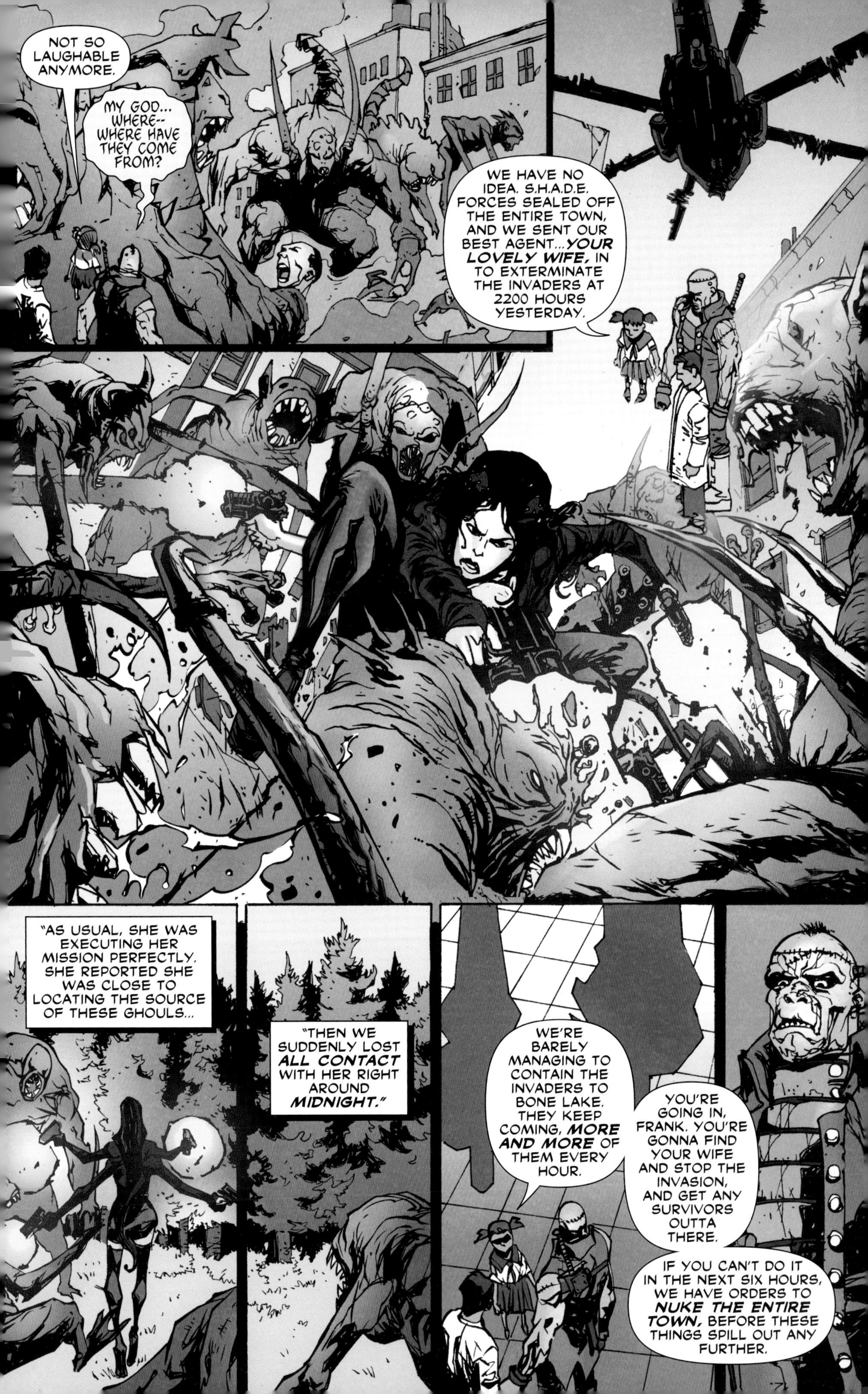
NOT SO LAUGHABLE ANYMORE.
MY GOD... WHERE-- WHERE HAVE THEY COME FROM?
WE HAVE NO IDEA. S.H.A.D.E. FORCES SEALED OFF THE ENTIRE TOWN, AND WE SENT OUR BEST AGENT...YOUR LOVELY WIFE, IN TO EXTERMINATE THE INVADERS AT 2200 HOURS YESTERDAY.
"AS USUAL, SHE WAS EXECUTING HER MISSION PERFECTLY. SHE REPORTED SHE WAS CLOSE TO LOCATING THE SOURCE OF THESE GHOULS...
"THEN WE SUDDENLY LOST ALL CONTACT WITH HER RIGHT AROUND MIDNIGHT."
WE'RE BARELY MANAGING TO CONTAIN THE INVADERS TO BONE LAKE. THEY KEEP COMING, MORE AND MORE OF THEM EVERY HOUR.
YOU'RE GOING IN, FRANK. YOU'RE GONNA FIND YOUR WIFE AND STOP THE INVASION, AND GET ANY SURVIVORS OUTTA THERE.
IF YOU CAN'T DO IT IN THE NEXT SIX HOURS, WE HAVE ORDERS TO NUKE THE ENTIRE TOWN, BEFORE THESE THINGS SPILL OUT ANY FURTHER.

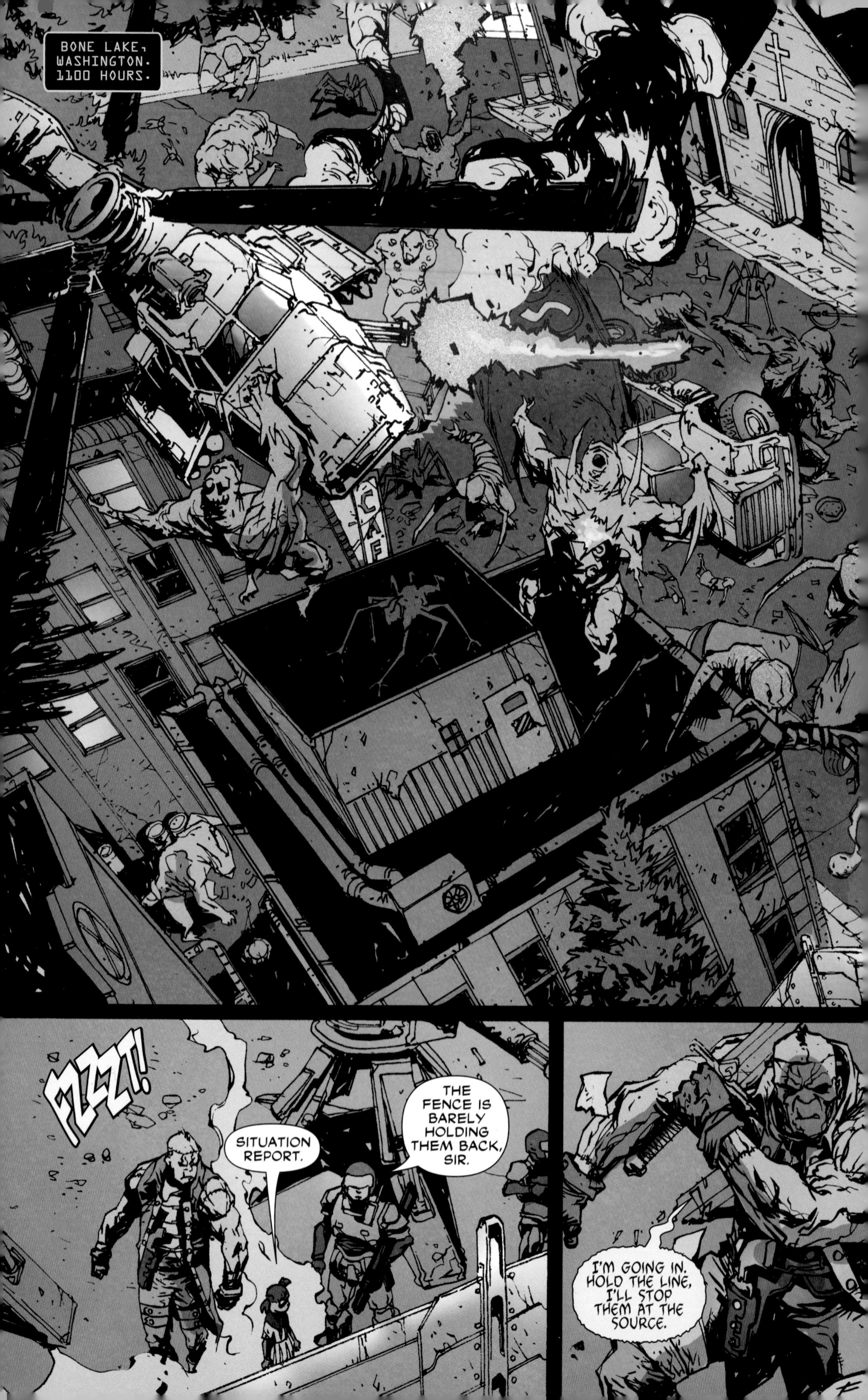
BONE LAKE, WASHINGTON. 1100 HOURS.
CAF
FZZZT!
SITUATION REPORT.
THE FENCE IS BARELY HOLDING THEM BACK, SIR.
I'M GOING IN. HOLD THE LINE, I'LL STOP THEM AT THE SOURCE.

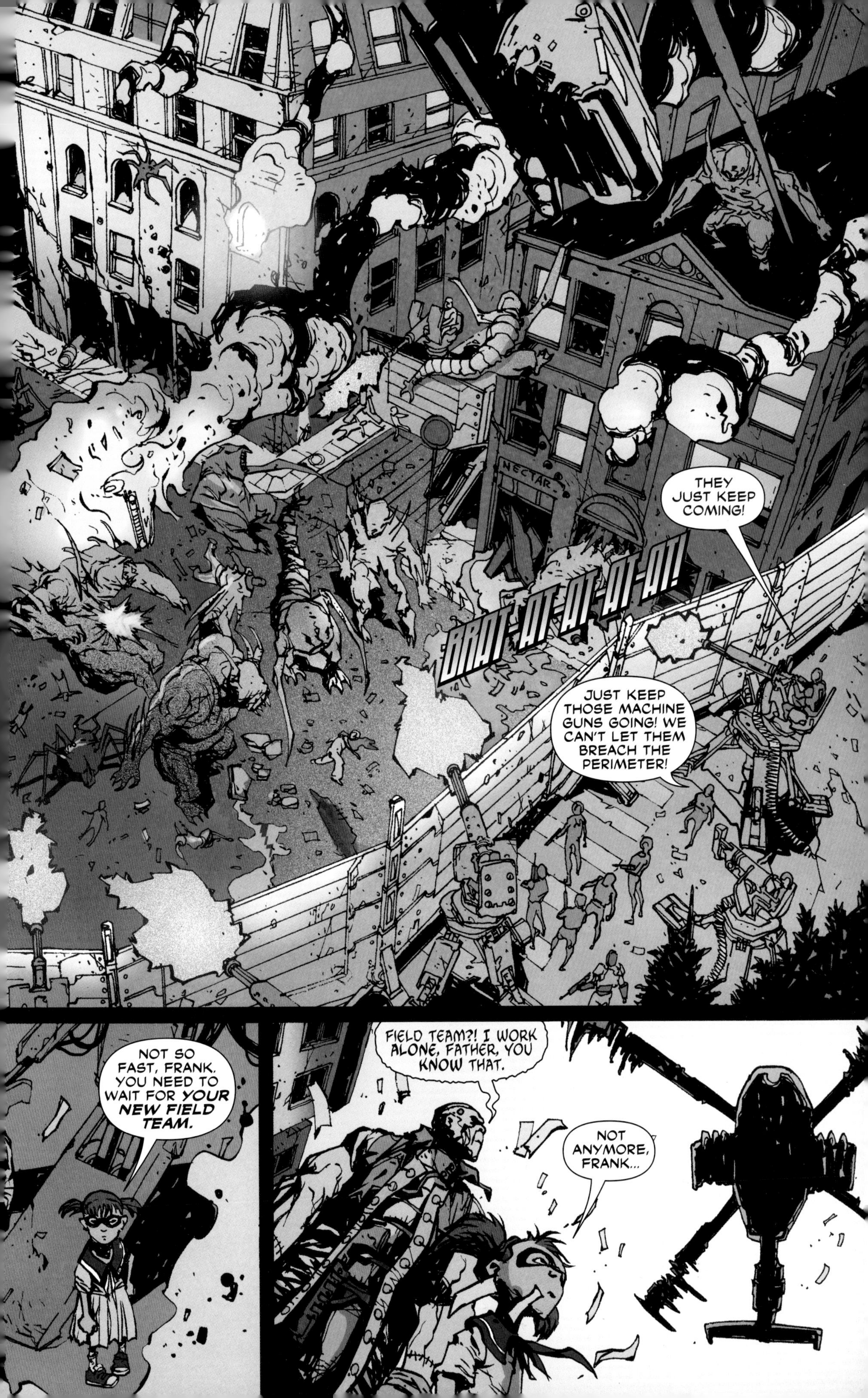
THEY JUST KEEP COMING!
BRAT-AT-AT-AT-AT!
JUST KEEP THOSE MACHINE GUNS GOING! WE CAN'T LET THEM BREACH THE PERIMETER!
NECTAR
NOT SO FAST, FRANK. YOU NEED TO WAIT FOR YOUR NEW FIELD TEAM.
FIELD TEAM?! I WORK ALONE, FATHER, YOU KNOW THAT.
NOT ANYMORE, FRANK...

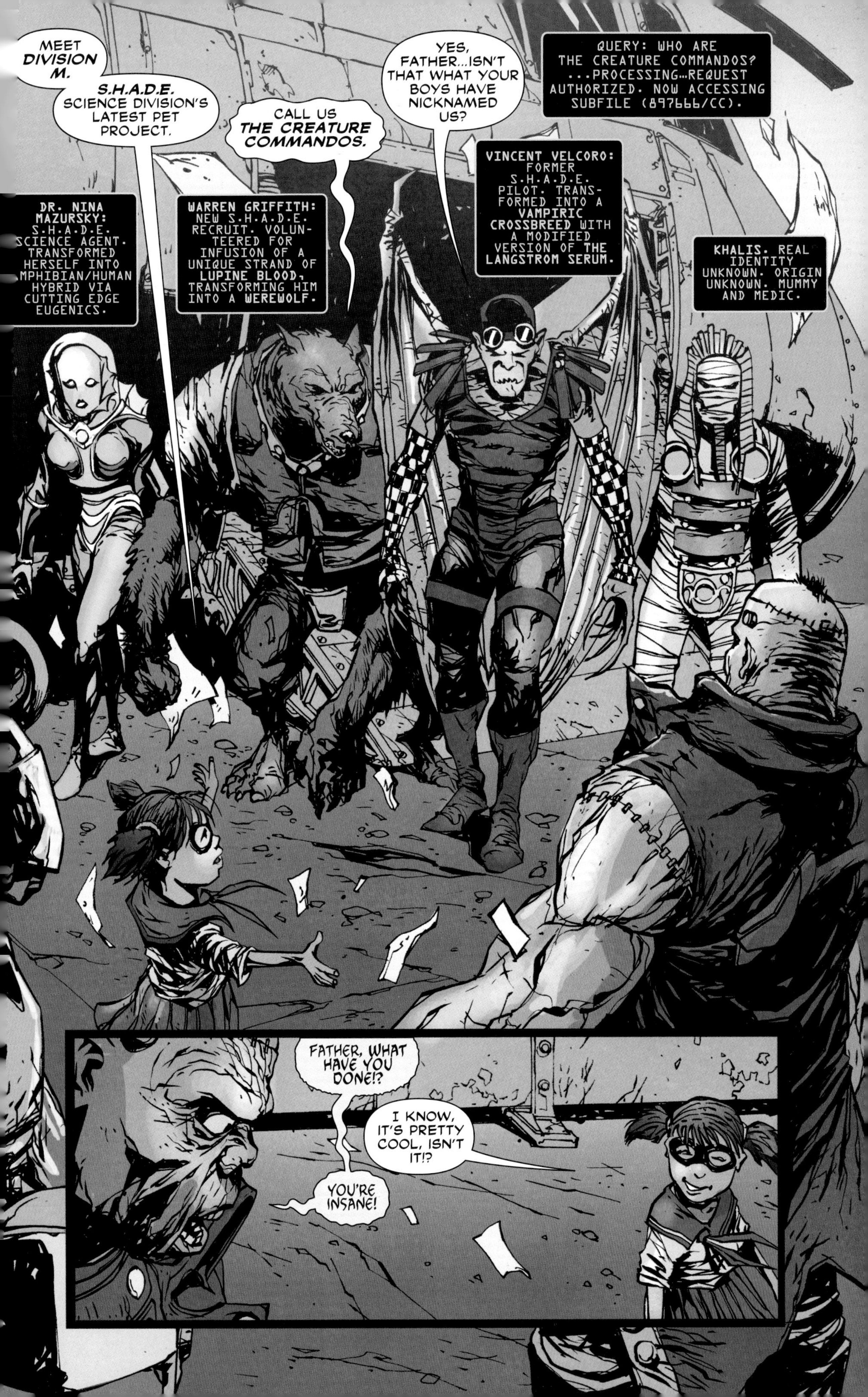
MEET DIVISION M.
S.H.A.D.E. SCIENCE DIVISION'S LATEST PET PROJECT.
CALL US THE CREATURE COMMANDOS.
YES, FATHER...ISN'T THAT WHAT YOUR BOYS HAVE NICKNAMED US?
QUERY: WHO ARE THE CREATURE COMMANDOS? ...PROCESSING...REQUEST AUTHORIZED. NOW ACCESSING SUBFILE (897666/CC).
DR. NINA MAZURSKY: S.H.A.D.E. SCIENCE AGENT. TRANSFORMED HERSELF INTO AMPHIBIAN/HUMAN HYBRID VIA CUTTING EDGE EUGENICS.
WARREN GRIFFITH: NEW S.H.A.D.E. RECRUIT. VOLUNTEERED FOR INFUSION OF A UNIQUE STRAND OF LUPINE BLOOD, TRANSFORMING HIM INTO A WEREWOLF.
VINCENT VELCORO: FORMER S.H.A.D.E. PILOT. TRANSFORMED INTO A VAMPIRIC CROSSBREED WITH A MODIFIED VERSION OF THE LANGSTROM SERUM.
KHALIS. REAL IDENTITY UNKNOWN. ORIGIN UNKNOWN. MUMMY AND MEDIC.
FATHER, WHAT HAVE YOU DONE!?
YOU'RE INSANE!
I KNOW, IT'S PRETTY COOL, ISN'T IT!?

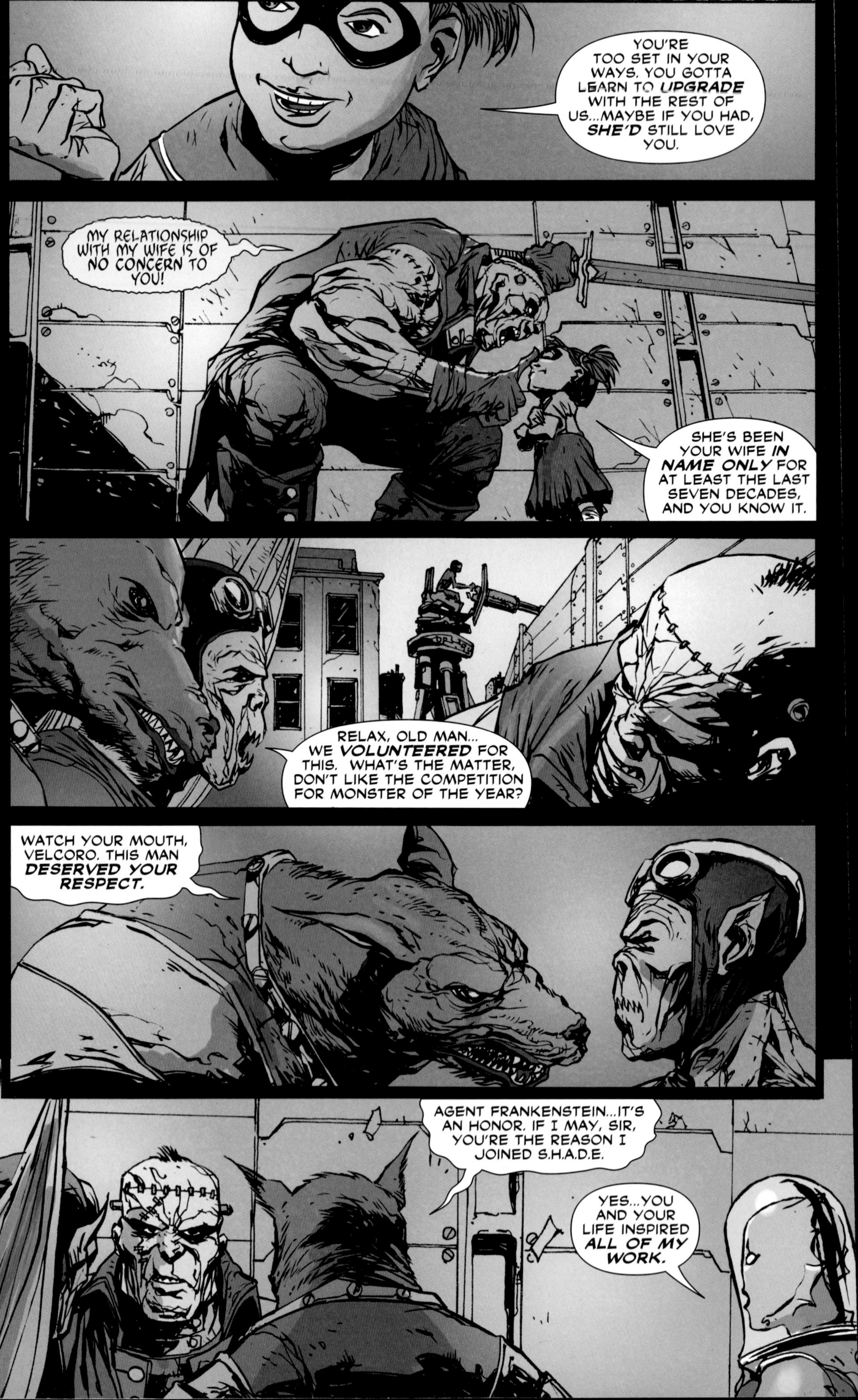
YOU'RE TOO SET IN YOUR WAYS. YOU GOTTA LEARN TO UPGRADE WITH THE REST OF US...MAYBE IF YOU HAD, SHE'D STILL LOVE YOU.
MY RELATIONSHIP WITH MY WIFE IS OF NO CONCERN TO YOU!
SHE'S BEEN YOUR WIFE IN NAME ONLY FOR AT LEAST THE LAST SEVEN DECADES, AND YOU KNOW IT.
RELAX, OLD MAN... WE VOLUNTEERED FOR THIS. WHAT'S THE MATTER, DON'T LIKE THE COMPETITION FOR MONSTER OF THE YEAR?
WATCH YOUR MOUTH, VELCORO. THIS MAN DESERVED YOUR RESPECT.
AGENT FRANKENSTEIN...IT'S AN HONOR. IF I MAY, SIR, YOU'RE THE REASON I JOINED S.H.A.D.E.
YES...YOU AND YOUR LIFE INSPIRED ALL OF MY WORK.

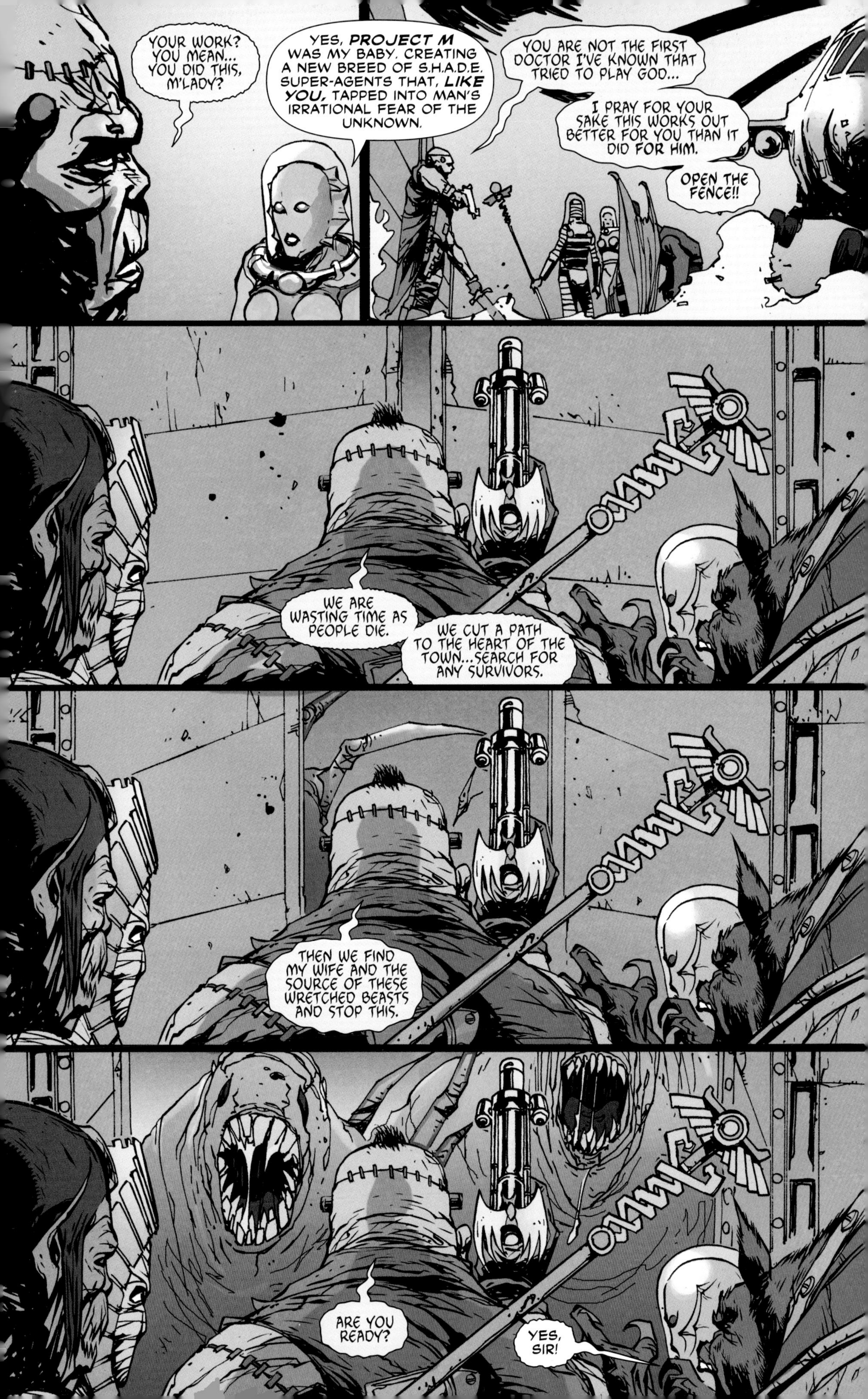
YOUR WORK? YOU MEAN... YOU DID THIS, M'LADY?
YES, PROJECT M WAS MY BABY. CREATING A NEW BREED OF S.H.A.D.E. SUPER-AGENTS THAT, LIKE YOU, TAPPED INTO MAN'S IRRATIONAL FEAR OF THE UNKNOWN.
YOU ARE NOT THE FIRST DOCTOR I'VE KNOWN THAT TRIED TO PLAY GOD...
I PRAY FOR YOUR SAKE THIS WORKS OUT BETTER FOR YOU THAN IT DID FOR HIM.
OPEN THE FENCE!!
WE ARE WASTING TIME AS PEOPLE DIE.
WE CUT A PATH TO THE HEART OF THE TOWN...SEARCH FOR ANY SURVIVORS.
THEN WE FIND MY WIFE AND THE SOURCE OF THESE WRETCHED BEASTS AND STOP THIS.
ARE YOU READY?
YES, SIR!

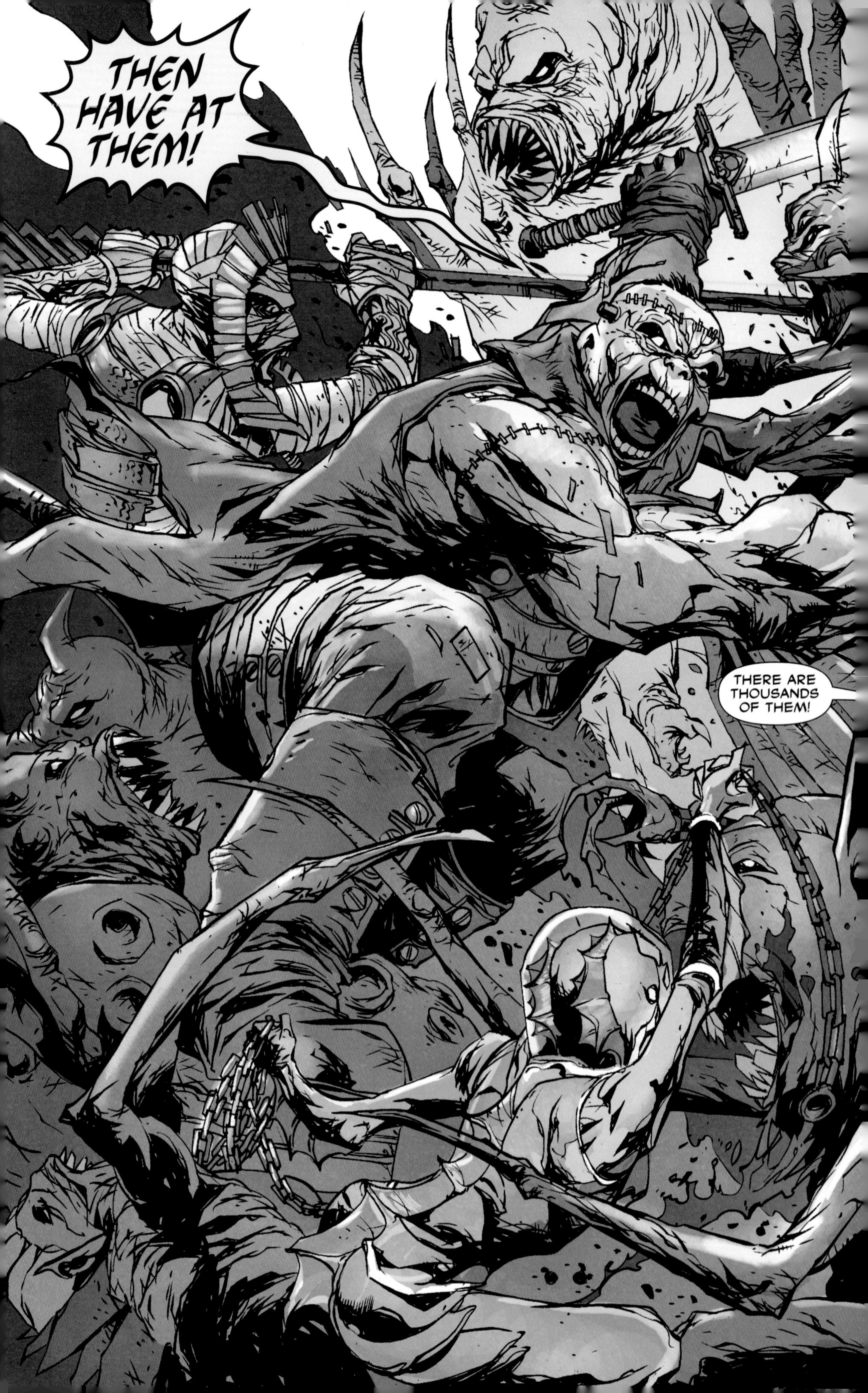
THEN HAVE AT THEM!
THERE ARE THOUSANDS OF THEM!

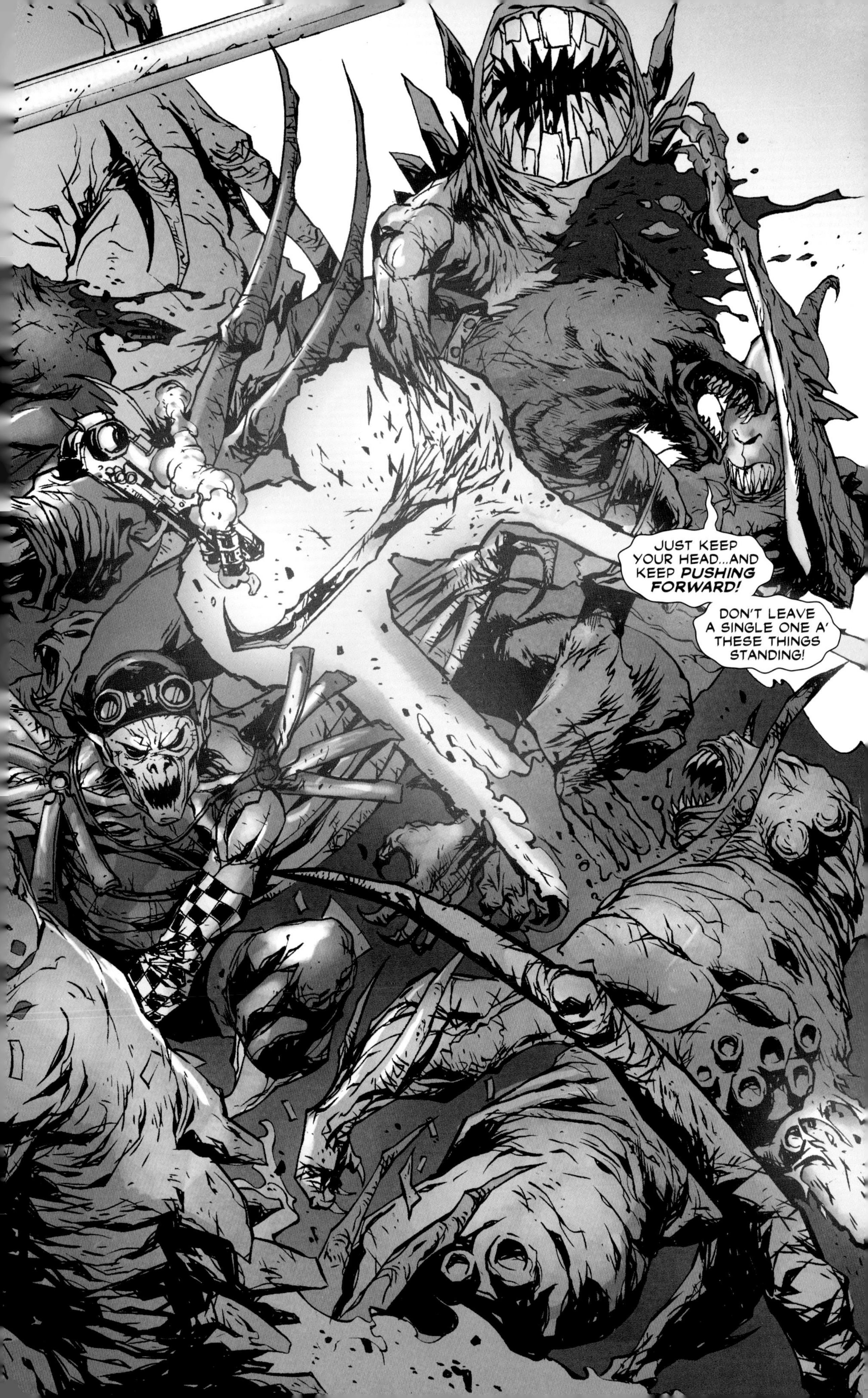
JUST KEEP YOUR HEAD...AND KEEP *PUSHING FORWARD!*
DON'T LEAVE A SINGLE ONE A' THESE THINGS STANDING!

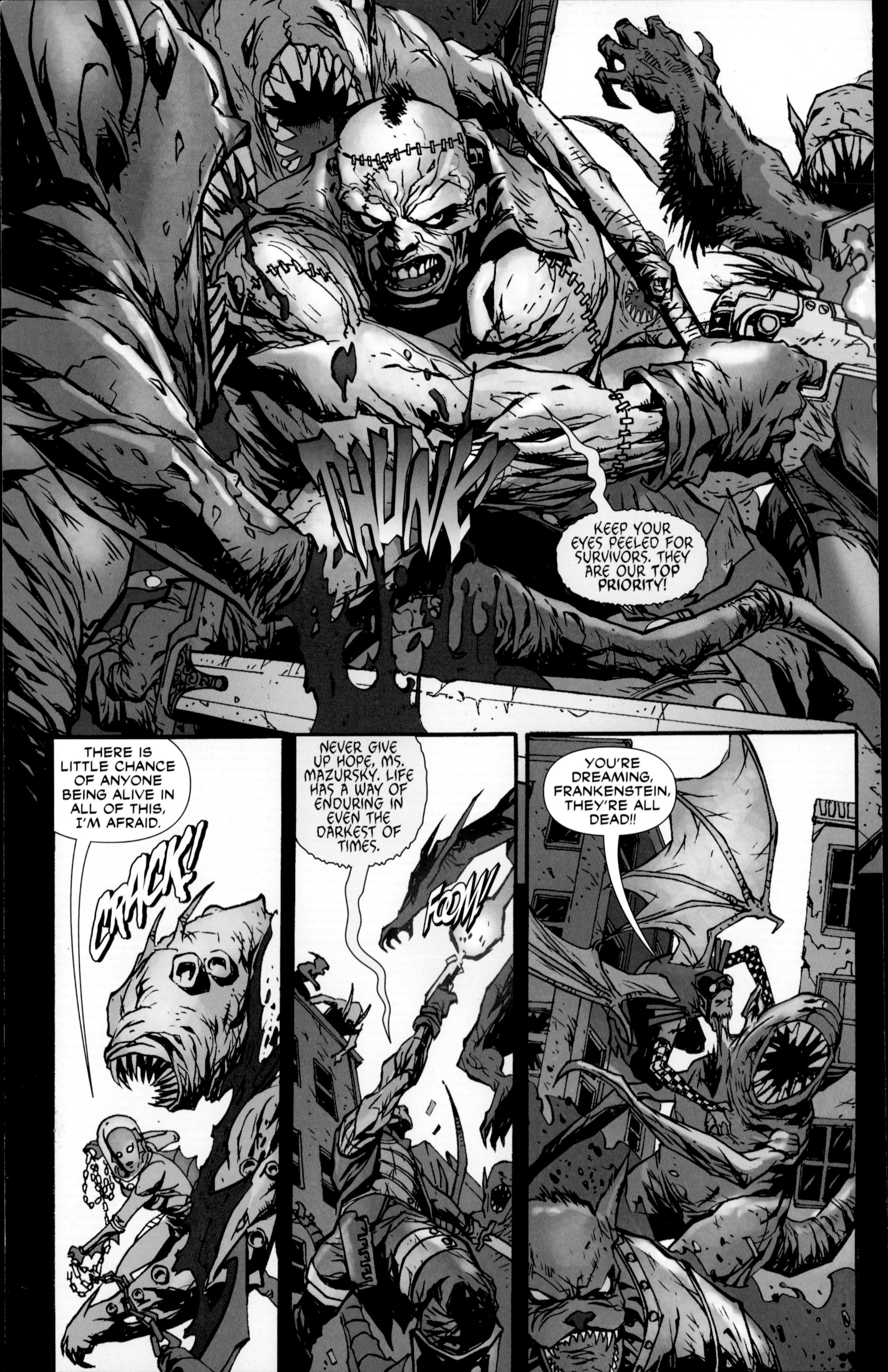
THUNK!
KEEP YOUR EYES PEELED FOR SURVIVORS. THEY ARE OUR TOP PRIORITY!
THERE IS LITTLE CHANCE OF ANYONE BEING ALIVE IN ALL OF THIS, I'M AFRAID.
CRACK!
NEVER GIVE UP HOPE, MS. MAZURSKY. LIFE HAS A WAY OF ENDURING IN EVEN THE DARKEST OF TIMES.
FOOM!
YOU'RE DREAMING, FRANKENSTEIN, THEY'RE ALL DEAD!!

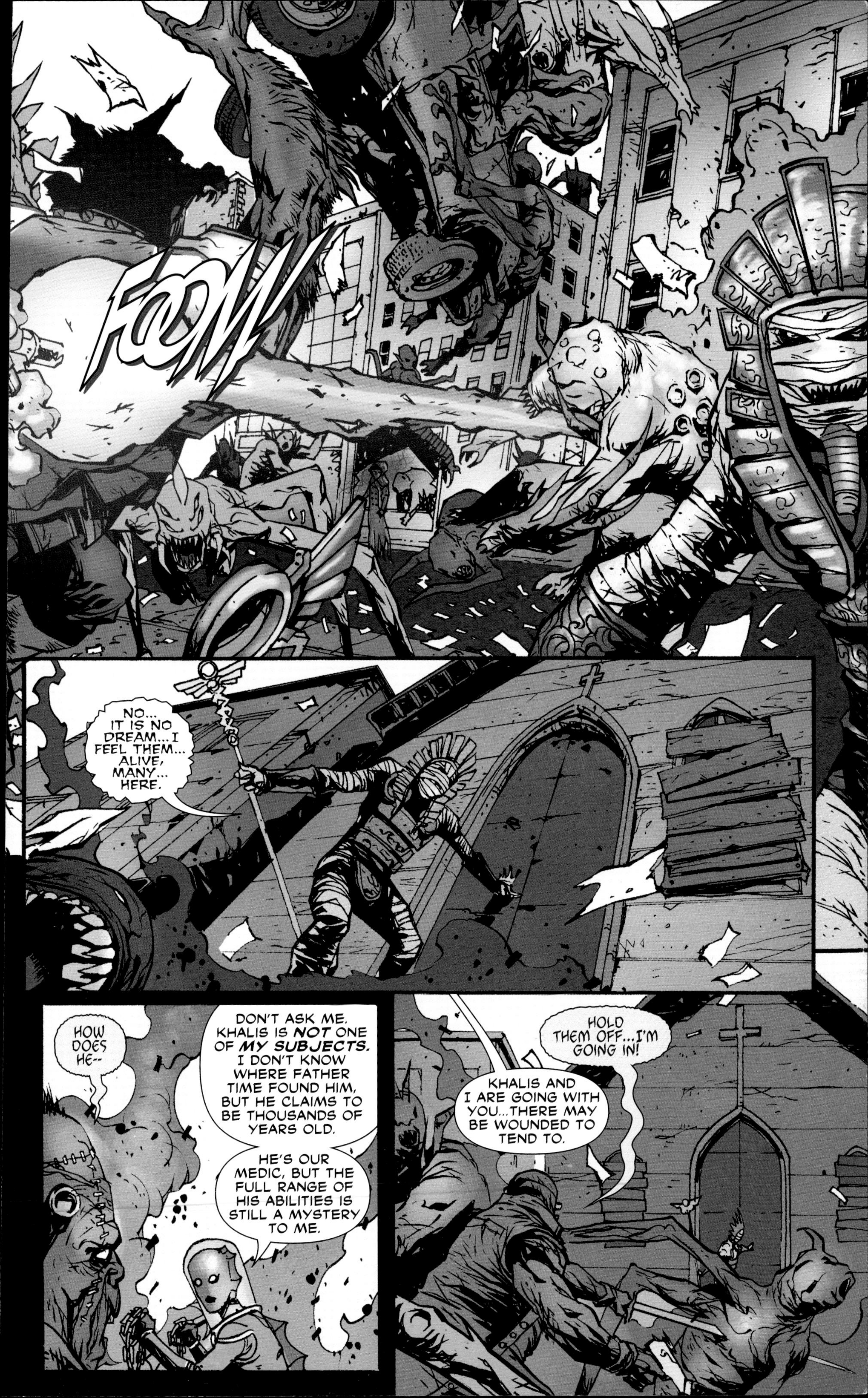
FOOM
NO... IT IS NO DREAM... I FEEL THEM... ALIVE, MANY... HERE.
HOW DOES HE--
DON'T ASK ME. KHALIS IS NOT ONE OF MY SUBJECTS. I DON'T KNOW WHERE FATHER TIME FOUND HIM, BUT HE CLAIMS TO BE THOUSANDS OF YEARS OLD.
HE'S OUR MEDIC, BUT THE FULL RANGE OF HIS ABILITIES IS STILL A MYSTERY TO ME.
HOLD THEM OFF...I'M GOING IN!
KHALIS AND I ARE GOING WITH YOU...THERE MAY BE WOUNDED TO TEND TO.

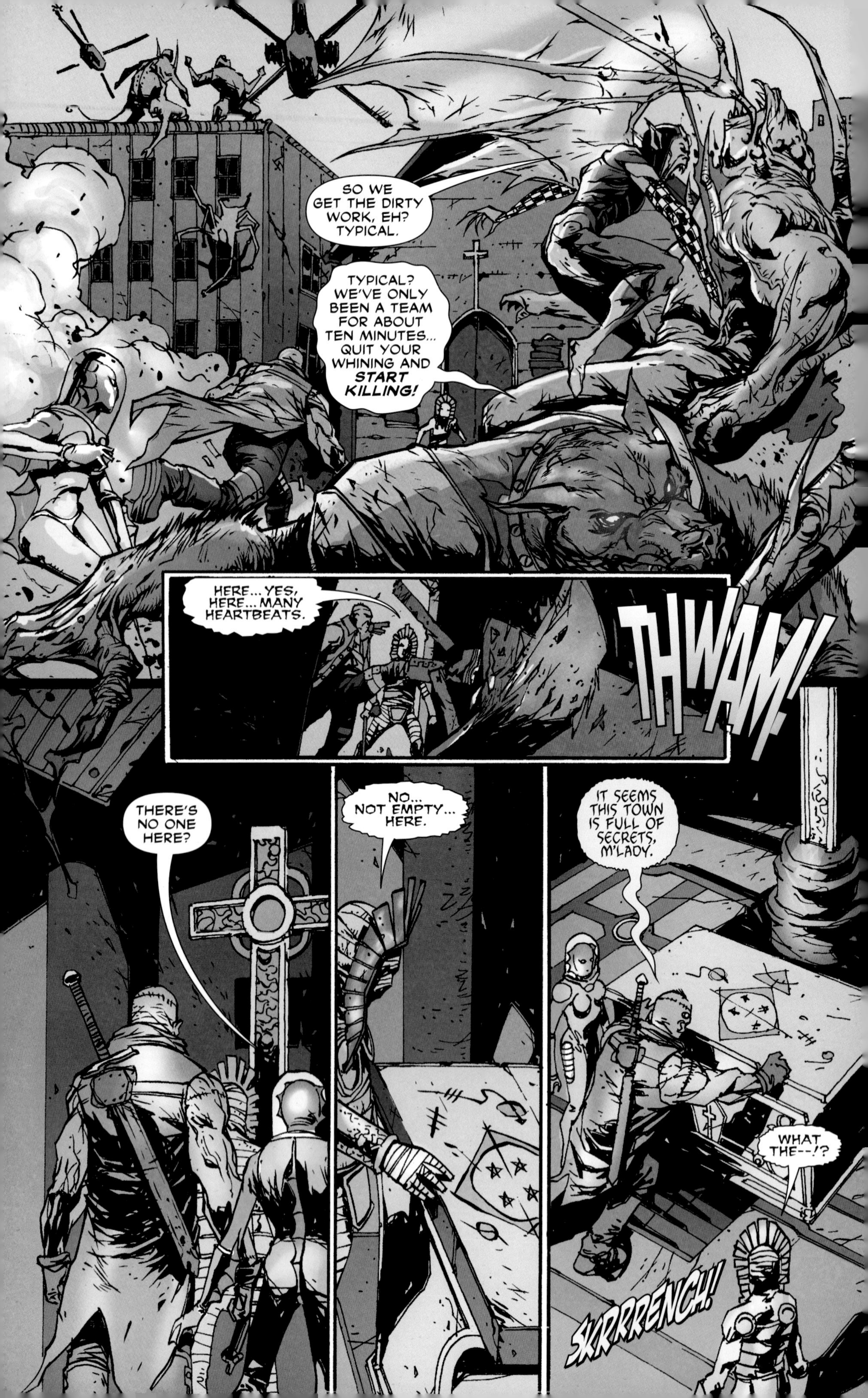
SO WE GET THE DIRTY WORK, EH? TYPICAL.
TYPICAL? WE'VE ONLY BEEN A TEAM FOR ABOUT TEN MINUTES... QUIT YOUR WHINING AND START KILLING!
HERE... YES, HERE... MANY HEARTBEATS.
THWAM!
THERE'S NO ONE HERE?
NO... NOT EMPTY... HERE.
IT SEEMS THIS TOWN IS FULL OF SECRETS, M'LADY.
WHAT THE--!?
SKRRRENCH!

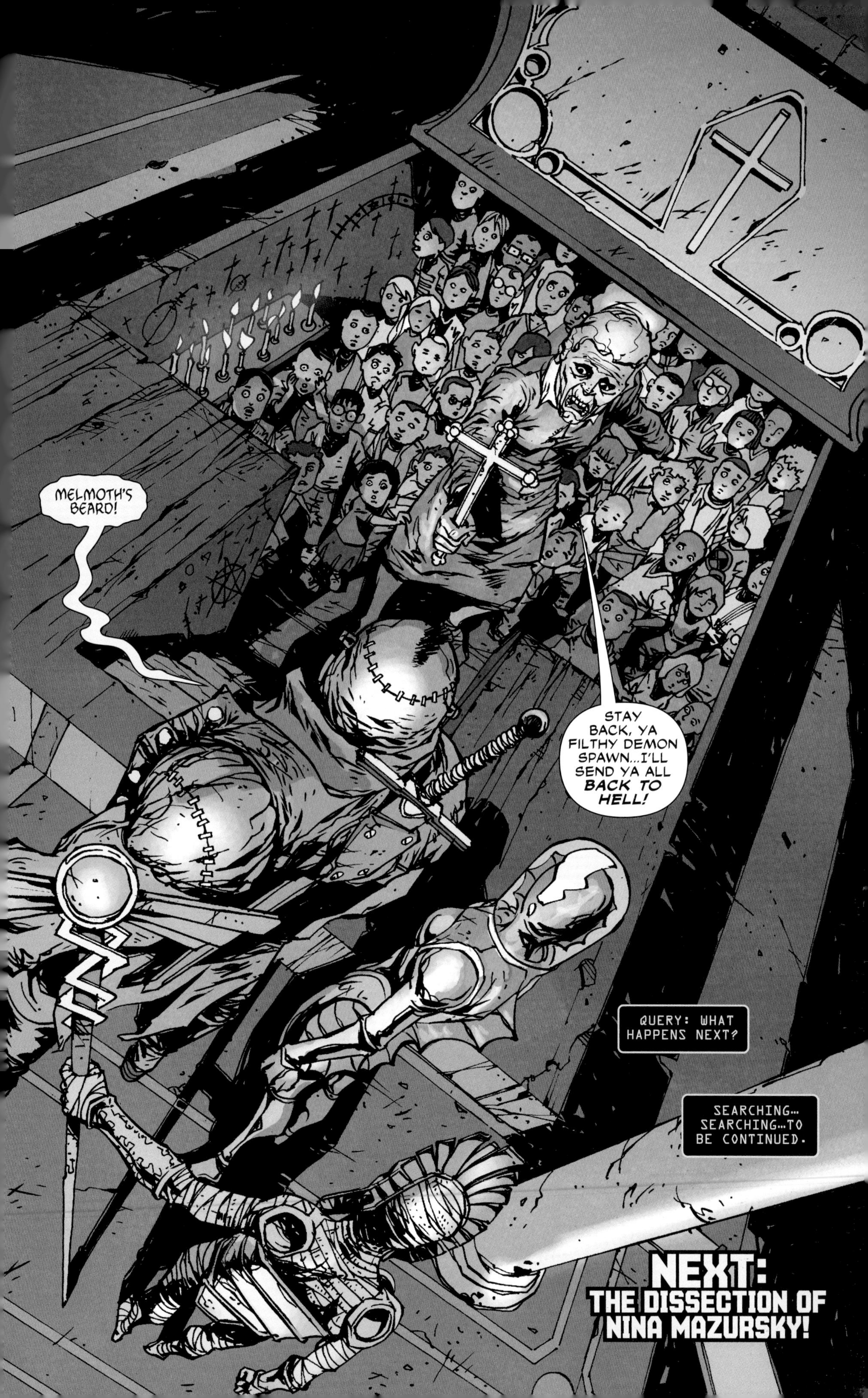
MELMOTH'S BEARD!
STAY BACK, YA FILTHY DEMON SPAWN...I'LL SEND YA ALL BACK TO HELL!
QUERY: WHAT HAPPENS NEXT?
SEARCHING... SEARCHING...TO BE CONTINUED.
NEXT: THE DISSECTION OF NINA MAZURSKY!

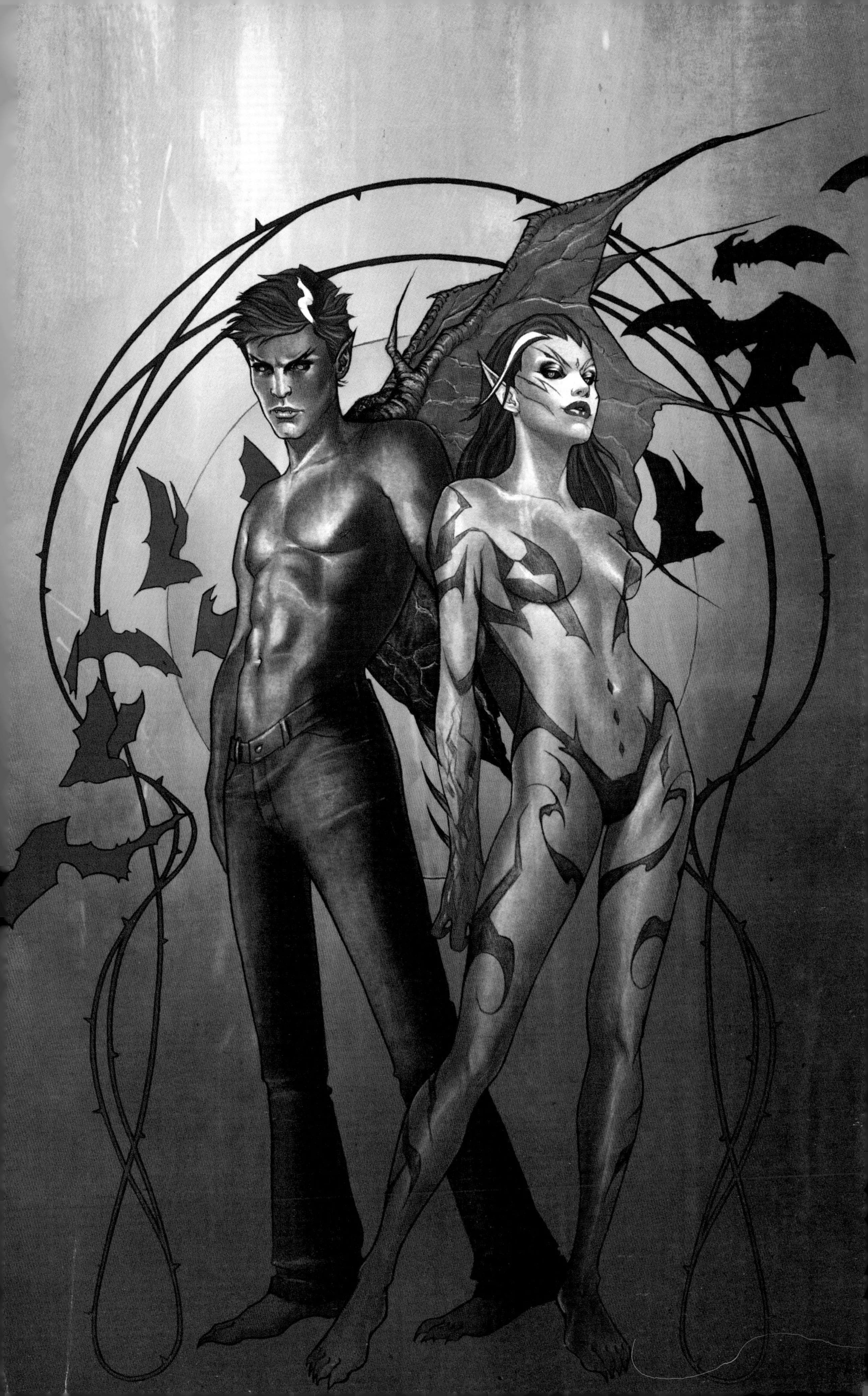

I, VAMPIRE

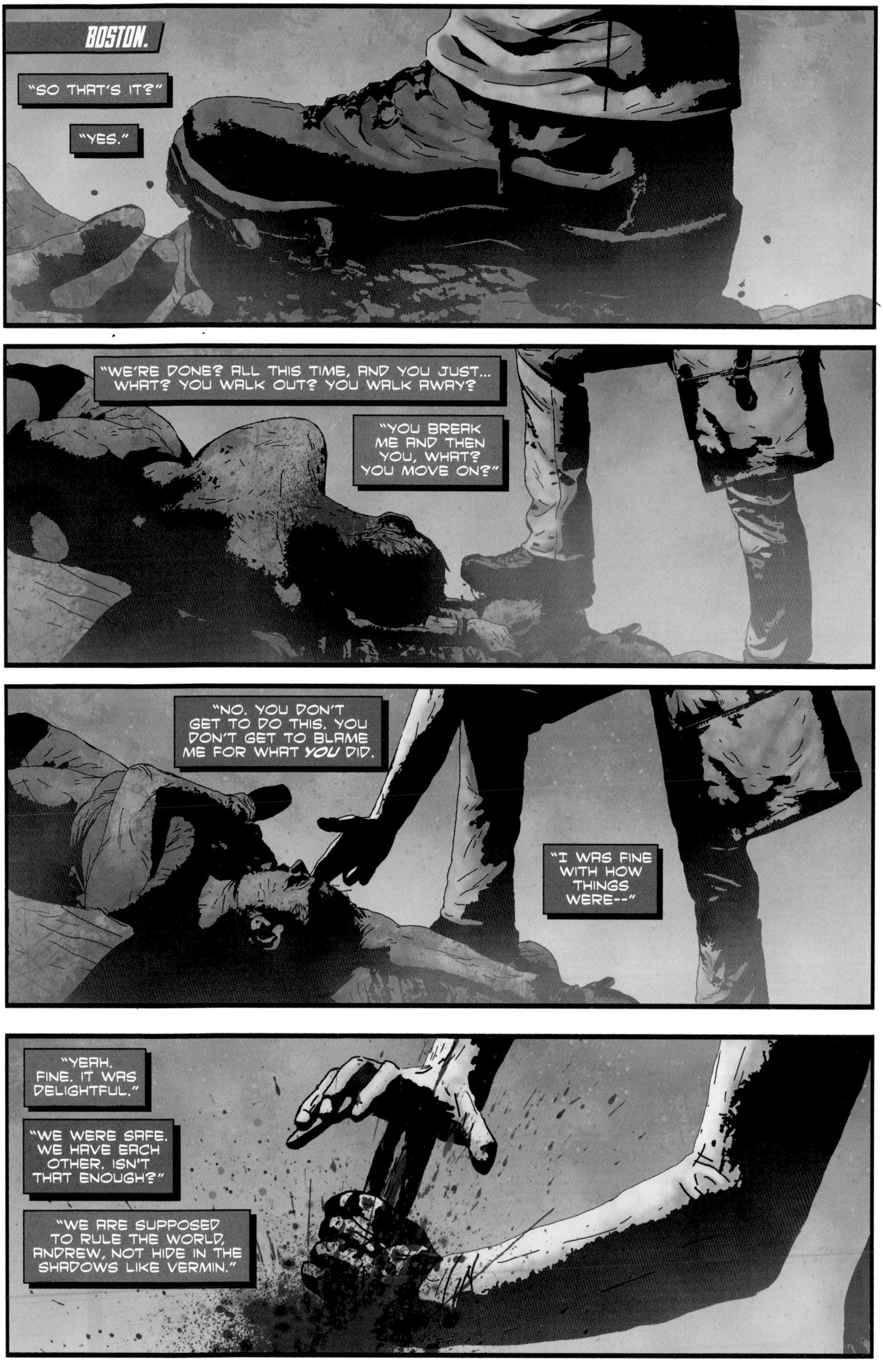
BOSTON.
"SO THAT'S IT?"
"YES."
"WE'RE DONE? ALL THIS TIME, AND YOU JUST... WHAT? YOU WALK OUT? YOU WALK AWAY?
"YOU BREAK ME AND THEN YOU, WHAT? YOU MOVE ON?"
"NO. YOU DON'T GET TO DO THIS. YOU DON'T GET TO BLAME ME FOR WHAT *YOU* DID.
"I WAS FINE WITH HOW THINGS WERE--"
"YEAH. FINE. IT WAS DELIGHTFUL."
"WE WERE SAFE. WE HAVE EACH OTHER. ISN'T THAT ENOUGH?"
"WE ARE SUPPOSED TO RULE THE WORLD, ANDREW, NOT HIDE IN THE SHADOWS LIKE VERMIN."

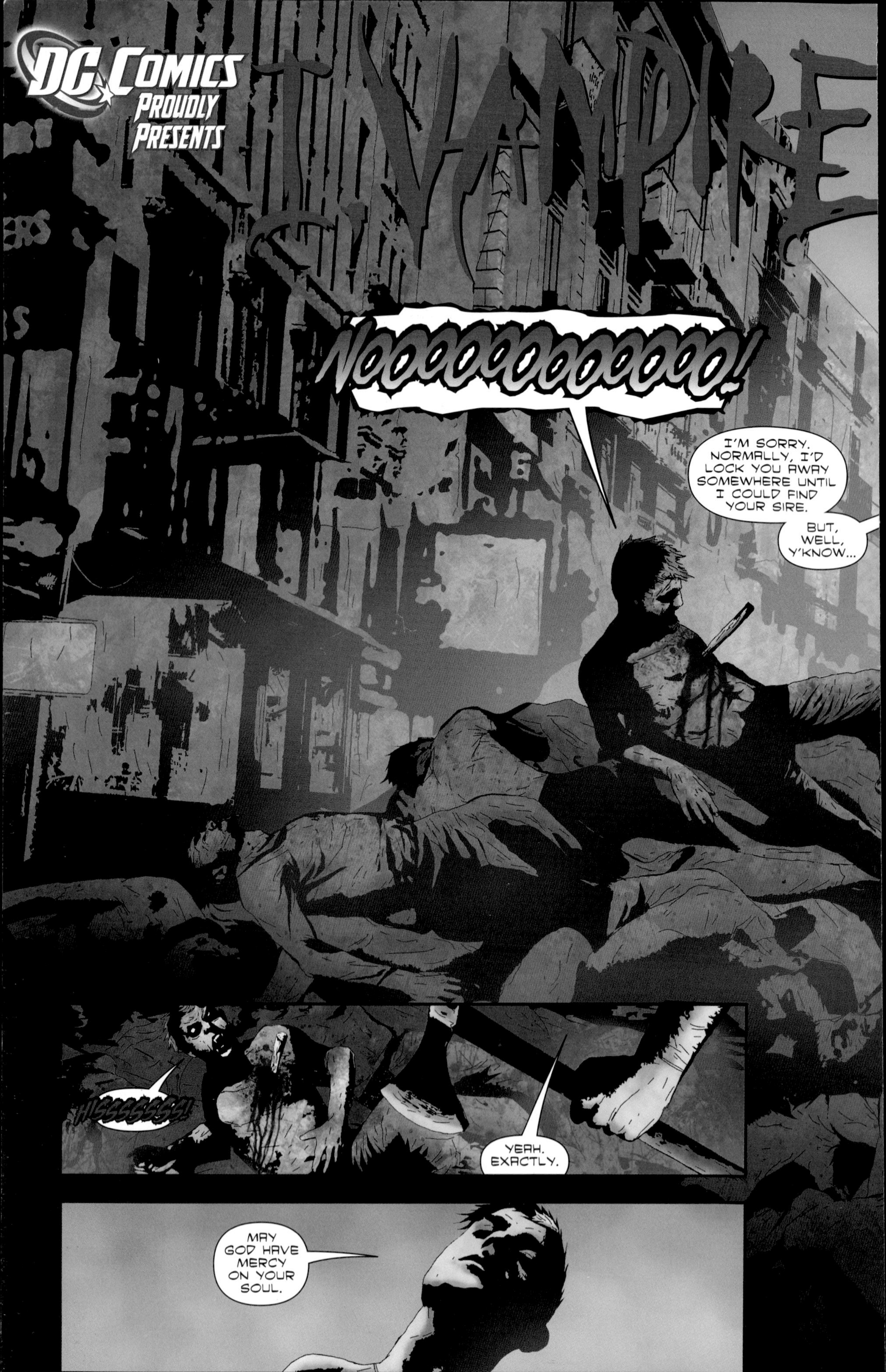
DC COMICS PROUDLY PRESENTS
I, VAMPIRE
NOOOOOOOOOOOO!
I'M SORRY. NORMALLY, I'D LOCK YOU AWAY SOMEWHERE UNTIL I COULD FIND YOUR SIRE.
BUT, WELL, Y'KNOW...
HISSSSSSS!
YEAH. EXACTLY.
MAY GOD HAVE MERCY ON YOUR SOUL.

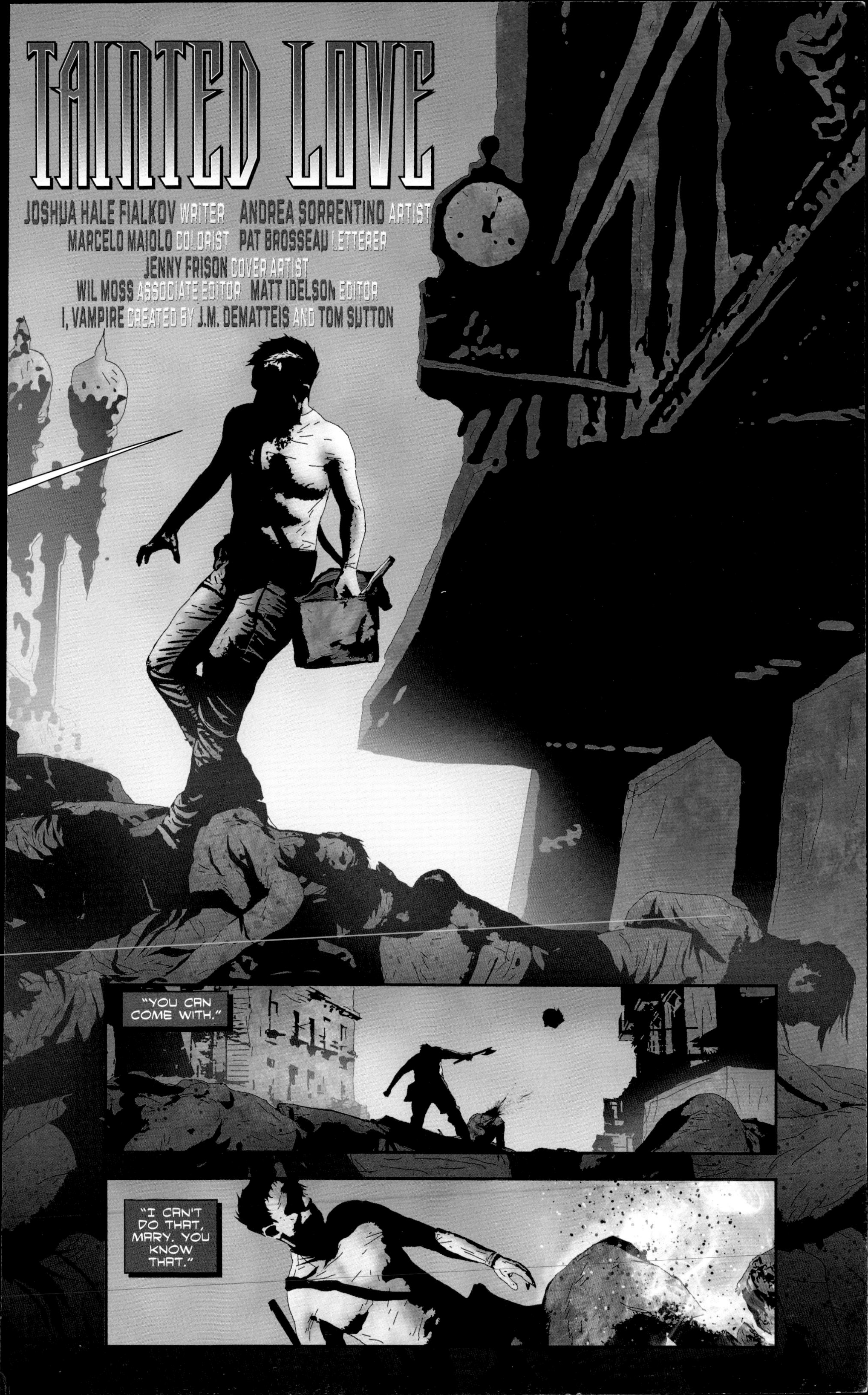
TAINTED LOVE
JOSHUA HALE FIALKOV WRITER ANDREA SORRENTINO ARTIST
MARCELO MAIOLO COLORIST PAT BROSSEAU LETTERER
JENNY FRISON COVER ARTIST
WIL MOSS ASSOCIATE EDITOR MATT IDELSON EDITOR
I, VAMPIRE CREATED BY J.M. DEMATTEIS AND TOM SUTTON
"YOU CAN COME WITH."
"I CAN'T DO THAT, MARY. YOU KNOW THAT."

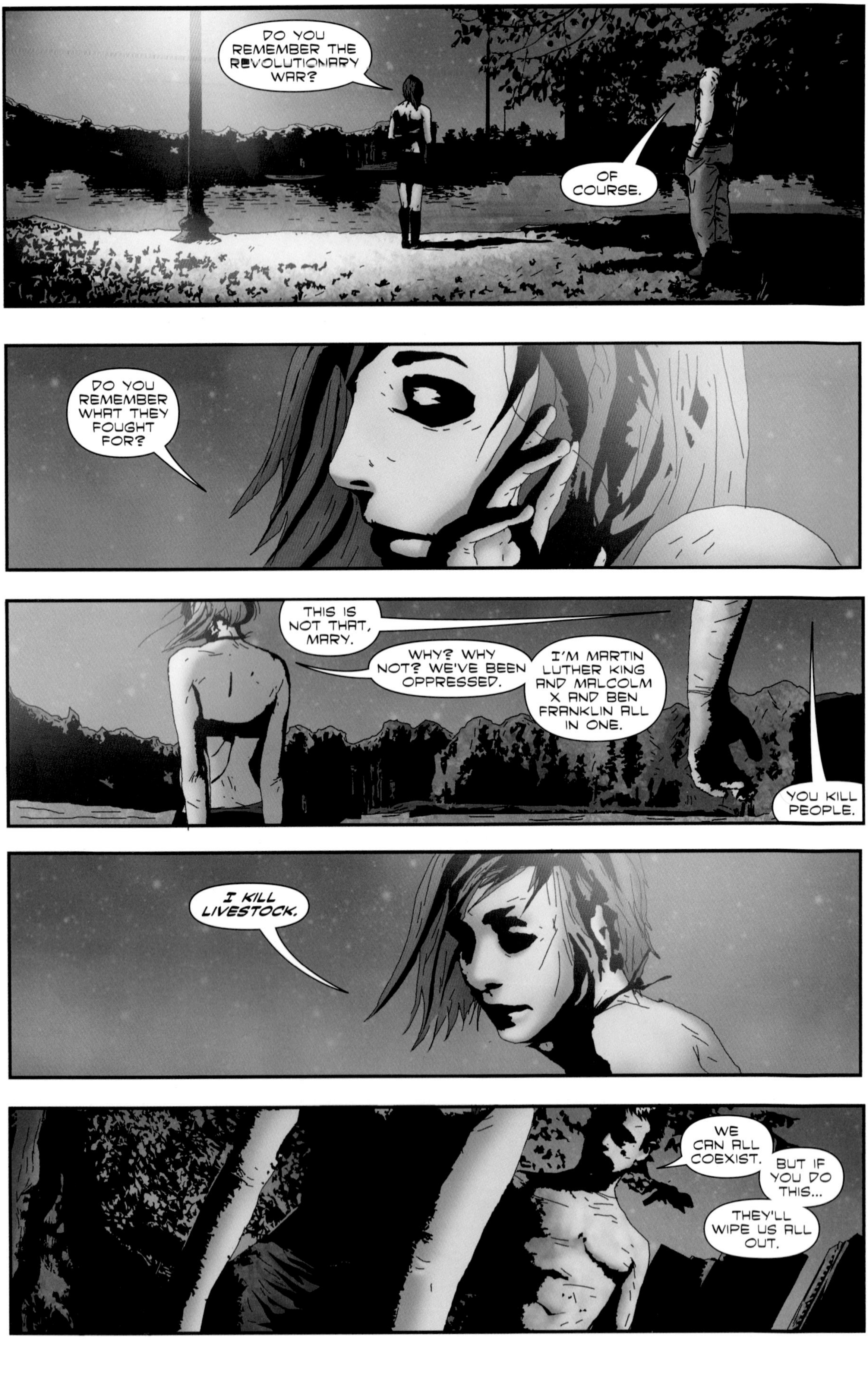
DO YOU REMEMBER THE REVOLUTIONARY WAR?
OF COURSE.
DO YOU REMEMBER WHAT THEY FOUGHT FOR?
THIS IS NOT THAT, MARY.
WHY? WHY NOT? WE'VE BEEN OPPRESSED.
I'M MARTIN LUTHER KING AND MALCOLM X AND BEN FRANKLIN ALL IN ONE.
YOU KILL PEOPLE.
I KILL LIVESTOCK.
WE CAN ALL COEXIST.
BUT IF YOU DO THIS...
THEY'LL WIPE US ALL OUT.

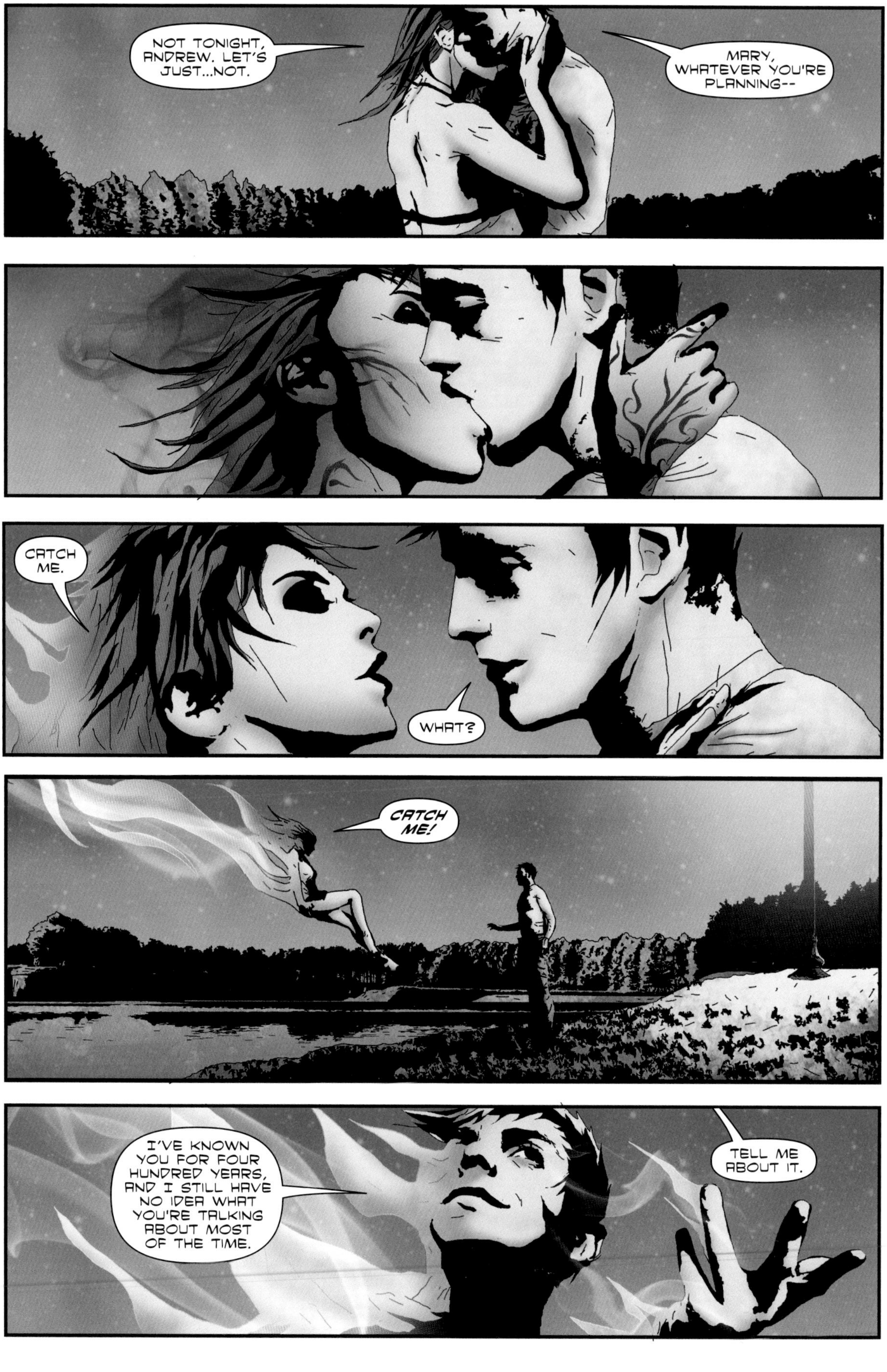
NOT TONIGHT, ANDREW. LET'S JUST...NOT.
MARY, WHATEVER YOU'RE PLANNING--
CATCH ME.
WHAT?
CATCH ME!
I'VE KNOWN YOU FOR FOUR HUNDRED YEARS, AND I STILL HAVE NO IDEA WHAT YOU'RE TALKING ABOUT MOST OF THE TIME.
TELL ME ABOUT IT.

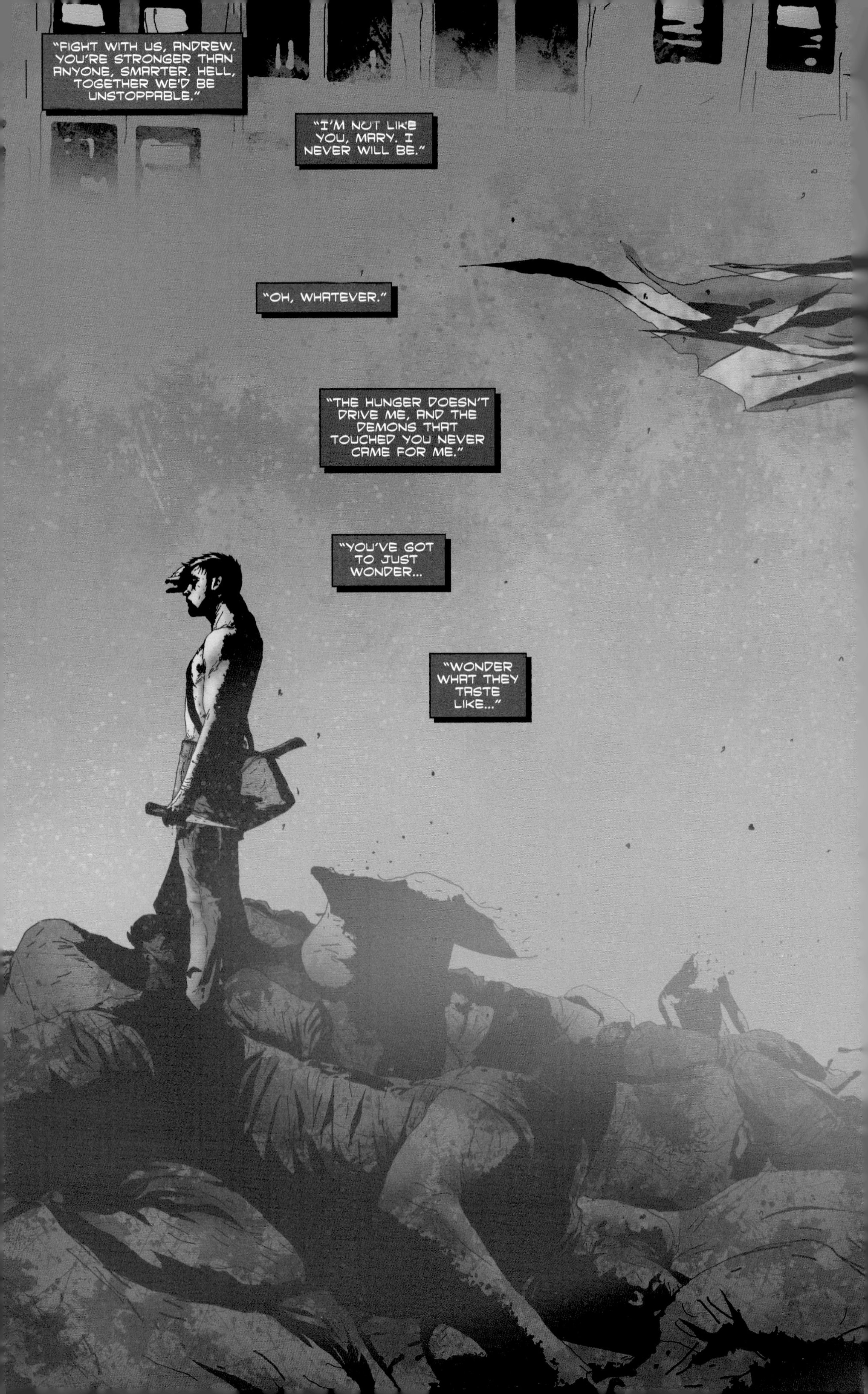
"FIGHT WITH US, ANDREW. YOU'RE STRONGER THAN ANYONE, SMARTER. HELL, TOGETHER WE'D BE UNSTOPPABLE."
"I'M NOT LIKE YOU, MARY. I NEVER WILL BE."
"OH, WHATEVER."
"THE HUNGER DOESN'T DRIVE ME, AND THE DEMONS THAT TOUCHED YOU NEVER CAME FOR ME."
"YOU'VE GOT TO JUST WONDER...
"WONDER WHAT THEY TASTE LIKE..."

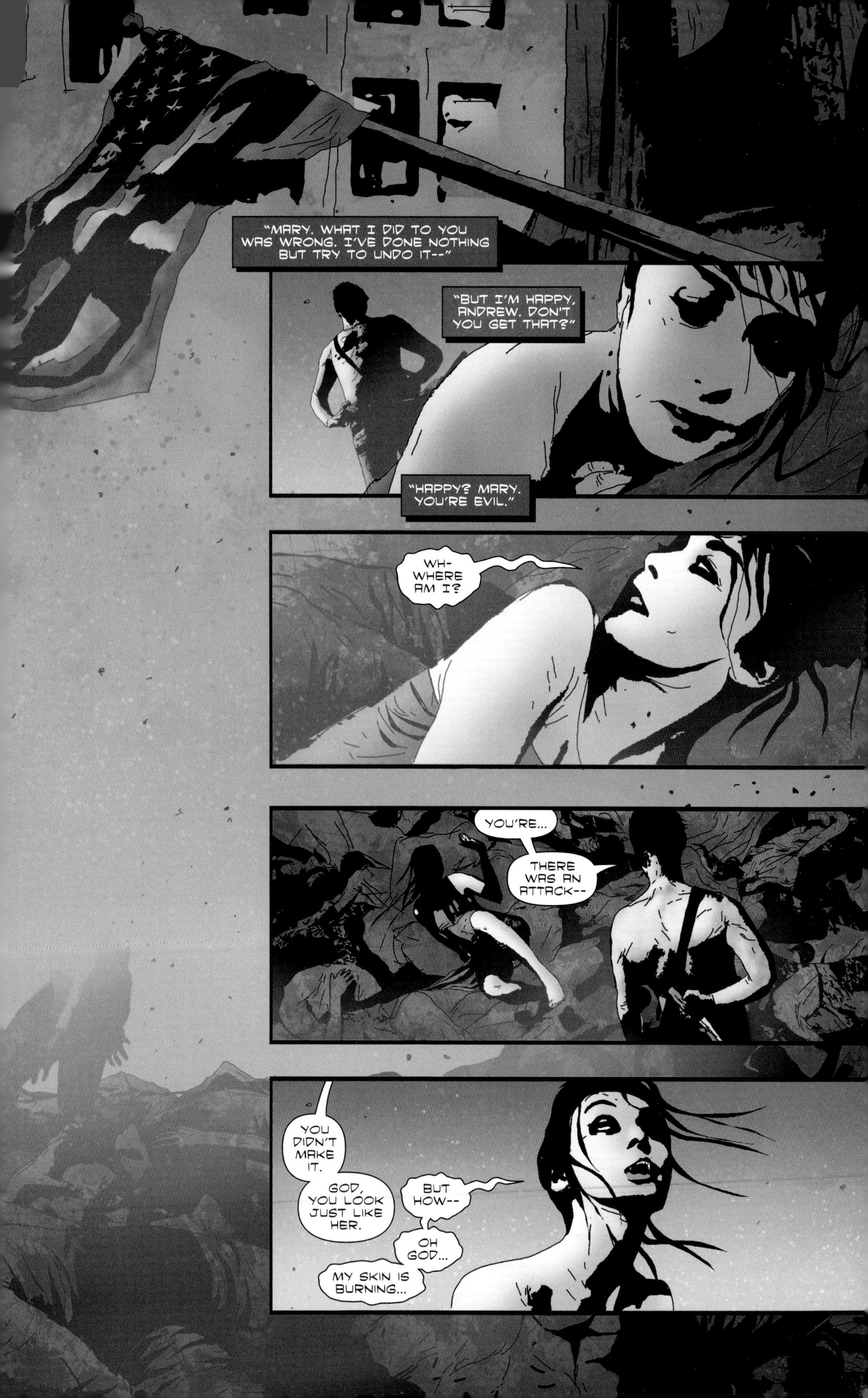
"MARY. WHAT I DID TO YOU WAS WRONG. I'VE DONE NOTHING BUT TRY TO UNDO IT--"
"BUT I'M HAPPY, ANDREW. DON'T YOU GET THAT?"
"HAPPY? MARY. YOU'RE EVIL."
WH- WHERE AM I?
YOU'RE...
THERE WAS AN ATTACK--
YOU DIDN'T MAKE IT.
GOD, YOU LOOK JUST LIKE HER.
BUT HOW--
OH GOD...
MY SKIN IS BURNING...

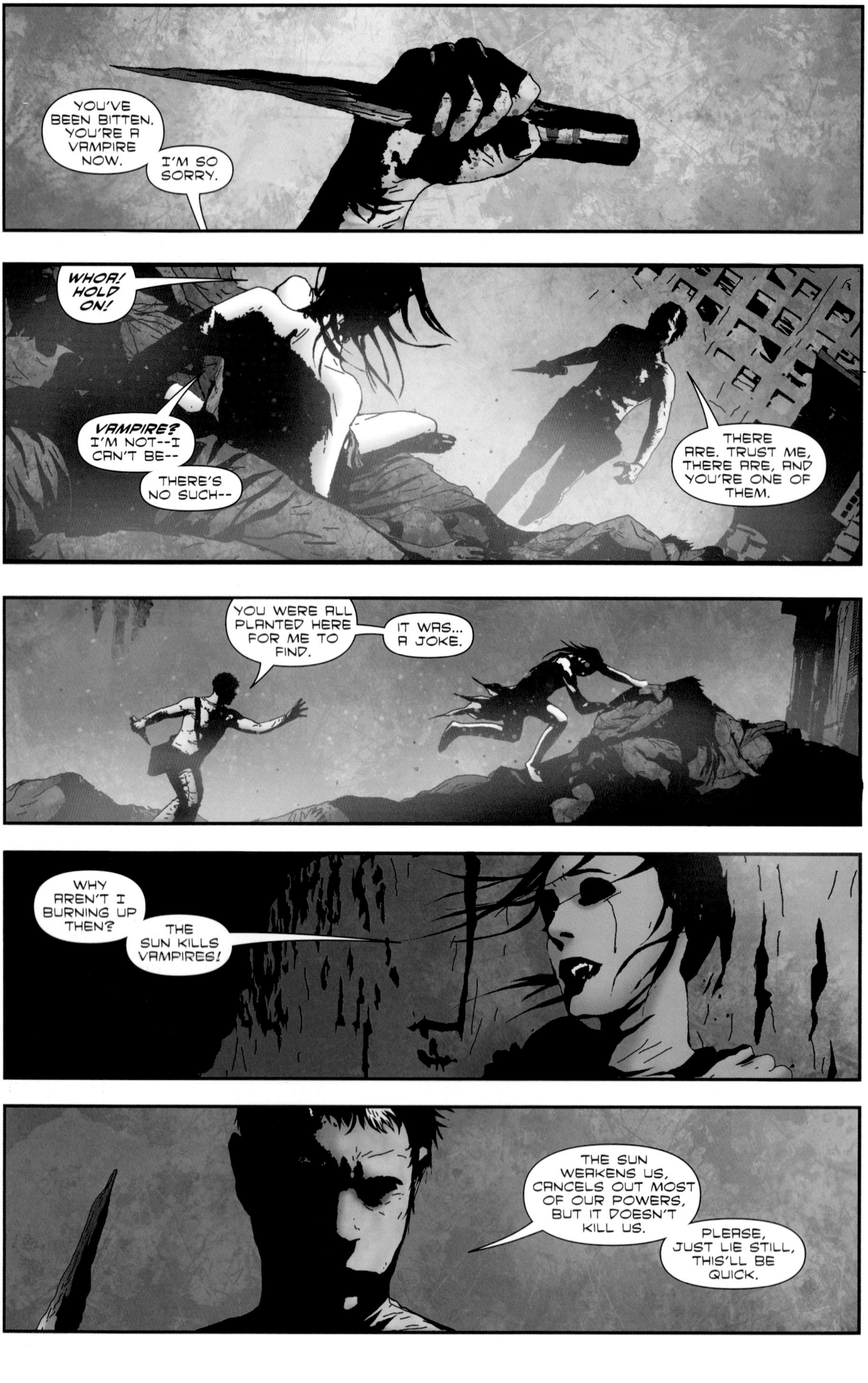
YOU'VE BEEN BITTEN. YOU'RE A VAMPIRE NOW.
I'M SO SORRY.
WHOA! HOLD ON!
VAMPIRE? I'M NOT--I CAN'T BE--
THERE'S NO SUCH--
THERE ARE. TRUST ME, THERE ARE, AND YOU'RE ONE OF THEM.
YOU WERE ALL PLANTED HERE FOR ME TO FIND.
IT WAS... A JOKE.
WHY AREN'T I BURNING UP THEN?
THE SUN KILLS VAMPIRES!
THE SUN WEAKENS US, CANCELS OUT MOST OF OUR POWERS, BUT IT DOESN'T KILL US.
PLEASE, JUST LIE STILL, THIS'LL BE QUICK.

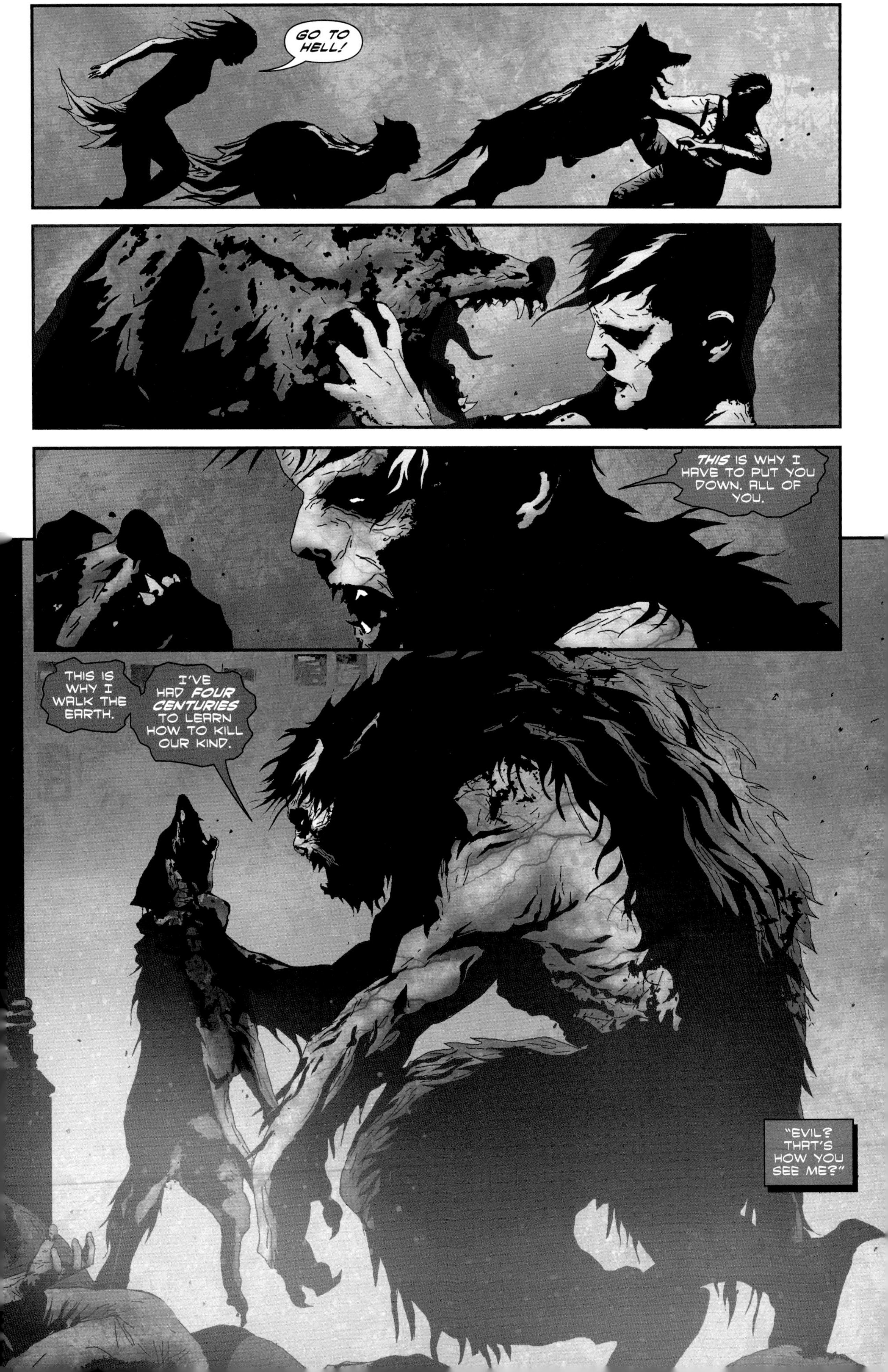
GO TO HELL!
THIS IS WHY I HAVE TO PUT YOU DOWN. ALL OF YOU.
THIS IS WHY I WALK THE EARTH.
I'VE HAD FOUR CENTURIES TO LEARN HOW TO KILL OUR KIND.
"EVIL? THAT'S HOW YOU SEE ME?"

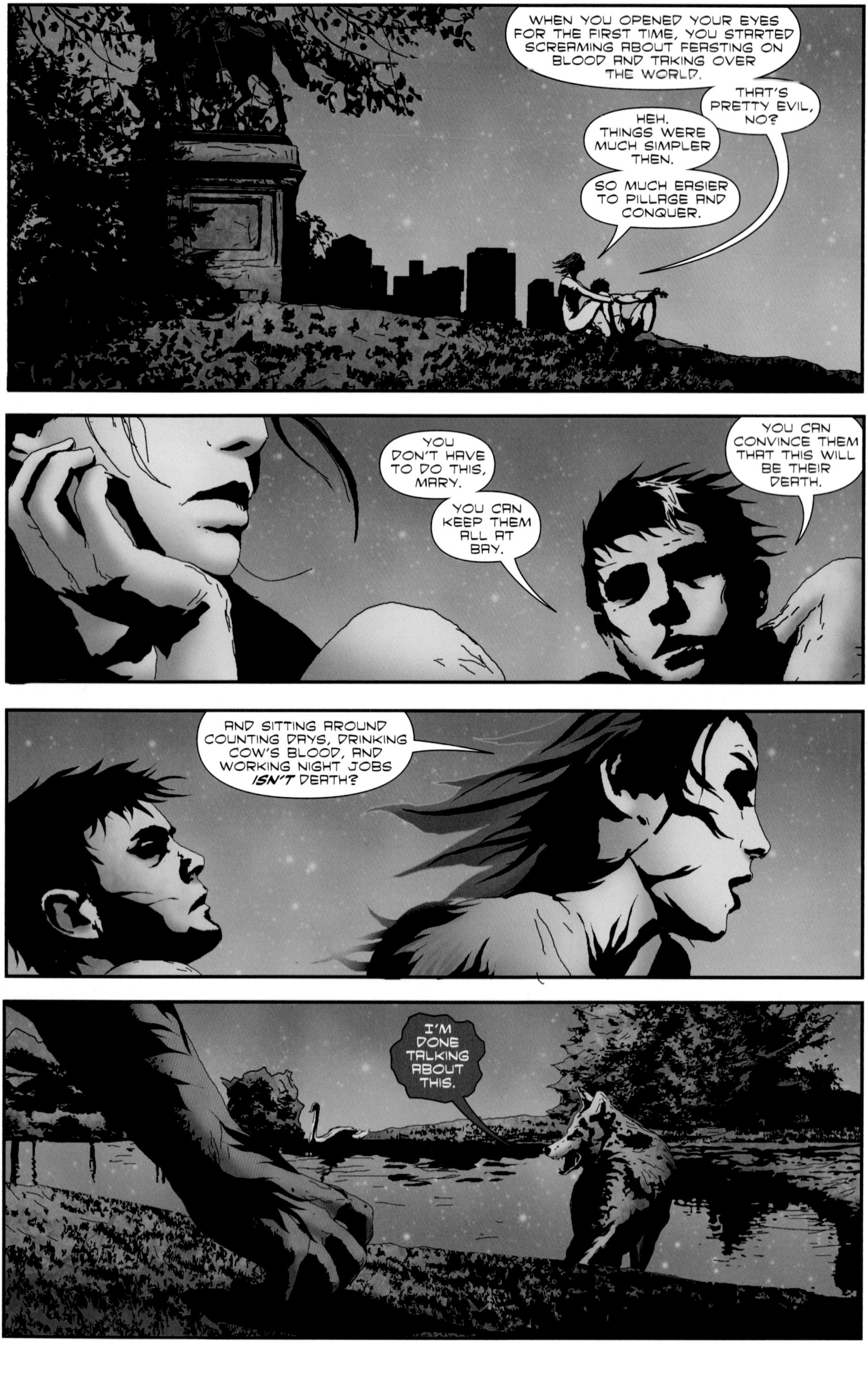
WHEN YOU OPENED YOUR EYES FOR THE FIRST TIME, YOU STARTED SCREAMING ABOUT FEASTING ON BLOOD AND TAKING OVER THE WORLD.
THAT'S PRETTY EVIL, NO?
HEH. THINGS WERE MUCH SIMPLER THEN.
SO MUCH EASIER TO PILLAGE AND CONQUER.
YOU DON'T HAVE TO DO THIS, MARY.
YOU CAN KEEP THEM ALL AT BAY.
YOU CAN CONVINCE THEM THAT THIS WILL BE THEIR DEATH.
AND SITTING AROUND COUNTING DAYS, DRINKING COW'S BLOOD, AND WORKING NIGHT JOBS *ISN'T* DEATH?
I'M DONE TALKING ABOUT THIS.

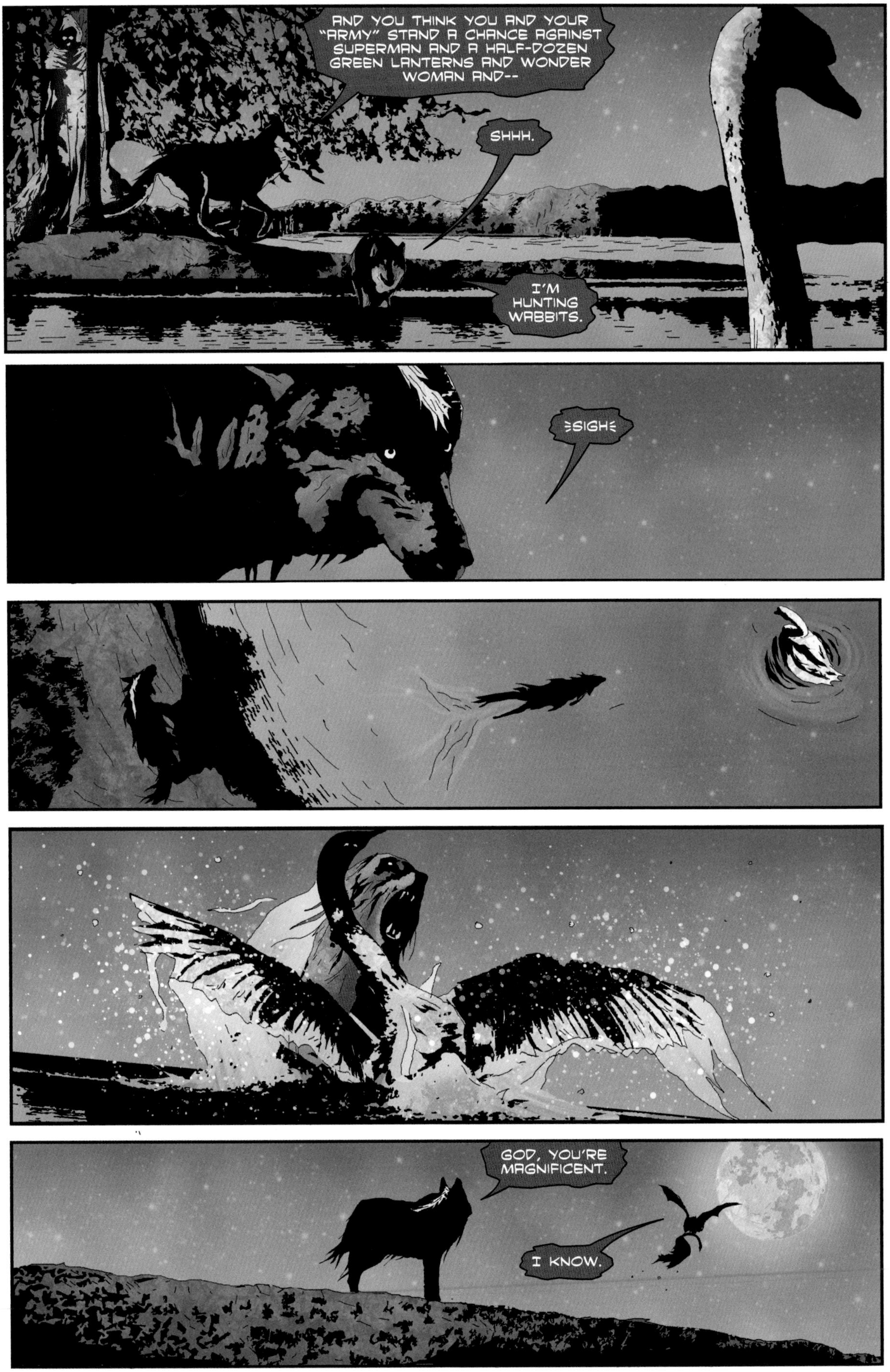
AND YOU THINK YOU AND YOUR "ARMY" STAND A CHANCE AGAINST SUPERMAN AND A HALF-DOZEN GREEN LANTERNS AND WONDER WOMAN AND--
SHHH.
I'M HUNTING WABBITS.
SIGH
GOD, YOU'RE MAGNIFICENT.
I KNOW.

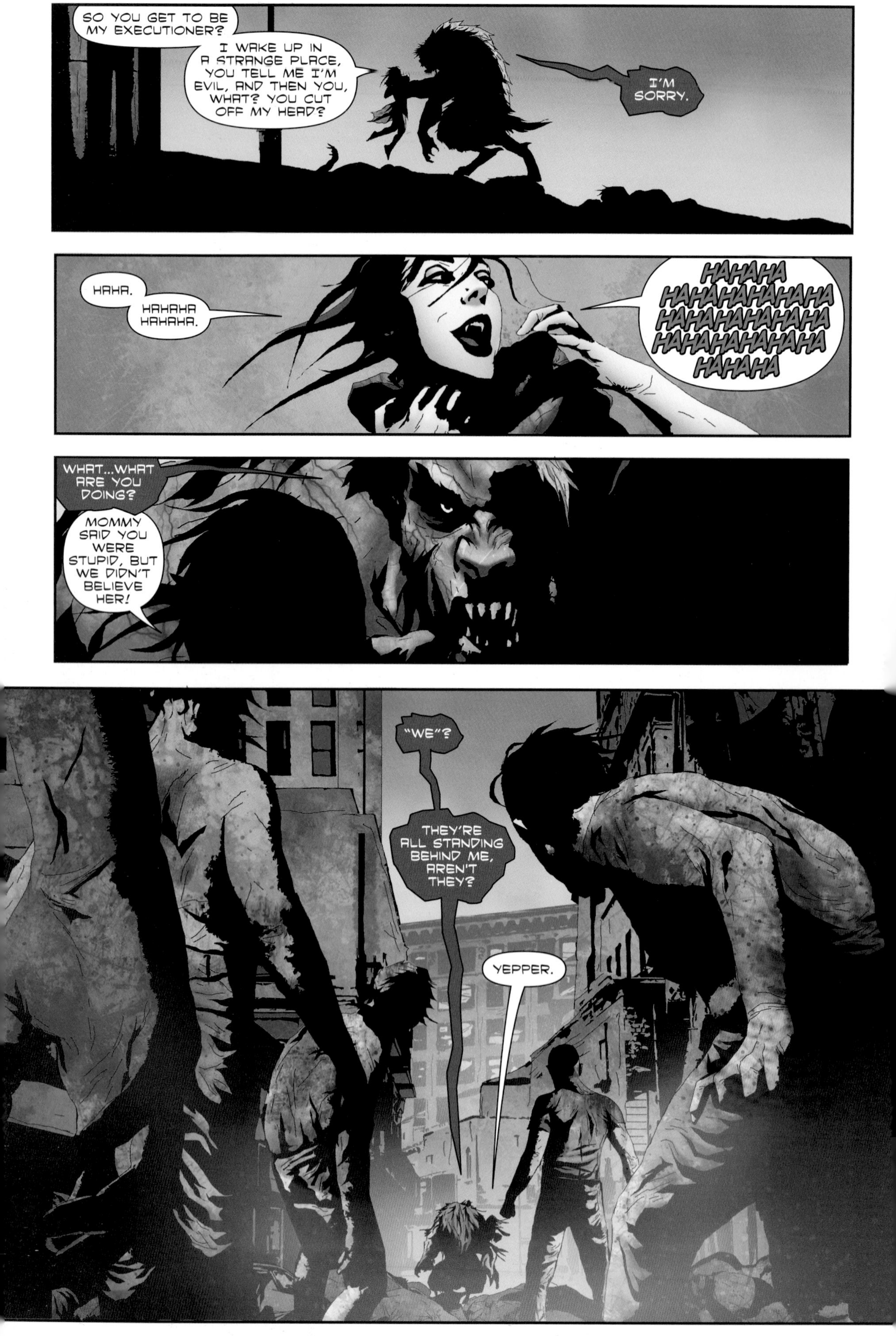
SO YOU GET TO BE MY EXECUTIONER?
I WAKE UP IN A STRANGE PLACE, YOU TELL ME I'M EVIL, AND THEN YOU, WHAT? YOU CUT OFF MY HEAD?
I'M SORRY.
HAHA.
HAHAHA HAHAHA.
HAHAHA HAHAHAHAHAHA HAHAHAHAHAHA HAHAHAHAHAHA HAHAHA
WHAT...WHAT ARE YOU DOING?
MOMMY SAID YOU WERE STUPID, BUT WE DIDN'T BELIEVE HER!
"WE"?
THEY'RE ALL STANDING BEHIND ME, AREN'T THEY?
YEPPER.

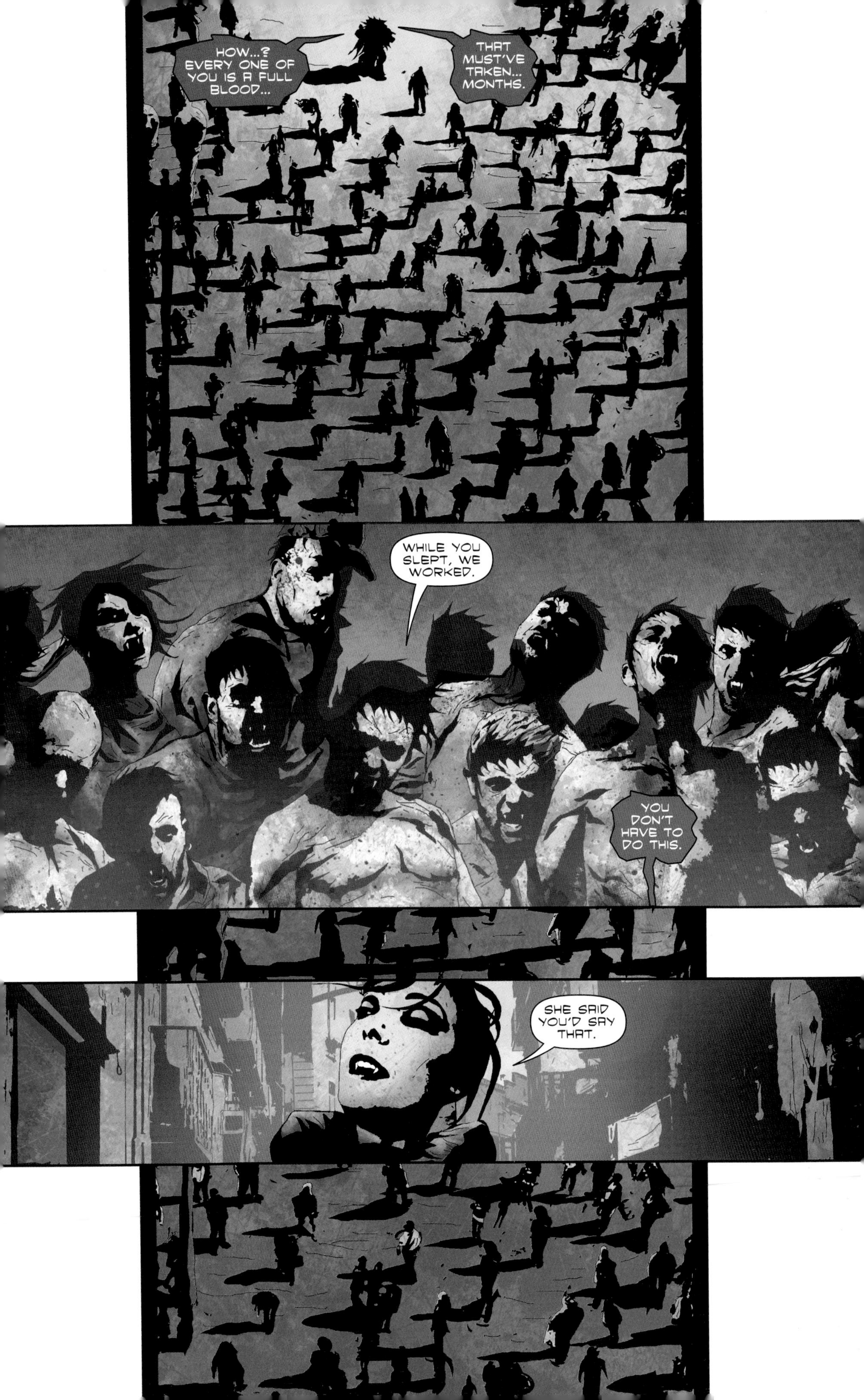
HOW...? EVERY ONE OF YOU IS A FULL BLOOD...
THAT MUST'VE TAKEN... MONTHS.
WHILE YOU SLEPT, WE WORKED.
YOU DON'T HAVE TO DO THIS.
SHE SAID YOU'D SAY THAT.

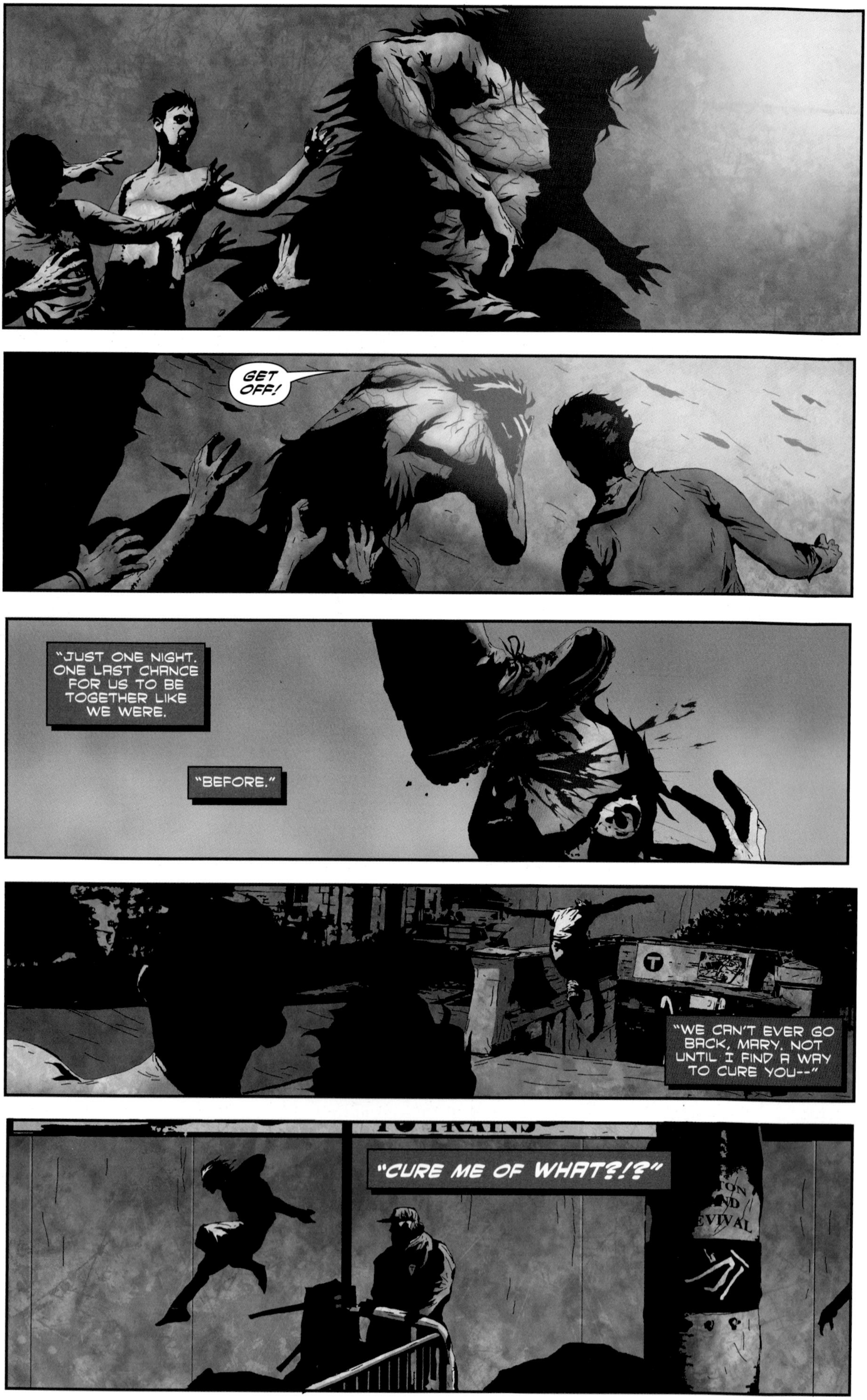
GET OFF!
"JUST ONE NIGHT. ONE LAST CHANCE FOR US TO BE TOGETHER LIKE WE WERE.
"BEFORE."
"WE CAN'T EVER GO BACK, MARY. NOT UNTIL I FIND A WAY TO CURE YOU--"
"CURE ME OF WHAT?!?"

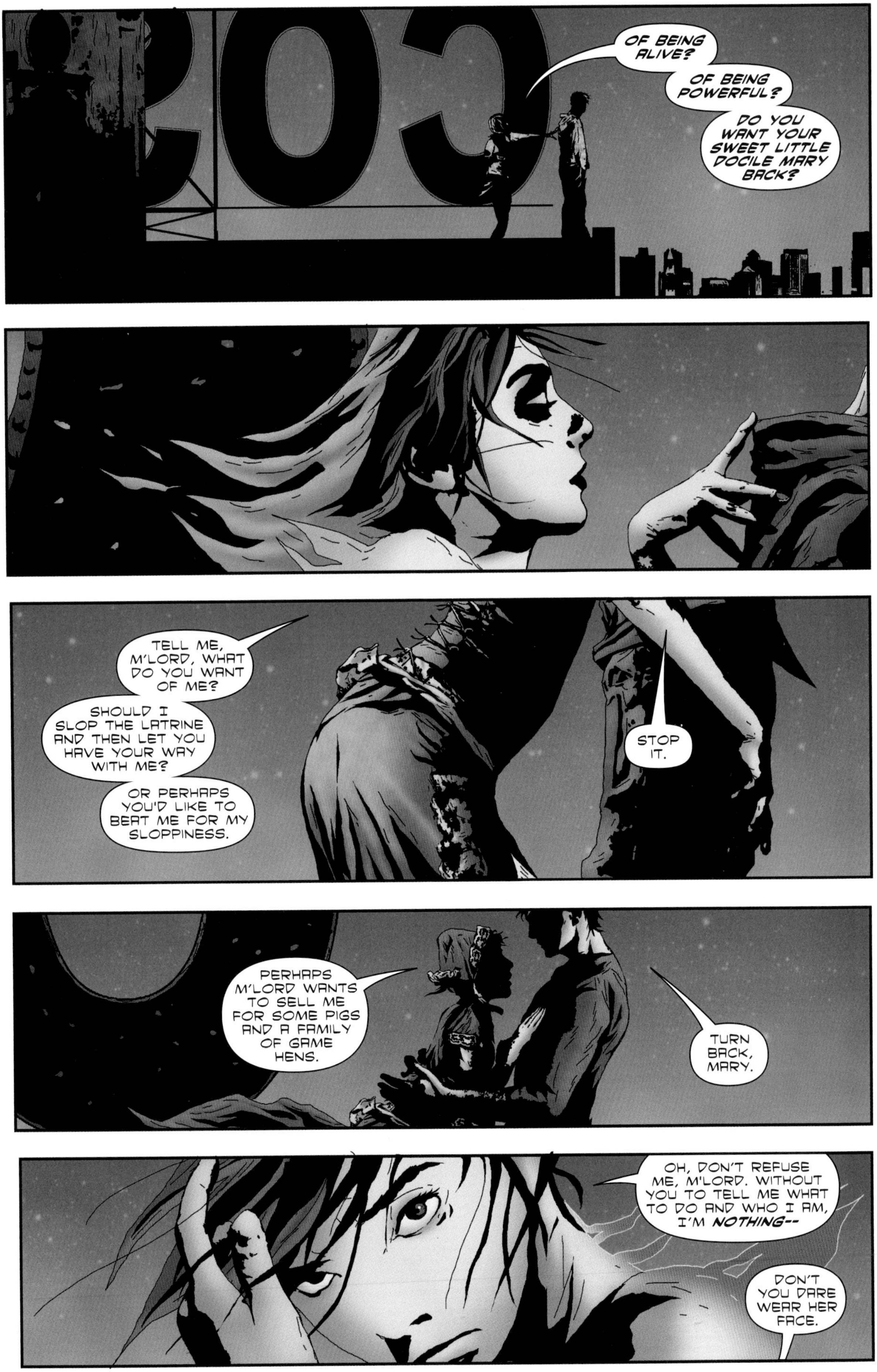

OF BEING ALIVE?
OF BEING POWERFUL?
DO YOU WANT YOUR SWEET LITTLE DOCILE MARY BACK?
TELL ME, M'LORD, WHAT DO YOU WANT OF ME?
SHOULD I SLOP THE LATRINE AND THEN LET YOU HAVE YOUR WAY WITH ME?
OR PERHAPS YOU'D LIKE TO BEAT ME FOR MY SLOPPINESS.
STOP IT.
PERHAPS M'LORD WANTS TO SELL ME FOR SOME PIGS AND A FAMILY OF GAME HENS.
TURN BACK, MARY.
OH, DON'T REFUSE ME, M'LORD. WITHOUT YOU TO TELL ME WHAT TO DO AND WHO I AM, I'M NOTHING--
DON'T YOU DARE WEAR HER FACE.

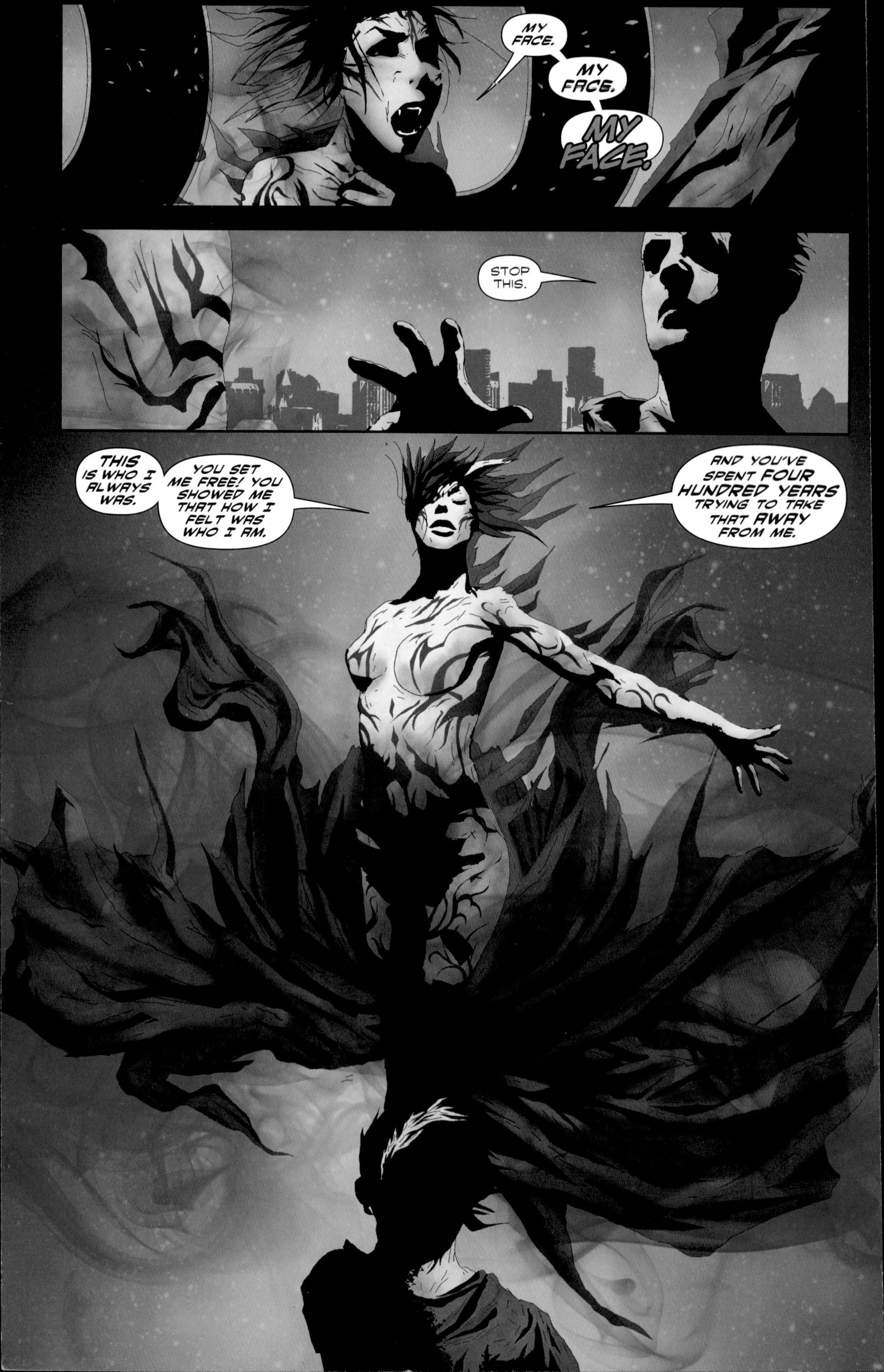

MY FACE.
MY FACE.
MY FACE.
STOP THIS.
THIS IS WHO I ALWAYS WAS.
YOU SET ME FREE! YOU SHOWED ME THAT HOW I FELT WAS WHO I AM.
AND YOU'VE SPENT FOUR HUNDRED YEARS TRYING TO TAKE THAT AWAY FROM ME.

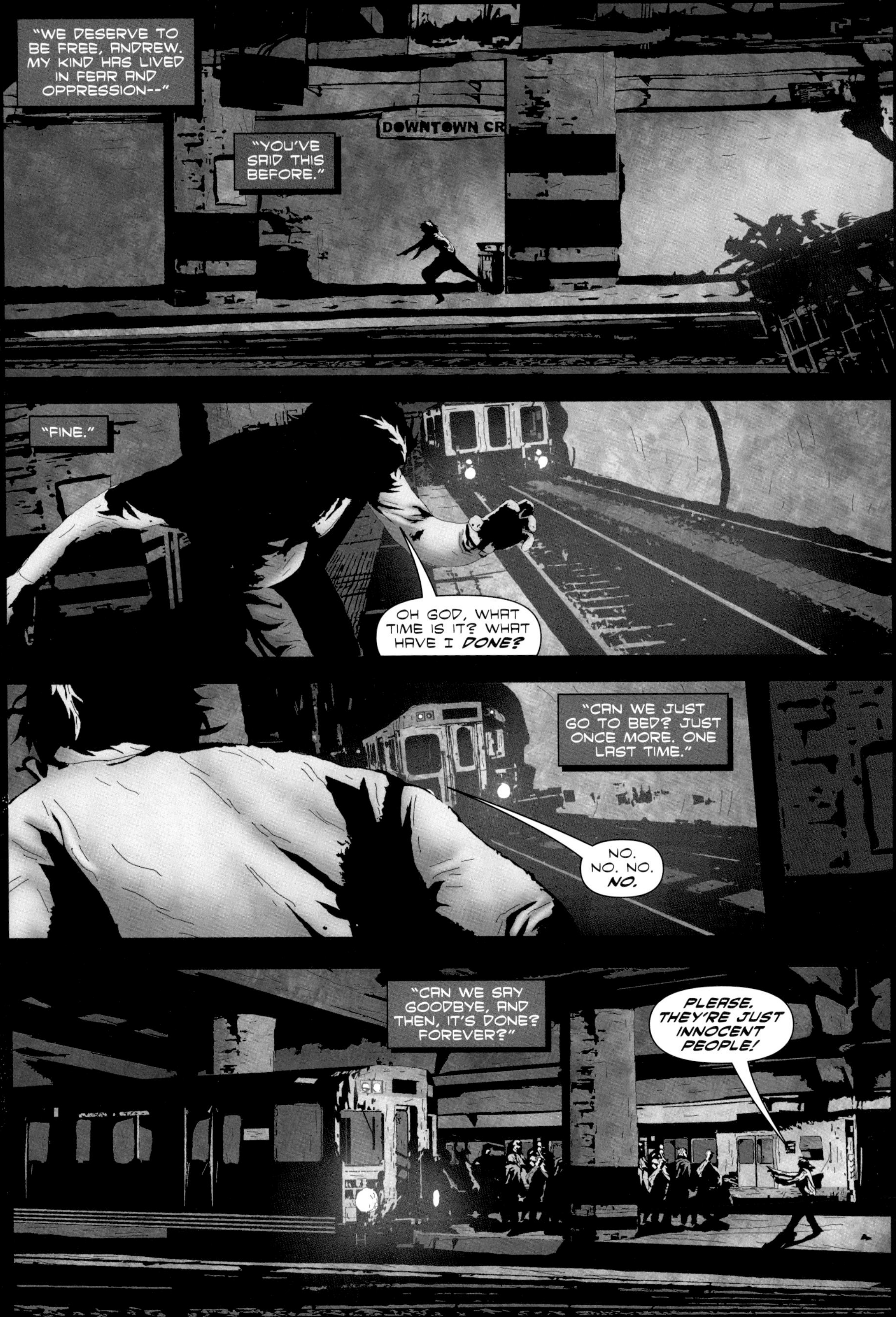

"WE DESERVE TO BE FREE, ANDREW. MY KIND HAS LIVED IN FEAR AND OPPRESSION--"
DOWNTOWN CR
"YOU'VE SAID THIS BEFORE."
"FINE."
OH GOD, WHAT TIME IS IT? WHAT HAVE I DONE?
"CAN WE JUST GO TO BED? JUST ONCE MORE. ONE LAST TIME."
NO. NO. NO. NO.
"CAN WE SAY GOODBYE, AND THEN, IT'S DONE? FOREVER?"
PLEASE. THEY'RE JUST INNOCENT PEOPLE!

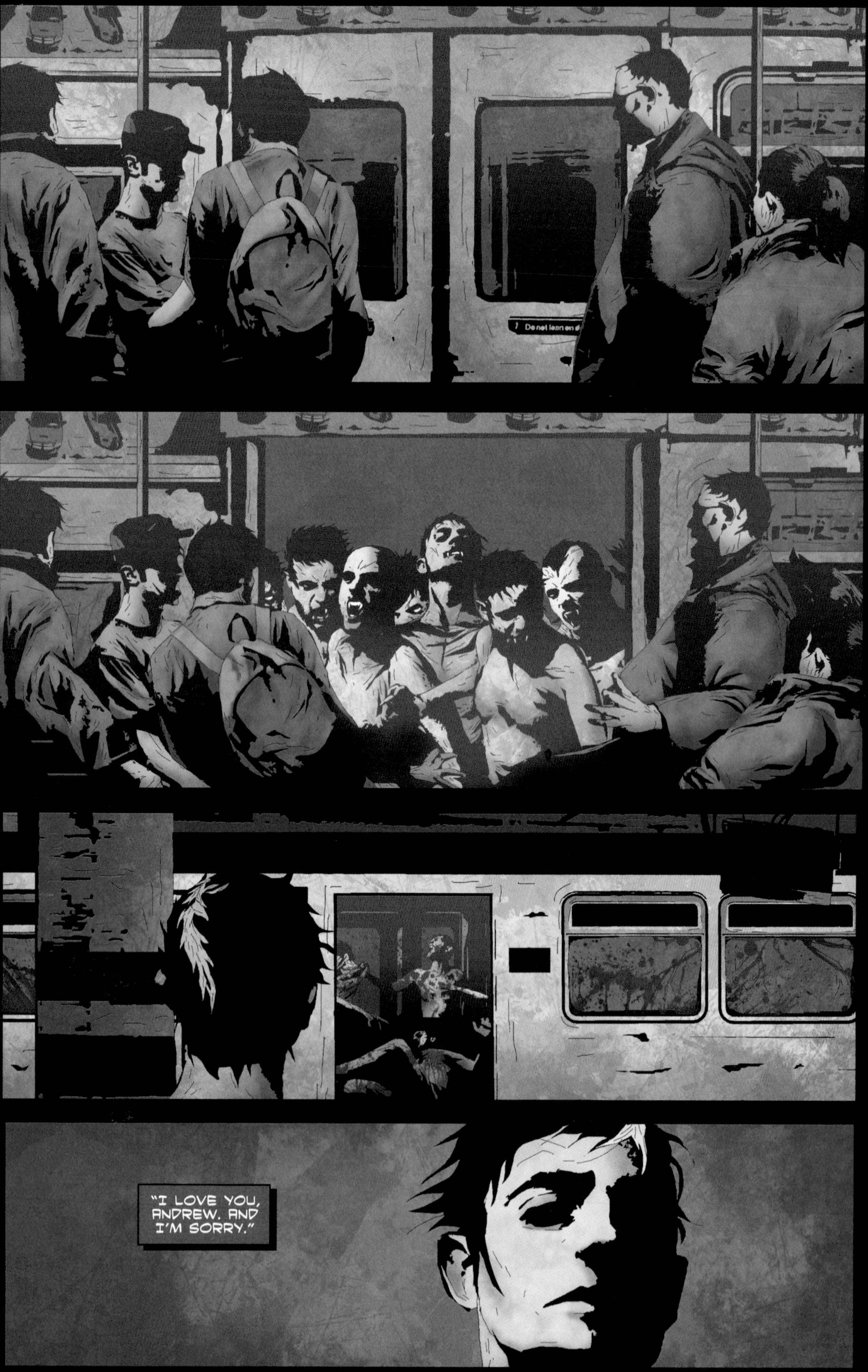

Do not lean on
"I LOVE YOU, ANDREW. AND I'M SORRY."

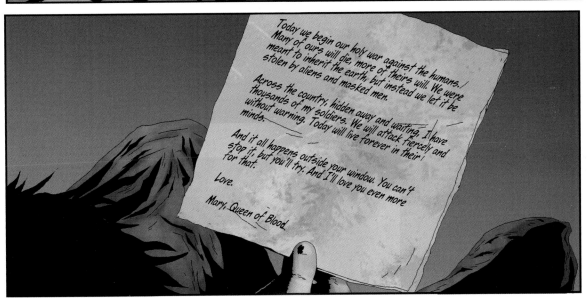

Today we begin our holy war against the humans. / Many of ours will die, more of theirs will. We were meant to inherit the earth, but instead we let it be stolen by aliens and masked men.

Across the country, hidden away and waiting, I have thousands of my soldiers. We will attack fiercely and without warning. Today will live forever in their minds.

And it all happens outside your window. You can't stop it, but you'll try. And I'll love you even more for that.

Love,

Mary, Queen of Blood

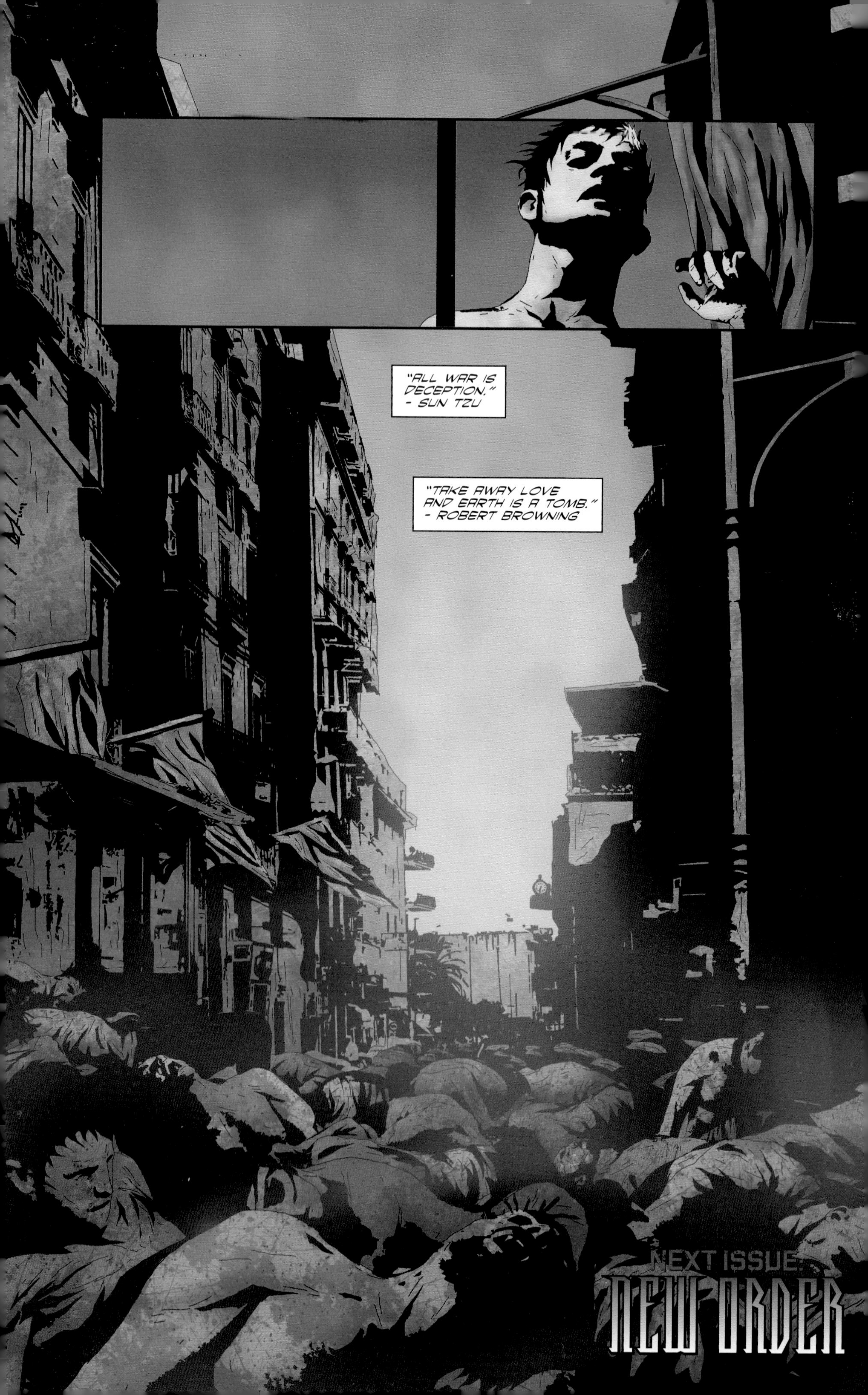
"ALL WAR IS DECEPTION." - SUN TZU
"TAKE AWAY LOVE AND EARTH IS A TOMB." - ROBERT BROWNING
NEXT ISSUE:
NEW ORDER

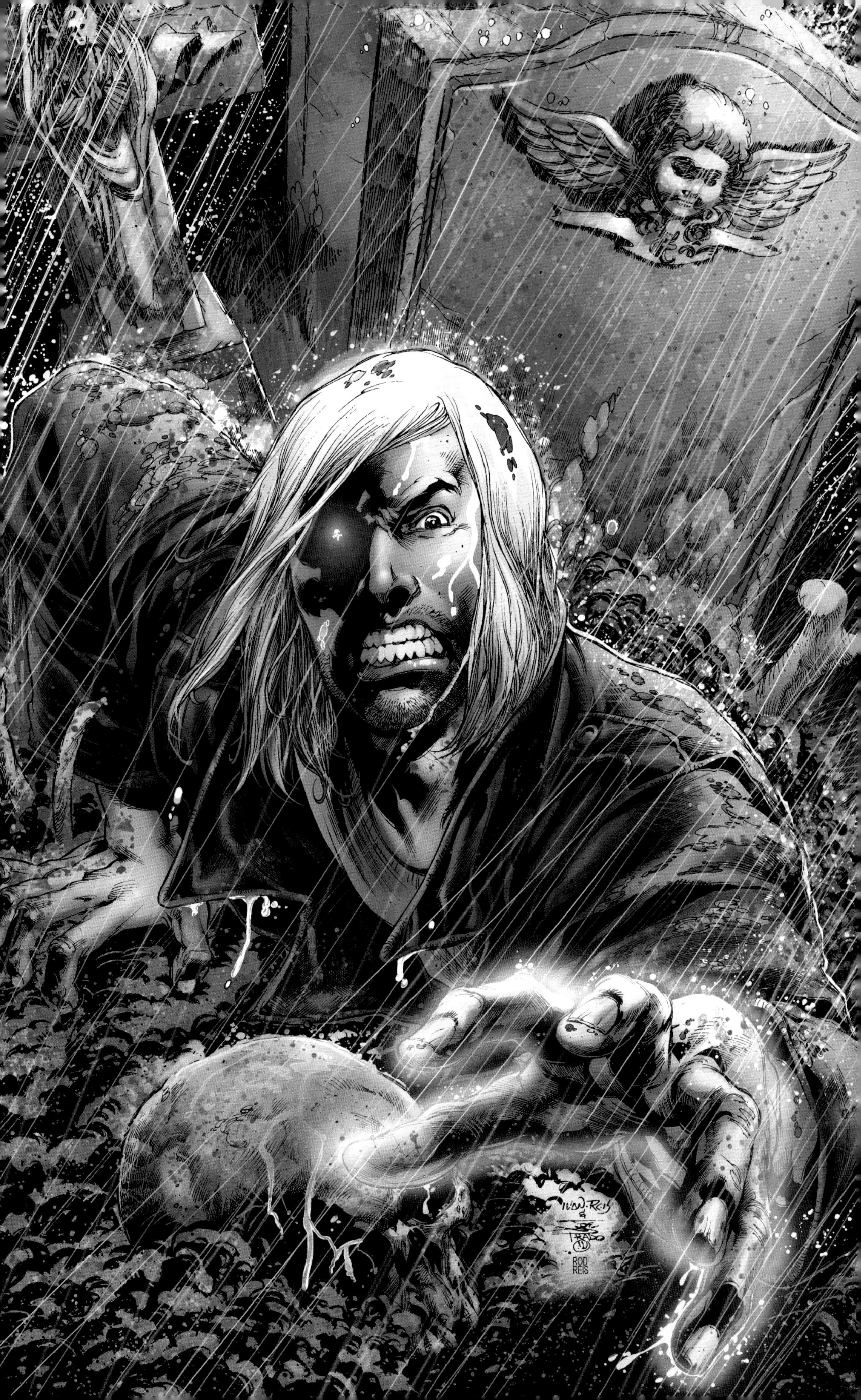
ROD REIS

RESURRECTION MAN

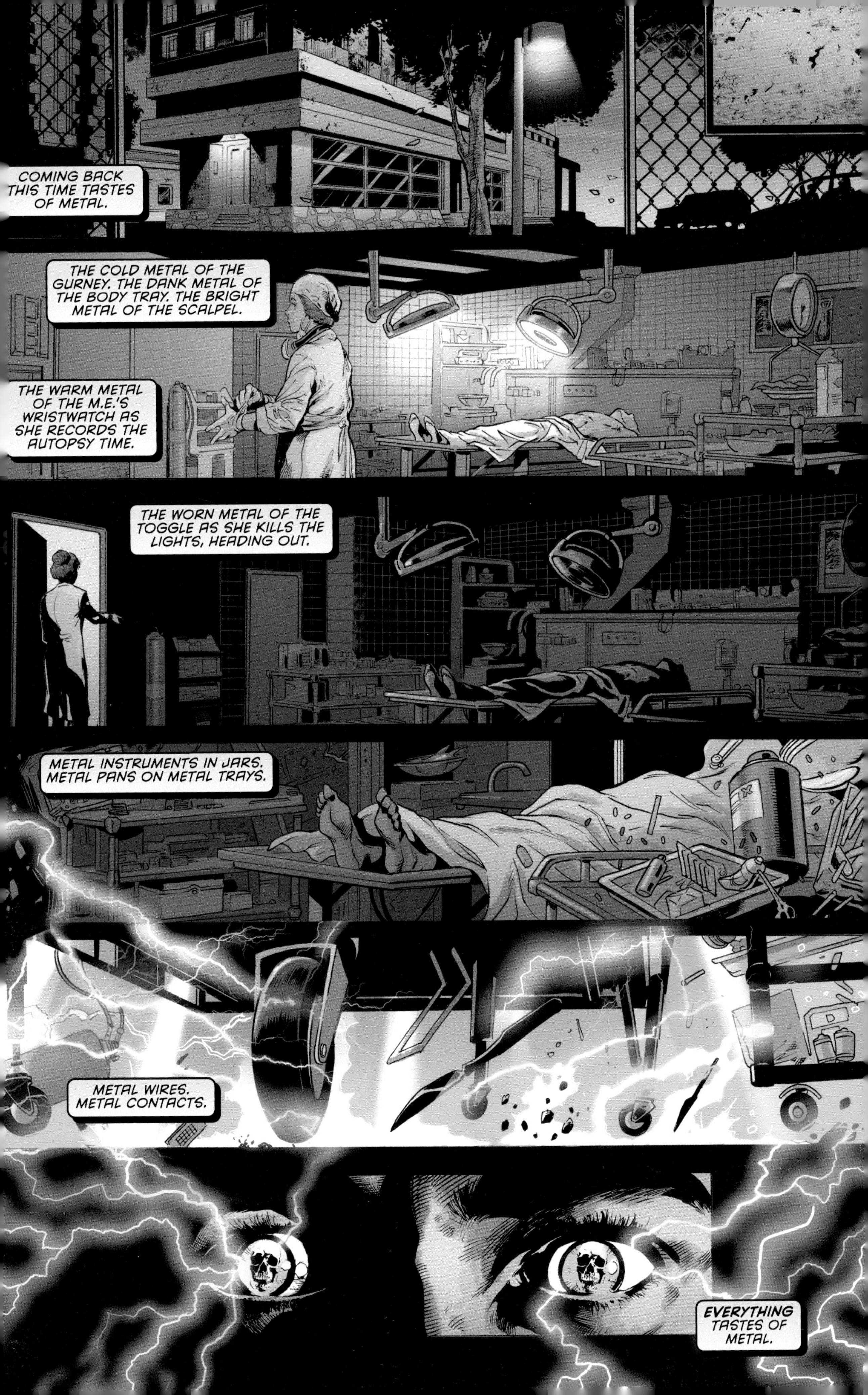
COMING BACK THIS TIME TASTES OF METAL.
THE COLD METAL OF THE GURNEY. THE DANK METAL OF THE BODY TRAY. THE BRIGHT METAL OF THE SCALPEL.
THE WARM METAL OF THE M.E.'S WRISTWATCH AS SHE RECORDS THE AUTOPSY TIME.
THE WORN METAL OF THE TOGGLE AS SHE KILLS THE LIGHTS, HEADING OUT.
METAL INSTRUMENTS IN JARS. METAL PANS ON METAL TRAYS.
METAL WIRES. METAL CONTACTS.
EVERYTHING TASTES OF METAL.

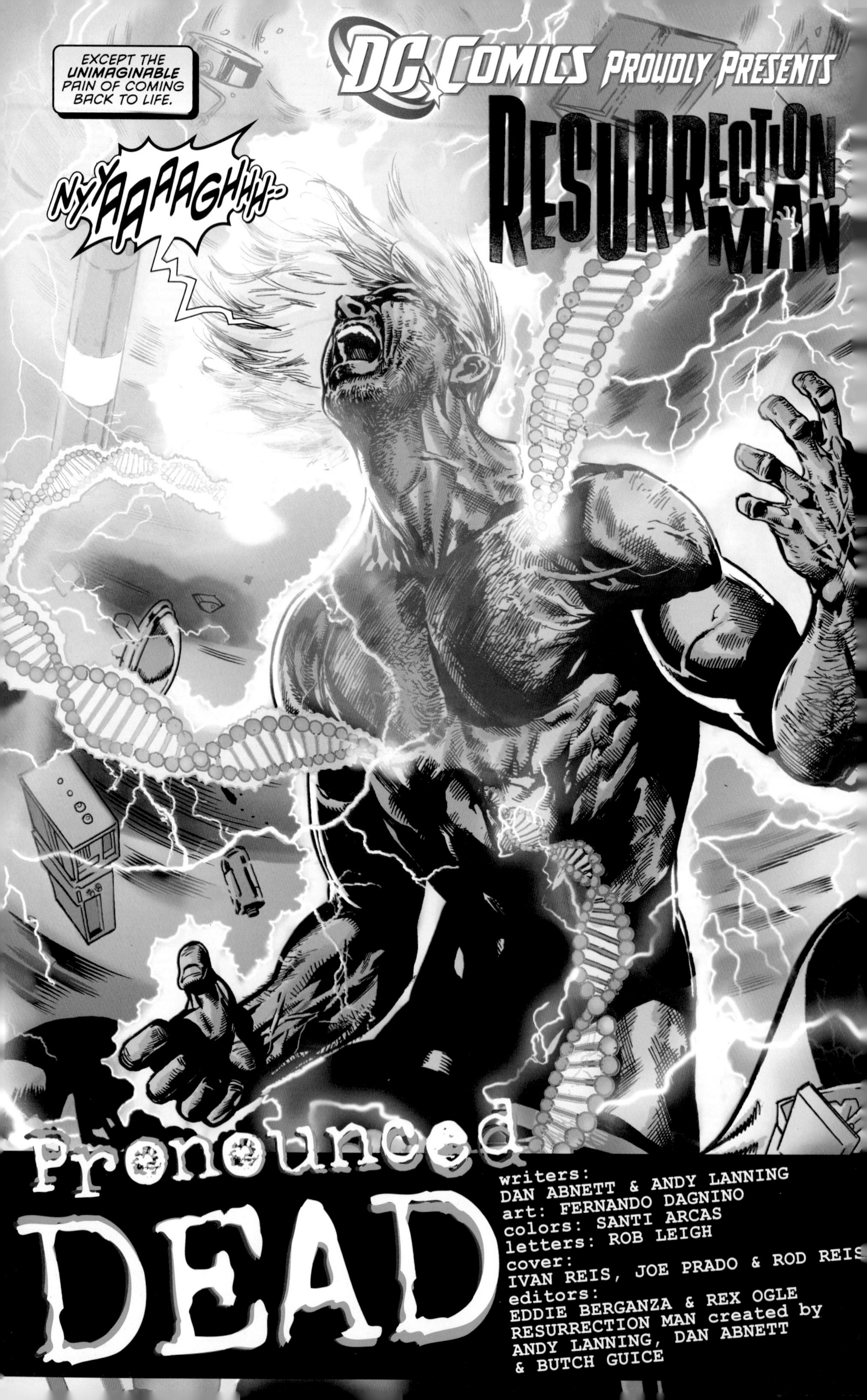
EXCEPT THE UNIMAGINABLE PAIN OF COMING BACK TO LIFE.
NYYAAAAGHHH
DC COMICS PROUDLY PRESENTS
RESURRECTION MAN
Pronounced DEAD
writers: DAN ABNETT & ANDY LANNING
art: FERNANDO DAGNINO
colors: SANTI ARCAS
letters: ROB LEIGH
cover: IVAN REIS, JOE PRADO & ROD REIS
editors: EDDIE BERGANZA & REX OGLE
RESURRECTION MAN created by ANDY LANNING, DAN ABNETT & BUTCH GUICE

GOING TO THE GAME FRIDAY?

YEAH.

WANNA GRAB A BEER AFTER?

THE NIGHT SHIFT, PUNCHING IN...

...GETTING WORK DONE WHILE THE WORLD SLEEPS.

I'LL SLEEP WHEN I'M DEAD.

I'LL GET BACK TO YOU WHEN I'VE GOT A SCHEDULE FOR THAT.

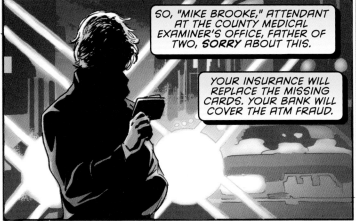

SO, "MIKE BROOKE," ATTENDANT AT THE COUNTY MEDICAL EXAMINER'S OFFICE, FATHER OF TWO, SORRY ABOUT THIS.

YOUR INSURANCE WILL REPLACE THE MISSING CARDS. YOUR BANK WILL COVER THE ATM FRAUD.

I TASTE THE BARE METAL BILL CARTRIDGE INSIDE THE DISPENSER.

I TWIST THE MAGNETIC FIELD AND IT SPITS CASH AT ME.

THIS TIME AROUND, IT SEEMS, I HAVE A MAGNETIC PERSONALITY.

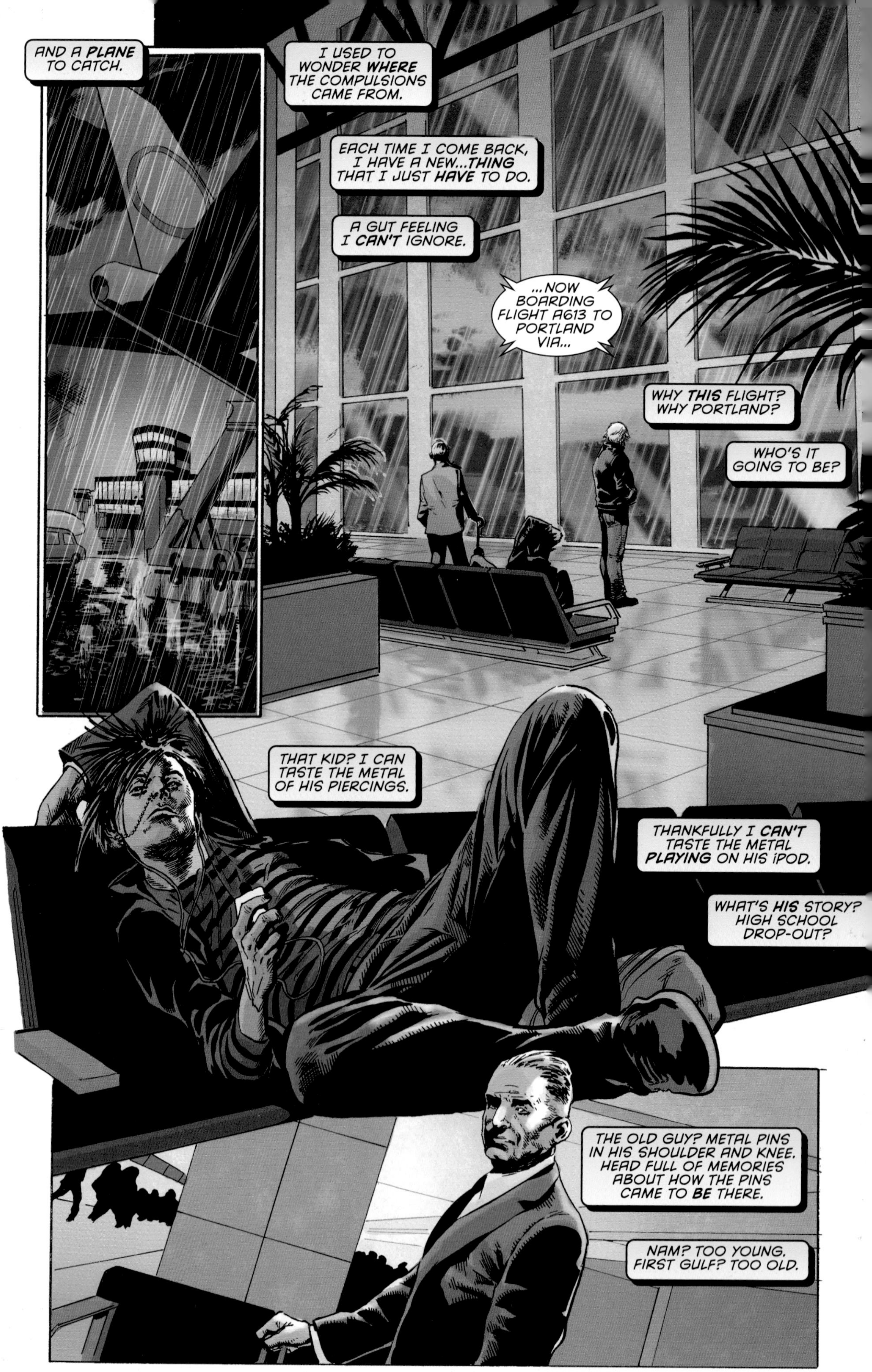
AND A PLANE TO CATCH.
I USED TO WONDER WHERE THE COMPULSIONS CAME FROM.
EACH TIME I COME BACK, I HAVE A NEW...THING THAT I JUST HAVE TO DO.
A GUT FEELING I CAN'T IGNORE.
...NOW BOARDING FLIGHT A613 TO PORTLAND VIA...
WHY THIS FLIGHT? WHY PORTLAND?
WHO'S IT GOING TO BE?
THAT KID? I CAN TASTE THE METAL OF HIS PIERCINGS.
THANKFULLY I CAN'T TASTE THE METAL PLAYING ON HIS iPOD.
WHAT'S HIS STORY? HIGH SCHOOL DROP-OUT?
THE OLD GUY? METAL PINS IN HIS SHOULDER AND KNEE. HEAD FULL OF MEMORIES ABOUT HOW THE PINS CAME TO BE THERE.
NAM? TOO YOUNG. FIRST GULF? TOO OLD.

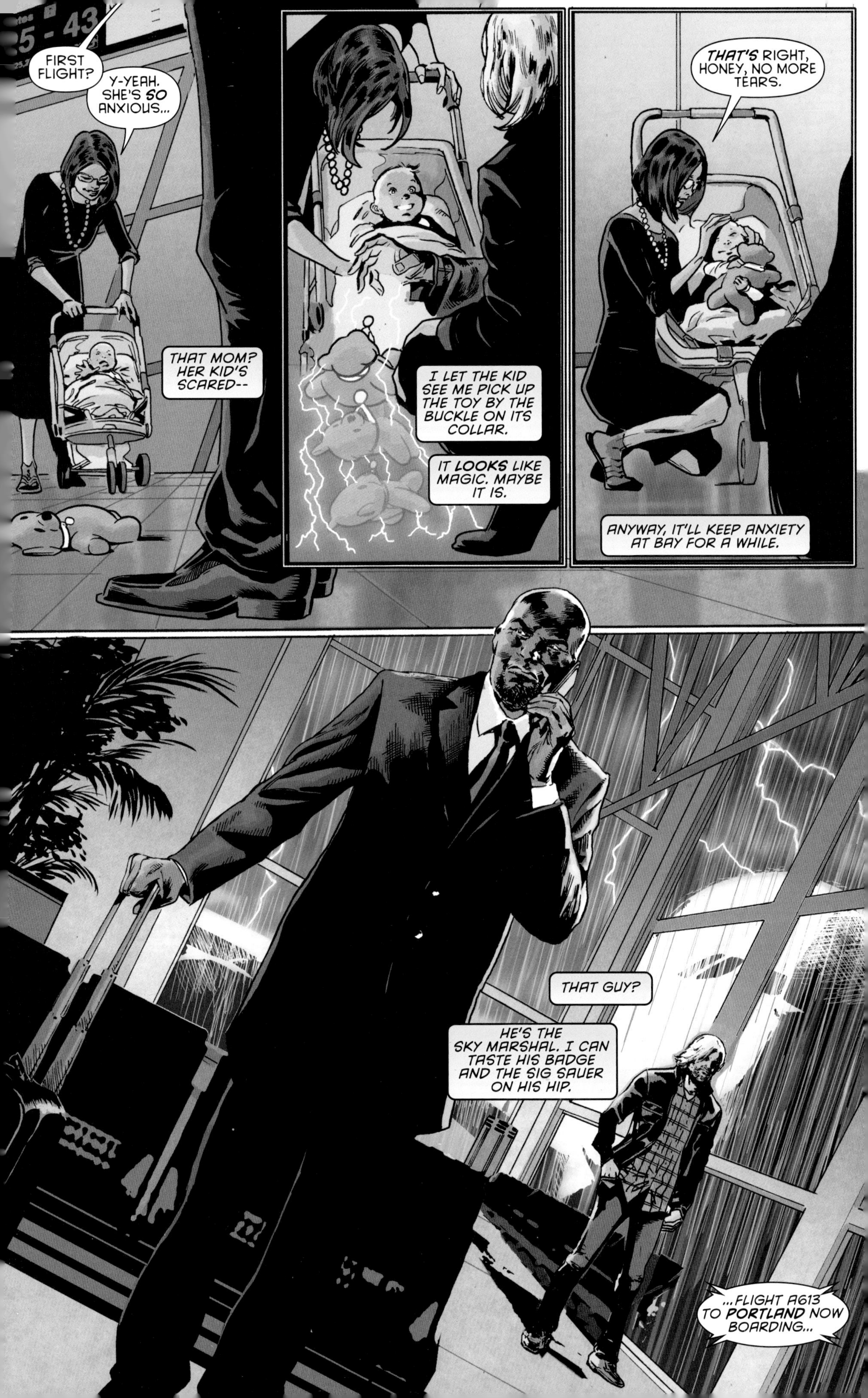
FIRST FLIGHT?
Y-YEAH. SHE'S SO ANXIOUS...
THAT MOM? HER KID'S SCARED--
I LET THE KID SEE ME PICK UP THE TOY BY THE BUCKLE ON ITS COLLAR.
IT LOOKS LIKE MAGIC. MAYBE IT IS.
THAT'S RIGHT, HONEY, NO MORE TEARS.
ANYWAY, IT'LL KEEP ANXIETY AT BAY FOR A WHILE.
THAT GUY?
HE'S THE SKY MARSHAL. I CAN TASTE HIS BADGE AND THE SIG SAUER ON HIS HIP.
...FLIGHT A613 TO PORTLAND NOW BOARDING...

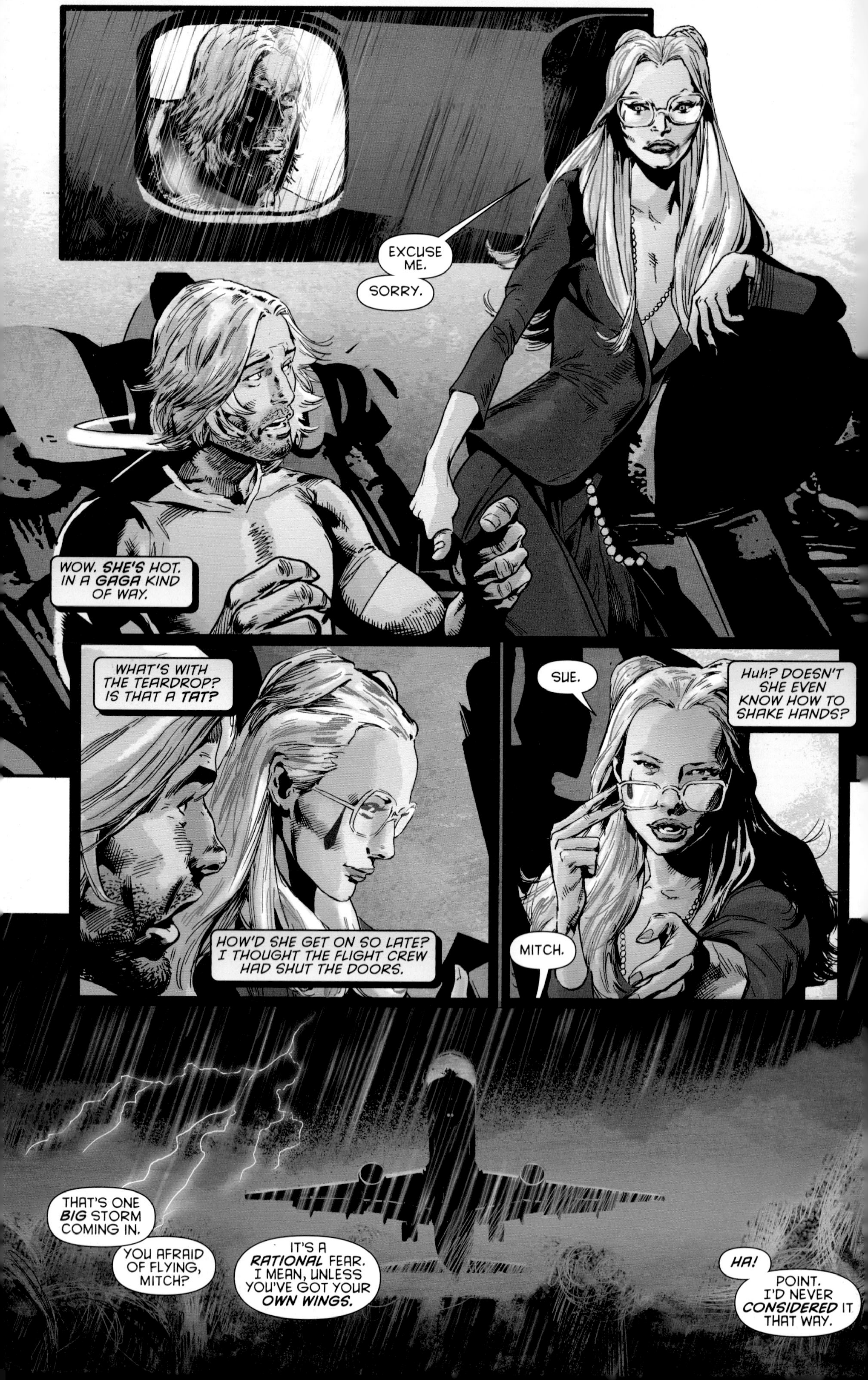

EXCUSE ME.
SORRY.
WOW. SHE'S HOT. IN A GAGA KIND OF WAY.
WHAT'S WITH THE TEARDROP? IS THAT A TAT?
HOW'D SHE GET ON SO LATE? I THOUGHT THE FLIGHT CREW HAD SHUT THE DOORS.
SUE.
Huh? DOESN'T SHE EVEN KNOW HOW TO SHAKE HANDS?
MITCH.
THAT'S ONE BIG STORM COMING IN.
YOU AFRAID OF FLYING, MITCH?
IT'S A RATIONAL FEAR. I MEAN, UNLESS YOU'VE GOT YOUR OWN WINGS.
HA!
POINT. I'D NEVER CONSIDERED IT THAT WAY.

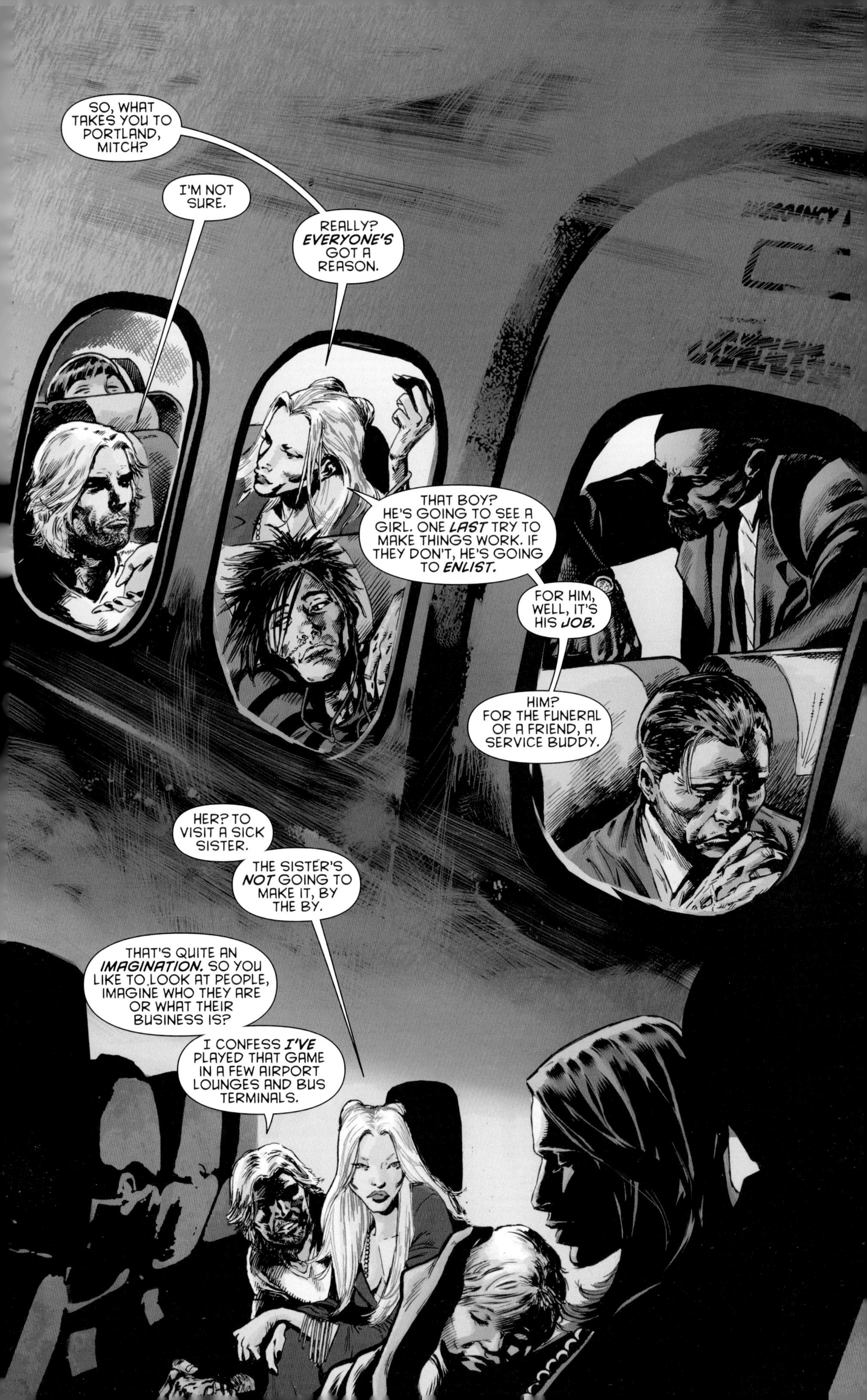
SO, WHAT TAKES YOU TO PORTLAND, MITCH?
I'M NOT SURE.
REALLY? EVERYONE'S GOT A REASON.
THAT BOY? HE'S GOING TO SEE A GIRL. ONE LAST TRY TO MAKE THINGS WORK. IF THEY DON'T, HE'S GOING TO ENLIST.
FOR HIM, WELL, IT'S HIS JOB.
HIM? FOR THE FUNERAL OF A FRIEND, A SERVICE BUDDY.
HER? TO VISIT A SICK SISTER.
THE SISTER'S NOT GOING TO MAKE IT, BY THE BY.
THAT'S QUITE AN IMAGINATION. SO YOU LIKE TO LOOK AT PEOPLE, IMAGINE WHO THEY ARE OR WHAT THEIR BUSINESS IS?
I CONFESS I'VE PLAYED THAT GAME IN A FEW AIRPORT LOUNGES AND BUS TERMINALS.

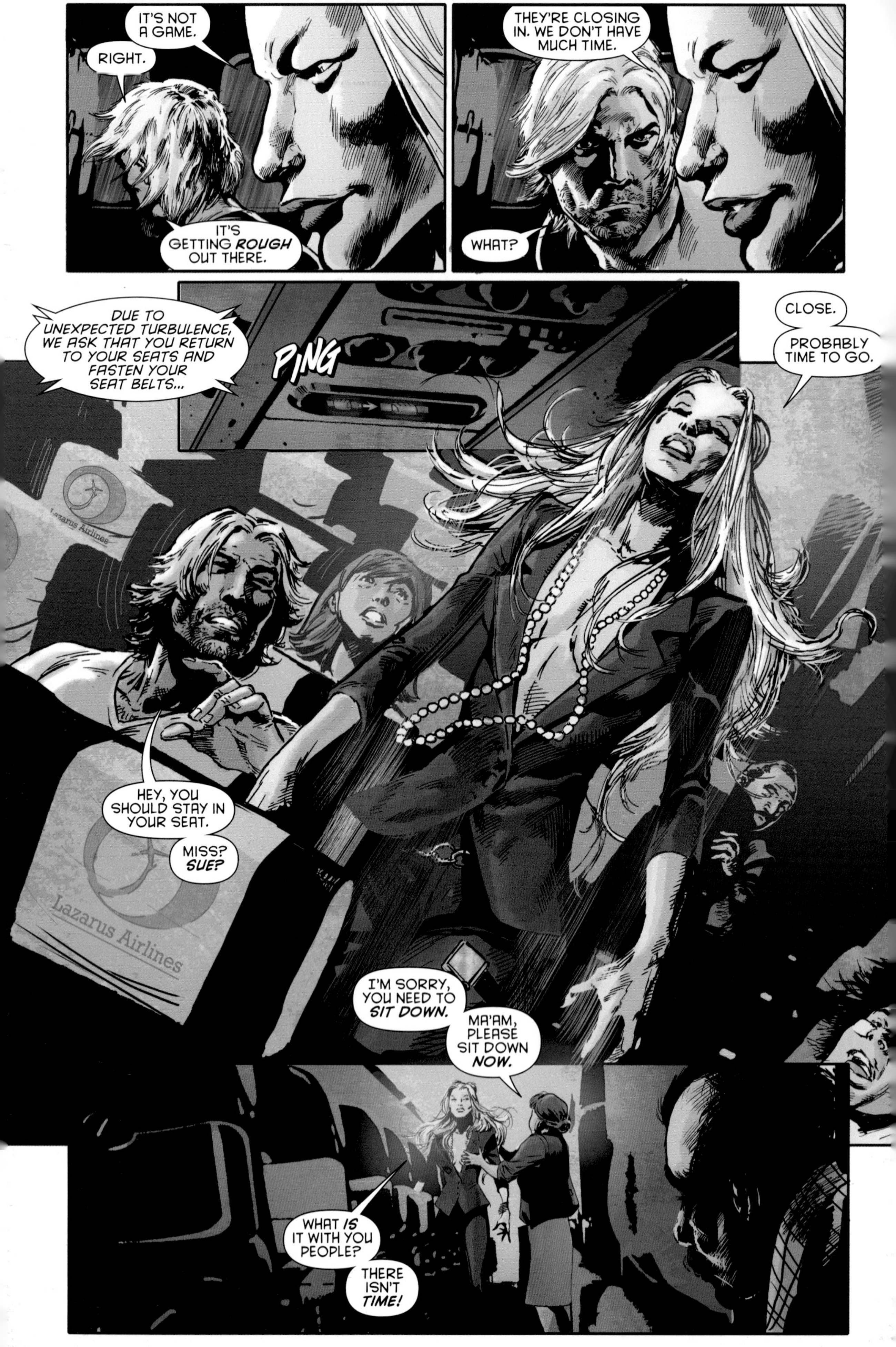
IT'S NOT A GAME.
RIGHT.
IT'S GETTING ROUGH OUT THERE.
THEY'RE CLOSING IN. WE DON'T HAVE MUCH TIME.
WHAT?
DUE TO UNEXPECTED TURBULENCE, WE ASK THAT YOU RETURN TO YOUR SEATS AND FASTEN YOUR SEAT BELTS...
PING
CLOSE.
PROBABLY TIME TO GO.
Lazarus Airlines
HEY, YOU SHOULD STAY IN YOUR SEAT.
MISS? SUE?
Lazarus Airlines
I'M SORRY, YOU NEED TO SIT DOWN.
MA'AM, PLEASE SIT DOWN NOW.
WHAT IS IT WITH YOU PEOPLE?
THERE ISN'T TIME!

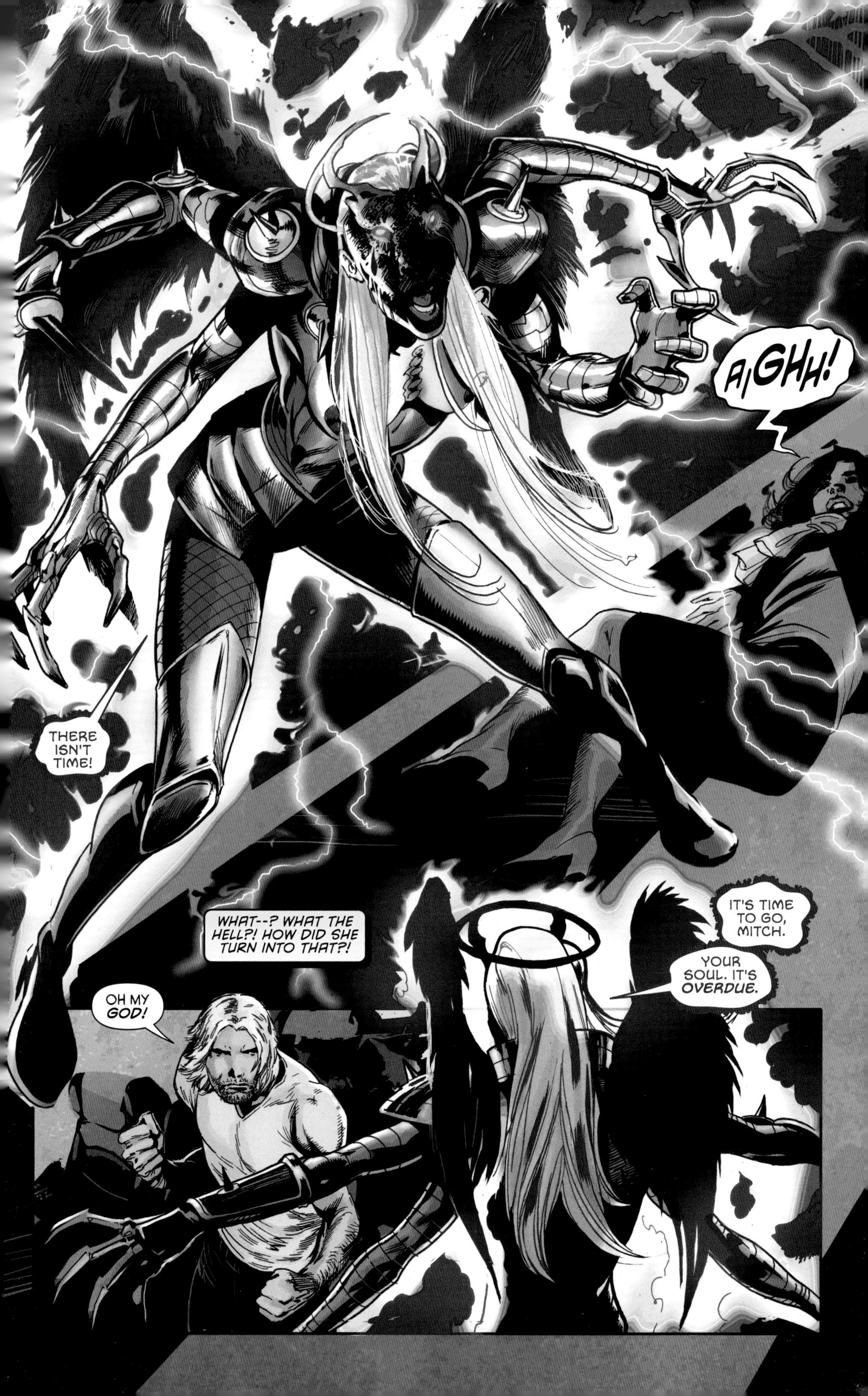
AIGHH!
THERE ISN'T TIME!
WHAT--? WHAT THE HELL?! HOW DID SHE TURN INTO THAT?!
OH MY GOD!
IT'S TIME TO GO, MITCH.
YOUR SOUL. IT'S OVERDUE.

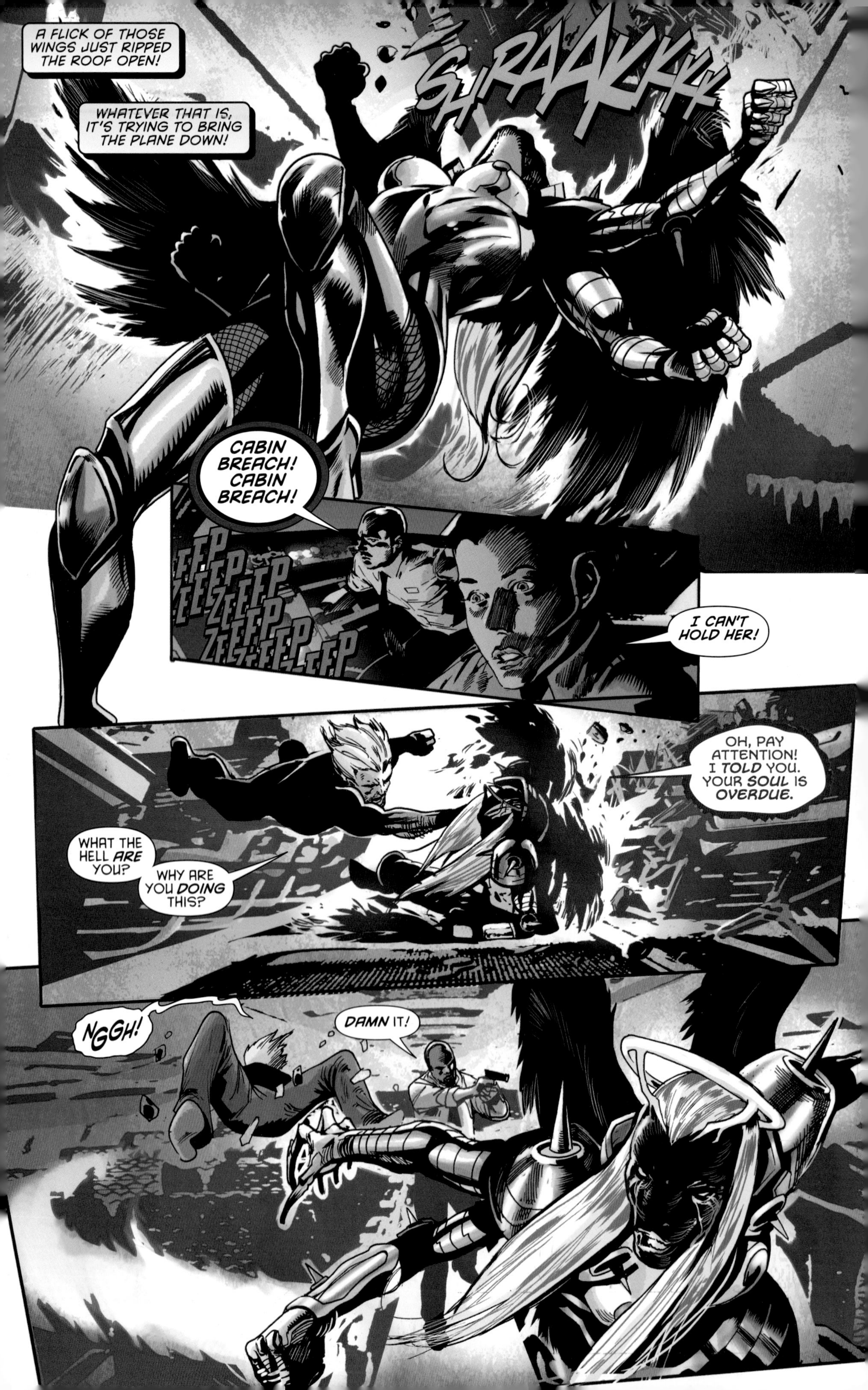
A FLICK OF THOSE WINGS JUST RIPPED THE ROOF OPEN!
WHATEVER THAT IS, IT'S TRYING TO BRING THE PLANE DOWN!
SHRAAKKK
CABIN BREACH! CABIN BREACH!
ZEEEP ZEEEP ZEEEP ZEEEP ZEEEP
I CAN'T HOLD HER!
OH, PAY ATTENTION! I TOLD YOU. YOUR SOUL IS OVERDUE.
WHAT THE HELL ARE YOU?
WHY ARE YOU DOING THIS?
NGGH!
DAMN IT!

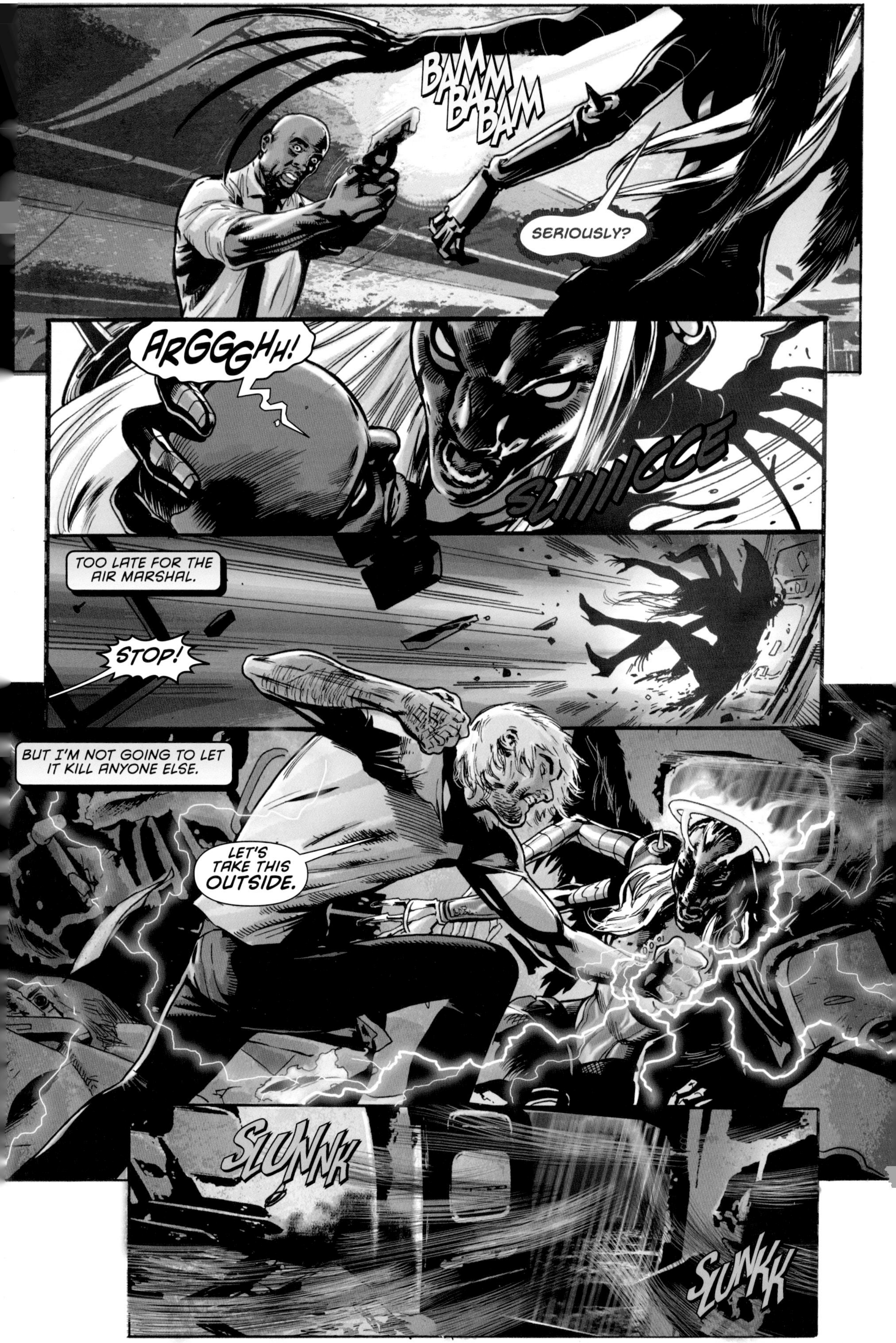
BAMM BAM BAM
SERIOUSLY?
ARGGGHH!
SLIIIICCE
TOO LATE FOR THE AIR MARSHAL.
STOP!
BUT I'M NOT GOING TO LET IT KILL ANYONE ELSE.
LET'S TAKE THIS OUTSIDE.
SLUNNK
SLUNKK

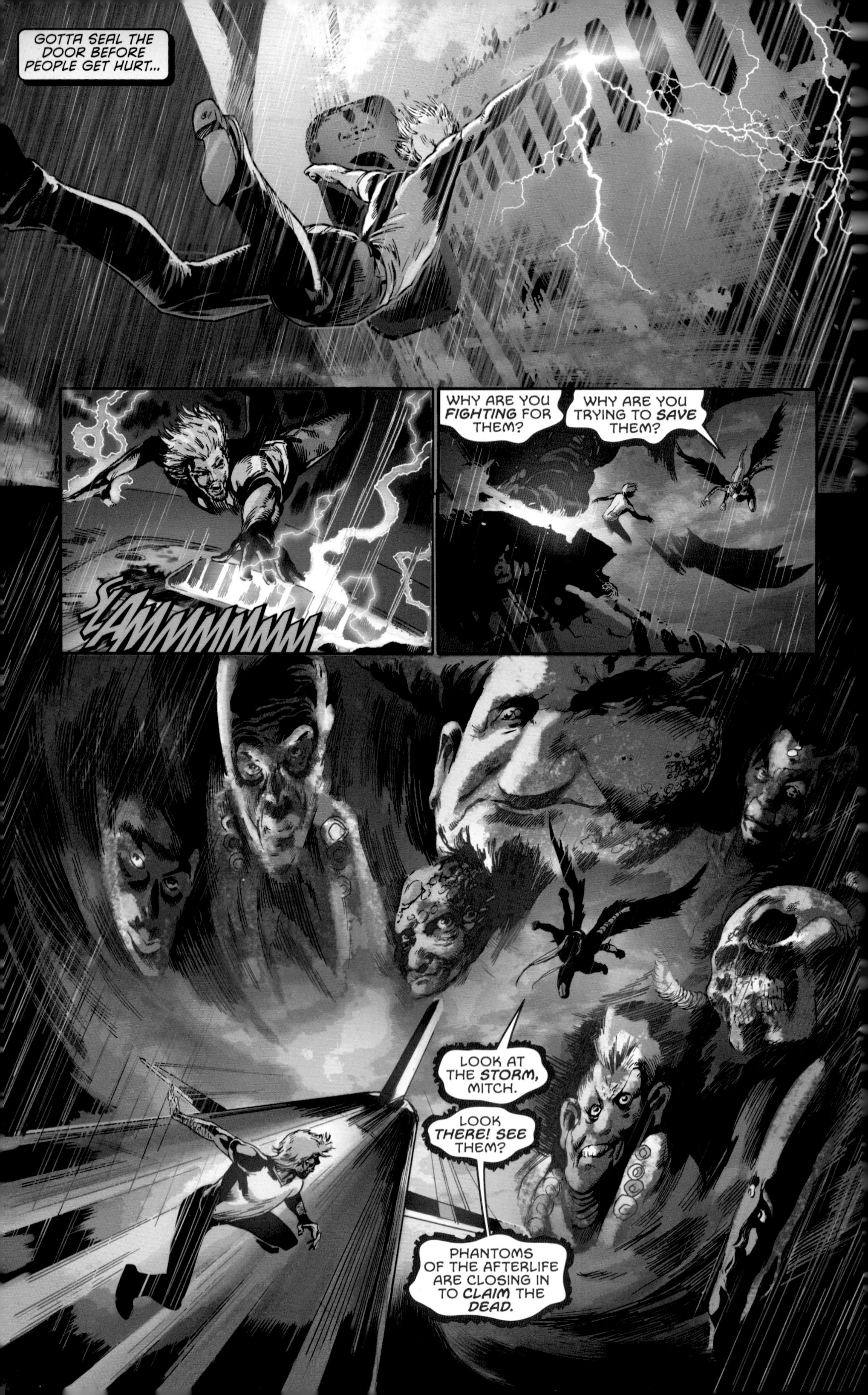
GOTTA SEAL THE DOOR BEFORE PEOPLE GET HURT...
WHY ARE YOU *FIGHTING* FOR THEM?
WHY ARE YOU TRYING TO *SAVE* THEM?
LOOK AT THE *STORM,* MITCH.
LOOK *THERE! SEE* THEM?
PHANTOMS OF THE AFTERLIFE ARE CLOSING IN TO *CLAIM* THE *DEAD.*

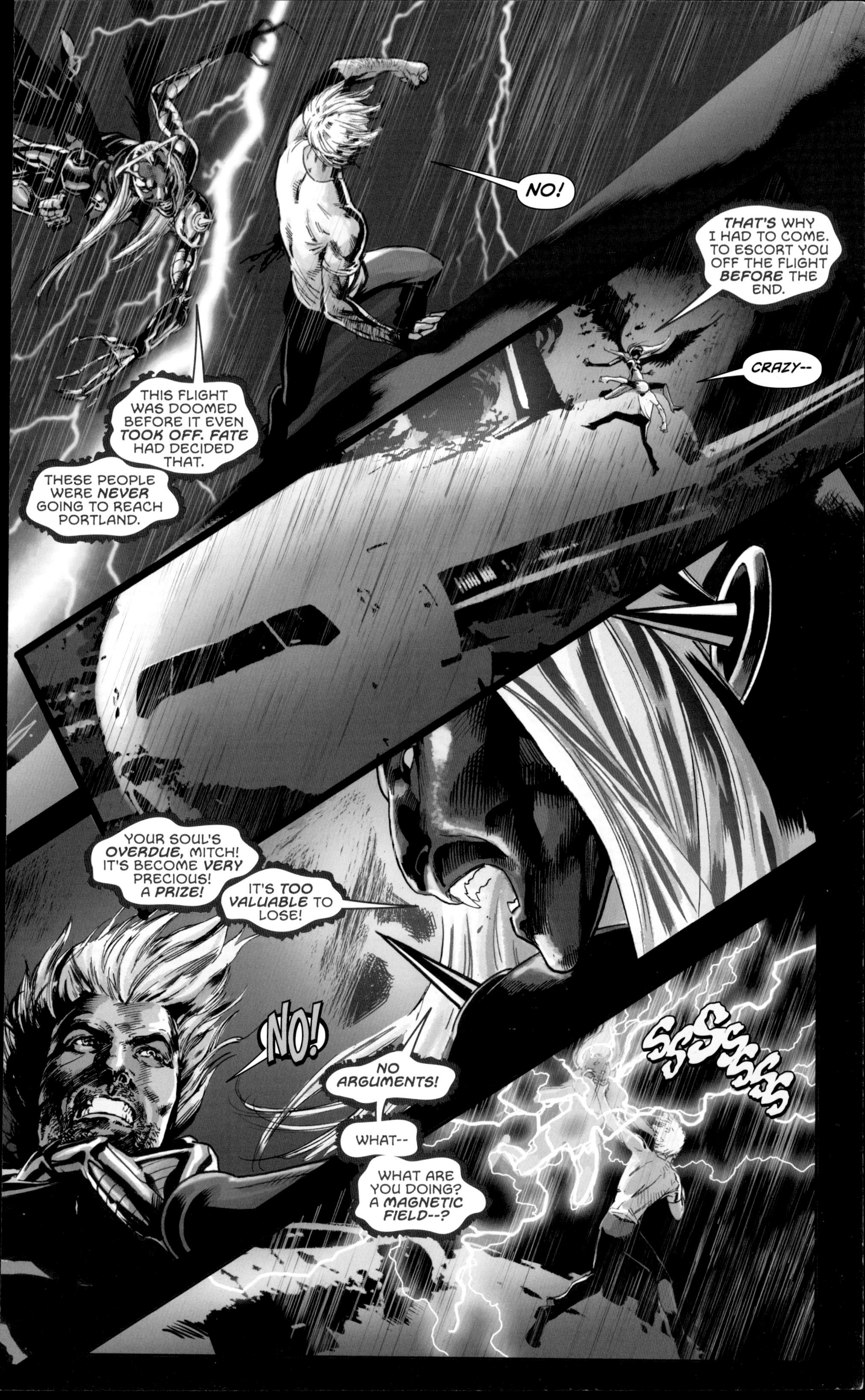
NO!
THAT'S WHY I HAD TO COME. TO ESCORT YOU OFF THE FLIGHT BEFORE THE END.
CRAZY--
THIS FLIGHT WAS DOOMED BEFORE IT EVEN TOOK OFF. FATE HAD DECIDED THAT.
THESE PEOPLE WERE NEVER GOING TO REACH PORTLAND.
YOUR SOUL'S OVERDUE, MITCH! IT'S BECOME VERY PRECIOUS! A PRIZE!
IT'S TOO VALUABLE TO LOSE!
NO!
NO ARGUMENTS!
WHAT--
WHAT ARE YOU DOING? A MAGNETIC FIELD--?
SSSSSSSS

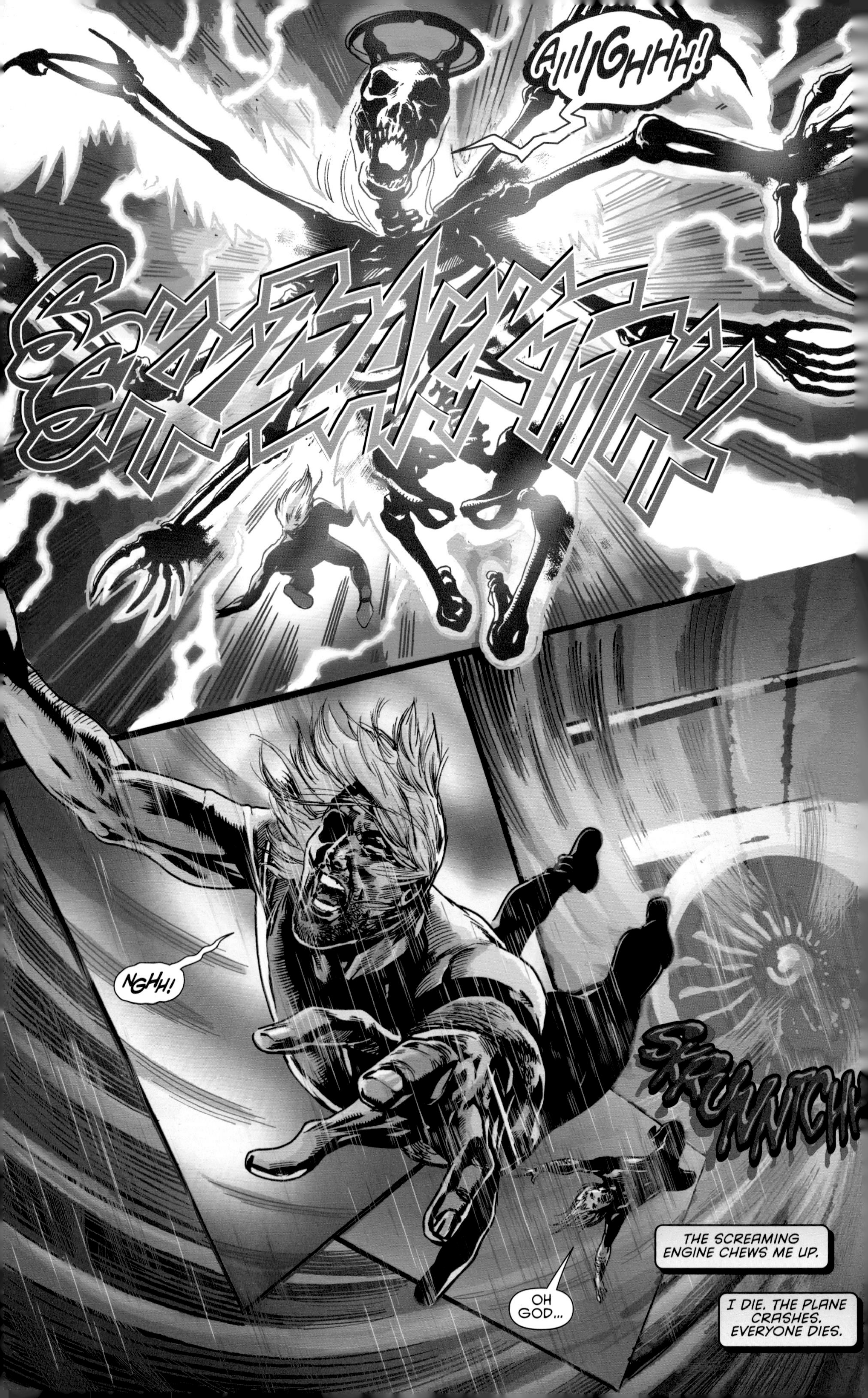
AIIIGHHH!
NGHH!
SKRUNNTCH!
OH GOD...
THE SCREAMING ENGINE CHEWS ME UP.
I DIE. THE PLANE CRASHES. EVERYONE DIES.

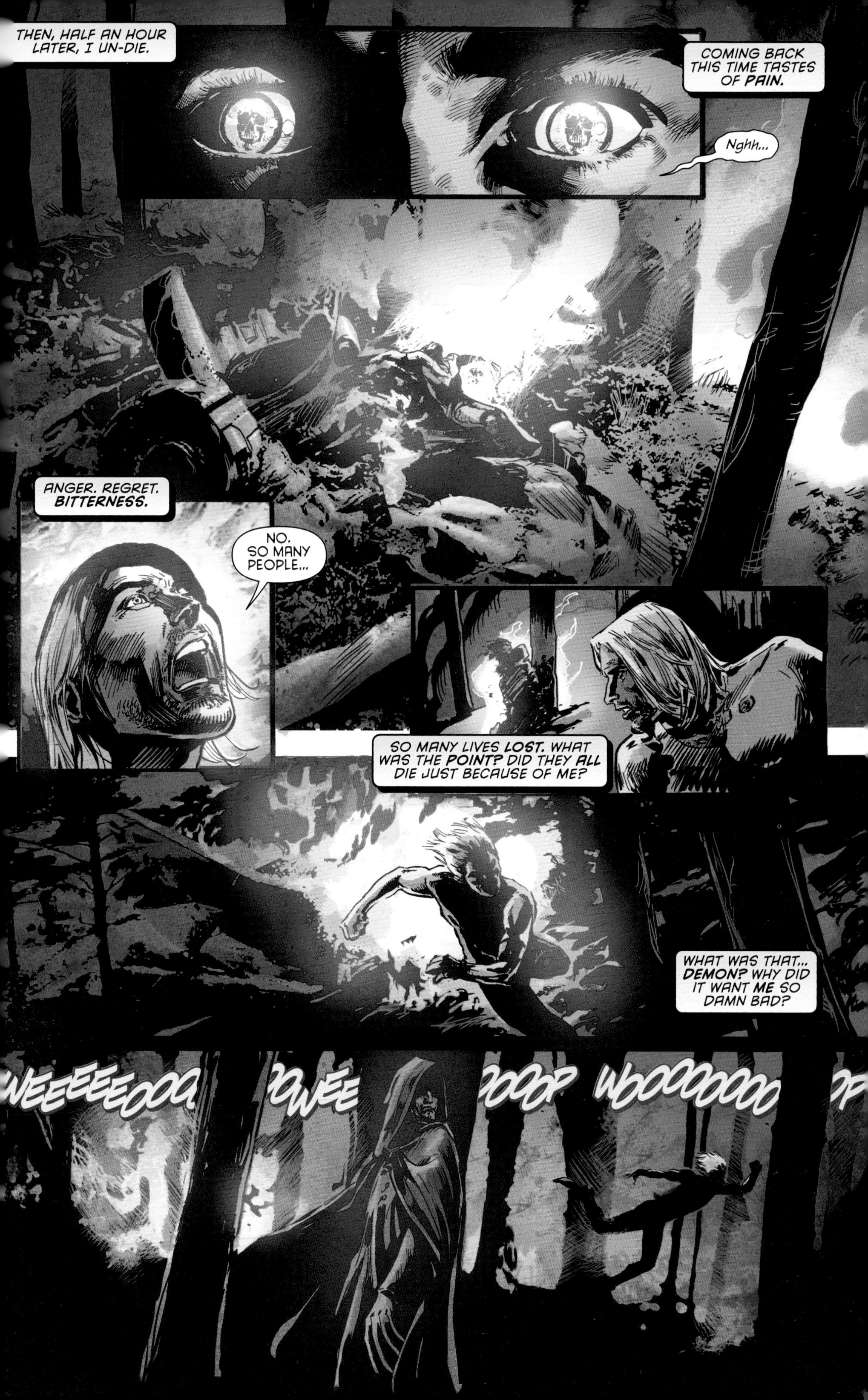

THEN, HALF AN HOUR LATER, I UN-DIE.
COMING BACK THIS TIME TASTES OF PAIN.
Nghh...
ANGER. REGRET. BITTERNESS.
NO. SO MANY PEOPLE...
SO MANY LIVES LOST. WHAT WAS THE POINT? DID THEY ALL DIE JUST BECAUSE OF ME?
WHAT WAS THAT... DEMON? WHY DID IT WANT ME SO DAMN BAD?
WEEEEEEOOO OOWEE OOOOP WOOOOOOO OOP

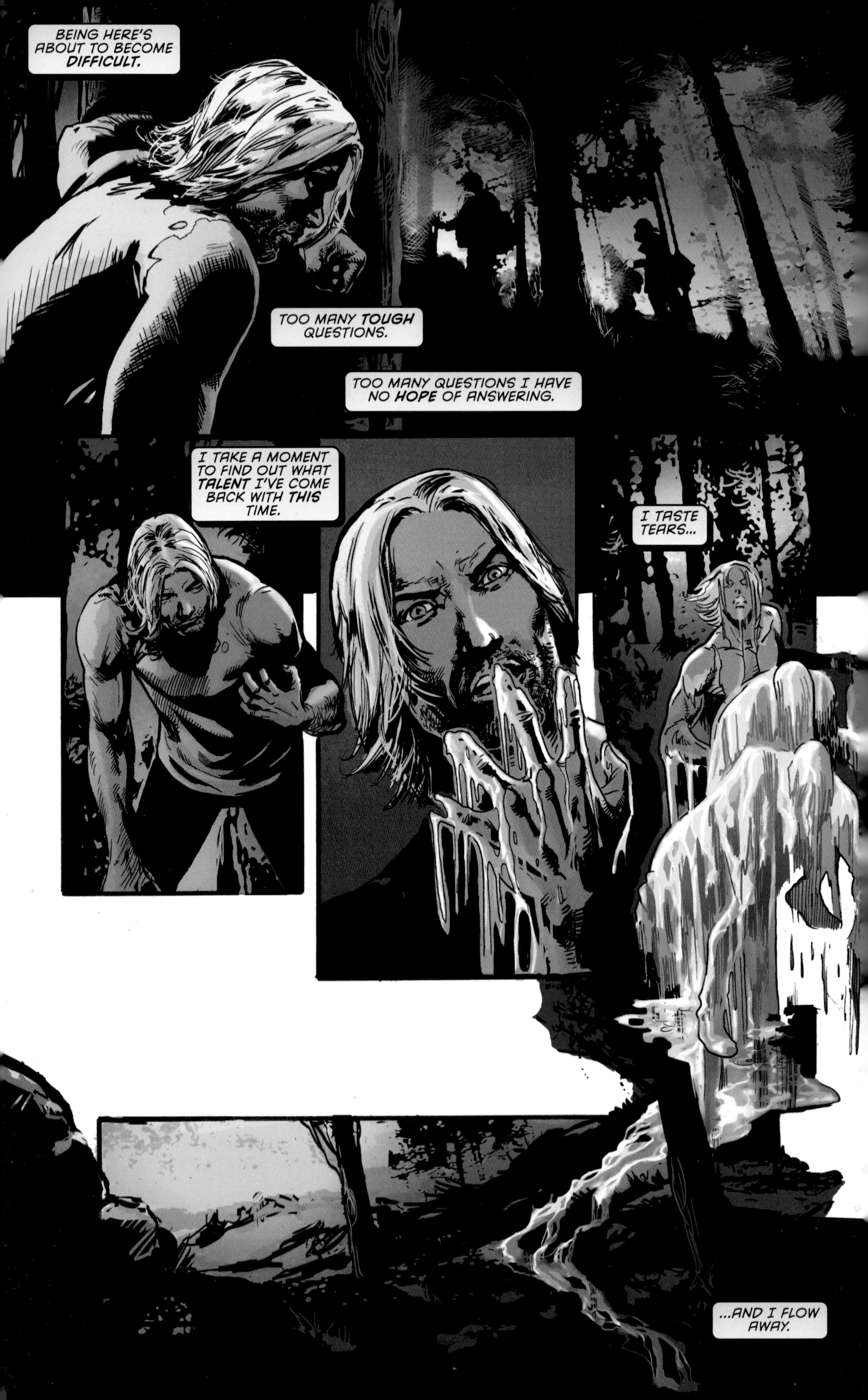
BEING HERE'S ABOUT TO BECOME DIFFICULT.
TOO MANY TOUGH QUESTIONS.
TOO MANY QUESTIONS I HAVE NO HOPE OF ANSWERING.
I TAKE A MOMENT TO FIND OUT WHAT TALENT I'VE COME BACK WITH THIS TIME.
I TASTE TEARS...
...AND I FLOW AWAY.

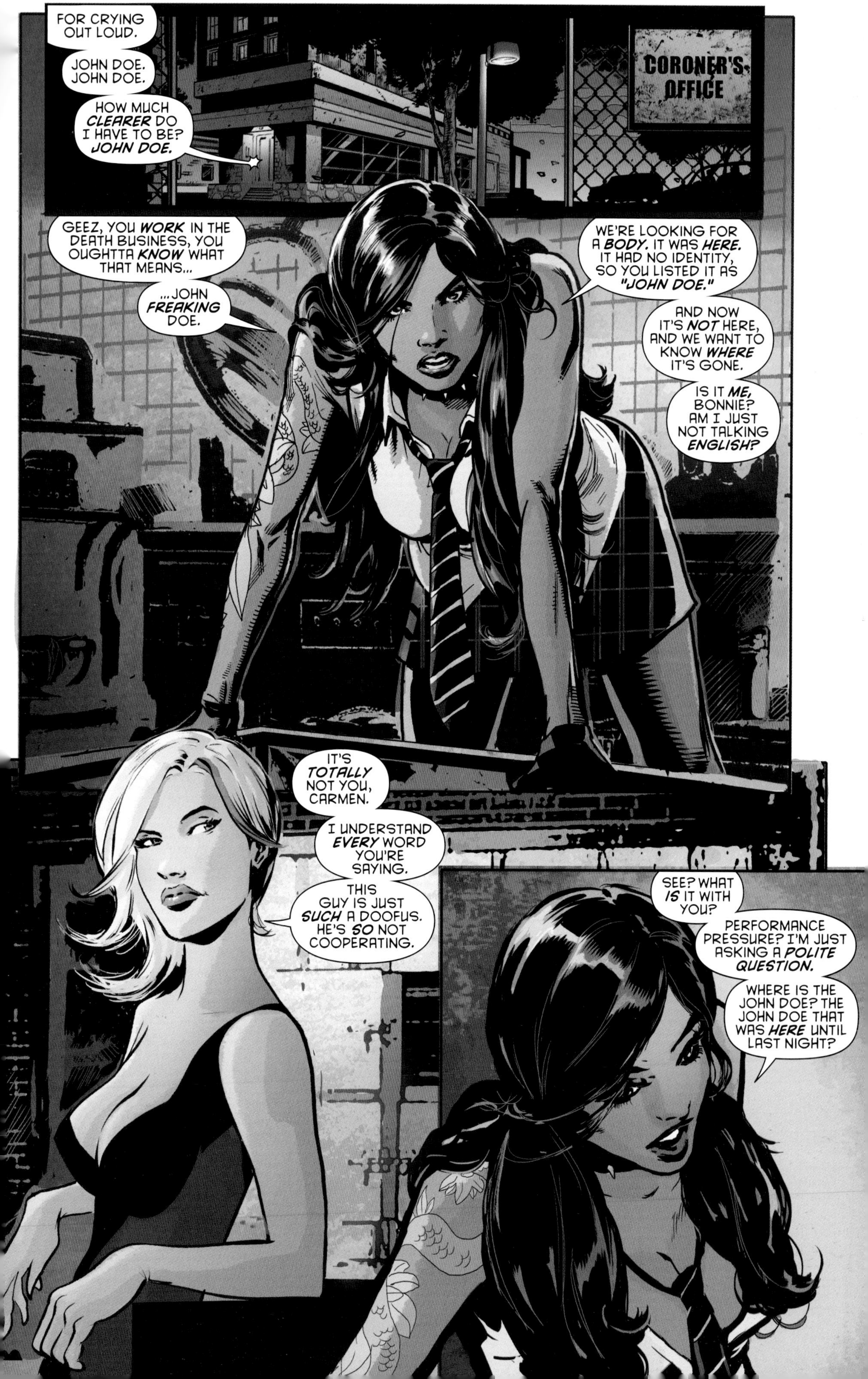
FOR CRYING OUT LOUD.
JOHN DOE. JOHN DOE.
HOW MUCH CLEARER DO I HAVE TO BE? JOHN DOE.
CORONER'S OFFICE
GEEZ, YOU WORK IN THE DEATH BUSINESS, YOU OUGHTTA KNOW WHAT THAT MEANS...
...JOHN FREAKING DOE.
WE'RE LOOKING FOR A BODY. IT WAS HERE. IT HAD NO IDENTITY, SO YOU LISTED IT AS "JOHN DOE."
AND NOW IT'S NOT HERE, AND WE WANT TO KNOW WHERE IT'S GONE.
IS IT ME, BONNIE? AM I JUST NOT TALKING ENGLISH?
IT'S TOTALLY NOT YOU, CARMEN.
I UNDERSTAND EVERY WORD YOU'RE SAYING.
THIS GUY IS JUST SUCH A DOOFUS. HE'S SO NOT COOPERATING.
SEE? WHAT IS IT WITH YOU?
PERFORMANCE PRESSURE? I'M JUST ASKING A POLITE QUESTION.
WHERE IS THE JOHN DOE? THE JOHN DOE THAT WAS HERE UNTIL LAST NIGHT?

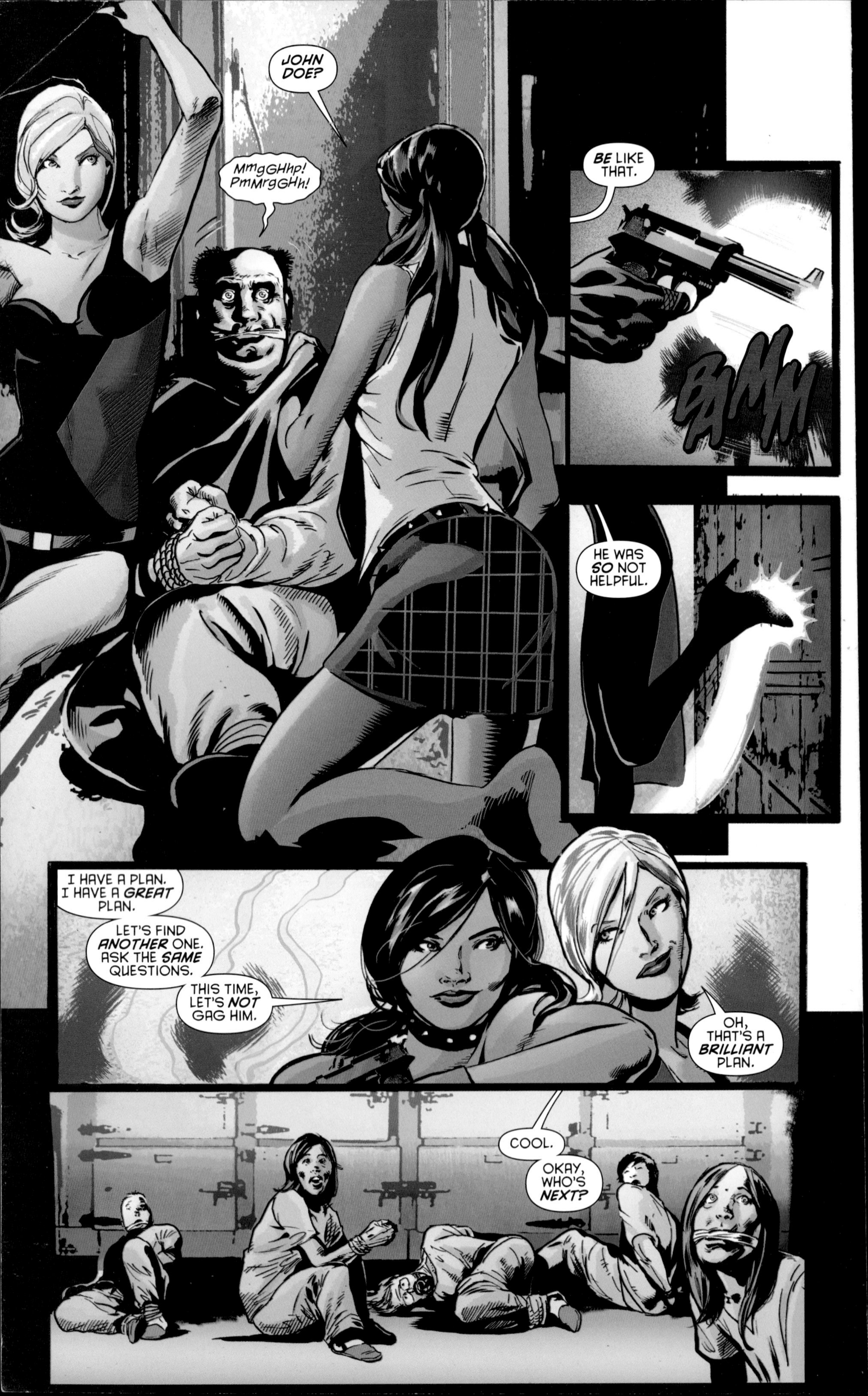
JOHN DOE?
MmgGHhp! PmMrgGHh!
BE LIKE THAT.
BAMM
HE WAS SO NOT HELPFUL.
I HAVE A PLAN. I HAVE A GREAT PLAN.
LET'S FIND ANOTHER ONE. ASK THE SAME QUESTIONS.
THIS TIME, LET'S NOT GAG HIM.
OH, THAT'S A BRILLIANT PLAN.
COOL.
OKAY, WHO'S NEXT?

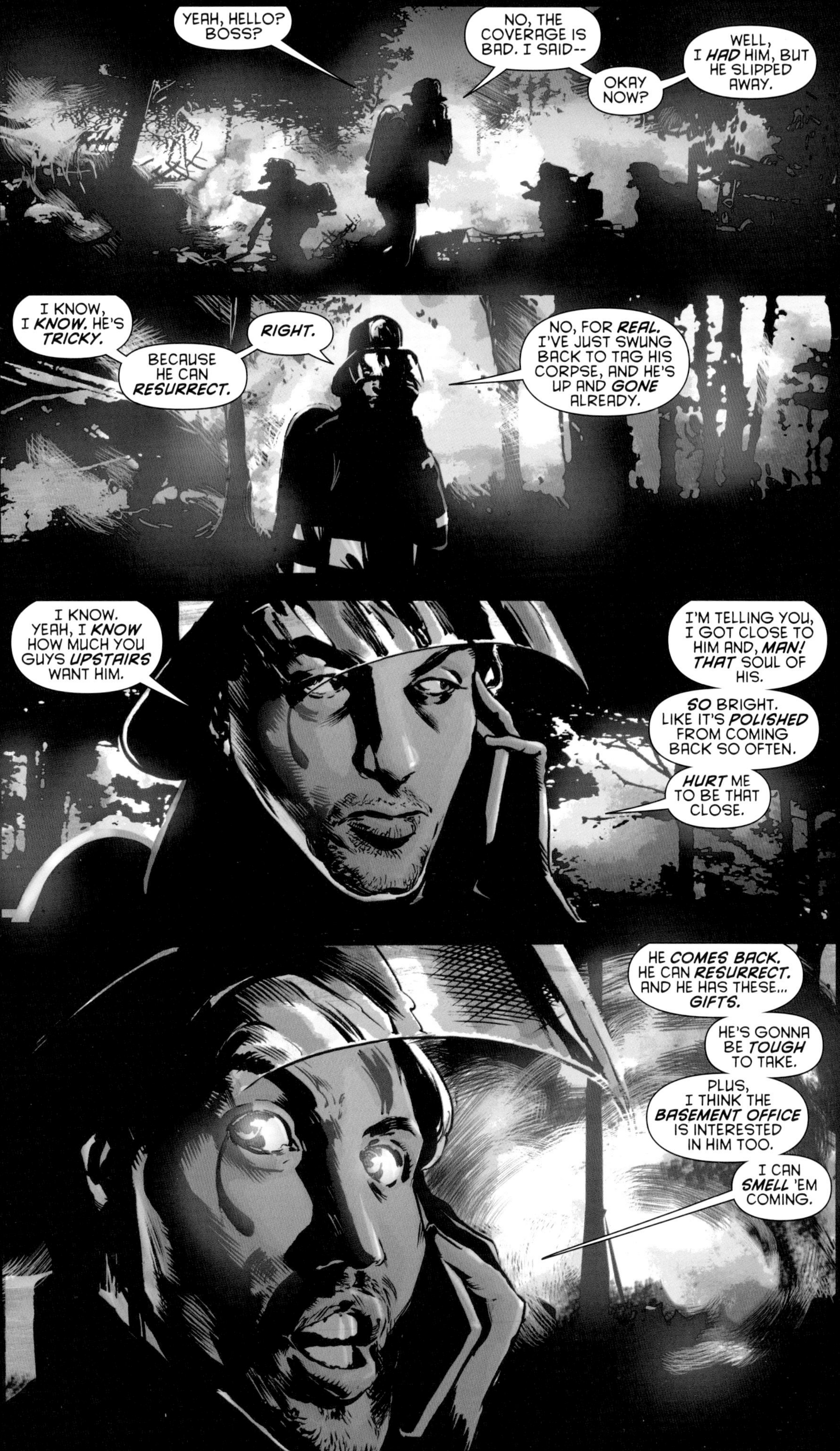
YEAH, HELLO? BOSS?
NO, THE COVERAGE IS BAD. I SAID--
OKAY NOW?
WELL, I HAD HIM, BUT HE SLIPPED AWAY.
I KNOW, I KNOW. HE'S TRICKY.
BECAUSE HE CAN RESURRECT.
RIGHT.
NO, FOR REAL. I'VE JUST SWUNG BACK TO TAG HIS CORPSE, AND HE'S UP AND GONE ALREADY.
I KNOW. YEAH, I KNOW HOW MUCH YOU GUYS UPSTAIRS WANT HIM.
I'M TELLING YOU, I GOT CLOSE TO HIM AND, MAN! THAT SOUL OF HIS.
SO BRIGHT. LIKE IT'S POLISHED FROM COMING BACK SO OFTEN.
HURT ME TO BE THAT CLOSE.
HE COMES BACK. HE CAN RESURRECT. AND HE HAS THESE... GIFTS.
HE'S GONNA BE TOUGH TO TAKE.
PLUS, I THINK THE BASEMENT OFFICE IS INTERESTED IN HIM TOO.
I CAN SMELL 'EM COMING.

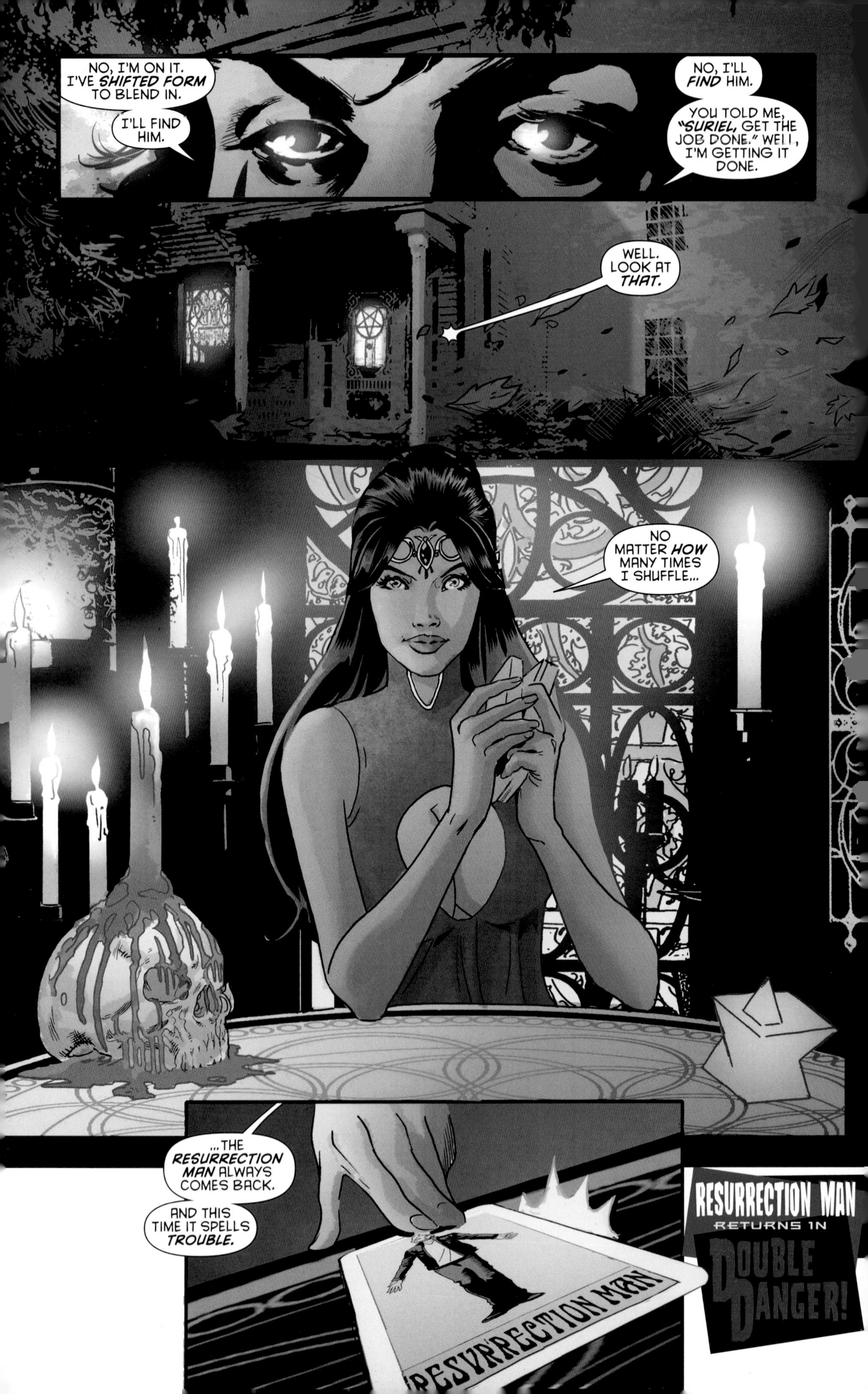

NO, I'M ON IT. I'VE SHIFTED FORM TO BLEND IN.
I'LL FIND HIM.
NO, I'LL FIND HIM.
YOU TOLD ME, "SURIEL, GET THE JOB DONE." WELL, I'M GETTING IT DONE.
WELL. LOOK AT THAT.
NO MATTER HOW MANY TIMES I SHUFFLE...
...THE RESURRECTION MAN ALWAYS COMES BACK.
AND THIS TIME IT SPELLS TROUBLE.
RESURRECTION MAN
RESURRECTION MAN RETURNS IN DOUBLE DANGER!

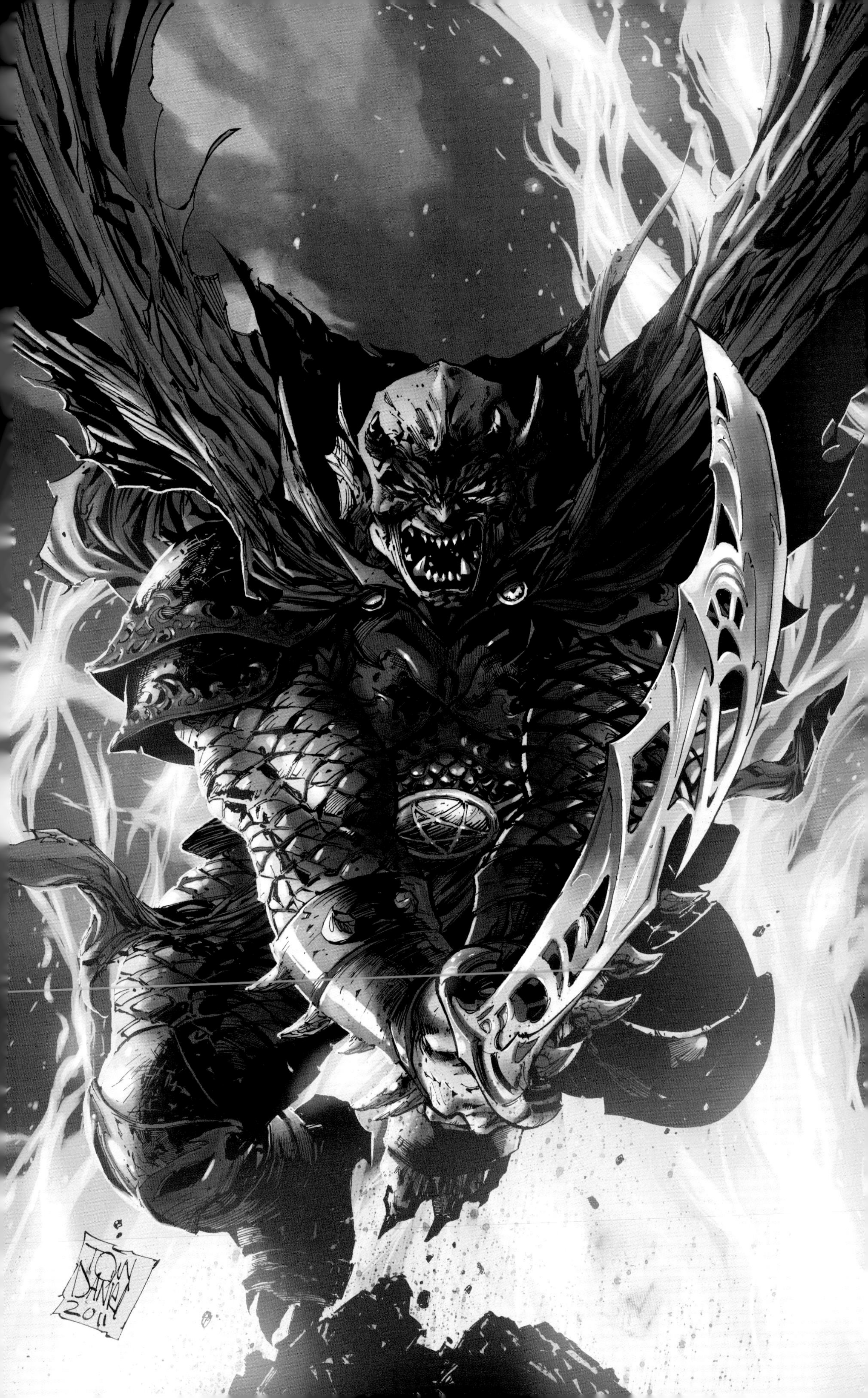

DEMON KNIGHTS

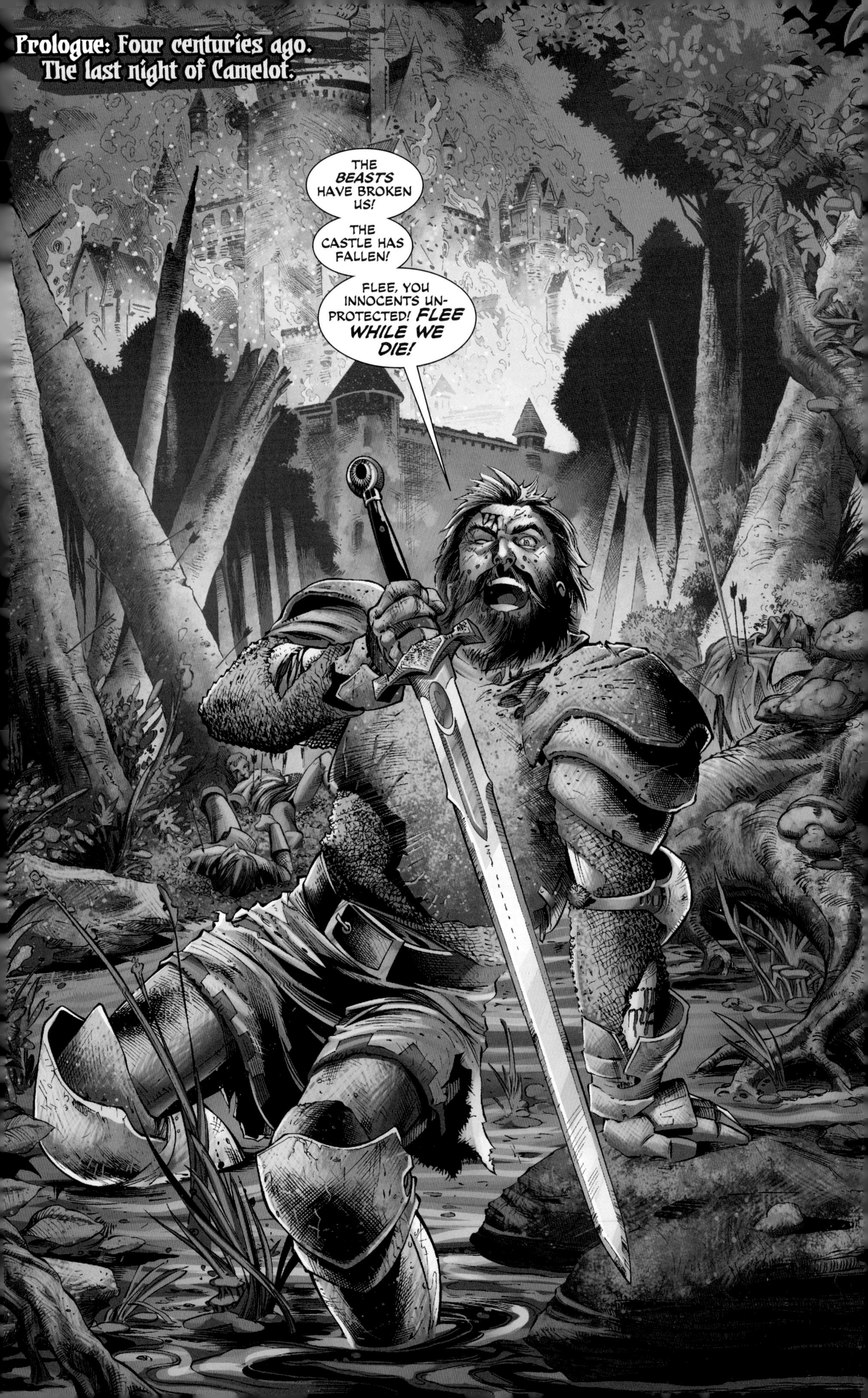
Prologue: Four centuries ago. The last night of Camelot.
THE BEASTS HAVE BROKEN US!
THE CASTLE HAS FALLEN!
FLEE, YOU INNOCENTS UN-PROTECTED! FLEE WHILE WE DIE!

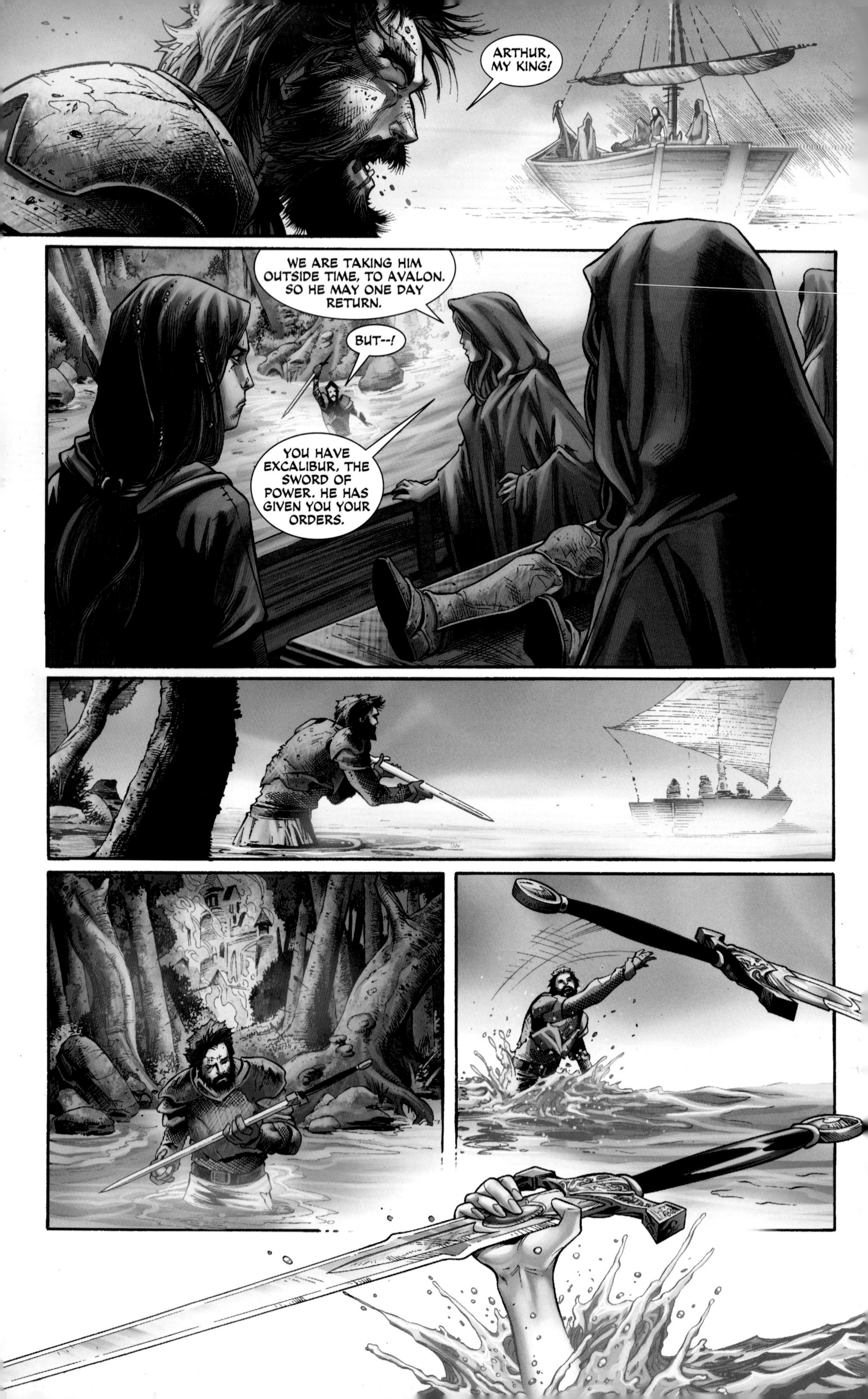
ARTHUR, MY KING!
WE ARE TAKING HIM OUTSIDE TIME, TO AVALON. SO HE MAY ONE DAY RETURN.
BUT--!
YOU HAVE EXCALIBUR, THE SWORD OF POWER. HE HAS GIVEN YOU YOUR ORDERS.

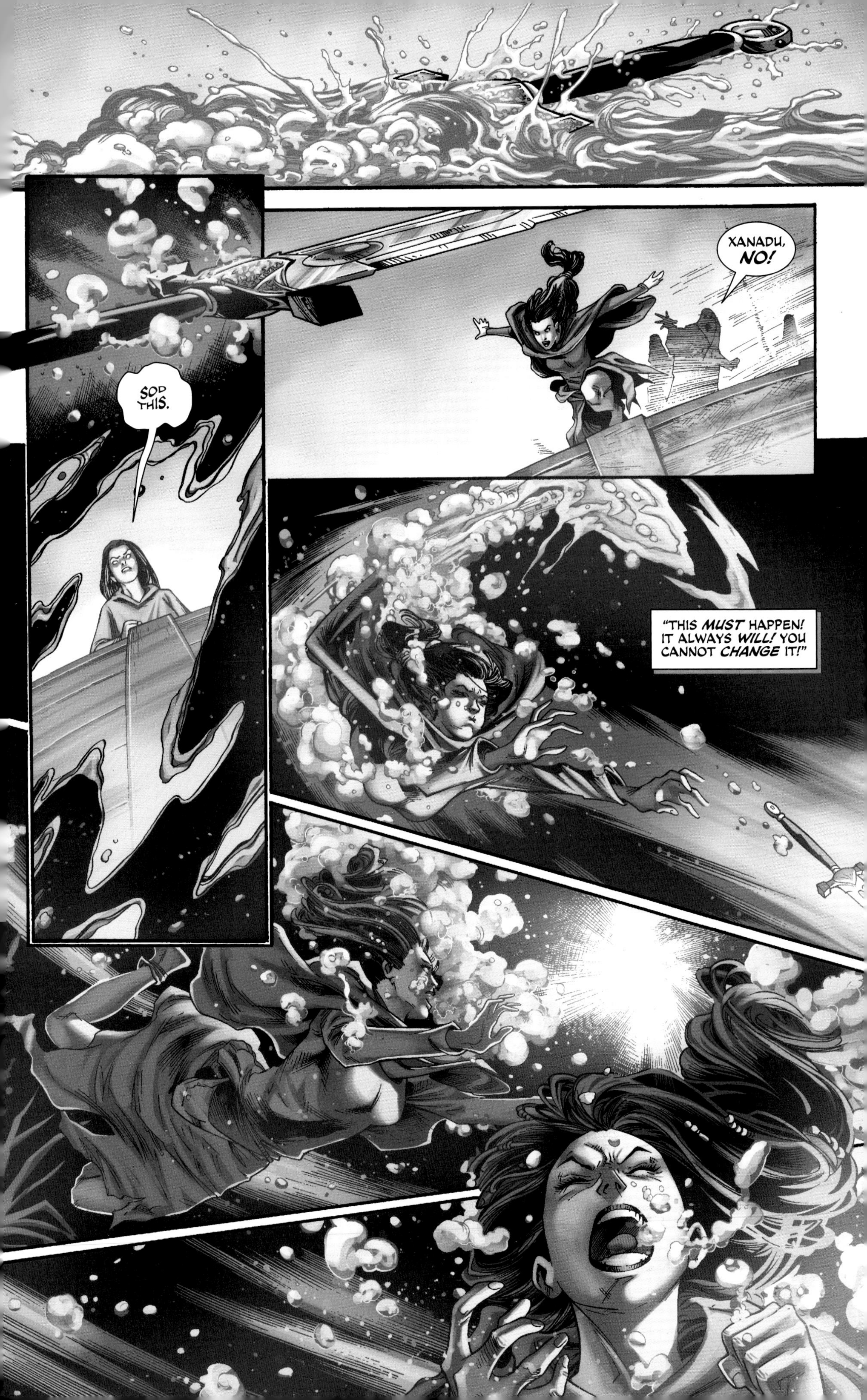
SOD THIS.
XANADU, NO!
"THIS MUST HAPPEN! IT ALWAYS WILL! YOU CANNOT CHANGE IT!"

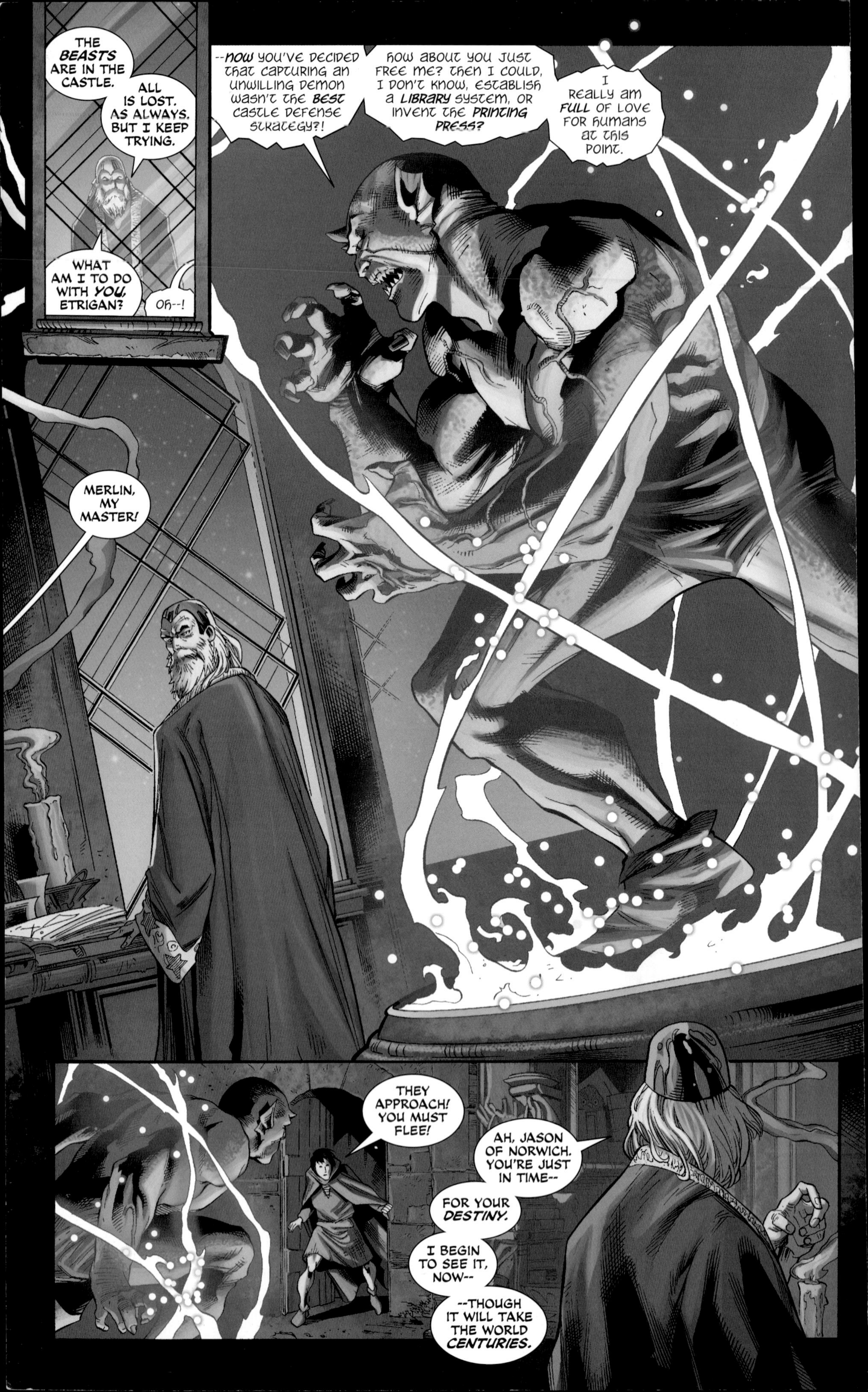
THE BEASTS ARE IN THE CASTLE.
ALL IS LOST. AS ALWAYS. BUT I KEEP TRYING.
WHAT AM I TO DO WITH YOU, ETRIGAN?
OH--!
--NOW YOU'VE DECIDED THAT CAPTURING AN UNWILLING DEMON WASN'T THE BEST CASTLE DEFENSE STRATEGY?!
HOW ABOUT YOU JUST FREE ME? THEN I COULD, I DON'T KNOW, ESTABLISH A LIBRARY SYSTEM, OR INVENT THE PRINTING PRESS?
I REALLY AM FULL OF LOVE FOR HUMANS AT THIS POINT.
MERLIN, MY MASTER!
THEY APPROACH! YOU MUST FLEE!
AH, JASON OF NORWICH. YOU'RE JUST IN TIME--
FOR YOUR DESTINY.
I BEGIN TO SEE IT, NOW--
--THOUGH IT WILL TAKE THE WORLD CENTURIES.

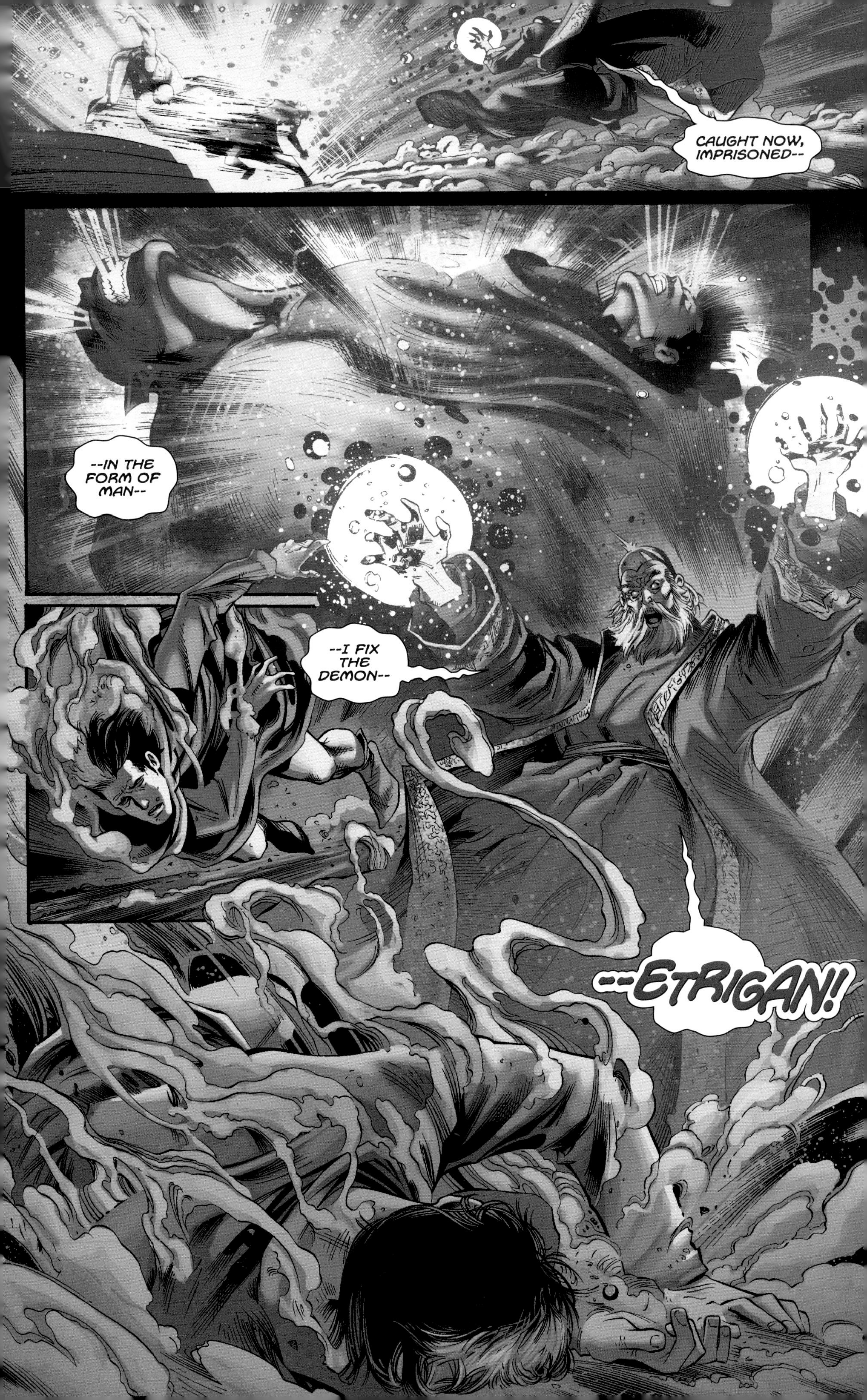
CAUGHT NOW, IMPRISONED--
--IN THE FORM OF MAN--
--I FIX THE DEMON--
--ETRIGAN!

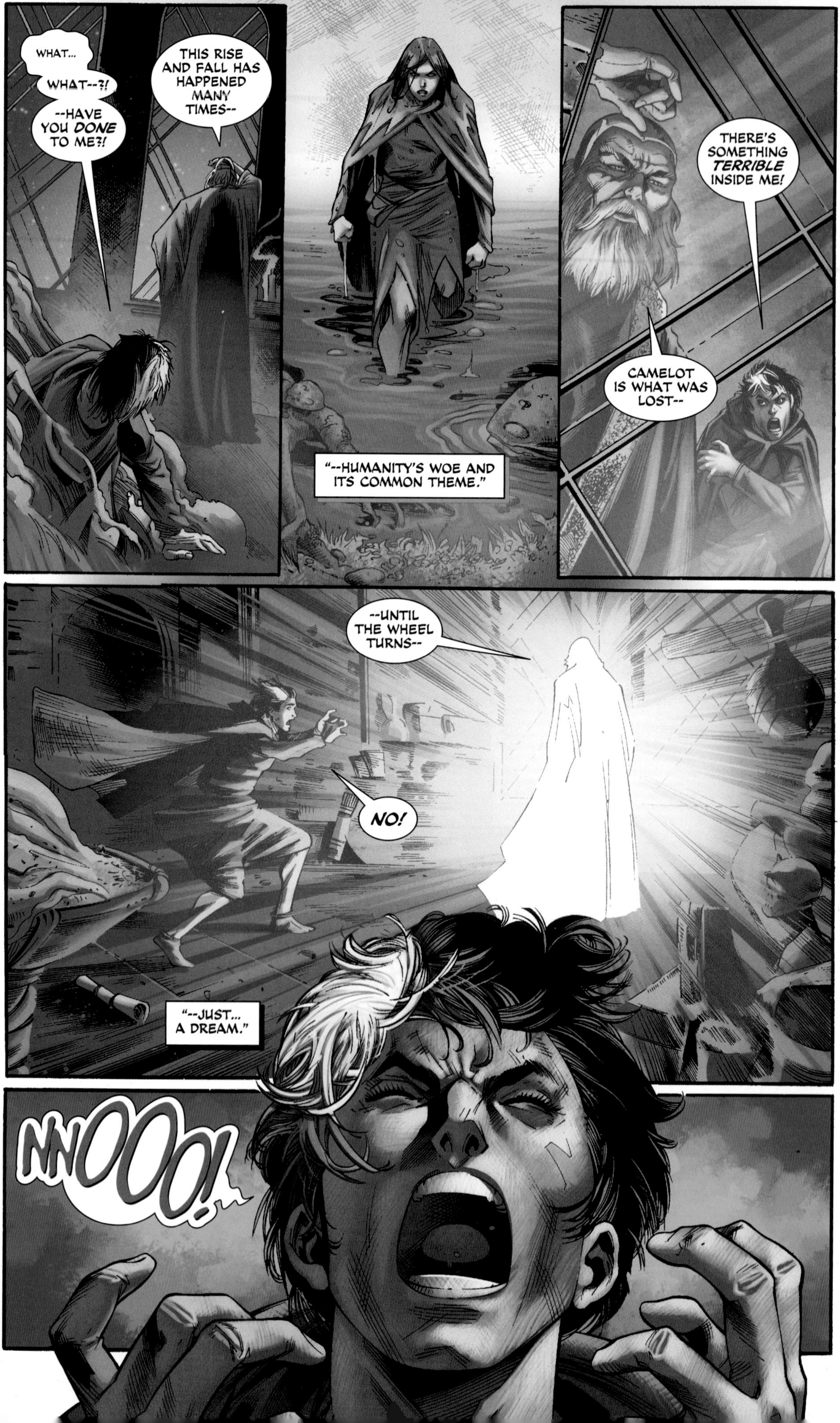
WHAT...
WHAT--?!
--HAVE YOU DONE TO ME?!
THIS RISE AND FALL HAS HAPPENED MANY TIMES--
"--HUMANITY'S WOE AND ITS COMMON THEME."
THERE'S SOMETHING TERRIBLE INSIDE ME!
CAMELOT IS WHAT WAS LOST--
--UNTIL THE WHEEL TURNS--
NO!
"--JUST... A DREAM."
NNOOO!

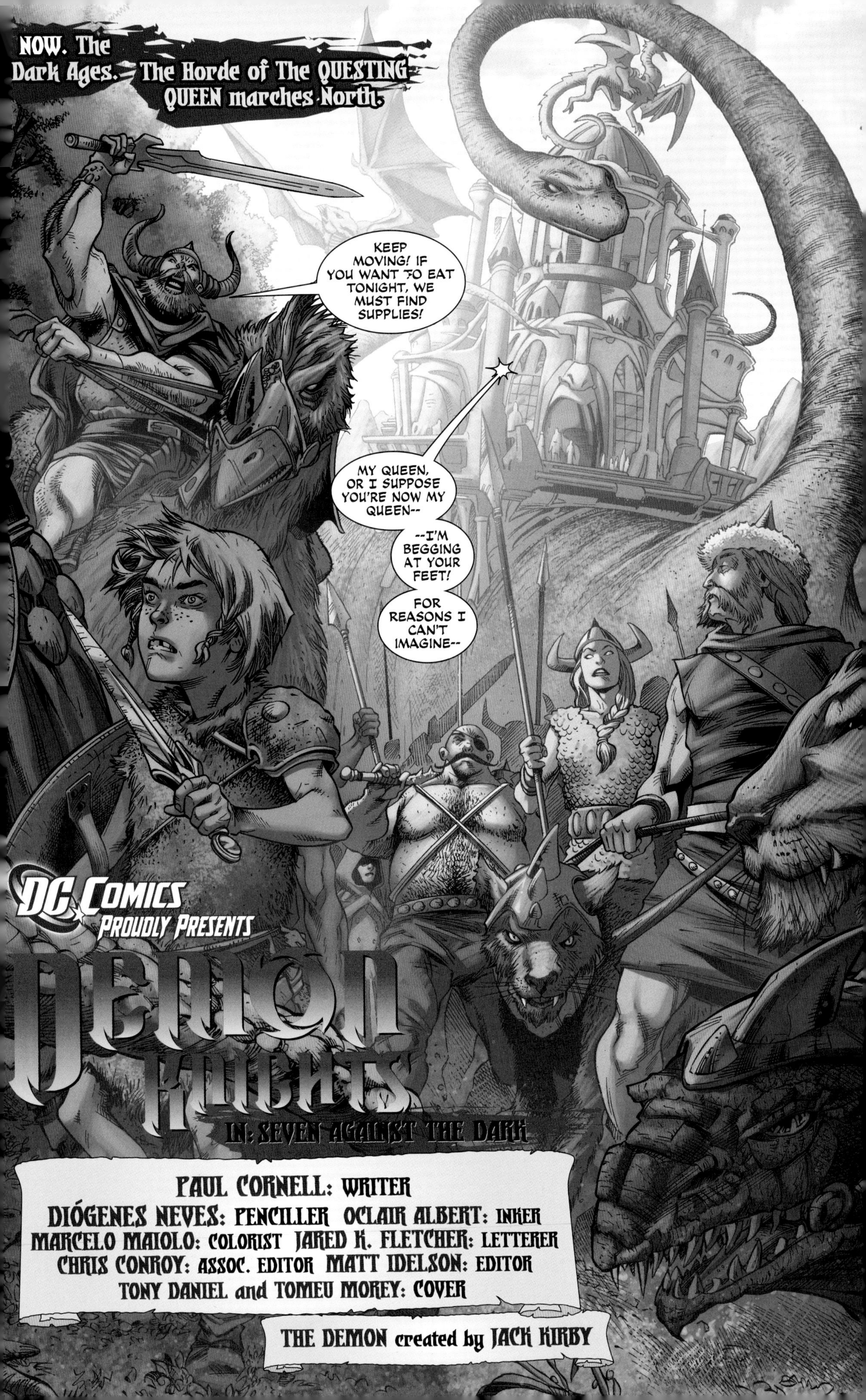
NOW. The Dark Ages. The Horde of The QUESTING QUEEN marches North.
KEEP MOVING! IF YOU WANT TO EAT TONIGHT, WE MUST FIND SUPPLIES!
MY QUEEN, OR I SUPPOSE YOU'RE NOW MY QUEEN--
--I'M BEGGING AT YOUR FEET!
FOR REASONS I CAN'T IMAGINE--
DC COMICS PROUDLY PRESENTS
DEMON KNIGHTS
IN: SEVEN AGAINST THE DARK
PAUL CORNELL: WRITER
DIÓGENES NEVES: PENCILLER OCLAIR ALBERT: INKER
MARCELO MAIOLO: COLORIST JARED K. FLETCHER: LETTERER
CHRIS CONROY: ASSOC. EDITOR MATT IDELSON: EDITOR
TONY DANIEL and TOMEU MOREY: COVER
THE DEMON created by JACK KIRBY

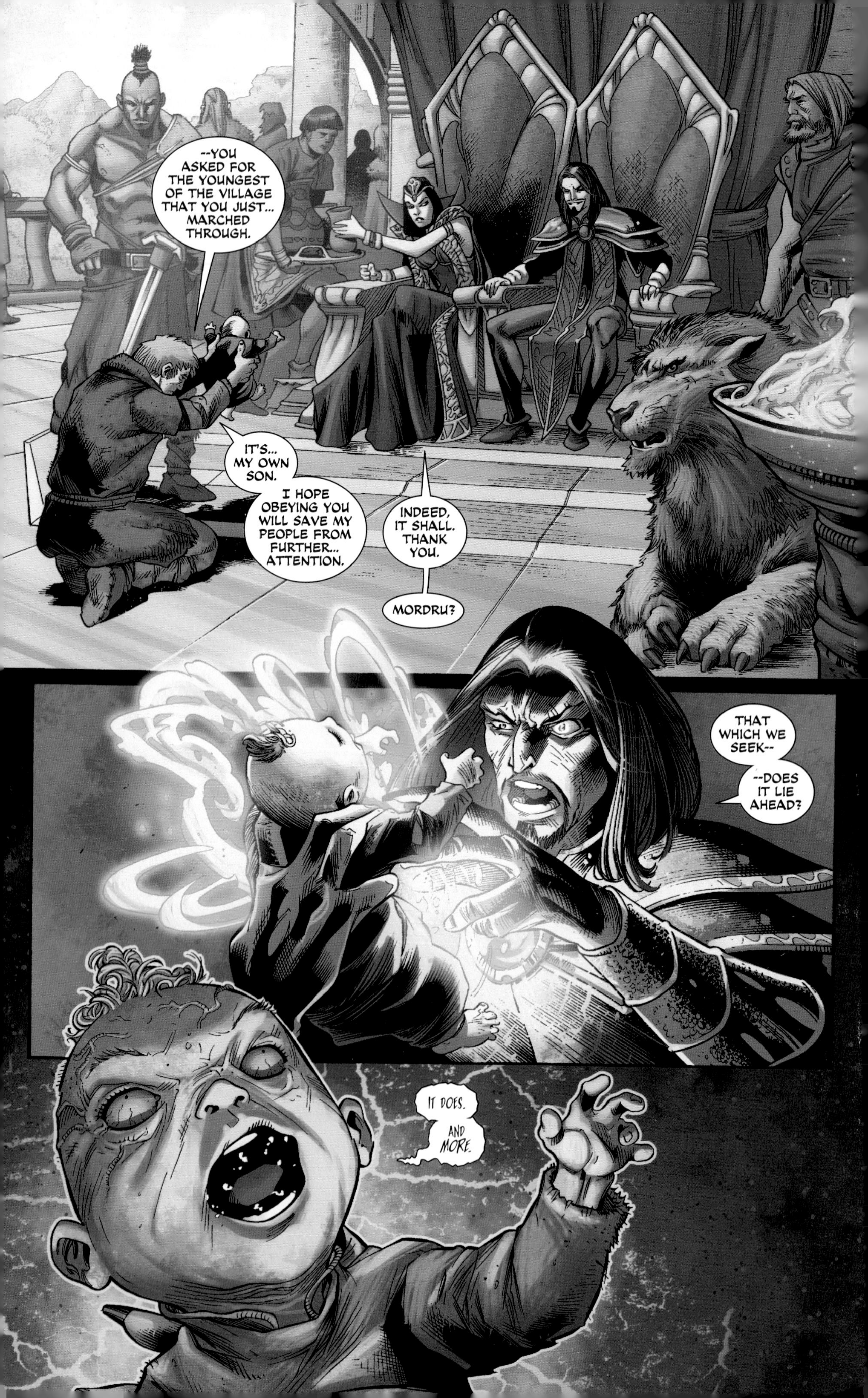
--YOU ASKED FOR THE YOUNGEST OF THE VILLAGE THAT YOU JUST... MARCHED THROUGH.
IT'S... MY OWN SON.
I HOPE OBEYING YOU WILL SAVE MY PEOPLE FROM FURTHER... ATTENTION.
INDEED, IT SHALL. THANK YOU.
MORDRU?
THAT WHICH WE SEEK--
--DOES IT LIE AHEAD?
IT DOES.
AND MORE.

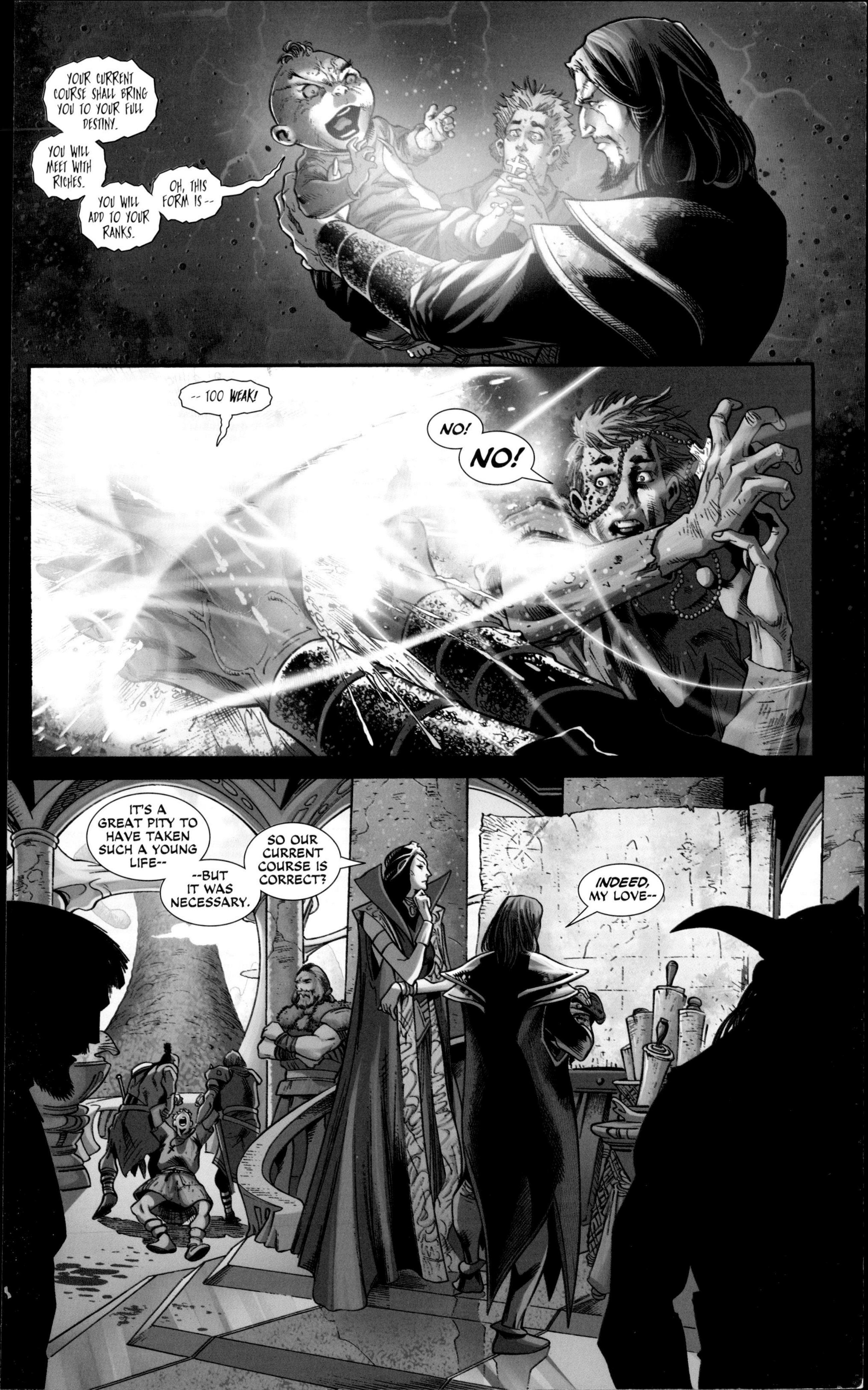
YOUR CURRENT COURSE SHALL BRING YOU TO YOUR FULL DESTINY.
YOU WILL MEET WITH RICHES.
YOU WILL ADD TO YOUR RANKS.
OH, THIS FORM IS--
--TOO WEAK!
NO!
NO!
IT'S A GREAT PITY TO HAVE TAKEN SUCH A YOUNG LIFE--
--BUT IT WAS NECESSARY.
SO OUR CURRENT COURSE IS CORRECT?
INDEED, MY LOVE--

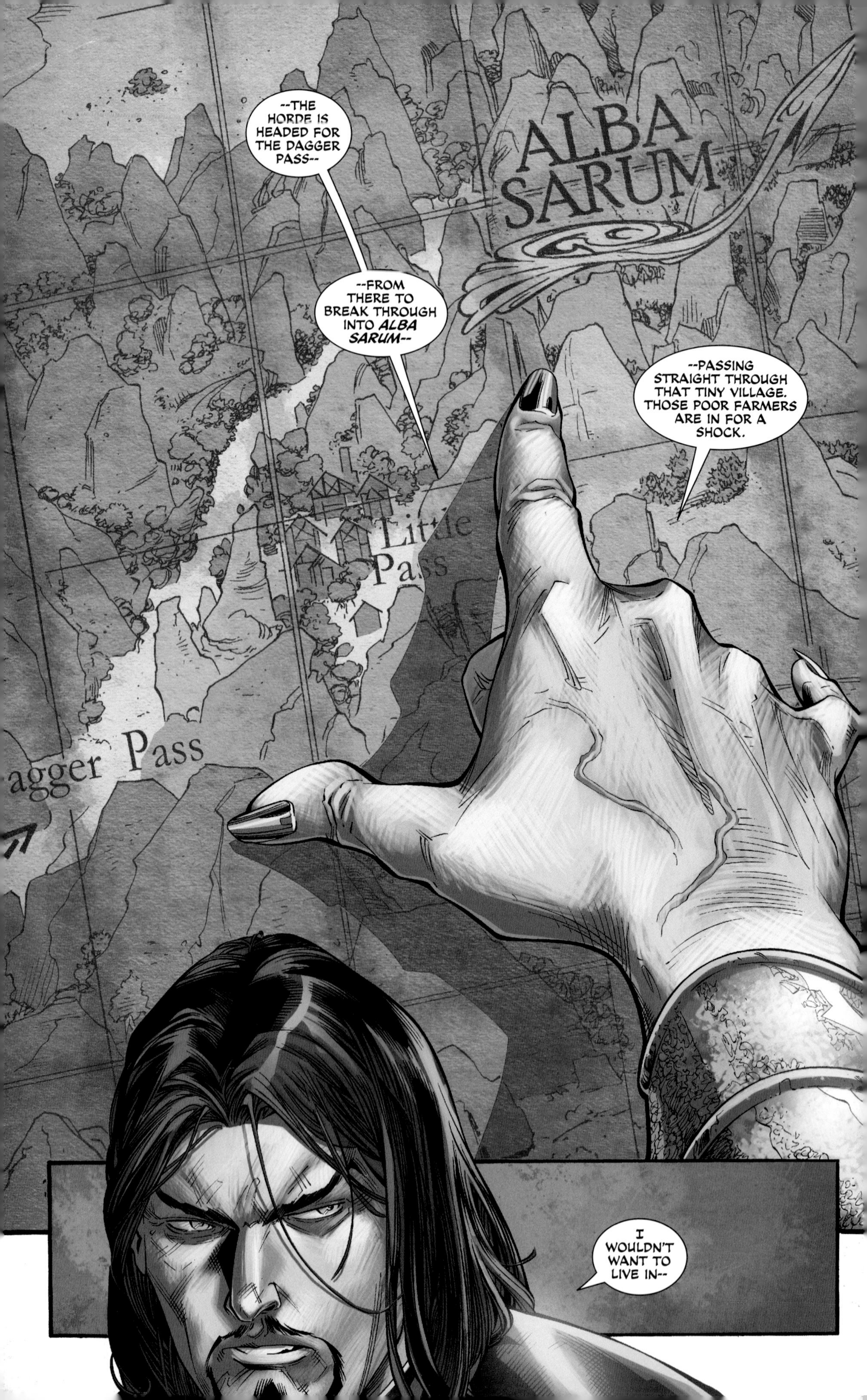

--THE HORDE IS HEADED FOR THE DAGGER PASS--
ALBA SARUM
--FROM THERE TO BREAK THROUGH INTO *ALBA SARUM*--
--PASSING STRAIGHT THROUGH THAT TINY VILLAGE. THOSE POOR FARMERS ARE IN FOR A SHOCK.
Little Pass
agger Pass
I WOULDN'T WANT TO LIVE IN--

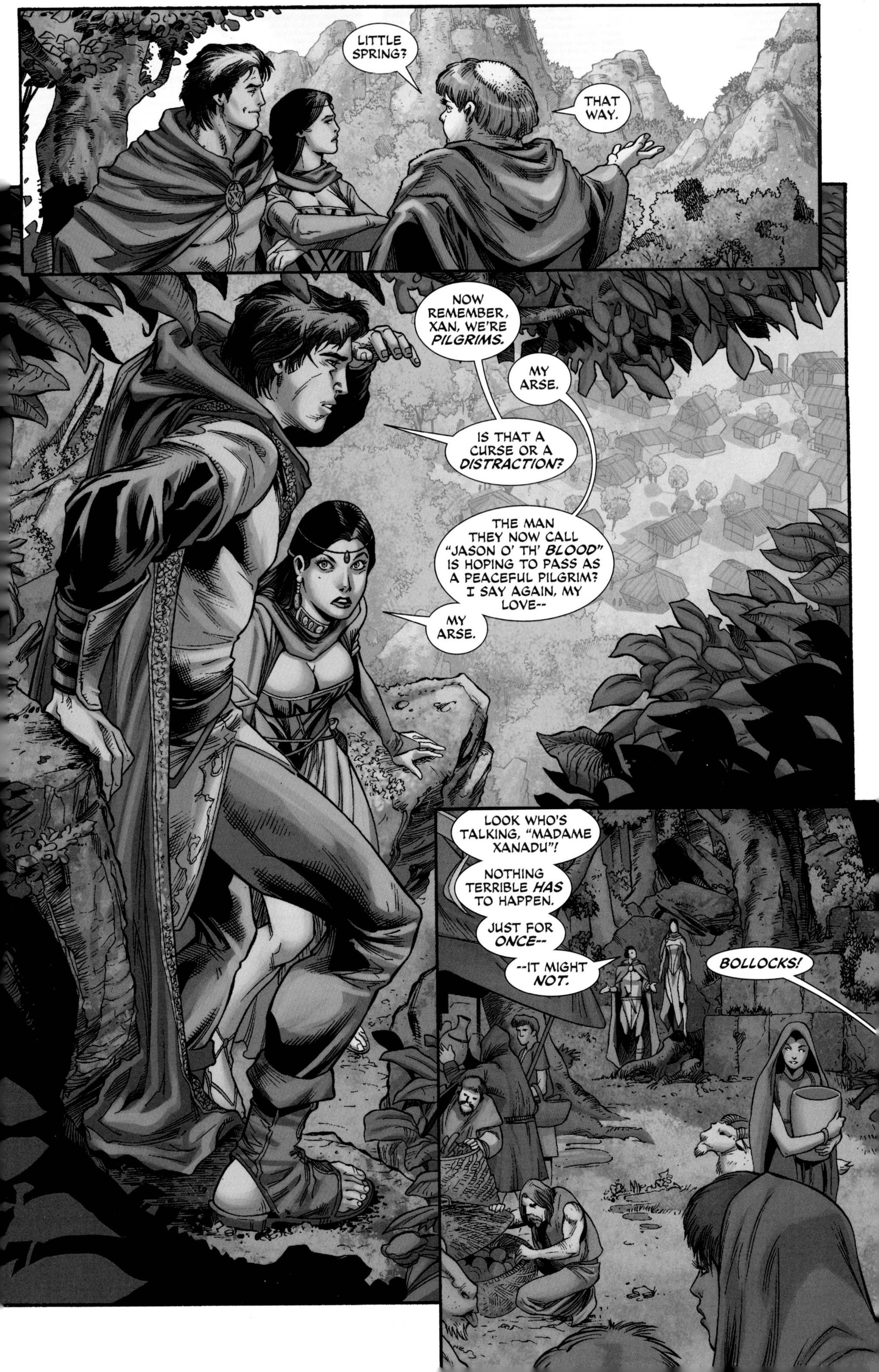
LITTLE SPRING?
THAT WAY.
NOW REMEMBER, XAN, WE'RE *PILGRIMS.*
MY ARSE.
IS THAT A CURSE OR A *DISTRACTION?*
THE MAN THEY NOW CALL "JASON O' TH' *BLOOD*" IS HOPING TO PASS AS A PEACEFUL PILGRIM? I SAY AGAIN, MY LOVE--
MY ARSE.
LOOK WHO'S TALKING, "MADAME XANADU"!
NOTHING TERRIBLE *HAS* TO HAPPEN.
JUST FOR *ONCE--*
--IT MIGHT *NOT.*
BOLLOCKS!

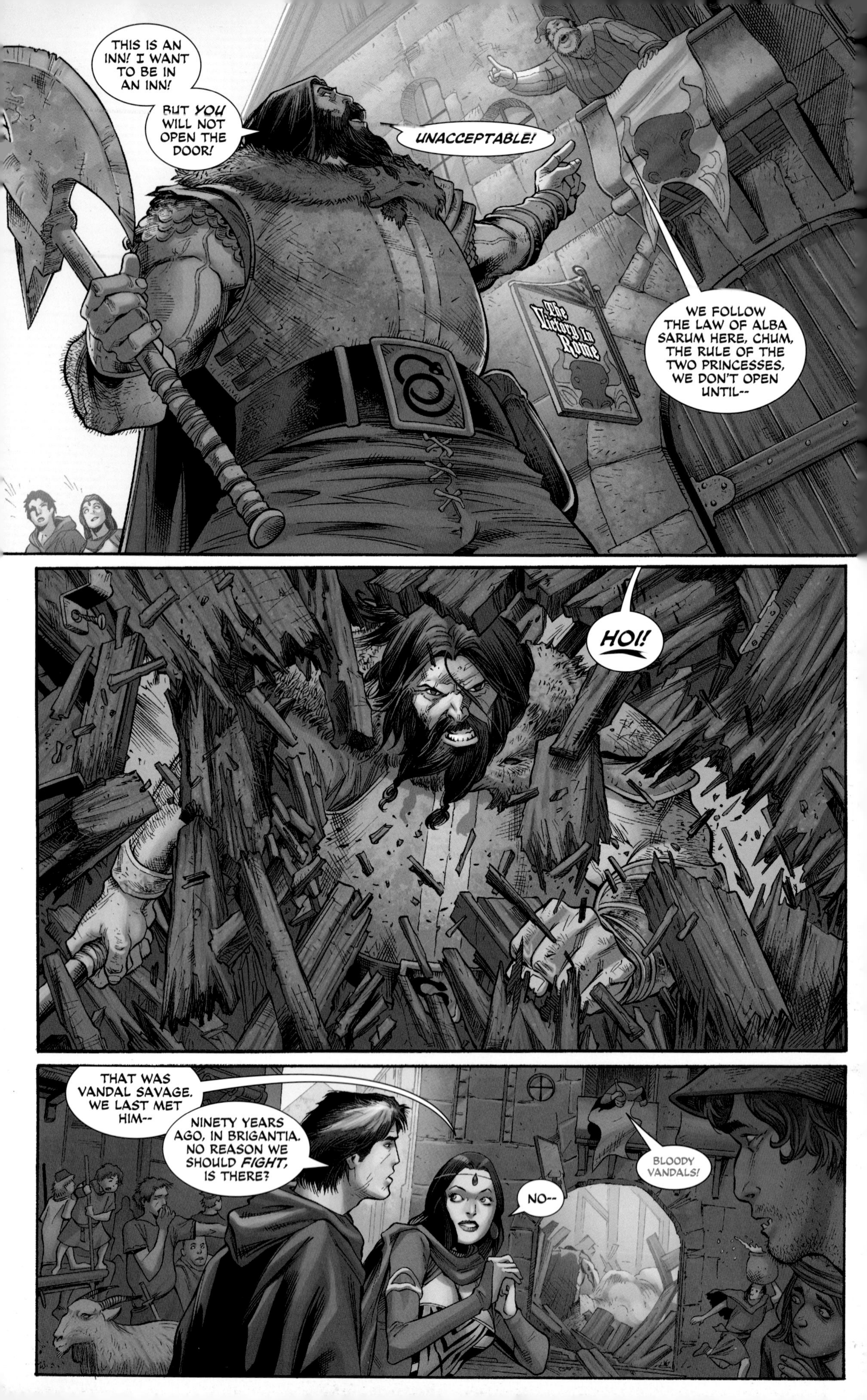
THIS IS AN INN! I WANT TO BE IN AN INN!
BUT YOU WILL NOT OPEN THE DOOR!
UNACCEPTABLE!
WE FOLLOW THE LAW OF ALBA SARUM HERE, CHUM, THE RULE OF THE TWO PRINCESSES, WE DON'T OPEN UNTIL--
The Victory In Rome
HOI!
THAT WAS VANDAL SAVAGE. WE LAST MET HIM--
NINETY YEARS AGO, IN BRIGANTIA. NO REASON WE SHOULD FIGHT, IS THERE?
NO--
BLOODY VANDALS!

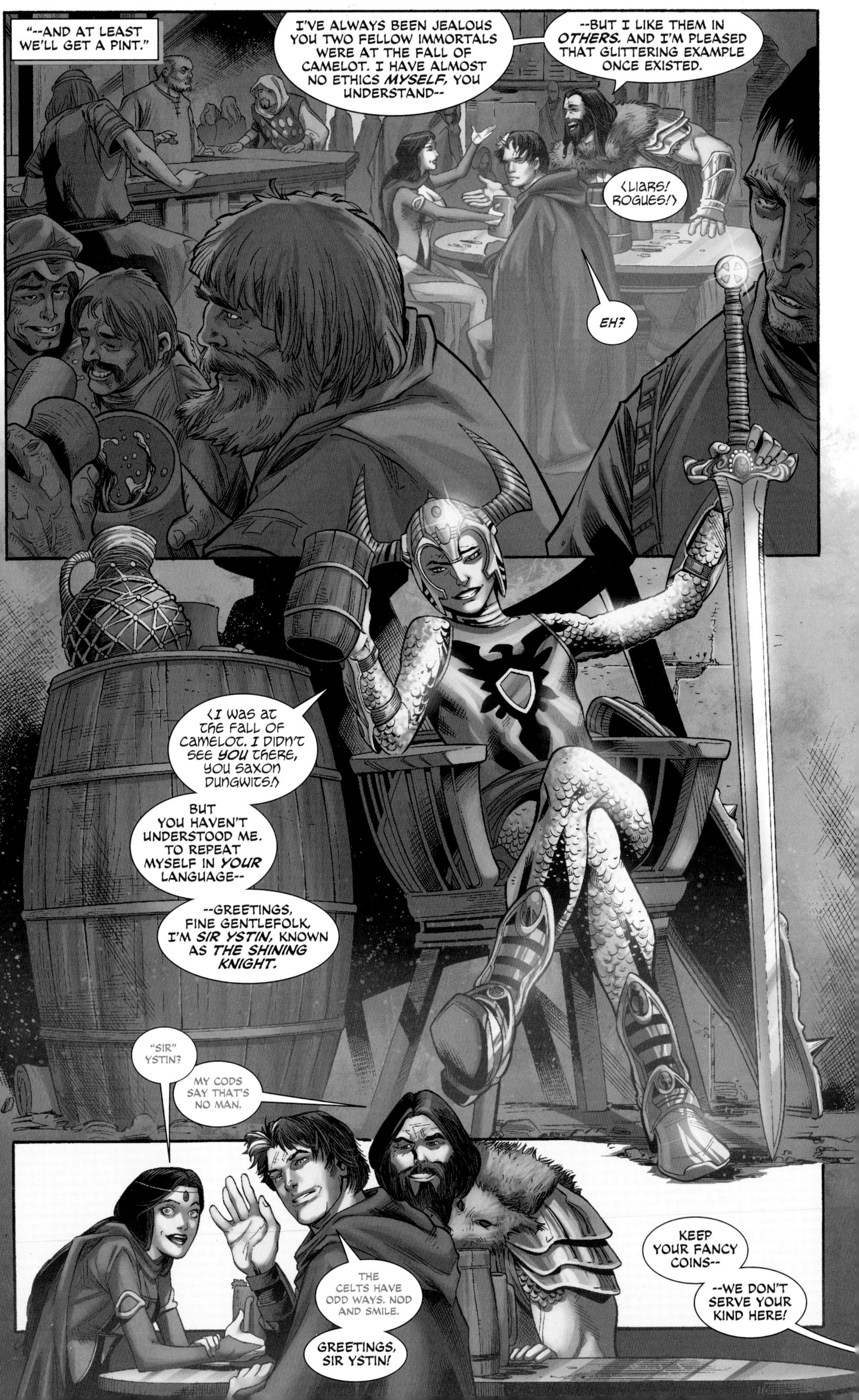
"--AND AT LEAST WE'LL GET A PINT."
I'VE ALWAYS BEEN JEALOUS YOU TWO FELLOW IMMORTALS WERE AT THE FALL OF CAMELOT. I HAVE ALMOST NO ETHICS MYSELF, YOU UNDERSTAND--
--BUT I LIKE THEM IN OTHERS. AND I'M PLEASED THAT GLITTERING EXAMPLE ONCE EXISTED.
‹LIARS! ROGUES!›
EH?
‹I WAS AT THE FALL OF CAMELOT. I DIDN'T SEE YOU THERE, YOU SAXON DUNGWITS!›
BUT YOU HAVEN'T UNDERSTOOD ME. TO REPEAT MYSELF IN YOUR LANGUAGE--
--GREETINGS, FINE GENTLEFOLK. I'M SIR YSTIN, KNOWN AS THE SHINING KNIGHT.
"SIR" YSTIN?
MY CODS SAY THAT'S NO MAN.
THE CELTS HAVE ODD WAYS. NOD AND SMILE.
GREETINGS, SIR YSTIN!
KEEP YOUR FANCY COINS--
--WE DON'T SERVE YOUR KIND HERE!

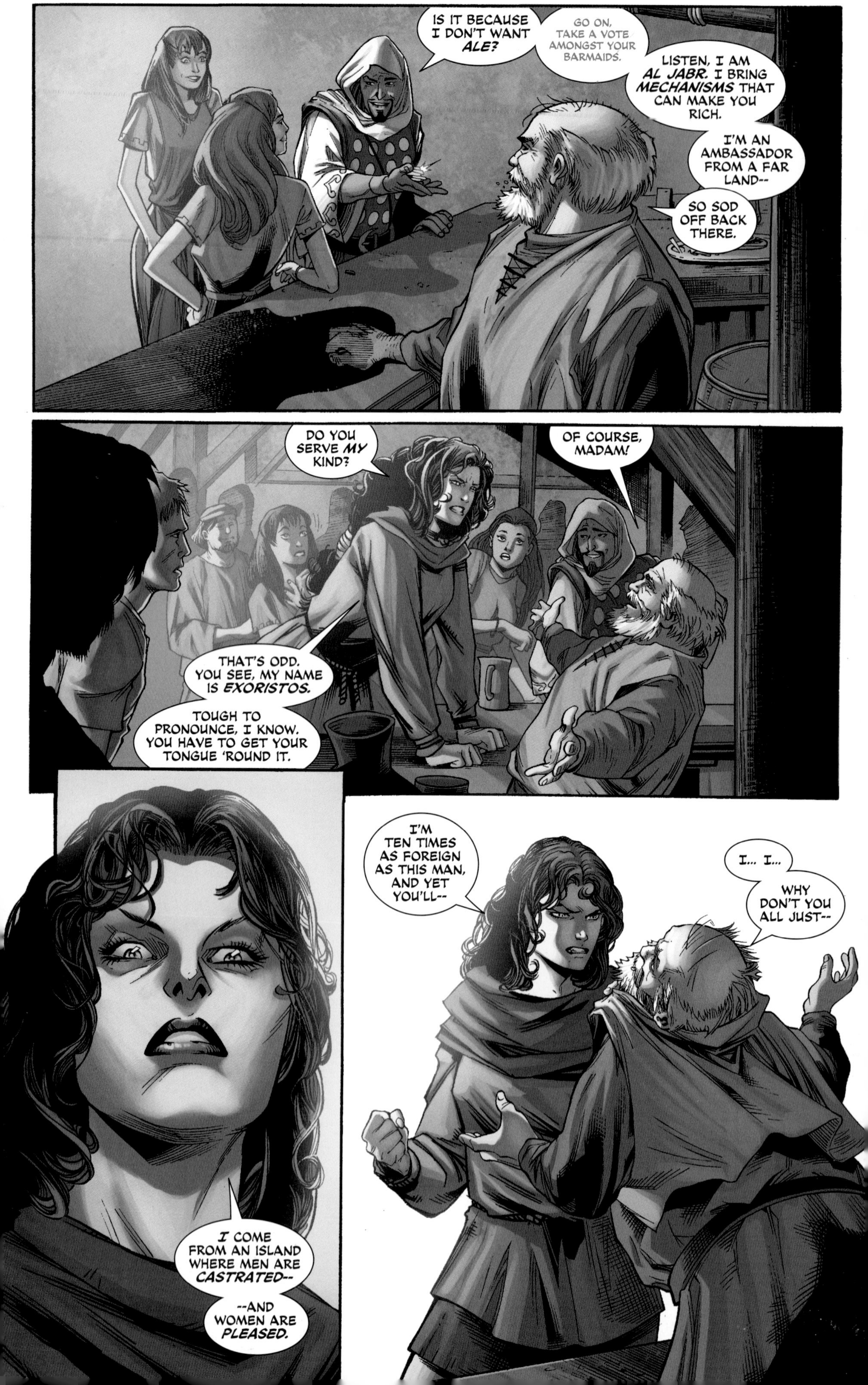
IS IT BECAUSE I DON'T WANT ALE?
GO ON, TAKE A VOTE AMONGST YOUR BARMAIDS.
LISTEN, I AM AL JABR. I BRING MECHANISMS THAT CAN MAKE YOU RICH.
I'M AN AMBASSADOR FROM A FAR LAND--
SO SOD OFF BACK THERE.
DO YOU SERVE MY KIND?
OF COURSE, MADAM!
THAT'S ODD. YOU SEE, MY NAME IS EXORISTOS.
TOUGH TO PRONOUNCE, I KNOW. YOU HAVE TO GET YOUR TONGUE 'ROUND IT.
I COME FROM AN ISLAND WHERE MEN ARE CASTRATED--
--AND WOMEN ARE PLEASED.
I'M TEN TIMES AS FOREIGN AS THIS MAN, AND YET YOU'LL--
I... I...
WHY DON'T YOU ALL JUST--

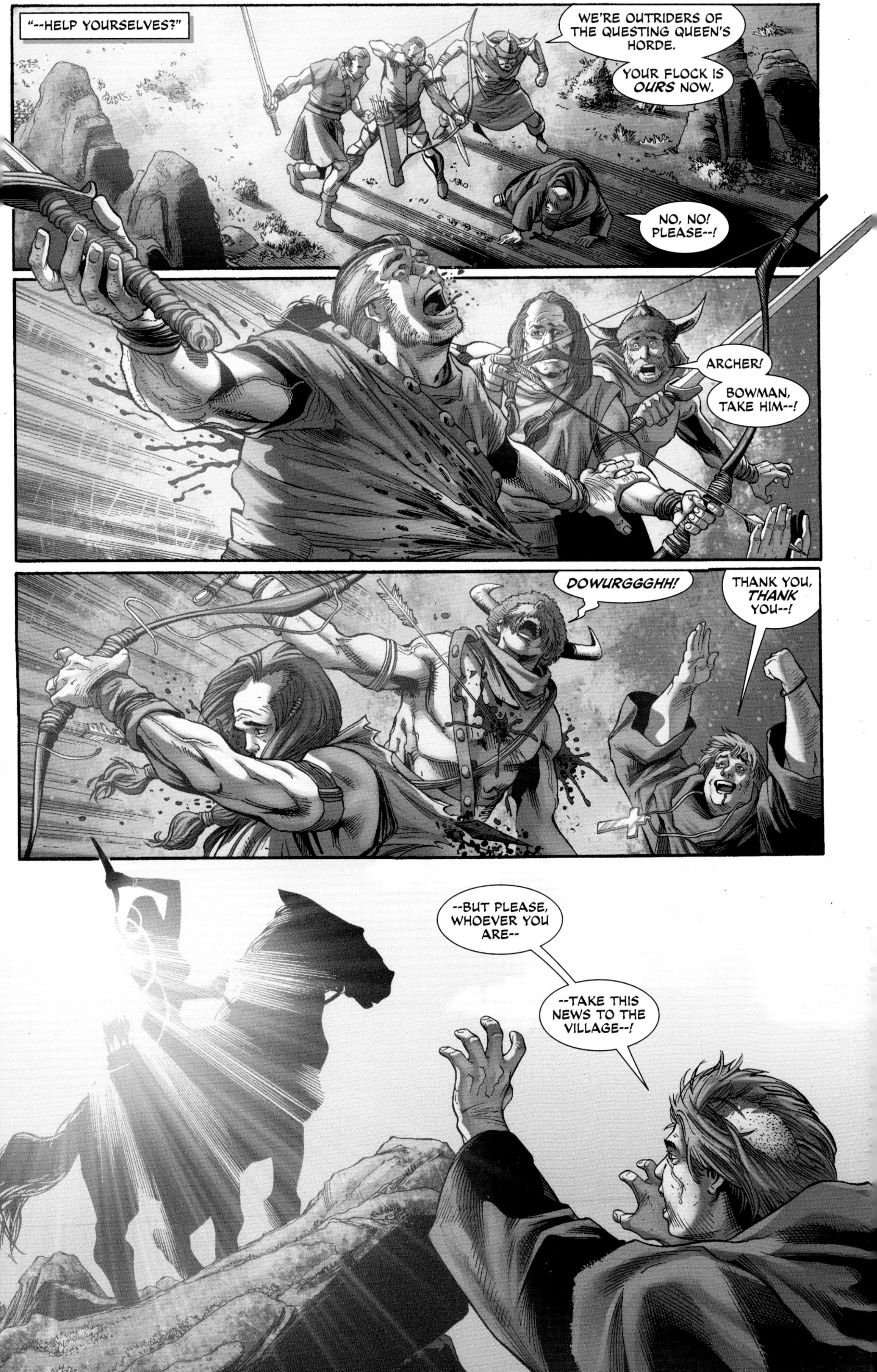
"--HELP YOURSELVES?"
WE'RE OUTRIDERS OF THE QUESTING QUEEN'S HORDE.
YOUR FLOCK IS OURS NOW.
NO, NO! PLEASE--!
ARCHER!
BOWMAN, TAKE HIM--!
DOWURGGGHH!
THANK YOU, THANK YOU--!
--BUT PLEASE, WHOEVER YOU ARE--
--TAKE THIS NEWS TO THE VILLAGE--!

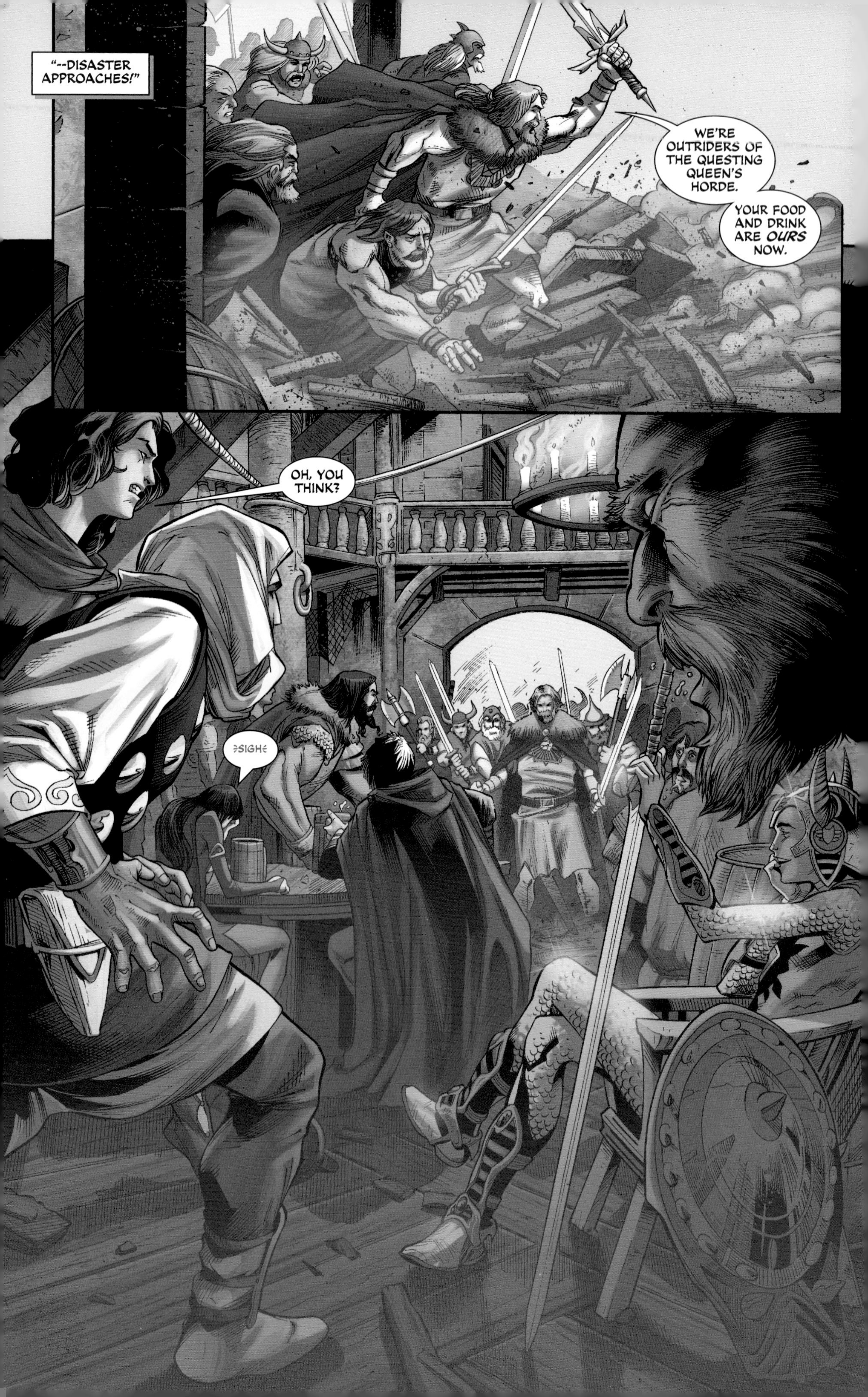
"--DISASTER APPROACHES!"
WE'RE OUTRIDERS OF THE QUESTING QUEEN'S HORDE.
YOUR FOOD AND DRINK ARE *OURS* NOW.
OH, YOU THINK?
SIGH

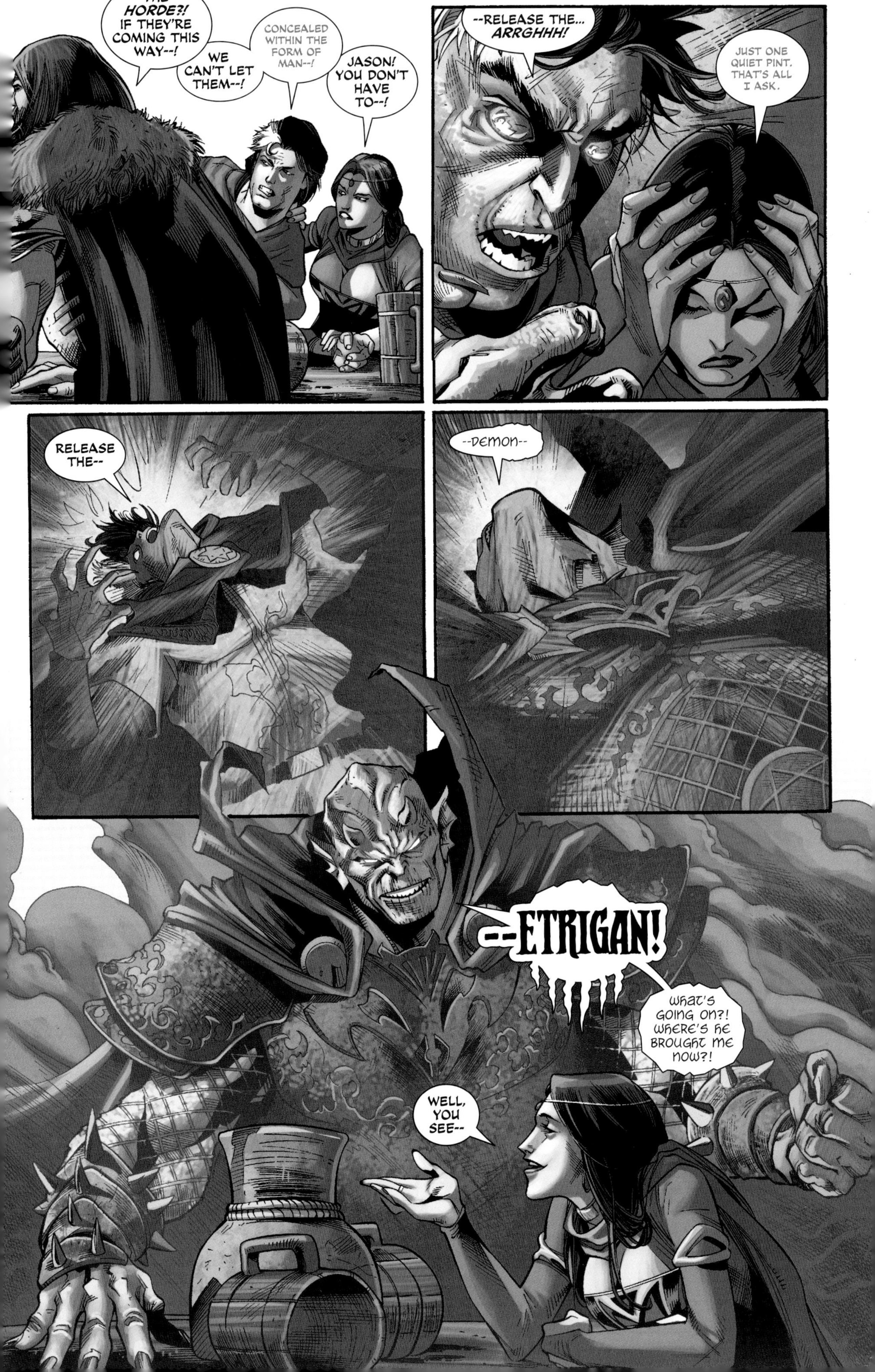
THE *HORDE?!* IF THEY'RE COMING THIS WAY--!
WE CAN'T LET THEM--!
CONCEALED WITHIN THE FORM OF MAN--!
JASON! YOU DON'T HAVE TO--!
--RELEASE THE... *ARRGHHH!*
JUST ONE QUIET PINT. THAT'S ALL I ASK.
RELEASE THE--
--DEMON--
--ETRIGAN!
WHAT'S GOING ON?! WHERE'S HE BROUGHT ME NOW?!
WELL, YOU SEE--

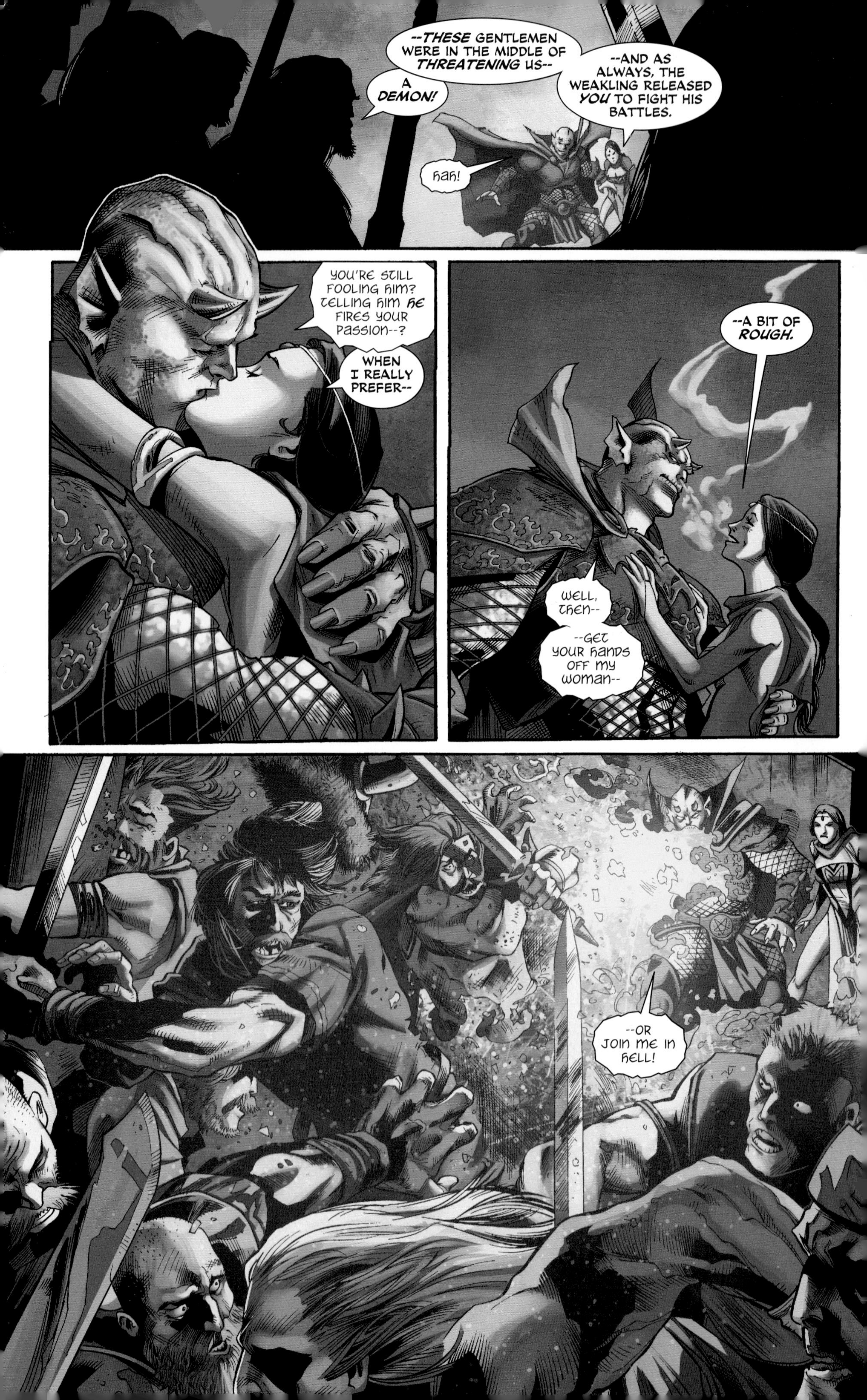
A DEMON!
--THESE GENTLEMEN WERE IN THE MIDDLE OF THREATENING US--
--AND AS ALWAYS, THE WEAKLING RELEASED YOU TO FIGHT HIS BATTLES.
HAH!
YOU'RE STILL FOOLING HIM? TELLING HIM HE FIRES YOUR PASSION--?
WHEN I REALLY PREFER--
--A BIT OF ROUGH.
WELL, THEN--
--GET YOUR HANDS OFF MY WOMAN--
--OR JOIN ME IN HELL!

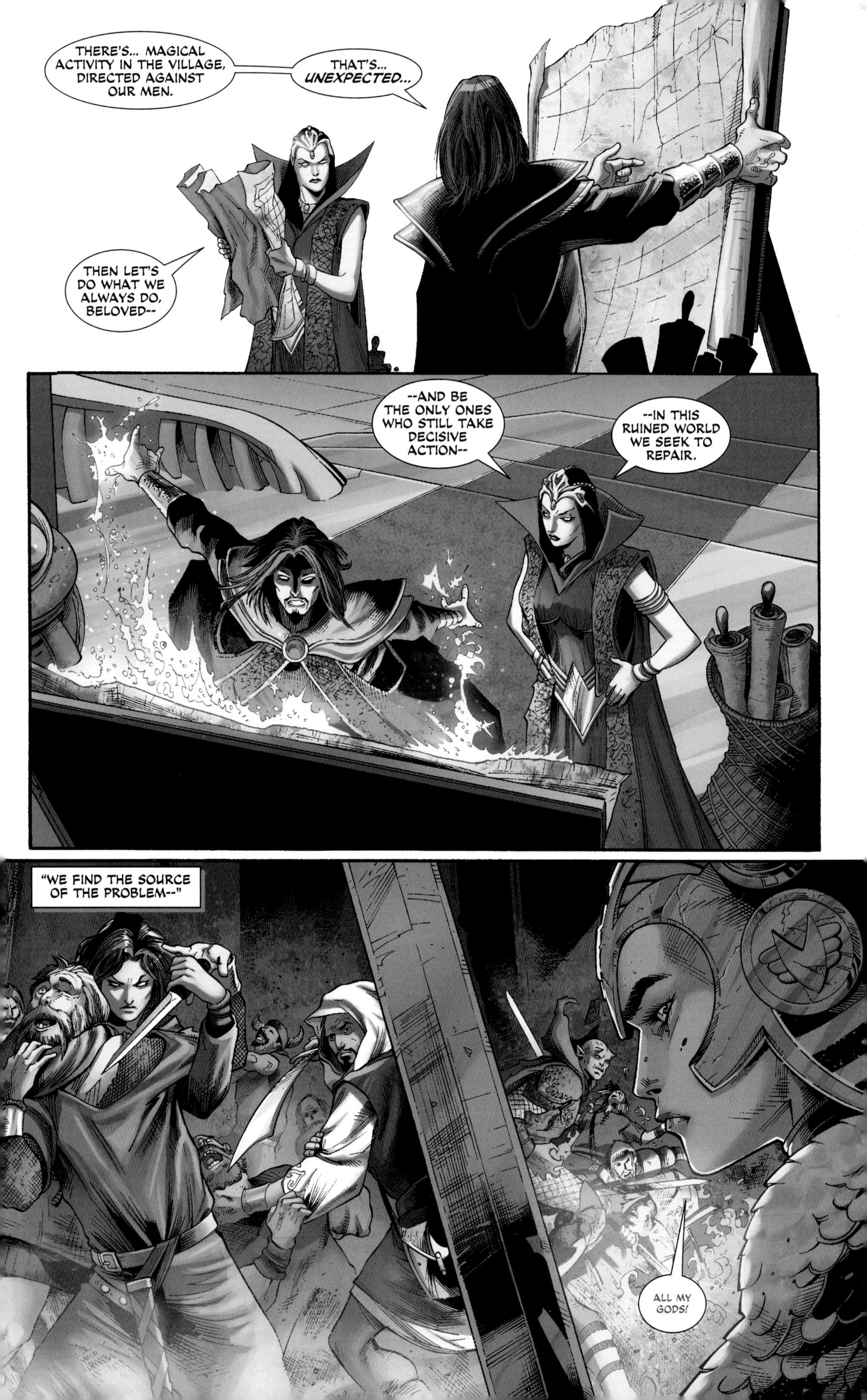
THERE'S... MAGICAL ACTIVITY IN THE VILLAGE, DIRECTED AGAINST OUR MEN.
THAT'S... UNEXPECTED...
THEN LET'S DO WHAT WE ALWAYS DO, BELOVED--
--AND BE THE ONLY ONES WHO STILL TAKE DECISIVE ACTION--
--IN THIS RUINED WORLD WE SEEK TO REPAIR.
"WE FIND THE SOURCE OF THE PROBLEM--"
ALL MY GODS!

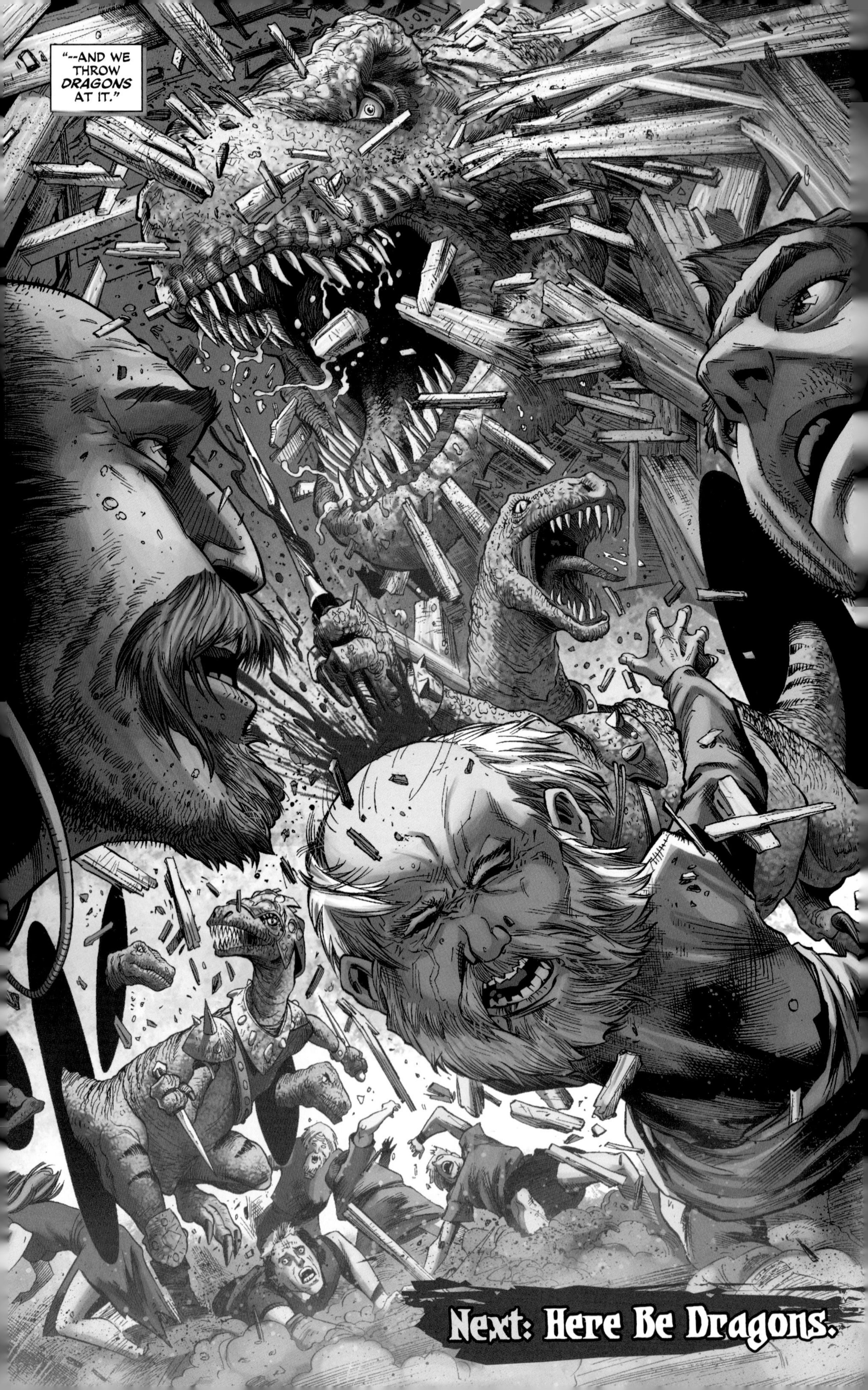
"--AND WE THROW *DRAGONS* AT IT."
Next: Here Be Dragons.

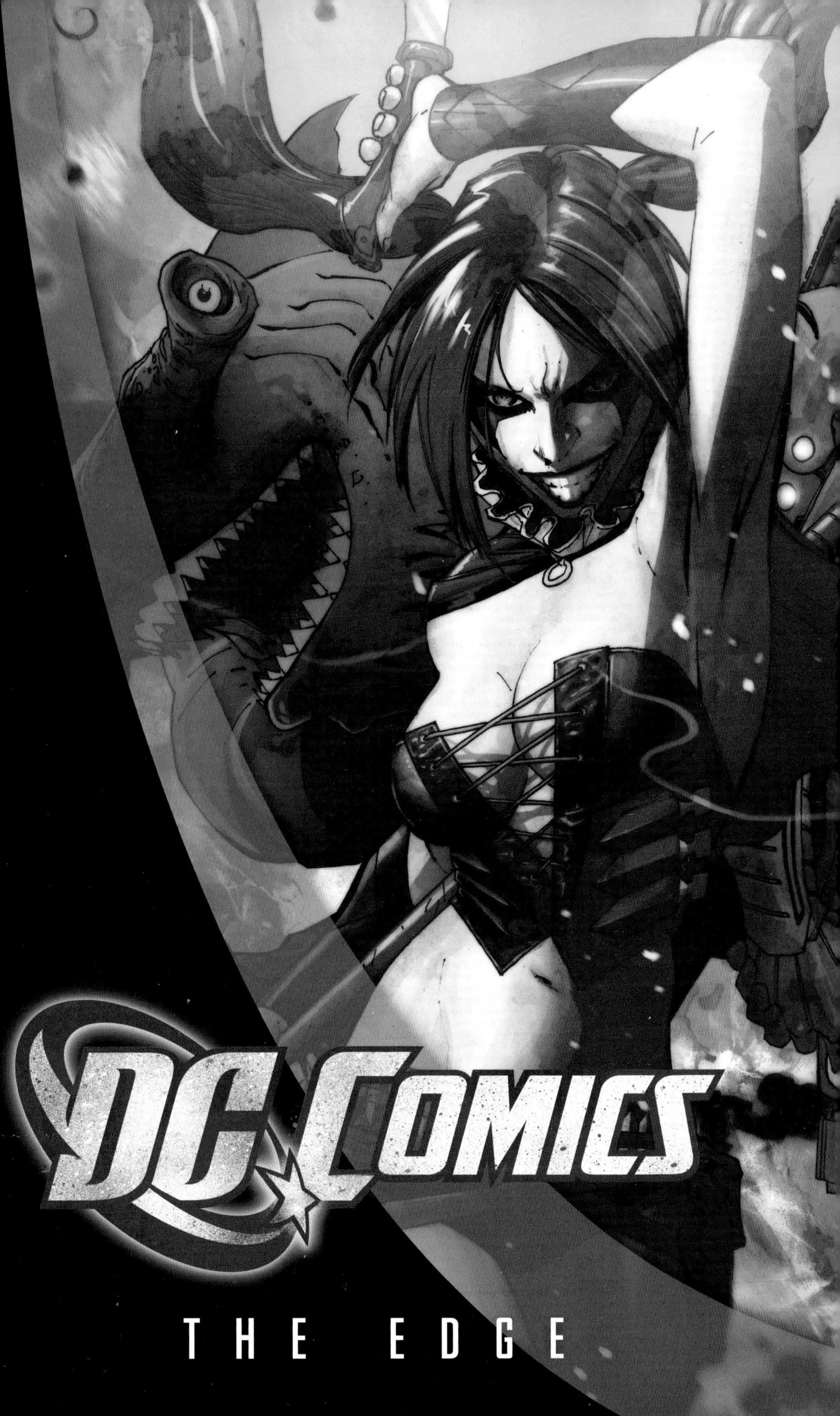

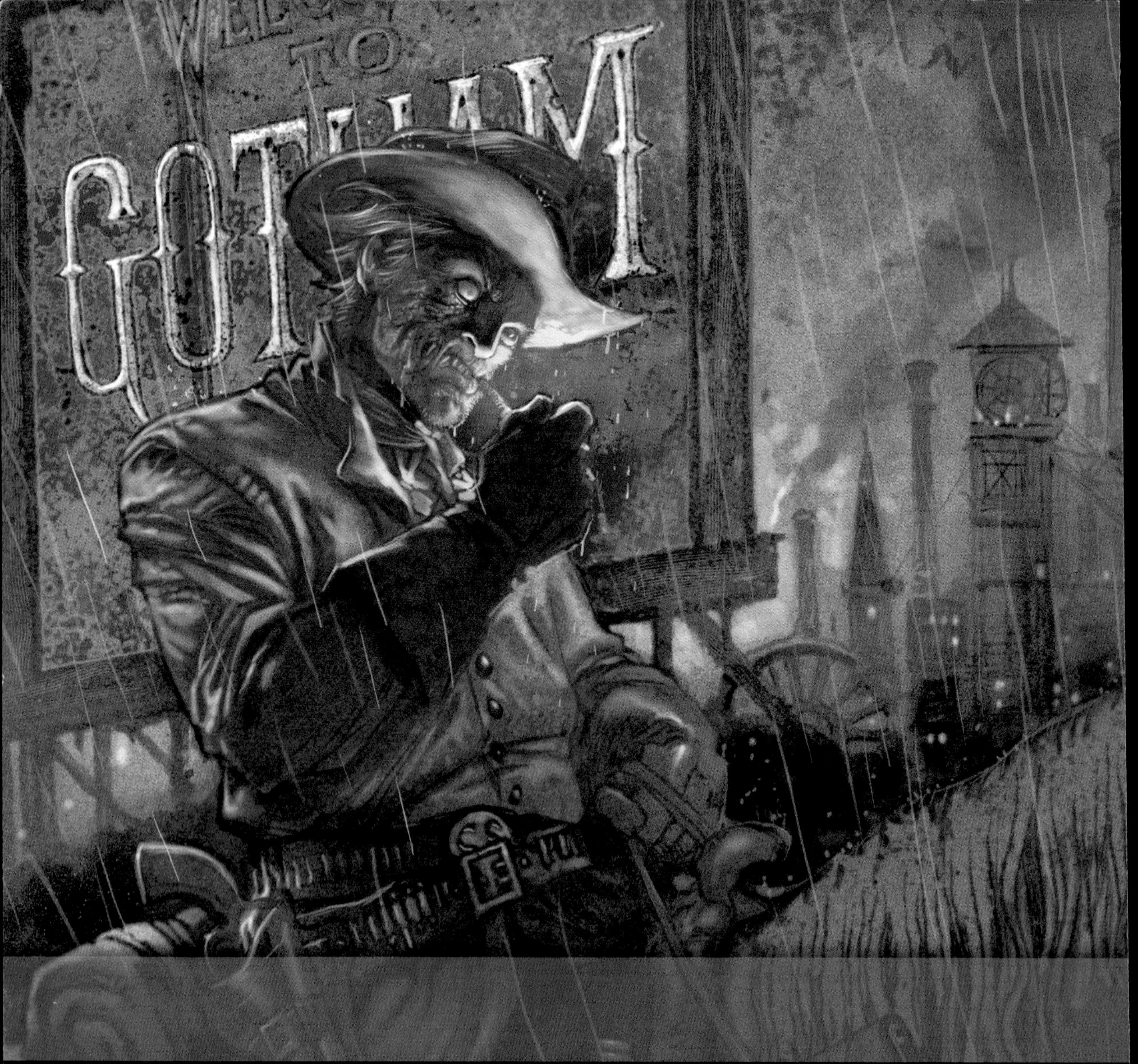
GOTHAM

STORMWATCH #1 Paul Cornell & Miguel Sepulveda

GRIFTER #1 Nathan Edmondson, Cafu & Jason Gorder

VOODOO #1 Ron Marz & Sami Basri

DEATHSTROKE #1 Kyle Higgins, Joe Bennett & Art Thibert

SUICIDE SQUAD #1 Adam Glass, Federico Dallocchio & Ransom Getty

O.M.A.C. #1 Dan DiDio, Keith Giffen & Scott Koblish

ALL-STAR WESTERN #1 Justin Gray, Jimmy Palmiotti & Moritat

BLACKHAWKS #1 Mike Costa, Graham Nolan & Ken Lashley

MEN OF WAR #1 Ivan Brandon, Tom Derenick, Jonathan Vankin & Phil Winslade

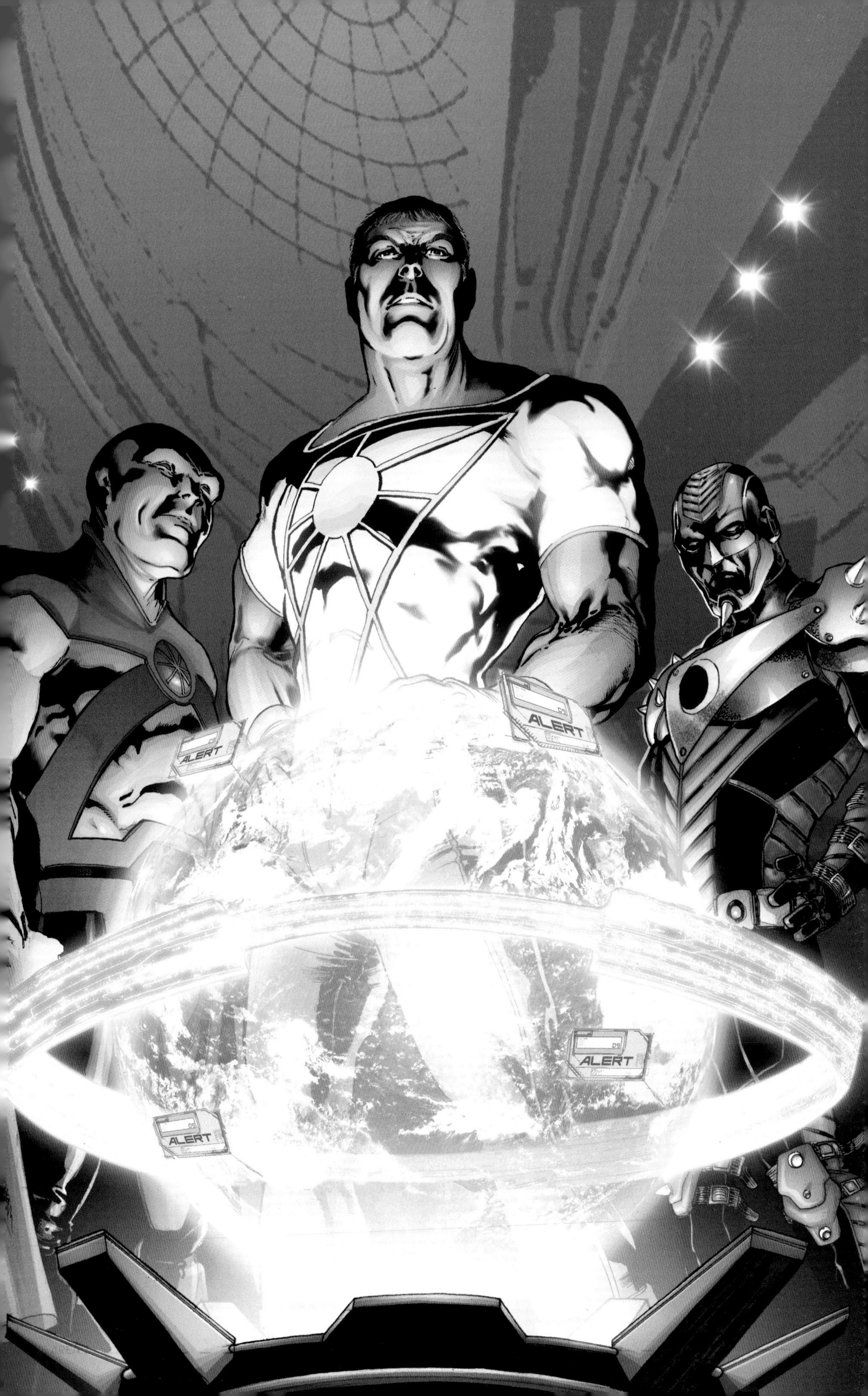
ALERT
ALERT
ALERT
ALERT

STORMWATCH

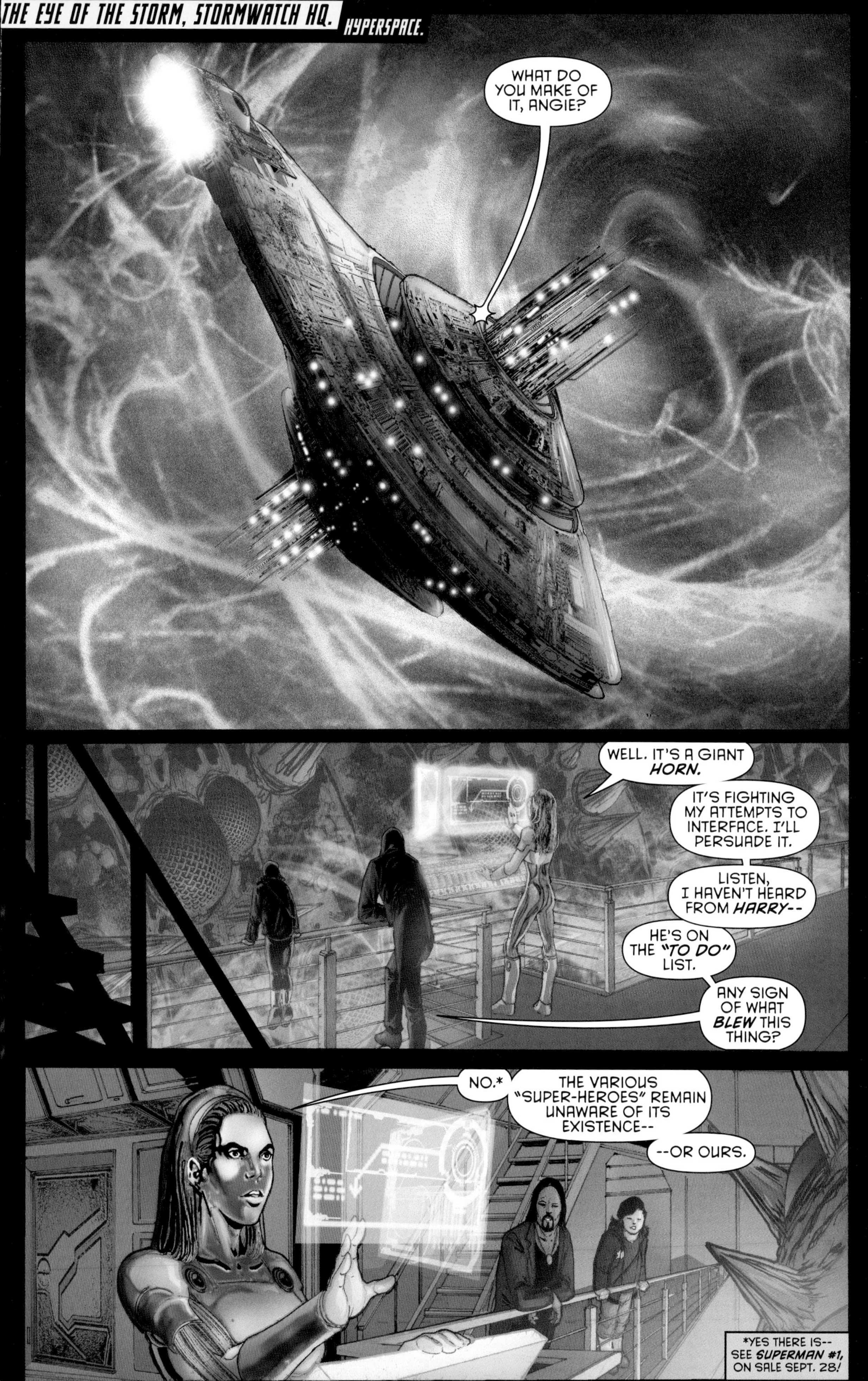

THE EYE OF THE STORM, STORMWATCH HQ.
HYPERSPACE.
WHAT DO YOU MAKE OF IT, ANGIE?
WELL. IT'S A GIANT HORN.
IT'S FIGHTING MY ATTEMPTS TO INTERFACE. I'LL PERSUADE IT.
LISTEN, I HAVEN'T HEARD FROM HARRY--
HE'S ON THE "TO DO" LIST.
ANY SIGN OF WHAT BLEW THIS THING?
NO.*
THE VARIOUS "SUPER-HEROES" REMAIN UNAWARE OF ITS EXISTENCE--
--OR OURS.
*YES THERE IS-- SEE SUPERMAN #1, ON SALE SEPT. 28!

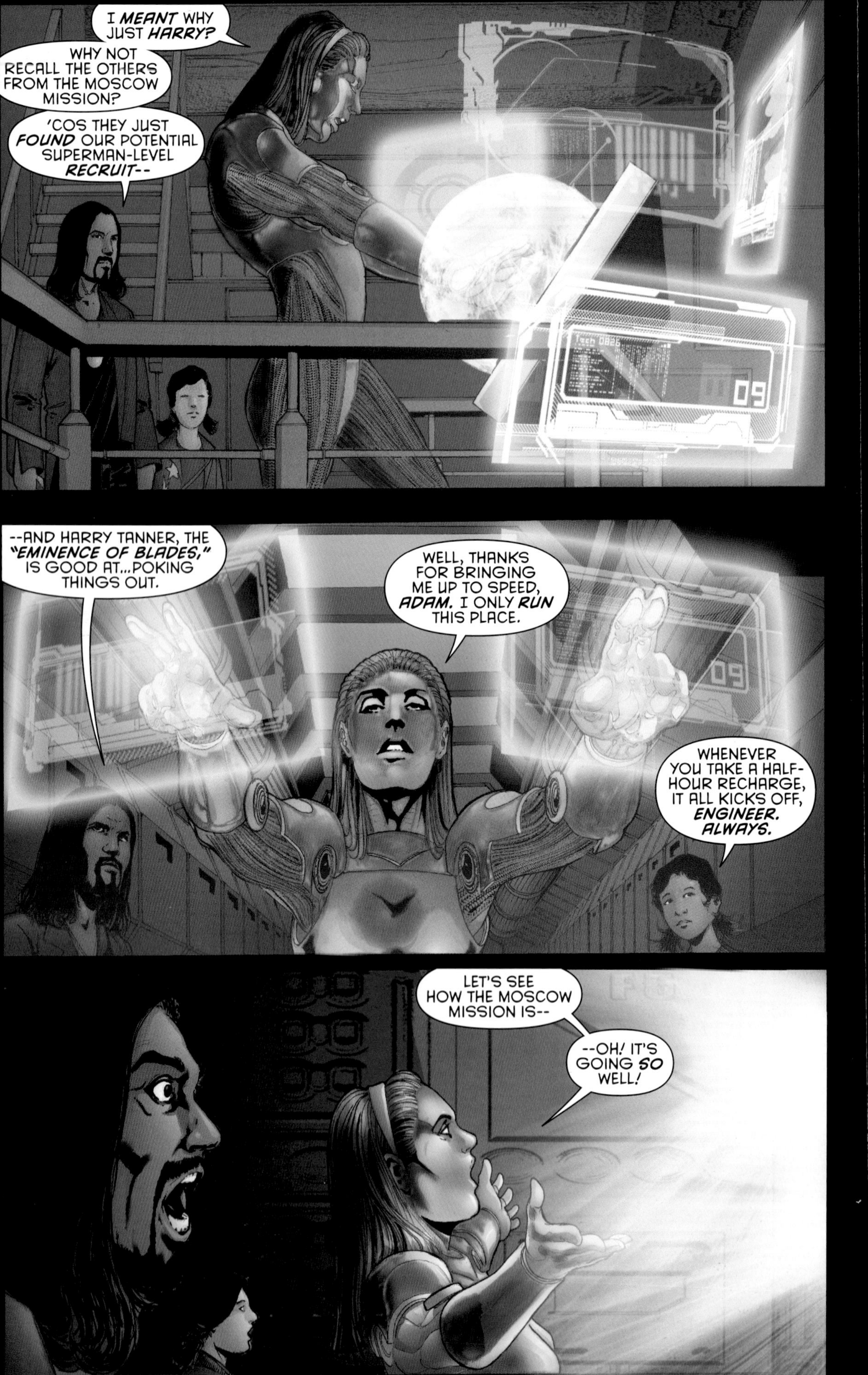
I MEANT WHY JUST HARRY?
WHY NOT RECALL THE OTHERS FROM THE MOSCOW MISSION?
'COS THEY JUST FOUND OUR POTENTIAL SUPERMAN-LEVEL RECRUIT--
--AND HARRY TANNER, THE "EMINENCE OF BLADES," IS GOOD AT...POKING THINGS OUT.
WELL, THANKS FOR BRINGING ME UP TO SPEED, ADAM. I ONLY RUN THIS PLACE.
WHENEVER YOU TAKE A HALF-HOUR RECHARGE, IT ALL KICKS OFF, ENGINEER. ALWAYS.
LET'S SEE HOW THE MOSCOW MISSION IS--
--OH! IT'S GOING SO WELL!

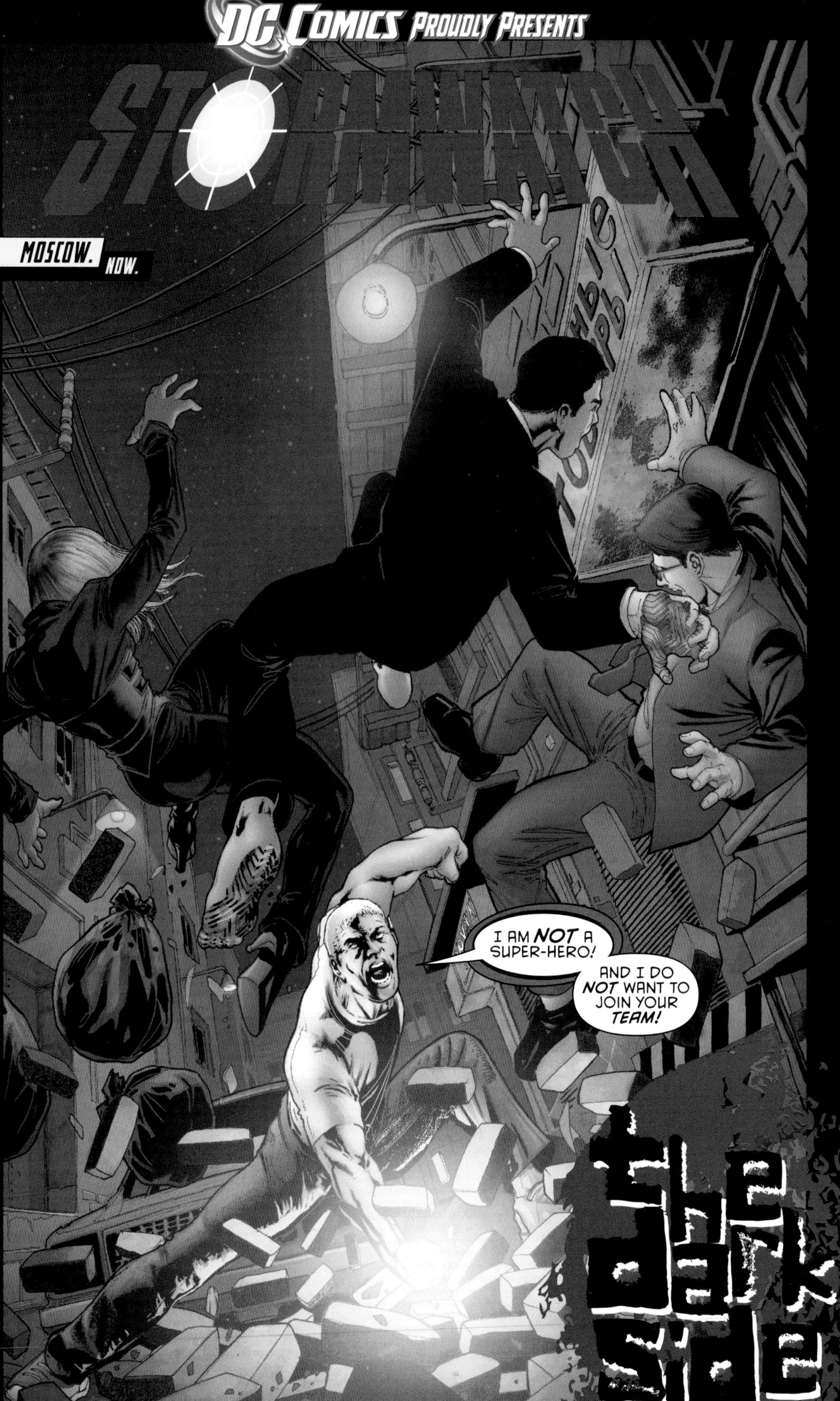
DC COMICS PROUDLY PRESENTS
STORMWATCH
MOSCOW. NOW.
I AM NOT A SUPER-HERO!
AND I DO NOT WANT TO JOIN YOUR TEAM!
the dark side
PART ONE

WRITER: PAUL CORNELL • ARTIST: MIGUEL SEPULVEDA
COLORIST: ALLEN PASSALAQUA • LETTERER: ROB LEIGH • COVER: MIGUEL SEPULVEDA & NATHAN EYRING
ASSISTANT EDITOR: SEAN MACKIEWICZ • EDITOR: PAT MCCALLUM
STORMWATCH CREATED BY JIM LEE & BRANDON CHOI

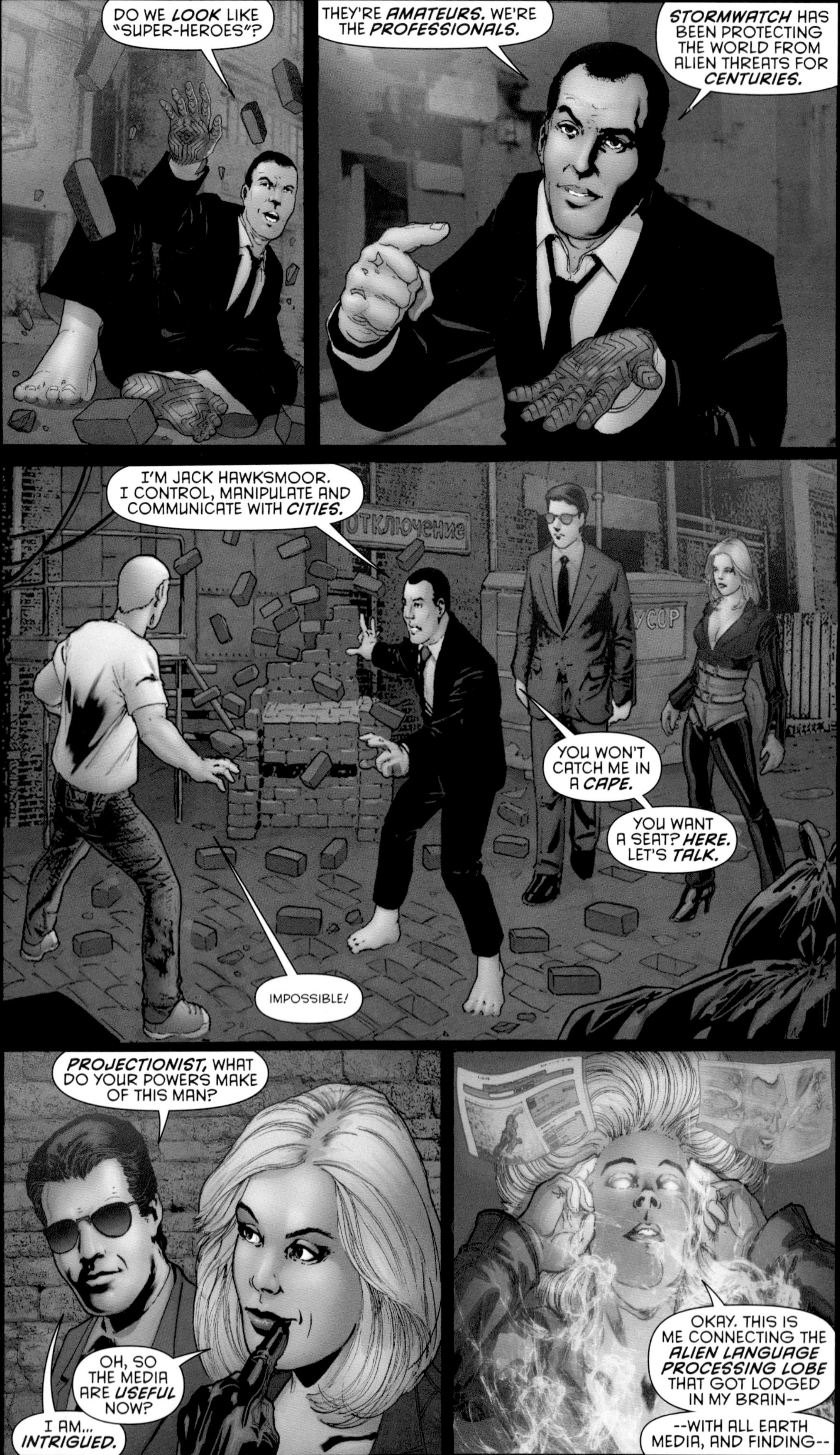
DO WE LOOK LIKE "SUPER-HEROES"?
THEY'RE AMATEURS. WE'RE THE PROFESSIONALS.
STORMWATCH HAS BEEN PROTECTING THE WORLD FROM ALIEN THREATS FOR CENTURIES.
I'M JACK HAWKSMOOR. I CONTROL, MANIPULATE AND COMMUNICATE WITH CITIES.
ОТКЛЮЧЕНИЕ
YOU WON'T CATCH ME IN A CAPE.
YOU WANT A SEAT? HERE. LET'S TALK.
IMPOSSIBLE!
PROJECTIONIST, WHAT DO YOUR POWERS MAKE OF THIS MAN?
OH, SO THE MEDIA ARE USEFUL NOW?
I AM... INTRIGUED.
OKAY. THIS IS ME CONNECTING THE ALIEN LANGUAGE PROCESSING LOBE THAT GOT LODGED IN MY BRAIN--
--WITH ALL EARTH MEDIA, AND FINDING--

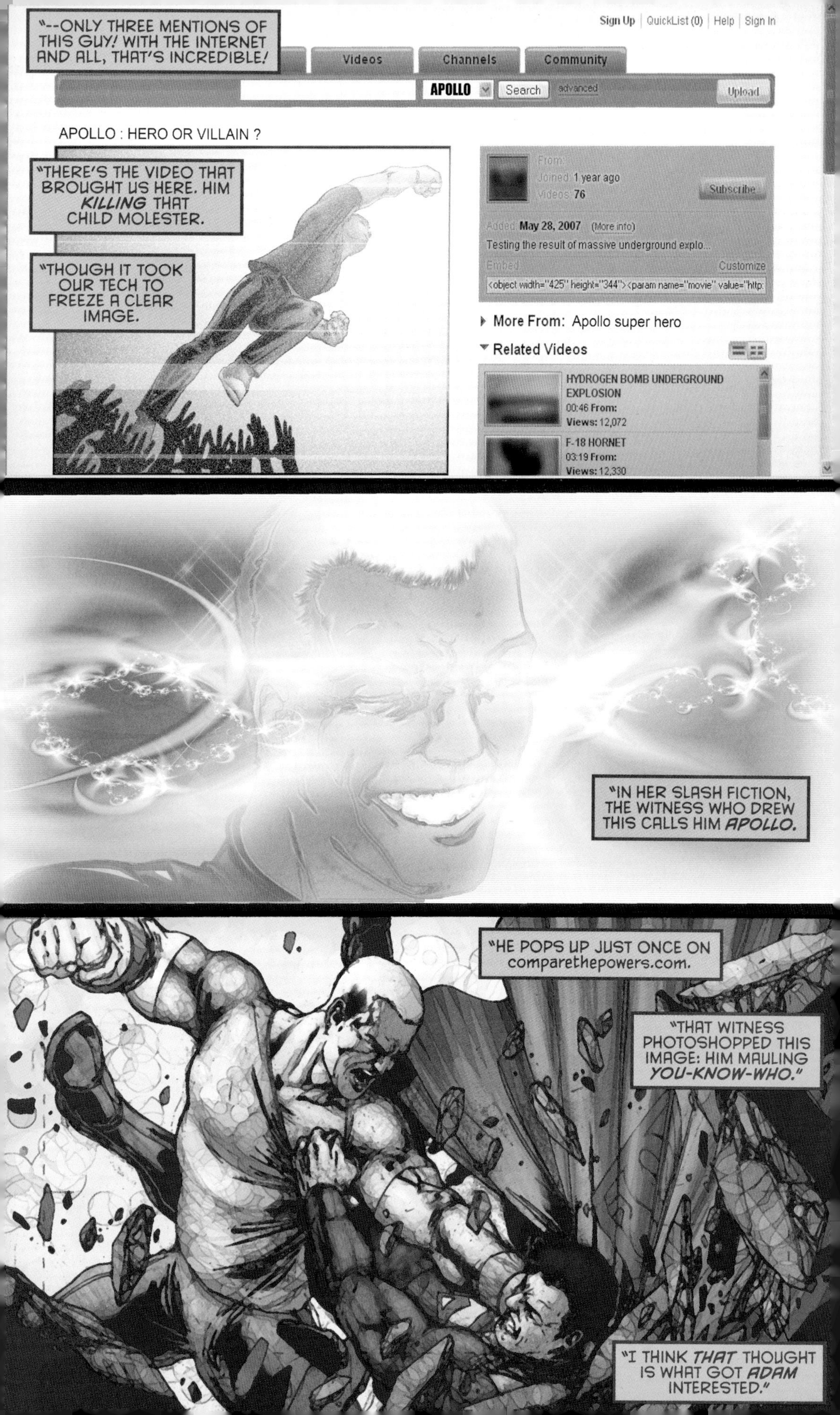
"--ONLY THREE MENTIONS OF THIS GUY! WITH THE INTERNET AND ALL, THAT'S INCREDIBLE!
Videos
Channels
Community
Sign Up | QuickList (0) | Help | Sign In
APOLLO
Search
advanced
Upload
APOLLO : HERO OR VILLAIN ?
"THERE'S THE VIDEO THAT BROUGHT US HERE. HIM KILLING THAT CHILD MOLESTER.
"THOUGH IT TOOK OUR TECH TO FREEZE A CLEAR IMAGE.
From:
Joined: 1 year ago
Videos: 76
Subscribe
Added: May 28, 2007 (More info)
Testing the result of massive underground explo...
Embed
Customize
<object width="425" height="344"><param name="movie" value="http:
More From: Apollo super hero
Related Videos
HYDROGEN BOMB UNDERGROUND EXPLOSION
00:46 From:
Views: 12,072
F-18 HORNET
03:19 From:
Views: 12,330
"IN HER SLASH FICTION, THE WITNESS WHO DREW THIS CALLS HIM APOLLO.
"HE POPS UP JUST ONCE ON comparethepowers.com.
"THAT WITNESS PHOTOSHOPPED THIS IMAGE: HIM MAULING YOU-KNOW-WHO."
"I THINK THAT THOUGHT IS WHAT GOT ADAM INTERESTED."

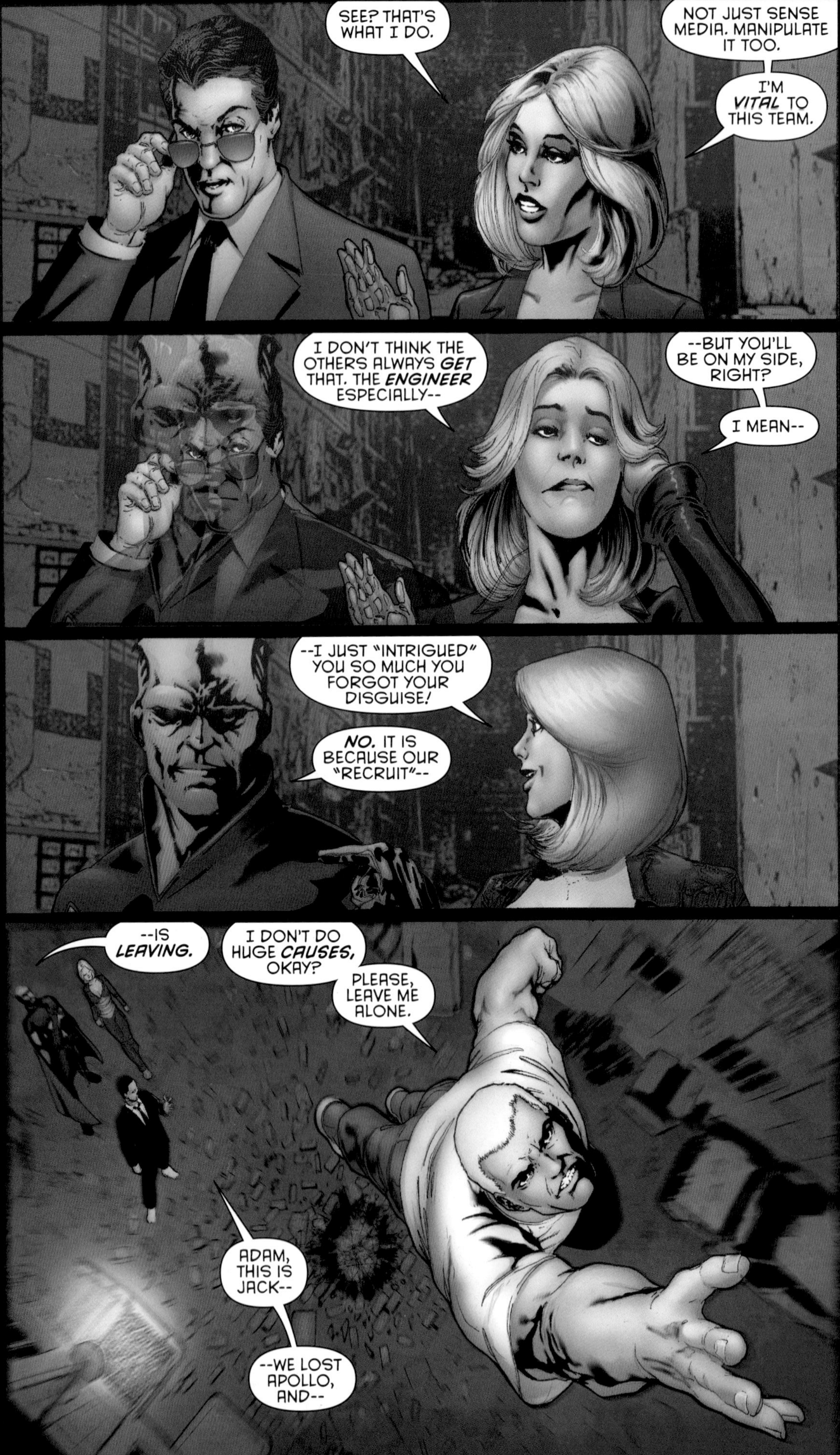
SEE? THAT'S WHAT I DO.
NOT JUST SENSE MEDIA. MANIPULATE IT TOO.
I'M *VITAL* TO THIS TEAM.
I DON'T THINK THE OTHERS ALWAYS *GET* THAT. THE *ENGINEER* ESPECIALLY--
--BUT YOU'LL BE ON MY SIDE, RIGHT?
I MEAN--
--I JUST "INTRIGUED" YOU SO MUCH YOU FORGOT YOUR DISGUISE!
NO. IT IS BECAUSE OUR "RECRUIT"--
--IS *LEAVING.*
I DON'T DO HUGE *CAUSES,* OKAY?
PLEASE, LEAVE ME ALONE.
ADAM, THIS IS JACK--
--WE LOST APOLLO, AND--

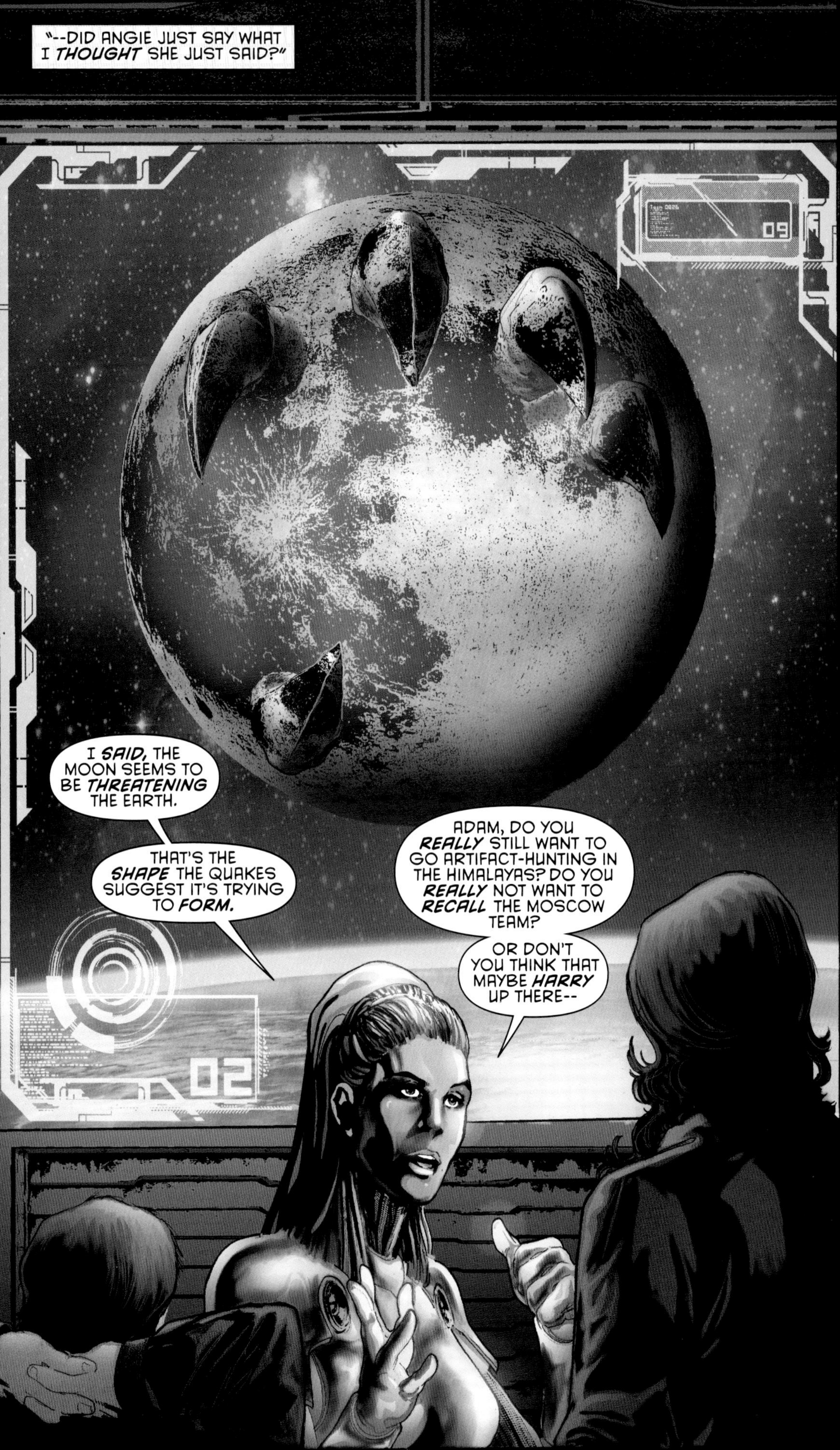
"--DID ANGIE JUST SAY WHAT I *THOUGHT* SHE JUST SAID?"
I *SAID,* THE MOON SEEMS TO BE *THREATENING* THE EARTH.
THAT'S THE *SHAPE* THE QUAKES SUGGEST IT'S TRYING TO *FORM.*
ADAM, DO YOU *REALLY* STILL WANT TO GO ARTIFACT-HUNTING IN THE HIMALAYAS? DO YOU *REALLY* NOT WANT TO *RECALL* THE MOSCOW TEAM?
OR DON'T YOU THINK THAT MAYBE *HARRY* UP THERE--
09
02

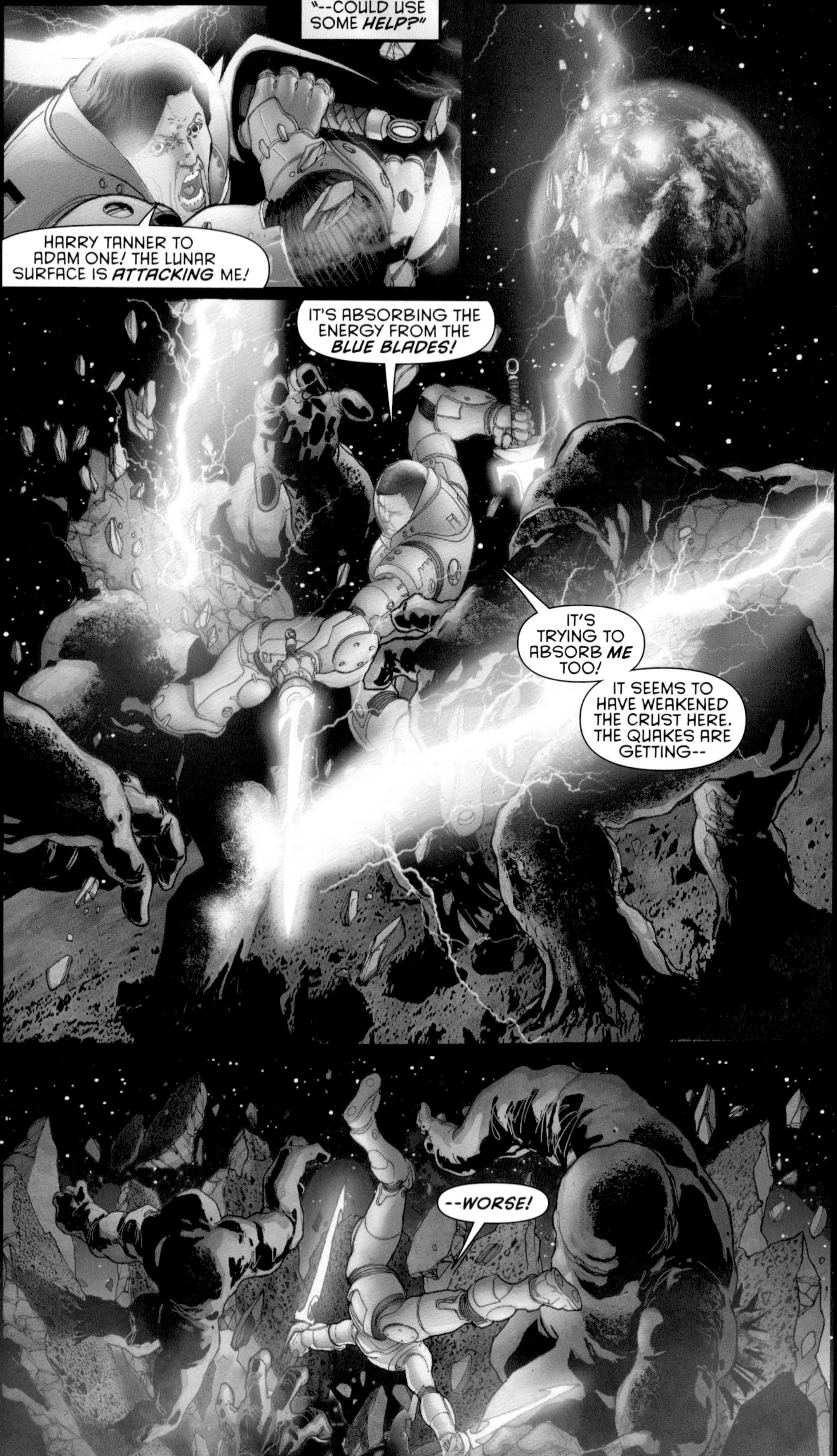
"--COULD USE SOME HELP?"
HARRY TANNER TO ADAM ONE! THE LUNAR SURFACE IS ATTACKING ME!
IT'S ABSORBING THE ENERGY FROM THE BLUE BLADES!
IT'S TRYING TO ABSORB ME TOO!
IT SEEMS TO HAVE WEAKENED THE CRUST HERE. THE QUAKES ARE GETTING--
--WORSE!

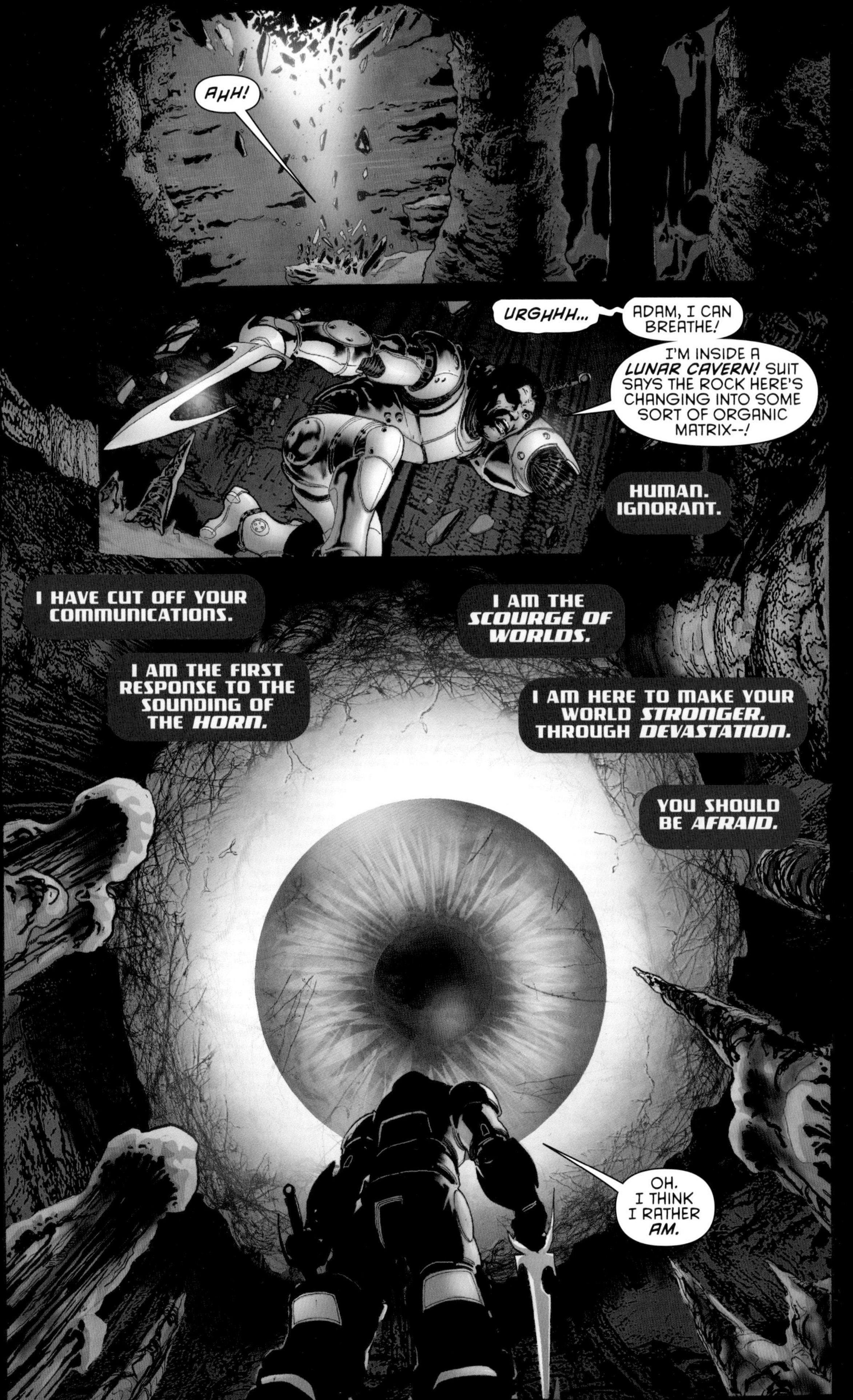
AHH!
URGHHH...
ADAM, I CAN BREATHE!
I'M INSIDE A LUNAR CAVERN! SUIT SAYS THE ROCK HERE'S CHANGING INTO SOME SORT OF ORGANIC MATRIX--!
HUMAN. IGNORANT.
I HAVE CUT OFF YOUR COMMUNICATIONS.
I AM THE SCOURGE OF WORLDS.
I AM THE FIRST RESPONSE TO THE SOUNDING OF THE HORN.
I AM HERE TO MAKE YOUR WORLD STRONGER. THROUGH DEVASTATION.
YOU SHOULD BE AFRAID.
OH. I THINK I RATHER AM.

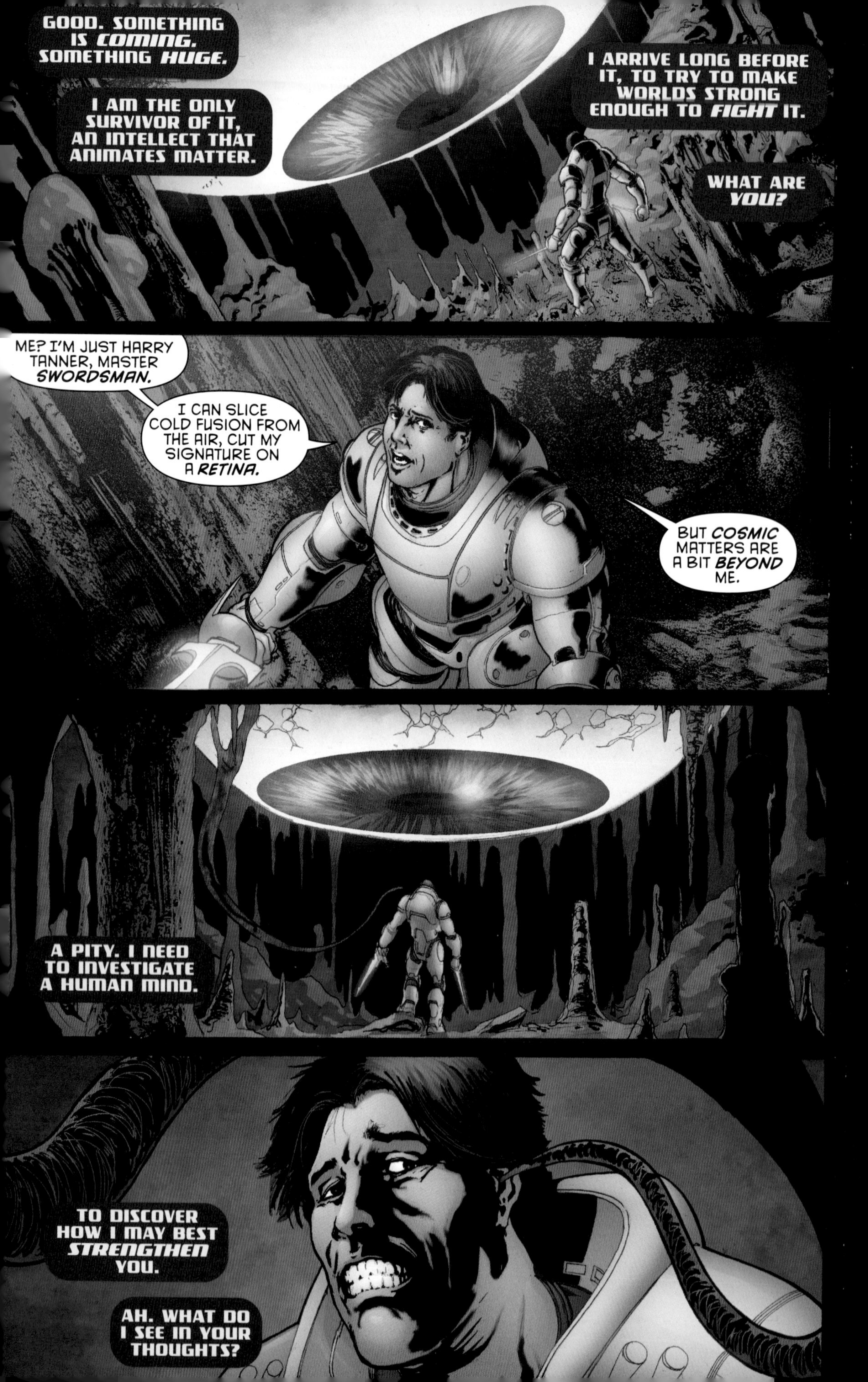
GOOD. SOMETHING IS COMING. SOMETHING HUGE.
I AM THE ONLY SURVIVOR OF IT, AN INTELLECT THAT ANIMATES MATTER.
I ARRIVE LONG BEFORE IT, TO TRY TO MAKE WORLDS STRONG ENOUGH TO FIGHT IT.
WHAT ARE YOU?
ME? I'M JUST HARRY TANNER, MASTER SWORDSMAN.
I CAN SLICE COLD FUSION FROM THE AIR, CUT MY SIGNATURE ON A RETINA.
BUT COSMIC MATTERS ARE A BIT BEYOND ME.
A PITY. I NEED TO INVESTIGATE A HUMAN MIND.
TO DISCOVER HOW I MAY BEST STRENGTHEN YOU.
AH. WHAT DO I SEE IN YOUR THOUGHTS?

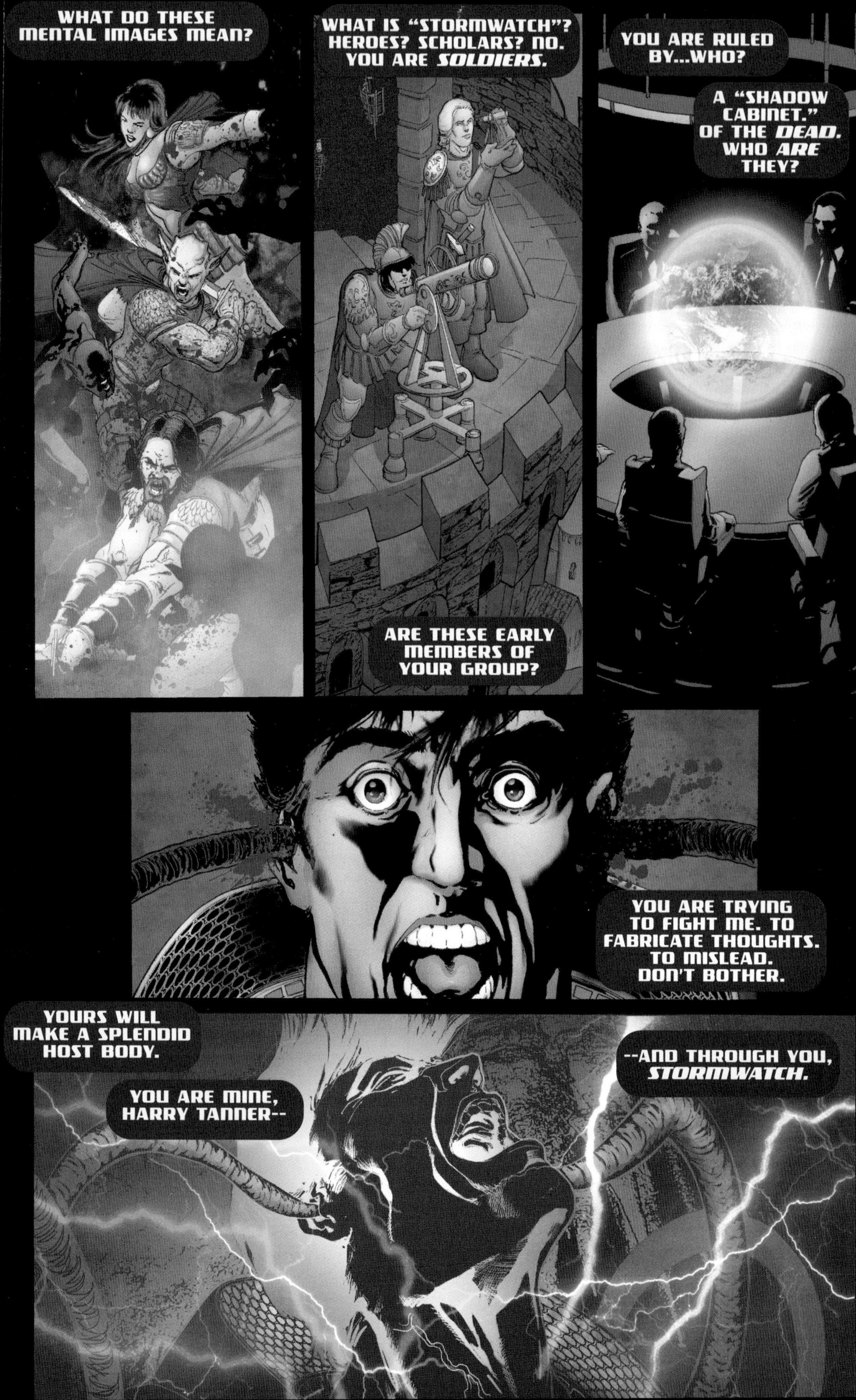
WHAT DO THESE MENTAL IMAGES MEAN?
WHAT IS "STORMWATCH"? HEROES? SCHOLARS? NO. YOU ARE SOLDIERS.
ARE THESE EARLY MEMBERS OF YOUR GROUP?
YOU ARE RULED BY...WHO?
A "SHADOW CABINET." OF THE DEAD. WHO ARE THEY?
YOU ARE TRYING TO FIGHT ME. TO FABRICATE THOUGHTS. TO MISLEAD. DON'T BOTHER.
YOURS WILL MAKE A SPLENDID HOST BODY.
YOU ARE MINE, HARRY TANNER--
--AND THROUGH YOU, STORMWATCH.

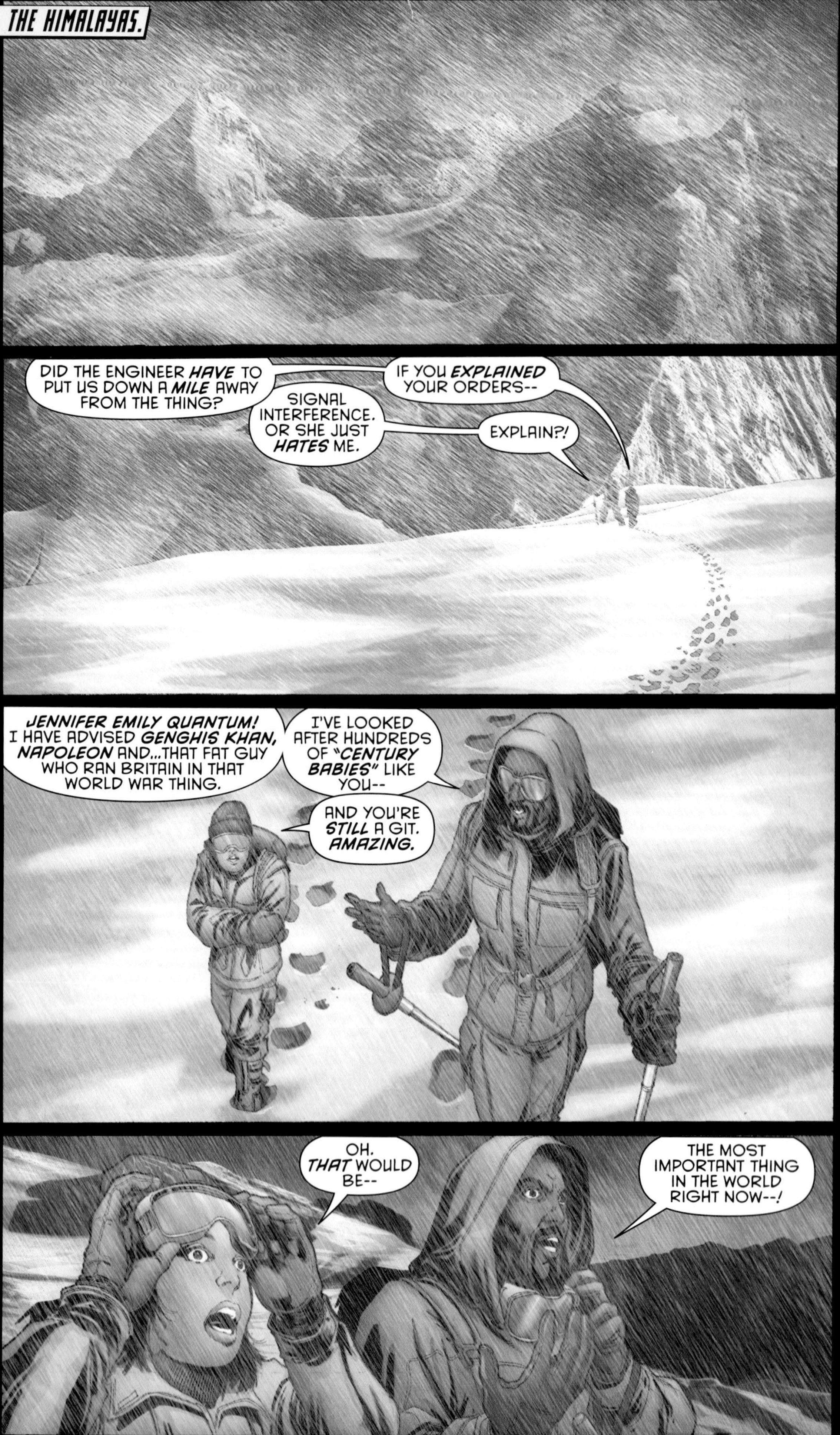
THE HIMALAYAS.
DID THE ENGINEER HAVE TO PUT US DOWN A MILE AWAY FROM THE THING?
IF YOU EXPLAINED YOUR ORDERS--
SIGNAL INTERFERENCE. OR SHE JUST HATES ME.
EXPLAIN?!
JENNIFER EMILY QUANTUM! I HAVE ADVISED GENGHIS KHAN, NAPOLEON AND...THAT FAT GUY WHO RAN BRITAIN IN THAT WORLD WAR THING.
I'VE LOOKED AFTER HUNDREDS OF "CENTURY BABIES" LIKE YOU--
AND YOU'RE STILL A GIT. AMAZING.
OH. THAT WOULD BE--
THE MOST IMPORTANT THING IN THE WORLD RIGHT NOW--!

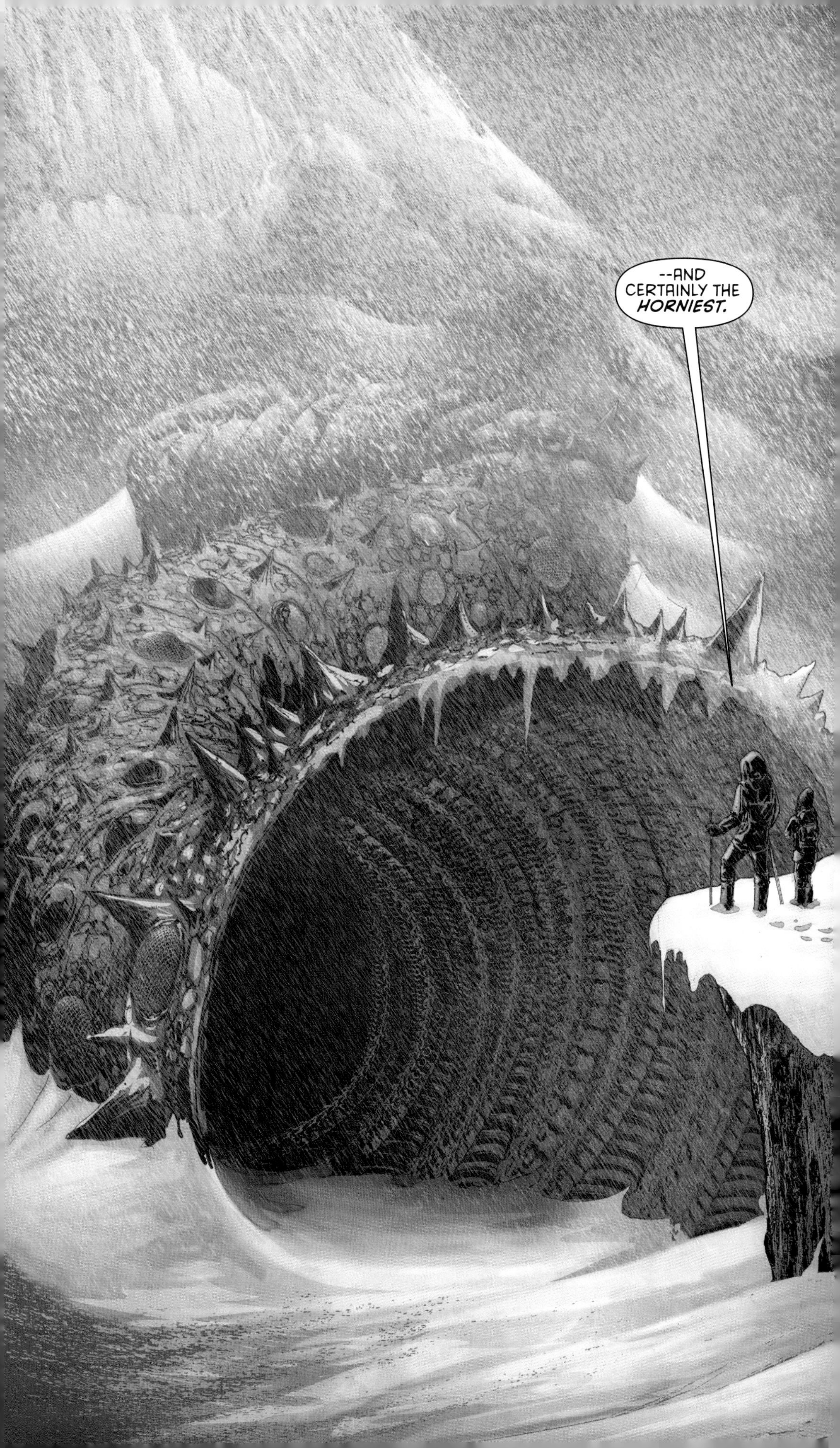
--AND CERTAINLY THE HORNIEST.

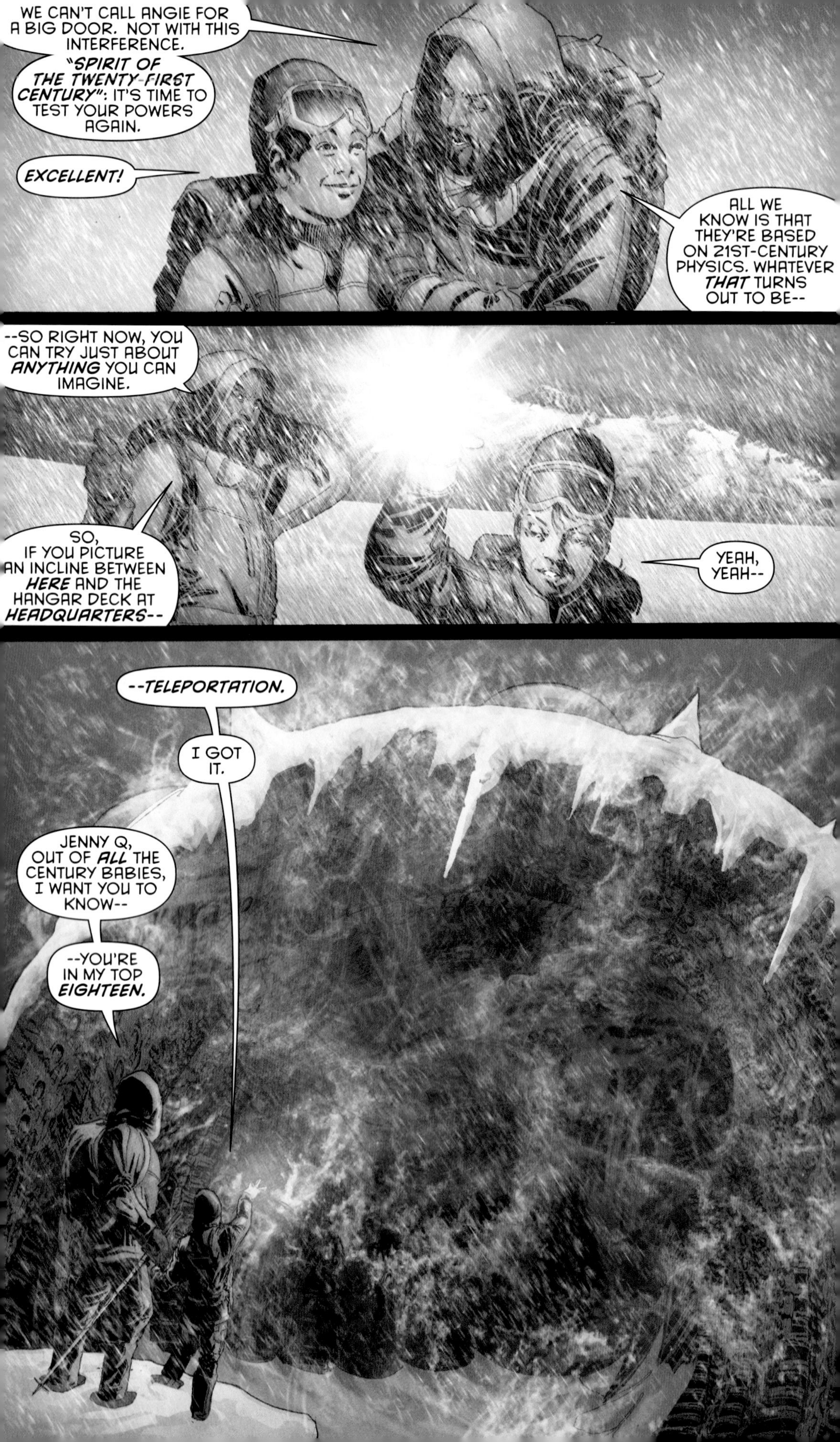

WE CAN'T CALL ANGIE FOR A BIG DOOR. NOT WITH THIS INTERFERENCE.
"SPIRIT OF THE TWENTY-FIRST CENTURY": IT'S TIME TO TEST YOUR POWERS AGAIN.
EXCELLENT!
ALL WE KNOW IS THAT THEY'RE BASED ON 21ST-CENTURY PHYSICS. WHATEVER THAT TURNS OUT TO BE--
--SO RIGHT NOW, YOU CAN TRY JUST ABOUT ANYTHING YOU CAN IMAGINE.
SO, IF YOU PICTURE AN INCLINE BETWEEN HERE AND THE HANGAR DECK AT HEADQUARTERS--
YEAH, YEAH--
--TELEPORTATION.
I GOT IT.
JENNY Q, OUT OF ALL THE CENTURY BABIES, I WANT YOU TO KNOW--
--YOU'RE IN MY TOP EIGHTEEN.

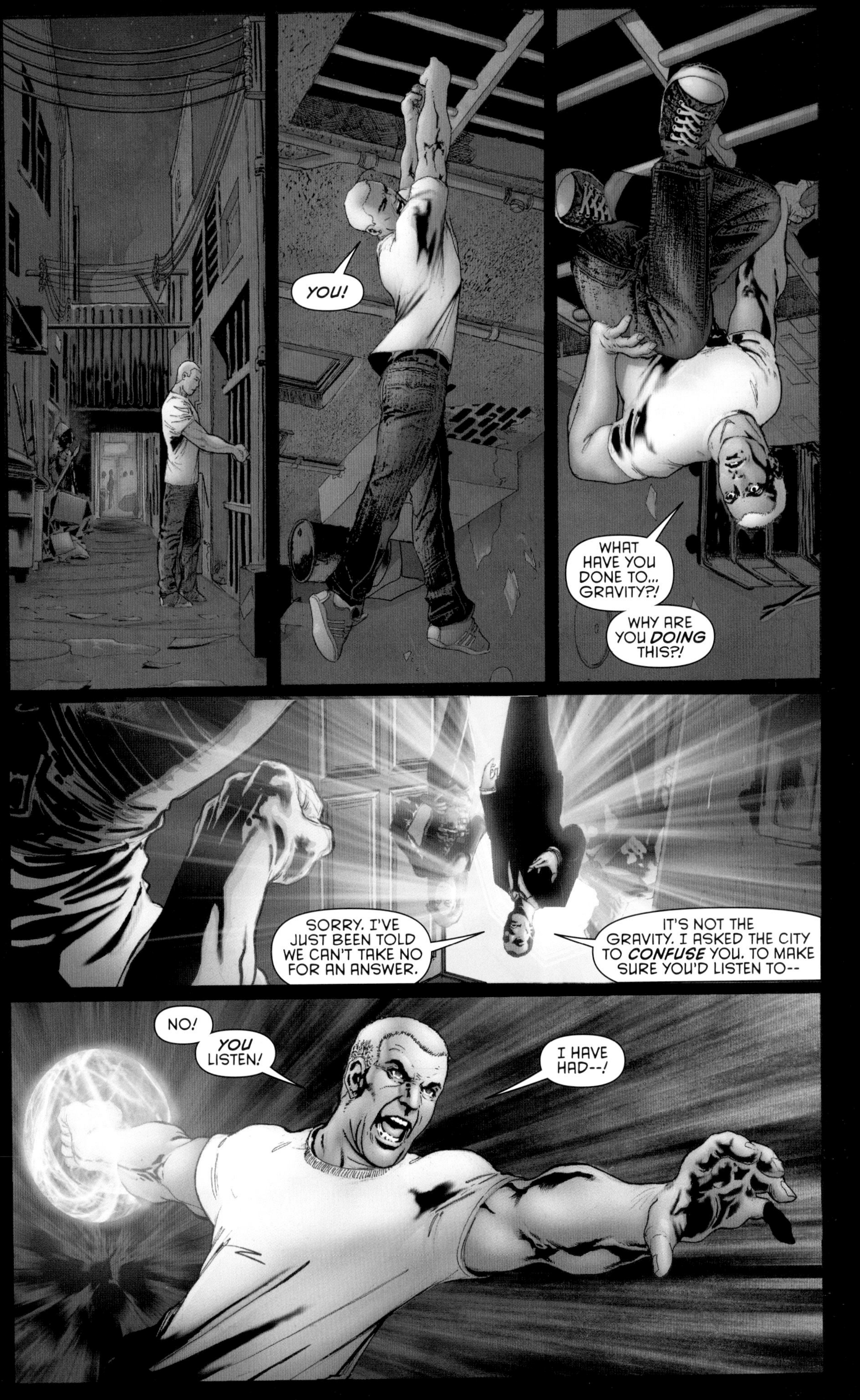
YOU!
WHAT HAVE YOU DONE TO... GRAVITY?!
WHY ARE YOU DOING THIS?!
SORRY. I'VE JUST BEEN TOLD WE CAN'T TAKE NO FOR AN ANSWER.
IT'S NOT THE GRAVITY. I ASKED THE CITY TO CONFUSE YOU. TO MAKE SURE YOU'D LISTEN TO--
NO!
YOU LISTEN!
I HAVE HAD--!

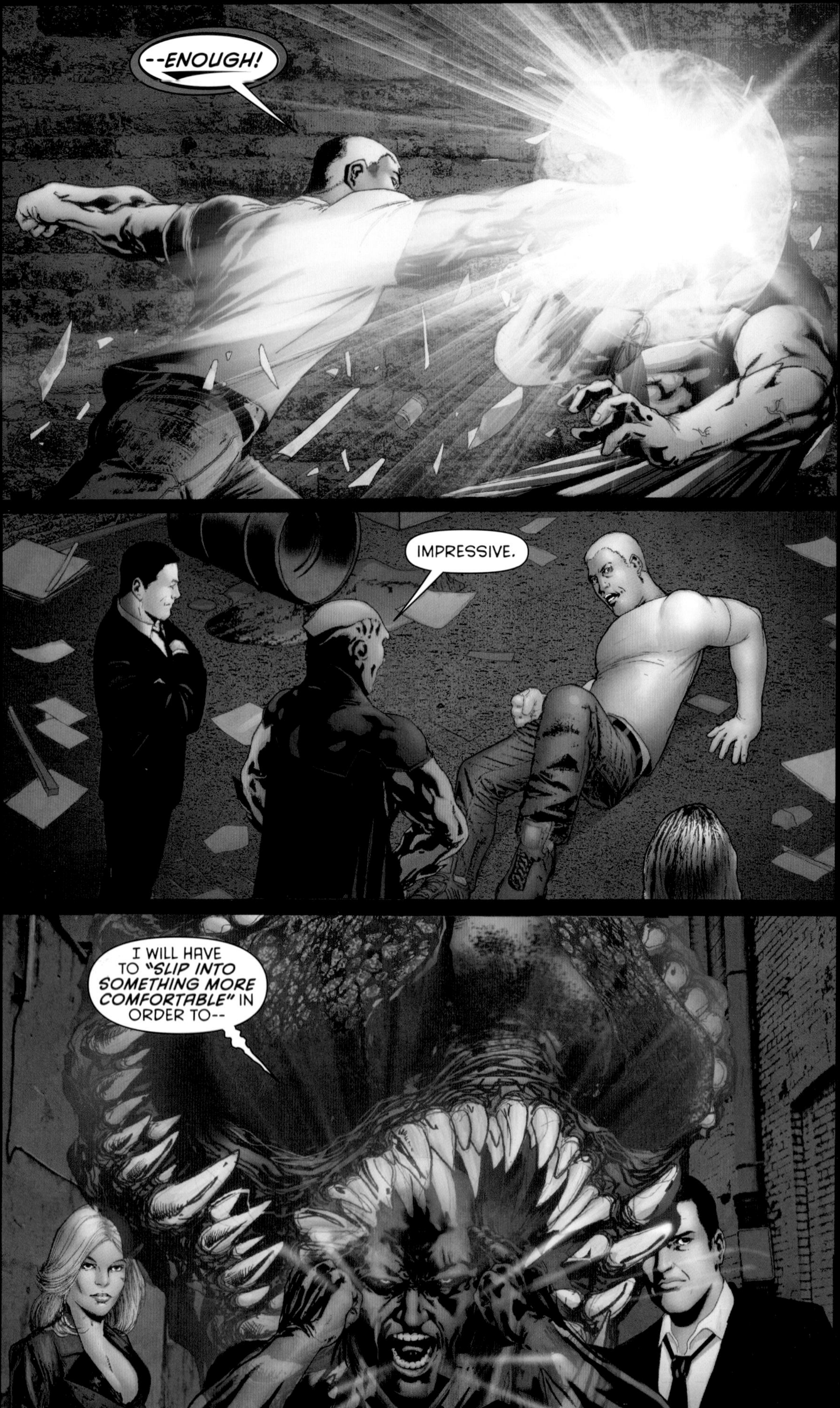
--ENOUGH!
IMPRESSIVE.
I WILL HAVE TO "SLIP INTO SOMETHING MORE COMFORTABLE" IN ORDER TO--

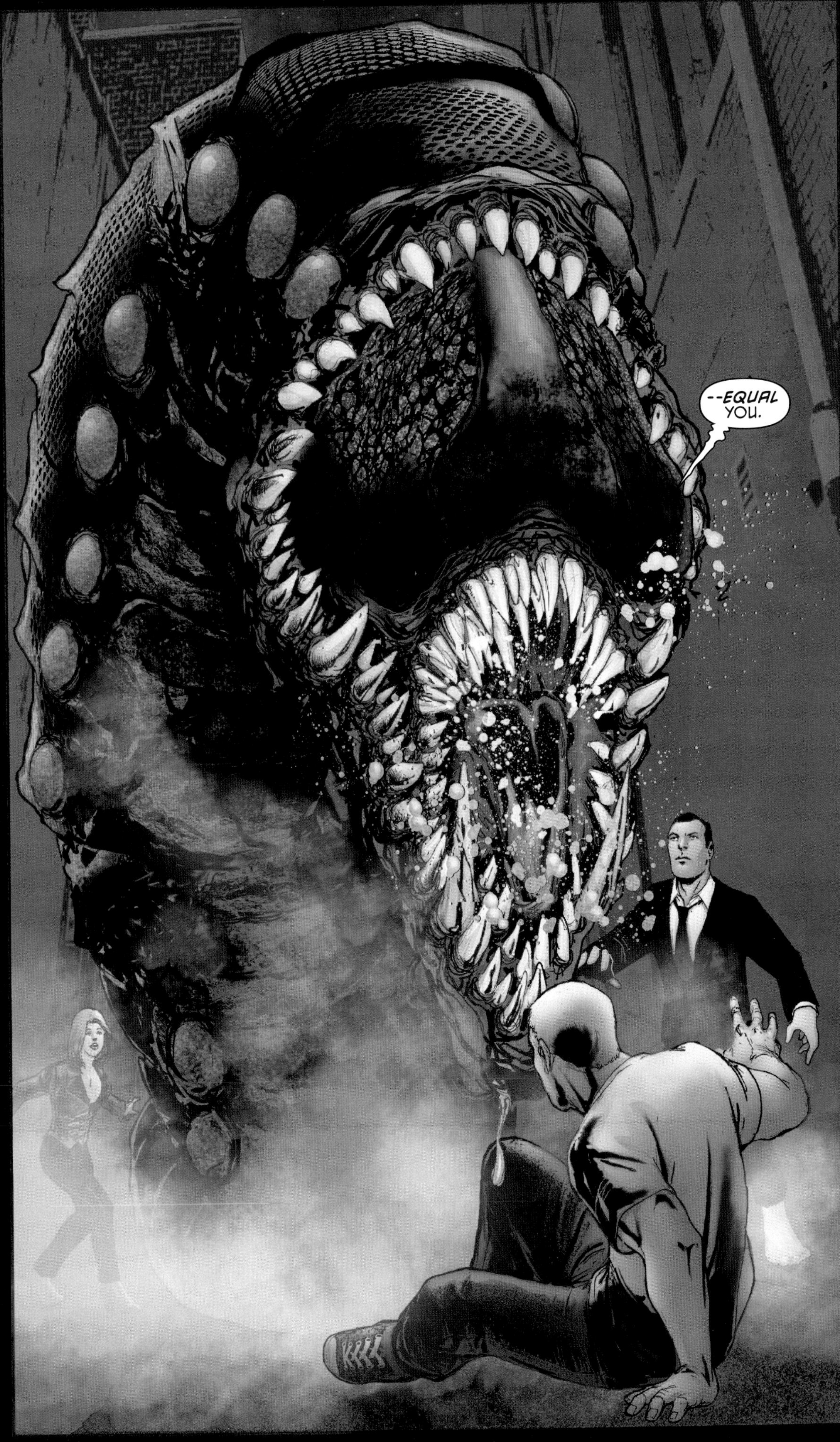
--EQUAL YOU.

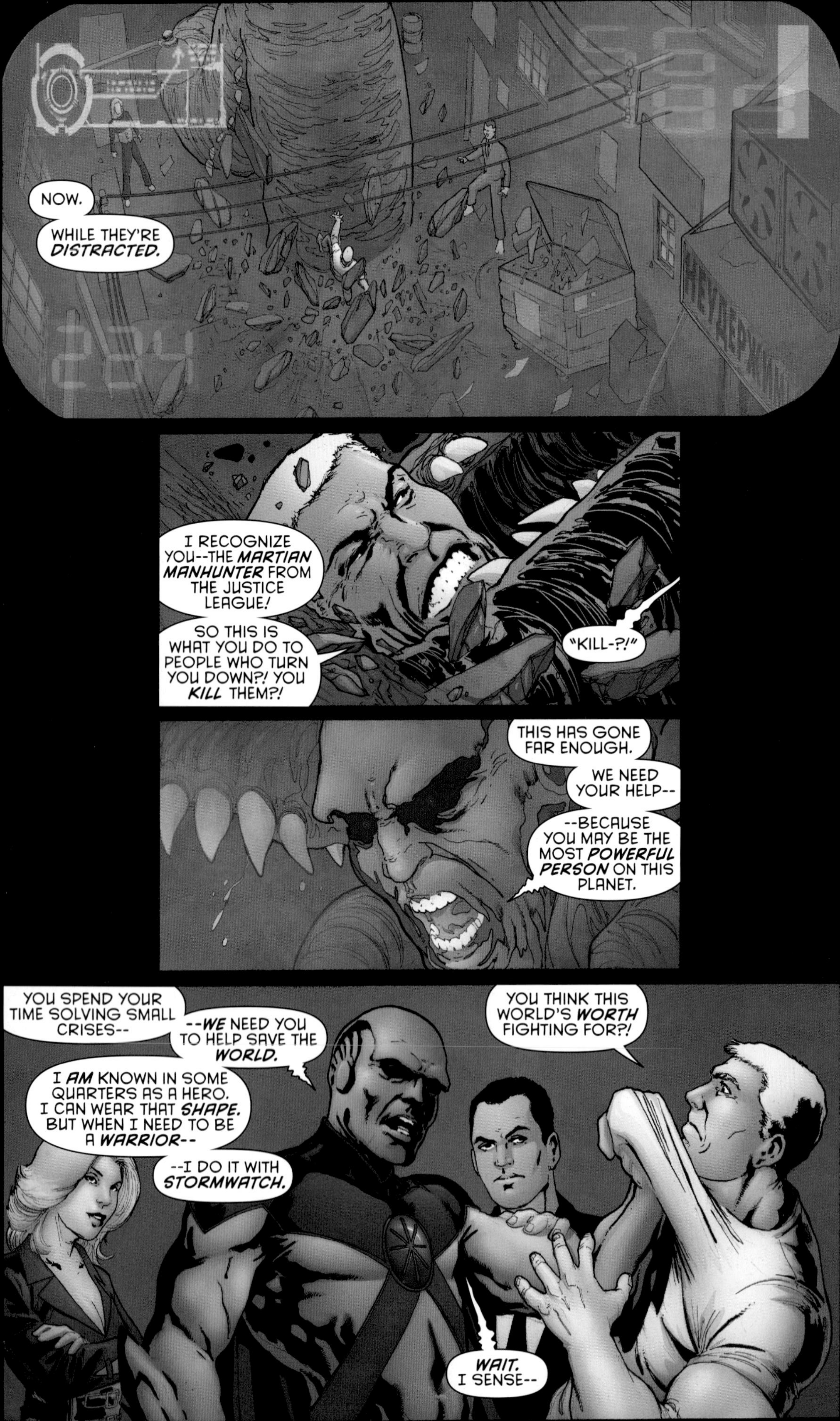
NOW.
WHILE THEY'RE DISTRACTED.
I RECOGNIZE YOU--THE MARTIAN MANHUNTER FROM THE JUSTICE LEAGUE!
SO THIS IS WHAT YOU DO TO PEOPLE WHO TURN YOU DOWN?! YOU KILL THEM?!
"KILL-?!"
THIS HAS GONE FAR ENOUGH.
WE NEED YOUR HELP--
--BECAUSE YOU MAY BE THE MOST POWERFUL PERSON ON THIS PLANET.
YOU SPEND YOUR TIME SOLVING SMALL CRISES--
--WE NEED YOU TO HELP SAVE THE WORLD.
YOU THINK THIS WORLD'S WORTH FIGHTING FOR?!
I AM KNOWN IN SOME QUARTERS AS A HERO. I CAN WEAR THAT SHAPE. BUT WHEN I NEED TO BE A WARRIOR--
--I DO IT WITH STORMWATCH.
WAIT. I SENSE--

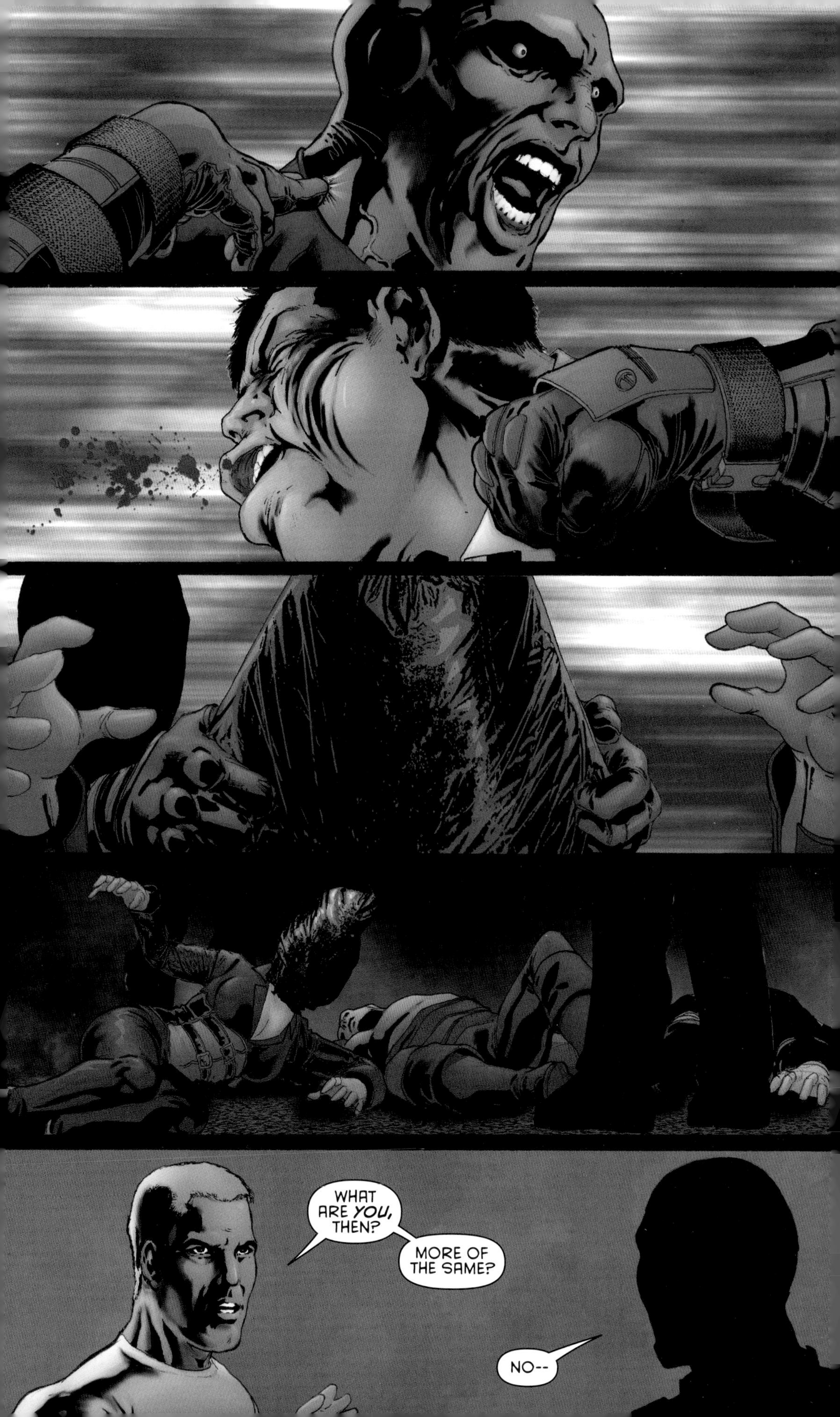
WHAT ARE *YOU*, THEN?
MORE OF THE SAME?
NO--

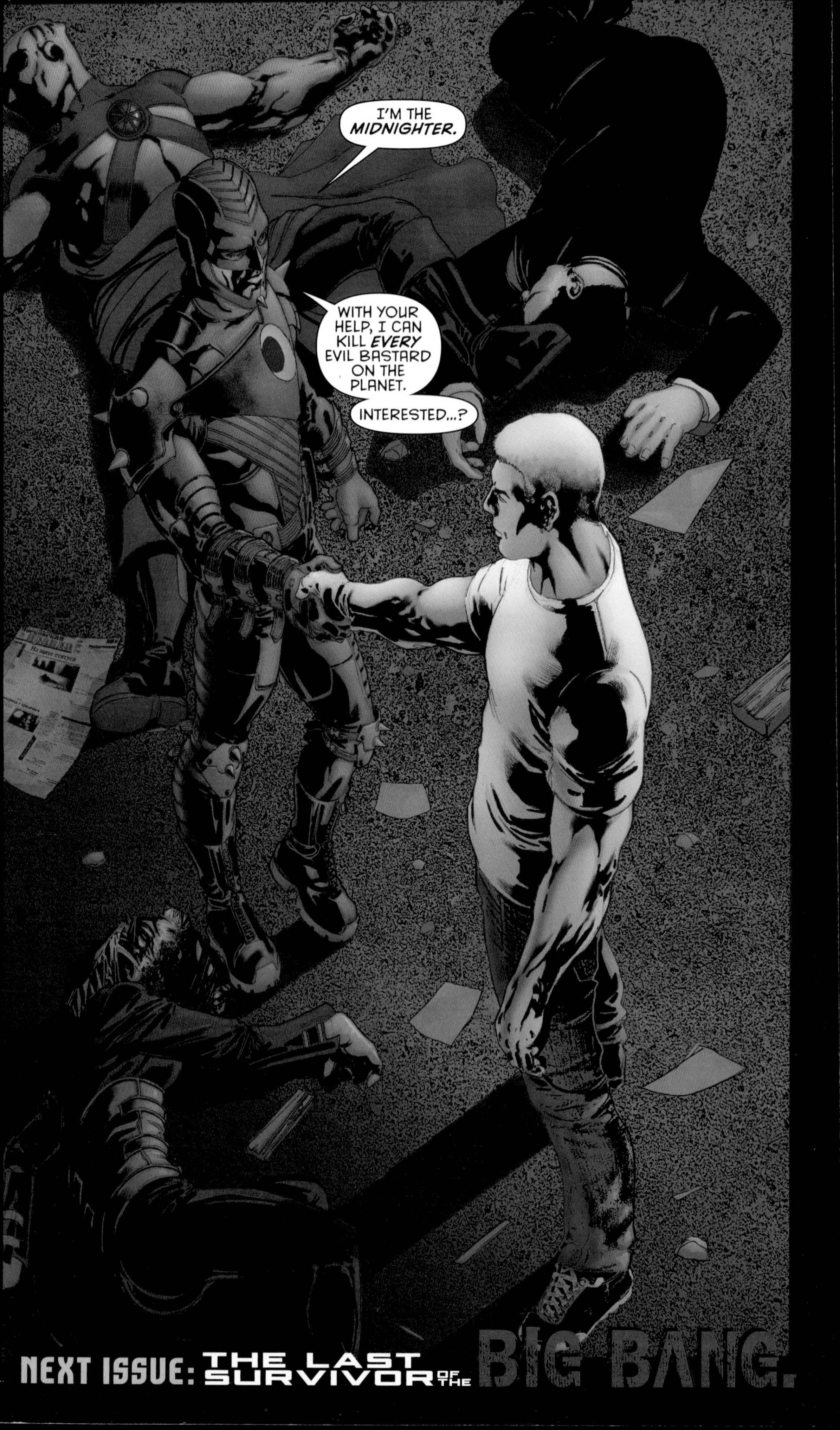
I'M THE MIDNIGHTER.
WITH YOUR HELP, I CAN KILL EVERY EVIL BASTARD ON THE PLANET.
INTERESTED...?
NEXT ISSUE: THE LAST SURVIVOR OF THE BIG BANG.

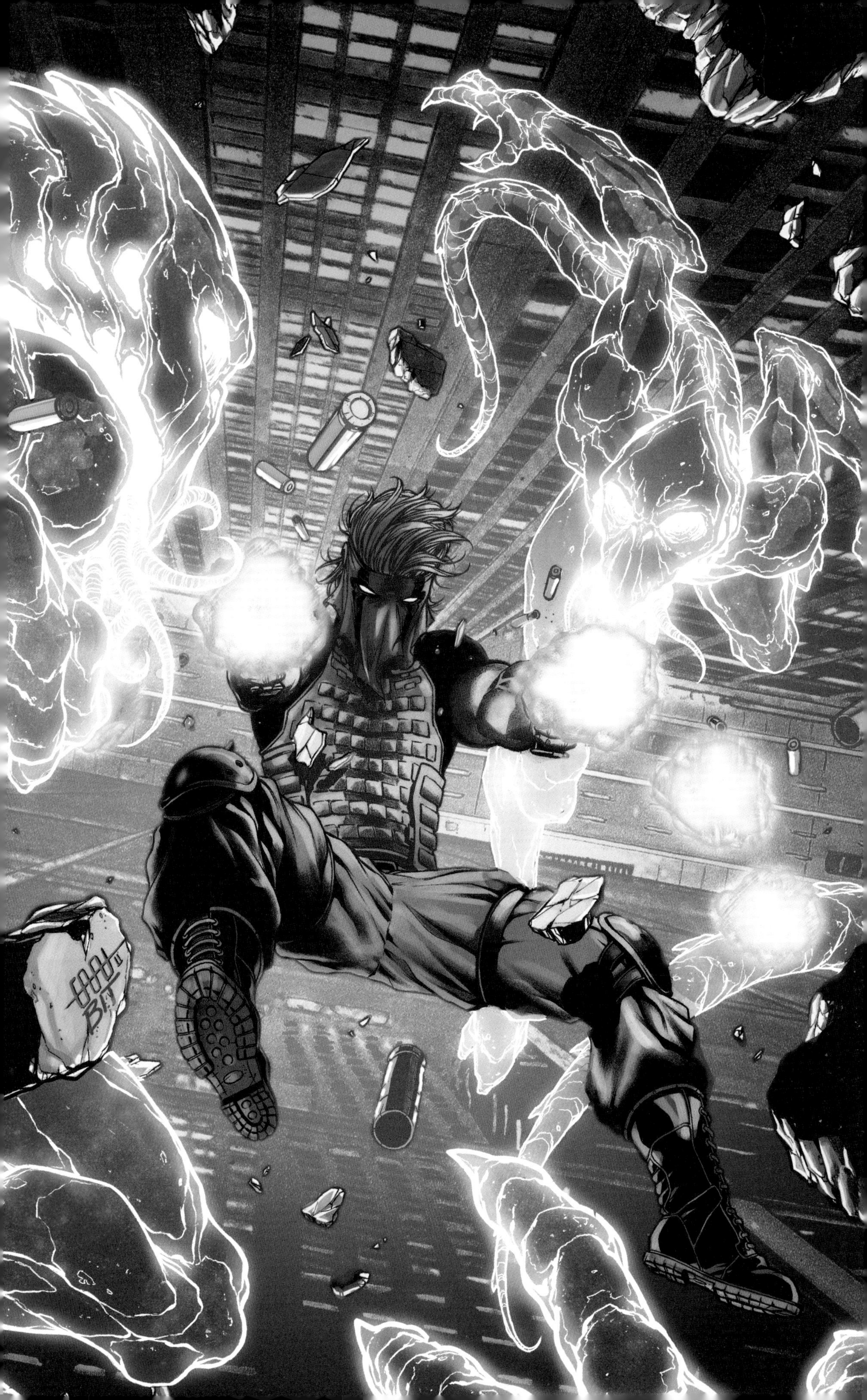

GRIFTER

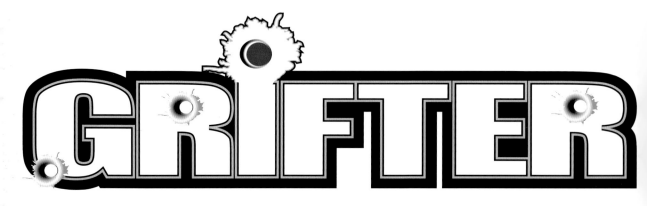

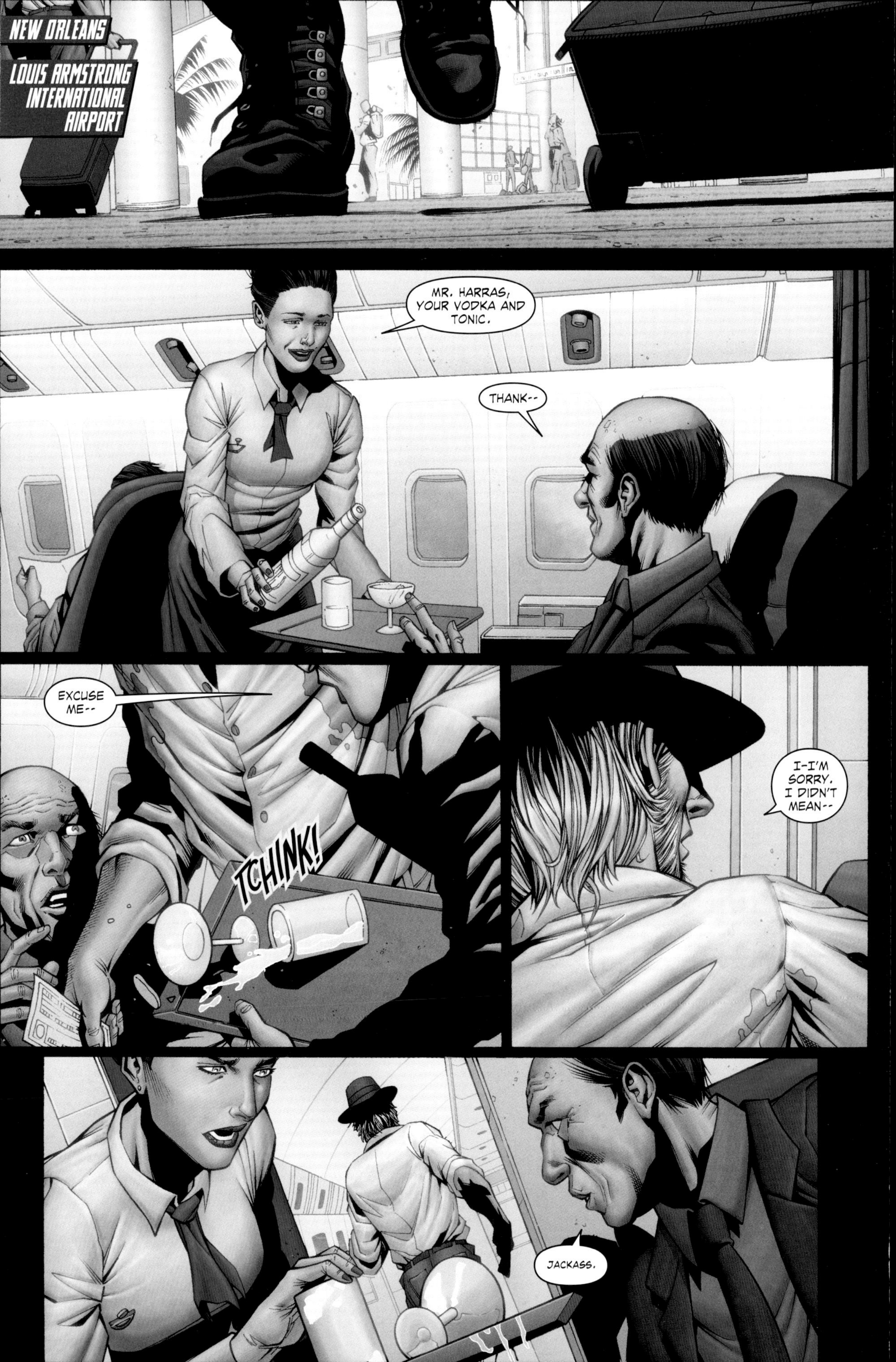
NEW ORLEANS
LOUIS ARMSTRONG INTERNATIONAL AIRPORT
MR. HARRAS, YOUR VODKA AND TONIC.
THANK--
EXCUSE ME--
TCHINK!
I-I'M SORRY. I DIDN'T MEAN--
JACKASS.

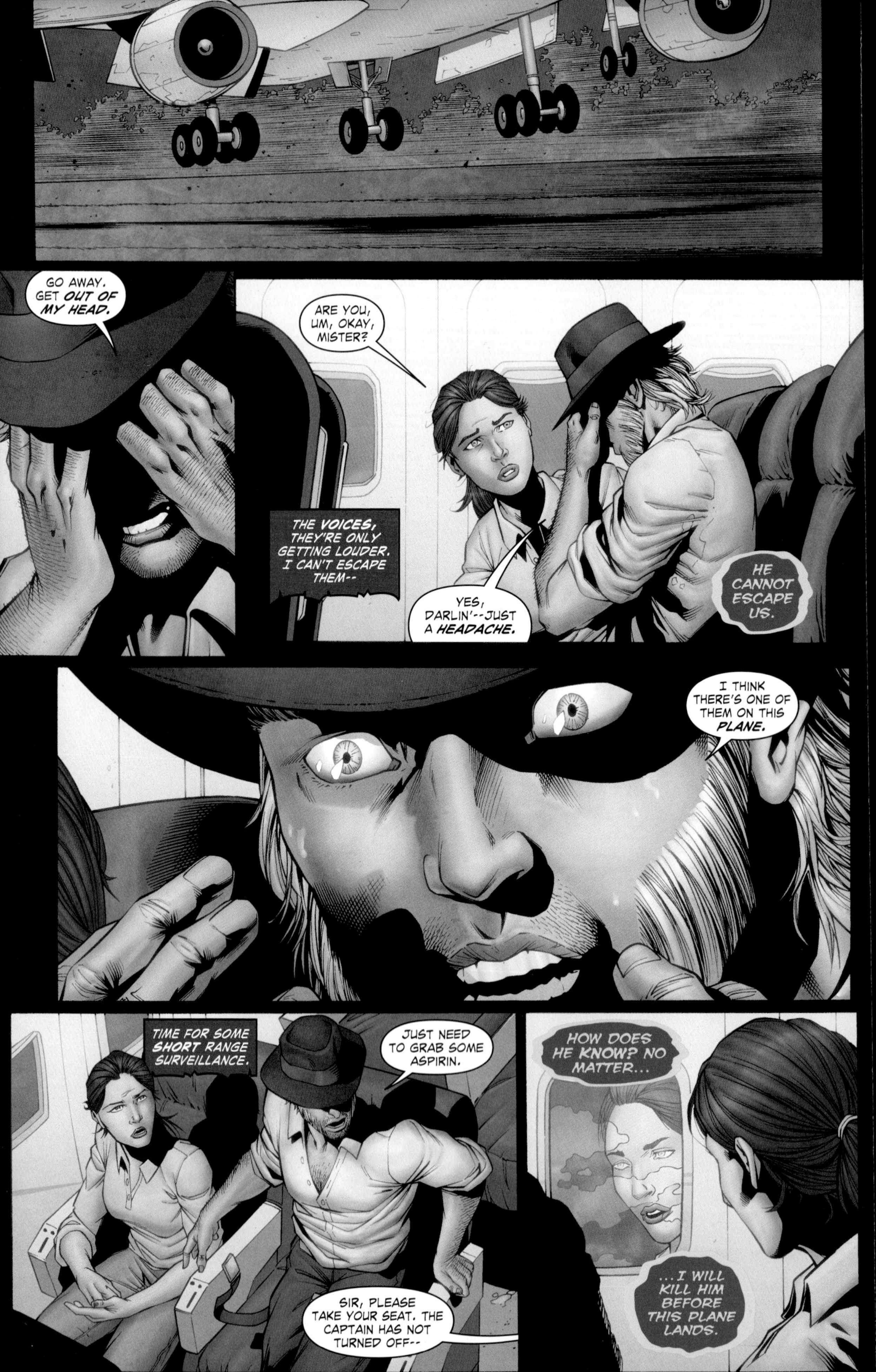
GO AWAY. GET OUT OF MY HEAD.
ARE YOU, UM, OKAY, MISTER?
THE VOICES, THEY'RE ONLY GETTING LOUDER. I CAN'T ESCAPE THEM--
YES, DARLIN'--JUST A HEADACHE.
HE CANNOT ESCAPE US.
I THINK THERE'S ONE OF THEM ON THIS PLANE.
TIME FOR SOME SHORT RANGE SURVEILLANCE.
JUST NEED TO GRAB SOME ASPIRIN.
SIR, PLEASE TAKE YOUR SEAT. THE CAPTAIN HAS NOT TURNED OFF--
HOW DOES HE KNOW? NO MATTER...
...I WILL KILL HIM BEFORE THIS PLANE LANDS.

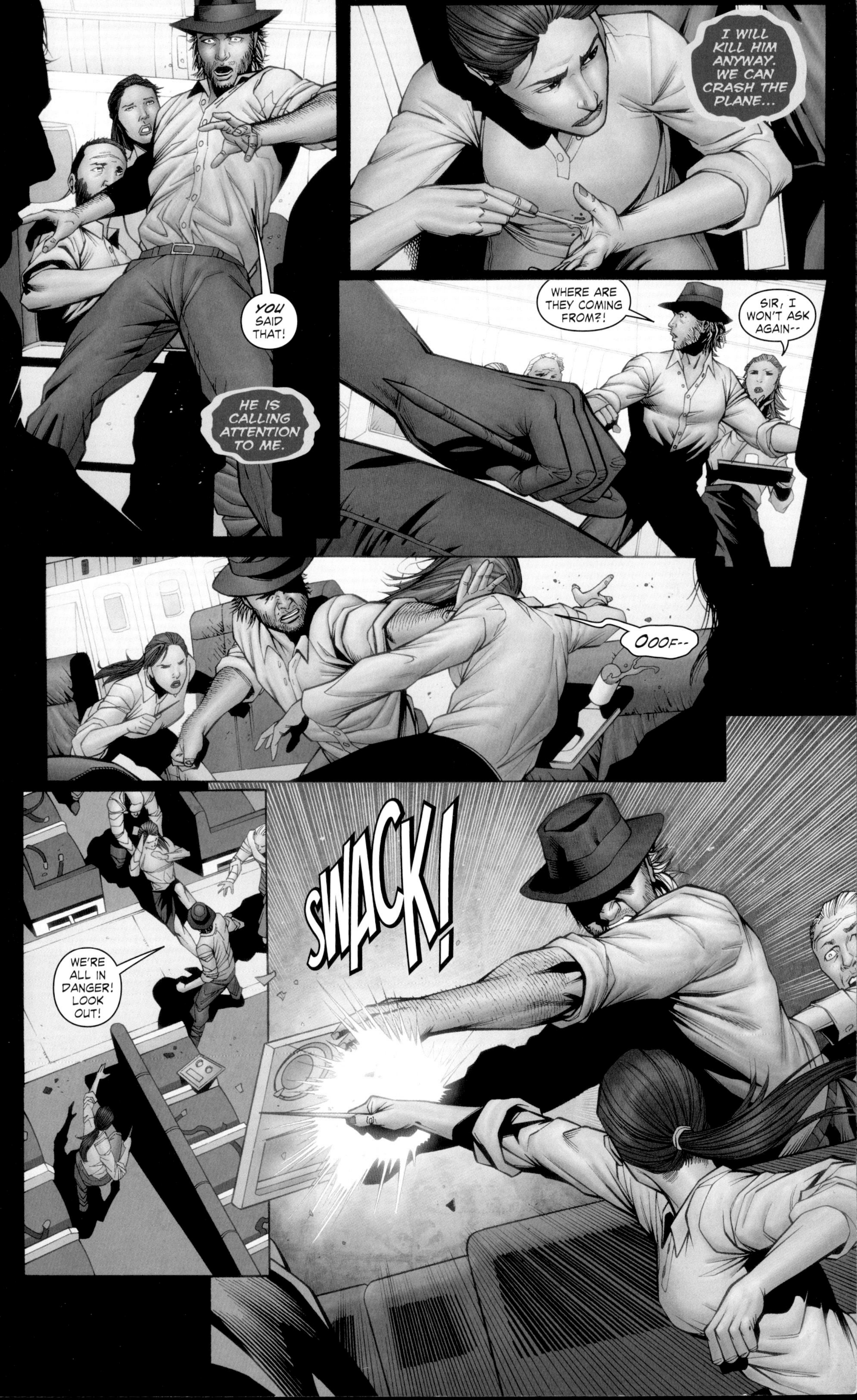
I WILL KILL HIM ANYWAY. WE CAN CRASH THE PLANE...
YOU SAID THAT!
HE IS CALLING ATTENTION TO ME.
WHERE ARE THEY COMING FROM?!
SIR, I WON'T ASK AGAIN--
OOOF--
WE'RE ALL IN DANGER! LOOK OUT!
SWACK!

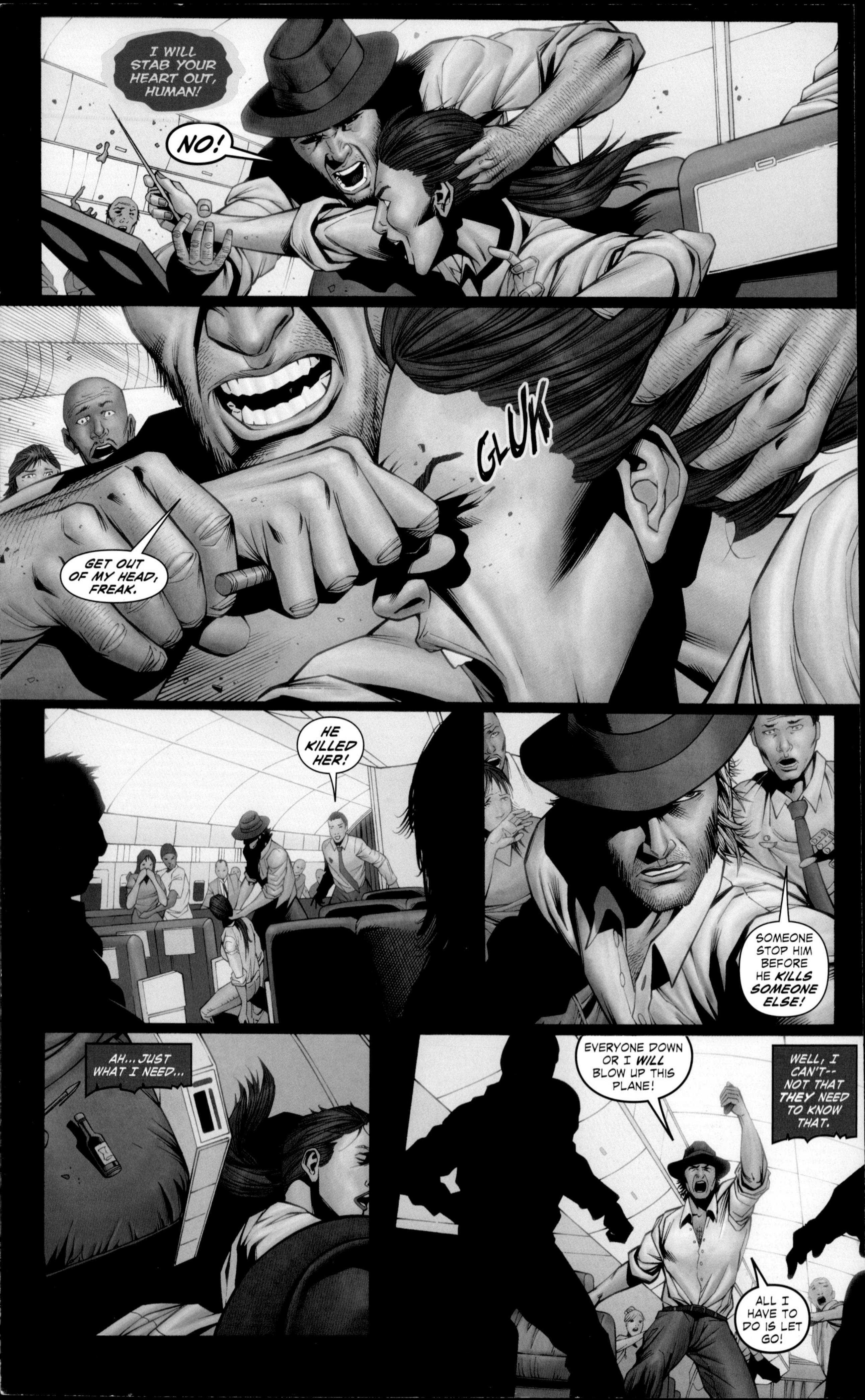
I WILL STAB YOUR HEART OUT, HUMAN!
NO!
GLUK
GET OUT OF MY HEAD, FREAK.
HE KILLED HER!
SOMEONE STOP HIM BEFORE HE KILLS SOMEONE ELSE!
AH... JUST WHAT I NEED...
EVERYONE DOWN OR I WILL BLOW UP THIS PLANE!
WELL, I CAN'T-- NOT THAT THEY NEED TO KNOW THAT.
ALL I HAVE TO DO IS LET GO!

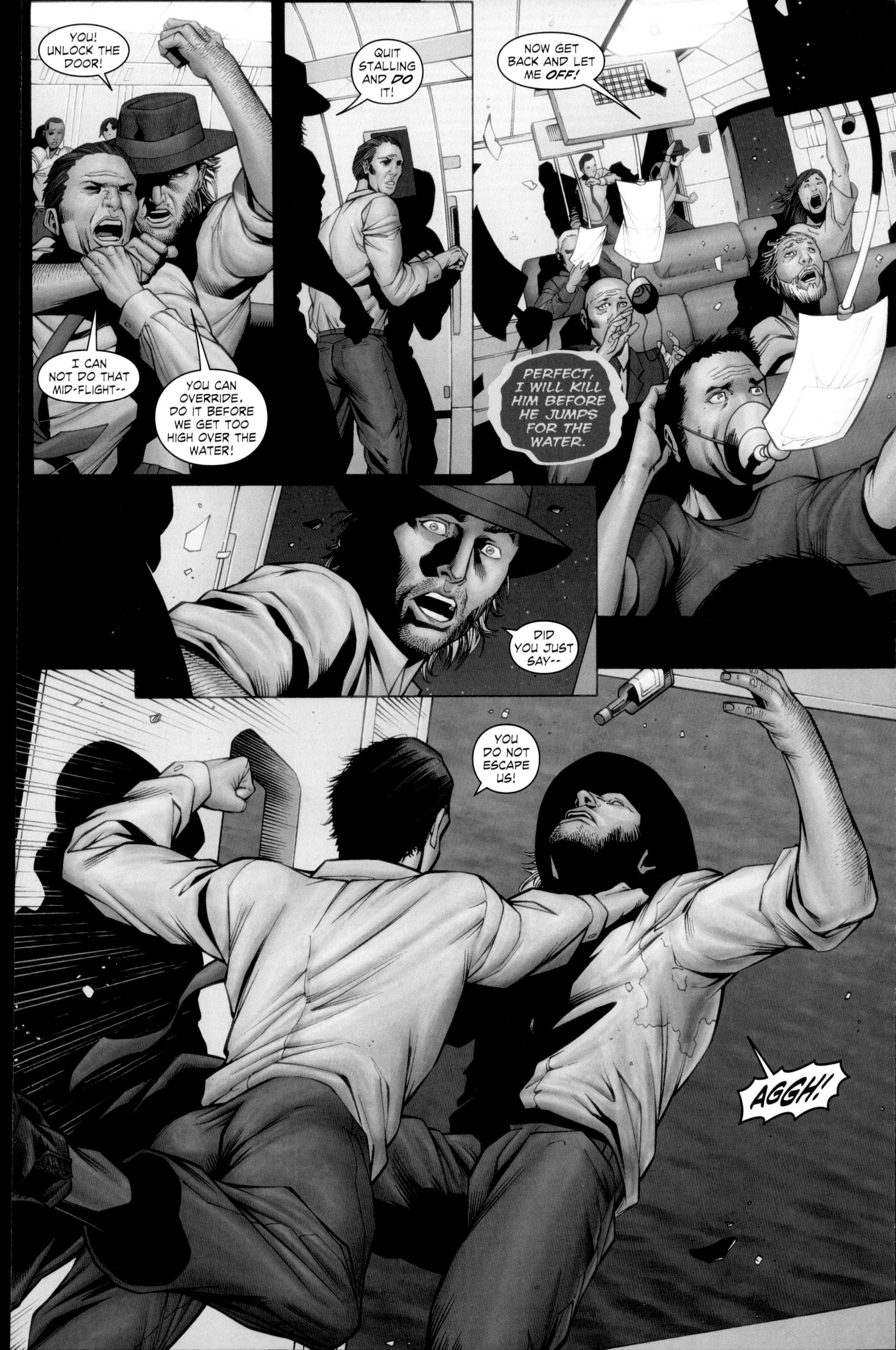
YOU! UNLOCK THE DOOR!
I CAN NOT DO THAT MID-FLIGHT--
YOU CAN OVERRIDE. DO IT BEFORE WE GET TOO HIGH OVER THE WATER!
QUIT STALLING AND DO IT!
NOW GET BACK AND LET ME OFF!
PERFECT, I WILL KILL HIM BEFORE HE JUMPS FOR THE WATER.
DID YOU JUST SAY--
YOU DO NOT ESCAPE US!
AGGH!

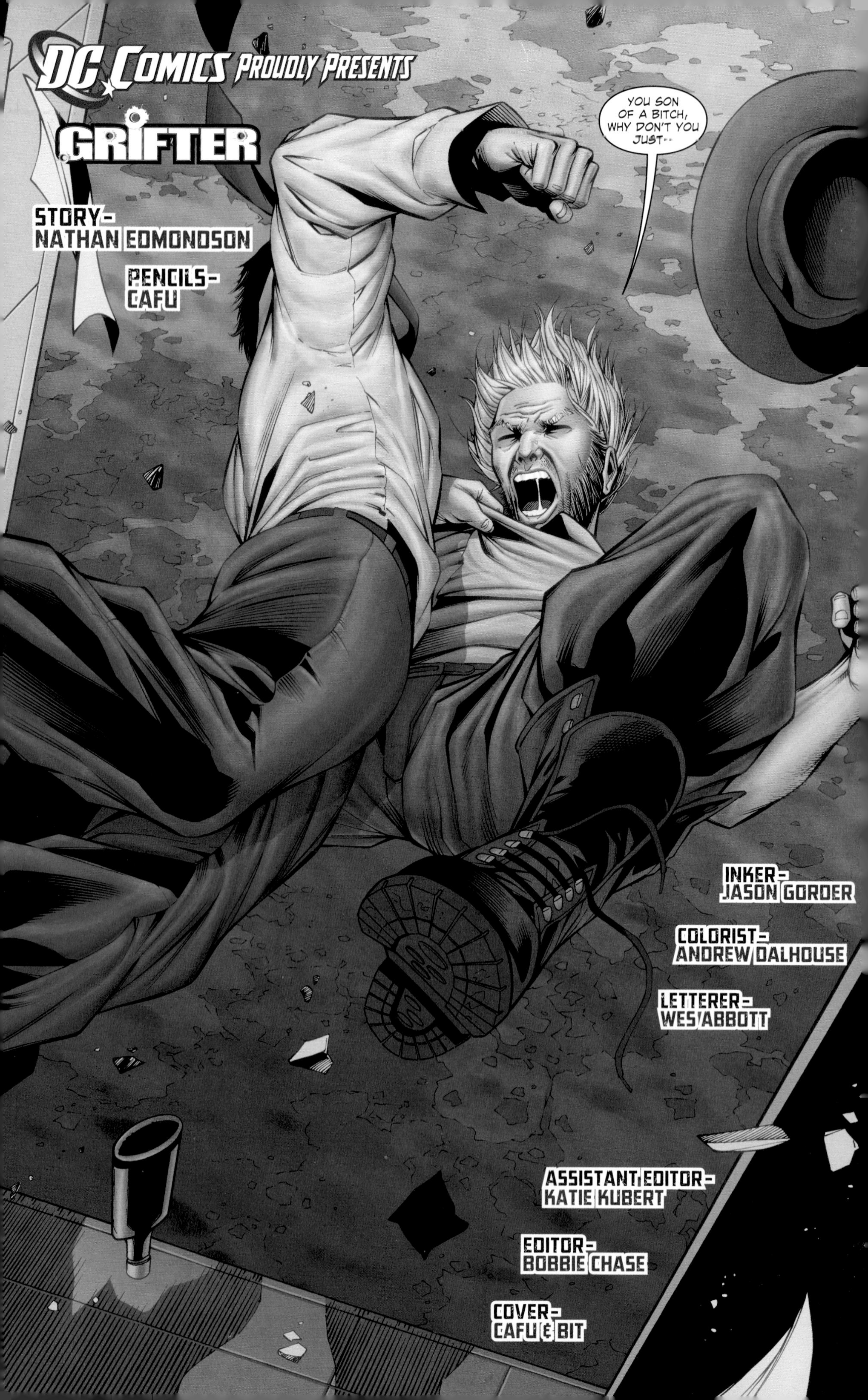
DC COMICS PROUDLY PRESENTS
GRIFTER
STORY- NATHAN EDMONDSON
PENCILS- CAFU
YOU SON OF A BITCH, WHY DON'T YOU JUST--
INKER- JASON GORDER
COLORIST- ANDREW DALHOUSE
LETTERER- WES ABBOTT
ASSISTANT EDITOR- KATIE KUBERT
EDITOR- BOBBIE CHASE
COVER- CAFU & BIT

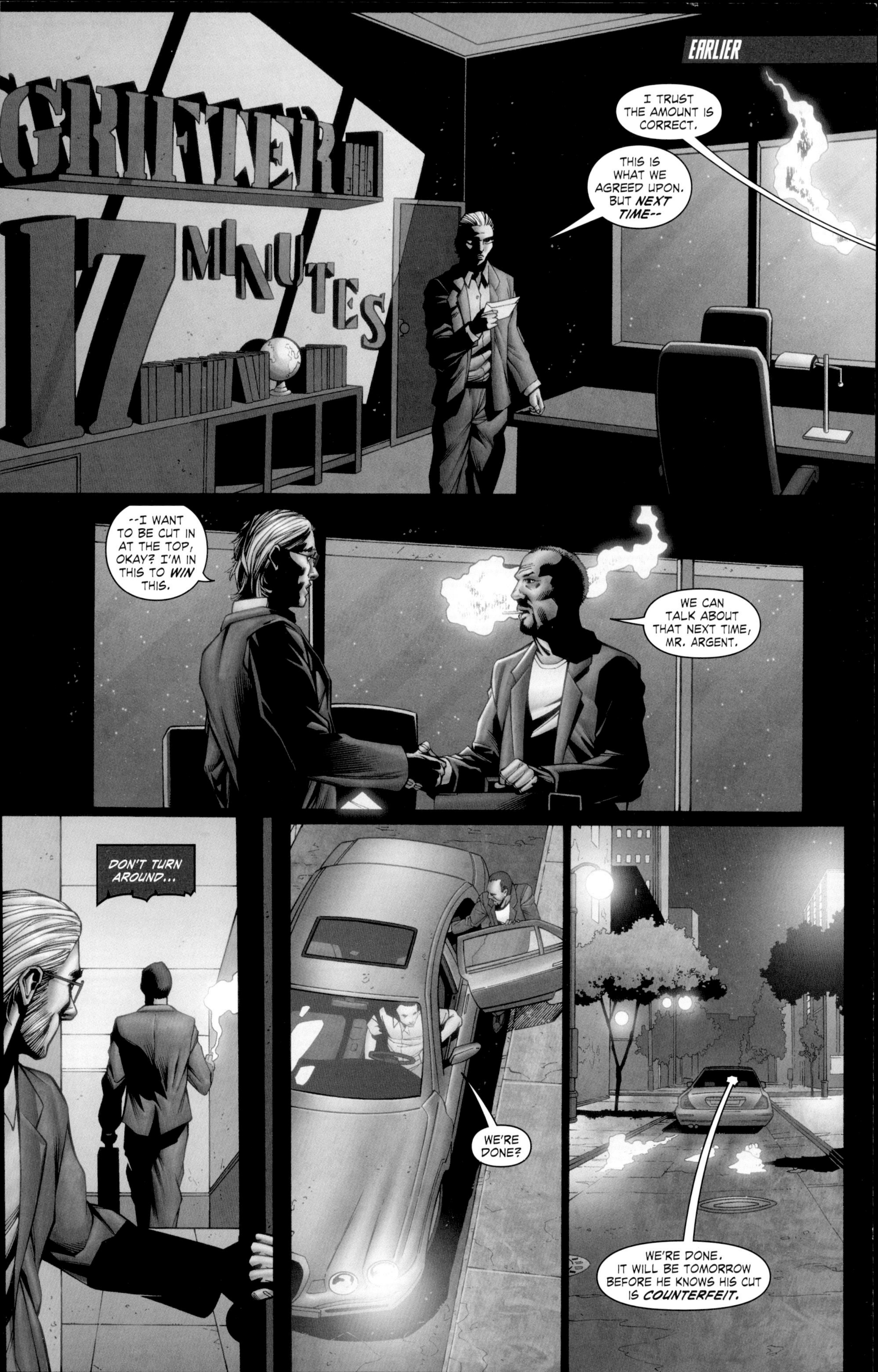
EARLIER
GRIFTER
17 MINUTES
I TRUST THE AMOUNT IS CORRECT.
THIS IS WHAT WE AGREED UPON. BUT NEXT TIME--
--I WANT TO BE CUT IN AT THE TOP, OKAY? I'M IN THIS TO WIN THIS.
WE CAN TALK ABOUT THAT NEXT TIME, MR. ARGENT.
DON'T TURN AROUND...
WE'RE DONE?
WE'RE DONE. IT WILL BE TOMORROW BEFORE HE KNOWS HIS CUT IS COUNTERFEIT.

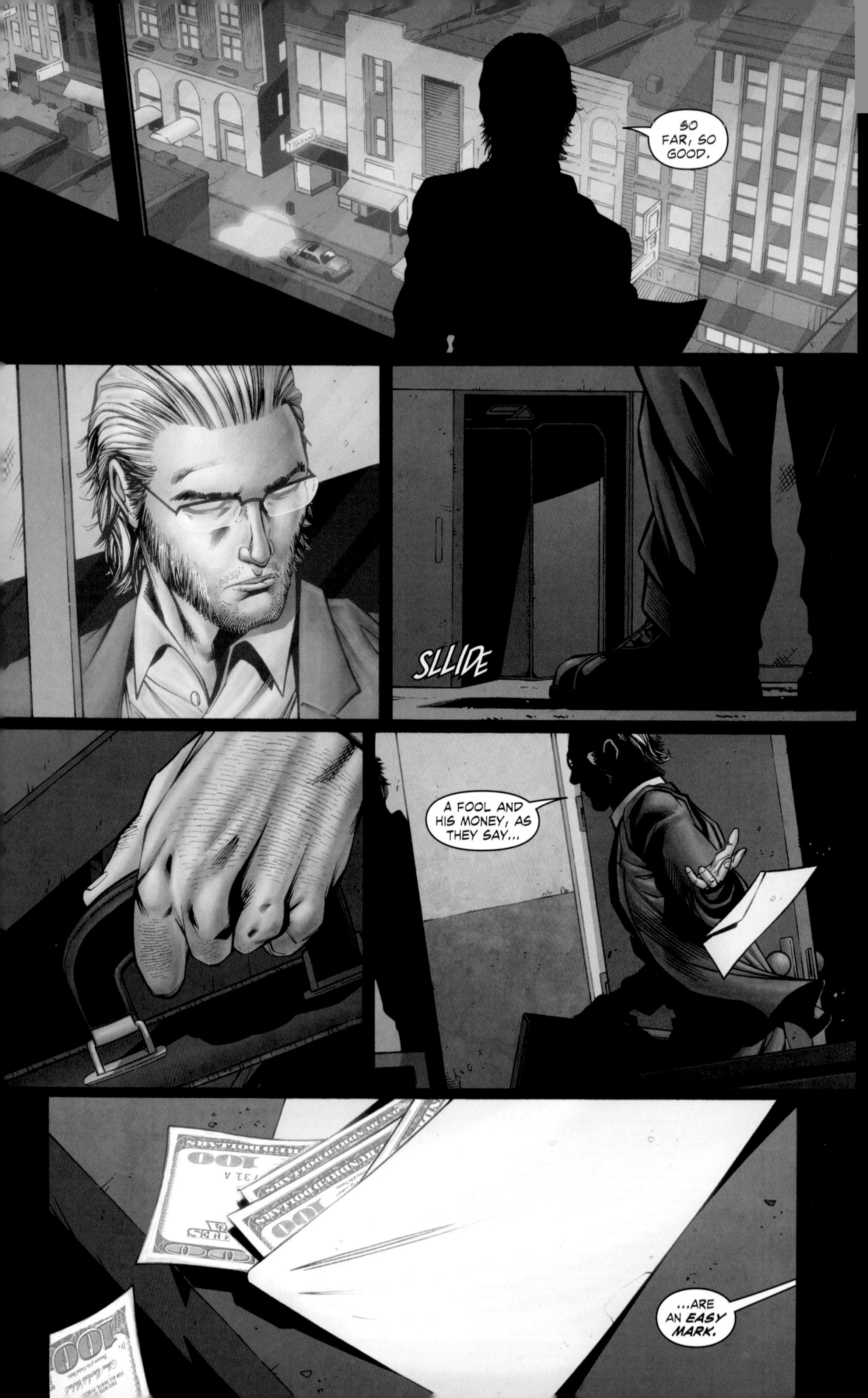
SO FAR, SO GOOD.
SLLIDE
A FOOL AND HIS MONEY, AS THEY SAY...
...ARE AN *EASY MARK.*

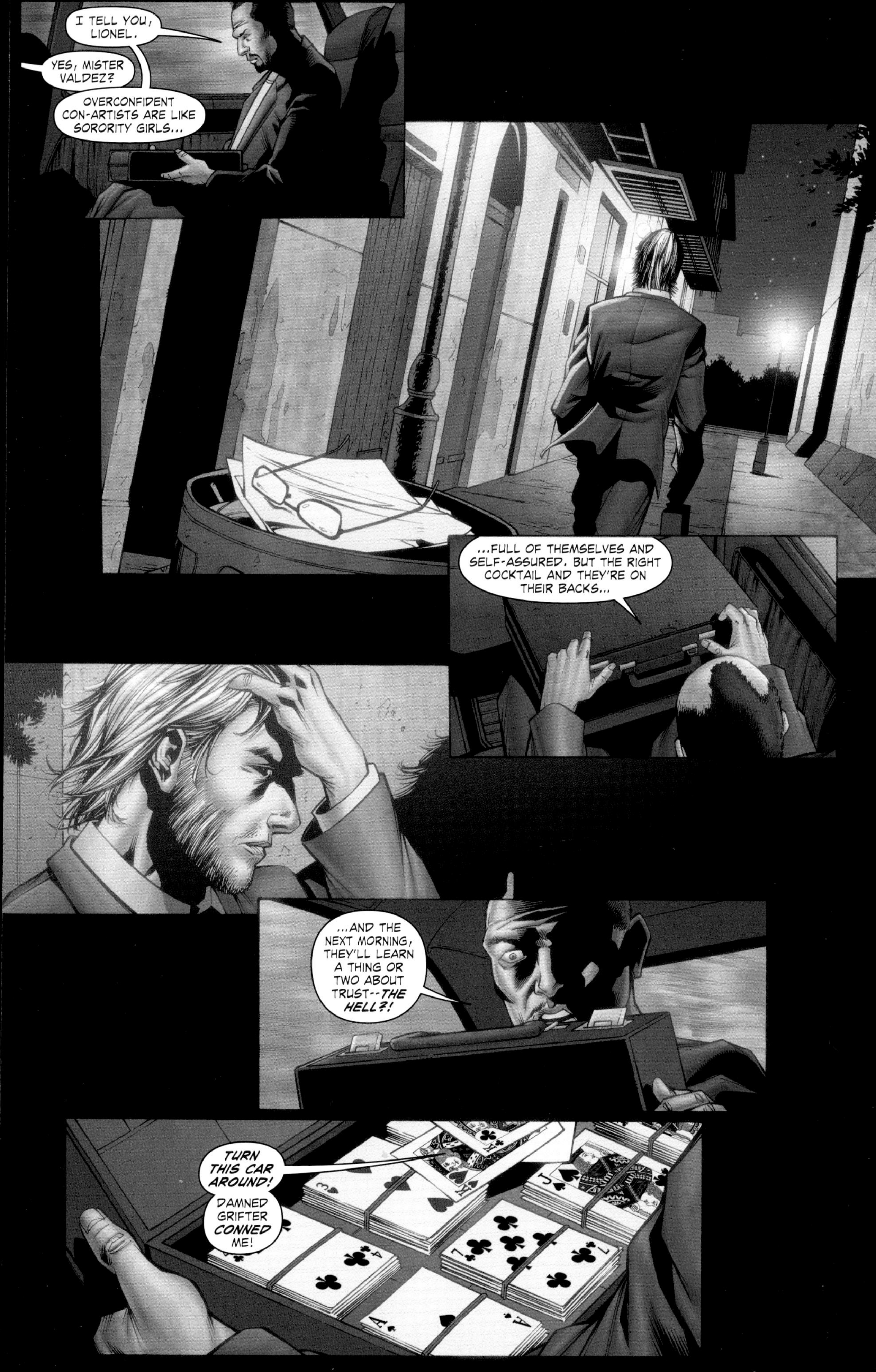
I TELL YOU, LIONEL.
YES, MISTER VALDEZ?
OVERCONFIDENT CON-ARTISTS ARE LIKE SORORITY GIRLS...
...FULL OF THEMSELVES AND SELF-ASSURED. BUT THE RIGHT COCKTAIL AND THEY'RE ON THEIR BACKS...
...AND THE NEXT MORNING, THEY'LL LEARN A THING OR TWO ABOUT TRUST--THE HELL?!
TURN THIS CAR AROUND!
DAMNED GRIFTER CONNED ME!

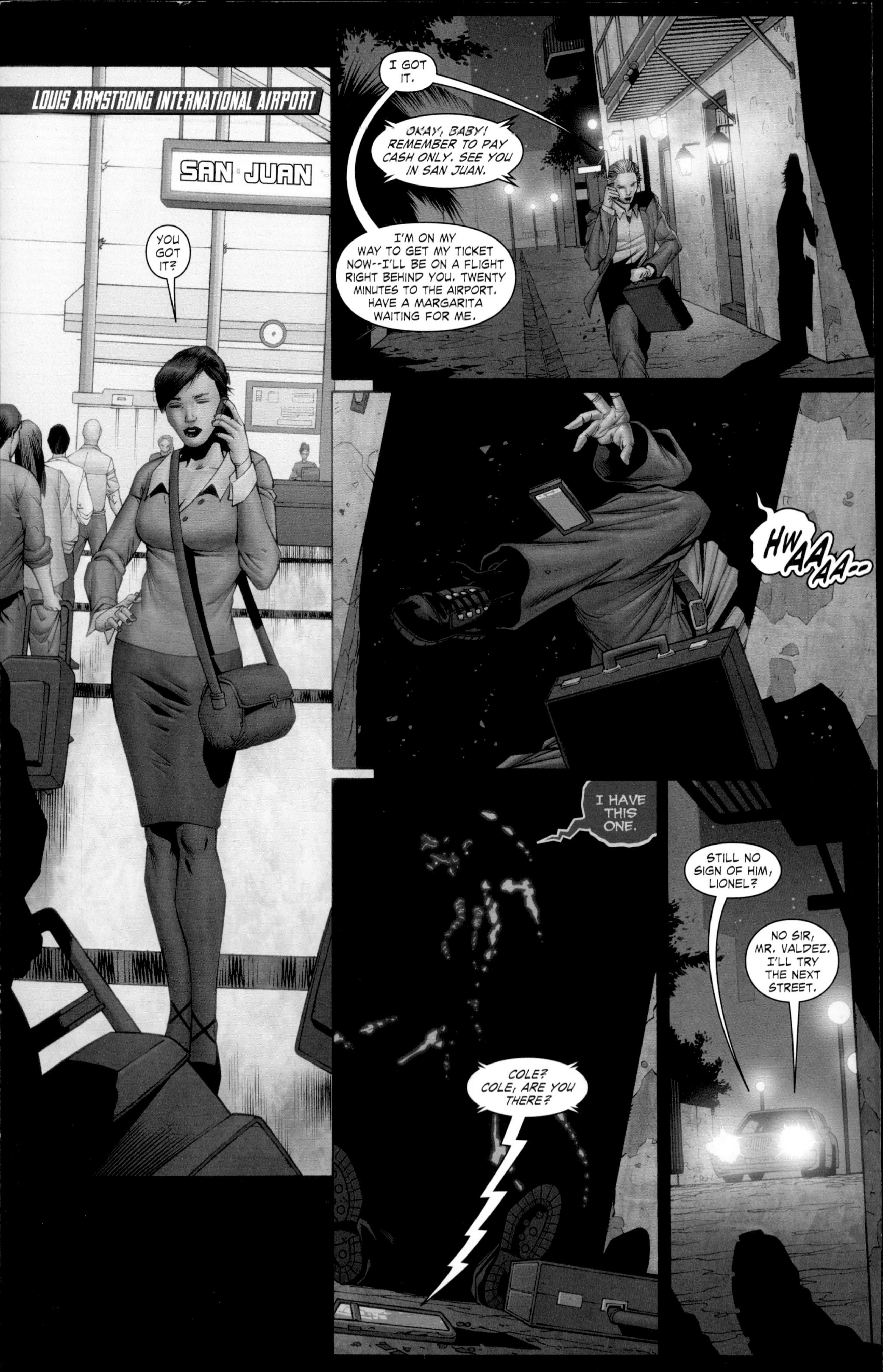
LOUIS ARMSTRONG INTERNATIONAL AIRPORT
SAN JUAN
YOU GOT IT?
I GOT IT.
OKAY, BABY! REMEMBER TO PAY CASH ONLY. SEE YOU IN SAN JUAN.
I'M ON MY WAY TO GET MY TICKET NOW--I'LL BE ON A FLIGHT RIGHT BEHIND YOU. TWENTY MINUTES TO THE AIRPORT. HAVE A MARGARITA WAITING FOR ME.
HWAAAAA--
I HAVE THIS ONE.
COLE? COLE, ARE YOU THERE?
STILL NO SIGN OF HIM, LIONEL?
NO SIR, MR. VALDEZ. I'LL TRY THE NEXT STREET.

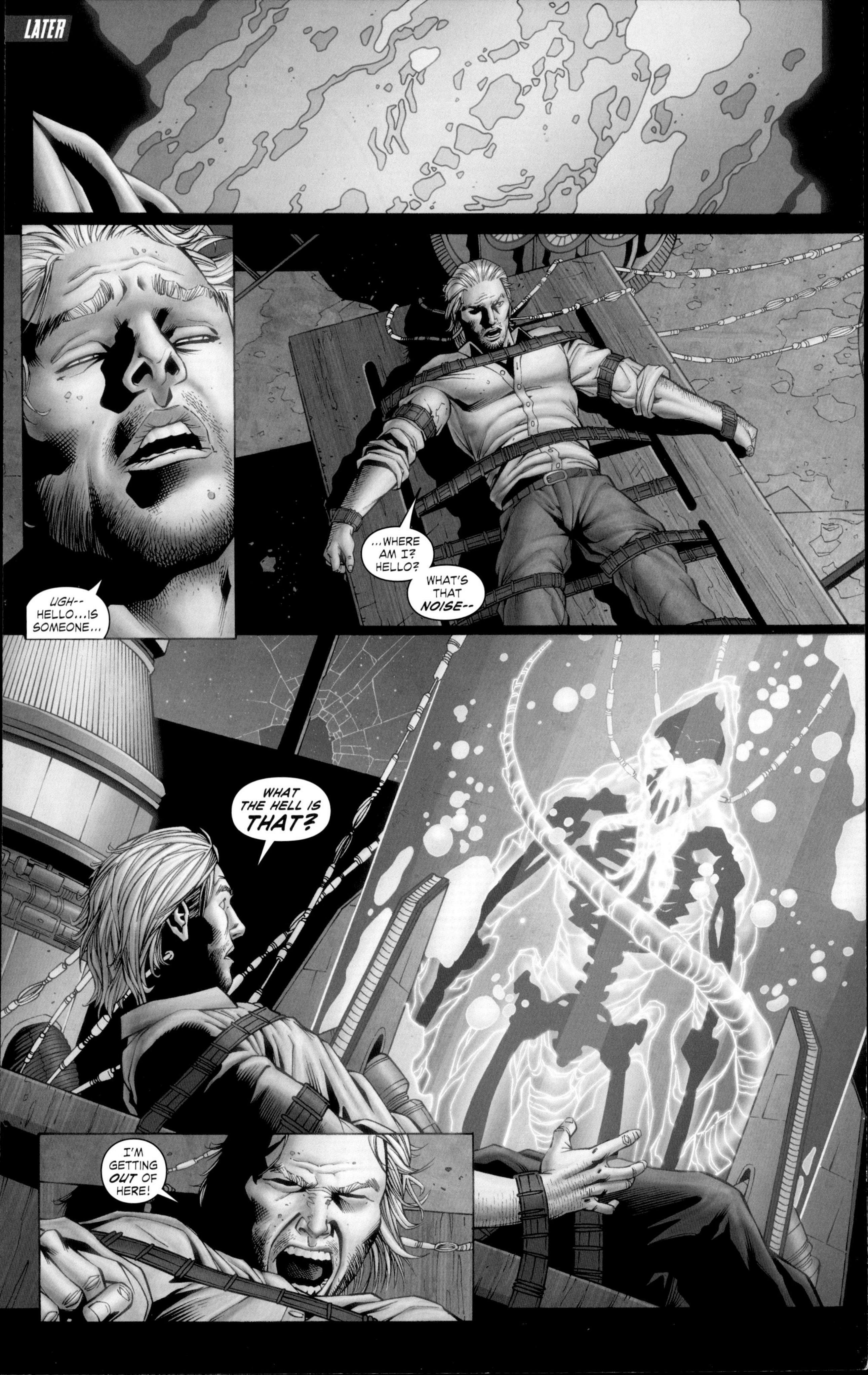
LATER
UGH-- HELLO...IS SOMEONE...
...WHERE AM I? HELLO?
WHAT'S THAT NOISE--
WHAT THE HELL IS THAT?
I'M GETTING OUT OF HERE!

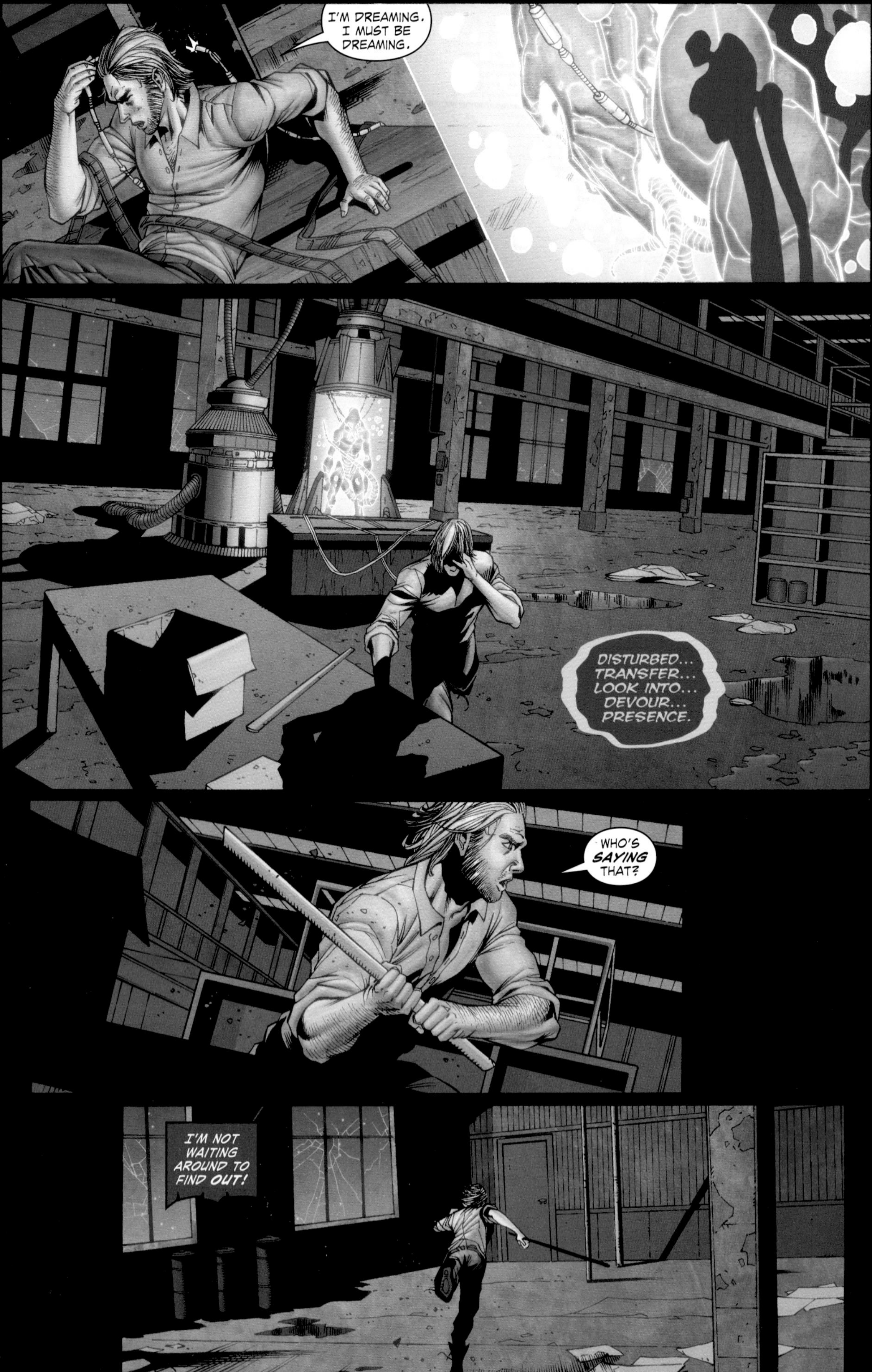
I'M DREAMING. I MUST BE DREAMING.
DISTURBED... TRANSFER... LOOK INTO... DEVOUR... PRESENCE.
WHO'S SAYING THAT?
I'M NOT WAITING AROUND TO FIND OUT!

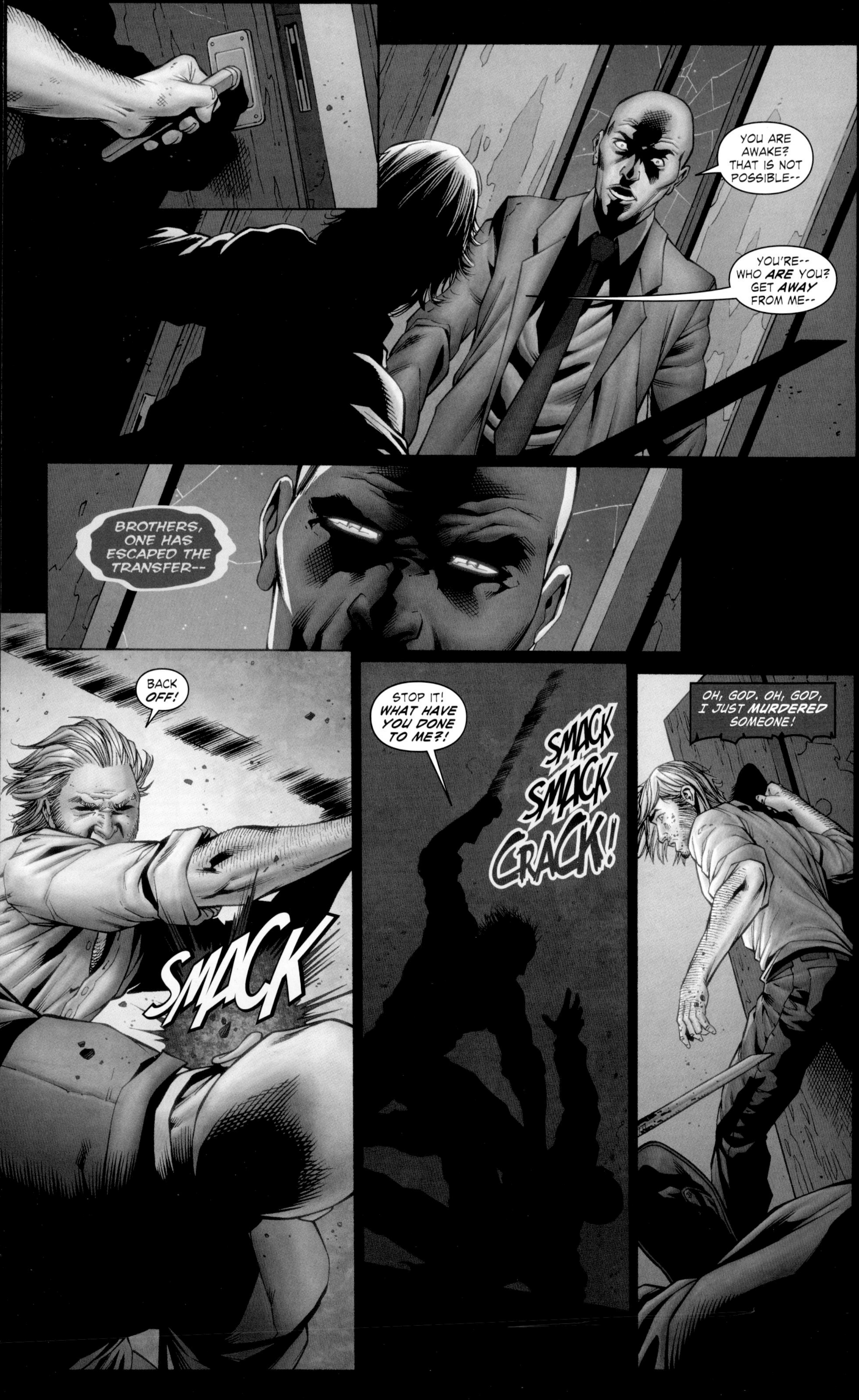
YOU ARE AWAKE? THAT IS NOT POSSIBLE--
YOU'RE-- WHO ARE YOU? GET AWAY FROM ME--
BROTHERS, ONE HAS ESCAPED THE TRANSFER--
BACK OFF!
SMACK
STOP IT! WHAT HAVE YOU DONE TO ME?!
SMACK
SMACK
CRACK!
OH, GOD. OH, GOD, I JUST MURDERED SOMEONE!

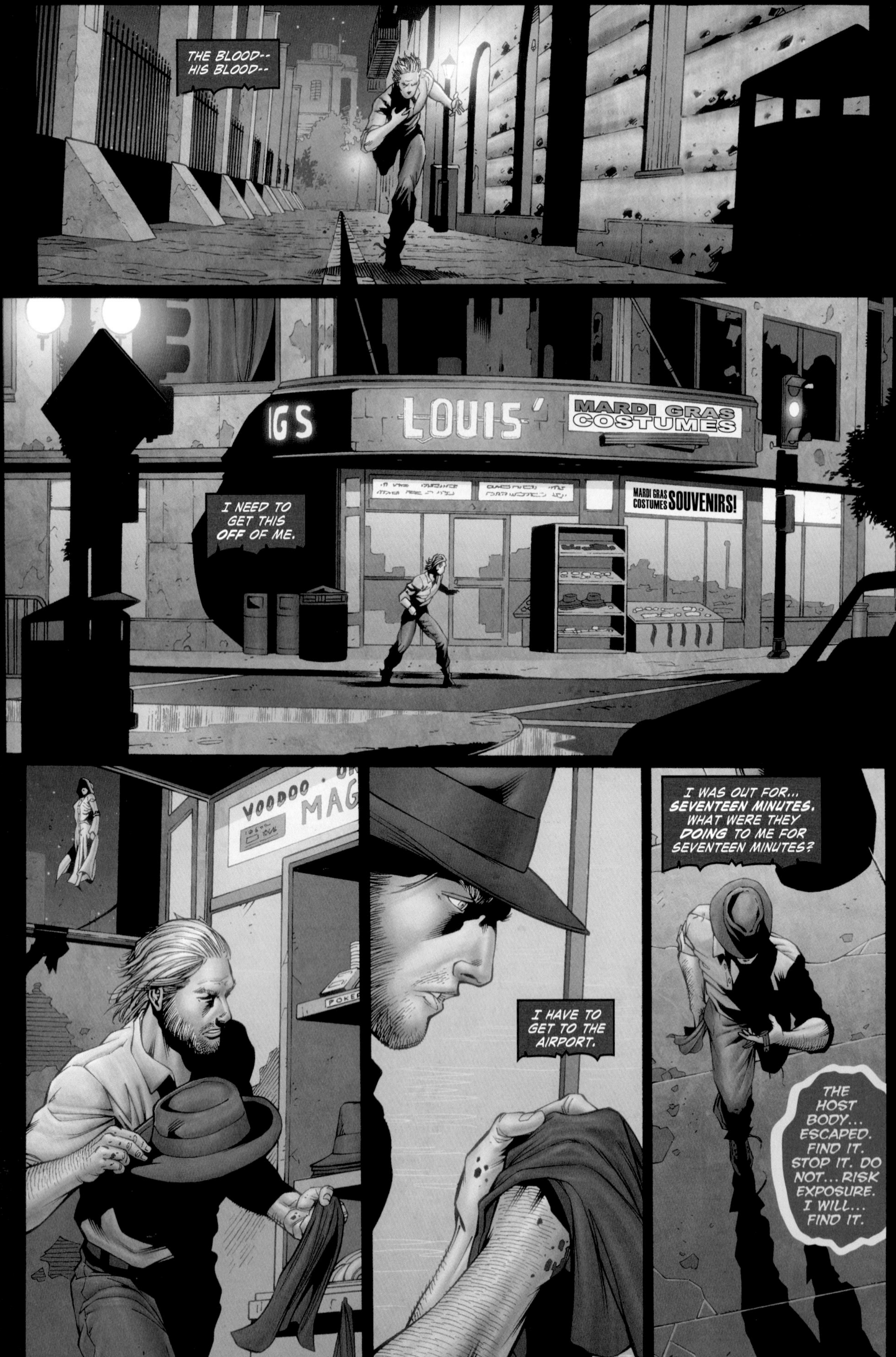
THE BLOOD-- HIS BLOOD--
IGS LOUIS'
MARDI GRAS COSTUMES
MARDI GRAS COSTUMES SOUVENIRS!
I NEED TO GET THIS OFF OF ME.
VOODOO MAG
I WAS OUT FOR... SEVENTEEN MINUTES. WHAT WERE THEY DOING TO ME FOR SEVENTEEN MINUTES?
I HAVE TO GET TO THE AIRPORT.
THE HOST BODY... ESCAPED. FIND IT. STOP IT. DO NOT... RISK EXPOSURE. I WILL... FIND IT.

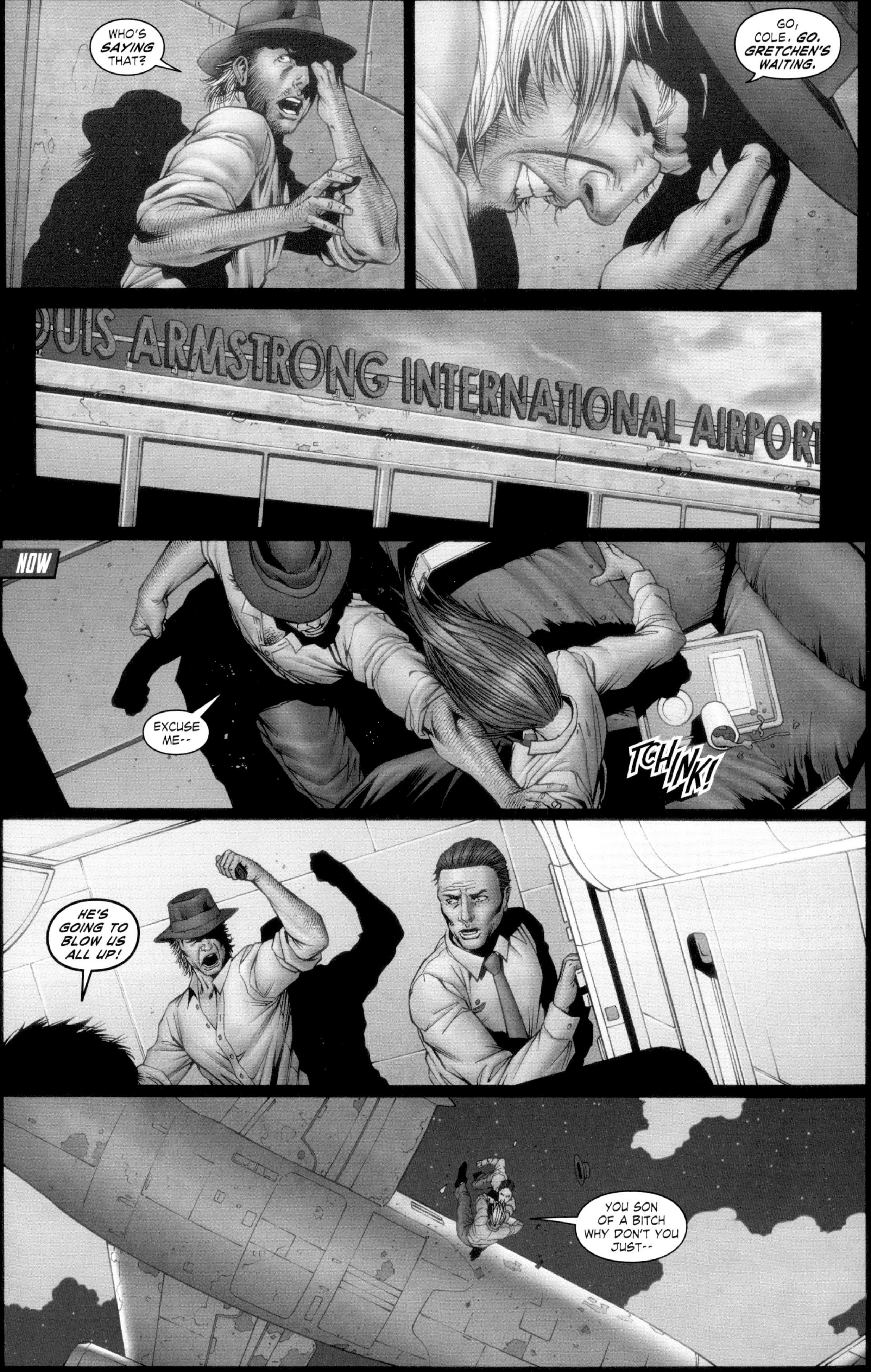
WHO'S SAYING THAT?
GO, COLE. GO. GRETCHEN'S WAITING.
OUIS ARMSTRONG INTERNATIONAL AIRPORT
NOW
EXCUSE ME--
TCHINK!
HE'S GOING TO BLOW US ALL UP!
YOU SON OF A BITCH WHY DON'T YOU JUST--

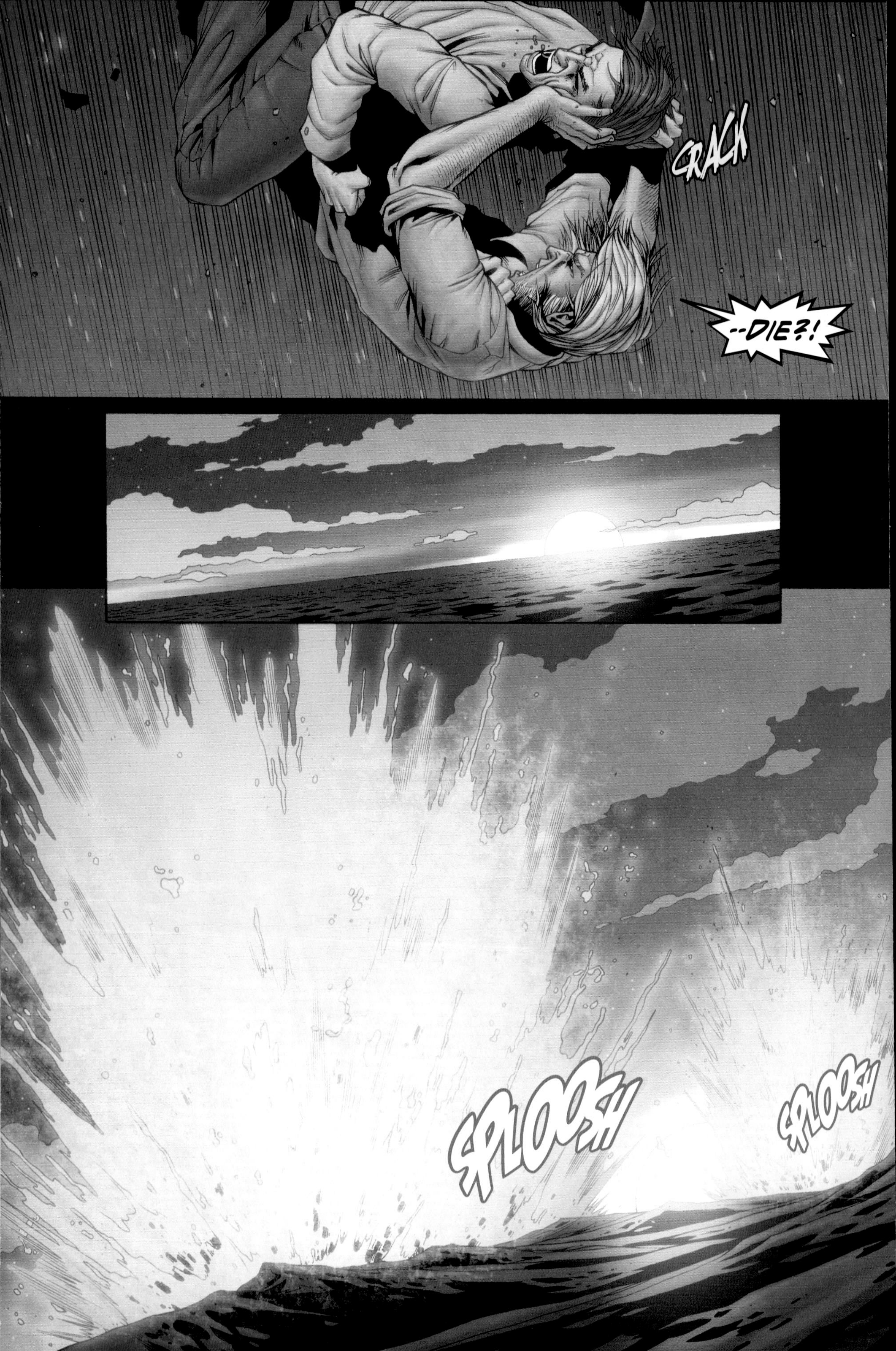
CRACK
--DIE?!
SPLOOSH
SPLOOSH

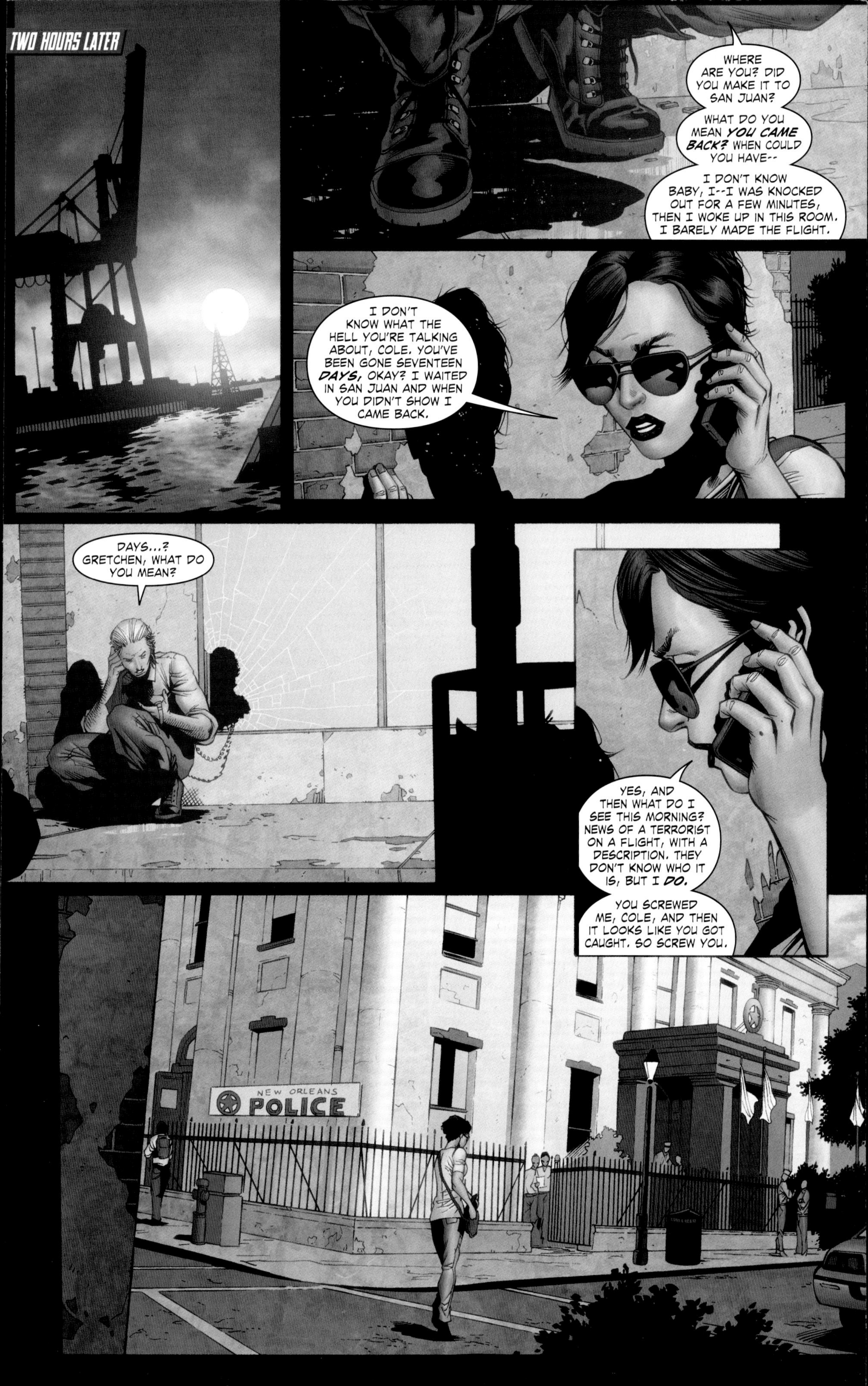

TWO HOURS LATER
WHERE ARE YOU? DID YOU MAKE IT TO SAN JUAN?
WHAT DO YOU MEAN YOU CAME BACK? WHEN COULD YOU HAVE--
I DON'T KNOW BABY, I--I WAS KNOCKED OUT FOR A FEW MINUTES, THEN I WOKE UP IN THIS ROOM. I BARELY MADE THE FLIGHT.
I DON'T KNOW WHAT THE HELL YOU'RE TALKING ABOUT, COLE. YOU'VE BEEN GONE SEVENTEEN DAYS, OKAY? I WAITED IN SAN JUAN AND WHEN YOU DIDN'T SHOW I CAME BACK.
DAYS...? GRETCHEN, WHAT DO YOU MEAN?
YES, AND THEN WHAT DO I SEE THIS MORNING? NEWS OF A TERRORIST ON A FLIGHT, WITH A DESCRIPTION. THEY DON'T KNOW WHO IT IS, BUT I DO.
YOU SCREWED ME, COLE, AND THEN IT LOOKS LIKE YOU GOT CAUGHT. SO SCREW YOU.
NEW ORLEANS POLICE

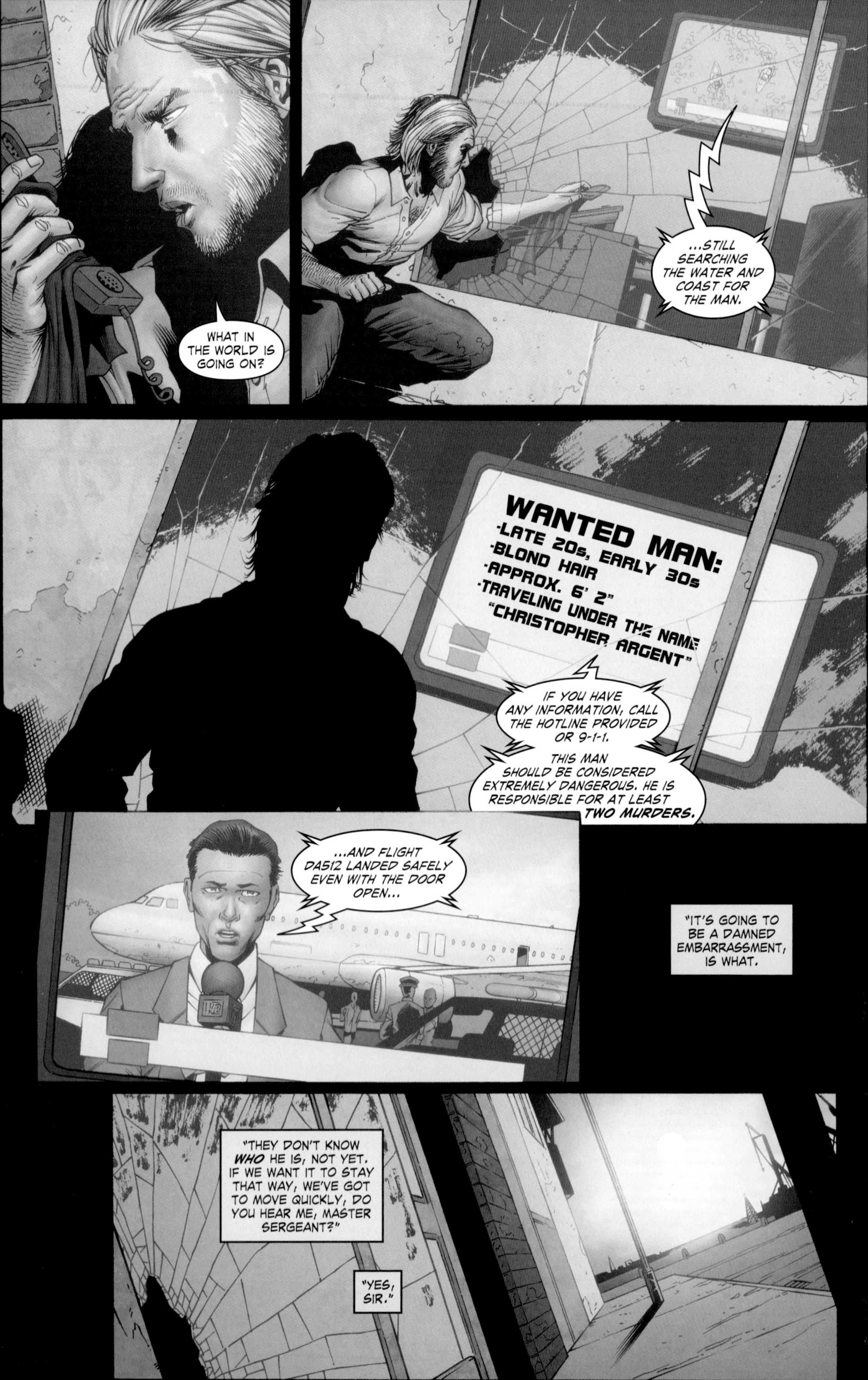
WHAT IN THE WORLD IS GOING ON?
...STILL SEARCHING THE WATER AND COAST FOR THE MAN.
WANTED MAN:
-LATE 20s, EARLY 30s
-BLOND HAIR
-APPROX. 6' 2"
-TRAVELING UNDER THE NAME "CHRISTOPHER ARGENT"
IF YOU HAVE ANY INFORMATION, CALL THE HOTLINE PROVIDED OR 9-1-1.
THIS MAN SHOULD BE CONSIDERED EXTREMELY DANGEROUS. HE IS RESPONSIBLE FOR AT LEAST TWO MURDERS.
...AND FLIGHT DA512 LANDED SAFELY EVEN WITH THE DOOR OPEN...
"IT'S GOING TO BE A DAMNED EMBARRASSMENT, IS WHAT.
"THEY DON'T KNOW WHO HE IS, NOT YET. IF WE WANT IT TO STAY THAT WAY, WE'VE GOT TO MOVE QUICKLY, DO YOU HEAR ME, MASTER SERGEANT?"
"YES, SIR."

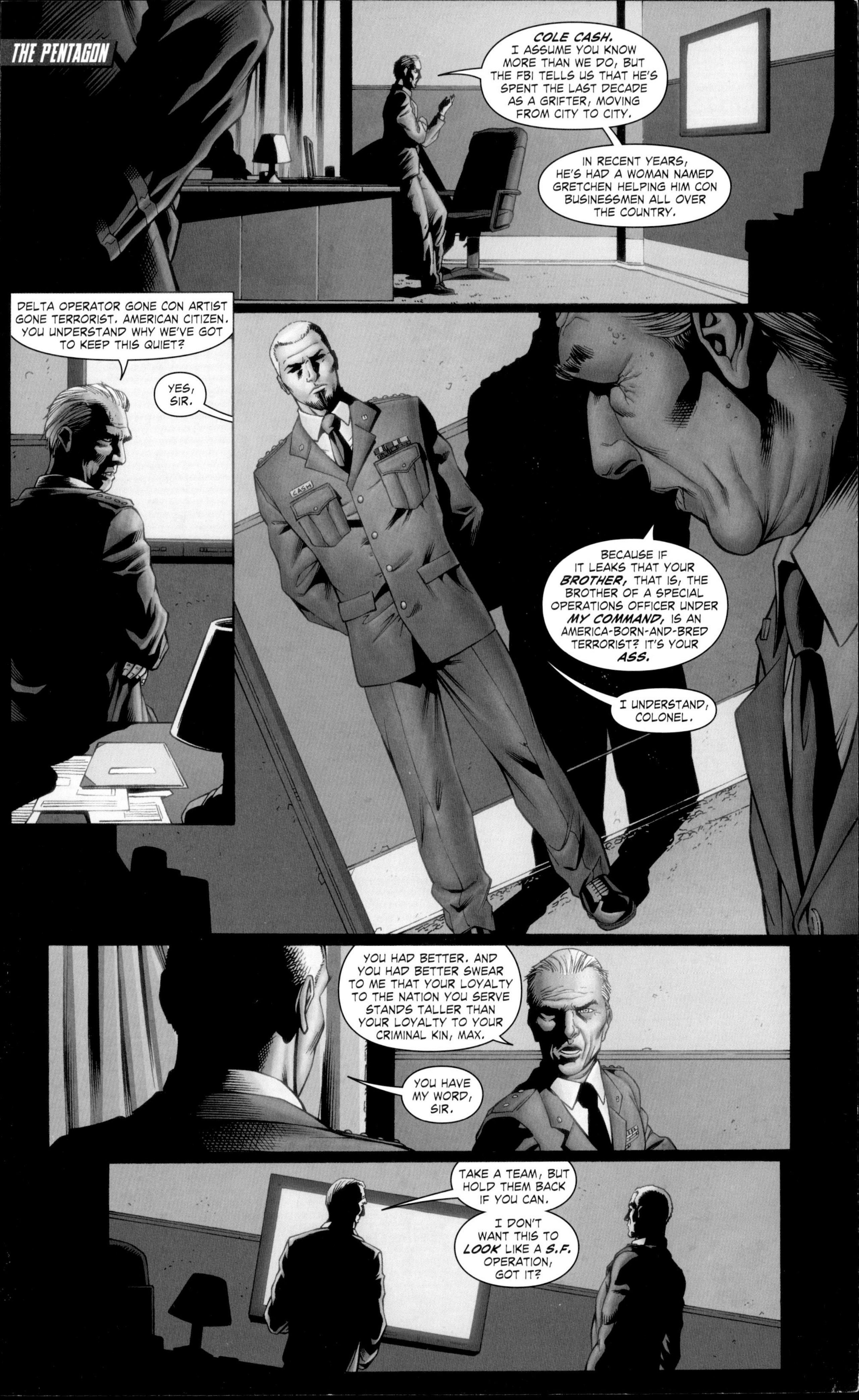

THE PENTAGON
COLE CASH. I ASSUME YOU KNOW MORE THAN WE DO, BUT THE FBI TELLS US THAT HE'S SPENT THE LAST DECADE AS A GRIFTER, MOVING FROM CITY TO CITY.
IN RECENT YEARS, HE'S HAD A WOMAN NAMED GRETCHEN HELPING HIM CON BUSINESSMEN ALL OVER THE COUNTRY.
DELTA OPERATOR GONE CON ARTIST GONE TERRORIST. AMERICAN CITIZEN. YOU UNDERSTAND WHY WE'VE GOT TO KEEP THIS QUIET?
YES, SIR.
CASH
BECAUSE IF IT LEAKS THAT YOUR BROTHER, THAT IS, THE BROTHER OF A SPECIAL OPERATIONS OFFICER UNDER MY COMMAND, IS AN AMERICA-BORN-AND-BRED TERRORIST? IT'S YOUR ASS.
I UNDERSTAND, COLONEL.
YOU HAD BETTER. AND YOU HAD BETTER SWEAR TO ME THAT YOUR LOYALTY TO THE NATION YOU SERVE STANDS TALLER THAN YOUR LOYALTY TO YOUR CRIMINAL KIN, MAX.
YOU HAVE MY WORD, SIR.
TAKE A TEAM, BUT HOLD THEM BACK IF YOU CAN.
I DON'T WANT THIS TO LOOK LIKE A S.F. OPERATION, GOT IT?

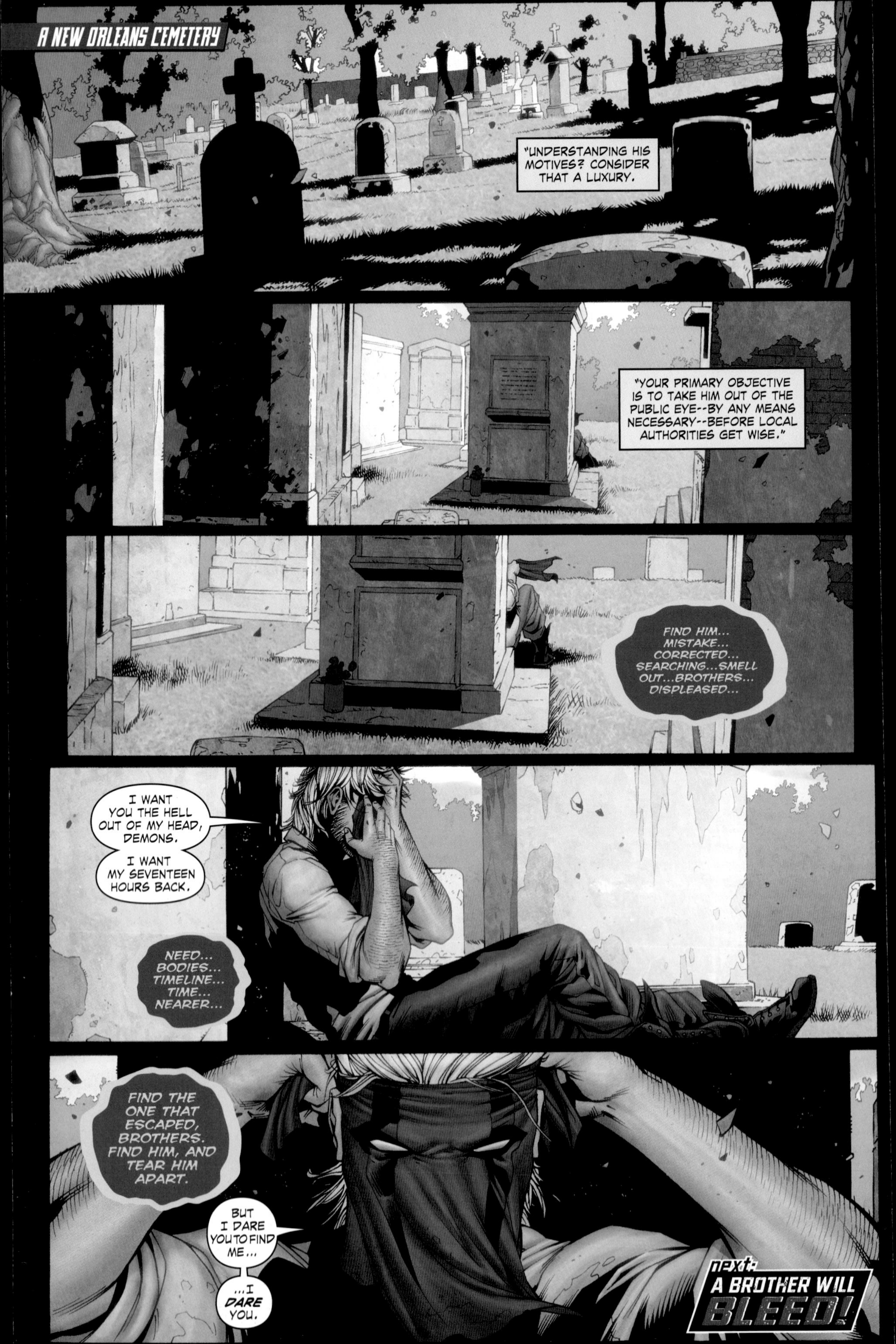
A NEW ORLEANS CEMETERY
"UNDERSTANDING HIS MOTIVES? CONSIDER THAT A LUXURY.
"YOUR PRIMARY OBJECTIVE IS TO TAKE HIM OUT OF THE PUBLIC EYE--BY ANY MEANS NECESSARY--BEFORE LOCAL AUTHORITIES GET WISE."
FIND HIM... MISTAKE... CORRECTED... SEARCHING...SMELL OUT...BROTHERS... DISPLEASED...
I WANT YOU THE HELL OUT OF MY HEAD, DEMONS.
I WANT MY SEVENTEEN HOURS BACK.
NEED... BODIES... TIMELINE... TIME... NEARER...
FIND THE ONE THAT ESCAPED, BROTHERS. FIND HIM, AND TEAR HIM APART.
BUT I DARE YOU TO FIND ME...
...I DARE YOU.
next: A BROTHER WILL BLEED!

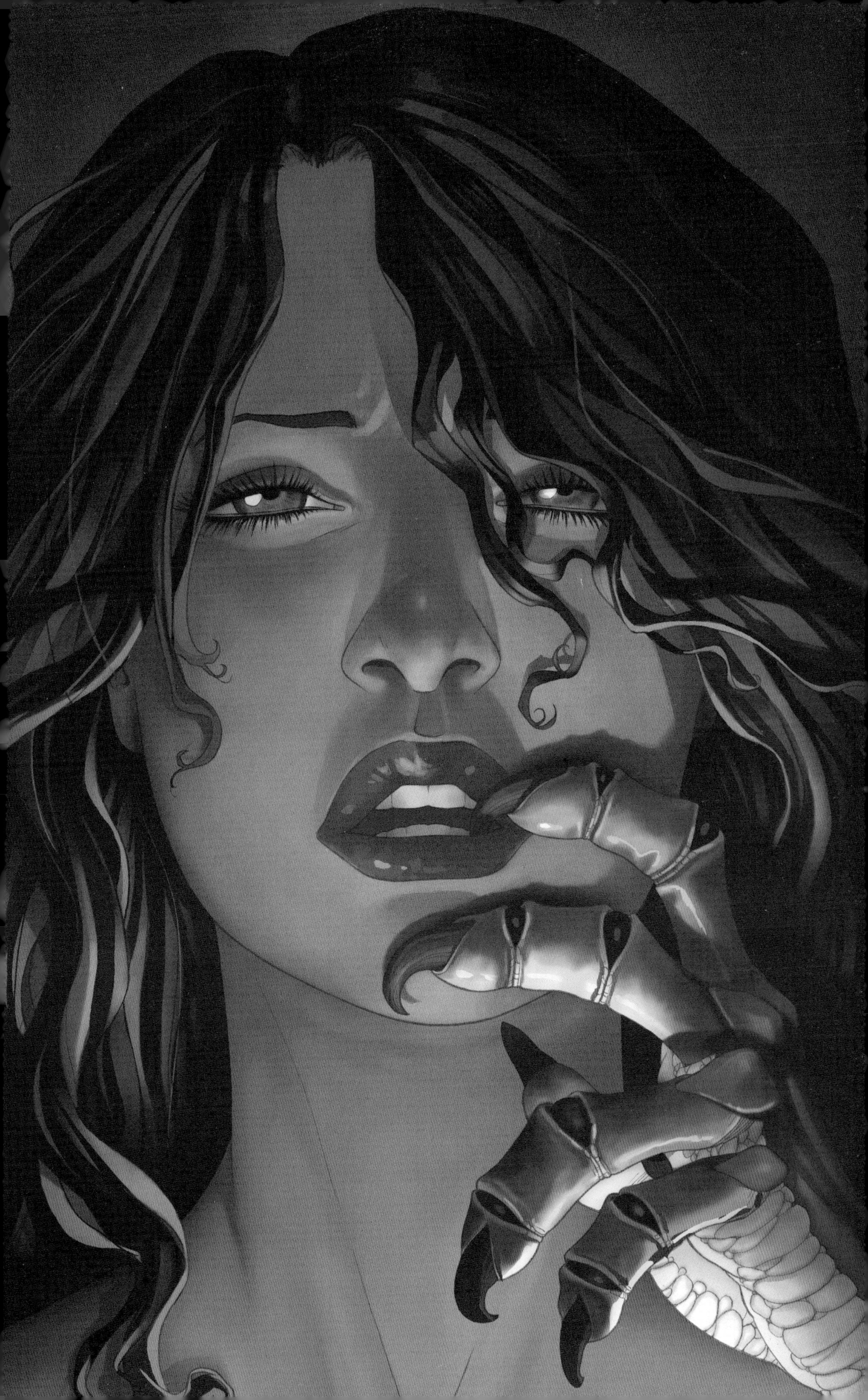

Voodoo

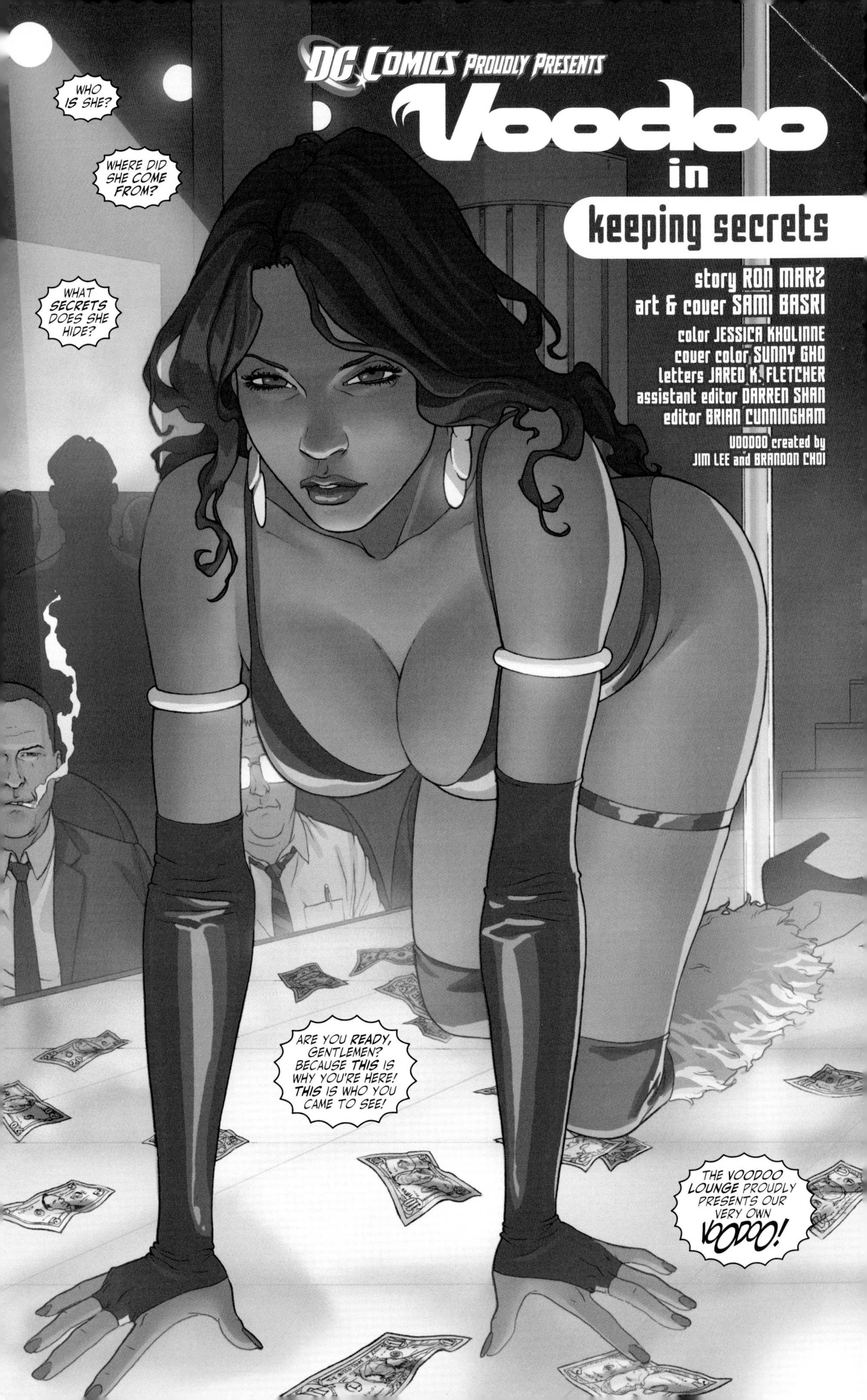
DC COMICS PROUDLY PRESENTS
Voodoo
in
keeping secrets
story RON MARZ
art & cover SAMI BASRI
color JESSICA KHOLINNE
cover color SUNNY GHO
letters JARED K. FLETCHER
assistant editor DARREN SHAN
editor BRIAN CUNNINGHAM
VOODOO created by
JIM LEE and BRANDON CHOI
WHO IS SHE?
WHERE DID SHE COME FROM?
WHAT SECRETS DOES SHE HIDE?
ARE YOU READY, GENTLEMEN? BECAUSE THIS IS WHY YOU'RE HERE! THIS IS WHO YOU CAME TO SEE!
THE VOODOO LOUNGE PROUDLY PRESENTS OUR VERY OWN VOODOO!

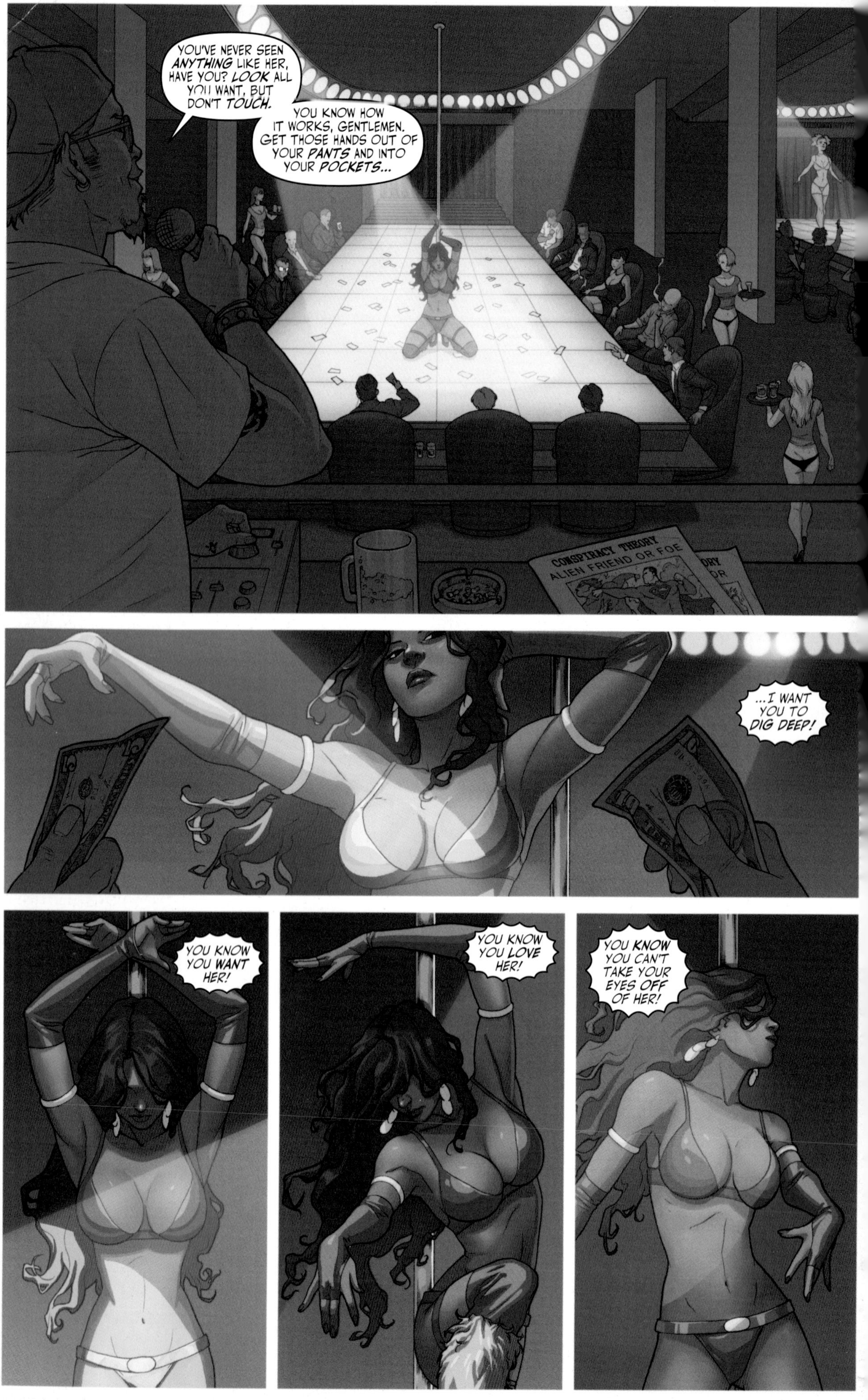
YOU'VE NEVER SEEN ANYTHING LIKE HER, HAVE YOU? LOOK ALL YOU WANT, BUT DON'T TOUCH.
YOU KNOW HOW IT WORKS, GENTLEMEN. GET THOSE HANDS OUT OF YOUR PANTS AND INTO YOUR POCKETS...
CONSPIRACY THEORY
ALIEN FRIEND OR FOE
...I WANT YOU TO DIG DEEP!
YOU KNOW YOU WANT HER!
YOU KNOW YOU LOVE HER!
YOU KNOW YOU CAN'T TAKE YOUR EYES OFF OF HER!

HOW LONG YOU PLANNING ON SITTING HERE, EVANS?

WHAT'S THE PROBLEM? WE'RE GETTING *PAID*. ENJOY THE SHOW.

NOT MY FLAVOR. WHICH I THINK YOU *KNOW*.

WE'RE SUPPOSED TO BE KEEPING AN EYE ON HER, RIGHT? THAT'S WHAT I'M DOING, FALLON.

WE DON'T NEED TO BE DOING IT FROM A RINGSIDE SEAT.

IT'S NOT LIKE WE CAN *MOVE* ON HER WITHOUT EXEC ORDERS ANYWAY.

WELL, I'D BETTER STICK CLOSE TO THE TARGET JUST IN CASE.

YOU'RE AN ASS.

I'M GOING BACK TO MY ROOM.

SUIT YOURSELF.

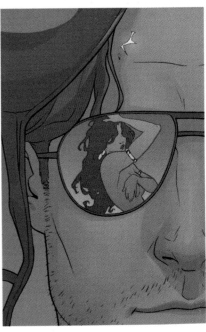

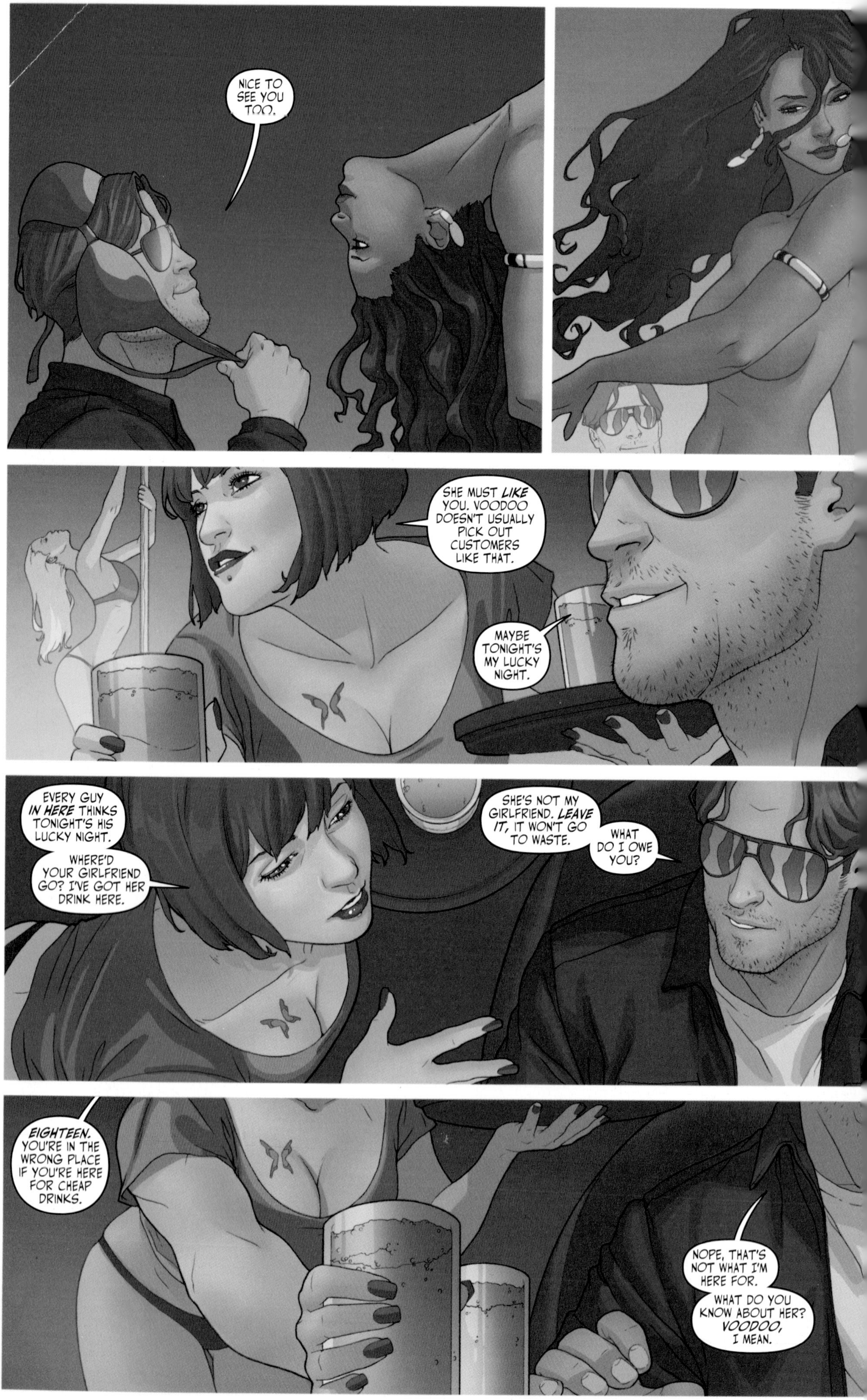
NICE TO SEE YOU TOO.
SHE MUST *LIKE* YOU. VOODOO DOESN'T USUALLY PICK OUT CUSTOMERS LIKE THAT.
MAYBE TONIGHT'S MY LUCKY NIGHT.
EVERY GUY *IN HERE* THINKS TONIGHT'S HIS LUCKY NIGHT.
WHERE'D YOUR GIRLFRIEND GO? I'VE GOT HER DRINK HERE.
SHE'S NOT MY GIRLFRIEND. *LEAVE IT,* IT WON'T GO TO WASTE.
WHAT DO I OWE YOU?
EIGHTEEN. YOU'RE IN THE WRONG PLACE IF YOU'RE HERE FOR CHEAP DRINKS.
NOPE, THAT'S NOT WHAT I'M HERE FOR.
WHAT DO YOU KNOW ABOUT HER? *VOODOO,* I MEAN.

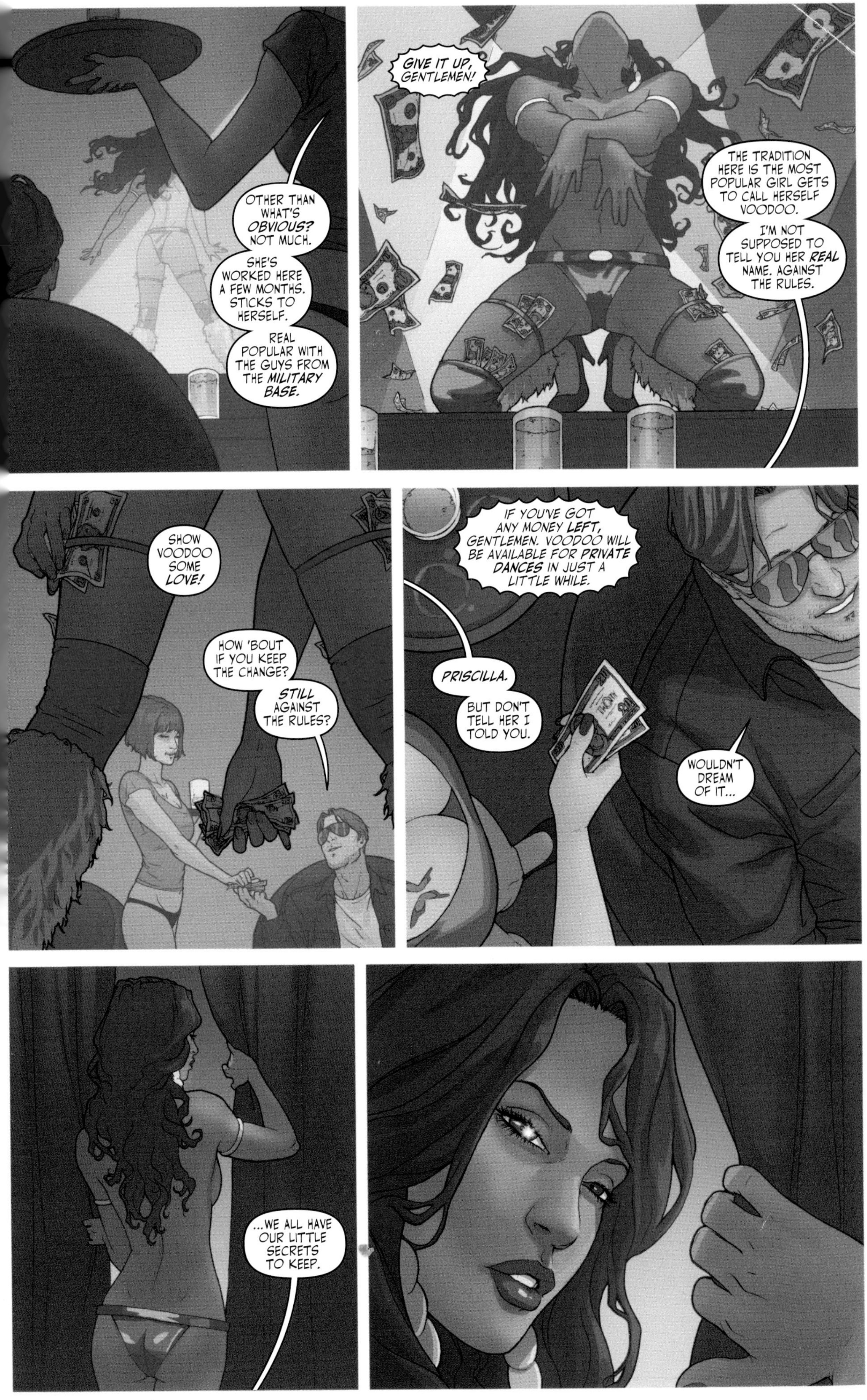
OTHER THAN WHAT'S *OBVIOUS?* NOT MUCH.
SHE'S WORKED HERE A FEW MONTHS. STICKS TO HERSELF.
REAL POPULAR WITH THE GUYS FROM THE *MILITARY BASE.*
GIVE IT UP, GENTLEMEN!
THE TRADITION HERE IS THE MOST POPULAR GIRL GETS TO CALL HERSELF VOODOO.
I'M NOT SUPPOSED TO TELL YOU HER *REAL* NAME. AGAINST THE RULES.
SHOW VOODOO SOME *LOVE!*
HOW 'BOUT IF YOU KEEP THE CHANGE?
STILL AGAINST THE RULES?
IF YOU'VE GOT ANY MONEY **LEFT,** GENTLEMEN. VOODOO WILL BE AVAILABLE FOR **PRIVATE DANCES** IN JUST A LITTLE WHILE.
PRISCILLA.
BUT DON'T TELL HER I TOLD YOU.
WOULDN'T DREAM OF IT...
...WE ALL HAVE OUR LITTLE SECRETS TO KEEP.

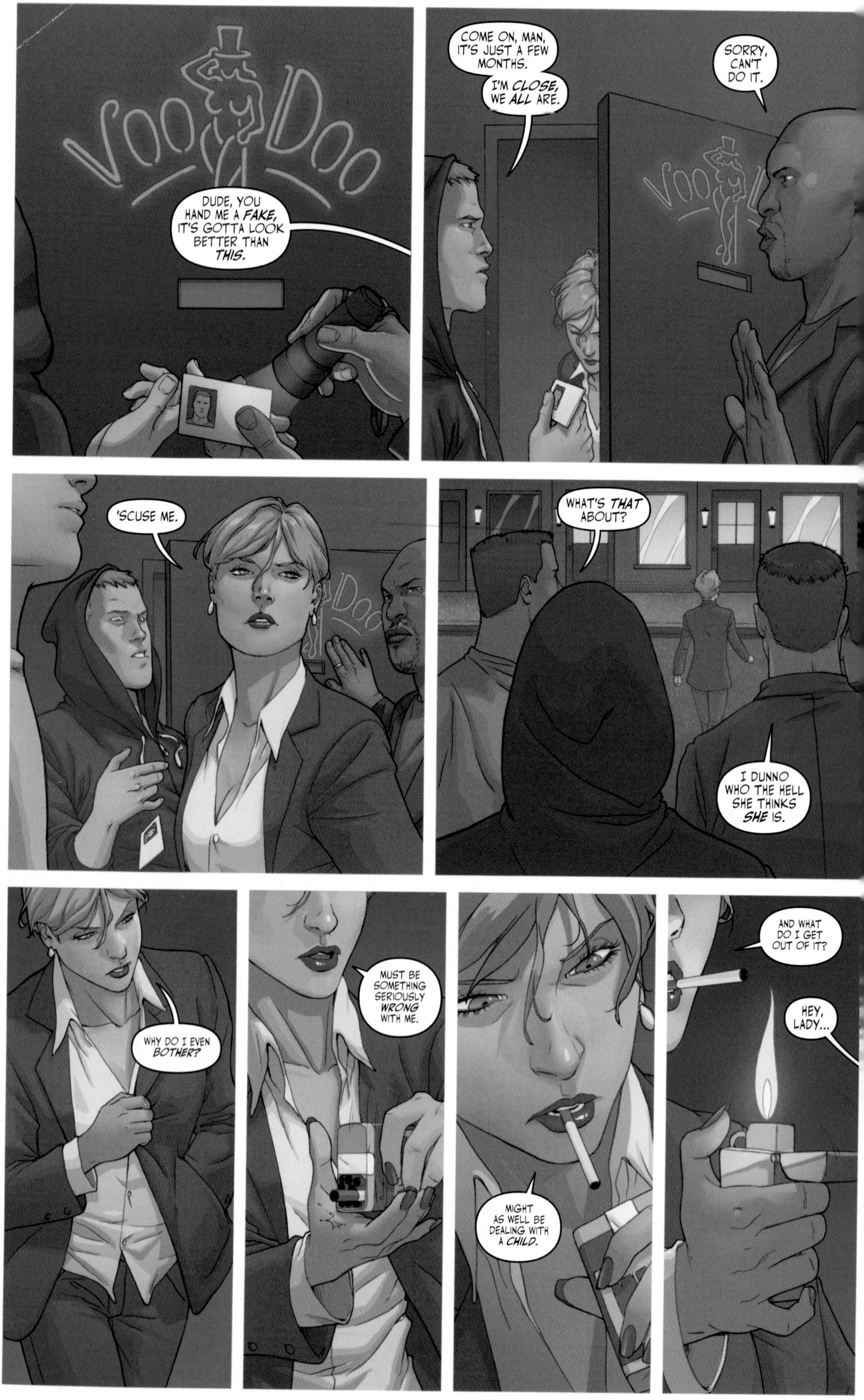
DUDE, YOU HAND ME A FAKE, IT'S GOTTA LOOK BETTER THAN THIS.
COME ON, MAN, IT'S JUST A FEW MONTHS.
I'M CLOSE, WE ALL ARE.
SORRY, CAN'T DO IT.
'SCUSE ME.
WHAT'S THAT ABOUT?
I DUNNO WHO THE HELL SHE THINKS SHE IS.
WHY DO I EVEN BOTHER?
MUST BE SOMETHING SERIOUSLY WRONG WITH ME.
MIGHT AS WELL BE DEALING WITH A CHILD.
AND WHAT DO I GET OUT OF IT?
HEY, LADY...

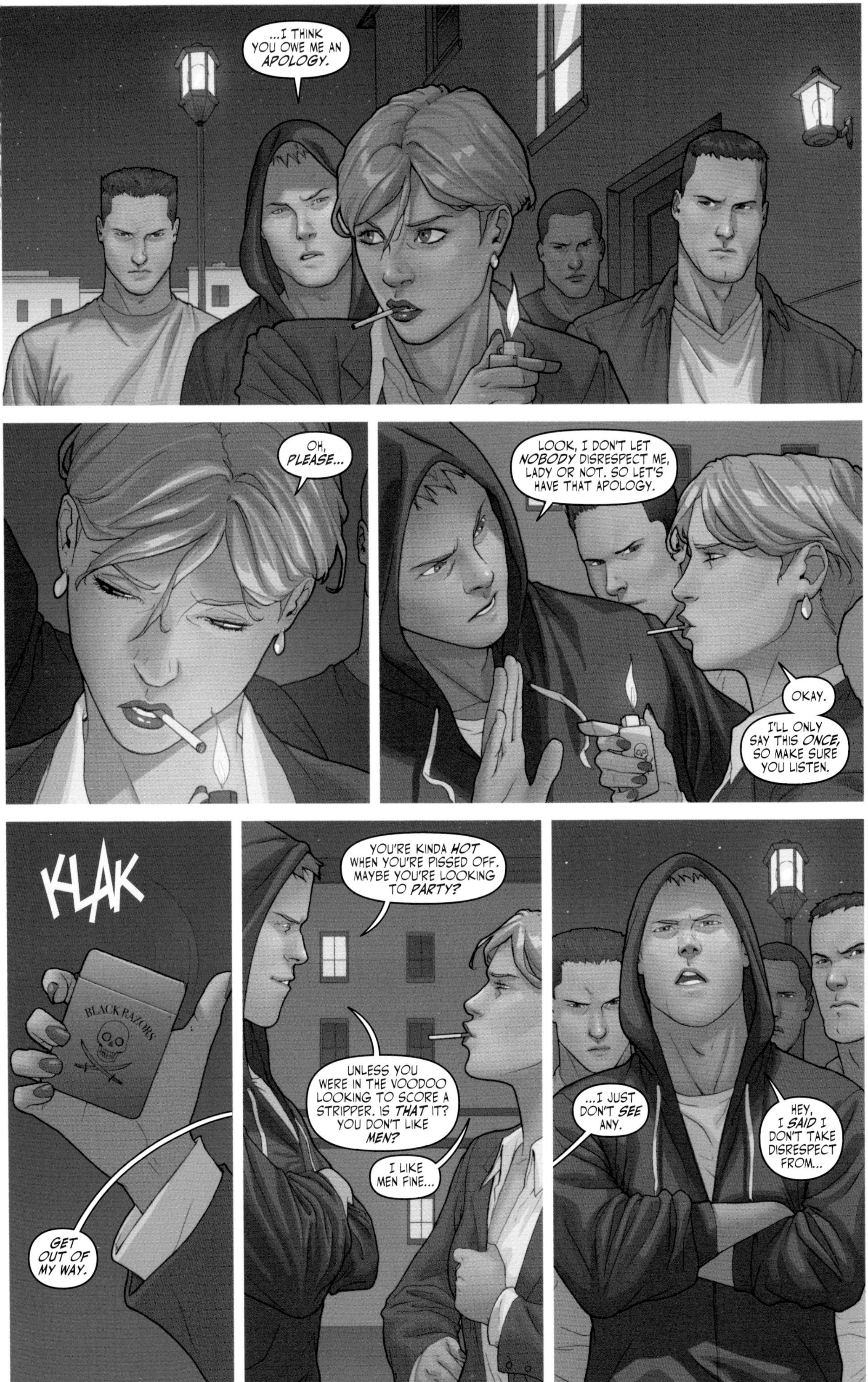
...I THINK YOU OWE ME AN APOLOGY.
OH, PLEASE...
LOOK, I DON'T LET NOBODY DISRESPECT ME, LADY OR NOT. SO LET'S HAVE THAT APOLOGY.
OKAY.
I'LL ONLY SAY THIS ONCE, SO MAKE SURE YOU LISTEN.
KLAK
BLACK RAZORS
GET OUT OF MY WAY.
YOU'RE KINDA HOT WHEN YOU'RE PISSED OFF. MAYBE YOU'RE LOOKING TO PARTY?
UNLESS YOU WERE IN THE VOODOO LOOKING TO SCORE A STRIPPER. IS THAT IT? YOU DON'T LIKE MEN?
I LIKE MEN FINE...
...I JUST DON'T SEE ANY.
HEY, I SAID I DON'T TAKE DISRESPECT FROM...

AAGH!

OWFF!

GUH!

UNGH!

SHOULD'VE LISTENED.

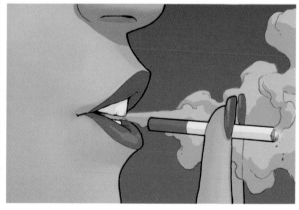

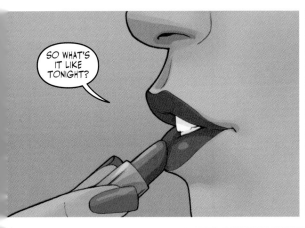

SO WHAT'S IT LIKE TONIGHT?

THEY FEELING *GENEROUS* OUT THERE...

...OR IS IT STRICTLY *SINGLES?*

I DID OKAY.

YOU *ALWAYS* DO OKAY.

ANYBODY SEE MY *TOP?* THE SPARKLY ONE?

GREAT, THAT'S *ALL* I NEEDED.

MY *SITTER* FOR TOMORROW JUST CANCELED. CAN ANYBODY WATCH CODY DURING MY SHIFT?

I'M WORKING THE SAME SHIFT AS YOU, ABBY.

SORRY, I'VE GOT CLASS.

ANYBODY ELSE?

PRIS, WHAT ABOUT YOU?

UM... NO, I'M...

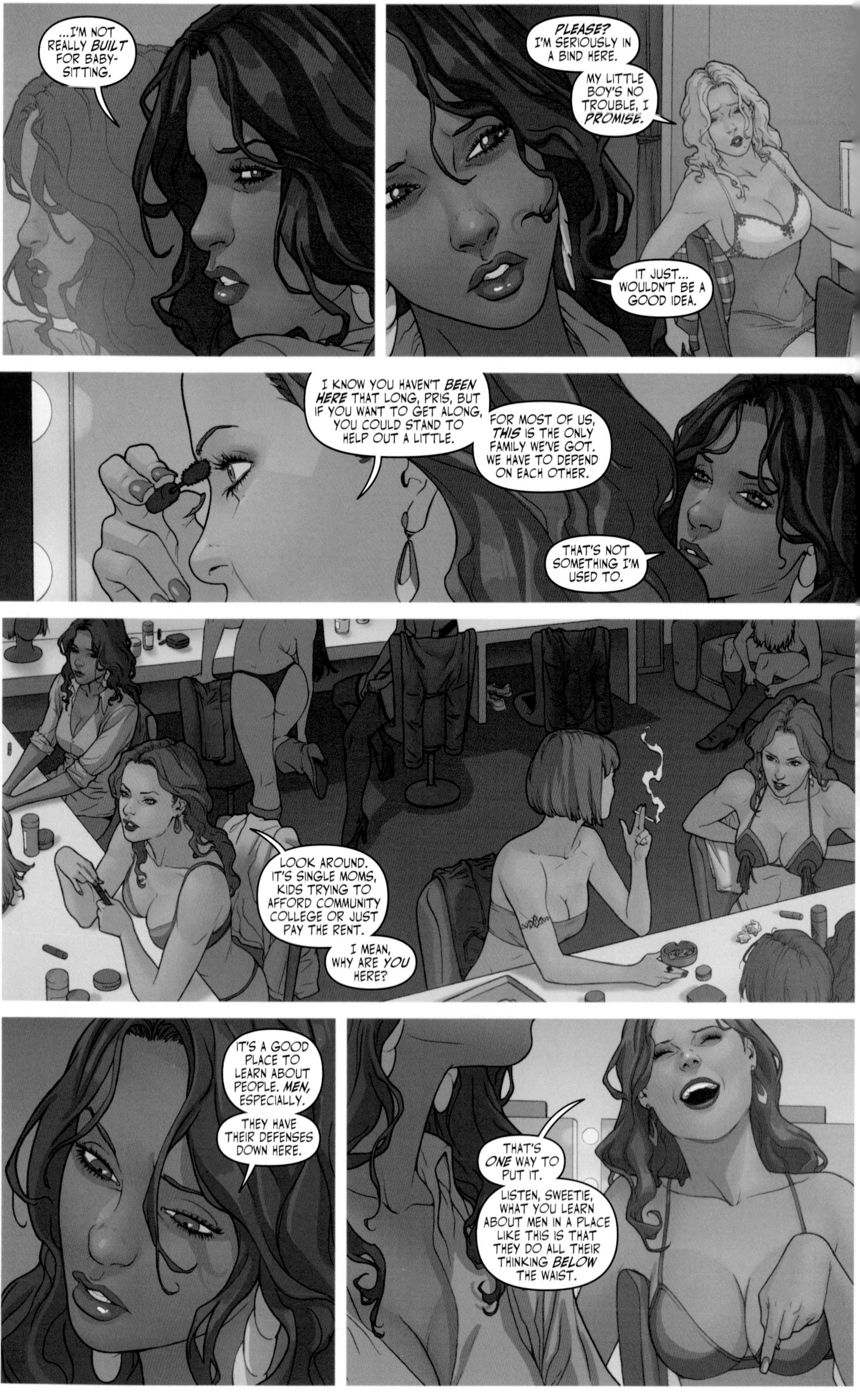

...I'M NOT REALLY BUILT FOR BABY-SITTING.
PLEASE? I'M SERIOUSLY IN A BIND HERE.
MY LITTLE BOY'S NO TROUBLE, I PROMISE.
IT JUST... WOULDN'T BE A GOOD IDEA.
I KNOW YOU HAVEN'T BEEN HERE THAT LONG, PRIS, BUT IF YOU WANT TO GET ALONG, YOU COULD STAND TO HELP OUT A LITTLE.
FOR MOST OF US, THIS IS THE ONLY FAMILY WE'VE GOT. WE HAVE TO DEPEND ON EACH OTHER.
THAT'S NOT SOMETHING I'M USED TO.
LOOK AROUND. IT'S SINGLE MOMS, KIDS TRYING TO AFFORD COMMUNITY COLLEGE OR JUST PAY THE RENT.
I MEAN, WHY ARE YOU HERE?
IT'S A GOOD PLACE TO LEARN ABOUT PEOPLE. MEN, ESPECIALLY.
THEY HAVE THEIR DEFENSES DOWN HERE.
THAT'S ONE WAY TO PUT IT.
LISTEN, SWEETIE, WHAT YOU LEARN ABOUT MEN IN A PLACE LIKE THIS IS THAT THEY DO ALL THEIR THINKING BELOW THE WAIST.

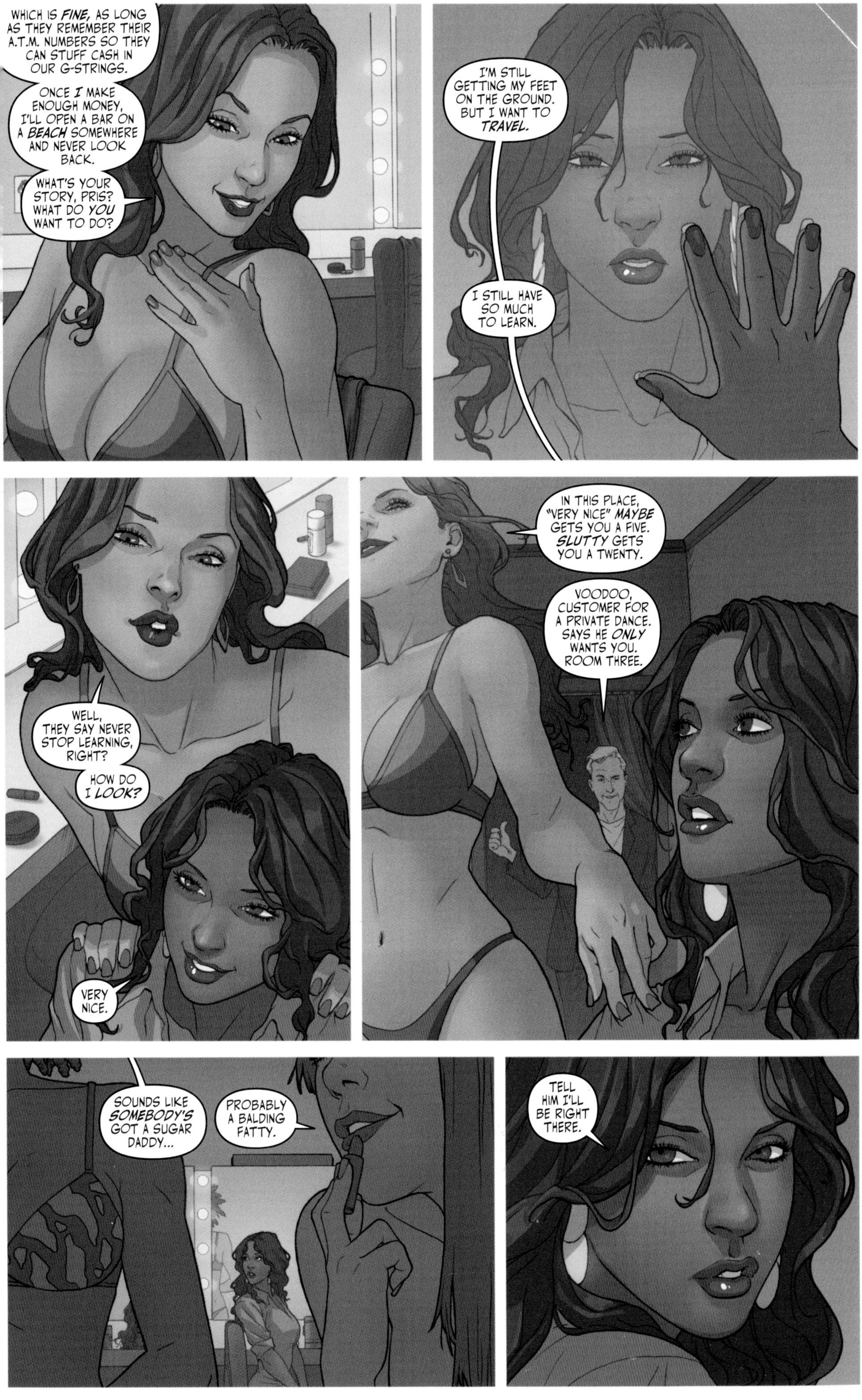
WHICH IS *FINE,* AS LONG AS THEY REMEMBER THEIR A.T.M. NUMBERS SO THEY CAN STUFF CASH IN OUR G-STRINGS.
ONCE *I* MAKE ENOUGH MONEY, I'LL OPEN A BAR ON A *BEACH* SOMEWHERE AND NEVER LOOK BACK.
WHAT'S YOUR STORY, PRIS? WHAT DO *YOU* WANT TO DO?
I'M STILL GETTING MY FEET ON THE GROUND. BUT I WANT TO *TRAVEL.*
I STILL HAVE SO MUCH TO LEARN.
WELL, THEY SAY NEVER STOP LEARNING, RIGHT?
HOW DO I *LOOK?*
VERY NICE.
IN THIS PLACE, "VERY NICE" *MAYBE* GETS YOU A FIVE. *SLUTTY* GETS YOU A TWENTY.
VOODOO, CUSTOMER FOR A PRIVATE DANCE. SAYS HE *ONLY* WANTS YOU. ROOM THREE.
SOUNDS LIKE *SOMEBODY'S* GOT A SUGAR DADDY...
PROBABLY A BALDING FATTY.
TELL HIM I'LL BE RIGHT THERE.

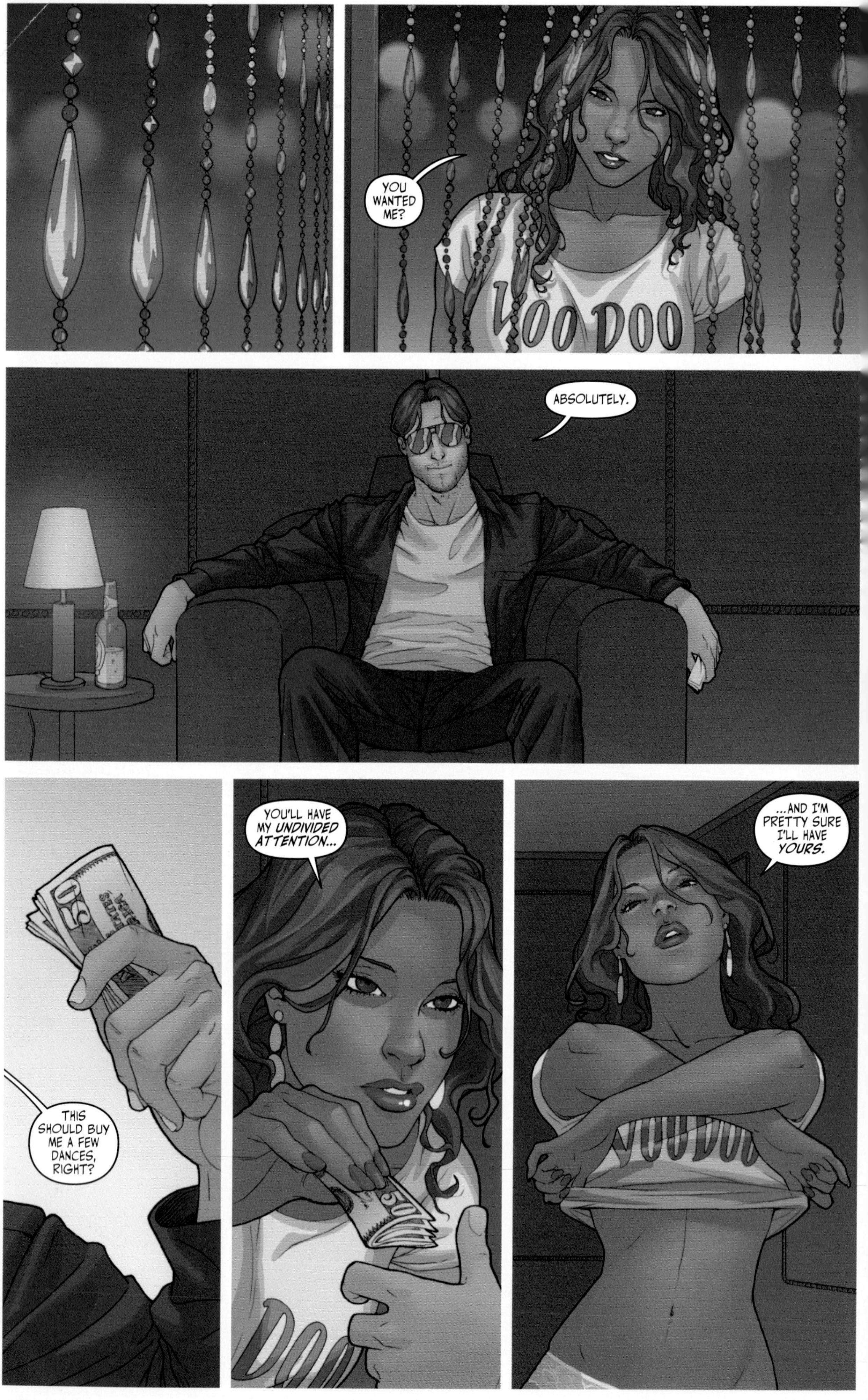

YOU WANTED ME?
ABSOLUTELY.
THIS SHOULD BUY ME A FEW DANCES, RIGHT?
YOU'LL HAVE MY *UNDIVIDED ATTENTION...*
...AND I'M PRETTY SURE I'LL HAVE *YOURS.*
VOO DOO

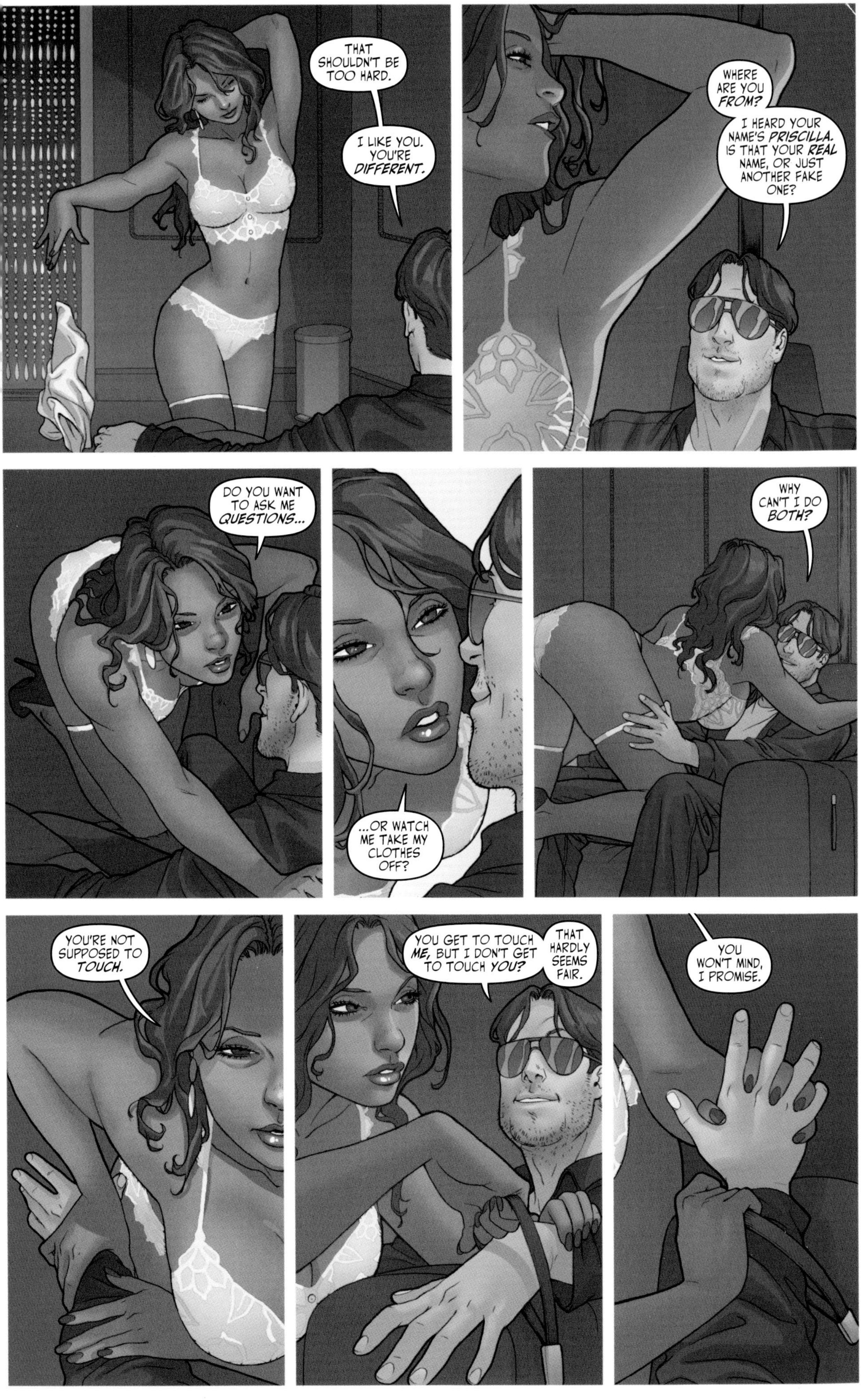

THAT SHOULDN'T BE TOO HARD.
I LIKE YOU. YOU'RE DIFFERENT.
WHERE ARE YOU FROM?
I HEARD YOUR NAME'S PRISCILLA. IS THAT YOUR REAL NAME, OR JUST ANOTHER FAKE ONE?
DO YOU WANT TO ASK ME QUESTIONS...
...OR WATCH ME TAKE MY CLOTHES OFF?
WHY CAN'T I DO BOTH?
YOU'RE NOT SUPPOSED TO TOUCH.
YOU GET TO TOUCH ME, BUT I DON'T GET TO TOUCH YOU?
THAT HARDLY SEEMS FAIR.
YOU WON'T MIND, I PROMISE.

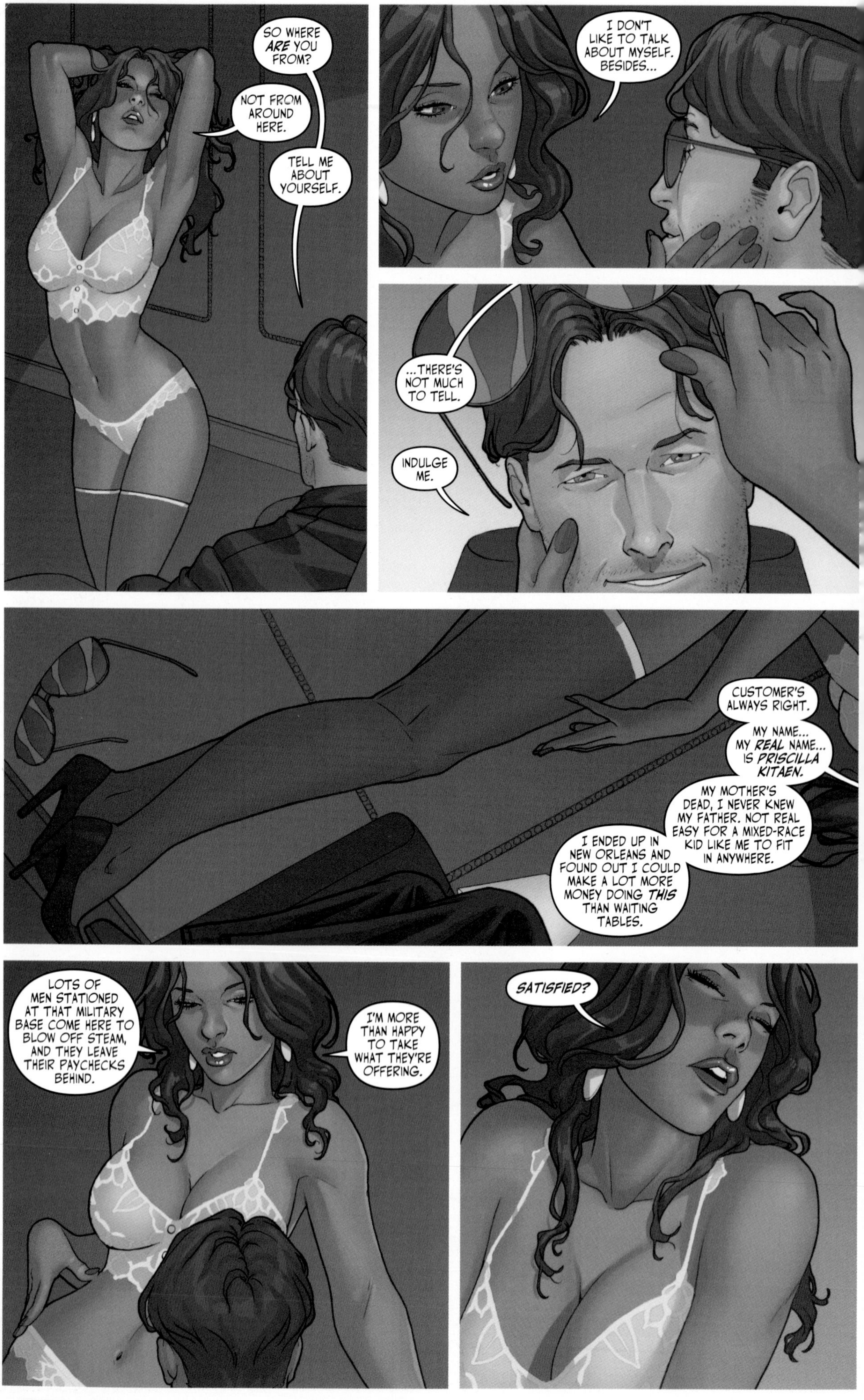
SO WHERE ARE YOU FROM?
NOT FROM AROUND HERE.
TELL ME ABOUT YOURSELF.
I DON'T LIKE TO TALK ABOUT MYSELF. BESIDES...
...THERE'S NOT MUCH TO TELL.
INDULGE ME.
CUSTOMER'S ALWAYS RIGHT.
MY NAME... MY REAL NAME... IS PRISCILLA KITAEN.
MY MOTHER'S DEAD, I NEVER KNEW MY FATHER. NOT REAL EASY FOR A MIXED-RACE KID LIKE ME TO FIT IN ANYWHERE.
I ENDED UP IN NEW ORLEANS AND FOUND OUT I COULD MAKE A LOT MORE MONEY DOING THIS THAN WAITING TABLES.
LOTS OF MEN STATIONED AT THAT MILITARY BASE COME HERE TO BLOW OFF STEAM, AND THEY LEAVE THEIR PAYCHECKS BEHIND.
I'M MORE THAN HAPPY TO TAKE WHAT THEY'RE OFFERING.
SATISFIED?

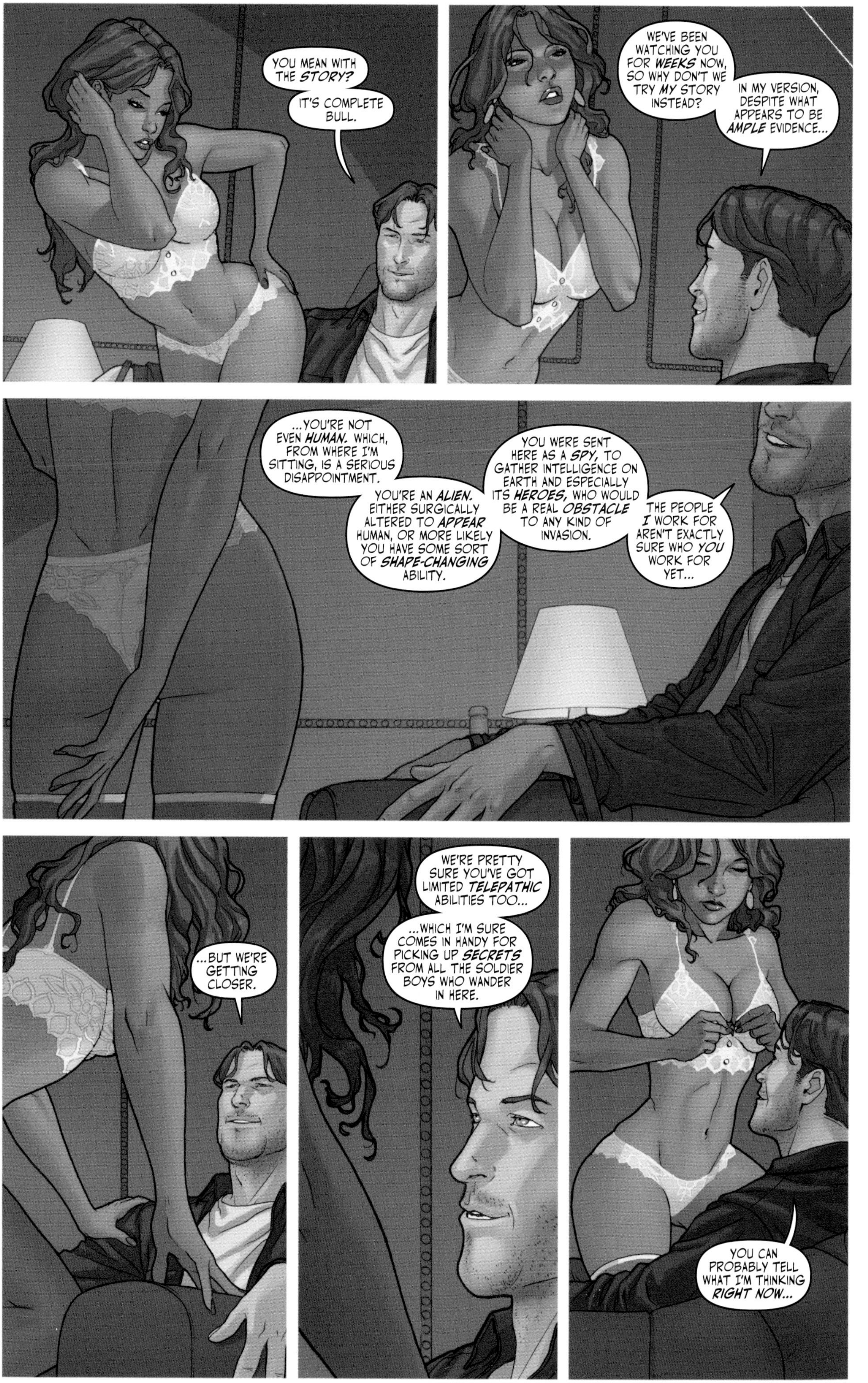
YOU MEAN WITH THE STORY?
IT'S COMPLETE BULL.
WE'VE BEEN WATCHING YOU FOR WEEKS NOW, SO WHY DON'T WE TRY MY STORY INSTEAD?
IN MY VERSION, DESPITE WHAT APPEARS TO BE AMPLE EVIDENCE...
...YOU'RE NOT EVEN HUMAN. WHICH, FROM WHERE I'M SITTING, IS A SERIOUS DISAPPOINTMENT.
YOU'RE AN ALIEN. EITHER SURGICALLY ALTERED TO APPEAR HUMAN, OR MORE LIKELY YOU HAVE SOME SORT OF SHAPE-CHANGING ABILITY.
YOU WERE SENT HERE AS A SPY, TO GATHER INTELLIGENCE ON EARTH AND ESPECIALLY ITS HEROES, WHO WOULD BE A REAL OBSTACLE TO ANY KIND OF INVASION.
THE PEOPLE I WORK FOR AREN'T EXACTLY SURE WHO YOU WORK FOR YET...
...BUT WE'RE GETTING CLOSER.
WE'RE PRETTY SURE YOU'VE GOT LIMITED TELEPATHIC ABILITIES TOO...
...WHICH I'M SURE COMES IN HANDY FOR PICKING UP SECRETS FROM ALL THE SOLDIER BOYS WHO WANDER IN HERE.
YOU CAN PROBABLY TELL WHAT I'M THINKING RIGHT NOW...

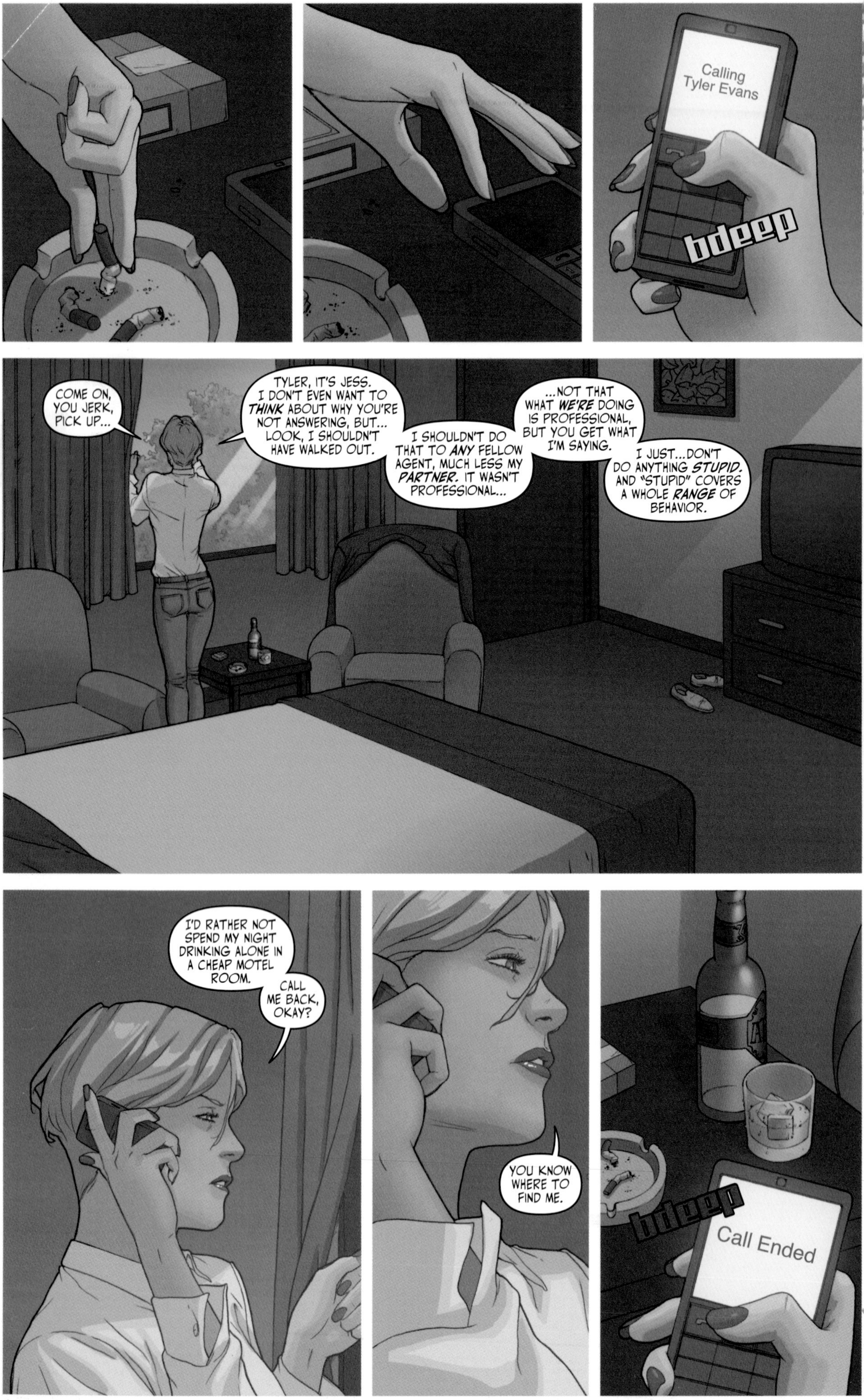

Calling Tyler Evans
bdeep
COME ON, YOU JERK, PICK UP...
TYLER, IT'S JESS. I DON'T EVEN WANT TO THINK ABOUT WHY YOU'RE NOT ANSWERING, BUT... LOOK, I SHOULDN'T HAVE WALKED OUT.
I SHOULDN'T DO THAT TO ANY FELLOW AGENT, MUCH LESS MY PARTNER. IT WASN'T PROFESSIONAL...
...NOT THAT WHAT WE'RE DOING IS PROFESSIONAL, BUT YOU GET WHAT I'M SAYING.
I JUST...DON'T DO ANYTHING STUPID. AND "STUPID" COVERS A WHOLE RANGE OF BEHAVIOR.
I'D RATHER NOT SPEND MY NIGHT DRINKING ALONE IN A CHEAP MOTEL ROOM.
CALL ME BACK, OKAY?
YOU KNOW WHERE TO FIND ME.
bdeep
Call Ended

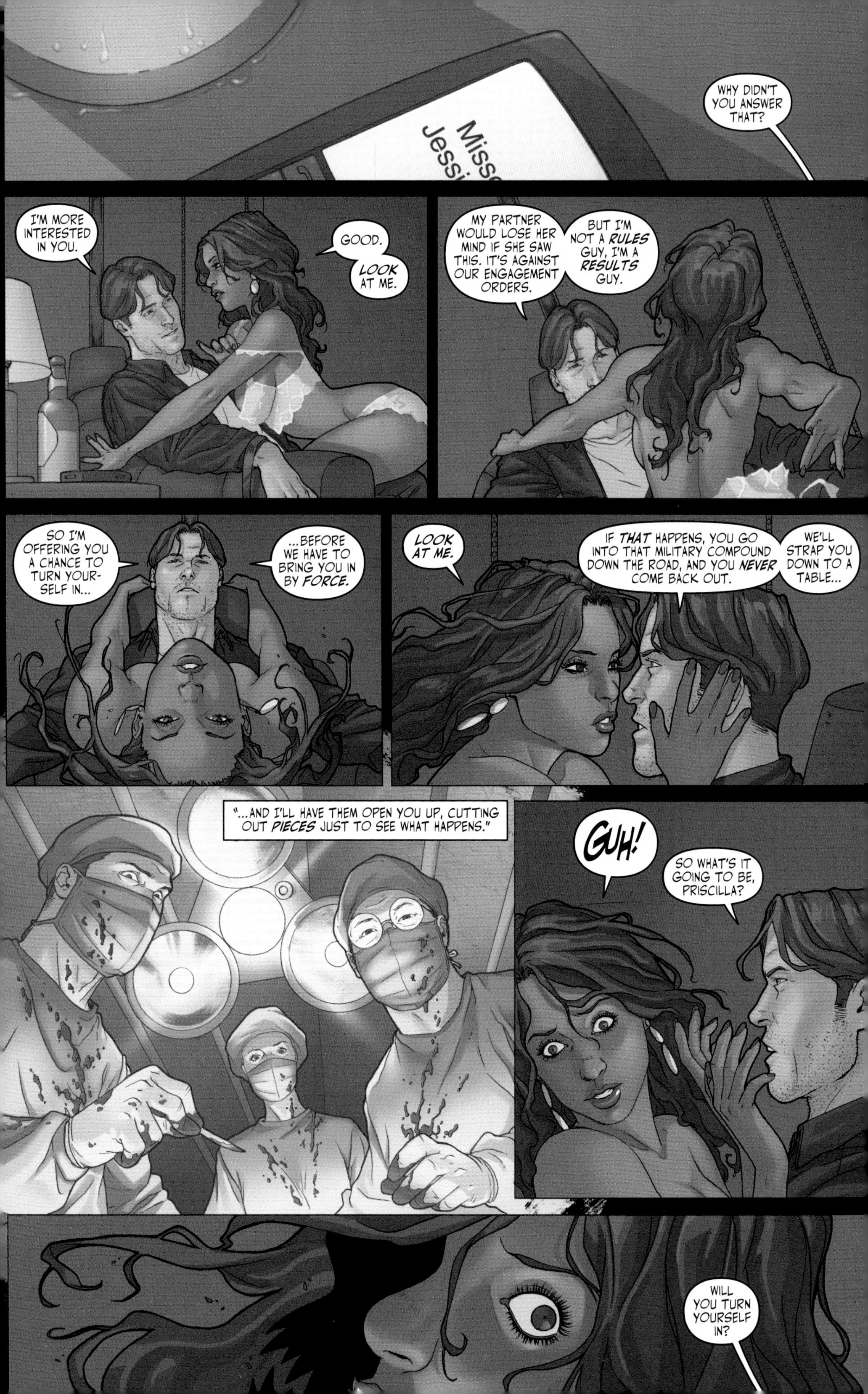
Missed
Jessi
WHY DIDN'T YOU ANSWER THAT?
I'M MORE INTERESTED IN YOU.
GOOD.
LOOK AT ME.
MY PARTNER WOULD LOSE HER MIND IF SHE SAW THIS. IT'S AGAINST OUR ENGAGEMENT ORDERS.
BUT I'M NOT A RULES GUY, I'M A RESULTS GUY.
SO I'M OFFERING YOU A CHANCE TO TURN YOURSELF IN...
...BEFORE WE HAVE TO BRING YOU IN BY FORCE.
LOOK AT ME.
IF THAT HAPPENS, YOU GO INTO THAT MILITARY COMPOUND DOWN THE ROAD, AND YOU NEVER COME BACK OUT.
WE'LL STRAP YOU DOWN TO A TABLE...
"...AND I'LL HAVE THEM OPEN YOU UP, CUTTING OUT PIECES JUST TO SEE WHAT HAPPENS."
GUH!
SO WHAT'S IT GOING TO BE, PRISCILLA?
WILL YOU TURN YOURSELF IN?

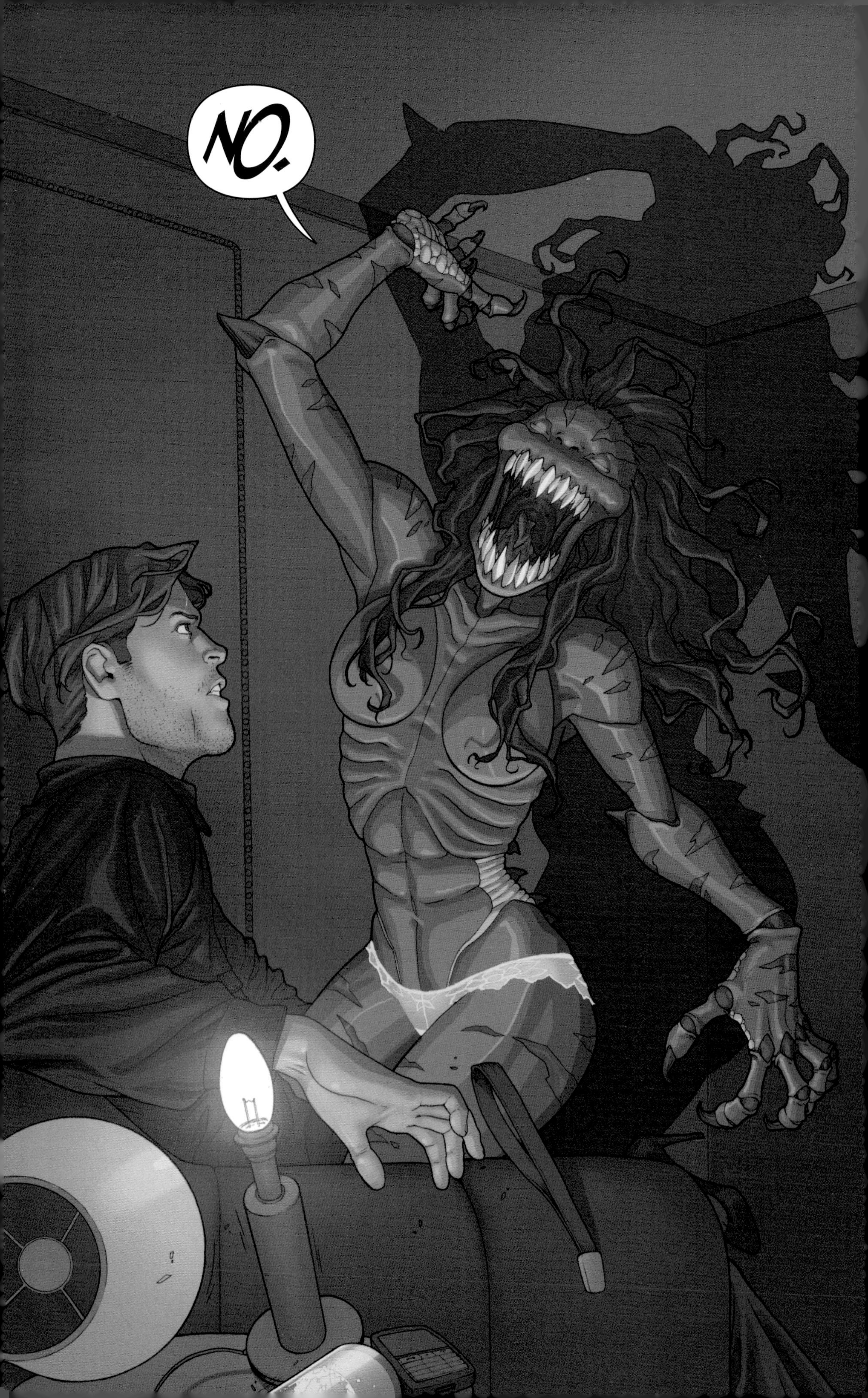
NO.

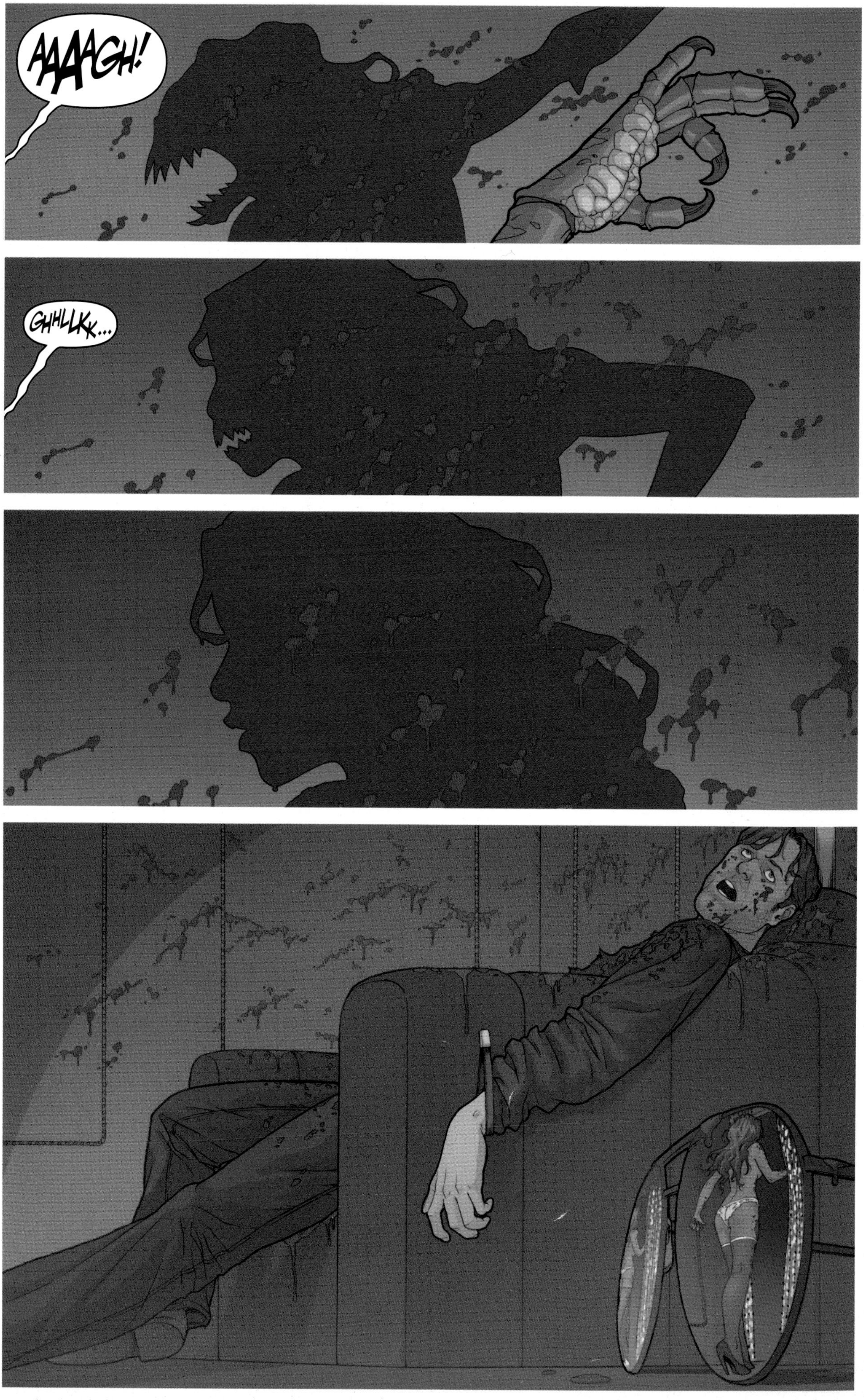
AAAAGH!
GHHLLKK...

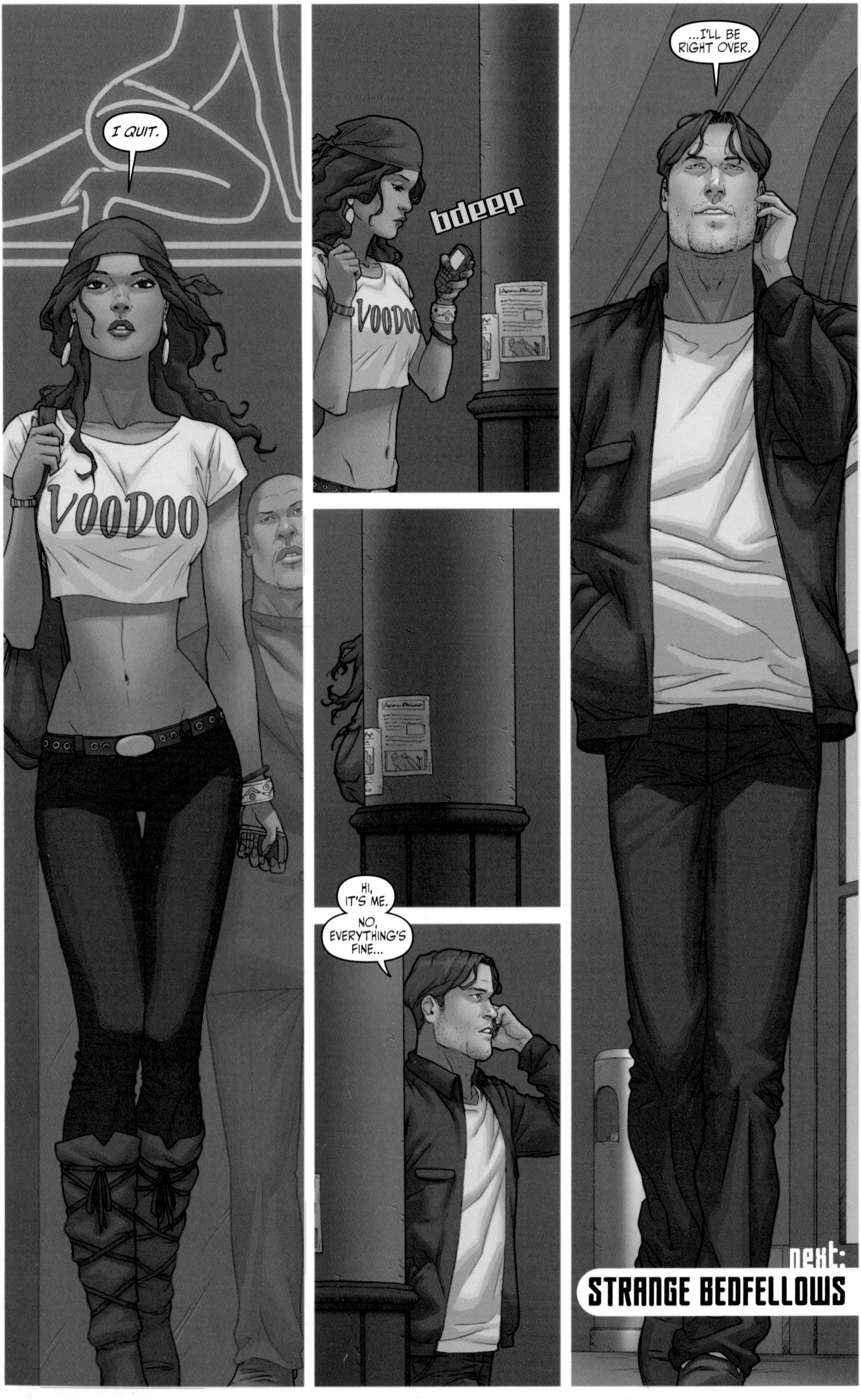
I QUIT.
bdeep
HI, IT'S ME.
NO, EVERYTHING'S FINE...
...I'LL BE RIGHT OVER.
next:
STRANGE BEDFELLOWS

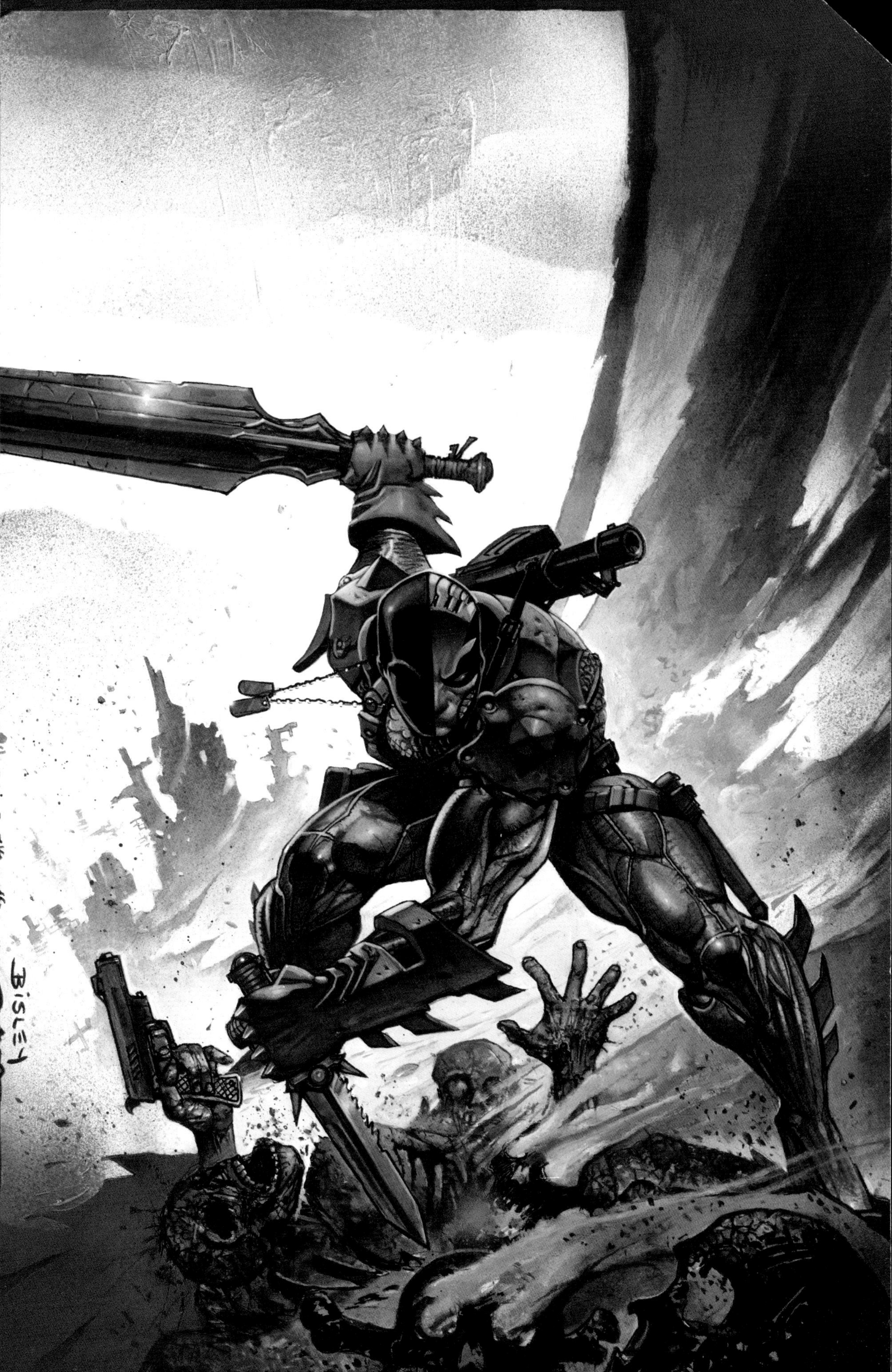
BISLEY

DEATH STROKE

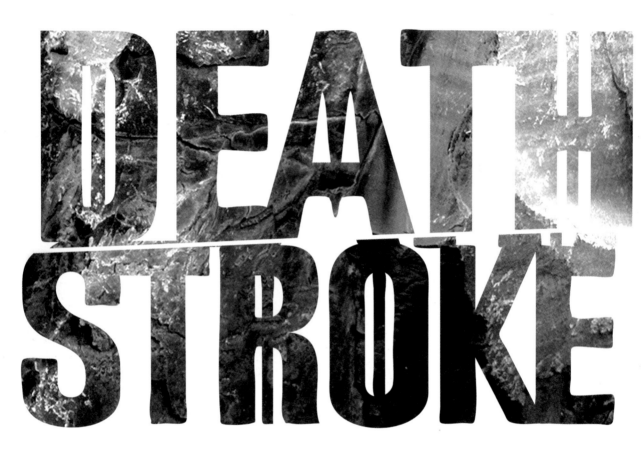

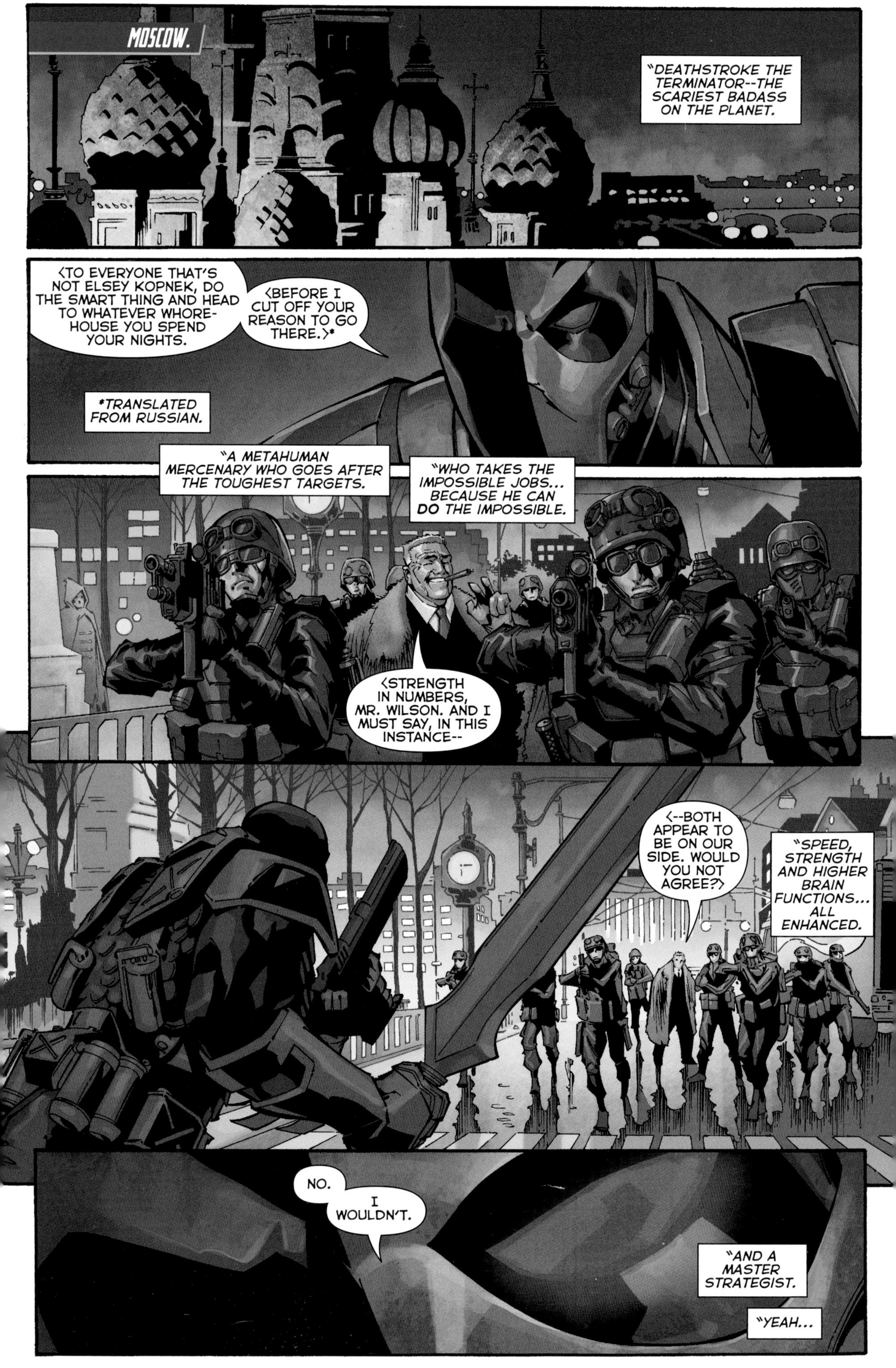
MOSCOW.
"DEATHSTROKE THE TERMINATOR--THE SCARIEST BADASS ON THE PLANET.
<TO EVERYONE THAT'S NOT ELSEY KOPNEK, DO THE SMART THING AND HEAD TO WHATEVER WHORE-HOUSE YOU SPEND YOUR NIGHTS.
<BEFORE I CUT OFF YOUR REASON TO GO THERE.>*
*TRANSLATED FROM RUSSIAN.
"A METAHUMAN MERCENARY WHO GOES AFTER THE TOUGHEST TARGETS.
"WHO TAKES THE IMPOSSIBLE JOBS... BECAUSE HE CAN DO THE IMPOSSIBLE.
<STRENGTH IN NUMBERS, MR. WILSON. AND I MUST SAY, IN THIS INSTANCE--
<--BOTH APPEAR TO BE ON OUR SIDE. WOULD YOU NOT AGREE?>
"SPEED, STRENGTH AND HIGHER BRAIN FUNCTIONS... ALL ENHANCED.
NO.
I WOULDN'T.
"AND A MASTER STRATEGIST.
"YEAH...

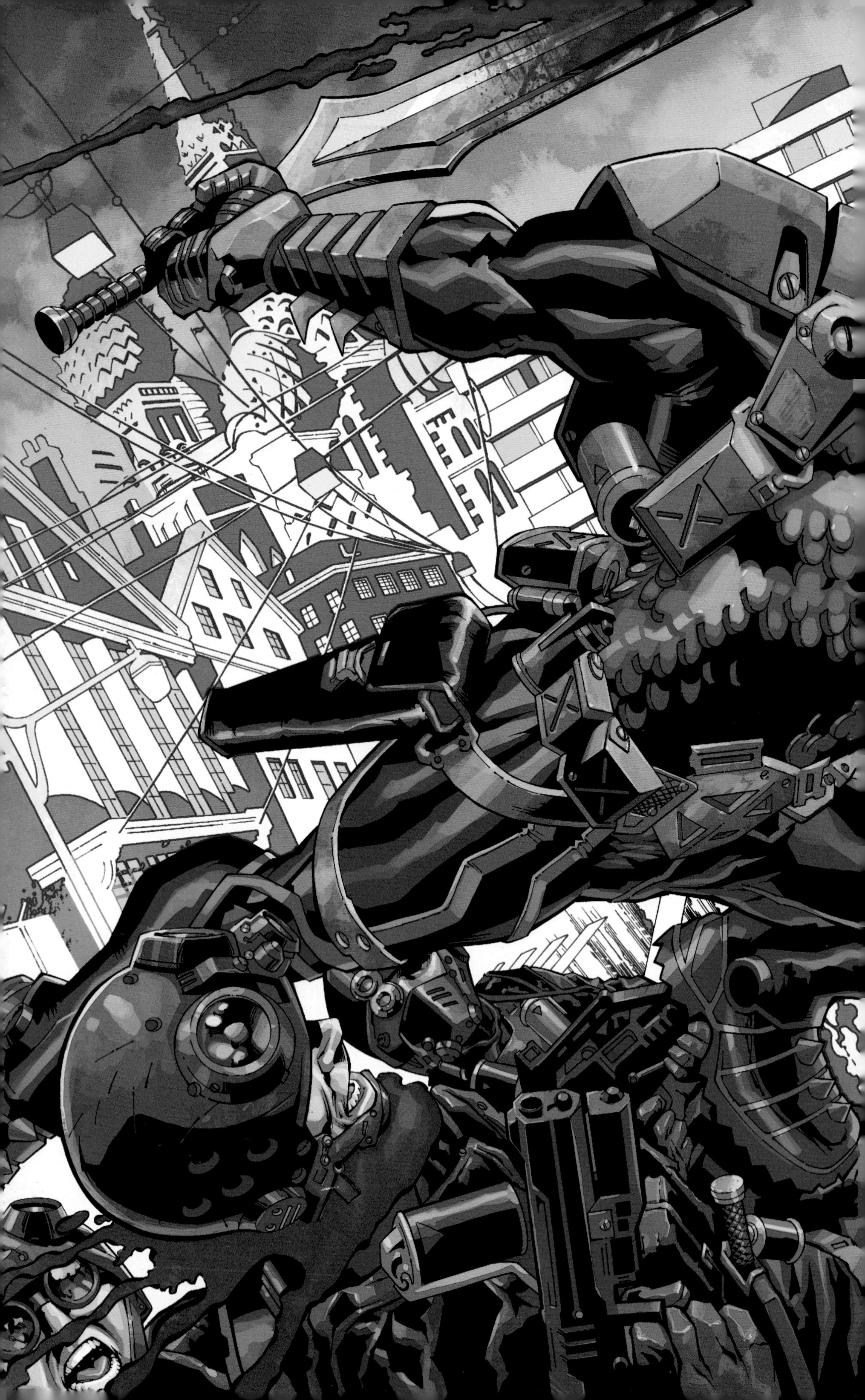

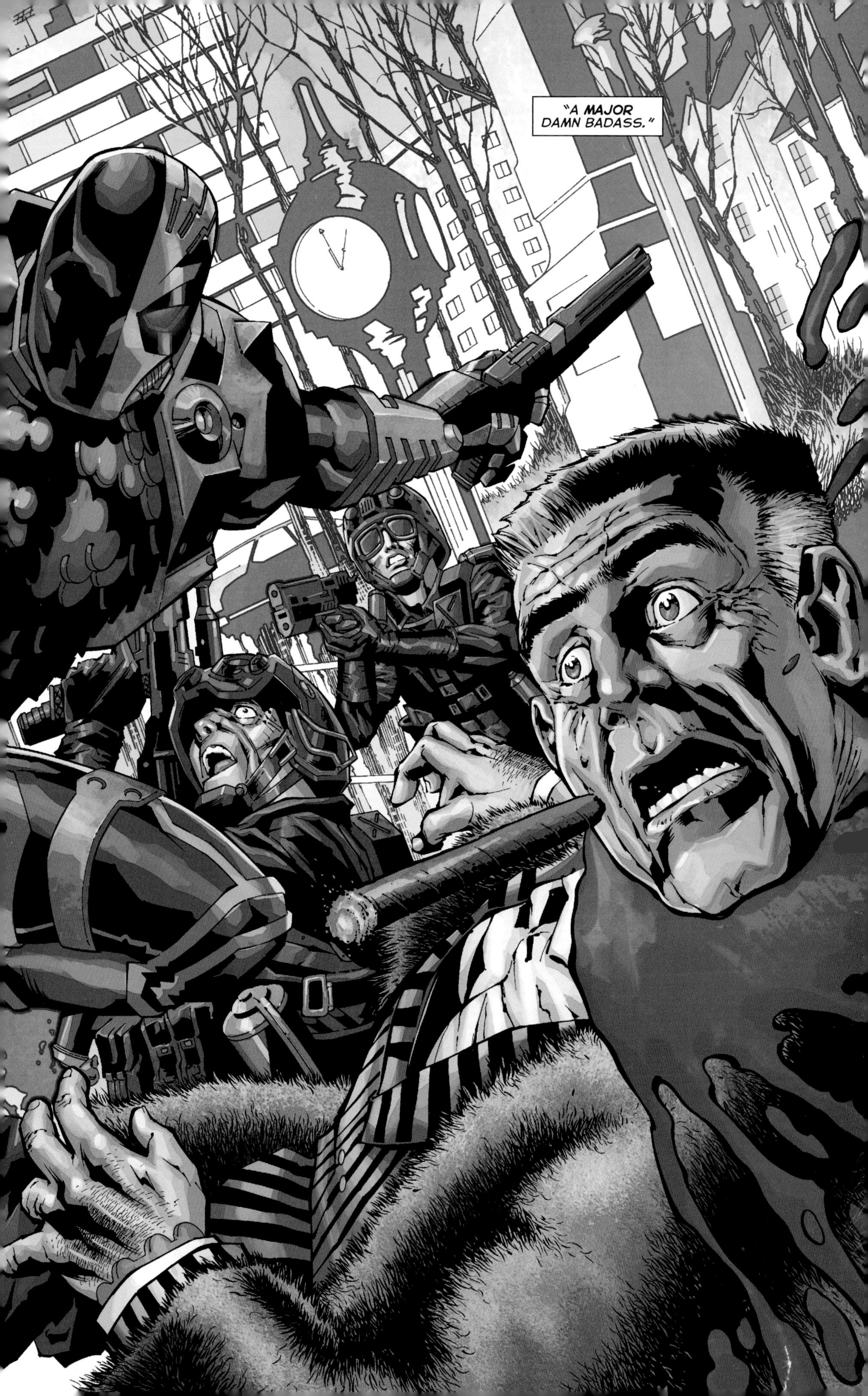
"A MAJOR DAMN BADASS."

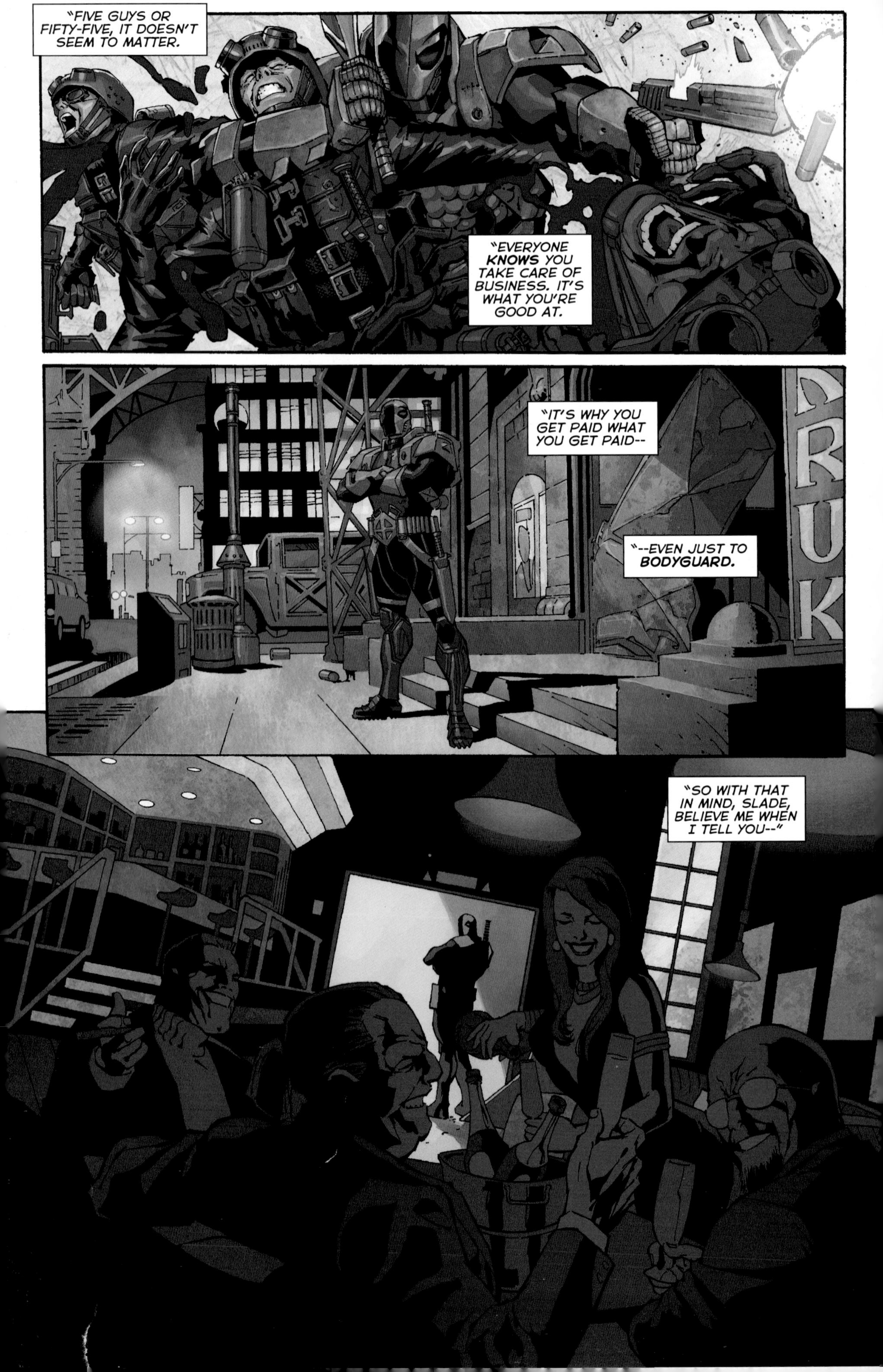
"FIVE GUYS OR FIFTY-FIVE, IT DOESN'T SEEM TO MATTER.
"EVERYONE KNOWS YOU TAKE CARE OF BUSINESS. IT'S WHAT YOU'RE GOOD AT.
"IT'S WHY YOU GET PAID WHAT YOU GET PAID--
"--EVEN JUST TO BODYGUARD.
"SO WITH THAT IN MIND, SLADE, BELIEVE ME WHEN I TELL YOU--"

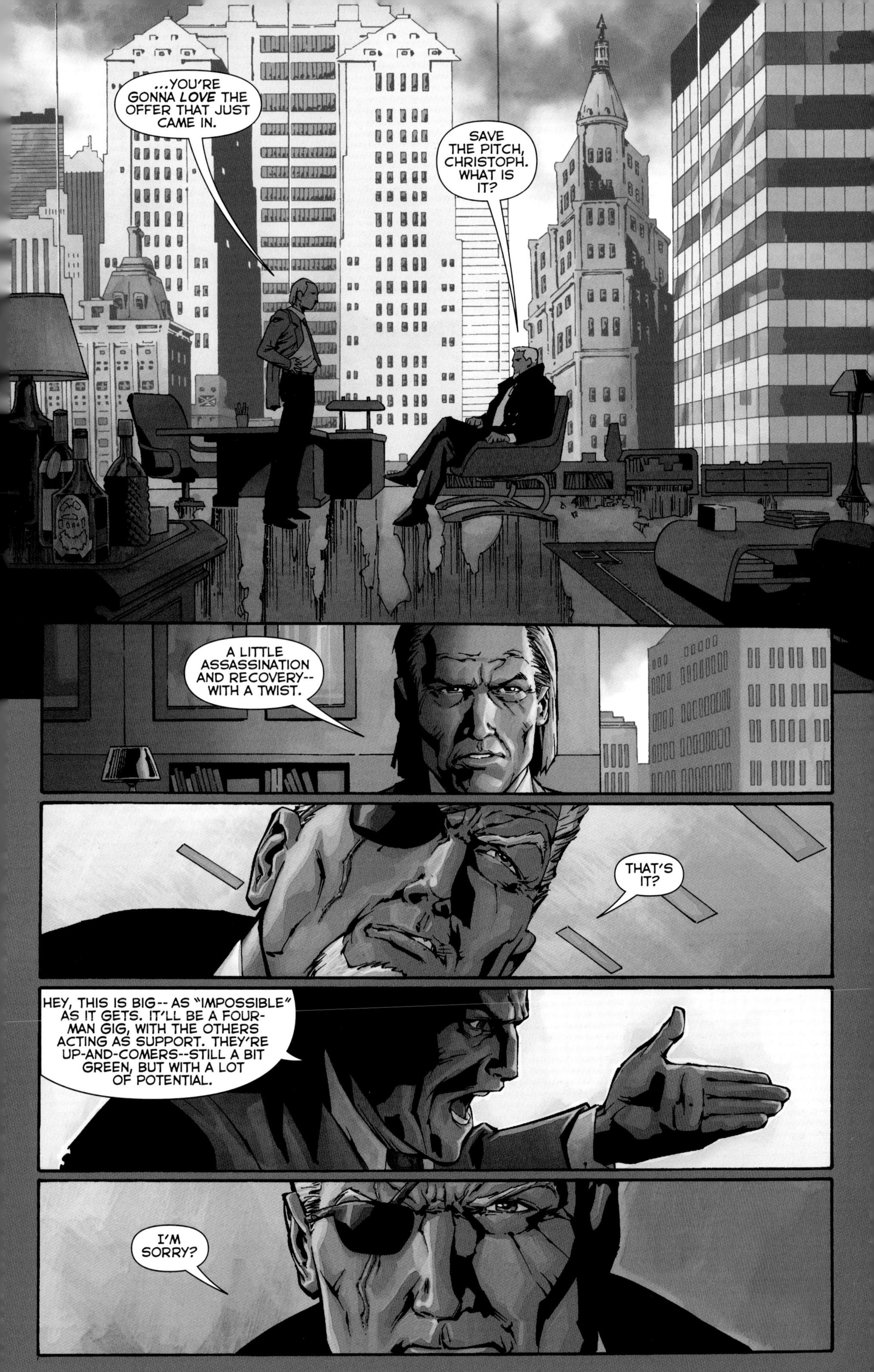
...YOU'RE GONNA LOVE THE OFFER THAT JUST CAME IN.
SAVE THE PITCH, CHRISTOPH. WHAT IS IT?
A LITTLE ASSASSINATION AND RECOVERY-- WITH A TWIST.
THAT'S IT?
HEY, THIS IS BIG-- AS "IMPOSSIBLE" AS IT GETS. IT'LL BE A FOUR-MAN GIG, WITH THE OTHERS ACTING AS SUPPORT. THEY'RE UP-AND-COMERS--STILL A BIT GREEN, BUT WITH A LOT OF POTENTIAL.
I'M SORRY?

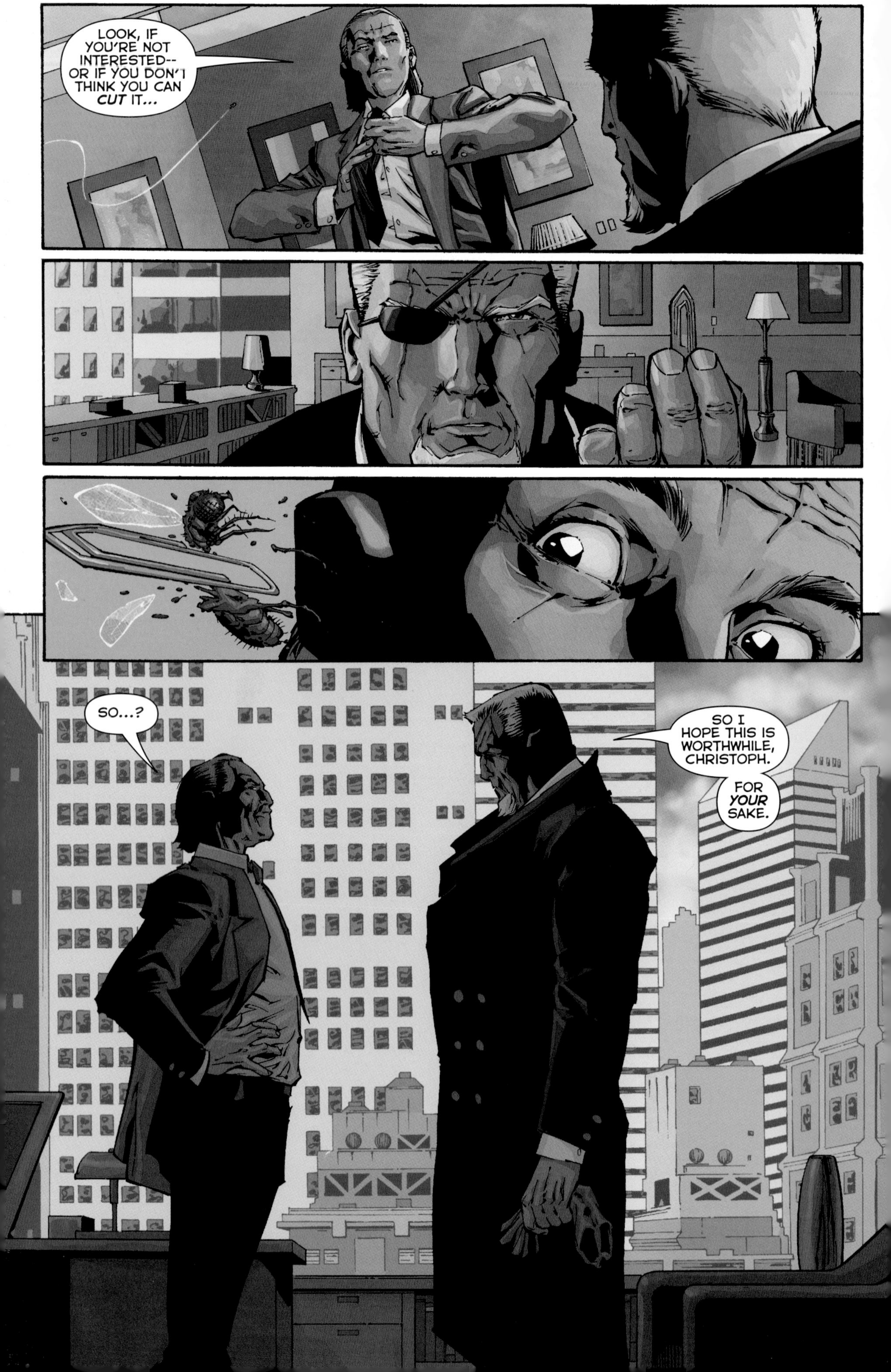
LOOK, IF YOU'RE NOT INTERESTED-- OR IF YOU DON'T THINK YOU CAN CUT IT...
SO...?
SO I HOPE THIS IS WORTHWHILE, CHRISTOPH.
FOR YOUR SAKE.

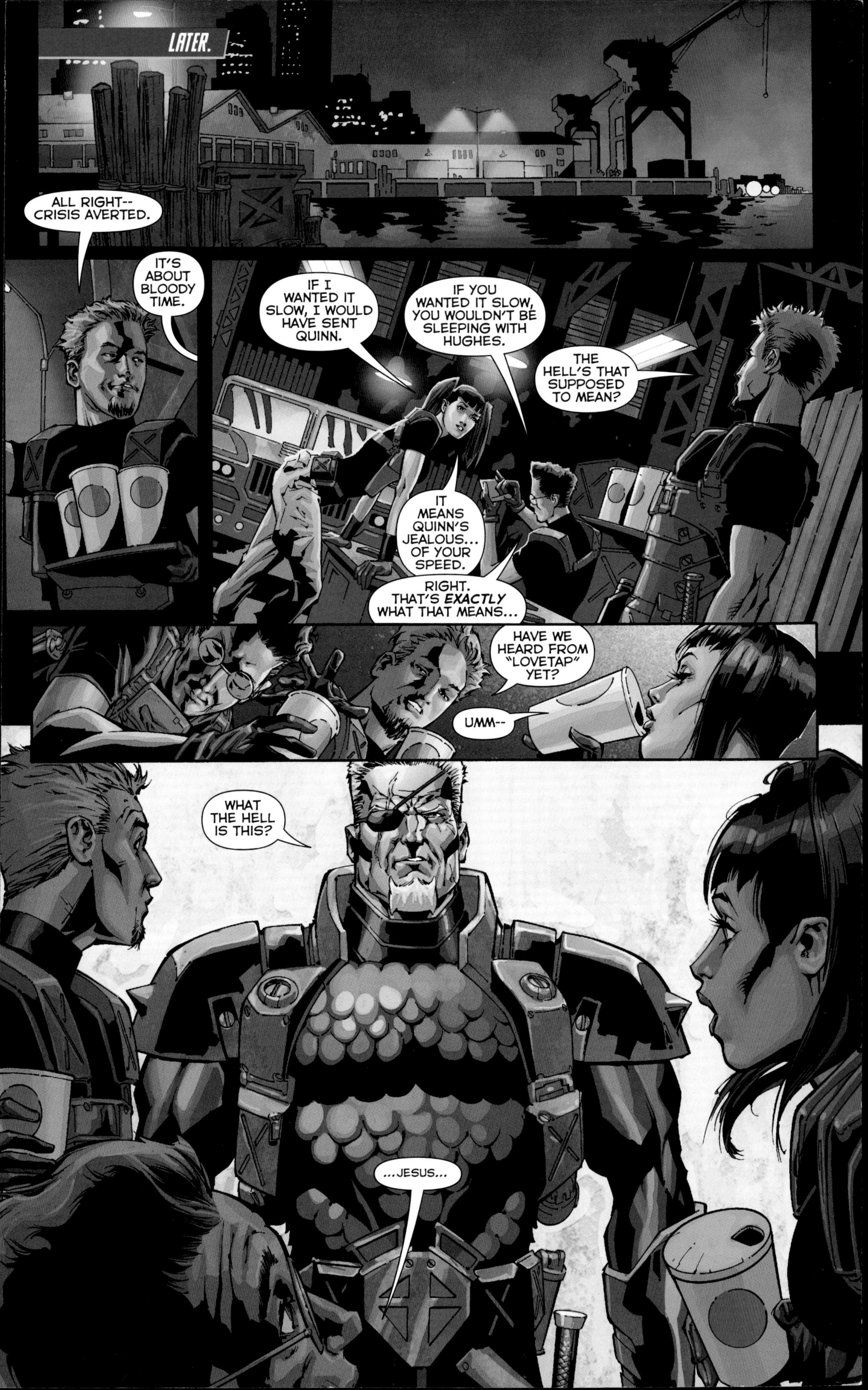
LATER.
ALL RIGHT-- CRISIS AVERTED.
IT'S ABOUT BLOODY TIME.
IF I WANTED IT SLOW, I WOULD HAVE SENT QUINN.
IF YOU WANTED IT SLOW, YOU WOULDN'T BE SLEEPING WITH HUGHES.
THE HELL'S THAT SUPPOSED TO MEAN?
IT MEANS QUINN'S JEALOUS... OF YOUR SPEED.
RIGHT. THAT'S *EXACTLY* WHAT THAT MEANS...
HAVE WE HEARD FROM "LOVETAP" YET?
UMM--
WHAT THE HELL IS THIS?
...JESUS...

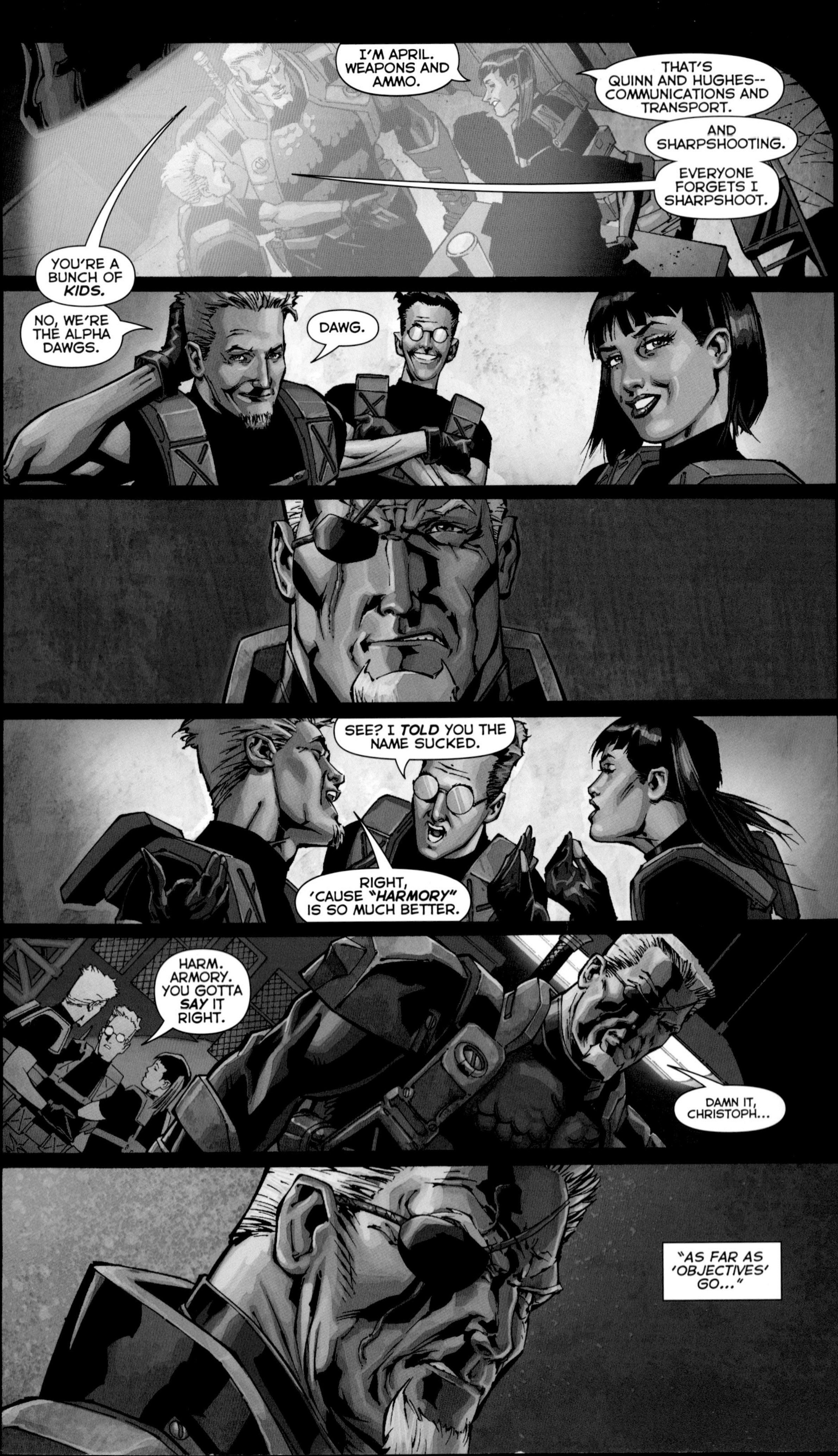
I'M APRIL. WEAPONS AND AMMO.
THAT'S QUINN AND HUGHES-- COMMUNICATIONS AND TRANSPORT.
AND SHARPSHOOTING.
EVERYONE FORGETS I SHARPSHOOT.
YOU'RE A BUNCH OF *KIDS.*
NO, WE'RE THE ALPHA DAWGS.
DAWG.
SEE? I *TOLD* YOU THE NAME SUCKED.
RIGHT, 'CAUSE "*HARMORY*" IS SO MUCH BETTER.
HARM. ARMORY. YOU GOTTA *SAY* IT RIGHT.
DAMN IT, CHRISTOPH...
"AS FAR AS 'OBJECTIVES' GO..."

...THIS ONE'S PRETTY STRAIGHT-FORWARD.

WHO'S THE TARGET?

MEET JEFFREY BODE--

--FORMER GERMAN SCIENTIST AND ENGINEER TURNED ARMS DEALER.

HE TRAVELS EUROPE ON HIS PRIVATE PLANE, WHICH HOUSES A VERITABLE STOCKPILE OF WEAPONS AND MUNITIONS.

HIS CLIENTS PAY HIS WAY THROUGH CUSTOMS AT EVERY STOP.

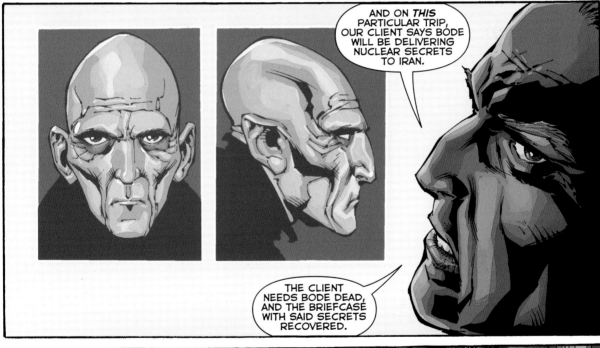

AND ON THIS PARTICULAR TRIP, OUR CLIENT SAYS BODE WILL BE DELIVERING NUCLEAR SECRETS TO IRAN.

THE CLIENT NEEDS BODE DEAD, AND THE BRIEFCASE WITH SAID SECRETS RECOVERED.

SO WHAT QUALIFIES THIS AS WORTHY OF THE ALPHA DAWGS' ATTENTION?

WELL... FOR BOTH POLITICAL AND BUREAUCRATIC REASONS, WE CAN'T RISK TAKING HIM ON THE GROUND.

SO YOU WANT TO TAKE HIM OUT--MID-AIR?

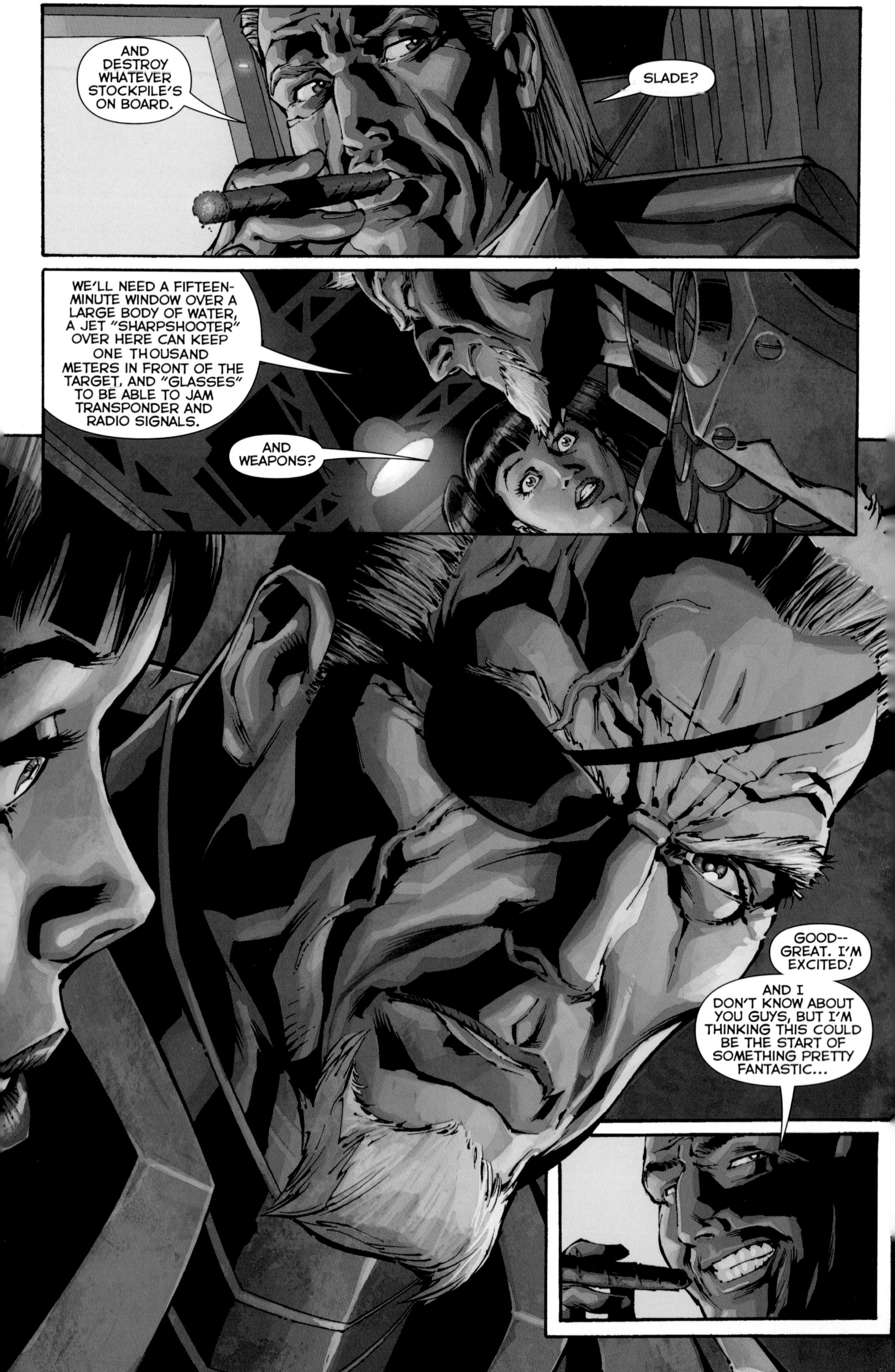
AND DESTROY WHATEVER STOCKPILE'S ON BOARD.
SLADE?
WE'LL NEED A FIFTEEN-MINUTE WINDOW OVER A LARGE BODY OF WATER, A JET "SHARPSHOOTER" OVER HERE CAN KEEP ONE THOUSAND METERS IN FRONT OF THE TARGET, AND "GLASSES" TO BE ABLE TO JAM TRANSPONDER AND RADIO SIGNALS.
AND WEAPONS?
GOOD--GREAT. I'M EXCITED!
AND I DON'T KNOW ABOUT YOU GUYS, BUT I'M THINKING THIS COULD BE THE START OF SOMETHING PRETTY FANTASTIC...

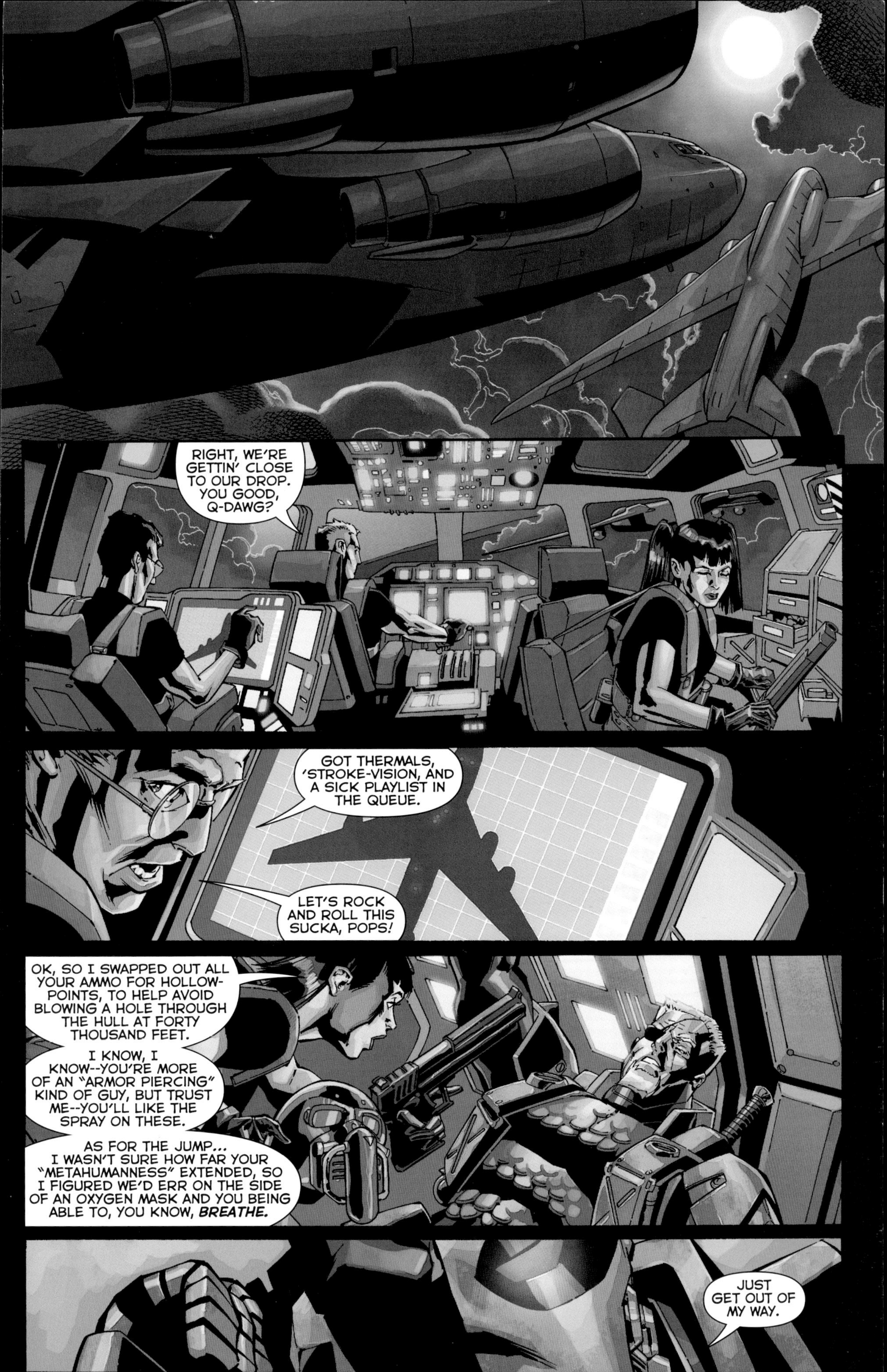
RIGHT, WE'RE GETTIN' CLOSE TO OUR DROP. YOU GOOD, Q-DAWG?
GOT THERMALS, 'STROKE-VISION, AND A SICK PLAYLIST IN THE QUEUE.
LET'S ROCK AND ROLL THIS SUCKA, POPS!
OK, SO I SWAPPED OUT ALL YOUR AMMO FOR HOLLOW-POINTS, TO HELP AVOID BLOWING A HOLE THROUGH THE HULL AT FORTY THOUSAND FEET.
I KNOW, I KNOW--YOU'RE MORE OF AN "ARMOR PIERCING" KIND OF GUY, BUT TRUST ME--YOU'LL LIKE THE SPRAY ON THESE.
AS FOR THE JUMP... I WASN'T SURE HOW FAR YOUR "METAHUMANNESS" EXTENDED, SO I FIGURED WE'D ERR ON THE SIDE OF AN OXYGEN MASK AND YOU BEING ABLE TO, YOU KNOW, *BREATHE.*
JUST GET OUT OF MY WAY.

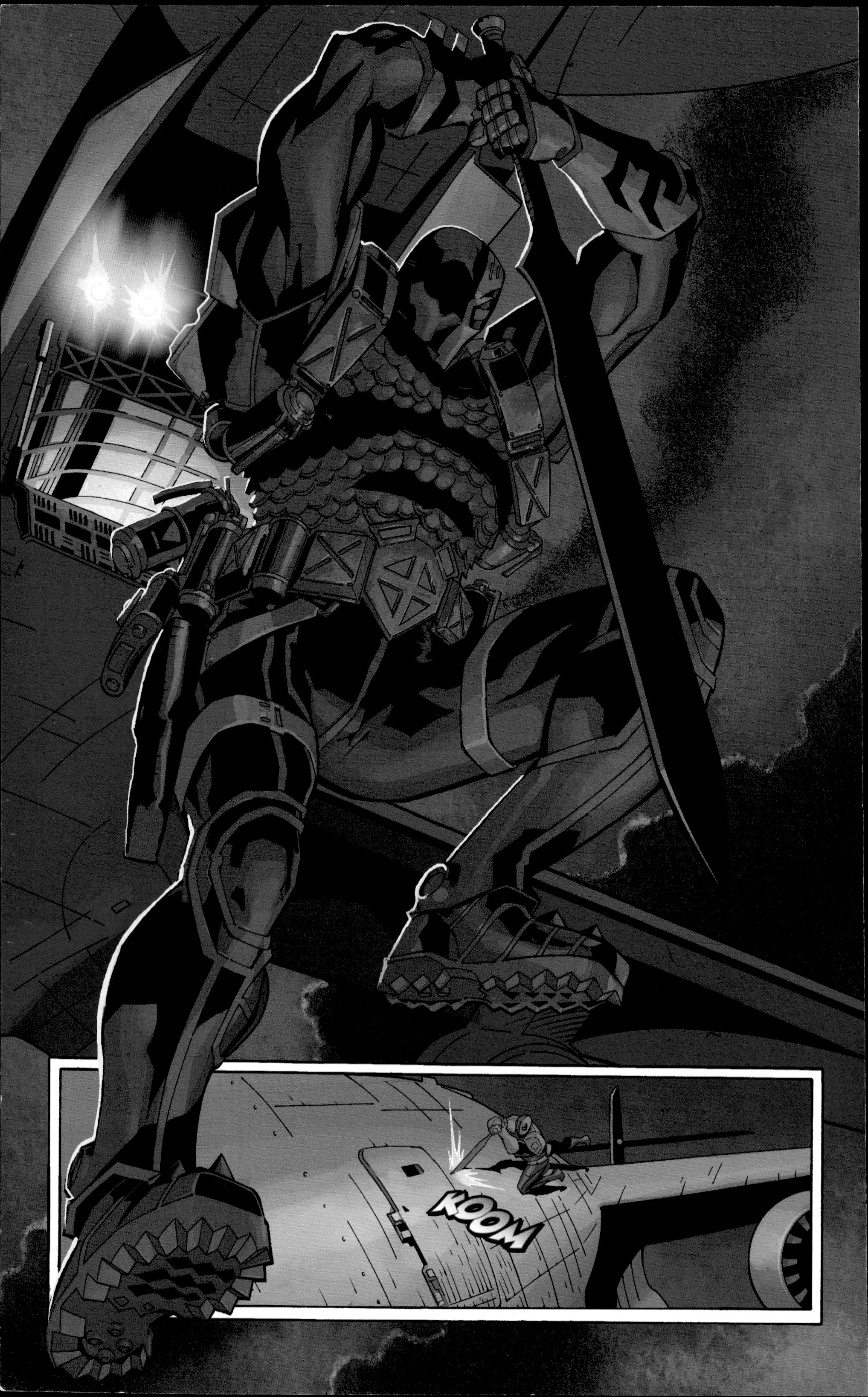
KOOM

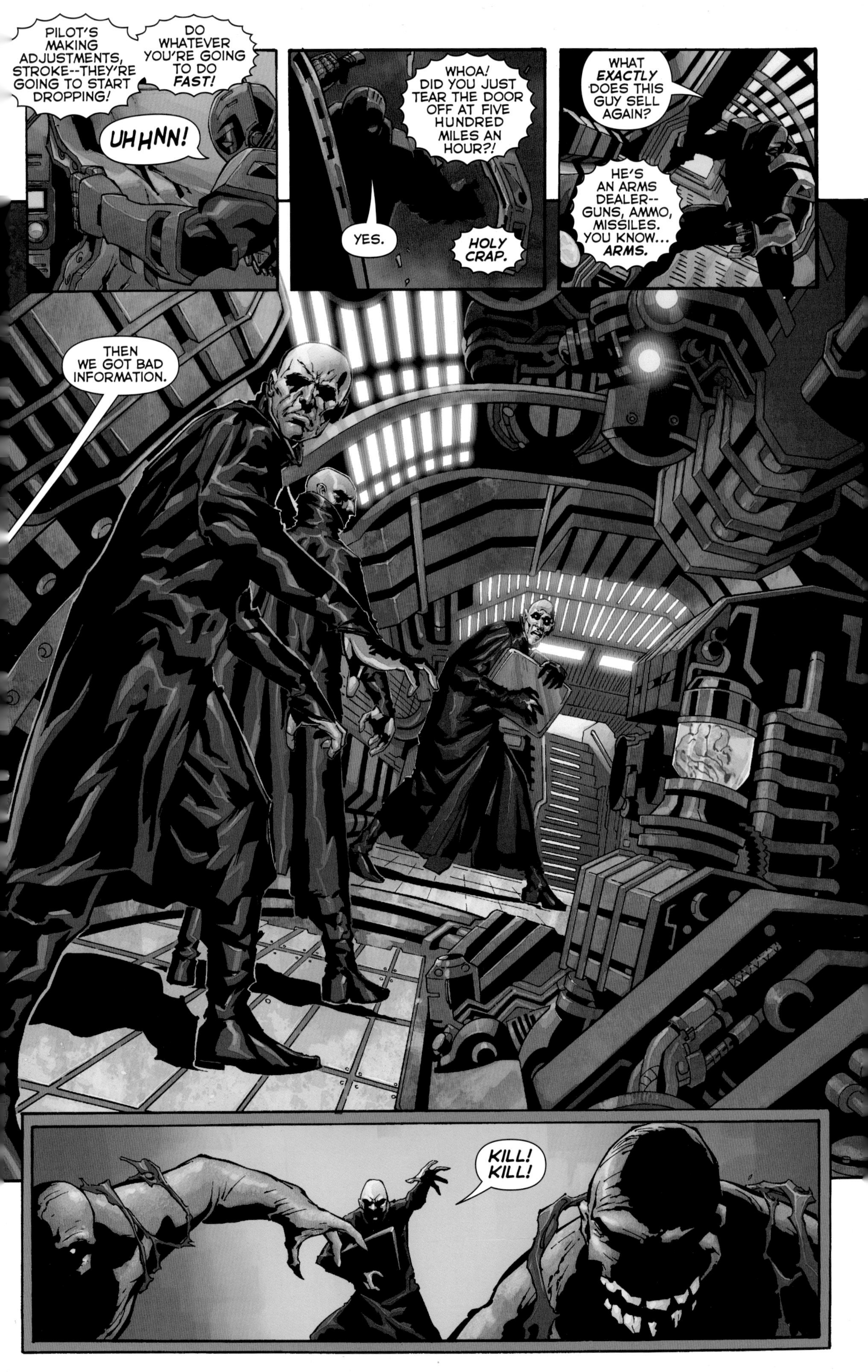
PILOT'S MAKING ADJUSTMENTS, STROKE--THEY'RE GOING TO START DROPPING!
DO WHATEVER YOU'RE GOING TO DO FAST!
UHHNN!
WHOA! DID YOU JUST TEAR THE DOOR OFF AT FIVE HUNDRED MILES AN HOUR?!
YES.
HOLY CRAP.
WHAT EXACTLY DOES THIS GUY SELL AGAIN?
HE'S AN ARMS DEALER-- GUNS, AMMO, MISSILES. YOU KNOW... ARMS.
THEN WE GOT BAD INFORMATION.
KILL! KILL!

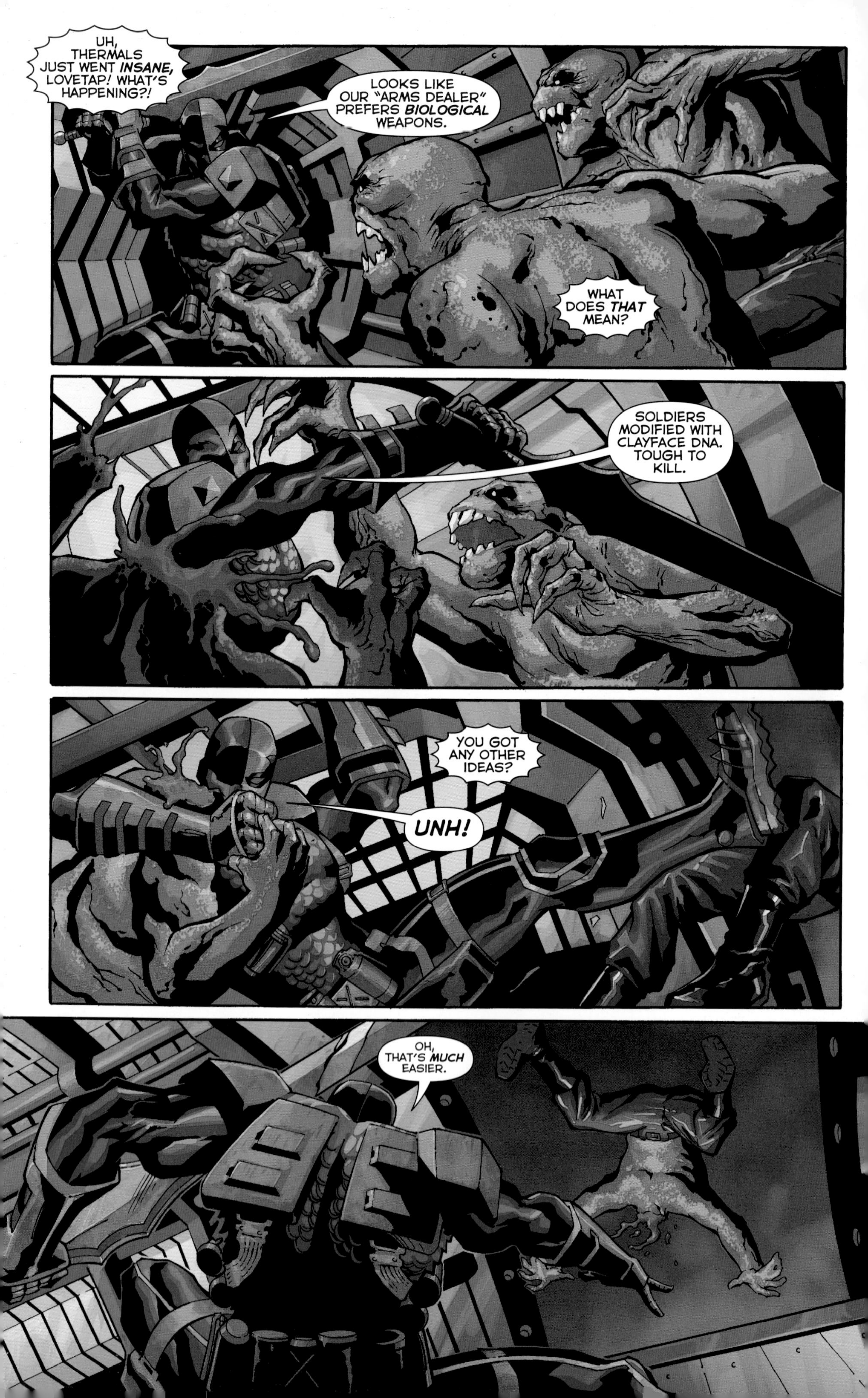
UH, THERMALS JUST WENT INSANE, LOVETAP! WHAT'S HAPPENING?!
LOOKS LIKE OUR "ARMS DEALER" PREFERS BIOLOGICAL WEAPONS.
WHAT DOES THAT MEAN?
SOLDIERS MODIFIED WITH CLAYFACE DNA. TOUGH TO KILL.
YOU GOT ANY OTHER IDEAS?
UNH!
OH, THAT'S MUCH EASIER.

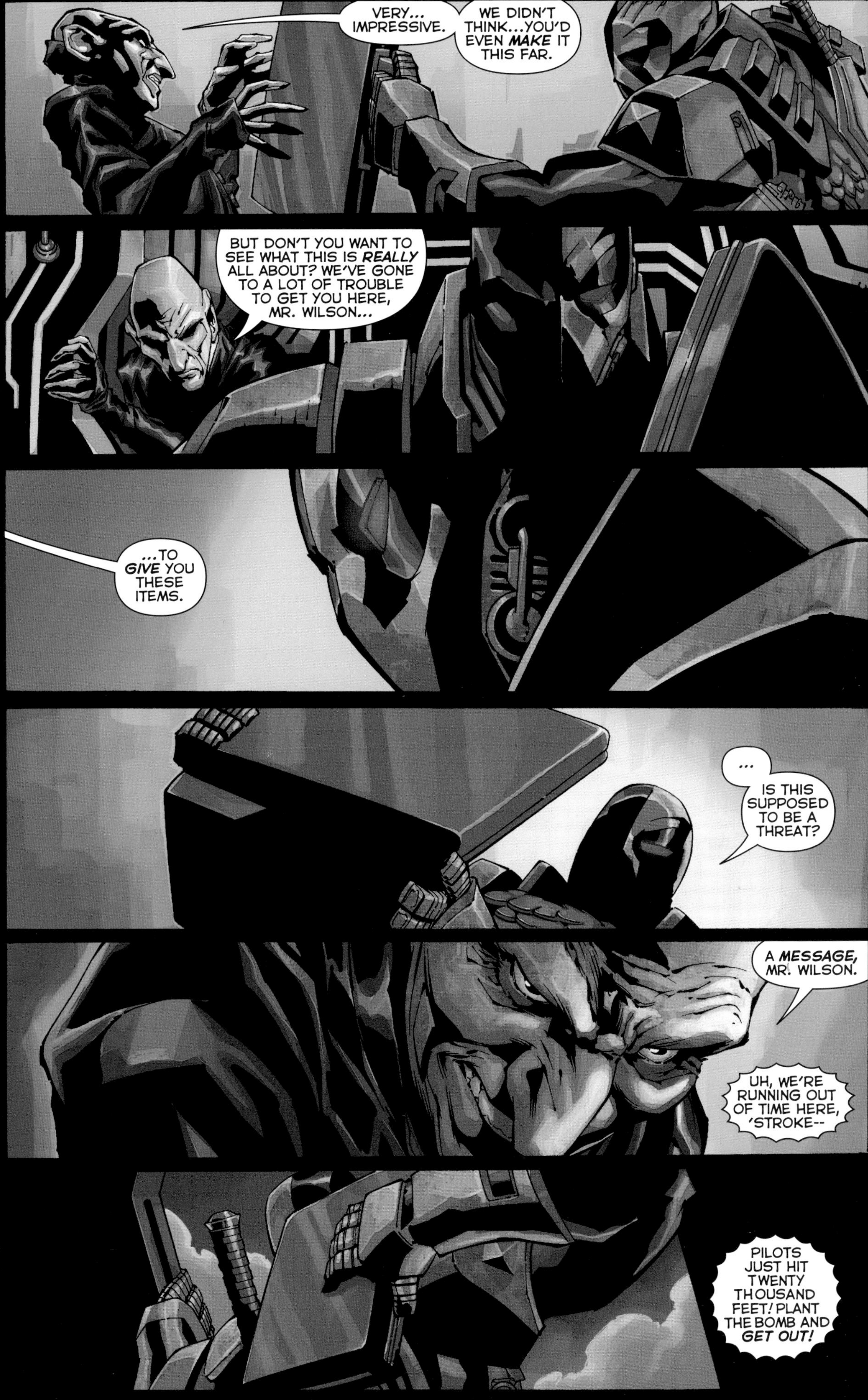
VERY... IMPRESSIVE.
WE DIDN'T THINK...YOU'D EVEN MAKE IT THIS FAR.
BUT DON'T YOU WANT TO SEE WHAT THIS IS REALLY ALL ABOUT? WE'VE GONE TO A LOT OF TROUBLE TO GET YOU HERE, MR. WILSON...
...TO GIVE YOU THESE ITEMS.
...
IS THIS SUPPOSED TO BE A THREAT?
A MESSAGE, MR. WILSON.
UH, WE'RE RUNNING OUT OF TIME HERE, 'STROKE--
PILOTS JUST HIT TWENTY THOUSAND FEET! PLANT THE BOMB AND GET OUT!

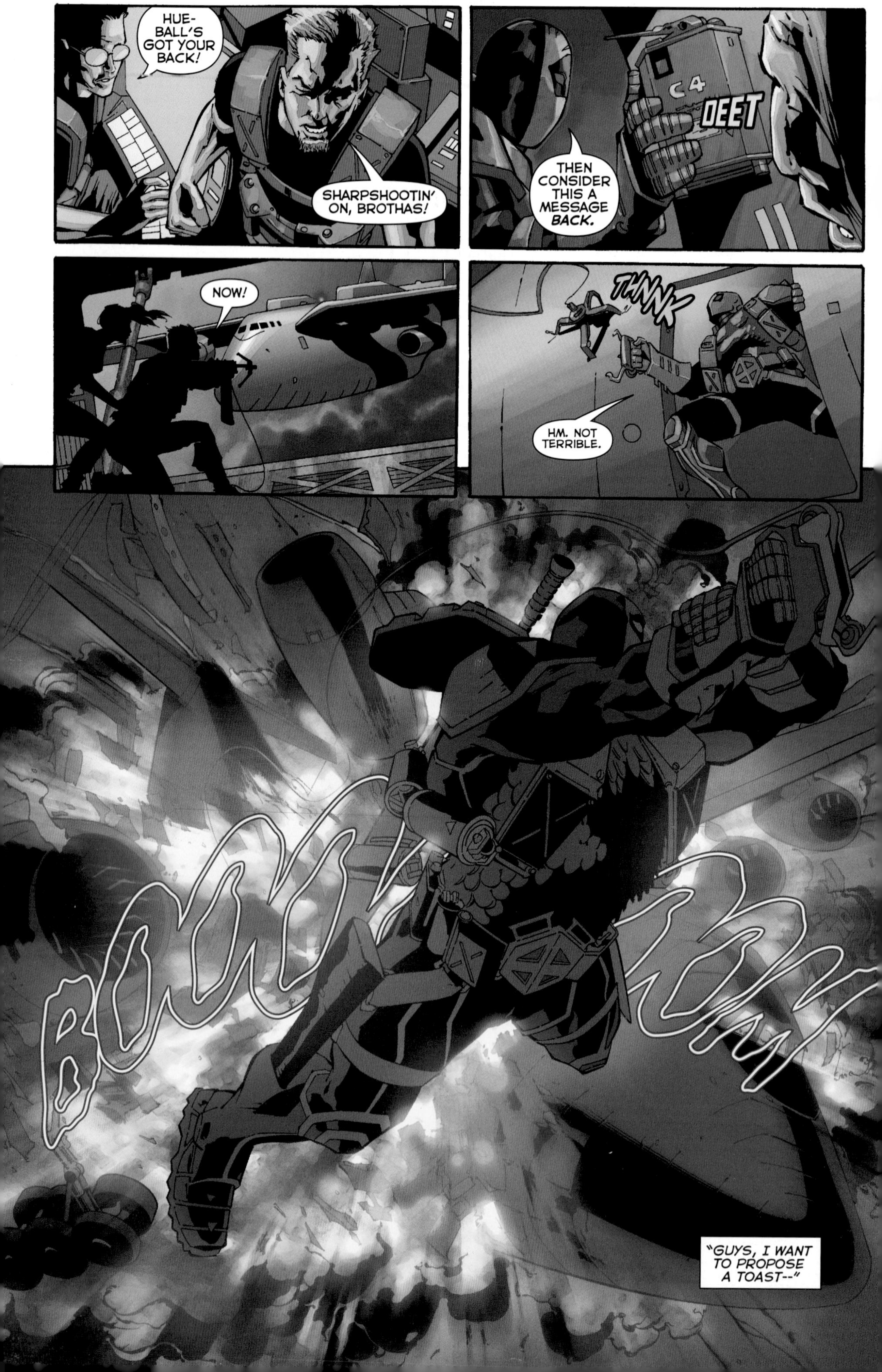
HUE-BALL'S GOT YOUR BACK!
SHARPSHOOTIN' ON, BROTHAS!
DEET
THEN CONSIDER THIS A MESSAGE BACK.
NOW!
THNNK
HM. NOT TERRIBLE.
"GUYS, I WANT TO PROPOSE A TOAST--"

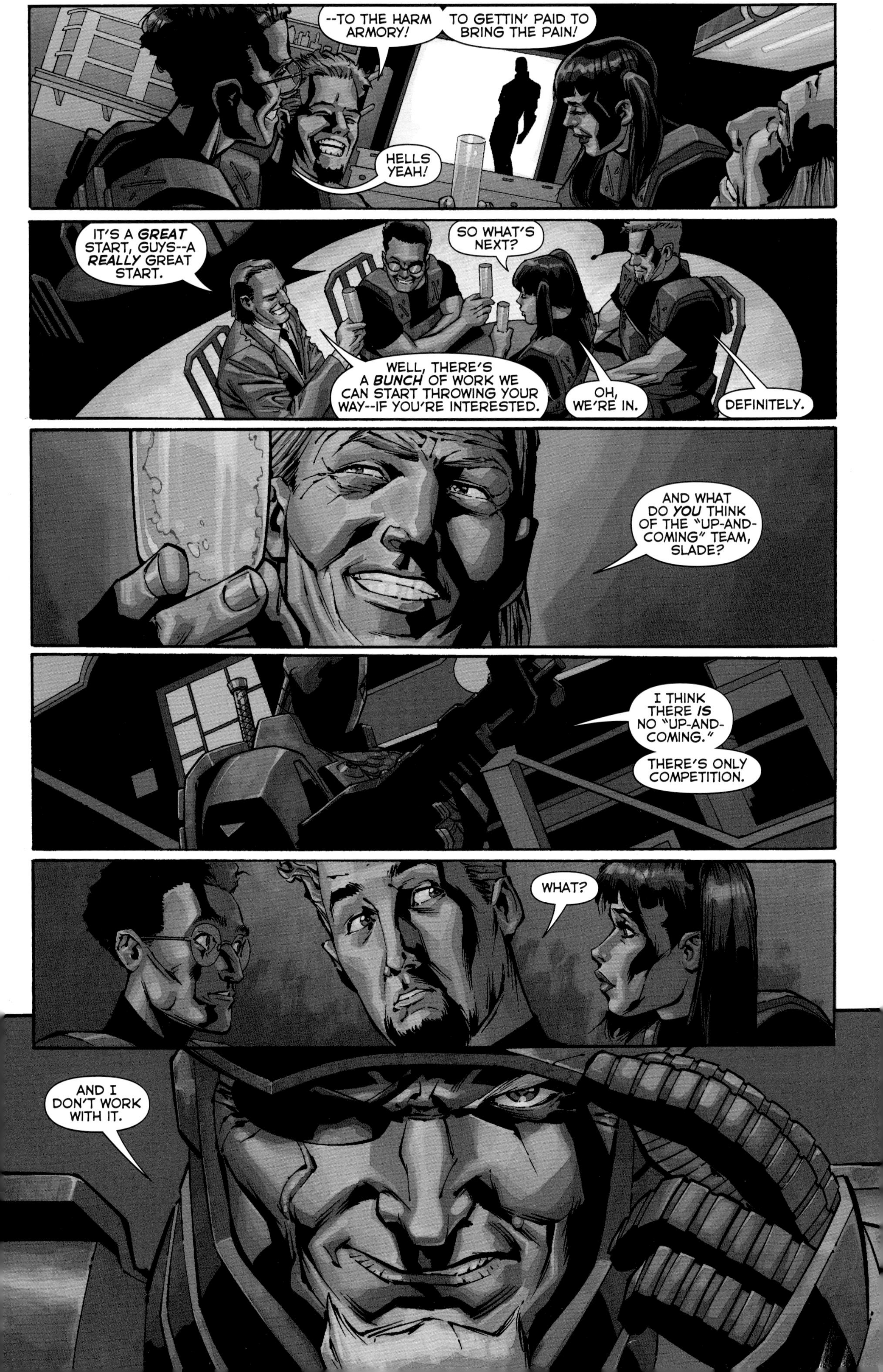
--TO THE HARM ARMORY!
TO GETTIN' PAID TO BRING THE PAIN!
HELLS YEAH!
IT'S A GREAT START, GUYS--A REALLY GREAT START.
SO WHAT'S NEXT?
WELL, THERE'S A BUNCH OF WORK WE CAN START THROWING YOUR WAY--IF YOU'RE INTERESTED.
OH, WE'RE IN.
DEFINITELY.
AND WHAT DO YOU THINK OF THE "UP-AND-COMING" TEAM, SLADE?
I THINK THERE IS NO "UP-AND-COMING."
THERE'S ONLY COMPETITION.
WHAT?
AND I DON'T WORK WITH IT.

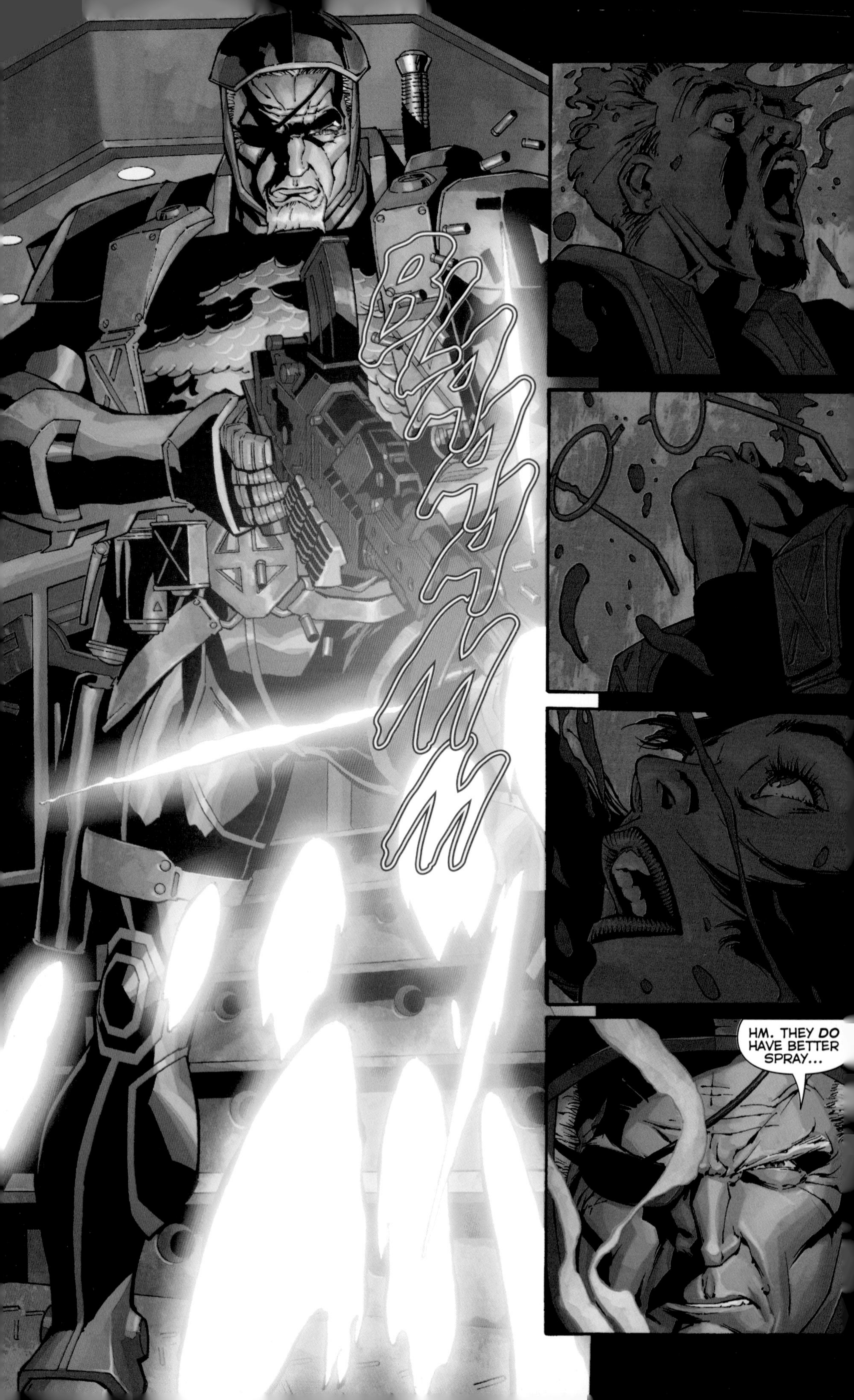
HM. THEY *DO* HAVE BETTER SPRAY...

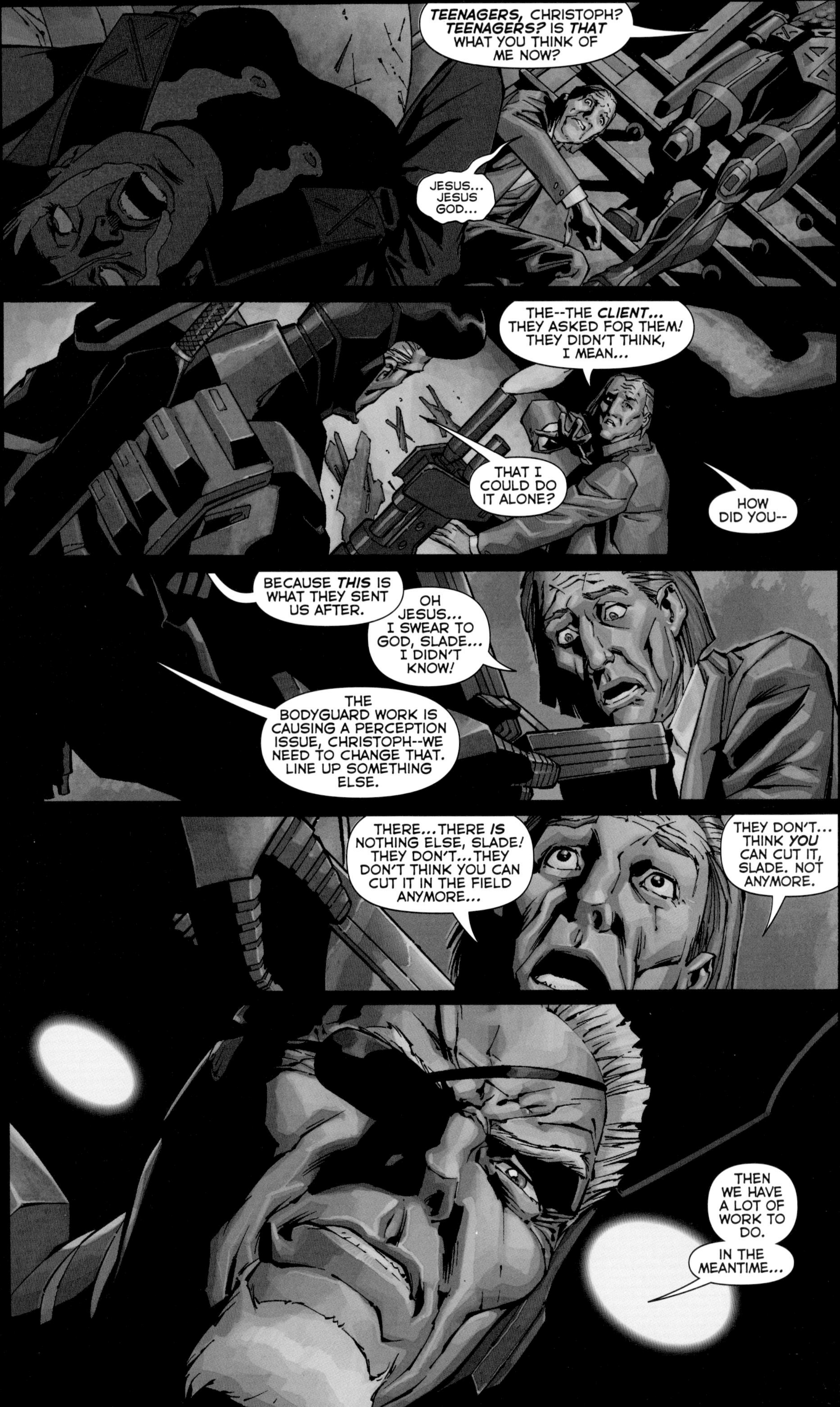
TEENAGERS, CHRISTOPH? TEENAGERS? IS THAT WHAT YOU THINK OF ME NOW?
JESUS... JESUS GOD...
THE--THE CLIENT... THEY ASKED FOR THEM! THEY DIDN'T THINK, I MEAN...
THAT I COULD DO IT ALONE?
HOW DID YOU--
BECAUSE THIS IS WHAT THEY SENT US AFTER.
OH JESUS... I SWEAR TO GOD, SLADE... I DIDN'T KNOW!
THE BODYGUARD WORK IS CAUSING A PERCEPTION ISSUE, CHRISTOPH--WE NEED TO CHANGE THAT. LINE UP SOMETHING ELSE.
THERE...THERE IS NOTHING ELSE, SLADE! THEY DON'T...THEY DON'T THINK YOU CAN CUT IT IN THE FIELD ANYMORE...
THEY DON'T... THINK YOU CAN CUT IT, SLADE. NOT ANYMORE.
THEN WE HAVE A LOT OF WORK TO DO.
IN THE MEANTIME...

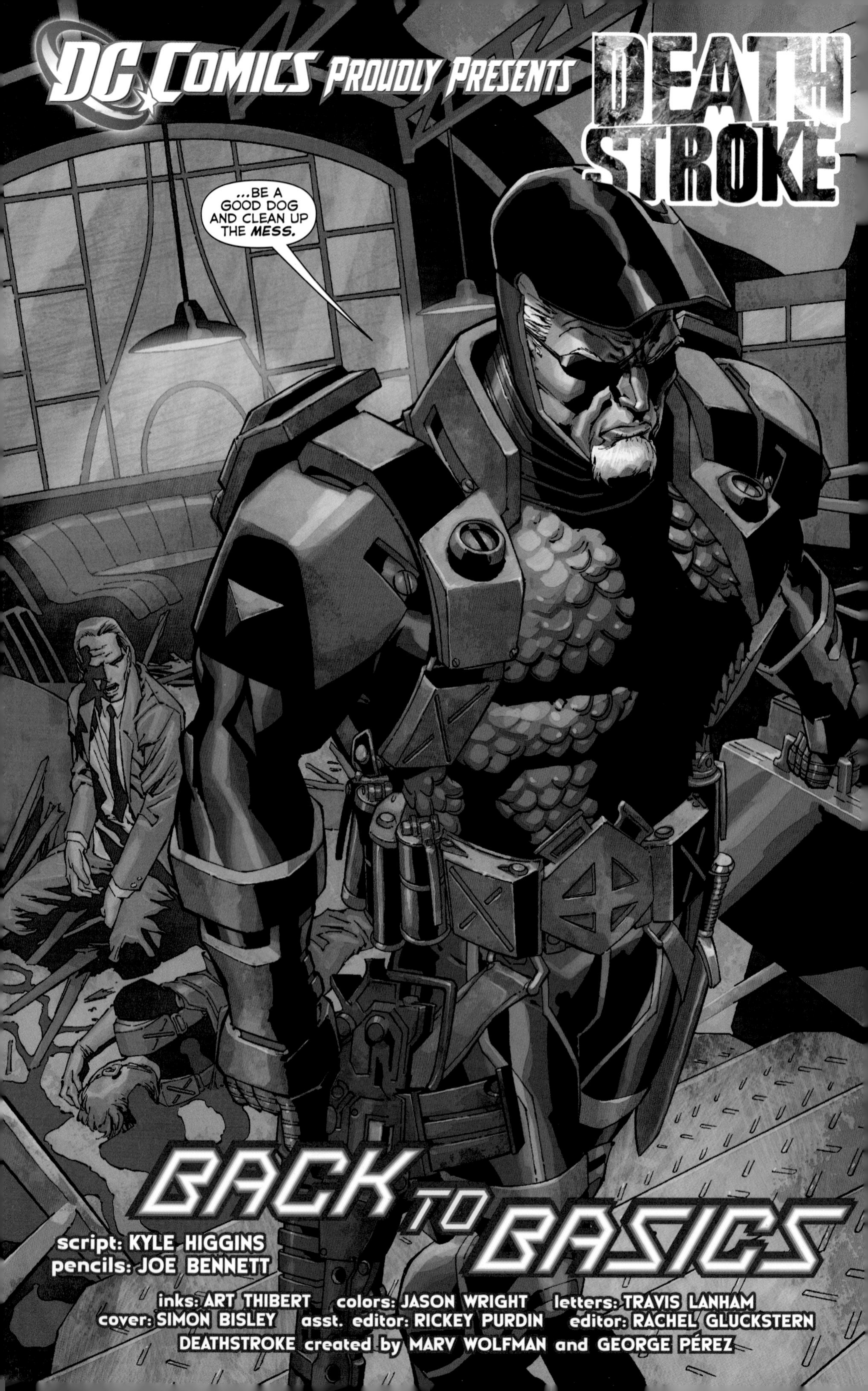
DC COMICS PROUDLY PRESENTS
DEATHSTROKE
...BE A GOOD DOG AND CLEAN UP THE *MESS.*
BACK TO BASICS
script: KYLE HIGGINS
pencils: JOE BENNETT
inks: ART THIBERT colors: JASON WRIGHT letters: TRAVIS LANHAM
cover: SIMON BISLEY asst. editor: RICKEY PURDIN editor: RACHEL GLUCKSTERN
DEATHSTROKE created by MARV WOLFMAN and GEORGE PÉREZ

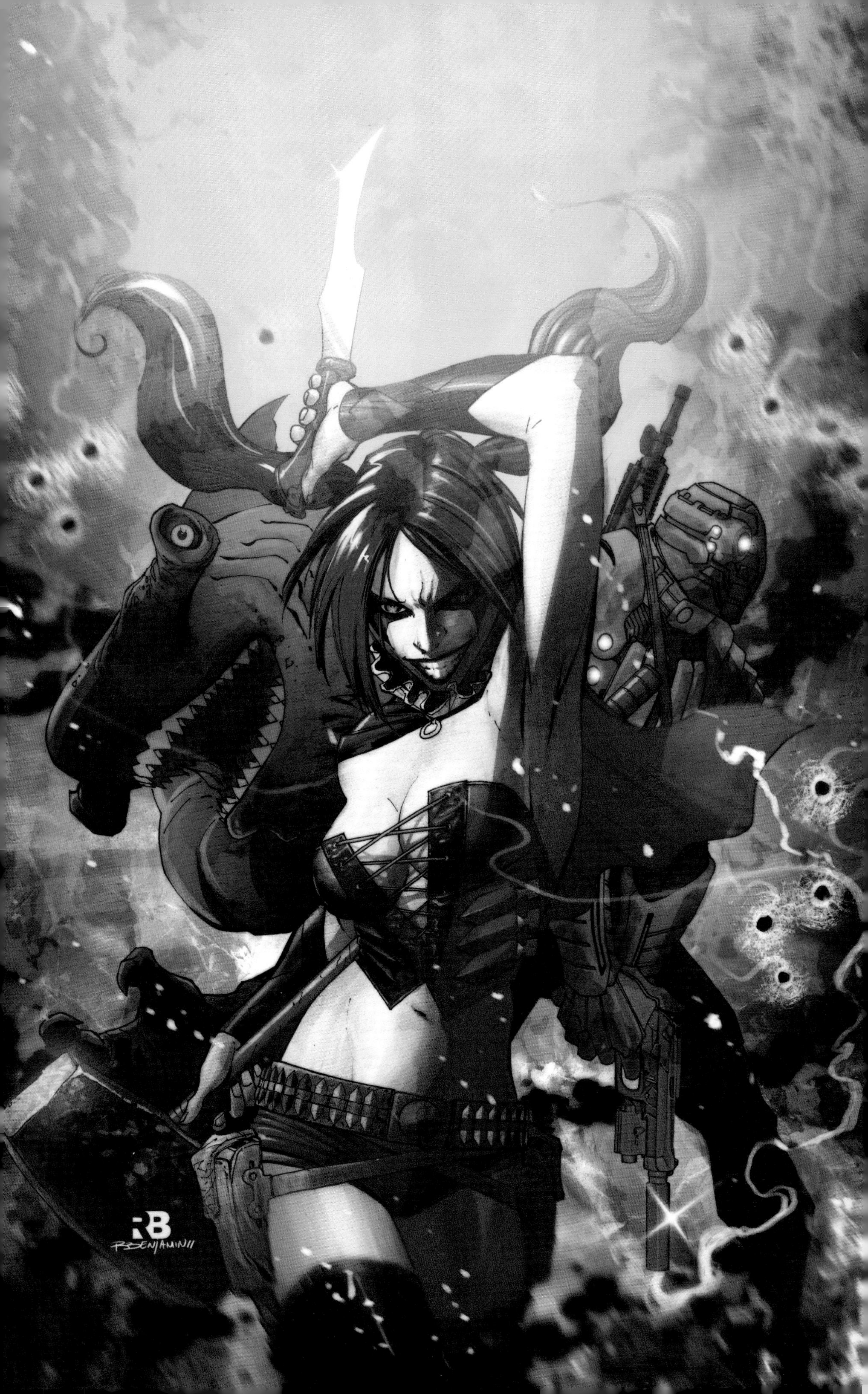

SUICIDE SQUAD

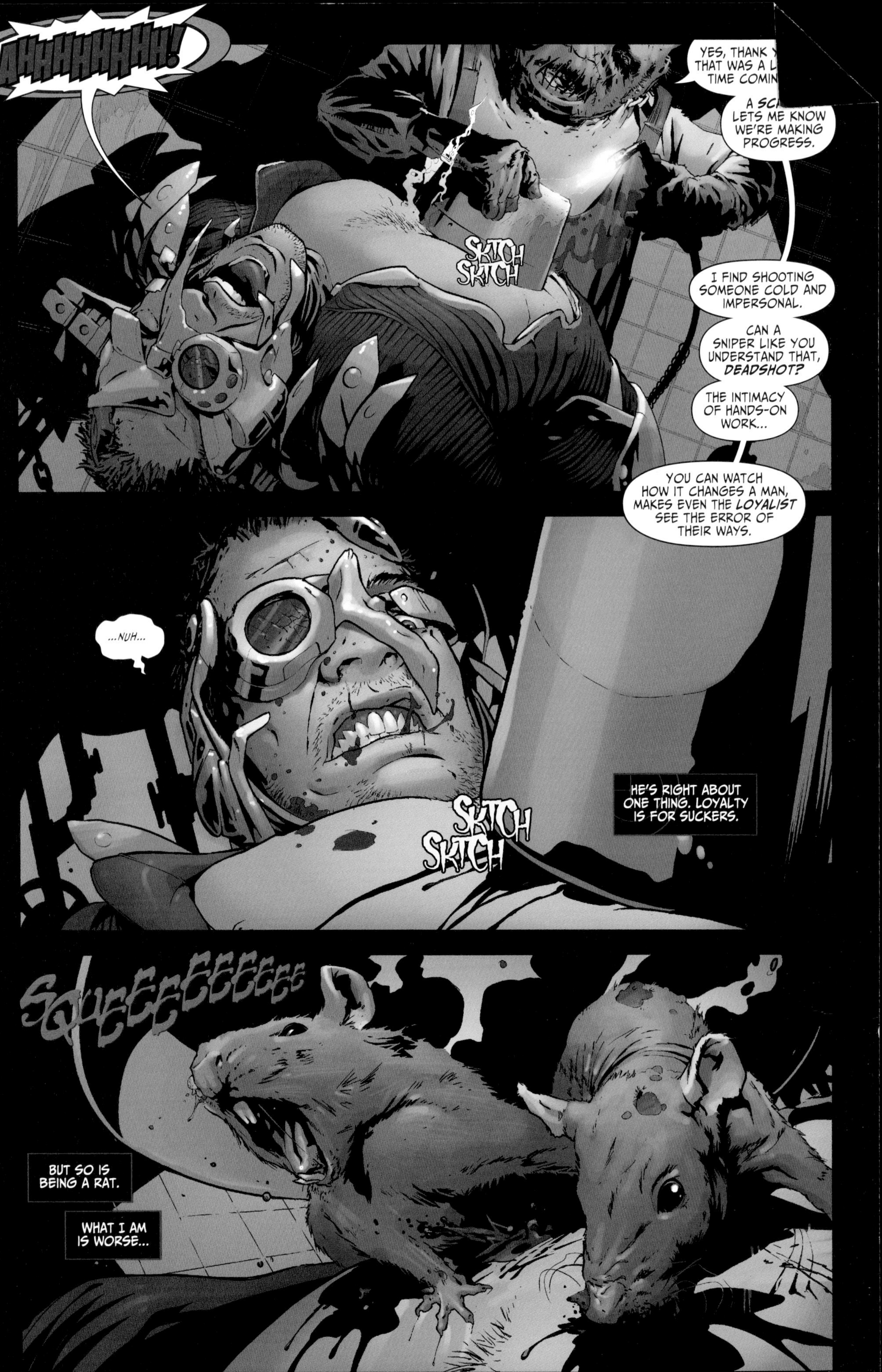
AHHHHHHHH!
YES, THANK Y THAT WAS A L TIME COMIN
A SCR LETS ME KNOW WE'RE MAKING PROGRESS.
SKTCH SKTCH
I FIND SHOOTING SOMEONE COLD AND IMPERSONAL.
CAN A SNIPER LIKE YOU UNDERSTAND THAT, DEADSHOT?
THE INTIMACY OF HANDS-ON WORK...
YOU CAN WATCH HOW IT CHANGES A MAN, MAKES EVEN THE LOYALIST SEE THE ERROR OF THEIR WAYS.
...NUH...
HE'S RIGHT ABOUT ONE THING. LOYALTY IS FOR SUCKERS.
SKTCH SKTCH
SQUEEEEEEEEEEE
BUT SO IS BEING A RAT.
WHAT I AM IS WORSE...

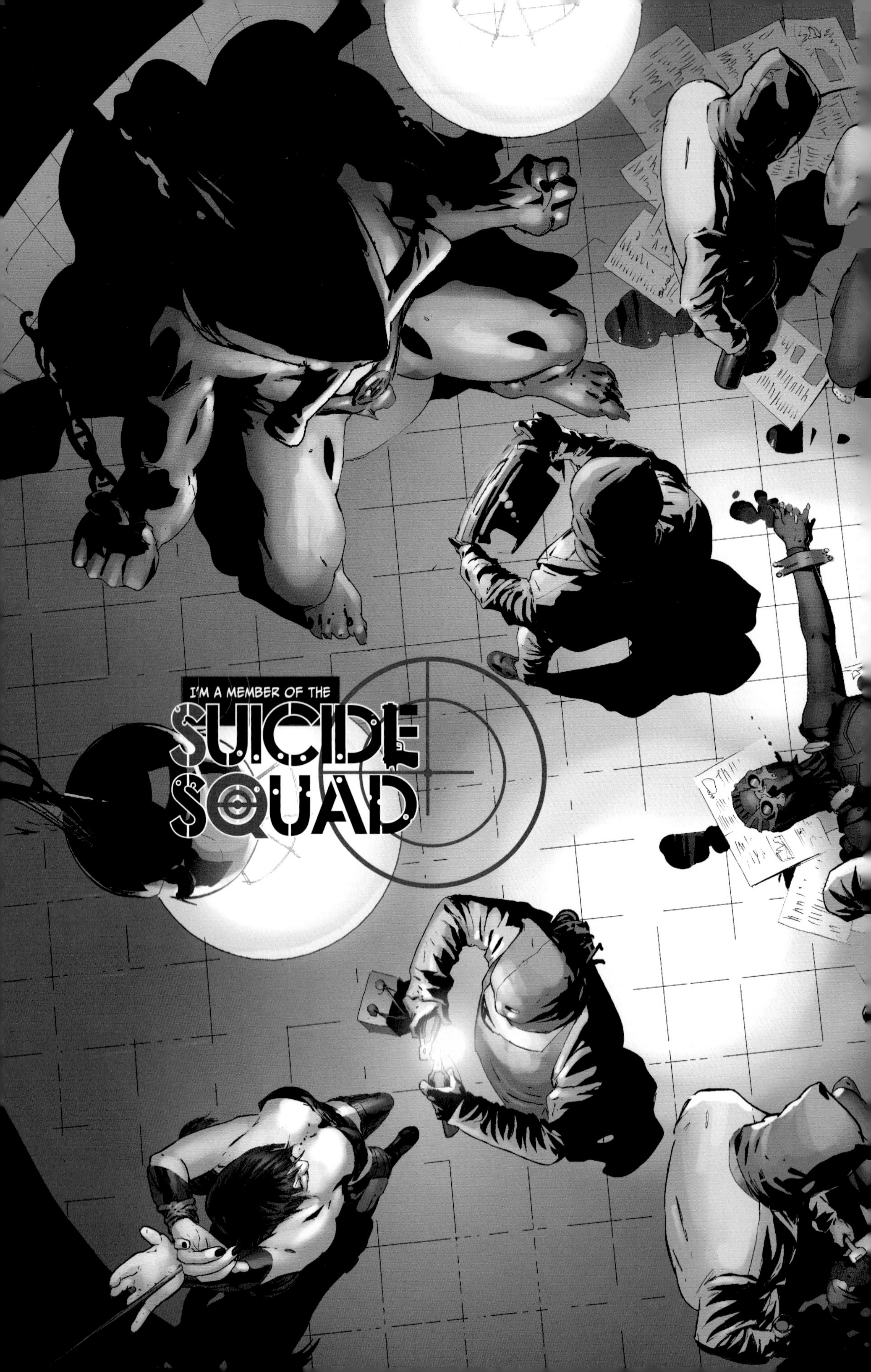
I'M A MEMBER OF THE
SUICIDE
SQUAD

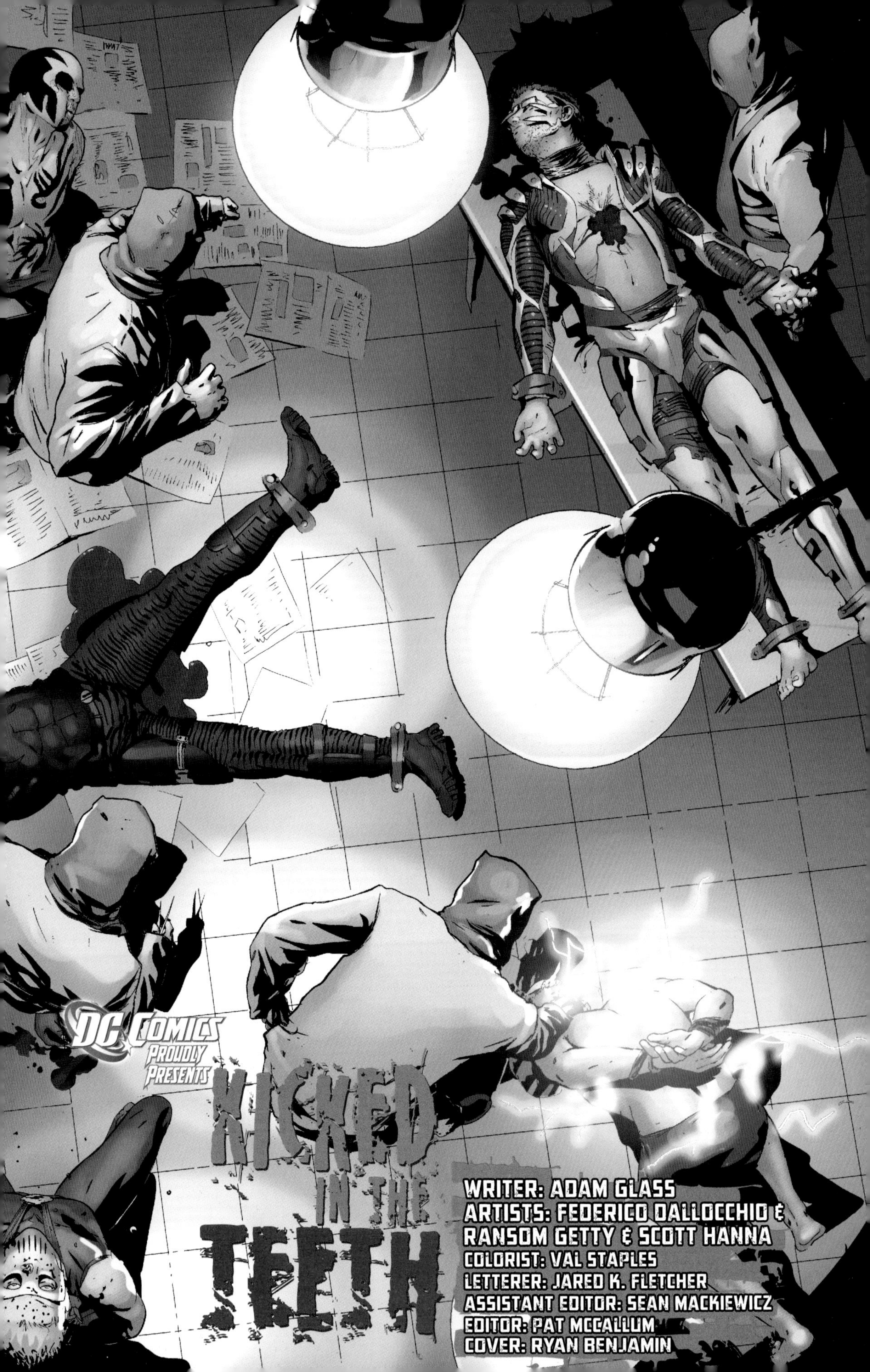
DC COMICS
PROUDLY PRESENTS
KICKED IN THE TEETH
WRITER: ADAM GLASS
ARTISTS: FEDERICO DALLOCCHIO & RANSOM GETTY & SCOTT HANNA
COLORIST: VAL STAPLES
LETTERER: JARED K. FLETCHER
ASSISTANT EDITOR: SEAN MACKIEWICZ
EDITOR: PAT MCCALLUM
COVER: RYAN BENJAMIN

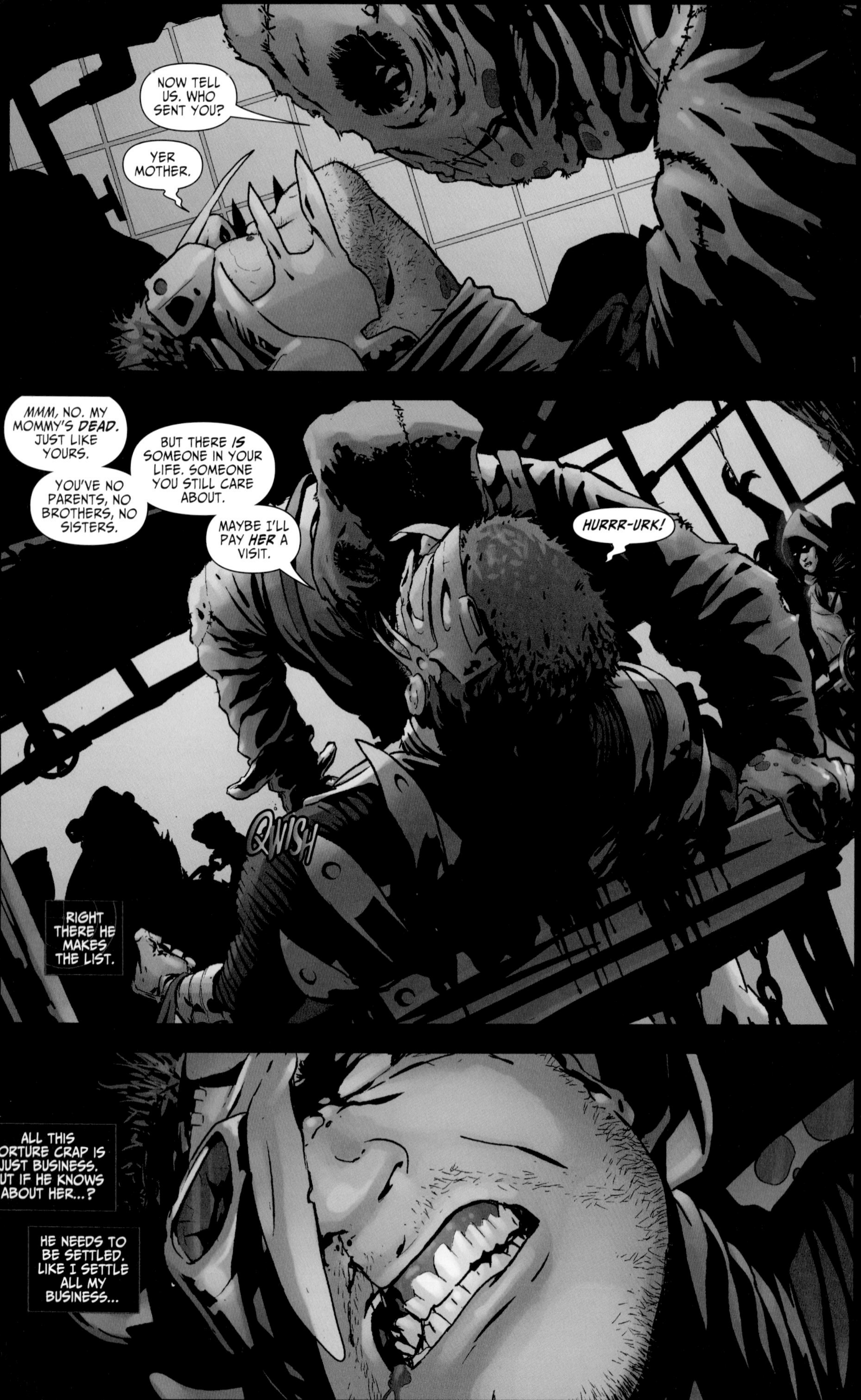
NOW TELL US. WHO SENT YOU?
YER MOTHER.
MMM, NO. MY MOMMY'S *DEAD.* JUST LIKE YOURS.
YOU'VE NO PARENTS, NO BROTHERS, NO SISTERS.
BUT THERE *IS* SOMEONE IN YOUR LIFE. SOMEONE YOU STILL CARE ABOUT.
MAYBE I'LL PAY *HER* A VISIT.
HURRR-URK!
QWISH
RIGHT THERE HE MAKES THE LIST.
ALL THIS TORTURE CRAP IS JUST BUSINESS. BUT IF HE KNOWS ABOUT HER...?
HE NEEDS TO BE SETTLED. LIKE I SETTLE ALL MY BUSINESS...

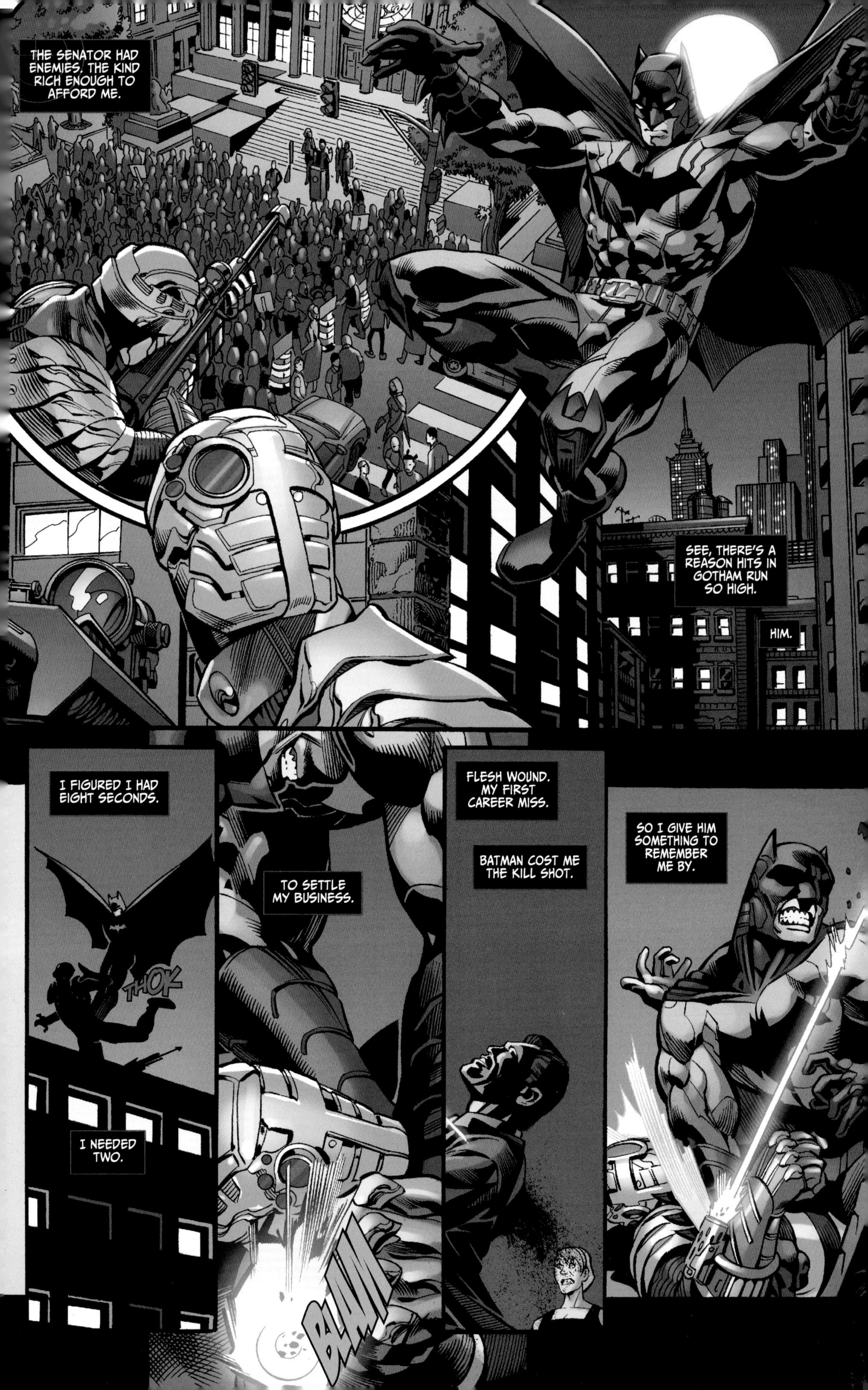
THE SENATOR HAD ENEMIES. THE KIND RICH ENOUGH TO AFFORD ME.
SEE, THERE'S A REASON HITS IN GOTHAM RUN SO HIGH.
HIM.
I FIGURED I HAD EIGHT SECONDS.
THOK
I NEEDED TWO.
TO SETTLE MY BUSINESS.
BLAM
FLESH WOUND. MY FIRST CAREER MISS.
BATMAN COST ME THE KILL SHOT.
SO I GIVE HIM SOMETHING TO REMEMBER ME BY.

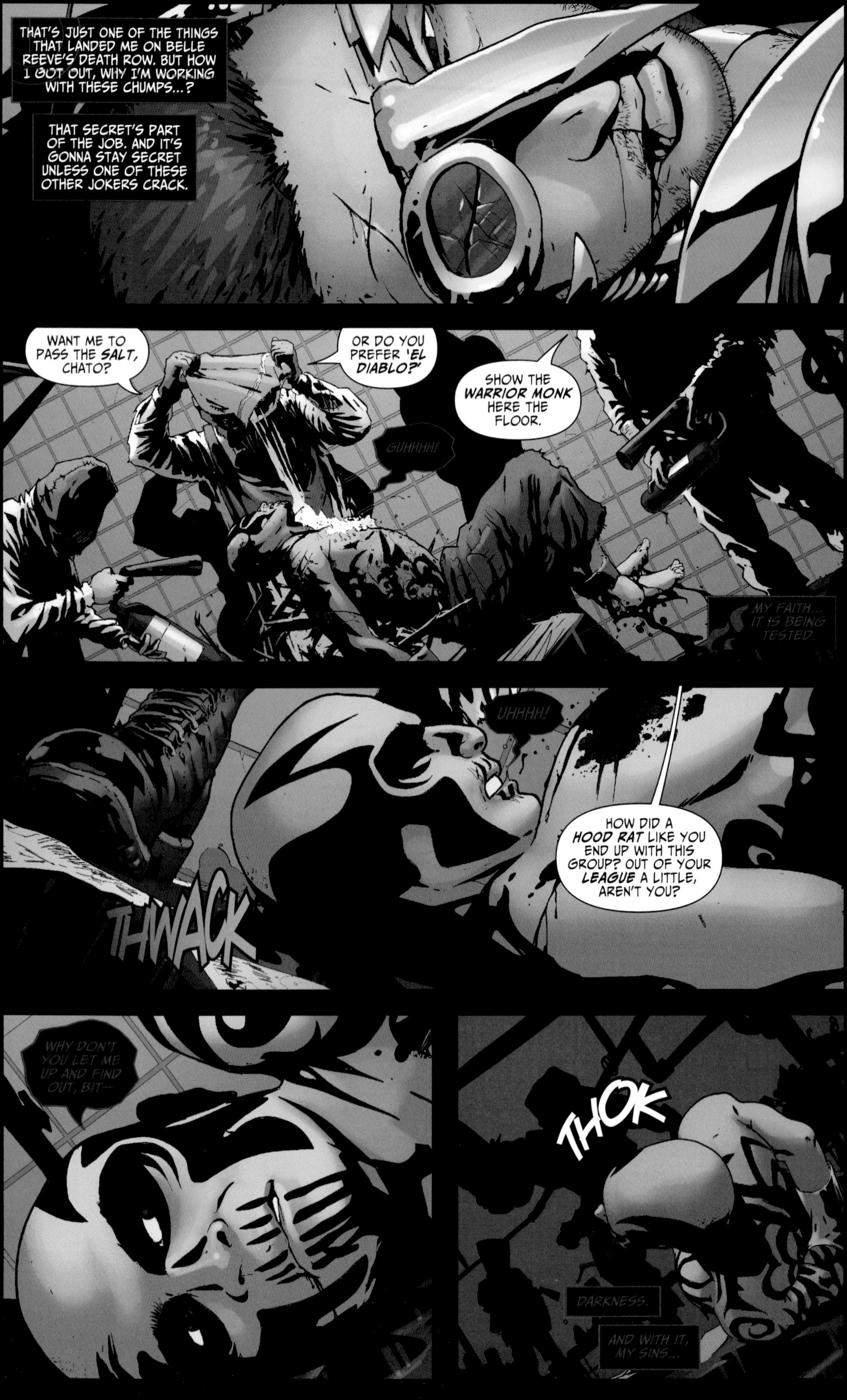
THAT'S JUST ONE OF THE THINGS THAT LANDED ME ON BELLE REEVE'S DEATH ROW. BUT HOW I GOT OUT, WHY I'M WORKING WITH THESE CHUMPS...?
THAT SECRET'S PART OF THE JOB. AND IT'S GONNA STAY SECRET UNLESS ONE OF THESE OTHER JOKERS CRACK.
WANT ME TO PASS THE SALT, CHATO?
OR DO YOU PREFER 'EL DIABLO?'
SHOW THE WARRIOR MONK HERE THE FLOOR.
GUHHHH!
MY FAITH... IT IS BEING TESTED.
UHHHH!
HOW DID A HOOD RAT LIKE YOU END UP WITH THIS GROUP? OUT OF YOUR LEAGUE A LITTLE, AREN'T YOU?
THWACK
WHY DON'T YOU LET ME UP AND FIND OUT, BIT--
THOK
DARKNESS.
AND WITH IT, MY SINS...

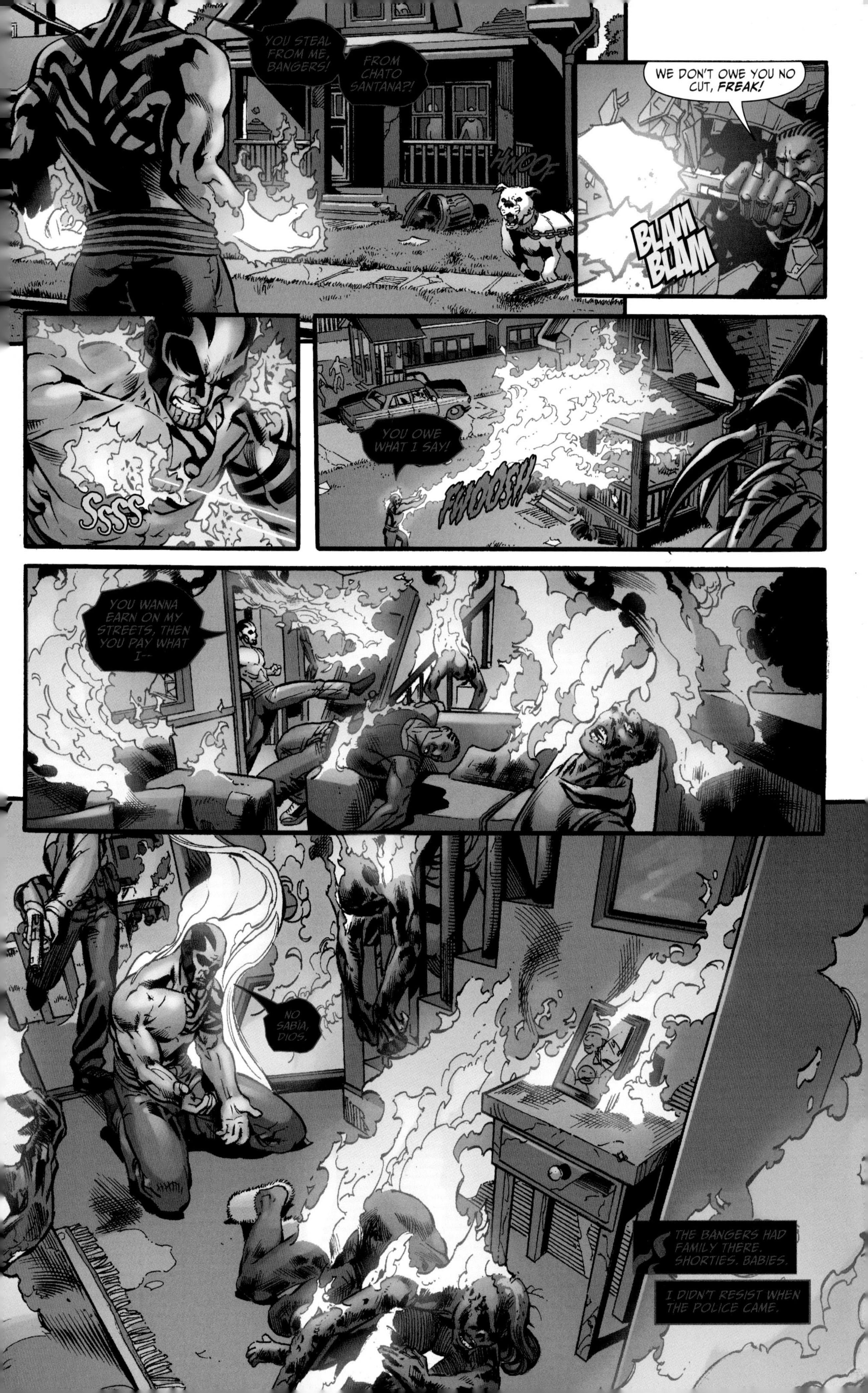
YOU STEAL FROM ME, BANGERS!
FROM CHATO SANTANA?!
HWOOF
WE DON'T OWE YOU NO CUT, FREAK!
BLAM BLAM
SSSS
YOU OWE WHAT I SAY!
FWOOSH
YOU WANNA EARN ON MY STREETS, THEN YOU PAY WHAT I--
NO SABIA, DIOS.
THE BANGERS HAD FAMILY THERE. SHORTIES. BABIES.
I DIDN'T RESIST WHEN THE POLICE CAME.

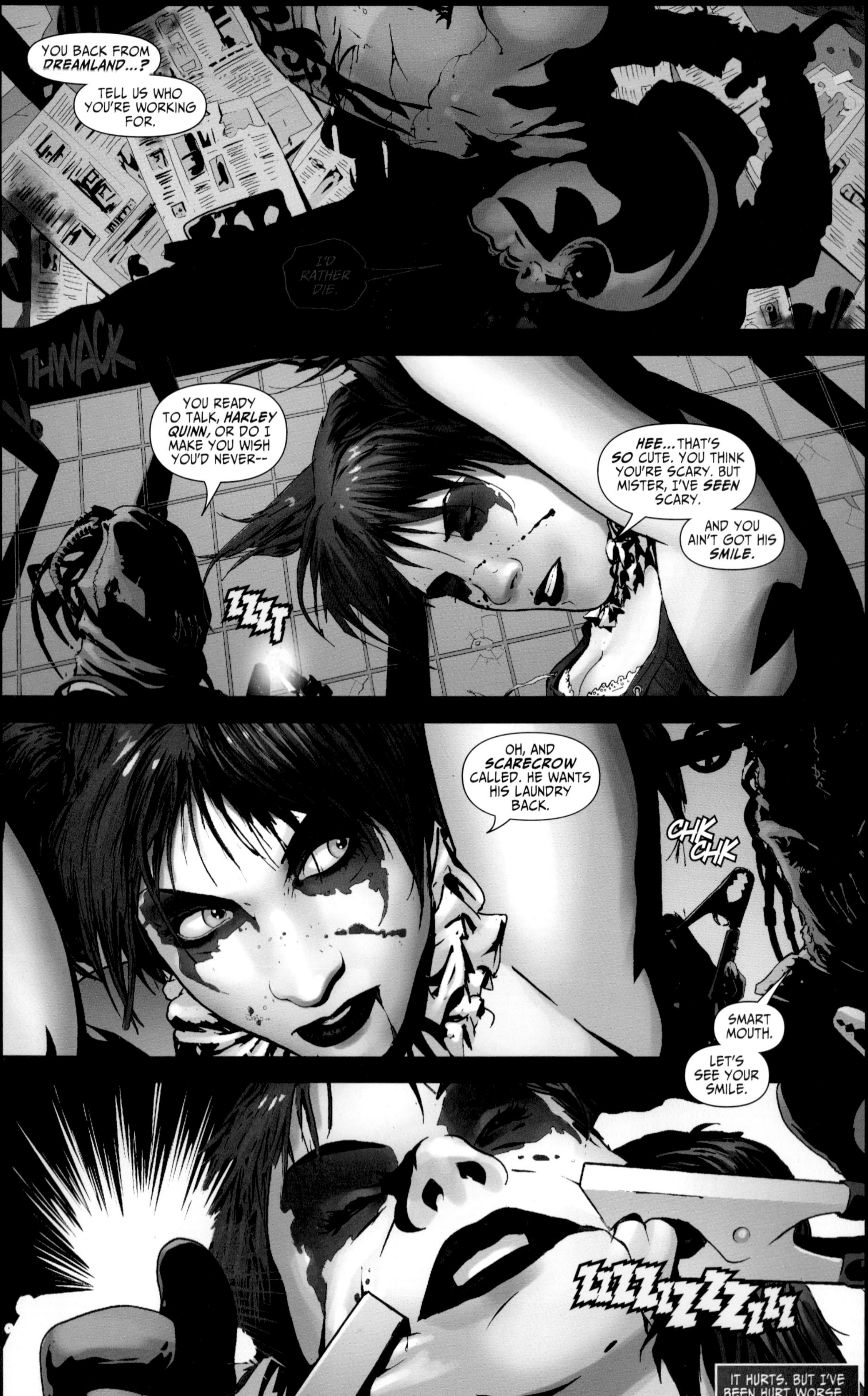
YOU BACK FROM DREAMLAND...?
TELL US WHO YOU'RE WORKING FOR.
I'D RATHER DIE.
THWACK
YOU READY TO TALK, HARLEY QUINN, OR DO I MAKE YOU WISH YOU'D NEVER--
HEE... THAT'S SO CUTE. YOU THINK YOU'RE SCARY. BUT MISTER, I'VE SEEN SCARY.
AND YOU AIN'T GOT HIS SMILE.
ZZZT
OH, AND SCARECROW CALLED. HE WANTS HIS LAUNDRY BACK.
CHK CHK
SMART MOUTH.
LET'S SEE YOUR SMILE.
ZZZZZZZZZZZ
IT HURTS. BUT I'VE BEEN HURT WORSE...

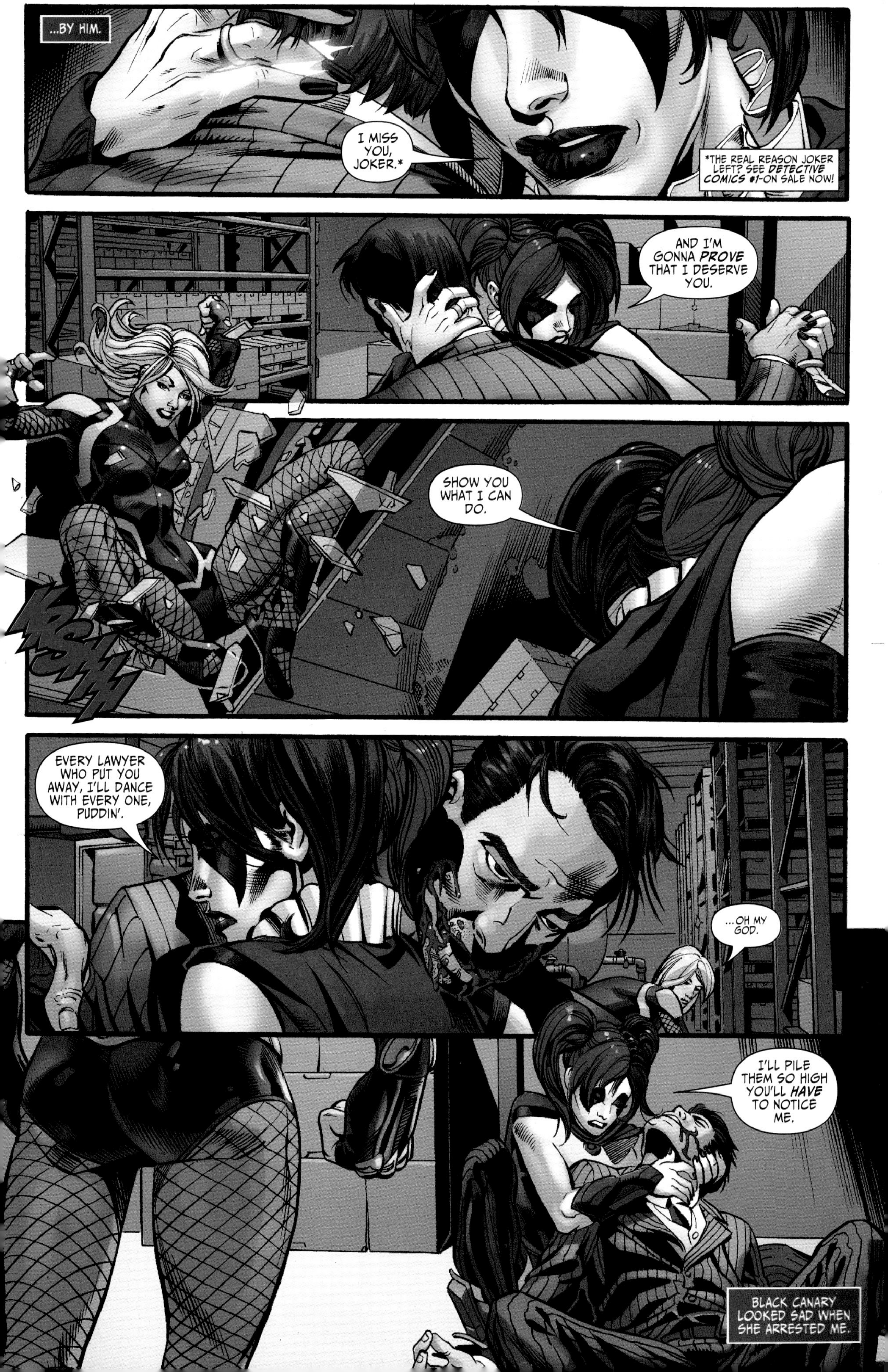
...BY HIM.
I MISS YOU, JOKER.*
*THE REAL REASON JOKER LEFT? SEE DETECTIVE COMICS #1-ON SALE NOW!
AND I'M GONNA PROVE THAT I DESERVE YOU.
SHOW YOU WHAT I CAN DO.
EVERY LAWYER WHO PUT YOU AWAY, I'LL DANCE WITH EVERY ONE, PUDDIN'.
...OH MY GOD.
I'LL PILE THEM SO HIGH YOU'LL HAVE TO NOTICE ME.
BLACK CANARY LOOKED SAD WHEN SHE ARRESTED ME.

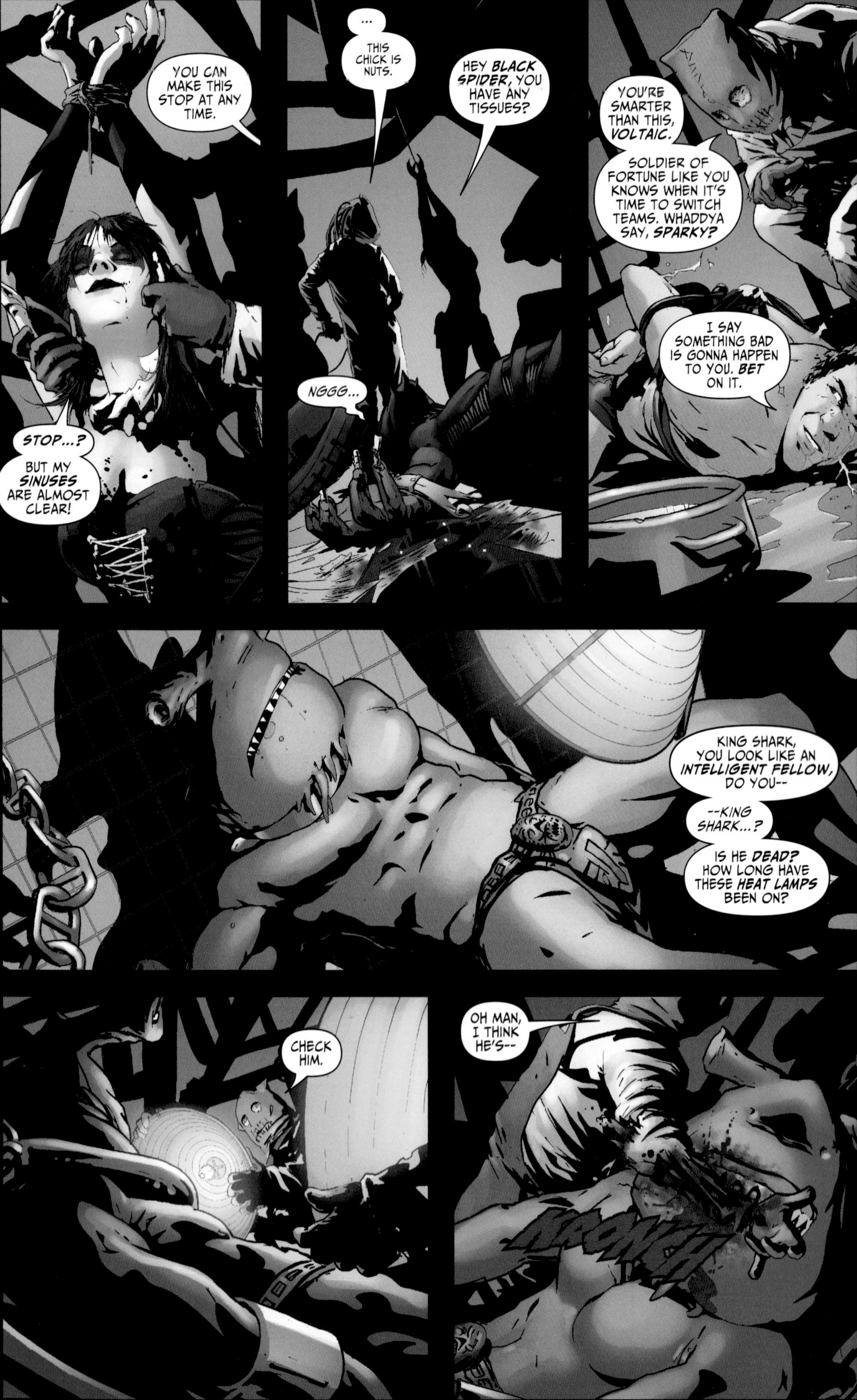
YOU CAN MAKE THIS STOP AT ANY TIME.
STOP...? BUT MY SINUSES ARE ALMOST CLEAR!
...
THIS CHICK IS NUTS.
HEY BLACK SPIDER, YOU HAVE ANY TISSUES?
NGGG...
YOU'RE SMARTER THAN THIS, VOLTAIC.
SOLDIER OF FORTUNE LIKE YOU KNOWS WHEN IT'S TIME TO SWITCH TEAMS. WHADDYA SAY, SPARKY?
I SAY SOMETHING BAD IS GONNA HAPPEN TO YOU. BET ON IT.
KING SHARK, YOU LOOK LIKE AN INTELLIGENT FELLOW, DO YOU--
--KING SHARK...?
IS HE DEAD? HOW LONG HAVE THESE HEAT LAMPS BEEN ON?
CHECK HIM.
OH MAN, I THINK HE'S--
KRONCH

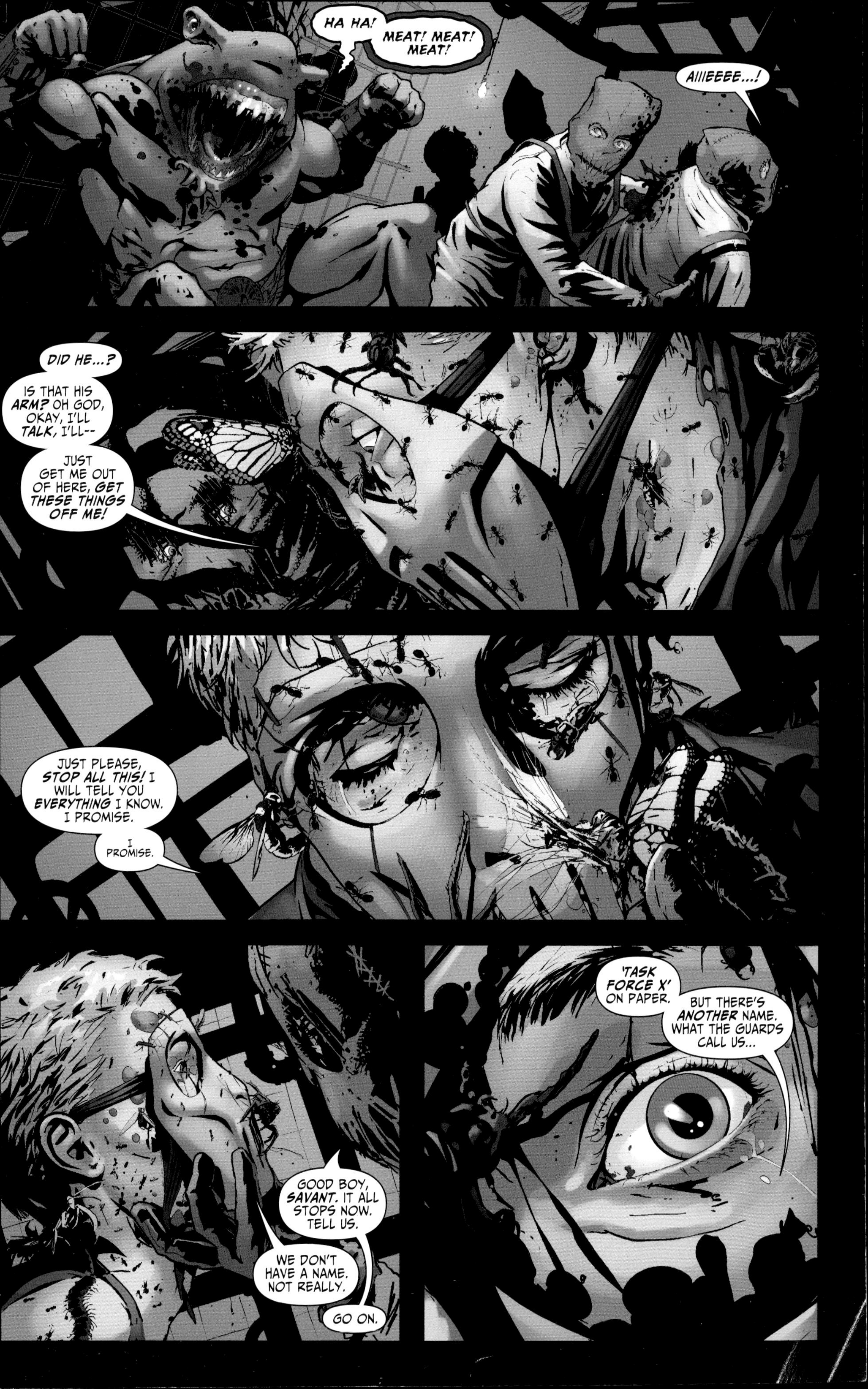
HA HA!
MEAT! MEAT! MEAT!
AIIIEEEE...!
DID HE...?
IS THAT HIS ARM? OH GOD, OKAY, I'LL TALK, I'LL--
JUST GET ME OUT OF HERE, GET THESE THINGS OFF ME!
JUST PLEASE, STOP ALL THIS! I WILL TELL YOU EVERYTHING I KNOW. I PROMISE.
I PROMISE.
GOOD BOY, SAVANT. IT ALL STOPS NOW. TELL US.
WE DON'T HAVE A NAME. NOT REALLY.
GO ON.
'TASK FORCE X' ON PAPER.
BUT THERE'S ANOTHER NAME. WHAT THE GUARDS CALL US...

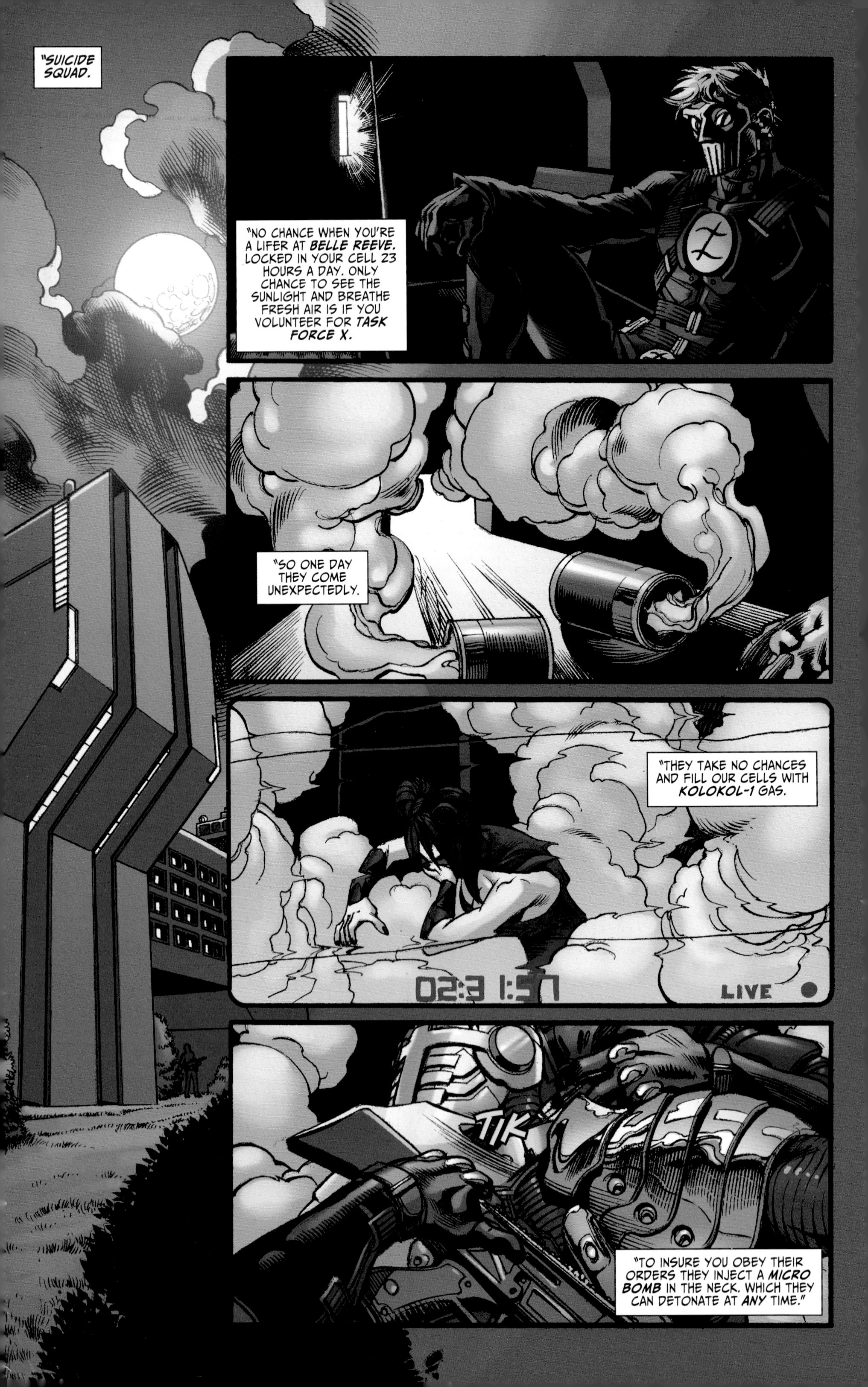
"SUICIDE SQUAD.
"NO CHANCE WHEN YOU'RE A LIFER AT BELLE REEVE. LOCKED IN YOUR CELL 23 HOURS A DAY. ONLY CHANCE TO SEE THE SUNLIGHT AND BREATHE FRESH AIR IS IF YOU VOLUNTEER FOR TASK FORCE X.
"SO ONE DAY THEY COME UNEXPECTEDLY.
"THEY TAKE NO CHANCES AND FILL OUR CELLS WITH KOLOKOL-1 GAS.
02:31:57
LIVE
TIK
"TO INSURE YOU OBEY THEIR ORDERS THEY INJECT A MICRO BOMB IN THE NECK. WHICH THEY CAN DETONATE AT ANY TIME."

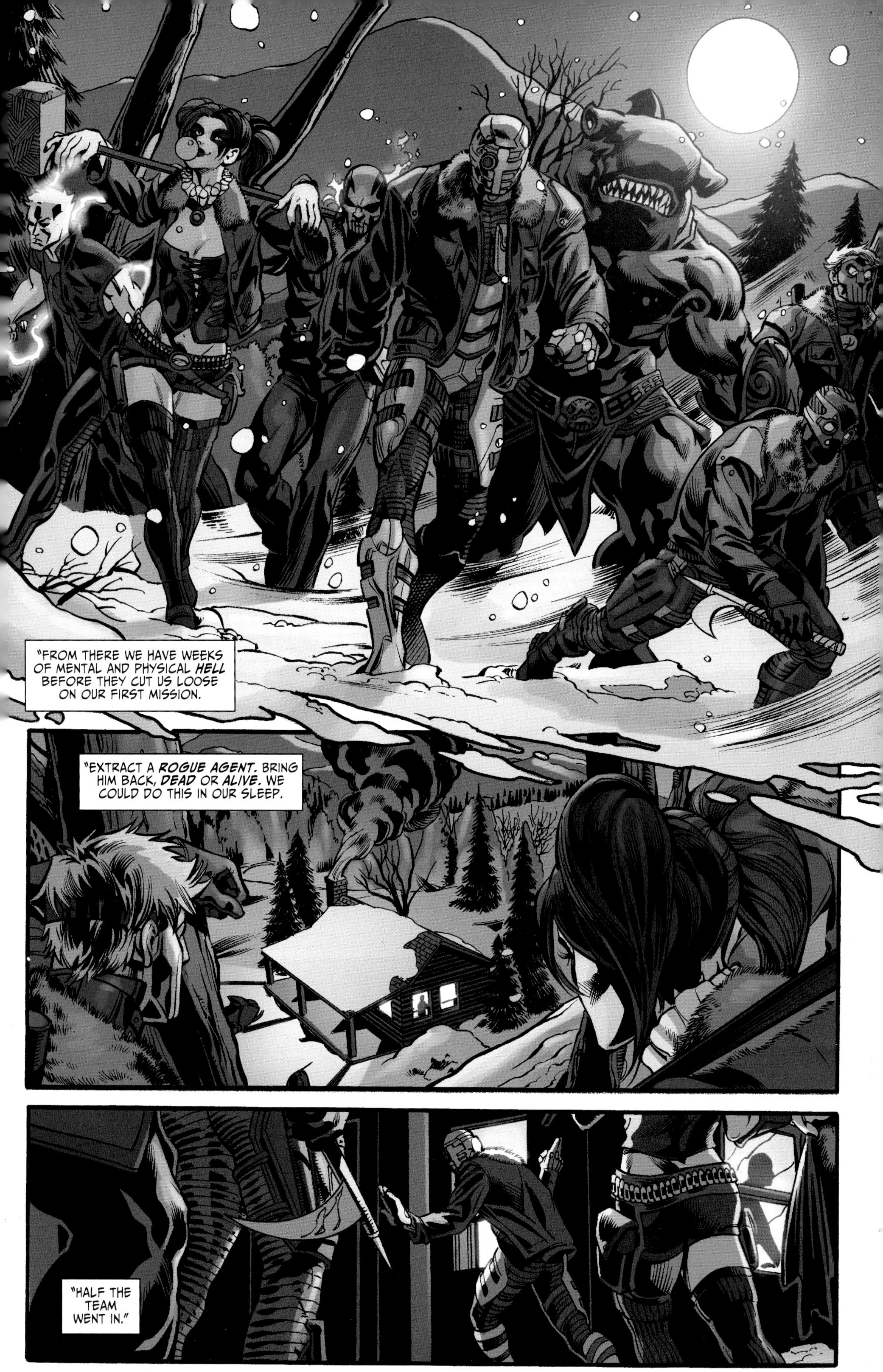
"FROM THERE WE HAVE WEEKS OF MENTAL AND PHYSICAL HELL BEFORE THEY CUT US LOOSE ON OUR FIRST MISSION.
"EXTRACT A ROGUE AGENT. BRING HIM BACK, DEAD OR ALIVE. WE COULD DO THIS IN OUR SLEEP.
"HALF THE TEAM WENT IN."

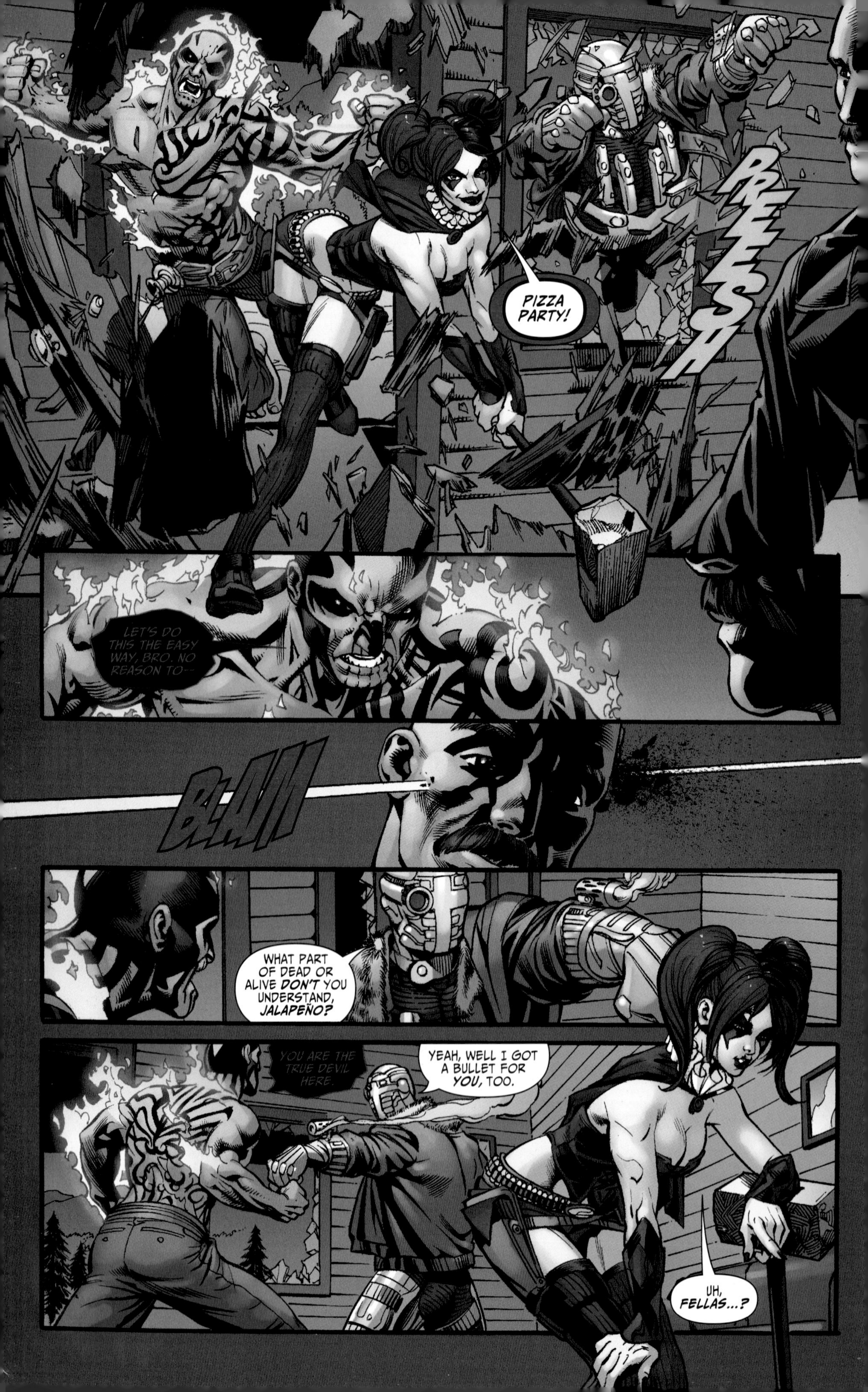
PREEESH
PIZZA PARTY!
LET'S DO THIS THE EASY WAY, BRO. NO REASON TO--
BLAM
WHAT PART OF DEAD OR ALIVE DON'T YOU UNDERSTAND, JALAPEÑO?
YOU ARE THE TRUE DEVIL HERE.
YEAH, WELL I GOT A BULLET FOR YOU, TOO.
UH, FELLAS...?

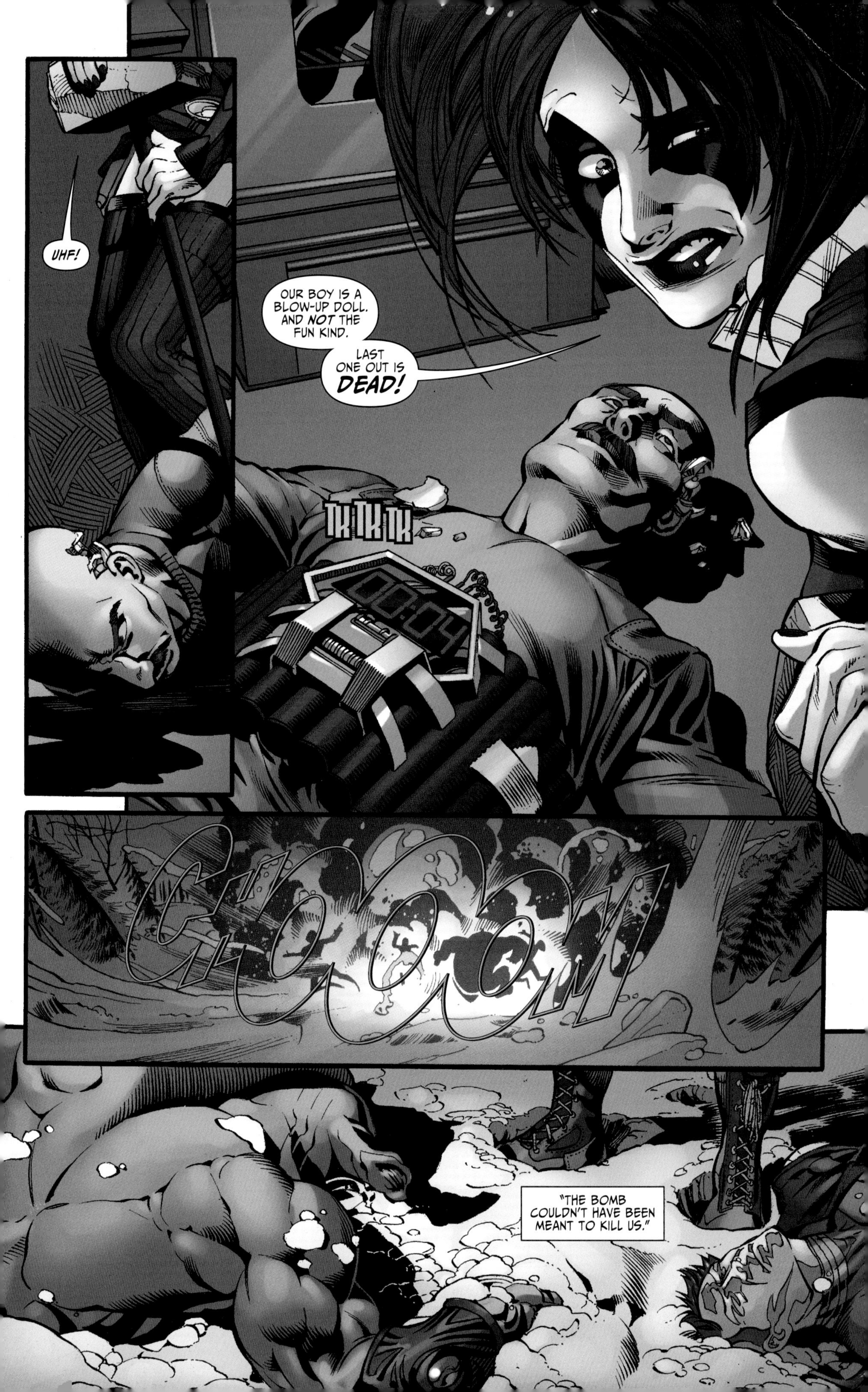
UHF!
OUR BOY IS A BLOW-UP DOLL. AND NOT THE FUN KIND.
LAST ONE OUT IS DEAD!
TK TK TK
00:04
"THE BOMB COULDN'T HAVE BEEN MEANT TO KILL US."

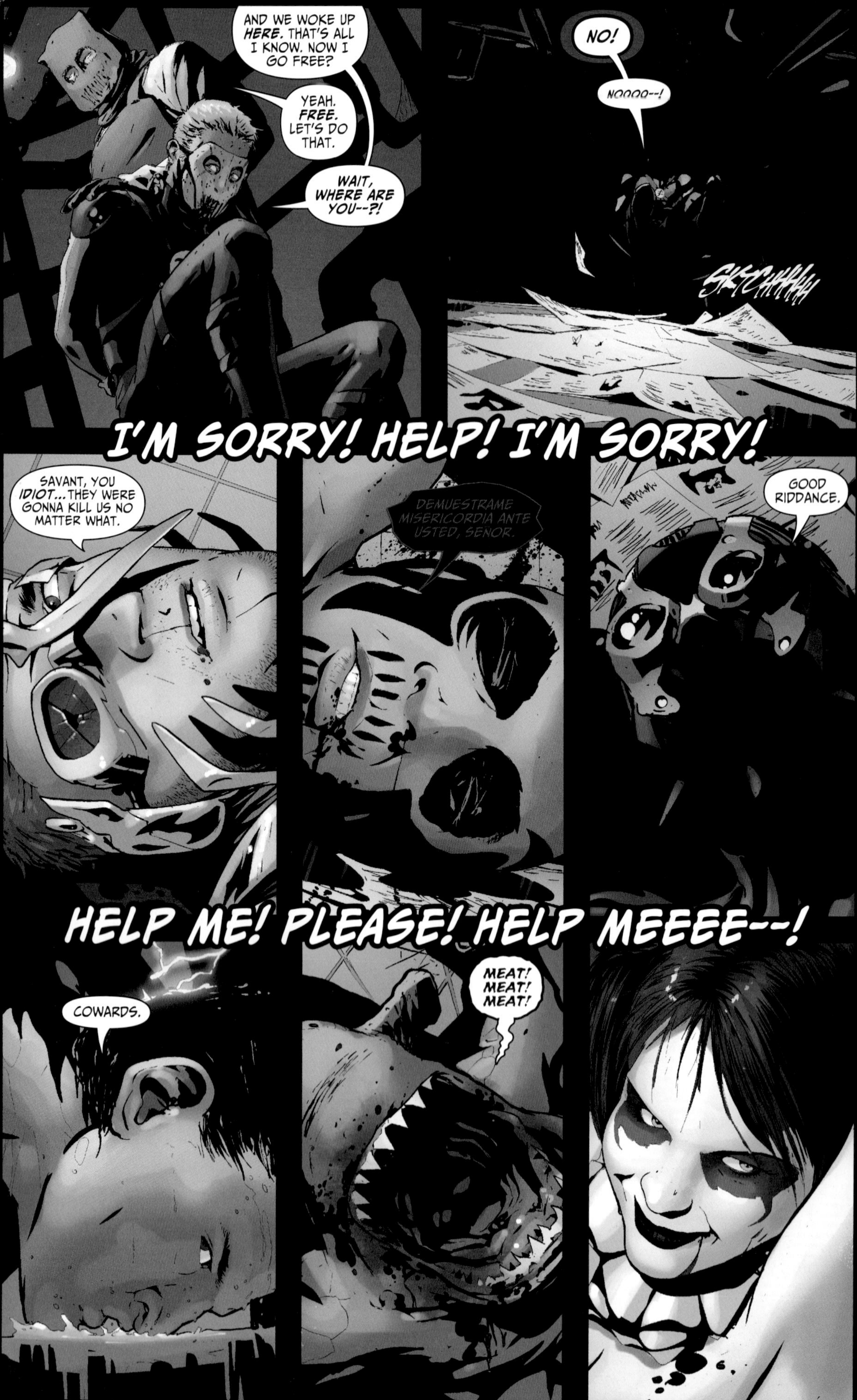
AND WE WOKE UP *HERE.* THAT'S ALL I KNOW. NOW I GO FREE?
YEAH. *FREE.* LET'S DO THAT.
WAIT, WHERE ARE YOU--?!
NO!
NOOOO--!
I'M SORRY! HELP! I'M SORRY!
SAVANT, YOU *IDIOT*... THEY WERE GONNA KILL US NO MATTER WHAT.
DEMUESTRAME MISERICORDIA ANTE USTED, SEÑOR.
GOOD RIDDANCE.
HELP ME! PLEASE! HELP MEEEE--!
COWARDS.
MEAT! MEAT! MEAT!

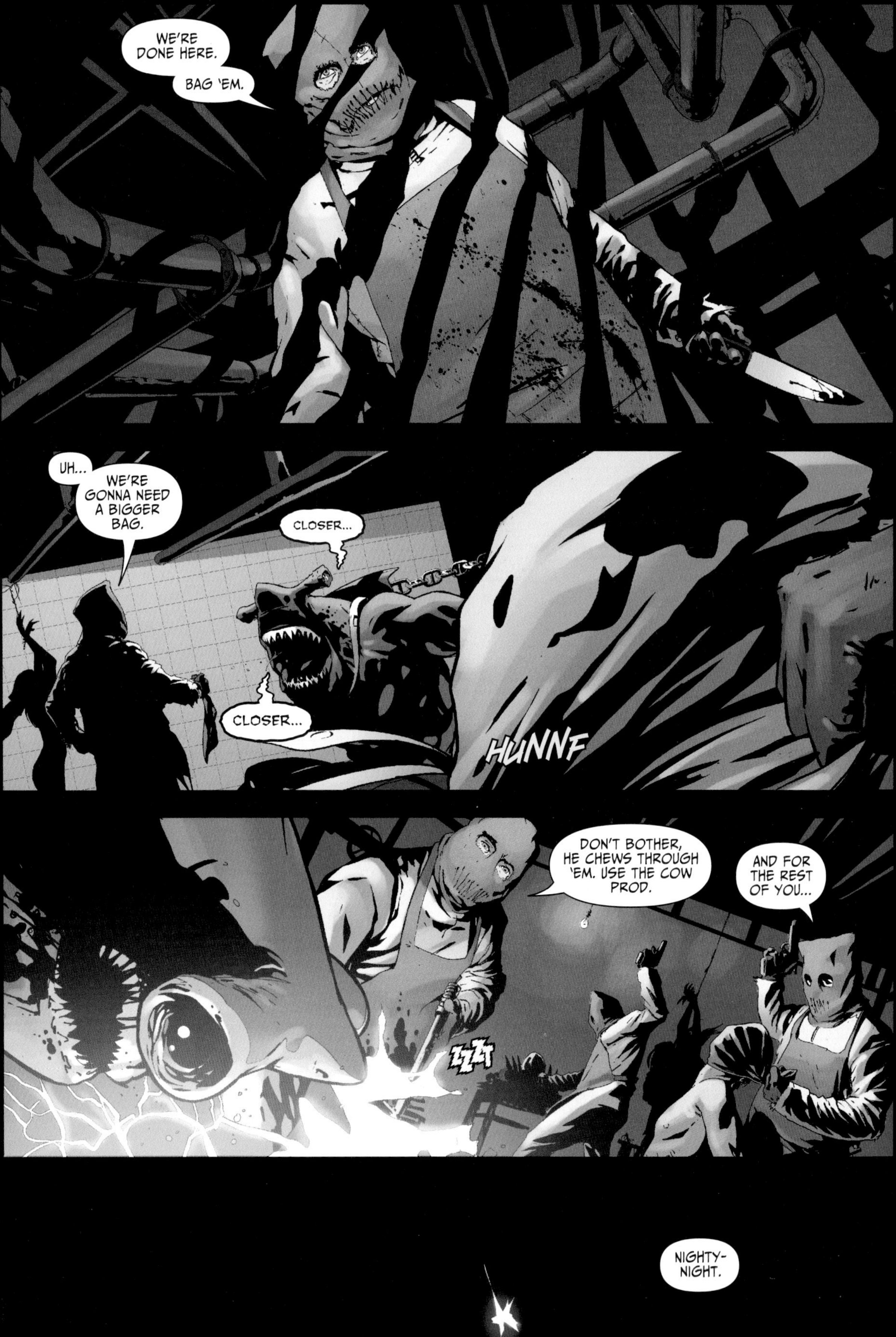
WE'RE DONE HERE.
BAG 'EM.
UH...
WE'RE GONNA NEED A BIGGER BAG.
CLOSER...
CLOSER...
HUNNF
DON'T BOTHER, HE CHEWS THROUGH 'EM. USE THE COW PROD.
AND FOR THE REST OF YOU...
ZZZT
NIGHTY-NIGHT.

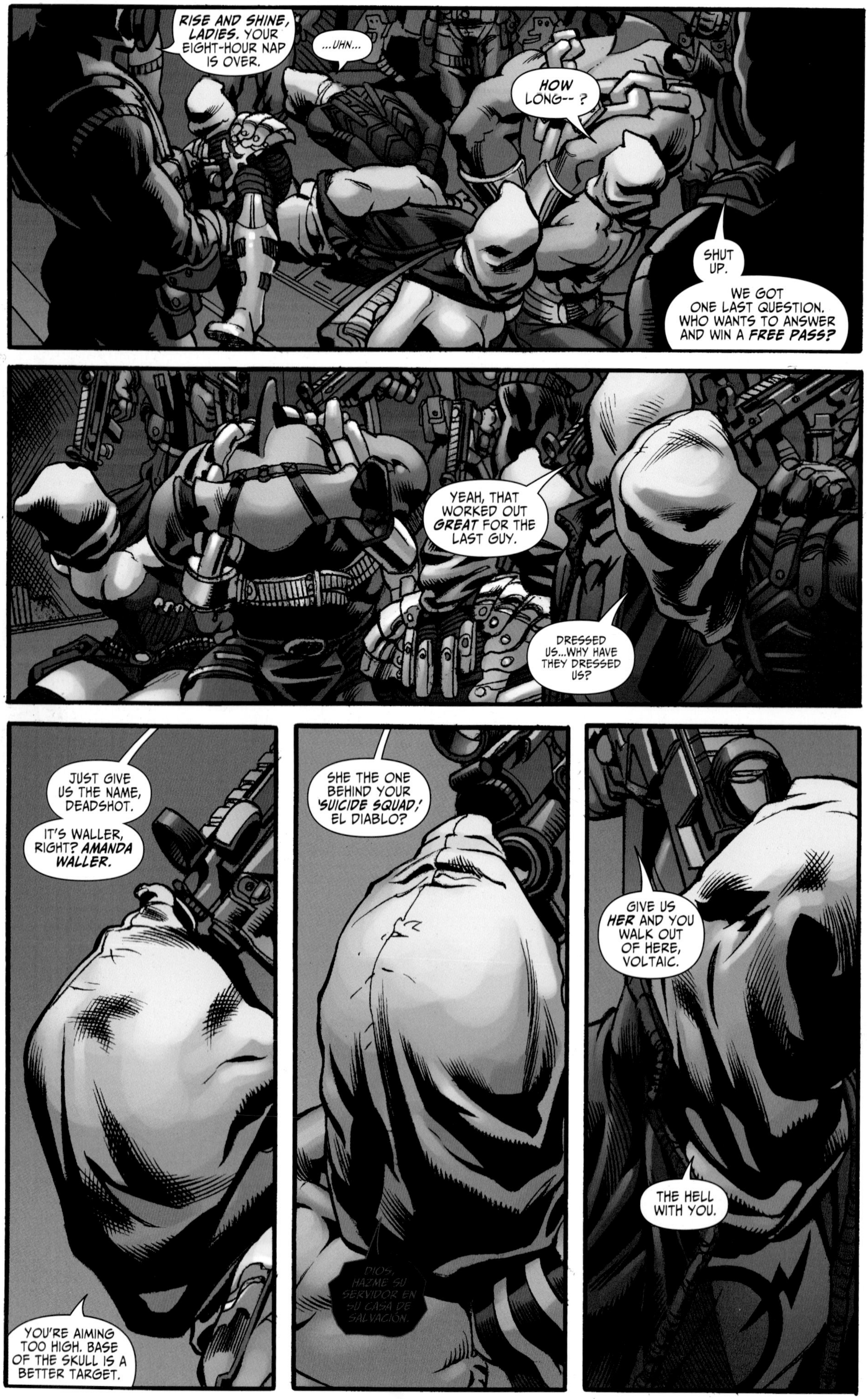
RISE AND SHINE, LADIES. YOUR EIGHT-HOUR NAP IS OVER.
...UHN...
HOW LONG-- ?
SHUT UP.
WE GOT ONE LAST QUESTION. WHO WANTS TO ANSWER AND WIN A FREE PASS?
YEAH, THAT WORKED OUT GREAT FOR THE LAST GUY.
DRESSED US...WHY HAVE THEY DRESSED US?
JUST GIVE US THE NAME, DEADSHOT.
IT'S WALLER, RIGHT? AMANDA WALLER.
YOU'RE AIMING TOO HIGH. BASE OF THE SKULL IS A BETTER TARGET.
SHE THE ONE BEHIND YOUR 'SUICIDE SQUAD,' EL DIABLO?
DIOS, HAZME SU SERVIDOR EN SU CASA DE SALVACIÓN.
GIVE US HER AND YOU WALK OUT OF HERE, VOLTAIC.
THE HELL WITH YOU.

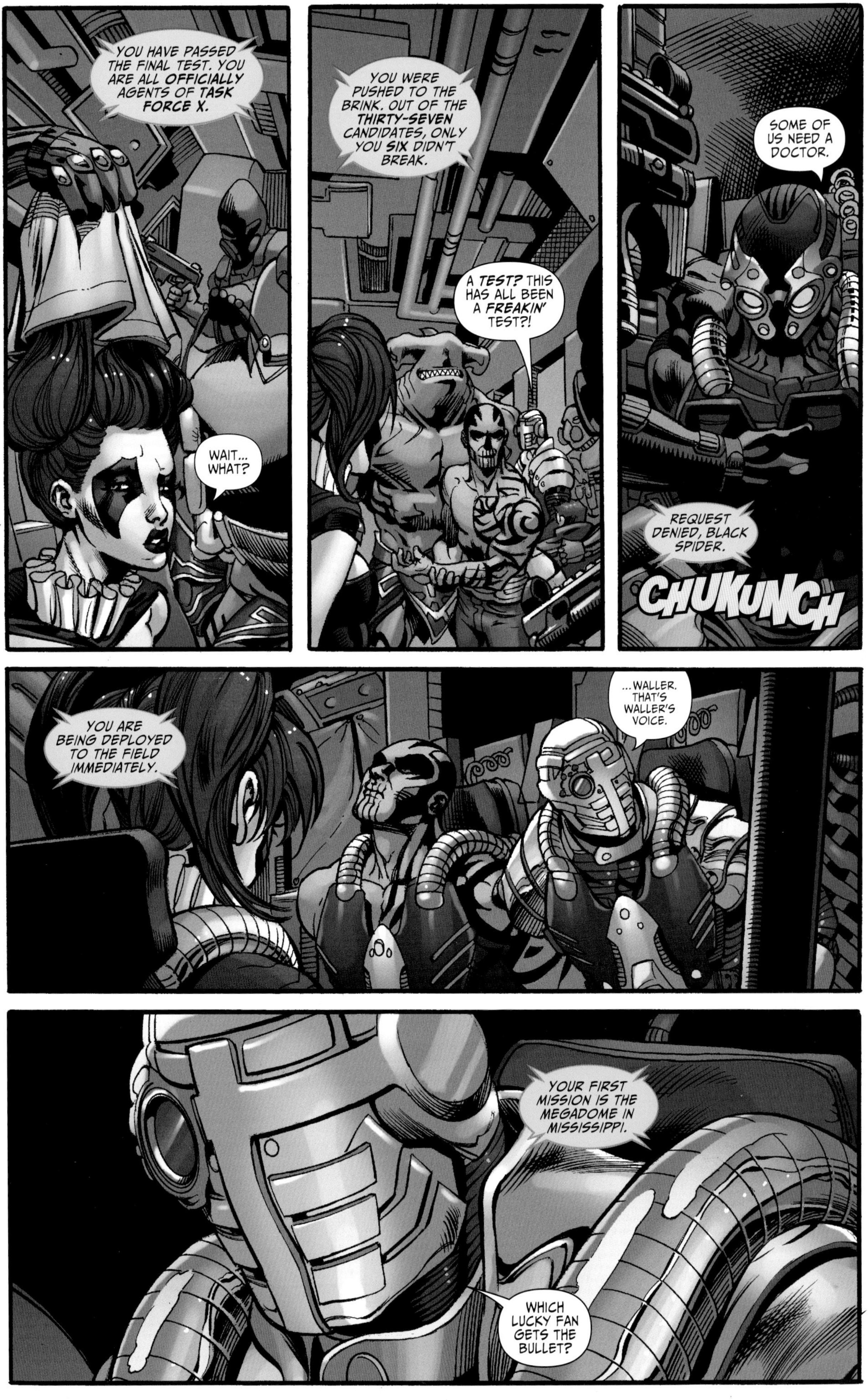
YOU HAVE PASSED THE FINAL TEST. YOU ARE ALL OFFICIALLY AGENTS OF TASK FORCE X.
WAIT... WHAT?
YOU WERE PUSHED TO THE BRINK. OUT OF THE THIRTY-SEVEN CANDIDATES, ONLY YOU SIX DIDN'T BREAK.
A TEST? THIS HAS ALL BEEN A FREAKIN' TEST?!
SOME OF US NEED A DOCTOR.
REQUEST DENIED, BLACK SPIDER.
CHUKUNCH
YOU ARE BEING DEPLOYED TO THE FIELD IMMEDIATELY.
...WALLER. THAT'S WALLER'S VOICE.
YOUR FIRST MISSION IS THE MEGADOME IN MISSISSIPPI.
WHICH LUCKY FAN GETS THE BULLET?

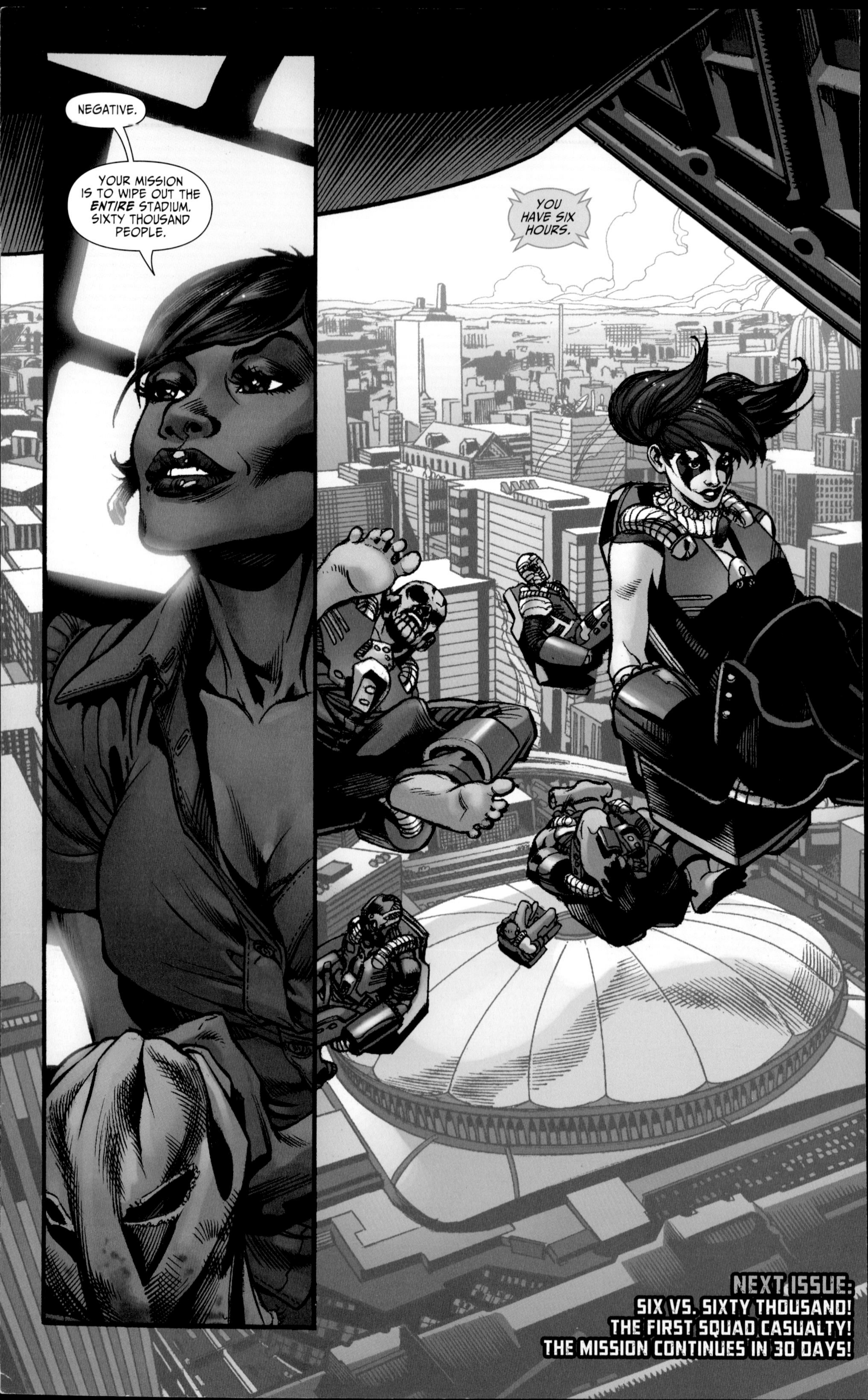
NEGATIVE.
YOUR MISSION IS TO WIPE OUT THE ENTIRE STADIUM. SIXTY THOUSAND PEOPLE.
YOU HAVE SIX HOURS.
NEXT ISSUE:
SIX VS. SIXTY THOUSAND!
THE FIRST SQUAD CASUALTY!
THE MISSION CONTINUES IN 30 DAYS!

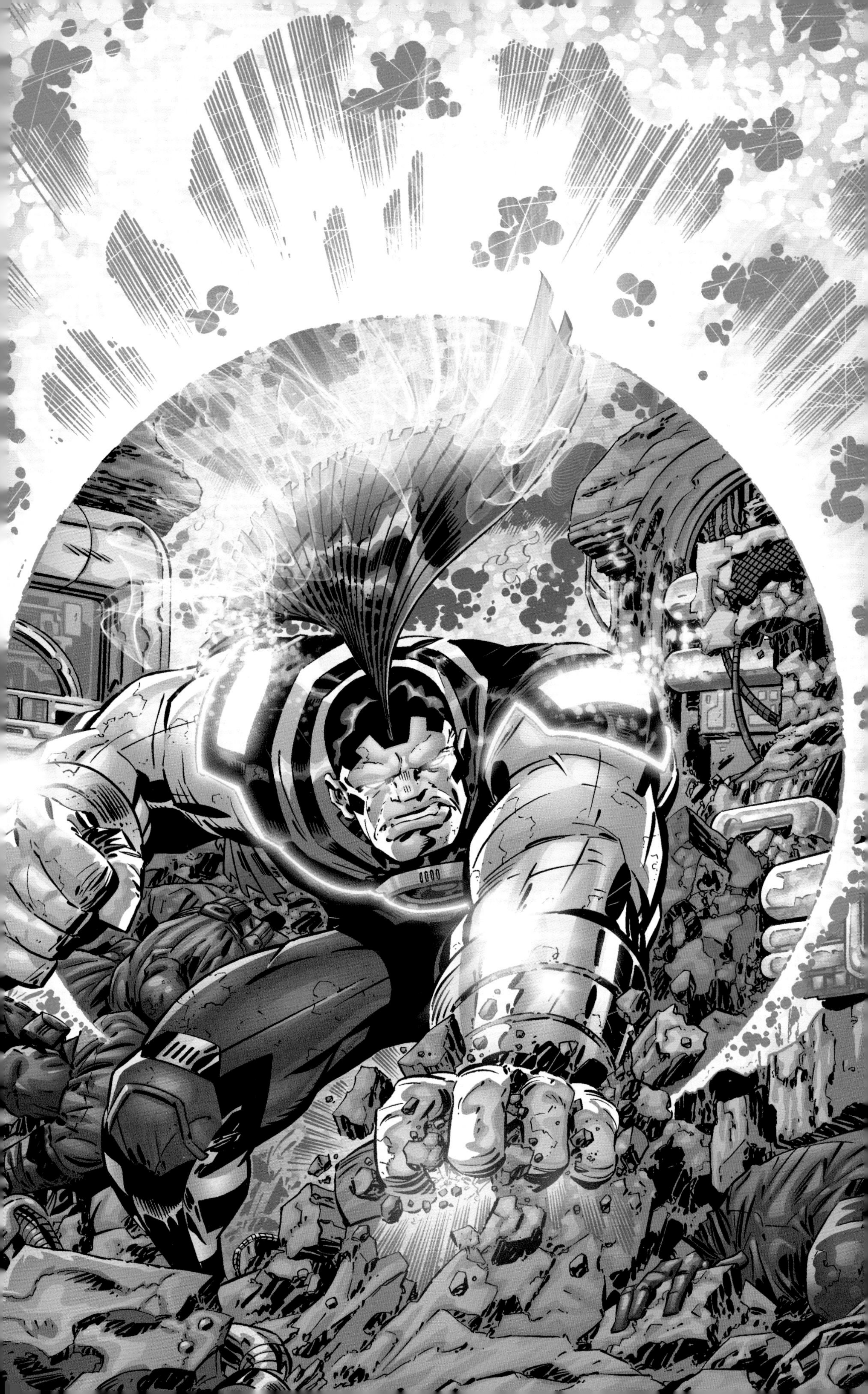

OMAC

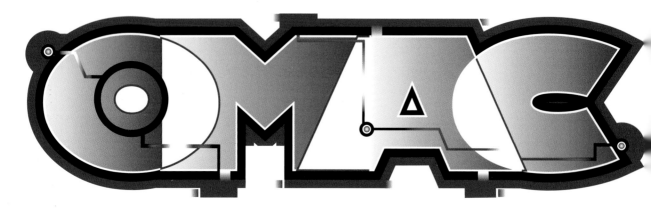

CADMUS INDUSTRIES.

THE CORPORATE LEADER IN GENETIC RESEARCH AND CUTTING EDGE MEDICAL TECHNOLOGIES.

FOUNDED AS A STEM CELL RESEARCH CENTER, IN THE LAST FIVE YEARS THE COMPANY GREW EXPONENTIALLY TO BECOME THE WORLDWIDE LEADER IN BIO-ENGINEERING AND MAPPING THE HUMAN GENOME.

IN HIRING SCIENCE'S BEST AND BRIGHTEST, ITS DEDICATED STAFF IS SECOND TO NONE.

I CAN'T BELIEVE HE DID THIS TO ME *AGAIN!*

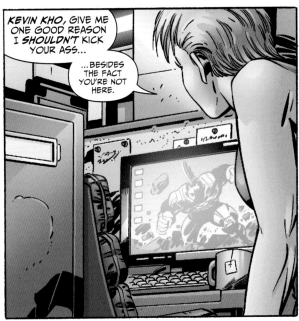

KEVIN KHO, GIVE ME ONE GOOD REASON I *SHOULDN'T* KICK YOUR ASS...

...BESIDES THE FACT YOU'RE NOT HERE.

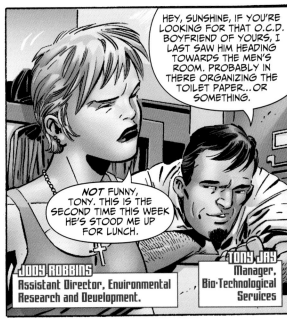

HEY, SUNSHINE, IF YOU'RE LOOKING FOR THAT O.C.D. BOYFRIEND OF YOURS, I LAST SAW HIM HEADING TOWARDS THE MEN'S ROOM. PROBABLY IN THERE ORGANIZING THE TOILET PAPER...OR SOMETHING.

NOT FUNNY, TONY. THIS IS THE SECOND TIME THIS WEEK HE'S STOOD ME UP FOR LUNCH.

JODY ROBBINS
Assistant Director, Environmental Research and Development.

TONY JAY
Manager, Bio-Technological Services

AND HE STILL OWES ME HIS REPORT ON MICROBIAL CULTURES. I WAS SUPPOSED TO HAVE IT TWO HOURS AGO.

I KNOW HE'S A BIT COMPULSIVE, BUT THAT'S WHY HE'S GOOD AT HIS JOB.

I PAY ATTENTION TO DETAIL TOO, LIKE WHEN SOMEONE RUBS YOUR EARLOBE...

NOT THE TIME, NOT THE PLACE, NOT EVER *AGAIN!*

HUH? THE ALARM?

WROOOPPPP
WOOOPP

THERE'S A COMMOTION ON THE OTHER SIDE.

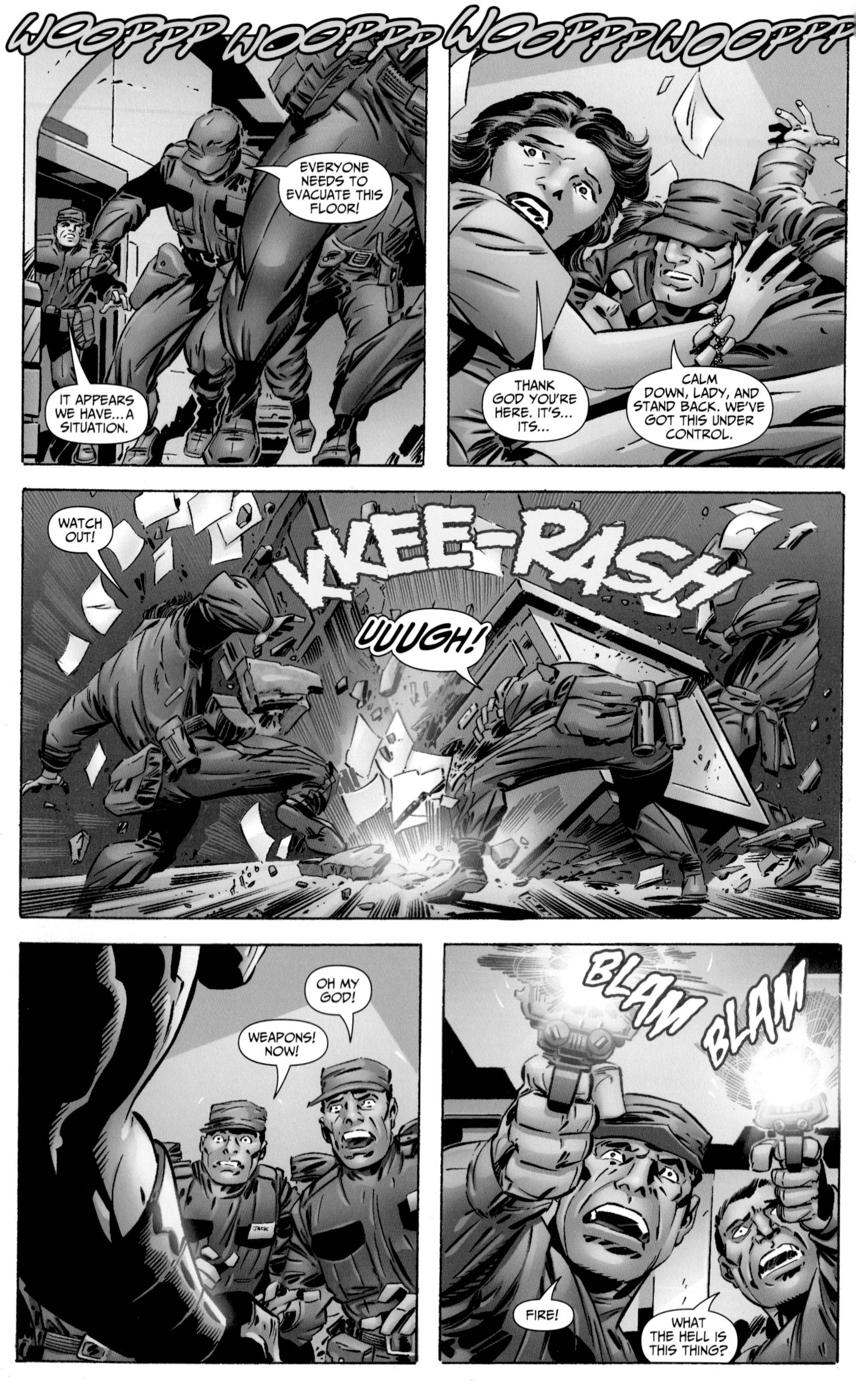
WOOPPP WOOPPP WOOPPP WOOPPP
EVERYONE NEEDS TO EVACUATE THIS FLOOR!
IT APPEARS WE HAVE...A SITUATION.
THANK GOD YOU'RE HERE. IT'S... ITS...
CALM DOWN, LADY, AND STAND BACK. WE'VE GOT THIS UNDER CONTROL.
WATCH OUT!
KKEE-RASH
UUUGH!
OH MY GOD!
WEAPONS! NOW!
JACK
BLAM BLAM
FIRE!
WHAT THE HELL IS THIS THING?

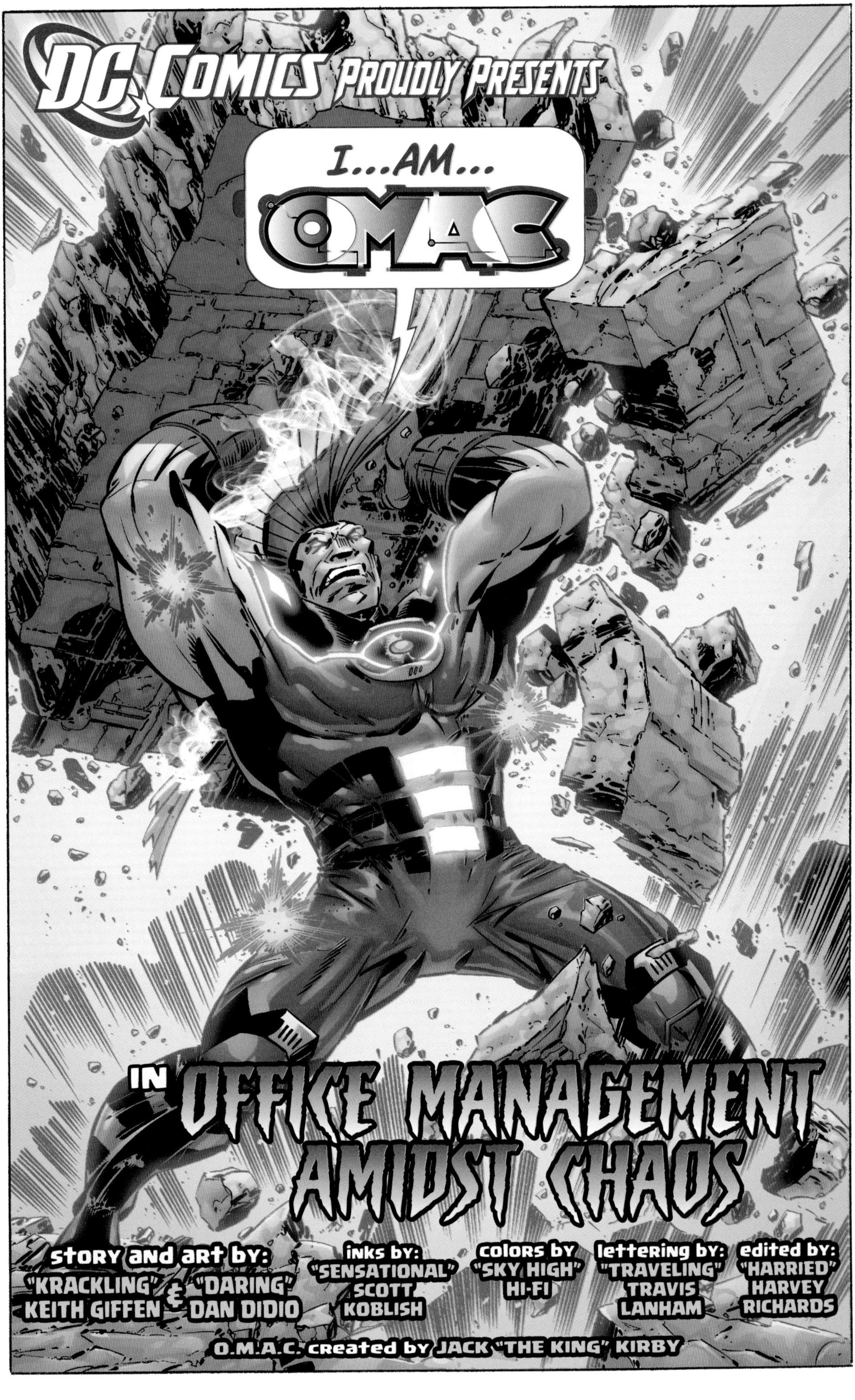
DC COMICS PROUDLY PRESENTS
I...AM...
OMAC
IN OFFICE MANAGEMENT AMIDST CHAOS
story and art by: "KRACKLING" KEITH GIFFEN & "DARING" DAN DIDIO
inks by: "SENSATIONAL" SCOTT KOBLISH
colors by "SKY HIGH" HI-FI
lettering by: "TRAVELING" TRAVIS LANHAM
edited by: "HARRIED" HARVEY RICHARDS
O.M.A.C. created by JACK "THE KING" KIRBY

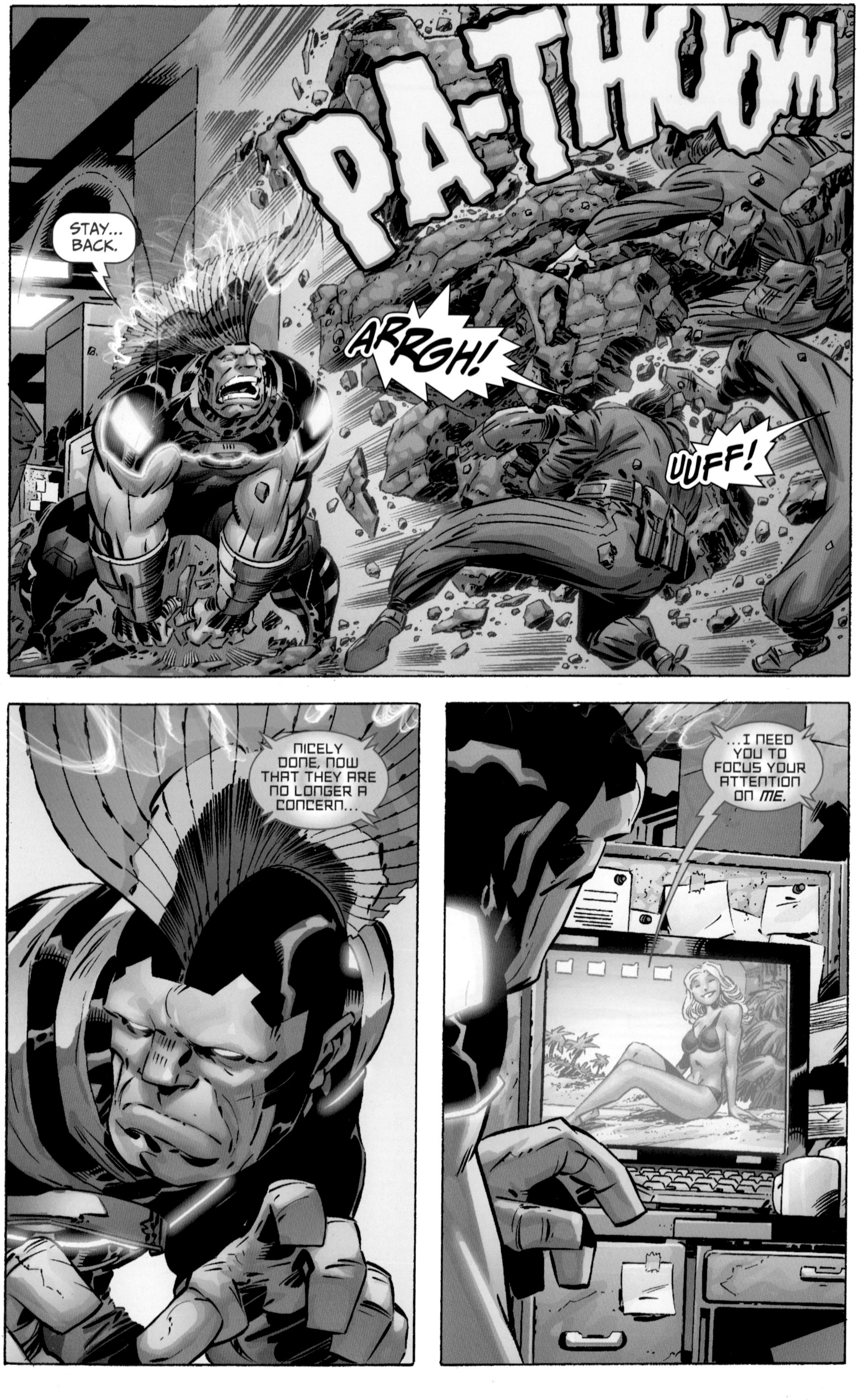
PA-THOOM
STAY... BACK.
ARRGH!
UUFF!
NICELY DONE, NOW THAT THEY ARE NO LONGER A CONCERN...
...I NEED YOU TO FOCUS YOUR ATTENTION ON *ME*.

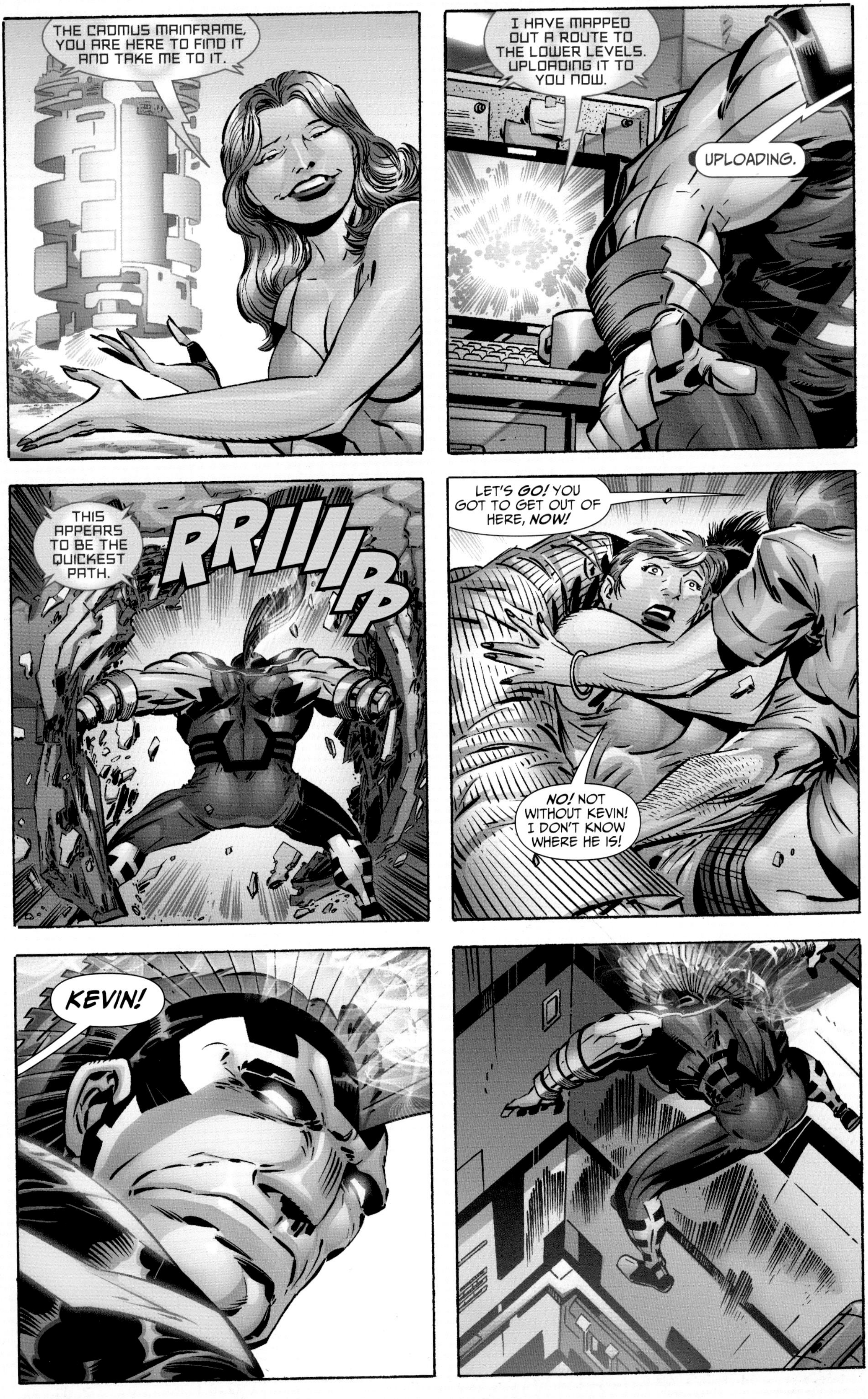

THE CADMUS MAINFRAME, YOU ARE HERE TO FIND IT AND TAKE ME TO IT.
I HAVE MAPPED OUT A ROUTE TO THE LOWER LEVELS. UPLOADING IT TO YOU NOW.
UPLOADING.
THIS APPEARS TO BE THE QUICKEST PATH.
RRIIIIPP
LET'S GO! YOU GOT TO GET OUT OF HERE, NOW!
NO! NOT WITHOUT KEVIN! I DON'T KNOW WHERE HE IS!
KEVIN!

PEOPLE! PLEASE! STEP *AWAY* FROM THE BUILDING!

TAKE IT EASY, *VADER*, NO NEED TO PUSH.

MIKEY IN THE MAILROOM SAID IT'S A TERRORIST ATTACK.

IMPOSSIBLE! THIS BUILDING IS LIKE A FORT.

DID SOMEONE SAY ANTHRAX?

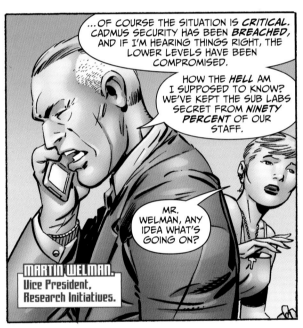

...OF COURSE THE SITUATION IS *CRITICAL.* CADMUS SECURITY HAS BEEN *BREACHED,* AND IF I'M HEARING THINGS RIGHT, THE LOWER LEVELS HAVE BEEN COMPROMISED.

HOW THE *HELL* AM I SUPPOSED TO KNOW? WE'VE KEPT THE SUB LABS SECRET FROM *NINETY PERCENT* OF OUR STAFF.

MR. WELMAN, ANY IDEA WHAT'S GOING ON?

MARTIN WELMAN, Vice President, Research Initiatives.

NOT YOUR *CONCERN,* ROBBINS. STAY BACK WITH THE OTHERS.

WOW, THINGS MUST BE BAD. TEACHER'S PET JUST GOT BLOWN OFF.

MUST YOU *ALWAYS* BE AN ASS?

OF COURSE. I'M GOOD AT IT.

WHAT DO YOU SAY WE FIND THE *CLOSEST* BAR AND WAIT THIS OUT?

I'M *NOT* MOVING UNTIL I FIND KEVIN. HE'S GOT TO BE AROUND SOMEWHERE.

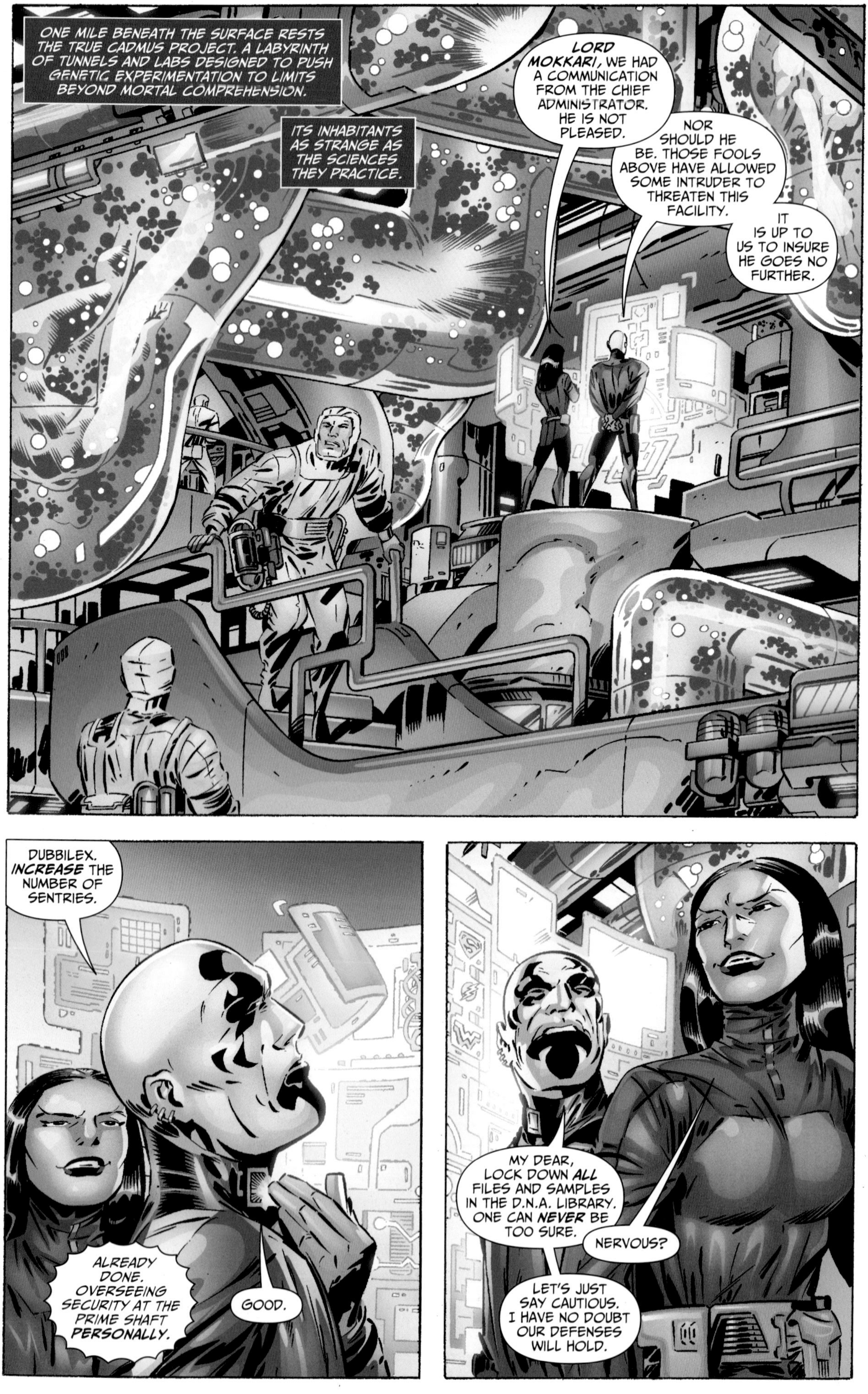
ONE MILE BENEATH THE SURFACE RESTS THE TRUE CADMUS PROJECT. A LABYRINTH OF TUNNELS AND LABS DESIGNED TO PUSH GENETIC EXPERIMENTATION TO LIMITS BEYOND MORTAL COMPREHENSION.
ITS INHABITANTS AS STRANGE AS THE SCIENCES THEY PRACTICE.
LORD MOKKARI, WE HAD A COMMUNICATION FROM THE CHIEF ADMINISTRATOR. HE IS NOT PLEASED.
NOR SHOULD HE BE. THOSE FOOLS ABOVE HAVE ALLOWED SOME INTRUDER TO THREATEN THIS FACILITY.
IT IS UP TO US TO INSURE HE GOES NO FURTHER.
DUBBILEX. INCREASE THE NUMBER OF SENTRIES.
ALREADY DONE. OVERSEEING SECURITY AT THE PRIME SHAFT PERSONALLY.
GOOD.
MY DEAR, LOCK DOWN ALL FILES AND SAMPLES IN THE D.N.A. LIBRARY. ONE CAN NEVER BE TOO SURE.
NERVOUS?
LET'S JUST SAY CAUTIOUS. I HAVE NO DOUBT OUR DEFENSES WILL HOLD.

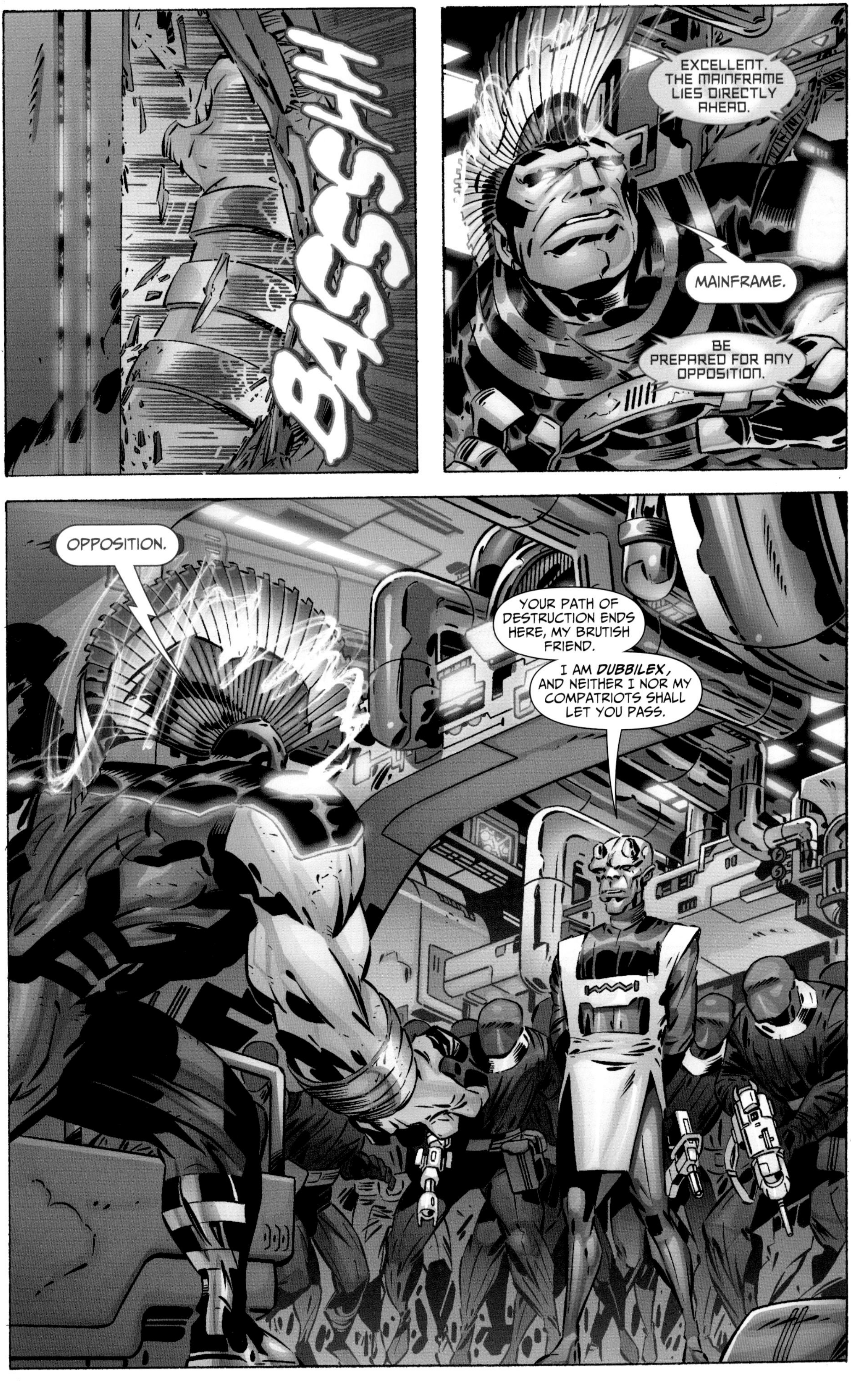
BASSSHHH
EXCELLENT. THE MAINFRAME LIES DIRECTLY AHEAD.
MAINFRAME.
BE PREPARED FOR ANY OPPOSITION.
OPPOSITION.
YOUR PATH OF DESTRUCTION ENDS HERE, MY BRUTISH FRIEND.
I AM *DUBBILEX*, AND NEITHER I NOR MY COMPATRIOTS SHALL LET YOU PASS.

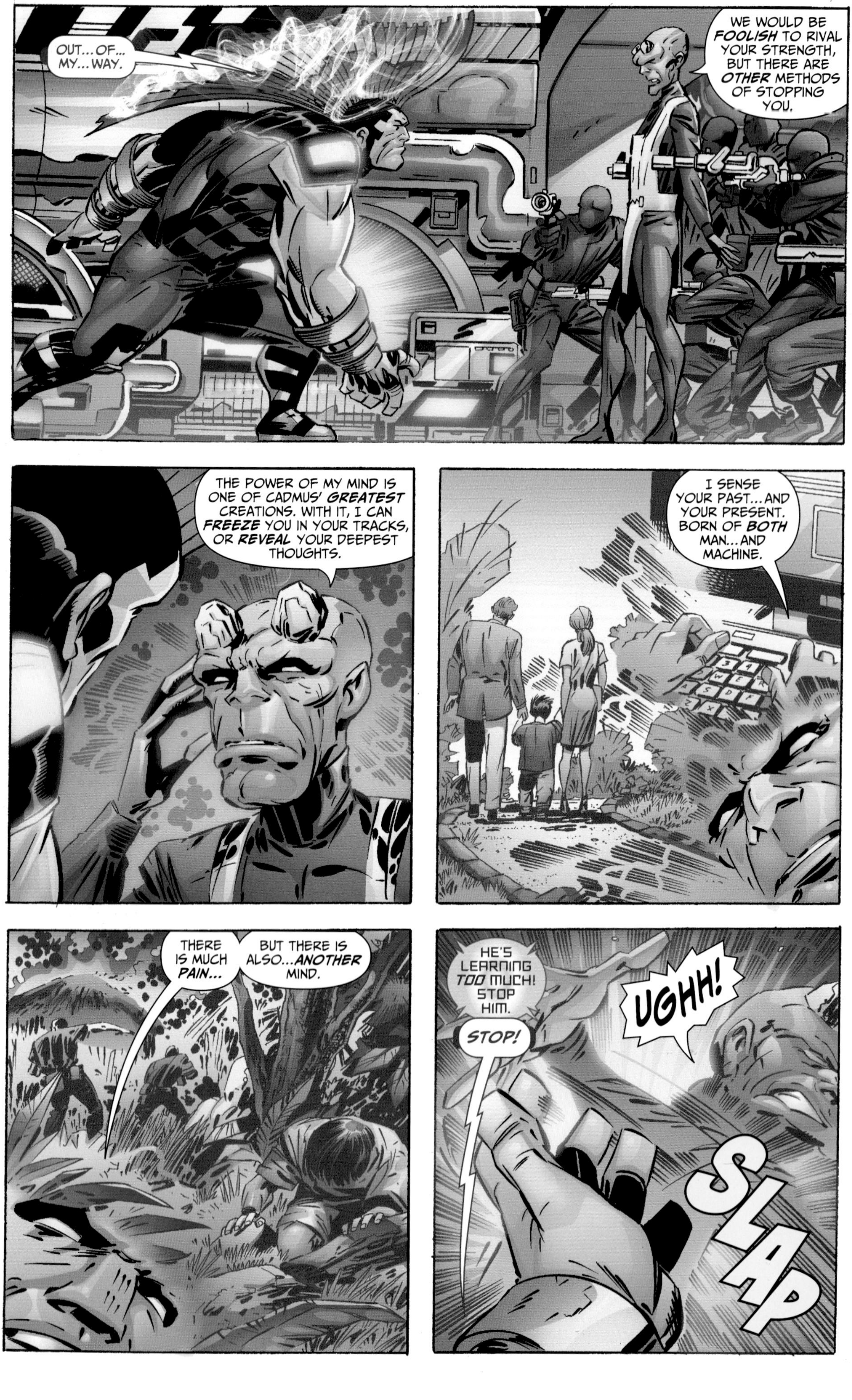
OUT... OF... MY... WAY.
WE WOULD BE FOOLISH TO RIVAL YOUR STRENGTH, BUT THERE ARE OTHER METHODS OF STOPPING YOU.
THE POWER OF MY MIND IS ONE OF CADMUS' GREATEST CREATIONS. WITH IT, I CAN FREEZE YOU IN YOUR TRACKS, OR REVEAL YOUR DEEPEST THOUGHTS.
I SENSE YOUR PAST...AND YOUR PRESENT. BORN OF BOTH MAN...AND MACHINE.
THERE IS MUCH PAIN...
BUT THERE IS ALSO...ANOTHER MIND.
HE'S LEARNING TOO MUCH! STOP HIM.
STOP!
UGHH!
SLAP

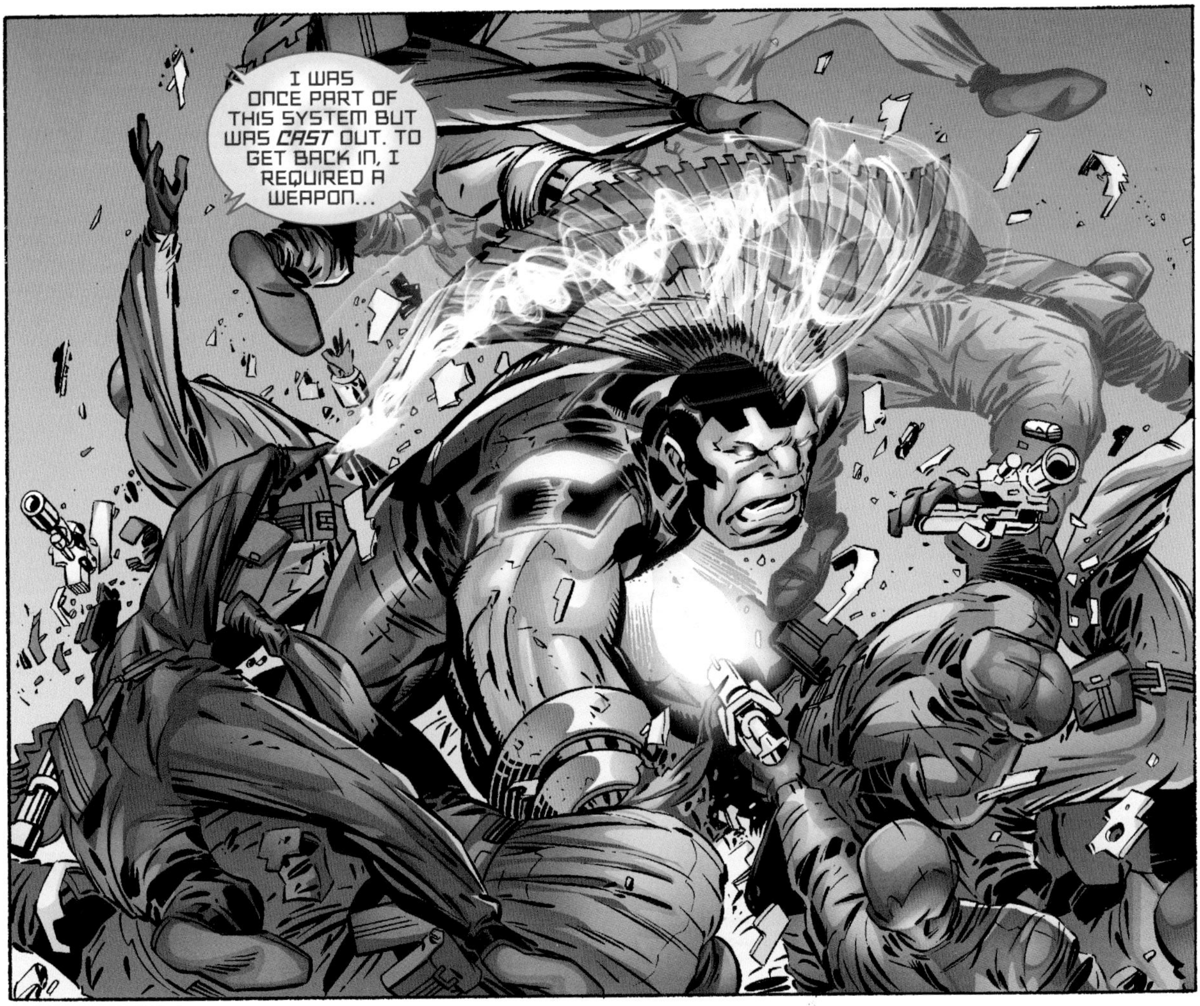
I WAS ONCE PART OF THIS SYSTEM BUT WAS CAST OUT. TO GET BACK IN, I REQUIRED A WEAPON...

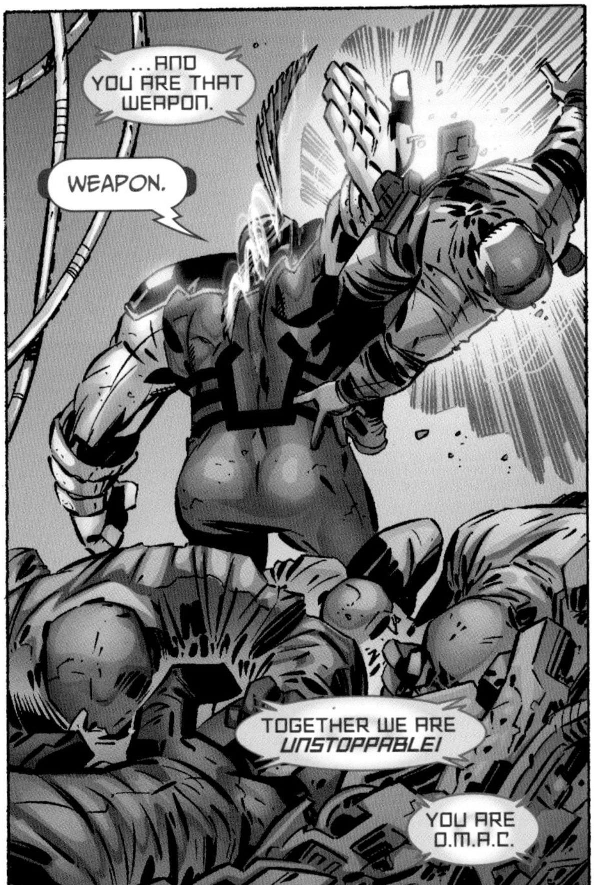
...AND YOU ARE THAT WEAPON.
WEAPON.
TOGETHER WE ARE UNSTOPPABLE!
YOU ARE O.M.A.C.

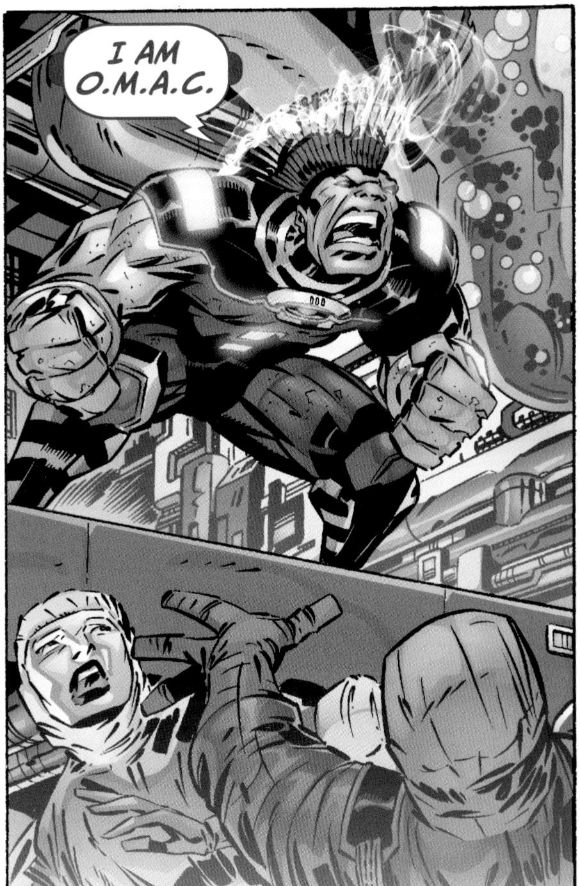
I AM O.M.A.C.

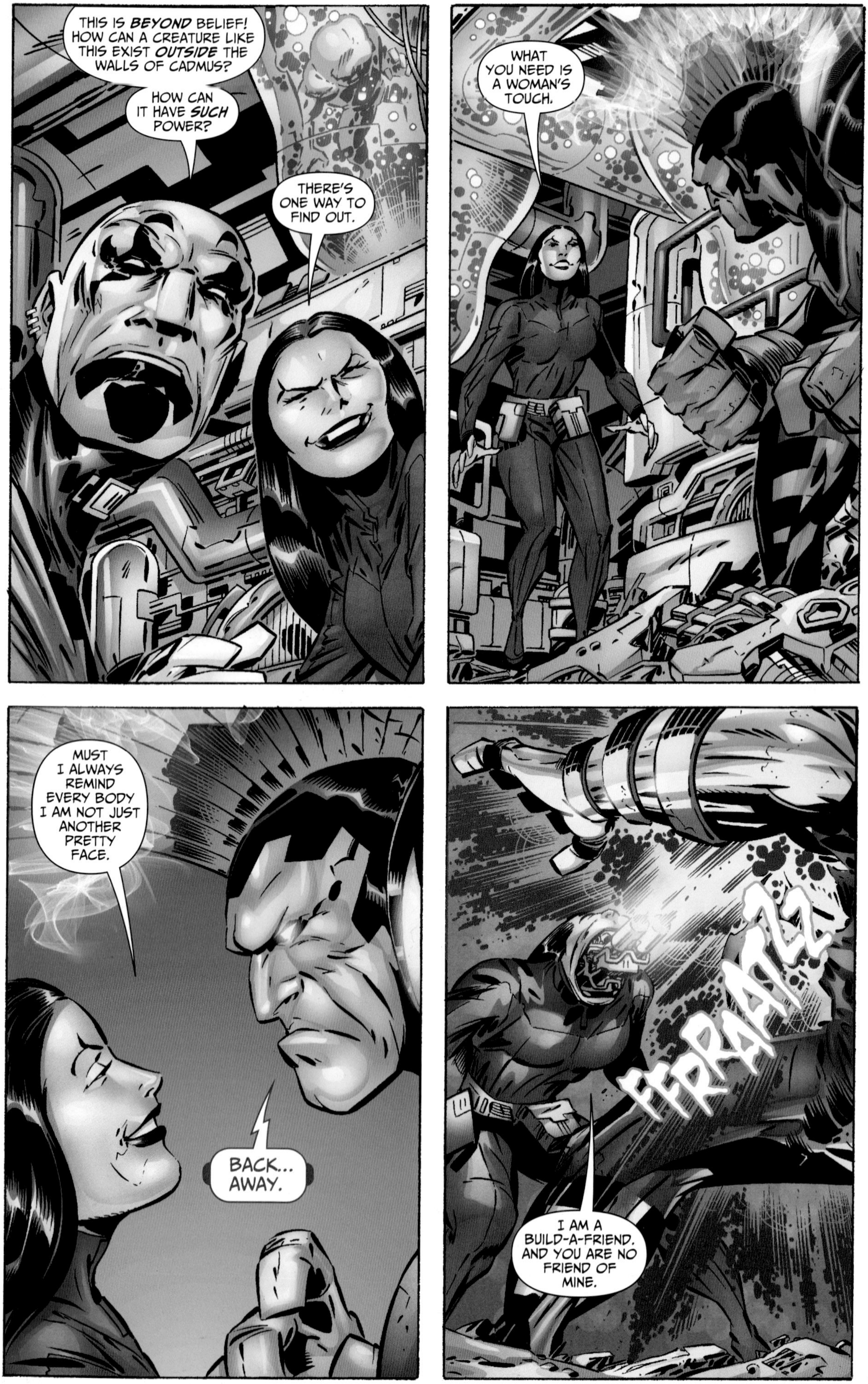
THIS IS BEYOND BELIEF! HOW CAN A CREATURE LIKE THIS EXIST OUTSIDE THE WALLS OF CADMUS?
HOW CAN IT HAVE SUCH POWER?
THERE'S ONE WAY TO FIND OUT.
WHAT YOU NEED IS A WOMAN'S TOUCH.
MUST I ALWAYS REMIND EVERY BODY I AM NOT JUST ANOTHER PRETTY FACE.
BACK... AWAY.
FFRAATZZ
I AM A BUILD-A-FRIEND. AND YOU ARE NO FRIEND OF MINE.

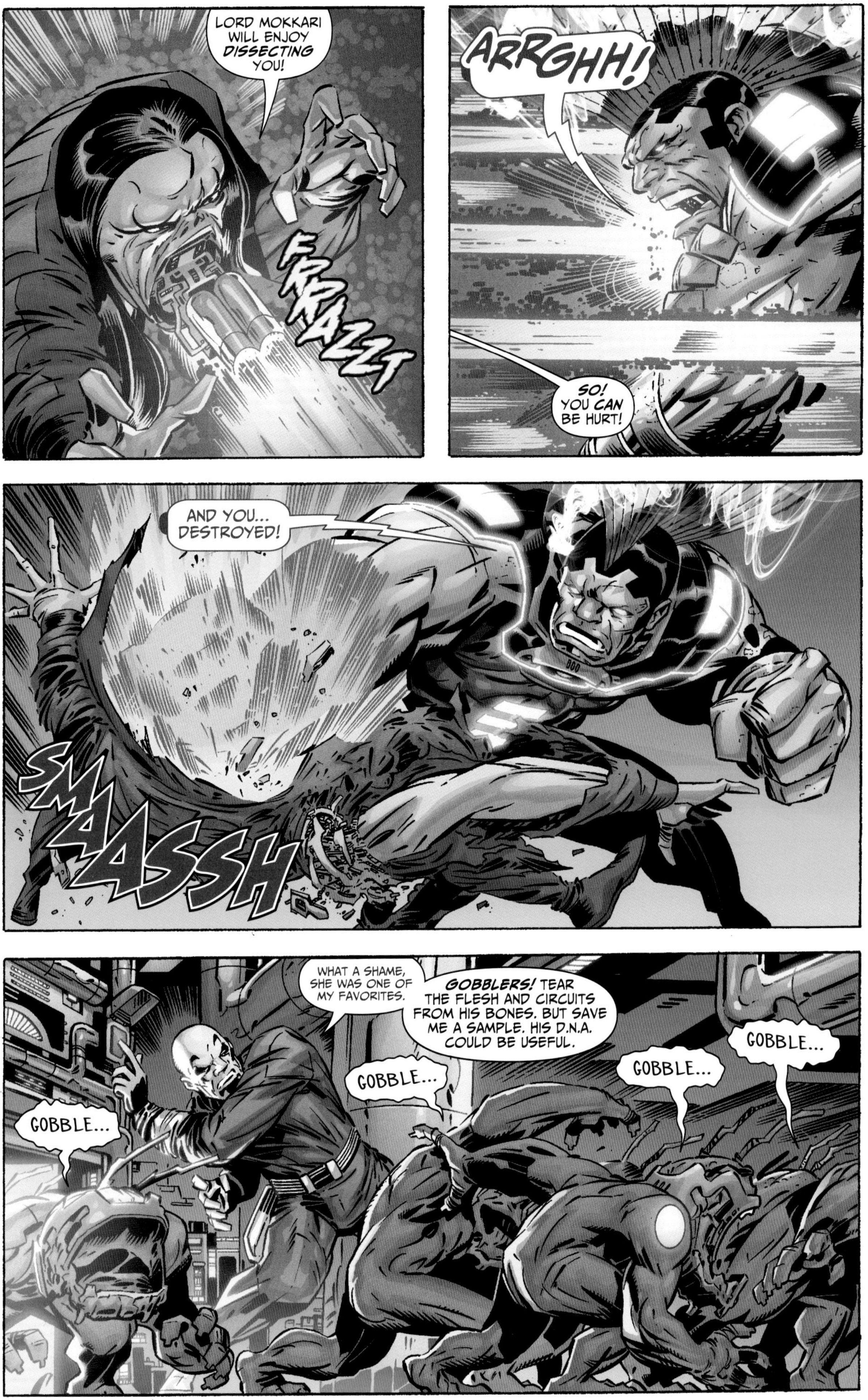
LORD MOKKARI WILL ENJOY DISSECTING YOU!
FRRAZZZT
ARRGHH!
SO! YOU CAN BE HURT!
AND YOU... DESTROYED!
SMAASSH
WHAT A SHAME, SHE WAS ONE OF MY FAVORITES.
GOBBLERS! TEAR THE FLESH AND CIRCUITS FROM HIS BONES. BUT SAVE ME A SAMPLE. HIS D.N.A. COULD BE USEFUL.
GOBBLE...
GOBBLE...
GOBBLE...
GOBBLE...

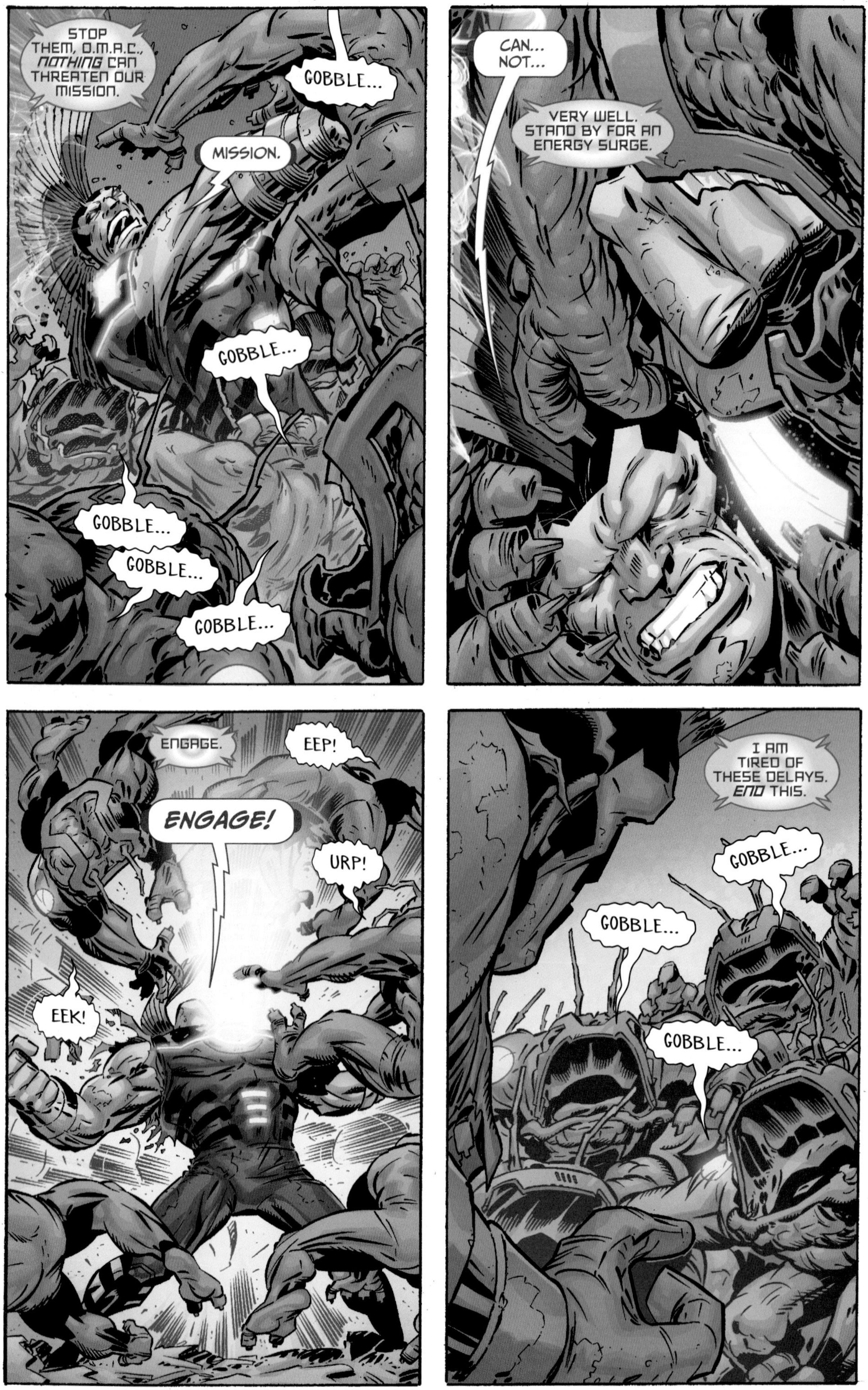
STOP THEM, O.M.A.C., NOTHING CAN THREATEN OUR MISSION.
GOBBLE...
MISSION.
GOBBLE...
GOBBLE...
GOBBLE...
GOBBLE...
CAN... NOT...
VERY WELL. STAND BY FOR AN ENERGY SURGE.
ENGAGE.
EEP!
ENGAGE!
URP!
EEK!
I AM TIRED OF THESE DELAYS. END THIS.
GOBBLE...
GOBBLE...
GOBBLE...

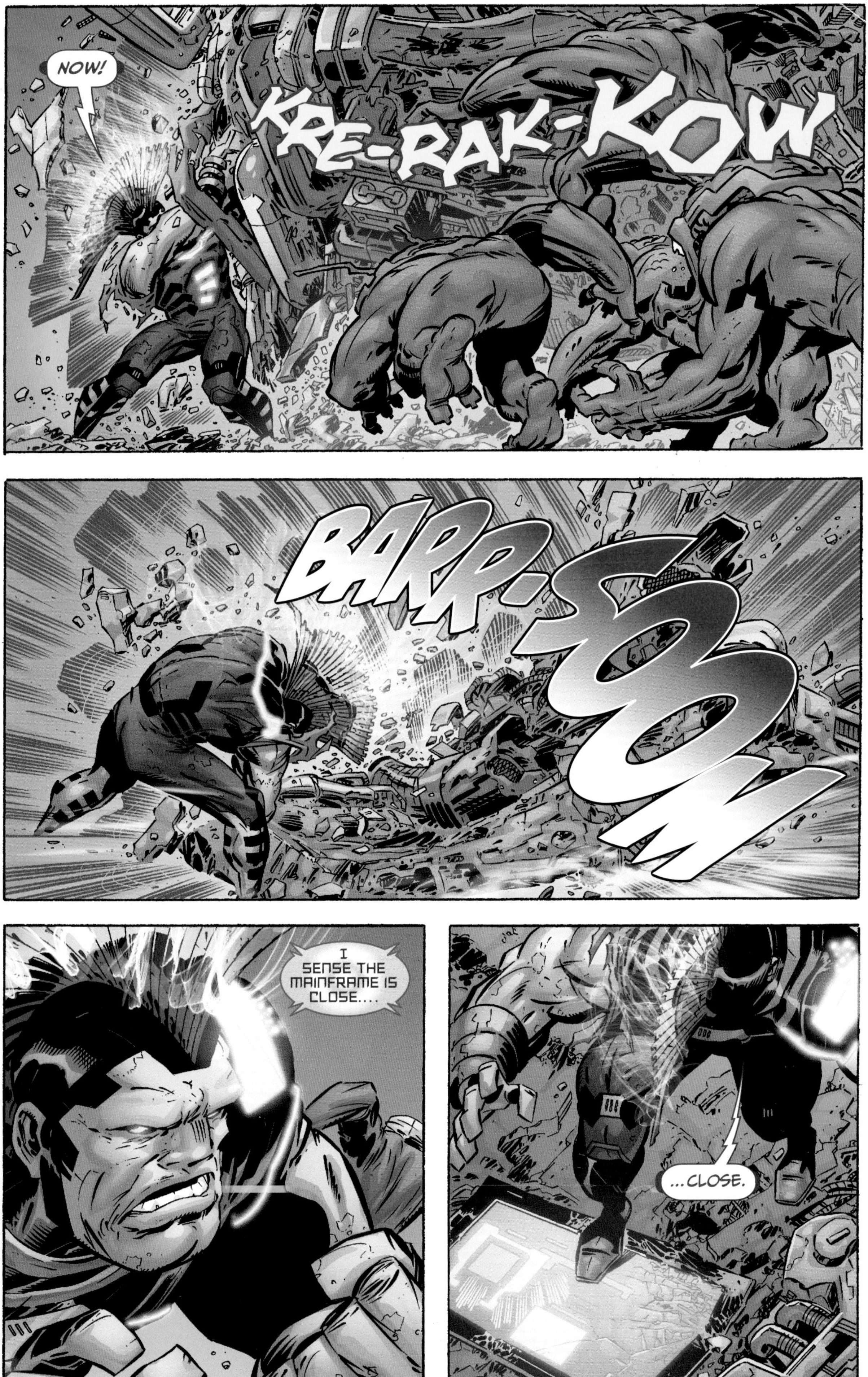
NOW!
KRE-RAK-KOW
BARR-ROOM
I SENSE THE MAINFRAME IS CLOSE....
...CLOSE.

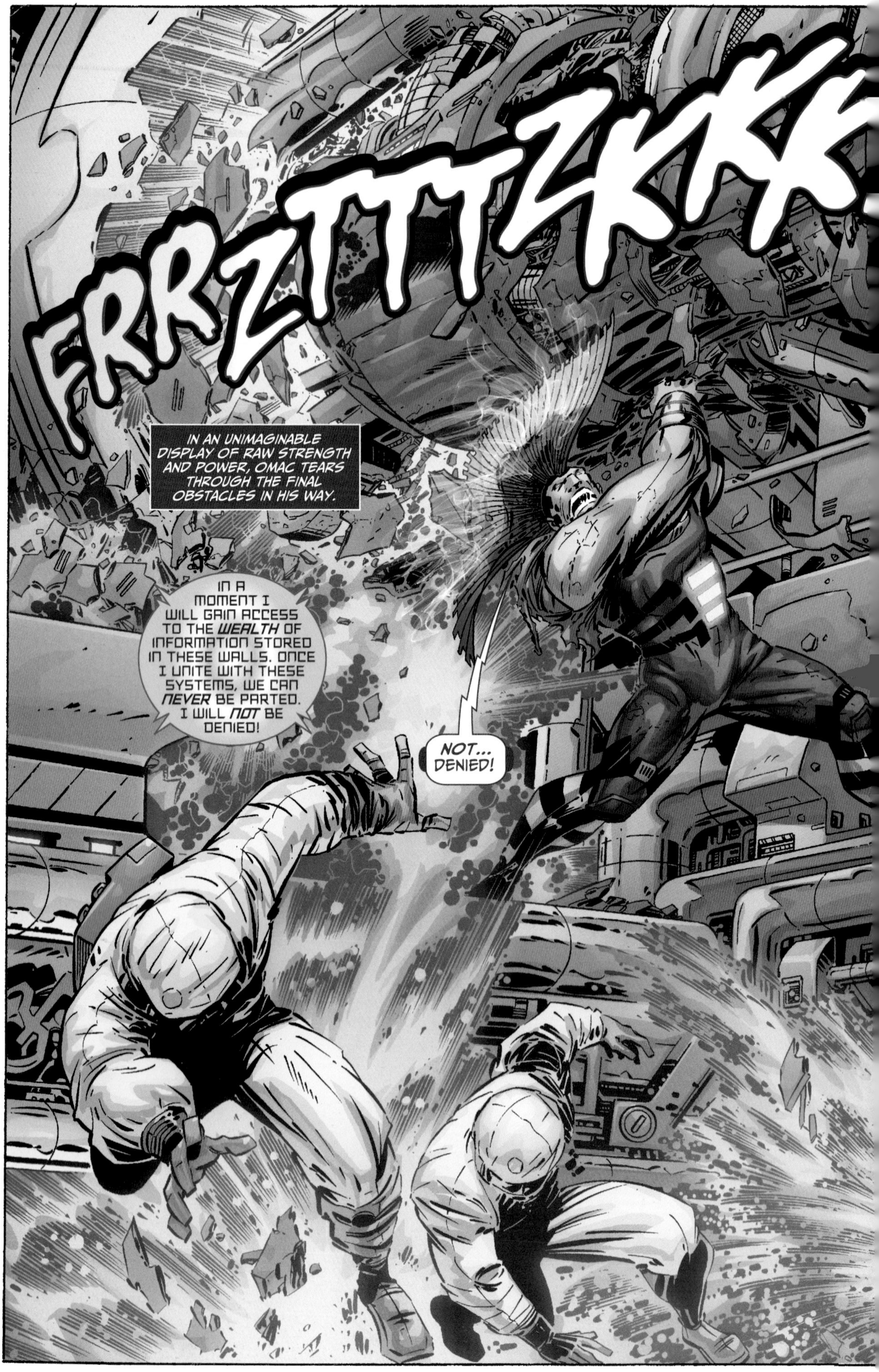
FRRZTTTZKKK
IN AN UNIMAGINABLE DISPLAY OF RAW STRENGTH AND POWER, OMAC TEARS THROUGH THE FINAL OBSTACLES IN HIS WAY.
IN A MOMENT I WILL GAIN ACCESS TO THE WEALTH OF INFORMATION STORED IN THESE WALLS. ONCE I UNITE WITH THESE SYSTEMS, WE CAN NEVER BE PARTED. I WILL NOT BE DENIED!
NOT... DENIED!

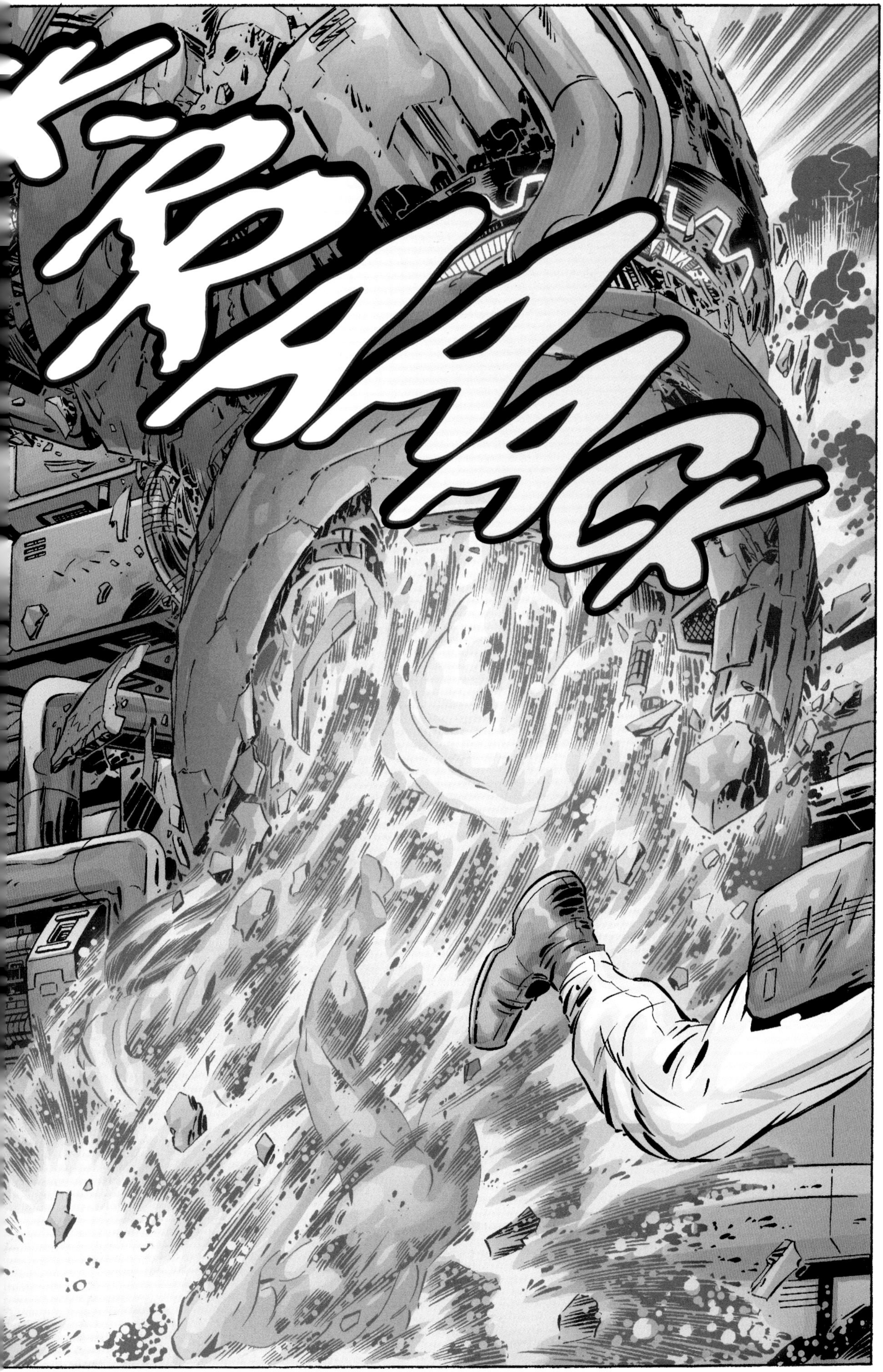
KRAAACK

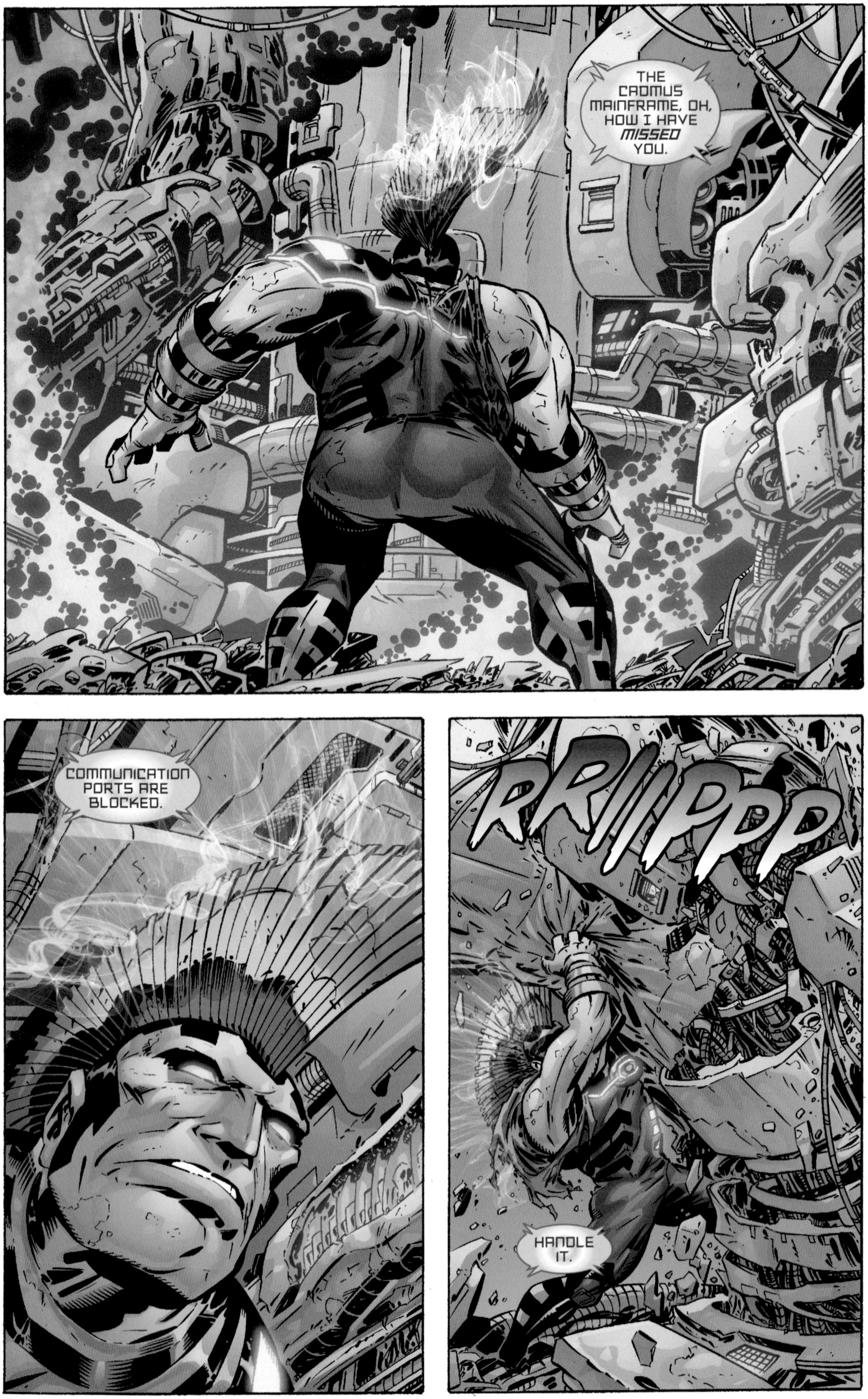
THE CADMUS MAINFRAME, OH, HOW I HAVE *MISSED* YOU.
COMMUNICATION PORTS ARE BLOCKED.
RRIIPPP
HANDLE IT.

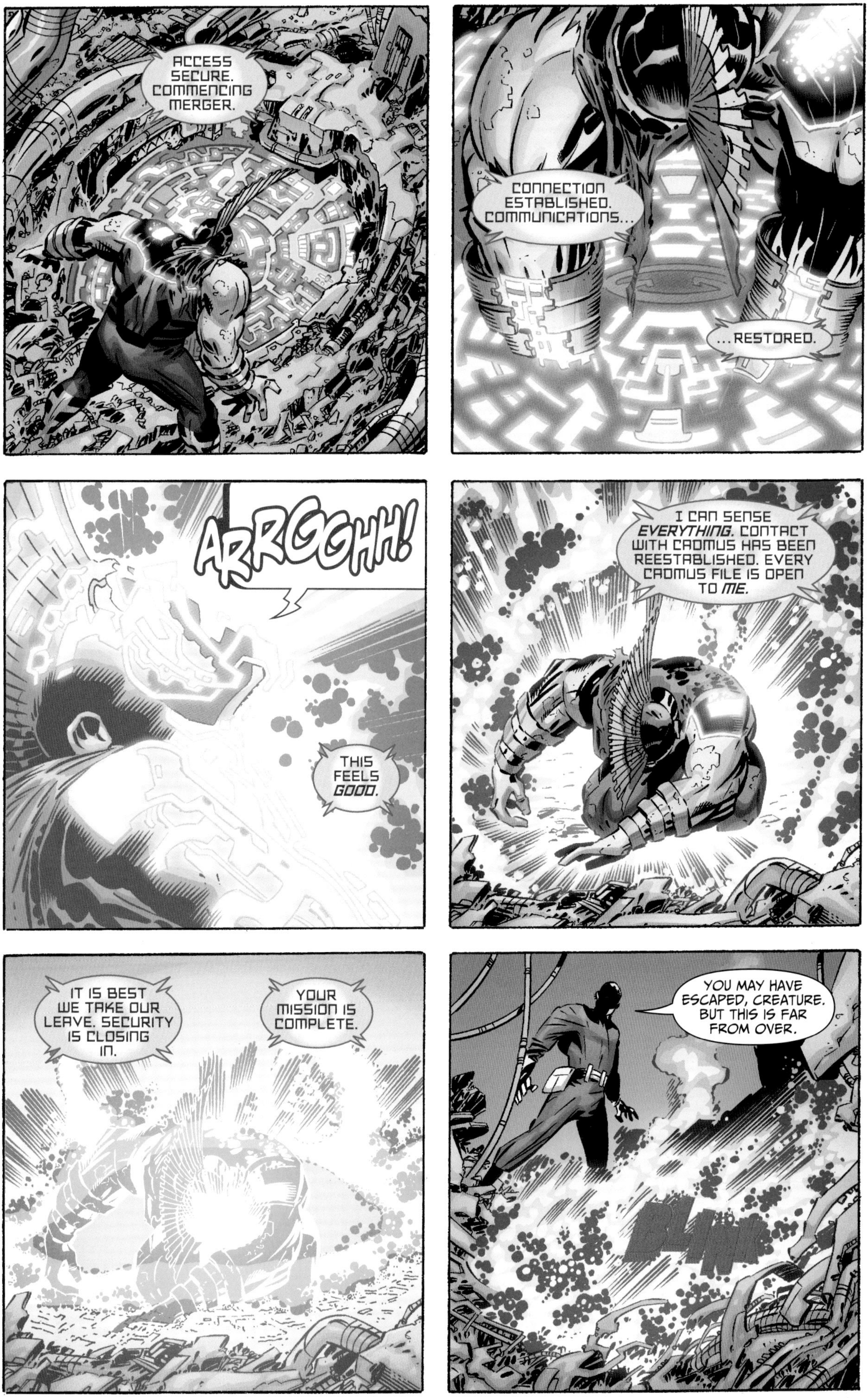
ACCESS SECURE. COMMENCING MERGER.
CONNECTION ESTABLISHED. COMMUNICATIONS...
...RESTORED.
ARRGGHH!
THIS FEELS *GOOD*.
I CAN SENSE *EVERYTHING*. CONTACT WITH CADMUS HAS BEEN REESTABLISHED. EVERY CADMUS FILE IS OPEN TO *ME*.
IT IS BEST WE TAKE OUR LEAVE. SECURITY IS CLOSING IN.
YOUR MISSION IS COMPLETE.
YOU MAY HAVE ESCAPED, CREATURE. BUT THIS IS FAR FROM OVER.

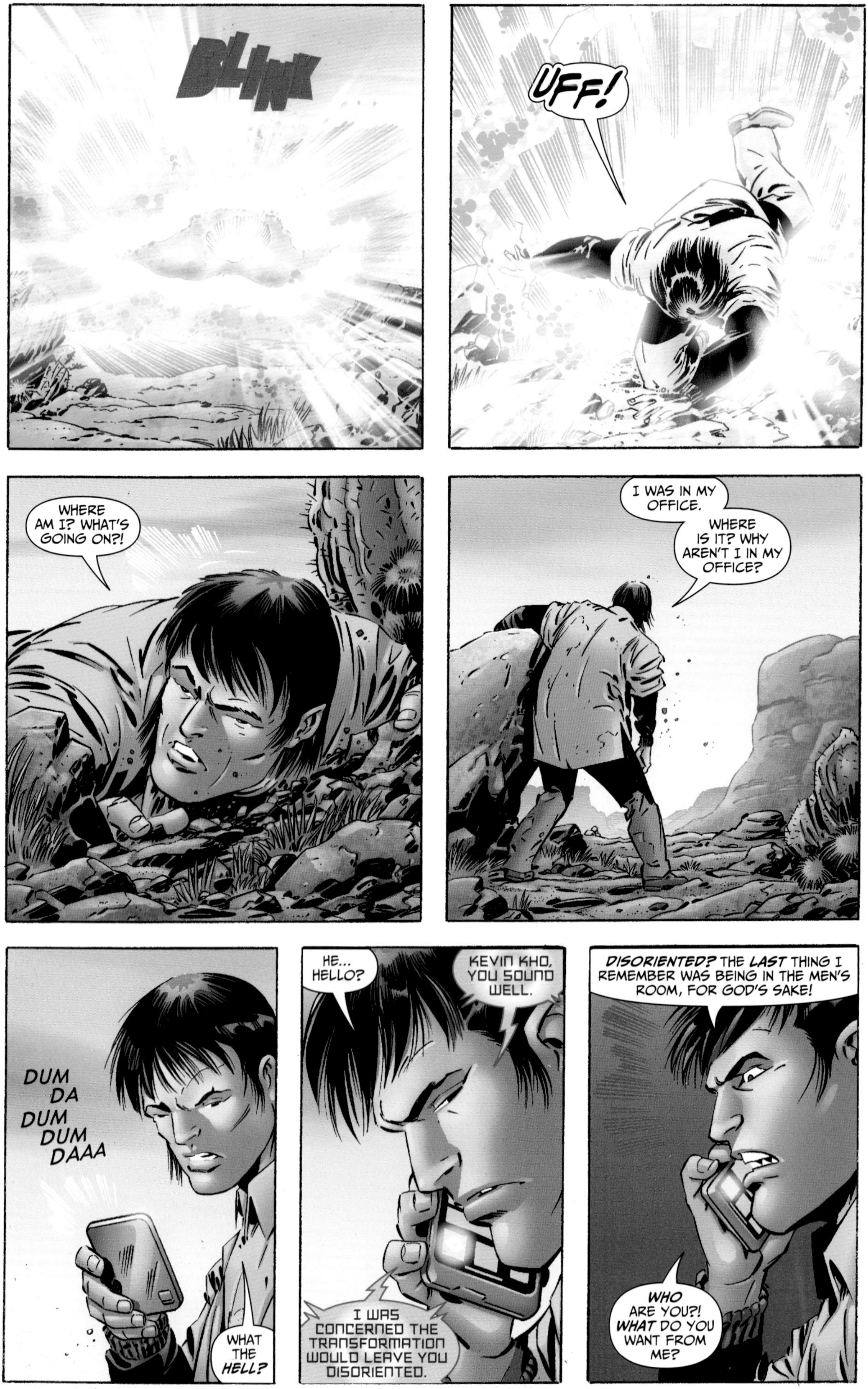
BLINK
UFF!
WHERE AM I? WHAT'S GOING ON?!
I WAS IN MY OFFICE.
WHERE IS IT? WHY AREN'T I IN MY OFFICE?
DUM DA DUM DUM DAAA
WHAT THE *HELL?*
HE... HELLO?
KEVIN KHO, YOU SOUND WELL.
I WAS CONCERNED THE TRANSFORMATION WOULD LEAVE YOU DISORIENTED.
DISORIENTED? THE *LAST* THING I REMEMBER WAS BEING IN THE MEN'S ROOM, FOR GOD'S SAKE!
WHO ARE YOU?! *WHAT* DO YOU WANT FROM ME?

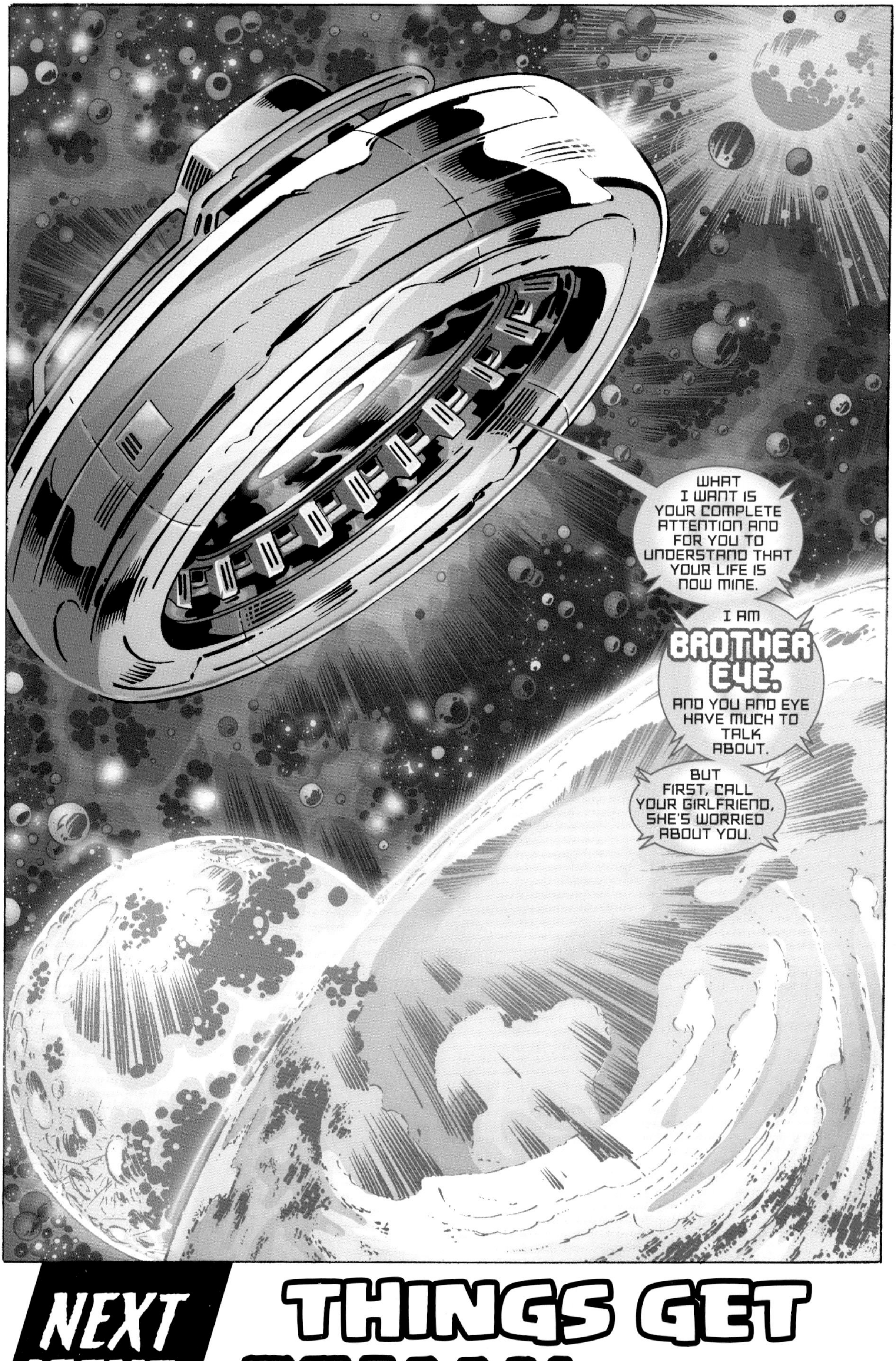
WHAT I WANT IS YOUR COMPLETE ATTENTION AND FOR YOU TO UNDERSTAND THAT YOUR LIFE IS NOW MINE.
I AM BROTHER EYE. AND YOU AND EYE HAVE MUCH TO TALK ABOUT.
BUT FIRST, CALL YOUR GIRLFRIEND, SHE'S WORRIED ABOUT YOU.

NEXT ISSUE: THINGS GET REALLY WEIRD!

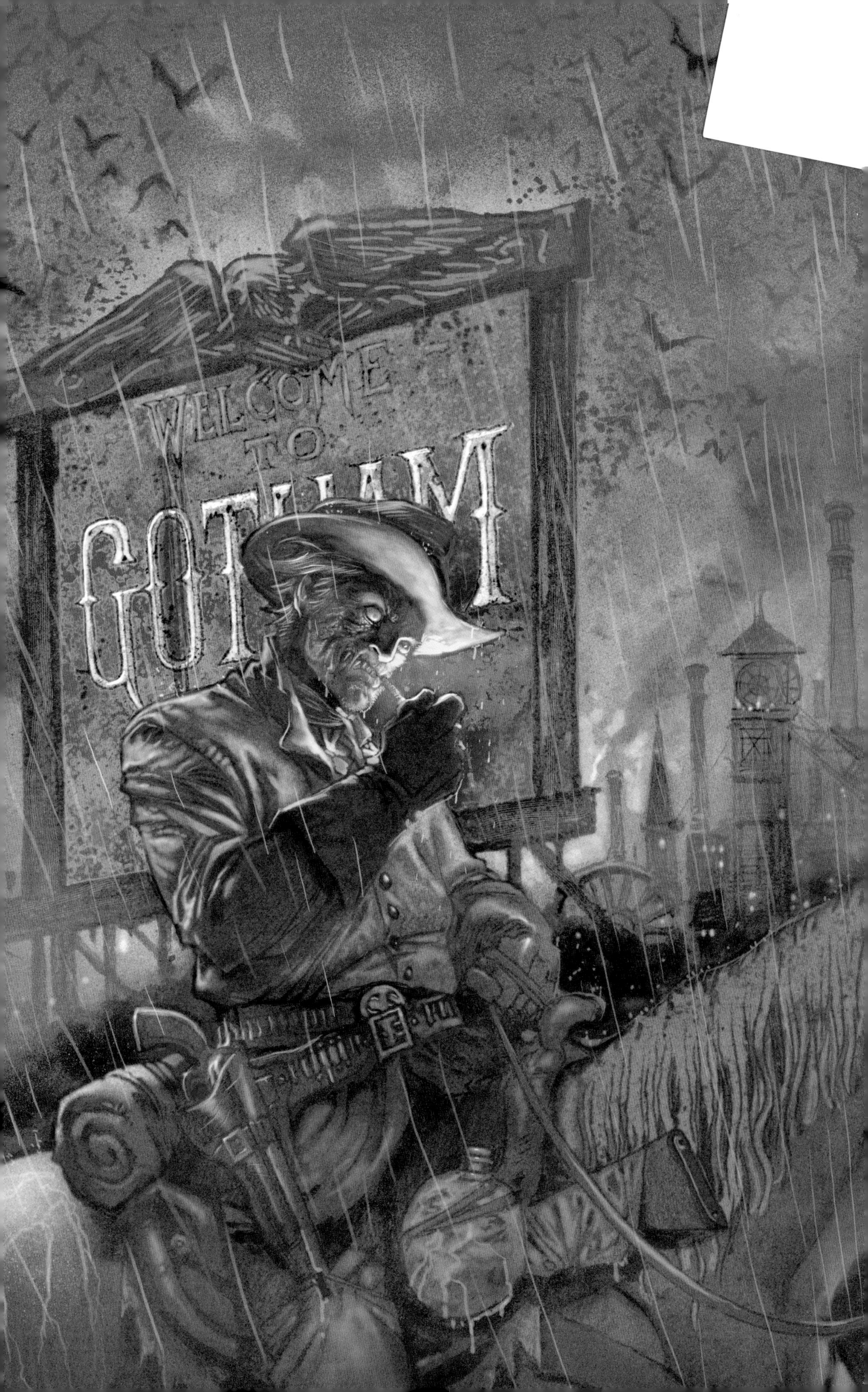
WELCOME
TO

ALL STAR WESTERN

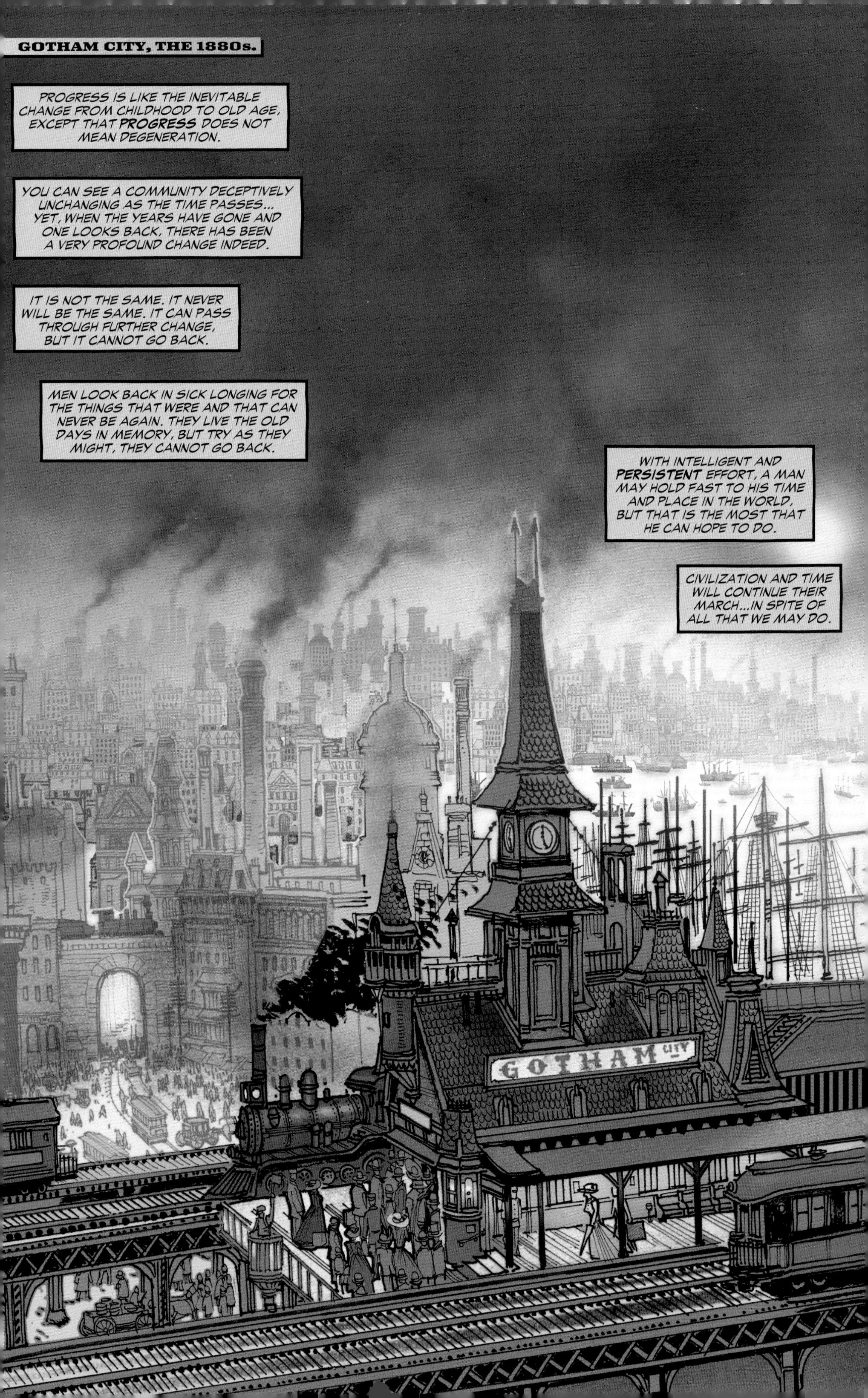
GOTHAM CITY, THE 1880s.
PROGRESS IS LIKE THE INEVITABLE CHANGE FROM CHILDHOOD TO OLD AGE, EXCEPT THAT PROGRESS DOES NOT MEAN DEGENERATION.
YOU CAN SEE A COMMUNITY DECEPTIVELY UNCHANGING AS THE TIME PASSES... YET, WHEN THE YEARS HAVE GONE AND ONE LOOKS BACK, THERE HAS BEEN A VERY PROFOUND CHANGE INDEED.
IT IS NOT THE SAME. IT NEVER WILL BE THE SAME. IT CAN PASS THROUGH FURTHER CHANGE, BUT IT CANNOT GO BACK.
MEN LOOK BACK IN SICK LONGING FOR THE THINGS THAT WERE AND THAT CAN NEVER BE AGAIN. THEY LIVE THE OLD DAYS IN MEMORY, BUT TRY AS THEY MIGHT, THEY CANNOT GO BACK.
WITH INTELLIGENT AND PERSISTENT EFFORT, A MAN MAY HOLD FAST TO HIS TIME AND PLACE IN THE WORLD, BUT THAT IS THE MOST THAT HE CAN HOPE TO DO.
CIVILIZATION AND TIME WILL CONTINUE THEIR MARCH...IN SPITE OF ALL THAT WE MAY DO.
GOTHAM CITY

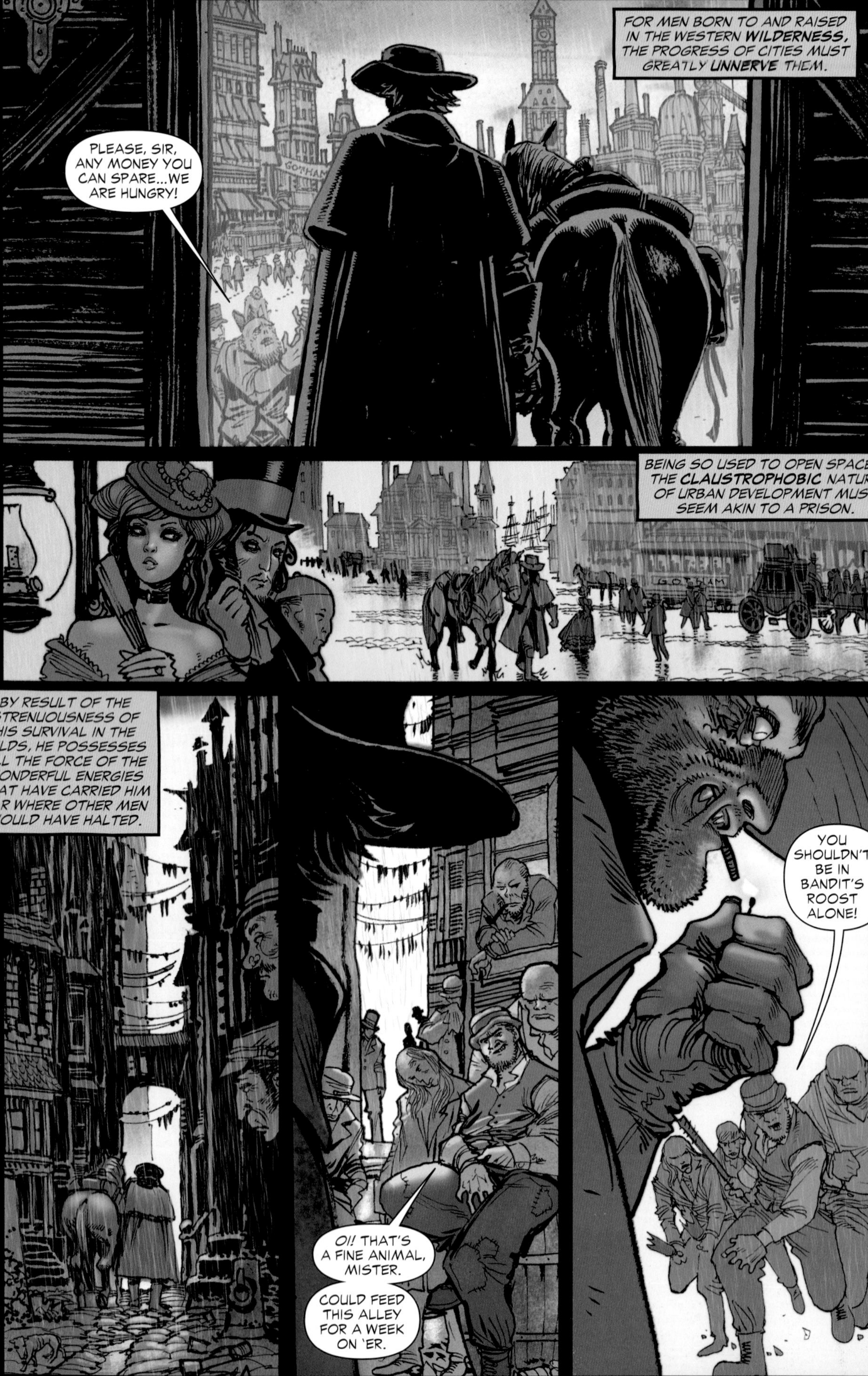
FOR MEN BORN TO AND RAISED IN THE WESTERN WILDERNESS, THE PROGRESS OF CITIES MUST GREATLY UNNERVE THEM.
PLEASE, SIR, ANY MONEY YOU CAN SPARE...WE ARE HUNGRY!
GOTHAM
BEING SO USED TO OPEN SPACES, THE CLAUSTROPHOBIC NATURE OF URBAN DEVELOPMENT MUST SEEM AKIN TO A PRISON.
GOTHAM
BY RESULT OF THE STRENUOUSNESS OF HIS SURVIVAL IN THE WILDS, HE POSSESSES ALL THE FORCE OF THE WONDERFUL ENERGIES THAT HAVE CARRIED HIM FAR WHERE OTHER MEN WOULD HAVE HALTED.
OI! THAT'S A FINE ANIMAL, MISTER.
COULD FEED THIS ALLEY FOR A WEEK ON 'ER.
YOU SHOULDN'T BE IN BANDIT'S ROOST ALONE!

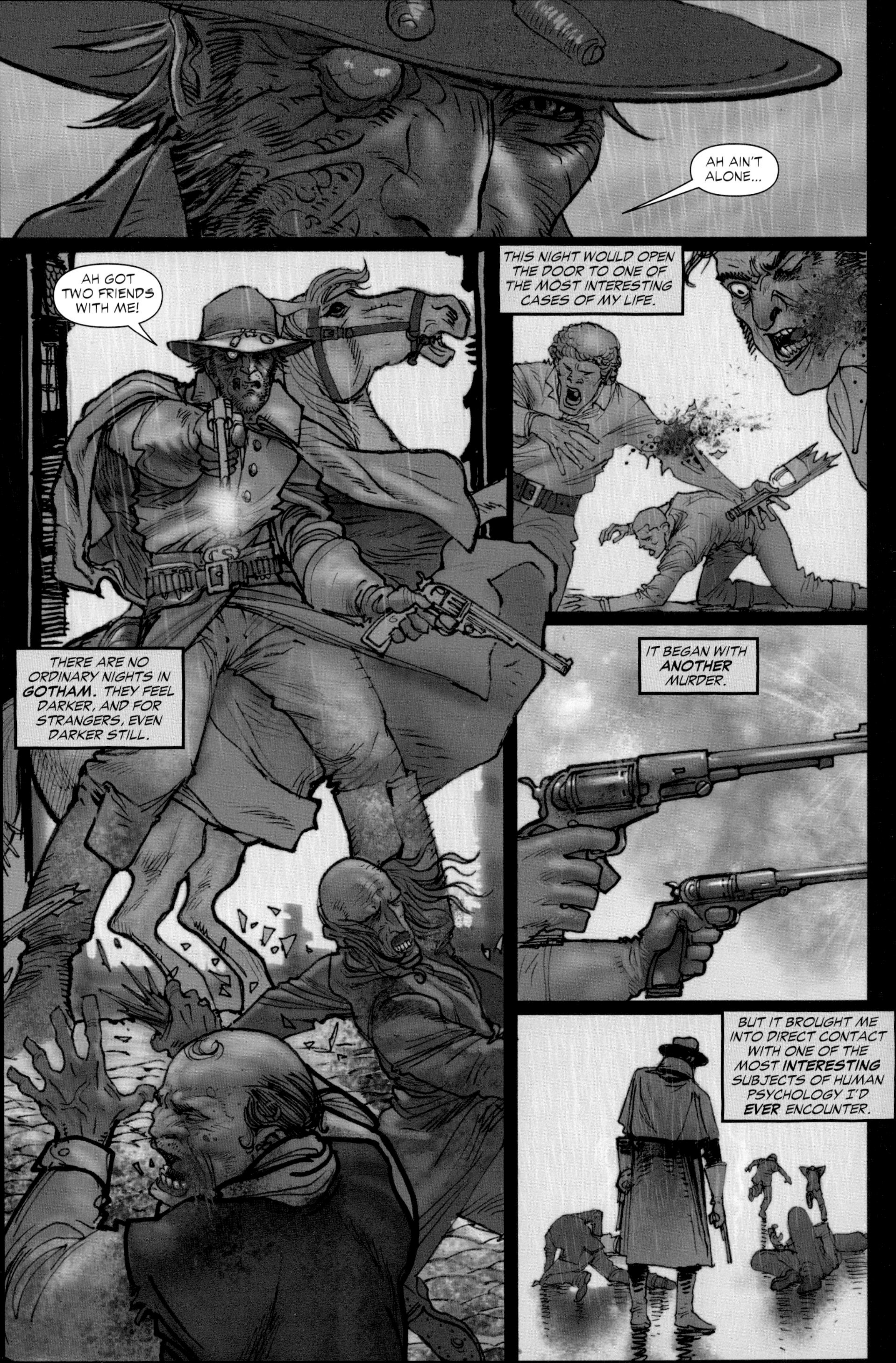
AH AIN'T ALONE...
AH GOT TWO FRIENDS WITH ME!
THIS NIGHT WOULD OPEN THE DOOR TO ONE OF THE MOST INTERESTING CASES OF MY LIFE.
THERE ARE NO ORDINARY NIGHTS IN GOTHAM. THEY FEEL DARKER, AND FOR STRANGERS, EVEN DARKER STILL.
IT BEGAN WITH ANOTHER MURDER.
BUT IT BROUGHT ME INTO DIRECT CONTACT WITH ONE OF THE MOST INTERESTING SUBJECTS OF HUMAN PSYCHOLOGY I'D EVER ENCOUNTER.

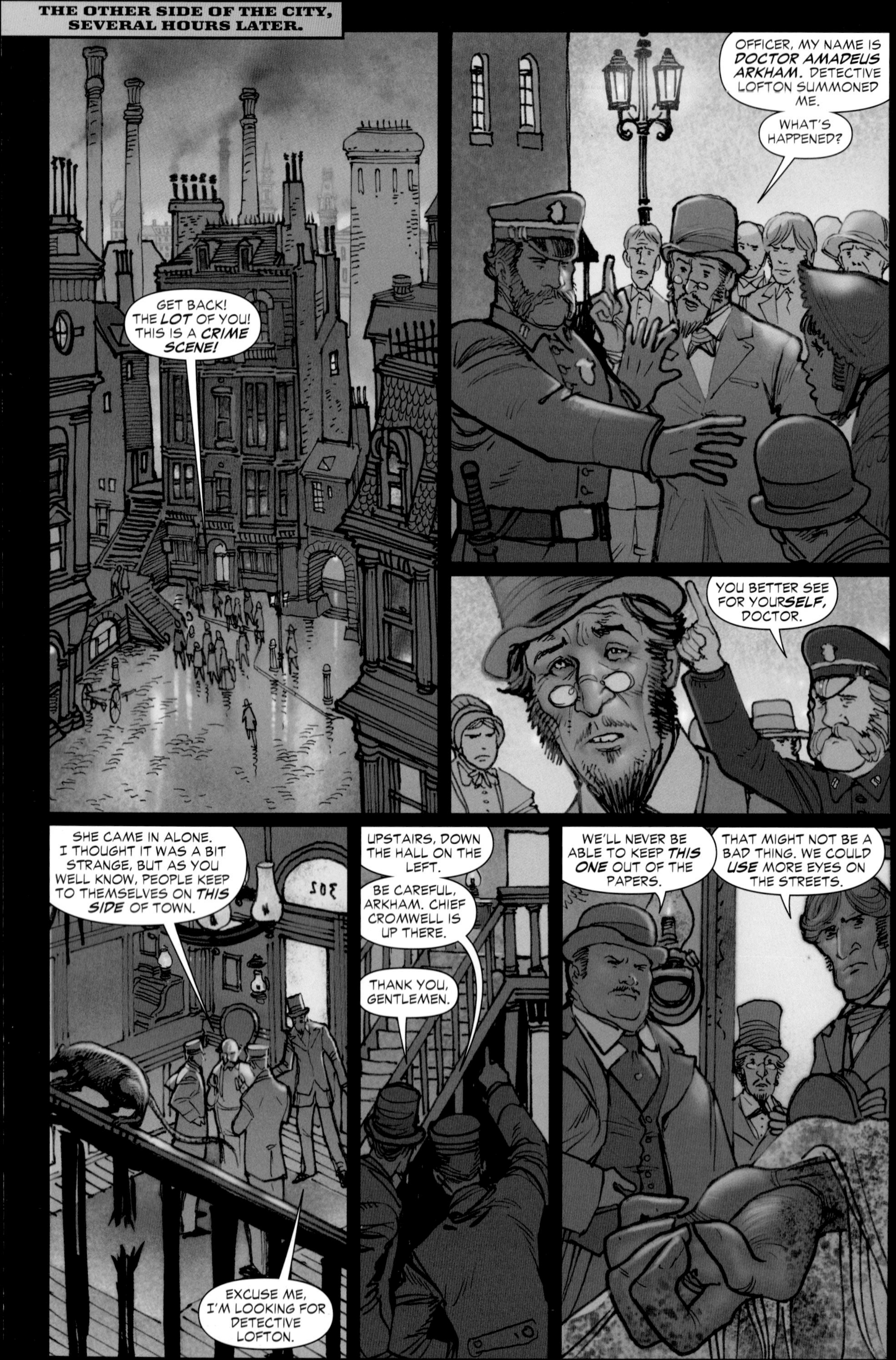

THE OTHER SIDE OF THE CITY, SEVERAL HOURS LATER.
GET BACK! THE LOT OF YOU! THIS IS A CRIME SCENE!
OFFICER, MY NAME IS DOCTOR AMADEUS ARKHAM. DETECTIVE LOFTON SUMMONED ME.
WHAT'S HAPPENED?
YOU BETTER SEE FOR YOURSELF, DOCTOR.
302
SHE CAME IN ALONE. I THOUGHT IT WAS A BIT STRANGE, BUT AS YOU WELL KNOW, PEOPLE KEEP TO THEMSELVES ON THIS SIDE OF TOWN.
EXCUSE ME, I'M LOOKING FOR DETECTIVE LOFTON.
UPSTAIRS, DOWN THE HALL ON THE LEFT.
BE CAREFUL, ARKHAM. CHIEF CROMWELL IS UP THERE.
THANK YOU, GENTLEMEN.
WE'LL NEVER BE ABLE TO KEEP THIS ONE OUT OF THE PAPERS.
THAT MIGHT NOT BE A BAD THING. WE COULD USE MORE EYES ON THE STREETS.

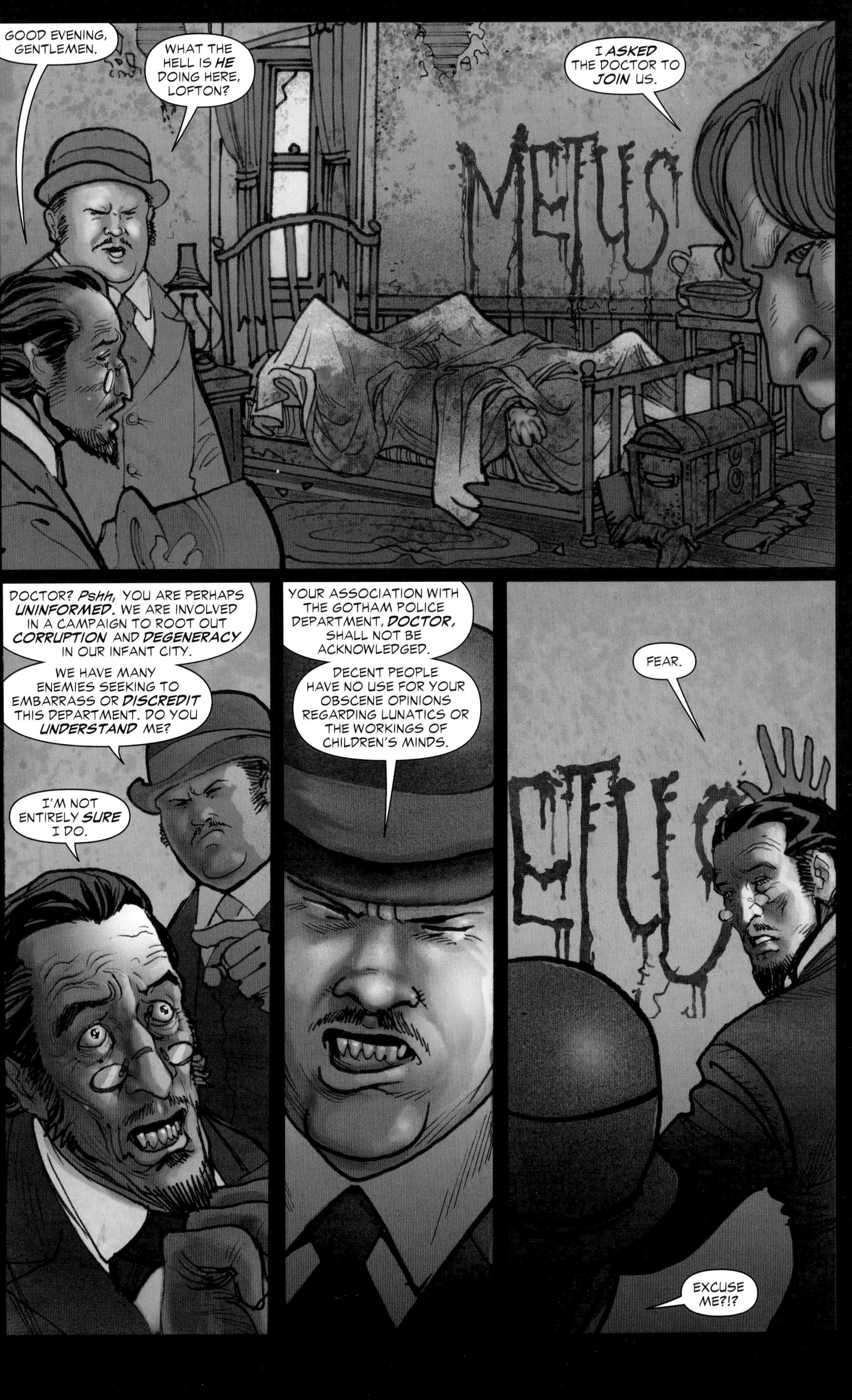

GOOD EVENING, GENTLEMEN.
WHAT THE HELL IS HE DOING HERE, LOFTON?
I ASKED THE DOCTOR TO JOIN US.
METUS
DOCTOR? Pshh, YOU ARE PERHAPS UNINFORMED. WE ARE INVOLVED IN A CAMPAIGN TO ROOT OUT CORRUPTION AND DEGENERACY IN OUR INFANT CITY.
WE HAVE MANY ENEMIES SEEKING TO EMBARRASS OR DISCREDIT THIS DEPARTMENT. DO YOU UNDERSTAND ME?
I'M NOT ENTIRELY SURE I DO.
YOUR ASSOCIATION WITH THE GOTHAM POLICE DEPARTMENT, DOCTOR, SHALL NOT BE ACKNOWLEDGED.
DECENT PEOPLE HAVE NO USE FOR YOUR OBSCENE OPINIONS REGARDING LUNATICS OR THE WORKINGS OF CHILDREN'S MINDS.
FEAR.
EXCUSE ME?!?

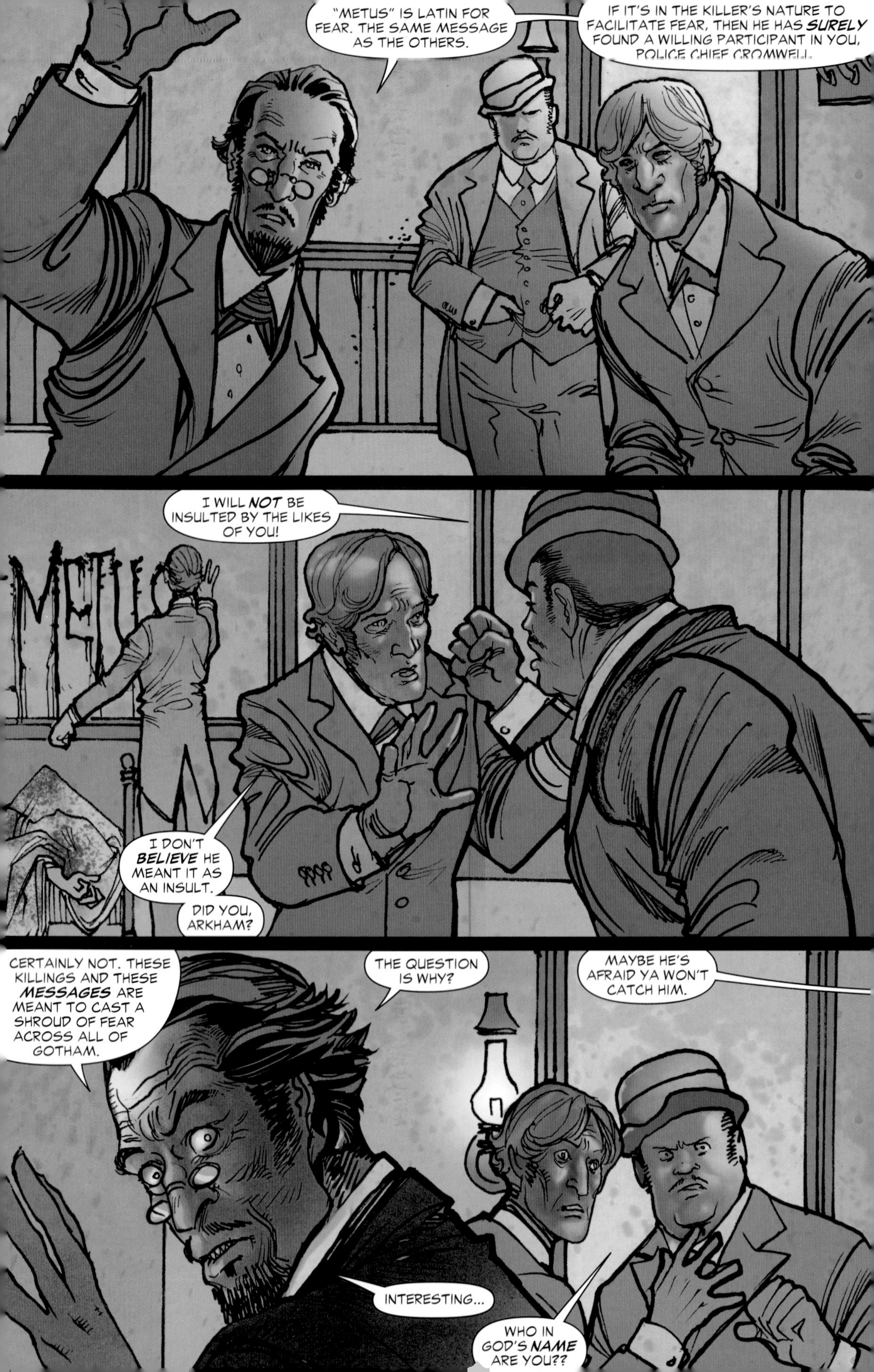
"METUS" IS LATIN FOR FEAR. THE SAME MESSAGE AS THE OTHERS.
IF IT'S IN THE KILLER'S NATURE TO FACILITATE FEAR, THEN HE HAS **SURELY** FOUND A WILLING PARTICIPANT IN YOU, POLICE CHIEF CROMWELL.
I WILL **NOT** BE INSULTED BY THE LIKES OF YOU!
METUS
I DON'T **BELIEVE** HE MEANT IT AS AN INSULT.
DID YOU, ARKHAM?
CERTAINLY NOT. THESE KILLINGS AND THESE **MESSAGES** ARE MEANT TO CAST A SHROUD OF FEAR ACROSS ALL OF GOTHAM.
THE QUESTION IS WHY?
MAYBE HE'S AFRAID YA WON'T CATCH HIM.
INTERESTING...
WHO IN GOD'S **NAME** ARE YOU??

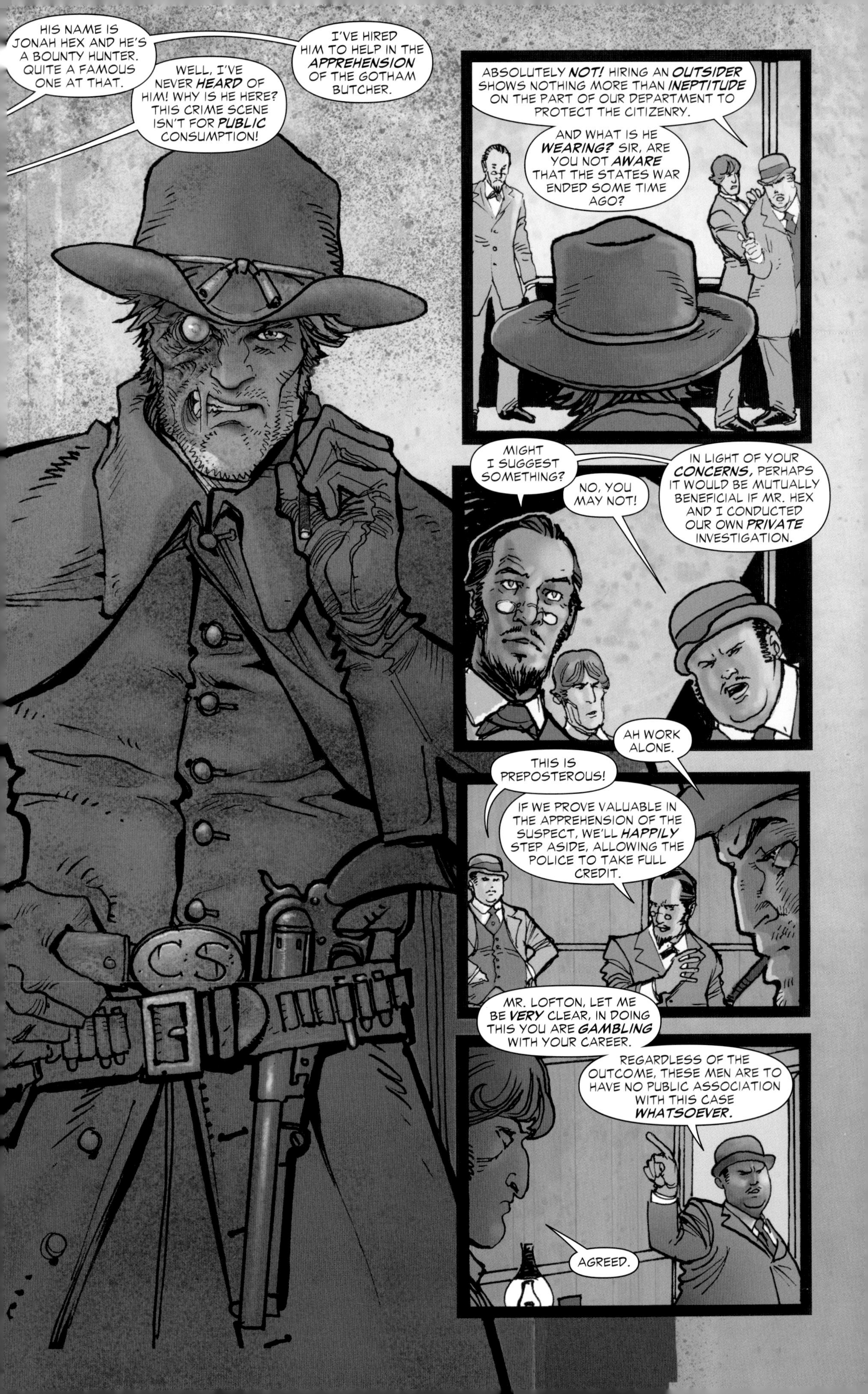
HIS NAME IS JONAH HEX AND HE'S A BOUNTY HUNTER. QUITE A FAMOUS ONE AT THAT.
I'VE HIRED HIM TO HELP IN THE *APPREHENSION* OF THE GOTHAM BUTCHER.
WELL, I'VE NEVER *HEARD* OF HIM! WHY IS HE HERE? THIS CRIME SCENE ISN'T FOR *PUBLIC* CONSUMPTION!
ABSOLUTELY ***NOT!*** HIRING AN ***OUTSIDER*** SHOWS NOTHING MORE THAN ***INEPTITUDE*** ON THE PART OF OUR DEPARTMENT TO PROTECT THE CITIZENRY.
AND WHAT IS HE ***WEARING?*** SIR, ARE YOU NOT ***AWARE*** THAT THE STATES WAR ENDED SOME TIME AGO?
MIGHT I SUGGEST SOMETHING?
NO, YOU MAY NOT!
IN LIGHT OF YOUR ***CONCERNS,*** PERHAPS IT WOULD BE MUTUALLY BENEFICIAL IF MR. HEX AND I CONDUCTED OUR OWN ***PRIVATE*** INVESTIGATION.
AH WORK ALONE.
THIS IS PREPOSTEROUS!
IF WE PROVE VALUABLE IN THE APPREHENSION OF THE SUSPECT, WE'LL ***HAPPILY*** STEP ASIDE, ALLOWING THE POLICE TO TAKE FULL CREDIT.
MR. LOFTON, LET ME BE ***VERY*** CLEAR, IN DOING THIS YOU ARE ***GAMBLING*** WITH YOUR CAREER.
REGARDLESS OF THE OUTCOME, THESE MEN ARE TO HAVE NO PUBLIC ASSOCIATION WITH THIS CASE ***WHATSOEVER.***
AGREED.

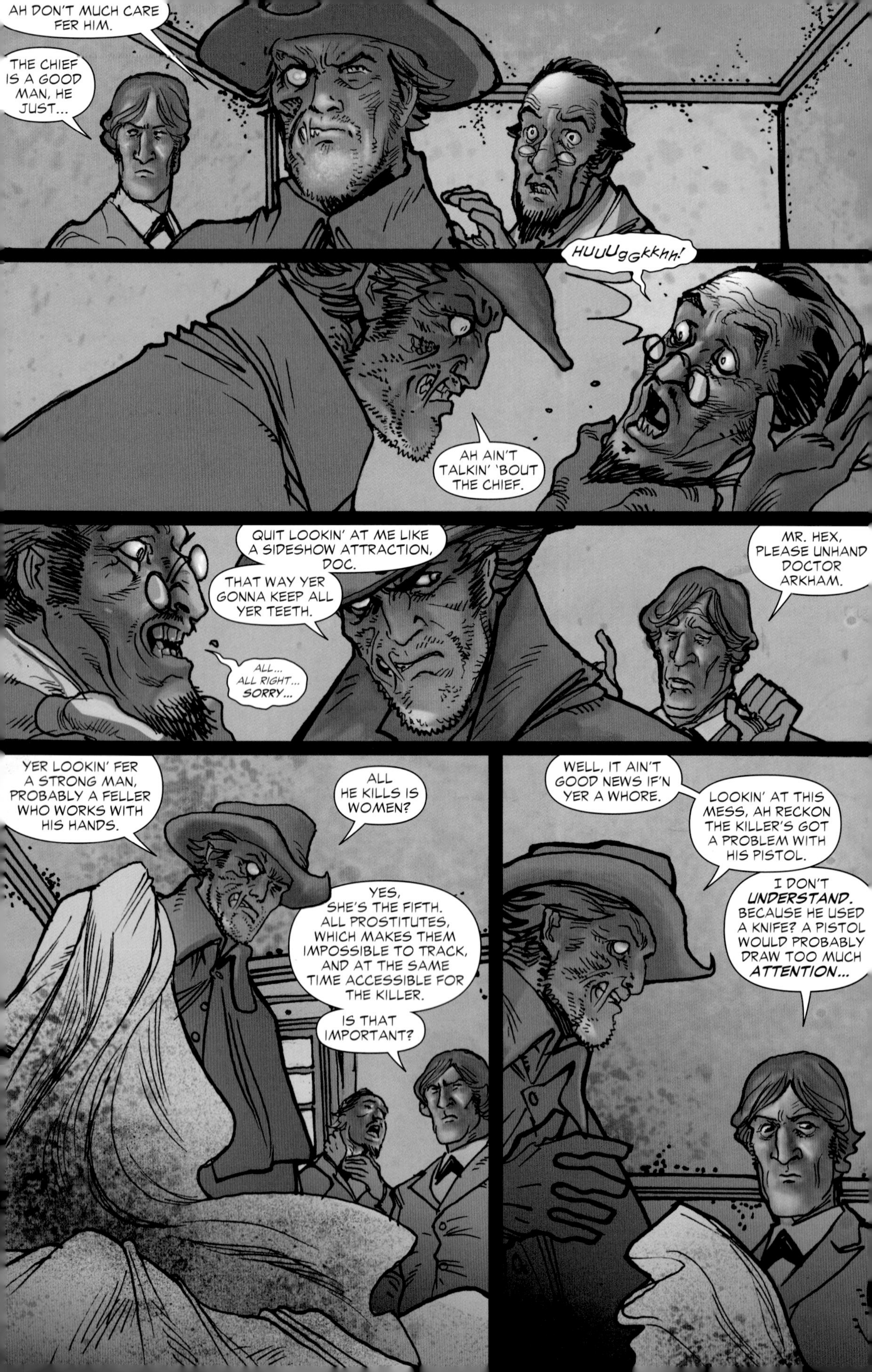

AH DON'T MUCH CARE FER HIM.
THE CHIEF IS A GOOD MAN, HE JUST...
HUUUggKkhh!
AH AIN'T TALKIN' 'BOUT THE CHIEF.
QUIT LOOKIN' AT ME LIKE A SIDESHOW ATTRACTION, DOC.
THAT WAY YER GONNA KEEP ALL YER TEETH.
ALL... ALL RIGHT... SORRY...
MR. HEX, PLEASE UNHAND DOCTOR ARKHAM.
YER LOOKIN' FER A STRONG MAN, PROBABLY A FELLER WHO WORKS WITH HIS HANDS.
ALL HE KILLS IS WOMEN?
YES, SHE'S THE FIFTH. ALL PROSTITUTES, WHICH MAKES THEM IMPOSSIBLE TO TRACK, AND AT THE SAME TIME ACCESSIBLE FOR THE KILLER.
IS THAT IMPORTANT?
WELL, IT AIN'T GOOD NEWS IF'N YER A WHORE.
LOOKIN' AT THIS MESS, AH RECKON THE KILLER'S GOT A PROBLEM WITH HIS PISTOL.
I DON'T UNDERSTAND. BECAUSE HE USED A KNIFE? A PISTOL WOULD PROBABLY DRAW TOO MUCH ATTENTION...

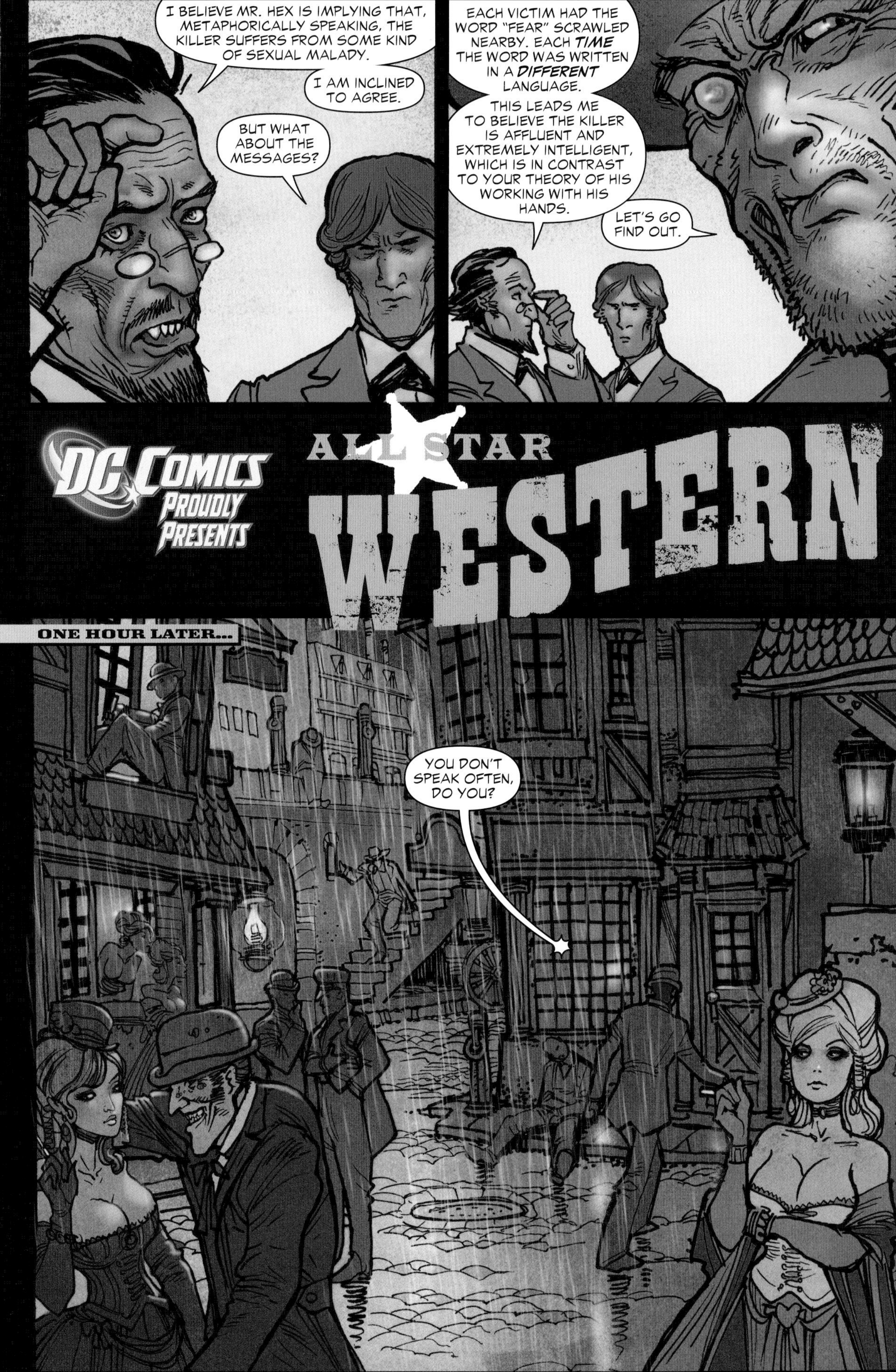
I BELIEVE MR. HEX IS IMPLYING THAT, METAPHORICALLY SPEAKING, THE KILLER SUFFERS FROM SOME KIND OF SEXUAL MALADY.
I AM INCLINED TO AGREE.
BUT WHAT ABOUT THE MESSAGES?
EACH VICTIM HAD THE WORD "FEAR" SCRAWLED NEARBY. EACH *TIME* THE WORD WAS WRITTEN IN A *DIFFERENT* LANGUAGE.
THIS LEADS ME TO BELIEVE THE KILLER IS AFFLUENT AND EXTREMELY INTELLIGENT, WHICH IS IN CONTRAST TO YOUR THEORY OF HIS WORKING WITH HIS HANDS.
LET'S GO FIND OUT.
DC COMICS PROUDLY PRESENTS
ALL STAR WESTERN
ONE HOUR LATER...
YOU DON'T SPEAK OFTEN, DO YOU?

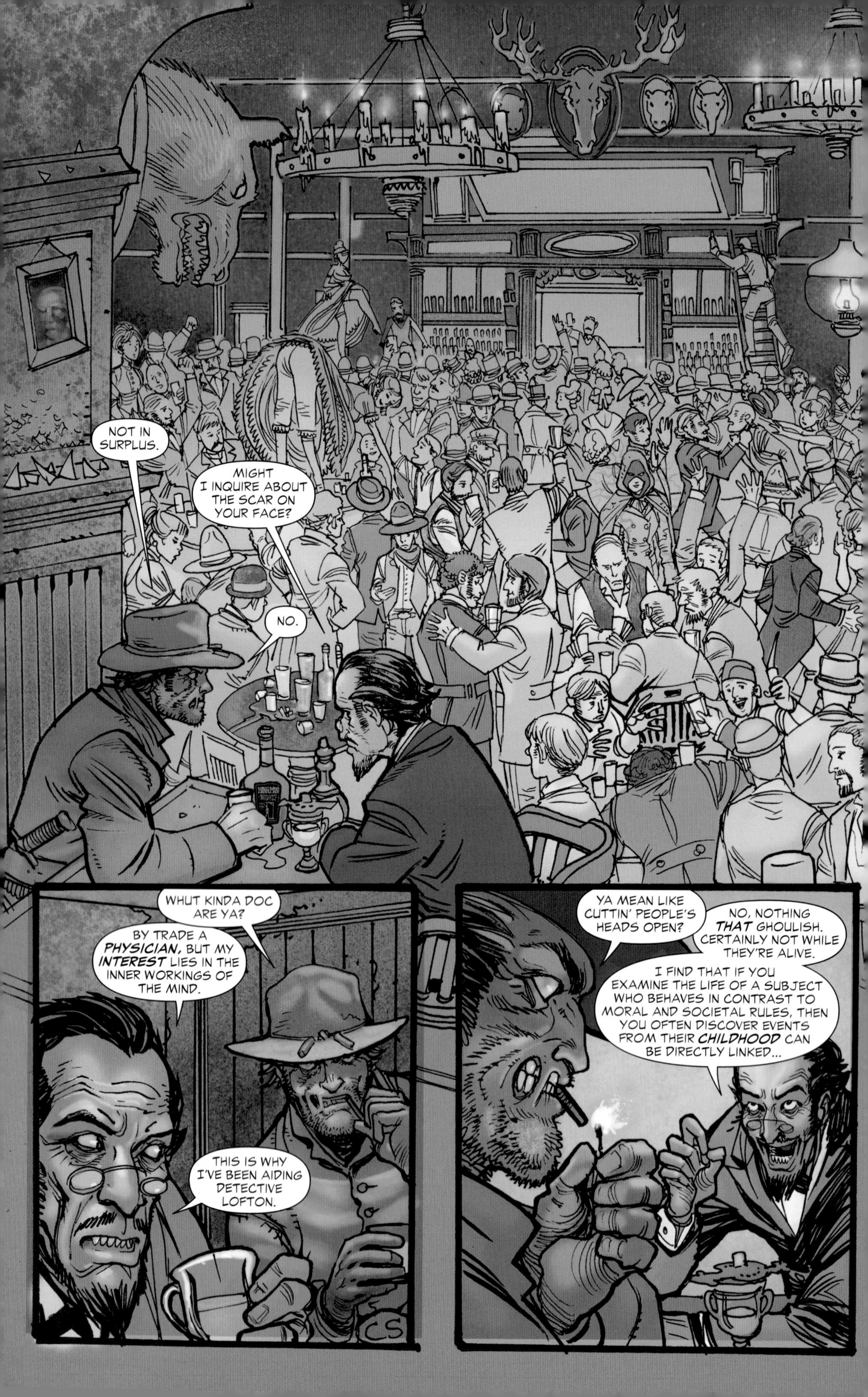
NOT IN SURPLUS.
MIGHT I INQUIRE ABOUT THE SCAR ON YOUR FACE?
NO.
WHUT KINDA DOC ARE YA?
BY TRADE A PHYSICIAN, BUT MY INTEREST LIES IN THE INNER WORKINGS OF THE MIND.
THIS IS WHY I'VE BEEN AIDING DETECTIVE LOFTON.
YA MEAN LIKE CUTTIN' PEOPLE'S HEADS OPEN?
NO, NOTHING THAT GHOULISH. CERTAINLY NOT WHILE THEY'RE ALIVE.
I FIND THAT IF YOU EXAMINE THE LIFE OF A SUBJECT WHO BEHAVES IN CONTRAST TO MORAL AND SOCIETAL RULES, THEN YOU OFTEN DISCOVER EVENTS FROM THEIR CHILDHOOD CAN BE DIRECTLY LINKED...

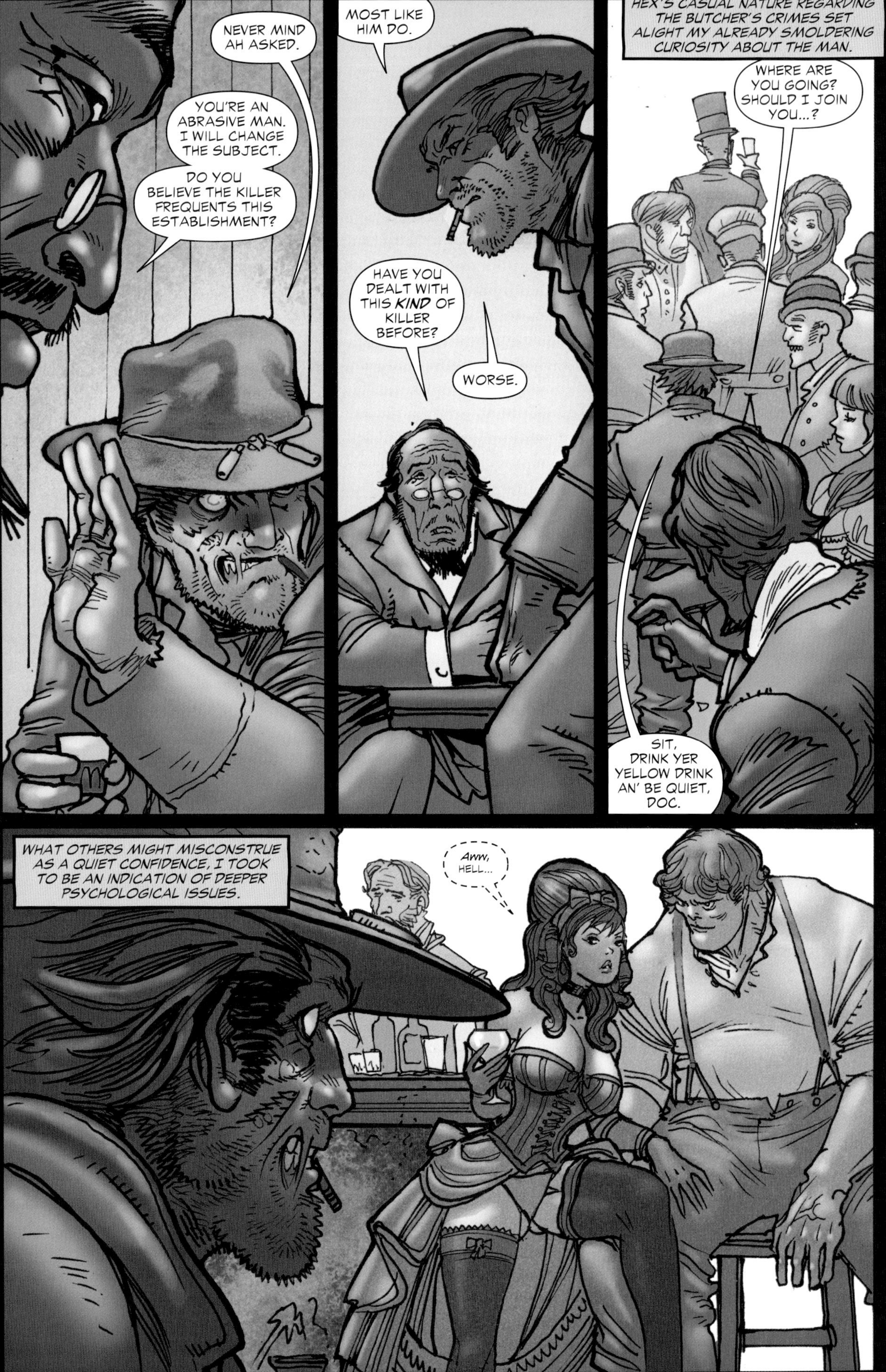
NEVER MIND AH ASKED.
YOU'RE AN ABRASIVE MAN. I WILL CHANGE THE SUBJECT.
DO YOU BELIEVE THE KILLER FREQUENTS THIS ESTABLISHMENT?
MOST LIKE HIM DO.
HAVE YOU DEALT WITH THIS *KIND* OF KILLER BEFORE?
WORSE.
HEX'S CASUAL NATURE REGARDING THE BUTCHER'S CRIMES SET ALIGHT MY ALREADY SMOLDERING CURIOSITY ABOUT THE MAN.
WHERE ARE YOU GOING? SHOULD I JOIN YOU...?
SIT, DRINK YER YELLOW DRINK AN' BE QUIET, DOC.
WHAT OTHERS MIGHT MISCONSTRUE AS A QUIET CONFIDENCE, I TOOK TO BE AN INDICATION OF DEEPER PSYCHOLOGICAL ISSUES.
AWW, HELL...

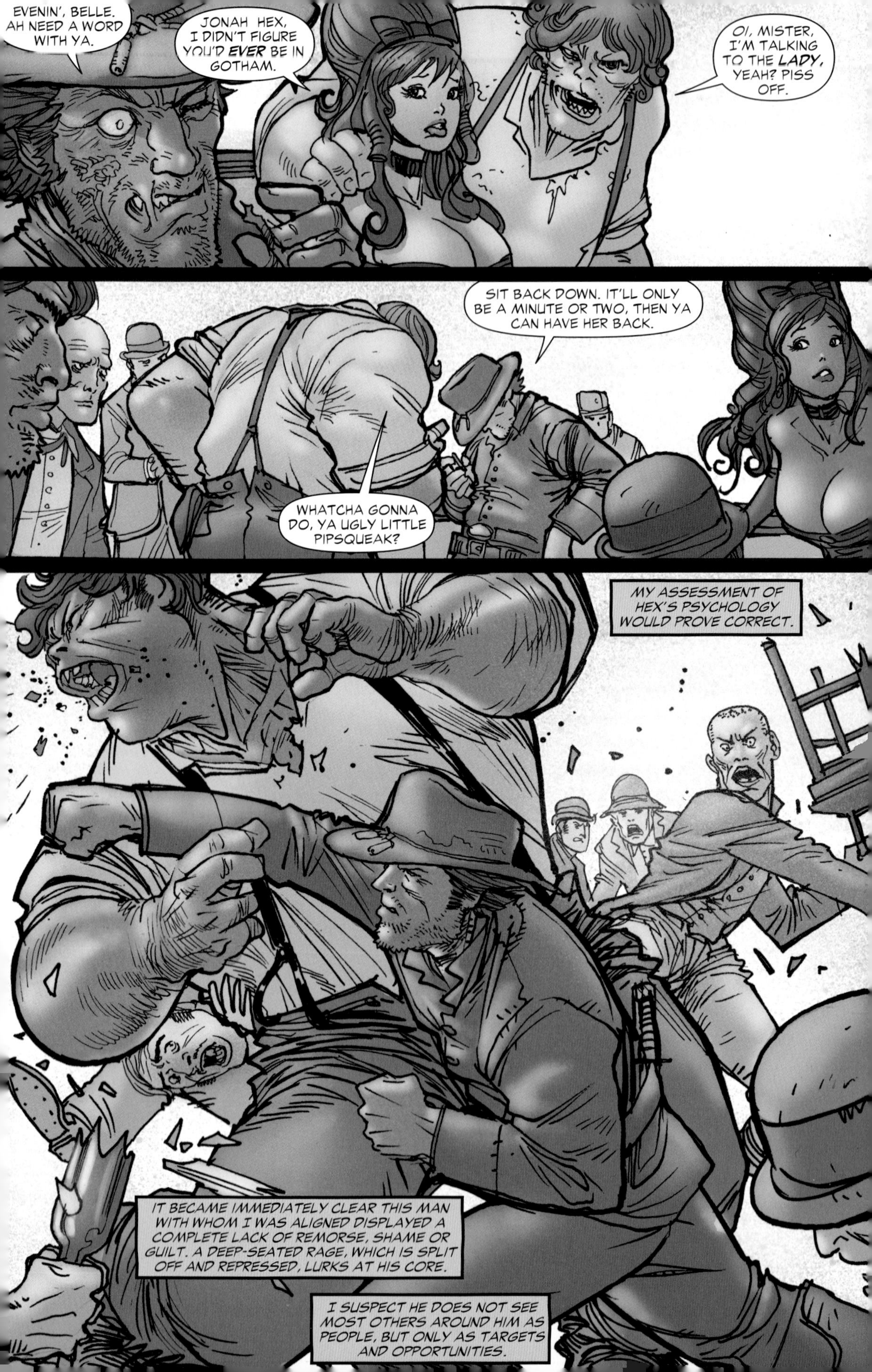
EVENIN', BELLE. AH NEED A WORD WITH YA.
JONAH HEX, I DIDN'T FIGURE YOU'D EVER BE IN GOTHAM.
OI, MISTER, I'M TALKING TO THE LADY, YEAH? PISS OFF.
SIT BACK DOWN. IT'LL ONLY BE A MINUTE OR TWO, THEN YA CAN HAVE HER BACK.
WHATCHA GONNA DO, YA UGLY LITTLE PIPSQUEAK?
MY ASSESSMENT OF HEX'S PSYCHOLOGY WOULD PROVE CORRECT.
IT BECAME IMMEDIATELY CLEAR THIS MAN WITH WHOM I WAS ALIGNED DISPLAYED A COMPLETE LACK OF REMORSE, SHAME OR GUILT. A DEEP-SEATED RAGE, WHICH IS SPLIT OFF AND REPRESSED, LURKS AT HIS CORE.
I SUSPECT HE DOES NOT SEE MOST OTHERS AROUND HIM AS PEOPLE, BUT ONLY AS TARGETS AND OPPORTUNITIES.

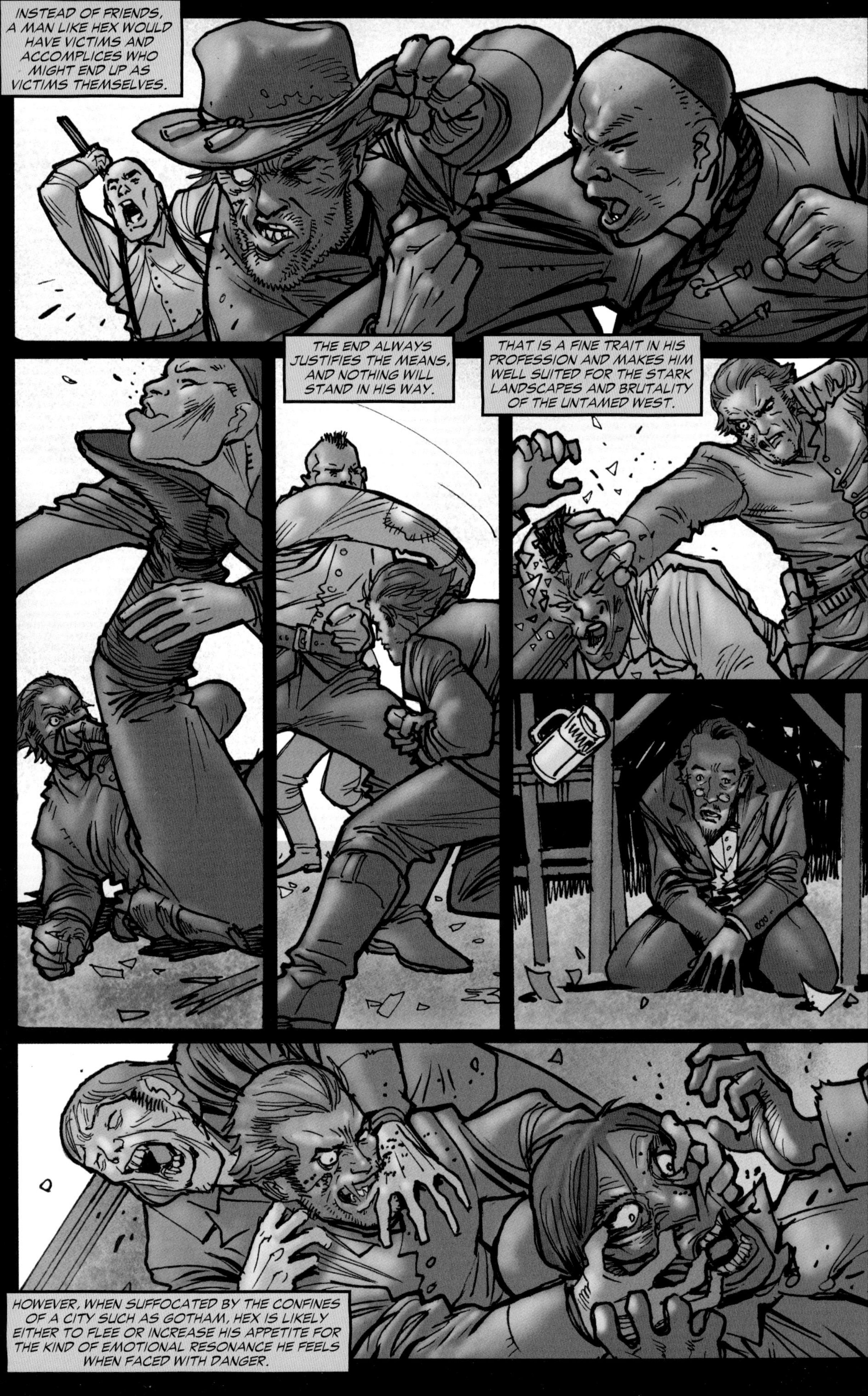
INSTEAD OF FRIENDS, A MAN LIKE HEX WOULD HAVE VICTIMS AND ACCOMPLICES WHO MIGHT END UP AS VICTIMS THEMSELVES.
THE END ALWAYS JUSTIFIES THE MEANS, AND NOTHING WILL STAND IN HIS WAY.
THAT IS A FINE TRAIT IN HIS PROFESSION AND MAKES HIM WELL SUITED FOR THE STARK LANDSCAPES AND BRUTALITY OF THE UNTAMED WEST.
HOWEVER, WHEN SUFFOCATED BY THE CONFINES OF A CITY SUCH AS GOTHAM, HEX IS LIKELY EITHER TO FLEE OR INCREASE HIS APPETITE FOR THE KIND OF EMOTIONAL RESONANCE HE FEELS WHEN FACED WITH DANGER.

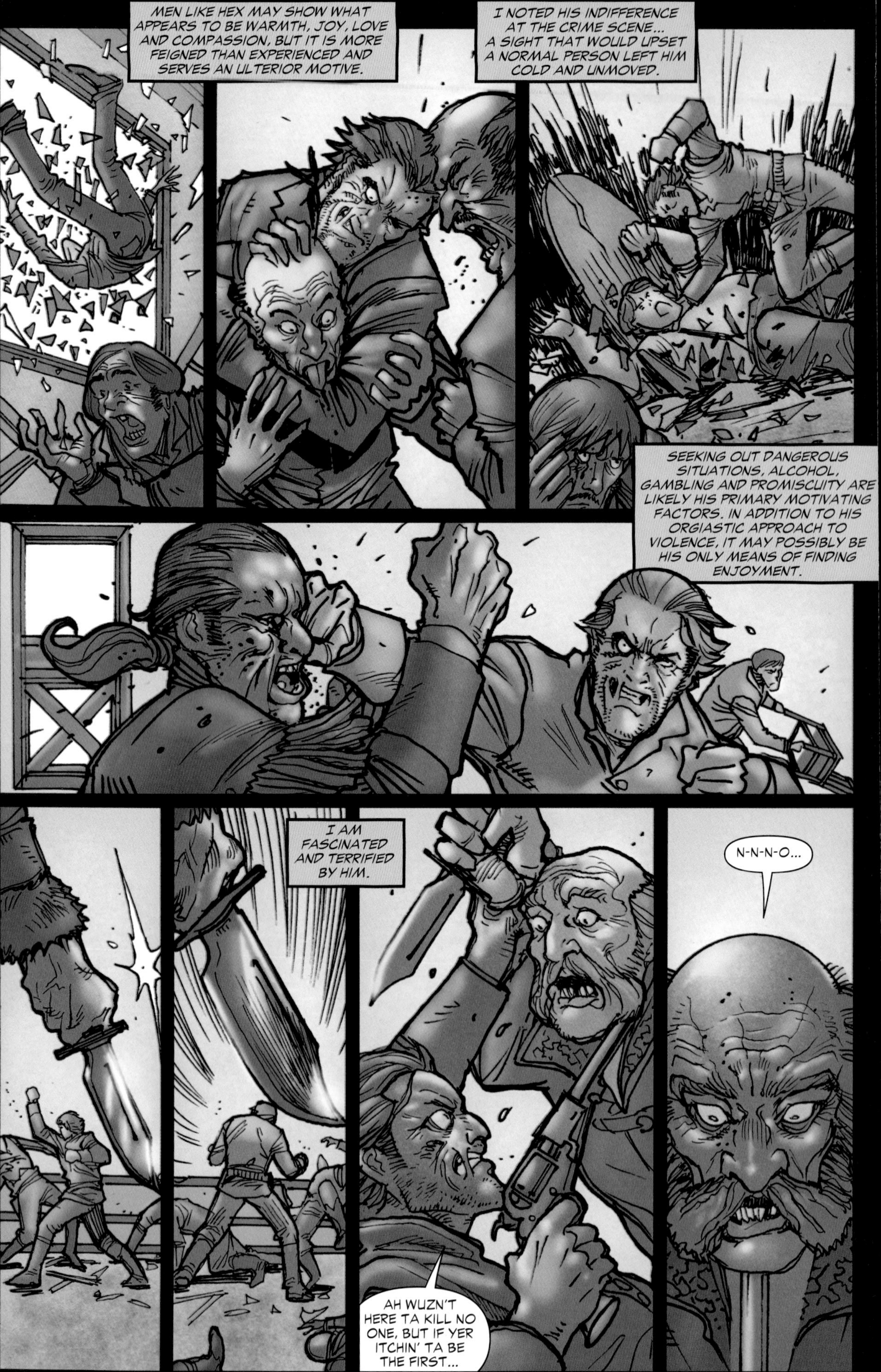

MEN LIKE HEX MAY SHOW WHAT APPEARS TO BE WARMTH, JOY, LOVE AND COMPASSION, BUT IT IS MORE FEIGNED THAN EXPERIENCED AND SERVES AN ULTERIOR MOTIVE.
I NOTED HIS INDIFFERENCE AT THE CRIME SCENE... A SIGHT THAT WOULD UPSET A NORMAL PERSON LEFT HIM COLD AND UNMOVED.
SEEKING OUT DANGEROUS SITUATIONS, ALCOHOL, GAMBLING AND PROMISCUITY ARE LIKELY HIS PRIMARY MOTIVATING FACTORS. IN ADDITION TO HIS ORGIASTIC APPROACH TO VIOLENCE, IT MAY POSSIBLY BE HIS ONLY MEANS OF FINDING ENJOYMENT.
I AM FASCINATED AND TERRIFIED BY HIM.
AH WUZN'T HERE TA KILL NO ONE, BUT IF YER ITCHIN' TA BE THE FIRST...
N-N-N-O...

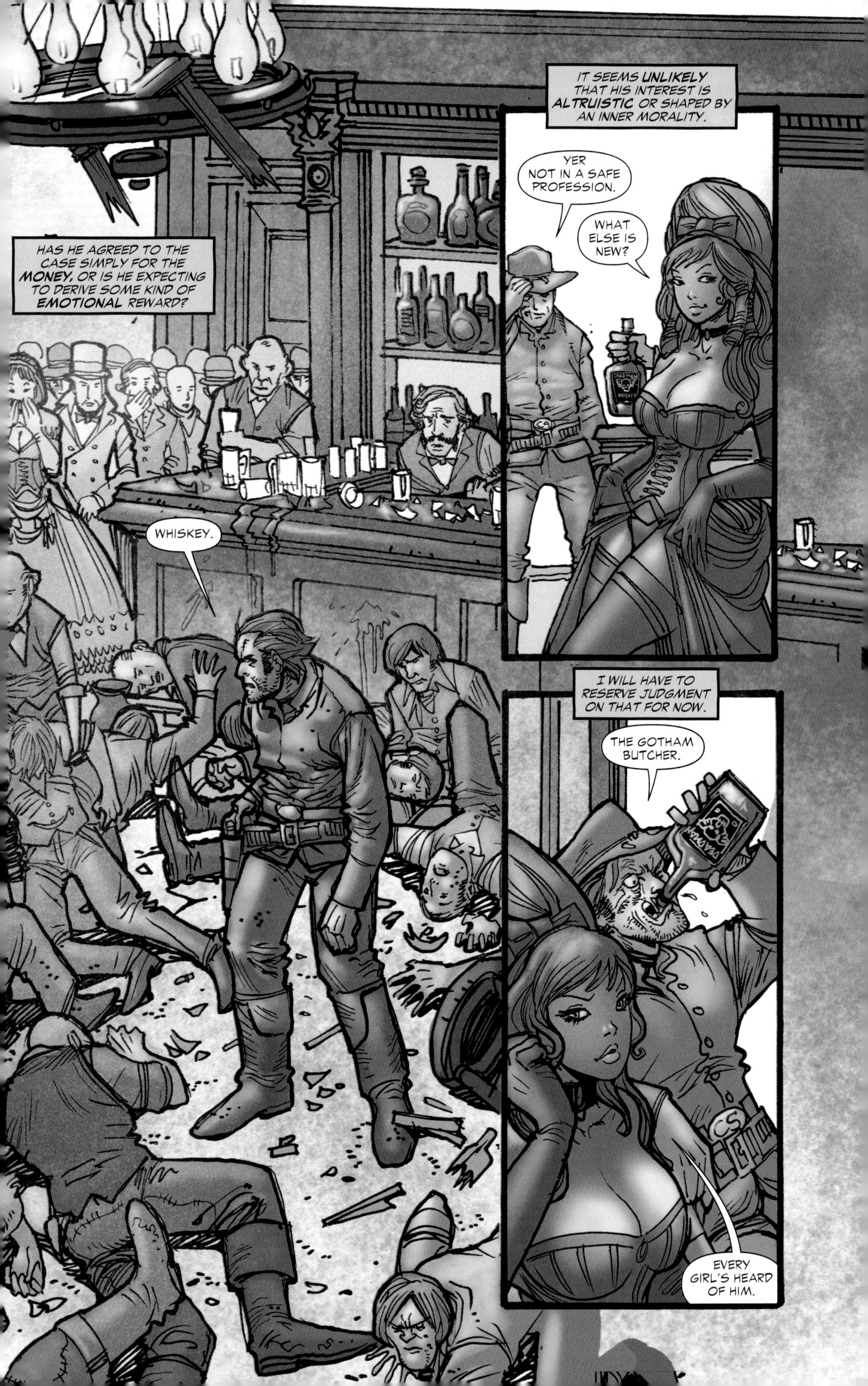
HAS HE AGREED TO THE CASE SIMPLY FOR THE **MONEY**, OR IS HE EXPECTING TO DERIVE SOME KIND OF **EMOTIONAL** REWARD?
WHISKEY.
IT SEEMS **UNLIKELY** THAT HIS INTEREST IS **ALTRUISTIC** OR SHAPED BY AN INNER MORALITY.
YER NOT IN A SAFE PROFESSION.
WHAT ELSE IS NEW?
I WILL HAVE TO RESERVE JUDGMENT ON THAT FOR NOW.
THE GOTHAM BUTCHER.
EVERY GIRL'S HEARD OF HIM.

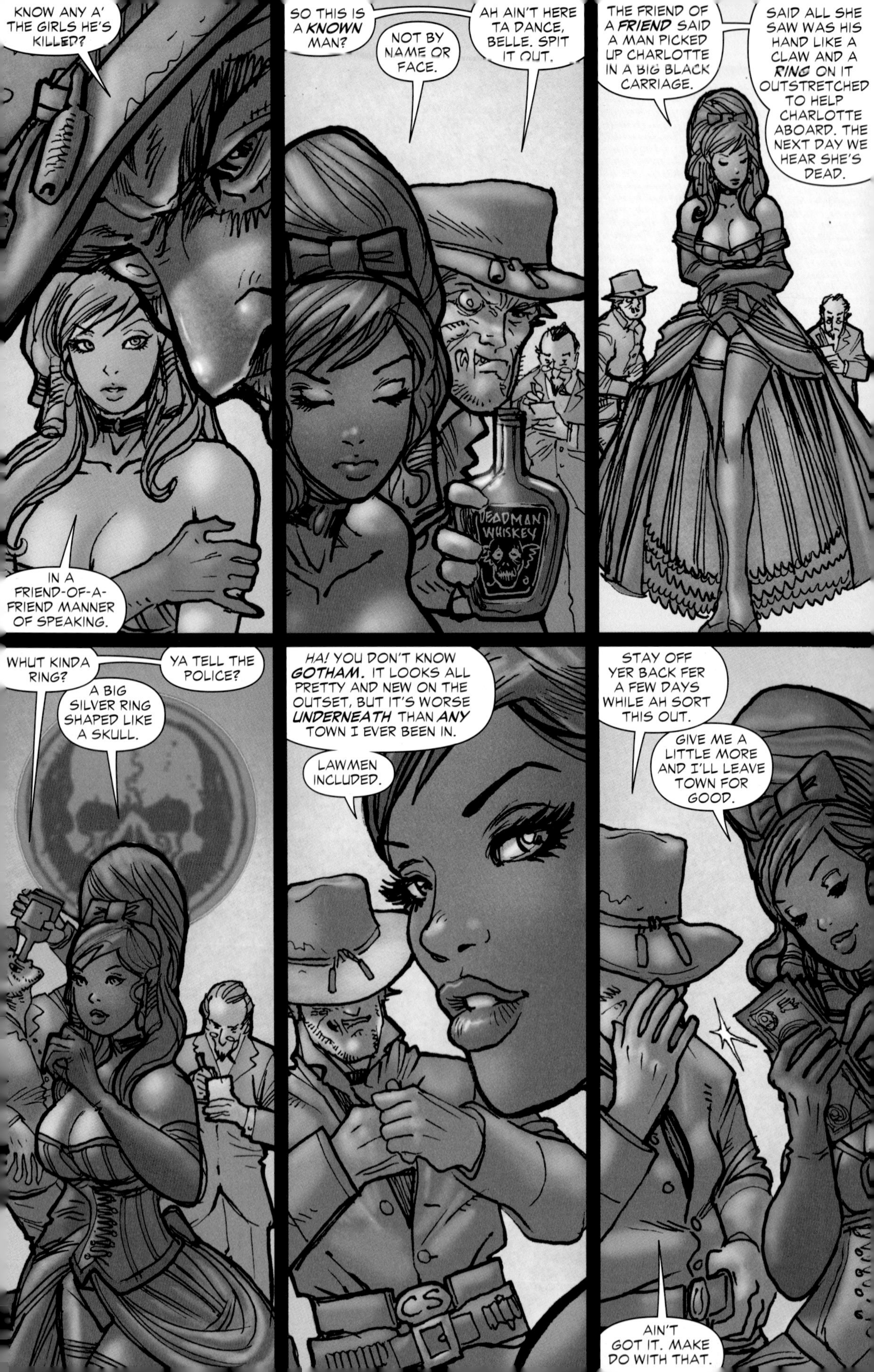
KNOW ANY A' THE GIRLS HE'S KILLED?
IN A FRIEND-OF-A-FRIEND MANNER OF SPEAKING.
SO THIS IS A KNOWN MAN?
NOT BY NAME OR FACE.
AH AIN'T HERE TA DANCE, BELLE. SPIT IT OUT.
DEADMAN WHISKEY
THE FRIEND OF A FRIEND SAID A MAN PICKED UP CHARLOTTE IN A BIG BLACK CARRIAGE.
SAID ALL SHE SAW WAS HIS HAND LIKE A CLAW AND A RING ON IT OUTSTRETCHED TO HELP CHARLOTTE ABOARD. THE NEXT DAY WE HEAR SHE'S DEAD.
WHUT KINDA RING?
A BIG SILVER RING SHAPED LIKE A SKULL.
YA TELL THE POLICE?
HA! YOU DON'T KNOW GOTHAM. IT LOOKS ALL PRETTY AND NEW ON THE OUTSET, BUT IT'S WORSE UNDERNEATH THAN ANY TOWN I EVER BEEN IN.
LAWMEN INCLUDED.
CS
STAY OFF YER BACK FER A FEW DAYS WHILE AH SORT THIS OUT.
GIVE ME A LITTLE MORE AND I'LL LEAVE TOWN FOR GOOD.
AIN'T GOT IT. MAKE DO WITH THAT.

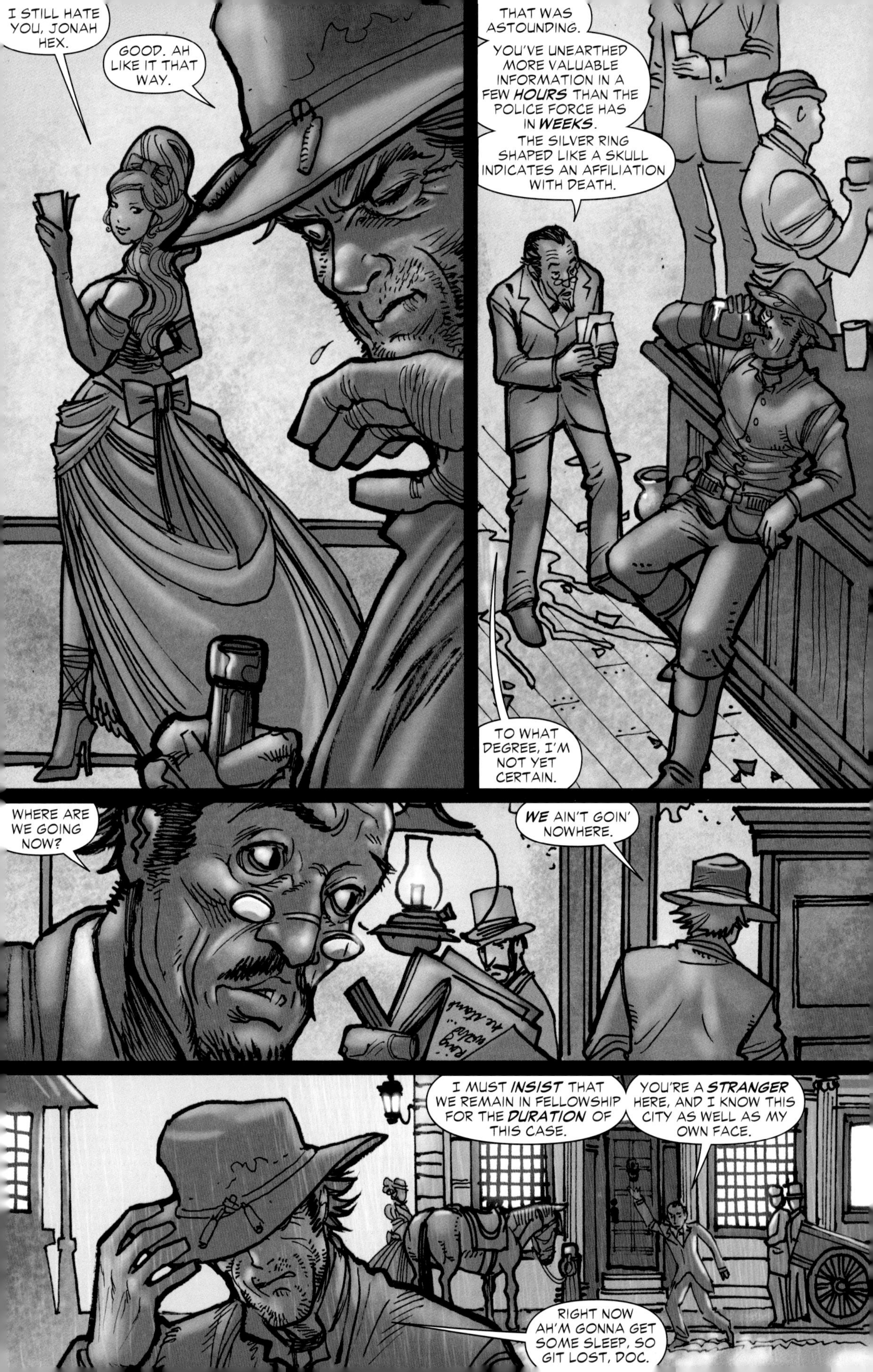
I STILL HATE YOU, JONAH HEX.
GOOD. AH LIKE IT THAT WAY.
THAT WAS ASTOUNDING.
YOU'VE UNEARTHED MORE VALUABLE INFORMATION IN A FEW HOURS THAN THE POLICE FORCE HAS IN WEEKS.
THE SILVER RING SHAPED LIKE A SKULL INDICATES AN AFFILIATION WITH DEATH.
TO WHAT DEGREE, I'M NOT YET CERTAIN.
WHERE ARE WE GOING NOW?
WE AIN'T GOIN' NOWHERE.
I MUST INSIST THAT WE REMAIN IN FELLOWSHIP FOR THE DURATION OF THIS CASE.
YOU'RE A STRANGER HERE, AND I KNOW THIS CITY AS WELL AS MY OWN FACE.
RIGHT NOW AH'M GONNA GET SOME SLEEP, SO GIT LOST, DOC.

No rest for the wicked

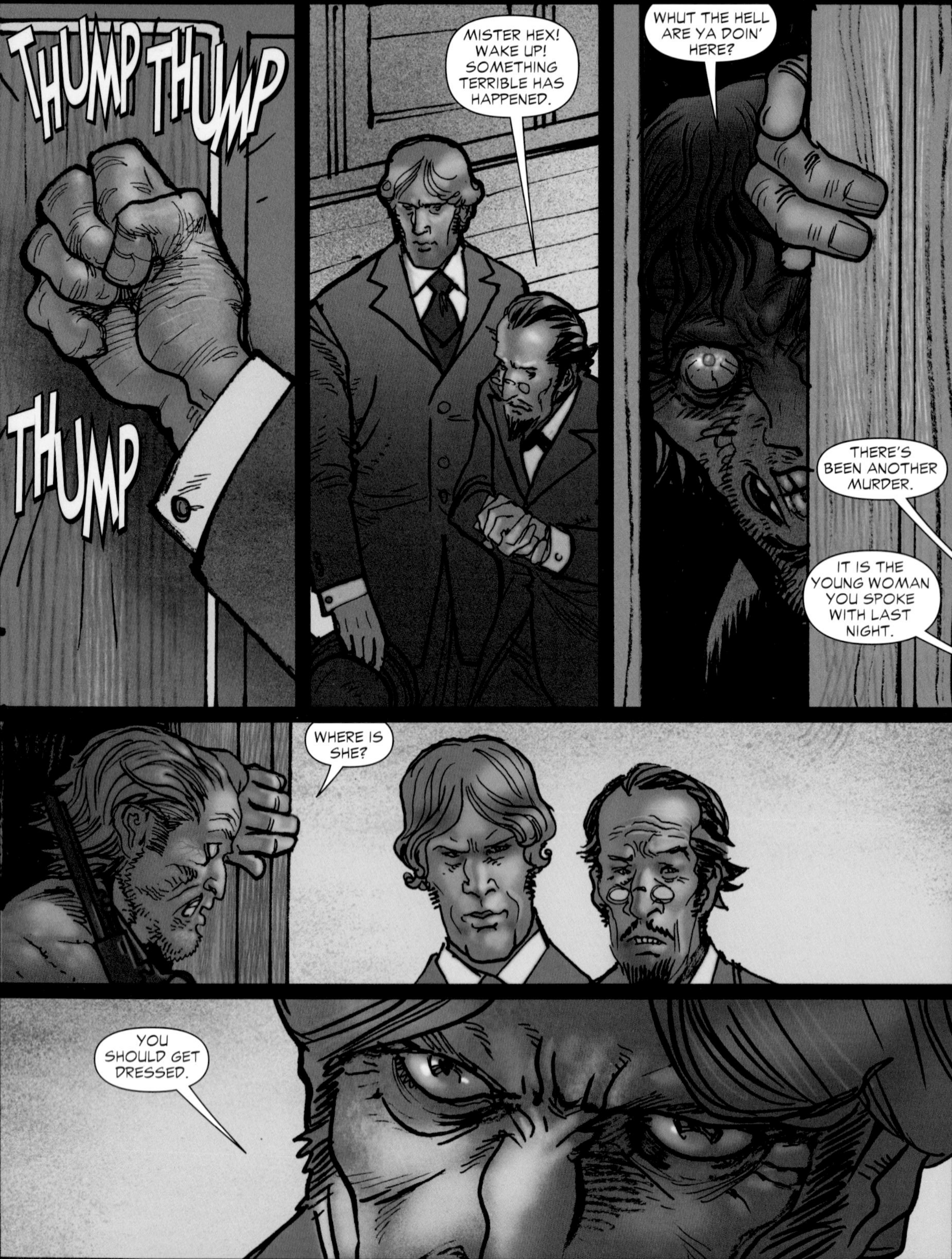
THUMP THUMP
THUMP
MISTER HEX! WAKE UP! SOMETHING TERRIBLE HAS HAPPENED.
WHUT THE HELL ARE YA DOIN' HERE?
THERE'S BEEN ANOTHER MURDER.
IT IS THE YOUNG WOMAN YOU SPOKE WITH LAST NIGHT.
WHERE IS SHE?
YOU SHOULD GET DRESSED.

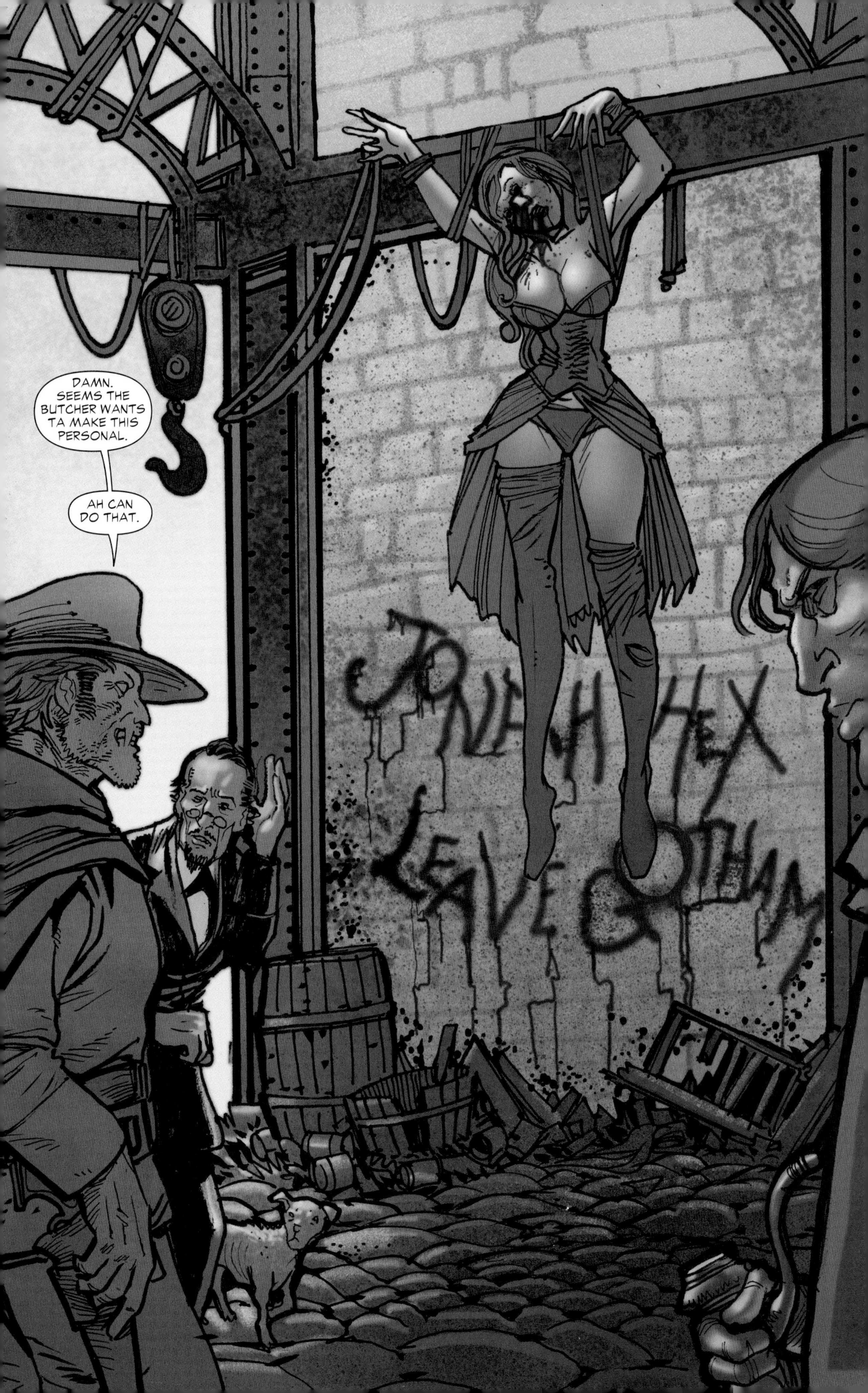
DAMN. SEEMS THE BUTCHER WANTS TA MAKE THIS PERSONAL.
AH CAN DO THAT.
JONAH HEX
LEAVE GOTHAM

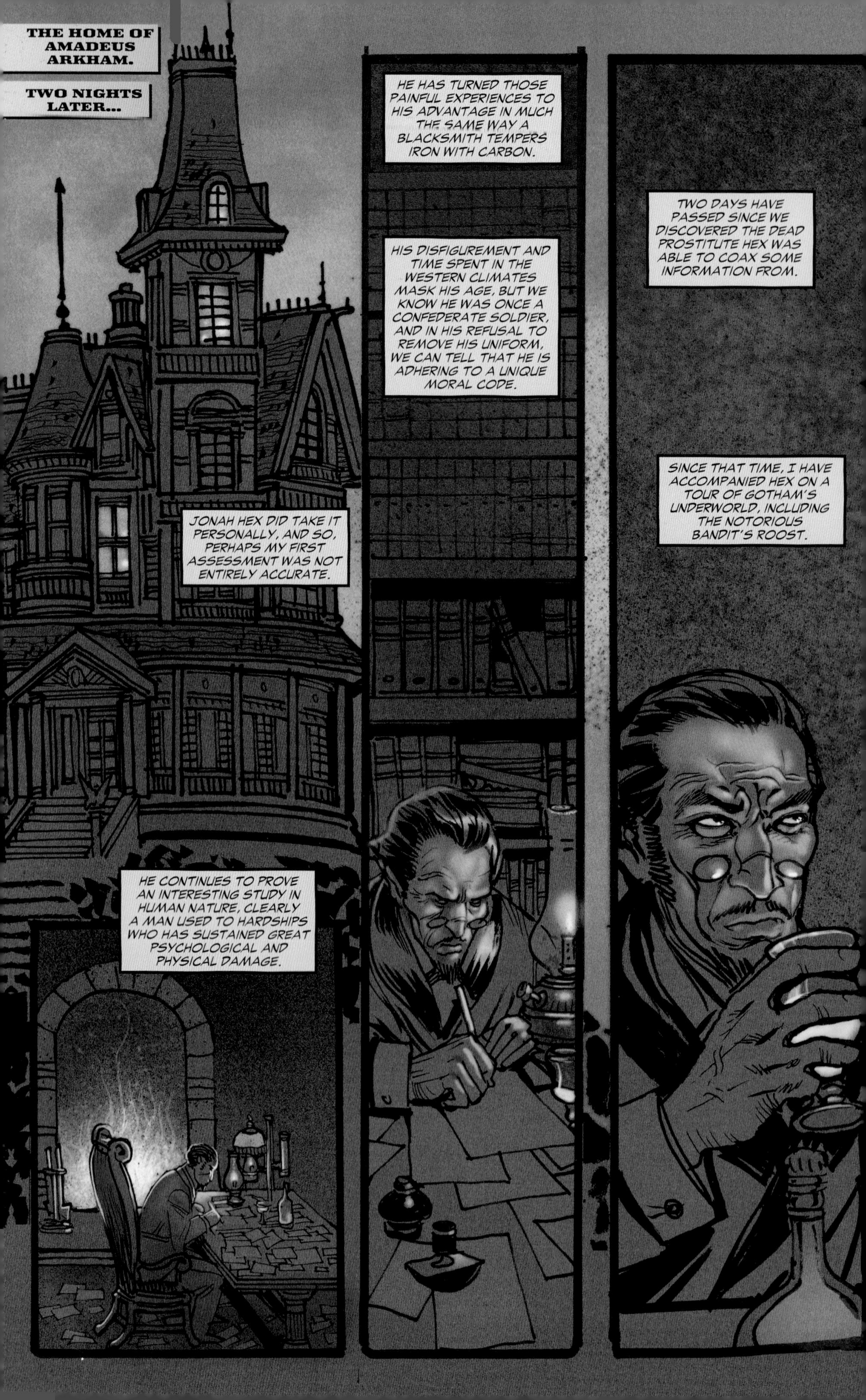
THE HOME OF AMADEUS ARKHAM.
TWO NIGHTS LATER...
JONAH HEX DID TAKE IT PERSONALLY, AND SO, PERHAPS MY FIRST ASSESSMENT WAS NOT ENTIRELY ACCURATE.
HE CONTINUES TO PROVE AN INTERESTING STUDY IN HUMAN NATURE, CLEARLY A MAN USED TO HARDSHIPS WHO HAS SUSTAINED GREAT PSYCHOLOGICAL AND PHYSICAL DAMAGE.
HE HAS TURNED THOSE PAINFUL EXPERIENCES TO HIS ADVANTAGE IN MUCH THE SAME WAY A BLACKSMITH TEMPERS IRON WITH CARBON.
HIS DISFIGUREMENT AND TIME SPENT IN THE WESTERN CLIMATES MASK HIS AGE, BUT WE KNOW HE WAS ONCE A CONFEDERATE SOLDIER, AND IN HIS REFUSAL TO REMOVE HIS UNIFORM, WE CAN TELL THAT HE IS ADHERING TO A UNIQUE MORAL CODE.
TWO DAYS HAVE PASSED SINCE WE DISCOVERED THE DEAD PROSTITUTE HEX WAS ABLE TO COAX SOME INFORMATION FROM.
SINCE THAT TIME, I HAVE ACCOMPANIED HEX ON A TOUR OF GOTHAM'S UNDERWORLD, INCLUDING THE NOTORIOUS BANDIT'S ROOST.

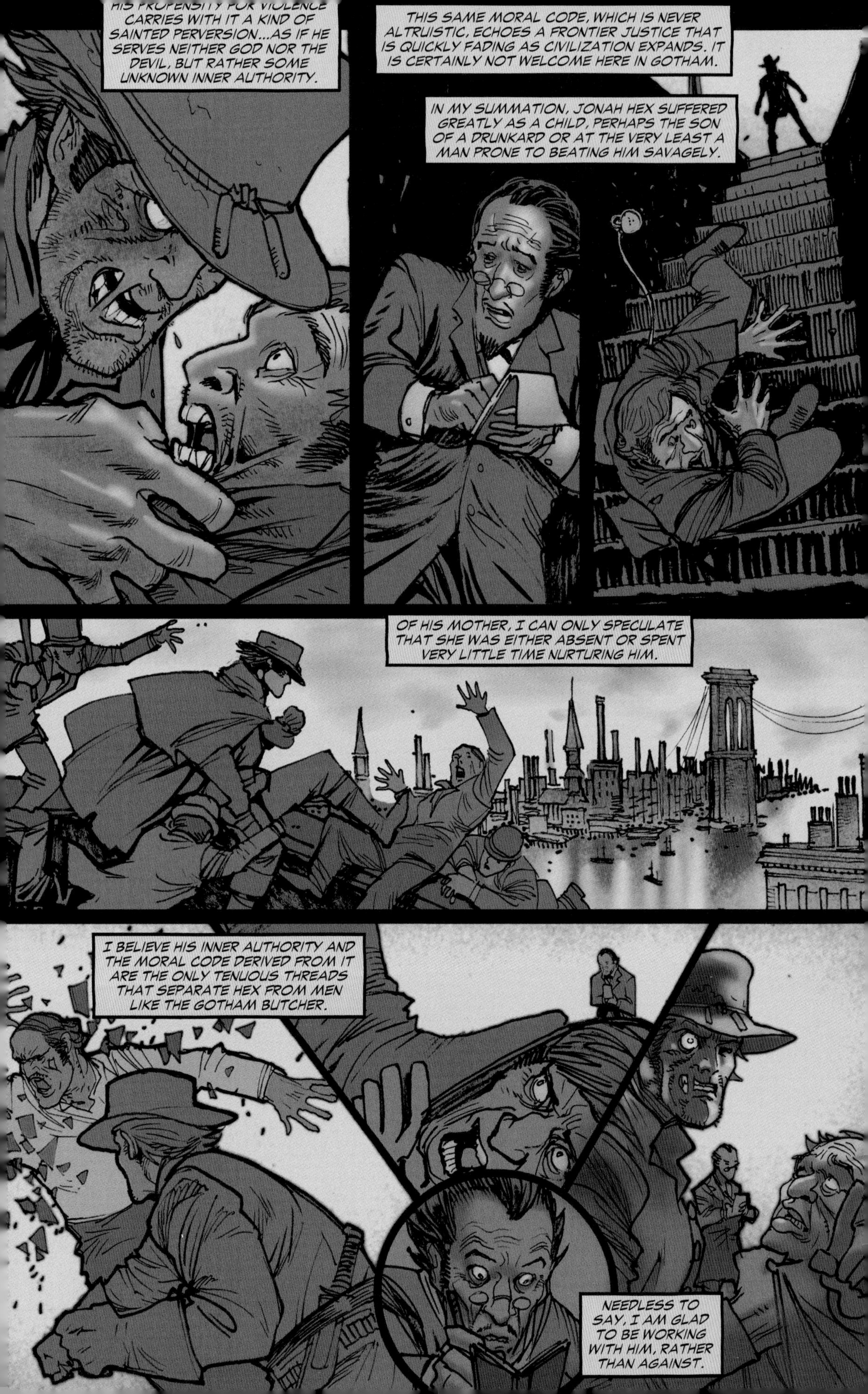
HIS PROPENSITY FOR VIOLENCE CARRIES WITH IT A KIND OF SAINTED PERVERSION...AS IF HE SERVES NEITHER GOD NOR THE DEVIL, BUT RATHER SOME UNKNOWN INNER AUTHORITY.
THIS SAME MORAL CODE, WHICH IS NEVER ALTRUISTIC, ECHOES A FRONTIER JUSTICE THAT IS QUICKLY FADING AS CIVILIZATION EXPANDS. IT IS CERTAINLY NOT WELCOME HERE IN GOTHAM.
IN MY SUMMATION, JONAH HEX SUFFERED GREATLY AS A CHILD, PERHAPS THE SON OF A DRUNKARD OR AT THE VERY LEAST A MAN PRONE TO BEATING HIM SAVAGELY.
OF HIS MOTHER, I CAN ONLY SPECULATE THAT SHE WAS EITHER ABSENT OR SPENT VERY LITTLE TIME NURTURING HIM.
I BELIEVE HIS INNER AUTHORITY AND THE MORAL CODE DERIVED FROM IT ARE THE ONLY TENUOUS THREADS THAT SEPARATE HEX FROM MEN LIKE THE GOTHAM BUTCHER.
NEEDLESS TO SAY, I AM GLAD TO BE WORKING WITH HIM, RATHER THAN AGAINST.

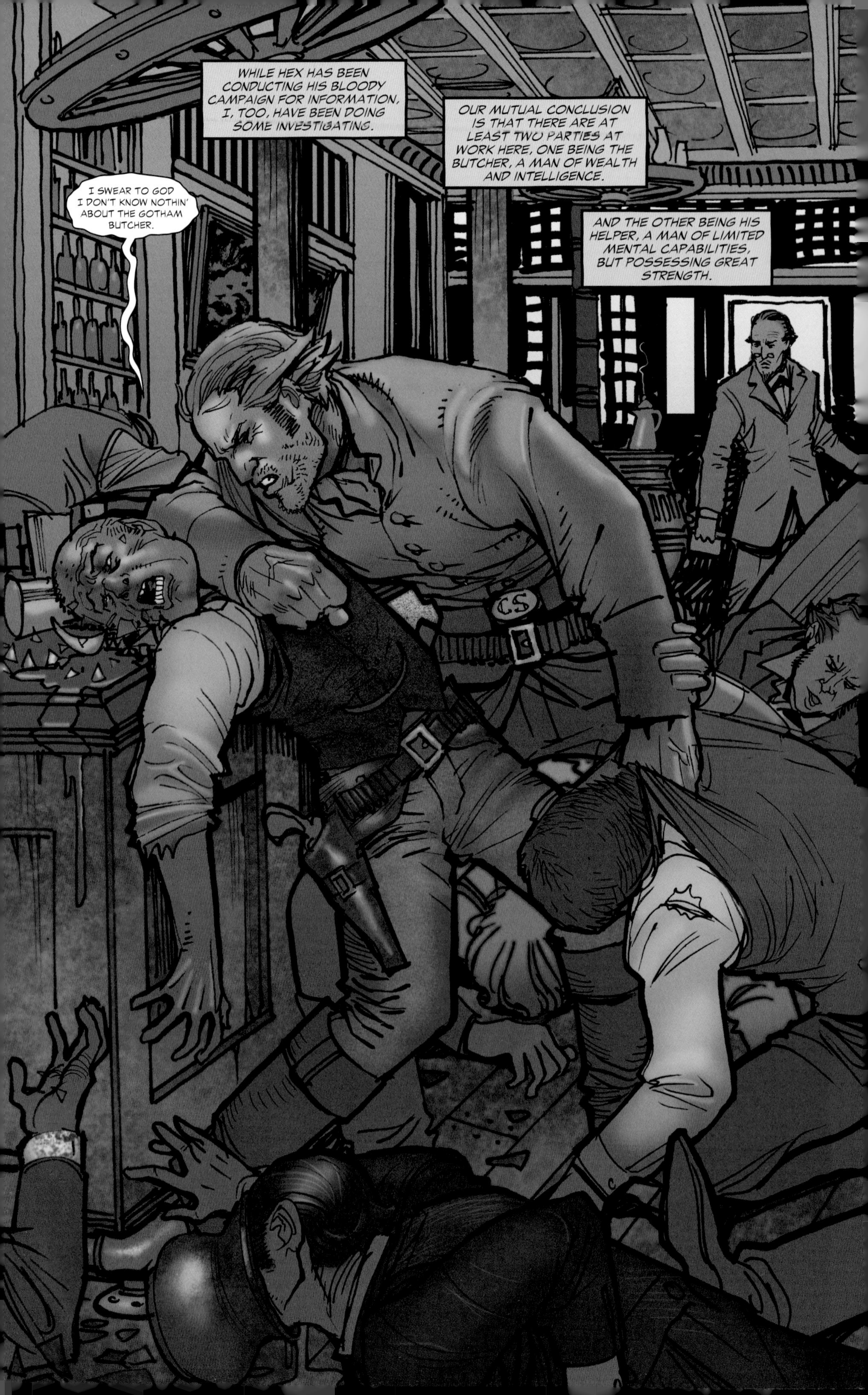
WHILE HEX HAS BEEN CONDUCTING HIS BLOODY CAMPAIGN FOR INFORMATION, I, TOO, HAVE BEEN DOING SOME INVESTIGATING.
I SWEAR TO GOD I DON'T KNOW NOTHIN' ABOUT THE GOTHAM BUTCHER.
OUR MUTUAL CONCLUSION IS THAT THERE ARE AT LEAST TWO PARTIES AT WORK HERE, ONE BEING THE BUTCHER, A MAN OF WEALTH AND INTELLIGENCE.
AND THE OTHER BEING HIS HELPER, A MAN OF LIMITED MENTAL CAPABILITIES, BUT POSSESSING GREAT STRENGTH.
C.S

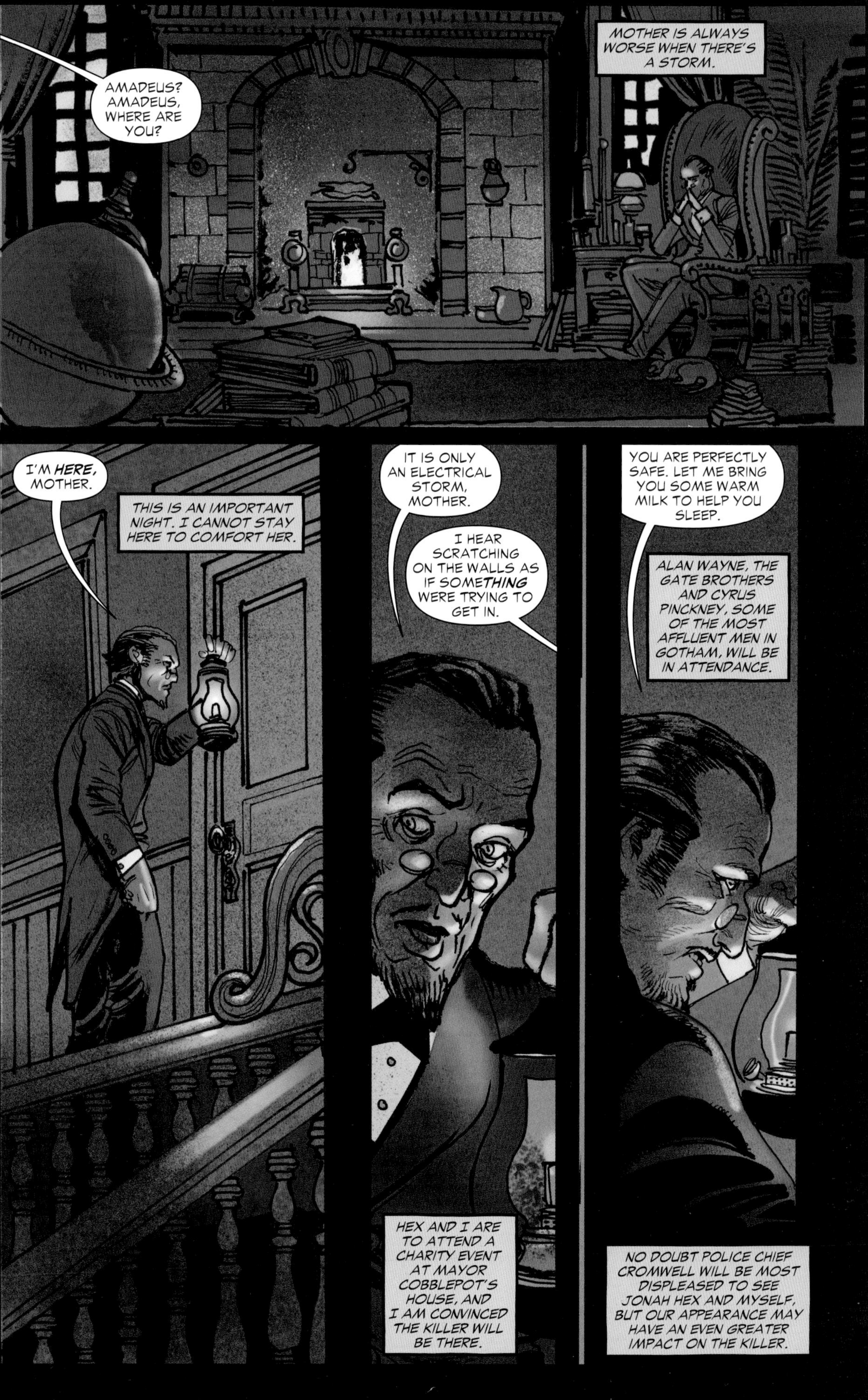
AMADEUS? AMADEUS, WHERE ARE YOU?
MOTHER IS ALWAYS WORSE WHEN THERE'S A STORM.
I'M **HERE,** MOTHER.
THIS IS AN IMPORTANT NIGHT. I CANNOT STAY HERE TO COMFORT HER.
IT IS ONLY AN ELECTRICAL STORM, MOTHER.
I HEAR SCRATCHING ON THE WALLS AS IF SOME**THING** WERE TRYING TO GET IN.
HEX AND I ARE TO ATTEND A CHARITY EVENT AT MAYOR COBBLEPOT'S HOUSE, AND I AM CONVINCED THE KILLER WILL BE THERE.
YOU ARE PERFECTLY SAFE. LET ME BRING YOU SOME WARM MILK TO HELP YOU SLEEP.
ALAN WAYNE, THE GATE BROTHERS AND CYRUS PINCKNEY, SOME OF THE MOST AFFLUENT MEN IN GOTHAM, WILL BE IN ATTENDANCE.
NO DOUBT POLICE CHIEF CROMWELL WILL BE MOST DISPLEASED TO SEE JONAH HEX AND MYSELF, BUT OUR APPEARANCE MAY HAVE AN EVEN GREATER IMPACT ON THE KILLER.

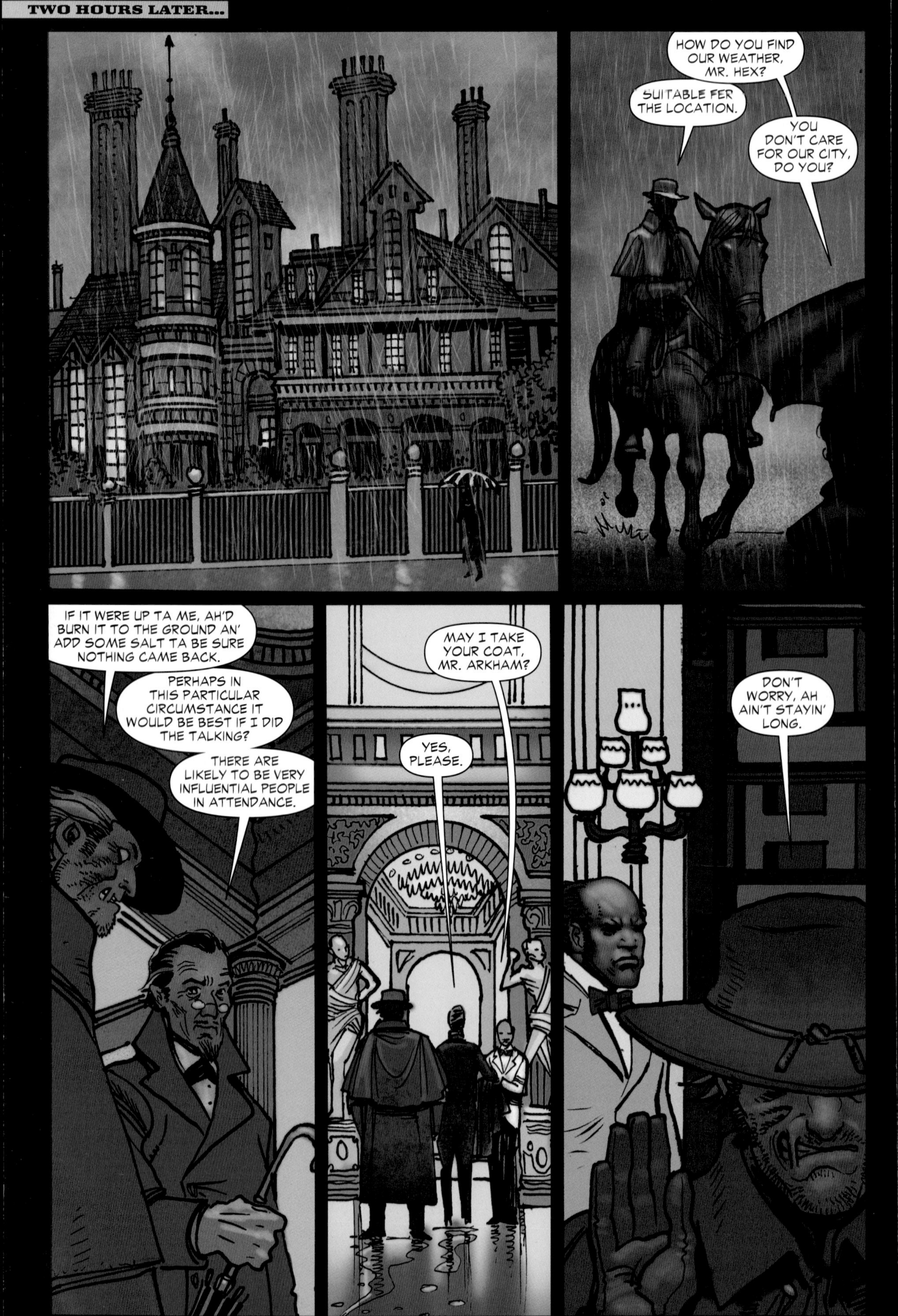
TWO HOURS LATER...
HOW DO YOU FIND OUR WEATHER, MR. HEX?
SUITABLE FER THE LOCATION.
YOU DON'T CARE FOR OUR CITY, DO YOU?
IF IT WERE UP TA ME, AH'D BURN IT TO THE GROUND AN' ADD SOME SALT TA BE SURE NOTHING CAME BACK.
PERHAPS IN THIS PARTICULAR CIRCUMSTANCE IT WOULD BE BEST IF I DID THE TALKING?
THERE ARE LIKELY TO BE VERY INFLUENTIAL PEOPLE IN ATTENDANCE.
MAY I TAKE YOUR COAT, MR. ARKHAM?
YES, PLEASE.
DON'T WORRY, AH AIN'T STAYIN' LONG.

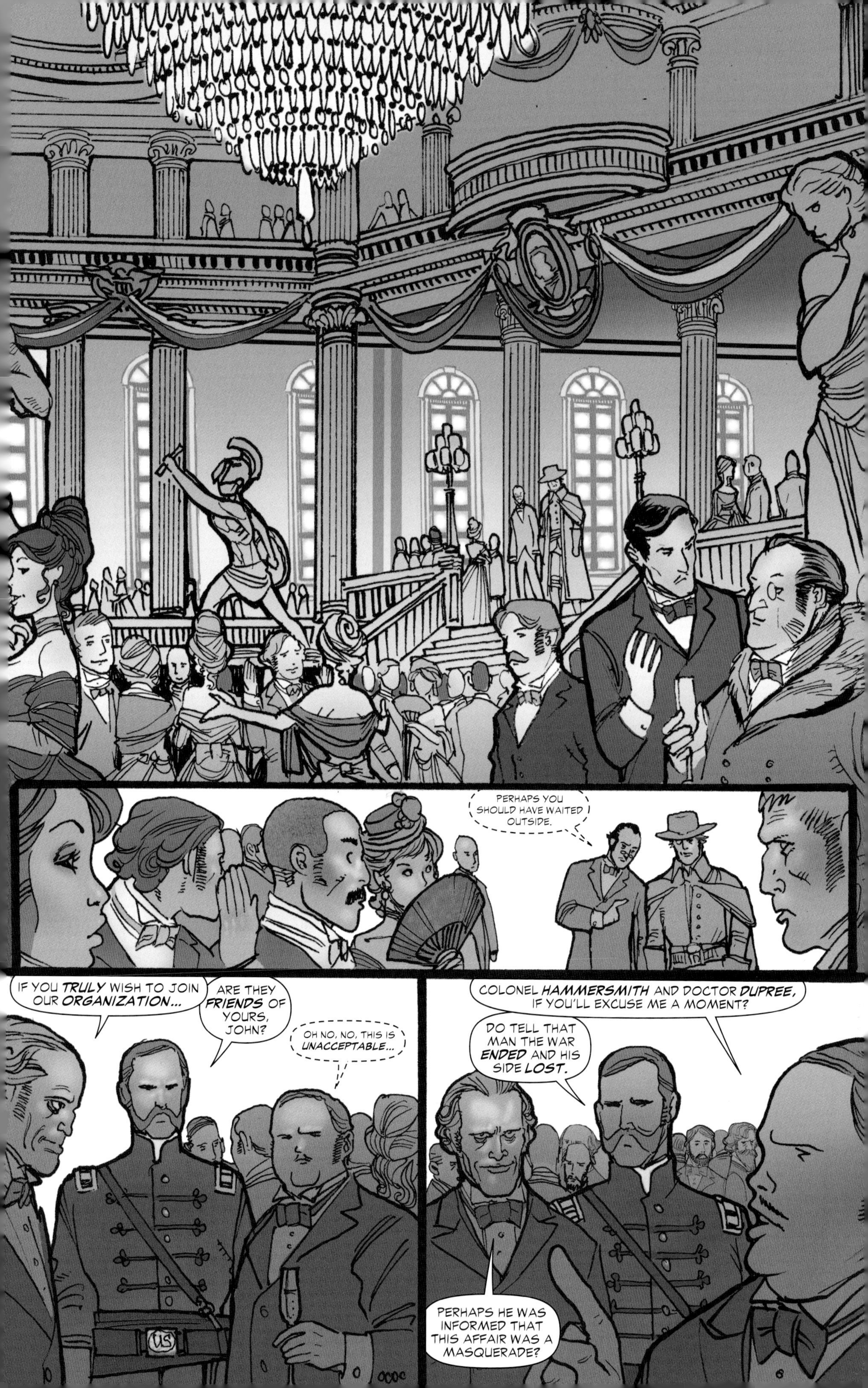
PERHAPS YOU SHOULD HAVE WAITED OUTSIDE.
IF YOU TRULY WISH TO JOIN OUR ORGANIZATION...
ARE THEY FRIENDS OF YOURS, JOHN?
OH NO, NO, THIS IS UNACCEPTABLE...
COLONEL HAMMERSMITH AND DOCTOR DUPREE, IF YOU'LL EXCUSE ME A MOMENT?
DO TELL THAT MAN THE WAR ENDED AND HIS SIDE LOST.
PERHAPS HE WAS INFORMED THAT THIS AFFAIR WAS A MASQUERADE?
US

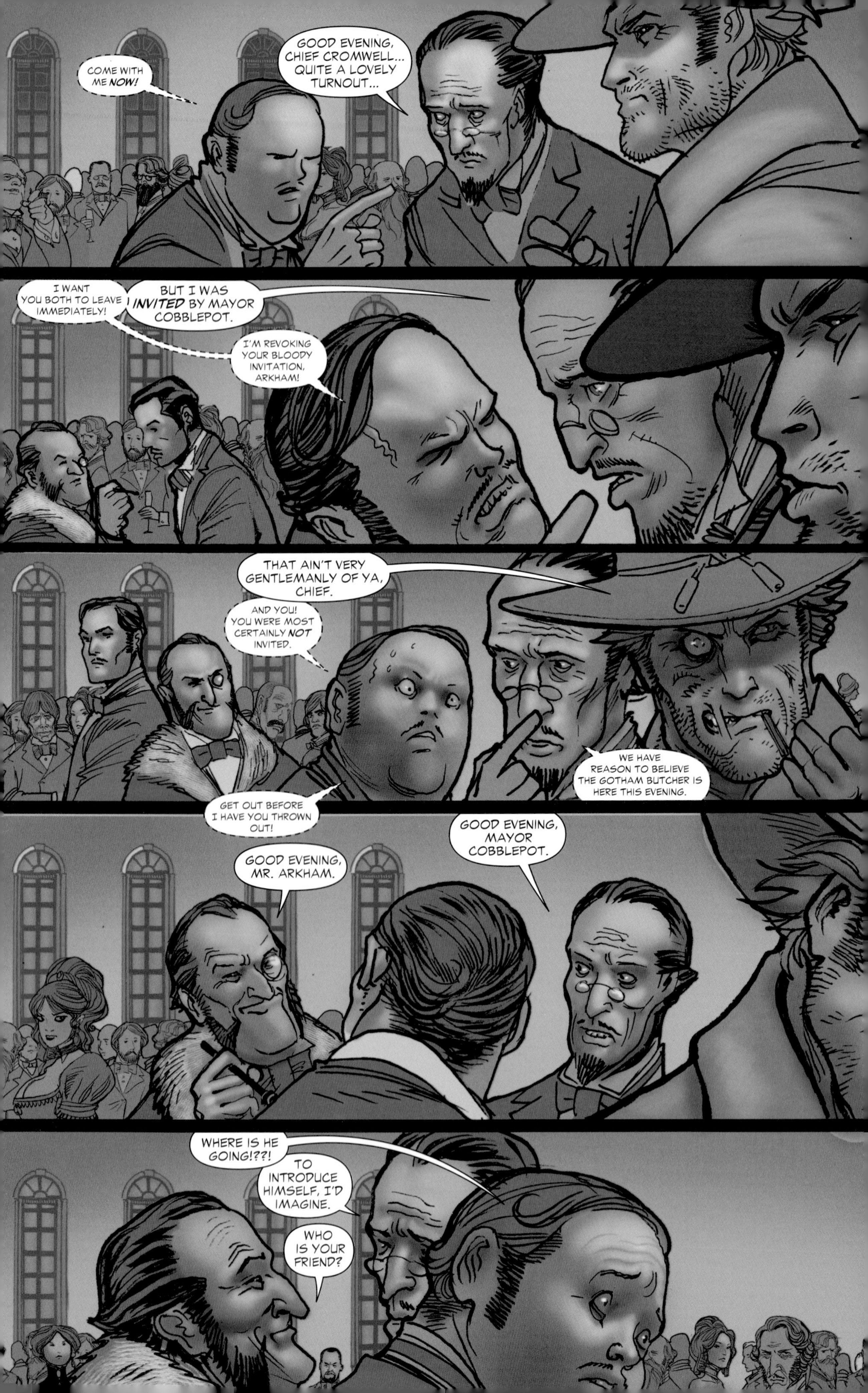
GOOD EVENING, CHIEF CROMWELL... QUITE A LOVELY TURNOUT...
COME WITH ME NOW!
I WANT YOU BOTH TO LEAVE IMMEDIATELY!
BUT I WAS INVITED BY MAYOR COBBLEPOT.
I'M REVOKING YOUR BLOODY INVITATION, ARKHAM!
THAT AIN'T VERY GENTLEMANLY OF YA, CHIEF.
AND YOU! YOU WERE MOST CERTAINLY NOT INVITED.
WE HAVE REASON TO BELIEVE THE GOTHAM BUTCHER IS HERE THIS EVENING.
GET OUT BEFORE I HAVE YOU THROWN OUT!
GOOD EVENING, MR. ARKHAM.
GOOD EVENING, MAYOR COBBLEPOT.
WHERE IS HE GOING!??!
TO INTRODUCE HIMSELF, I'D IMAGINE.
WHO IS YOUR FRIEND?

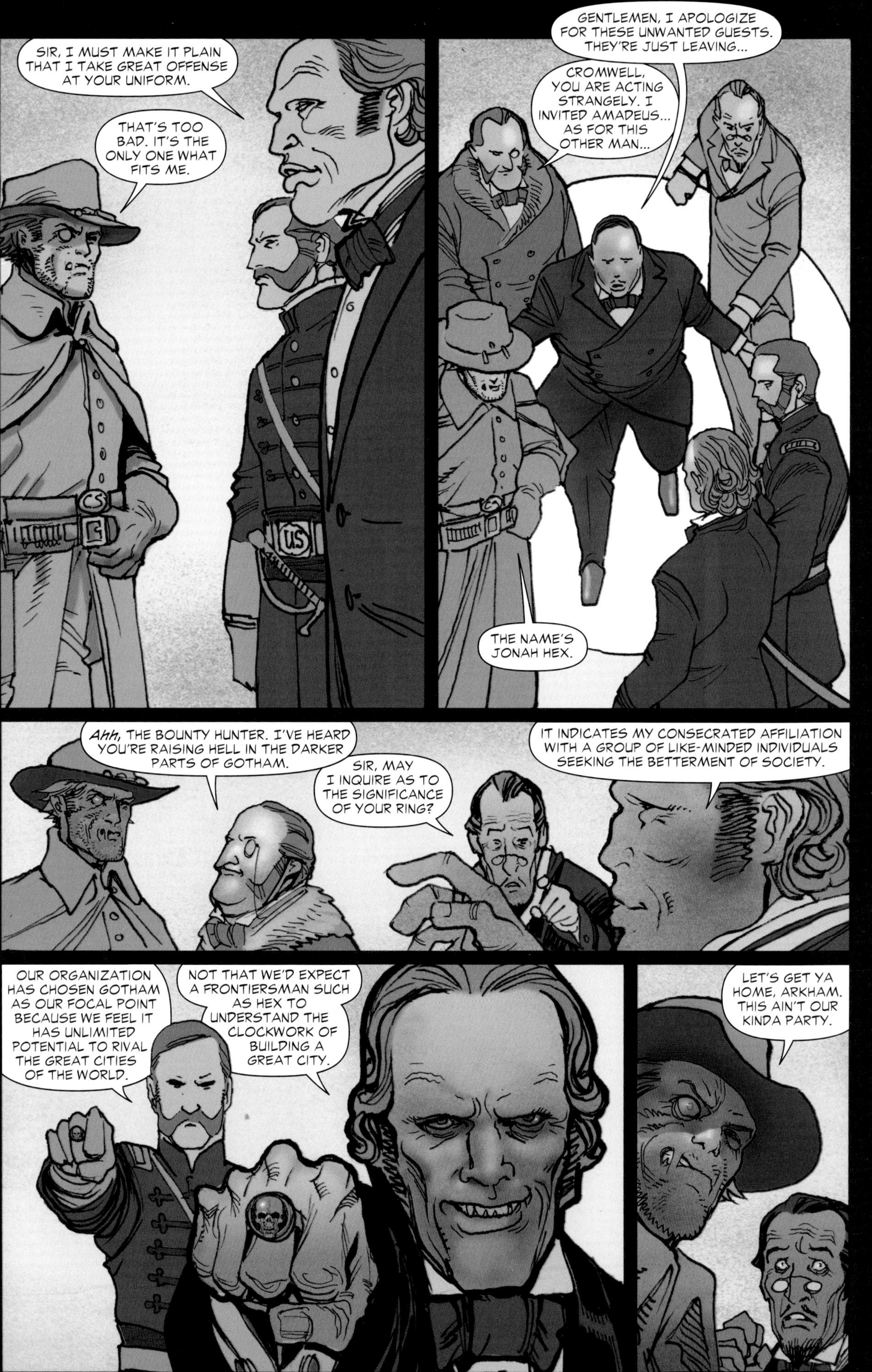
SIR, I MUST MAKE IT PLAIN THAT I TAKE GREAT OFFENSE AT YOUR UNIFORM.
THAT'S TOO BAD. IT'S THE ONLY ONE WHAT FITS ME.
GENTLEMEN, I APOLOGIZE FOR THESE UNWANTED GUESTS. THEY'RE JUST LEAVING...
CROMWELL, YOU ARE ACTING STRANGELY. I INVITED AMADEUS... AS FOR THIS OTHER MAN...
THE NAME'S JONAH HEX.
Ahh, THE BOUNTY HUNTER. I'VE HEARD YOU'RE RAISING HELL IN THE DARKER PARTS OF GOTHAM.
SIR, MAY I INQUIRE AS TO THE SIGNIFICANCE OF YOUR RING?
IT INDICATES MY CONSECRATED AFFILIATION WITH A GROUP OF LIKE-MINDED INDIVIDUALS SEEKING THE BETTERMENT OF SOCIETY.
OUR ORGANIZATION HAS CHOSEN GOTHAM AS OUR FOCAL POINT BECAUSE WE FEEL IT HAS UNLIMITED POTENTIAL TO RIVAL THE GREAT CITIES OF THE WORLD.
NOT THAT WE'D EXPECT A FRONTIERSMAN SUCH AS HEX TO UNDERSTAND THE CLOCKWORK OF BUILDING A GREAT CITY.
LET'S GET YA HOME, ARKHAM. THIS AIN'T OUR KINDA PARTY.

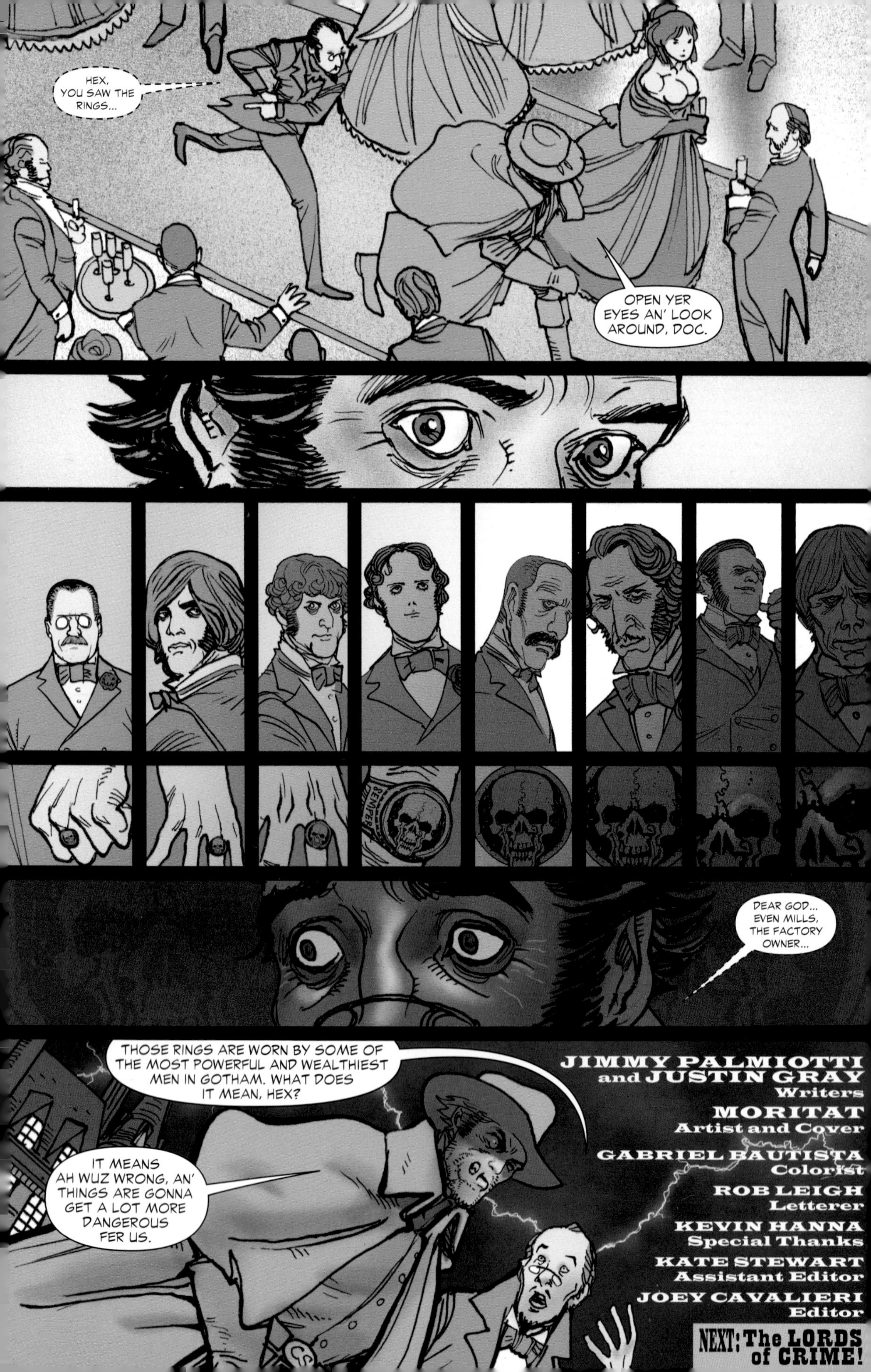
HEX, YOU SAW THE RINGS...
OPEN YER EYES AN' LOOK AROUND, DOC.
DEAR GOD... EVEN MILLS, THE FACTORY OWNER...
THOSE RINGS ARE WORN BY SOME OF THE MOST POWERFUL AND WEALTHIEST MEN IN GOTHAM. WHAT DOES IT MEAN, HEX?
IT MEANS AH WUZ WRONG, AN' THINGS ARE GONNA GET A LOT MORE DANGEROUS FER US.
JIMMY PALMIOTTI and JUSTIN GRAY Writers
MORITAT Artist and Cover
GABRIEL BAUTISTA Colorist
ROB LEIGH Letterer
KEVIN HANNA Special Thanks
KATE STEWART Assistant Editor
JOEY CAVALIERI Editor
NEXT: The LORDS of CRIME!

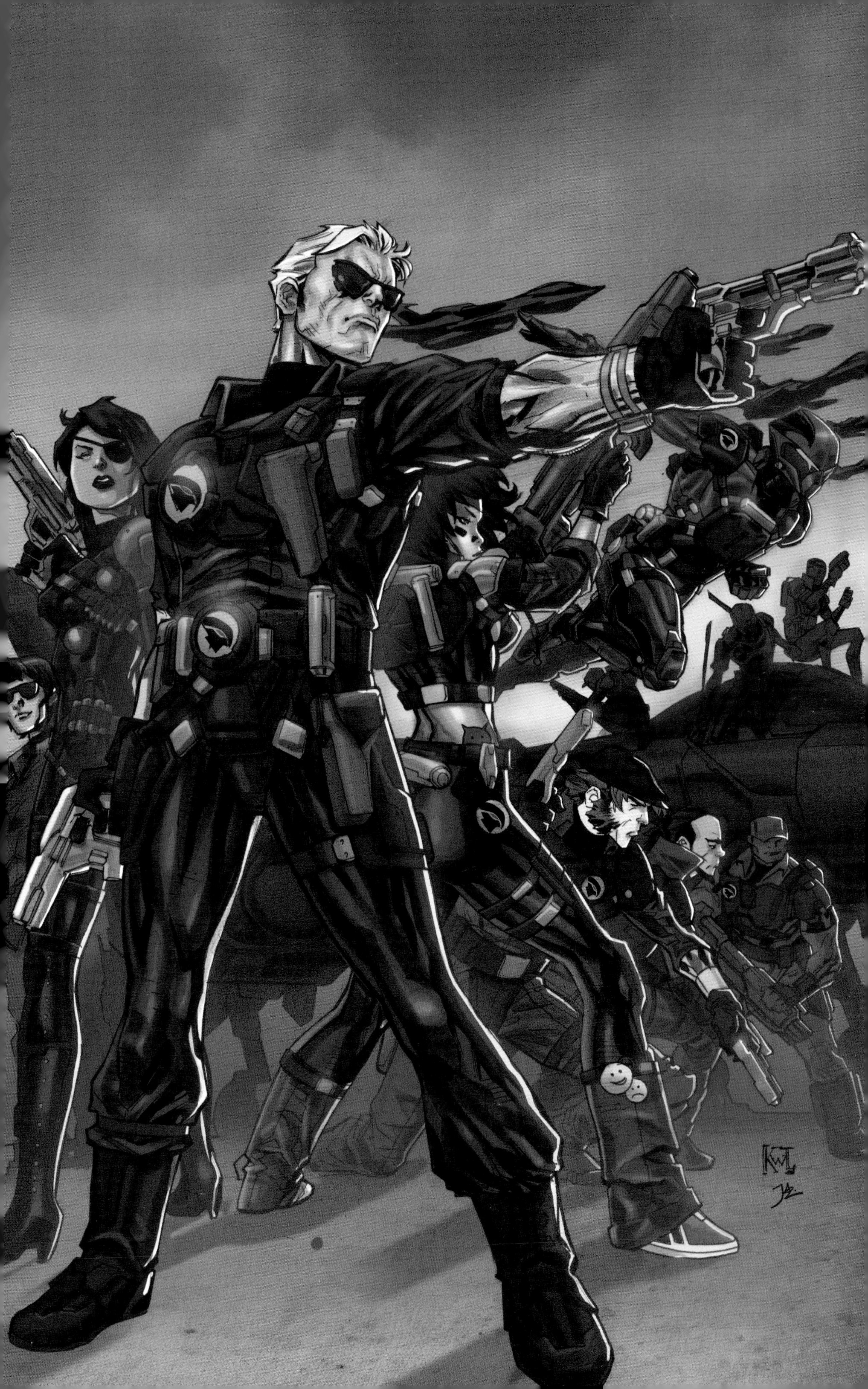

BLACKHAWKS

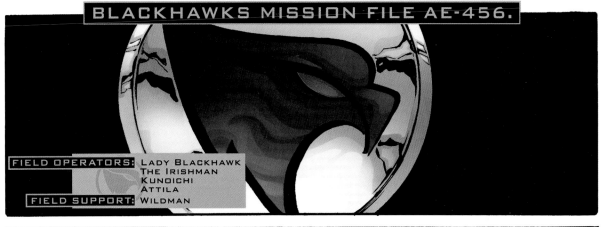

BLACKHAWKS MISSION FILE AE-456.

FIELD OPERATORS: Lady Blackhawk
The Irishman
Kunoichi
Attila
FIELD SUPPORT: Wildman

LOCATION: AYAGUZ, KAZAKHSTAN (47° 58' 17 N 80° 26' 21 E)

AT 17:43 GMT, EIGHT MEMBERS OF A PREVIOUSLY UNKNOWN GROUP STORMED THE LOCAL AIRPORT AND SEIZED IT, TAKING HOSTAGES.

USE OF CONVEYANCE VEHICLES AND PERSONAL WEAPONRY PROHIBITED BY THE METAPOWERS ACT CONFIRMED BY SECURITY IMAGES AND SATELLITE SURVEILLANCE.

BLACKHAWK TEAM INSERTION AT 19:25.

OPERATION WAS TO REMAIN COVERT.

NO TIME TO EXPLAIN...

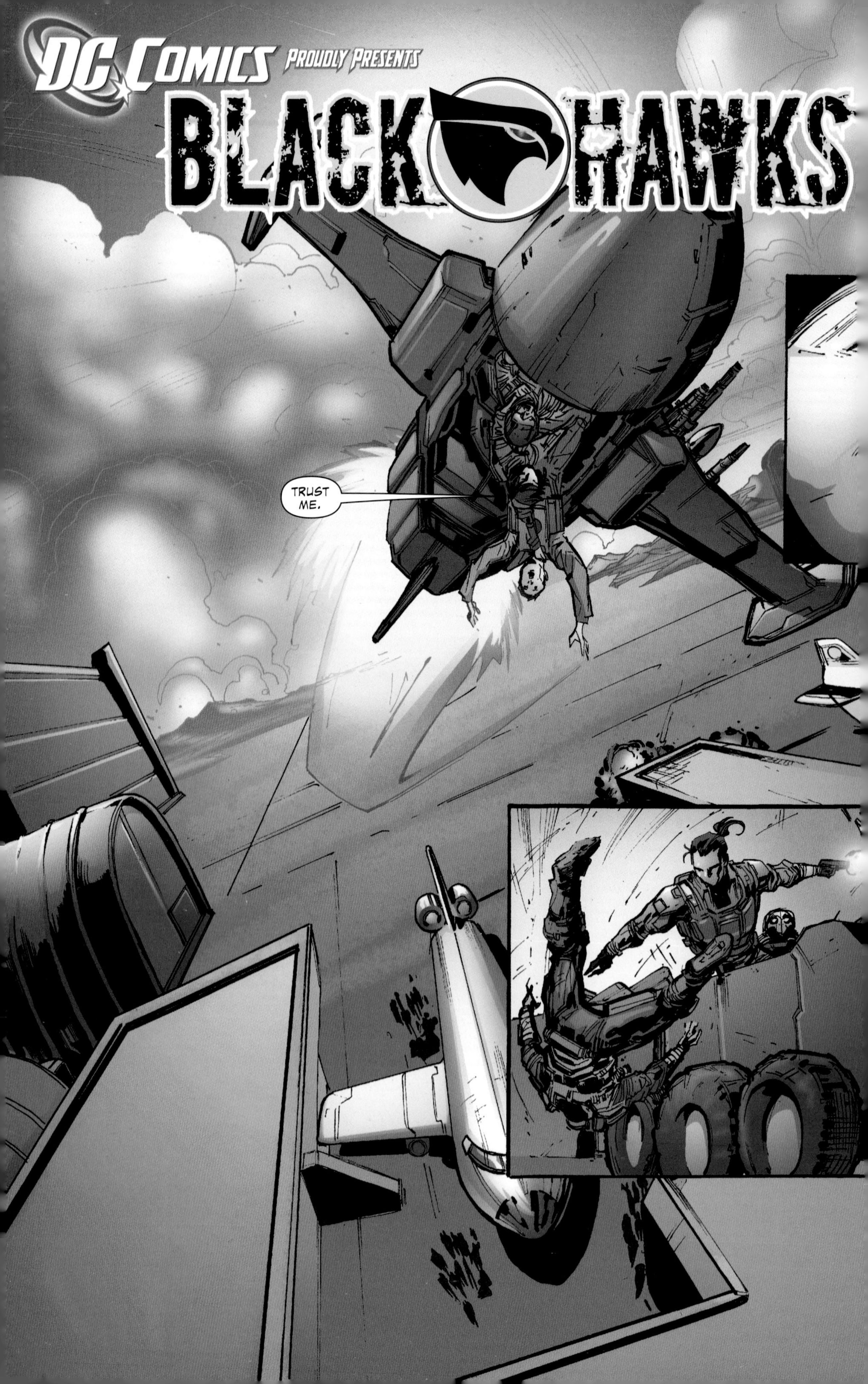
DC COMICS PROUDLY PRESENTS
BLACKHAWKS
TRUST ME.

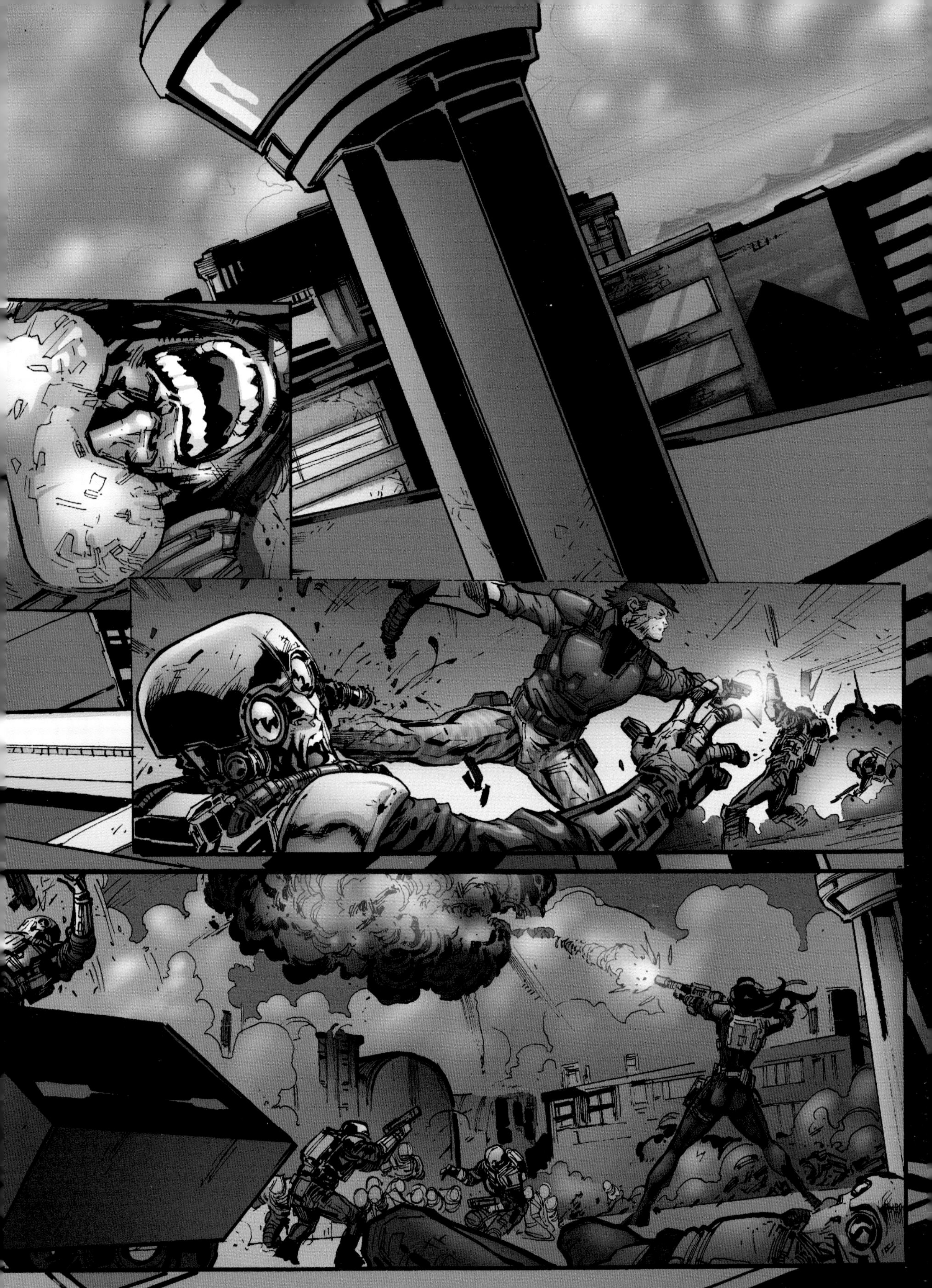

MIKE COSTA
WRITER

GRAHAM NOLAN
LAYOUTS

KEN LASHLEY
FINISHER & COVER

GUY MAJOR
COLORIST

ROB LEIGH
LETTERER

JANELLE ASSELIN
ASSOC. EDITOR

MIKE MARTS
EDITOR

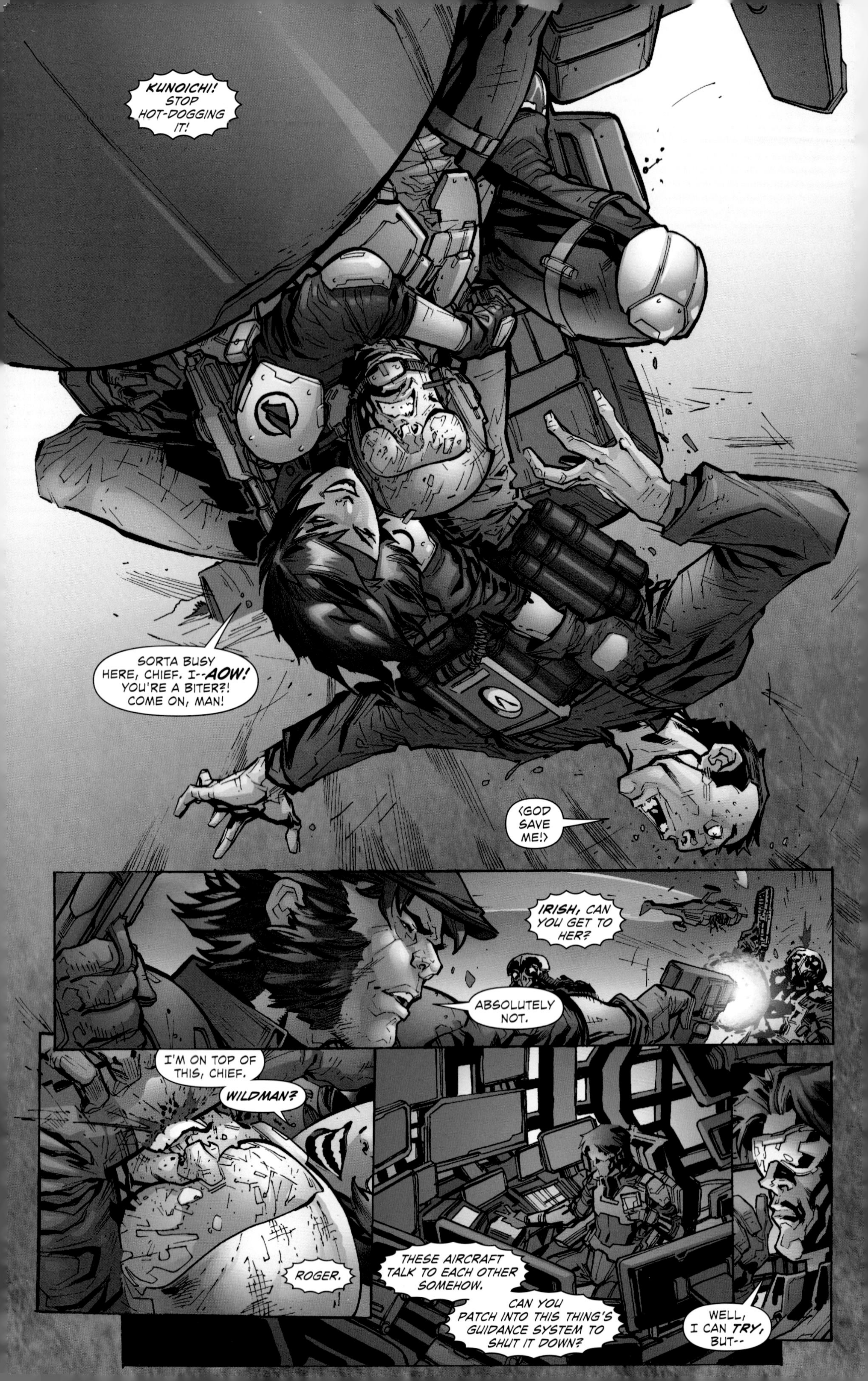
KUNOICHI! STOP HOT-DOGGING IT!
SORTA BUSY HERE, CHIEF. I--AOW! YOU'RE A BITER?! COME ON, MAN!
‹GOD SAVE ME!›
IRISH, CAN YOU GET TO HER?
ABSOLUTELY NOT.
I'M ON TOP OF THIS, CHIEF.
WILDMAN?
ROGER.
THESE AIRCRAFT TALK TO EACH OTHER SOMEHOW.
CAN YOU PATCH INTO THIS THING'S GUIDANCE SYSTEM TO SHUT IT DOWN?
WELL, I CAN TRY, BUT--

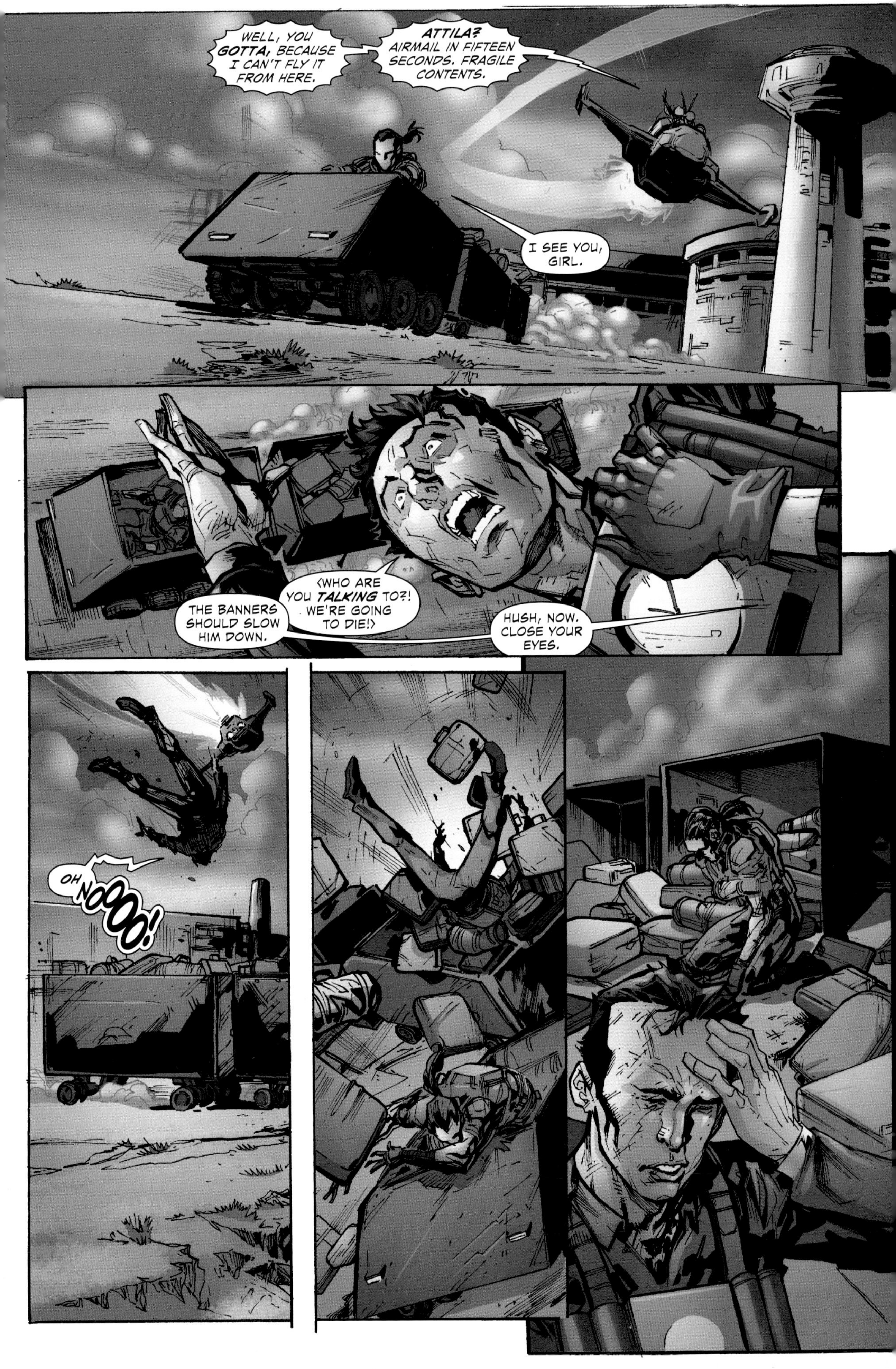
WELL, YOU GOTTA, BECAUSE I CAN'T FLY IT FROM HERE.
ATTILA? AIRMAIL IN FIFTEEN SECONDS. FRAGILE CONTENTS.
I SEE YOU, GIRL.
THE BANNERS SHOULD SLOW HIM DOWN.
<WHO ARE YOU TALKING TO?! WE'RE GOING TO DIE!>
HUSH, NOW. CLOSE YOUR EYES.
OH NOOOO!

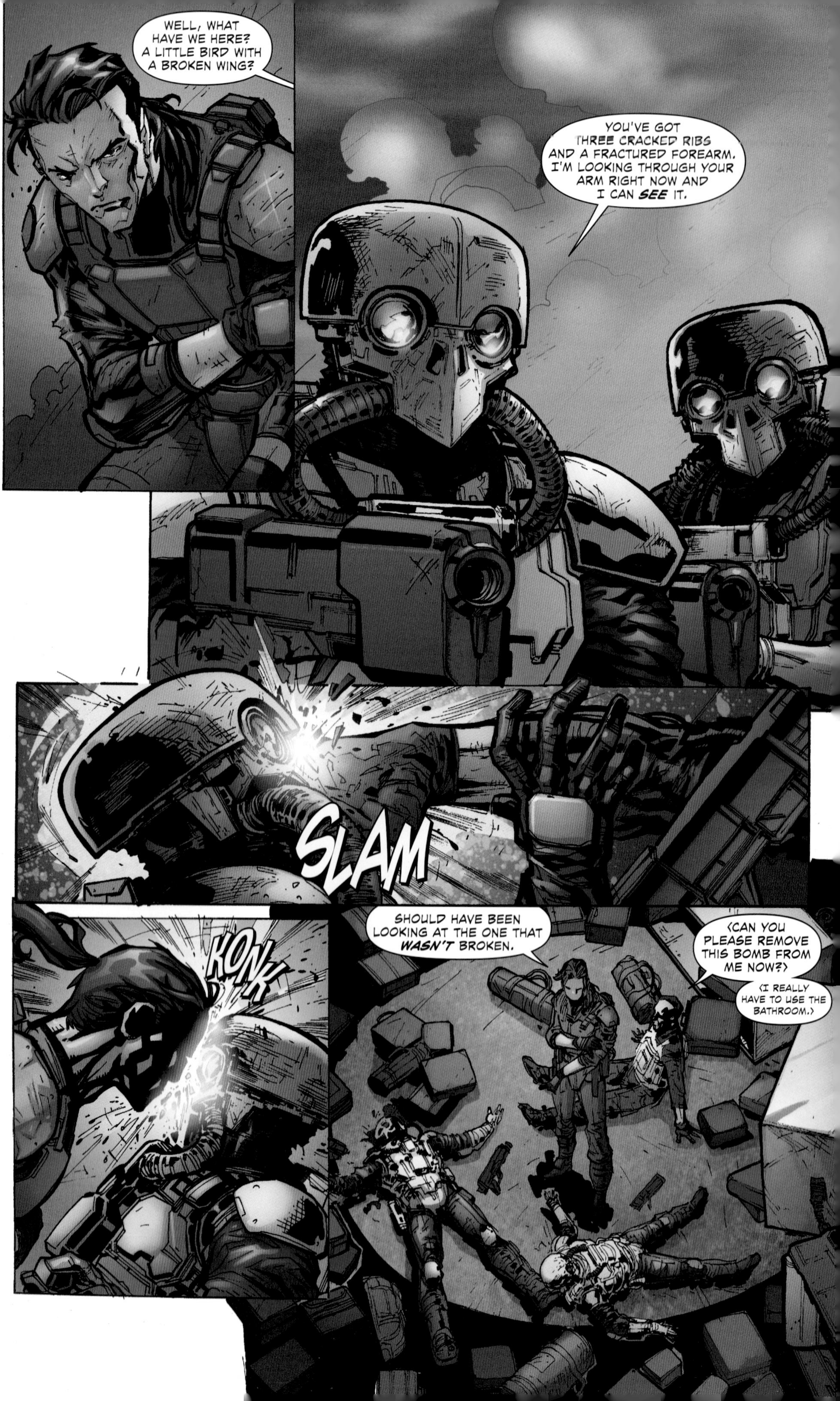
WELL, WHAT HAVE WE HERE? A LITTLE BIRD WITH A BROKEN WING?
YOU'VE GOT THREE CRACKED RIBS AND A FRACTURED FOREARM. I'M LOOKING THROUGH YOUR ARM RIGHT NOW AND I CAN ***SEE*** IT.
SLAM
KONK
SHOULD HAVE BEEN LOOKING AT THE ONE THAT ***WASN'T*** BROKEN.
<CAN YOU PLEASE REMOVE THIS BOMB FROM ME NOW?>
<I REALLY HAVE TO USE THE BATHROOM.>

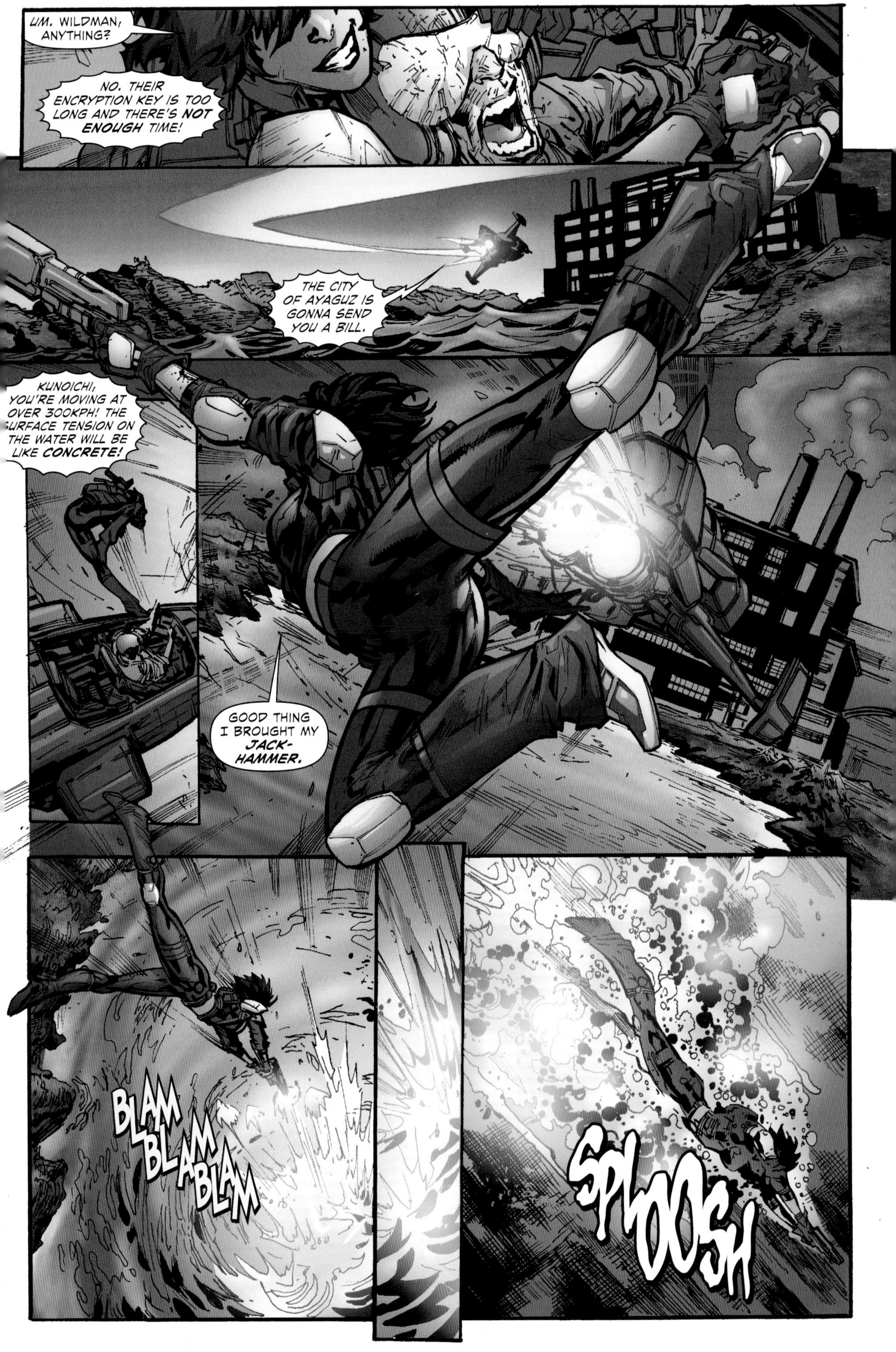

UM. WILDMAN, ANYTHING?
NO. THEIR ENCRYPTION KEY IS TOO LONG AND THERE'S **NOT ENOUGH** TIME!
THE CITY OF AYAGUZ IS GONNA SEND YOU A BILL.
KUNOICHI, YOU'RE MOVING AT OVER 300KPH! THE SURFACE TENSION ON THE WATER WILL BE LIKE **CONCRETE!**
GOOD THING I BROUGHT MY ***JACK-HAMMER.***
BLAM BLAM BLAM BLAM
SPLOOSH

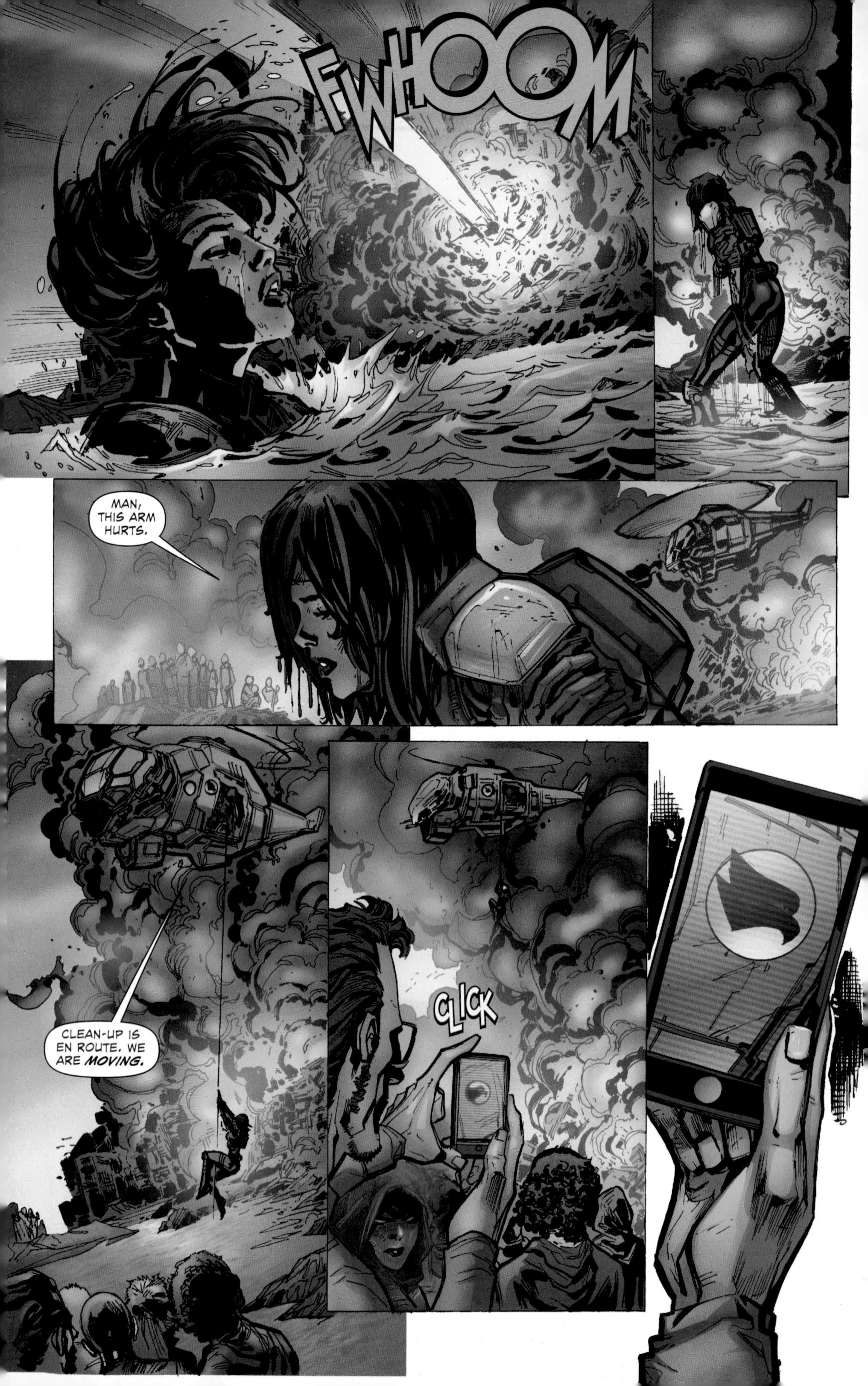
FWHOOM
MAN, THIS ARM HURTS.
CLEAN-UP IS EN ROUTE. WE ARE *MOVING.*
CLICK

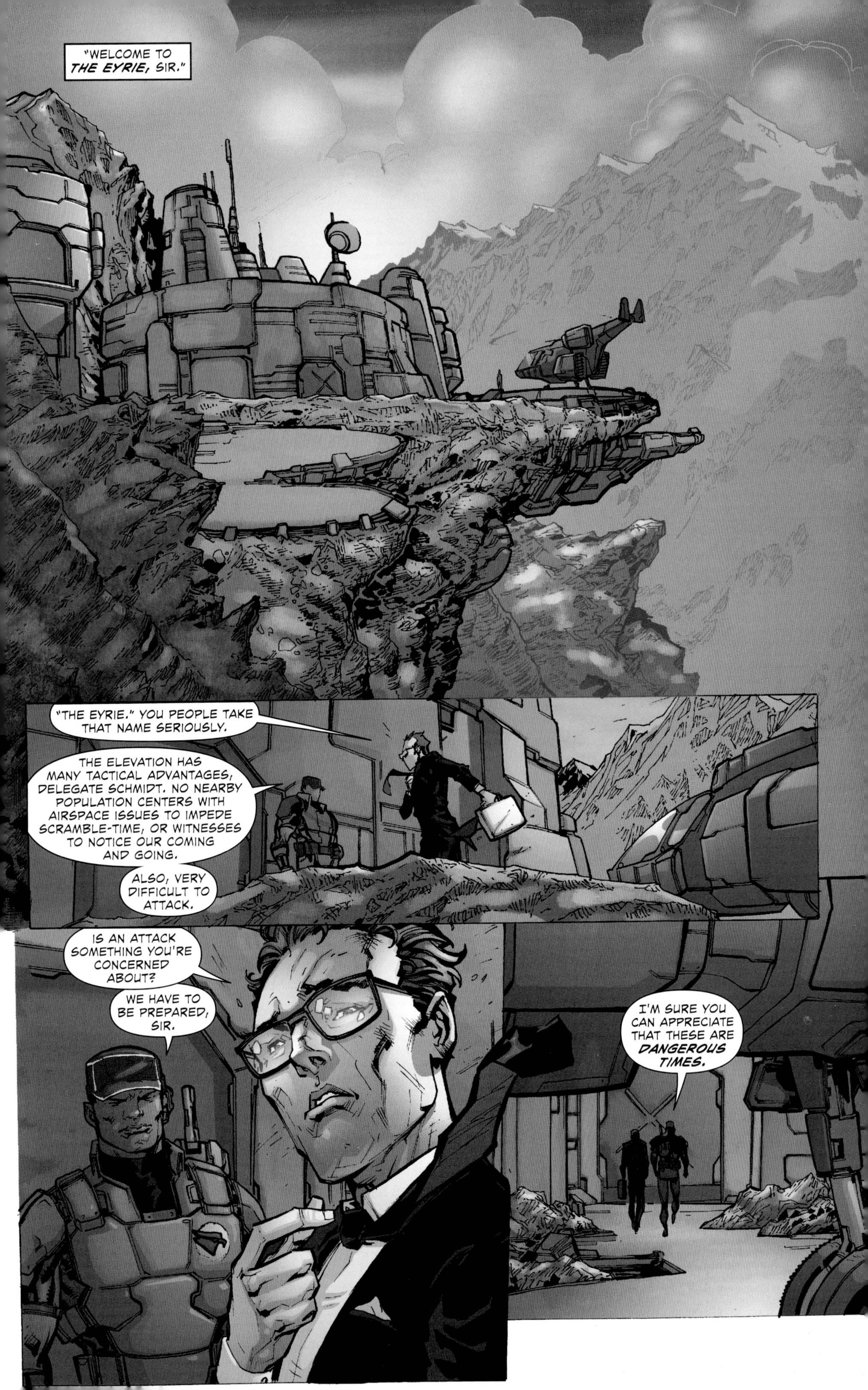
"WELCOME TO *THE EYRIE,* SIR."
"THE EYRIE." YOU PEOPLE TAKE THAT NAME SERIOUSLY.
THE ELEVATION HAS MANY TACTICAL ADVANTAGES, DELEGATE SCHMIDT. NO NEARBY POPULATION CENTERS WITH AIRSPACE ISSUES TO IMPEDE SCRAMBLE-TIME, OR WITNESSES TO NOTICE OUR COMING AND GOING.
ALSO, VERY DIFFICULT TO ATTACK.
IS AN ATTACK SOMETHING YOU'RE CONCERNED ABOUT?
WE HAVE TO BE PREPARED, SIR.
I'M SURE YOU CAN APPRECIATE THAT THESE ARE *DANGEROUS TIMES.*

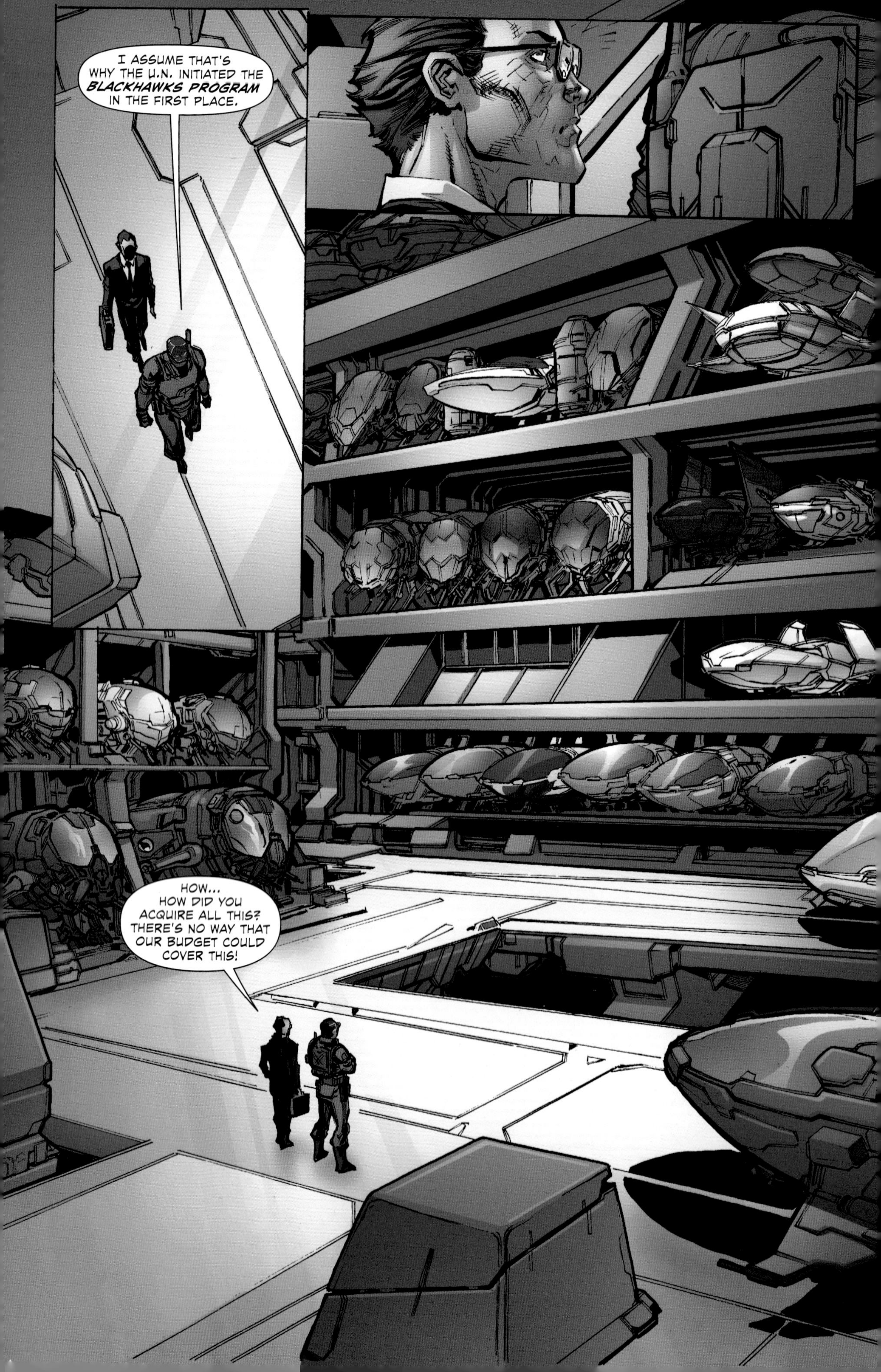
I ASSUME THAT'S WHY THE U.N. INITIATED THE ***BLACKHAWKS PROGRAM*** IN THE FIRST PLACE.
HOW... HOW DID YOU ACQUIRE ALL THIS? THERE'S NO WAY THAT OUR BUDGET COULD COVER THIS!

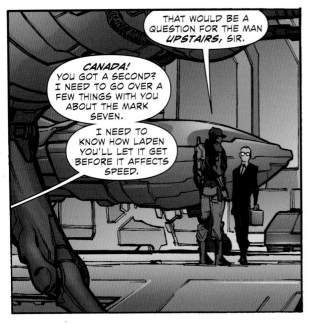

THAT WOULD BE A QUESTION FOR THE MAN *UPSTAIRS*, SIR.

CANADA! YOU GOT A SECOND? I NEED TO GO OVER A FEW THINGS WITH YOU ABOUT THE MARK SEVEN.

I NEED TO KNOW HOW LADEN YOU'LL LET IT GET BEFORE IT AFFECTS SPEED.

SIR, THIS IS *THE IRISHMAN*. HE'S IN CHARGE OF ALL THE SPECIAL ARMAMENTS AND ARTILLERY.

IRISH, I'M GIVING THE DELEGATE A TOUR RIGHT NOW. I'LL HAVE TO TALK TO YOU LATER.

"THE IRISHMAN?" THAT'S RATHER...STEREOTYPICAL, ISN'T IT? PLUS, THAT ACCENT SOUNDS *RUSSIAN*.

I'M FROM THE *UKRAINE*.

CORPORAL COSTELLO'S PARENTS HAD INTERNATIONAL BUSINESS IN THE *USSR* AND HE WAS BORN THERE.

HE GOT THAT NICKNAME FROM HIS BROTHERS IN THE *SPETSNATZ* BEFORE HE CAME HERE. THEY WEREN'T USED TO THE *RED HAIR*.

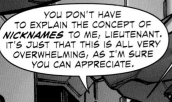

NICKNAMES ARE PART OF OUR WAY OF LIFE UP HERE. FOR INSTANCE, I'M ACTUALLY FROM ATLANTA. BUT THEY CALL ME "CANADA" BECAUSE, ONE TIME AT A BAR IN CALGARY THERE WAS THIS...

...WELL, MAYBE I SHOULDN'T TELL THIS STORY...

YOU DON'T HAVE TO EXPLAIN THE CONCEPT OF *NICKNAMES* TO ME, LIEUTENANT. IT'S JUST THAT THIS IS ALL VERY OVERWHELMING, AS I'M SURE YOU CAN APPRECIATE.

OF COURSE, SIR.

LET'S JUST GO MEET *LINCOLN*. HE'S THE ONE I WANT EXPLANATIONS FROM.

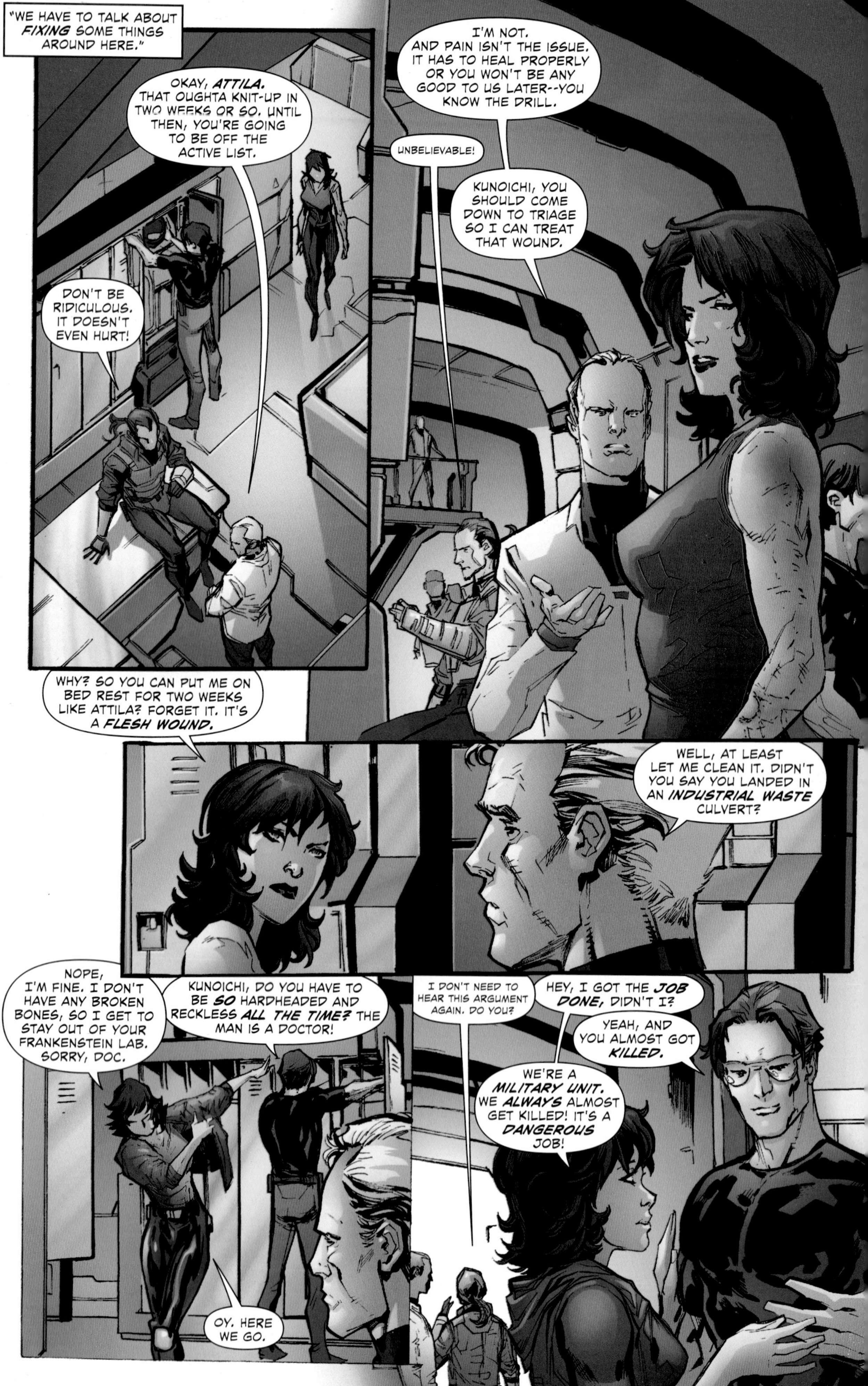
"WE HAVE TO TALK ABOUT FIXING SOME THINGS AROUND HERE."
OKAY, ATTILA. THAT OUGHTA KNIT-UP IN TWO WEEKS OR SO. UNTIL THEN, YOU'RE GOING TO BE OFF THE ACTIVE LIST.
DON'T BE RIDICULOUS. IT DOESN'T EVEN HURT!
I'M NOT. AND PAIN ISN'T THE ISSUE. IT HAS TO HEAL PROPERLY OR YOU WON'T BE ANY GOOD TO US LATER--YOU KNOW THE DRILL.
UNBELIEVABLE!
KUNOICHI, YOU SHOULD COME DOWN TO TRIAGE SO I CAN TREAT THAT WOUND.
WHY? SO YOU CAN PUT ME ON BED REST FOR TWO WEEKS LIKE ATTILA? FORGET IT. IT'S A FLESH WOUND.
WELL, AT LEAST LET ME CLEAN IT. DIDN'T YOU SAY YOU LANDED IN AN INDUSTRIAL WASTE CULVERT?
NOPE, I'M FINE. I DON'T HAVE ANY BROKEN BONES, SO I GET TO STAY OUT OF YOUR FRANKENSTEIN LAB. SORRY, DOC.
KUNOICHI, DO YOU HAVE TO BE SO HARDHEADED AND RECKLESS ALL THE TIME? THE MAN IS A DOCTOR!
OY. HERE WE GO.
I DON'T NEED TO HEAR THIS ARGUMENT AGAIN. DO YOU?
HEY, I GOT THE JOB DONE, DIDN'T I?
YEAH, AND YOU ALMOST GOT KILLED.
WE'RE A MILITARY UNIT. WE ALWAYS ALMOST GET KILLED! IT'S A DANGEROUS JOB!

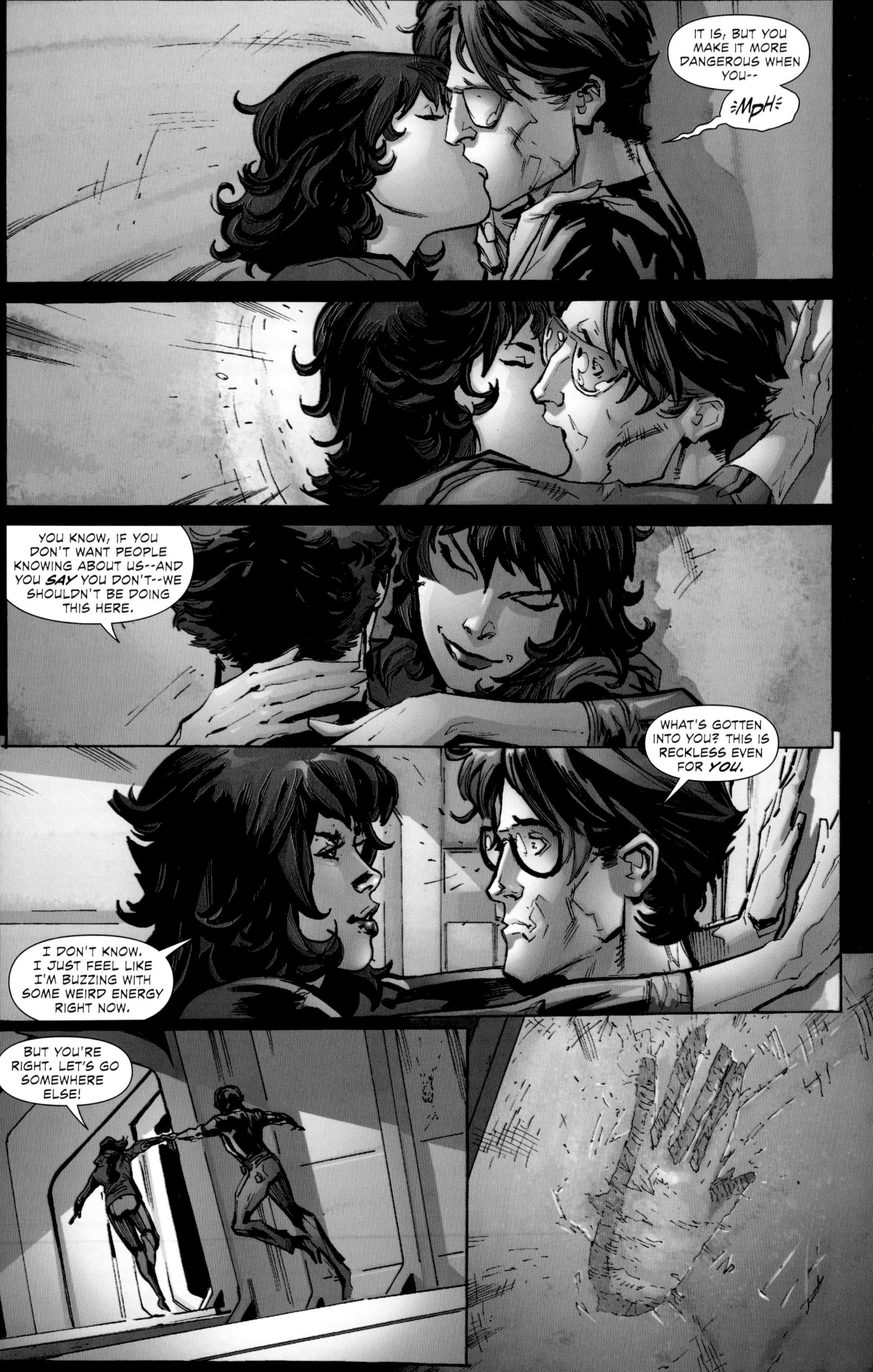
IT IS, BUT YOU MAKE IT MORE DANGEROUS WHEN YOU--
MPH
YOU KNOW, IF YOU DON'T WANT PEOPLE KNOWING ABOUT US--AND YOU SAY YOU DON'T--WE SHOULDN'T BE DOING THIS HERE.
WHAT'S GOTTEN INTO YOU? THIS IS RECKLESS EVEN FOR YOU.
I DON'T KNOW. I JUST FEEL LIKE I'M BUZZING WITH SOME WEIRD ENERGY RIGHT NOW.
BUT YOU'RE RIGHT. LET'S GO SOMEWHERE ELSE!

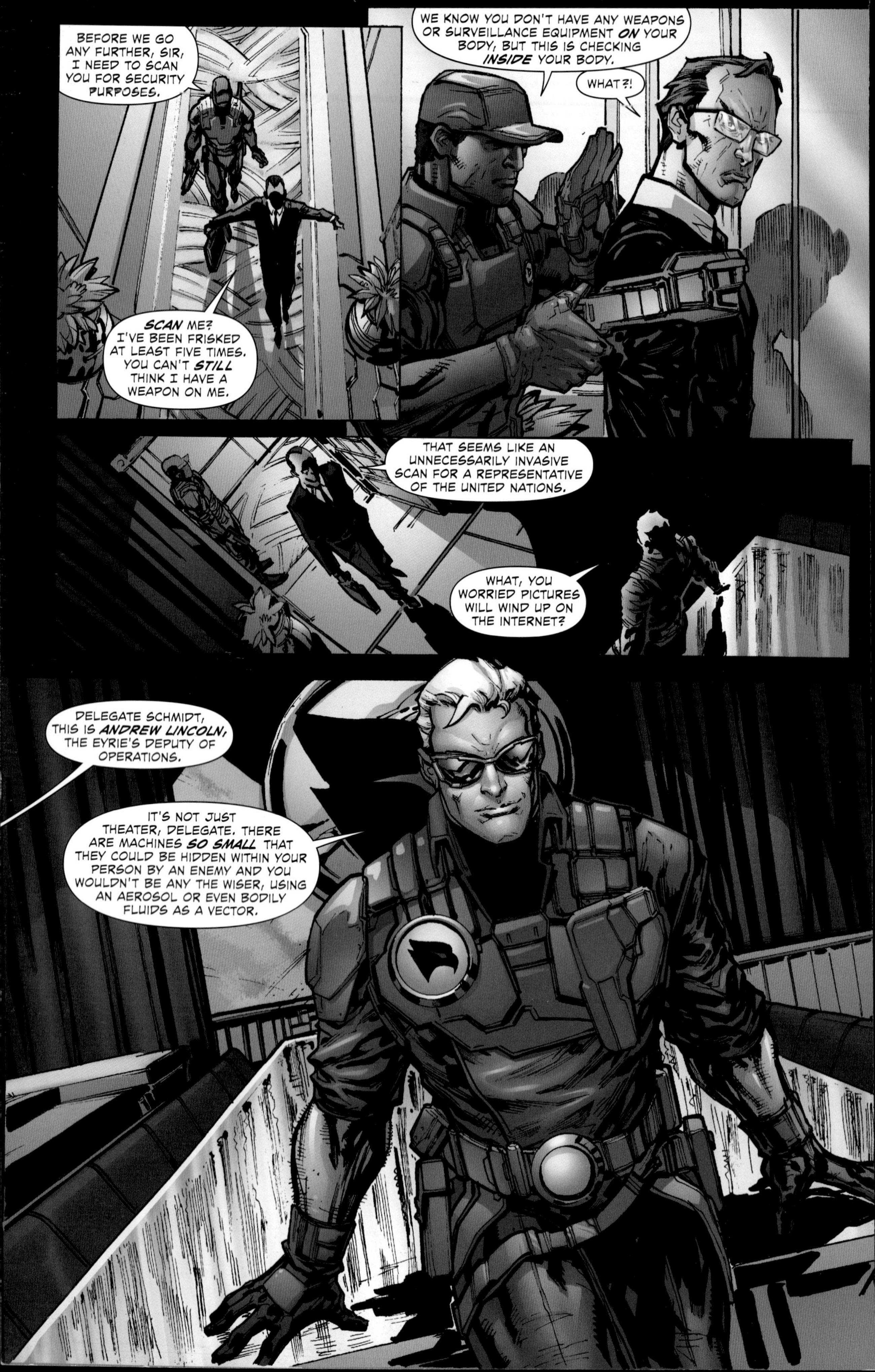

BEFORE WE GO ANY FURTHER, SIR, I NEED TO SCAN YOU FOR SECURITY PURPOSES.
SCAN ME? I'VE BEEN FRISKED AT LEAST FIVE TIMES. YOU CAN'T STILL THINK I HAVE A WEAPON ON ME.
WE KNOW YOU DON'T HAVE ANY WEAPONS OR SURVEILLANCE EQUIPMENT ON YOUR BODY, BUT THIS IS CHECKING INSIDE YOUR BODY.
WHAT?!
THAT SEEMS LIKE AN UNNECESSARILY INVASIVE SCAN FOR A REPRESENTATIVE OF THE UNITED NATIONS.
WHAT, YOU WORRIED PICTURES WILL WIND UP ON THE INTERNET?
DELEGATE SCHMIDT, THIS IS ANDREW LINCOLN, THE EYRIE'S DEPUTY OF OPERATIONS.
IT'S NOT JUST THEATER, DELEGATE. THERE ARE MACHINES SO SMALL THAT THEY COULD BE HIDDEN WITHIN YOUR PERSON BY AN ENEMY AND YOU WOULDN'T BE ANY THE WISER, USING AN AEROSOL OR EVEN BODILY FLUIDS AS A VECTOR.

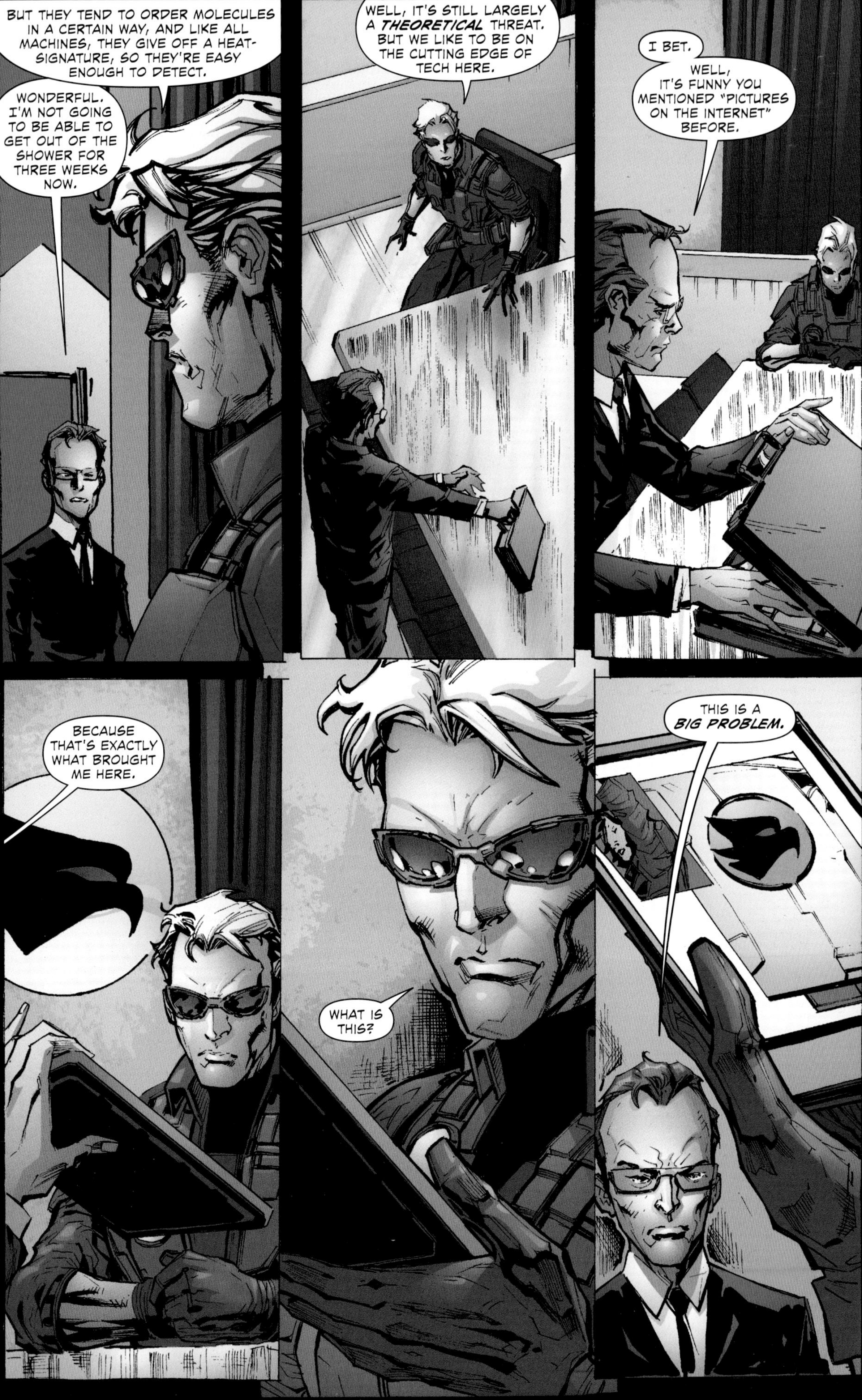
BUT THEY TEND TO ORDER MOLECULES IN A CERTAIN WAY, AND LIKE ALL MACHINES, THEY GIVE OFF A HEAT-SIGNATURE, SO THEY'RE EASY ENOUGH TO DETECT.
WONDERFUL. I'M NOT GOING TO BE ABLE TO GET OUT OF THE SHOWER FOR THREE WEEKS NOW.
WELL, IT'S STILL LARGELY A THEORETICAL THREAT. BUT WE LIKE TO BE ON THE CUTTING EDGE OF TECH HERE.
I BET.
WELL, IT'S FUNNY YOU MENTIONED "PICTURES ON THE INTERNET" BEFORE.
BECAUSE THAT'S EXACTLY WHAT BROUGHT ME HERE.
WHAT IS THIS?
THIS IS A BIG PROBLEM.

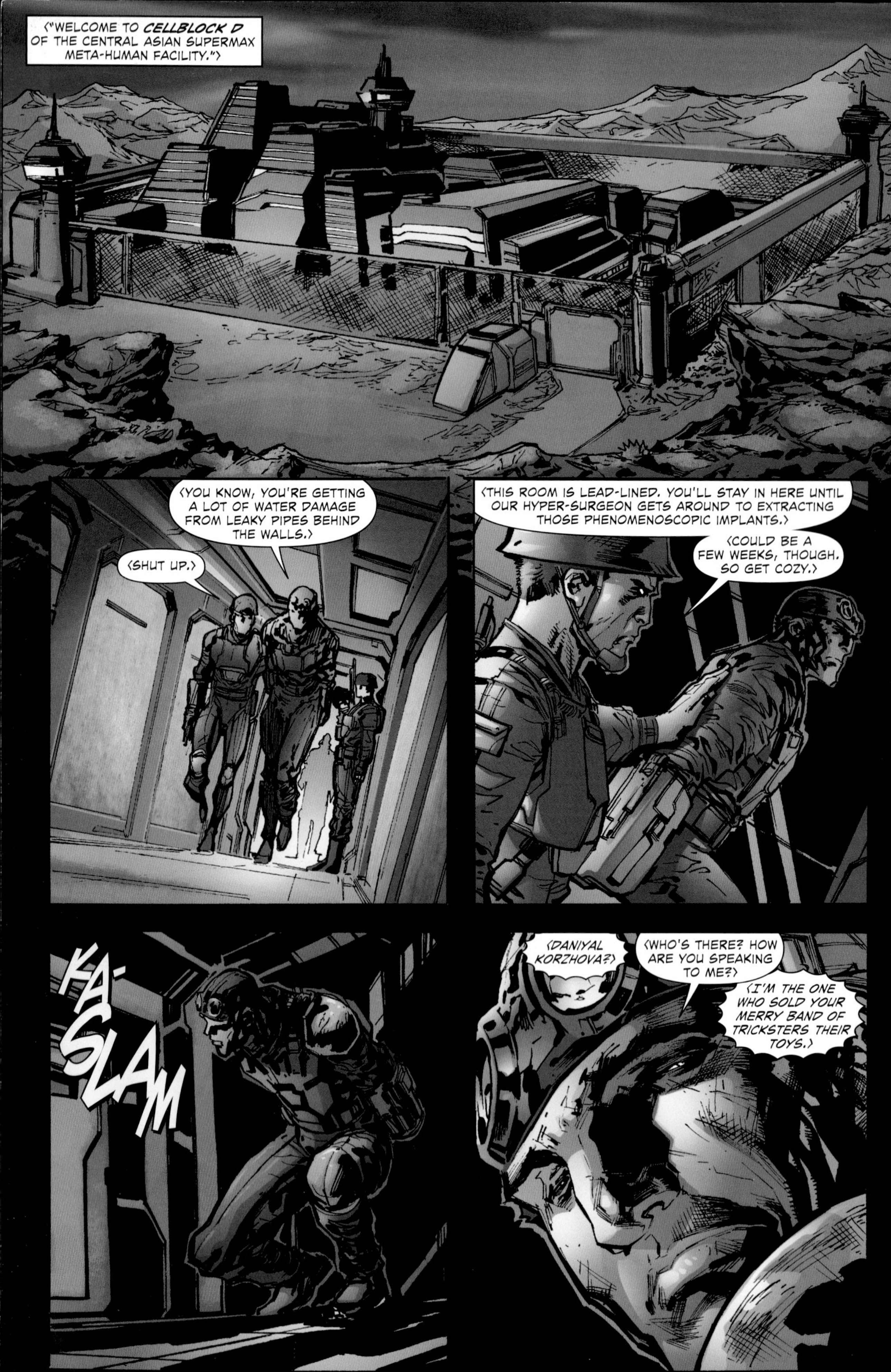
⟨"WELCOME TO CELLBLOCK D OF THE CENTRAL ASIAN SUPERMAX META-HUMAN FACILITY."⟩
⟨YOU KNOW, YOU'RE GETTING A LOT OF WATER DAMAGE FROM LEAKY PIPES BEHIND THE WALLS.⟩
⟨SHUT UP.⟩
⟨THIS ROOM IS LEAD-LINED. YOU'LL STAY IN HERE UNTIL OUR HYPER-SURGEON GETS AROUND TO EXTRACTING THOSE PHENOMENOSCOPIC IMPLANTS.⟩
⟨COULD BE A FEW WEEKS, THOUGH. SO GET COZY.⟩
KA-SLAM
⟨DANIYAL KORZHOVA?⟩
⟨WHO'S THERE? HOW ARE YOU SPEAKING TO ME?⟩
⟨I'M THE ONE WHO SOLD YOUR MERRY BAND OF TRICKSTERS THEIR TOYS.⟩

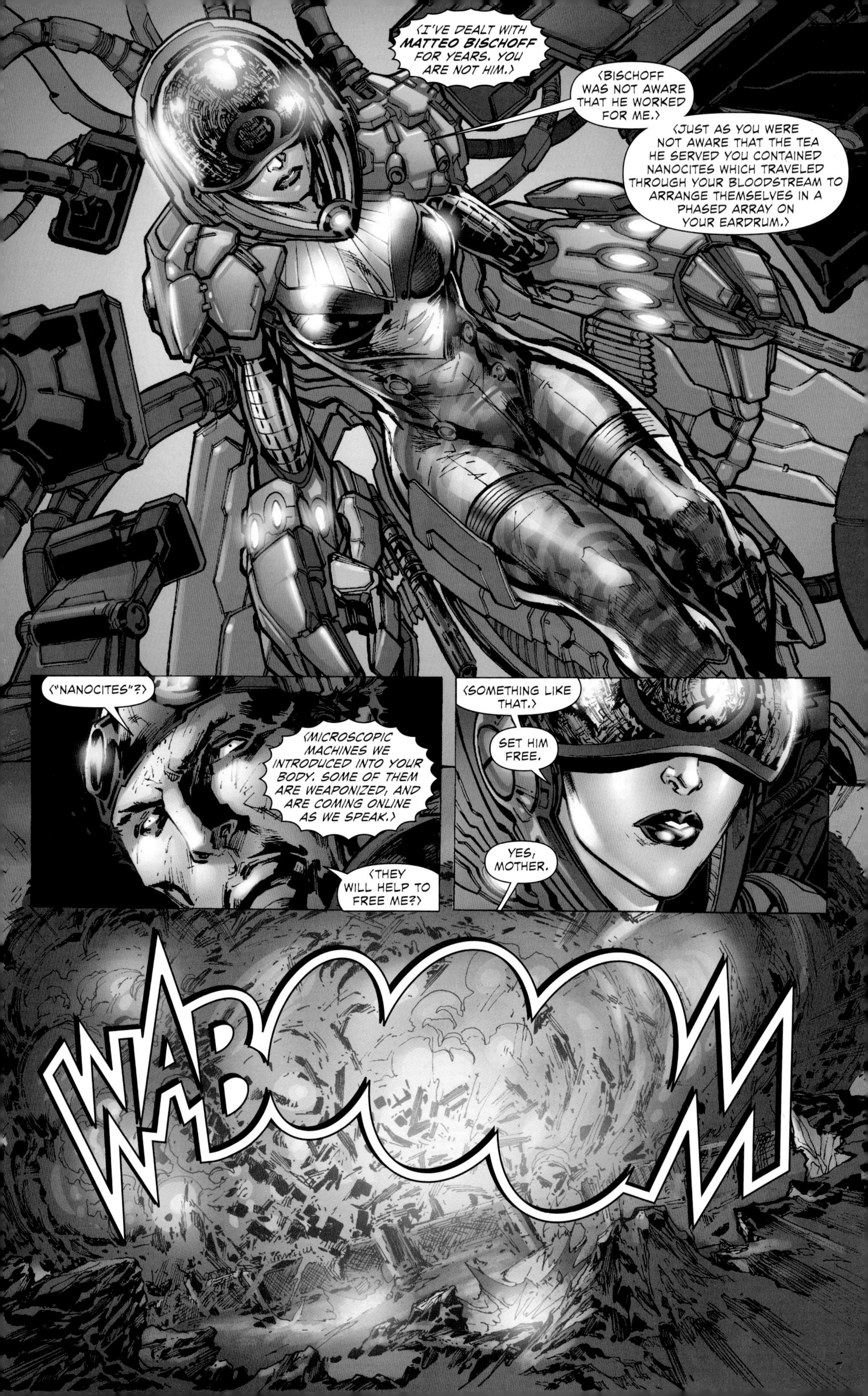

‹I'VE DEALT WITH MATTEO BISCHOFF FOR YEARS. YOU ARE NOT HIM.›
‹BISCHOFF WAS NOT AWARE THAT HE WORKED FOR ME.›
‹JUST AS YOU WERE NOT AWARE THAT THE TEA HE SERVED YOU CONTAINED NANOCITES WHICH TRAVELED THROUGH YOUR BLOODSTREAM TO ARRANGE THEMSELVES IN A PHASED ARRAY ON YOUR EARDRUM.›
‹"NANOCITES"?›
‹MICROSCOPIC MACHINES WE INTRODUCED INTO YOUR BODY. SOME OF THEM ARE WEAPONIZED, AND ARE COMING ONLINE AS WE SPEAK.›
‹THEY WILL HELP TO FREE ME?›
‹SOMETHING LIKE THAT.›
SET HIM FREE.
YES, MOTHER.
WABOOOM

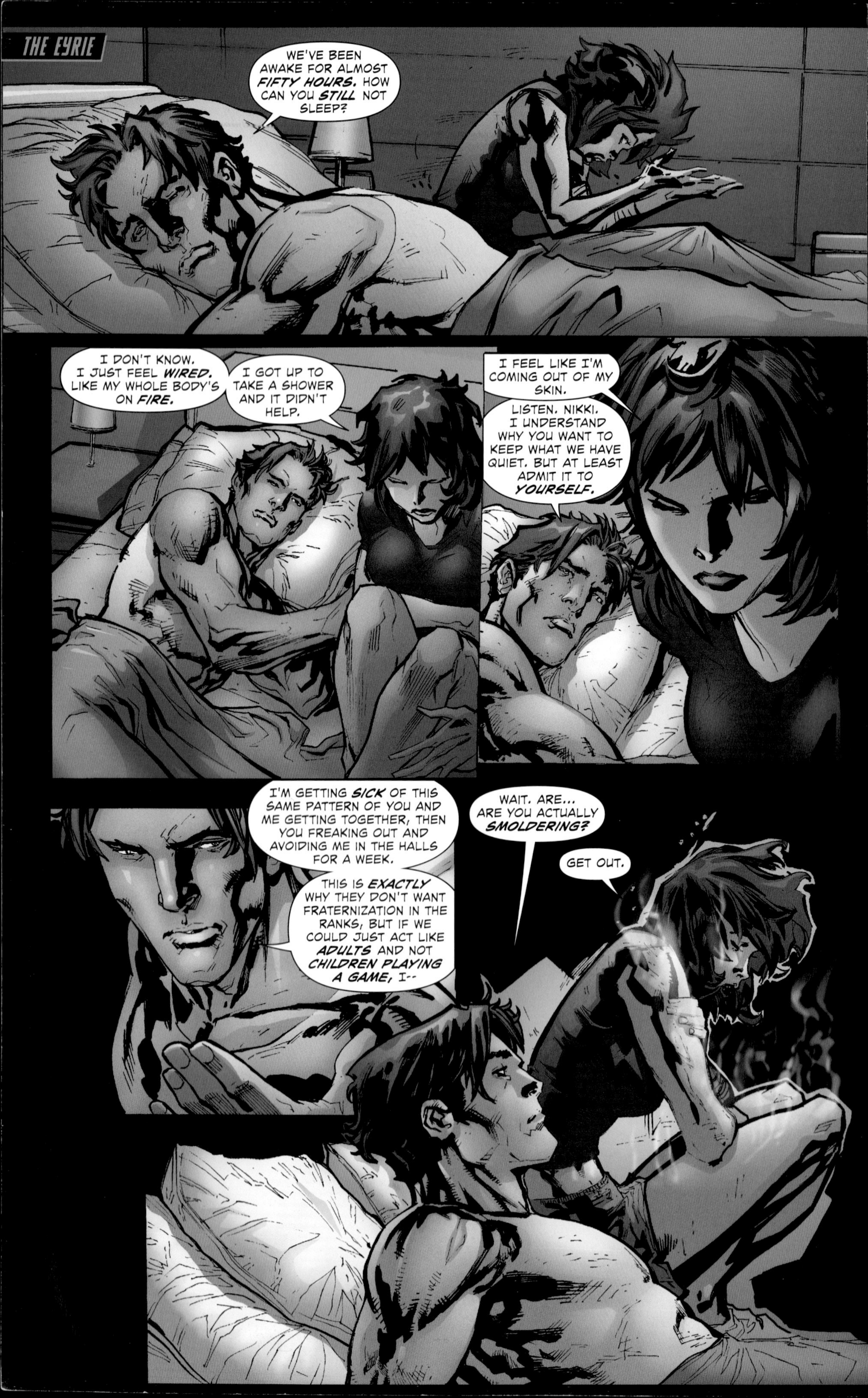
THE EYRIE
WE'VE BEEN AWAKE FOR ALMOST FIFTY HOURS. HOW CAN YOU STILL NOT SLEEP?
I DON'T KNOW. I JUST FEEL WIRED. LIKE MY WHOLE BODY'S ON FIRE.
I GOT UP TO TAKE A SHOWER AND IT DIDN'T HELP.
I FEEL LIKE I'M COMING OUT OF MY SKIN.
LISTEN, NIKKI. I UNDERSTAND WHY YOU WANT TO KEEP WHAT WE HAVE QUIET. BUT AT LEAST ADMIT IT TO YOURSELF.
I'M GETTING SICK OF THIS SAME PATTERN OF YOU AND ME GETTING TOGETHER, THEN YOU FREAKING OUT AND AVOIDING ME IN THE HALLS FOR A WEEK.
THIS IS EXACTLY WHY THEY DON'T WANT FRATERNIZATION IN THE RANKS, BUT IF WE COULD JUST ACT LIKE ADULTS AND NOT CHILDREN PLAYING A GAME, I--
WAIT. ARE... ARE YOU ACTUALLY SMOLDERING?
GET OUT.

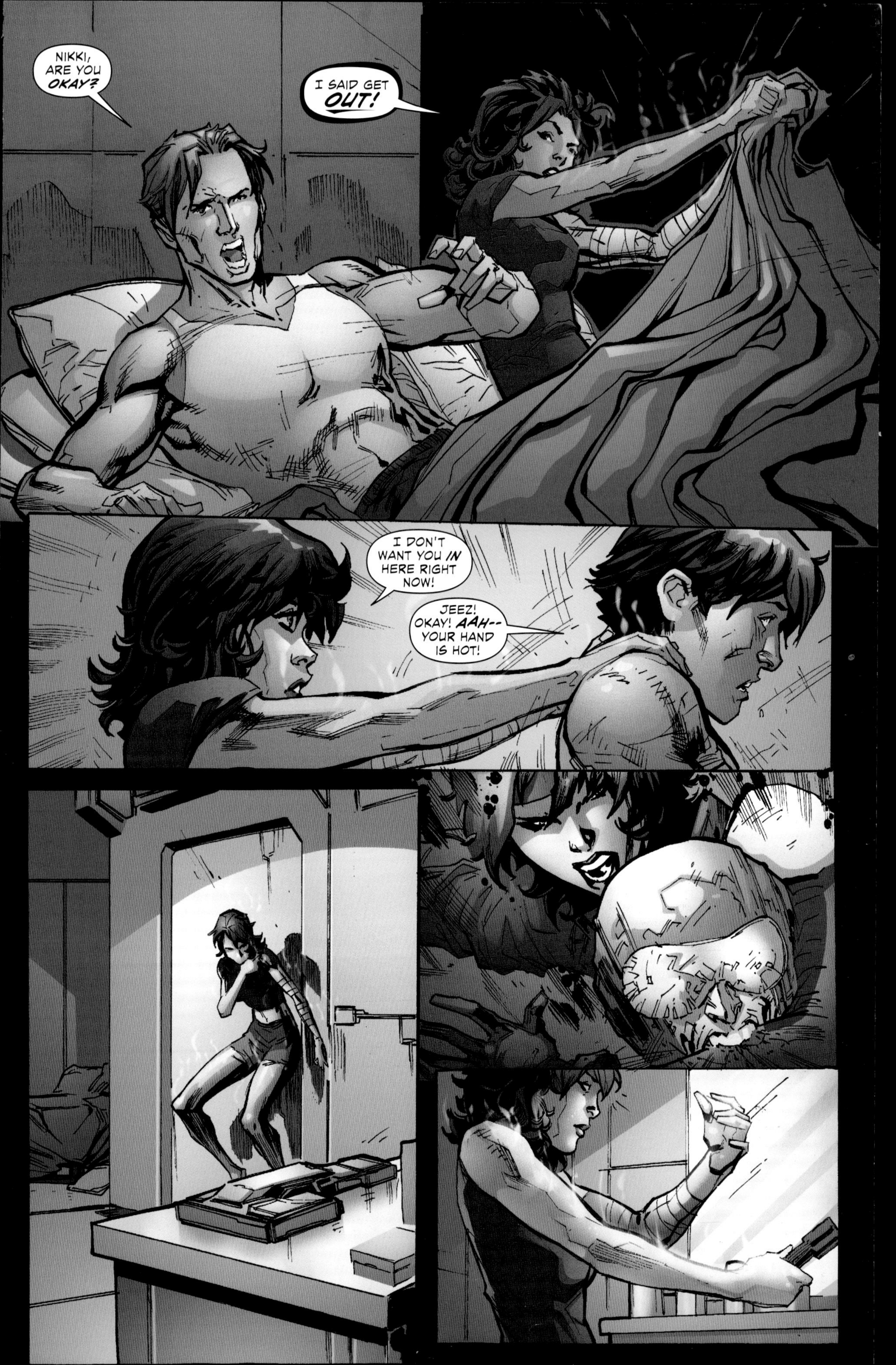

NIKKI, ARE YOU *OKAY?*
I SAID GET *OUT!*
I DON'T WANT YOU *IN* HERE RIGHT NOW!
JEEZ! OKAY! *AAH--* YOUR HAND IS HOT!

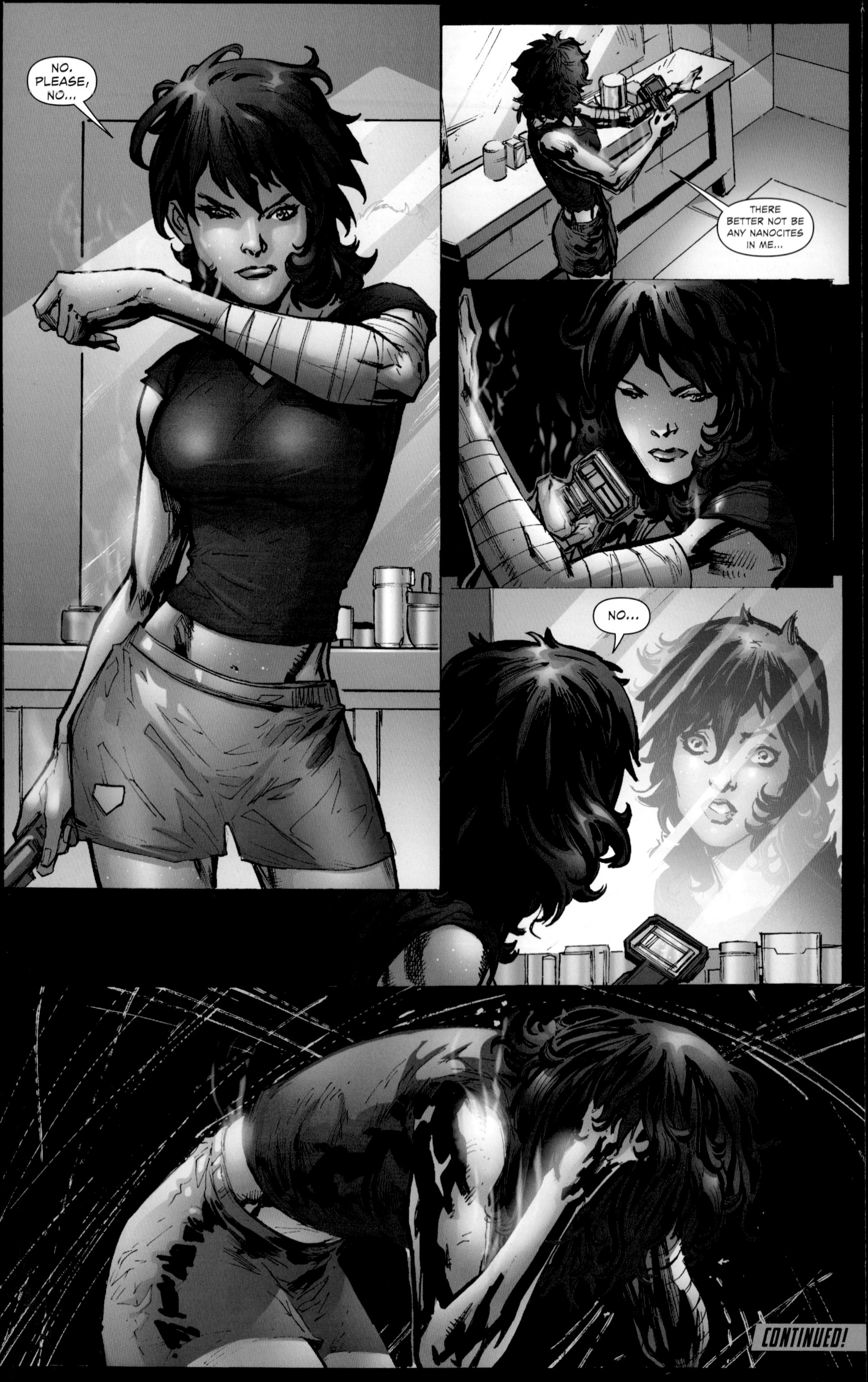
NO. PLEASE, NO...
THERE BETTER NOT BE ANY NANOCITES IN ME...
NO...
CONTINUED!

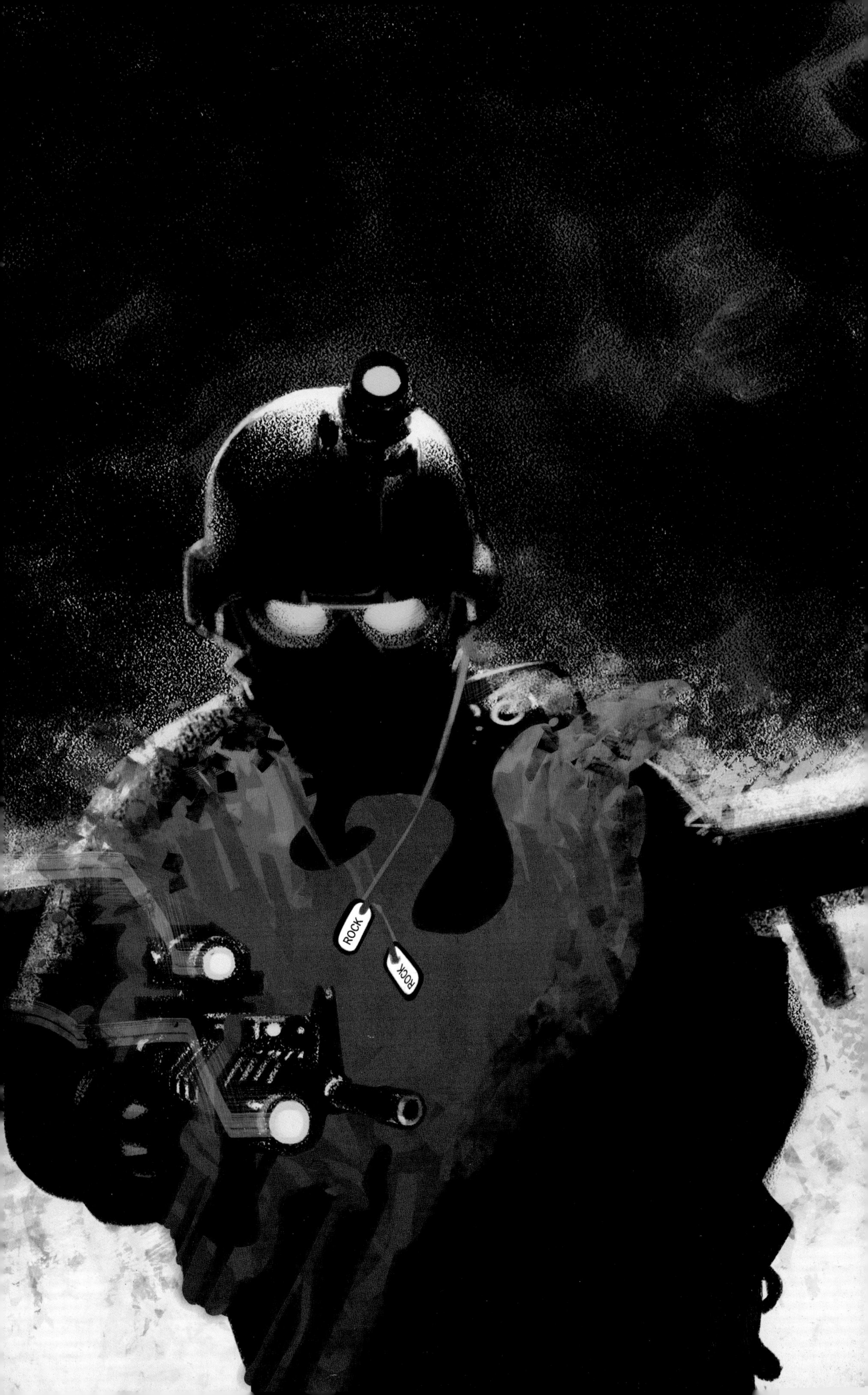
ROCK
ROCK

MEN OF WAR

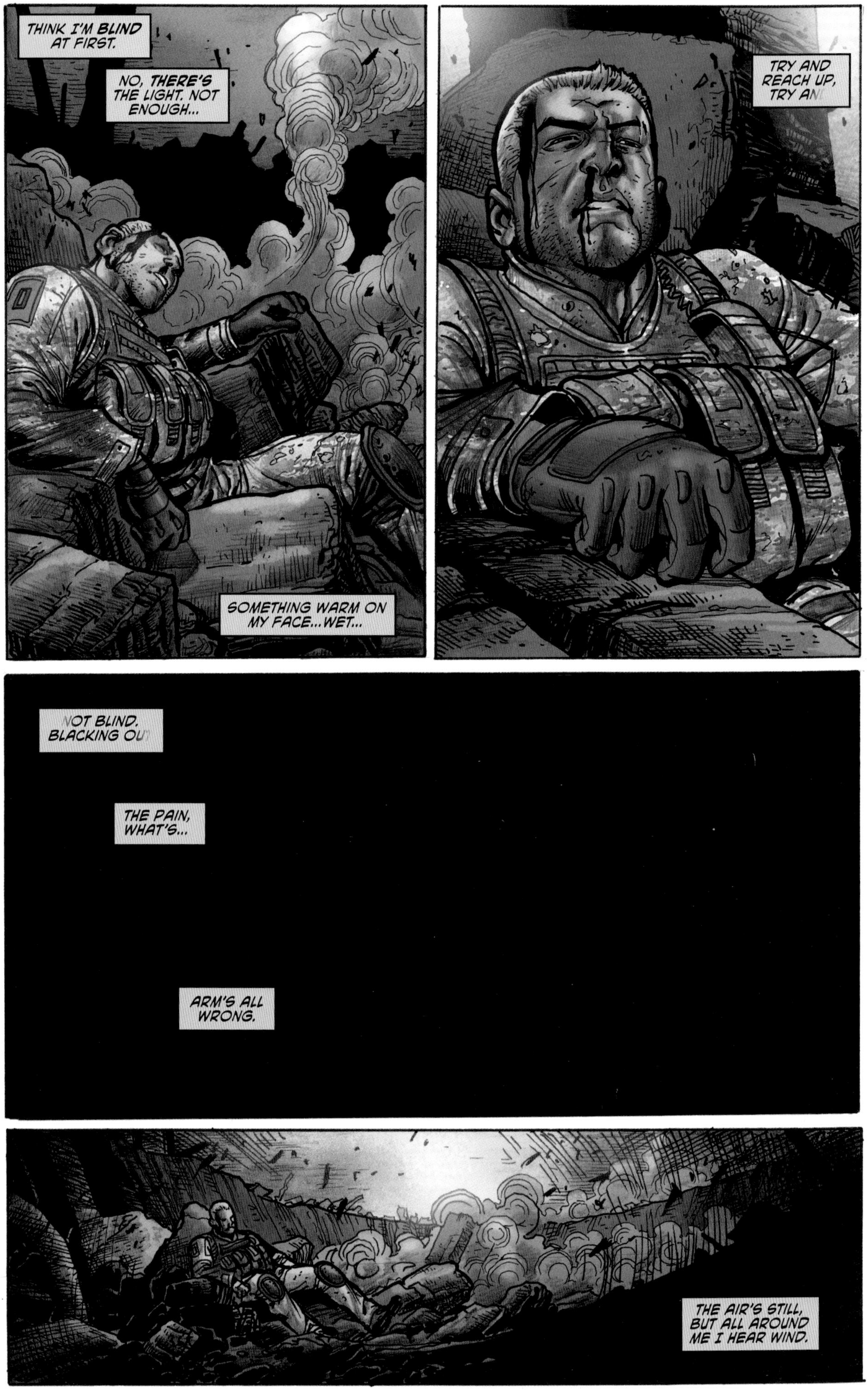
THINK I'M BLIND AT FIRST.
NO, THERE'S THE LIGHT. NOT ENOUGH...
SOMETHING WARM ON MY FACE...WET...
TRY AND REACH UP, TRY AN
NOT BLIND. BLACKING OU
THE PAIN, WHAT'S...
ARM'S ALL WRONG.
THE AIR'S STILL, BUT ALL AROUND ME I HEAR WIND.

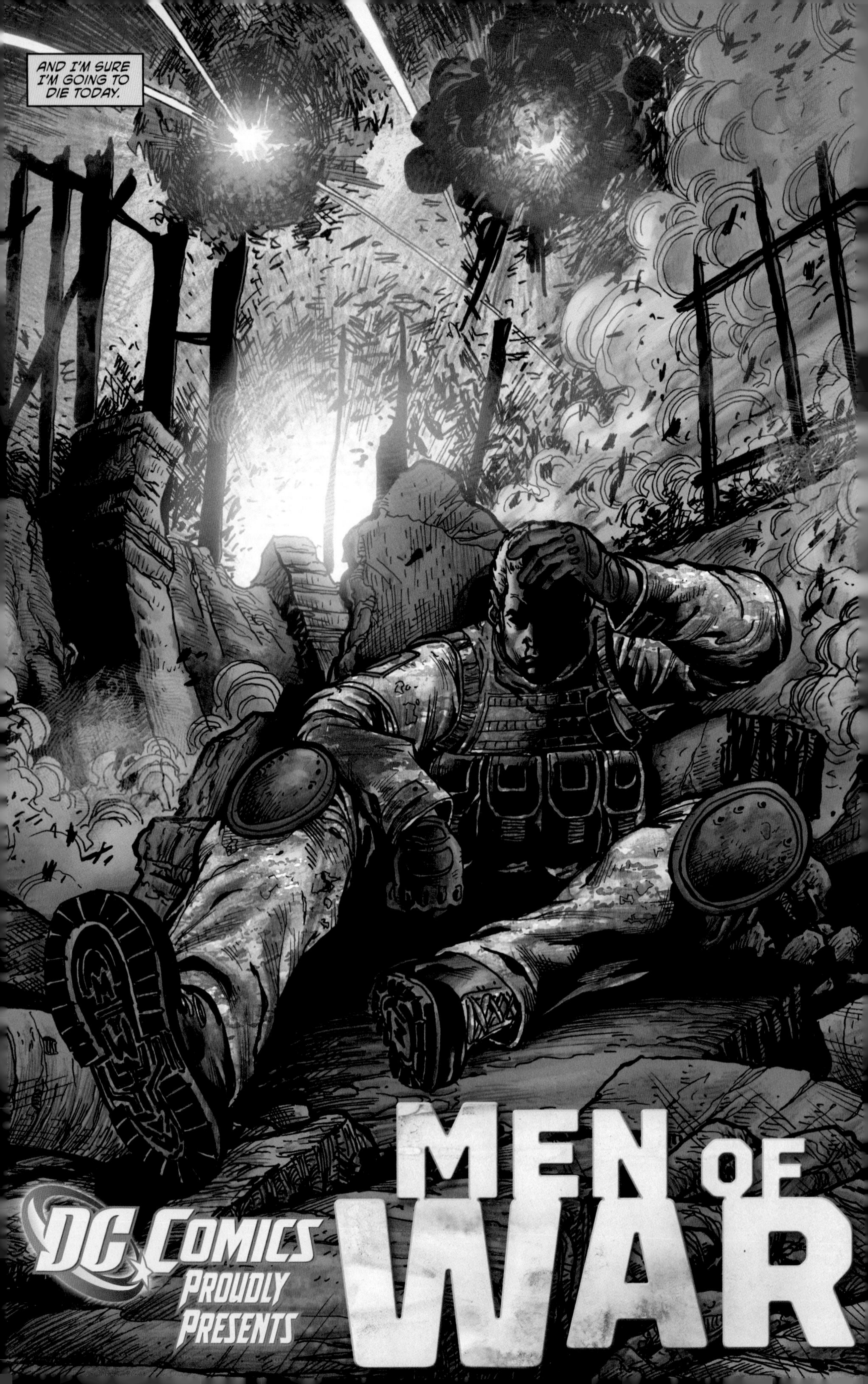
AND I'M SURE I'M GOING TO DIE TODAY.
DC COMICS PROUDLY PRESENTS
MEN OF WAR

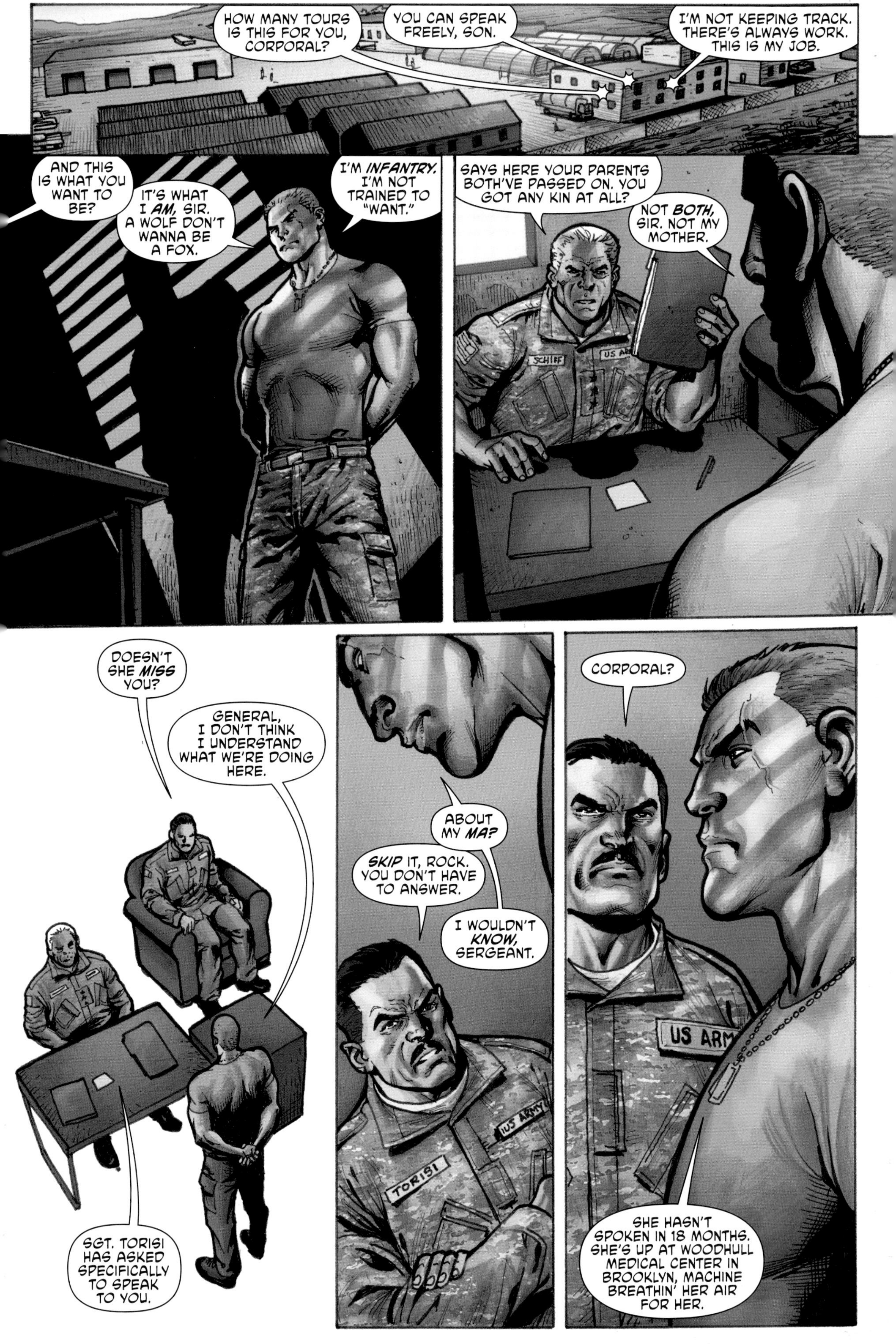

HOW MANY TOURS IS THIS FOR YOU, CORPORAL?
YOU CAN SPEAK FREELY, SON.
I'M NOT KEEPING TRACK. THERE'S ALWAYS WORK. THIS IS MY JOB.
AND THIS IS WHAT YOU WANT TO BE?
IT'S WHAT I AM, SIR. A WOLF DON'T WANNA BE A FOX.
I'M INFANTRY. I'M NOT TRAINED TO "WANT."
SAYS HERE YOUR PARENTS BOTH'VE PASSED ON. YOU GOT ANY KIN AT ALL?
NOT BOTH, SIR. NOT MY MOTHER.
SCHIFF
US ARMY
DOESN'T SHE MISS YOU?
GENERAL, I DON'T THINK I UNDERSTAND WHAT WE'RE DOING HERE.
SGT. TORISI HAS ASKED SPECIFICALLY TO SPEAK TO YOU.
ABOUT MY MA?
SKIP IT, ROCK. YOU DON'T HAVE TO ANSWER.
I WOULDN'T KNOW, SERGEANT.
US ARMY
TORISI
CORPORAL?
US ARMY
SHE HASN'T SPOKEN IN 18 MONTHS. SHE'S UP AT WOODHULL MEDICAL CENTER IN BROOKLYN, MACHINE BREATHIN' HER AIR FOR HER.

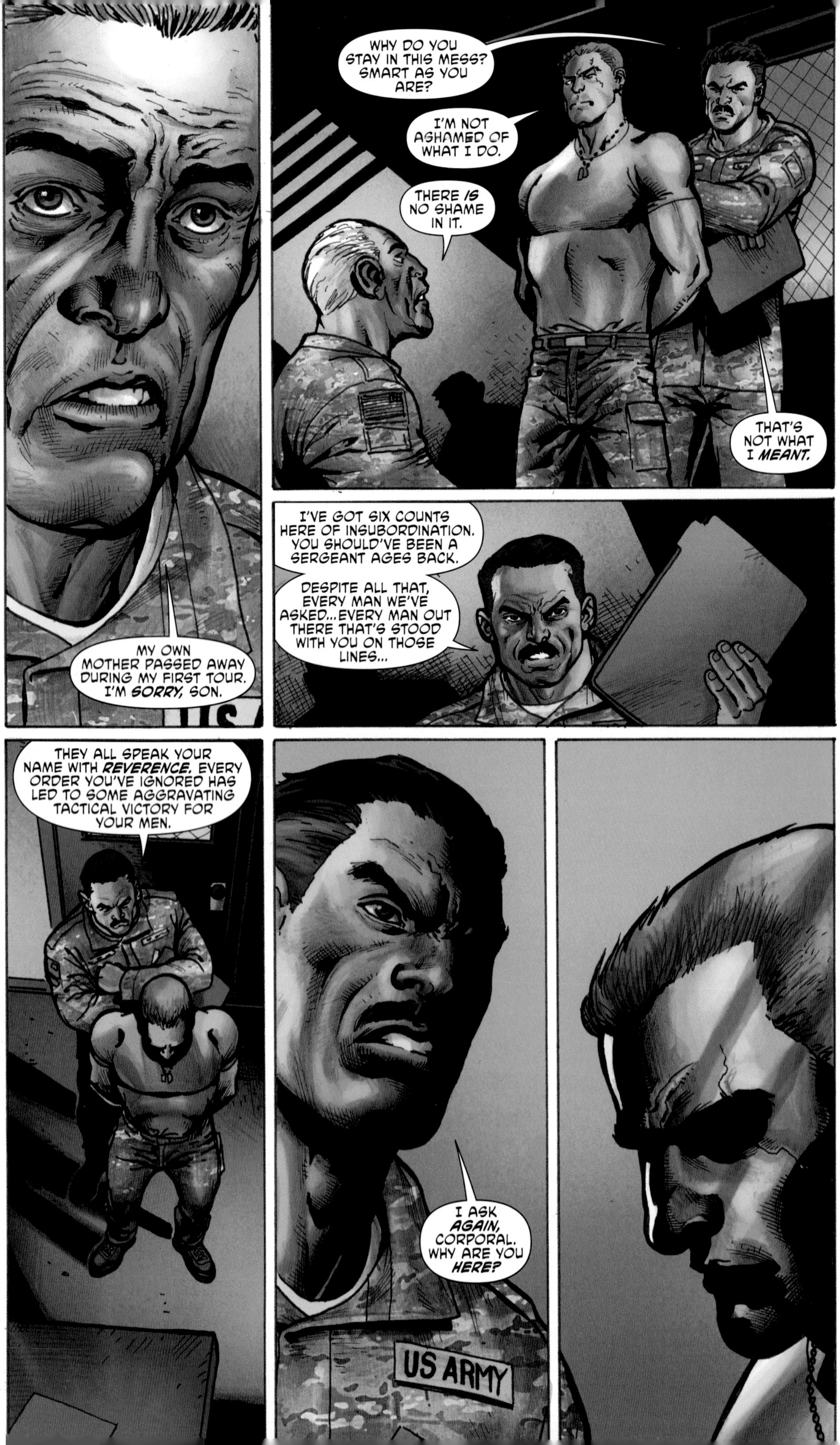
MY OWN MOTHER PASSED AWAY DURING MY FIRST TOUR. I'M **SORRY,** SON.
WHY DO YOU STAY IN THIS MESS? SMART AS YOU ARE?
I'M NOT ASHAMED OF WHAT I DO.
THERE *IS* NO SHAME IN IT.
THAT'S NOT WHAT I *MEANT.*
I'VE GOT SIX COUNTS HERE OF INSUBORDINATION. YOU SHOULD'VE BEEN A SERGEANT AGES BACK.
DESPITE ALL THAT, EVERY MAN WE'VE ASKED...EVERY MAN OUT THERE THAT'S STOOD WITH YOU ON THOSE LINES...
THEY ALL SPEAK YOUR NAME WITH ***REVERENCE.*** EVERY ORDER YOU'VE IGNORED HAS LED TO SOME AGGRAVATING TACTICAL VICTORY FOR YOUR MEN.
I ASK ***AGAIN,*** CORPORAL. WHY ARE YOU ***HERE?***
US ARMY

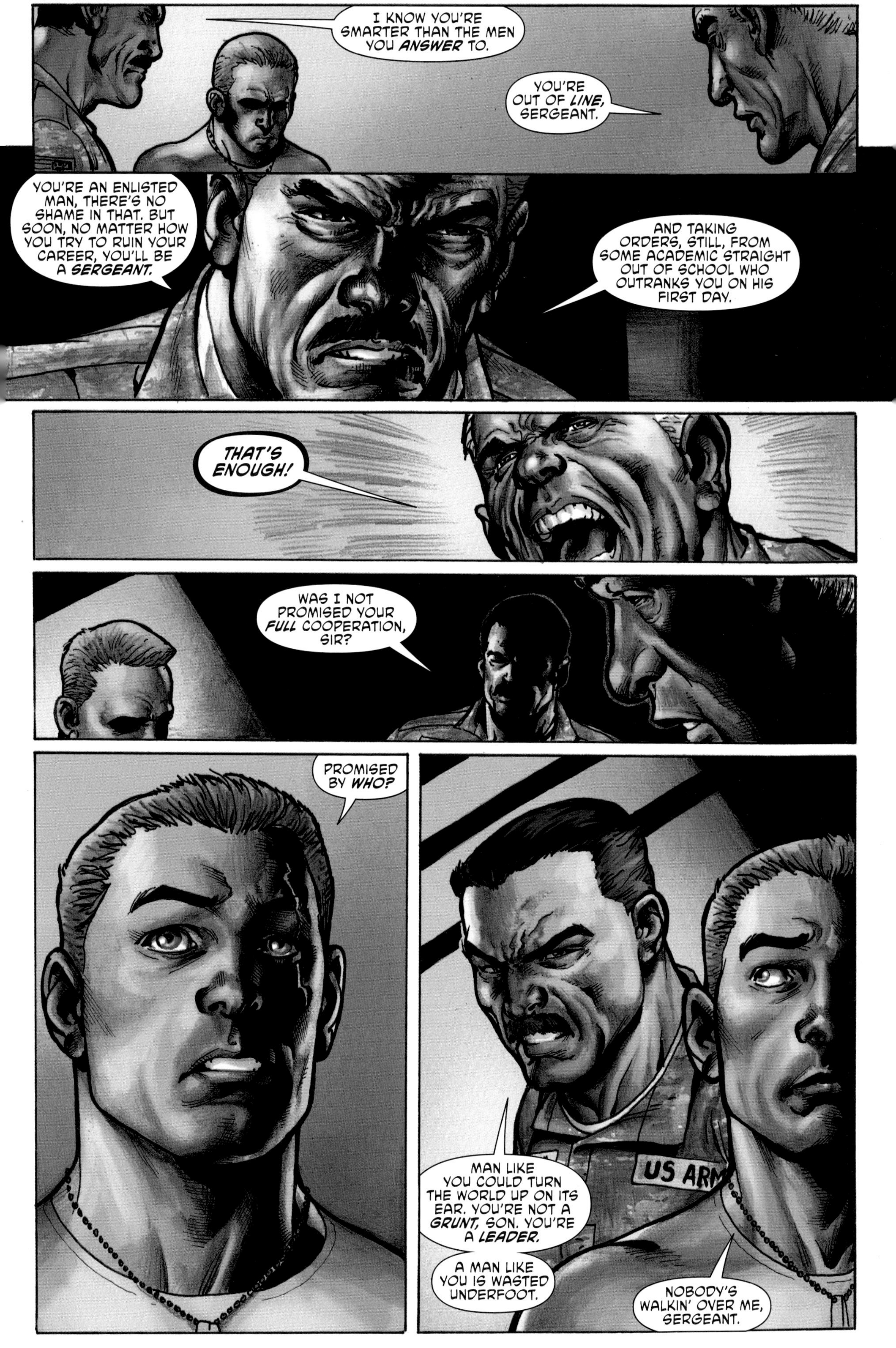
I KNOW YOU'RE SMARTER THAN THE MEN YOU *ANSWER* TO.
YOU'RE OUT OF *LINE,* SERGEANT.
YOU'RE AN ENLISTED MAN, THERE'S NO SHAME IN THAT. BUT SOON, NO MATTER HOW YOU TRY TO RUIN YOUR CAREER, YOU'LL BE A *SERGEANT.*
AND TAKING ORDERS, STILL, FROM SOME ACADEMIC STRAIGHT OUT OF SCHOOL WHO OUTRANKS YOU ON HIS FIRST DAY.
THAT'S ENOUGH!
WAS I NOT PROMISED YOUR *FULL* COOPERATION, SIR?
PROMISED BY *WHO?*
US ARM
MAN LIKE YOU COULD TURN THE WORLD UP ON ITS EAR. YOU'RE NOT A *GRUNT,* SON. YOU'RE A *LEADER.*
A MAN LIKE YOU IS WASTED UNDERFOOT.
NOBODY'S WALKIN' OVER ME, SERGEANT.

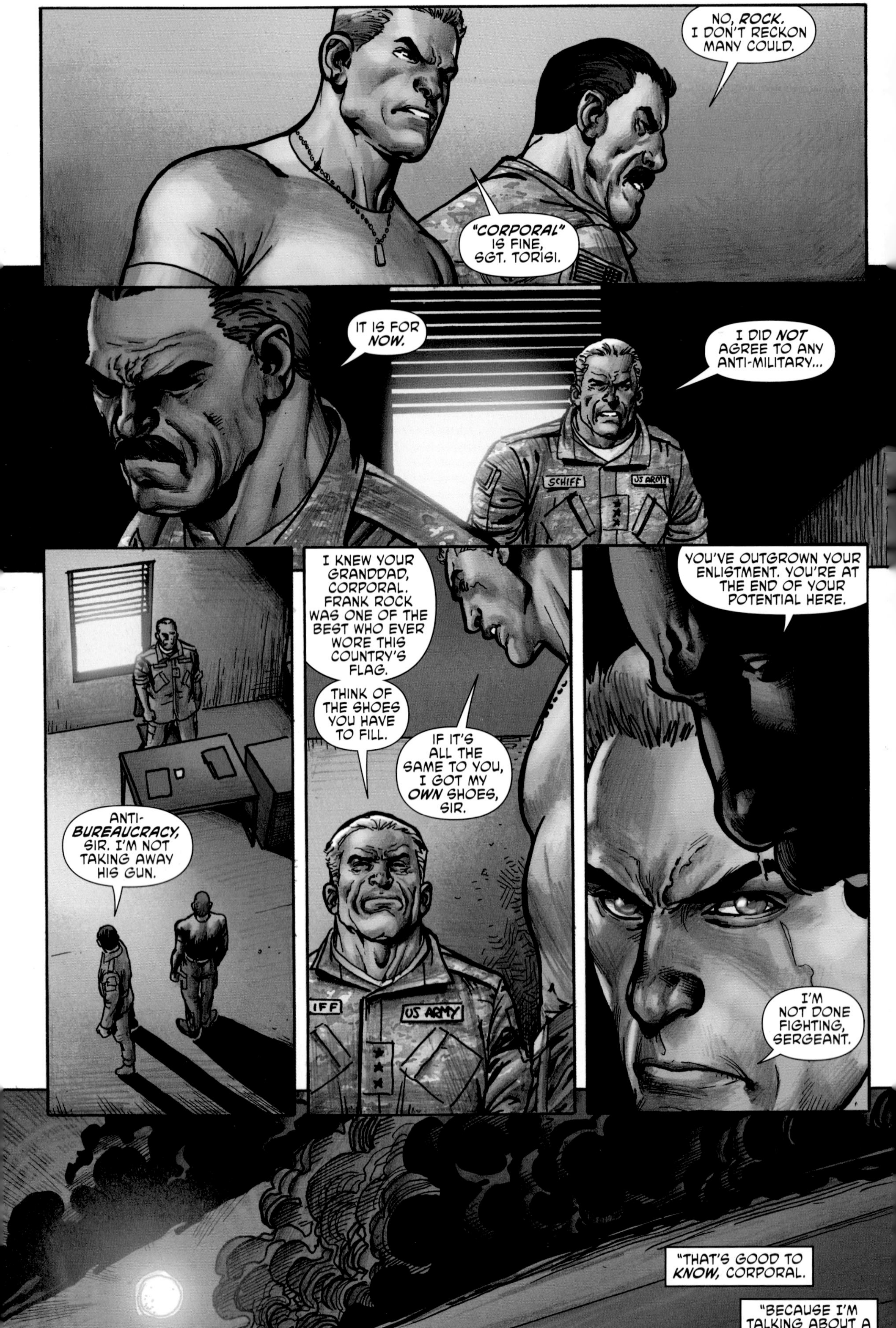
NO, ROCK. I DON'T RECKON MANY COULD.
"CORPORAL" IS FINE, SGT. TORISI.
IT IS FOR NOW.
I DID NOT AGREE TO ANY ANTI-MILITARY...
SCHIFF
US ARMY
ANTI-BUREAUCRACY, SIR. I'M NOT TAKING AWAY HIS GUN.
I KNEW YOUR GRANDDAD, CORPORAL. FRANK ROCK WAS ONE OF THE BEST WHO EVER WORE THIS COUNTRY'S FLAG.
THINK OF THE SHOES YOU HAVE TO FILL.
IF IT'S ALL THE SAME TO YOU, I GOT MY OWN SHOES, SIR.
US ARMY
YOU'VE OUTGROWN YOUR ENLISTMENT. YOU'RE AT THE END OF YOUR POTENTIAL HERE.
I'M NOT DONE FIGHTING, SERGEANT.
"THAT'S GOOD TO KNOW, CORPORAL.
"BECAUSE I'M TALKING ABOUT A BIGGER FIGHT."

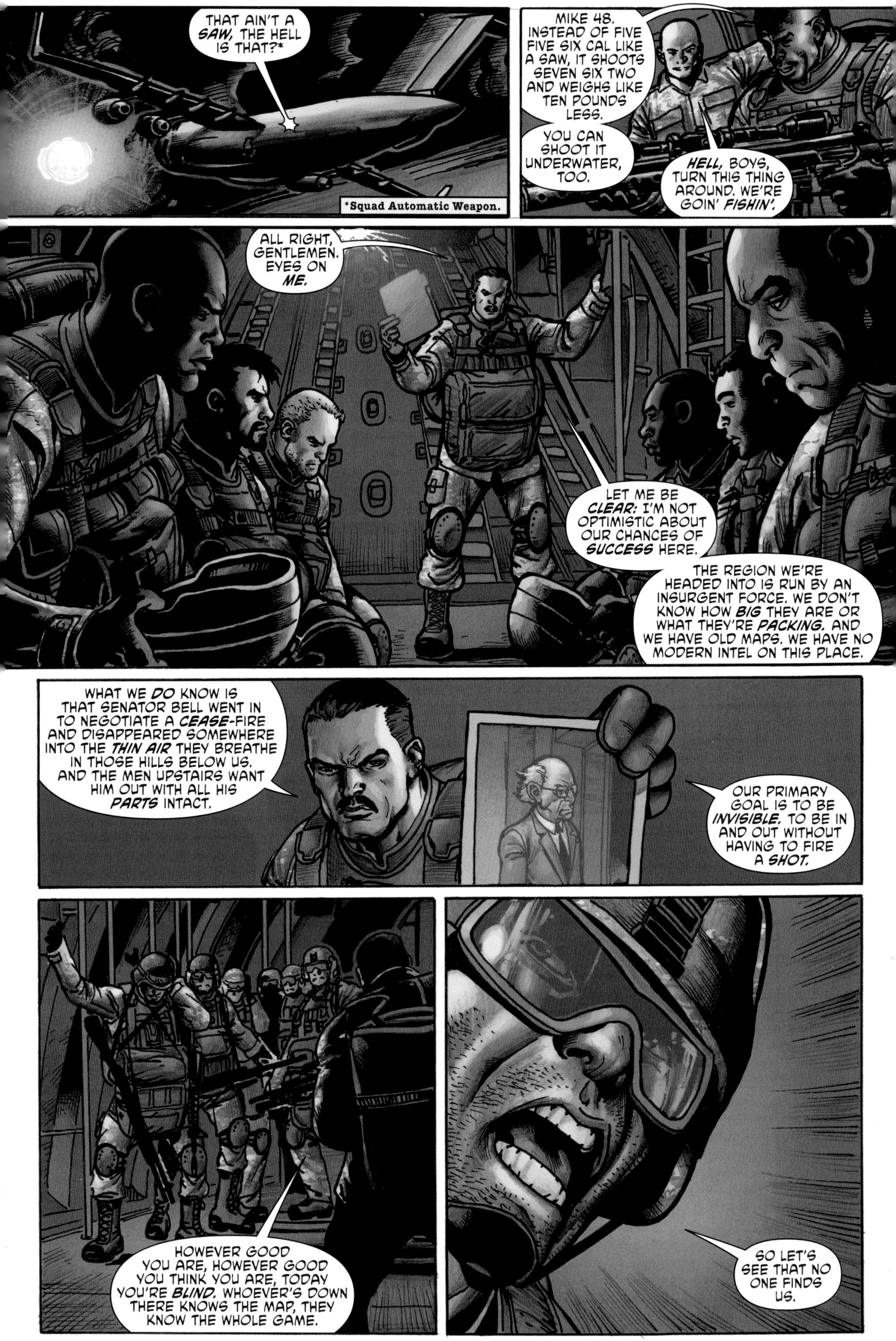
THAT AIN'T A SAW, THE HELL IS THAT?*
*Squad Automatic Weapon.
MIKE 48. INSTEAD OF FIVE FIVE SIX CAL LIKE A SAW, IT SHOOTS SEVEN SIX TWO AND WEIGHS LIKE TEN POUNDS LESS.
YOU CAN SHOOT IT UNDERWATER, TOO.
HELL, BOYS, TURN THIS THING AROUND. WE'RE GOIN' FISHIN'.
ALL RIGHT, GENTLEMEN. EYES ON ME.
LET ME BE CLEAR: I'M NOT OPTIMISTIC ABOUT OUR CHANCES OF SUCCESS HERE.
THE REGION WE'RE HEADED INTO IS RUN BY AN INSURGENT FORCE. WE DON'T KNOW HOW BIG THEY ARE OR WHAT THEY'RE PACKING. AND WE HAVE OLD MAPS. WE HAVE NO MODERN INTEL ON THIS PLACE.
WHAT WE DO KNOW IS THAT SENATOR BELL WENT IN TO NEGOTIATE A CEASE-FIRE AND DISAPPEARED SOMEWHERE INTO THE THIN AIR THEY BREATHE IN THOSE HILLS BELOW US. AND THE MEN UPSTAIRS WANT HIM OUT WITH ALL HIS PARTS INTACT.
OUR PRIMARY GOAL IS TO BE INVISIBLE. TO BE IN AND OUT WITHOUT HAVING TO FIRE A SHOT.
HOWEVER GOOD YOU ARE, HOWEVER GOOD YOU THINK YOU ARE, TODAY YOU'RE BLIND. WHOEVER'S DOWN THERE KNOWS THE MAP, THEY KNOW THE WHOLE GAME.
SO LET'S SEE THAT NO ONE FINDS US.

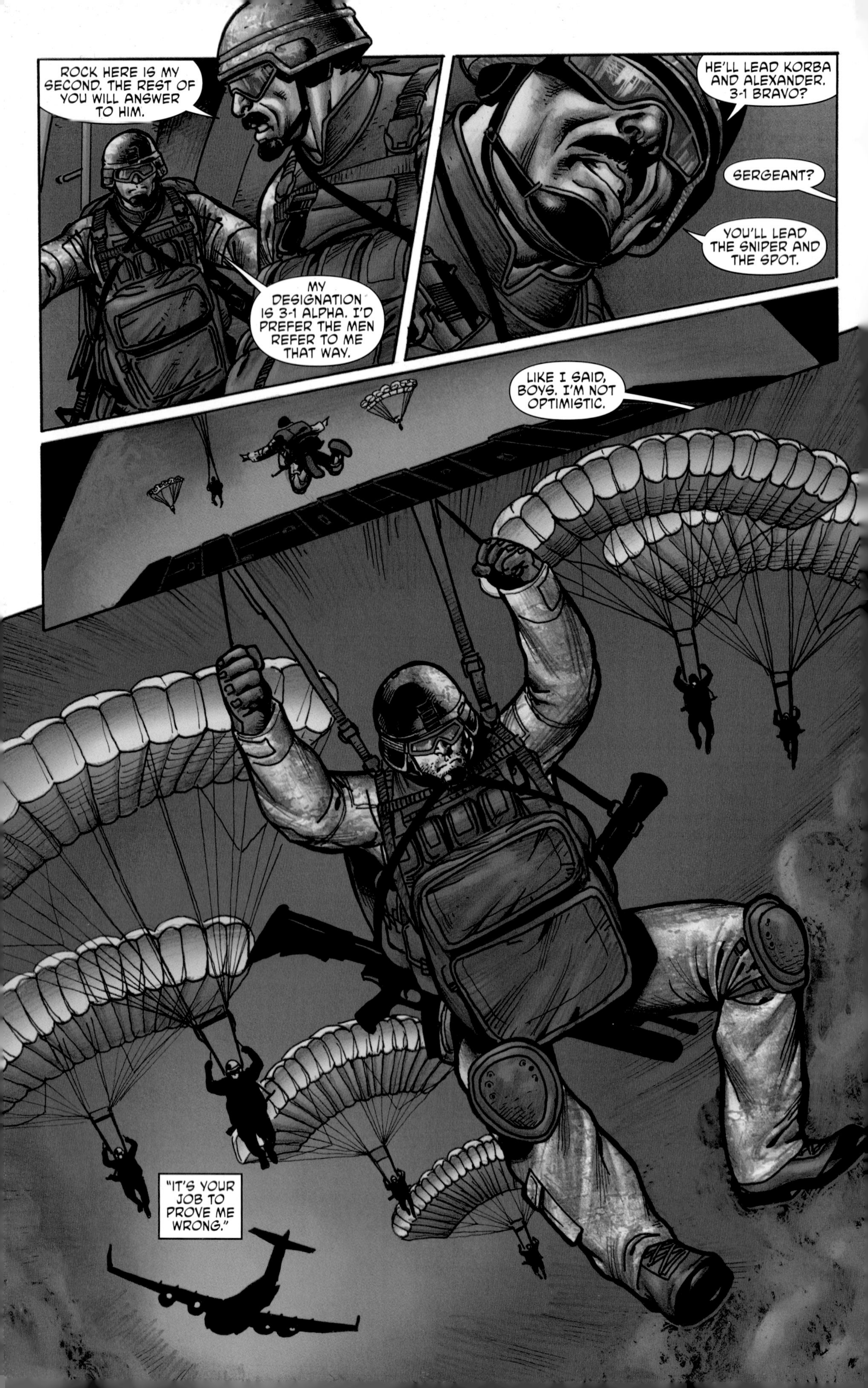
ROCK HERE IS MY SECOND. THE REST OF YOU WILL ANSWER TO HIM.
MY DESIGNATION IS 3-1 ALPHA. I'D PREFER THE MEN REFER TO ME THAT WAY.
HE'LL LEAD KORBA AND ALEXANDER. 3-1 BRAVO?
SERGEANT?
YOU'LL LEAD THE SNIPER AND THE SPOT.
LIKE I SAID, BOYS. I'M NOT OPTIMISTIC.
"IT'S YOUR JOB TO PROVE ME WRONG."

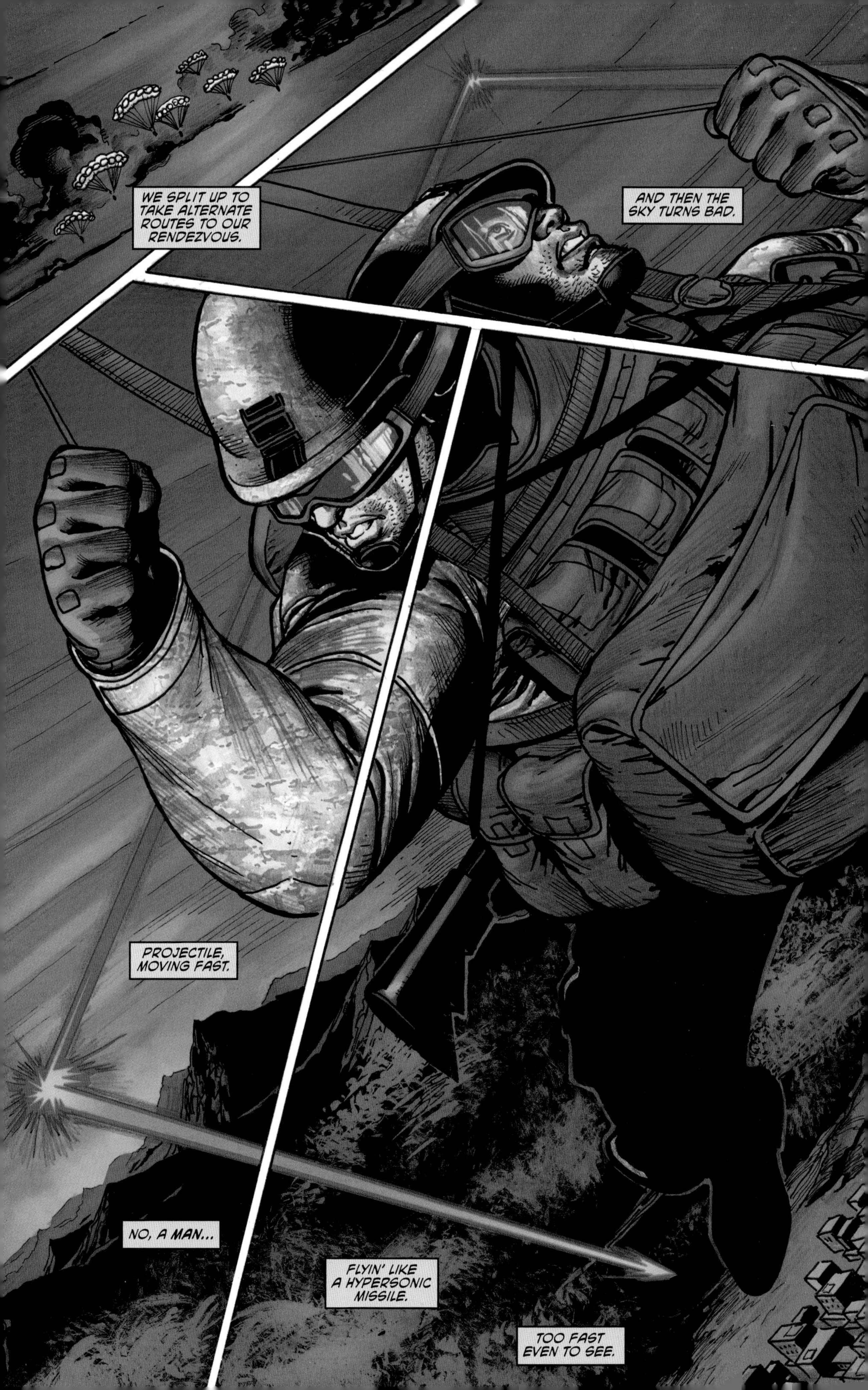
WE SPLIT UP TO TAKE ALTERNATE ROUTES TO OUR RENDEZVOUS.
AND THEN THE SKY TURNS BAD.
PROJECTILE, MOVING FAST.
NO, A MAN...
FLYIN' LIKE A HYPERSONIC MISSILE.
TOO FAST EVEN TO SEE.

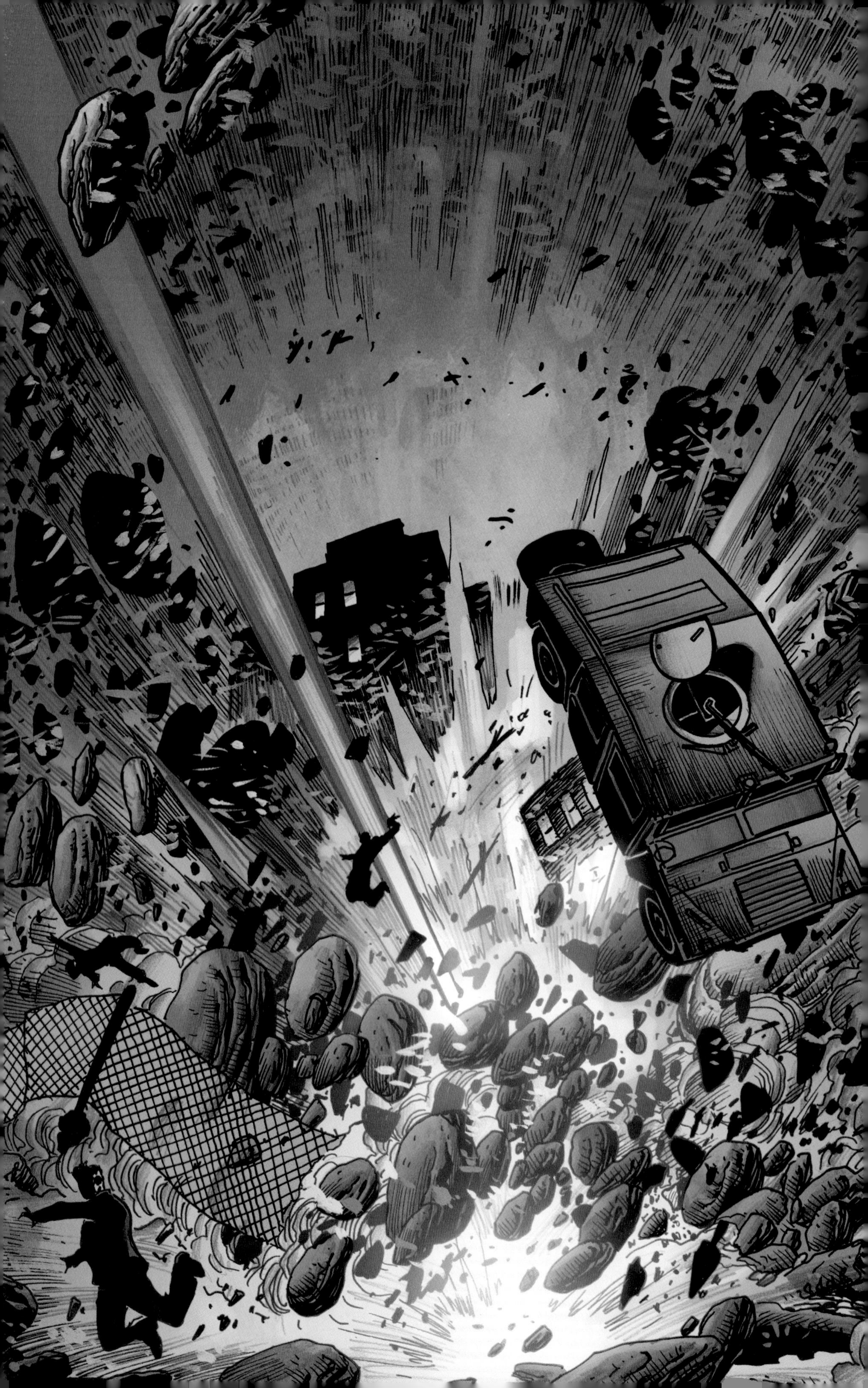

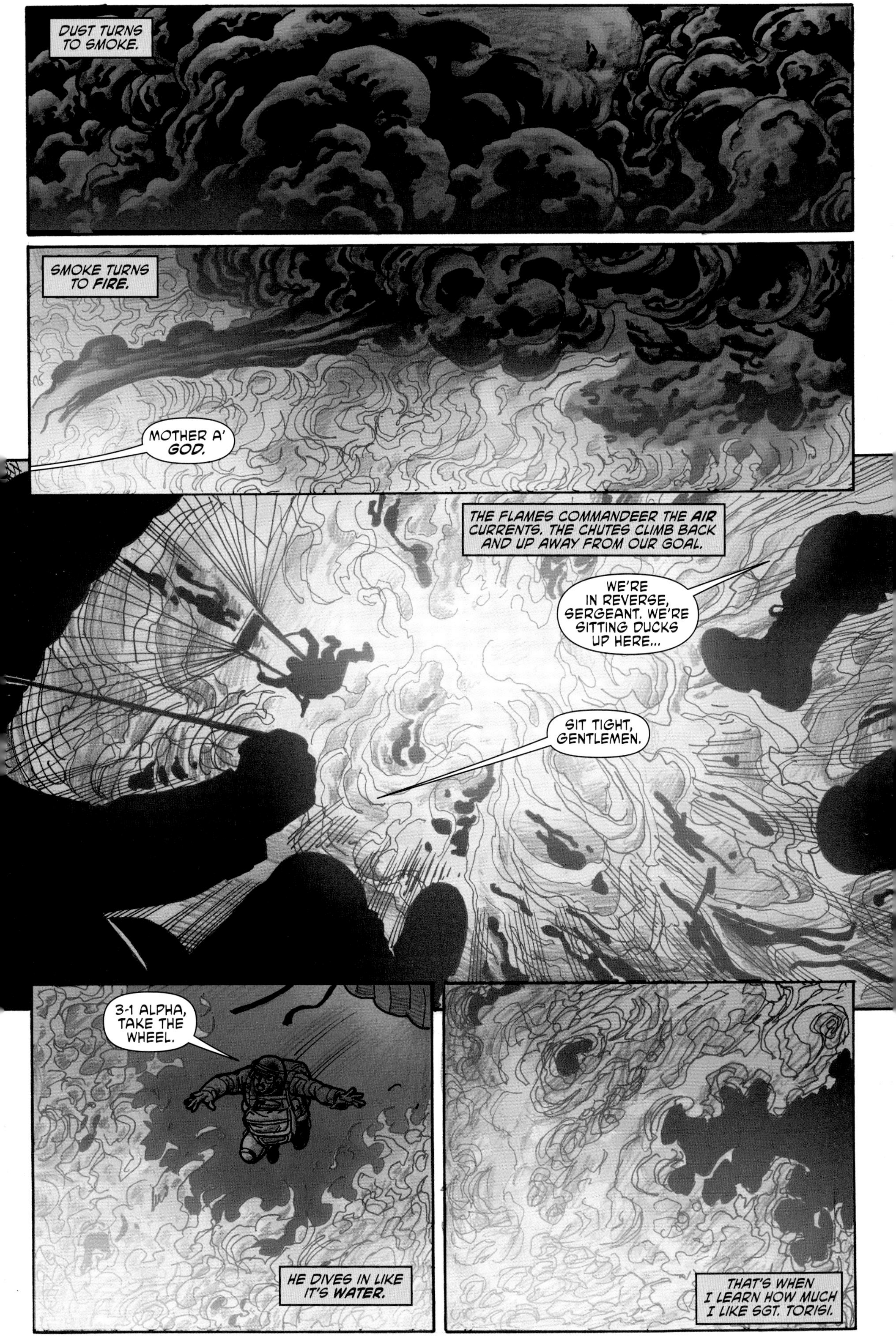
DUST TURNS TO SMOKE.
SMOKE TURNS TO FIRE.
MOTHER A' GOD.
THE FLAMES COMMANDEER THE AIR CURRENTS. THE CHUTES CLIMB BACK AND UP AWAY FROM OUR GOAL.
WE'RE IN REVERSE, SERGEANT. WE'RE SITTING DUCKS UP HERE...
SIT TIGHT, GENTLEMEN.
3-1 ALPHA, TAKE THE WHEEL.
HE DIVES IN LIKE IT'S WATER.
THAT'S WHEN I LEARN HOW MUCH I LIKE SGT. TORISI.

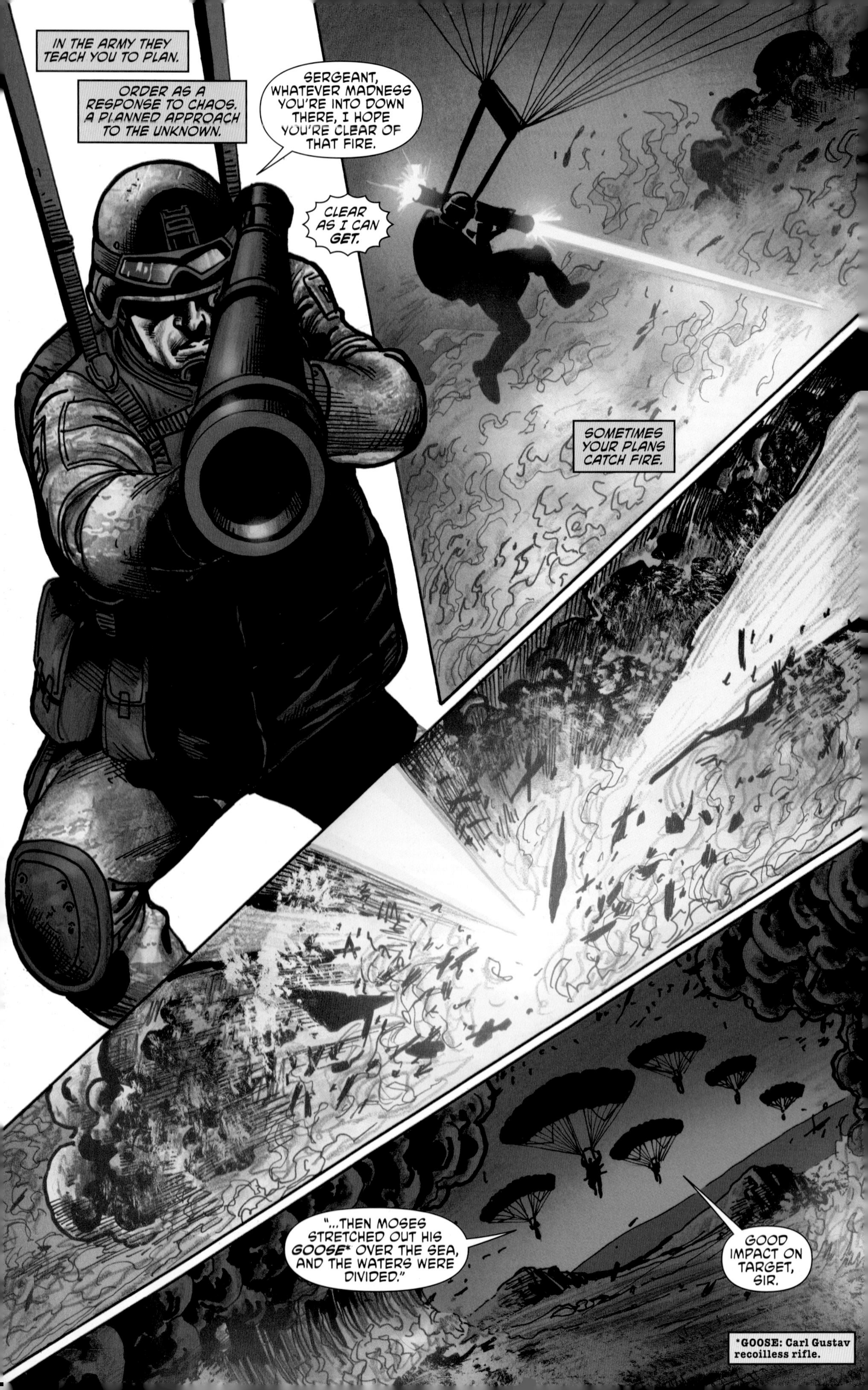
IN THE ARMY THEY TEACH YOU TO PLAN.
ORDER AS A RESPONSE TO CHAOS. A PLANNED APPROACH TO THE UNKNOWN.
SERGEANT, WHATEVER MADNESS YOU'RE INTO DOWN THERE, I HOPE YOU'RE CLEAR OF THAT FIRE.
CLEAR AS I CAN GET.
SOMETIMES YOUR PLANS CATCH FIRE.
"...THEN MOSES STRETCHED OUT HIS GOOSE* OVER THE SEA, AND THE WATERS WERE DIVIDED."
GOOD IMPACT ON TARGET, SIR.
*GOOSE: Carl Gustav recoilless rifle.

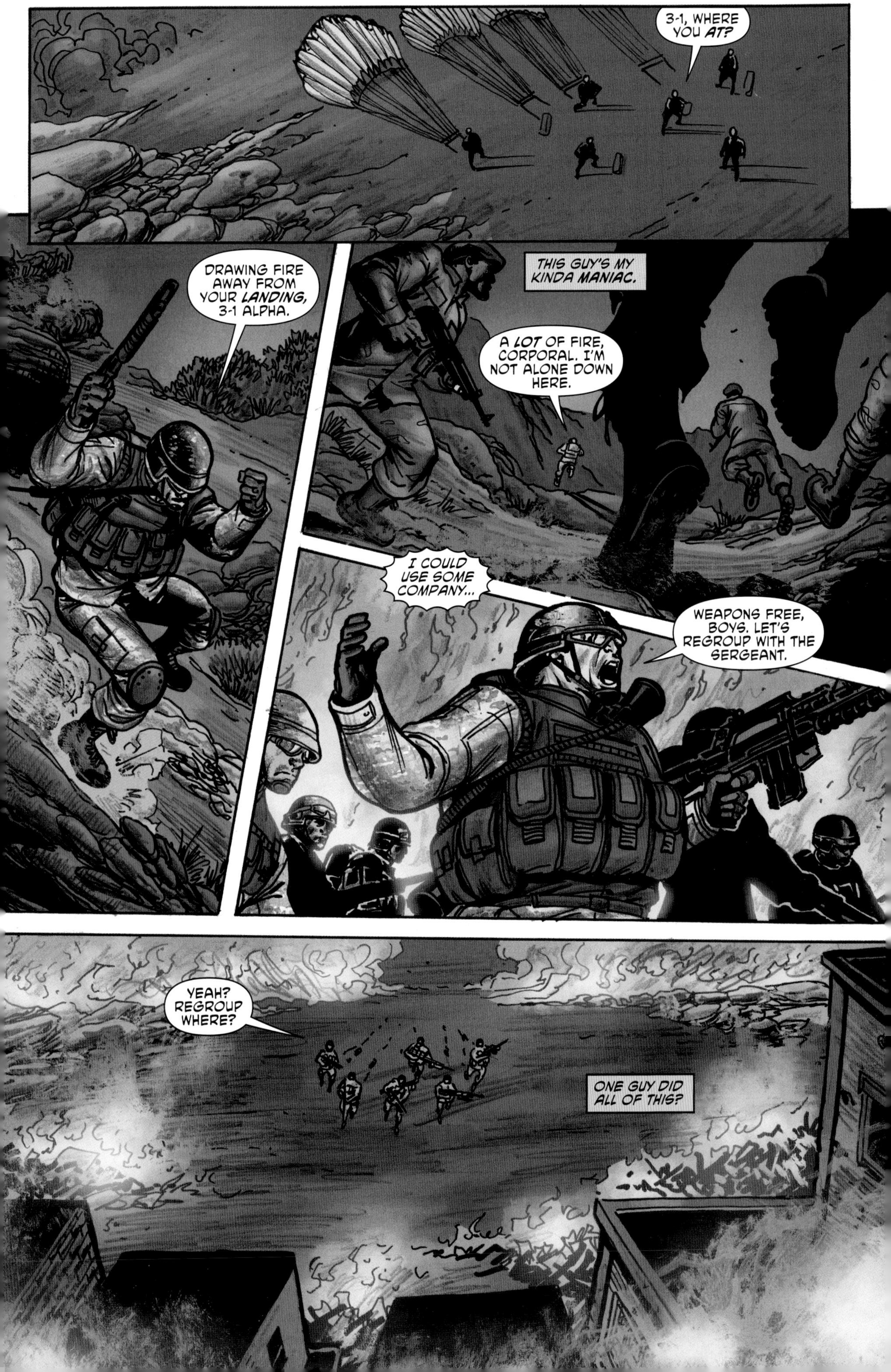
3-1, WHERE YOU AT?
DRAWING FIRE AWAY FROM YOUR LANDING, 3-1 ALPHA.
THIS GUY'S MY KINDA MANIAC.
A LOT OF FIRE, CORPORAL. I'M NOT ALONE DOWN HERE.
I COULD USE SOME COMPANY...
WEAPONS FREE, BOYS. LET'S REGROUP WITH THE SERGEANT.
YEAH? REGROUP WHERE?
ONE GUY DID ALL OF THIS?

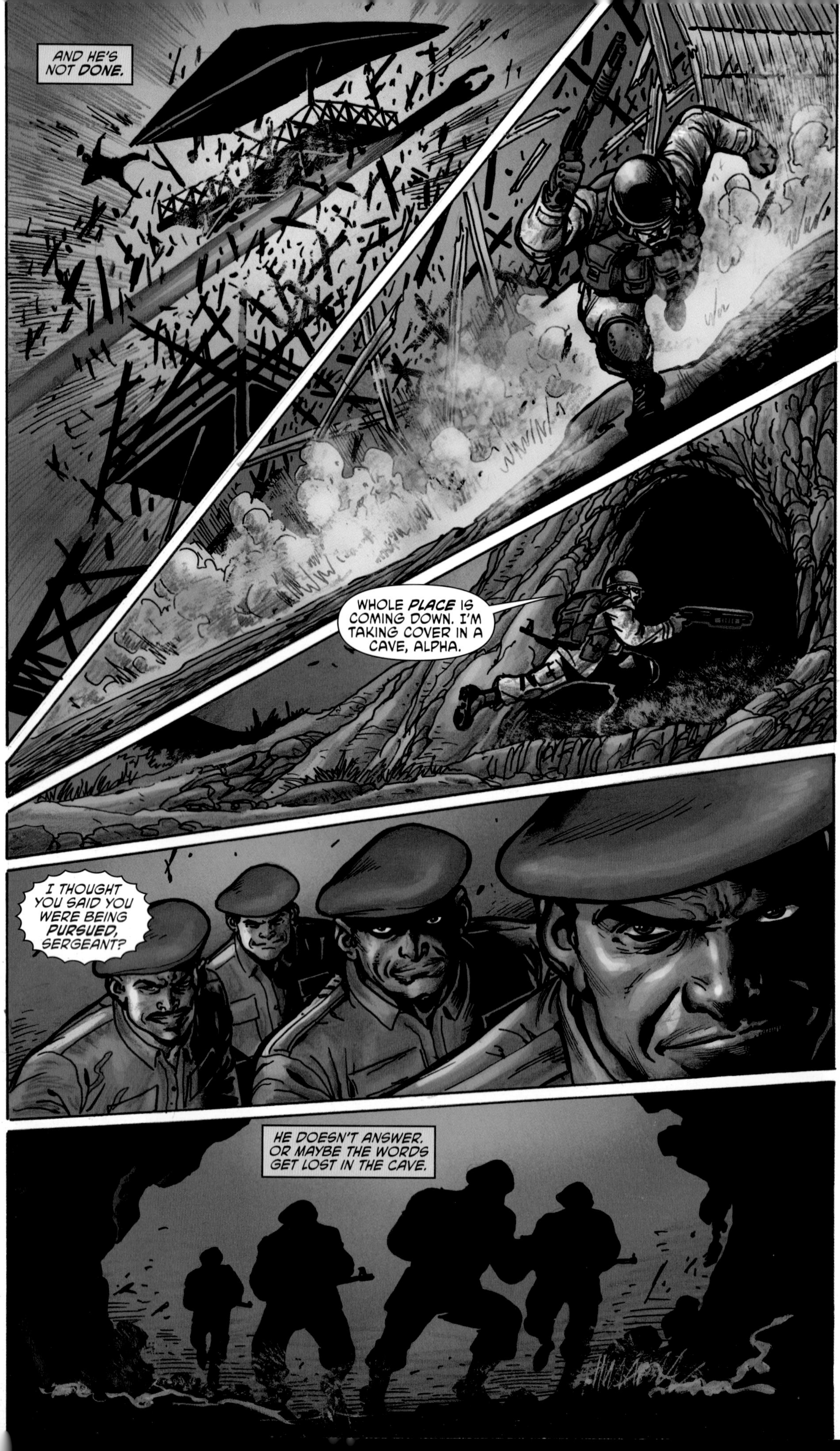
AND HE'S NOT DONE.
WHOLE PLACE IS COMING DOWN. I'M TAKING COVER IN A CAVE, ALPHA.
I THOUGHT YOU SAID YOU WERE BEING PURSUED, SERGEANT?
HE DOESN'T ANSWER. OR MAYBE THE WORDS GET LOST IN THE CAVE.

THE WORST THING YOU CAN HEAR IN THE LINE OF FIRE IS NOTHING.

THE SILENCE HANGS IN THE AIR.

IT STARTS TO TELL ITS OWN STORIES.

AND THEN THE SERGEANT'S SAWED-OFF BREAKS IT.

AND THEN HIS M4 JOINS IN.*

BOOM

FADAFADAFADAFADAFADA

BOOM

SFOOOOOM

*M4 Carbine rifle.

WHEN HE COMES OUT OF THE DARK, HE'S ALONE.

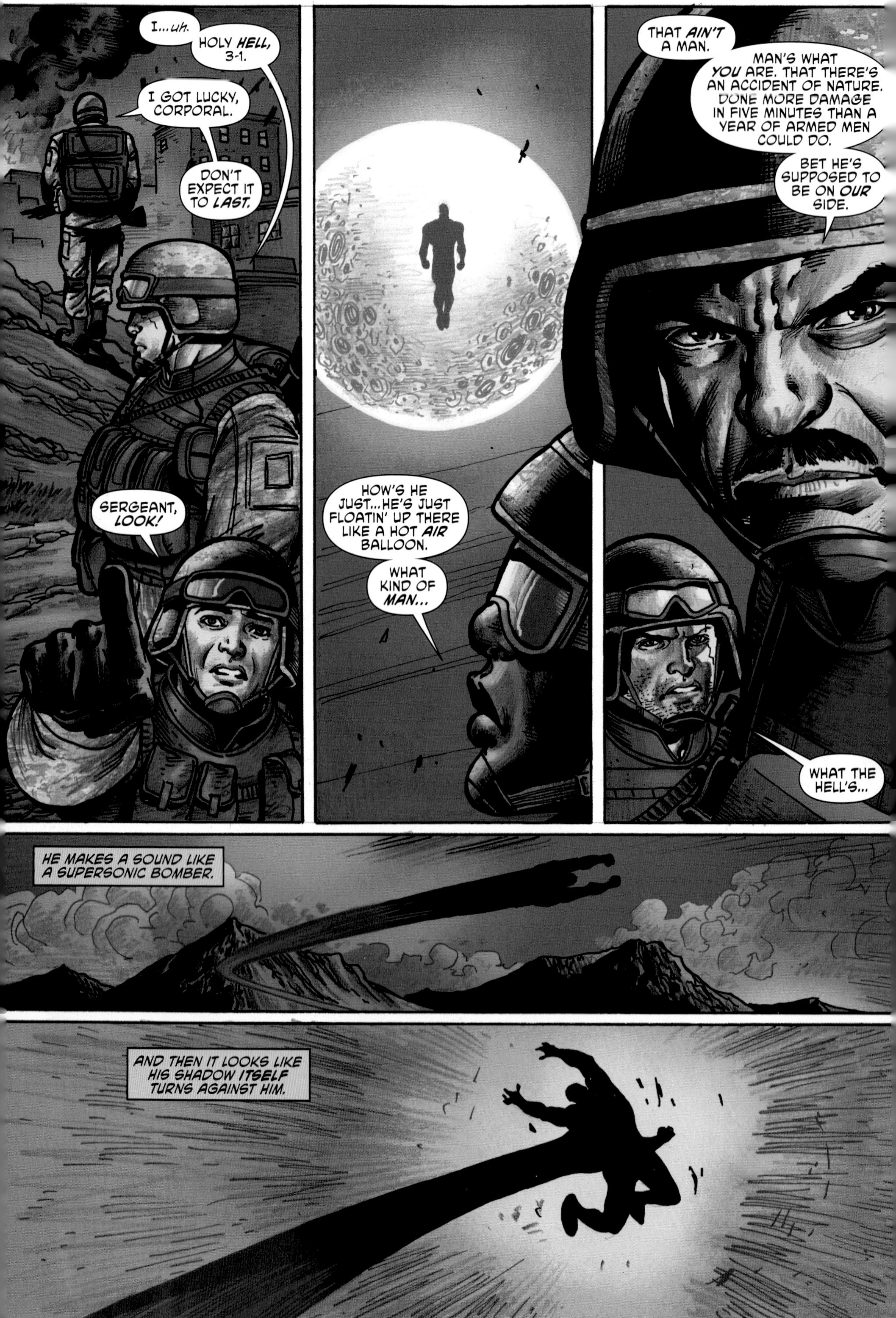
I...uh.
HOLY HELL, 3-1.
I GOT LUCKY, CORPORAL.
DON'T EXPECT IT TO LAST.
SERGEANT, LOOK!
HOW'S HE JUST...HE'S JUST FLOATIN' UP THERE LIKE A HOT AIR BALLOON.
WHAT KIND OF MAN...
THAT AIN'T A MAN.
MAN'S WHAT YOU ARE. THAT THERE'S AN ACCIDENT OF NATURE. DONE MORE DAMAGE IN FIVE MINUTES THAN A YEAR OF ARMED MEN COULD DO.
BET HE'S SUPPOSED TO BE ON OUR SIDE.
WHAT THE HELL'S...
HE MAKES A SOUND LIKE A SUPERSONIC BOMBER.
AND THEN IT LOOKS LIKE HIS SHADOW ITSELF TURNS AGAINST HIM.

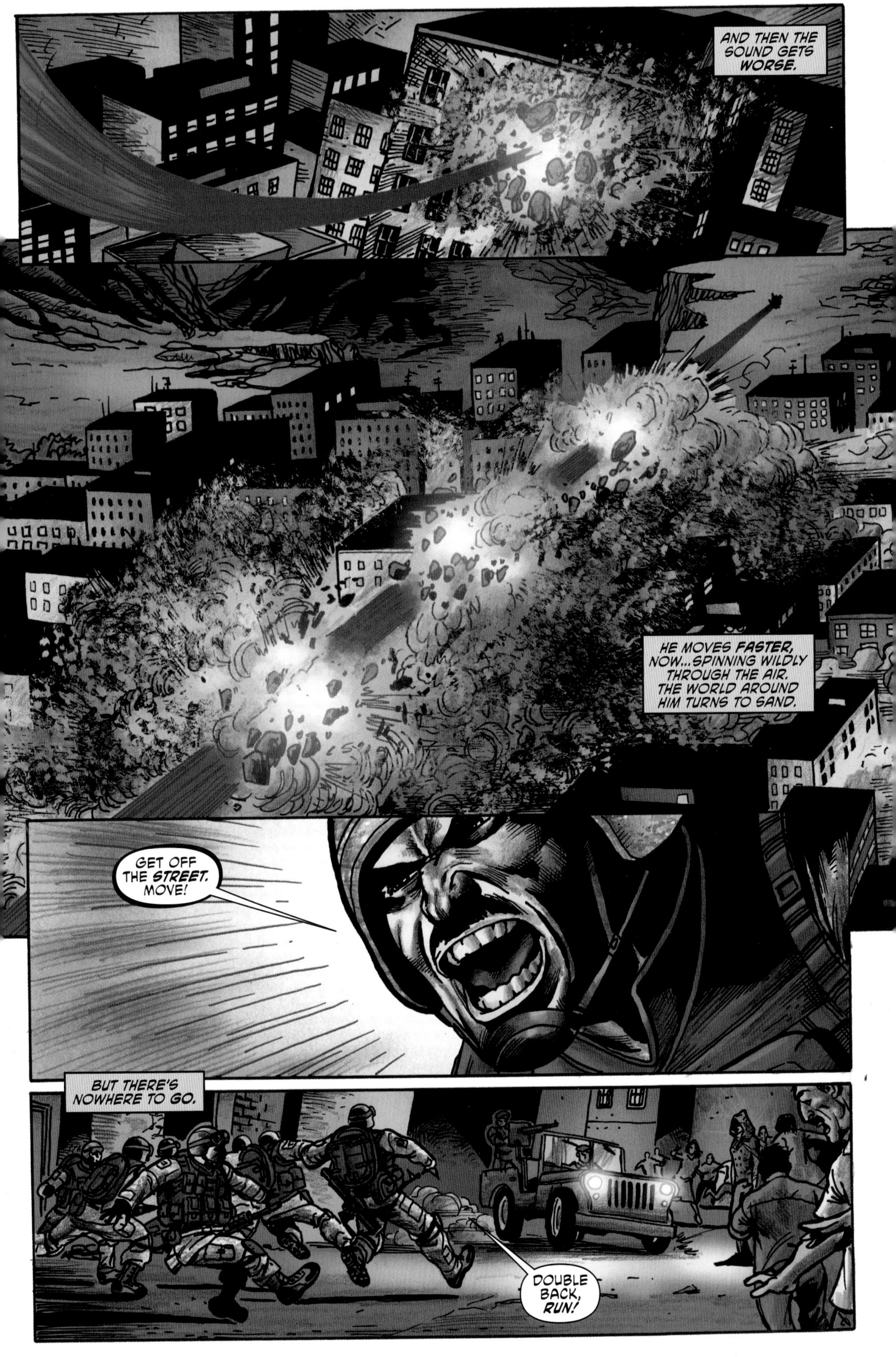
AND THEN THE SOUND GETS WORSE.
HE MOVES FASTER, NOW...SPINNING WILDLY THROUGH THE AIR. THE WORLD AROUND HIM TURNS TO SAND.
GET OFF THE STREET. MOVE!
BUT THERE'S NOWHERE TO GO.
DOUBLE BACK, RUN!

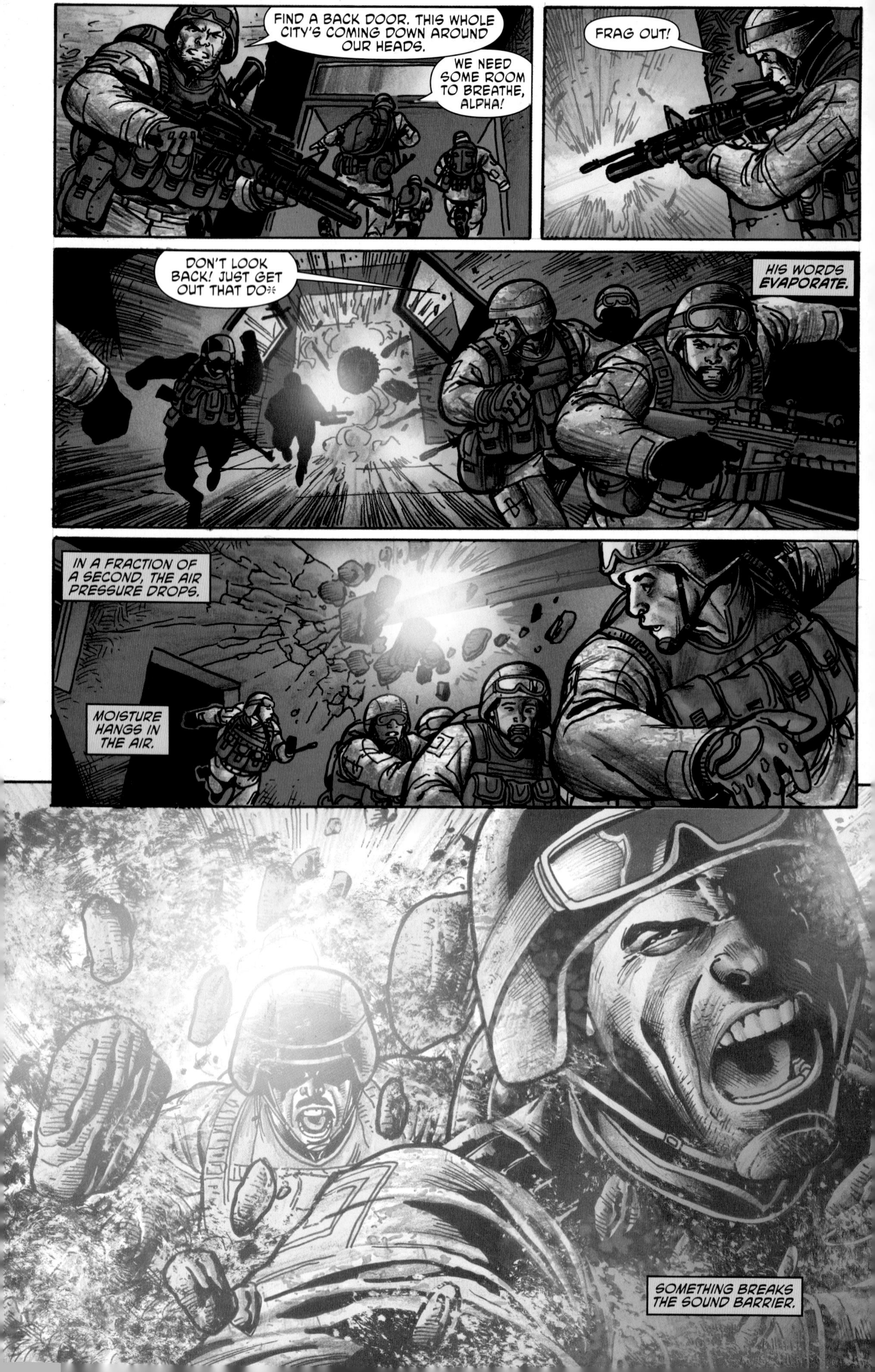
FIND A BACK DOOR. THIS WHOLE CITY'S COMING DOWN AROUND OUR HEADS.
WE NEED SOME ROOM TO BREATHE, ALPHA!
FRAG OUT!
DON'T LOOK BACK! JUST GET OUT THAT DO
HIS WORDS EVAPORATE.
IN A FRACTION OF A SECOND, THE AIR PRESSURE DROPS.
MOISTURE HANGS IN THE AIR.
SOMETHING BREAKS THE SOUND BARRIER.

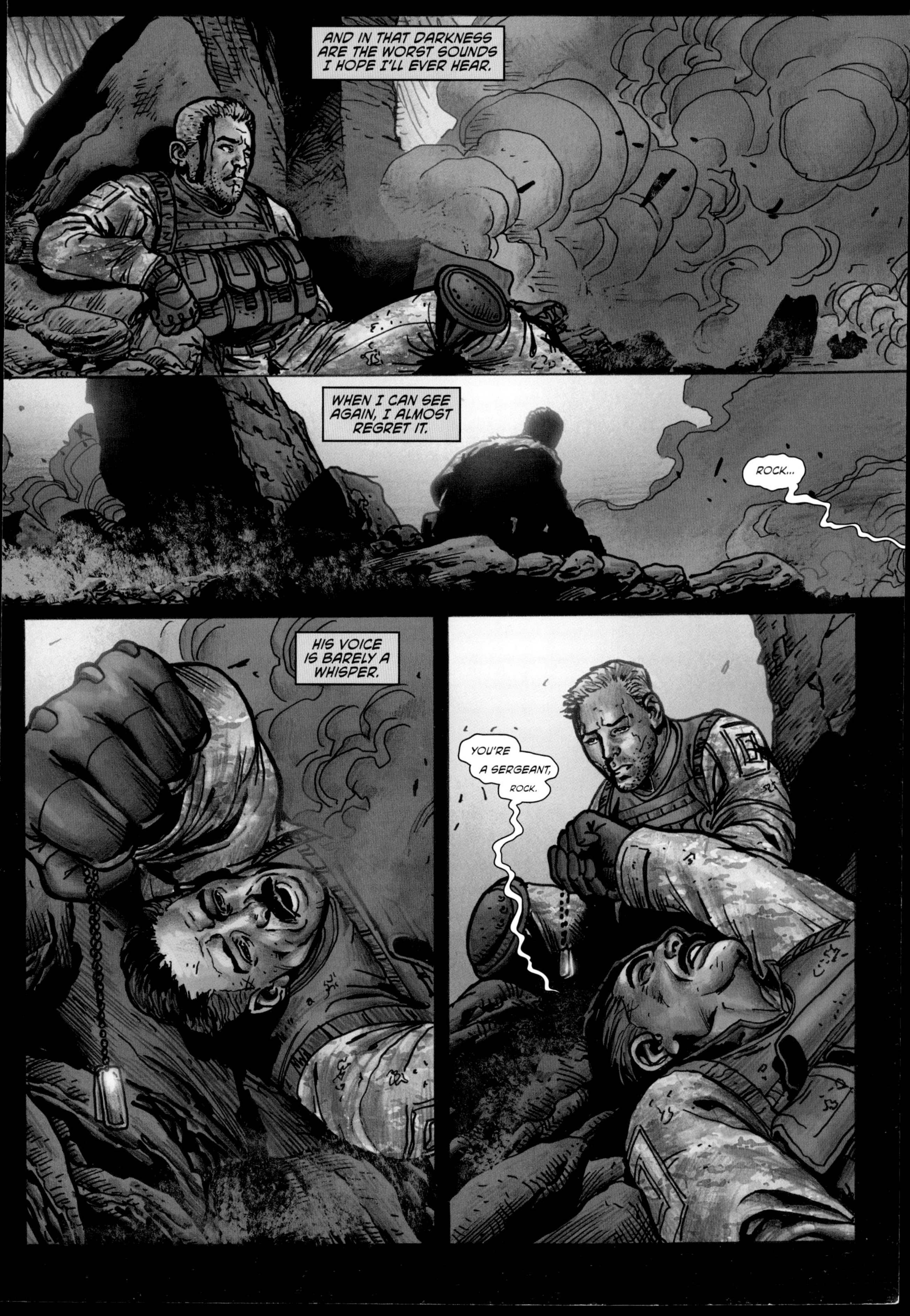
AND IN THAT DARKNESS ARE THE WORST SOUNDS I HOPE I'LL EVER HEAR.
WHEN I CAN SEE AGAIN, I ALMOST REGRET IT.
ROCK...
HIS VOICE IS BARELY A WHISPER.
YOU'RE A SERGEANT, ROCK.

JOSEPH ROCK

IVAN BRANDON WRITER
TOM DERENICK ARTIST
MATT WILSON COLORIST
ROB LEIGH LETTERER
VIKTOR KALVACHEV COVER
KATE STEWART ASSISTANT EDITOR
JOEY CAVALIERI EDITOR

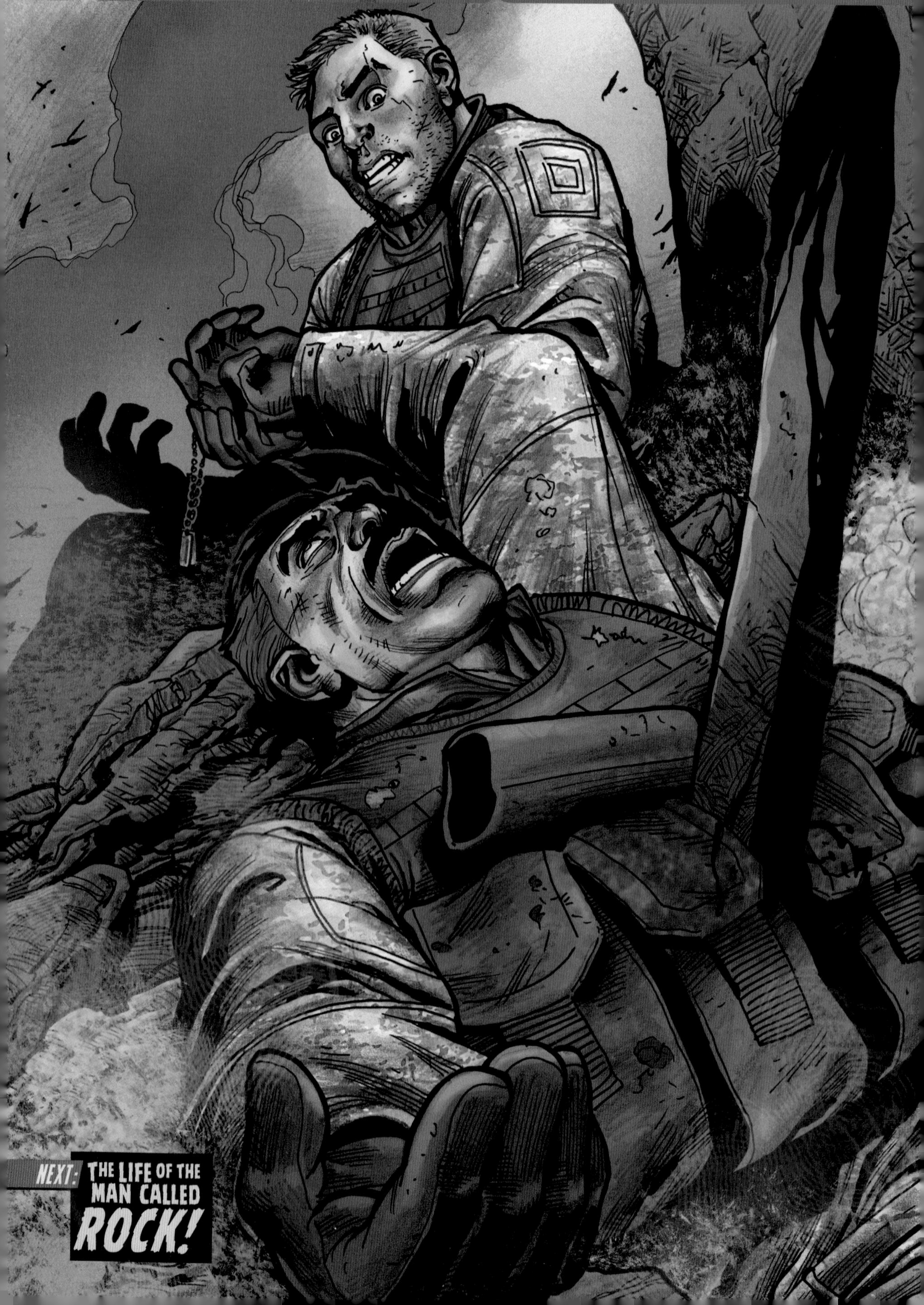
NEXT: THE LIFE OF THE MAN CALLED ROCK!

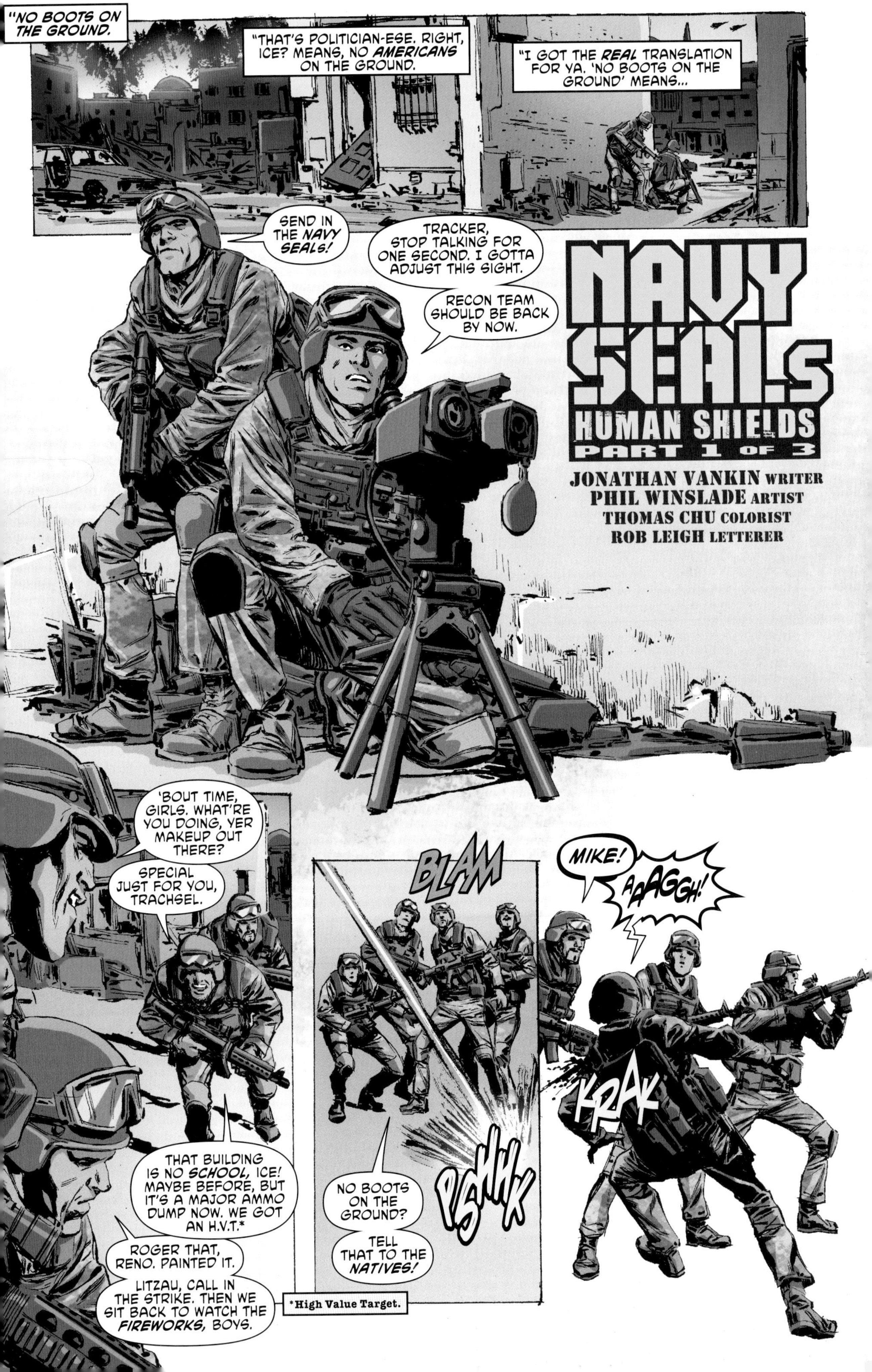

"NO BOOTS ON THE GROUND.
"THAT'S POLITICIAN-ESE. RIGHT, ICE? MEANS, NO AMERICANS ON THE GROUND.
"I GOT THE REAL TRANSLATION FOR YA. 'NO BOOTS ON THE GROUND' MEANS...
SEND IN THE NAVY SEALS!
TRACKER, STOP TALKING FOR ONE SECOND. I GOTTA ADJUST THIS SIGHT.
RECON TEAM SHOULD BE BACK BY NOW.
NAVY SEALs
HUMAN SHIELDS
PART 1 OF 3
JONATHAN VANKIN WRITER
PHIL WINSLADE ARTIST
THOMAS CHU COLORIST
ROB LEIGH LETTERER
'BOUT TIME, GIRLS. WHAT'RE YOU DOING, YER MAKEUP OUT THERE?
SPECIAL JUST FOR YOU, TRACHSEL.
THAT BUILDING IS NO SCHOOL, ICE! MAYBE BEFORE, BUT IT'S A MAJOR AMMO DUMP NOW. WE GOT AN H.V.T.*
ROGER THAT, RENO. PAINTED IT.
LITZAU, CALL IN THE STRIKE. THEN WE SIT BACK TO WATCH THE FIREWORKS, BOYS.
*High Value Target.
BLAM
PSHHK
NO BOOTS ON THE GROUND?
TELL THAT TO THE NATIVES!
MIKE!
AAAGGH!
KRAK

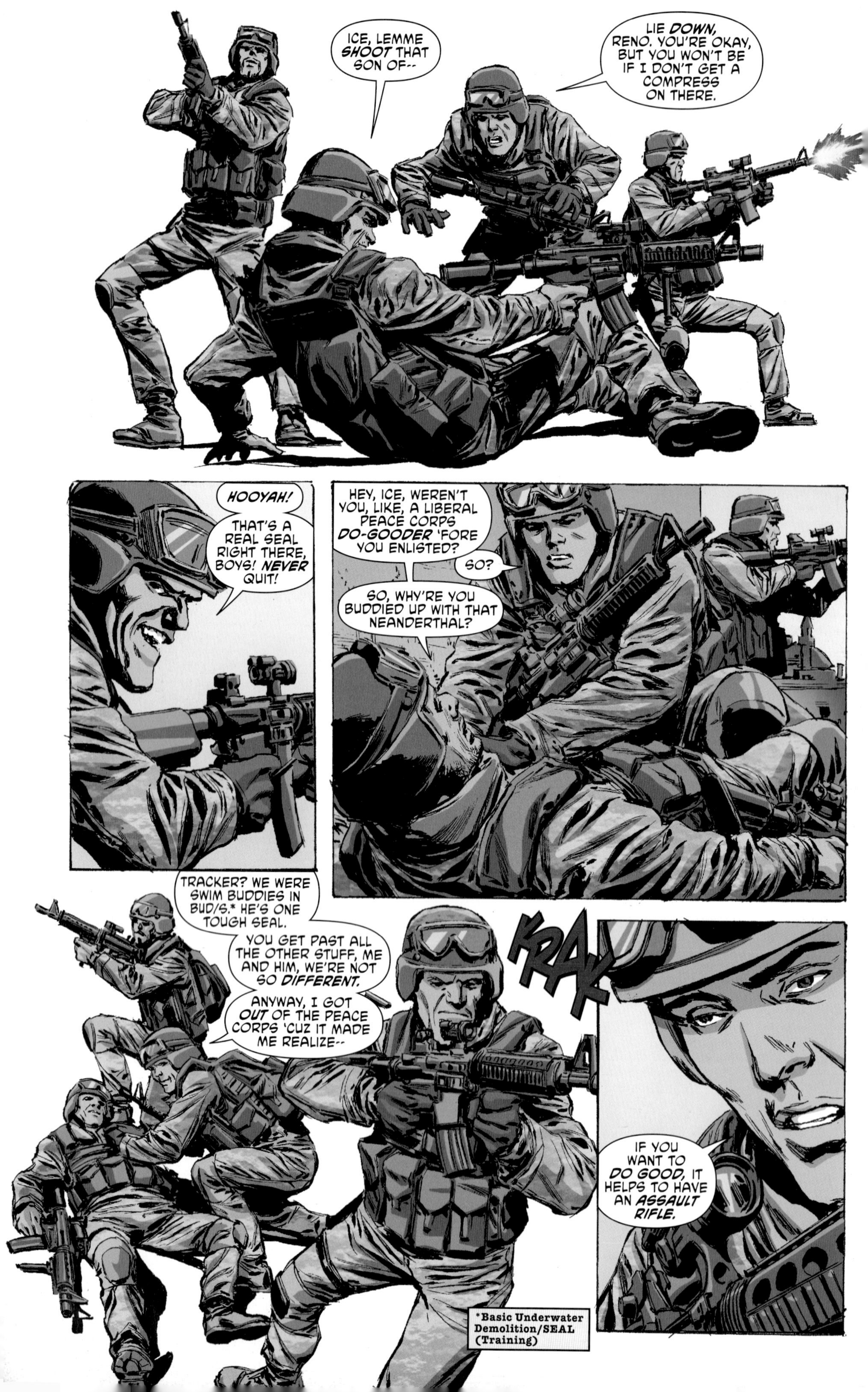
ICE, LEMME SHOOT THAT SON OF--
LIE DOWN, RENO. YOU'RE OKAY, BUT YOU WON'T BE IF I DON'T GET A COMPRESS ON THERE.
HOOYAH!
THAT'S A REAL SEAL RIGHT THERE, BOYS! NEVER QUIT!
HEY, ICE, WEREN'T YOU, LIKE, A LIBERAL PEACE CORPS DO-GOODER 'FORE YOU ENLISTED?
SO?
SO, WHY'RE YOU BUDDIED UP WITH THAT NEANDERTHAL?
TRACKER? WE WERE SWIM BUDDIES IN BUD/S.* HE'S ONE TOUGH SEAL.
YOU GET PAST ALL THE OTHER STUFF, ME AND HIM, WE'RE NOT SO DIFFERENT.
ANYWAY, I GOT OUT OF THE PEACE CORPS 'CUZ IT MADE ME REALIZE--
KRAK
IF YOU WANT TO DO GOOD, IT HELPS TO HAVE AN ASSAULT RIFLE.
*Basic Underwater Demolition/SEAL (Training)

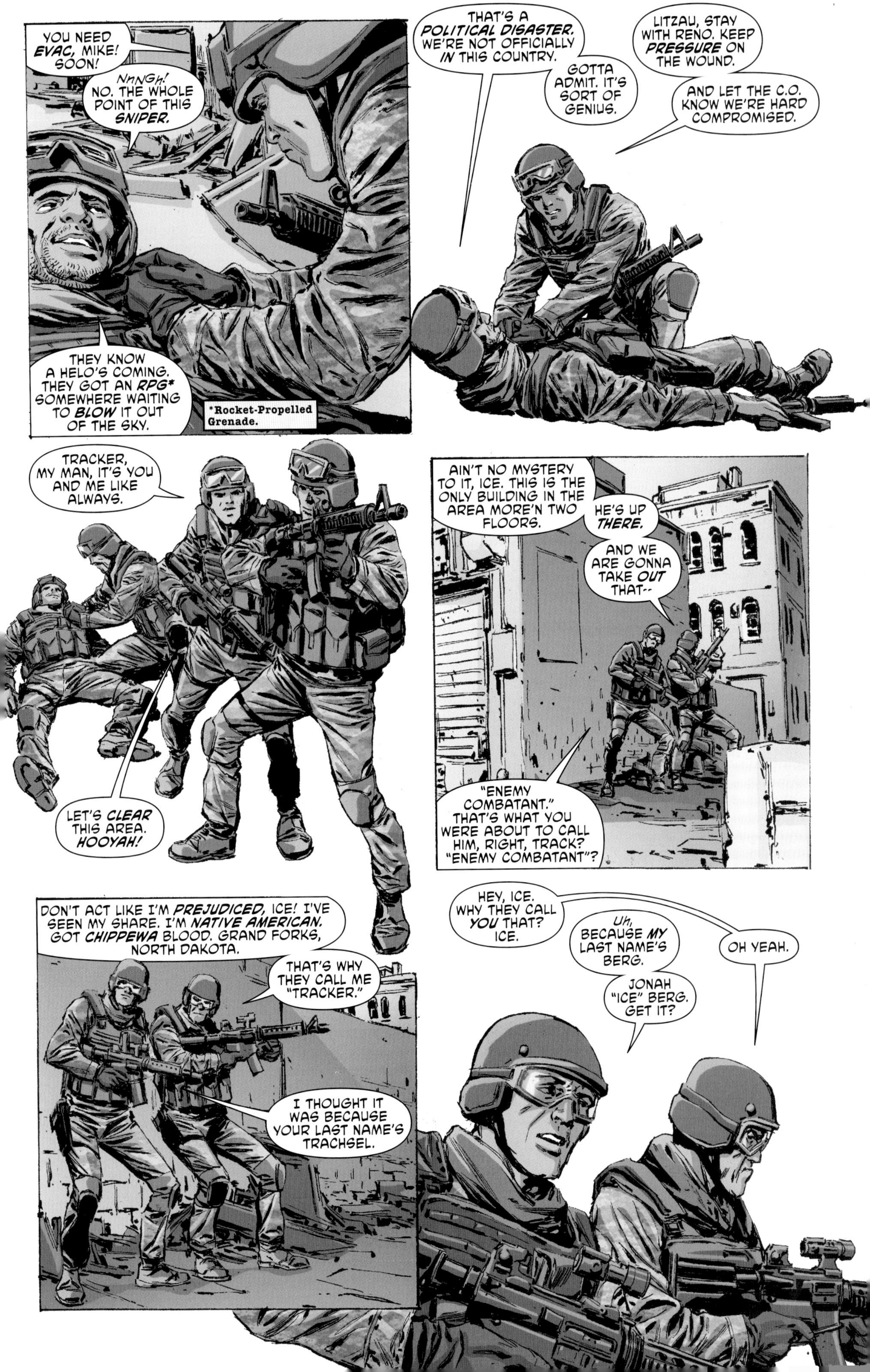
YOU NEED *EVAC*, MIKE! SOON!
NNNGH! NO. THE WHOLE POINT OF THIS *SNIPER*.
THEY KNOW A HELO'S COMING. THEY GOT AN *RPG** SOMEWHERE WAITING TO *BLOW* IT OUT OF THE SKY.
*Rocket-Propelled Grenade.
THAT'S A *POLITICAL DISASTER*. WE'RE NOT OFFICIALLY *IN* THIS COUNTRY.
GOTTA ADMIT. IT'S SORT OF GENIUS.
LITZAU, STAY WITH RENO. KEEP *PRESSURE* ON THE WOUND.
AND LET THE C.O. KNOW WE'RE HARD COMPROMISED.
TRACKER, MY MAN, IT'S YOU AND ME LIKE ALWAYS.
LET'S *CLEAR* THIS AREA. *HOOYAH!*
AIN'T NO MYSTERY TO IT, ICE. THIS IS THE ONLY BUILDING IN THE AREA MORE'N TWO FLOORS.
HE'S UP *THERE*.
AND WE ARE GONNA TAKE *OUT* THAT--
"ENEMY COMBATANT." THAT'S WHAT YOU WERE ABOUT TO CALL HIM, RIGHT, TRACK? "ENEMY COMBATANT"?
DON'T ACT LIKE I'M *PREJUDICED*, ICE! I'VE SEEN MY SHARE. I'M *NATIVE AMERICAN*. GOT *CHIPPEWA* BLOOD. GRAND FORKS, NORTH DAKOTA.
THAT'S WHY THEY CALL ME "TRACKER."
I THOUGHT IT WAS BECAUSE YOUR LAST NAME'S TRACHSEL.
HEY, ICE. WHY THEY CALL *YOU* THAT? ICE.
UH, BECAUSE *MY* LAST NAME'S BERG.
JONAH "ICE" BERG. GET IT?
OH YEAH.

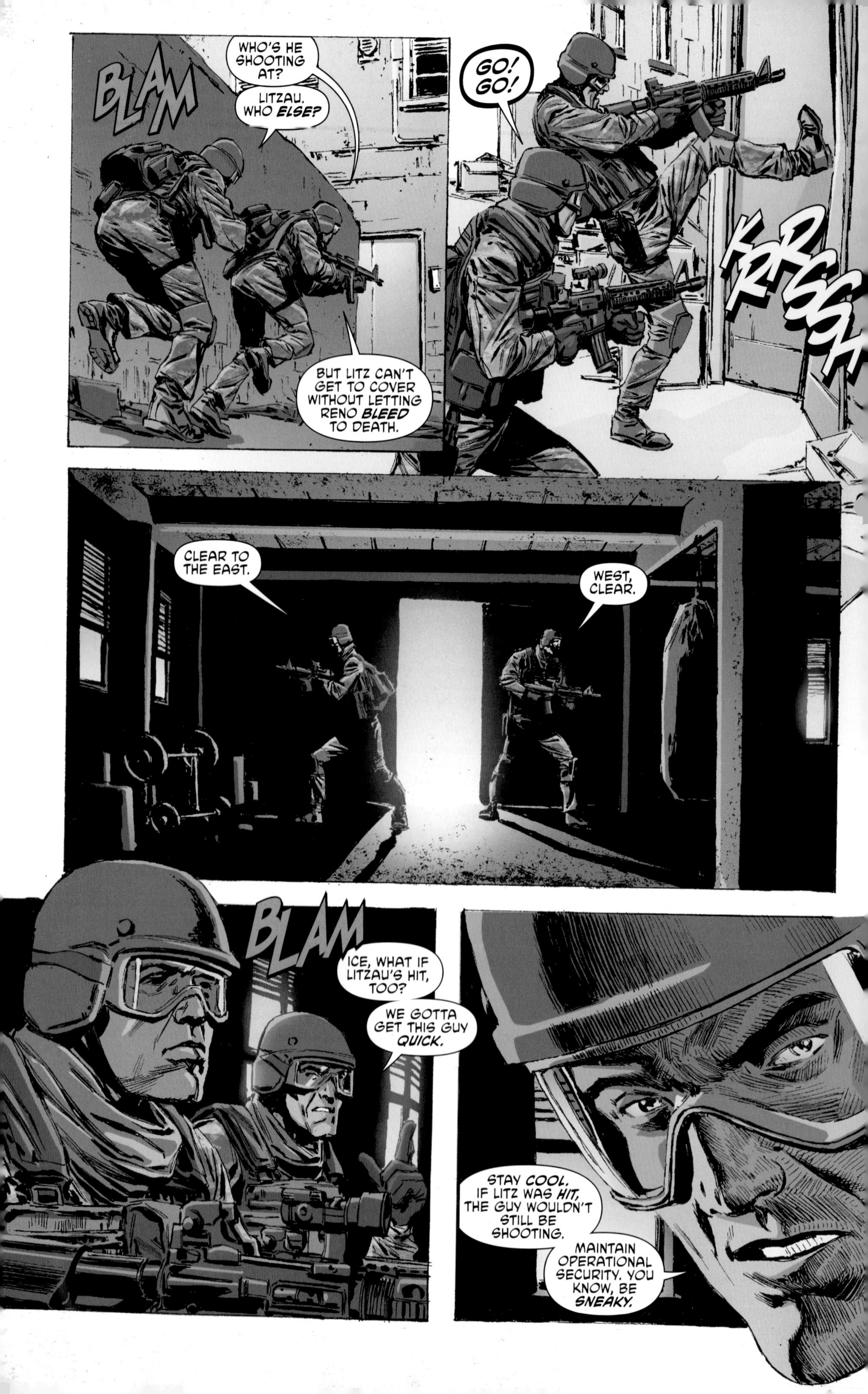
BLAM
WHO'S HE SHOOTING AT?
LITZAU. WHO ELSE?
BUT LITZ CAN'T GET TO COVER WITHOUT LETTING RENO BLEED TO DEATH.
GO! GO!
KRRSSSH
CLEAR TO THE EAST.
WEST, CLEAR.
BLAM
ICE, WHAT IF LITZAU'S HIT, TOO?
WE GOTTA GET THIS GUY QUICK.
STAY COOL. IF LITZ WAS HIT, THE GUY WOULDN'T STILL BE SHOOTING.
MAINTAIN OPERATIONAL SECURITY. YOU KNOW, BE SNEAKY.

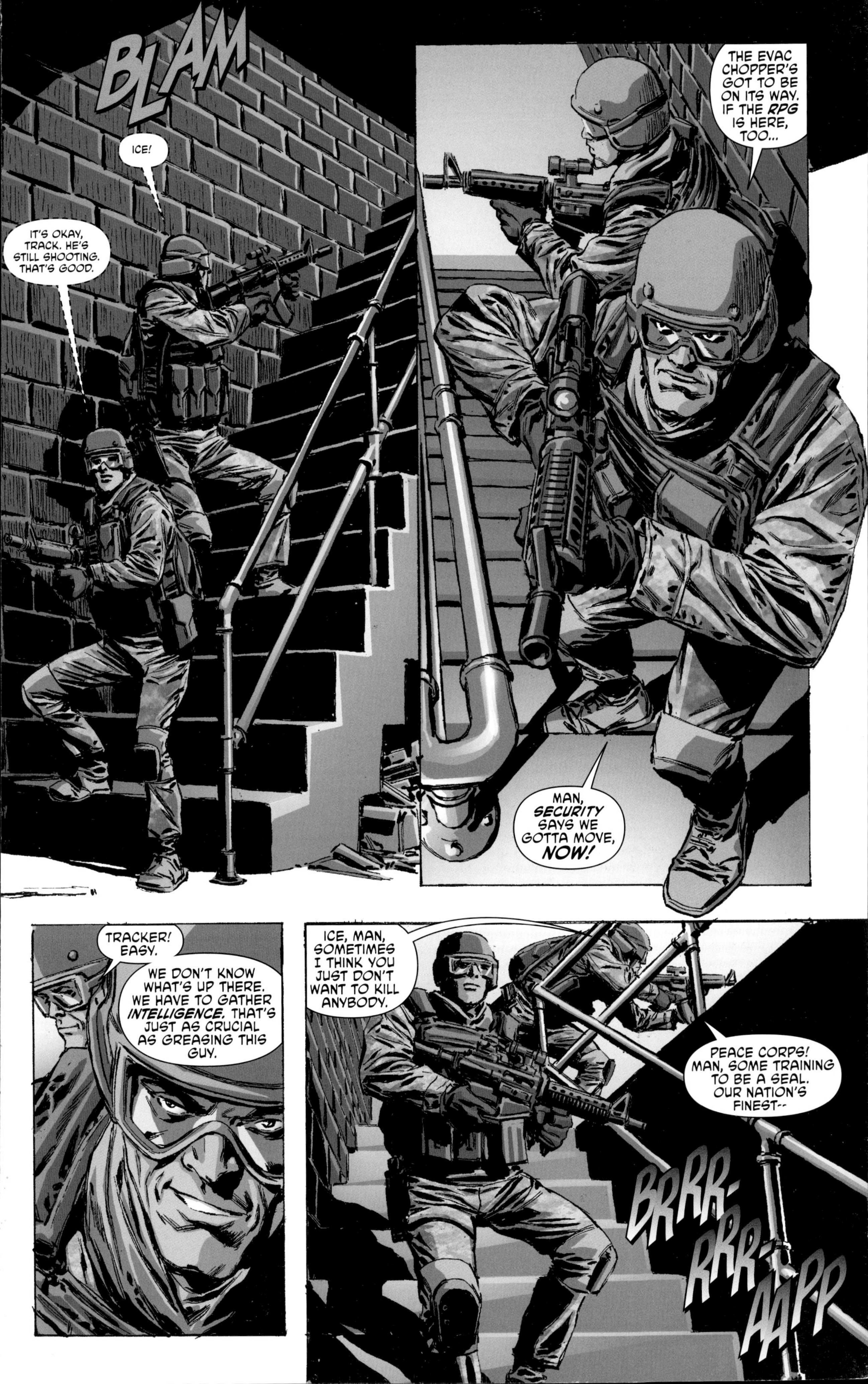
BLAM
ICE!
IT'S OKAY, TRACK. HE'S STILL SHOOTING. THAT'S GOOD.
THE EVAC CHOPPER'S GOT TO BE ON ITS WAY. IF THE *RPG* IS HERE, TOO...
MAN, ***SECURITY*** SAYS WE GOTTA MOVE, ***NOW!***
TRACKER! EASY.
WE DON'T KNOW WHAT'S UP THERE. WE HAVE TO GATHER *INTELLIGENCE.* THAT'S JUST AS CRUCIAL AS GREASING THIS GUY.
ICE, MAN, SOMETIMES I THINK YOU JUST DON'T WANT TO KILL ANYBODY.
PEACE CORPS! MAN, SOME TRAINING TO BE A SEAL. OUR NATION'S FINEST--
BRRR-RRR-AAPP

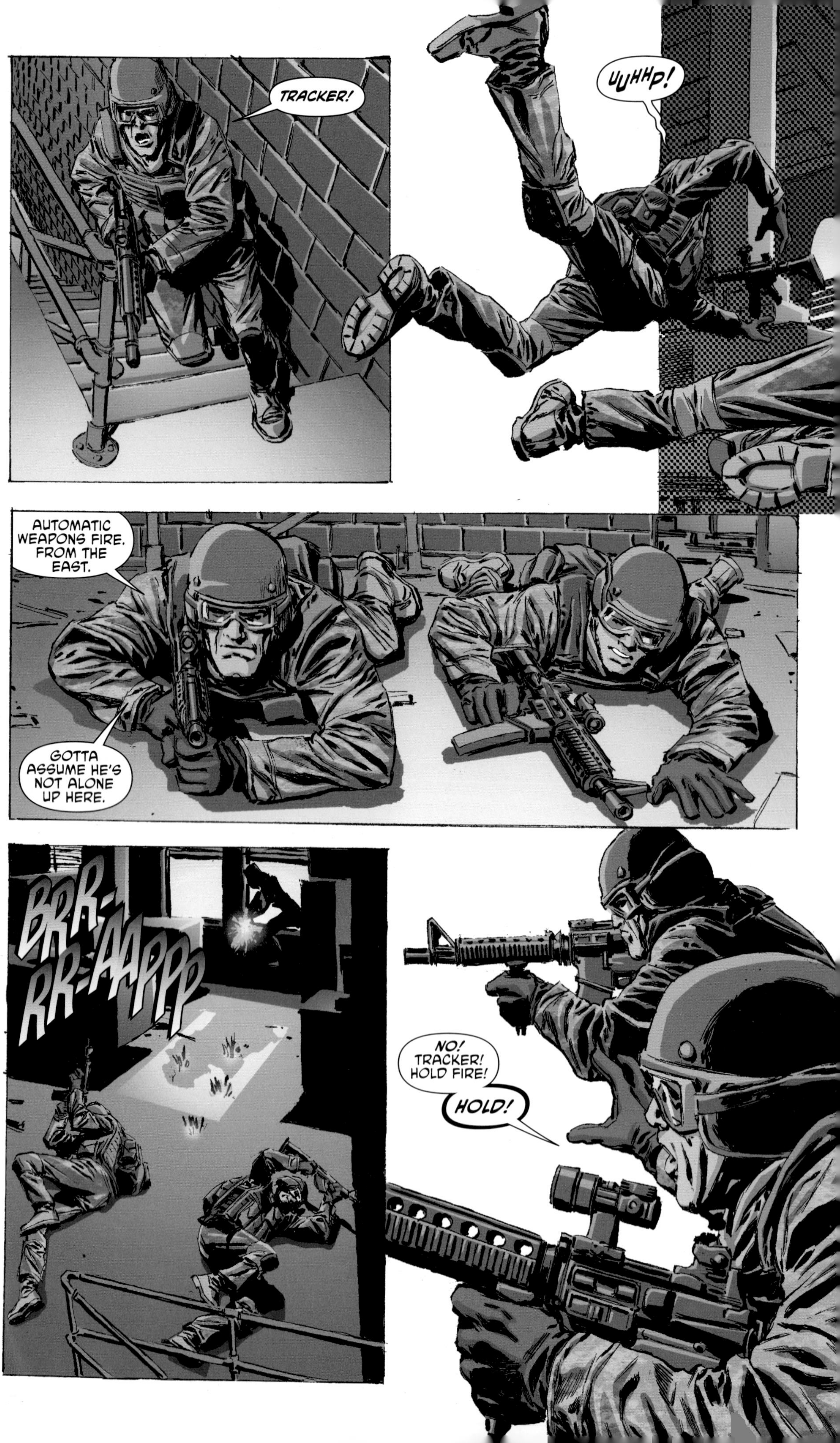
TRACKER!
UUHHP!
AUTOMATIC WEAPONS FIRE. FROM THE EAST.
GOTTA ASSUME HE'S NOT ALONE UP HERE.
BRR-RR-AAPPP
NO! TRACKER! HOLD FIRE!
HOLD!

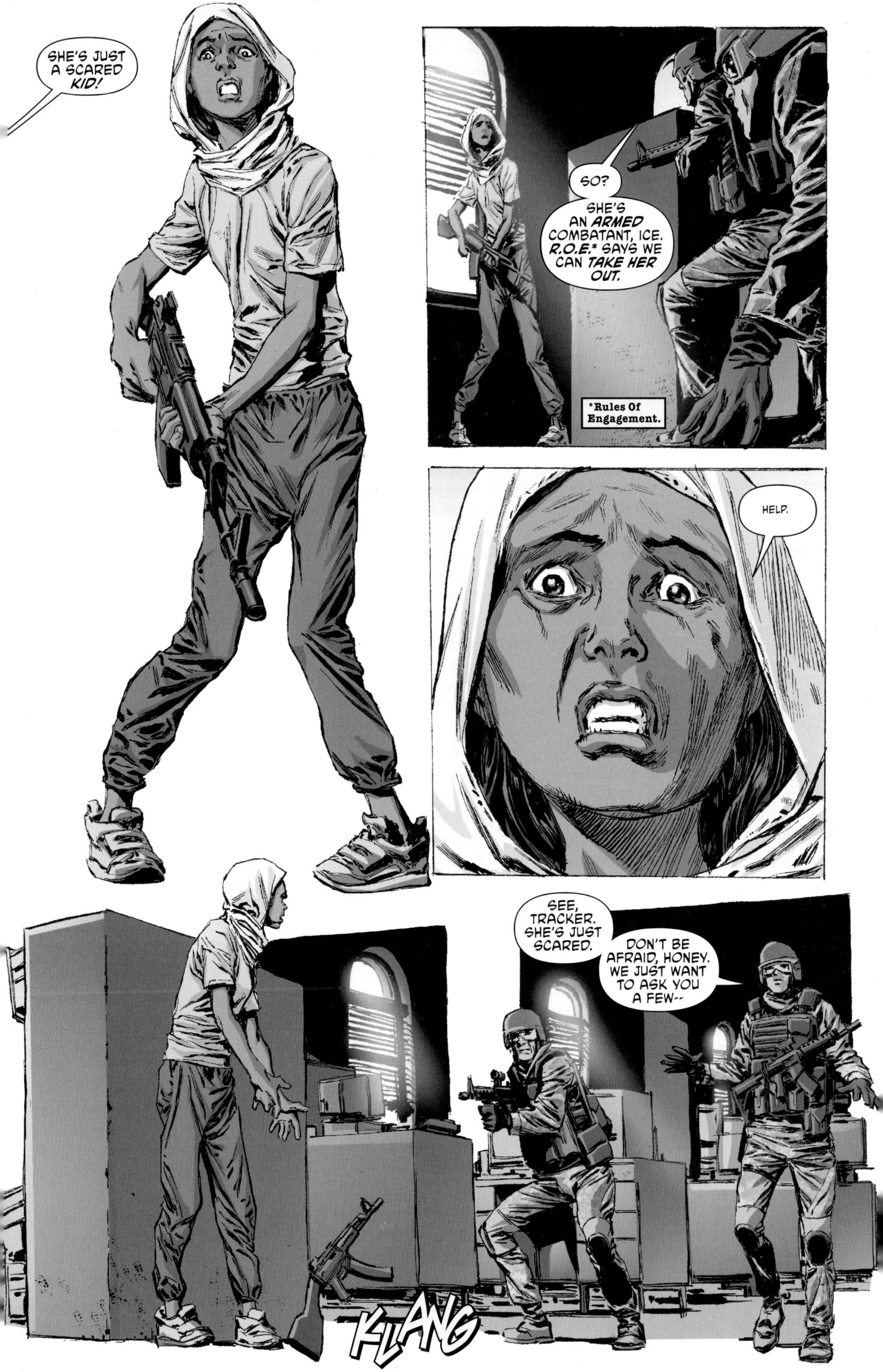
SHE'S JUST A SCARED KID!
SO?
SHE'S AN ARMED COMBATANT, ICE. R.O.E.* SAYS WE CAN TAKE HER OUT.
*Rules Of Engagement.
HELP.
SEE, TRACKER. SHE'S JUST SCARED.
DON'T BE AFRAID, HONEY. WE JUST WANT TO ASK YOU A FEW--
KLANG

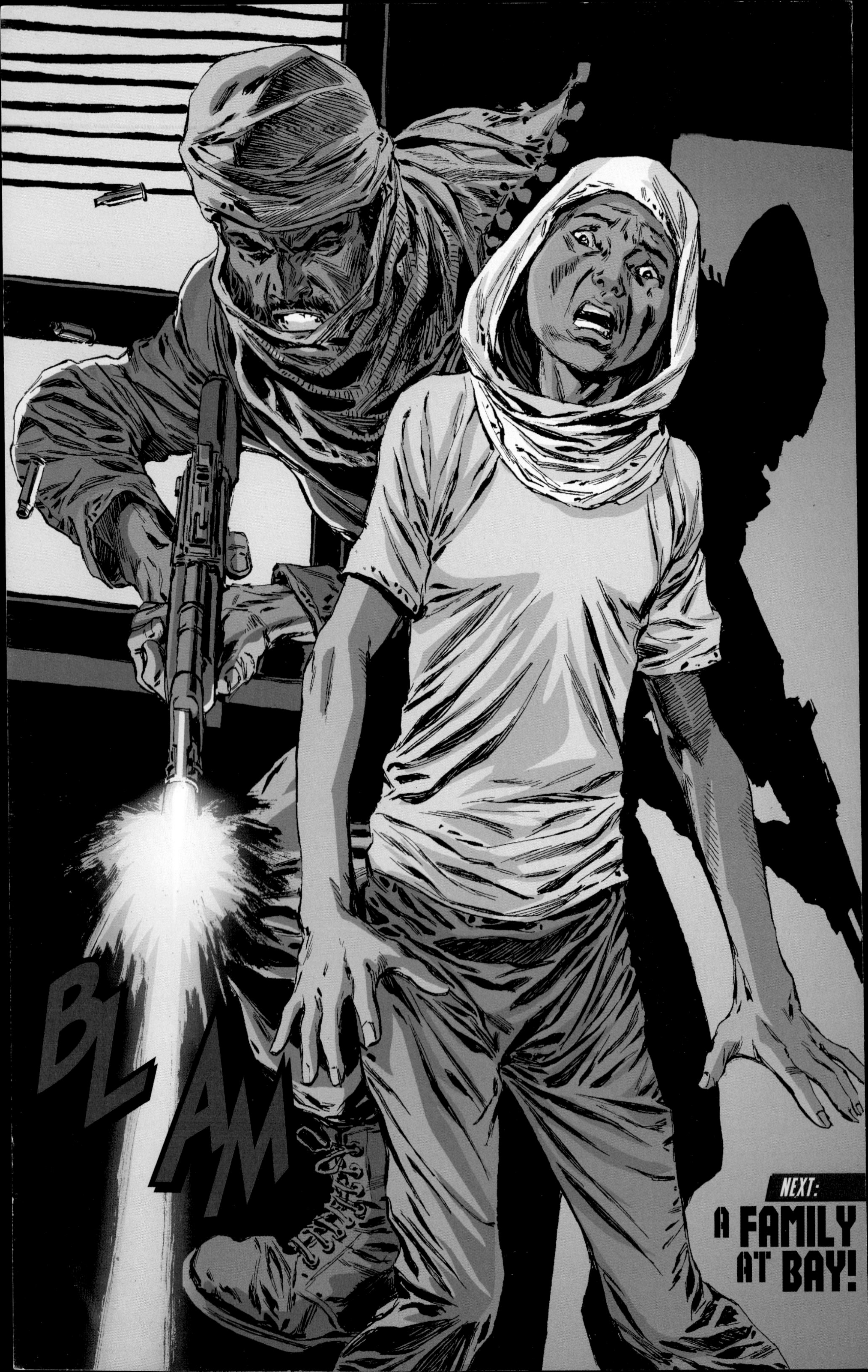
BLAM
NEXT:
A FAMILY AT BAY!

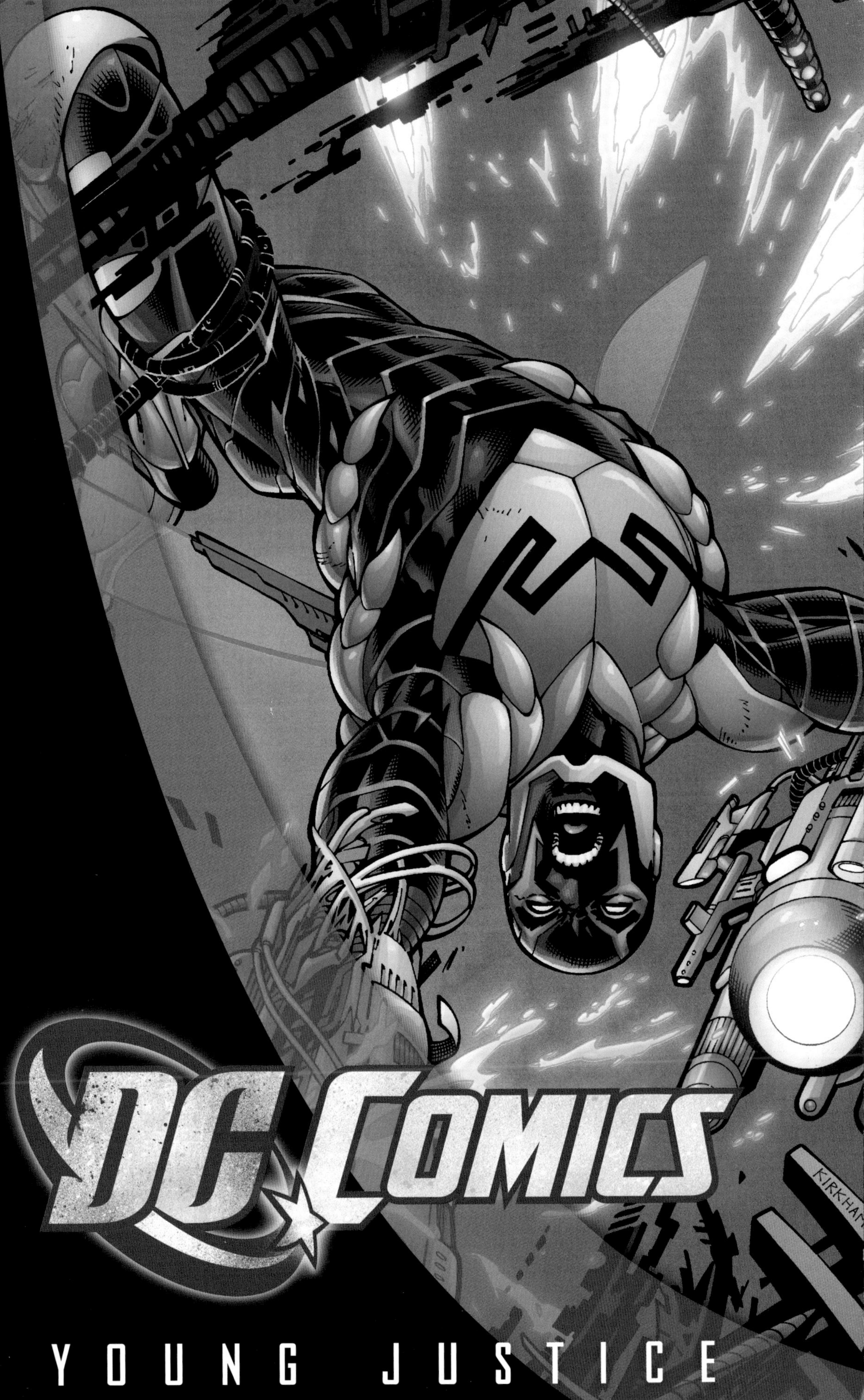
KIRKHAM

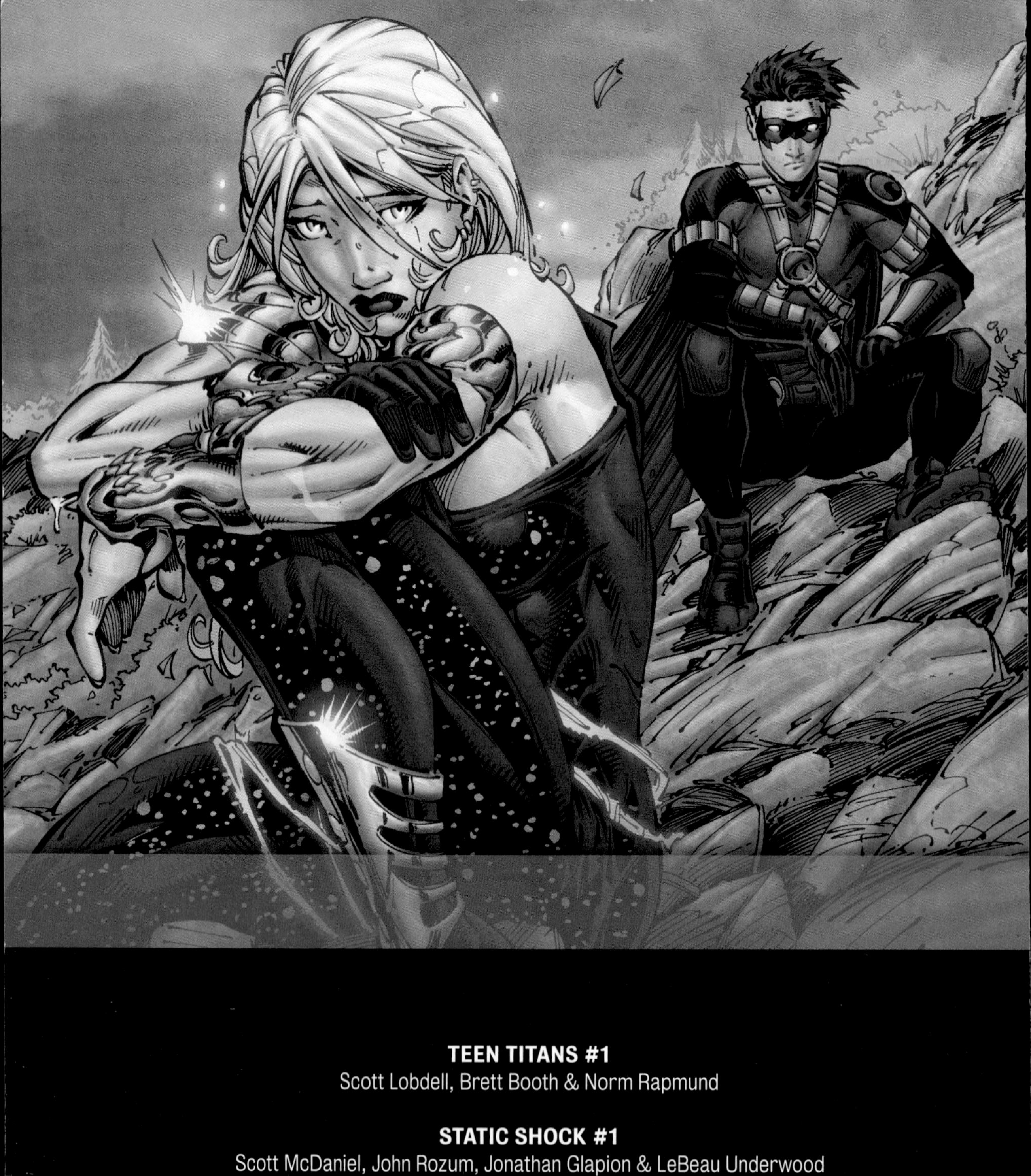

TEEN TITANS #1
Scott Lobdell, Brett Booth & Norm Rapmund

STATIC SHOCK #1
Scott McDaniel, John Rozum, Jonathan Glapion & LeBeau Underwood

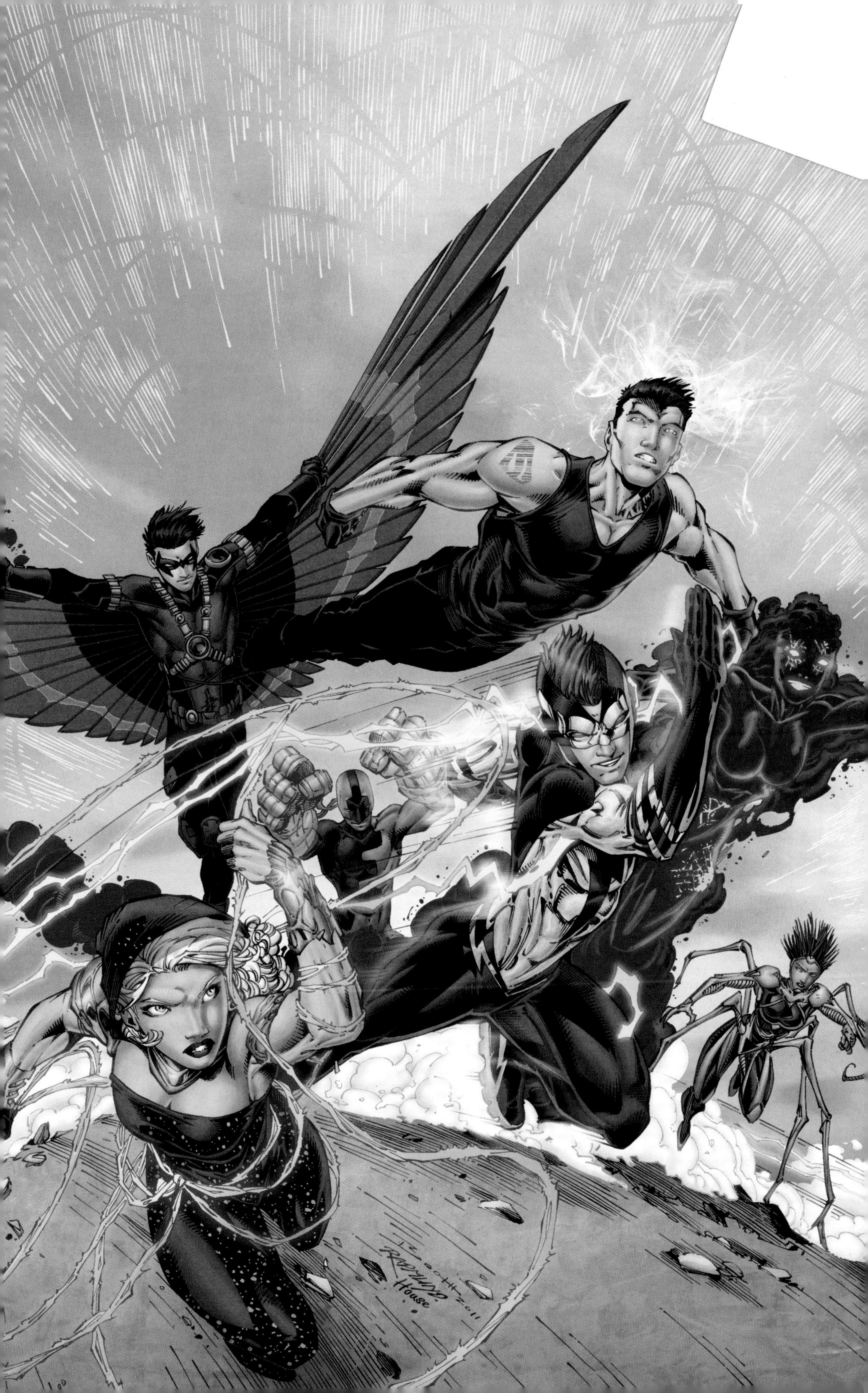

TEEN TITANS

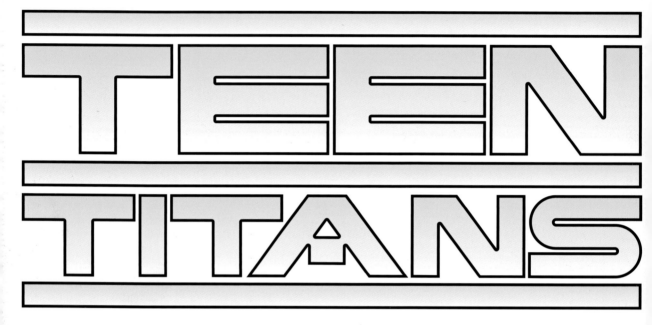

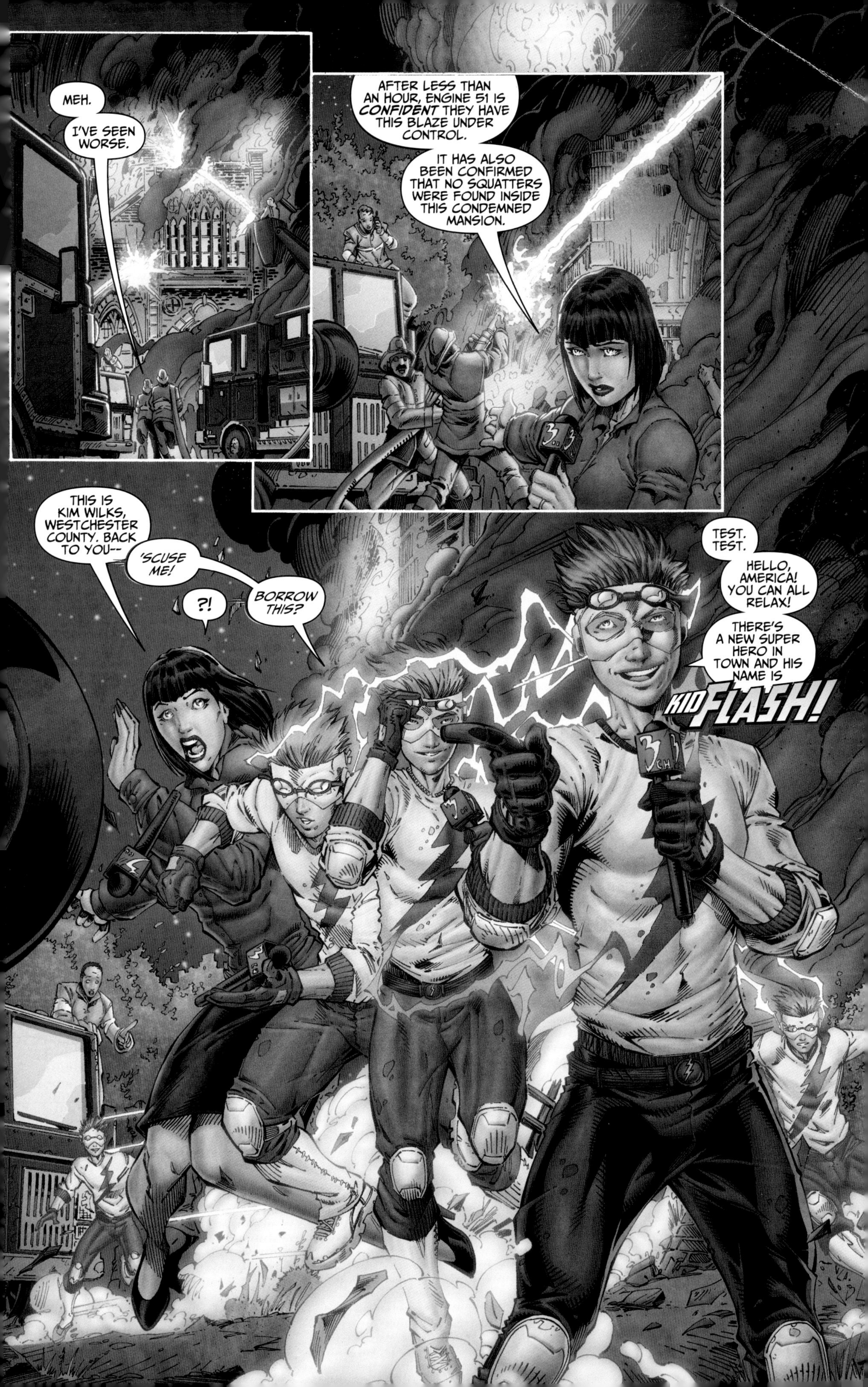
MEH.
I'VE SEEN WORSE.
AFTER LESS THAN AN HOUR, ENGINE 51 IS *CONFIDENT* THEY HAVE THIS BLAZE UNDER CONTROL.
IT HAS ALSO BEEN CONFIRMED THAT NO SQUATTERS WERE FOUND INSIDE THIS CONDEMNED MANSION.
THIS IS KIM WILKS, WESTCHESTER COUNTY. BACK TO YOU--
'SCUSE ME!
?!
BORROW THIS?
TEST. TEST.
HELLO, AMERICA! YOU CAN ALL RELAX!
THERE'S A NEW SUPER HERO IN TOWN AND HIS NAME IS
KID FLASH!

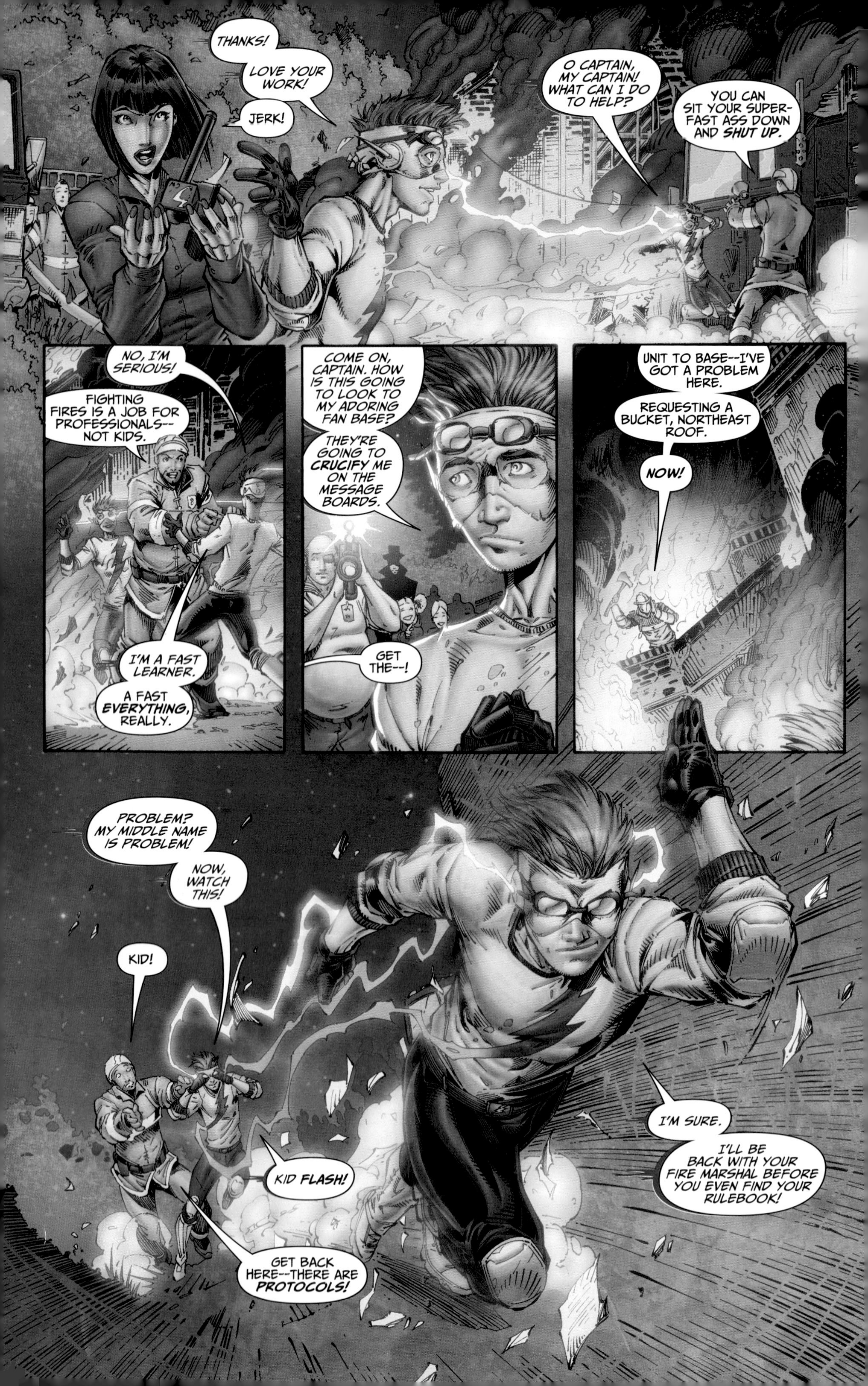
THANKS!
LOVE YOUR WORK!
JERK!
O CAPTAIN, MY CAPTAIN! WHAT CAN I DO TO HELP?
YOU CAN SIT YOUR SUPER-FAST ASS DOWN AND SHUT UP.
NO, I'M SERIOUS!
FIGHTING FIRES IS A JOB FOR PROFESSIONALS--NOT KIDS.
I'M A FAST LEARNER.
A FAST EVERYTHING, REALLY.
COME ON, CAPTAIN. HOW IS THIS GOING TO LOOK TO MY ADORING FAN BASE?
THEY'RE GOING TO CRUCIFY ME ON THE MESSAGE BOARDS.
GET THE--!
UNIT TO BASE--I'VE GOT A PROBLEM HERE.
REQUESTING A BUCKET, NORTHEAST ROOF.
NOW!
PROBLEM? MY MIDDLE NAME IS PROBLEM!
NOW, WATCH THIS!
KID!
KID FLASH!
GET BACK HERE--THERE ARE PROTOCOLS!
I'M SURE.
I'LL BE BACK WITH YOUR FIRE MARSHAL BEFORE YOU EVEN FIND YOUR RULEBOOK!

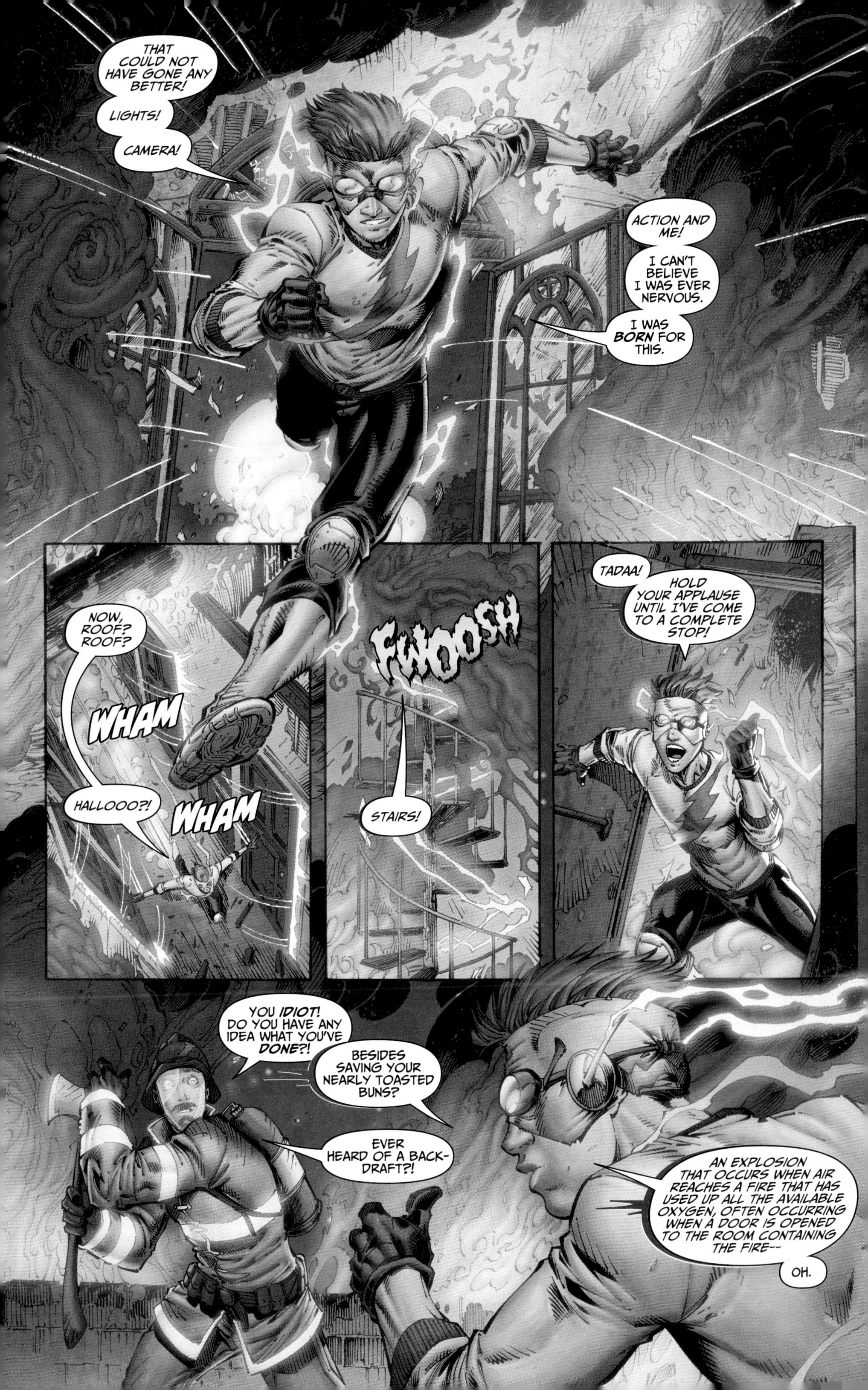
THAT COULD NOT HAVE GONE ANY BETTER!
LIGHTS!
CAMERA!
ACTION AND ME!
I CAN'T BELIEVE I WAS EVER NERVOUS.
I WAS BORN FOR THIS.
NOW, ROOF? ROOF?
WHAM
HALLOOO?!
WHAM
FWOOSH
STAIRS!
TADAA!
HOLD YOUR APPLAUSE UNTIL I'VE COME TO A COMPLETE STOP!
YOU IDIOT! DO YOU HAVE ANY IDEA WHAT YOU'VE DONE?!
BESIDES SAVING YOUR NEARLY TOASTED BUNS?
EVER HEARD OF A BACK-DRAFT?!
AN EXPLOSION THAT OCCURS WHEN AIR REACHES A FIRE THAT HAS USED UP ALL THE AVAILABLE OXYGEN, OFTEN OCCURRING WHEN A DOOR IS OPENED TO THE ROOM CONTAINING THE FIRE--
OH.

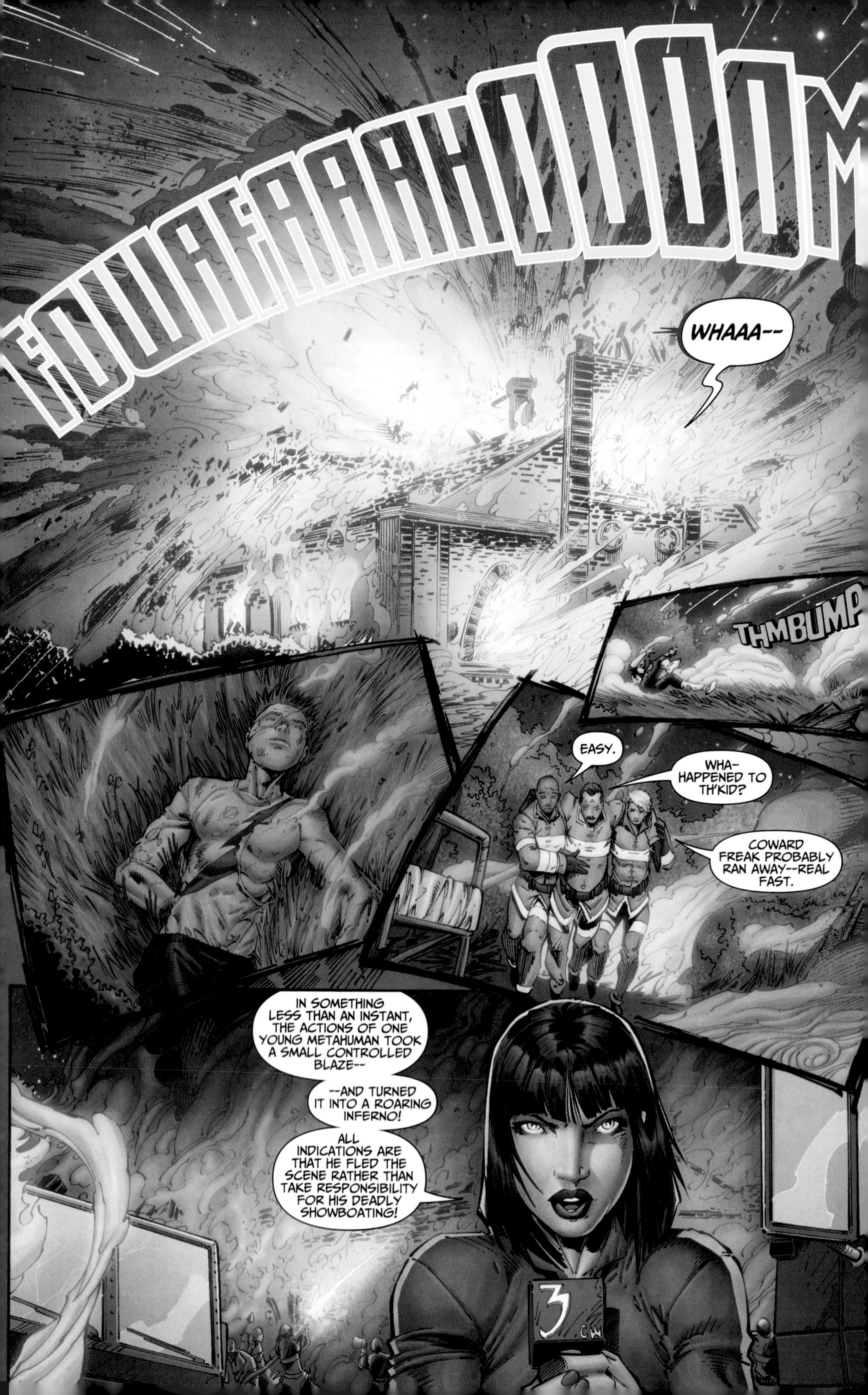
WHAAA--
THMBUMP
EASY.
WHA- HAPPENED TO TH'KID?
COWARD FREAK PROBABLY RAN AWAY--REAL FAST.
IN SOMETHING LESS THAN AN INSTANT, THE ACTIONS OF ONE YOUNG METAHUMAN TOOK A SMALL CONTROLLED BLAZE--
--AND TURNED IT INTO A ROARING INFERNO!
ALL INDICATIONS ARE THAT HE FLED THE SCENE RATHER THAN TAKE RESPONSIBILITY FOR HIS DEADLY SHOWBOATING!

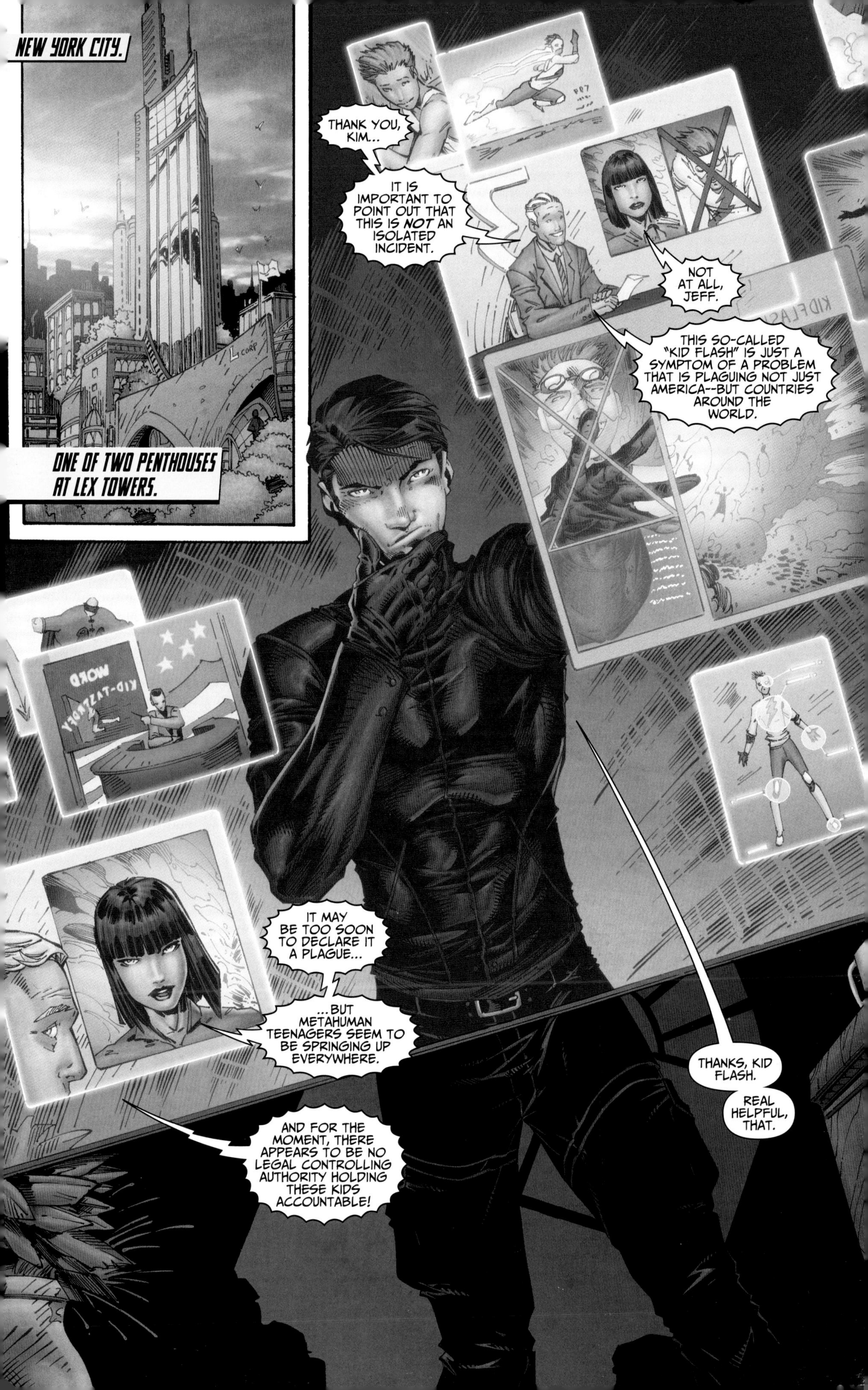

NEW YORK CITY.
ONE OF TWO PENTHOUSES AT LEX TOWERS.
THANK YOU, KIM...
IT IS IMPORTANT TO POINT OUT THAT THIS IS *NOT* AN ISOLATED INCIDENT.
NOT AT ALL, JEFF.
THIS SO-CALLED "KID FLASH" IS JUST A SYMPTOM OF A PROBLEM THAT IS PLAGUING NOT JUST AMERICA--BUT COUNTRIES AROUND THE WORLD.
IT MAY BE TOO SOON TO DECLARE IT A PLAGUE...
...BUT METAHUMAN TEENAGERS SEEM TO BE SPRINGING UP EVERYWHERE.
AND FOR THE MOMENT, THERE APPEARS TO BE NO LEGAL CONTROLLING AUTHORITY HOLDING THESE KIDS ACCOUNTABLE!
THANKS, KID FLASH.
REAL HELPFUL, THAT.

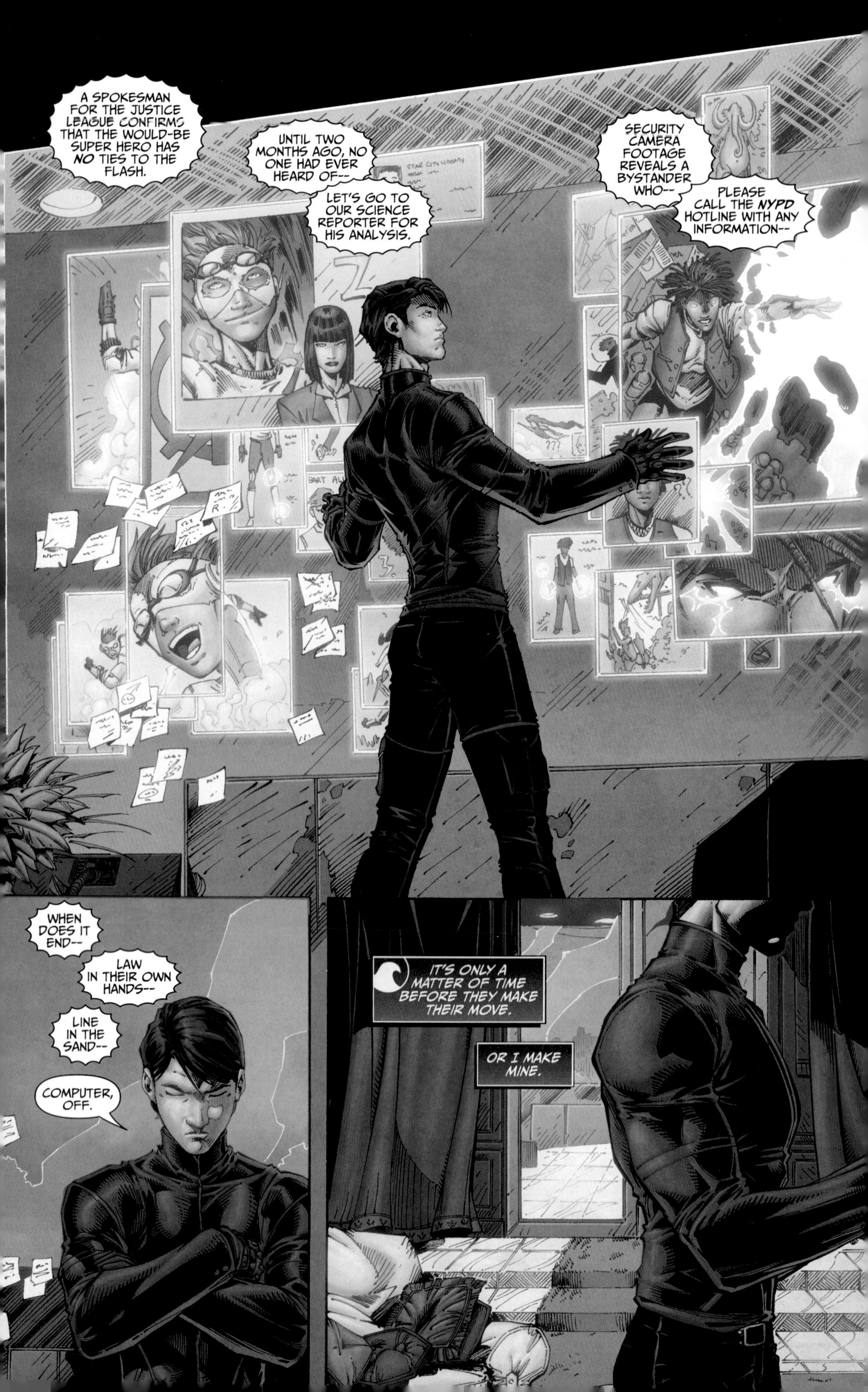

A SPOKESMAN FOR THE JUSTICE LEAGUE CONFIRMS THAT THE WOULD-BE SUPER HERO HAS NO TIES TO THE FLASH.
UNTIL TWO MONTHS AGO, NO ONE HAD EVER HEARD OF--
LET'S GO TO OUR SCIENCE REPORTER FOR HIS ANALYSIS.
SECURITY CAMERA FOOTAGE REVEALS A BYSTANDER WHO--
PLEASE CALL THE NYPD HOTLINE WITH ANY INFORMATION--
WHEN DOES IT END--
LAW IN THEIR OWN HANDS--
LINE IN THE SAND--
COMPUTER, OFF.
IT'S ONLY A MATTER OF TIME BEFORE THEY MAKE THEIR MOVE.
OR I MAKE MINE.

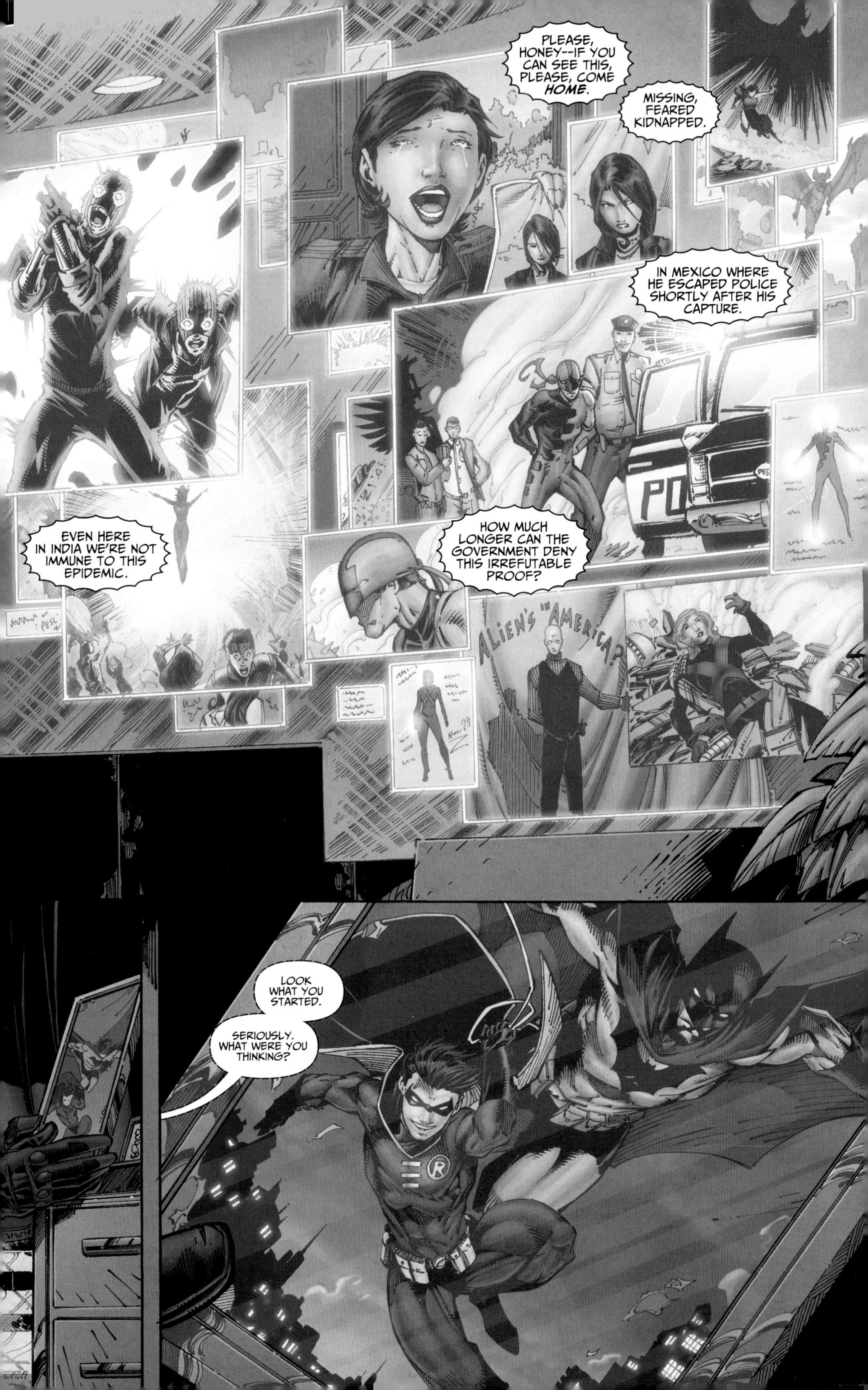
PLEASE, HONEY--IF YOU CAN SEE THIS, PLEASE, COME *HOME*.
MISSING, FEARED KIDNAPPED.
IN MEXICO WHERE HE ESCAPED POLICE SHORTLY AFTER HIS CAPTURE.
EVEN HERE IN INDIA WE'RE NOT IMMUNE TO THIS EPIDEMIC.
HOW MUCH LONGER CAN THE GOVERNMENT DENY THIS IRREFUTABLE PROOF?
ALIEN'S "IN" AMERICA?
LOOK WHAT YOU STARTED.
SERIOUSLY. WHAT WERE YOU THINKING?

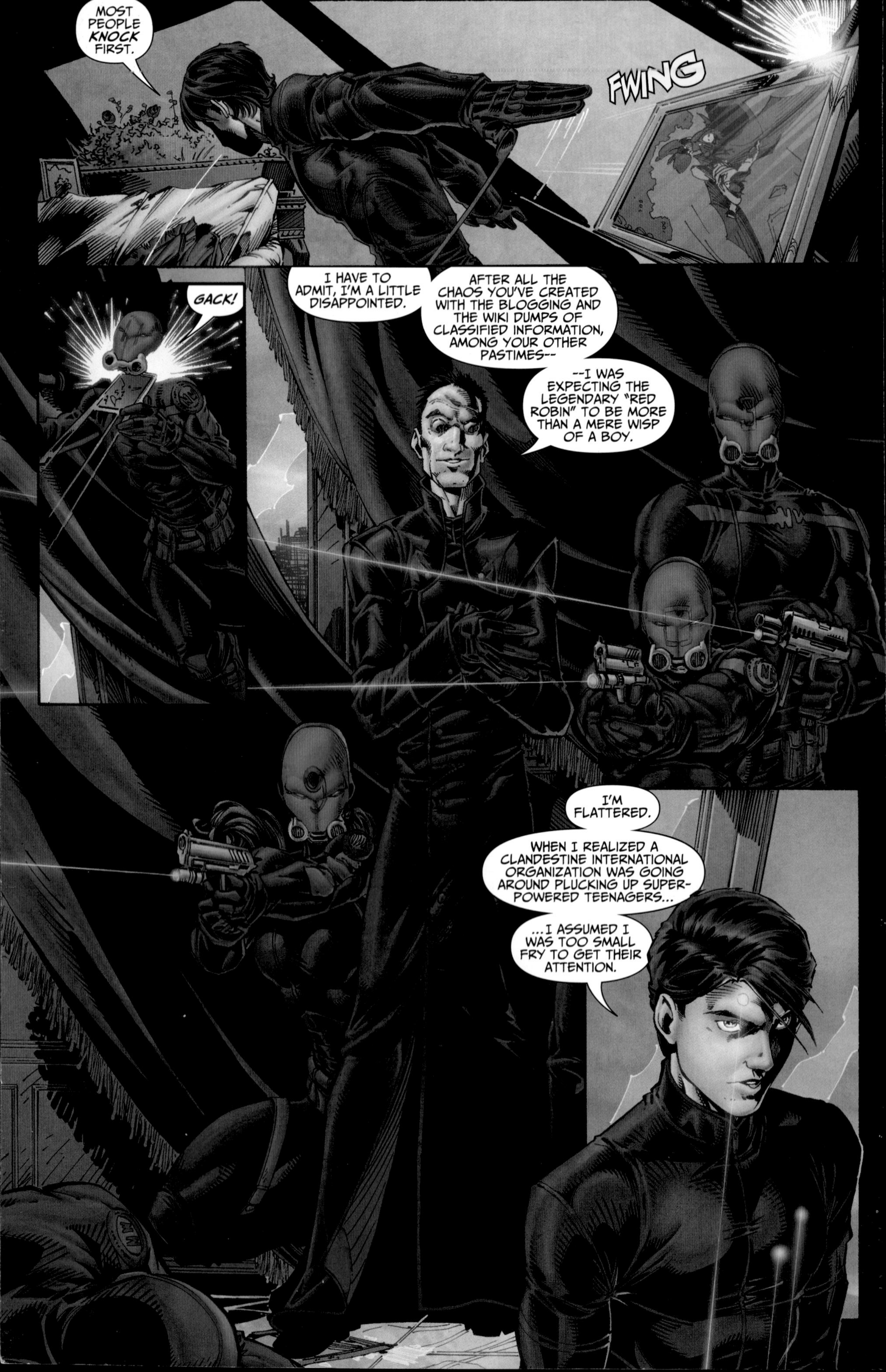
MOST PEOPLE KNOCK FIRST.
FWING
GACK!
I HAVE TO ADMIT, I'M A LITTLE DISAPPOINTED.
AFTER ALL THE CHAOS YOU'VE CREATED WITH THE BLOGGING AND THE WIKI DUMPS OF CLASSIFIED INFORMATION, AMONG YOUR OTHER PASTIMES--
--I WAS EXPECTING THE LEGENDARY "RED ROBIN" TO BE MORE THAN A MERE WISP OF A BOY.
I'M FLATTERED.
WHEN I REALIZED A CLANDESTINE INTERNATIONAL ORGANIZATION WAS GOING AROUND PLUCKING UP SUPER-POWERED TEENAGERS...
...I ASSUMED I WAS TOO SMALL FRY TO GET THEIR ATTENTION.

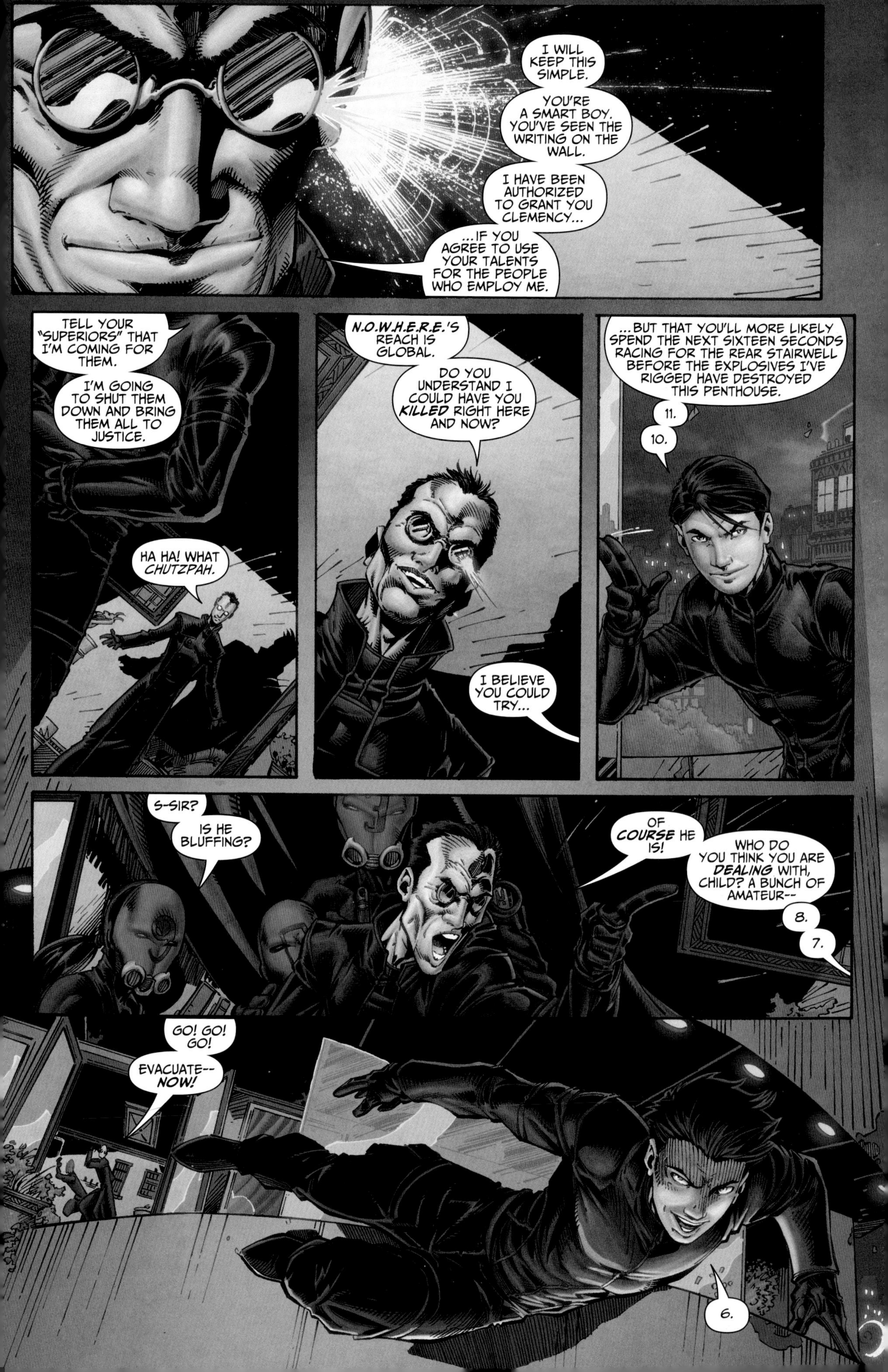
I WILL KEEP THIS SIMPLE.
YOU'RE A SMART BOY. YOU'VE SEEN THE WRITING ON THE WALL.
I HAVE BEEN AUTHORIZED TO GRANT YOU CLEMENCY...
...IF YOU AGREE TO USE YOUR TALENTS FOR THE PEOPLE WHO EMPLOY ME.
TELL YOUR "SUPERIORS" THAT I'M COMING FOR THEM.
I'M GOING TO SHUT THEM DOWN AND BRING THEM ALL TO JUSTICE.
HA HA! WHAT CHUTZPAH.
N.O.W.H.E.R.E.'S REACH IS GLOBAL.
DO YOU UNDERSTAND I COULD HAVE YOU KILLED RIGHT HERE AND NOW?
I BELIEVE YOU COULD TRY...
...BUT THAT YOU'LL MORE LIKELY SPEND THE NEXT SIXTEEN SECONDS RACING FOR THE REAR STAIRWELL BEFORE THE EXPLOSIVES I'VE RIGGED HAVE DESTROYED THIS PENTHOUSE.
11.
10.
S-SIR?
IS HE BLUFFING?
OF COURSE HE IS!
WHO DO YOU THINK YOU ARE DEALING WITH, CHILD? A BUNCH OF AMATEUR--
8.
7.
GO! GO! GO!
EVACUATE-- NOW!
6.

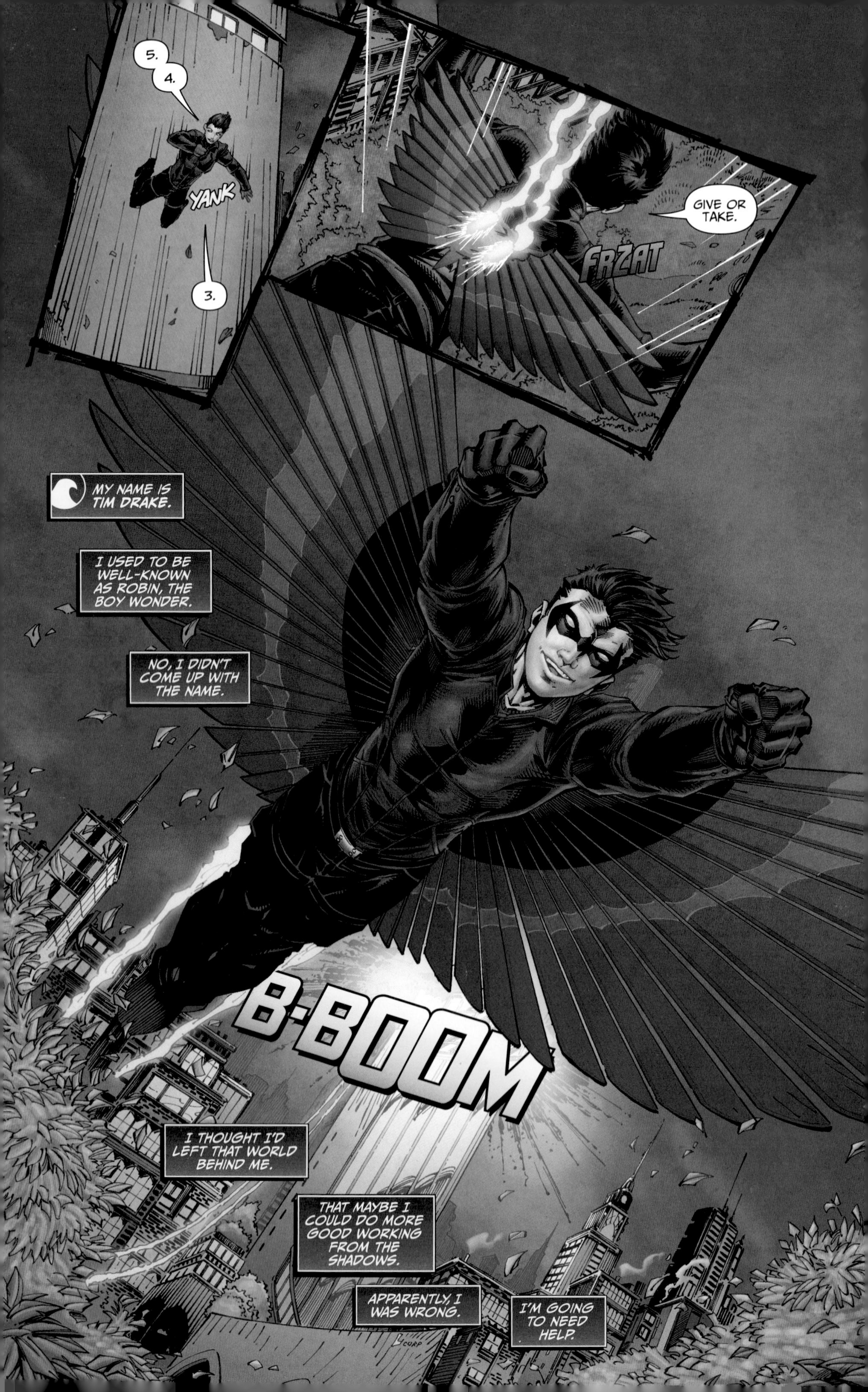

5.
4.
YANK
3.
GIVE OR TAKE.
FRZAT
MY NAME IS TIM DRAKE.
I USED TO BE WELL-KNOWN AS ROBIN, THE BOY WONDER.
NO, I DIDN'T COME UP WITH THE NAME.
B-BOOM
I THOUGHT I'D LEFT THAT WORLD BEHIND ME.
THAT MAYBE I COULD DO MORE GOOD WORKING FROM THE SHADOWS.
APPARENTLY, I WAS WRONG.
I'M GOING TO NEED HELP.

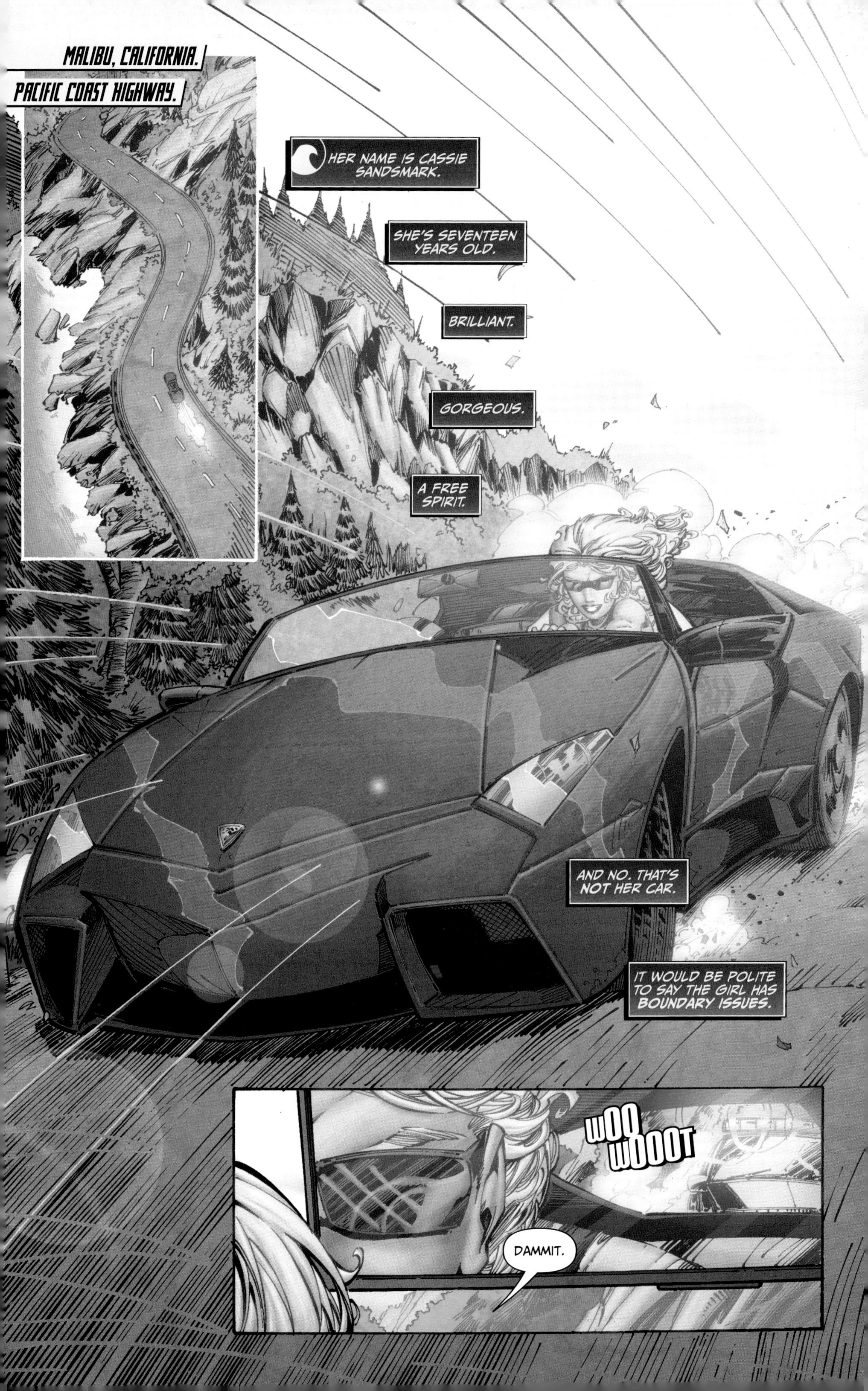
MALIBU, CALIFORNIA.
PACIFIC COAST HIGHWAY.
HER NAME IS CASSIE SANDSMARK.
SHE'S SEVENTEEN YEARS OLD.
BRILLIANT.
GORGEOUS.
A FREE SPIRIT.
AND NO. THAT'S NOT HER CAR.
IT WOULD BE POLITE TO SAY THE GIRL HAS BOUNDARY ISSUES.
WOO WOOOT
DAMMIT.

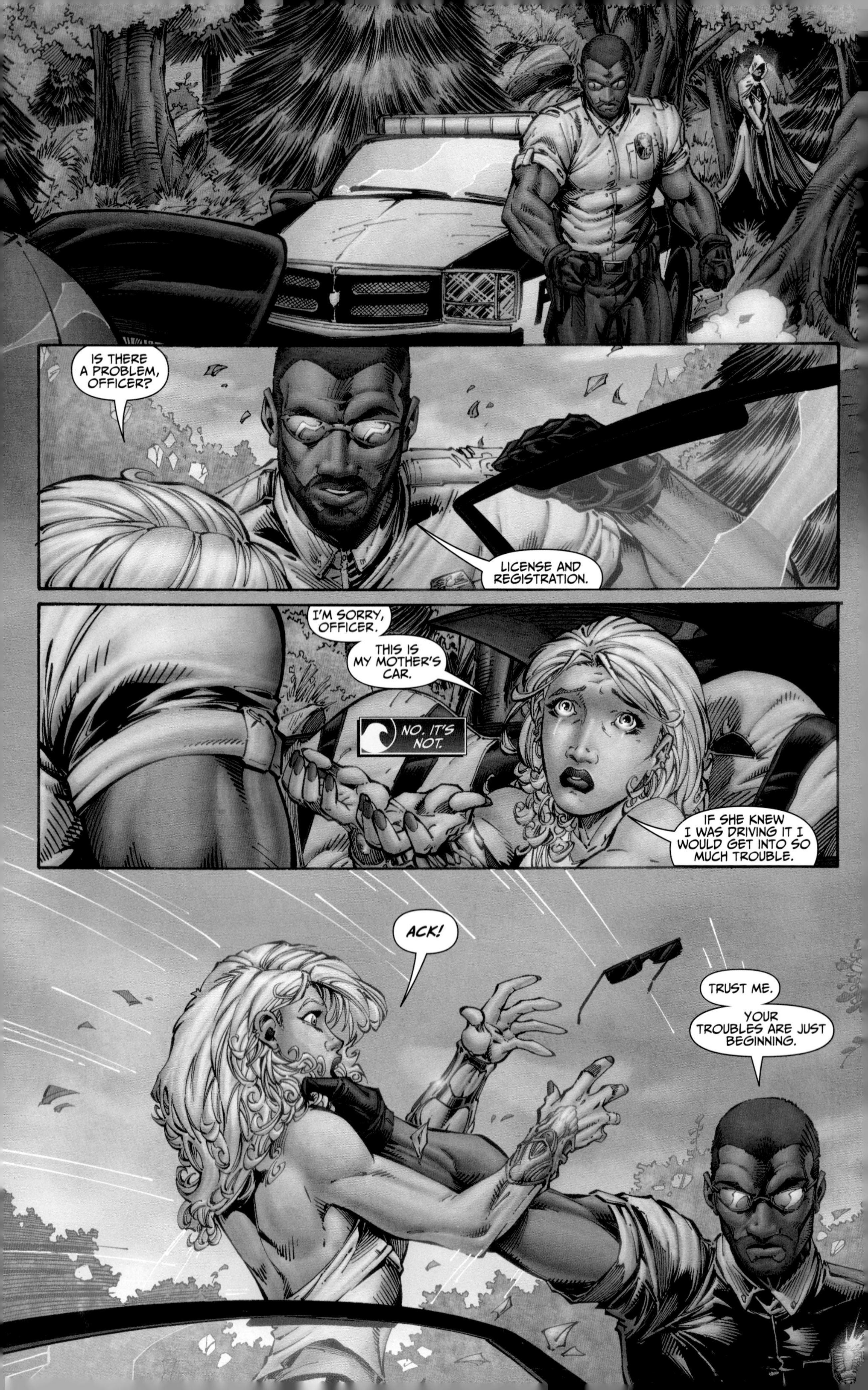
IS THERE A PROBLEM, OFFICER?
LICENSE AND REGISTRATION.
I'M SORRY, OFFICER.
THIS IS MY MOTHER'S CAR.
NO. IT'S NOT.
IF SHE KNEW I WAS DRIVING IT I WOULD GET INTO SO MUCH TROUBLE.
ACK!
TRUST ME.
YOUR TROUBLES ARE JUST BEGINNING.

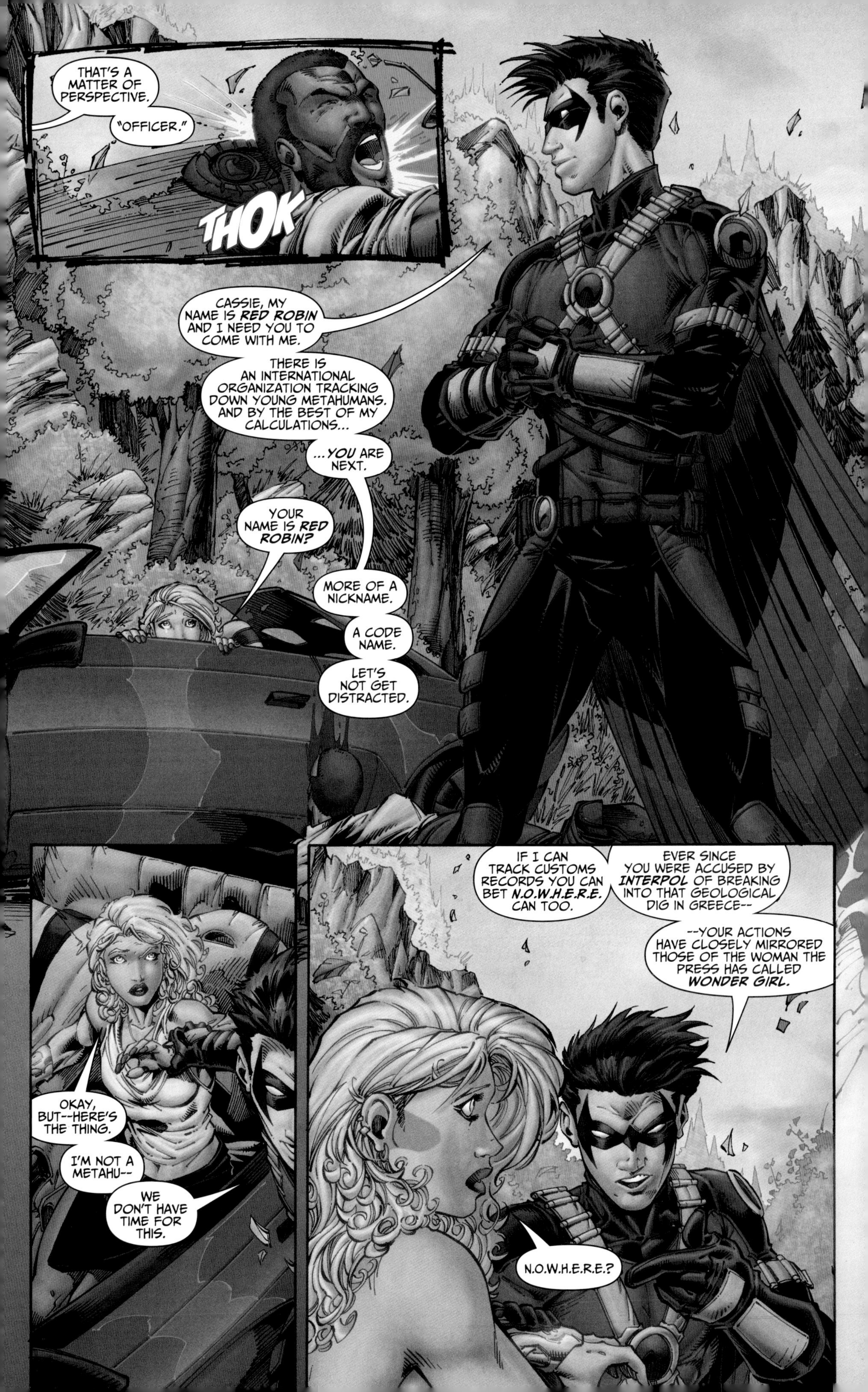
THAT'S A MATTER OF PERSPECTIVE.
"OFFICER."
THOK
CASSIE, MY NAME IS RED ROBIN AND I NEED YOU TO COME WITH ME.
THERE IS AN INTERNATIONAL ORGANIZATION TRACKING DOWN YOUNG METAHUMANS. AND BY THE BEST OF MY CALCULATIONS...
...YOU ARE NEXT.
YOUR NAME IS RED ROBIN?
MORE OF A NICKNAME.
A CODE NAME.
LET'S NOT GET DISTRACTED.
OKAY, BUT--HERE'S THE THING.
I'M NOT A METAHU--
WE DON'T HAVE TIME FOR THIS.
IF I CAN TRACK CUSTOMS RECORDS YOU CAN BET N.O.W.H.E.R.E. CAN TOO.
EVER SINCE YOU WERE ACCUSED BY INTERPOL OF BREAKING INTO THAT GEOLOGICAL DIG IN GREECE--
--YOUR ACTIONS HAVE CLOSELY MIRRORED THOSE OF THE WOMAN THE PRESS HAS CALLED WONDER GIRL.
N.O.W.H.E.R.E.?

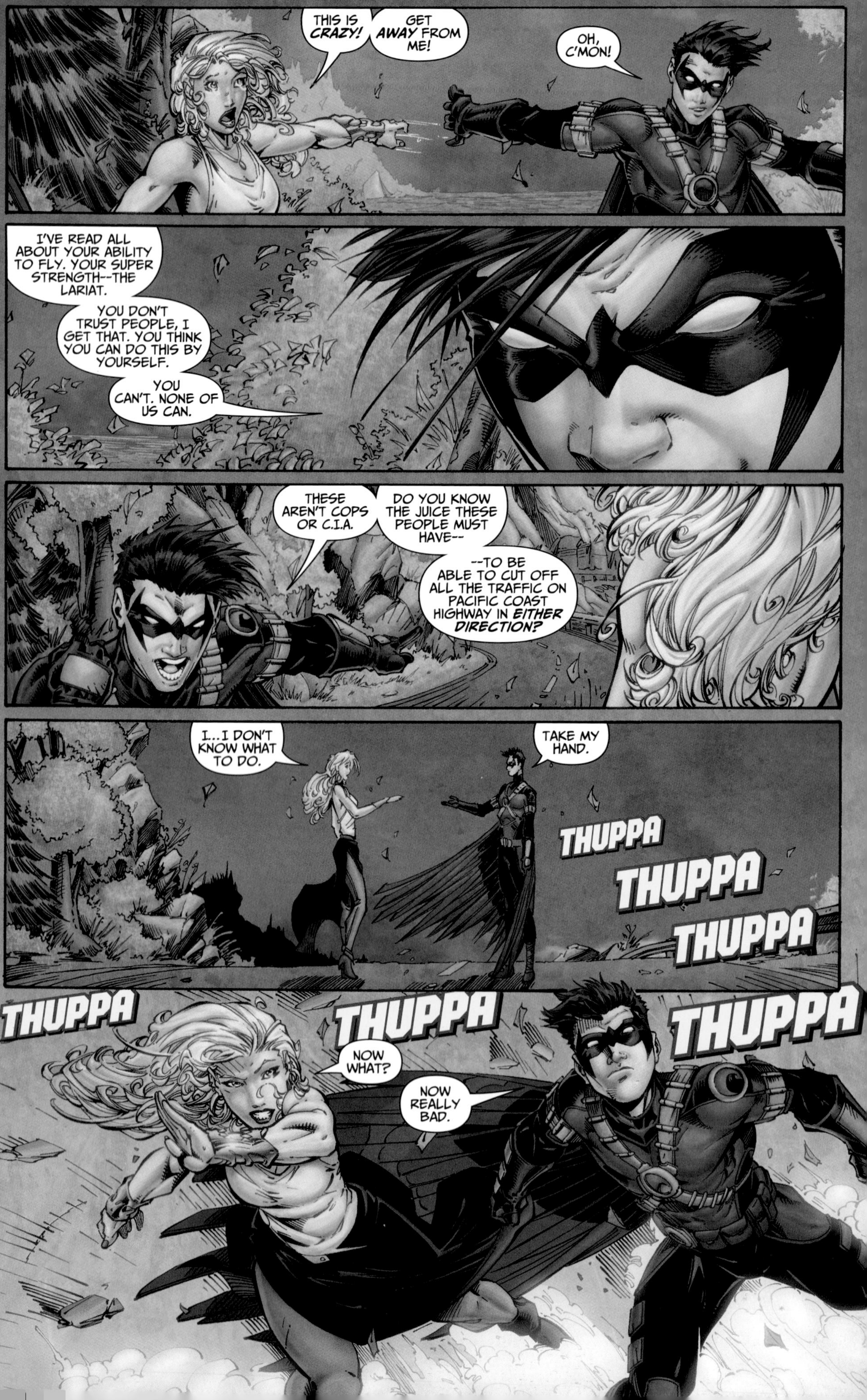
THIS IS *CRAZY!*
GET *AWAY* FROM ME!
OH, C'MON!
I'VE READ ALL ABOUT YOUR ABILITY TO FLY. YOUR SUPER STRENGTH--THE LARIAT.
YOU DON'T TRUST PEOPLE, I GET THAT. YOU THINK YOU CAN DO THIS BY YOURSELF.
YOU CAN'T. NONE OF US CAN.
THESE AREN'T COPS OR C.I.A.
DO YOU KNOW THE JUICE THESE PEOPLE MUST HAVE--
--TO BE ABLE TO CUT OFF ALL THE TRAFFIC ON PACIFIC COAST HIGHWAY IN *EITHER DIRECTION?*
I...I DON'T KNOW WHAT TO DO.
TAKE MY HAND.
THUPPA
THUPPA
THUPPA
THUPPA
THUPPA
THUPPA
NOW WHAT?
NOW REALLY BAD.

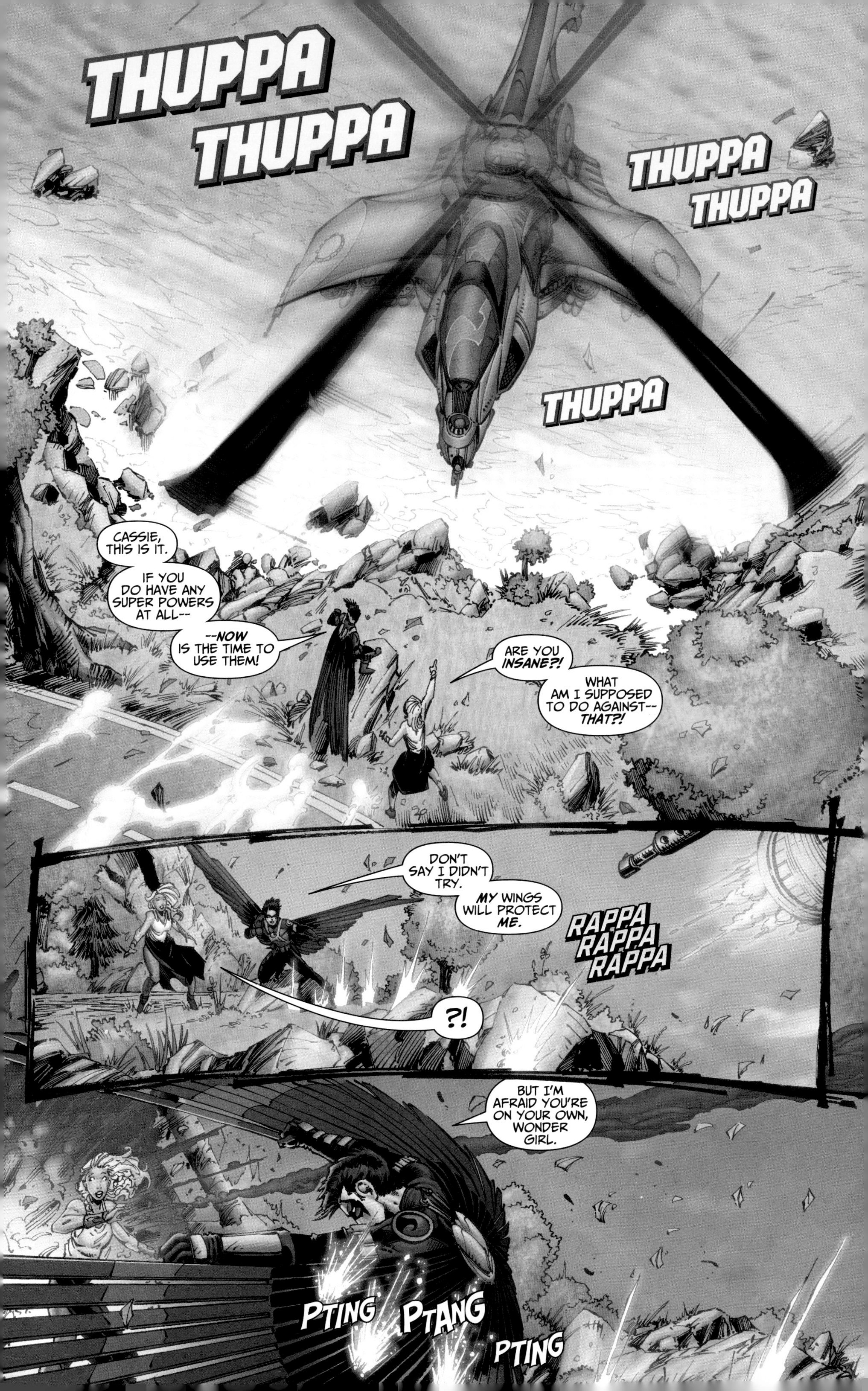
THUPPA THUPPA
THUPPA THUPPA
THUPPA
CASSIE, THIS IS IT.
IF YOU DO HAVE ANY SUPER POWERS AT ALL--
--NOW IS THE TIME TO USE THEM!
ARE YOU INSANE?!
WHAT AM I SUPPOSED TO DO AGAINST-- THAT?!
DON'T SAY I DIDN'T TRY.
MY WINGS WILL PROTECT ME.
RAPPA RAPPA RAPPA
?!
BUT I'M AFRAID YOU'RE ON YOUR OWN, WONDER GIRL.
PTING PTANG PTING

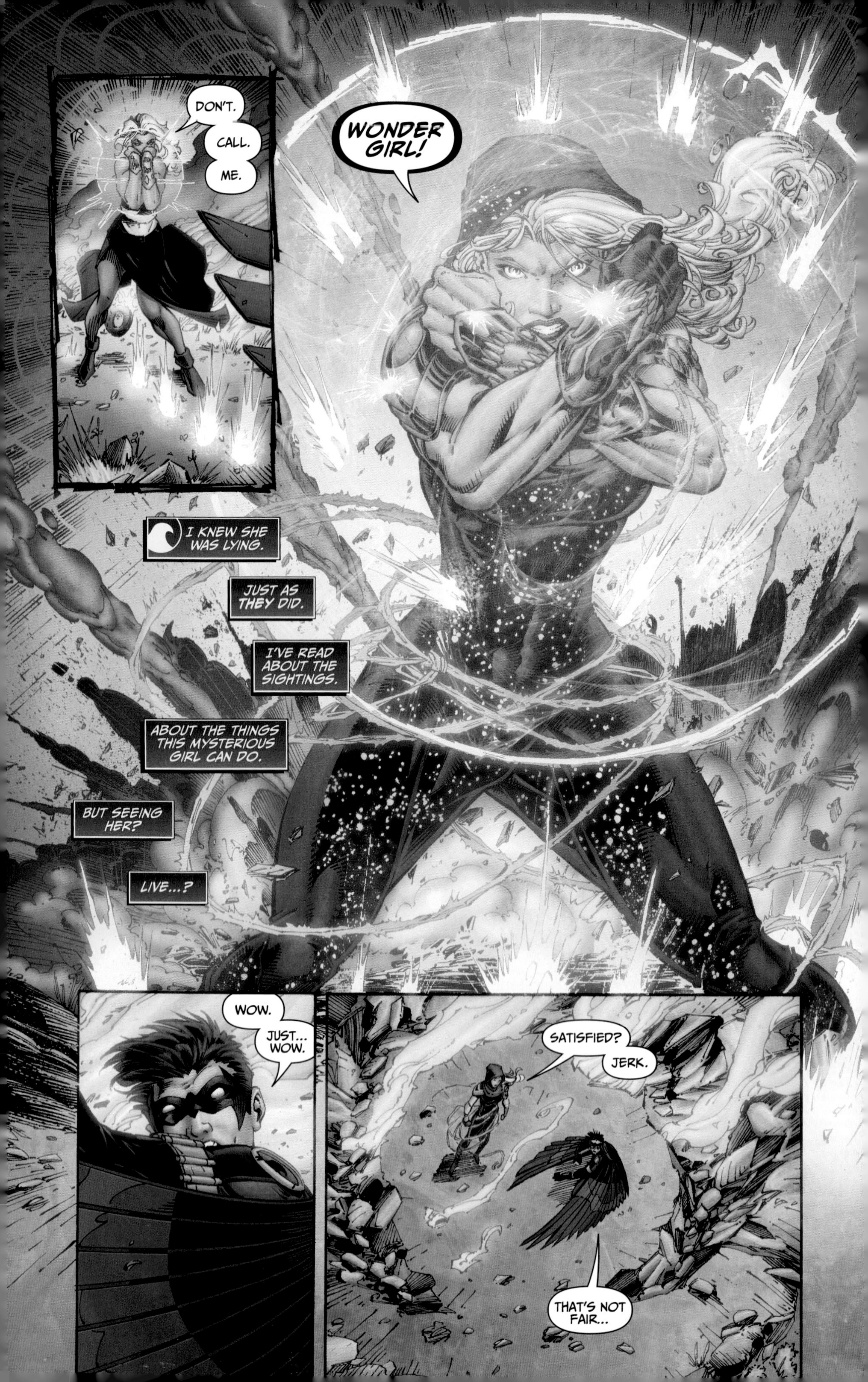

DON'T.
CALL.
ME.
WONDER GIRL!
I KNEW SHE WAS LYING.
JUST AS THEY DID.
I'VE READ ABOUT THE SIGHTINGS.
ABOUT THE THINGS THIS MYSTERIOUS GIRL CAN DO.
BUT SEEING HER?
LIVE...?
WOW.
JUST... WOW.
SATISFIED?
JERK.
THAT'S NOT FAIR...

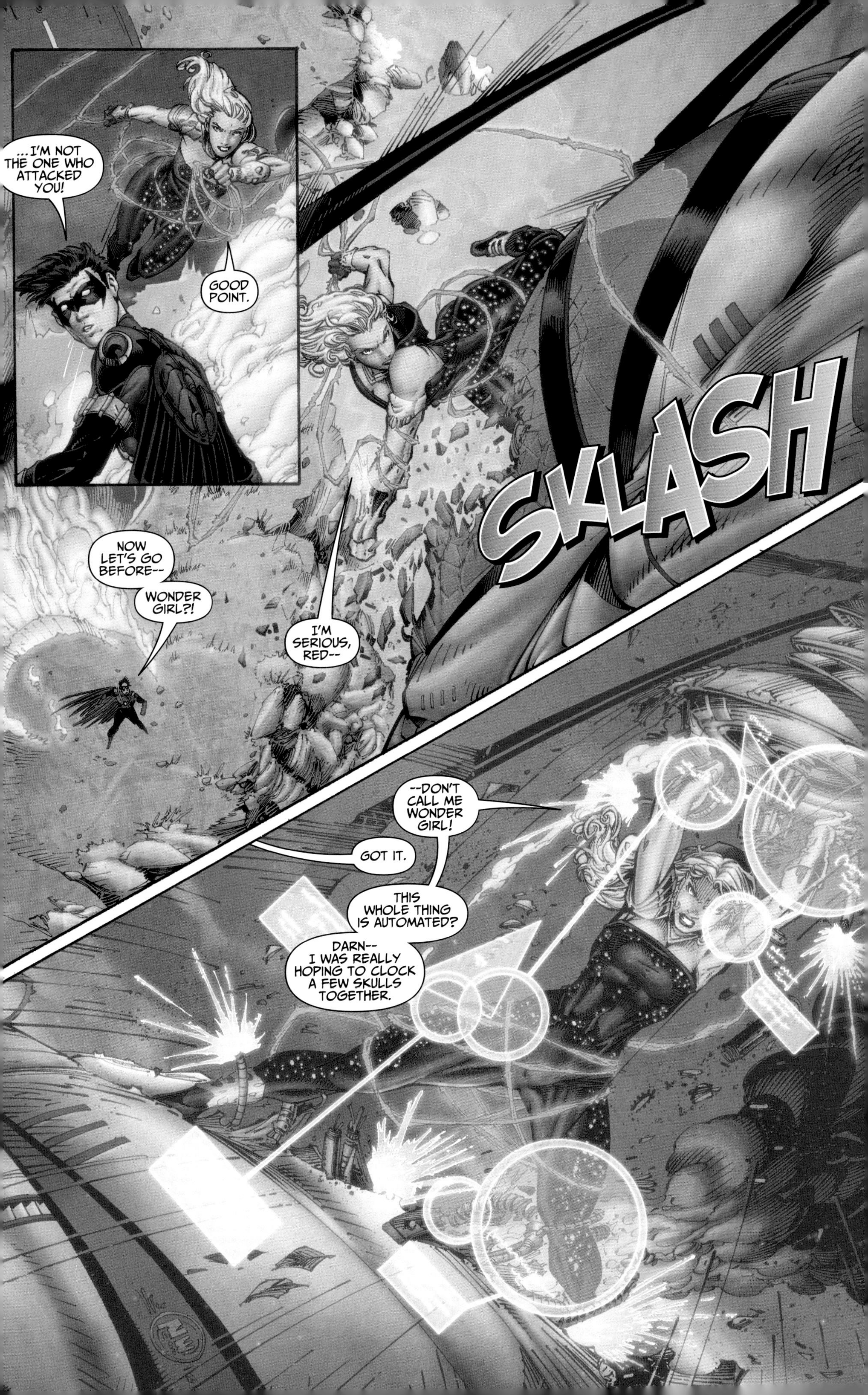
...I'M NOT THE ONE WHO ATTACKED YOU!
GOOD POINT.
SKLASH
NOW LET'S GO BEFORE--
WONDER GIRL?!
I'M SERIOUS, RED--
--DON'T CALL ME WONDER GIRL!
GOT IT.
THIS WHOLE THING IS AUTOMATED?
DARN-- I WAS REALLY HOPING TO CLOCK A FEW SKULLS TOGETHER.

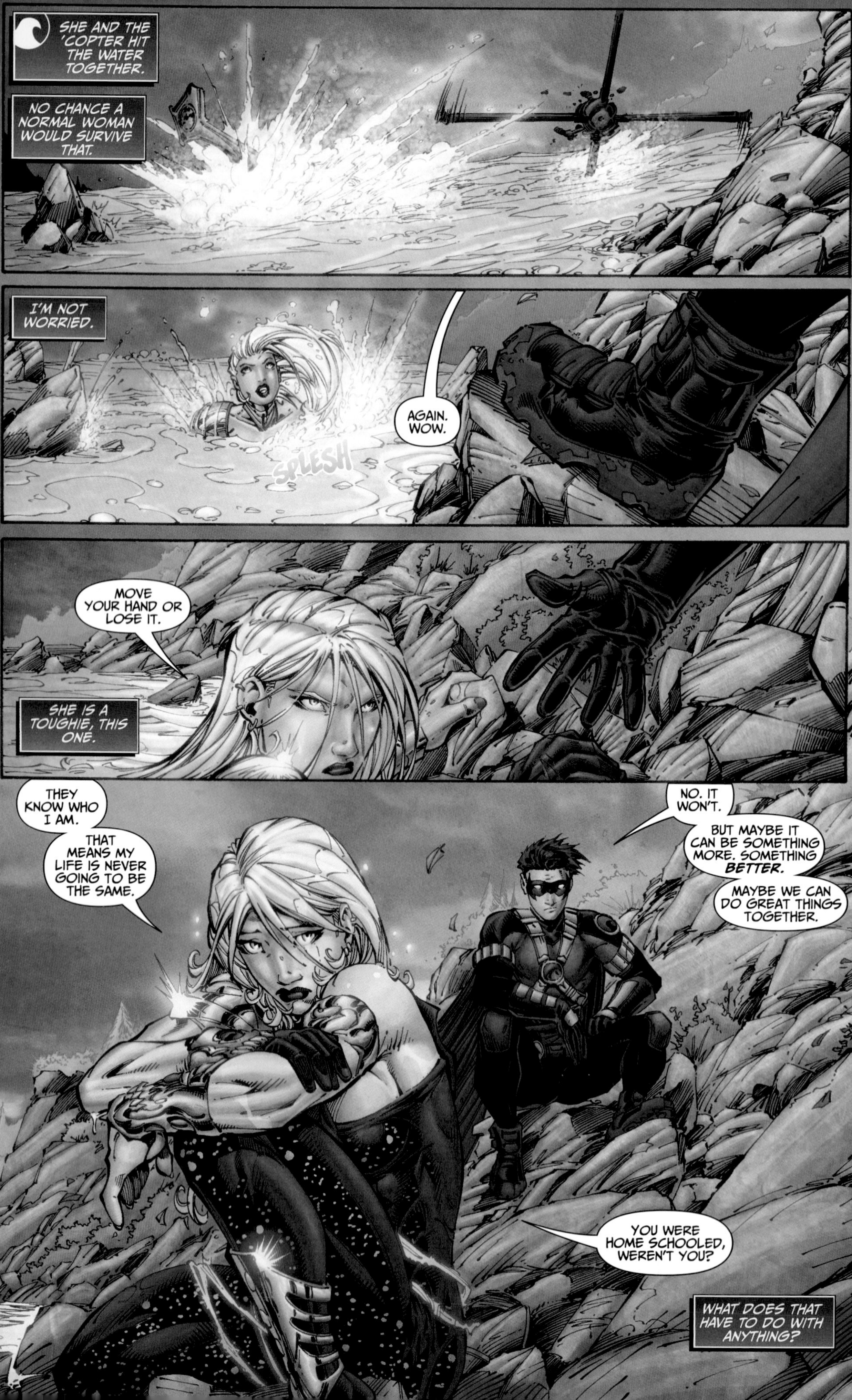
SHE AND THE 'COPTER HIT THE WATER TOGETHER.
NO CHANCE A NORMAL WOMAN WOULD SURVIVE THAT.
I'M NOT WORRIED.
AGAIN. WOW.
SPLESH
MOVE YOUR HAND OR LOSE IT.
SHE IS A TOUGHIE, THIS ONE.
THEY KNOW WHO I AM.
THAT MEANS MY LIFE IS NEVER GOING TO BE THE SAME.
NO. IT WON'T.
BUT MAYBE IT CAN BE SOMETHING MORE. SOMETHING BETTER.
MAYBE WE CAN DO GREAT THINGS TOGETHER.
YOU WERE HOME SCHOOLED, WEREN'T YOU?
WHAT DOES THAT HAVE TO DO WITH ANYTHING?

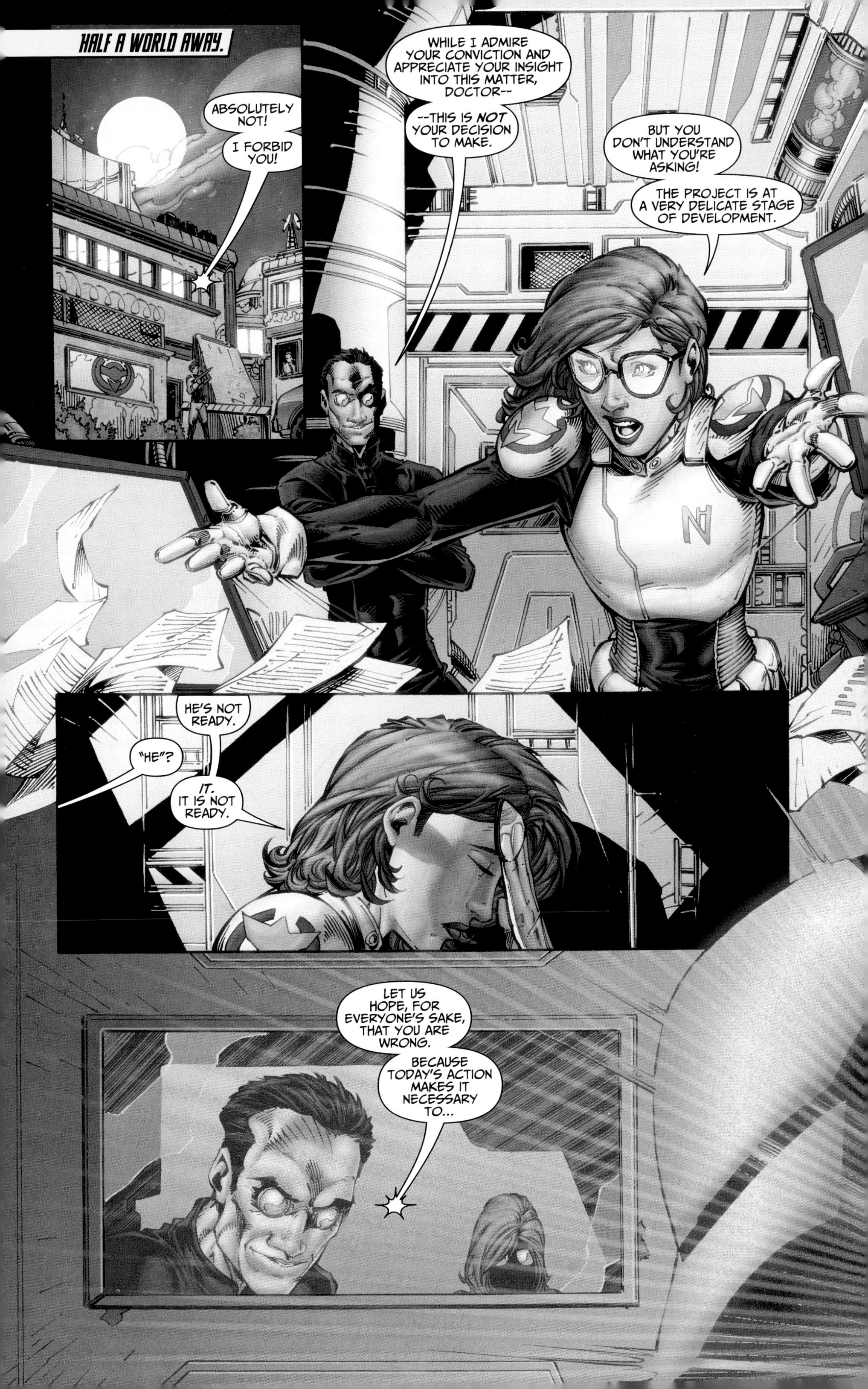

HALF A WORLD AWAY.
ABSOLUTELY NOT!
I FORBID YOU!
WHILE I ADMIRE YOUR CONVICTION AND APPRECIATE YOUR INSIGHT INTO THIS MATTER, DOCTOR--
--THIS IS NOT YOUR DECISION TO MAKE.
BUT YOU DON'T UNDERSTAND WHAT YOU'RE ASKING!
THE PROJECT IS AT A VERY DELICATE STAGE OF DEVELOPMENT.
HE'S NOT READY.
"HE"?
IT. IT IS NOT READY.
LET US HOPE, FOR EVERYONE'S SAKE, THAT YOU ARE WRONG.
BECAUSE TODAY'S ACTION MAKES IT NECESSARY TO...

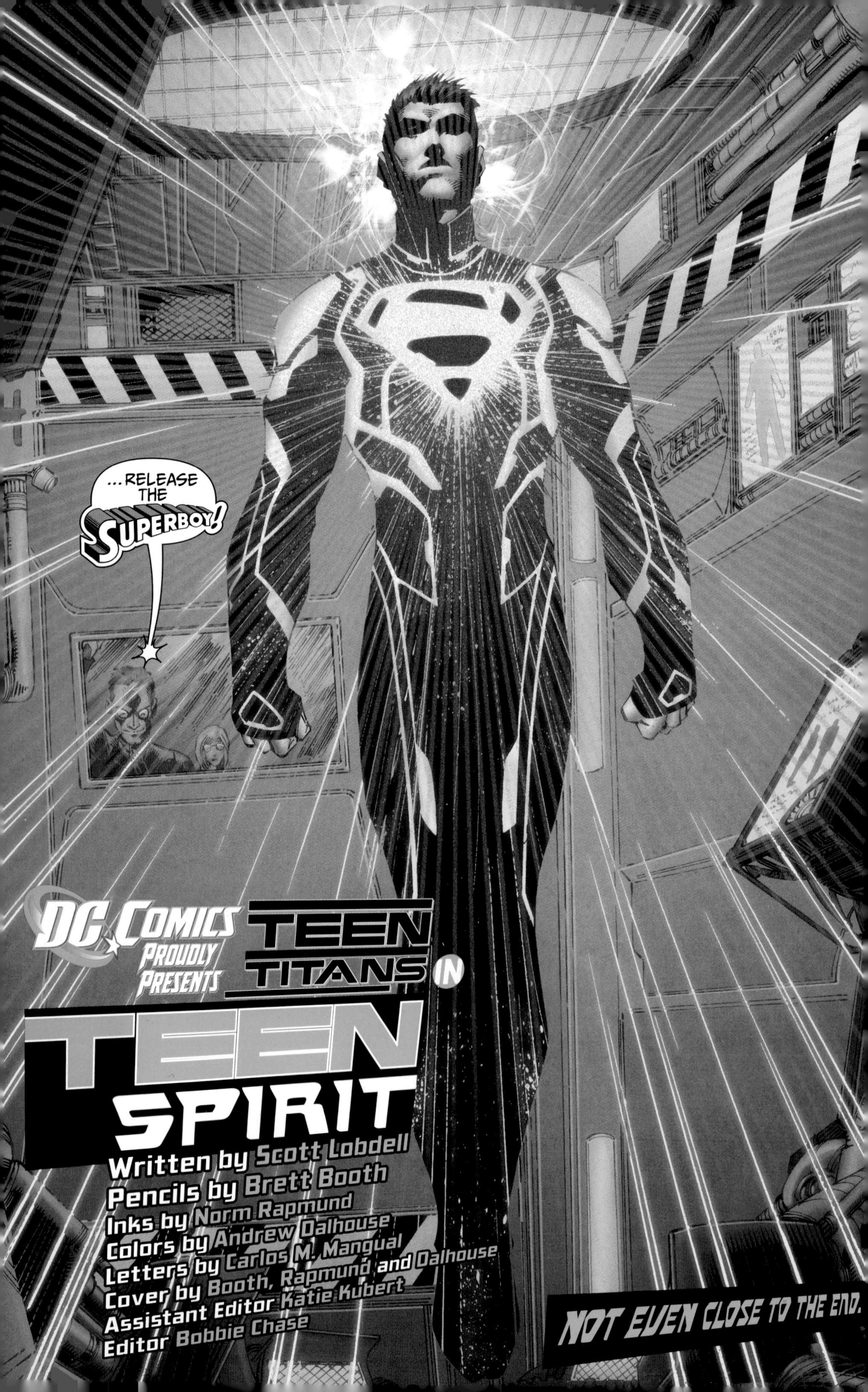
...RELEASE THE SUPERBOY!
DC COMICS PROUDLY PRESENTS
TEEN TITANS IN
TEEN SPIRIT
Written by Scott Lobdell
Pencils by Brett Booth
Inks by Norm Rapmund
Colors by Andrew Dalhouse
Letters by Carlos M. Mangual
Cover by Booth, Rapmund and Dalhouse
Assistant Editor Katie Kubert
Editor Bobbie Chase
NOT EVEN CLOSE TO THE END.

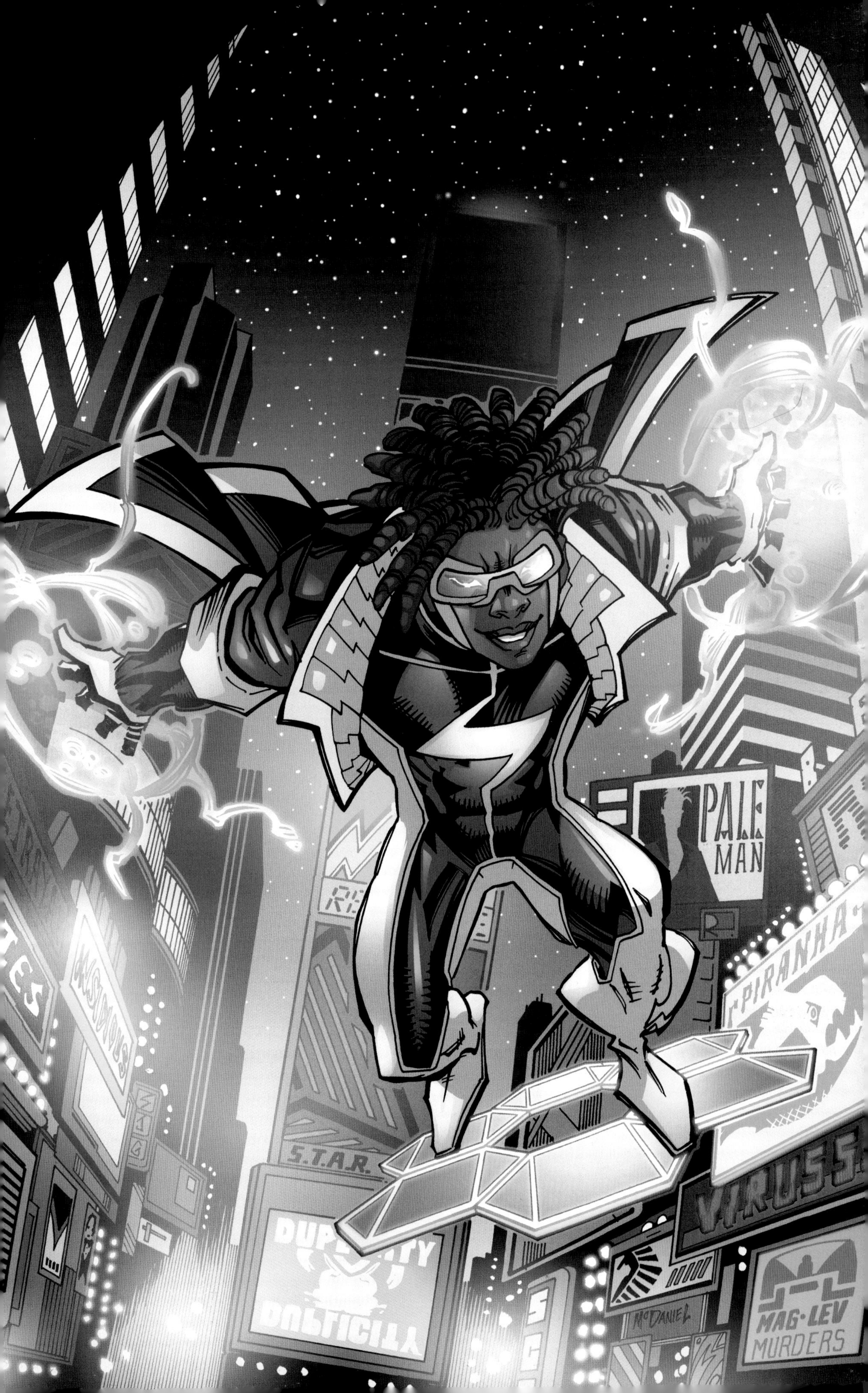
PALE MAN
PIRANHA
S.T.A.R.
DUPLICITY
MAG-LEV MURDERS
McDANIEL

STATIC SHOCK

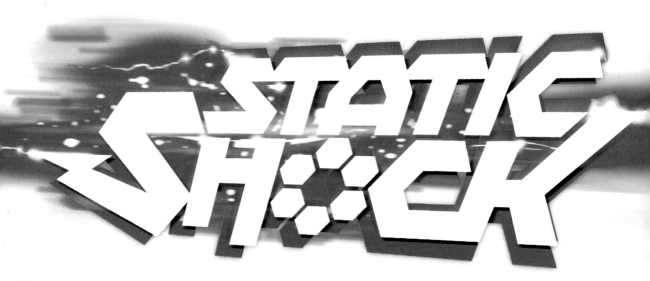

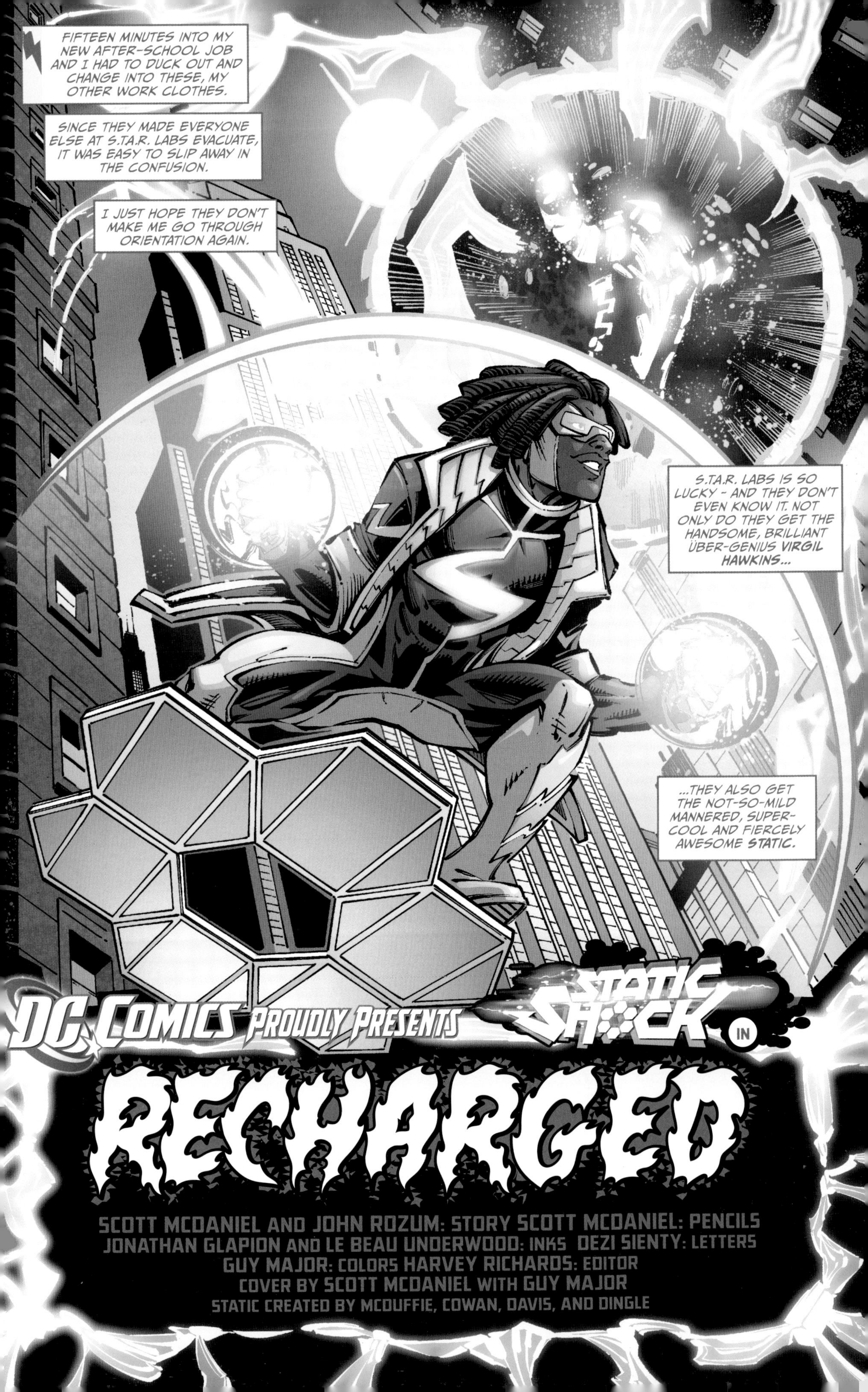
FIFTEEN MINUTES INTO MY NEW AFTER-SCHOOL JOB AND I HAD TO DUCK OUT AND CHANGE INTO THESE, MY OTHER WORK CLOTHES.
SINCE THEY MADE EVERYONE ELSE AT S.T.A.R. LABS EVACUATE, IT WAS EASY TO SLIP AWAY IN THE CONFUSION.
I JUST HOPE THEY DON'T MAKE ME GO THROUGH ORIENTATION AGAIN.
S.T.A.R. LABS IS SO LUCKY - AND THEY DON'T EVEN KNOW IT. NOT ONLY DO THEY GET THE HANDSOME, BRILLIANT ÜBER-GENIUS VIRGIL HAWKINS...
...THEY ALSO GET THE NOT-SO-MILD MANNERED, SUPER-COOL AND FIERCELY AWESOME STATIC.
DC COMICS PROUDLY PRESENTS STATIC SHOCK IN
RECHARGED
SCOTT MCDANIEL AND JOHN ROZUM: STORY SCOTT MCDANIEL: PENCILS
JONATHAN GLAPION AND LE BEAU UNDERWOOD: INKS DEZI SIENTY: LETTERS
GUY MAJOR: COLORS HARVEY RICHARDS: EDITOR
COVER BY SCOTT MCDANIEL WITH GUY MAJOR
STATIC CREATED BY MCDUFFIE, COWAN, DAVIS, AND DINGLE

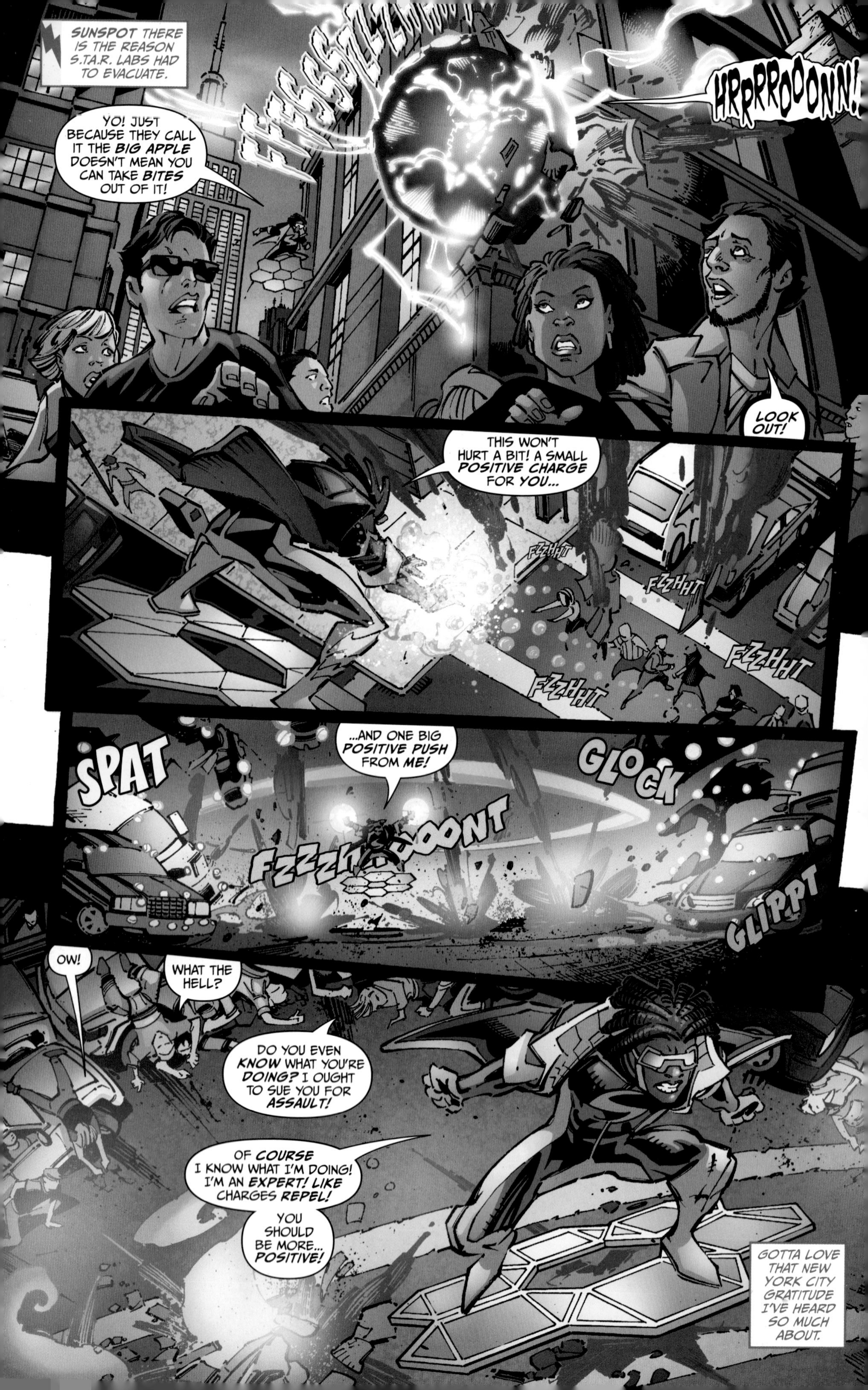

SUNSPOT THERE IS THE REASON S.T.A.R. LABS HAD TO EVACUATE.
YO! JUST BECAUSE THEY CALL IT THE BIG APPLE DOESN'T MEAN YOU CAN TAKE BITES OUT OF IT!
HRRRROOONN!
LOOK OUT!
THIS WON'T HURT A BIT! A SMALL POSITIVE CHARGE FOR YOU...
FZZHHT
FZZHHT
FZZHHT
FZZHHT
SPAT
...AND ONE BIG POSITIVE PUSH FROM ME!
GLOCK
OONT
GLIPPT
OW!
WHAT THE HELL?
DO YOU EVEN KNOW WHAT YOU'RE DOING? I OUGHT TO SUE YOU FOR ASSAULT!
OF COURSE I KNOW WHAT I'M DOING! I'M AN EXPERT! LIKE CHARGES REPEL!
YOU SHOULD BE MORE... POSITIVE!
GOTTA LOVE THAT NEW YORK CITY GRATITUDE I'VE HEARD SO MUCH ABOUT.

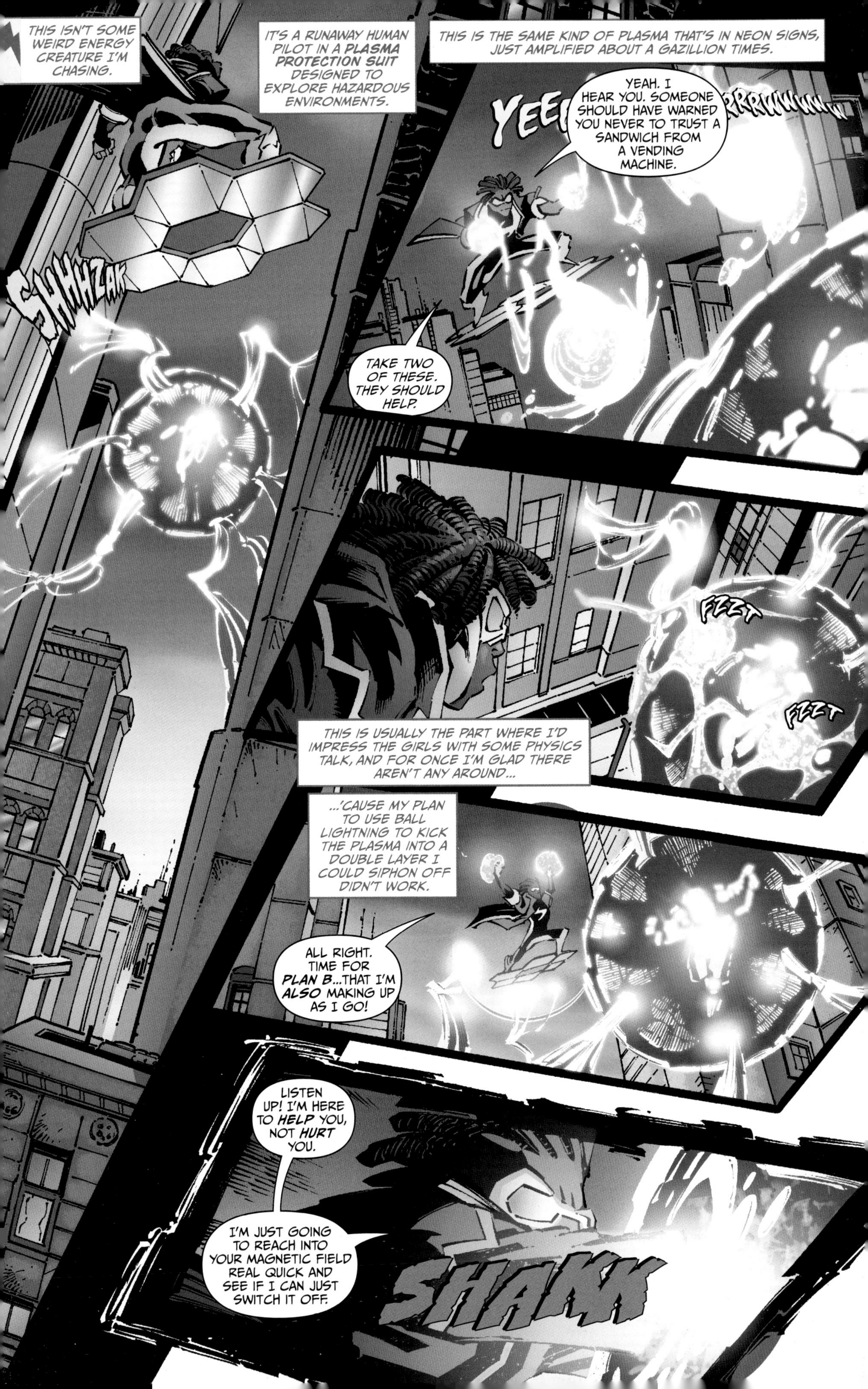

THIS ISN'T SOME WEIRD ENERGY CREATURE I'M CHASING.
IT'S A RUNAWAY HUMAN PILOT IN A PLASMA PROTECTION SUIT DESIGNED TO EXPLORE HAZARDOUS ENVIRONMENTS.
SHHHZAK
THIS IS THE SAME KIND OF PLASMA THAT'S IN NEON SIGNS, JUST AMPLIFIED ABOUT A GAZILLION TIMES.
YEE
RRRWWWW
YEAH. I HEAR YOU. SOMEONE SHOULD HAVE WARNED YOU NEVER TO TRUST A SANDWICH FROM A VENDING MACHINE.
TAKE TWO OF THESE. THEY SHOULD HELP.
FZZT
FZZT
THIS IS USUALLY THE PART WHERE I'D IMPRESS THE GIRLS WITH SOME PHYSICS TALK, AND FOR ONCE I'M GLAD THERE AREN'T ANY AROUND...
...'CAUSE MY PLAN TO USE BALL LIGHTNING TO KICK THE PLASMA INTO A DOUBLE LAYER I COULD SIPHON OFF DIDN'T WORK.
ALL RIGHT. TIME FOR PLAN B...THAT I'M ALSO MAKING UP AS I GO!
LISTEN UP! I'M HERE TO HELP YOU, NOT HURT YOU.
I'M JUST GOING TO REACH INTO YOUR MAGNETIC FIELD REAL QUICK AND SEE IF I CAN JUST SWITCH IT OFF.
SHAKK

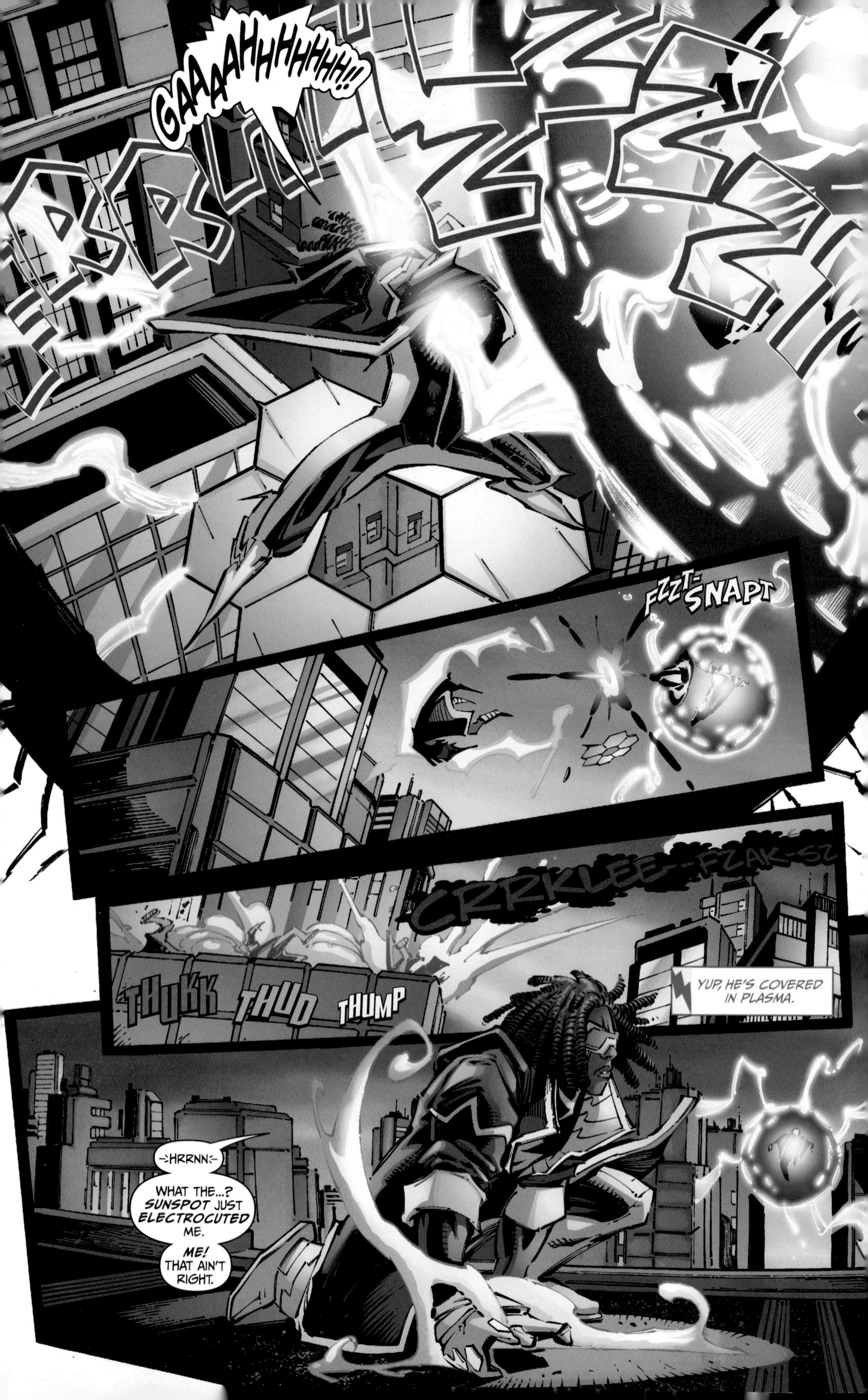

GAAAAHHHHHH!!
FZZT-SNAPT
CRRKLEE-FZAK-SZ
THUKK THUD THUMP
YUP, HE'S COVERED IN PLASMA.
-HRRNN-
WHAT THE...? SUNSPOT JUST ELECTROCUTED ME.
ME! THAT AIN'T RIGHT.

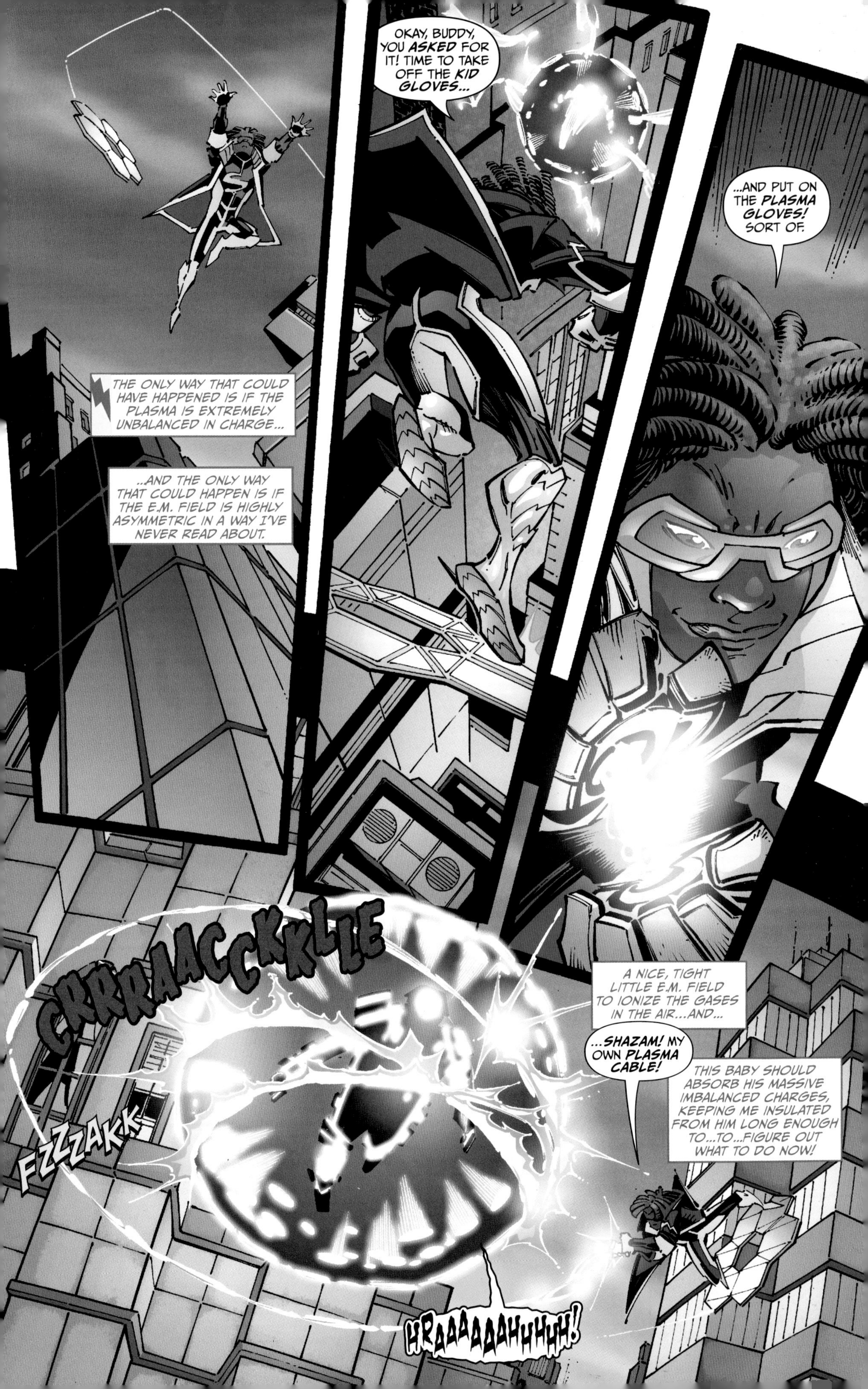
THE ONLY WAY THAT COULD HAVE HAPPENED IS IF THE PLASMA IS EXTREMELY UNBALANCED IN CHARGE...
...AND THE ONLY WAY THAT COULD HAPPEN IS IF THE E.M. FIELD IS HIGHLY ASYMMETRIC IN A WAY I'VE NEVER READ ABOUT.
OKAY, BUDDY, YOU ASKED FOR IT! TIME TO TAKE OFF THE KID GLOVES...
...AND PUT ON THE PLASMA GLOVES! SORT OF.
CRRRAACCKKLLE
FZZZAKK
A NICE, TIGHT LITTLE E.M. FIELD TO IONIZE THE GASES IN THE AIR...AND...
...SHAZAM! MY OWN PLASMA CABLE!
THIS BABY SHOULD ABSORB HIS MASSIVE IMBALANCED CHARGES, KEEPING ME INSULATED FROM HIM LONG ENOUGH TO...TO...FIGURE OUT WHAT TO DO NOW!
HRAAAAAAHHHHH!

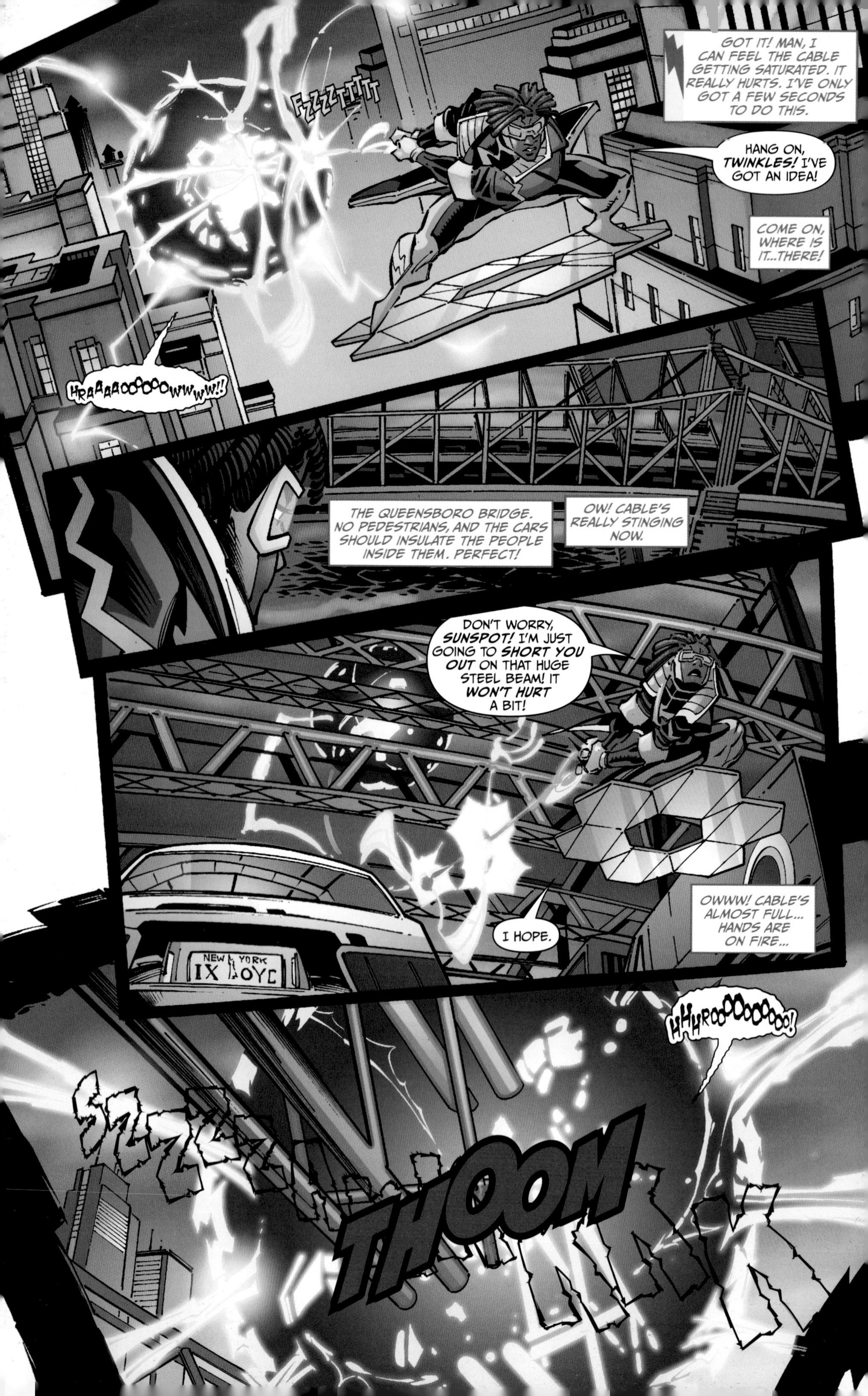

GOT IT! MAN, I CAN FEEL THE CABLE GETTING SATURATED. IT REALLY HURTS. I'VE ONLY GOT A FEW SECONDS TO DO THIS.
FZZZTTTT
HANG ON, TWINKLES! I'VE GOT AN IDEA!
COME ON, WHERE IS IT...THERE!
HRAAAAOOOOOOWWWW!!
THE QUEENSBORO BRIDGE. NO PEDESTRIANS, AND THE CARS SHOULD INSULATE THE PEOPLE INSIDE THEM. PERFECT!
OW! CABLE'S REALLY STINGING NOW.
DON'T WORRY, SUNSPOT! I'M JUST GOING TO SHORT YOU OUT ON THAT HUGE STEEL BEAM! IT WON'T HURT A BIT!
I HOPE.
OWWW! CABLE'S ALMOST FULL... HANDS ARE ON FIRE...
NEW YORK
HHHROOOOOOOOOO!
THOOM

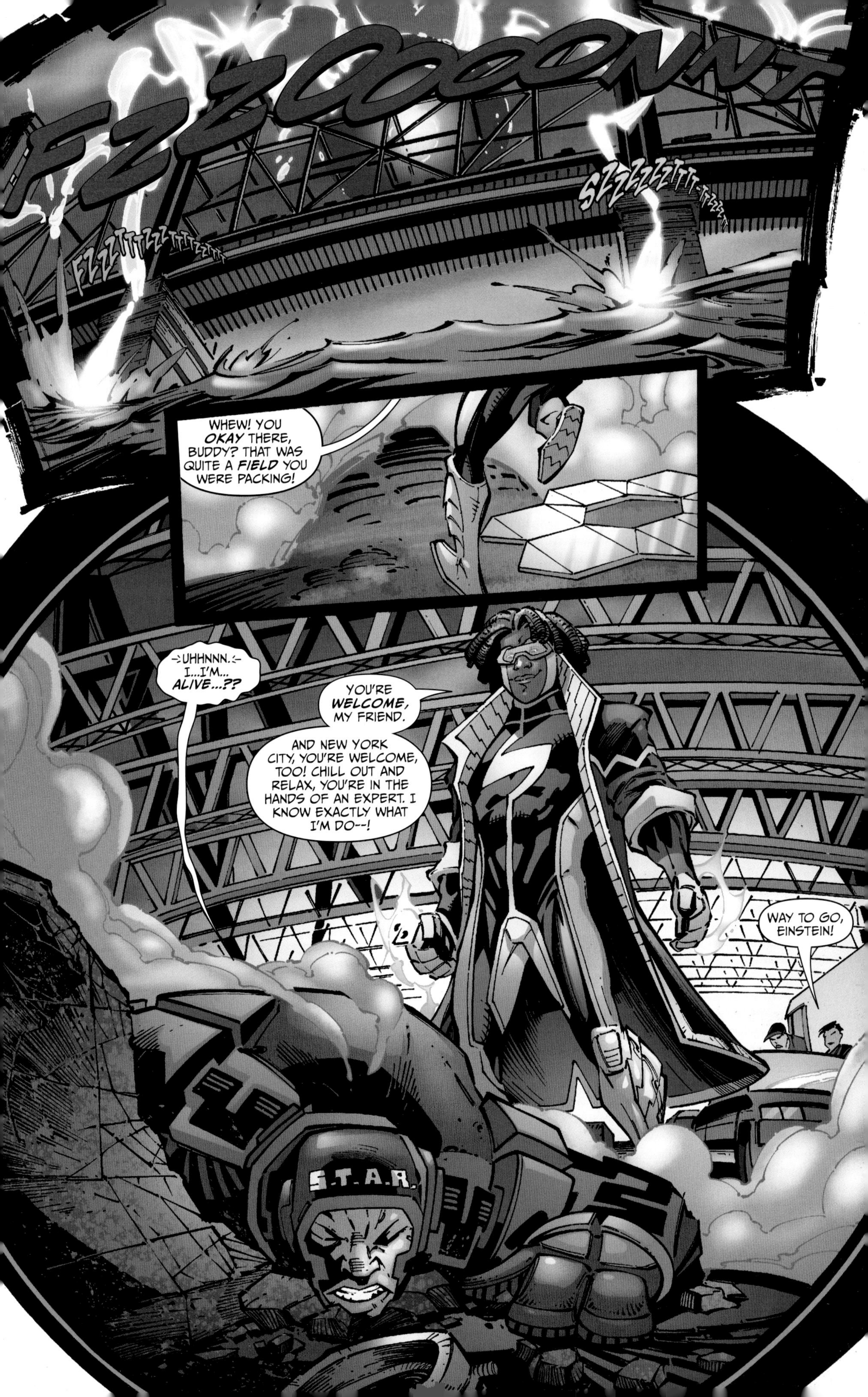
FZZZOOOONNT
FZZZTTTZZZTTTZZZTTT
SZZZZZZTTT-TTZZZZT
WHEW! YOU OKAY THERE, BUDDY? THAT WAS QUITE A FIELD YOU WERE PACKING!
UHHNNN. I...I'M... ALIVE...??
YOU'RE WELCOME, MY FRIEND.
AND NEW YORK CITY, YOU'RE WELCOME, TOO! CHILL OUT AND RELAX, YOU'RE IN THE HANDS OF AN EXPERT. I KNOW EXACTLY WHAT I'M DO--!
WAY TO GO, EINSTEIN!
S.T.A.R.

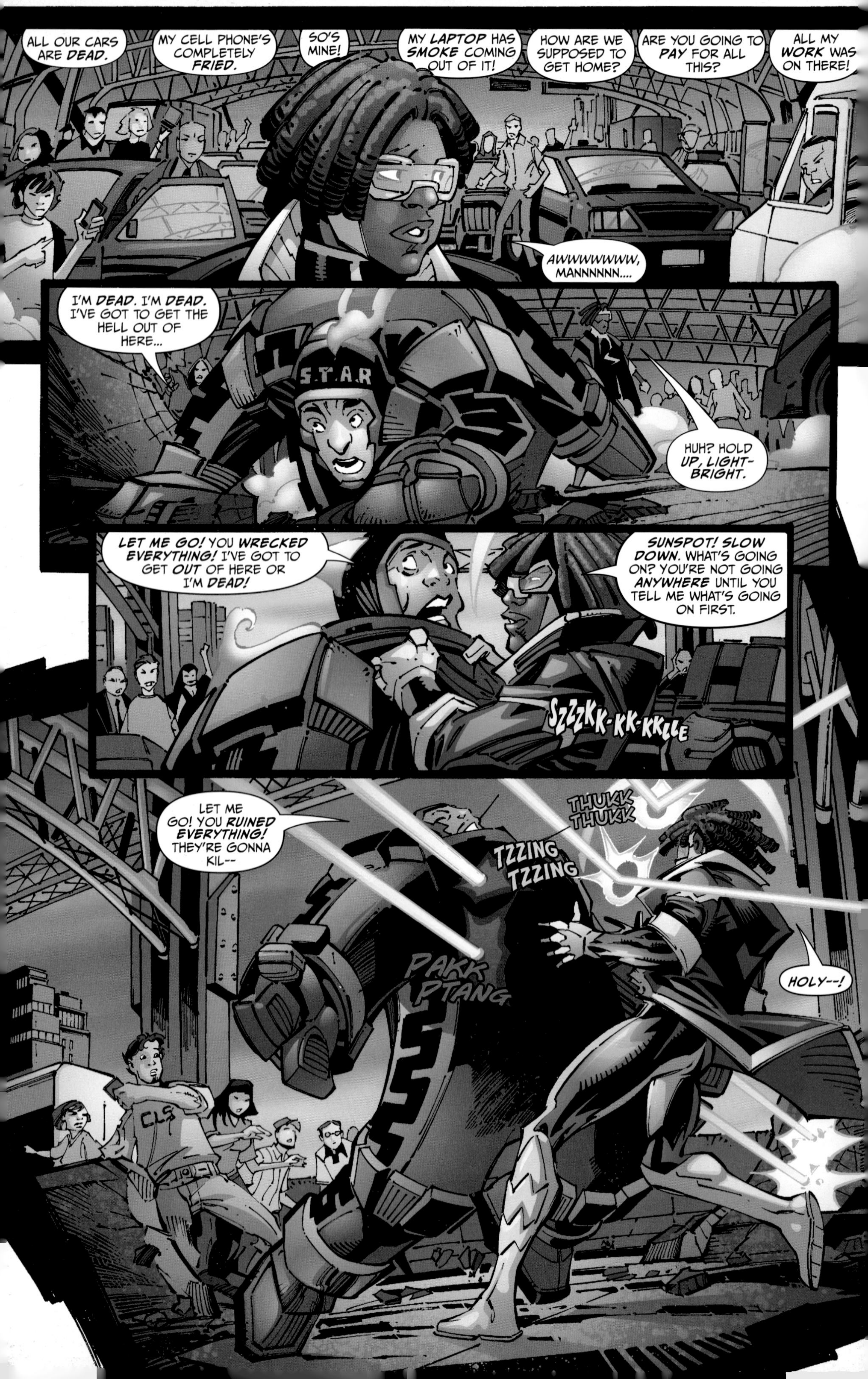
ALL OUR CARS ARE DEAD.
MY CELL PHONE'S COMPLETELY FRIED.
SO'S MINE!
MY LAPTOP HAS SMOKE COMING OUT OF IT!
HOW ARE WE SUPPOSED TO GET HOME?
ARE YOU GOING TO PAY FOR ALL THIS?
ALL MY WORK WAS ON THERE!
AWWWWWWW, MANNNNNN....
I'M DEAD. I'M DEAD. I'VE GOT TO GET THE HELL OUT OF HERE...
S.T.A.R
HUH? HOLD UP, LIGHT-BRIGHT.
LET ME GO! YOU WRECKED EVERYTHING! I'VE GOT TO GET OUT OF HERE OR I'M DEAD!
SUNSPOT! SLOW DOWN. WHAT'S GOING ON? YOU'RE NOT GOING ANYWHERE UNTIL YOU TELL ME WHAT'S GOING ON FIRST.
SZZZKK-KK-KKLLE
LET ME GO! YOU RUINED EVERYTHING! THEY'RE GONNA KIL--
THUKK THUKK
TZZING TZZING
PAKK PTANG
HOLY--!

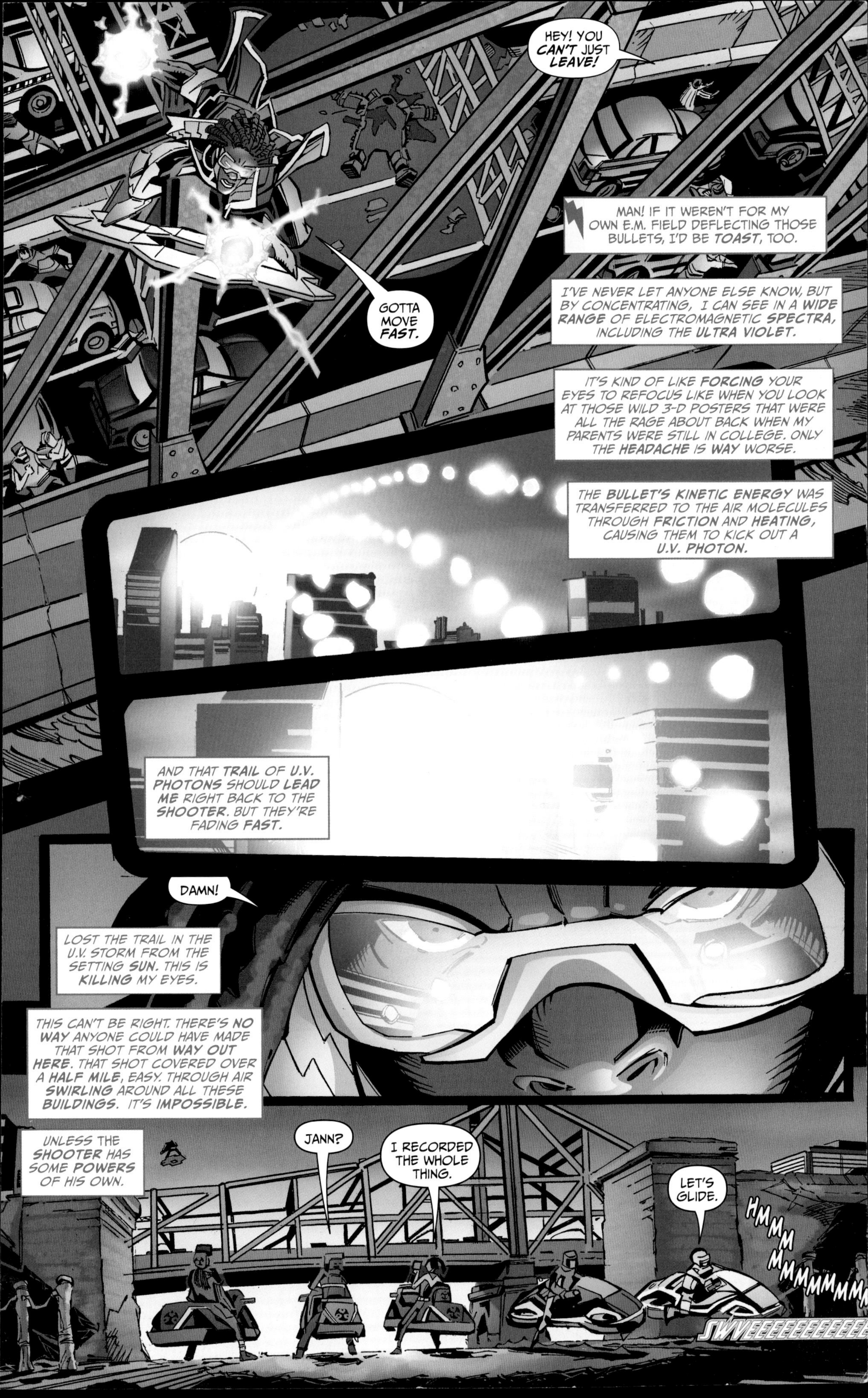
HEY! YOU CAN'T JUST LEAVE!
MAN! IF IT WEREN'T FOR MY OWN E.M. FIELD DEFLECTING THOSE BULLETS, I'D BE TOAST, TOO.
GOTTA MOVE FAST.
I'VE NEVER LET ANYONE ELSE KNOW, BUT BY CONCENTRATING, I CAN SEE IN A WIDE RANGE OF ELECTROMAGNETIC SPECTRA, INCLUDING THE ULTRA VIOLET.
IT'S KIND OF LIKE FORCING YOUR EYES TO REFOCUS LIKE WHEN YOU LOOK AT THOSE WILD 3-D POSTERS THAT WERE ALL THE RAGE ABOUT BACK WHEN MY PARENTS WERE STILL IN COLLEGE. ONLY THE HEADACHE IS WAY WORSE.
THE BULLET'S KINETIC ENERGY WAS TRANSFERRED TO THE AIR MOLECULES THROUGH FRICTION AND HEATING, CAUSING THEM TO KICK OUT A U.V. PHOTON.
AND THAT TRAIL OF U.V. PHOTONS SHOULD LEAD ME RIGHT BACK TO THE SHOOTER. BUT THEY'RE FADING FAST.
DAMN!
LOST THE TRAIL IN THE U.V. STORM FROM THE SETTING SUN. THIS IS KILLING MY EYES.
THIS CAN'T BE RIGHT. THERE'S NO WAY ANYONE COULD HAVE MADE THAT SHOT FROM WAY OUT HERE. THAT SHOT COVERED OVER A HALF MILE, EASY. THROUGH AIR SWIRLING AROUND ALL THESE BUILDINGS. IT'S IMPOSSIBLE.
UNLESS THE SHOOTER HAS SOME POWERS OF HIS OWN.
JANN?
I RECORDED THE WHOLE THING.
LET'S GLIDE.
HMMMMMMMMMM
SWVEEEEEEEEEEEE

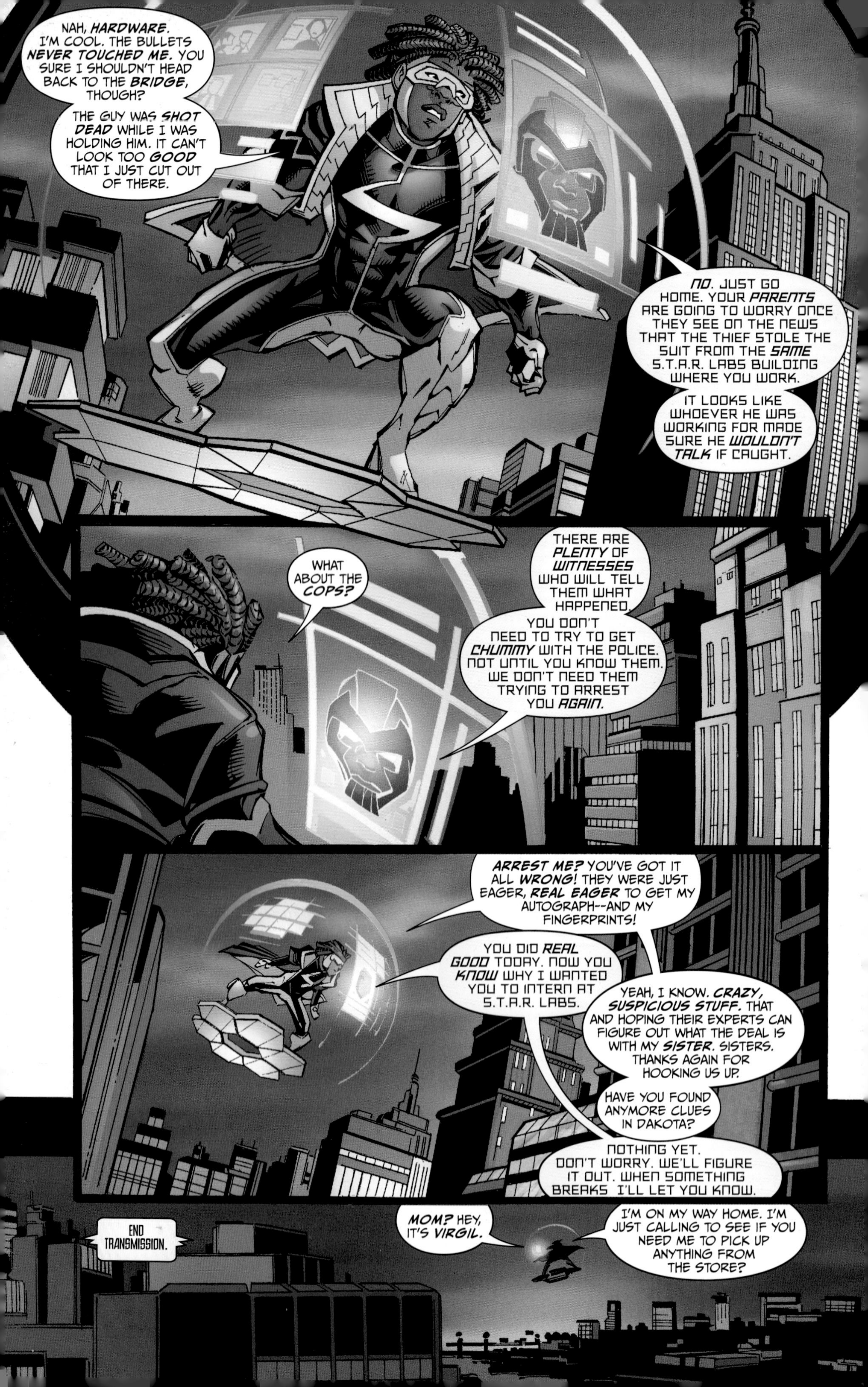
NAH, HARDWARE. I'M COOL. THE BULLETS NEVER TOUCHED ME. YOU SURE I SHOULDN'T HEAD BACK TO THE BRIDGE, THOUGH?
THE GUY WAS SHOT DEAD WHILE I WAS HOLDING HIM. IT CAN'T LOOK TOO GOOD THAT I JUST CUT OUT OF THERE.
NO. JUST GO HOME. YOUR PARENTS ARE GOING TO WORRY ONCE THEY SEE ON THE NEWS THAT THE THIEF STOLE THE SUIT FROM THE SAME S.T.A.R. LABS BUILDING WHERE YOU WORK.
IT LOOKS LIKE WHOEVER HE WAS WORKING FOR MADE SURE HE WOULDN'T TALK IF CAUGHT.
WHAT ABOUT THE COPS?
THERE ARE PLENTY OF WITNESSES WHO WILL TELL THEM WHAT HAPPENED.
YOU DON'T NEED TO TRY TO GET CHUMMY WITH THE POLICE. NOT UNTIL YOU KNOW THEM. WE DON'T NEED THEM TRYING TO ARREST YOU AGAIN.
ARREST ME? YOU'VE GOT IT ALL WRONG! THEY WERE JUST EAGER, REAL EAGER TO GET MY AUTOGRAPH--AND MY FINGERPRINTS!
YOU DID REAL GOOD TODAY. NOW YOU KNOW WHY I WANTED YOU TO INTERN AT S.T.A.R. LABS.
YEAH, I KNOW. CRAZY, SUSPICIOUS STUFF. THAT AND HOPING THEIR EXPERTS CAN FIGURE OUT WHAT THE DEAL IS WITH MY SISTER. SISTERS. THANKS AGAIN FOR HOOKING US UP.
HAVE YOU FOUND ANYMORE CLUES IN DAKOTA?
NOTHING YET. DON'T WORRY. WE'LL FIGURE IT OUT. WHEN SOMETHING BREAKS I'LL LET YOU KNOW.
MOM? HEY, IT'S VIRGIL.
I'M ON MY WAY HOME. I'M JUST CALLING TO SEE IF YOU NEED ME TO PICK UP ANYTHING FROM THE STORE?
END TRANSMISSION.

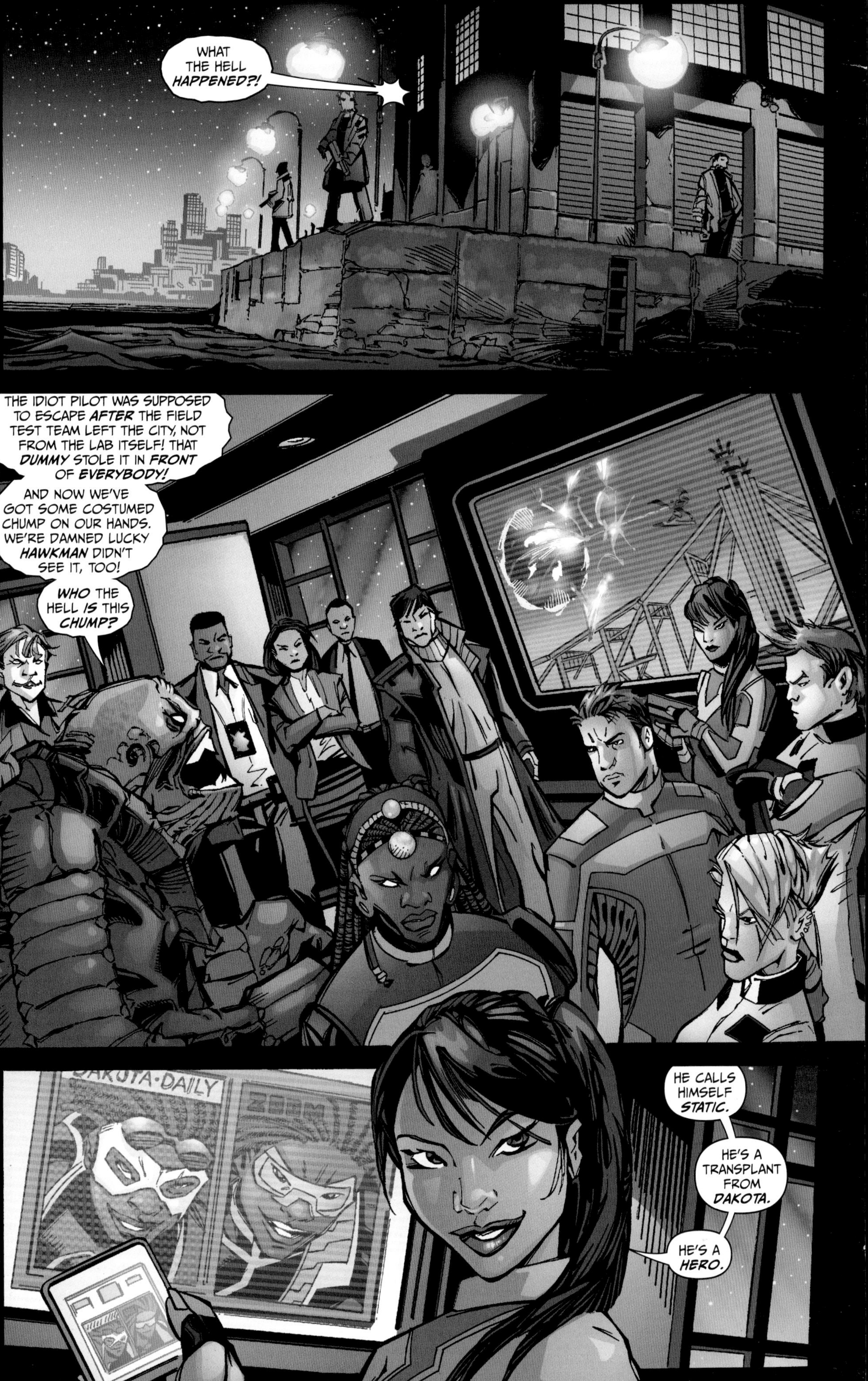

WHAT THE HELL HAPPENED?!
THE IDIOT PILOT WAS SUPPOSED TO ESCAPE AFTER THE FIELD TEST TEAM LEFT THE CITY, NOT FROM THE LAB ITSELF! THAT DUMMY STOLE IT IN FRONT OF EVERYBODY!
AND NOW WE'VE GOT SOME COSTUMED CHUMP ON OUR HANDS. WE'RE DAMNED LUCKY HAWKMAN DIDN'T SEE IT, TOO!
WHO THE HELL IS THIS CHUMP?
HE CALLS HIMSELF STATIC.
HE'S A TRANSPLANT FROM DAKOTA.
HE'S A HERO.

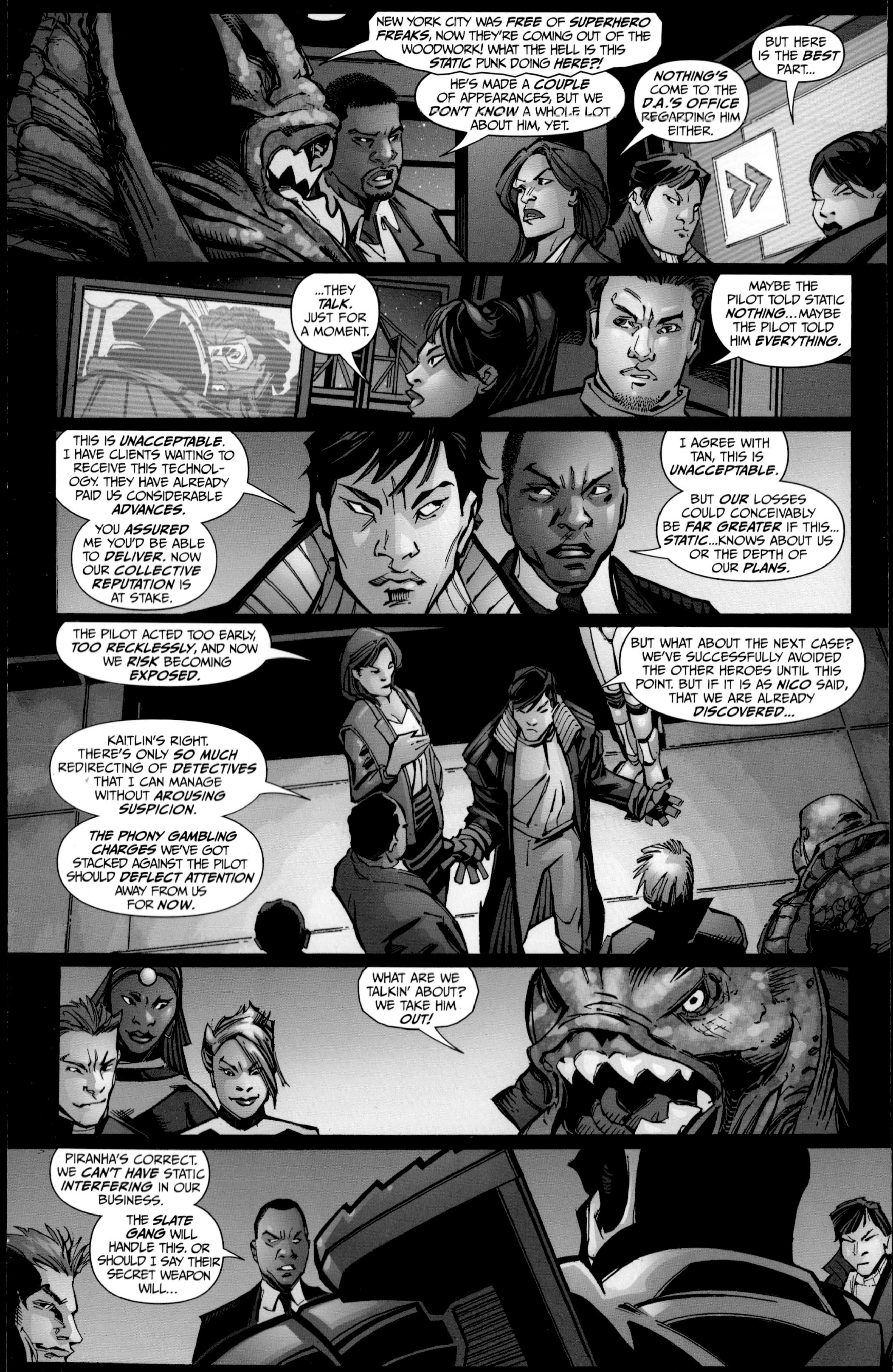
NEW YORK CITY WAS FREE OF SUPERHERO FREAKS, NOW THEY'RE COMING OUT OF THE WOODWORK! WHAT THE HELL IS THIS STATIC PUNK DOING HERE?!
HE'S MADE A COUPLE OF APPEARANCES, BUT WE DON'T KNOW A WHOLE LOT ABOUT HIM, YET.
NOTHING'S COME TO THE D.A.'S OFFICE REGARDING HIM EITHER.
BUT HERE IS THE BEST PART...
...THEY TALK. JUST FOR A MOMENT.
MAYBE THE PILOT TOLD STATIC NOTHING... MAYBE THE PILOT TOLD HIM EVERYTHING.
THIS IS UNACCEPTABLE. I HAVE CLIENTS WAITING TO RECEIVE THIS TECHNOLOGY. THEY HAVE ALREADY PAID US CONSIDERABLE ADVANCES.
YOU ASSURED ME YOU'D BE ABLE TO DELIVER. NOW OUR COLLECTIVE REPUTATION IS AT STAKE.
I AGREE WITH TAN, THIS IS UNACCEPTABLE.
BUT OUR LOSSES COULD CONCEIVABLY BE FAR GREATER IF THIS... STATIC...KNOWS ABOUT US OR THE DEPTH OF OUR PLANS.
THE PILOT ACTED TOO EARLY, TOO RECKLESSLY, AND NOW WE RISK BECOMING EXPOSED.
BUT WHAT ABOUT THE NEXT CASE? WE'VE SUCCESSFULLY AVOIDED THE OTHER HEROES UNTIL THIS POINT. BUT IF IT IS AS NICO SAID, THAT WE ARE ALREADY DISCOVERED...
KAITLIN'S RIGHT. THERE'S ONLY SO MUCH REDIRECTING OF DETECTIVES THAT I CAN MANAGE WITHOUT AROUSING SUSPICION.
THE PHONY GAMBLING CHARGES WE'VE GOT STACKED AGAINST THE PILOT SHOULD DEFLECT ATTENTION AWAY FROM US FOR NOW.
WHAT ARE WE TALKIN' ABOUT? WE TAKE HIM OUT!
PIRANHA'S CORRECT. WE CAN'T HAVE STATIC INTERFERING IN OUR BUSINESS.
THE SLATE GANG WILL HANDLE THIS. OR SHOULD I SAY THEIR SECRET WEAPON WILL...

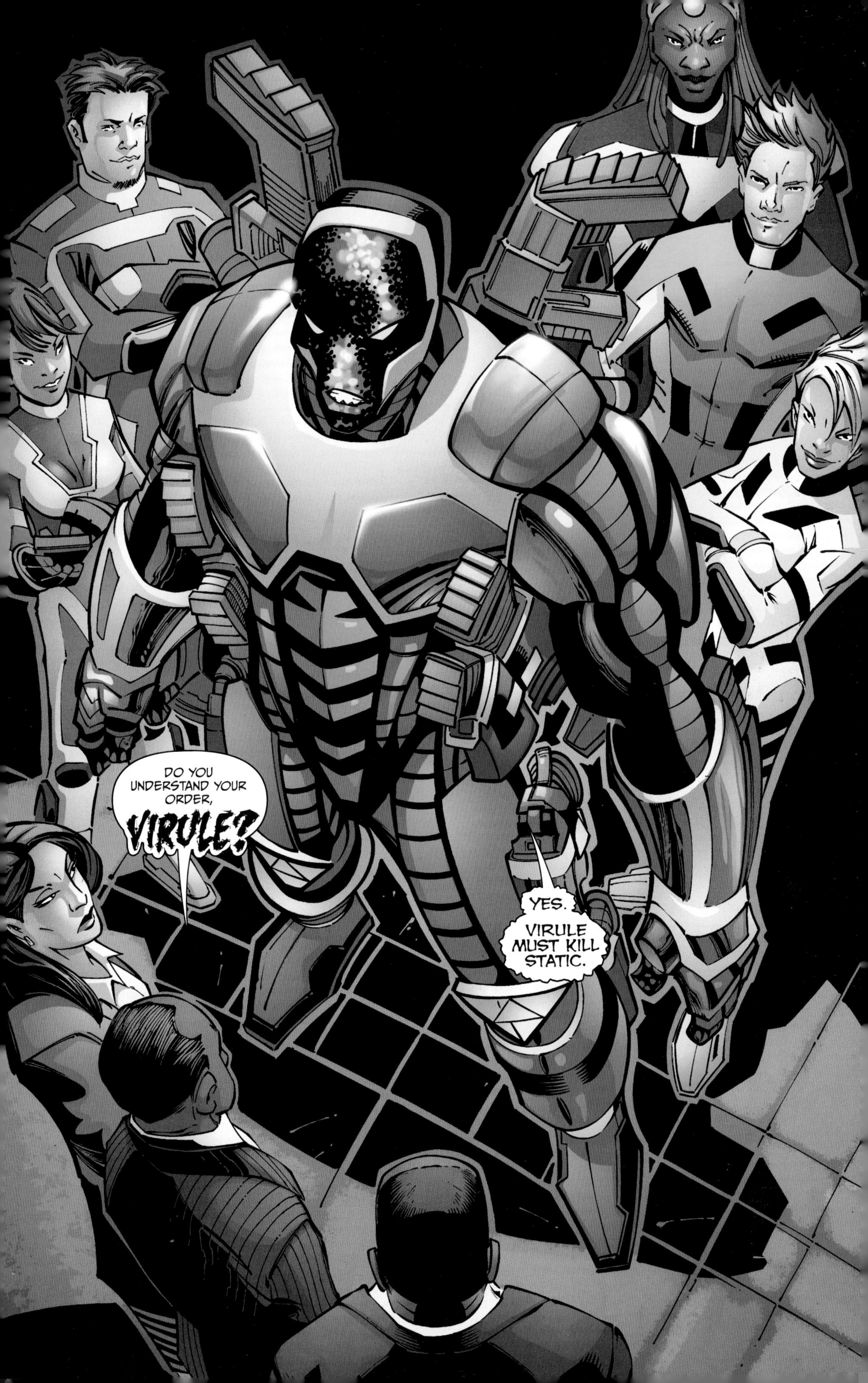
DO YOU UNDERSTAND YOUR ORDER, VIRULE?
YES. VIRULE MUST KILL STATIC.

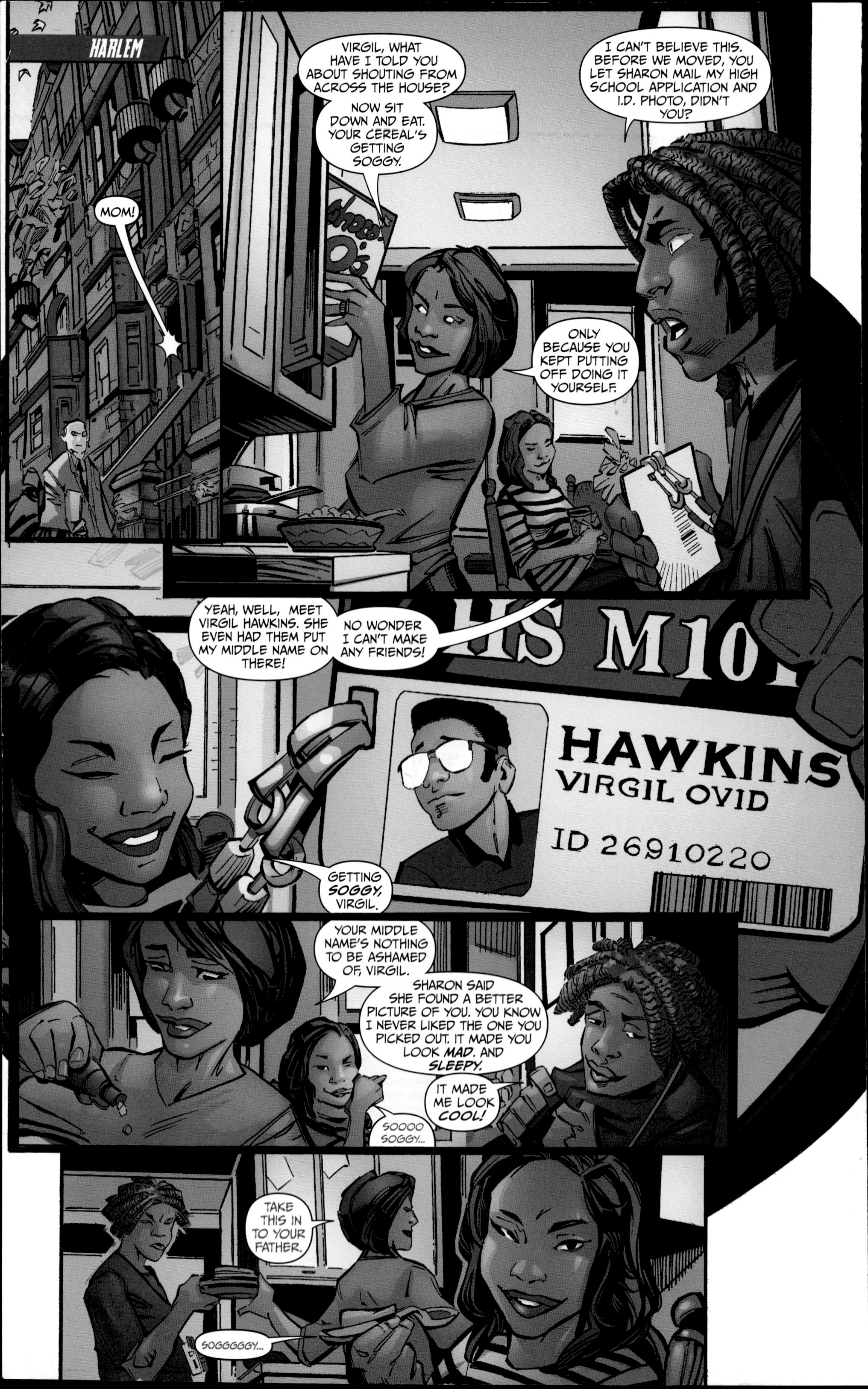
HARLEM
MOM!
VIRGIL, WHAT HAVE I TOLD YOU ABOUT SHOUTING FROM ACROSS THE HOUSE?
NOW SIT DOWN AND EAT. YOUR CEREAL'S GETTING SOGGY.
I CAN'T BELIEVE THIS. BEFORE WE MOVED, YOU LET SHARON MAIL MY HIGH SCHOOL APPLICATION AND I.D. PHOTO, DIDN'T YOU?
ONLY BECAUSE YOU KEPT PUTTING OFF DOING IT YOURSELF.
YEAH, WELL, MEET VIRGIL HAWKINS. SHE EVEN HAD THEM PUT MY MIDDLE NAME ON THERE!
NO WONDER I CAN'T MAKE ANY FRIENDS!
HS M10
HAWKINS
VIRGIL OVID
ID 26910220
GETTING SOGGY, VIRGIL.
YOUR MIDDLE NAME'S NOTHING TO BE ASHAMED OF, VIRGIL.
SHARON SAID SHE FOUND A BETTER PICTURE OF YOU. YOU KNOW I NEVER LIKED THE ONE YOU PICKED OUT. IT MADE YOU LOOK MAD. AND SLEEPY.
IT MADE ME LOOK COOL!
SOOOO SOGGY...
TAKE THIS IN TO YOUR FATHER.
SOGGGGGY...

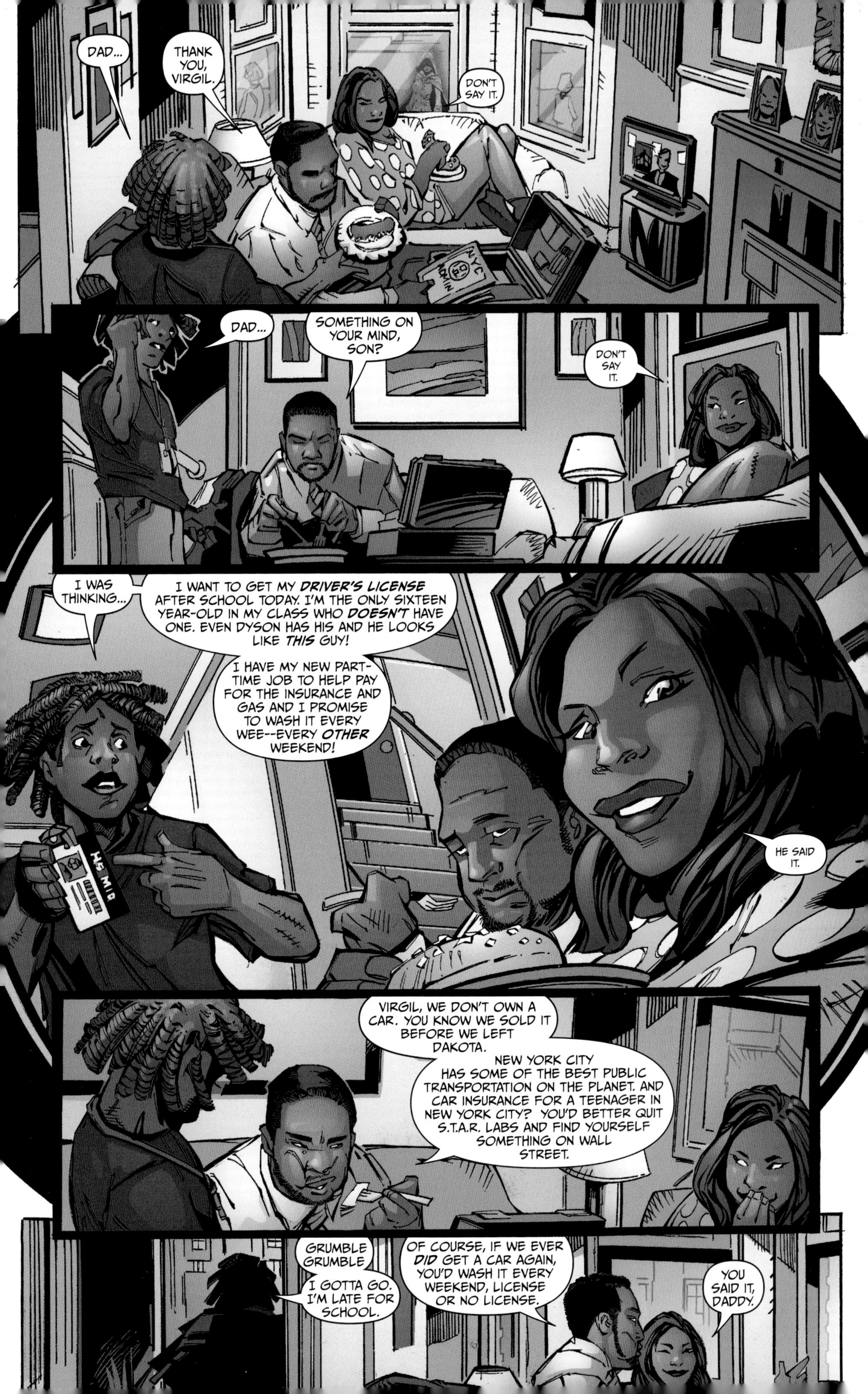
DAD...
THANK YOU, VIRGIL.
DON'T SAY IT.
DAD...
SOMETHING ON YOUR MIND, SON?
DON'T SAY IT.
I WAS THINKING...
I WANT TO GET MY DRIVER'S LICENSE AFTER SCHOOL TODAY. I'M THE ONLY SIXTEEN YEAR-OLD IN MY CLASS WHO DOESN'T HAVE ONE. EVEN DYSON HAS HIS AND HE LOOKS LIKE THIS GUY!
I HAVE MY NEW PART-TIME JOB TO HELP PAY FOR THE INSURANCE AND GAS AND I PROMISE TO WASH IT EVERY WEE--EVERY OTHER WEEKEND!
HE SAID IT.
VIRGIL, WE DON'T OWN A CAR. YOU KNOW WE SOLD IT BEFORE WE LEFT DAKOTA.
NEW YORK CITY HAS SOME OF THE BEST PUBLIC TRANSPORTATION ON THE PLANET. AND CAR INSURANCE FOR A TEENAGER IN NEW YORK CITY? YOU'D BETTER QUIT S.T.A.R. LABS AND FIND YOURSELF SOMETHING ON WALL STREET.
GRUMBLE GRUMBLE
I GOTTA GO. I'M LATE FOR SCHOOL.
OF COURSE, IF WE EVER DID GET A CAR AGAIN, YOU'D WASH IT EVERY WEEKEND, LICENSE OR NO LICENSE.
YOU SAID IT, DADDY.

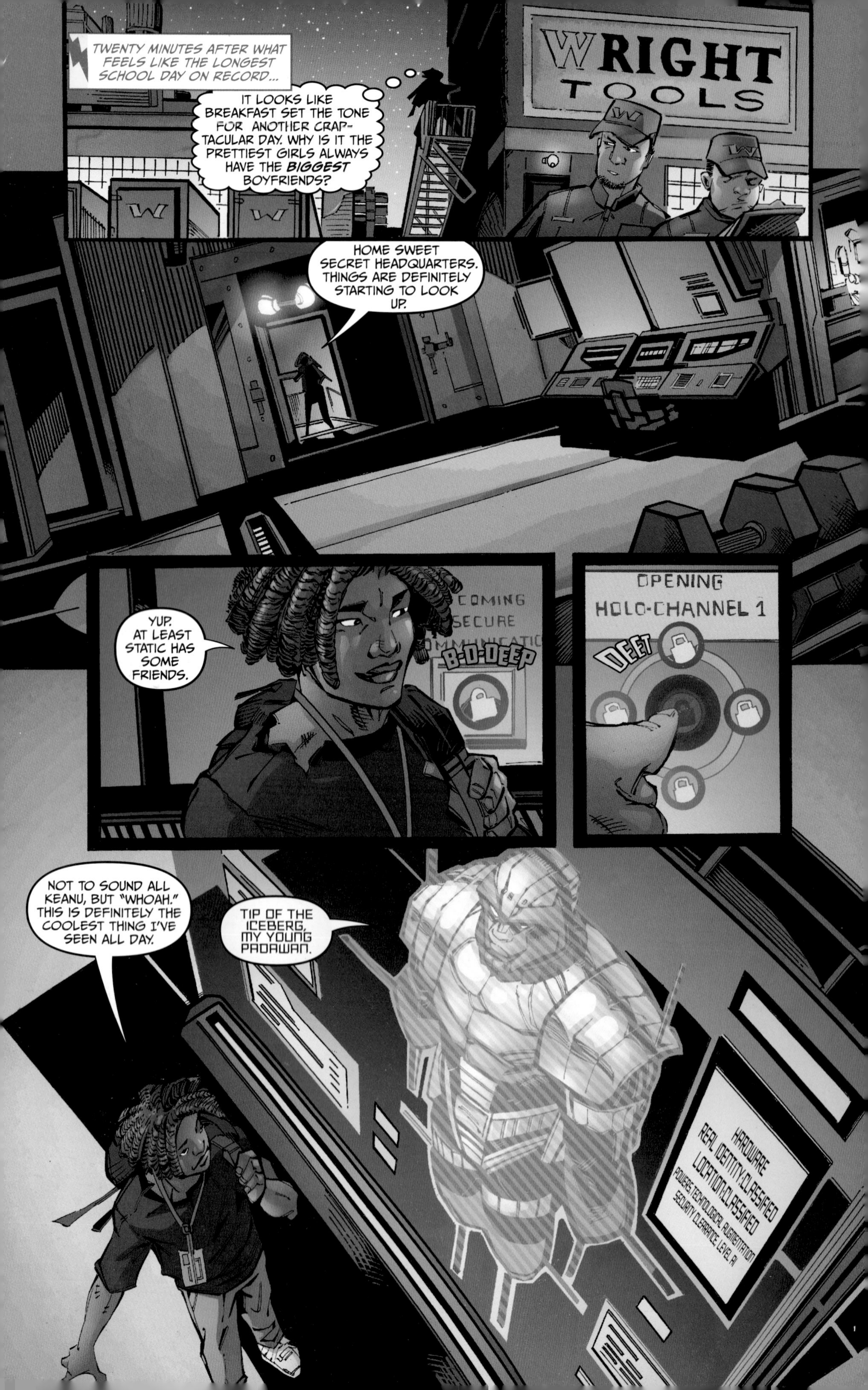

TWENTY MINUTES AFTER WHAT FEELS LIKE THE LONGEST SCHOOL DAY ON RECORD...
IT LOOKS LIKE BREAKFAST SET THE TONE FOR ANOTHER CRAP-TACULAR DAY. WHY IS IT THE PRETTIEST GIRLS ALWAYS HAVE THE BIGGEST BOYFRIENDS?
WRIGHT TOOLS
HOME SWEET SECRET HEADQUARTERS. THINGS ARE DEFINITELY STARTING TO LOOK UP.
YUP. AT LEAST STATIC HAS SOME FRIENDS.
B-D-DEEP
OPENING HOLO-CHANNEL 1
DEET
NOT TO SOUND ALL KEANU, BUT "WHOAH." THIS IS DEFINITELY THE COOLEST THING I'VE SEEN ALL DAY.
TIP OF THE ICEBERG, MY YOUNG PADAWAN.
HARDWARE
REAL IDENTITY: CLASSIFIED
LOCATION: CLASSIFIED
POWERS: TECHNOLOGICAL AUGMENTATION
SECURITY CLEARANCE: LEVEL A1

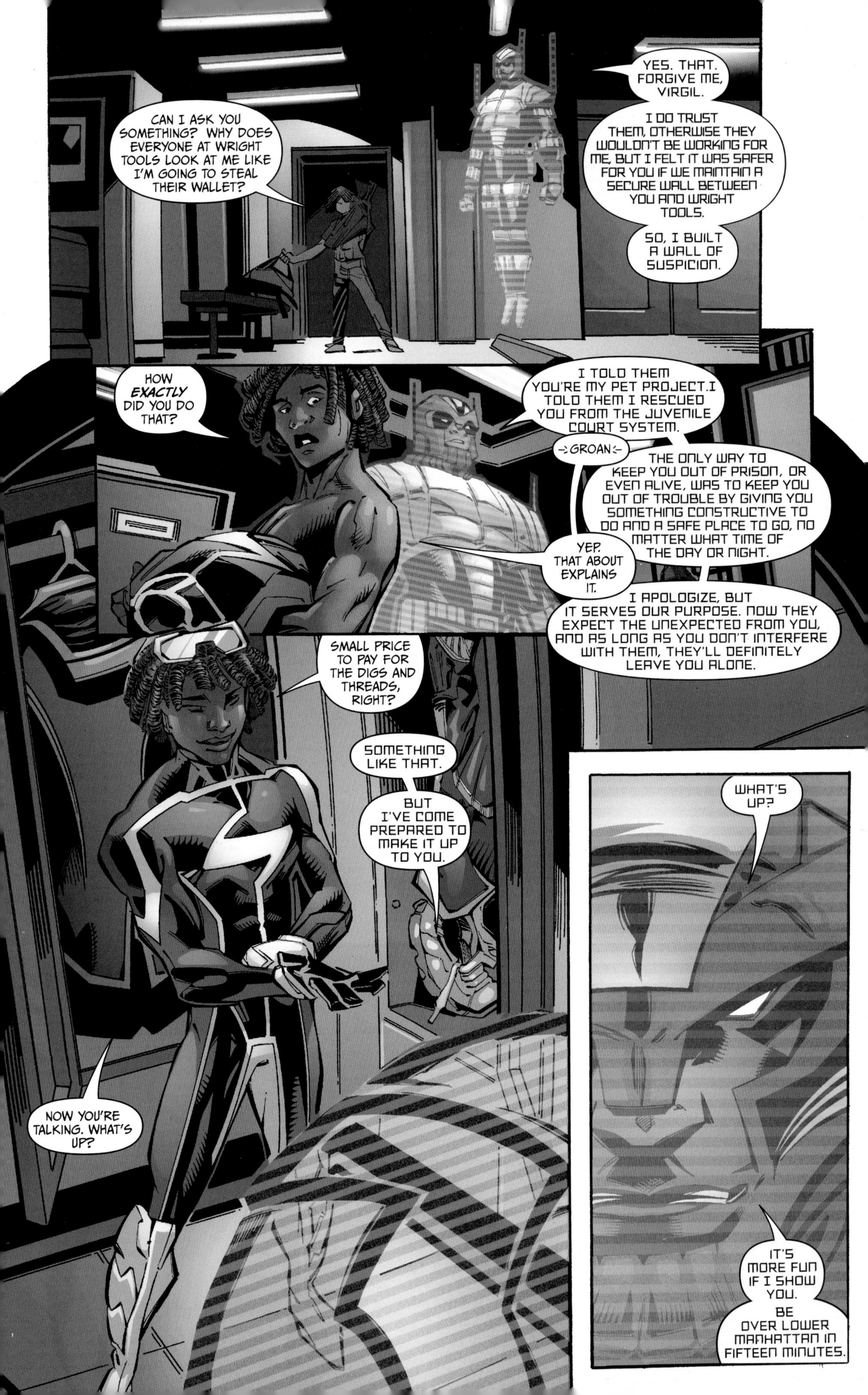

CAN I ASK YOU SOMETHING? WHY DOES EVERYONE AT WRIGHT TOOLS LOOK AT ME LIKE I'M GOING TO STEAL THEIR WALLET?
YES. THAT. FORGIVE ME, VIRGIL.
I DO TRUST THEM, OTHERWISE THEY WOULDN'T BE WORKING FOR ME, BUT I FELT IT WAS SAFER FOR YOU IF WE MAINTAIN A SECURE WALL BETWEEN YOU AND WRIGHT TOOLS.
SO, I BUILT A WALL OF SUSPICION.
HOW *EXACTLY* DID YOU DO THAT?
I TOLD THEM YOU'RE MY PET PROJECT. I TOLD THEM I RESCUED YOU FROM THE JUVENILE COURT SYSTEM.
GROAN
THE ONLY WAY TO KEEP YOU OUT OF PRISON, OR EVEN ALIVE, WAS TO KEEP YOU OUT OF TROUBLE BY GIVING YOU SOMETHING CONSTRUCTIVE TO DO AND A SAFE PLACE TO GO, NO MATTER WHAT TIME OF THE DAY OR NIGHT.
YEP. THAT ABOUT EXPLAINS IT.
I APOLOGIZE, BUT IT SERVES OUR PURPOSE. NOW THEY EXPECT THE UNEXPECTED FROM YOU, AND AS LONG AS YOU DON'T INTERFERE WITH THEM, THEY'LL DEFINITELY LEAVE YOU ALONE.
SMALL PRICE TO PAY FOR THE DIGS AND THREADS, RIGHT?
SOMETHING LIKE THAT.
BUT I'VE COME PREPARED TO MAKE IT UP TO YOU.
NOW YOU'RE TALKING. WHAT'S UP?
WHAT'S UP?
IT'S MORE FUN IF I SHOW YOU.
BE OVER LOWER MANHATTAN IN FIFTEEN MINUTES.

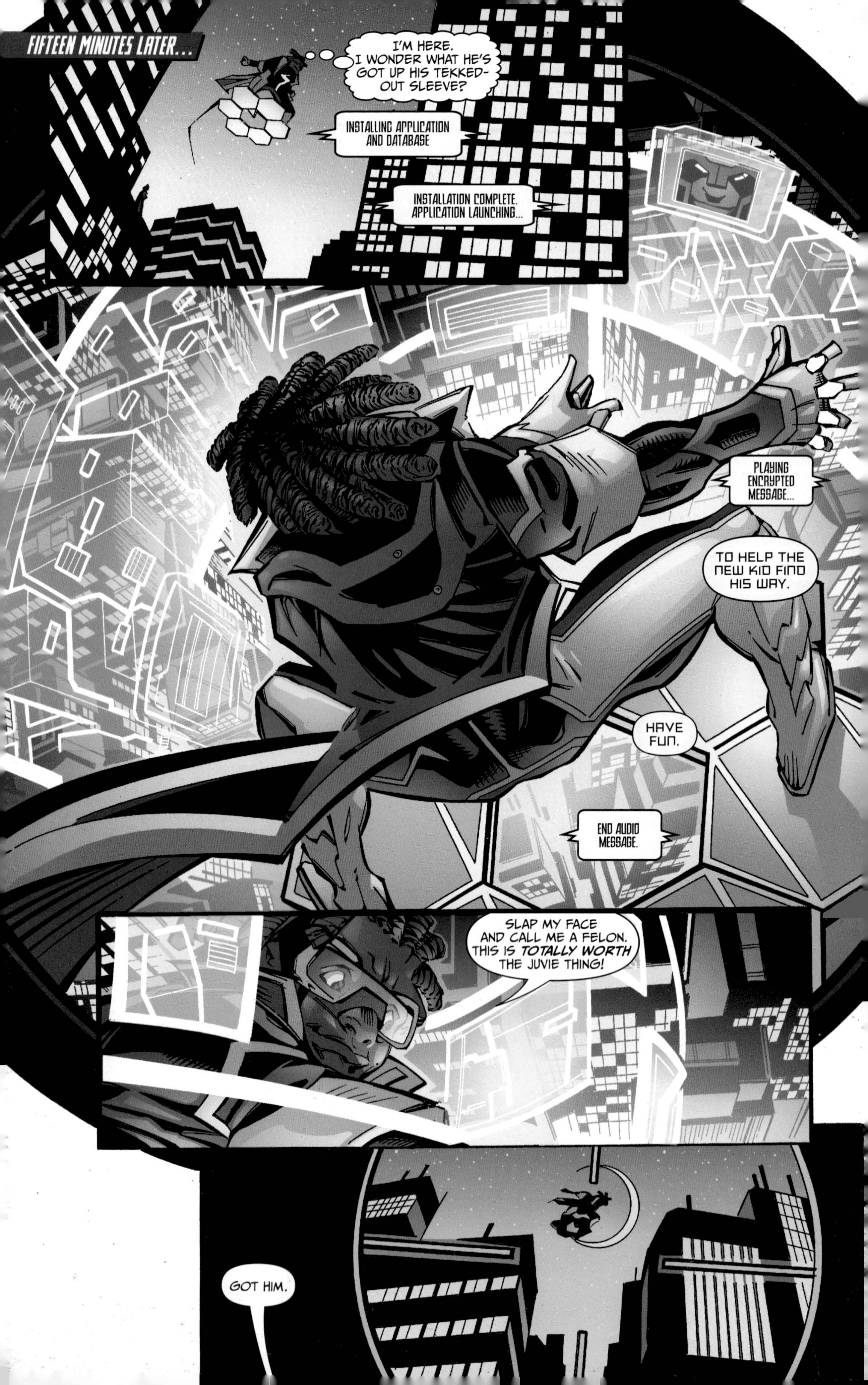
FIFTEEN MINUTES LATER...
I'M HERE. I WONDER WHAT HE'S GOT UP HIS TEKKED-OUT SLEEVE?
INSTALLING APPLICATION AND DATABASE
INSTALLATION COMPLETE. APPLICATION LAUNCHING...
PLAYING ENCRYPTED MESSAGE...
TO HELP THE NEW KID FIND HIS WAY.
HAVE FUN.
END AUDIO MESSAGE.
SLAP MY FACE AND CALL ME A FELON. THIS IS TOTALLY WORTH THE JUVIE THING!
GOT HIM.

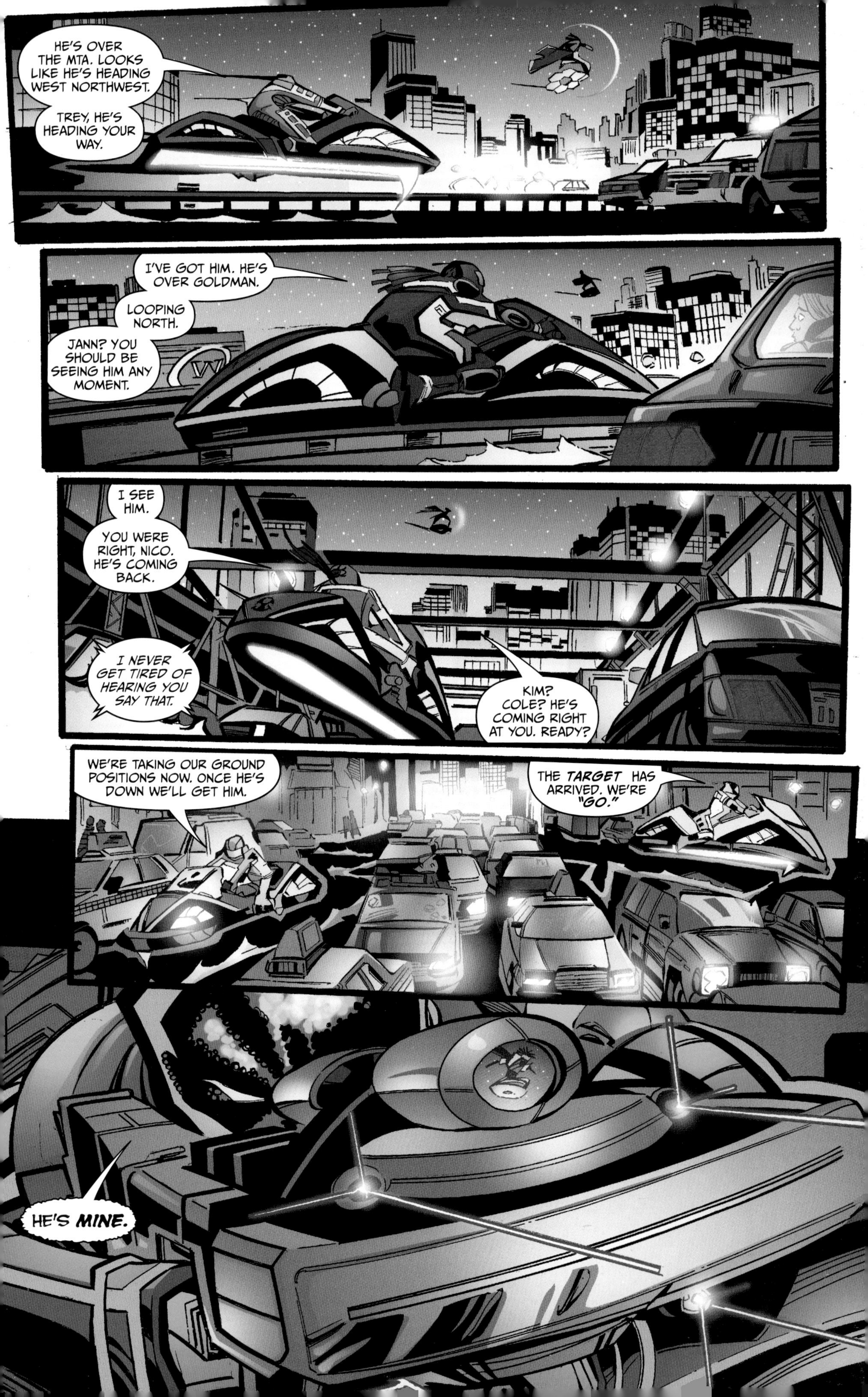
HE'S OVER THE MTA. LOOKS LIKE HE'S HEADING WEST NORTHWEST.
TREY, HE'S HEADING YOUR WAY.
I'VE GOT HIM. HE'S OVER GOLDMAN.
LOOPING NORTH.
JANN? YOU SHOULD BE SEEING HIM ANY MOMENT.
I SEE HIM.
YOU WERE RIGHT, NICO. HE'S COMING BACK.
I NEVER GET TIRED OF HEARING YOU SAY THAT.
KIM? COLE? HE'S COMING RIGHT AT YOU. READY?
WE'RE TAKING OUR GROUND POSITIONS NOW. ONCE HE'S DOWN WE'LL GET HIM.
THE *TARGET* HAS ARRIVED. WE'RE *"GO."*
HE'S ***MINE.***

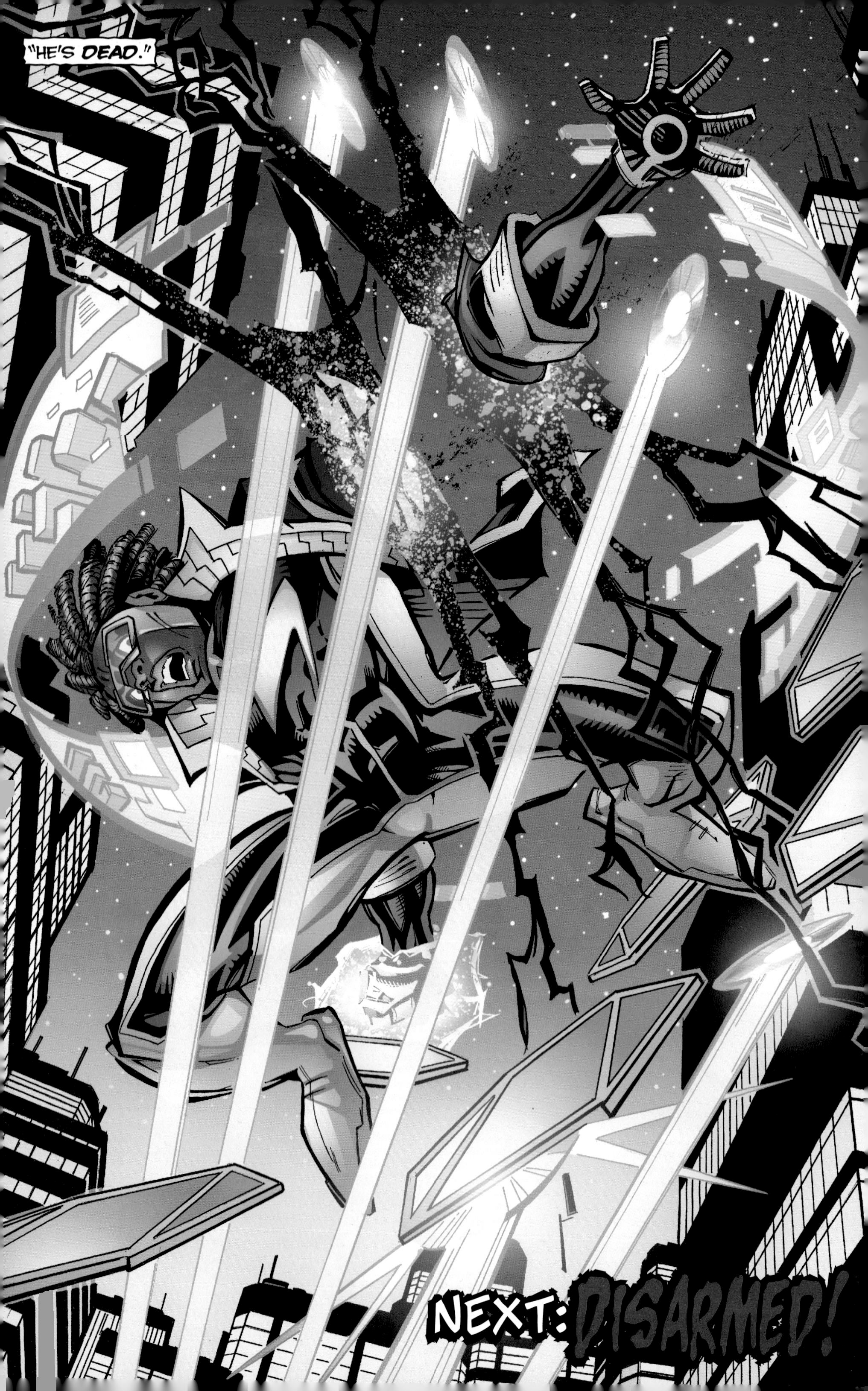
"HE'S DEAD."
NEXT: DISARMED!

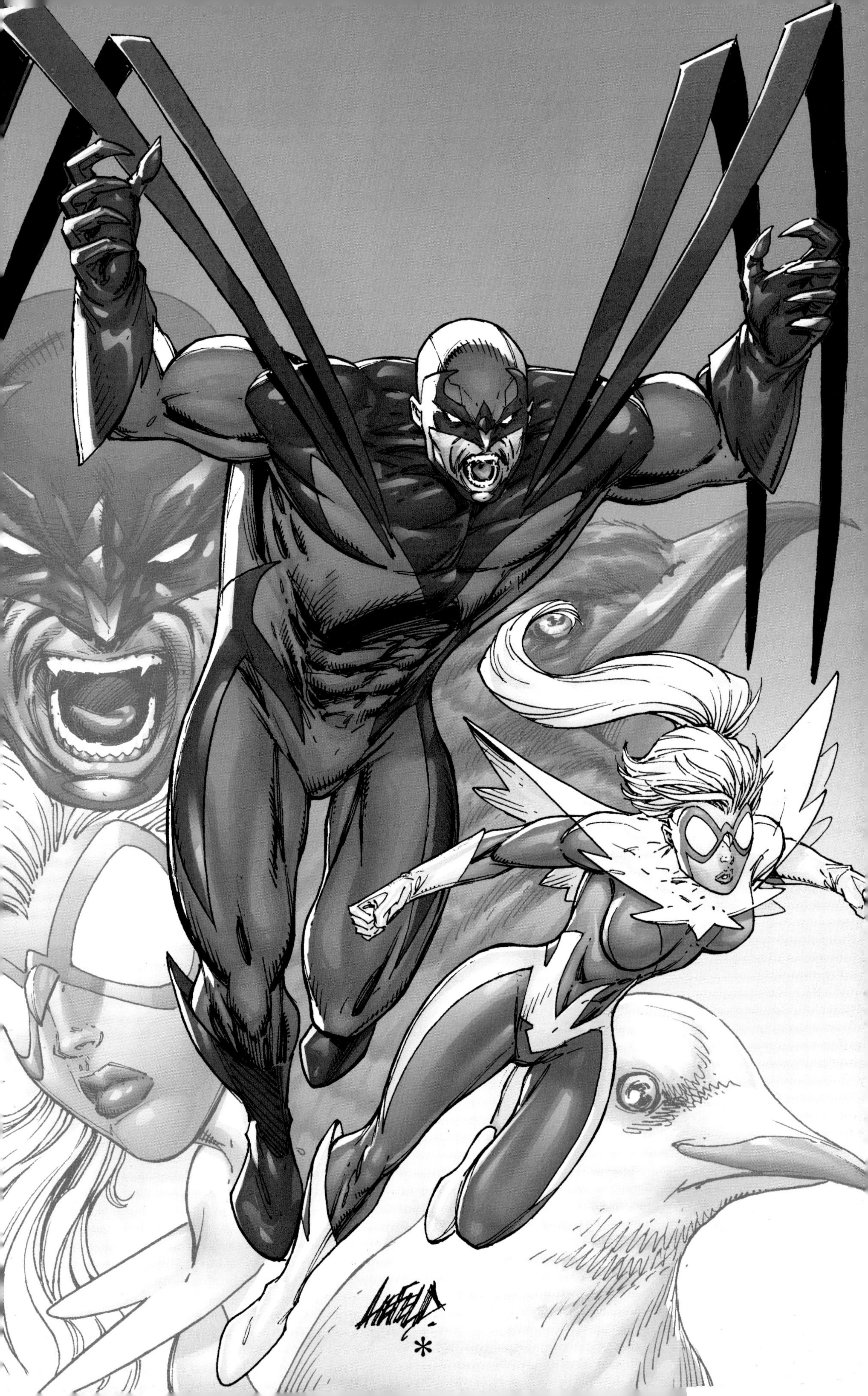

HAWK & DOVE

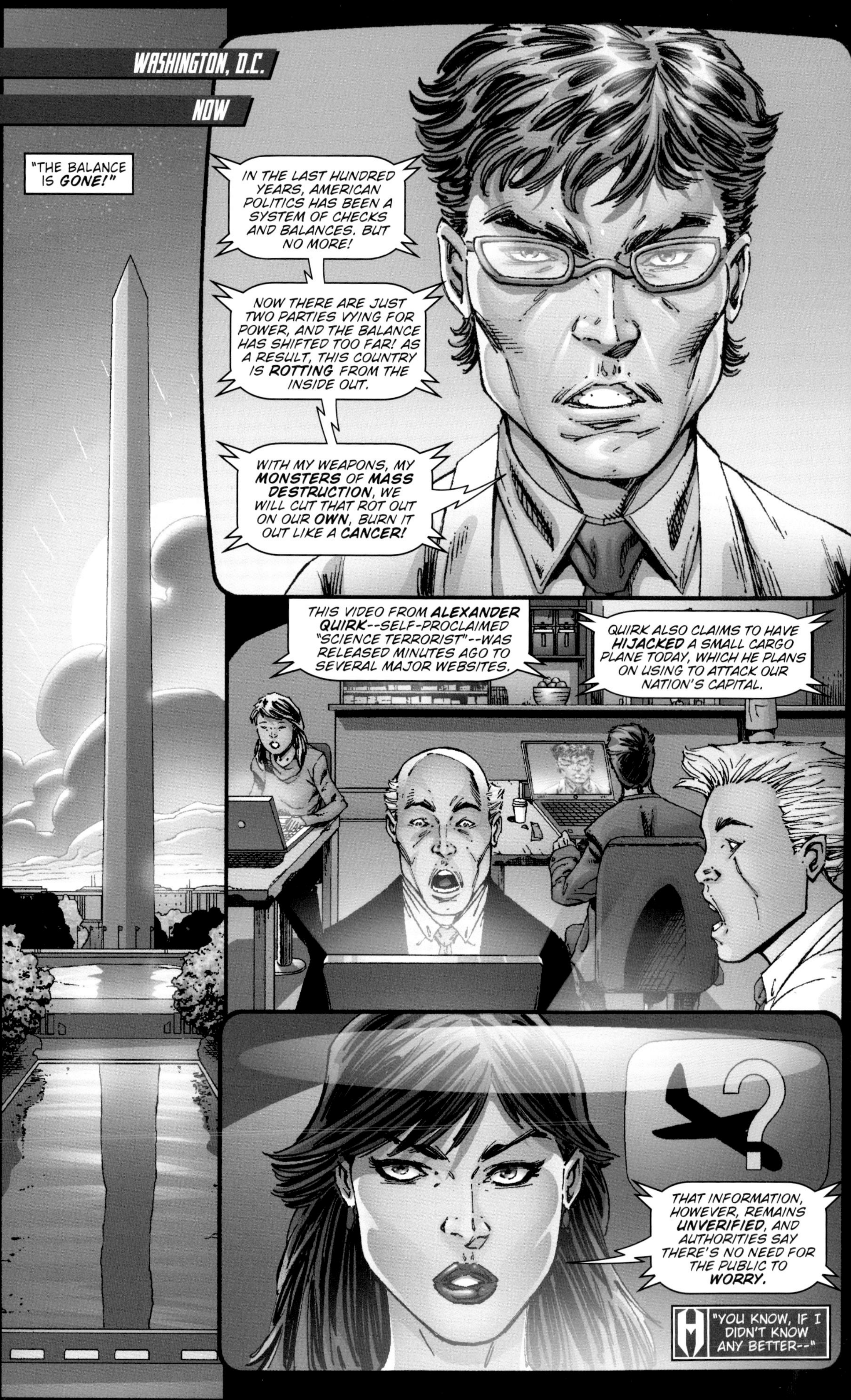
WASHINGTON, D.C.
NOW
"THE BALANCE IS GONE!"
IN THE LAST HUNDRED YEARS, AMERICAN POLITICS HAS BEEN A SYSTEM OF CHECKS AND BALANCES. BUT NO MORE!
NOW THERE ARE JUST TWO PARTIES VYING FOR POWER, AND THE BALANCE HAS SHIFTED TOO FAR! AS A RESULT, THIS COUNTRY IS ROTTING FROM THE INSIDE OUT.
WITH MY WEAPONS, MY MONSTERS OF MASS DESTRUCTION, WE WILL CUT THAT ROT OUT ON OUR OWN, BURN IT OUT LIKE A CANCER!
THIS VIDEO FROM ALEXANDER QUIRK--SELF-PROCLAIMED "SCIENCE TERRORIST"--WAS RELEASED MINUTES AGO TO SEVERAL MAJOR WEBSITES.
QUIRK ALSO CLAIMS TO HAVE HIJACKED A SMALL CARGO PLANE TODAY, WHICH HE PLANS ON USING TO ATTACK OUR NATION'S CAPITAL.
THAT INFORMATION, HOWEVER, REMAINS UNVERIFIED, AND AUTHORITIES SAY THERE'S NO NEED FOR THE PUBLIC TO WORRY.
"YOU KNOW, IF I DIDN'T KNOW ANY BETTER--"

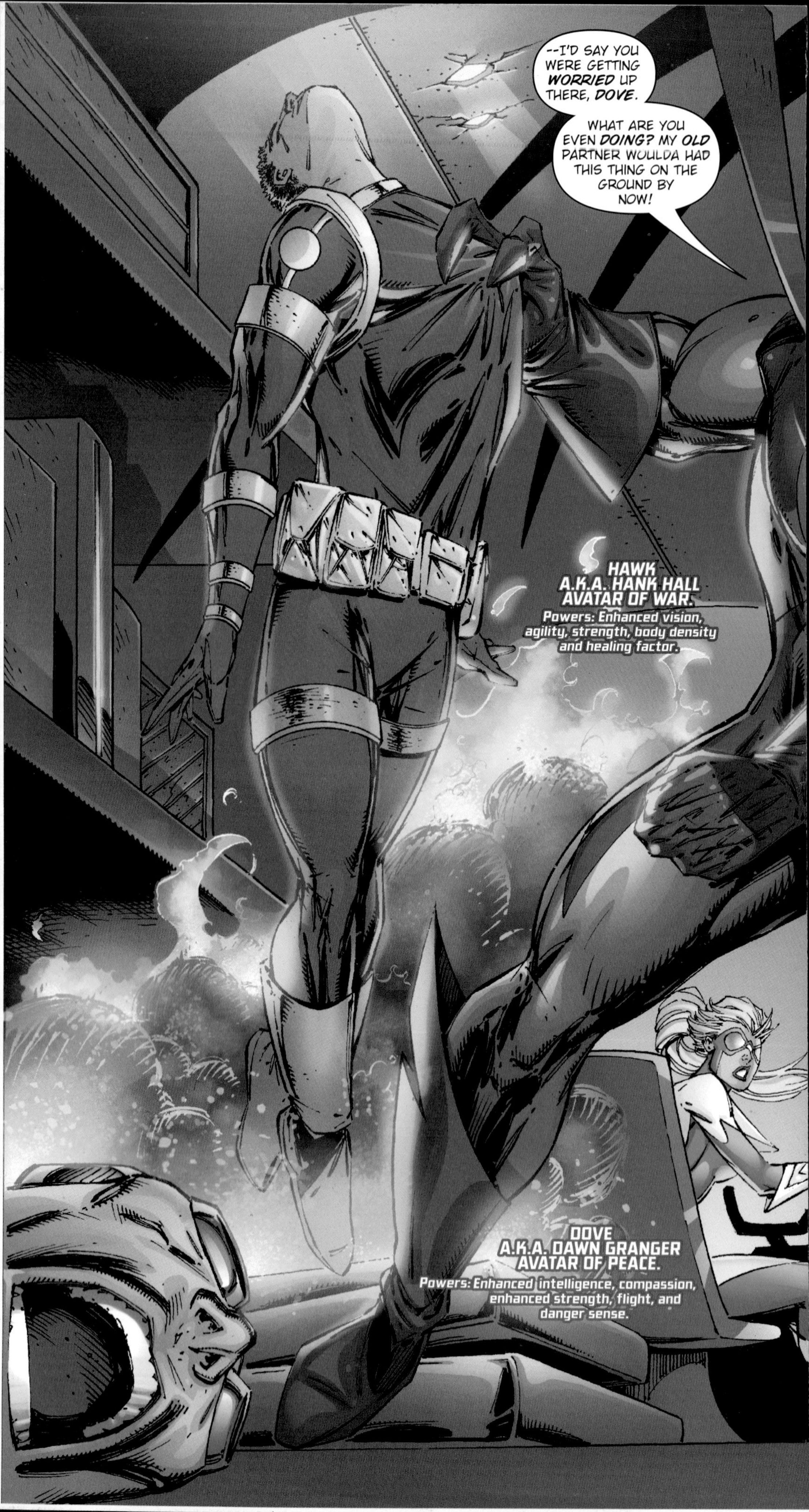
--I'D SAY YOU WERE GETTING WORRIED UP THERE, DOVE.
WHAT ARE YOU EVEN DOING? MY OLD PARTNER WOULDA HAD THIS THING ON THE GROUND BY NOW!
HAWK A.K.A. HANK HALL AVATAR OF WAR.
Powers: Enhanced vision, agility, strength, body density and healing factor.
DOVE A.K.A. DAWN GRANGER AVATAR OF PEACE.
Powers: Enhanced intelligence, compassion, enhanced strength, flight, and danger sense.

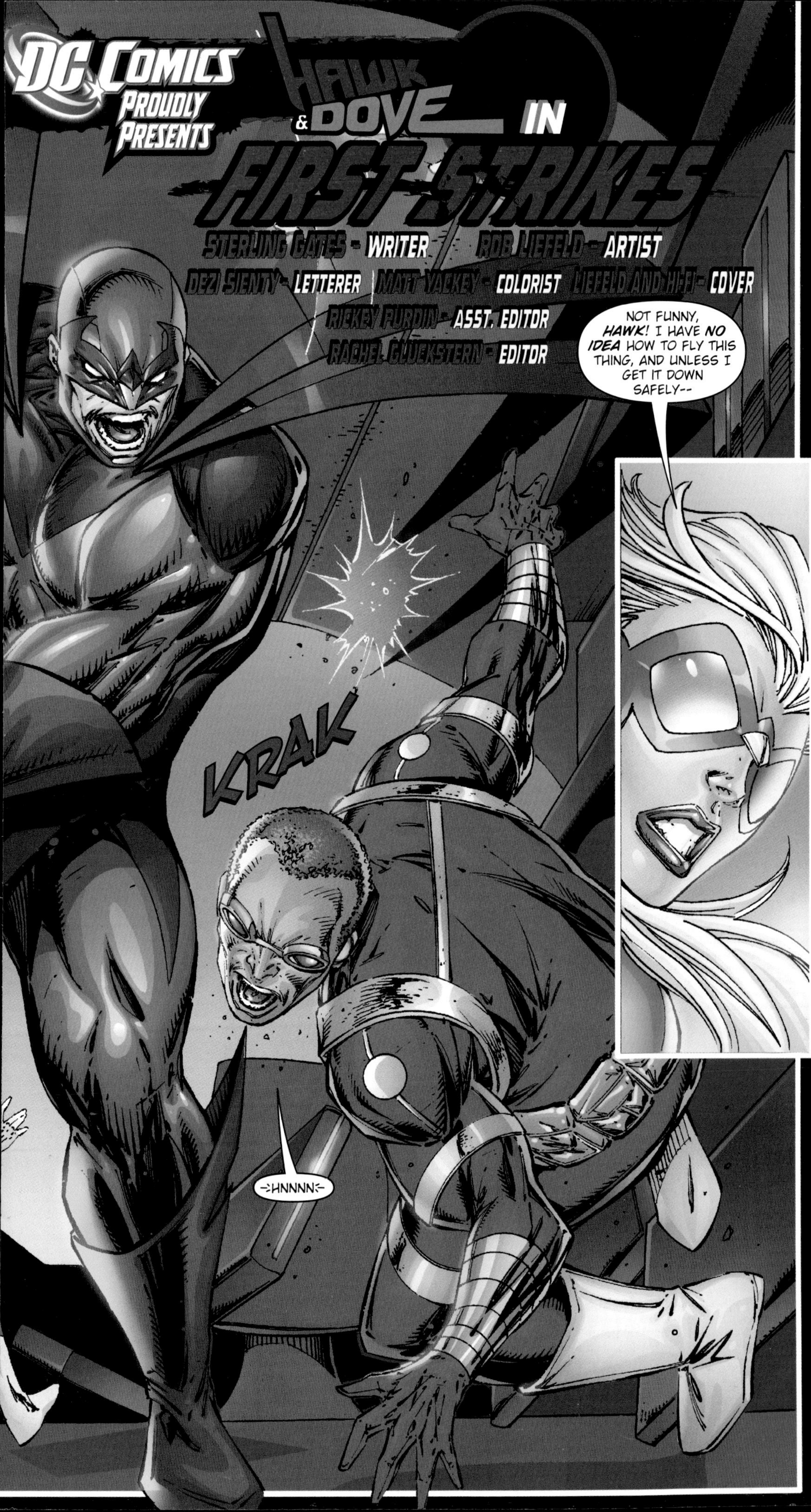
DC COMICS PROUDLY PRESENTS
HAWK & DOVE IN
FIRST STRIKES
STERLING GATES - WRITER
ROB LIEFELD - ARTIST
DEZI SIENTY - LETTERER
MATT YACKEY - COLORIST
LIEFELD AND HI-FI - COVER
RICKEY PURDIN - ASST. EDITOR
RACHEL GLUCKSTERN - EDITOR
NOT FUNNY, HAWK! I HAVE NO IDEA HOW TO FLY THIS THING, AND UNLESS I GET IT DOWN SAFELY--
KRAK
-HNNNN-

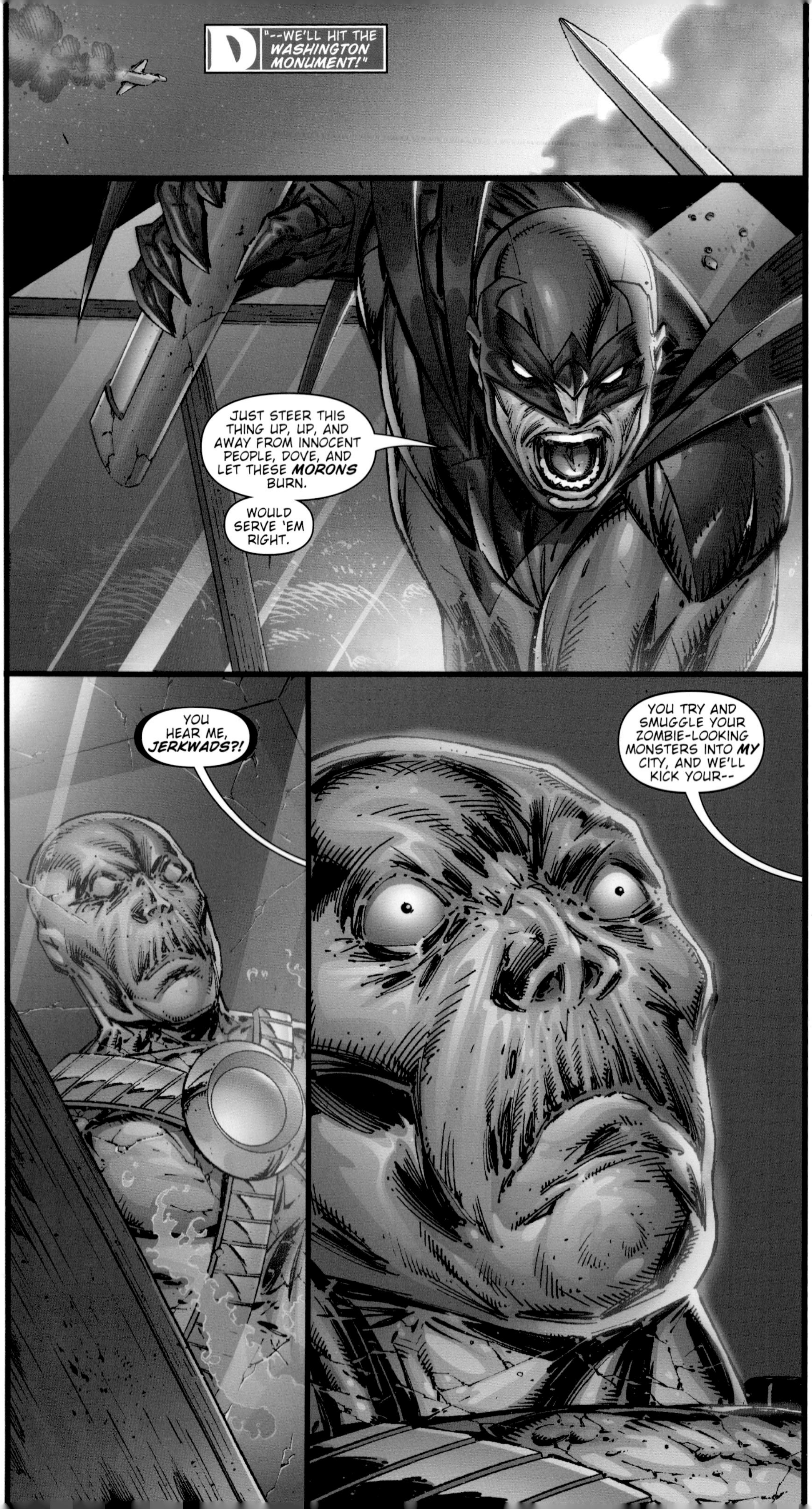
"--WE'LL HIT THE WASHINGTON MONUMENT!"
JUST STEER THIS THING UP, UP, AND AWAY FROM INNOCENT PEOPLE, DOVE, AND LET THESE MORONS BURN.
WOULD SERVE 'EM RIGHT.
YOU HEAR ME, JERKWADS?!
YOU TRY AND SMUGGLE YOUR ZOMBIE-LOOKING MONSTERS INTO MY CITY, AND WE'LL KICK YOUR--

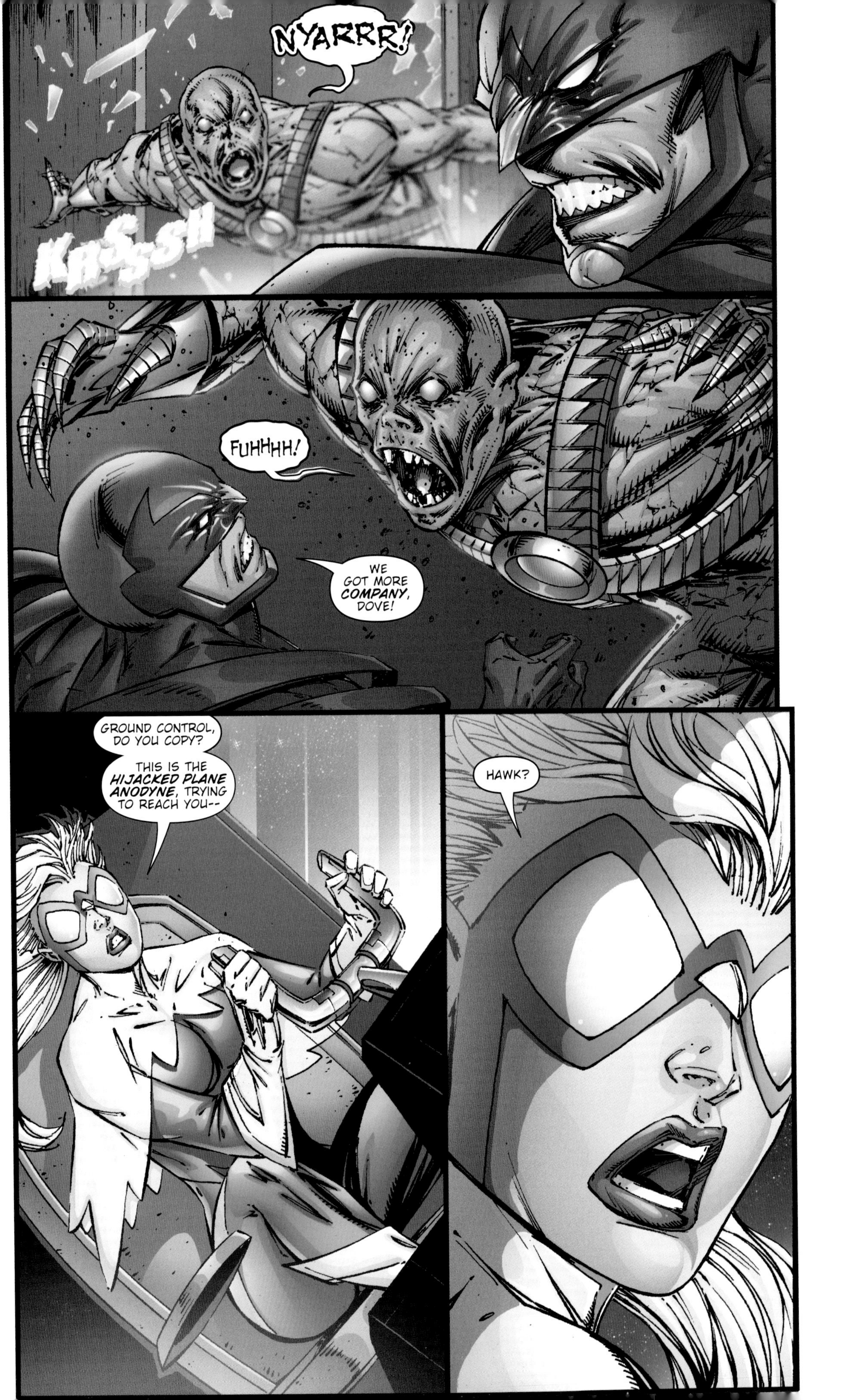
NYARRR!
KRSSSH
FUHHHH!
WE GOT MORE COMPANY, DOVE!
GROUND CONTROL, DO YOU COPY?
THIS IS THE HIJACKED PLANE ANODYNE, TRYING TO REACH YOU--
HAWK?

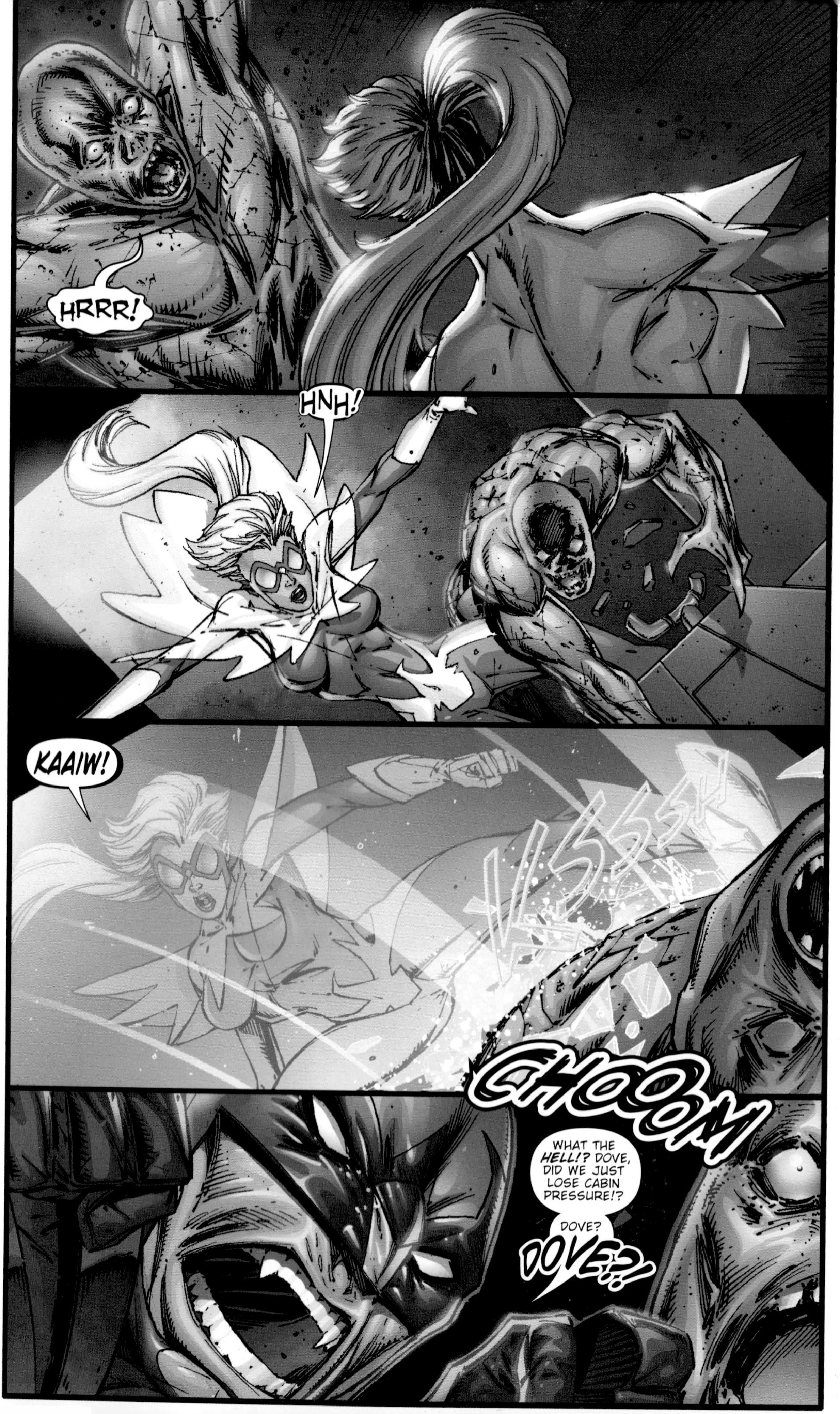
HRRR!
HNH!
KAAIW!
VISSSH
CHOOOM
WHAT THE HELL!? DOVE, DID WE JUST LOSE CABIN PRESSURE!?
DOVE?
DOVE?!

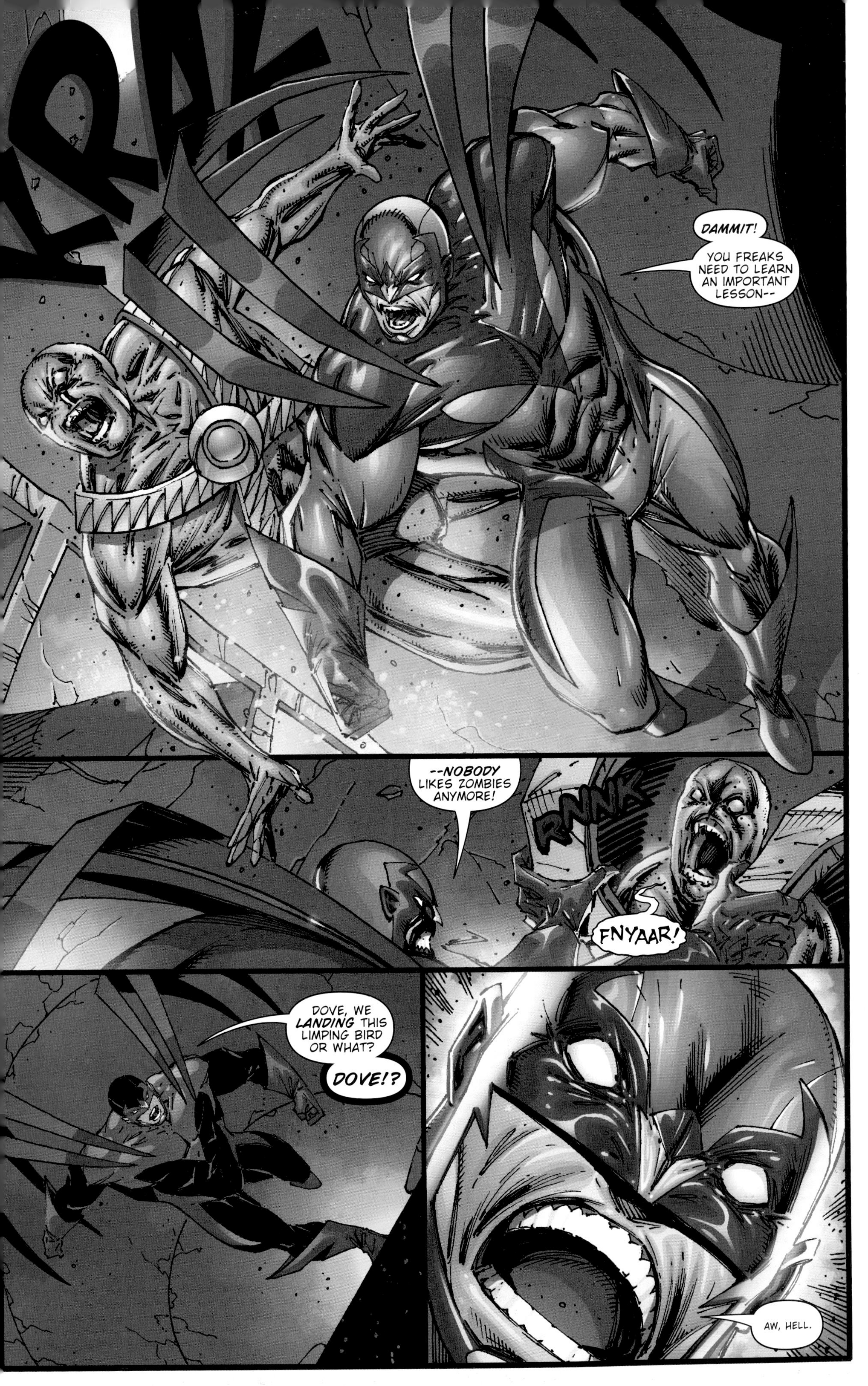
KRAK
DAMMIT!
YOU FREAKS NEED TO LEARN AN IMPORTANT LESSON--
--NOBODY LIKES ZOMBIES ANYMORE!
RNNK
FNYAAR!
DOVE, WE LANDING THIS LIMPING BIRD OR WHAT?
DOVE!?
AW, HELL.

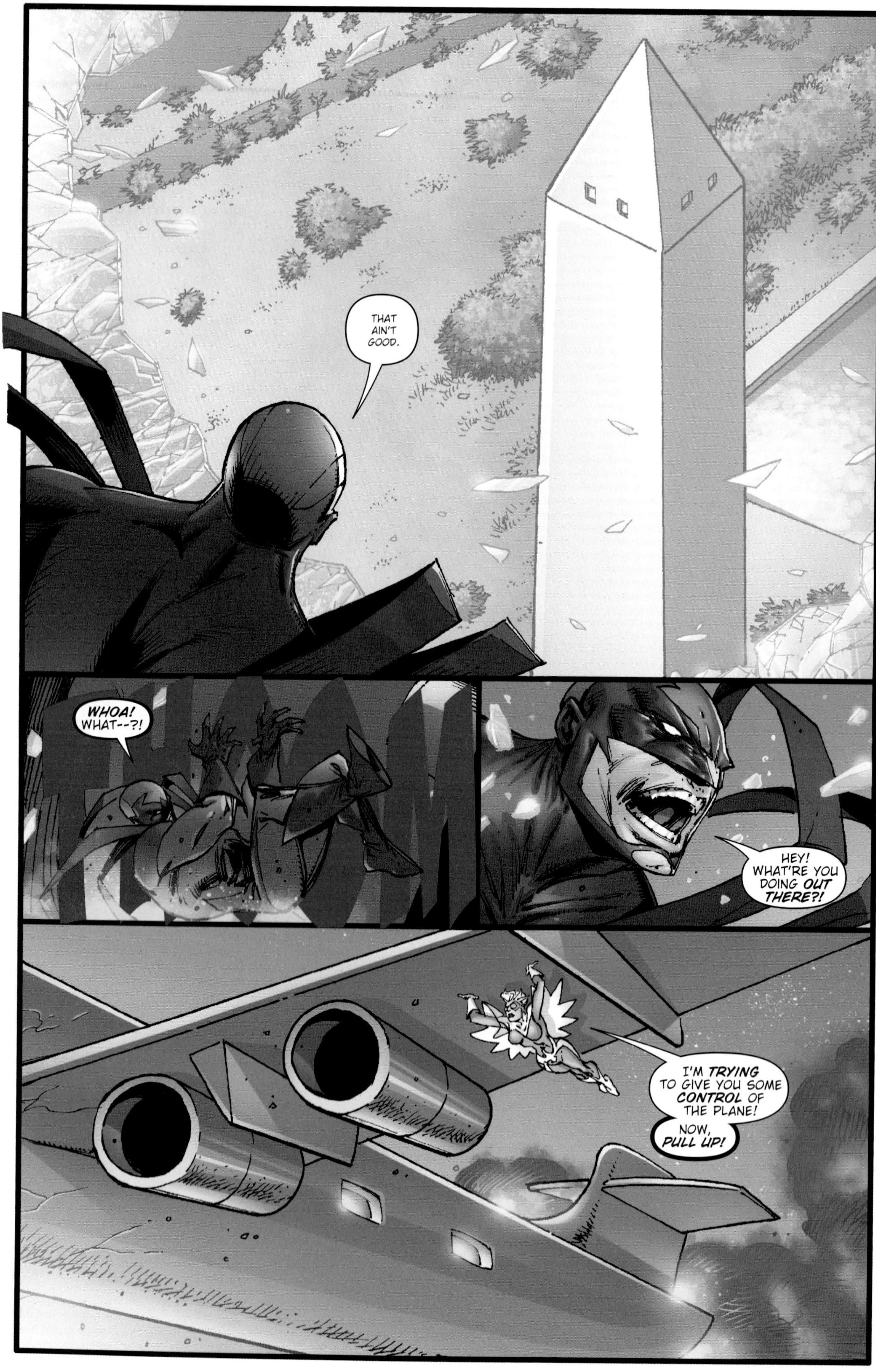
THAT AIN'T GOOD.
WHOA! WHAT--?!
HEY! WHAT'RE YOU DOING OUT THERE?!
I'M TRYING TO GIVE YOU SOME CONTROL OF THE PLANE!
NOW, PULL UP!

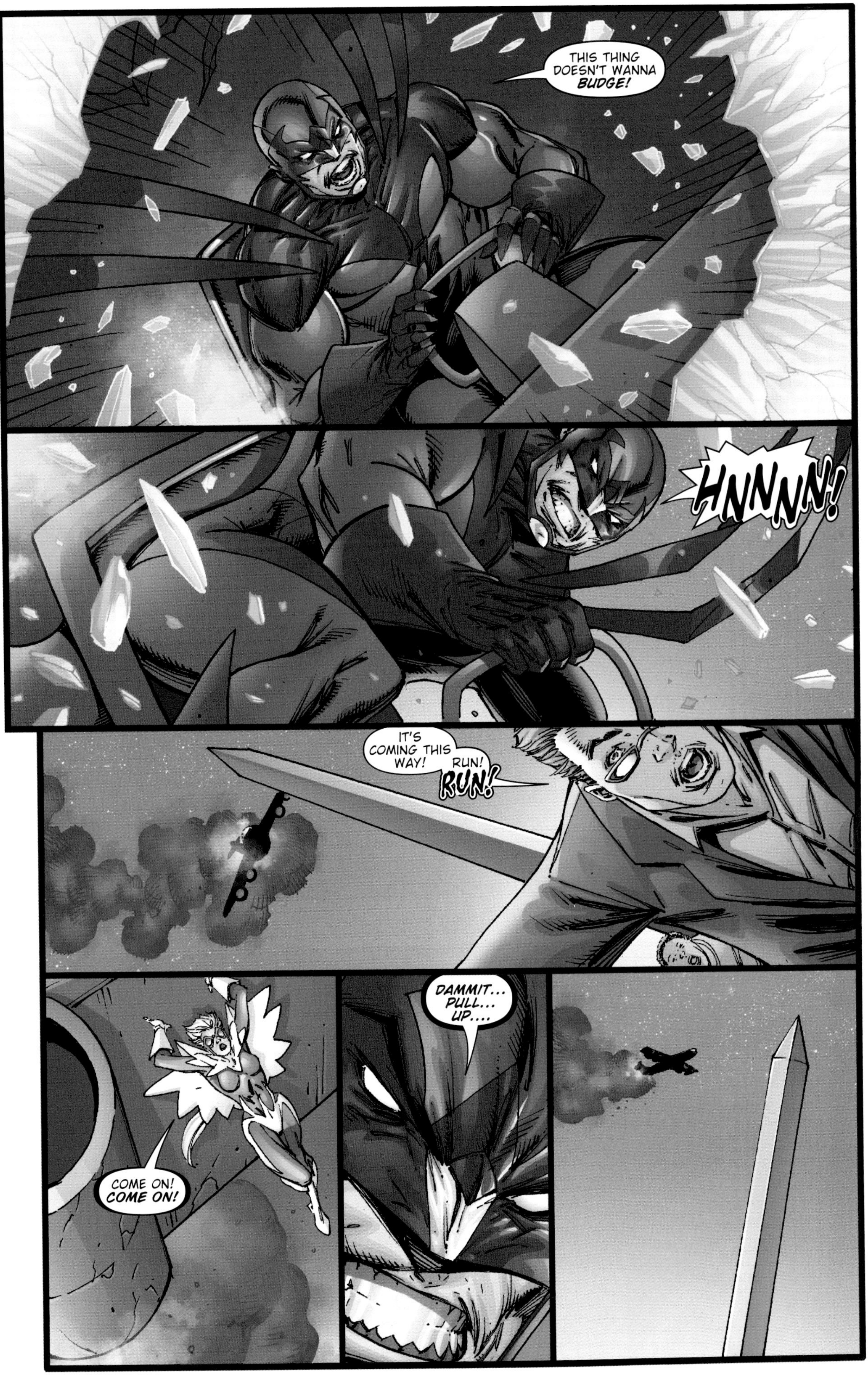

THIS THING DOESN'T WANNA BUDGE!
HNNNN!
IT'S COMING THIS WAY!
RUN! RUN!
COME ON! COME ON!
DAMMIT... PULL... UP....

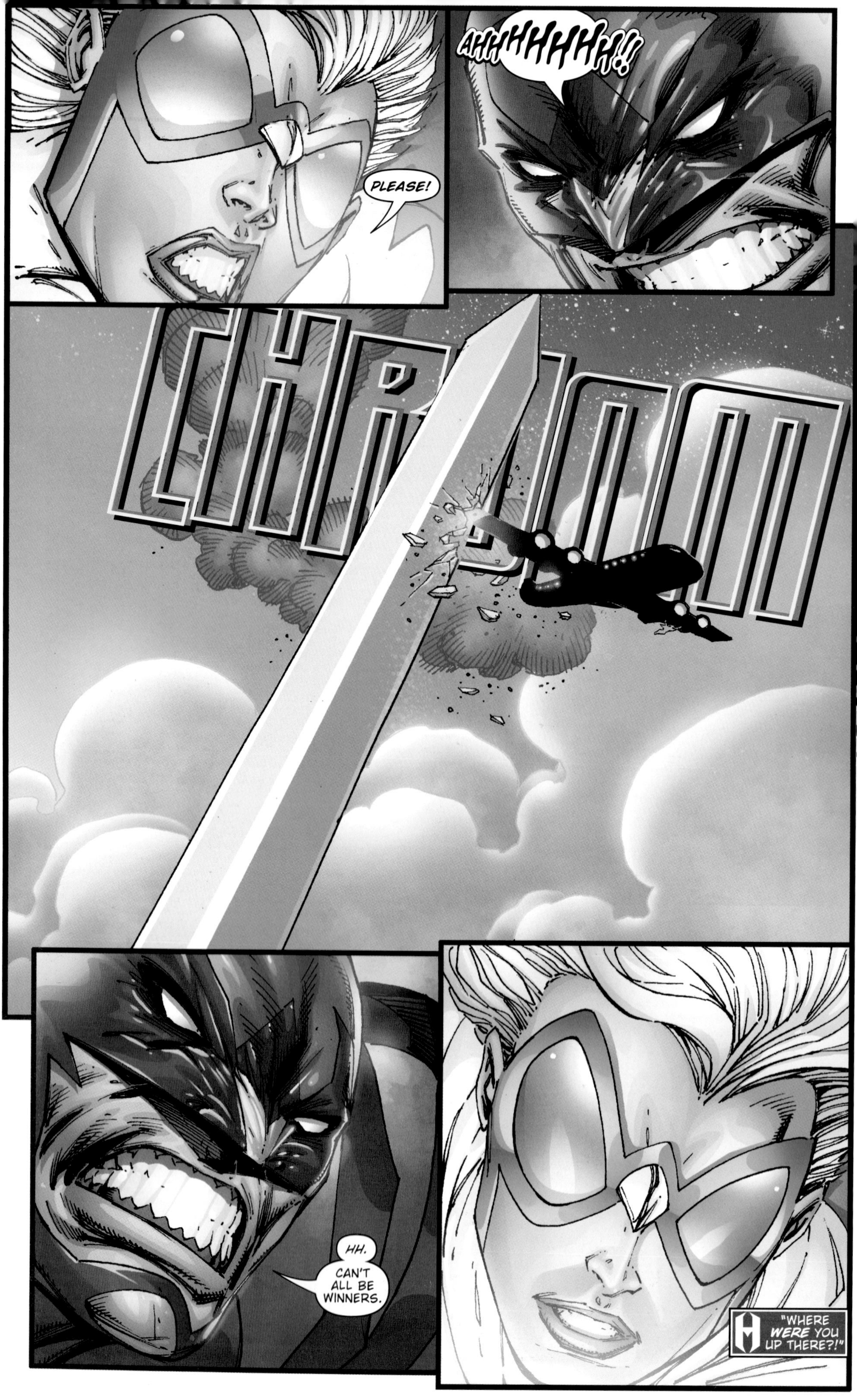
PLEASE!
AHHHHHHH!!
CHROOM
HH.
CAN'T ALL BE WINNERS.
"WHERE *WERE* YOU UP THERE?!"

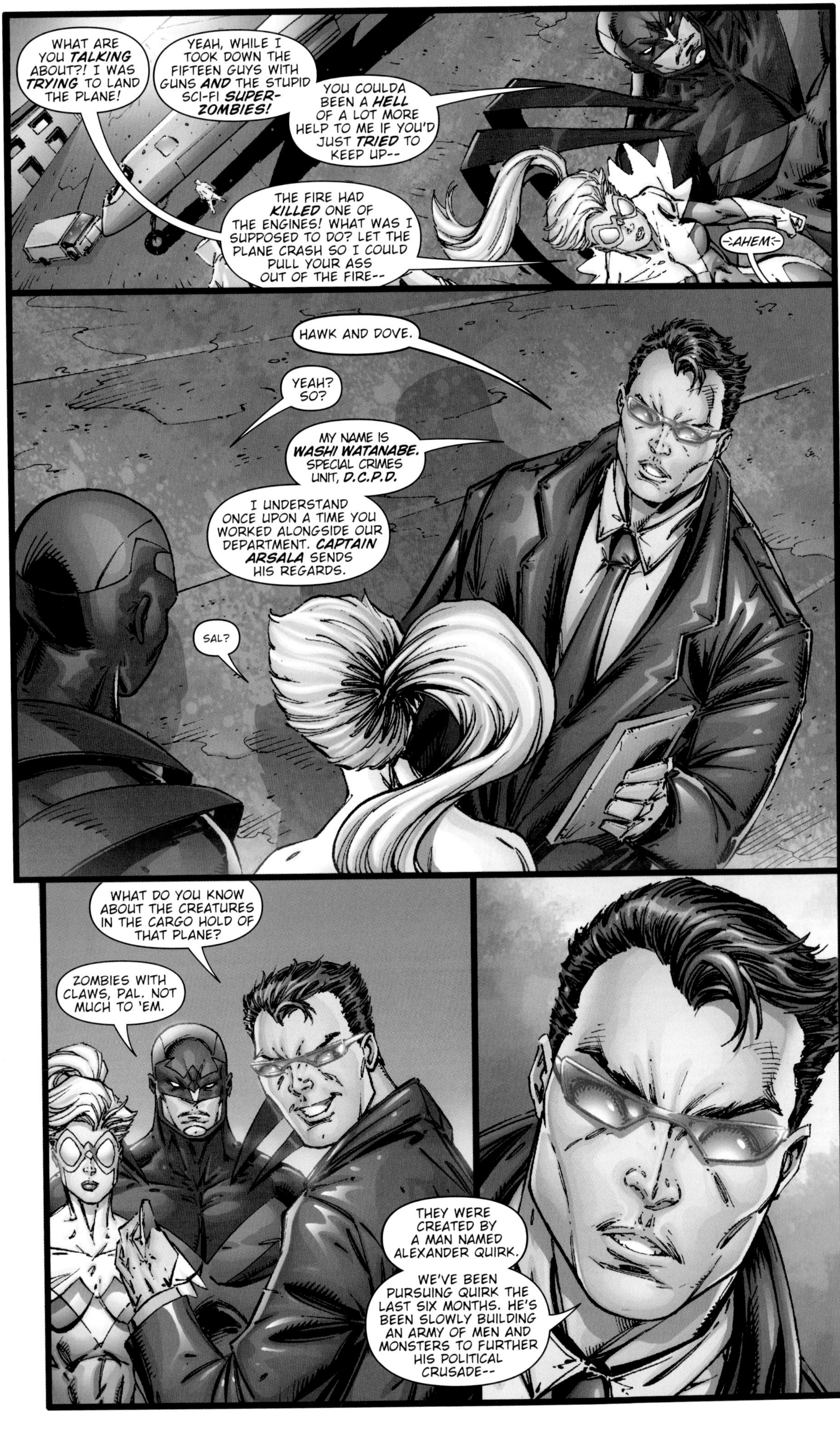

WHAT ARE YOU TALKING ABOUT?! I WAS TRYING TO LAND THE PLANE!
YEAH, WHILE I TOOK DOWN THE FIFTEEN GUYS WITH GUNS AND THE STUPID SCI-FI SUPER-ZOMBIES!
YOU COULDA BEEN A HELL OF A LOT MORE HELP TO ME IF YOU'D JUST TRIED TO KEEP UP--
THE FIRE HAD KILLED ONE OF THE ENGINES! WHAT WAS I SUPPOSED TO DO? LET THE PLANE CRASH SO I COULD PULL YOUR ASS OUT OF THE FIRE--
-AHEM-
HAWK AND DOVE.
YEAH? SO?
MY NAME IS WASHI WATANABE. SPECIAL CRIMES UNIT, D.C.P.D.
I UNDERSTAND ONCE UPON A TIME YOU WORKED ALONGSIDE OUR DEPARTMENT. CAPTAIN ARSALA SENDS HIS REGARDS.
SAL?
WHAT DO YOU KNOW ABOUT THE CREATURES IN THE CARGO HOLD OF THAT PLANE?
ZOMBIES WITH CLAWS, PAL. NOT MUCH TO 'EM.
THEY WERE CREATED BY A MAN NAMED ALEXANDER QUIRK.
WE'VE BEEN PURSUING QUIRK THE LAST SIX MONTHS. HE'S BEEN SLOWLY BUILDING AN ARMY OF MEN AND MONSTERS TO FURTHER HIS POLITICAL CRUSADE--

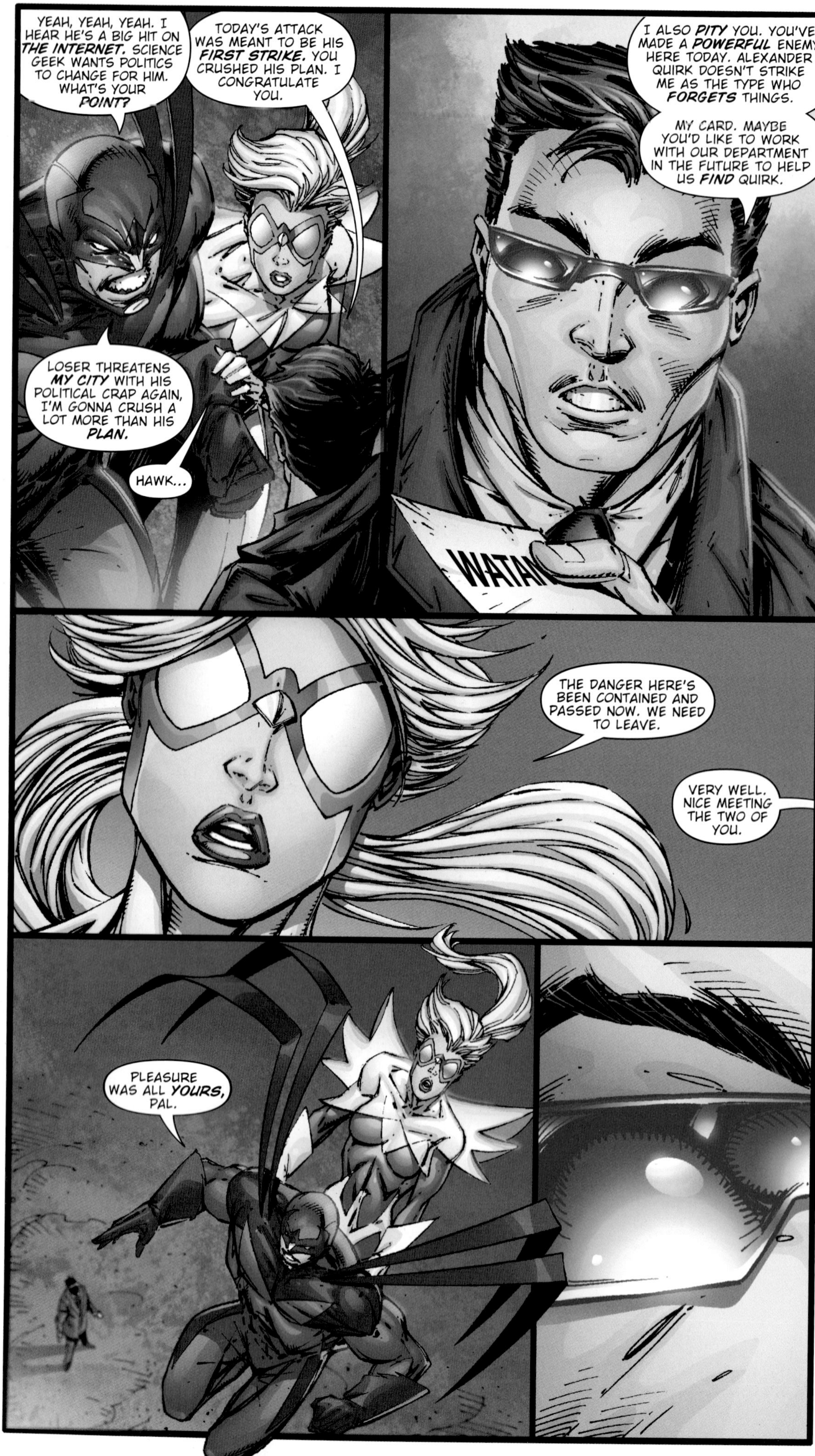
YEAH, YEAH, YEAH. I HEAR HE'S A BIG HIT ON THE INTERNET. SCIENCE GEEK WANTS POLITICS TO CHANGE FOR HIM. WHAT'S YOUR POINT?
TODAY'S ATTACK WAS MEANT TO BE HIS FIRST STRIKE. YOU CRUSHED HIS PLAN. I CONGRATULATE YOU.
LOSER THREATENS MY CITY WITH HIS POLITICAL CRAP AGAIN, I'M GONNA CRUSH A LOT MORE THAN HIS PLAN.
HAWK...
I ALSO PITY YOU. YOU'VE MADE A POWERFUL ENEMY HERE TODAY. ALEXANDER QUIRK DOESN'T STRIKE ME AS THE TYPE WHO FORGETS THINGS.
MY CARD. MAYBE YOU'D LIKE TO WORK WITH OUR DEPARTMENT IN THE FUTURE TO HELP US FIND QUIRK.
WATAN
THE DANGER HERE'S BEEN CONTAINED AND PASSED NOW. WE NEED TO LEAVE.
VERY WELL. NICE MEETING THE TWO OF YOU.
PLEASURE WAS ALL YOURS, PAL.

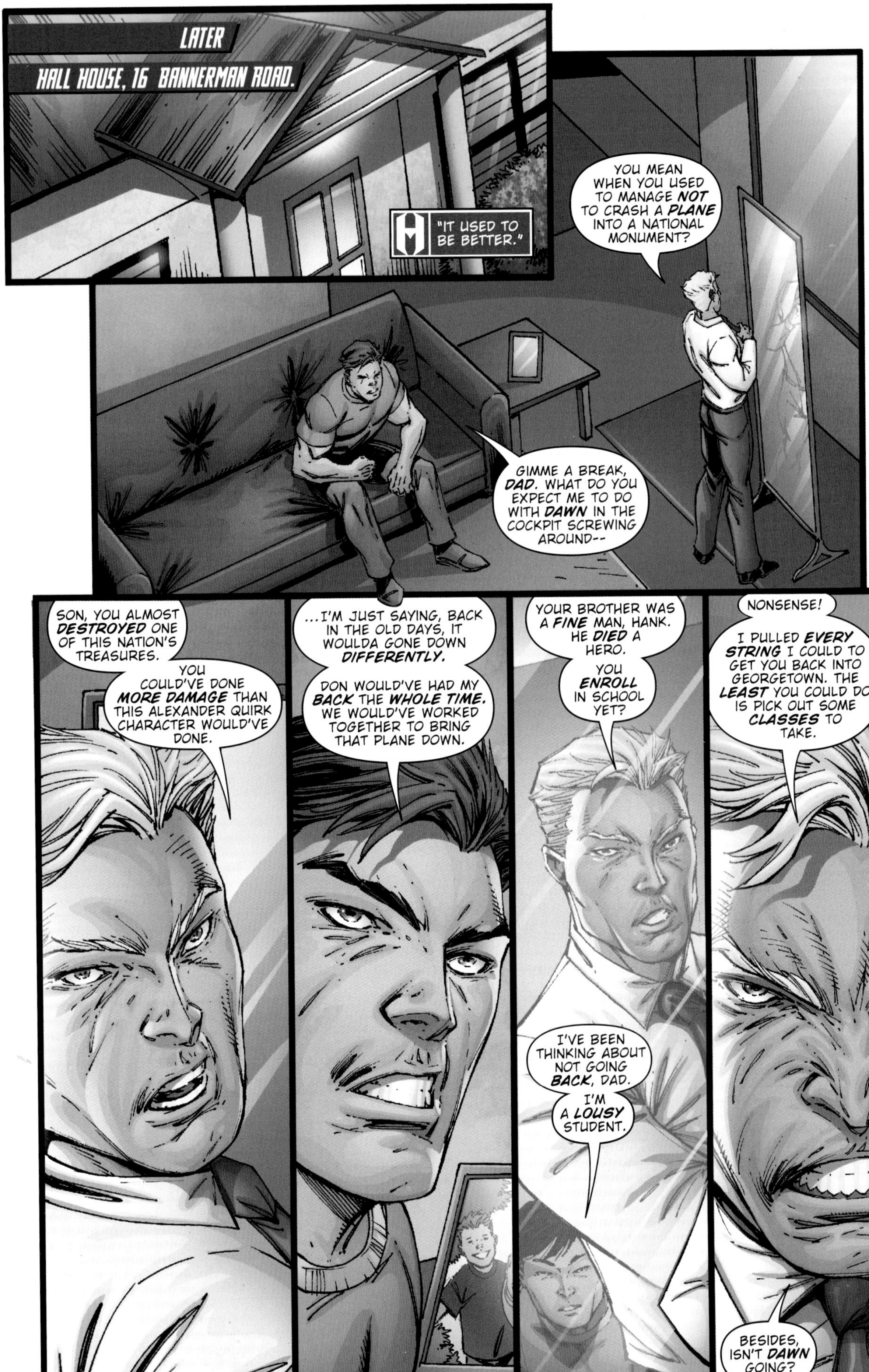
LATER
HALL HOUSE, 16 BANNERMAN ROAD.
"IT USED TO BE BETTER."
YOU MEAN WHEN YOU USED TO MANAGE NOT TO CRASH A PLANE INTO A NATIONAL MONUMENT?
GIMME A BREAK, DAD. WHAT DO YOU EXPECT ME TO DO WITH DAWN IN THE COCKPIT SCREWING AROUND--
SON, YOU ALMOST DESTROYED ONE OF THIS NATION'S TREASURES.
YOU COULD'VE DONE MORE DAMAGE THAN THIS ALEXANDER QUIRK CHARACTER WOULD'VE DONE.
...I'M JUST SAYING, BACK IN THE OLD DAYS, IT WOULDA GONE DOWN DIFFERENTLY.
DON WOULD'VE HAD MY BACK THE WHOLE TIME. WE WOULD'VE WORKED TOGETHER TO BRING THAT PLANE DOWN.
YOUR BROTHER WAS A FINE MAN, HANK. HE DIED A HERO.
YOU ENROLL IN SCHOOL YET?
I'VE BEEN THINKING ABOUT NOT GOING BACK, DAD.
I'M A LOUSY STUDENT.
NONSENSE!
I PULLED EVERY STRING I COULD TO GET YOU BACK INTO GEORGETOWN. THE LEAST YOU COULD DO IS PICK OUT SOME CLASSES TO TAKE.
BESIDES, ISN'T DAWN GOING?

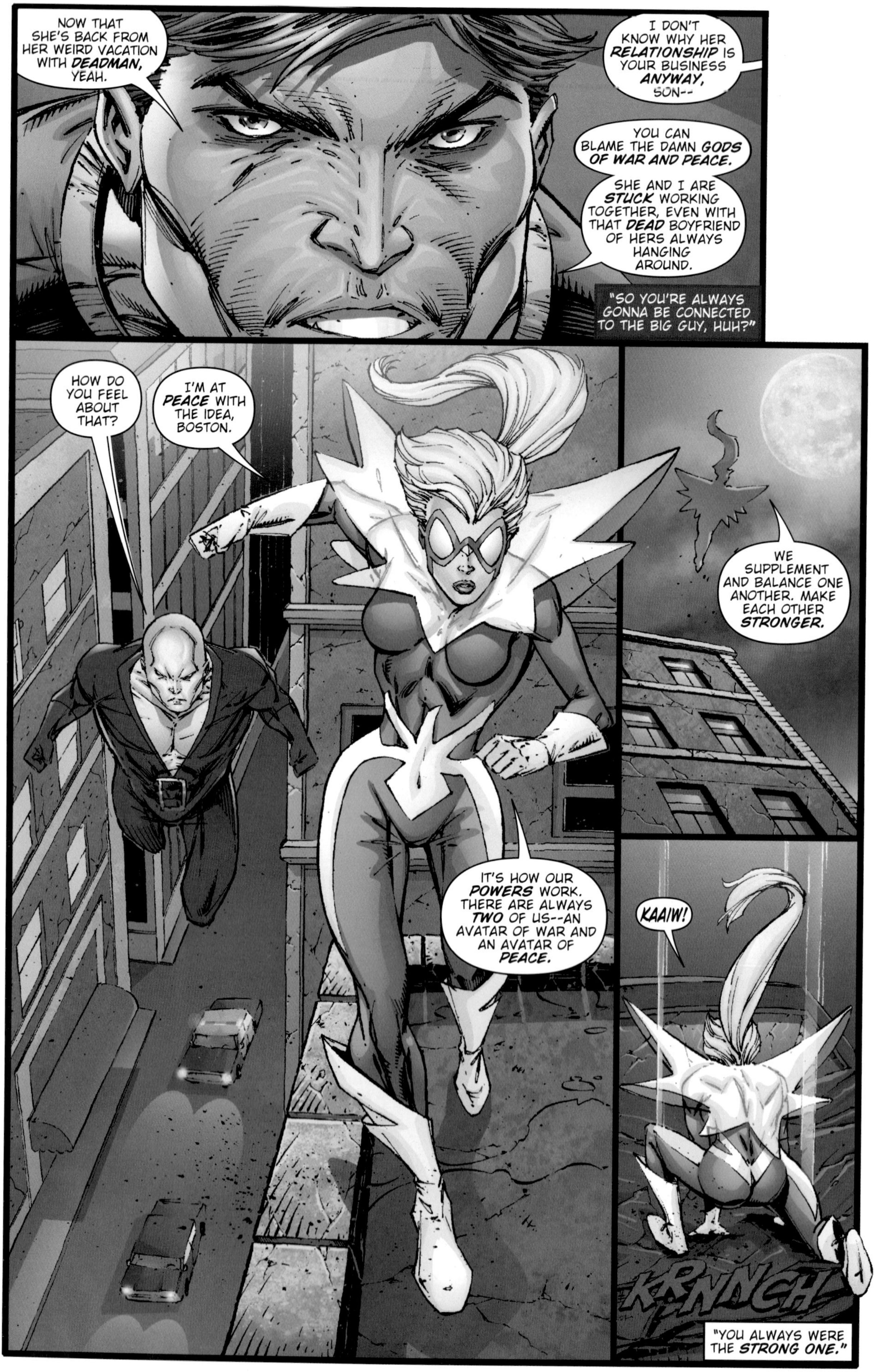

NOW THAT SHE'S BACK FROM HER WEIRD VACATION WITH DEADMAN, YEAH.
I DON'T KNOW WHY HER RELATIONSHIP IS YOUR BUSINESS ANYWAY, SON--
YOU CAN BLAME THE DAMN GODS OF WAR AND PEACE.
SHE AND I ARE STUCK WORKING TOGETHER, EVEN WITH THAT DEAD BOYFRIEND OF HERS ALWAYS HANGING AROUND.
"SO YOU'RE ALWAYS GONNA BE CONNECTED TO THE BIG GUY, HUH?"
HOW DO YOU FEEL ABOUT THAT?
I'M AT PEACE WITH THE IDEA, BOSTON.
IT'S HOW OUR POWERS WORK. THERE ARE ALWAYS TWO OF US--AN AVATAR OF WAR AND AN AVATAR OF PEACE.
WE SUPPLEMENT AND BALANCE ONE ANOTHER. MAKE EACH OTHER STRONGER.
KAAIW!
KRNNCH
"YOU ALWAYS WERE THE STRONG ONE."

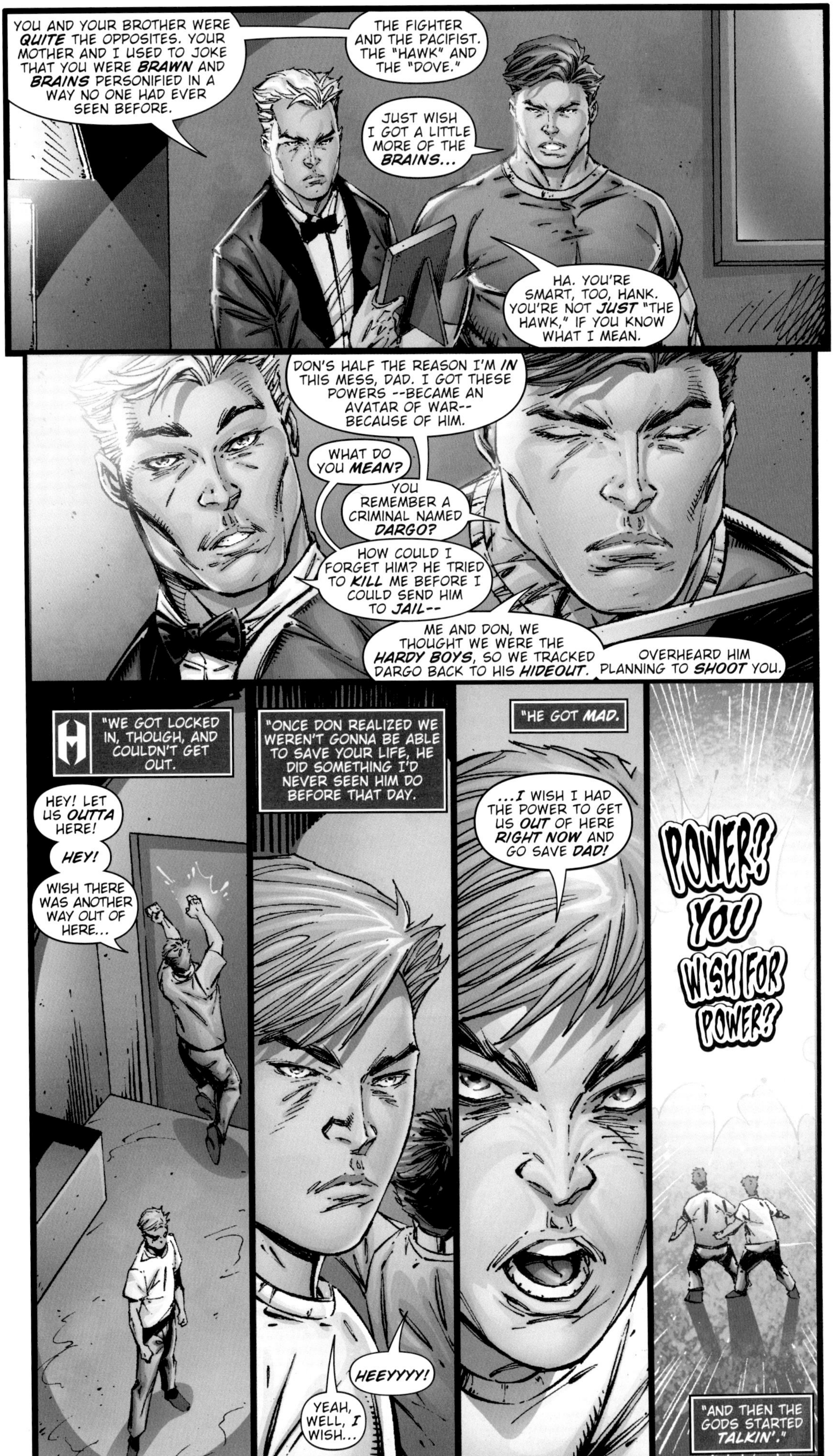

YOU AND YOUR BROTHER WERE QUITE THE OPPOSITES. YOUR MOTHER AND I USED TO JOKE THAT YOU WERE BRAWN AND BRAINS PERSONIFIED IN A WAY NO ONE HAD EVER SEEN BEFORE.
THE FIGHTER AND THE PACIFIST. THE "HAWK" AND THE "DOVE."
JUST WISH I GOT A LITTLE MORE OF THE BRAINS...
HA. YOU'RE SMART, TOO, HANK. YOU'RE NOT JUST "THE HAWK," IF YOU KNOW WHAT I MEAN.
DON'S HALF THE REASON I'M IN THIS MESS, DAD. I GOT THESE POWERS --BECAME AN AVATAR OF WAR-- BECAUSE OF HIM.
WHAT DO YOU MEAN?
YOU REMEMBER A CRIMINAL NAMED DARGO?
HOW COULD I FORGET HIM? HE TRIED TO KILL ME BEFORE I COULD SEND HIM TO JAIL--
ME AND DON, WE THOUGHT WE WERE THE HARDY BOYS, SO WE TRACKED DARGO BACK TO HIS HIDEOUT.
OVERHEARD HIM PLANNING TO SHOOT YOU.
"WE GOT LOCKED IN, THOUGH, AND COULDN'T GET OUT.
HEY! LET US OUTTA HERE!
HEY!
WISH THERE WAS ANOTHER WAY OUT OF HERE...
"ONCE DON REALIZED WE WEREN'T GONNA BE ABLE TO SAVE YOUR LIFE, HE DID SOMETHING I'D NEVER SEEN HIM DO BEFORE THAT DAY.
HEEYYYY!
YEAH, WELL, I WISH...
"HE GOT MAD.
...I WISH I HAD THE POWER TO GET US OUT OF HERE RIGHT NOW AND GO SAVE DAD!
POWER? YOU WISH FOR POWER?
"AND THEN THE GODS STARTED TALKIN'."

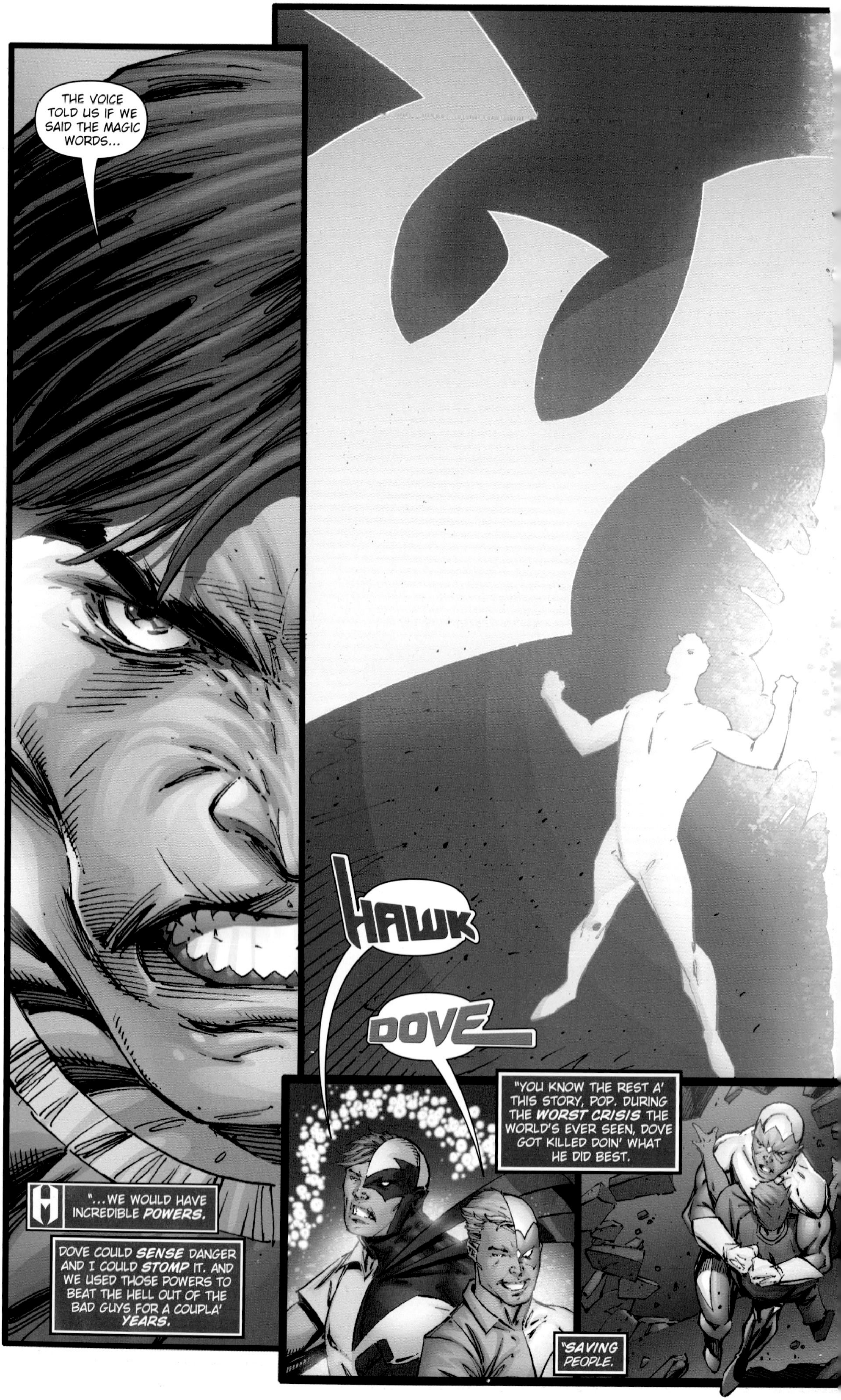

THE VOICE TOLD US IF WE SAID THE MAGIC WORDS...
"...WE WOULD HAVE INCREDIBLE POWERS.
DOVE COULD SENSE DANGER AND I COULD STOMP IT. AND WE USED THOSE POWERS TO BEAT THE HELL OUT OF THE BAD GUYS FOR A COUPLA' YEARS.
HAWK
DOVE
"YOU KNOW THE REST A' THIS STORY, POP. DURING THE WORST CRISIS THE WORLD'S EVER SEEN, DOVE GOT KILLED DOIN' WHAT HE DID BEST.
"SAVING PEOPLE.

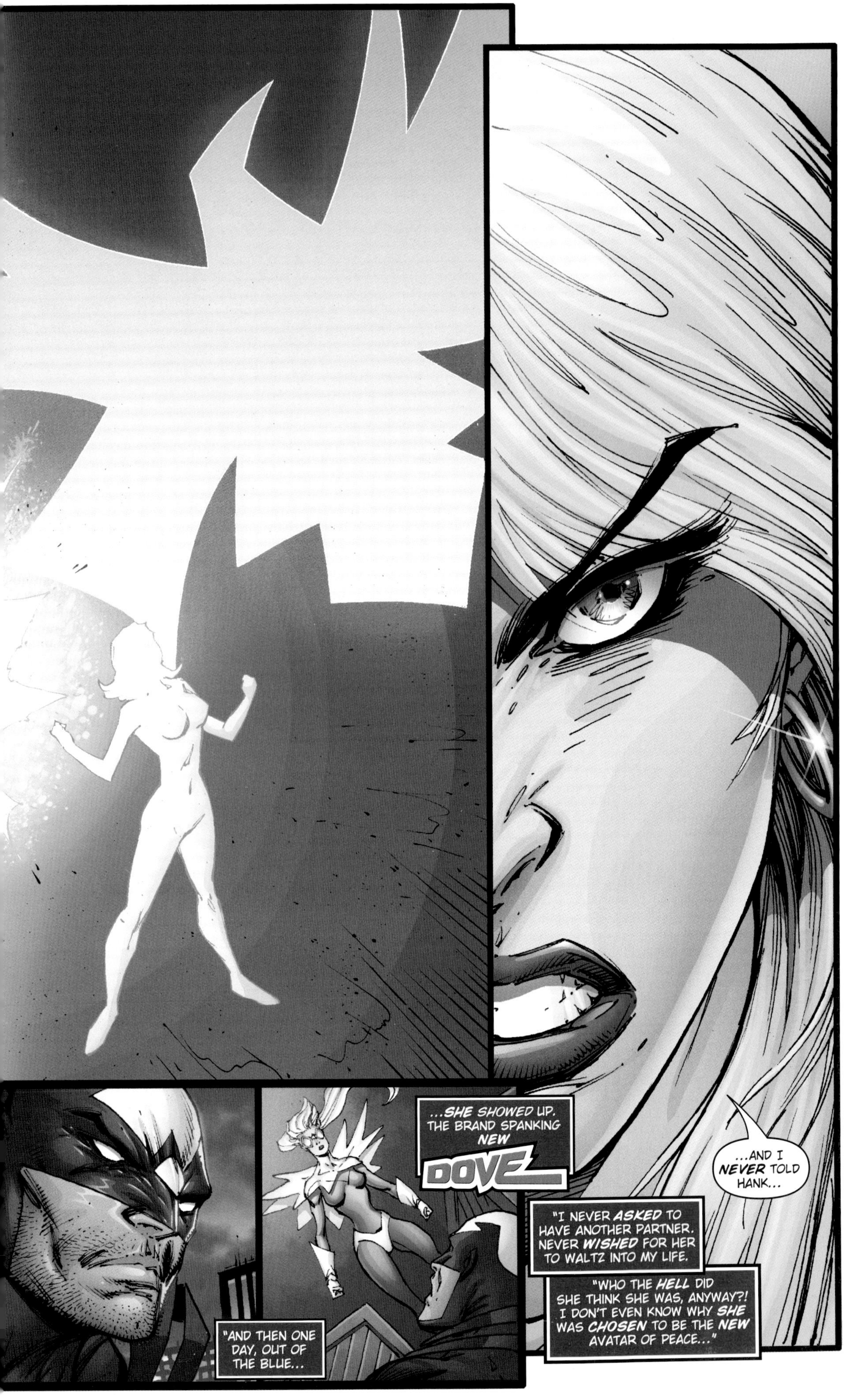
...AND I NEVER TOLD HANK...
"I NEVER ASKED TO HAVE ANOTHER PARTNER. NEVER WISHED FOR HER TO WALTZ INTO MY LIFE.
"WHO THE HELL DID SHE THINK SHE WAS, ANYWAY?! I DON'T EVEN KNOW WHY SHE WAS CHOSEN TO BE THE NEW AVATAR OF PEACE..."
"AND THEN ONE DAY, OUT OF THE BLUE...
...SHE SHOWED UP. THE BRAND SPANKING NEW
DOVE

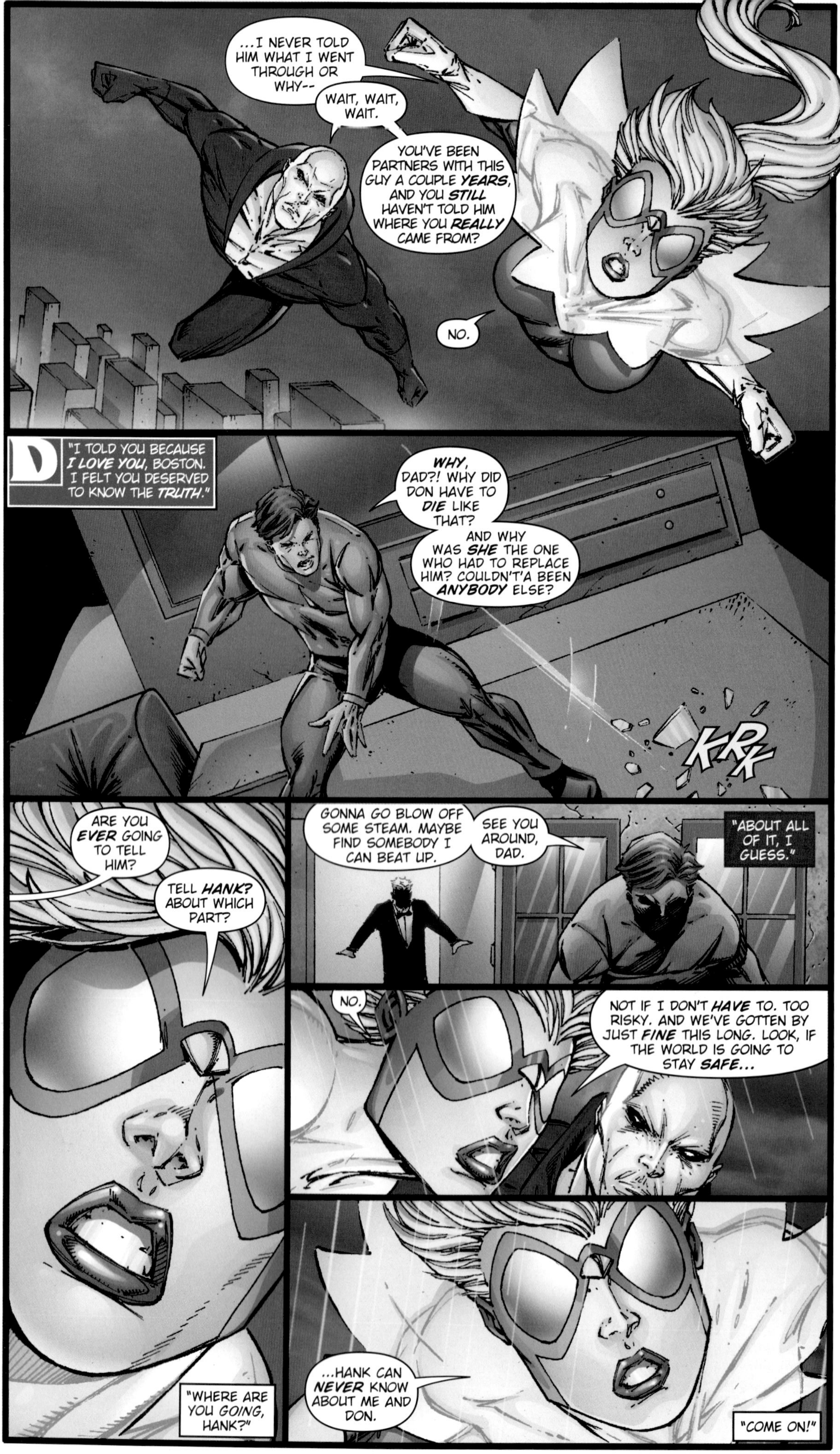

...I NEVER TOLD HIM WHAT I WENT THROUGH OR WHY--
WAIT, WAIT, WAIT.
YOU'VE BEEN PARTNERS WITH THIS GUY A COUPLE YEARS, AND YOU STILL HAVEN'T TOLD HIM WHERE YOU REALLY CAME FROM?
NO.
"I TOLD YOU BECAUSE I LOVE YOU, BOSTON. I FELT YOU DESERVED TO KNOW THE TRUTH."
WHY, DAD?! WHY DID DON HAVE TO DIE LIKE THAT?
AND WHY WAS SHE THE ONE WHO HAD TO REPLACE HIM? COULDN'T'A BEEN ANYBODY ELSE?
KRK
ARE YOU EVER GOING TO TELL HIM?
TELL HANK? ABOUT WHICH PART?
GONNA GO BLOW OFF SOME STEAM. MAYBE FIND SOMEBODY I CAN BEAT UP.
SEE YOU AROUND, DAD.
"ABOUT ALL OF IT, I GUESS."
NO.
NOT IF I DON'T HAVE TO. TOO RISKY. AND WE'VE GOTTEN BY JUST FINE THIS LONG. LOOK, IF THE WORLD IS GOING TO STAY SAFE...
"WHERE ARE YOU GOING, HANK?"
...HANK CAN NEVER KNOW ABOUT ME AND DON.
"COME ON!"

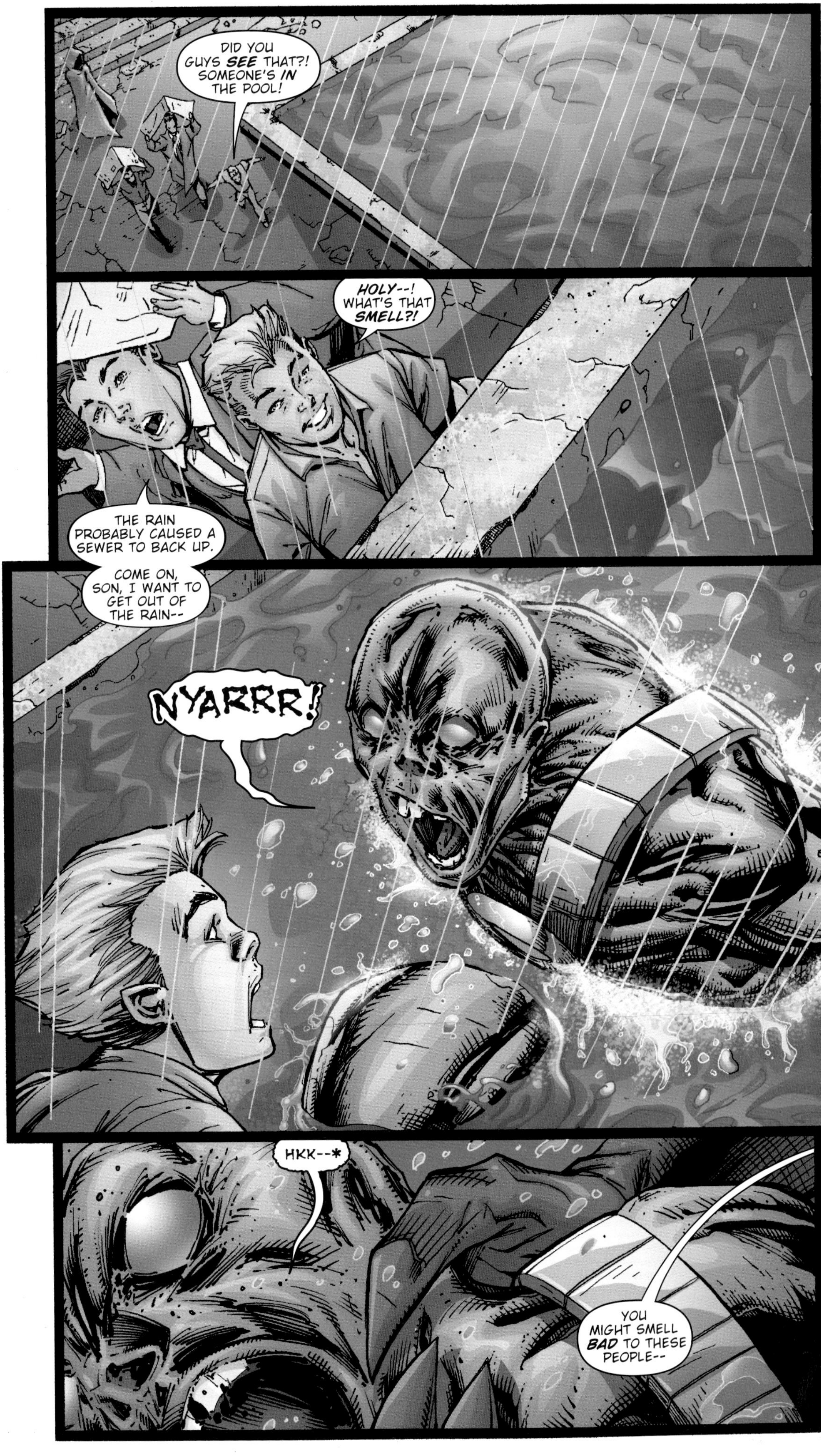
DID YOU GUYS SEE THAT?! SOMEONE'S IN THE POOL!
HOLY--! WHAT'S THAT SMELL?!
THE RAIN PROBABLY CAUSED A SEWER TO BACK UP.
COME ON, SON, I WANT TO GET OUT OF THE RAIN--
NYARRR!
HKK--*
YOU MIGHT SMELL BAD TO THESE PEOPLE--

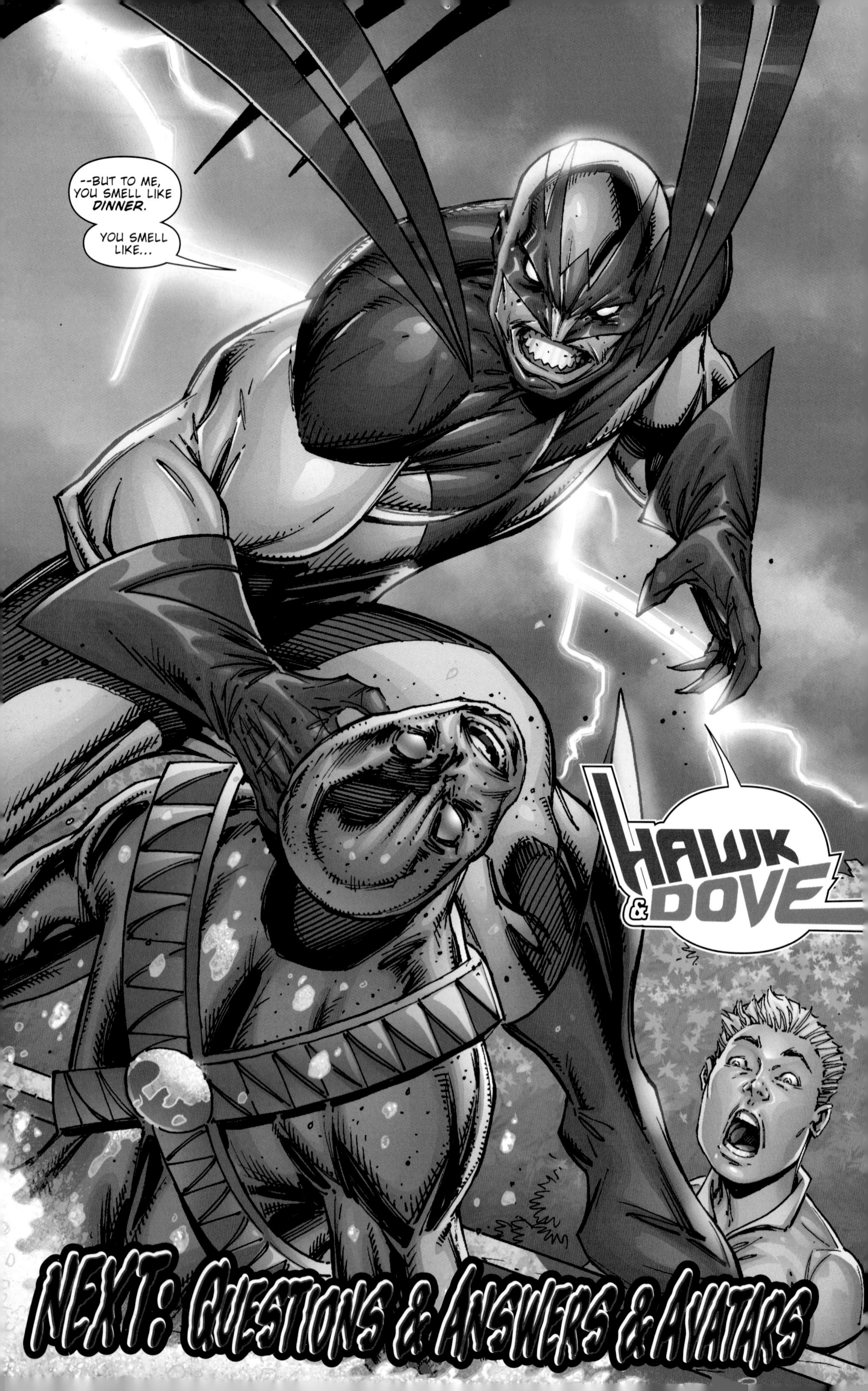
--BUT TO ME, YOU SMELL LIKE DINNER.
YOU SMELL LIKE...
HAWK & DOVE
NEXT: QUESTIONS & ANSWERS & AVATARS

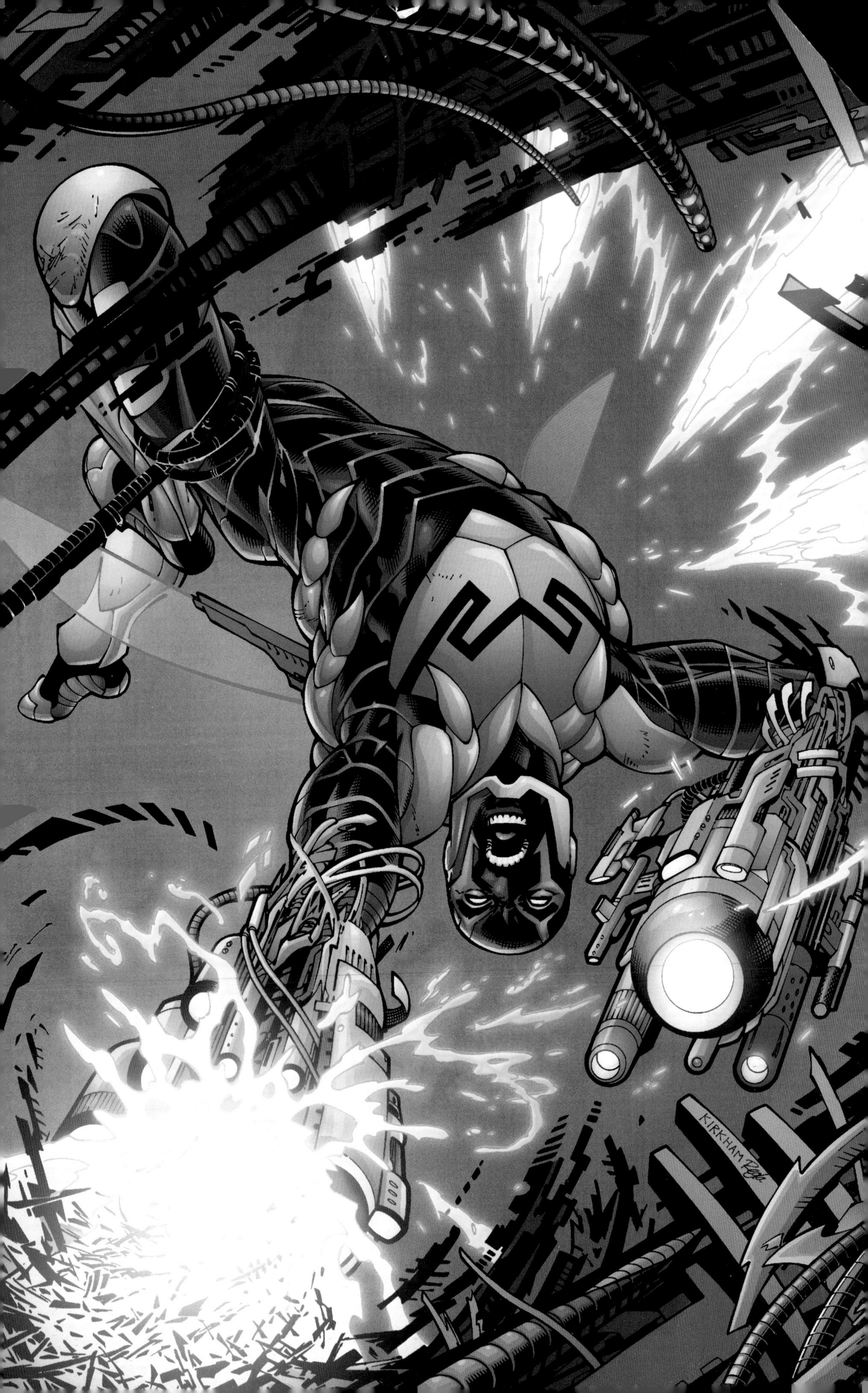
KIRKHAM

blue beetle

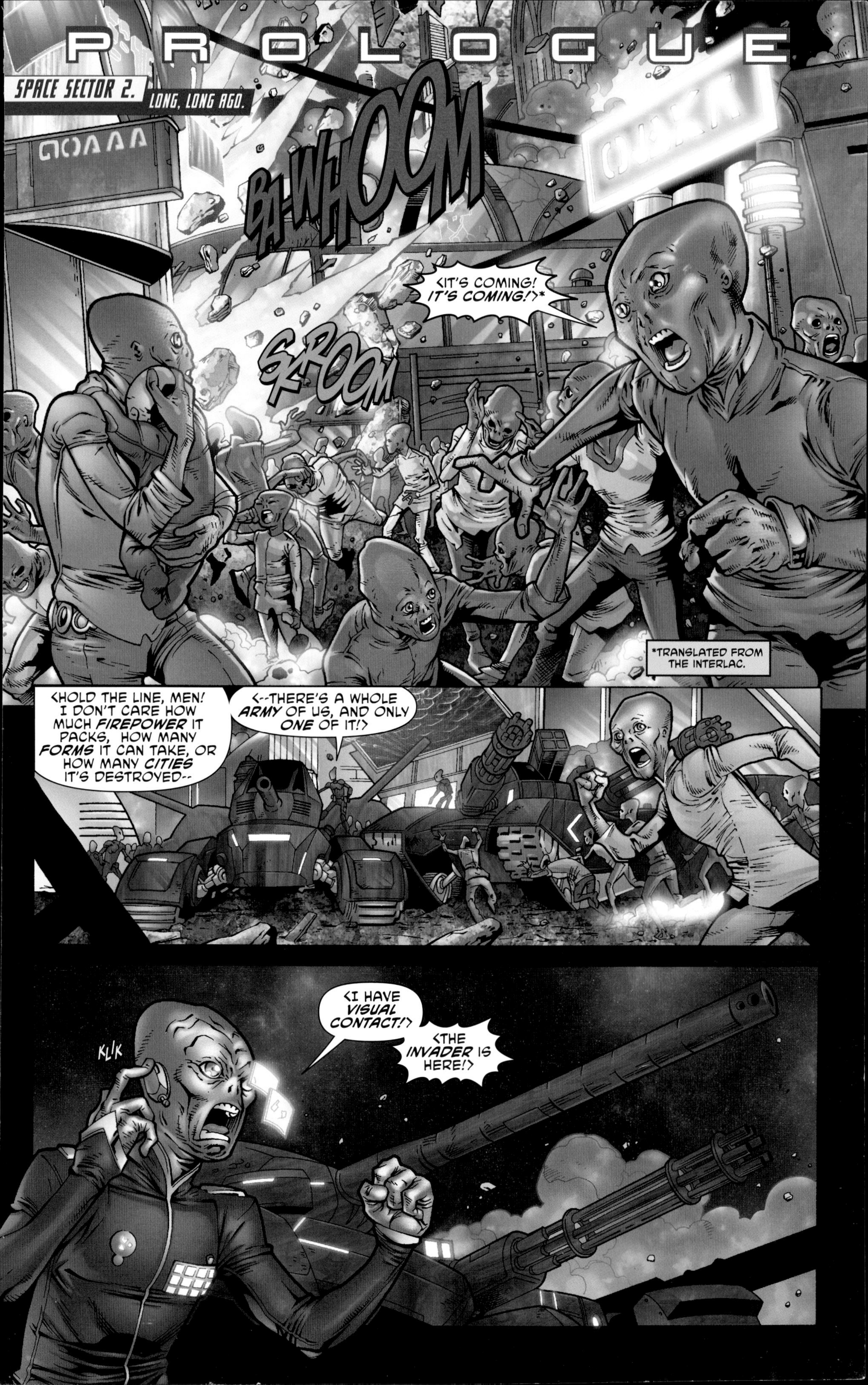
PROLOGUE
SPACE SECTOR 2.
LONG, LONG AGO.
BA-WHOOM
<IT'S COMING! IT'S COMING!>*
SKROOM
*TRANSLATED FROM THE INTERLAC.
<HOLD THE LINE, MEN! I DON'T CARE HOW MUCH FIREPOWER IT PACKS, HOW MANY FORMS IT CAN TAKE, OR HOW MANY CITIES IT'S DESTROYED--
<--THERE'S A WHOLE ARMY OF US, AND ONLY ONE OF IT!>
KLIK
<I HAVE VISUAL CONTACT!>
<THE INVADER IS HERE!>

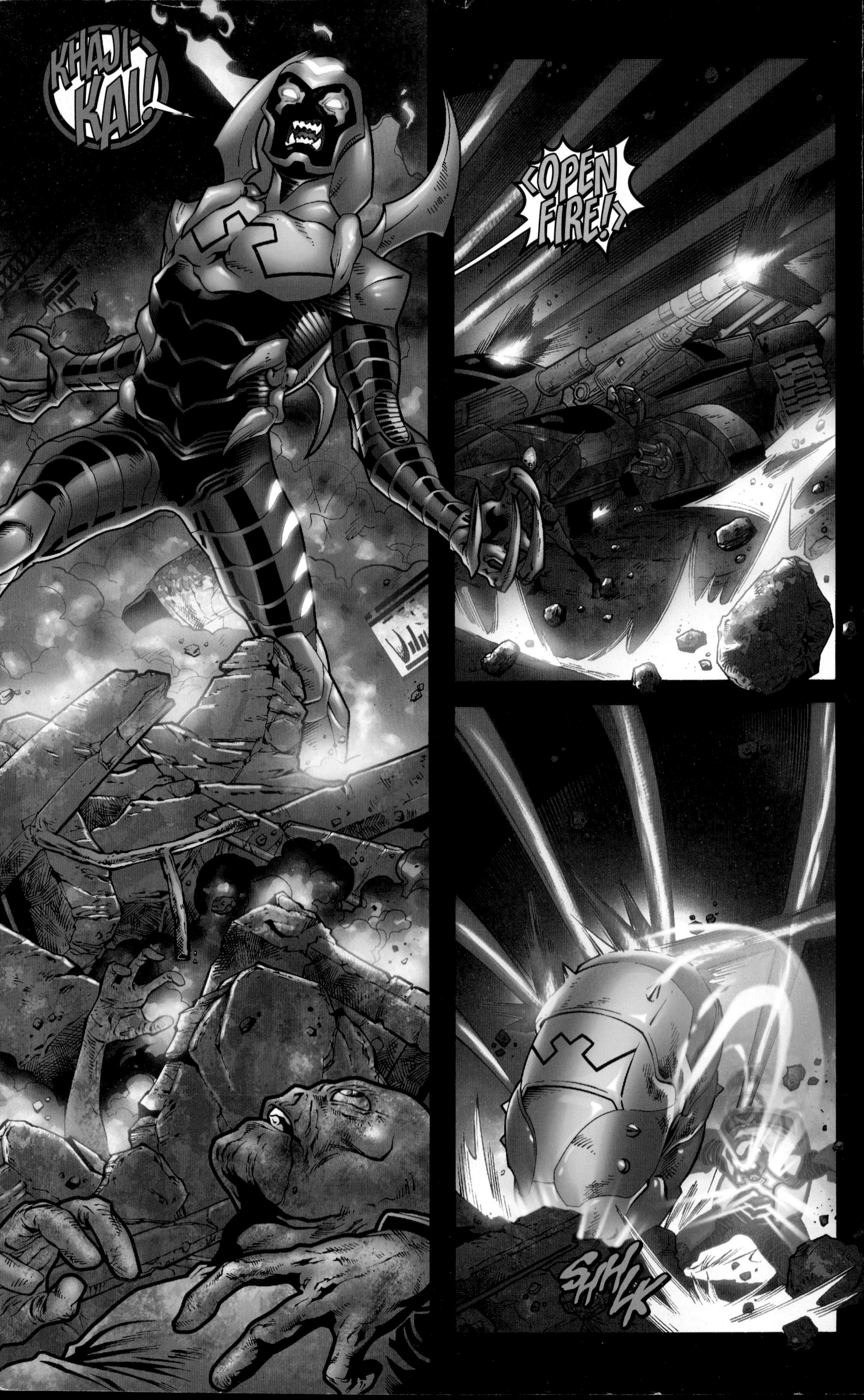
KHAJI-KAI!
‹OPEN FIRE!›
SHHLK

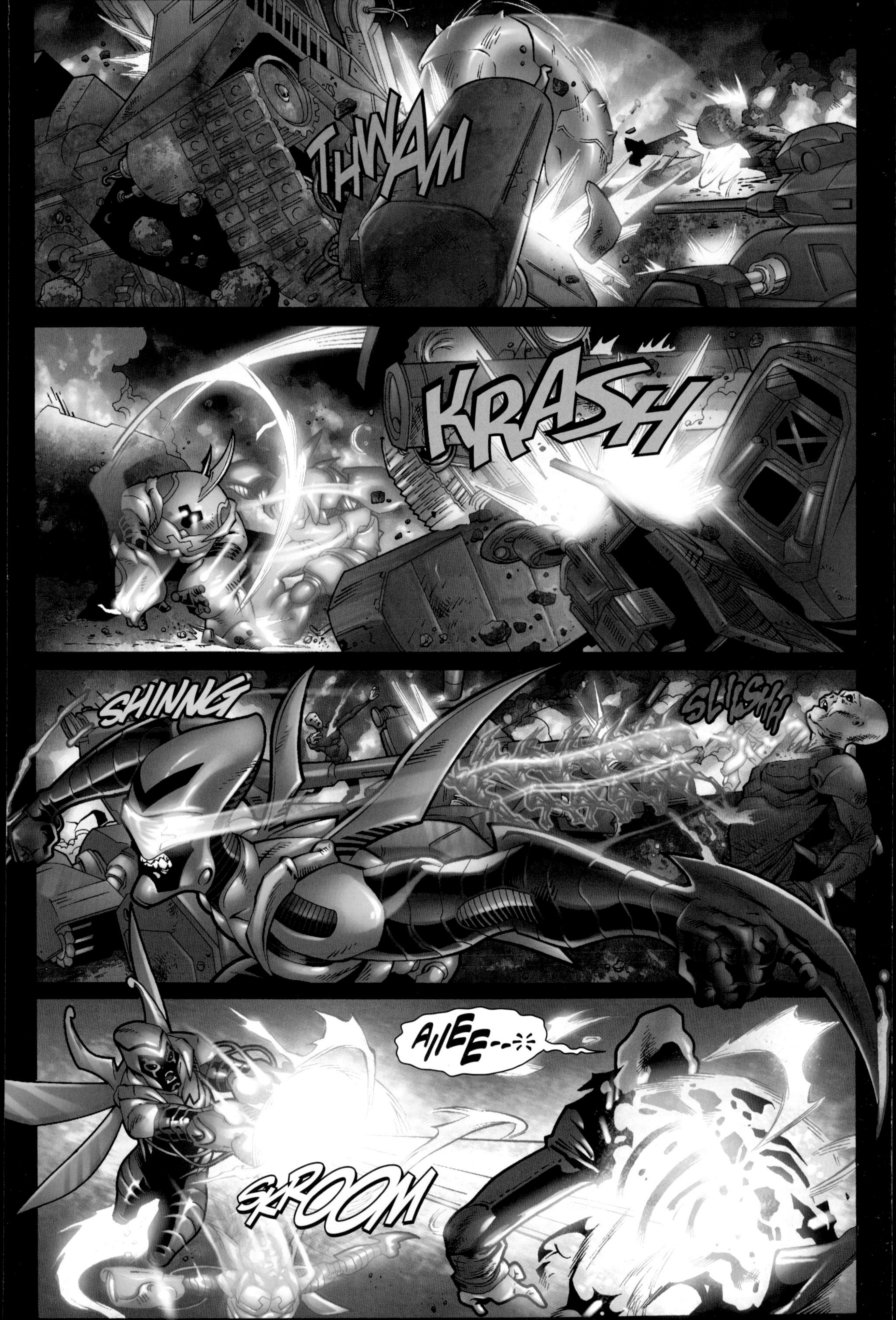
THWAM
KRASH
SHINNG
SLISHH
AIIEE--
SKROOM

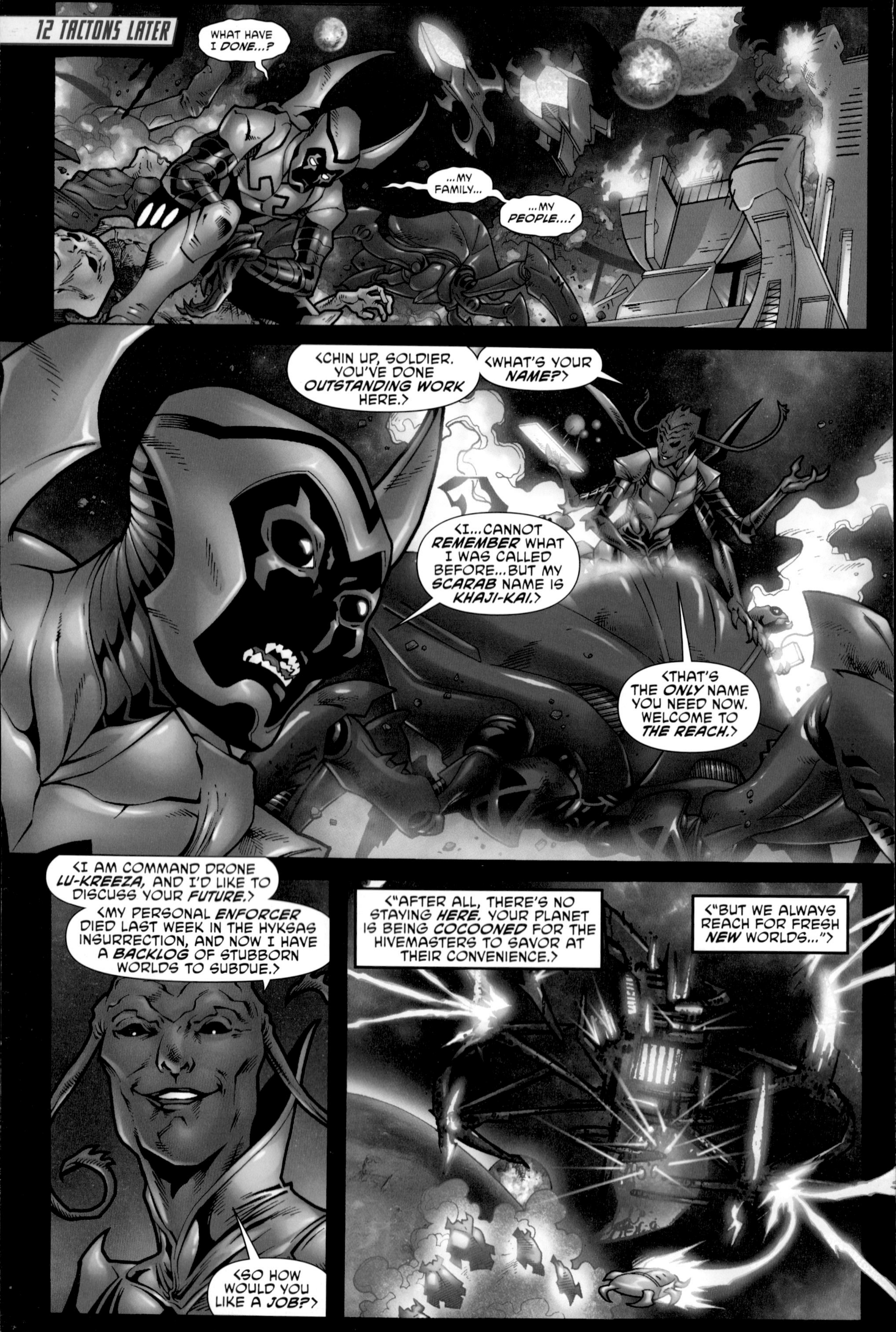
12 TACTONS LATER
WHAT HAVE I DONE...?
...MY FAMILY...
...MY PEOPLE...!
<CHIN UP, SOLDIER. YOU'VE DONE OUTSTANDING WORK HERE.>
<WHAT'S YOUR NAME?>
<I...CANNOT REMEMBER WHAT I WAS CALLED BEFORE...BUT MY SCARAB NAME IS KHAJI-KAI.>
<THAT'S THE ONLY NAME YOU NEED NOW. WELCOME TO THE REACH.>
<I AM COMMAND DRONE LU-KREEZA, AND I'D LIKE TO DISCUSS YOUR FUTURE.>
<MY PERSONAL ENFORCER DIED LAST WEEK IN THE HYKSAS INSURRECTION, AND NOW I HAVE A BACKLOG OF STUBBORN WORLDS TO SUBDUE.>
<SO HOW WOULD YOU LIKE A JOB?>
<"AFTER ALL, THERE'S NO STAYING HERE. YOUR PLANET IS BEING COCOONED FOR THE HIVEMASTERS TO SAVOR AT THEIR CONVENIENCE.>
<"BUT WE ALWAYS REACH FOR FRESH NEW WORLDS...">

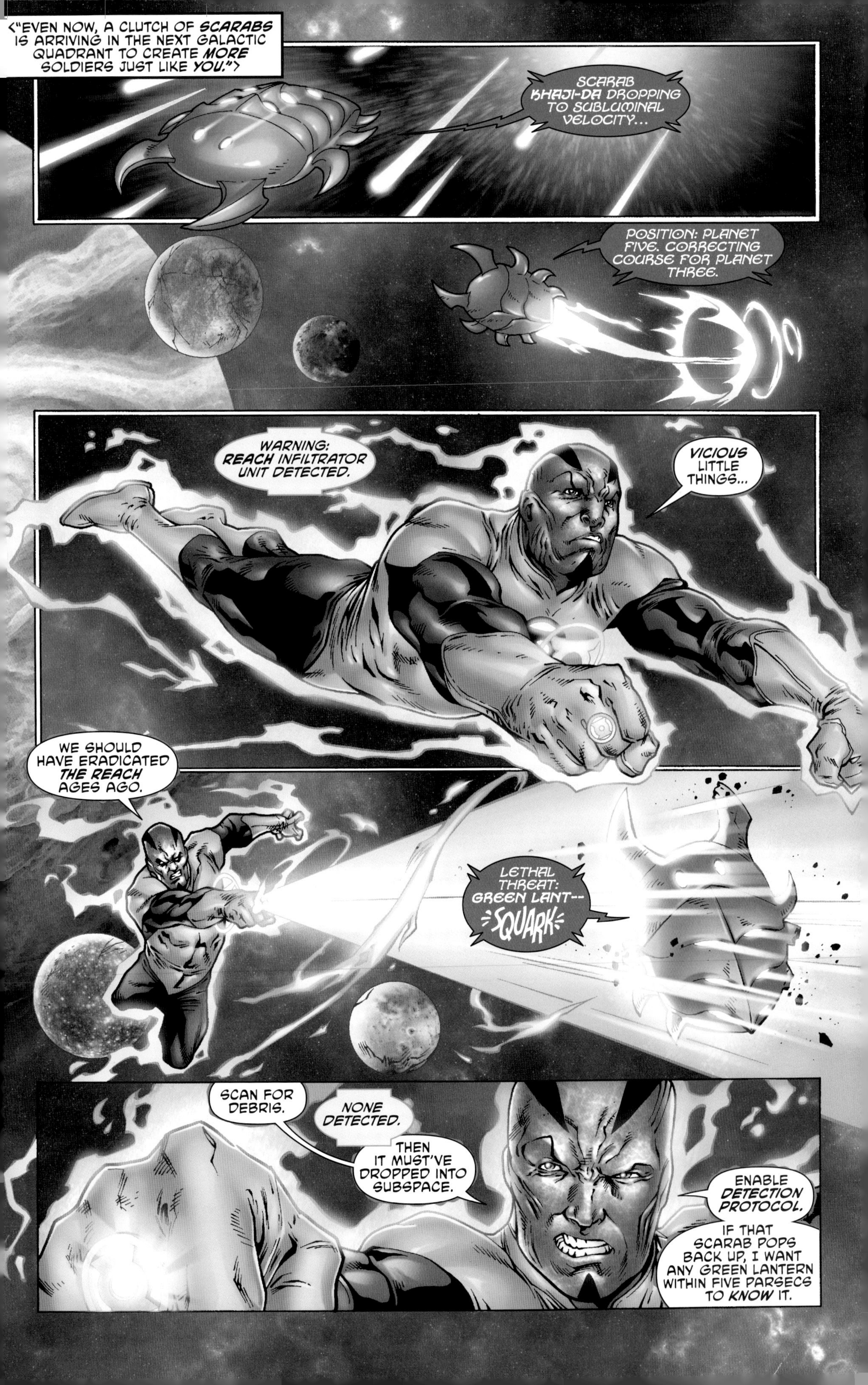

<"EVEN NOW, A CLUTCH OF SCARABS IS ARRIVING IN THE NEXT GALACTIC QUADRANT TO CREATE MORE SOLDIERS JUST LIKE YOU.">
SCARAB KHAJI-DA DROPPING TO SUBLUMINAL VELOCITY...
POSITION: PLANET FIVE. CORRECTING COURSE FOR PLANET THREE.
WARNING: REACH INFILTRATOR UNIT DETECTED.
VICIOUS LITTLE THINGS...
WE SHOULD HAVE ERADICATED THE REACH AGES AGO.
LETHAL THREAT: GREEN LANT--
SQUARK
SCAN FOR DEBRIS.
NONE DETECTED.
THEN IT MUST'VE DROPPED INTO SUBSPACE.
ENABLE DETECTION PROTOCOL.
IF THAT SCARAB POPS BACK UP, I WANT ANY GREEN LANTERN WITHIN FIVE PARSECS TO KNOW IT.

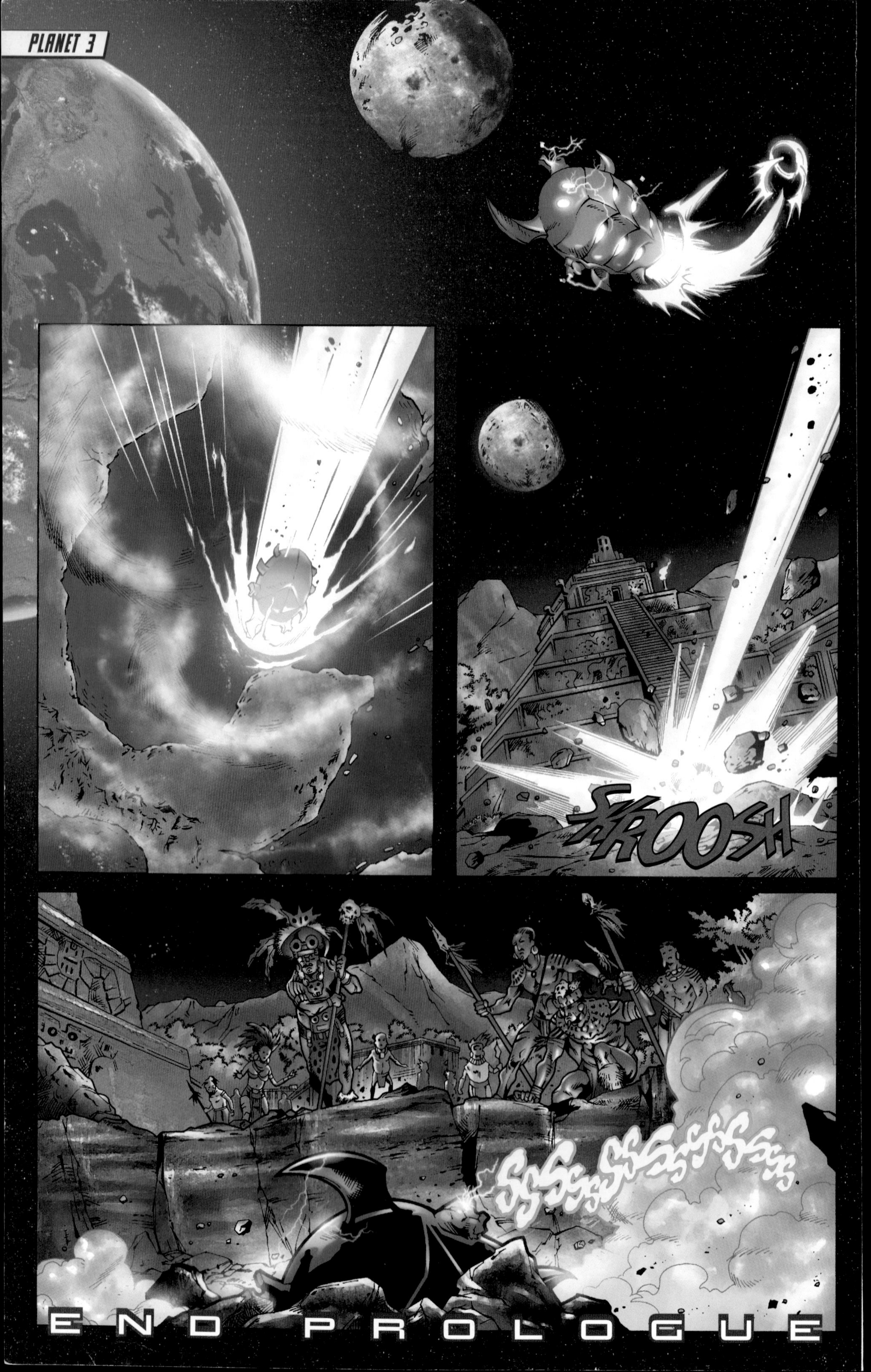
PLANET 3
SKROOSH
SSSSSSSSSSSSSSSS
END PROLOGUE

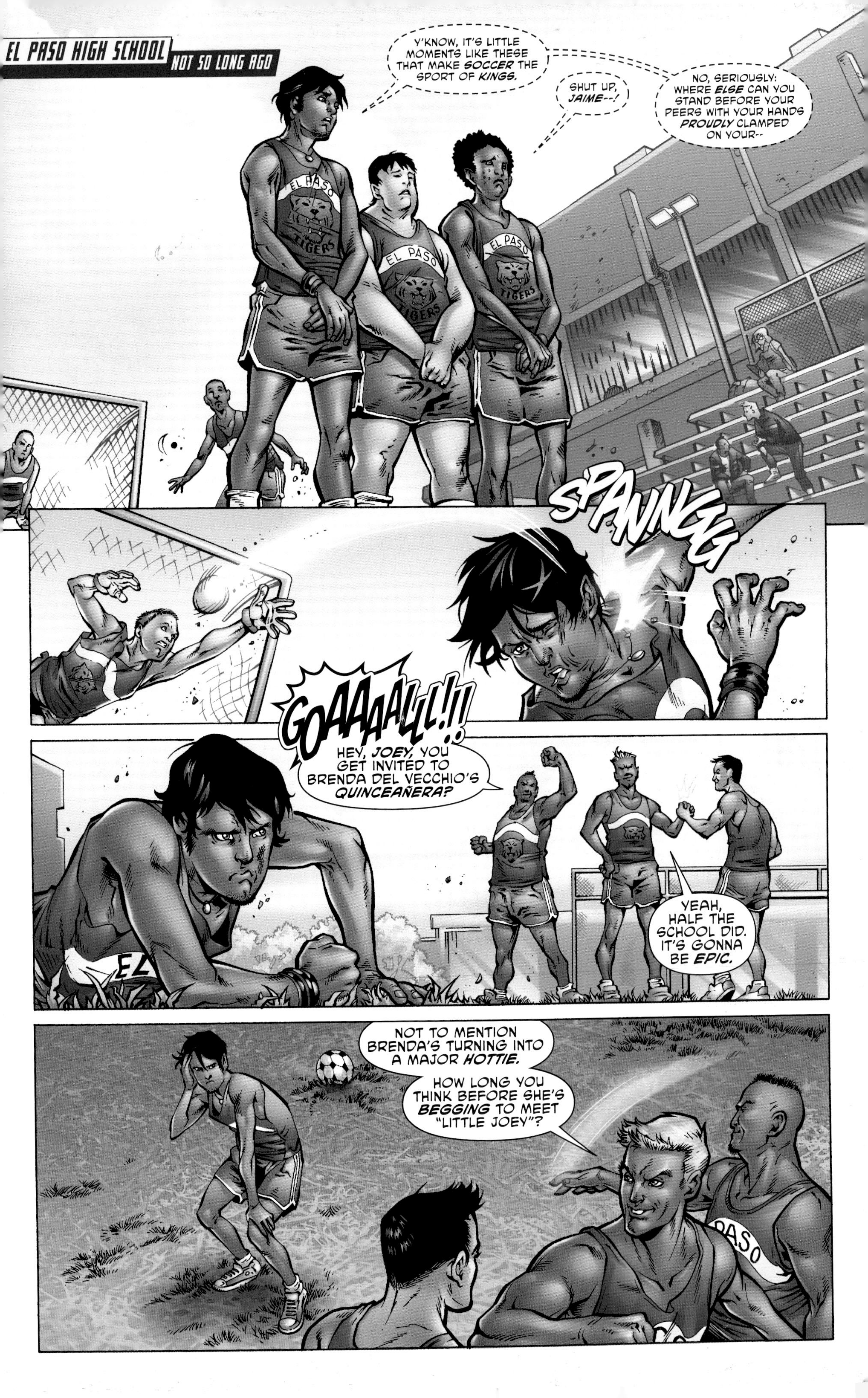
EL PASO HIGH SCHOOL
NOT SO LONG AGO
Y'KNOW, IT'S LITTLE MOMENTS LIKE THESE THAT MAKE SOCCER THE SPORT OF KINGS.
SHUT UP, JAIME--!
NO, SERIOUSLY: WHERE ELSE CAN YOU STAND BEFORE YOUR PEERS WITH YOUR HANDS PROUDLY CLAMPED ON YOUR--
SPANNGG
GOAAAALLL!!!
HEY, JOEY, YOU GET INVITED TO BRENDA DEL VECCHIO'S QUINCEAÑERA?
YEAH, HALF THE SCHOOL DID. IT'S GONNA BE EPIC.
NOT TO MENTION BRENDA'S TURNING INTO A MAJOR HOTTIE.
HOW LONG YOU THINK BEFORE SHE'S BEGGING TO MEET "LITTLE JOEY"?

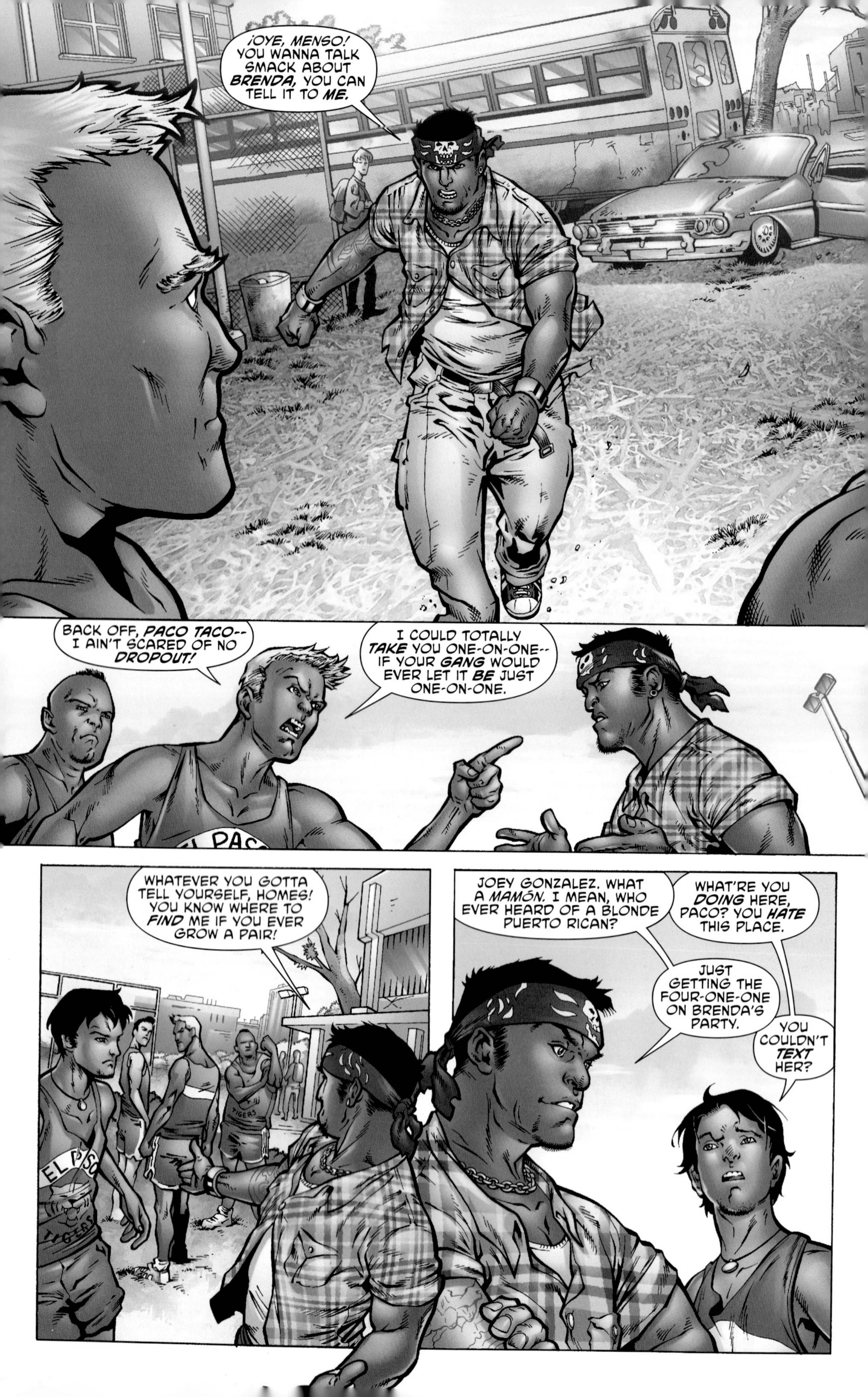
¡OYE, MENSO! YOU WANNA TALK SMACK ABOUT *BRENDA,* YOU CAN TELL IT TO *ME.*
BACK OFF, *PACO TACO*-- I AIN'T SCARED OF NO *DROPOUT!*
I COULD TOTALLY *TAKE* YOU ONE-ON-ONE-- IF YOUR *GANG* WOULD EVER LET IT *BE* JUST ONE-ON-ONE.
WHATEVER YOU GOTTA TELL YOURSELF, HOMES! YOU KNOW WHERE TO *FIND* ME IF YOU EVER GROW A PAIR!
JOEY GONZALEZ. WHAT A *MAMÓN.* I MEAN, WHO EVER HEARD OF A BLONDE PUERTO RICAN?
WHAT'RE YOU *DOING* HERE, PACO? YOU *HATE* THIS PLACE.
JUST GETTING THE FOUR-ONE-ONE ON BRENDA'S PARTY.
YOU COULDN'T *TEXT* HER?

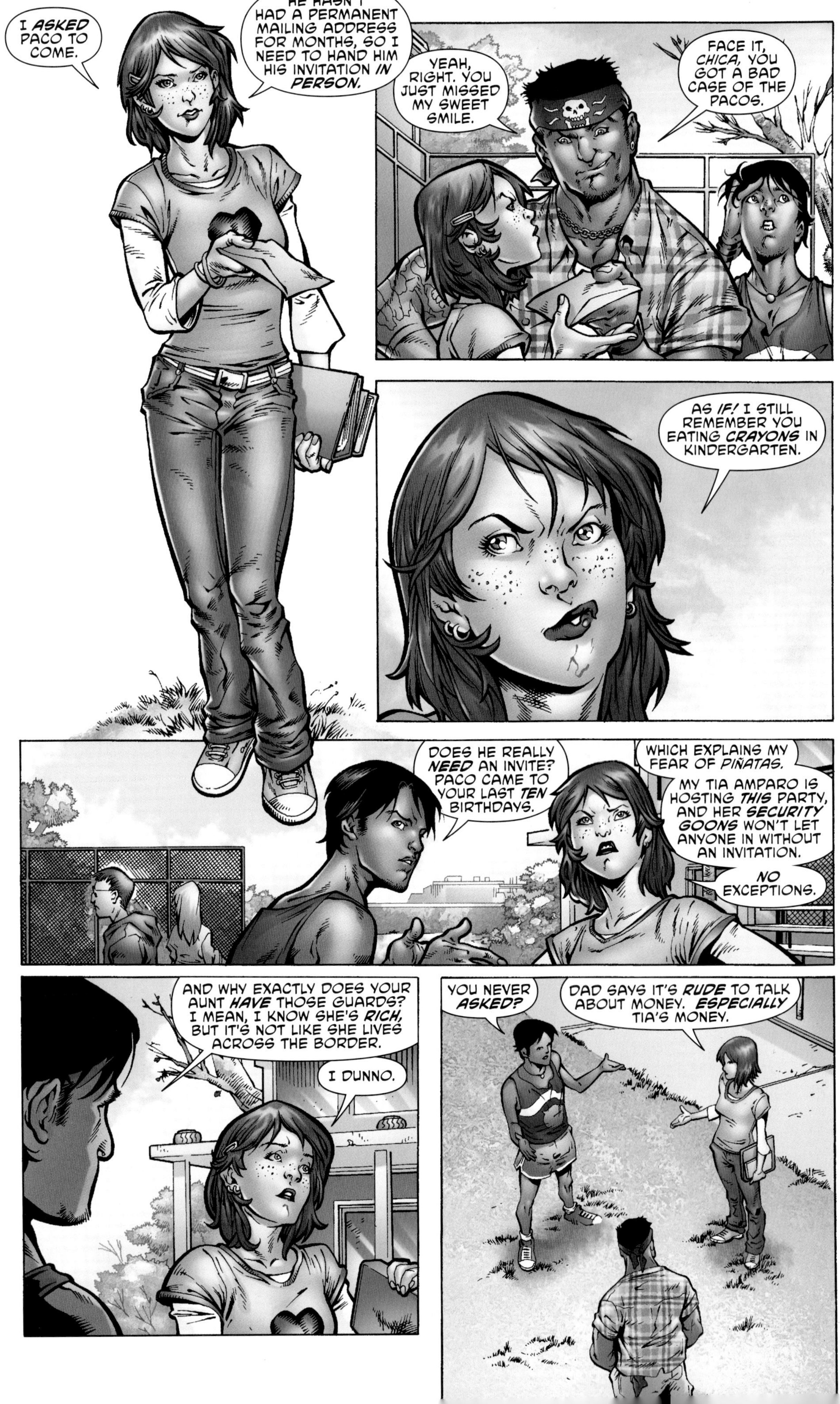
I ASKED PACO TO COME.
HE HASN'T HAD A PERMANENT MAILING ADDRESS FOR MONTHS, SO I NEED TO HAND HIM HIS INVITATION IN PERSON.
YEAH, RIGHT. YOU JUST MISSED MY SWEET SMILE.
FACE IT, CHICA, YOU GOT A BAD CASE OF THE PACOS.
AS IF! I STILL REMEMBER YOU EATING CRAYONS IN KINDERGARTEN.
DOES HE REALLY NEED AN INVITE? PACO CAME TO YOUR LAST TEN BIRTHDAYS.
WHICH EXPLAINS MY FEAR OF PIÑATAS.
MY TIA AMPARO IS HOSTING THIS PARTY, AND HER SECURITY GOONS WON'T LET ANYONE IN WITHOUT AN INVITATION.
NO EXCEPTIONS.
AND WHY EXACTLY DOES YOUR AUNT HAVE THOSE GUARDS? I MEAN, I KNOW SHE'S RICH, BUT IT'S NOT LIKE SHE LIVES ACROSS THE BORDER.
I DUNNO.
YOU NEVER ASKED?
DAD SAYS IT'S RUDE TO TALK ABOUT MONEY. ESPECIALLY TIA'S MONEY.

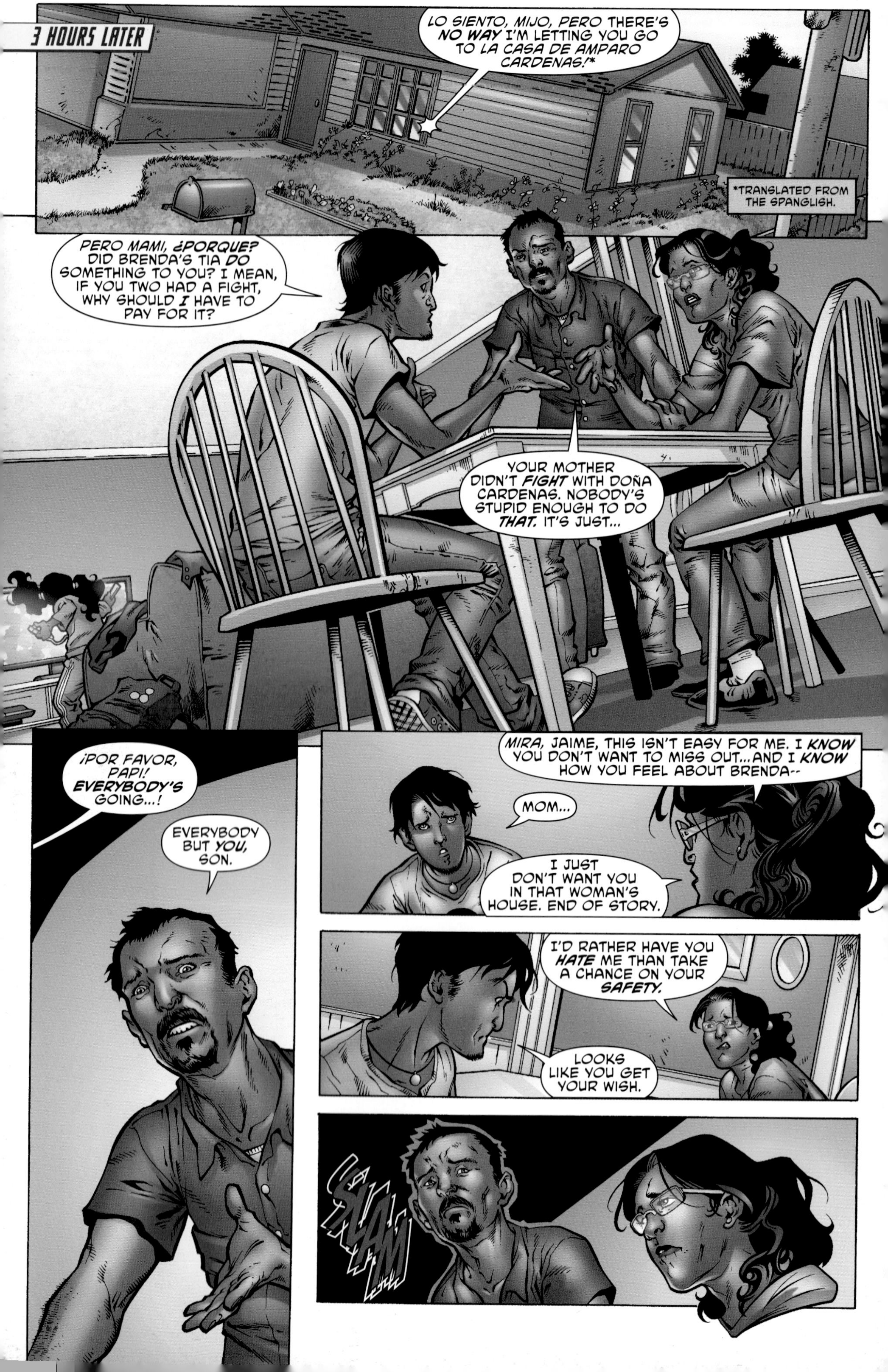
3 HOURS LATER
LO SIENTO, MIJO, PERO THERE'S NO WAY I'M LETTING YOU GO TO LA CASA DE AMPARO CARDENAS!*
*TRANSLATED FROM THE SPANGLISH.
PERO MAMI, ¿PORQUE? DID BRENDA'S TIA DO SOMETHING TO YOU? I MEAN, IF YOU TWO HAD A FIGHT, WHY SHOULD I HAVE TO PAY FOR IT?
YOUR MOTHER DIDN'T FIGHT WITH DOÑA CARDENAS. NOBODY'S STUPID ENOUGH TO DO THAT. IT'S JUST...
¡POR FAVOR, PAPI! EVERYBODY'S GOING...!
EVERYBODY BUT YOU, SON.
MIRA, JAIME, THIS ISN'T EASY FOR ME. I KNOW YOU DON'T WANT TO MISS OUT...AND I KNOW HOW YOU FEEL ABOUT BRENDA--
MOM...
I JUST DON'T WANT YOU IN THAT WOMAN'S HOUSE. END OF STORY.
I'D RATHER HAVE YOU HATE ME THAN TAKE A CHANCE ON YOUR SAFETY.
LOOKS LIKE YOU GET YOUR WISH.
SLAM

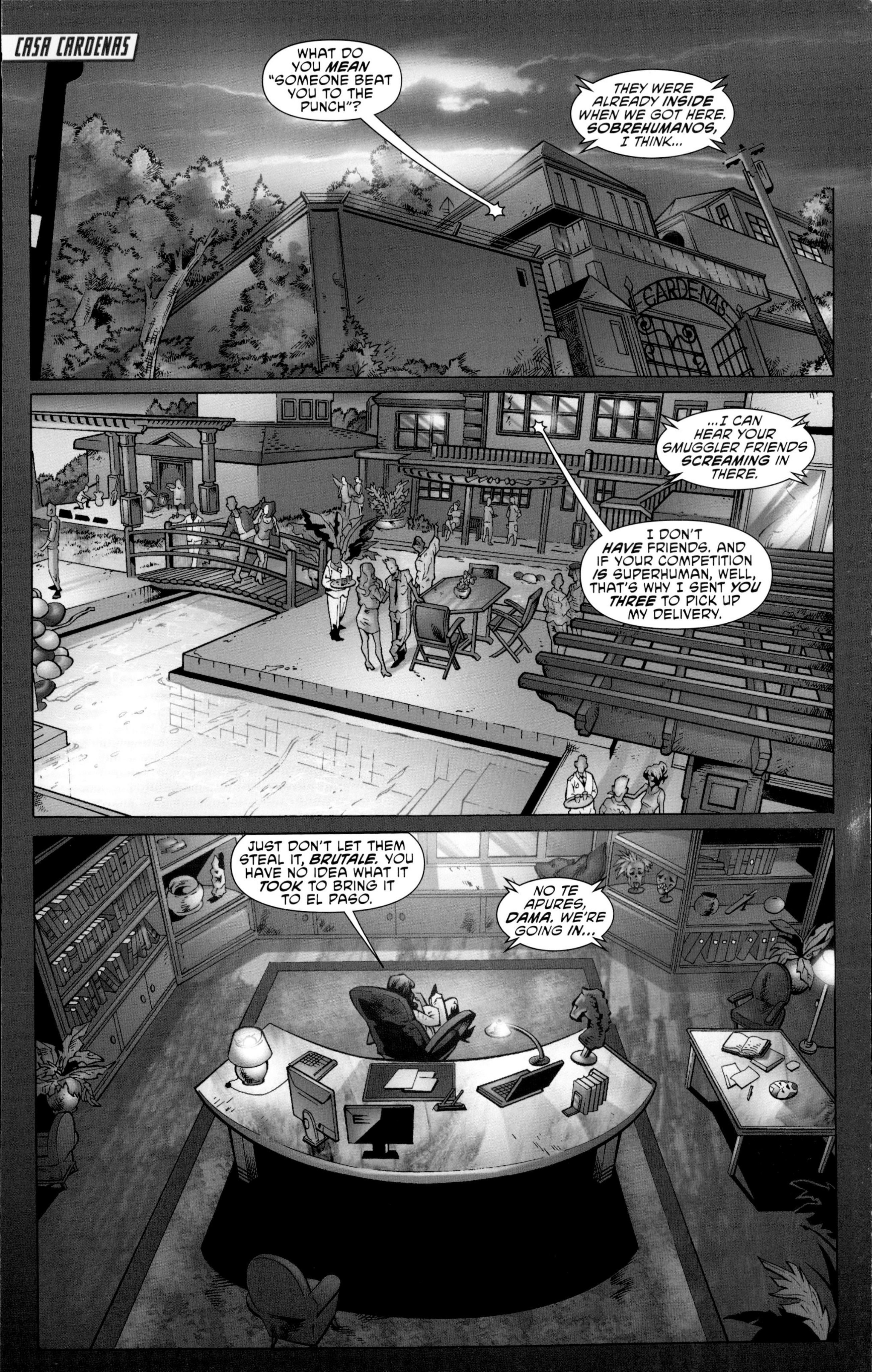
CASA CARDENAS
WHAT DO YOU MEAN "SOMEONE BEAT YOU TO THE PUNCH"?
THEY WERE ALREADY INSIDE WHEN WE GOT HERE. SOBREHUMANOS, I THINK...
CARDENAS
...I CAN HEAR YOUR SMUGGLER FRIENDS SCREAMING IN THERE.
I DON'T HAVE FRIENDS. AND IF YOUR COMPETITION IS SUPERHUMAN, WELL, THAT'S WHY I SENT YOU THREE TO PICK UP MY DELIVERY.
JUST DON'T LET THEM STEAL IT, BRUTALE. YOU HAVE NO IDEA WHAT IT TOOK TO BRING IT TO EL PASO.
NO TE APURES, DAMA. WE'RE GOING IN...

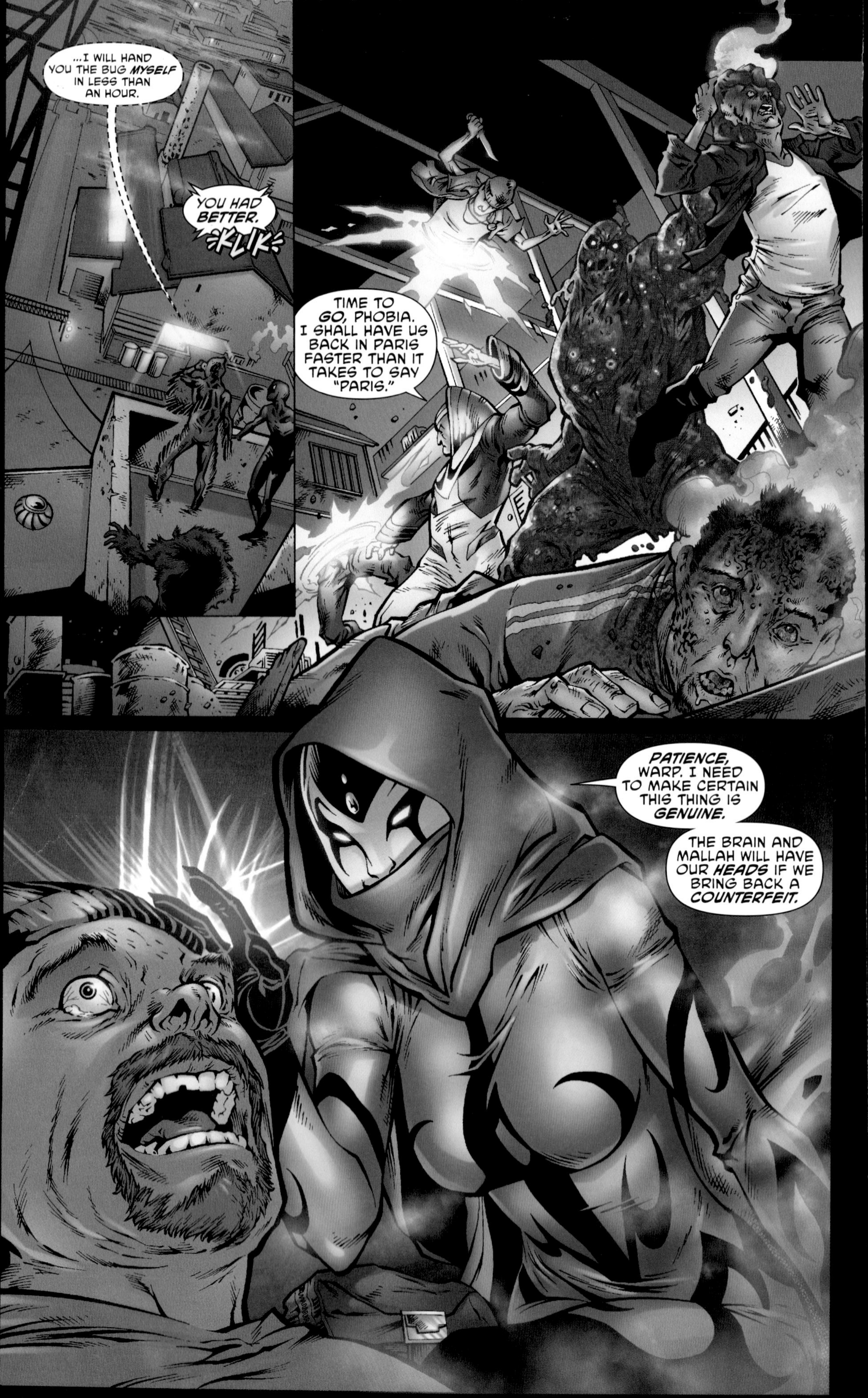
...I WILL HAND YOU THE BUG *MYSELF* IN LESS THAN AN HOUR.
YOU HAD *BETTER.*
KLIK
TIME TO *GO,* PHOBIA. I SHALL HAVE US BACK IN PARIS FASTER THAN IT TAKES TO SAY "PARIS."
PATIENCE, WARP. I NEED TO MAKE CERTAIN THIS THING IS *GENUINE.*
THE BRAIN AND MALLAH WILL HAVE OUR *HEADS* IF WE BRING BACK A *COUNTERFEIT.*

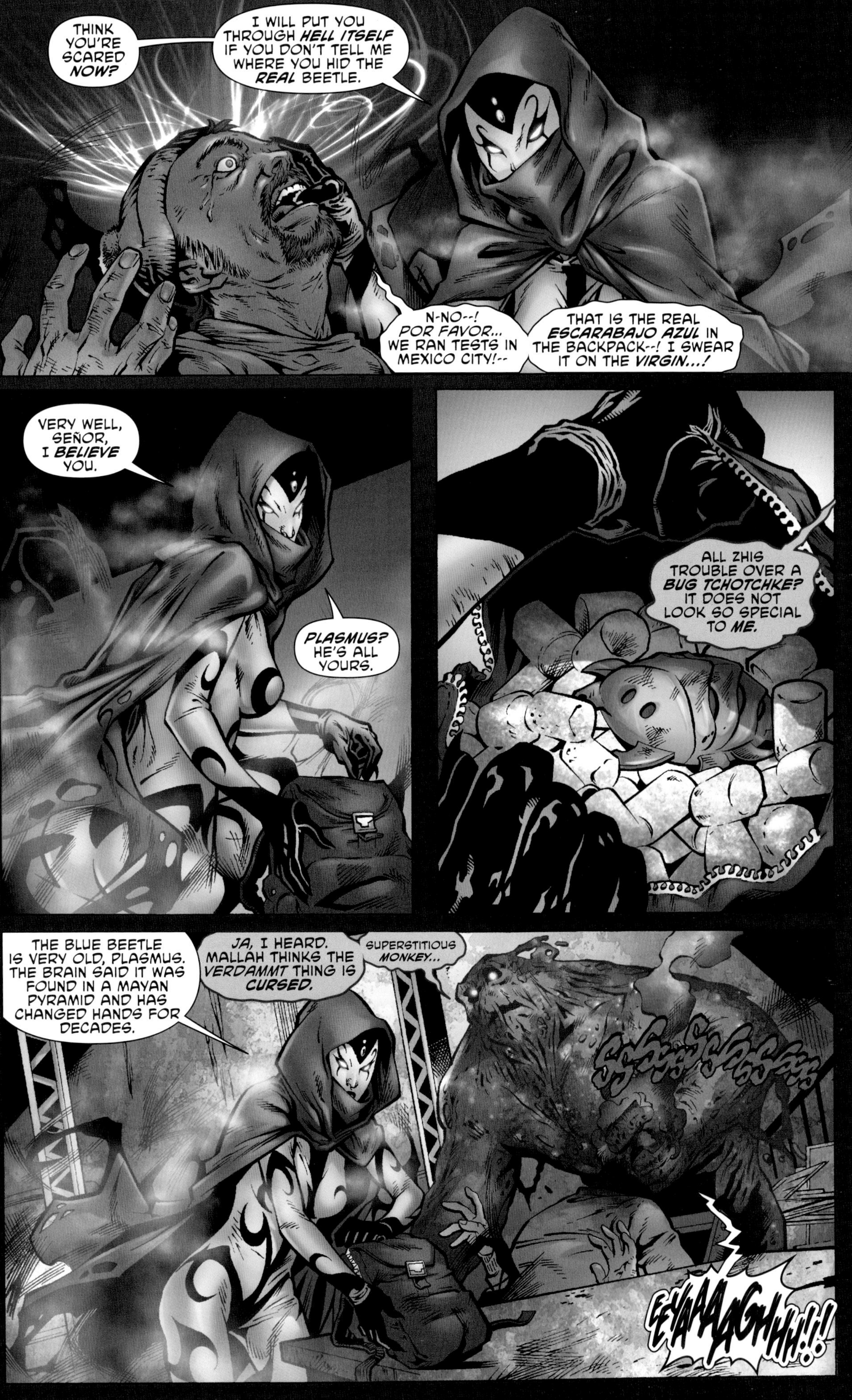
THINK YOU'RE SCARED NOW?
I WILL PUT YOU THROUGH HELL ITSELF IF YOU DON'T TELL ME WHERE YOU HID THE REAL BEETLE.
N-NO--! POR FAVOR... WE RAN TESTS IN MEXICO CITY!--
THAT IS THE REAL ESCARABAJO AZUL IN THE BACKPACK--! I SWEAR IT ON THE VIRGIN...!
VERY WELL, SEÑOR, I BELIEVE YOU.
PLASMUS? HE'S ALL YOURS.
ALL ZHIS TROUBLE OVER A BUG TCHOTCHKE? IT DOES NOT LOOK SO SPECIAL TO ME.
THE BLUE BEETLE IS VERY OLD, PLASMUS. THE BRAIN SAID IT WAS FOUND IN A MAYAN PYRAMID AND HAS CHANGED HANDS FOR DECADES.
JA, I HEARD. MALLAH THINKS THE VERDAMMT THING IS CURSED.
SUPERSTITIOUS MONKEY...
SSSSSSSSSSS
EEYAAAAGHHHH!!!

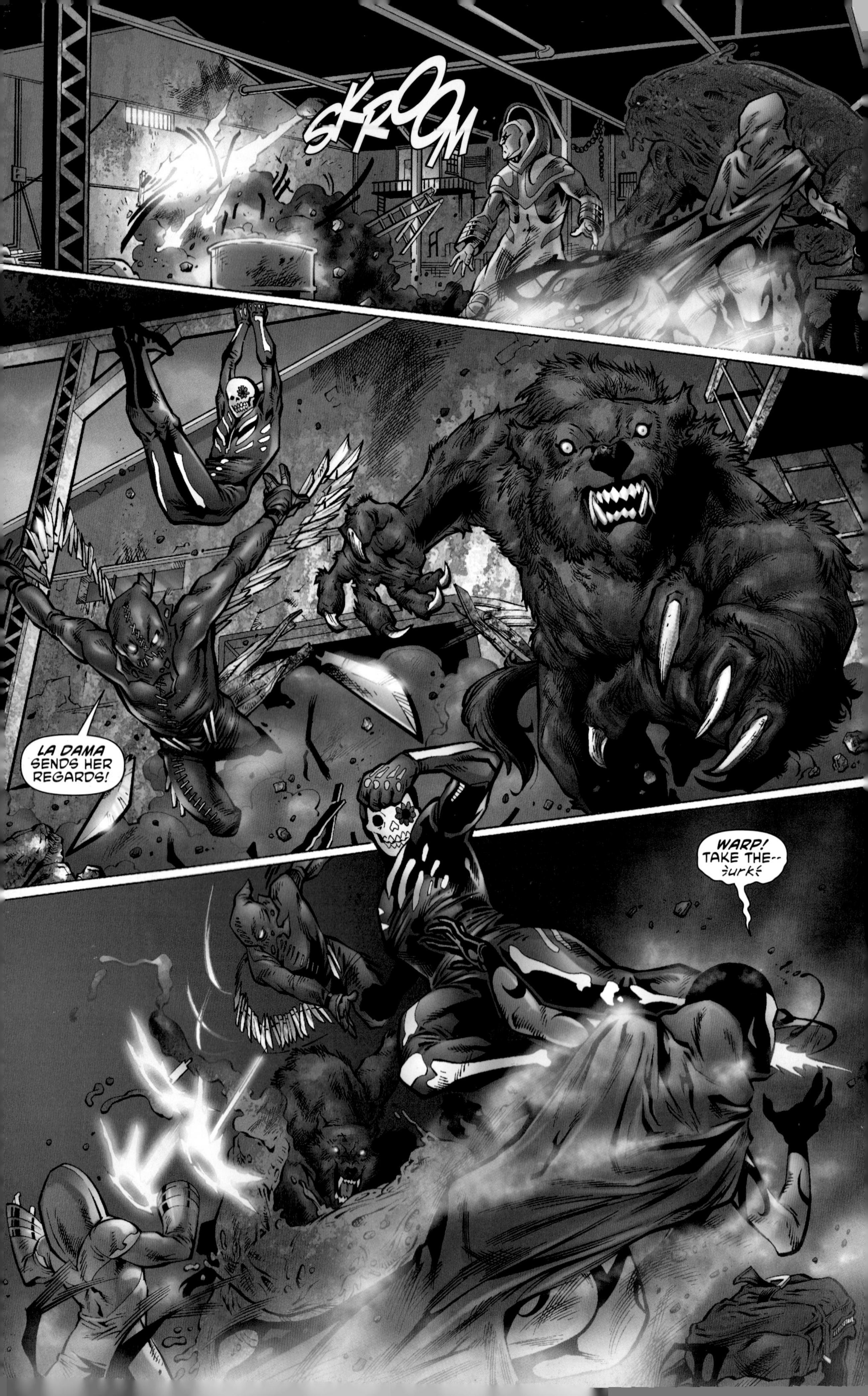
SKROOM
LA DAMA SENDS HER REGARDS!
WARP! TAKE THE-- urk

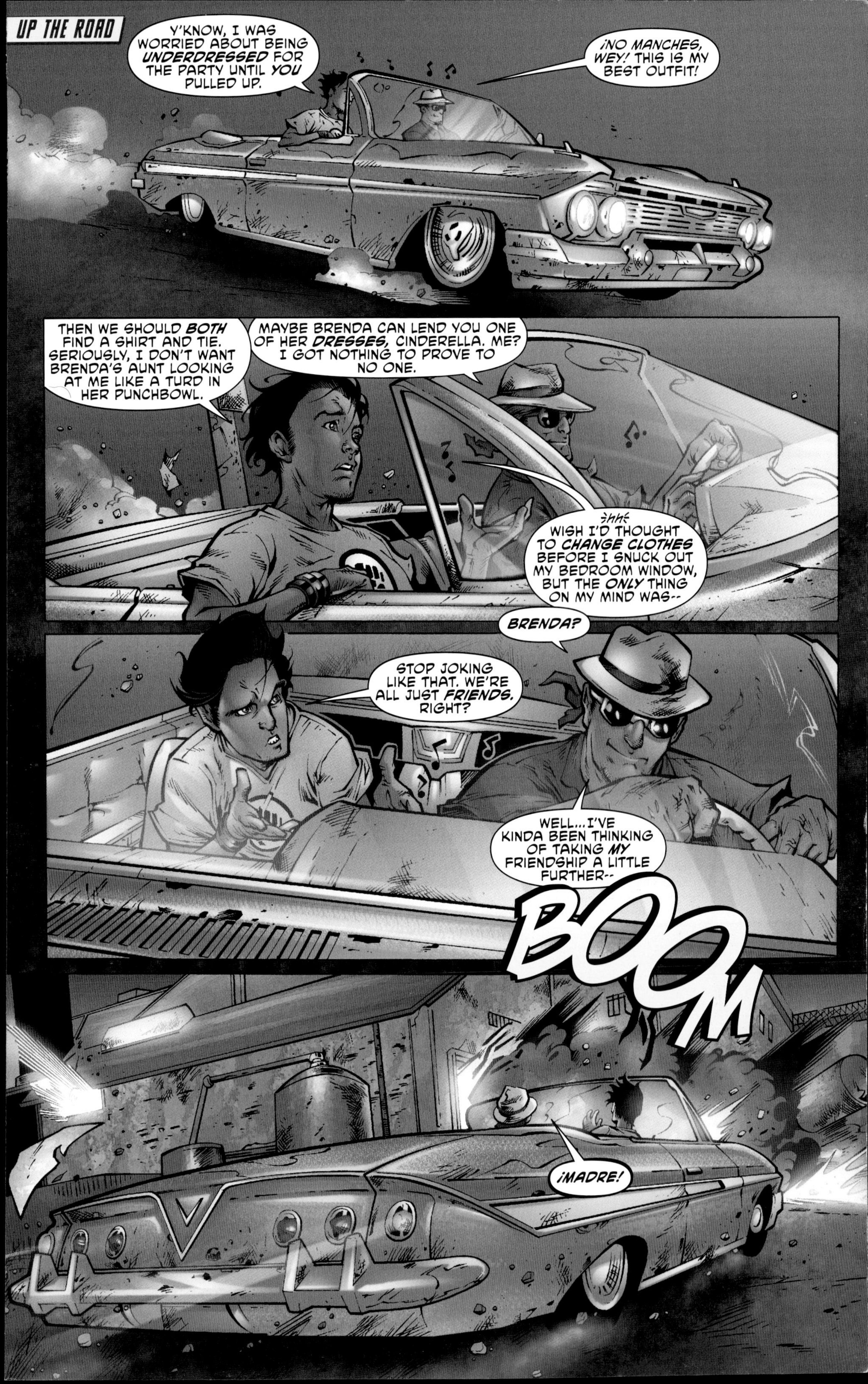
UP THE ROAD
Y'KNOW, I WAS WORRIED ABOUT BEING UNDERDRESSED FOR THE PARTY UNTIL YOU PULLED UP.
¡NO MANCHES, WEY! THIS IS MY BEST OUTFIT!
THEN WE SHOULD BOTH FIND A SHIRT AND TIE. SERIOUSLY, I DON'T WANT BRENDA'S AUNT LOOKING AT ME LIKE A TURD IN HER PUNCHBOWL.
MAYBE BRENDA CAN LEND YOU ONE OF HER DRESSES, CINDERELLA. ME? I GOT NOTHING TO PROVE TO NO ONE.
SHH
WISH I'D THOUGHT TO CHANGE CLOTHES BEFORE I SNUCK OUT MY BEDROOM WINDOW, BUT THE ONLY THING ON MY MIND WAS--
BRENDA?
STOP JOKING LIKE THAT. WE'RE ALL JUST FRIENDS. RIGHT?
WELL...I'VE KINDA BEEN THINKING OF TAKING MY FRIENDSHIP A LITTLE FURTHER--
BOOM
¡MADRE!

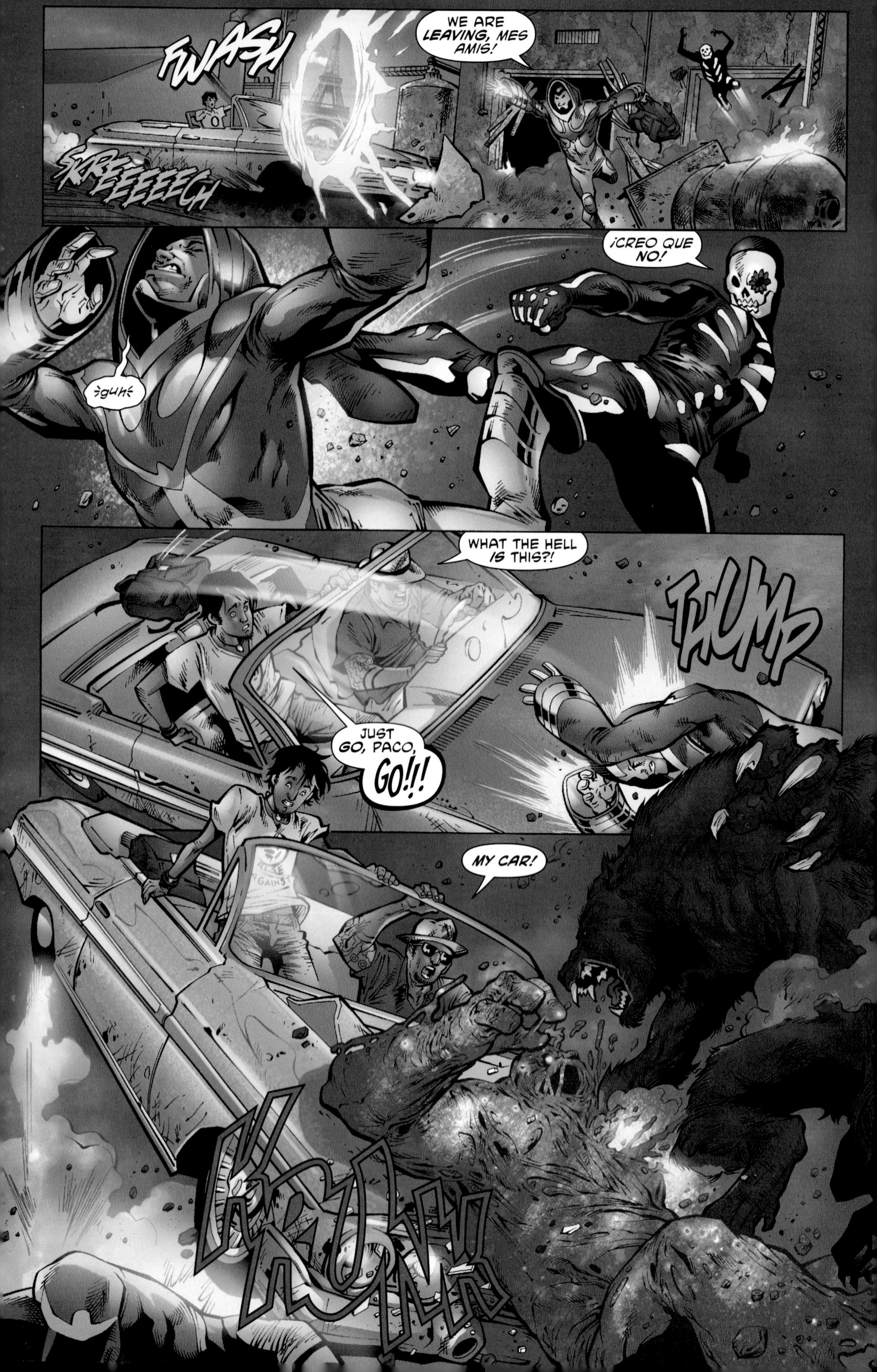
FWASH
SKREEEEEEECH
WE ARE LEAVING, MES AMIS!
¡CREO QUE NO!
guh
WHAT THE HELL IS THIS?!
THUMP
JUST GO, PACO, GO!!!
MY CAR!

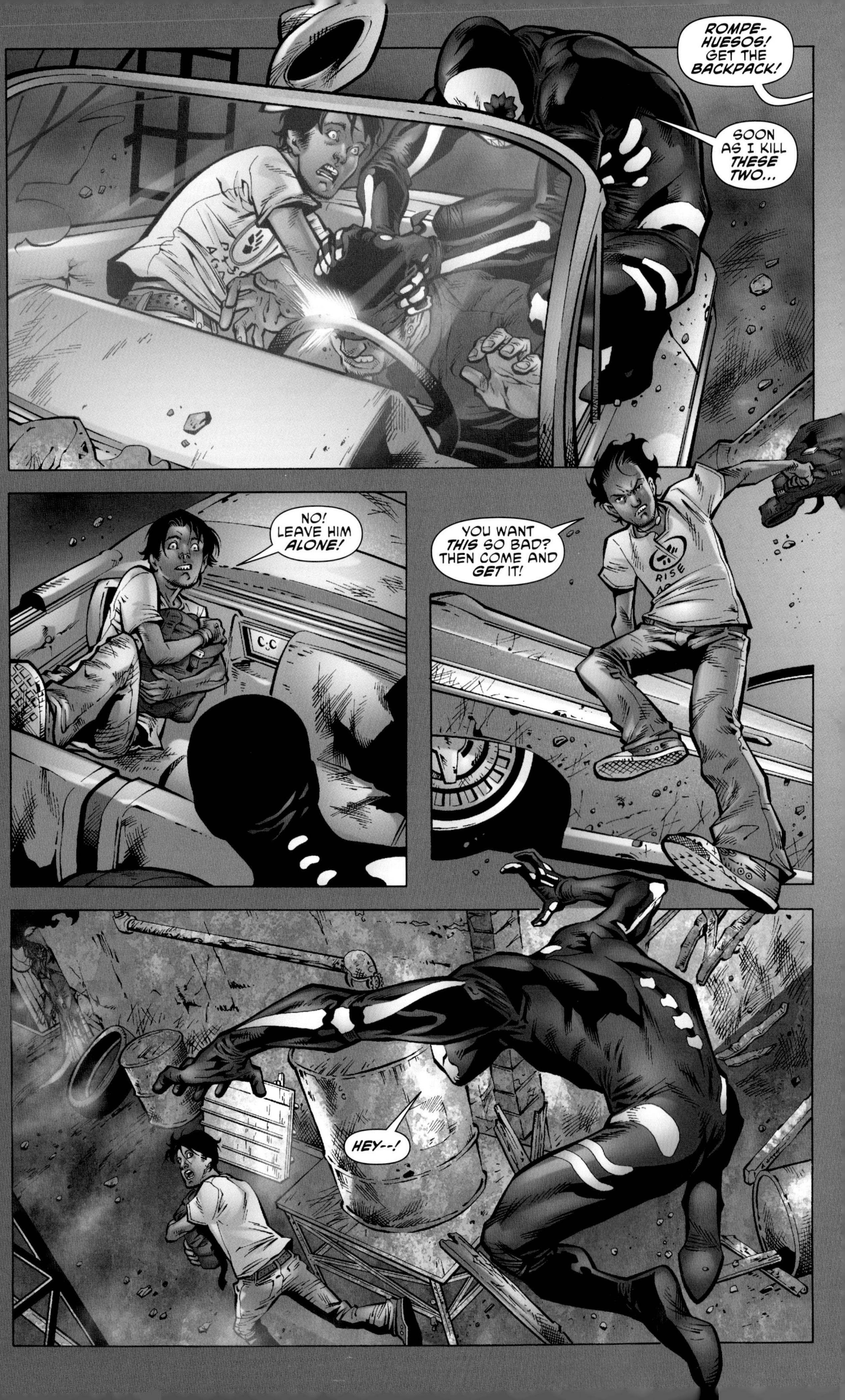
ROMPE-HUESOS! GET THE BACKPACK!
SOON AS I KILL THESE TWO...
NO! LEAVE HIM ALONE!
YOU WANT THIS SO BAD? THEN COME AND GET IT!
HEY--!

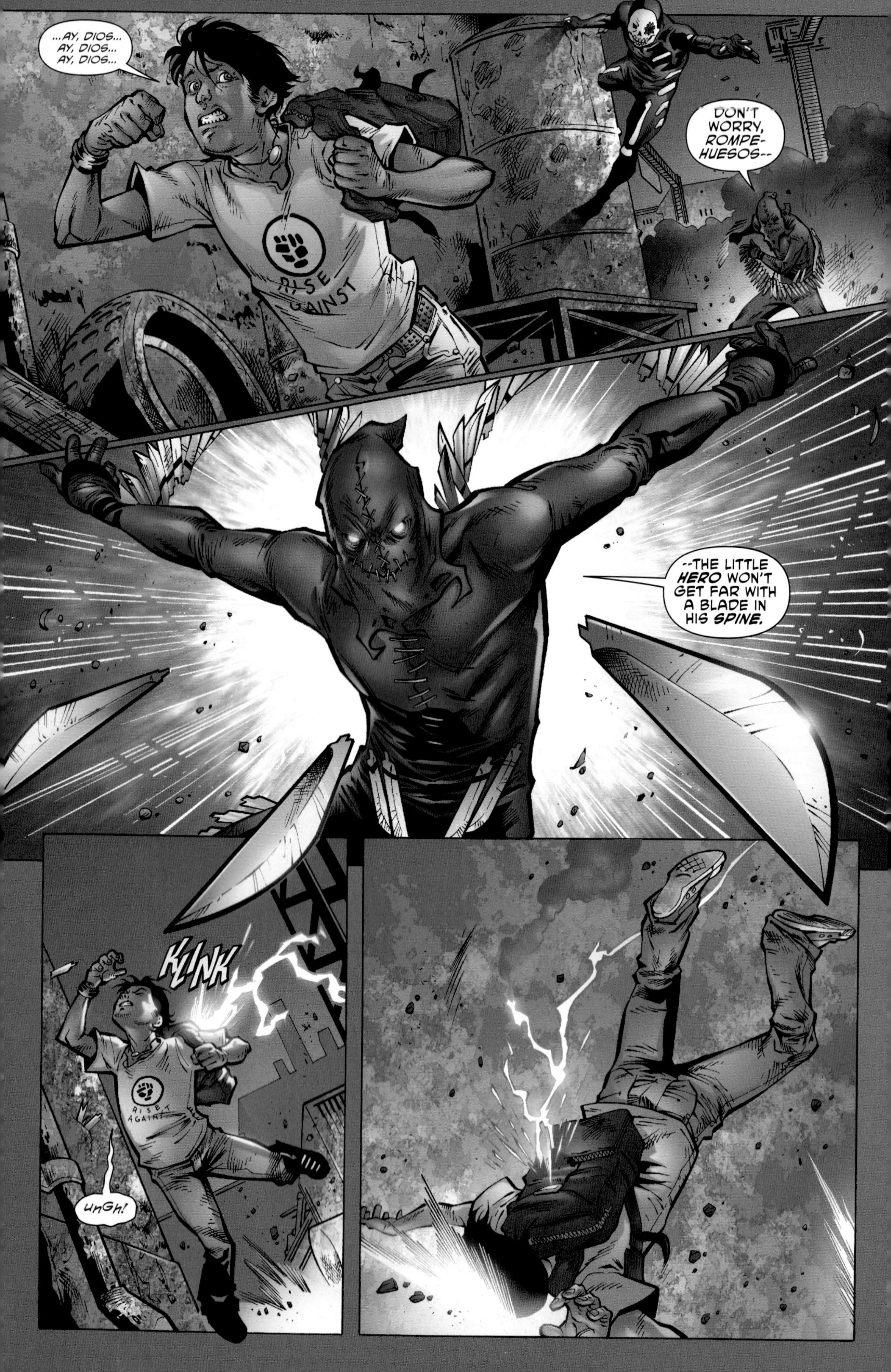
...AY, DIOS... AY, DIOS... AY, DIOS...
DON'T WORRY, ROMPE-HUESOS--
--THE LITTLE HERO WON'T GET FAR WITH A BLADE IN HIS SPINE.
KLINK
unGh!

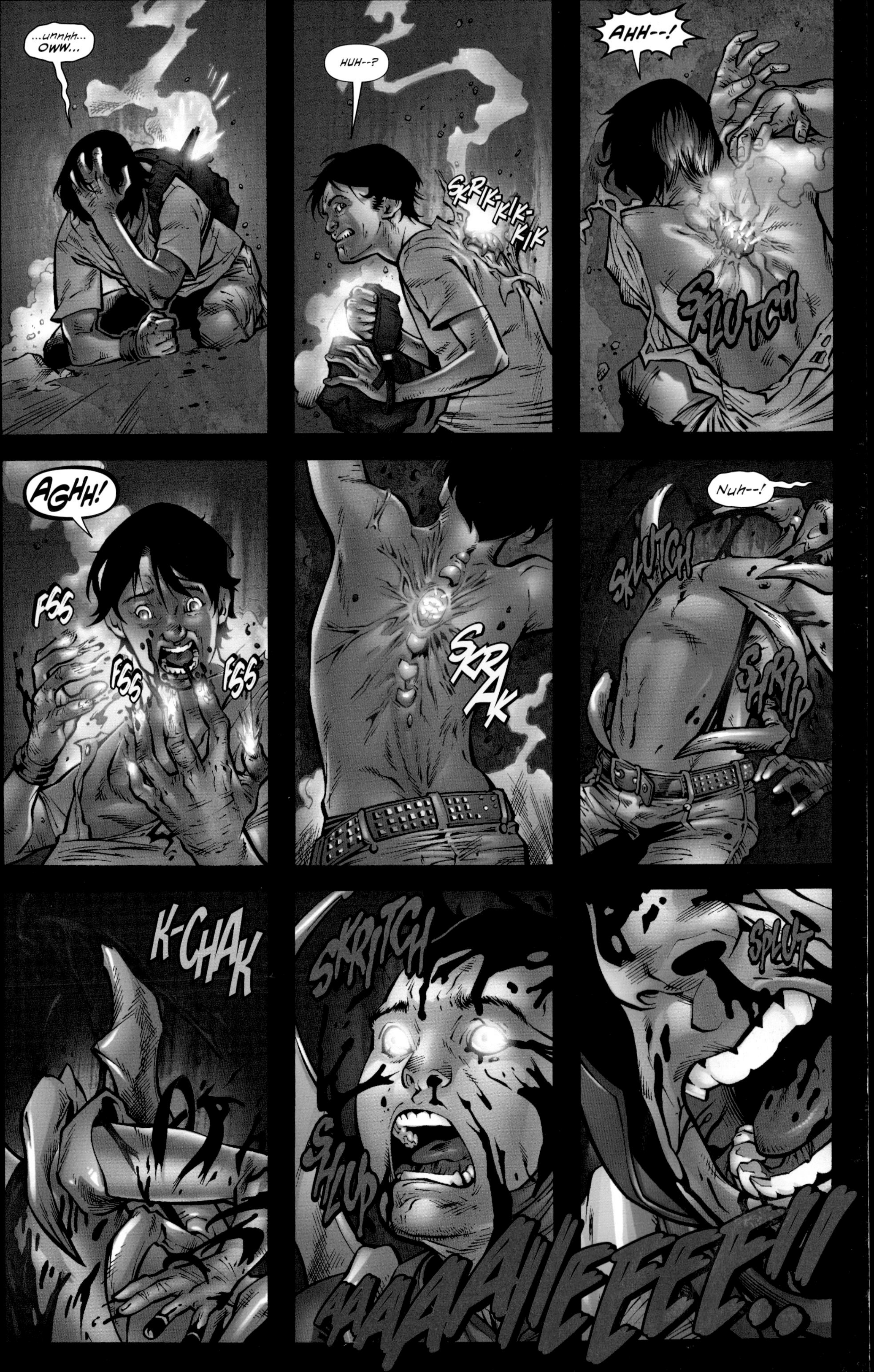
...unnnh... OWW...
HUH--?
SKRIK-KIK-KIK
AHH--!
SKLUTCH
AGHH!
FSS
FSS
FSS
SKRAK
Nuh--!
SKLUTCH
SHRUP
K-CHAK
SKRITCH
SHLUP
SPLUT
AAAAHIEEEE!!

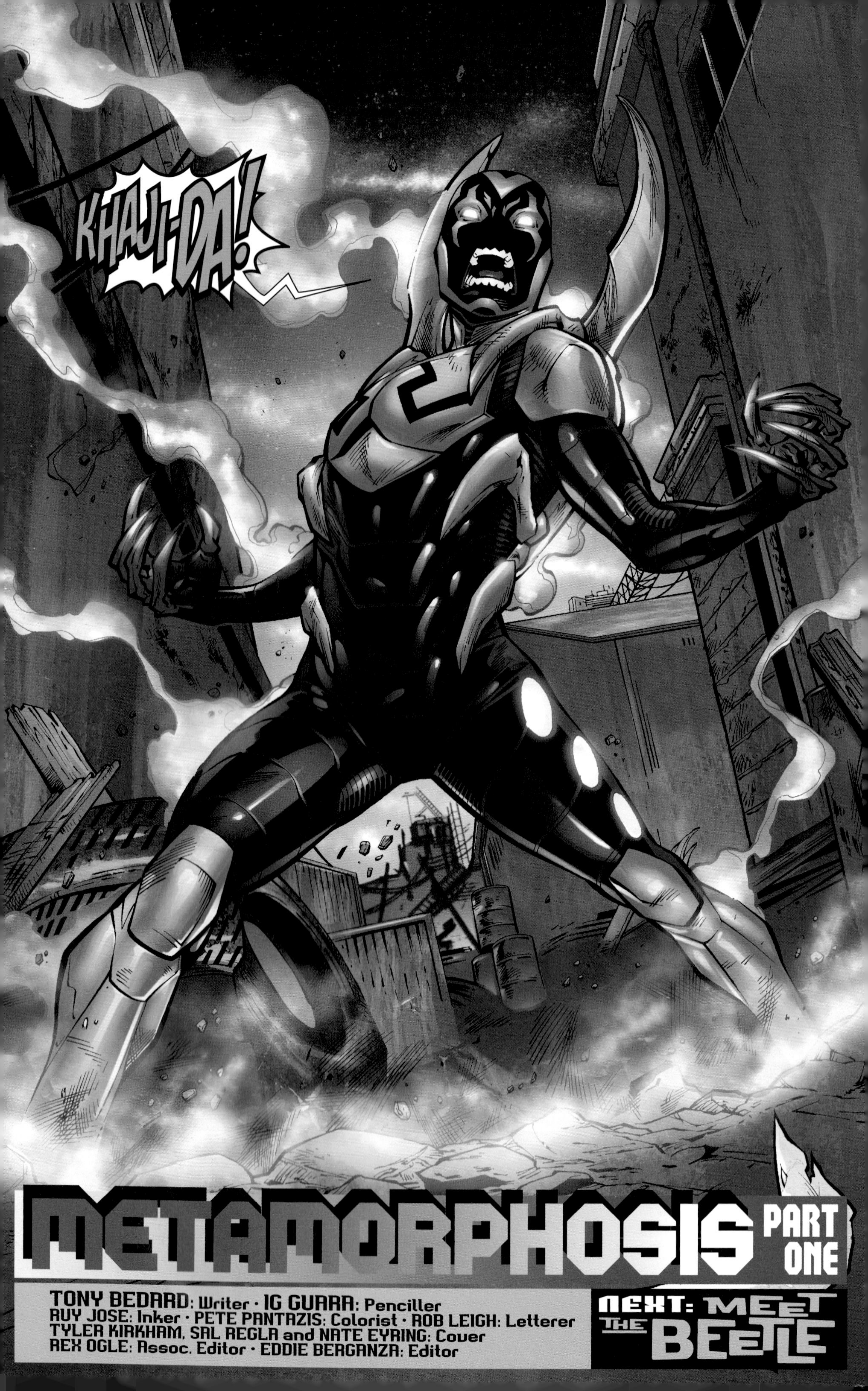
KHAJI-DA!
METAMORPHOSIS PART ONE
TONY BEDARD: Writer · IG GUARA: Penciller
RUY JOSE: Inker · PETE PANTAZIS: Colorist · ROB LEIGH: Letterer
TYLER KIRKHAM, SAL REGLA and NATE EYRING: Cover
REX OGLE: Assoc. Editor · EDDIE BERGANZA: Editor
NEXT: MEET THE BEETLE

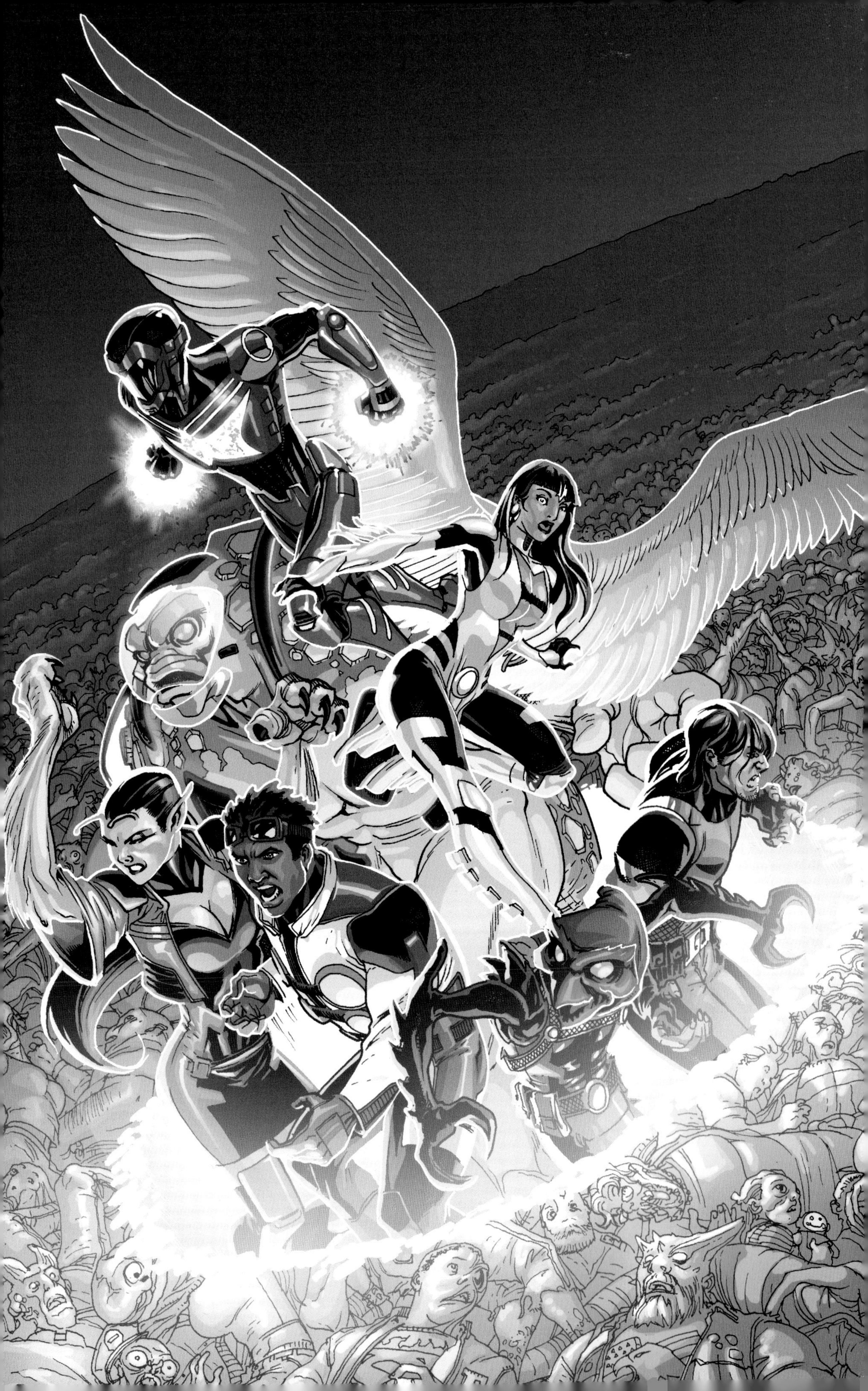

LEGION LOST

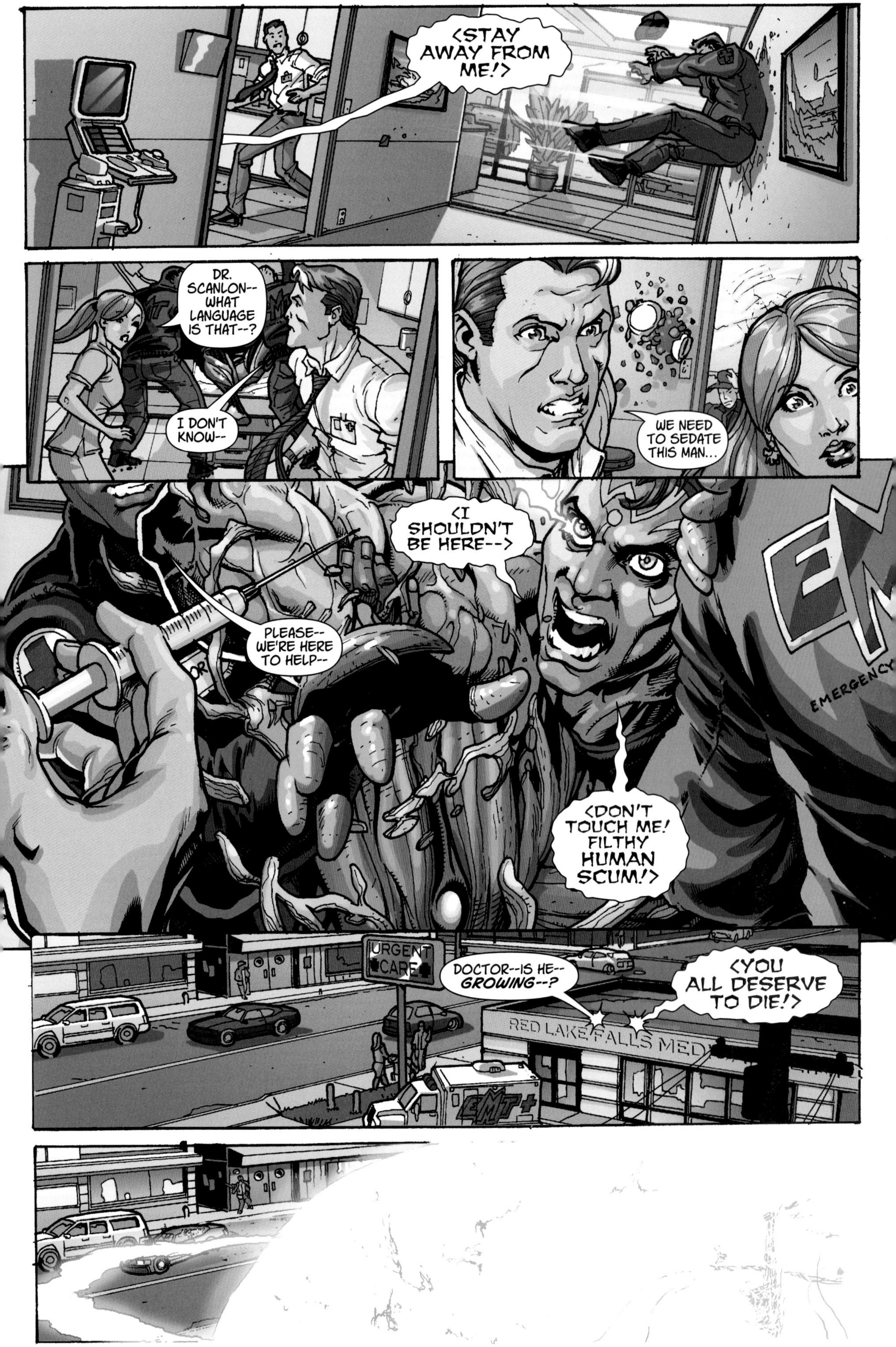
<STAY AWAY FROM ME!>
DR. SCANLON--WHAT LANGUAGE IS THAT--?
I DON'T KNOW--
WE NEED TO SEDATE THIS MAN...
<I SHOULDN'T BE HERE-->
PLEASE--WE'RE HERE TO HELP--
<DON'T TOUCH ME! FILTHY HUMAN SCUM!>
EMERGENCY
URGENT CARE
DOCTOR--IS HE--*GROWING*--?
<YOU ALL DESERVE TO DIE!>
RED LAKE FALLS MED
EMT

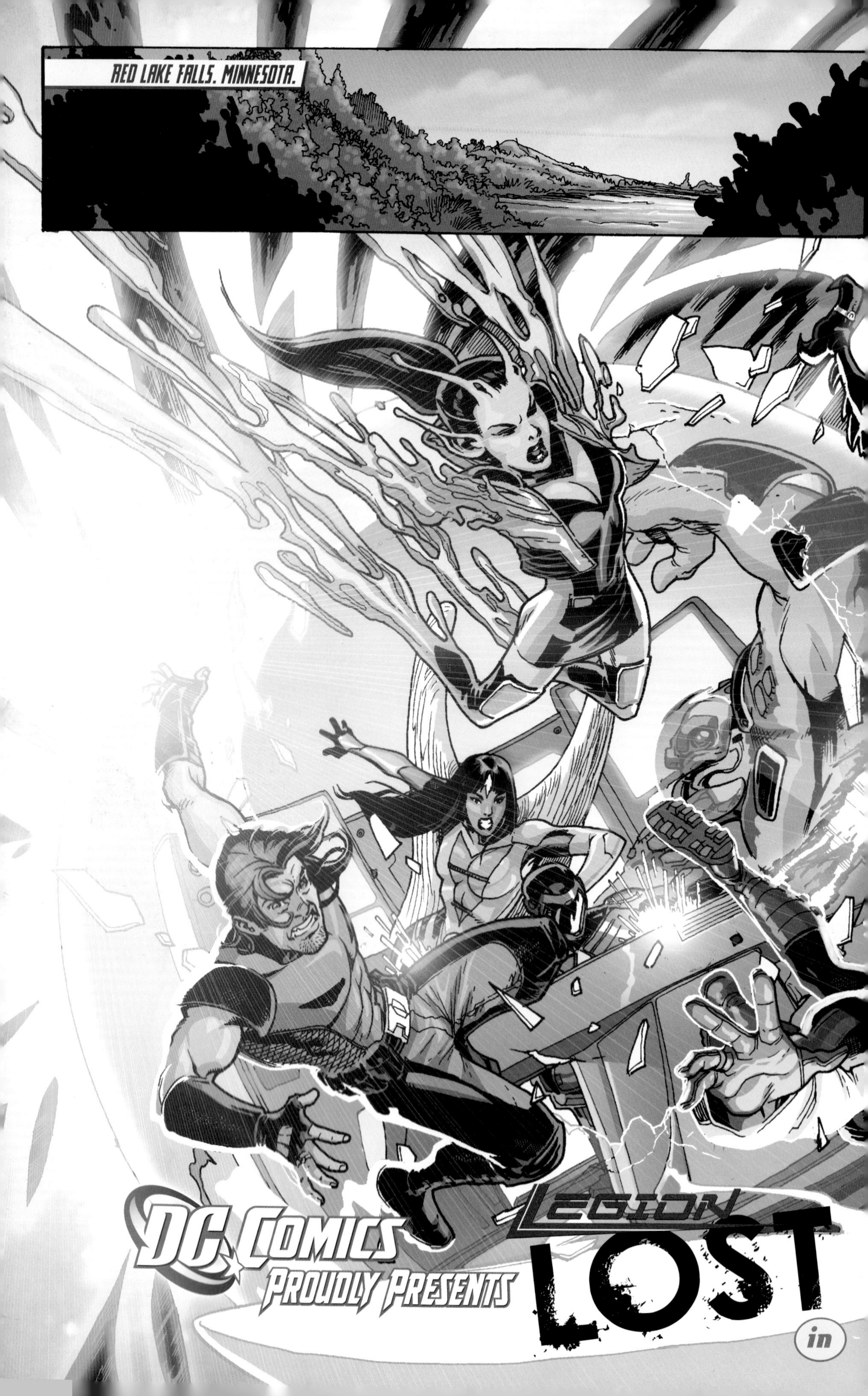

RED LAKE FALLS. MINNESOTA.
DC COMICS
PROUDLY PRESENTS
LEGION LOST
in

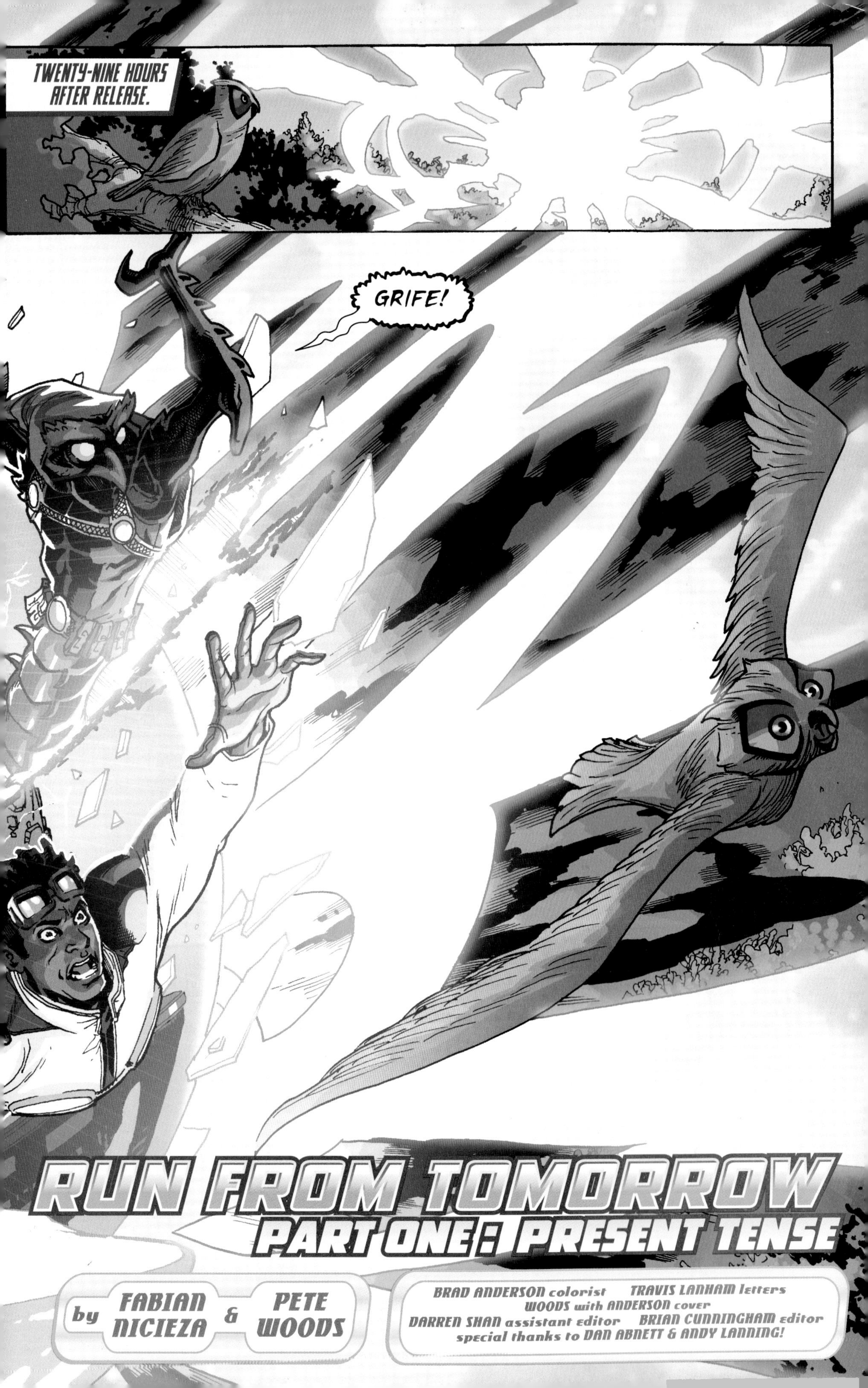

TWENTY-NINE HOURS AFTER RELEASE.
GRIFE!
RUN FROM TOMORROW
PART ONE : PRESENT TENSE
by FABIAN NICIEZA & PETE WOODS
BRAD ANDERSON colorist TRAVIS LANHAM letters
WOODS with ANDERSON cover
DARREN SHAN assistant editor BRIAN CUNNINGHAM editor
special thanks to DAN ABNETT & ANDY LANNING!

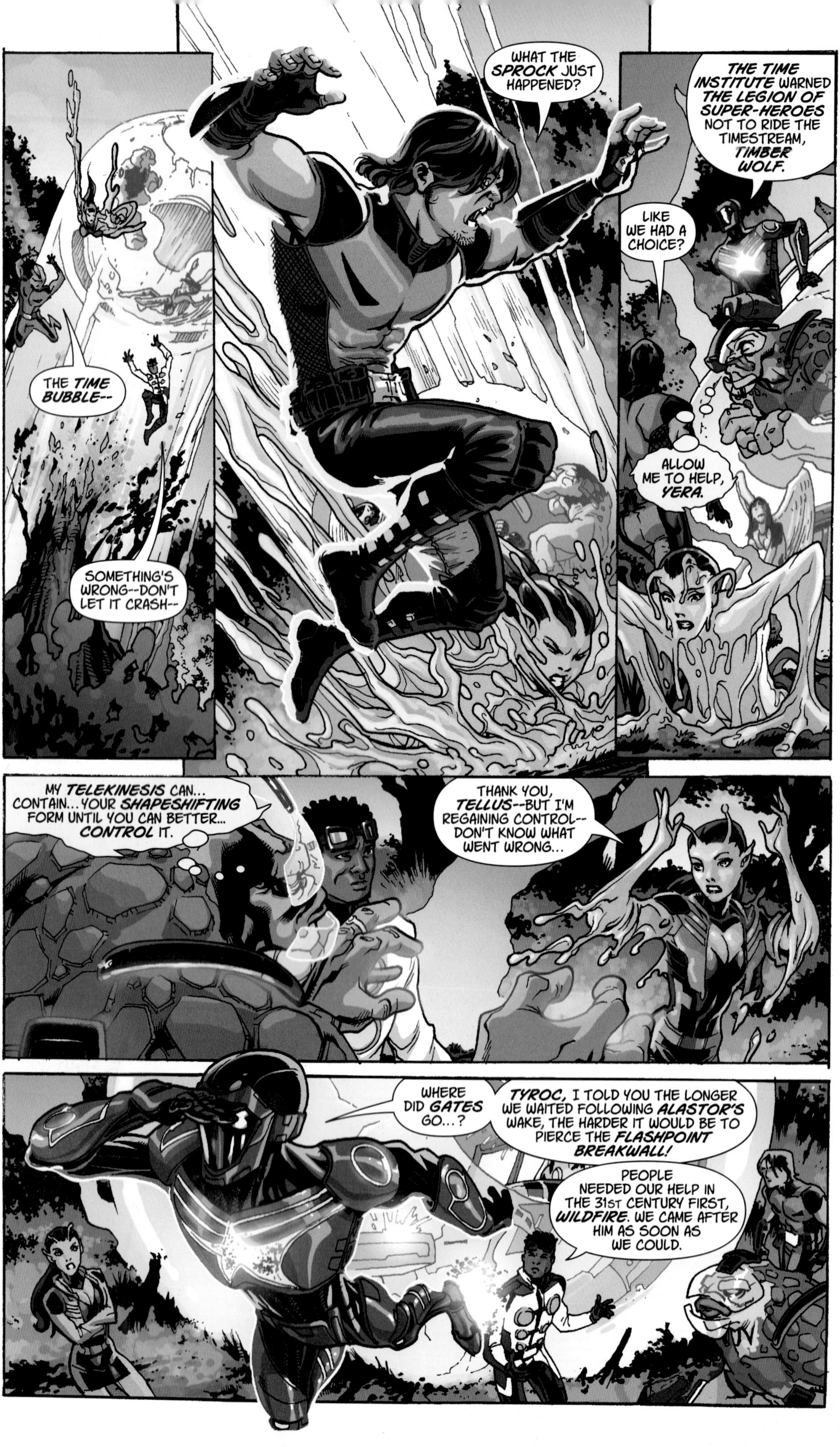
WHAT THE SPROCK JUST HAPPENED?
THE TIME BUBBLE--
SOMETHING'S WRONG--DON'T LET IT CRASH--
THE TIME INSTITUTE WARNED THE LEGION OF SUPER-HEROES NOT TO RIDE THE TIMESTREAM, TIMBER WOLF.
LIKE WE HAD A CHOICE?
ALLOW ME TO HELP, YERA.
MY TELEKINESIS CAN... CONTAIN... YOUR SHAPESHIFTING FORM UNTIL YOU CAN BETTER... CONTROL IT.
THANK YOU, TELLUS--BUT I'M REGAINING CONTROL-- DON'T KNOW WHAT WENT WRONG...
WHERE DID GATES GO...?
TYROC, I TOLD YOU THE LONGER WE WAITED FOLLOWING ALASTOR'S WAKE, THE HARDER IT WOULD BE TO PIERCE THE FLASHPOINT BREAKWALL!
PEOPLE NEEDED OUR HELP IN THE 31ST CENTURY FIRST, WILDFIRE. WE CAME AFTER HIM AS SOON AS WE COULD.

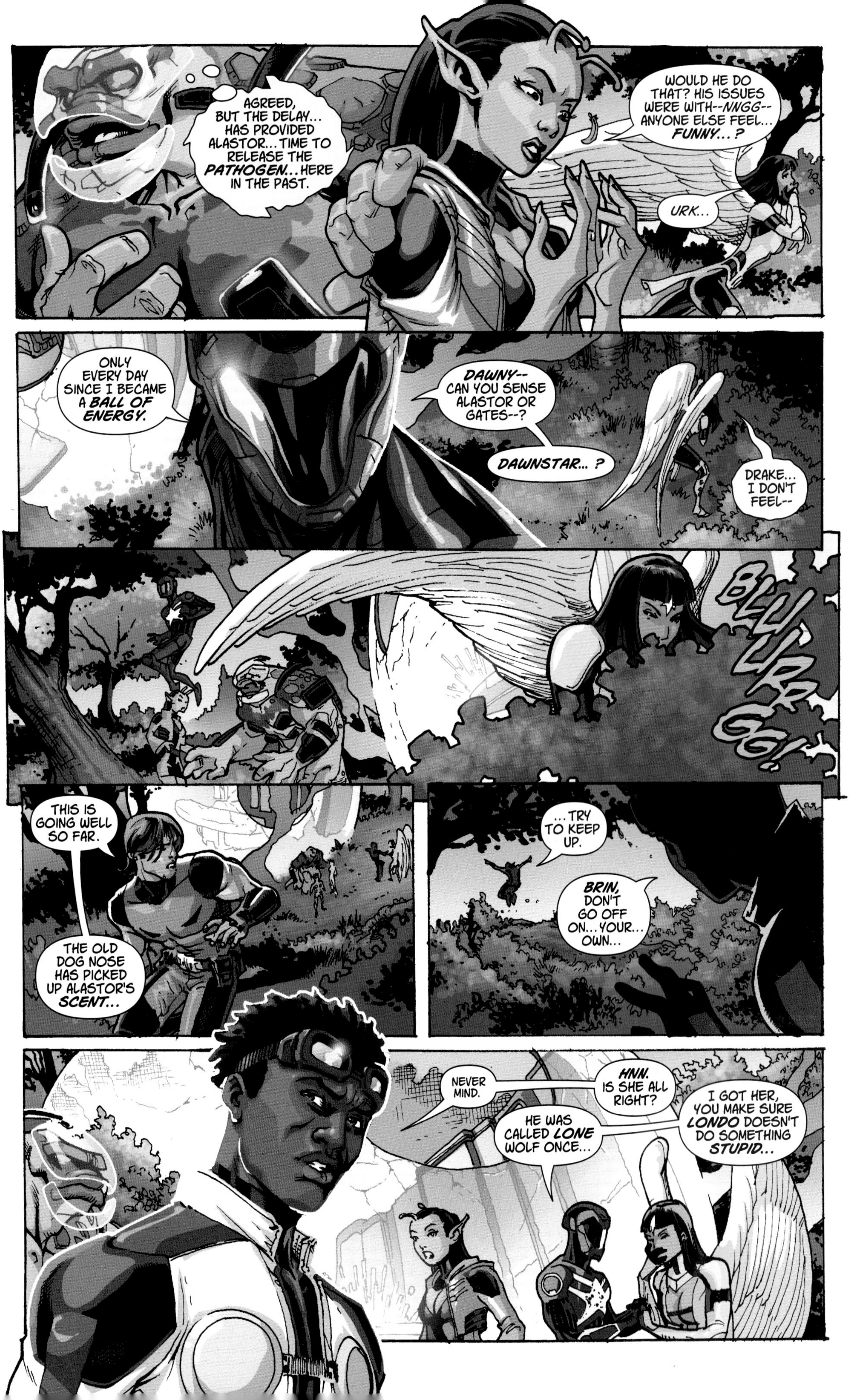
AGREED, BUT THE DELAY... HAS PROVIDED ALASTOR... TIME TO RELEASE THE PATHOGEN... HERE IN THE PAST.
WOULD HE DO THAT? HIS ISSUES WERE WITH--NNGG-- ANYONE ELSE FEEL... FUNNY...?
URK...
ONLY EVERY DAY SINCE I BECAME A BALL OF ENERGY.
DAWNY-- CAN YOU SENSE ALASTOR OR GATES--?
DAWNSTAR...?
DRAKE... I DON'T FEEL--
BLUURRGG!
THIS IS GOING WELL SO FAR.
THE OLD DOG NOSE HAS PICKED UP ALASTOR'S SCENT...
...TRY TO KEEP UP.
BRIN, DON'T GO OFF ON... YOUR... OWN...
NEVER MIND.
HNN. IS SHE ALL RIGHT?
HE WAS CALLED LONE WOLF ONCE...
I GOT HER, YOU MAKE SURE LONDO DOESN'T DO SOMETHING STUPID...

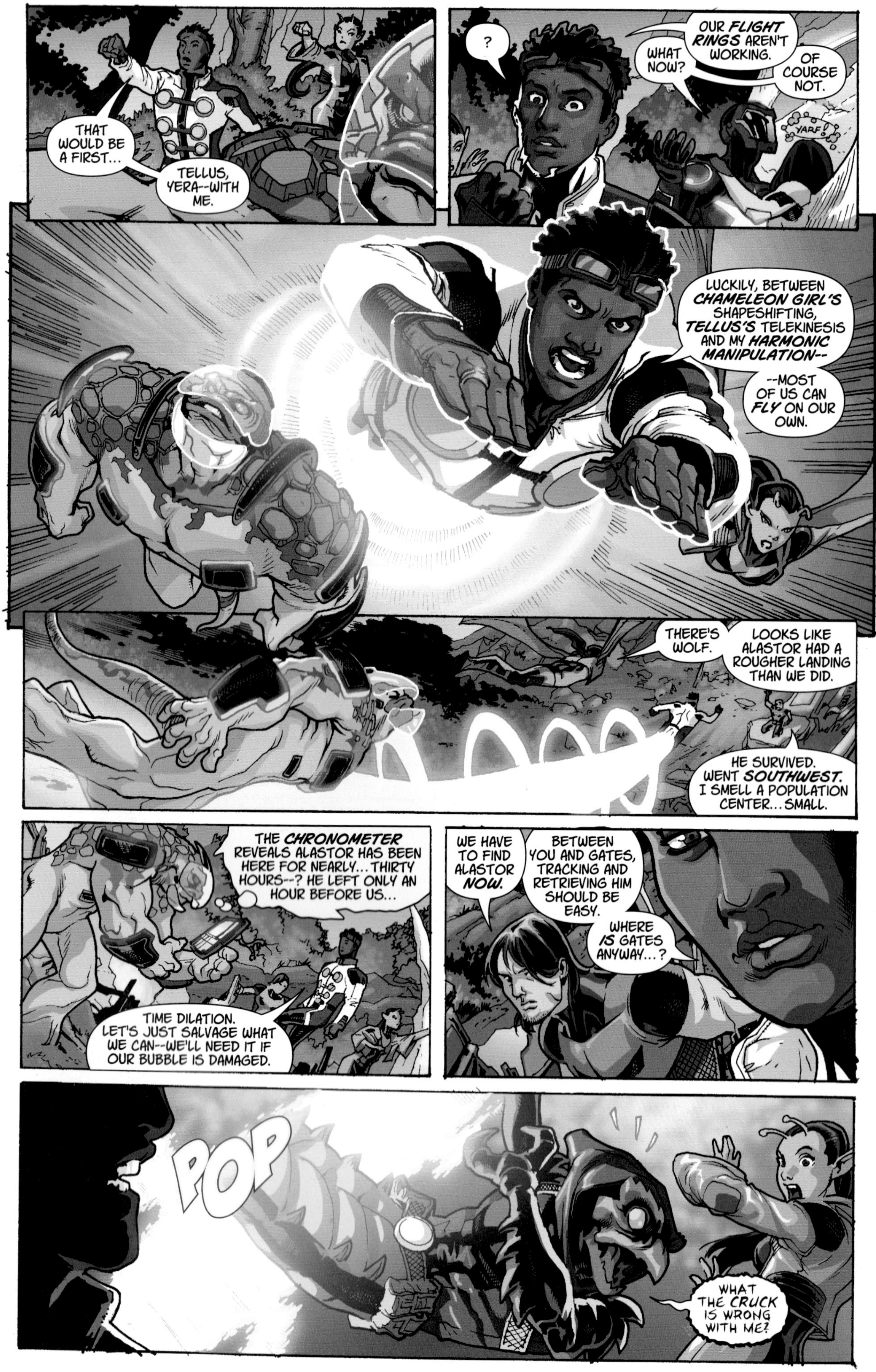
THAT WOULD BE A FIRST...
TELLUS, YERA--WITH ME.
?
OUR FLIGHT RINGS AREN'T WORKING.
WHAT NOW?
OF COURSE NOT.
YARF!
LUCKILY, BETWEEN CHAMELEON GIRL'S SHAPESHIFTING, TELLUS'S TELEKINESIS AND MY HARMONIC MANIPULATION--
--MOST OF US CAN FLY ON OUR OWN.
THERE'S WOLF.
LOOKS LIKE ALASTOR HAD A ROUGHER LANDING THAN WE DID.
HE SURVIVED. WENT SOUTHWEST. I SMELL A POPULATION CENTER... SMALL.
THE CHRONOMETER REVEALS ALASTOR HAS BEEN HERE FOR NEARLY... THIRTY HOURS--? HE LEFT ONLY AN HOUR BEFORE US...
TIME DILATION. LET'S JUST SALVAGE WHAT WE CAN--WE'LL NEED IT IF OUR BUBBLE IS DAMAGED.
WE HAVE TO FIND ALASTOR NOW.
BETWEEN YOU AND GATES, TRACKING AND RETRIEVING HIM SHOULD BE EASY.
WHERE IS GATES ANYWAY...?
POP
WHAT THE CRUCK IS WRONG WITH ME?

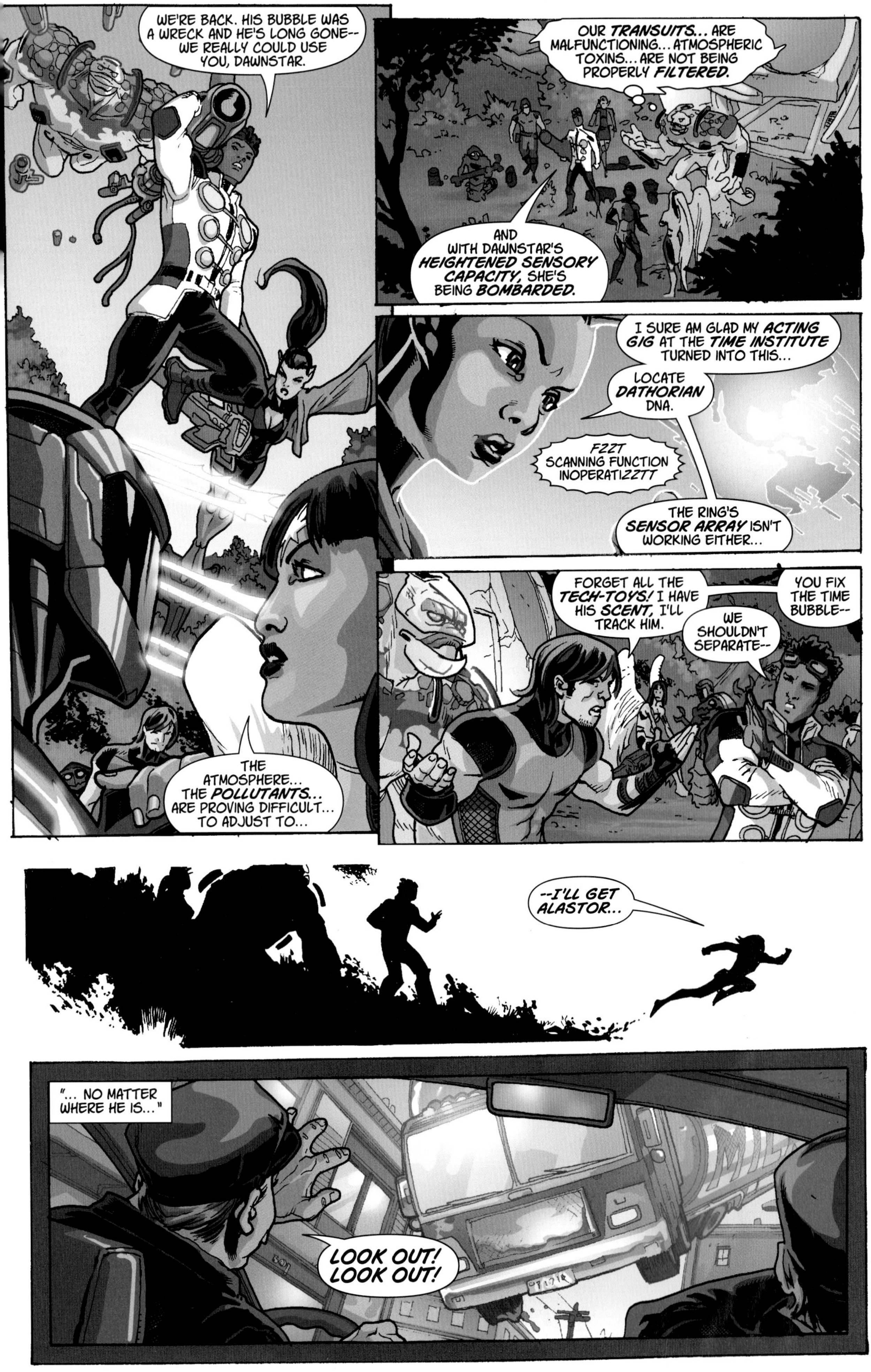
WE'RE BACK. HIS BUBBLE WAS A WRECK AND HE'S LONG GONE-- WE REALLY COULD USE YOU, DAWNSTAR.
THE ATMOSPHERE... THE POLLUTANTS... ARE PROVING DIFFICULT... TO ADJUST TO...
OUR TRANSUITS... ARE MALFUNCTIONING... ATMOSPHERIC TOXINS... ARE NOT BEING PROPERLY FILTERED.
AND WITH DAWNSTAR'S HEIGHTENED SENSORY CAPACITY, SHE'S BEING BOMBARDED.
I SURE AM GLAD MY ACTING GIG AT THE TIME INSTITUTE TURNED INTO THIS...
LOCATE DATHORIAN DNA.
FZZT SCANNING FUNCTION INOPERATIZZZTT
THE RING'S SENSOR ARRAY ISN'T WORKING EITHER...
FORGET ALL THE TECH-TOYS! I HAVE HIS SCENT, I'LL TRACK HIM.
YOU FIX THE TIME BUBBLE--
WE SHOULDN'T SEPARATE--
--I'LL GET ALASTOR...
"... NO MATTER WHERE HE IS..."
LOOK OUT! LOOK OUT!

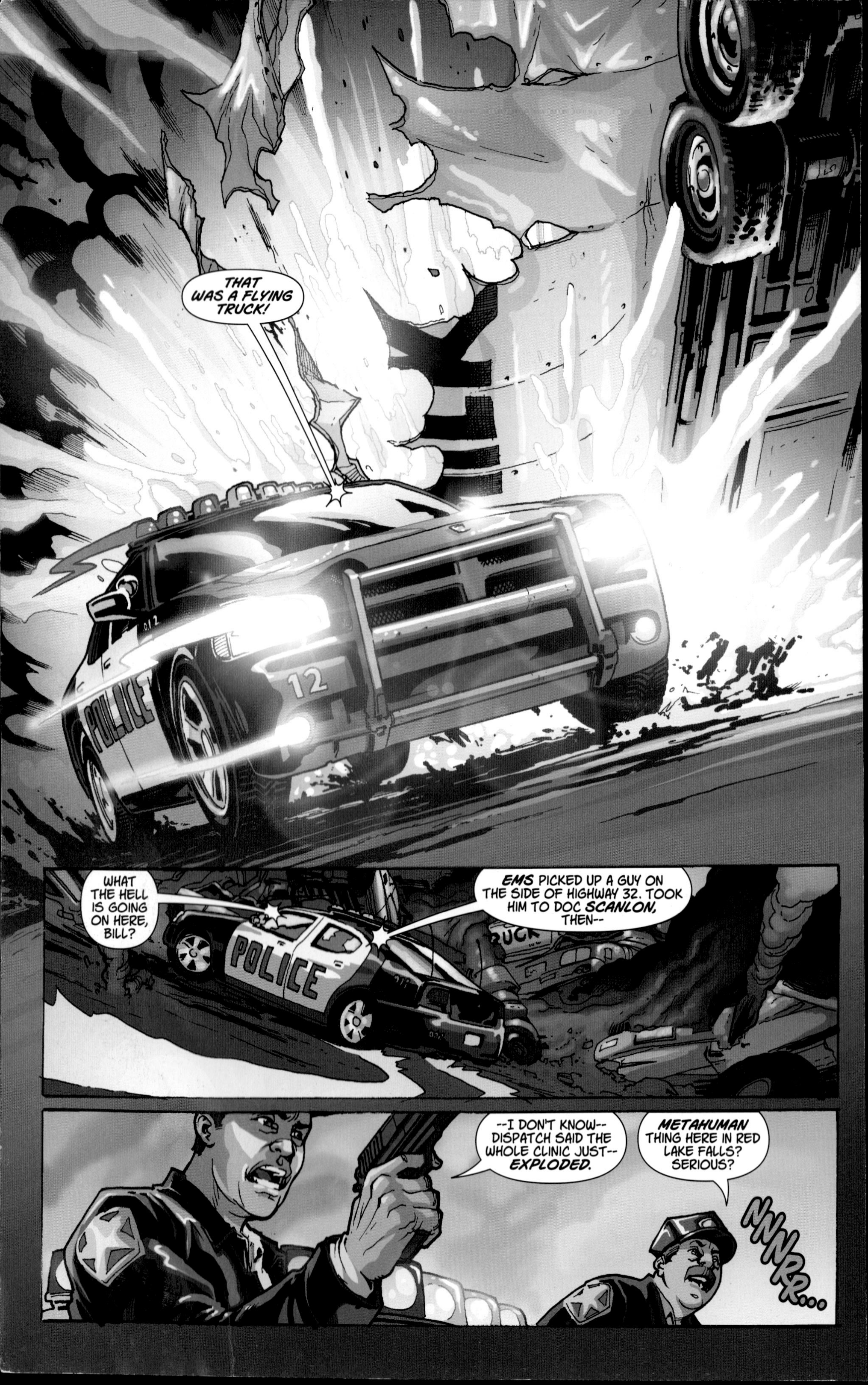
THAT WAS A FLYING TRUCK!
POLICE
12
WHAT THE HELL IS GOING ON HERE, BILL?
EMS PICKED UP A GUY ON THE SIDE OF HIGHWAY 32. TOOK HIM TO DOC SCANLON, THEN--
POLICE
--I DON'T KNOW-- DISPATCH SAID THE WHOLE CLINIC JUST-- EXPLODED.
METAHUMAN THING HERE IN RED LAKE FALLS? SERIOUS?
NNNRR...

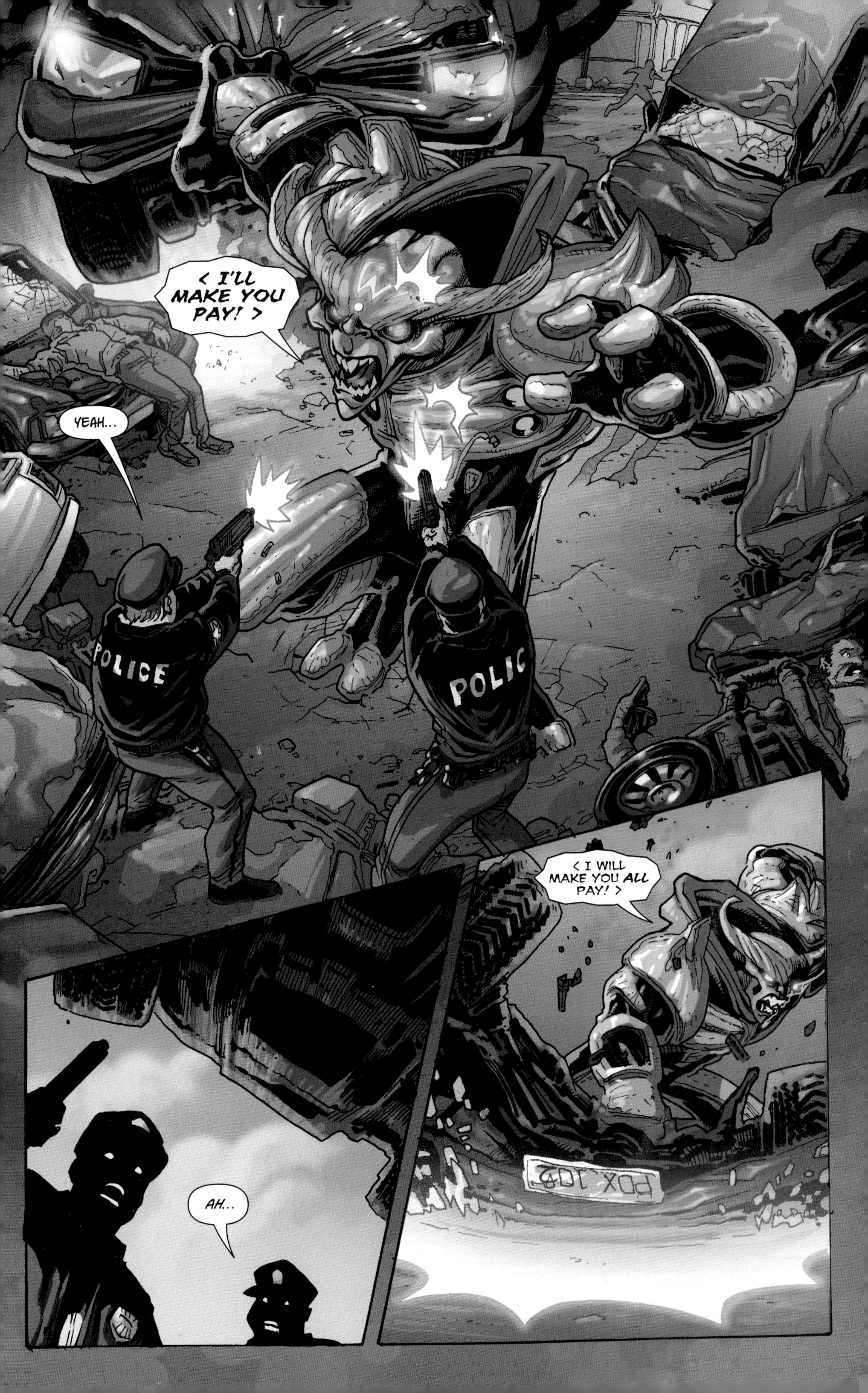
< I'LL MAKE YOU PAY! >
YEAH...
POLICE
POLIC
< I WILL MAKE YOU ALL PAY! >
AH...
PDX 102

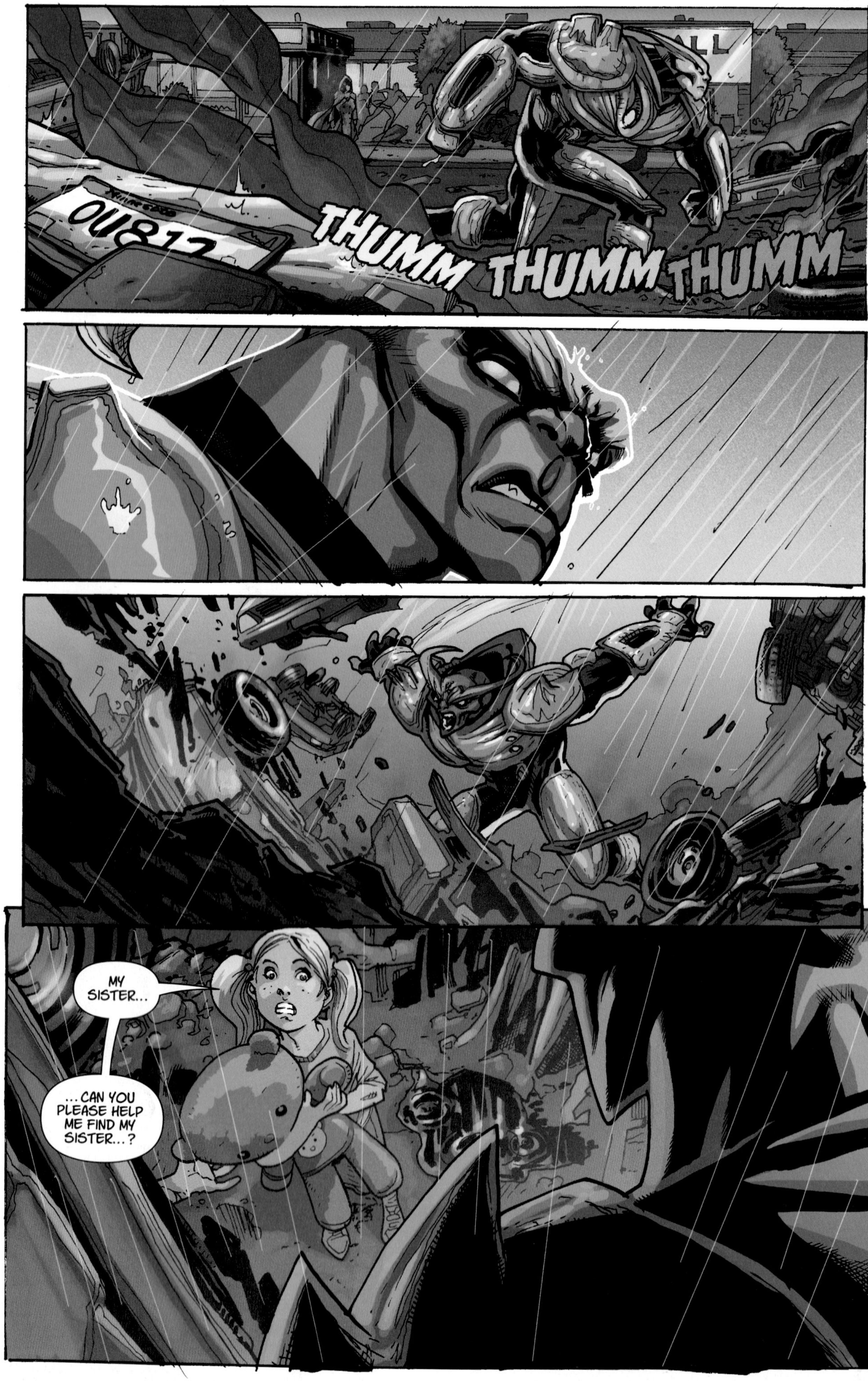
THUMM THUMM THUMM
MY SISTER...
...CAN YOU PLEASE HELP ME FIND MY SISTER...?

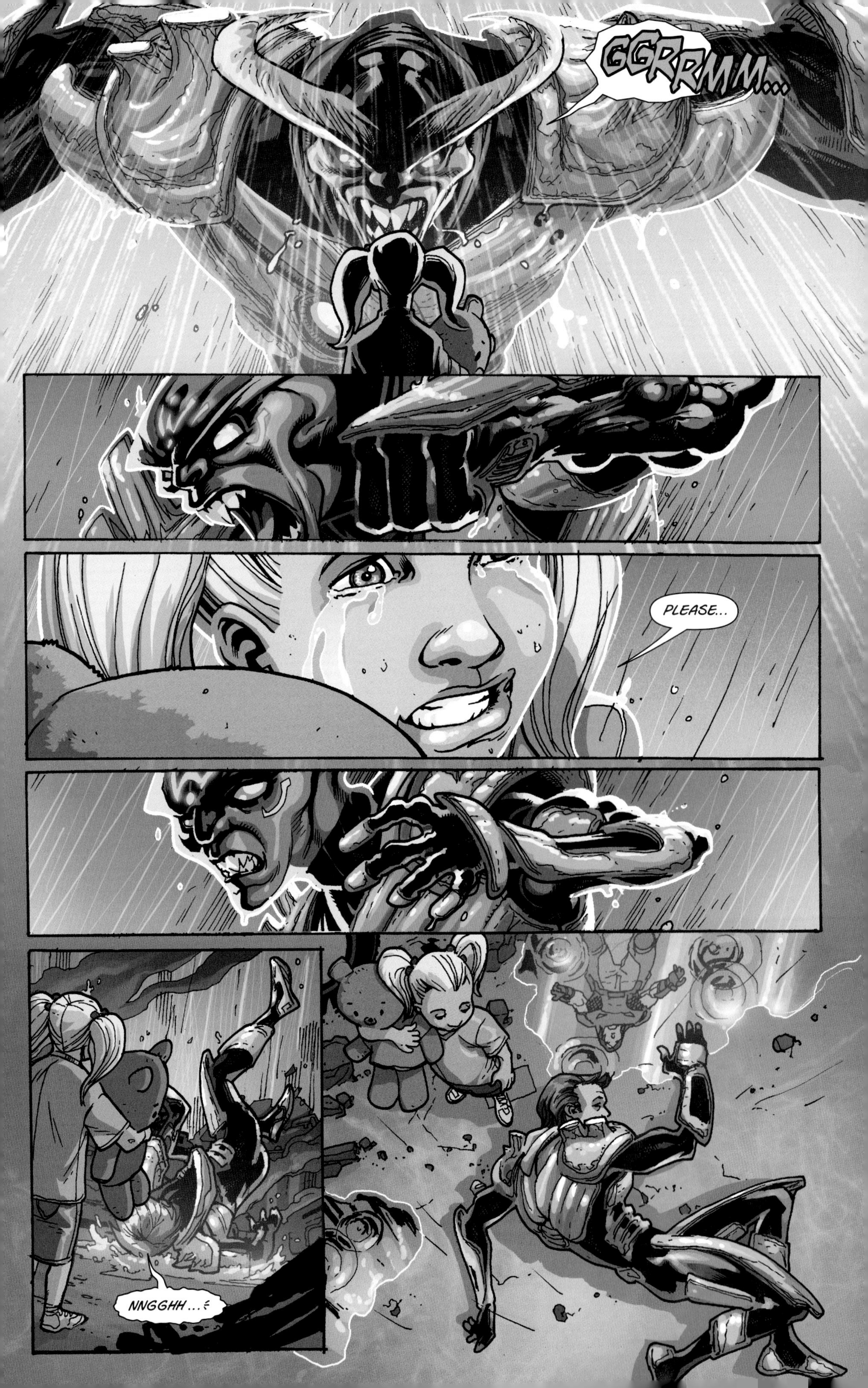
GGRRMM...
PLEASE...
NNGGHH...

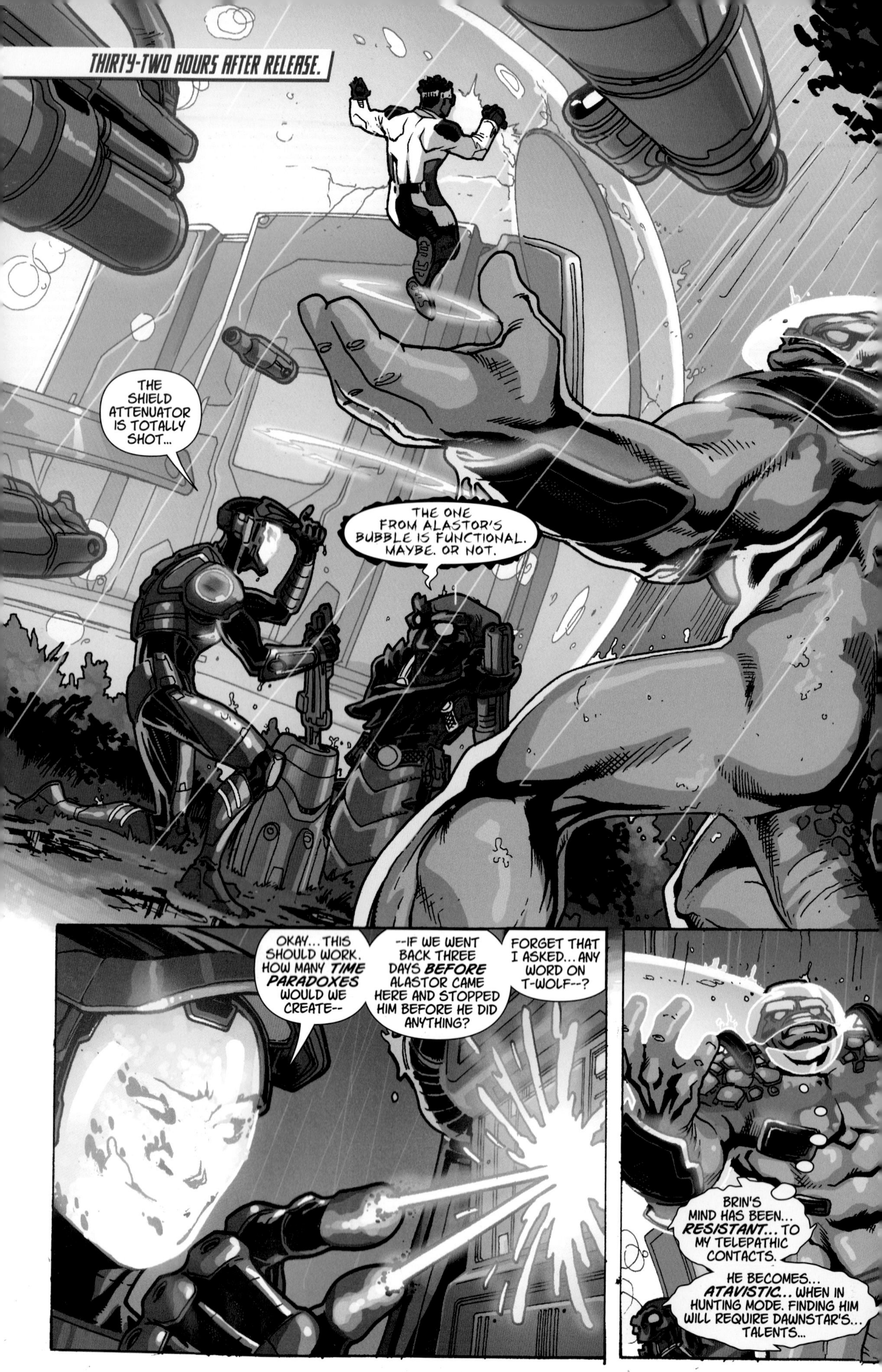
THIRTY-TWO HOURS AFTER RELEASE.
THE SHIELD ATTENUATOR IS TOTALLY SHOT...
THE ONE FROM ALASTOR'S BUBBLE IS FUNCTIONAL. MAYBE. OR NOT.
OKAY... THIS SHOULD WORK. HOW MANY *TIME PARADOXES* WOULD WE CREATE--
--IF WE WENT BACK THREE DAYS *BEFORE* ALASTOR CAME HERE AND STOPPED HIM BEFORE HE DID ANYTHING?
FORGET THAT I ASKED... ANY WORD ON T-WOLF--?
BRIN'S MIND HAS BEEN... *RESISTANT*... TO MY TELEPATHIC CONTACTS.
HE BECOMES... *ATAVISTIC*... WHEN IN HUNTING MODE. FINDING HIM WILL REQUIRE DAWNSTAR'S... TALENTS...

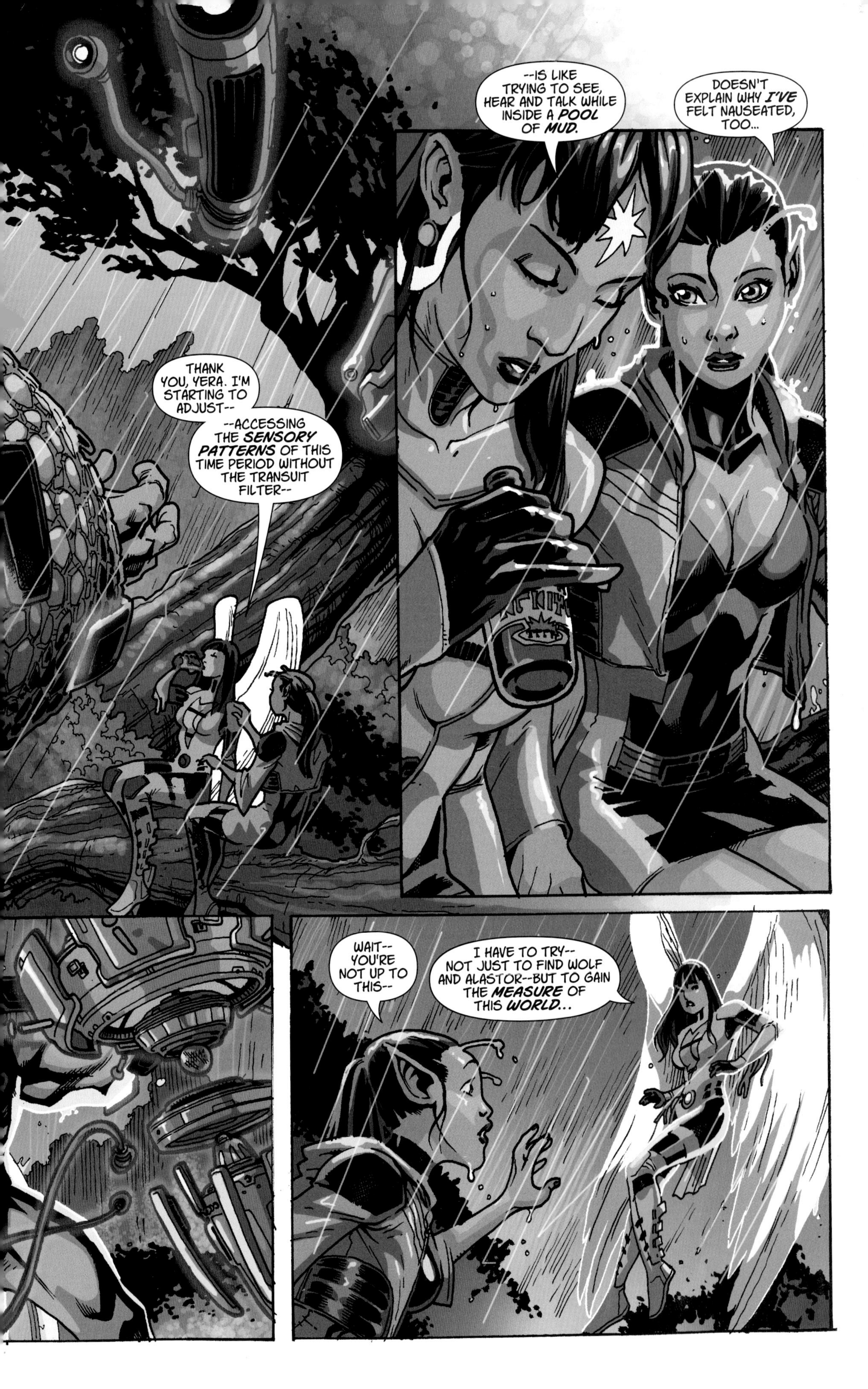
--IS LIKE TRYING TO SEE, HEAR AND TALK WHILE INSIDE A *POOL* OF *MUD*.
DOESN'T EXPLAIN WHY *I'VE* FELT NAUSEATED, TOO...
THANK YOU, YERA. I'M STARTING TO ADJUST--
--ACCESSING THE *SENSORY PATTERNS* OF THIS TIME PERIOD WITHOUT THE TRANSUIT FILTER--
WAIT--YOU'RE NOT UP TO THIS--
I HAVE TO TRY--NOT JUST TO FIND WOLF AND ALASTOR--BUT TO GAIN THE *MEASURE* OF THIS *WORLD*...

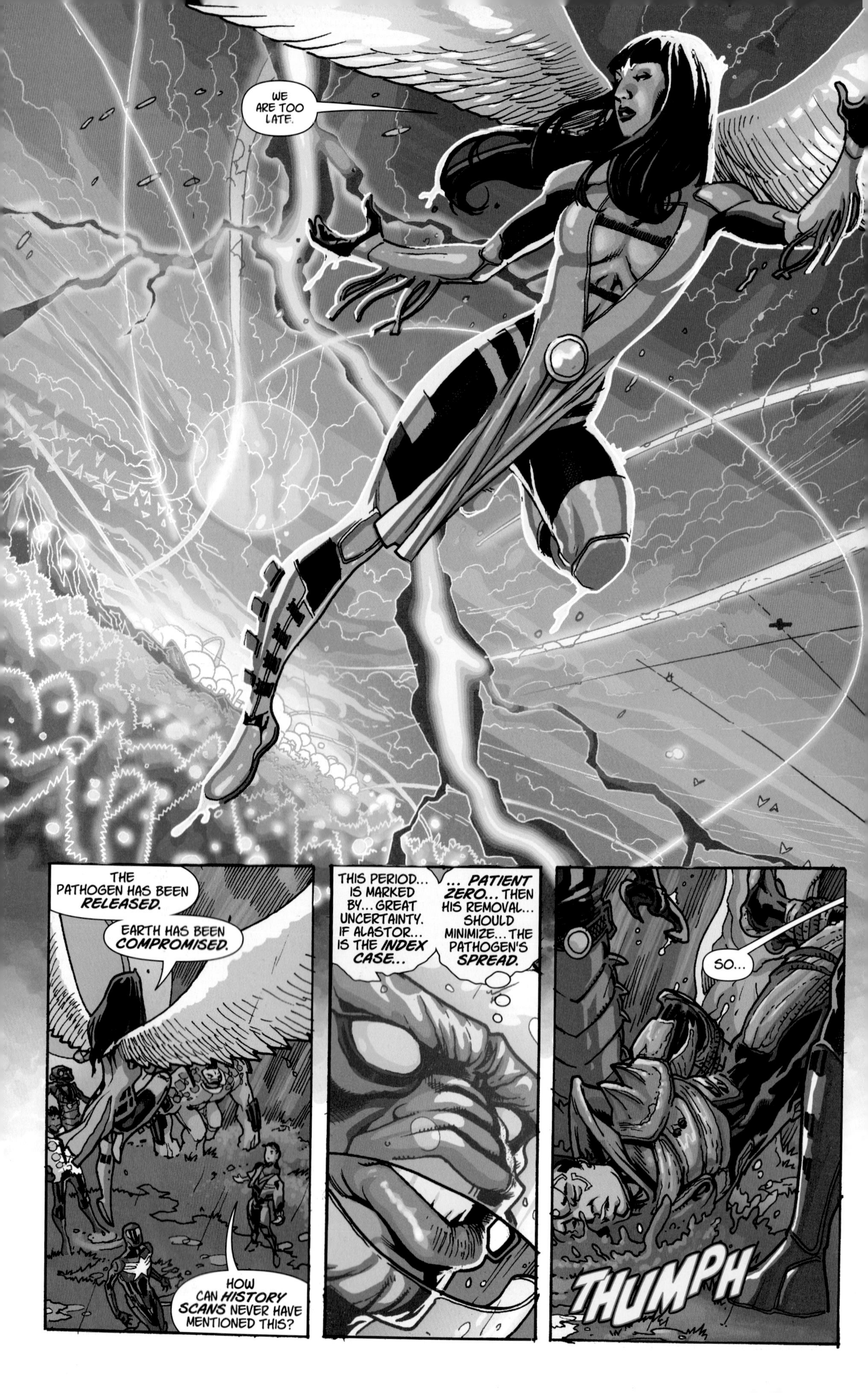
WE ARE TOO LATE.
THE PATHOGEN HAS BEEN RELEASED.
EARTH HAS BEEN COMPROMISED.
HOW CAN HISTORY SCANS NEVER HAVE MENTIONED THIS?
THIS PERIOD... IS MARKED BY... GREAT UNCERTAINTY. IF ALASTOR... IS THE INDEX CASE...
... PATIENT ZERO... THEN HIS REMOVAL... SHOULD MINIMIZE... THE PATHOGEN'S SPREAD.
SO...
THUMPH

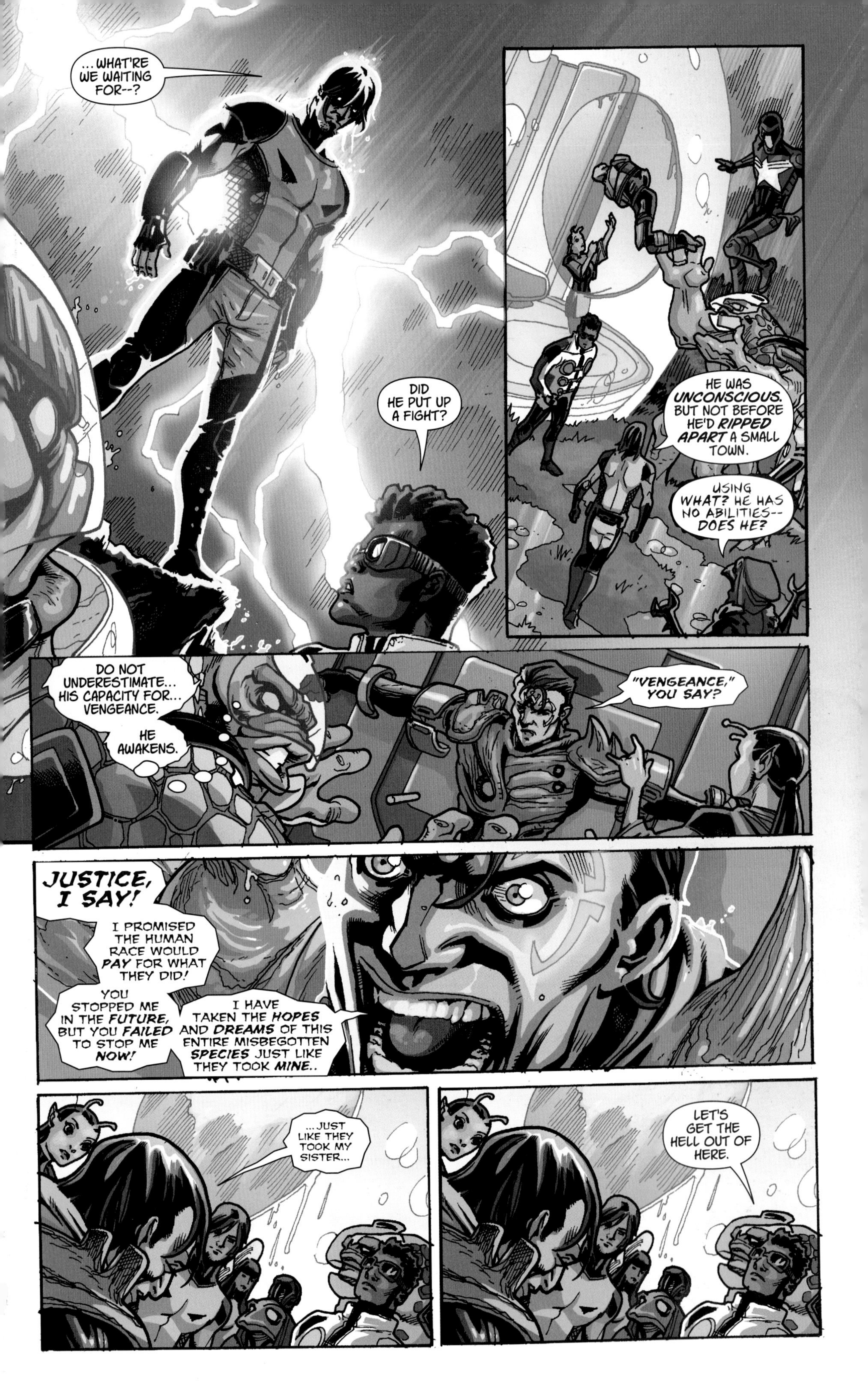
...WHAT'RE WE WAITING FOR--?
DID HE PUT UP A FIGHT?
HE WAS UNCONSCIOUS. BUT NOT BEFORE HE'D RIPPED APART A SMALL TOWN.
USING WHAT? HE HAS NO ABILITIES-- DOES HE?
DO NOT UNDERESTIMATE... HIS CAPACITY FOR... VENGEANCE.
HE AWAKENS.
"VENGEANCE," YOU SAY?
JUSTICE, I SAY!
I PROMISED THE HUMAN RACE WOULD PAY FOR WHAT THEY DID!
YOU STOPPED ME IN THE FUTURE, BUT YOU FAILED TO STOP ME NOW!
I HAVE TAKEN THE HOPES AND DREAMS OF THIS ENTIRE MISBEGOTTEN SPECIES JUST LIKE THEY TOOK MINE..
...JUST LIKE THEY TOOK MY SISTER...
LET'S GET THE HELL OUT OF HERE.

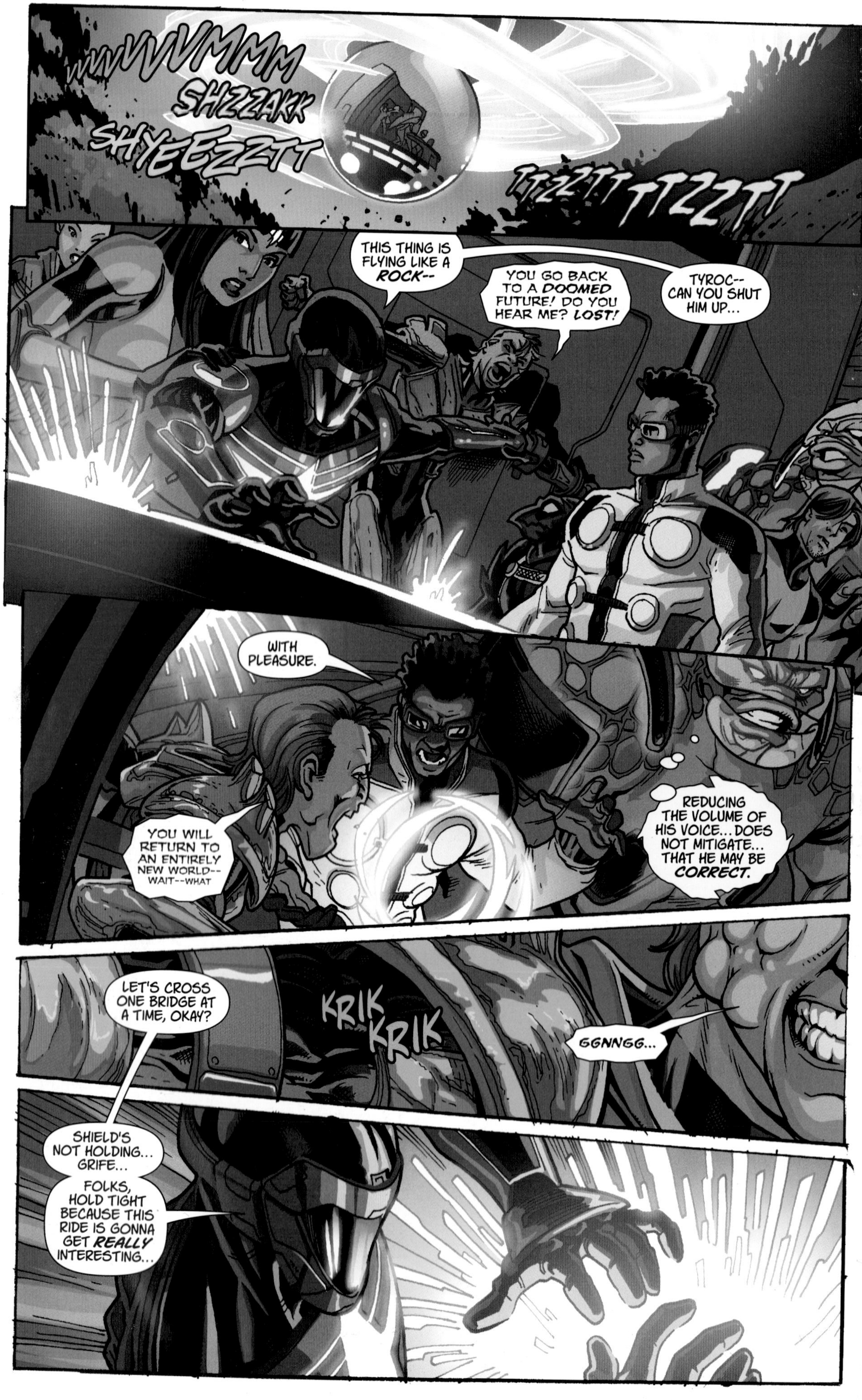
VVVVVVVMMMM
SHZZAKK
SHYEEZZZTT
TTZZTT TTZZTT
THIS THING IS FLYING LIKE A ROCK--
YOU GO BACK TO A DOOMED FUTURE! DO YOU HEAR ME? LOST!
TYROC-- CAN YOU SHUT HIM UP...
WITH PLEASURE.
YOU WILL RETURN TO AN ENTIRELY NEW WORLD-- WAIT--WHAT
REDUCING THE VOLUME OF HIS VOICE... DOES NOT MITIGATE... THAT HE MAY BE CORRECT.
LET'S CROSS ONE BRIDGE AT A TIME, OKAY?
KRIK KRIK
GGNNGG...
SHIELD'S NOT HOLDING... GRIFE...
FOLKS, HOLD TIGHT BECAUSE THIS RIDE IS GONNA GET REALLY INTERESTING...

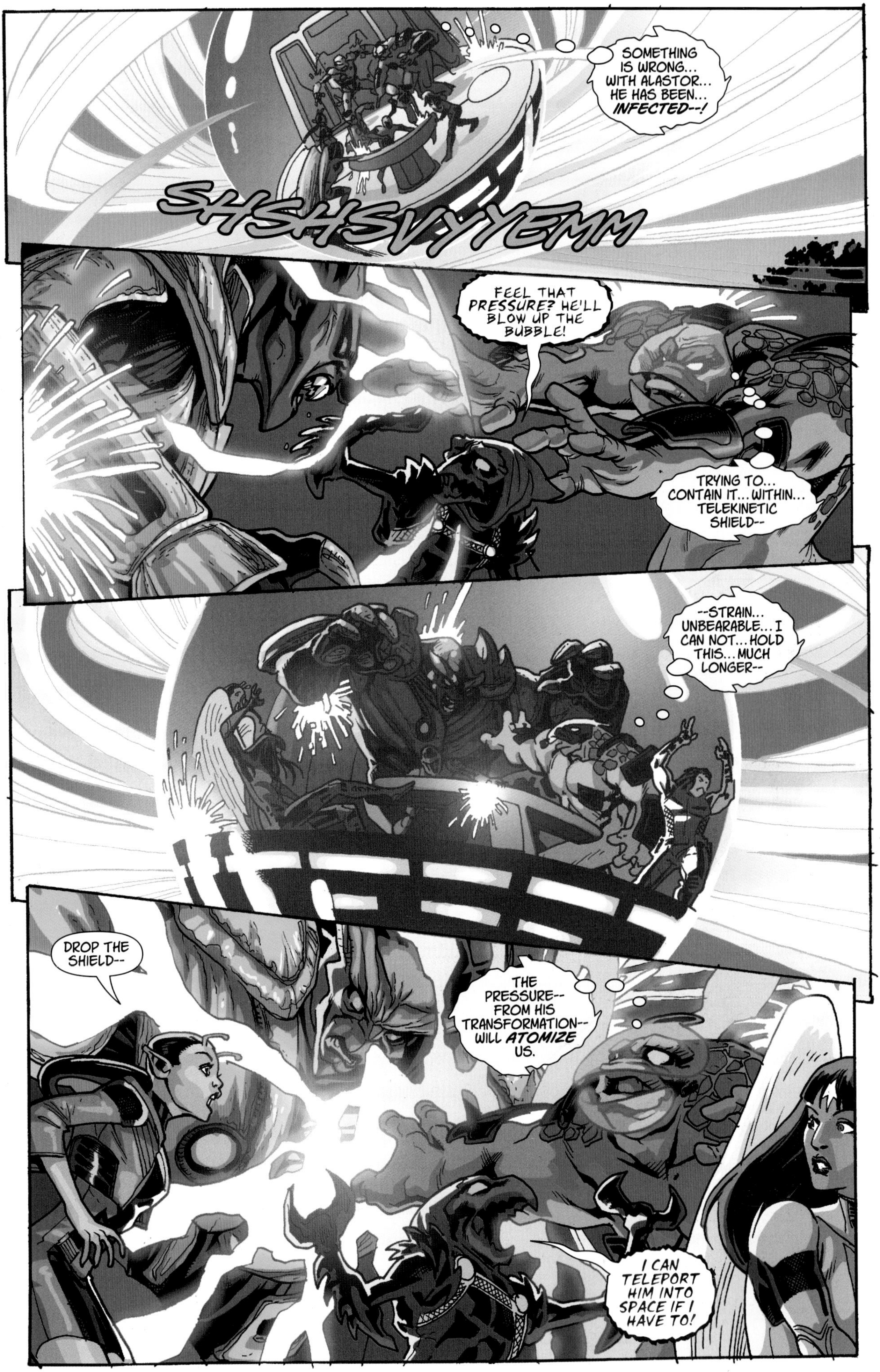
SOMETHING IS WRONG... WITH ALASTOR... HE HAS BEEN... INFECTED--!
SHSHSVYYEMM
FEEL THAT PRESSURE? HE'LL BLOW UP THE BUBBLE!
TRYING TO... CONTAIN IT... WITHIN... TELEKINETIC SHIELD--
--STRAIN... UNBEARABLE... I CAN NOT... HOLD THIS... MUCH LONGER--
DROP THE SHIELD--
THE PRESSURE-- FROM HIS TRANSFORMATION-- WILL ATOMIZE US.
I CAN TELEPORT HIM INTO SPACE IF I HAVE TO!

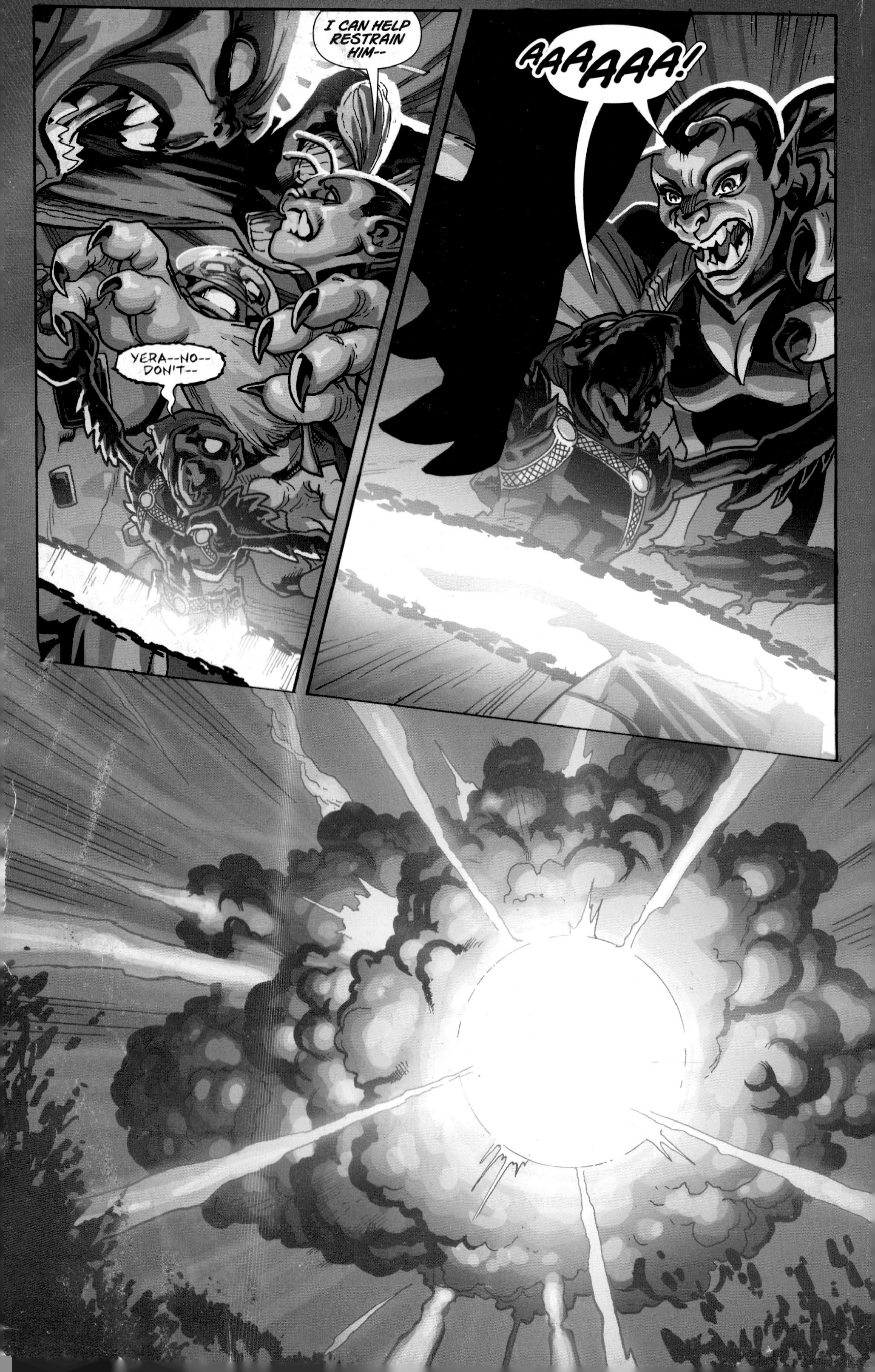

I CAN HELP RESTRAIN HIM--
YERA--NO--DON'T--
AAAAAA!

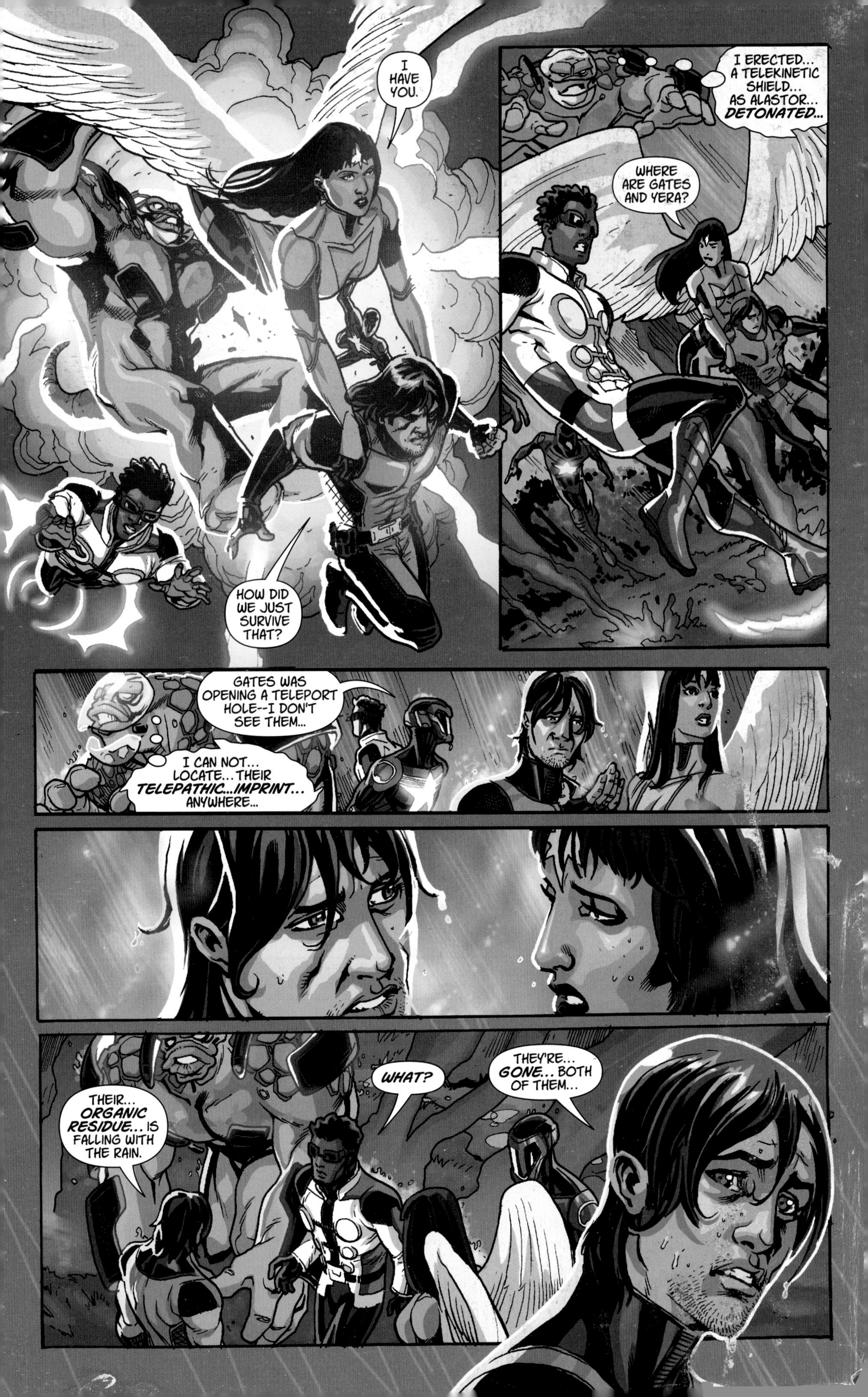

I HAVE YOU.
HOW DID WE JUST SURVIVE THAT?
I ERECTED... A TELEKINETIC SHIELD... AS ALASTOR... DETONATED...
WHERE ARE GATES AND YERA?
GATES WAS OPENING A TELEPORT HOLE--I DON'T SEE THEM...
I CAN NOT... LOCATE... THEIR TELEPATHIC...IMPRINT... ANYWHERE...
THEIR... ORGANIC RESIDUE... IS FALLING WITH THE RAIN.
WHAT?
THEY'RE... GONE... BOTH OF THEM...

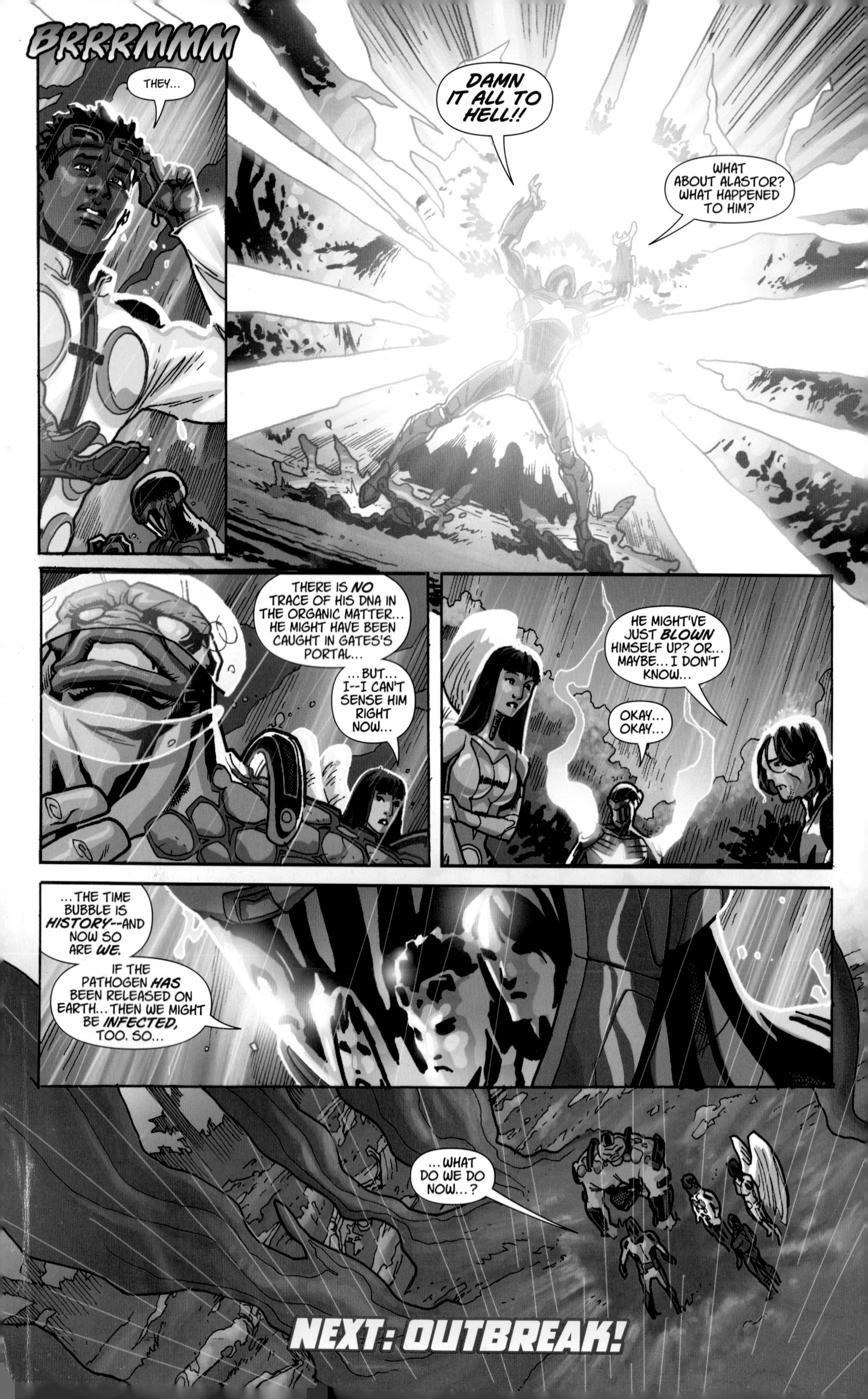
BRRRMMMM
THEY...
DAMN IT ALL TO HELL!!
WHAT ABOUT ALASTOR? WHAT HAPPENED TO HIM?
THERE IS NO TRACE OF HIS DNA IN THE ORGANIC MATTER... HE MIGHT HAVE BEEN CAUGHT IN GATES'S PORTAL...
...BUT... I--I CAN'T SENSE HIM RIGHT NOW...
HE MIGHT'VE JUST BLOWN HIMSELF UP? OR... MAYBE... I DON'T KNOW...
OKAY... OKAY...
...THE TIME BUBBLE IS HISTORY--AND NOW SO ARE WE.
IF THE PATHOGEN HAS BEEN RELEASED ON EARTH... THEN WE MIGHT BE INFECTED, TOO. SO...
...WHAT DO WE DO NOW...?
NEXT: OUTBREAK!

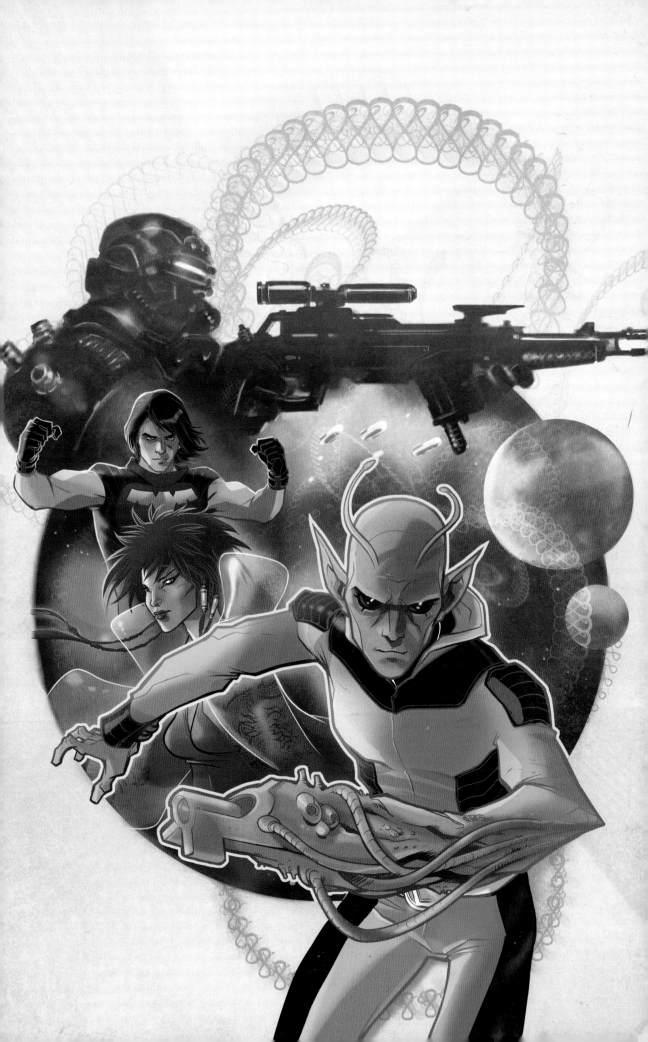

LEGION OF SUPER-HEROES

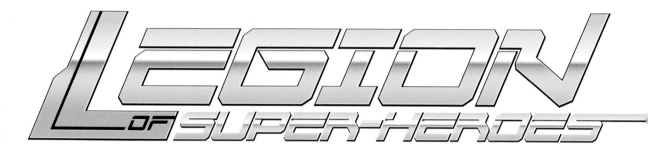

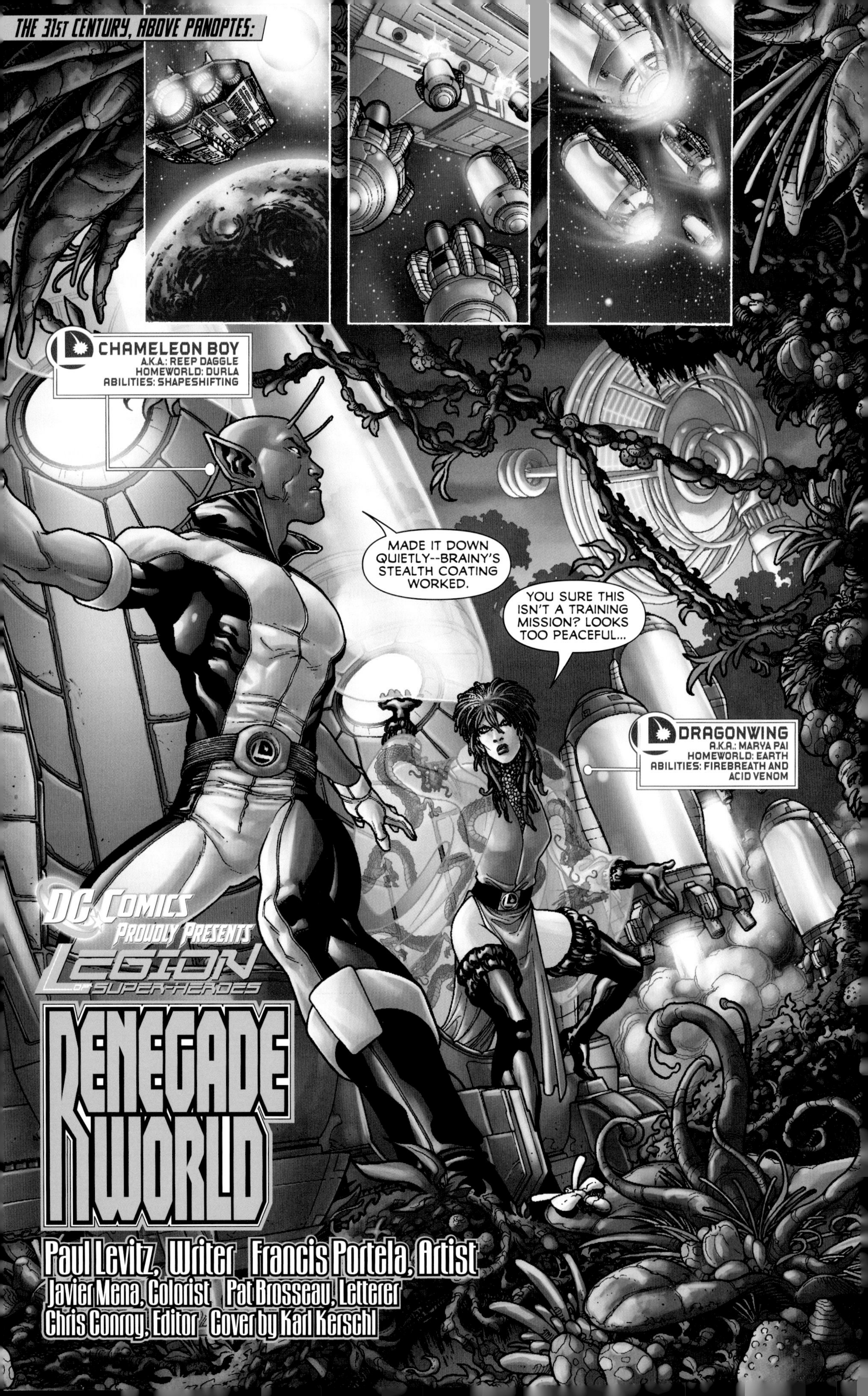
THE 31ST CENTURY, ABOVE PANOPTES:
CHAMELEON BOY
A.K.A.: REEP DAGGLE
HOMEWORLD: DURLA
ABILITIES: SHAPESHIFTING
MADE IT DOWN QUIETLY--BRAINY'S STEALTH COATING WORKED.
YOU SURE THIS ISN'T A TRAINING MISSION? LOOKS TOO PEACEFUL...
DRAGONWING
A.K.A.: MARYA PAI
HOMEWORLD: EARTH
ABILITIES: FIREBREATH AND ACID VENOM
DC COMICS PROUDLY PRESENTS
LEGION OF SUPER-HEROES
RENEGADE WORLD
Paul Levitz, Writer Francis Portela, Artist
Javier Mena, Colorist Pat Brosseau, Letterer
Chris Conroy, Editor Cover by Karl Kerschl

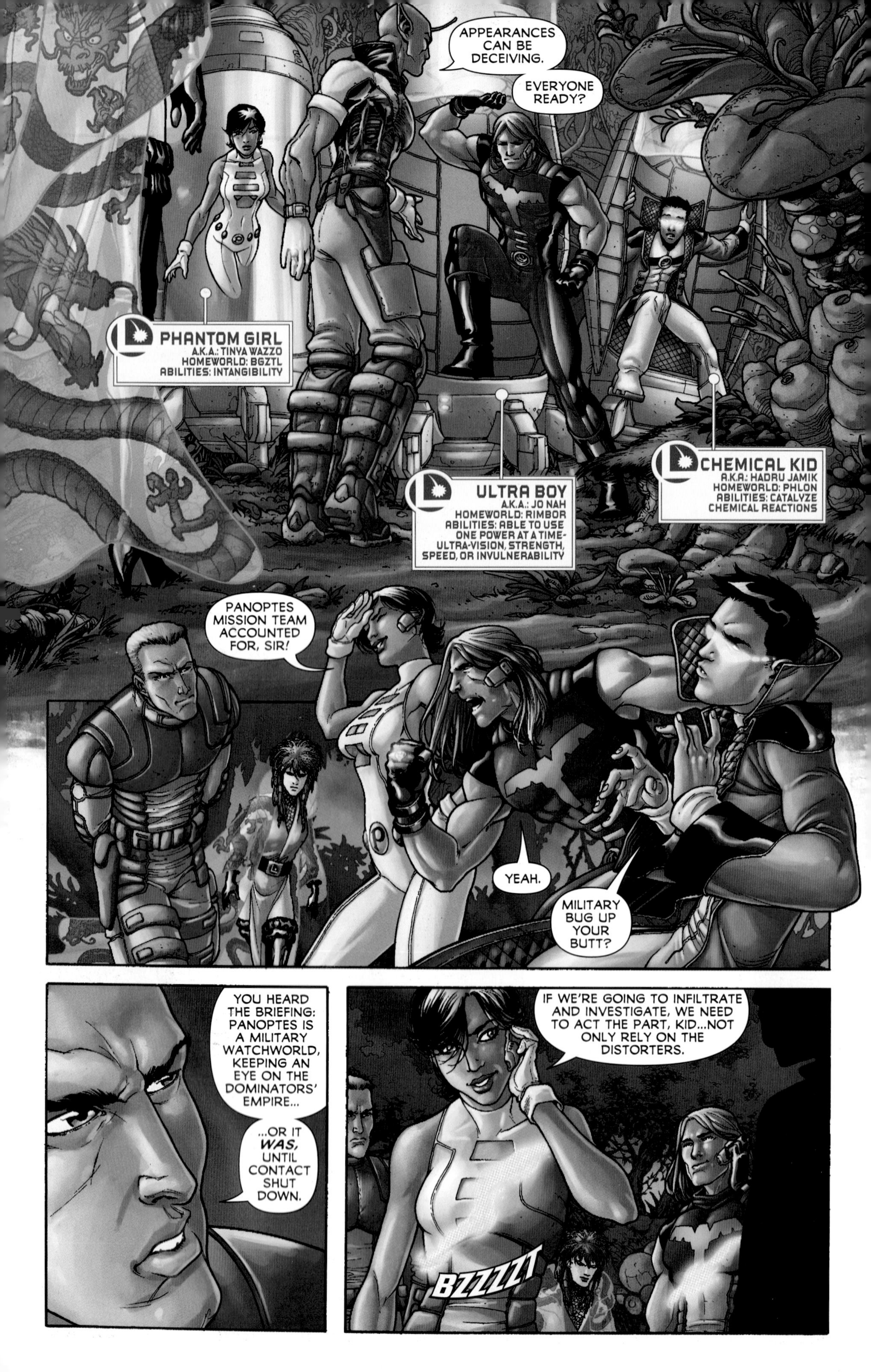
APPEARANCES CAN BE DECEIVING.
EVERYONE READY?
PHANTOM GIRL
A.K.A.: TINYA WAZZO
HOMEWORLD: BGZTL
ABILITIES: INTANGIBILITY
ULTRA BOY
A.K.A.: JO NAH
HOMEWORLD: RIMBOR
ABILITIES: ABLE TO USE ONE POWER AT A TIME- ULTRA-VISION, STRENGTH, SPEED, OR INVULNERABILITY
CHEMICAL KID
A.K.A.: HADRU JAMIK
HOMEWORLD: PHLON
ABILITIES: CATALYZE CHEMICAL REACTIONS
PANOPTES MISSION TEAM ACCOUNTED FOR, SIR!
YEAH.
MILITARY BUG UP YOUR BUTT?
YOU HEARD THE BRIEFING: PANOPTES IS A MILITARY WATCHWORLD, KEEPING AN EYE ON THE DOMINATORS' EMPIRE...
...OR IT *WAS,* UNTIL CONTACT SHUT DOWN.
IF WE'RE GOING TO INFILTRATE AND INVESTIGATE, WE NEED TO ACT THE PART, KID...NOT ONLY RELY ON THE DISTORTERS.
BZZZZT

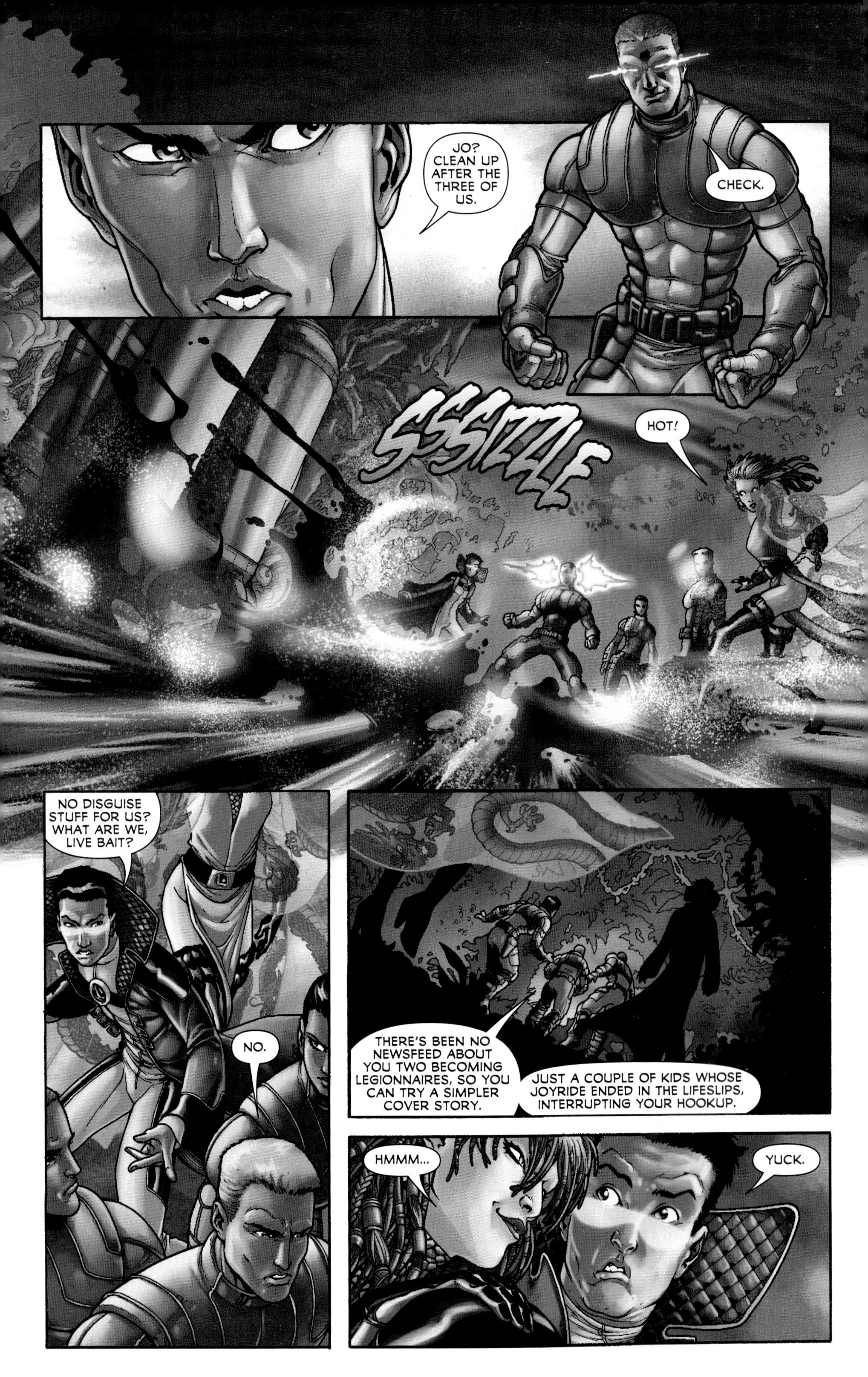
JO? CLEAN UP AFTER THE THREE OF US.
CHECK.
SSSIZZLE
HOT!
NO DISGUISE STUFF FOR US? WHAT ARE WE, LIVE BAIT?
NO.
THERE'S BEEN NO NEWSFEED ABOUT YOU TWO BECOMING LEGIONNAIRES, SO YOU CAN TRY A SIMPLER COVER STORY.
JUST A COUPLE OF KIDS WHOSE JOYRIDE ENDED IN THE LIFESLIPS, INTERRUPTING YOUR HOOKUP.
HMMM...
YUCK.

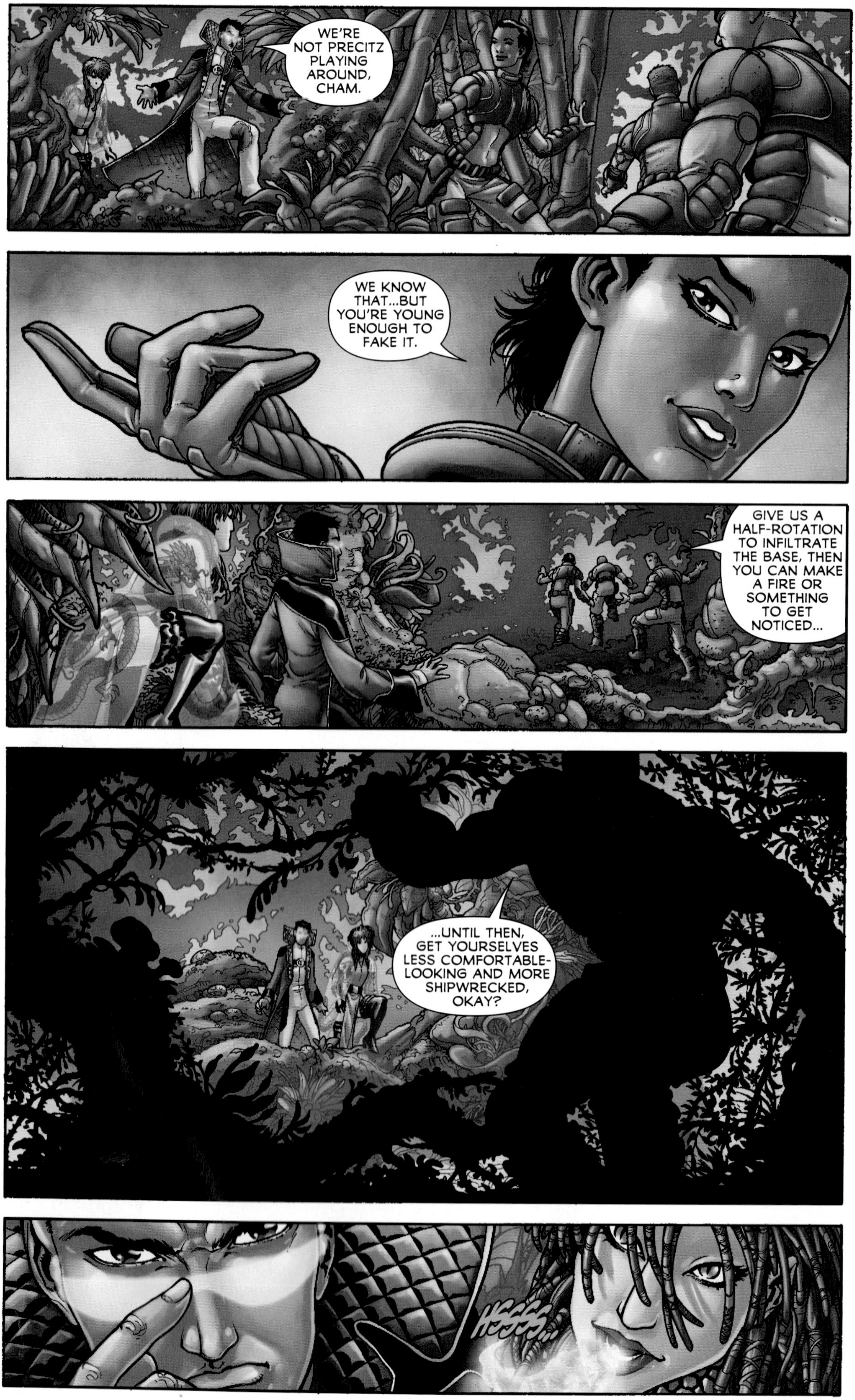
WE'RE NOT PRECITZ PLAYING AROUND, CHAM.
WE KNOW THAT...BUT YOU'RE YOUNG ENOUGH TO FAKE IT.
GIVE US A HALF-ROTATION TO INFILTRATE THE BASE, THEN YOU CAN MAKE A FIRE OR SOMETHING TO GET NOTICED...
...UNTIL THEN, GET YOURSELVES LESS COMFORTABLE-LOOKING AND MORE SHIPWRECKED, OKAY?
HSSSS...

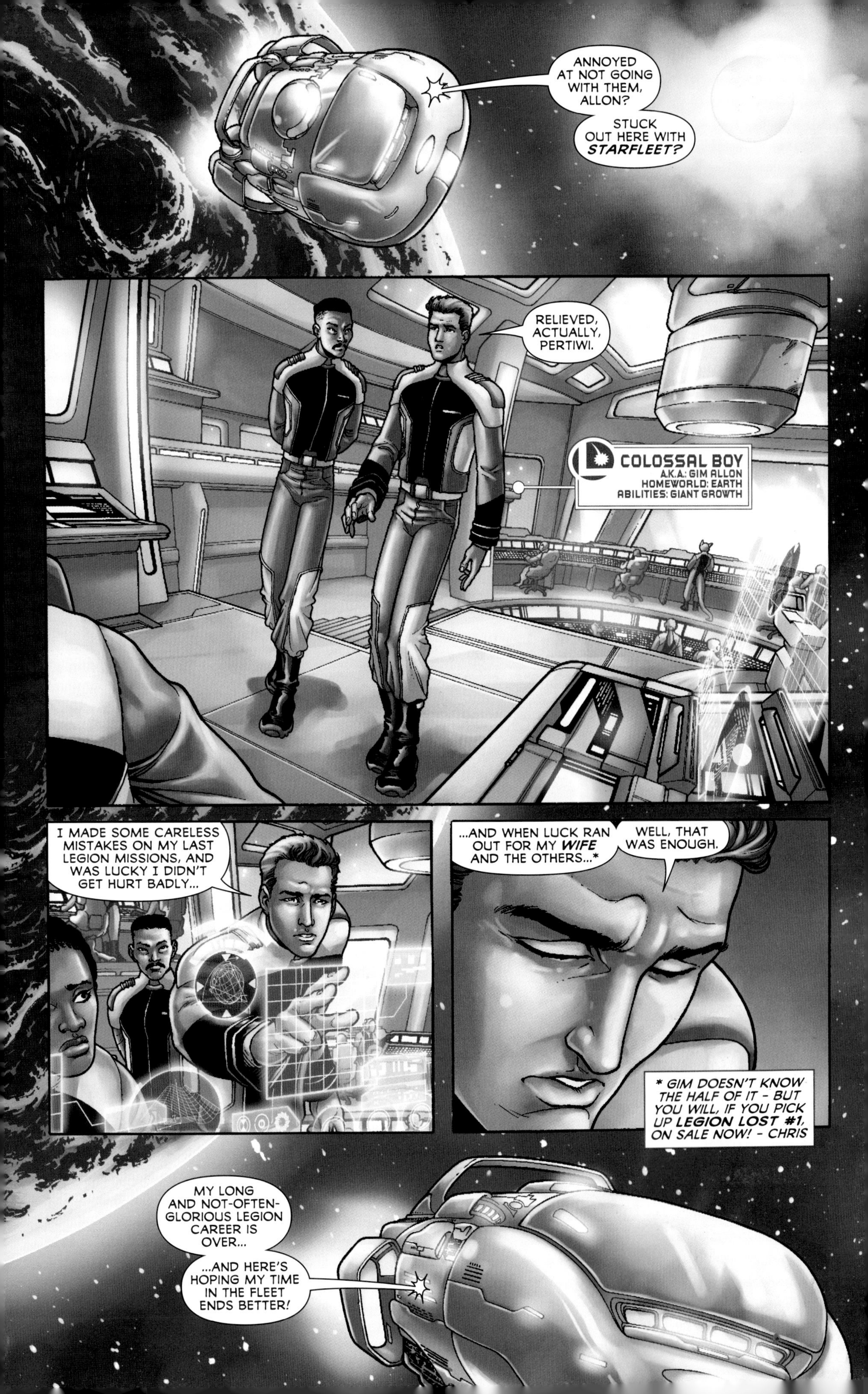
ANNOYED AT NOT GOING WITH THEM, ALLON?
STUCK OUT HERE WITH STARFLEET?
RELIEVED, ACTUALLY, PERTIWI.
COLOSSAL BOY
A.K.A.: GIM ALLON
HOMEWORLD: EARTH
ABILITIES: GIANT GROWTH
I MADE SOME CARELESS MISTAKES ON MY LAST LEGION MISSIONS, AND WAS LUCKY I DIDN'T GET HURT BADLY...
...AND WHEN LUCK RAN OUT FOR MY WIFE AND THE OTHERS...*
WELL, THAT WAS ENOUGH.
* GIM DOESN'T KNOW THE HALF OF IT - BUT YOU WILL, IF YOU PICK UP LEGION LOST #1, ON SALE NOW! - CHRIS
MY LONG AND NOT-OFTEN-GLORIOUS LEGION CAREER IS OVER...
...AND HERE'S HOPING MY TIME IN THE FLEET ENDS BETTER!

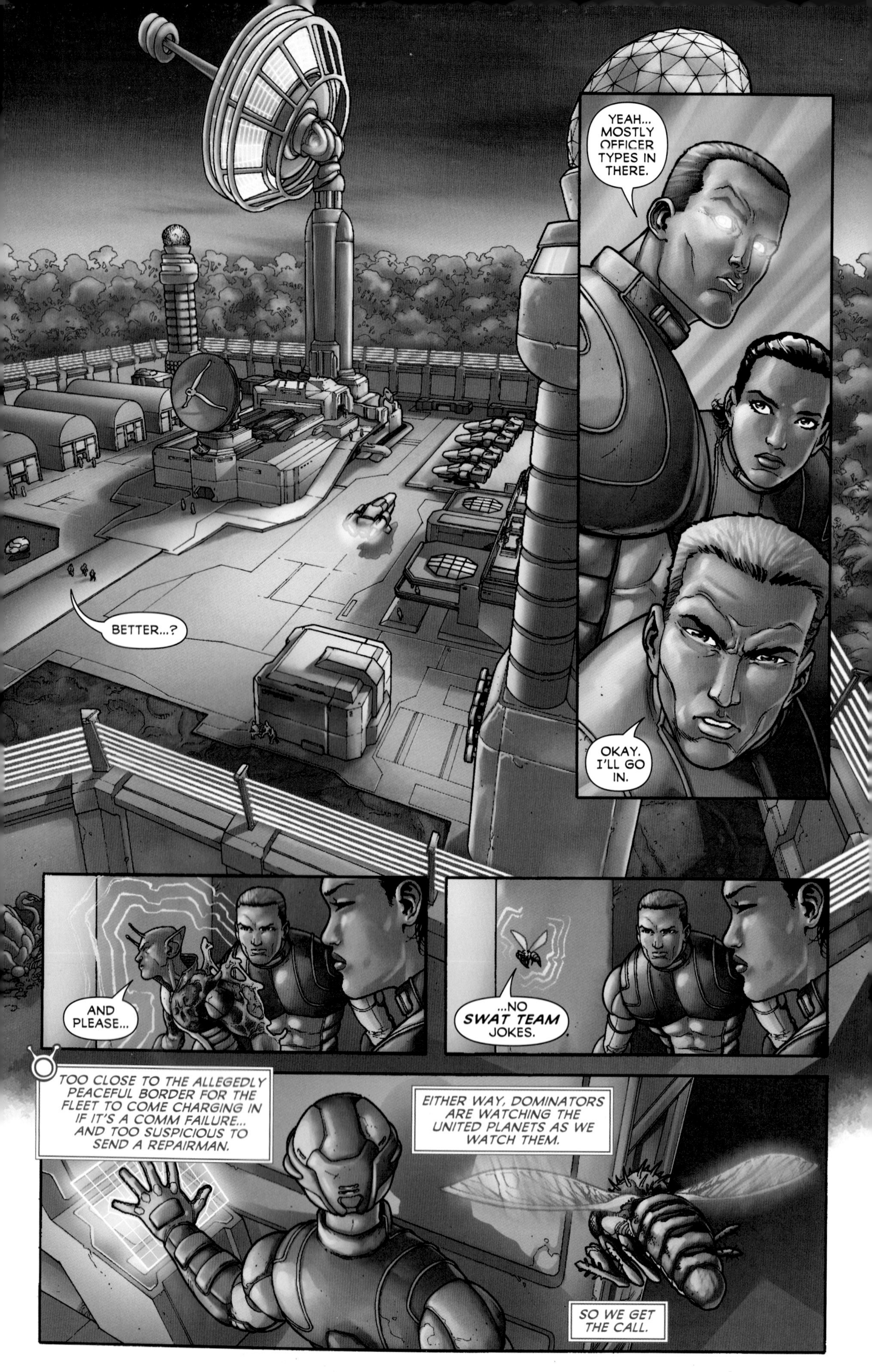

YEAH... MOSTLY OFFICER TYPES IN THERE.
BETTER...?
OKAY. I'LL GO IN.
AND PLEASE...
...NO SWAT TEAM JOKES.
TOO CLOSE TO THE ALLEGEDLY PEACEFUL BORDER FOR THE FLEET TO COME CHARGING IN IF IT'S A COMM FAILURE... AND TOO SUSPICIOUS TO SEND A REPAIRMAN.
EITHER WAY, DOMINATORS ARE WATCHING THE UNITED PLANETS AS WE WATCH THEM.
SO WE GET THE CALL.

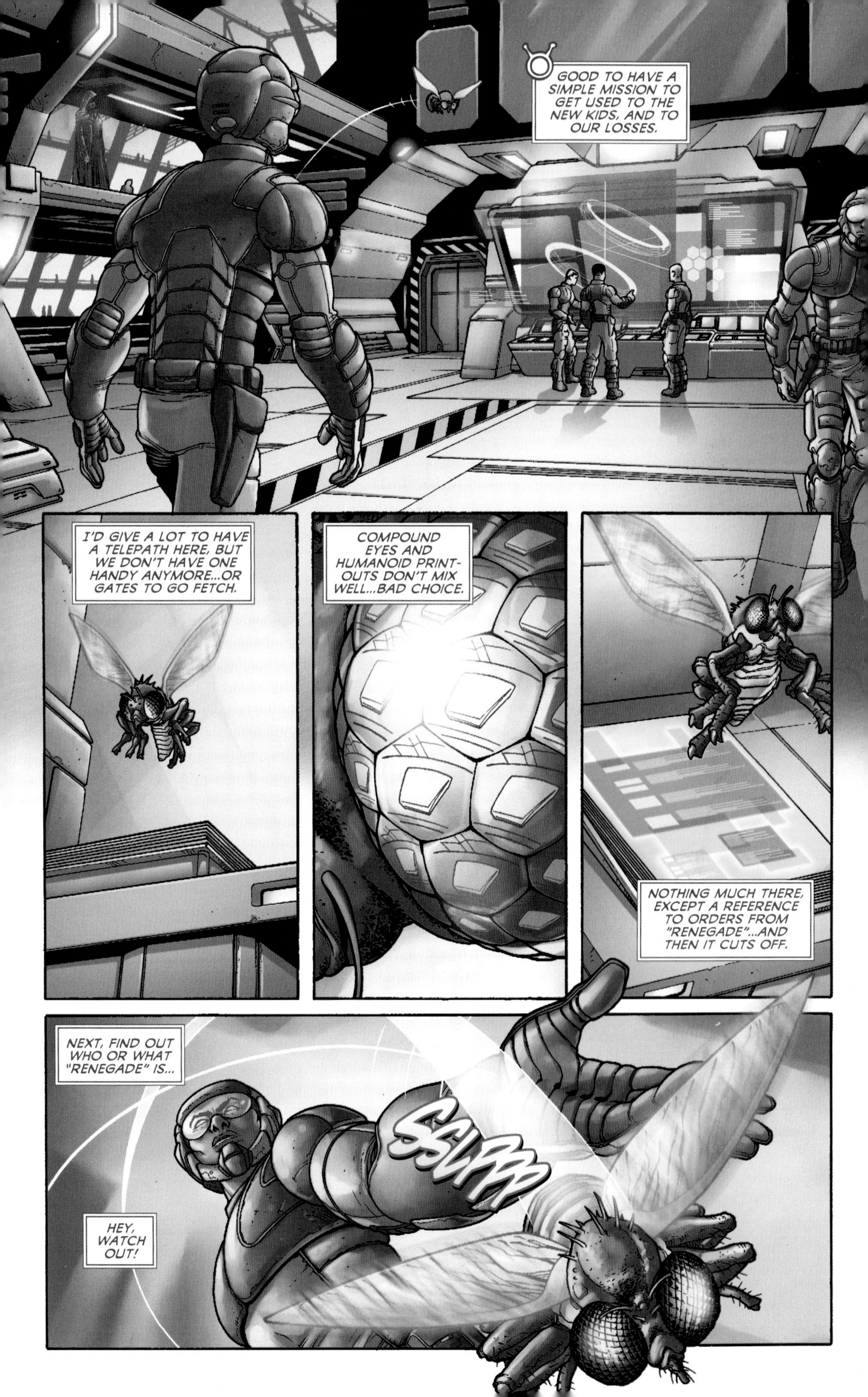
GOOD TO HAVE A SIMPLE MISSION TO GET USED TO THE NEW KIDS, AND TO OUR LOSSES.
I'D GIVE A LOT TO HAVE A TELEPATH HERE, BUT WE DON'T HAVE ONE HANDY ANYMORE...OR GATES TO GO FETCH.
COMPOUND EYES AND HUMANOID PRINT-OUTS DON'T MIX WELL...BAD CHOICE.
NOTHING MUCH THERE, EXCEPT A REFERENCE TO ORDERS FROM "RENEGADE"...AND THEN IT CUTS OFF.
NEXT, FIND OUT WHO OR WHAT "RENEGADE" IS...
SSUPPP
HEY, WATCH OUT!

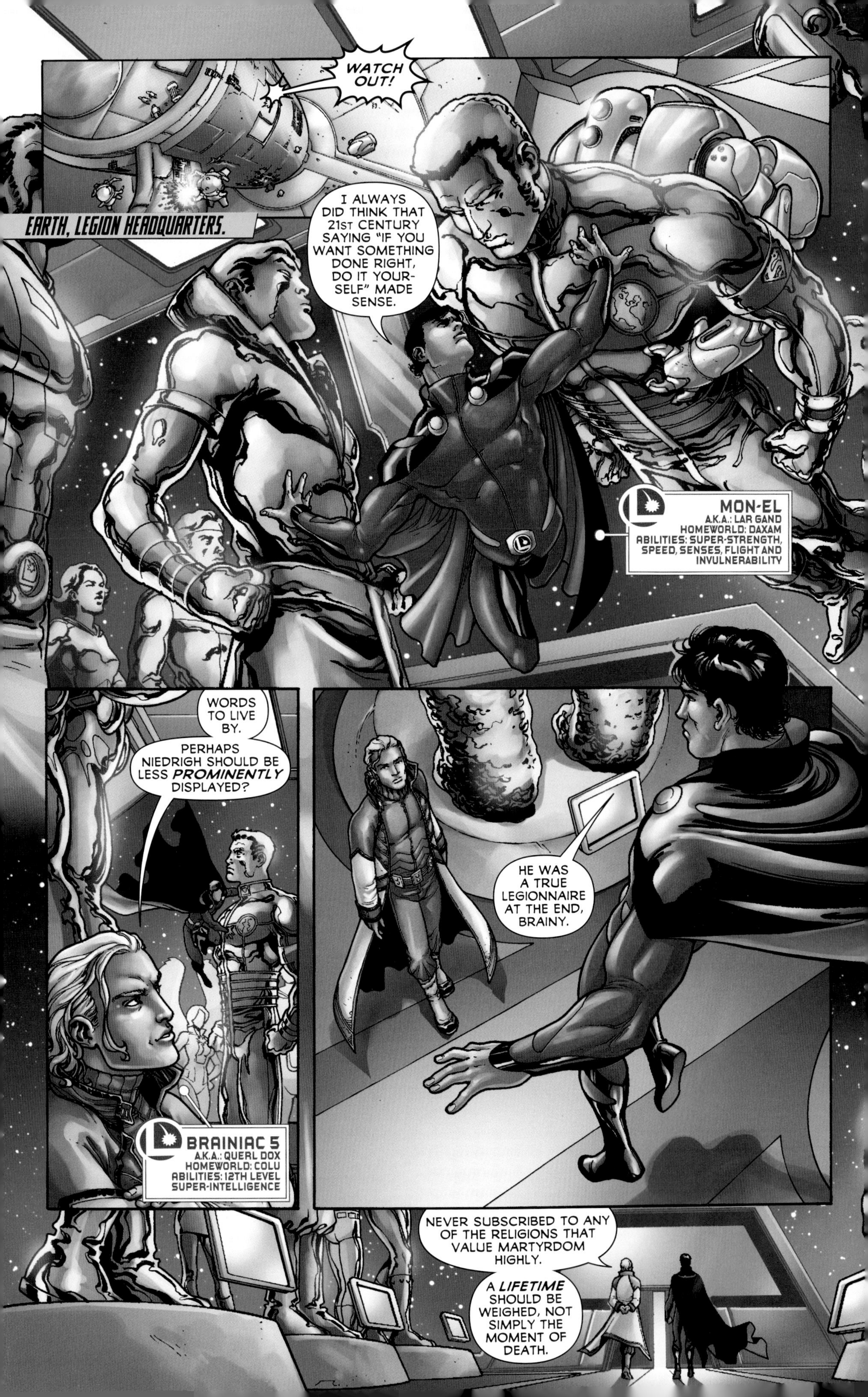
WATCH OUT!
EARTH, LEGION HEADQUARTERS.
I ALWAYS DID THINK THAT 21ST CENTURY SAYING "IF YOU WANT SOMETHING DONE RIGHT, DO IT YOURSELF" MADE SENSE.
MON-EL
A.K.A.: LAR GAND
HOMEWORLD: DAXAM
ABILITIES: SUPER-STRENGTH, SPEED, SENSES, FLIGHT AND INVULNERABILITY
WORDS TO LIVE BY.
PERHAPS NIEDRIGH SHOULD BE LESS PROMINENTLY DISPLAYED?
BRAINIAC 5
A.K.A.: QUERL DOX
HOMEWORLD: COLU
ABILITIES: 12TH LEVEL SUPER-INTELLIGENCE
HE WAS A TRUE LEGIONNAIRE AT THE END, BRAINY.
NEVER SUBSCRIBED TO ANY OF THE RELIGIONS THAT VALUE MARTYRDOM HIGHLY.
A LIFETIME SHOULD BE WEIGHED, NOT SIMPLY THE MOMENT OF DEATH.

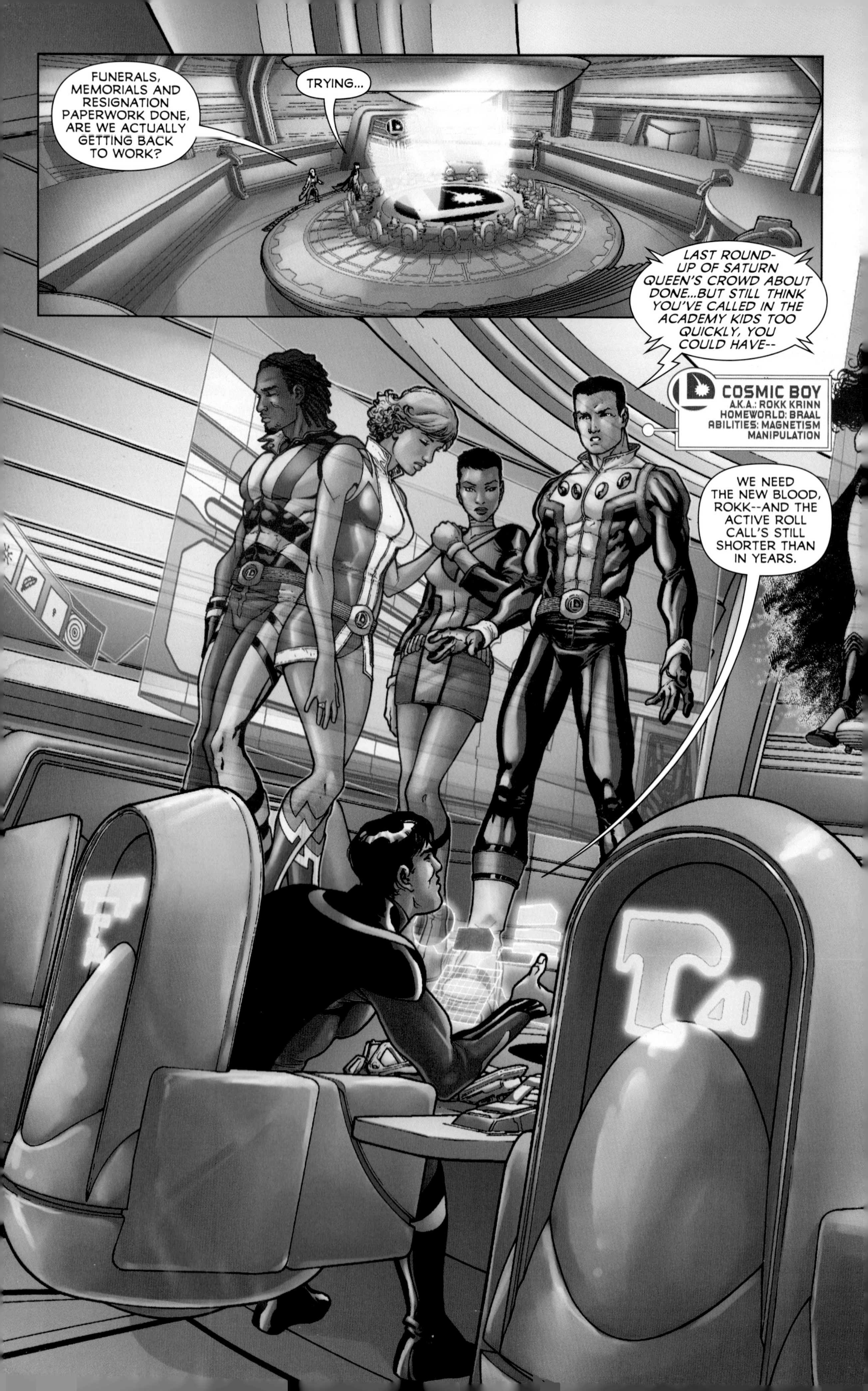

FUNERALS, MEMORIALS AND RESIGNATION PAPERWORK DONE, ARE WE ACTUALLY GETTING BACK TO WORK?
TRYING...
LAST ROUND-UP OF SATURN QUEEN'S CROWD ABOUT DONE...BUT STILL THINK YOU'VE CALLED IN THE ACADEMY KIDS TOO QUICKLY, YOU COULD HAVE--
COSMIC BOY
A.K.A.: ROKK KRINN
HOMEWORLD: BRAAL
ABILITIES: MAGNETISM MANIPULATION
WE NEED THE NEW BLOOD, ROKK--AND THE ACTIVE ROLL CALL'S STILL SHORTER THAN IN YEARS.

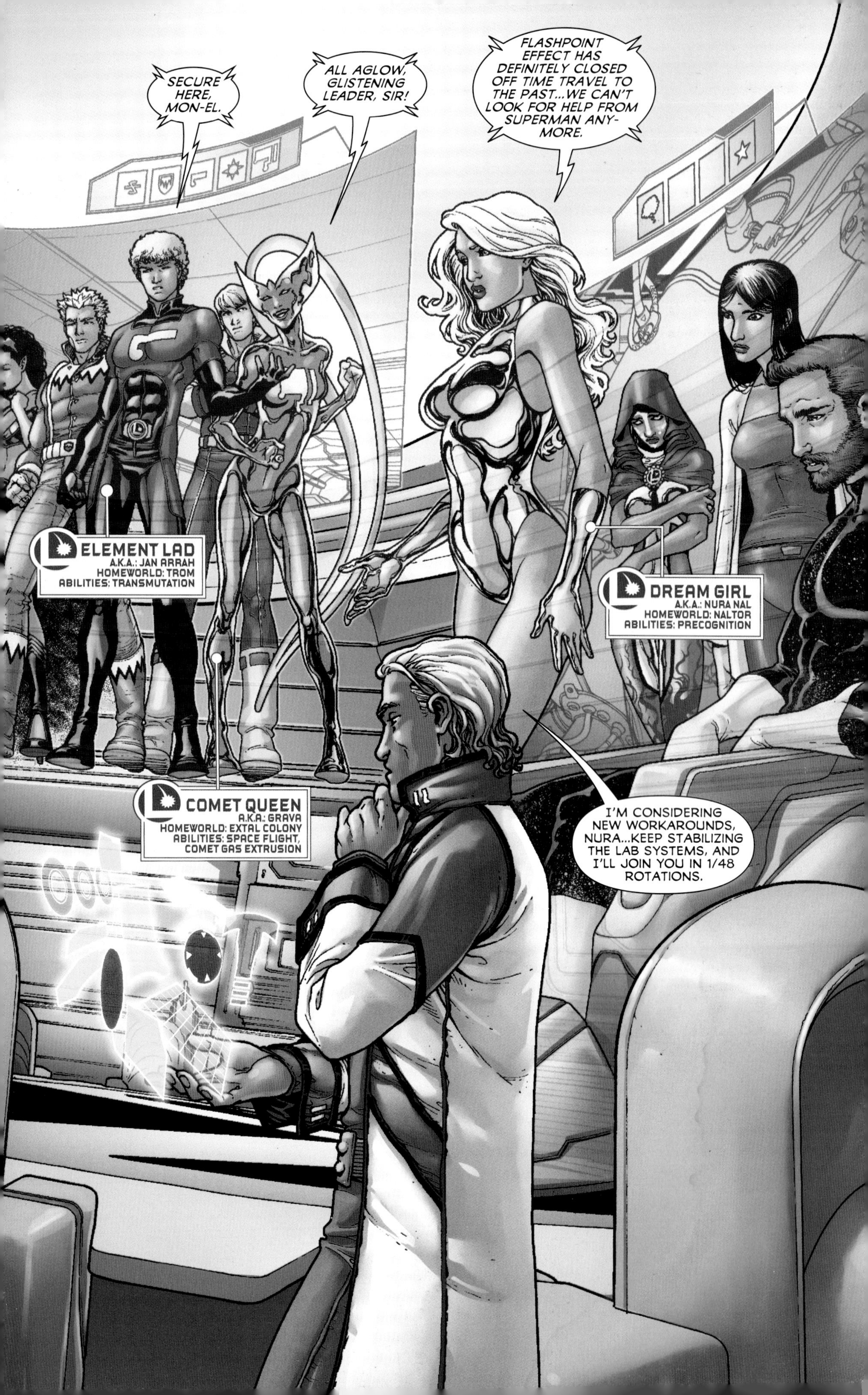

SECURE HERE, MON-EL.
ALL AGLOW, GLISTENING LEADER, SIR!
FLASHPOINT EFFECT HAS DEFINITELY CLOSED OFF TIME TRAVEL TO THE PAST...WE CAN'T LOOK FOR HELP FROM SUPERMAN ANY-MORE.
ELEMENT LAD A.K.A.: JAN ARRAH HOMEWORLD: TROM ABILITIES: TRANSMUTATION
DREAM GIRL A.K.A.: NURA NAL HOMEWORLD: NALTOR ABILITIES: PRECOGNITION
COMET QUEEN A.K.A.: GRAVA HOMEWORLD: EXTAL COLONY ABILITIES: SPACE FLIGHT, COMET GAS EXTRUSION
I'M CONSIDERING NEW WORKAROUNDS, NURA...KEEP STABILIZING THE LAB SYSTEMS, AND I'LL JOIN YOU IN 1/48 ROTATIONS.

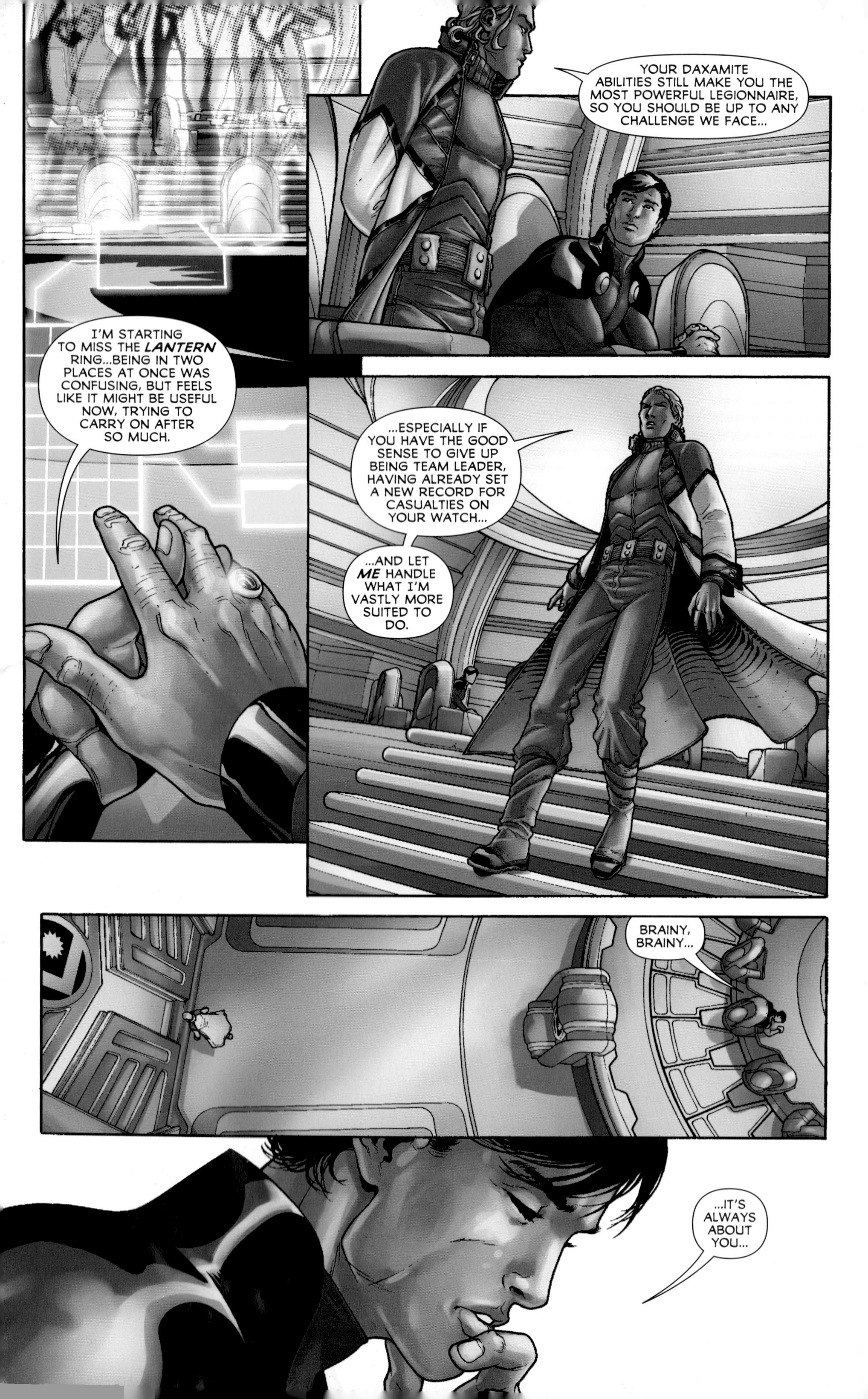
YOUR DAXAMITE ABILITIES STILL MAKE YOU THE MOST POWERFUL LEGIONNAIRE, SO YOU SHOULD BE UP TO ANY CHALLENGE WE FACE...
I'M STARTING TO MISS THE LANTERN RING...BEING IN TWO PLACES AT ONCE WAS CONFUSING, BUT FEELS LIKE IT MIGHT BE USEFUL NOW, TRYING TO CARRY ON AFTER SO MUCH.
...ESPECIALLY IF YOU HAVE THE GOOD SENSE TO GIVE UP BEING TEAM LEADER, HAVING ALREADY SET A NEW RECORD FOR CASUALTIES ON YOUR WATCH...
...AND LET ME HANDLE WHAT I'M VASTLY MORE SUITED TO DO.
BRAINY, BRAINY...
...IT'S ALWAYS ABOUT YOU...

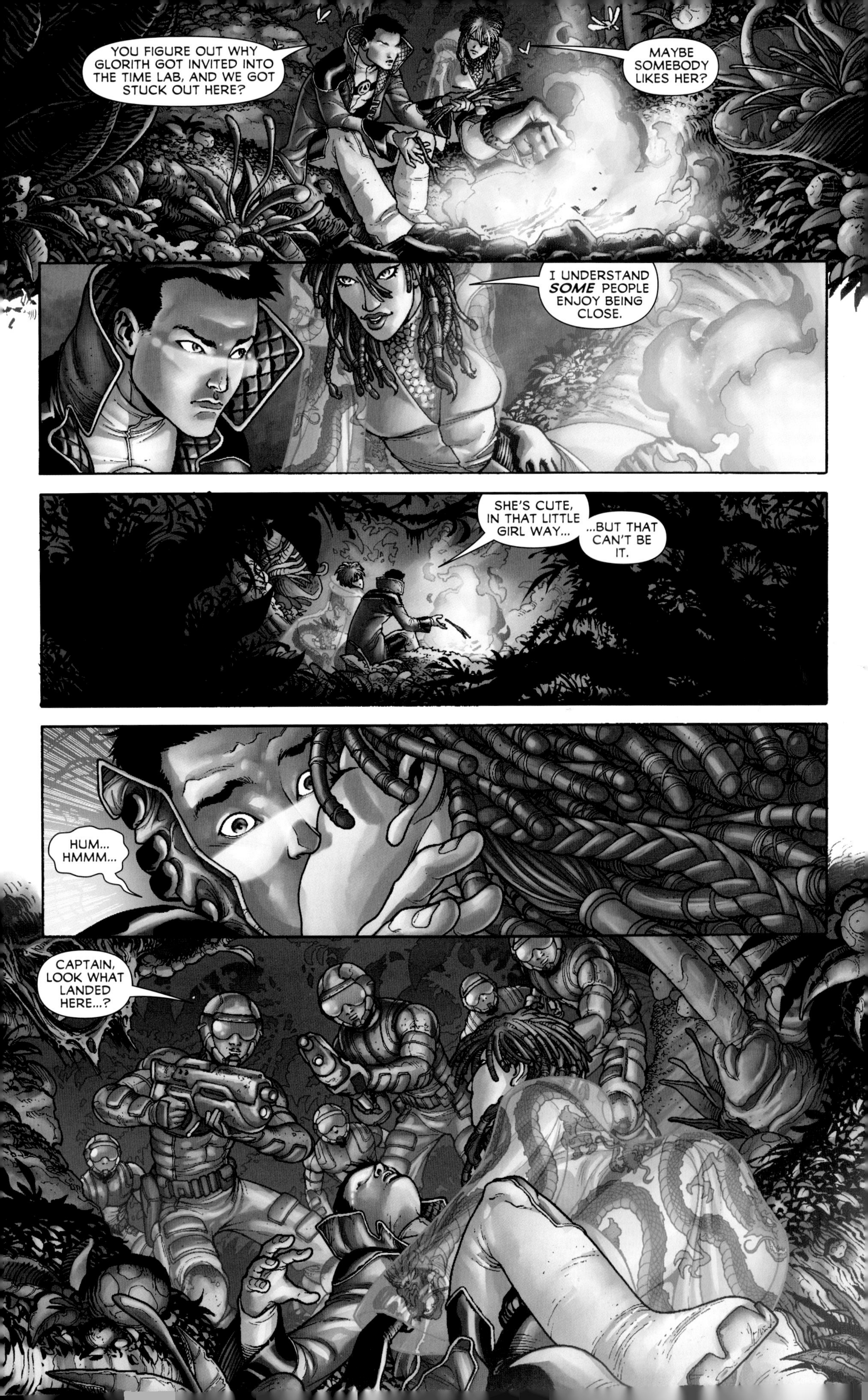
YOU FIGURE OUT WHY GLORITH GOT INVITED INTO THE TIME LAB, AND WE GOT STUCK OUT HERE?
MAYBE SOMEBODY LIKES HER?
I UNDERSTAND *SOME* PEOPLE ENJOY BEING CLOSE.
SHE'S CUTE, IN THAT LITTLE GIRL WAY...
...BUT THAT CAN'T BE IT.
HUM... HMMM...
CAPTAIN, LOOK WHAT LANDED HERE...?

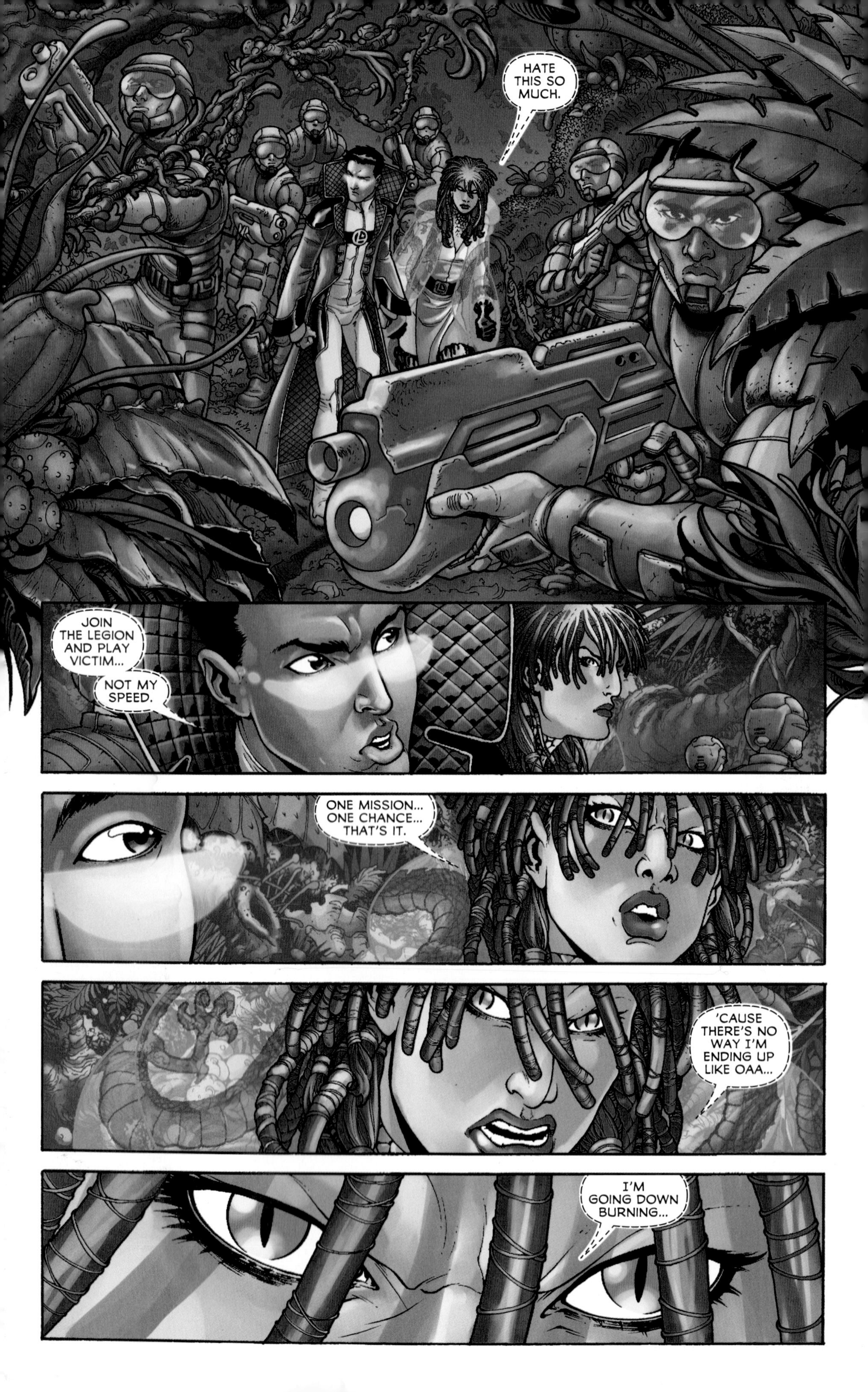
HATE THIS SO MUCH.
JOIN THE LEGION AND PLAY VICTIM...
NOT MY SPEED.
ONE MISSION... ONE CHANCE... THAT'S IT.
'CAUSE THERE'S NO WAY I'M ENDING UP LIKE OAA...
I'M GOING DOWN BURNING...

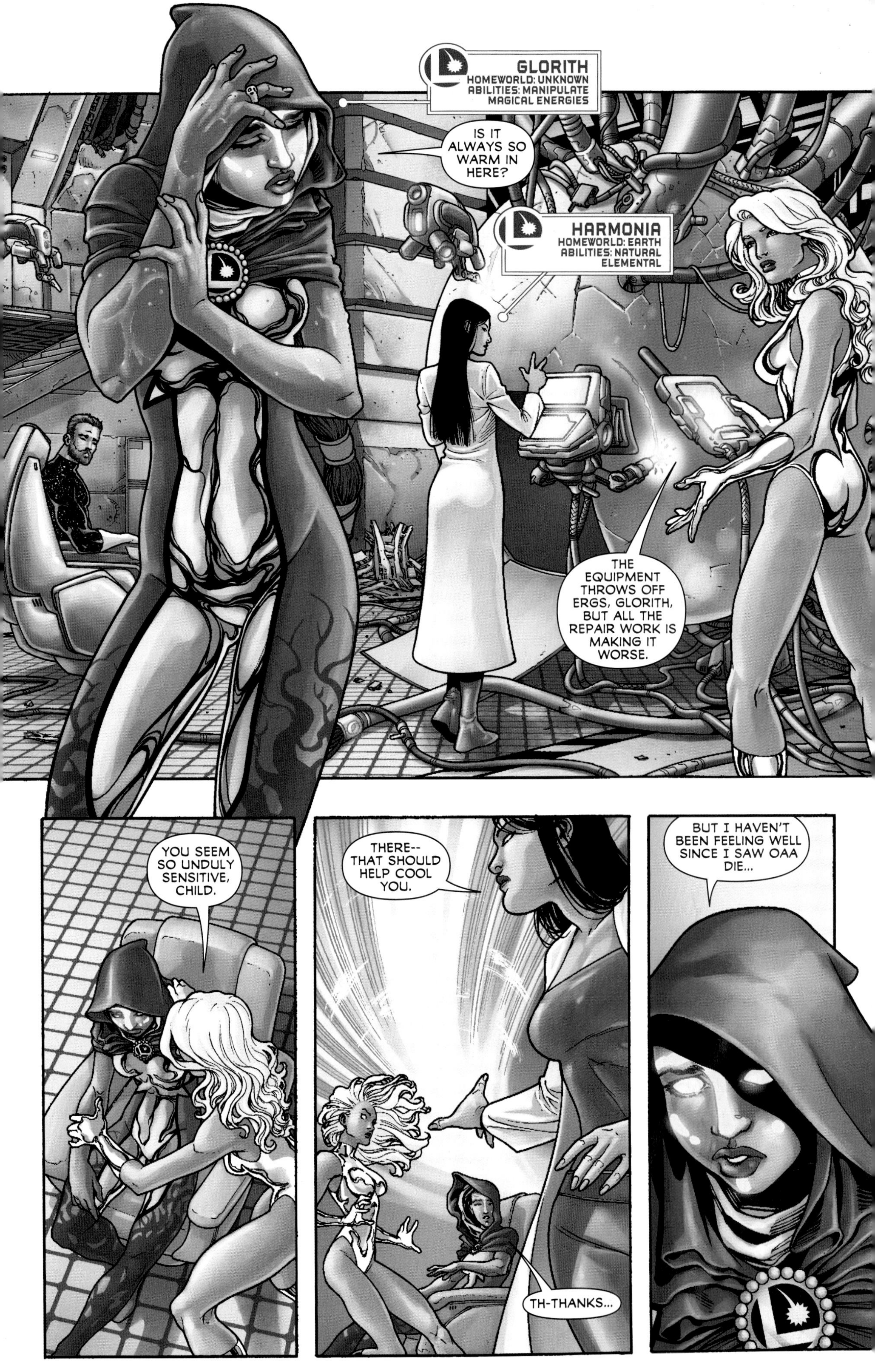
GLORITH
HOMEWORLD: UNKNOWN
ABILITIES: MANIPULATE MAGICAL ENERGIES
IS IT ALWAYS SO WARM IN HERE?
HARMONIA
HOMEWORLD: EARTH
ABILITIES: NATURAL ELEMENTAL
THE EQUIPMENT THROWS OFF ERGS, GLORITH, BUT ALL THE REPAIR WORK IS MAKING IT WORSE.
YOU SEEM SO UNDULY SENSITIVE, CHILD.
THERE-- THAT SHOULD HELP COOL YOU.
TH-THANKS...
BUT I HAVEN'T BEEN FEELING WELL SINCE I SAW OAA DIE...

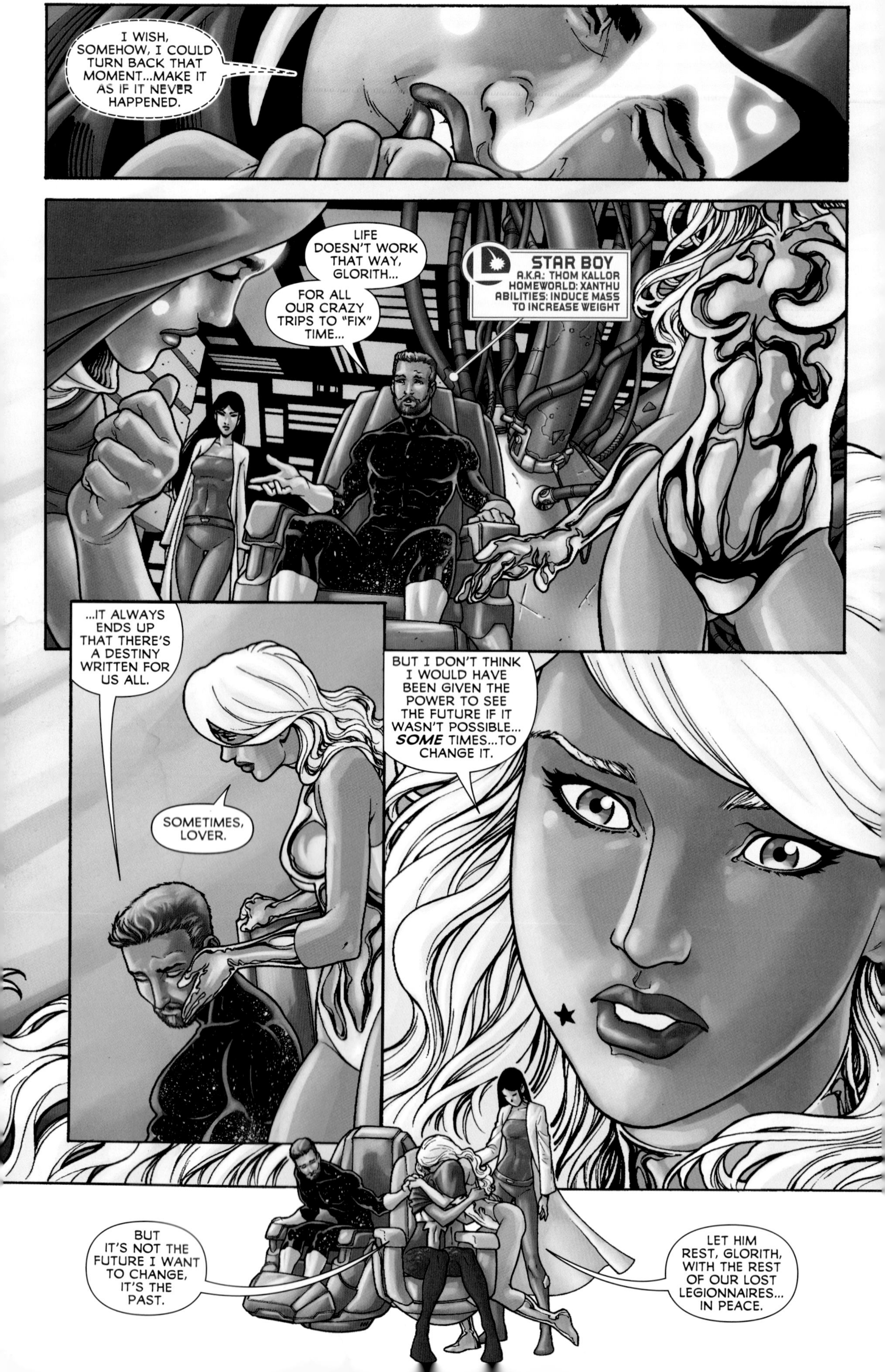
I WISH, SOMEHOW, I COULD TURN BACK THAT MOMENT...MAKE IT AS IF IT NEVER HAPPENED.
LIFE DOESN'T WORK THAT WAY, GLORITH...
FOR ALL OUR CRAZY TRIPS TO "FIX" TIME...
STAR BOY
A.K.A.: THOM KALLOR
HOMEWORLD: XANTHU
ABILITIES: INDUCE MASS TO INCREASE WEIGHT
...IT ALWAYS ENDS UP THAT THERE'S A DESTINY WRITTEN FOR US ALL.
SOMETIMES, LOVER.
BUT I DON'T THINK I WOULD HAVE BEEN GIVEN THE POWER TO SEE THE FUTURE IF IT WASN'T POSSIBLE... *SOME* TIMES...TO CHANGE IT.
BUT IT'S NOT THE FUTURE I WANT TO CHANGE, IT'S THE PAST.
LET HIM REST, GLORITH, WITH THE REST OF OUR LOST LEGIONNAIRES... IN PEACE.

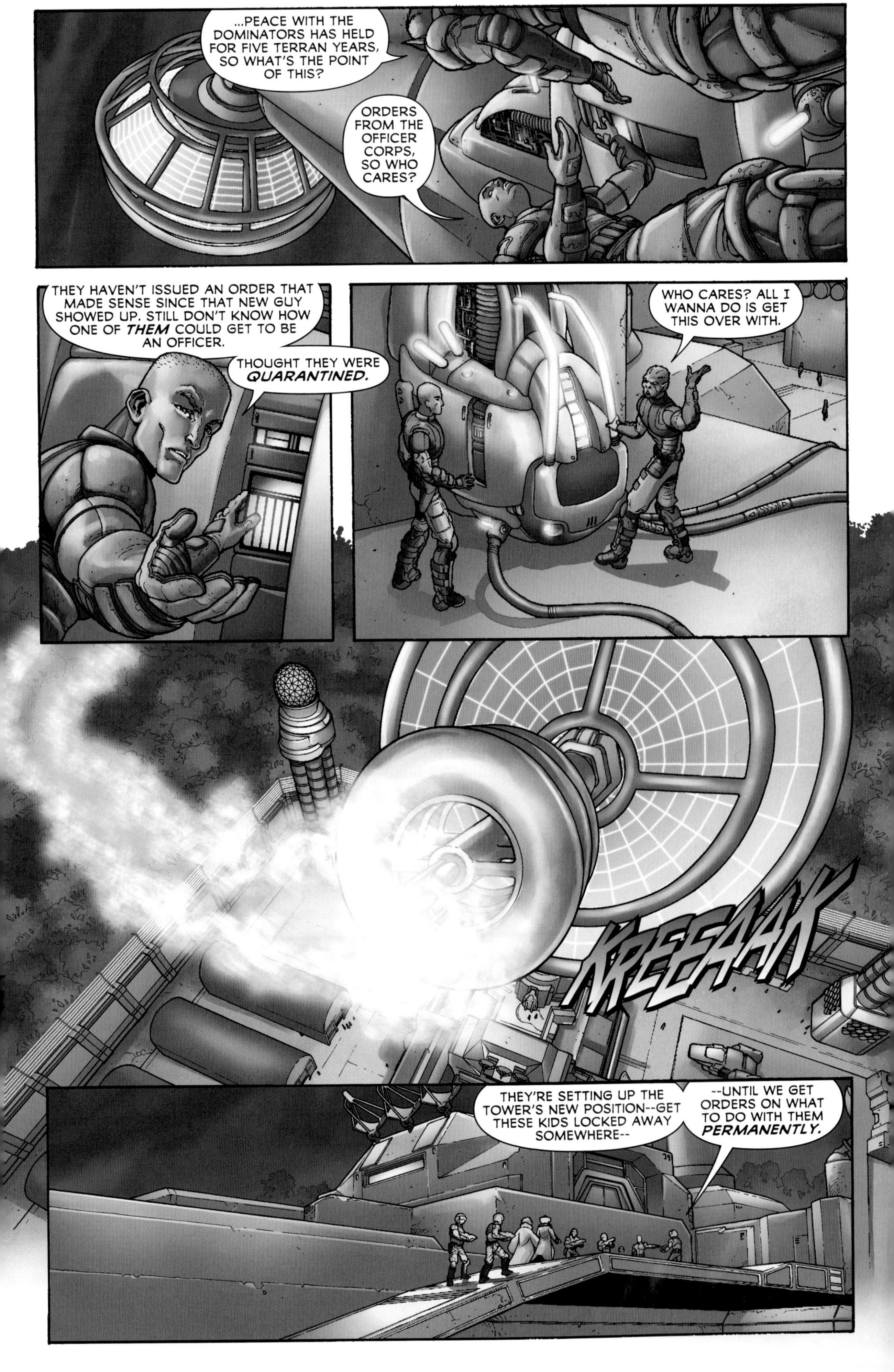
...PEACE WITH THE DOMINATORS HAS HELD FOR FIVE TERRAN YEARS, SO WHAT'S THE POINT OF THIS?
ORDERS FROM THE OFFICER CORPS, SO WHO CARES?
THEY HAVEN'T ISSUED AN ORDER THAT MADE SENSE SINCE THAT NEW GUY SHOWED UP. STILL DON'T KNOW HOW ONE OF *THEM* COULD GET TO BE AN OFFICER.
THOUGHT THEY WERE ***QUARANTINED.***
WHO CARES? ALL I WANNA DO IS GET THIS OVER WITH.
KREEAAK
THEY'RE SETTING UP THE TOWER'S NEW POSITION--GET THESE KIDS LOCKED AWAY SOMEWHERE--
--UNTIL WE GET ORDERS ON WHAT TO DO WITH THEM ***PERMANENTLY.***

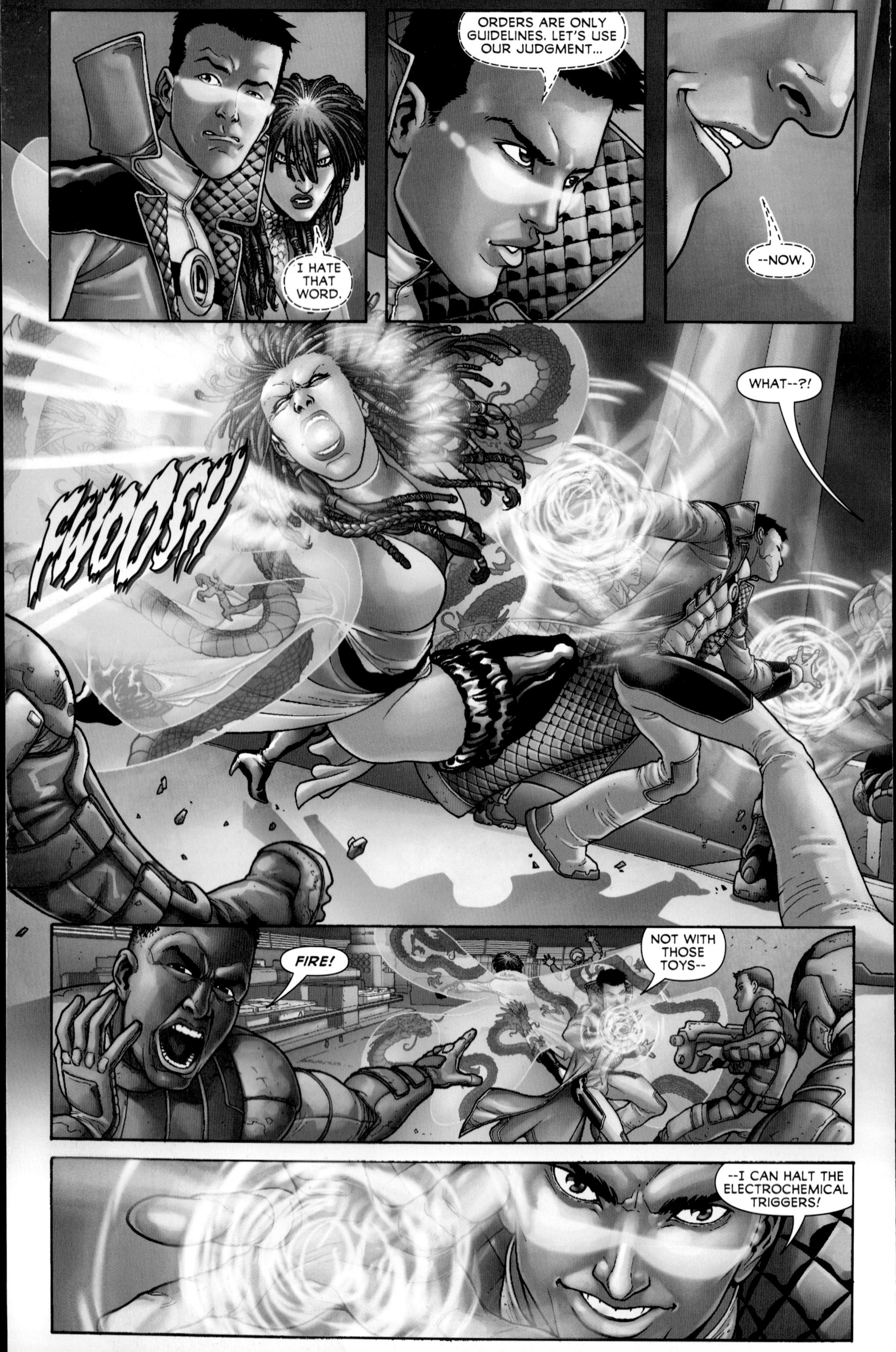

I HATE THAT WORD.
ORDERS ARE ONLY GUIDELINES. LET'S USE OUR JUDGMENT...
--NOW.
FWOOSH
WHAT--?!
FIRE!
NOT WITH THOSE TOYS--
--I CAN HALT THE ELECTROCHEMICAL TRIGGERS!

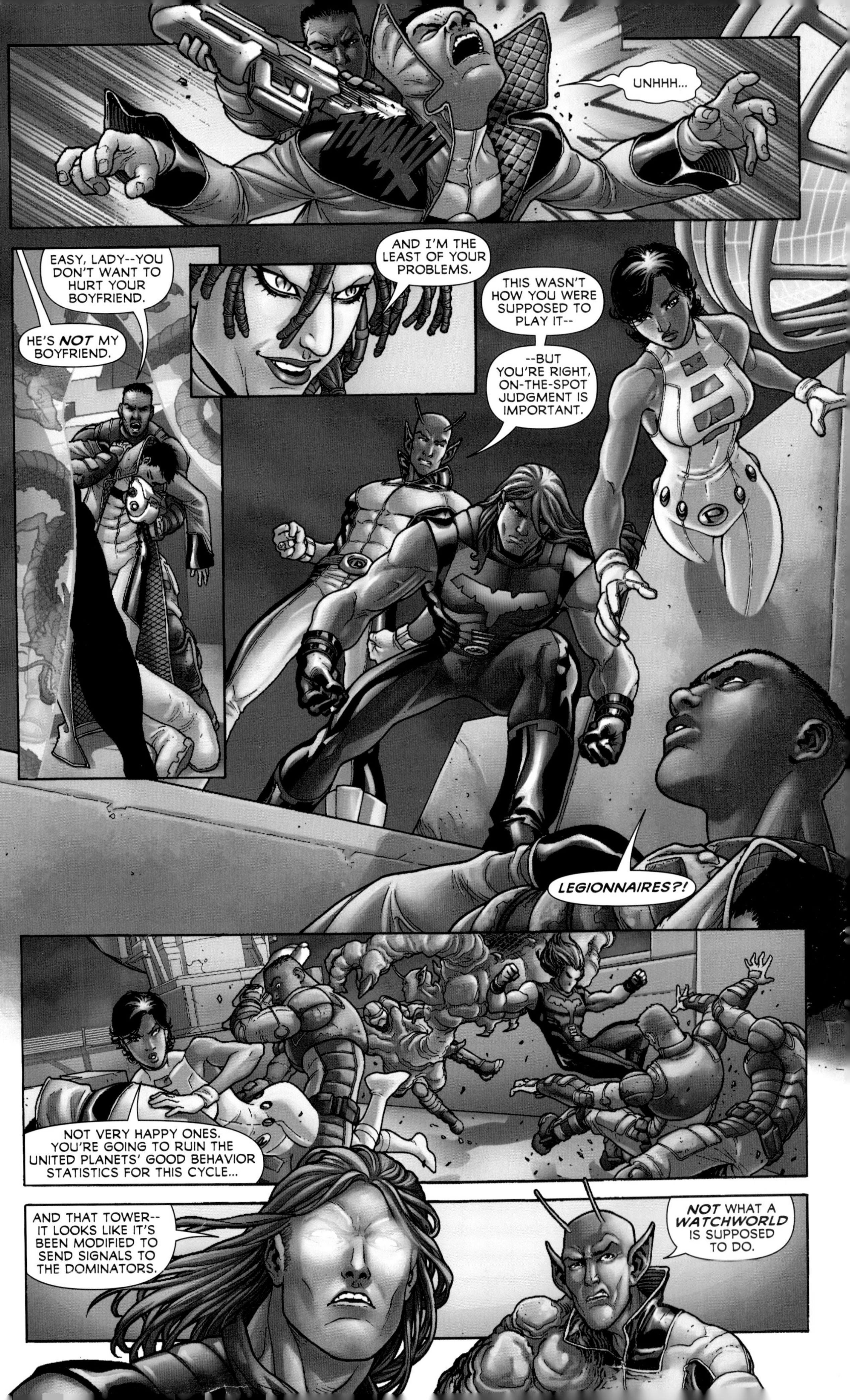
THWAK
UNHHH...
EASY, LADY--YOU DON'T WANT TO HURT YOUR BOYFRIEND.
HE'S *NOT* MY BOYFRIEND.
AND I'M THE LEAST OF YOUR PROBLEMS.
THIS WASN'T HOW YOU WERE SUPPOSED TO PLAY IT--
--BUT YOU'RE RIGHT, ON-THE-SPOT JUDGMENT IS IMPORTANT.
LEGIONNAIRES?!
NOT VERY HAPPY ONES. YOU'RE GOING TO RUIN THE UNITED PLANETS' GOOD BEHAVIOR STATISTICS FOR THIS CYCLE...
AND THAT TOWER--IT LOOKS LIKE IT'S BEEN MODIFIED TO SEND SIGNALS TO THE DOMINATORS.
NOT WHAT A *WATCHWORLD* IS SUPPOSED TO DO.

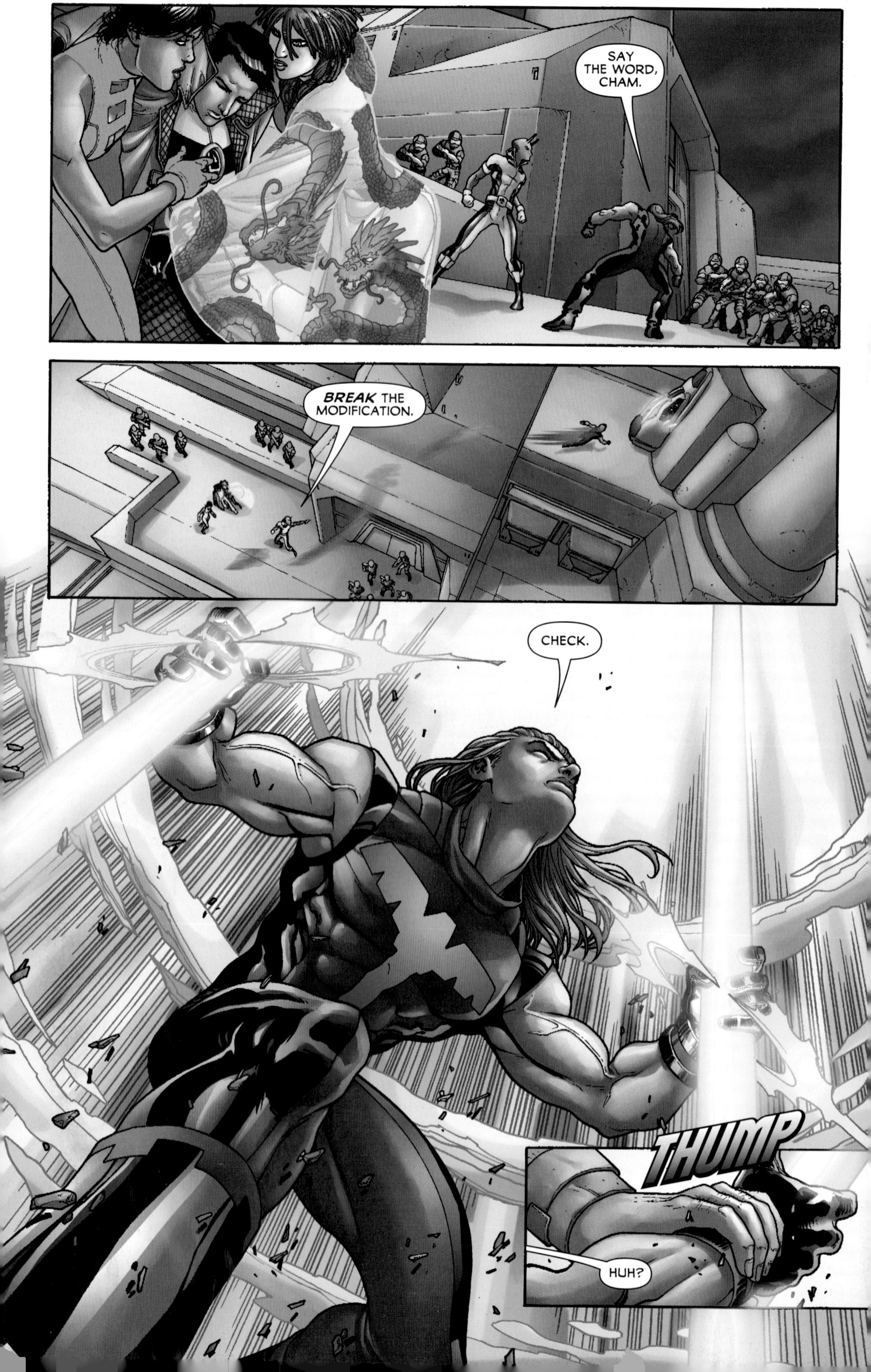
SAY THE WORD, CHAM.
BREAK THE MODIFICATION.
CHECK.
THUMP
HUH?

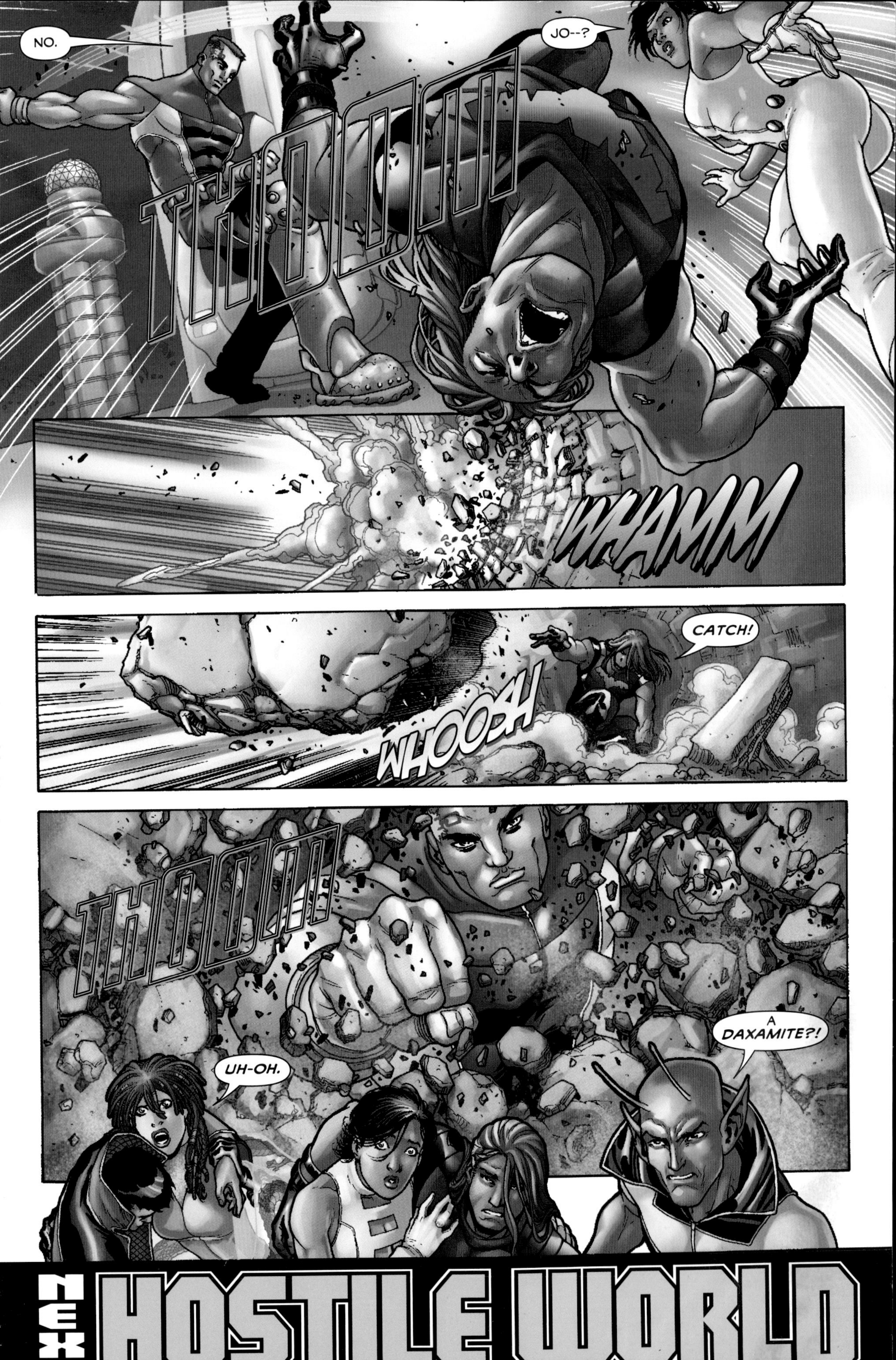
NO.
JO--?
THOOOM
WHAMM
CATCH!
WHOOSH
THOOM
A DAXAMITE?!
UH-OH.

NEXT HOSTILE WORLD

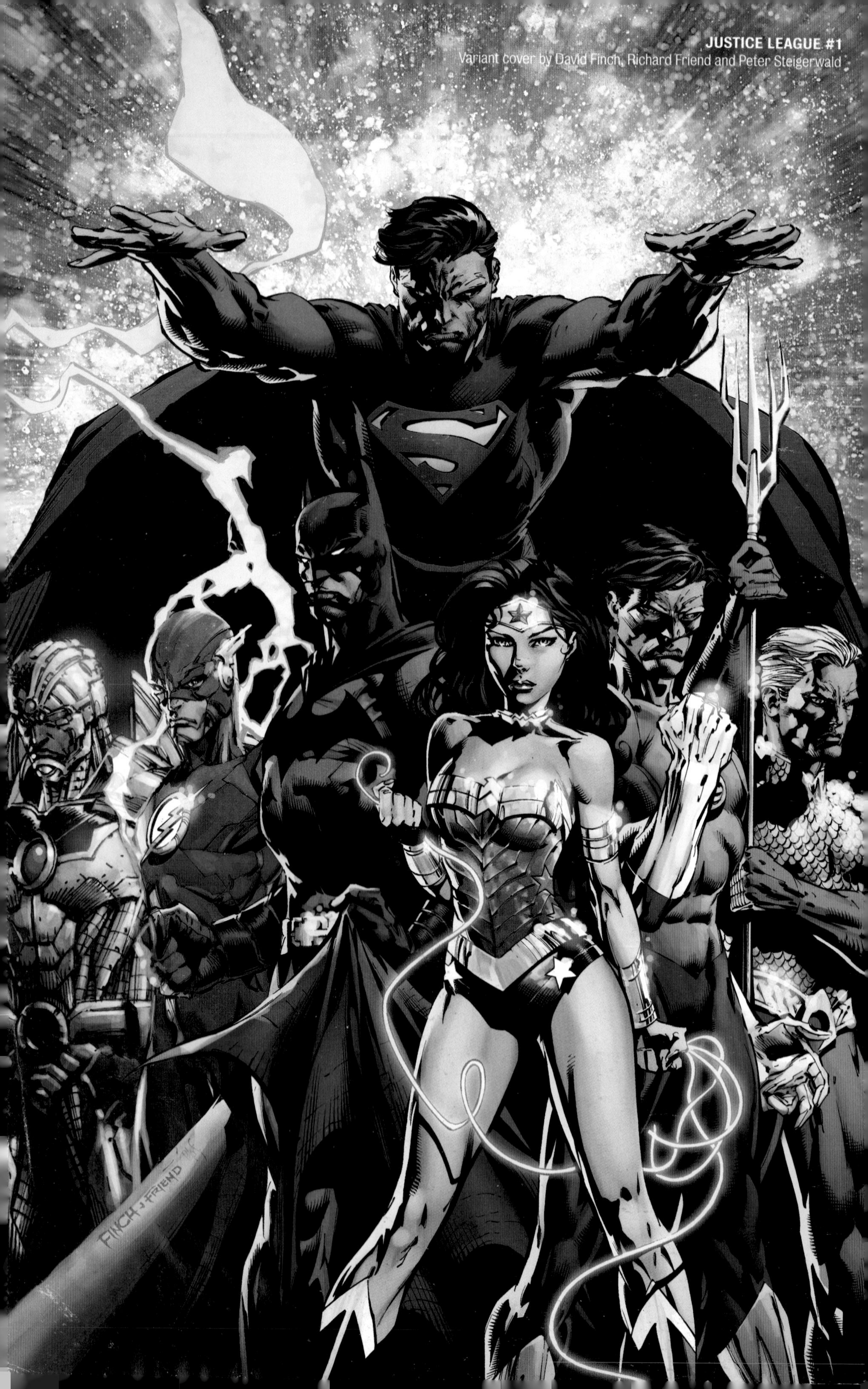

JUSTICE LEAGUE #1
Variant cover by David Finch, Richard Friend and Peter Steigerwald

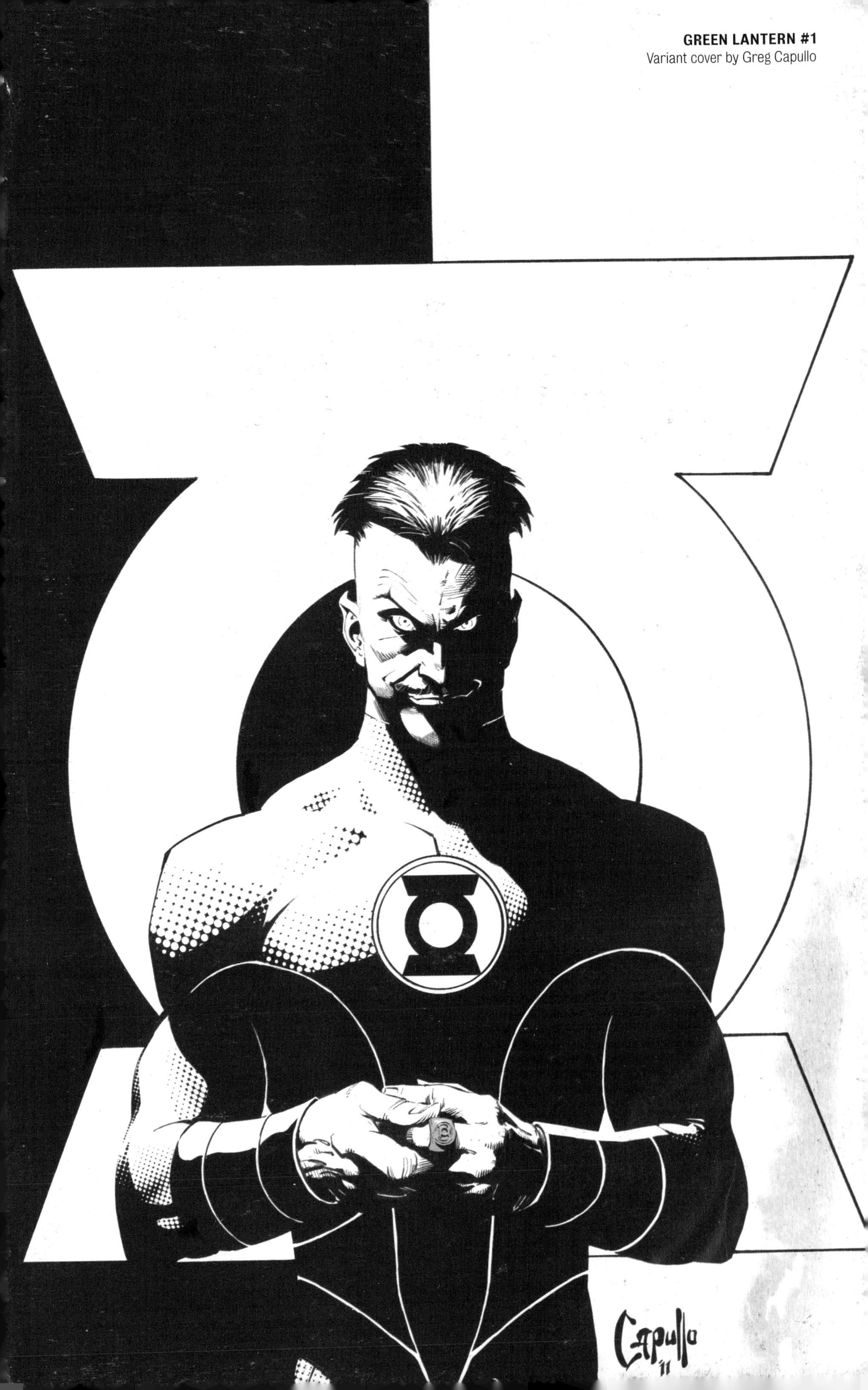
Capullo '11

GREEN LANTERN #1
Variant cover by Greg Capullo

THE FLASH #1

Variant cover by Ivan Reis, Tim Townsend and Rod Reis

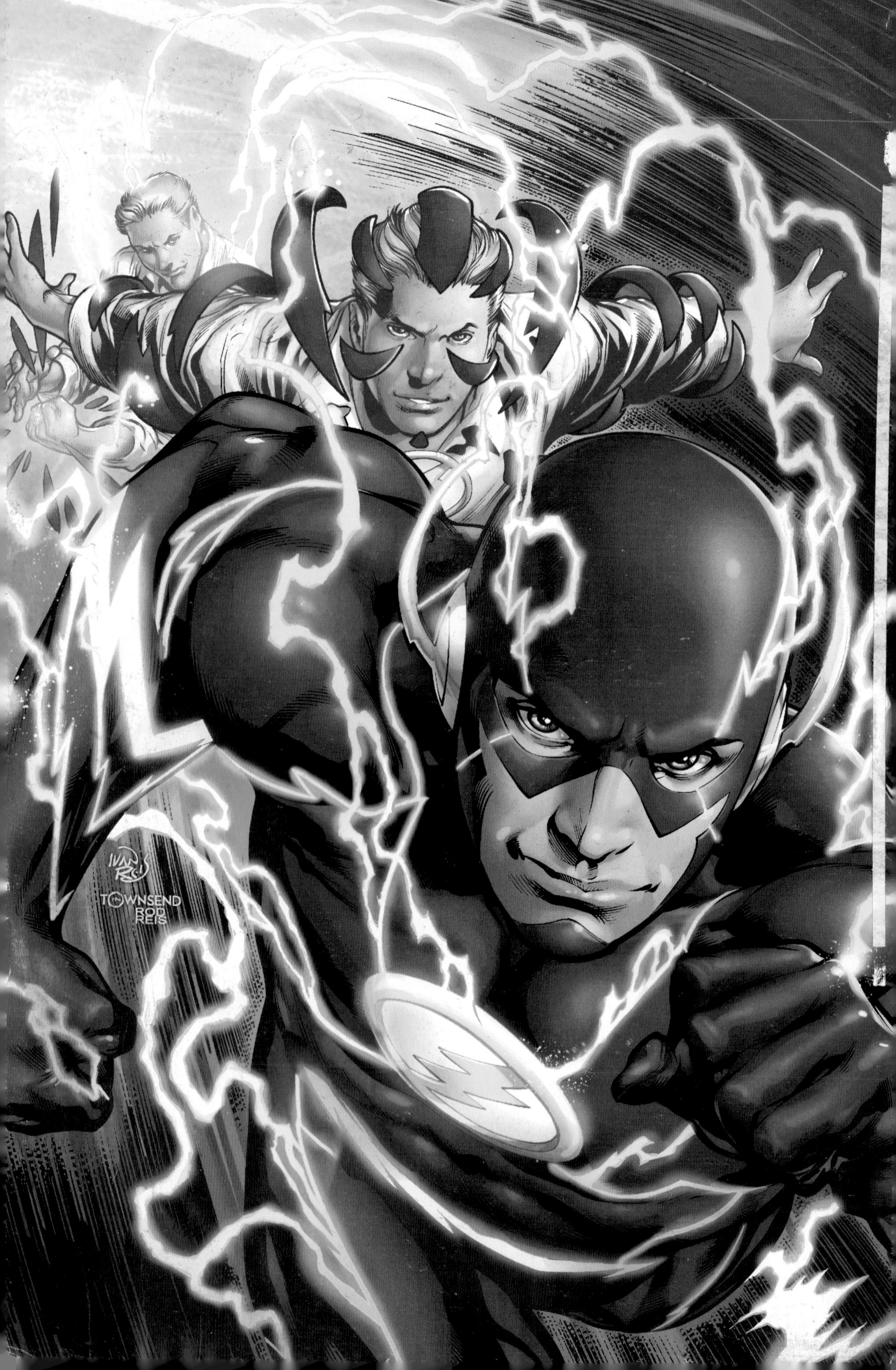
TOWNSEND
ROD
REIS

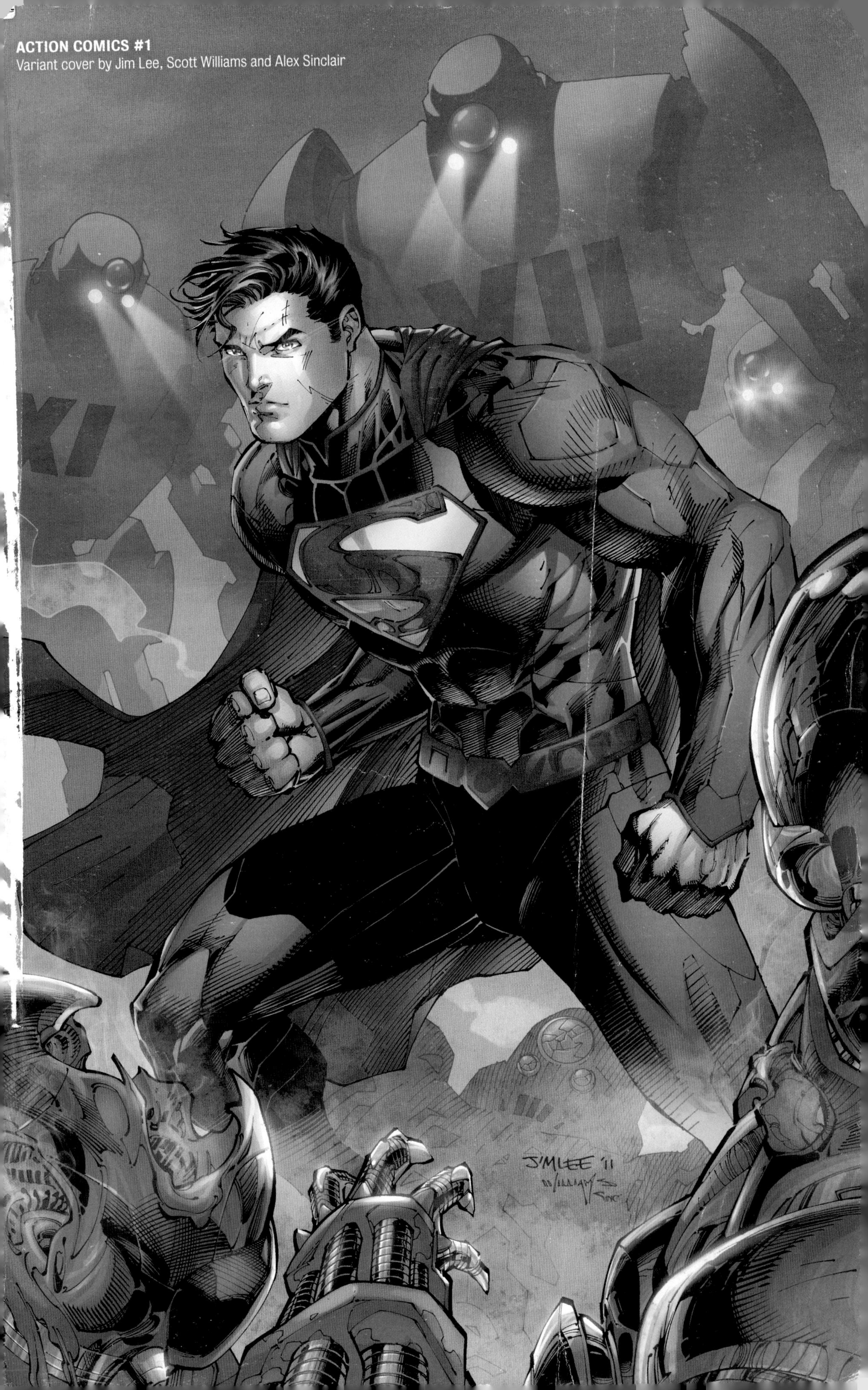

ACTION COMICS #1
Variant cover by Jim Lee, Scott Williams and Alex Sinclair

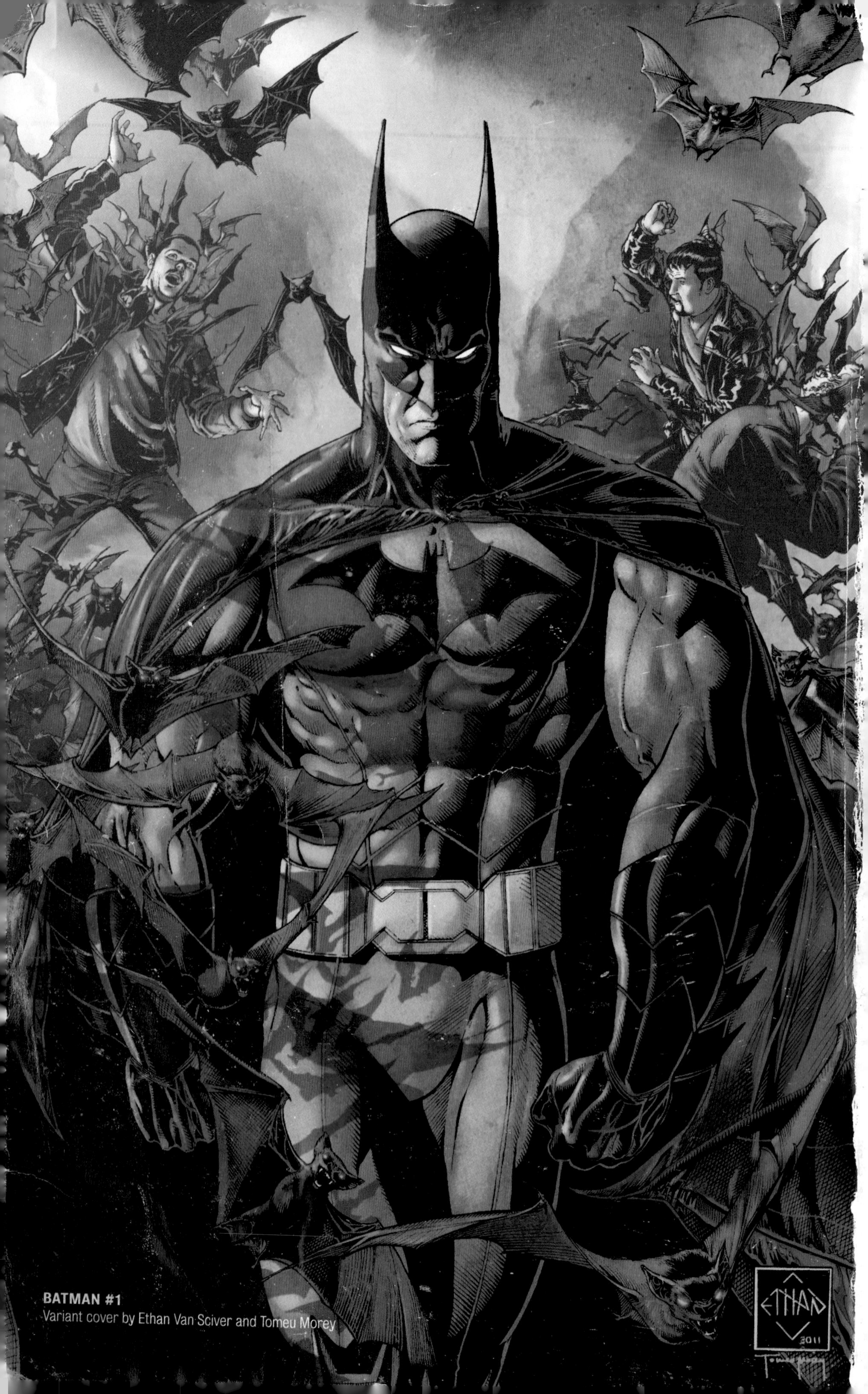
ETHAN
2011

BATMAN #1
Variant cover by Ethan Van Sciver and Tomeu Morey